Scotland

AN ENCYCLOPEDIA OF PLACES & LANDSCAPE

Scotland

AN ENCYCLOPEDIA OF PLACES & LANDSCAPE

David Munro
Bruce Gittings

HarperCollins Publishers
Westerhill Road, Bishopbriggs,
Glasgow G64 2QT

www.collins.co.uk

First published 2006

The publisher acknowledges the generous assistance of The Robertson Trust with the publication of this book

A catalogue record for this book is available from the British Library

ISBN-10 0-00-472466-6
ISBN-13 0-00-472466-9

Printed and bound in Thailand

Preface

The concept of a topographical dictionary, systematically describing the places in which we live and the landscape that surrounds us is not a new one. Indeed, there was a strong Scottish tradition in the 19th century of producing and publishing such works of reference. Yet this tradition did not continue. For more than a century, the principal reference work of this type on Scotland has remained Francis Groome's *Ordnance Gazetteer of Scotland*, first produced in 1885, with its final edition produced posthumously in 1903. The reasons for this are partly due to a change in fashion, with tourist guides and other thematic works becoming popular, but partly also due to the enormity of the task. This book was conceived by David Munro (of the Royal Scottish Geographical Society) and Bruce Gittings (of the University of Edinburgh) in 1995, realising that there was no single source which described the towns and villages, bens and glens, notable buildings and industrial sites of our small country. Realising the vision has taken considerable time and much work.

In selecting entries to go into the book, the significance of the location has been assessed and all cities, towns and villages in Scotland have generally been included, with details of populations, industry and attractions. For larger towns and cities we also included separate entries for areas or features of particular importance. For reasons of space, some smaller settlements have had to be omitted. At the back of the book there are 32 pages of colour mapping, served by a separate index. Within the body of the book there are town plans and maps of the individual local government divisions (currently as council areas).

At almost the same time as a traditional paper-based publication was envisaged, the web was just beginning to be recognised as an exciting new medium. Gittings and Munro have become web pioneers by realising the need for consistent and factually-correct material on the web, rather than the uncontrolled free-for-all which, while it has its place and value, is not ideal as a work of reference. The use of the web has had several effects: firstly it enabled the editors to have the satisfaction of publishing material as work progressed, avoiding the otherwise dispiriting process of setting out on a 10-year project with no results to show until the end. Secondly it allowed omissions and errors to come to light as the project proceeded and for these to be resolved. However, the web with its almost infinite space allowed much more material to be prepared than could possibly be published in paper form, particularly in terms of the thousands of colour photographs which have been included. Therefore what is presented here is a selection of a selection, edited and specially prepared as a consistent single volume.

Thus, as well as this book, the Gazetteer for Scotland website at www.scottish-places.info now contains over 13,000 entries and a wide selection of illustrations. In addition to places, the website contains biographies of famous Scots and brief histories of clans and families, connecting both of these to the landscape and settlements. In addition, the website is able to develop in a manner impossible for a book, and will be able to include new entries beyond those presented here. The editors would be grateful if all suggestions and corrections could be sent by email to feedback@scottish-places.info

Sources

Entries have been compiled using a range of primary and secondary sources collected by the editors. A selected bibliography is included at the back of the book. Other sources include:

- local- and central-government publications;
- tourist authority publications;
- leaflets, websites or other sources relating to particular features or tourist attractions;
- letters or telephone calls to specific organisations posing particular questions;
- original investigation of places through the use of historical documents or visits on the ground (ground survey);
- out-of-copyright sources (effectively works published before 1900, or in the case of UK Crown Copyright, works published before 1950);
- US National Imagery and Mapping Agency (NIMA) Geographic Names Database (GNDB);
- Sketch maps are redrawn from the New (2nd) Series Ordnance Survey mapping (out-of-copyright) and where necessary updated on the basis of non-copyright sources and ground investigation, including US National Imagery and Mapping Agency (NIMA) Digital Orthorectified Imagery (DOI-10), which contains data (c) CNES/SPOT Image 1992-1994 available under unrestricted licence;
- Population figures are Crown copyright. Data supplied by General Register Office for Scotland.

Conventions Adopted

We have principally used SI (metric) units throughout, with their imperial equivalents afterwards in brackets. There are two exceptions; distances are given in miles first because that is the system used for roads in the United Kingdom and weights are given in tons, because the metric equivalent (the tonne) is only just over 1% larger.

English names have been used for settlements in the Gaelic areas, principally because the Gaelic names are unfamiliar to those outside the Gaeltacht, but Gaelic names are given as alternatives.

Acknowledgements

Completing a project of this magnitude has involved the assistance of many and the authors are grateful to them all.

The Robertson Trust and Carnegie Trust for the Universities of Scotland provided funding for the project, for which we are most grateful. We have also been supported by the Royal Scottish Geographical Society and the University of Edinburgh.

Kenny Macleod has provided invaluable assistance in terms of collating information and assisting in the preparation of the book and writing of entries. David Tidswell, Alice Froggatt and Tom Armitage also assisted with the process of collation and writing. Anona Lyons was principally responsible for the cartography. The following have also assisted in the creation of the web site associated with this project (the Gazetteer for Scotland): Mike Forster, Tom Armitage, Tomasz Chojnacki, Nick Clark, Karen Clarke, Andrew Crooks, Carleen Ghio, David Halsey, Chris Harris, Scott Krueger, Ian Parnaby, Simon Ricketts and Jie Yang. Without Steve Dowers's computing expertise, given freely over the years, this project would have been much the poorer. Last, but not least, Margaret Wilkes has greatly improved our attention to detail and given much encouragement.

At Harper Collins, Christopher Riches has shown immense patience with our slow progress and Ian Brooke must be praised, as well as thanked, for his thorough, intelligent and careful copy-editing.

Bruce Gittings, Edinburgh
David Munro, Glasgow
May 2006

Contents

The Landscapes of Scotland

Scotland in so many ways represents a unique landscape, or series of unique landscapes, both physical and cultural. For such a small country, the physical landscape is one of remarkable diversity, from the rich farmland of the east and southwest to the grandeur of the glens and mountains of the Highlands. This landscape has formed as a result of the evolving climate over hundreds of thousands of years and the diversity of the underlying geology, with all ages of rocks exposed from the ancient Pre-Cambrian basement to fossil-bearing Cretaceous chalk, and ample evidence of the action of glaciers. This geology also gave rise to natural resources, such as coal and iron-ore, which ensured the rapid development of the country and its cities during the Industrial Revolution leading to, for example, the ship-building industry on the Clyde.

While it is perhaps stereotypical to suggest that Scotland hits above its weight in terms of its contribution to the world, there is no doubt that following the Act of Union in 1707 and recovery from its disastrous colonial experiment on the Darien Peninsula in Central America, this modest country became a centre of the Industrial Revolution and the focus of a flowering of intellectual thought that was the Scottish Enlightenment. The notables who lived at this time not only did much to interpret the physical, cultural and social landscape of Scotland, but contributed much to fields as diverse as the sciences, technology, economics, medicine, literature and the arts. The landscape was critical to many of these developments: exploited by industrialists, providing a rich laboratory for geologists, and inspiring artists, composers and philosophers.

The Physical Landscape

Occupying the northern third of mainland Great Britain and bounded to the west and north by nearly 800 islands, Scotland has one of the most distinctive outlines of any country in the world. The map of Scotland is instantly recognisable, highlighting as it does the contrast between the regular east coast with its wide estuaries and the deeply indented fjord-like western seaboard.

For such a small country, Scotland has a remarkably long coastline. Measured from Mean High Water, which extends into estuaries until the normal tidal limit, Scotland's mainland coastline measures 4174 miles (6718 km). If you take into account the main islands of the north and west, the coastline increases in length to 11,550 miles (18,588 km), a figure that represents 8% of the coastline of Europe.

The Islands of Scotland

Island	*Area (hectares)*	*Area (sq. miles)*
Lewis and Harris	216,428	835.63
Skye	167,261	645.80
Shetland Mainland	96,660	373.21
Mull	91,123	351.83
Islay	62,016	239.44
Orkney Mainland	51,369	198.34
Arran	42,859	165.48
Jura	36,740	141.85
North Uist	32,321	124.79
South Uist	31,016	119.75
Yell	21,078	81.38
Eigg	15,598	60.22
Hoy	14,374	55.50
Bute	12,184	47.04
Unst	11,883	45.88
Tiree	7822	30.20
Benbecula	7747	29.91
Coll	7530	29.07
Raasay	7200	27.80
Barra	5807	22.42
Rousay	5617	21.69
Sanday	5143	19.86
South Ronaldsay	4928	19.03
Westray	4691	18.11
Colonsay	4465	17.24
Fetlar	4077	15.74
Stronsay	3626	14.00
Luing	3604	13.92
Shapinsay	2817	10.87
Bressay	2753	10.63
Eday	2752	10.63
Lismore	2186	8.44
Great Bernera	2078	8.02
West Burra	1952	7.53
Whalsay	1941	7.50
Muckle Roe	1741	6.72
Gigha	1397	5.39
Seil	1394	5.38
Great Cumbrae	1155	4.46
Vatersay	1137	4.39
Berneray	1085	4.19
Burray	1011	3.90
Flotta	953	3.68
Iona	851	3.29
Grimsay	849	3.28
Papa Westray	847	3.27
Fair Isle	758	2.93
North Ronaldsay	746	2.88
Eriskay	718	2.77
Scalpay	689	2.66
East Burra	494	1.91
Trondra	274	1.06
Housay	217	0.84
Easdale	23	0.09
Scotland (total)	**7797068.11**	**30104.64**

While the geology of Scotland is intensely complicated when examined in detail, the mainland can be divided into three parts: a northern and southern upland area and a rift valley in the centre. Known as the Highlands, Southern Uplands and Central Lowlands respectively, these areas are separated by great fault lines that follow a southwest to northeast trend.

The Highlands, which lie to the north and west of the Highland Boundary Fault, are generally composed of hard, old crystalline metamorphic rocks that are relatively resistant to erosion but have, nonetheless, been deeply excavated by valley glaciers. In the west, Ben Nevis rises 4409 feet (1344 metres) directly from sea level, while more centrally, the Cairngorm Mountains form a plateau-like area more than 4000 feet (1218 metres) above sea level.

To the south of the Southern Upland Boundary Fault lie the Southern Uplands, an area of low, rounded hills which stretch across the country, rising to 2766 feet (843 metres) at the Merrick in the Galloway Hills to the west. In the east, the Cheviot Hills provide a boundary zone between Scotland and England.

The Central Lowlands, which form a great rift valley, slipped downward thousands of feet when the Earth's mantle cracked along two boundary fault zones. Geological deposits, including the coal and iron ore that subsequently fuelled the Industrial Revolution, were laid down during the Carboniferous age and preserved from later erosion.

Any geological map of Scotland, whether it covers a large or small area, is a kaleidoscope of colour that reflects the wide diversity of rocks that lie beneath our feet. The rich variety of landforms that make up Scotland's scenery stimulated the pioneering work of some of the world's first geologists including Roderick Murchison, Archibald Geikie, John MacCulloch and James Hutton, author of *The Theory of the Earth* (1788) and father of modern geology. In 1835 Britain became the first country in the world to establish a national geological survey, with much of the early work being undertaken in Scotland by the Victorian geologists John Horne and Benjamin Peach.

The shaping of Scotland's scenery is a story of drifting continents, mountain building, erosion and glaciation that goes back nearly three billion years. Amongst the oldest rocks in the world, banded Lewisian gneiss of the Precambrian period, can be found in the Inner and Outer Hebrides and along a narrow coastal strip extending southwards from Cape Wrath to Kyle of Lochalsh. There it forms a knobbly terrain of bare rock knolls between pools of peaty water. This ancient rock was forged in the lower reaches of the Earth's crust from molten material, including granite and gabbro, which rose from the mantle beneath and was later transformed into gneiss by intense heat and pressure caused by the movement of crustal plates about 2600 million years ago. These rocks finally reached the surface of the Earth 1100 million years ago after 15 km of early crust had been eroded, mainly under tropical, semi-desert conditions.

As soon as it was exposed, this ancient Lewisian landscape was buried again under a 7-km-deep blanket of Torridonian river sediments that were themselves subsequently eroded to reveal today's distinctive mountains of Torridonian sandstone, like Suilven in Assynt. A number of these peaks in Sutherland and Wester Ross are capped by hard, white quartzite derived from quartz-rich sands that were laid down by tidal currents in shallow seas at the beginning of the Cambrian period, 545 million years ago. Many of the sandstones and limestones of this period originated as beach deposits at a time when Scotland lay on the edge of the continent of Laurentia which had slowly drifted northwards from south polar regions into tropical latitudes. The muds, silts and sands that were laid down on the continental edge show evidence of early life forms, some of which can be found in the limestone at Durness in northwest Sutherland.

During much of its early geological history Scotland was separated from England and Wales by the vast Iapetus Ocean. Around 500 million years ago, however, the continents of Laurentia, Baltica and Avalonia began to converge. The eventual closure of the Iapetus Ocean took place about 410 million years ago when the continents collided and Scotland, a disparate group of islands, was brought into contact with England. The violent process of collision resulted in a great upheaval known as the Caledonian orogeny. This gave rise to some of Scotland's most familiar landmarks including the Highland Boundary Fault which extends from Bute in the southwest to Stonehaven in the northeast, separating older Dalradian metamorphic rock to the north from younger pebbly conglomerates and softer sandstones to the south. Great mountain ranges as high as the Himalayas were formed from molten magma injected upwards into the Earth's crust. The Cairngorms, Ben Nevis and many other mountains in the Scottish Highlands were sculpted from granite formed at this time but later exposed by erosion.

During the Devonian period 360–440 million years ago, rivers brought great volumes of sediment down into a huge lake on the edge of which the Orkney Islands were born and in the Old Red Sandstone that was created, 'fish beds' provide today's geologists with evidence of primitive fish and early plants. The age of the coal swamps began with the onset of the Carboniferous period, when Scotland lay on the Equator. In the Midland Valley,

Top 25 Mountains by Height

Ben Nevis	1344 m
Ben Macdui	1309 m
Braeriach	1296 m
Cairn Toul	1293 m
Sgor an Lochain Uaine	1258 m
Cairn Gorm	1245 m
Aonach Beag	1234 m
Aonach Mor	1221 m
Carn Mor Dearg	1220 m
Ben Lawers	1214 m
Beinn a' Bhuird – South Top	1177 m.
Beinn a' Bhuird – North Top	1197 m
Carn Eige	1183 m
Beinn Mheadhoin	1182 m
Mam Sodhail	1181 m
Stob Choire Claurigh	1177 m
Ben More	1174 m
Leabaidh an Daimh Bhuidhe	1171 m
Stob Binnein	1165 m
Beinn Bhrotain	1157 m
Derry Cairngorm	1155 m
Lochnagar	1155 m
Sgurr nan Ceathreamhnan	1151 m
Bidean nam Bian	1150 m
Sgurr na Lapaich	1150 m

decaying vegetation was compressed to form coal deposits while volcanoes continued to erupt, creating hills such as East and West Lomond in Fife, Arthur's Seat, Castle Rock and Calton Hill in Edinburgh, and Berwick Law and the Bass Rock in East Lothian. At the same time, layer upon layer of basalt lava poured into the valley to form the Campsie Fells and Gargunnock Hills. Desert conditions prevailed over much of Scotland for the next 70 million years during the Permian, turning the landscape into a great desert that would eventually provide modern builders with easily worked red sandstone.

The eventual separation of North America around 65 million years ago caused a stretching and thinning of the Earth's crust near the margin of the emerging Atlantic Ocean, allowing molten lava to break through in a line extending from St Kilda in the north down through Skye, Rum, Ardnamurchan and Mull to Arran and Ailsa Craig. Fingal's Cave on the island of Staffa and the flat lava fields of the Treshnish Isles are typical creations of this period which also saw an immense amount of volcanic activity with swarms of dykes radiating outwards in all directions. Molten rock under the lava fields later solidified to form a rock known as gabbro which is best seen in the Black Cuillins of Skye. The neighbouring Red Cuillins were formed when melting gabbro came into contact with the lower crust to create red granite.

During the remainder of the Tertiary period that followed, physical and chemical forces removed more than a mile (1.6 km) of rock, most of the sediment draining eastwards into the North Sea where 3000 m accumulated, filling in a great tear in the sea floor between Norway and Britain. The oil and gas that has been extracted from the North Sea since the 1970s comes from these sediments. The uplands were deeply weathered at this time, but more resistant rocks remained, leaving a legacy of granite tors such as those found at the Barns of Bynack and Beinn a' Bhuird in the Cairngorm Mountains.

Scotland experienced a succession of alternating cooler and warmer periods during a period commonly known as the Ice Age which lasted for 2.4 million years. Ice moving with great force smoothed bare rock, removed weathered debris and scoured out over 500 mountain hollows or corries in the Highlands. Valleys were deepened to form rock basins now occupied by freshwater lochs and more than 100 fjord-like sea lochs were created on the west coast. Large quantities of debris were deposited over the landscape as the ice moved or as it melted in situ and sea-level change in late-glacial and post-glacial times gave rise to raised beaches around the Scottish coastline. Typical landscapes of erosion include the striated rocks of Lewis and Harris, U-shaped valleys such as Glen Sannox on Arran and the crag-and-tail feature on which Edinburgh's Old Town stands. Landscapes of deposition include the drumlins over which the city of Glasgow is spread, the hummocky moraines of the Valley of a Hundred Hills in Torridon and the suites of esker ridges to be found in mid-Strathspey. In the past 30,000 years most of the country was covered in a great depth of ice on two occasions, a final major readvance centred on Rannoch Moor taking place during the last cold period around 12,500 years ago. About 11,500 years ago, the climate warmed up rapidly and the last remaining glaciers melted, allowing soils to stabilise and vegetation to clothe the landscape once again.

Scotland's Climate

Lying as it does between 55° and 60° north, Scotland is one of the boreal or northern countries of Europe. Its capital, Edinburgh, is nearer to the Arctic than it is to the Mediterranean but the corresponding latitudes of North America are sparsely inhabited frozen wastes. The effect of latitude is ameliorated by the fact that Scotland has a maritime climate influenced by the surface conditions of the North Atlantic Ocean which imports vast amounts of heat from equatorial regions. The Gulf Stream flows northwards and eastwards from the Gulf of Mexico past the eastern coast of Florida before fanning out across the North Atlantic where it becomes the North Atlantic Drift. As a result, the coastal waters of Scotland are relatively warm in comparison to other sea areas at high latitudes. This effect is most striking in winter and most beneficial to those parts of the country exposed to polar maritime air currents.

It is often said that on many a day Scotland experiences the weather of all seasons of the year within twenty-four hours. Fine, mild weather may occur in mid-winter, frost in late May and an August excursion into the hills may be marked by wintry storms. The climatic regime is indeed one of frequent change resulting from the interplay of air systems, especially the alternating warm and cold fronts from the North Atlantic that move west to east across the country. Change can take place over relatively short distances too, since the rain-bearing systems generally come from the west and release large amounts of precipitation when they encounter the mountains of the west coast. Situated at the foot of Ben Nevis, Fort William is one of the wettest places in Scotland with a precipitation of about 120 inches (3000 mm) a year. Further east, lowland areas benefit from the 'rain shadow' effect, experiencing 25–30 inches (700–800 mm) of precipitation a year. This has had a profound effect on settlement and agriculture. In the west, high rainfall combined with exposure to the prevailing southwesterly winds has produced a settlement pattern where few houses are situated and few fields are cultivated above an altitude of 300 feet. By contrast, 50 miles to the east grain crops are found growing at elevations near 1000 feet above sea level.

While infinite variability is a characteristic of Scottish weather, the general climatic regime can be characterised by statistical means round which such fluctuations in temperature, rainfall and wind speed oscillate. The mean annual temperature ranges from 7°C in Shetland to almost 9°C in the south. More significant are the figures for the period with a mean temperature above 6°C, the most generally accepted threshold of vegetation growth. At sea-level this ranges from five to six months in the north and northwest to seven to eight months on the low ground elsewhere. Summer mean temperatures reach only 12°C in the north and 14°C in the south, with low daily ranges, 5°C in the north and 8°C in the south. At the same time, the east of Scotland is cooler than the west owing to the reduced effect of the Gulf Stream and the cooler surface temperature of the North Sea. Winter temperatures fall to an average of 4°C in the east and 5°C in the west, with a range in both places of less than 5°C. Away from the coast temperature falls with height at an average rate of about 0.7°C per 100 metres for the maximum temperature and 0.5°C for the minimum temperature. In spring, summer and autumn the effect of latitude predominates and temperatures in Scotland are a few degrees lower than in England. The maximum temperature in the lowlands ranges from an average of 6°C in winter to 18°C in summer. The coldest temperature ever recorded was -27.2°C at Braemar on 10 January 1982 and at Altnaharra on 30 December 1995. The highest recorded temperature was 32.9°C at Greycrook in the Scottish Borders on 9 August 2003.

In general, snow becomes more common with altitude and occurs most often when continental air is drawn over the North Sea. Braemar in the eastern Grampian Mountains experiences an average of 59 snow days per year while the Western Isles and low lying coastal areas have an average of less than 10 days, rising to 15 and 20 days in the north and northeast.

Situated at a relatively high latitude, Scotland experiences a marked contrast between summer and winter day length. Although winter days are very short, summer days are long with an extended twilight. In the far north there is no complete darkness on midsummer day, Lerwick in Shetland having about four hours more daylight than London. The sunniest places for the year as a whole tend to be the outer estuaries of the Firths of Tay and Forth, with Dunbar having the highest average annual sunshine total in Scotland. The record for the maximum amount of sunshine in a month, however, is held by Tiree which had an average of 10.6 hours of sunshine per day in May 1946 and May 1975. While Tiree could boast of 329 hours of sunshine in May, it is generally true that in May and June the west coast is the sunniest part of Scotland.

The marginality and variability of the Scottish climate is reflected not only in the limitations and hazards faced by farmers and horticulturalists today but also in the rural and urban landscapes that have evolved over many centuries. In the past, traditional housing was always carefully sited, usually taking every little advantage of aspect, shelter and warm soil. Each season had its own cycle of activity. For example, in the Highlands, livestock was moved, often long distances, from the fermtoun to summer grazings in a system of transhumance that maximised access to fodder. During the Agricultural Revolution farmers modified the environment to cope with wind and rain by planting shelter belts and draining fields. High-walled gardens attached to mansion houses created their own microclimate as did the small walled enclosures known as plantiecrues in the Northern and Western Isles where the wind blows relentlessly, particularly in winter when the highest frequency of gales occurs. Likewise, the cleits of St Kilda took advantage of the drying power of the wind while the houses of coastal fishing villages were often built gable end facing wind and storm.

The Vegetation of Scotland

Radio-carbon dating and pollen analysis have provided scientists with the tools to investigate vegetational history and climatic change from the time when Scotland was covered by ice during the last glacial period to the present day. The great majority of species now considered as native to Scotland are assumed to have been established by migration from Europe across the land bridge which existed until some 8000 years ago at a time when the land was significantly lower in relation to sea level than it is now.

About 10,000 years ago juniper and other shrubs covered the tundra as the climate became less cold. A thousand years later birches followed by hazel began to form forests in southern Scotland. After a further one thousand years birch had spread to the far north of Scotland. About 7500 years ago elm began to appear in southern Scotland and 800 years later oak trees started to grow. Both of these species spread through the Central Lowlands into northern Scotland while Scots pine advanced across the Highlands to create what came to be known as the Caledonian Forest.

In these forests, soils began to develop as tree roots reached down, bringing up nutrients, and rotting leaves added organic matter to the harsh post-glacial soils. Wetter conditions in the Atlantic and Sub-Atlantic periods 7000 years and 2000 years ago contributed to the development of vast areas of peat on poorly drained soils and on shallow gradients, particularly at higher altitudes. Evidence for the retreat of pine and birch forest at these times is found in the remains of tree stumps preserved in peat. Thick deposits of peat have accumulated during the past 2000 years over wide areas of the Highlands and hills of southern Scotland. It is estimated that blanket peat of more than one metre in depth covers 14% of Scotland.

Two broad types of vegetation association – broadleaf deciduous forest and heather and upland grass moor – have been categorised as 'natural.' Human activity has, however, exerted profound modifying effects on most of the vegetation of Scotland. Where slope and exposure are not severe, drainage is not impeded and soils tend to be basic rather than acidic, the climax vegetation on brown forest soils is open broadleaf deciduous forest dominated by oak, ash and sycamore – along with Scots pine and grass groundcover in the Highlands. In upland areas where the growing season is shorter, subarctic heath and moorland occur. Coarse grasses and sedges characterise the wetter and more exposed west while in the drier east heaths and heathers bring to the hills a late summer and autumn purple so closely identified with Scotland.

At elevations above 3000 feet (914 metres), as on the Cairngorm plateau, Arctic tundra vegetation prevails and on a few favoured spots, such as the higher slopes of Ben Lui and Ben Lawers, alpine plants are found that are relicts of late glacial times. In lowland areas the vegetation mosaic includes a variety wetlands, saltmarshes, meadowlands and coastal sand dune communities, each with its own assemblage of plant species.

Even though Scotland's natural forest cover has been significantly reduced as a result of man's activities and climatic change, the landscape is today covered with mile upon mile of coniferous woodlands. Some of these were planted by enlightened landowners since the 18th century, but the planting of trees on a grand scale dates from 1919 when the government of the United Kingdom established the Forestry Commission after a serious shortage of wood threatened national security during World War I. In the earlier years European larch was the main species, but after World War II the faster-growing Sitka Spruce was found to be ideal for the wetter western moorlands. Since the 1970s, amenity, wildlife and recreation have been just as important to the forester as timber and in recent times the restoration of ancient woodlands and the planting of the Millennium Forest in central Scotland have developed as important environmental projects designed to enhance the landscape and biodiversity.

Scotland's Freshwater Lochs and Rivers

Scotland is known for its lochs which number more than 30,000 in total. On a regional basis, the Western Isles have the highest number of standing fresh waters smaller than 25 hectares in surface area owing to the abundance of small lochans in the glaciated landscape. In terms of area and volume, the west and northeast Highlands together account for 50% and 66% of the total respectively and include nine of Scotland's 13 largest lochs. In the uplands, Scotland's freshwater lochs are typically nutrient-poor and of low pH, reflecting the widespread occurrence of acidic rocks often overlain by acidic glacial sediments and waterlogged soils or peat. By contrast, the freshwater lochs of the Scottish lowlands are more rich in nutrients, influenced as they are by more easily weathered sedimentary rocks and human activity.

Fed by an annual rainfall that produces a net discharge of 71 billion cubic metres per year, Scotland has a dense network of streams and rivers. The west and northeast Highlands contain the highest numbers of running waters as a result of local climate and topography. Watercourses there tend to be small and steep, responding rapidly to rainfall and snowmelt. Most of the larger rivers, with lower gradients and more delayed response to precipitation, flow eastwards into the North Sea. Of these, the River Tay has the highest recorded discharge of any river in the UK with an average flow of 164 cubic metres per second. The other chief rivers of Scotland – the Tweed, Clyde, Forth, Dee and Spey – transport less water, with average flows in the range 50–100 cubic metres per second.

Lochs by Area

Loch	*Sq. miles*	*Sq. km*
Lomond	27.45	71
Ness	21.78	56.4
Awe	14.85	38.5
Maree	11.03	28.6
Morar	10.3	26.7
Tay	10.19	26.39
Shin	8.7	22.53
Shiel	7.56	19.58
Rannoch	7.37	19.09
Ericht	7.21	18.67

Lochs by Depth

Loch	*Sq. miles*	*Sq. km*
Morar	310	1017
Ness	230	754
Lomond	190	623
Lochy	162	531
Ericht	156	512
Tay	155	508
Katrine	151	495
Rannoch	134	440
Treig	133	436
Shiel	128	420

Rivers by Length

River	*miles*	*km*
Tay	120	193
Clyde	106	171
Spey	100	160
Tweed	97	156
Dee	85	137
Don	82	132
Nith	70	112
Forth	66	106
Findhorn	62	99
Deveron	61	98

Peopling the Landscape

People have lived in Scotland since at least 7500 BC, initially as hunter gatherers dependent on plant and animal foods from the land and sea. These Mesolithic nomads did not build permanent houses or monuments of stone and have left behind only scant traces such as stone flakes, the scorched remains of a hearth or domestic rubbish in the form of shell middens. The earliest known settlements are at Kinloch on the island of Rum, Tentsmuir in east Fife and Biggar in Upper Clydesdale. Population density was low during this early period of settlement, each group of hunter-gatherers numbering 10–20 people and occupying an area of 400 square miles (1000 square km). At this density, between one and four groups would have controlled the coastal plains and the northern sides of the Lammermuir, Moorfoot and Pentland Hills from Edinburgh to Berwick-upon-Tweed.

From around 4000 BC people began to adopt agriculture and build greater burial and ritual monuments. Forest-clearing began as the population grew and new technologies like pottery and, much later, bronze, augmented the use of bone, wood, stone and other naturally occurring materials. The most characteristic surviving burial structures from the period between 4000 and 3500 BC are the chambered tombs of the west and north of Scotland, such as the long cairn at Camster in Caithness. These were built to serve as a link between the living community, their dead ancestors and the land itself. At a later period ritual became less centred on the land and more on the movements of the sun and moon, with large timber and stone rings, such as the circles at Stenness in Orkney and Callanish in the Western Isles, being erected. Houses at this time were either isolated or in very small settlements such as that discovered on the west coast of Orkney at Skara Brae, the most famous Neolithic settlement in Britain, but by 3000 BC centres for more widespread groups were becoming important and settlements increased in size.

The sites chosen by prehistoric settlers tended to concentrate on the more freely drained lower slopes and gravel ridges. Dense vegetation and unstable stony topography affected the choices of early house builders, while times of improved climate encouraged settlers to move further up the hillside. The early inhabitants of Scotland depended on a thorough knowledge of the surrounding land not only to find food and material resources but also to travel and navigate. This was not always easy in a landscape with much dense woodland. For this reason early settlers often favoured coastlands, major waterways or obvious routeways. Two thousand years ago, in the Iron Age, pressure on the land increased and defence became an important factor. During this period hill forts, crannogs or lake dwellings and great towers or brochs such as the broch at Mousa in Shetland, made their appearance.

While the Romans never properly colonised Scotland, they did venture north on several occasions with a view to conquest. Agricola recognised the strategic importance of the Forth–Clyde isthmus during his campaigns of AD 80–85 and some time later in AD 142 the Romans established a new frontier line along the Antonine Wall. Aided by aerial photography, Roman forts, signal stations, ramparts, ditches, roads and military camps have been identified from the Southern Uplands northwards to Strathmore in Angus, but outstanding amongst the Roman remains surviving to the present day is the massive fort at Ardoch near Braco in Perthshire.

During the first millennium AD there was considerable movement of peoples in Scotland. The Iron Age Picts encountered by the Romans, came under pressure from new immigrant groups including the Scots from northern Ireland, the Angles from Frisia and later the Norsemen who came first as raiders then as settlers. All of these groups contributed language and cultural traits as well as new structures in the landscape. Of these, the most fascinating are the many pagan and Christian symbol stones largely found in the east, most notably at Aberlemno in Angus.

The welding of Scotland into a political whole proceeded from the union of the Scots and Picts under Kenneth MacAlpin in AD 843. Both church and state subsequently played their part in breaking down Scottish isolation and developing a national identity. David I (1124–53) brought Anglo-Norman nobles, new religious orders and feudal institutions into Scotland with a view to modernising the country, and from the 12th century castles, ranging from simple fortified tower houses to great royal strongholds, and cathedrals, monasteries and churches made their appearance in the landscape.

A semi-pictorial impression of the pre-Improvement landscape of rural Scotland comes from the military maps of William Roy between 1747 and 1755 which depict treeless upland moorlands and lowland heaths, and agricultural hamlets or fermtoun settlements surrounded by unenclosed fields. The arable land was divided into a constantly cropped infield and an outfield that was occasionally left fallow to be manured by grazing livestock. The fields in the infield were often further divided into individual strips or rigs in a system known as 'run-rig' which allocated shares to each tenant. In addition, tenants also held rights in areas of common grazing. The characteristic form of nuclear settlement in both the Highlands and Lowlands was the multiple tenancy or joint farm comprising three to eight tenancies. They worked their leases under middlemen known as tacksmen and paid their rent in kind or, in the Highlands and islands, as military service to the clan chief. These multiple tenants were often supplemented by a few cottars working as farm labourers.

Between 1661 and 1695 the Scottish Parliament enacted legislation empowering landlords to sweep away the old systems of run-rig and common grazing and rearrange and enclose their lands. The process of agricultural improvement gathered momentum in the 18th and 19th centuries as landowners saw the potential to generate an income from farm rents. Coupled with a dramatic and unsustainable increase in the rural population of Scotland, following the virtual elimination of smallpox and the introduction of the potato as a staple crop, the reorganisation process was often a painful one involving, at worst, wholesale forced eviction or 'clearance' to make

Island Populations

Island	*2001 Census*	*1991 Census*
Lewis and Harris	19,918	21,737
Skye	9251	8868
Shetland Mainland	17,575	17,596
Mull	2696	2708
Islay	3457	3538
Orkney Mainland	15,339	15,128
Arran	5058	4474
Jura	188	196
North Uist	1320	1459
South Uist	1818	2106
Yell	957	1075
Eigg	133	179
Hoy	392	477
Bute	164	172
Unst	720	1055
Tiree	770	768
Benbecula	1249	1803
Coll	113	106
Raasay	194	163
Barra	1078	1244
Rousay	267	291
Sanday	478	533
South Ronaldsay	854	943
Westray	563	704
Colonsay	58	41
Fetlar	81	126
Stronsay	358	382

Island	*2001 Census*	*1991 Census*
Luing	220	182
Shapinsay	300	322
Bressay	357	363
Eday	131	141
Lismore	146	140
Great Bernera	136	141
West Burra	784	857
Whalsay	1034	1041
Muckle Roe	104	115
Gigha	233	262
Seil	560	506
Great Cumbrae	1434	1393
Vatersay	94	72
Berneray	384	352
Burray	7228	7,354
Flotta	110	143
Iona	125	130
Grimsay	201	215
Papa Westray	65	85
Fair Isle	86	90
North Ronaldsay	70	92
Eriskay	69	67
Scalpay	322	382
East Burra	121	166
Trondra	133	117
Housay	76	85
Easdale	66	72

way for sheep farmers or deer forests and, at best, a relocation from the old fermtoun to a new crofting township to begin a new life. For many, migration to the industrial cities of central Scotland or emigration to the New World were the only options for a better life, but it was not until the late 19th and early 20th centuries that rural depopulation began to make its mark. Despite the Crofting Act of 1886, which preserved the crofting system in the north and northwest, whole island communities off the west coast, most notably St Kilda in 1930, were abandoned after generations of occupation.

Rural depopulation has largely come to an end as a result of better transport, the development of dormitory villages and the growth of rural industries including forestry and tourism. In some places the trend has been reversed, most notably in Highland Council Area where the population increased by 2.4% between 1991 and 2001.

The Administrative Landscape

At the national scale, disregarding invasions and other conflagrations, Scotland was an independent and separate state until the Union of the Crowns in 1603, when the Scottish monarch James VI inherited the throne of England and Wales as James I. The states continued to operate quite separately, although under the same king, until the Act of Union of 1707 which created the United Kingdom, dissolved the Scottish Parliament and gave full authority over Scotland to an enlarged parliament in Westminster. Scotland was run from London until 1999, although an Edinburgh-based Scottish Office had been given increasing autonomy from the late 1930s.

The provision of local government is a rather more complicated picture. The parish was most likely the earliest form of local administration, existing from medieval times, supporting a church and a priest, within a diocese run by a bishop, who ultimately took his authority from Rome. Post-Reformation, the Church hierarchy was replaced by a presbytery, but the function of parishes otherwise continued. As early as 1617, attempts were made to regularise boundaries and ensure consistent coverage, yet even in 1871 there was at least one area of Scotland which fell outside the parish system. In the 19th century the differing needs of church and state brought the advent of civil parishes (*quoad civilia*), which were an integral part of local government until 1975 and are still used as units of registration for births, deaths and marriages. These are now distinguished from ecclesiastical parishes (*quoad sacra*) which persist, although they differ from one denomination to another and are subject to regular mergers as congregations decline and churches close. In addition, there are also agricultural parishes which are used as the basis for agricultural-production statistics.

Counties have also existed since medieval times, initially for judicial purposes (the sheriffdom) but the Local Government Act (Scotland) of 1889 created county councils and also reorganised parishes such that they all lay within defined county boundaries without the detached portions which had previously existed. The only

The Relationship between post-1995 Council Areas and pre-1974 Counties

Council Area	*Old County*
Aberdeen City	Aberdeenshire, Kincardineshire
Aberdeenshire	Aberdeenshire, Moray (Elginshire), Angus (Forfarshire), Banffshire, Kincardineshire, Morayshire
Angus	Angus (Forfarshire)
Argyll & Bute	Argyllshire, Bute, Dumbartonshire
City of Edinburgh	West Lothian (Linlithgowshire), East Lothian (Haddingtonshire), Midlothian (Edinburghshire)
Clackmannanshire	Clackmannanshire, Perthshire
Dumfries & Galloway	Ayrshire, Dumfriesshire, Kirkcudbrightshire, Wigtownshire, Selkirkshire, Roxburghshire
Dundee City	Angus (Forfarshire), Perthshire
East Ayrshire	Ayrshire
East Dunbartonshire	Dumbartonshire, Lanarkshire, Stirlingshire
East Lothian	East Lothian (Haddingtonshire), Berwickshire, Midlothian (Edinburghshire)
East Renfrewshire	Ayrshire, Lanarkshire, Renfrewshire
Falkirk	Stirlingshire, West Lothian (Linlithgowshire)
Fife	Fife, Kinross-shire, Clackmannanshire, Perthshire
Glasgow City	Dumbartonshire, Renfrewshire, Lanarkshire
Highland	Argyllshire, Caithness, Nairn, Moray (Elginshire), Inverness-shire, Ross & Cromarty, Sutherland
Inverclyde	Renfrewshire
Midlothian	Midlothian (Edinburghshire), Peebles-shire
Moray	Banffshire, Moray (Elginshire)
North Ayrshire	Ayrshire, Bute
North Lanarkshire	Dumbartonshire, Lanarkshire, Stirlingshire, West Lothian (Linlithgowshire)
Orkney	Orkney
Perth & Kinross	Clackmannanshire, Kinross-shire, Perthshire, Dumbartonshire, Fife, Angus (Forfarshire)
Renfrewshire	Lanarkshire, Renfrewshire
Scottish Borders	Berwickshire, Dumfriesshire, Midlothian (Edinburghshire), Peebles-shire, Roxburghshire, Selkirkshire, Lanarkshire
Shetland	Shetland
South Ayrshire	Ayrshire, Wigtownshire, Kirkcudbrightshire
South Lanarkshire	Lanarkshire, Peebles-shire West Lothian (Linlithgowshire),
Stirling	Dumbartonshire, Stirlingshire, Perthshire
W. Dunbartonshire	Dumbartonshire
West Lothian	Lanarkshire, West Lothian (Linlithgowshire) Midlothian (Edinburghshire)
Western Isles	Ross & Cromarty, Inverness-shire

exception was in Ross and Cromarty which were so intertwined that the two older counties were joined as one. At this time, municipal government was confirmed in the form of burghs and police burghs. Burghs had also existed from medieval times, often with sweeping powers based on trading privileges.

In the 1920s some names changed: Forfarshire became Angus; Linlithgowshire became West Lothian; Edinburghshire became Midlothian; and so on. The creation of counties of cities separated the cities from their hinterlands, resulting in, for example, Edinburgh's no longer being in Midlothian, though it has long been regarded as the 'Heart of Midlothian'. Further reform came in 1929, with the abolition of the parish council and increased powers for the so-called large burghs. The universities remained completely outside the system of local government, having their own constitutions and, remarkably, returning their own members of parliament until 1950. Counties and burghs were abolished in 1975, when a two-tier system of regions and districts was introduced (along with three unitary island authorities). These divisions lasted only twenty years, until replaced once again in 1996 by 32 unitary council areas, which is what remains today. Confusingly, counties are still used by the Post Office for the delivery of letters, for biological recording (called vice counties) and for land registration, each having differing boundaries!

The administrative landscape of Scotland, much simplified in the above explanation, is one of moving boundaries, changing names and juggling responsibilities, in a manner unimaginable in many other countries of the world.

The Urban Landscape

While a handful of small urban centres certainly functioned in Scotland during the first millennium AD it was not until the introduction of feudal institutions in

The Relationship between Regions and District Councils (1974–95) and post-1995 Council Areas

Region	*Admin centre*	*Area (sq. km)*	*District councils*	*Post 1995*
Borders Region	Newton St Boswells	4,662	Berwickshire, Roxburgh, Ettrick & Lauderdale, Tweeddale	Borders council area retained
Central Region	Stirling	2,590	Clackmannan, Falkirk, Stirling	Clackmannan, Falkirk & Stirling exist as separate council areas
Dumfries & Galloway Region	Dumfries	6,475	Annandale & Eskdale, Nithsdale, Stewartry, Wigtown	Dumfries & Galloway council area retained
Fife Region	Glenrothes	1,308	Dunfermline, Kirkcaldy, North-East Fife	Fife council area retained
Grampian Region	Aberdeen	8,550	Aberdeen, Banff & Buchan, Gordon, Kincardine & Deeside, Moray	Divided between Aberdeen City, Aberdeenshire and Moray council areas
Highland Region	Inverness	26,136	Badenoch & Strathspey, Caithness, Inverness, Lochaber, Nairn, Ross & Cromarty, Skye & Lochalsh, Sutherland	Highland council area retained
Lothian Region	Edinburgh	1,756	East Lothian, Edinburgh, Midlothian, West Lothian	East Lothian, City of Edinburgh, Midlothian and West Lothian exist as separate council areas
Strathclyde Region	Glasgow	13,856	Argyll & Bute, Bearsden & Milngavie, Clydebank, Clydesdale, Cumbernauld & Kilsyth, Cumnock & Doone Valley, Cunninghame, Dumbarton, East Kilbride, Eastwood, Glasgow, Hamilton, Inverclyde, Kilmarnock & Loudoun, Kyle & Carrick, Monklands, Motherwell, Renfrew, Strathkelvin	New council areas established for Argyll & Bute, East Ayrshire, North Ayrshire, South Ayrshire, Renfrewshire, East Renfrewshire, North Lanarkshire, South Lanarkshire, East Dunbartonshire, West Dunbartonshire, Inverclyde, Glasgow City
Tayside Region	Dundee	7,668	Angus, Dundee, Perth & Kinross	Angus, Dundee City and Perth & Kinross exist as separate council areas
Island Authorities				
Orkney Islands Council	Kirkwall	974		Council area retained
Shetland Islands Council	Lerwick	1,427		Council area retained
Western Isles Council	Stornoway	2,901		Council area retained

the early 12th century that there is evidence of the creation of towns, many of which survive to the present day. The church, the castle and the burgh town were all interlinked in an ambitious scheme of national development undertaken by King David I and his successors. Royal castles and associated royal burgh towns were the basis of the king's feudal power, religious orders were granted sites for their abbeys and allowed to establish ecclesiastical burghs and the king's vassals or barons were granted land and given the opportunity to develop burghs of barony. The burghs, which were given special trading privileges, fostered economic development through the stimulation of trade and industry, providing the king with a revenue from taxes and rent. The distribution of these burgh towns correlates strongly with geographical factors favouring communication and defence. Where these features were backed by a rich agricultural hinterland the result was a burgh that prospered. Stirling, with its prominent castle, developed at a strategic crossing point on the River Forth, Dundee was founded near the mouth of an estuary by William the Lion in 1180 and Dumfries developed as a river port on an important routeway from south to north in the western border between Scotland and England.

By the year 1200 there were 38 burgh towns in Scotland, most situated in the east where agricultural produce was exported to the Low Countries and Flanders. During the next 200 years the pace of urban development slackened with the creation of just 32 burghs. As the medieval burgh town prospered and expanded, there rose to power a merchant oligarchy known as burgesses whose landholdings or burgage plots formed an essential element of the medieval townscape still seen today in towns like St Andrews. The period from 1400 to the Union of the Parliaments in 1707 witnessed a rapid growth in the number of burghs of barony created for the benefit of landowners rather than merchant burgesses. With their limited privileges, these towns served as local market centres or way stations on principal routeways. During this late medieval period burgh town development intensified and new urban forms were created through the infilling of burgage plots behind the street frontage, the building of higher tenement houses or the occupation of the wide market place with permanent buildings. Of particular significance was the release of large quantities of land in and around ecclesiastical burghs after the Reformation in the 1560s. By the beginning of the 18th century the urban settlement forms in Scotland included not only burgh towns but also rural fermtouns, kirktons and castletons of varying size mostly created by medieval burghal laws that promoted exclusive marketing monopolies.

During the 18th century the Improving movement began to transform the rural landscape, introducing both regularly enclosed farms and new settlements that were not dependent on royal grants. Some of these settlements were linked to rural activities, providing a home and place of employment for estate workers, while others were designed to promote fishing or textile manufacturing industries. Between 1735 and 1850 about 150 new planned villages were created, their regular layout contrasting with the unordered forms of older pre-Improvement settlements. The earliest planned villages originated in the replanning of existing settlements, mostly in the east, but after 1770 the distribution of villages changed dramatically as new settlements were founded throughout the country. After 1850, the conditions which had made planned villages a profitable form of landed investment were steadily eroded as industrialisation in

Top 50 Towns & Cities by Population (2001 & 1991)

Town/City	*2001 Census*	*1991 Census*	*Town/City*	*2001 Census*	*1991 Census*
Glasgow	629,501	658,379	Wishaw	28,565	29,574
Edinburgh	430,082	400,632	Bearsden	27,967	27,707
Aberdeen	184,788	182,133	Bishopbriggs	23,118	23,825
Dundee	154,674	157,808	Arbroath	22,785	23,680
Paisley	74,170	73,925	Newton Mearns	22,637	19,342
East Kilbride	73,796	70,579	Musselburgh	22,112	20,261
Livingston	50826	42,178	Elgin	20,829	19,338
Cumbernauld	49,664	49,507	Bellshill	20,705	21,624
Hamilton	48,546	49,988	Dumbarton	20,527	21,797
Kirkcaldy	46,912	47,274	Kirkintilloch	20,281	20,624
Ayr	46,431	47,962	Renfrew	20,251	20,764
Greenock	45,467	49,267	Polmont	19,563	17,866
Kilmarnock	43,588	43,207	Clarkston	19,136	18,899
Perth	43,450	41,724	Alloa	18,989	18,842
Coatbridge	41,170	43,467	Peterhead	17,947	18,413
Inverness	40,949	40,918	Grangemouth	17,771	18,528
Dunfermline	39,229	39,068	Blantyre	17,328	18,584
Glenrothes	38,679	38,320	Barrhead	17,244	16,753
Airdrie	36,326	36,842	Port Glasgow	16,617	19,426
Irvine	33,090	33,406	Johnstone	16,468	18,280
Stirling	32,673	29,768	Buckhaven	16,391	16,918
Falkirk	32,379	31,399	Stenhousemuir	16,311	16,711
Dumfries	31,146	31,936	Giffnock	16,178	16,190
Motherwell	30,311	30,769	Kilwinning	15,908	15,317
Clydebank	29,858	29,171	Viewpark	15,841	15,044

the larger towns of central Scotland and better transport undermined local markets. In 1755 there were four towns in Scotland with over 10,000 inhabitants comprising some 9% of the total population. In 1821 these figures had increased to 13 towns and 25% of the population. At this time seven out of ten Scots could still be regarded as rural dwellers, but by 1851 32.2% of the country's population lived in towns of 10,000 or more and by 1891 the proportion was nearly 50%. In the space of a century Scotland had changed from an essentially rural society to a predominantly industrial society with a constant stream of migration from the countryside to urban centres.

Associated with the coalfields of West Fife, Clackmannan, the Lothians, Ayrshire and Lanarkshire, it was largely the Central Lowlands that saw the full impact of the industrial revolution. Canals were dug from the end of the 18th century and the railway network spread from the middle of the 19th century.

Factories and densely packed tenement housing dominated the urban landscapes of Glasgow, Edinburgh, Dundee and Aberdeen until 1914. A challenge to planners since then has been the legacy of dereliction, social deprivation and visual squalor. Since 1945 the urban scene has been transformed by land reclamation, urban-regeneration schemes and the creation of 'New Towns' such as Cumbernauld, East Kilbride, Irvine and Glenrothes as well as the expansion of nearly every large and small burgh in Scotland.

In more recent times, unlike the rest of the United Kingdom, the population of Scotland has fallen. Low birth and death rates have combined with outward migration to create an ageing population. In addition to this, while Edinburgh in the wake of devolution continues to enjoy a modest growth rate, there has been a general redistribution of population from the older industrial cities to the small burgh towns and villages situated within commuting distance of centres of employment. Between 1991 and 2001, for example, the population of Glasgow dropped from 658,379 to 629,501, representing a 4.4% decline in a continuing process that began over half a century ago. The stagnant state of Scotland's population since the early 1980s contrasts markedly with the rapid pace of population growth in the 19th century when Scotland's population expanded from 1.6 million in 1801 to 3.2 million in 1861. While the landscape of Scotland remains largely rural in aspect, the population of Scotland today, concentrated as it is in the Central Lowlands, is essentially an urban one.

A Modernising Landscape

The Scottish landscape continues to develop. The pressure on housing and a desire for the rural idyll has seen significant expansion of hamlets and villages which lie in the growing hinterland of the cities. While industrial areas such as the docklands of Glasgow and Edinburgh, and the huge brown-field site which was the Ravenscraig Steelworks, have been re-used for housing, pressure on the green-belt and rural development remain controversial. Equally controversial is the quest to meet an insatiable requirement for energy. The North Sea oil industry, not even 40 years old, could already be in decline. Yet its mark on the landscape is profound: immense facilities such as Grangemouth and Mossmorran, together with a network of oil and gas pipelines which criss-cross the country, thankfully buried from view. Deep mining for coal, once a mainstay of the Scottish economy which employed 150,000 men, has withered from the 1960s and ceased completely with the closure of Longannet Colliery in 2002. However, as deep mining declined, so open-cast mining has boomed, with a considerable impact on the landscape. While landscape restoration is mandatory, significant areas of Fife, Lanarkshire, Ayrshire and the Lothians are being changed forever, although in some cases this is but a further reworking of an already post-industrial landscape. The changing economics of electricity generation and the push towards environmentally-friendly energy has seen older coal-fired power stations like Kincardine being demolished, nuclear stations such as Hunterston 'A', Chapelcross and Dounreay being decommissioned and wind farms such as Dun Law and Black Law, being developed. Yet controversy also surrounds both the number and location of these new power stations, with commercial interests and environmental prerogatives vying with local communities, who in some cases enthusiastically welcome these developments, while others are vehemently opposed. It is perhaps interesting to reflect on the impact on the landscape of wind farms compared to the grand hydro-power schemes constructed between the 1920s and the 1960s and the visual impact of the network of electricity pylons which form the national power grid.

By the time of the re-establishment of the Scottish Parliament in 1999, land ownership and accessibility had become a key debate. An essentially feudal system of ownership was ended by the Land Reform (Scotland) Act of 2003, which also established a public right of access and a community right to buy the land on which they live. Public access has opened areas of the Scottish landscape for the first time, while community ownership has the potential for better management and sustainable exploitation of areas which, in some cases, have been allowed to decline for decades. While the value of sporting estates has, to some extent, ensured that heather moorland is managed for grouse, woodland for pheasant and the rivers for salmon and lochs for trout, land reform could have as significant an effect on the Scottish landscape as was brought about by the plantation forests established by the Forestry Commission from the 1920s. Through the National Parks Act (2000), the Scottish Parliament has also brought a greater degree of protection to the landscape by establishing the first national parks in Scotland, with Loch Lomond and the Trossachs being designated in 2002 and the Cairngorms the following year.

Despite this focus on the countryside, traditional farming is in decline, with many crops and animal production proving increasingly uneconomic due to the accumulated disasters of BSE and foot-and-mouth disease, taken alongside decreasing agricultural subsidies. Inactivity in the form of European Union-supported set-aside is becoming an increasing trend in the countryside, with notable examples of diversification into tourism or more unusual produce (eg. llamas, deer or ostrich farming, or the production of hemp, cheese or ice-cream), together with direct contact with an increasingly discerning public through farmer's markets. Set-aside has been shown to have remarkable benefits in terms of biodiversity, and is one of a host of measures targeted at improving the environment. Significant progress in solving the environmental problems left by past industries has been made over the last 30 years through regulation, cultural change and the pro-active involvement of environmental organisations and community groups. Tackling pollution in rivers and estuaries in the more populated parts of the country has seen marked improvement in water quality and the return of fish to rivers where they have been absent for decades. Eutrophication of lochs, due to over-use of fertilisers in the countryside and point-source discharges of effluent from settlements, has also been addressed – a notable example being the much-studied Loch Leven National Nature Reserve.

Charities such as the John Muir Trust and the Royal Society for the Protection of Birds have become significant land-owners, encouraged by their members to take direct action in the protection of wilderness areas through ownership and management. The National Trust for Scotland (NTS) also has substantial land holdings, including ownership of several important landscape features such as Ben Lomond, Ben Lawers, Kintail, Torridon, Mar Lodge, the Grey Mare's Tail, the Corrieshalloch Gorge, St. Abb's Head and the islands of Iona, Staffa, Fair Isle and St Kilda. In terms of the built environment, the NTS is responsible for a diverse portfolio of country seats, former industrial buildings, cottages, town houses, palaces and gardens, while Historic Scotland, a government agency, manage a range of archaeological sites, ruined castles and abbeys on behalf of the public. The designation of listed buildings and conservation areas and the availability of grants for building maintenance and restoration also serves to protect the built environment and prevent the degradation of our architectural heritage. In the past, many fine buildings, such as Hamilton Palace in Lanarkshire and Panmure House in Angus, were lost in the name of progress or because their upkeep was too costly. Today, protection and support through grant aid has brought about the restoration of ruined castles and towers for renewed habitation.

Thus, despite its being steeped in history and tradition, the Scottish landscape continues to evolve.

Glossary

A-listed building *(category A-listed building)* The highest category of preservation afforded to buildings of national or international importance, through their architectural or historic interest or being a little-altered example of a particular period, style or building type. The listing is carried out by Historic Scotland on behalf of the Scottish Executive.

abhainn *(aibhne, amhuinn, aimhne)* A river (Gaelic).

achadh *(achaidh, ach, auch)* A field (Gaelic).

agricultural parish The agricultural parish is a statistical unit in the United Kingdom used as the basis for collecting data on farms, livestock, crops and yields.

ailean *(ailein, ailean)* A green spot, meadow or enclosure (Gaelic).

aisle A term often used to describe a burial place or an enclosed and covered burial place adjoining a church.

ald *(alt, ault, auld)* A burn or stream (Gaelic).

aonach *(aonaich)* A moor or market-place (Gaelic).

ard *(aird)* A height or promontory (Gaelic).

ashlar A finely dressed stone block with a smooth surface and squared edges, often used on the facade of buildings.

auchtenpart An ancient measure of land often used in the Highlands to describe the eighth part of a davoch (see davoch).

auchter *(uachdar, uachdair)* Top, upper part (Gaelic), as in Auchtermuchty.

bac *(bhaic, bacaichean)* A bank, peat bank (Gaelic).

bad *(bhaid)* A tuft or a place (Gaelic).

bagh *(bhaig)* A bay (Gaelic).

baile *(bhaile)* A town, a hamlet or homestead (Gaelic).

ban *(bhan, bhain, baine, bana)* Fair, white (Gaelic).

bard *(baird)* An enclosed meadow, though it also means poet (Gaelic).

barony A large manor or estate created in the Middle Ages within which the baron held his own court.

barrow An earthen mound covering a burial chamber.

bartizan A parapet or battlement of a castle or fortress.

basalt A fine-grained igneous rock derived from volcanic lava that can spread rapidly to form extensive sheets or sills. It can also crack when cooling into hexagonal columns as at Fingal's Cave on the island of Staffa.

beag *(bheag, bhig, bige, beaga)* Little (Gaelic).

bealach *(bhealaich)* A pass between hills (Gaelic).

beinn *(bheinn, beinne)* Mountain or ben (Gaelic).

bigging A word of Norse origin that usually refers to a building or farmsteading.

bing A waste-heap lying beside a mine. Although often landscaped or removed, the Oil Shale Bings of West Lothian are particularly prominent landscape features, some of which are protected as Scheduled Ancient Monuments.

binnean *(binnin)* Small and peaked mountain (Gaelic).

black house A long house comprising a byre and dwellinghouse, typical of houses built in the Highlands and Islands of Scotland.

blar *(blair)* Cleared space, plain (Gaelic).

bleachfields A place for bleaching cloth, a process designed to whiten textile fabrics.

bothy A cottage for farm workers.

brae A Scots word for a slope or hillside.

braiding The process whereby a river is continually forced to divide into several channels with islands separating them. The banks of these water-courses tend to be unstable, and consequently the channel is very wide in relation to its depth.

breac *(bhreac, bhric, brice, breaca)* Speckled (Gaelic).

broch A prehistoric building in the shape of a circular tower. Also a term used in the north east to describe a burgh or town.

Bronze Age A period of human settlement in the British Isles dating from 1900 BC to 500 BC. Hill forts, hut circles, burial mounds, ritual monuments and ancient field patterns are landscape features from this period which was characterized by the use of bronze, an alloy of copper and tin, to manufacture implements.

buidhe *(bhuidhe)* Yellow (Gaelic).

burgess plot A strip of land in a medieval town owned by a merchant or burgess. The plot would include the site of a house as well as room for a market stall and a small amount of enclosed land for grazing a cow or growing vegetables.

burgh *(Pron. Bur-uh)* An urban settlement in Scotland, the burgh, from medieval times, possessed a charter granting trading privileges and the right to regulate its own affairs. A Royal Burgh, which was either created by the crown or upgraded from another status, such as a burgh of barony, had exclusive trading privileges and was represented in the Scottish Parliament. By 1707 there were 70 royal burghs , most of these being sea-ports. Burghs of barony were granted by the crown to secular landowners for the purpose of creating market centres. Over 300 burghs of barony were created between 1450 and 1707. A burgh of regality, enjoying wide powers in criminal and civil law, was granted to a leading Scottish noble with a large estate, the main function being to maintain law and order on behalf of the crown. In 1832–33 royal burghs and many burghs of barony were designated as parliamentary burghs with elected town councils. In the 19th and 20th centuries police burghs were created in towns which used local or national acts of parliament to adopt an elected town council. In 1930 burghs were divided into large and small burghs and counties of cities and in 1974 burghs were abolished and replaced by district councils which were later replaced by the current local government authorities in 1996.

but and ben An agricultural building that usually comprises two rooms that provide living quarters for people and livestock.

butt An irregular parcel of land often abutting adjacent parcels at right angles.

byre A cow-shed or farm building for keeping cattle.

cairn *(carn)* A heap of stones, forming a marker or memorial, or a rocky place (Gaelic).

cala *(caladh)* Harbour (Gaelic).

Caledonian Forest The name given to the native pinewood forest that developed in the Highlands of Scotland after the end of the last Ice Age. Only fragments of this forest remain, the largest remnants being found at Rannoch, Mar, Strathspey, Cannich and Feshie.

Caledonian orogeny A period of mountain-building in northwest Europe between c.430 and 360 million years ago.

camas *(chamais)* A channel, a bay or a bend (Gaelic).

Cambrian The earliest period of the Palaeozoic era stretching from c.570 to 500 million years ago.

caol *(caolas, chaolais)* A narrow, strait, firth or kyle (Gaelic).

Carboniferous A period of the Palaeozoic era extending from c.345 to 280 million years ago. In addition to mountain building, sediments of sandstone, limestone and coal were formed at this time.

carse Flat fertile land adjacent to a river is often referred to as carse land, as in the Carse of Gowrie adjacent to the Tay.

castleton A fermetoun settlement associated with a castle.

cattle tryst A meeting place for cattle drovers or a market place.

ceann A promontory or head (Gaelic) (in English, ken or kin).

ceapoch A tillage plot (Gaelic) (in English, keppoch).

chancel The space around the altar of a church for the clergy and sometimes the choir, often enclosed by a screen or railing. It is at the eastern end of a church.

choir The eastern end of a cruciform church; that part of a church where services are sung.

cill *(cille, ceall)* A church or burying-place (Gaelic).

cirque *see* corrie.

civil parish *(quoad civilia parish)* Between 1845 and 1860 civil *(quoad civilia)* parishes were established with elected parochial boards, these parishes continuing as units of local government until 1975. Civil parishes remain a statistical unit used for the recording of births, deaths and marriages

clach *(cloiche)* Stone (Gaelic).

clachan A Highland word used to describe a settlement with a church.

cleit *(chleit)* Rocky prominence (Gaelic).

close An open or covered passage or courtyard extending off a main thoroughfare which gives access to a number of residences or other buildings.

cluain *(cluaine)* A green plain or pasture (Gaelic).

cnap *(chnaip)* A hillock (Gaelic).

cnoc *(chunie, cnocan)* A round hill (Gaelic).

coinneach *(choinnich)* Moss (Gaelic).

coir *(coire, choire)* Round hollow in mountainside, a corrie or cirque (Gaelic).

col A depression or pass in a mountainous area (Gaelic).

collegiate church church of medieval times founded to support a community of priests, often to sing mass or pray for the soul of the founder. They may also have been founded in connection with the pre-Reformation universities, for example at Aberdeen or St Andrews.

commendator The individual (usually a Bishop) who was entrusted with the property and money of an abbey. After the Reformation, the commendators were lay individuals or former abbots who inherited the wealth of the abbey when it was dissolved.

commonty The name for common lands in Scotland owned by one or more proprietors with communal rights, e.g. peat cutting or grazing, shared with others. During the 18th and 19th centuries most commonties were divided by agreement or at the instance of any one party under the Division of Commonty Act 1695.

conglomerate A rock composed of rounded fragments of stone in a cement of hardened clay or sand. Conglomerates were often formed at the mouths of rivers.

conservation areas Areas of special architectural or historic interest, the character or appearance of which is desirable to preserve or enhance. In Scotland, these areas are designated by local authorities under the Planning (Listed Buildings and Conservation Areas) (Scotland) Act 1997.

consumption dyke A drystone dyke enclosure erected where an excess of stones derived from glacial deposits covers the land. They are most commonly found in Aberdeenshire.

coppice A type of deciduous woodland of small trees or bushes which were regularly trimmed back to stumps (or stools) from which fresh shoots regenerate. Coppice woodland was cut over either periodically or under a strict rotation to provide wood for fuel or industrial use as in the tanning and charcoal industries. Former coppice woodland can be seen around Loch Lomond.

Corbett A mountain peak with a summit lying between 2500 and 3000 feet (762 m and 914.4 m) and with an ascent of at least 500 feet (152.4 m) on all sides. The list of 220 peaks was compiled by John Rooke Corbett, a district valuer based in Bristol and keen member of the Scottish Mountaineering Club, who completed the Munros and Tops in 1930.

corrie Also known as a cirque or cwm, a corrie takes the form of a semi-circular bowl-shaped hollow at the head of a valley that was, during the Ice Age, a collecting ground for ice.

cottown A settlement, often set apart from a township, occupied by cottars who were landless people allowed to settle on the common land and cultivate a small area of land in return for their labour.

Council Area The local authority divisions currently used in Scotland. In 1996, a unitary system of Council Areas replaced the two-tier Regions and Districts in accordance with the Local Government (Scotland) Act 1994. There are 32 Council Areas, including the three island authorities of the Western Isles, Orkney and Shetland.

County A local government sub-division which existed in various forms in Scotland until 1974. Over the years a large number of changes were made to the counties. Particularly major changes took place in 1889, when the 'old counties' were replaced involving some changes of name together with significant boundary changes. There were 33 counties. Their geographical extent was not always logical, with the We stern Isles being split between the mainland counties of Inverness-shire and Ross and Cromarty.

covenanter A supporter of the National Covenant of 1638, which demanded the restoration of the Presbyterian system for church governance over the Episcopalian system being promoted by King Charles I. Armed conflict broke out in 1639 and continued on-and-off until 1688.

crag and tail A glacial landform created when a glacier overrides hard rock (the crag) which protects softer rocks in its lee to form a gently sloping ridge (the tail).

craig A rock (Gaelic).

crannog A prehistoric lake dwelling.

croach *(crocaich)* Branched (Gaelic).

croft A small-holding held by a sub-tenant in a township. The crofter derives income from employment in addition to farming a few acres of land. The crofting community today is found mostly in the Highlands and Islands of Scotland. The Crofting Acts of 1886 and after established the rights of crofters in the crofting counties of Inverness, Argyll, Ross and Cromarty, Caithness, Sutherland, Orkney and Shetland.

croich *(criche)* A boundary.

cross-slab A type of Pictish symbol stone which takes the form of a shaped stone slab which is carved in relief with a cross and sometimes other symbols. Cross-slabs largely date from AD c.800–1000.

Crown Charter A charter of land or privileges granted by the monarch.

crowstep Also known as corbiestep, the crowstep is a form of building gable with rectangular, stepped stones that take the place of a sloping cope or skew.

cru (cro) A small enclosure, usually in Shetland.

cruach *(chruach, chruaich)* A heap or stack (Gaelic).

cruachan A haunch (Gaelic).

cuil A nook or recess (Gaelic).

cuith *(cuithe)* A pit or narrow glen (Gaelic).

cul *(chiul, chuile)* Back or hill-back (Gaelic).

culdee One of a brotherhood of monks living in small cells in Scotland from the 8th century. Their name is a latinised form of the Old Irish word for a servant or companion of God.

cup and ring marked stones Natural rocks on which small hollows have been pecked out in prehistoric times. In some cases the hollows are surrounded by single or multiple rings.

Dalradian The name given to metamorphosed rocks, mostly schists, lying to the north of the Highland Boundary Fault and named after the ancient Scots kingdom of Dalriada. Precambrian and younger, the Dalradian schists overlay the older Moine schists in the southern and eastern Highlands. Dalradian rocks provide evidence of some of the earliest life-forms in Scotland as well as glacial activity when Scotland was positioned close to the South Pole.

damh *(daimh)* An ox or stag (Gaelic).

davoch An ancient measure of land often used in the Highlands and reflecting an agricultural unit, often the arable area of a township. In the 18th century the davoch equalled 96 Scots acres.

dearg *(dheirg)* Red (Gaelic).

deer forest A wild tract of land frequented by deer, but not necessarily woodland or forest.

derry *(dhoire, doire)* A grove or hollow (Gaelic).

dip slope A dip slope occurs where the slope of land mirrors the slope of underlying rock strata.

Disruption, the A period of conflict in the Church of Scotland over patronage, or the appointment of ministers by landowners, culminated in the Disruption of 1843 when 451 ministers out of a total of 1200 left their manses and their livings to establish the Free Church under the leadership of Thomas Chalmers.

District A second-order local authority sub-division used in Scotland between 1974 and 1995. There were nine regional authorities, divided into 53 districts, plus three unitary island authorities.

doire *see* derry.

dolerite A type of coarse-grained basic igneous rock like basalt.

Donald A hill in the Scottish Lowlands with a height above 2000 feet (609.6 m). The highest of the 86 hills and 133 tops listed by Percy Donald is Merrick which rises to 2765 feet (843 m) in Glentrool Forest Park, Dumfries and Galloway.

donjon *see* keep.

Doric A Greek architectural style characterised by its simplicity and massive strength.

dormer window A window which projects vertically from a roof and lights an attic room contained within the roof.

dovecote Also known as doocot, the dovecote is a pigeon house or loft either in a separate building or incorporated in the roof gable of a building.

drove road A route used by cattle drovers driving cattle from the Highlands and Islands to the markets or trysts of southern Scotland and England.

drum *(droma, druim)* A ridge, the back (Gaelic).

drumlin An elongated mound of boulder clay deposited in an area of low relief following glaciation. Drumlins can be up to a mile (1–2 km) in length and 60 m (200 feet) in height. Its long axis lies parallel to the line of ice flow.

drystane dyke A stone wall built without mortar. Unfashioned stones are used to construct such walls.

duba *(dub)* A Scots word describing a pool of foul water (Gaelic).

dubh *(dhubh, dhuibhe, dubha)* Black (Gaelic).

dun *(duin, dhuin)* A fortress, castle or a mound (Gaelic).

dyke A term used in Scotland to describe a stone wall. A drystane dyke is a wall without mortar.

each *(eich)* Horse (Gaelic).

eas *(easa, easan)* Waterfall or rough ravine (Gaelic).

ecclesiastical parish *(quoad sacra parish)* Ecclesiastical *(quoad sacra)* parishes were areas of land whose inhabitants were obliged to pay a proportion of their produce or income to the Church

eilean *(eilein, eileanan)* Island or islands (Gaelic).

Enlightenment, the A period during the late 18th century when a belief in reason and human progress prompted the arts and sciences to flourish in Scotland.

enterprise zone Designed to encourage private enterprise, enterprise zones are areas designated for industrial or other economic development.

Episcopalian A system of governance in the Protestant church, prevalent in the Church of England, which is based on hierarchical management by archbishops and bishops, under the authority of the monarch. King Charles I unsuccessfully tried to impose this system on Scotland in the early 17th C. Contrasts with the Presbyterian system.

escarpment A continuous line of steep slopes at the edge of a plateau. A steep slope is also known as a scarp slope.

esker A sinuous ridge comprising material deposited by water that is derived from melted ice and flows in a channel either under or through an ice sheet.

estuary A semi-enclosed body of water which has a free connection with the open sea and within which the seawater is measurably diluted by freshwater from the surrounding land.

fad *(fhad, fhada, fada)* Long, a long mountain (Gaelic).

faire Watching (Gaelic).

faoghail *(faodhail)* A ford in a sea channel (Gaelic).

fas Growth or vegetation (Gaelic).

fauld (fold) A small area of the medieval outfield periodically enclosed and cultivated.

fault A geological fault arises from the fracturing of the Earth's surface. This causes rocks to be displaced vertically, horizontally or at some intermediate angle.

faur Cold (Gaelic).

fear *(fhir, fir)* A man (Gaelic).

fearn *(fhearna)* Alder tree (Gaelic).

fell *(fjall, fjell)* A rough hill, as in Goatfell (Scandinavian).

fermetoun A fermetoun, or farm town, is the name given to a typical Scottish nucleated settlement whose function was originally associated with agriculture, usually with joint tenancies. Each family has a house, kail-yard (vegetable patch), barn or byre, communally managed arable land and hill pasture. Compare this type of settlement with the planned village of the18th and 19th centuries.

feu Land held in perpetuity in payment of a yearly sum. The feuar is the one who takes land in feu. In the 16th–18th centuries many tenancies were converted to feu holdings. Tenants can now buy out the feu and become freeholders.

firth A Scots word for an estuary, that is a wide tidal channel at the mouth of a river, formed as a flooded river valley. For example, the Firth of Forth.

forfeited estates Estates of Jacobite landowners were sequestered by the Crown after the collapse of the Jacobite Rising in the spring of 1746. Most of the estates were later sold by public auction, but thirteen estates in or near the

Highlands were annexed by the Crown and managed directly by Commissioners for the purpose of promoting improved agriculture, industry and the erection of planned villages.

fortalice A small fortress or fortified building.

fosse A ditch or moat.

fraoch Heather (Gaelic).

freestone A type of stone without pronounced laminations.

fuaran *(fhuarain)* A well or spring (Gaelic).

gabbro A dark granular igneous rock of crystalline texture. Good examples can be found on the island of Skye.

gait A main street, usually with a prefix describing its use, direction or destination, for example Marketgait.

garbh *(gharbh, ghairbh, garba)* Rough (Gaelic).

garth A small enclosure.

geal *(gheal, ghil, gile, geala)* White (Gaelic).

geo An inlet in a coastal cliff face created by wave erosion.

girnal A granary.

glacial erratic A rock which has been transported by a glacier or ice sheet and deposited in an area of different geology to that of its source. During the last Ice Age rocks from Ailsa Craig in the Firth of Clyde were moved as far south as Lancashire in England.

glais A stream.

glas *(ghlas, ghlais, glaise, glasa)* Grey or green (Gaelic).

gleann *(ghlinne)* A narrow valley, dale or glen (Gaelic).

glebe A small area of arable land attached or near to a parish minister's manse (house) formerly given to him as a supplement to his stipend.

glen *(gleann, ghlinne)* A narrow valley (Gaelic).

gneiss A hard and ancient metamorphic rock found in many areas of the Highlands and Islands. The Lewisian gneiss of the Northwest Highlands and Western Isles are amongst the oldest rocks to be found in Scotland.

gorm *(ghorm, ghuirme, guirme)* Blue (Gaelic).

Graham A mountain peak with a height between 2000 and 2499 feet (610m and 761m) with a drop of at least 150 metres (493 ft) on all sides.

grange An ecclesiastical manor, created from wasteland and set at some distance from the parent monastery and typical of the farming system developed by the Cistercian Order in the 11th–13th centuries.

granite A hard igneous rock of crystalline texture often used in building as in Aberdeen, the 'Granite City'.

greywacke A grey, gritty hard sandstone.

haaf A Shetland term for the deep sea.

hagi (hoga) A Shetland term for hill pasture.

harl Also known as roughcast, harl is a protective facing applied to the outside of a stone wall. It comprises two or three applications of lime, or lime and cement, mixed with sand and small aggregate, the final coat being cast or thrown on.

haugh land A Scots word for low level land beside a stream or river that is flooded from time to time.

head dyke a turf or stone wall separating the infield and outfield of a township or farm from the grazings on the open hill.

henge A neolithic earthwork monument comprising a ditch with an embankment, sometimes enclosing circles of stone or timber uprights.

Highland Clearances The general term given to the removal of tenants and the destruction of townships in the Highlands and Islands by landowners and their agents during the 18th and 19th centuries to make room for sheep.

Historic Scotland A government agency charged with the protection of Scotland's built heritage, in the form of buildings and ancient monuments. Historic Scotland is also responsible for a programme of archaeology to protect ancient sites and landscapes. Historic Scotland work closely with the Royal Commission on the Ancient and Historical Monuments of Scotland, which is charged with the recording and interpretation of heritage sites.

howe (Scots) A hollow, valley or low-lying flat tract of land, as in the Howe of Fife.

howff (hauff) A place of resort, an inn or tavern.

hypocaust The underfloor heating system of Roman buildings, especially evident in their bath houses.

ice-house An underground store built to contain winter ice and/or snow which can be used to preserve food in the warm months of the summer.

igneous rock A type of rock, such as granite, which originated as molten magma beneath the earth's surface. An igneous intrusion occurs when magma forces its way through pre-existing rocks and then solidifies below the surface of the ground. Extrusive igneous rocks are formed when magma erupts onto the earth's surface as lava.

inbhir *(inbhire)* (Gaelic) A meeting of rivers or the place where a river meets the sea (in English, inver).

inbye All of the pasture land of a township or farm within the head dyke, some of which has been improved.

infield-outfield system Infield referred to the best arable or corn land surrounding a township in pre-enclosure days. The outfield referred to poorer quality land further away from the township that was less frequently cultivated.

innis *(innse)* In Gaelic an island, the meadow by a river or a resting place for cattle (in English, inch)

iolair *(iolaire)* Eagle (Gaelic).

Ionic A Greek architectural style characterised by pillars surmounted with scrolled features.

iosal *(isle)* Low (Gaelic).

Iron Age A period of human settlement in the British Isles following the Bronze Age and beginning *c.*500 BC.

Jacobite A follower of the Stuart dynasty after Catholic King James VII (or James II of England) was deposed in 1689. Supporters of James Francis Edward Stuart brought about the Jacobite Rebellion of 1715 and supporters of his son Prince Charles Edward Stuart (or Bonnie Prince Charlie) rose in 1745.

joint tenure A form of land holding in which the members of a township or clachan held and worked their land in common.

Jurassic The middle period of the Mesozoic era from 135 to 205 million years ago, marked by rapid sea-level rise and the flooding of much of Scotland.

kail-yard A Scots word for a vegetable patch associated with a fermetoun holding.

kame A landform comprising a mound of stratified sands and gravels formed by meltwater from a decaying glacier or ice sheet. Kame terraces develop between the ice and a valley wall.

keep The main tower of a castle.

kettle A depression in the land created by the melting of a block of ice buried by overlying sediments. Kettle holes, initially filled with meltwater, often form small lochs.

kirk A church (Scots, derived from *kirkja*, Scandinavian).

kirkton A fermetoun settlement associated with a church, as in Kirkton of Auchterhouse.

knock-and-lochan A type of landscape resulting from the erosion of a relatively low-lying area of hard rock by an ice sheet which scours the area and produces numerous depressions in areas of geological weakness. Following the retreat of the ice, the hollows (lochans) become filled with water or peat bogs. The lochans are separated from each other by low rounded landforms smoothed by the action of ice. This type of landscape is associated with the northwest Highlands and the Western Isles, particularly the landscapes of Lewisian gneiss.

laccolith An intrusion of igneous rock which spreads along bedding planes below the surface of the ground forcing the overlying strata into a dome shape.

lag *(luig)* A hollow (Gaelic).

laigh land A low-lying moist meadow land.

laird A Scots word for the owner of an estate.

lairig *(lairige)* A pass (Gaelic).

laomuinn A beacon (in English, lomond).

law A hill (Scots), for example Dundee Law or Norman's Law.

leac *(lice, lic)* Flat stones (Gaelic).

learg *(leirge)* A plain or hillside (Gaelic).

leathad *(leathaid)* A slope (Gaelic).

leathann *(laethainn, leathan, leathain)* Broad (Gaelic).

liath *(leith, leithe)* Grey (Gaelic).

limestone A type of sedimentary rock with a carbonate of lime constituent and often with fossil content.

linn *(linne)* A Scots word describing either a waterfall or the pool at the base of the fall as in Linn of Dee.

lios Garden.

loan Most often referring to a narrow street or lane between corn fields along which cows are driven to and from the pasture, a loan can also describe a small paddock.

local authority Syonymous with local government

Local Nature Reserve (LNR) A Local Nature Reserve is an area of special local natural interest, which is set up to protect nature and allow access for people to enjoy and appreciate the natural environment.

loch *(locha, lochan, lochain)* A lake or lakelet (Gaelic). An inland water body, or in the case of a sea-loch, one open to the sea.

loft A gallery in a church with special purpose. For example, an organ loft, where the organ is situated, or the laird's loft, a private space for the land-owner and his family.

loggia An Italian term for a small sheltered space facing outwards from a building, in the form of a gallery or balcony, lying behind a row of columns.

loinn *(loinne)* An enclosure, land (Gaelic).

long *(luinge)* A ship (Gaelic).

loupin-on-stone A short stone stair used to assist a rider in mounting his horse.

lub *(luib)* A bend (Gaelic).

lynchet A man-made terrace on a hill-side, usually running parallel to the contours and associated with ancient agricultural practice from the Iron Age or earlier.

machair *(machar)* a sandy plain. A Gaelic word referring to a distinctive type of coastal grassland found in the north and west of Scotland, which is associated with calcareous sand, blown inland by prevailing winds from beaches and mobile dunes. The machair is associated with long established agricultural practices, which include fertilising with kelp and low intensity cultivation. It is recognised as a unique habitat for birds and plants.

madadh *(mhadaidh)* A dog, wolf or fox (Gaelic).

magh *(mhaigh, mhaga)* A plain or a field (Gaelic).

mam *(mhaim)* A gently rising hill (Gaelic).

maol *(maoile)* Bare top (Gaelic).

march A Scots word for a boundary. A march stone marks the boundary between one property and another and the 'Riding of the Marches' is an event that takes place annually in and around some Border towns.

meadhon *(mheadhoin)* Middle (Gaelic).

meall *(mhill)* A lump, applied to a round hill (Gaelic).

meander A sinuous bend in the channel of a slow-flowing river.

meltwater channel A valley or gulley created by erosion resulting from running water derived from melting glacier ice.

mercat cross Literally 'market cross', a stone monument erected at the centre of a Burgh as the focus of trading activity and ceremony.

merkland A measure of land introduced in the 12th century, a merk or mark's worth of land was valued at thirteen shillings and fourpence per annum.

Mesolithic The name given to the middle period of the Stone Age which lasted in the British Isles from 7500 to 3000 BC. The first people to settle in Scotland after the Ice Age were from this period.

milton A fermetoun settlement associated with a mill, as in Milton of Balgonie.

moine *(mointeach, monadh)* A peat, mossy ground (Gaelic).

moine The name given to metamorphosed Precambrian rocks, mostly schists, of the northwest Highlands north of the Highland Boundary Fault. Overlain by younger Dalradian schists, the moine schists have been thrust northwestwards over older rocks such as Lewisian gneiss and Torridonian sandstone (the Moine Thrust).

mol *(mal)* Shingle beach (Gaelic).

monadh A hill or mountain (Gaelic).

mor *(mhor, mhoir, moire)* Large, great (Gaelic).

moraine A landform associated with various types of debris deposited at the edges of glaciers or ice sheets.

mort safe An iron frame placed over the coffin or grave in the 17th and 18th centuries to discourage resurrectionists, who attempted to steal recently buried bodies to sell to anatomists in the medical schools.

mort-house A cemetery building built to house the hearse or hand cart used to carry coffins at funerals.

moss A word used to desribe an area of peatland or poorly-drained land.

motte A mound forming the site of a former castle or fort.

mudstone An unstratified, fine-grained, clay-like, compact sedimentary rock.

muir A Scots word for grass or heather moorland.

mull *(muli, mool)* A promontory (Scandinavian).

Munro A mountain peaks over 3000 feet (914.4 m) in height, with 'sufficient separation' from associated summits of a similar height. Such associated summits are known as Munro Tops. The list of Munros, first compiled by Sir Hugh Munro in 1891, now comprises 279 separate mountains and 517 tops. Periodically revised by the Scottish Mountaineering Club, 'Munro's Tables' are essential reading for the ever-growing number of 'Munro baggers'. The ascent of all the Munros was first achieved by the Revd A. E. Robertson in 1901 and the first ascent of all the Munros in a single journey of 1639 miles was undertaken by Hamish Brown in 1974.

Munro top A subsidiary summit of a Munro, which while exceeding 3000 feet (914 m) is not sufficiently far from the main peak to qualify as a Munro.

Murdo A mountain peak over 3000 feet (914.4 m) in height with a drop of at least 30 metres (98 ft) on all sides. The list of 444 Murdos, which comprises all 277 Munros, 160 of the 517 Munro tops and seven other summits, was compiled by hillwalker Murdo Munro and first published in 1995.

National Nature Reserves Areas of land set aside for nature where the main purpose of management is the conservation of habitats and species of national and international significance. Scotland has 73 National Nature Reserves.

National Park Legislation to create National Parks in Scotland was passed in August 2002 by the Scottish Parliament and parks have been established in Loch Lomond and the Trossachs and the Cairngorms. In Scotland, National Parks have been established to deliver better management of some of Scotland's special areas of outstanding natural and cultural heritage.

National Trust for Scotland (NTS) Founded in 1931, the National Trust for Scotland is an independent conservation charity that protects and promotes Scotland's natural and cultural heritage. Over 100 historic houses, castles, gardens, battlefields, monuments, mountains and coastal areas are in the Trust's care.

Natural Scenic Areas Scotland's only national landscape conservation designation, the Natural Scenic Areas are those areas of land considered of national significance on the basis of their outstanding scenic interest or unsurpassed attractiveness.

Neolithic A name given to the later or more culturally advanced Stone Age.

ness *(nes, nis)* A headland, promontory or cape (Scandinavian).

New Town One of five planned settlements created to alleviate the over-population of the Glasgow conurbation, an area suffering industrial decline, and attract people to new employment opportunities. The new towns were Glenrothes (1948), East Kilbride (1949), Cumbernauld (1956), Livingston (1962) and Irvine (1966). Each was run by a government-appointed new-town corporation (rather than an elected local authority) until their special status ended in 1995.

Norse period (or Viking period) A period of human settlement in the British Isles dating from around AD 900–1300, coming after the Iron Age.

nucleated settlement A type of settlement where buildings are formed into a group around a nucleus.

nunatak A word of Inuit origin, referring to rocky peaks projecting above the surface of an ice sheet.

ob *(oba, oban)* A bay (Gaelic).

odhar *(odhair, uidhre, idhir)* Dun-coloured (Gaelic).

ogam (ogham) An ancient Celtic alphabet of straight lines meeting or crossing a central line for ease of cutting in stone. It was in use in Ireland by the second century AD.

oitir *(oitire)* Sand bank (Gaelic).

ord *(uird)* Round hill (Gaelic).

Ordnance Survey A UK government agency charged with the mapping of Scotland, England and Wales (but not Northern Ireland) since the 18th century. Today, they provide definitive paper and computerised mapping on a commercial basis.

Ordovician A period of the earth's history from 440 to 510 million years ago when thick layers of sediments were laid down on the ocean floor.

os *(ois, osa)* A river mouth or outlet (Gaelic).

outfield an extension of arable cultivation beyond the infield or corn lands of medieval settlements, the outfield was manured by livestock then cropped for a restricted period. It formed part of an openfield system that lay within the head-dyke or outer enclosing wall.

outset An enclosure in the hill pasture or commonty derived from the Old Norse *saeter* which referred to farm or homestead.

pairc *(pairce)* A park or field (Gaelic).

Palaeozoic A period of the Earth's history comprising the Cambrian and Permian eras.

Palladian A classical style of architecture introduced by Andrea Palladio (1518–80) modelled on Vitruvius, a Roman architect under the Emperor Augustus (31 BC–AD 14).

parish First created in medieval times to support the church, ecclesiastical (quoad sacra) parishes were areas of land whose inhabitants were obliged to pay a proportion of their produce or income to the Church. In the 17th century the crown divided Scotland into burghs, sheriffdoms and parishes for the purpose of taxation. Between 1845 and 1860 civil (quoad civilia) parishes were establish ed with elected parochial boards, these parishes continuing as units of local government until 1975. The agricultural parish is a statistical unit in the United Kingdom used as the basis for collecting data on farms, livestock, crops and yields.

parliamentary church (Telford church) One of several churches built in the North and West of Scotland by the government, the Telford or parliamentary churches were new buildings erected in areas in need of a church to celebrate victory in the Napoleonic Wars. Parliamentary Commissioners were appointed in 1823 to build 'Additional Places of Worship in the Highlands and Islands of Scotland'. Constructed to a simple plan prepared by noted engineer Thomas Telford (1757–1834), the churches were plain T-shaped structures with cast-iron windows and each had its own manse. There were thirty-two of these churches built in the late 1820s at a total cost exceeding £50,000.

pediment A term deriving from Classical architecture for a triangular structure above a door or window.

peridotite A coarse-grained igneous rock containing olivine and other ferro-magnesian minerals.

Perpendicular A late English style of Gothic architecture common in the 14th to mid-16th centuries.

Picts One of the four peoples who eventually coalesced to make Scotland during the first millennium AD, the Picts were first mentioned in two different Latin sources in 297 AD. The term Picti (painted ones) for this grouping of Celtic tribes may well have been a Latin nick-name given by Roman soldiers but the Scots called them Cruithni. The Picts left in the landscape a large number of remarkable symbol stones.

pet (pit) A farm or piece of land, sometimes a hollow.

plantiecrui (planticrub, plantiecote, plantiecruive) A drystone enclosure built to protect cabbage plants throughout the winter in Shetland.

policy in Scotland a policy is the name given to the designed landscape surrounding a mansion house.

poll *(phuill)* A pool or pit (Gaelic).

porphyry A type of rock containing feldspar crystals embedded in a compact mass of dark red or purple.

port A gateway or entrance to a mediaeval Scots town.

Precambrian The oldest era in the earth's history dating from 550 to 3 billion years ago during which great thicknesses of sediments accumulated in Scotland. The oldest rocks in Scotland, the Lewisian gneisses, date from this period.

Presbyterian A democratic system of governance in the Protestant church based on the wishes of the elders of the congregation, along with individual ministers. Policy is formulated at an annual general assembly, held in Edinburgh. Developed at the time of the Reformation in the mid-16th century, the Presbyterian system persists in the Church of Scotland to the present day. Contrasts with the Episcopalian system.

Presiding Officer The speaker in the Scottish Parliament, responsible for chairing the parliamentary sessions, ensuring procedure is followed and maintaining order.

raineach *(rainich)* A fern (Gaelic).

raised beach a coastal deposit of sand, shingle and broken shells lying above the highest level of the spring tides, the product of past wave action at a time when the sea level was higher. Raised beaches are the result of fluctuations in sea-level since the end of the last Ice Age.

ramh *(raimh)* An oar (Gaelic).

rathad *(rathaid)* A road or way (Gaelic).

reamhar *(reamhair, reamhra)* Thick or fat (Gaelic).

Reformation A 15th- and 16th-century movement in Western Europe that aimed at reforming some doctrines and practices of the Roman Catholic Church and resulted in the establishment of the Protestant churches.

regality A mediaeval jurisdiction much wider than a barony that was abolished in 1747. The Lord of Regality formerly held court under licence from the Crown.

region A first-order local authority sub-division used in Scotland between until 1995. There were nine regional authorities, each divided into districts, plus three unitary island authorities. This system of regions and districts replaced the counties in 1974.

reidh *(reidhe)* Smooth, level or plain (Gaelic).

riabhach *(riabhaich)* Brindled or greyish (Gaelic).

ridge and Furrow A landscape feature formed as a result of ploughing, the soil from the furrow being thrown up by the plough to form a ridge that varied in height according to the type of soil and plough.

rigg A narrow division of land laid out in mediaeval times. Riggs are often preserved in today's settlement patterns, for example in Haddington and Linlithgow.

righ *(righe)* King (Gaelic).

roinn *(roinne)* A point or promontory (Gaelic).

Roman period A period of human settlement in the British Isles dating from AD 43 to around AD 450, the Roman Period occurs within what is otherwise called the Iron Age. The Romans were in Scotland between AD 79 and c.AD 200.

Romanesque A style of architecture characterised by round arches and vaults marking the transition from Roman to Gothic architecture.

room (rouming) A term for a piece of cultivated arable land.

roup A Scots word for an auction.

Royal Commission on the Ancient and Historical Monuments of Scotland (RCAHMS) The government body concerned with the recording and interpretation of sites, monuments and buildings connected with Scotland's past. RCAHMS works closely with Historic Scotland, who are charged with the maintenance and protection of heritage sites.

Royal Society for the Protection of Birds (RSPB) A voluntary British conservation charity established in 1889, the RSPB aims to protect bird species, both indigenous and migratory, and their habitats. The RSPB began working in Scotland in 1904 and now owns or manages over 40 reserves and tracts of land in Scotland, including Abernethy Forest, Insh Marshes and Lochwinnoch.

ruadh Red or reddish (Gaelic).

rudha *(rubha)* A spit, headland or promontory (Gaelic).

runrig A medieval system of cultivation associated with the infield and outfield system rather than a number of large arable field. Ridges or riggs in each field were allocated to each member of the township, thus the land was equally divided in value and extent. Runrig was widespread in Scotland until the reorganisation of land in the 18th and 19th centuries.

SSSI (Site of Special Scientific Interest) A Site of Special Scientific Interest designated to protect the best wildlife, plant, rock or landform sites. There are 1447 SSSIs in Scotland covering an area of 1,007,260 hectares. Sites are notified under the Wildlife and Conservation Act 1982.

saeter *(setter, setr)* An Old Norse word referring to a farm or homestead, often an outset or secondary settlement associated with the summer hill pasture.

sail *(saile)* Heel or salt water (Gaelic).

sandstone A sedimentary rock composed of fine grains of sand of a quartz variety laid down originally as marine sediments.

scattald An area of common land found in Shetland.

schist A fissile metamorphic rock.

Scots acre A former measurement of land area equivalent to 1.26 standard acres, the Scots acre was divided into 4 roods and 40 falls.

Scots mile A linear measure, 80 chains or 1,976 yards in length.

Scots Pine *Pinus sylvestris* is the only native British pine, it was the main species of the Caledonian Pine Forest, which once covered much of Scotland, but only fragments remain.

Scottish Baronial A style of architecture drawing on features of medieval fortified buildings in Scotland applied by architects like David Bryce in the 19th century.

Scottish Enlightenment A period, primarily during the second half of the 18th century, when literature, arts and sciences flourished in Scotland.

Scottish Environmental Protection Agency (SEPA) A government body charged with protecting and improving the environment principally through the regulation of water quality, effluent discharges and disposal of waste.

Scottish Executive The government in Scotland, the Scottish Executive exercises significant (but not universal) powers devolved from the United Kingdom Parliament in London. The Executive is responsible to the Scottish Ministers, led by the First Minister.

Scottish ministers The powers of government in Scotland are vested in the Scottish ministers and executed on their behalf by the Scottish Executive. The Scottish ministers have limits to their powers, with some responsibilities remaining with the United Kingdom government in Scotland.

Scottish Natural Heritage (SNH) A government body charged with the protection of Scotland's natural environment. SNH was formed through merger of the Nature Conservancy Council for Scotland with the Countryside Commission for Scotland in 1991.

sea loch A water body with one end open to the sea. A fjord.

sedimentary A type of rock, such as sandstone, composed of sediments that have been derived from existing rocks which have been broken and eroded, then transported by water, wind or glacier ice.

sgeir *(sgeire)* A sea rock (Gaelic).

sgor *(sgorr)* Rocky peak (Gaelic).

shieling A term used to described areas of summer grazing or the seasonally occupied buildings of shepherds. The shieling system is associated with the transhumance of livestock from the arable land of the fermetoun to the hill pastures.

sill An intrusion of igneous rock formed by flowing lava that spreads nearly horizontally between rock strata.

Silurian A period of the Earth's history from 410 to 440 million years ago when which continents collided and Scotland united with England.

sithean *(sithein)* A hillock, fairy knoll (Gaelic).

skerry *(skeir, sker)* Rocky outcrops at sea (Scandinavian).

skew A sloping cope at the gable end of a house. A skewputt is a form of rooftop ornamentation found on the skew.

sleac *(slic)* Flat stones (Gaelic).

slochd *(sloc, sluichd)* Deep or hollow (Gaelic).

sneachd *(sneachdha)* Snow (Gaelic).

socach *(socaich)* Snout or projecting place (Gaelic).

souming and rouming A term used to describe grazing rights in the hill pasture (souming) based on winter carrying capacity in the township arable land (Rouming).

souterrain An early Iron Age semi-underground structure often paved and with stone walls. These structures possibly served as byres or stores.

srath *(sratha)* A valley in Gaelic (in English, strath).

sron *(sroine)* A nose or point in Gaelic (in English, stron).

sruth *(srutha, sruthan, sruthain)* A current, a stream or a streamlet (Gaelic).

stac *(staca)* A steep conical hill (Gaelic).

stell An enclosure for sheep.

stewartry In Scotland, the jurisdiction of a steward; also, the lands under such jurisdiction.

stob A point (Gaelic).

stuc A peak (Gaelic).

suidhe A resting place (Gaelic).

tack The Scots word for a lease, the tacksman being the holder of the lease.

tairbeart *(tairbeirt, tarbert, tarbet)* A narrow isthmus (Gaelic).

tarsuinn Tranverse, across (Gaelic).

tenement The name given to a small holding or a multi-story building erected on a small piece of ground. The medieval tenements of Edinburgh, built on burgess plots, were amongst the earliest high-rise buildings in Europe.

Tertiary A 60-million-year period of volcanic activity associated with the opening of the Atlantic Ocean that began 65 million years ago. During this period granites, gabbros, basalt and other igneous rocks were formed, mostly in the west of Scotland. Ailsa Craig, Goatfell on Arran, the island of Staffa, Ben More on Mull and the Cuillins of Skye are examples of prominent features created during the Tertiary period.

thanage The land held by a thane (a feudal lord or baron in Scotland).

tigh *(tighe, tay, ti)* A house (Gaelic).

tobar *(tobair, tober)* A well (Gaelic).

toft (toftin) A small holding.

tolbooth The administrative centre of a Burgh, which usually included the Council Chamber, prison and tax office.

tombolo A coastal feature, produced by the deposition of sand and shingle, which joins the mainland to an island.

top A subsidiary hill or mountain with a drop of 100 feet (30.5 m) on all sides or elevations of sufficient topographical interest with a drop of 100 feet (30.5 m) and 50 feet (15.2 m) on all sides. Munro Tops are those tops associated with Munros. The grouping of 'tops' into 'hills' is calculated on the basis that tops are no more than 17 units from the main top of the 'hill', a unit being one-twelfth of a mile measured either along the connecting ridge or one of 50 feet (15.2 m) contour between the lower top and the connecting col.

tor A prominent rock feature in granite landscapes formed since the last Ice Age as a result of weathering to create exposed rectangular tower-like structures. Examples in Scotland include the Barns of Bynack in the Cairngorms.

torc *(tuirc)* A boar (Gaelic).

torr *(torra)* A heap, hill or castle (Gaelic).

tower house A compact fortified house, smaller than that which could be regarded as a castle.

township A collection of houses surrounded by cultivated arable land at one time contained within a town dyke beyond which livestock were grazed on common pasture.

trachyte A fine grained igneous rock.

traigh A beach (Gaelic).

trunk road A term used, especially in the United Kingdom, to describe a main road.

tuff A sedimentary rock composed of angular fragments of lava in a finer matrix.

tulach *(tulaich)* A knoll or a hillock (Gaelic).

uachdar *(uachdair)* Top, upper part (Gaelic).

uaine Green or blue (Gaelic).

uamh *(uamha, uaigh, uaighe)* A cave (Gaelic).

udal *(odel, udel)* The Old Norse system of land tenure in the Northern Isles. Udallers or little heritors conveyed their estates to their successors by a title called Udal Succession.

uig A nook, hollow or bay (Gaelic).

uisg *(uisge)* Water (Gaelic).

unconformity First noted by the geologist James Hutton, an unconformity is a major break in the stratigraphical sequence of rocks.

uruisg A goblin or brownie (Gaelic).

vaulted ceiling A ceiling of composed of arches in stone (in the strict sense), wood or plaster in medieval architecture. The simplest is the tunnel or barrel vault, which is a continuous semi-circualr arch. The more complex forms include Gothic Cross or Groin vaults.

vennel An alley or narrow lane.

voe An inlet, bay or estuary, most commonly in the Shetland or Orkney islands.

wadset A Scots word for a mortgage, the holder of a wadset being a wadsetter.

ward A division of a city or town, especially an electoral district, for administrative and representative purposes. A district of some Scottish counties corresponding roughly to the hundred or the wapentake.

watershed The line separating head-streams which flow into different drainage basins.

wave-cut platform The worn stump of rock strata, often exposed at low water, left when cliff rock has been cut back by wave erosion.

wheelhouse (aisled round house) A type of Iron-age house found in northwest Scotland, Shetland and the Western Isles, a wheelhouse (sometimes known as an aisled round house) comprises a circular drystone building, with the internal walls arranged like the spokes of a wheel.

whinstone The name given to various types of hard stone that are difficult to work.

wick *(vik)* A bay or creek (Scandinavian).

wynd A lane running from a main thoroughfare.

yett A hinged wrought metal gate protecting the entrance to a building (usually a tower or castle).

A' Bhuidheanach Bheag *Perth and Kinross* A mountain in the southern Grampians, A' Bhuidheanach Bheag rises to 936 m (3070 ft) to the east of Loch Ericht and the A9.

A' Chabag The Gaelic name for Kebock Head in the Western Isles.

A' Chailleach *Highland* A summit in the Monadhliath Mountains, A' Chailleach ('the old woman') rises to 930 m (3050 ft), 4 miles (6.5 km) northwest of Newtonmore in Badenoch.

A' Chailleach *Highland* The most westerly mountain of the Fannichs, in the Ross and Cromarty district, A' Chailleach rises to 999 m (3277 ft).

A' Chill *Highland* A'Chill is located on the southern coastline of the island of Canna in the Inner Hebrides. Lying to the west of Canna Harbour, the settlement overlooks the island of Sanday to the south.

A' Chràlaig *Highland* A mountain in southwest Highland Council area, A' Chràlaig ('basket' or 'creel') rises to 1120 m (3674 ft) to the north of Loch Cluanie. This mountain is also known as Garbh Leac.

A' Chùli *Argyll and Bute* An island in the Firth of Lorn, A' Chùli lies between Garbh Eileach and Eileach an Naoimh in the Garvellachs (Isles of the Sea).

A' Ghlas-bheinn *Highland* A mountain in the Lochalsh district of Highland Council area, A' Ghlas-bheinn rises to 918 m (3011 ft) to the northwest of Beinn Fhada (Ben Attow) and 4 miles (6.5 km) east of Loch Duich.

A' Mhaighdean *Highland* A mountain of Wester Ross, A' Mhaighdean ('the maiden') rises to 967 m (3172 ft) in the wilderness of Letterewe, 4 miles (6.5 km) north of Loch Maree and southeast of Fionn Loch. It is one of the remotest of Scotland's peaks.

A' Mharconaich *Perth and Kinross* A flat plateau in the southwest Grampians, A' Mharconaich rises to 975 m (3198 ft) to the east of Loch Ericht and 6 miles (10 km) southwest of Dalwhinnie.

Aa Skerry *Shetland* A large rock off the southwest coast of the Shetland Mainland, Aa Skerry lies in an area known as The Deeps, a half-mile (1 km) west of Roe Ness.

Abbey Craig *Stirling* A wooded basaltic knoll in eastern Stirling Council area, Abbey Craig rises to 91 m (300 ft) above the River Forth to the east of the city of Stirling. It forms a glacial crag-and-tail feature and on its summit stands the 67 m/220 ft-high Wallace Monument, a memorial to Sir William Wallace (*c.*1272–1305) erected in 1869 to a design by the architect John T. Rochhead.

Abbey Green An alternative name for Lesmahagow in South Lanarkshire.

Abbey Head *Dumfries and Galloway* A headland on the Solway Firth coast of Dumfries and Galloway, Abbey Head lies 2 miles (3 km) to the south of Dundrennan. The Abbey Burn enters the firth here at Abbey Burnfoot.

Abbey St Bathans *Scottish Borders* The village of Abbey St Bathans is located on the banks of the Whiteadder Water, 5 miles (8 km) north of Duns within the Scottish Borders. The Monynut Water and the burns of Weir and Eller both join the Whiteadder at Abbey St Bathans. The nunnery of St Mary was founded here in the 12th century by Ada, Countess of Dunbar, and remains from it have been incorporated into the church building. The village sits in fertile lowland with wooded lower slopes surrounding the area. A copper mine was opened nearby in 1828, but it was relatively unsuccessful and was closed soon afterwards.

Abbey Strand *City of Edinburgh* A short street at the eastern end of Edinburgh's Royal Mile, Abbey Strand leads directly to the Palace of Holyroodhouse. It formerly marked the outer extent of the precincts of Holyrood Abbey (the ruins of which stand next to the palace) and hence the boundary of 'sanctuary', which is still indicated by brass studs and the letter 'S' in the road. Fugitives took refuge in the Strand, although mostly it was debtors who sought the protection of the area, a practice that continued until 1880, when debtors' prisons were abolished. The author and 'opium eater' Thomas De Quincey regularly took advantage of the privilege between 1833 and 1840. The fugitives' stay would not have been entirely unpleasant since there were various taverns in the vicinity. Today the buildings that remain in Abbey Strand date from the 16th and 17th centuries and include a fine example of a refurbished fore-stair. On the old Abbey Courthouse wall is a fine restored panel bearing the arms of Scotland and the monogram of King James IV.

Abbeyhill *City of Edinburgh* A small district of Edinburgh, centred to the south of London Road, a half-mile (1 km) east of Princes Street, Abbeyhill lies on a ridge that extends east from Calton Hill to Meadowbank. The district takes its name from Holyrood Abbey, which lies in ruins next to the Palace of Holyroodhouse. A road called Abbeyhill leads north from the abbey. Flatted cottages in seven parallel streets, known as the 'Colonies', were built *c.*1870 by the Edinburgh Co-operative Building Company with the aim of providing low-cost housing for working people. Between the abbey and New Calton Burial Ground is a small modern housing estate (built in 1967), centred on Abbeyhill Crescent. Previously the site of a foundry, Abbeyhill is today a largely residential area with shops and small high-technology businesses. The east-coast railway to London leaves Edinburgh through Abbeyhill, as does the A1 trunk road.

Abbot House *Fife* The oldest house in Dunfermline, situated in the Maygate at the centre of the burgh, Abbot House was built on the line of the old abbey wall. Constructed in the 16th century after the Reformation, it was probably built for Robert Pitcairn, commendator (lay administrator) of the old abbey estates, and was probably never the home of an abbot. In 1994 the building was opened as a museum tracing the story of the town from Pictish times to the present day.

Abbotrule *Scottish Borders* A hamlet to the south of Teviotdale, Abbotrule is located on the Forderlee Burn, 2 miles (3 km) northeast of the village of Bonchester Bridge and 8 miles (13 km) east of Hawick. The ruins of a church lie to the southeast. The hamlet once lay within the Abbotrule Estate, which extended to 960 ha (2372 acres).

Abbots Deuglie *Perth and Kinross* In the Middle Ages the abbots of Cambuskenneth on the River Forth held title to the land around Abbots Deuglie, a hamlet of Perth and Kinross situated in the Ochil Hills a mile (1.5 km) to the west of Glenfarg. Glendeuglie, Abbots Deuglie and Wester Deuglie lie on a minor road leading over the hill from Glenfarg to Invermay and Forgandenny. Glenfarg Reservoir to the west was created in 1912.

Abbotsford House *Scottish Borders* Abbotsford House, the home of the novelist Sir Walter Scott (1771–1832), stands on the south bank of the River Tweed, 1.5 miles (2.5 km) southeast of Galashiels and 2 miles (3 km) west of Melrose in the Scottish Borders. With his great love of the Border country, Scott, who saw himself as a Tweeddale laird, bought a farmhouse and land from a local minister in 1811 for £4000. It was originally called Cartleyhole, but Scott, with his keen sense of history, renamed it Abbotsford in honour of the monks of Melrose who had originally owned the land. Scott and his family moved to the farmhouse in 1812, but almost immediately he made plans to build a larger property, to be funded by the success of his writing. By purchasing adjacent properties, Scott extended the estate to 566 ha (1399 acres) and commissioned the architect William Atkinson to draw up plans for a new house. In 1822 the original farmhouse was demolished and the core of the current house was completed by 1824. The Scottish baronial-style design incorporated copies of architectural features of historical interest such as a gateway from Linlithgow Palace, roof designs from Rosslyn Chapel, a mantelpiece from Melrose Abbey and oak panelling from the Auld Kirk, Dunfermline. Scott also built on the estate various cottages in which he accommodated friends. He landscaped the grounds, planting a large number of trees. Abbotsford is filled with Scott's enormous collection of historical curiosities, including Rob Roy's purse, a tumbler once owned by Robert Burns and a lock of Bonnie Prince Charlie's hair, together with weapons, armour and paintings. Notable visitors to Abbotsford during Scott's lifetime included the English author Maria Edgeworth, the American essayist Washington Irving and the poets William Wordsworth and Thomas Moore. After Scott's death in 1832, tourists came to Abbotsford in increasing numbers. Royal visitors have included Queen Victoria (1867) and King George V, Queen Mary, and the Duke and Duchess of York (later to become King George VI and Queen Elizabeth) in 1923.

Abbotsinch Airport A former name of Glasgow Airport in Renfrewshire.

Abdie *Fife* A parish in northwest Fife that stretches from Newburgh on the Firth of Tay to Lindores Loch, Abdie includes the village of Lindores and the hamlet of Grange of Lindores, and in its churchyard near Grange of Lindores is a 7th-century Pictish symbol stone. Buried in the same churchyard are John Bethune (d.1839) and his brother Alexander (d.1843) who are remembered as local poets. There is also a monument to Sir Frederick Lewis Maitland (1777–1839), captain of the British warship HMS *Bellerophon*, which took the defeated Napoleon on board in 1815 prior to his exile in St Helena.

Aberarder *Highland* A settlement on the northwestern side of Loch Laggan, 4 miles (6.5 km) southwest of Kinloch Laggan in Highland Council area, Aberarder sits on the main road from Spean Bridge to Newtonmore.

Aberargie *Perth and Kinross* A small village at the head of Glen Farg in Perth and Kinross, Aberargie lies a mile (1.5 km) to the west of Abernethy and 2 miles (3 km) southeast of Bridge of Earn at the junction of the A912 and A913. Nearby are Glenfarg House and the Baiglie Inn. Aberdargie is an alternative version of the name.

Abercairny *Perth and Kinross* On 12 September 1842 Queen Victoria alighted from the train 'for a moment' just to visit Abercairny, a Gothic-style mansion house in the process of being built. Situated to the south of the A85, 4 miles (6.5 km) east of Crieff in the parish of Fowlis Wester, Perth and Kinross, Abercairny stands on an estate held by the Moray family since the end of the 13th century. Milton of Abercairny lies to the north.

Aberchalder *Highland* A village at the northeastern end of Loch Oich, Aberchalder lies close to the Caledonian Canal, 5 miles (8 km) southwest of Fort Augustus in Highland Council area. At nearby Aberchalder Lodge, Prince Charles Edward Stewart (Bonnie Prince Charlie) gathered over 2000 men in August 1745 for his march to the Scottish Lowlands. The small settlements of Easter and Wester Aberchalder lie some distance away, to the east of Loch Mhòr, 13 miles (21 km) northeast of Aberchalder.

Aberchalder Burn *Highland* A stream located east of Loch Ness in Highland Council area, Aberchalder Burn flows westwards from Carn na Saobhaidhe through the settlements of Easter and Wester Aberchalder before emptying into Loch Mhòr.

Aberchirder *Aberdeenshire* A small town in Marnoch parish, northwest Aberdeenshire, Aberchirder lies on the A97 between Banff and Huntly in the valley of the Burn of Auchintoul, which flows southwards to join the River Deveron near Marnoch Lodge. Known locally as Foggieloan, the name of an earlier fermetoun nearby, it was founded as a planned estate village in 1764 by Alexander Gordon of Auchintoul, whose grandfather was a general in Peter the Great's Russian army. Extending down from the top of a hill, it has a regular plan of streets around a central square. There is a walk round Cleanhill Wood at the southern end of the town and nearby are the Bridge of Marnoch (1806), Old Marnoch Kirk (1792) and standing stones (1800 BC), as well as the 16th-century Innes stronghold of Crombie Castle and mid-15th-century Kinnairdy Castle, linked with the Innes and Gregory families. Aberchirder, which has several church buildings, was associated with the Disruption of 1843 that created the Free Church of Scotland.

Abercorn *West Lothian* A hamlet on the Hopetoun Estate in West Lothian, Abercorn lies 3 miles (5 km) west of South Queensferry. Restored in 1893, its noteworthy parish church incorporates 12th-century and post-Reformation architecture. In the churchyard are the remains of an 8th-century stone cross and some unusual 17th-century gravestones, together with the burial vault of the Dalyells of the Binns, built in 1623. The parish of Abercorn (or Aebercurnig) is mentioned by the Venerable Bede as early as AD 696, being the site of a monastery and residence of a bishop. An excavation close to the church in 1963 revealed evidence of the monastery. By 1160 the parish had become part of the Barony of Aberlady. By then there was a castle, which passed to the Graemes and, following the death of John the Graeme at Falkirk (1298), to the 'Black' Douglases. The castle was besieged and destroyed by King James II in 1455, never to be rebuilt. In the 16th century the Crown bestowed Abercorn on Claud Hamilton (*c*.1543–1622). Despite being forfeited by the Hamiltons, who had remained loyal to Mary, Queen of Scots, it was restored to them by her son King James VI who created Claud the 1st Baron Paisley in 1587 and his son the 1st Earl of Abercorn. The village and estate then passed through the Mures, Lindsays and Setons before being sold in 1678 to John Hope, whose widow, Margaret, and son, Charles (later the 1st Earl of Hopetoun), began in 1699 the construction of Hopetoun House just to the east of the village.

Abercrombie *Fife* A farming hamlet in the East Neuk of Fife, Abercrombie lies a mile (1.5 km) north of St Monans. Abercrombie farmhouse, dating from 1892, stands on the site of a mansion built in the 13th century by a Richard Cocus. Close by is Balcaskie House. In the Chapel Wood between the village and the house stand the ruins of Abercrombie Church, which was gifted to the monks of Dunfermline in the 12th century and consecrated in October 1247 by David de Bernham, Bishop of St Andrews. For many years the burial place of the Abercrombies, this building was abandoned in 1646 when the seat of the former parish of Abercrombie moved to St Monans.

Aberdalgie *Perth and Kinross* A hamlet with a church (1773) in a parish of the same name, Aberdalgie lies on the southern slopes of the Gask Ridge which overlooks the valley of the River Earn, 2 miles (3 km) southwest of Perth in Perth and Kinross. Close by are Aberdalgie House and Milltown of Aberdalgie, and a mile (1.5 km) to the southwest is the home of the earls of Kinnoull, Dupplin Castle, a Tudor-style building that replaced an earlier structure destroyed by fire in 1827.

Aberdargie An alternative name for Aberargie in Perth and Kinross.

Aberdeen *Area: 186 sq. km (72 sq. miles)* The third-largest city in Scotland, Aberdeen lies 150 miles (241 km) north of Edinburgh, for the most part occupying land between the mouths of the River Dee and the River Don which flow eastwards into the North Sea from the Grampians. Founded in the 7th or 8th century, the seaport of Aberdeen is known as 'The Granite City', a name that reflects its handsome grey granite architecture. Since the 1970s its proximity to the North Sea oil and gas fields has earned it the title of Scotland's 'oil capital'. Also known as the 'Flower of Scotland', Aberdeen has long been famous for its outstanding parks, gardens and floral displays that include 2 million

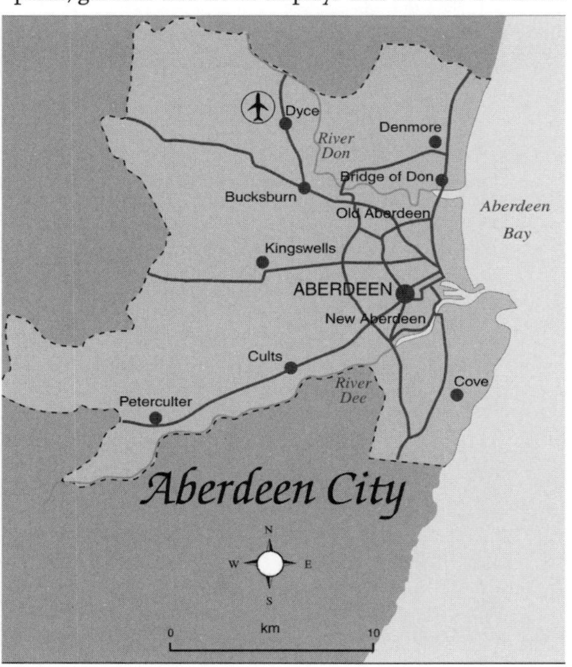

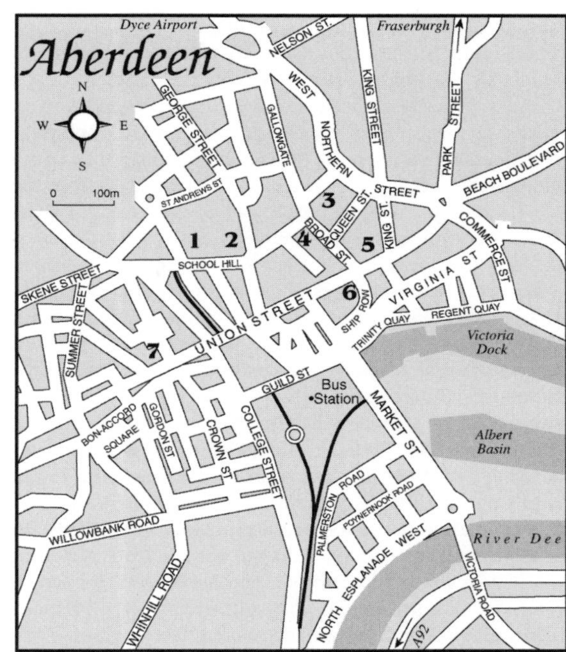

1 *Aberdeen Art Gallery*
2 *Robert Gordon University*
3 *Marischal College*
4 *Provost Skene's House*
5 *The Tolbooth Museum*
6 *Provost Ross's House*
7 *Music Hall*

roses, 11 million daffodils and 3 million crocuses. Granted a royal charter by William the Lion in 1179, Aberdeen grew up as two separate burghs – Old Aberdeen at the mouth of the Don, and New Aberdeen, a fishing and trading settlement where the Denburn entered the Dee estuary. In 1495 William Elphinstone, Bishop of Aberdeen, founded King's College to teach theology, medicine and the liberal arts. Named in honour of King James IV, its first principal was the distinguished historian and humanist, Hector Boece (*c.*1465–1536). In 1593 the Protestant George Keith (*c.*1553–1623), 5th Earl Marischal, founded the University of Marischal College, which boasts the world's second-largest granite building. The two universities were eventually united in 1860. Robert Gordon's College, which was founded in 1750 and became a noted centre for the teaching of education, was constituted as a university in 1992.

Formerly part of the county of Aberdeenshire, Aberdeen City was one of five district councils created in 1975 within the two-tier Grampian Region. In 1996 Aberdeen City became a separate local government area as one of the new unitary local authorities established under local government reform. The city's coat of arms, depicting three castles, and its motto – *'Bon Accord'* – are said to date from the time of King Robert the Bruce and the massacre of English troops in the neighbourhood. The motto was the watchword to initiate the campaign and the arms represent three castles that stood on three hills around which Aberdeen developed, namely Castle Hill, the Port or Windmill Hill (Gallowgate) and St Catherine's Hill. Robert the Bruce granted his hunting lands on the Forest of Stocket to the citizens of Aberdeen. These 'Freedom Lands' provided revenue that was eventually applied to creating the city's Common Good Fund. Sites of interest in Old Aberdeen include St Machar's Cathedral, King's College Chapel and the Cruickshank Botanical Gardens. In the centre of New Aberdeen are several buildings of interest, including Aberdeen Art Gallery; the Music Hall (1822); James Dun's House (18th century); Provost Skene's House, built in the 16th century and the city's oldest surviving house; Tolbooth Museum, built between 1616 and 1629 as a prison; the Gordon Highlanders Museum; Aberdeen Maritime Museum; and Provost Ross's House (1593). Dominated by oil- and gas-related industries, engineering, fish processing, papermaking, textiles, information technology and construction and transport industries, Aberdeen City has industrial sites to the south of the Dee at West Tullos, East Tullos, Altens, Wellington Road and Lochside; to the south of the Don at Mastrick, St Machar and Mugiemoss Road; and to the north of the Don at Bridge of Don, Denmore and Dyce. In 1971 there were 94,700 people employed in the city. By 1998 this figure had risen to 150,000, a third of whom worked in oil-related industries. Aberdeen is Scotland's primary fish-processing centre, and at its Offshore Technology Park and Science and Technology Park innovative research is undertaken by a range of private companies whose work complements the research carried out by Aberdeen's two universities and eight scientific institutes. Today Aberdeen is a centre of administration, education and industry, with a seaport, trade and ferry links to the Northern Isles, Scandinavia and the mainland Europe. It is one of Scotland's leading fishing ports and also a coastal resort with a 2-mile/3-km-long beach, a Beach Leisure Centre, a golf complex on the King's Links, and Pittodrie Stadium, the home of Aberdeen Football Club. Throughout the year the city hosts a number of festivals including a Winter Festival and an International Youth Festival.

Aberdeen Airport *Aberdeen City* Located at Dyce, 7 miles (11 km) northwest of Aberdeen, Aberdeen Airport is one of seven in the UK operated by the denationalised British Airports Authority, BAA plc. Opened originally in 1934, it now incorporates the world's largest commercial heliport, servicing the North Sea oil industry, with 390,000 passengers per year. In total, the airport handles 2.7 million passengers annually, is served by at least 13 airlines and has a single runway of 1829 m (6000 ft).

Aberdeen Art Gallery *Aberdeen City* Situated on Schoolhill in the centre of the Aberdeen, Aberdeen Art Gallery houses a collection of Impressionist, Victorian, Scottish and 20th-century British paintings, as well as collections of silver and glass.

Aberdeen Maritime Museum *Aberdeen City* Built at a cost of £4 million and opened in 1997, Aberdeen Maritime Museum is located in Shiprow near Aberdeen City docks. It tells the story of Aberdeen's links with the sea from the days of sail and clipper ships to the latest oil and gas exploration technology. The museum includes a range of interactive exhibits and models, including an 8.5-m/28-ft-high model of the Murchison oil production platform and the 19th-century assembly taken from Rattray Head lighthouse.

Aberdeenshire *Area: 6317 sq. km (2439 sq. miles)* A former county of northeast Scotland and now a unitary local authority, Aberdeenshire Council area was separated from the City of Aberdeen in 1996, although its administration remains in Aberdeen. It includes the

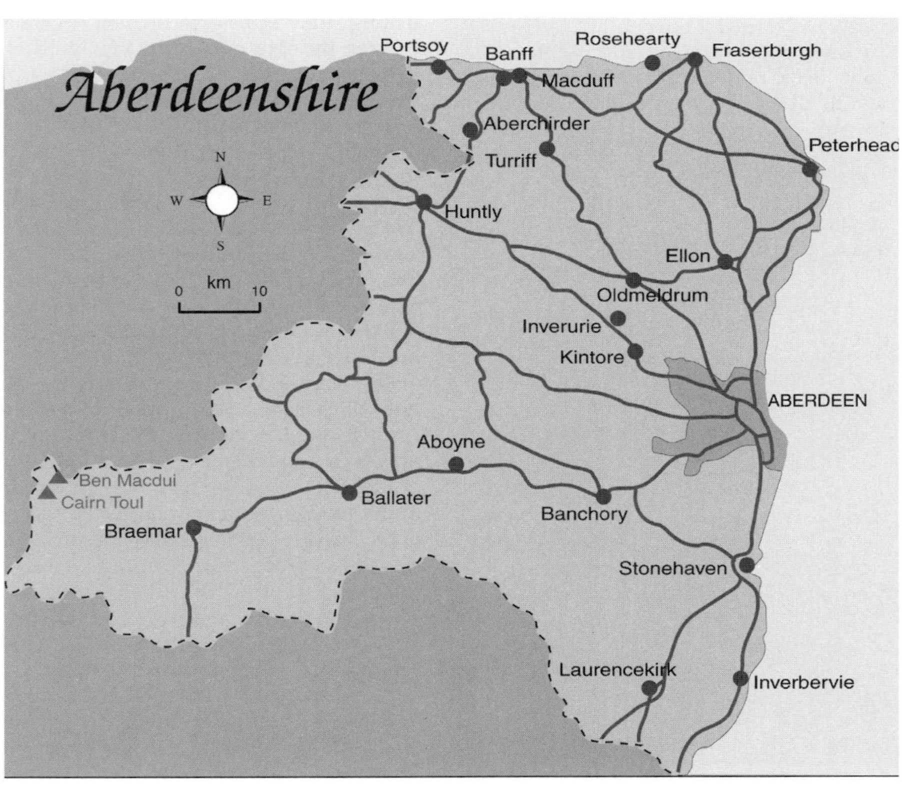

districts of Buchan, Formartine, Cromar and Strathbogie. Lying between the Grampians and the North Sea, which washes its northern and eastern coasts, rural Aberdeenshire is best known for its beef cattle, coastal fishing villages and many historic castles. Aberdeenshire is also home to major paper, food and drink, tourism and oil-related industries. It is watered by the Dee, Don, Ythan and Deveron rivers, and its chief towns are Fraserburgh, Banff, Inverurie, Stonehaven and Peterhead, which is Europe's premier white-fish port.

Aberdeenshire Canal Designed by John Rennie (1761–1821), the 17-lock Aberdeenshire Canal once extended 18 miles (29 km) from Aberdeen Harbour to Port Elphinstone. It was built to transport agricultural produce, timber and stone from rural Aberdeenshire to the port, while taking manure and lime inland. Work began in 1796 and the canal was opened in 1805. Never a great economic success, it was bought by the Great North of Scotland Railway Company in 1845 and abandoned by 1854 so that a railway line could be built along the route. Today little of the canal remains, but it is perhaps most obvious just to the southeast of Hatton of Fintray.

Aberdeenshire Farming Museum, the *Aberdeenshire* Situated within Aden Country Park, between Old Deer and Mintlaw, 9 miles (14 km) west of Peterhead, the Aberdeenshire Farming Museum is one of the most visited attractions in northeast Scotland and comprises the North East of Scotland Agricultural Heritage Centre and Hareshowe Working Farm. Located in an unusual early 19th-century curved steading building, the heritage centre tells the story of the Aden Estate, northeast farming life and agricultural innovations through displays and audiovisual presentations. The steading had become derelict during the 20th century but was renovated in 1983 by Banff and Buchan District Council. Hareshowe of Ironside is a typical small Buchan farm steading. Once located 9 miles (14 km) from Aden Country Park and owned by the Barron family from 1935 until the late 1980s, it was dismantled stone by stone and rebuilt on its present site in 1990–91. The farm was returned to its mid-1950s character. Guided tours are offered in addition to demonstrations of kitchencraft in the farmhouse and traditional working practices on the 8 ha (20 acres) of farmland. Hareshowe was opened as a museum on 3 May 1991 by its former owner, Margaret Barron.

Aberdour *Fife* A small resort town on the Firth of Forth between Inverkeithing and Burntisland, Aberdour sits on a narrow headland that protects the mouth of the Dour Burn. It was formerly two towns: Wester Aberdour, a burgh of barony created in 1501, and Easter Aberdour, a burgh of regality designated in 1638. Once a thriving fishing community, it is now a summer resort with a fine beach (Silver Sands), an 18-hole golf course and historic landmarks that include 14th-century Aberdour Castle, 17th-century Aberdour House, Aberdour Station (1890) and St Fillan's Kirk, whose Romanesque nave and chancel date from the 12th century. During the summer months there is a ferry from Aberdour Harbour to the island of Inchcolm. Stone for chippings and hardcore is quarried nearby.

Aberdour Bay *Aberdeenshire* An inlet on the Moray Firth coast of Aberdeenshire, Aberdour Bay lies between the headlands of Strathangles Point and Quarry Head, due north of the village of New Aberdour. It receives the Dour, a tributary of the Tore Burn, and its cliffs are pitted with caves. The ruined Castle of Dundarg, a promontory fort, overlooks the bay.

Aberdour Castle *Fife* A ruined keep, Aberdour Castle lies near Aberdour on the Firth of Forth. It was in the possession of the Mortimer family and later passed to Thomas Randolph, the Earl of Moray (d.1332) and then to the Douglas earls of Morton in 1342. It comprises a 14th-century E-plan tower house with later extensions, and its grounds include a 16th-century beehive dovecote, a well, gardens and walled terraces. It passed into state care in 1924. In 1725, the Douglas family moved to nearby Aberdour House, which was formerly known as Cuttlehill.

Aberfeldy *Perth and Kinross Pop: 1895* A town in central Perth and Kinross, Aberfeldy lies on the southern side of the River Tay 13 miles (21 km) southwest of Pitlochry. It stands astride the Urlar Burn, a mile (1.5 km) to the north of the Falls of Moness, which are said to have inspired Robert Burns, who visited the town in 1787, to write the 'Birks of Aberfeldy'. The Tay is crossed here by a magnificent 112-m/367-ft-long five-arched bridge built in 1733 by the military road builder General Wade to a design by William Adam. A monument erected near the bridge in 1887 commemorates the raising of the Black Watch Regiment here in 1740. In the late 18th century Aberfeldy developed around small woollen mills. It later flourished as a summer resort. Today, in addition to timeshare tourist accommodation, the town has a working water mill (restored in 1987), a distillery, a recreation centre and an 18-hole golf course.

Aberfeldy Water Mill *Perth and Kinross* Located in Mill Street, Aberfeldy, Perth and Kinross, Aberfeldy Water Mill is a working meal mill. Originally built in 1825, it was opened to the public in 1987 following an award-winning restoration by Tom Rodger, a miller from Cupar in Fife. The mill takes water from the Moness Burn in the Birks of Aberfeldy through a 460-m/500-yd-long lade that runs under the town, emerging to power a 4.6 m (15 ft) overshot mill wheel. The mill wheel turns two 1.3 m (57 in) French burr millstones, each weighing 1.5 tons (1.52 tonnes), which visitors can see grinding oats. The restoration project received a Civic Trust commendation (1988) and a conservation award from the Royal Institute of Chartered Surveyors and *The Times* newspaper (1989).

Aberfoyle *Stirling* A tourist centre at the gateway to the Highlands, Aberfoyle lies 20 miles (32 km) northwest of Stirling and 25 miles (40 km) north of Glasgow at a key point in the A821 loop road known as the 'Trossachs Trail'. To the south are the pasture lands of the Forth Valley and to the north the dramatic Duke's Pass, which cuts through the Queen Elizabeth Forest Park. Situated on the River Laggan, the old village or 'Clachan at Aberfoyle' was one of the settings in Walter Scott's novel *Rob Roy* (1817), the site now being occupied by the Bailie Nicol Jarvie Inn which was erected by the Duke of Montrose. The ruins of the old parish church (1774) survive, as do the remains of Milton Mill (1667) to the west. Nearby Duchray Castle was built in the 16th century by the Grahames of Duchray and Rednock. Walter Scott popularised this part of Scotland, which developed as a holiday centre during the 19th century. The village has tourist facilities, including an 18-hole golf course and the Scottish Wool Centre.

Abergeldie Castle *Aberdeenshire* A tower house built in the 16th century, Abergeldie Castle is located on the southern bank of the River Dee, 2 miles (3 km) east of Balmoral Castle. It was much modernised in the 20th century and is used as a 'shooting-box' and summer residence by the Prince of Wales.

Aberlady *East Lothian* Located on the southern coast of the Firth of Forth, Aberlady lies 17 miles (27 km) east of Edinburgh and 5 miles (8 km) north of Haddington. A former port for Haddington, situated next to Aberlady Bay, it had a pier and harbour until the mid-19th century, when the Peffer Burn and the bay silted up to create salt marshes and mud flats. The old custom house, Haddington House, remains to this day at Aberlady Point. Other buildings nearby include Luffness House, Gosford House, Kilspindie Castle, the parish church (with a 15th-century tower) and the ruins of a Carmelite nunnery (13th century). The Mercat Cross stands in the middle of this elongated village which possesses several 18th- and 19th-century cottages. There is an 18-hole golf course.

Aberlady Bay *East Lothian* Located on the Firth of Forth coastline of East Lothian, to the south of Gullane Point and Gullane Bay, Aberlady Bay is 6 miles (10 km) southwest of North Berwick. The village of Aberlady lies on the bay. The bay, with its salt marshes and mud flats, is a designated nature reserve and a noted wintering ground for wild geese.

Aberlady Point *East Lothian* Located less than a half-mile (1 km) to the east of Craigielaw Point lies the headland of Aberlady Point. Projecting into the Firth of Forth, this point faces the Aberlady Bay Local Nature Reserve. The settlement of Craigielaw lies directly to the south.

Aberlemno *Angus* Situated on the B9134 midway between Forfar and Brechin in Angus, the village of Aberlemno has within its bounds four of Scotland's best Pictish carved monuments. Three stones stand by the roadside, the most easterly probably being the earliest. It is an unshaped stone with prehistoric cup marks, incised on one face with a serpent, a double disc and Z-rod, and a mirror and comb. The small centre stone carries indistinct traces of a crescent and a curving line, but the most dramatic is the immense 3 m (10 ft) cross-slab. On the front of this monument a cross is carved in high relief, its shaft being flanked by angels, animals and panels of interlace. On the back of the stone can be seen Pictish symbols, a hunting scene and a depiction of David rending the jaws of the lion. A fourth stone in the churchyard is intricately carved with interlace patterns cleverly intertwined with animals. The back of the cross-slab features the only known battle scene in Pictish art, a scene thought to depict the Battle of Nechtansmere which took place 6 miles (10 km) to the south in AD 685. Aberlemno village is divided into three separate sections known respectively as Crosston, Kirkton and Flemington.

Aberlour *Moray Pop: 785* A village in central Moray, Aberlour is situated 15 miles (24 km) south of Elgin on the right bank of the River Spey where it is joined by the Burn of Aberlour. Also known more fully as Charlestown of Aberlour, it is named after Charles Grant of Wester Elchies, who in 1812 laid out the village in its present plan comprising a mile/1.5km-long High Street with a square to the west. The new village replaced the earlier community of Skirdustan, of which the ruined St Drostan's Kirk is all that remains. Buildings of note include the remains of the Aberlour Orphanage founded in 1875 by Canon Jupp, and the Fleming Institute which was designed by William Reid and gifted to the burgh by James Fleming, a local banker. Also of interest are two bridges: an old pack-horse bridge crossing the Burn of Aberlour and, crossing the Spey, a more modern steel suspension footbridge built by James Abernethy in 1902. To the northeast of the village stands Aberlour House, built in 1838 to a design by William Robertson for Alexander Grant, a local farmer's son who made his fortune in the West Indies and returned to Scotland to buy the ancestral home of the Gordons of Aberlour. To the south, Ben Rinnes rises to a height of 840 m (2755 ft). Aberlour, which has tourist facilities, is noted for fishing on the Spey, shortbread and the whisky produced at nearby Glenallachie Distillery, within whose grounds is a well dedicated to St Drostan.

Aberlour, Burn of *Moray* The Burn of Aberlour (or Lour Burn) rises in headwaters that flow down from the northeastern slopes of Ben Rinnes in Moray. It passes through the settlements of Milltown of Edinville and Charlestown of Aberlour before joining the River Spey.

Abernethy *Perth and Kinross* The village of Abernethy is located 3 miles (5 km) west of Newburgh in Perth and Kinross. Located within the village is a round tower that rises to a height of 22.5 m (74 ft) and is similar to the one in Brechin. It has characteristics similar to the round towers that can be found in Ireland and dates from AD 850 to AD 950. A museum of local history opened in 2000. To the northeast of the village at Carpow, on the southern banks of the River Tay, lie the remains of a Roman fortress and naval base. The hamlets of Glenfoot and Aberargie were once part of the same parish as Abernethy.

Abernethy Forest *Highland* One of Scotland's largest areas of native pinewood, Abernethy Forest extends from the valley of the River Spey in Strathspey southwards into the Cairngorm Mountains. Situated 6 miles (10 km) south of Grantown on Spey, the forest includes the lochs of Garten and Mallachie. Tore Hill (338 m/1109 ft) is the highest point in the forest. The settlements of Boat of Garten and Nethybridge lie within its bounds, and at Loch Garten there is the first osprey nesting site to be made accessible to the public, via a well-equipped observation centre managed by the RSPB. Formerly a source of timber managed by the Strathspey Estate, 2296 ha (5674 acres) of Abernethy Forest are now designated as a National Nature Reserve with management geared to encouraging natural regeneration of Scots pine. The area is also important for its invertebrate fauna, which include no fewer than 350 species of beetle, 11 species of dragonfly and over 280 species of moths and butterflies.

Abernyte *Perth and Kinross* The hamlet of Abernyte lies in a fold of the Sidlaw Hills within a parish of the same name and is situated on the B953, 11 miles (18 km) east northeast of Perth. An old fermetoun settlement, it takes a linear shape and overlooks the Abernyte Burn.

Abertaff House *Highland* The oldest secular building in Inverness, dating from 1593, Abertaff House was originally built as a town house for the Frasers of Lovat. It is now the regional headquarters of the National Trust for Scotland.

Abertay Sands *Angus* The Abertay Sands stretch eastwards into the North Sea for nearly 8 miles (13 km) from the mouth of the River Tay at Tayport in Fife. The Tentsmuir Sands extend southwards towards the mouth of the River Eden. The Arbroath-built Abertay light vessel was placed on station at the eastern end of Abertay Sands in 1877 and was for ten years the only manned lightship in Scottish waters.

Aberuchill *Perth and Kinross* A laird's house in Perth and Kinross, Aberuchill lies to the south of the River Earn, 2 miles (3 km) southwest of Comrie. The original fortalice was built in the late 16th century by Colin, second son of Campbell of Lawers, who received a Crown charter in 1596. This building was enlarged with Scottish baronial-style additions in the 19th century.

Aberuthven *Perth and Kinross* A linear village of Strathearn in southwest Perth and Kinross, Aberuthven stands on the right bank of the Ruthven Water, 3 miles (5 km) northeast of Auchterarder. Once noted for its cattle fairs, it developed in the 18th and 19th centuries as a centre of the weaving industry.

Abhainn an t-Srath Chuileannaich *Highland* A remote river of central Ross-shire in the northern Highlands, the Abhainn an t-Srath Chuileannaich (alternatively Abhainn an t-Srath Chuilionaich) rises as the Glasha Burn in the Freevater Forest, flowing northeast and east before turning southeast through Strath Cuileannach. It becomes the Black Water before entering the River Carron just to the northeast of Amat Lodge.

Abhainn Bruachaig *Highland* A river rising on the slopes of Fionn Bheinn in Wester Ross, the Abhainn Bruachaig flows 12 miles (19 km) southwestwards to empty into Loch Maree near Taagan, which lies 2 miles (3 km) northwest of Kinlochewe.

Abhainn Crò Chlach *Highland* The Abhainn Crò Chlach rises on the northern slopes of Carn Bàn and flows 6 miles (10 km) north to join the upper reaches of the River Findhorn in the Badenoch district of Highland Council area.

Abhainn Cuileig *Highland* A river rising from the northern end of Loch a' Bhraoin in Wester Ross, the Abhainn Cuileig flows 3 miles (5 km) northeast to join the River Droma to form the River Broom, a mile (1.5 km) to the north of the Corrieshalloch Gorge.

Abhainn Dromm The Gaelic name for the River Droma in Highland Council area.

Abhainn Duibhe *Perth and Kinross* Rising in hills to the southeast of Rannoch Moor in Perth and Kinross, the Abhainn Duibhe flows northeastwards for 5 miles (8 km) through Gleann Duibhe to join the River Gaur 2 miles (3 km) west of Loch Rannoch.

Abhainn na Frithe *Highland* A stream in the Sutherland district of Highland Council area, Abhainn na Frithe rises in the Borrobol Forest and flows east to join the River Helmsdale 2 miles (3 km) south of Burnfoot.

Abhainn na Glasa *Highland* Rising on the slopes of Beinn Tharsuinn in Easter Ross, Abhainn na Glasa flows south, east, then southeast to empty into Loch Morie, 9 miles (14 km) north of Dingwall.

Abhainn Righ *Highland* A river rising on the slopes of Beinn na Gucaig in the Lochaber district of Highland Council area, Abhainn Righ flows through Glen Righ, south and then west, to empty into Loch Linnhe at the Corran Narrows.

Abhainn Shira *Argyll and Bute* A stream on Rannoch Moor, Abhainn Shira flows east from Loch Dochard for 4 miles (6.5 km) to enter Loch Tulla to the north of Glen Orchy in the northeastern corner of Argyll and Bute.

Abhainnsuidhe *or* **Abhainn Suidhe** Alternative names for Amhuinnsuidhe in the Western Isles.

Abington *South Lanarkshire* A settlement adjacent to the M74/A74(M) from Carlisle to Glasgow, Abington lies 11 miles (18 km) southwest of Biggar. The A702 to Edinburgh joins the M74 at Abington. The River Clyde flows north past the village.

Aboyne *Aberdeenshire* A resort town in Royal Deeside, Aboyne lies on the northern side of the River Dee on the A93, 32 miles (51 km) west of Aberdeen. Laid out after 1670, when it received a burgh charter, its grey granite buildings surround a large central green. It was originally called Charleston of Aboyne in honour of Charles Gordon, 1st Earl of Aboyne, who obtained the charter and who in 1671 rebuilt part of Aboyne Castle, an important stronghold to the north of the town protecting the roads that converge there. With the arrival of the railway in 1853 (closed in 1966), Aboyne developed as a resort town largely at the hands of Sir Cunliffe Brooks of Glentanar whose daughter married the 11th Marquess of Huntly. Today the town has a wide range of tourist facilities that include an 18-hole golf course, bowling green, all-weather tennis courts, fishing and shooting, water-skiing on Aboyne Loch and gliding at the Deeside Gliding Club 3 miles (5 km) to the west. Places of interest nearby include the Muir of Dinnet National Nature Reserve, the former royal hunting grounds of the Forest of Birse, Potarch Park, and the Braeloine Visitor Centre in the Forest of Glentanar. Robert Burns' song 'O'er the Water to Charlie' refers to John Ross, the Jacobite boatman who ferried travellers across the Dee at Aboyne before the building of a bridge in 1828. Each September since 1867, the town has hosted the Aboyne Highland Games.

Abriachan *Highland* The settlement of Abriacahan sits on the western bank of Loch Ness in the Inverness district of Highland Council area, about 3 miles (5 km) southwest of the northern end of the loch. Four miles (6.5 km) to the south lie Drumnadrochit and Castle Urquhart.

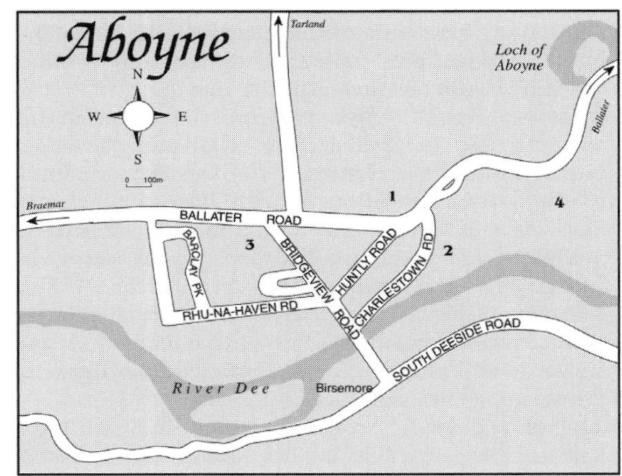

1 *Victory Centre*
2 *The Mart*
3 *Community Centre*
4 *Hospital*

Abronhill *North Lanarkshire* Abronhill is a northern suburb of the town of Cumbernauld in North Lanarkshire. It is located 2 miles (3 km) northeast of the town centre.

Acha *Argyll and Bute* The crofting settlement of Acha on the island of Coll in the Inner Hebrides lies 3 miles (5 km) southwest of Arinagour.

Achadh Mòr An alternative name for Achmore in the Western Isles.

Achadun Castle *Argyll and Bute* Located on the northern coastline of Lismore, overlooking Loch Linnhe and Bernera, the ruins of Achadun Castle date from the 13th century. The castle was held by the bishops of Argyll until the mid-16th century. Three miles (5 km) to the northeast lies the settlement of Achnacroish.

Achahoish *Argyll and Bute* A village in Knapdale, Achahoish lies at the head of Loch Caolisport, 7 miles (11 km) southwest of Ardrishaig. To the southwest of the village at Ellary is St Columba's Cave.

Achaidh na h-Inich, Loch *Highland* A small loch in the Lochalsh district of Highland Council area, Loch Achaidh na h-Inich lies 2 miles (3 km) south of Plockton. To the northwest is Loch Lundie, and Beinn Raimh rises 2 miles (3 km) to the east.

Achairn Burn *Highland* Rising on the slopes of the Hill of Yarrows in Caithness, the Achairn Burn flows north then east past Pulgadon, before turning north to join the Wick River, 3 miles (5 km) west of Wick.

Achalader *Perth and Kinross* A settlement in Perth and Kinross, Achalader lies to the north of the A923, 3 miles (5 km) west of Blairgowrie.

Achaleven *Argyll and Bute* A settlement on the south shore of Loch Etive, Achaleven lies a half-mile (1 km) east of Connel in Argyll and Bute.

Achall, Glen *Highland* A valley in Wester Ross, Glen Achall carries the water of the River Rhidorroch westwards to Loch Achall near Ullapool.

Achall, Loch *Highland* A loch in Wester Ross, Loch Achall lies 2 miles (3 km) east of Ullapool. It is fed by the River Rhidorroch and Allt a'Ghiubhais, and is drained by the Ullapool River, which flows west to Loch Broom.

Achallader *Argyll and Bute* A settlement in northeast Argyll and Bute, Achallader lies on a tributary of the Water of Tulla, 3 miles (5 km) northeast of Bridge of Orchy. Loch Tulla lies a mile (1.5 km) southwest, and a mile (1.5 km) to the southeast is Beinn Achaladair. Black Duncan of Cowal, one of the Campbells of Glenorchy, built one of his seven castles here, the remains of which can still be seen next to Achallader Farm.

Achamore House *Argyll and Bute* Located at the southern end of the island of Gigha in the Inner Hebrides, Achamore House and Gardens lie to the south of the settlement of Ardminish. Lt-Col Sir James Horlick, who bought the island in 1944, created at Achamore one of the finest gardens on the west coast and gifted to the National Trust for Scotland his fine collection of plants. The gardens, which are open to the public, include many species of rhododendron and azalea, as well as tropical plants that take advantage of the warming effects of the Gulf Stream.

Achanalt *Highland* A small settlement in Strath Bran, Ross and Cromarty, Achanalt lies 4 miles (6.5 km) west of the head of Loch Luichart. Achanalt has a station on the railway from Inverness to Kyle of Lochalsh. The River Bran flows to the south.

Achanalt, Loch *Highland* A small loch in Strath Bran, Ross and Cromarty, Loch Achanalt lies on the course of the River Bran 3 miles (5 km) west of the head of Loch Luichart.

Achandunie *Highland* A settlement of Easter Ross, Achandunie lies on the banks of the Alness River, a mile (1.5 km) north of Alness.

Achany *Highland* The rural settlement of Achany lies to the west of the River Shin in Highland Council area. Situated in Achany Glen, the village lies 3 miles (5 km) south of Lairg and the head of Loch Shin.

Achany Glen *Highland* A wooded glen in Sutherland, Highland Council area, Achany Glen occupies the valley of the River Shin between Loch Shin and the River Oykel. At the Shin Falls to the north of Inveran, salmon can be seen swimming in the pool below the falls from an observation platform. Achany House, a Munro family seat situated at the centre of the glen, dates from *c.*1810, with conical drum towers added in 1885.

Achaphubuil *Highland* The linear settlement of Achaphubuil lies a mile (1.5 km) southeast of Corpach, across the Narrows of Loch Eil, in Highland Council area. Two miles (3 km) west, across Loch Linnhe, lies Fort William.

Acharacle *Highland* The straggling village of Acharacle in the Lochaber region of Highland Council area is situated 2 miles (3 km) north of Salen at the western end of Loch Shiel. A popular tourist resort, it is noted for salmon fishing and hill walking. The Loch Shiel Spring Festival and the Jacobite Steam Train to Mallaig are also popular attractions. Acharacle is surrounded by mountains, with Beinn Resipol rising to 845 m (2774 ft) nearby.

Acharn *Highland* A scattered settlement of Morvern in Highland Council area, Acharn lies 4 miles (6.5 km) northeast of Lochaline. It is situated on the River Aline where it rises from Loch Arienas.

Acharn *Perth and Kinross* A village in Kenmore parish, Perth and Kinross, Acharn lies on the southern shore of Loch Tay, 2 miles (3 km) southwest of Kenmore. The village was built for estate workers in the early 1800s, and the water of the Acharn Burn was harnessed by a mill that was converted into a craft centre in the 1970s. Its six-spoke overshot wheel has been retained. Nearby at Croft-na-Caber is the Scottish Crannog Centre with its reconstruction of a prehistoric lake dwelling.

Acharn Burn *Perth and Kinross* A stream in Perth and Kinross, the Acharn Burn rises on Creagan na Beinne in the hills to the north of Glen Almond. It flows northwards for 5 miles (8 km) before entering the southern side of Loch Tay near the village of Acharn. A steep walk southwards up the burn leads to a wooded gorge with a series of waterfalls with a total height of 24.5 m (80 ft). The falls were visited in 1803 by William Wordsworth and his sister, Dorothy, who noted in her diary the 'very beautiful prospect' of Loch Tay.

Acharole, Burn of *Highland* A stream in northeast Caithness, the Burn of Acharole rises in the Flow Country to the west of Wick. It flows northeast to join the Strath Burn before it enters Loch Watten.

Acharosson *Argyll and Bute* The settlement of Acharosson lies 4 miles (6.5 km) northwest of Tighnabruaich in Argyll and Bute.

Achateny Water *Highland* A small stream on the

Ardnamurchan peninsula, the Achateny Water rises as the Allt an Doire Dharaich and flows north, through the settlement of Achateny, before emptying into the sea at Port Bàn.

Achavanich *Highland* A small settlement in eastern Caithness, Achavanich lies at a road junction 6 miles (10 km) north of Latheron and to the west of Stemster Hill. A school here once served children from the surrounding crofts, and a rare U-shaped setting of 36 Neolithic standing stones lies to the east of the road.

Achduart *Highland* A settlement overlooking Loch Broom in Wester Ross, Achduart lies a half-mile (1 km) east of the headland of Rubha Dubh Ard and 4 miles (6.5 km) southeast of Achiltibuie.

Acheninver *Highland* A small settlement in the Coigach district of Wester Ross, Acheninver is located 6 miles (10 km) northwest of Ullapool. Acheninver overlooks Horse Sound and Horse Island near the mouth of Loch Broom.

Achentoul *Highland* A settlement at the head of the Strath of Kildonan in eastern Sutherland, Achentoul lies to the east of the Bannock Burn, a mile (1.5 km) north of Kinbrace. Built c.1900, Auchentoul Lodge overlooks a wide expanse of moorland to the north of Kinbrace. Achentoul Forest lies to the north.

Achfary *Highland* A settlement in northwest Sutherland, Achfary lies at the northern end of Loch More, 6 miles (10 km) southeast of Laxford Bridge. Strath Stack extends northwestwards and to the west lies Reay Forest. The settlement was developed around a shooting lodge in the 1800s by the dukes of Sutherland and then the 1st Duke of Westminster. The timber-clad Achfary School was built in 1953 in an English rustic style.

Achgarve *Highland* A locality in Wester Ross, Highland Council area, Achgarve lies on a peninsula to the west of Gruinard Bay, 3 miles (5 km) north of Aultbea.

Achiltibuie *Highland* A linear settlement in Coigach district of Wester Ross, the crofting township of Achiltibuie lies on Badentarbat Bay 10 miles (16 km) north-northwest of Ullapool. It overlooks the Summer Isles at the mouth of Loch Broom and is a centre of fishing, hillwalking and tourism. The Summer Isles Hotel grows its own vegetables in a hydroponicum, without soil.

Achilty, Loch *Highland* A small loch in Easter Ross, Loch Achilty lies between Loch Garve and Loch Achonachie, 3 miles (5 km) west of Strathpeffer and 6 miles (10 km) west of Dingwall in the shadow of Torr Achilty.

Achinduich *Highland* A settlement in central Sutherland, Achinduich lies 4 miles (6.5 km) south of Lairg on the eastern side of Achany Glen. Shin Falls on the River Shin and the remains of a Neolithic double-ring stone circle are close by. Auchinduich House dates from c.1800.

Achinhoan *Argyll and Bute* A handful of buildings on the Kintyre peninsula, Achinhoan lies a half-mile (1 km) west of Achinhoan Head and 3 miles (5 km) southeast of Campbeltown.

Achinhoan Head *Argyll and Bute* A headland on the east coast of the Kintyre peninsula, Achinhoan Head extends into the Kilbrannan Sound a half-mile (1 km) east of the settlement of Achinhoan and 4 miles (6.5 km) southeast of Campbeltown.

Achintee *Highland* A hamlet of Wester Ross, Achintee lies at the head of Loch Carron on the course of the River Taodail. The settlement is on the West Highland railway line, with a station just to the north at Strathcarron.

Achintraid *Highland* A settlement of Wester Ross, Achintraid lies at the head of Loch Kishorn, 3 miles (5 km) northeast of Plockton.

Achlain *Highland* A locality in Glen Moriston, Achlain lies on the southern bank of the River Moriston to the west of Loch Ness.

Achlaise, Lochan na h- *Highland* A small loch on Rannoch Moor, southern Highland Council area, Lochan na h-Achlaise lies between Loch Bà and Loch Tulla to the east of Black Mount.

Achlyness *Highland* A linear crofting township, Achlyness lies at the head of Loch Inchard, in northwest Sutherland, 2 miles (3 km) west of Rhiconich.

Achmelvich *Highland* A small settlement at the southern end of Achmelvich Bay on the west coast of Sutherland, Achmelvich lies 3 miles (5 km) to the northwest of Lochinver. On a rocky headland stands the Hermit's Castle, a modern single-roomed concrete building erected by an architect as a retreat in 1950.

Achmore *Highland* A small settlement in the Lochalsh district, Achmore lies on the Allt Cadh an Eas a mile (1.5 km) southwest of Stromeferry.

Achmore *Stirling* A locality in northern Stirling Council area, Achmore lies at the western end of Loch Tay, a mile (1.5 km) to the east of Killin. Queen Victoria is said to have been rowed to Achmore from Taymouth Castle at the east end of the loch in 1842, and in 1873 the Earl of Breadalbane converted 'a nice little cottage' here into the more stately Achmore House.

Achmore *Western Isles* A village in central Lewis, Achmore (Gael: *Achadh Mòr*) lies 7 miles (11 km) to the west of Stornoway on the road to Carloway and Callanish. Nearby is the site of an ancient circle with a radius of 41 m (135 ft) first uncovered by peat-cutting in the 1930s.

Achnaba *Argyll and Bute* A settlement on the western shore of Loch Fyne, Achnaba lies 3 miles (5 km) southeast of Lochgilphead.

Achnacarnin *Highland* A scattered crofting community in the Assynt district of western Sutherland, Achnacarnin lies 3 miles (5 km) southeast of the Point of Stoer and 7 miles (11 km) northwest of Lochinver. To the east lies Clashnessie Bay.

Achnacarry *Highland* Achnacarry, home of the Camerons of Locheil (chiefs of the Clan Cameron) since the 1660s, is situated between Loch Arkaig and Loch Lochy in southern Highland Council area. The present house, which dates from 1802, was designed by James Gillespie Graham and replaced an earlier building burned down in 1746 as a reprisal for the 'gentle Locheil's' role in the Jacobite Rising. During World War II, Achnacarry was used as a Commando training centre. There is a museum dedicated to the Clan Cameron in the settlement of Achnacarry, which lies 5 miles (8 km) northwest of Spean Bridge.

Achnacloich *Argyll and Bute* A settlement in the Lorn district of Argyll and Bute, Achnacloich on the south shore of Loch Etive lies 3 miles (5 km) east of Connel. To the south lies the Fearnoch Forest.

Achnacloich *Highland* Located on the western coast of the Sleat peninsula of the isle of Skye, the small village of Achnacloich lies on the Gillean Burn as it enters

Tarskavaig Bay. The settlement of Tarskavaig lies immediately to the north.

Achnaconeran *Highland* The crofting settlement of Achnaconeran lies a half-mile (1 km) northwest of Invermoriston and the River Moriston, in the Inverness district of Highland Council area.

Achnacroish *Argyll and Bute* The settlement of Achnacroish lies on the eastern coast of the island of Lismore in Loch Linnhe. It faces onto the Lynn of Lorn.

Achnadrish *Argyll and Bute* A settlement at the north end of the island of Mull in the Inner Hebrides, Achnadrish lies 4 miles (6.5 km) southwest of Tobermory on the road to Dervaig.

Achnafauld *Perth and Kinross* A small farming settlement of Perth and Kinross at the southeast end of Loch Freuchie in Glen Quaich, Achnafauld lies on a minor road to the west of Amulree, 9 miles (14 km) north of Crieff.

Achnagarron *Highland* A settlement in Easter Ross, Achnagarron is located on the A9 2 miles (3 km) northwest of Invergordon.

Achnaha *Highland* A crofting community on the Ardnamurchan peninsula, Achnaha is situated 3 miles (5 km) north of Kilchoan and 2 miles (3 km) east of the Point of Ardnamurchan.

Achnaha *Highland* Overlooking the Sound of Mull, the village of Achnaha is situated on the shore of the Morvern peninsula, below Fiunary Forest, 2 miles (3 km) west of Lochaline.

Achnahaird *Highland* A small linear settlement of the Coigach district of Wester Ross, Achnahaird lies southwest of Achnahaird Bay. The headland of Rubha Coigeach lies 4 miles (6.5 km) to the northwest.

Achnahanat *Highland* A scattered crofting community of Strath Oykel in southeast Sutherland, Achnahanat lies 7 miles (11 km) northwest of Bonar Bridge.

Achnairn *Highland* Located 4 miles (6.5 km) north of Lairg in central Sutherland, the small settlement of Achnairn lies on the eastern side of Loch Shin.

Achnalea *Highland* A village in Lochaber, southwest Highland Council area, Achnalea lies in Glen Tarbert, 2 miles (3 km) east of Strontian.

Achnamara *Argyll and Bute* A settlement in Knapdale, Achnamara lies on an inlet on the eastern side of Loch Sween, 5 miles (8 km) south of Crinan.

Achnamoine *Highland* A locality in north-central Caithness a half-mile (1 km) east of Spittal and 5 miles (8 km) southeast of Halkirk.

Achnamoine, Loch *Highland* A loch in east-central Sutherland, Loch Achnamoine lies on the course of the River Helmsdale 4 miles (6.5 km) west of Kinbrace.

Achnasheen *Highland* A settlement in Wester Ross, Achnasheen lies on the River Bran at the western end of Strath Bran, 9 miles (14 km) southeast of Kinlochewe and 30 miles (48 km) west of Dingwall. It is situated at the junction of two roads built by the engineer Thomas Telford in the early 1800s. A railway station was built here in 1870.

Achnashellach *Highland* A locality in Glen Carron in Wester Ross, Achnashellach lies on the West Highland Railway to the northeast of Loch Carron. Achnashellach Forest extends to the north and south of the A890 between Achnasheen and Lochcarron.

Achnastank *Moray* A small settlement to the southeast of Ben Rinnes in Moray, Achnastank is situated 5 miles (8 km) southwest of Dufftown between the Burn of Faval and the Corriehabbie Burn.

Achonachie, Loch *Highland* A reservoir in Strath Conon, Easter Ross, Loch Achonachie lies on the course of the River Conon 3 miles (5 km) southwest of Strathpeffer and to the south of Loch Achilty.

Achosnich *Highland* The crofting community of Achosnich lies 3 miles (5 km) northwest of Kilchoan on the Ardnamurchan peninsula. The settlement of Achnaha lies 2 miles (3 km) to the northeast.

Achosnich *Highland* A small settlement in Easter Ross, Achosnich lies 5 miles (8 km) northwest of Dornoch in the valley of the River Evelix.

Achranich *Highland* A small settlement on the Morvern peninsula, southwest Highland Council area, Achranich lies near Ardtornish at the head of Loch Aline close to the mouth of the Rannoch River.

Achray, Loch *Stirling* A small loch in the Trossachs district of Stirling Council area, Loch Achray lies between Loch Venachar and Loch Katrine, 7 miles (11 km) west of Callander. It has a surface area of 82 ha (202 acres) and a mean depth of 11 m (36 ft).

Achreamie *Highland* A settlement on the northern coast of Caithness, Achreamie lies 2 miles (3 km) east of the Dounreay Atomic Energy Establishment.

Achriabhach *Highland* A settlement in Lochaber, southwest Highland Council area, Achriabhach is located in Glen Nevis, 5 miles (8 km) southeast of Fort William.

Achriesgill *Highland* A settlement on the west coast of Sutherland, Achriesgill lies at the head of Loch Inchard, a mile (1.5 km) north of Rhiconich.

Achrimsdale *Highland* A settlement in eastern Sutherland, Highland Council area, Achrimsdale lies 2 miles (3 km) north of Brora.

Achtoty *Highland* A township in northern Sutherland, Highland Council area, Achtoty lies near Torrisdale Bay, 3 miles (5 km) west of Bettyhill.

Achtriochtan, Loch *Highland* A loch at the western end of Glen Coe, Loch Achtriochtan lies on the course of the River Coe, between the peaks of the Three Sisters to the south and the Aonach Eagach ridge to the north. The village of Glencoe is situated 3 miles (5 km) to the west.

Ackergill *Highland* A locality in eastern Caithness, Ackergill lies 2 miles (3 km) northwest of Wick. The five-storeyed Ackergill Tower, dating from the 15th century and once the seat of the Earls Marischal, is now used as a conference centre. It was remodelled in the Scottish baronial style by David Bryce in 1851. Close by are a pair of 18th-century dovecotes and the elegant farm buildings of Ackergill Mains farmsteading.

Adabrock *Western Isles* One of a collection of crofting townships located in the Ness district at the northern tip of Lewis in the Outer Hebrides, Adabrock (Gael: *Adabroc*) lies immediately to the south-southeast of Lionel, a half-mile (1 km) southwest of Port of Ness.

Adam House *City of Edinburgh* Located towards the eastern end of Chambers Street in Edinburgh, this remarkable mock-Georgian building lies on the site of Adam Square, which was demolished to make way for South Bridge and Chambers Street itself. The square included the Watt Institute and School of Arts (which eventually became Heriot-Watt University), but perhaps more notably the home of the influential Adam family of architects. Adam House was completed in 1954 and represented the first postwar building for the University of Edinburgh. The architect was Sir William Kininmonth (1904–88). Today the university uses Adam House for exhibitions, examinations and as an Edinburgh Festival venue.

Add, Lochan *Argyll and Bute* A small loch located 2 miles (3 km) to the east of Kilmartin, Lochan Add lies a half-mile (1 km) west of Loch Leathan.

Add, River *Argyll and Bute* A river of central Argyll and Bute, the Add rises in hills 7 miles (11 km) north of Lochgilphead. Flowing south and west, it passes the settlement of Drimvore and Dunadd Fort before entering Crinan Loch at Bellanoch.

Addiewell *West Lothian* A small industrial village in West Lothian, Addiewell lies to the south of the Breich Water, 2 miles (3 km) south of Blackburn. The village developed in association with the oil-shale industry. James 'Paraffin' Young (1811–83) opened mines and built a refinery here in the 1860s for his Light and Mineral Oil Company. The plant operated until the 1930s and the landscape retains evidence of the industry in the form of a large bing, now managed as a reserve by the Scottish Wildlife Trust. Addiewell has an industrial estate, a primary school and an unstaffed railway station on the line from Glasgow Central to Edinburgh.

Aden Country Park *Aberdeenshire* A recreational area in the Buchan district of northern Aberdeenshire, Aden Country Park occupies an area of 93 ha (230 acres) between the villages of Old Deer and Mintlaw, 10 miles (16 km) west of Peterhead. Part of a former wooded estate, it now comprises the Aberdeenshire Farming Museum, a wildlife centre, caravan park and camping site. The now-ruined Aden House was built in 1832 on the site of a former castle that was a stronghold of the Keith and Russell families. The South Ugie Water passes through the park.

Advie *Highland* A small settlement in Strathspey, Advie lies just south of the River Spey, 10 miles (16 km) northeast of Grantown-on-Spey.

Advocate's Close *City of Edinburgh* Located off Edinburgh's High Street, opposite St Giles Cathedral, Advocate's Close takes its name from Sir James Stewart, the first Lord Advocate of Scotland, who served in this role between 1692 and 1713 and had his house in the close. The earliest building was completed for a merchant called Clement Cor in 1590, and over the doorway are two inscriptions: *Spes Altera Vitae* ('another hope of life') and 'Blissit be God of al his Giftis'. Through the close is Adam Bothwell's House (*c.*1630), named after a Bishop of Orkney who was responsible for running the abbey and estates of Holyrood after the Reformation.

Advocates' Library *City of Edinburgh* Lying to the rear of the Signet Library behind Parliament Square in Edinburgh's old town is the Advocates' Library, which is visible from George IV Bridge. The library was founded in 1682 by Sir George Mackenzie of Rosehaugh and was originally located in Parliament Square, later occupying the Upper Library of what is now the Signet Library. The current building was begun in 1829 by William Henry Playfair (1789–1857) and contained many rare and exceptional books. It was originally conceived to be much more than simply a legal library and was an important resource at the time of the Enlightenment. David Hume (1711–76) was a keeper of the library, and its facilities were greatly praised by the likes of Thomas Carlyle (1795–1881) and Sir Walter Scott (1771–1832). In 1925, the majority of the collection was gifted to form the core of the new National Library of Scotland, which today lies between the Advocates' Library and George IV Bridge. The law books were retained for the use of the advocates and the library remains an actively used legal resource to the present day.

Ae *Dumfries and Galloway* A forestry village in Dumfries and Galloway, Ae lies on the Water of Ae where it emerges from the Forest of Ae, 8 miles (13 km) north of Dumfries.

Ae, Forest of *Dumfries and Galloway* Located within the Galloway Forest Park, the Forest of Ae lies to the north of Dumfries in the catchment of the Water of Ae. Predominantly a coniferous forest, the Forest of Ae has a number of waymarked cycle routes. There is also an open-air collection of historic forestry ploughs, some of which were used locally by the Clarks of Parkgate.

Ae, Water of *Dumfries and Galloway* A river of Dumfries and Galloway, the Water of Ae rises to the east of Queensberry and flows generally southeastwards through the Forest of Ae before joining the Kinnel Water near Templand, 2 miles (3 km) north of Lochmaben. It has a total length of 16 miles (26 km), and its chief tributaries are the Deer, Bran, Capel, Windyhill, Goukstane, Black Linn and Garrel burns.

Ae Bridgend *Dumfries and Galloway* A locality in Dumfries and Galloway, Ae Bridgend is situated on the A701 at a crossing on the Water of Ae, 7 miles (11 km) north of Dumfries. The Barony College lies on the opposite side of the Water of Ae.

Affleck *Angus* A locality lying just to the west of Monikie in southeast Angus and 4 miles (6.5 km) north of Monifieth, which includes Affleck Castle, said to be one of the finest surviving tower houses in the country. This L-plan tower was built around 1460. It comprises thick walls suppporting four storeys topped by a garret that is surrounded by a parapet. For a time known as Auchinleck Castle, Affleck was originally home to the family of the same name, who were closely associated with the Lindsay family. In the 17th century the castle passed to the Reids, but they forfeited the property in 1746 as they had been Jacobites. The castle has been unoccupied since *c.*1760, when a new house was built nearby. Press reports in 2004 indicated that Hollywood actor Ben Affleck believed this castle belonged to his ancestors.

Affric, Glen *Highland* One of the most attractive glens in Scotland, Glen Affric extends in a northeast–southwest alignment to the west of Loch Ness and southwest of Cannich in Highland Council area. It occupies the valley of the River Affric which is formed to the west by the junction of headstreams that rise on the slopes of Aonach Meadhoin and Beinn Fhada (Ben Attow) in Kintail. The Affric flows through Loch Affric and Loch Beinn a' Mheadhoin before joining the Abhainn Deabhag to form the River Cannich. There are fine stands of native pinewood currently being managed to create one of the largest continuous tracts of native Scots pine forest in Scotland. The Affric–Beauly scheme for hydro-electric power generation extends to the east.

Afton Water *East Ayrshire* Celebrated in a famous song by Robert Burns, the Afton Water today flows north from Afton Reservoir in East Ayrshire, emptying into the River Nith near New Cumnock. It is 9 miles (14 km) long.

Agie, Burn of *Highland* The Burn of Agie rises from a small lochan on the southwestern slopes of Stob Poitre Coire Ardair in southern Highland Council area. Flowing north and passing through the Forest of Braeroy, it joins the River Roy 2 miles (3 km) east of Turret Bridge in the upper reaches of Glen Roy.

Aignish *Western Isles* A crofting township at the entrance to the Eye peninsula on the east coast of Lewis in the Outer Hebrides, Aignish (Gael: *Aignis*) lies a half-mile (1 km) northwest of Knock and 4 miles (6.5 km) east of Stornoway.

Aikwood Tower *Scottish Borders* Restored in 1992 by Lord Steel of Aikwood, Aikwood Tower (also Oakwood Tower) lies in the valley of the Ettrick Water 4 miles (6.5 km) southwest of Selkirk. Built in 1535 for the Scott family on land granted by James V, it passed to the Murrays, then back to the Scotts. The building is four storeys high with an attic and corner cap-houses; the adjoining byre is used for exhibitions of local works.

Ailnack, Water of *Moray* The Water of Ailnack rises in the uplands of Moray, flowing northeastwards through the Cairngorm Mountains to meet the River Avon near Delnabo. The Water of Caiplich is one of its headwaters.

Ailort, Loch *Highland* A sea loch opening out into the Sound of Arisaig, Loch Ailort lies between the Ardnish peninsula and Moidart to the south. The settlement of Lochailort lies near its head.

Ailsa Craig *South Ayrshire* This distinctive dome-shaped island rock lies 10 miles (16 km) off the coast of South Ayrshire and rises sharply from the Firth of Clyde to a height of 340 m (1114 ft). Ailsa Craig, which derives its name from the Gaelic for 'fairy rock', is 1200 m (1300 yd) long and 800 m (900 yd) wide, with an area of 100 ha (247 acres). It is also known as Paddy's Milestone owing to its position as a landmark en route from Ireland. The island was the heart of an ancient volcano, its rock exhibiting fine columnar structure and renowned as the source of a superior microgranite used to fashion curling stones. By the late 19th century the island had a population of 29 people working in the quarries or in the lighthouse, which was built in 1883–6 by Thomas Stevenson and his nephew David. Since the closure of the quarries and automation of the light, Ailsa Craig has been inhabited only by a sizeable and important colony of sea birds. The island is home to one of the largest gannet colonies in the world, with more than 70,000 birds, and is designated as a European Special Protection Area. The island is accessible by boat from Girvan.

Ailsh, Loch *Highland* A loch at the head of Glen Oykel in southwest Sutherland, Loch Ailsh lies 8 miles (13 km) southeast of Inchnadamph. It is the source of the River Oykel, which flows southeastwards to the Dornoch Firth. The peak of An Stuc lies to the southeast, while to the north lies the Benmore Forest.

Ainort, Loch *Highland* A sea loch on the east coast of the isle of Skye, 6 miles (10 km) northwest of Broadford, Loch Ainort opens into the Caolas Scalpay opposite the island of Scalpay.

Aird *Dumfries and Galloway* A village in Dumfries and Galloway, Aird is situated 2.5 miles (4 km) east of Stranraer and a mile (1.5 km) west of Castle Kennedy. A mile (1.5 km) to the west is Bridge of Aird.

Aird *Western Isles* A crofting township of the Eye peninsula in eastern Lewis, Aird lies above the bay of Bagh Phort Bholair, 8 miles (13 km) east of Stornoway.

Aird, the *Highland* Located on the northeast coastline of the isle of Skye, at the northernmost extremity of the Trotternish peninsula, the Aird includes the headlands of Rubha Hunish and Rubha na t-Aiseig to the east. Tulm Island and Duntulm Bay lie to the west, while at its southwest end lies Duntulm Castle.

Aird, the *Highland* The region to the south of the Beauly Firth lying between the River Beauly and Loch Ness is known as the Aird. It comprises high wooded ground rising to 316 m (1037 ft) at Cnoc na Moine and includes the settlements of Kiltarlity and Kirkhill.

Aird an Runair *Western Isles* The westernmost point of North Uist in the Outer Hebrides, the headland of Aird an Runair lies 3 miles (5 km) southwest of Balmartin.

Aird Kilfinichen *Argyll and Bute* A headland on the north shore of Loch Scridain on the island of Mull, Aird Kilfinichen lies to the west of Kilfinichen Bay.

Aird Leimhe A Gaelic name for Ardslave in the Western Isles.

Aird Mhidhinis The Gaelic name for Ardveenish in the Western Isles.

Aird of Coigach *Highland* An area in the Coigach district of Wester Ross, the Aird of Coigach lies to the north of Loch Bad a'Ghaill, 10 miles (16 km) north of Ullapool.

Aird of Kinloch *Argyll and Bute* A promontory at the head of Loch Scridain on the island of Mull, the Aird of Kinloch separates the loch from the smaller Loch Beg.

Aird of Sleat *Highland* A settlement on the island of Skye in the Inner Hebrides, Aird of Sleat lies near the southern tip of the Sleat peninsula, 4 miles (6.5 km) southwest of Armadale.

Aird Ranish *Western Isles* A bulbous peninsula on the east coast of Lewis in the Outer Hebrides, Aird Ranish (also Aird Raerinish, Gael: *Aird Ranais* or *Aird Raerinis*) lies between Loch Grimshader in the north and Loch Leurbost in the south. The settlements of Ranish and Crossbost lie across the narrow neck of the peninsula, which terminates at Ranish Point.

Aird Shleibhe A Gaelic name for Ardslave in the Western Isles.

Aird Uig *Western Isles* A crofting township on the west coast of Lewis in the Outer Hebrides, Aird Uig (also Aird Uige) lies a half-mile (1 km) south of Gallan Head, 24 miles (38 km) west of Stornoway. RAF Aird Uig, to the north of the settlement, was once the site of an important communications and monitoring station. While a small part of the facility is still used by NATO, the buildings of the associated military camp have either been turned to civilian use or lie disused.

Airdbhair, Loch *Highland* A sea loch on the northwest coast of Sutherland, Loch Airdbhair forms an inlet on the south side of Eddrachillis Bay. A broch is located at the head of the loch where it is joined by the Allt na Claise. The settlement of Ardvar lies on the northeast shore of the loch.

Airdrie *North Lanarkshire* Located in the Monklands district of North Lanarkshire to the east of Coatbridge and 11 miles (18 km) east of Glasgow, the former industrial town of Airdrie developed from a farmsteading in the 17th century through the efforts of Robert Hamilton (1650–1701) who helped create a market established in 1695. In the 18th century it became a centre for handloom weaving and in 1821 it achieved the status of a burgh, one of the last in Scotland to be granted a charter. In the 19th century Airdrie expanded, with coal mining, oil-shale extraction and cotton milling, the area around it supplying much of the ironstone that supported the foundries at Coatbridge. Engineering and the production of beer, railway wagons, bricks and paper were also important industries. Now largely a residential settlement with knitwear, liqueur and cosmetics industries, Airdrie lost its burgh status in 1975 when it became part of Monklands district. Notable buildings include the Sir John Wilson Town Hall (1912), the Wellwynd Church (1847), the West Parish Church (1834), St Margaret's RC Church (1839), Airdrie Town House (1826), Cairnhill House (1841), Airdrie Academy (1895) and the Weavers' Cottages Museum.

Airdriehill *North Lanarkshire* Located to the northeast of Airdrie, Airdriehill sits on a small hill to the west of Plains.

Airds Bay *Argyll and Bute* Located at the southwestern end of the district of Appin in Argyll and Bute, Airds Bay forms an inlet of the Lynn of Lorn to the north of the mouth of Loch Creran, immediately southwest of Port Appin.

Airds Bay *Argyll and Bute* A bay on the southern shore of Loch Etive in Argyllshire, Airds Bay lies to the east of Airds Point and less than a mile (1.5 km) north of the settlement of Taynuilt. Bonawe lies to the east.

Airds Moss *East Ayrshire* An area of blanket bog in the Muirpark Uplands, Airds Moss lies to the north of Cumnock. It extends northwards to the River Ayr and comprises a mantle of peat characterised by bog moss and other wetland species.

Airds of Kells *Dumfries and Galloway* A hamlet in Dumfries and Galloway, Airds of Kells lies to the north of the River Dee and west of the southern end of Loch Ken, 5 miles (8 km) south of New Galloway.

Airds Point *Dumfries and Galloway* A small headland on the Solway Firth coast of Dumfries and Galloway, Airds Point lies to the southwest of Balcary Point nearly 3 miles (5 km) southeast of Auchencairn. Big Airds Hill rises behind the point, and to the east and west are rocky coastal features given the names Lot's Wife and Adam's Chair.

Airds Point *Dumfries and Galloway* A headland of Dumfries and Galloway, Airds Point lies near the mouth of the River Nith, 6 miles (10 km) south of Dumfries.

Airidh a' Bhruaich The Gaelic name for Arivruaich in the Western Isles.

Airie Burn *Dumfries and Galloway* A stream in Dumfries and Galloway, the Airie Burn rises from Loch Skerrow and flows northeastwards for nearly 2 miles (3 km) before joining the Black Water of Dee.

Airieland *Dumfries and Galloway* A locality in Dumfries and Galloway, Airieland lies by the B727, 3 miles (5 km) south of Castle Douglas. To the south, on the lower slopes of Screel Hill, is the Airieland Moor.

Airigh, Gleann *Argyll and Bute* Located in the heart of the Minard Forest, 5 miles (8 km) northeast of Lochgilphead in Argyll and Bute, Gleann Airigh carries the middle section of the River Add from the foothills of Beinn Laoigh to the flood plains of Mòine Mhòr.

Airlie *Angus* A hamlet with a primary school in western Angus, Airlie is located in a parish of the same name 4.5 miles (7 km) northeast of Alyth and 5 miles (8 km) southwest of Kirriemuir. Kirkton of Airlie is situated a half-mile (1 km) to the north and Airlie Castle lies 2 miles (3 km) to the northwest at the junction of the Melgam Water with the River Isla. The original castle was built by Walter Ogilvy of Lintrathen following a grant made to him in 1432 by James I, but it was destroyed in 1640 by the 8th Earl of Argyll, when James Ogilvy, the 1st Earl of Airlie, refused to sign the National Covenant. Although it was never rebuilt, a country house was constructed over the ruins in 1793. This was restored during the 20th century and remains occupied.

Airntully *Perth and Kinross* A farming and commuter village in Perth and Kinross, Airntully lies to the west of the River Tay, 8 miles (13 km) north of Perth. It is an old fermetoun village that thrived on cottage weaving in the 18th century. Although it has a relatively unspoiled charm today, the anonymous writer of the *Old Statistical Account of the Parish of Kinclaven* in the 1790s was not impressed by the backward state of the village, commenting that, 'The county of Perth, were it possessed of no other spot of a similar description, should allow Arntully [sic] to remain in its present state, that a proper contrast might be drawn, between a neat modern village, and one upon the old construction'.

Airor *Highland* A locality on the coast of Knoydart, Airor looks out over the Sound of Sleat to Skye. Airor Island lies just off the coast.

Airth *Falkirk* The largest village of northern Falkirk Council area, Airth lies on the A905 road close to the River Forth beneath a wooded escarpment to the north of the Bowtrees roundabout. The 18th-century core of the village, which includes a Market Cross (1697), is a designated conservation area. On the south slope of Airth Hill are a ruined church once associated with Holyrood Abbey and Airth Castle, a 16th-century castle with an early 19th-century facade by David Hamilton (1768–1843), now a hotel and conference centre. In 1633 the earldom of Airth was conferred upon William Graham of Monteith, but the title became extinct in 1694.

Airthrey *Stirling* A locality in Stirling Council area, Airthrey lies at the western end of the Ochil Hills, immediately southeast of Bridge of Allan. The policies of the former Airthrey Estate, focusing on Airthrey Park and Airthrey Loch, were landscaped by a pupil of 'Capability' Brown, and Airthrey Castle was built to a design by Robert Adam for the Haldane family in 1791. The lands of Airthrey now form the campus of the University of Stirling, which was founded here in 1967.

Aisgernis The Gaelic name for Askernish in the Western Isles.

Aith *Shetland* A remote township on the western coast of Mainland Shetland, Aith or Aithsting lies at the head of Aith Voe. In addition to being a fishing centre, it has a marina, lifeboat station and school.

Aithsting *Shetland* A district and old parish in west Mainland Shetland, Aithsting includes the village of Aith and lies to the south and west of Aith Voe at the neck of the Walls peninsula.

Aithsetter *Shetland* A hamlet on the east coast of the

Mainland of Shetland, Aithsetter lies in the district and old parish of Cunningsburgh, a half-mile (1 km) northeast of the village of the same name.

Akran, Loch *Highland* A small loch to the east of Strath Halladale in northeast Sutherland, Loch Akran lies 3 miles (5 km) southwest of the settlement of Reay. It is the source of the Akran Burn, which connects with the Halladale River.

Aladale, Glen *Highland* A narrow glen in Moidart, southwest Highland Council area, Glen Aladale occupies the valley of the Glenaladale River which is formed by the meeting of the Coire Reidh and the Allt a' Chuirn below Croit Bheinn. It flows southeastwards into Loch Sheil.

Alcaig *Highland* A village in Easter Ross, Alcaig lies a mile (1.5 km) southeast of Dingwall.

Aldclune *Perth and Kinross* A hamlet in Moulin parish, Perth and Kinross, Aldclune lies on the left bank of the River Garry, 2 miles (3 km) east-southeast of Blair Atholl.

Aldie *Aberdeenshire* A locality to the northwest of Cruden Bay in Aberdeenshire, Aldie is situated on the southeast-facing slope of the Hill of Aldie overlooking the Laeca Burn. North Aldie lies a half-mile (1 km) to the north.

Aldie *Perth and Kinross* A locality in southeast Perth and Kinross, the name Aldie is associated with Aldie Castle and the farms of Easter Aldie, Wester Aldie, Parks of Aldie and Hilton of Aldie, all lying on a ridge to the east of Powmill. Aldie Castle is believed to have been acquired by the powerful Mercer family, merchants in Perth, about the middle of the 14th century and named after Aldia Murray, daughter of Sir William Murray of Tullibardine. The present fortified keep, restored between the 1930s and 1960s, dates largely from the 16th and 17th centuries. A village near the castle known as the Muckle Toon of Aldie disappeared some time before the beginning of the 19th century.

Aldie, Glen *Highland* A narrow wooded glen in Easter Ross, Glen Aldie occupies the valley of the Aldie Water which flows in a loop round Tain to join the Dornoch Firth.

Aldinna Loch *South Ayrshire* A small loch of South Ayrshire, Aldinna Loch lies 3 miles (5 km) northwest of Shalloch on Minnoch. It is one of many small lochs that feed Loch Bradan and Loch Riecawr.

Aldochlay *Argyll and Bute* A settlement on the western shore of Loch Lomond, Aldochlay lies a mile (1.5 km) south of Luss, on the eastern edge of Argyll and Bute Council area. It lies within the Loch Lomond and Trossachs National Park and looks out to the island of Inchtavannach.

Aldourie Castle *Highland* Aldourie Castle sits at the northeastern end of Loch Ness, 2 miles (3 km) north of Dores in the Inverness district of Highland Council area. Built in the 17th century, this tower house is said to be haunted by a ghost known as 'the Gray Lady'.

Ale Water *Scottish Borders* A tributary of the River Teviot in Scottish Borders, the Ale Water rises on the northwestern slopes of Henwoodie Hill in Roberton parish. It flows northeast and east for 24 miles (38 km) to meet the Teviot just south of Ancrum village. It passes through Ashkirk and Lilliesleaf.

Alemoor Loch *Scottish Borders* A small loch in Roberton parish in Scottish Borders, Alemoor lies on the course of the Ale Water.

Alexandria *West Dunbartonshire* Situated to the south of Loch Lomond and 3 miles (5 km) north of Dumbarton on the west bank of the River Leven, Alexandria developed from a simple grocer's shop established on the site in the early 18th century. The settlement is named after Lieutenant Alexander Smollet, who was born there and died in 1799 at the Battle of Alkmaar. It expanded to form an industrial town with a narrow north–south street plan that eventually connected with other villages such as Balloch and Jamestown, and in 1836 a bridge over the Leven linked Alexandria with Bonhill. Bleaching, dyeing and printing brought early prosperity to the town, and between 1905 and 1913 the Argyll Motor Works was the largest car production plant in Europe. The factory, later used by the Admiralty to produce torpedoes, now houses a motor museum. Alexandria is now largely a commuter settlement with rail links to Glasgow, its textile industry replaced by whisky distilling and light industry on the Vale of Leven Industrial Estate.

Alford *Aberdeenshire* Situated amid fertile farmland to the south of the Coreen Hills in Aberdeenshire, the village of Alford lies in the Howe of Alford near the River Don, 23 miles (37 km) west of Aberdeen. Originally an agricultural kirkton settlement with a fair, Alford developed as the terminus of the Alford Valley Railway which opened in 1859. In addition to its cattle market (which closed in the 1980s) and agricultural engineering, Alford became a commuter settlement following the North Sea oil boom of the 1970s. In the 1980s a country park was established in the policies of Haughton House, and the Grampian Transport Museum, a short section of the Alford Valley Railway and Alford Heritage Centre were opened. Alford was the site of the defeat of the Covenanters by the Marquess of Montrose in 1645.

Aline, Loch *Highland* An inlet of the Sound of Mull on the coast of the Morvern peninsula, Loch Aline extends 3 miles (5 km) inland from Lochaline to Kinlochaline Castle at the head of the loch. The River Aline, which rises from Loch Arienas, enters the loch near the castle, as does the River Rannoch, which joins it from Loch Tearnait in the east. There is a ferry link from Lochaline to Fishnish on the island of Mull.

Aline, River *Highland* A river of the Morvern peninsula, the River Aline flows south from Loch Arienas, past Kinlochaline Castle to empty into Loch Aline.

Allachy, Water of *Aberdeenshire* A headstream of the Water of Tanar in the Grampians, the Water of Allachy rises in the Aberdeenshire parish of Aboyne and Glentanar. It flows generally northwards towards Royal Deeside from the back of the Hill of Cat on the border between Angus and Aberdeenshire. For most of its course it flows through the Forest of Glen Tanar, joining the Tanar a mile (1.5 km) to the southwest of Glen Tanar House.

Alladale, Glen *Highland* The valley of the River Alladale in Easter Ross, Glen Alladale lies 10 miles (16 km) west of Bonar Bridge. The Alladale River rises in the Freevater Forest and flows 4 miles (6.5 km) east to join the Abhainn a' Ghlinne Mhoir near Alladale Lodge, where it becomes the River Carron.

Allan, Strath *Perth and Kinross/Stirling* The wide valley of Strath Allan follows the course of the Allan Water from Blackford in the northeast to Dunblane in the southwest and includes the settlements of Braco and Greenloaning.

Allan Water *Scottish Borders* A tributary of the River Teviot in Scottish Borders, the Allan Water is formed at the meeting of the Skelfhill and Priesthaugh burns, which rise on Langtae Hill and Cauldcleuch Head near the border with Dumfries and Galloway. It flows northwestwards for 5 miles (8 km) before joining the Teviot 4 miles (6.5 km) southwest of Hawick.

Allan Water *Scottish Borders* An affluent of the River Tweed, the Allan Water rises near Langshaw in Scottish Borders and flows south through the Fairydean to join the Tweed to the west of Gattonside.

Allan Water *Stirling* A river of central Scotland, the Allan Water rises in the Ochil Hills to the south of Blackford in Perth and Kinross. After its descent from the hills into Strath Allan, it flows southwestwards and southwards into Stirling Council area, where it joins the River Forth immediately south of Bridge of Allan. Its total length is 22 miles (35 km).

Allanbank *North Lanarkshire* A small settlement on the southern bank of the South Calder Water, Allanbank lies between the villages of Bonkle and Allanton.

Allandale *Falkirk* A village in Falkirk Council area, Allandale lies to the west of Bonnybridge on the B816, close to the Forth and Clyde Canal, the line of the Antonine Wall and the main railway line. It comprises three parts: Allandale Cottages in the east, Dundas Cottages in the west, and the 20th-century artisan dwellings that form a conservation area.

Allanfearn *Highland* A settlement in eastern Highland Council area, Allanfearn lies 4 miles (6.5 km) east of Inverness.

Allangrange *Highland* A locality on the Black Isle, Allangrange lies 2 miles (3 km) southwest of Munlochy.

Allanton *North Lanarkshire* A village in the valley of the South Calder Water, Allanton lies 4 miles (6.5 km) northwest of Wishaw and 2 miles (3 km) north of Bonkle. It developed in the 20th century in association with the nearby Kingshills Colliery. The mine finally closed in 1973, although open-cast workings remain to the southeast.

Allanton *South Lanarkshire* A commuter settlement 2 miles (3 km) to the southeast of Hamilton, Allanton sits between the M74 and Chatelherault Country Park. Strathclyde Country Park lies 2 miles (3 km) to the north.

Allargue *Aberdeenshire* Situated in the upper valley of the River Don in Aberdeenshire, Allargue House and Inn lie at the foot of Allargue Hill close to Cock Bridge.

Allean Forest *Perth and Kinross* A forest in Tay Forest Park, Allean lies at the east end of Loch Tummel, to the north and west of the Queen's View. Woodland walks combine varied terrain and tree species with archaeological sites, including a partly restored 18th-century clachan or farmstead.

Allermuir *Midlothian* A summit at the northern end of the Pentland Hills, Allermuir rises to 493 m (1617 ft) above the village of Swanston on the southern outskirts of Edinburgh.

Alligin Shuas *Highland* A locality in Wester Ross, Alligin Shuas lies close to the northern shore of Upper Loch Torridon and southwest of Beinn Alligin.

Alloa *Clackmannanshire* The administrative centre of Clackmannanshire Council area, Alloa is situated on the north bank of the River Forth 7 miles (11 km) east of Stirling. The settlement developed at a ford and ferry crossing defended in medieval times by Alloa Tower, which was built on land acquired by the Erskine family around 1360. Other buildings of interest include the Burgh Chambers (1874), now replaced by the new Council Offices at Greenfield; Alloa Town Hall, built in 1888–98 to a design by Paul Waterhouse for John Thomson Paton, director of Paton's Alloa mills; the old Church of St Mungo with its graveyard and 17th-century tower; St Mungo's Parish Church, built to a design by James Gillespie Graham in 1819 and one of Scotland's finest neo-perpendicular Gothic hall kirks; Bauchop's House, built in 1695 by noted local stonemason Tobias Bauchop; and the Mar Inn, built in the 18th century beside a thriving harbour and reputedly a haunt of the locally born artist David Allan whose father was shoremaster. Alloa developed as a port in the late-18th and 19th centuries in association with expanding textile, sawmilling, rope-making, sail-making, shipbuilding, distilling, brewing (which dates from 1784), coal and glass-making industries. Although its port trade declined after World War I, glassware, distilling and brewing are still important industries. Lime Tree Walk, created in 1714 between the harbour and the town, formed part of an extensive designed landscape largely created by John Erskine, 6th Earl of Mar, who was responsible for establishing the deep-water port with its independent Customs House. Alloa has a trade centre and Riverbank Industrial Estate, as well as a museum and gallery (Speirs Centre).

Alloa Tower *Clackmannanshire* Located in the centre of Alloa in Clackmannanshire, Alloa Tower is one of the largest surviving medieval towers in Scotland. Completed in 1497 and significantly modified in the early 18th century, Alloa Tower is the ancestral home of the Erskine family, earls of Mar and Kellie. Original features of special interest are the oak roof beams, groin vaulting and a domed Italianate staircase. The Erskines were custodians of the young Mary, Queen of Scots, and John Erskine, 1st Earl of Mar (*c*.1510–77), was Regent of Scotland, while another John, 6th Earl of Mar (1645–1733), was involved in the Jacobite Rising of 1715. Now managed

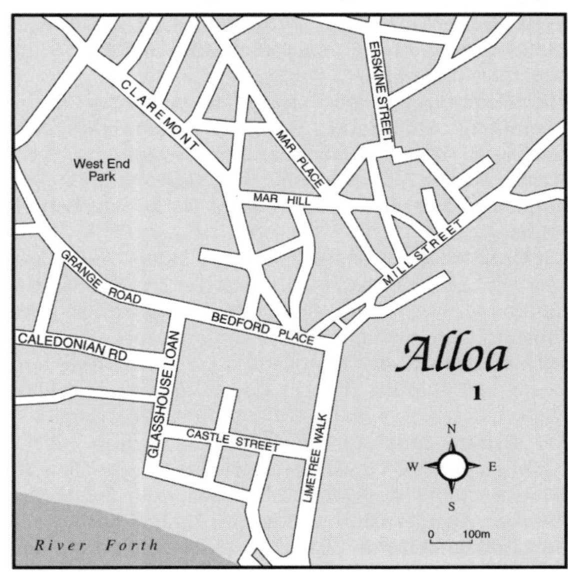

1 *Alloa Tower*

by the National Trust for Scotland, an eight-year restoration was completed and opened in 1997 by Queen Elizabeth II to mark the tower's 500th anniversary.

Alloway *South Ayrshire* A locality on the River Doon to the south of Ayr in South Ayrshire, Alloway is best known as the birthplace in 1759 of the poet Robert Burns. The Burns Museum possesses some of his original papers while the Land o' Burns Centre also has a display of his life and works. Nearby are the Auld Brig o' Doon, Alloway Kirk and the Burns Monument.

Allt a' Chaoil Reidhe *Highland* A stream in the Ben Alder Forest, Badenoch, the Allt a' Chaoil Reidhe flows northeast to empty into the southern end of Loch Pattack.

Allt a' Gheallaidh *Moray* A stream rising in the uplands of Moray, the Allt a' Gheallaidh flows 5 miles (8 km) southeastwards through Glen Gheallaidh and Scootmore Forest to join the River Spey near that river's confluence with the River Avon.

Allt a' Mhuilinn *Highland* A stream in northeast Sutherland, the Allt a' Mhuilinn rises in Caol-loch and flows east to join the River Halladale 5 miles (8 km) south of Melvich.

Allt an Stacain *Argyll and Bute* A river in eastern Argyll and Bute, the Allt an Stacain rises to the north of Lochan Shira and flows west to become the Cladich River 2 miles (3 km) southeast of the settlement of Cladich.

Allt Arder *Moray* A burn in the Grampians, the Allt Arder rises at the back of the Hill of Slackmore in the uplands of Moray. Joined by the Blarnish Burn, it flows southeastwards to join the River Spey near Knockando.

Allt Beochlich *Argyll and Bute* Rising in a small loch to the north of Cruach Mhòr in the Lorn district of Argyll and Bute, Allt Beochlich flows 3 miles (5 km) east to empty into Loch Awe.

Allt Bhlàraidh *Highland* A river in the Levishie Forest, southern Highland Council area, the Allt Bhlàraidh rises in Loch Liath and flows southeastwards through the Bhlàraidh Reservoir before joining the River Moriston at Bhlàraidh.

Allt Bhran *Highland* A river in Badenoch, the Allt Bhran rises in the Grampians to the east of Gaick Forest. It flows northwest to join the River Tromie, 6 miles (10 km) south of Kingussie.

Allt Chomhraig *Highland* A stream rising in the Grampian Mountains, the Allt Chomhraig flows northeast through Glen Chomhraig to join the River Feshie 6 miles (10 km) northeast of Kingussie.

Allt Chriosdain An alternative name for Burn of Loin in Moray.

Allt Connie *Aberdeenshire* A stream in the Grampians, the Allt Connie rises on the slopes of Carn Bhac on the border with Perth and Kinross. It flows northeast for 4 miles (6.5 km) to join the River Dee at Inverey.

Allt Conait *Perth and Kinross* A short stream in western Perth and Kinross, the Allt Conait links the Loch na Daimh Reservoir with the River Lyon in Glen Lyon.

Allt Cristie Mor *Aberdeenshire* A stream in the Grampians, the Allt Cristie Mor rises in the Glen Ey Forest on the slopes of Carn Bhac near the border between Aberdeenshire and Angus. It flows northwards to join the Allt Connie, and then continues north to join the River Dee at Inverey.

Allt Cuaich *Highland* Flowing from the southern end of Loch Cuaich in Badenoch, the Allt Cuaich flows west and then northwest to join the River Truim 2 miles (3 km) north of Dalwhinnie.

Allt Darrarie *Aberdeenshire* A stream in the eastern Grampians of Aberdeenshire, the Allt Darrarie rises between the Watery Hill and the Black Hill of Mark close to the border between Aberdeenshire and Angus. It flows north round the Black Hill to join the River Muick just east of Loch Muick.

Allt Easach *Argyll and Bute* A stream on the Kintyre peninsula, the Allt Easach rises on Sgreadan Hill and flows a mile (1.5 km) southwest to join the Glenlussa Water a half-mile (1 km) south of Lussa Loch.

Allt Eigheach *Perth and Kinross* A stream in the southwest Grampians, the Allt Eigheach rises to the north of Rannoch Moor and flows south for nearly 8 miles (13 km) before entering Loch Eigheach a mile (1.5 km) east of Rannoch Station.

Allt Ghlas *Perth and Kinross* A stream in highland Perth and Kinross, the Allt Ghlas rises on the slopes of Stob an Aonaich Mhoir to the east of Loch Ericht. It flows south for nearly 5 miles (8 km) to join the River Ericht where it emerges from the southern end of Loch Ericht.

Allt Ghlinn Thaitneich *Perth and Kinross* A stream in east highland Perth and Kinross, the Allt Ghlinn Thaitneich flows southeast through Gleann Thaitneich from its source in Loch nan Eun, eventually joining the Glen Lochsie Burn to form the Shee Water near Spittal of Glenshee.

Allt Glas Choire *Perth and Kinross* A stream of Atholl in highland Perth and Kinross, the Allt Glas Choire rises in the southern Grampians near the border with Highland Council area. It flows 7 miles (11 km) southwards to join the River Garry and is joined by the Allt a' Chireachain.

Allt Laire *Highland* A stream in the Lochaber district of Highland Council area, the Allt Laire rises to the west of Loch Treig and flows 6 miles (10 km) northeast to empty into Loch Moy, 5 miles (8 km) east of Roybridge.

Allt Lorgy *Highland* A stream in Strathspey, the Allt Lorgy rises on Carn Dearg Mòr and flows northeast to join the River Dulnain a mile (1.5 km) west of Carrbridge.

Allt Mhoille *Argyll and Bute* Rising to the south of Beinn a' Chochuil in the district of Lorn, the Allt Mhoille flows southeast to join the River Strae just before it empties into the head of Loch Awe.

Allt na Caim *Highland* A stream in the Lochaber district of Highland Council area, Allt na Caim flows 3 miles (5 km) south from Loch na Sgeallaig to empty into the head of the Blackwater Reservoir.

Allt nan Achaidhean *Highland* A stream to the west of Kinbrace in east-central Sutherland, the Allt nan Achaidhean rises on Cnoc an Liath-bhaid Mhòir and flows southeast to become the Abhainn na Frithe, 2 miles (3 km) northeast of the settlement of Altanduin.

Allt nan Caorach *Highland* A stream in Easter Ross, Allt nan Caorach rises on Ben Wyvis and flows 6 miles (10 km) east to join the River Glass 3 miles (5 km) northwest of Evanton.

Allt Odhar *Highland* Rising in the Monadhliath Mountains 6 miles (10 km) southwest of Loch Killin, the Allt Odhar flows 4 miles (6.5 km) northeast to join the River Killin.

Allt Riabhach *Highland* Rising on Meallan Odhar to the

south of Glen Affric in the Inverness district of Highland Council area, Allt Riabhach flows 6 miles (10 km) northeast to form the Abhainn Deabhag at the Pladda Falls.

Allt Ruadh *Highland* A stream in Badenoch, the Allt Ruadh rises on the northwest slopes of Carn Bàn Mòr and flows northeast to join the River Feshie to the east of Kingussie.

Allt Shallainn *Perth and Kinross* Rising in the Talla Bheith Forest, 6 miles (10 km) northwest of Kinloch Rannoch, the Allt Shallainn flows northeast to empty into the southern end of Loch Garry.

Allt Tolaghan *Argyll and Bute* A stream of northeast Argyll and Bute rising to the west of Glen Orchy, the Allt Tolaghan flows northeast to join Abhainn Shira just before it empties into Loch Tulla.

Alltain Duibh, Loch an *Highland* An inlet on the west coast of Coigach in Wester Ross, Loch an Alltain Duibh separates the Summer Isles of Isle Ristol and Eilean Mullagrach from the mainland, 2 miles (3 km) north of Achiltibuie.

Alltnacaillich *Highland* A settlement in Strath More, northern Sutherland, Alltnacaillich lies 3 miles (5 km) south of Loch Hope. To the south is the Dun Dornaigill Broch.

Alltsigh *Highland* A locality on the western side of Loch Ness, Alltsigh lies 8 miles (13 km) northeast of Fort Augustus. A river of the same name rises on the eastern slopes of Carn a' Mheallain Odhair and flows down through Alltsigh to join Loch Ness.

Almond, Glen *Perth and Kinross* Glen Almond, the valley of the River Almond in Perth and Kinross, extends southeast and east from the source of the Almond south of Loch Tay to the junction of the Almond with the River Tay just north of Perth. For part of its middle course the Almond flows through the Sma' Glen and Buchanty Spout before meandering past Trinity College and through the former industrial village of Almondbank. Trinity College, now a boarding school, was founded in 1843 as a theological college of the Scottish Episcopal Church.

Almond, River A river of east-central Scotland, the Almond rises on the eastern flank of the Cant Hills, a mile (1.5 km) north of Shotts in North Lanarkshire. From there, it flows past Harthill and then through West Lothian, which represents the majority of its catchment. The river flows east past Whitburn and on through Blackburn before being joined by the Breich Water near Seafield. It then continues through the old village and new town of Livingston before meeting the Linhouse Water, another main tributary, at Mid Calder. By this stage the river is flowing in a steep-sided gorge. Continuing northeast, the Almond is crossed by the Union Canal on a sizeable aqueduct, and then by the M8, before entering the City of Edinburgh. Just to the north of Newbridge the M9 crosses the river which flows onwards to Kirkliston and then alongside Edinburgh Airport, under the Cramond Brig and past Barnton, before draining into the Firth of Forth at Cramond, which marks the end of its 28-mile (45-km) course. The Almondell and Calder Wood Country Park forms a notable recreational resource centred on the river to the east of Livingston. The river has long been a victim of pollution, with the bleaching of flax in the 18th century, and oil-shale and coal mining in the 19th and 20th centuries, together making it one of Scotland's most polluted rivers. From the late 20th century, the river has been subject to an integrated management plan, with the aim of improving the water quality.

Almond, River *Perth and Kinross* A river of Perth and Kinross, the River Almond rises to the south of Loch Tay and flows generally eastwards for 30 miles (45 km) before joining the River Tay just east of Almondbank.

Almondbank *Perth and Kinross* A village in the parish of Methven, Perth and Kinross, Almondbank, as its name suggests, sits on the River Almond, 4 miles (6.5 km) northwest of Perth. Once a textile centre with bleachfields, Almondbank is now a residential satellite of Perth and the site of Royal Naval Aircraft Workshops established here during World War II.

Almorness Point *Dumfries and Galloway* A headland on the Solway Firth coast, Almorness Point lies opposite Hestan Island at the end of a narrow peninsula separating the Rough Firth from Auchencairn Bay.

Alness *Highland* Located 3 miles (5 km) west of Invergordon in Easter Ross, Alness sits astride the Alness River where it enters the Cromarty Firth. In recent times the town has grown to be the largest in the district due to an influx of light industries. Although agriculture, forestry, sawmilling and distilling have always offered employment in the area, it is the development of the Alness Point Business Park, with emphasis on software development and the creation of a British Telecom helpdesk operation, that have contributed significantly to the growth of the town. The business park was built on the site of a wartime flying-boat training base, and a memorial commemorating this fact was unveiled in 2001. Although not a tourist centre, there is excellent salmon and sea-trout fishing to be found in the area and a small 9-hole golf course is located outside the town.

Alness River *Highland* Also known as the Averon, the Alness River rises in headstreams to the northwest of Alness in Easter Ross, Highland Council area. It flows down to meet the Cromarty Firth at Alness Point.

Alsh, Loch *Highland* A sea loch near the west coast of Highland Council area between the island of Skye and the mainland, Loch Alsh opens out northwestwards to the Inner Sound via Kyle Akin and southwards to the Sound of Sleat via Kyle Rhea. The settlements of Balmacara and Kyle of Lochalsh lie on its shore.

Altabrug, Loch *Western Isles* A small loch on the west coast of the island of South Uist in the Western Isles, Loch Altabrug lies 8 miles (13 km) north of Lochboisdale. The scattered community of Stoneybridge lies immediately to the west, with Loch Fada to the east.

Altandhu *Highland* A settlement on the Rubha Mòr peninsula, Wester Ross, Altandhu (also Alltan Dubh) lies 4 miles (6.5 km) northwest of Achiltibuie.

Altanduin *Highland* A settlement in east-central Sutherland, Altanduin lies to the west of the Strath of Kildonan, 4 miles (6.5 km) south of Loch Achnamoine.

Altass *Highland* A small settlement in central Sutherland, Altass lies in Strath Oykel, 6 miles (10 km) southwest of Lairg.

Altgaltraig *Argyll and Bute* A locality a mile (1.5 km) southeast of Colintraive on the eastern shore of the Kyles of Bute, Altgaltraig includes Upper and Lower Altgaltraig.

Alticry *Dumfries and Galloway* A locality in the Machars, Dumfries and Galloway, Alticry lies near the eastern coast of Luce Bay, 6 miles (10 km) northwest of Port William.

Altimeg Hill *South Ayrshire* A hill in the Deer How 4 miles (6.5 km) southeast of Ballantrae, Altimeg Hill rises to 340 m (1115 ft) near the border with Dumfries and Galloway.

Altnabreac *Highland* A locality in western Caithness, Altnabreac lies by the Sleach Water on the railway line 9 miles (14 km) east of Forsinard and 23 miles (37 km) west of Wick. It sits in the extensive Altnabreac Moss in the heart of the Flow Country. For a short while in the 1970s the peat moss was exploited by the Hydro Board, which established a peat-burning power station here. A remote railway station serving the Highland Line was established here in 1874, and in 1895 the Sinclairs of Ulbster built a hunting lodge at nearby Lochdhu.

Altnaharra *Highland* A village in northern Sutherland, Altnaharra lies at the western end of Loch Naver, 13 miles (21 km) south of Tongue. There are numerous examples of former settlement in the area, including hut circles, heaps of clearance stones and field terraces. An inn was built here *c.*1820 and by the 1840s the village had developed into a small angling resort.

Altrieve Burn *Scottish Borders* A stream to the east of St Mary's Loch in Scottish Borders, the Altrieve Burn or Altrive, rises on Peat Law and flows southeastwards to join a stream known as Altrieve Lake, a tributary of the Yarrow Water. Altrieve Rig rises to 459 m (1505 ft) to the north of the stream, and the farm of Altrieve was the last home of the poet and writer James Hogg, the 'Ettrick Shepherd' (1770–1835).

Alturlie Point *Highland* A triangular-shaped headland in the inner Moray Firth, Alturlie Point lies 5 miles (8 km) northeast of Inverness.

Altyre *Moray* Situated within a wooded landscape 2 miles (3 km) to the south of Forres in Moray, Altyre Estate is the family home of the Gordon Cummings, the descendants of the great family of Comyn. Altyre House, which was renovated by Sir William Gordon Cumming at the end of the 19th century with John Kinross as its architect, was demolished in 1962. At the centre of the estate is Blairs House, designed by W. L. Carruthers in 1895, and an Italianate farmsteading, possibly the work of Archibald Simpson, is nearby. Altyre also gives its name to woodlands and the surrounding parish, which united with Rafford in 1651. The remains of Altyre Kirk date from the 13th century.

Alva *Clackmannanshire* A Hillfoots town in Clackmannanshire, Alva is situated in the Devon Valley at the foot of the Ochil Hills between Menstrie and Tillicoultry. The town developed during the 18th and 19th centuries in association with textile mills powered by the Alva Burn that flows down from the hills. In the 1880s there were nine spinning mills, all powered by steam and water. Knitwear is still produced, and a working mill displays the craft of woollen making at the Mill Trail Visitor Centre. Other industries include publishing, engineering and industrial supplies. Recreational facilities exist at the Cochrane Park, which is the venue for the annual Alva Highland Games, and there are walks up the Silver Glen and in the nearby Ochil Hills Woodland Park on the lower slopes of Wood Hill. St Serf's Parish Church was established in the 12th century, the present building dating from 1632. In its churchyard is a fine mausoleum of the Johnstone family built in 1790 by Robert and James Adam, who were employed in the remodelling of Alva House.

Alves *Moray* A small agricultural village of Moray, Alves lies just to the north of the A96 between Forres and Elgin. The village today comprises Alves itself and Crook of Alves. In the locality are North Alves, Wester Alves, Alves Wood to the southwest and New Alves to the southeast. The old village lay to the north at Kirkton where the Old Kirk (1769) surrounded by its churchyard lies abandoned. The parish church to the southwest was built in 1878 as a Free Church and in the village there is a Gothic-style school dating from 1895. The Aberdeen–Inverness railway runs a half-mile (1 km) to the south, but Alves station has closed. To the east, on top of the Knock of Alves, the octagonal Duke of York Tower (1827) stands within the remains of a prehistoric fort.

Alvie *Highland* A village in Badenoch, Alvie lies in a parish of the same name between Loch Alvie and the River Spey, 3 miles (5 km) south of Aviemore. A granite column on Tor Alvie commemorates the 5th Duke of Gordon (1770–1836).

Alwhat *East Ayrshire/Dumfries and Galloway* A peak on the border between East Ayrshire and Dumfries and Galloway, Alwhat rises to 628 m (2060 ft) east of Windy Standard and 10 miles (16 km) southwest of Sanquhar. Blacklorg and Blackcraig Hill rise to the north.

Alyth *Perth and Kinross* An ancient town in the Braes of Angus, Alyth sits on the Burn of Alyth 5 miles (8 km) east of Blairgowrie on the northern edge of the valley of Strathmore close to Perthshire's eastern boundary with Angus. Created a burgh with a market in 1488, Alyth developed in association with cattle droving and the wool, jute and linen trades. Its Market Cross dates from 1670 and in the Norman-style Parish Church (1839) there is a Pictish stone. The Alyth Arches stand on the site of the 6th-century Church of St Moluag. A folk museum features displays on local agrarian history, and the Alyth Hotel was the home of the inventor James Sandy (b.1766) who devised the invisible hinge. Near the town is Bamff House, incorporating a 16th-century tower house, and to the northeast on Barry Hill stands an Iron Age fort that also has traditional associations with the King Arthur legend. There is an 18-hole golf course and walks through the Den of Alyth and along the Drovers' Road that skirts the Hill of Alyth (294 m/966 ft). Sawmilling, agricultural machinery and the manufacture of glass are modern industries associated with the town. The much smaller planned village of New Alyth stands on the Blairgowrie–Kirriemuir road to the southwest.

Alyth, Burn of *Perth and Kinross* A stream in Perth and Kinross, the Burn of Alyth rises in the Forest of Alyth, 6 miles (10 km) northwest of Alyth. It flows southeast through the town of Alyth before meeting the River Isla at Inverquiech, 2 miles (3 km) east of Alyth. There is a pathway through the Den of Alyth, the deep-set wooded glen of the Burn of Alyth to the west of Alyth.

Alyth, Forest of *Perth and Kinross* An area of deer forest between the Black Water and the River Isla, Perth and Kinross, the Forest of Alyth was designated a royal hunting reserve in the 12th century.

Am Balg *Highland* A group of uninhabited islets off the coast of northwest Sutherland, Am Balg lies a mile (1.5 km) northwest of the Am Buachaille headland.

Am Baile The Gaelic name for Balla in the Western Isles.

Am Barradhu *Argyll and Bute* A headland on the island of Tiree, Am Barradhu lies to the east of Hynish, on the southeast coast of the island.

Am Basteir *Highland* A summit on the Cuillin Ridge, at the north end of the Cuillins, on the isle of Skye, Am Basteir rises to 935 m (3067 ft) and dominates the head of Corrie a' Bhasteir. The easiest approach to the summit is along the eastern ridge from Bealach a' Bhasteir. The name is derived from the Gaelic for 'obscure'.

Am Beidhneag An alternative name for Bynack More on the border of Highland and Aberdeenshire.

Am Bodach *Highland* One of four peaks known as the 'Ring of Steall' that form a horseshoe around Coire a' Mhail in the Mamores of Lochaber, Am Bodach rises to a height of 1034 m (3392 ft) to the north of Kinlochleven. Am Bodach's eastern face is particularly steep, especially above the head of Coire na Bà. The name Am Bodach derives from the Gaelic for 'the old man'.

Am Bràigh Riabhach The Gaelic name for Braeriach on the border of Highland and Aberdeenshire.

Am Buachaille *Highland* A headland in northwest Sutherland, Am Buachaille lies 7 miles (11 km) southwest of Cape Wrath and the southern end of Sandwood Bay. The islets of Am Balg are located a mile (1.5 km) to the northwest.

Am Faochagach *Highland* A mountain in the northwest Highlands, Am Faochagach rises to 954 m (3129 ft) to the north of Loch Glascarnoch. It is a massive, rounded hill whose upper flanks have steep slopes leading to a flat summit dome. Its name is derived from the Gaelic for 'place of the shells'.

Am Fraoch Eilean *Argyll and Bute* A small uninhabited island in the Sound of Islay, Am Fraoch Eilean lies a mile (1.5 km) from Ardfin at the southern tip of the island of Jura. To the east lies Brosdale Island.

Amat *Highland* A deer forest and lodge in Easter Ross, Amat lies at the meeting of the Black Water with the River Carron, 10 miles (16 km) west of Bonar Bridge. The pinewoods of Amat represent one of the largest remnants of the ancient Caledonian Forest and as such are designated as a Site of Special Scientific Interest (SSSI).

Amhuinnsuidhe *Western Isles* A locality with a castle on the remote B886, which runs west through North Harris, Amhuinnsuidhe (also Abhainnsuidhe or Abhainn Suidhe) lies 8 miles (13 km) northwest of Tarbert. Amhuinnsuidhe Castle dates from 1868. Built in the Scottish baronial style by architect David Bryce (1803-76) for Charles Murray, the 7th Earl of Dunmore (1841–1907), this fine country house looks out into Loch Leosavay, an opening in West Loch Tarbert. Sir James Barrie (1860–1937) wrote the first draft of his play *Mary Rose* here. Later owned by the Bulmer family, of cider fame, the castle was separated from much of its North Harris estate following the buyout of the estate by the local community in 2002. The castle is now used for corporate and sporting events.

Amisfield Park *East Lothian* Located a half-mile (1 km) northeast of Haddington, Amisfield Park is today home to the Haddington Golf Club. Amisfield House, regarded as the finest example of orthodox Palladian architecture in Scotland, was built *c.*1755 by Isaac Ware for Francis Charteris, 5th Earl of Wemyss and March. It was extended in 1785, but was demolished in 1928. Some of the sandstone from Amisfield House was reused to build a school at Prestonpans, the Vert Hospital in Haddington and Longniddry Golf Clubhouse. Originally part of the lands of a 12th-century Cistercian nunnery, the estate was used for the Tyneside Games, held annually for 20 years from 1833. Haddington Golf Club was established here in 1865. The park was occupied by the military during the Jacobite Rebellion (1745–46) and the Napoleonic Wars (1793–1815); the house was used as officers' quarters during World War I; and the park was used again during World War II. A modern clubhouse for the Haddington Golf Club now occupies the site of the house, but the stable block (1785) by John Henderson remains, along with an icehouse, temple, walled garden and grand gate piers situated at the west entrance from Haddington. The land was sold to Haddington Town Council in 1960; and housing estates were developed at Amisfield Mains and Amisfield Park.

Amisfield Town *Dumfries and Galloway* A settlement of Dumfries and Galloway, Amisfield Town lies on the Amisfield Burn, 5 miles (8 km) northeast of Dumfries. To the northwest is Amisfield Castle, a former stronghold of the Charteris family.

Ample, Glen *Stirling* A narrow valley in northeast Stirling Council area, Glen Ample stretches south to Loch Lubnaig from Edinample on the south side of Loch Earn. The Burn of Ample, which flows for much of the length of Glen Ample, is fed by streams from Ben Vorlich and Stuc a' Chroin.

Amulree *Perth and Kinross* A hamlet to the west of Strathbraan, Amulree lies close to the geographical centre of Scotland. Situated on open moorland by the River Quaich 9 miles (14 km) southwest of Dunkeld, it was once a cattle tryst. Its drovers' inn was a 'King's House' on the 18th-century Wade military road before becoming a coaching inn, and its church was founded in 1744 as a mission of the Scottish Society for the Propagation of Christian Knowledge.

An Cabar *Highland* A southwestern summit of Ben Wyvis in Easter Ross, An Cabar rises to a height of 947 m (3106 ft).

An Caisteal *Stirling* A mountain in northwest Stirling Council area, An Caisteal rises to a height of 995 m (3264 ft) to the south of Crianlarich. Its name is derived from the Gaelic for 'the castle'.

An Cala Garden *Argyll and Bute* A garden on the south coast of the island of Seil, the An Cala Garden lies a mile (1.5 km) east of Easdale. The garden is famed for its collections of rhododendron, hydrangea, camellia and rhabdotum.

An Cnoc The Gaelic name for Knock in the Western Isles.

An Cnoc Ard The Gaelic name for Knockaird in the Western Isles.

An Coileachan *Highland* A peak of the Fannich ridge, in Ross and Cromarty, An Coileachan rises to a height of 923 m (3028 ft) to the north of Loch Fannich. The name An Coileachan is derived from the Gaelic for 'the little cock'.

An Dubh Sgeir *Highland* A rocky reef in the Sea of the Hebrides, An Dubh Sgeir lies 2 miles (3 km) off the northwest coast of Skye, west of Idrigill Point and MacLeod's Maidens.

An Gallan Uigeach The Gaelic name for Gallan Head in the Western Isles.

An Garbh-eilean *Highland* An uninhabited islet off the north coast of Sutherland, An Garbh-eilean (Garve Island) lies 4 miles (6.5 km) east of Cape Wrath. The headland of Cleit Dhubh lies immediately to the south.

An Gead Loch *Highland* A small loch in Wester Ross, An Gead Loch lies 12 miles (19 km) east of Loch Carron. It is linked by a stream to nearby Loch Monar.

An Gearanach *Highland* A summit in the Mamores of Lochaber, An Gearanach rises to 985 m (3231 ft) to the north of Kinlochleven. It is one of four peaks collectively known as the 'Ring of Steall' that form a horseshoe around Coire a' Mhail. It is located on a short narrow ridge, projecting in a northerly direction from Stob Coire a' Chairn. The northern flank of the peak falls steeply down to Glen Nevis. The name An Gearanach is derived from the Gaelic for 'the complainer'.

An Gleann Ur The Gaelic name for New Valley in the Western Isles.

An Grianan *Highland* A mountain in northwest Sutherland, An Grianan rises to a height of 467 m (1532 ft) 5 miles (8 km) northeast of Kinlochbervie. It sits to the west of the peaks of Creag Riabhach 485 m (1591 ft) and Meall na Moine 464 m (1522 ft) and east of Sandwood Loch.

An Leth Meadhanach The Gaelic name for South Boisdale in the Western Isles.

An Riabhachan *Highland* A mountain to the north of Glen Cannich, An Riabhachan rises to 1129 m (3703 ft) to the north of Loch Mullardoch. Its summit ridge is long and level, with corries to the north and south. Its name is derived from the Gaelic for 'the brindled greyish one'.

An Ruadh-stac *Highland* A mountain in Wester Ross, An Ruadh-stac rises to 892 m (2926 ft) 4 miles (6.5 km) north of Loch Carron. The peaks of Ben Damph and Maol Chean-dearg rise to the north.

An Scriodan *North Ayrshire* A headland on the north coastline of the island of Arran, An Scriodan lies between the Rubha Creagan Dubha headland to the west and the Cock of Arran. The settlement of Lochranza lies a mile (1.5 km) to the southwest.

An Sgarsoch *Aberdeenshire/Perth and Kinross* A remote peak in the Grampians, An Sgarsoch rises to 1006 m (3300 ft) in the centre of the headwaters of the River Feshie, Geldie Burn and Tarf Water, on the border between Aberdeenshire and Perth and Kinross.

An Sgurr *Highland* A mountain in Wester Ross, An Sgurr rises to 392 m (1286 ft) between Loch Carron and Loch Kishorn. The peak of Bad a' Chreamha lies to the south.

An Socach *Aberdeenshire* A summit in the Grampians, An Socach forms a long curved ridge rising to 944 m (3097 ft) 8 miles (13 km) southwest of Braemar. Its name is derived from the Gaelic for 'the projecting place' or 'the snout'.

An Socach *Highland* A mountain to the west of Glen Affric, An Socach rises to 920 m (3018 ft) 2 miles (3 km) southwest of Mam Sodhail.

An Socach *Highland* A mountain to the north of Glen Cannich, An Socach rises to 1069 m (3506 ft) between Loch Mullardoch and Loch Monar. It is an isolated peak, with the main access to the summit being via a continuation westward from its neighbour, An Riabhachan. The summit ridge encloses a corrie, Coire Mham.

An Stuc *Perth and Kinross* A northern summit of Ben Lawers, An Stuc rises to 1118 m (3668 ft) to the north of Loch Tay on land owned by the National Trust for Scotland 10 miles (16 km) northeast of Killin. This peak is particularly steep-sided on the east overlooking Lochan nan Cat and its name is derived from the Gaelic for 'rocky cone'.

An t-Ob The Gaelic name for Leverburgh in the Western Isles.

An Tairbeart The Gaelic name for Tarbert in the Western Isles.

An Teallach *Highland* A prominent mountain massif of Torridonian sandstone in Wester Ross, An Teallach lies to the south of Little Loch Broom. Rising to 1062 m (3483 ft), it has two peaks, Bidein a' Ghlas Thuill (the higher) and Sgurr Fiona (1059 m/3474 ft). The An Teallach massif is the most extensive of the former nunataks that rose above the last ice sheet in northwest Scotland which reached a maximum altitude of *c.*760 m (2500 ft) around the massif 22,000 years ago. An earlier thick ice sheet of unknown age reached a maximum of about *c.*900 m (3000 ft).

An Torc *Highland/Perth and Kinross* A summit in the southern Grampians, An Torc (also known as the Boar of Badenoch) rises to 739 m (2424 ft) between Loch Ericht and the Pass of Drumochter. Located on the border of Highland Council area and Perth and Kinross, this is one of a group of peaks, including Gael Charn and A' Mharconaich.

Anaboard Burn *Highland* A stream on the Dava Moor, Anaboard Burn rises to the west of the settlement of Anaboard and flows east then north to become the Dorback Burn 2 miles (3 km) northeast of Lochindorb.

Anaheilt *Highland* A small settlement in Sunart, southwest Highland Council area, Anaheilt lies just north of Strontian.

Ancrum *Scottish Borders* A village of Teviotdale in Scottish Borders, Ancrum lies 3 miles (5 km) northwest of Jedburgh near the junction of the Ale Water with the Teviot. New or Nether Ancrum replaced the old market centre of Old Ancrum to become a burgh of barony in 1639. Ancrum House on the site of Old Ancrum was demolished *c.*1970. The Harestanes Visitor Centre lies to the east. The village gives its name to the earldom of Ancrum.

Ancrum Moor *Scottish Borders* Located at the side of the A68, 2 miles (3 km) north of the village of Ancrum and 2.5 miles (4 km) southeast of St Boswells, Ancrum Moor was the site of a battle between the Scots and the English in 1544. Here Archibald Douglas, the 6th Earl of Angus (1489–1557), routed a much larger English army under Sir Ralph Evers and Sir Brian Latoun, who were both left dead on the field of combat. The fight followed the burning of Melrose and its abbey, at the heart of Douglas's territory.

Anderston *Glasgow City* From its origins as a weavers' village in the 1720s, Anderston merged with the city of Glasgow as the city developed in the 18th century east and west along the banks of the River Clyde. Anderston began to spread westwards as Bridgeton grew eastwards, its name being derived from the principal landowners of the area, the Anderson family of Stobcross. The village became an industrial centre with the growth of Glasgow's cotton industry, and by 1824 it had become a burgh of barony, although by 1846 it had been incorporated into the city. Anderston is home to the Finnieston Crane, a prominent landmark on the Glasgow skyline. Situated on the western fringes of the city centre, Anderston is the focal point for major riverside development, including the Scottish Exhibition and Conference Centre and the Clyde Auditorium, with associated modern hotels.

Angel's Peak An alternative name for Sgor an Lochain Uaine in Aberdeenshire.

Angus *Area: 2181 sq. km (842.3 sq. miles)* Its eastern coast washed by the North Sea, Angus stretches northwards from Dundee on the Firth of Tay to the high peaks of the Braes of Angus which rise to more than 915 m (3000 ft) in the eastern Grampians. Between the Grampians and the Sidlaw Hills in the south lies the wide and fertile valley of Strathmore which has some of the best agricultural land in Scotland and is particularly renowned for its cattle breeding, seed potatoes and soft fruit. Across this great valley flows the River South Esk on its way to the Montrose Basin, an inlet of the North Sea rich in wildlife. Forfar (the administrative centre), Brechin, Montrose, Arbroath and Carnoustie, with its championship golf course, are the main towns, and among the region's many historic landmarks are Glamis Castle and the birthplace in Kirriemuir of J. M. Barrie, the author of *Peter Pan*. Formerly known as Forfarshire, Angus was a Scottish county until it constituted one of the three districts of Tayside region between 1975 and 1996. The earldom of Angus was one of the seven original Celtic earldoms, Angus passing in the 13th century through the heiress Matilda to the Anglo-Norman Umfravilles, a line that expired in 1381. In 1389, King Robert II granted the earldom to the Douglas family, the Douglas earls of Angus being known as the 'Red' Douglases to distinguish them from the 'Black' Douglases. The 11th Earl was created Marquess of Douglas in 1633 and his title passed eventually to the dukes of Hamilton. Angus being essentially a rich agricultural area, its seven towns have a long tradition of both manufacturing and service industry. From Montrose southwards, fine beaches have promoted the development of links golf courses and resort towns, while the prosperity of Dundee has encouraged the growth of commuter settlements in the interior. Engineering, malting, distilling, food processing, fishing and oil-related industries are also important to the economy.

Angus Folk Museum *Angus* Located in the village of Glamis, 5 miles (8 km) southwest of Forfar in Angus, the Angus Folk Museum comprises six cottages and a farmsteading that illustrate the daily life of the rural communities of Angus in the 18th century. It is administered by the National Trust for Scotland.

Anguston *Aberdeen City* A locality in the far west of Aberdeen City Council area, Anguston lies to the north of the Gormack Burn, 2 miles (3 km) northwest of Peterculter and 9 miles (14 km) west-southwest of Aberdeen. It comprises the hamlet of Mid-Anguston together with farms at Upper Anguston, Nether Anguston, Easter Anguston and the Howe of Anguston.

Ankerville Corner *Highland* A small settlement at a road junction in Easter Ross, Ankerville Corner lies to the east of Nigg Bay, nearly 3 miles (5 km) north of the village of Nigg. At nearby Ankerville, an 18th-century warehouse was converted into attractive dormered cottages c.1900.

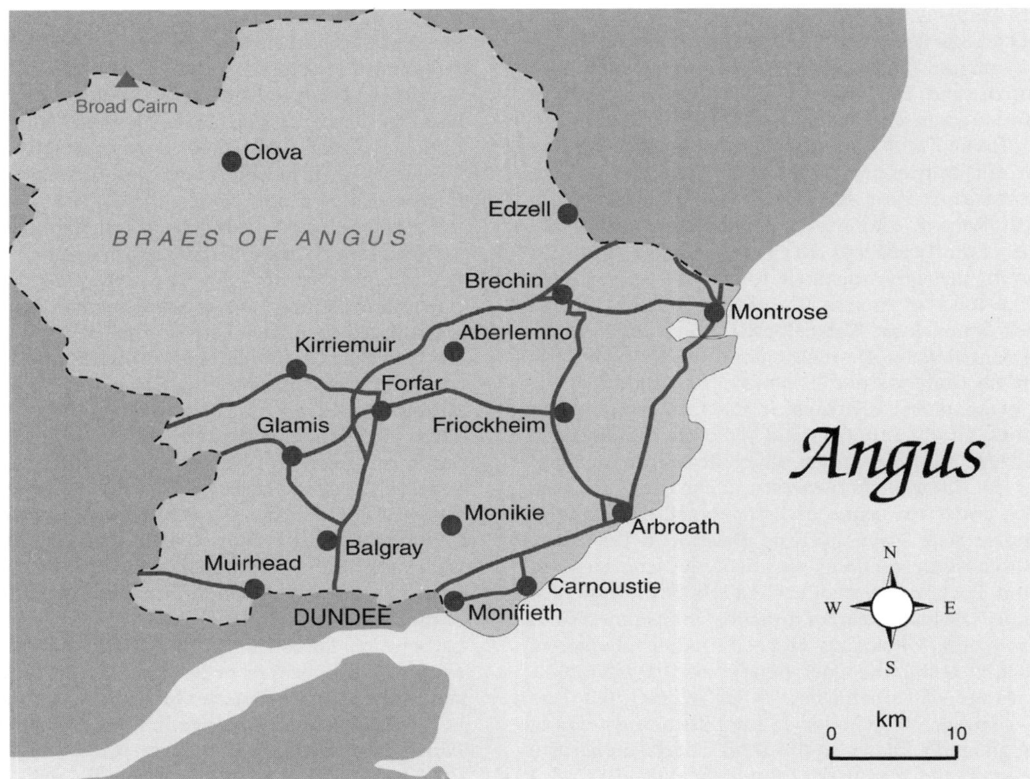

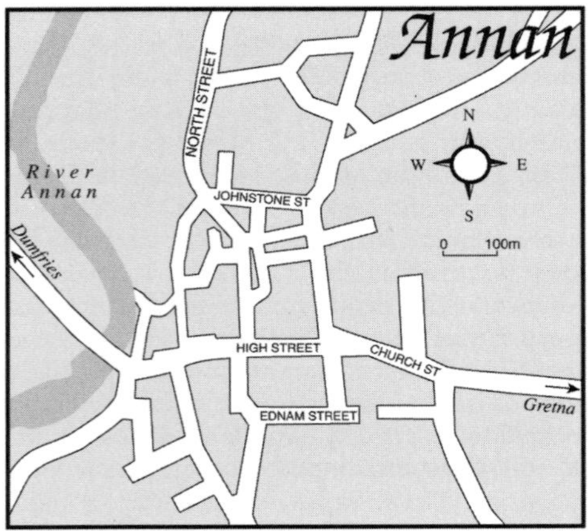

Annan *Dumfries and Galloway* Situated on the Solway Firth at the mouth of the River Annan in Dumfries and Galloway, the burgh of Annan lies 17 miles (25 km) southeast of Dumfries. Emerging as a burgh of barony in the 12th century, Annan was the site of a medieval hospital and a castle built by the Bruce family. It was elevated to the status of a royal burgh in 1532 but was described by Daniel Defoe in the 1720s as 'in a state of irrevocable decay'. The founding of a cotton mill in 1785 signalled a turn in Annan's fortunes, and during the 19th century it developed as a port with shipbuilding, engineering and whisky-distilling industries. During the 20th century pharmaceuticals, knitwear, chipboard and food-processing industries developed, and between 1975 and 1996 Annan was the administrative centre of Annandale and Eskdale District. Buildings of note include the Town Hall (1878), Erskine Church (1835), Old Annan Academy and Annan Bridge, built by Robert Stevenson in 1824–6. The African explorer Hugh Clapperton and the evangelist Edward Irving were born in Annan, and the writer Thomas Carlyle, born in Ecclefechan, was schooled at the Academy.

Annan, River *Dumfries and Galloway/Scottish Borders* A river of Dumfries and Galloway, the River Annan rises in headstreams near Hartfell on the boundary with Scottish Borders and within a short distance of the sources of the Tweed and the Clyde. It flows 49 miles (78 km) south through Annandale to join the Solway Firth near the town of Annan. Its main tributaries are the Birnock Water, Evan Water, Moffat Water, Whamphray Water, Kinnel Water, Dryfe Water and the Water of Milk.

Annandale *Dumfries and Galloway* The middle of the three geographical divisions of the former county of Dumfriesshire in Dumfries and Galloway, Annandale is the valley of the River Annan, which flows from north to south with Nithsdale to the west and Eskdale to the east. In 1124, under the name of Estra-Hanet, the lands of Annandale were given by King David I to the Bruce family, whose descendants eventually became kings of Scotland. Lochmaben was the chief seat of the Bruces at that time. The title of Earl of Annandale was conferred in 1643 upon the Johnstones of Lochwood, a member of this family being the poet Ben Jonson (1572–1637). A marquessate of Annandale created in 1701 fell into abeyance in 1792. The hollow in the hills to the north of Moffat generally known as the Devil's Beef Tub used to be known as the Marquess of Annandale's Beef Stand, a reminder of the days when stolen cattle were kept here by the reivers of Annandale.

Annat *Argyll and Bute* A settlement on the north shore of Loch Awe, Annat lies a half-mile (1 km) south of Kilchrenan.

Annat *Highland* A small settlement in Wester Ross, Annat lies at the head of Upper Loch Torridon, a mile (1.5 km) south of Torridon.

Annat Bay *Highland* A wide bay in Wester Ross, Annat Bay lies on the south side of Loch Broom where it widens out towards the sea. The settlement of Achmore sits at the western end of the bay.

Annathill *North Lanarkshire* A locality to the southwest of Condorrat near Cumbernauld, Annathill includes the lands of Annathill Farm, Annathill, South Medrox and North Medrox.

Annbank *South Ayrshire* A village in the Kyle district of South Ayrshire, Annbank lies to the north of the River Ayr 5 miles (8 km) east of Ayr. It sits close to the East Ayrshire border and was originally a mining community with a rail link to Ayr harbour. Located in attractive countryside amid dairy farms, there is a wildlife reserve nearby at Enterkine Estate.

Annet Burn *Stirling* The Annet Burn rises in the hills of Kilmadock parish to the northeast of Callander in Stirling Council area. It flows southeastwards in two headstreams down the southern slopes of Uamh Bheag and on through the Braes of Doune before joining the River Teith below Burn of Cambus. It is 6 miles (10 km) long and has a number of attractive cascades.

Annick Water *North Ayrshire* A river in the Cunninghame district of North Ayrshire, the Annick Water is formed by the merging of headstreams from Long Loch and the Corsehouse Reservoir near Stewarton. It flows south and west to join the River Irvine at the southern edge of the town of Irvine.

Anniesland *Glasgow City* A district of northwest Glasgow, Anniesland lies at the western end of Great Western Road between Knightswood and Maryhill. Although Great Western Road was extended as far as Anniesland Toll by 1850, there were few houses in this large agricultural area prior to development of industry in the late 19th century. In nearby Temple a gasworks was founded to serve the emerging northwest suburbs, but it was not until the arrival of the railway that the middle classes moved into villas and tenements here.

Anstruther *Fife* Situated on the Firth of Forth in the East Neuk of Fife, the resort town of Anstruther comprises the settlements of Anstruther Easter and Wester and the old fishing village of Cellardyke (formerly Nether or Lower Kilrenny). Anstruther Easter, which became a burgh of barony in 1572 and a royal burgh in 1587, lies between Caddys Burn on the east and the Dreel Burn on the west. It has a skyline once dominated by the Chalmers Memorial Church (1847), named after Thomas Chalmers, the first moderator of the United Free Church, who was born here in 1780. This building was abandoned in 1982 and destroyed by fire in 1991. The harbour of Anstruther Easter was the capital of the winter herring fleet prior to World War I, and close to it stands the Scottish Fisheries Museum which was opened in 1969. Other significant landmarks include St Adrian's Parish Church (1634), the Mercat Cross (1677), the Old Corn Mill (1702) and Melville Manse, built in 1590 by the

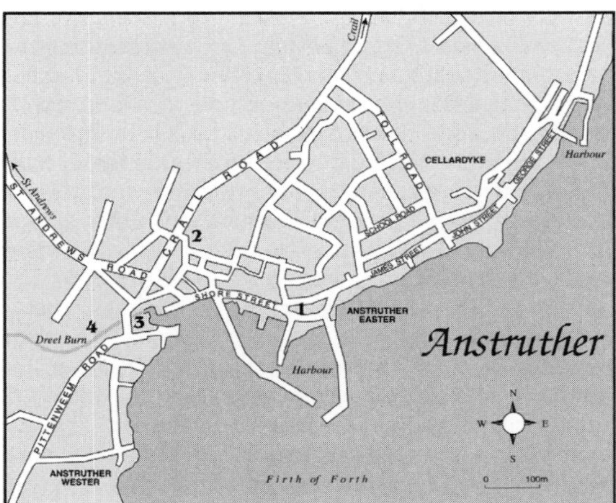

1 *Scottish Fisheries Museum*
2 *St Adrian's Parish Church*
3 *St Adrian's Church Hall*
4 *Old Corn Mill*

diarist the Revd James Melville. There are also fragments of Dreel Castle, built in 1663 by Sir Philip Anstruther and visited by Charles II who described its tower room as 'a craw's nest'. This castle was the meeting place of the notorious 'Beggars' Benison of Anstruther' secret society, a 'Scottish Society of an erotic and convivial nature composed of the Nobility and Gentry of Anstruther' founded in 1739. Anstruther Wester, situated to the west of the Dreel Burn, was designated a burgh of barony in 1154 and a royal burgh in the 1580s. Among many fine old merchants' houses stands the former parish church of St Nicholas (now St Adrian's Church Hall) with its 16th-century bell tower. An attractive coastal village with many interesting old buildings, Anstruther was designated a conservation area in 1972. For visitors there are sea-angling, diving, swimming and bowling facilities, as well as a nine-hole golf course, and boat trips to the Isle of May.

Antonine Wall A Roman defensive fortification between the firths of Forth and Clyde in central Scotland, the Antonine Wall was built in honour of Emperor Antoninus Pius by Lollius Urbicus, the Governor of Britain, around AD 143. It established a frontier to the north of Hadrian's Wall in England, with the intention of restraining the Pictish tribes to the north. However, residual hostile tribes in the Southern Uplands of Scotland forced more than one retreat to the safety of Hadrian's Wall, and the Antonine Wall was probably completely abandoned by AD 180. The wall is 37 miles (60 km) in length, extending from Old Kilpatrick to Bo'ness but is best observed to the southwest of Falkirk.

Antonshill *Falkirk* A northwestern suburb of Stenhousemuir in Falkirk Council area, Antonshill lies to the south of Bellsdyke Hospital and the motorway junction between the M876 and the M9.

Anwoth *Dumfries and Galloway* A settlement in a parish of the same name in the Vale of Fleet, Anwoth lies a mile (1.5 km) to the west of Gatehouse of Fleet. An ancient fort on Trusty's Hill was occupied by the Picts who carved a series of symbol stones in a rock beside the entrance passage.

Aoistail, Gleann *Argyll and Bute* A valley in the northern half of the island of Jura, Gleann Aoistail carries the Abhainn Ghleann Aostail south towards the head of Loch Tarbert.

Aonach air Chrith *Highland* A mountain at the western end of Glen Loyne on the eastern section of the South Glen Shiel Ridge, Aonach air Chrith rises to 1021 m (3349 ft). Its name derives from the Gaelic for 'trembling hill'.

Aonach Beag *Highland* A mountain of Lochaber, Aonach Beag (Gaelic, 'little ridge') rises to 1234 m (4049 ft) to the east of Ben Nevis and the south of Aonach Mor. Aonach Beag is connected to Carn Mòr Dearg by a high bealach or pass at 830 m (2723 ft), its summit ridge running east to west.

Aonach Beag *Highland* A mountain in Badenoch, Aonach Beag rises to 1114 m (3655 ft) to the west of Ben Alder and Loch Ericht. Three clear-cut ridges converge to form the summit which has a small flat plateau. One of four Munros on the ridge between Strath Ossian and Loch Pattack, its name is derived from the Gaelic for 'little ridge'.

Aonach Buidhe *Highland* A mountain in the Killilan Forest, Aonach Buidhe rises to a height of 899 m (2949 ft) 3 miles (5 km) northwest of the western end of Loch Mullardoch in Glen Cannich.

Aonach Eagach *Highland* A mountain ridge on the north side of Glen Coe, Aonach Eagach rises to 967 m (3172 ft) at Sgorr nam Fiannaidh at the western end of the ridge.

Aonach Meadhoin *Highland* One of the Five Sisters of Kintail, Aonach Meadhoin rises to 1001 m (3284 ft) to the west of Loch Cluanie. Its summit is on a small level plateau and its name is derived from the Gaelic for 'middle hill'.

Aonach Mòr *Highland* A mountain in Lochaber, Aonach Mòr (Gaelic, 'big broad ridge') rises to 1221 m (4006 ft) 5 miles (8 km) east of Fort William and 2 miles (3 km) northeast of Ben Nevis. Although lower than its neighbour Aonach Beag, it is named the big ridge because of its greater bulk. Aonach Mòr is connected to Aonach Beag by a high bealach or pass at 1050 m (3445 ft).

App, Water of *South Ayrshire* A river in the Carrick district of South Ayrshire, the Water of App rises on Beneraird and flows southwest for 4 miles (6.5 km) through Glen App into Finnart Bay on the northeast shore of Loch Ryan.

Appin *Argyll and Bute/Highland* A district on the indented coastline of Loch Linnhe straddling the boundary between Argyll and Bute and Highland Council area, Appin lies to the north of Oban and Benderloch and to the south of Loch Leven. Its principal settlements are Portnacroish and Port Appin, where a ferry connects with the island of Lismore. The name Appin refers to the abbey lands that, in this case, associated with Lismore, and the locality is linked to the infamous Appin Murder, the killing of Colin Campbell of Glenure in the 18th century.

Appin *Argyll and Bute* A village in the Strath of Appin, Appin lies at the head of the road to Port Appin, 9 miles (14 km) southwest of Ballachulish.

Appin, Strath of *Perth and Kinross* A valley at the eastern end of Glen Lyon in Perth and Kinross, the Strath of Appin extends northwards from Appin of Dull, following the course of the Keltney Burn.

Appin Burn *Dumfries and Galloway* A stream in Dumfries and Galloway, the Appin Burn rises on the eastern side of Colt Hill on the border between Penpont and Carsphairn parishes. It flows nearly 2 miles (3 km) southeastwards to join the Shinnel Water 4 miles (6.5 km) northwest of Moniaive.

Appin of Dull *Perth and Kinross* A locality of Strath Tay in Perth and Kinross, the Appin of Dull comprises the rich flatlands of the River Tay to the south of Dull and between Loch Tay and Aberfeldy. The name Appin refers to the abbey lands that, in this case, associated with a great abbey, the foundation of St Adamnan, that is said to have flourished here.

Applecross *Highland* A village on the coast of Wester Ross, Applecross occupies a remote location on a peninsula between Loch Torridon and Loch Kishorn. It was inaccessible by road until the late 18th century and can now be reached via the long coastal road from Shieldaig (completed in 1982) or the Bealach na Bà (the Pass of the Cattle), which at 625 m (2035 ft) is one of the highest roads in Scotland. In the 7th century AD St Maelrubha, an Irish monk, founded a community here that continued for two centuries but was destroyed by Viking invaders. A few relics of that early period remain in the church, which was built in 1817, and in the churchyard are a Celtic cross-slab and the remains of a 15th-century chapel. A naval base for testing torpedoes was established here in the 1970s.

Applecross Bay *Highland* A bay on the coast of Wester Ross, Applecross Bay forms an inlet on the eastern shore of the the Inner Sound, opposite the island of Raasay. The Applecross River empties into the bay to the north of the settlement of Applecross, which lies at the southern end of the bay.

Applecross Forest *Highland* A large deer forest in Wester Ross, Applecross Forest lies east of the settlement of Applecross. It is traversed in the north by the Applecross River.

Applegarth Town *Dumfries and Galloway* A small hamlet of Annandale in Dumfries and Galloway, Applegarth Town lies on the east bank of the River Annan close to its junction with the Nethercleugh Burn, 3 miles (5 km) northwest of Lockerbie.

Arabella *Highland* A linear estate village in Easter Ross, Highland Council area, Arabella lies to the north of Nigg Bay, 9 miles (14 km) northeast of Invergordon. It takes its name from the first wife of Hugh Rose of Glastullich, who bought the estate *c.*1800.

Aray, Glen *Argyll and Bute* A narrow glen in Argyll and Bute, Glen Aray occupies the valley of the River Aray which empties into the head of Loch Fyne at Inveraray. The settlements of Ladyfield, Drimfern, Sallachry and Tulloch are also located in the glen.

Arbigland *Dumfries and Galloway* An estate in Dumfries and Galloway, Arbigland lies on the Solway Firth coast to the southeast of Kirkbean. The classically styled Arbigland House was built in 1755 by the improving laird and gentleman architect William Craik (1703–98), and a small dower house called the House on the Shore was built in 1936 by Kathleen Blackett-Swiny. The founder of the United States Navy, John Paul Jones, whose father was a gardener at Arbigland, was born in a cottage in the grounds on 6 July 1747. The gardens at Arbigland are open to the public at selected times during the summer months.

Arbirlot *Angus* A village in an Angus parish of the same name, Arbirlot lies on the Elliot Water, 2 miles (3 km) west of Arbroath. Occupied by handloom weavers and farmers in the 18th and 19th centuries, Arbirlot once had a meal mill, a slaughterhouse and two schools. A nature trail by the Elliot Water links Arbirlot with the former railway junction of Elliot on the Angus coast. Kelly Castle, which overlooks the Elliot Water, comprises a four-storey tower of the 16th century set within a 19th-century courtyard. It was a stronghold of the Mowbray family until forfeited to the Stewarts in the early 14th century, and was restored by the Earl of Dalhousie in the 19th century.

Arbroath *Angus* A fishing port and resort town on the North Sea coast of Angus, Arbroath sits at the mouth of the Brothock Burn 17 miles (27 km) northeast of Dundee. Formerly known as Aberbrothock, it became a royal burgh in 1599. Its most notable building is Arbroath Abbey, which was completed in 1233 and was the scene of the signing of the Declaration of Arbroath in 1320. In addition to its activities as a port, the burgh developed in the 18th and 19th centuries as a centre of linen weaving, spinning, bleaching and tanning. In 1875 there were 154 fishing boats and 34 spinning mills and factories as well as tanning, shipbuilding and chemical industries. The modern economy depends on engineering, oil-related industries, fishing, boatbuilding and the manufacture of metal products and textiles. The town, the largest in Angus, remains an important fishing port and holiday resort on the Angus Tourist Route, with the Signal Tower Museum of town history, bathing on the West Links, a sports centre and a golf course. Established in 1935, Kerr's Miniature Railway on the West Links Park is the oldest in Scotland. Arbroath was the home town of music-hall

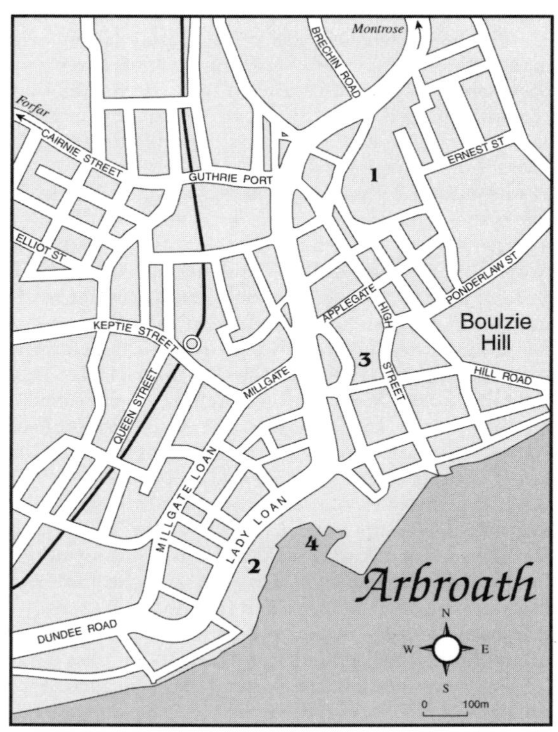

1 *Arbroath Abbey*
2 *Signal Tower Museum*
3 *Market Place*
4 *Harbour*

entertainer Sir Harry Lauder (1870–1950) until the age of 14, and of Adam Shanks (1801–1845), inventor of the lawnmower. Arbroath is particularly associated with a variety of smoked haddock known as Arbroath Smokies.

Arbroath Abbey *Angus* An historic monument in the royal burgh of Arbroath, Angus, Arbroath Abbey was originally founded for the grey-clad monks of the order of Tiron in 1178 by King William the Lion. It was St Thomas of Canterbury's apparent supernatural intervention in the capture of King William at Alnwick in 1174 that prompted him to establish the abbey after his return from imprisonment in Normandy. The presbytery at the eastern end was the first part of the building completed by the king's death in 1214 and it was here that he was buried nineteen years before the final consecration of the abbey in 1233. The Declaration of Arbroath, which confirmed the nobility's support of Scottish independence from English domination, was signed at the abbey in 1320.

Arbuthnot Museum *Aberdeenshire* Located in the town of Peterhead in Aberdeenshire, the Arbuthnot Museum highlights the maritime past of Aberdeenshire's principal fishing port and complements the collection at Peterhead Maritime Heritage. Exhibitions and photographs highlight not only the history of Peterhead but also include Inuit Indian artefacts, displays on Arctic animals and whaling, and one of the largest coin collections in the north of Scotland.

Arbuthnott *Aberdeenshire* A parish of southeastern Aberdeenshire, Arbuthnott lies to the east of the Highland Boundary Fault, between the Howe of the Mearns and the North Sea. It is traversed by the Bervie Water and has a landscape of rolling farmland that rises to 216 m (710 ft) at Bruxie Hill. Close to the Bervie Water and 2 miles (3 km) northwest of Inverbervie is St Ternan's Church, a red sandstone building, the oldest part of which dates from the 13th century. Restored in 1896 by A. Marshall Mackenzie, with stained-glass windows by Daniel Cottier, St Ternan's is one of the few parish churches in Scotland that dates from pre-Reformation times and is still in use for public worship. St Ternan is believed to have been born to a Pictish family in the Mearns during the 5th century AD. He went on to become abbot of a monastic settlement in Leinster in Ireland before returning to northeast Scotland, where he established a religious community in Banchory. James Sibbald, Vicar of Arbuthnott, completed a famous religious book known as the *Missal of Arbuthnott* in 1492, and Alexander Arbuthnott, the first Protestant minister of the parish, went on to become Moderator of the General Assembly of the Church of Scotland and first Protestant principal of King's College, Aberdeen. The church incorporates the Lady Chapel, which is the burial aisle of the Arbuthnott family, and a bell tower built in 1500 by Sir Robert Arbuthnott of that ilk. The novelist of the Mearns, James Leslie Mitchell (d.1935), better known by his pen-name Lewis Grassic Gibbon, is buried in the churchyard, and nearby is the family croft of Bloomfield. Attached to the Parish Hall in the village of Arbuthnott is the Grassic Gibbon Centre, a visitor centre dedicated to the life and times of this famous Scottish writer, built by the community in 1991. To the west is Arbuthnott House, home of the Arbuthnott family which has been associated with this area for over 800 years.

Arched House, The *Dumfries and Galloway* Located in Ecclefechan 6 miles (10 km) southeast of Lockerbie in Dumfries and Galloway, The Arched House was the birthplace of the Scottish writer and historian Thomas Carlyle (1795–1881). Built by his father and uncle in 1795, the property, now in the care of the National Trust for Scotland, houses a collection of Carlyle's belongings and portraits, as well as being furnished in a style reflective of his time.

Archer Beck *Dumfries and Galloway* A stream in Liddesdale, southeast Dumfries and Galloway, Archer Beck rises 4 miles (6.5 km) southeast of Langholm and flows south to join the Liddel Water on the English border just southeast of Rowanburn.

Archers' Hall *City of Edinburgh* Located on the western side of Buccleuch Street in Edinburgh, Archers' Hall was built in 1777 by Alexander Laing (d.1823) for the Royal Company of Archers. The hall was extended to the south in 1900 by A.F. Balfour Paul. The Royal Company of Archers was granted its charter by Queen Anne in 1704. Since King George IV visited Edinburgh in 1822, the company has provided the bodyguard for the sovereign while in Scotland, although today their role is entirely ceremonial. Members of the company practise on the Meadows and each year compete for the 'Edinburgh Arrow'. Inside Archers' Hall are paintings of notable members, including one of James, 5th Earl of Wemyss, Captain-General of the Company (1743–56), which is thought to be the work of Allan Ramsay. Today, members comprise senior military officers, politicians and members of the nobility, including Baron Lang of Monkton, the Earl of Airlie, the Duke of Buccleuch and Queensberry, the Earl of Dalkeith, the Earl of Elgin and Kincardine, the Marquess of Lothian and the Duke of Montrose.

Archerfield Estate *East Lothian* A 405 ha (1000 acre) estate lying to the east of Dirleton in East Lothian, Archerfield was the home of the Nisbet family prior to its purchase by the 14th Duke of Hamilton in 1963. Part of the estate, along with Archerfield House, an 18th-century Adam mansion, was sold in 2001 for housing and residential development. The estate is said to have been so named because it was where the archers of King Edward I's invading army of 1298 camped. Archerfield House was built in 1733, probably to a design by William Adam. The interior was remodelled by Robert Adam in 1790, with new ceilings and fine marble chimney-pieces. The most notable Nisbet family member was Mary Nisbet, wife of Thomas, 7th Earl of Elgin of 'Elgin Marbles' fame, who had an infamous liaison with Robert Ferguson of Raith (1767–1840), which resulted in divorce. Towards the end of the 19th century the family made their home at Biel near Stenton and Archerfield was let out to, among others, Herbert Asquith, the prime minister. The house was later abandoned.

Archiestown *Moray* Founded in 1760 by Sir Archibald Grant of Monymusk in an attempt to improve the desolate Moor of Ballintomb, the Moray village of Archiestown lies to the south of Elchies Forest, 4 miles (6.5 km) west of Craigellachie. It comprises a main street with a square at its centre. Many of the houses were destroyed by an accidental fire in 1783 and the village never grew to any great extent. It is today a conservation area and is regularly well placed in the Moray Best-Kept

Village Competition. There is a village hall, a post office and hotels, in addition to furniture making at Burnside of Ballintomb to the west.

Ard, Loch *Stirling* A loch in the Trossachs district of Stirling Council area, Loch Ard lies to the north of Loch Ard Forest, 3 miles (5 km) west of Aberfoyle. The River Forth flows from the eastern end of the loch. Loch Ard has an area of 243 ha (600 acres) and a mean depth of 13.5 m (44 ft). Sir Walter Scott, in his novel *Rob Roy* (1817), described the loch as 'an enchanting sheet of water'. On the south shore are the remains of a castle built by Murdoch Stewart (*c*.1362–1425), 2nd Duke of Albany, Regent of Scotland.

Ardailly *Argyll and Bute* Located a mile (1.5 km) southwest of the settlement of Tarbert on the island of Gigha in Argyll and Bute, Ardailly lies to the south of the island's highest point, Creag Bhàn.

Ardalanish *Argyll and Bute* Situated on the southern coast of the Ross of Mull in Argyll and Bute, the settlement of Ardalanish is located 2 miles (3 km) south of Bunessan at the southern end of the island of Mull. Immediately to the south lies the headland of Rubh' Ardalanish.

Ardanaiseig *Argyll and Bute* The settlement of Ardanaiseig is located 3 miles (5 km) southwest of Lochawe across the northwestern arm of Loch Awe. The Ardanaiseig Gardens are located nearby.

Ardarroch *Highland* A settlement in Wester Ross, Ardarroch lies at the head of Loch Kishorn, 3 miles (5 km) west of Lochcarron.

Ardbeg *Argyll and Bute* A hamlet adjoining Port Bannatyne on the northeastern coast of the isle of Bute, Ardbeg lies to the south of Ardbeg Point. Ardbeg and Port Bannatyne combine to form a holiday resort that extends from Kames Bay in the north to Rothesay in the south.

Ardbeg *Argyll and Bute* A settlement on the south coast of the island of Islay, Ardbeg lies 3 miles (5 km) east of Port Ellen. A distillery here produces malt whisky.

Ardcharnich *Highland* A locality in Wester Ross, Ardcharnich is situated on the eastern side of Loch Broom, 5 miles (8 km) southeast of Ullapool.

Ardchattan *Argyll and Bute* A parish in the Lorn district of Argyll and Bute, Ardchattan lies to the northeast of Oban by Loch Etive. It contains fourteen Munro summits, the highest being Ben Cruachan, and on the north shore of Loch Etive are the remains of a Valliscaulian priory founded in 1231 by Duncan Macdougal of Lorn. Robert the Bruce is said to have held a parliament here in 1308, the last in which business was conducted in the Gaelic language. Cromwell's soldiers burned the priory in 1654. The priory is surrounded by 1.6 ha (4 acres) of garden.

Ardchiavaig *Argyll and Bute* The settlement of Ardchiavaig is located on the southern coast of the Ross of Mull, on the island of Mull. The settlement of Bunessan is located 2 miles (3 km) to the north.

Ardchonnel *Argyll and Bute* The settlement of Ardchonnel is located a mile (1.5 km) south of Connel, in the Lorn district of Argyll and Bute.

Ardchonnell *Argyll and Bute* A settlement located on the east shore of Loch Awe opposite Dalavich, Ardchonnell lies on the edge of the Eredine Forest 9 miles (14 km) northeast of Ford.

Ardchronie *Highland* A settlement of Easter Ross, Ardchronie is situated at the northwest end of the Dornoch Firth, 2 miles (3 km) south of Bonar Bridge.

Ardchullarie More *Stirling* A locality in east-central Stirling Council area, Ardchullarie More is situated on the east side of Loch Lubnaig, 5 miles (8 km) northwest of Callander. A house here was the retreat of the African explorer James Bruce of Kinnaird (1730–94) while he was writing an account of his journey in 1768 to the source of the Blue Nile, which he mistakenly believed to be the source of the main Nile. His *Travels to Discover the Source of the Nile* was published in Edinburgh in 1790.

Ardchyle *Stirling* A hamlet in Glen Dochart, northwest Stirling Council area, Ardchyle with its old schoolhouse lies on the main road from Killin to Crianlarich, near the foot of Gleann Dubh.

Ardclach *Highland* A locality in Highland Council area, Ardclach lies on the River Findhorn, 16 miles (26 km) east of Inverness. A two-storey fortified bell tower stands on the hill above the parish church of Ardclach. Built in 1655, it summoned worshippers to church and gave warning in times of danger.

Ardeer *North Ayrshire* A peninsula of North Ayrshire, Ardeer extends southeast from Stevenston with its southern tip facing the new town of Irvine. It is approximately 2 miles (3 km) in length and 1.5 miles (2.5 km) at its widest point. To the west, it forms the northern part of Irvine Bay, an inlet of the Firth of Clyde, and to the east the mouth of the River Garnock. At its southern tip lay the only British dynamite-manufacturing plant built by Alfred Nobel, the Swedish inventor of the explosive and originator of the Nobel prizes.

Ardelve *Highland* A settlement in western Highland Council area, Ardelve lies on the northern side of Loch Alsh near the mouth of Loch Long and a half-mile (1 km) west of Dornie.

Arden *Argyll and Bute* Located at the southeast edge of Argyll and Bute Council area, Arden is situated on the southwest shore of Loch Lomond. Balloch lies 3 miles (5 km) to the southeast.

Ardencaple *Argyll and Bute* A settlement situated on the northern shoreline of the island of Seil, a mile (1.5 km) west of Clachan Bridge and a mile (1.5 km) north of An Cala Garden.

Ardentallen *Argyll and Bute* A settlement located on the northern shore of Loch Feochan to the south of Oban in the district of Lorn, a mile (1.5 km) northeast of Kilninver across the loch.

Ardentinny *Argyll and Bute* A village of Argyll and Bute, Ardentinny lies near the mouth of Glen Finart on the western shore of Loch Long, 4 miles (6.5 km) north of Strone Point. Stronchullin Hill rises to the southwest of the village.

Ardeonaig *Stirling* A hamlet with a hotel in northeast Stirling Council area, Ardeonaig lies on the southern side of Loch Tay, 5 miles (8 km) east of Killin. It is situated at the mouth of the Finglen Burn where it enters Loch Tay and was once a ferry crossing point.

Ardersier *Highland* A settlement on the inner Moray Firth, Ardersier lies 10 miles (16 km) northeast of Inverness and just north of Inverness Airport. Founded by the Campbells of Cawdor, who created a burgh of barony here in 1623, and formerly known as Campbelltown, Ardersier was the southern terminus of a ferry from the Middle Ages that linked with Chanonry Point on the Black Isle. The nearby oil-rig platform construction and repair site was developed in the 1970s to serve the North Sea oil industry.

Ardessie *Highland* A locality in Wester Ross, Ardessie lies on the south shore of Little Loch Broom, 2 miles (3 km) northwest of Dundonnell.

Ardfern *Argyll and Bute* A yachting centre on the western side of Loch Craignish, Ardfern lies 25 miles (40 km) south of Oban.

Ardfin *Argyll and Bute* A hamlet at the southern tip of the island of Jura in the Inner Hebrides, Ardfin lies to the west of Jura House, 3 miles (5 km) southeast of Craighouse.

Ardgay *Highland* A village in the parish of Kincardine, Ross-shire, Ardgay lies on the railway line between Tain and Lairg, at the head of the Dornoch Firth, 13 miles (21 km) west of Dornoch.

Ardgour *Highland* A mountainous area of Lochaber in Highland Council area, Ardgour lies to the east of Sunart and is bounded by Loch Eil to the north, Loch Linnhe to the east, Loch Shiel to the west and Loch Sunart and Glen Tarbert to the south. The highest peak is Sgurr Dhomhnuill (888 m/2913 ft). The uplands of Ardgour are mostly drained eastwards to Loch Linnhe by streams that flow down through glens such as Glen Gour, Glen Scaddle and the Cona Glen, and on the shore of Loch Sunart is the former mining settlement of Strontian. At the Corran Narrows on Loch Linnhe there is a ferry crossing.

Ardhallow *Argyll and Bute* A village on the Cowal peninsula, Ardhallow lies on the Firth of Clyde 3 miles (5 km) southwest of Dunoon and a mile (1.5 km) north of Innellan.

Ardheslaig *Highland* A locality in Wester Ross, Ardheslaig lies close to the shore of Loch Shieldaig, 3 miles (5 km) northwest of Shieldaig.

Ardindrean *Highland* A hamlet in Wester Ross, Ardindrean lies on the west shore of Loch Broom, 3 miles (5 km) north of Inverbroom.

Ardivachar Rocks *Western Isles* A rocky reef close to Ardivachar Point, the Ardivachar Rocks are situated to the northwest of the island of South Uist. The settlement of Aird a' Mhachair lies immediately to the south.

Ardjachie Point *Highland* A small headland jutting into the Dornoch Firth, Ardjachie Point lies to the northwest of Tain in Easter Ross.

Ardkinglas *Argyll and Bute* Giving the impression of an old tower house extended in the 18th century, Ardkinglas was built as a fine Edwardian sporting lodge between 1906 and 1908 by the architect Sir Robert Lorimer (1864–1929). It lies on Loch Fyne, opposite Inveraray Castle, home of the dukes of Argyll. The estate of Ardkinglas was granted by Sir Colin Campbell to his youngest son in 1396 and a castle existed in the late 16th century, although it was demolished by the mid-18th century. The house that replaced the original castle was recorded as being derelict when Dorothy Wordsworth visited it in 1822. Sir Andrew Noble purchased the estate in 1905 and immediately commissioned Lorimer to build a house. The rooms are of fine quality; principal among them is the oak-panelled Jacobean-style saloon which boasts a massive carved granite fireplace, a fine plasterwork ceiling with a central painted panel illustrating Apollo, and tapestry hangings. On the first floor, the dining room leads out to an unusual loggia that looks onto the loch. Ardkinglas has several interesting 'modern' conveniences, including a shower cage designed by Lorimer. It was also one of the first country houses to have electricity incorporated at the time of building rather than as an afterthought. The tiled kitchen remains exactly as it was when built. The gardens at Ardkinglas, established in 1875, contain one of the finest collections of rhododendrons and conifers in the UK.

Ardlamont *Argyll and Bute* The settlement of Ardlamont lies at the southeastern tip of the Cowal peninsula, 4 miles (6.5 km) south of Tighnabruaich. Immediately to the south lie Ardlamont Bay and Ardlamont Point.

Ardle, River *Perth and Kinross* A river in eastern Perth and Kinross, the River Ardle rises in headstreams which flow down Gleann Fearnach and Glen Brerachan. It flows 13 miles (21 km) southeastwards along Strath Ardle before joining the Black Water at Bridge of Cally to become the River Ericht.

Ardler *Perth and Kinross* A small village on the eastern boundary of Perth and Kinross, Ardler is situated 3 miles (5 km) east of Coupar Angus, to the east of the A94. The village was founded in the 1830s by the radical thinker George Kinloch, who planned to develop a marketing centre for Strathmore on the railway line linking Dundee and Coupar Angus. Originally naming it Washington after the American president, Kinloch intended the streets to take the names of well-known political and philosophical heroes from William Wallace to Benjamin Franklin. Kinloch did not live to see the completion of the village, which failed to prosper.

Ardlui *Argyll and Bute* A settlement in Glen Falloch, Ardlui lies on the western shore of Loch Lomond, 7 miles (11 km) north of Tarbet and 10 miles (16 km) southeast of Crianlarich. There is an old droving inn at Inverarnan nearby, and a pier at the north end of the loch once served the West Highland Railway.

Ardlussa *Argyll and Bute* A settlement located on the east coast of Jura in the Inner Hebrides, Ardlussa lies a mile (1.5 km) northeast of Inverlussa at the mouth of the Lussa River. Ardlussa looks onto the Sound of Jura.

Ardmaddy *Argyll and Bute* A settlement on the east shore of Loch Etive, Ardmaddy lies at the mouth of Glen Kinglass 6 miles (10 km) northeast of Taynuilt.

Ardmaddy Bay *Argyll and Bute* A square-shaped inlet of Seil Sound, Ardmaddy Bay lies 4 miles (6.5 km) southwest of Kilninver and 8 miles (13 km) south of Oban. Ardmaddy Castle, a former seat of the marquesses of Breadalbane, lies to the north.

Ardmair *Highland* A settlement in Wester Ross, Ardmair lies nearly 3 miles (5 km) north of Ullapool.

Ardmaleish *Argyll and Bute* A settlement on the island of Bute, Ardmaleish lies to the north of Kames Bay and west of Ardmaleish Point.

Ardmaleish Point *Argyll and Bute* A headland on the eastern coast of the island of Bute, Ardmaleish Point extends into the eastern arm of the Kyles of Bute opposite the mouth of Loch Striven.

Ardmeanach An old name for the Black Isle in Highland.

Ardmenish *Argyll and Bute* A settlement on the island of Jura, Ardmenish lies to the north of Lowlandman's Bay on the east coast of the island.

Ardmiddle House *Aberdeenshire* Situated on the River

Deveron, Ardmiddle House lies 3 miles (5 km) west of Turriff in Aberdeenshire. Ardmiddle Mains and Hillhead of Ardmiddle lie to the southeast.

Ardminish *Argyll and Bute* A settlement on the island of Gigha, Ardminish looks out over Ardminish Bay, an inlet of the Sound of Gigha. A ferry service connects with Tayinloan on the Kintyre peninsula. To the south of the village lie Achamore House and Gardens.

Ardmolich *Highland* A settlement in Moidart, western Highland Council area, Ardmolich lies in Glen Moidart at the east end of Loch Moidart.

Ardmore *Argyll and Bute* The settlement of Ardmore is located 2 miles (3 km) northwest of Cardross on a peninsula that extends into the Firth of Clyde. Ardmore faces Greenock across the Firth of Clyde.

Ardmore *Highland* A settlement in Eddertoun parish, Easter Ross, Ardmore lies on the southern shore of the Dornoch Firth, 5 miles (8 km) northwest of Tain. It developed as a small port in the 19th century servicing small ships carrying coal and lime.

Ardmore Point *Argyll and Bute* A headland on the southeastern coast of the island of Islay in the Inner Hebrides, Ardmore Point extends into the sea 5 miles (8 km) northeast of Ardbeg. The settlement of Ardmore lies to the east.

Ardmore Point *Argyll and Bute* A headland at the north end of the island of Mull, Ardmore Point extends into the Sound of Mull 3 miles (5 km) north of Tobermory.

Ardmore Point *Highland* A headland on the coast of northwest Sutherland, Ardmore Point lies on the eastern side of the entrance to Loch Laxford.

Ardmore Point *Highland* A headland on the island of Skye, Ardmore Point extends into the sea on the west side of the Vaternish peninsula. It encloses Ardmore Bay.

Ardmore Point *Highland* A headland on the north coast of Sutherland, Ardmore Point juts into the Pentland Firth 4 miles (6.5 km) to the northeast of Bettyhill.

Ardmucknish Bay *Argyll and Bute* A wide inlet opening out into the Firth of Lorn, Ardmucknish Bay lies to the west of Benderloch, between the headlands of Rubha Garbh-aird and Dunstaffnage. The settlements of Kiel Crofts, Ledaig and South Ledaig lie on the bay, together with the Connel Airfield. The waters of Loch Etive enter the south of the bay through the Falls of Lora, and to the west Dunstaffnage Bay forms an inlet protected by Eilean Mòr and Eilean Beag.

Ardnacross Bay *Argyll and Bute* A sandy bay on the eastern side of the Kintyre peninsula, Ardnacross Bay opens out onto the Kilbrannan Sound opposite the island of Arran. The settlement of Peninver lies to the west of the bay.

Ardnagoine *Highland* A largely seasonal settlement on Tanera Mòr, the largest of the Summer Isles, Ardnagoine is located to the north of The Anchorage.

Ardnagrask *Highland* A settlement in Easter Ross, Ardnagrask lies a mile (1.5 km) southwest of Muir of Ord.

Ardnamurchan *Highland* Occupying an area of 81,000 ha (200,000 acres) on the western coast of Highland Council area, the sparsely populated Ardnamurchan peninsula extends westwards from Sunart. It is separated from the Morvern peninsula by Loch Sunart, and from Mull by the Sound of Mull. There is a ferry link between Kilchoan and Tobermory on Mull, and near Kilchoan is Mingarry Castle, a former stronghold of the Macleans of Ardnamurchan, a sept of the Macdonald Lords of the Isles. To the west are the remnants of a large volcanic crater created over 60 million years ago when the North American and European plates of the Earth's crust separated to form the Atlantic Ocean.

Ardnamurchan, Point of *Highland* The western headland of the Ardnamurchan peninsula in Highland Council area at the Point of Ardnamurchan (meaning 'point of the great ocean') is the westernmost point on the UK mainland at 6 degrees 28 minutes west. A lighthouse was built here in 1849 by engineer Alan Stevenson (1807–65).

Ardnarff *Highland* A locality in Wester Ross, Ardnarff lies on the southern side of Loch Carron, 2 miles (3 km) east of Stromeferry.

Ardnastang *Highland* A settlement in Sunart, southwest Highland Council area, Ardnastang lies on the northern side of Loch Sunart, a mile (1.5 km) west of Strontian.

Ardnave *Argyll and Bute* A settlement located at the north end of the island of Islay, a mile (1.5 km) southwest of Ardnave Point and a half-mile (1 km) to the west of the mouth of Loch Gruinart.

Ardnish *Highland* A flat headland of the Arisaig peninsula, Ardnish juts southwards into the Sound of Arisaig, separating Loch nan Uamh from Loch Ailort.

Ardno *Argyll and Bute* A hamlet on the northeast shore of Loch Fyne, Ardno lies at the mouth of Hell's Glen, 5 miles (8 km) northwest of Lochgoilhead.

Ardoch *Perth and Kinross* A locality near Braco in southwest Perth and Kinross, Ardoch is the site of one of the most important surviving monuments of the Roman period in Britain. A fort with remarkably preserved earthworks and a series of six overlapping marching camps have been identified as important military installations built by the Roman Army at various times between AD 80 and AD 200.

Ardoch Burn *Stirling* A stream in Kilmadock parish, Stirling Council area, the Ardoch Burn rises in headstreams beyond the Braes of Doune. It flows southwards for 7 miles (11 km) before joining the River Teith between Doune and Dunblane. Kilbryde Castle, a former seat of the Grahams and later the Campbells of Aberuchill, stands on a rocky promontory on the banks of the Ardoch.

Ardochrig *South Lanarkshire* An agricultural settlement of South Lanarkshire, Ardochrig lies 4 miles (6.5 km) northwest of Strathaven, 5 miles (8 km) south of East Kilbride and 2.5 miles (4 km) southeast of Auldhouse.

Ardoe House *Aberdeenshire* Situated on the south side of the River Dee in Aberdeenshire, Ardoe House lies a mile (1.5 km) to the south of Cults and southwest of Aberdeen. The house was built in 1878 in the Scottish baronial style and was designed by James Matthews for the Aberdeen soap-maker Alexander Ogston.

Ardovie *Angus* A residence of northeast Angus, Ardovie House lies on the edge of Montreathmont Moor, 3 miles (5 km) south of Brechin.

Ardpatrick *Argyll and Bute* A settlement of southwest Knapdale, Ardpatrick lies 9 miles (14 km) southwest of Tarbert near Ardpatrick Point.

Ardpatrick Point *Argyll and Bute* Located at the southwestern extremity of the Knapdale district of Argyll and Bute, Ardpatrick Point forms a headland at the western end of West Loch Tarbert.

Ardrishaig *Argyll and Bute* A settlement at the mouth of Loch Gilp, an inlet of Loch Fyne in Argyll and Bute, Ardrishaig lies 2 miles (3 km) south of Lochgilphead at the northern end of the Kintyre peninsula. The village developed in association with the herring-fishing industry and as the eastern terminus of the Crinan Canal, which was dug between 1793 and 1801 and engineered by John Rennie. Steamboat connections were made with Oban and Glasgow, and a distillery was in production at Glendarroch between 1831 and 1937. Fish farming, forestry, hydro-electricity and servicing an oil depot have maintained the population of Ardrishaig in modern times.

Ardross *Highland* A small settlement in Easter Ross, Ardross lies to the west of the Struie Road, 2 miles (3 km) north of Alness. Ardross Castle, a former seat of the Munros, was remodelled in Scottish baronial style in 1880 for Charles William Dyson Perrins (1864–1958), the Worcester sauce millionaire.

Ardross Castle *Fife* The ruined 14th-century castle of Ardross is located on the northern coast of the Firth of Forth, between the settlements of Elie and St Monans. It was a stronghold of the Dischington family until the 12th century.

Ardrossan *North Ayrshire* Situated on the north side of Irvine Bay, an inlet of the Firth of Clyde, Ardrossan lies 5 miles (8 km) northwest of Irvine. Founded as a resort in 1805 by the Earl of Eglinton, its deep-water harbour was suitable for steamboats connecting with Arran, Belfast, the Isle of Man and Campbeltown. Ardrossan also became a seaport for the export of coal, iron and chemicals, although it never realised its ambition to be a terminus on the proposed Glasgow, Paisley and Ardrossan Canal. Created a burgh in 1846, one of the last to be established in Scotland, Ardrossan became a centre of railway engineering, shipbuilding and oil refining. It still maintains a ferry link with Arran (dating from 1834) and the Isle of Man (dating from 1892), and timber bound for the paper mill at Irvine is imported. There are three railway stations at Ardrossan. Offshore is the Horse Isle nature reserve.

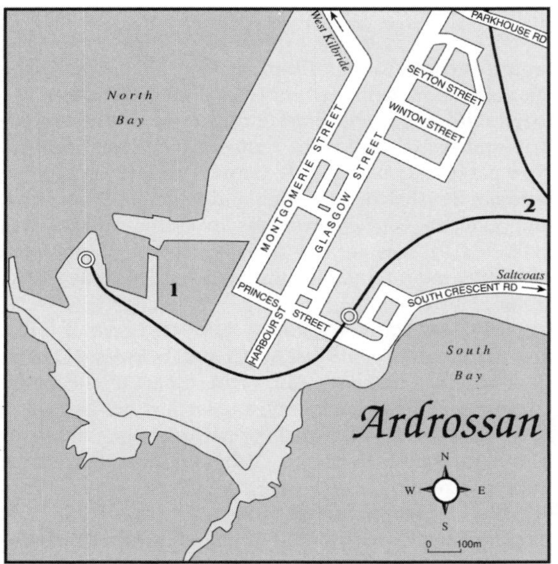

1 *Ardrossan Harbour* 2 *North Ayrshire Museum*

Ardshealach *Highland* A settlement in Sunart, southwest Highland Council area, Ardshealach lies at the southwestern extremity of Loch Shiel.

Ardslave *Western Isles* One of a succession of scattered settlements strung along the rocky east coast of South Harris in the Outer Hebrides, Ardslave (Gael: *Aird Shleibhe* or *Aird Leimhe*) lies between Manish and Beacravik, 5 miles (8 km) northeast of Rodel.

Ardslignish *Highland* A locality on the south side of the Ardnamurchan peninsula, southwest Highland Council area, Ardslignish lies 2 miles (3 km) west of Glenborrodale.

Ardtalla *Argyll and Bute* Situated on the east coast of the island of Islay, Ardtalla lies immediately north of Claggain Bay and to the south of the headland of Rubha Liath. Port Ellen lies 9 miles (14 km) to the southwest. A single-track road leads from Ardbeg 7 miles (11 km) north to Ardtalla.

Ardtalnaig *Perth and Kinross* A hamlet in central Perth and Kinross, Ardtalnaig lies on the south side of Loch Tay, 6 miles (10 km) southwest of Kenmore. There is a footpath over the hills to Glen Almond.

Ardtarig *Argyll and Bute* A settlement on the Cowal peninusla, Ardtarig is located 8 miles (13 km) northwest of Dunoon on the northeast shore of Loch Striven.

Ardtoe *Highland* A locality on the coast of Moidart, southwest Highland Council area, Ardtoe lies 3 miles (5 km) northwest of Acharacle, near the mouth of Kentra Bay. A sea fish marine unit of the Sea Fish Industry Authority is based here. Newton of Ardtoe lies to the east.

Ardtornish *Highland* A settlement of Morvern, Ardtornish lies at the head of Loch Aline, near the mouth of the Rannoch River and immediately to the north of Achranich.

Ardtornish Point *Highland* A basalt headland of the Morvern peninsula, Ardtornish Point extends into the Sound of Mull to the west of Ardtornish Bay. The ruins of a former stronghold of the Lords of the Isles stand on the headland which lies 2 miles (3 km) south of the village of Ardtornish at the head of Loch Aline.

Ardtun *Argyll and Bute* A scattered community of the island of Mull, Ardtun is located on the Ross of Mull peninsula to the northeast of Bunessan.

Arduaine *Argyll and Bute* A locality on the western coastline of Argyll and Bute, 20 miles (32 km) south of Oban, Arduaine overlooks Loch Melfort to the north and the island of Shuna to the southwest. Kilmelford lies 4 miles (6.5 km) northeast. Arduaine Gardens occupy an area of 8 ha (20 acres) in a sheltered position on the Sound of Jura. Taking advantage of the warming effect of the Gulf Stream, James Arthur Campbell started planting here in 1898. Essex businessmen Edmund and Harry Wright bought Arduaine in 1971 and after restoring and developing the garden gave it to the National Trust for Scotland in 1992.

Ardullie *Highland* A locality in Easter Ross, Ardullie lies at the northern end of the road bridge over the Cromarty Firth from the Black Isle built in 1980. Ardullie Lodge, dating from the 17th century, was a house of the Munro family until the late 1970s.

Ardvar *Highland* A settlement in the Assynt district of western Sutherland, Ardvar lies on the east side of Loch Airdbhair, 5 miles (8 km) west of Unapool.

Ardvasar *Highland* A village on the island of Skye in the Inner Hebrides, Ardvasar lies on the eastern coast of the Sleat peninsula a half-mile (1 km) southwest of Armadale.

Ardveenish *Western Isles* A small settlement on the east coast of Barra in the Outer Hebrides, Ardveenish (Gael: *Aird Mhidhinis*) lies on the northern shore of Bay Hirivagh, a half-mile (1 km) east-northeast of Northbay and 4.5 miles (7 km) northeast of Castlebay. Ardveenish has a pier for fishing boats. A sizeable shellfish-processing factory and the small Barra Power Station are located here.

Ardverikie *Highland* A locality in Badenoch, Ardverikie lies on the southern shore of Loch Laggan, 3 miles (5 km) southwest of Kinloch Laggan. Ardverikie deer forest extends to the south and Ardverikie House, a 19th-century shooting lodge, was visited by Queen Victoria in 1847 and considered by her as a possible Highland home before finding Balmoral. More recently, Ardverikie has been used as a location in the film *Mrs Brown* (1997), which explored the relationship between Victoria and her Highland servant, John Brown, starring Judi Dench and Billy Connolly. It has also featured as 'Glenbogle' in the recent BBC television series *Monarch of the Glen*. The estate extends to 12,141 ha (30,000 acres) and provides fishing and deer stalking. Ardverikie Wall provides challenging climbing.

Ardvorlich *Perth and Kinross* A hamlet of southwest Perth and Kinross, Ardvorlich lies on the south side of Loch Earn, 3 miles (5 km) southeast of Lochearnhead. The mansion house of the Stewarts of Ardvorlich was the Darnlinvarach of Sir Walter Scott's novel *The Legend of Montrose* (1819).

Ardvreck Castle *Highland* A ruined castle in the Assynt district of Sutherland, Ardvreck Castle is situated on a peninsula that juts out into Loch Assynt near Inchnadamph. It was built by the Macleods, who gained control of Assynt in the 13th century. In 1650 the laird of Assynt was responsible for the capture of James Graham, Marquess of Montrose, after his defeat at the Battle of Carbisdale. Montrose was held prisoner at Ardvreck prior to his being despatched to Edinburgh and the gallows. Ardvreck was subsequently acquired by the Mackenzies who built nearby Calda House, both Ardvreck and Calda later being destroyed by fire.

Ardwell *Dumfries and Galloway* A locality in the Rhinns of Galloway, Ardwell lies on Chapel Rossan Bay, an inlet of Luce Bay, 9 miles (14 km) southeast of Portpatrick. The gardens of Ardwell House are open to the public during the spring and summer, and to the west of the peninsula are the farms of High and Low Ardwell. Doon Castle on Ardwell Point to the southwest of High Ardwell is one of four remaining brochs on the western coast of Galloway.

Ardwell *Moray* A small settlement in Moray, Ardwell lies near the confluence of the Black Water and the River Deveron, 2 miles (3 km) north of Cabrach.

Ardyne Burn *Argyll and Bute* Rising in the foothills of Corlarach Hill on the Cowal peninsula, the Ardyne Burn flows northwest then southwest, passing to the east of the settlements of Blairbuie and Knockdow, before emptying into the Kyles of Bute less than a mile (1.5 km) to the east of Ardyne Point.

Arecloch Forest *South Ayrshire* The Arecloch Forest is located 4 miles (6.5 km) southwest of Barrhill in South Ayrshire. The Water of Tig rises within the Arecloch Forest.

Argaty *Stirling* A locality in central Stirling Council area, Argaty lies a mile (1.5 km) to the north of Doune. Argaty House dates from the 1800s, with Scottish baronial-style additions in the 1860s and 1920s.

Argrennan House *Dumfries and Galloway* A mansion house in Dumfries and Galloway, Argrennan lies in the valley of the River Dee, 4 miles (6.5 km) southwest of Castle Douglas. Dating from 1818 and formerly known as Deebank, it was designed by James Gillespie Graham.

Argyle Street *Glasgow City* Running west from the High Street at Glasgow Cross, Argyle Street is one of Glasgow's longest streets and extends to Kelvingrove Park in the West End. Originally named St Thenew's Gait, it was renamed Argyle Street in 1751 after the Duke of Argyll. Though it was developed as a site for housing for the Glasgow merchants in the 18th century, it is now one of the principal shopping thoroughfares in the city and houses some of the city's finest examples of 19th-century shopping architecture, for example the Argyle Arcade and warehouse developments at the junction with Buchanan Street.

Argyll and Bute *Area: 7021 sq. km (2711 sq. miles)* Situated on the heavily indented Atlantic seaboard of western Scotland, Argyll and Bute Council area is a land of lochs, mountains and islands. Within its bounds lie the Cowal peninsula and the long peninsula known as the Mull of Kintyre, Lochs Awe, Fyne and Etive, and many of the inner isles of Scotland including Mull, Coll, Tiree, Islay, Jura, Colonsay, Gigha, Lismore and Bute. Its main settlements are Lochgilphead, Campbeltown, Oban, Dunoon, Inveraray, Arrochar, Helensburgh and Tobermory. Argyll and Bute is the second-largest of Scotland's unitary local authorities by area, yet it is the eleventh-smallest in terms of population. Local industries include forestry, farming, fishing and fish farming. Tourism is of great importance, and attractions include picturesque scenery, sizeable mountains, ancient castles and whisky distilleries. The numerous distilleries include those at Oban and Campbeltown, but it is the distilleries on the island of Islay that are particularly noted for the rich peaty qualities of their malts. The region includes a significant number of native Gaelic speakers, approaching 10 per cent of the population.

Argyllshire *Argyll and Bute* A former county of western Scotland, Argyllshire is the home of the Clan Campbell. Now part of Argyll and Bute Council area, it was divided between Strathclyde and Highland regions between 1975 and 1996. Its county town was Inveraray, and its area extended to 8055 sq. km (3110 sq. miles) of indented coastline, mountainous countryside and islands in the Inner Hebrides.

Argyll Forest Park *Argyll and Bute* An area of forest and mountain in southeast Argyll and Bute, Argyll Forest Park occupies much of the northern part of the Cowal peninsula between Loch Long and Loch Fyne. Opened in 1935, it was the first National Forest Park to be created for public recreation in the UK. It has an area of 24,282 ha (60,000 acres).

Argyll's Bowling Green *Argyll and Bute* A physiographic district and range of peaks of south-central Argyll and Bute, Argyll's Bowling Green lies between Loch Long and Loch Goil and rises to 787m

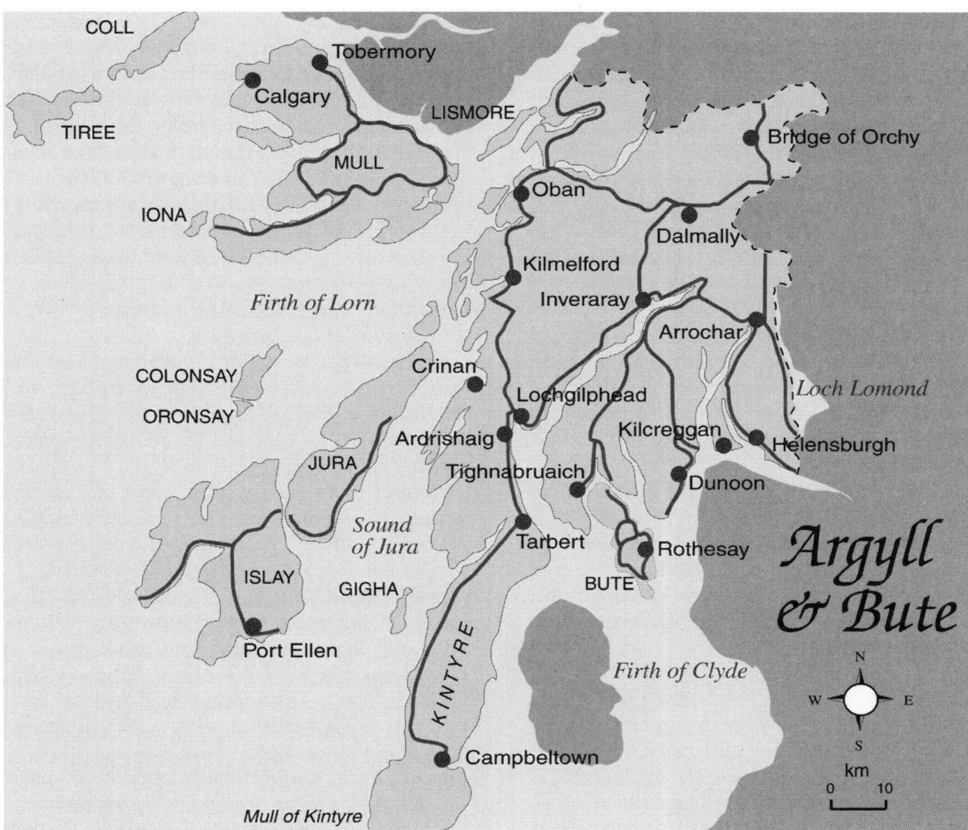

(2582 ft) at the Brack which lies to the south of Glen Croe. The name Argyll's Bowling Green is a misnomer: the area is far from flat and the name is actually a corruption of the Gaelic *Baile na Greine* or 'sunny hamlet'. The lower slopes are covered by the Ardgartan Forest, part of the Argyll Forest Park.

Argyll's Lodgings *Stirling* Argyll's Lodgings is located in the historic old town of Stirling and is arguably the most striking of Scotland's surviving 17th-century town houses. Built by the founder of Nova Scotia, Sir William Alexander (1567–1640), the house passed into the hands of the Argyll family when he died. Comprising rooms furnished with period furniture, it is now in the care of Historic Scotland.

Aridhglas *Argyll and Bute* The settlement of Aridhglas is located on the Ross of Mull, on the southwest coast of the island of Mull. Situated on the main route between Bunessan and Fionnphort, Aridhglas lies 2 miles (3 km) to the east of Fionnphort and a mile (1.5 km) south of the headland of Rubha nan Cearc.

Arienas, Loch *Highland* A loch on the Morvern peninsula, southwest Highland Council area, Loch Arienas lies to the north of Fiunary Forest and Ardtornish.

Arileod *Argyll and Bute* A settlement on the western coastline of the island of Coll, Arileod lies 4 miles (6.5 km) southwest of Arinagour.

Arinagour *Argyll and Bute* The principal settlement and main port of the island of Coll, Arinagour is located at the head of Loch Eatharna on the island's east coast 5 miles (8 km) from the northern tip of the island.

Arisaig *Highland* A village in South Morar, southwest Highland Council area, Arisaig lies 7 miles (11 km) south of Mallaig at the head of Loch nan Ceall. Looking out to Skye and the Small Isles, Arisaig lies on the 'Road to the Isles' and was a stopping-off place for steamers. In 1901 a station was opened on the railway from Fort William to Mallaig, bringing tourists to the area. The 9-hole Traigh golf course lies to the north, and there are ferries from here to the Small Isles in the summer months. Arisaig House to the east was built in the 19th century by Lord Cranston.

Arisaig *Highland* A district of South Morar, southwest Highland Council area, Arisaig forms a peninsula that extends into the sea to the south of Mallaig. Its coast has fine sandy beaches, and its chief settlements are the townships of Arisaig, Back of Keppoch, Portnaluchaig, Morroch, Rhumach and Druimindarroch. The peninsula has many associations with St Maelrubha and with Prince Charles Edward Stewart (Bonnie Prince Charlie) who landed at Loch nan Uamh in July 1745 and eventually escaped to France from there in 1746.

Arisaig, Sound of *Highland* Separating the Arisaig and Moidart peninsulas of southwest Highland Council area, the Sound of Arisaig extends west from the Ardnish peninsula. Loch Ailort and Loch nan Uamh open out into the sound on either side of Ardnish.

Ariundle *Highland* A National Nature Reserve in the Sunart district of southwest Highland Council area, Ariundle lies to the west of Strontian. It is the focal point of the Sunart Oakwoods Project, a scheme to regenerate the original native broadleaved woodland. Until 1920

Ariundle was part of the Sunart Estate owned by the Riddell family. It was acquired by the Forestry Commission and largely given over to the planting of commercial conifers until 1997 when the emphasis changed to conservation.

Arivruaich *Western Isles* A crofting township of southern Lewis in the Outer Hebrides, Arivruaich (Gael: *Airidh a' Bhruaich*) lies at the junction of Tob Cheann Tarabhaigh and Loch Seaforth, 3 miles (5 km) west of the head of the latter and 12.5 miles (20 km) northeast of Tarbert.

Arkaig, Loch *Highland* A loch in Lochaber, Loch Arkaig lies 10 miles (16 km) north of Fort William and extends for 12 miles (19 km) in an east–west direction to the west of Loch Lochy.

Arkle *Highland* A mountain in northwest Sutherland, Arkle rises to 787 m (2582 ft) 4 miles (6.5 km) east of Laxford Bridge.

Arklet, Loch *Stirling* A loch in Buchanan parish, central Stirling Council area, Loch Arklet lies between Loch Katrine and Loch Lomond, 12 miles (19 km) northwest of Aberfoyle. It drains westwards to Loch Lomond and receives a number of streams, the largest of which, the Corriearklet Burn, flows southwards to Loch Arklet from the slopes of Beinn a' Choin.

Arkleton *Dumfries and Galloway* A locality in eastern Dumfries and Galloway, Arkleton lies on the Ewes Water, 3 miles (5 km) north of Langholm. Arkleton Hill rises to the northeast.

Armadale *Highland* A settlement in northern Sutherland, Highland Council area, Armadale lies 5 miles (8 km) east of Bettyhill and close to Armadale Bay which receives the Armadale Burn.

Armadale *Highland* A ferry port on the Sleat peninsula in the southeast of the isle of Skye. Armadale Bay lies immediately to the north, with the early 19th-century Armadale Castle and the Clan Donald Centre a half-mile (1 km) beyond. Armadale receives a ferry across the Sound of Sleat from Mallaig.

Armadale *West Lothian* Armadale is a long, linear town situated 2 miles (3 km) west of Bathgate. Armadale is known locally as the Dale. In the 1850s this rural hamlet developed into a major industrial site through the exploitation of local deposits of coal, ironstone, limestone and brick clay. Several quarries, steelworks and tile, brick and fire-brick yards operated in the early 20th century and with the demise of mining, industrial estates were established in the 1970s. Originally known as Barbauchlaw, indicating an area for boar hunting, the lands were bought by Sir William Honeyman in 1790 and named after the settlement on his estates in Sutherland. Later, as a stop on the Edinburgh–Glasgow 'Great Road', Armadale added an inn and a tollhouse; the railway arrived in 1855, taking coal and ironstone to the Monkland Iron Company's Works. Its unusual public house, The Goth (1911), was designed on the Swedish Gothenburg System, which sought to reduce alcohol consumption by providing ample coffee and food.

Armadale Bay *Highland* A small bay on the north coast of Sutherland, Armadale Bay lies between Ardmore Point to the west and Strathy Point to the east. The Armadale Burn flows northwards into the bay from Loch Buidhe Mòr.

Armadale Castle *Highland* The former seat of the Macdonalds of Sleat, who with the Macleods of Dunvegan were the hereditary chiefs of the island of Skye, Armadale Castle (1815) replaced an earlier building on the shore that was visited by Dr Johnson and James Boswell in 1773. Today the main associated attractions are the Armadale Castle Gardens, Clan Donald Centre and Museum of the Isles which look out onto the Sound of Sleat at Armadale Bay. The 16 ha (40 acre) garden is set within the 8094 ha (20,000 acre) Armadale Estate, and there are woodland walks in the area.

Armadillo, the An informal name for the Clyde Auditorium in Glasgow City.

Arnabost *Argyll and Bute* A settlement on the island of Coll, Argyll and Bute, Arnabost is located 2 miles (3 km) northwest of Arinagour and 5 miles (8 km) northeast of Arileod. It is the junction for routes between Sorisdale, Clabhach and Arinagour.

Arncroach *Fife* A small hamlet in Carnbee parish, eastern Fife, Arncroach lies 3 miles (5 km) north of St Monans. Kellie Castle, the home of the architect Sir Robert Lorimer (1864–1929), lies to the east.

Arndilly House *Moray* Built for David Macdowall Grant in 1750, Arndilly House lies to the north of Craigellachie in Moray. It is situated by the River Spey at the foot of Ben Aigan, on whose western slopes is the Wood of Arndilly. The house was enlarged in neo-Jacobean style by Thomas Mackenzie in 1850. A Pictish symbol stone is built into the west gable.

Arngask *Perth and Kinross* A parish of southeast Perth and Kinross, Arngask extends over an eastern portion of the Ochil Hills with the village of Glenfarg as its focal point. The old church of Arngask, originally a chapel of the Barclays of Balvaird and last used in 1951, stands on a hill overlooking Glenfarg to which it is connected across the M90 by a bridge. Prior to 1891 the parish lay within the three counties of Fife, Kinross and Perth.

Arnhall *Aberdeenshire* A hamlet and mansion house in Fettercairn parish, southern Aberdeenshire, Arnhall lies in the Howe of the Mearns a mile (1.5 km) to the east of Edzell.

Arnhall Castle *Stirling* The remains of Arnhall Castle, a former seat of the Dow family, lie within the policies of Keir House, 4 miles (6.5 km) northwest of Stirling. Built in 1617, the building was incorporated into the Stirling of Keir Estate by marriage.

Arnicle *Argyll and Bute* Located on the Barr Water on the Kintyre peninsula, Argyll and Bute, Arnicle lies 3 miles (5 km) northeast of Glenbarr. The peaks of Beinn Bhreac and Beinn an Tuirc rise to the east.

Arnisdale *Highland* A village on the north shore of Loch Hourn, Arnisdale lies 8 miles (13 km) southeast of Glenelg.

Arnisdale, River *Highland* A river in western Highland Council area, the River Arnisdale flows westwards through Glen Arnisdale to enter Loch Hourn at Corran.

Arnish *Highland* A settlement on the island of Raasay, Arnish lies 3 miles (5 km) from the northern end of the island and overlooks Loch Arnish, an inlet of the Sound of Raasay to the west.

Arnish, Loch *Highland* A sea loch on the west coast of the island of Raasay, Loch Arnish forms a wide inlet between Manish Point in the south and Ard an Torrain in the north.

Arnish Point *Western Isles* Arnish Point lies at the west entrance to Stornoway Harbour on the east coast of the island of Lewis. A Stevenson lighthouse (1852) sits atop the point, while a half-mile (1 km) north lies Stornoway.

Arniston House *Midlothian* This magnificent Palladian mansion lies in a beautiful country setting in Midlothian, 1.5 miles (2.5 km) southwest of Gorebridge. It was begun in 1726 by the noted architect William Adam (1689–1748) for Robert Dundas, the 2nd Lord Arniston. The estate had been acquired by the Dundas family in 1571, and it was Robert's grandfather who first lived there and founded a legal dynasty. Arniston House was built in two phases and was eventually completed by John Adam (1721–92) in 1755 for the 4th Lord Arniston, half-brother of Henry Dundas, Viscount Melville. William Adam's *tour de force* here is the fine two-storey hall blending baroque, classical and rococo styles. A system of Corinthian pillars rises to the level of the gallery, above which they are richly decorated with fruit and flowers. The younger Adam constructed the west side of the house and was also responsible for fine plaster interiors in the dining and drawing rooms. The house contains fine porcelain and an exceptional collection of portraiture, including works by Sir Henry Raeburn (1756–1823) and Allan Ramsay (1713–84).

Arnol *Western Isles* A crofting township on the Isle of Lewis in the Outer Hebrides, Arnol lies between Carloway and Barvas on the northwest coast. The Blackhouse Museum is an example of the Tigh Dubh or drystone-walled thatched cottage typical of Lewis.

Arnol, River *Western Isles* A river on the Isle of Lewis in the Outer Hebrides, the Arnol rises among the lochs to the south of the village of Arnol and flows north through Loch Arnol to empty into Port Arnol. The settlements of Arnol and Bragor lie on either side of the river.

Arnprior *Stirling* A linear ridge-top village overlooking the Lake of Menteith, Arnprior is situated on the A811, 14 miles (22 km) west of Stirling. It developed as a service centre for the surrounding agricultural community.

Aros *Argyll and Bute* A locality on the north coast of the island of Mull, Aros lies 4 miles (6.5 km) southwest of Tobermory, with Loch Frisa to the west and Speinne Mòr rising to the southeast.

Aros Castle *Argyll and Bute* With commanding views over the Sound of Mull, Aros Castle is located at the mouth of the Aros River, where it enters Salen Bay on the northeast coast of the island of Mull. Little remains of this 13th-century castle which was once home to the Lords of the Isles and was protected by a fosse and drawbridge. It is believed that treasure from a sunken Spanish galleon is buried among the ruins. and it was at Aros Castle in 1608 that Lord Ochiltree gathered together the Highland chiefs for dinner aboard his ship before imprisoning them and taking them south to Blackness, Dumbarton and Stirling.

Aros River *Argyll and Bute* A river on the island of Mull, the Aros is formed by the joining of the Ledmore River and the Eas Corrach to the south of Loch Frisa. Flowing east through Glen Aros, it empties into the Sound of Mull a mile (1.5 km) north of Salen.

Arran *North Ayrshire* Sheltered from the Atlantic by the Kintyre peninsula and separated from mainland Scotland by the Firth of Clyde to the east and the Sound of Bute to the north, the mountainous island of Arran has a circumference of 55 miles (88 km), an area of 42,800 hectares (105,718 acres), and rises to a height of 874 m (2866 ft) at Goatfell. There are ferry links from Ardrossan to Brodick and, during the summer, from Claonaig on the Kintyre peninsula to Lochranza. The island's principal settlements include Brodick, Lamlash, Whiting Bay, Blackwaterfoot, Pirnmill and Lochranza, and among its historic attractions are Brodick Castle and Gardens, Arran Heritage Museum, the stone circles on Machrie Moor, Auchagallon stone circle, Kilpatrick Dun, Torr a' Chaisteil Fort, Torrylin Cairn and Lochranza Castle. A road completes the circumference of the island, which is traversed from east to west through mountain glens by the String Road, built by Thomas Telford in 1817, and to the south the Ross Road. A mecca for geologists, Arran lies on the Highland Boundary Fault and has examples of rock formations from many periods. It was frequently visited by the 18th-century geologist James Hutton, whose discovery of an unconformity here helped consolidate his theories of igneous geology. Tourism, farming, forestry and the production of dairy products and whisky are the chief industries on the island. Its population grew from 4472 in 1991 to 5045 in 2001.

Arrochar *Argyll and Bute* A town at the head of Loch Long, Arrochar lies a mile (1.5 km) west of Tarbet on Loch Lomond. With a railway station on the West Highland Line and easily accessible by road and water, it has developed into a focal point for climbers heading for Ben Arthur (the Cobbler), Beinn Narnain and Beinn Ime, all situated to the northwest. In 1263, King Haakon of Norway launched his Armada against Scotland, which ultimately led to his defeat at the Battle of Largs. Many of his Viking longships sailed up Loch Long, where they were dragged across the isthmus between Arrochar and Tarbet, thereby allowing the invaders further penetration into mainland Scotland.

Arrochar Alps *Argyll and Bute* The Arrochar Alps are a picturesque and rugged range of mountains in the southern Highlands, lying to the north and west of Arrochar and to the west of Loch Lomond. The range lies within the Loch Lomond and Trossachs National Park and includes four Munros, six Corbetts and three other mountains. The Munros are Beinn Ime (1101 m/3317 ft), Ben Vorlich (943 m/3094 ft), Beinn Narnain (926 m/3038 ft) and Ben Vane (915 m/3002 ft). The Corbetts are Beinn an Lochain (901 m/2956 ft), Ben Arthur (also known as the Cobbler; 884 m/2901 ft), Beinn Luibhean (857 m/2812 ft), Ben Donich (847 m/2779 ft), Binnein an Fhidhleir (817 m/2681 ft) and the Brack (787 m/2582 ft). The other significant hills are Beinn Chorranach (888 m/2914 ft), A' Chrois (848 m/2782 ft) and Cruach Tairbeirt (415 m/1349 ft). The proximity of the Arrochar Alps to Glasgow has ensured that they are popular with hill-walkers and climbers.

Arron, Loch *Dumfries and Galloway* A tiny loch in the Galloway Forest Park, Dumfries and Galloway, Loch Arron lies to the northeast of Glen Trool, between Loch Enoch to the north and Loch Neldricken to the south.

Artfield Fell *Dumfries and Galloway* A hill in Dumfries and Galloway, Artfield Fell rises to 274 m (888 ft) in the Galloway Hills, 6 miles (10 km) northeast of Glenluce.

Arthur, Loch *Dumfries and Galloway* A small loch in Dumfries and Galloway, Loch Arthur lies to the east of

Beeswing, 6 miles (10 km) southwest of Dumfries. There are the remains of a crannog, or ancient lake dwelling, at its western end.

Arthur's Seat *City of Edinburgh* The remains of an ancient volcano that erupted under water, Arthur's Seat is located within Holyrood Park in the centre of Edinburgh. Although only 251 m (823 ft) high, Arthur's Seat is a notable landmark, dominating the city. Known also as the Lion's Head, Arthur's Seat is the highest of a series of peaks that take the form of a crouched lion. Geologically what remains is a basalt lava plug that choked the neck of a volcano that would have been active around 335 million years ago. The action of glaciation has cut into its heart, making it one of the most accessible exposures of an ancient volcano.

Artney, Glen *Perth and Kinross* A narrow valley of central Perth and Kinross, Glen Artney stretches over 8 miles (13 km) northeastwards from Glenartney Lodge to Cultybraggan. For all its length it follows the course of the Water of Ruchill, which joins the River Earn at Comrie. The Forest of Glen Artney, which lies between Glen Artney and Loch Earn, was once part of the royal deer forest of Strath Earn, supplying venison to the sovereigns of Scotland. The glen was immortalised in Sir Walter Scott's *The Lady of the Lake* (1810): 'The stag at eve had drunk his fill, Where danced the moon on Monan's rill, And deep his midnight lair had made, In lone Glenartney's hazel shade.'

Ascaig, Loch *Highland* A small loch in eastern Sutherland, Loch Ascaig lies to the west of the Strath of Kildonan, 12 miles (19 km) northwest of Helmsdale.

Ascog *Argyll and Bute* A settlement on the east coast of the isle of Bute, Ascog lies 2 miles (3 km) southeast of Rothesay to the east of Loch Ascog. The village overlooks the Firth of Clyde and offers views east to Great Cumbrae and the Scottish mainland.

Ascrib Islands *Highland* Situated in Loch Snizort, the uninhabited Ascrib Islands form a chain lying between the Vaternish and Trotternish peninsulas of northern Skye.

Ashavat, Loch *Western Isles* A small loch of North Harris in the Outer Hebrides, Loch Ashavat is the source of the Abhainn Eabhal, which flows south to empty into Loch Chloistair.

Ashfield *Stirling* Designated a conservation village in 1976, Ashfield is a hamlet 2 miles (3 km) north of Dunblane. Comprising terraced stone houses surrounding a village green, it was built in the 19th century for those working at the local mill.

Ashgill *South Lanarkshire* A settlement in the Clyde Valley, Ashgill lies 2 miles (3 km) southeast of Larkhall and 7 miles (11 km) northwest of Lanark. This former mining village lies between the M74 and the upper reaches of the River Clyde.

Ashie, Loch *Highland* A reservoir in Glen More, central Highland Council area, Loch Ashie lies just over 6 miles (10 km) southwest of Inverness, to the east of Loch Ness.

Ashiestiel *Scottish Borders* A locality in the Ettrick district of Scottish Borders, Ashiestiel lies on the south side of the River Tweed, 4 miles (6.5 km) east of Innerleithen. Ashiestiel House was the home of Sir Walter Scott before he moved to Abbotsford House in 1811. To the southwest, Ashiestiel Hill rises to 401 m (1315 ft).

Ashintully Castle *Perth and Kinross* A castle of Strath Ardle in east-central Perth and Kinross, Ashintully Castle dates from 1583, when it was built by Andrew Spalding. The building was restored in the 1830s, with further modifications in the late 19th century and early 20th century.

Ashkirk *Scottish Borders* A village in Scottish Borders, Ashkirk lies in the upper valley of the Ale Water, 4 miles (6.5 km) south of Selkirk. A former agricultural milltown, it is now largely a commuter settlement.

Askernish *Western Isles* A crofting community in southwest South Uist in the Outer Hebrides, Askernish (Gael: *Aisgernis*) lies around Loch an Eilein, 4 miles (6.5 km) northwest of Lochboisdale.

Askival *Highland* The highest point on the island of Rum in the Small Isles, Askival rises to 812 m (2663 ft). To the south it overlooks the Sound of Rum and the island of Eigg.

Asknish House *Argyll and Bute* A mansion at the head of Loch Gair, a western spur of Loch Fyne, Asknish House lies a half-mile (1 km) north of Lochgair and a mile (1.5 km) southeast of Loch Glashan.

Assel, Water of *South Ayrshire* A stream rising on Kirkland Hill in South Ayrshire, the Water of Assel flows west then south for 4.5 miles (7 km) to join the Duisk River at Asselfoot.

Assembly Hall of the Church of Scotland *City of Edinburgh* Lying behind the frontage of New College at the top of the Mound in Edinburgh, the Assembly Hall was erected for the Free Church of Scotland, which had separated from the established Church in the Disruption of 1843. It was built as the Free High Kirk in 1859 by David Bryce (1803–76), with alterations in 1901 by J.M. Dick Peddie. When the United Free Church merged with the Church of Scotland in 1929, the building became a meeting place for the General Assembly, which meets annually in May. The General Assembly, which comprises ministers, elders and lay members, is the governing body of the Church. The first General Assembly of the Church of Scotland took place in Magdalen Chapel in the Cowgate in 1560 and included the Protestant reformer John Knox (*c.*1513–72). In the 19th century, the Assembly moved to Victoria Hall, which became the Highland Tolbooth Kirk and recently the Edinburgh Festival Centre (the Hub). The Assembly Hall was subject to temporary alterations in 1999 to accommodate the debating chamber of the revived Scottish Parliament before it moved to its permanent home in 2004.

Assynt *Highland* A mountainous and rocky district of western Sutherland, Assynt includes numerous lochs, such as Loch Assynt, and prominent peaks such as Canisp, Suilven, Quinag, Conival and the massif of Ben More Assynt. The anglers' resort of Inchnadamph and the fishing port of Lochinver are the chief settlements, the remainder of the thinly scattered population occupying crofts in townships such as Nedd, Drumbeg, Culkein, Stoer and Clachtoll. In 1993 the crofters here were among the first in the Highlands to purchase the estate on which they lived.

Assynt, Loch *Highland* A loch in the Assynt district of western Sutherland, Loch Assynt extends 6 miles (10 km) northwest from Inchnadamph. The ruined Ardvreck Castle stands on a peninsula jutting into the loch.

Athelstaneford *East Lothian* Located 3 miles (5 km) northeast of Haddington, the East Lothian village of Athelstaneford takes its name from a perhaps mythical battle between the Saxon King Athelstane and the Pictish King Hungus, which is supposed to have taken place in the 9th century. The Scottish Flag Heritage Centre in the village commemorates the battle and the appearance of the Cross of St Andrew in the sky which inspired the Picts and became the flag of Scotland. Athelstaneford has changed little since it was constructed as a model village in the late 18th century by Sir David Kinloch of Gilmerton to improve the housing conditions of local farm-workers who were provided with well-proportioned housing and a sizeable garden for a nominal rent. A weaving industry was established in the village, which became noted for a striped cloth, although this has now disappeared. John Home (1722–1808), the playwright, was minister at Athelstaneford between 1847 and 1857, and the painter Archibald Skirving (1749–1819) was born here.

Atholl *Perth and Kinross* The district of Atholl lies at the heart of Scotland, occupying largely mountainous country in highland Perth and Kinross. It stretches from Rannoch Moor in the west to Glen Isla in the east and to the River Almond in the south. Among its high peaks are Schiehallion (1083 m/3547 ft) and Beinn a' Ghlo (1121 m/3671 ft), and chief among its rivers are the Tay, Tummel, Garry, Ardle and Braan. At its centre is Blair Atholl and Blair Castle, seat of the dukes of Atholl, a branch of the Murray family. The district is noted for a delicacy known as Atholl Brose which is made from whisky, honey and eggs.

Atholl, Forest of *Perth and Kinross* An area of deer forest in highland Perth and Kinross, the Forest of Atholl extends over 40,470 ha (100,000 acres) of rugged mountain landscape. Once more extensively wooded than it is today, the Forest of Atholl is first recorded in the 12th century as a baronial forest with special rights and privileges.

Attadale *Highland* A settlement in western Highland Council area, Attadale lies on the eastern side of Loch Carron, 2 miles (3 km) south of the head of the loch. The River Attadale flows down to join the loch here. The Attadale deer forest lies to the east, and to the north lie Attadale House and Attadale Station on the railway line from Inverness to Kyle of Lochalsh.

Attadale, River *Highland* The River Attadale rises on the slopes of Carn Geuradainn in Wester Ross and flows 4 miles (6.5 km) southwest to empty into Loch Carron at the settlement of Attadale.

Auchagallon *North Ayrshire* A locality on the west coast of Arran, Auchagallon is the site of a Bronze Age burial cairn and stone circle comprising 15 red sandstone blocks. The circle has a diameter of 14.3 m (47 ft).

Auchbreck *Moray* A small settlement in Glenlivet, Auchbreck lies to the east of the River Livet at the junction of the B9009 and B9008, 8 miles (13 km) north of Tomintoul.

Auchedly *Aberdeenshire* Situated immediately south of the River Ythan, 3 miles (5 km) northwest of Ellon in north-central Aberdeenshire, Auchedly is a scattered community comprising Auchedly, South Auchedly, Mains of Auchedly and Mill of Auchedly.

Auchenblae *Aberdeenshire* A village in southeast Aberdeenshire, Auchenblae lies in the Howe of the Mearns, 5 miles (8 km) north of Laurencekirk. It developed in the 18th and 19th centuries as a textile and market centre with cattle and horse fairs. The most noted of these fairs was the three-day Paddy Fair or Paldy Fair which takes its name from Palladius, an early saint whose bones were brought to Auchenblae by the Mearns missionary St Ternan. On a knoll at the south end of the village is St Palladius's Chapel, and in the present church can be found a Pictish stone that is one of the earliest cross-slabs in the area. There is a memorial here to the Protestant martyr George Wishart (1513–1546).

Auchenbowie *Stirling* A village in St Ninian's parish, southeast Stirling Council area, Auchenbowie lies on the Auchenbowie burn, 2 miles (3 km) southwest of Bannockburn. Auchenbowie House was once the home of a cadet branch of the Clan Munro.

Auchenbrack *Dumfries and Galloway* A locality in north-central Dumfries and Galloway, Auchenbrack lies near the head of the valley of the Shinnel Water to the north of Moniaive.

Auchenbreck *Argyll and Bute* A village on the Cowal peninsula, Auchenbreck lies 3 miles (5 km) southeast of Clachan of Glendaruel. The Auchenbreck Burn joins the River Ruel a half-mile (1 km) to the east of the village.

Auchencairn *Dumfries and Galloway* A hamlet in east-central Dumfries and Galloway, Auchencairn lies between the Forest of Ae and the River Nith, 6 miles (10 km) north of Dumfries.

Auchencairn *Dumfries and Galloway* A village in the Dumfries and Galloway parish of Rerrick, Auchencairn is situated close to Auchencairn Bay, an inlet of the Solway Firth, 10 miles (16 km) east of Kirkcudbright.

Auchencairn Bay *Dumfries and Galloway* A bay on the Solway Firth coast of southern Dumfries and Galloway, Auchencairn Bay is the westernmost of a series of river-mouth inlets that include the Rough Firth and Orchardton Bay. The Torr peninsula separates Auchencairn Bay from Orchardton Bay, and the village of Balcary overlooks the bay. Hestan Island lies at the mouth of the bay, whose sands at low tide are traversed by the channel of a stream known as the Auchencairn Lane.

Auchencastle *Dumfries and Galloway* A country-house hotel near Beattock in Dumfries and Galloway, Auchencastle was originally built as a private mansion in 1869.

Auchencrow *Scottish Borders* A village in the Berwickshire district of Scottish Borders, Auchencrow lies on the southeastern edge of the Lammermuir Hills, 7 miles (11 km) west of Eyemouth.

Auchendinny *Midlothian* A small village located on the steep slopes of the valley of River North Esk, 1.25 miles (2 km) northwest of Penicuik. Auchendinny has long been associated with paper production, and the Dalmore Mill, which began operation in 1837, remains. The Penicuik branch of the Peebles Railway once served the mill, and a tunnel is extant. The village had a station on the same line, which opened in 1872 but closed in 1951. The early 18th-century Auchendinny House is a fine Palladian villa by Sir William Bruce (1630–1710).

Auchengray *South Lanarkshire* The village of Auchengray is located near the northeastern border of South Lanarkshire Council area, 5 miles (8 km) north of Carnwath and 6 miles (10 km) southwest of West Calder. The village was a stop on the Caledonian Railway on its route from Carlisle to Edinburgh.

Auchenheath *South Lanarkshire* A settlement on the River Nethan, Auchenheath lies a mile (1.5 km) east of Blackwood and Kirkmuirhill and 4 miles (6.5 km) west of Lanark. Situated to the east of the M74, nearby places of interest include Black Hill Fort and Craignethan Castle.

Auchenhessnane *Dumfries and Galloway* A locality in Nithsdale, Auchenhessnane lies to the west of the Scaur Water, 4 miles (6.5 km) west of Thornhill.

Auchenlarrie *Dumfries and Galloway* A locality in southwest Dumfries and Galloway, Auchenlarrie lies at the northern end of Wigtown Bay, 5 miles (8 km) southwest of Gatehouse of Fleet.

Auchenlochan *Argyll and Bute* A hamlet of the Cowal peninsula, Auchenlochan lies on the Kyles of Bute a mile (1.5 km) south of Tighnabruaich opposite the island of Bute. Loch Riddon lies to the northeast.

Auchenmalg *Dumfries and Galloway* A locality in southwest Dumfries and Galloway, Auchenmalg lies close to Auchenmalg Bay, a small inlet of Luce Bay lying to the east of the Mull of Sinniness, 3 miles (5 km) southeast of Glenluce.

Auchenreoch Loch *Dumfries and Galloway* A small loch in central Dumfries and Galloway, Auchenreoch Loch lies just southwest of Crocketford and 6 miles (10 km) northeast of Castle Douglas. It is the source of the Spottes Burn which flows south to join the Urr Water at the Haugh of Urr.

Auchentiber *North Ayrshire* A hamlet located close to the eastern border of North Ayrshire, Auchentiber lies on the A736, 3 miles (5 km) west of Stewarton.

Auchentroig *Stirling* A locality in western Stirling Council area, Auchentroig and neighbouring Wester Auchentroig are situated a mile (1.5 km) to the west of Buchlyvie.

Auchenvey Burn *Dumfries and Galloway* A stream in central Dumfries and Galloway, the Auchenvey Burn rises on Larglear Hill to the south of Garcrogo Forest and 8 miles (13 km) north of Castle Douglas. It flows eastwards into Arvie and Corsock lochs.

Auchincruive *South Ayrshire* A settlement and country estate in South Ayrshire, Auchincruive lies to the southeast of St Quivox and about 3 miles (5 km) northeast of Ayr. It is now home to a campus of the Scottish Agricultural College and Research Institute, previously the West of Scotland Agricultural College, established in 1930 and amalgamated into the current institution in 1990. At the centre of the estate is Oswald Hall, which was designed by Robert Adam and was home to Richard Oswald, responsible for negotiating a preliminary treaty following the American War of Independence. Today it serves as a conference centre.

Auchindachy *Moray* A small settlement in Strath Isla, Auchindachy is situated 2 miles (3 km) southeast of Keith on the River Isla. Its existence is linked to a mill on the river and to the opening of a railway station here. To the north is the farm of Mains of Auchindachy.

Auchindoun Castle *Moray* The ruins of Auchindoun Castle stand on a hill overlooking the River Fiddich to the southeast of Dufftown in Moray. A former Gordon family stronghold dating from the 15th century, Auchindoun was destroyed in 1592 as a reprisal for the murder of the Bonnie Earl of Moray by the Marquess of Huntly.

Auchindrain *Argyll and Bute* A restored township to the west of Loch Fyne, Auchindrain lies 5 miles (8 km) southwest of Inveraray. The abandoned settlement was restored in 1975 as an open-air museum, demonstrating West Highland life in the 19th century.

Auchindrean *Highland* A settlement in Strath More, Wester Ross, Auchindrean lies to the west of the River Broom, 10 miles (16 km) southeast of Ullapool.

Auchingilloch *South Lanarkshire* A hill in South Lanarkshire, Auchingilloch rises to a height of 462 m (1515 ft), 6 miles (10 km) south of Strathaven. It is the source of the Glengavel Water.

Auchinleck *East Ayrshire* Situated on high ground north of the Lugar Water 5 miles (8 km) southeast of Mauchline in East Ayrshire, the village of Auchinleck (often pronounced Affleck) has been associated with the Boswell family since the early 16th century. Nearby stands Auchinleck House, commissioned in 1760. Dr Johnson visted James Boswell here in 1773 and engaged in heated debate with Boswell's father. The parish church displays portraits of the author James Boswell and William Murdoch (or Murdock), who developed gas lighting. Its Boswell Aisle (1754) is now the Boswell Museum.

Auchinloch *North Lanarkshire* A settlement of North Lanarkshire, Auchinloch lies immediately to the south of Lenzie and 2 miles (3 km) south of Kirkintilloch. The settlement comprises Wester Auchinloch, Auchinloch and Easter Auchinloch. A half-mile (1 km) to the northwest lies the small loch of Gadloch.

Auchinstarry *North Lanarkshire* Located a mile (1.5 km) northeast of the North Lanarkshire settlement of Twechar, Auchinstarry lies to the south of the Forth and Clyde Canal. To the north lie the upper reaches of the River Kelvin and the town of Kilsyth. Between Auchinstarry and Croy, which lies a half-mile (1 km) to the southeast, are the remains of a Roman fort and two beacon platforms associated with the Antonine Wall.

Auchintore *Highland* A locality in Lochaber, Highland Council area, Auchintore lies on the eastern shore of Loch Linnhe, a mile (1.5 km) southwest of Fort William.

Auchiries *Aberdeenshire* A locality in Cruden parish, eastern Aberdeenshire, Auchiries lies a mile (1.5 km) to the northeast of Cruden Bay.

Auchleeks House *Perth and Kinross* A locality in Glen Errochty, highland Perth and Kinross, Auchleeks House lies on the Errochty Water, 9 miles (14 km) west of Blair Atholl. It was built in a classical style for Robert Robertson in the early 19th century.

Auchleven *Aberdeenshire* A village in the parish of Premnay, central Aberdeenshire, Auchleven lies on the Gadie Burn 2 miles (3 km) south of Insch. Once a textile village with a carding and spinning mill, the village was given easier access to the south with the building of a bridge across the burn in 1836. To the southeast Hermit Seat rises to 477 m (1564 ft). On its northwest-facing slope above the village stand the ruins of Licklyhead Castle.

Auchlochan *South Lanarkshire* The settlement of Auchlochan is located within South Lanarkshire, 2 miles (3 km) south of Lesmahagow on the banks of the River Nethan. To the southwest of the village, the Logan Water joins the River Nethan.

Auchlyne *Stirling* A locality in northwest Stirling Council area, Auchlyne lies close to the northern bank of the River Dochart between the Auchlyne West and

Auchlyne East Burns that descend from the Breadalbane Hills. Four miles (6.5 km) northeast is the settlement of Killin. A mansion house with a walled garden dates from 1760, and nearby are the ruins of a chapel.

Auchmacoy *Aberdeenshire* A locality in Aberdeenshire, Auchmacoy lies 3 miles (5 km) east of Ellon close to where the Burn of Auchmacoy meets the River Ythan. It comprises an estate with a mill, landscaped policies, a dovecote and a mansion house built in the 1830s by the Buchans, a family associated with the area since the early 14th century.

Auchmithie *Angus* Perched on an exposed cliff 50 m (150 ft) above its tiny harbour, the small red sandstone fishing village of Auchmithie lies in St Vigeans parish on the North Sea coast of Angus. It originated the Arbroath Smokie, which was supplied by local fishermen to Arbroath 3 miles (5 km) to the south. Once popular with smugglers who made use of local caves in the red sandstone cliffs, Auchmithie was the Musselcrag that featured in Sir Walter Scott's novel *The Antiquary* (1816).

Auchmuirbridge *Fife/Perth and Kinross* Situated on the boundary between Fife and Perth and Kinross, the hamlet of Auchmuirbridge lies adjacent to a bridge that crosses the River Leven. The present bridge, which replaced an earlier bridge across the old course of the River Leven, was constructed in 1830 to traverse the new and straighter channel created as part of the ambitious Leven Improvement Scheme. This scheme involved the partial drainage of Loch Leven to the west and the creation of a 4-mile/6.5-km-long channel that came to be known as 'the Cut'. The water of the Arnot Burn, which flows down from the Lomond Hills to meet the River Leven at Auchmuirbridge, was used to power a corn mill.

Auchnacraig *Argyll and Bute* A settlement on the southeast coast of the island of Mull, Auchnacraig lies a half-mile (1 km) north of Port Donain and a mile (1.5 km) southwest of the headland at Grass Point.

Auchnafree *Perth and Kinross* A small settlement of central Perth and Kinross, Auchnafree is situated in an isolated location near the head of Glen Shervie in Glen Almond, 8 miles (13 km) northwest of Crieff.

Auchnagatt *Aberdeenshire* A hamlet on the Ebrie Burn in Old Deer parish, central Aberdeenshire, Auchnagatt lies on the A948 between Ellon and New Deer. It developed in the 19th century with the opening of a station on the former Aberdeen and Fraserburgh Railway, which now forms the route of the Fortmartine and Buchan Way.

Auchnangoul *Argyll and Bute* A settlement on the west side of Loch Fyne, Auchnangoul lies 3 miles (5 km) southwest of Inveraray. The Douglas Water flows through the village into Loch Fyne.

Auchter Bridgend An old name for part of Bonkle in North Lanarkshire.

Auchterarder *Perth and Kinross* A village and parish lying to the north of the Ochil Hills in southwest Perth and Kinross, Auchterarder stretches out along a mile (1.5 km)-long main street that is lined on both sides with shops selling a wide range of tourist goods. Formerly situated on the main road from Perth to Stirling but now bypassed, the village has a long history dating back to the 13th century, when it was founded by Gilbert, Earl of Strathearn. Its ruined castle is said to have been a royal hunting lodge established by Malcolm Canmore in the 11th century, and the village itself was for a time a burgh. Disaster struck in 1715 when the settlement was destroyed by Jacobite soldiers retreating from the Battle of Sheriffmuir, but emerging from the ashes the new Auchterarder became a thriving textile town. In 1834 the parish of Auchterarder was the scene of one of the first disputes that gave rise to the Disruption of 1843, when the church congregation refused to accept the minister nominated by the landowner. Today, the Auchterarder Heritage Museum in Glenruthven Mill not only explores the history of the village but also has on display Scotland's only working textile steam engine. Gleneagles railway station nearby serves both the Gleneagles Hotel and Auchterarder, which has its own 18-hole golf course. In addition to tourism, Auchterarder is now a centre for building, transport, agricultural engineering and personnel services.

Auchtercairn *Highland* A settlement in Wester Ross, Auchtercairn lies on the north shore of the Gair Loch, 4 miles (6.5 km) southwest of Poolewe.

Auchterderran *Fife* A village and parish in western Fife to the south of Kinglassie, Auchterderran is traversed by the River Ore. Its landscape was dramatically altered by over a century of coal mining that developed from the early 19th century and resulted in the former hamlets of Auchterderran, Cardenden, Bowhill and Dundonald all merging into one great mining township. No longer dependent on coal mining, Auchterderran now has a diverse range of industries that include mechanical engineering and the manufacture of electrical equipment, clothing, bagpipes and building materials. Well remembered local writers from the mining community include the poets Joe Corrie (1894–1968) and John Pindar (1837–1905), who has a memorial in the parish church. The ancient church of Auchterderran was given by Bishop Fothad to the Culdees of the old Celtic Church in the 11th century, but the present parish church, enlarged in 1890, dates from 1789.

Auchtergaven *Perth and Kinross* A parish to the south of Dunkeld in Perth and Kinross, Auchtergaven's chief settlement is the village of Bankfoot, which also used to be known as Auchtergaven. The poet Robert Nicoll (1814–37) was born at Little Tullybelton.

Auchterhead Muir *North Lanarkshire/South Lanarkshire* An afforested moorland tract on the border between North and South Lanarkshire, Auchterhead Muir lies 4 miles (6.5 km) east of Wishaw. The area is traversed from east to west by the Auchter Water, a tributary of the South Calder Water, and represents the highest point in the parish of Cambusnethan.

Auchterhouse *Angus* A hamlet in a parish of the same name in Angus, Auchterhouse sits on the south-facing slopes of the Sidlaw Hills, 5 miles (8 km) northwest of Dundee. The 17th-century tower house of Auchterhouse, which was a possession of the Ogilvies and then, in the late 20th century, the Mansion House Hotel, stands close to an earlier structure known as the Wallace Tower. Auchterhouse Country Sports, a centre for shooting, fishing and archery, lies a mile (1.5 km) to the northwest, and the Kirkton of Auchterhouse is located a similar distance to the east.

Auchtermuchty *Fife* A burgh town in northeast Fife at the junction of the A91 and A983, 7 miles (11 km) west of Cupar. The name is derived from the Gaelic *uachdarmuc*,

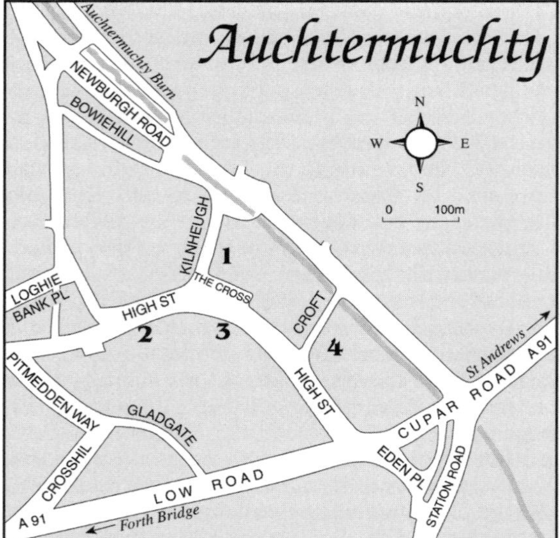

1 *Town House*
2 *Macduff House*
3 *Boar's Head (Forest Hills Hotel)*
4 *Parish Church*

meaning the 'high ground of the wild boar', its adjacent woods and swamps being the scene of royal boar hunts in ancient times. The town was granted a royal charter in 1517, and in the 18th and 19th centuries it was a flourishing centre of weaving, bleaching, distilling and sawmilling. Today its industries produce knitwear, furniture, postcards, structural steelwork, electrochemical sensors, electronic weighing equipment, crafts and food products. Amid a townscape of red pantiles, crow-stepped gables, and the occasional thatched roof (originally using the rushes of Lindores Loch), fine buildings include Macduff House (1597), the Town House (1728), the Parish Church (1779–81) and the Boar's Head (a 19th-century coaching inn, now called the Forest Hills Hotel). The old-world streets of Auchtermuchty featured in the recent TV series *Dr Finlay's Casebook*, and among the town's most famous sons are the accordionist and bandleader Jimmy Shand and the internationally popular singing duo The Proclaimers.

Auchterneed *Highland* A hamlet to the north of Strathpeffer in Easter Ross, Auchterneed was established by the Cromarty Estate in the mid-19th century to absorb people removed from the nearby glens. In legend it is associated with the annual ball of the Gaels which was held on the Raven's Rock, a place where they are said to have learned the secret art of mouth music played to them by the captured King of the Ravens.

Auchtertool *Fife* A village in a parish of the same name that lies between Kirkcaldy and Cowdenbeath in southwest Fife. Formerly on lands held by the Bishop of Dunkeld and now incorporating the small satellite settlement of Newbigging, the village once stood at the junction of roads linking Dunfermline to Kirkcaldy and the Kinghorn ferry to Perth. The solitary parish church to the west of the village was rebuilt in 1833, and to the north stand the ruins of Hallyards which was erected by Sir James Kirkcaldy of Grange, Lord High Treasurer to James V. Candleford House, a former manse, and Auchtertool House were both built in the early 19th century. A distillery was also established in the 19th century, but today Auchtertool is a centre of farming and engineering with a primary school and a nursing home.

Auchtertyre *Highland* A locality in Kintail, western Highland Council area, Auchtertyre lies between Dornie and Kyle of Lochalsh below Auchtertyre Hill.

Auchtoo *Stirling* Sometimes spelt Achtow or Auchtubh, this former crofting township lies at the head of Strathyre on the glen road leading to Loch Voil in the parish of Balquhidder.

Auckengill *Highland* Auckengill is a scattered farming community located 6 miles (10 km) south of John o' Groats on the east coast of Caithness. Places of interest include the John Nicolson Museum (now the Northlands Viking Centre), statues erected nearby by the 19th-century Caithness antiquarian John Nicolson, and a broch.

Auldearn *Highland* A small village in a parish of the same name in eastern Highland Council area, Auldearn lies to the east of the River Nairn, 2 miles (3 km) east of Nairn. It takes its name from the old castle of Eren (Old Eren), built here in the mid-12th century. This was William the Lion's (1143–1214) stronghold during his expeditions in the north and it was here that Robert the Bruce accepted the surrender of the rebellious men of Ross. Although Auldearn was an early Scottish burgh, it lost its status *c.*1190 with the founding of Nairn close by. Amid the earthworks of the old castle on a hill overlooking Auldearn stands the white-harled Boath Dovecote, which was built in the 17th century to serve Boath House. This private mansion to the northeast of the village was rebuilt in the 1820s for Sir James Dunbar to a Gothic-style design by the architect Archibald Simpson of Aberdeen. The dovecote and medieval motte were presented to the National Trust for Scotland in 1947 by Brigadier J. Muirhead of Boath. Auldearn is perhaps best remembered as the site of a battle fought in May 1645 on boggy ground to the southwest of the village. Here the Royalist forces of the Marquess of Montrose routed a Covenanting army led by Sir John Hurry. The battle is recalled in local place names such as Dead Wood and in memorial stones in the north porch of the parish church, which dates from 1757. This building replaced an earlier church dedicated to St Colm or Columba, who is said to have had a chapel here in the 6th century and whose name was also commemorated until the 1880s in the local St Colm's annual fair.

Auldgirth *Dumfries and Galloway* A village in Nithsdale, north-central Dumfries and Galloway, Auldgirth lies on the River Nith 8 miles (13 km) northwest of Dumfries.

Auldhouse *South Lanarkshire* Located 3 miles (5 km) south of East Kilbride in South Lanarkshire, the small farming settlement of Auldhouse sits at a crossroads and comprises cottages, a primary school and a public house.

Auliston Point *Highland* Auliston Point forms a headland at the entrance to Loch Sunart on the coast of the Morvern peninsula. Tobermory lies 3 miles (5 km) to the southwest on the opposite side of the Sound of Mull.

Ault a' chruinn *Highland* A settlement in Kintail, western Highland Council area, Ault a' chruinn lies at the head of Glen Shiel and at the southeastern end of Loch Duich.

Aultbea *Highland* A small crofting settlement in Wester Ross, Aultbea lies on the east shore of Loch Ewe, 8 miles (13 km) north of Poolewe, looking out towards the Isle of

Ewe. During the two World Wars Aultbea was used as a deep-water sheltered anchorage for ships of the Home Fleet; in World War II the Arctic convoys heading for Russia assembling here. In postwar years a naval refuelling base was maintained.

Aultdearg *Highland* A hunting lodge in Ross-shire, Highland Council area, Auldearg lies to the north of Strath Bran, 3 miles (5 km) northwest of Loch Luichart.

Aultgrishin *Highland* A locality on the coast of Wester Ross, Aultgrishan lies just south of Melvaig on a peninsula to the west of Loch Ewe.

Aultmore *Moray* A small settlement with a distillery, Aultmore lies on the B9016 2 miles (3 km) northwest of Keith. The Burn of Aultmore (or Altmore) flows southwards past the settlement to join the River Isla near Fife Keith.

Aultnagoire *Highland* A settlement in the Great Glen, Aultnagoire lies to the east of Loch Ness in Farigaig Forest and 3 miles (5 km) northeast of Foyers in Highland Council area.

Aultnamain Inn *Highland* A locality in Easter Ross, Aultnamain Inn lies on the Struie Road, 8 miles (13 km) southeast of Bonar Bridge

Auquharney House *Aberdeenshire* Situated by the Water of Cruden in eastern Aberdeenshire, Auquharney House lies due west of Hatton and 6 miles (10 km) northeast of Ellon.

Auskerry *Orkney* A small, flat, red sandstone islet of the Orkney Islands, Auskerry is situated in the North Sea 3 miles (5 km) south of Stronsay, from which it is separated by the Auskerry Sound. Auskerry has an area of 85 ha (210 acres). A standing stone and medieval chapel are signs of early settlement, but in the 1960s when the lighthouse was automated, the island was abandoned. An inlet known as Hunters' Geo was a favourite place for hunting seals in the past.

Auskerry Sound *Orkney* The Auskerry Sound is a stretch of sea in the Orkney Islands that separates the islet of Auskerry from the island of Stronsay to the north.

Avelshay, Point of *Orkney* The Point of Avelshay is located at the southern end of the island of Rousay in the Orkney Islands. It overlooks the island of Wyre to the south and Wyre Sound.

Aven, Water of *Aberdeenshire* A river of Royal Deeside in Aberdeenshire, the Water of Aven flows down from its source in a small lochan in the Grampians on the border with Angus. It follows a northeasterly course, eventually joining the Water of Feugh west of Strachan.

Avenuehead *Stirling* A locality in southern Stirling Council area, Avenuehead is situated 3 miles (5 km) south of Stirling opposite the entrance to the avenue leading to Auchenbowie House.

Averon River An alternative name for the Alness River in Highland.

Avich, Loch *Argyll and Bute* A small loch to the west of Loch Awe, Loch Avich lies 2 miles (3 km) northwest of Dalavich. The River Avich rises in Loch Avich and flows a mile (1.5 km) eastwards into Loch Awe.

Aviemore *Highland* A modern resort town in Strathspey, Aviemore lies to the west of the River Spey, 27 miles (43 km) southeast of Inverness. During the 19th century it developed from a scattered crofting township into a railway junction when the Highland Railway opened a direct line to Inverness in 1892. Prior to that, an inn or 'Kingshouse' on the 18th-century military road had existed here. During the 1960s Aviemore expanded dramatically in association with the development of skiing in the Cairngorm Mountains to the east, and attempts were made to make the town an all-year resort with the building of hotels and other facilities. The Aviemore Centre was developed from 1964, and in 1973 a railway preservation society reopened part of the old Highland line to Boat of Garten, providing journeys by steam train. The Rothiemurchus Estate and Glenmore Forest Park to the east offer a range of activities from watersports, walking and birdwatching to fishing, canoeing and mountain biking.

Avoch *Highland* A village in Easter Ross, Avoch (pronounced 'auch') lies on the inner Moray Firth at the mouth of the Killen Burn, 2 miles (3 km) west of Fortrose. Said to have originated following the wreck of a galleon from the Spanish Armada of 1588, Avoch developed as a fishing village that produced sailcloth and textiles in the 18th and 19th centuries. Its harbour was built in 1814 to a design by Thomas Telford and in 1894 the Fortrose branch of the former Highland Railway connected with the settlement. The station was closed to passenger traffic in 1951 and to goods services in 1960. Fishing thrived until the 1970s, but today the harbour of Avoch is mainly used by pleasure craft.

Avoch Bay *Highland* An inlet of the inner Moray Firth on the southeastern coast of the Black Isle, in Easter Ross, Avoch Bay lies to the east of the village of Avoch.

Avon, Loch *Moray* Situated at an altitude of 903 m (2377 ft) in the remoteness of the central Cairngorm Mountains, Loch Avon (Loch A'an) is the source of the River Avon that flows eastwards through Glen Avon. Cairn Gorm rises steeply to the north and Ben Macdui to the southwest.

Avon, River *North Lanarkshire, Falkirk and West Lothian* The River Avon issues from the Fannyside Lochs in the northeastern corner of North Lanarkshire, some 3 miles (5 km) east of Cumbernauld. It is 19 miles (31 km) in length and flows east into Falkirk Council area, passing to the north of Slamannan and then on through Avonbridge. The river then swings slowly northwards and proceeds along a shallow valley through the Muiravonside Country Park. It passes below the Union Canal, which is conveyed over the river by the Avon Aqueduct, the largest in Scotland, and then under the Edinburgh–Glasgow railway, which is carried by a substantial 23-arch viaduct, immediately to the west of Linlithgow. The Avon then turns northwest past the Birkhill Clay Mine before entering the Firth of Forth at the Grangemouth Oil Refinery between Grangemouth and Bo'ness. From approximately a half-mile (1 km) to the east of Avonbridge until a similar distance northwest of Linlithgow, the river forms the boundary between the Falkirk and West Lothian council areas. Its main tributaries are the Polness Burn, Barbauchlaw Burn and the Ballencrieff Water. The Avon crisscrosses the course of the Roman Antonine Wall.

Avon, River *Moray* A river of northeast Scotland, mostly in Moray, the Avon rises in the Cairngorm Mountains and flows 22 miles (35 km) east and north from Loch Avon to join the River Spey at Ballindalloch.

Avon Water *South Lanarkshire* The Avon Water, a tributary of the River Clyde mostly in South Lanarkshire, rises 6 miles (10 km) to the southeast of Galston on the Weddle Hill, East Ayrshire. It flows northeast, passing south of the settlement of Strathaven and through Larkhall. It continues past Cadzow Castle and Chatelherault Country Park until a mile (1.5 km) east of Hamilton, near Birkenshaw, it joins the River Clyde.

Avonbridge *Falkirk* A small village in Falkirk Council area, Avonbridge lies 5 miles (8 km) south of Falkirk and a similar distance east of Slamannan. The settlement takes its name from its position as a crossing point of the River Avon.

Awe, Loch *Argyll and Bute* A loch in Argyll and Bute to the southeast of Oban, Loch Awe extends 24 miles (39 km) from northeast to southwest and is the longest freshwater loch in Scotland. It receives the Orchy and Strae rivers in the northeast, as well as numerous short streams that flow in from all sides. The loch drains through the Pass of Brander via a northwestern arm and the River Awe into Loch Etive, and its waters serve the hydro-electric power station at Cruachan to the north. In addition to numerous ancient crannogs, there are the remains of Inishail Chapel and the two former Campbell strongholds of Kilchurn and Finharn. Close to the shores of Loch Awe are a number of small settlements, including Lochawe, Port Sonachan, Ford, Dalavich, Inverinan and Taychreggan.

Awe, Loch *Highland* A small loch in western Sutherland, Loch Awe is located 4 miles (6.5 km) south of Loch Assynt and the settlement of Inchnadamph and a mile (1.5 km) north of Ledmore.

Awe, River *Argyll and Bute* A river of Argyll and Bute, the Awe flows from the northwest arm of Loch Awe into Loch Etive at the settlement of Bonawe. Flowing through the Pass of Brander, it has a length of 3 miles (5 km).

Awhirk *Dumfries and Galloway* A small settlement in the Rhinns of Galloway, Awhirk lies at a road junction 3 miles (5 km) southeast of Portpatrick.

Ayr *South Ayrshire* Situated at the mouth of the River Ayr as it flows into Ayr Bay on the Firth of Clyde, the town of Ayr is 42 miles (67 km) southwest of Glasgow. A popular resort town today, Ayr is the administrative centre of South Ayrshire and the heart of the 'Burns Country' which is associated with the poet Robert Burns (1759–96). He is commemorated in the town with a monument in Burns Statue Square as well as in a local museum and at the Auld Brig (c.1491). Formerly known as Inverayr, Ayr was developed around a castle built in 1197 by William the Lion for the purpose of subduing the revolts of the men of Galloway. In 1230, Alexander II founded a Dominican friary, the first of its kind in Scotland. In 1297 William Wallace burned the Barbs of Ayr, a military barracks of Edward I of England, and in 1298 Robert the Bruce destroyed the castle. The town received its royal charter in 1205, and in 1315 the Scottish Parliament met to decide the succession to the throne in the Church of St John, a building later sacked by Cromwell. In medieval times Ayr developed as a shipbuilding centre and major port, trading in, among other things, fish, wine, textiles, leather and metal goods. The tobacco trade was important in the 18th century, and with the building of a wet dock in 1883 Ayr benefited from an extensive trade in coal in addition to its emerging role as a steamer port linked to the railway system. Modern industries include quarrying for construction and the manufacture of furnishing fabrics, electronics and computers. A racecourse was established in 1770 and today Ayr hosts National Hunt and flat racing. Buildings of interest include Loudon Hall (1534), the Wallace Tower (1832), the Court House and Regional Buildings (c.1820) and the New Church of St John (1654–56), where Burns was baptised in 1759.

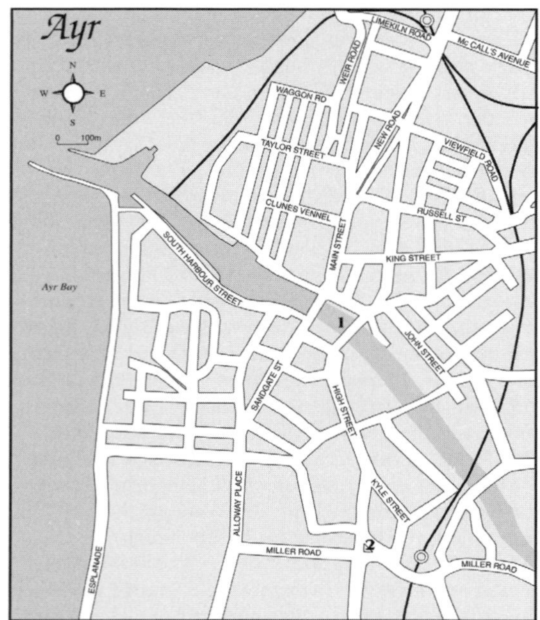

1 *Auld Brig* 2 *Burns Statue Square*

Ayr, Heads of *South Ayrshire* A headland on the South Ayrshire coast, the Heads of Ayr extends into the sea 4 miles (6.5 km) south of Ayr. It is regarded as being at the southern extremity of the Firth of Clyde. A Butlin's holiday camp was opened here in the 1930s.

Ayr, River *South Ayrshire and East Ayrshire* A river of South and East Ayrshire, the River Ayr rises in headstreams that include the Ponesk Burn and a stream rising from the Glenbuck Water, near the border with South Lanarkshire. Flowing west, it passes through the settlements of Sorn and Catrine before entering South Ayrshire. Here it meanders through lowlands south of Annbank and Auchincruive before emptying into Ayr Bay at Ayr.

Ayr Bay *South Ayrshire* Stretching from Troon in the north to the Heads of Ayr in the south, Ayr Bay is a wide, west-facing bay on the South Ayrshire coastline. At the centre of the bay is the town of Ayr.

Ayre, Point of *Orkney* A headland on the eastern coast of Mainland Orkney, the Point of Ayre extends into the sea opposite the island of Copinsay 4 miles (6.5 km) south of Mull Head.

Ayre Point *Orkney* A headland lying on the southeastern coastline of the island of Fara, in the Orkney Islands. Ayre Point extends into Weddell Sound to the north of the island of Flotta.

Ayre of Cara *Orkney* A beach lying at the northern end of South Ronaldsay in the Orkney Islands, the Ayre of Cara lies to the southeast of the causeway linking South Ronaldsay with Burray to the north.

Ayrshire A former county of southwest Scotland situated on the Firth of Clyde, Ayrshire comprised the ancient divisions of Cunninghame in the north, Kyle in the centre and Carrick in the south, these three areas being separated by the Irvine and Doon rivers. The chief settlements were the county town of Ayr, Irvine, Kilmarnock and Prestwick. In 1974 the county was incorporated into Strathclyde Region and in the local government reorganisation of 1996 it emerged as North, East and South Ayrshire Council Areas.

Ayton *Scottish Borders* A village in eastern Scottish Borders, Ayton lies 6 miles (10 km) northwest of Berwick-upon-Tweed near the Eye Water. It developed in association with a medieval castle founded nearby in the 12th century and destroyed in the 1490s. In the 18th century local industries such as sawmilling, papermaking and bleaching contributed to the growth of Ayton. Between 1846 and 1963 a railway station to the east served the village, and in 1981 Ayton was bypassed by the A1.

Ayton Castle *Scottish Borders* Located to the northwest of Ayton in eastern Scottish Borders, Ayton Castle lies 3 miles (5 km) southwest of Eyemouth and 7 miles (11 km) north of Berwick-upon-Tweed. Built by James Gillespie Graham in 1841 and extended in 1860 by David Bryce, it replaced a castle that was often held by the English in their raids into Scotland. A stronghold of the Aytoun, Home and Fordyce families, it was burned to the ground in 1834.

Aywick *Shetland* A locality on the east coast of the island of Yell, Aywick comprises the settlements of North Aywick and South Aywick, around the bay of Ay Wick, with the Loch of North Aywick to the north.

Ba, Loch *Highland* A loch on Rannoch Moor to the southeast of Glen Coe in Highland Council area, the irregularly shaped Loch Ba lies on the River Ba 6 miles (10 km) north of Bridge of Orchy.

Ba, River *Highland* A river in the Lochaber district of southern Highland Council area, the Ba rises south of Clach Leathad to the south of Glen Etive and flows eastwards onto Rannoch Moor, passing through Loch Buidhe, Lochan na Stainge and Loch Ba before emptying into Loch Laidon, which straddles the border between Highland Council area and Perth and Kinross.

Bac Beag *Argyll and Bute* One of the Treshnish Isles off the northwest coast of Mull in the Inner Hebrides, the basalt island of Bac Beag lies to the south of Lunga and Bac Mòr (Dutchman's Cap).

Bac Mòr *Argyll and Bute* An island in the Inner Hebrides, Bac Mòr lies at the southwest end of the Treshnish Isles between the islands of Lunga and Bac Beag. Also known as Dutchman's Cap, its distinctive outline comprises a volcanic cone surrounded by grass-covered lava.

Baca Ruadh *Highland* A mountain on the island of Skye in the Inner Hebrides, Baca Ruadh rises to 637 m (2089 ft) on the Trotternish peninsula 3 miles (5 km) northwest of the Storr and 9 miles (14 km) north of Portree.

Bachelors' Club, The *South Ayrshire* A 17th-century thatched house in Tarbolton, 5 miles (8 km) east of Prestwick, The Bachelors' Club was the house where the poet Robert Burns (1759–96) met with his friends in 1780 to form a debating society. The Bachelors' Club was also the place where Burns joined the Freemasons and attended dancing classes. The house is furnished with period items.

Bachnagairn Falls *Angus* Located near the head of the River South Esk on the northern border of Angus, the picturesque Bachnagairn Falls drop 18 m (60 ft) through precipitous rocks above Glen Clova on the steep slopes of Broad Cairn.

Back *Western Isles* A crofting township on the east coast of Lewis, Back lies 6 miles (10 km) northeast of Stornoway in the Outer Hebrides. To the south is the village of Coll and to the north is Gress.

Back Burn *South Lanarkshire* Rising in the foothills of Dunside Rig, the Back Burn flows north and east to empty into the southern end of the Kype Reservoir in South Lanarkshire.

Backies *Highland* A settlement in eastern Sutherland, Backies lies a mile (1.5 km) north of Golspie. There are the remains of an ancient tower nearby that is thought to be Norse in origin.

Backlass *Highland* A settlement in northeast Caithness, Backlass lies 2 miles (3 km) west of Watten, between Loch Watten and the Loch of Toftingall. The Backlass Stone Circle is closeby.

Backmuir of New Gilston *Fife* A hamlet on the northern border of Largo parish in the East Neuk of Fife, Backmuir of New Gilston lies 5 miles (8 km) north of Upper Largo.

Back of Keppoch *Highland* A locality in Arisaig, southwest Highland Council area, Back of Keppoch lies a mile (1.5 km) northwest of the settlement of Arisaig.

Badachro *Highland* A settlement in Wester Ross, Badachro lies on the River Badachro 5 miles (8 km) southwest of Gairloch on the southern edge of the Gair Loch in the Ross and Cromarty district of Highland Council area.

Badbea *Highland* A deserted settlement on the east coast of Caithness, Badbea lies 4 miles (6.5 km) northeast of Helmsdale. It was built in the early 19th century to accommodate families evicted from Largwell, who then subsequently emigrated to New Zealand. A memorial to the former residents was erected in 1912.

Badcall *Highland* A village on the west coast of Sutherland, Badcall lies on the north side of Loch Inchard, a mile (1.5 km) east of Kinlochbervie.

Badcall Bay *Highland* An inlet of the larger Eddrachillis Bay on the west coast of Sutherland, Badcall Bay lies to the south of Scourie. The townships of Upper and Lower Badcall lie to the west and east of the bay.

Badcaul *Highland* A village in Wester Ross, Badcaul lies 5 miles (8 km) northwest of Dundonnell on the southwest shore of Little Loch Broom.

Baddidarroch *Highland* A crofting township in the Assynt district of western Sutherland, Baddidarroch (Baddidarach) lies on the north shore of Loch Inver, a half-mile (1 km) northwest of the village of Lochinver.

Baddinsgill Burn *Scottish Borders* Rising in the Pentland Hills to the northwest of West Linton in Scottish Borders, the Baddinsgill Burn flows down from the eastern slopes of Colzium Hill to join the Lyne Water just south of Baddinsgill Reservoir. Baddinsgill House and Farm lie by an old drovers' road over the hills.

Baddoch Burn *Aberdeenshire* A tributary of the Clunie Water in southern Aberdeenshire, the Baddoch Burn rises near the border between Angus and Aberdeenshire to the west of Glen Clunie. It flows northeast to join the Clunie 4 miles (6.5 km) north of The Cairnwell.

Badenloch, Loch *Highland* A loch in northern Sutherland, Loch Badenloch, along with Loch nan Clàr and Loch Rimsdale, forms a body of water near the head of Strathnaver. Badenloch Lodge and Forest lie to the east.

Back of Keppoch *Highland* A locality in Arisaig, southwest Highland Council area, Back of Keppoch lies a mile (1.5 km) northwest of the settlement of Arisaig.

Badachro *Highland* A settlement in Wester Ross, Badachro lies on the River Badachro 5 miles (8 km) southwest of Gairloch on the southern edge of the Gair Loch in the Ross and Cromarty district of Highland Council area.

Badbea *Highland* A deserted settlement on the east coast of Caithness, Badbea lies 4 miles (6.5 km) northeast of Helmsdale. It was built in the early 19th century to accommodate families evicted from Largwell, who then subsequently emigrated to New Zealand. A memorial to the former residents was erected in 1912.

Badcall *Highland* A village on the west coast of Sutherland, Badcall lies on the north side of Loch Inchard, a mile (1.5 km) east of Kinlochbervie.

Badcall Bay *Highland* An inlet of the larger Eddrachillis Bay on the west coast of Sutherland, Badcall Bay lies to the south of Scourie. The townships of Upper and Lower Badcall lie to the west and east of the bay.

Badcaul *Highland* A village in Wester Ross, Badcaul lies 5 miles (8 km) northwest of Dundonnell on the southwest shore of Little Loch Broom.

Baddidarroch *Highland* A crofting township in the Assynt district of western Sutherland, Baddidarroch (Baddidarach) lies on the north shore of Loch Inver, a half-mile (1 km) northwest of the village of Lochinver.

Baddinsgill Burn *Scottish Borders* Rising in the Pentland Hills to the northwest of West Linton in Scottish Borders, the Baddinsgill Burn flows down from the eastern slopes of Colzium Hill to join the Lyne Water just south of Baddinsgill Reservoir. Baddinsgill House and Farm lie by an old drovers' road over the hills.

Baddoch Burn *Aberdeenshire* A tributary of the Clunie Water in southern Aberdeenshire, the Baddoch Burn rises near the border between Angus and Aberdeenshire to the west of Glen Clunie. It flows northeast to join the Clunie 4 miles (6.5 km) north of The Cairnwell.

Badenloch, Loch *Highland* A loch in northern Sutherland, Loch Badenloch, along with Loch nan Clàr and Loch Rimsdale, forms a body of water near the head of Strathnaver. Badenloch Lodge and Forest lie to the east.

Badenoch *Highland* An ancient district to the south of Strathspey in the heart of the Highlands, Badenoch extends over the upper reaches of the River Spey between the Monadhliath Mountains to the west and the Cairngorm Mountains to the east. That part of the Spey valley formerly controlled by the Clan Chattan, the area was also a centre of power for the Comyns and then the Stewarts, of whom the most famous was Alexander Stewart (1343–1405), known as the 'Wolf of Badenoch'. Other families of the district include the Grants, Gordons, Macintoshes and Macphersons. The chief town is Kingussie, which lies 3 miles (5 km) northeast of Newtonmore. The name retained a formal usage in the Badenoch and Strathspey District Council until local government reorganisation in 1996.

Badenoch and Strathspey *Highland* A former local government area in the central Highlands, Badenoch and Strathspey was a district of Highland Regional Council between 1974 and 1996. Its administrative centre was Kingussie.

Badentarbat Bay *Highland* A bay on the coast of the Coigach district in Wester Ross, Badentarbat Bay forms a sheltered inlet between the mainland at Achiltibuie and the Summer Isles, 12 miles (19 km) northwest of Ullapool. There are the remains of a former salmon-fishing station.

Badenyon *Aberdeenshire* A settlement in southwest Aberdeenshire, Badenyon lies at the head of Glenbuchat, to the north of Ladylea Hill, 4 miles (6.5 km) north of Strathdon. Badenyon is celebrated in the song *John o' Badenyon* written by the ecclesiastical historian the Revd John Skinner (1721–1807).

Badicaul *Highland* The settlement of Badicaul is located a mile (1.5 km) north of Kyle of Lochalsh on the road to Plockton and commands views over the Inner Sound towards the islands of Pabay, Scalpay and Skye in the Inner Hebrides.

Badlipster *Highland* A settlement in northeast Caithness, Badlipster lies to the south of the Strath Burn, 3 miles (5 km) south of Watten.

Badnaban *Highland* A small settlement on the west coast of Assynt in western Sutherland, Badnaban lies on the south shore of Loch Inver, 2 miles (3 km) southwest of Lochinver.

Badninish *Highland* A locality in eastern Sutherland, Badninish lies 4 miles (6.5 km) northwest of Dornoch.

Badrallach *Highland* A township in Wester Ross, Badrallach lies on the north side of Little Loch Broom, 4 miles (6.5 km) northwest of Dundonnell.

Bagh a' Chaisteil The Gaelic name for Castlebay in the Western Isles.

Bagh a Tuath The Gaelic name for North Bay on Barra in the Western Isles.

Bagh Bhatasaigh The Gaelic name for Vatersay Bay in the Western Isles.

Bagh Shiarabhagh The Gaelic name for Northbay in the Western Isles.

Baghasdail, Loch The Gaelic name for Loch Boisdale in the Western Isles.

Baghasdal The Gaelic name for North Boisdale in the Western Isles.

Bail Ur na Fleisirin The Gaelic name for Fleisirin in the Western Isles.

Baile an Truiseil The Gaelic name for Ballantrushal in the Western Isles.

Baile Mhartainn The Gaelic name for Balmartin in the Western Isles.

Baile Mòr *Argyll and Bute* A village on the east coast of the island of Iona, in the Inner Hebrides, Baile Mòr looks southeast over the Sound of Iona to Fionnphort on the Ross of Mull. The village was the site of a 6th-century monastery, and nearby there are 13th-century remains and a 15th-century Celtic cross (MacLean's Cross). The cathedral of Iona is located to the north of the village.

Baile Mhanaich An alternative name for Balivanich in the Western Isles.

Baile nan Cailleach The Gaelic name for Nunton in the Western Isles.

Bailebhainich An alternative Gaelic name for Balivanich in the Western Isles.

Baillie McMorran's House *City of Edinburgh* Lying at the back of Riddle's Court off the Lawnmarket in Edinburgh are the remains of the 16th-century house of Baillie John McMorran, one of Edinburgh's wealthiest citizens of the time. McMorran built two L-shaped blocks in 1590, his own home being on the south and west sides. The house passed to McMorran's brother and hosted a fine banquet in 1598 given by the town council to honour King James VI and his queen. The houses, which were extended and refitted in the 17th century, were converted as a university residence in 1889 by Patrick Geddes who carved his motto *Vivendo Discimus* ('By living we learn') in the court. The buildings were adapted as an adult education centre by Lothian Regional Council in the late 20th century.

Baillieston *Glasgow City* A residential eastern suburb of the city of Glasgow, Baillieston lies to the north of the River Clyde, 7 miles (11 km) east of the city centre. Formerly a mining village, Baillieston was annexed to the city of Glasgow in 1975. With the building of motorways in the 1960s the Baillieston interchange was constructed. Nearby is Baillieston House.

Baintown *Fife* Less than a mile (1.5 km) north of Kennoway in central Fife is the settlement of Baintown, which lies immediately west of Bonnybank and the A916 from Kennoway to Cupar.

Baird Institute Museum *East Ayrshire* Located within the town of Cumnock in East Ayrshire, the Baird Institute Museum has an eclectic collection of exhibits, ranging from displays of Mauchline box ware and Cumnock pottery to exhibits on the social and industrial history of the area. A room within the building is dedicated to James Keir Hardie (1856–1915), the founder of the Labour Party.

Balado *Perth and Kinross* A small modern settlement in Perth and Kinross, Balado is situated a mile (1.5 km) to the west of Kinross on the A977 from Kinross to Kincardine. Prior to the building of the village in the 1980s, the name Balado was associated with Balado House and the farms of Balado Farm West, Middle Balado and Easter Balado. An 18th-century high-arched bridge crosses the South Queich here, and to the north of the village is the Balado Bridge NATO Communications Facility, known locally as the 'Golf Ball'. Gravel-extraction and later chicken-farming industries have developed nearby, and in recent years the popular T in the Park music festival has been located on a site used as an airfield during World War II.

Balagich Hill An alternative name for Ballageich Hill in East Renfrewshire.

Balavil *Highland* A locality in Badenoch, Balavil lies close to the River Spey, 2 miles (3 km) northeast of Kingussie. Balavil House was the home of James Macpherson (1736–96), author of the *Ossian* poems.

Balbeg *Highland* A locality in the Great Glen, Highland Council area, Balbeg lies to the west of Loch Ness, 4 miles (6.5 km) south of Drumnadrochit.

Balbeggie *Perth and Kinross* A village of east-central Perth and Kinross, Balbeggie lies astride the A94 from Perth to Coupar Angus, 2 miles (3 km) northeast of Scone. Perth Airport lies a mile (1.5 km) to the southwest.

Balbirnie Park *Fife* A 168-ha (415-acre) country park to the northwest of Markinch in central Fife, Balbirnie Park has within its bounds an outstanding collection of rhododendrons, an 18-hole golf course, a caravan park and the Balbirnie Craft Centre where clothing, furniture and other craft articles are made by hand. It was once part of a large estate dating from the 14th century, and its focal point is the impressive Balbirnie House, which was converted into a deluxe hotel in 1989. Built by the Balfour family in the 17th century, the house was given a Greek neoclassical frontage in the period 1777–82 and substantially enlarged between 1815 and 1819. At the north end of the park lies the 3000-year-old Balbirnie Stone Circle, excavated in 1970-1 and relocated some 125 m (410 ft) from its original position in order to make way for road widening.

Balblair *Highland* A locality on the Black Isle, Easter Ross, Balblair lies on the coast of the Cromarty Firth opposite Invergordon. Chartered as a burgh of barony in 1677, Balblair developed at a ferry crossing close to an early chapel.

Balcary *Dumfries and Galloway* A locality in southern Dumfries and Galloway, 9 miles (14 km) southeast of Castle Douglas, Balcary comprises a fishing settlement with a small harbour adjacent to Balcary Bay, Balcary Point and Balcary Hill.

Balcary Point *Dumfries and Galloway* A headland on the Solway Firth coast, Balcary Point lies at the mouth of Auchencairn Bay, 10 miles (16 km) south of Castle Douglas.

Balcaskie House *Fife* A mansion house with a garden and fine views looking out over the Firth of Forth, Balcaskie House is situated in the East Neuk of Fife a mile (1.5 km) north of St Monans. Originally the site of a tower house, Balcaskie was remodelled by Sir William Bruce, Surveyor-General of the Royal Works in Scotland, who owned the property from 1665 to 1684. In 1698 Balcaskie came into the hands of the Anstruthers, who still live in the house. Bruce's garden was the first formally designed private garden to be created in Scotland. The driveway from the west was designed by W.S. Gilpin in 1826–7. There is a stunning sightline from the garden to the windmill at St Monans, with Bass Rock beyond.

Balchladich *Highland* A township in the Assynt district of western Sutherland, Balchladich lies 2 miles (3 km) north of Clachtoll near Clashnessie.

Balchraggan *Highland* A settlement in the Aird, Easter Ross, Balchraggan lies 2 miles (3 km) southeast of Beauly.

Balchraggan *Highland* A locality on the west side of Loch Ness, Balchraggan lies 7 miles (11 km) northeast of Drumnadrochit.

Balchrick *Highland* A small township in northwest Sutherland, Balchrick lies near the coast, 3 miles (5 km) northwest of Kinlochbervie.

Balcomie Links *Fife* Blasted by winds blowing off the North Sea, Balcomie Links lies immediately west of Fife Ness at the eastern extremity of Fife. To the southwest is Crail and 7 miles (11 km) northwest is St Andrews, the home of golf. The Balcomie Golf Course, first used by the Crail Golfing Society in 1895, is a classic example of a coastal links set within landscaped parkland. The Crail Golfing Society, founded in 1786, is the seventh-oldest golf club in the world. Close by, the late 16th-century Balcomie Castle, with its five-storey tower, ranges and walled garden, stands within a complex that includes a 19th-century mansion and modern farmstead. The gatehouse at Balcomie still bears the arms of the Learmounth and Myretoun familes who once lived here. It was at Balcomie that Mary of Guise was welcomed in June 1538 when she landed in Scotland on her way to marry James V at St Andrews.

Balconie Point *Highland* A small headland on the Cromarty Firth in Easter Ross, Balconie Point lies near the mouth of the Allt Grand to the south of Alness Bay.

Balcurvie *Fife* An old settlement of Markinch parish in south-central Fife, Balcurvie lies immediately north of the village of Windygates, of which it is now a part.

Baldinnie *Fife* The old fermetoun hamlet of Baldinnie in the parish of Ceres, eastern Fife, lies to the east of the village of Ceres at a road junction on the B940 linking Largoward with Cupar, which is 4 miles (6.5 km) to the northwest. The farms of Lower Baldinnie, Over Baldinnie and Percy Baldinnie occupy land to the north and east.

Baldinnies *Perth and Kinross* A locality in Strath Earn, central Perth and Kinross, Baldinnies lies a mile (1.5 km) to the northeast of Dunning, just south of the River Earn.

Baldoon Castle *Dumfries and Galloway* Baldoon Castle is located near Wigtown, in southern Dumfries and Galloway. The ruined, ivy-covered remains of the castle are said to be haunted by the ghost of Janet Dalrymple, the daughter of Sir James Dalrymple, who walks the ruins on the anniversary of her untimely death. This story inspired Sir Walter Scott's *Bride of Lammermoor* (1819).

Baldovie *Dundee City* A village on the northeast edge of Dundee, Baldovie lies on the Fithie Burn north of Broughty Ferry. It has an industrial estate with offshore oil-related industries, and a major waste-to-energy facility that opened in 1999 to replace an incinerator that closed in 1996.

Baledgarno *Perth and Kinross* A neat 18th-century planned village in the Braes of the Carse, eastern Perth and Kinross, Baledgarno lies unsignposted on the Rossie Priory Estate, a mile (1.5 km) north of Inchture and 8 miles (13 km) west-southwest of Dundee. It comprises a row of single-storey estate workers' cottages, a 19th-century school, a factor's house and a steading.

Baledmund *Perth and Kinross* A locality in highland Perth and Kinross, Baledmund House lies to the north of the village of Moulin near Pitlochry.

Balemartine *Argyll and Bute* A settlement on the south coast of the island of Tiree in the Inner Hebrides, Balemartine lies at the southern end of Hynish Bay. Scarinish lies 4 miles (6.5 km) to the northeast, and 2 miles (3 km) south are the Skerryvore Museum and the Skerryvore Lighthouse.

Balephuil *Argyll and Bute* A settlement on the island of Tiree in the Inner Hebrides, Balephuil lies on the east side of Balephuil Bay, 2 miles (3 km) west of the settlement of Balemartine.

Balerno *City of Edinburgh* A former mill village to the west of Edinburgh, Balerno lies on the left bank of the Water of Leith. Incorporated into the city in 1975, it is now a largely residential commuter suburb of the city. Notable buildings include Cockburn House (1672) and the early 17th-century Malleny House, administered by the National Trust for Scotland. A rail link from Edinburgh was created in 1874, but passenger trains stopped in 1943 and the line finally closed in the 1960s.

Balerominmore *Argyll and Bute* A settlement on the southeast coast of the island of Colonsay in the Inner Hebrides, Balerominmore lies 2 miles (3 km) south of Scalasaig.

Baleshare *Western Isles* A low-lying island in the Outer Hebrides, Baleshare lies to the west of North Uist, to which it is connected at low tide. A 350-m (383-yd) causeway was built in 1962 to provide a permanent connection. There are two settlements on the island, Samala on the east and Teananachar to the west. To the north is Kirkibost Island.

Balfarg *Fife* A residential area on the north side of Glenrothes in central Fife, Balfarg lies to the north of Cadham and west of Balbirnie Park. Prior to the building of modern houses, a prehistoric henge monument was excavated to reveal grave pits and artefacts. Originally comprising rings of massive upright timbers and stone, the 60-m/65-yd-wide earthwork still remains. This prehistoric site is linked to the nearby Balbirnie Stone Circle and dates from the 3rd and 2nd millennia BC.

Balfour *Orkney* A small village on the Orkney island of Shapinsay, Balfour was built in the mid-19th century by the son of John Balfour of Trenabie on Westray, the MP for Orkney and Shetland who had made a fortune in India. He imported craftsmen and weavers to the village and in the 1880s dammed the nearby marshland to provide water for a mill. To the south is Balfour Castle, built by John Balfour in 1848.

Balfour Monument *East Lothian* Located by the roadside, high on an escarpment overlooking Traprain Law, 2.5 miles (4 km) southwest of East Linton, the Balfour Monument takes the form of a sizeable obelisk built of red sandstone and dedicated to James Balfour (1820–56), the father of both the British prime minister Arthur Balfour (1848–1930) and the embryologist Francis Balfour (1851–82).

Balfron *Stirling* A dormitory village in southwest Stirling Council area, Balfron is situated on the A875, 18 miles (29 km) west of Stirling and 16 miles (26 km) north of Glasgow. A key rural settlement, it has shops, a health centre and a secondary school. The old clachan of Balfron developed into a textile-weaving village in the late 18th century. Buildings of note include the Old Manse (1789), the Parish Church (1832), Clachan House (1766) and Ballindalloch House. The architect Alexander (Greek) Thomson (1817–75) was a native of Balfron.

Balfluig Castle *Aberdeenshire* Balfluig, an L-shaped castle near Alford in central Aberdeenshire, was built by the Forbes family in the 1550s. Sold to the Farquharsons in 1753, it was used as a farmhouse before being abandoned. Restoration work began in 1966.

Balgavies Loch *Angus* A wetland area in central Angus, situated on the Lunan Water between Forfar and Friockheim, Balgavies Loch is home to a wide variety of resident and migrant birds.

Balgay Park *Dundee City* A public park in west-central Dundee, Balgay Park comprises a hill on top of which stand a cemetery and the only public observatory in Britain. Opened in 1935, the observatory was endowed with money bequeathed by John Mills, a local manufacturer. Balgay Park, along with the adjacent Lochee Park, was opened in 1871 by the Earl of Dalhousie and was intended to improve the health of mill workers who lived and worked in poor conditions.

Balgonar *Fife* A hamlet and estate in western Fife, Balgonar lies less than a mile (1.5 km) north of Saline on a minor road that leads to Hill End at the eastern end of the Cleish Hills. Saline Hill rises to the east and to the southwest is the farm of West Balgonar.

Balgonie Castle *Fife* A 15th-century tower house on the south bank of the River Leven, Balgonie Castle is situated a mile (1.5 km) to the southeast of Markinch in central Fife. Associated with the Sibbald and Lundy families and once occupied by Rob Roy Macgregor (1671–1734), its most famous owner was the Covenanting General Sir Alexander Leslie, who fought with Gustavus Adolphus in the Thirty Years' War. He bought the estate in 1635, six years before being created 1st Earl of Leven and Lord Balgonie. Restoration of the tower began in the late 1970s. A turbine house using water from the River Leven was built nearby in 1922 by the Balgonie Colliery Company. The turbine was used as a source of power by a local paper mill in the 1980s and was brought back into action in the 1990s by a private power-generating company.

Balgowan *Highland* A locality in Badenoch, Balgowan lies in the upper valley of the River Spey, 7 miles (11 km) southwest of Newtonmore.

Balgown *Highland* A locality on the Trotternish peninsula at the north end of the island of Skye, Balgown lies 4 miles (6.5 km) north of Uig.

Balgray *Angus* A hamlet in southern Angus, Balgray lies 5 miles (8 km) north of Dundee on the southern edge of the Sidlaw Hills.

Balgrochan *East Dunbartonshire* Once a separate village, Balgrochan now forms a northern part of the settlement of Torrance in East Dunbartonshire. It lies 3 miles (5 km) north of Bishopbriggs.

Balhall *Angus* A locality in Strathmore to the west of Kirkton of Menmuir and 6 miles (10 km) northwest of Brechin in Angus, Balhall comprises Balhall Lodge, once the home of Viscount Arbuthnott, and three farms: Mains of Balhall, Milton of Balhall and Bogton of Balhall. Here Sir John Lyon of Glamis (*c.*1340–82) was killed in a duel with Sir James Lindsay of Crawford.

Balhary *Perth and Kinross* A small settlement of eastern Perth and Kinross, Balhary lies 2 miles (3 km) southeast of Alyth in Strathmore.

Balholmie *Perth and Kinross* A house in eastern Perth and Kinross, Balholmie overlooks the River Tay just south of Cargill, 5 miles (8 km) southwest of Coupar Angus.

Baligill Head *Highland* A headland on the north coast of Sutherland, Baligill Head extends into the Pentland Firth near the township of Baligill, a former centre of woollen milling, to the northwest of Melvich. Baligill Loch lies to the south.

Balintore *Angus* A hamlet with a castle in the Braes of Angus, Balintore lies in the valley of the Quharity Burn, 7 miles (11 km) northwest of Kirriemuir.

Balintore *Highland* A village on the Tarbat peninsula of Easter Ross, Balintore lies on the Moray Firth, 12 miles (19 km) northeast of Invergordon. A former fishing village with a harbour built in the 1890s, Balintore expanded after 1978 when oil from the Beatrice Field was brought ashore for processing by a pipeline linked to nearby Shandwick.

Balintraid *Highland* An industrial locality in Easter Ross, Balintraid lies on the Cromarty Firth, 2 miles (3 km) northeast of Invergordon. Its development in the 1970s was associated with the North Sea oil industry.

Balivanich *Western Isles* A village of Benbecula in the Western Isles, Balivanich (Gael: *Balivanish, Baile Mhanaich, Bail' a' Mhanaich* or *Bailebhainich*) lies to the west of the causeway linking Benbecula to North Uist. The name, meaning 'town of the monks', relates to a monastery established here in the 6th century and the remains of Teampull Chaluim Chille can be seen to the south of the village. An airfield to the north, built during World War II, was later the control centre for a rocket range established in 1957 at the height of the Cold War. In 2002 the airport benefited from a £500,000 upgrade to support the test programme for the Eurofighter that is using the range facilities. There are air links with Barra and Stornoway, a community school, an office of the North of Scotland College of Agriculture and a seafood-processing factory. The size of the village has grown and declined with the fortunes of the military facilities.

Balkissock *South Ayrshire* Located south of the Water of Tig, the settlement of Balkissock lies 3 miles (5 km) east of Ballantrae in the Carrick district of South Ayrshire.

Balla *Western Isles* The southernmost of an agglomeration of townships that forms the major settlement on the island of Eriskay in the Outer Hebrides, Balla (Gael: *Am Baile*) lies in the northwest of the island 5 miles (8 km) south of Lochboisdale on South Uist. The township of Rubha Bàn lies immediately to the north.

Ballachulish *Highland* A locality in the Lochaber district of southern Highland Council area, Ballachulish comprises the settlements of Ballachulish, South Ballachulish and North Ballachulish. The village of Ballachulish, formerly known as Laroch, lies on the south side of Loch Leven to the west of Glen Coe. Slate has been quarried near here since the 16th century. On either side of the strait, where the mouth of Loch Leven narrows, stand the villages of North and South Ballachulish. The two settlements were linked by ferry until 1975, when a roadbridge across the loch was completed. A monument on the south side of Loch Leven marks the spot where James Stewart was hanged for the murder in May 1752 of Colin Campbell of Glenure, and a stone in the forest between South Ballachulish and Kentallen indicates the site of the famous 'Appin Murder', which features in Robert Louis Stevenson's novel *Kidnapped* (1886).

Ballagan Water An alternative name for the Blane Water in Stirling Council area.

Ballageich Hill *East Renfrewshire* Also known as *Balagich*, Ballageich Hill rises to 330 m (1084 ft) in southeast East Renfrewshire. Eaglesham is 4 miles (6.5 km) to the northeast and the Bennan Loch Reservoir lies a half-mile (1 km) to the west.

Ballantrae *South Ayrshire* Situated on Ballantrae Bay at the mouth of the River Stinchar, the resort town of Ballantrae lies 13 miles (21 km) south of Girvan. Created a burgh of barony in 1541, it developed in medieval times in association with a hospice for pilgrims and a castle built by the Kennedy family in the 15th century. Ballantrae was for many years a fishing port, with smuggling a popular activity along the deserted coastline nearby. Robert Louis Stevenson (1850–94), author of *The Master of Ballantrae* (1888), is said to have been stoned here in 1876 by locals who, he alleged, were upset by his clothing.

Ballantrushal *Western Isles* A crofting township on the northwest coast of Lewis in the Outer Hebrides, Ballantrushal (also Ballantrushel, Gael: *Baile an Truiseil*) lies a half-mile (1 km) to the southwest of Shader and 3 miles (4 km) northeast of Barvas. The Trushel Stone, Scotland's largest prehistoric standing stone, is located here.

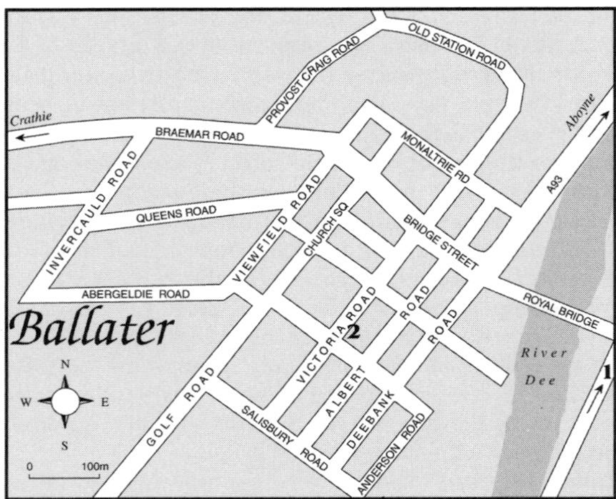

1 *To the Pananich Mineral Wells*
2 *The Old Royal Station*

Ballater *Aberdeenshire* A small resort town in the Royal Deeside parish of Glenmuick, Tullich and Glengairn, western Aberdeenshire, Ballater lies on the River Dee 43 miles (69 km) west of Aberdeen. It developed as a spa resort in the 1770s, first to accommodate visitors to the Pananich Mineral Wells, and later with the arrival of the railway in 1866 (closed 1966). Largely built of reddish granite, its houses are laid out in a regular pattern around a central church green. The town lies amid dramatic mountain and forest scenery at an altitude of 213 m (700 ft) above sea level and is today a centre for wayfaring and orienteering, with tourist and sporting facilities including an 18-hole golf course. The Pass of Ballater to the north of the town is an ice-worn ravine linking Milton of Tullich in the east to Bridge of Gairn.

Ballaterach *Aberdeenshire* A farm in western Aberdeenshire situated to the south of the River Dee 3 miles (5 km) east of Ballater, Ballaterach is associated with the poet Lord Byron (1788–1824) who spent part of his childhood here.

Ballathie *Perth and Kinross* A hamlet in east-central Perth and Kinross, Ballathie lies on the west bank of the River Tay, 10 miles (16 km) north of Perth. Ballathie House, now a hotel, was built for Major General Richardson of Tullybelton in the mid-19th century.

Ballchraggan *Highland* A village in Easter Ross, Ballchraggan lies 5 miles (8 km) south of Tain.

Ballechin *Perth and Kinross* A small settlement of Strathtay in central Perth and Kinross, Ballechin lies 3 miles (5 km) southwest of Pitlochry, to the north of the River Tay.

Ballencrieff *East Lothian* A village of East Lothian, Ballencrieff is located 3 miles (5 km) northwest of Haddington and a mile (1.5 km) south of Aberlady. Ballencrieff Castle, situated 2 miles (3 km) southeast of Aberlady in the shadow of the Garleton Hills, was built by John Murray in 1586. It was the birthplace in 1721 of General James Murray, who became the first British Governor of Canada. The castle, which was visited by Dr Samuel Johnson and James Boswell in 1773, was destroyed by fire in 1868 but was restored in the 1990s and is now a family home and hotel.

Ballengeich *Stirling* Ballengeich is the name given to a steep pass to the west of Stirling Castle. King James V (1512–42) wandered the countryside disguised as the 'Gudeman of Ballengeich'.

Balliemore *Argyll and Bute* The chief settlement of the island of Kerrera in the Firth of Lorn, Balliemore lies 2 miles (3 km) southwest of the headland of Rubh' a'Bhearnaig and 2 miles (3 km) southwest of Oban.

Balliemore *Argyll and Bute* Located in the northwestern corner of the Argyll Forest Park at the northern end of the Cowal peninsula, the settlement of Balliemore lies 2 miles (3 km) south of Strachur and 3 miles (5 km) northwest of the head of Loch Eck.

Ballikinrain Castle *Stirling* The original Ballikinrain Castle was built in 1868 for Sir Archibald Orr-Ewing to a design by David Bryce, master of the Scottish baronial style. It is situated in Strathendrick, southwest Stirling Council area, between Fintry and Killearn, and was rebuilt after a fire in 1913.

Ballimore *Argyll and Bute* Located on the west side of the Cowal peninsula, Ballimore lies close to the eastern shore of Loch Fyne, 8 miles (13 km) northwest of Tighnabruaich.

Ballimore *Stirling* A locality in the Stirling parish of Balquhidder, Ballimore lies on the Calair Burn in Glen Buckie, 2 miles (3 km) south of Balquhidder.

Ballinbreich *Fife* A farm in the parish of Flisk on the northern shores of Fife, Ballinbreich lies to the east of Newburgh looking out onto the Firth of Tay. Close by stand the ruins of a castle built in the 14th century by the Leslies, who acquired the lands of the barony of Balnebrich in 1312.

Ballindalloch *Moray* A small, scattered settlement in Moray, Ballindalloch lies to the west of the River Avon a half-mile (1 km) north of Bridge of Avon. Nearby is Ballindalloch Castle.

Ballindalloch Castle *Moray* Ballindalloch Castle, known as the 'Pearl of the North', is located on the Speyside Way, at the confluence of the rivers Spey and Avon, 9 miles (14 km) northeast of Grantown-on-Spey and the same distance west-southwest of Dufftown. It has been the home of the Macpherson-Grant family since 1546. Originally a tower house, built on the Z-plan, it has been developed into a comfortable country house. In 1645, the castle required major restoration after it was plundered and burned by James Graham, 1st Marquess of Montrose. General James Grant, hero of the American War of Independence, added two new wings to the house in 1770, one to house his favourite French chef. Further extensions and a major refurbishment were begun in 1850 under the direction of the architect Thomas MacKenzie. Between 1965 and 1967 one of the wings added in the 19th century was demolished and the castle modernised. Ballindalloch Estate is the home of one of the oldest cattle herds in the world, the famous Aberdeen Angus herd established by Sir George Macpherson-Grant in 1860 from a number of beasts bred by William McCombie. Within the grounds are a 17th-century dovecote and an early-20th-century rock garden.

Ballindean *Perth and Kinross* A settlement of southeast Perth and Kinross, Ballindean with Ballindean House and West Ballindean lies at the foot of the Braes of the Carse, to the west of Baledgarno between Perth and Dundee.

Ballingry *Fife* A small town to the south of Benarty Hill in western Fife, the old Kirkton of Ballingry developed as a mining settlement after 1870. Its ancient church, rebuilt in 1831, features in Sir Walter Scott's novel *The Abbot* (1820). A gas plant and former opencast mine lie to the east at Westfield.

Ballinloan Burn *Perth and Kinross* A stream in central Perth and Kinross, the Ballinloan Burn rises in the hills to the north of Strath Braan. It flows southeastwards for 4 miles (6.5 km) before joining the River Braan 2 miles (3 km) west of Inver.

Ballinluig *Perth and Kinross* A village of Logierait parish in central Perth and Kinross, Ballinluig lies on the River Tummel adjacent to the A9, 4 miles (6.5 km) southeast of Pitlochry. It developed in the 19th century at a junction of the Highland Railway with a branch leading to Aberfeldy. Nearby at Cuil-an-Daraich is the Childhood Heritage Centre and Toy Museum.

Ballintuim *Perth and Kinross* A village of Strathardle in eastern Perth and Kinross, Ballintuim lies by the River Ardle on the A924 to Kirkmichael from Blairgowrie, 3 miles (5 km) northwest of Bridge of Cally.

Balloch *Highland* A commuter village in eastern Highland Council area, Balloch lies to the northeast of Culloden, 4 miles (6.5 km) east of Inverness.

Balloch *North Lanarkshire* A suburb of the new town of Cumbernauld, Balloch lies 2 miles (3 km) west of the town centre.

Balloch *Perth and Kinross* A small settlement in central Perth and Kinross, Balloch lies adjacent to a small loch of the same name, 3 miles (5 km) southwest of Crieff.

Balloch *West Dunbartonshire* Situated immediately north of Alexandria and 5 miles (8 km) north of Dumbarton in West Dunbartonshire, the village of Balloch lies at the south end of Loch Lomond on the east bank of the River Leven. The earls of Lennox built a castle here in 1238, and Balloch became a small ferry port. In 1816 David Napier's *Marion* was the first pleasure steamer to operate on Loch Lomond from Balloch, and in 1850 Balloch Pier became the terminus of a railway from Dumbarton. Balloch flourished in association with the development of tourism and is today a focal point for leisure craft and the location of the Loch Lomond and the Trossachs National Park Gateway Centre at Loch Lomond Shores.

Balloch Castle *West Dunbartonshire* Located within the grounds of Balloch Castle Country Park, near Balloch in West Dunbartonshire, Balloch Castle dates from 1808, when it was built for the Vale of Leven textile magnate John Stirling. The former mansion house, originally called Tullichewan Castle, is now used as a visitor centre for the country park. An earlier castle near this site was built by the earls of Lennox in 1238, and the surrounding moat is still visible.

Balloch, the *Aberdeenshire* A hill in north Aberdeenshire, the Balloch rises to 366 m (1200 ft) at Meikle Balloch in a bend of the River Isla. The Bin Forest lies on its eastern slopes.

Ballochmorrie *South Ayrshire* The settlement of Ballochmorrie is located 2 miles (3 km) northwest of Barrhill and 3 miles (5 km) southeast of Pinwherry in South Ayrshire. The River Duisk flows to the east.

Ballochroy *Argyll and Bute* A locality on the northwest coast of Kintyre, Ballochroy lies 4 miles (6.5 km) northeast of Tayinloan. Nearby is a group of standing stones. The Ballochroy Burn flows west through the Ballochroy Glen into the Sound of Gigha.

Ballogie *Aberdeenshire* An estate in the southern Aberdeenshire parish of Birse, Ballogie lies on the Burn of Cattie to the southeast of Aboyne in Royal Deeside.

Ballone Castle *Highland* Located south of Tarbat Ness headland in Easter Ross, Ballone Castle is a 16th-century Z-plan tower house built by the Dunbars of Easter Tarbat. It lay ruinous for many years before being restored in the 1990s by a local architect, Lachlan Stewart, as a family home.

Ballygown *Argyll and Bute* A village of northwest Mull in the Inner Hebrides, Ballygown lies on Ballygown Bay, an inlet on the northern shoreline of Loch Tuath. The village faces the island of Ulva and lies between the settlements of Fanmore and Kilbrenan.

Ballygrant *Argyll and Bute* A village on the island of Islay in the Inner Hebrides, Ballygrant lies to the west of Loch Ballygrant and 3 miles (5 km) southwest of Port Askaig.

Ballyhaugh *Argyll and Bute* A locality on the island of Coll in the Inner Hebrides, Ballyhaugh lies at the northern end of Hogh Bay, 3 miles (5 km) west of Arinagour. Arnabost lies 3 miles (5 km) to the northeast.

Ballyoukan House *Perth and Kinross* A mansion house in Strathtay, Perth and Kinross, Ballyoukan House lies to the east of the River Tummel nearly 2 miles (3 km) south of Pitlochry.

Balmacaan Forest *Highland* An extensive area of deer forest to the south of Glen Urquhart, Balmacaan Forest lies to the west of Loch Ness. Balmacaan House is associated with the earls of Seafield.

Balmacara *Highland* A scattered village on the west coast of Highland Council area, Balmacara sits on Balmacara Bay on the north shore of Loch Alsh. The 2750 ha (6795 acre) crofting estate of Balmacara was bequeathed to the National Trust for Scotland in 1946 by Lady Hamilton, and in 1954 Lochalsh House was conveyed to the Trust. The restoration of Balmacara Square and the management of the surrounding native pinewoods have been important conservation projects carried out by the Trust in association with other bodies.

Balmaclellan *Dumfries and Galloway* A village of the Glenkens district of central Dumfries and Galloway, Balmaclellan lies east of the Water of Ken and 2 miles (3 km) northeast of New Galloway. The parish church dates from 1772, and in its kirkyard are stones commemorating Robert Grierson, a Covenanter martyred in 1683, and the family of Robert Paterson, the original of Sir Walter Scott's novel *Old Mortality* (1816). Just over a mile (1.5 km) to the northeast stands Barscobe Castle, which was built in 1684 by William Maclellan.

Balmaghie *Dumfries and Galloway* A parish and mansion house in south-central Dumfries and Galloway, Balmaghie lies to the west of the River Dee and Castle Douglas. Balmaghie House is said to stand on lands acquired by an Irish chieftain called M'Ghie whose descendants were granted charters by the Stewart kings. There is a deer park close by.

Balmaha *Stirling* A settlement in western Stirling Council area, Balmaha is situated at the southeastern end of Loch Lomond, 4 miles (6.5 km) west of Drymen. It is a centre of tourism, yachting, farming and forestry, and lies within the Loch Lomond and the Trossachs National Park. From here the West Highland Way heads northwards up the eastern side of Loch Lomond through the Pass of Balmaha to Rowardennan. Strathcashel Point to the north contains the remains of an ancient enclosure, and a crannog or Iron Age lake dwelling lies just offshore. Garadhban Forest lies immediately to the north on the slopes of Conic Hill.

Balmalcolm *Fife* An 18th-century farming and weaving village in Kettle parish, central Fife, Balmalcolm is situated on the A92 between Kettlebridge and Pitlessie. It is a centre of local farm produce.

Balmalloch *North Lanarkshire* Formerly a separate village, Balmalloch now forms a northwestern suburb of Kilsyth.

Balmangan *Dumfries and Galloway* A locality in southern Dumfries and Galloway, Balmangan lies 5 miles (8 km) southwest of Kirkcudbright at the head of Balmangan Bar on the west side of Kirkcudbright Bay. The remains of a 16th-century tower house lie opposite Balmangan Farm.

Balmanno Castle *Perth and Kinross* Lying in the shadow of the Ochil Hills near the Perthshire hamlet of Dron and a mile (1.5 km) south of Bridge of Earn is Balmanno Castle, a 16th-century L-plan tower house built *c.*1570 for George Auchinleck, shortly after the family had acquired the surrounding estate. In 1915, a splendid restoration was undertaken by architect Sir Robert Lorimer for William Millar, a Glasgow shipowner, as his summer residence. Completion was delayed by World War I, but like his previous restorations at Kellie and Earlshall Castles, Lorimer's work was of extremely high quality and undertaken with great care. Externally he added extra wings to form a courtyard. Lorimer allowed himself to dabble in the Gothic style, while incorporating internal details from Holyrood Palace, the restoration of which was the work of Sir William Bruce (1630–1710). Lorimer also furnished the house in every detail, using items he had commissioned as well as commercial pieces purchased around the country.

Balmartin *Western Isles* A crofting township on the west coast of North Uist in the Outer Hebrides, Balmartin (Gael: *Baile Mhartainn*) lies to the north of Loch Hosta, a mile (1.5 km) northeast of Tigharry.

Balmeanach Bay *Highland* An inlet on the east coast of the island of Skye in the Inner Hebrides, Balmeanach Bay lies opposite the south end of Raasay. Balmeanach township and the Braes lie to the west.

Balmedie *Aberdeenshire* An eastern Aberdeenshire settlement on the A92, Balmedie lies 7 miles (11 km) north of Aberdeen. Between Balmedie and the coast is a 5-mile/8-km-long survey baseline measured by the Ordnance Survey in 1817. Balmedie Country Park, with its boardwalks and visitor centre, extends over an area of sand dunes. The remains of an icehouse and World War II pillboxes can be found here.

Balmerino *Fife* A small fishing village and former port on the Firth of Tay, northern Fife, Balmerino lies 6 miles (10 km) southwest of Newport-on-Tay. Balmerino Abbey, a Cistercian monastery founded in 1229 by the widowed queen of William the Lion, was destroyed during the Reformation, but in 1936 its remains were given into the care of the National Trust for Scotland by the Earl of Dundee. A Spanish chestnut tree here is one of the oldest of its kind in the country. The village was designated a conservation area in 1987.

Balminnoch *Dumfries and Galloway* A locality in southwest Dumfries and Galloway, Balminnoch lies to the north of Loch Heron, 6 miles (10 km) northeast of Glenluce.

Balmoral Castle *Aberdeenshire* A royal residence in western Aberdeenshire, Balmoral Castle is located 8 miles (13 km) east of Braemar in the gently wooded valley of the River Dee. It is one of relatively few royal residences actually owned by the Royal Family. King Robert II (1316–90) had a hunting lodge in the vicinity, and Sir Malcolm Drummond built a tower on the same site. The Earl of Huntly bought the estate in the 15th century and it changed hands twice more before being purchased by Prince Albert for Queen Victoria in 1852. He paid £31,500 for the 9700-ha (24,000-acre) estate. The castle was built in 1855 by William Smith, the city architect for Aberdeen. Prince Albert was closely involved in the planning of both house and grounds. Over the years the Royal Family has improved and developed the house and estate. The Duke of Edinburgh has most recently enlarged the flower garden and created a water garden.

Balmore *East Dunbartonshire* Located a half-mile (1 km) west of Torrance and 3 miles (5 km) east of Milngavie in East Dunbartonshire, the village of Balmore lies to the north of the city of Glasgow. Immediately to the south of the village are the River Kelvin, which flows west and south to the River Clyde, and remains of the Antonine Wall.

Balmore *Highland* A settlement in Ardclach parish, eastern Highland Council area, Balmore lies by the Loch of Boath, 7 miles (11 km) south of Nairn.

Balmossie *Dundee City* A residential district and ancient chapelry of eastern Dundee City, on the border of Angus Council area, Balmossie lies around the Dighty Water between Broughty Ferry and Monifieth, adjacent to Barnhill. The chapel once stood on a crag opposite Balmossie Mill, but the ruin was razed to the ground *c.*1762. Suburban housing has been developed here since the 1970s and Balmossie Halt opened to the south on the East Coast main-line railway in 1962.

Balmule *Fife* Situated in Dunfermline parish less than a half-mile (1 km) north of Townhill in western Fife, the estate of Balmule once belonged to Sir Henry Wardlaw, who was chamberlain to Anne of Denmark (1574–1619), wife of King James VI (1566–1625).

Balmullo *Fife* A village in the parish of Leuchars in eastern Fife, Balmullo is situated on the eastern slopes of Lucklaw Hill 2 miles (3 km) west of Leuchars. Now largely a dormitory settlement, it was once a weaving village. Balmullo was the home of the picture-postcard cartoonist Martin Anderson ('Cynicus') whose red sandstone Cynicus Castle was demolished in 1939, seven years after his death. A prominent red sandstone quarry, a source of red pathway chippings, lies to the west.

Balmyle *Perth and Kinross* A mansion house in Strath Ardle, eastern Perth and Kinross, Balmyle lies to the east of the River Ardle, 9 miles (14 km) northwest of Blairgowrie.

Balnaboth *Angus* The settlement of Balnaboth is located in Angus, 9 miles (14 km) northwest of Kirriemuir. The Balnaboth Estate lies close by and extends to an area of 2226 ha (5500 acres). Held by the Ogilvy family since 1470, the estate's principal building is Balnaboth House, which dates from the late 16th century.

Balnacarn *Highland* A locality in Glen Moriston to the west of Loch Ness, Balnacarn lies on the Allt Baile nan Carn, a tributary of the River Moriston, 8 miles (13 km) northwest of Fort Augustus.

Balnafoich *Highland* A settlement in Strathnairn, Balnafoich lies on the River Nairn, 7 miles (11 km) south of Inverness.

Balnagown Castle *Highland* The 15th-century tower house of Balnagown Castle (Balnagowan Castle) in Easter Ross stands on the south bank of the Balnagown River, 2 miles (3 km) northeast of Invergordon. Extended in the 17th century and again in the Scottish Gothic style in 1838, the castle was originally the seat of the Clan Ross. Both the castle and the 12,145-ha (30,000-acre) Balnagown Estate were purchased in 1973 by Mohammed Al Fayed, the Egyptian businessman and owner of Harrods department store in London.

Balnagown River *Highland* A river of Easter Ross, the Balnagown River is formed by the meeting of the Allt Dearg and the Strathrory River 6 miles (10 km) northeast of Invergordon. It flows eastwards past Balnagown Castle before entering Nigg Bay to the southeast of Milton.

Balnaguard *Perth and Kinross* A village of Strathtay in central Perth and Kinross, Balnaguard lies to the south of the River Tay where it is joined by the Balnaguard Burn, near the junction of the Tay and Tummel rivers.

Balnahard *Argyll and Bute* Located on the west coast of the island of Mull in the Inner Hebrides, Balnahard lies a mile (1.5 km) south of Clachandhu and south of the entrance to Loch na Keal. To the west lies the island of Inch Kenneth.

Balnain *Highland* A settlement in Glen Urquhart to the west of Loch Ness, Balnain lies 4 miles (6.5 km) west of Drumnadrochit.

Balnain House *Highland* Situated by the River Ness on Huntly Street, Inverness, Balnain House was built by a merchant in 1726. It was used as a field hospital for Hanoverian troops during the Battle of Culloden in 1746 and in the 1880s it became the Highland base of the Ordnance Survey. After restoration by the National Trust for Scotland in 1993, the building housed a music heritage centre until it closed in 2001

Balnakeil *Highland* A village in Durness parish, northern Sutherland, Balnakeil lies on the broad Balnakeil Bay which forms an inlet between Cape Wrath and Loch Eriboll. Balnakeil House was built in the 1700s by the Mackay Lords of Reay, and Balnakeil Church, reconstructed in 1727, dates from the early 17th century. In the churchyard there is a memorial to Rob Doun (Robert Calder Mackay, 1714–78), the drover and Gaelic poet. A World War II military encampment has been converted into a craft village.

Balnakeil Bay *Highland* A sizeable bay of northwest Sutherland, Balnakeil Bay lies at the mouth of the Kyle of Durness, between Cape Wrath and Loch Eriboll, 1.25 miles (2 km) northwest of Durness. The eastern shore of the bay is formed by the dune-covered peninsula of Faraid Head.

Balnakeilly *Perth and Kinross* A neoclassical mansion house in highland Perth and Kinross, Balnakeilly lies to the north of the village of Moulin, a mile (1.5 km) northeast of Pitlochry. It was built in 1821.

Balnald *Perth and Kinross* A house in eastern Perth and Kinross, Balnald is located in Strath Ardle, a mile (1.5 km) southwest of Kirkmichael. Dating from 1886, it includes a farmhouse, steading and sawmill that incorporates an earlier grain mill.

Balnapaling *Highland* A settlement in Easter Ross, Balnapaling lies on the north side of the Cromarty Firth opposite Cromarty.

Balone *Fife* A mile (1.5 km) to the west of St Andrews in eastern Fife lies the hamlet of Balone, a farming and commuter settlement with camping and caravan facilities.

Balornock *Glasgow City* Located south of Springburn Park, to the north of Glasgow city centre, Balornock developed in the 19th century in response to the housing needs of those working at the St Rollox Railway Works. Like nearby Sighthill, Cowlairs and Colston, it pre-dates the settlement of Springburn. Extended in the 1930s by Glasgow City Corporation, much of the earlier Victorian housing was replaced in the 1960s.

Balquhidder *Stirling* The kirkton or village of Balquhidder is situated in the parish of Balquhidder, western Stirling Council area, at the east end of Loch Voil, but the name is also applied to the Braes of Balquhidder, an area celebrated in a song by Robert Tannahill (1774–1810), that extends along the lochside. Once the home of the Clan MacLaren, it came to be more closely associated with the Macgregors, especially Rob Roy Macgregor (1671–1734), who lies buried adjacent to the roofless old church of the parish along with his wife and two sons.

Balta *Shetland* An island to the east of Unst in the Shetland Islands, Balta is situated at the mouth of Balta Sound. It has an area of 80 ha (198 acres) and three hills, the highest of which at 44 m (144 ft) is Muckle Head. Antiquities on the island include a ruined broch at South Sail and the remains of a chapel formerly dedicated to the Norse saint Sunniva.

Baltasound *Shetland* The chief township of Unst in the Shetland Islands, Baltasound is situated at the head of Balta Sound, which is protected at its mouth by the island of Balta. The sound used to be the centre of the northern herring-fishing industry and could boast a seasonal population of over 10,000 in its heyday. Today Baltasound, with its two hotels and airstrip, serves the North Sea oil industry as well as being an outlet for talc. The settlement's Swedish Church was built in 1910. Just to the north is the unique and well-furnished Unst Bus Shelter.

Balthayock *Perth and Kinross* A locality in eastern Perth and Kinross, Balthayock lies at the western end of the Carse of Gowrie, 3 miles (5 km) east of Perth. Balthayock Castle, a former stronghold of the Blairs restored in 1870, dates from the 14th century. The derelict mansion house of Balthayock also dates from 1870 and has architectural details associated with the building of railways.

Balvag, River *Stirling* A river of Strathyre in western Stirling Council area, the River Balvag issues from the eastern end of Loch Voil by the village of Balquhidder. It meanders east then south for nearly 5 miles (8 km) before entering the north end of Loch Lubnaig.

Balvaird Castle *Perth and Kinross* Situated in southeast Perth and Kinross between Gateside and Bridge of Earn, the L-shaped tower house of Balvaird Castle sits atop an exposed ridge, overlooking Glen Farg. The Murrays of

Balvaird were the forebears of the family that eventually acquired the titles of Lord Balvaird, Viscount Stormont and Earl of Mansfield. The Murray family abandoned this castle in favour of Scone in 1685, and although it subsequently served as accommodation for farm workers, Balvaird had fallen into disrepair by 1845. Acquired by Historic Scotland in 1974, it has been restored.

Balvarran *Perth and Kinross* A mid-18th-century house in Strath Ardle, eastern Perth and Kinross, Balvarran is situated to the east of the River Ardle, 2 miles (3 km) northwest of Kirkmichael. It has a porch and entrance hall designed by Robert Lorimer in 1895.

Balvenie Castle *Moray* The ruined courtyard castle of Balvenie is located to the north of Dufftown. Originally a Comyn family seat dating from the 13th century, it was formerly known as Mortlach Castle. Granted to John Stewart, 1st Earl of Atholl, in 1459, it remained in Stewart hands until 1610. Occupied by Jacobites after the Battle of Killiecrankie in 1689, Balvenie Castle was later garrisoned by Government forces during the Jacobite Rebellion of 1745–6. After the Battle of Culloden in 1746, it was finally abandoned. Notable visitors have included King Edward I of England, Mary, Queen of Scots, and the Marquess of Montrose, who sought refuge here in 1644.

Balvicar *Argyll and Bute* A village on the east coast of the island of Seil in Argyll and Bute, Balvicar lies on Balvicar Bay, facing the Sound of Seil, 2 miles (3 km) south of Clachan Bridge, the 'Bridge over the Atlantic' that links the Scottish mainland with the island of Seil.

Balvraid *Highland* A settlement in western Highland Council area, Balvraid lies in Gleann Beag, 3 miles (5 km) southeast of Glenelg. The Glenelg brochs lie to the west.

Balvraid *Highland* A locality in eastern Highland Council area, Balvraid lies on the Allt Bruachaig, 5 miles (8 km) southeast of Moy and a mile (1.5 km) northeast of Tomatin.

Bamff *Perth and Kinross* A locality in eastern Perth and Kinross, Bamff lies to the north of the Hill of Alyth, 3 miles (5 km) northwest of the town of Alyth. It comprises Bamff House, Little Bamff and Newton of Bamff. Bamff House, originally a tower house dating from the 1580s, was remodelled in the 1830s for Sir James Ramsay by the architect William Burn.

Banavie *Highland* A locality in Lochaber, southwest Highland Council area, Banavie lies on the Caledonian Canal, 2 miles (3 km) north of Fort William.

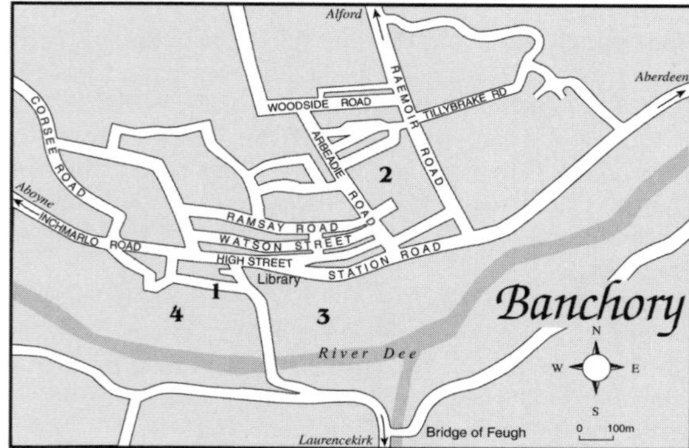

1 *Banchory Museum*
2 *Banchory Academy*
3 *King George V Playing Field*
4 *Golf Course*

Banchory *Aberdeenshire* A resort town in Royal Deeside, Banchory is situated on the north bank of the River Dee, 18 miles (29 km) west of Aberdeen. Built on river terraces that slope down to the Dee, Banchory lies at a junction of roads linking Aberdeen with Upper Deeside, Deeside with Strathmore to the south via Cairn o' Mount, and Deeside with Strathbogie to the north. Founded in 1805 and formerly included in Kincardineshire, Banchory developed during the 19th century as a tourist resort and in the late 20th century also as a commuter settlement for those working in Aberdeen. Through local meetings of the Strathspey and Reel Society and the Accordion and Fiddle Club, the people of Banchory keep alive a strong musical tradition that is associated with the locally born composer of fiddle music, James Scott Skinner (1843–1927), whose life and work is commemorated in Banchory Museum. In addition to tourism-related facilities there are craft, woollen, food-processing, building and timber industries in Banchory.

Banchory-Devenick *Aberdeenshire* Situated to the south of the River Dee in the southeast Aberdeenshire parish of the same name, Banchory-Devenick is a scattered commuter settlement on the outskirts of Aberdeen.

Bandirran *Perth and Kinross* A locality in eastern Perth and Kinross, Bandirran is situated to the southwest of Dunsinane Hill, 7 miles (11 km) northeast of Perth. It comprises the hamlet of Bandirran, a mansion house and Southtown of Bandirran.

Banff *Aberdeenshire* Formerly the county town of Banffshire, the northern Aberdeenshire seaport and resort of Banff lies at the mouth of the River Deveron where it flows into the Moray Firth. Built on a series of terraces rising up to a cliff top, Banff became a royal centre by the end of the 12th century. In medieval times it was linked to the North Hanseatic league of trading towns, and in 1372 was created a royal burgh. It remained a prosperous commercial and fishing port until the end of the 19th century and has many well-preserved merchants' buildings dating from the 17th and 18th centuries. At the heart of the burgh are the Plainstanes, a fine group of buildings that includes the Town House (1764–7), Tolbooth (1796), 16th-century Mercat Cross and Biggar Fountain (1878). The original castle of Banff, built to defend the coast against Viking attack, was rebuilt in the 18th century by James Ogilvy, 3rd Earl of Seafield. The Carmelites built a monastery here in the 14th century. Banff High Street lies along an upper ridge while Low Street sits at the level of the River Deveron. The lower part of the town can be reached by the narrow and precipitous Water Path that leads to the High Shore, at the west end of which stand the ruins of the late-medieval Church of St Mary. At the north end of the High Shore is the harbour which was originally built by the engineer John Smeaton in 1770–5. From the south, Banff is entered across a seven-span bridge built in 1799 by Smeaton for the 2nd Earl of Fife as an imposing approach to Duff House, which lies amid acres of parkland. The young Lord Byron (1788–1824) frequently visited relatives in Banff, and the poet Robert Southey (1774–1843), visiting in 1819, described the 'clean, fresh town, open to the sea breezes and the country air'. Dr Samuel Johnson (1709–84), overnighting at the Black Bull Inn en route to the Western Isles, could not get enough

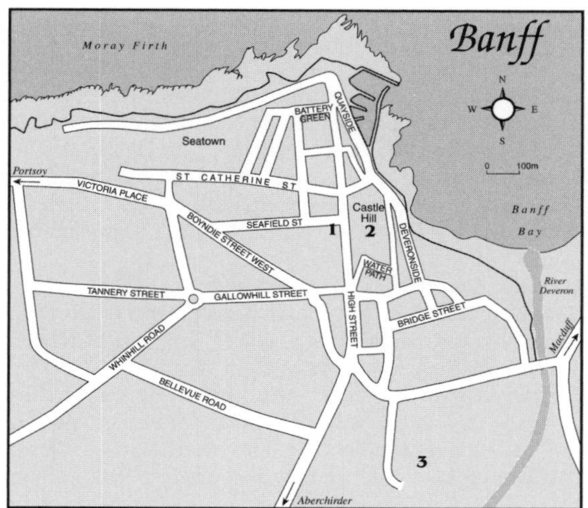

1 *Plainstanes Town House*
2 *Banff Castle, Site of*
3 *Duff House*

of this fresh air, noting that 'the necessity of ventilating human habitations has not yet been found by our northern neighbours'. Highlighting the social history and natural development of the town, the Banff Museum is located on the High Street. Collections in the museum include instruments that belonged to the astronomer James Ferguson (1710–1776) and the natural-history collection of Thomas Edward (1814–1886). Today the town is a popular resort, with a sailing club and an 18-hole golf course.

Banff Bay *Aberdeenshire* An inlet of the Moray Firth on the coast of Aberdeenshire, Banff Bay lies at the mouth of the River Deveron between Banff and Macduff.

Banffshire A former county of northeast Scotland lying between Morayshire to the west and Aberdeenshire to the east, Banffshire extended northwards from the Cairngorm Mountains to the coast of the Moray Firth. Watered by the River Spey and River Deveron, its county town was Banff. In 1974 it was incorporated into the Banff and Buchan District of Grampian Region and in the local government reorganisation of 1996 was divided between Moray and Aberdeenshire Council Areas.

Bank of Scotland Head Office *City of Edinburgh* The headquarters of the Bank of Scotland stand on the Mound in Edinburgh, perched above East Princes Street Gardens. It was initiated while Henry Dundas, Viscount Melville (1742–1811), was Governor of the Bank and was built by the architects Robert Reid (1774–1856) and Richard Crichton between 1802 and 1806 at a cost of £43,000. Complaints about the rear of the building as it was seen from the developing New Town, together with the need for enlargement, resulted in David Bryce (1803–76) being asked to submit plans in 1862 for its augmentation. New wings were added on both sides of the building, each topped by domes. These, together with a grand replacement central dome combined with other stylistic features, created a fine public building. The interior was also remodelled by Bryce and subsequently in 1929 and 1981, but it remains a grand symbol of the wealth of Scotland's oldest bank, which was established by an Act of the Scottish Parliament in 1695. The oldest surviving UK clearing bank, it was originally located in Old Bank Close in the Lawnmarket, before making the short move to its new site on the Mound. In addition to its banking functions, the building incorporates a small museum, opened in 1987. Exhibits include coins and banknotes (and their forgeries), a 17th-century bullion chest, and maps, watercolours and engravings of old Edinburgh. In 2001, the Bank of Scotland merged with the Halifax Building Society to become HBOS Plc. This building remains the headquarters of the group.

Bankend *Dumfries and Galloway* A village of Nithsdale, southern Dumfries and Galloway, Bankend lies to the west of the Lochar Water, 6 miles (10 km) southeast of Dumfries.

Bankend *South Lanarkshire* A locality in South Lanarkshire Council area, Bankend lies 2 miles (3 km) west of Coalburn. It comprises North and South Bankend and was closely associated with the nearby open-cast coal mine at Coalburn.

Bankfoot *Perth and Kinross* A village in central Perth and Kinross, Bankfoot lies to the west of the A9, 5 miles (8 km) southeast of Dunkeld. The minor poet Robert Nicoll was born at nearby Tullybelton in 1814.

Bankhead *Aberdeen City* A settlement in Aberdeen City Council area, Bankhead lies on the River Don between Bucksburn and Stoneywood, 3 miles (5 km) northwest of the centre of Aberdeen.

Bankhead *Dumfries and Galloway* A locality in Rerrick parish, southern Dumfries and Galloway, Bankhead lies a mile (1.5 km) to the northeast of Dundrennan on the A711.

Bankhead *South Lanarkshire* A former country estate of South Lanarkshire, Bankhead is now a district of Rutherglen.

Banknock *Falkirk* A village in Falkirk Council area, Banknock is situated on the Bonny Water to the west of the A80 and north of the Forth and Clyde Canal. The Bankier Distillery lies on its western edge.

Bankrugg *East Lothian* The hamlet of Bankrugg is located 3 miles (5 km) east of East Saltoun in East Lothian. The Newhall Burn flows to the east.

Bankshill *Dumfries and Galloway* A hamlet in southeast Dumfries and Galloway, Bankshill lies to the south of the Water of Milk in the hills of Tundergarth parish, 4 miles (6.5 km) east of Lockerbie.

Bannockburn *Stirling* A residential area in southeast Stirling Council area, Bannockburn is 2 miles (3 km) south of Stirling. The original village developed in the 18th and 19th centuries as a centre for coal mining and textile manufacture, specialities being the production of carpets and tartan. The National Trust for Scotland's Bannockburn Heritage Centre, opened in 1987, is associated with one of Scotland's most historic sites. On a battlefield nearby, King Robert the Bruce routed the army of King Edward II of England in June 1314 to win freedom for the Scots from English domination. A few yards from the centre is the famous Borestone site, which by tradition was Bruce's command post before the battle. The site is enclosed by a rotunda that focuses on the approach route of the English army intent on capturing Stirling Castle. The rotunda was inaugurated by Queen Elizabeth II in June 1964, when she also unveiled the statue of Bruce by Pilkington Jackson. In 1930 a committee under the 10th Earl of Elgin and Kincardine, head of the Bruce family, successfully raised funds to purchase 23.5 ha (58 acres) of the site of the battlefield. This land was eventually gifted in 1960 to the National Trust for Scotland, which acquired further land. The Bannock Burn Valley is a major open space within the Stirling conurbation.

Banton *North Lanarkshire* A locality in North Lanarkshire, Banton lies 2 miles (3 km) east of Kilsyth and 2 miles (3 km) west of Banknock. Banton comprises the village of Banton as well as the hamlets of High Banton and Craigs. Banton Loch separates the village from nearby Kilsyth, while to the south flows the Forth and Clyde Canal.

Baosbheinn *Highland* A peak in Wester Ross, Highland Council area, Baosbheinn lies to the north of Loch a'Bhealaich, east of Loch a'Ghobhainn and 5 miles (8 km) north of Upper Loch Torridon. It rises to 875 m (2870 ft) at the heart of the Shieldaig Forest.

Bar Hill *East Dunbartonshire* Bar Hill rises to 155 m (508 ft) a half-mile (1 km) to the northeast of the village of Twechar in East Dunbartonshire. Situated in forested land next to the village, the hill overlooks the ruins of a Roman fort.

Barabhas The Gaelic name for Barvas in the Western Isles.

Barassie *South Ayrshire* A village on the South Ayrshire coast of the Firth of Clyde, Barassie lies a mile (1.5 km) to the north of Troon. Established in the mid-1830s as a railway settlement at the junction of two railway lines, it initially developed as a centre of railway-carriage and wagon repair. An 18-hole golf course was founded in 1887, and in the 20th century Barassie expanded as a northern suburb of Troon, with the development of the Barassie Garden Village. Barassie became a weekend retreat for the people of Kilmarnock, earning itself the alternative name of New Kilmarnock.

Barbaraville *Highland* A settlement in Easter Ross, Barbaraville lies on the shore of Nigg Bay, 3 miles (5 km) northeast of Invergordon.

Barcaldine *Argyll and Bute* The scattered village of Barcaldine is located in the Benderloch district of Argyll and Bute, near the southern shore of Loch Creran, 5 miles (8 km) north of Connel. Two miles (3 km) to the southeast, Beinn Bhreac (*Ben Vrackie*) rises to 708 m (2342 ft).

Barcaldine Castle *Argyll and Bute* The L-shaped tower house of Barcaldine Castle, sometimes known as the Black Castle because of its dark stones, is located to the west of the village of Benderloch in Argyll and Bute. It was built in 1609 for Sir Duncan Campbell of Glenorchy ('Duncan of the Seven Castles') and remained a Campbell stronghold until it was abandoned in 1735, when the family moved to Barcaldine House. In the late 19th century the family returned and restored the castle. Campbell descendants still occupy the tower. In 1691 MacIan of Glencoe was detained here by the weather on his way to Inveraray to sign the oath of allegiance to King William III, a delay that ultimately led to the Massacre of Glencoe the following year.

Barcloy Hill *Dumfries and Galloway* A hill in southern Dumfries and Galloway, Barcloy Hill forms a headland at the mouth of the Rough Firth where it meets the Solway Firth. Rockcliffe lies a mile (1.5 km) to the northwest, and Barcloymill and West Barcloy lie within the shadow of the hill.

Bardowie *East Dunbartonshire* A hamlet in East Dunbartonshire, Bardowie lies 2 miles (3 km) southeast of Milngavie and 6 miles (10 km) north of Glasgow. It is situated to the southeast of Bardowie Loch and Bardowie Castle, while to the southwest runs the River Kelvin, a tributary of the River Clyde. The 16th-century tower of Bardowie Castle was a stronghold of the Hamiltons.

Barevan *Highland* A medieval kirkton in eastern Highland Council area, Barevan with its old church lies to the south of the River Nairn, a mile (1.5 km) south of Nairn.

Bargaly *Dumfries and Galloway* An estate with a mansion house in Minnigaff parish, central Dumfries and Galloway, Bargaly lies 3 miles (5 km) east of Newton Stewart. Bargaly House dates from 1691.

Bargany *South Ayrshire* A locality in South Ayrshire, Bargany lies on the Water of Girvan 2 miles (3 km) west of Dailly and 4 miles (6.5 km) northeast of Girvan. Bargany village has all but disappeared, but Bargany House and Estate have been extensively redeveloped, the main attractions being the wooded walks and gardens with rhododendrons.

Bargatton Loch *Dumfries and Galloway* A small loch in southern Dumfries and Galloway, Bargatton Loch lies 6 miles (10 km) north of Kirkcudbright, between Ringford and Laurieston.

Bargeddie *North Lanarkshire* Located northeast of the junction of the M73 and M8, Bargeddie is a small town of North Lanarkshire. Situated 2 miles (3 km) west of Coatbridge, Bargeddie grew, along with neighbouring Cuilhill and Drumpark, in association with the mining of coal. In the late 1940s a major housing estate was created to accommodate an influx of residents from Glasgow and the surrounding areas.

Bargrennan *Dumfries and Galloway* A hamlet in Galloway, Bargrennan lies by the River Cree on the A714 to Girvan, 9 miles (14 km) northwest of Newton Stewart. To the northeast is the Glentrool Forest Park. Between Bargrennan and Glentrool Village is located the White Cairn, a chambered cairn dating from the 3rd millennium BC. Bargrennan lies on the Southern Upland Way.

Barhapple Loch *Dumfries and Galloway* A small loch in southwest Dumfries and Galloway, Barhapple Loch lies just south of the A75 road, 4 miles (6.5 km) east of Glenluce. It receives the Dergoals Burn.

Barharrow *Dumfries and Galloway* A locality in southern Dumfries and Galloway, Barharrow is situated at a road junction, 2 miles (3 km) south of Gatehouse of Fleet.

Barlae *Dumfries and Galloway* A locality in southwest Dumfries and Galloway, Barlae lies on the A75 road where it crosses the Tarf Water, 10 miles (16 km) southwest of Newton Stewart.

Barlanark *Glasgow City* A residential area to the northeast of Glasgow city centre, Barlanark was developed in response to the city's postwar housing needs. In 1946 over 2300 four- and five-apartment houses were built around Barlanark House, which had been constructed by David Hamilton in 1822 and was demolished in 1972. These tenements are characterised by brick balconies.

Barmolloch *Argyll and Bute* The isolated locality of Barmolloch lies to the east of Kilmartin and 8 miles (13 km) north of Lochgilphead. It sits on the Socach Burn between Loch Ederline to the north and Loch Leathan to the south. Beinn Bhàn rises to 319 m (1046 ft) to the west.

Barmore Island *Argyll and Bute* A headland in eastern Knapdale, Barmore Island extends into Loch Fyne 2 miles (3 km) north of Tarbert. It is predominantly wooded and rises to a height of 62 m (204 ft).

Barmurrie *Dumfries and Galloway* A locality in the Glenkens district of Dumfries and Galloway, Barmurrie lies on the A712, a mile (1.5 km) east of Balmaclellan.

Barnabarroch *Dumfries and Galloway* A hamlet in Dalbeattie Forest, southern Dumfries and Galloway, Barnabarroch lies to the east of the Urr Water, 3 miles (5 km) south of Dalbeattie.

Barnacarry *Argyll and Bute* Situated on the east shore of Loch Fyne opposite Minard Castle, the settlement of Barnacarry lies 8 miles (13 km) southwest of Strachur and a mile (1.5 km) southwest of Castle Lachlan.

Barnbarroch *Dumfries and Galloway* A mansion house dating from 1780 in the Machars district of Dumfries and Galloway, Barnbarroch lies 3 miles (5 km) southwest of Wigtown.

Barnbougle Castle *City of Edinburgh* Situated one-third of a mile (0.5 km) north of Dalmeny House on the south shore of the Firth of Forth, Barnbougle Castle was the original home of the earls of Rosebery. It is a 13th-century tower house, abandoned for the more comfortable surroundings of Dalmeny in 1817. An original plan by Robert Adam (1728–92) was intended to extend and modernise the castle, but the family preferred a new site set back from the exposed location by the river. In 1881 the 5th Earl of Rosebery, who became prime minister, rebuilt the castle as a retreat.

Barnhill *Dundee City* A residential suburb of Dundee, lying adjacent to its eastern border with Angus at Monifieth and to the east of Broughty Ferry, Barnhill is constrained by the Dichty Water to the north and east.

Barnhourie *Dumfries and Galloway* A sandbank in the Solway Firth, Barnhourie lies just south of the Mersehead Sands on the south coast of Dumfries and Galloway, to the south of Dumfries.

Barnkirk Point *Dumfries and Galloway* A promontory on the Solway Firth coast, Barnkirk Point is located at the mouth of the River Annan, a mile (1.5 km) south of the town of Annan.

Barns Ness *East Lothian* A headland on the coast of East Lothian, Barns Ness extends into the North Sea 3 miles (5 km) southeast of Dunbar. A lighthouse designed by D. A. Stevenson was built here in 1901.

Barnton *City of Edinburgh* A residential northwestern suburb of Edinburgh, Barnton lies to the west of Silverknowes and Davidson's Mains. Numerous bungalows and sizeable villas dating from 1900 to 1930 surround older buildings such as the Whitehouse (*c*.1615) and Barnton House (*c*.1640), which was restyled by Robert Adam in 1790 and demolished *c*.1900. The Barnton Estate provided land for the prestigious Royal Burgess and Bruntsfield golf clubs, which moved here from Musselburgh and the south side of Edinburgh respectively. Postwar housing developments have significantly expanded the suburb, and close by at Barnton Quarry are the remains of a secret command centre dating from the Cold War.

Barnweil Monument, the *South Ayrshire* Situated on a hilltop to the north of Ayr, the Barnweil Monument marks the spot where William Wallace (*c*.1272–1305) commanded a battle against the English. He trapped the English Army in Ayr and allegedly set all the barns in the surrounding area alight, encircling the enemy.

Barony, the *Dumfries and Galloway* Occupying 240 ha (96 acres) of farm and woodland estate in Dumfries and Galloway, the Barony lies on the Water of Ae, 8 miles (13 km) north of Dumfries, just south of the village of Parkgate. In addition to the working estate, the Barony also comprises the Barony College, a college providing vocational training for land-based industries, and the Barony Centre, a conference facility. Originally built in 1834, the Jacobean-style house was converted to a modern college 1984–91.

Barony, the *Fife* A locality on the south shore of the River Tay in northern Fife, the Barony defines the old extent of the Barony of Ballinbreich, which was acquired by the Leslies in 1312. The minor coastal road from Newburgh that follows the Tay eastwards through Flisk parish is known as the Barony Road.

Barony Church *Glasgow City* A former church on the High Street in Glasgow, the Barony Church takes its name from the Barony parish, which extends over the East End of the city centre. The red-sandstone Barony Church was completed in 1890, replacing an older 18th-century church. Designed by Sir J. J. Burnet, it is an example of the architectural style known as Scottish Gothic Revival. It is now used as the ceremonial hall for the University of Strathclyde, where graduation ceremonies and other official functions are held.

Barr *Argyll and Bute* The settlement of Barr is located 4 miles (6.5 km) east of Bowmore on Islay in the Inner Hebrides. It sits on the River Laggan, 2 miles (3 km) southwest of its source on the slopes of Sgorr nam Faoileann.

Barr *Highland* A settlement on the Morvern peninsula, Barr lies to the west of Loch Teacuis, 8 miles (13 km) northwest of Lochaline.

Barr *South Ayrshire* A remote village in the Carrick district of South Ayrshire, Barr lies on the Stinchar River, 6 miles (10 km) southeast of Girvan. It forms a compact settlement with the Changue Forest to the east.

Barra *Western Isles* The largest of the islands to the south of the Uists in the Outer Hebrides, Barra (Gael: *Barraigh*) is the homeland of the MacNeils, whose ownership of the island dates from 1427, when Alexander, Lord of the Isles, granted Gilleonan MacNeil a charter. It is joined to Vatersay by a narrow causeway and has a total area of 6173 ha (15,247 acres). Overlying gneiss, an ancient metamorphic rock, is a landscape shaped by glaciation to give a rocky east coast and a west coast with fine sandy bays backed by machair. There are five hills, the highest being Heaval (383 m/1180 ft), on whose slopes stands a white Carrara marble statue of the Madonna and Child. Castlebay is the chief settlement. Developed as a herring port by James Methuen in 1869, it looks out onto the picturesque Kisimul Castle, seat of the MacNeils of Barra. The island of Barra is thought to be named after the 6th-century Irish missionary St Barr or Finbar, a disciple of St Columba reputedly sent to the island to replace a priest who had been eaten by the inhabitants. There are ferry links to Lochboisdale, Oban and Mallaig from Castlebay, and to Eriskay and Ludag on South Uist from Eoligarry in the north. Flights from Glasgow land on the sandy Tràigh Mhòr or Cockle Strand at the north end of the island.

Barra, Sound of *Western Isles* The Sound of Barra is the name given to the sea channel that separates the island of Barra from South Uist to the north. The islands of Fuday, Lingay and Eriskay lie within the sound.

Barra Head *Western Isles* Barra Head (Gael: *Ceann Bharraigh*) forms a cape on the south coast of the island of Berneray in the Western Isles. It lies 12 miles (19 km) to the southwest of the island of Barra and represents the southernmost point of the Outer Hebrides. Because of this position, the entire island is sometimes referred to as Barra Head.

Barraigh The Gaelic name for Barra in the Western Isles.

Barrapoll *Argyll and Bute* Located in the western half of the island of Tiree in the Inner Hebrides, Barrapoll lies 3 miles (5 km) southeast of the headland of Rubha Chraiginis. One mile (1.5 km) to the east is the settlement of Heylipoll.

Barras, the *Glasgow City* Established on a site near the Barrier's Gate, the old city gate of Glasgow, the Barras has been a part of the city's heritage since the early 1920s. Principally an area of market stalls, it has expanded to include ten markets and in excess of 1000 stalls and shops. It is also the location of the Barrowland Ballroom.

Barr Castle *East Ayrshire* Located in Galston town centre, East Ayrshire, Barr Castle is a Norman keep built by the Lockhart family in the 12th and 13th centuries. George Wishart and John Knox both preached here in the 16th century after being banned from preaching in church during the early years of the Reformation.

Barr Mòr *Argyll and Bute* A hill in Argyll and Bute, Barr Mòr rises to 255 m (836 ft) on the east side of Glen Shira, 3 miles (5 km) northeast of the town of Inveraray. Two miles (3 km) to the south, Strone Point extends into the head of Loch Fyne.

Barr Point *Dumfries and Galloway* A small promontory on the east coast of Luce Bay, southwest Dumfries and Galloway, Barr Point lies a mile (1.5 km) to the south of the village of Elrig and nearly 2 miles (3 km) northwest of Port William.

Barrel of Butter *Orkney* A small rock just appearing above the surface of the water in Scapa Flow in the Orkney Islands, the Barrel of Butter is said to derive its name from the annual rent of a barrel of butter once paid to the local laird in return for permission to kill seals on the rock.

Barrhead *East Renfrewshire* An industrial town in East Renfrewshire, Barrhead lies on the Levern Water, 7 miles (11 km) southwest of Glasgow. It developed from a number of smaller villages in the late 18th century in association with the textile industry, in particular bleaching, cotton spinning and calico printing. It was created a burgh in 1894. Its stoneware industry became widely known through its links with the Shanks firm of sanitary engineers. Copper was mined from volcanic rocks at the nearby Boylestone Quarry, and in the late 20th century industries included waterproofing and the manufacture of soft leather and pet foods. The Barrhead Community Museum houses displays highlighting the natural and social history of the surrounding area.

Barrhill *South Ayrshire* Situated 12 miles (19 km) southeast of Girvan on the Duisk River in South Ayrshire and at an elevation of around 135 m (450 ft), the village of Barrhill developed in association with local mills, the expansion of the road system and the arrival of the railway in 1877. Nearby is the Convent of Kildonan. Since the 1960s, afforestation has offered employment.

Barrie's Birthplace *Angus* A two-storey building at 9 Brechin Road, Kirriemuir, was the birthplace in 1860 of the playwright J. M. Barrie, creator of *Peter Pan*. Gifted to the National Trust for Scotland in 1937, it is furnished as it might have been when Barrie lived there. The adjacent house features a display of Barrie's literary and theatrical works, and a wash house outside is said to have been his first theatre. In 1930 J. M. Barrie was given the freedom of Kirriemuir. He later presented the town with a cricket pavilion and the camera obscura on Kirrie Hill.

Barrisdale *Highland* A locality in Knoydart, southwest Highland Council area, Barrisdale lies on Barrisdale Bay, an inlet of Loch Hourn. The River Barrisdale, which flows down through Glen Barrisdale, joins the bay here.

Barrisdale, Glen *Highland* A narrow glen in Knoydart, Highland Council area, Glen Barrisdale forms a river valley between Slat Bheinn and Meall nan Eun which opens out into Barrisdale Bay, an inlet on the south side of Loch Hourn.

Barrnacarry Bay *Argyll and Bute* An inlet on the eastern side of the Firth of Lorn, Barrnacarry Bay lies to the south of the island of Kerrera at the mouth of Loch Feochan.

Barrock *Highland* A locality in northern Caithness, Barrock lies to the south of the main road between John o' Groats and Thurso, southeast of Dunnet Head. Its sizeable Free Church dates from 1844. The mid-19th-century Barrock House, situated to the west of the Burn of Lyth, 9 miles (14 km) northwest of Wick, is associated with a branch of the Sinclair family.

Barrowland Ballroom, the *Glasgow City* Located in the East End of Glasgow City Centre, the Barrowland Ballroom is surrounded by the Barras market. Formerly Glasgow's leading ballroom, it is now a music venue with a capacity of over 3000 and is generally regarded as the city's best venue for rock and pop concerts.

Barry *Angus* A village in the Angus coastal parish of the same name, Barry is situated on the Pitairlie Burn, 2 miles (3 km) west of Carnoustie. To the south lie Barry Links and to the north is the restored Barry Mill.

Barry Links *Angus* An area of low-lying sand dunes, Barry Links are located between Monifieth and Carnoustie and extend out into the mouth of the Firth of Tay behind Buddon Ness. The links are largely occupied by a military training area and the largest rifle range in Scotland, associated with Barry Buddon Army Camp. At the northeastern side of the links is the Carnoustie Championship golf course. Much of the area is designated a Site of Special Scientific Interest (SSSI) to protect its sand-dune systems, and the vegetation is of European importance and proposed as a Special Area of Conservation. The Dundee-Aberdeen railway forms the northern boundary of the links.

Barry Mill *Angus* A working 19th-century meal mill, Barry Mill is situated to the north of Barry village near Carnoustie. Rebuilt in 1814 following a fire, a mill has operated on this site since at least 1539. Barry Mill was the last water-powered meal mill to operate in Angus, producing oatmeal until the 1970s and animal feed until 1982. Damage to the mill lade brought an end to commercial operations and the buildings were subsequently acquired by the National Trust for Scotland in 1988. Now fully restored, the mill once again produces animal fodder.

Barry Sands *Angus* A sand bank off the Barry Links at the mouth of the Tay estuary.

Barsalloch Point *Dumfries and Galloway* A headland on the east coast of Luce Bay, southwest Dumfries and Galloway, Barsalloch Point lies over a mile (1.5 km) to the southeast of Port William.

Barshaw Park *Renfrewshire* An area of parkland in Paisley, Barshaw Park has a small boating pond as well as a putting green, tennis, crazy golf and miniature railway. A Nature Corner houses a variety of small animals and birds.

Barvas *Western Isles* A significant crofting township on the northwest coast of Lewis in the Western Isles, Barvas (Gael: *Barabhas*) lies in a parish of the same name, on the River Barvas, 11 miles (18 km) northwest of Stornoway. The settlement comprises Barvas itself, with its Gaelic-medium primary school, two churches and a post office, together with Upper Barvas (Gael: *Barabhas Uarach*) to the north-northeast and Lower Barvas (Gael: *Barabhas Iarach*) to the west, adjacent to Loch More Barvas.

Barvas, Aird *Western Isles* Aird Barvas is a small headland on the west coast of the Isle of Lewis in the Western Isles. Lying a half-mile (1 km) south of Rubha Leathann, it extends into the sea 2 miles (3 km) north of the settlement of Barvas.

Barvas, River *Western Isles* Flowing through the settlement of Barvas on the west coast of the Isle of Lewis in the Outer Hebrides, the Barvas River passes through Loch More Bharvais before emptying into the sea.

Barvick Burn *Perth and Kinross* A stream in central Perth and Kinross, the Barvick Burn rises in hills to the east of Loch Turret and flows southeastwards to join the Turret Water 2 miles (3 km) northwest of Crieff. Near its confluence with the Turret it cascades over the Falls of Barvick.

Bass Rock *East Lothian* A steep-sided island lying 1.5 miles (2.5 km) off the East Lothian coast, 3.5 miles (5.5 km) northeast of North Berwick, Bass Rock rises sharply to 107 m (350 ft). Geologically, the rock is a volcanic plug of Lower Carboniferous age and thus similar to the other notable physiographic features of Edinburgh and East Lothian, such as North Berwick Law. James Hutton (1726–97) first recognised the rock as an igneous intrusion, and Hugh Miller (1802–56) wrote an extensive monograph on the geology of the rock, having visited in 1847. St Baldred lived on the rock in the 7th century and a chapel, now ruined, was built on the site of his cell. Owned by the Lauder family from 1316, it was sold in 1671 to the Government, which rebuilt an older fortress as a prison to confine first Covenanters – including Alexander Peden (*c.*1626–86) and John Blackadder (1615–86) – and then Jacobites. In 1691 Jacobite prisoners seized the fortress in the name of the exiled King James VII while their captors were unloading a delivery of coal. Reinforced and supplied by the French, and provided with a ship with which they plundered passing boats, the Jacobites held out until 1694. They finally surrendered, having secured 'most honourable terms', and the fort was subsequently demolished in 1701, although some remnants can still be seen. In 1706, ownership of Bass Rock passed to Sir Hew Dalrymple of North Berwick. Today, Bass Rock supports a lighthouse and sustains approximately 80,000 gannets which form the largest single-rock gannetry in the world. Indeed, the North Atlantic gannet is more formally named *Morus bassana* after the rock. The colony can be studied by remote-controlled cameras at the Scottish Seabird Centre in North Berwick.

Bastard, the *Argyll and Bute* A hill overlooking the southeast coast of the Kintyre peninsula in Argyll and Bute, the Bastard rises to 188 m (616 ft) to the northeast of Glen Hervie and 5.5 miles (9 km) south-southeast of Campbeltown. There is a dun on its eastern slopes.

Bathgate *West Lothian* An industrial town in West Lothian, Bathgate is situated north of the M8, 18 miles (29 km) southwest of Edinburgh. The town was established as a burgh of barony in 1661 and had seven annual fairs. During the 17th century Huguenots from France settled here, bringing their weaving skills with them. Jarvey Street is named after one of these families (Jarves). The renowned scientist James 'Paraffin' Young (1811–83) developed the world's first oil refinery here, extracting paraffin from the oil-shale fields to the east of Bathgate. The resulting economic boom subsided in the early 1870s with the import of cheap crude oil from the USA. By the mid-19th century, Bathgate had developed into a settlement comprising an old town on the slopes of the Bathgate Hills and a new town to the south, designed on a regular plan with elegant villas. In the 20th century, engineering and the manufacture of motor vehicles dominated the industrial landscape. Bathgate Heritage Museum (or Bennie Museum), housed in the oldest row of cottages in the town, tells the story of Bathgate's industrial past. Sir James Young Simpson, who introduced chloroform as an anaesthetic, was born in Bathgate in 1811, as was John Newlands, who bought land and slaves in Jamaica and founded the old Bathgate Academy, now part of West Lothian College of Further Education.

Bathgate Hills *West Lothian* A range of low rolling hills in West Lothian, the Bathgate Hills rise to a height of 305 m (1000 ft) at the Knock and largely comprise ash and lava piled up by volcanic activity during the Carboniferous era over 340 million years ago. In 1998 the oldest known fossil reptile was discovered in the East Kirkton limestone quarry. Ballencrieff Water rises among the hills.

Bauds of Cullen *Moray* An area of heathland between Findochty and Cullen in Moray, the Bauds of Cullen is bounded to the south by the Bauds Wood. The word 'baud' refers to thick broom or whin vegetation.

Baugh *Argyll and Bute* A settlement on the east coast of the island of Tiree in the Inner Hebrides, Baugh lies a mile (1.5 km) southwest of Scarinish and 2 miles (3 km) east of Crossapoll. To the southwest lies Hynish Bay, while to the west is the island's airport.

Bawsinch Nature Reserve *City of Edinburgh* Lying immediately to the south of Duddingston Loch in Edinburgh, the Bawsinch Nature Reserve is managed and partially owned by the Scottish Wildlife Trust. Covering 26 ha (64 acres), the reserve was an industrial wasteland associated with the Innocent Railway and a nearby brewery. It is now designated a Site of Special Scientific Interest (SSSI) and includes trees and scrub together with several small ponds. Hides managed by the trust provide excellent bird-watching over Duddingston Loch.

Baxters Visitor Centre *Moray* Situated in Mosstodloch to the west of Fochabers in Moray, the food-processing and canning factory of Baxters of Speyside produces a famous brand of Royal Game Soup and other delicacies. Originally located in Spey Street, Fochabers, the factory was transferred to Mosstodloch in 1916. A visitor centre, opened in 1986, includes a demonstration theatre, an audio-visual programme and a reconstruction of the original shop.

Bayble *Western Isles* A locality on the southeast coast of the Eye Peninsula of Lewis in the Outer Hebrides, Bayble (Gael: *Phabail* or *Pabail*) is located 6 miles (10 km) east of Stornoway and comprises the hamlets of Upper Bayble (Gael: *Pabail Uarach*) and Lower Bayble (Gael: *Pabail Iarach*), together with a rocky bay divided by a pier into Upper Bayble Bay (Gael: *Bagh Phabail Uarach*) and Lower Bayble Bay (Gael: *Bagh Phabail Iarach*), and Beinn Phabail, which rises to 88 m (288 ft) to the west.

Bayhirivagh An alternative name for Northbay in the Western Isles.

Bayhead *Western Isles* A hamlet on the southwest coast of North Uist in the Outer Hebrides, Bayhead (Gael: *Ceann a' Bhaigh*) lies on an inlet of the same name, 1.25 miles (2 km) north of Kirkibost Island. It is the largest of the settlements that comprise the locality of Paible, and the Gaelic-medium Paible School, which provides primary and secondary education to pupils between the ages of 5 and 14, is located here.

Beacrabhaic The Gaelic name for Beacravik in the Western Isles.

Beacravik *Western Isles* One of a succession of scattered settlements strung along the rocky east coast of South Harris in the Outer Hebrides, Beacravik (Gael: *Beacrabhaic*) lies between Geocrab and Ardslave, 5.5 miles (9 km) northeast of Rodel.

Beag, Gleann *Highland* A valley in Ross-shire, eastern Highland Council area, Gleann Beag lies to the west of Bonar Bridge. It carries the Abhainn a' Ghlinne Bhig northeastwards into Gleann Mòr, where it joins the River Carron.

Beag, Gleann *Highland* A valley to the south of Glenelg in western Highland Council area, Gleann Beag carries a stream westwards into Port a'Gharaidh, an inlet of the Sound of Sleat.

Beag, Gleann *Perth and Kinross* A valley at the head of Glen Shee, in northeast Perth and Kinross, Gleann Beag extends northeast from the Spittal of Glenshee for 5 miles (8 km) to the Cairnwell on the Aberdeenshire border. The A93 follows the route of an old military road through the glen to Braemar, which also contains the Allt a' Ghlinne Bhig, a tributary of the Shee Water.

Beag, Loch *Highland* A small sea loch on the west coast of the island of Skye in the Inner Hebrides, Loch Beag forms an inlet at Bracadale near the mouth of Loch Harport.

Bealach na Ba *Highland* A mountain pass in Wester Ross, the Bealach na Ba (Pass of the Cattle) carries the highest road in Scotland from Loch Kishorn over Meall Gorm to Applecross. It rises to 626 m (2053 ft) above sea level and is characterised by hairpin bends and steep gradients. It offers views to the islands of Skye and Raasay.

Beannach, Loch *Highland* Situated to the south of the Ben Armine Forest in central Sutherland, Loch Beannach lies to the north of the River Brora, 3 miles (5 km) east of Dalnessie.

Beannach, Loch *Highland* A small loch in the Assynt district of western Sutherland, Loch Beannach lies to the west of Loch Assynt, 3 miles (5 km) northeast of Lochinver.

Beannacharain, Loch *Highland* Also known as Loch Beannach, Loch Beannacharain lies on the course of the River Meig in Ross-shire, Highland Council area. Situated in the Strathconan Forest, it lies due west of Inverchoran.

Beannacharan, Loch *Highland* A small deep loch on the course of the River Farrar in Highland Council area, Loch Beannacharan lies in Glen Strathfarrar to the west of Struy.

Bearnaraigh The Gaelic name for Berneray in the Western Isles.

Bearnaraigh The Gaelic name for Great Berneray in the Western Isles.

Bearnock *Highland* A settlement in Glen Urquhart to the west of Loch Ness, Bearnock lies 6 miles (10 km) west of Drumnadrochit.

Bearsden *East Dunbartonshire* A residential suburb of Glasgow, Bearsden lies on the line of the Antonine Wall 5 miles (8 km) northwest of the city centre. The River Kelvin flows to the east and the Forth and Clyde Canal passes to the south. Designated a parliamentary burgh in 1958, it was originally a small kirkton. During the 20th century Bearsden expanded as a residential suburb with rail links to central Glasgow. Buildings of interest include Bearsden Academy, Boclair Academy, the former Canniesburn Hospital and the Schaw Home (now the Lynedoch Nursing Home), which was built in 1895 as a convalescent home for patients from Glasgow Royal Infirmary. The former Notre Dame Roman Catholic Teaching College was renamed St Andrew's College in 1981 and has now been absorbed into the University of Glasgow.

Beattock *Dumfries and Galloway* A former railway village in Annandale, eastern Dumfries and Galloway, Beattock lies on the Evan Water, 2 miles (3 km) southwest of Moffat and 18 miles (29 km) northeast of Dumfries. The number of ancient forts in the neighbourhood testifies to its strategic importance from the Iron Age to medieval times, but its development in more recent times is linked to rail and road transport. The notoriously steep Beattock Bank proved difficult for northbound stagecoaches travelling on Thomas Telford's new road from Carlisle to Glasgow in the early 19th century, and was no less problematic for the steam trains of the Caledonian Railway which followed this route from 1847. Between 1883 and 1954 a branch line from Beattock served the spa town of Moffat, and by 1965 the village had been largely bypassed by the new A74 which was later upgraded to a motorway. Buildings of interest include the parish church (1798), the Beattock Outdoor Centre (1875), Beattock House (1870), 16th-century Lochhouse Tower and the site of a Roman fortlet at Milton, a mile (1.5 km) to the south.

Beaufort Castle *Highland* A Scottish baronial-style mansion in Kiltarlity parish, Easter Ross, Beaufort Castle lies on the right bank of the River Beauly 13 miles (21 km) west of Inverness and commands wide views across the Aird. Built in 1882 and formerly a seat of the Frasers of

Lovat, it is said to be the thirteenth building on the site. Earlier castles were destroyed by Cromwell's forces and the Duke of Cumberland. In 1995 the 24-bedroom castle was bought by Stagecoach bus tycoon Anne Gloag.

Beauly *Highland* Situated amid rich and fertile farmland in Easter Ross, Beauly lies 10 miles (16 km) west of Inverness. With wooded hills as a backdrop and the mouth of the River Beauly opening out into an estuary, Beauly is well named. In 1230 John Bisset established here a priory for the French order of Valliscaulian monks. It was these monks who allegedly named the place 'Beau Lieu' or 'beautiful place'. Remains of the priory survive, and 4 miles (6.5 km) southwest of Beauly stands Beaufort Castle, the former seat of the Frasers of Lovat. About 1760 the Forfeited Estates Commission laid out a new village to house demobilised soldiers. The settlement attracted those cleared from Highland estates and became a market centre for cattle and sheep as well as an outlet for timber. In 1811 Telford's Lovat Bridge across the River Beauly provided access to the far north of Scotland, and in 1862 the railway arrived. Today Beauly is a centre for tourism and craft-based industries.

Beauly, River *Highland* A river in central Highland Council area, the River Beauly is formed by the meeting of the River Glass and the River Farrar at Struy. It meanders northeastwards for 16 miles (26 km) before opening out into the Beauly Firth. There are spectacular falls at Kilmorack, and on its banks stand the town of Beauly and Beaufort Castle.

Beauly Firth *Highland* An inlet of the Moray Firth in Highland Council area, the Beauly Firth forms a basin 7 miles (11 km) long between Inverness and Beauly. It receives the River Beauly entering at its western end and the Caledonian Canal at its mouth.

Bedrule *Scottish Borders* A village of Teviotdale in Scottish Borders, Bedrule lies on the Rule Water, 4 miles (6.5 km) southwest of Jedburgh. Nearby are the remains of a stronghold of the Turnbulls.

Bee, Loch *Western Isles* A large inland loch located at the north end of South Uist in the Outer Hebrides, Loch Bee (Gael: *Loch Bi*) has many small islets and is crossed by a causeway. This was originally constructed in the 18th century, but now carries the A865 which connects the islands of North Uist and Benbecula with South Uist. The loch is separated from the sea by flood gates opening into Loch Sheilavaig, to the southeast, and at Clachan, to the north.

Beecraigs Country Park *West Lothian* A country park in the Bathgate Hills offering a wide range of leisure and recreational facilities, Beecraigs lies 2 miles (3 km) south of Linlithgow. Occupying over 370 ha (913 acres) of woodland, water and open spaces, its highest point is Cockleroy Hill (Hill of Kings).

Beeswing *Dumfries and Galloway* A hamlet in New Abbey parish, southern Dumfries and Galloway, Beeswing lies between Loch Arthur and a stream known as the Kirkgunzeon Lane, midway between Dumfries and Dalbeattie. Formerly known as Lochend, the village took its present name from an inn that was bought in the mid-19th century by local racehorse owner Robert Orde. Orde renamed the Lochend Inn after Beeswing, a championship racehorse that won 51 races in eight seasons. The village eventually came to be known by that name, although the church is still called Lochend Church.

Beg, Loch *Argyll and Bute* A small loch on the southwest coast of the island of Mull in the Inner Hebrides, Loch Beg forms a bay sheltered by the Aird of Kinloch at the head of Loch Scridain. The Coladoir River empties into Loch Beg at a point known as An Leth-onn, an area of marshlands and pebble beaches.

Beich Burn *Stirling* The Beich Burn rises in the hills between Loch Tay and Loch Earn. It flows 6 miles (10 km) southwestwards through Glen Beich before entering Loch Earn at Dalveich.

Bein Inn *Perth and Kinross* A noted hostelry in southern Perth and Kinross dating from the days of coaching, the Bein Inn lies in the wooded valley of Glen Farg on the old Great North Road midway between Milnathort and Perth, at its junction with a road leading over the hill past Balvaird Castle to Gateside in Fife.

Beinn a' Bheithir *Highland* The horseshoe-shaped ridge of Beinn a' Bheithir (Ben Vair) is situated in the Lochaber district of southwest Highland Council area to the southwest of Ballachulish. Its highest peak is Sgorr Dhearg, which rises to 1024 m (3359 ft). To the west is Sgorr Dhonuill (1001 m/3284 ft).

Beinn a' Bhuird *Aberdeenshire* The 'table hill' of Beinn a' Bhuird forms a large plateau in the centre of the Grampians to the southeast of Glen Avon on the border between Aberdeenshire and Moray Council areas. Its North Top rises to a height of 1197 m (3927 ft), while its South Top reaches 1179 m (3867 ft).

Beinn a' Chàisgein Beag *Highland* A mountain in Wester Ross, Beinn a' Chàisgein Beag rises to 680 m (2230 ft) between Fionn Loch and Loch na Sealga. Beinn a' Chàisgein Mòr rises 3 miles (5 km) to the south.

Beinn a' Chàisgein Mòr *Highland* A mountain in Wester Ross, Beinn a' Chàisgein Mòr rises to 857 m (2811 ft) between Fionn Loch and Loch na Sealga. Beinn a' Chàisgein Beag rises 3 miles (5 km) to the north.

Beinn a' Chaisteil *Highland* A mountain in Easter Ross, Beinn a' Chaisteil rises to 787 m (2582 ft) 2 miles (3 km) east of the head of Loch Vaich.

Beinn a' Chaolais *Argyll and Bute* The smallest of the Paps of Jura, Beinn a' Chaolais rises to a height of 734 m (2408 ft) at the western end of the range.

Beinn a' Chaorainn *Aberdeenshire/Angus* A cone-shaped summit in the Grampians, Beinn a' Chaorainn rises to 1083 m (3552 ft) to the south of Glen Avon. It is connected to Beinn Bhreac, 3 miles (5 km) to the south, by a vast medium-level plateau originally called Mòine Bhealaidh but now referred to as Yalla Moss.

Beinn a' Chaorainn *Highland* Beinn a' Chaorainn rises to 1049 m (3442 ft) to the northeast of Loch Moy in the Lochaber district of Highland Council area. Its summit has three tops, the middle one being the highest.

Beinn a' Charnain *Western Isles* Rising to 196 m (446 ft), Beinn a' Charnain is the highest peak on the island of Pabbay in the Western Isles.

Beinn a' Chlachair *Highland* Beinn a' Chlachair rises to 1087 m (3566 ft) to the south of Loch Laggan in Badenoch. Its name is derived from the Gaelic for the 'stonemason's hill'.

Beinn a' Chlaidheimh *Highland* A sandstone mountain to the north of Kinlochewe in Wester Ross, Beinn a' Chlaidheimh rises to a height of 916 m (3005 ft). Its name is derived from the Gaelic for 'hill of the sword'.

Beinn a' Chleibh *Stirling/Argyll and Bute* A mountain to the southwest of Ben Lui, on the border between Stirling and Argyll and Bute Council areas, Beinn a' Chleibh rises to 916 m (3005 ft).

Beinn a' Chochuill *Argyll and Bute* A mountain to the east of Loch Etive, Beinn a' Chochuill rises to 980 m (3215 ft). Its name is derived from the Gaelic for 'hill of the hood'.

Beinn a' Chreachain *Perth and Kinross* Rising to 1081 m (3547 ft) to the north of Loch Lyon in western Perth and Kinross, Beinn a' Chreachain is the highest peak in the Bridge of Orchy range.

Beinn a' Chroin *Stirling* A mountain in northwest Stirling Council area, Beinn a' Chroin rises to 940 m (3084 ft) to the south of Crianlarich. Its summit is located at the eastern end of a half-mile/1-km-long ridge and its name is derived from the Gaelic for 'hill of danger'.

Beinn a' Ghlo *Perth and Kinross* A mountain massif in the southern Grampians, Beinn a' Ghlo rises to the northeast of Blair Atholl, in highland Perth and Kinross. Its highest peak is Carn nan Gabhar which rises to 1129 m (3704 ft) to the south of Glen Tilt. Other tops to the southwest are Braigh Coire Chruinn-bhalgain (1069 m/3507 ft) and Carn Liath (975 m/3199 ft).

Beinn a' Mhanaich *Argyll and Bute* Beinn a' Mhanaich rises to a height of 709 m (2326 ft) 3 miles (5 km) northeast of Garelochead.

Beinn Achaladair *Perth and Kinross/Argyll and Bute* A mountain to the south of Rannoch Moor, Beinn Achaladair (Achallader) rises to 1038 m (3406 ft) to the east of Loch Tulla on the border of Perth and Kinross and Argyll and Bute.

Beinn Alligin *Highland* A mountain in Wester Ross, Beinn Alligin rises about 2 miles (3 km) to the north of Upper Loch Torridon. It comprises two peaks: Sgurr Mhòr (985 m/3231 ft) and Tom na Gruagaich (920 m/3018 ft).

Beinn an Armuinne The Gaelic name for Ben Armine in Highland.

Beinn an Dothaidh *Argyll and Bute* Forming the continuation of a ridge that extends northwards from Beinn Dorain, Beinn an Dothaidh rises to 1004 m (3294 ft) to the east of Bridge of Orchy.

Beinn an Eoin *Highland* A mountain ridge in Wester Ross, Beinn an Eoin rises to 855 m (2804 ft) 5 miles (8 km) from the head of Upper Loch Torridon.

Beinn an Eoin *Highland* A mountain in central Sutherland, Beinn an Eoin rises to 544 m (1784 ft) 4 miles (6.5 km) north of Oykel Bridge.

Beinn an Oir *Argyll and Bute* Rising to a height of 785 m (2571 ft) on the island of Jura in the Inner Hebrides, Beinn an Oir is the highest of the peaks of the Paps of Jura, which also include Beinn Shiantaidh and Beinn a' Chaolais.

Beinn an Tuirc *Argyll and Bute* The highest peak on the Kintyre peninsula, Beinn an Tuirc rises to 454 m (1491 ft) on the southern edge of the Carradale Forest, 4 miles (6.5 km) to the southwest of the settlement of Carradale. A 680-ha (1680-acre) wind farm comprising 50 turbines was established on the hill in 2002.

Beinn Bhalgairean *Argyll and Bute* A mountain rising to 636 m (2086 ft) 3 miles (5 km) southeast of Dalmally, Beinn Bhalgairean is the source of the Teatle Water and tributaries of the River Fyne.

Beinn Bhàn *Argyll and Bute* A mountain ridge of Islay, Argyll and Bute, Beinn Bhàn is located in the southern half of the island, 8 miles (13 km) northeast of Port Ellen. It reaches a height of 471 m (1545 ft) at a cairn located at the northeastern end of the ridge.

Beinn Bhàn *Highland* A mountain in Wester Ross, Beinn Bhàn rises to 896 m (2939 ft), 6 miles (10 km) south of Shieldaig and 5 miles (8 km) east of Applecross.

Beinn Bhàn *Highland* A mountain in Lochaber, Beinn Bhàn rises to 796 m (2611 ft), 3 miles (5 km) west of the southwest end of Loch Lochy.

Beinn Bhàn *Highland* A mountain in Morvern, Beinn Bhàn rises to 400 m (1312 ft), 3 miles (5 km) north of Lochaline. It is surrounded by Fiunary Forest.

Beinn Bharrain The Gaelic name for Ben Varren in North Ayrshire.

Beinn Bheag *Argyll and Bute* A mountain on the Cowal peninsula, Beinn Bheag rises to 618 m (2027 ft) in the Argyll Forest Park to the west of Lock Eck.

Beinn Bheag *Highland* A mountain in the Lochalsh district of Highland Council area, Beinn Bheag rises to 619 m (2030 ft) 2 miles (3 km) southwest of Loch Monar.

Beinn Bheag *Highland* Twin summits in Wester Ross, Beinn Bheag rises 7 miles (11 km) northeast of Kinlochewe and 3 miles (5 km) east of Lochan Fada. The eastern summit is the taller, reaching a height of 668 m (2191 ft), while the western summit rises to 615 m (2017 ft).

Beinn Bheigeir *Argyll and Bute* The highest peak on the island of Islay in the Inner Hebrides, Beinn Bheigeir rises to of 491 m (1610 ft) 3 miles (5 km) southwest of McArthur's Head, which lies on the island's east coast, and 6 miles (10 km) north of Ardbeg.

Beinn Bheoil *Highland* A mountain in Badenoch, Beinn Bheoil rises to 1019 m (3343 ft) to the west of Loch Ericht. Its name is derived from the Gaelic for 'hill of the mouth'.

Beinn Bhreac *Aberdeenshire* Rising to a height of 931 m (3054 ft) to the east of Glen Derry in the Grampians of western Aberdeenshire, the summit of Beinn Bhreac is covered by peat bogs, turf and endless pools of water, giving rise to its name which is derived from the Gaelic for 'speckled hill'. It is connected to Beinn a' Chaorainn by a vast medium-level plateau originally called Mòine Bhealaidh, but now referred to as Yalla Moss.

Beinn Bhreac *Argyll and Bute* Beinn Bhreac rises to a height of 467 m (1532 ft) at the northern end of the island of Jura in the Inner Hebrides, 4 miles (6.5 km) northwest of the settlement of Lussagiven.

Beinn Bhreac *Highland* A ridge on the island of Skye in the Inner Hebrides, Beinn Bhreac rises to 329 m (1079 ft) 3 miles (5 km) northwest of the settlement of Dunvegan. A lower northern summit reaches 314 m (1030 ft).

Beinn Bhreac *Highland* A mountain in Wester Ross, Beinn Bhreac rises to 624 m (2047 ft) 3 miles (5 km) northwest of Beinn Alligin and 6 miles (10 km) north of Shieldaig.

Beinn Bhrotain *Aberdeenshire* The granite peak of Beinn Bhrotain rises to a height of 1157 m (3796 ft) to the west of Glen Dee in the Grampians, western Aberdeenshire. It is connected by a col called Adha nam Fiann to the neighbouring mountain, Monadh Mòr. East of the summit there is a large expanse of sandy gravel almost devoid of vegetation, although rare arctic-alpine plants can be found near the cliffs at An Garbh Choire. The name of the peak is derived from the Gaelic for 'hill of (the mastiff) Brotan'.

Beinn Bhuidhe *Argyll and Bute* A mountain to the north of Loch Fyne in Argyll and Bute, the isolated peak of Beinn Bhuidhe rises to 948 m (3110 ft). Its name is derived from the Gaelic for 'yellow hill'.

Beinn Bhuidhe *Argyll and Bute* Beinn Bhuidhe rises to 412 m (1351 ft) 3 miles (5 km) southeast of the settlement of Salen, on the island of Mull in the Inner Hebrides. It forms part of a chain that includes Beinn na h-Uamha to the west and Beinn na Lus to the east.

Beinn Bhuidhe Mhòr *Highland* Beinn Bhuidhe Mhòr rises to 548 m (1797 ft) 4 miles (6.5 km) east of the settlement of Daviot in the Inverness district of Highland Council area.

Beinn Ceitlein *Highland* A sizeable mountain mass located to the south of Glen Etive in southern Highland Council area, Beinn Ceitlein rises to 832 m (2729 ft) 5 miles (8 km) northeast of the head of Loch Etive.

Beinn Chabhair *Stirling* A mountain in northwest Stirling Council area, Beinn Chabhair rises to 933 m (3061 ft) to the northeast of Loch Lomond. Its name is derived from the Gaelic for 'hill of the hawk'.

Beinn Chaluim The Gaelic name for Ben Challum in Stirling Council area.

Beinn Cheathaich *Stirling* A peak in the Breadalbane Hills, northwest Stirling Council area, Beinn Cheathaich rises to 937 m (3074 ft) between Glen Dochart and Glen Lochay.

Beinn Chlianaig *Highland* Beinn Chlianaig rises to a height of 721 m (2365 ft) to the south of Glen Spean in the Lochaber district, 2 miles (3 km) southeast of Roybridge, between the River Spean and Allt Laire, both of which flow into Loch Moy.

Beinn Cleith Bric The Gaelic name for Ben Klibreck in Highland.

Beinn Damh The Gaelic name for Ben Damph in Highland.

Beinn Dearg *Highland* A mountain in Wester Ross, Beinn Dearg rises to 914 m (2998 ft) 3 miles (5 km) north of the head of Upper Loch Torridon.

Beinn Dearg *Highland* Beinn Dearg rises to a height of 1084 m (3556 ft) in Wester Ross, 6 miles (10 km) southeast of the head of Loch Broom. The peaks of Meall nan Ceapraichean and Eididh nan Clach Geala rise to the north and Cona' Mheall to the east.

Beinn Dearg *Highland* A summit in northwest Sutherland, Beinn Dearg rises to 423 m (1387 ft) 6 miles (10 km) south of Cape Wrath.

Beinn Dearg *Perth and Kinross* A peak in the southern Grampians, Beinn Dearg rises to 1008 m (3307 ft) to the west of Glen Tilt in highland Perth and Kinross. On the route to the summit there are a number of cairns, some of which have historical references. The Lady March Cairn, which Lady March is reported to have initiated in the 19th century during a picnic lunch, is now over 2 m (6.5 ft) high. The Carn Mhic Shimidh, further up the mountain, commemorates a battle between the Murrays of Atholl and the intruding Frasers. The cairn marks the spot where Simon Lovat, chief of the Frasers, was killed. The name Beinn Dearg is derived from the Gaelic for 'red hill', which alludes to the reddish screes on the flanks of the mountain.

Beinn Dearg Mhòr *Highland* A mountain in Wester Ross, Beinn Dearg Mhòr rises to 908 m (2978 ft) in the Fisherfield Forest 4 miles (6.5 km) southwest of An Teallach. Loch na Sealga is 2 miles (3 km) northeast.

Beinn Dhorain *Highland* Beinn Dhorain rises to a height of 626 m (2060 ft) 3 miles (5 km) north of the settlement of Lothbeg near the east coast of Sutherland. The Glen Loth River rises on its slopes.

Beinn Dorainn *Argyll and Bute* A prominent conical mountain in northeast Argyll and Bute, Beinn Dorainn rises to 1076 m (3530 ft) to the southeast of the Bridge of Orchy.

Beinn Dronaig *Highland* Beinn Dronaig rises to a height of 796 m (2611 ft) on the southwestern side of Loch Calavie, in the Lochalsh district of Highland Council area. To the west lies the Attadale Forest.

Beinn Dubhchraig *Stirling* Rising to a height of 978 m (3209 ft) in the Tyndrum Hills to the west of Crianlarich in Stirling Council area, Beinn Dubhchraig is an eastward extension of Ben Lui. It has a steep southern face with broken crags below its level summit ridge, and its name is derived from the Gaelic for 'black rock hill'.

Beinn Each *Stirling* Located 5 miles (8 km) northwest of Callander, in western Stirling Council area, the mountain range of Beinn Each reaches a height of 810 m (2660 ft).

Beinn Edra *Highland* A mountain on the island of Skye in the Inner Hebrides, Beinn Edra rises to 611 m (2004 ft) on the Trotternish peninsula, 3 miles (5 km) east of Uig and 3 miles (5 km) west of the headland of Rubha nam Brathairean.

Beinn Eibhinn *Highland* Rising to a height of 1101 m (3611 ft) 2 miles (3 km) east of Loch Guilbinn on the border between the districts of Lochaber and Badenoch, Beinn Eibhinn forms a continuous ridge with the peaks of Aonach Beag (1114 m/3655 ft) and Gael Charn (1132 m/3714 ft).

Beinn Eighe *Highland* A mountain mass in Wester Ross, Beinn Eighe rises to a height of 1010 m (3313 ft) to the south of Loch Maree. Its highest peak is named Ruadh-stac Mòr, and a subsidiary peak to the southwest, Sàil Mhòr, rises to 981 m (3219 ft). In 1951, Beinn Eighe was designated the UK's first national nature reserve.

Beinn Eunaich *Argyll and Bute* A mountain in Argyll and Bute, Beinn Eunaich rises to 989 m (3245 ft) on the ridge connecting Loch Etive to Glen Strae. A band of porphyry on the northeast shoulder of this peak interrupts the granite of which the main mass of the mountain is composed. Its name is thought to be derived from the Gaelic for a 'fowling hill'.

Beinn Fhada *Highland* Beinn Fhada (also known as Ben Attow) rises to a height of 1032 m (3386 ft) to the north of the Five Sisters of Kintail. Its name is derived from the Gaelic for 'long hill', which seems appropriate since it stretches for 5 miles (8 km), a distance equivalent to the length of the Five Sisters.

Beinn Fhada *Highland* A mountain mass lying to the south of Glen Coe, Beinn Fhada is the easternmost of the Three Sisters and comprises multiple tops located along a ridge, the highest reaching 931 m (3054 ft). Following the ridge to the southwest, climbers reach Stob Coire Sgreamhach (1072 m/3517 ft), and turning to the northwest the ridge continues to the mass of Bidean nam Bian (1150 m/3773 ft), the highest mountain in the range.

Beinn Fhionnlaidh *Argyll and Bute* Rising to a height of 959 m (3146 ft) at the head of Loch Etive in Argyll and Bute, Beinn Fhionnlaidh forms a 4-mile (6.5-km) ridge running east to west. The ridge itself is bare, with numerous boulders, erratics and multiple false summits. Its name is derived from the Gaelic for 'Finlay's Hill'.

Beinn Fhionnlaidh *Highland* A remote mountain peak at the head of Glen Cannich, Beinn Fhionnlaidh rises to 1005 m (3297 ft) to the south of Loch Mullardoch. Its summit is topped by a large circular cairn that was used as a benchmark by the Ordnance Survey in the 1840s.

Beinn Freiceadain *Highland* A hill of north-central Caithness, Beinn Freiceadain overlooks Loch Shurrery from the east, 2.5 miles (4 km) west of Scotscalder station. It rises to 238 m (780 ft). A large Iron Age hillfort lies on its summit, representing the most northerly hillfort of any size on the British mainland.

Beinn Ghlas *Perth and Kinross* A summit to the north of Loch Tay in west Perth and Kinross, Beinn Ghlas (Ben Glas) rises to 1103 m (3619 ft) on the southwest shoulder of Ben Lawers. Its name is derived from the Gaelic for 'green-grey hill'.

Beinn Ghobhlach *Highland* A mountain in Wester Ross, Beinn Ghobhlach rises to 635 m (2083 ft) on the headland between Loch Broom and Little Loch Broom, 5 miles (8 km) west of Ullapool.

Beinn Ghuilean *Argyll and Bute* A hill on the Kintyre peninsula 2 miles (3 km) south-southeast of Campbeltown, Beinn Ghuilean rises to 352 m (1155 ft) and offers views over Campbeltown Loch, Davaar Island, the Kilbrannan Sound and the Firth of Clyde.

Beinn Heasgarnich *Perth and Kinross* A mountain in Breadalbane, western Perth and Kinross, Beinn Heasgarnich rises to 1078 m (3537 ft) in the Glen Lochay hills between Loch Lyon and the Forest of Mamlorn.

Beinn Iadain *Highland* A peak on the Morvern peninsula, Beinn Iadain rises to 571 m (1873 ft) 7 miles (11 km) north of Lochaline and 3 miles (5 km) south of Loch Sunart.

Beinn Ime *Argyll and Bute* A mountain to the north of the Cowal peninsula, Beinn Ime is the highest of the Arrochar Alps. Rising to 1011 m (3317 ft) to the north of Ben Arthur (The Cobbler), it has a large cairn on its summit. The north and east flanks leading to the summit are steep and rugged, while the southern flank in contrast is grassy. Its name is derived from the Gaelic for 'butter hill'.

Beinn Iutharn Mhòr *Aberdeenshire/Perth and Kinross* A summit in the southeast Grampians, Beinn Iutharn Mhòr rises to 1045 m (3428 ft) to the southwest of Braemar, on the border between Aberdeenshire and Perth and Kinross. Its name is derived from the Gaelic for 'big hill of the edge'.

Beinn Làir *Highland* A mountain in Wester Ross, Beinn Làir rises to 860 m (2821 ft) in the Letterewe Forest a mile (1.5 km) west of the head of Lochan Fada and 2 miles (3 km) south of Fionn Loch.

Beinn Laoghall The Gaelic name for Ben Loyal in Highland.

Beinn Laoigh The Gaelic name for Ben Lui in Stirling Council area.

Beinn Leoid *Highland* Beinn Leoid (*Ben Leoid*) rises to a height of 792 m (2598 ft) 6 miles (10 km) northeast of the settlement of Inchnadamph and 6 miles (10 km) southeast of Unapool in northwest Sutherland.

Beinn Liath Mhòr *Highland* Located southeast of Torridon in Wester Ross, Beinn Liath Mhòr rises to a height of 925 m (3034 ft) in the Coulin Forest. The summit ridge of this peak is very long and curved and is composed of quartzite. The summit is at the northern end. The name is the Gaelic for 'big grey hill'.

Beinn Liath Mhòr Fannaich *Highland* A summit to the east of the main Fannich ridge in Wester Ross, Beinn Liath Mhòr Fannaich rises to 954 m (3129 ft) to the north of Loch Fannich. Its name is derived from the Gaelic for 'big grey hill of Fannich'.

Beinn Lochain *Argyll and Bute* A mountain range on the Cowal peninsula, Beinn Lochain rises to 703 m (2306 ft) 3 miles (5 km) west of Lochgoilhead. It commands views to the east of Loch Goil and to the south towards the Argyll Forest Park.

Beinn Mhanach *Perth and Kinross* Beinn Mhanach rises to a height of 953 m (3127 ft) between the Orchy Hills and Loch Lyon in western Perth and Kinross. Its name is derived from the Gaelic for 'monk hill'.

Beinn Mheadhoin *Moray* A summit in the Cairngorm Mountains, Beinn Mheadhoin rises to 1182 m (3878 ft) to the southeast of Loch Etchachan and to the northeast of Ben Macdui. Its summit is capped by a large granite tor with a cairn. Its name is thought to derive from the Gaelic for 'middle hill'.

Beinn Mheadhonach *Western Isles* A hill in the Outer Hebrides, Beinn Mheadhonach rises to 397 m (1302 ft) on the Isle of Lewis, a mile (1.5 km) south of Loch Grunavat and 4 miles (6.5 km) north of the head of Loch Resort.

Beinn Mhealaich *Highland* A summit in eastern Sutherland, Beinn Mhealaich rises to 592 m (1942 ft) 4 miles (6.5 km) west of Helmsdale. It is the source of the River Loth, which flows through Glen Loth to meet the North Sea at Lothbeg Point.

Beinn Mhòr *Argyll and Bute* A mountain on the Cowal peninsula, Beinn Mhòr rises to 741 m (2430 ft) in the heart of the Argyll Forest Park, 2 miles (3 km) west of Loch Eck. It offers views over Loch Eck, Loch Tarsan and south towards the island of Bute.

Beinn Mhòr *Western Isles* A peak on the island of South Uist in the Outer Hebrides, Beinn Mhòr forms a northwest-to-southeast ridge rising to 620 m (2034 ft), 2 miles (3 km) north of Loch Eynort. It has a lower top of 608 m (1995 ft) to the northwest.

Beinn Mhòr *Western Isles* A mountain in the Outer Hebrides, Beinn Mhòr rises to 572 m (1876 ft) in the Park district of southeast Lewis. It overlooks the sea lochs of Seaforth, Claidh and Shell.

Beinn na Caillich *Highland* Beinn na Caillich is a peak of southeast Skye, in Highland Council area. Located 2 miles (3 km) southeast of Kyleakin, it reaches a height of 733 m (2404 ft) and offers views over Loch Alsh. To the southwest rises the peak of Sgurr na Coinnich. Another Beinn na Caillich, of almost the same height, lies 11 miles (18 km) to the west.

Beinn na Caillich *Highland* A Graham peak located towards the centre of the isle of Skye, in Highland Council area, Beinn na Caillich rises to 732 m (2401 ft) 2.5 miles (4 km) west of Broadford. The mountain is linked to Beinn Dearg Mhòr (709 m/2325 ft) by a high pass. Another Beinn na Caillich is located 11 miles (18 km) to the east.

Beinn na Faoghla The Gaelic name for Benbecula in the Western Isles.

Beinn na h-Uamha *Argyll and Bute* A top of the Beinn Bhuidhe mountain range on the island of Mull, Beinn na h-Uamha rises to 386 m (1266 ft) 3 miles (5 km) southeast of Salen.

Beinn na Lap *Highland* Beinn na Lap rises to a height of 935 m (3068 ft) to the north of Loch Ossian in the Lochaber district of Highland Council area. Its name is derived from the Gaelic for 'mottled hill'.

Beinn na' Leac *Highland* A hill on the island of Raasay in the Inner Hebrides, Beinn na' Leac rises to 319 m (1046 ft) 2 miles (3 km) northeast of East Suisnish. It offers views over the Inner Sound.

Beinn na Lus *Argyll and Bute* A top on the Beinn Bhuidhe range on the island of Mull in the Inner Hebrides, Beinn na Lus rises to 408 m (1339 ft) 3 miles (5 km) southeast of Salen.

Beinn na Seilg *Highland* A summit on the Ardnamurchan peninsula, Beinn na Seilg rises to 342 m (1122 ft) 2 miles (3 km) west of the settlement of Kilchoan.

Beinn nam Bad Mòr *Highland* A hill in northern Caithness, Beinn nam Bad Mòr rises to 290 m (951 ft) between Loch Scye and Loch Caluim to the south of Dounreay.

Beinn nan Aighenan *Argyll and Bute* Beinn nan Aighenan rises to a height of 960 m (3150 ft) to the southeast of the head of Loch Etive in northeast Argyll and Bute. Its name is derived from the Gaelic for 'hill of the hinds'.

Beinn nan Eun *Highland* A mountain in Easter Ross, Beinn nan Eun rises to 742 m (2434 ft) 5 miles (8 km) north of Ben Wyvis.

Beinn nan Ramh *Highland* A mountain in Wester Ross, Beinn nan Ramh rises to 711 m (2332 ft) 8 miles (13 km) northeast of Kinlochewe. Loch Fannich lies 2 miles (3 km) to the east.

Beinn Narnain *Argyll and Bute* A mountain in the Arrochar Alps to the northwest of Loch Long, Beinn Narnain rises to 926 m (3038 ft). It has a level plateau summit with a triangulation point, and its name is derived from the Gaelic for 'middle hill'.

Beinn Odhar *Argyll and Bute/Stirling* A mountain on the border between Argyll and Bute and Stirling Council areas, Beinn Odhar rises to 901 m (2955 ft) to the south of Beinn Dorain and north of the settlements of Clifton and Tyndrum.

Beinn Reithe *Argyll and Bute* A summit on the Cowal peninsula, Beinn Reithe rises to 653 m (2142 ft) 3 miles (5 km) southeast of Lochgoilhead.

Beinn Resipol *Highland* A mountain in Sunart, Beinn Resipol rises to 845 m (2774 ft) between Loch Sunart and Loch Shiel

Beinn Sgeireach *Highland* A mountain in northern Sutherland, Beinn Sgeireach rises to 476 m (1562 ft) 7 miles (11 km) northwest of Lairg and 3 miles (5 km) west of Loch Shin.

Beinn Sgreamhaidh *Highland* Beinn Sgreamhaidh rises to a height of 435 m (1427 ft) 2 miles (3 km) west of Loch Shin and a mile (1.5 km) south of Strath an Loin in the Sutherland district of Highland Council area.

Beinn Sgritheall An alternative name for Ben Screel in Highland.

Beinn Sgulaird *Argyll and Bute* A granite mountain in the Benderloch district of northern Argyll and Bute, Beinn Sgulaird rises to 937 m (3074 ft) to the east of Loch Creran and south of Glen Ure.

Beinn Shiantaidh *Argyll and Bute* The second-largest of the Paps of Jura, Beinn Shiantaidh rises to a height of 755 m (2476 ft) at the east end of the range.

Beinn Smeoral *Highland* Beinn Smeoral rises to a height of 486 m (1594 ft) 6 miles (10 km) northwest of Brora, on the east coast of Sutherland district.

Beinn Spionnaidh *Highland* Beinn Spionnaidh rises to a height of 772 m (2532 ft) at the head of Loch Eriboll, 2 miles (3 km) northwest of the settlement of Polla, in northern Sutherland.

Beinn Stumanadh *Highland* Beinn Stumanadh rises to a height of 527 m (1729 ft) a mile (1.5 km) east of Loch Loyal in northern Sutherland. To the northeast is the Borgie Forest.

Beinn Suidhe *Argyll and Bute* Beinn Suidhe rises to a height of 675 m (2214 ft) 6 miles (10 km) west of Bridge of Orchy and a mile (1.5 km) south of Loch Dochard.

Beinn Talaidh *Argyll and Bute* A mountain at the centre of the island of Mull in the Inner Hebrides, Beinn Talaidh rises to 761 m (2496 ft) 5.5 miles (9 km) west of Craignure and 6 miles (10 km) north of Lochbuie.

Beinn Tarsuinn *North Ayrshire* A mountain on the island of Arran, Beinn Tarsuinn rises to 825 m (2706 ft) 5 miles (8 km) northwest of Brodick. It is one of two mountains on the island by the same name, the other rising to 554 m (1817 ft) 4 miles (6.5 km) south of Lochranza.

Beinn Tarsuinn *Highland* A remote peak capped with quartzite in Wester Ross, Beinn Tarsuinn rises to 936 m (3071 ft) 7 miles (11 km) north of Kinlochewe. Its name is derived from the Gaelic for 'transverse hill'.

Beinn Teallach *Highland* Beinn Teallach rises to a height of 915 m (3001 ft) to the north of Loch Moy in Lochaber. Its eastern and northern corries are steep-sided, in contrast to the southern and western corries which have gentler slopes. Its name is derived from the Gaelic for 'forge hill'.

Beinn Tharsuinn *Highland* A mountain ridge in the West Monar Forest, Beinn Tharsuinn lies 9 miles (14 km) southwest of Achnasheen and has three summits at 795 m (2608 ft), 817 m (2680 ft) and 863 m (2831 ft).

Beinn Tharsuinn *Highland* A mountain in Easter Ross, Beinn Tharsuinn rises to 692 m (2270 ft) 8 miles (13 km) south of Bonar Bridge and 6 miles (10 km) northwest of Alness.

Beinn Tharsuinn *Highland* A mountain in southern Sutherland, Beinn Tharsuinn rises to 714 m (2342 ft) 13 miles (21 km) north of Garve and immediately west of Diebidale Forest.

Beinn Tighe *Highland* The second-highest peak on the island of Eigg in the Small Isles, Beinn Tighe rises to 315 m (1033 ft) a mile (1.5 km) southeast of the headland of Rubha an Fhasaidh.

Beinn Trilleachan *Argyll and Bute/Highland* A mountain on the border between Argyll and Bute and Highland Council areas, Beinn Trilleachan rises to 839 m (2752 ft) to the north of Loch Etive and southwest of Beinn Sgulaird.

Beinn Tulaichean *Stirling* A mountain in northwest Stirling Council area, Beinn Tulaichean rises to 946 m (3104 ft) to the southeast of Crianlarich. It forms a long north-south ridge with Cruach Arsrain and is generally regarded as a peak of the latter rather than a separate mountain. Its name is derived from the Gaelic for 'hill of the hillocks'.

Beinn Udlaidh *Argyll and Bute* A mountain in northeast

Argyll and Bute, Beinn Udlaidh rises to 840 m (2755 ft) 4 miles (6.5 km) northwest of Tyndrum and 5 miles (8 km) south of Bridge of Orchy. It commands views of Glen Orchy to the north.

Beinn Udlamain *Perth and Kinross* The highest of the Drumochter mountains in highland Perth and Kinross, the plateau summit of Beinn Udlamain rises to 1011 m (3317 ft) to the east of Loch Ericht. On the ridge to the summit, a line of fence posts marks the boundary between the former counties of Perthshire and Inverness-shire. Its name is derived from the Gaelic for 'gloomy mountain'.

Beinn Uidhe *Highland* A mountain in the Assynt district of western Sutherland, Beinn Uidhe rises to 740 m (2427 ft) 3 miles (5 km) northeast of Inchnadamph.

Beinn Ulbhaidh *Highland* A mountain with three summits in Sutherland, Beinn Ulbhaidh rises to 493 m (1617 ft) to the south of Strath Oykel.

Beinne Bàine, Loch na *Highland* A small loch in Highland Council area, Loch na Beinne Bàine lies between Glen Moriston and Glen Affric. It is the source of a headwater of the River Glass.

Beith *North Ayrshire* The small textile town of Beith is situated 19 miles (31 km) southwest of Glasgow and to the east of Kilbirnie Loch. Its industries have included the manufacture of golf clubs, furniture, fishing nets, thread and plastics. Dairy farming, engineering and quarrying have also been important industries. It is served by railway stations at Glengarnock and Lochwinnoch.

Beldorney Castle *Aberdeenshire* A 16th-century Z-shaped castle, Beldorney Castle lies west of the River Deveron, in northwest Aberdeenshire, close to the border with Moray, 6 miles (10 km) west of Huntly and a similar distance east of Dufftown. Originally a stronghold of the Ogilvies, the castle has passed through the hands of the Gordon, Lyon, Buchan and Grant families. It was modernised in the 19th century and restored in the 20th century and remains in domestic use.

Belhaven *East Lothian* A western part of the settlement of Dunbar in East Lothian, Belhaven lies at the eastern end of Belhaven Bay. The Belhaven Brewery was founded in 1719 and remains the oldest surviving independent brewery in Scotland and one of the oldest in Britain. It is likely that brewing was originally carried out by Benedictine monks on the land around 'Bele' (now Belhaven) granted to them by King David I (c.1080–1153). Remains within the current buildings suggest a brewery existed on the site from at least the 16th century and records show that Belhaven ale was supplied to soldiers garrisoned at nearby Dunbar Castle in the 1550s. On tasting the ale as he passed through the area, James Boswell (1740–95) noted that it was 'the best small beer I ever had'. Although primarily serving the local population, the beer had, by the 19th century, established a reputation as far afield as London and even Vienna, where it found favour with the Austrian emperor. The brewery buildings were reconstructed after fires in 1814 and 1887.

Belhaven Bay *East Lothian* An inlet of the North Sea on the coast of East Lothian, Belhaven Bay is located to the west of the settlements of Belhaven and Dunbar. The River Tyne flows into the bay, and the John Muir Country Park extends along its coastline.

Belhelvie *Aberdeenshire* A village in the eastern Aberdeenshire parish of the same name, Belhelvie lies to the west of Balmedie, 7 miles (11 km) north of Aberdeen. The village was home to the Revd Alexander Forsyth (1769–1848), parish minister and inventor of the percussion cap.

Bellabeg *Aberdeenshire* A small roadside settlement in Strathdon, western Aberdeenshire, Bellabeg lies on the north side of the River Don opposite the village of Strathdon. The Lonach Highland Gathering and Games are held annually in the Bellabeg Park on the fourth Saturday in August. On the day of the Gathering the Men of Lonach in full Highland dress and carrying pikes and Lochaber battle-axes march to the park, visiting the homes of the Patrons of the Gathering en route. The event concludes in the evening with the Lonach Highland Ball.

Belladrum *Highland* A locality in the Aird, Easter Ross, Belladrum lies 3 miles (5 km) south of Beauly.

Bellahouston Park *Glasgow City* An area of parkland in Glasgow, Bellahouston Park lies to the south of Govan and the M8. It occupies an area of 71 ha (175 acres) and was the site of the 1938 Empire Exhibition which was attended by over 13 million visitors. The 91-m/300-ft-tall Tait Tower was to be a permanent reminder of the exhibition for the people of Glasgow, but with the onset of World War II it was demolished. Little evidence of the exhibition exists today. The park was also the site of a Mass during the visit of Pope John Paul II in 1982. To the north of the park lies the House for an Art Lover, which was built in 1996 as a realisation of Charles Rennie Mackintosh's design for a *Haus Eines Kunstfreundes*.

Bellanoch *Argyll and Bute* Located on the southwestern side of the Crinan Canal and on Crinan Loch, the hamlet of Bellanoch lies 2 miles (3 km) southeast of the village of Crinan. A five-span cast-iron bridge built in 1851 crosses the River Add, which joins Loch Crinan at Bellanoch. The Knapdale Forest extends southwards.

Belloch *Argyll and Bute* A settlement on the Kintyre peninsula, Belloch lies a mile (1.5 km) east of Glenacardoch Point and a mile (1.5 km) north of Glenbarr.

Bellochantuy *Argyll and Bute* A settlement on the Kintyre peninsula, Bellochantuy lies at the south end of Bellochantuy Bay, 9 miles (14 km) northwest of Campbeltown.

Bell Rock *Angus* A reef in the North Sea, 11 miles (18 km) southeast of Arbroath on the Angus coast and east of the entrance to the Firth of Tay. Formerly also known as Inchcape, this dangerous reef came to be known as the Bell Rock when an Abbot of Arbroath set up a bell here to warn sailors of the hazard. Southey's ballad *The Inchcape Rock* (1802) tells how the wrecker Sir Ralph the Rover cut down the bell and a year later himself perished on the reef. The Bell Rock lighthouse represents one of the major engineering feats of the early 19th century; it was designed by Robert Stevenson and came into service in 1811. The lighthouse tower was built of four types of stone. Granite from Cairngall Quarry near Peterhead was used for the foundation stones, while the main tower had an outer skin of granite from Rubislaw Quarry, Aberdeen, and a core of Old Red Sandstone from Mylnefield Quarry, Kingoodie. Sandstone from Craigleith Quarry (Edinburgh) was used to finish the cornice and parapet around the light.

Bell's Bridge, the *Glasgow City* The Bell's Bridge was built in 1988 to connect the Scottish Exhibition and Conference Centre with the Glasgow Garden Festival, held the same year. The bridge can rotate on its south pier to allow larger vessels to reach the upper Clyde.

Bell's Cherrybank Centre *Perth and Kinross* A 2.8-ha (7-acre) garden on the western edge of Perth, Bell's Cherrybank Gardens is home to the Bell's National Heather Collection, comprising over 900 varieties of heather, the largest collection of its kind in the UK. The garden was created in 1984 by the Bell's whisky distilling company, whose headquarters once lay adjacent, and is now owned by Scotland's Garden Trust. In 2002, the garden was gifted to the trust by Diageo plc, the multinational company that owns Bell's. Cherrybank provides a headquarters for Scotland's Garden Trust which is developing an adjacent site into a National Garden for Scotland.

Bellsbank *East Ayrshire* A detached portion of the East Ayrshire village of Dalmellington, Bellsbank lies just to the east of the River Doon and comprises a post-World War II public housing estate built to accommodate miners. While it supports a school, post office, church and hotel, Bellsbank has suffered considerably since the closure of the mines, with an unemployment rate that reached 37 per cent in the 1990s, the highest in Scotland.

Bellshill *North Lanarkshire* A town in North Lanarkshire, Bellshill lies to the north of the South Calder Water, 9 miles (14 km) southeast of Glasgow. It includes the suburbs of Orbiston, Hattonrig, Mossend and Milnwood. Formerly a weaving village, Bellshill developed as a mining town with the arrival of the railway in the mid-19th century. Many of its sandstone buildings date from the late-Victorian era, with the notable exception of the parish church (1762). Nearby are Strathclyde Country Park, Strathclyde Business Park, the Eurocentral industrial estate, and a railway terminal for Channel Tunnel traffic opened in 1994.

Bellside *North Lanarkshire* The hamlet of Bellside is located 2 miles (3 km) northwest of Newmains, and with Parkside forms the eastern end of the settlement known as Cleland. To the south of the hamlet flows the South Calder Water.

Bellsquarry *West Lothian* A hamlet in West Lothian, Bellsquarry now forms a district of the new town of Livingston.

Bellymack *Dumfries and Galloway* A locality in southern Dumfries and Galloway, Bellymack lies due east of Laurieston on the B795.

Belmaduthy *Highland* A settlement on the Black Isle, Easter Ross, Belmaduthy lies a mile (1.5 km) north of Munlochy.

Belmont *Shetland* The ferry port for the island of Unst in the Shetland Islands, Belmont is situated at the southwestern corner of the island. Its ferry service links with Gutcher on the neighbouring island of Yell. The nearby Belmont House was built in 1777.

Belmont *South Ayrshire* A suburb of Ayr, Belmont lies to the south of Ayr town centre.

Belmont Castle *Perth and Kinross* Dating chiefly from the 15th century, Belmont Castle lies to the south of the settlement of Meigle in eastern Perth and Kinross. It was the home of Sir H. Campbell Bannerman (1836–1908), Liberal prime minister 1905–08.

Belnahua *Argyll and Bute* An island in the Firth of Lorn, Belnahua lies to the east of the Garvellachs and a mile (1.5 km) northwest of Luing. Famed for its slate, the only remains of this industry are the slate workers' cottages and the quarry cuttings.

Belses *Scottish Borders* A locality in Ancrum parish in Scottish Borders, Belses lies nearly 8 miles (13 km) northeast of Hawick. It once had a railway station serving Ancrum village.

Belston *South Ayrshire* A settlement in South Ayrshire, Belston lies 3 miles (5 km) east of Ayr on the main route from Ayr to Cumnock. One mile (1.5 km) to the east lies the settlement of Joppa.

Beltie Burn *Aberdeenshire* A river of central Aberdeenshire, the Beltie Burn rises in Kincardine O'Neil parish on the slopes of Benaquhallie. It flows southwards past Torphins to join the River Dee 2 miles (3 km) west of Banchory.

Bemersyde House *Scottish Borders* A country house in Scottish Borders, Bemersyde lies 1 mile (1.5 km) northeast of Newtown St Boswells close to the River Tweed. The house incorporates a rectangular tower, built around 1535, burned ten years later and subsequently restored. The tower was greatly extended in the 18th century. Sir Walter Scott (1771–1832) was a frequent visitor and much enjoyed the view from nearby Bemersyde Hill (Scott's View). In 1921 the house was bought by the Government and presented by the nation to Field Marshal Douglas Haig (1861–1928), commander of the Western Front during World War I. The gardens are regularly open during the summer.

Ben Aden *Highland* A mountain in Lochaber, Ben Aden rises to 885 m (2920 ft) a mile (1.5 km) to the north of Sgurr na Ciche, Sgurr nan Coireachan and Garbh Chioch Mhòr and 2 miles (3 km) west of the head of Loch Quoich.

Ben Aigan *Moray* A hill rising to a height of 471 m (1546 ft) to the east of the River Spey in Moray, Ben Aigan lies to the east of Rothes and northeast of Craigellachie. The Spey flows along the foot of its western and northern slopes, and within the Wood of Arndilly there are forest cycle routes.

Ben Alder *Highland* A mountain in Badenoch, the vast summit plateau of Ben Alder rises to 1148 m (3757 ft) to the west of Loch Ericht. Almost 4 sq. km (1.5 sq. miles) of the Ben Alder plateau is above 1000 m (3300 ft) in height. Stone polygons associated with permafrost can be found. Its name is derived from the Gaelic for 'hill of the rock water'.

Ben Alisky *Highland* A mountain in Caithness, Ben Alisky rises to 348 m (1141 ft) 4 miles (6.5 km) southwest of Loch More.

Ben An *Stirling* A mountain in the Trossachs, Ben An rises to 461 m (1512 ft) 4 miles (6.5 km) north of Aberfoyle, between Glen Finglas Reservoir and Loch Katrine. Loch Achray is a mile (1.5 km) to the south.

Ben Armine *Highland* A mountain in central Sutherland, Ben Armine (Gael: *Beinn an Armuinne*) rises to 704 m (2309 ft) 5 miles (8 km) southeast of Loch Choire and northeast of Lairg. Ben Armine Forest extends to the south.

Ben Arthur *Argyll and Bute* A mountain in the Arrochar Alps, Ben Arthur rises to 884 m (2901 ft) 3 miles (5 km) west of Arrochar and 2 miles (3 km) northwest of the head of Loch Long. It is also known as the Cobbler, a name derived from its resemblance, when seen from

Tarbert, to a cobbler bent over his work. Ben Arthur overlooks Glen Croe to the south.

Ben Aslak *Highland* A mountain at the southeast end of the island of Skye in the Inner Hebrides, Ben Aslak rises to 610 m (2001 ft) 4 miles (6.5 km) south of Kyleakin. It commands views over the Sound of Sleat to the Sandaig Islands, while to the southwest rise the peaks of Beinn na Seamraig and Beinn Bhreac.

Ben Attow An alternative name for Beinn Fhada in Highland.

Ben Auskaird *Highland* A mountain in northwest Sutherland, Ben Auskaird rises to 386 m (1266 ft) 4 miles (6.5 km) southeast of the village of Scourie.

Ben Avon *Aberdeenshire/Moray* A summit in the Grampian Mountains on the border of Aberdeenshire and Moray, Ben Avon lies 5 miles (8 km) north of Braemar. It has five tops over 914 m (3000 ft), the highest being Leabaidh an Daimh Bhuidhe at 1171 m (3842 ft). Ben Avon has a number of interesting geomorphological features, including massive granite tors, some of which can be seen from a great distance.

Ben Buie *Argyll and Bute* A mountain on the island of Mull in the Inner Hebrides, Ben Buie rises to 717 m (2352 ft) a mile (1.5 km) north of Lochbuie. Creach Beinn rises a mile (1.5 km) to the east.

Ben Challum *Stirling* A mountain in northwest Stirling, Ben Challum (Gael: *Beinn Chaluim*), rising to a height of 1025 m (3363 ft), is the most prominent peak at the head of Glen Lochay and is located 4 miles (6.5 km) east of Tyndrum. A large cairn overlooking the steep and rocky north face is the true summit. Its name is derived from the Gaelic for 'Malcolm's Hill'.

Ben Chonzie *Perth and Kinross* A mountain to the north of Comrie in central Perth and Kinross, Ben Chonzie rises to 931 m (3054 ft). Its name is derived from the Gaelic for 'hill of moss'.

Ben Cleuch *Clackmannanshire* The highest point of the Ochil Hills in central Scotland, Ben Cleuch rises to a height of 721 m (2363 ft) to the north of Tillicoultry in Clackmannanshire.

Ben Cruachan *Argyll and Bute* A mountain in northern Argyll and Bute, Ben Cruachan rises to a height of 1126 m (3694 ft) 4 miles (6.5 km) east of Bonawe. The name is derived from the Gaelic for 'stacky hill'. It is of classic mountain form with four ridges culminating in a sharp peak. The main ridge running east to west is littered with boulders. Within the mountain a hydro-electric power station pumps water from Loch Awe to the Cruachan Reservoir, which is enclosed in the southern corrie.

Ben Damph *Highland* A mountain in Wester Ross, Ben Damph (Gael: *Beinn Damh*) rises to 902 m (2959 ft) 2 miles (3 km) east of Loch Damh and 3 miles (5 km) south of the head of Upper Loch Torridon. The Ben-damph Forest extends northwards.

Ben Donich *Argyll and Bute* A mountain on the Cowal peninsula, Ben Donich rises to 847 m (2779 ft) 2 miles (3 km) north of Lochgoilhead and 2.5 miles (4 km) southwest of Ben Arthur (the Cobbler). It lies between Glen Croe and the Ardgoil Estate.

Ben Garrisdale *Argyll and Bute* A mountain at the north end of the island of Jura in the Inner Hebrides, Ben Garrisdale rises to 365 m (1197 ft) 2 miles (3 km) south of the settlement of Glengarrisdale and Glengarrisdale Bay.

Ben Glas The anglicised name for Beinn Ghlas in Perth and Kinross.

Ben Griam Beg *Highland* A mountain in northeast Sutherland, Ben Griam Beag rises to 580 m (1903 ft) west of Strath Halladale, a mile (1.5 km) east of Loch Druim a'Chliabhain and 2 miles (3 km) northeast of Ben Griam More.

Ben Griam More *Highland* A mountain in northeast Sutherland, Ben Griam More rises to 590 m (1935 ft) to the west of Strath Halladale, a mile (1.5 km) south of Loch Druim a'Chliabhain and 3 miles (5 km) northeast of Loch nan Clar.

Ben Gulabin *Perth and Kinross* A Corbett peak at the head of Glen Shee in northeast Perth and Kinross, Ben Gulabin rises to 806 m (2643 ft) 1.25 miles (2 km) north of Spittal of Glenshee and 17 miles (27 km) north-northwest of Blairgowrie.

Ben Hee *Highland* A mountain in Sutherland, Ben Hee rises to 873 m (2863 ft) 9 miles (14 km) west of Altnaharra.

Ben Hiant *Highland* A mountain on the Ardnamurchan peninsula, Ben Hiant rises to 528 m (1732 ft) 3 miles (5 km) east of Kilchoan and 3 miles (5 km) west of Glenbeg.

Ben Hope *Highland* A mountain in northern Sutherland, Ben Hope rises to 927 m (3040 ft) to the east of Loch Hope and southwest of Tongue.

Ben Horn *Highland* A mountain in eastern Sutherland, Ben Horn rises to 521 m (1706 ft) a mile (1.5 km) east of Loch Horn and 4 miles (6.5 km) northeast of Golspie.

Ben Hutig *Highland* A mountain on the north coast of Sutherland, Ben Hutig rises to 408 m (1338 ft) 7 miles (11 km) northwest of Tongue.

Ben Hynish *Argyll and Bute* The highest point on the Inner Hebridean island of Tiree, Ben Hynish rises to 141 m (462 ft) in the southwest of the island and is topped by a radar-tracking station.

Ben Killilan *Highland* A mountain in the Lochalsh district of Highland Council area, Ben Killilan rises to 753 m (2470 ft) a mile (1.5 km) northeast of the settlement of Killilan and 2 miles (3 km) northeast of the head of Loch Long. Faochaig rises 3 miles (5 km) to the east in the Killilan Forest.

Ben Klibreck *Highland* A mountain massif in Sutherland, Highland Council area, Ben Klibreck (Gael: *Beinn Cleith Bric*) rises to 961 m (3154 ft) to the south of Loch Naver. The Klibreck Burn flows north to join the loch just east of Klibreck.

Ben Lawers *Perth and Kinross* Rising to a height of 1214 m (3984 ft) to the north of Loch Tay in central Perth and Kinross, Ben Lawers is the highest peak in the southern Highlands. On its summit stand the remains of a 7-m/23-ft-high cairn built in 1878 in an attempt to raise the mountain to a height in excess of 1219 m (4000 ft). On a clear day there are views west to the Atlantic and east to the North Sea. The National Trust for Scotland purchased 3452 ha (8530 acres) on the southern slopes in 1950, and a visitor centre was opened in 1972. In 1966 a further 1348 ha (3331 acres) of the Tarmachan Range to the west was acquired. In 1975 the area was designated a National Nature Reserve.

Ben Ledi *Stirling* A mountain to the north of the Trossachs, Ben Ledi rises to 879 m (2883 ft) between the Glen Finglas Reservoir and Loch Lubnaig, 4 miles (6.5 km) northwest of Callander.

Ben Lee *Highland* A mountain on the island of Skye in

the Inner Hebrides, Ben Lee rises to 445 m (1460 ft) a mile (1.5 km) west of the settlement of Peinchorran. It offers views east to the island of Raasay.

Ben Leoid The anglicised name for Beinn Leoid in Highland.

Ben Lomond *Stirling* Rising to a height of 974 m (3195 ft) from the eastern shore of Loch Lomond, Ben Lomond lies at the heart of Loch Lomond and the Trossachs National Park. In 1984 the National Trust for Scotland acquired 2173 ha (5369 acres) of mountain land, including Ben Lomond and the summits of Ptarmigan, Sròn Aonaich and Beinn Uird. This property, along with adjacent Forestry Commission land, was designated the Ben Lomond National Memorial Park in December 1995 as a tribute to those who gave their lives in the service of their country.

Ben Loyal *Highland* A significant Corbett of northern Sutherland, Ben Loyal (Gael: *Beinn Laoghall*) comprises at least eight tops, rising to a height of 764 m (2506 ft) at An Caisteal. The mountain is located 2 miles (3 km) west of Loch Loyal and 5 miles (8 km) south of Tongue.

Ben Lui *Stirling* A mountain in northwest Stirling Council area, Ben Lui (Gael: *Beinn Laoigh*) rises to 1130 m (3702 ft) to the south of the River Lochy, 6 miles (10 km) southeast of Dalmally. In profile, it is of classic mountain form with five ridges radiating outwards to produce four corries. The name Ben Lui is derived from the Gaelic for 'hill of the calf'.

Ben Macdui *Moray* Rising to 1309 m (4296 ft) at the centre of the Cairngorm Mountains, Ben Macdui is the second-highest peak in Scotland. Its name is said to be derived from the Gaelic for 'hill of the black pig'. The plateau area between Ben Macdui and Cairn Gorm is unique in Britain, with a varied subarctic terrain that, with the peak itself, includes extensive granite boulder fields, corries, cliffs and buttresses. A stone hut just east of the summit, known locally as the Sapper's Bothy, was originally said to have been used by military surveyors. Once thought to have been the highest peak in Scotland, a trigonometrical station was set up in 1847 by the Ordnance Survey which settled the argument. Ben Macdui is said to be haunted by a giant ghost called, in Gaelic, Am Fear Liath Mòr ('The Big Grey Man'). It is reported that when the Victorian mountaineer Professor N.J. Collie was alone at the summit he heard footsteps in the snow and was so scared that he fled from the top.

Ben Meabost *Highland* A mountain in Strathaird on the island of Skye in the Inner Hebrides, Ben Meabost rises to a height of 346 m (1135 ft) 2 miles (3 km) northeast of the settlement of Elgol.

Ben Mòr Coigach *Highland* A mountain in the Coigach area of Wester Ross, Ben Mòr Coigach rises to a height of 743 m (2437 ft) 7 miles (11 km) northwest of Ullapool.

Ben More *Argyll and Bute* The highest peak on the island of Mull in the Inner Hebrides, Ben More rises to 966 m (3168 ft) 7 miles (11 km) southwest of Salen.

Ben More *Stirling* A mountain in northwest Stirling Council area, Ben More rises to 1174 m (3852 ft) to the south of Glen Dochart and east of Crianlarich.

Ben More Assynt *Highland* A mountain in the Assynt district of western Sutherland, Ben More Assynt rises to 998 m (3247 ft) 4 miles (6.5 km) southeast of Inchnadamph.

Ben Nevis *Highland* A granite mountain rising to a height of 1344 m (4409 ft) to the east of Fort William in Lochaber, Ben Nevis is the highest peak not only in Scotland but in Great Britain. In association with Carn Mòr Dearg to the northeast it forms a vast northwest-facing horseshoe. The northeast face of the mountain is possibly the most interesting, with a grand array of cliffs composed of tough rocks that are suitable for climbing. The Tower and Castle ridges and the imposing North-east Brothers are also popular with summer climbers. The 2-mile/3-km-long, 610-m/2000-ft-high headwall is the most formidable rock face in Britain and provides the most challenging ice and snow climbing in the country. On the northeast ridge of Ben Nevis stand the ruins of a weather observatory that was manned between 1883 and 1904. A pony track was created to provide access to the observatory where Nobel prize-winning physicist Charles Wilson (1869–1959) developed his ideas for the cloud chamber, which made the tracks of ionising particles – atoms – visible. William Speirs Bruce, leader of the Scottish National Antarctic Expedition (1902-04), worked in the observatory and learned to ski here. For a while the observatory operated as a temperance hotel, and in 1911 a Model T Ford was driven to the summit. The first recorded ascent of Ben Nevis was in 1771 by the botanist James Robertson. Other early ascents were made by the African explorer Mungo Park (1771–1806) and the poet John Keats (1795–1821). Ben Nevis became popular with tourists following the opening of the West Highland Railway to Fort William in 1894, and in the following year the first Ben Nevis Hill Race was was run from foot to summit and back again. This event now takes place each year in September. An international Peace Cairn was erected on Ben Nevis by Bert Bissell from Dudley, who made his 104th ascent of the mountain on his 90th birthday in 1992. In 2000 Ben Nevis was acquired by the John Muir Trust.

Ben Oss *Stirling* A mountain in northwest Stirling Council area, Ben Oss rises to 1029 m (3376 ft) to the southeast of Ben Lui, 4 miles (6.5 km) southwest of Tyndrum. Its summit takes the shape of a whaleback ridge running from southwest to northeast and its name is derived from the Gaelic for 'loch outlet hill'.

Ben Raah *Western Isles* Rising to a height of 267 m (876 ft), Ben Raah is the highest peak on the island of Taransay in the Outer Hebrides.

Ben Rinnes *Moray* A mountain in northeast Scotland, Ben Rinnes rises to a height of 840 m (2755 ft) 5 miles (8 km) southwest of Dufftown in Moray. It is bounded to the west and north by the valleys of the Rivers Avon and Spey respectively.

Ben Screel *Highland* A mountain in West Highland Council area, Ben Screel (Gael: *Beinn Sgritheall*) rises steeply from the north shore of Loch Hourn to a height of 981 m (3195 ft). Its name is derived from the Gaelic for 'hill of screes'.

Ben Stack *Highland* A mountain to the west of Loch Stack in northwest Sutherland, Ben Stack rises to 721 m (2365 ft) 3.5 miles (5.5 km) southeast of Laxford Bridge and 1.5 miles (3 km) northwest of Achfary.

Ben Stack *Western Isles* A hill at the southern end of the island of Eriskay in the Outer Hebrides, Ben Stack rises to 122 m (400 ft) and offers views south over the Sound of Barra to Barra and the neighbouring islands of Fuday, Gighay and the Stack Islands.

Ben Starav *Highland* A mountain on the southern boundary of Highland Council area to the south of Glen Coe, Ben Starav rises to 1078 m (3537 ft) to the east of Loch Etive.

Ben Strome *Highland* A mountain in northwest Sutherland, Ben Strome rises to 426 m (1397 ft) a mile (1.5 km) northeast of Kylestrome and 2 miles (3 km) north of Unapool.

Ben Tarbert *Western Isles* A hill on South Uist in the Outer Hebrides, Ben Tarbert rises to 168 m (551 ft) 5 miles (9 km) southeast of Hornish Point and a mile (1.5 km) northwest of the settlement of Loch Sgioport.

Ben Tee *Highland* A mountain in Lochaber, Ben Tee rises to 901 m (2955 ft) 2.5 miles (4 km) northwest of the settlement of Kilfinnan at the head of Loch Lochy.

Ben Tianavaig *Highland* A mountain on the island of Skye in the Inner Hebrides, Ben Tianavaig rises to 413 m (1355 ft) 3 miles (5 km) southeast of Portree.

Ben Vair The anglicised name for Beinn a' Bheithir in Highland.

Ben Vane *Argyll and Bute* A mountain in the Arrochar Alps to the north of Loch Long, Ben Vane rises to 915 m (3002 ft) 4 miles (6.5 km) northwest of Arrochar.

Ben Vane *Stirling* A mountain peak in western Stirling Council area, Ben Vane rises to 820 m (2685 ft) to the west of Loch Lubnaig. The Calair Burn, which rises on its slopes, flows north into Balquhidder.

Ben Varren *North Ayrshire* A mountain in the northwest of the island of Arran, Ben Varren (Gael: *Beinn Bharrain*) rises to 796 m (2365 ft) 2 miles (3 km) southeast of the settlement of Pirnmill. It has a second top at a height of 715 m (2345 ft).

Ben Venue *Stirling* A mountain in the Trossachs district of western Stirling Council area, Ben Venue rises to 727 m (2385 ft) a mile (1.5 km) southeast of the foot of Loch Katrine, near the Pass of Achray. The settlement of Aberfoyle lies 4 miles (6.5 km) to the southeast.

Ben Vorlich *Argyll and Bute* The most northerly of the Arrochar Alps to the north of Loch Long, Ben Vorlich rises to 943 m (3094 ft) to the west of the head of Loch Lomond.

Ben Vorlich *Stirling/Perth and Kinross* A conical mountain on the border between Stirling and Perth and Kinross Council areas, Ben Vorlich rises to 985 m (3232 ft) to the south of Loch Earn.

Ben Vrackie *Perth and Kinross* A mountain in highland Perth and Kinross, Ben Vrackie rises to 841 m (2758 ft) 3 miles (5 km) north of Pitlochry.

Ben Wyvis *Highland* A mountain massif in Easter Ross, Ben Wyvis rises to 1046 m (3431 ft) at Glas Leathad Mòr, 8 miles (13 km) northwest of Dingwall, 2.5 miles (4 km) southwest of Wyvis Forest and 4 miles (6.5 km) southwest of Loch Glass.

Benarty Hill *Perth and Kinross* A hill rising to 356 m (1168 ft) to the south of Loch Leven in Perth and Kinross, Benarty forms a long ridge separating that region from Fife. Known locally as the 'sleeping giant', its summit is capped by quartz dolorite rocks. An outlier called Vane Hill forms part of the RSPB Vane Farm Nature Reserve.

Benbecula *Western Isles* Nestled between North and South Uist in the Western Isles, Benbecula (Gael: *Beinn na Faoghla*) is a low flat windswept island with a solitary hill that rises to 124 m (409 ft) at Rueval. It has an area of 8235 ha (20,340 acres) comprising machair in the west and peat moorland in the east, and its main settlement is at Baile Mhanaich. An army base established here in 1958 was extended in 1971 to house military personnel servicing the South Uist rocket range, and to the northeast lies the island's airfield. The total population numbers about 1300. In 1896 a harbour was built at Peter's Port in the narrows between Benbecula and the island of Wiay which is a bird sanctuary. In 1960 Queen Elizabeth the Queen Mother opened a causeway over the North Ford connecting with North Uist and in 1982 another causeway was extended across the sands of South Ford linking the island to South Uist. At 5 miles (8 km) in length, the North Ford Causeway is the longest in the Western Isles. It clips the western end of the island of Grimsay and runs over various smaller islands en route. Antiquities on Benbecula include the ruins of the Clan Ranald stronghold of Borve Castle, Teampull Bhuirgh and the 14th-century nunnery of Nunton Chapel. It was from Benbecula that Prince Charles Edward Stewart (Bonnie Prince Charlie) sailed 'over the sea to Skye' in April 1746 and it was from Lady Clanranald at Nunton House that he acquired the clothes with which he disguised himself as a maidservant to Flora Macdonald. The MacDonalds of Clan Ranald owned the island until 1839, when it passed to Colonel Gordon of Cluny, whose estate held the island until 1942. Benbecula Airport is situated by the B892 at the northwest end of the island. It consists of two runways of 1681 m (5515 ft) and 1200 m (3937 ft) respectively.

Benderloch *Argyll and Bute* A settlement on the western edge of a district of the same name, Benderloch lies on Ardmucknish Bay, 3 miles (5 km) north of Connel.

Benderloch *Argyll and Bute* An ancient district of Argyllshire, Benderloch is the name given to that part of Argyll and Bute bordered by Loch Etive to the south and Loch Creran to the north. The main peaks of the area are Beinn Bhreac, Beinn Molurgainn and Beinn Mheadhonach. The settlement of Benderloch lies on its western edge.

Beneraird *South Ayrshire/Dumfries and Galloway* A hill on the border between South Ayrshire and Dumfries and Galloway, Beneraird rises to 439 m (1440 ft) 4 miles (6.5 km) southeast of Ballantrae. It is the source of the Water of App.

Bengairn *Dumfries and Galloway* A hill in southern Dumfries and Galloway, Bengairn rises to 391 m (1282 ft) northwest of Auchencairn and 6 miles (10 km) south of Castle Douglas.

Benholm *Aberdeenshire* A scattered rural settlement in the southeast Aberdeenshire parish of the same name, Benholm lies near the North Sea coast to the southwest of Inverbervie. It comprises the hamlets of Benholm, Nether Benholm, Stone of Benholm and Benholm Mill, the only surviving water-powered meal mill in the Kincardine area of Aberdeenshire.

Benloch Burn *Dumfries and Galloway* A stream rising on the southwestern slope of Cairnsmore of Carsphairn, the Benloch Burn flows westwards to join the Water of Deugh, a mile (1.5 km) to the north of Carsphairn.

Benmore *Argyll and Bute* A settlement on the Cowal peninsula, Argyll and Bute, Benmore lies to the south of Loch Eck, 6 miles (10 km) northwest of Dunoon. The Younger Botanic Garden is located here.

Bennachie *Aberdeenshire* A red granite mountain

range in the eastern Grampians, Bennachie rises to a height of 528 m (1733 ft) 5 miles (8 km) west of Inverurie. It comprises the distinctive tor peaks of Oxen Craig, Watch Craig and the Mither Tap. The Mither Tap o' Bennachie (518 m/1700 ft) is flanked by a stone-walled fort dating from the Iron Age.

Bennane Head *South Ayrshire* The headland of Bennane Head extends into the Firth of Clyde at the northern end of Ballantrae Bay, 11 miles (18 km) southwest of Girvan in South Ayrshire. The cannibal Sawney Bean lived here with his family in the 15th century.

Bennan Head *North Ayrshire* A headland at the southern tip of Arran, Bennan Head extends into the Firth of Clyde 7 miles (11 km) southwest of Lamlash. There are views southeast to the island of Pladda and south to Ailsa Craig.

Bennan Loch Reservoir *East Renfrewshire* The Bennan Loch Reservoir is located 4 miles (6.5 km) southwest of Eaglesham and a half-mile (1 km) west of Ballageich Hill in East Renfrewshire. The reservoir is home to the Bennan Angling Club.

Bennie Museum *West Lothian* The Bennie Museum in Bathgate, West Lothian, is housed in two adjoining 18th-century cottages. Displays include collections of early photographs and glass from the former Bathgate glassworks, plus exhibits on two local men, Sir James Young Simpson (1811–70), who introduced chloroform as an anaesthetic, and James 'Paraffin' Young (1811–83), which highlight the social and industrial history of the area.

Benslie *North Ayrshire* A hamlet of North Ayrshire, Benslie lies to the east of the Lugton Water 2 miles (3 km) east of Kilwinning and 2.5 miles (4 km) northeast of Irvine.

Bentfoot *North Lanarkshire* A locality to the west of the Forestburn Reservoir in North Lanarkshire, Bentfoot lies to the north of the M8.

Bentpath *Dumfries and Galloway* A hamlet of Eskdale in eastern Dumfries and Galloway, Bentpath lies on the River Esk, 5 miles (8 km) northwest of Langholm. A monument to Thomas Telford (1757–1834) overlooks the river to the west.

Benvie *Dundee City* A village in Liff and Benvie parish on the western border of the Dundee City, Benvie lies on the Invergowrie Burn to the north of the Dundee–Perth road. The old parish church lies ruined and a Pictish cross-slab of the 9th century, formerly in the churchyard, is now in the McManus Galleries in Dundee. Benvie Manse was the birthplace in 1748 of the mathematician and geologist John Playfair.

Beoraid, Loch *Highland* A narrow, deep loch in South Morar, Loch Beoraid lies between Loch Morar and Loch Eilt. It is fed from the east by the Allt a' Choire and drains northwards into Loch Morar via the Meoble.

Beoraidbeg *Highland* A small settlement in Morar, Beoraidbeg lies 2 miles (3 km) south of Mallaig.

Bernera *Highland* A locality in the Lochalsh district, Bernera lies on Glenelg Bay opposite the island of Skye. The Bernera military barracks was one of four established after the 1745 Jacobite Rising, its main purpose being to control the narrow crossing from the mainland to Skye. Now a ruin, it once accommodated up to 200 soldiers, the garrison being finally withdrawn c.1800.

Berneray *Western Isles* The 'bear island' or 'Bjorn's Island', Berneray (Gael: *Bearnaraigh*) is the southernmost island of the Outer Hebrides. Often referred to as Barra Head, this wedge-shaped island comprises 204 ha (504 acres) of granite and gneiss rock. Robert Stevenson (1772–1850) used the local granite to build the island's lighthouse above Skate Point in 1833. Here, Berneray's west-facing sea cliffs take the full force of Atlantic waves, a storm in 1836 allegedly moving a two-tonne rock a distance of some 1.5 m (5 ft). Two fortified mounds near the 193-m (633-ft) summit of the island are amongst more than 80 excavated archaeological sites. Last inhabited by lighthouse keepers in the 1970s, the island had a population of 36 in 1891. There is no regular access to the island today, but there are anchorages on the north shore. Most of Berneray is given over to sheep grazing.

Berneray *Western Isles* Joined by a causeway to the northern tip of North Uist in the Outer Hebrides, but forming part of the parish of Harris, the island of Berneray (Gael: *Eilean Bhearnaraigh*) is largely composed of gneiss overlaid with fertile sandy soil. With an area of 1085 ha (2681 acres), the island rises to a height of 93 m (305 ft) at Beinn Shleibhe (Moor Hill) and 85 m (278 ft) at Borve Hill. At the centre of the island between the two hills lies the freshwater Loch Bhruist, and on the east coast in the sea loch known as Bays Loch there is a harbour built in the 1980s with EU funding. Settlement is largely concentrated in the east at Borve and Ruisgarry, sheep farming and fishing being the main occupations. Berneray, which is associated with the Clan MacLeod and the Harris Estate, was the birthplace of the 'Cape Breton Giant' Angus MacAskill (1825–63), who claimed to be one of the world's tallest and strongest men. The oldest building on the island is the Gunnery of MacLeod, which was the birthplace of the Gaelic scholar Norman MacLeod (1614–1705). Notable antiquities include the Chair Stone, a legendary place of execution, and the Clach Mhòr standing stone, built on a site that is associated with St Columba and St Maolrubha. There is a car ferry link with North Uist and a passenger ferry connection with North Uist and Harris.

Berneray, Sound of *Western Isles* The Sound of Berneray forms a strait in the Outer Hebrides separating the island of Berneray from North Uist to the south. The island of Eilean na Cloiche lies in the sound.

Berneray, Sound of *Western Isles* The Sound of Berneray forms a strait separating the island of Mingulay from the island of Berneray to the south, at the southernmost end of the Outer Hebrides.

Bernice *Argyll and Bute* The settlement of Bernice is located on the western shore of Loch Eck, at the foot of the Bernice Glen, 4 miles (6.5 km) south of Invernoaden. Beinn Bheag rises to the northeast and Beinn Mhòr to the southwest.

Bernisdale *Highland* A township on the island of Skye in the Inner Hebrides, Bernisdale lies near the head of Loch Snizort Beag, 2 miles (3 km) northwest of Skeabost.

Berriedale *Highland* A small village in a sheltered location on the east coast of Caithness, Highland Council area, Berriedale lies 20 miles (32 km) northeast of Brora at a point where the Berriedale Water and Langwell Water meet before joining the sea. An Iron Age broch stands on nearby Ousdale Head, and 18th/19th-century Langwell House overlooks the village associated with the Duke of

Portland's estate. On a cliff top overlooking the beach stand the ruins of Berriedale Castle, whose twin towers have been dubbed the 'Duke's Candlesticks'. Former fishermen's cottages line the shore, and the parish church and manse of Berriedale date from 1826 when they were built to a standard parliamentary design by Thomas Telford. Caithness Spring water is bottled here, and a wind generator erected in the 1980s is to be found in Glen Langwell. Also in the glen is a walled garden that is open to the public during the summer.

Berriedale Water *Highland* A river of Caithness, the Berriedale Water rises in headstreams to the east of Strath Halladale and the Strath of Kildonan. It flows 17 miles (27 km) east and southeast through deep wooded valleys, joining the Langwell Water at Berriedale just before entering the North Sea.

Berryscaur *Dumfries and Galloway* A locality in Annandale, southeast Dumfries and Galloway, Berryscaur lies on the Caldwell Burn near its confluence with the Dryfe Water, 6 miles (10 km) north of Lockerbie.

Bervie Bay *Aberdeenshire* An inlet on the North Sea coast of Aberdeenshire, Bervie Bay lies at the mouth of the Bervie Water by the town of Inverbervie.

Bervie Water *Aberdeenshire* A river of southeast Aberdeenshire, the Bervie Water rises in the eastern Grampians and follows an S-shaped course through the Howe of the Mearns to enter the North Sea at Bervie Bay.

Berwickshire A former county of southeast Scotland, Berwickshire extended southwards from the Lammermuir Hills to the lower course of the River Tweed on the border with England. Its county town was Duns. In 1974 it was incorporated into the new Borders Region as Berwickshire District and in the local government reorganisation of 1996 remained part of the Scottish Borders Council Area.

Bethelnie *Aberdeenshire* A locality in the Aberdeenshire parish of Meldrum, Bethelnie lies to the west of the A947 from Oldmeldrum to Fyvie and comprises Bethelnie and North Bethelnie. A fine farmsteading dating from 1872 and the ruined old parish church are located here, and on the Core Hill of Bethelnie (244 m/803 ft) to the south is a radio mast.

Bettyhill *Highland* Named after Elizabeth, Countess of Sutherland (1765–1839), wife of George Granville Leveson-Gower, 1st Duke of Sutherland, Bettyhill lies at the head of Torrisdale Bay on the north coast of Sutherland, 9 miles (14 km) southwest of Strathy Point. Situated at the head of Strathnaver, it was one of sixty-four communities that populated the area before the Sutherland clearances in the early 19th century and was one of the few to remain populated. To the east of the village is the Strathnaver Crofting Museum which documents the history of this area. There are fine sandy beaches nearby.

Beul An Toim *Western Isles* Beul An Toim is the name given to the sea channel that separates the island of Baleshare in the Western Isles from the island of Benbecula to the south. Even at low tide this channel remains open.

Bhacsaigh The Gaelic name for Vacsay in the Western Isles.

Bhainne, Loch a' *Highland* A small loch in Lochaber, Loch a' Bhainne lies 3 miles (5 km) northwest of Invergarry. It drains through waterfalls as the Allt a' Bhainne, a stream that joins the outlet from Loch Lundie to flow into the River Garry as the Aldernaig Burn.

Bhaltos The Gaelic name for Valtos in the Western Isles.

Bhatarsaigh The Gaelic name for Vatersay in the Western Isles.

Bhealaich, Loch a' *Highland* A small loch in Sutherland, Loch a' Bhealaich lies to the northwest of Ben Armine Forest. It drains northeastwards into Loch Choire, its ultimate outlet being via the Mallart to Loch Naver.

Bhealaich, Loch a' *Highland* A small loch in Kintail, Loch a' Bhealaich lies to the northeast of Beinn Fhada. It drains northwards to Glen Elchaig, passing over the dramatic Falls of Glomach, one of the highest waterfalls in the UK.

Bhealaich, Loch a' *Highland* Situated in the heart of Shieldaig Forest in Wester Ross, Loch a' Bhealaich lies between Loch Torridon and Loch Maree. It drains northwestwards through smaller lochs into Gair Loch.

Bhlàir, Loch a' An alternative name for Loch Blair in Highland.

Bhotarsaigh The Gaelic name for Votersay in the Western Isles.

Bhragair The Gaelic name for Bragar in the Western Isles.

Bhraoin, Loch a' *Highland* A loch in Wester Ross, Highland Council area, Loch a' Bhraoin lies 7 miles (11 km) south of the head of Loch Broom. The Abhainn Cuileig flows from its eastern end to form the River Broom at its junction with the Abhainn Dromm.

Bhrodainn, Loch *Highland* A loch in Badenoch, Loch Bhrodainn lies in the Gaick Forest, 7 miles (11 km) east of Dalwhinnie.

Bhrollum, Loch *Western Isles* Located on the heavily indented southeastern coastline of the Isle of Lewis in the Western Isles, Loch Bhrollum lies 2 miles (3 km) east of Loch Claidh and 4 miles (6.5 km) southwest of Loch Shell.

Bhruthaich, Loch An alternative name for Loch Bruicheach in Highland.

Bhuirgh The Gaelic name for Borve in the Western Isles.

Bi, Loch The Gaelic name for Loch Bee in the Western Isles.

Bi, Lochan na *Argyll and Bute* A small loch in Glen Lochy, Argyll and Bute, Lochan na Bi lies to the south of the A85 to Dalmally, nearly 2 miles (3 km) west of Tyndrum. The River Lochy issues from its western end.

Bianasdail, Gleann *Highland* A valley in Wester Ross, Gleann Bianasdail carries the Abhainn an Fhasaigh from Lochan Fada southwards into Loch Maree.

Bidean a' Choire Sheasgaich *Highland* A remote mountain in Wester Ross, Bidean a' Choire Sheasgaich rises to 945 m (3100 ft) to the east of Strathcarron. Its name is derived from the Gaelic for 'peak of the corrie of the barren cattle'.

Bidean nam Bian *Highland* The highest mountain in the former county of Argyllshire, Bidean nam Bian rises to a height of 1150 m (3766 ft) to the south of Glen Coe. Part of a larger estate in the care of the National Trust for Scotland, it comprises a north-facing ridge of three corries that are known as the Three Sisters.

Bidein a' Ghlas Thuill *Highland* Bidein a' Ghlas Thuill is the higher summit of the An Teallach massif in Wester Ross. Rising to a height of 1062 m (3483 ft), its name is derived from the Gaelic for 'peak of the greenish-grey hollow'.

Biel *East Lothian* A hamlet in East Lothian, Biel lies on the Biel Water a half-mile (1 km) northeast of Stenton and a half-mile (1 km) northwest of Pitcox.

Bield, the *Scottish Borders* A locality in the Tweeddale district of Scottish Borders, the Bield lies between The Crook Inn and Tweedsmuir in the valley of the River Tweed. It was the site of an inn and in the late 17th century the Covenanters planned to capture Graham of Claverhouse here. On a hill nearby is the site of Oliver Castle, a former stronghold of the Frasers.

Bieldside *Aberdeen City* A commuter village west of Aberdeen, Bieldside lies between Cults and Peterculter on the A93 to the north of the River Dee, 4 miles (6.5 km) southwest of Aberdeen city centre.

Big Balcraig *Dumfries and Galloway* A locality in the Machars, Dumfries and Galloway, Big Balcraig lies to the north of the Monreith Burn, 3 miles (5 km) east of Port William.

Biggar *South Lanarkshire* A market town and commercial centre in South Lanarkshire, Biggar lies 14 miles (22 km) southeast of Lanark. William Wallace and Sir Walter Newbigging defeated Edward I of England at the Battle of Biggar in 1297, and in 1451 Biggar gained burgh status. It developed in association with cattle markets and the textile and brewing industries. Today its industries include engineering and the distribution of fine foods. The Church of St Mary (1546), one of the last pre-Reformation churches in Scotland, stands on the site of the earlier Church of St Nicholas. In its graveyard are buried the ancestors of the 19th-century Liberal prime minister William Gladstone. Notable buildings include the Gladstone Court Museum, the Greenhill Covenanters' House (17th-century), the Moat Park Heritage Centre, the Gasworks Museum, the Albion Motor Museum and the Victorian Puppet Theatre, which still offers performances. John Brown, author of *Rab and his Friends*, was born in Biggar in 1810 and the author Hugh MacDiarmid lived nearby at Brownsbank Cottage.

Biggar Water *South Lanarkshire* A stream rising as the Biggar Burn at the southern end of the Pentland Hills in the South Lanarkshire parish of Biggar, the Biggar flows south and southwest past the town of Biggar before turning east to continue for 5 miles (8 km) as the Biggar Water. It passes through the village of Broughton and joins the Tweed near Drumelzier. The Pentland Hills are separated from the Culter Hills to the south by the Biggar Gap, a glacial breach that forms a flat hollow 7 miles (11 km) in length, linking the Clyde and Tweed valleys. This glacial breach was probably formed by ice moving eastwards during the Ice Age.

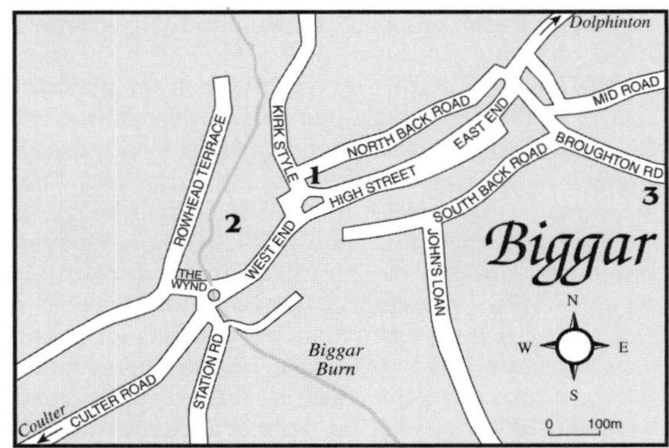

1 *Church of St Mary*
2 *Biggar Museums Trust*
3 *Biggar Puppet Theatre*

Bighouse Hill *Highland* A small hill in northern Sutherland, Bighouse Hill rises to 145 m (476 ft) in Strath Halladale to the west of the River Halladale, 4 miles (6.5 km) south of Melvich.

Big Scare *Dumfries and Galloway* A rocky islet in Luce Bay, southwest Dumfries and Galloway, the Big Scare lies to the southwest of the Little Scares, which together form a group known as the Scares.

Big Water of Fleet *Dumfries and Galloway* A river of southwest Dumfries and Galloway, the Big Water of Fleet rises in headstreams to the south of Loch Grannoch in the Galloway Hills. It flows southeastwards to join the Little Water of Fleet to become the Water of Fleet, 3 miles (5 km) northwest of Gatehouse of Fleet. The Big Water of Fleet is crossed by a 20-span viaduct built for the Portpatrick Railway which opened in 1861.

Bigton *Shetland* A small village on the southwest coast of Mainland Shetland, Bigton looks westwards towards St Ninian's Isle, 2 miles (3 km) west of Levenwick.

Bilbster *Highland* A locality in northeast Caithness, Bilbster lies on the A882 between Wick and Loch Watten. Bilbster House dates from the 18th century.

Bilston *Midlothian* A former Midlothian mining village lying on the A701 a mile (1.5 km) southwest of Loanhead. Opposite lay the Bilston Glen Colliery, one of the deepest mines in Europe, which had an extensive network of underground roadways extending to the former Monktonhall Colliery 5 miles (8 km) to the northeast. Bilston Glen closed in 1989 having flooded during the miners' strike and the site has subsequently been redeveloped as a business park. The massive A-listed Bilston Glen Viaduct lies to the east.

Bin, the *Aberdeenshire* A hill in northern Aberdeenshire, the Bin rises to a height of 313 m (1027 ft) in the Bin Forest, a mile (1.5 km) to the north of Huntly.

Bin of Cullen, the *Moray* A hill in Moray, the Bin of Cullen rises to a height of 324 m (1053 ft) 2 miles (3 km) southwest of Cullen. The Little Bin, which rises to 247 m (802 ft), lies to the east.

Bingham *City of Edinburgh* A housing estate in southeast Edinburgh, Bingham lies to the north of Niddrie and the Southern District railway line and to the east of Duddingston House and golf course. Council houses were first erected here in the 1950s. Private housing has been developed to the east at the Jewel.

Binks, the *City of Edinburgh* A rock formation in the Firth of Forth, just west of South Queensferry harbour. The rocks form a natural jetty and until c.1812 it was from this jetty that passengers embarked to travel over the Firth of Forth to Fife on the Queen's Ferry. The ferry took its name from St Margaret (1045–93), queen of Malcolm III, who endowed ships to take pilgrims over the river on the route north to St Andrews.

Binn, the *Fife* Rising abruptly to a height of 193 m (632 ft) behind the Fife coastal town of Burntisland, the Binn (Hill) has two craggy summits. Little remains of the village of the Binn that stood on the eastern slopes. Founded in 1878 by James 'Paraffin' Young, this village was built to house those working in the shale-oil industry started here by Young. The import of cheap American oil brought this small industry to an end in

1892, and by 1913 there were only 16 people left in the village. During World War I the houses and school were used to house Admiralty workers and troops, but in 1954 the last inhabitant left the village.

Binnein Beag *Highland* A conical peak of the Mamore ridge to the northeast of Kinlochleven in Lochaber, Highland Council area, Binnein Beag rises to 940 m (3083 ft) southwest of the larger Binnein Mòr. Its name is the Gaelic for 'small peak' and surrounding its summit are scree slopes.

Binnein Mòr *Highland* Located at the eastern end of the Mamore ridge to the northeast of Kinlochleven in Lochaber, Binnein Mòr rises to a height of 1128 m (3700 ft) and is the highest of the range. Its name is derived from the Gaelic for 'big peak'. It has a classic mountain form with ridges and corries meeting at the summit. A spur carries the main ridge southwest to Na Gruagaichean.

Binns, the An alternative name for House of the Binns in West Lothian.

Birdston *East Dunbartonshire* A settlement in East Dunbartonshire, Birdston lies a mile (1.5 km) north of Kirkintilloch and a mile (1.5 km) south of Milton of Campsie.

Birichen *Highland* A settlement in eastern Sutherland, Highland Council area, Birichen is located 3 miles (5 km) northwest of Dornoch.

Birkenshaw *North Lanarkshire* A settlement of northwest North Lanarkshire, Birkenshaw lies to the northeast of the junction of the M73 and M74, west of the settlement of Tannochside.

Birkenshaw *South Lanarkshire* A small community in South Lanarkshire, Birkenshaw lies on the Avon Water 2 miles (3 km) south of Larkhall. Originally a small estate, it grew, like many of the surrounding settlements, with the discovery of coal.

Birkhall *Aberdeenshire* An estate with a fine mansion house in Royal Deeside, Aberdeenshire, Birkhall is situated on the River Muick to the southwest of Ballater. The property was acquired from the Aberdalgie family by Prince Albert. It became the Deeside home of Queen Elizabeth the Queen Mother and later of Prince Charles. A fine wire suspension bridge erected in 1880 crosses the River Muick here.

Birkhill *Angus/Dundee City* A dormitory settlement lying next to Muirhead 4.5 miles (7 km) northwest of the centre of Dundee, on the border of Angus Council area and Dundee City. Birkhill has a primary school, opened in 1993. Camperdown Park lies immediately to the southeast.

Birkhill *Dumfries and Galloway* A locality in the Moffat valley, eastern Dumfries and Galloway, Birkhill lies on the Moffat Water, 3 miles (5 km) south of St Mary's Loch.

Birks of Aberfeldy, the *Perth and Kinross* A woodland to the south of Aberfeldy in central Perth and Kinross, the Birks of Aberfeldy straddle the steep-sided gorge of the Moness Burn which flows northwards to meet the River Tay. A nature trail follows the scenic route through oak, beech and birch (birk) trees to the spectacular Falls of Moness. The name of the wood derives from a reference in a poem composed by Robert Burns (1759–1796): 'The hoary cliffs are crowned wi' flowers, White o'er the linns the burnie pours, And rising, weets wi' misty showers The birks of Aberfeldy.'

Birnam *Perth and Kinross* A mid-Victorian village in central Perth and Kinross, Birnam lies near the junction of the Braan and Tay rivers just south of Dunkeld. The village owes its development to the arrival of the railway, its station being the northern terminus of the Highland Railway until the 1890s. Its finely ornamented station still serves Birnam and Dunkeld. Turreted mansion houses overlook the grand Birnam Hotel. Smaller boarding houses, which were built to welcome tourists of all levels of income in the 19th century, abound. A feature today is the Beatrix Potter Garden which is associated with the author of children's books who spent holidays near here and was strongly influenced by the landscape. On Birnam Hill stands a fort known locally as Duncan's Camp, said to have been the scene of courts held by King Duncan whose murder at the hands of Macbeth – along with the famed Birnam Woods – appears in Shakespeare's *Macbeth*.

Birness *Aberdeenshire* A scattered rural settlement to the northeast of Ellon in Aberdeenshire, Birness comprises the hamlets of Milltown of Birness, Nether Mill of Birness, Knaps of Birness, Mains of Birness and Toll of Birness.

Birnie Kirk *Moray* Once one of the seats of the bishops of Moray, Birnie Kirk is one of the oldest places of worship in Moray. It is situated on a prominent mound 2 miles (3 km) south of Elgin on a side road. In its kirkyard is a Pictish stone on which are carved the images of an eagle, a notched rectangle and a Z-rod. Restored by A. Marshall Mackenzie in 1891, the church is dedicated to St Brendan.

Birnie Loch Nature Reserve *Fife* A local nature reserve in the Howe of Fife to the south of the A91 and the village of Collessie. It was created in 1991 from the restored workings of Kinloch Quarry and donated to the people of Fife by the family of J. S. Baird & Sons in association with Pioneer Aggregates (UK) Ltd.

Birns Water *East Lothian* The Birns Water is a tributary of the River Tyne in East Lothian. Rising in the Lammermuir Hills to the west of Lammer Law, the Birns Water flows in a northwesterly direction before heading north to join the River Tyne at a point 4 miles (6.5 km) southeast of Tranent.

Birrens *Dumfries and Galloway* The site of a Roman fort in southeast Dumfries and Galloway, Birrens lies to the southeast of Lockerbie, just north of the Mein Water. Dating from the 1st and 2nd centuries AD, it was in 1895 the first Roman fort in Scotland to be extensively excavated. Birrens Roman fort was originally known as Blatobulgium.

Birsay *Orkney* A settlement and parish at the northwest corner of the Orkney Mainland, Birsay looks out onto Birsay Bay and the grass-covered tidal island known as the Brough of Birsay with its early Christian and Norse settlements. Known as the 'garden of Orkney', the farmland of Birsay produces oats and barley. Buildings of interest include the Barony Mill and the ruins of Earl Stewart's Palace, which was the home of the earls of Orkney before they moved to Kirkwall in the 12th century.

Birse *Aberdeenshire* A village in the Aberdeenshire parish of the same name, Birse is situated 2 miles (3 km) southeast of Aboyne by the Burn of Birse, which flows north to meet the River Dee here. Birse Castle lies some distance to the south near the Water of Feugh, which flows eastwards through the Forest of Birse.

Birse, Forest of *Aberdeenshire* Created a royal forest in the 12th century, the Forest of Birse occupies a part of the eastern Grampians between the River Dee and the border between Aberdeenshire and Angus. The Water of Feugh rises in the Forest of Birse.

Bishop Burn *Dumfries and Galloway* A stream in the Machars district of Dumfries and Galloway, the Bishop Burn rises to the southwest of Newton Stewart. It flows southeastwards for 6 miles (10 km) before entering Wigtown Bay just over a mile (1.5 km) to the northeast of Wigtown.

Bishopbriggs *East Dunbartonshire* Situated 3 miles (5 km) north of Glasgow and south of the Forth and Clyde Canal, the town of Bishopbriggs has devloped since the 18th century in association with coal mining, brick making, quarrying, engineering and publishing. A rail-connected oil and gas depot established in the 1970s closed in the 1990s. A prison is located at Low Moss. Prior to being incorporated into Strathkelvin District in 1975, Bishopbriggs had for just over a decade been a burgh town. It now has a retail and industrial park at Westerhill.

Bishopton *Dumfries and Galloway* A locality in the Machars, Dumfries and Galloway, Bishopton lies immediately northwest of Whithorn, which was formerly a bishopric.

Bishopton *Renfrewshire* A large dormitory village situated on the Clyde estuary 6 miles (10 km) northwest of Paisley, Bishopton grew from a village of less than 300 inhabitants in 1959 to its present population following the development of rail and road links with Glasgow. Local industries include a tyre factory and the Royal Ordnance Factory, built in 1937 to utilise the expertise in munitions manufacture established during World War I at the nearby Georgetown Filling Factory which employed over 10,000 workers in 1917. The lands nearby, owned by the bishopric of Glasgow in the 14th century, were later held by the Brisbane family and, from 1703, by the lords of Blantyre. Notable buildings include Bishopton House (17th-century, recast 1916–20), Gleddoch House (1926–7), Drums (1770, repaired 1898–1900 for the Lithgow family), Formakin (1903) by Robert Lorimer and now within a country park, and Dargavel House (16th-century) within the Royal Ordnance Factory grounds.

Blà Bheinn The Gaelic name for Blaven in Highland.

Black Burn *Dumfries and Galloway* A stream in the northern Machars of southwest Dumfries and Galloway, the Black Burn rises in moorland 7 miles (11 km) west of Newton Stewart. It follows a circuitous route eastwards to join the River Bladnoch 2 miles (3 km) north of Shennanton.

Black Burn *Moray* A stream in Moray, the Black Burn rises in headwaters to the west and northwest of Dallas. It flows northeastwards past Monaughty Forest to join the River Lossie just west of Elgin.

Black Cart Water *Renfrewshire* The Black Cart Water rises from Castle Semple Loch, Renfrewshire, and flows north and east before joining the White Cart Water 3 miles (5 km) north of Paisley. One mile (1.5 km) further north this river joins the River Clyde.

Black Castle An alternative name for Barcaldine Castle in Argyll and Bute.

Black Crofts *Argyll and Bute* The hamlet of Black Crofts is located on the northern shore of Loch Etive, a mile (1.5 km) east of Ledaig Point.

Black Cuillins, the *Highland* Located in south-central Skye, the Black Cuillins are the highest mountains on the island. Forming a great massif, these mountains include the Cuillin Ridge and twelve Munros, the highest being Sgurr Alasdair at 993 m (3258 ft). The mountains provide challenging climbing. They can be accessed from Glen Brittle in the west, where there is a youth hostel, from Sligachan in the north and from Elgol in the south. Geologically, the Black Cuillins represent the exposed core of an early Tertiary volcanic complex, associated with the opening of the North Atlantic Ocean. Their dark colour comes from the basic igneous rock of which they are composed – primarily gabbro and peridotite. This colour contrasts with the Red Cuillins, to the east.

Black Devon *Fife/Clackmannanshire* A river of Fife and Clackmannanshire that rises on Outh Muir in the Cleish Hills to the north of Dunfermline, the Black or South Devon flows 15 miles (24 km) west and southwest before joining the River Forth southeast of Alloa. West of Forest Mill, its water is diverted into the Gartmorn Dam Reservoir.

Black Esk *Dumfries and Galloway* A river in eastern Dumfries and Galloway, the Black Esk rises in Eskdalemuir Forest to the south of Ettrick Pen. It flows south through the Black Esk Reservoir, which was created in 1962, then generally southeastwards before joining the White Esk to become the River Esk just south of Castle O'er.

Black Head *Dumfries and Galloway* A promontory on the west coast of the Rhinns of Galloway in southwest Dumfries and Galloway, Black Head lies at the southern end of Killantringan Bay, 2 miles (3 km) northwest of Portpatrick.

Black Hill *South Lanarkshire* Black Hill, 2 miles (3 km) east of Blackwood in South Lanarkshire, is the site of a Bronze Age burial cairn and an Iron Age fortress occupying a strategic site offering views along the valley of the River Clyde. It is now in the care of the National Trust for Scotland.

Black Isle *Highland* Not an island at all, the Black Isle forms a peninsula in Easter Ross between the Beauly Firth and the Cromarty Firth. Formerly known as Ardmeanach, it is said to be 'black' because it seldom takes the white of winter snow. Measuring 12 miles (19 km) in length by 7 miles (11 km) at its widest, the Black Isle comprises fertile farmland surrounding a central forested ridge. At its northeastern tip is the small town of Cromarty, birthplace of the writer, stonemason and geologist Hugh Miller who is noted for his studies of the local Old Red Sandstone rocks and their fossils. The largest settlement is the cathedral burgh of Fortrose, which lies at the head of the Chanonry Point looking out onto the Moray Firth. The Black Isle is relatively flat, the highest point, in the centre, being Mount Eagle which reaches a height of 256 m (840 ft).

Black Laggan Ward *Dumfries and Galloway* A hill of Dumfries and Galloway, the Black Laggan Ward rises to a height of 318 m (1042 ft) to the south of Loch Dee and west of Clatteringshaws Loch.

Black Law *Scottish Borders* A hill in the Ettrick district of Scottish Borders, Black Law rises to 696 m (2285 ft) 4 miles (6.5 km) northwest of St Mary's Loch.

Black Loch *Dumfries and Galloway* A loch in the Rhinns of Galloway, southwest Dumfries and Galloway, the Black Loch lies to the east of the White Loch, 3 miles (5 km) east of Stranraer. The remains of Castle Kennedy lie on its southwestern shore.

Black Mount *Highland/Argyll and Bute* An upland area and a deer forest at the western end of Rannoch Moor on the border between Highland Council area and Argyll and Bute, the Black Mount extends over an area of boggy moorland 4 miles (6.5 km) north of Bridge of Orchy.

Black Mount *South Lanarkshire* Located between the settlements of Dolphinton and Walston on the southern slopes of the Medwin Water valley, the Black Mount rises to a height of 516 m (1692 ft). The settlement of Dunsyre is located a mile (1.5 km) to the north.

Black Sark *Dumfries and Galloway* A stream in southeast Dumfries and Galloway near the English border, the Black Sark is a small tributary of the River Sark.

Black Watch Memorial *Dundee City* A monument to the north of Dundee off the main road from Dundee to Forfar, the Black Watch Memorial was erected in memory of those men recruited from Dundee to serve in the Black Watch Regiment. The memorial is in the form of a soldier in Black Watch service uniform looking down over the city.

Black Watch Regimental Museum *Perth and Kinross* Located in Balhousie Castle in Perth, the Black Watch Regimental Museum is part of the Regimental Headquarters of the Black Watch (Royal Highland Regiment), which originated as one of the independent companies of Highlanders created in the 1720s to police the Scottish Highlands in the aftermath of the first Jacobite Rising. The original six companies were amalgamated in 1739 to form the Highland Regiment of Foot.

Black Water *Dumfries and Galloway* A stream in Dumfries and Galloway, the Black Water rises in headstreams in Dalry parish. It flows westwards for 6 miles (10 km) to join the Water of Deugh at the northern end of the Glenkens district.

Black Water *Highland* A stream in southern Highland Council area, the Black Water rises on the slopes of Carn Dearg to the south of Loch Ossian. It flows south then west into the eastern end of the Blackwater Reservoir.

Black Water *Highland* A short stretch of river in Easter Ross, the Black Water represents the lower reaches of the Abhainn an t-Srath Chuileannaich, to the north of the Amat Forest. The river flows east-southeast for 1.5 miles (2.5 km) before entering the River Carron to the east of Amat Lodge.

Black Water *Moray* A stream in the uplands of Moray, the Black Water rises on the northwestern slope of Threestone Hill to the west of the Cabrach Road. It flows north and east to join the River Deveron at Dalriach.

Black Water of Dee An alternative name for the River Dee in Dumfries and Galloway.

Blackacre *Dumfries and Galloway* A locality in southeast Dumfries and Galloway, Blackacre lies on the eastern edge of the Forest of Ae, 10 miles (16 km) northeast of Dumfries.

Blackadder Water *Scottish Borders* A river in Scottish Borders, the Blackadder Water rises in headstreams in the Lammermuir Hills. It flows southeastwards to the town of Greenlaw then turns northeast to continue on before meeting the Whiteadder to the southwest of Chirnside. Its total length is 6 miles (10 km).

Blackburn *Aberdeenshire* A village in eastern Aberdeenshire, Blackburn lies on the A96 road between Aberdeen and Kintore at its junction with the B979. The history and heritage of the area is reflected through the work of local and international sculptors whose work is on display in Kirkhill Forest to the east of Blackburn. Initiated in 1995 by Forest Enterprise, the Tyrebagger Sculpture Project takes its name from Tyrebagger Hill which rises to 250 m (821 ft) in Kirkhill Forest.

Blackburn *West Lothian* A small industrial town 5 miles (8 km) west of Livingston in West Lothian, Blackburn originally developed as a cotton-manufacturing centre. In the mid-19th century it became a centre for coal mining. Its small population expanded rapidly from 4302 in 1961 to around 9000 by 1965 as a result of employment opportunities in Bathgate to the north and through in-migration following the inception of the Glasgow Overspill Plan. The closure of the British Leyland plant in 1986 brought decline to the area, along with the destruction of many homes built during the 1960s. The railway station at Bathgate was reopened in 1986, and the 30-minute journey to Edinburgh now attracts commuters to live in Blackburn.

Blackdog *Aberdeenshire* A locality on the east coast of Aberdeenshire 2 miles (3 km) north of Aberdeen, Blackdog lies at the mouth of the Blackdog Burn which falls into the North Sea here. An offshore rock is known as the Blackdog Rock.

Blackford *Aberdeenshire* A scattered rural settlement to the west of Rothienorman in Aberdeenshire, Blackford comprises the settlements of Blackford and Mill of Blackford which lie to the north of the Hill of Rothmaise.

Blackford *City of Edinburgh* A small residential area of southern Edinburgh, lying to the northeast of Blackford Hill. The Craigmillar Park golf course can be found here, and the King's Buildings Campus of the University of Edinburgh is nearby.

Blackford *Perth and Kinross* A village of Strathallan, southwest Perth and Kinross, Blackford lies in the parish of the same name adjacent to the A9 road between Stirling and Perth. Destroyed by retreating Jacobites in January 1716 shortly after the Battle of Sheriffmuir, the village was subsequently rebuilt in a linear form. It was a noted centre of brewing in the Middle Ages, a trade enhanced in 1488 when James IV stopped to taste the ale and gave it his approval. Whisky was later produced here but today Blackford is better known as a source of leading brands of bottled mineral water. Alexander Buchan (1829–1907), the 'Father of modern meteorology', taught in the local school during the 1860s.

Blackford Glen *City of Edinburgh* Blackford Glen lies between Blackford Hill and the Braid Hills on the south side of Edinburgh, where it forms an eastward extension of the Hermitage of Braid containing the Braid Burn. The glen provides a popular walk for local residents and access to the Agassiz Rock, a feature that provided the Swiss geologist Louis Agassiz (1807–73) with evidence for the action of glaciers on the landscape, the first time this had been noted in Scotland. Agassiz was taken to Blackford by the newspaper editor and amateur geologist Charles Maclaren (1782–1866), and although other interpretations for this particular site have been put forward, Agassiz provided the stimulus for geologists to identify evidence of glacial action throughout Scotland. Andesite was removed from Blackford Hill Quarry, accessible through the glen, to be used as road metal. The quarry, closed in 1953, is used as a depot by the City Council Roads Department.

Blackford Hill *City of Edinburgh* Blackford Hill lies 2 miles (3 km) south of the centre of Edinburgh and rises to 164 m (539 ft). Prominently located on the hill is the green-domed Royal Observatory, which includes the Institute for Astronomy of the University of Edinburgh. The grand red sandstone archway at the entrance to Observatory Road was built in 1887 to commemorate Sir George Harrison, Lord Provost and MP for Edinburgh South, who had died two years previously. It was Harrison who had facilitated the purchase of 43 ha (107 acres) of the hill by the city in 1884 to make it available as a public park. Blackford Hill is composed of Lower Devonian volcanic rocks, lying between Upper Devonian sandstones, representing the northernmost extent of those found in the Pentland Hills. Thus, geologically, this hill is rather different from the Carboniferous volcanic plugs and intrusions that form the remainder of Edinburgh's hills (with the exception of the Braid Hills). Also of geological interest is Agassiz Rock, situated close by in Blackford Glen, the first recognisable evidence of the action of glaciers to be found in Scotland. The residential area of Blackford lies to the northeast. Blackford Pond to the northwest lies adjacent to Cluny Gardens, and to the southwest are the Hermitage of Braid and the Braid Hills.

Blackfriars Chapel *Fife* A ruined building in the grounds of Madras College, South Street, St Andrews, Blackfriars Chapel is all that remains of the medieval St Andrews house of the Dominicans or Blackfriars, probably founded in the 14th century.

Blackhall *Aberdeenshire* A largely forested estate in Deeside, Aberdeenshire, Blackhall lies to the south of the River Dee, 2 miles (3 km) west of Banchory.

Blackhall *City of Edinburgh* A sizeable suburban residential area of northwest Edinburgh, centred on the Queensferry Road (which is known as Hillhouse Road as it passes through Blackhall), Blackhall is situated to the northeast of Corstorphine Hill. Speculative building took place from the 1920s. To the south is the 16th-century Craigcrook Castle. Blackhall (or Maidencraig) and Craigcrook quarries produced sandstone used in building the New Town of Edinburgh; the former begins just to the west of the much larger Craigleith Quarry, the latter lying to the southwest towards Corstorphine Hill.

Blackhope Burn *Dumfries and Galloway* Rising in headstreams on the southeastern slope of Hart Fell in eastern Dumfries and Galloway, the Blackhope Burn flows down to join the Moffat Water at Capplegill.

Blacklunans *Perth and Kinross* A small settlement in eastern Perth and Kinross, Blacklunans lies at the southern foot of Mount Blair on the Black Water, adjacent to the A93 from Blairgowrie to Braemar.

Blackness *Falkirk* A village at the eastern extremity of Falkirk Council area, Blackness lies 4 miles (6.5 km) northeast of Linlithgow, on the south shore of the Firth of Forth overlooking Blackness Bay. Formerly a port for Linlithgow, until superseded by Bo'ness in 1680, it developed in the shadow of Blackness Castle, from which it is separated by parkland. Nothing of the original settlement survives. Today, Blackness consists of a 19th-century core, with a small public housing estate to the east (c.1960). To the west is Blackness House, which was the seat of the Wedderburn family. Blackness Castle, which stands on a promontory to the northeast of the village, was built in the 1440s and was one of the chief strongholds of central Scotland in late-medieval times. Under the Articles of Union it was one of the four castles in Scotland that had to be left fortified. In 1870 it became an ammunition depot and in the 1920s it was restored. Today the castle is in the care of Historic Scotland.

Blackridge *West Lothian* A village in West Lothian, Blackridge lies between Bathgate and Airdrie, 2 miles (3 km) west of Armadale. The village developed in association with mining and quarrying, and over 76 per cent of its population occupies public housing. A cycleway follows the route of the former railway line.

Blackshaw *Dumfries and Galloway* A locality in southeast Dumfries and Galloway, Blackshaw lies on the Solway Firth, 8 miles (13 km) southeast of Dumfries.

Blacksmill Burn *Scottish Borders* A burn that rises on a hill of the same name in the Lammermuirs, eastern Scottish Borders, Blacksmill Burn flows northeastwards to join the Dye Water near Longformacus.

Blackwater Forest *Moray* A remote upland deer forest area of Moray, the Blackwater Forest lies in the Grampians between Glen Suidhe and the Cabrach Road to the south of Dufftown.

Blackwater Lodge *Moray* A shooting lodge in the uplands of Moray, Blackwater Lodge is situated by the Black Water to the northeast of Blackwater Forest. It is approached from the Cabrach Road to the south of Dufftown.

Blackwater Reservoir *Highland* A reservoir in southern Highland Council area, the Blackwater Reservoir lies to the north of Rannoch Moor and east of Kinlochleven. It extends 8 miles (13 km) east–west and is drained by the River Leven into Loch Leven. It is fed by the Black Water.

Blackwaterfoot *North Ayrshire* A settlement on the west coast of Arran, Blackwaterfoot lies on Drumadoon Bay, where it is joined by the Black Water, 9 miles (14 km) southwest of Brodick.

Blackwood *Dumfries and Galloway* A locality in Nithsdale, Dumfries and Galloway, Blackwood lies at the junction of the Clauchrie Burn with the River Nith, 8 miles (13 km) northwest of Dumfries.

Blackwood *South Lanarkshire* The village of Blackwood lies adjacent to Kirkmuirhill between the M74 and the River Nethan, 6 miles (10 km) west of Lanark. Nearby are the village of Auchenheath and the Black Hill Fort.

Bladnoch *Dumfries and Galloway* A village in the Machars of Dumfries and Galloway, Bladnoch lies on the River Bladnoch, a mile (1.5 km) southwest of Wigtown. Bladnoch Distillery, dating from 1817, has as its motif the broad-leaved helleborine, a rare orchid found in the oak woodland alongside the river.

Bladnoch, River *Dumfries and Galloway* A river of Dumfries and Galloway, the Bladnoch rises in Kirkcowan parish to the west of Newton Stewart and flows generally southeastwards before entering Wigtown Bay just south of Wigtown.

Blaich *Highland* A village in Ardgour, southwest Highland Council area, Blaich lies on the south side of Loch Eil, 6 miles (10 km) west of Fort William.

Blainslie *Scottish Borders* A locality in Lauderdale, Blainslie lies by the Leader Water, 3 miles (5 km) south of Lauder. The hamlet of Nether Blainslie is surrounded by farms at New Blainslie, South Blainslie, Middle Blainslie and Upper Blainslie.

Blair, Loch *Highland* A small loch in Lochaber, Loch Blair (Gael: *Loch a' Bhlàir*) drains southwards into Loch Arkaig.

Blair Atholl *Perth and Kinross* A village in highland Perth and Kinross, Blair Atholl lies at the junction of the Rivers Tilt and Garry 34 miles (55 km) north of the city of Perth. The village, which has hotels, camping and caravan facilities, and a nine-hole golf course, is well situated for walks into the Grampians via Glen Tilt, the Minigaig Pass and Old Struan Path. Tourist attractions include a working corn mill, a country museum and the imposing white-harled Blair Castle, which dates from the 13th century and is the seat of the dukes of Atholl. The Duke of Atholl has the distinction of having the only remaining private army in Europe, the Atholl Highlanders, which holds parades from time to time at the castle. The last of the earls of Atholl of the royal Celtic line died before 1211 and the earldom was passed through the female line to David of Strathbogie, whose family forfeited the title following its opposition to Robert the Bruce (1274–1329). After being held by King Robert II (1316–90) and his son Walter, the earldom was given in 1457 to King James II's maternal half-brother, John Stewart of Balvenie. The title eventually passed to the Murrays of Tullibardine by marriage in 1629. For his support of the Royalist cause during the Civil War, the 5th Earl was created Marquess of Atholl and in 1702 his son was created 1st Duke of Atholl by Queen Anne for his loyalty to the Government against the Jacobites. The celebrated fiddler Neil Gow (1727–1807) was musician to the 2nd, 3rd and 4th dukes of Atholl.

Blair Castle *Perth and Kinross* Located in Strath Garry, just to the north of Blair Atholl, a village that served the castle, Blair Castle was largely rebuilt in its present form in 1869 for John Murray, the 7th Duke of Atholl (1840–1917). The distinctive whitewashed edifice in the Scottish baronial style was the work of architect David Bryce (1803–76). Blair Castle has undergone many changes since the 13th century, expanding the fortunes of the Atholls and altering its appearance to suit the style of the day. Today, little can be seen externally of these earlier works. A tower was first erected *c.*1269 by the Comyns of Badenoch during an incursion into Atholl territory while the Earl of Atholl was away. Following a complaint to King Alexander III (1241–86), the site was reclaimed and has been a home to the earls, then dukes, of Atholl continuously since then. The original tower was significantly extended in the 15th and 16th centuries, although much was destroyed by Oliver Cromwell (1599–1654) while trying to extract James Graham, Marquess of Montrose (1612–50), who was garrisoned there. His cousin, John Graham of Claverhouse, who occupied the castle in 1689, was brought back after his death at the Battle of Killiecrankie and lies buried nearby. During the '45 Jacobite Rebellion, Bonnie Prince Charlie stayed here briefly on his way south after raising his standard at Glenfinnan. In 1746, the castle was occupied by Government troops and besieged by Lord George Murray, Jacobite brother of the 2nd Duke, the last siege of any castle in Britain. Other historic figures who have stayed at Blair include Edward III, James V, Mary, Queen of Scots, Napoleon III, Empress Eugenie, Queen Victoria and Edward VII. Today, the castle is maintained through a charitable trust following the death of the bachelor 10th Duke. Situated in parkland, approached by an avenue of lime trees, it is home to a fine collection of arms, furniture, and portraits by Henry Raeburn (1756–1823) and Allan Ramsay (1713–84).

Blair Drummond *Stirling* An estate in the valley of the River Forth, Blair Drummond lies a mile (1.5 km) to the south of Doune and 4 miles (6.5 km) northwest of Stirling. The present three-storeyed Scottish baronial-style house, designed by J. C. Walker and built in 1868–72, replaced an earlier mansion created by Alexander McGill in 1715. The house was sold in 1977 to the Camphill Trust who use it to care for handicapped people. During the 18th century Blair Drummond was the home of Henry Home, Lord Kames (1696–1792), an enlightened landlord who set about clearing the deep moss of the carse lands with a view to agricultural improvement. The scheme was initiated in 1766 and within a few decades the greater part of Blair Drummond and Flanders Moss had been converted to productive farmland by Lord Kames and his improving neighbours. Lord Kames was a law lord and leading figure of the Scottish Enlightenment during the second half of the 18th century, one of his most notable publications being his *Essays on the Principles of Morality and Natural Religion* (1751). Within the policies of the estate are a stable block (1835) with a clock tower added in 1871, a 19th-century icehouse, an octagonal storehouse (1800), Tudor lodges and the Mill of Torr, which had originally been designed to raise water from the River Teith to wash away peat moss. Today over 1500 acres of the policy lands at Blair Drummond are given over to Scotland's only safari and leisure park, established in the 1970s.

Blairadam *Fife/Perth and Kinross* A locality on the border between Fife and Perth and Kinross near Kelty, Blairadam comprises the mansion house and policies of Blairadam and Blairadam Forest. The architect William Adam bought the estate of Blair Crambeth in the 1730s and built Blairadam House in 1733. The policies of the house, known as Blairadam Park, were developed by William Adam's sons James, John and Robert, and include a walled garden, coach house and estate cottages. Sir Walter Scott was one of a group of nine antiquarians who met at Blairadam in the early years of the 19th century. Hosted by Lord Chief Commissioner William Adam, the so-called Blairadam Club gathered at the house on Friday evenings, before taking a ride to some historical scene on the Saturday. On Sundays they attended the service at nearby Cleish Church, which now contains memorials to the Adam family.

Blairgowrie *Perth and Kinross* A town in the valley of Strathmore, eastern Perth and Kinross, Blairgowrie is situated amid fertile farmland 16 miles (26 km) northeast of Perth at the southern entry to Glen Shee. Known locally as 'Blair', Blairgowrie lies on the River Ericht, which flows south to join the River Isla nearby. It expanded from being a mere village following the establishment of water-powered textile mills, the arrival of the railway in 1855 and the development of Scotland's fruit-growing industry which is centred on Blairgowrie. Today the town has further developed to become a tourist resort with an emphasis on outdoor activities linked to skiing, walking, hang-gliding and pony trekking in Glenshee and the surrounding area. Indoor activities are catered for in the Blairgowrie Recreation Centre and the town has three golf courses. Keathbank Mill houses an heraldic workshop and heraldry museum, together with Scotland's largest working water wheel and a model railway. Additional industries include printing, food services, fish farming and the manufacture of agricultural machinery, paper bags and animal feedstuffs.

Blairhall *Fife* A former mining village in western Fife, Blairhall is situated to the southwest of Comrie. It was founded in 1911 to house miners at an adjacent colliery and has a primary school and a community leisure centre. Nearly a mile (1.5 km) to the south beyond Shiresmill and to the west of the Bluther Burn stands the handsome 17th-century laird's house of Blairhall which was the birthplace (c.1630) of Sir William Bruce (later of Balcaskie and then Kinross), Surveyor-General to Charles II.

Blairhoyle *Stirling* A locality in Stirling Council area, Blairhoyle lies 2 miles (3 km) east of Port of Menteith.

Blairingone *Perth and Kinross* A village in southern Perth and Kinross close to the border with Clackmannanshire, Blairingone straddles the A977 from Kinross to the Kincardine Bridge. It developed as a single-street mining village in the 19th century and has a primary school and church (1838). The earls of Tullibardine are said to have had a family seat near here on a site known as the Palace Brae. Opencast mining is still carried out nearby.

Blairlogie *Stirling* An attractive Hillfoots village, Blairlogie is situated beneath the great cliff of Dumyat between Stirling and Menstrie. One of central Scotland's earliest conservation villages, Blairlogie comprises a cluster of 17th–19th-century cottages. The minister of Logie Parish between 1598 and 1609 was the poet Alexander Hume, whose most famous poem was *Of The Day Estivall.*

Blairmore *Argyll and Bute* The holiday village of Blairmore is located at the entrance to Loch Long, a mile (1.5 km) north of Strone Point.

Blairmore *Highland* A locality in central Sutherland, Highland Council area, Blairmore lies to the north of Strath Fleet, just north of Rogart.

Blairmore *Highland* A small township in northwest Sutherland, Blairmore lies near Balchrick, 3 miles (5 km) northwest of Kinlochbervie.

Blairquhan *South Ayrshire* The settlement of Blairquhan is located a mile (1.5 km) northwest of Straiton in South Ayrshire. It lies on a tributary of the Water of Girvan. Blairquhan Castle is a Tudor-Gothic-style mansion built by the Edinburgh-based architect William Burn (1789–1870). The castle was commissioned by Sir David Hunter Blair, son of the banker and Lord Provost of Edinburgh, Sir James Hunter Blair (1741–87), and built on an estate bought by his trustees following the untimely death of his father. The estate included a castle that had been a Kennedy stronghold built in 1346 and extended in 1573. The old castle, which had become ruinous, was removed and in 1821 the foundation stone of the new pile was laid by Sir Alexander Boswell of Auchinleck, son of the biographer and traveller James Boswell (1740–95). Completed in 1824, the house is surrounded by an estate of some 810 ha (2000 acres) which was planned from 1803 by Sir David himself. He diverted the Water of Girvan to bring it closer to the house, and created a walled garden, glasshouse and pinetum, which includes a specimen of giant sequoia brought from North America in the mid-19th century. Today, the castle remains in the Hunter Blair family and is actively marketed as a venue for conferences and corporate entertainment.

Blairs, Loch of *Moray* A small loch on the Altyre Estate in Moray, the Loch of Blairs lies in a wooded landscape 2 miles (3 km) south of Forres.

Blairs Ferry *Argyll and Bute* A settlement on the western shore of the Kyles of Bute, Blairs Ferry faces the island of Bute, 2 miles (3 km) south of Tighnabruaich.

Blane Water *Stirling* The Blane (or Ballagan) Water rises in the Campsie Fells and flows south then west through Strathblane village before turning northwestwards through the Blane Valley to join the Endrick Water near Killearn. Its total length is about 10 miles (16 km).

Blanefield *Stirling* A dormitory village for Glasgow, Blanefield is situated in the Blane Valley next to Strathblane on the A81 at the southern extremity of Stirling Council area.

Blanerne *Scottish Borders* A locality in Berwickshire in Scottish Borders, Blanerne Castle and estate lie to the north of Edrom and the Whiteadder Water, 3 miles (5 km) west of Chirnside.

Blantyre *South Lanarkshire* A settlement in South Lanarkshire, Blantyre lies on the River Clyde, 3 miles (6.5 km) north of East Kilbride and 8 miles (12 km) southeast of Glasgow. A priory attached to Jedburgh was established here in the 13th century for the Augustinian canons, and in 1598 High Blantyre was chartered as a burgh of barony. In 1785 a large water-powered cotton mill was established at Low Blantyre just over a mile (1.5 km) northeast of High Blantyre, and a model village was created to house the textile workers. The explorer David Livingstone was born in a mill tenement in Low Blantyre in 1813. High Blantyre developed in association with coal mining in the 19th century, and in the 20th century the settlement further expanded with industries including quarrying, engineering and the manufacture of concrete products. Modern industry is centred on the Auchenraith industrial site and the Hamilton International Technology Park. The David Livingstone Centre, established in 1923, is now in the care of the National Trust for Scotland.

Blar a' Chaorainn *Highland* A locality in Lochaber, Blar a' Chaorainn lies on the old military road from Kinlochleven to Fort William, 5 miles (8 km) south of Fort William.

Blargie *Highland* A locality in Badenoch, Blargie lies to the north of the River Spey and west of Laggan, 7 miles (11 km) southwest of Newtonmore.

Blarmachfoldach *Highland* A small settlement in Lochaber, Blarmachfoldach lies on the old military road from Kinlochleven to Fort William, 3 miles (5 km) south of Fort William.

Blaven *Highland* A mountain on the eastern edge of the Black Cuillins on the isle of Skye in the Inner Hebrides, Blaven (Gael: *Blà Bheinn*) rises to a height of 928 m (3045 ft) at the head of Loch Slapin, 6 miles (10 km) west of Broadford. The greater part of the peak comprises dark-coloured gabbro rock.

Blebocraigs *Fife* A village in Kemback parish, western Fife, Blebocraigs is situated on a ridge overlooking the Kinness Burn, 5 miles (8 km) west of St Andrews. It was originally an estate village whose inhabitants quarried red sandstone in the surrounding area.

Blelack House *Aberdeenshire* A house of 18th-century origin in the Cromar district of central Aberdeenshire, Blelack lies just southeast of Newkirk and 6 miles (10 km) northwest of Aboyne. Partly destroyed in 1745, it was largely rebuilt in the 1850s as a Victorian shooting lodge.

Blervie Castle *Moray* The ruins of Blervie Castle in Moray lie 2 miles (3 km) southeast of Forres. Built in the 16th century, the castle was a stronghold of the Dunbar family. Nearby is the Edwardian mansion of Blervie House, built in 1910 to a design by J. M. Dick Peddie.

Bloch Hill *Dumfries and Galloway* A summit in southeast Dumfries and Galloway, Bloch Hill rises to 268 m (878 ft) nearly 3 miles (5 km) southwest of Langholm.

Blotchnie Fiold *Orkney* Rising to 251 m (821 ft) above Brinyan at the southeastern end of the Orkney island of Rousay, Blotchnie Fiold is the highest hill on the island.

Bluemull Sound *Shetland* A channel separating the Shetland islands of Yell and Unst, Bluemull Sound extends north–south and is 0.75 mile (1.25 km) wide. A vehicle ferry crosses the sound at its southern end joining Gutcher and Belmont, while also providing a service to the island of Fetlar, which lies 4 miles (6.5 km) to the south-southeast. The island of Linga lies in the sound.

Blyth Bridge *Scottish Borders* A village in Scottish Borders, Blyth Bridge lies on the Tarth Water, 10 miles (16 km) northwest of Peebles. Situated at a river crossing, it has an old water mill.

Blythswood Square *Glasgow City* Near the centre of Glasgow, Blythswood Square was created for the city's merchants in 1823 by the developer William Garden and his architect John Brash. The area of Blythswoodhill had originally been laid out by William Harley in 1804, but when he became bankrupt Garden took over. Garden himself was declared bankrupt and the rest of the development was completed by his trustees. It is now an area of offices, clubs and restaurants. The east side of the square was occupied by the Royal Scottish Automobile Club until 2002, when its premises were sold for conversion to a luxury hotel.

Bo Bàn *Western Isles* Little more than a rocky outlier, Bo Bàn is situated 2 miles (3 km) north of the island of Scarp, which lies off the northwest coast of North Harris in the Western Isles.

Boar of Badenoch An alternative name for An Torc on the border of Highland and Perth and Kinross.

Boar's Head Rock *Moray* The Boar's Head Rock is an islet at the centre of Spey Bay, an inlet of the Moray Firth that extends from Portknockie to Lossiemouth. It lies 4 miles (6.5 km) southeast of Lossiemouth.

Boar's Raik *Fife* The Cursus Apri or Boar's Raik was the name given in the Middle Ages to the territory immediately surrounding St Andrews in the parishes of St Andrew and St Leonard, Cameron, Dunino, Ceres and Kemback. It referred to the land originally granted to the church of the apostle St Andrew. 'Raik' is an old Scots word that was often applied to an extent of grazing for sheep or cattle, but in this context may have been applied to land where wild boars were hunted.

Boarhills *Fife* A village in eastern Fife, Boarhills lies on the Kenly Water 3 miles (5 km) southeast of St Andrews. Interesting buildings include the Parish School (1815), Boarhills Church (1867), Kenly Bridge (1793), 17th-century Kenly Dovecote, 16th-century Peekie Bridge and Kenly Green House, which was built to an Adam design in 1791.

Boat of Garten *Highland* A village in Strathspey, Highland Council area, Boat of Garten lies on the west side of the River Spey, 6 miles (10 km) northeast of Aviemore. A former ferry crossing, Boat of Garten developed as a railway village when the Inverness and Perth Junction Railway opened its main line from Forres to Dunkeld in 1863. Three years later Boat of Garten became a junction on the opening of the Great North of Scotland Railway line to Nethy Bridge and beyond. With the advent of tourism, an 18-hole golf course was established in 1898. Passenger rail travel ceased in 1965, but in 1973 the Strathspey Railway Society reopened the line from Boat of Garten to Aviemore for tourist use, the former station being used as their headquarters. At nearby Loch Garten nature reserve is an osprey nesting site with viewing facilities.

Boath *Highland* A locality in Easter Ross, Boath lies on the River Alness to the west of Ardross, 5 miles (8 km) northwest of Alness.

Boath Doocot *Highland* A 17th-century dovecote on the site of an ancient motte, Boath Doocot lies on the edge of the village of Auldearn near Nairn, Highland Council area. It was gifted to the National Trust for Scotland in 1947. On 9 May 1645 the Covenanters were defeated near here by the Marquess of Montrose.

Bod an Deamhain An alternative name for the Devil's Point.

Bodach Mòr *Highland* A mountain of the Freevater Forest in the Sutherland district of Highland Council area, Bodach Mòr lies 7 miles (11 km) west of the head of Strathcarron and reaches a height of 822 m (2696 ft).

Boddam *Aberdeenshire* A fishing village on the Buchan coast of Aberdeenshire, Boddam lies 3 miles (5 km) south of Peterhead by the promontory of Buchan Ness, on which stands Boddam Lighthouse, dating from 1827. Officially designated a port in 1845 by Act of Parliament, two harbours were developed at Boddam to the north and south of Buchan Ness. Further down the coast lie the ruins of Boddam Castle, the former seat of the Keiths of Ludquarn.

Boddam *Shetland* A village at the southern end of the Mainland of Shetland, Boddam lies some 4 miles (6.5 km) north of Sumburgh. Situated next to a working horizontal water mill of Norse design is the Croft House Museum, a showcase of Shetland rural life in the 19th century.

Boddin Point *Angus* A headland at the north end of Lunan Bay, Angus, Boddin Point is the site of an old harbour, 18th-century limekilns, a 19th-century salmon-fishing station, an icehouse and a bothy.

Bodesbeck Burn *Dumfries and Galloway* A stream in

Dumfries and Galloway, the Bodesbeck Burn rises between Bodesbeck Law and White Shank. It flows down to join the Moffat Water at Bodesbeck Farm opposite Capplegill. James Hogg (1770–1835), the 'Ettrick Shepherd', tells in *The Brownie of Bodesbeck* how the legendary brownies laboured to make this farm the best in the district until the farmer one night left out for them an inedible mess of bread and milk.

Bodesbeck Law *Dumfries and Galloway* A hill in Dumfries and Galloway, Bodesbeck Law rises to 662 m (2173 ft) to the east of the Moffat Water, 7 miles (11 km) northeast of Moffat.

Bogallan *Highland* A settlement on the Black Isle, Highland Council area, Bogallan lies 2 miles (3 km) southwest of Munlochy.

Bogend *South Ayrshire* Situated a mile (1.5 km) northeast of Symington in South Ayrshire, Bogend lies between the settlements of Whitelees and Coodham.

Boghead *South Lanarkshire* The small village of Boghead lies a mile (1.5 km) southwest of Kirkmuirhill and 2 miles (3 km) southwest of Blackwood in South Lanarkshire, close to the M74.

Bogie, Water of *Aberdeenshire* A river of Aberdeenshire, the Water of Bogie rises in headstreams in the parish of Auchindoir and Kearn to the north of Lumsden. It flows northeastwards through Rhynie to become the River Bogie. Continuing northwards through Strathbogie, it eventually joins the River Deveron just north of Huntly.

Bogniebrae *Aberdeenshire* The site of an inn in Strathbogie, Aberdeenshire, Bogniebrae lies to the west of the Burn of Forgue, at the junction of the A97 with the B9002. Nearby are Yonder Bognie and Mains of Bognie.

Bogrie Hill *Dumfries and Galloway* A hill in Dumfries and Galloway, Bogrie Hill rises to 432 m (1417 ft) above Bogrie Moor to the south of Moniaive.

Bogroy *Highland* A crofting settlement in Strathspey, Highland Council area, Bogroy lies near the Dulnain River, just west of Carrbridge.

Bogside *North Lanarkshire* Bogside is a southwestern district of the town of Kilsyth in North Lanarkshire.

Bogue *Dumfries and Galloway* A hamlet in the Glenkens district of Dumfries and Galloway, Bogue lies 1.5 miles (2.5 km) east of St John's Town of Dalry and 3 miles (5 km) northeast of New Galloway.

Bohenie *Highland* A locality in Glen Roy, Highland Council area, Bohenie lies nearly 2 miles (3 km) northeast of Roybridge.

Bohuntine *Highland* Situated in Glen Roy, Highland Council area, Bohuntine lies to the west of the River Roy and north of Roybridge.

Boisdale, Loch *Western Isles* Located in the southeast of South Uist in the Western Isles, Loch Boisdale (Gael: *Loch Baghasdail*) forms a large sea loch with several small islands, on one of which, Calvay, stands a lighthouse and the ruined remains of a castle. The settlement of Lochboisdale lies at the head of the loch.

Boleskine *Highland* A locality in the Great Glen, Highland Council area, Boleskine lies to the east of Loch Ness in the neighbourhood of Foyers. Boleskine House was home to the satanist Aleister Crowley (1875–1947).

Bolfracks *Perth and Kinross* A locality in Perth and Kinross, Bolfracks overlooks the River Tay 2 miles (3 km) southwest of Aberfeldy. Bolfracks House, situated in the shadow of Bolfracks Hill, is an 18th-century farmsteading with a Gothic-style frontage created in the early 19th century for the 2nd Marquess of Breadalbane, owner of nearby Taymouth Castle.

Bolshan *Angus* A hamlet and estate in the Angus parish of Kinnell, Bolshan lies 5 miles (8 km) to the south of Brechin and 2 miles (3 km) northeast of Friockheim. Said to have been a gift from the Abbot of Brechin to the Abbot of Arbroath in 1127, Bolshan was the site of a castle that had been removed by the 18th century. Bolshan has associations with the Ogilvie family and the Maules, who became the earls of Panmure.

Bolton *East Lothian* Lying to the west of the Gifford Water in East Lothian, 2.5 miles (4 km) south of Haddington, is the village of Bolton. It consists of a group of buildings on an elevated site, the most notable being the handsome Parish Church (1809), the former school (1838) and an 18th-century dovecote. Bolton is best known as the last home of the poet Robert Burns's younger brother Gilbert, his sister Annabella and their mother, Agnes Broun. Gilbert moved from Ayrshire on the death of his brother, working at Morham West Mains, 2.5 miles (4 km) to the east, before becoming factor to Lord Blantyre at Lennoxlove. He took up residence in a house at Grant's Braes and his mother and sister came to live with him. The location of that house is marked by a roadside memorial a mile (1.5 km) north of the village, and Burns' Mother's Well lies nearby. Gilbert oversaw the building of Bolton Parish Church, and the family lie buried together in the churchyard. The parish is now united with nearby Saltoun. Lennoxlove House, now home of the dukes of Hamilton, lies 2 miles (3 km) to the north.

Bombie *Dumfries and Galloway* A settlement in the former Stewartry of Kirkcudbright, Bombie lies to the south of the Gribdae Burn, 2 miles (3 km) east of Kirkcudbright. Bombie Hill rises to the south.

Bonaly Reservoir *City of Edinburgh* A reservoir lying 3 miles (5 km) to the southwest of Wester Hailes and 6 miles (10 km) southwest of Edinburgh city centre, Bonaly Reservoir is one of a number of reservoirs supplying the city with water.

Bonar Bridge *Highland* A village in Easter Ross, Highland Council area, Bonar Bridge lies on a narrow strip of land between the Kyle of Sutherland and Dornoch Firth. It is situated at a crossing and road junction that was developed in the early 19th century. An iron bridge over the Kyle, built by Thomas Telford, was erected in 1811–12. Washed away in 1892, this bridge was replaced by a structure designed by William Arrol, and in 1973 a third Bonar Bridge was built. A railway was brought to Bonar Bridge Station at nearby Ardgay in 1864, and with the advent of tourism, hotels and a golf course appeared.

Bonawe *Argyll and Bute* Located on Airds Bay on the southern shore of Loch Etive, the village of Bonawe lies a mile (1.5 km) northeast of Taynuilt. To the northeast of the village lies the site of the Bonawe Iron Furnace, an 18th-century industrial site where cannons and shot were produced, and across the loch lies the settlement of Bonawe Quarries.

Bonawe Iron Furnace *Argyll and Bute* The Bonawe Iron Furnace is located on the south side of Loch Etive, just northeast of the village of Taynuilt. This charcoal-fuelled iron furnace was founded in 1753 and is the most complete example of this type of building in Britain. It operated until 1874, producing cannon and shot for the Navy. Now under the ownership of Historic Scotland, it houses displays on the making of iron.

Bonawe Quarries *Argyll and Bute* The settlement of Bonawe Quarries is located on the northern shore of Loch Etive, a mile (1.5 km) north of Bonawe and 2 miles (3 km) northeast of Taynuilt.

Bonchester Bridge *Scottish Borders* A hamlet to the south of Teviotdale in Scottish Borders, Bonchester Bridge lies on the Rule Water, 6 miles (10 km) southeast of Hawick. Bonchester Hill, which is topped by the ramparts of an Iron Age fort, rises to 322 m (1059 ft) to the east.

Bo'ness *Falkirk* A town in Falkirk Council area, situated on a nose of land jutting into the Firth of Forth, Bo'ness is short for Borrowstounness – the Burgh Town on the Ness. Recognised as a port in 1601, it became one of Scotland's leading ports in the early 18th century when the customs house was moved from nearby Blackness. It exported coal and slag to the Low Countries and Scandinavia and imported timber from the Baltic and clay and flint from Devon and Cornwall for use in Dr John Roebuck's Bridgeness pottery. The town also developed as a prosperous shipbuilding, whaling and fishing port, its inhabitants being known as 'Garvies', a local name for sprats. A decline in the fortunes of Bo'ness followed the collapse of the tobacco trade and the completion in 1790 of the Forth and Clyde Canal, which resulted in trade moving to Grangemouth. Shipbreaking, coal mining and the manufacture of pit props became important local industries in the 19th century, the waste slag from coal mines being used to reclaim land from the Forth, an idea developed by the local geologist Henry M. Cadell (1860–1934). Buildings of interest include Kinneil House, Bo'ness Town Hall (1904) and Bridgeness Tower, which was formerly a windmill and an observatory. Part of the Roman Antonine Wall known as Graham's Dyke passes through the town, which now incorporates the districts of Corbiehall, Castleloan, Deanfield, Maidenpark, Kinneil, Borrowstoun Mains, Borrowstoun, Newtown, Grangepans, Grahamsdyke, Carriden and Bridgeness. The Scottish Railway Preservation Society operates steam-hauled trains on the Bo'ness and Kinneil Railway which stretches for 3.5 miles (5.5 km) from Bo'ness to Birkill Clay Mine, where 300-million-year-old fossils can be seen in underground tunnels.

Bonhill *West Dunbartonshire* Situated on the east bank of the River Leven opposite Alexandria, Bonhill is a former textile town best known for bleaching and dyeing. Sir James Smollett, grandfather of the novelist Tobias Smollett (1721–71), was granted the lands of Bonhill in 1660. The town was well known for its halfpenny toll bridge (1836) which was named the 'Bawbee Bridge'. Nearby are the settlements of Alexandria and Renton.

Bonjedward*Scottish Borders* A hamlet in Scottish Borders, Bonjedward lies 2 miles (3 km) north of Jedburgh near the junction of the River Teviot with the Tweed.

Bonkle *North Lanarkshire* The settlement of Bonkle is located 3 miles (5 km) northwest of Wishaw in North Lanarkshire. Originally the two separate settlements of Auchter Bridgend and Bonkle, the latter name now applies to the area from the Auchter Water to the settlement of Bonkle. The village is believed to date from 1775, when the first cottages are thought to have been built. There was a close association with the Stuarts of Allanton, many residents of the village working on the Allanton Estate, a country estate that extended to 810 ha (2000 acres).

Bonnavoulin *Highland* A settlement on the Morvern peninsula, Bonnavoulin lies 2 miles (3 km) southeast of Auliston Point.

Bonnington Linn *South Lanarkshire* A waterfall situated a mile (1.5 km) upstream of New Lanark in the Clyde Valley, Bonnington Linn is 11 m (36 ft) high and is used as a source of hydro-electric power via the Bonnington Power Station.

Bonnybank *Fife* Less than a mile (1.5 km) to the north of Kennoway in Fife, the settlement of Bonnybank straddles the A916 from Kennoway to Cupar.

Bonnybridge *Falkirk* A village in Falkirk Council area, Bonnybridge is situated on the Bonny Water and the Forth and Clyde Canal, 4 miles (6.5 km) west of Falkirk. It developed in the 19th century in association with a paper mill, sawmill and iron foundries. High Bonnybridge, with its industrial estate, lies to the south, and to the west is a sand and gravel quarry. Rough Castle, the most complete of the surviving Roman forts on the Antonine Wall, is nearby.

Bonnyrigg *Midlothian* A small town in Midlothian, Bonnyrigg is located 6 miles (10 km) southeast of Edinburgh in the parishes of Cockpen and Lasswade. Bonnyrigg was a mining village until the 1920s and had a carpet factory that was demolished in 1994. The village

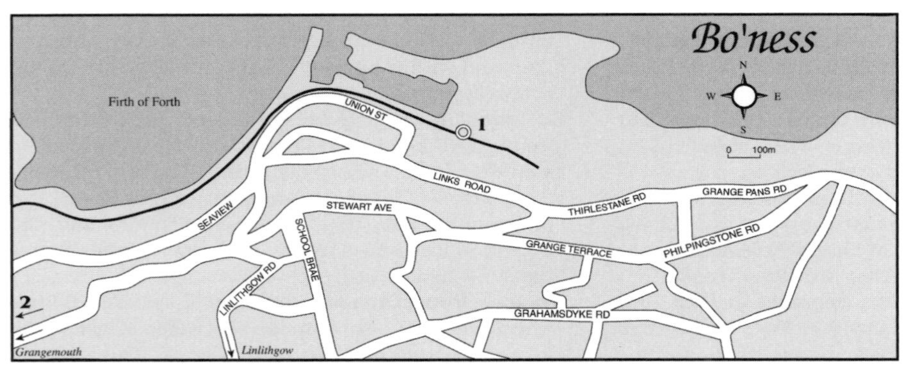

1 *Scottish Railway Exhibition*
2 *Kinneil House*

centre mostly dates from the 19th century, though buildings at the main crossroads were built in the 1960s. In 1929 it united with Lasswade. In nearby Polton are buildings from the 18th and 19th centuries, including De Quincey Cottage (home of the writer Thomas De Quincey, from 1840 until his death in 1859), Blairesk Hall (*c*.1818) and Midfield House (18th century, reconstructed 1914).

Bonshaw Tower *Dumfries and Galloway* A 16th-century tower house in southeast Dumfries and Galloway, Bonshaw Tower sits by the Kirtle Water, 5 miles (8 km) northwest of Gretna Green. It was a stronghold of the Irvines who inherited the property from the Corries in the 15th century.

Boondreigh Water *Scottish Borders* A stream in Scottish Borders, the Boondreigh Water rises on Twin Law in the Lammermuirs. It flows 7 miles (11 km) southwards to join the Leader Water southeast of Lauder.

Boquhan *Stirling* A small hamlet and estate in Stirling Council Area, Boquhan lies a mile (1.25 km) southwest of Balfron, on the opposite bank of the Endrick Water, and 1.25 miles (2 km) northeast of Killearn. Lying to the east, Boquhan Old House dates from 1784.

Boraraigh The Gaelic name for Boreray between Harris and North Uist in the Western Isles.

Bore Stone, the *City of Edinburgh* Mounted on the wall of the former Morningside Parish Church, on Morningside Road in Edinburgh, is the Bore Stone. The stone is popularly believed to have supported the royal standard when the Scottish Army mustered on the Borough Muir before the Battle of Flodden in 1513. This claim has been challenged, and it may be that the stone was actually a simple boundary marker of a nearby estate.

Boreland *Dumfries and Galloway* A village of Annandale in Dumfries and Galloway, Boreland lies on the Boreland Burn, 9 miles (14 km) northeast of Lockerbie.

Boreraig *Highland* A settlement on the island of Skye in the Inner Hebrides, Boreraig (sometimes Borreraig) lies on the western shore of Loch Dunvegan, 2 miles (3 km) south of Dunvegan Head. Boreraig is intimately connected with the MacCrimmons, the famed hereditary pipers to MacLeod of Dunvegan, who established a piping college here. It is also a name given to another locality on Skye to the north of Loch Eishort.

Boreray *Western Isles* The uninhabited island of Boreray is in the St Kilda group of islands that lie 52 miles (83 km) west of North Harris in the Western Isles. Situated 3 miles (5 km) northeast of St Kilda, this island is little more than a rock outlier with steep cliffs that are home to nesting sea birds. Owned by the National Trust for Scotland, it has an area of 77 ha (190 acres) and a height of 384 m (1260 ft). The island of Stac an Armin lies to the north.

Boreray *Western Isles* An uninhabited island in the Sound of Harris in the Outer Hebrides, Boreray (Gael: *Boraraigh*) lies 1.25 miles (2 km) north of North Uist and 2 miles (3 km) west of Berneray and is approximately 1.5 miles (2.5 km) long by a mile (1.5 km) wide. The sizeable Loch Mòr fills much of the middle of the island, and its highest point is Mullach Mòr in the north, which rises to 56 m (184 ft). Until the 19th century, the island was the property of the MacLeans of Boreray. It has been uninhabited since the 1960s and the ruins of its abandoned village lie on its eastern shore. The island is today used for grazing by the islanders of Berneray.

Borghastan The Gaelic name for Borrowston in the Western Isles.

Borgh The Gaelic name for Borve in the Western Isles.

Borgie *Highland* A settlement in northern Sutherland, Borgie lies on the River Borgie to the west of Bettyhill. An original crofting settlement that was cleared for sheep in the 19th century was resettled *c*.1919.

Borgie, River *Highland* A river of Sutherland, Highland Council area, the Borgie flows 6 miles (10 km) northeastwards from Loch Loyal (*Loch Laoghal*) to Torrisdale Bay, an inlet of the Pentland Firth.

Borgue *Dumfries and Galloway* A village of southern Dumfries and Galloway, Borgue is situated 4 miles (6.5 km) southwest of Kirkcudbright. The 'Bard of Galloway', William Nicholson, was born at Tannymas in Borgue in August 1783.

Borgue *Highland* A settlement on the east coast of Caithness, Highland Council area, Borgue lies on the A9, 3 miles (5 km) south of Dunbeath.

Borneskitaig *Highland* A locality at the northern end of the island of Skye in the Inner Hebrides, Bornaskitaig lies 5 miles (8 km) to the north of Uig near the Ru Bornaskitaig headland.

Borness *Dumfries and Galloway* A locality in southern Dumfries and Galloway, Borness lies close to Borness Point on the Solway Firth and 6 miles (10 km) southwest of Kirkcudbright.

Borralan, Loch *Highland* A small loch in the Assynt district of western Sutherland, Loch Borralan lies just southeast of Ledmore.

Borrobol Lodge *Highland* A late 19th-century shooting lodge in eastern Sutherland, Highland Council area, Borrobol Lodge lies near the junction of Srath na Frithe and the Strath of Kildonan, 14 miles (22 km) northwest of Helmsdale.

Borrowston *Western Isles* A crofting township on the west coast of Lewis in the Outer Hebrides, Borrowston (Gael: *Borghastan*) lies on the north shore of Loch Carloway, a half-mile (1 km) west of Carloway. Ben Borrowston rises to 85 m (278 ft) immediately to the west.

Borrowston House *Aberdeenshire* Situated on the River Dee by Kincardine O'Neil in Aberdeenshire, Borrowston House lies 7 miles (11 km) west of Banchory.

Borrowstounness An alternative name for Bo'ness in Falkirk.

Borthwick *Midlothian* A hamlet lying 2 miles (3 km) southeast of Gorebridge. The 15th-century Borthwick Castle, now a hotel, was visited by Mary, Queen of Scots (1542–87) shortly after her third marriage. The picturesque Borthwick Parish Church dates from the mid-19th century.

Borthwick Castle *Midlothian* A twin-towered castle on the eastern flank of the hamlet of Borthwick in Midlothian, Borthwick Castle lies 2 miles (3 km) southeast of Gorebridge. It was built by Sir William Borthwick in 1430 on the site of an earlier tower and is noted for its exceptionally strong walls, which are up to 4.3 m (14 ft) thick. It is said that prisoners, with their hands tied, were invited to jump the 4-m (12-ft) gap between the massive towers of this U-plan keep. Those who succeeded were freed, those who did not would no longer be in need of the hospitality of the house! Mary,

Queen of Scots visited the castle in 1567, soon after her unpopular marriage to James Hepburn, Earl of Bothwell. The couple were besieged by a force of 1000, led by some of Mary's most senior nobles, who implicated Bothwell in the murder of her second husband, Henry Stewart, Lord Darnley. Mary was able to negotiate with the force, allowing Bothwell to slip away, and she escaped the following day dressed as a pageboy. The opposition quickly caught up with Mary who, within days, was forced into compromise and captivity at Carberry Hill. The Parliamentarian army of Oliver Cromwell attacked Borthwick in 1650 and brought about its swift surrender. Damage to the stonework, caused by cannon, can still be seen. The castle was abandoned not long after the visit of Cromwell's forces but was fully restored between 1890 and 1914. During World War II, Borthwick was used as a secret repository for various national treasures. In 1973 this fine castle was converted into a hotel.

Borthwick Water *Scottish Borders* A tributary of the River Teviot in Scottish Borders, the Borthwick Water rises as headstreams in Craik Forest near the border with Dumfries and Galloway. It flows 16 miles (26 km) northeastwards to join the Teviot 2 miles (3 km) above Hawick. A Roman road followed the course of the Borthwick Water from Craik Cross, its ultimate destination being Tweedmouth.

Borve *Highland* A village on the island of Skye in the Inner Hebrides, Borve lies 4 miles (6.5 km) northwest of Portree.

Borve *Western Isles* A settlement on the northwest coast of Lewis in the Outer Hebrides, Borve (Gael: *Bhuirgh*) lies on the Abhainn Bhuirgh, midway between Barvas and the Butt of Lewis. It comprises the townships of Five Penny Borve (Gael: *Coig Peighinnean Bhuirgh*) to the west, Melbost Borve (Gael: *Mealabost Bhuirgh*) to the north and Bail 'Ard Bhuirgh to the east.

Borve *Western Isles* A locality on the west coast of South Harris in the Outer Hebrides, Borve (Gael: *Na Buirgh*) lies 5.5 miles (9 km) north of Leverburgh. The location comprises a few scattered crofts, Borve Lodge, which was once the home of Lord Leverhulme, and a cemetery, with the tiny Loch Borve to the northeast and the remains of Dun Buirgh to the southeast.

Borve *Western Isles* A scattered crofting settlement on the southeast coast of the island of Berneray in the Outer Hebrides, Borve (Gael: *Borgh*) lies between Borve Hill and Loch Borve. The causeway connecting Berneray to North Uist and the pier that receives the ferry from Leverburgh are located a half-mile (1 km) to the south.

Borve *Western Isles* A crofting township on the west coast of Barra in the Outer Hebrides, Borve (Gael: *Borgh*) lies 2 miles (3 km) north-northwest of Castlebay. A pair of standing stones are located by the roadside.

Bothwell *South Lanarkshire* A settlement in South Lanarkshire, Bothwell lies 2 miles (3 km) east of Blantyre on the opposite side of the River Clyde, 2 miles (3 km) north of Hamilton and adjacent to the M74. Associated with the coal, iron and steel industries that predominated in the area in the late 19th and early 20th centuries, the town grew in association with nearby Hamilton and Blantyre. To the southeast of the town is the site of Bothwell Bridge Battlefield.

Bothwell Bridge Battlefield *South Lanarkshire* Located a mile (1.5 km) to the southeast of Bothwell and next to the M74 lies the battlefield of the Battle of Bothwell Bridge. It was here in 1679 that the Covenanter movement, after their success at the Battle of Drumclog, had gathered to establish their next move. While here they were attacked by the combined forces of Graham of Claverhouse, the Duke of Monmouth and the Earl of Linlithgow. Although few of the Covenanters were killed in battle, many died after capture and over 200 were shipwrecked while being transported in *The Crown of London*.

Bothwell Castle *South Lanarkshire* Located a mile (1.5 km) northwest of the town of Bothwell, Bothwell Castle stands on a rocky outcrop that overlooks the River Clyde. Of strategic importance, it was built by the Moray family in the 13th century, after Walter de Moray inherited the estates of Bothwell through marriage (1242). The Morays intended to build a fine castle, with a large courtyard, but only part was complete when the Wars of Independence began and Bothwell was taken by the English (1296). It changed hands several times and was subject to a succession of damaging sieges, the most notable of which was in 1301, when King Edward I captured the castle using a huge siege engine. The most interesting feature of the castle is the immense 'Great Donjon', or round tower, which the Morays were able to complete. This stands 27.4 m (90 ft) high, has walls that reach 4.6 m (15 ft) thick and has been described as 'the grandest ruin of its kind in Scotland' (MacGibbon and Ross, 1887). In 1337, after the last siege, the castle was dismantled by the Scots Army to prevent further English occupation. Around 1362, Bothwell passed through marriage to Archibald 'the Grim' Douglas, who undertook significant rebuilding to repair the destruction it had suffered. When the 'Black' Douglas family fell from favour in 1455, the castle became the property of the Crown. In 1489, it was given to Patrick Hepburn, the 2nd Lord Hailes, but very soon afterwards was exchanged with the 'Red' Douglas earls of Angus in return for Hermitage Castle in Scottish Borders, although the Hepburns were later known as the earls of Bothwell. In 1669, the castle passed to the Douglas earls of Forfar who built a fine Palladian mansion just to the east, which was demolished in 1926 having been undermined by coal mining. By the 19th century the property had passed to the earls of Home, who remain the owners, although the ruins have been in the care of the State since 1935.

Bothwellhaugh *South Lanarkshire* A locality and former mining village, Bothwellhaugh was, from medieval times, the name given to a tract of low-lying pasture-land wrapped around a bend in the River Clyde lying to the east of the town of Bothwell. Originally the site of a Roman fort, the area much later became part of the Duke of Hamilton's estates. The duke ensured rapid development when he allowed the Hamilton Palace Colliery to be sunk here in 1884 to exploit the rich coal measures lying beneath the surface. Other pits lay to the west, north and east. The village of Bothwellhaugh, known locally as 'the Pailis' after the mine, became one of the largest mining villages in the Clyde Valley. It included two churches, two schools, a Miner's Welfare Association, Cooperative store, 450 dwellings and allotment gardens, all in the shadow of a large bing, but not a solitary public house as alcohol was prohibited. At its peak the colliery employed 1400 workers and produced 2000 tonnes of coal per day. It was this colliery that undermined Hamilton Palace, necessitating its demolition in the 1920s. The pit closed in 1959 and the village quickly declined, with many houses lying empty. With the community lost, the last of the people were dispersed in the early 1960s and the remainder of the village demolished in 1966. The area lay derelict until much of it was flooded when Strathclyde Loch was created within Strathclyde Country Park in the early 1970s. The M74 was routed immediately to the west of the site. The only traces of the village today are a memorial cairn, with memorabilia and displays in the Countryside Ranger Service Visitor Centre in the country park. James Hamilton of Bothwellhaugh assassinated the Regent Moray in Linlithgow in 1570.

Bottle Island *Highland* One of the Summer Isles, Bottle Island lies off the coast of Wester Ross, a mile (1.5 km) south of Eilean Dubh. To the west is Priest Island and to the south Gruinard.

Bottomcraig *Fife* A small hamlet in the parish of Balmerino, northern Fife, Bottomcraig lies between the villages of Balmerino and Gauldry.

Bousd *Argyll and Bute* A settlement on the north coast of the island of Coll in the Inner Hebrides, Bousd lies 4 miles (6.5 km) northeast of Arinagour.

Bovain *Stirling* A locality in Glen Dochart, northwest Stirling Council area, Bovain lies on a minor road to the north of the River Dochart, 2 miles (3 km) southwest of Killin. From the 14th century, Bovain was the seat of the chief of the Clan MacNab.

Bow Burn *Dumfries and Galloway* A stream in Dumfries and Galloway, the Bow Burn rises on the slopes of Cairnsmore of Carsphairn. It flows generally southwestwards to join the Water of Deugh 2 miles (3 km) northwest of Carsphairn.

Bow of Fife *Fife* A hamlet with a red-spired church (1843) in the parish of Monimail, central Fife, the Bow of Fife is situated 3 miles (5 km) west of Cupar at a point where the estates of Melville, Over Rankeillour and Nether Rankeillour meet. It lies on a bend of the Daft Burn which flows southwards to meet the River Eden.

Bowbeat Hill *Midlothian/Scottish Borders* A hill on the border of Midlothian and Scottish Borders, Bowbeat Hill is one of the Moorfoot Hills. It rises to 626 m (2053 ft) 3 miles (5 km) east of Eddleston and 5 miles (8 km) northeast of Peebles. A wind farm opened here in 2002.

Bowdun Head *Aberdeenshire* A headland on the North Sea coast of southeast Aberdeenshire, Bowdun Head lies directly north of Dunnottar Castle on the north side of Castle Haven.

Bowermadden *Highland* A scattered settlement in Caithness, northeastern Highland Council area, Bowermadden lies 4 miles (6.5 km) southeast of Castletown.

Bowershall *Fife* A small agricultural hamlet in Dunfermline parish, western Fife, Bowershall is situated a mile (1.5 km) north of Townhill and just over 2 miles (3 km) north of Dunfermline.

Bowertower *Highland* A locality in Caithness, northeastern Highland Council area, Bowertower lies to the south of the B876, 5 miles (8 km) south of Castletown.

Bowhill *Scottish Borders* Located 3 miles (5 km) west of Selkirk, Bowhill is a seat of the dukes of Buccleuch. Built in the early 18th century, Bowhill underwent two major face-lifts: firstly into a neoclassical villa at the hands of William Atkinson, who was the architect at Sir Walter Scott's Abbotsford, and later by William Burn (1789–1870). Scott (1771–1832) was a close friend and distant relation of the 4th Duke of Buccleuch. The estate had been owned by the Scotts since the 12th century. However, it passed in 1690 to the Murray family, who built the original house. It was bought back by the 2nd Duke of Buccleuch in 1745. The 4th Duke added substantially to the house from 1812, asking architect William Atkinson initially to build on to the south aspect, but then adding new flanking wings (1819). The 5th Duke commissioned William Burn to remodel further and extend the house (1831), and Burn continued to tinker with it until his death. The result was an extensive if somewhat rambling house with an enormous 133-m (437-ft) frontage. The house contains a fine collection of French furniture, porcelain (including Meissen and Sèvres), and portraiture by Reynolds, Gainsborough, Van Dyck, Raeburn and Lely. One room includes memorabilia relating to the Duke of Monmouth, the son of King Charles II, who married the Duchess of Buccleuch but was executed in 1685. The furnishings and art have been enhanced by items drawn from the Buccleuchs' former homes of Dalkeith Palace and Montagu House (London) which have been put to other uses. A notable piece of furniture thus moved is 'General Monk's Bed', transferred to Bowhill from Dalkeith.

Bowling *West Dunbartonshire* Located on the northern bank of the River Clyde, 3 miles (5 km) east of Dumbarton, Bowling sits at the foot of the Kilpatrick Hills. Situated on the road from Glasgow to Dumbarton, it developed in association with mills and a brewery in the 18th century and received a boost in 1790 when it was chosen as the western terminus of the Forth and Clyde Canal, which was built for the transport of coal and iron. The trials of the pioneer steamship *Comet* took place here in 1812 and port facilities were developed. A shipyard was opened in 1825 and Clyde steamers linked Bowling with Lochgilphead. Today Bowling is largely a commuter settlement with leisure yachting facilities.

Bowmont Water *Scottish Borders* A stream in Scottish Borders, the Bowmont Water rises in headstreams in the Cheviots. It flows generally northwards past Town Yetholm and Kirk Yetholm, crossing the English Border to join the Till near Flodden.

Bowmore *Argyll and Bute* A fishing village with whisky distillery on the island of Islay, Bowmore lies on the eastern shore of Loch Indaal, 10 miles (16 km) north of Port Ellen. The former settlement of Loggan, chartered as a burgh of barony in 1614, was replaced by a new planned village called Bowmore laid out in 1767–8 by Daniel Campbell of Islay. A unique circular church was built and the equally unique Islay parliament, which had originally convened at Kinlaggan, met here from 1718 to 1843. Bowmore's harbour, which had served Glasgow steamers, had silted up by the 1920s, but its pier was used as a flying-boat base during World War II. In addition to whisky distilling there are textile, craft and dairy-produce industries.

Bowriefauld *Angus* A hamlet of central Angus, Bowriefauld is located a half-mile (1 km) southwest of Letham and a similar distance southeast of Dunnichen.

Boyken Burn *Dumfries and Galloway* A stream in Eskdale, Dumfries and Galloway, the Boyken Burn rises in the hills to the south of Castle O'er Forest and flows eastwards to join the River Esk just south of Bentpath.

Boyndie *Aberdeenshire* A settlement in an Aberdeenshire parish of the same name, Boyndie lies between the Burn of Boyndie and the Moray Firth coast, 3 miles (5 km) west of Banff. An RAF station was established to the west of Boyndie during World War II.

Boyndie Bay *Aberdeenshire* An inlet of the Moray Firth on the coast of Aberdeenshire, Boyndie Bay stretches westwards from Banff to Whitehills.

Boyndlie House *Aberdeenshire* Situated in northern Aberdeenshire, Boyndlie House lies 6 miles (10 km) southwest of Fraserburgh. It is a seat of a branch of the Forbes family.

Boyne Castle *Aberdeenshire* The remains of Boyne Castle are located on the Burn of Boyne, southeast of Boyne Bay on the northern coast of Aberdeenshire. Situated between Portsoy and Banff, the castle is 16th century in origin.

Braal Castle *Highland* A 15th-century keep, Braal (or *Brawl*) Castle is located on the west bank of the River Thurso on the northeast side of Halkirk in the Caithness district of Highland Council area.

Braan, River *Perth and Kinross* A river of Perth and Kinross, the Braan emerges from the eastern end of Loch Freuchie, to the west of Amulree. It flows 11 miles (18 km) eastwards through Strath Braan to join the River Tay at Dunkeld. Nearly 3 miles (5 km) from its mouth at Rumbling Bridge, the river falls into a deep gorge.

Brabster *Highland* A settlement in Caithness, Highland Council area, Brabster lies 5 miles (8 km) to the southwest of Duncansby Head.

Bracadale *Highland* A village on the west coast of the isle of Skye, Highland Council area, Bracadale lies near the shore of Loch Bracadale, 10 miles (16 km) north of the Cuillins.

Bracadale, Loch *Highland* A sea loch on the west coast of the isle of Skye, Highland Council area, Loch Bracadale opens out at the mouth of Loch Harport opposite Ardtreck Point. The village of Bracadale lies to the north, and the loch is fed by the Allt Mòr.

Brack, Loch *Dumfries and Galloway* A small loch in Dumfries and Galloway, Loch Brack lies on the slopes of Traquhain Hill in Corriedoo Forest, 4 miles (6.5 km) northeast of New Galloway.

Brackland, Falls of An alternative name for the Falls of Bracklinn in Stirling Council area.

Brackletter *Highland* A settlement in the Great Glen, Highland Council area, Brackletter lies to the south of the River Spean, a mile (1.5 km) west of Spean Bridge.

Brackley *Highland* A locality in Highland Council area, Brackley is situated at a road junction near Loch Flemington, 3 miles (5 km) southeast of Ardersier and 10 miles (16 km) northeast of Inverness.

Bracklinn, Falls of *Stirling* A series of dramatic waterfalls on the Keltie Water to the northeast of Callander, the Falls of Bracklinn are approached along a woodland walk from a car park by the Callander Crags at Callander. They are also referred to as the Falls of Brackland.

Braco *Perth and Kinross* A village in southwestern Perth and Kinross, Braco is situated on the River Knaik 6 miles (10 km) northeast of Dunblane. On the northern edge of the village is the site of the great Roman fortress of Ardoch and its associated marching camps. The 16th-century tower house of Braco Castle is located to the northwest of the settlement. An agricultural show is held annually.

Bracora *Highland* A settlement in North Morar, Highland Council area, Bracora lies on the north shore of Loch Morar, 4 miles (6.5 km) southeast of Mallaig.

Bracorina *Highland* The settlement of Bracorina lies on the north shore of Loch Morar, a mile (1.5 km) to the east of Bracora in North Morar, Highland Council area.

Bradan, Loch *South Ayrshire* A reservoir in South Ayrshire, Loch Bradan is the source of a tributary of the Water of Girvan, which flows through Blairquhan. The loch is located within the Glentrool Forest Park, 7 miles (11 km) southwest of Dalmellington.

Brae *Highland* A locality in Strath Oykel, Easter Ross, Brae lies 4 miles (6.5 km) east of Oykel Bridge.

Brae *Shetland* A township on the Mainland island of Shetland, Brae is situated 22 miles (35 km) north of Lerwick on the neck of land that separates Sullom Voe from Busta Voe. The road diverges here for the oil terminal at Sullom Voe.

Braegrum *Perth and Kinross* A settlement of Perth and Kinross, Braegrum lies on the A85 from Perth to Crieff, a mile (1.5 km) west of Methven.

Braehead *South Lanarkshire* The village of Braehead is located 7 miles (11 km) northeast of Lanark, 3 miles (5 km) northwest of Carnwath in South Lanarkshire.

Braehead Centre *Renfrewshire* Located halfway between Glasgow city centre and Glasgow Airport on the south bank of the River Clyde, the Braehead Centre is Scotland's premier shopping centre. It was opened in 1999 and has over 100 stores on two floors. It also has leisure facilities, including an ice rink for skating and curling, an indoor arena and the Clydebuilt Maritime Heritage Centre.

Braelangwell Lodge *Highland* A former shooting lodge of the Rosses of Balnagown dating from the 1740s, Braelangwell Lodge lies in Strathcarron to the west of Bonar Bridge.

Braemar *Aberdeenshire* A settlement in Upper Deeside, western Aberdeenshire, Braemar is situated at an altitude of 335 m (1100 ft) above sea level, 59 miles (95 km) west of Aberdeen and 50 miles (80 km) north of Perth. It comprises the villages of Castleton of Braemar and Auchindryne on either side of the Clunie Water, which joins the River Dee immediately to the north. The village is a winter-sports and tourist centre, giving access to some of Scotland's finest mountain scenery, and plays host to the annual Braemar Gathering in September, an event held in the Princess Royal Park and usually attended by members of the royal family. The original castle of Braemar, known as Kindrochit or Bridge-head, was a hunting lodge of King Robert II during the late 14th century. The present castle was built in 1628 by the Earl of Mar to check the rising power of the Farquharsons, who later came to own the building in 1732. Following the second Jacobite Rising, it was restored as a Hanoverian garrison by the architect John Adam. In 1715 the Earl of Mar raised the Jacobite standard on a mound where the

Invercauld Hotel now stands, and in 1881 Robert Louis Stevenson wrote *Treasure Island* (1883) while staying in a cottage in Braemar. The modern development of Braemar as a resort dates from 1852, when Prince Albert purchased the nearby Balmoral Estate from the Earl of Fife. Queen Victoria's frequent visits to Deeside and the eventual penetration of Upper Deeside by a railway drew large numbers of visitors to this scenic location with its dry and bracing climate.

Braemore *Highland* A locality in central Sutherland, Braemore lies to the west of Achany Glen, 3 miles (5 km) southwest of Lairg.

Braemore Lodge *Highland* A mid-19th-century shooting lodge in eastern Caithness, Braemore Lodge lies in the valley of the Berriedale Water to the west of Dunbeath. The lodge stands on the site of a former chapel.

Braeriach *Highland/Aberdeenshire* Rising to a height of 1296 m (4252 ft), Braeriach is the second-highest peak in the Cairngorms. Located west of Lairig Ghru and Glen Dee on the border of Highland Council area and Aberdeenshire, Braeriach offers fine views towards Aviemore. It has a crescent-shaped peak created by three symmetrical northern corries that have red granite cliffs just below the summit. Its name is derived from the Gaelic for 'the brindled upland'.

Braes of Angus *Angus* Rising up from the wide valley of Strathmore in Angus, the Braes of Angus form the southeastern edge of the Grampian Mountains. The Ardler, Shee, Isla, Prosen, South Esk and North Esk Rivers cut down through the Braes of Angus, forming deep valleys.

Braes of Balquhidder *Stirling* A range of hills in the Balquhidder district of Stirling Council area, the south-facing Braes of Balquhidder rise to the north of Loch Doine and Loch Voil to the west of Balquhidder village. The Braes are cut deep by burns such as the Allt Carnaig, Monachyle Burn and Allt Gleann Crotha, which flow down from the high peaks that separate Glen Dochart from Balquhidder.

Braes of the Carse *Perth and Kinross* The Braes of the Carse is the name given to the south-facing foothills of the Sidlaw Hills fringing the Carse of Gowrie between Perth and Dundee. The villages of Kilspindie, Rait, Kinnaird and Baledgarno are among the main settlements of the Braes.

Bragar *Western Isles* A sizeable crofting township on the northwest coast of Lewis in the Outer Hebrides, Bragar (Gael: *Bhragair*) lies 1.25 miles (2 km) west-southwest of Arnol and 2 miles (3 km) east-northeast of Shawbost. Bragar benefits from a primary school, and there is a whalebone arch in the centre of the village. Erected in 1920, the arch comprises the jawbone of a whale that beached locally.

Brahan Castle *Highland* The ruined remains of Brahan Castle are located in Easter Ross, 4 miles (6.5 km) southwest of Dingwall. The castle was built in the 17th century and was the stronghold of the earls of Seaforth, chiefs of the Clan Mackenzie, before it was demolished in 1953.

Braid *City of Edinburgh* A residential district of southern Edinburgh, Braid is centred on the Hermitage of Braid and was formed by the feuing of the Braid Estate from the late 19th century. The name Braid may derive from the De Brad family who were associated with the area from the time of King David I (*c.*1080–1153) until 1305. Braid Castle existed from the 12th century to the 18th century, a new country house eventually being completed at the Hermitage of Braid in 1785 for Charles Gordon of Cluny. Much to the disgust of the author Robert Louis Stevenson, large villas were built to the north of the Braid Burn between 1877 and 1905, under the direction of the feuing architect Sir Robert Rowand Anderson. The district was further extended to the south on the slopes of the Braid Hills with the building of bungalows during the inter-war period. The Braid district was the location of the last execution in Scotland for highway robbery. Thomas Kelly and Henry O'Neill were hanged in 1815, and the two slabs that formed the base for the gallows can still be seen at the junction of Braid Road and Comiston Terrace.

Braid Burn *City of Edinburgh* Formed by the meeting of headwaters rising in the Pentland Hills, the Braid Burn flows for 9 miles (14 km) northeast through the city of Edinburgh before becoming the Figgate Burn northeast of Duddingston and completing its final mile (1.5 km) before draining into the Firth of Forth at Portobello.

Braid Hills *City of Edinburgh* The Braid Hills rise in a pair of summits of 206 m (675 ft) and 166 m (546 ft) 2.5 miles (4 km) south of the centre of Edinburgh. The area was established as a park by the city fathers in 1890, and two municipal golf courses are now draped over the hills which serve as an important part of Edinburgh's green belt and a wildlife refuge. Geologically, the Braid Hills are composed of Lower Devonian volcanic rocks similar to those in the Pentland Hills to the south.

Braidwood *South Lanarkshire* A commuter village in South Lanarkshire, Braidwood is located 2 miles (3 km) south of Carluke and 7 miles (11 km) northwest of Carstairs Junction. Once a centre of limestone production, Braidwood was an ancient barony that belonged to the earls of Douglas, the earls of Angus and the Lockharts of Carnwath, among others. Close to the village is Hallbar Tower, a 16th-century fortification that was built in response to a 1593 Act of Parliament and the threat posed by Border reivers.

Braigh Coire Chruinn-bhalgain *Perth and Kinross* One of three tops on the Beinn a' Ghlo massif, Braigh Coire Chruinn-bhalgain rises to a height of 1070 m (3510 ft) northeast of Blair Atholl, Perth and Kinross. Its name is the Gaelic for 'upland of the corrie of round blisters'.

Braigh na h-Aoidhe The Gaelic name for Branahuie in the Western Isles.

Bran, River *Highland* A river in Easter Ross, the River Bran rises in Loch a' Chroisg and flows 10 miles (16 km) eastwards through Strath Bran to enter Loch Achanalt, Loch a' Chuilinn and then Loch Luichart.

Bran, Strath *Highland* A valley in Ross-shire, Highland Council area, Strath Bran extends east–west from Loch Luichart to Achnasheen following the course of the River Bran. Both the railway from Dingwall to Kyle of Lochalsh and the A832 run through the valley.

Bran Burn *Dumfries and Galloway* A headstream of the Water of Ae in Dumfries and Galloway, the Bran Burn rises on the slopes of Queensberry, from where it flows south and southeast.

Branahuie *Western Isles* A small crofting township in eastern Lewis in the Outer Hebrides, Branahuie (Gael: *Braigh na h-Aoidhe*) lies to the south of Melbost and Stornoway Airport and 2.5 miles (4 km) east of Stornoway.

Branault *Highland* A settlement on the Ardnamurchan peninsula, Branault lies 5 miles (8 km) northeast of Kilchoan.

Brander, Pass of *Argyll and Bute* A narrow pass in the Lorn district of Argyll and Bute, the Pass of Brander links the head of Loch Awe with Loch Etive to the northwest. It is occupied by the course of the River Awe, with Ben Cruachan rising to the north.

Branderburgh *Moray* Situated immediately north of Lossiemouth on the coast of the Moray Firth, Branderburgh and its harbour were built *c*.1830 when the new town of Lossiemouth and the harbour by the Seatown could not cope with the increased volume of boats. The grid-plan settlement was designed by George MacWilliam and named after local landowner Colonel Brander of Pitgaveny. The Fishery and Community Museum contains scale models of fishing boats and a reconstruction of the study of Britain's first Labour prime minister, Ramsay MacDonald, who was born in Lossiemouth in 1866.

Brandy, Loch *Angus* A small loch in Angus, Loch Brandy is located nearly 610 m (2000 ft) above sea level on the western slopes of the Green Hill above Glen Clova.

Branklyn Garden *Perth and Kinross* A small garden in the eastern outskirts of the city of Perth, Branklyn Garden is located on the Dundee road to the east of the River Tay. Described as 'the finest two acres of private garden in the country', it was bequeathed to the National Trust for Scotland in 1967 by chartered land agent John T. Renton CBE who, with his wife, began planting on the site of a former orchard in 1922. The garden contains an outstanding collection of rhododendrons, alpines, and herbaceous and peat-garden plants.

Branny, Burn of *Angus* A small stream in Angus, the Burn of Branny rises in the Grampians and flows southwards for nearly 5 miles (8 km) before uniting with the Water of Mark and the Water of Lee to form the River North Esk.

Branxholme Castle *Scottish Borders* Owned by the dukes of Buccleuch, Branxholme Castle overlooks the River Teviot, 3 miles (5 km) southwest of Hawick. Branxholme has been the hereditary seat of the Scotts of Buccleuch since the middle of the 15th century and was the centre of power in Upper Teviotdale on one of the key historic routes south to England. The original tower was burned in 1532 by the Earl of Northumberland and then blown up in 1570 during the invasion of the Earl of Surrey. Most of what can be seen today dates from rebuilding between 1571 and 1574 begun by Sir Walter Scott of Branxholme and completed by his widow, although one substantial corner tower remains from the previous structure. The author Sir Walter Scott (1771–1832), a close friend and distant relative of the 4th Duke of Buccleuch, set his narrative poem *Lay of the Last Minstrel* (1805) at Branxholme.

Branxholme Easter Loch *Scottish Borders* A small loch in Scottish Borders, Branxholme Easter Loch lies 2 miles (3 km) west of Branxholme and 4 miles (6.5 km) southwest of Hawick. Its outlet feeds into the Newmill Burn.

Branxholme Wester Loch *Scottish Borders* Situated a mile (1.5 km) to the southwest of Branxholme Easter Loch in Scottish Borders, Branxholme Wester Loch is the source of the Newmill Burn, a tributary of the River Teviot.

Brawl *Highland* A township in northern Sutherland, Highland Council area, Brawl lies to the east of Armadale and south of Strathy Point.

Brawl Castle An alternative name for Braal Castle in Highland.

Breac, Loch *Highland* A small loch to the southeast of Ben Alisky in Caithness, Highland Council area, Loch Breac lies at the head of the Raffin Burn, a tributary of the Dunbeath Water.

Breac, Loch nam *Highland* A small loch in Caithness, Highland Council area, Loch nam Breac lies between Strathnaver and Strath Halladale. It is the source of the Uair, which flows northwards.

Breac Dearga, Loch nam *Highland* A small loch to the west of Loch Ness in Highland Council area, Loch nam Breac Dearga lies 3 miles (5 km) to the northeast of Invermoriston.

Breachacha Castle *Argyll and Bute* A castle on the south coast of the island of Coll in Argyll and Bute, Breachacha Castle is located next to Glendyke, 5 miles (8 km) southwest of the settlement of Arinagour. Overlooking Loch Breachacha, the castle was built in the 14th century and was a MacLean clan stronghold. An 18th-century mansion house stands nearby.

Breaclaich, Lochan *Stirling* A reservoir in the hills to the south of Loch Tay, Lochan Breaclaich lies 4 miles (6.5 km) southeast of Killin in Stirling Council area. The Allt Breachlaich drains northwards from the reservoir, emptying into Loch Tay between Firbush Point and Fiddlers Bay.

Breaclete *Western Isles* A hamlet located at the centre of the island of Great Bernera on the west coast of Lewis in the Outer Hebrides, Breaclete (Gael: *Breacleit*) lies 5 miles (8 km) southwest of Carloway. The Bernera Museum, a modern community centre and a primary school are located here. Loch Breaclete lies immediately to the southeast.

Breacleit The Gaelic name for Breaclete in the Western Isles.

Breadalbane *Perth and Kinross/Stirling* A mountainous district of western Perth and Kinross and northwest Stirling Council area, Breadalbane extends from Strathfillan in the west to Strathtay in the east. It includes Glen Dochart and Loch Tay with the mountains to the north and south, and is associated with the Clan Campbell, one of whom, Sir John Campbell, was created Earl of Breadalbane in 1677. In the 19th century Breadalbane, focused on Taymouth Castle near Kenmore, formed one of the largest estates in Scotland, extending 100 miles (160 km) from Easdale on the coast of Argyllshire to Aberfeldy in the east. Located at the Falls of Dochart in Killin, the Breadalbane Folklore Centre provides information on the life and legends of Breadalbane, which is also known as the High Country of Scotland. Established in a restored water mill, the centre highlights the folk traditions of the Gaelic people of the Highlands, as well as the clans of the area, including the clans MacGregor, MacLaren, MacNab and Campbell. The Breadalbane Hydro-Electric Power Scheme, centred on Loch Earn, Loch Lyon and Loch Tay, incorporates seven power stations built by the North of Scotland Hydro-Electric Board in 1956.

Breakish *Highland* A small township on the isle of Skye, Highland Council area, Breakish lies 2 miles (3 km) east of Broadford on the road from Kyleakin. The campaigning *West Highland Free Press* was founded here in 1972.

Breanais The Gaelic name for Brenish in the Western Isles.

Breascleit *Western Isles* A township of Lewis in the Western Isles, Breascleit lies to the east of East Loch Roag, 12 miles (19 km) west of Stornoway. Local industries include fish processing and the manufacture of pharmaceuticals.

Brechin *Angus* A burgh town in the valley of Strathmore, Angus, Brechin is situated on the River South Esk 9 miles (14 km) west of Montrose. It was the cathedral town of the pre-Reformation diocese of Brechin and developed from the 12th century when the bishop was granted permission to hold a weekly market on Sundays. In 1641 Brechin was raised to the status of a royal burgh. Brechin Cathedral, which incorporates one of only two surviving 11th-century round towers in Scotland, was built in a Gothic style in the 13th century. It replaced an earlier religious centre from which the Culdee monks of the Celtic church had ministered to the local communities of Angus and the Mearns. Buildings of historic and architectural interest include Brechin Castle, the Town House and Museum (1789), Gardner Memorial Church (1897–8), Fox Maule Ramsay Memorial Fountain, Public Library (1891–3), Den Burn Works (1864), Mechanics Institute (1838), the chapel of Maison Dieu Hospital built as an almshouse in 1267 by Lord William de Brechin, and several gabled merchants' houses from the 18th century. The station and goods yard built for the Caledonian Railway Company in 1895 and closed in 1981 have been restored by the Brechin Railway Preservation Society which runs steam trains along 4 miles (6.5 km) of track eastwards to Bridge of Dun. Brechin is also a considerable industrial centre, with textiles, distilling, engineering, packaging and food canning. The Brechin Castle Centre on the Haughmuir includes a 25-ha (62-acre) country park and the 'Pictavia' exhibition exploring the world of the Picts. Brechin was the birthplace of the physicist Sir Robert Alexander Watson-Watt (1892–1973), who was associated with the development of radar.

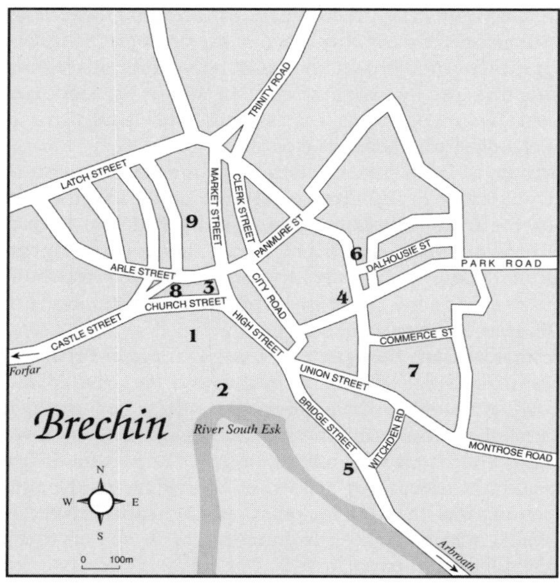

1 *Brechin Cathedral*
2 *Brechin Castle*
3 *Town House*
4 *Gardner Memorial Church*
5 *Leisure Centre*
6 *Public Library and Museum*
7 *Den Burn Works*
8 *Mechanics Institute*
9 *The Chapel of Maison Dieu Hospital*

Brechin Castle *Angus* Situated on the western outskirts of Brechin on a crag overlooking the River South Esk, Brechin Castle is the seat of the earls of Dalhousie. A castle built by the Maules existed here in the 13th century, but for nearly 300 years Brechin was a royal stronghold. In the 16th century it passed to the Erskine earls of Mar, but in 1634 it was purchased by the Maules who were later created earls of Panmure. Much of the present building was erected in the 18th century. There is a visitor centre and the 'Pictavia' exhibition in its grounds.

Breckonside *Dumfries and Galloway* A former stronghold of the Johnstons in Dumfries and Galloway, the ruined 16th-century tower of Breckonside lies near Moffat in Annandale.

Bredsie An alternative name for Broadsea in Aberdeenshire.

Breibhig The Gaelic name for Breivig in the Western Isles.

Breibhig The Gaelic name for Brevig in the Western Isles.

Breich *West Lothian* A village in West Lothian, Breich lies close to the Breich Water, 2 miles (3 km) east of Fauldhouse. A former railway station served coal mines and quarries in the area.

Brein, Glen *Highland* A valley of Strath Errick to the east of Loch Ness in Highland Council area, Glen Brein occupies the course of the Allt Breinag which flows from Glendoe Forest northwards out of the Monadhliath Mountains to meet the River Feehlin at Whitebridge, 3 miles (5 km) south of Foyers.

Breivig *Western Isles* A small crofting township, with a harbour, on the east coast of Lewis in the Outer Hebrides, Breivig (Gael: *Breibhig*) lies a half-mile (1 km) south of Back, a mile (1.5 km) southeast of Coll and 5 miles (8 km) northeast of Stornoway.

Brenfield Point *Argyll and Bute* The headland of Brenfield Point is located on the western side of Loch Fyne, Argyll and Bute. The settlement of Ardrishaig lies 2 miles (3 km) to the north.

Brenish *Western Isles* A remote crofting township on the west coast of Lewis in the Outer Hebrides, Brenish (sometimes Breanish, Gael: *Breanais*) is located between Islivig and Mealasta, 6 miles (10 km) southwest of Timsgarry. Aird Brenish lies a mile (1.5 km) to the west-northwest.

Brenish, Aird *Western Isles* A headland on the west coast of Lewis in the Western Isles, Aird Brenish (*Aird Breanais*) is located a mile (1.5 km) northwest of the settlement of Brenish.

Bressay *Shetland* Offering shelter to the port of Lerwick, the island of Bressay lies to the east of Mainland Shetland. Extending over an area of 3106 ha (7672 acres), the island is largely composed of Old Red Sandstone which has provided the flagstone slates and building stone for many of Shetland's dwellings. The highest point on the island is the Ward of Bressay, which rises to 226 m

(741 ft). Early antiquities include the Bressay Stone, a Pictish cross-slab with Ogam inscriptions. A ferry links Lerwick with Maryfield on Bressay, in the north of which is Gardie House, built in 1724. The island's total population fell from 904 in 1841 to 384 in 2001.

Brevig *Western Isles* A small crofting township with a jetty on the east coast of the island of Barra in the Outer Hebrides, Brevig (Gael: *Breibhig*) lies on Brevig Bay, 1.5 miles (2.5 km) east of Castlebay.

Brewlands *Angus* A locality in Glen Isla, Angus, Brewlands lies to the west of the River Isla, opposite Kirkton of Glenisla. The Brewlands Hall, a centre of local activity and the venue for the Glen Isla Games Ball, stands beside the modern Brewlands Bridge. This replaced an old single-span structure that can still be found downstream amid trees.

Bridge End *Shetland* A hamlet on the island of West Burra, off the west coast of the Shetland Mainland, Bridge End is located at the end of the road bridge that connects to the neighbouring island of East Burra. There is an outdoor centre here, and the settlements of Grunasound and Toogs lie immediately to the north.

Bridge of Alford *Aberdeenshire* A village in the Howe of Alford, Aberdeenshire, Bridge of Alford lies on the River Don, a mile (1.5 km) northwest of Alford.

Bridge of Allan *Stirling* A largely residential town, Bridge of Allan is situated between the Allan Water and the wooded western end of the Ochil Hills. The earliest record of a bridge here is from 1520. The remains of a predecessor to the present bridge are still visible in the river, with its former parapet running towards an old corn mill (1710) that was part of the clachan of Bridgend, a community that eventually grew into Bridge of Allan. The village developed during the 19th century as a spa resort, succeeding the clachan of Bridgend and the nearby settlement of Pathfoot which was the focal point of copper mining on the Airthrey Estate from the 16th century until 1815. The spa was developed by Sir Robert Abercrombie, who was aware of the growing number of people visiting the Trossachs, popularised by Sir Walter Scott. The settlement expanded from 1846 with the arrival of the railway, its prosperity being reflected in a growing number of fine Victorian villas and public buildings, including the Fountain of Niniveh, Museum Hall and Holy Trinity Church (1860). Robert Louis Stevenson and Charles Dickens are among the many writers who visited Bridge of Allan during its heyday as a spa. The Pullar Memorial Park, which is the setting for the town's War Memorial, was donated to the community in 1923 by Edmund Pullar, and the beautiful grounds of the Airthrey Estate below the Ochils are the setting for the University of Stirling which was founded in 1967. Bridge of Allan also has a leisure centre, sporting facilities, a golf club, a library and hotels.

Bridge of Balgie *Perth and Kinross* A hamlet in Glen Lyon, central Perth and Kinross, Bridge of Balgie lies on the River Lyon at the junction of the Glen Lyon road with the road leading south by Ben Lawers to Loch Tay.

Bridge of Brown *Highland/Moray* A small settlement on the border between Highland and Moray Council areas, Bridge of Brown lies in Glen Brown on the old military road from Grantown-on-Spey to Tomintoul. It once had a school serving the local farming community.

Bridge of Cally *Perth and Kinross* A village of eastern Perth and Kinross, Bridge of Cally lies at the junction of the A93 and A924, 5 miles (8 km) northwest of Blairgowrie. Here the River Ardle combines with the Black Water to form the River Ericht. The village is a winter resort at a 'gateway' to the Highlands, accommodating skiers using winter sporting facilities in Glenshee.

Bridge of Canny *Aberdeenshire* A locality in Royal Deeside, Aberdeenshire, Bridge of Canny lies 3 miles (5 km) west of Banchory at the junction of the Burn of Canny with the River Dee.

Bridge of Dee *Aberdeen City* Crossing the River Dee at what was once the southern boundary of the city of Aberdeen, the Bridge of Dee is a seven-arched bridge dating from 1520. Built following a bequest of £20,000 by Bishop William Elphinstone who died in 1514, the bridge was completed by Bishop Gavin Dunbar. It was the site of a battle in 1639 between the Royalists under Viscount Aboyne and the Covenanters who were led by the Marquess of Montrose. Restored in 1718–21 and widened in the 19th century, the bridge still features the original 16th-century piers, coats of arms and passing places. There are interesting riverside walks nearby.

Bridge of Dee *Dumfries and Galloway* A village of Dumfries and Galloway, Bridge of Dee lies at a crossing of the River Dee, 2 miles (3 km) southwest of Castle Douglas.

Bridge of Don *Aberdeen City* Once an industrial village in the parish of Old Machar in the city of Aberdeen, Bridge of Don has grown substantially and is now regarded as a district of Aberdeen. It is situated to the north of the River Don, opposite what is known as Old Aberdeen. To the east are located the Offshore Technology Park, an industrial estate and Aberdeen Exhibition and Conference Centre, and to the southwest is the Aberdeen Science and Technology Park. Food-processing, construction, transport, engineering and oil-related industries predominate. The original five-arched bridge crossing the River Don at the northern boundary of the City of Aberdeen was built in 1825. Its construction was financed by a bequest made in 1605 by Sir Alexander Hay, who left funds to maintain the Auld Brig o' Balgownie which stands close by.

Bridge of Dun *Angus* A locality in the Angus parish of Dun, Bridge of Dun lies on the River South Esk just west of the Montrose Basin and 4 miles (6.5 km) east of Brechin. The magnificent Gothic-style three-arched stone bridge that crosses the South Esk here was built 1785–7. Here, too, is the eastern terminus of the Brechin Railway Preservation Society.

Bridge of Earn *Perth and Kinross* A village of Perth and Kinross, Bridge of Earn sits by the River Earn, 4 miles (6.5 km) south of Perth. A dormitory village for Perth, it developed in association with bridges crossing the River Earn where tolls were once collected. The present bridge was built *c.*1822. The growth of the village in the 19th century was linked to the popularity of nearby Pitkeathly Wells, which ceased to function as a spa in 1949. Established during World War II to cope with an expected influx of casualties after the D-Day landings, Bridge of Earn Hospital was one of Perthshire's leading hospitals and a major source of employment until it was closed in 1993. Transferred to the National Health Service in 1948, the hospital was built on a farm named Oudenarde, which was named after one of the Duke of Marlborough's victories in 1708.

Bridge of Ericht *Perth and Kinross* A small settlement of Perth and Kinross, Bridge of Ericht lies near the mouth of the River Ericht at the northwest end of Loch Rannoch. A hydro-electric power station lies immediately to the east.

Bridge of Forss *Highland* A small locality in northern Caithness, Highland Council area, Bridge of Forss lies a mile (1.5 km) to the east of Lybster and 6 miles (10 km) west of Thurso. An early 19th-century two-arched bridge crosses the Forss Water here.

Bridge of Gairn *Aberdeenshire* A small settlement in Royal Deeside, Aberdeenshire, Bridge of Gairn lies a mile (1.5 km) northwest of Ballater close to the junction of the River Gairn with the River Dee, and the A93 Deeside road with the A939 road northwards to Strathdon and the Lecht Road.

Bridge of Gaur *Perth and Kinross* A hamlet in Perth and Kinross, Bridge of Gaur lies immediately southeast of a bridge that crosses the River Gaur before entering the western end of Loch Rannoch. The three-arched granite bridge crossing the Gaur was built in 1838 by Sir Neil Menzies to commemorate the accession of Queen Victoria.

Bridge of Lossie *Moray* A small settlement in Moray, Bridge of Lossie lies on the River Lossie to the south of Dallas village.

Bridge of Orchy *Argyll and Bute* A village in northeast Argyll and Bute to the south of Rannoch Moor, Bridge of Orchy lies at the head of Glen Orchy, 6 miles (10 km) north of Tyndrum. A bridge over the River Orchy was built here in 1751 during the construction of a military road. An inn erected in the settlement became a stance for drovers, and was visited by Dorothy Wordsworth in 1803.

Bridge of Tilt *Perth and Kinross* A settlement immediately north of Blair Atholl, Perth and Kinross, Bridge of Tilt sits on the River Tilt which flows southwards off the Cairngorms to meet the River Garry near here.

Bridge of Weir *Renfrewshire* A small town in Renfrewshire, Bridge of Weir lies 6 miles (10 km) west of Paisley. Established near the Bridge of Weir in 1792, the village developed in association with cotton-milling and tanning industries. The former cotton mills were established between 1790 and 1840 on the River Gryfe. The Bridge of Weir Leather Company, founded in 1905, produces leather seats for cars, and the town has become a popular holiday resort with golf and fishing facilities. Notable buildings include Castle Terrace (1882 by Robert Raeburn and formerly the Ranfurly Hotel), St Machar's Church (1877–8) and Ranfurly Castle (15th century), which was built for the Knox family and is on the golf course.

Bridgegate, the *Glasgow City* Stretching from the Saltmarket area of Glasgow to Victoria Bridge, the Bridgegate (or Briggait) was home to many of the city's 17th-century merchants. As the merchants moved westwards, so the area became home to an influx of Irish immigrants. In the 1870s the City of Glasgow Union Railway swept away many of the original buildings, and although attempts have been made to regenerate the area, it is still one of the poorer districts of the city centre.

Bridgend *Argyll and Bute* A settlement on the island of Islay in the Inner Hebrides, Bridgend lies at the head of Loch Indaal, 6 miles (10 km) southwest of Port Askaig.

Bridgend *Argyll and Bute* The settlement of Bridgend is located in the valley of the River Add, 3 miles (5 km) north of Lochgilphead.

Bridgend *Dumfries and Galloway* A locality in Annandale, Dumfries and Galloway, Bridgend lies on the River Annan, 2 miles (3 km) north of Moffat.

Bridgend *Fife* A village in Ceres parish, central Fife, Bridgend lies 2 miles (3 km) southeast of Cupar on the left bank of the Ceres Burn adjacent to the northwest end of the old town of Ceres.

Bridgend *Perth and Kinross* A largely residential suburb of Perth, Bridgend lies to the east of the River Tay facing the bridge built by the engineer John Smeaton between 1766 and 1770.

Bridgend *West Lothian* A village of West Lothian, Bridgend is located a half-mile (1 km) south of Philpstoun and 2.5 miles (4 km) east-southeast of Linlithgow.

Bridgend of Lintrathen *Angus* A hamlet in the Angus parish of Lintrathen, Bridgend of Lintrathen lies on the Melgam Water just east of the Loch of Lintrathen, 6 miles (10 km) northeast of Alyth. The parish church dates from 1802.

Bridgeness *West Lothian* A former village that now forms an eastern suburb of Bo'ness, Bridgeness lies a mile (1.5 km) east of that town. It is here that the Antonine Wall ends, and Roman camps have been found immediately to the south and to the east at Carriden.

Bridgeton *Glasgow City* An eastern district of Glasgow, Bridgeton (originally Bridgetown) developed on a site formerly known as Barrowfield following the construction of Rutherglen Bridge in 1776. The market here became the main street of Bridgeton and after 1782 a large area was laid out in a grid plan, the road junction taking the name Bridgeton Cross. In 1814 the land to the south by the River Clyde was designated Europe's first public park as Glasgow Green. Bridgeton expanded in the 19th century to become an industrial suburb with textile, engineering, pottery and carpet-manufacturing industries. In 1846 Bridgeton was incorporated into the City of Glasgow. Many of Bridgeton's former industrial buildings were demolished in the 1960s in advance of Scotland's largest urban-renewal initiative, the Glasgow Eastern Area Renewal (GEAR) scheme. The Templeton Carpet Factory remains as the Templeton Business Centre and as flats.

Briga Head *Highland* A headland on the north coast of Caithness, Highland Council area, Briga Head extends into the sea on the west coast of the Dunnet Head peninsula, 3 miles (5 km) northwest of Dunnet.

Brighouse Bay *Dumfries and Galloway* An inlet of Wigtown Bay on the Solway Firth, Dumfries and Galloway, Brighouse Bay lies to the west of the Mull of Ross, 4 miles (6.5 km) southwest of Kirkcudbright.

Brightons *Falkirk* A settlement in Falkirk Council area, Brightons is situated to the south of the Union Canal and Polmont.

Brighty, Glen *Angus* A glen in Glenisla parish, Angus, Glen Brighty lies to the east of Cairnwell near the border between Angus and Aberdeenshire. Its stream joins the River Isla near its head.

Brig o' Balgownie *Aberdeen City* Crossing a gorge of

the River Don in Old Aberdeen, the Auld Brig o' Balgownie was erected c.1290 either by Bishop Cheyne or Robert the Bruce. It has a single Gothic arch with a span of 20.5 m (67 ft) and stands 10.5 m (34.5 ft) above a deep salmon pool which was mentioned by Byron in *Don Juan*. In 1605 Sir Alexander Hay left lands with a yearly income to keep the Auld Brig in good repair. It was from this fund that the new Bridge of Don was built in 1825.

Brig o' Doon *South Ayrshire* A late mediaeval single-arch bridge on the south side of Alloway, South Ayrshire, the Brig o' Doon was made famous in the poem *Tam o' Shanter* by Robert Burns (1759-96). Rebuilt in the 18th century, it crosses the River Doon near the Tam o' Shanter Experience and is now managed as part of the Burns National Heritage Park. The bridge gave its name to the Broadway musical *Brigadoon* by Lerner and Loewe, which opened in 1947 and went on to become a successful Hollywood film (1954).

Brig o' Turk *Stirling* A small scattered village, Brig o' Turk is situated on the 'Trossachs Trail' of attractions in the Trossachs and is 24 miles (38 km) northwest of Stirling. Its inhabitants comprise commuters and those employed in the forestry, farming, tourism and water industries. Overlooking the village are the peaks of Ben Venue and Ben An, and nearby are Lochs Venachar and Achray. The name Brig o' Turk derives from Gaelic and means 'bridge of the wild boar'.

Brims *Orkney* A scattered settlement on the south coast of the island of Hoy in Orkney, Brims is located 9 miles (14 km) northeast of Dunnet Head. The Longhope lifeboat station was once located here. The original shed was built in 1874 next to the isthmus that connects Hoy to the South Walls peninsula and permitted lifeboats to be launched either into Longhope to the north or Aith Voe to the south. A new station was built further south in 1906 which served until 1999 and is now the Longhope Lifeboat Museum.

Brims Ness *Highland* A headland on the north coast of Caithness, Brims Ness extends into the Pentland Firth 5 miles (8 km) west of Thurso.

Brin, River *Highland* A tributary of the River Nairn in eastern Highland Council area, the Brin is formed by the meeting of the An Leth-allt and the Allt na Beinne. It flows northwards to join the Nairn near Brinmore. Brin House and Brin Mains lie to the north on the opposite side of the River Nairn.

Bring Deeps *Orkney* A body of water lying between the Mainland of Orkney and the island of Hoy to the south, the Bring Deeps opens eastwards into Scapa Flow, northwestwards into Hoy Sound and northwards into Clestrain Sound.

Brinyan *Orkney* A settlement at the southeast end of the Orkney island of Rousay, Brinyan (Brinian) is the island's chief landing place. To the north Blotchnie Fiold rises to 250 m (821 ft), and to the west are found numerous prehistoric sites including the Knowe of Yarso cairn, Midhowe broch and chambered tomb and Taversoe Tuick chambered tomb.

Britannia Panopticon Music Hall *Glasgow City* The second-oldest theatre in Scotland after the Dumfries Theatre Royal, and the oldest and most originally intact early-Victorian music hall, the Britannia Music Hall occupies the first and second floors of a former warehouse building on Glasgow's Trongate. Grade-A listed, the theatre was in regular use until the 1930s and gave Stan Laurel his comedy debut in 1906. Actor Cary Grant, using his original name Archie Leach, performed here early in his career. It was also used to house a zoo, waxworks, a freak show and a carnival, and showed regular films from 1896. The projection box dates from 1904 and is one of the oldest in the country. Closed to the public, the building has lain hidden since 1938 and has only recently been brought to the public's attention through its inclusion in the BBC's *Restoration* TV programme in 2003. The Britannia Panopticon Music Hall Trust has been founded to restore and reopen the building.

British Golf Museum *Fife* A museum of golf history in St Andrews, the 'home of golf', the British Golf Museum is situated on the West Sands next to the Old Course and the Royal and Ancient Golf Club. Opened in 1996, it traces the 500-year history of the game using multimedia and touch-screen displays.

Brittle, Glen *Highland* A narrow glen on the west coast of the island of Skye in the Inner Hebrides, Glen Brittle occupies the valley of the River Brittle which flows from the Cuillins into Loch Brittle.

Brittle, Loch *Highland* A sea loch on the west coast of the island of Skye, Highland Council area, Loch Brittle lies to the west of the Cuillins, between Loch Eynort and Soay Sound. The River Brittle enters the loch from the north through Glen Brittle.

Broad Bay *Western Isles* A large bay on the east coast of the Isle of Lewis in the Outer Hebrides, Broad Bay (Gael: *Loch a' Tuath*) stretches from Tolsta Head, 8 miles (13 km) northeast of Stornoway, to Tiumpan Head at the northern end of the Eye peninsula, and extends inland as far as the settlement of Laxdale.

Broad Cairn *Aberdeenshire/Angus* Located southwest of Loch Muick and on the border of Aberdeenshire and Angus, Broad Cairn rises to a height of 998 m (3274 ft) at the head of a glaciated valley to the south of Lochnagar.

Broad Head *Dumfries and Galloway* A hill in Eskdale, Dumfries and Galloway, Broad Head rises to 492 m (1614 ft) to the east of Castle O'er Forest.

Broad Law *Scottish Borders* A hill in the Tweeddale district of Scottish Borders, Broad Law rises to 840 m (2756 ft), 4 miles (6.5 km) east of Tweedsmuir. The Megget and Talla reservoirs lie to the southwest and southeast respectively.

Broadford *Highland* A township on the island of Skye, Broadford lies at the head of Broadford Bay, where it is joined by Strath Suardal, 6 miles (10 km) west of Kyleakin. It was the site of a cattle tryst in the 18th and 19th centuries. A road was constructed through Broadford to Portree 1806–12 and the village was expanded for the settlement of veteran soldiers from the Napoleonic Wars. A pier was erected for steamers and fishing boats in the mid-19th century, a hospital was built in 1971 and a small industrial estate opened in the 1980s. Fish farming and processing, tourism and quarrying are the chief industries.

Broadford Bay *Highland* An inlet on the east coast of the island of Skye, Highland Council area, Broadford Bay looks out into the Inner Sound towards the islands of Scalpay, Longay and Pabay. It receives the Broadford River, which enters the bay at the township of Broadford.

Broadsea *Aberdeenshire* A former fishing village in the

Buchan district of Aberdeenshire, Broadsea (or *Bredsie*) is now a northwest part of Fraserburgh. It has views looking out to the North Sea beyond a headland known as Clubbie Craig.

Broadsea Bay *Dumfries and Galloway* A bay on the west coast of the Rhinns of Galloway, Broadsea Bay extends northwards from Black Head, 2 miles (3 km) northwest of Portpatrick.

Brocair The Gaelic name for Broker in the Western Isles.

Broch, the An alternative name for Fraserburgh in Aberdeenshire.

Broch of Gurness *Orkney* An Iron Age broch situated on the Aiker Ness peninsula, 17 miles (27 km) northwest of Kirkwall on Mainland Orkney. The site was occupied continuously from the early Christian era to the Viking age.

Brochel *Highland* A locality on the east coast of the island of Raasay in the Inner Hebrides, Brochel lies on the edge of Raasay Forest. Nearby is a ruined castle of the Macleods of Raasay.

Brodick *North Ayrshire* Situated on Brodick Bay, an inlet on the east coast of the island of Arran, Brodick is the chief settlement and main port of entry to the island for travellers to and from the mainland ferry port of Ardrossan. There are also seasonal ferries to Rothesay on the island of Bute. The village of Invercloy came to be known as Brodick in the 1890s, and during the 20th century it developed in association with tourism. Brodick Castle, on the northern outskirts of Brodick, is the ancient seat of the dukes of Hamilton. A fortified tower dating from the 13th century was extended in the 16th century and again by Cromwell in the 17th century. In 1844 Princess Marie of Baden, wife of the 11th Duke of Hamilton, added an extension. Her granddaughter, Lady Mary Louise, the Duchess of Montrose, lived in the castle until 1957, and in the following year Brodick Castle came into the stewardship of the National Trust for Scotland. The gardens and policies at Brodick form a country park.

Brodie Castle *Moray* Set in parkland 3 miles (5 km) to the west of Forres in Moray, Brodie Castle dates from 1567, although the Brodie family were first granted land here by Malcolm IV in 1160. Damaged in 1645 during the campaigns of the Marquess of Montrose, Brodie is a Z-plan structure with additions made in the 17th and 19th centuries. The building, with its contents and 70 ha (175 acres) of policies, was transferred into the care of the National Trust for Scotland in 1980. It contains fine French furniture, English, Continental and Chinese porcelain, and a fine collection of paintings, ranging from 17th-century Dutch to 18th/19th-century English watercolours and Scottish Colourists. There is an extensive daffodil collection and an attractive woodland walk.

Broker *Western Isles* One of several contiguous crofting townships located at the eastern end of the Eye peninsula on the east coast of Lewis in the Outer Hebrides, Broker (Gael: *Brocair*) lies immediately to the east of Cnoc Amhlaigh, a half-mile (1 km) west of Portvoller and a mile (1.5 km) southwest of Tiumpan Head.

Brookfield *Renfrewshire* A dormitory village of Renfrewshire that lies 1.25 miles (2 km) northwest of Johnstone and a mile (1.5 km) northeast of Kilbarchan, Brookfield developed from the beginning of the 20th century. Merchiston Hospital, occupying the former Merchiston House, lies immediately to the east.

Broom, Loch *Highland* A sea loch in Wester Ross, Highland Council area, Loch Broom extends southeastwards inland from the Minch for 7 miles (11 km). The 18th-century planned village of Ullapool lies on its eastern shore and beyond its mouth are a scattering of islands known as the Summer Isles.

Broom, River *Highland* A river of Wester Ross, Highland Council area, the Broom is formed by the meeting of the Abhainn Dromm and the Abhainn Cuileig just south of Braemore. It flows northwards through Strath More for 5 miles (8 km) before entering the southern end of Loch Broom.

Broomholm *Dumfries and Galloway* A locality in eastern Dumfries and Galloway, the estate and mansion of Broomholm lie on the River Esk, 2 miles (3 km) southeast of Langholm.

Broomielaw, The *Glasgow City* Named after the Brumelaw Croft, a stretch of land along the River Clyde, the Broomielaw extends from Victoria Bridge to Anderston Quay in Glasgow. Originally the main port of Glasgow, it was remodelled by Thomas Telford as a steamboat quay for the thousands of immigrants who came over from Ireland in the mid-19th century. It was also the place where many of the citizens of Glasgow embarked on their holidays, as they sailed 'doon the watter' on paddle steamers heading for the resorts of the Clyde.

Brora *Highland* A small town on the east coast of Sutherland, Highland Council area, Brora lies at the mouth of the River Brora. Originally known as Inverbrora, it was chartered as a burgh of barony in 1345. A seam of Jurassic coal, mined in the 16th century to fuel local saltpans, was worked until 1974 and was the only coal mine in Britain to mine Jurassic rather than Carboniferous coal. The mine latterly also produced bricks manufactured from the overlying Oxford clay shales. The settlement was laid out in its present form in 1811 and a new harbour built in 1814. The arrival of the railway in 1871 and the creation of an engineering works boosted the local mining, quarrying, distilling, textile-manufacturing and tourism industries, and in 1898 an 18-hole golf course was created. Woollen and tweed manufacture was a significant employer until 2003, with the closure of Hunters of Brora. Tourism remains important alongside the provision of goods and services to the surrounding agricultural communities.

Brora, Loch *Highland* A loch in eastern Sutherland, Loch Brora lies on the River Brora, 4 miles (6.5 km) northwest of Brora. It is nearly 4.5 miles (7 km) in length.

Brora, River *Highland* A river of east Sutherland, the Brora rises in headstreams to the east of Loch Shin. It flows generally southeastwards for 26 miles (42 km) through Strath Brora before entering the North Sea at Brora. For nearly 4.5 miles (7 km) it widens to form Loch Brora.

Brother Loch *East Renfrewshire* The Brother Loch is a small loch in East Renfrewshire located 4 miles (6.5 km) south of Barrhead.

Broubster *Highland* A small settlement of Caithness, Broubster lies on the Forss Water, 5 miles (8 km) south of Lybster and a mile (1.5 km) west of Loch Calder. The Broubster Leans, or Leans of Achaeter, to the east is an area of transition mire and quaking bog considered to be one of the best of its kind in the United Kingdom.

Brough *Highland* A small settlement in northeast Caithness, Brough lies 2 miles (3 km) southeast of Dunnet Head to the north of St John's Loch.

Brough *Shetland* A village on the Shetland island of Whalsay, Brough is situated on the northwest coast 2 miles (3 km) north of the port of Symbister. There is a lighthouse nearby at Suther Ness, and a narrow neck of land links with Kirk Ness, on which stands a church.

Brough of Birsay *Orkney* A tidal island lying off the northwestern tip of Mainland Orkney. Rising to high cliffs in the west, it has an area of 56 ha (138 acres) and can be reached at low tide across an artificial causeway. At the foot of the slope are the remains of a settlement of early Christian and Viking times. There are interesting domestic and ecclesiastical remains here, as well as fine examples of Norse hall-houses.

Broughton *Edinburgh City* A former village and barony on the northern outskirts of old Edinburgh, Broughton was absorbed into the city with the building of the New Town in the 18th and 19th centuries. Street names such as Broughton Street and Broughton Place are reminders of the old village which lay on the road linking Edinburgh to North Leith. The poet Christopher Grieve, alias Hugh MacDiarmid, was a student teacher at Broughton High School, which moved to a new location west of Inverleith Park in the 1960s.

Broughton *Scottish Borders* A village located 11 miles (18 km) southwest of Peebles on the Biggar Water in Scottish Borders, Broughton is noted for its ruined church which includes a cell allegedly occupied by a 7th-century missionary. Sir Basil Spence built Broughton Place (1938) on the site of the burned home of Sir John Murray of Broughton (1715–77). Born in Broughton, Murray acted as Prince Charles Edward Stewart's secretary but gave evidence against him after the failure of the 1745 Rising. The John Buchan Centre opened in 1988 in the old kirk and celebrates the famous author of numerous books, including *The Thirty-Nine Steps* (1915). The Greenmantle Brewery, established in 1979, produces bottled ale.

Broughton House *Dumfries and Galloway* Located on the High Street of Kirkcudbright in Dumfries and Galloway, and overlooking the estuary of the River Dee, Broughton House is an 18th-century town house first occupied by the Murrays of Broughton and Cally. It was purchased by the artist E. A. Hornel, one of the founders of the 'Glasgow Boys' art movement in Scotland. He added an art gallery and studio to the house which contains many of his works of art as well as a collection of rare Scottish books, including limited editions of works by Robert Burns.

Broughty Castle *Dundee City* Situated on the north bank of the River Tay, by the harbour in Broughty Ferry, Broughty Castle was built in 1498 by Andrew, 3rd Lord Gray. It was reconstructed by the noted architect Sir Robert Rowand Anderson in 1861 and now houses a museum featuring displays on local history, arms and armour, seashore life and the former Dundee whaling industry.

Broughty Ferry *Dundee City* A small port and residential suburb to the east of Dundee, Broughty Ferry is situated on the north bank of the Firth of Tay opposite Tayport in Fife, to which it was formerly linked by ferry. Once a fishing village and ferry port, Broughty Ferry developed as a residential and resort town during the 19th century, when many of its fine villas were erected by jute industrialists from Dundee. Incorporated with the City of Dundee in 1913, it has a fine seafront, harbour and esplanade. Guarding the mouth of the Tay estuary, the 15th-century Broughty Castle overlooks the harbour.

Brown, Burn of *Moray* Rising in the Cairngorm Mountains to the west of Tomintoul, the Burn of Brown flows north through Glen Brown and Bridge of Brown to meet other streams that form the Burn of Lochy, a tributary of the River Avon.

Brown Caterthun *Angus* The site of an Iron Age hillfort at Menmuir in central Angus, the Brown Caterthun forms a complex earthwork of enclosures and ramparts, 4 miles (6.5 km) northwest of Brechin.

Brownhills *Fife* A hamlet in east Fife, Brownhills lies just beyond the junction of the A917 with the B9131, a mile (1.5 km) south of St Andrews.

Brownsbank Cottage *South Lanarkshire* Brownsbank Cottage was the home of the great Scottish writer Hugh MacDiarmid (Christopher Grieve, 1892–1978). Located near the town of Biggar, South Lanarkshire, it overlooks the Peeblesshire Hills to the south and was acquired by the Biggar Museum Trust in 1992. Containing original interiors with portraits and photographs, the cottage is now home to a writer-in-residence.

Broxburn *East Lothian* The hamlet of Broxburn is located to the east of Dunbar in East Lothian. The Dunbar battlefield of 1650 lies immediately to the south, while the earlier Battle of Dunbar, which took place in 1296, is located a mile (1.5 km) to the southwest.

Broxburn *West Lothian* A settlement in West Lothian, Broxburn is located on the Union Canal, 2 miles (3 km) northeast of Livingston. Formerly situated on the main Edinburgh–Glasgow road, it developed in the 19th century into a centre-point for transporting people and goods by canal, road and rail. The Union Canal (1821) was laid out to the west of Broxburn, while the railway (1849) lies to its south. The discovery of coal, iron and shale oil resulted in an increase in population and the creation of gigantic waste bings that surround the area. Many buildings survive from the mid- and late-Victorian era, while much housing to the south (the Old Town) dates from the late 1960s. The local economy is supported by light industries as well as a large chicken farm and the manufacture of food and drink products.

Broxmouth *East Lothian* A locality on the coast of East Lothian, Broxmouth lies to the east of the village of Broxburn, 2 miles (3 km) southeast of Dunbar. Broxmouth House was originally built as a dower house for Margaret, widow (d.1683) of the 3rd Earl of Roxburghe. Rebuilt in the 18th century, the house is surrounded by a designed landscape laid out around a series of long-distance vistas inspired by French baroque gardens.

Bru The Gaelic name for Brue in the Western Isles.

Bruach Mairi The Gaelic name for Marybank in the Western Isles.

Bruach na Frithe *Highland* A peak on the Cuillin Ridge on the island of Skye in the Inner Hebrides, Bruach na Frithe rises to 958 m (3143 ft) and is the only peak in the Cuillins to support a triangulation pillar. The name Bruach na Frithe is the Gaelic for 'slope of the deer forest'.

Bruairnis The Gaelic name for Bruernish in the Western Isles.

Bruan *Highland* A settlement on the east coast of Caithness, Bruan lies 5 miles (8 km) northeast of Lybster.

Bruar *Perth and Kinross* A settlement of northern Perth and Kinross, Bruar sits by the Bruar Water near its junction with the River Garry, 3 miles (5 km) west of Blair Atholl. The Clan Donnachaidh Centre and House of Bruar shopping complex attract visitors who also have the chance to enjoy a woodland walk to the Falls of Bruar. The planting of larch, pine and beech to enhance the walk is attributed to the Duke of Atholl following the 'Humble Petition of Bruar Water', delivered to him by Robert Burns in 1787.

Bruar, Glen *Perth and Kinross* The valley of the Bruar Water in highland Perth and Kinross, Glen Bruar extends 8 miles (13 km) northwards from Glen Garry into the southern flank of the Grampian Mountains.

Bruar Lodge *Perth and Kinross* Remotely located in Glen Bruar, highland Perth and Kinross, Bruar Lodge is a shooting lodge of the Forest of Atholl situated on the southern edge of the Grampian Mountains, 6 miles (10 km) north of Calvine.

Bruar Water *Perth and Kinross* Rising in the southern Grampians of Perth and Kinross, Bruar Water flows southwards for 8 miles (13 km) before joining the River Garry at Bruar, where a wooded walk leads to the Falls of Bruar.

Brucklay Castle *Aberdeenshire* The ruined remains of Brucklay Castle lie 3 miles (5 km) northeast of New Deer in Aberdeenshire. The castle was built in the 17th century and later modernised.

Brue *Western Isles* A linear crofting township on the northwest coast of Lewis in the Outer Hebrides, Brue (Gael: *Bru*) lies between the coastal lochs of Eirearaigh and More Barvas, 2 miles (3 km) east-northeast of Arnol and a similar distance west of Barvas.

Bruernish *Western Isles* A crofting and fishing hamlet on the east coast of Barra in the Outer Hebrides, Bruernish (Gael: *Bruairnis*) lies on the south shore of North Bay, 4 miles (6.5 km) northeast of Castlebay.

Bruicheach, Loch *Highland* A small loch to the north of Glen Urquhart to the east of Loch Ness, Loch Bruicheach (*Loch Bhruthaich*) lies between Strathglass and Glen Convinth.

Bruichladdich *Argyll and Bute* Located on the island of Islay, Argyll and Bute, Bruichladdich lies on the eastern shore of Loch Indaal, directly opposite the settlement of Bowmore. Port Charlotte lies 2 miles (3 km) to the south. Bruichladdich is home to one of the many Islay malt whisky distilleries. It was established in 1881.

Brunton *Fife* Hidden within the folding hills of northern Fife to the east of Norman's Law lies the old fermetoun village of Brunton. Surviving as a cottage weaving village in the 18th and 19th centuries, Brunton is now an attractive commuter settlement. The village once had a meal mill, and nearby stand the remains of a Free Church built in 1843.

Bruntsfield Links *City of Edinburgh* An area of parkland on the south side of Edinburgh, Bruntsfield Links lies immediately to the south of the Meadows, separating the districts of Bruntsfield and Marchmont. Extending to 14 ha (35 acres), the links are notable as the site of the world's first golf courses, the game having been played here since the 15th century and perhaps earlier. No fewer than six golf clubs began on the links; however, all had moved elsewhere by the 19th century. The Royal Burgess (founded 1735) and the Bruntsfield Links Golfing Society (founded 1761) are now located in the Barnton district of the city, while the Honourable Company of Edinburgh Golfers (founded 1744) is now based at the championship-standard Muirfield course at Gullane (East Lothian). Bruntsfield Links form the last remaining fragment of the Burgh (Borough) Muir which once stretched from the Borough Loch (South Loch) to Blackford Hill. The Borough Muir was given to the city in 1508 by King James IV and on several occasions provided the marshalling ground for the Scottish Army. At other times the Muir provided rough grazing for cattle. The name lives on in Boroughmuir High School, located nearby in Viewforth.

Brydekirk *Dumfries and Galloway* A village of Annandale in Dumfries and Galloway, Brydekirk lies on the River Annan, 3 miles (5 km) north of Annan.

Brylach Hill *Moray* Brylach Hill lies 3 miles (5 km) northwest of Rothes in Moray. Overlooking the Glen of Rothes, the peak rises to a height of 325 m (1066 ft).

Buachaille Etive Beag *Highland* A ridge in Lochaber, Buachaille Etive Beag ('the little herdsman of Etive') lies to the south of Glen Coe and to the west of Buachaille Etive Mòr. Its summit is Stob Dubh, which rises to 958 m (3142 ft) at the southwest end of the ridge.

Buachaille Etive Mòr *Highland* A mountain mass at the eastern end of Glen Coe in Lochaber, Buachaille Etive Mòr ('the big herdsman of Etive') rises to 1022 m (3352 ft) at its northeastern summit, Stob Dearg. Situated within property owned by the National Trust for Scotland, it boasts some of the finest climbing in the Highlands.

Bualadubh *Western Isles* A settlement lying close to the north coast of South Uist, Bualadubh (Gael: *Buaile Dubh*) lies immediately to the west of the A865 and forms an eastern extension of Iochdar. The Iochdar Primary School is located here.

Bualintur *Highland* A township in southwestern Skye, Highland Council area, Bualintur lies at the head of Loch Brittle to the west of the Cuillins.

Buccleuch *Scottish Borders* A locality in Scottish Borders, Buccleuch lies on the Rankle Burn, a tributary of the Tweed, 12 miles (19 km) west of Hawick. The original stronghold of the dukes of Buccleuch once stood here.

Buchan *Aberdeenshire* A district of northeast Aberdeenshire, Buchan lies between the Ythan and the Deveron rivers with an extensive coastline that includes the fisher towns of Fraserburgh and Peterhead. Sometimes the district of Formartine between the Don and the Ythan is also considered part of Buchan. The coast is often dramatic, as at the Bullers of Buchan, but the interior is largely flat agricultural land rising only to 230 m (755 ft) at Mormond Hill to the west of the Loch of Strathbeg. It has been described as the 'Land of Cakes' and the 'Land of Plenty' because of its rich farmland and prosperous coastal towns.

Buchan Ness *Aberdeenshire* A headland on the North Sea coast of Aberdeenshire, Buchan Ness extends into the sea due east of Boddam, 3 miles (5 km) south of Peterhead.

Buchanan Castle *Stirling* Situated immediately west of the village of Drymen in southwest Stirling Council area, the remains of Buchanan Castle stand within landscaped policies. The Grahams of Montrose moved here from

Mugdock in the 1640s, although the present building dates only from 1854. Also in the policies are a lodge designed by William Playfair, an icehouse, stables, High Mains farmhouse, and the Old House, which dates from 1724.

Buchanan Smithy *Stirling* A small settlement in Stirling Council area, Buchanan Smithy lies just north of Buchanan Castle, less than a mile (1.5 km) to the northwest of Drymen.

Buchanan Street *Glasgow City* Buchanan Street is the main shopping thoroughfare of Glasgow, running north–south in the city centre to link Argyle Street and Sauchiehall Street. It was first feued in 1777 and was named after a wealthy tobacco merchant, Andrew Buchanan. A successful Victorian shopping centre, it was one of the few main streets in Glasgow to avoid tramcars, although motor cars were allowed. At its southern end sits St Enoch's Square, the St Enoch's Underground Station and St Enoch's Shopping Centre, while to the north lies the Buchanan Galleries Shopping Centre and Buchanan Street Underground Station. The street was pedestrianised in 1978 and landscaped in 2000.

Buchanty *Perth and Kinross* A small settlement in Glen Almond, Perth and Kinross, Buchanty lies in the parish of Fowlis Wester, at a crossing of the River Almond a mile (1.5 km) east of the southern end of the Sma' Glen and 10 miles (16 km) northeast of Crieff. The river, which flows through a succession of turbulent gorges, is crossed here by a 17th-century high-arched bridge that looks onto deep pools and the swirling water of Buchanty Spout.

Buchany *Stirling* A small roadside settlement in Stirling Council area, Buchany lies to the north of the River Teith, a mile (1.5 km) to the northwest of Doune.

Buchat, Water of *Aberdeenshire* Rising on the eastern flanks of the Ladder Hills in the eastern Grampians, the Water of Buchat flows southeastwards for nearly 10 miles (16 km) through Glenbuchat before joining the River Don near Glenbuchat Castle.

Buchlyvie *Stirling* A village in Stirling Council area, Buchlyvie lies 15 miles (24 km) west of Stirling and 2 miles (3 km) south of the River Forth. Now bypassed by the main road to Loch Lomond, Buchlyvie was in the 18th century a minor industrial settlement situated on a military road. Designated a burgh of barony in 1672, it became a railway junction in 1882. The railways closed in 1959. The village comprises a single wide main street with 18th- and 19th-century cottages.

Buck, the *Aberdeenshire* A mountain in the eastern Grampians, the Buck rises to 721 m (2367 ft) 7 miles (11 km) west of Lumsden in Aberdeenshire. The Cabrach Road to the north links Rhynie with Dufftown.

Buckhaven *Fife* A town in Wemyss parish, Fife, Buckhaven is situated on the Firth of Forth between East Wemyss and Methil. Once a thriving weaving village and fishing port, it was reported as having in 1831 the second-largest fishing fleet in Scotland with a total of 198 boats. The fishing declined during the 19th century but in the 1860s Buckhaven developed as a mining town. Although coal waste blackened its beaches and silted up its harbour, it later became a Fife coast holiday resort. Said to be descended from Norsemen who settled there in the 9th century, its fisherfolk bought an Episcopal Church in St Andrews in 1869 and transported it stone by stone to Buckhaven. Restored in the 1980s, this building was turned into a theatre. Buckhaven Museum features the history of the fishing industry and other temporary exhibitions.

Buckie *Moray* A fisher town in the Moray parish of Rathven, Buckie is situated on the Moray Firth at the mouth of the Burn of Buckie, 8 miles (13 km) northeast of Fochabers. Once described as 'the largest purely fishing village in Scotland', Buckie developed in the 19th century as the head of the fishery district between Banff and Findhorn. In 1877 John Gordon of Cluny constructed a harbour (Cluny Harbour) at a cost of £60,000. In 1881 its fishing craft numbered 333, employing 1320 men and boys. By 1913, Buckie had the largest steam-drifter fleet in Scotland. The settlement, which is divided by the Burn of Buckie into Nether Buckie (or Buckpool) to the west and Easter Buckie to the east, includes the communities of Yardie, Ianstown, Gordonsburgh and Portlessie (originally Rottinslough), which were incorporated between 1901 and 1903. In the 1780s Cosmo Gordon of Cluny laid out a new town, New Buckie, in the form of a long street focused on a square overlooked by North Parish Church (1880) with its open crown spire. The history of the local fishing industry is told in the Maritime Heritage Centre (The Buckie Drifter), and in the Anson Gallery are works by the marine artist Peter Anson. The town has marine industries, and for the visitor there are facilities including hotels and an 18-hole golf course.

Bucksburn *Aberdeen City* A settlement in the parish of Newhills in the city of Aberdeen, Bucksburn is situated 4 miles (6.5 km) northwest of Aberdeen city centre at the junction of the A96 and A947. A centre of paper making, food processing and the manufacture of protective clothing, it comprises the former hamlets of Auchmill and Buxburn. The Craibstone Estate is the northeastern base for the Scottish Agricultural College's agricultural and horticultural advisory services and the home of the Rowett Research Institute, a centre for the study of animal nutrition.

Buddon Burn *Angus* A stream of southeast Angus, the Buddon Burn rises in the Sidlaw Hills and flows southeast to enter the Tay estuary between Monifieth and Buddon Artillery Camp. Barry Links lie to the east.

Buddon Ness *Angus* A headland on the North Sea coast of Angus, Buddon Ness forms the southeasternmost extremity of Barry Links at the mouth of the Tay estuary to the south of Carnoustie and east of Broughty Ferry. A map of the east coast of Scotland compiled by John Marr in the 1680s shows the promontory of 'Botannais' with a 'Small Light' near its tip. In 1884, because the entrance channel was altering with the slow movement of the sandbanks, the lower Buddon lighthouse tower was moved 49 m (53 yd) to the north of its old site.

Buidhe, Loch *Highland* A small loch at the eastern end of Rannoch Moor, Loch Buidhe lies on the southern border of Highland Council area on the course of the River Bà, 5 miles (8 km) north of Bridge of Orchy.

Buidhe, Loch *Highland* A small loch in eastern Sutherland, Highland Council area, Loch Buidhe lies at the head of the Torboll River, 5 miles (8 km) northeast of Bonar Bridge.

Buidhe Bheinn *Highland* A mountain in Lochaber, Buidhe Bheinn rises to 879 m (2883 ft) to the north of Kinloch Hourn.

Builg, Loch *Aberdeenshire* A loch in the Grampians, Loch Builg lies between the valleys of the River Gairn and the upper River Avon. It has a depth of 10–20 m (33–66 ft). The Builg Burn flows northwards from the loch to meet the Avon near Inchrory.

Builg Burn *Moray* A stream in the uplands of Moray, the Builg Burn flows north from Loch Builg to join the upper River Avon near Inchrory.

Buldoo *Highland* A small settlement on the north coast of Caithness, Buldoo lies just east of Dounreay.

Buldoo *Highland* A locality on the east coast of Caithness, Highland Council area, Buldoo lies close to Latheron and is noted for its 17th-century bell tower which was used to summon the scattered congregation of Latheron to the church below.

Bullers of Buchan *Aberdeenshire* A small settlement situated 2 miles (3 km) northeast of Cruden Bay in Aberdeenshire, Bullers of Buchan takes its name from the famous coastal granite cliff feature nearby. Here the sea rushes through a natural archway into a cavern with a vertical opening 30 m (100 ft) high known as the Pot. In 1773 James Boswell and Samuel Johnson visited the Bullers, which Boswell described as a 'monstrous cauldron'. Johnson remarked on the dramatic sight 'which no man can see with indifference who has either sense of danger or delight in rarity'. The coastline to the south was frequented by Bram Stoker, the creator of *Dracula*, who was inspired by the ruins of New Slains Castle.

Bun Abhainn-eadar, Loch *Western Isles* A northern extension of West Loch Tarbert, Loch Bun Abhainn-eadar lies on the southwest coastline of the island of North Harris in the Western Isles.

Bunacaimb *Highland* A small settlement in South Morar, Bunacaimb lies just north of Arisaig.

Bunarkaig *Highland* A locality in Lochaber, Bunarkaig lies on the northwest shore of Loch Lochy, 10 miles (16 km) north of Fort William.

Bunaveneadar *Western Isles* A small settlement of North Harris in the Outer Hebrides, Bunaveneadar (also Bunavoneader, Gael: *Bun Abhainn Eadarra*) lies at the mouth of the Eadar River (Abhainn Eadarra) where it enters Loch Bun Abhainn-eadar, an inlet in West Loch Tarbert, 3 miles (5 km) northwest of Tarbert.

Bun a' Mhuillinn The Gaelic name for Bunmhullin in the Western Isles.

Bun Abhainn Eadarra The Gaelic name for Bunaveneadar in the Western Isles.

Bunchrew *Highland* A locality in the Aird, Easter Ross, Bunchrew lies on the south side of the Beauly Firth, 5 miles (8 km) west of Inverness.

Bundalloch *Highland* A settlement in Kintail, Bundalloch lies on the east shore of Loch Long, 2 miles (3 km) northeast of Dornie.

Bunessan *Argyll and Bute* Located on the Ross of Mull in the southwest corner of the island of Mull, Argyll and Bute, Bunessan lies at the head of the sea loch of Loch na Lathaich, a half-mile (1 km) south of the settlement of Ardtun. It lies on the route to Fionnphort, the ferry terminal for Iona, and has an anchorage, lobster fishing and a boatyard.

Bunloinn Forest *Highland* A deer forest at the eastern end of Glen Loyne in Highland Council area, Bunloinn Forest lies between Loch Cluanie and Loch Loyne near the head of Glen Moriston.

Bunmhullin *Western Isles* A small settlement on the north coast of the island of Eriskay in the Outer Hebrides, Bunmhullin (Gael: *Bun a' Mhuillinn*) overlooks the Sound of Eriskay a half-mile (1 km) east of Haun.

Bunnahabhainn *Argyll and Bute* Located on the isolated northeast coast of the island of Islay in the Inner Hebrides, Bunnahabhainn lies at the southern end of Bunnahabhainn Bay and overlooks the Sound of Islay to the island of Jura. Port Askaig lies 3 miles (5 km) to the south of the village. Bunnahabhainn is home to one of the many Islay malt whisky distilleries, established in 1881.

Buntait *Highland* A scattered settlement in Highland Council area, Buntait lies to the east of Strathglass, 4 miles (6.5 km) east of Cannich.

Burdiehouse *Edinburgh City* A village on the southern outskirts of Edinburgh, Burdiehouse lies to the south of Liberton. Its original name is said to have been Bordeaux House, a place of residence for some of Mary, Queen of Scots's retinue in 1561. Limestone was formerly quarried and burned in kilns nearby that are still extant.

Burg *Argyll and Bute* A settlement located within a district of the same name and located in the Ardmeanach area of the island of Mull, Burg lies 3 miles (5 km) east of the headland of Rubh' a' Chaoil.

Burgar Hill *Orkney* A hill in the parish of Evie on the northeast Mainland of Orkney, on which three experimental wind turbine aero-generators were built in 1983.

Burghead *Moray* A fishing village in the Moray parish of Duffus, Burghead is situated on a headland overlooking the Moray Firth, 8 miles (13 km) northwest of Elgin. The promontory, which has been occupied since prehistoric times and was a major centre of Pictland, is crowned by the remains of a Pictish fort incorporating a rock-hewn chamber known as the Well. The modern grid-iron town behind the promontory largely dates from the development of the harbour after 1805. The harbour trades in timber, and for the tourist there are facilities including a camping and caravan site and a museum. The ancient midwinter Yule-fire festival known as 'Burning the Clavie' is continued by the local community, or 'Brochers' as they call themselves, on 11 January (Old Yule Night) each year. The Clavie crew, led by the Clavie King, take it in turn to carry through the streets the blazing tar-barrel or Clavie, which is made from a whisky barrel and set alight with a burning peat.

Burghead Bay *Moray* A wide sweeping bay on the Moray Firth coast, Burghead Bay has Burghead at its eastern extremity and the mouth of the River Findhorn at its western end.

Burleigh Castle *Perth and Kinross* A former stronghold of the Balfours of Burleigh, keepers of Falkland Palace, Burleigh Castle lies on the eastern outskirts of Milnathort in Perth and Kinross. Two towers remain, one being topped by an unusual square cap-house bearing the date 1582. The Balfours abandoned the castle when the estate was forfeited to the Crown as a result of their participation in the 1715 Jacobite Rising. The building is now in the care of Historic Scotland.

Burn, the *Aberdeenshire* A house in Fettercairn parish, South Aberdeenshire, the Burn was built on the left bank of the River North Esk in 1791 by Lord Adam Gordon. Situated in Glen Esk, 2 miles (3 km) north of Edzell, it is used today as a conference retreat.

Burn of Cambus *Stirling* A small roadside settlement in Stirling Council area, Burn of Cambus lies on the Burn of Cambus at the entrance to Doune Lodge, just over a mile (1.5 km) northwest of Doune and 10 miles (16 km) northwest of Stirling. Milton of Cambus lies further up the burn.

Burnbank *South Lanarkshire* A fomer mining village in South Lanarkshire, Burnbank is now a northwestern suburb of Hamilton. It was the birthplace of football manager Jock Stein (1922–85) and boxer Walter McGowan (b.1942).

Burnbrae *North Lanarkshire* The hamlet of Burnbrae is located a mile (1.5 km) south of Shotts, North Lanarkshire. A small, scattered community, it lies to the west of the upper reaches of the South Calder Water directly west of the settlement of Stane.

Burncrooks Reservoir *Stirling* Situated in the Kilpatrick Hills on the southwestern border of Stirling Council area, the Burncrooks Reservoir lies 6 miles (10 km) northeast of Dumbarton. It drains northeastwards into the Blane Water.

Burnfoot *Dumfries and Galloway* A hamlet in Eskdale, Dumfries and Galloway, Burnfoot lies 3 miles (5 km) northwest of Langholm.

Burnfoot *Perth and Kinross* A hamlet in Glendevon, Perth and Kinross, Burnfoot lies opposite the main settlement of Glendevon, close to the junction of the River Devon with the outflow from Glenquey Reservoir.

Burnhaven *Aberdeenshire* An Aberdeenshire fishing village on the North Sea coast, Burnhaven is situated at the southern end of Peterhead Bay, 2 miles (3 km) south of Peterhead. The village was created in the 19th century by George Mudie of Meethill.

Burnhead *Dumfries and Galloway* A village of Nithsdale in Dumfries and Galloway, Burnhead lies to the west of the River Nith, a mile (1.5 km) west of Thornhill.

Burnhead *Dumfries and Galloway* A hamlet of Nithsdale in eastern Dumfries and Galloway, Burnhead lies to the west of the River Nith, 6 miles (10 km) northwest of Dumfries. Burnhead should not be confused with a village of the same name that is located 7 miles (11 km) to the north-northwest.

Burnhouse *North Ayrshire* A hamlet of North Ayrshire, Burnhouse is located at a crossroads on the A736, 1.5 miles (2.5 km) west of Dunlop. The border between North Ayrshire and East Ayrshire follows the course of the Lugton Water just to the east.

Burnmouth *Scottish Borders* A hamlet on the Berwickshire coast of Scottish Borders, Burnmouth lies at the foot of cliffs 6 miles (10 km) northwest of Berwick-upon-Tweed. A harbour was built in 1830, and a station on top of the cliffs, opened in 1846, operated until 1962. The settlement now comprises fishermen's houses and holiday cottages.

Burns House *Dumfries and Galloway* Located in the town of Dumfries, Dumfries and Galloway, Burns House was where the poet Robert Burns (1759–96) spent the last years of his life. Retaining much of its 18th-century character and relics from the period, the house is now a museum with items including the chair in which Burns wrote many of his later works.

Burns House Museum *East Ayrshire* Located in the village of Mauchline in North Ayrshire, the Burns House Museum was one of the homes of the poet Robert Burns (1759–96). Inside there are collections of Burns' memorabilia, Mauchline box ware, and curling stones made nearby.

Burns Monument *City of Edinburgh* A monument on Calton Road in central Edinburgh, the Burns Monument overlooks the Calton New Burial Ground on the south flank of Calton Hill. The monument was built in 1830 by the architect Thomas Hamilton (1784–1858), following the design of his earlier memorial at the bard's birthplace in Alloway in South Ayrshire.

Burns Monument *South Ayrshire* Completed in 1823, the Burns Monument in Alloway, South Ayrshire, was the first monument built to honour Scotland's national poet, Robert Burns (1759–96). Created by Thomas Hamilton in a Grecian style, it has a platform halfway up that commands views over the surrounding area, including Brig o' Doon. The monument was financed through public subscription. By 1819 over £1500 had been raised, enabling work to begin a year later on 25 January, the birthday of Robert Burns.

Burns' Mother's Well *East Lothian* On the roadside between Haddington and Bolton, a mile (1.5 km) from the latter village, lies a well dedicated to Agnes Broun (1732–1820), mother of Scotland's national poet, Robert Burns (1759–96). Burns' mother had come to live with her son Gilbert (1760–1827) after he took the job of a farm-worker on the Lennoxlove Estate. It was at this spring that Agnes had taken water for the family. The dedication reads as follows: 'Drink of the pure crystals and not only be ye succoured but also refreshed in the mind. Agnes Broun, 1732–1820. To the mortal and immortal memory and in noble tribute to her, who not only gave a son to Scotland but to the whole world and whose own doctrines he preached to humanity that we might learn.' The well was restored in 1932 by William Baxter FSA (Scot). The Burns' former home at Grant's Braes is marked by a roadside monument, some 90 m (100 yd) southwest of the well.

Burnside *Fife* A hamlet by the A91 leading eastwards through Fife to Cupar and St Andrews, Burnside is situated a mile (1.5 km) to the southwest of Gateside close to the River Eden, which once powered a corn mill there. Road tolls were collected here prior to the formation of county road boards in 1878.

Burnside of Duntrune *Angus* A hamlet of southern Angus, Burnside of Duntrune lies on the Fithie Burn a half-mile (1 km) north of the boundary with Dundee and 1.25 miles (2 km) west-southwest of Kellas. Duntrune House (built 1826) lies to the east.

Burnswark Hill *Dumfries and Galloway* A landmark of lower Annandale in Dumfries and Galloway, Burnswark Hill rises to 277 m (910 ft) 3 miles (5 km) north of Ecclefechan. On its twin summits are the remains of an Iron Age fort dating from 600 BC, with impressive ramparts of later 2nd-century AD Roman forts to the north and south of it.

Burntisland *Fife* A Fife coastal town on the Firth of Forth, Burntisland lies 10 miles (16 km) east of the Forth Rail Bridge. Occupying a natural harbour, Burntisland is said to have been chosen by Agricola as a Roman naval base as early as AD 83. Given to Dunfermline Abbey in the 12th century, a castle, church and kirkton were established close to the harbour. The town was granted a royal charter by James V in 1541 and developed as a naval base and a port trading initially in fish and later in coal. In addition to brewing and distilling, which was carried on from 1786 to 1916, Burntisland was a centre of shipbuilding for half a century, between 1918 and 1968. The aluminium works founded in 1917 are still a major employer, in addition to marine service industries. In 1850 the first rail ferry in the world, the *Leviathan*, came into operation, linking Burntisland and Granton on the opposite side of the Firth of Forth. It was the concept of Thomas Bouch who was later to be responsible for the design of the ill-fated Tay Railway Bridge. Local landmarks include Rossend Castle, which dates from the 12th century; the Burgh Chambers (1843); Burntisland Library and Museum; Mary Somerville's house (1595), once the home (1786–1817) of a daughter of one of Lord Nelson's captains and pioneer of women's education who gave her name to Oxford's first college for women, founded in 1879; and the octagonal-towered St Columba's Church, said to be the first church built after the Reformation and where the General Assembly of the Church of Scotland, meeting in 1601, decided to publish the new authorised or 'King James' version of the Bible. On the Binn Hill just above Burntisland, James 'Paraffin' Young started shale-oil production and founded a village in 1878. Annual events in Burntisland include a fair, Highland games and the crowning of a 'Summer Queen' on the Links. A popular summer resort, Burntisland has a caravan site, bowling green, football ground and 18-hole golf course.

Burravoe *Shetland* A hamlet on the southeast tip of the Shetland island of Yell, Burravoe lies on an inlet of the same name. Its notable buildings include the fine St Colman's Church and the 17th-century Old Haa, which was the former laird's house and monitored traffic into the harbour.

Burray *Orkney* One of a ring of islands surrounding Scapa Flow in Orkney, Burray is sandwiched between the Mainland of Orkney to the north and South Ronaldsay to the south. It is connected to both of these islands as well as the smaller islets of Lamb Holm and Glimps Holm by the Churchill Barriers, which were erected during World War II after the sinking of HMS *Royal Oak*, to prevent German U-Boats entering Scapa Flow. Irregularly shaped and with an area of 1007 ha (22487 acres), the island is separated from the Mainland of Orkney by Holm Sound, from South Ronaldsay by Water Sound and from the small island of Hunda to the west by Hunda Sound. Echnaloch Bay in the northwest opens out into Scapa Flow, and fringing the bay facing eastwards is a fine long beach backed by the Links. Of archeological interest are the ruins of a broch at Northfield and the remains of St Lawrence's Church. Farming and the production of knitwear are the main economic activities, and there is a bird sanctuary at Ness on the eastern tip of the island.

Burrell Collection, the *Glasgow City* A collection of treasures gifted to the City of Glasgow by Sir William Burrell, shipowner and art collector, in 1944, the Burrell Collection is located in a purpose-built gallery within Pollok Country Park. After much wrangling over where the collection should be located, it was, in 1967, finally agreed that it should be housed in a specially designed building situated in the park. Designed by Barry Gasson, John Meunier and Brit Anderson of the Cambridge University School of Architecture, the gallery was finally opened to the public in 1983. The building is clad in Locharbriggs red sandstone, which is combined with glass and stainless steel. The collection comprises 19th-century paintings, including works by Degas, Cezanne, Renoir, MacTaggart and Whistler; North European medieval art, including stained glass, tapestries and sculptures; European post-medieval art, comprising silver, table glass and needlework; Oriental art, including Chinese ceramics, Japanese prints, and bronzes and jade; Near-East carpets from areas between India and Turkey; and ancient artefacts from Egypt, Greece, Rome, Assyria and Mesopotamia.

Burrelton *Perth and Kinross* A village of Perth and Kinross, Burrelton is situated on the A94, 2 miles (3 km) southwest of Coupar Angus. Woodside lies adjacent to the north.

Burrow Head *Dumfries and Galloway* A headland on the Solway Firth coast, Burrow Head is the southernmost point of the Machars peninsula, extending into the firth 2 miles (3 km) southwest of Isle of Whithorn.

Burwick *Orkney* A hamlet on the southwest coast of the island of South Ronaldsay, Burwick lies on the inlet of Bur Wick and looks out onto the Pentland Firth. A passenger ferry links with John o' Groats during the summer.

Busby *East Renfrewshire* A settlement that forms a southern residential suburb of Glasgow, Busby lies on the White Cart River 6 miles (10 km) south of the city centre. It once straddled the border between the old counties of Renfrewshire and Lanarkshire and had chemical works, cotton mills, a paper mill and bleachfields. Greenbank House, built in 1765, a mile (1.5 km) to the west of Busby, was acquired by the National Trust for Scotland in 1976.

Busta *Shetland* A hamlet in the west of the Delting district of Mainland Shetland, Busta looks out onto Busta Voe a mile (1.5 km) southwest of Brae. The island of Muckle Roe lies a half-mile (1 km) to the southwest and Mavis Grind and the district of Northmavine a mile (1.5 km) to the north.

Bute *Argyll and Bute* Extending southwards into the Firth of Clyde, the island of Bute lies between the Cowal peninsula and the island of Arran. It has an area of 12,168 ha (30,055 acres) and is largely owned by the Bute Estate. Its population was 7228 in 2001. Loch Fad, which cuts diagonally across the centre of the island, forms part of the Highland Boundary Fault, separating a wild, hilly landscape of Dalradian schists to the north from the more productive arable land on old red sandstone to the south. Bute has a unique long-tailed field mouse, and a trial reintroduction of the European beaver took place here in 1875. Rothesay, the main town on the island, is linked by ferry to Wemyss Bay, and Rhubodach, at the northern tip of Bute, is connected by ferry to Colintraive on the opposite side of the narrow Kyles of Bute. Places of interest include Mount Stuart House and Gardens, Rothesay Castle, Kames Castle, St Blane's Chapel, St Mary's Chapel, Bute Museum, and the settlements of Port Bannatyne, Kerrycroy, Kingarth and Kilchattan Bay.

Buteshire A former county of west central Scotland, Buteshire comprised the island of Bute in the Firth of Clyde with Rothesay as its county town. In 1974 it was incorporated into the Argyll and Bute District of Strathclyde Region and in the local government reorganisation of 1996 remained part of Argyll and Bute Council Area.

Butt of Lewis *Western Isles* The northernmost tip of the Isle of Lewis in the Outer Hebrides (Gael: *Rubha Robhanais*).

Butterstone *Perth and Kinross* A village of Perth and Kinross, Butterstone lies on the A923 from Dunkeld to Blairgowrie, 3 miles (5 km) northeast of Dunkeld. It stands to the north of the small Loch of Butterstone.

Butterstone, Loch of *Perth and Kinross* A loch 2 miles (3 km) to the northwest of Dunkeld in Perth and Kinross, the Loch of Butterstone is one of a group of three small lochs, the others being the Loch of Lowes and the Loch of Craiglush. They lie at the head of the valley of the Lunan Burn, which flows east and southeast to join the River Isla near Coupar Angus.

Bynack Burn *Aberdeenshire* A stream in southwest Aberdeenshire, the Bynack Burn rises in the Grampians close to the border between Angus and Aberdeenshire. It flows northeastwards to join the River Dee near the White Bridge.

Bynack Lodge *Aberdeenshire* A former shooting lodge in the Glen Ey Forest, Bynack Lodge is situated on the Bynack Burn in the Grampian uplands of southwest Aberdeenshire.

Bynack More *Aberdeenshire/Highland* A mountain peak in the eastern Cairngorm Mountains, Bynack More rises to 1090 m (3575 ft) above Glen Avon, on the border between Aberdeenshire and Highland Council areas. Formerly called Am Beidhneag, it is capped by granite tors known as the Barns of Bynack.

Byre Burn *Dumfries and Galloway* A stream in Eskdale, Dumfries and Galloway, the Byre Burn rises on the slopes of Bruntshiel Hill and flows south to join the River Esk to the north of Canonbie. Limestone was burned at the Byreburn Limeworks in the mid-19th century.

Byreburnfoot *Dumfries and Galloway* A former coal-mining village in Eskdale, Dumfries and Galloway, Byreburnfoot lies to the north of Canonbie near the River Esk.

Caaf Water *North Ayrshire* A river of North Ayrshire, the Caaf Water emerges from the southern end of the Caaf Reservoir and flows south and then east for 3 miles (5 km) to join the River Garnock to the south of the settlement of Dalry.

Cabrach *Argyll and Bute* A locality at the southern end of the island of Jura, Cabrach lies 3 miles (5 km) southwest of Craighouse and a half-mile (1 km) north of the settlement of Ardfin and Jura House.

Cabrach, the *Moray* A sparsely populated, heath-covered upland plateau area of southeast Moray, the Cabrach lies between Dufftown and the settlements of Rhynie and Lumsden. Watered by the upper streams of the Deveron River and by the Black Water, the Cabrach is centred on the hamlet of Cabrach and is traversed by an old pony whisky route known as the Cabrach Road. The parish church of Cabrach dates from 1786, and the bridge over the Allt Deveron was built in 1820. The Buck of the Cabrach rises to 721 m (2368 ft) on the border between Moray and Aberdeenshire.

Cadboll Point *Highland* A headland on the Moray Firth coast of Easter Ross, Cadboll Point extends into the sea east of Cadboll and north of the settlement of Hilton of Cadboll.

Cadder *East Dunbartonshire* A hamlet on the west bank of the Forth and Clyde Canal, Cadder lies 2 miles (3 km) north of Bishopbriggs in East Dunbartonshire. To the north are the remains of the Antonine Wall and an associated Roman fort.

Cadderlie *Argyll and Bute* A settlement on the north side of Loch Etive, Cadderlie lies in the Benderloch district of Argyll and Bute, 2 miles (3 km) northeast of Bonawe Quarries.

Caddonfoot *Scottish Borders* A small settlement of the central Scottish Borders, Caddonfoot sits at the mouth of the Caddon Water as it empties into the River Tweed, 3 miles (5 km) west of Galashiels.

Caddon Water *Scottish Borders* A stream in north-central Scottish Borders, Caddon Water rises on Windlestraw Law, 4 miles (6.5 km) north of Innerleithen. It flows generally southeastwards to join the Tweed near Caddonfoot.

Cadham *Fife* A planned village in central Fife 1.25 miles (2 km) west of Markinch, Cadham is now part of Glenrothes New Town. It was originally built during the 1920s on land bought from the Balbirnie Estate to house employees of the Tullis Russell paper mill. Planned as a spacious low-density housing development with a rural rather than urban character, it was designated a conservation area in 1985.

Cadzow *South Lanarkshire* A southern suburb of Hamilton in South Lanarkshire, Cadzow was the name of the parish of Hamilton until 1455.

Cadzow Castle *South Lanarkshire* Situated on the banks of the Avon Water, in the grounds of Chatelherault Country Park, Cadzow Castle lies 2 miles (3 km) southeast of the centre of Hamilton in South Lanarkshire. Now maintained by Historic Scotland, Cadzow Castle was built in the 13th century and was a royal residence for Alexander II and Alexander III. It is said to have been a hunting lodge of the ancient kings of Strathclyde, and it was here that Mary, Queen of Scots stayed after her dramatic escape from Loch Leven Castle in 1568.

Caen Burn *Highland* Rising in the foothills of Cnoc na Maolie in eastern Sutherland, the Caen Burn flows south for 2 miles (3 km), passing through the settlement of Caen before emptying into the River Helmsdale.

Caenlochan Glen *Angus* A small glen in the Grampians, Caenlochan Glen lies to the east of Glas Maol and at the head of Glen Isla. The glen forms part of a 759-ha (1876-acre) nature reserve established in 1986.

Caerlaverock Castle *Dumfries and Galloway* One of the finest castles in Scotland, Caerlaverock Castle lies near the mouth of the River Nith on the Solway Firth coast of Dumfries and Galloway, 8 miles (13 km) southwest of Dumfries. Built by the Maxwells in the 12th century, it has a triangular design and is one of the few castles in Scotland to have a protective moat. Additional features of this red sandstone fortress include a twin-towered gatehouse and the Nithsdale Lodging, a splendid Renaissance range dating from 1638. Attacked many times, its garrison of 60 men withstood a siege by 3000 troops of Edward I of England in 1300. In all, it withstood five sieges and was dismantled three times. Caerlaverock was finally abandoned in 1634, following an attack by Covenanting forces. It remained in Maxwell hands until 1946, when it was given over to State care. The salt marshes nearby, which are an important wintering ground for geese and wildfowl, are protected as a National Nature Reserve with an area of 7703 ha (19,034 acres).

Cagar Feosaig *Highland* A mountain of eastern Sutherland, Cagar Feosaig rises to 377 m (1237 ft) a mile (1.5 km) northeast of the settlement of Backies on the southwest shore of Loch Brora.

Cailleach Head *Highland* A headland at the northwestern extremity of a peninsula separating Loch Broom and Little Loch Broom in Wester Ross, Cailleach Head looks out over Priest Island and the Summer Isles.

Caiplich, Water of *Moray* A stream that rises in the Cairngorm Mountains to the southeast of Abernethy Forest, the Water of Caiplich flows east before turning sharply north around a rock outcrop known as the Castle, when it becomes the Water of Ailnack.

Caiplie Caves *Fife* Midway between Kilrenny and Crail on the Fife Coastal Walk, the red sandstone was cut out by waves in post-glacial times when the lower raised beach was being formed. Monks and pilgrims en route to St Andrews carved crosses in the caves, and today local children still try to throw stones through the hole in the southwesterly cliff in an attempt to make a wish come true. The farm of Caiplie stands on the upper beach level between the coast and the A917.

Cairinis A Gaelic name for Carinish in the Western Isles.

Caird Park *Dundee City* Located to the north of Dundee city centre, Caird Park occupies 106 ha (262 acres) that include two golf courses (nine- and 18-hole) and an athletics track. Mains Castle is located in the park.

Cairn Bannoch *Aberdeenshire/Angus* A mountain to the west of Loch Muick on the border between Angus and Aberdeenshire, Cairn Bannoch rises to 1012 m (3320 ft) above a glaciated valley south of Lochnagar. Its name is derived from the Gaelic for 'peaked hill', which is appropriate since its summit takes the form of a cone-shaped granite tor.

Cairn Burn *Scottish Borders* Rising in Harlaw Muir, the Cairn Burn flows for 5 miles (8 km) southwest towards West Linton, Scottish Borders. The burn flows into the Lyne Water a mile (1.5 km) south of West Linton at the nearby settlement of Broomlee Centre.

Cairn Catto *Aberdeenshire* A locality in Buchan, northeast Aberdeenshire, Cairn Catto lies 4 miles (6.5 km) southwest of Peterhead. There are a number of prehistoric cairns and burial chambers in the immediate area.

Cairn Cattoch *Moray* A peak of northern Moray, Cairn Cattoch lies 3 miles (5 km) southwest of the settlement of Rothes and rises to 369 m (1210 ft).

Cairn Dulnan *Highland* A mountain of the southern Monadliath Mountains of south-central Highland Council area, Cairn Dulnan (also *Carn Dulnan*) rises to 742 m (2434 ft) 6 miles (10 km) north of Kingussie.

Cairn Gorm *Highland/Moray* Giving its name to the Cairngorm Mountains, the highest mass in the Grampians rises to 1245 m (4085 ft) on the border between Highland and Moray council areas. The granite peaks of the Cairngorms, created over 400 million years ago, have eroded to their present rounded tops that support an Arctic alpine flora and fauna. During the 1960s the north-facing corries of Coire na Ciste and Coire Cas were developed as ski pistes, and a chairlift was created to take skiers to a middle station at 1080 m (3543 ft) and a top station 164 m (538 ft) from the summit. In 2001 an all-season funicular was established to take tourists to the summit of Cairn Gorm.

Cairn Head *Dumfries and Galloway* A headland on the Solway coast of Dumfries and Galloway, Cairn Head lies at the southern end of Portyerrock Bay, a mile (1.5 km) north of Isle of Whithorn.

Cairn-mon-earn *Aberdeenshire* A hill in the Durris Forest, eastern Aberdeenshire, Cairn-mon-earn rises to 378 m (1241 ft) to the south of the River Dee and just east of the road from Stonehaven to Banchory. It has a television transmission mast on its summit.

Cairn o' Mount *Aberdeenshire* A hill of southern Aberdeenshire, Cairn o' Mount rises to 455 m (1492 ft) 4 miles (6.5 km) north of Fettercairn and 10 miles (16 km) south-southwest of Banchory. The B974, which follows the route of an 18th-century military road and connects lower Deeside with the Howe of the Mearns and Strathmore, reaches its highest point at Cairn o' Mount, where there is a roadside viewpoint to the south.

Cairn of Claise *Aberdeenshire/Angus* Located northeast of the Cairnwell Pass, on the border of Aberdeenshire and Angus, Cairn of Claise rises to 1064 m (3491 ft). Its name is derived from the Gaelic for 'hill of the hollow'.

Cairn of Get, the *Highland* A Neolithic chambered cairn in eastern Caithness, Highland Council area, the Cairn of Get lies 11 miles (18 km) south of Wick. Excavated in 1866, the cairn dates from the 4th or 3rd millennium BC.

Cairn Table *South Lanarkshire/East Ayrshire* The hill of Cairn Table rises to 593m (1945 ft) 3 miles (5 km) southeast of Muirkirk on the border of South Lanarkshire and East Ayrshire. It is the source of the Duneaton Water.

Cairn Toul *Highland/Aberdeenshire* Rising to a height of 1293 m (4241 ft) in the Cairngorm Mountains, Cairn Toul (Gael: *Carn an t-Sabhail*) lies on the border between Highland and Aberdeenshire council areas. Its name is derived from the Gaelic for 'peak of the barn'.

Cairn Water *Dumfries and Galloway* A stream in central Dumfries and Galloway, Cairn Water is formed at the meeting of the Dalwhat Water and Castlefairn Water just east of Moniaive. It flows southeastwards for 12 miles (19 km) before joining the Old Water to become the Cluden Water.

Cairn William *Aberdeenshire* A hill in west-central Aberdeenshire, Cairn William rises to 448 m (1468 ft) 2 miles (3 km) northwest of Monymusk.

Cairnbaan *Argyll and Bute* Situated on the Crinan Canal, the village of Cairnbaan lies 2 miles (3 km) northwest of Lochgilphead in Argyll and Bute. One mile (1.5 km) to the east, the prehistoric rock carvings known as the Cairnbaan Cup and Ring Marks are in the care of Historic Scotland.

Cairnbawn, Loch An alternative name for Loch a' Chàirn Bhàin in Highland.

Cairnbulg *Aberdeenshire* A small fishing village on the North Sea coast of Buchan in northeast Aberdeenshire, Cairnbulg lies at the east end of Fraserburgh Bay. Cairnbulg Castle lies on the Water of Philorth 2 miles (3 km) southeast of Fraserburgh. Thought to date from the 13th century, and restored in the 19th century, it was a stronghold of the Comyn family. Cairnbulg Point forms a headland just northwest of Inverallochy at the western end of Fraserburgh Bay.

Cairncross *Scottish Borders* A small hamlet of eastern Scottish Borders, Cairncross is located 2 miles (3 km) southwest of Coldingham and to the south of the course of the Ale Water.

Cairndow *Argyll and Bute* The hamlet of Cairndow lies at the mouth of the Kinglas Water as it empties into Loch Fyne in Argyll and Bute. Located 11 miles (18 km) east of Inveraray, the hamlet sits near the head of the loch. Originally associated with an inn, Cairndow developed in the 1950s with the creation of the Clachan Hydro-Electric scheme. Today the village is noted for the farming of oysters and for the gardens of Ardkinglas.

Cairness House *Aberdeenshire* Situated southwest of St Combs in the Buchan parish of Lonmay, northeast Aberdeenshire, is the unusual Grecian-style Cairness House, built for Charles Gordon of Buthlaw in 1791–7 to a design by James Playfair. Completed by Sir John Soane after Playfair's death, it cost £25,000 to build.

Cairneyhill *Fife* A former linen-weaving village in western Fife, Cairneyhill lies on the A994, 3 miles (5 km) west of Dunfermline. In addition to a small industrial estate, there is a golf range, garden centre and a church, formerly United Presbyterian, built in 1752.

Cairngarroch *Dumfries and Galloway* A small settlement of western Dumfries and Galloway, Cairngarroch lies a mile (1.5 km) east of Cairngarroch Bay, on the west coast of the Rhinns of Galloway.

Cairngorms National Park Designated in 2003, the Cairngorms National Park is Scotland's second national park. It extends over parts of Aberdeenshire, Angus, Highland and Moray council areas, from Strathspey in the north to the Angus glens in the south and Dinnet in the east to Laggan in the west. Towns within its boundary include Newtonmore, Kingussie, Aviemore, Grantown-on-Spey, Tomintoul, Ballater and Braemar. The population living in the park is 15,000. The Cairngorms National Park includes within its bounds the Cairngorm and Glenshee ski areas, the forests of Abernethy, Glenmore and Rothiemurchus and the high peaks of the Cairngorm Mountains rising to 1309 m (4296 ft) at Ben Macdui, the second-highest mountain in Britain.

Cairnhall *Dumfries and Galloway* A small settlement of central Dumfries and Galloway, Cairnhall lies 6 miles (10 km) northwest of Dumfries.

Cairnharrow *Dumfries and Galloway* A hill in southwest Dumfries and Galloway, Cairnharrow rises to 456 m (1497 ft) 4 miles (6.5 km) southeast of Creetown.

Cairnholly *Dumfries and Galloway* The site of a prehistoric chambered cairn in southwest Dumfries and Galloway, Cairnholly lies in the hills between Gatehouse of Fleet and Creetown in Kirkdale Glen. The two tombs date from the 3rd millennium BC.

Cairnie, Burn of *Aberdeenshire* A stream of Strathbogie in northwest Aberdeenshire, the Burn of Cairnie rises in hills to the northwest of Huntly and flows northeastwards through the Bin Forest and past the villages of Cairnie and Ruthven before joining the River Isla at Littlemill on the border with Moray.

Cairnkinna Hill *Dumfries and Galloway* A summit in Penpont parish, northern Dumfries and Galloway, Cairnkinna Hill rises to 555 m (1819 ft) 5 miles (8 km) south of Sanquhar.

Cairnpapple Hill *West Lothian* One of the most important prehistoric sites in Scotland, Cairnpapple Hill rises to 310 m (1017 ft) southeast of Torphichen in West Lothian. Five periods of settlement stretching over 3000 years are represented by a series of monuments that include a henge monument and burial pits containing beaker ware, a large cairn built over two Bronze Age cist burials, and assorted burials from varying periods.

Cairnryan *Dumfries and Galloway* Formerly known as Macherie, the village of Cairnryan in southwest Dumfries and Galloway lies on the east side of Loch Ryan, 5 miles (8 km) north of Stranraer. The modern port was developed during World War II when part of the famous Mulberry Harbour used at the Normandy landings on D-Day was made here. The Dutch-style Lochryan House was built by the Agnew family in 1701, the same year that the settlement was created a burgh of barony. There has been a ferry link with Larne in Northern Ireland since the early 1960s, and the aircraft carriers HMS *Eagle* and *Ark Royal* were broken up in Cairnryan's ship-breaking yard in the 1970s.

Cairns of Coll *Argyll and Bute* Two rocks that rise out of the sea 2 miles (3 km) off the northeast coast of the island of Coll in the Inner Hebrides.

Cairnsmore of Carsphairn *Dumfries and Galloway* A mountain in northwest Dumfries and Galloway, Cairnsmore of Carsphairn rises to 797 m (2612 ft) nearly 4 miles (6.5 km) northeast of Carsphairn. It is also known as Cairnsmore of Deugh.

Cairnsmore of Fleet *Dumfries and Galloway* A range of hills of volcanic origin rising to the east of Newton Stewart in central Dumfries and Galloway, Cairnsmore of Fleet, which is designated as a National Nature Reserve, has two summits: Minnigaff (771 m/2331 ft) and Kirkmabreck (656 m/2152 ft). Cairnsmore of Fleet features in John Buchan's novel *The Thirty-Nine Steps* (1915). Several plane crashes in the 1940s and one in the 1970s are commemorated with a plaque close to the summit of Minnigaff.

Cairnwell, the *Perth and Kinross/Aberdeenshire* Located in northeast Perth and Kinross, on the boundary with Aberdeenshire, the Cairnwell rises to 933 m (3061 ft) and is easily accessible via a nearby road, so much so that the paths leading to its summit are greatly eroded. The Cairnwell chairlift, part of the adjacent Glenshee Ski Centre, ascends to within 50 m (164 ft) of the summit.

Cairnwell Pass *Perth and Kinross* A mountain pass on the border of Aberdeenshire and Perth and Kinross Council areas, the Cairnwell Pass carries the A93 road from Spittal of Glenshee to Braemar and is the highest main road in Britain, reaching a height of 670 m (2199 ft). To the west lies the peak of the Cairnwell, and the Glenshee Ski Centre is located here.

Caithness *Highland* A former county of northeast Scotland extending to 177,596 ha (438,833 acres), Caithness was a pendicle of the Norse earldom of Orkney that was erected into a Scottish earldom in the Middle Ages. The earldom passed to Henry Sinclair in 1379, and in 1468 the King of Denmark and Norway pledged his Crown rights to James III as security for the dowry of his daughter, Margaret. While King James acquired rights over Orkney, the Sinclairs remained earls of Caithness. With a coastline of 105 miles (168 km), Caithness is bounded to the west and south by Sutherland, and to the north and east by the Pentland Firth and the Moray Firth. Its highest point is Morvern (705 m/2313 ft) and its chief settlements are Wick, the former county town, and Thurso. Between 1975 and 1996 Caithness was a district of Highland Region with much-extended boundaries.

Caiy Stane *City of Edinburgh* Located on Caiystane View, a street in the residential district of Fairmilehead in Edinburgh, is the prehistoric Caiy Stane. Variously known as the Kel, Cat or Camus Stane, it is a substantial block of red standstone, standing some 2.75 m (9 ft) tall, with a breadth of 1.6 m (5 ft). The rear of the stone includes a line of six cup marks. The Caiy Stane may have been erected as early as the Neolithic period (3000 BC) to denote a ritual or burial place. Records of other nearby monuments suggest the area continued to be used for burial in the Bronze Age. It has also been suggested that the stone is a monument to a battle between the Picts and the Romans, or perhaps more recently involving the army of Oliver Cromwell. The stone was given to the National Trust for Scotland in 1936.

Cakemuir Castle *Midlothian* Situated 4 miles (6.5 km) southeast of Pathhead, in the Lammermuir Hills, Midlothian, Cakemuir Castle is said to have derived its name from giving shelter and hospitality to pilgrims on their way to Melrose Abbey. This four-storey tower was built in the mid-16th century on the site of an earlier structure. The tower was extended to the southwest in the 18th century and, like so many others, was baronialised towards the end of the 19th century. It was modernised by Rowand Anderson, Paul & Partners in 1926 and again by Neil & Hurd in the 1950s.

Calair Burn *Stirling* Rising in headstreams in the hills to the south of Loch Voil in the Balquhidder district of Stirling Council area, the Calair Burn flows east to Glen Buckie before turning north on its way to join the River Balvag at the east end of Loch Voil.

Calanais A Gaelic name for Callanish in the Western Isles.

Calavie, Loch *Highland* A small loch in the Lochalsh district of Highland Council area, Loch Calavie lies between the peaks of Beinn Dronaig and Lurg Mhòr, 3 miles (5 km) southwest of Loch Monar.

Calbhaigh The Gaelic name for Calvay in the Western Isles.

Calbha Mòr The Gaelic name for Calva More in Highland.

Calbost *Western Isles* A scattered crofting township on the east coast of Lewis in the Outer Hebrides, Calbost lies in the South Lochs district, between Loch Erisort and Loch Ouirn, a mile (1.5 km) south of Marvig.

Calcruchie An alternative name for Castle Stewart in Dumfries and Galloway.

Calder, Loch *Highland* A large loch in the Caithness district of Highland Council area, Loch Calder lies 5 miles (8 km) southwest of Thurso. Served by runoff water from Loch Olginey to the south, the loch is 2 miles (3 km) in length and a mile (1.5 km) wide. The runoff of Forss Water flows north from Loch Calder to enter the Pentland Firth at Crosskirk Bay.

Calder, River *Highland* A river of Strathspey, the River Calder is formed from three runoff streams from the Monadhliath Mountains and flows east for 3 miles (5 km) to join the River Spey to the south of Newtonmore.

Calder, River *North Ayrshire/Renfrewshire* Rising as the Calder Water on the northern slopes of the North Burnt Hill in North Ayrshire, the Calder flows east into Renfrewshire before widening west of Clyde Muirshiel Country Park to become the River Calder. It continues southeast towards Castle Semple Loch, entering the loch at a point southeast of Lochwinnoch.

Calder Burn *Highland* Rising in the foothills of Carn Dearg, east of the settlement of Laggan, Calder Burn flows north for 5 miles (8 km) through Glen Buck to skirt the southern edge of Aberchalder before emptying into Loch Oich in the Great Glen.

Calder House *West Lothian* This fine 16th-century mansion is located in Mid Calder next to the Kirk of Calder. It remains the home of the Sandilands family who were given the Barony of Calder in the 14th century and created the Lords Torphichen in 1579. It was at Calder House that John Knox (c.1513–72) celebrated the first Protestant communion in 1556. Another notable visitor to Calder House was the Polish composer Frederick Chopin during his visit to Scotland in 1848.

Calder Water *South Lanarkshire* The Calder Water rises on the northeast slopes of the Laird's Seat to the south of East Kilbride in South Lanarkshire. It flows northeast, becoming the Rotten Calder after receiving the Rotten Burn 2 miles (3 km) southeast of East Kilbride. Passing through Calderglen Country Park, the river continues in a northeasterly direction before joining the River Clyde a mile (1.5 km) west of Uddingston, having completed a course of 9 miles (14 km).

Calder Water *South Lanarkshire* The Calder Water rises as the Calder Burn and joins the Avon Water from the west, at a point a half-mile (1 km) from Caldermill and 3 miles (5 km) southwest of Strathaven.

Calderbank *North Lanarkshire* Located between Coatbridge and Chapelhall in North Lanarkshire, the village of Calderbank is separated from Chapelhall to the east by the North Calder Water. To the west of the village lie the remains of the Monklands Canal. Calderbank was established as a company village to house workers in the iron and steel industry, the first purpose-built steelworks in Scotland being erected in the village in 1887. During the 1930s, when reorganisation of the industry resulted in the closing of the steelworks, much of the village was destroyed and replaced with more modern housing. Only the church and several Main Street buildings remain from the earlier period.

Caldercruix *North Lanarkshire* A village of North Lanarkshire, Caldercruix is located on the North Calder Water, 2 miles (3 km) northeast of Plains and 4 miles (6.5 km) northeast of Airdrie. Hillend Reservoir lies a half-mile (1 km) to the east of the village. Taking its name from the 'crooks' or windings on the river, Caldercruix developed in the 19th century in association with mining and paper making.

Calderglen Country Park *South Lanarkshire* A country park in South Lanarkshire, Calderglen is located a mile (1.5 km) southeast of East Kilbride town centre. It comprises 121 ha (300 acres) of parkland, country walks, a children's zoo and sports facilities centred around Torrance House, which is now privately owned. The park lies on the course of the Calder Water, on which there are a number of waterfalls.

Caldermill *South Lanarkshire* The hamlet of Caldermill is located 3 miles (5 km) to the southwest of Strathaven, on the banks of the Calder Water in South Lanarkshire.

Caledonian Canal *Highland* Linking Loch Lochy, Loch Oich and Loch Ness, the Caledonian Canal forms a waterway through the Great Glen that provides a safer and shorter route to the north of Scotland. Built by the engineer Thomas Telford, it was opened in October 1822. Between Fort William and the canal's northern terminus at Clachnaharry just west of Inverness, there are 29 locks, the most famous being a series of eight locks at Banavie known as Neptune's Staircase. Reconstructed in the 1840s, the canal's locks were mechanised in the 1960s. The total length of the canal, which comprises 38 miles (61 km) of natural lochs and 22 miles (35 km) of canal cuttings, is 60 miles (96 km). The summit level at Loch Oich is 32 m (106 ft).

Calf of Cava *Orkney* The Calf of Cava forms a headland at the northern end of the small island of Cava in the Orkney Islands. There is a lighthouse on the headland. To the west is the Bring Deeps and to the east Scapa Flow.

Calf of Eday *Orkney* An uninhabited island of the Orkney Islands, the Calf of Eday is situated to the northeast of the island of Eday from which it is separated by Calf Sound. The island, with an area of 243 ha (300 acres), has a number of prehistoric chambered cairns, close to which lie the remains of a saltworks that provided Orkney with most of its salt during the 18th and 19th centuries.

Calf of Flotta *Orkney* A small uninhabited island in the Orkney Islands, the Calf of Flotta is located off the northeast coast of the island of Flotta and is separated from this island by Calf Sound.

Calf of Linga *Shetland* The Calf of Linga is a small uninhabited islet located off the northeast coast of the island of East Linga in the Shetland Islands.

Calf Sound *Orkney* A stretch of water in the Orkney Islands, the Calf Sound separates Calf of Eday from the northeast coast of the island of Eday.

Calf Sound *Orkney* A stretch of water separating the Calf of Flotta from Roan Head on the northeast coast of the island of Flotta in the Orkney Islands.

Calgary *Argyll and Bute* A hamlet with a hotel, Calgary lies on a fine sandy bay in the northwest corner of the island of Mull. Calgary gave its name to the city of Calgary in Alberta, Canada. The road south from the village has spectacular views of the Treshnish Isles and Coll, while to the north it offers views of Ardnamurchan and Skye. The people of Calgary and the surrounding area were largely 'cleared' in 1822.

Calgary Bay *Argyll and Bute* A sheltered bay on the northwest coast of the island of Mull in Argyll and Bute, Calgary Bay looks west towards Coll and Tiree. The settlement of Calgary lies at the head of the bay.

Calgary Point *Argyll and Bute* A headland on the southwest coast of the island of Coll, Calgary Point extends into Caolas Bàn, a stretch of water separating Coll from Gunna to the southwest.

Calgow *Dumfries and Galloway* A locality in southwest Dumfries and Galloway, Calgow lies between Larg Hill and the River Cree, 2 miles (3 km) southeast of Newton Stewart.

Caliach Point *Argyll and Bute* A headland on the northwest coast of the island of Mull, Caliach Point lies 3 miles (5 km) northwest of Calgary and 10 miles (16 km) northwest of Tobermory.

California *Falkirk* A village in central Falkirk Council area, California is situated 3 miles (5 km) south of Falkirk in an upland agricultural landscape. Wetlands to the north and west are designated wildlife habitats.

Callakille *Highland* Also known as Kalnakill, the small township of Callakille lies on the Inner Sound, over 6 miles (10 km) north of Applecross in Wester Ross.

Callander *Stirling* Often hailed as the 'Gateway to the Highlands', Callander is a small town situated at the junction of the Leny River and the River Teith, 18 miles (29 km) northwest of Stirling. It lies immediately south of the Highland Boundary Fault and east of the Pass of Leny, a main route into the Highlands. The settlement, which is historically a meeting point between Highlander and Lowlander, owes its modern development to the Commissioners for Forfeited Estates who planned the layout of the village in the wake of the 1745 Jacobite Rising on lands formerly owned by the Drummond family. It expanded as a tourist resort in the 19th century and remains today a leading centre of tourist activity with its Rob Roy and Trossachs Centre located in the former St Kessog's Church. Callander featured as Tannochbrae in the 1960s' TV series of *Dr Finlay's Casebook*. There are walks to the Bracklinn Falls on the Keltie Water to the east, and to the west a footpath and cycle track follow the line of the former Callander and Oban Railway.

Callanish *Western Isles* A village on the west coast of Lewis in the Outer Hebrides, Callanish (*Calanais*) lies at the head of East Loch Roag, 13 miles (21 km) west of Stornoway. On a low ridge close by is one of Scotland's most spectacular prehistoric ceremonial centres, comprising a small circle of 13 standing stones which form the focus of four rows of stones to the north, south, east and west. Within the circle is a tall pillar, 4.75 m (16 ft) in height, beside a small chambered tomb.

Callater Burn *Aberdeenshire* A stream in the Grampian Mountains, the Callater Burn rises on the border between Aberdeenshire and Angus and flows northwest through Glen Callater and Loch Callater before joining the Clunie Water 2 miles (3 km) south of Braemar.

Callendar House *Falkirk* Set within Callendar Park, a mile (1.5 km) east of Falkirk town centre, Callendar House dates from the 14th century. It was home to the Livingstons of Callendar for almost 400 years, and to William Forbes who bought the estate in the 1780s. Originally a fortified castle, it was visited by Mary, Queen of Scots, whose guardian was the 5th Lord Livingston, as well as being seized by troops loyal to Cromwell. In the 19th century it was restored and remodelled in the chateau style that is evident today. Permanent displays open to the public include features on the story of the house and the social history of Falkirk during the Industrial Revolution. Falkirk Museums Services and a History Research Centre are based here. The Roman Antonine Wall passes through the park, which also contains Callendar Park Technical College.

Callievar Hill *Aberdeenshire* A hill in the Howe of Alford, central Aberdeenshire, Callievar Hill (also Coiliochbhar Hill) rises in a bend of the River Don, 4 miles (6.5 km) west of Alford.

Calligarry *Highland* A small settlement on the island of Skye, Calligarry is situated near Ardvasar on the Sleat peninsula.

Callop River *Highland* Flowing generally northwards for 5 miles (8 km), the Callop River empties into the head of Loch Shiel in Lochaber district, Highland Council area, to the east of the settlement of Glenfinnan.

Cally, Glen *Angus* A small glen in the Braes of Angus, Glen Cally lies between Glen Prosen and Glen Clova.

Cally House *Perth and Kinross* A mansion house in Strathardle, north-central Perth and Kinross, Cally House lies by the River Ardle, just over a mile (1.5 km) northwest of Bridge of Cally. To the northeast, the Hill of Cally rises to 349 m (1064 ft).

Cally Park *Dumfries and Galloway* An estate in southern Dumfries and Galloway, Cally Park lies within the Fleet Forest, a mile (1.5 km) to the south of Gatehouse of Fleet. The remains of Cally House lie close to Cally Lake.

Calrossie *Highland* A locality in Easter Ross, Calrossie lies a mile (1.5 km) to the northeast of Nigg.

Calternish *Western Isles* A locality on the northeast coast of South Uist in the Outer Hebrides, Calternish (also Caltanish and Caltinish, Gael: *Caltanais*) lies between Loch Carnan and Loch Sheilavaig, 14 miles (22 km) north of Lochboisdale. Craig Calternish rises to 30 m (98 ft) on the coast, and Strom Calternish forms a narrow rocky channel at the head of Loch Sheilavaig.

Calton Hill *City of Edinburgh* Rising to 108 m (355 ft) to the east end of Princes Street in the centre of Edinburgh, Calton Hill is not the highest of the city's hills, yet it occupies a dramatic setting with views to Leith, the Firth of Forth and Fife to the north, and Holyrood Park to the south. Remarkable for its eclectic assortment of architecture, Calton Hill is largely responsible for Edinburgh's soubriquet as 'The Athens of the North'. Geologically the hill is volcanic in origin, dating from the Lower Carboniferous age (335 million years ago), similar to Arthur's Seat and Castle Rock. Buildings and monuments of note include the Nelson Monument (1816), built in the shape of a telescope; the unfinished National Monument (1822), modelled on the Parthenon but otherwise known as 'Edinburgh's disgrace'; the City Observatory, comprising Observatory House (1776), the Old Observatory (1818) and the City Dome (1895); and monuments to philosopher Dugald Stewart (1753–1828) and mathematician John Playfair (1748–1819), both designed by William Playfair (1789–1857). There is a monument commemorating the success of the vigil for the return of the Scottish Parliament.

Caluim, Loch *Highland* Located within northwest Caithness district, Highland Council area, Loch Caluim lies 2 miles (3 km) southeast of Loch Scye and 2 miles (3 km) southwest of Loch Shurrery.

Calva More *Highland* The larger of two small uninhabited islands, Calva More (Gael: *Calbha Mòr*) lies within Eddrachillis Bay off the west coast of Sutherland. The settlement of Badcall is situated 3 miles (5 km) to the north.

Calvay *Western Isles* The small island of Calvay (Gael: *Calbhaigh*) lies at the mouth of Loch Boisdale, a sea loch of South Uist in the Outer Hebrides. The island rises to 23 m (75 ft) and a lighthouse stands on its east coast, while the remains of a castle are located on the northwest shore. Another island of Calvay lies in the Sound of Eriskay to the south.

Calvay *Western Isles* A small uninhabited island in the Sound of Eriskay, Calvay (Gael: *Calbhaigh*) rises to 21 m (68 ft) at the eastern end of the sound. Another island of Calvay lies at the mouth of Loch Boisdale to the north.

Calve Island *Argyll and Bute* A small uninhabited island located at the entrance to Tobermory Bay, Calve Island lies on the east coast of Mull.

Calvie, Glen *Highland* A small and partially forested valley of Easter Ross, Glen Calvie extends south near the head of Strathcarron and conveys the Water of Glencalvie from Glen Diebidale in the south for 2 miles (3 km) to its junction with the River Carron.

Calvine *Perth and Kinross* A village of northern Perth and Kinross, Calvine lies 4 miles (6.5 km) west of Blair Atholl near the confluence of the Errochty Water and the River Garry, which is crossed by a three-arched stone railway viaduct. The artist Samuel John Peploe (1871–1935) painted in this locality.

Cam Chriochan *Perth and Kinross* A stream rising from a small loch and flowing south for 3 miles (5 km), the Cam Chriochan empties into the foot of Loch Ericht, within the Rannoch Forest of Perth and Kinross.

Cam Loch *Highland* Located at the southern edge of Sutherland, the Cam Loch lies immediately to the north of Loch Veyatie, to which it is joined at its southern extremity by the Abhainn Mòr river. The settlement of Elphin lies to the south and Inchnadamph is 6 miles (10 km) to the north.

Camasericht *Perth and Kinross* A locality in northwest Perth and Kinross, Camusericht lies at the western end of Loch Rannoch. Camusericht Lodge is immediately west of Bridge of Ericht, and Camusericht Farm lies further west, beyond Rannoch Lodge.

Camas Fearna *Highland* Located on the southern coastline of the Ardnamurchan peninsula, Camas Fearna forms a small bay 6 miles (10 km) southwest of the settlement of Tarbert.

Camas nan Geall *Highland* Located on the southern coastline of the Ardnamurchan peninsula, Camas nan Geall forms a small bay 7 miles (11 km) southwest of the settlement of Tarbert.

Camastianavaig *Highland* A township on the isle of Skye, Camastianavaig (Gael: *Camustinivaig*) lies on Tianavaig Bay, 3 miles (5 km) southeast of Portree.

Camasunary Bay *Highland* Located on the south coast of the isle of Skye, Camasunary Bay lies on the shore of Loch Scavaig 8 miles (13 km) southwest of Broadford. It is regarded as one of the finest bays on the island. Deriving from the Gaelic for 'Bay of the Fair Shieling' (pasture), Camasunary Bay has a small bothy for hillwalkers.

Camault Muir *Highland* A scattered crofting settlement of Inverness district, Highland Council area, Camault Muir is located 4 miles (6.5 km) south of Beauly and immediately to the south of Kiltarlity. The Bruaich Burn flows to the west of the settlement.

Cambo *Fife* An estate on the east coast of Fife near Kingsbarns, Cambo developed as a country park during the early 1980s. Extending over 648 ha (1600 acres) of countryside and seashore, its house was a medieval stronghold of the Norman de Cambhous family and later of the Myretouns who held it from 1364 to 1668, when it was bought by Sir Charles Erskine, Lord Lyon King of Arms. The estate's East New Hall Steading was built in the 18th century and converted to a visitor centre in the 1980s. The park has nature trails, picnic sites, play areas and educational facilities. Cambo House, with its walled garden, was rebuilt in 1879 after being destroyed by fire.

Cambo Sands *Fife* The Cambo Sands lie immediately to the north of Cambo Ness, 3 miles (5 km) north of Crail on the east coast of Fife. The sands extend to encircle some nearby rocky islets. The settlement of Kingsbarns lies immediately to the west.

Cambus *Clackmannanshire* A small village in western Clackmannanshire, Cambus lies to the north of the River Forth where it is joined by the River Devon, 2 miles (3 km) west of Alloa. Whisky distilling, which here dates from 1806, continues.

Cambusavie *Highland* A locality in southeast Sutherland, Highland Council area, Cambusavie lies to the west of Loch Fleet, 6 miles (10 km) to the north of Dornoch. It comprises a farm and the site of a former hospital on opposite sides of the A9. The hospital, closed in 1989, was built near the Mound Station in 1906 as the Sutherland County Infectious Diseases Hospital. The various isolation wards were built of wood frames and corrugated iron.

Cambusbarron *Stirling* Separated from the Stirling conurbation by the M80, Cambusbarron is an ancient village and former spinning and woollen manufacturing settlement of southeast Stirling Council area. The Parkvale and Hayford mills, the latter founded by the Smiths in 1860 and still surviving, once employed more than 1000 people. The Bruce Memorial Church (1910) stands on the site of a chapel where Robert the Bruce is said to have taken sacrament on the eve of the Battle of Bannockburn (1314).

Cambushinnie Hill *Perth and Kinross* Cambushinnie Hill rises to 268 m (878 ft) to the north of Strathallan and 2 miles (3 km) west of Braco in Perth and Kinross.

Cambuskenneth *Stirling* A hamlet on the River Forth, Cambuskenneth lies a mile (1.5 km) to the east of Stirling. The imposing three-storeyed campanile is all that survives of Cambuskenneth Abbey, which was founded for Augustinian canons in 1147 by King David I. Closely linked to the royal castle of Stirling, the abbey grew to immense wealth and importance in medieval times, and it was here that King James III was buried after his death at the Battle of Sauchieburn (1488).

Cambuslang *South Lanarkshire* Situated to the east of Rutherglen and south of the River Clyde in South Lanarkshire, Cambuslang developed from a small handloom weaving village in the 18th century to a centre of heavy industry in the 20th century. In 1742, before its expansion in association with coal mining and the manufacture of textiles and iron, it was the centre of an evangelical revival that came to be known as the 'Cam'uslang Wark'. Led by the Revd William McCulloch and the Revd John Robe and assisted by the English Methodist preacher George Whitefield, this mass movement had, for a short while, 30,000 adherents. By the 1980s the redevelopment of derelict industrial areas was underway with the establishment of an investment park, South Lanarkshire College and Scotland's first indoor kart-racing track. Modern industries include the manufacture of steel. Cambuslang was the birthplace of horticulturalist John Claudius London (1783–1843) and rock singer James (Midge) Ure (b.1953).

Cambusnethan *North Lanarkshire* Originally a separate village, Cambusnethan is now an eastern suburb of the town of Wishaw in North Lanarkshire.

Cambuswallace *South Lanarkshire* A northern district of Biggar in South Lanarkshire, Cambuswallace was the name of an estate located a mile (1.5 km) northeast of Biggar.

Camelon *Falkirk* A settlement in Falkirk Council area, Camelon lies to the west of Falkirk between the River Carron and the Forth and Clyde Canal. Roman remains associated with the Antonine Wall have been excavated in the area, and Scotland's 'second national drink', Barr's Irn Bru, is produced here. Just west of Camelon, the Falkirk Wheel, opened in 2002, links the Forth and Clyde Canal to the Union Canal.

Cameron *Fife* A parish in eastern Fife that contains a pattern of dispersed farmsteads as well as the settlements of Denhead, Lathones and Radernie, Cameron is associated with Kate Dalrymple who was immortalised by the peasant poet William Watt (1792–1859) and is thought to have lived in a cottage by the Cameron Burn. This burn now flows eastwards out of Cameron Reservoir to meet the Kenly Water east of Stravithie.

Cameron Bridge *Fife* A settlement at a bridge over the River Leven just south of Windygates in southern Fife, Cameron Bridge is situated 2 miles (3 km) west of Leven. It was the first upstream crossing of the river when the ford at Leven was flooded. An earlier bridge was rebuilt in 1870, and a distillery was established here by the Haig family in the early 19th century.

Cameron Reservoir *Fife* A small reservoir in eastern Fife, Cameron Reservoir lies 4 miles (6.5 km) southwest of St Andrews. It is the source of the Cameron Burn, a tributary of the Kenly Water, and is the main water supply for St Andrews.

Cameron Toll *City of Edinburgh* A locality at the south end of Dalkeith Road on the south side of Edinburgh, Cameron Toll was originally the site of a tollhouse built in the early 19th century to collect road tolls. Today, Cameron Toll comprises an immense roundabout, traversed by the former Southern District Railway between Newington and Craigmillar but is better known for its large modern shopping centre. The late 18th-century Cameron House lies to the east.

Cameronian Museum *South Lanarkshire* Located a half-mile (1 km) to the northeast of Hamilton in South Lanarkshire, the Cameronian Museum occupies the former riding school of the dukes of Hamilton, built by architect William Burn in 1842. The 26th (or Cameronian) Regiment of Foot was raised in Douglas (South Lanarkshire) in 1689 by the Marquess of Douglas. It was recruited from Covenanters and took its name from the most famous of their number, Richard Cameron, 'The Lion of the Covenant'. The museum was opened in 1983.

Camerory *Highland* A settlement in Strathspey, Camerory lies on the edge of Dava Moor, 3 miles (5 km) north of Grantown-on-Spey.

Camgharaidh, Gleann *Highland* Located within Lochaber district, Highland Council area, Gleann Camgharaidh carries the waters of Allt Camgharaidh northeast to empty into Loch Arkaig, a mile (1.5 km) from its head.

Camghouran *Perth and Kinross* A hamlet in the Black Wood of Rannoch close to the south shore of Loch

Rannoch, Camghouran lies on the Allt Camghouran, 7 miles (11 km) west of Kinloch Rannoch, Perth and Kinross.

Camieston *Scottish Borders* A small settlement located within the central Scottish Borders, Camieston lies a mile (1.5 km) south of Newtown St Boswells.

Camlachie *Glasgow City* A district of Glasgow, Camlachie lies a mile (1.5 km) east of Glasgow Cross, between Dennistoun to the north and Bridgeton to the south. In the 18th century the waters of the Molendinar and Camlachie Burns coupled with the discovery of coal-fuelled industrial development resulted in the establishment of textile mills, a brewery and chemical works. Much of the area's industrial past has been replaced by modern housing.

Camore *Highland* A settlement in southeast Sutherland, Highland Council area, Camore lies nearly 2 miles (3 km) northwest of Dornoch.

Campbeltown *Argyll and Bute* The chief town and port of the Kintyre peninsula of Argyll and Bute, Campbeltown sits at the head of Campbeltown Loch, 30 miles (48 km) south of Tarbert. A former seat of the kings of Dalriada, the site was granted by King James V to the Campbells of Argyll, who were charged with maintaining royal power and authority in this rebellious corner of Scotland. The Campbells later created Kilkerran Castle and renamed the existing small settlement Campbeltown. Lowlanders from Ayrshire and Renfrewshire settled in the town in the 17th century, enhancing its status as a burgh of barony (1667) and a royal burgh (1700). The town developed in association with coal mining, herring fishing, boat building and whisky distilling, all of which went into decline at the beginning of the 20th century. Of the 36 distilleries that once operated in Campbeltown, only a handful survive. Now an agricultural service centre and tourist resort with a small shipyard and food-processing industries, Campbeltown has the oldest surviving cinema in Scotland and a local museum. Campbeltown or Machrihanish Airport is situated to the northwest.

Campbeltown Loch *Argyll and Bute* A sea loch on the southeast coast of the Kintyre peninsula, Campbeltown Loch forms an inlet of the Kilbrannan Sound. Campbeltown lies at its head and at its mouth is Davaar Island.

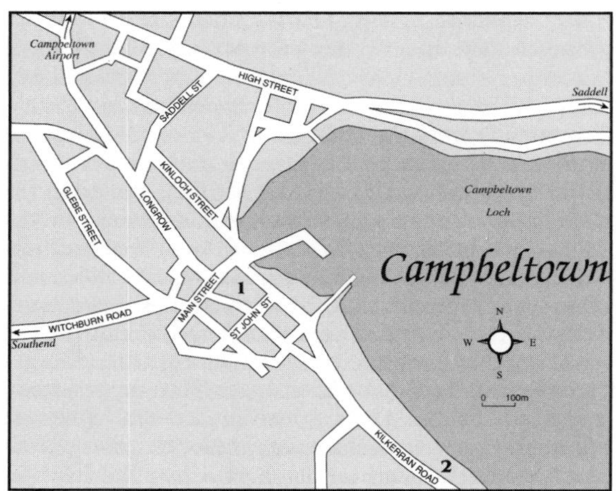

1 *Campbeltown Museum* 2 *Kilkerran Castle*

Camperdown Park *Dundee City* A public park on the northern outskirts of Dundee, Camperdown Park comprises the house and former policies of the earls of Camperdown. Camperdown House was designed by the Edinburgh architect William Burn and completed in 1828 for Robert Duncan, Earl of Camperdown and son of Admiral Duncan who defeated the French at the Battle of Camperdown in 1797. Opened as a public park in 1946, it has a wildlife centre and an 18-hole golf course. This is the largest of Dundee's parklands.

Camphill Reservoir *North Ayrshire* Located some 3 miles (5 km) west of Kilbirnie in North Ayrshire, the Camphill Reservoir lies due south of Muirhead Reservoir and is the source of the Rye Water.

Cample *Dumfries and Galloway* Located a mile (1.5 km) southeast of Thornhill in Dumfries and Galloway, the settlement of Cample lies on the course of the Cample Water in Nithsdale.

Cample Water *Dumfries and Galloway* A stream in northern Dumfries and Galloway, the Cample Water rises on Wedder Law in the Lowther Hills. It flows southwards for 8 miles (13 km) before joining the River Nith a mile (1.5 km) south of Thornhill.

Camps *West Lothian* A small village of West Lothian, Camps lies a half-mile (1 km) north of Kirknewton and a half-mile (1 km) northeast of East Calder.

Camps Water *South Lanarkshire* The Camps Water flows from the Camps Reservoir, 3 miles (5 km) to the east of Crawford in South Lanarkshire. A tributary of the River Clyde, it flows west from the reservoir to join the Clyde to the north of Crawford.

Campsie *East Dunbartonshire* A village of East Dunbartonshire, Campsie (also Clachan of Campsie) lies 2 miles (3 km) northwest of Lennoxtown on a tributary of the Glazert Water, which joins the River Kelvin.

Campsie Fells *Stirling/East Dunbartonshire* A range of hills in southern Stirling Council area and East Dunbartonshire, the Campsie Fells lie between the Endrick Water and the valley of Strathblane, which separates the Campsies from the Kilpatrick Hills to the west. The highest point in the range is Earl's Seat, which rises to 578 m (1897 ft). Erosion along the line of a geological faultline known as the Campsie Fault has left tiers of rock representing some 30 lava flows dating from the Carboniferous period. The headwaters of the River Kelvin rise in the Campsie Fells.

Campsie Glen *East Dunbartonshire* A valley on the south side of the Campsie Fells, Campsie (or Kirkton) Glen lies immediately north of the Clachan of Campsie in East Dunbartonshire. A tributary of the Glazert Water flows through the glen to meet the River Kelvin.

Campsie Linn *Perth and Kinross* At the waterfall of Campsie Linn, 5 miles (8 km) north of Perth in Perth and Kinross, the River Tay begins to widen as it meanders southwards. Taymount House and Home Farm lie immediately west.

Camptoun *East Lothian* A small village of East Lothian, Camptoun is situated a mile (1.5 km) west of Athelstaneford and 3 miles (5 km) northeast of Haddington.

Camptown *Scottish Borders* A small settlement of Scottish Borders, Camptown lies on the course of the Jed Water, 5 miles (8 km) south of Jedburgh.

Camrie Burn *Dumfries and Galloway* A stream in

Dumfries and Galloway, the Camrie Burn rises on Camrie Fell, 2 miles (3 km) north of Glenluce. It flows southwestwards past Glenluce Abbey to join the Water of Luce.

Camserney *Perth and Kinross* The hamlet of Camserney lies on a burn of the same name at the eastern end of the Appin of Dull, 3 miles (5 km) west of Aberfeldy in Perth and Kinross. It overlooks the River Tay to the south and comprises a number of thatched, cruck-framed cottages. This former crofting township once boasted a meal mill, sawmill, carpet factory and wheelwright mill that made bobbins for the textile industry of Dundee.

Camster *Highland* A locality on open moorland in eastern Caithness, Camster comprises the settlements of Upper and Lower Camster which lie to the southwest of Wick. The Camster Burn rises to the east of Upper Camster, and near Lower Camster are the Grey Cairns of Camster, two of the best-preserved Neolithic chambered cairns in Britain. Dating from the 4th and 3rd millennium BC, the round cairn is 18 m (59 ft) in diameter, and the long cairn 69.5 m (228 ft) in length, both having been excavated in 1865.

Camusnagaul *Highland* A small settlement in Lochaber, southern Highland Council area, Camusnagaul lies on the Ardgour peninsula opposite Fort William, to which it is linked by a ferry.

Camusteel *Highland* A hamlet in Wester Ross, Camusteel lies 2 miles (3 km) south of Applecross.

Camusterrach *Highland* A small settlement located on the west coast of Wester Ross, Camusterrach lies 3 miles (5 km) south of Applecross overlooking the Inner Sound.

Camustinivaig An alternative name for Camastianavaig in Highland.

Candleriggs *Glasgow City* A street in the Merchant City district of Glasgow, Candleriggs takes its name from the trade once carried out there, namely the production of candles. It was one of the main roads linking the Trongate and the River Clyde to the north of the city. In the 1990s it underwent partial regeneration, the old Candleriggs Indoor Market being renovated for retail and café/bistro use.

Canisbay *Highland* A settlement in a parish of the same name in northeast Caithness, Canisbay lies on the Pentland Firth, 2 miles (3 km) west of John o' Groats. The medieval St Drostan's Church with its saddle-back west tower has in its porch a tombstone commemorating members of the Dutch Grot or Groat family who settled in Caithness in the late 15th century and whose descendants operated a ferry to Orkney. John Groat, who held a pennyland in nearby Duncansby from the Earl of Caithness, gave his name to John o' Groats.

Canisp *Highland* A mountain of Assynt, Canisp rises to 846 m (2775 ft) within the Glencanisp Forest, 4 miles (6.5 km) southwest of Inchnadamph. The peak of Suilven rises 3 miles (5 km) to the west.

Canna *Highland* The most westerly of the Small Isles in the Inner Hebrides, Canna lies to the northwest of Rum, between Skye and South Uist. Accessed by ferry from Mallaig, Canna is 5 miles (8 km) long and 1.5 miles (2.5 km) wide. Geologically the island is a lava platform comprising terraced Tertiary basalt rock. It has a rich fertile soil and rises to 210 m (689 ft) at Carn a' Ghaill. This combination of good soils and a sheltered harbour, linked to the island's position at a crossroads between the Outer Hebrides and the mainland of Scotland and between Skye and the islands of Argyll to the south, has made Canna an important island with a long and continuous settlement dating from the Bronze Age. There are over 1000 archeological features on the island whose earliest historical records are linked with St Columba, to whom a monastery on the island was dedicated. The last private owner of Canna was Dr John Lorne Campbell who bought the island in 1938 and subsequently gifted it to the National Trust for Scotland in 1981. Included in the gift was Dr Campbell's extensive and unique library of Gaelic language and literature. The population of the island, which had risen to 436 in 1821 from around 230 in the mid-18th century, fell to 127 in 1861 as a result of clearances and the failure of the kelp industry. By 2000 there were only 15 people on the island. Canna is part of the Small Isles National Scenic Area, all the island apart from the farm and inbye croft land being designated a Site of Special Scientific Interest (SSSI). Its cliffs are noted for their large numbers of breeding sea birds, the colony of shag being the largest in Scotland. Buildings of interest include the remains of the former township of A' Chill, the remnants of the 7th-century St Columba's Chapel, Canna House, the medieval cairn tower at An Coroghon, and St Edward's Church, which is now a study centre for visitors. At its southeast end, Canna is linked to the island of Sanday by a bridge and a reef.

Canna, Sound of *Highland* The Sound of Canna in the Small Isles of Highland separates the islands of Canna and Sanday from Rum to the southeast.

Cannich *Highland* A village in the centre of Highland Council area, Cannich stands at the confluence of the Rivers Glass and Cannich in Glen Cannich, 8 miles (13 km) west of Drumnadrochit. Originally a small farming village, it grew in the 20th century with the development of the nearby hydro-electric power station at Fasnakyle. Situated amid great hillwalking country, Cannich lies at the point where Glens Urquhart, Cannich and Affric all meet. Places of interest include the prehistoric Corrimony cairn in Glen Urquhart, the dam on Loch Mullardoch (the longest in Scotland) and the Dog Falls of Glen Affric. One of the largest remnants of ancient Caledonian pine forest lies to the southwest and west.

Cannich, River *Highland* Rising from the eastern end of Loch Mullardoch, Highland Council area, the River Cannich flows in an easterly direction, passing through a number of small lochs, before joining the River Glass a mile (1.5 km) northeast of the settlement of Cannich.

Canonbie *Dumfries and Galloway* A village of Eskdale in southeast Dumfries and Galloway, Canonbie lies on the River Esk, 5 miles (8 km) southeast of Langholm. In the Middle Ages there was an Augustinian priory in the village, and in the 19th and 20th centuries coal and lime were mined in the neighbourhood. Nearby Holehouse Tower was a stronghold of the Armstrongs, and 2 miles (3 km) to the north on a promontory overlooking the Esk once stood Johnnie Armstrong's Tower of Gilnockie.

Canongate, The *City of Edinburgh* Forming a westerly extension of the High Street in the Old Town of Edinburgh, The Canongate comprises the lower part of the Royal Mile linking Edinburgh Castle to the Palace of Holyroodhouse. It stretches towards the palace from the junction of St Mary's Street with the High Street, the site of the Netherbow Port or eastern entry through the medieval city walls. It was through this entrance that the Augustinian canons of Holyrood Abbey entered and left the city. Forming a separate burgh outwith the walls of Edinburgh, the more spacious Canongate was favoured by the nobility who set up residence here. A number of fine mansions built by these families survive today, including Huntly House (c.1570), now a museum, Moray House (1625), Acheson House (1633) and Queensberry House (1681), which now forms part of the Scottish Parliament complex. Built in 1591, the Canongate Tolbooth, now a museum, was the administrative centre of the burgh that united with Edinburgh in 1856. As the New Town gained in popularity as a residential area, the Canongate declined. Many of the buildings that exist today are 20th-century reconstructions, the result of restoration schemes initially prompted by John Crichton Stuart, 4th Marquess of Bute (1881–1947).

Canonmills *City of Edinburgh* A district of northwest Edinburgh, Canonmills lies between the New Town and the residential suburb of Inverleith. It developed as a village with mills on the Water of Leith, which is known locally as the Puddocky Burn. Once situated on royal land, it was gifted by David I to the Augustinian canons of Holyrood Abbey who worked the mills. The bakers of Canongate were obliged by law to grind their corn here. Robert Louis Stevenson (1850–94) was born in Howard Place, and the composer Frederick Chopin (1810–49) stayed in Warriston Crescent.

Cantick Head *Orkney* A headland of the island of Hoy in the Orkney Islands, Cantick Head lies at the eastern end of the South Walls peninsula, a mile (1.5 km) southeast of Hackness. Overlooking the Cantick Sound, Cantick Head lies to the south of the bay of Kirk Hope. A Stevenson-built lighthouse stands on the headland.

Cantraywood *Highland* A locality in eastern Highland Council area, Cantraywood lies just southwest of Croy, 6 miles (10 km) east of Inverness. Nearby are the settlements of Cantray and Cantraydoune.

Canty Bay *East Lothian* A small inlet on the northern coast of East Lothian, Canty Bay lies 2 miles (3 km) east of North Berwick.

Caol *Highland* A village in Lochaber, southern Highland Council area, Caol lies at the head of Loch Linnhe, just over a mile (1.5 km) north of Fort William.

Caol Ila *Argyll and Bute* A locality on Loch nam Bàn, immediately to the north of Port Askaig on the east coast of the island of Islay, Caol Ila gives its name to a distillery producing malt whisky, established in 1826.

Caol-loch *Highland* A small narrow loch of eastern Sutherland, Caol-loch lies 3 miles (5 km) southeast of the southern end of the Strathy Forest and 3 miles (5 km) west of Dalhalvaig in Strath Halladale.

Caolas *Argyll and Bute* Located at the eastern end of the island of Tiree, the scattered settlement of Caolas lies a mile (1.5 km) west of the headland of Rubha Dubh. A standing stone is situated a half-mile (1 km) southwest of Caolas.

Caolas a' Mhorain *Western Isles* Caolas a' Mhorain is the name given to the stretch of sea in the Outer Hebrides that separates the island of Boreray from North Uist to the south.

Caolas Bhatarsaigh The Gaelic name for the Sound of Vatersay in the Western Isles.

Caolas Mòr *Argyll and Bute* A channel in the Inner Hebrides, Caolas Mòr separates the island of Oronsay at the southern end of Colonsay from rocky islets to the south, the principal islet being Eilean Ghaoideamal.

Caolas Orasaigh The Gaelic name for the Sound of Orosay in the Western Isles.

Caolas Phabaigh The Gaelic name for the Sound of Pabay in the Western Isles.

Caolas Scalpaigh The Gaelic name for Kyles Scalpay in the Western Isles.

Caolas Stocinis The Gaelic name for Kyles Stockinish in the Western Isles.

Caolisport, Loch *Argyll and Bute* A sea loch on the coast of Knapdale, Loch Caolisport extends 5 miles (8 km) southwest into the Sound of Jura from Achahoish. St Columba's Cave is on its north shore near Ellary.

Capel Mounth *Aberdeenshire* The Capel Mounth forms an old route that crosses over the hills from the top end of Glen Clova in Angus to Ballater in Aberdeenshire by way of Glen Muick.

Capel Water *Dumfries and Galloway* A stream in northern Dumfries and Galloway, the Capel Water rises as the Capel Burn in the Lowther Hills to the west of Queensberry. It flows southwards into the Forest of Ae where it joins the Water of Ae.

Caplaw *East Renfrewshire* A settlement in East Renfrewshire, Caplaw lies 4 miles (6.5 km) southwest of Paisley to the south of the Gleniffer Braes and east of Whittliemuir Midton Loch.

Cappercleuch *Scottish Borders* A small settlement of Ettrick in southeast Scottish Borders, Cappercleuch lies to the west of St Mary's Loch, 16 miles (26 km) northeast of Moffat. In 1978 the Megget Dam was built 2 miles (3 km) to the west, impounding the Megget Reservoir, the longest reservoir in southwest Scotland.

Capplegill *Dumfries and Galloway* A locality in the Moffat Hills of northern Dumfries and Galloway, Capplegill lies in the valley of the Moffat Water, 5 miles (8 km) northeast of Moffat.

Caputh *Perth and Kinross* An estate village with blue and white painted buildings in central Perth and Kinross, Caputh lies on the A984 from Dunkeld to Meikleour, 4 miles (6.5 km) east of Dunkeld. Immediately south, the River Tay is crossed by the Victoria Bridge, which was built in 1887 by Sir William Arrol for William Cox of Snaigow and Foggyley. Its girders are of identical design to the ones used on the Tay Rail Bridge at Dundee. The church at Caputh dates from 1798.

Cara *Argyll and Bute* An uninhabited island of the Inner Hebrides, Cara lies to the south of Gigha and is separated from the Kintyre peninsula by the Sound of Gigha. The island has an area of 61 ha (153 acres) and rises to 56 m (184 ft) at the Mull of Cara. Legend has it that in an attic of Cara House lives the 'Brownie of Cara', the ghost of a Macdonald murdered by the Campbells. Cara was frequented by the smugglers of Gigha, Jura and Islay during the 18th century.

Carberry Hill *East Lothian* A hill rising to 122 m (400 ft) 2.5 miles (4 km) south of Musselburgh in East Lothian, Carberry Hill was the site, on 15 June 1567, of a stand-off between the armies of Mary, Queen of Scots, led by her husband, James Hepburn, Earl of Bothwell, and a confederation of Protestant lords under the leadership of James Douglas, Earl of Morton. Mary was taken to

Loch Leven Castle to begin a long period of captivity, and Bothwell left the scene for Dunbar en route to the Continent.

Carberry Tower *East Lothian* A 16th-century tower house 2.5 miles (4 km) south of Musselburgh in East Lothian, Carberry Tower was a stronghold of the Elphinstone, Blair of Lochwood, Dickson and Fullerton families. It was converted into a Scottish baronial-style country seat in 1819 with later extensions in 1860 and 1909. It was here that Mary, Queen of Scots surrendered to her Protestant lords in June 1567. Sydney, the 16th Lord Elphinstone, married Mary Frances Bowes-Lyon, daughter of Claude, 14th Earl of Strathmore (1855–1944), and sister of Queen Elizabeth, the Queen Mother. When King George VI visited the Palace of Holyroodhouse, the queen would bring her daughters to stay at Carberry. Their bedroom is now referred to as the Queen's Room. When the widowed Lady Elphinstone died in 1961 she gave the property to the Church of Scotland to be used as a youth and conference centre. The Church built a chapel in the grounds in 1965, and in 1996 both the tower and the surrounding estate were purchased by the Carberry Trust, an ecumenical charity.

Carbeth *Stirling* An estate in Strathblane parish, southwest Stirling Council area, Carbeth lies 2 miles (3 km) west of Strathblane. Carbeth is the site of the largest 'hut' community in Scotland, a form of social experiment providing city dwellers with weekend accommodation in the countryside. Established after World War I, controversy raged when tenant rents were increased in the 1990s.

Carbisdale Castle *Highland* Situated in a commanding position overlooking the Kyle of Sutherland, Carbisdale Castle lies a half-mile (1 km) north of Culrain in Easter Ross. The castle was built by the dowager Duchess of Sutherland between 1906 and 1917. In 1945 Carbisdale was gifted to the Scottish Youth Hostel Association (SYHA) to form one of the grandest hostels in the world. It features a fine gallery of Italian marble statues.

Carbost *Highland* A township on the island of Skye, Carbost lies on the south shore of Loch Harport, 10 miles (16 km) southwest of Portree. The Carbost Burn joins Loch Harport here, and the Talisker whisky distillery is located on the northwestern edge of the village.

Cardenden *Fife* A former mining town on the Carden Burn in the parish of Auchterderran, western Fife, Cardenden incorporates the settlements of Auchterderran, Bowhill and Dundonald and was the home of the poet Joe Corrie (1894–1968), who gave his name to the Corrie Centre. Cardenden was also the birthplace in 1960 of the award-winning crime writer Ian Rankin. Carden Tower was built in the 16th century by the Mertyne family of Medhope. In a field at Cardenbarns to the south of Cardenden, the last duel to take place in Scotland was fought on 2 August 1826 between David Landale, a Kirkcaldy bleacher, and George Morgan, an agent of the Bank of Scotland. Local industries include engineering and the manufacture of alloy castings.

Cardonald *Glasgow City* A residential suburb of Glasgow, Cardonald is located to the southwest of the city centre on the former Cardonald Estates, which were created in the 15th century from the lands of Crookston for the illegitimate son of the Earl of Lennox. By the 18th century the estate had been subdivided into farms and associated country houses, and in the 1930s Glasgow Corporation and the Scottish Special Housing Association (SSHA) built flatted cottages across the ridge of Cardonald and down into South Cardonald. Cardonald College was built in the 1970s, and in 1994 the Mirror Group newspapers moved from Anderston Quay to a new plant at Cardonald.

Cardoness Castle *Dumfries and Galloway* The ruined remains of Cardoness Castle are located a mile (1.5 km) southwest of Gatehouse of Fleet in southwest Dumfries and Galloway. Built in the 15th century, the four-storey tower house overlooks the Water of Fleet and was the ancestral home of the MacCulloch clan. Disputes between the MacCullochs and Gordons resulted in abandonment of the castle in 1697.

Cardon Hill *South Lanarkshire* Cardon Hill rises to 675 m (2215 ft) close to the border between Scottish Borders and South Lanarkshire, 4 miles (6.5 km) southeast of Biggar.

Cardow *Moray* A distillery settlement in Moray, Cardow lies to the north of Knockando on the Malt Whisky Trail. Established in 1824 by the Cummings of Cardow, the Cardhu Distillery was extended in 1885.

Cardrona *Scottish Borders* A commuter village in the central Scottish Borders, Cardrona lies in the valley of the River Tweed, 3 miles (5 km) southeast of Peebles. The village has been subject to significant planned development from the late 1990s, which has brought more than 180 new executive homes, a luxury 150-bedroom hotel and a country club. Cardrona House (1840) lies to the south below a wooded hill on which stand the remains of an earlier tower.

Cardross *Argyll and Bute* A kirkton settlement on the north side of the Firth of Clyde, 3 miles (5 km) northwest of Dumbarton in Argyll and Bute, Cardross developed as a residential village centred around its 17th-century church. King Robert the Bruce is said to have died from leprosy in Cardross Castle in 1329, and the novelist Tobias Smollett was born here in 1721. Darleith House, a mile (1.5 km) to the north, was built in 1510 by the Darleith family, one of whom was Lord Darnley, husband of Mary, Queen of Scots. St Peter's Seminary, a Catholic College built in 1966 but closed by 1980, lies ruined to the northeast, despite a campaign to restore this fine building.

Careston *Angus* A locality with a 15th-century castle, school and church, Careston lies in the Angus parish of the same name, 5 miles (8 km) west of Brechin. The parish, sometimes known as Caraldston, is said to have taken its name from a stone commemorating a Danish chieftain.

Carfraemill *Scottish Borders* A village of Berwickshire in Scottish Borders, Carfraemill lies at a road junction 4 miles (6.5 km) north of Lauder.

Carfin *North Lanarkshire* A former mining village in North Lanarkshire, Carfin village lies 2 miles (3 km) northeast of Motherwell, a mile (1.5 km) southeast of New Stevenston and a mile (1.5 km) southwest of Newarthill. The Carfin Grotto of Our Lady of Lourdes was opened in 1922 as a copy of the shrine of Our Lady of Lourdes in France.

Cargen *Dumfries and Galloway* A locality in Nithsdale,

southern Dumfries and Galloway, Cargen lies between the Crooks Pow and Cargen Pow, 3 miles (5 km) south of Dumfries. The Cargen Pow joins the River Nith near here, and to the north and south are Cargen Holm and Flotts of Cargen.

Cargenbridge *Dumfries and Galloway* A settlement of Nithsdale in southern Dumfries and Galloway, Cargenbridge lies on the Cargen Pow, nearly 2 miles (3 km) southwest of Dumfries. A plastics factory was built here in 1939.

Cargen Water *Dumfries and Galloway* A stream in southern Dumfries and Galloway, the Cargen Water rises 4 miles (6.5 km) southwest of Dumfries. It flows northeast then southeast through Cargenbridge before joining the River Nith a mile (1.5 km) south of Dumfries.

Cargill *Perth and Kinross* A hamlet in eastern Perth and Kinross, Cargill lies on the River Tay 5 miles (8 km) southwest of Coupar Angus. Its church dates from 1831.

Carie *Perth and Kinross* A roadside hamlet overlooking the north shore of Loch Tay, central Perth and Kinross, Carie lies 7 miles (11 km) northeast of Killin. A ferry used to ply from the nearby shore to Ardeonaig on the south side of the loch.

Carie *Perth and Kinross* A locality in Perth and Kinross, Carie lies at the mouth of the Carie Burn where it enters the south side of Loch Rannoch, 4 miles (6.5 km) west of Kinloch Rannoch. During the 18th century the Forfeited Estates Commissioners operated a sawmill here, converting timber extracted from the Black Wood of Rannoch.

Carim Lodge *Stirling* A locality at the western end of the Ochil Hills in Stirling Council area, Carim Lodge lies 4 miles (6.5 km) southwest of Blackford.

Carinish *Western Isles* A hamlet in the southwest of North Uist in the Outer Hebrides, Carinish (Gael: *Cairinis* or *Chairinis*) is located 7.5 miles (12 km) southwest of Lochmaddy. Carinish benefits from a Gaelic-medium primary school, and a village hall built in 1957 and significantly upgraded in 2001. Carinish was once the terminal of the ferry to Benbecula, but the ferry was replaced by the North Ford Causeway, which opened in 1960. In 1601, the Battle of Carinish saw the defeat of a raiding part of MacLeods from Skye by the resident MacDonalds. The ruins of the early 13th-century Temple of the Trinity (Gael: *Teampall na Trionaid*) lies a quarter-mile (0.5 km) to the southwest.

Carlabhagh The Gaelic name for Carloway in the Western Isles.

Carlabhagh, Loch The Gaelic name for Loch Carloway in the Western Isles.

Carleatheran *Stirling* Rising to a height of 486 m (1595 ft), Carleatheran is the highest point in the Gargunnock Hills of southern Stirling Council area.

Carleton Castle *South Ayrshire* The ruined remains of Carleton Castle are located to the south of the settlement of Lendalfoot in South Ayrshire.

Carlops *Scottish Borders/Midlothian* A village on the boundary between Scottish Borders and Midlothian, Carlops lies to the east of the Pentland Hills on the North Esk, 6 miles (10 km) southwest of Penicuik and 2.5 miles (4 km) north-northeast of West Linton. Founded in 1784, the village developed in association with cotton weaving and the mining of coal and limestone. In the late 19th century its industry declined and it became a health resort, also relying on links with the Edinburgh poet Allan Ramsay (1681–1758).

Carlingheugh Bay *Angus* A large bay on the North Sea coast of Angus, Carlingheugh Bay is located to the northeast of Arbroath at the northern end of the Seaton Cliffs Nature Trail. Overlooked by red sandstone cliffs, the bay's raised beach was once the site of a small settlement. At the head of the bay are remnants of an old boathouse, and in former times the fisherwomen of nearby Auchmithie came here to collect seaweed. At the southern end of the bay is a rock feature known as the Three Sisters.

Carlingwark Loch *Dumfries and Galloway* A loch in southern Dumfries and Galloway, Carlingwark Loch lies just south of Castle Douglas. Iron Age crannogs or lake dwellings have been discovered.

Carlock Hill *South Ayrshire* A hill of South Ayrshire, Carlock Hill rises to 319 m (1046 ft) to the west of Glen App and 3 miles (5 km) south of Ballantrae.

Carloway *Western Isles* A crofting township at the head of Loch Carloway on the northwest coast of the Isle of Lewis in the Outer Hebrides, Carloway (*Carlabhagh*) is noted for its fine example of a Pictish broch situated to the southwest. One of 500 brochs around the coasts of north and west Scotland, the massive stone tower of Dun Carloway Broch has been in State guardianship since 1887. It dates from between 100 BC and AD 300, and has double drystone walls rising to 9 m (30 ft). There are chambers at ground level that connect with progressively narrower galleries at higher levels. Excavation of the site in 1972 revealed hearths, ash and pottery, suggesting a secondary period of occupation between 400 and 700 AD, and it is said that the broch was used as a stronghold by the Morison clan in the 17th century during the feud between the Morisons of Ness and the Macauleys of Uig.

Carloway, Loch *Western Isles* A sea loch on the west coast of the Isle of Lewis in the Outer Hebrides, Loch Carloway (*Carlabhagh*) forms an inlet at the mouth of East Loch Roag. Lying to the west of Carloway village, the loch is fed by the Carloway River.

Carluke *South Lanarkshire* Situated on a high plateau at an elevation of 198 m (650 ft), Carluke overloooks the middle reaches of the River Clyde in South Lanarkshire. It lies on the Jock's Burn, 6 miles (10 km) northwest of Lanark, and in 1662 was chartered as a royal burgh, also known as Kirkstyle. A Roman road passed this way, and a number of tower houses were built in the locality. Carluke developed in the 18th, 19th and 20th centuries in association with corn milling, cotton weaving, coal mining and the manufacture of bricks, glass, confectionery and jam. Miltonhead, a mile (1.5 km) to the southwest, was the birthplace in 1721 of the military surveyor General William Roy, and Milton Lockhart, 2 miles (3 km) to the west, was the home of John Lockhart, the biographer of Sir Walter Scott. In 1897 the remains of Milton Lockhart House were transported to Japan and re-erected near Tokyo. Peter Kid, one of Carluke's 17th-century Covenanting ministers, was imprisoned on the Bass Rock.

Carlungie *Angus* A locality to the north of the Dundee–Arbroath road in southeast Angus, Carlungie is noted for its L-shaped underground souterrain dating from the 1st-2nd centuries AD. Discovered in 1949, it was excavated by F. T. Wainwright between 1950 and 1951.

Carmacoup *South Lanarkshire* A settlement in South Lanarkshire, Carmacoup is located a mile (1.5 km) southwest of Glespin and 3 miles (5 km) southwest of Douglas.

Carmel Water *East Ayrshire/North Ayrshire* Rising from Burnfoot Reservoir, East Ayrshire, the Carmel Water flows south and west, passing through Kilmaurs and Crosshouse into North Ayrshire. Here it flows west to join the River Irvine to the south of Dreghorn.

Carmichael *South Lanarkshire* A settlement in South Lanarkshire, Carmichael lies 3 miles (5 km) west of Thankerton and 7.5 miles (11 km) west of Biggar. Associated with the Carmichael family for over 700 years, its inhabitants took the name as their surname and as the name of the village. Today, the Carmichael Estates are still held by Richard Carmichael of Carmichael, Chief of the Clan Carmichael.

Carmichael Burn *South Lanarkshire* Rising amid forest land on Longmoor Hill, South Lanarkshire, the Carmichael Burn flows northeast then northwest to join the River Clyde at a point 2 miles (3 km) northwest of the settlement of Carmichael.

Carminish Islands, The *Western Isles* A group of rocks and islets off the southeast coast of the island of South Harris in the Outer Hebrides, the Carminish Islands lie between South Harris and the island of Ensay, to the southwest of Rubha Charnain and 3 miles (5 km) northwest of Renish Point.

Carmunnock *Glasgow City* A village situated within the southern green belt of Glasgow, Carmunnock lies 3 miles (5 km) northwest of East Kilbride and 3 miles (5 km) southwest of Rutherglen. This ancient settlement, which is associated with the early Christian missionary St Cadoc, has a medieval street plan set within the lands of an estate held by Lord Hamilton until 1700 and then the Stuarts of Castlemilk.

Carmyle *Glasgow City* A southeast district of Glasgow, Carmyle lies on the north bank of the River Clyde, 4 miles (6.5 km) southeast of the city centre and south of Mount Vernon. Dating from the 13th century, the village of Carmyle developed in association with meal mills established by the bishops of Glasgow. It later expanded with the building of a muslin factory in 1761, and in the 1780s iron-smelting works were founded following the discovery of ironstone in the area. In 1829 the Clyde Ironworks was the first to use the hot-blast process invented by James Neilson.

Carmyllie *Angus* A village in an Angus parish of the same name, Carmyllie, more fully Milton of Carmyllie, lies on the B971, 5 miles (8 km) west of Arbroath. Paving and building stone from the nearby quarries was exported worldwide and, because it was shipped from Arbroath, came to be known as 'Arbroath stone'. The reaping machine was invented in Carmyllie in 1826 by the parish minister, the Revd Patrick Bell.

Carn a' Bhacain *Aberdeenshire* A hill in the eastern Grampians of Aberdeenshire, Carn a' Bhacain rises to 738 m (2422 ft) to the south of Corgarff.

Carn a' Chlamain *Perth and Kinross* Located west of Glen Tilt and within the Forest of Atholl in Perth and Kinross, Carn a' Chlamain rises to 963 m (3159 ft). Its name is derived from the Gaelic for 'hill of the kite (or buzzard)'.

Carn a' Choire Bhoidheach *Aberdeenshire* Located southwest of Lochnagar in western Aberdeenshire, Carn a' Choire Bhoidheach rises to a flat summit at a height of 1110 m (3642 ft). Its name is derived from the Gaelic for 'hill of the beautiful corrie'.

Carn a' Ghaill *Highland* A hill on the island of Canna in the Inner Hebrides, Carn a' Ghaill is the highest point on the island and rises to 210 m (690 ft). It lies a half-mile (1 km) north of the settlement of A'Chill.

Carn a' Gheoidh *Aberdeenshire/Perth and Kinross* A mountain in the eastern Grampians, Carn a' Gheoidh rises to 975 m (3198 ft) to the west of The Cairnwell, on the border between Aberdeenshire and Perth and Kinross Council areas. Spittal of Glenshee is 4 miles (6.5 km) to the south. The mountain's name is derived from the Gaelic for 'hill of the goose'.

Carn a' Mhaim *Aberdeenshire* With a Gaelic name signifying 'peak of the large rounded hill', Carn a' Mhaim rises to 1037 m (3402 ft) in the southern Cairngorms, west of the Lairig Ghru and south of Ben Macdui. Predominantly composed of granite, it tapers to a long ridge in the north. The River Dee lies immediately to the west.

Carn an Fhidhleir *Aberdeenshire/Highland/Perth and Kinross* Rising to a height of 994 m (3261 ft) in the centre of the headwaters of the Feshie, Geldie and Tarf, Carn an Fhidhleir (also *Carn Ealar*) lies on the borders of Aberdeenshire, Highland and Perth and Kinross council areas. Its name is derived from the Gaelic for 'hill of the fiddler'.

Carn an Righ *Perth and Kinross* A mountain in the central Grampians, Carn an Righ rises to 1029 (3376 ft) between Glen Shee and Glen Tilt in Perth and Kinross. Its name is derived from the Gaelic for 'hill of the king'.

Carn an t-Sabhail A Gaelic name for Cairn Toul on the border of Highland and Aberdeenshire.

Carn an t-Sagairt Mòr *Aberdeenshire* A mountain in the eastern Grampians, Carn an t-Sagairt Mòr (also Carn Taggart) rises to 1047 m (3434 ft) southwest of Lochnagar and southeast of Braemar in Aberdeenshire. Its name is derived from the Gaelic for 'big hill of the priest'.

Carn an Tuirc *Aberdeenshire* A mountain in the eastern Grampians, Carn an Tuirc rises to 1019 m (3343 ft) northeast of Cairnwell Pass in southern Aberdeenshire. Its name is derived from the Gaelic for 'hill of the boar'.

Carn Aosda *Aberdeenshire* A mountain in the eastern Grampians, Carn Aosda rises to 917 m (3008 ft) at the north end of Glen Shee in southern Aberdeenshire. Its name is derived from the Gaelic for 'hill of age'.

Carn Bhac *Aberdeenshire/Perth and Kinross* A mountain in the eastern Grampians, Carn Bhac rises to 946 m (3104 ft) southeast of Braemar, on the border between Aberdeenshire and Perth and Kinross Council areas. Its summit is northeast of the southwestern top, and its name is derived from the Gaelic for 'hill of peat banks'.

Carn Dearg *Highland/Perth and Kinross* A mountain in the southwest Grampians, Carn Dearg rises to 941 m (3086 ft) to the east of Loch Ossian on the border between Highland and Perth and Kinross Council areas. With Sgor Gaibhre it forms a rounded massif with a number of open corries known to be frequented by some of the largest herds of red deer in Scotland. The name Carn Dearg is derived from the Gaelic for 'red hill'.

Carn Dearg *Highland* Rising to 1034 m (3392 ft) to the west of Loch Ericht, Carn Dearg is one of four peaks on the ridge between Strath Ossian and Loch Pattack, in southern Highland Council area.

Carn Dearg *Highland* A mountain of the Monadhliath range, Carn Dearg rises to 945 m (3100 ft) to the west of Newtonmore in Badenoch. A buttress below the summit has a sheer drop of 100 m (328 ft).

Carn Dearg *Highland* A locality in Wester Ross, Carn Dearg lies on the north shore of Gair Loch, 3 miles (5 km) west of Gairloch. There is a youth hostel.

Carn Ealar An alternative name for Carn an Fhidhleir on the borders of Aberdeenshire, Highland, and Perth and Kinross.

Carn Ealasaid *Aberdeenshire* A mountain in the Grampians, Carn Ealasaid rises to 792 m (2598 ft) to the north of the River Don and northeast of Cock Bridge in eastern Aberdeenshire.

Carn Eas *Aberdeenshire* A mountain in the eastern Grampians of Aberdeenshire, Carn Eas rises to the south of Ben Avon in two peaks, the larger of which is 1089 m (3319 ft) above sea level. The River Gairn rises on its eastern slopes, and to the south the Invercauld Forest stretches to the River Dee.

Carn Eige *Highland* A mountain in the northwest Highlands, Carn Eige rises to 1183 m (3881 ft) northwest of Loch Affric in central Highland Council area. It is one of the highest mountains north of the Great Glen. Its name is derived from the Gaelic for 'file hill'.

Carn Ghluasaid *Highland* Rising to a height of 957 m (3140 ft) north of Loch Cluanie, in central Highland Council area, Carn Ghluasaid has a flat and stony summit. Its name is derived from the Gaelic for 'hill of movement'.

Carn Gorm *Perth and Kinross* Rising to a height of 1029 m (3376 ft) Carn Gorm is one of four peaks that combine to form a horseshoe-shaped ridge extending 6 miles (10 km) from east to west on the north side of Glen Lyon in western Perth and Kinross. The summit cairn is found about 100 m (328 ft) southwest of the Ordnance Survey triangulation point.

Carn Liath *Highland* Rising to a height of 1006 m (3300 ft) to the northwest of Loch Laggan in the Badenoch and Strathspey district of Highland Council area, Carn Liath forms a flat, stony plateau. Its name is derived from the Gaelic for 'grey hill'.

Carn Liath *Perth and Kinross* One of the three peaks of the Beinn a' Ghlo massif, Carn Liath rises to 975 m (3199 ft) northeast of Blair Atholl in central Perth and Kinross Council area.

Carn Mairg *Perth and Kinross* A mountain in western Perth and Kinross, Carn Mairg is the highest of four peaks that form a 6-mile/10-km-long horseshoe-shaped ridge, on the north side of Glen Lyon. It rises to 1042 m (3419 ft) 4 miles (6.5 km) south of Kinloch Rannoch.

Carn Mòr *Aberdeenshire* The highest summit of the Ladder Hills in the eastern Cairngorms of Aberdeenshire, Carn Mòr rises to 804 m (2637 ft) to the east of Glenlivet.

Carn Mòr Dearg *Highland* A mountain in Lochaber, Carn Mòr Dearg rises to 1220 m (4003 ft) to the southwest of Ben Nevis, to which it is connected by a narrow ridge. The name Carn Mòr Dearg is derived from the Gaelic for 'big red hill'.

Carn na Cailliche *Moray* A hill of central Moray, Carn na Cailliche lies 3 miles (5 km) north of Upper Knockando and reaches a height of 404 m (1325 ft).

Carn na Caim *Highland/Perth and Kinross* A mountain in the southern Grampians, Carn na Caim rises to 941 m (3087 ft) east of Dalwhinnie, on the border between Highland and Perth and Kinross Council areas. Its name is derived from the Gaelic for 'cairn of the curve'.

Carn nan Gabhar *Perth and Kinross* A mountain in the southern Grampians, Carn nan Gabhar rises to 1121 m (3671 ft) northeast of Blair Atholl in northern Perth and Kinross. The highest of the three mountains of the Beinn a' Ghlo massif, Carn nan Gabhar is also the most remote.

Carn nan Gobhar *Highland* A mountain rising to a height of 992 m (3255 ft) west of Cannich, in the Inverness district of Highland Council area, Carn nan Gobhar derives its name from the Gaelic for 'hill of the goats'.

Carn Sgulain *Highland* A mountain in the Badenoch district of central Highland Council area, Carn Sgulain rises to 920 m (3018 ft) in the Monadhliath range, northwest of Kingussie.

Carn Taggart An alternative name for Carn an t-Sagairt Mòr in Aberdeenshire.

Carna *Highland* An island in Loch Sunart at the mouth of Loch Teacuis, an inlet of the Morvern peninsula, Carna is 213 ha (526 acres) in area and reaches a height of 169 m (554 ft) at Cruachan Charna in the centre of the island. A small population farms the land.

Carnach *Western Isles* A small crofting settlement in the extreme southeast of North Harris, Carnach lies immediately to the east of Kyles Scalpay, 4.5 miles (7 km) southeast of Tarbert.

Carnan, Loch *Western Isles* A sea loch on the northeast coast of the island of South Uist in the Outer Hebrides, Loch Carnan lies between Bagh nam Faoileann to the north and Loch Sgioport to the south.

Carnassarie *Argyll and Bute* A locality with a castle, Carnassarie lies a mile (1.5 km) north of Kilmartin and 3 miles (5 km) from the head of Loch Craignish. Built by John Carswell, the castle passed to the Campbells of Auchinbreck in 1572 and was finally destroyed in 1685 when its owner, Sir Douglas Campbell, joined forces with the 9th Earl of Argyll in the Monmouth Rising and the Royalist forces of MacLaine of Torloisk blew up the castle. It is now under the guardianship of Historic Scotland.

Carnbee *Fife* A settlement and parish in the East Neuk of Fife, the lands of Carnbee were once owned by the Melvilles of Raith whose church, rebuilt in 1793, was possessed in pre-Reformation times by the Abbey of Dunfermline. The parish also contains the hamlet of Arncroach, and rises to 182 m (557 ft) at Kellie Law and 212 m (600 ft) at Cassingray.

Carnbo *Perth and Kinross* A village of southeast Perth and Kinross, Carnbo lies on the lower south-facing slopes of the Ochil Hills, 4 miles (6.5 km) west of Milnathort. A former tollhouse here used to extract road-toll money from cattle drovers who crossed the Ochils by this route.

Carnegie Birthplace Museum *Fife* Situated near the centre of Dunfermline in western Fife, at No. 2 Moodie Street, is an 18th-century pantiled weaver's cottage where Andrew Carnegie (1835–1918), the industrialist and benefactor, was born. Now a museum, it was extended in 1925 with the construction of the adjacent Memorial Building designed by James Shearer.

Carnethy Hill *Midlothian* The second-highest summit of the Pentland Hills, Carnethy Hill rises to 576 m (1890 ft)

3 miles (5 km) northwest of Penicuik towards the northern boundary of Midlothian Council area. Loganlea Reservoir lies on its northwest flank.

Carnock *Fife* A village in Carnock parish, western Fife, Carnock is situated on the Carnock Burn 2.5 miles (4 km) northwest of Dunfermline. The village is said to be named after St Cearnock, one of the disciples of St Ninian. It has a parish church built in 1840, but nearby in the old kirkyard stand the ruins of the original 12th-century parish church, which was rebuilt in 1602 by the salt manufacturer Sir George Bruce of Culross. There is a fine gravestone with Latin and Hebrew inscriptions commemorating John Row (1568–1646), who was minister of the parish and the Church of Scotland's first historian.

Carnoustie *Angus* A residential and resort town on the North Sea coast of Angus, Carnoustie is situated 11 miles (18 km) east of Dundee. It is the youngest of the seven Angus burghs and owes its development to the prosperity of Dundee and to golf. Its spacious sandy golfing links include the championship Burnside and Buddon Links courses, the British Open first being played here in 1931. Westhaven and Easthaven on the outskirts of Carnoustie were fishing villages. The local economy is also dependent on engineering and the manufacture of machinery, maltings and light service industries. Carnoustie Gala Week is an annual summer event.

Carntyne *Glasgow City* A suburb of Glasgow to the east of the city centre and adjacent to Robroyston, Carntyne was developed during the inter-war years as a housing renewal scheme.

Carnwadric *Glasgow City* A residential suburb of Glasgow to the south of the city centre, Carnwadric was developed in the 1920s as cottage-flat housing. Five high-rise buildings were erected in the mid-1960s.

Carnwath *South Lanarkshire* A village of Clydesdale, Carnwath stands at an altitude of 220 m (770 ft) in the River Clyde valley, 7 miles (11 km) east of Lanark. In a commanding position, its 12th-century motte was the largest in Lanarkshire. A medieval church was made collegiate in 1424 by Sir Thomas Sommerville, whose family remained in the locality until the 16th century. Carnwath became a burgh of barony in 1451 and later developed in association with road and rail facilities. Now a commuter settlement, it has businesses associated with coaches, clinical research and the manufacture of dairy produce.

Carolside *Scottish Borders* A house and estate on the Leader Water in the north-central Scottish Borders, Carolside lies to the north of Earlston.

Carradale *Argyll and Bute* A village on the east coast of the Kintyre peninsula, Carradale lies 11 miles (18 km) northeast of Campbeltown. In the 19th century it developed as a small resort with steamer connections and a fishing harbour, and in the 20th century the neighbouring hills of Kintyre were extensively afforested. In 1990 the Carradale fishing vessel *Antares* was accidentally sunk by a naval submarine on manoeuvres. The author Naomi Mitchison lived at Carradale House until her death in 1999.

Carradale Bay *Argyll and Bute* A bay on the east side of the Kintyre peninsula, Carradale Bay lies between the settlements of Whitestone to the south and Carradale to the north. Carradale Garden is located near the bay, while at the eastern end is Carradale Point. There are splendid views across the Kilbrannan Sound to the island of Arran.

Carradale Point *Argyll and Bute* A headland located on the east coast of the Kintyre peninsula, Argyll and Bute, Carradale Point lies a mile (1.5 km) south of the settlement of Carradale at the eastern end of Carradale Bay. The point forms a rocky prominence on which stand the remains of an ancient fortification.

Carradale Water *Argyll and Bute* A river rising in the lochans and foothills of Narachan Hill on the Kintyre peninsula, the Carradale Water flows south through the Carradale Forest before emptying into the Kilbrannan Sound at the settlement of Dippen on Carradale Bay.

Carrbridge *Highland* A resort village of Strathspey, Carrbridge lies on the Dulnain Water 7 miles (11 km) north of Aviemore. Now bypassed by the main road from Perth to Inverness, the village dates from the early 19th century when it developed in association with tree planting on the Strathspey Estate. The remains of the original Carr Bridge built in 1717 still stand. The Landmark Visitor Centre features displays on the history and natural history of the Highlands.

Carrick *Argyll and Bute* A small settlement on the Kintyre peninsula, Carrick is located a half-mile (1 km) north of Port Ann and 3 miles (5 km) east of Lochgilphead.

Carrick *Argyll and Bute* A resort village on the western shore of Loch Goil, Argyll and Bute, Carrick lies 2 miles (3 km) north of the junction of Loch Goil with Loch Long. The 15th-century Carrick Castle was a stronghold of the Clan Campbell.

Carrick *South Ayrshire* The southernmost of the three ancient districts of Ayrshire, Carrick occupies an area of upland to the south of Ayr and the River Doon. Its highest point is Polmaddie Hill (565 m/1853 ft), and its chief settlements are the villages of Barr and North and South Balloch. The chief seat of the earldom of Carrick, which dates from the 12th century, was Turnberry Castle on the Ayrshire coast. The title, now held by the Prince of Wales, was passed by marriage to the father of King Robert the Bruce in 1271.

Carrick Forest *Dumfries and Galloway/South Ayrshire* Situated at the northern end of the Galloway Forest Park in Dumfries and Galloway and South Ayrshire, Carrick Forest lies to the west of Loch Doon and southwest of Dalmellington. A waymarked cycle route links Loch Doon to the village of Barr.

Carrifran Glen *Scottish Borders* A valley in the Moffat Hills of Scottish Borders, Carrifran Glen lies 5 miles (8 km) northwest of Moffat. Here a broken bow (the Rotten Bottom Bow) discarded by a hunter 6000 years ago was discovered by a hillwalker in 1990. Subsequent pollen studies of peat cores have provided a 10,000-year record of the vegetation in the valley, reaching back to the end of the Ice Age. This prompted environmental enthusiasts to initiate a scheme to restore the Carrifran Glen to its former wooded state.

Carrington *Midlothian* A picturesque agricultural hamlet of rural Midlothian, Carrington lies 2 miles (3 km) west of Gorebridge and 2.5 miles (4 km) southeast of Rosewell. The former parish church, with its square tower, dates from 1711. Arniston House, which dates from the mid-

18th century, lies a half-mile (1 km) to the southeast. To the northeast lies the mausoleum of the Ramsays of Whitehill, built in the early 18th century. The hamlet is also known as Primrose, the family name of the earls of Rosebery.

Carron *Falkirk* A settlement in northern Falkirk Council area, Carron lies to the north of the River Carron and west of Carronshore. It was the site of Scotland's first large-scale iron foundry, established in 1760 by the Cadell family in partnership with the English industrialists Samuel Garbett and Dr John Roebuck. The ironworks utilised the nearby seam of coal and ironstone at Bo'ness.

Carron *Moray* The Moray township of Carron lies nearly 6 miles (10 km) southwest of Craigellachie on the River Spey in what has been described as 'one of the most beautiful little glens in Scotland'. It surrounds Dailuaine Distillery, founded in 1851 by William Mackenzie and located close to a former railway line that now forms part of the Speyside Way. To the east is Carron House.

Carron, Loch *Highland* A sea loch on the coast of Wester Ross, Loch Carron extends northeastwards from the southern end of the Inner Sound, north of Kyle of Lochalsh. Stromeferry lies near its mouth.

Carron, River *Dumfries and Galloway* A river of Nithsdale in northern Dumfries and Galloway, the River Carron rises in the Lowther Hills and flows southwards for 9 miles (14 km) to join the River Nith at Carronbridge.

Carron, River *Highland* A river in Easter Ross, the Carron is formed at the junction of the Alladale River and the Abhainn a' Ghlinne Mhoir. It flows for 12 miles (19 km) eastwards through Strathcarron to join the Dornoch Firth near Bonar Bridge.

Carron, River *Highland* A river in Wester Ross, the Carron rises on the slopes of Carn Beag in Ledgowan Forest. It flows 12 miles (19 km) southwest through Glen Carron to enter the head of Loch Carron near Achintee.

Carron, River *Stirling* The River Carron rises in the Carron Bog in the uplands of Stirling Council area. It flows eastwards for 20 miles (32 km) through the Carron Valley Reservoir and the settlements of Denny and Larbert before entering the River Forth at Grangemouth.

Carron Valley Reservoir *Stirling/Falkirk* Situated to the east of the Campsie Fells in Stirling and Falkirk council areas, the Carron Valley Reservoir forms part of the upper reaches of the River Carron.

Carron Water *Aberdeenshire* A stream of eastern Aberdeenshire, the Carron Water rises in Fetteresso Forest on the eastern edge of the Grampians. It flows eastwards to enter the North Sea at Stonehaven.

Carronbridge *Dumfries and Galloway* A village of Nithsdale in Dumfries and Galloway, Carronbridge lies just over a mile (1.5 km) northwest of Thornhill near the confluence of the Carron Water and the River Nith. Drumlanrig Castle is northwest of the village.

Carronshore *Falkirk* A settlement in northern Falkirk Council area, Carronshore lies to the north of the River Carron and east of Carron.

Carrutherstown *Dumfries and Galloway* A village of Annandale in Dumfries and Galloway, Carrutherstown lies close to the A75 from Dumfries to Annan, 8 miles (13 km) southeast of Dumfries.

Carsaig *Argyll and Bute* A scattered community in the south of the island of Mull, Carsaig lies on Carsaig Bay 2 miles (3 km) west of the entrance to Loch Buie.

Carscreugh *Dumfries and Galloway* A locality in southwest Dumfries and Galloway, Carscreugh lies 2 miles (3 km) northeast of Glenluce. A ruined tower near here was built in 1680 for James Dalrymple, Lord Stair, who had married the daughter of James Ross of Balneil, owner of an earlier building on the site that once belonged to Glenluce Abbey.

Carse of Forth Also known as the Carse of Stirling, the Carse of Forth is the name given to the fertile land on either side of the River Forth from Grangemouth in the east to the upper reaches of the River Forth, near the Lake of Menteith, in the west. Extending over an area of 100 sq. km (39 sq. miles) and with a total length of 30 miles (48 km), it is the most extensive of Scotland's alluvial flood plains. From 1767, agricultural improvements resulted in large areas of raised bog peat, up to 6 m (20 ft) thick, being cleared from the Drip Moss, the Moss of Ochtertyre and Blairdrummond Moss. The only substantial remains of this peat cover are at Flanders Moss near Kippen.

Carse of Gowrie *Perth and Kinross* The flat 'kerselands' of the Carse of Gowrie, rarely exceeding a height of 15 m (50 ft) above sea level, occupy a narrow strip of land in southeast Perth and Kinross between the Tay estuary in the south and the Sidlaw Hills to the north. Traversed by the main road linking Perth and Dundee, the rich farmlands of the Carse are sheltered from cold north winds. During the post-glacial period this area was under water, but in the 18th century it was extensively drained by local landowners who planted orchards of apples, plums and pears. The chief settlements of the Carse of Gowrie are Errol, Inchture, Longforgan, Leetown and Glencarse.

Carse of Lecropt *Stirling* The fertile lands of the Carse of Lecropt in central Stirling Council area lie to the west of Bridge of Allan between the River Teith, just north of its junction with the Forth, and the policy lands of Keir House. The parish church of Lecropt looks down on the carse lands from high ground to the west of the Allan Water.

Carse of Stirling An alternative name for Carse of Forth.

Carsebreck *Perth and Kinross* A locality close to the Allan Water in southwest Perth and Kinross, Carsebreck and its adjacent curling pond lie 2 miles (3 km) west of Blackford.

Carsegowan *Dumfries and Galloway* A locality in the Machars, southwest Dumfries and Galloway, Carsegowan lies on the edge of the Carsegowan Moss, 3 miles (5 km) north of Wigtown.

Carsehope Burn *South Lanarkshire* Rising in the area known as the Carsehope Middens close to the border with Dumfries and Galloway, the Carsehope Burn flows north and east, past the peak of Ballencleuch Law. It joins the Daer Water at a point a half-mile (1 km) southwest of the head of the Daer Reservoir, South Lanarkshire.

Carsethorn *Dumfries and Galloway* A residential hamlet on the Solway Firth, Carsethorn lies at the mouth of the River Nith, 10 miles (16 km) south of Dumfries. It was created c.1815 with a steamer pier for Dumfries and a harbour master's house. After the steamer service ceased, Carsethorn became a centre for salmon fishing.

Carskey *Argyll and Bute* A small village at the south end of the Kintyre peninsula in Argyll and Bute, Carskey (also Carskiey) is situated at the mouth of the Breakerie Water where it enters Carskey Bay.

Carsluith *Dumfries and Galloway* A hamlet in Dumfries and Galloway, Carsluith lies on the shore of Wigtown Bay, 3 miles (5 km) south of Creetown. Last occupied in 1748, Carsluith Castle was a stronghold of the Cairns, Lindsay and Brown families.

Carsphairn *Dumfries and Galloway* An 18th-century village at an altitude of 180 m (590 ft) above sea level in northern Dumfries and Galloway, Carsphairn lies on the Water of Deugh, 10 miles (16 km) southeast of Dalmellington. The village is a centre for outdoor pursuits, particularly hillwalking, and there is a heritage centre. In the churchyard are the burial enclosure of the Macadams of Waterhead and the headstone of the Covenanting martyr Roger Dunn (d. 1689). Copper, lead, silver and zinc were discovered to the west at Woodhead, and mines were operated from the 19th century until the late 1950s.

Carsphairn Lane *Dumfries and Galloway* A stream in western Dumfries and Galloway, Carsphairn Lane rises between Loch Doon and Cairnsmore of Carsphairn. It flows southeastwards for 5 miles (8 km) to join the Water of Deugh at Carsphairn.

Carstairs *South Lanarkshire* A village in South Lanarkshire, Carstairs lies 4 miles (6.5 km) east of Lanark, close to the site of the Roman fort of Castledykes. Chartered as a burgh of barony in 1765, its Tudor Gothic-style mansion, designed in 1821–4 by William Burn for Henry Monteith, became a nursing home in the 1970s. The medieval castle of Castleterrs, which belonged to the bishops of Glasgow, has disappeared but its church (1794) contains a 15th-century crucifixion stone. The village of Carstairs Junction lies a mile (1.5 km) to the southeast.

Carstairs Junction *South Lanarkshire* A village and railway junction in South Lanarkshire, Carstairs Junction lies a mile (1.5 km) southeast of Carstairs and 5 miles (8 km) east of Lanark. The village developed in association with the Caledonian Railway, whose station here was opened in 1848 at a major junction on the routes between Glasgow and Edinburgh. It was here that coaches were attached or detached en route to different destinations, at what was one of the most important junctions on the Scottish railway network. Electrification of the line to Edinburgh in 1991 and the introduction of fast through trains removed the need for combining and splitting trains. In the 1920s a State Hospital for the criminally insane was built nearby.

Carter Fell *Scottish Borders* A mountain ridge on the border between Scotland and England, Carter Fell runs in a northeast to southwest direction 6 miles (10 km) northeast of Kielder. It reaches a height of 556 m (1824 ft).

Carterhope Burn *Scottish Borders* A stream in the Tweedsmuir district of Scottish Borders, Carterhope Burn rises on Hart Fell near the border with Dumfries and Galloway. It flows northwards into Fruid Reservoir.

Cartland *South Lanarkshire* The hamlet of Cartland lies 2 miles (3 km) northwest of the centre of Lanark, from which it is separated by the Mouse Water. Lee Castle, built c.1817 by James Gillespie Graham and once home to the Lockharts of Lee, lies 0.75 mile (1.15 km) to the west.

Carvie, Water of *Aberdeenshire* A stream in west-central Aberdeenshire, the Water of Carvie rises in hills to the north of Ballater and flows northwards to join the River Don at Candacraig.

Cashlie *Perth and Kinross* A locality in Glen Lyon, Perth and Kinross, Cashlie lies on the River Lyon, 2 miles (3 km) east of Loch Lyon. The farm of Cashlie (Castles) lies close to the remains of four Iron Age forts: Caisteal cona Bhacain, Bhacain, the Castle of the Red Man, and Cambuslaie. In legend, these were four of the twelve castles in 'the crooked glen of stones' attributed to Fingal.

Castle Bay *Western Isles* A bay on the south coast of the island of Barra in the Outer Hebrides, Castle Bay (Gael: *Bagh a' Chaisteil*) looks south towards Vatersay. The town of Castlebay is located at the head of the bay, while Kisimul Castle lies on an islet in the bay.

Castle Campbell *Clackmannanshire* Standing on an elevated position overlooking Dollar in Clackmannanshire, Castle Campbell, formerly known as the Castle of Gloom, was held by the Stewarts until the late 15th century when it passed by marriage to the Campbells. In 1489 an Act of Parliament was passed permitting the four-storey tower house then built to be renamed Castle Campbell. Held by them for nearly three centuries, it was the principal Campbell stronghold in the Lowlands. The castle was extended in the 16th century, but in 1654 it was attacked and badly damaged, making it unfit to be used as a garrison by Cromwell's English soldiers. George, 6th Duke of Argyll, sold the land and buildings in the early 19th century. In 1948 the castle was taken into the care of the Ministry of Works. Today, the castle is managed by Historic Scotland.

Castle Douglas *Dumfries and Galloway* A village in the Stewartry, south-central Dumfries and Galloway, Castle Douglas lies on the edge of Carlingwark Loch, 18 miles (29 km) southwest of Dumfries. Previously known as Causewayend and later Carlingwark, the settlement was rebuilt and renamed in 1789 by Sir William Douglas of Gelston, who obtained a charter for his burgh two years later in 1791. Castle Douglas began to prosper as a post town with a cotton mill, a foundry, a branch of the Paisley Union Banking Company and a fair. During the 20th century it developed as a tourist and local service centre, its through railway having operated between 1859 and 1965. In addition to a livestock market and slaughterhouse, modern industries include knitwear and the manufacture of dairy equipment. Castle Douglas is the headquarters of the Galloway Cattle Society and has a nine-hole golf course.

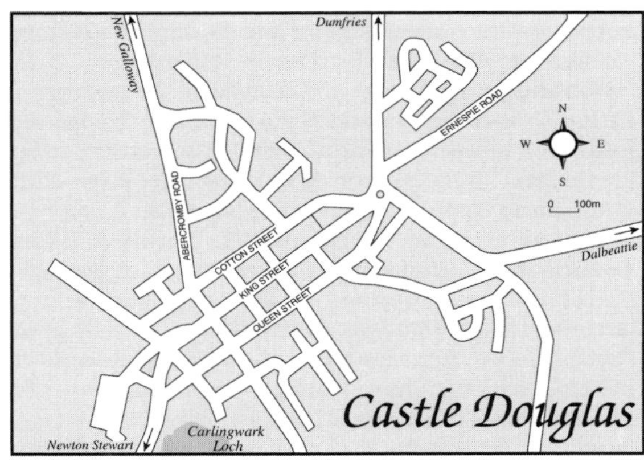

Castle Forbes *Aberdeenshire* The seat of the Forbes family, Castle Forbes lies southwest of Bennachie, on the River Don by Keig in the Howe of Alford, Aberdeenshire. Originally called Putachie, the house was built in the early 19th century to a design by Archibald Simpson.

Castle Fraser *Aberdeenshire* Described as the most elaborate Z-plan castle in Scotland, Castle Fraser lies near Sauchen in east-central Aberdeenshire, 16 miles (26 km) west of Aberdeen. Begun in 1575 by Michael Fraser and incorporating an earlier fortalice, it was not completed until 1636. The castle was given into the care of the National Trust for Scotland in 1976 and a formal garden was recreated in the old walled garden.

Castle Girnigoe *Highland* A former stronghold of the Sinclairs, the ruins of Castle Girnigoe crown a rocky peninsula 3 miles (5 km) north-northeast of Wick on the northeast coast of Caithness in Highland Council area. Close by are the remains of Castle Sinclair.

Castle Grant *Highland* The former seat of the chiefs of the Clan Grant in Strathspey, Castle Grant lies immediately north of Grantown-on-Spey. It was originally known as Castle Freuchie.

Castle Haven *Aberdeenshire* A bay on the North Sea coast of south-central Aberdeenshire, Castle Haven lies between Bowdun Head and the headland on which stands Dunnottar Castle.

Castle Haven Bay *Dumfries and Galloway* A bay on the Solway coast of Dumfries and Galloway, Castle Haven lies 2 miles (3 km) west of Borgue and 6 miles (10 km) south of Gatehouse of Fleet. On its shore stands a restored broch dating from the Iron Age. It is similar to types of fortification found in Argyll and Bute.

Castle Huntly *Perth and Kinross* Located just to the southwest of Longforgan, 10 miles (16 km) west of Dundee and a similar distance east of Perth, Castle Huntly is one of only two open prisons in Scotland (the other being HM Prison Noranside). Built in 1452, the castle was built on a rock in the middle of the Carse of Gowrie for the Gray family, to replace their castle at Fowlis. It was purchased by Patrick Lyon, 1st Earl of Kinghorne (1575–1615). In 1647 it became a residence of Patrick, 1st Earl of Strathmore, who extended the castle and made many improvements. It was further extended in the 18th and 19th centuries. The North Gate, rebuilt at the present location in 1783, is noteworthy. Castle Huntly was purchased as a borstal in 1947 and has subsequently been extended to include a prisoner accommodation block, kitchens, a gymnasium, and an employment complex that places prisoners on local and community projects.

Castle Kennedy *Dumfries and Galloway* A village in the Rhinns of Galloway, southwest Dumfries and Galloway, Castle Kennedy lies 4 miles (6.5 km) east of Stranraer to the south of the Black and White Lochs. From 1861 Castle Kennedy developed in association with the Portpatrick Railway. The village takes its name from a castle built in 1607 by the 5th Earl of Cassilis. Fine landscaped policies, which incorporated the two lochs, were later laid out by the Earl of Stair, but the castle was destroyed during the 1715 Jacobite Rising.

Castle Knowe An alternative name for Fast Castle in Scottish Borders.

Castle Lachlan *Argyll and Bute*A castle on the east shore of Loch Fyne, 10 miles (16 km) southwest of Inveraray, Castle Lachlan is the home of the Maclachlan chiefs. It was built *c.*1790 near the site of an earlier tower.

Castle Leod *Highland* Originally built as a tower house in the 12th century, Castle Leod lies a half-mile (1 km) north of Strathpeffer in the Ross and Cromarty district of Highland Council area. A five-storey keep remodelled in 1606 by Sir Roderick Mackenzie, it is the ancestral seat of the Mackenzie earls of Cromarty.

Castle Loch *Dumfries and Galloway* A loch in eastern Dumfries and Galloway, Castle Loch lies immediately south of Lochmaben. The ruined Lochmaben Castle, a former stronghold of the powerful Bruces of Annandale, lies on its southern shore. The loch is a nature reserve.

Castle Loch *Dumfries and Galloway* A loch in southwest Dumfries and Galloway, Castle Loch lies on the Gargrie Moor to the west of Mochrum Loch, 6 miles (10 km) southeast of Glenluce.

Castle Menzies *Perth and Kinross* A 16th-century castle in Strathtay, central Perth and Kinross, Castle Menzies lies to the west of Weem, near Aberfeldy. It takes the form of a Z-plan tower and replaces a castle that was burned to the ground in 1502. Situated in the ancient Menzies homeland and owned by the Clan Menzies chiefs until 1918, it is now in the care of the Menzies Clan Society. Of particular interest are the great hall, with its ceiling commemorating the Union of 1707, Prince Charlie's Room, where the Young Pretender slept for two nights, and an anteroom with a collection of memorabilia. The west wing was added in 1840 and was designed by William Burn.

Castle O'er *Dumfries and Galloway* Also known as Castle Over or Castle Overbie, the hamlet of Castle O'er lies in the heart of the Castle O'er Forest near the junction of the White and Black Esk, 9 miles (14 km) northwest of Langholm in Eskdale, eastern Dumfries and Galloway. An Iron Age hillfort near here dates from the 1st millennium BC.

Castle of Craighouse A former name for Castlecraig on the Black Isle in Highland.

Castle of Mey *Highland* A castle in the Caithness district of Highland Council area, the Castle of Mey stands on the shores of the Pentland Firth, 6 miles (10 km) west of John o' Groats and 9 miles (14 km) east of Thurso. The castle was the principal Scottish residence of the late Queen Elizabeth, the Queen Mother, who purchased it in 1952, shortly after the death of her husband, King George VI. When she bought the castle from Captain Imbert-Terry it was in a state of neglect. Over a number of years it was restored and electric lighting and heating installed. The castle was built on a Z-plan between 1566 and 1572 by George Sinclair, 4th Earl of Caithness. The Sinclairs, who originally called their family seat Barrogil, extended the castle in the 18th century and again in 1819, when architect William Burn added the porch and Scottish baronial features.

Castle of Park *Aberdeenshire* A Z-plan tower in Aberdeenshire, the Castle of Park is located a half-mile (1 km) southwest of Cornhill. Built in 1536, it now houses holiday homes, an art gallery and a restaurant.

Castle of St John *Dumfries and Galloway* The Castle of St John is alternatively known as the Chapel or Stranraer Castle and is located in the centre of Stranraer in western Dumfries and Galloway. Restored by Wigtown District Council and open to the public since 1990, the castle was built in 1510 by Ninian Adair of Kilhurst, one of the most powerful lairds of Wigtownshire. It passed to the Kennedys in 1591, was a Dalrymple of Stair property from 1680, and eventually passed to public ownership in 1815 when it was purchased by the burgh of Stranraer. Standing four storeys tall, it was used as the town gaol between 1815 and 1907.

Castle Semple Loch *Renfrewshire* Castle Semple Loch is located to the east of Lochwinnoch in Renfrewshire and is part of the Castle Semple Water Country Park. This park is part of the larger Clyde Muirshiel Country Park.

Castle Semple Water Country Park *Renfrewshire* Centred round Castle Semple Loch, the Castle Semple Water Country Park is located to the east of Lochwinnoch in Renfrewshire. A centre for rowing, sailing and canoeing, it also incorporates the RSPB Lochwinnoch Nature Reserve.

Castle Stalker *Argyll and Bute* A tower house on an islet in Loch Laich on the Appin coast in Argyll and Bute, Castle Stalker dates from the 15th century, and was built by Duncan Stewart whose family held ownership until 1765. It lay in a ruinous state until 1965 when restoration work was undertaken.

Castle Stewart *Dumfries and Galloway* A former stronghold of the Stewarts in Dumfries and Galloway, Castle Stewart lies just west of the River Cree, 3 miles (5 km) northwest of Newton Stewart. It was named after Colonel William Stewart who made a fortune in the 17th century as a mercenary soldier fighting under Gustavus Adolphus of Sweden. On his return to Scotland he bought the estate, which was then called Calcruchie.

Castle Stuart *Highland* A tower house in eastern Highland Council area, Castle Stuart lies near Inverness Airport (Dalcross Airport), 5 miles (8 km) northeast of Inverness. Dating from 1625, it was a stronghold of the earls of Moray.

Castle Sween *Argyll and Bute* A ruined castle in Knapdale, Castle Sween looks onto Loch Sween, 8 miles (13 km) southwest of Crinan. It has been derelict since 1647, when it was destroyed by MacDonald of Colkitto. The castle dates from the 12th century, with improvements and extensions in the late 15th century. It was occupied by the MacSweens in the early 14th century and later by Hector MacNeill on behalf of the Lords of the Isles and Colin Campbell, 1st Earl of Argyll, who held it for King James III. It is now under the guardianship of Historic Scotland.

Castle Toward *Argyll and Bute* A Gothic-style mansion on the Cowal peninsula, Castle Toward lies at the eastern entrance to the Kyles of Bute opposite Rothesay, just over a mile (1.5 km) west of Toward Point and 8 miles (13 km) southwest of Dunoon. It was built in 1821 near the ruined castle of the Lamonts, Lords of Cowal, and now operates as an outdoor activity centre. Toward Hill rises to the north.

Castle Urquhart *Highland* Located a mile (1.5 km) east of Drumnadrochit at the eastern end of Glen Urquhart, Castle Urquhart stands on a highly defensible rocky promontory overlooking Loch Ness, with commanding views along the Great Glen to Inverness in the northeast and Fort Augustus in the southwest. The most recent structure is a ruined early 17th-century tower, but other ruins and archaeological remains suggest much earlier settlement. There are traces of Iron Age fortifications, and the site was certainly a defensive structure in the 6th century when St Columba visited the area and apparently encountered a sea creature. Ownership of the site passed from the Durwards to the Comyns in the 13th century, and the castle was occupied by Edward I in 1296 and 1303. Castle Urquhart was regularly attacked by the MacDonalds of the Isles and was occupied by Covenanters (1645) and then Jacobites (1689), before being destroyed by the Government (1691) to prevent its use as a Jacobite stronghold.

Castlebay *Western Isles* The chief settlement on the island of Barra in the Outer Hebrides, Castlebay (Bagh a' Chaisteil) became an active herring-fishing port in the 19th century when James Methuen developed associated curing and packing industries at the head of the sheltered Castle Bay at the southern end of the island. To the west of the bay is Kisimul Castle, the restored seat of the MacNeils of Barra. Today Castlebay has shops, schools, hotels, a tourist office, a cottage hospital and Dualchas, the Barra heritage centre.

Castlecary *North Lanarkshire* A village in northeast North Lanarkshire, Castlecary is situated to the west of the A80 and south of the Forth and Clyde Canal. A Roman fort on the Antonine Wall was excavated here in 1902, and nearby stands a castle dating from the 15th century.

Castlecraig *Highland* A locality in the parish of Nigg in Easter Ross, Castlecraig lies on the Moray Firth, 2 miles (3 km) east of Nigg Ferry. The remains of a castle date from the 12th century, when William the Lion is said to have established a stronghold here to maintain law and order.

Castlecraig *Highland* The site of a former stronghold of the Urquharts on the Black Isle, the ruins of Castlecraig (also Castle of Craighouse) overlook the Cromarty Firth opposite Evanton. Known originally as the Castle of Craighouse, it was for a while the principal residence of the bishops of Ross. After the Reformation, it is said to have been occupied by Donald Monro, at one time Archdeacon of the Isles and author of *A Description of the Western Isles, 1547*, the earliest personal account of the isles on record.

Castlefairn *Dumfries and Galloway* A locality in central Dumfries and Galloway, Castlefairn lies on the Castlefairn Water, 4 miles (6.5 km) southwest of Moniaive.

Castlefairn Water *Dumfries and Galloway* A stream in central Dumfries and Galloway, the Castlefairn Water rises on the border between Dalry and Glencairn parishes. It flows generally eastwards before joining the Dalwhat Water near Moniaive to form the Cairn Water.

Castlehill *Highland* A locality in northern Caithness, Highland Council area, Castlehill lies adjacent to Castletown on the Pentland Firth, 4 miles (6.5 km) east of Thurso. The dairy of a large farmsteading operates as an interpretative centre for the Castlehill Quarries that once produced Caithness flagstones that were shipped out from the Castlehill Harbour. The wide triangular quay was designed by James Bremner *c.*1820.

Castlehill *City of Edinburgh* The westernmost section of Edinburgh's Royal Mile, Castlehill rises steeply over the short distance between the Lawnmarket and the Esplanade of Edinburgh Castle. Notable buildings on Castlehill include the Hub Festival Centre (previously St John's Highland Tolbooth Church, by Augustus Pugin), the former Ragged School (set up in 1850 by reformer

Thomas Guthrie) and the old Castlehill Reservoir (now the Tartan Weaving Mill and Exhibition). The Outlook Tower and Ramsay Gardens, which lie immediately to the north, are both associated with visionary town planner Professor Sir Patrick Geddes (1854–1932).

Castlehill Point *Dumfries and Galloway* A headland in Dumfries and Galloway, Castlehill Point lies at the mouth of the Rough Firth, a mile (1.5 km) to the southeast of Rockcliffe. The Urr Water joins the Solway Firth opposite the point.

Castlehill Tower *Scottish Borders* In the valley of the Manor Water, about 4 miles (6.5 km) south of Peebles in Scottish Borders, Castlehill or Castle Hill of Manor was built by the Lowis family, who held the property from the early 15th century. The property was later held by the Veitches, Baillies of Jerviswood, the earls of March, the Burnets of Barns and the Tweedies of Quarter.

Castlemilk *Dumfries and Galloway* A locality in Annandale, eastern Dumfries and Galloway, Castlemilk lies on the Water of Milk, 3 miles (5 km) south of Lockerbie.

Castlemilk *Glasgow City* A residential district of Glasgow, Castlemilk lies to the south of the River Clyde between Carmunnock and Busby. A 13th-century castle was rebuilt here in 1460 by the Stuarts and named after their estate to the south of Lockerbie in Dumfriesshire. In 1938 the land was bought by Glasgow Corporation, and the Castlemilk housing estate was developed from 1953 as one of the city's four new peripheral suburbs. Lack of employment and social deprivation resulted in a fall in population from 37,000 in 1971 to 18,000 in 1991. A regeneration strategy has focused on the creation of improved housing and the development of local arts.

Castlesea Bay *Angus* An inlet of the North Sea on the coast of Angus, Castlesea Bay is located between Arbroath and Auchmithie.

Castleton *Argyll and Bute* A small settlement of central Argyll and Bute, Castleton is located 3 miles (5 km) southeast of Lochgilphead, between Loch Gilp and Loch Fyne. The islands of Eilean Mòr and Liath Eilean lie off the coast.

Castletown *Highland* A village in northern Caithness, Castletown lies 4 miles (6.5 km) east of Thurso. Linear in shape, the village was planned c.1802 by Sheriff James Traill in association with the development of the nearby Castlehill flagstone quarries. Eventually laid out in 1824 and initially employing 100 quarriers, the industry expanded to employ nearly 500 workers by 1900, the flagstone being exported to pave streets all over the UK and as far afield as New Zealand and South America. By 1925 the natural-flagstone industry of Caithness had been superseded by precast concrete paving. Sheriff Traill's house in Castletown was burned down in 1970, but a public hall and reading room gifted to the people of Olrig parish in 1867 by Margaret Traill, daughter of Sheriff Traill, remains. Now disused, the Gothic-style Old Church of Castletown dates from 1840. In addition to livestock haulage, the largest local industry is now the manufacture of domestic and commercial freezers.

Castramont *Dumfries and Galloway* A locality in Dumfries and Galloway, Castramont lies 3 miles (5 km) north of Gatehouse of Fleet. The Castramont Burn flows down from the Fell of Laghead to join the Water of Fleet at Aikyhill below Castramont Wood and is known as the Doon of Castramont. Castramont Wood is a fine example of an old oak woodland.

Cat Law *Angus* A hill in the Braes of Angus, Cat Law rises to 671m (2201 ft) between Glen Prosen and Glen Isla, 6 miles (10 km) northwest of Kirriemuir.

Cat, Lochan nan *Perth and Kinross* Occupying a north-facing corrie that looks out over Loch an Daimh, Lochan nan Cat is situated near the summit of Stuchd an Lochain, to the north of Glen Lyon in northwest Perth and Kinross.

Cat, Lochan nan *Perth and Kinross* A small corrie loch in central Perth and Kinross, Lochan nan Cat lies between the summits of Ben Lawers and Meall Garbh. It is the source of the Lawers Burn which flows down to Loch Tay.

Catacol Bay *North Ayrshire* Catacol Bay forms an inlet of the Kilbrannan Sound on the northwest coastline of the island of Arran, North Ayrshire. It has a long sandy beach, and the waters that flow through Glen Catacol empty into the sound through the bay.

Cathcart *Glasgow City* An ancient parish that now forms a suburb of Glasgow, Cathcart lies 3 miles (5 km) south of the city centre on the White Cart Water. From the 17th century Cathcart developed in association with the manufacture of cardboard, snuff and textiles, and in 1886 the marine engineering firm of G. and J. Weir Ltd, latterly known as the Weir Group, was established. The arrival of the Cathcart District Railway in 1884 led to the expansion of Cathcart as a residential area within commuting distance of the city centre, and in 1912 Cathcart was incorporated into Glasgow. Its business park is the operational headquarters of Scottish Power.

Cathcartstone Visitor Centre *East Ayrshire* Located in Dalmellington, East Ayrshire, the Cathcartstone Visitor Centre comprises a row of converted weavers' cottages whose exhibits highlight the importance of weaving within the area.

Catlodge *Highland* A hamlet in southern Badenoch, Catlodge lies to the east of Loch Laggan, 7 miles (11 km) north of Dalwhinnie near the junction of the Allt Breakachy with the River Spey. One of General Wade's mid-18th-century military roads passes through the settlement.

Catrine *East Ayrshire* A village in East Ayrshire, Catrine lies on the River Ayr, 2 miles (3 km) southeast of Mauchline. Formerly a centre for spinning and cotton milling, its spinning mills acquired the first large power loom in Scotland in 1814.

Cattadale *Argyll and Bute* A settlement on the island of Islay in Argyll and Bute, Cattadale lies on a tributary of the Laggan Water, 4 miles (6.5 km) east of Bowmore.

Catterline *Aberdeenshire* A former fishing village on the southeast coast of Aberdeenshire, Catterline stands on a cliff top at the end of a narrow road 4 miles (6.5 km) north of Inverbervie. Lime and coal used to be shipped into its sheltered anchorage. Two miles (3 km) further up the coast lie the remains of the once-thriving fishing community of Crawton.

Cattie, Burn of *Aberdeenshire* A stream in south-central Aberdeenshire, the Burn of Cattie rises in the Forest of Birse to the south of Aboyne. It flows northeastwards to join the River Dee.

Cauldcleuch Head *Scottish Borders* A hill in southwest Scottish Borders, Cauldcleuch Hill rises to 608 m (1010 ft) 10 miles (16 km) southwest of Hawick.

Cauldhame *Stirling* A village in southwest Stirling Council area, Cauldhame lies immediately southwest of the village of Kippen in the shadow of the Gargunnock Hills.

Cauldron Linn *Clackmannanshire/Perth and Kinross* The name given to a series of waterfalls in a deep and narrow gorge of the River Devon near Rumbling Bridge on the border between Clackmannanshire and Perth and Kinross. Its water-hollowed rocks were described by Thomas Pennant in 1769 as being 'formed into great circular cavities like cauldrons'.

Caulkerbush *Dumfries and Galloway* A village in south-central Dumfries and Galloway, Caulkerbush is situated on the Caulkerbush Burn and at a road junction just over 6 miles (10 km) southeast of Dalbeattie.

Caulside *Dumfries and Galloway* A hamlet in Eskdale, eastern Dumfries and Galloway, Caulside (formerly *Cauldside*) lies close to the English border, just over 3 miles (5 km) northeast of Canonbie.

Causamul Rocks *Western Isles* A small group of rocky islets off the west coast of North Uist in the Outer Hebrides, the Causamul Rocks lie 2 miles (3 km) west of the headland of Aird an Runair.

Causeway End *Dumfries and Galloway* A locality in southwest Dumfries and Galloway, Causeway End lies due west of the Moss of Cree, 3 miles (5 km) south of Newton Stewart.

Causewayhead *Stirling* A settlement in Stirling Council area, Causewayhead lies at the foot of Abbey Craig, at the eastern end of the causeway that leads southwestwards across the River Forth to Stirling. It lies on a bend of the River Forth in the shadow of the Wallace Monument, a mile (1.5 km) south of Bridge of Allan. Stone and coal were once mined in the neighbourhood.

Cava *Orkney* A low grassy island in the Orkney Islands, Cava lies on the western side of Scapa Flow, to the east of Hoy. It has an area of 107 ha (264 acres) and is today mainly used for grazing. The Calf of Cava is a small northern peninsula with a lighthouse.

Cavens *Dumfries and Galloway* A locality in Dumfries and Galloway, Cavens lies just south of Kirkbean and 12 miles (19 km) south of Dumfries.

Cawdor *Highland* A name associated with a thanage mentioned in Shakespeare's *Macbeth*, the castle and hamlet of Cawdor are situated on the Allt Dearg, a tributary of the River Nairn, 13 miles (21 km) east of Inverness, Highland Council area. Cawdor developed in association with the castle, a stronghold of the Campbells, which was rebuilt as a stone tower *c*.1372 and extended in the mid-15th century. The Royal Brackla whisky distillery, located to the east, was founded in 1812 by William Fraser.

Ceabhagh The Gaelic name for Keava in the Western Isles.

Ceann a Bhaigh The Gaelic name for Kennavay in the Western Isles.

Ceann a' Bhaigh The Gaelic name for Bayhead in the Western Isles.

Ceann a' Deas Loch Baghasdail An alternative Gaelic name for South Lochboisdale in the Western Isles.

Ceann a' Gharaidh The Gaelic name for Kennagary in the Western Isles.

Ceann Bharraigh The Gaelic name for Barra Head in the Western Isles.

Ceann Ear *Western Isles* The largest of the Heisker or Monach Islands in the Outer Hebrides, Ceann Ear lies 7 miles (11 km) southwest of Aird an Runair on the west coast of North Uist and has an area of 357 ha (883 acres). The group comprises five uninhabited islands. Ceann Ear is connected at low tide by sandbanks to Shivinish and hence to Ceann Iar, the largest island of the group.

Ceann Hulabhig, Loch An alternative Gaelic name for Loch Kinhoulavig in the Western Isles.

Ceann Hulavig, Loch An alternative Gaelic name for Loch Kinhoulavig in the Western Isles.

Ceann Iar *Western Isles* The largest of the Heisker or Monach Islands in the Outer Hebrides, Ceann Iar lies 8 miles (13 km) southwest of Aird an Runair on the west coast of North Uist. It is one of three uninhabited islands connected at low tide by sandbanks, the others being Ceann Ear and Shivinish. The island reaches a high point of 19 m (62 ft).

Ceann Mòr The Gaelic name for Kenmore in the Western Isles.

Cearsiadar The Gaelic name for Kershader in the Western Isles.

Cearstaigh The Gaelic name for Kearstay in the Western Isles.

Ceathramh Meadhanach The Gaelic name for Middlequarter in the Western Isles.

Ceileagraigh The Gaelic name for Killegray in the Western Isles.

Cellardyke *Fife* An old fishing village on the Firth of Forth, Cellardyke forms the eastern part of the settlement of Anstruther. Formerly known as Lower Kilrenny or Sillerdyke, its present name was coined, it is said, by the fishermen of Kilrenny who once kept their fishing gear in cellars near the harbour. They also built dykes on the cliff top to keep stray animals away from their fishing nets laid out to dry on the green. Although the fishing industry is long gone, the 16th-century harbour (Skinfasthaven), which was rebuilt in 1829–31 by Joseph Mitchell, is still used by pleasure boats. Close to the Town Hall stands Kilrenny Cross (1642) and beyond the harbour lies a bathing pool known locally as the Cardinal's Steps, after Cardinal Beaton of St Andrews who had a seaside residence here in the 16th century. Cellardyke was designated a conservation area in 1977. The arrival of the 'Sea Queen' each August is a survival of the old sea-harvest thanksgiving festivals that used to take place in coastal fishing villages.

Cellar Head *Western Isles* A headland on the northeast coast of the Isle of Lewis in the Outer Hebrides, Cellar Head lies 6 miles (10 km) north of Tolsta Head.

Celtic Park *Glasgow City* A football stadium in Glasgow, Celtic Park (sometimes called Parkhead after the district in which it stands) is located on Kerrydale Street, off London Road, about 2 miles (3 km) east of the city centre. Celtic Park is the home of Celtic Football Club. Established in 1888, the club was the idea of Brother Walfrid, the leader of a teaching institute in Glasgow. He wished to create a club similar to Edinburgh's Hibernian Football Club with the purpose of raising money for the Poor Children's Dinner Table charity that he had established. The name chosen for the club was Celtic, as it conveyed the Irish and Scottish roots of the community. In 1890 the club was admitted into the Scottish League.

Central Mosque and Islamic Centre *Glasgow City* Glasgow's Central Mosque and Islamic Centre is located on the south bank of the River Clyde within the Gorbals. Completed in 1984, it is the focal point for the estimated 30,000 Muslims in Glasgow and the surrounding area.

Central Station *Glasgow City* Opened in 1879 as a terminus for southbound passenger trains, Glasgow's Central Station originally had nine platforms, but with an increase in passenger numbers was extended and expanded by four more platforms in the period 1901–05. This Edwardian station is probably one of the grandest in the country, and some of Glasgow's best-loved landmarks are associated with it. The Shell, a World War I shell that was converted into a charity bowl, is one of Glasgow's best-known meeting points, while another is the Heilan'man's Umbrella, the area beneath the railway bridge that crosses Argyle Street and was frequented by travellers from the Highlands and islands.

Ceos The Gaelic name for Keose in the Western Isles.

Ceres *Fife* Once described as 'the most attractive village in Scotland', Ceres lies amid fertile farmland in northeast Fife, 3 miles (5 km) southeast of Cupar. Mentioned as early as the 12th century, it was created a burgh of barony in 1620 under the Hopes of Craighall, developing as a centre of farming, weaving and brewing. Unlike most Scottish villages, its attractive pantiled cottages stand around a green, the scene of annual games that are the oldest in Scotland. These games celebrate the return of the men of Ceres from the Battle of Bannockburn in 1314. There is a Bannockburn Memorial by the village green and an old bridge over the Ceres Burn leads to the Fife Folk Museum, which was opened in 1968 by the Central and North Fife Preservation Society. Built into a wall in the main street is the seated figure of the Revd Thomas Buchanan, the last church provost in 1578.

Cessford *Scottish Borders* A hamlet with a 15th-century castle, Cessford is located 5.5 miles (9 km) east-northeast of Jedburgh and 6 miles (10 km) south of Kelso. Cessford lies on the St Cuthbert's Way long-distance footpath.

Cessford Castle *Scottish Borders* The ruined remains of Cessford Castle lie near the settlement of Cessford, 11 miles (18 km) southeast of Newtown St Boswells in Scottish Borders. Built in the 15th century to an L-shaped plan, the castle was a stronghold of the Kerrs of Cessford, a sept of the Kerr clan, the family of the dukes of Roxburgh and marquesses of Lothian.

Cessnock Water *East Ayrshire* A river of East Ayrshire, the Cessnock Water rises on the western slopes of Distinkhorn (386 m/1266 ft) not far from the boundary with South Lanarkshire. The river flows southwest to a point a half-mile (1 km) northeast of Mauchline where it turns northwest for 3 miles (5 km) then westwards before briefly forming the border between East Ayrshire and South Ayrshire. It then turns northwest once again and finally northeast past Hurlford to join the River Irvine 2.5 miles (4 km) east of Kilmarnock, having completed a course of 14 miles (22 km).

Chabet Water *Moray* Rising in hills to the north of Tomintoul in Moray, the Chabet Water flows northwards to join the River Avon at Ballcorach.

Chaipaval *Western Isles* A mountain of South Harris in the Outer Hebrides, Chaipaval rises to 365 m (1197 ft) on a southwestern peninsula of the island, some 2 miles (3 km) southeast of the headland of Toe Head. A secondary peak of 339 m (1112 ft) rises to the northwest.

Chairinis A Gaelic name for Carinish in the Western Isles.

Chàirn Bhàin, Loch a' *Highland* A sea loch on the west coast of the Sutherland district of Highland Council area, Loch a' Chairn Bhain (also Loch Cairnbawn) forms an inlet at the head of Eddrachillis Bay 3 miles (5 km) west of Kylestrome, where it joins the lochs of Glendhu and Glencoul.

Challoch *Dumfries and Galloway* A hamlet in Penninghame parish, Dumfries and Galloway, Challoch sits near a bend in the River Cree, 2 miles (3 km) northwest of Newton Stewart.

Chalmadale, Glen *North Ayrshire* A valley at the northern end of the island of Arran, North Ayrshire, Glen Chalmadale extends northwest from north Glen Sannox towards Loch Ranza on the island's northwest coast.

Chanlock Burn *Dumfries and Galloway* A stream in Dumfries and Galloway, the Chanlock Burn rises in hills to the southwest of Sanquhar. It flows 6 miles (10 km) east to join the Scaur Water 5 miles (8 km) northwest of Penpont Bridge.

Chanonry Point *Highland* A headland on the east coast of the Black Isle in Easter Ross, Chanonry Point extends into the Cromarty Firth opposite Fort George. Chanonry, the former name of the town of Fortrose that lies at its head, refers to the canonry of Ross which was the residence of a bishop.

Chapel *Fife* A hamlet in the hills of central Fife, a mile (1.5 km) south of Kettlebridge, Chapel was the birthplace in 1794 of the eminent surgeon James Moncrieff Arnon.

Chapel Finian *Dumfries and Galloway* The foundations are all that is left of Chapel Finian, a 10th-11th century AD chapel that lies on the east side of Luce Bay in the Machars of Dumfries and Galloway. It stands on an old raised beach at Corwall port and probably takes its name from the Irish St Finian who was educated at Whithorn and died c.579 AD. The site may have been a landing place for Irish pilgrims to St Ninian's shrine.

Chapel of Garioch *Aberdeenshire* A village of the Garioch district in Aberdeenshire, Chapel of Garioch lies in a parish of the same name at a road junction 3 miles (5 km) northwest of Inverurie. The parish church dates from 1813.

Chapel Rossan *Dumfries and Galloway* A locality in the Rhinns of Galloway, Dumfries and Galloway, Chapel Rossan lies on Chapel Rossan Bay adjacent to Ardwell and 9 miles (14 km) south of Stranraer. There is a 19th-century Gothic-style house.

Chapel Rossan Bay *Dumfries and Galloway* A small inlet on the west side of Luce Bay, Dumfries and Galloway, Chapel Rossan Bay lies by Chapel Rossan and Ardwell on the southeast coast of the Rhinns of Galloway.

Chapelcross Nuclear Power Station *Dumfries and Galloway* Located near Annan in Dumfries and Galloway, Chapelcross is one of the oldest nuclear power stations in the United Kingdom, and the first in Scotland. Operational since 1959, it comprises four 50-megawatt Magnox reactors and a processing plant. The Magnox reactors, so called because magnesium alloy was used to contain the fuel rods, were designed to produce weapons-grade plutonium for the military as well as power for the civilian market. It closed in 2004 and is being decommissioned.

Chapelhall *North Lanarkshire* A village of North Lanarkshire, Chapelhall is located 2 miles (3 km) southeast of Airdrie and is separated from Calderbank to the west by the North Calder Water. Formerly a centre for the manufacture of steel, Chapelhall has a country park and an industrial estate.

Chapelhill *Perth and Kinross* A small linear settlement in the Carse of Gowrie, Chapelhill lies between St Madoes and Leetown, 7 miles (11 km) east of Perth.

Chapelknowe *Dumfries and Galloway* A hamlet in Dumfries and Galloway, Chapelknowe lies close to the Logan Water, 6 miles (10 km) southwest of Canonbie.

Chapelton *South Lanarkshire* The farming settlement of Chapelton is located 3 miles (5 km) northwest of Strathaven and 5 miles (8 km) southwest of Hamilton in South Lanarkshire.

Chapeltown *Moray* The Chapeltown of Glenlivet lies nearly 3 miles (5 km) east of Knockandhu in the uplands of Moray. Now a distillery village, it was once a remote refuge for persecuted Catholics and for whisky smugglers at the heart of the Braes of Glenlivet. The old school was closed in 1960 after a century in use. In the Catholic Church of Our Lady of Perpetual Succour is a memorial to Abbe Paul Macpherson (1756–1846), a pupil of the nearby Scalan Seminary, who was engaged in 1812 by the British Government to warn Pope Pius VII of his imminent rescue from the fortress of Savona, where he had been held by Napoleon.

Charr, Water of *Aberdeenshire/Angus* A stream in the eastern Grampians of Aberdeenshire, the Water of Charr rises on Sturdy Hill on the border between Aberdeenshire and Angus. It flows north to meet the Water of Dye at Charr.

Charing Cross *Glasgow City* A district at the centre of Glasgow's West End, Charing Cross lies between the residential areas of Garnethill and Woodlands and the industrial area of Anderston. Named after Charing Cross in London, the district has some of Glasgow's most elegant buildings, including Charing Cross Mansions (1891), St George's Mansions (1901) and the Mitchell Library (1911). Transport policy in the 1960s resulted in the development of the M8 motorway extension to the Kingston Bridge cutting through the heart of Charing Cross and effectively creating a barrier to development between the city and the West End.

Charleston *Angus* A planned hamlet of central Angus, Charleston (more fully Charleston of Glamis) lies a half-mile (1 km) south of Glamis. The hamlet was developed in the 1830s.

Charlestown *Highland* A village on the Black Isle in Easter Ross, Highland Council area, Charlestown lies on the north shore of the Beauly Firth, a mile (1.5 km) west of the Kessock Bridge. The village was laid out in 1812 by Sir Charles Mackenzie of Kilcoy.

Charlestown *Fife* A planned industrial village founded c.1770 by Charles, 5th Earl of Elgin (1732–71), Charlestown lies on the Fife coast, 2 miles (3 km) southwest of Dunfermline. The village is laid out in the shape of an elongated 'E', its focal point being the Scottish baronial-style Queen's Hall built to a design by Robert Rowand Anderson in 1887 to celebrate the golden jubilee of Queen Victoria. The original inhabitants were engaged in working coal and limestone. Conservation areas were established in 1974 and 1984.

Charlestown of Aberlour An alternative name for Aberlour in Moray.

Chartershall *Stirling* A settlement in Stirling Council area, Chartershall lies on the Bannock Burn 2 miles (3 km) south of Stirling. Chartershall, with its bridge dating from 1747, was once a nail-making community.

Chatelherault Country Park *South Lanarkshire* A country park extending over 200 ha (494 acres) 2 miles (3 km) southwest of Hamilton in South Lanarkshire, Chatelherault was formerly part of the estate of the Duke of Hamilton surrounding Hamilton Palace. The palace was demolished but Chatelherault hunting lodge, built for the 5th Duke of Hamilton, and an Iron Age fort survive. Also within the park are a deep gorge of the Avon Water overlooked by 13th-century Cadzow Castle, oak trees dating from the 15th century, and a rare breed of white cattle bred by the dukes of Hamilton and perhaps descended from the ancient wild cattle of Scotland. The park was opened in 1987 by the Duke of Gloucester.

Cherrybank Gardens An alternative name for Bell's Cherrybank Centre in Perth and Kinross.

Chester Hill *Scottish Borders* A small hill in Scottish Borders, Chester Hill lies near the North Sea coast just south of Burnmouth. It is topped by an Iron Age hillfort.

Chesters *Scottish Borders* A locality in Scottish Borders, Chesters lies on the Jed Water, 2 miles (3 km) east of Hobkirk.

Chesthill *Perth and Kinross* A locality in Glen Lyon, Perth and Kinross, Chesthill House overlooks the River Lyon, 3 miles (5 km) west of Fortingall. This was the home of Robert Campbell of Glenlyon who commanded the Campbells at the infamous massacre of the Macdonalds at Glencoe in 1692.

Cheviot Hills, the *Scottish Borders* A range of hills on the border between Scotland and England, the Cheviot Hills extend for 35 miles (56 km) northeast to southwest and rise to a height of 815 m (2676 ft) at the Cheviot, which lies just south of the border. The range gives its name to a breed of sheep.

Children's Village, the *East Lothian* Lying prominently on a hillside just to the southeast of Humbie in East Lothian and 4 miles (6.5 km) south of Pencaitland, the Children's Village was built in 1905 in the form of a series of cottages administered by the Algrade Trust to house disabled children. The village closed in 1999. The buildings are listed for their special architectural and historical interest.

Chill Donnain, Loch The Gaelic name for Loch Kildonan in the Western Isles.

Chilleine, Gleann a' *Perth and Kinross* A narrow valley in Perth and Kinross, Gleann a' Chilleine extends a distance of 4 miles (6.5 km) southeastwards from the south side of Loch Tay at Ardtalnaig. It follows the course of the Allt a' Chilleine which rises between the steep-sided Dunan Hill and the Shee of Ardtalnaig.

Chirnside *Scottish Borders* A village of Berwickshire in Scottish Borders, Chirnside lies to the north of the Whiteadder Water, 9 miles (14 km) west of Berwick-upon-Tweed. It has a 12th-century church and a paper mill established in 1842.

Chiscan *Argyll and Bute* A small settlement on the Kintyre peninsula, Argyll and Bute, Chiscan lies on the west bank of the Chiscan Water 2 miles (3 km) west of Campbeltown.

Chisholme *Scottish Borders* An estate in Scottish

Borders, Chisholme lies to the south of the Borthwick Water, 5 miles (8 km) southwest of Hawick.

Chno Dearg *Highland* A mountain rising to a height of 1046 m (3432 ft) southeast of Loch Treig in the Lochaber district of Highland Council area, the flat summit of Chno Dearg (also *Cnoc Dearg*) is covered in boulders. Its name is derived from the Gaelic for 'red nut' or 'red hill'.

Chomraidh, Gleann *Perth and Kinross* Extending southwestwards for nearly 3 miles (5 km) from Bridge of Gaur at the west end of Loch Rannoch in Perth and Kinross, Gleann Chomraidh follows the course of the Allt Chomraidh, a stream that rises in Rannoch Forest.

Chon, Loch *Stirling* A loch in the Trossachs district of Stirling Council area, Loch Chon lies to the south of Loch Katrine, 11 miles (18 km) west of Aberfoyle. It is surrounded on three sides by the Loch Ard Forest and is drained southeastwards towards Loch Ard via the smaller Loch Dhu and the Water of Chon.

Christ Church *Western Isles* A chapel located on the uninhabited Hebridean island of Ensay in the Sound of Harris, Christ Church dates from the 12th century although little is known of its early history. In ruins by the beginning of the 20th century, it was beautifully restored as a private chapel by Jessie Scott, a sister of the laird of the island who was resident at the nearby Ensay House. It was used from 1909 and services continued periodically until 1935 when the chapel was made over to the Scottish Episcopal Church with a small endowment for its maintenance on condition that it was used for at least two services annually. The church fell into disrepair but was restored and rededicated in 1973.

Chryston *North Lanarkshire* Situated 8 miles (13 km) northeast of Glasgow between the Garnkirk Burn and the Bothlin Burn, the village of Chryston lies adjacent to the hamlet of Muirhead and southwest of Moodiesburn in North Lanarkshire. The Crow Wood Golf Course is west of the village and nearby are the remains of Bedlay Castle.

Churchill Barriers *Orkney* A set of four barriers created from blocks of concrete and stone, the Churchill Barriers were designed to protect the eastern approaches to Scapa Flow in the Orkney Islands. The barriers, extending about 1.5 miles (2.5 km) in length, cross four sounds, linking Mainland Orkney with the islands of Lamb Holm, Glimps Holm, Burray and South Ronaldsay. The barriers were built during World War II on the orders of Prime Minister Winston Churchill,after a German U-boat penetrated the flow in October 1939 and sank the British battleship *Royal Oak* with the loss of over 800 lives. Taking several years to complete, the barriers form a series of causeways topped by a roadway. Over 66,000 huge blocks of concrete were laid on a foundation of more than quarter of a million tonnes of rock, the blocks preventing the tide from sweeping over the road.

Ciaran, Loch *Argyll and Bute* Located on the Kintyre peninsula, Loch Ciaran lies a mile (1.5 km) south of Clachan in Argyll and Bute. An outlet stream flows from the loch to enter the mouth of West Loch Tarbert to the north of Ronachan Point.

Cill Donnain The Gaelic name for Kildonan in the Western Isles.

Cille Bhrighde The Gaelic name for Kilbride in the Western Isles.

Cille Pheadair The Gaelic name for Kilpheder in the Western Isles.

Cilmalieu *Highland* A settlement in Lochaber, southern Highland Council area, Cilmalieu (also *Kilmalieu*) lies on the west shore of Loch Linnhe, 3 miles (5 km) northeast of Glengalmadale.

Cioch na h-Oighe *North Ayrshire* A mountain rising to 661 m (2168 ft) on the island of Arran in North Ayrshire, Cioch na h-Oighe lies 6 miles (10 km) north of Brodick. Goatfell rises immediately to the south.

Circebost The Gaelic name for Kirkibost in the Western Isles.

Ciribhig The Gaelic name for Cirivig in the Western Isles.

Cirivig *Western Isles* A crofting township on the west coast of Lewis in the Outer Hebrides, Cirivig (Gael: *Ciribhig*) lies on the south shore of Loch Carloway, forming a southwestern extension of the village of Carloway.

Ciste Dhubh *Highland* One of four Munros on a ridge known as the North Glen Shiel Range, Ciste Dhubh rises to 979 m (3212 ft) to the east of the Lochalsh district of Highland Council area. Its name is derived from the Gaelic for 'black chest'.

Citizens' Theatre, The *Glasgow City* A theatre in the Gorbals district of Glasgow, the Citizens' Theatre lies south of the city centre and the River Clyde. It was established in 1943 by the Scottish playwright James Bridie as a home for Scottish dialect works. Renovated in 1978, much of its original facade was removed, though the stone statues of Shakespeare, Burns and the four Muses have been retained and are now placed in the foyer.

City Chambers *City of Edinburgh* Located on Edinburgh's High Street, the City Chambers is a grand building built around three sides of a piazza, fronted by an arched colonnade that frames a statue of Alexander and Bucephalus by Sir John Steell (1804–91). The building was designed by John Adam (1721–92) between 1753 and 1761 over several of the medieval High Street 'closes', including Mary King's Close. Originally intended to be a Royal Exchange where the Edinburgh merchant community would transact their business, the merchants preferred to meet in the High Street and the building was acquired by the city council in the 19th century as the centre of administration for the City of Edinburgh.

City Chambers *Glasgow City* Located on the eastern side of George Square, Glasgow City Chambers was built by a London Scot, William Young, in the Italian Renaissance style and opened in 1888 by Queen Victoria. It was intended to convey the wealth and importance of Glasgow as the second city of the Empire. The interior reflects the opulence of Victorian Glasgow, with staircases and galleries of marble, mosaics and tiles. Today, the City Chambers is the centre of administration of Glasgow City Council.

City Square *Dundee City* A somewhat austere pedestrianised square in the centre of Dundee, lying off the High Street. It was laid out in 1931 following the controversial decision to demolish William Adam's fine Town House (1731) which had previously stood on the site. The colonnade of this old building, known as the 'pillars', had been the meeting place for generations of Dundonians. The Caird Hall, with its massive pillared colonnade, forms the southern aspect of the square, and the City Chambers lies on its western side. Such was the austerity of the square that it was used in 1983 as a substitute for Moscow during the filming of the Alan Bennett play *An Englishman Abroad.* More recently improved by the addition of fountains and flowerbeds, the square still forms the very heart of the city.

Clabhach *Argyll and Bute* A scattered settlement on the northwest coast of the island of Coll in Argyll and Bute, Clabhach lies 3 miles (5 km) northwest of Arinagour. To the north is Grishipoll Point and to the west the headland of Rubha Hogh.

Clachaig *Argyll and Bute* A settlement of the Cowal peninsula, Clachaig lies on the Little Eachaig River 5 miles (8 km) northwest of Dunoon.

Clachaig Water *Argyll and Bute* A river of the Kintyre peninsula, Argyll and Bute, the Clachaig Water rises in hills in the Carradale Forest. It flows south-southwest to enter the sea at Muasdale, 4 miles (6.5 km) south of Tayinloan.

Clachan *Argyll and Bute* A village on the Kintyre peninsula, Argyll and Bute, Clachan lies near the mouth of West Loch Tarbert, 10 miles (16 km) southwest of Tarbert. Associated with the Clan Alasdair, Clachan has a number of carved stones depicting clan chiefs. Loup Hill, which lies 1.5 miles (2.5 km) to the northeast, was the site of the last major battle on Kintyre. Government troops defeated soldiers loyal to King James VII here in May 1689.

Clachan Bridge *Argyll and Bute* A modest single-arch bridge connecting the west coast of the mainland with Seil Island over the Clachan Sound, the Clachan Bridge is located 8 miles (13 km) southwest of Oban. Built in 1792 by engineer Thomas Telford (1757–1834), the bridge finds fame as the 'Bridge over the Atlantic'.

Clachan Mòr *Argyll and Bute* A scattered settlement on the island of Tiree, Argyll and Bute, Clachan Mòr is situated 5 miles (8 km) northwest of Scarinish, on the northern coast.

Clachan of Campsie An alternative name for Campsie in East Dunbartonshire.

Clachan of Glendaruel *Argyll and Bute* A settlement on the Cowal peninsula in Argyll and Bute, Clachan of Glendaruel lies on the River Ruel in Glendaruel, 4 miles (6.5 km) north of the head of Loch Riddon. In the churchyard are the Kilmodan Sculptured Stones, a collection of West Highland carved grave slabs under Historic Scotland protection.

Clachan-Seil *Argyll and Bute* Situated on the eastern coast of the island of Seil, Argyll and Bute, the small village of Clachan-Seil lies a mile (1.5 km) south of the Clachan Bridge, a hump-backed road bridge sometimes known as the 'Bridge over the Atlantic', connecting Seil with the mainland of Argyll.

Clachan Strachur An alternative name for Strachur in Argyll and Bute.

Clachaneasy *Dumfries and Galloway* A locality in Dumfries and Galloway, Clachaneasy lies on the River Cree, 6.5 miles (11 km) northwest of Newton Stewart.

Clachnaben *Aberdeenshire* A hill in the eastern Grampians, Clachnaben rises to 589 m (1932 ft) between Glen Dye and the Water of Aven, 5 miles (8 km) southwest of Strachan in Deeside.

Clachnaharry *Highland* A former fishing village on The Aird, Highland Council area, Clachnaharry lies 2 miles (3 km) west of Inverness on the south shore of the Beauly Firth. The village is said to derive its name from the 'watchman's stone' which refers to nearby rocks used as a lookout post by the townsfolk of Inverness. A monument here commemorates a battle between the Clan Munro and the Clan Chattan in 1387.

Clachtoll *Highland* A crofting township in Assynt, Highland Council area, Clachtoll lies on the west coast of Sutherland, 5 miles (8 km) northwest of Lochinver. A broch on the edge of the sea dates from the late 1st millennium BC.

Clackmannan *Clackmannanshire* A town in the Clackmannanshire parish of Clackmannan, Clackmannan is situated to the north of the River Forth, 2 miles (3 km) southeast of Alloa. Dominated by its church and tower, the settlement lies on a ridge that rises out of the surrounding carse land. At the centre of the town stands the stone or 'Clack' that gives the place its name. Thought to have been sacred to the pre-Christian sea-god Mannan, the stone has been moved from its original site. Adjacent to the stone is the ancient Mercat Cross and a bell tower, all that remains of the Tolbooth, built in 1592. The parish church, said to have been founded in the 5th century by St Serf, was rebuilt to a design by James Gillespie Graham in 1815, and on the King's Seat Hill stands Clackmannan Tower, which has a commanding view over the Forth estuary. Occupying a strategic site, the fortified tower was built in the 12th century to serve as one of a number of royal residences for King Malcolm IV. In the late 14th century the tower was given to the Bruces, who built the present structure and extended it in the 16th and 17th centuries. In a later mansion house occupied by the Bruce family until 1791, but later demolished, Mrs Bruce of Clackmannan, the last laird's widow, is said to have 'knighted' Robert Burns in 1787 with the sword of King Robert the Bruce. Among other favoured guests, she is also said to have dubbed the lexicographer the Revd John Jamieson, editor of the *Etymological Dictionary of the Scottish Language.* Clackmannan was the county town of Clackmannanshire until 1822 when it was superseded by the faster-growing Alloa. The merchant and minor poet William Burns was born in Clackmannan in 1825.

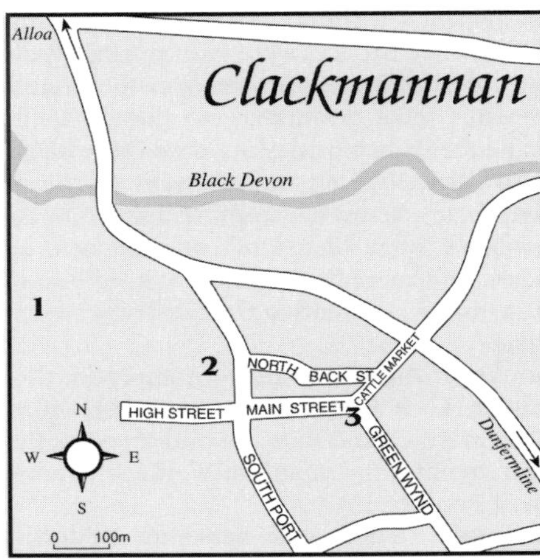

1 *Clackmannan Tower*
2 *Parish Church*
3 *Tolbooth and Clack Stone*

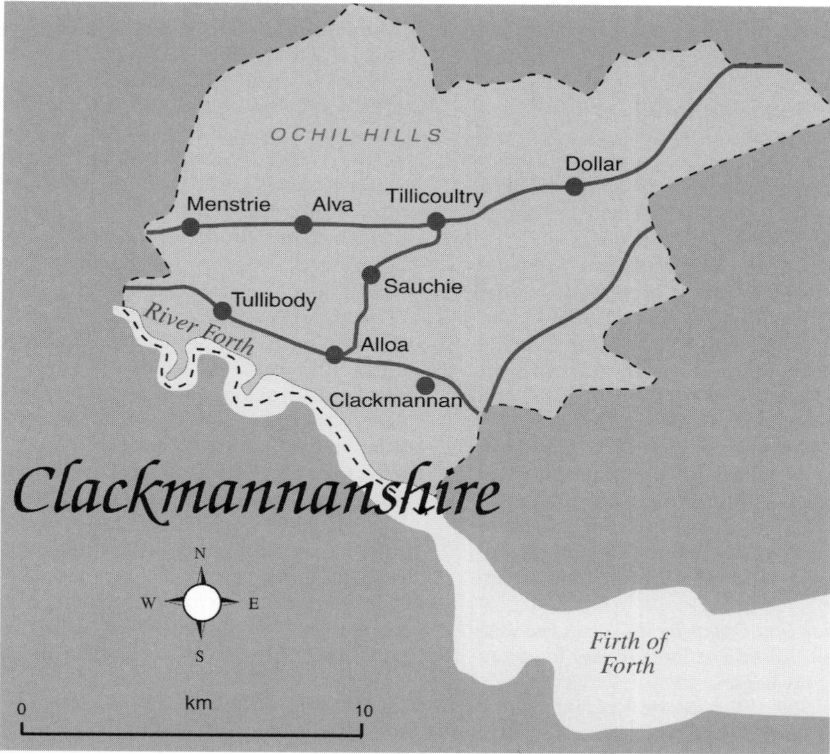

Clackmannanshire *Area: 158 sq. km (61 sq. mi)* Affectionately remembered as the 'Wee County', Clackmannanshire was Britain's smallest county prior to its inclusion in Central Region between 1975 and 1996. A local government area once again, Clackmannanshire is the second-smallest, after Dundee City, of Scotland's new unitary authorities. Clackmannanshire occupies territory between the Ochil Hills to the north, which rise to heights of more than 600 m (2000 ft), and the River Forth to the south. It largely comprises a lowland plain forming the valleys of the River Forth and of the River Devon, which joins the Forth near Cambus. Alloa, which is the centre of administration, outgrew the former county town of Clackmannan in 1822. The rich alluvial soils of the area support valuable agricultural land, and underlying coal measures have contributed to a mining economy that stretches back over several centuries. Settlements along the River Forth have developed as strategic ford or ferry crossing points, while the Hillfoot villages from Menstrie to Dollar have grown to their present size as textile towns formerly dependent on sheep grazing on upland pastures and water power derived from burns dropping down from the Ochil Hills. Other industries of importance have included brewing, distilling, paper making and glass making.

Cladh Hallan Bronze Age Settlement *Western Isles* The remains of a Bronze Age village on the machair of South Uist, Cladh Hallan is located 1.25 miles (2 km) west-northwest of Daliburgh. Here archaeological excavations between 1989 and 2002 uncovered the remains of a settlement from around 1000 BC. Scientists from the University of Sheffield discovered a rich assemblage of artefacts, including tools, jewellery and pottery, with a cooking pot retaining evidence of milk protein. Uniquely, one house contained two human burials where the bodies appear to have been mummified. These represented the first mummified remains ever to be found in Britain. Investigation revealed that the bodies seem to have been preserved by placing them in the acid environment of a peat bog for a short period of time before being retained perhaps as objects of veneration.

Cladich *Argyll and Bute* A scattered settlement of Argyll and Bute, Cladich lies on the Cladich River 5 miles (8 km) southwest of Dalmally. The Cladich River is joined by the Archan River before passing into Loch Awe.

Claggain Bay *Argyll and Bute* A bay on the east coast of the island of Islay in Argyll and Bute, Claggain Bay faces the island of Gigha, 4 miles (6.5 km) south of the headland of McArthur's Head.

Claggan *Highland* A settlement in Morvern, southwest Highland Council area, Claggan lies between Loch Aline and Loch Arienas, 2 miles (3 km) north of Ardtornish.

Claidh, Loch *Western Isles* A sea loch on the southeast coast of Harris in the Outer Hebrides, Loch Claidh lies to the east of Loch Seaforth on the heavily indented coastline of the Park district.

Claigan *Highland* A small settlement in the northwest of the isle of Skye, Claigan lies to the east of Loch Dunvegan, 4 miles (6.5 km) north of Dunvegan.

Clan Armstrong Trust Museum, the *Dumfries and Galloway* Located at Castleholm in Langholm, Dumfries and Galloway, the Clan Armstrong Trust Museum holds extensive genealogical records as well as many artefacts and memorabilia associated with the Armstrong Clan.

Clan Cameron Museum *Highland* The Clan Cameron Museum is located at Achnacarry, near Spean Bridge in

Highland Council area. In addition to featuring Clan Cameron history, there are exhibitions on the 1745 Jacobite Rising and the Queen's Own Cameron Highlanders Regiment.

Clan Donnachaidh Museum *Perth and Kinross* Situated at Bruar Falls in northern Perth and Kinross, the Clan Donnachaidh Museum lies 4 miles (6.5 km) north of Pitlochry and a mile (1.5 km) south of Blair Atholl. A display tells the story of the Donnachaidh or Robertson Clan associated with this part of Atholl.

Clan Gunn Heritage Centre and Museum *Highland* The Clan Gunn Heritage Centre and Museum is located in Latheron in Highland Council area and is dedicated to the Clan Gunn, one of Scotland's oldest clans. Exhibits highlight the clan's Norse origins through to the present day. The centre is also home to the most comprehensive record of Clan Gunn genealogy in the world.

Clan Macpherson Museum *Highland* The Clan Macpherson Museum is housed in the Main Street of Newtonmore in Highland Council area and highlights the history of the Clan Macpherson and associated families. There are also relics associated with Prince Charles Edward Stewart (Bonnie Prince Charlie) on display.

Clanyard Bay *Dumfries and Galloway* A bay on the west coast of the Rhinns of Galloway, Clanyard Bay forms an inlet to the south of Port Logan.

Claonaig *Argyll and Bute* A small settlement on the Kintyre peninsula of Argyll and Bute, Claonaig lies 2 miles (3 km) west of Skipness and 8 miles (13 km) south of Tarbert. Claonaig Bay lies to the south. A summer ferry sails to Lochranza on Arran.

Clarebrand *Dumfries and Galloway* A hamlet in Dumfries and Galloway, Clarebrand is situated between the River Dee and the Urr Water, 2 miles (3 km) north of Castle Douglas.

Clarencefield *Dumfries and Galloway* A village in Ruthwell parish, Dumfries and Galloway, Clarencefield lies 9 miles (14 km) southeast of Dumfries.

Clarkston *East Renfrewshire* A commuter settlement on the southern outskirts of Glasgow, Clarkston lies 5 miles (8 km) south of Glasgow city centre and 6 miles (10 km) southeast of Paisley in East Renfrewshire. Located between Clarkston and nearby Newton Mearns is the National Trust for Scotland property of Greenbank House and Gardens.

Clashmore *Highland* A small settlement in eastern Sutherland, Highland Council area, Clashmore lies to the north of the Dornoch Firth, 4 miles (6.5 km) west of Dornoch. It once had a cattle market, and nearby is Skibo Castle.

Clashnessie *Highland* A crofting township in Assynt, Highland Council area, Clashnessie, near the Point of Stoer on the west coast of Sutherland, lies 7 miles (11 km) north of Lochinver. The ruins of a horizontal mill can be found on a burn near here.

Clathy *Perth and Kinross* A village in Perth and Kinross, Clathy lies to the north of the Roman road on the Gask ridge, 8 miles (13 km) southwest of Perth. Nearby are the houses of Clathypark, Clathybeg and Clathymore.

Clatt *Aberdeenshire* The Aberdeenshire village of Clatt, more fully known as Kirktown of Clatt, is situated on the Gadie Burn at the foot of the Coreen Hills, 2 miles (3 km) east of Rhynie. Designated a burgh of barony in 1501 by James IV, this tiny settlement had its own provost and baillies in addition to being the birthplace of the Bard of Corgarff, Wullie Gray. The village is a noted craft-making centre with a rural exhibition.

Clatteringshaws Loch *Dumfries and Galloway* One of a number of lochs associated with the Galloway Hydro-Electric Power Scheme, Dumfries and Galloway, Clatteringshaws Loch lies in the Galloway Forest Park, 5 miles (8 km) west of New Galloway. On the adjacent Moss Raploch stands Bruce's Stone, said to be the site where King Robert the Bruce rested after fighting the English here in 1307. The stone was gifted to the National Trust for Scotland by the Earl of Mar in 1932. There is a Forest Wildlife Centre, and across the main road from the loch is the entrance to the Raiders' Road, a 10-mile (16-km) forest road linking with the A762 near Mossdale. This route was popularised by S.R. Crockett in his novel of cattle rustling entitled *The Raiders* (1894).

Clatto Country Park *Dundee City* A country park to the northwest of Dundee city centre, Clatto Country Park is dominated by a 10-ha (24-acre) expanse of water, the former Clatto Reservoir, with surrounding picnic area, footpaths and a beach.

Clauchlands Point *North Ayrshire* A headland at the northern end of Lamlash Bay on the east coast of the island of Arran, Clauchlands Point lies to the north of Holy Island.

Clauchrie Burn *Dumfries and Galloway* Rising in the Aucherhairn Height of Dumfries and Galloway, the Clauchrie Burn flows south to join the River Nith a mile (1.5 km) south of Blackwood.

Clava Chambered Cairns *Highland* A late-Neolithic monument near Culloden, the Clava Cairns lie 6 miles (10 km) east of Inverness. The site comprises two chambered cairns and a ring cairn in a row, each surrounded by a circle of stones.

Clava Viaduct *Highland* Located some 6 miles (10 km) east of Inverness, the Clava Viaduct conveys the Perth–Inverness railway line 39 m (128 ft) above the valley of the River Nairn. Built between 1893 and 1898, this impressive viaduct is some 549 m (600 yd) in length and consists of 29 red sandstone arches. The viaduct was built by Sir John Fowler, designer of the Forth Railway Bridge, and Murdoch Paterson. Nearby are the prehistoric chambered cairns of Clava.

Claverhouse *Dundee City* A settlement of north Dundee City, Claverhouse lies on the Dighty Water, 3 miles (5 km) northeast of the centre of Dundee. A monument marks the site of a former mansion house that was the home of John Graham of Claverhouse, 1st Viscount Dundee (c.1649–89).

Claygate *Dumfries and Galloway* A village of Eskdale in Dumfries and Galloway, Claygate is situated 4 miles (6.5 km) southeast of Langholm.

Clayock *Highland* A locality in Caithness, Highland Council area, Clayock lies on the A882 between Thurso and Wick.

Claypotts Castle *Dundee City* The 'Tower Fortalice and Mannor Place' of Claypotts was built between 1569 and 1588 by John Strachan or Strathauchin, representing a cadet branch of Strachan of Angus and Thornton in the Mearns. It is situated close to the junction of the A92 and B978 between Dundee and Broughty Ferry. Erected in a Z-plan style, it has three storeys and circular wings. At the beginning of the 17th century the estate passed to the newly created Barony of Lindores and the Strachans moved north to Balhousie after selling Claypotts to Sir William Graham of Ballunie in 1601. The Claypotts Estate was eventually sold to the Grahams of Claverhouse, reverting to the Crown in 1689 when Claverhouse lands were declared forfeit after the Battle of Killiecrankie. The property was granted by royal charter in 1694 to James, 2nd Marquess of Douglas. Claypotts Castle was placed under the guardianship of the Commissioners of Works in 1926. Outside is a demonstration garden.

Cleadale *Highland* A small settlement on the island of Eigg, Highland Council area, Cleadale lies on the northwest side of the island.

Clearburn Loch *Scottish Borders* A small loch in the Ettrick district of Scottish Borders, Clearburn Loch lies to the east of the Ettrick Water on the old border between Selkirk and Roxburgh.

Cleaven Dyke *Perth and Kinross* To the north of the River Tay, just northwest of the village of Meikleour, the great bank and flanking ditches of the Cleaven Dyke run for a mile (1.5 km) across the landscape of Perth and Kinross. Once thought to have been a Roman feature associated with the nearby fort at Inchtuthill, this site is now identified as a Neolithic monumental construction dating from the late 5th to the mid-4th millennium BC.

Cleekhimin *North Lanarkshire* A small, scattered community in North Lanarkshire, Cleekhimin lies between Motherwell and Carfin.

Cleish *Perth and Kinross* An attractive hamlet in a parish of the same name in Perth and Kinross, Cleish lies 2 miles (3 km) west of the M90 and 3 miles (5 km) southwest of Kinross. Its fuller name, Kirkton of Cleish, describes its location adjacent to the parish church that stands on raised ground. Granted by the Earl of Fife to the Church of the Holy Trinity of Dunfermline in the early 13th century, Cleish Kirk was redesigned in 1775 by the architect John Adam of nearby Blairadam. After a fire in 1832 it was totally rebuilt, and in 1897 a tower was added to celebrate the diamond jubilee of Queen Victoria. There are memorials to the Adams of Blairadam, a fragment of a 9th-century cross slab, an almshouse, sanctuary crosses and the graves of Ebenezer Michie (d.1813), a friend of the poet Robert Burns, and the parish minister, the Revd W. Wallace Duncan, whose wife, Mary Lundie Duncan, penned the Cleish Hymn – 'Jesus, tender shepherd, hear me'. Visited by Sir Walter Scott and other members of the Blairadam Club, the church is the 'Kirk of Cleish Bothan' featured in the introduction to Scott's novel *The Abbot* (1820). Other buildings of interest in and around the settlement, which is a designated conservation area, include 16th-century Cleish Castle, 18th-century Cleish House and Cleish Public School (1835).

Cleish Hills *Perth and Kinross/Fife* A range of hills on the border between Perth and Kinross and Fife Council areas, the Cleish Hills rise to a height of 378 m (1240 ft) at Dumglow. The reservoirs of Loch Glow and the Black Loch lie within the range, and the remains of an ancient vitrified hillfort can be found on the summit of Dummiefarline which overlooks the village of Cleish. Fine sandstone quarried in the past for building is capped by basalt here.

Cleland *North Lanarkshire* A village of North Lanarkshire, Cleland lies 3 miles (5 km) east of Motherwell. The village is joined to the north by the settlement of Parkside, while to the east it is joined to Bellside. The South Calder Water flows to the south of Cleland.

Cleongart *Argyll and Bute* A scattered settlement on the west coast of the Kintyre peninsula, Argyll and Bute, Cleongart lies a mile (1.5 km) northeast of Bellochantuy.

Clephanton *Highland* A settlement to the east of Inverness in Highland Council area, Clephanton lies to the west of the River Nairn, 7 miles (11 km) southwest of Nairn.

Clerkhill Burn *Dumfries and Galloway* A stream in Eskdale, Dumfries and Galloway, Clerkhill Burn is formed by the meeting of the Windsheil Grain and the Harewood Burn. It skirts the south side of Clerk Hill before joining the White Esk opposite Eskdalemuir.

Clermiston Tower *City of Edinburgh* Located close to the summit of Corstorphine Hill in west Edinburgh, Clermiston Tower (also known as Scott Tower or Corstorphine Hill Tower) was built in 1871 by William Macfie of Dreghorn to commemorate the centenary of the birth of the novelist Sir Walter Scott (1771–1832). The tower is maintained by the city council. It is opened on request and the 101 steps up to the cap-house and viewing gallery are worth the climb for the spectacular views across Edinburgh, north to the Firth of Forth and south to the Pentland Hills.

Cleughbrae *Dumfries and Galloway* A locality in Nithsdale, Dumfries and Galloway, Cleughbrae lies on the A75 between Mouswald and Collin, 6 miles (10 km) southeast of Dumfries.

Clickimin Loch *Shetland* A small loch on the Shetland Mainland, Clickimin Loch is situated immediately west of Lerwick. On a rocky islet is the 20-m/32-ft-diameter Clickimin Broch, a Pictish fortification occupied from c.700 BC to the 5th or 6th centuries AD. Originally a Bronze Age farmstead, the site developed into an Iron Age ring fort, then a broch and later into a wheelhouse settlement. During the winter months the loch is visited by large numbers of wildfowl, and close by are a campsite and leisure complex.

Cliff *Western Isles* A small settlement in the west of Lewis in the Outer Hebrides, Cliff (Gael: *Cliobh*) lies a mile (1.5 km) southwest of Valtos.

Clifton *Stirling* A village on the northwest border of Stirling Council area, Clifton lies immediately north of Tyndrum at the head of Glen Lochy and at the junction of the A82 and A85. The village developed in the 1830s in association with local lead mines on the Breadalbane Estate.

Clifton Park *Scottish Borders* An estate on the Bowmont Water in Scottish Borders, Clifton Park lies just northwest of Morebattle.

Climpy *South Lanarkshire* The settlement of Climpy is located a mile (1.5 km) northwest of Forth in South Lanarkshire.

Cliobh The Gaelic name for Cliff in the Western Isles.

Clisham *Western Isles* Rising to 799 m (2622 ft) in North Harris, Clisham is the highest hill in the Outer Hebrides.

Clivocast *Shetland* A settlement on the south coast of the island of Unst, Clivocast looks out over Skuda Sound to the island of Uyea, to the east of the village of Uyeasound.

Clo Mòr Cliffs *Highland* Representing the highest sea cliffs on the British mainland, the Clo Mòr cliffs rise to 281 m (920 ft) on the north coast of Scotland, 4 miles (6.5 km) east of Cape Wrath and 6 miles (10 km) northwest of Durness. The cliffs provide sanctuary for a significant colony of breeding sea birds.

Cloch Lighthouse *Inverclyde* The Cloch Lighthouse is located on Cloch Point, Inverclyde, 3 miles (5 km) southwest of Gourock, on the Firth of Clyde's eastern coast directly opposite Dunoon. Built in 1797, it was designed by Thomas Smith.

Clola *Aberdeenshire* A settlement in Old Deer parish, Aberdeenshire, Clola lies on the A952, 3 miles (5 km) south of Mintlaw.

Closeburn *Dumfries and Galloway* A village of Nithsdale in Dumfries and Galloway, Closeburn lies to the east of the River Nith, 11 miles (18 km) northwest of Dumfries. Closeburn Castle, a former stronghold of the Kirkpatricks, dates from c.1380–1420, with an adjoining mansion of a later period.

Clousta *Shetland* A small and scattered hamlet in the Aithsting district on the west coast of the Shetland Mainland, Clousta lies at the head of the Voe of Clousta 15 miles (24 km) northwest of Lerwick.

Clova *Angus* Also known as Milton of Clova, this Angus settlement stands on the left bank of the South Esk River in Glen Clova, 15 miles (24 km) north of Kirriemuir.

Clova *Aberdeenshire* A settlement of Aberdeenshire, Clova lies 6 miles (10 km) southwest of the village of Rhynie and to the east of Clova Hill.

Clova, Glen *Aberdeenshire/Angus* A glen in the southern Grampians, Glen Clova occupies the valley of the River South Esk which rises on the slopes of Broad Cairn near the border with Aberdeenshire and flows southeastwards into the valley of Strathmore below the Braes of Angus. Cortachy Castle once guarded the entrance to the glen, and near its head is the hamlet of Clova, close to which are the ruins of another castle. Glen Clova once formed a main route from Angus over the Grampians to Aberdeenshire.

Clovenfords *Scottish Borders* A hamlet in Scottish Borders, Clovenfords lies on the Caddon Water, 3 miles (5 km) west of Galashiels. The novelist Sir Walter Scott (1771–1832) often visited Clovenfords, and William and Dorothy Wordsworth stayed at the inn in September 1803. A railway station operated between 1866 and 1962.

Clovullin *Highland* A village of Ardgour in Lochaber, Highland Council area, Clovullin lies on the west side of Loch Linnhe near the Corran Narrows.

Cloy, Glen *North Ayrshire* Carrying the waters of the Gleann Dubh, Glen Cloy runs in a northwesterly direction to pass to the west of the settlement of Brodick, Arran, North Ayrshire.

Cluanie, Loch *Highland* A reservoir occupying the greater part of Glen Cluanie in the west Highlands, Loch Cluanie lies to the north of Glen Loyne. A dam at its eastern end provides a head of water as part of the Garry-Moriston Hydro-Electric Scheme. The River Moriston issues from the loch and the A87 runs along its northern shore.

Cluanie Inn *Highland* Formerly known as the Rhiabuie Inn, the Cluanie Inn in western Highland Council area lies in upper Glen Moriston at the west end of Loch Cluanie. Here the old 18th-century military road linking Fort Augustus with Bernera was joined by a road over the hills to Glen Garry built by Thomas Telford in the early 19th century. The expansion of Loch Loyne and Loch Cluanie by the building of hydro-electric dams in the 1950s and 1960s caused the Telford road to be diverted eastwards.

Clubbiedean Reservoir *City of Edinburgh* A reservoir lying 2 miles (3 km) east of Balerno and 6 miles (10 km) southwest of Edinburgh city centre, Clubbiedean Reservoir is one of a network of reservoirs that supplies the city with water. To the east of the reservoir lie Bonaly Country Park and Bonaly Reservoir.

Cluden Water *Dumfries and Galloway* A river in Dumfries and Galloway, the Cluden Water is formed by the meeting of the Cairn Water and the Old Water near Drumpark. It flows southeast for 6 miles (10 km) to join the River Nith on the northern outskirts of Dumfries.

Clugston Loch *Dumfries and Galloway* A small loch in Dumfries and Galloway, Clugston Loch lies to the west of the River Bladnoch, 2 miles (3 km) southeast of Kirkcowan.

Clunas *Highland* A locality to the east of Inverness in Highland Council area, Clunas lies 3 miles (5 km) southeast of Cawdor. Nearby is the Clunas Reservoir.

Clune *Highland* A settlement in Strath Dearn, Highland Council area, Clune lies on the River Findhorn, 3 miles (5 km) southwest of Tomatin.

Clunes *Highland* A locality in Lochaber, southern Highland Council area, Clunes lies on the west side of Loch Lochy, 7 miles (11 km) north of Spean Bridge.

Clunes Lodge *Perth and Kinross* A neo-Tudor-style shooting lodge in Glen Garry, Perth and Kinross, Clunes Lodge lies close to the A9 from Perth to Inverness, a mile (1.5 km) northwest of Calvine. It was built in 1866.

Clunie *Perth and Kinross* A settlement on the west shore of the Loch of Clunie, eastern Perth and Kinross, Clunie lies in the parish of Stormont, 4 miles (6.5 km) west of Blairgowrie. On a knoll by the village are traces of a building said to have been used as a base for hunting in the nearby royal forest of Clunie. On an artificial island in the loch are the ruins of Clunie Castle, a tower house of the bishops of Dunkeld built on the site of an Iron Age crannog or lake dwelling. Robert Crichton, the last pre-Reformation bishop, handed the property to his near relative Robert Crichton of Eliock whose son James, better known as the Admirable Crichton (1560–c.1585), spent his childhood there. The parish church, rebuilt in 1840, has within its churchyard a mausoleum with a 12th- or early 13th-century Romanesque doorway that probably belonged to one of the earlier churches on that site.

Clunie, Loch of *Perth and Kinross* A small secluded loch in eastern Perth and Kinross, Loch of Clunie lies in the valley of the Lunan Burn, 3 miles (5 km) west of Blairgowrie. The ruins of Clunie Castle, a former tower house of the bishops of Dunkeld, occupies a small island in the loch, and the hamlet of Clunie lies on its southwest shore.

Clunie Water *Aberdeenshire* A river in the Grampians, the Water of Clunie rises in headstreams that flow from the northern slopes of The Cairnwell. It flows northwards through Glen Cluny to meet the River Dee at Braemar. It joins with the Baddoch Burn and the Callater Burn.

Cluny *Fife* A former mining village in Auchterderran parish, Fife, Cluny is situated to the south of the River Ore at the junction of the A910 from Kirkcaldy to Lochgelly with the B922 to Kinglassie.

Cluny *City of Edinburgh* A small residential area of southern Edinburgh, Cluny lies to the south of Morningside and to the west of Blackford Hill, on what was part of the Braid Estate. At its centre is Morningside (or Cluny) Parish Church, which came to public attention as the location for the funeral of Labour Party leader John Smith (1938-94), who lived nearby.

Clunybridge *Fife* A small settlement on the River Ore, Fife, Clunybridge lies on the B922 between the villages of Cluny and Kinglassie.

Cluny Castle *Aberdeenshire* Situated in Cluny parish, Aberdeenshire, the grey granite Cluny Castle lies just over a mile (1.5 km) to the south of Monymusk. A stronghold of the Gordon family built in the 15th century, Cluny was rebuilt in the 19th century in its present style.

Cluny House *Perth and Kinross* A mansion house dating from the 1820s in Strathtay, Perth and Kinross, Cluny House lies to the north of the River Tay, 2 miles (3 km) northeast of Aberfeldy. It has a fine 2.4-ha (6-acre) Himalayan woodland garden laid out in 1950 and managed on principles of natural regeneration without the use of weedkillers.

Clyde, Firth of The River Clyde widens at its mouth to form an estuary named the Firth of Clyde. It extends westwards from Dumbarton to Gourock and then south to the island of Ailsa Craig off the South Ayrshire coast. The Cowal peninsula lies to the west of the Firth of Clyde, which surrounds the islands of Great Cumbrae and Little Cumbrae between Bute and the mainland.

Clyde, River A river opening out into a wide firth in west-central Scotland, the Clyde rises at an altitude of 472 m (1550 ft) in the Lowther Hills in South Lanarkshire. It flows north then turns west near Carstairs Junction, passing through the former industrial village of New Lanark where the Falls of Clyde form a spectacular view much painted by artists. Flowing northwestwards through Clydesdale, the river continues on through the heart of Glasgow and past Clydebank, where over 35,000 ships were built in the 19th and 20th centuries. After it is crossed by the Erskine Bridge, the Clyde widens to form the Firth of Clyde, having flowed a distance of 106 miles (171 km).

Clyde Auditorium, the *Glasgow City* Built by Sir Norman Foster in the 1990s and one of the principal concert venues in the country, this £30-million building dominates the north bank of the River Clyde to the west of the Kingston Bridge and Glasgow city centre. An extension to the Scottish Exhibition and Conference Centre complex, it has gained the nickname of 'the Armadillo' owing to its resemblance to the animal of the same name. Silver in colour, it compliments the Glasgow Science Centre located on the south bank of the river. The Finnieston Crane lies directly to the east.

Clyde Muirshiel Regional Park Covering 275 sq. km (106 sq. miles) of countryside in Inverclyde, Renfrewshire and North Ayrshire, the Clyde Muirshiel Regional Park extends from Greenock southwards along the Clyde coast to West Kilbride and inland to Lochwinnoch. The park centre is located at Barnbrock, 4 miles (6.5 km) north of Lochwinnoch, and there are other centres at Castle Semple, Muirshiel and Cornalees. Formally designated in 1990, the park protects areas of mixed woodland, wetland, moorland, lochs and coastline and offers outdoor adventure activity courses such as canoeing, sailing, trail-biking and hill-walking. The RSPB Lochwinnoch Nature Reserve lies within the park, and a cycle route from Glasgow to Irvine passes Castle Semple.

Clyde Walkway, the *Glasgow City/Lanarkshire* A long-distance walkway linking the centre of Glasgow to New Lanark in South Lanarkshire, the Clyde Walkway extends a distance of 40 miles (64 km) through the scenic Clyde Valley.

Clydebank *West Dunbartonshire* An industrial town on the River Clyde to the west of Glasgow, Clydebank developed from a small village to a major shipbuilding centre during the 19th century. It was originally known as Barns o' Clyde, but its name was changed in 1882 to Clydebank, the name of the shipyard established by J. and G. Thomson in 1872. Famous ships built by Thomson's and John Brown & Co. included the *Lusitania* (1906), *Queen Mary* (1934), *Queen Elizabeth* (1938) and the *Queen Elizabeth II* or *QE2* (1967). Other industries associated with the early development of the town were engineering, distilling and the manufacture of chemicals. The US-owned Singer sewing-machine factory, opened in 1884, was the largest factory in Europe in the 1950s, when it employed 17,000 workers. It closed in 1979. In March 1941 two air raids resulted in the destruction of more than one-third of the town's houses, and 96 per cent of the population were evacuated for a time. Clydebank now has an industrial park, a College of Further Education and a Business Creation Centre.

Clydesdale *South Lanarkshire* Clydesdale, which gives its name to a breed of working horse, is the name given to the valley that carries the middle section of the River Clyde in South Lanarkshire. It stretches from just south of Carstairs Junction northwards to Motherwell, and although broad at either end of the valley, it narrows at Hyndford Bridge and Lanark, where there are many waterfalls, including Bonnington Linn and Corra Linn. The World Heritage settlement of New Lanark is located in Clydesdale.

Clynder *Argyll and Bute* A linear villa settlement of the Rosneath peninsula in southern Argyll and Bute, Clynder lies immediately to the northwest of Rosneath, facing onto the Gare Loch, 1.25 miles (2 km) west of Rhu. Originally known as Rosebank, it was once noted for boatbuilding but now serves as a commuter village.

Clyne *Highland* A kirkton in eastern Sutherland, Highland Council area, Clyne or Clynekirkton lies to the west of Brora. The roofless former parish church of Clyne dates from 1775 and was last used in 1921, after which Brora became the parish centre of worship.

Clynelish *Highland* A locality in Sutherland, Highland Council area, Clynelish lies a mile (1.5 km) northwest of Brora. A model farm complex with farmhouse, steading, threshing mill, dairy, laundry and cottages, it was designed in 1865 by William Fowler, and a distillery erected here by the Marquess of Stafford and the Countess of Sutherland dates from 1819. The distillery was expanded in 1896 by the Leith whisky blenders

Ainslie and Co., and in 1967 a new distillery was built alongside the old one.

Clyth *Highland* A scattered settlement in eastern Caithness, Clyth lies between the sea and the moorland interior to the east of Lybster, 8 miles (13 km) southwest of Wick. Upper Clyth, West Clyth, East Clyth, the Hill of Clyth, Clyth Mains and Clyth Shore are all associated settlements lying to the west of Clyth Ness. Clythness Lighthouse was built by D. A. Stevenson in 1916, and nearby are the remains of a 19th-century fish store and curing house.

Cnip The Gaelic name for Kneep in the Western Isles.

Cnoc Amhlaigh *Western Isles* One of several contiguous crofting townships lying at the eastern end of the Eye peninsula on the east coast of Lewis in the Outer Hebrides, Cnoc Amhlaigh (literally, Knock MacAulay) is located immediately to the east of Fleisirin, 1.25 miles (2 km) southwest of Tiumpan Head.

Cnoc Dearg An alternative name for Chno Dearg in Highland.

Cnoc Moy *Argyll and Bute* A hill at the southwest end of the Kintyre peninsula, Argyll and Bute, Cnoc Moy is 6 miles (10 km) northwest of Southend and 5 miles (8 km) north of the headland of the Mull of Kintyre. Rising to a height of 446 m (1463 ft), it overlooks the settlement of Largybaan to the south.

Coalburn *South Lanarkshire* A village of South Lanarkshire, Coalburn lies on the Coal Burn, a tributary of the Douglas Water, 3 miles (5 km) south of Lesmahagow. It developed from the 1850s as a railway settlement associated with local coal mines. With the closure of the last colliery in 1965 and the railway in 1971, the village population declined from a peak of nearly 2,300. An opencast mine was opened nearby in 1987.

Coalsnaughton *Clackmannanshire* A former mining village in Clackmannanshire, situated a mile (1.5 km) to the south of Tillicoultry, which it overlooks.

Coaltown of Balgonie *Fife* A late 18th-century mining and weaving village in south-central Fife, Coaltown of Balgonie is situated on a ridge between the Ore and Leven rivers to the east of Glenrothes and south of Markinch. The village has a primary school and a Miners' Institute. To the northeast is Balgonie Castle.

Coaltown of Burnturk *Fife* A hamlet in Kingskettle parish, central Fife, Coaltown of Burnturk lies in rolling hills 2 miles (3 km) east of the village of Kingskettle. Limestone is quarried nearby.

Coaltown of Wemyss *Fife* A former mining village to the north of the coastal town of West Wemyss in Fife, Coaltown of Wemyss lies 3 miles (5 km) northeast of Kirkcaldy. Originally divided into Easter and Wester settlements, the villages grew together during the 1860s when the Wemyss Coal Company created a 'model' mining village for workers at the nearby Bell pit. The semi-detached miners' cottages now form part of a conservation area designated in 1980. The village has a primary school.

Coatbridge *North Lanarkshire* An industrial town in North Lanarkshire, Coatbridge lies 9 miles (14 km) east of Glasgow and 3 miles (5 km) west of Airdrie in the parish of Old Monkland. It developed in the 19th century in association with the exploitation of central Scotland's largest deposits of coal and iron, and at one time boasted 'more blast furnaces than any other town in Scotland'. From humble origins by a bridge crossing the North Calder Water on the Colts Estate, it developed into the ninth-largest town in Scotland. The construction of the Monkland Canal between Calderbank and Glasgow, opened in 1788, preceded the discovery of ironstone by David Mushet and William Dixon c.1800 and the invention of the blast furnace by James Neilson in 1828. In 1826 a wagonway crossed the Airdrie to Glasgow road by a bridge that was known as Coatbridge. The settlement took this name and within 20 years no fewer than 60 furnaces were in operation. Other industries associated with the early industrial development of Coatbridge included locomotive repair, engineering and the manufacture of bricks. In 1988 the remains of Summerlee Ironworks were opened as the Summerlee Heritage Centre, and in 1991 an ice and water attraction known as The Time Capsule was opened. Notable buildings in Coatbridge include Gartsherrie Church (1839), Cartysherrie Academy (1845), the Carnegie Library (1905), St Patrick's Church (1896), the remains of the fire-damaged Municipal Buildings (1894) and Coats Parish Church (1874).

Coatdyke *North Lanarkshire* A suburb of Airdrie in North Lanarkshire, Coatdyke is located a mile (1.5 km) west of the town centre.

Coats Observatory *Renfrewshire* The Coats Observatory is located in the Oakshaw area of Paisley, Renfrewshire. Designed and built by John Honeyman in 1883 and funded by the wealthy thread-making Coats family, the Victorian observatory houses astronomical and meteorological data. It has a satellite picture receiver and a public telescope.

Cobairdy *Aberdeenshire* A settlement of Strathbogie in Aberdeenshire, Cobairdy comprises an estate with a mansion house and farms, including a home farm and the farm of Boghead of Cobairdy, situated in Forgue parish to the west of the A97, 4 miles (6.5 km) northeast of Huntly.

Cobbinshaw Reservoir *West Lothian* A reservoir in West Lothian, Cobbinshaw lies to the west of the Pentland Hills. It receives the Cobbinshaw Burn that rises in Cobbinshaw Moss.

Cobbler, the An alternative name for Ben Arthur in Argyll and Bute.

Cobleland *Stirling* A locality on the eastern edge of Loch Ard Forest, Stirling Council area, Cobleland lies on the upper reaches of the River Forth, a mile (1.5 km) to the north of Gartmore and just over a mile (1.5 km) to the south of Aberfoyle.

Cochill, Glen *Perth and Kinross* Situated between Strathbraan and Strathtay in Perth and Kinross, Glen Cochill is occupied by the Cochill Burn which rises in Loch na Craige and Loch Hoil and flows southwards to join the River Braan a mile (1.5 km) northeast of Amulree. A segment of General Wade's 18th-century military road passes through the glen.

Cock Bridge *Aberdeenshire* A locality in the uplands of Aberdeenshire between the valleys of the rivers Dee and Spey, Cock Bridge is situated on the upper reaches of the River Don, on the road from Ballater to Grantown-on-Spey. A hill known as The Cock and 16th-century Corgarff Castle lie immediately south.

Cockburnspath *Scottish Borders* A village of Berwickshire in Scottish Borders, Cockburnspath lies close to the North Sea coast, 7 miles (11 km) southeast of Dunbar, and is the eastern finishing point of the long-distance Southern Upland Way.

Cockenzie *East Lothian* A settlement of East Lothian on the south side of the Firth of Forth, Cockenzie lies between Prestonpans and Longniddry and a mile (1.5 km) west of Port Seton, with which it now forms a burgh. The natural harbour of Cockenzie, which served the ancient Seatoun, was improved in 1830 as a coal and fishing port. A wagonway built in 1722 to carry coal from Tranent to Cockenzie became the first railway to be used in warfare during the Jacobite Rebellion of 1745. Fishing and mining continue in the locality, whose skyline is dominated by the 1200 megawatt coal-fired Cockenzie Power Station which opened in 1967. Cockenzie House, built in the late 17th century, was the home of the Cadell family, one of whom, Francis Cadell (1822–79), navigated the Murray River in Australia in 1852.

Cockle Strand *Western Isles* The plane from Glasgow to Barra in the Outer Hebrides makes a dramatic landing at a unique airfield, the Cockle Strand, or Tràigh Mhòr. A wide sweeping beach at the north end of the island of Barra, the Cockle Strand is the world's only tidal beach airport with scheduled airline services. In times of famine the cockles here were removed by the Barra folk in cart-loads. Located 5 miles (8 km) north-northeast of Castlebay, Barra Airport was opened in 1936. It handles between 8000 and 9000 passengers per year.

Cock of Arran *North Ayrshire* The Cock of Arran is the name given to a headland located at the northern end of the island of Arran, North Ayrshire.

Coe, Glen *Highland* One of the most famous glens in the Scottish Highlands, Glen Coe forms a narrow defile 10 miles (16 km) long between Loch Leven and Rannoch Moor. The main road from Glasgow to Fort William passes through wild scenery that provides some of the finest hill walking and climbing in Scotland. The hills surrounding Glen Coe are internationally important as a geological site that demonstrates the phenomenon of a volcano collapsing in on itself. The glen is also an important botanical site, noted especially for its native woodland and arctic alpine flora. In the 1930s 5180 ha (12,800 acres) of the glen were purchased by the National Trust for Scotland with the help of an appeal launched by Percy Unna, President of the Scottish Mountaineering Club, and in 1976 a visitor centre was opened at Clachaig. An Torr Woodland and Inverigan campsite were purchased by the Trust in the 1990s and a native woodland restoration scheme initiated. In 2002 the National Trust opened a new visitor centre near the campsite. It was near Inverigan that the massacre of the Macdonalds by the Campbells took place in 1692.

Coeffin Castle *Argyll and Bute* Located on the island of Lismore in Argyll and Bute, the ruined remains of Coeffin Castle are situated on the island's northwest coast overlooking Loch Linnhe. Built in the 13th century, possibly by the MacDougalls of Lorn, the castle stood on the site of a Viking fortress.

Coigach *Highland* A district of Wester Ross in Highland Council area, Coigach forms a large peninsula to the north of Loch Broom that terminates in the Rubha Coigeach headland. In the southeast Ben Mòr Coigach rises to 743 m (2438 ft). Achiltibuie is the chief settlement.

Coignafearn Forest *Highland* A deer forest in the Monadhliath Mountains, Highland Council area, Coignafearn Forest lies at the head of Strath Dearn. The area is watered by the headstreams of the River Findhorn, and there is a lodge at Coignafearn to the south of Tomatin.

Coig Peighinnean The Gaelic name for Fivepenny in the Western Isles.

Coilacriech *Aberdeenshire* A roadside settlement by the River Dee in Aberdeenshire, Coilacriech lies on the A93, 3 miles (5 km) west of Ballater in Royal Deeside.

Coilantogle *Stirling* A locality in Stirling Council area, Coilantogle lies at the east end of Loch Venachar, 2 miles (3 km) southwest of Callander. A former ford on the River Teith, it was mentioned by Sir Walter Scott in *The Lady of the Lake* (1810) as 'Clan Alpine's outmost guard'.

Coiliochbhar Hill An alternative name for Callievar Hill in Aberdeenshire.

Coillore *Highland* A settlement on the island of Skye, Highland Council area, Coillore lies to the southeast of Loch Beag, a mile (1.5 km) southeast of Bracadale.

Coiltry *Highland* A locality in the Great Glen, southern Highland Council area, Coiltry lies 3 miles (5 km) southwest of Fort Augustus.

Col The Gaelic name for Coll in the Western Isles.

Colaboll *Highland* A settlement in Sutherland, Highland Council area, Colaboll lies on the northeastern shore of Loch Shin, 3 miles (5 km) northwest of Lairg.

Coladoir River *Argyll And Bute* A river on the island of Mull in the Inner Hebrides, the Coladoir River rises in Glen More and flows west to enter the head of Loch Scridain.

Colbost *Highland* A scattered settlement in the northwest of the isle of Skye, Colbost lies 2 miles (3 km) northwest of Dunvegan.

Coldbackie *Highland* A locality on the north coast of Sutherland, Highland Council area, Coldbackie lies at the head of Tongue Bay, 2 miles (3 km) north of Tongue. The small bay is dominated by a sheer conglomerate red sandstone cliff. Skullomie Harbour nearby is said to have been built for the use of the people of Tongue.

Coldingham *Scottish Borders* A village of Berwickshire in Scottish Borders, Coldingham lies close to the North Sea coast, 3 miles (5 km) northwest of Eyemouth. There are the remains of a Benedictine priory founded in 1098 by King Edgar and linked to the canons regular of Durham. Coldingham was made a burgh of barony in 1638 and survived as a stopping-off place on the main coastal road. Coldingham Moor lies to the northwest, and to the east on Coldingham Bay is the village of St Abbs, formerly known as Coldingham Shore.

Coldingham Bay *Scottish Borders* An inlet of the North Sea on the coast of Scottish Borders, Coldingham Bay lies at the mouth of the Buskin Burn to the east of Coldingham.

Coldstream *Scottish Borders* A settlement of Berwickshire in Scottish Borders, Coldstream lies at an important crossing on the River Tweed, 14 miles (22 km) southwest of Berwick-upon-Tweed. A Cistercian priory was founded here in the 12th century by Earl Gospatric, and its inn was often used by royalty before crossing the Tweed at low water, prior to the building of a bridge. Both the English and Scots forded here several times during the centuries of conflict between the two nations, led by Edward I (1296), Robert the Bruce, James IV (1513),

Montrose (1640), and General Monk (1660). Monk established the headquarters of his regiment here in 1659, although it was raised at Berwick-upon-Tweed. On 1 January 1660 the force set out for London on its famous march, resulting in the restoration of Charles II. Only in 1670, after the death of Monk, was the regiment named after the starting point of the march. The Coldstream Museum highlights the history of the regiment and is located on the site of the original headquarters. In 1611 the Home family acquired the Hirsel on the outskirts of the town which received a charter as a burgh of barony in 1621. Burgh status was lost in 1975. In addition to tourism, local industries include paper making and agricultural engineering. Coldstream also has a cottage hospital and tourist facilities, including a nine-hole golf course that lies within the adjacent Hirsel Country Park.

Coldwakning Burn *South Lanarkshire* Rising to the northwest of the settlement of Stobieside in South Lanarkshire, the Colwakning Burn flows east through the village of Coldwakning before heading south then north. It joins the Glengavel Water at a point to the north of Gilmourton.

Colenden *Perth and Kinross* A settlement in Perth and Kinross, Colenden is situated on the east side of the River Tay, a mile (1.5 km) east of Luncarty and 3 miles (5 km) north of Perth.

Colfin *Dumfries and Galloway* A settlement on the Rhnins of Galloway, Colfin lies 4 miles (6.5 km) east of Portpatrick.

Colgrain *Argyll and Bute* A small, scattered community of Argyll and Bute, Colgrain lies 2 miles (3 km) northwest of Cardross and 2 miles (3 km) southeast of Helensburgh. It looks out over the Firth of Clyde.

Colgrave Sound *Shetland* A channel to the east of the Shetland island of Yell, the Colgrave Sound separates that island from Fetlar. The island of Hascosay lies in the channel, which has a maximum width of 4 miles (6.5 km).

Colinsburgh *Fife* A planned village in the East Neuk of Fife, Colinsburgh lies 2 miles (3 km) northwest of Elie. It was built in 1705 for disbanded soldiers by Colin, 3rd Earl of Balcarres (1652–1722). The village has a Town Hall dating from 1895 and the Galloway Library built in 1903. To the north lies Balcarres House, an L-plan tower house built in 1595 by the Lindsay family and later extended in the 19th century by the architects William Burn and David Bryce.

Colinton *City of Edinburgh* Originally a ford and mill village lying in a steep-sided valley cut by the Water of Leith, some 4 miles (6.5 km) southwest of central Edinburgh, Colinton has grown into a sizeable and desirable residential suburb of the city. The mills produced textiles, snuff and paper. The Bank of Scotland's first banknotes were said to have been printed on paper manufactured in Colinton. Today, the road crosses the river high above the old village, with Spylaw Street descending to the old village, the historic Colinton Parish Church and Colinton Dell. In 1874 the Caledonian Railway built a spur from Slateford to Balerno, with a station at Colinton. Passenger services ceased in 1943 and the line finally closed when goods trains stopped in the 1960s. Colinton Castle was destroyed by Oliver Cromwell in 1650 but repaired, only to be partially demolished on the instructions of painter Alexander Nasmyth (1758–1801) to create a picturesque ruin. Redford Barracks lie on Colinton Road, just to the east of the old village. Philanthropist James Gillespie (1726–97) had his home and business in the village. The author Robert Louis Stevenson (1850–94) is known to have been a regular visitor to the village, his maternal grandfather having been the parish minister. The architect Sir Robert Rowand Anderson (1834–1921) also lived here and worked on various buildings in the village. There are cottage-style villas on Colinton Road by another noted architect, Sir Robert Lorimer (1864–1929). Today, Colinton is a designated conservation area.

Colinton Dell *City of Edinburgh* Colinton Dell is a steep-sided gorge and wildlife refuge on the Water of Leith, just north of the old village of Colinton. It extends from Colinton Parish Church towards Slateford along the Water of Leith Walkway and has an area of 10 ha (24 acres). The Dell includes mature and ancient mixed woodland, and the protection afforded by the high banks and thick undergrowth makes it a natural habitat for wildlife, including numerous bird species and amphibians, voles, weasels, stoats and occasionally roe deer. Today, walkways and a cycle path take visitors to the ruined Redhall Mill and past Kate's Mill, where paper for the Bank of Scotland's first banknotes is said to have been made.

Colinton Parish Church *City of Edinburgh* Lying close to the Water of Leith in the old village of Colinton is St Cuthbert's Parish Church. Founded as the Church of Halis (Hailes) around 1095 by Ethelred, third son of Malcolm Canmore and Queen Margaret, but not dedicated until 1248, the church was possibly destroyed during the Earl of Hertford's invasion (1544) and certainly replaced around 1650, most likely having been damaged by the army of Oliver Cromwell. It was rebuilt again in 1771 and altered in 1837 by architect David Bryce (1803–76), who built the tower. The church was rebuilt for the final time in 1908, by Sydney Mitchell, and the interior redesigned in a neo-Byzantine style. New halls, function rooms and offices were built alongside the church in 1998. Dr Lewis Balfour, maternal grandfather of author Robert Louis Stevenson (1850–94), was minister here between 1823 and 1860, and is buried in the kirkyard, which contains several 17th- and 18th-century memorials, including the mausoleum of philanthropist James Gillespie (1726–97). The earliest memorial has been placed in the church and dates from 1593.

Colintraive *Argyll and Bute* A village on the Cowal peninsula of Argyll and Bute, Colintraive lies on the eastern side of the Kyles of Bute opposite the settlement of Rhubodach on the island of Bute, to which it is linked by a ferry.

Coll *Argyll and Bute* An island of the Inner Hebrides, Coll lies to the northwest of Mull and northeast of Tiree. Its principal settlement and ferry port is Arinagour, which lies 19 miles (31 km) west of Tobermory. The island, which rises to 104 m (341 ft) at Ben Hogh, is just over 12 miles (19 km) long and between 1 and 3 miles (1.5 and 5 km) wide. It has an area of 7723 ha (19,075 acres) and mostly comprises metamorphic schist covered with grass and heather. The island was unable to support a population of 1440 in 1841, and the Maclean chieftain of Coll encouraged half the population to emigrate to Australia and Canada before selling the island to John

Lorne Stewart in 1856. Having at first promoted the clearance of the island, the Stewarts later repopulated the island with Ayrshire dairy farmers who marketed a well-known variety of cheese. The 15th-century Breachacha Castle was restored by the Project Trust, a youth training scheme. Coll has an airstrip and is linked by ferry to Tiree, Oban and Tobermory. Its population in 2001 was 164.

Coll *Western Isles* A crofting township in the Outer Hebrides, Coll (Gael: *Col*) lies 5.5 miles (9 km) northeast of Stornoway on the east side of Lewis. Upper Coll (Gael: *Col Uarach*) lies to the southwest, separated by two streams, the River Coll (Gael: *Abhainn Chuill*) and Gil Thaisader.

Coll, River *Western Isles* Rising from Loch an Eilein on the Isle of Lewis in the Outer Hebrides, the River Coll (Gael: *Abhainn Chuil*) flows 3 miles (5 km) southeast past the settlement of Coll (also *Col*) to enter a bay on the north coast of Loch a' Tuath.

Collace *Perth and Kinross* A settlement of eastern Perth and Kinross, Collace lies on the north side of the Sidlaw Hills, 8 miles (13 km) northeast of Perth. It comprises the two separate locations of Collace and Kirkton of Collace. To the east the King's Seat rises to 377 m (1105 ft), Black Hill to 360 m (1181 ft) and Dunsinane Hill to 308 m (1012 ft), on whose summit stands Macbeth's Castle. In 1991 a national controversy arose following a planning application to extend Collace Quarry to within 274 m (900 ft) of the castle.

Collafirth *Shetland* A settlement comprising North and South Collafirth, Collafirth lies to the west of the wide sea loch of Colla Firth, an inlet of Yell Sound on the east coast of Northmavine on Mainland Shetland, 39 miles (63 km) north of Lerwick.

Collafirth *Shetland* A small settlement on the east coast of the Shetland Mainland, Collafirth lies at the head of the Colla Firth, an inlet to the south of Dales Voe, 24 miles (38 km) north of Lerwick.

Collaster, Loch of *Shetland* A small loch lying close to the north coast of the west Mainland of Shetland, the Loch of Collaster is located a half-mile (1 km) east of Norby.

College of St Leonard *Fife* Refounded as a college of the University of St Andrews in 1512 by Archbishop Alexander Stewart and Prior John Hepburn, the original Hospital of St Leonard was attached to a nearby priory. The buildings were abandoned after the union of the college with St Salvator's in 1747 but still comprise a complete group that includes a church and hall on the north side and a residential range on the south, with a gatehouse at its east end. The chapel of the college is the old Parish Church of St Leonard that was reroofed by the university in 1910 and refurnished 1948–52. All the buildings other than the church now belong to St Leonard's School, which was founded in 1877 and moved to this site in 1882.

College of St Salvator *Fife* The College of St Salvator at the University of St Andrews is situated between North Street and The Scores. It was founded in 1450 by Bishop James Kennedy (c.1408–1465), who is remembered annually in a colourful student end-of-term event known as the Kate Kennedy Pageant. Its main frontage is still virtually intact, with its great tower, Jacobean-style college buildings and collegiate church, all of which comprise one of St Andrews' most magnificent architectural compositions. The tower, to which a spire was added in 1550, is 38 m (125 ft) tall and contains the original bells of the college. Within the college is the tomb of Bishop Kennedy, which dates from c.1460 and is said to be the finest example of medieval craftsmanship in Britain. St Salvator's was united with the College of St Leonard in 1747.

Collessie *Fife* An attractive hamlet with narrow lanes in northeast Fife, Collessie is situated on a minor road just north of the A91, 5 miles (8 km) west of Cupar. Overlooking the Howe of Fife, its ancient parish church (rebuilt 1838–9) stands on a hillock at the centre of a settlement containing several well-preserved 17th-, 18th- and 19th-century weaving cottages, some with thatched roofs. Designated a conservation area in 1986, it has a primary school dating from 1846.

Collieston *Aberdeenshire* A former fishing village on the North Sea coast of Aberdeenshire, Collieston lies 3 miles (5 km) north of the estuary of the Ythan River at the northern end of the Sands of Forvie. Once famous for its 'speldings' or haddocks dried in the rock, and much frequented by smugglers, Collieston is now largely given over to tourists during the summer months. The village was visited by T. E. Lawrence (Lawrence of Arabia) who, on leave from RAF duty, rented a cottage that he described as 'the nearest hovel to the high-tide mark'.

Collin *Dumfries and Galloway* A village in Dumfries and Galloway, Collin lies to the east of the Lochar Water, 3 miles (5 km) east of Dumfries.

Colliston *Angus* A roadside village in St Vigeans parish, eastern Angus, Colliston lies on the A933 from Arbroath to Brechin. Nearby Colliston Castle is said to have been built in 1542 by Cardinal Beaton for his son-in-law, John Guthrie.

Colmonell *South Ayrshire* Situated on the River Stinchar in South Ayrshire, the village of Colmonell (pronounced com-mon-ell) lies 10 miles (16 km) south of Girvan. Nearby are the remains of several castles, including Kirkhill (1589), Craigneil (13th century) and Knockdolian. The area is associated with the Kennedys of Bargany.

Colonel's Bed, the *Aberdeenshire* Located in the central Grampians of Aberdeenshire, to the west of Glen Clunie and 6 miles (10 km) southwest of Braemar, the Colonel's Bed forms a gorge on the Ey Burn, a tributary of the River Dee.

Colonsay *Argyll and Bute* An island of the Inner Hebrides in Argyll and Bute, Colonsay lies to the west of Jura and south of Mull. Rising to a maximum height of 143 m (469 ft), the island is 8 miles (13 km) long and from 1 to 3 miles (1.5 and 5 km) wide, with an area of 4336 ha (10,710 acres). At its southern end, Colonsay is linked to the island of Oronsay by a wide expanse of sand known as The Strand, which can be crossed on foot at low tide. The island's fertile soils, derived from ancient sandstone and limestone, support a rich diversity of natural plantlife as well as a range of exotic trees and shrubs imported to Kiloran Gardens near Colonsay House after Colonsay was acquired by Lord Strathcona in 1905. Prior to that date Colonsay had been owned by the MacNeills, who in 1700 had exchanged lands in Knapdale with the island's owners, the Campbells of Argyll. In the 15th century the owners of the island had been the Macphees or MacDuffys, archivists to the Lords of the Isles, later to be ousted by the Macdonalds, who were in turn dispossesed by the Campbells. From a peak of 387 in 1881, the island's population has steadily declined to its present level of 108 in 2001. In 1965 a ferry pier was built at Scalasaig, the main settlement on Colonsay.

Colonsay Airport *Argyll and Bute* Little more than a grass landing strip on the west coast of the island of Colonsay in Argyll and Bute, Colonsay Airport lies near the settlement of Machrins. The airfield extends for 505 m (1656 ft).

Colpy *Aberdeenshire* A settlement in Culsalmond parish, Aberdeenshire, Colpy lies on the Colpy Burn, 3 miles (5 km) north of Insch and just west of Kirkton of Culsalmond.

Coltfield *Moray* A hamlet in Alves parish, Moray, Coltfield lies 4 miles (6.5 km) south of Burghead.

Colt Hill *Dumfries and Galloway* A summit in the Galloway Hills, Dumfries and Galloway, Colt Hill rises to 598 m (1962 ft) to the northwest of Tynron at the head of the Shinnel Water.

Colvend *Dumfries And Galloway* A small village with a hall, school and early church, Colvend lies to the south of the White Loch, 5 miles (8 km) southeast of Dalbeattie.

Colzium House *North Lanarkshire* A mansion house in the grounds of Colzium Lennox Estate in Kilsyth, Colzium House was gifted to the community in 1937. It houses a local-history museum and is surrounded by planned gardens with collections of conifers and shrubs. Nearby there is a medieval icehouse.

Comely Bank *City of Edinburgh* A residential district on the north side of Edinburgh, Comely Bank lies between Inverleith to the north and Dean to the south, with Stockbridge to the east and Craigleith to the west. The former Comely Bank Estate was the property of Sir William Fettes, founder of Fettes College, which was built on the gentle slope of Comely Bank to a design by David Bryce and opened in 1870. Residents of Comely Bank in the 19th century included the landscape painter John Ewbank (1779–1847) and the physician Sir James Young Simpson (1811–70).

Comers *Aberdeenshire* A small settlement in Midmar parish, Aberdeenshire, Comers lies to the north of the Hill of Fare, 4 miles (6.5 km) west of Echt.

Comiston Spring House *City of Edinburgh* Built in 1676 and located in a private garden off Fox Spring Crescent in Edinburgh, the Comiston Spring House gathered water from the four Comiston springs and routed it to the Old Town of Edinburgh. Comiston was the first source of water to be conveyed to the Castlehill Reservoir, and pipes made of elm were used. The four springs were named after animals and birds – fox, swan, peewit (lapwing) and hare. The entry of each into the spring house was marked by a lead sculpture of the appropriate creature. The original sculptures are now on display in the Museum of Edinburgh in the Canongate.

Compass Hill *Highland* A hill at the eastern end of the island of Canna, Highland Council area, Compass Hill rises to 140 m (459 ft) east of Carn a' Ghaill.

Comrie *Perth and Kinross* A village in highland Perth and Kinross, Comrie lies 7 miles (11 km) west of Crieff where the broad valley of Strathearn narrows at the confluence of the Ruchill Water and River Lednock with the River Earn. Its name is derived from the Gaelic for the 'confluence of streams'. In AD 79 Agricola built one of his Highland line of forts here, calling the place Victoria. It later developed as a kirktown that expanded in 1796 with the influx of dispossessed Highland crofters who came from Glenlednock to work in the village's distillery and two breweries or as handloom weavers. Between the Earn and Ruchill lies The Ross, a former crofting and weaving community that is still accessed by a stone bridge built in 1792. To the south of the Earn is the 'suburb' of Dalginross, formerly a separate village. Nicknamed the 'Shakey Toun', Comrie has long been associated with earth tremors because of its situation on the Highland Boundary Fault. First recorded in 1597, a major series of quakes were reported in 1789, and in 1840 the world's first seismometers were erected here. A more sophisticated recording station, Earthquake House, was built in a field in The Ross in 1869. A prominent landmark is the White Church (1805), which is now used as a community centre and is the focal point of the New Year Flambeaux procession that was originally performed to drive evil spirits from the village. At the head of Glenlednock are a reservoir and hydro-electric dam, and on the summit of Dunmore overlooking Comrie is a monument built in 1812 to commemorate the 1st Lord Melville, Henry Dundas, who was Lord Advocate and Home Secretary under William Pitt the Younger. To the west of the village is Aberuchill Castle (1602) and to the south are the former prisoner of war camp at Cultybraggan and the Auchingarrich Wildlife and Highland Cattle Centre. There are scenic walks to the north towards the Deil's Cauldron waterfall and Laggan Wood. The village has hotels, a caravan park, bowling green, public library and a nine-hole golf course.

Comrie *Fife* A mining village in western Fife, Comrie lies immediately west of Oakley on the A907 between Dunfermline and Alloa. The community developed in the 1930s and 1940s after the sinking of the Comrie mine. To the south of the village the Comrie Burn flows westwards to meet the Bluther Burn.

Comrie Castle *Perth and Kinross* A ruined 16th-century tower house at the eastern end of Glen Lyon in Perth and Kinross, Comrie Castle stands by the River Lyon to the south of Coshieville. It was a stronghold of the Menzies family and last occupied in 1748.

Con, Loch *Perth and Kinross* A small loch in highland Perth and Kinross, Loch Con lies between Loch Errochty and Glen Garry. It is the source of the Allt Con, which flows a short distance southwards past Sròn Choin to Loch Errochty.

Cona' Mheall *Highland* A mountain in the Ross and Cromarty district of Highland Council area, Cona' Mheall rises to 978 m (3208 ft) north of Loch Glascarnoch and 14 miles (22 km) northwest of Dingwall. Its name is derived from the Gaelic for 'hill of the dog'.

Concraigie *Perth and Kinross* A hamlet in eastern Perth and Kinross, Concraigie lies to the west of the Loch of Clunie, 4 miles (6.5 km) west of Blairgowrie.

Condorrat *North Lanarkshire* A suburb of Cumbernauld, North Lanarkshire, Condorrat is located 2 miles (3 km) southwest of Cumbernauld town centre.

Conglass Water *Moray* Rising in headstreams to the southeast of the village of Tomintoul in Moray, the Conglass Water flows northwestwards through Tomintoul to join the River Avon to the north of Strathavon Lodge.

Conheath *Dumfries and Galloway* A locality in Nithsdale, Dumfries and Galloway, Conheath lies just east of the River Nith, 4 miles (6.5 km) southeast of Dumfries.

Conic Hill *Stirling* An elongated hill of western Stirling Council area, Conic Hill lies on the Highland Boundary Fault, which gives it its shape, a mile (1.5 km) northeast of Balmaha and Loch Lomond. The hill comprises multiple summits along a ridge, the highest rising to 361 m (1184 ft). The West Highland Way loops around the northern flank of the hill.

Conie Water *Argyll and Bute* The Conie Water rises in the foothills of the Slate, a peak at the south of the Kintyre peninsula, Argyll and Bute. Flowing eastwards, it enters the Conie Glen and flows south towards Southend. It enters the sea at a point to the south of Southend.

Conival *Highland* A mountain of Assynt in the Sutherland district of Highland Council area, Conival rises to 987 m (3238 ft), southeast of Inchnadamph and adjacent to Ben More Assynt. Its name is derived from the Gaelic for 'hill of the dog'.

Connel *Argyll and Bute* A small settlement in the Lorn district of Argyll and Bute, Connel is situated at the mouth of Loch Etive, 5 miles (8 km) northeast of Oban. It is joined to North Connel, on the north side of the entrance to the loch, by the Connel Bridge. The Falls of Lora lie immediately to the north.

Connell, Loch *Dumfries and Galloway* A small loch in Dumfries and Galloway, Loch Connell lies at the northern end of the Rhinns of Galloway, just west of Kirkcolm. It is the source of the Craigoch Burn.

Connel Bridge *Argyll and Bute* Joining the settlements of Connel and North Connel, the Connel Bridge lies across the entrance to Loch Etive, Argyll and Bute. Built in 1901, it is the second-largest cantilever bridge in Britain.

Conon Bridge *Highland* A village in Easter Ross, Highland Council area, Conon Bridge lies at the western end of the Black Isle, 2 miles (3 km) south of Dingwall. The River Conon, which flows into the head of the Cromarty Firth here, was crossed by a five-arched bridge built in 1809, and in 1814 a new road from the south created a junction at which the village, originally called Conan, grew up. The village expanded in the 20th century in association with the Cromarty Firth naval base, and in modern times Conon Bridge is sustained by a fish-freezing plant and as a commuter settlement with easy access to Inverness. The combined settlements of Conon Bridge and Maryburgh, with a combined population of 8555, are often referred to as Cononbridge.

Conon, River *Highland* A river in Easter Ross, the River Conon is formed by the meeting of the Meig and Sheen Rivers. It continues 12 miles (19 km) eastwards through Strathconon to join the Cromarty Firth near Conon Bridge. To the north of Little Scatwell at the foot of Loch Luichart are the Falls of Conon. The river's waters form part of an extensive hydro-electric scheme developed between 1946 and 1961.

Cononish, River *Stirling* A river rising as the Allt Coire Laoigh between Ben Lui and Ben Oss, the River Cononish flows northeast to join other headwaters of the River Fillan, 2 miles (3 km) south of Tyndrum in northwest Stirling Council area.

Constantine's Cave *Fife* A shallow cave on the east coast of Fife, Constantine's Cave lies to the east of Crail and just south of Fife Ness. King Constantine was reputedly killed by the Vikings here in AD 874.

Contin *Highland* A village in Easter Ross, Highland Council area, Contin lies on the Black Water, 4 miles (6.5 km) southwest of Strathpeffer. It developed in the 20th century in association with tourism and the creation of the nearby Torr Achilty hydro-electric power station.

Coodham *South Ayrshire* A settlement of South Ayrshire, Coodham is located a mile (1.5 km) northeast of Symington. To the south lie the settlements of Bogend and Whitelees.

Cook's Cairn *Moray* A peak rising to 755 m (2478 ft) in the Blackwater Forest, Moray, Cook's Cairn lies between the Livet and Blackwater rivers to the west of the Cabrach Road.

Cookney A small settlement in Aberdeenshire, Cookney lies 2 miles (3 km) west of Muchalls and 5 miles (8 km) north of Stonehaven, on the edge of the Red Moss. Its church was built c.1817 as a chapel of ease.

Cooran Lane *Dumfries and Galloway* A river in Dumfries and Galloway, the Cooran Lane rises in headstreams on the west side of the Rhinns of Kells. It flows southwards to join the Black Water of Dee to the northeast of Loch Dee.

Copinsay *Orkney* An uninhabited island situated in the North Sea to the east of Mainland Orkney, Copinsay rises steeply from the west to cliffs in the east and is surrounded by skerries and reefs. It is connected to Corn Holm by a rocky saddle known as Isle Rough and extends to 73 ha (180 acres). Corn Holm is in turn linked to the smaller islets of Ward Holm and Black Holm by reefs, and to the north Copinsay is separated by the Horse Sound from a grass-topped 18-m/59-ft-high stack known as the Horse of Copinsay. Designated the James Fisher Memorial Island in 1972, Copinsay is an RSPB nature reserve noted for its birdlife.

Coppay *Western Isles* Rising to a height of 35 m (114 ft), this uninhabited and rocky island lies a mile (1.5 km) west of the headland of Toe Head, on the western coastline of South Harris in the Outer Hebrides.

Copshaw Holm An alternative name for Newcastleton in Scottish Borders.

Cor Water *Scottish Borders* A stream in the Tweeddale district of Scottish Borders, the Cor Water forms a headstream of the River Tweed.

Corgarff *Aberdeenshire* A remote location in the Grampians of Aberdeenshire, Corgarff lies close to the upper reaches of the River Don on a road that links the Dee Valley with Strathspey. A 16th-century castle close by was used as a military barracks in the 18th century.

Cornhill *Aberdeenshire* A village of northwest Aberdeenshire, Cornhill lies to the east of the Burn of Boyne, 5 miles (8 km) south of Portsoy. Originally a burgh of barony, Cornhill is now a farming village that holds a weekly livestock market. Knock Hill, 7 miles (11 km) southwest of the village, is the site of an annual cross-country race.

Cornish Loch *South Ayrshire* A small loch in South Ayrshire, Cornish Loch is located 9 miles (14 km) southwest of Dalmellington.

Cornton *Stirling* A settlement on the River Forth, Cornton lies between Stirling and Bridge of Allan. It has a community centre and business park, and to the north is HM Prison Cornton Vale, the only women's prison in

Scotland, constructed in the 1970s on the site of a former male borstal institution.

Corntown *Highland* A settlement in Easter Ross, Highland Council area, Corntown lies a half-mile (1 km) northeast of Conon Bridge.

Corpach *Highland* A village in Lochaber, Highland Council area, Corpach lies at the southern end of the Caledonian Canal and at the head of Loch Linnhe, 2 miles (3 km) north of Fort William. A pulp mill operated here between 1965 and 1980, and a paper mill was established in 1966. Timber is exported from Corpach. In 1995 the Treasures of the Earth Visitor Centre featuring gemstones and geology was opened.

Corr Eilean *Argyll and Bute* An island of Argyll and Bute in the Sound of Jura, Corr Eilean lies at the mouth of Loch Sween, a mile (1.5 km) south of Danna Island and a half-mile (1 km) to the east of Eilean Mòr.

Corr, Loch *Argyll and Bute* A small loch on the island of Islay in Argyll and Bute, Loch Corr lies near the northwest coast of the island, a mile (1.5 km) south of the headland of Tòn Mhòr.

Corra Linn *South Lanarkshire* A spectacular waterfall situated a half-mile (1 km) upstream of New Lanark in the Clyde Valley, Corra Linn is 28 m (92 ft) high and, along with Bonnington Linn, is used as a source of hydro-electric power via the Bonnington Power Station.

Corran *Highland* A settlement in Lochaber, Highland Council area, Corran lies on the northeast shore of Loch Hourn, a mile (1.5 km) southeast of Arnisdale.

Corran *Highland* Where Loch Linnhe is pinched to form the Corran Narrows to the south of Fort William in Lochaber, southern Highland Council area, a vehicle ferry crosses to the small settlement of Corran on the Ardgour peninsula, which here forms the western shore of the loch.

Correen Hills *Aberdeenshire* A range of slate hills in Aberdeenshire, the Correen Hills rise to a height of 518 m (1699 ft) at Lord Arthur's Cairn between Alford and Rhynie.

Corrie *North Ayrshire* A resort village on the east coast of the island of Arran, North Ayrshire, Corrie lies on a raised beach 4 miles (6.5 km) north of Brodick. The village and its pier developed in the 19th century in association with the quarrying and export of local stone. The old fermetoun settlement of High Corrie lies to the west. Notable buildings include the villa of Cromla and Corrie Parish Church (1886).

Corrie *Dumfries and Galloway* A hamlet in eastern Dumfries and Galloway, Corrie is situated to the east of the Corrie Water, 4 miles (6.5 km) northeast of Lockerbie.

Corrie Common *Dumfries and Galloway* A village in the parish of Hutton and Corrie, Corrie Common lies to the east of the Corrie Water, 5 miles (8 km) northeast of Lockerbie. Hart Fell rises to the northeast.

Corrie Water *Dumfries and Galloway* A stream in northeast Dumfries and Galloway, the Corrie Water rises in Castle O'er Forest. It flows southwestwards to join the Water of Milk east of Lockerbie.

Corriearklet *Stirling* A locality in Stirling Council area, Corriearklet lies midway between Inversnaid on the east shore of Loch Lomond and Stronachlachar on the west shore of Loch Katrine. It is situated by the Corriearklet Burn which flows down from the back of Beinn a' Choin to enter Loch Arklet near here.

Corrieshalloch Gorge *Highland* The spectacular Corrieshalloch Gorge is located 1.5 miles (2.5 km) south of Braemore and 12 miles (19 km) southeast of Ullapool in Highland Council area. The gorge exceeds a mile (1.5 km) in length and is 61 m (200 ft) deep. Within this steep-sided ravine the Abhainn Dromm plunges 46 m (150 ft) over the Falls of Measach. The area was designated a National Nature Reserve (NNR) in 1967 and confirmed as a Site of Special Scientific Interest (SSSI) in 1984, having both geological and botanical interest. The gorge is the result of rapid erosion of hard metamorphic Moine schists by glacial melt-waters 10–13,000 years ago, which exploited local fractures in the rock. A rich flora of ferns, mosses and liverworts can be found on the walls of the gorge and the boulders of the river bed. The woodland above the gorge includes a further diversity of tree and plant species. The suspension footbridge a short distance downstream from the falls was built by Sir John Fowler (1817–98), architect of the Forth Railway Bridge, who bought the Braemore Lodge and estate in 1867 and owned it for more than 30 years. The gorge, together with 14 ha (35 acres) of land surrounding it, was given to the National Trust for Scotland in 1945. A further 13 ha (32 acres) adjacent were acquired from the Forestry Commission in 1994.

Corrieyairack Pass *Highland* A pass at the southwestern end of the Monadhliath Mountains in Highland Council area, the Corrieyairack Pass follows a routeway from the upper reaches of the River Spey north of Loch Laggan to the head of Glen Tarff which feeds into the Great Glen. The 18th-century military road builder General Wade followed this route, which rises to 764 m (2507 ft), in constructing a road to Fort Augustus. To the north of the pass, Corrieyairack Hill rises to 896 m (2922 ft).

Corrigall Farm Museum *Orkney* A restored mid-19th-century farmstead, Corrigall Farm Museum is located near Harray on Mainland Orkney. Open during the summer, it comprises special exhibitions on farming and rural life, including a grain-drying kiln, a hand mill and weaving loom. Nearby is the only working example of an Orcadian horizontal water mill.

Corrimony *Highland* A settlement in Glen Urquhart, Highland Council area, Corrimony lies 8 miles (13 km) west of Loch Ness. The Corrimony Chambered Cairn, which forms a well-preserved passage grave, dates from the 3rd millennium BC. A ring of 11 standing stones surrounds the cairn.

Corrow *Argyll and Bute* Little more than a few buildings, Corrow lies at the northern end of Loch Goil, a mile (1.5 km) southwest of Lochgoilhead in Argyll and Bute.

Corry *Highland* A settlement on the island of Skye, Highland Council area, Corry lies on the west side of Broadford Bay, just north of Broadford.

Corrybrough *Highland* A locality in Strathdearn, Corrybrough lies on the River Findhorn a mile (1.5 km) east of Tomatin. A house here was a seat of the Macqueen family.

Corryhabbie Hill *Moray* A mountain rising to 781 m (2562 ft) in the Glenfiddich Forest, Moray, Corryhabbie Hill is traversed from Glenfiddich by a routeway known as Morton's Way.

Corrykinloch *Highland* A settlement in Sutherland, Highland Council area, Corrykinloch lies at the northwest end of Loch Shin.

Corryvreckan, Strait of *Argyll and Bute* Barely a mile (1.5 km) wide, the Strait of Corryvreckan forms a narrow passage between the islands of Jura and Scarba. Taking its name from the Gaelic for 'Breacon's Cauldron', it is best known for its dangerous whirlpool that is caused by the surging tide. Exaggerated tales of mermaids and sea monsters are associated with the strait.

Corse *Aberdeenshire* A locality in Aberdeenshire, Corse lies on the Corse Burn, 5 miles (8 km) east of Huntly. Corse Hill rises to the south and the remains of Corse Castle, a former stronghold of the Forbes family, stand between the road and the burn. The lands of Corse once formed part of the barony of Coull and O'Neill, which was bestowed upon Patrick Forbes, armour-bearer to King James III, in 1476. The property eventually fell into the hands of the Forbes family of Craigievar, which lies 2 miles (3 km) to the northeast. Also in the locality are Corse House, Mains of Corse, Newton of Corse and Wester Corse.

Corse Hill *Aberdeenshire* Rising to a height of 422 m (1383 ft), Corse Hill lies to the south of the village of Corse in Aberdeenshire.

Corse Hill *East Renfrewshire/South Lanarkshire* Located on the border of East Renfrewshire and South Lanarkshire, Corse Hill rises to 376 m (1234 ft) 4 miles (6.5 km) south of Eaglesham.

Corserine *Dumfries and Galloway* A hill rising to 813 m (2337 ft) in Dumfries and Galloway, Corserine is the highest peak in the Rhinns of Kells to the northwest of New Galloway.

Corsewall Point *Dumfries and Galloway* A headland at the northwestern tip of the Rhinns of Galloway, Dumfries and Galloway, Corsewall Point looks out to the Atlantic. One mile (1.5 km) inland lie the remains of 15th-century Corsewall Castle, a former stronghold of the Stewarts of Dreghorn.

Corsindae *Aberdeenshire* A locality in the Aberdeenshire parish of Cluny, Corsindae lies to the east of the Corsindae Burn, 4 miles (6.5 km) west of Dunecht. It comprises the hamlets of Corsindae, Mains of Corsindae and Milton of Corsindae.

Corsock *Dumfries and Galloway* A village in Dumfries and Galloway, Corsock lies on the Urr Water, 8 miles (13 km) east of New Galloway.

Corsock Loch *Dumfries and Galloway* A small loch in Dumfries and Galloway, Corsock Loch lies just south of the hamlet of Corsock and west of the Urr Water, 9 miles (14 km) north of Castle Douglas.

Corstorphine *City of Edinburgh* A suburb of Edinburgh, Corstorphine lies 4 miles (6.5 km) west of the city centre. Until the 20th century it was an agricultural village separated from Edinburgh by open countryside. It comprised the new or high village developed on St John's Road along the main route between Edinburgh and Glasgow and the old village lying a little to the south. A chapel, founded *c.*1400 by Sir Adam Forrester, became a collegiate church, dedicated to St John the Baptist in 1429. The 14th-century Corstorphine Castle was dismantled in the 18th century and now lies in ruins. The only remnant is its 16th-century dovecote, surviving in Dovecot Road. In 1920, Corstorphine was incorporated within the boundaries of the City of Edinburgh.

Corstorphine Hill *City of Edinburgh* Rising to a height of 161 m (531 ft) to the north of the Corstorphine district of western Edinburgh, Corstorphine Hill comprises the eroded remnants of a dolerite sill, a body of igneous rock injected between pre-existing sediments. The dolerite is used for surfacing roads, and siltstone once proved ideal as flagstones. Well-formed cup markings, probably dating from the Bronze Age, were discovered in 1991, and in 2000 Corstorphine Hill was designated a Regionally Important Geological Site in addition to its earlier designations as a local nature reserve, listed wildlife site and nature conservation site. Near to its summit is Clermiston Tower (also known as Corstorphine Hill Tower or Scott Tower), and on its northern slopes are Edinburgh Zoo, Corstorphine Hospital and Murrayfield Hospital.

Cortachy *Angus* A hamlet in the Braes of Angus, Cortachy lies on the River South Esk, 4 miles (6.5 km) north of Kirriemuir. Cortachy Castle has been the seat of the Ogilvy earls of Airlie since 1473, and the church at Cortachy was rebuilt in 1828. To the northwest on Tulloch Hill is the Airlie Monument, a copy of one of the towers of Airlie Castle erected in memory of David Ogilvy, 9th Earl of Airlie, who was killed in the Boer War.

Cortachy Castle *Angus* A grand whitewashed baronial edifice of northern Angus, which is the seat of the earls of Airlie, Cortachy Castle sits on the River South Esk guarding the entrance to Glen Clova, 3 miles (5 km) north of Kirriemuir. It comprises a much-altered 15th-century courtyard castle, built on the Z-plan. The first castle on this site was built *c.*1330 and was the property of the Stewart earls of Strathearn. In 1473, King James III granted the lands to Sir Walter Ogilvy, who was most likely responsible for beginning the current structure. Three original round towers survive; one is unusual, with a rectangular watch-room at the top, corbelled out on a W-shaped support. In 1641, the castle was damaged by Archibald Campbell, Marquess of Argyll. It was restored but then burned in 1651 by Oliver Cromwell in revenge for the Ogilvys' support for Charles II, who had spent a night in the King's Room the previous year. The castle and its estates were forfeited to the Crown following the Ogilvys' support for the Jacobite Rebellion of 1745 and subsequently occupied by Government troops but later returned to the family. In 1871 it was extended by the architect David Bryce. The castle is said to be haunted by a drummer, who is heard when a member of the family nears death.

Coruisk, Loch *Highland* A remote freshwater loch on the island of Skye in the Inner Hebrides, Loch Coruisk (Gael: *Cor' uisge*) extends deep into the heart of the Cuillins. It is connected to the sea (Loch na Cuilce and then Loch Scavaig) by the short Scavaig River which crosses a narrow ice-smoothed rock barrier. The loch is situated in one of the most spectacular glaciated valleys in Britain. Its name means 'the water cauldron', and during wet weather waterfalls cascade down on all sides. The loch is accessible only by sea or a lengthy, but well-trodden, walk.

Corwar House *South Ayrshire* The settlement of Corwar House is located 3 miles (5 km) southeast of Barrhill in South Ayrshire. It lies on the A714 between Newton Stewart and Girvan.

Coshieville *Perth and Kinross* A hamlet in the Strath of Appin, Perth and Kinross, Coshieville lies on the Keltney Burn, 5 miles (8 km) west of Aberfeldy. In the 18th century the Coshieville Hotel was a 'Kingshouse' occupied by officers of General Wade's road-making force, the track on which he built his road following an old cattle-droving route to the ford of Lyon at Comrie Castle. A fair was formerly held at Coshieville on the last Thursday of October and another in December to sell cattle and sheep reared in the district.

Cothall *Aberdeenshire* A settlement of east-central Aberdeenshire, Cotthall lies on the River Don immediately to the north of the boundary with Aberdeen City, 2 miles (3 km) north-northwest of Dyce. The remains of St Meddan's Church lie to the west.

Cottown *Aberdeenshire* A small settlement in west-central Aberdeenshire, Cottown lies to the east of the Burn of Craig, a half-mile (1 km) east of Rhynie.

Cottown *Aberdeenshire* A scattered settlement in the Formartine district of Aberdeenshire, Cottown lies 4 miles (6.5 km) northeast of Fyvie.

Cottown *Perth and Kinross* A small hamlet in the Carse of Gowrie, Cottown lies just to the south of Chapelhill, 7 miles (11 km) east of Perth. The restored former schoolhouse retains its thatched roof.

Cougie *Highland* A locality in the Guisachan Forest, Highland Council area, Cougie lies on the Allt Riabhach, 10 miles (16 km) southwest of Cannich and south of Glen Affric.

Coul House *Highland* The former seat of a cadet branch of the Mackenzie family, Coul House lies near Contin in Easter Ross. Built in 1819–21, the present house is possibly the third building to be erected by the Mackenzies on this site. Major-General Sir Alexander Mackenzie was Provincial Commander-in-Chief of Bengal for the East India Company. The house is now a hotel.

Coul Point *Argyll and Bute* The headland of Coul Point lies on the western coastline of the island of Islay, Argyll and Bute. It lies 2 miles (3 km) west of Loch Gorm and a mile (1.5 km) west of Machrie.

Coulaghailtro *Argyll and Bute* A settlement near the west coast of Knapdale in Argyll and Bute, Coulaghailtro lies a mile (1.5 km) north of Kilberry and 9 miles (14 km) east of Tarbert.

Coulags *Highland* A settlement in Glen Carron, Wester Ross, Highland Council area, Coulags lies 3 miles (5 km) northeast of the head of Loch Carron.

Coull *Aberdeenshire* A hamlet in the Cromar district of Aberdeenshire, Coull is situated 3 miles (5 km) northwest of Aboyne between the Burn of Tarland and Coull Hill. Close by are the ruins of Coull Castle, a former stronghold of the Durward family, of whom it was said that on a Durward dying, the church bell of Coull would toll of its own accord.

Coulport *Argyll and Bute* A village on the east shore of Loch Long in Argyll and Bute, Coulport lies 4 miles (6.5 km) north of Cove opposite Ardentinny, with which it was once linked by ferry. The Kibble Palace now in the Glasgow Botanic Gardens was located in Coulport in 1872. A nuclear weapons store of the Clyde Naval Base was brought here during the Cold War.

Coulter *South Lanarkshire* A village of South Lanarkshire, Coulter (also Culter) lies on the Culter Water 3 miles (5 km) south of Biggar. Its church dates from 1810. The Coulter Motte Hill, 2 miles (3 km) to the north, is the site of a castle dating from the 11th century.

Coultra *Fife* A settlement of northeast Fife, Coultra lies on high ground to the west of Gauldry. Ardie Hill rises to the south, and to the north the land drops down to the Tay estuary.

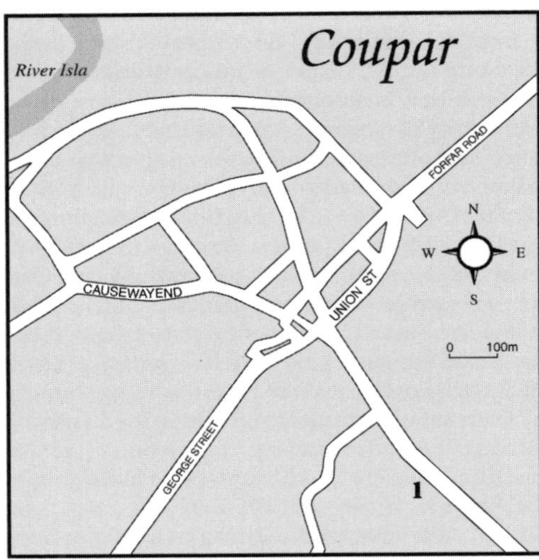

1 *Roman Camp*

Coupar Angus *Perth and Kinross* A market town in eastern Perth and Kinross, Coupar Angus is situated at a crossroads on the south bank of the River Isla in the centre of the fertile valley of Strathmore. The site of a Roman camp lies to the southeast of the centre. A Cistercian abbey, of which only part of the gateway survives, was founded here by King Malcolm IV *c.*1164. A stream that divides the town in two was formerly the boundary between Perthshire and Angus, the older part of the town being in the Angus portion and giving rise to the name Coupar Angus. The town was revitalised in the 19th century as a market town, manufacturing centre and communication hub following the creation of the turnpike roads and the arrival of the railway. Interesting buildings from this period include a tollhouse, tannery, weaving mill, maltings and station. Modern industries include printing and the manufacture of food products, agricultural chemicals and farm machinery. There are recreational facilities in the Larghan Victory Park.

Cour *Argyll and Bute* A small settlement on the western coast of the Kintyre peninsula, Argyll and Bute, Cour looks out over the Kilbrannan Sound to the island of Arran. Situated on Cour Bay, it is 3 miles (5 km) north of Grogport. Cour Island lies southeast of the village.

Courance *Dumfries and Galloway* A village in Dumfries and Galloway, Courance lies to the west of the Kinnel Water, 7 miles (11 km) northwest of Lockerbie.

Courteachan *Highland* A settlement in North Morar, Highland Council area, Courteachan is situated across the harbour to the east of Mallaig.

Cousland *Midlothian* Lying 2.5 miles (4 km) east of Dalkeith and 2 miles (3 km) west of Ormiston, and just within the northern boundary of Midlothian, is the village of Cousland. The name derives quite literally from the Scots for the 'land of cows'. The ruined Cousland Castle dates from the 13th century but was destroyed when the Duke of Somerset invaded in 1547. The smiddy, in continuous use since it was built in the early 18th century, has been preserved by the Cousland

Smiddy Trust. Lime was worked on a significant scale just to the north of the village from medieval times until the early 1970s. Today the village benefits from a primary school (built in the late 1960s to replace the original of c.1850) and a post office. An active community association is based around the village hall, which was built in 1930 as the Miners' Institute.

Cove *Aberdeen City* A commuter settlement and fishing village in the Aberdeen City parish of Nigg, Cove (Cove Bay) lies between the A956 and the North Sea coast, 5 miles (8 km) south of Aberdeen city centre. To the north is the Altens Industrial Estate, with fish-processing, printing, engineering and oil-related industries.

Cove *Argyll and Bute* A linear settlement of Argyll and Bute on the east shore of Loch Long, Cove extends along to merge with Kilcreggan a mile (1.5 km) to the south.

Cove *Highland* A village in Wester Ross, Highland Council area, Cove lies on the west side of Loch Ewe, 7 miles (11 km) northwest of Poolewe.

Cove Bay An alternative name for Cove in Aberdeen City.

Covesea *Moray* The resort settlement of Covesea with its Silver Sands Leisure Park is located on the northern coast of Moray, 3 miles (5 km) west of Lossiemouth and 3 miles (5 km) east of Burghead. Directly off the coast lie the Covesea Skerries, a group of small islands and rocks that are marked by a lighthouse dating from 1846. Stone quarried nearby was used to build St Machar's Cathedral in Aberdeen.

Cowal *Argyll and Bute* A district of Argyll and Bute, Cowal forms a peninsula indented by sea lochs that lies between Loch Long on the Firth of Clyde in the east and Loch Fyne in the west. It is separated from the island of Bute by the Kyles of Bute. The principal settlements are Dunoon, Tighnabruaich and Ardbeg, and many of its coastal villages are popular holiday resorts. Its rural hinterland is largely given over to sheep farming and forestry, the Argyll Forest Park occupying land in the vicinity of Loch Eck. The highest peak on the peninsula is Beinn an Lochain (901 m/2955 ft).

Cowcaddens *Glasgow City* A district of Glasgow, Cowcaddens is situated close to the M8 and the Port Dundas industrial area. Its 19th-century tenements were largely demolished as part of an urban regeneration scheme designed to promote cultural and educational facilities in the heart of Glasgow. Glasgow Caledonian University, the Scottish Piping Centre, the Royal Scottish Academy of Music and Drama, the Scottish Media Group, the Theatre Royal and Buchanan Bus Station are all in this so-called Arts and Media Quarter.

Cowdenbeath *Fife* A former mining town in western Fife, Cowdenbeath lies to the southwest of Lochgelly on the railway line from Dunfermline to Cupar. Originally a small agricultural settlement with a coaching halt on the route north to Perth, Cowdenbeath expanded rapidly with the development of the western Fife iron and coal fields between 1850 and 1914. The population grew during this period from 1000 to 25,000 but declined to its present level following the pit closures of the 1960s. Cowdenbeath now supports a wide range of light industries, including engineering, textiles, food processing, construction and plant hire, on its Woodend, Glenfield and Thistle industrial estates, and the town is a focal point of coach and bus networks. There is a community leisure centre, community education centre, vocational training centre and a stock car-racing circuit (Cowdenbeath Racewall).

Cowdens *Perth and Kinross* A mansion house in Strathearn, Perth and Kinross, Cowdens is situated in Madderty parish, nearly 2 miles (3 km) south of Fowlis Wester.

Cowgate *City of Edinburgh* A district of Edinburgh on the southwest margin of the Old Town, the Cowgate was originally a routeway used to drive cattle from Holyrood to the Grassmarket. Once a fashionable area, it declined in the 19th century. Unlike the Royal Mile, which runs parallel to it, the Cowgate was not subject to renewal schemes that involved the demolition of old run-down buildings. More recent regeneration has attempted to restore older buildings, including the Magdalen Chapel (1544), Tailors' Hall (1621), St Cecilia's Hall (1763) and the former Argyle Brewery. A major fire destroyed some less historic buildings in 2002.

Cowgill Reservoirs *South Lanarkshire* The Cowgill Reservoirs, Cowgill Upper and Lower, are located 2 miles (3 km) southeast of Lamington in South Lanarkshire. The Lower Cowgill is the source of the Cow Gill, a stream that flows north and east to join the Culter Water.

Cowhythe Head *Aberdeenshire* A headland on the Moray Firth coast of Aberdeenshire, Cowhythe Head separates Strathmarchin Bay from Boyne Bay, just over a mile (1.5 km) to the east of Portsoy.

Cowie *Aberdeenshire* A former fishing village on the coast of Aberdeenshire, Cowie is situated on the north shore of Stonehaven Bay at the northern end of the burgh town of Stonehaven. A castle, said to have been built by Malcom III (Canmore) and held by the Fraser thanes of Cowie, once stood on a promontory overlooking the sea, and nearby are the ruins of a chapel associated with the 7th-century St Nathalan. The castle, which was the guardian of a coastal route known as the Cowie Mounth, was one of three royal castles in this part of Aberdeenshire defending key routeways, the others being Kincardine and Durris. The original village of Cowie on Megray Hill above the present Cowie House was destroyed by the Marquess of Montrose in 1645 and rebuilt on a coastal site at the mouth of the Cowie Water. Today Cowie is a commuter village and tourist resort comprising rows of cottages with colourful doors and window frames.

Cowie *Stirling* One of the three 'Eastern Villages' of Stirling Council area, Cowie is situated to the southeast of Bannockburn. A former coal-mining settlement that was also associated with stone quarrying, Cowie's economy now depends on small-scale industry and the manufacture of paperboard and other related timber products.

Cowie Water *Aberdeenshire* A stream in Aberdeenshire, the Cowie Water rises on the western border of Glenbervie parish. It flows 13 miles (21 km) eastwards before reaching the sea near Stonehaven.

Cowlairs *Glasgow City* An area of Glasgow, located near the centre of Springburn, which was synonymous with railways. It was here that the Edinburgh and Glasgow Railway Co. established its workshops in 1842. For the next 125 years, the workshops here produced rolling stock for the rail network in the UK.

Cowlatt, Burn of the *Moray* Rising in the Loch of the Cowlatt in Knockando parish, Moray, the Burn of the

Cowlatt flows eastwards to join the Knockando Burn north of Upper Knockando.

Coxton Tower *Moray* Located near the village of Lhanbryde in Moray, Coxton Tower dates from 1641. It is a four-storey tower house with a single vaulted room on each floor linked by a narrow spiral stair within the wall thickness. The roof of the tower is made of stone slabs and there are two circular bartizan towers.

Coyle, Water of *East Ayrshire* The Water of Coyle rises 3 miles (5 km) north of Dalmellington in East Ayrshire. Flowing north and west, it passes through the settlements of Littlemill and Sundrum before joining the River Ayr, a mile (1.5 km) northwest of Belston. Old King Cole is said to have held his musical courts by this stream in the 5th century.

Coylton *South Ayrshire* A settlement in South Ayrshire, Coylton lies 5 miles (8 km) east of Ayr on the A70 to Cumnock. It comprises the farm villages of Low Coylton, Hillhead (formerly New Coylton) and Joppa and has grown substantially as a residential settlement since the 1970s, although it does not yet have all the facilities of a modern town.

Coylumbridge *Highland* A locality with a hotel in Strathspey, Highland Council area, Coylumbridge lies 2 miles (3 km) to the east of Aviemore on the edge of Glenmore Forest Park. It developed as a centre of winter sports from the mid-1960s.

Cradhlastadh The Gaelic name for Crowlista in the Western Isles.

Craggan *Highland* A locality in Strathspey, Highland Council area, Craggan lies by the River Spey, a mile (1.5 km) to the southwest of Grantown-on-Spey. It comprises the settlements of Upper and Wester Craggan.

Cragganmore Distillery *Moray* A Speyside malt, Cragganmore is produced at the Cragganmore Distillery in Ballindalloch, Moray, 14 miles (22 km) northeast of Grantown-on-Spey and 10 miles (16 km) southwest of Aberlour. The distillery offers tours of the facilities, exhibitions and a local shop. It is regarded as one of the classic malts.

Craggie *Highland* A locality to the southeast of Inverness, Highland Council area, Craggie lies a half-mile (1 km) east of Daviot where the Craggie Burn joins the River Nairn. It comprises Craggie, Easter Craggie and Craggiemore.

Craichie *Angus* A hamlet of south-central Angus, Craichie lies a mile (1.5 km) south-southwest of Dunnichen and 2 miles (3 km) southwest of Letham. Craichie has grown considerably through new housing built in the latter part of the 20th century and in 2003–4.

Craig *Highland* A small settlement in Wester Ross, Highland Council area, Craig lies on the northeast shore of Loch Torridon, 4 miles (6.5 km) southeast of Redpoint.

Craig *Highland* A settlement in Glencarron, Highland Council area, Craig lies in Wester Ross, 10 miles (16 km) southwest of Achnasheen.

Craig *Perth and Kinross* A locality in Strathmore, eastern Perth and Kinross, the name Craig is associated with the old farm towns of Easter Craig, Nether Craig and New Craig which lie between the Burn of Auchrannie and the Loch of Lintrathen.

Craig a Barns A forest-covered craggy hill in Strath Tay, Perth and Kinross, Craig a Barns rises to 337m (1105 ft) above the River Tay to the northwest of Dunkeld. In the 18th century tree seed was scattered amongst the crags with the aid of a cannon.

Craig Castle *Aberdeenshire* A 16th-century castle in Aberdeenshire, Craig Castle lies on the Burn of Craig just over a mile (1.5 km) to the north of Lumsden. It was a seat of a branch of the Gordon family.

Craig Head *Moray* A promontory on the Moray Firth coast, Craig Head lies at the foot of Law Hillock, due west of Findochty in Moray.

Craig Lea *Perth and Kinross* A hill rising to a height of 529 m (1736 ft) to the north of Glenalmond in Perth and Kinross, Craig Lea rises steeply to the west of the Milton Burn, 2 miles (3 km) northwest of Harrietfield.

Craig Rossie *Perth and Kinross* A forested hill rising to 411 m (1349 ft) on the northern edge of the Ochil Hills, 2 miles (3 km) east of Auchterarder in Perth and Kinross, Craig Rossie overlooks the valley of Strathearn.

Craigan Roan *Moray* A rock in Spey Bay, Moray, Craigan Roan lies directly off Portgordon and shelters the harbour behind.

Craiganour Lodge *Perth and Kinross* A shooting lodge on the north side of Loch Rannoch, Perth and Kinross, Craiganour lies 2 miles (3 km) west of Kinloch Rannoch. A prehistoric standing stone known as the Craiganour Stone or Clach na h-Jobairte, stands on top of an ancient barrow nearby.

Craigdam *Aberdeenshire* A locality in the Formartine district of Aberdeenshire, Craigdam lies a mile (1.5 km) to the southwest of Tarves and northeast of Oldmeldrum.

Craigdarroch Water *Dumfries and Galloway* A stream in Dumfries and Galloway, the Craigdarroch Water rises as the Craiglearan and Stronshalloch burns. It flows eastwards to join the Castlefairn Water at Moniaive.

Craigdews *Dumfries and Galloway* A locality in Dumfries and Galloway, Craigdews lies on the Queen's Way from New Galloway to Newton Stewart, to the southwest of Clatteringshaws Loch.

Craige, Loch na *Perth and Kinross* A small loch in Glen Cochill, Perth and Kinross, Loch na Craige lies on the old military road 2 miles (3 km) south of Aberfeldy.

Craigearn *Aberdeenshire* A village to the south of the River Don in Aberdeenshire, Craigearn lies a mile (1.5 km) to the south of Kemnay and east of Monymusk.

Craigellachie *Moray* Situated at the junction of the Fiddich and Spey rivers in Moray, Craigellachie is a terraced village that looks towards Craigellachie Rock, the traditionally lower boundary of Strathspey and the lands of the Clan Grant whose war-cry is 'Stand fast Craigellachie!' It lies on the Malt Whisky Trail at the junction of the A95 and A941, 2 miles (3 km) east of Aberlour and 3 miles (5 km) south of Rothes, and is the home of a cooperage that makes casks for the whisky industry. The Spey is crossed here by the 48-m/150-ft-span of the Craigellachie Bridge, built between 1812 and 1815 by Thomas Telford. This is thought to be the oldest surviving iron bridge in Scotland and one of the finest in the UK. The village has two parks, Highland Park and Fiddich Park. There are fine woodland walks.

Craigencross *Dumfries and Galloway* A locality in the Rhinns of Galloway, Dumfries and Galloway, Craigencross lies at a road junction a mile (1.5 km) to the southeast of Leswalt, close to the western shore of Loch Ryan.

Craigend *Perth and Kinross* A village in Perth and

Kinross, Craigend is situated between the River Earn and the River Tay, a mile (1.5 km) to the south of Perth. It lies on the former main road to Perth from the south and near a former railway junction.

Craigend Castle *Stirling* The ruined Craigend Castle lies in Mugdock Country Park, 2 miles (3 km) north of Milngavie. Built in 1815, this mansion was designed in the Regency Gothic style by Alexander Ramsay (c.1777–1847). It was home to the Smith, Buchanan, Outram and Yarrow families, and in the mid-20th century was the site of the short-lived Craigend Zoo. The stables were converted to the Mugdock Park Visitor Centre, completed in 1996.

Craigendoran *Argyll and Bute* An eastern suburb of Helensburgh in Argyll and Bute, Craigendoran developed following the building of a pier served by steamers of the North British Railway from 1882.

Craigens *East Ayrshire* A hamlet of East Ayrshire, Craigens lies between Netherthird and the Kilmarnock–Dumfries railway line, a mile (1.5 km) southeast of Cumnock.

Craigentinny *City of Edinburgh* A residential district of Edinburgh, Craigentinny lies 2.5 miles (4 km) east of the city centre, between Restalrig and the Firth of Forth. The district developed on the estates of 17th-century Craigentinny House, once owned by the eccentric politician William (Christie) Miller (1789–1848). Miller's ostentatious mausoleum, known locally as the 'Craigentinny Marbles', lies in Craigentinny Crescent.

Craighall *Perth and Kinross* A locality in eastern Perth and Kinross, Craighall lies on the River Ericht, 2 miles (3 km) north of Blairgowrie.

Craighead Inn *Moray* A locality in upland Moray, Craighead Inn lies on the Burn of Tervie to the south of Ben Rinnes, between Tomintoul and Dufftown.

Craighouse *Argyll and Bute* A settlement on the east coast of the island of Jura, Argyll and Bute, Craighouse is located 3 miles (5 km) north of the southern tip of the island. The village spreads around a small bay and looks out onto the Small Isles of the Sound of Jura. The Isle of Jura whisky distillery is located to the south of the village.

Craigie *Perth and Kinross* A village in eastern Perth and Kinross, Craigie lies immediately southeast of the Loch of Clunie, 3 miles (5 km) west of Blairgowrie.

Craigie *South Ayrshire* A village of South Ayrshire, Craigie lies 4 miles (6.5 km) south of Kilmarnock.

Craigie *South Ayrshire* Craigie is the name given to an eastern suburb of the town of Ayr in South Ayrshire.

Craigie Horticultural Centre *South Ayrshire* Built in 1996 and located within the Craigie Estate in Ayr, South Ayrshire, the Craigie Horticultural Centre houses collections of exotic plants from the Mediterranean, South America and Australia. There is also an educational visitor centre within the grounds.

Craigieburn *Dumfries and Galloway* A 795-ha (1964-acre) forest plantation in the Moffat Hills of Dumfries and Galloway, Craigieburn lies on hilly ground to the east of Moffat and offers fine views over Annandale and the Moffat Water from a height of 450 m (1470 ft).

Craigievar Castle *Aberdeenshire* A tower house built in 1626 by William Forbes, Craigievar Castle lies to the south of the village of Muir of Fowlis near Alford in central Aberdeenshire. Forbes, an Aberdeen merchant who had made his fortune trading with the Baltic, created a six-storey tower house with turrets, cupolas and corbelling. It escaped later alterations and remained in the hands of the Forbes family for most of its history. The interior is wholly Jacobean with vaulted ceilings and wood panelling. Craigievar's ancient charm made it an early tourist attraction whose reputation was enhanced by a visit from Queen Victoria and Prince Albert together with many of the crowned heads of Europe who were their guests. Craigievar Castle, along with 121 ha (300 acres) of land, was acquired by the National Trust for Scotland in 1963.

Craigleith *East Lothian* A small island off the East Lothian coast, Craigleith lies near the mouth of the Firth of Forth a mile (1.5 km) north of North Berwick harbour. It rises to 24 m (80 ft) and was purchased by Sir Hew Dalrymple from North Berwick Town Council in 1814. Craigleith is noted for its sea birds, including cormorants, shags, guillemots and puffins, which can be studied by remotely controlled cameras at the Scottish Seabird Centre in North Berwick. Geologically, Craigleith is a laccolith, a dome-shaped igneous intrusion composed of essexite, a rock popular for the manufacture of curling stones.

Craigleith *City of Edinburgh* A district to the west of Edinburgh city centre, Craigleith lies between Comely Bank and Blackhall. The Craigleith Quarry formerly provided much of the fine sandstone used in the building of Edinburgh's New Town in the 18th and 19th centuries. First worked to provide stone for Edinburgh Castle in the 17th century, Craigleith stone was last used in 1895 during the construction of Leith Docks. The monolithic Ionic columns at the front of the University of Edinburgh's Old College represent the largest single pieces of stone cut from the quarry. The quarry site has been redeveloped as a large shopping centre.

Craiglemine *Dumfries and Galloway* A locality in the southern Machars of Dumfries and Galloway, Craiglemine lies 2 miles (3 km) west of Whithorn.

Craiglethy *Aberdeenshire* A rocky reef off the North Sea coast of southeast Aberdeenshire, Craiglethy lies to the south of Trelung Ness, 3 miles (5 km) south of Stonehaven.

Craiglockhart *City of Edinburgh* A suburban district of Edinburgh located 2.5 miles (4 km) southwest of the city centre, Craiglockhart lies between the A70 and the Craiglockhart Hills. Consisting principally of pre- and post-war private bungalows, the area developed around the 12th-century Craiglockhart Tower that once stood on the lands of the Lockhart family. To the east, on the flanks of Wester Craiglockhart Hill, is the Craiglockhart Campus of Napier University. Previously the Craiglockhart College of Education, the campus was built as the Craiglockhart Hydropathic Institution (1880) in the Italianate style. The institution became the Convent of the Sacred Heart and was also used as a military hospital during World War I: the poets Siegfried Sassoon and Wilfred Owen convalesced here after having been injured on the Western Front. The mid-18th-century Redhall House, with its pedimented frontage and porch supported on Ionic columns, was built for George Inglis, who owned a paper mill at Auchendinny. Craiglockhart House (1830) is a Tudor-Gothic-style pile in Craiglockhart Dell Road, built by the noted surgeon

Professor Alexander Monro (1773–1859). The Craiglockhart Sports Centre, in 'Happy Valley', hosts international tennis competitions. The Water of Leith and Craiglockhart Dell lie on its western margin. A steep-sided wooded valley on the Water of Leith, Craiglockhart Dell connects along the Water of Leith walkway with Colinton Dell to the southwest. In the Dell is the early-19th-century Gothic grotto of Craiglockhart House and, towards Colinton, the remains of Redhall Mill, a mid-19th-century sawmill.

Craiglush, Loch of *Perth and Kinross* One of a group of small lochs at the head of the valley of the Lunan Burn in eastern Perth and Kinross, the Loch of Craiglush lies a mile (1.5 km) to the northeast of Dunkeld. It is connected to the Loch of Lowes.

Craigmaroinn *Aberdeenshire* A rocky reef on the North Sea coast of Aberdeenshire, Craigmaroinn lies just south of Portlethen.

Craigmill *Stirling* A village in Stirling Council area, Craigmill lies to the south of Abbey Craig and immediately east of Causewayhead, 2 miles (3 km) northeast of Stirling. A burn flows down through Craigmill to meet the River Forth nearby.

Craigmillar *City of Edinburgh* A district of southeast Edinburgh, Craigmillar was originally associated with the substantial 15th-century Craigmillar Castle which lies 3 miles (5 km) south of the city centre. In the 1930s a large public housing estate was developed to the south of the brewery complex at Peffermill to provide homes for families displaced from run-down housing in the Old Town. Two tower blocks were erected in the 1960s, by which time Craigmillar was itself suffering from environmental decay and social deprivation. The Scottish Office designated Craigmillar a priority area for community regeneration in 1996, and by 2001 significant redevelopment had taken place, creating more than 1000 new homes, a health centre and a business centre. The Craigmillar Festival Society, founded in the 1960s, is an early example of a community support group formed with the objective of improving social and environmental conditions. Now a major employer in the district, it organises employment training schemes in addition to an annual arts festival.

Craigmillar Castle *City of Edinburgh* Often overlooked in favour of the more famous Edinburgh Castle, Craigmillar Castle is a substantial and historically important ruin, lying only 3 miles (5 km) from the centre of Edinburgh. Although a building existed on this site from the 13th century, the present fortress dates from the mid-15th century, when it was the home of the Preston family. King James V stayed at Craigmillar in 1517. The castle suffered at the hands of the Earl of Hertford during the English invasion of 1544, and Mary, Queen of Scots sought seclusion here after the murder in 1566 of her secretary, David Rizzio, at Holyrood Palace. Craigmillar was also where Mary's nobles, including the Earl of Bothwell and William Maitland, plotted the demise of her second husband, Lord Darnley. In 1660 the castle was bought by Sir John Gilmour, who extended and significantly modernised it. It was abandoned in the 18th century and given to the nation by the Gilmour family in 1946. It is now maintained by Historic Scotland.

Craigmyle House *Aberdeenshire* A house in Aberdeenshire, Craigmyle House lies just east of Torphins and 6 miles (10 km) northwest of Banchory. It was built in 1676 by a branch of the Burnett family. The house was extended and modernised by Sir Robert Lorimer in 1902 for R. P. Robertson-Glasgow.

Craigneil *South Ayrshire* A settlement of South Ayrshire, Craigneil lies to the north of the River Stinchar a half-mile (1 km) southwest of Colmonell and 4 miles (6.5 km) east of Ballantrae Bay.

Craignethan Castle *South Lanarkshire* A castle of South Lanarkshire, Craignethan is located high above the River Nethan, a mile (1.5 km) west of Crossford and 6 miles (10 km) northwest of Lanark. The castle was built around 1530 by the powerful Sir James Hamilton of Finnart. He had travelled in Europe, learning about military architecture and fortification. In constructing the castle, he made best use of its strategic location, protected by steep slopes on three sides. When Finnart fell from favour and was executed for treason, the castle was taken by King James V. On his death it passed back to the Hamiltons in the person of James, the 2nd Earl of Arran. It was lost once again when Arran opposed the marriage of Mary, Queen of Scots to Lord Darnley and was briefly banished to France, but was retaken in 1568 by Arran's son, Lord Claud Hamilton. At a time of power struggles and political intrigue, the Hamiltons supported Mary's cause and she was sheltered here after she escaped from Loch Leven Castle, where she was imprisoned following her abdication. The young Claud Hamilton set off with Mary, heading for Dumbarton Castle, but was intercepted at Langside by James Stewart, the Earl of Moray and Regent. Moray then came to Craignethan to demand its surrender. Hamilton returned and retook his castle, continuing to oppose the nobles who ran the country. In 1579, with Mary's cause lost, James Douglas, the 4th Earl of Morton, who was by then Regent, moved decisively against the Hamiltons. They fled Craignethan, which was torn down to prevent re-occupation. Craignethan came to the fore once again in the 19th century as the Tillietudlem Castle of Sir Walter Scott's *Old Mortality* (1816). The castle was given to the State in 1949 by Sir Alec Douglas-Home and is now in the care of Historic Scotland. A caponier, or stone-vaulted artillery chamber, unique in Britain, was discovered in 1962.

Craigneuk *North Lanarkshire* An eastern suburb of Motherwell, Craigneuk lies at the southern edge of the site of the former Ravenscraig Steelworks, a mile (1.5 km) from Motherwell town centre. The settlement of Shieldmuir lies immediately to the south.

Craignish *Argyll and Bute* A peninsula of Argyll and Bute, Craignish extends southwards from Arduaine towards Craignish Point opposite the northern tip of Jura. To the southeast is Loch Craignish and to the northwest Asknish Bay. Craignish Castle, a former stronghold of the Campbells, lies towards the end of the peninsula.

Craignish, Loch *Argyll and Bute* A sea loch on the coast of Argyll and Bute, Loch Craignish lies at the northern end of the Sound of Jura and on the southeastern side of the Craignish peninsula. Several islands lie within the loch, the largest being Eilean Righ, Eilean Mhic Chrion and Island Macaskin. The village of Ardfern and the hamlets of Corranmore and Kirkton lie on its northwestern shore. Standing stones and burial cairns can be found at the head of the loch.

Craignure *Argyll and Bute* Located on Craignure Bay on the eastern coast of the island of Mull, Argyll and Bute, the village of Craignure looks out over the Sound of Mull, the entrance to Loch Linnhe and the island of Lismore. Ferry services operate between Craignure and Oban on the mainland. The Mull and West Highland Railway operates from the village to Torosay Castle to the south.

Craigo *Angus* A village in Angus, Craigo lies on the River North Esk, 5 miles (8 km) northwest of Montrose. It prospered until the 1870s as a textile village with a bleachfield and flax-spinning mill.

Craigower *Perth and Kinross* A hill in Perth and Kinross overlooking the Pass of Killiecrankie, Craigower rises to 450 m (1300 ft) 10 miles (16 km) north of Dunkeld. In 1947 4.5 ha (11 acres) were gifted to the National Trust for Scotland by Mrs M. D. Ferguson of Baledmund in memory of her father, Captain G. A. Wisley. From the summit there are fine panoramic views in all directions. A pathway to the summit of this hill has been extended to form the Dunmore Trail in memory of John, Earl of Dunmore (1939-80) and his father Viscount Fincastle who was killed in action in 1940.

Craigowl Hill *Angus* A summit of the Sidlaw Hills in Angus, Craigowl Hill rises to 455 m (1492 ft) northeast of Kirkton of Auchterhouse.

Craigrothie *Fife* A small village in eastern Fife, Craigrothie is situated on the Craigrothie Burn 4 miles (6.5 km) south of Cupar. The village was once a coaching stop on the route to Cupar and horses were changed at the nearby Chance Inn or 'Change Inn'. To the south is Struthers Castle, which dates from the end of the 14th century. In 1663 the title of Lord Struthers was conferred on the 1st Earl of Lindsay by Charles II, who later visited the castle.

Craigruie *Stirling* A locality in the Braes of Balquhidder, Stirling Council area, Craigruie lies on the north side of Loch Voil, due west of Balquhidder Lodge.

Craigs *Argyll and Bute* Little more than a group of farm buildings, Craigs is located on the Kintyre peninsula of Argyll and Bute, 3 miles (5 km) northwest of Campbeltown. Campbeltown Airport lies 2 miles (3 km) to the southwest.

Craigston Castle *Aberdeenshire* Built between 1604 and 1607 by John Urquhart, the Tutor of Cromarty, so called because he tutored the father of Sir Thomas Urquhart, the translator of Rabelais. Craigston Castle lies 4 miles (6.5 km) northeast of Turriff in Aberdeenshire. Externally it is characterised by its white tower, while internally the wood carvings in the drawing room depict biblical themes.

Craigton *Angus* A village in eastern Angus, Craigton lies to the east of Monikie Reservoir, 5 miles (8 km) northwest of Carnoustie.

Craigton *Angus* A small hamlet of western Angus, Craigton lies in Strathmore, 4 miles (6.5 km) southwest of Kirriemuir and 5 miles (8 km) east of Alyth. The name is a contraction of Craigton of Airlie, and the hamlet of Airlie lies a mile (1.5 km) to the west-southwest.

Craik Forest *Scottish Borders* An area of forest in Scottish Borders, Craik Forest lies to the south of Buccleuch on the border with Dumfries and Galloway. The Borthwick Water rises on Craik Cross Hill and the Rankle Burn flows northwards from Black Knowe.

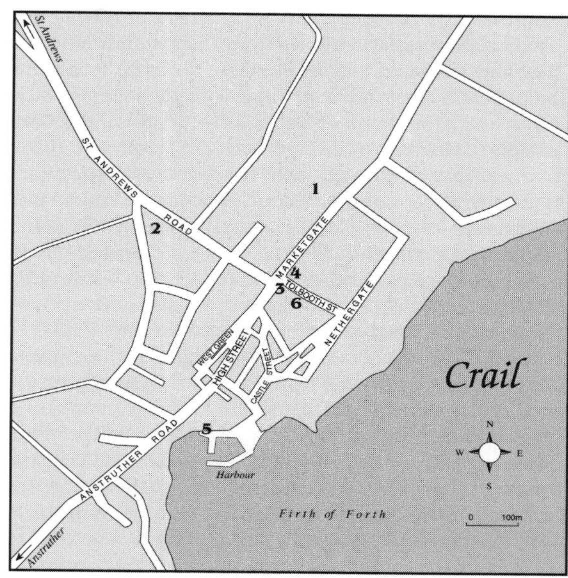

1 *St Mary's Church*
2 *Pictish cross slab*
3 *Market Cross*
4 *Tolbooth*
5 *Customs House*
6 *Crail Museum*

Crail *Fife* A seaside resort and fishing village on the Firth of Forth, eastern Fife, Crail lies 10 miles (16 km) southeast of St Andrews. Once an important seaport exporting salt, fish, mutton and woollens to the Continent, the picturesque village of Crail is the easternmost of the coastal settlements in the East Neuk of Fife. It once had a royal castle that was the occasional residence of David I in the 12th century and was confirmed as a royal burgh by Robert the Bruce in 1310. Close to the harbour lies the oldest part of Crail, with its narrow streets and houses huddled together as protection against the harsh sea wind. On higher ground to the east, the upper part of the town has a more formal layout, reflecting the growth and expansion that took place in late medieval times when local merchants prospered. The burgh's chief landmarks include: St Mary's Church, which dates from the 12th century and contains an 8th-century Pictish cross slab; the 17th-century Market Cross; the 16th/18th-century Tolbooth, whose tower contains a Dutch bell that is rung every night at 10 o'clock to remind villagers of the curfew that once marked the time for fires and lights to be put out; the 17th-century Customs House; and Crail Museum and Heritage Centre, established by Crail Preservation Society in 1979. Crail, with its 18-hole Balcomie Links golf course, has a golfing society founded in 1786, and nearby is the HMS *Jackdaw* airfield which operated as a Royal Naval Air Station during World War II and is now used for go-karting and microlight flying. Local industries include crab and lobster fishing and the manufacture of chemicals.

Crailing *Scottish Borders* A village of Teviotdale in Scottish Borders, Crailing lies on the Oxnam Water, 4 miles (6.5 km) northeast of Jedburgh.

Cramalt Burn *Scottish Borders* A stream in the Tweedsmuir Hills in Scottish Borders, the Cramalt Burn is a tributary of the Megget Water rising on Cramalt Craig.

Cramond *City of Edinburgh* A former iron-milling and oyster-fishing village on the Firth of Forth, Cramond was probably a Roman port in the 1st century AD. It is still a picturesque area and is popular with day-trippers who can cross to the Dalmeny estate at the mouth of the River Almond. Notable buildings include Cramond Tower (15th century), Cramond House (1680), late 18th-century terraced cottages, and Cramond Kirk (15th century, with a stunning interior). There is a footpath to the old mills.

Cranshaws *Scottish Borders* A village of Berwickshire in Scottish Borders, Cranshaws lies on the Whiteadder Water, 9 miles (14 km) northwest of Duns. Cranshaws Castle was a stronghold of the Douglas family.

Cranstackie *Highland* A mountain in northwest Sutherland, Cranstackie rises to 802 m (2631 ft) to the west of the head of Loch Eriboll.

Craobh Haven *Argyll and Bute* Located 2 miles (3 km) south of Arduaine and 20 miles (32 km) south of Oban, the village of Craobh Haven was established in the early 1980s as a response to housing and tourism needs in mid-Argyll. Overlooking the island of Shuna, the inshore islands form a natural harbour and are now used as a yacht marina. To the northwest lie the islands of Luing, Seil and Torsay.

Crarae *Argyll and Bute* Situated on the western shore of Loch Fyne, Crarae lies a mile (1.5 km) north of Minard, 2 miles (3 km) southwest of Furnace and 9 miles (14 km) southwest of Inveraray, Argyll and Bute. The village is dissected by the Crarae Burn, which flows into the loch at Crarae Point. Nearby Crarae Gardens were created as a forest garden extending over 20 ha (50 acres) of native oak woodland. The gardens include a Himalayan Gorge containing over 400 exotic shrubs and trees, a clan garden highlighting plants associated with Scotland's clans, and four country trails. In 2002 the gardens were acquired by the National Trust for Scotland.

Crask Inn *Highland* A settlement in Strath Tirry, Sutherland, Highland Council area, Crask Inn lies on the north side of the Srath a' Chraisg burn, 8 miles (13 km) south of Altnaharra.

Crask of Aigas *Highland* A locality in Easter Ross, Highland Council area, Crask of Aigas lies on the River Beauly, 5 miles (8 km) southwest of Beauly.

Crathes Castle *Aberdeenshire* A castle of Royal Deeside, Crathes Castle lies to the east of Banchory in Aberdeenshire. Robert the Bruce gifted the lands of Ley in 1323 to the Burnett family, who built the fortified tower house in 1553–96. Some of the rooms retain their original painted ceilings, and in the Great Hall is the ancient Horn of Leys, a symbol of the grant made by King Robert. The walled gardens incorporate herbaceous borders and great yew hedges that are fine examples of topiary dating from as early as 1702. The property of Crathes, comprising 215 ha (531 acres), was given to the National Trust for Scotland in 1951.

Crathie *Aberdeenshire* A locality in Royal Deeside, central Aberdeenshire, Crathie is situated on the A93 close to the River Dee and to Balmoral Castle, which is accessed via a bridge built by Prince Albert. The main feature of Crathie is its church which dates from 1895 and is attended by members of the royal family when staying at Balmoral. In the churchyard of Crathie Kirk is the grave of John Brown, Queen Victoria's 'devoted and faithful attendant'.

Crathie Point *Aberdeenshire* A headland on the Moray Firth coast of Aberdeenshire, Crathie Point lies nearly 2 miles (3 km) east of Cullen. The remains of Findlater Castle are nearby.

Cravadale, Loch *Western Isles* Loch Cravadale is located on the western coastline of North Harris in the Outer Hebrides. North-facing, this sea loch lies 2 miles (3 km) northeast of the settlement of Huisinis.

Crawford *South Lanarkshire* A village of South Lanarkshire, Crawford is located on the upper reaches of the River Clyde at the junction of the Camps and Midlock Waters with the Clyde 2 miles (3 km) southeast of Abington. The M74 passes to the west of the village.

Crawfordjohn *South Lanarkshire* A village of South Lanarkshire, Crawfordjohn lies to the north of the Duneaton Water, a tributary of the River Clyde, 3 miles (5 km) west of Abington and 7 miles (11 km) northeast of Leadhills. Curling stones produced here are thought to be the best in the world. Located in a former church, the Crawfordjohn Heritage Venture is a museum dedicated to the history of hill farming.

Crawfordton *Dumfries and Galloway* A house and estate in Dumfries and Galloway, Crawfordton lies a mile (1.5 km) to the east of Moniaive.

Crawick *Dumfries and Galloway* A hamlet of northern Dumfries and Galloway, Crawick is situated a half-mile (1 km) to the northwest of Sanquhar.

Crawick Water *Dumfries and Galloway* A stream of Dumfries and Galloway, the Crawick Water rises in the Lowther Hills. It flows southwestwards to join the River Nith at Crawick near Sanquhar.

Crawton *Aberdeenshire* All that remains of the once-thriving fishing community of Crawton on the southeast Aberdeenshire coast to the north of Catterline is Crawton Farm, which lies to the north of Crawton Bay. Following nearly fifty years of decline, Crawton was finally deserted by its last inhabitant in 1927 and now all that survive on the cliff top above the shingle beach are the ruins of twenty-three houses and a school. In its heyday, thirty Crawton men fished twelve boats and the village had its own fish merchant.

Crawton Ness *Aberdeenshire* A headland on the North Sea coast of southeast Aberdeenshire, Crawton Ness lies at the north end of Crawton Bay, 4 miles (6.5 km) south of Stonehaven.

Cray *Perth and Kinross* A locality in Glen Shee, eastern Perth and Kinross, Cray lies on the Shee Water at the foot of Mount Blair.

Creach Bheinn *Argyll and Bute* A mountain in the Benderloch district of Argyll and Bute, Creach Bheinn rises to 810 m (2657 ft) 2 miles (3 km) southeast of the head of Loch Creran. The peaks of Beinn Bhreac and Beinn Molurgainn rise to the south.

Creach Bheinn *Argyll and Bute* A mountain in the Ardmeanach area of the island of Mull, Argyll and Bute, Creach Bheinn rises to 491 m (1610 ft) a mile (1.5 km) east of the headland of Aird na h-Iolaire.

Creag a' Mhaim *Highland* One of seven peaks on the South Glen Shiel Ridge, Creag a' Mhaim rises to 1021 m (3350 ft) in the Inverness district of Highland Council area. Its name is derived from the Gaelic for 'rock of the large rounded hill'.

Creag Ghoraidh The Gaelic name for Creagorry in the Western Isles.

Creag Island *Argyll and Bute* Creag Island is an islet

located off the south coast of the island of Lismore, less than a mile (1 km) to the south of Eileann Dubh and to the west of Pladda Island, Argyll and Bute.

Creag Leacach *Angus* Located in the southwest corner of the Mounth plateau in Angus, Creag Leachan rises to 987 m (3238 ft). Its name is derived from the Gaelic for 'slabby rock', an apt description of the ridge leading to the summit which is covered in scree and boulders.

Creag Meagaidh *Highland* A mountain rising to a height of 1128 m (3703 ft) to the north of Loch Moy in the Lochaber district of Highland Council area. Creag Meagaidh derives its name from the Gaelic for 'bog land rock'. Management of the native pinewood on the slopes of the mountain aims to encourage natural regeneration.

Creag Mhòr An alternative name for Meall nan Aighean in Highland.

Creag Mhòr *Perth and Kinross/Stirling* A mountain rising to a height of 1047 m (3434 ft) to the northeast of Tyndrum on the border between Perth and Kinross and Stirling, Creag Mhòr lies within the Forest of Mamlorn. Its summit is formed at the apex of three distinct ridges, two of which enclose Coire Cheathaich at the head of Glen Lochay. Its name is derived from the Gaelic for 'big rock'.

Creag na Faoilinn *Highland* Located at the head of Loch Eriboll near the northern coastline of Highland Council area, the peak of Creag na Faoilinn rises to 286 m (938 ft). The valley of Strath Beag runs south from the foothills of Creag na Faoilinn.

Creag nan Damh *Highland* One of seven peaks on the South Glen Shiel Ridge, Creag nan Damh rises to 918 m (3012 ft) on the edge of Lochalsh district of Highland Council area. Its name is derived from the Gaelic for 'rock of the stags'.

Creag Pitridh *Highland* A mountain to the south of Loch Laggan in the Badenoch and Strathspey district of Highland Council area, Creag Pitridh rises to 924 m (3031 ft) and is noticeably smaller than its neighbours. Creag Pitridh's distinguishable features include a pointed summit and broken crags on its west face. The name is derived from the Gaelic for 'Petrie's hill'.

Creag Uchdag *Perth and Kinross* A hill rising to 879 m (2887 ft) to the south of Loch Tay in Perth and Kinross, Creag Uchdag overlooks Loch Lednock Reservoir to the south.

Creagan *Argyll and Bute* Located on the northern shore of Loch Creran, Argyll and Bute, the settlement of Creagan is separated from South Creagan by a small bridge that crosses the narrows of the loch. Three miles (5 km) to the northwest lies the settlement of Portnacroish.

Creagorry *Western Isles* A hamlet of southern Benbecula in the Outer Hebrides, Creagorry (Gael: *Creag Ghoraidh*) lies on the approaches to the South Ford causeway which provides the link to South Uist, a mile (1.5 km) southeast of Liniclate. There has been an inn here (now the Creagorry Hotel) since the 19th century.

Creca *Dumfries and Galloway* A village of Annandale in Dumfries and Galloway, Creca lies between the River Annan and the Kirtle Water, 3 miles (5 km) northeast of Annan.

Cree, River *South Ayrshire/Dumfries and Galloway* A river of Dumfries and Galloway, the Cree issues from Loch Moan on the border with South Ayrshire. It flows southwards for 25 miles (40 km) through the Galloway Forest Park before entering Wigtown Bay.

Creebank *Dumfries and Galloway* A locality in Dumfries and Galloway, Creebank is situated in the upper reaches of the River Cree, 9 miles (14 km) northwest of Newton Stewart.

Creebank Burn *Dumfries and Galloway* A tributary of the River Cree in Dumfries and Galloway, the Creebank Burn rises in Glentrool Forest.

Creebridge *Dumfries and Galloway* A village of Dumfries and Galloway with a woollen mill, Creebridge lies a half-mile (1 km) east of Newton Stewart and the River Cree.

Creetown *Dumfries and Galloway* A village in the Stewartry, Dumfries and Galloway, Creetown lies on the east bank of the River Cree, 6 miles (10 km) southeast of Newton Stewart. It dates from 1785, when a cotton mill was erected by James McCulloch of Barholm. In 1791 Creetown was created a burgh of barony. The majority of its houses have been built using local granite that was also shipped from the area in large quantities in the 19th century. Local attractions include a Heritage Museum and a Gem Rock Museum.

Creggans *Argyll and Bute* A locality with an inn on the east shore of Loch Fyne in Argyll and Bute, Creggans lies a mile (1.5 km) northwest of Strachur and 5 miles (8 km) south of Inveraray on the opposite side of the loch.

Creich *Fife* A village in a parish now linked with Flisk, Kilmany and Monimail, Creich lies in the hills of northern Fife, to the northeast of Brunton. The surrounding woodlands were once the hunting grounds of the earls of Fife, and within a farmsteading stand the ruins of a dovecote (1723) and castle once occupied by the Beatons of Balfour, hereditary stewards of Fife. Mary Beaton of Creich was one of the 'four Maries' who attended Mary, Queen of Scots. To the east is the ruined 14th-century St Devenic's Church of Creich, with its 16th-century aisle.

Creise *Highland* A mountain to the west of Rannoch Moor, Creise rises to 1100 m (3609 ft) on the south side of Glen Etive.

Creran, Glen *Argyll and Bute* A wooded valley in Argyll and Bute, Glen Creran carries the River Creran southwest to Loch Baile Mhic Chailein and out to Loch Creran.

Creran, Loch *Argyll and Bute* A sea loch of Argyll and Bute, Loch Creran forms a sea arm of Loch Linnhe extending into the Benderloch area for almost 7 miles (11 km) from the Lynn of Lorn, the strait separating Lismore from the mainland, to the foot of Glen Creran, a half-mile (1 km) southwest of Glasdrum.

Cretshengan *Argyll and Bute* Little more than a collection of farm buildings, Cretshengan is located 2 miles (3 km) north of Kilberry near the western coastline of the Kintyre peninsula, Argyll and Bute.

Creuch Hill *Inverclyde* A hill rising to a height of 441 m (1447 ft) 5 miles (8 km) south of Greenock, Creuch Hill is the highest point in Inverclyde. It lies within the Clyde Muirshiel Regional Park.

Crianlarich *Stirling* A village at the junction of Glen Falloch with Strath Fillan in western Stirling Council area, Crianlarich developed at the junction of three railways, two of which survive: Glasgow–Oban and Glasgow–Fort William. Crianlarich is also at the junction of the northbound A82 that skirts Loch Lomond and the A85 Perth–Oban road. The village is a centre for forestry, the surrounding farming community and tourism, and has hotels and a youth hostel. Three miles (5 km) to the west are the scant remains of a chapel dedicated to St Fillan by Robert the Bruce as an offering for the victory at Bannockburn. St Fillan's Bell was preserved in the churchyard for nearly a thousand years and the St Fillan crozier, known as the Quigrich, was in the custody of its hereditary keepers, the Dewars, until it passed, along with the bell, to the Royal Museum of Scotland in Edinburgh.

Crichope Linn *Dumfries and Galloway* A waterfall in Dumfries and Galloway, Crichope Linn lies on the Crichope Burn which flows into the Cample Water to the east of Thornhill.

Crichton Castle *Midlothian* A ruined castle overlooking the Tyne Water, 5 miles (8 km) southeast of Dalkeith in Midlothian. Crichton Castle belonged to Sir William Crichton, Lord Chancellor of Scotland in the 15th century. In 1440 the castle came under siege and shortly afterwards was remodelled to make it less vulnerable. In the 16th century the castle was home to James Hepburn, 4th Earl of Bothwell, the husband of Mary, Queen of Scots. In the late 16th century an unusual inner courtyard, resembling an Italian piazza, was created.

Crieff *Perth and Kinross* A resort town at the southern edge of highland Perth and Kinross, Crieff lies 12 miles (19 km) west of Perth, overlooking the River Earn which is joined here by the River Turret. Formerly the administrative centre of Strathearn, the original settlement was known to the Celtic earls of Strathearn as 'Cref'. The later village of Drummond, destroyed by the Jacobites in 1716, was rebuilt after 1731 on a grid plan by James Drummond, 3rd Duke of Perth, who encouraged handloom weaving. Although the Drummond Estates were subsequently forfeited to the Crown following the 1745 Jacobite Rebellion, the Forfeited Estates Commissioners encouraged the development of bleaching, tanning, paper making and other industries. Between 1672 and 1770, prior to the establishment of the Falkirk Tryst, Crieff was also the centre of Scotland's largest cattle market and the hub of a system of drove roads. During the early 19th century, whisky distilling, malting and woollen manufacture were the chief industries. Later in the century Crieff became one of Scotland's most notable holiday resorts, taking advantage of its sheltered, sunny location on the south-facing slope of the Knock. The railway arrived in 1856, Morrison's Academy was founded in 1859 and the Hydropathic Establishment (Crieff Hydro) opened its doors in 1868. The town remains an important resort and rural service centre, with hotels, a visitor centre, factory shop outlets, Highland Tryst Museum, two 18-hole golf courses and the Glenturret Distillery, Scotland's oldest Highland malt whisky distillery (1775). Local crafts include the manufacture of pottery and glassware, and there are recreational facilities in the Macrosty Park. Crieff Highland Gathering has been held annually since 1870.

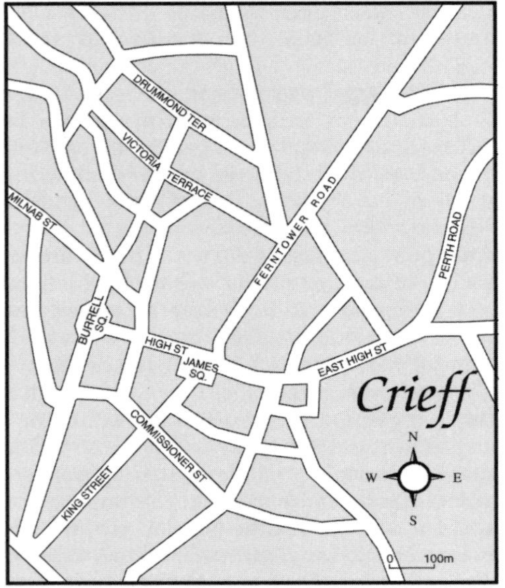

Criffell *Dumfries and Galloway* A hill in Dumfries and Galloway, Criffell rises to 569 m (1867 ft) 2 miles (3 km) south of New Abbey. The prominent Criffell Ridge forms an elevated tract of land some 15 miles (24 km) in length and is composed of granite rock that has resisted weathering more readily than the surrounding rock. At its summit is a pile of stones called Douglas's Cairn.

Crimond *Aberdeenshire* A Buchan village in northeast Aberdeenshire, Crimond lies to the south of the Loch of Strathbeg, 8 miles (13 km) northwest of Peterhead. An RAF station was created here during World War II.

Crinan *Argyll and Bute* Situated 6 miles (10 km) northwest of Lochgilphead, the village of Crinan sits at the northern end of the canal to which it gives its name. The Crinan Canal links Loch Crinan in the north with Ardrishaig and Loch Fyne in the south. Northwest across the bay stands Duntrune Castle, which dates from the 12th century.

Crinan, Loch *Argyll and Bute* A sea loch of Argyll and Bute, Loch Crinan lies on the Sound of Jura at the seaward end of the Crinan Canal and overlooking the island of Jura. The settlement of Crinan lies at the southern end of the loch, while Lochgilphead is 6 miles (10 km) southeast.

Crinan Canal *Argyll and Bute* The Crinan Canal on the west coast of Scotland affords passage by boat from Loch Fyne to the Sound of Jura. Its creation in the early 19th century gave herring boats and other coastal shipping quicker and safer passage to the Hebrides from the Firth of Clyde, thus avoiding the longer and more dangerous route around the Mull of Kintyre. In the late 18th century both James Watt (1736–1819) and John Rennie (1761–1821) undertook separate surveys of the proposed route, demonstrating the merits of the Crinan scheme over an alternative scheme linking East and West Loch Tarbert to the south. In 1793, John Campbell, 5th Duke of Argyll (1723–1806), was elected to run the canal company. He appointed Rennie as chief engineer, but progress was hindered by problems related to the effects of the tides. Opened in 1801, the 15-lock canal is 9 miles (14 km) in length and rises to a maximum height of 21 m (68 ft). Henry Bell's steamship *Comet* ran a regular service between Glasgow and Fort William, and Queen Victoria passed through the canal in 1847. However, as ship sizes grew, the canal became less important for trade and subsequently developed as a tourist link between Glasgow and the islands. Today it is a favourite destination for pleasure craft.

Crindledyke *North Lanarkshire* A small, scattered settlement of North Lanarkshire, Crindledyke lies a mile (1.5 km) east of Newmains. It is bordered to the north by the village of Bonkle, while to the south lies the village of Cathburn.

Crionaig *Western Isles* The area known as Crionaig is located in the southern section of the Isle of Lewis, in the Outer Hebrides. Rising to a height of 470 m (1542 ft), the Crionaig peak lies 3 miles (5 km) south of the head of the sea loch of Loch Shell.

Crocketford *Dumfries and Galloway* A village in Dumfries and Galloway, Crocketford lies at a road junction 8 miles (13 km) northeast of Castle Douglas. It is also known as Ninemile Bar, a name that dates from the establishment of a road toll bar here in the 18th century, 9 miles (14 km) from Dumfries.

Croe, Glen *Argyll and Bute* Glen Croe marks the northern boundary of the Cowal peninsula, Argyll and Bute. Bordered by Ben Arthur and Ben Donich, the glen carries the water from the Croe Water southeast to the head of Loch Long. The main route west, the A83, follows the glen, and it is at the northern end of the glen that the Rest and Be Thankful is located.

Croft-na-Caber *Perth and Kinross* A locality on the south shore of Loch Tay, Croft-na-Caber lies a half-mile (1 km) southwest of Kenmore. A reconstruction of a crannog, or prehistoric lake dwelling, was opened as the Scottish Crannog Centre in 1997. It is managed by the Scottish Trust for Underwater Archaeology.

Croftamie *Stirling* A small village in western Stirling Council area, Croftamie lies 3 miles (5 km) southwest of Drymen within Loch Lomond and the Trossachs National Park and the Loch Lomond Regional Park. It developed around a railway station in the 19th century.

Croggan *Argyll and Bute* A village of southeast Mull, Croggan lies on the south side of the narrow entrance to Loch Spelve from the Sound of Lorn.

Croick *Highland* A locality in Sutherland, Highland Council area, Croick lies in Strathcarron on the Allt an t-Srath Chuileannaich. Its T-plan parliamentary church was erected in 1827 to a design by Thomas Telford. Eighty people took refuge in its kirkyard in May 1845 after being evicted from their homes in Glencalvie to make way for a sheep farm.

Croig *Argyll and Bute* A township on the north coast of the island of Mull, Argyll and Bute, Croig lies on the shore of Loch a' Chumhainn 2 miles (3 km) northwest of Dervaig. Caliach Point lies 3 miles (5 km) to the west.

Cromar *Aberdeenshire* A district of Aberdeenshlre, Cromar lies between the middle reaches of the River Dee to the south and the Grampians to the north, with the village of Tarland at its centre.

Cromarty *Highland* A village at the northern tip of the Black Isle at the entrance to the Cromarty Firth in Highland Council area, Cromarty lies 15 miles (24 km) northeast of Inverness. Its natural harbour was known to the Vikings as Sikkerssand and later it developed as a trading post with royal burgh status (1264) and a royal castle nearby. Its importance waned in the 16th century when a ferry link to Nigg was established. In 1772 Sir George Ross of Pitkerie bought Cromarty with a view to redeveloping the harbour, encouraging industry and promoting fishing. He also built Cromarty's Gaelic Church and Cromarty House. The construction of better roads to the north and a decline in the fishing industry again turned Cromarty into a backwater until the 1970s, when it became a dormitory settlement for those working in oil-related industries. Hugh Miller (1802–56), the geologist and naturalist, writer and folklorist, was born in Cromarty. His birthplace is in the care of the National Trust for Scotland. Cromarty Courthouse houses an award-winning museum highlighting life past and present within the town.

Cromarty A dispersed ancient county of Highland Scotland, Cromarty comprised the estates of the Mackenzies of Tarbat, who became the Earls of Cromarty from 1703. The nucleus of the county was around the county town, also Cromarty, on Black Isle on the south shore of the Cromarty Firth, together with tracts of land scattered through the adjacent Ross-shire, extending to Loch Broom on the west coast. Cromarty was united with Ross-shire, to form Ross and Cromarty in 1889.

Cromarty Firth *Highland* An inlet of the Moray Firth in Highland Council area, the Cromarty Firth separates the mainland of Easter Ross from the Black Isle. It extends 18 miles (29 km) west and southwest to Dingwall from its mouth between the headlands known as the Sutors of Cromarty. Invergordon was an important naval harbour during both World Wars, and sheltered deep-water facilities here have been used more recently in the construction and repair of North Sea oil rigs.

Crombie *Fife* A small village in western Fife, Crombie lies on the A985 3 miles (5 km) west of Dunfermline. Originally an agricultural settlement, it developed during the 20th century in association with naval and marine facilities at Crombie Pier immediately to the south. The former parish of Crombie was united with Torryburn in 1622.

Crombie Country Park *Angus* A 102-ha (252-acre) country park with a loch and 4 miles (6.5 km) of woodland trails, Crombie Country Park lies to the west of Arbroath in Angus. Opened in 1983, it has a children's adventure play area. The loch, which was created in a former quarry between 1866 and 1868, provided additional water for Dundee, the works at nearby Monikie proving inadequate by then. Crombie was last used to supply water to Carnoustie in 1981.

Crombie Water *Moray* Rising in the Braes of Glenlivet, the Crombie Water flows north to meet the River Livet opposite Tombae, skirting the Bochel on its way.

Cromdale *Highland* A village in Strathspey, Highland Council area, Cromdale lies on the River Spey, 3 miles (5 km) northeast of Grantown-on-Spey. The village developed in association with forest planting on the Strathspey Estate in the early 19th century. The Hills of Cromdale rise to 710 m (2329 ft) to the south. A Government army defeated a force of Jacobites at the Haughs of Cromdale in 1690, an event later commemorated in a popular ballad by James Hogg, the 'Ettrick Shepherd' (1770–1835).

Cromor The Gaelic name for Cromore in the Western Isles.

Cromore *Western Isles* A remote crofting township with a modest jetty on the east coast of the island of Lewis in the Outer Hebrides, Cromore (Gael: *Cromor*) is located on a hammerhead-shaped peninsula at the mouth of Loch Erisort.

Crongart, Loch *South Ayrshire* A loch in South Ayrshire, Loch Crongart lies 3 miles (5 km) to the east of Barrhill. It is the source of the Feoch Burn, a tributary of the River Duisk.

Crook of Devon *Perth and Kinross* Situated in the parish of Fossoway in Perth and Kinross, the village of Crook of Devon straddles the A977 from Kinross to the Kincardine Bridge. It lies at a point where the River Devon takes a sharp turn westwards after flowing eastwards from the Ochil Hills and comprises the Old Crook, Tulliebole Mill and Waulkmill areas. Fossoway and Tulliebole Church at the west end of the village dates from 1729, and built into a nearby dyke is a large sandstone boulder known as the Bull Stone, possibly associated with the pastime of bull baiting. Crook of Devon was the scene of famous witchcraft trials in the 1660s, the witches being burned to death in a field known as 'Lamblairs'.

Crookedholm *East Ayrshire* The eastern Ayrshire village of Crookedholm lies 2 miles (3 km) east of Kilmarnock, at the junction of the River Irvine with the old road to Hurlford.

Crooked Loch *Scottish Borders* A small loch in Scottish Borders, the Crooked Loch lies on the old Selkirkshire–Roxburghshire county border, 8 miles (13 km) west of Hawick.

Crookston Castle *Glasgow City* Crookston Castle is located in the Pollok district of Glasgow, some 5 miles (8 km) south of the city centre and overlooking the Levern Water, just before its confluence with the White Cart Water. The castle was most likely built in the late 14th century and was long the property of the Stewarts of Darnley, including Henry Stewart (1545–67), who was second husband to Mary, Queen of Scots. The castle had been besieged by King James IV in 1489 and significantly damaged. The ruin passed through various hands, including the dukes of Montrose, who sold it to the Maxwells of Pollok in 1757. This family partially restored the castle to commemorate the visit of Queen Victoria to Glasgow in 1847. The poets Robert Burns (1759–96), William Motherwell (1797–1835) and Robert Tannahill (1774–1810) have all mentioned the castle in their works, while Sir Walter Scott (1771–1832) suggested Queen Mary watched the Battle of Langside (1568) from its towers, although the topography makes this impossible. In 1931, Crookston was the first property acquired by the National Trust for Scotland, having been presented by Sir John Stirling Maxwell (1866–1956), one of its founder members. Today, its maintenance is the responsibility of Historic Scotland.

Cros The Gaelic name for Cross in the Western Isles.

Crosbost The Gaelic name for Crossbost in the Western Isles.

Cross *Western Isles* One of several closely associated crofting townships lying in the Ness district at the northern tip of Lewis in the Outer Hebrides, Cross (Gael: *Cros*) is located immediately to the southwest of Swainbost and to the northeast of North Dell. Cross benefits from a primary school.

Cross Water of Luce *South Ayrshire/Dumfries and Galloway* A river of Dumfries and Galloway, the Cross Water of Luce forms the eastern headwater of the Water of Luce which flows southwards into Luce Bay. The Cross Water of Luce rises in South Ayrshire and flows southwards, joining the Main Water of Luce near New Luce to form the Water of Luce.

Crossaig *Argyll and Bute* The settlement of Crossaig lies on the eastern shore of Kintyre in Argyll and Bute, 5 miles (8 km) north of Grogport. Overlooking the Kilbrannan Sound, Crossaig offers views to the island of Arran. To the north of the village lies Crossaig Glen and its associated river.

Crossapol *Argyll and Bute* A small settlement on the southwestern coast of the island of Coll in Argyll and Bute, Crossapol has views across Crossapol Bay.

Crossapoll *Argyll and Bute* A settlement located on Hynish Bay, on the south coast of the island of Tiree in Argyll and Bute, Crossapoll lies 3 miles (5 km) southwest of Scarinish.

Crossbost *Western Isles* A linear crofting and fishing village in the Lochs district of the island of Lewis, Crossbost (Gael: *Crosbost*) lies at the mouth of Loch Leurbost immediately to the southwest of Ranish, a half-mile (1 km) southeast of Leurbost and 6 miles (10 km) south-southwest of Stornoway. With Ranish, Crossbost occupies the neck of Aird Ranish. The settlement benefits from two churches, including the Lochs Parish Church, and a pier.

Crossford *South Lanarkshire* Located near the confluence of the rivers Clyde and Nethan, the small village of Crossford lies 3 miles (5 km) southwest of Carluke and 5 miles (8 km) northwest of Lanark in South Lanarkshire. Nearby lie the ruins of Craignethan Castle.

Crossford *Fife* A village in western Fife, Crossford lies on the A994 a mile (1.5 km) west of Dunfermline. A former weaving village, Crossford is said to take its name from the ford crossed by monks on their way between the abbeys of Dunfermline and Culross. To the southeast lies the 18-hole Pitfirrane golf course of the Dunfermline Golf Club, whose clubhouse was the mansion of the Halkett family, owners of the former Pitfirrane Estate until 1951.

Crossgatehall *East Lothian* Located on the western edge of East Lothian close to the border with Midlothian, Crossgatehall is a hamlet 3 miles (5 km) northeast of Dalkeith. The 16th-century house of Carberry Tower is located a mile (1.5 km) to the northwest.

Crossgates *Fife* A former coal-mining village in western Fife, Crossgates sits on a road junction 2 miles (3 km) south of Cowdenbeath. In the days of cattle droving the blacksmiths of Crossgates made shoes for cattle, and in the 18th century coal from the surrounding area was first transported by wagonway to St David's Harbour on Inverkeithing Bay.

Crosshill *Fife* A former burgh of barony (1511) situated to the east of Loch Ore in Ballingry parish, western Fife, Crosshill developed as a mining town in the late 19th century when it merged with Lochore to the north and Glencraig to the south. The village has a business centre with building, decorating and employment services. Lochore Meadows Country Park lies to the west, and the Bronze Age Harelaw Cairn stands on a hill to the east.

Crosshill *Glasgow City* A residential suburb of Glasgow, Crosshill lies to the south of the city centre. Created a police burgh in 1871, it became part of Glasgow in 1891.

Crosshill *South Ayrshire* Located 3 miles (5 km) southeast of Maybole in South Ayrshire, Crosshill is a planned village without the strict layout associated with planned settlements. With the development of feuing in 1808, land was taken up and many single-storey cottages were built by Irish immigrants attracted by the growth of handloom weaving. Although a few were altered or demolished, there are still original cottages to be found on Dalhowan Street.

Crosshouse *East Ayrshire* A sizeable village near the western boundary of East Ayrshire, Crosshouse lies on the Carmel Water, 2 miles (3 km) west of Kilmarnock and a similar distance south-southwest of Kilmaurs. Once at the centre of coal-mining and brick-making industries, Crosshouse later became important for its enormous Massey-Ferguson tractor plant, although this entered receivership in 1977. Crosshouse Hospital, which lies immediately to the east of the village, opened in 1984 and is the principal general hospital for East and North Ayrshire. Born in Crosshouse was Andrew Fisher (1862–1928), who became prime minister of Australia on three occasions. He has a memorial in the village.

Crosskirk *Highland* A locality on the north coast of Caithness, Highland Council area, Crosskirk is located on Crosskirk Bay, 5 miles (8 km) west of Thurso. On a cliff overlooking the sea stands the roofless 12th-century St Mary's Chapel, one of the oldest ecclesiastical buildings in Caithness.

Crossmichael *Dumfries and Galloway* A village of Dumfries and Galloway, Crossmichael lies to the east of Loch Ken, 3.5 miles (6 km) northwest of Castle Douglas. The village once had a cross around which was held the Michaelmas Fair.

Crossmount *Perth and Kinross* A mid-18th-century mansion house in the Rannoch district of Perth and Kinross, Crossmount lies to the south of Dunalastair Water, 3 miles (5 km) east of Kinloch Rannoch.

Crossraguel Abbey *South Ayrshire* Located 2 miles (3 km) southwest of Maybole in South Ayrshire, Crossraguel Abbey dates from the 13th century and was founded by the 1st Earl of Carrick. It was extended in the 15th and 16th centuries. The Cross of Riaghill was a great standing cross that was located nearby. The well-preserved ruined abbey is now in the care of Historic Scotland.

Crossroads *East Ayrshire* As its name suggests, the hamlet of Crossroads sits at the junction of the Kilmarnock–Mauchline and Galston–Ayr roads, 4 miles (6.5 km) southeast of Kilmarnock. Cessnock Water, a tributary of the River Irvine, runs close by.

Crosswood Reservoir *West Lothian* A reservoir in West Lothian on the west side of the Pentland Hills, Crosswood Reservoir lies on the Crosswood Burn.

Crovie *Aberdeenshire* A fishing village comprising a single row of cottages on the Moray Firth coast of Aberdeenshire, Crovie lies immediately north of Gardenstown on the east shore of Gamrie Bay.

Crow Road *East Dunbartonshire/Stirling* The road north from Lennoxtown in East Dunbartonshire to Fintry in Stirling Council area is known as the Crow Road. It passes over high ground between the Campsie Fells and the Kilsyth Hills. At a sharp bend 2 miles (3 km) north of Lennoxtown there are fine views over west-central Scotland.

Crowlin Islands *Highland* A group of three uninhabited islands in the Inner Sound, the Crowlin Islands lie between Skye and the mainland, from which they are separated by the Caolas Mòr. The island group comprises Eilean Mòr ('big island'), Eilean Meadhonach ('middle island') and Eilean Beag ('little island') and has an area of 229 ha (567 acres). At low tide the islands are connected by reefs.

Crowlista *Western Isles* A small and remote crofting township on the north side of Uig Bay in the far west of Lewis in the Outer Hebrides, Crowlista (Gael: *Cradhlastadh*) lies a mile (1.5 km) west of Timsgarry and 25 miles (40 km) west of Stornoway.

Crows *Dumfries and Galloway* A locality in the Machars, Dumfries and Galloway, Crows lies on the Crows Burn to the east of Crows Moss, 4 miles (6.5 km) west of Wigtown.

Croy *Highland* A settlement to the east of Inverness in Highland Council area, Croy lies on the River Nairn, a mile (1.5 km) southeast of Inverness Airport.

Croy *North Lanarkshire* The village of Croy is located a mile (1.5 km) south of Kilsyth in North Lanarkshire. To the northeast of the village on Croy Hill are remnants of the Antonine Wall, including a Roman fort and two beacon platforms.

Cruach an t-Sorchain *Argyll and Bute* A hill on the Kintyre peninsula in Argyll and Bute, Cruach an t-Sorchain rises to 343 m (1125 ft) 2 miles (3 km) south of the settlement of Tarbert.

Cruach Ardrain *Stirling* Rising to a height of 1046 m (3432 ft) southeast of Crianlarich in Stirling Council area, Cruach Ardrain is one of a number of mountains encircling the village. The name is derived from the Gaelic for 'stack of the high part'.

Cruach Lusach *Argyll and Bute* A mountain in the Knapdale area of Argyll and Bute, Cruach Lusach rises to 466 m (1528 ft). It overlooks Loch Fyne to the east and Loch Sween to the west.

Cruach na Caol-bheinn *Argyll and Bute* A hill to the east of Gartavaich on the Kintyre peninsula, Argyll and Bute, the hill of Cruach na Caol-bheinn rises to 264 m (866 ft).

Cruachan Hydro Power Station *Argyll and Bute* Located at the north end of Loch Awe, 5 miles (8 km) southeast of Taynuilt, Cruachan is a 400 megawatt pumped-storage power station. One of the first of this type of station built in the world, it raises water to a high reservoir during off-peak periods and then releases it again to generate additional power during times of peak demand. Much of the station is actually buried deep within Ben Cruachan and a guided tour takes visitors almost 1000 m (3280 ft) underground. The station has been operational since 1966 and was built and run by the North of Scotland Hydro-Electric Board, but was transferred to Scottish Power on privatisation in 1990.

Cruden, Bay of *Aberdeenshire* An inlet on the North Sea coast of Aberdeenshire, Bay of Cruden lies at the mouth of the Water of Cruden and stretches southwards from the harbour at Port Erroll to a rocky reef known as The Skares.

Cruden, Water of *Aberdeenshire* A stream in eastern Aberdeenshire, the Water of Cruden rises on the Hill of Auchleuchries, 4 miles (6.5 km) northeast of Ellon. It flows eastwards to enter the North Sea at Cruden Bay.

Cruden Bay *Aberdeenshire* A resort on the Buchan coast of Aberdeenshire, Cruden Bay lies to the north of the Bay of Cruden near the mouth of the Water of

Cruden, 7 miles (11 km) south of Peterhead. Originally known as Invercruden, the village was renamed in 1924. Cruden Bay once had rail connections that brought holidaymakers to its grand railway hotel and golf links by the bay. A short distance to the southeast lies the harbour of Port Erroll, the former Ward of Cruden. To the north stand the cliff-top ruins of the New, or second, Slains Castle, the ancestral home of the earls of Errol built in 1597 by Francis Hay, the 9th Earl. Johnson and Boswell stayed here on the night of 24 August 1773, Boswell recording that Johnson thought the prospect here 'the noblest he had ever seen'. Two miles (3 km) further north is the roofless cave known as the Bullers of Buchan. Since 1975 crude oil from the Forties field in the North Sea has been pumped ashore at Cruden Bay.

Cruggleton Bay An alternative name for Rigg Bay in Dumfries and Galloway.

Cruick Water *Angus* A stream in Angus, the Cruick Water rises on Mowat's Seat in the Braes of Angus. It flows south into the valley of Strathmore then east to join the River North Esk at Stracathro. It has a total length of 16 miles (26 km).

Cruickshank Botanical Gardens *Aberdeen City* Established in 1898, the 4.5-ha (11-acre) Cruickshank Botanical Gardens of the University of Aberdeen are located in the Chanonry of Old Aberdeen. In addition to a water garden and exotic trees, the gardens have collections of alpines, succulents and rock plants.

Cruise Burn *Dumfries and Galloway* A stream in Dumfries and Galloway, the Cruise Burn is a tributary of the Water of Luce, which it joins just south of New Luce.

Cuaig *Highland* A settlement in Wester Ross, Cuaig lies on the coast of the Inner Sound opposite the island of Rona, Highland Council area.

Cubbie Roo's Castle *Orkney* Said to be the remains of the oldest stone castle in Scotland, Cubbie Roo's Castle stands on the small Orkney island of Wyre. It dates from the mid-12th century and was probably the stronghold of the Norseman Kolbein Hruga (Cubbie Roo), who is recorded in the *Orkneyinga Saga* as having a seat here.

Cuidhtinis The Gaelic name for Quidinish in the Western Isles.

Cuileannach, Strath *Highland* A remote and partially forested valley of Ross in the northern Highlands, Strath Cuileannach lies to the north of the head of Strath Carron and runs northwest–southeast for 5.5 miles (9 km). The valley contains the Abhainn an t-Srath Chuileannaich in its middle and lower reaches.

Cuillins, the *Highland* A range of mountains located in the southern part of the isle of Skye in Highland Council area, the Cuillins are a favourite walking and rock-climbing area. The name is believed to be derived from the legendary Irish hunter Cu Chulainn, who is said to have come from Ireland to Skye in two strides. The main body of the Cuillins is known as the Black Cuillins, with the lower Red Cuillins lying just to the east. The highest peak of the group is Sgurr Alasdair, at 992 m (3255 ft).

Cul Beag *Highland* A mountain in northwest Highland Council area, Cul Beag rises to 769 m (2523 ft) 8 miles (13 km) north of Ullapool.

Cul Mòr *Highland* A mountain in northwest Highland Council area, Cul Mòr rises to 849 m (2785 ft) in Drumrunie Forest, 9 miles (14 km) north of Ullapool.

Culardoch *Aberdeenshire* A mountain in the eastern Grampians, Culardoch rises to 900 m (2953 ft) to the north of the River Dee, 7 miles (11 km) northeast of Braemar.

Culbin Sands *Moray* Now an area of conifer forest, the Culbin Sands originally comprised barren sand dunes stretching westwards along the Moray Firth coast from the mouth of the River Findhorn. Described as the 'Scottish Sahara', the Culbin Sands were said to have been part of a fertile coastal estate owned by the Kinnaird family that was overwhelmed by sandstorms in 1694. Erosion probably resulted from the harvesting of marram grass for roof thatch, a practice that was forbidden by an Act of the Scottish Parliament in 1695. Attempts to reclaim the Culbin Sands in the 18th century failed, and it was not until the Forestry Commission acquired the land in 1922 and planted trees that the area was stabilised.

Culblean Hill *Aberdeenshire* A hill in Aberdeenshire, Culblean Hill rises to 604 m (1983 ft) to the north of the River Dee, 3 miles (5 km) northeast of Ballater.

Culbokie *Highland* The 'Haunted Nook' of Culbokie lies on the Black Isle, Highland Council area, 5 miles (8 km) northeast of Conon Bridge. The Findon Burn lies to the east of the village.

Culburnie *Highland* A settlement in The Aird, Highland Council area, Culburnie lies between the River Beauly and the Boblainy Forest, 5 miles (8 km) southwest of Beauly.

Culcabock *Highland* A settlement in Highland Council area, Culcabock forms an eastern suburb of Inverness.

Culcharry *Highland* A settlement to the east of Inverness in Highland Council area, Culcharry lies 4 miles (6.5 km) south of Nairn.

Culcraigie Loch *Dumfries and Galloway* A small loch in Dumfries and Galloway, Culcraigie Loch lies 4 miles (6.5 km) north of Kirkcudbright. It is the source of the Spout Burn which flows southeastwards to meet the Tarff Water.

Culcreuch Castle *Stirling* A former stronghold of the Galbraith family who built it in the 15th century, Culcreuch Castle lies within a 647-ha (1600-acre) country park to the northeast of Fintry in southern Stirling Council area. A pinetum in the park was planted in 1842.

Culkein *Highland* A small township of Assynt in western Sutherland, Culkein lies on the north coast of a peninsula that culminates in the Point of Stoer.

Cullen *Moray* A resort town in Moray, Cullen is situated on Cullen Bay, an inlet of the Moray Firth, 25 miles (40 km) east of Elgin. The original royal burgh charter was granted in 1455 to Inverculan, a settlement that stood near the Cullen Water adjacent to the old kirk of St Mary of Cullen. This church foundation can be traced back to 1327, when King Robert the Bruce endowed a chaplaincy for his second wife who had died there. It was rebuilt in 1543 by Alexander Ogilvie of Findlater, whose monument occupies the full height of the chancel wall. Old Cullen was moved to higher ground some time in the Middle Ages, and in 1811 the Earl of Seafield commissioned a plan for a new town. The first house was built in 1820 and gradually the whole of Old Cullen was removed to the new site with its regular grid plan and central square. Occupying a hillside overlooking Cullen Bay, the New Town or Uptown of Cullen looks down on the Seatown of Cullen, an old fishing settlement largely comprising one-storey cottages. The adjacent harbour, originally designed in 1736 by William Adam for the Earl of Findlater, was rebuilt in 1817 and 1823 and extended in 1834. Nearby on Castle Hill stands Cullen House, first built in 1600 by the Earl of Findlater who moved his seat from Findlater Castle, the ruins of which lie 2 miles (3 km) to the east of Cullen on a cliff top overlooking the sea. Noted architects including William Adam, James Adam, James Playfair and David Bryce were all at various times involved in creating and embellishing one of Scotland's finest houses and designed landscapes. The burgh developed as a holiday resort with the coming of the railway, which also resulted in the creation of the fine viaduct that spans the main street. Cullen, with its long fishing tradition, gives its name to a rich creamy haddock soup known as Cullen Skink. The Bin of Cullen rises to 320 m (1050 ft) to the southwest, and on the shore of Cullen Bay are three sandstone rock stacks known as the Three Kings of Cullen.

Cullen Bay *Moray* A bay of the Moray Firth coast, Cullen Bay is situated between Scar Nose to the west and Logie Head to the east. The port of Cullen lies on its shore.

Cullicudden *Highland* A scattered settlement on the Black Isle, Highland Council area, Cullicudden lies on the southeastern side of the Cromarty Firth opposite Evanton. It is said to take its name from a small tasteless fish known as a cuddy that used to be caught in large quantities in a small creek on the shore. The old church, which stands on a slope running down to the Cromarty Firth, was built in 1606.

Cullipool *Argyll and Bute* A village on the northwest coast of the island of Luing in Argyll and Bute, Cullipool looks out over the Firth of Lorn towards the Garvellach Islands to the west and Mull to the north.

Culloch Burn *Dumfries and Galloway* A stream in Dumfries and Galloway, the Culloch Burn is a tributary of the Kirkgunzeon Lane, east of Haugh of Urr and 2 miles (3 km) north of Dalbeattie.

Culloden *Highland* A locality 4 miles (6.5 km) east of Inverness in Highland Council area, Culloden comprises a sizeable commuter settlement, Culloden House, Culloden Forest and Culloden Muir, the scene of a battle fought on 16 April 1746 at which the Highland army of Prince Charles Edward Stewart (Bonnie Prince Charlie) was defeated by the Government forces of the Duke of Cumberland. This was the last battle to be fought on British soil. A National Trust for Scotland visitor centre houses a permanent Jacobite exhibition, and also in the Trust's care are the Graves of the Clans, the Well of the Dead, the Memorial Cairn, the Cumberland Stone, the Field of the English, and Old Leanach Cottage, which survived the battle being fought around it. Built in 1772–83, Culloden House between Smithton and Balloch belonged to the Forbes family.

Culmalzie *Dumfries and Galloway* A locality in the Machars, Dumfries and Galloway, Culmalzie lies at a road junction 4 miles (6.5 km) southwest of Wigtown.

Culnacraig *Highland* A township in Wester Ross, Highland Council area, Culnacraig lies on the northern shore of Loch Broom, 5 miles (8 km) southeast of Achiltibuie. Ben Mòr Coigach rises to the northeast.

Culnaknock *Highland* A settlement on the northeast coast of the island of Skye, Highland Council area, Culnaknock lies 3 miles (5 km) south of Staffin.

Culrain *Highland* A locality in Sutherland, Highland Council area, Culrain lies 3 miles (5 km) northwest of Bonar Bridge, to the west of the Kyle of Sutherland.

Culross *Fife* An attractive example of an old Scottish burgh in western Fife, Culross is situated on the Firth of Forth 7 miles (11 km) west of Dunfermline. Created a royal burgh in 1588, Culross was the legendary birthplace of St Kentigern (or St Mungo). An abbey was founded here in 1217 by Malcolm, 7th Earl of Fife, and during the 17th century salt panning, coal mining, weaving and trade with the Low Countries from the foreshore port of Sandhaven were developed, chiefly by the enterprising local merchant Sir George Bruce. Another famous product of the town at that time was the iron baking girdle. The town is rich in 17th- and 18th-century cobbled lanes and buildings, many of which have been restored by the National Trust for Scotland. Among the main historic landmarks are: The Palace, built by Sir George Bruce in the 16th century; 13th-century Culross Abbey, a Cistercian foundation; the Town House (1626); and The Study (1633), with its corbelled top storey.

Culroy *South Ayrshire* A hamlet of South Ayrshire, Culroy lies on the B7024 between Ayr and Maybole, 3 miles (5 km) north of Maybole.

Culter An alternative name for Coulter in South Lanarkshire.

Culter Burn *Aberdeen City* A small river in the far west of Aberdeen City, the Culter Burn represents the lower reaches of the Leuchar Burn. The Culter Burn flows south and receives the Gormack Burn before turning east to form the boundary between Aberdeen City and Aberdeenshire. It joins the River Dee at Peterculter.

Culter Hills *South Lanarkshire/Scottish Borders* A range of hills on the border between South Lanarkshire and Scottish Borders, the Culter Hills are separated from the Tweedsmuir Hills by the River Tweed. Rising to a height of 748 m (2454 ft) at Culter Fell, the hills are the source of the Culter Water which flows northwest from Culter Waterhead Reservoir to join the River Clyde near Symington. The northern boundary of the Culter Hills is formed by the Biggar Water and the Biggar Gap.

Culter Water *South Lanarkshire* A stream in South Lanarkshire, the Culter Water rises in hills to the south of Biggar, passes through the Culter Waterhead Reservoir and flows for 6 miles (10 km) northwest through Coulter before joining the Clyde.

Cultercullen *Aberdeenshire* A hamlet in the Aberdeenshire parish of Foveran, Cultercullen lies a mile (1.5 km) east of Udny Station and 15 miles (24 km) north of Aberdeen.

Cults *Aberdeen City* A village of Aberdeen City, situated on the A93 close to the River Dee, 4 miles (6.5 km) southwest of Aberdeen city centre. It is now largely a commuter settlement for Aberdeen.

Cultybraggan *Perth and Kinross* A locality at the entrance to Glen Artney in Perth and Kinross, Cultybraggan lies 2 miles (3 km) south of Comrie by the Water of Ruchill. Now used as a military camp, it was established during World War II to house up to 4000 German prisoners of war. The modern military camp lies close to the site of a much earlier Roman fort that guarded the mouth of the glen.

Culzean Bay *South Ayrshire* Culzean Bay is located on

the coastline of South Ayrshire and extends from Culzean Country Park, which sits at its southern end, to Dunure at the northern end. Culzean Castle looks northwards over the bay, while Dunure Castle looks to the south.

Culzean Castle *South Ayrshire* A castle and country park near Maybole on the coast of South Ayrshire, Culzean is one of Scotland's leading tourist attractions. Culzean Castle was built in 1772–90 by Robert Adam for David, 10th Earl of Cassilis. It stands on a dramatic cliff top overlooking the Firth of Clyde on a site associated with the Kennedy family since the 14th century. The Eisenhower Room in the castle commemorates General Eisenhower's links with Scotland. Surrounding the castle is parkland landscaped by Alexander Nasmyth (1758–1840). In 1945 Culzean was gifted to the National Trust for Scotland, and in 1969 228 ha (563 acres) were designated as Scotland's first country park.

Cumberhead *South Lanarkshire* The settlement of Cumberhead is located 4 miles (6.5 km) southwest of Lesmahagow in South Lanarkshire.

Cumbernauld *North Lanarkshire* One of Scotland's five New Towns and the only New Town designated in Britain in the 1950s, Cumbernauld developed close to an earlier textile and mining village of the same name. It was designated a New Town on 9 December 1955 with plans to house 50–80,000 people, primarily relocated from Glasgow. Situated 13 miles (21 km) northeast of Glasgow and 5 miles (8 km) south of Kilsyth, it lies north of the Luggie Water, south of the Forth and Clyde Canal and the River Kelvin, and east of Broadwood Loch. Its economy is centred on retail and high-tech industries, mostly located in large industrial parks to the west of the town. Residential districts include Balloch, Eastfield, Carrickstone, Seafar, Carbrain, Condorrat, Dalshannan, Deadridge, Westfield and Abronhill.

Cuminestown *Aberdeenshire* A planned village in Buchan founded in 1763 by the 'improving' laird Joseph Cumine of Auchry, Cuminestown is situated in Aberdeenshire, 5 miles (8 km) east of Turriff. Comprising a single street, it lies in a designed landscape to the south of Auchry House, from which it is separated by the Burn of Monquhitter. Joseph Cumine obliged his feuars to keep a book of worthwhile improvements and rewarded hard workers with a dram of whisky at regular meetings held in the local inn. The poet William Ingram was born here in 1765 and the artist James Cowie was a son of the village who used local views as backgrounds to many of his works. The village today has a small industrial estate.

Cumlewick *Shetland* A locality with a harbour on the east coast of the Mainland of Shetland, Cumlewick lies on a small peninsula, a half-mile (1 km) south of Stove and 12 miles (19 km) south-southwest of Lerwick. Cumlewick Ness lies a half-mile (1 km) to the south.

Cummertrees *Dumfries and Galloway* A settlement in Dumfries and Galloway, Cummertrees lies by the Pow Water, 3 miles (5 km) west of Annan.

Cummingstown *Moray* Consisting of a single street of stone cottages, the Moray village of Cummingstown lies between Burghead and Lossiemouth overlooking the Moray Firth. It was established in 1808 by Sir William Gordon-Cumming to house masons working in the nearby stone quarries.

Cumnock *East Ayrshire* An ancient market town and former mining settlement of East Ayrshire, Cumnock (originally Old Cumnock) is situated at the confluence of the River Glaisnock with the Lugar Water, 16 miles (26 km) east of Ayr. Created a burgh of barony in 1509 for the Dunbars, earls of March, it developed in the 18th century in association with coal mining, weaving and the production of gas. Snuffboxes, pottery and farm machinery were also manufactured in Cumnock, and ironstone was mined between 1873 and 1906. In the 20th century, yarn spinning and the manufacture of shoes, farm implements, carpets and knitwear sustained the town, although unemployment was high by the 1990s. The more recent introduction of electronics industries and opencast mining maintains the industrial base of Cumnock. The town has a museum (which includes a snuffbox collection), the Mercat Cross (square shaft, dating from 1509), and the Town Hall, which opens onto a statue of Keir Hardie (1856–1915), a founder of the Labour Party and union organiser and journalist in Cumnock.

Cunninghame *North Ayrshire/South Ayrshire* One of the ancient divisions of Ayrshire, Cunninghame extends over the greater part of North Ayrshire and part of South Ayrshire. In the 12th and 13th centuries the De Morville family, High Constables of Scotland, held most of this land which is watered by the Rye, Caaf, Dusk, Garnock, Lugton and Annick. From 1975 to 1996 Cunninghame formed a district of Strathclyde Region.

Cunninghamhead *North Ayrshire* A former mining hamlet at the head of a narrow tract of North Ayrshire extending northeastwards into East Ayrshire, Cunninghamhead is located 2 miles (3 km) west of Kilmaurs and a similar distance northeast of Perceton. The Annick Water flows just to the north of the settlement.

Cunningsburgh *Shetland* A village on the Mainland of Shetland, Cunningsburgh lies on the east coast 8 miles (13 km) south-southeast of Lerwick. A district and old parish of the same name extends across the island, and the Cunningsburgh Hills form a ridge running nearly parallel with the coast. An agricultural show is held in Cunningsburgh each August.

Cupar *Fife* A burgh town in northeast Fife, Cupar lies on the River Eden at the east end of the Howe of Fife, 12 miles (19 km) west of St Andrews. The former county town of Fife and seat of the Sheriff of Fife, Cupar received its royal charter in 1328, along with the right to trade through a port near Guardbridge on the coast. The town subsequently developed as an administrative and agricultural market centre, functions that continued until 1975 when Glenrothes became the new county town and 1994 when the local market was closed. Its castle, the seat of the earls of Fife, was the scene in 1535 of the first performance of *Ane Pleasant Satyre of the Thrie Estaitis* by Sir David Lindsay, a courtier of James V born at the Mount to the northwest of Cupar. Historic buildings include Preston Lodge, the 17th-century town house of the Prestons of Airdrie; the 17th-century Chancellor's House which was the birthplace of John Campbell, who became Lord Chancellor in 1859; the County Buildings (*c.*1812–17); the Corn Exchange; the Mercat Cross (1683); the Duncan Institute (1870); and the Old Parish Church (St Michael of Tarvit). Between 1926 and the 1970s Scotland's only sugar beet factory operated outside

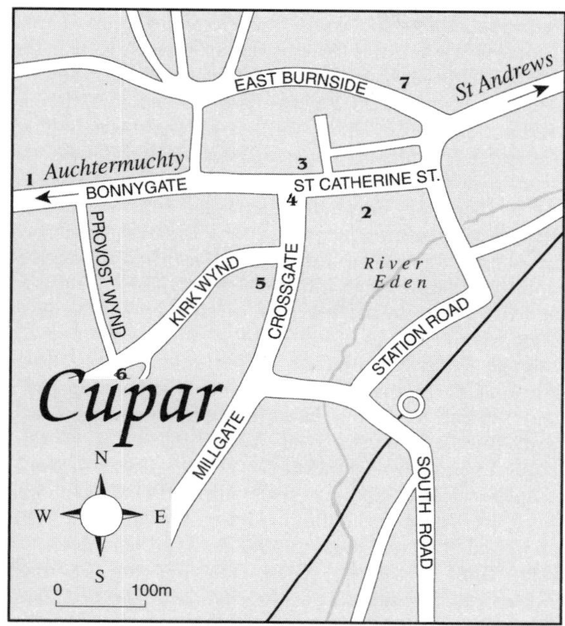

1 *Preston Lodge*
2 *County Buildings*
3 *Corn Exchange*
4 *Mercat Cross*
5 *Duncan Institute*
6 *Old Parish Church*
7 *Eden Park Leisure Centre*

Cupar. Today Cupar has newspaper, printing, grain-milling, food-processing, chemical, furniture and construction industries, some of which are located to the east of the town in the Prestonhall and Cupar trading estates. It is also the home of Elmwood College (horticulture and farming) and the Bell-Baxter High School, which evolved from the Madras Academy (founded in 1831 by Andrew Bell) and an educational institute 'for young ladies' (founded in 1871 by Lady Baxter of Kilmaron Castle to the north of Cupar). The town has a sports centre (Eden Park Leisure Centre), a nine-hole golf course and the Douglas Bader Garden for the disabled.

Cupar Muir *Fife* A village in the parish of Cupar, northeast Fife, Cupar Muir lies between Cupar and Springfield. It was once associated with the quarrying of stone and more famously with a confrontation in 1559 between the French troops of Mary of Guise (mother of Mary, Queen of Scots) and the forces of the Protestant Lords of the Congregation. A truce that ultimately led to the withdrawal of the French was a turning point in the Reformation struggle.

Cur, River *Argyll and Bute* Rising in the foothills of Beinn Lochain, Argyll and Bute, the Cur flows east then south, passing through the Argyll Forest Park and the settlements of Balliemore and Invernoaden before flowing into Lock Eck.

Curachan *Western Isles* Curachan is one of a number of rocks that lie 5 miles (8 km) northeast of the settlement of Castlebay, off the east coast of Barra in the Outer Hebrides.

Currie *City of Edinburgh* A western suburb of Edinburgh, Currie was formerly one of several villages along the Water of Leith on the north side of the Pentland Hills. Currie had several mills in the past, including those for producing paper and snuff. Notable buildings include Lennox Tower (15th century), the Kirk (1784, on the site of a pre-Reformation church and with painted false windows) and the Glenburn Hotel (1887) by Sir R. Rowand Anderson. The rail line between Edinburgh and Currie operated between 1874 and the 1960s, although passenger traffic ceased in 1943. The campus of Heriot Watt University lies to the north.

Cushnie *Aberdeenshire* A locality in northern Aberdeenshire, Cushnie lies 2 miles (3 km) south of Gardenstown. The farms of Easter Cushnie, South Cushnie and Little Cushnie are nearby.

Cushnie, Glen of *Aberdeenshire* A small glen in Aberdeenshire, the Glen of Cushnie occupies the valley of the Cushnie Burn which rises on the Socach to the north of Tarland and flows east then north into the Howe of Alford where it meets the River Don.

Cuthill *Highland* A locality on the north shore of the Dornoch Firth in Highland Council area, Cuthill overlooks the Dornoch Sands, 4 miles (6.5 km) west of Dornoch.

Cuween Hill *Orkney* A hill on the Mainland of Orkney, to the south of Kirkwall, Cuween Hill is the site of an ancient chambered tomb.

Daaey *Shetland* A small uninhabited island of the Shetland Islands, Daaey lies off the north coast of the island of Fetlar opposite the headland of Urie Ness.

Daer Water *South Lanarkshire* Rising on Queensberry Hill in the Lowther Hills, South Lanarkshire, the Daer Water flows north for 10 miles (16 km) through the Daer Reservoir before joining the Potrail Water near Elvanfoot to form the upper reaches of the River Clyde. It is the longest headstream of the Clyde.

Dail The Gaelic name for Dell in the Western Isles.

Dail *Argyll and Bute* Situated on the north shore of Loch Etive, Argyll and Bute, Dail lies 6 miles (10 km) northeast of the village of Taynuilt.

Dail bho Dheas The Gaelic name for South Dell in the Western Isles.

Dail bho Thuath The Gaelic name for North Dell in the Western Isles.

Dailly *South Ayrshire* The name of two villages on the Water of Girvan in South Ayrshire. Old Dailly grew by an ancient ford 3 miles (5 km) northeast of Girvan. This settlement was superseded by New Dailly, a planned village 3 miles (5 km) to the north erected in the 1760s close to coal mines that were worked until the 1960s. A coal pit at nearby Dalquharran caught fire in 1849 and burned for half a century. Near the ford at Old Dailly stands the Baron's Stone, a granite boulder 12 m (36 ft) in circumference and estimated to weigh 37 tonnes. Carried down by glaciers from the hills above Loch Doon, this glacial erratic was anciently a place of assembly and seat of justice. Extensive postwar housing in New Dailly replaced many of the older run-down buildings.

Daimh, Loch an *Perth and Kinross* A reservoir in western Perth and Kinross, Loch an Daimh lies to the north of Glen Lyon. At its western end it receives the Eas Daimh which flows into the loch through Gleann Daimh, and at its eastern end it is connected to the River Lyon by the Allt Conait.

Daimh, Loch an *Highland* Located to the southeast of the Rhidorroch Forest in Wester Ross, Loch an Daimh is a small loch lying 9 miles (14 km) east of Ullapool.

Dairsie *Fife* A linear village in eastern Fife, Dairsie is situated on the A91, 3 miles (5 km) east of Cupar. Formerly known as Dairsiemuir or Osnaburgh (after a coarse German linen), its 18th/19th-century cottages were once occupied by linen weavers, many of whom came from Flanders. In addition to its weaving, Dairsie benefited from the development of the turnpike road in the early 19th century. The village has a modern primary school (1970) and the Dairsie Memorial Hall (1922). To the south, near the River Eden, are St Mary's Old Parish Church (1621), the restored late 16th-century Dairsie Castle and the massive triple-arched Dairsie Bridge (c.1530).

Dal, Loch na *Highland* An inlet of the Sound of Sleat, Loch na Dal is located at the head of the Sleat peninsula on the southeast coast of the island of Skye, Highland Council area.

Dalabrog The Gaelic name for Daliburgh in the Western Isles.

Dalavich *Argyll and Bute* A village of Argyll and Bute, Dalavich lies on the west shore of Loch Awe, 8 miles (13 km) southwest of Taychreggan. Built as a forestry village in the 1950s, it lies in the shadow of Inverliever Forest. A road over the hills to Kilmelford passes Loch Avich. Marble was once quarried nearby and, more recently, holiday chalets and cycle routes have been developed in the area.

Dalbeattie *Dumfries and Galloway* A planned village in Dumfries and Galloway, Dalbeattie lies in the valley of the Urr Water, 14 miles (22 km) southwest of Dumfries and adjacent to Dalbeattie Forest. In 1325 nearby Buittle was chartered as a burgh of barony near the site of Buittle Place, which had been the home of Lady Devorgilla (c.1209–90), mother of John Balliol, the pretender to the Scottish throne. In the 17th century there was a Mill of Dalbety on a stream known as the Kirkgunzeon Lane, but it was not until the 1780s that the village of Dalbeattie appeared when Alexander Copeland established a water-powered paper mill here. In the 19th century local grey granite was quarried and shipped out, first by boat from Craignair Bridge and later by rail. Stone blocks were cut for the building of Liverpool Docks, the Thames Embankment and the Eddystone Lighthouse, as well as for export throughout the world, but by the 1970s most of Dalbeattie's granite was in the form of road chippings. Dalbeattie has a museum situated in the High Street.

Dalbeattie Forest *Dumfries and Galloway* Located in the hills to the south of Dalbeattie in Dumfries and Galloway, Dalbeattie Forest contains waymarked cycle routes with fine views over the Solway coast.

Dalchalm *Highland* A settlement on the east coast of Sutherland, Highland Council area, Dalchalm lies a mile (1.5 km) north of Brora.

Dalchreichart *Highland* A settlement in Glen Moriston, Highland Council area, Dalchreichart lies north of the River Moriston, 6 miles (10 km) northwest of Fort Augustus.

Dalchruin *Perth and Kinross* A settlement in Glen Artney, Perth and Kinross, Dalchruin lies on the Water of Ruchill, 4 miles (6.5 km) southwest of Comrie.

Dalclathick *Perth and Kinross* A settlement in Glen Artney, Perth and Kinross, Dalclathick lies on the north side of the Water of Ruchill, 4 miles (6.5 km) southwest of Comrie.

Dalcross *Highland* A locality in Highland Council area, Dalcross lies 6 miles (10 km) east of Inverness near the Moray Firth coast. In 1855 a railway station on the new Inverness and Nairn Railway was opened at Dalcross, and during World War II a military airfield was built to the north. Originally known as Dalcross, this airfield was from 1946 developed as a Scottish Airways service, acting as a stopover between Aberdeen and Stornoway. Renamed Inverness Airport in 1953, Dalcross developed in association with the expansion of internal air services and the creation of an industrial estate. The churchyard at Petty is the burial place of the Macintosh lairds of Dalcross.

Dalcrue *Perth and Kinross* A settlement on the River Almond, Perth and Kinross, Dalcrue is situated nearly 2 miles (3 km) to the northeast of Methven and 2 miles (3 km) to the northwest of Almondbank. It is also sometimes known as Dalcruvie. The elegant 24-m (80-ft) single-arched bridge across the Almond at Dalcrue was built in 1832–7 by William Henry Playfair, who also designed Dalcrue House in 1832 for Lord Lynedoch.

Dale, Glen *Highland* Glen Dale lies on the most northwesterly peninsula of the island of Skye, Highland Council area. Running 7 miles (11km) north, it carries the waters of the Hamara River as it flows to Loch Pooltiel, which lies some 5 miles (8 km) south of Dunvegan Head.

Dalelia *Highland* A locality in Lochaber, Highland Council area, Dalelia lies on the north shore of Loch Shiel, 3 miles (5 km) southeast of Kinlochmoidart.

Dalgarven Mill Museum *North Ayrshire* Located on the River Garnock, 2 miles (3 km) north of Kilwinning in North Ayrshire, Dalgarven Mill is home to the Museum of Ayrshire Country Life and Costume, with collections of tools, furniture and room settings unique either to Ayrshire or to country life. Also within the grounds are an antiques centre and cafe.

Dalgety Bay *Fife* A commuter settlement on the Fife coast between Inverkeithing and Aberdour, Dalgety Bay looks out over Dalgety Bay, an inlet of the Firth of Forth. Its development largely dates from 1962, prior to the opening of the Forth Road Bridge two years later. Built on the lands of the former Donibristle Estate, it was the first private development of a new town in Scotland. Historic buildings include the 13th-century St Bride's Church, the refurbished Donibristle Stables and Dalgety Kirk (1830). To the north lies Donibristle Industrial Park.

Dalginross *Perth and Kinross* A southern extension of Comrie in Strathearn, Perth and Kinross, Dalginross lies to the south of the River Earn at its junction with the Water of Ruchill. A Roman fort and camp have been identified to the southwest. The expansion of Comrie took place in the late 18th century with the influx of dispossessed Highland crofters who came to work in local textile, brewing and distilling industries.

Dalguise *Perth and Kinross* A village in central Perth and Kinross, Dalguise lies to the west of the River Tay, 5 miles (8 km) northwest of Dunkeld. The Dalguise Estate was given to the church of Dunkeld by William the Lion and later fell into the hands of the Stewart family. Dating from 1753 with later additions, Dalguise House was rented for eleven summers between 1871 and 1881 by Rupert Potter, father of the writer Beatrix Potter

(1866–1943). The nearby Dalguise railway viaduct on the Perth–Inverness line was built in 1861–3 to a design by the engineer Joseph Mitchell.

Dalhalvaig *Highland* A village of Caithness, Highland Council area, Dalhalvaig lies in Strath Halladale, 6 miles (10 km) south of Melvich.

Dalhousie Castle *Midlothian* Located a mile (1.5 km) west of Newtongrange in Midlothian, on the banks of the River South Esk, Dalhousie Castle was originally built in the 13th century and was unsuccessfully besieged by King Henry IV of England in 1400. It was extended in distinctive pink sandstone around 1450 and further enlarged in 1633 to form a Renaissance house for Lord Ramsay, the Earl of Dalhousie. The castle was again altered in 1825 by the architect William Burn (1789–1870), when an entrance hall was created on several levels. Since the early 20th century, the earls of Dalhousie have chosen to live at one of their other homes, Brechin Castle. Dalhousie Castle was leased to a series of tenants and was a boarding school, before being converted to a hotel in 1972. Many features of the original castle still exist, including its dungeons, and a major restoration has been undertaken.

Daliburgh *Western Isles* A scattered hamlet on the island of South Uist in the Outer Hebrides, Daliburgh (Gael: *Dalabrog*) is located among small lochans 2.5 miles (4 km) northwest of Lochboisdale. Daliburgh benefits from a community hall, a hotel and a Gaelic-medium combined primary and junior secondary school. The former Daliburgh hospital, which closed in 2001, has been redeveloped as a care unit for the elderly.

Daljarrock *South Ayrshire* A locality with a hotel in South Ayrshire, Daljarrock lies a half-mile (1 km) north of Pinwherry and 5 miles (8 km) south of Girvan.

Dalkeith *Midlothian* Situated 6 miles (10 km) southeast of Edinburgh, the town of Dalkeith lies on a ridge between the Rivers North and South Esk. Created a burgh of barony (1401) and burgh of regality (1540) while under the control of the earls of Morton, Dalkeith passed to the Buccleuchs in the mid-17th century. The settlement, which grew southwestwards from its 12th-century castle, had in the 17th century one of Scotland's largest markets in its exceptionally broad High Street. In 1831 Dalkeith was linked to Edinburgh by a railway line that transported coal, minerals and agricultural produce, and two decades later, in 1853, the Corn Exchange, the largest interior grain market in Scotland, was built. Other notable buildings include the 13th-century Collegiate Church of St Nicholas, the Tolbooth (1648), Watch Towers (1827 and 1829), early 19th-century iron mills and Dalkeith House (sometimes 'Palace'), which replaced the castle in the late 16th century and was rebuilt in the early 18th century. George IV stayed in Dalkeith House on his visit to Scotland in 1822 and Queen Victoria spent her first night in Scotland here in 1842. The building is now leased to the University of Wisconsin and the estate forms a country park extending to 344 ha (850 acres). Born in Dalkeith were the poet John Roland (1575), the politician Henry Dundas, 1st Viscount Melville (1742), and the artist John Kay (1742). William Gladstone delivered a famous speech in Dalkeith during the election campaign of 1880 that resulted in the defeat of Disraeli's government.

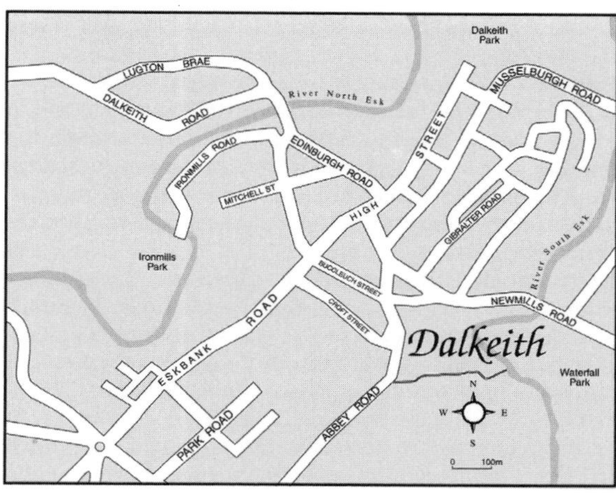

Dall *Perth and Kinross* A locality on the south shore of Loch Rannoch, Perth and Kinross, Dall is situated 5 miles (8 km) west of Kinloch Rannoch in a clearing in the Black Wood of Rannoch that lies east of the Dall Burn. The baronial-style Dall House, later Rannoch School, dates from 1854 and was designed by Thomas Mackenzie.

Dallas *Moray* A small village with a single street, Dallas lies on the River Lossie, 9 miles (14 km) southwest of Elgin in Moray. It was relocated to its present site in 1811, a medieval mercat cross in the kirkyard being the remnant of an earlier kirkton settlement. The church dates from 1793 and Dallas Lodge from 1901. A half-mile (1 km) to the north stand the remains of Tor Castle, built in 1400 by Sir Thomas Cumming of Altyre.

Dallas Forest *Moray* Dallas Forest is an area of forested land lying 2 miles (3 km) north of the settlement of Dallas in Moray. The Hill of the Wangie rises to a height of 319 m (1047 ft) within the forest.

Dallas, Loch *Moray* Situated in the uplands of Moray, Loch Dallas lies in hills to the southwest of the village of Dallas. It drains westwards to the River Divie.

Dall Burn *Perth and Kinross* A stream in Perth and Kinross, the Dall Burn rises to the north of Glen Lyon and flows 6 miles (10 km) north and northeast through Rannoch Forest to join Loch Rannoch near Rannoch School.

Dalmahoy *City of Edinburgh* A former seat of the earls of Morton, Dalmahoy House lies nearly 2 miles (3 km) southeast of Ratho on the western edge of the City of Edinburgh. Owned by the Dalmahoy family from the 13th century to the 17th century, Dalmahoy Estate was acquired next by the Dalrymples and then in the mid-18th century by the 17th Earl of Morton. Dalmahoy was developed as a golf and country club in the late 20th century.

Dalmally *Argyll and Bute* A village of Argyll and Bute, Dalmally lies at the junction of Glen Orchy, Glen Lochy and Glen Strae, near the point where the River Orchy flows into Loch Awe. Its whitewashed octagonal church was built in 1811 by the 4th Earl of Breadalbane, and in the 19th century the village developed in association with the railway and tourist steamers on Loch Awe. In the 20th century a livestock market and agricultural show emerged, and between 1962 and 1966 the Cruachan Hydro Power Station was created 5 miles (8 km) to the west. On a hill overlooking Dalmally stands a monument to the Gaelic poet Duncan Bàn Macintyre (1724–1812).

Dalmarnock *Glasgow City* An industrial district of the city of Glasgow, Dalmarnock lies to the north of the River Clyde, 2 miles (3 km) east of the city centre on the border with South Lanarkshire. Once a largely rural area, a dyehouse for Turkey red dye was established here in 1788, and by 1860 an ironworks, gasworks, sewage works and power station had opened.

Dalmarnock Bridge *Glasgow City/South Lanarkshire* Dalmarnock Bridge on the River Clyde links the South Lanarkshire settlement of Rutherglen with the Glasgow district of Dalmarnock. Built in 1891, it was the first flat bridge in Glasgow and replaced timber bridges that had stood at this site since 1821. In 1997 it underwent reinforcement and refurbishment while retaining much of its original Gothic-style parapet and ornamental panelling.

Dalmary *Stirling* A locality in the Trossachs district of Stirling Council area, Dalmary lies on the Kelty Water, a mile (1.5 km) to the south of Gartmore.

Dalmellington *East Ayrshire* A village of East Ayrshire, Dalmellington is situated near Bigton Loch in the valley of the River Doon, 15 miles (24 km) southwest of Ayr. Chartered as a burgh of barony in 1607, it developed in association with coal mining and the manufacture of textiles. In 1856 a railway from Ayr to Dalmellington was built to serve an ironworks opened in 1847 by the Dalmellington Iron Company at Waterside, 3 miles (5 km) to the northwest. The village expanded in the 20th century with the opening of more collieries, but in 1968 and 1978 first the railway then the last coal mine closed. A collection of industrial steam and diesel locomotives and rolling stock can be seen at the Scottish Industrial Railway Centre, created on the site of the former Minnivey steep drift mine by the Ayrshire Railway Preservation Society. An ancient hillfort lies at the centre of Dalmellington, whose economy is now more closely linked to opencast mining and afforestation in the surrounding area.

Dalmeny *City of Edinburgh* A planned village on the Dalmeny Estate, Dalmeny lies to the east of South Queensferry and west of the city of Edinburgh, close to the A90 approaching the Forth Bridge. Its fine 12th-century Norman church and stone cottages were built around a square, the whole village now being designated a conservation area. In the 1930s, both the church and village were renovated by volunteers, miners' cottages having been razed and their occupants moved to modern public housing nearby in 1938. Built in 1814–17 for the 3rd Earl of Rosebery to a design by William Wilkins, Dalmeny House was the first Tudor Gothic Revival house in Scotland. Archibald, 5th Earl of Rosebery, who collected items associated with Napoleon now on display in the house, supported William Gladstone's Midlothian campaign in 1880 and was himself prime minister in 1894–5. Dalmeny House replaced the former residence of Barnbougle Castle on the shores of the Firth of Forth, which had been a stronghold of the Primrose family since 1662. Barnbougle had originally been a keep of the Moubrays, Norman knights and crusaders who had come with William the Conqueror to Britain.

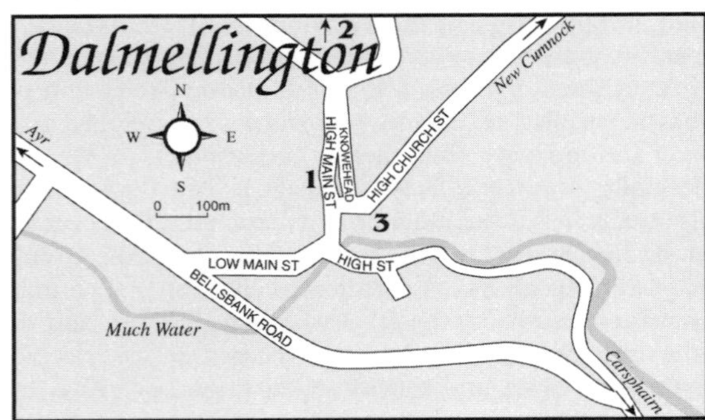

1 *Cathcarstone Visitor Centre*
2 *Scottish Industrial Railway Centre*
3 *Hill Fort*

Dalmoak Castle *West Dunbartonshire* A castle in Dumbarton, West Dunbartonshire, Dalmoak Castle is more a castellated Gothic-style mansion house than a fortified castle. The present building was erected in 1869, although it is believed that a building has stood here since the mid-15th century. Currently a private nursing home, it has a five-bay facade of coupled windows, a large stained-glass window and battlemented parapets with a central tower rising behind.

Dalmore *Highland* A locality with a distillery in Easter Ross, Highland Council area, Dalmore lies just southeast of Alness on the shore of the Cromarty Firth.

Dalnabreck *Highland* A settlement in Sunart, southwestern Highland Council area, Dalnabreck lies near the southwest end of Loch Shiel, 2 miles (3 km) east of Acharacle.

Dalnacardoch *Perth and Kinross* A lodge and deer forest in Glen Garry, Perth and Kinross, Dalnacardoch lies on the River Garry, 15 miles (24 km) northwest of Pitlochry. The Lodge, dating from 1774, was built as an inn by order of George III.

Dalnahaitnach *Highland* A locality in Strathspey, Dalnahaitnach lies on the Dulnain River, 4 miles (6.5 km) southwest of Carrbridge.

Dalnamein Forest *Perth and Kinross* A deer forest in highland Perth and Kinross, Dalnamein occupies the slopes of Sròn a' Chleirich in the much larger Forest of Atholl in the southern Grampians.

Dalnashaugh Inn *Moray* A locality overlooking the River Avon in Moray, Dalnashaugh lies immediately south of Bridge of Avon at the junction of the B9008 and A95.

Dalnaspidal *Perth and Kinross* A lodge in Perth and Kinross, Dalnaspidal lies in Glen Garry, 20 miles (32 km) northwest of Pitlochry. Loch Garry lies to the south. The lodge, built by the Duke of Atholl, takes its name from an ancient inn on the site. Bonnie Prince Charlie stayed here in August 1745 and an unamused Queen Victoria and Prince Albert stopped by on 9 October 1861 to have 'a shabby pair of horses put in, with a shabby driver driving from the box'.

Dalness *Highland* A settlement in Lochaber, southwestern Highland Council area, Dalness lies in Glen Etive, to the south of Glen Coe.

Dalqueich *Perth and Kinross* A farming and commuter hamlet in the southern foothills of the Ochil Hills, Perth and Kinross, Dalqueich lies on the North Queich, 3 miles (5 km) northwest of Kinross.

Dalquharran *South Ayrshire* A settlement on the Water of Girvan in South Ayrshire, Dalquharran lies to the north of Dailly. The 15th-century Dalquharran Castle lies in a ruinous state between the village and the later, 18th-century castle built for the Kennedys by Robert Adam (1728–92).

Dalreach *Perth and Kinross* A mansion house in Strath Ardle, Perth and Kinross, Dalreach lies on the River Ardle, 7 miles (11 km) northeast of Pitlochry.

Dalriada *Argyll and Bute* An ancient kingdom in the western Highlands, Dalriada extended over an area roughly equivalent to modern Argyll and Bute. It was established in the early 5th century by the Scots from Ireland with major centres at Dunadd and Dunstaffnage. Kenneth I, 36th king of Dalriada, moved his capital to Scone to escape the Viking raids and, according to legend, took with him the ancestral enthroning-stone blessed by St Patrick known as the Stone of Destiny. In AD 843 Kenneth MacAlpin united the kingdoms of the Scots and Picts to the north of the Clyde and Forth.

Dalroy *Highland* A locality in Highland Council area, Dalroy lies on the River Nairn, 8 miles (13 km) east of Inverness.

Dalry An alternative name for St John's Town of Dalry in Dumfries and Galloway.

Dalry *North Ayrshire* A village of North Ayrshire situated 11 miles (18 km) northwest of Kilmarnock on the River Garnock, Dalry developed in association with textile, iron, engineering, coal and brick-making industries. A factory producing vitamin C and food colorants was opened in the 1980s.

Dalrymple *East Ayrshire* A village of East Ayrshire, Dalrymple lies on the River Doon 5 miles (8 km) south of Ayr. Its main features lie on its two short streets, notably the bridge on the Girvan–Edinburgh road which was built in 1849, and single-storey whitewashed cottages with dormers, some of which date back to the early 19th century.

Dalserf *South Lanarkshire* A village of South Lanarkshire, Dalserf is situated on the River Clyde 2 miles (3 km) east of Larkhall and 7 miles (11 km) southeast of Hamilton. The area was formerly associated with the mining of ironstone, sandstone and coal.

Dalswinton *Dumfries and Galloway* A village of Nithsdale in Dumfries and Galloway, Dalswinton lies to the north of the River Nith, 6 miles (10 km) northwest of Dumfries. Nearby are Dalswinton Tower, a former stronghold of the Comyn family, and Dalswinton House, which was built by the entrepreneur Patrick Miller (1731–1815), landlord of Robert Burns who farmed at Ellisland. Thanks to Miller's initiative, the threshing mill and drill plough were introduced to Scotland and the first turnip seeds were sent to him by King Gustav of Sweden – hence the name 'swede' for turnip. He also designed an armament called the carronade, which was later used against the French navy, and on Dalswinton Loch in 1788 he launched the world's first steamboat. Evidence from aerial photographs suggests that Dalswinton was the site of a large Agricolan Roman fort that was destroyed and later replaced by a cavalry fort downstream at Carzield.

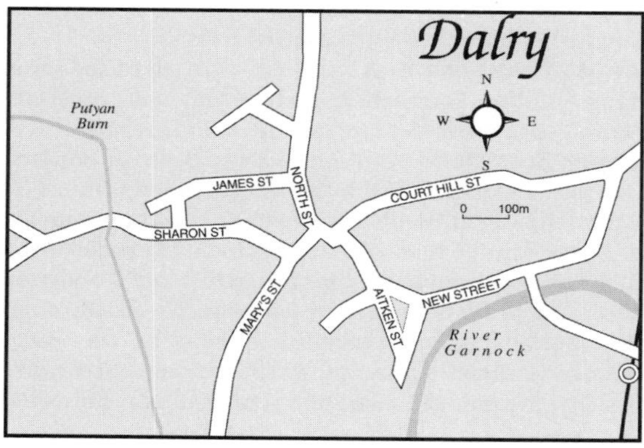

Dalton *Dumfries and Galloway* A village of Annandale in Dumfries and Galloway, Dalton lies in a parish of the same name, 6 miles (10 km) northwest of Annan. It is the largest of the Royal Four Towns of Lochmaben.

Dalvadie *Dumfries and Galloway* A locality in the Rhinns of Galloway, Dumfries and Galloway, Dalvadie is situated a mile (1.5 km) to the northwest of Sandhead and 6 miles (10 km) south of Stranraer.

Dalveen Pass *Dumfries and Galloway* A routeway through the Lowther Hills, Dumfries and Galloway, the Dalveen Pass lies in the valley of the Carron Water, 6 miles (10 km) north of Carronbridge.

Dalveich *Stirling* A locality in northeastern Stirling Council area, Dalveich lies on the north shore of Loch Earn, 2 miles (3 km) east of Lochearnhead. It is situated at the mouth of the Beich Burn which flows down to meet Loch Earn here.

Dalvey House *Moray* A mansion house built by Sir Archibald Grant in the 1770s, Dalvey House lies to the west of Forres in Moray.

Dalwhat Water *Dumfries and Galloway* A river of Dumfries and Galloway, the Dalwhat Water rises in the uplands of Penpont parish. It flows southeastwards to join the Castlefairn Water at Moniaive, where it becomes the Cairn Water.

Dalwhinnie *Highland* A settlement in Badenoch, Highland Council area, Dalwhinnie lies at the head of Glen Truim and near the north end of Loch Ericht. Formerly a meeting point for cattle drovers, Dalwhinnie became a road junction during the period of military road building in the 1720s, and a bridge was built over the River Truim here. With the opening of the Inverness and Perth Junction (later Highland) Railway's main line in 1863, a station was built and Dalwhinnie became a centre for the shipment of sheep to be taken south for sale. A distillery, built here in 1898 at the height of a whisky boom, was the first in Scotland to become American-owned.

Damff, Glen *Angus* A small glen in the Braes of Angus, Glen Damff lies to the north of the Backwater Reservoir between Glen Prosen and Glen Isla. Its stream joins that of Glen Taitney before entering the north end of the reservoir.

Damh, Loch *Highland* A loch of Wester Ross, Loch Damh (also Loch Damph) lies to the south of Upper Loch Torridon and 2.5 miles (4 km) southeast of Shieldaig. Ben Damph (902 m/2959 ft) rises to the east.

Damnaglaur *Dumfries and Galloway* A locality at the southern end of the Rhinns of Galloway, Dumfries and Galloway, Damnaglaur lies at a road junction a mile (1.5 km) to the southwest of Drummore.

Danderhall *Midlothian* A former mining village on the northern boundary of Midlothian, Danderhall lies a half-mile (1 km) northeast of the Edinburgh suburb of

Gilmerton and 2 miles (3 km) northwest of Dalkeith. The village comprises a preponderance of public housing. Coal mines once operated at Edmonstone to the northwest, Sheriffhall to the southeast and Woolmet immediately to the east, with Monktonhall beyond Woolmet, which was worked between 1953 and 1998, the last deep mine in the Lothians.

Danna, Island of *Argyll and Bute* Not an island, but a peninsula of Argyll and Bute, Danna Island is connected to the mainland by a narrow isthmus separating Loch Sween from the Sound of Jura.

Danskine *East Lothian* A settlement of East Lothian, Danskine lies 3 miles (5 km) southeast of Gifford. Danskine Loch lies just to the northwest and Danskine Burn descends from here into the Yester Estate.

Darnaway Castle *Moray* The seat of the earls of Moray, Darnaway Castle lies 3 miles (5 km) southwest of Forres in Moray in the midst of an extensive forested landscape. It was once the centre of the powerful Province of Moray, the original castle being associated with the Dunbar, Gordon and Douglas families before being acquired by the Stuarts in 1562. The new house, built in the style of a Gothic French mansion, was designed by Alexander Laing for the 9th Earl of Moray in 1802. The castle has a fine collection of family portraits, and the story of the Darnaway Estate is told in the visitor centre at Tearie, 2.5 miles (4 km) west of Forres.

Darnick *Scottish Borders* A village of Scottish Borders, Darnick lies on the River Tweed just west of Melrose. Darnick Tower was built in the 15th century by the Heiton family.

Darvel *East Ayrshire* One of the three so-called 'valley burghs' of East Ayrshire, Darvel is situated at the confluence of the River Irvine and Glen Water, 9 miles (14 km) east of Kilmarnock. The village of Darvel has been associated with the production of polyester, carpets and lace. The discoverer of penicillin, Sir Alexander Fleming (1881–1955), grew up at Lochfield Farm nearby.

Darwin Mounds A spectacular coral reef off the northwest coast of Scotland, the Darwin Mounds cover 98 sq. km (38 sq. miles) more than 1000 m (3280 ft) under the sea, in the Rockall Trough, 120 miles (192 km) off Cape Wrath. Discovered in 1998, they are regarded as Britain's finest cold-water coral reef, which the UK Government committed to protect in 2001.

Dava *Highland* A locality in Strathspey, Highland Council area, Dava lies to the east of Lochindorb on Dava Moor near the border with Moray, 7 miles (11 km) northwest of Grantown-on-Spey.

Davaar Island *Argyll and Bute* Located in Kilbrannan Sound at the mouth of Campbeltown Loch, Davaar Island lies towards the southern end of the Kintyre peninsula in Argyll and Bute. It is connected to the mainland at low tide by a shingle causeway. At the north of the island is a Stevenson-built lighthouse, while to the south, in Crucifixion Cave, one of the island's seven caves, is a painting of the crucifixion of Christ.

Davan, Loch *Aberdeenshire* A small loch in Deeside, Aberdeenshire, Loch Davan lies immediately north of Loch Kinord, 6 miles (10 km) west of Aboyne.

David Livingstone Centre, The *South Lanarkshire* Created in the 1920s and opened by the Duchess of York (later Queen Elizabeth the Queen Mother), the National Memorial to David Livingstone in Blantyre, South Lanarkshire, celebrates the life and work of the African missionary-explorer David Livingstone, who was born in Blantyre in 1813. Established at his birthplace in a mill house by the River Clyde, the centre is now in the care of the National Trust for Scotland.

Davidson's Mains *City of Edinburgh* An old village of Edinburgh lying 3 miles (5 km) northwest of the city centre, Davidson's Mains developed around the junction between the roads from Leith and Edinburgh to Cramond and South Queensferry. Originally known as Muttonhole, the structure of the village, together with many of its older buildings, was saved by the re-routing of the Queensferry Road to the south in 1823. The name Davidson's Mains is derived from the wealthy Davidson family, which traded with the Continent and lived at nearby Muirhouse. The village remained a relatively isolated farming community until the early 20th century, but first the railway (which formerly came this way to Barnton) and then other forms of public transport brought suburban expansion. To the west are the estates of Barnton House (now demolished) and Lauriston Castle, largely now parkland or golf courses. To the north are the housing schemes of Silverknowes and Muirhouse, and to the south Blackhall and Corstorphine Hill.

Davidston, Burn of *Moray* A stream in Moray, the Burn of Davidston rises to the east of Dufftown. It flows northwards to join the River Isla at Auchindachy, 2 miles (3 km) southwest of Keith.

Davington *Dumfries and Galloway* A small village in Eskdale, Dumfries and Galloway, Davington lies on the White Esk, 6 miles (10 km) south of Ettrick. A meteorological observatory was built near here in 1904–07, taking advantage of the clear, unpolluted country air. Also close by is the Kagu Samye Ling Tibetan Centre developed around an old farmhouse at Garwaldwaterfoot from 1967.

Davington Burn *Dumfries and Galloway* A stream in eastern Dumfries and Galloway, the Davington Burn is a tributary of the River Esk to the north of Langholm.

Daviot *Highland* A locality with a church and school in Strath Nairn, Highland Council area, Daviot lies near the A9 and the River Nairn, 5 miles (8 km) southeast of Inverness. An ancient hillfort here was replaced by a 15th-century keep that was in turn replaced by Daviot House. The settlement developed in association with its mill, and in the 1890s a station nearby was temporarily the northern terminus of the Highland Railway's main line from Aviemore to Inverness. A quarry nearby provided material for the building of the A9 road. Novelist Alistair MacLean (1922–87) was brought up in the manse at Daviot, his father being the parish minister.

Daviot *Aberdeenshire* A village in a parish of the same name in the Formartine district of Aberdeenshire, Daviot lies 4 miles (6.5 km) northwest of Inverurie.

Dawyck *Scottish Borders* An estate in Scottish Borders, Dawyck lies near Stobo in the Tweed Valley, 8 miles (13 km) southwest of Peebles. Tree planting by the Nasmyths of Dawyck in the mid-17th century included some of the first horse chestnuts, European larches and Lombardy poplars in Scotland. There are landscaped walks through the specialist garden established here by the Royal Botanic Garden, Edinburgh, which includes the world's first cryptogamic sanctuary and reserve of non-flowering plants.

Deadwaters *South Lanarkshire* A settlement of South Lanarkshire, Deadwaters lies 2 miles (3 km) west of Kirkmuirhill, on the Kype Water.

Dean Bridge *City of Edinburgh* Linking Queensferry Road and Queensferry Street to the northwest of Edinburgh city centre, the impressive sandstone Dean Bridge was built by Thomas Telford in 1832. It carries a road 32 m (106 ft) above the steep valley of the Water of Leith and is 136 m (447 ft) long.

Dean Castle *East Ayrshire* Located a mile (1.5 km) north of Kilmarnock town centre, East Ayrshire, Dean Castle comprises a 14th-century keep and 15th-century palace with dungeon, battlements and banqueting hall, all of which have been accurately restored. The ancestral home of the Boyd family, the castle houses a collection of arms, armour and medieval musical instruments. There are also tapestries and some artefacts associated with Robert Burns (1759–96).

Dean Gallery *City of Edinburgh* Located close to Edinburgh's New Town, the Dean Gallery represents a conversion of the Dean Orphan Hospital by architects Terry Farrell and Partners. Administered by the Scottish National Gallery of Modern Art, the gallery was designed to house the Paolozzi Gift of sculpture and graphic art. In addition, significant holdings of Dada and Surrealist work, previously rarely seen in their entirety, are displayed. The collection includes many celebrated works by artists such as Dali, Duchamp, Ernst, Giacometti, Magritte, Man Ray, Miró, Picasso, Tanguy and Delvaux. The gallery also includes a library and archive of artists' books, manuscripts and papers. The architects have sympathetically redeveloped the institutional interior of the orphanage, which was designed by Thomas Hamilton in 1831, while maintaining the exterior unaltered.

Dean Water *Angus* A stream in Strathmore, the Dean Water flows westwards for 10 miles (16 km) from the Loch of Forfar in Angus before entering the River Isla near Meigle in Perth and Kinross.

Deans *West Lothian* A suburb of the new town of Livingston in West Lothian, Deans developed from a farmsteading into a village in the early 1870s in association with oil-shale mining. It has a community school and industrial park.

Deanshaugh *Perth and Kinross* A locality in Strathbraan, Perth and Kinross, Deanshaugh lies near the junction of the Cochil Burn with the River Braan, nearly 2 miles (3 km) northeast of Amulree and 7 miles (11 km) southwest of Dunkeld.

Deanston *Stirling* A village of Stirling Council area, Deanston lies on the River Teith a mile (1.5 km) to the west of Doune, from which it is separated by the Wood of Doune. The village developed in association with a cotton mill established here in 1785. This mill came under the management in 1807 of James Smith (1789-1850), an enlightened entrepreneur and philanthropist. Lochills Industrial Estate supports light industry.

Deas, Taobh *Western Isles* Taobh Deas is the name given to the southwest-facing slope of the mountain ridge of Chaipaval on the western coast of the island of South Harris in the Western Isles. The ruined remains of a chapel lie at the southeastern extremity of the slope.

Deasker *Western Isles* An islet in the Outer Hebrides, Deasker lies 3 miles (5 km) north of the Heisker Islands and 3 miles (5 km) southwest of the headland of Aird an Runair on the western coastline of North Uist in the Western Isles.

Dechmont *West Lothian* A village of central West Lothian, Dechmont lies 1.25 miles (2 km) west of Uphall and 2 miles (3 km) north of Livingston, immediately to the north of the M8 motorway. Dechmont developed in conjunction with the Bangour Hospitals which are located just to the west.

Dee, Glen *Aberdeenshire* A glen in the eastern Grampians of Aberdeenshire, Glen Dee occupies the upper reaches of the River Dee between its source in the Pools of Dee just west of Ben Macdui to the Chest of Dee, where it turns eastwards towards Linn of Dee and Braemar. The Corrour Bothy lies in the glen.

Dee, Linn of *Aberdeenshire* A series of cascades on the upper reaches of the River Dee in Aberdeenshire, nearly 7 miles (11 km) west of Braemar, the Linn of Dee forms a rugged and rocky narrow neck in the river some 275 m (300 yd) long.

Dee, Loch *Dumfries and Galloway* A loch in the Galloway Forest Park, Dumfries and Galloway, Loch Dee lies 3 miles (5 km) east of Loch Trool and 5 miles (8 km) west of Clatteringshaws Loch, to which it is linked by the Black Water of Dee (River Dee).

Dee, River Rising in the Cairngorm Mountains to the west of Ben Macdui, the River Dee flows south from the Pools of Dee through Glen Dee before turning east at the Chest of Dee for the remainder of its course through Royal Deeside. It eventually enters the North Sea at Footdee in the city of Aberdeen and has a total length of 85 miles (137 km). To the west of Braemar it forms a cascade known as the Linn of Dee, and on its course it passes Braemar, Ballater, Aboyne, Banchory and Peterculter.

Dee, River *Dumfries and Galloway* A river of Dumfries and Galloway, the River Dee rises in Loch Dee to the east of Glentrool. It flows nearly 19 miles (31 km) southeastwards through Clatteringshaws Loch and the smaller Stroan Loch before entering Loch Ken opposite Parton. The river continues southwards from Loch Ken for another 15 miles (24 km), flowing past Threave Castle to Kirkcudbright and on into Kirkcudbright Bay. It has a total course from its source of just over 38 miles (61 km). In its upper reaches before reaching Loch Ken, its dark waters have also given rise to it being named the Black Water of Dee.

Deebank An alternative name for Argrennan House in Dumfries and Galloway.

Deecastle *Aberdeenshire* A hunting lodge of the Earl of Aboyne built on the site of a former settlement, Deecastle is situated on a hillock on the south side of the River Dee opposite the Muir of Dinnet, Aberdeenshire.

Deep Sea World *Fife* A marine aquarium in North Queensferry opened in 1994 as a tourist and educational facility featuring an underwater viewing tunnel and audiovisual presentations.

Degnish Point *Argyll and Bute* A headland on the northern shore of Loch Melfort, Argyll and Bute, Degnish Point offers views across the loch to the National Trust for Scotland garden at Arduaine, while to the east and south can be seen the islands of Luing and Shuna.

Delgaty Castle *Aberdeenshire* Situated 2 miles (3 km)

northeast of Turriff in Aberdeenshire, Delgaty (or Delgatie) Castle was for over three centuries a stronghold of the Hays of Erroll prior to its purchase in 1762 by Peter Garden of Troup, whose son sold it on to James, 2nd Earl of Fife.

Dell *Western Isles* A locality on the northwest coast of Lewis in the Outer Hebrides, Dell (Gael: *Dail*) lies around the Dell River, 3.5 miles (6 km) south-southwest of the Butt of Lewis. The location comprises the village of South Dell (Gael: *Dail bho Dheas*), with the smaller North Dell (Gael: *Dail bho Thuath*) lying to the east, adjacent to Cross, and Aird Dell (Gael: *Aird Dhail*) to the northwest.

Dell Mill *Western Isles* A restored 19th-century grain mill, the Dell Mill is located in the settlement of North Dell on the Isle of Lewis in the Western Isles. Inside the mill there is a full range of equipment and machinery and also interpretive displays on the history of the mill and local grain production.

Dell River *Western Isles* A stream on the Isle of Lewis in the Western Isles, the Dell River rises in Loch nan Atrabhat and flows 5 miles (8 km) northeast before entering the sea at a point 3 miles (5 km) southwest of the Butt of Lewis. The Dell separates the settlements of South and North Dell.

Dell Rock *Western Isles* A rocky islet off the northwest coast of the Isle of Lewis in the Western Isles, Dell Rock lies some 2 miles (3 km) northwest of the settlements of North and South Dell and a mile (1.5 km) northwest of the mouth of the River Dell.

Delliefure *Highland* A locality in Strathspey, Highland Council area, Delliefure lies to the north of the River Spey, 4 miles (6.5 km) northeast of Grantown-on-Spey.

Delnabo *Moray* A settlement of Upper Strathavon in Moray, Delnabo lies at the junction of the Water of Ailnack with the River Avon, a mile (1.5 km) to the southwest of Tomintoul. In 1647 George Gordon, the 2nd Marquess of Huntly, a supporter of King Charles II, was captured here by Cromwell's soldiers, and over a year later executed in Edinburgh. A corn mill operated here in the 18th century, and from 1850 to 1858 George Smith of Minmore took over Delnabo as the Cairngorm Distillery to supplement Glenlivet Distillery before its enlargement. The turreted Delnabo House dates from the 19th century.

Delny *Highland* A locality in Easter Ross, Highland Council area, Delny lies 3 miles (5 km) northeast of Invergordon.

Delting *Shetland* A district and old parish in the northwest of the Shetland Mainland, Delting includes the settlements of Burravoe, Collafirth, Voe and the Sullom Voe oil terminal.

Delvine *Perth and Kinross* An estate in Caputh parish, Perth and Kinross, Delvine lies to the east of Dunkeld near the left bank of the River Tay. The site of the Roman fort of Inchtuthill lies between Delvine House and Gardens to the southeast of the village of Spittalfield.

Den of Lindores *Fife* A hamlet in Abdie parish, northwestern Fife, Den of Lindores is situated at the junction of the A913 and B936, 2 miles (3 km) southeast of Newburgh. To the northwest stand the ruins of Denmylne Castle, a fortified house of the Balfour family, and nearby are Lindores Loch and the old monastic farms of Grange of Lindores, Ormiston, Berryhill and Hilton.

Denbrae *Fife* An estate in Logie parish, northeastern Fife, Denbrae was one of the estates owned by Sir William Fettes, Lord Provost of Edinburgh, whose bequest created the Edinburgh school known as Fettes College.

Denhead *Dundee City* A former village now incorporated into the city of Dundee, Denhead (also Denhead of Gray) is situated in Liff and Benvie parish to the northwest of the city. It once had a sizeable spinning mill.

Denhead *Fife* A hamlet of Cameron parish in eastern Fife, Denhead is situated to the east of Drumcarrow Craig, 3 miles (5 km) southwest of St Andrews.

Denholm *Scottish Borders* A village of Roxburghshire in Scottish Borders, Denholm lies on the Teviot, 5 miles (8 km) northeast of Hawick. It forms a square round a green, at the centre of which is a monument to the scholar-poet John Leyden (1775–1811), who was born in Denholm. Also born in the village in 1837 was Sir James Murray, editor of the *New English Dictionary*. Now a centre of knitwear production, Denholm's inhabitants once manufactured stockings, farmed the land and, for over fifty years in the 19th century, quarried stone nearby.

Denmore *Aberdeen City* A commuter and industrial settlement in the Aberdeen parish of Old Machar, Denmore is situated to the north of Bridge of Don on the A92.

Denmylne Castle *Fife* One mile (1.5 km) to the southeast of Newburgh in northern Fife and opposite the entrance to a large quarry stand the ruins of Denmylne Castle, built by Sir Alexander Balfour in the 15th century on the site of an early fortress of the earls of Fife. One of that family was Sir James Balfour of Kinnaird, Lord Lyon King of Arms and a noted collector of manuscripts. The castle was abandoned in 1772 when the estate was sold.

Dennistoun *Glasgow City* A district of Glasgow situated to the east of the city centre, Dennistoun was originally occupied by Glasgow city merchants who built villas here as an alternative to the more highly priced suburbs to the west. Urban development and the building of tenements date from the 1860s. To the north is Alexandra Park, with its boating pond, gardens, nine-hole golf course and walkways, laid out by the City Improvement Trust in 1866. Comedians Ricky Fulton (1924–2004) and Dorothy Paul (b.1937) were both born in Dennistoun, which was also the home of singer Lulu (b.1948) and poet William Miller (1810–72), author of the nursery rhyme *Wee Willie Winkie*.

Denny *Falkirk* A town in Falkirk Council area, Denny lies to the south of the River Carron. The Little Denny and Drumbowie Reservoirs, which are fed by the Little Denny Burn, lie to the southwest, and to the west near Fankerton is the Strathcarron Hospice.

Dennyloanhead *Falkirk* A village in Falkirk Council area, Dennyloanhead is situated between the A80 and the Bonny Water. There are extensive bonded warehouses to the south.

Dens *Aberdeenshire* A scattered settlement amid the open rolling landscape of Buchan, Dens straddles a stream called the West Den, 3 miles (5 km) southwest of Peterhead in Aberdeenshire. It comprises Dens, Little Dens, Meikle Dens and the Oldtown of Meikle Dens. To the south is Cairn Catto, a long burial cairn dating from the 4th–3rd millennia BC.

Derculich *Perth and Kinross* A locality in Strath Tay, Perth and Kinross, Derculich lies 3 miles (5 km) northeast of Aberfeldy on the north side of the River Tay. Derculich House has its origins in a farmhouse that was extended in the Scottish baronial style in the mid-19th century. The Derculich Burn flows down some 2 miles (3 km) from its source in Loch Derculich to meet the River Tay near here.

Dernaglar Loch *Dumfries and Galloway* A small loch in Dumfries and Galloway, Dernaglar Loch lies to the south of the A75 from Newton Stewart to Stranraer, 4 miles (6.5 km) east of Glenluce. It receives a stream that rises on Knock Fell and drains the Knock Moss to the south, and is itself drained by the Lannygore Burn which links it to the Tarff Water to the east.

Derry, Loch *Dumfries and Galloway* A small loch in Dumfries and Galloway, Loch Derry lies between Craigairie Fell and the River Bladnoch, 9 miles (14 km) northeast of Glenluce.

Derry Cairngorm *Aberdeenshire* Located east of Ben Macdui and south of Loch Etchachan in the Cairngorms in Moray, Derry Cairngorm rises to a height of 1155 m (3789 ft) and is characterised by an extensive granite boulder field. It derives its name from the Gaelic for 'blue peak of the (oak) thicket'.

Derry Lodge *Aberdeenshire* The remains of a shooting lodge on the Mar Estate in the eastern Grampians, Aberdeenshire, Derry Lodge lies at the head of Glen Lui near the junction of the Lui Beg Burn and the Derry Burn, which join here to form the Lui Water.

Derry Water *Aberdeenshire* A stream in the eastern Grampians, the Derry Water rises from Loch Etchachan on the northeastern slopes of Ben Macdui. It flows nearly 7 miles (11 km) southwards through Glen Derry to join the Lui Water at Derry Lodge to the west of Braemar.

Dervaig *Argyll and Bute* A village on the island of Mull, Dervaig lies at the head of Loch Cuan, nearly 9 miles (14 km) southwest of Tobermory.

Deskford *Moray* A kirkton settlement in Moray, Deskford lies 2 miles (3 km) south of Cullen. Created a burgh of barony in 1698, the former Deskford Tower was a seat of the earls of Findlater and Seafield. Its church dates from 1551. A new village was built in the 1760s but industry failed to prosper and the village, now largely occupied by commuters, never expanded.

Deskry Water *Aberdeenshire* A stream in the eastern Grampians, Aberdeenshire, the Deskry Water rises in the hills to the south of Strathdon on the slopes of Morven. It flows 9 miles (14 km) northeastwards past the Forest of Bunzeach and forms a loop before joining the River Don at Deskry. Deskryshiel Lodge lies by the Deskry Water at the foot of Birk Hill.

Dessarry, Glen *Highland* Glen Dessarry lies within Lochaber district, Highland Council area, immediately to the southeast of Garbh Choich Mhòr. It carries the waters of the River Dessarry in a southeasterly direction to join the River Pean in Glen Pean, a half-mile (1 km) west of the head of Loch Arkaig.

Dessarry, River *Highland* A river of Lochaber in the Inverness-shire district of Highland Council area, the River Dessarry rises in mountains at the eastern end of Knoydart. It flows nearly 6 miles (10 km) through Glen Dessarry to join the River Pean before entering the west end of Loch Arkaig.

Destitution Road *Highland* Built during the 1840s to provide employment during times of famine, the Destitution Road was the name given to a number of roads in Wester Ross, especially the road between Loch Maree and Braemore.

Deucheran Hill *Argyll and Bute* A hill within the Carradale Forest on the Kintyre peninsula, Deucheran Hill rises to 330 m (1082 ft) 3 miles (5 km) west of Grogport and 15.5 miles (25 km) north-northwest of Campbeltown. The Deucheran Hill Wind Farm opened here in 2001.

Deugh, Water of *Dumfries and Galloway/East Ayrshire* A river of Dumfries and Galloway, the Water of Deugh rises on the eastern slopes of Windy Standard to the north of Cairnsmore of Carsphairn on the border with East Ayrshire. It flows west then south to Carsphairn, where it turns in a southeasterly direction before flowing into the head of Kendoon Loch. It has a total length of 20 miles (32 km).

Deveron, River *Moray* Rising in the uplands of Moray to the west of the Cabrach Road, the River Deveron flows 61 miles (98 km) northeastwards to join the sea at Banff Bay, which lies between the towns of Banff and Macduff. On its way it passes through the town of Huntly.

Devil's Beef Tub *Dumfries and Galloway* A dramatic hollow in the hills to the north of Moffat in Dumfries and Galloway, the Devil's Beef Tub can be viewed from the A701 as it twists downwards into Moffat. Located near the border between Annandale in the south and Tweeddale in the north, it is dominated by the Great Hill, which rises to 465 m (1527 ft). At the bottom of the hollow is a martyred Covenanter's grave. The Devil's Beef Tub was also known as the Marquess of Annandale's Beef Stand on account of its use by the men of Annandale as a place to hide stolen cattle.

Devil's Elbow, the *Perth and Kinross* The Devil's Elbow was the name given to the steeply climbing double hairpin bend on the old road through Gleann Beag near its highest point at the Cairnwell Pass. In the space of 5 miles (8 km) the height above sea level doubles from 335 m (1100 ft) at Spittal of Glen Shee to 670 m (2200 ft) at the highest point on the road from Blairgowrie to Braemar. The old road is now bypassed by a wider modern road without such dramatic bends.

Devil's Mill *Clackmannanshire/Perth and Kinross* The name of a waterfall on the River Devon at Rumbling Bridge on the border between Clackmannanshire and Perth and Kinross.

Devil's Point, the *Aberdeenshire* Rising to a height of 1004 m (3294 ft) north of Glen Geusachan in Aberdeenshire, the Devil's Point acquired its name after a visit by Queen Victoria. The Devil's Point was offered as an alternative to the Gaelic name of Bod an Deamhain, translated as 'The Devil's Penis', to avoid embarrassment.

Devil's Staircase *Highland* A difficult section on the old military road between the head of Loch Leven and the head of Glen Coe, the Devil's Staircase rises to 672 m (2206 ft).

Devon, Glen *Perth and Kinross* A valley in the Ochil Hills, Glen Devon extends eastwards from the source of the River Devon to the Yetts o' Muckhart. The river is dammed to form two reservoirs, and at the centre of the glen, on the road to Gleneagles, are the hamlet, castle and parish church of Glendevon.

Devon, River *Perth and Kinross/Clackmannanshire* A river rising on Blairdenon Hill in the Ochil Hills at an altitude of 548 m (1800 ft), the Devon flows east and southeast through Glendevon, takes a sharp turn to the southwest at Crook of Devon and then continues westwards along the foot of the Ochils until it reaches the River Forth to the west of Alloa. Its upper reaches have been dammed to form reservoirs (Upper Glendevon, Lower Glendevon and Castlehill), and at Rumbling Bridge it passes through a narrow ravine with a series of waterfalls with names such as the Devil's Mill and Cauldron Linn. The last song by Robert Burns, *Fairest maid on Devon banks, Crystal Devon, winding Devon,* was written in July 1796 and recalls Charlotte Hamilton of Mauchline whom he had seen at nearby Harviestoun nine years earlier. During the 18th and 19th centuries the water of the Devon was used by textile mills and bleachfields, many of which were developed by Dunfermline industrialists.

Devonside *Clackmannanshire* A hamlet in central Clackmannanshire, Devonside is situated on high ground overlooking the River Devon and the Hillfoots town of Tillicoultry. Knitwear is manufactured at the Devonpark Mills.

Dhu, Glen *Highland* A remote valley, sea loch and deer forest of the Assynt district of the northwest Highlands, Glen Dhu (Gael: *Gleann Dubh*) carries the Abhainn a' Ghlinne Dhuibh west into Loch Glendhu 3 miles (5 km) south of Achfary and 4 miles (6.5 km) east of Kylesku. The Glendhu Forest lies to the north and Loch Glendhu flows west for 3 miles (5 km) before becoming Loch a' Chairn Bhain to the west of Kylesku, which in turn drains into Eddrachillis Bay.

Diabaig *Highland* A locality to the east of Loch Torridon in Wester Ross, Diabaig comprises the larger settlement of Lower Diabaig, with its whitewashed cottages on the north shore of Loch Diabaig, and to the east, Upper Diabaig which lies on Loch Diabaigas Airde.

Diebidale, Glen *Highland* A valley in Easter Ross, Highland Council area, Glen Diebidale lies at the head of Glen Calvie, 10 miles (16 km) southwest of Bonar Bridge.

Digg *Highland* A settlement on the northeast coast of the isle of Skye, Highland Council area, Digg lies on the west side of Staffin Bay.

Dighty Water *Angus* A stream in southeastern Angus, the Dighty (or Dichty) Water rises in the Sidlaw Hills to the northwest of Dundee. It flows southeastwards to enter the Tay estuary between Broughty Ferry and Monifieth.

Dingwall *Highland* A burgh town in Easter Ross, Highland Council area, Dingwall lies at the head of the Cromarty Firth, 10 miles (16 km) northwest of Inverness. Its name is derived from the Scandinavian for 'parliament in the valley'. An important market centre, Dingwall gained royal burgh status in 1226 and was the seat of the sheriffdom of Ross from 1265. The former county town of Ross and Cromarty, it was from 1975 to 1996 the administrative centre of the Ross and Cromarty district of Highland Region. The medieval Tulloch Castle, a stronghold of the Clan Ross, was replaced by a mansion, and the town's harbour eventually silted up. Linen spinning arrived in the 18th century, and a century later Dingwall prospered as a road and railway junction with livestock markets. North Sea oil-related development in the 1970s boosted the population by 5000 within a decade. Dingwall has a museum and hosts a Highland traditional-music festival in the summer in addition to a Highland games. Buildings of note include the 18th-century Town House and St Clement's Church (1801). Foulis Castle, seat of the chiefs of the Clan Munro, lies to the northeast.

Dinnet *Aberdeenshire* A village in Aberdeenshire, Dinnet lies in Royal Deeside, midway between Aboyne and Ballater. The Burn of Dinnet, which issues from Loch Davan, joins the River Dee here. To the north of the Dee and west of the village is the Muir of Dinnet Nature Reserve which protects oak woodland.

Dinvin *Dumfries and Galloway* A locality in the Rhinns of Galloway, Dumfries and Galloway, Dinvin lies a mile (1.5 km) to the northeast of Portpatrick.

Dinwoodie Mains *Dumfries and Galloway* A locality in Annandale, Dumfries and Galloway, Dinwoodie Mains lies to the east of the River Annan, 6 miles (10 km) north of Lockerbie. Dinwoodie Tollhouse, on the old Glasgow to Carlisle road (A74), was designed in the 1820s by Thomas Telford.

Dippin Head *North Ayrshire* A headland on the southeast coast of the island of Arran, North Ayrshire, Dippen Head lies 2 miles (3 km) south of Whiting Bay. Dippin Bay lies to the southwest and the settlement of Dippin lies a half-mile (1 km) inland.

Dipple *South Ayrshire* A hamlet of South Ayrshire, Dipple is located 2 miles (3 km) south of Turnberry and sits on the Firth of Clyde coast.

Dippool Water *South Lanarkshire* The Dippool Water rises to the west of Auchengray in South Lanarkshire. It flows south and west to join the Mouse Water 2 miles (3 km) north of Carstairs. The Mouse Water eventually joins the River Clyde a mile (1.5 km) northwest of Lanark.

Dirleton *East Lothian* Regarded as one of Scotland's most picturesque villages, Dirleton is located 2 miles (3 km) east-northeast of Gullane and 2 miles (3 km) west-southwest of North Berwick in East Lothian. Dominated by the 13th-century Dirleton Castle, which is now in the care of Historic Scotland, Dirleton includes neat rows of cottages around a large village green. In the northwest corner of the green is an old schoolhouse, and a fine parish church dating from 1661, but extended in 1825. The Castle Inn (*c.*1820) is by the noted architect William Burn.

Dirleton Castle *East Lothian* Constructed originally by the De Vaux family around 1225, Dirleton Castle was one of the most formidable castles of its time. However, it was captured by an English army under Bishop Anthony Bek of Durham in 1298 and was recovered only by Robert the Bruce in 1311. Bruce pulled down much of the castle to ensure the English armies could not make future use of it. Rebuilt in the 14th century by the Halyburton family, who added a new gatehouse, kitchen and great hall, the castle was further augmented by the Ruthven family in the 15th century, and passed to Sir Thomas Erskine (1566–1639) for his loyalty to James VI during the Gowrie Conspiracy of 1600. However, it was destroyed once again by General Monk in 1650. It passed to the Nisbet family in 1663, but was quickly abandoned as a residence in favour of their new and more comfortable house at Archerfield. The castle and surrounding garden are now in the care of Historic Scotland and substantial ruins remain, including the drawbridge, chapel, pit-prison, a well-preserved beehive dovecote and the world's longest herbaceous border.

Discovery Point *Dundee City* Situated at Discovery Quay on the waterfront of the city of Dundee, Discovery Point is the home of Captain Scott's famous RRS *Discovery*, one of the last wooden three-masted ships to be built in Britain and the first to be constructed specifically for scientific research. Built in Dundee, the *Discovery* was launched in 1901 as the research vessel of the British National Antarctic Expedition. Adjacent to the ship is a visitor centre that features displays on the history of Captain Scott's first Antarctic expedition of 1901-04. The Polarama Room, opened by the explorer Sir Ranulph Fiennes in 1999, is an interactive gallery that explores the geography of Antarctica.

Divie, River *Moray* A river of Moray, the Divie rises in headstreams on Dava Moor and flows 12 miles (19 km) northwards before joining the River Findhorn near Doune of Relugas.

Dobbie's Loan *Glasgow City* Dobbie's Loan gained its name from the local landowner, John Dobbie, and is believed to have formed part of the route of an old Roman road from Dumbarton to Glasgow. It stretched from Glasgow Cathedral to Garscube in the north of the city and was originally used as the main thoroughfare for cattle drovers on their way to the markets on Glasgow Green. As Port Dundas developed, so did the importance of Dobbie's Loan, and even after the decline in the fortunes of the Forth and Clyde Canal it remained an important business location, although much smaller than it once was. It now acts as a feeder road to the M8.

Dochard, Loch *Argyll and Bute* A small loch of Argyll and Bute, Loch Dochard is located a mile (1.5 km) north from the peak of Beinn Suidhe, 4 miles (6.5 km) west of Loch Tulla and 4 miles (6.5 km) south of Aonach Mòr.

Dochart, Falls of *Stirling* The Falls of Dochart form the most scenic and most photographed section of the River Dochart in Glen Dochart, Stirling Council area. Situated by a bridge leading into the village of Killin at the western end of Loch Tay, the falls cascade around the island of Inchbuie (or Innes Buie), the traditional burial place of the Clan MacNab.

Dochart, Glen *Stirling* A valley in northern Stirling Council area, Glen Dochart stretches eastwards from the junction of Strath Fillan and Glen Falloch at Crianlarich to Killin, following the course of the River Dochart which flows through Loch Dochart and Loch Iubhair.

Dochart, Loch *Stirling* A loch in northwestern Stirling Council area, Loch Dochart lies at the western end of Glen Dochart, a mile (1.5 km) to the east of Crianlarich and in the shadow of Ben More. On a small wooded island in the loch stand the ruins of a castle, a former stronghold of the Campbells of Lochawe, described by Dorothy Wordsworth in September 1803 as 'a place of retirement and peace'.

Dochart, River *Striling* A river of Breadalbane in Stirling Council area, the Dochart flows eastwards for 13 miles (21 km) from Loch Dochart at the head of Glen Dochart through to Loch Tay at Killin.

Docherty, Glen *Highland* Glen Docherty lies in Wester Ross, 5 miles (8 km) west of Achnasheen, and runs towards the settlement of Kinlochewe.

Dochgarroch *Highland* A settlement in the Great Glen, Highland Council area, Dochgarroch lies on the Caledonian Canal at the head of Loch Ness, 4 miles (6.5 km) southwest of Inverness.

Doe, Glen *Highland* Glen Doe lies to the west of the Monadhliath Mountains and east of Loch Ness, in the Inverness district of Highland Council area. It carries the waters of the Allt Doe north to empty into the loch, a mile (1.5 km) from its head.

Doe, River *Highland* A river rising in the mountains to the south of Loch Affric in Highland Council area, the River Doe flows southeastwards through Glen Doe to join the River Moriston 2 miles (3 km) east of Loch Cluanie.

Dog Hillock *Angus* A hill in the southern Grampians, Dog Hillock rises to 722 m (2369 ft) at the head of Glen Ogil in the Braes of Angus. The Trusty Burn, a headstream of the Noran Water, rises on its southern slopes.

Dogton Stone *Fife* An ancient stone bearing a Celtic cross and other sculptures situated in a field to the south of Dogton Farm by Kinglassie, the Dogton Stone is said to mark the inroads of the Danes in the 9th century.

Doine, Loch *Stirling* A small loch in the Balquhidder district of Stirling Council area, Loch Doine lies immediately west of Loch Voil to which it is joined.

Doll *Highland* A settlement on the east coast of Sutherland, Highland Council area, Doll lies a mile (1.5 km) to the southwest of Brora.

Doll, Glen *Angus* A small glen in the southern Grampians, Glen Doll lies at the head of Glen Clova in Angus. It is a starting point for walks into the mountains. Jock's Road extends from here to Braemar. The White Water, which flows through Glen Doll, joins the River South Esk at Braedownie.

Dollar *Clackmannanshire* A Hillfoots village in Clackmannanshire, Dollar lies to the east of Tillicoultry and north of the River Devon. An earlier village was destroyed in 1645 by the Marquess of Montrose while attacking the Covenanting stronghold of Castle Campbell,

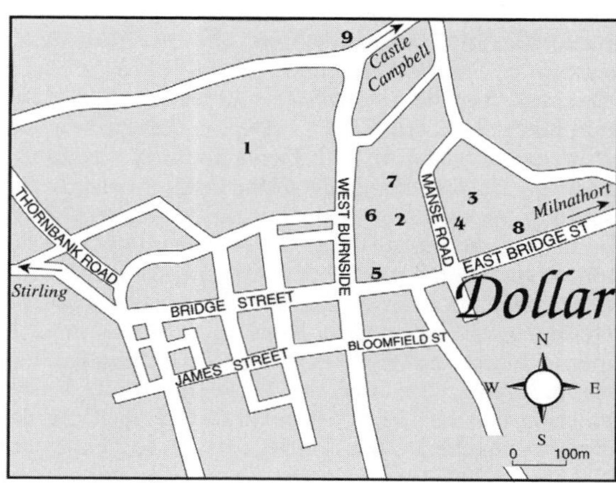

1 *Dollar Academy*
2 *Old School House*
3 *Old Parish Church*
4 *Mort House*
5 *Spence Memorial Clock*
6 *Mylne Bridge*
7 *Argyle Cottage*
8 *Parish Church*
9 *Museum*

which stands on an eminence in Dollar Glen overlooking the Devon Valley. The village expanded in the 19th century with the building of the turnpike road (1806), the development of a textile mill, the Brunt Mill (1822), and the building of Dollar Academy (1818–20) to a design by William Playfair for the trustees of John McNabb (1732–1802), a local herd-boy who rose to fortune as a sea captain and bequeathed money to build a school in Dollar. Interesting buildings include the Old School House, Old Parish Church and Mort House, Spence Memorial Clock, Mylne Bridge, Argyle Cottage, Parish Church (1841) and Museum. During the 20th century the village grew with the development of both public and private housing.

Dollar Glen *Clackmannanshire* A wooded glen on the Ochil Hills geological fault above the village of Dollar, Dollar Glen provides spectacular walks from the village to Castle Campbell. Maintained by the National Trust for Scotland, 22 ha (54 acres) of the glen was designated a Site of Special Scientific Interest (SSSI) in 1989 to protect its diverse habitats and important geological features.

Dollar Law *Scottish Borders* A hill in the Ettrick district of Scottish Borders, Dollar Law rises to 817 m (2680 ft) 10 miles (16 km) southwest of Peebles.

Dolphingstone *East Lothian* A hamlet lying beside the A1 in East Lothian, Dolphingstone lies a mile (1.5 km) to the southwest of Prestonpans and 1.5 miles (2.5 km) west of Tranent. It came to prominence in 2001 when a significant mining-related collapse occurred at what became known as the Dolphingstone Subsidence Site, endangering the main railway line south and resulting in it being rerouted some 500 m (547 yd) to the south. Mines were active nearby from at least the 18th century until the middle of the 20th century, including the Dolphin stone and Bankton collieries. Just to the south are the ruins of the 17th-century Dolphingstone Castle, which is said to have briefly hosted Oliver Cromwell but of which little remains except a dovecote.

Dolphinton *South Lanarkshire* A village of South Lanarkshire, Dolphinton is located 7 miles (11 km) northeast of Biggar and 27 miles (43 km) southwest of Edinburgh. The local manor belonged in the 12th century to Dolfine, elder brother of the 1st Earl of Dunbar.

Domhain, Gleann *Argyll and Bute* A valley of Argyll and Bute, Gleann Domhain carries the Barbreck River southwest from Lagalochan to the head of Loch Craignish. It extends southwest for almost 6 miles (10 km).

Don, Loch *Argyll and Bute* Located on the southeastern coast of the island of Mull to the south of Craignure, Loch Don forms a large inlet of the Firth of Lorn. To the south of the mouth of the loch is the headland of Grass Point, while to the north lies the settlement of Gorten.

Don, River *Aberdeenshire* A river of Aberdeenshire, the Don rises in headstreams in the northeastern Grampians between Glen Avon and Cock Bridge. It follows a circuitous route eastwards for 82 miles (132 km) through Strathdon and the Howe of Alford before entering the North Sea just north of Old Aberdeen. Its chief tributaries are the Conrie, Carvie, Leochel, Ernan, Nochty, Bucket, Kindy and Ury. In 1750 the Don's lower reaches were channelled towards the sea, moving its confluence with the sea northwards.

Donibristle *Fife* An estate in Dalgety parish in south-central Fife situated between Inverkeithing and Dalgety Bay, Donibristle looks out over the Firth of Forth. Originally owned by the abbots of Inchcolm, the property fell at the Reformation to Sir James Stuart of Doune whose son, the 'Bonny' Earl of Moray, was killed on the seashore below the castle in 1592, an event commemorated in an old Scots ballad. The mansion of Donibristle now forms part of the modern residential development of Dalgety Bay, the Moray Estates having sold the property to developers in the 1960s for the purpose of creating a new town. The former Donibristle colliery and its associated village were associated with a mining disaster in August 1901 when eight miners died. An airfield at Donibristle was opened in 1917 as a base for the Royal Naval Air Service. During World War II, as HMS *Merlin*, it was used as a Royal Navy aircraft repair yard. After the war it was renamed HMS *Cochrane*, and with closure in 1959 it was converted into Hillend and Donibristle industrial estates.

Doon, Loch *East Ayrshire* A loch and reservoir in East Ayrshire, Loch Doon lies at the head of the River Doon, 4 miles (6.5 km) south of Dalmellington.

Doon, River *East Ayrshire/Dumfries and Galloway* A river rising in Loch Doon on the border between East Ayrshire and Dumfries and Galloway, the River Doon flows north through the Ness Glen and into Bogton Loch before continuing north and west. It passes through the settlements of Patna and Skeldon before finally entering Ayr Bay at Doonfoot, a mile (1.5 km) northwest of Alloway.

Doon Castle *Dumfries and Galloway* The name given to a Pictish broch in the Rhinns of Galloway, Dumfries and Galloway, Doon Castle stands on Ardwell Point, a low rocky promontory just south of Sandhead. It is one of the best preserved of a small number of brochs in western Galloway that date from the 1st century AD.

Doonfoot *South Ayrshire* A suburb of the town of Ayr in South Ayrshire, Doonfoot is located on the Firth of Clyde coastline at the mouth of the River Doon.

Doonie Point *Aberdeenshire* A headland on the North Sea coast of Aberdeenshire, Doonie Point lies a mile (1.5 km) to the south of Muchalls and 6 miles (10 km) north of Stonehaven.

Dorback Burn *Moray* Emerging from the northern end of Lochindorb, the Dorback Burn flows 8 miles (13 km) northwards through Moray to meet the River Divie, before joining the River Findhorn which drains to the Moray Firth.

Dorback Burn *Highland* A stream in Strathspey, Highland Council area, the Dorback Burn rises in headstreams in the Braes of Abernethy. It flows west and north to join the River Nethy near Lettoch, to the southeast of Nethy Bridge. Dorback Lodge was built in the 19th century as a shooting lodge on the Strathspey Estate.

Dores *Highland* A village in the Great Glen, Highland Council area, Dores lies on the east side of Loch Ness at the southern end of Strath Dores.

Dornal, Loch *South Ayrshire/Dumfries and Galloway* A loch on the border of South Ayrshire and Dumfries and Galloway, Loch Dornal lies 5 miles (8 km) southeast of Barrhill and adjacent to Loch Maberry, which sits to the southwest. To the northwest is Drumlamford Loch.

Dornie *Highland* A former fishing village in the Kintail district of Wester Ross, Highland Council area, Dornie lies on the east side of the entrance to Loch Long, 8 miles (13 km) east of Kyle of Lochalsh. Prior to the building of

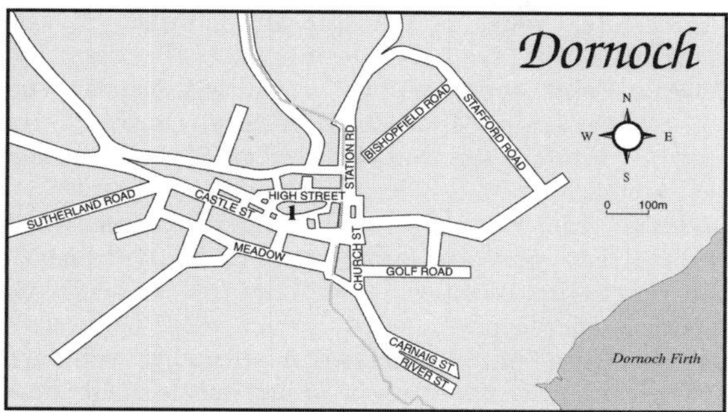

1 *Dornoch Cathedral*

a bridge in the 1930s, a ferry linked Dornie with Ardelve. An ancient centre of Highland Catholicism, the Duchess of Leeds founded a convent and church here in the 19th century. Nearby is the restored Macrae stronghold of Eilean Donan Castle.

Dornoch *Highland* The former county town of Sutherland, Dornoch lies at the mouth of the Dornoch Firth, 22 miles (35 km) north of Dingwall. Thought to have been home to a community of the early Celtic Church, its church was first recorded in 1140 during the reign of David I. St Gilbert of Moray, elected Bishop of Caithness in 1222, moved the seat of the Diocese of Caithness to Dornoch for safety in 1224 and built a cathedral prior to his death in 1245. Gilbert was the last Scotsman to be canonised before the Reformation. Destroyed during a clan feud in 1570, the cathedral, now the parish church, was restored by Elizabeth, Countess of Sutherland, in 1835–7. There is a memorial to philanthropist Andrew Carnegie (1835–1918) who lived nearby at Skibo Castle. Noted for its fine beaches and golf links, Dornoch developed as a tourist resort after the arrival of the Dornoch Light Railway in 1902. This linked the town with the Highland Railway station at The Mound, a distance of 7 miles (11 km), until 1960. Buildings of note include the Deanery (c.1840), Dornoch Castle Hotel, Dornoch Academy (1964), the Carnegie Building (1902) and the County Buildings and Court House (1850–60).

Dornoch Firth *Highland* An estuary between the Easter Ross and Sutherland districts of Highland Council area, the Dornoch Firth receives the River Oykel, which is joined by the Shin near Carbisdale Castle. The estuary opens into the Kyle of Sutherland just south of Carbisdale, then narrows at Bonar Bridge before continuing eastwards to the sea beyond Dornoch Point near the burgh of Dornoch on the east coast. The Meikle ferry that once crossed the narrows was the scene of a skirmish in 1746 on the eve of the Battle of Culloden, and a tragedy in 1809 when an overcrowded ferry boat capsized with the loss of 70 lives. In 1991 a bridge across the firth was opened by Queen Elizabeth the Queen Mother, shortening the A9 route from Inverness to Wick.

Dornock *Dumfries and Galloway* A village of Annandale in Dumfries and Galloway, Dornock lies close to the Solway Firth, 3 miles (5 km) east of Annan.

Douglas *South Lanarkshire* A village of South Lanarkshire, Douglas lies on the Douglas Water, 11 miles (18 km) southwest of Lanark. It developed in medieval times in association with a castle that was the seat of the Black Douglas earls, including James Douglas, the loyal supporter of King Robert the Bruce. Chartered as a burgh of barony in 1458, Douglas later thrived as a centre of coal mining and the manufacture of cotton goods. Scotland's first wind farm was established in 1994 on Hagshaw Hill, 2 miles (5 km) to the west. Douglas has its own heritage museum. Little remains of the 18th-century Douglas Castle, which was destroyed in the mid-20th century after a coal seam opened underneath; it was used by Sir Walter Scott (1771–1832) for his novel *Castle Dangerous* (1832).

Douglas, Glen *Argyll and Bute* A valley in Argyll and Bute, Glen Douglas carries the Douglas Water from Tullich Hill east to the settlement of Inverbeg at Loch Lomond.

Douglas Water *Argyll and Bute* A river of Argyll and Bute, the Douglas Water rises in the foothills of Tullich Hill, east of Loch Long. It flows east through Glen Douglas to Loch Lomond, which it enters at the settlement of Inverbeg.

Douglas Water *Argyll and Bute* Rising in a small loch a mile (1.5 km) south of the peak of An Suidhe, the Douglas Water flows north, south then east to enter Loch Fyne 3 miles (5 km) south of Inveraray.

Douglas Water *South Lanarkshire* A small hamlet to the east of the river Douglas Water in South Lanarkshire, Douglas Water lies a mile (1.5 km) from Rigside, 3 miles (5 km) northeast of Uddington and 3 miles (5 km) east of the M74.

Douglas Water *South Lanarkshire* A river of South Lanarkshire, the Douglas Water rises 7 miles (11 km) southwest of Douglas and flows 20 miles (32 km) northeast, passing through Douglas and Douglas Water. It joins the River Clyde 3 miles (5 km) south of Lanark and 2 miles (3 km) south of the New Lanark Heritage Centre and the Falls of Clyde.

Douglastown *Angus* A hamlet of central Angus, Douglastown lies in Strathmore at the foot of the Sidlaw Hills, 2 miles (3 km) northeast of Glamis and 3 miles (5 km) southwest of Forfar. Douglastown was built in the early 1790s around a flax mill managed for a time by James Ivory (1765–1842), who went on to become a noted mathematician.

Dounby *Orkney* A village on the Mainland of Orkney, Dounby lies to the north of the Loch of Harray, 14 miles (22 km) northwest of Kirkwall. It developed at a crossroads in the 18th century and has a market and facilities serving the surrounding farming community. Between 1939 and 1940 an RAF fighter base operated at Skeabrae, just over a mile (1.5 km) to the west.

Doune *Stirling* An historic village situated on the River Teith where it is joined by the Ardoch Burn, Doune lies close to Doune Castle on the A84, 7 miles (11 km) northwest of Stirling. Once known for its manufacture of pistols, a trade introduced by Thomas Cadell in 1646, Doune is now a dormitory village and centre of tourism. Among its buildings of historic and architectural interest are Kilmadock Parish Church (1822), the Market Cross (1620), the Moray Institute and the Bridge of Teith (1535). Nearby are an Arts and Antique Centre and the Doune Ponds, which were developed from an abandoned sand and gravel quarry.

Doune Castle *Stirling* Located a half-mile (1 km) southeast of the village of Doune, above the confluence of the Rivers Teith and Ardoch, Doune Castle is one of the most significant and best-preserved examples of

14th-century military architecture in Scotland. The triangular site is naturally well defended, being protected on two sides by the rivers and on the third by a deep moat. The castle was built at a strategic crossroads by Robert Stewart (c.1340–1419), 1st Duke of Albany and comprises an impressive curtain wall enclosing a large court dominated by a square gatehouse tower. Doune passed to King James I when he executed Stewart's son, Murdoch, the 2nd Duke of Albany (c.1362–1425), and became the home of a succession of dowager queens, before passing to the Earls of Moray. The castle fell to the Jacobites in 1745. Ruined and roofless by the end of the 18th century, it remained in this sad state until the 14th Earl undertook repairs in 1883. The castle was used as the backdrop for the film *Monty Python and the Holy Grail* (1975). In 1984 the castle was given to the Secretary of State for Scotland on a 999-year lease and has subsequently been in the care of Historic Scotland.

Doune Hill *Argyll and Bute* A hill of Argyll and Bute, Doune Hill rises to a height of 734 m (2408 ft) between Glen Douglas and Glen Luss, to the west of Loch Lomond.

Dounepark *South Ayrshire* Dounepark is the name given to a southern district of Girvan, South Ayrshire.

Dounie *Highland* A locality in Sutherland, Highland Council area, Dounie lies in Strathcarron, 2 miles (3 km) west of Bonar Bridge. The remains of An Dun broch lie close by near the River Carron.

Dounreay *Highland* A location on the north coast of Caithness in Highland Council Area, 10 miles (16 km) west of Thurso, Dounreay is principally recognised as the site of the Dounreay Nuclear Power Development Establishment. Located at Lower Dounreay and opened in 1954, this nuclear-power facility was built on a former World War II airfield, a site chosen for its remoteness from the largest cities of the UK. It was designed to find ways of producing cheaper energy, and fuel reprocessing began in 1958. In 1962 it was the first fast-breeder reactor in the world to supply energy to the public electricity supply. A second prototype fast reactor began operating in 1974 and by the late 1970s nearly 3500 people were employed. A reduction in staffing began in 1989 when the government decided to wind down the Fast Breeder Reactor programme and in 1994 the experimental reactor was closed. The remains of the 16th century Dounreay Castle, once home to the Mackay Lords of Reay, lies within the nuclear plant and was. A small farming settlement lies 1.25 miles (2 km) to the southeast at Upper Dounreay.

Dowally *Perth and Kinross* A roadside village in Strath Tay, Perth and Kinross, Dowally lies by the A9, 5 miles (8 km) northwest of Dunkeld. Dowally Kirk dates from 1818, replacing an earlier church that once served the independent parish of Dowally. A stream flows down from Dowally Loch to meet the River Tay near here.

Dowhill *Perth and Kinross* An estate in the Cleish Hills, Perth and Kinross, Dowhill includes the ruined Dowhill Castle, a former stronghold of the Lindsays dating from the 16th century, and Dowhill House, formerly Barns House, which dates from 1710.

Downan Point *South Ayrshire* A coastal feature of South Ayrshire, Downan Point forms a headland at the south end of Ballantrae Bay.

Downhill *Perth and Kinross* A locality in Perth and Kinross, Downhill lies to the west of the River Tay, immediately north of Luncarty and 4 miles (6.5 km) north of Perth.

Downie Point *Aberdeenshire* Forming a headland on the North Sea coast of Aberdeenshire, Downie Point extends into the sea midway between Stonehaven and Dunnottar.

Downies *Aberdeenshire* A commuter settlement and former fishing village with a small harbour in eastern Aberdeenshire, Downies lies on a cliff top 5 miles (8 km) south of Aberdeen.

Dowrie Burn *Aberdeenshire* A stream in southern Aberdeenshire, the Dowrie Burn is formed near Fettercairn by the meeting of the Burn of Garroll, Crichie Burn and Burn of Balnakettle, which rise in the Braes of Angus. It flows southeastwards across the Howe of the Mearns to join the Luther Water to the east of Luthermuir. The stream passes through an area of intensive pig farming.

Draffan *South Lanarkshire* A settlement of South Lanarkshire, Draffan is located 4 miles (6.5 km) southeast of Larkhall and a mile (1.5 km) west of the M74.

Dreghorn *North Ayrshire* A large village in North Ayrshire, Dreghorn lies 3 miles (5 km) east of Irvine, between the River Irvine and the Annick Water. It developed in the 19th century in association with coal mining and the manufacture of bricks, and was the birthplace in 1845 of John Boyd Dunlop, inventor of the pneumatic tyre.

Drem *East Lothian* A small village in East Lothian surrounded by fertile farmland, Drem lies 4 miles (6.5 km) north of Haddington in the shadow of an ancient hillfort called the Chesters. It is situated on the main railway line to England at its junction with a branch line to North Berwick. An airfield established here during World War I became a significant fighter base during World War II, its fighter planes intercepting German raids over Britain en route to the naval base at Rosyth. RAF Drem also gave its name to a lighting system used to enable aircraft to take off and land in bad weather and at night that was pioneered at the airfield.

Dreumasdal The Gaelic name for Drimsdale in the Western Isles.

Driesh *Angus* A mountain in the Mounth plateau above Glen Doll in Angus, Driesh rises to a height of 947 m (3107 ft). Its slopes are covered in coniferous forests and its name is derived from the Gaelic word dris, which means 'bramble' or 'thorn bush'.

Drimsdale *Western Isles* A small crofting settlement on the west coast of South Uist in the Outer Hebrides, Drimsdale (Gael: *Dreumasdal*) lies a quarter-mile (0.5 km) south of Loch Stilligary and 12 miles (19 km) north-northwest of Lochboisdale. Drimsdale House was once a manse.

Drip *Stirling* A locality in Stirling Council area, Drip lies 3 miles (5 km) northwest of Striling and comprises the scattered settlements of West Drip, Dripend and Hill of Drip, all of which lie on the reclaimed Drip Moss. The five-arched Old Drip Bridge over the River Forth dates from 1790, with a tollhouse built in 1820. The road heading northwestwards from Stirling between the Rivers Teith and Forth is known as the Drip Road.

Drochil Castle *Scottish Borders* A massive Z-plan castle in Scottish Borders, Drochil Castle lies between the Tarth and Lyne Waters, 7 miles (11 km) southwest of

Peebles. It was built by James Douglas, 4th Earl of Morton, Regent of Scotland, but was not completed before his execution in 1581 for his part in the death of Henry, Lord Darnley, husband of Mary, Queen of Scots.

Drolsay, Loch *Argyll and Bute* A small loch located a mile (1.5 km) west of Loch Cam, in the northern half of the island of Islay in Argyll and Bute, Loch Drolsay is one of three small lochs that lie 5 miles (8 km) northeast of Bowmore.

Droma, River *Highland* A runoff stream from Loch Droma in Wester Ross, the River Droma (Gael: *Abhainn Dromm*) flows 4 miles (6.5 km) northwest to join the Abhainn Cuileig and form the River Broom. The Corrieshalloch Gorge lies on the course of this river.

Dron *Perth and Kinross* A locality in Strathearn, Perth and Kinross, Dron lies on the River Farg in the northern foothills of the Ochil Hills, a mile (1.5 km) to the southeast of Bridge of Earn. The former parish church of Dron with its pinnacled tower dates from 1824. Adjacent are the former manse, built in 1810, a school of the same period, and Balmanno Castle, built c.1580 and restored by Sir Robert Lorimer in 1916–21 for the Glasgow shipowner William Miller. Sir Walter Scott (1771–1832) thought the vista across Strathearn from Dron Hill one of the most beautiful views in the world. On the slopes of Dron Hill rests a block of whinstone known as the Rocking Stone of Dron.

Drongan *East Ayrshire* A village of East Ayrshire, Drongan lies to the south of the A70, midway between Ayr and Cumnock. Much expanded by public housing in the 1950s, it developed in association with coal mining.

Dronley *Angus* A village in the Angus parish of Auchterhouse, Dronley lies on the Dronley Burn, 4 miles (6.5 km) northwest of the centre of Dundee.

Dronner's Dyke *Angus* An earthwork in the Montrose Basin, Dronner's Dyke was raised in 1670 by the entrepreneur Robert Raitt, with the assistance of Dutch engineers, in an attempt to reclaim the northern part of the basin. Raitt had gained title to the substantial area of agricultural land that would have been created, but the project was abandoned after the embankment was badly damaged in a storm. Almost a mile (1.5 km) in length, the dyke runs west to east across the centre of the basin and remains visible today at low tide.

Druchtag Motte *Dumfries and Galloway* A medieval earthwork in the Machars district of Dumfries and Galloway, the Druchtag Motte lies just north of Mochrum. It forms a steep-sided mound and has a summit area 20 m (65 ft) in diameter. Druchtag once formed part of the barony of Mochrum of Druchtag held for a time by the McCullochs of Druchtag.

Druidibeg, Loch *Western Isles* Located at the north end of the island of South Uist in the Western Isles, Loch Druidibeg lies 4 miles (6.5 km) northwest of the peak of Beinn Mhòr. It is the site of a nature reserve.

Druimarbin *Highland* A settlement in Highland Council area, Druimarbin lies on the east side of Loch Linnhe, 2 miles (3 km) southwest of Fort William.

Druimindarroch *Highland* A locality in Arisaig, southwestern Highland Council area, Druimindarroch lies on the north side of Loch nan Uamh, between Loch Ailort and Arisaig.

Druim Shionnach *Highland* One of seven peaks on the South Glen Shiel ridge in the Inverness district of Highland Council area, Druim Shionnach rises to a height of 987 m (3238 ft). Its name is derived from the Gaelic for 'trembling hill'.

Drum *Perth and Kinross* A village in Perth and Kinross, Drum is situated a mile (1.5 km) to the east of Crook of Devon and 4 miles (6.5 km) west of Kinross. Also known as Drum of Tulliebole, it lies to the west of 16th-century Tulliebole Castle, home of the Moncreiffes of Tulliebole.

Drum Castle *Aberdeenshire* Located 2.5 miles (4 km) west of Peterculter and a mile (1.5 km) north of the River Dee, the robust square tower at Drum was built in the late 13th century. Drum was granted by Robert the Bruce (1274–1329) to his standard bearer, William de Irwyn, in 1323. The property has changed little in the intervening time, although the architect David Bryce (1803–76) undertook some modernisation in 1871. Drum remained a possession of the Irvine family until 1975, when it was bequeathed to the National Trust for Scotland.

Drum of Tulliebole An alternative name for Drum in Perth and Kinross.

Drumbeg *Highland* A scattered crofting township in the Assynt district of western Sutherland, Highland Council area, Drumbeg lies near the south shore of Eddrachillis Bay. The school and schoolhouse date from 1878 and a library gifted by Millicent, Duchess of Sutherland, was erected in 1909. In addition to a post office and hotel, there is a fish farm.

Drumblade *Aberdeenshire* A hamlet on the Burn of Forgue in the Strathbogie district of Aberdeenshire, Drumblade is situated in a parish of the same name 2 miles (3 km) east of Huntly.

Drumbrae *Stirling* A locality in Stirling Council area at the western end of the Ochil Hills, Drumbrae is situated on high ground overlooking Bridge of Allan.

Drumbuie *Highland* A locality in Highland Council area, Drumbuie lies between Kyle of Lochalsh and Plockton. In the 1970s an attempt to develop this site in association with the exploitation of North Sea oil and gas was successfully opposed by the local crofters and the National Trust for Scotland.

Drumburn *Dumfries and Galloway* A locality in Dumfries and Galloway, Drumburn lies on the Drum Burn which flows down from the Criffell massif to enter Drum Bay, an inlet of the Solway Firth. Kirkbean lies 2 miles (3 km) to the south and New Abbey is 3 miles (5 km) north.

Drumchapel *Glasgow City* A residential area on the northwest periphery of the city of Glasgow, Drumchapel lies 6 miles (10 km) northwest of the city centre. Formerly known as Chapelton, the village of Drumchapel expanded following the purchase of the Garscadden Estate by Glasgow Corporation in 1939, although it was not until the late 1940s that housing development got underway. By 1971 Drumchapel's population reached a peak of 34,000, but with a lack of services and local employment opportunities 'The Drum' came to be synonymous with poverty and vandalism.

Drumchastle *Perth and Kinross* A locality between Loch Rannoch and Loch Tummel, Perth and Kinross, Drumchastle lies on a burn flowing southwards into Dunalastair Water, a mile (1.5 km) to the east of Kinloch Rannoch.

Drumclog *South Lanarkshire* A village of South Lanarkshire, Drumclog lies in the valley of the Avon

Water, 5 miles (8 km) east of Darvel and 6 miles (10 km) southwest of Strathaven. Originally comprising the rural farmtowns of Low and High Drumclog, a village developed close to a railway station opened in 1905. Sand and gravel are quarried nearby, and a mile (1.5 km) to the northwest near High Drumclog is a monument commemorating the Battle of Drumclog in 1679 at which the Covenanters defeated Government forces under Graham of Claverhouse.

Drumcoltran Castle *Dumfries and Galloway* Located near the village of Kirkgunzeon in Dumfries and Galloway, Drumcoltran Tower is an L-shaped tower house constructed for the Maxwell family in 1550. Still occupied in the 1890s, it is now in the care of Historic Scotland.

Drumeldrie *Fife* A hamlet in east Fife, Drumeldrie lies 2 miles (3 km) east of Lower Largo on the A917 to Elie.

Drumelzier *Scottish Borders* A village in a parish of the same name in Scottish Borders, Drumelzier lies on the Drumelzier Burn near its confluence with the River Tweed, 8 miles (13 km) southwest of Peebles. Drumelzier Law rises to 669 m (2191 ft), and nearby is Drumelzier Castle, a former stronghold of the Tweedie family. Merlin the magician is said to be buried near the meeting of the Powsail Burn with the Tweed.

Drumfearn *Highland* A settlement on the isle of Skye, Highland Council area, Drumfearn lies at the head of the Sleat peninsula, 5 miles (8 km) south of Broadford.

Drumfergue *Aberdeenshire* A locality in the Strathbogie district of Aberdeenshire, Drumfergue lies on the Hill of Drumfergue in Clashindarroch Forest, 5 miles (8 km) south of Huntly.

Drumgelloch *North Lanarkshire* A former village of New Monkland parish, Drumgelloch is now an eastern suburb of Airdrie.

Drumguish *Highland* A locality in Badenoch, Highland Council area, Drumguish lies on the south side of the River Spey, 2 miles (3 km) southeast of Kingussie.

Drumin *Moray* A small settlement in Strathavon, Moray, Drumin lies close to the confluence of the River Livet with the Avon. On a bluff overlooking the two rivers stand the ruins of Drumin Castle, which guarded the entrance to Speyside from the Lecht. Dating from the 14th century, it was once in the possession of Sir Alexander Stewart, the Wolf of Badenoch (*c*.1343–1406), who also owned the strongholds of Lochindorb and Loch-an-Eilean. The farmhouse at Drumin (1818), now a museum of country life, was the home of James Skinner, factor to successive dukes of Gordon from 1824 to 1873. Skinner was a grandson of the well-known violinist and composer of Strathspey reels, William Marshall (1748–1833), himself a factor to the Duke of Gordon.

Drumjohn *Dumfries and Galloway* A locality in Dumfries and Galloway, Drumjohn lies to the east of Loch Doon between Carsphairn and Dalmellington.

Drumlamford *South Ayrshire* Drumlamford House on the western shore of Loch Dornal lies 5 miles (8 km) southeast of Barrhill in South Ayrshire. Drumlamford Loch lies a half-mile (1 km) to the northwest of the house.

Drumlanrig Castle *Dumfries and Galloway* Located in Upper Nithsdale, 16 miles (26 km) west of Moffat and 18 miles (29 km) north-northwest of Dumfries, Drumlanrig is a seat of the dukes of Buccleuch and Queensberry. Drumlanrig was built on the site of a 14th-century castle of the 'Black' Douglas family where King James VI was entertained in 1617 on his return to Scotland. The family was rewarded for supporting the Stewart monarchy, and William Douglas (1637–95), 1st Duke and 3rd Earl of Queensberry, ordered the construction of the present castle as a dwelling more appropriate to his status, a project that nearly bankrupted him in the process. Drumlanrig was built between 1679 and 1691, probably by James Smith (*c*.1645–1731), perhaps with the assistance of his father-in-law, Robert Mylne (1633–1710), the king's master mason. Internal wood panelling and carving are a notable feature, and the rich oak staircase and balustrade represents one of the first of its kind in Scotland. Bonnie Prince Charlie visited while retreating north late in 1745, and his bedroom can be seen today. The Buccleuchs brought to the home a magnificent collection of furniture and art, with works by Holbein and Rembrandt, and a Leonardo that was stolen in 2003. Today, the castle is surrounded by extensive estates deriving income from farming and forestry.

Drumlithie *Aberdeenshire* A picturesque village with a school in southeastern Aberdeenshire, Drumlithie lies 7 miles (11 km) southwest of Stonehaven at the northern end of the Howe of the Mearns. In the 18th century the village had a thriving handloom-weaving industry, a reminder of this period being the bell tower of 1777 whose bell called the weavers to work. A large standing stone that, legend has it, must be kept whitewashed at all times, stands in a field at nearby Mill of Mondynes, allegedly marking the spot where King Duncan II was slain in 1094.

Drumly Harry, Falls of *Angus* A cascade on the Noran Water in Angus, the Falls of Drumly Harry are located to the south of Glen Ogil and to the north of Tannadice.

Drummond, Pond of *Perth and Kinross* A small loch in Strathearn, Perth and Kinross, the Pond of Drummond lies a mile (1.5 km) to the northwest of Muthill near Drummond Castle. It empties into the River Earn through the Bennybeg Pond.

Drummond Castle *Perth and Kinross* An estate in central Perth and Kinross, Drummond Castle lies 3 miles (5 km) southwest of Crieff and 1.5 miles (2.5 km) northwest of Muthill. The castle, which dates from *c*.1490, comprises an old tower built by John, 1st Lord Drummond, Steward of Strathearn and Justice-General to James IV. Much damaged by Cromwell's forces in the mid-17th century and again during the second Jacobite Rebellion in 1745, Drummond Castle had been extended by the architect John Mylne. It was rebuilt in the mid-19th century. On the opposite side of the paved courtyard stands a mansion house erected in 1688 by the 4th Earl of Perth, who employed John Reid, author of the first Scottish book on gardening, to design a garden. The garden was reshaped into a vast formal parterre in the 1840s for Clementina Sarah Drummond and her husband, the 21st Baron Willoughby de Eresby. Queen Victoria planted copper beech trees when she visited Drummond Castle in 1842.

Drummond Hill *Perth and Kinross* A forested hill in Breadalbane, Perth and Kinross, Drummond Hill rises to 458 m (1492 ft) at the northeastern end of Loch Tay, separating the valleys of the Tay and the Lyon which meet at the eastern end of the hill. There are 10 miles (16 km) of forest walks open to the public.

Drummore *Dumfries and Galloway* The village of Drummore in Dumfries and Galloway overlooks Luce Bay and lies towards the southern tip of the Rhinns of Galloway, 17 miles (27 km) south of Stranraer. Most of its buildings date from the 19th century, including the Ship Inn (*c.* 1860), the Queen's Hotel and the harbour (*c.*1845).

Drummossie Muir *Highland* An area of partly forested moorland to the southeast of Inverness in Highland Council area, Drummossie Muir lies to the west of the River Nairn and southeast of Culloden. It was in the centre of Drummossie Muir that the Battle of Culloden was fought in 1746.

Drummuie *Highland* A locality to the west of Golspie in eastern Sutherland, Highland Council area, Drummuie comprises a group of buildings dating from *c.*1809 which, until the 1960s, was associated with the Sutherland Technical School, now the technical annexe to Golspie High School. The technical school was established in 1903 by Millicent, Duchess of Sutherland, and was the first school in Scotland to provide free residential education for the sons of crofters from isolated communities in the Highlands and Islands.

Drummuir Castle *Moray* A former home of the Duff family, Drummuir Castle lies between Newmill and Dufftown in Moray. The present castellated Gothic-style building was designed by Thomas Mackenzie for Admiral Duff in 1847. It replaced the earlier and more modest Kirkton House.

Drumnadrochit *Highland* A locality in the Great Glen, Highland Council area, Drumnadrochit lies on the River Enrick at the east end of Glen Urquhart and at the head of Urquhart Bay, an inlet on the west side of Loch Ness. A post office was established here in 1835, and its hotel became popular in the 19th century, the area's prosperity being linked to the exploitation of the Loch Ness Monster legend. In addition to visitor centres focusing on the monster, there is an oatcake bakery.

Drumoak *Aberdeenshire* A parish in Aberdeenshire, Drumoak lies to the west of Peterculter and north of the River Dee. Drum Castle lies at the centre of the parish.

Drumochter, Pass of *Highland* Located 5 miles (8 km) south of Dalwhinnie, the Pass of Drumochter represents the highest point on both the A9 road and the railway on the route from Perth to Inverness. In fact, at 452 m (1484 ft), it is the highest point on any railway in Britain. At one time, two engines were required to haul trains to the summit, and the speed was sufficiently slow that many of the passengers would alight from the train and walk to the summit.

Drumoig *Fife* A golf club and village with golf practice ranges, Drumoig is situated close to the A92 near Pickletillem in northeast Fife. Established in phases from 1996 on a greenfield site, Drumoig includes a hotel, an exclusive private housing development and the Scottish National Golf Centre, which provides facilities for amateur golfers.

Drumpellier Country Park *North Lanarkshire* A country park in Monklands parish, North Lanarkshire, Drumpellier lies a mile (1.5 km) to the northwest of Coatbridge. It has lakeside walks and other recreational facilities.

Drumtochty Castle *Aberdeenshire* A mansion house in the Glen of Drumtochty in Aberdeenshire, Drumtochty Castle lies on the Luther Water north of Laurencekirk, 4 miles (6.5 km) west of Glenbervie.

Drumtroddan *Dumfries and Galloway* A locality in the Machars of Dumfries and Galloway, Drumtroddan lies to the north of the White Loch of Myerton, 2 miles (3 km) east of Port William. Standing stones and cup-and-ring markings on outcrops of greywacke date from the 2nd millennium BC.

Drumuie *Highland* A linear settlement on the island of Skye in the Inner Hebrides, Drumuie lies 3 miles (5 km) northwest of Portree at the southern end of the Trotternish peninsula.

Drumuillie *Highland* A locality in Strathspey, Highland Council area, Drumuillie lies to the north of the River Spey, a mile (1.5 km) north of Boat of Garten.

Drumvaich *Stirling* A roadside location in Stirling Council area, Drumvaich lies by the River Teith on the A820, 4 miles (6.5 km) northwest of Doune.

Drunkie, Loch *Stirling* A small loch in the Trossachs district of Stirling Council area, Loch Drunkie lies between Loch Venachar to the north and the Menteith Hills to the south. To the west it is bounded by Achray Forest.

Drunzie *Perth and Kinross* A locality in south Perth and Kinross, the adjacent settlements of Drunzie and Drunzie Feus lie just over a mile (1.5 km) to the south of Glenfarg on the old toll road from Milnathort to Glenfarg.

Dry Burn *East Lothian* A river of East Lothian, the Dry Burn rises in the Lammermuir Hills and flows in a northeasterly direction towards the North Sea. It passes through the settlement of Skateraw, entering the North Sea at a point 4 miles (6.5 km) southeast of Dunbar.

Drybridge *North Ayrshire* A small village on a sharp bend in the River Irvine on the southern border of North Ayrshire, Drybridge lies a mile (1.5 km) south-southeast of Dreghorn and 1.25 miles (2 km) north of Dundonald. Drybridge takes its name from a bridge built in 1811 to carry the road over the horse-drawn Kilmarnock and Troon Railway. The railway still passes by at the southern margin of the village but Drybridge station closed in 1969.

Drybridge *Moray* A village on the Burn of Buckie in Moray, Drybridge lies 2 miles (3 km) south of Buckie on the Moray Firth coast.

Dryburgh *Scottish Borders* A small settlement in Scottish Borders, Dryburgh lies a half-mile (1 km) north of St Boswells. The remains of Dryburgh Abbey are nearby, and to the north is a large statue of William Wallace (*c.*1274–1305), erected in 1814.

Dryburgh Abbey *Scottish Borders* One of the four great abbeys of Scottish Borders, Dryburgh Abbey lies on a loop of the River Tweed, 5 miles (8 km) southeast of Melrose and 4 miles (6.5 km) south of Earlston. Built in the 12th century by David I, it is now in a ruinous condition, although it is still fairly complete. Sir Walter Scott (1771–1832) and Field Marshal Earl Haig (1861–1928) are buried here. The abbey is now in the care of Historic Scotland.

Dryfe Water *Dumfries and Galloway* A river of Annandale, Dumfries and Galloway, the Dryfe Water rises on the southern slope of Loch Fell, just over 5 miles (8 km) east of Moffat. It flows south and southwestwards for more than 18 miles (29 km) before joining the River Annan 2 miles (3 km) west of Lockerbie. It gives its name to Dryfesdale, the name of an Annandale parish whose church is located in Lockerbie.

Drymen *Stirling* A village of Strathendrick in Stirling Council area, Drymen lies 3 miles (5 km) east of the southeast corner of Loch Lomond, just north of the Endrick Water and 20 miles (32 km) north-northwest of Glasgow. The village was enhanced in the 1640s with the arrival of the Grahams of Montrose, who built Buchanan Castle to the west. Further development took place following the construction of the military road from Stirling to Dumbarton in the 18th century. The parish church dates from 1771, and the village has two golf courses. The Scottish dramatist James Bridie (1888–1951) lived in Drymen.

Drynoch *Highland* A small settlement on the island of Skye, Drynoch lies at the head of Loch Harport, 5 miles (8 km) southeast of Bracadale.

Drynoch, Glen *Highland* Located on the island of Skye, Highland Council area, Loch Drynoch lies west of the head of Loch Harport, into which the waters of the River Drynoch flow.

Dualchas *Western Isles* Located in Castlebay on the island of Barra, in the Outer Hebrides, Dualchas (The Barra Heritage and Cultural Centre) houses a collection of local photographs and artefacts, all relevant to the history of Barra.

Dualt Burn *Stirling* A stream in southern Stirling Council area, the Dualt Burn rises on Auchineden Hill to the west of Strathblane. It flows 3 miles (5 km) northeastwards before joining the Blane Water, a tributary of the Endrick Water.

Duart Bay *Argyll and Bute* A bay on the east coast of the island of Mull, Argyll and Bute, Duart Bay forms an inlet of the Sound of Mull, 2 miles (3 km) southeast of Craignure. To the east of the bay lie Duart Point and Duart Castle, while to the west sits the mansion house of Torosay Castle, accessible from Craignure by the Mull and West Highland Railway.

Duart Castle *Argyll and Bute* A Maclean stronghold on the island of Mull, Duart Castle overlooks the Sound of Mull, 2 miles (3 km) southeast of Craignure. Built to guard the entrance to the sound in the 13th century, it was destroyed during the Jacobite Rising and lay in ruins until it was restored in the early 20th century. The castle has displays on the ship *The Swan*, Oliver Cromwell's flagship which sank nearby in 1653. Duart Castle, a seat of the chiefs of the Clan Maclean, has featured in a number of films, including *Entrapment* starring Sean Connery (2000).

Dubbieside An alternative name for Innerleven in Fife.

Dubford *Aberdeenshire* A locality in northern Aberdeenshire, Dubford is situated in Gamrie parish at a road junction a mile (1.5 km) south of Gardenstown.

Dubh, Gleann *Stirling* A small valley in the Balquhidder district of Stirling Council area, Gleann Dubh lies in the hills to the south of Loch Voil. Headstreams of the Calair Burn drain from Gleann Dubh.

Dubh Artach *Argyll and Bute* An isolated mass of basalt rock in the Torran reef, Dubh Artach (also Dhu Heartach) lies in the Atlantic Ocean, 16 miles (26 km) southwest of the Ross of Mull. A lighthouse was erected with some difficulty in 1870 by David and Thomas Stevenson.

Dubh Loch *Angus* A small loch in the Grampians, Dubh Loch is located between Lochnagar and Broad Cairn in Aberdeenshire. It is linked by the Abhainn an Dubh Loch to Loch Muick, which lies to the east at the head of Glen Muick.

Dubh Loch *Argyll and Bute* A loch in Argyll and Bute, Dubh Loch lies on the course of the River Shira at the head of Glen Shira, 2.5 miles (4 km) northeast of Inveraray.

Dubh-Lochain, Loch an *Highland* A small loch at the centre of the Knoydart peninsula in the west Highlands, Loch an Dubh-Lochain lies at the head of Gleann Meadail and is the source of the Inverie River which flows west to Inverie Bay on Loch Nevis.

Dubh Lochan *Moray* A small loch in the Cairngorm Mountains, the Dubh Lochan or 'black lochan' lies in the valley of the Lairig an Laoigh at the foot of Beinn Mheadhoin. Its waters drain northeastwards into the upper reaches of the River Avon.

Dubh Sgeir *Argyll and Bute* A rock islet in the Firth of Lorn in Argyll and Bute, Dubh Sgeir lies a mile (1.5 km) south of Bach Island, a mile (1.5 km) southwest of Kerrera and 3 miles (5 km) east of the southeastern coast of the island of Mull.

Dubh Sgeir *Argyll and Bute* A group of rocks in the Firth of Lorn, Dubh Sgeir lies a half-mile (1 km) to the west of Seil and less than a mile (1 km) northeast of Insh Island.

Duchally *Highland* A settlement in Sutherland, Highland Council area, Duchally lies on the east side of Glen Cassley, 6 miles (10 km) west of Loch Shin.

Duchal Moor *Inverclyde* An area of upland moorland in Inverclyde, Duchal Moor is ringed by hills of the Clyde Muirshiel Regional Park, including Hyndal Hill, Dunnairbuck Hill, Laird's Seat, Knockminwood Hill, Creuch Hill, North Burnt Hill and South Burnt Hill. To the south is Queenside Muir and to the north the Loch Thom and Gryfe reservoirs. The area is traversed by power lines and includes a disused narrow-gauge railway.

Duchray Water *Stirling* A headstream of the River Forth in the Trossachs district of Stirling Council area, the Duchray Water rises in the Queen Elizabeth Forest Park to the east of Loch Lomond. It flows nearly 14 miles (22 km) eastwards past Duchray Castle, a former stronghold of the Grahams, before joining the Forth, a mile (1.5 km) west of Aberfoyle.

Duddingston *City of Edinburgh* A former village, now a suburb of southeast Edinburgh, Duddingston lies on the south side of Holyrood Park, 1.5 miles (2.5 km) from the city centre. Designated a conservation area, it has retained much of its essential village character. Although Bronze Age artefacts were found in Duddingston Loch in 1778 and Iron Age cultivation terraces are clearly visible on the slopes of Arthur's Seat, the settlement dates from the founding of a church here in the 12th century. In the 18th century Duddingston was noted for its production of coarse linen cloth known as 'Duddingston Hardings'. In addition to the old church, notable buildings include Duddingston House, built in the 1760s by Sir William Chambers; Bonnie Prince Charlie's Cottage, an early 18th-century building where the prince held council before the Battle of Prestonpans in 1745; and the Sheep's Heid Inn, one of the oldest inns in Scotland, whose landlord in 1580 was presented with an embellished ram's head by King James VI. Duddingston Loch, a bird sanctuary since 1925, was used, when frozen in winter, as an ice rink by the Duddingston Curling Society. Also popular with skaters, it features in a famous painting of *The Revd Walker Skating on Duddingston Loch* attributed to Sir Henry Raeburn (1756–1823).

Dudhope Castle *Dundee City* Dudhope Castle, one of Dundee's oldest buildings, is set dramatically on an escarpment overlooking the city, beneath Dundee Law. The original house was built in the 13th century and was home of the Scrymageour family, appointed Hereditary Constables of Dundee by William Wallace (*c.*1274–1305). The original building was replaced around 1460 and then by the current structure in 1580. In 1683, both the castle and the office of Hereditary Constable were acquired by John Graham of Claverhouse, 'Bonnie Dundee', the Jacobite commander who died at the Battle of Killiecrankie in 1689. The castle was used as a barracks between 1796 and 1881, and shortly thereafter was purchased by Dundee Town Council, who made the estate a public park. The castle has been used for various cultural and community purposes, most recently being refurbished to become the Dundee Business School of the University of Abertay.

Duff House *Aberdeenshire* A baroque country house in Aberdeenshire, Duff House lies on the west bank of the River Deveron, just southeast of Banff. Regarded as one of William Adam's greatest designs, it was built in 1735 for William Duff, Lord Braco and later 1st Earl of Fife. Lord Braco quarrelled with the architect, primarily over the cost, and never lived in the house. In 1906, Duff House was gifted to the town councils of Banff and Macduff by the Duke of Fife, and during World War II it housed German prisoners of war. Following an extensive restoration, in 1995 it became an outstation of the National Galleries of Scotland. Among its fine collection of paintings, furniture and works of art are El Greco's *St Jerome in Penitence* and Jacob Gerrits Cuyp's *Dutch Family Group*.

Dufftown *Moray* A small town in the Moray parish of Mortlach, Dufftown lies near the junction of the Dullan Water with the River Fiddich, 17 miles (27 km) south of Elgin. Founded in 1817 by James Duff, 4th Earl of Fife, to give employment after the Napoleonic Wars, Dufftown is laid out in the form of a crooked-armed cross with a Clock Tower (1839) at its centre. Now used as a tourist information centre, this building was formerly a jail and the Burgh Chambers. The planned village of Dufftown replaced the ancient settlement of Mortlach on the banks of the Dullan Water, whose church is said to have been founded in AD 566 by St Moluag. Described as the 'Malt Whisky Capital', Dufftown has seven distilleries: Balvenie (1890), Dufftown Glenlivet (1896), Glendullan (1897), Glenfiddich (1887), Mortlach (1823), Convalmore (1869) and Pittyvaich (1973). Nearby are the old parish church of Mortlach and the ruins of 15th-century Auchindoun Castle, which was destroyed in 1592 in revenge for the murder of the Bonnie Earl of Moray. The Dufftown Gala and Highland Games are held annually at the end of July.

Duffus *Moray* Moved to its present site in 1811, the Moray village of Duffus, or New Duffus, consists of two parallel streets of harled cottages situated a mile (1.5 km) to the southeast of Hopeman on the Moray Firth coast. The village of Old Duffus lay beside Duffus Castle, whose ruins stand on top of a hill another mile (1.5 km) to the southeast. This Norman-style motte and bailey keep dates from 1151 and once looked down on Spynie Loch. The castle was abandoned in the 18th century in favour of Duffus House, which was built for Archibald Dunbar of Thunderton. The roofless St Peter's Church (1226) stands within a kirkyard that contains many fine memorial stones. To the east is Gordonstoun School, established on the former Gordonstoun Estate by Dr Kurt Hahn in 1934, and to the west is Inverugie House, built in 1864 to a design by Alexander Reid.

Duibhe Bheag *Perth and Kinross* A stream in the Rannoch district of Perth and Kinross, the Duibhe Bheag rises in headstreams in Rannoch Forest and flows 2 miles (3 km) northeastwards to join the Abhainn Duibhe.

Duich, Loch *Highland* A loch in the Lochalsh district of Highland Council area, Loch Duich extends 5 miles (8 km) northwestwards from the head of Glen Shiel into Loch Alsh. Eilean Donan Castle lies near its mouth.

Dùin, Loch an *Perth and Kinross/Highland* A small loch in the southern Grampians, Loch an Dùin straddles the border between Perth and Kinross and Highland council areas, 5 miles (8 km) north of Glen Garry.

Dùin, Loch an *Western Isles* A small lochan on the west coast of South Harris in the Western Isles, Loch an Dùin lies 5 miles (8 km) north of Leverburgh.

Duirinish *Highland* A settlement near the west coast of Highland Council area, Duirinish lies between Kyle of Lochalsh and Plockton.

Duirinish *Highland* A remote hammerhead-shaped peninsula and district of the isle of Skye, the Duirinish peninsula lies on the far west of the island, 12 miles (19 km) west of Portree. Duirinish lies between Loch Dunvegan and Loch Bracadale and terminates at Dunvegan Head in the north and Idrigill Point in the south. The distinctive mountains known as MacLeod's Tables rise in the centre of the peninsula.

Duisdalemore *Highland* A settlement on the island of Skye, in the Inner Hebrides, Duisdalemore (Gael: *Duisdealmor*) lies on the east side of the Sleat peninsula, 8 miles (13 km) south of Broadford.

Duisker *Western Isles* A rocky outcrop in the Atlantic Ocean, Duisker lies 2 miles (3 km) north of the island of Scarp, off the west coast of North Harris in the Western Isles.

Duisk River *South Ayrshire* Rising from a small loch near Drumlamford Loch southeast of Barrhill in South Ayrshire, the Duisk River flows north and west to join the River Stinchar southwest of Pinwherry.

Duisky *Highland* A settlement in Ardgour, southern Highland Council area, Duisky lies on the south shore of Loch Eil, 6 miles (10 km) west of Fort William across Loch Linnhe.

Duke of Gordon's Monument *Moray* On top of Lady Hill, which rises to the southwest of Elgin, is a 24-m/80-ft-high monument erected in 1839 in honour of the 5th Duke of Gordon, the first commander of the Gordon Highlanders Regiment. The duke's statue was placed on the pillar in 1855. From the top of the hill there are views across Elgin to the Cairngorms, and at the foot of the hill lies Anderson's Institution.

Duke's Road, the *Stirling* A 4-mile (6.5-km) stretch of road over the hills from Aberfoyle to the Trossachs in Stirling Council area. In the early 19th century, after the Trossachs had been popularised by writers and poets such as Sir

Walter Scott and William Wordsworth, the Duke of Montrose built a road, the so-called 'Duke's Road', that would provide easier access from the south for tourists.

Dull *Perth and Kinross* A village in Strath Tay, Perth and Kinross, Dull lies at the eastern end of the Appin of Dull, 3 miles (5 km) west of Aberfeldy. Once a much larger settlement, Dull was the site of a monastery that is said to have been the first seat of learning in Scotland. Given the title Abthanedum of Dull by King Edgar, the monastery was granted by the Bishop of Dunkeld to the Priory of St Andrews at the opening of the University of St Andrews. The monastery was also a sanctuary, and one of the four sanctuary crosses still survives in the middle of the village. Tradition associates Dull with St Adamnan, who lived and preached in Glen Lyon in the latter half of the 7th century. It is alleged that on his death he requested his body to be carried down the glen on a bier and that when the first thong or dul securing the bier broke, there he was to be buried, a church built and a college of learning founded. Another legend attributes the founding of the college in the 1st century AD to Menseteus, an ancestor of the Menzies family. In 1966 the parish of Dull was united with the parish of Weem.

Dullan Water *Moray* A river of Moray that rises to the south of Ben Rinnes as the Burn of Favar and the Corryhabie Burn which join at Milltown of Laggan. It flows 3 miles (5 km) northeastwards to meet the River Fiddich at Dufftown.

Dullatur *North Lanarkshire* A village of North Lanarkshire, Dullatur is located 2 miles (3 km) northwest of Cumbernauld. Sections of the Antonine Wall lie to the north of the village, while a half-mile (1 km) to the west are the remains of a Roman fort. Cumbernauld Village lies a mile (1.5 km) to the southeast.

Dulnain, River *Highland* A river rising to the north of Kingussie in the Monadhliath Mountains, the Dulnain flows 28 miles (45 km) southeast to join the River Spey near Dulnain Bridge, 3 miles (5 km) southwest of Grantown-on-Spey. It passes through Carrbridge where it is crossed by the remains of a packhorse bridge built in 1717 and said to be the oldest stone bridge in the Highlands.

Dulnain Bridge *Highland* A village in Strathspey, Highland Council area, Dulnain Bridge lies near the junction of the River Dulnain with the River Spey, 2 miles (3 km) southwest of Grantown-on-Spey. A bridge, rebuilt in 1791, was first built in 1754 on the military road between Forres and Corgarff. Swept away by the Moray flood of 1829, the second bridge was replaced in 1830 by Joseph Mitchell. The settlement later developed in association with tourism, the former castle at nearby Muckrach being converted into a shooting lodge and then a hotel.

Dulsie *Highland* A locality in Highland Council area, Dulsie lies on the River Findhorn, 12 miles (19 km) south of Nairn. A bridge over the river was erected here during the building of the military road from Grantown-on-Spey to Fort George in the 1720s.

Dumbarton *West Dunbartonshire* Former capital of the ancient kingdom of Strathclyde, Dumbarton lies at the mouth of the River Leven, which flows south from Loch Lomond to enter the Firth of Clyde 16 miles (26 km) northwest of Glasgow. A prominent landmark on the north side of the Clyde is Dumbarton Rock, an isolated

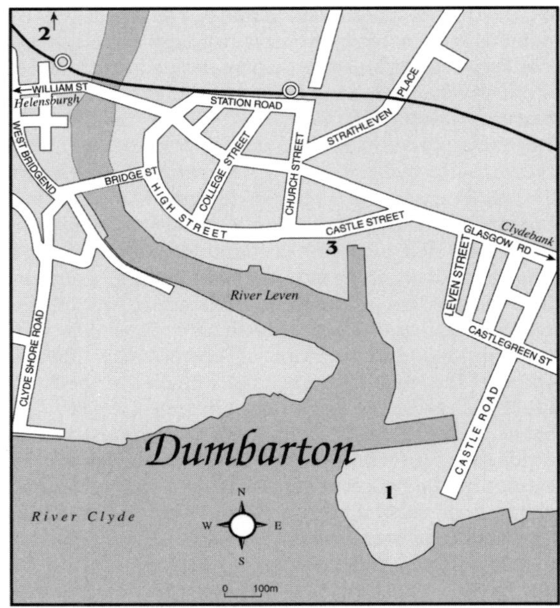

1 *Dumbarton Castle and Rock*
2 *Dalmoak Castle*
3 *Denny Ship Model Experiment Tank (Scottish Maritime Museum)*

73-m/240-ft-high volcanic plug that was first fortified in the 5th century AD. Created a royal burgh in 1222, Dumbarton developed in association with its royal castle, which became the centre of the earldom of Lennox in the 16th century. In the 17th century its port flourished with the sugar, indigo and tobacco trade, and in 1765 the River Leven was finally bridged as the last link in the network of military roadbuilding. In the 19th century, Dumbarton prospered as a centre for shipbuilding, the first pleasure steamers on Loch Lomond being built here. In 1869 the famous clipper *Cutty Sark* was constructed by Scott and Linton and completed by William Denny and Bros, builders of the first ocean-going merchant vessel with a steel hull. Dennys also produced the Sunderland flying boat between 1939 and 1945, and in 1963 a hovercraft for service on the Thames. Other industries associated with the burgh have included iron founding, boiler making, whisky distilling and the manufacture of glass.

Dumbarton Castle *West Dunbartonshire* The castle stands on Dumbarton Rock, a basalt rock prominence on the north bank of the River Clyde. The castle was built on the site of a Roman fort and was the ancient capital of Strathclyde. It was also a royal seat, briefly being the home of Mary, Queen of Scots before she departed to France at the age of five in preparation for her eventual marriage to the Dauphin. From the 17th century it was used as a garrison and fortress. The castle is now in the care of Historic Scotland.

Dumbiedykes *City of Edinburgh* With perhaps the best outlook of any public housing estate, Dumbiedykes in central Edinburgh lies in the shadow of Salisbury Crags to the south of the Canongate and opposite the Scottish Parliament in Holyrood Road. Built between 1959 and 1964 to a design by the City Architect's Department, this compact estate consists of 650 residences, including two multistorey tower blocks. Although the fabric of the houses has decayed to some extent and the immediate environment lacks services, Dumbiedykes remains a popular place to live. The location has ensured that the tenants' 'right to buy' has been exercised and thus many of the flats are now in private ownership.

Dumbuck *West Dunbartonshire* A locality on the southeast margin of Dumbarton, just to the north of the A82, Dumbuck lies adjacent to the village of Milton. The sizeable Dumbuck Quarry to the north has removed much of Dumbuck Hill.

Dumfries *Dumfries and Galloway* A market town and the administrative centre of Dumfries and Galloway, Dumfries sits close to the Solway Firth at the mouth of the River Nith, 35 miles (56 km) northwest of Carlisle and 90 miles (145 km) southwest of Edinburgh. When it was chartered as a royal burgh in 1186 Dumfries was already the site of a Benedictine nunnery called Lincluden Priory, founded by the Lord of Galloway in 1170. A royal castle, long since gone, was erected in the 13th century, and in 1306 Robert the Bruce slew the Red Comyn in a Franciscan friary founded here in 1266. Dumfries developed as a centre of trade, local merchants taking particular advantage of the free trade in tobacco offered by the Union of the Parliaments of Scotland and England in 1707. The livestock trade and textile manufacture developed during the 17th and 18th centuries, hosiery and tweed mills being major employers in the 19th century. In 1928 Dumfries incorporated the burgh of Maxweltown on the west side of the Nith, and in the 1990s the former Crichton Hospital complex, established in 1839, was adapted for use as a university campus linked to Paisley and Glasgow universities, as well as Bell College of Hamilton and the Dumfries and Galloway College. Buildings of interest include Dumfries Academy (1897), Devorgilla's Bridge (c.1430), Moorhead's Hospital (1753), Burns House, home of the poet Robert Burns from 1793 until his death in 1796, and St Michael's Church (1749), in whose churchyard Burns was buried. A windmill built in 1798 and now a museum was converted into an observatory and camera obscura in 1836 to coincide with an appearance of Halley's Comet. In Dock Park, site of the original harbour of Dumfries, stands a monument to John Law Hume and Thomas Mullin who died on the *Titanic*. The actor John Laurie was born in Dumfries in 1897, as was Angus Mackay (1813–59), piper to Queen Victoria.

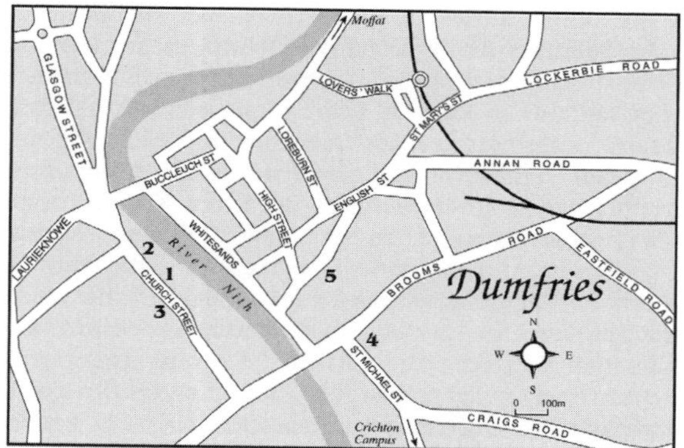

1 *Robert Burns Centre*
2 *Old Bridge House Museum*
3 *Dumfries Museum*
4 *St Michael's Church*
5 *Burns House*

Dumfries and Galloway *Area: 6439 sq. km (2486 sq. miles)* A local government area of southwest Scotland, whose coast of rocky headlands and sandy bays is washed to the south by the Solway Firth and to the west by the North Channel, which separates Scotland from Ireland.

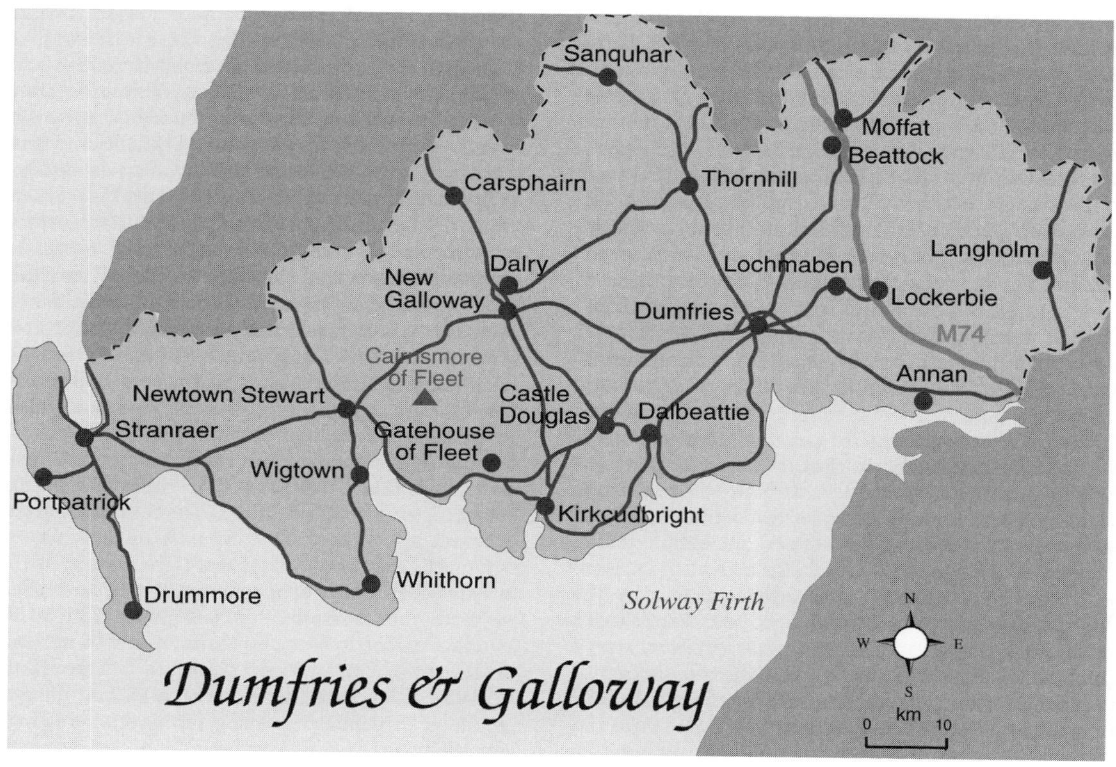

The rolling hills of the Southern Uplands are drained to the Solway Firth by the Rivers Nith, Annan and Esk, whose valleys form the three districts of Nithsdale, Annandale and Eskdale. Some 30 per cent of Scotland's dairy cattle comes from Dumfries and Galloway, and textiles, engineering and food processing are important industries in towns such as Dumfries, Kirkcudbright, Wigtown, Newton Stewart, New Galloway, Moffat, Lockerbie, Annan, Castle Douglas, Dalbeattie and the ferry port of Stranraer. Bordered to the north and east by South Ayrshire, East Ayrshire, South Lanarkshire and Scottish Borders, it comprises the former counties of Dumfries, Kirkcudbright and Wigtown. Its administrative centre is Dumfries.

Dumgoyne *Stirling* A locality with a distillery in Strathblane, Stirling Council area, Dumgoyne lies on the western edge of the Campsie Fells, 2 miles (3 km) south of Killearn. It is also the name of a prominent hill nearby, 427m (1401 ft), formed by an old volcanic neck, popular with walkers.

Dumyat *Stirling* A peak at the western end of the Ochil Hills, Dumyat rises to a height of 418 m (1373 ft), 5 miles (8 km) east of Bridge of Allan in Stirling Council area.

Dun See Bridge of Dun and House of Dun in Angus.

Dun *Western Isles* Dun is the southernmost island of the St Kilda group in the Atlantic Ocean, located 54 miles (86 km) west of the island of South Harris and 35 miles (56 km) west of North Uist, Western Isles. Lying off the southern end of St Kilda, Dun is uninhabited, steep-sided and barren. The only inhabitants of the island are sea birds.

Dun-aarin *Western Isles* Little more than a rock in the Sound of Harris, Dun-aarin (or Dun-arn) lies a quarter-mile (0.5 km) northeast of Gilsay and 1.25 miles (2 km) southwest of Renish Point at the south of Harris.

Dun Carloway *Western Isles* A small settlement surrounding Carloway Broch, Dun Carloway (Gael: *Dun Charlabhaigh*) is located on the west coast of Lewis in the Outer Hebrides, 1.25 miles (2 km) southwest of Carloway from which it is separated by Cirvig. Loch Carloway lies a half-mile (1 km) to the north.

Dun Charlabhaigh The Gaelic name for Dun Carloway in the Western Isles.

Dun Criech *Highland* A small hill, the site of an ancient fort, Dun Creich rises to 112 m (368 ft) on the northern shore of the Dornoch Firth, 3 miles (5 km) southeast of Bonar Bridge in the Sutherland district of Highland Council area.

Dun Eistean *Western Isles* A small islet surrounded by rocky slopes on the northeast coast of Lewis in the Outer Hebrides, Dun Eistean (sometimes Dun Eistein or Dun Uisdean) was the ancient stronghold of the Morrisons of Ness. Lying a quarter-mile (0.5 km) northeast of Knockaird and first occupied in medieval or perhaps even prehistoric times, it was here the Morrisons made their last stand against the MacLeods in the 16th century. Although little remains of the fort, this scheduled ancient monument was subject to archaeological investigations by the University of Glasgow between 2000 and 2004, and a bridge to the island was opened in 2002 to improve access. The island is now owned by the Clan Morrison Society.

Dun Law *Scottish Borders* A hill rising to 393 m (1289 ft) in Scottish Borders, Dun Law lies between Fala and Carfraemill, just to the south of Soutra, at the western end of the Lammermuir Hills. Dere Street, the old Roman Road that runs from Northumberland to the River Forth, skirts the hill to the west and the modern A68 lies to the east. Dun Law is the site of a sizeable wind farm, commissioned in 2000 by Scottish Power.

Dun Uisdean An alternative name for Dun Eistean in the Western Isles.

Dun's Dish *Angus* A small loch in eastern Angus, Dun's Dish lies 3 miles (5 km) to the east of Brechin near the House of Dun.

Dunadd *Argyll and Bute* A rocky outcrop topped by an ancient hillfort in central Argyll and Bute, Dunadd lies in the valley of the River Add, a mile (1.5 km) west of Kilmichael Glassary and 4 miles (6.5 km) east of Crinan. Defended by four walls, the fort was created in the 1st millennium AD. On a rock at its summit are the carved figure of a boar, the outline of a footprint, a hollowed-out basin and several lines of Ogam script. The basin and footprint have been interpreted as part of the royal ritual associated with the crowning of the kings of Dalriada. The carved boar is of Pictish origin.

Dunalastair *Perth and Kinross* By the River Tummel, Perth and Kinross, Dunalastair Estate lies between Loch Tummel and Loch Rannoch, 3 miles (5 km) west of Tummel Bridge. Dunalastair (or Mount Alexander), was for many years the home of the Robertsons of Struan, chiefs of the Clan Donnachaidh. Dunalastair Reservoir to the west is part of the Tummel hydro-electric scheme and was created in the 1930s by the damming of the River Tummel flowing eastwards out of Loch Rannoch. The ruined Scottish baronial-style Dunalastair House dates from 1852.

Dunan *Perth and Kinross* A locality to the west of Loch Rannoch, Perth and Kinross, Dunan lies on the River Gaur, 3 miles (5 km) east of Rannoch Station.

Dun-arn An alternative name for Dun-aarn in the Western Isles.

Dunaskin Open-Air Museum *East Ayrshire* Located at Waterside, near Patna, in East Ayrshire, the Dunaskin Open-Air Museum celebrates the industrial history of Ayrshire, in particular its ironworks, brick works and coal mining. The museum, which has audiovisual presentations, has displays of industrial machinery and historic buildings, including a reconstructed 19th-century cottage.

Dunaverty Rock *Argyll and Bute* A rocky headland near Southend at the southern tip of the Kintyre peninsula, Dunaverty Rock (also known as Bloody Rock) looks out over beaches and a golf course. A former stronghold of the Macdonalds that once stood here was the scene of a massacre in 1647, when 300 people were put to death by Covenanters under General Leslie.

Dunbar *East Lothian* A resort town on the North Sea coast of East Lothian, Dunbar lies 10 miles (16 km) east of Haddington, nearly halfway between Edinburgh and Berwick-upon-Tweed. Now bypassed by the A1, it owes its origins to a natural harbour that is overlooked by Dunbar Castle which stands on a defensible rock. The castle, once a Northumbrian stronghold, was given to the 1st Earl of Dunbar in 1070 by Malcolm Canmore. Two centuries later, a convent and priory were established by Patrick, 5th Earl of Dunbar. Burgh status soon followed, and the 9th Earl founded Scotland's first collegiate church here in 1342. In 1445 Dunbar became a royal burgh and ten years later its

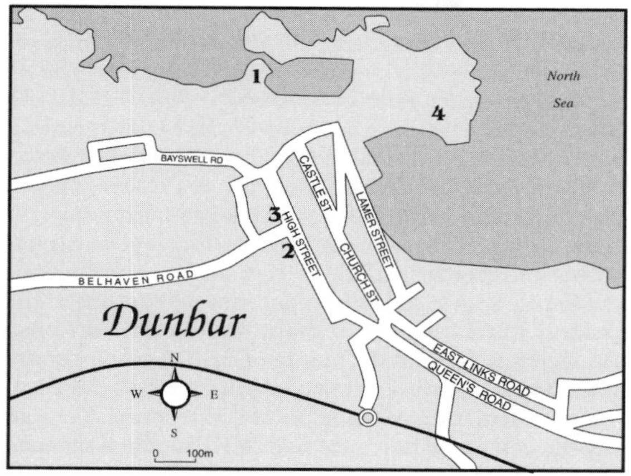

1 *Dunbar Castle*
2 *Dunbar Town House Museum*
3 *John Muir Birthplace*
4 *Lifeboat Station*

castle was forfeited to the Crown. A fishing and trading port for several centuries, Dunbar's harbour was rebuilt in 1650 with a grant of £300 from Oliver Cromwell, whose troops had taken the town following a battle just to the southeast. During the 18th century Dunbar grew in association with whaling, distilling, brewing, the export of coal and the manufacture of textiles. In the late 19th century it developed as a holiday resort with golf courses. Buildings of note include the parish church (1812–21), the mid-17th-century Tolbooth, and Lauderdale House (1790–2), which was designed by Robert and James Adam. Dunbar was the birthplace of the conservationist John Muir (1838–1914), whose achievements are remembered at his birthplace, the John Muir Centre, and in the naming of a coastal country park designated nearby in 1982.

Dunbartonshire A former county of west central Scotland, Dunbartonshire lay between the Clyde Estuary, Loch Long and Loch Lomond with a detached part to the northeast of Glasgow between Stirlingshire and Lanarkshire. Its county town was Dumbarton. In 1974 it was incorporated in Strathclyde Region as Dumbarton District and in the local government reorganisation of 1996 emerged as East Dunbartonshire and West Dunbartonshire Council Areas.

Dunbeath *Highland* A village forming a terrace of mid-19th-century cottages on the eastern coast of Caithness, Highland Council area, Dunbeath lies at the mouth of the Dunbeath Water, which enters a wide bay 20 miles (32 km) southwest of Wick. The cliffs on the south side of the bay are topped by Dunbeath Castle, which was built for Sir George Crichton, Lord High Admiral of Scotland. The modern bridge over the Dunbeath Water erected in 1989 supersedes the single-arch bridge built by Thomas Telford c.1815. The former school has been converted into a heritage centre. At Portormin Harbour, which dates from 1892, there are the remains of a fishing store, icehouse and salmon fishers' bothy. Neil Gunn, author of the *Para Handy* stories, was born in Dunbeath in 1891. In addition to tourism, lobster fishing and livestock transportation provide employment.

Dunbeath Bay *Highland* A bay on the east coast of Caithness, Dunbeath Bay lies to the southeast of the village of Dunbeath. It receives the Dunbeath Water, which rises 11 miles (18 km) to the west.

Dunbeg *Argyll and Bute* A hamlet on the south side of Dunstaffnage Bay in Argyll and Bute, Dunbeg is located 2.5 miles (4 km) northeast of Oban. The settlement was created in the early 1950s to accommodate the staff at the Dunstaffnage Marine Laboratory, which lies around the bay to the north. The 13th-century Dunstaffnage Castle lies a half-mile (1 km) to the north.

Dunblane *Stirling* An ancient burgh situated in the valley of the Allan Water 6 miles (10 km) north of Stirling, Dunblane is said to have been founded in AD 602 by the Celtic missionary St Blane who lived on the dun, or hillfort, behind the town. After St Blane's death in AD 640, Dunblane became a stronghold of the old Celtic Church, whose clergy began to build the cathedral tower that forms the lower storeys of the building erected much later, in the 13th century. The town developed at a crossing on the Allan Water, reaching a peak of prosperity in 1500 when King James IV gave it the status of a city. After the Reformation landowners took back land that had been held by the Church, and, starved of funds, the cathedral became ruinous. At the same time, the town declined to the level of a weaving village. During the 19th century Dunblane's fortunes were revived when it became a noted tourist resort, and between 1889 and 1893 the cathedral was renovated. The Cathedral Museum houses religious relics, and the Leighton Library, founded by Robert Leighton (1611–84), Bishop of Dunblane, is the oldest private library in Scotland. The Darn Walk (Daurinn or Water Road), a riverside walk, links Dunblane with Bridge of Allan, and a walk in the opposite direction extends to the Laighills Park. Ochlochy Park, a former common grazing to the east of the Perth Road, was gifted to Dunblane in 1942. The town has sporting facilities and an 18-hole golf course.

Dunbog *Fife* A village in northern Fife, Dunbog lies 3 miles (5 km) east of Newburgh, to the south of the A913 to Cupar.

Dunbuy *Aberdeenshire* A small rocky islet on the North Sea coast of Aberdeenshire, Dunbuy is situated 1.5 miles (2.5 km) to the northeast of Cruden Bay.

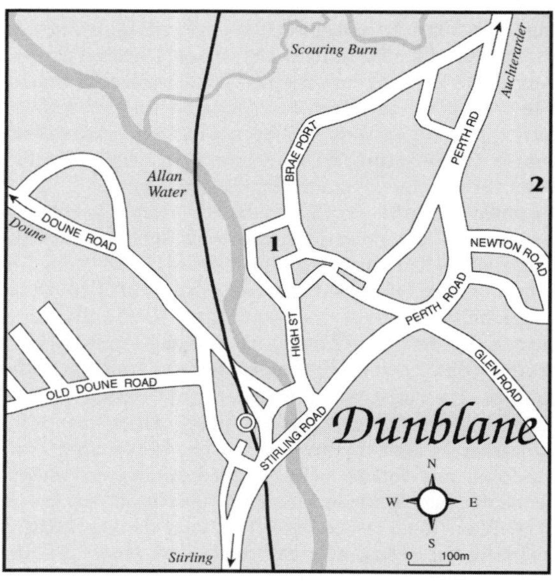

1 *Dunblane Cathedral*
2 *Dunblane Hydro*

Duncangill Head *South Lanarkshire* A mountain plateau with three distinct summits, Duncangill Head rises to a height of 560 m (1837 ft) 5 miles (8 km) east of Abington in South Lanarkshire.

Duncansby Head *Highland* A promontory on the coast of Caithness, Highland Council area, Duncansby Head forms the northeastern extremity of mainland Scotland, 2 miles (3 km) east of John o' Groats. Its sandstone cliffs, which rise to a height of 64 m (210 ft), are alive with sea birds, and offshore are three rocky islets known as the Stacks of Duncansby. A lighthouse was erected here in 1924.

Duncanston *Aberdeenshire* A settlement of west-central Aberdeenshire, Duncanston (also Duncanstone) lies 4 miles (6.5 km) west of Insch.

Duncanston *Highland* A settlement on the Black Isle, Highland Council area, Duncanston lies 3 miles (5 km) east of Conon Bridge.

Duncow *Dumfries and Galloway* A village of Nithsdale in Dumfries and Galloway, Duncow lies on the Duncow Burn between the River Nith and the Park Burn, 5 miles (8 km) north of Dumfries. The remains of an old windmill tower can be found here.

Duncraig Castle *Highland* A Scottish baronial-style mansion situated a half-mile (1 km) east of Plockton in the Lochalsh district of Highland Council area, Duncraig Castle was built in 1866 by Sir Alexander Matheson (1805-86) who made his fortune in China. It came into the hands of Inverness-shire County Council, who used it as a college of domestic science. After falling into disrepair, Duncraig was bought by an English family whose account of living together while restoring the castle featured in a BBC television series in 2004.

Duncrievie *Perth and Kinross* A village of Arngask parish in the Ochil Hills, Perth and Kinross, Duncrievie lies a mile (1.5 km) to the south of the village of Glenfarg on a former toll road linking Glenfarg with Milnathort to the south. It comprises 18th-century cottages and farm buildings. Nearby is the farm of Hilton of Duncrievie.

Dundaff Linn *South Lanarkshire* A waterfall on the River Clyde, Dundaff Linn is situated just upstream of New Lanark in South Lanarkshire. It is 3 m (10 ft) high and was a source of water for mills in the village. Diverted from a weir above the falls into the mill race, water was drawn into the village to waterwheels located under the four cotton mills. The weir has been restored by the New Lanark Conservation Trust to power an original 1930s' water turbine and generate hydro electricity.

Dundarave Castle *Argyll and Bute* Located 3 miles (5 km) east of Inveraray in Argyll and Bute, Dundarave Castle is a well-maintained L-plan tower dating from the 16th century. It was built as a seat of the Clan MacNaughton.

Dundas Castle *City of Edinburgh* Situated a mile (1.5 km) to the south of South Queensferry, Dundas Castle comprises a 19th-century mansion built beside a 15th-century tower. The original L-plan castle was built around 1425 and features a corbelled parapet, slit windows and, inside, barrel-vaulted rooms. In 1818 a castellated neo-Tudor mansion was built beside the tower by William Burn (1789–1870). The interior is primarily Jacobean, the result of a refurbishment c.1900. In the grounds is an unusual grand Renaissance fountain with a sundial (1623) and an 18th-century round dovecote.

Dundee *Dundee City Area: 65.15 sq. km (25.15 sq. miles)* A university city in the Midland Valley of Scotland, Dundee is situated 22 miles (35 km) east of Perth between the Firth of Tay and the Sidlaw Hills, and connected to Fife by rail and road bridges. Designated a city in 1889, it incorporated Broughty Ferry to the east in 1913. Formerly in the county of Angus, Dundee was the administrative centre of Tayside Region from 1975 to 1996, when it became a unitary local government authority. It is the smallest of the unitary authorities but the fourth-largest city in Scotland. Located on 'one of the finest natural sites of any city in the British Isles', Dundee is situated at the mouth of the Tay estuary where it occupies a south-facing natural harbour sheltered to the landward side by hills. To the west is the Carse of Gowrie and to the north the Sidlaw Hills, which separate Dundee from the valley of Strathmore. The centre of the city is dominated by Dundee Law, which rises to a height of 174 m (571 ft). The original settlement developed round a natural harbour between Castle Rock to the east and St Nicholas Craig in the west. In medieval times Dundee traded wool, sheepskins and cattle hides, with continental markets supplying in return quality textiles, metal goods and wine. The town was given the status of a burgh and developed as a 'new town' between 1178 and 1190 by Earl David, son of William I, the Lion. It prospered for many years as the third of Scotland's royal burghs after Edinburgh and Aberdeen. The city was destroyed by General Monk in 1651 and later its harbour was devastated by a storm. For nearly a century and a half thereafter the city's fortunes waned. During the 19th

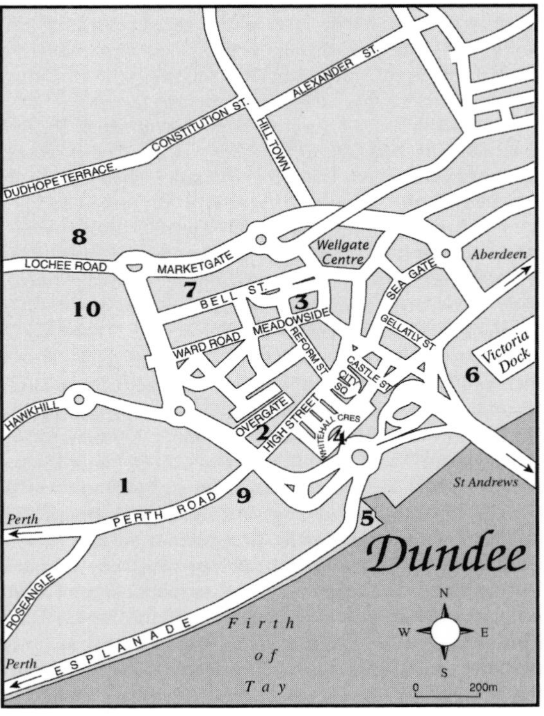

1 *University of Dundee*
2 *St Mary's Tower*
3 *McManus Galleries*
4 *Caird Hall*
5 *Discovery Point*
6 *Frigate* Unicorn
7 *Abertay University*
8 *Dudhope Park*
9 *Dundee Contemporary Art Centre*
10 *Verdant Works*

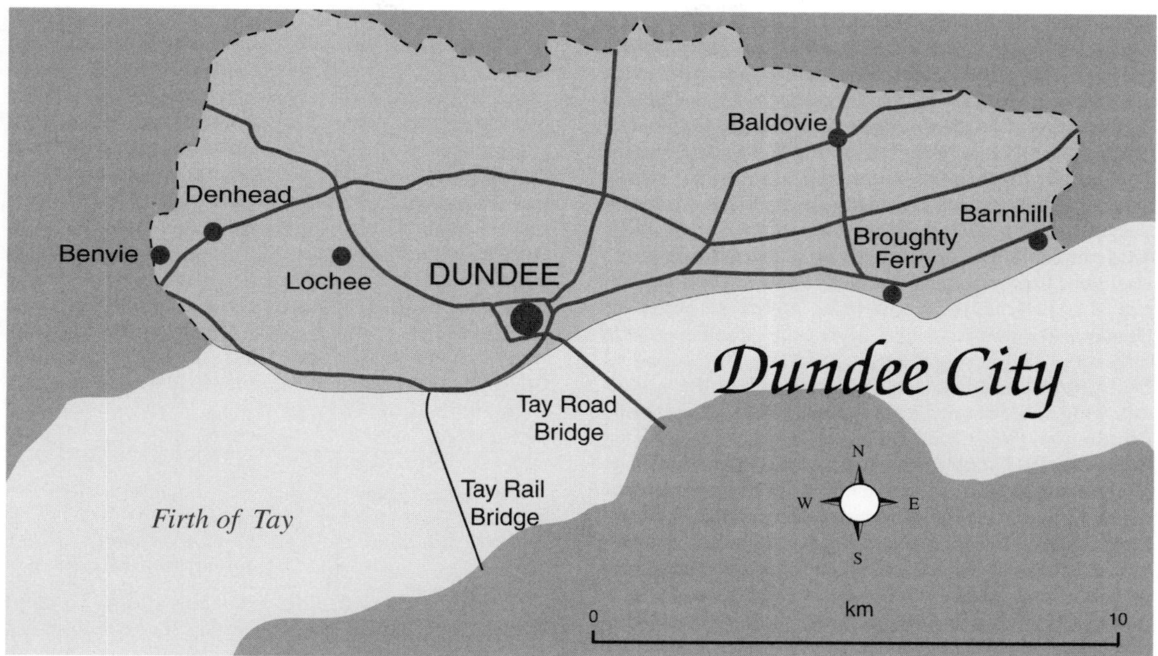

century Dundee again grew rapidly as a result of the whaling and fishing trade, shipbuilding, textile manufacture and the import from Bengal of jute, which was processed in mills employing large numbers of people. Between 1841 and 1881 the city's population rose from 63,700 to 140,000. By the latter half of the 19th century Dundee was investing vast sums of money in the development of the USA, with bankers such as Robert Fleming (1845–1933) investing in railways, ranches and the country's westward expansion. Dundee was also noted for its jam, produced from 1797 by the Keiller family, and its journalism, which came to be dominated in the 20th century by D. C. Thomson and Company, publishers of, among others, the *Courier and Advertiser, Sunday Post, People's Friend, Scots Magazine*, and the *Beano* and *Dandy* children's comics. Today D. C. Thomson is the only major magazine and newspaper house in Scotland to be controlled by Scots in Scotland. Dundee's port, dock and industrial estate facilities are important to the North Sea offshore oil industry. Chief among the city's industries are printing, publishing, food processing and the manufacture of tyres, carpets, electronics, computers and clothing. The principal industrial estates are located at the Technology Park, West Pitkerro, Baldovie, Wester Gourdie, Kingsway East, Dryburgh, Claverhouse and the Riverside. Dundee Airport is situated on land reclaimed from the River Tay just 1.5 miles (2.5 km) from the centre of the city. Once noted for its three 'Js' – jute, jam and journalism – Dundee is now promoted as the 'City of Discovery', a title that reflects not only its links with exploration and Captain Scott's research ship *Discovery*, but the city's post-industrial role as a centre of scientific research, education and tourism. Chief among the city's teaching and research establishments are the University of Dundee, which was founded as University College in 1881 and incorporated with St Andrews until 1967, the University of Abertay, Dundee, Dundee College, and Duncan of Jordanstone College of Art. Information technology and biomedical research are chief among the areas of excellence. The city has several fine parks and golf courses, as well as buildings of historic and architectural interest that include the Verdant Works Jute Mill, Baxter's Mills, St Mary's Tower, St Paul's Episcopal Church, St Andrew's Parish Church (1772), the Albert Institute (1867), Caird Hall, McManus Galleries, Dundee Contemporary Arts, Dudhope Castle, Mills Observatory, Camperdown House, the Mains of Fintry Castle, Claypotts Castle and the Wishart Arch, the last surviving gateway into the old town. Other places of interest include The Howff, formerly the garden of the Greyfriars Monastery, Shaw's Dundee Sweet Factory, Olympia Leisure Centre, Victoria Dock, in which is anchored the frigate HMS *Unicorn*, the oldest British warship still afloat, and Discovery Point, home of Captain Scott's RRS *Discovery*. Dundee was the birthplace of the historian Hector Boece (c.1465-1536), Admiral Adam Duncan of Camperdown (1731–1804), John Graham of Claverhouse, 1st Viscount Dundee (c.1649–89) and the poet William MacGonagall (1830–1902).

Dundee Law *Dundee City* Taking its name from an old Scots word for a hill, Dundee Law (or the Law) is a conical mass of volcanic basalt forming the highest point in the city of Dundee. It rises to a height of 174 m (571 ft). An Iron Age hillfort once occupied the site on which now stands a memorial to the dead of World War I erected in 1923. The beacon of the memorial is lit on four occasions each year: 25 September, in memory of the Battle of Loos where many local men serving in the Black Watch lost their lives; 24 October, for United Nations Day; Remembrance Sunday; and 11 November, Armistice Day.

Dundeugh Castle *Dumfries and Galloway* A ruined castle in Dumfries and Galloway, Dundeugh lies in woodland at the foot of Dundeugh Hill at the south end of Kendoon Loch, where the Polmaddy Burn meets the Water of Ken.

Dundonald *South Ayrshire* A sizeable village located towards the north of South Ayrshire, Dundonald lies 4 miles (6.5 km) northeast of Troon and a similar distance west of Kilmarnock. Once associated with weaving and coal mining, it has more recently been associated with nylon manufacture, quarrying and food distribution. The most prominent feature is the 14th-century Dundonald Castle, which stands on a round hill to the west of the village.

Dundonnell *Highland* A locality in Wester Ross, Highland Council area, Dundonnell lies at the southern end of Little Loch Broom, 12 miles (19 km) southwest of Ullapool. It owes its origin to an inn established here following the completion in 1851 of the so-called Destitution Road between Dingwall and Aultbea, built following the potato famine of 1846. The white-harled Dundonnell House dates from 1767.

Dundreggan *Highland* A settlement in Glen Moriston, Highland Council area, Dundreggan lies 7 miles (11 km) west of Invermoriston. Dundreggan deer forest extends northwards from the glen.

Dundrennan *Dumfries and Galloway* An attractive village in Dumfries and Galloway, Dundrennan lies a mile (1.5 km) from the Solway coast and 6 miles (10 km) east of Kirkcudbright. It is built partly from stones taken from the ruins of nearby Dundrennan Abbey.

Dundrennan Abbey *Dumfries and Galloway* Located at Dundrennan in Dumfries and Galloway, Dundrennan Abbey was founded in 1142 by King David I and Fergus, Lord of Galloway, but was not completed until the 1180s. It stands in a small, secluded valley, a typical location for Cistercian foundations. Now in the care of Historic Scotland, it is believed that Mary, Queen of Scots spent her last night in Scotland here.

Dunduff Castle *South Ayrshire* A tower house located 1 mile (2 km) northeast of Dunure in South Ayrshire, Dunduff Castle lies near the village of Fisherton. Dating from the 15th century, it was built to an L-shaped plan and abandoned in 1696. Restored in 1989, this castle was a stronghold of the Kennedy family.

Duneaton Water *South Lanarkshire/East Ayrshire* Duneaton Water rises on the slopes of Cairn Table, on the border of South Lanarkshire with East Ayrshire. Flowing east, it passes to the south of Crawfordjohn before joining the River Clyde at Abington.

Dunecht *Aberdeenshire* A village on an estate of the same name, Dunecht lies on the Kinnernie Burn, 12 miles (19 km) west of Aberdeen, beyond the Loch of Skene. Dunecht House, dating from 1820, is a seat of the earls of Crawford and Balcarres.

Dunfallandy *Perth and Kinross* A locality in Strath Temmel, Perth and Kinross, Dunfallandy lies on the west side of the River Tummel, a mile (1.5 km) to the south of Pitlochry. The Dunfallandy Stone, a well preserved Pictish cross slab dating from the 8th century AD, is situated on the hillside, a short walk from the road to Logierait.

Dunfermline *Fife* A burgh town in western Fife, Dunfermline is situated 4 miles (6.5 km) northwest of the Forth Road and Rail bridges. Now the third-largest town in Fife, Dunfermline has a history extending back over a thousand years to the foundation of a chapel by priests of the Celtic Church. It became an important Scottish centre when Malcolm Canmore moved his court here

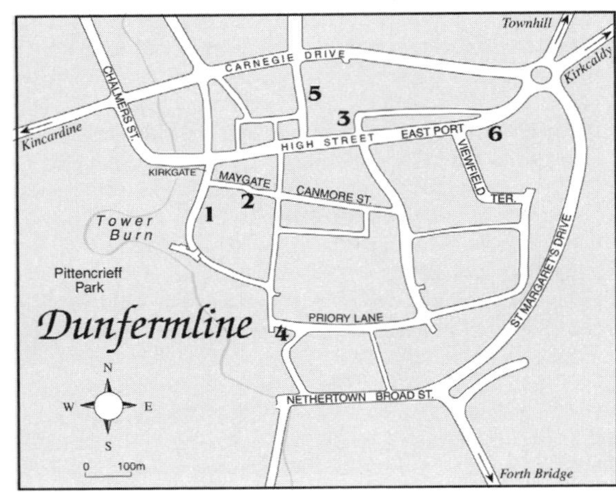

1 *Dunfermline Abbey*
2 *Abbot's House Museum*
3 *Kingsgate Centre*
4 *Carnegie Birthplace Museum*
5 *Erskine Church*
6 *Carnegie Hall*

from Forteviot and built a fortress c.1065. Canmore's second wife, Queen Margaret, established the town as an ecclesiastical centre, founding a Benedictine priory that was elevated to the status of an abbey in 1128. In 1250 Queen Margaret was canonised and her tomb in the abbey became a shrine. The importance of Dunfermline declined after the Reformation in the 16th century, although James VI gave it a royal charter in 1588 prior to presenting the abbey to his wife as a wedding present. The town's economic fortunes were revived during the 18th and 19th centuries with the development of the textile industry, producing linen, cotton, woollen and damask goods. From 1975 to 1996 it was the administrative centre of Dunfermline District. Today Dunfermline forms the heart of the so-called 'Bridgehead Dunfermline' economic development area and has industries that include printing, financial services and the manufacture of soft drinks, textiles, clothing, electronics and oil-drilling equipment. Some of these industries are now located in the Elgin Street and Albany Industrial Estates and in the larger Pitreavie Business Park to the south of the burgh. Places of interest include the Abbot House Museum and the Carnegie Birthplace Museum. The town, which is the home of the Carnegie Dunfermline Trust (1903), has many public parks, playing fields and community centres, in addition to the Carnegie Centre swimming baths, the football park of Dunfermline Football Club and three 18-hole golf courses. Queen Margaret and Lynebank Hospitals lie to the east, and retail parks have been developed near the town centre and at Halbeath to the east.

Dunfermline Abbey *Fife* Situated at the centre of Dunfermline in western Fife, Dunfermline Abbey stands on a ridge that falls steeply on the south and west to the course of the Tower Burn, which flows through Pittencrieff Park. The original Benedictine priory was founded in the 1070s by Queen Margaret on the site of an earlier chapel of the Celtic Church, and in 1128 her son David I extended the building and increased its status by making it an abbey. The western part of the present building is the nave of the abbey church built by David I between 1128 and 1150. The eastern end, with the tower bearing the words 'King Robert the Bruce', is the new parish kirk that was built on part of the ruins of the old abbey in 1818–21. In medieval times the abbey became a major ecclesiastical centre and was the burial place of several Scottish monarchs, including Malcolm Canmore, his wife Queen Margaret and Robert the Bruce, whose tomb was rediscovered in 1818. Queen Margaret was canonised in 1250 and a chapel and shrine were built at the east end and centre of the abbey. In 1303 the abbey was destroyed by Edward I of England, who recognised the significance of the site as a focal point of Scottish nationalism. Partially rebuilt, it was further damaged during the Reformation in the 16th century. The adjacent royal palace of Dunfermline grew out of the guesthouse of the abbey after its closure during the Reformation and was given as a wedding present to Anne of Denmark by her husband James VI in 1588. Prior to the Union of the Crowns in 1603, Anne of Denmark stayed here from time to time, and in 1600 her son, later to become Charles I, was born here.

Dunfermline Coaltown A former name for Townhill in Fife.

Dungavel *South Lanarkshire* A settlement in South Lanarkshire, Dungavel lies 5 miles (8 km) southwest of Strathaven. It developed in association with HM Prison Dungavel, originally Dungavel House, the shooting lodge of the dukes of Hamilton. The prison, which housed category 'C' offenders serving a maximum sentence of twelve years, closed in July 2000, only to reopen the following year as a specialist centre for asylum-seekers.

Dungeon, Loch *Dumfries and Galloway* A small loch in Dumfries and Galloway, Loch Dungeon lies on the eastern slopes of the Rhinns of Kells in Galloway Forest Park.

Dunglass *East Lothian/Scottish Borders* A locality near the North Sea coast of East Lothian, Dunglass lies a half-mile (1 km) northwest of Cockburnspath and 7 miles (11 km) southeast of Dunbar on the border between East Lothian and Scottish Borders council areas. A church was founded here in 1450 for a college of canons by Sir Alexander Hume.

Dunino *Fife* A village within a parish of the same name, Dunino is situated in eastern Fife, 4 miles (6.5 km) southeast of St Andrews to the south of the Kenly Water. Dunino Church, which dates from 1826, stands in a rural setting and has fine stained-glass windows.

Dunipace *Falkirk* A town in Falkirk Council area, Dunipace lies to the north of the Rivers Carron and Denny, to which it is linked by the Denny Bridge. There are two public parks at Tygetshaugh and Herbertshire Castle.

Dunira *Perth and Kinross* An estate in Strathearn, Perth and Kinross, Dunira lies to the north of the River Earn, 2 miles (3 km) northwest of Comrie. Dunira House was built in 1851–2 for Sir David Dundas, replacing an earlier mansion built for Viscount Melville. The mansion house has been demolished but a restored sawmill with a waterwheel remains on the estate.

Dunkeld *Perth and Kinross* An ancient burgh town in Perth and Kinross, Dunkeld is situated on the River Tay 15 miles (24 km) north of Perth. A monastery is thought to have been founded here before AD 700 by St Adamnan, the biographer of St Columba, whose relics were brought here from the west when Kenneth Macalpin united the kingdoms of the Picts and Scots in AD 846 and made Dunkeld and Scone his joint capitals. Dunkeld Cathedral was built over a 250-year period between the mid-13th and early 16th centuries. After the destruction of the town during the 1689 Battle of Dunkeld, the centre of the burgh was moved eastwards to its present position and the cathedral grounds were incorporated into the grounds of a house of the dukes of Atholl. Stanley Hill, a wooded backdrop to the village, is an artificial mound in the form of a fortification raised in 1730 by the Duke of Atholl. The National Trust for Scotland now owns 20 houses in the burgh, including the Ell Shop, which takes its name from the ell or weaver's measure fixed to the wall outside. The Canadian statesman Alexander Mackenzie (1822–92) lived in Dunkeld, which was also visited on several occasions by the author Beatrix Potter, who is remembered in the Beatrix Potter Garden created in nearby Birnam in 1991. The 208-m/227-yd-long Dunkeld Bridge over the Tay was built in 1809 as a toll bridge by Thomas Telford, who was surveyor and engineer to the Commission for Highland Roads and Bridges. A popular tourist centre, Dunkeld has antique shops, art galleries, a visitor centre, golf course and Museum of the Scottish Horse Regiment.

Dunkeld Cathedral *Perth and Kinross* This pre-Reformation cathedral is located on the north bank of the River Tay, just behind the centre of Dunkeld. Built between 1260 and 1501, on a site that supported a wattle monastery from the 6th century, the cathedral was rebuilt in stone by Kenneth Macalpin, King of the Scots, in AD 846. The current building, which is a mixture of Gothic and Norman styles, is dedicated to St Columba, who is said to have preached on the site for six months, and whose relics are thought to be buried under the chancel steps, having been transported from Iona by Kenneth Macalpin to avoid their loss to marauding Vikings. The tomb of the 'Wolf of Badenoch', Alexander Stewart, Earl of Buchan (1343–1405), is also here, and the sacristy contains early carved stones, including the 9th-century Apostles Stone. The cathedral has had a turbulent history, being partially destroyed in 1560 following the post-Reformation removal of Roman Catholic 'idolatry'. In 1689, following the Jacobite victory at Killiecrankie, the cathedral and much of Dunkeld was devastated by fire. Restorations have been undertaken over the years, most notably of the choir in 1908 and 1975. The cathedral remains an active church, within the community of the Church of Scotland. Visitors can see the Black Watch Regimental Memorial, and in the Chapterhouse Museum, the SHE Bible (1611), stone remnants of the original monastery and the tombstone of the fiddler Neil Gow (1727–1807).

Dunlop *East Ayrshire* A commuter village in the Cunninghame district of East Ayrshire, Dunlop lies 2 miles (3 km) north of Stewarton. Centred on an area noted for its dairy farming, Dunlop gives its name to a cheese produced locally. Other industries include concrete fabrication, sawmilling and the production of animal feed-stuffs. The village has a primary school, village hall and a railway station on the line from Glasgow to Kilmarnock. Dunlop is home to the curling champion Rhona Martin (b.1966), who led the gold medal-winning team in the Winter Olympics of 2002.

Dunlugas *Aberdeenshire* A locality and house in Alvah parish, northwestern Aberdeenshire, Dunlugas lies on the east bank of the River Deveron, 4 miles (6.5 km) northwest of Turriff. The granite mansion house of Dunlugas was built in 1793.

Dunman *Dumfries and Galloway* A hill of Dumfries and Galloway, Dunman lies 3 miles (5 km) southwest of Drummore. Rising to a height of 160 m (535 ft), there are the remains of an ancient fort on its southern slopes.

Dunmore *Falkirk* A residential village in Falkirk Council area, Dunmore is situated on the River Forth just over 2 miles (3 km) northeast of Airth. Built in the 19th century to house workers on the estate of the Earl of Dunmore, it comprises attractive stone cottages on three sides of a village green. It was designated a conservation area in 1977. The Dunmore Pineapple is a folly built in 1761 in the shape of a pineapple and used as a garden retreat. The building was gifted to the National Trust for Scotland in 1974 with the aid of the Landmark Trust, which leased and restored the building and walls, creating a holiday home.

Dunnet *Highland* A locality in northern Caithness, Highland Council area, Dunnet lies on the road between Thurso and John o' Groats, 5 miles (8 km) south of Dunnet Head, the most northerly point on the Scottish mainland. In addition to tourist facilities, including a hotel and caravan site, there is a museum and visitor centre. The celebrated cartographer, Revd Timothy Pont, was the minister of Dunnet from 1601 to 1614.

Dunnichen *Angus* A locality in Angus, Dunnichen lies at the foot of Dunnichen Hill and at a meeting of five roads, 4 miles (6.5 km) southeast of Forfar. Dunnichen House was the home of the 18th-century agricultural improver George Dempster, who built the nearby village of Letham. Outside the church, also built by George Dempster, is a replica Pictish symbol stone, the original 7th-century Dunnichen Stone having been moved to Dundee. Also near the church is a stone commemorating the triumph of the Picts over invading Northumbrians in AD 685 at the Battle of Dunnechtan. Another battle is remembered at nearby Camperdown Well, which honours Admiral Duncan's famous naval victory over the Dutch in 1797. Dempster's church replaced an earlier foundation dedicated to St Constantine, a Scottish king whose name degenerated locally into Cowsland or Causnan, a name associated with Causnan's Well and the St Causnan's Fair, which used to be held every March.

Dunnideer Hill *Aberdeenshire* One mile (1.5 km) to the west of Insch in Aberdeenshire, Dunnideer Hill rises to 268 m (876 ft) above the Shevock. The ramparts of a hillfort dating from the 1st millennium BC are clearly visible, and on top of the hill are the remains of the Castle of Dunnideer, built c.1260.

Dunninald Castle *Angus* A mansion and estate located 2 miles (3 km) south-southwest of Montrose. The third in a sequence of buildings erected in the vicinity, Dunninald Castle was built in the Gothic Revival style to the designs of architect James Gillespie Graham (1776–1855) for Peter Arklay in 1824. Little remains of the first fortified building, Black Jack's Castle, erected in the 15th century for the Gray family. The second structure, an earlier Dunninald Castle dating from the 17th century, was also home to the Grays. Dunninald Castle lies in a planned landscape dating from 1740, which includes a walled garden. Still a family home, the property is open to the public.

Dunning *Perth and Kinross* A village of Strathearn, Perth and Kinross, Dunning is situated on the site of an ancient settlement to the north of the Ochil Hills, 7 miles (11 km) southwest of Perth. Dunning is associated with St Serf, an early Christian saint who is said to have slain a dragon here and to have established Dunnyne, one of his favourite foundations. St Serf died at Dunning and was allegedly buried at Culross. Dating from the mid-12th century, the impressive Norman steeple of St Serf's Church dominates the village. Rebuilt in 1811, this building incorporates an ancient stone bearing a Celtic cross, pointing to the existence of an even earlier church on the site. The 9th-century Dupplin Cross, which formerly stood near Dupplin Castle, is now located within the church. In January 1716 Jacobite soldiers burned the village, an event marked by the planting of a thorn tree that was eventually blown down in 1936 but subsequently replaced twice. The village was rebuilt in the 1790s by John, 8th Baron Rollo, who also laid out adjacent land to the south at Newton of Pitcairns for weavers' cottages. Following the development of the weaving industry, the population of Dunning reached a peak of 2200 in the mid-19th century. Thereafter, the village declined and its important livestock market was removed to Perth. Antiquities nearby include a standing stone, the site of a Roman marching camp and a monument to Maggie Walls, who was 'burnt here – as a witch' in 1657.

Dunnottar Castle *Aberdeenshire* The ruins of Dunnottar Castle sit on a rocky headland on the outskirts of Stonehaven in Aberdeenshire. The castle was the seat of the Keiths until 1716, the 10th Earl losing the castle for his support of the Jacobite uprising. Eventually sold to the Viscountess Cowdray, it remains the property of her descendants. Entered by way of two tunnels from the entrance pathway, the castle sits amid a grassed courtyard with its own bowling green and kirkyard. The oldest remains are those of the chapel, which date from the mid-14th century. In 1651 the Scottish regalia were deposited here for safekeeping during the British Civil War. The castle was subsequently besieged by Cromwell's troops and the regalia were smuggled out, to be hidden under the floorboards of the parish church at Kinneff to the south.

Dunollie Castle *Argyll and Bute* A former stronghold of the MacDougalls, the ruined Dunollie Castle stands on the Argyll coast a mile (1.5 km) north of Oban.

Dunoon *Argyll and Bute* Situated at a focal point in the Firth of Clyde, Dunoon lies at the southern tip of the Cowal peninsula, 28 miles (45 km) northwest of Glasgow. Its castle was the seat of the Lord High Steward of Scotland from 1370, and an old cattle track terminated at Dunoon where ferries made the crossing to Cloch Point and Rothesay. In 1795 a new planned village was laid out for the 5th Duke of Argyll by James Craig, designer of Edinburgh's New Town. In 1820 a pier was constructed and a ferry link to Gourock established. In the 19th century, with the advent of paddle steamers, Dunoon established itself as a holiday resort, and in the 20th century it developed in association with car ferries and a US Navy submarine base operated on the Holy Loch

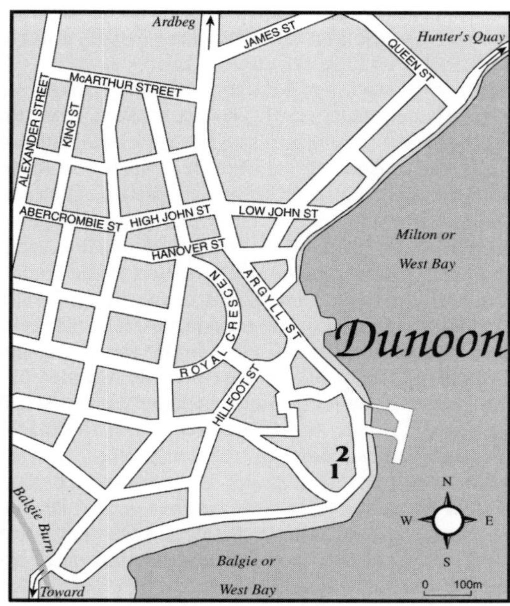

1 *Castle* 2 *Dunoon and Cowal Heritage Centre*

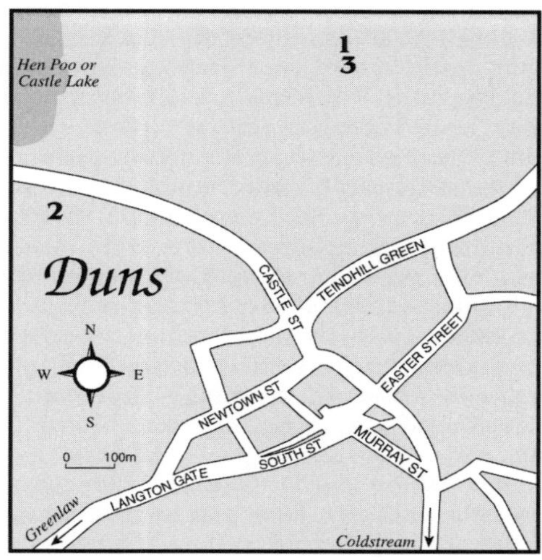

1 *Duns Law* 3 *Covenanters' Stone*
2 *Duns Castle*

from 1961 to 1992. A Celtic cross commemorates a massacre of the Lamonts by the Marquess of Argyll in 1646 and a memorial celebrates the life of Robert Burns' Highland Mary, who came from the nearby village of Auchnamore.

Dunphail House *Moray* Built for Major Charles Cumming Bruce in 1828, Dunphail House to the south of Forres in Moray was designed in Italianate style by William Playfair. The ruined Dunphail Castle nearby was a stronghold of the Comyn family.

Dunragit *Dumfries and Galloway* A village in the Rhinns of Galloway, Dumfries and Galloway, Dunragit lies on the A75, 6 miles (10 km) southeast of Stranraer. In 1979 the 12-acre Glenwhan Garden and Nursery nearby was created out of a bracken- and gorse-covered hillside.

Dunrobin Castle *Highland* The ancestral home of the earls and dukes of Sutherland, Dunrobin Castle stands on a prominent position looking out to sea, a half-mile (1 km) northeast of Golspie on the Sutherland coast of Highland Council area. The oldest part of the building dates from *c.*1275, its name first appearing in 1401 when it is thought to have been called Robin's Castle after Robert, 6th Earl of Sutherland. Extended in 1662 and 1672, Dunrobin was briefly held by the Jacobites in 1745. In 1845 the castle was remodelled by the architect Sir Charles Barry in the style of a fairy-tale French chateau, and in 1921, following a fire, the interior was reconstructed by Sir Robert Lorimer. It was under the 1st Duke of Sutherland that the infamous Sutherland clearances took place in the early 19th century. An earldom presently differs from a dukedom in that an earldom can pass through the female line, an event that took place in 1963 on the death of the 5th Duke.

Dunrossness *Shetland* A district and old parish, Dunrossness lies in the far south of the Shetland Mainland, 15 miles (24 km) south-southwest of Lerwick. Dunrossness has good agricultural land and its economy benefits from Sumburgh Airport.

Duns *Scottish Borders* Originally associated with an Iron Age hillfort, the small market town of Duns lies on the Merse of Berwickshire in Scottish Borders, 15 miles (24 km) west of Berwick-upon-Tweed. The former hilltop fort was replaced by a castle built in 1320 by Robert the Bruce at the foot of the hill and protected on three sides by swampland. Duns developed as a livestock market town and was county town of Berwickshire from 1551 until 1975 and administrative centre of Berwickshire District until 1996. Duns Castle includes part of a 14th-century tower constructed by Randolph, Earl of Moray, and rebuilt in 1820; the grounds now form a park with a bird sanctuary. On Duns Law stands the Covenanters' Stone, commemorating the encampment of General Sir Alexander Leslie and the Covenanting army in 1639 as they prepared to oppose Charles I in Berwick. Duns is also the most likely birthplace of John Duns Scotus (*c.*1265–1308), known as the Subtle Doctor, and one of Europe's great philosophers, who argued that religion depended on faith rather than reason. A bust of him stands in the public park, while a cairn is at his reputed birthplace of Pavilion Lodge, Duns Castle. Other prominent men born in the area include the motor-racing champion Jim Clark (1936–68), whose Memorial Room includes his trophies, the theologian Thomas Boston (1676–1732) and the astronomer Abraham Robertson (1751-1826).

Dunsapie Hill *City of Edinburgh* A small hill overlooking Dunsapie Loch in Edinburgh's Holyrood Park, Dunsapie Hill rises to the east of the Lion's Head of Arthur's Seat.

Dunsapie Loch *City of Edinburgh* A small artificial loch located between Dunsapie Hill and Arthur's Seat in Edinburgh's Holyrood Park. Created at the initiative of Prince Albert, Consort to Queen Victoria, in 1844, it is fed with water from Alnwickhill in the south of the city. Today, lying alongside the road at about 110 m (361 ft) above sea level, the loch forms a popular location within the park which is often the starting point for an ascent to the top of Arthur's Seat. It supports plentiful wildfowl.

Dunscore *Dumfries and Galloway* A village of Nithsdale in Dumfries and Galloway, Dunscore lies in a parish of the same name between the Cairn Water and the River Nith, 9 miles (14 km) northwest of Dumfries. Dunscore was the birthplace of Jane Haining (1897–1944), a missionary to the Jewish mission in Hungary and the only Scot to die in the Nazi death camp at Auschwitz.

Dunshelt *Fife* A village in Auchtermuchty parish in the Howe of Fife, Dunshelt is situated on the north bank of the River Eden, on the B936, a mile (1.5 km) southeast of Auchtermuchty. Sometimes known as Daneshalt or Dunshalt, it developed in the 18th and 19th centuries as a meal-milling and textile-manufacturing village on the Myers Estate. To the northwest stands Myers Castle, which was restored in the 1960s. It was built by John Scrymgeour, Master of the King's Works, who was employed in the construction of Falkland Palace to the south.

Dunsinane Hill *Perth and Kinross* A summit of the Sidlaw Hills in eastern Perth and Kinross, Dunsinane Hill rises to a height of 308 m (1012 ft) 8 miles (13 km) northeast of Perth. A hillfort on Dunsinane is locally known as Macbeth's Castle.

Dunskey Castle *Dumfries and Galloway* The ruined remains of Dunskey Castle in Dumfries and Galloway lie on the coast of the Rhinns of Galloway, a half-mile (1 km) south of Portpatrick. The castle was built in the 15th century and was designed as an L-plan tower house.

Dunstaffnage Castle *Argyll and Bute* The substantial ruined remains of Dunstaffnage Castle lie on a headland to the north of the village of Dunbeg, 2 miles (3 km) north of Oban in Argyll and Bute. Maintaining a strategic position on the Firth of Lorn at the mouth of Loch Etive, Dunstaffnage was built in the 13th century by the MacDougalls. In 1309 it was taken by Robert the Bruce who gave it to the Campbells, who held it intermittently until 1858. Dunstaffnage was previously one of the seats of the ancient kingdom of Dalriada from the 7th to the 9th centuries. It was abandoned as the Vikings took control of the Inner Hebrides and parts of Argyll.

Dunsyre *South Lanarkshire* A village of South Lanarkshire, Dunsyre is located near the South Medwin Water, 6 miles (10 km) east of Carnwath and 20 miles (32 km) southwest of Edinburgh. Once a seat of a barony, its kirk was a frequent retreat for Covenanters in the late 17th century.

Duntocher *West Dunbartonshire* A small town situated on the Cochne Water 9 miles (14 km) northwest of Glasgow, Duntocher takes its name from a small fort at the western end of the Roman Antonine Wall. In the 18th century ironworks were established and in the 19th century Duntocher became a cotton-spinning village, attracting migrants from Ireland and the Highlands. The Auchentoshan distillery was founded in 1817.

Duntreath Castle *Stirling* Abandoned in the 18th century, Duntreath Castle was a stronghold of the Edmonstones whose lands lay within the powerful earldom of Lennox. The family returned in the 1860s and restored the building which lies in Strathblane, Stirling Council area, a mile (1.5 km) to the northwest of Blanefield.

Duntrune Castle *Argyll and Bute* Duntrune Castle stands on the north shore of Loch Crinan, a half-mile (1 km) north of the settlement of Crinan in Argyll and Bute. The enclosure of the castle dates from the 13th century, while the tower house dates from the 16th century. Restoration in the late 18th century and modernisation in the 1950s has maintained this seat of the Malcolm family in a habitable condition.

Duntulm *Highland* A locality near the tip of the Trotternish peninsula on the island of Skye, Duntulm lies on Score Bay, 6 miles (10 km) north of Uig. There are the ruins of an ancient church and the 15th-century Macdonald stronghold of Duntulm Castle, which was abandoned in 1732.

Dunure *South Ayrshire* A fishing village on the Carrick coast of South Ayrshire, Dunure looks out to the Firth of Clyde, 6 miles (10 km) southwest of Ayr. A castle near here was a stronghold of the earls of Cassillis, but it was not until the building of a harbour for fishing and coastal trade that the village developed to any size. The opening of a railway station in 1906 brought tourists. To the south at Croy on an inclined section of the road is the Electric Brae (see entry).

Dunvegan *Highland* A village in northwestern Skye, Highland Council area, Dunvegan lies at the head of Loch Dunvegan just south of Dunvegan Castle, the seat of the Clan Macleod. The village of Dunvegan once had daily steamers to Oban.

Dunvegan Castle *Highland* Located 22 miles (35 km) west of Portree on the eastern shore of Loch Dunvegan, northwestern Skye, Highland Council area, Dunvegan Castle is the ancestral home of the chiefs of the Clan Macleod. Claimed to be the oldest inhabited castle in Scotland, parts of Dunvegan date from the 9th century. The most famous of the artefacts held in the castle is the 'Fairy Flag', a sacred banner that legend states will bring success to the clan chief who unfurls it in times of need.

Dunwan Dam *East Renfrewshire* Located on moorland 2 miles (3 km) southwest of Eaglesham, the Dunwan Dam is one of a number of reservoirs in the area of East Renfrewshire known as the Eaglesham Moors.

Dupplin Castle *Perth and Kinross* A mansion house in Strathearn, Perth and Kinross, Dupplin Castle lies 5 miles (8 km) southwest of Perth. Built in 1828–32, it replaced an earlier castle destroyed by fire, the seat of the Hay earls of Kinnoull. Nearby stood a stone cross marking the site of a battle that took place in August 1332 at which Edward Balliol defeated the Earl of Mar. The Dupplin Cross is now located in St Serf's Church in Dunning.

Dupplin Loch *Perth and Kinross* A small loch at the eastern end of the Gask Ridge, Dupplin Loch is situated on the Dupplin Estate, 5 miles (8 km) southwest of Perth.

Dura Den *Fife* An attractive wooded gorge between Dairsie and Pitscottie in northeastern Fife, Dura Den occupies part of the valley of the Ceres Burn which flows northwards to join the River Eden east of Cupar. Extensive fossil fish deposits were first discovered here c.1859 by the Newburgh minister and geologist John Anderson (1796–1864). For many years the burn powered jute-spinning mills.

Durisdeer *Dumfries and Galloway* A village on the western edge of the Lowther Hills in Dumfries and Galloway, Durisdeer lies on the Kirk Burn, 6 miles (10 km) north of Thornhill. The parish church contains the vault of the 1st Duke of Queensberry. Durisdeer Hill rises to 569 m (1861 ft) nearby, and a 4-mile (6.5-km) right of way called the Well Path links Durisdeer with the

Dalveen Pass. A Roman fortlet once guarded the road climbing out of Nithsdale into the hills.

Durn, Burn of *Aberdeenshire* A stream in northern Aberdeenshire, the Burn of Durn rises on the eastern slopes of the Hill of Summertown, 4 miles (6.5 km) southeast of Cullen. It flows northeastwards past Durn Hill to join the Moray Firth at Portsoy.

Durn Hill *Aberdeenshire* A hill in northern Aberdeenshire, Durn Hill rises to 199 m (653 ft) a mile (1.5 km) to the southwest of Portsoy. The trenches of an Iron Age hillfort can be seen near its summit.

Durness *Highland* A remote and scattered crofting township in northwestern Sutherland, Highland Council area, Durness lies to the northwest of Loch Eriboll and 13 miles (21 km) northeast of Laxford Bridge. There is a 12th-century church, and a craft village was established in former RAF huts in 1964 at Balnakeil. Two miles (3 km) to the east is the Smoo Cave, a series of large limestone caverns. The area offers unlimited sea-trout fishing opportunities as well as walking and sailing. One of the highlights of the year is the Durness Highland Gathering, which usually takes place at the end of July.

Duror, Glen *Highland/Argyll and Bute* Glen Duror is a valley lying on the border of Lochaber district, Highland Council area, with Argyll and Bute. Carrying the waters of the River Duror westwards, it feeds the river into Loch Linnhe at Cuil Bay.

Dusk Water *North Ayrshire* Rising at the western edge of East Renfrewshire, the Dusk Water flows west and south through North Ayrshire for 9 miles (14 km) before joining the River Garnock 2 miles (3 km) north of Kilwinning.

Dutchman's Cap, the A hill on the island of Bac Mòr in the Treshnish Isles in Argyll and Bute, the Dutchman's Cap rises to a height of 87 m (284 ft).

Duthie Park *Aberdeen City* Situated on Riverside Drive, Aberdeen, Duthie Park is named after Lady Charlotte Duthie who gifted the land to the city. The park, which was opened by Princess Beatrice in 1883, includes extensive gardens, a rose hill, boating pond, bandstand and play area, as well as the Winter Gardens, which are Europe's largest indoor gardens.

Duthil *Highland* A settlement in a parish of the same name in Strathspey, Highland Council area, Duthil lies near the junction of the Duthil Burn with the Dulnain River, a tributary of the Spey.

Dwarfie Stane *Orkney* A large block of red sandstone on the Orkney island of Hoy, the Dwarfie Stane lies in a valley to the southeast of Ward Hill and beneath the Dwarfie Hamars (*hamars* means 'crags'). Comprising a passage and two hollowed-out chambers, it is thought to be the only example in Britain of a rock-cut chamber tomb and dates from around 3000 BC.

Dyce *Aberdeen City* An industrial village of Aberdeen, Dyce lies on the west bank of the River Don, 5 miles (8 km) northwest of Aberdeen city centre. Dating from the 1860s, when it became an important junction of the main railway line from Aberdeen to Inverness and the Buchan and Formartine Railway, its modern expansion has been linked to the opening of Aberdeen Airport here in 1935 and the development of North Sea oil and gas industries since the 1970s. Food-processing, engineering, plant-hire, telecommunications, transport and oil-related industries are to be found at the Wellheads, Stoneywood, Farburn, Kirkhill, Raiths, Dyce Drive and Pitmedden Road industrial estates. The ancient ruined church of Dyce, dedicated to St Fergus, overlooks the gorge of Cothall and contains a Pictish symbol stone and cross slab dating from the 7th and 9th centuries AD.

Dye, Glen *Aberdeenshire* A glen in the eastern Grampians of Aberdeenshire, Glen Dye occupies the valley of the Water of Dye, which rises on the slopes of Mount Battock on the border between Aberdeenshire and Angus. The Dye flows eastwards, turning northwards at Spital Burn on the Cairn o' Mount Road. It continues northeastwards through the glen before joining the Water of Feugh near Strachan in Deeside.

Dyke *Moray* A picturesque Moray village situated immediately east of Brodie Castle, Dyke lies on the left bank of the Muckle Burn between the Culbin Forest to the north and the A96 Inverness–Aberdeen road to the south. In the kirkyard of Dyke Church is the burial place of the Brodies of Brodie, and on rising ground at the north end of the village is a school built in Elizabethan style in 1877.

Dykehead *North Lanarkshire* A scattered settlement lying to the south of Shotts in North Lanarkshire, Dykehead lies 5 miles (8 km) northeast of Wishaw. The South Calder Water flows to the south of the settlement.

Dykehead *Stirling* A village at the centre of Flanders Moss in Stirling Council area, Dykehead lies just north of a bend on the River Forth on the B8034 between Port of Menteith and Arnprior. To the east stand the 18th-century farmhouse of Brucehill, with its U-plan steading entered by a stone archway, and Cardross House, which was built after the Reformation by the Erskines of Cardross. The three-arched Cardross Bridge over the River Forth was built in 1774 from the revenues of lands forfeited to the Crown after the Jacobite Rising of 1745.

Dysart *Fife* An ancient burgh town on the south coast of Fife, Dysart lies to the northeast of Kirkcaldy, with which it was incorporated in 1930. Said to be named after the cave or 'desert' used as a retreat by St Serf, the town received its royal charter in 1587. Once an important coal-mining and salt-panning centre, it had by the 18th century developed a reputation for the manufacture of linen and nails and as a port trading with the Netherlands. Modern industries include meat processing and the manufacture of soft drinks. After years of decline, some of its shorefront buildings (Pan Ha') were restored in 1969 by the National Trust for Scotland under its Little Houses Improvement Scheme. Other interesting buildings include St Serf's Tower (16th century), the Tolbooth (1567), Dysart House (1756), and the birthplace (now a museum) of John McDouall Stuart (1815–66), the first explorer to complete the return journey traversing Australia from south to north in 1861–2.

Eachaig, River *Argyll and Bute* A small river of Argyll and Bute, the River Eachaig flows south from Loch Eck for over 5 miles (8 km) through Strath Eachaig before entering the Holy Loch.

Eaglesfield *Dumfries and Galloway* A long linear village in Dumfries and Galloway, Eaglesfield lies to the west of the Kirtle Water, 3 miles (5 km) east of Ecclefechan.

Eaglesham *East Renfrewshire* A village in East

Renfrewshire, Eaglesham is situated 9 miles (14 km) south of Glasgow and 5 miles (8 km) southwest of East Kilbride. The original village held a weekly market until the mid-17th century, but the present layout of two rows of houses separated by trees, a meadow and a stream was created in 1796 for the workers at the Earl of Eglinton's cotton factory. Work halted when the factory burned down in 1876. Notable structures include Eaglesham Old and Carswell Parish Church (1788), a monument to two Covenanters shot in May 1685, the ruins of Polnoon Castle (14th century) and Eaglesham House. In 1941 the German Nazi leader Rudolf Hess landed by parachute near this house, possibly on a peace mission. In 1960 Eaglesham became the first Scottish village listed as a place of special historical interest.

Eaglesham Moors *East Renfrewshire* An area of moorland stretching south to Fenwick Moors from Eaglesham in East Renfrewshire, Eaglesham Moors surrounds reservoirs including the Dunwan Dam, Bennan Loch and Lochgoin. Ballageich Hill rises to the southwest.

Earadale Point *Argyll and Bute* Located on the southwestern coastline of the Kintyre peninsula, the headland of Earadale Point lies 4 miles (6.5 km) southwest of Machrihanish.

Earl's Burn *Stirling* From its source in the Earlsburn Reservoirs in the Gargunnock Hills, Stirling Council area, the Earl's Burn flows more than 6 miles (10 km) southeastwards to join the River Carron at Muirmill, 5 miles (8 km) northwest of Denny.

Earl's Palace, The *Orkney* Located in Kirkwall on Mainland Orkney, the Earl's Palace was built in the 16th century for the Stewart earls. The palace is regarded as one of the most accomplished pieces of Renaissance architecture in Scotland. After the executions of Earl Robert and his son Patrick the palace fell into disrepair. By 1745 the roof had been stripped and the slates sold. It has remained roofless since. Nearby is St Magnus Cathedral, and the ruins of the Bishop's Palace.

Earl's Seat *East Dunbartonshire/Stirling* Rising to a height of 578 m (1897 ft) on the border between Stirling and East Dunbartonshire council areas, Earl's Seat is the highest point in the Campsie Fells.

Earlsferry *Fife* A royal burgh overlooking the Firth of Forth, Earlsferry lies at the western end of a line of settlements that extend along the Fife coast from Elie. It derives its name both from the ferries that used to arrive here from North Berwick and other ports on the Lothian coast, and from Macduff, the Thane or Earl of Fife who is said to have taken refuge from Macbeth in a cave at Kincraig Point before being ferried across the Firth of Forth to Dunbar. There are the remains of a hospice for pilgrims to St Andrews run by Cistercian nuns, and golf has been played on the Earlsferry Links since the 16th century. Today Earlsferry is a popular residential resort.

Earlsford *Aberdeenshire* A hamlet in the Formartine district of Aberdeenshire, Earlsford lies on a burn 2 miles (3 km) northwest of Tarves. Haddo House lies to the east.

Earlshall Castle *Fife* An L-plan tower house in northeast Fife to the east of Leuchars, Earlshall Castle was built in 1546 by Sir William Bruce of Earlshall (not the architect of the same name). Today it lies next to the runway at RAF Leuchars. Earlshall was restored from a ruinous state in 1891–8 by Sir Robert Lorimer (1864–1929) under the patronage of its owner W. R. M. Mackenzie. Situated amid wooded parkland, the house has a garden with topiary yew chessmen that were rescued by Lorimer as mature trees from an abandoned Edinburgh garden.

Earlston *Scottish Borders* A village of Lauderdale in Scottish Borders, Earlston lies to the east of the Leader Water, 3 miles (5 km) north of Newton St Boswells. Created a burgh of barony in 1489, its peel tower dates from the 16th century. An earlier tower and estate were owned by the 13th-century seer Thomas Learmont of Ercildoune (Earlston), or Thomas the Rhymer. Modern industries include the manufacture of textiles and farm machinery.

Earlstoun Loch *Dumfries and Galloway* A loch in the valley of Glenkens, Dumfries and Galloway, Earlstoun Loch is formed by a widening of the Water of Ken a mile (1.5 km) to the northwest of St John's Town of Dalry. Earlstoun Linn falls into the loch at its head, and on its eastern shore stand Earlstoun House and Earlstoun Castle, which was built by the Sinclair family in the mid-16th century. In 1615 the castle passed to Alexander Gordon of Airds.

Earn, Loch *Perth and Kinross* Occupying an east–west valley at the western end of Strath Earn in central Perth and Kinross, Loch Earn lies 30 miles (48 km) west of Perth and 6 miles (10 km) due south of the Killin end of Loch Tay. Situated at an elevation of 93 m (306 ft) above sea level, it is 6.5 miles (11 km) long and has an area of 6.3 sq. km (3.91 sq. miles) and a mean depth of 42 m (138 ft). The River Earn, which issues from its eastern end, joins the River Tay near Bridge of Earn, just south of Perth. Leisure activities on the loch include sailing, water skiing and fishing, facilities being located at the settlements of Lochearnhead and Auchraw at the western end and at St Fillans at the eastern end.

Earn, River *Perth and Kinross* A river of Perth and Kinross, the Earn emerges from the eastern end of Loch Earn at St Fillans. It flows 32 miles (51 km) eastwards through Strath Earn, eventually meeting the River Tay at the head of the Firth of Tay near Bridge of Earn. On its course it passes the settlements of Comrie and Crieff, and is crossed by fine bridges at Kinkell, Dalreoch, Dupplin and Bridge of Earn.

Earn, Strath *Perth and Kinross* A strath of Perth and Kinross, Strath Earn extends over the basin of the River Earn and its tributaries, from Balquhidder in the west to the Firth of Tay in the east. It is over 30 miles (48 km) long and averages 8 miles (13 km) wide. Historically Strath Earn was the seat of a Celtic earldom and formed with Menteith the ancient province of Fortrenn. It later formed a stewartry in the lands of the earls of Perth and gave its name to one of the dukedoms held by Queen Victoria's father. The principal settlements of Strath Earn are (west to east) Lochearnhead, St Fillans, Comrie, Crieff, Muthill, Auchterarder, Dunning, Forteviot, Forgandenny, Bridge of Earn and Abernethy.

Earn Water *East Renfrewshire* Rising from lochs on the Eaglesham Moors, the Earn Water is a tributary of the White Cart Water, which it joins at Waterfoot, East Renfrewshire.

Earsairidh The Gaelic name for Earsary in the Western Isles.

Earsary *Western Isles* A crofting township on the southeast coast of Barra in the Outer Hebrides, Earsary (sometimes Ersary, Gael: *Earsairidh*) is located 3 miles (5 km) east-northeast of Castlebay.

Earshaigs *Dumfries and Galloway* A forest plantation in Dumfries and Galloway, Earshaigs lies on the Southern Upland Way 4 miles (6.5 km) west of Beattock. Forming part of the Moffat Forest, it offers walks with fine views to the Lowther Hills. The ponds at Earshaigs are home to wildfowl, including Canada geese.

Earthquake House *Perth and Kinross* Situated in a field in The Ross at the western end of the 'Shakey Toun' of Comrie in Perth and Kinross, the Earthquake House was built in 1874 for the British Association's Committee for the Investigation of Scottish and Irish Earthquakes. A small, square building, it contains a model of the original Mallet seismometer alongside modern seismological instruments installed by the British Geological Survey. Earthquake House is positioned on the Highland Boundary Fault, the first earthquake having been recorded here in 1597. A major series of 70 shocks was noted in 1789 and the world's first seismometers were set up in Comrie in 1840.

Easaigh The Gaelic name for Ensay in the Western Isles.

Easdale *Argyll and Bute* An island of Argyll and Bute in the Firth of Lorn, Easdale lies off the west coast of Seil, 10 miles (16 km) south of Oban. It has an area of 24 ha (59 acres). Slate was quarried here from the 17th century until the early 20th century when the sea flooded the workings. The industry is featured in the Easdale Island Folk Museum which occupies some former cottages of the quarriers.

Easdale Sound *Argyll and Bute* Easdale Sound is the name given to the narrow channel of water that separates the island of Easdale from Seil, on the western coastline of Argyll and Bute.

Eassie *Angus* A locality in western Angus, Eassie lies in the valley of Strathmore, 2 miles (3 km) west of Glamis. Outside the old church of Eassie, just north of the A94 from Forfar to Coupar Angus, stands a Pictish cross slab dating from the 8th century. The farmhouse of Castleton of Eassie is enclosed within the earthwork remains of a 12th/13th-century castle. Eassie lies within the united parishes of Eassie and Nevay, Eassie lying to the northeast and Nevay to the southwest.

East Ayrshire *Area: 1251 sq. km (483 sq. miles)* Stretching northwards from Loch Doon in the Southern Uplands to Cunninghame in the Central Lowlands, East

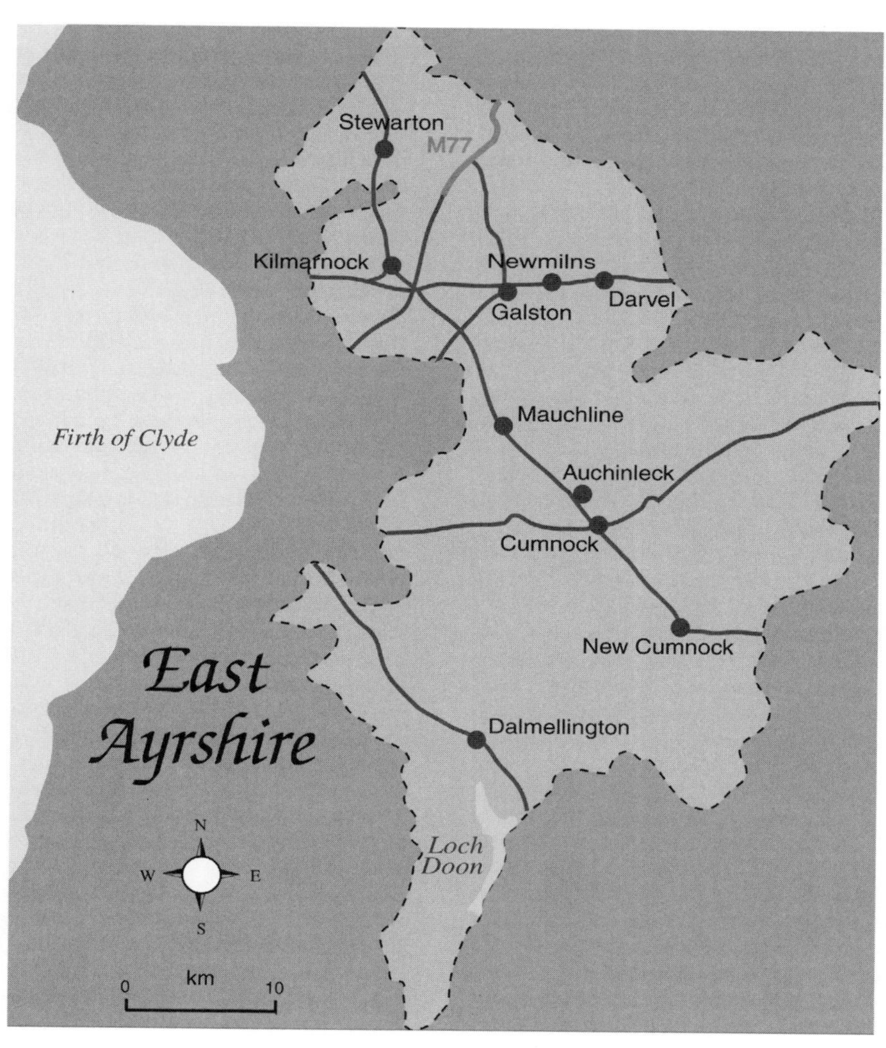

Ayrshire became a separate local government area in 1996. Between 1975 and 1996 it formed the districts of Kilmarnock and Loudon and Cumnock and Doon Valley in Strathclyde Region. Watered by the Rivers Irvine, Annick, Cessnock, Afton and Doon, it is bounded by Dumfries and Galloway, East Renfrewshire, North Ayrshire, South Ayrshire and South Lanarkshire council areas, and its principal towns are Kilmarnock (administrative centre), Cumnock, New Cumnock, Mauchline, Stewarton, Galston, Newmilns, Darvel, Auchinleck and Dalmellington. Nearly 70 per cent of East Ayrshire is devoted to agriculture, and largely given over to dairy farming and the production of beef and sheep. Many of the settlements developed during the 19th century in association with coal mining and the manufacture of textiles.

East Barns *East Lothian* A hamlet of East Lothian, East Barns is located 2 miles (3 km) southeast of Broxburn and a half-mile (1 km) south of the headland of Barns Ness. The main East Coast railway line runs immediately to the south.

East Burra *Shetland* An island situated to the west of the south Mainland of Shetland, from which it is separated by the Clift Sound. Linked to West Burra by a road bridge, the island has an area of 540 ha (1334 acres).

East Calder *West Lothian* A village of West Lothian, East Calder lies near the River Almond, 12 miles (19 km) southeast of Edinburgh and a mile (1.5 km) east of Mid Calder. Comprising a long main street, its notable buildings include the roofless 16th-century St Cuthbert's Parish Church, abandoned in 1750, and the Gothic-style Parish Church (1888). Ormiston Hall (1851) to the east stands on the site of the former Ormiston Hill House (17th-century). The minor poet Alexander Rodger (1784–1846) was born in East Calder. Nearby are the Almondell, Calderwood and Polkemmet Country Parks, which occupy former estates along the course of the Almond.

East Dunbartonshire *Area: 171 sq. km (66 sq. miles)* A small local government area in the Central Lowlands, East Dunbartonshire lies between Glasgow and the Campsie Fells. From 1975 until 1996 it comprised the districts of Strathkelvin and Bearsden and Milngavie in Strathclyde Region. Its principal settlements on the northern periphery of Glasgow are Kirkintilloch (administrative centre), Bearsden, Milngavie, Bishopbriggs and Lennoxtown. Over 75 per cent of the land is given over to farming, the remainder being largely urban.

East Haven *Angus* A fishing village of southeast Angus, East Haven is located on the North Sea coast, 5 miles (8 km) southwest of Arbroath. Originally the village comprised two rows of cottages known as the Long Row and Shore Row, the Long Row later being cut off from the sea by the railway line.

East Kilbride *South Lanarkshire* A planned New Town in South Lanarkshire, East Kilbride lies on the Kittoch Water high on an exposed upland plateau 12 miles (19 km) south of Glasgow and 10 miles (16 km) southeast of Paisley. The sixth-largest town in Scotland, it was designated on 6 May 1947 in the Clyde Valley Regional Plan as Scotland's first New Town, with a target population of 45,000 designed to

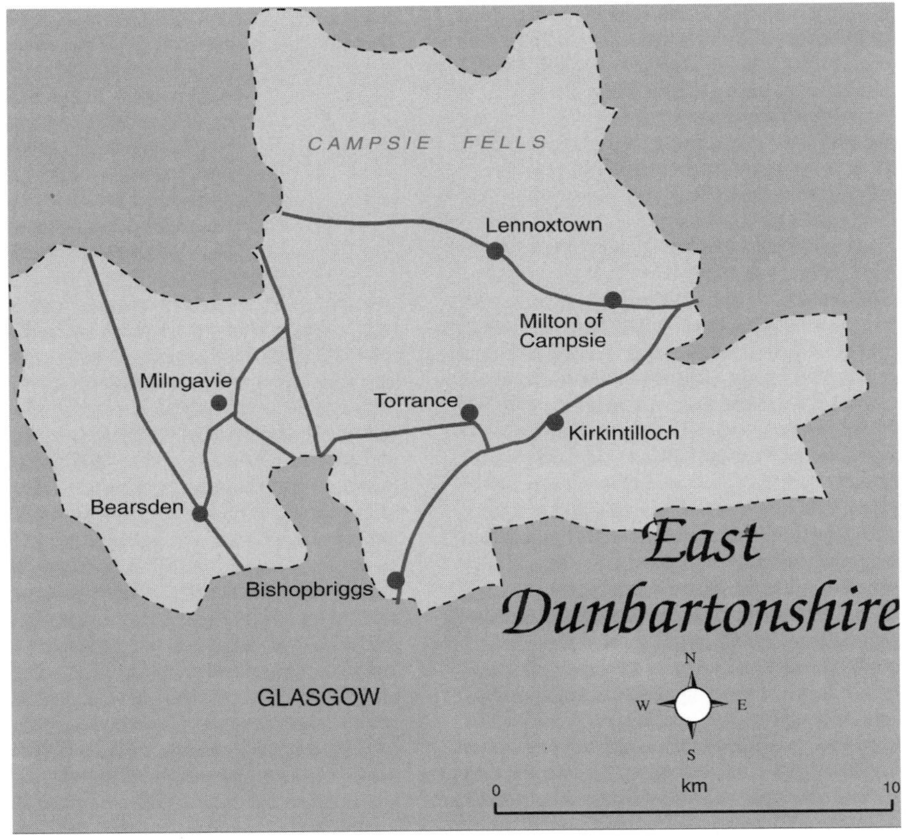

absorb overspill from Glasgow. An earlier settlement, with a 12th-century church dedicated to St Bride or Bridget, evolved as a farming village, and it was here that the Scottish Society of Friends, or Quakers, first met in 1653. East Kilbride later developed as a weaving village, primarily producing muslin and spinning cotton, although much of this industry moved east to take advantage of the water power generated by the Rotten Calder Water which cuts through a deep valley. Other early industries associated with East Kilbride included coal mining, limestone quarrying, clock making and the manufacture of boots, cement and tiles. The anatomist William Hunter, who studied at Glasgow University and bequeathed to the city the Hunterian Museum, was born in Long Calderwood House, now a museum itself, in 1718. Since work began on the new town in 1948, East Kilbride has developed its own identity and is notable for maintaining an average of more than one job per household. Between 1975 and 1996 it was the administrative centre of a district of Strathclyde Region, with engineering, electronic and computer-technology industries located at the Peel Science Park, Scottish Enterprise Technology Park and Kelvin South Business Park. Buildings of note include the ruined 15th-century Craigneith Castle, 13th-century Mains Castle and 14th-century Torrance House, which stands in the Calderglen Country Park near an 18-hole golf course. The Scottish Museum of Country Life is located at Wester Kittochside Farm near the industrial suburb of College Milton.

East Linton *East Lothian* Located on the River Tyne, 22 miles (35 km) east of Edinburgh, East Linton's 16th-century bridge over the gorge established the village's importance on the Edinburgh–Dunbar road. It later prospered through its road and rail connections but today is bypassed by the A1. In the 17th and 18th centuries East Linton developed as an agricultural centre and mill town with corn and textile mills. It had a cattle market and weekly hiring markets for migrant labourers. Buildings of interest in the area include Preston Mill, said to be the oldest working water mill in Scotland, Phantassie Doocot and the Museum of Flight at East Fortune. Hailes Castle, 2 miles (3 km) to the south, was probably built by the earls of Dunbar in the 13th or 14th centuries. It incorporates a 16th-century chapel and was held by the Gourlay and Hepburn families before its destruction in 1650 by Cromwell's forces. Preston Kirk, with its 13th-century chancel, is the burial place of the Smeaton family and the agriculturalist Andrew Meikle, who invented the threshing machine and worked at nearby Phantassie. The artist John Pettie (1839–93) was brought up in East Linton.

East Loch Roag *Western Isles* East Loch Roag is a large sea loch located on the west coast of the island of Lewis in the Outer Hebrides. The island of Great Bernera separates East Loch Roag from West Loch Roag. Situated within the loch are a number of islands, including Little Bernera, Vacasay Island and Keava.

East Loch Tarbert *Argyll and Bute* A sea loch on the east coast of the Kintyre peninsula, East Loch Tarbert forms a small inlet of Loch Fyne. The village of Tarbert, which is linked by ferry to Portavadie in the summer, lies at the head of the loch. To the southwest is the much longer West Loch Tarbert which separates Kintyre from Knapdale. Legend has it that Magnus Barelegs, son of King Olaf of Norway, had his men drag his ship across the narrow isthmus between East and West Loch Tarbert in 1098, enabling him to claim that Kintyre was an island and therefore a Viking possession.

East Lomond *Fife* Rising to a height of 482 m (1471 ft) in the Lomond Hills, western Fife, the volcanic summit of East Lomond forms a conspicuous landmark on the skyline above the new town of Glenrothes. Skirted by a pathway that traverses Fife Regional Park, there are the remains of old limekilns on the hill's southern slopes.

East Lothian *Area: 666 sq. km (257 sq. miles)* Stretching eastwards from Edinburgh in east-central Scotland, East Lothian has a coastline that is washed to the north by the Firth of Forth and to the east by the North Sea. It is

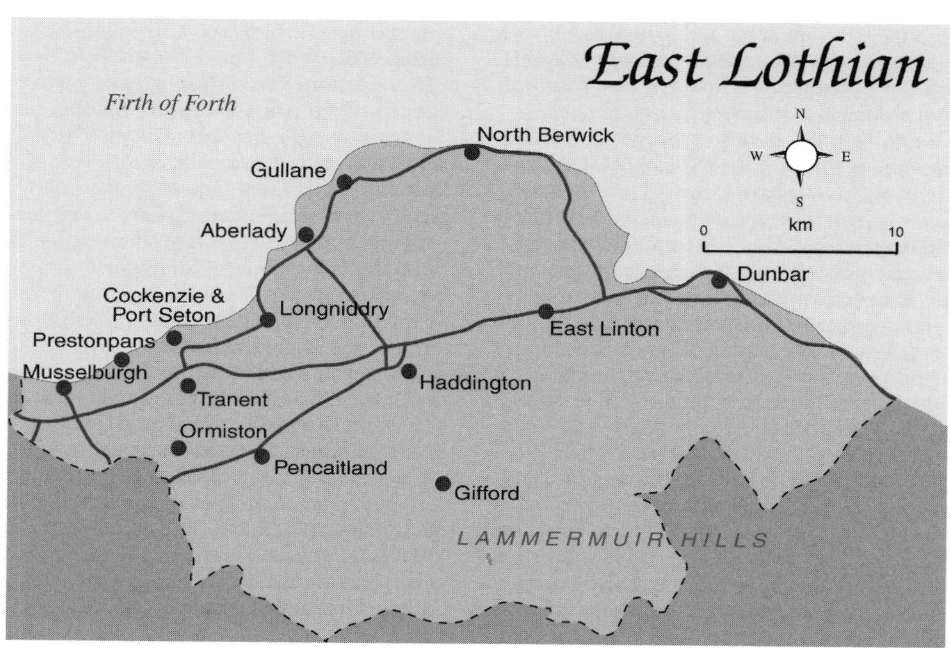

bounded to the south by the Lammermuir Hills, which rise to 535 m (1755 ft) at Meikle Says Law on the boundary with Scottish Borders. Its chief towns are Musselburgh, Haddington (administrative centre), Tranent, Dunbar, North Berwick, Aberlady and Gullane. Formerly known as Haddingtonshire, East Lothian was one of the four districts of Lothian region between 1975 and 1996. Two parallel geological fault lines 1.5 miles (2.5 km) apart traverse East Lothian from southwest to northeast. These are the Dunbar–Gifford fault and the Lammermuir fault. To the north of the former, the landscape is characterised by rolling farmland and sandy beaches, and the distinctive pyramid of Berwick Law (187 m/613 ft) and the whale-backed Traprain Law (224 m/734 ft) which are of volcanic origin. To the south of the latter, sandstone, limestone and conglomerate predominate, giving rise to notable coastal cliff formations that are home to colonies of sea birds. East Lothian is bisected by one main river, the Tyne, which flows southwest–northeast to meet the North Sea west of Dunbar. It is joined by numerous tributaries that flow down from the Lammermuirs where there are three reservoirs, the largest being Whiteadder. To the west the River Esk makes a brief appearance en route to join the Firth of Forth at Musselburgh, and in the east near Stenton is Pressmennan Loch, created in 1819. East Lothian benefits from a mild climate with some of the lowest rainfall in Scotland. Over 57 per cent of the area is given over to arable farming, the remainder largely comprising woodland (8 per cent), grassland (12 per cent) and moorland (9 per cent). Tourism, quarrying, power generation, electronics, scientific research and printing are also important to the economy. There are 21 designated Sites of Scientific Interest, including locations such as the Bass Rock and Danskine Loch, in addition to Aberlady Bay Local Nature Reserve and John Muir Country Park. Religious foundations such as Nunraw Abbey and the Collegiate Church of Haddington indicate the growth of church landholdings during the Middle Ages, and country houses such as Lennoxlove and Yester represent important lairded estates of a later period. East Lothian was in the forefront of the agricultural revolution during the 18th and 19th centuries, when landowners reclaimed land, enclosed fields, introduced crop rotations and created planned estate villages such as Ormiston.

East Neuk of Fife *Fife* The East Neuk or eastern 'corner' of Fife is the name generally given to that part of the Fife coast lying between St Andrews and Lundin Links. Claiming some of the most fertile farmland in Fife, it includes attractive picture-postcard fishing villages and former ports such as Crail, Anstruther, Pittenweem, St Monans, Elie, Earlsferry and Upper and Lower Largo. In medieval times much of Scotland's sea trade with France, the Low Countries and Scandinavia was conducted through the ports of the East Neuk, and in later years many of these coastal villages were home to large fishing fleets.

East Pilton *City of Edinburgh* Lying between Ferry Road in Edinburgh and Granton and West Pilton on the south shore of the Firth of Forth is the public housing estate of East Pilton. Laid out in 1930 as part of Edinburgh's plan to clear slums from the Old Town and provide the tenants with modern housing, the estate comprises two- and three-storey flats. It has long been regarded as offering a better quality of life than its more modern sister estate of West Pilton because of the effective provision of shops and other social facilities.

East Plean *Stirling* A former mining settlement in southeast Stirling Council area, East Plean lies 4 miles (6.5 km) southeast of Stirling.

East Renfrewshire *Area: 168 sq. km (65 sq. miles)* A small local government area in west-central Scotland, East Renfrewshire lies to the south of Glasgow (from where it is administered) and Renfrewshire. It reaches towards moorland and farming country through the city suburbs of Newton Mearns, Giffnock, Barrhead, Neilston, Uplawmoor and Clarkston, which grew dramatically after World War II and are among the largest fifty towns in Scotland. Designated in 1996, East Dunbartonshire was previously a district of Strathclyde and prior to 1975 was a part of the former county of Renfrewshire. There are several lochs and reservoirs in the council area, including Bennan Loch and Long Loch; rivers that pass through or act as a border include the White Cart Water and Earn Water. The council area's highest point is Corse Hill (376 m/1233 ft). East Renfrewshire is the sixth-smallest council area in size, the ninth-smallest in population, and the tenth-highest in density, with 71 per cent of its land devoted to agriculture, most of which is improved grassland. About one-sixth of its territory is developed, primarily for urban use.

East Tarbert Bay *Argyll and Bute* East Tarbert Bay is one of two bays located on either side of the settlement of Tarbert, which stands on a narrow neck of land at the northern end of the island of Gigha in Argyll and Bute. To the east, on the opposite side of the Sound of Gigha, is the Kintyre peninsula and to the west is West Tarbert Bay.

East Wemyss *Fife* A village of Fife, East Wemyss lies on the Firth of Forth 3 miles (5 km) northeast of Kirkcaldy. Formerly known as Castleton, it stands close to the ruins of 16th-century Macduff's Castle, which was the home of the Wemyss family before they built Wemyss Castle. The village takes its name from the weems or caves in the sandstone cliffs which contain Pictish and early Christian symbols. Between 1898 and 1967 the majority of the people in East Wemyss relied on the nearby Michael Coal Pit for employment. The largest pit in Scotland at nationalisation in 1946, it was closed after an undersea fire caused the death of nine miners. East Wemyss was the birthplace in 1908 of the accordionist and bandleader Jimmy Shand.

East Whitburn *West Lothian* A village in West Lothian, East Whitburn lies immediately to the south of the M8 motorway, a quarter-mile (0.5 km) east of Whitburn and 1.5 miles (2.5 km) west of Blackburn.

Easter Balgedie *Perth and Kinross* An agricultural hamlet of Perth and Kinross, Easter Balgedie sits at the foot of the Bishop Hill midway between the villages of Kinnesswood and Wester Balgedie, with views looking out over Loch Leven. There are the remains of a former United Presbyterian Church built in 1821.

Easter Elchies *Moray* A distillery village of Moray, Easter Elchies overlooks the left bank of the River Spey, a mile (1.5 km) to the west of Craigellachie. The old Grant family house of Easter Elchies, which dates from 1700, was restored for The Macallan distillery. Macallan (St Colin) takes its name from a former parish of the same name that united with Knockando in the late 16th century.

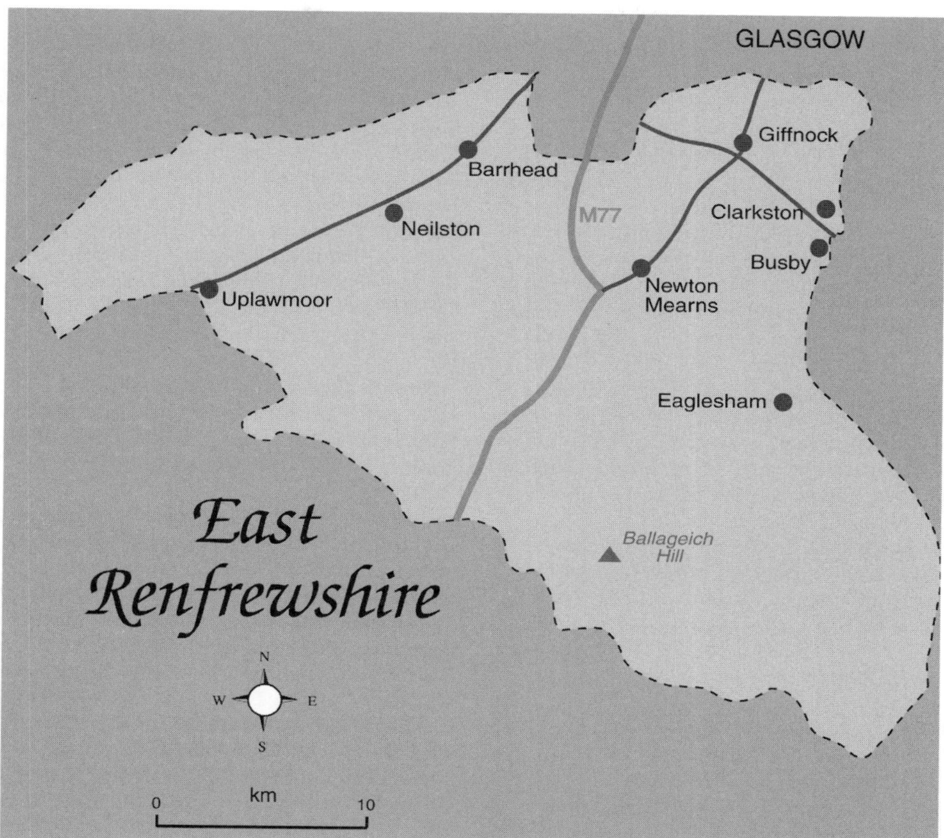

Easter Gaulrig *Moray* The upland Moray farm of Easter Gaulrig overlooks the left bank of the River Avon to the south of Tomintoul in the Grampians.

Easter Pitcorthie *Fife* A farm to the east of Colinsburgh in Carnbee parish, eastern Fife, Easter Pitcorthie is the site of a 2.4-m/8-ft-high standing stone decorated with thirty-three cup-markings and two dumbbell-shaped motifs located 350 m (383 yd) from the farmhouse. During the 19th century cremated bones were discovered at the base of the standing stone, which dates from the 2nd millennium BC.

Easter Road Park *City of Edinburgh* Home of Hibernian Football Club, Easter Road Park is located to the northeast of Edinburgh city centre. The club was established in 1875 by Irish immigrants who gave the team the name Hibernian, the Roman name for Ireland. Hibernian Football Club, locally known as Hibs, joined the Scottish League in 1876 and moved to their present ground in 1880. Hibs have been league champions four times, most recently in 1952, and Scottish Cup winners twice, in 1887 and 1902. There is a close city rivalry with Heart of Midlothian Football Club, which is located at Tynecastle Stadium in the city's western suburbs.

Easter Ross *Highland* An area of the eastern Highlands lying between the Cromarty and Dornoch firths, Easter Ross forms the eastern part of the old county of Ross-shire. The topography varies from the mountains surrounding Glen Glass and Strath Rusdale in the west to the low-lying agricultural land in the east. The major settlements of Easter Ross are Tain, Invergordon, Alness and Dingwall.

Easterhouse *Glasgow City* A district of Glasgow, Easterhouse lies to the east of the city centre and north of the M8. It developed initially in association with the creation of the Monklands Canal and the extension of a rail link from Glasgow to Coatbridge in 1871. A station named Easterhouse was opened at Swinton a half-mile (1 km) north of Baillieston. Incorporated into the City of Glasgow from Lanarkshire in 1938, Easterhouse was developed as a housing estate in the 1950s but without a town centre. A Township Centre was opened in 1973 with sport, library and shopping facilities, but the settlement came to be associated with high unemployment, poverty and deprivation. In the 1990s the Greater Easterhouse Development Company was formed to help attract industry to the area.

Eastfield *North Lanarkshire* A small village in North Lanarkshire, Eastfield lies directly west of Harthill and south of the M8.

Eastfield *North Lanarkshire* A suburb of Cumbernauld in North Lanarkshire, Eastfield lies a mile (1.5 km) west of the town centre.

Eastriggs *Dumfries and Galloway* A small village extended in 1916–18 to accommodate munitions workers, Eastriggs is located midway between Annan and Gretna on the B721.

Eastwood *East Renfrewshire* A parish and previously a district of Strathclyde Region, Eastwood lies on the southern periphery of the Glasgow conurbation, to the east of Barrhead. Now in East Renfrewshire, Eastwood remains a Scottish parliamentary constituency.

Eatharna, Loch *Argyll and Bute* A sea loch on the east

coast of the island of Coll in Argyll and Bute, Loch Eatharna forms a bay on which stands Arinagour, the chief settlement and ferry terminal of the island. The small islands of Eilean Eatharna and Eilean Ornsay lie at the mouth of the loch.

Ecclefechan *Dumfries and Galloway* A village of Annandale in Dumfries and Galloway, Ecclefechan lies in the valley of the Mein Water, a tributary of the River Annan, 5 miles (8 km) north of Annan and 8 miles (13 km) northwest of the English border. Of early origin, the settlement developed on either side of the main road from Carlisle to Glasgow, and established its own markets and fairs. Although it is now bypassed by the M74, it retains its linear form. The Arched House, birthplace of the historian and social reformer Thomas Carlyle (1795–1881), has been maintained by the National Trust for Scotland since 1936. Carlyle is buried in the local churchyard, where the grave of Archibald Arnott (1772–1855), Napoleon's doctor on St Helena, can also be found.

Eccles *Scottish Borders* A hamlet in the Berwickshire parish of the same name in Scottish Borders, Eccles lies 5 miles (8 km) southeast of Greenlaw. A Cistercian nunnery, founded here in 1155, was destroyed during a raid in 1545.

Ecclesgreig A former name for St Cyrus in Aberdeenshire.

Ecclesiamagirdle *Perth and Kinross* A locality in Strathearn, Perth and Kinross, Ecclesiamagirdle lies in the northern foothills of the Ochil Hills, a mile (1.5 km) to the southwest of Bridge of Earn. It derives its name from the now ruined chapel of St Gill or Gillan, one of St Columba's harpists. Close by are a small loch, a dovecote and Ecclesiamagirdle House, which was built in 1684.

Ecclesmachan *West Lothian* A village in a parish of the same name in West Lothian, Ecclesmachan lies 2 miles (3 km) southwest of Winchburgh. It takes its name from the Church of St Machan. The noted surgeon Robert Liston (1794–1847) was the son of the parish minister.

Echt *Aberdeenshire* A commuter village in mid-Aberdeenshire, Echt lies at a road junction to the northeast of the Hill of Fare and 12 miles (19 km) west of Aberdeen. It used to be the scene of cattle, horse and hiring fairs.

Eck, Loch *Argyll and Bute* A narrow loch on the Cowal peninsula, Argyll and Bute, Loch Eck extends over 6 miles (10 km) northwest to southeast in the heart of the Argyll Forest Park, 7 miles (11 km) north of Dunoon. The peaks of Beinn Bheag and Beinn Mhòr rise to the east of the loch, which is fed by the River Eachaig.

Eday *Orkney* A long narrow island in the Orkney Islands, Eday lies to the west of the southern tip of Sanday, from which it is separated by Eday Sound. It has an area of 2773 ha (6849 acres) and comprises a spine of peat-covered hills that rise to 101 m (331 ft) at Ward Hill in the south. Eday's fine yellow sandstone was used in the building of St Magnus Cathedral in Kirkwall, and its peat has been exported to a number of distilleries throughout Scotland. Carrick House at the north end of the island was built in 1633 by the Earl of Carrick, and among sites of archaeological interest are several prehistoric burned mounds, field boundaries, chambered cairns and the Stone of Setter, one of the finest standing stones in Orkney. Also to be found on Eday are the ruins of Iron Age houses, a small Norse castle at Stackel Brae and a 17th-century saltworks. The notorious pirate John Gow ran aground here in 1725 in his ship *Revenge* and was arrested. The island, whose population fell from a total of 944 in 1841 to 121 in 2001, is accessed by ferry from Kirkwall and the neighbouring islands, landing at the Bay of Backaland. There is also an airstrip, known as London Airport.

Edderton *Highland* A hamlet in a parish of the same name in Easter Ross, Highland Council area, Edderton lies on the south shore of the Dornoch Firth, 5 miles (8 km) northwest of Tain. Nearby are the Balblair Distillery and Edderton Hill, which rises to a height of 328 m (1000 ft).

Eddleston *Scottish Borders* A village in a parish of the same name in Scottish Borders, Eddleston lies by the Eddleston Water, 4 miles (6.5 km) north of Peebles. The Eddleston Water flows south to join the Tweed at Peebles.

Eddlewood *South Lanarkshire* A southern suburb of Hamilton in South Lanarkshire, Eddlewood lies adjacent to the districts of Meikle Earnock and Cadzow. It was once one of the many colliery villages in the area.

Eddrachillis Bay *Highland* An inlet on the northwest coast of Sutherland in Highland Council area, Eddrachillis Bay lies to the north of Assynt at the mouth of Loch a' Chairn Bhain. The neighbouring parish of Eddrachillis includes the settlement of Scourie.

Eden, River *Fife* The northernmost of the two principal rivers of Fife, the Eden is formed by the joining of the Carmore and Beattie burns at Burnside to the west of Gateside. It flows eastwards across the Howe of Fife through Strathmiglo and Cupar on its way to meet the North Sea 2 miles (3 km) north of St Andrews. It has a total length of nearly 30 miles (48 km), and its fall of around 90 m (300 ft) was once used to provide mills with water power. The Eden is joined by the Ceres Burn at Cupar and by the Moonzie Burn and Motray Water at Guardbridge, where it opens out into a wide estuary that was designated a local nature reserve in 1978. The tidal sand and mud flats, salt marshes, reed beds and sand-dune grassland of the Eden Estuary Nature Reserve are host to high densities of wintering bird populations, which include nationally important numbers of shelduck, internationally significant numbers of bar-tailed godwits and the most northerly wintering flock of black-tailed godwits.

Eden Water *Scottish Borders* A river of Scottish Borders, the Eden Water rises to the east of Lauder and flows 23 miles (37 km) east, south and east again to join the River Tweed near the village of Ednam.

Edendon Water *Perth and Kinross* A stream of Highland Perth and Kinross, the Edendon Water rises in the southern Grampians 5 miles (8 km) east of the Pass of Drumochter. It flows directly southwards for 6 miles (10 km) through the Forest of Atholl before joining the River Garry at Edendon Bridge, 8 miles (13 km) northwest of Calvine.

Ederline, Loch *Argyll and Bute* A small loch of Argyll and Bute, Loch Ederline lies to the south of the village of Ford, 3 miles (5 km) northeast of Kilmartin. It receives water from Loch Leathan, 3 miles (5 km) to the south and drains north towards Loch Awe.

Edgelaw Reservoir *Midlothian* Situated 2 miles (3 km)

west of Temple in Midlothian, Edgelaw Reservoir is one of a network of reservoirs supplying Edinburgh with water.

Edinample *Stirling* A locality in Stirling Council area, Edinample lies on the south side of Loch Earn near the mouth of the Burn of Ample, which flows down from the slopes of Ben Vorlich and Stuc a' Chroin over the Falls of Edinample to enter the loch 2 miles (3 km) southeast of Lochearnhead. The restored 16th-century Z-plan Edinample Castle was a stronghold of the Campbells of Breadalbane.

Edinbane *Highland* A crofting township on the north coast of the island of Skye, Edinbane lies at the head of Loch Greshornish on the road between Portree and Dunvegan. It has a sports centre, hospital, tourist facilities and fishing industries.

Edinburgh *City of Edinburgh Area: 260 sq. km (100.5 sq. miles)* Edinburgh, the capital of Scotland, is a major political, administrative, cultural, commercial and tourist centre known throughout the world for its Festival, which was first held in August 1947. A unitary authority since 1996, the City of Edinburgh comprises the city proper and its hinterland to the west and south. It occupies a dramatic hilly location on the south side of the Firth of Forth in east-central Scotland, extending from just west of South Queensferry to Joppa in the east and southwards to the Pentland Hills. West Lothian, Midlothian and East Lothian are its nearest neighbours, and it is the ninth-smallest, although second-most-populous, of Scotland's 32 local government areas. Forty-two per cent of the land in the council area is under agricultural use. Described as the 'Athens of the North' because of its neoclassical architecture and its cultural achievements in the 18th century, Edinburgh is said, like Rome, to be built on seven hills – Castle Hill, Calton Hill, Arthur's Seat, Salisbury Crags, Craiglockhart Hill, Blackford Hill and the Braid Hills. The city's hilly landscape derives from a succession of volcanic and erosional activity that dates back 350 million years to the Carboniferous period, when a volcano erupted and poured forth lava that cooled to form hard durable rock. Thick beds of sediment were laid down over millions of years underwater and renewed volcanic activity 285 million years ago intruded thick layers of molten rock between the sedimentary strata to create features such as Salisbury Crags. The horizontal strata were later tilted and folded by violent earthquakes. Subsequent erosion, particularly during the last Ice Age, selectively eroded softer sedimentary rock, leaving the harder volcanic rocks as hills. All these hills have a tail to the east, forming a 'crag and tail' feature, the best example being that of Castle Hill and the Royal Mile. Although there is some evidence that communities of hunter-gatherers were present along the valley of the Water of Leith from at least 5000 BC, the hilltops of Edinburgh supported fortifications from about 1000 BC. The historic core of the city is centred on one of these hills, Castle Hill, and the Royal Mile which formed the main artery of the medieval city, linking the castle to the Abbey and later the Palace of Holyroodhouse, now the official residence of the monarch when visiting Scotland. The New Town to the north, which was created from 1767, is

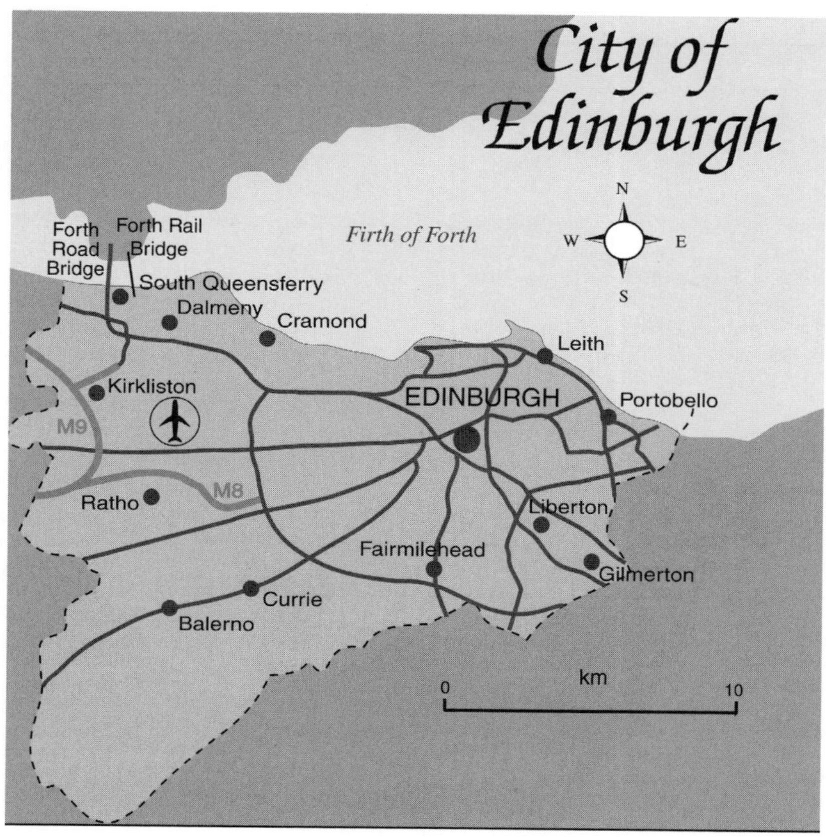

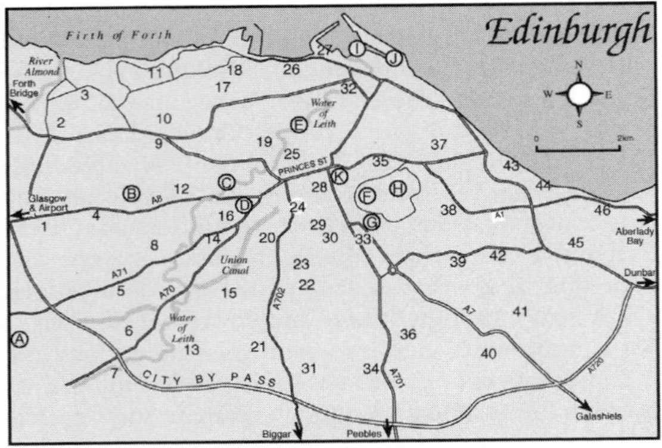

A *Heriot-Watt University*
B *Edinburgh Zoo*
C *Gallery of Modern Art*
D *Haymarket Station*
E *Royal Botanic Garden*
F *Holyrood Park*
G *Royal Commonwealth Pool*
H *Arthur's Seat*
I Britannia
J *Victoria Quay*
K *Waverley Station*

1 *Gyle*
2 *Barnton*
3 *Cramond*
4 *Corstorphine*
5 *Sighthill*
6 *Wester Hailes*
7 *Juniper Green*
8 *Stenhouse*
9 *Blackhall*
10 *Davidson's Mains*
11 *Muirhouse*
12 *Murrayfield*
13 *Colinton*
14 *Gorgie*
15 *Craiglockhart*
16 *Dalry*
17 *Pilton*
18 *Grandon*
19 *Comely Bank*
20 *Merchiston*
21 *Oxgangs*
22 *Blackford*
23 *Morningside*
24 *Tollcross*
25 *New Town*
26 *Trinity*
27 *Newhaven*
28 *Old Town*
29 *Marchmont*
30 *Grange*
31 *Fairmilehead*
32 *Leith*
33 *Newington*
34 *Kaimes*
35 *Abbeyhill*
36 *Liberton*
37 *Restalrig*
38 *Duddingston*
39 *Craigmillar*
40 *Gilmerton*
41 *Edmonstone*
42 *Niddrie*
43 *Portobello*
44 *Joppa*
45 *Newcraighall*
46 *Newhailes*

characterised by streets, squares and crescents all laid out in a regular geometric plan, many with elegant Georgian facades. As Edinburgh expanded throughout the 18th, 19th and 20th centuries, it absorbed surrounding villages such as Duddingston, Corstorphine, Liberton, Colinton and Juniper Green, and in 1920 the port of Leith at the mouth of the Water of Leith was amalgamated with the city. Created a royal burgh in the 12th century, Edinburgh became capital of Scotland only in 1532 when James V brought the country's central administration and courts to the city. Although Parliament met regularly in Edinburgh from 1466, the building known as Parliament Hall was not erected until 1639, some 36 years after the royal court had moved south to London following the Union of the Crowns. With the Union of the Parliaments in 1707, Edinburgh lost its status as a political centre until 1999, when a Scottish Parliament was re-established. In

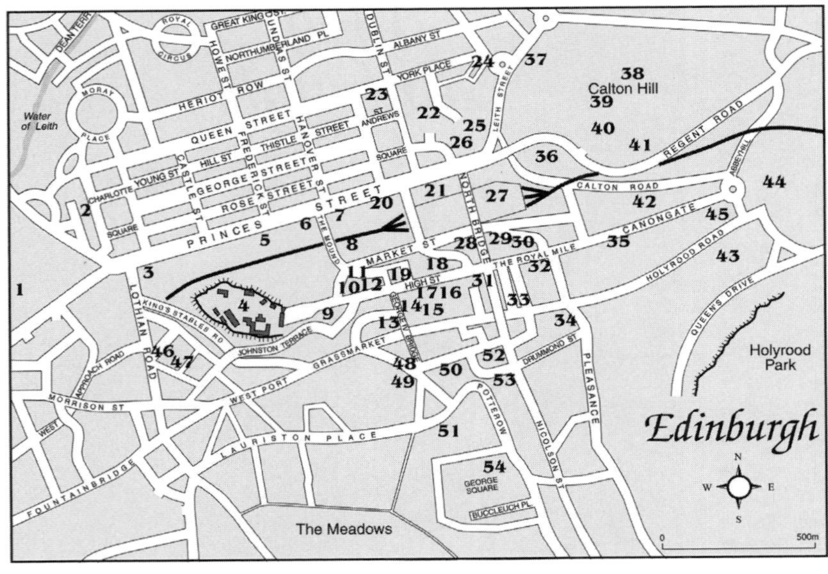

1 *St Mary's Cathedral (Episc.)*
2 *West Register House*
3 *St John's Church (Episc.)*
4 *Castle*
5 *Princes Street Gardens*
6 *Floral Clock*
7 *Royal Scottish Academy*
8 *National Gallery of Scotland*
9 *Scottish Whisky Heritage Centre*
10 *Outlook Tower/ Camera Obscura*
11 *Assembly Hall*
12 *Gladstone's Lane*
13 *Public Library*
14 *National Library of Scotland*
15 *Parliament House/ Supreme Courts*
16 *Mercat Cross*
17 *St Giles*
18 *City Chambers*
19 *High Court*
20 *Scott Monument*
21 *Waverley Market*
22 *Bus Station*
23 *Scottish National Portrait Gallery*
24 *St Mary's Cathedral*
25 *St James Centre*
26 *Register House*
27 *Waverley Station*
28 *City Art Centre*
29 *Brass Rubbing Centre*
30 *John Knox's House*
31 *Tron Kirk/Info. Centre*
32 *Museum of Childhood*
33 *St Cecilia's Hall*
34 *Flodden Wall*
35 *Huntly House Museum*
36 *St Andrew's House*
37 *Playhouse Theatre*
38 *Calton Hill*
39 *National Monument*
40 *Nelson Monument*
41 *Royal High School*
42 *Canongate Kirk*
43 *Dynamic Earth*
44 *Palace of Holyrood House/ Holyrood Abbey*
45 *Scottish Parliament*
46 *Usher Hall*
47 *Royal Lyceum Theatre*
48 *Greyfriars' Bobby*
49 *Greyfriars Kirk*
50 *Royal Museum of Scotland*
51 *McEwan Hall*
52 *Old College*
53 *Festival Theatre*
54 *University of Edinburgh*

addition to the castle and palace, chief among the city's buildings of architectural and historic note are St Giles Kirk, founded by Alexander II c.1120, Canongate Tolbooth (1591), Tron Kirk (1647), John Knox's House, the City Chambers, Craigmillar Castle, Lauriston Castle, Ramsay Gardens, the Scott Monument (1846), St Mary's Metropolitan Cathedral (1813), George Heriot's School (1659), Edinburgh Academy (1824), Donaldson's School (1841), Fettes College (1870), the Usher Hall (1914), the Royal Scottish Academy (1826), the National Gallery of Scotland (1854), the Scottish National Portrait Gallery (1895), the Scottish National Gallery of Modern Art (formerly John Watson's Hospital, 1828) and the Royal Museum of Scotland (1854). Among many notable people born in Edinburgh were the writers James Boswell (1740–95), Sir Walter Scott (1771–1832), Robert Louis Stevenson (1850–94) and Sir Arthur Conan Doyle (1859–1930), the artist Sir Henry Raeburn (1756–1823), the physicist James Clerk Maxwell (1831–79) and film star Sir Sean Connery (b.1930). Edinburgh has three universities: the University of Edinburgh, founded in 1583; Heriot-Watt University, founded as The School of Arts in 1821, later renamed Heriot-Watt College in 1879 and given university status in 1966; and Napier University, a former college given university status in 1992. A major centre for education and scientific research, Edinburgh is also a centre for financial services and industries such as the manufacture of food, drink and electronics.

Edinburgh Airport *City of Edinburgh* Located 7 miles (11 km) west of Edinburgh and 46 miles (74 km) east of Glasgow, Edinburgh Airport is operated by the British Airports Authority, BAA plc. It was originally the Turnhouse Royal Air Force base, but began handling civilian traffic in 1947. The old terminal building, opened in 1954, located to the northeast and on the opposite side of the runway to the current terminal, which opened in 1977 and now handles annually more than 7.9 million passengers, who are served by 39 different airlines with over 112,000 air transport movements each year. It is said to be Scotland's fastest growing airport. and a dramatic 57-m-(187-feet-) high air traffic control tower was completed in 2005 at a cost of £11 million and has become a notable landmark. It has three runways; the two main runways are 2560m (8399 feet) and 1828m (6000 feet) in length respectively. The much shorter third runway is used for small aircraft.

Edinburgh Castle *City of Edinburgh* Situated on a volcanic plug at the head of a crag-and-tail feature in the centre of Edinburgh, Edinburgh Castle is one of Scotland's leading tourist attractions. This remarkable fortress and former royal residence is visited annually by approximately one million people. Managed by Historic Scotland on behalf of the Government, the castle retains a military garrison. The site of the castle was probably first occupied in the Iron Age, although it is first documented in the 6th century. The present building dates from the mid-14th century. St Margaret, the wife of Malcolm III, died in the castle in 1093. The tiny Norman St Margaret's Chapel, built in her memory and the oldest building in the castle precinct, was spared on the several occasions the castle was razed. The royal apartments include a small wood-panelled room where in 1566 Mary, Queen of Scots gave birth to a son, who would become King James VI. The Honours of Scotland – the Crown, the Sceptre and the Sword of State – together with the Stone of Destiny, are on view in the Crown Room. Nearby is the Scottish National War Memorial, designed by Robert Lorimer shortly after World War I. Since 1861, a gun has been fired each day, except Sunday, from the castle at precisely 1.00 pm. The Castle Esplanade is the venue of the Edinburgh Military Tattoo, which takes place annually in August and comprises a programme of music, marching and historical re-enactments.

Edinburgh Zoo *City of Edinburgh* Situated 3 miles (5 km) west of the centre of Edinburgh, on Corstorphine Road, Edinburgh Zoo is owned by the Royal Zoological Society of Scotland. The society, a charitable organisation committed to the conservation of threatened wildlife worldwide, was founded in 1909. At 32 ha (80 acres) in size, with more than 1600 animals, 120 staff and almost 500,000 visitors per annum, it is Scotland's largest and most popular wildlife attraction. Edinburgh Zoo was one of the first in Britain to display animals in their natural surroundings and was completed in 1927 to the design of Sir Patrick Geddes (1854–1932). The zoo includes the world's largest penguin pool. The notable penguin colony was established by Edward Salvesen (1857–1942), who imported the birds from Antarctica on his family's whaling ships and became the first president of the society.

Edinkillie *Moray* A hamlet in a parish of the same name in Moray, Edinkillie lies on the River Divie, 8 miles (13 km) south of Forres.

Ednam *Scottish Borders* A village in a parish of the same name in the Roxburgh district of Scottish Borders, Ednam lies on the Eden Water, 3 miles (5 km) north of Kelso. It was the birthplace of James Thomson (1700–48), author of *The Seasons*, and the hymn-writer H. F. Lyte (1793–1847).

Edradour Distillery *Perth and Kinross* Established in 1825, the Edradour Distillery is located in Milton of Edradour, 2 miles (3 km) east of Pitlochry in Perth and Kinross. It takes its name from the burn that flows through it and claims to be the smallest distillery in Scotland. Edradour retains its original still house and boasts the only old-style refrigerator wort-cooler still in use today.

Edradynate *Perth and Kinross* An estate in Strathtay, Perth and Kinross, Edradynate lies on the north side of the River Tay, 3 miles (5 km) northeast of Aberfeldy.

Edrom *Scottish Borders* A village of Berwickshire in Scottish Borders, Edrom lies near the Whiteadder Water, 3 miles (5 km) northeast of Duns. In Edrom churchyard are the remains of a fine Norman chancel arch from a church built in the early 12th century by Thor Longus.

Edzell *Angus* A village and resort between Strathmore and the Howe of the Mearns in Angus, Edzell lies between the Whishop Burn and the River North Esk 6 miles (10 km) north of Brechin. The original village of Edzell, which stood near Edzell Castle and the old kirkyard, appears in the written 13th-century records of Arbroath Abbey as Edale or Adele. The present village was previously known as Slateford, describing a crossing over the North Esk. When the new church was built by Lord Panmure in 1818, Slateford became known as Edzell. The Dalhousie Arch which straddles the road at the entrance to the village, was built by tenants of the Dalhousie Estate in 1889 to commemorate the deaths of the Earl and Countess of Dalhousie, who had been held in high esteem. Buildings of historic and architectural interest include the Inglis Memorial Hall, gifted to the village in 1898 by Colonel Robert Inglis, head of the London Stock Exchange, who had it built in memory of his parents. Bank House in the High Street was originally the British Linen Bank in which James Guthrie, poet and banker, lived and worked. Guthrie, who was appointed by the Union Bank to start a branch in Edzell, took an active interest in the welfare of the village, introducing gas, establishing markets and presiding over the Highland Games. A suspension bridge known as the Shakkin' Brig was built over the North Esk in 1900, and a golf club was established in 1895. Edzell Muir and Pirner's Brig are favourite picnic spots, and walks follow the river from Gannochy Bridge to the Rocks of Solitude.

Edzell Castle *Angus* The ruined castle of Edzell stands close to the village of Edzell, 5 miles (8 km) north of Brechin in Angus. It dates from the early 16th century, when the L-plan tower section was built. Additions were made in the early 17th century, but it is generally regarded that the work was never finished as the northeast section is incomplete rather than ruined. There have been various owners of the castle, which is now retained by the descendants of the Earl of Dalhousie and maintained by Historic Scotland. Various artefacts within the castle are of interest, but the main attraction is the magnificent garden.

Egilsay *Orkney* The island of Egilsay, with a population of 37 in 2001, lies in the Orkney Islands to the east of the larger island of Rousay, from which it is separated by Rousay Sound. Extending to 581 ha (1435 acres), the island had a population of 190 in 1840. Its most noted landmark is the ruined 12th-century Church of St Magnus with its 15-m (49-ft) round tower. A monument nearby commemorates the murder of St Magnus here in 1117.

Eglinton Castle *North Ayrshire* Eglinton Castle is situated a mile (1.5 km) southeast of Kilwinning next to the River Lugton in North Ayrshire. It was built in 1796 by John Paterson for Hugh Montgomerie (1739–1819), 12th Earl of Eglinton, a member of the Seton family. The new building replaced a 17th-century castle that had previously occupied the site. The castle was ruined by the 1920s and used for commando training during World War II.

Eididh nan Clach Geala *Highland* A mountain in Wester Ross to the southeast of Ullapool and north of Loch Glascarnoch, Eididh nan Clach Geala rises to a height of 927 m (3401 ft). On the summit there are two cairns, the northwest one being the true summit. Just below this on the northwest side, white quartzite boulders can be found, possibly the 'web of white stones' that gives the mountain its Gaelic name.

Eigg *Highland* An island of the Small Isles in the Inner Hebrides, Eigg lies over 7 miles (11 km) southwest of Mallaig on the mainland of Highland Council area. It is separated from the island of Rum by the Sound of Rum, and from the island of Muck by the Sound of Eigg. Its area is 2967 ha (7329 acres) and its highest point is the prominent conical peak of An Sgurr (393 m/1291 ft), the largest residual mass of columnar pitchstone lava in the UK. The low-lying ground to the south overlies basalt, while the northern cliffs are of sandstone that erodes into curious shapes at the Camas Sgiotaig beach, renowned for its 'singing' sands. In 1840 the fossilised remains of a 180-million-year-old plesiosaur were discovered in shales in the northeast corner of the island. The island's chief settlements are Kildonnan, Galmisdale, Cleadale and Laig on the Bay of Laig. The Macdonalds of Eigg sold the island in 1829 and successive absentee landowners held the island until 1997, when it was purchased by the community. The population of Eigg has fallen to its present level of 67 from a total of nearly 550 in the 1840s. At Kildonnan an ancient Celtic cross slab stands near the ruins of a 14th-century church that was built on the site of a monastery founded by St Donan in the 7th century. There are ferry links with the other Small Isles and the mainland from Galmisdale. Kenneth MacLeod, composer of songs such as *The Road to the Isles*, was born on Eigg in 1872.

Eigheach, Loch *Perth and Kinross* A loch on Rannoch Moor in highland Perth and Kinross, Loch Eigheach lies on the River Gaur midway between Loch Laidon in the west and Loch Rannoch in the east. It receives the Allt Eigheach from the north. The loch has been artificially enlarged as part of the Tummel–Garry hydro-electric scheme.

Eil, Loch *Highland* A sea loch in southwest Highland Council area, Loch Eil extends nearly 7 miles (11 km) from west to east, opening into the northern end of Loch Linnhe at the southern end of the Caledonian Canal and opposite Fort William. It gives its name, Locheil, to the style of the chiefs of the Clan Cameron.

Eildon Hills *Scottish Borders* Surrounded by prosperous farming country, the legacy of 18th- and 19th-century farm improvement, the three volcanic peaks of the Eildon Hills rise to a height of 422 m (1385 ft) to the south of Melrose in the middle Tweed valley of Scottish Borders. The eroded remnants of a volcanic vent dating from the Carboniferous period (360–286 million years ago), the Eildons are capped by an Iron Age fort and a geographical indicator. In legend, the area around the Eildon Hills is associated with King Arthur, and the wizard Michael Scott (c.1175–c.1234), who is attributed with the splitting of the Eildon Hills.

Eileach an Naoimh *Argyll and Bute* The southernmost of the Garvellachs, a group of islands in the Firth of Lorn, Argyll and Bute, Eileach an Naoimh is a narrow island a mile (1.5 km) in length, with an area of 56 ha (138 acres). Now uninhabited, there are the remains of beehive cells and a monastery established in the 6th century by St Brendan.

Eilean a' Bhuic *Highland* Eilean a' Bhuic is one of the smaller islands of the Summer Isles, a group of islands located off the western coast of Highland Council area. Lying between Eilean Fada Mòr and Sgeir nam Feusgan, the island's name is derived from the Gaelic for 'buck island'.

Eilean a' Char *Highland* An island of the Summer Isles, a group of islands off the coast of Wester Ross, Highland Council area, Eilean a' Char lies to the north of Tanera Beg. Its name is derived from the Gaelic for 'island of seal flesh'.

Eilean a' Chleirich The Gaelic name for Priest Island in Wester Ross.

Eilean Balnagowan *Highland* A small island in Loch Linnhe, Eilean Balnagowan lies off the coast of Appin to the southwest of the mouth of Loch Leven and Cuil Bay.

Eilean Beag *Highland* The smallest of the Crowlin Islands between Skye and the mainland, Eilean Beag lies to the north of Eilean Meadhonach. Extending over an area of only 3 ha (7.5 acres), it is linked to Eilean Meadhonach by a reef at low tide.

Eilean Bhacasaigh The Gaelic name for Vacasay Island in the Western Isles.

Eilean Bhearnaraigh The Gaelic name for Berneray, to the north of North Uist, in the Western Isles.

Eilean Chaluim Chille *Western Isles* An uninhabited island in the Outer Hebrides, Eilean Chaluim Chille lies at the mouth of Loch Erisort on the eastern coast of the Isle of Lewis. At the southern end of the island lie the remains of St Columba's Church (Gael: *Eaglais Chalium Chille*).

Eileanan Chearabhaig The Gaelic name for the Keiravagh Islands in the Western Isles.

Eilean Chearstaigh The Gaelic name for Eilean Kearstay in the Western Isles.

Eilean Choinaid *Highland* An island in the Summer Isles group off the coast of Wester Ross, Highland Council area, Eilean Choinaid lies between Eilean Fada Mòr and Eilean a' Char. Its name is dervied from the Gaelic for 'big green slab'.

Eilean Donan *Highland* A rocky islet at the mouth of Loch Duich in Wester Ross, Highland Council area, Eilean Donan is the site of the picturesque castle of the Clan Macrae, which dates from the 13th century. Garrisoned by Spanish Jacobite troops in the abortive rebellion of 1719, Eilean Donan Castle was blown up by an English man o' war but later restored. It incorporates a memorial to the Clan Macrae who held it as hereditary constables on behalf of the Mackenzies of Kintail. The islet is joined to the mainland by a causeway.

Eilean Dubh Beag *Argyll and Bute* Located immediately to the north of the larger Eilean Dubh Mòr, in the Firth of Lorn, Argyll and Bute, Eilean Dubh Beag comprises a single hill that rises to a height of 40 m (131 ft). This uninhabited island has an area of 15 ha (37 acres).

Eilean Dubh Mòr *Argyll and Bute* Located between the Garvellachs and Luing, in the Firth of Lorn, Argyll and Bute, Eilean Dubh Mòr is an uninhabited island with an area of 65 ha (161 acres). It is essentially a single mound-shaped hill (53 m/174 ft) with a promontory to the northeast. To the north and attached at low tide by a rocky outcrop is the smaller island of Eilean Dubh Beag.

Eilean Fada Mòr *Highland* One of the Summer Isles, Eilean Fada Mòr lies off the coast of Wester Ross, Highland Council area. The island is linked to Tanera Mòr by a bank of fine coral sand that is visible only at low tide. Its name is derived from the Gaelic for 'big long island'.

Eilean Iubhaird The Gaelic name for Eilean Iuvard in the Western Isles.

Eilean Iuvard *Western Isles* An island at the mouth of Loch Shell on the east coast of Lewis in the Outer Hebrides, Eilean Iuvard (Gael: *Eilean Iubhaird* or *Eilean Iubhard*) lies a mile (1.5 km) south of Lemreway in the Park district. The island extends to 125 ha (309 acres) with high ground at opposite ends rising in the east to 76 m (249 ft). Maintaining a small population in the past, it is today uninhabited. Prince Charles Edward Stewart (Bonnie Prince Charlie) spent four days here in 1746 while attempting to escape to the continent.

Eilean Kearstay *Western Isles* An uninhabited island in East Loch Roag, Eilean Kearstay (Gael: *Eilean Chearstaigh*) lies at the southeast tip of Great Bernera a mile (1.5 km) west of Callanish on the Isle of Lewis. The island extends to 77 ha (190 acres) and rises to 37 m (121 ft) at a point towards the north of the island marked by a conspicuous cairn. In 1990 the island was sold by the laird of Great Bernera to two Australians who celebrated with a party on the island that included among the guests the Australian consul. Within three years the island had been sold once again.

Eilean Leathan A small island, the largest of the Stack Islands in the Outer Hebrides, Eilean Leathan is located at the southeast end of the Sound of Barra, a half-mile (1 km) south of Eriskay. The island rises to 45 m (147 ft) towards the south, close to Weaver's Castle. Also known as Castle Stalker, Caisteal a' Bhrebider or Caisteal an Reubadair, this small square ruined tower was home to a notorious pirate called MacNeil who raided ships and looted wrecks.

Eilean Macaskin *Argyll and Bute* The long narrow island of Eilean Macaskin lies at the entrance to Loch Craignish in Argyll and Bute. Covering an area of 50 ha (124 acres), this island has been uninhabited since the late 19th century, except for the sheep that graze its eastern side. Its western side is dominated by the steep sides to the island's central ridge that reaches a height of 65 m (213 ft). A line of skerries extends from the south of the island into the Sound of Jura.

Eilean Meadhonach *Highland* The second-largest of the Crowlin Islands between Skye and the mainland, Eilean Meadhonach extends over an area of 50 ha (124 acres). It is separated from Eilean Mòr by a narrow channel that is only 50 m (164 ft) wide at high tide.

Eilean Molach The Gaelic name for Ellen's Isle.

Eilean Molach *Western Isles* An uninhabited islet of the Western Isles, Eilean Molach lies off the headland of Aird Mhòr Mangurstadh on the western coastline of the Isle of Lewis, 4 miles (6.5 km) west of Timsgearraidh (or Timsgarry).

Eilean Mòr *Highland* The easternmost of the three Crowlin Islands between Skye and the mainland, Eilean Mòr extends over an area of 170 ha (420 acres). Largely used as grazing for sheep, the island rises to a height of 114 m (374 ft) at Meall a' Chois.

Eilean Mòr *Western Isles* The largest of the remote Flannan Islands, Eilean Mòr rises to 88 m (288 ft) immediately to the northwest of Eilean Tighe and 21 miles (33 km) northwest of Gallan Head on the west coast of the Isle of Lewis. The Flannan Isles Lighthouse lies on its northern shore, the island being uninhabited since the lighthouse was automated in 1971.

Eilean Mullagrach *Highland* A small island of the Summer Isles in Wester Ross, Eilean Mullagrach is the most northerly of the group and extends to 73 ha (180 acres).

Eilean na Cille *Western Isles* A small low-lying island in Bagh nam Faoilean to the southeast of Benbecula, Eilean na Cille lies at the end of the B891, which is conveyed from Benbecula over a series of causeways and islets. The road terminates at the jetty at Peter's Port.

Eilean nan Ron *Highland* An uninhabited island on the north coast of Sutherland, Eilean nan Ron lies just to the east of the mouth of Tongue Bay, 4.5 miles (7 km) northwest of Bettyhill and 6 miles (10 km) northeast of

Tongue. The island is just over a mile (1.5 km) in length and rises steeply to 76 m (249 ft). Formerly populated, the island is now a Site of Special Scientific Interest (SSSI), with its rocky shore supporting a breeding colony of grey seals. The smaller islands of Eilean Iosal and Meall Holm (or Meall Thailm) lie immediately to the northwest.

Eilean Odhar *Argyll and Bute* A rocky islet off the north coast of the island of Coll in the Inner Hebrides, Eilean Odhar lies to the west of Feall Bay.

Eilean Ornsay *Argyll and Bute* An uninhabited rocky island off the west coast of the island of Coll in the Inner Hebrides, Eilean Ornsay lies near the entrance to Loch Eatharna and is joined to the main island at low tides.

Eilean Rarsaidh *Highland* A small islet in Loch Hourn in the Lochaber district of Highland Council area, Eilean Rarsaidh lies off the northern shore of the loch, 2 miles (3 km) west of the settlement of Arnisdale.

Eilean Righ *Argyll and Bute* The largest island in Loch Craignish, a sea loch on the coast of Argyll and Bute, Eilean Righ has an area of 86 ha (213 acres). Taking its name from the Gaelic for 'island of the king', there are the remains of two Iron Age forts. Sir Reginald Johnston (1874–1938), tutor to Pu Yi, the last Emperor of China, owned the island and spent his retirement here.

Eilean Tighe *Western Isles* The smaller of the two main islands in the remote Flannan Islands group, Eilean Tighe rises to 59 m (193 ft) immediately to the southeast of Eilean Mòr and 21 miles (33 km) northwest of Gallan Head on the west coast of the Isle of Lewis.

Eilean Thoraidh The Gaelic name for Torray in the Western Isles.

Eilein, Loch an *Highland* A small loch in Rothiemurchus Forest, Badenoch, Loch an Eilein lies 3 miles (5 km) south of Aviemore. There is a visitor centre with exhibitions on the management of native Scots pine and on a small island stand the remains of a 15th-century castle.

Einacleit The Gaelic name for Enaclate in the Western Isles.

Einich, Loch *Highland* A loch in a spectacular setting in the Cairngorm Mountains, Loch Einich lies at the head of the U-shaped glaciated valley of Gleann Einich. Cairn Toul and Braeriach rise to the east.

Eireasort, Loch The Gaelic name for Loch Erisort in the Western Isles.

Eirisgeigh The Gaelic name for Eriskay in the Western Isles.

Eishken *Western Isles* An estate settlement of the Park district of Lewis in the Outer Hebrides, Eishken (Gael: *Eisgein*) lies on the north shore of Loch Shell at the centre of the Eishken Estate, 14 miles (22 km) southwest of Stornoway.

Eishort, Loch *Highland* A sea loch on the coast of the isle of Skye, Loch Eishort forms an inlet to the north of the Sleat peninsula.

Elcho Castle *Perth and Kinross* Located at Easter Elcho near Rhynd in Perth and Kinross, Elcho Castle was built in the latter half of the 16th century for the Wemyss family, whose descendants still own it, although it is now in the care of Historic Scotland. Overlooking the River Tay, the tower-shaped castle has many original features, including the ruins of the courtyard, the chapel and a round tower with a kiln.

Elderslie *Renfrewshire* A settlement in Renfrewshire, west-central Scotland, Elderslie lies 4 miles (6.5 km) west of Paisley. Best known as the birthplace of Sir William Wallace *c.*1272, it developed in the 19th century in association with the Glenpatrick paper mill, the Gleniffer distillery, coal mining and the manufacture of textiles. Carpet making eventually became an important industry. Notable buildings include the early 19th-century Wallace Tavern, the Moat House (1903) and the Library, a former school dating from 1799.

Eldrig, Loch *Dumfries and Galloway* A small loch in Dumfries and Galloway, Loch Eldrig lies in the parish of Penninghame, nearly 5 miles (8 km) west of Newton Stewart. Eldrig Hill rises to 98 m (322 ft) to the west and Eldrig Moss extends southwards.

Eldrig Loch *Dumfries and Galloway* A small loch in Dumfries and Galloway, Eldrig Loch lies 10 miles (16 km) west of Newton Stewart. Eldrig Fell rises to 226 m (741 ft) to the south and the Loch Strand links the loch with the Tarf Water to the southwest.

Electric Brae, the *South Ayrshire* Located 3 miles (5 km) northwest of Maybole and a mile (1.5 km) south of Dunure in South Ayrshire, the Electric Brae or Croy Brae is a well-known stretch of road where the configuration of the land gives the impression that a vehicle can freewheel uphill.

Elgin *Moray* The administrative centre of Moray, the royal burgh of Elgin lies on a bend of the River Lossie, 26 miles (42 km) east of Inverness. Known locally as a city because of its ruined cathedral, Elgin was named after Helgyn, the Norse general who founded it in the 10th century. It was one of the first Scots burghs created in the 12th century by David I and received a further royal charter from Alexander II. In 1224, Elgin became the cathedral seat of the bishopric of Moray when the Cathedral of the Holy Trinity was finally given a permanent site. Occupying a strategic site on the route from Aberdeen to Inverness, its ruined castle was the reputed scene of the murder of Duncan I by Macbeth in 1040. The town has a classic medieval layout with a high street and associated burgage plots stretching between the castle and cathedral and widening out in the middle to contain the market and high kirk. On the castle motte at the west end a monument to the Duke of Gordon (1839) now dominates the skyline. Most of Elgin's buildings were erected after the suppression of the Jacobite Risings of the 18th century, but a few earlier structures include Alexander Leslie's 17th-century Tower, Braco's Banking House (1684) and Thunderton House, built in the 16th century as a 'Great Lodging' of the Scottish kings to replace the castle. The first cathedral was destroyed by fire in 1270 and its successor was razed to the ground in 1390 by Alexander Stewart, Earl of Buchan, better known as the Wolf of Badenoch. Fine buildings from the Georgian era include the neoclassical Gray's Hospital (1815–19) and the Elgin Institution (1830–33). Following the arrival of the railway in the mid-19th century, the size of the burgh doubled. New Elgin to the south was created as a working-class suburb, while the middle-class suburb of Bishopsmill grew up to the north. Today Elgin thrives as a centre of administration, education, tourism and trade, with agricultural service and textile industries.

Elgol *Highland* A township on the isle of Skye, Highland

Council area, Elgol lies 10 miles (16 km) southwest of Broadford at the end of a peninsula. Nearby are Prince Charlie's Cave and the Spar Cave.

Elie *Fife* A coastal resort and residential town in the East Neuk of Fife, Elie lies 2.5 miles (4 km) southwest of St Monans on the edge of a sickle-shaped bay with sandy beaches. Stretching for a mile (1.5 km) around the bay, it comprises from east to west the once separate settlements of Elie, Liberty, Williamsburgh and Earlsferry, which were united as the burgh of Elie and Earlsferry in 1929. The town takes its name from the Ailie or island of Ardross which formed a natural harbour accessible only at low tide, and in 1589 received its royal charter from James VI. Elie subsequently developed as an important centre of commerce, boat building, fishing and weaving. Its harbour, built in the 16th century, is now a haven for yachts and small craft and is one of few harbours in Scotland to be run by a private company for the people of the burgh. Elie has many interesting 17th-, 18th- and 19th-century buildings. The parish church was built by Sir William Scott of Ardross in the 1630s, prior to the disjunction of Elie from the parish of Kilconquhar in 1641. To the east overlooking Ruby Bay stand the ruins of The Lady's Tower, built as a seaside summerhouse for Janet Fall, Lady Anstruther. Elie rubies are actually small, red, semi-precious pyrope garnets which can be found on the beach, having weathered out of the Carboniferous igneous rocks. Among Elie's most famous sons is the golfer James Braid, who won the British Open Championship five times between 1901 and 1910. In addition to having two golf courses, Elie is today a centre for bowling, tennis, sailing and windsurfing.

Ellen's Isle *Stirling* A small wooded islet at the eastern end of Loch Katrine, Ellen's Isle (or Eilean Molach) lies in the shadow of Ben Venue. Often used in the distant past as a refuge by Highland fugitives, it gained a certain romantic appeal after it featured in Sir Walter Scott's *Lady of the Lake* (1810).

Elliot *Angus* A locality and former railway junction on the southern outskirts of Arbroath, Elliot lies on the A92, but the railway now passes through without stopping. Elliot Junction once connected the Dundee–Aberdeen mainline to a railway built by Fox Maule Ramsay (1801–74), 11th Earl of Dalhousie, to connect with quarries beyond Carmyllie. The junction was the scene of a rail crash on 30 December 1906 when an express hit a local train in a blizzard, killing 22 people. The station closed in 1967. Today, the Arbroath Artisan Golf Club is located at Elliot.

Elliot Water *Angus* A river in southeast Angus, the Elliot Water rises to the west of Carmyllie in the Sidlaw Hills. It flows southeastwards through Arbirlot village before entering the North Sea to the southwest of Arbroath.

Ellisland *Dumfries and Galloway* A locality in Dumfries and Galloway, Ellisland lies 6.5 miles (11 km) north-northwest of Dumfries. Before moving to Dumfries, the poet Robert Burns (1759–96) farmed Ellisland for a brief period from 1788 to 1791, and while there wrote *Tam o' Shanter* and *Auld Lang Syne*. There is an audiovisual display in the granary and nearby there are riverside walks.

Ellon *Aberdeenshire* A market town at the centre of rich farming land in eastern Aberdeenshire, Ellon is situated at a crossing of the River Ythan 17 miles (27 km) north of Aberdeen. Once the main settlement of the Pictish province of Buchan, it was the scene of courts held in the Middle Ages by the Comyn earls of Buchan who dispensed justice at the Moot or Earl's Hill, a site now marked by a monument beside the car park in Market Street. Ellon was one of the settlements burned in the so-called 'Harrying of Buchan', following the defeat of the Comyns near Oldmeldrum by Robert the Bruce in 1308. Close by is Ellon Castle, rebuilt by the 4th Earl of Aberdeen in 1780, with its terraced garden created by Bailie James Gordon in 1706. The ancient Parish Church of St Mary, bestowed on Kinloss Abbey in 1310, was superseded by a new church in 1777 that was itself renovated in 1876. The town has a library, community centre, swimming pool and sporting and recreational facilities, including an 18-hole golf course. Still a market town with associated agricultural-engineering industries, Ellon expanded in the 1970s to accommodate workers in the oil industry. The Ythan Raft Race from Ellon to Logie Buchan takes place each summer.

Elphin *Highland* A hamlet in the Assynt district of Sutherland, Highland Council area, Elphin lies 7 miles (11 km) south of Inchnadamph. Marble is quarried nearby.

Elphinstone *East Lothian* A village in East Lothian, Elphinstone lies 2 miles (3 km) south of Tranent. In 1545 the Protestant martyr George Wishart was brought to Elphinstone Tower from Ormiston before being transported to St Andrews for trial and execution.

Elrig *Dumfries and Galloway* A hamlet in Dumfries and Galloway, Elrig lies between Elrig Loch and Luce Bay, 3 miles (5 km) north of Port William. The House of Elrig was home to Gavin Maxwell (1914–69), author of *Ring of Bright Water*.

Elrig Loch *Dumfries and Galloway* A small loch in Dumfries and Galloway, Elrig Loch lies to the east of Luce Bay, 2 miles (3 km) north of Mochrum. The Old Mill Burn flows south from the loch, through the village of Elrig, to enter Luce Bay between Barr Point and Milton Point.

Elsrickle *South Lanarkshire* A small village in South Lanarkshire, Elsrickle lies 3 miles (5 km) north of Biggar at the southern end of the Pentland Hills. It was formerly known as Elridgehill.

Elvan Water *South Lanarkshire* Rising in the Lowther Hills of South Lanarkshire, Elvan Water flows east for 7 miles (11km) before joining the River Clyde a half-mile (1 km) north of Elvanfoot.

Elvanfoot *South Lanarkshire* Situated at the confluence of Elvan Water and the River Clyde southeast of Douglas at an elevation of 274 m (900 ft), Elvanfoot is arguably the first village on the Clyde, nearest its source. It developed as a road and rail junction, with a branch line to the lead mines of Leadhills and Wanlockhead operating from 1901 to 1939. It possesses a fine 19th-century church and a tollhouse that was visited by Robert Burns (1759–96).

Elwick *Orkney* The chief anchorage of the island of Shapinsay in the Orkney Islands, the village of Elwick lies at the head of Elwick Bay on the southern coast of the island. There is a ferry link with Kirkwall from here and nearby is the Scottish baronial-style Balfour Castle, built in 1848 by John Balfour of Trenabie on Westray to a design by the architect David Bryce.

Embo *Highland* A former fishing village on the east coast of Sutherland, Highland Council area, Embo lies 2.5 miles (4 km) northeast of Dornoch. An anchor on the beach probably came from the Prussian barque *Vesta* that was wrecked here in 1876.

Enaclate *Western Isles* A small crofting township on the west shore of Little Loch Roag, Eneclate (Gael: *Einacleit*) is located in western Lewis in the Outer Hebrides, 7 miles (11 km) southwest of Callanish.

Endrick Water *Stirling* A river in Stirling Council area, the Endrick Water rises in headstreams in the Gargunnock Hills to the south of Kippen. Formed by the confluence of the Backside and Burnfoot burns, it flows south towards the Carron Valley Reservoir before turning west to meander nearly 30 miles (48 km) past Fintry, Balfron and Drymen. It eventually enters the southeast end of Loch Lomond, its largest tributary being the Blane Water. The valley through which it passes is known as Strathendrick or 'Sweet Innerdale'.

Enoch *Dumfries and Galloway* A locality in the Rhinns of Galloway, Dumfries and Galloway, Enoch lies nearly 2 miles (3 km) northeast of Portpatrick.

Enoch, Loch *Dumfries and Galloway* A small loch in Galloway Forest Park, Dumfries and Galloway, Loch Enoch lies to the east of the summit of Merrick. It is the source of the Pulskaih Burn and the Eglin Lane.

Enochdhu *Perth and Kinross* A settlement at the head of Strath Ardle, Perth and Kinross, Enochdhu (also Ennochdhu) lies on the River Ardle, 6 miles (10 km) northeast of Pitlochry. An early 19th-century house here was converted into the Kindrogan Field Centre in 1963 for the Scottish Field Studies Association.

Ensay *Western Isles* A significant island in the Sound of Harris, Ensay (Gael: *Easaigh*) lies to the north of Killegray and 2 miles (3 km) west of Leverburgh on Harris. The island rises to 49 m (160 ft) and extends to 186 ha (460 acres). Until the 1970s it supported a small number of people who were latterly associated with the seasonal grazing of sheep. Although the island is still used in the summer for grazing, there is now no permanent resident population. The Edwardian Ensay House, once home to the Stewart family, was renovated in 1991 as holiday accommodation. To the north is the 12th-century Christ Church chapel, also renovated and occasionally used for services by the Scottish Episcopal Church. There is a small jetty on the southeast shore of the island.

Enterkin Burn *Dumfries and Galloway* A stream in Dumfries and Galloway, the Enterkin Burn rises on the slopes of Lowther Hill. It flows southwards for 6 miles (10 km) to join the River Nith at Enterkinfoot.

Enterkinfoot *Dumfries and Galloway* A village in Durisdeer parish, Dumfries and Galloway, Enterkinfoot lies at the foot of the Enterkin Burn, 6 miles (10 km) north of Thornhill.

Eoligarry *Western Isles* A scattered hamlet on the Eoligarry peninsula in northern Barra in the Outer Hebrides, Eoligarry (Gael: *Eolaigearraidh*) lies in the lee of Ben Eoligarry 2 miles (3 km) north of Ardmore. The settlement extends across a network of minor roads and has a pier on the Sound of Fuday, which was once the terminal of the ferry from Eriskay. Barra's airport, Cockle Strand, lies on Tràigh Mòr 1.25 miles (2.5 km) to the southwest.

Eorodale *Western Isles* One of a collection of crofting townships in the Ness district at the northern tip of the island of Lewis in the Outer Hebrides, Eorodale (Gael: *Eorodal*) lies immediately to the south-southeast of Adabrock, a half-mile (1 km) south-southwest of Port of Ness.

Eoropie *Western Isles* The northernmost of several closely associated crofting townships lying in the Ness district at the northern tip of Lewis in the Outer Hebrides, Eoropie (Gael: *Eoropaidh*) is located immediately to the northwest of Fivepenny, a mile (1.5 km) south of the Butt of Lewis. The restored medieval Teampall Mholuaidh lies a short walk to the northeast.

Eorsa *Argyll and Bute* An island in Loch na Keal, a sea loch on the west coast of Mull, Argyll and Bute, Eorsa is uninhabited except for grazing sheep. The island, which occupies an area of 101 ha (250 acres), was used as a deep-water naval anchorage for the Grand Fleet during World War I.

Erchless Castle *Highland* A castle situated at the foot of Strathglass, near the settlement of Struy by the Rivers Glass and Farrar, 8 miles (13 km) southwest of Beauly, Highland Council area, Erchless is the ancestral home of the Chisholm family. It was built in the 17th century as an L-plan tower house and underwent much alteration in the 19th century.

Eriboll *Highland* A township in northern Sutherland, Highland Council area, Eriboll lies on the east shore of Loch Eriboll, a sea loch that opens out into the Pentland Firth.

Eriboll, Loch *Western Isles* A sizeable and deep sea loch on the north coast of Scotland, Loch Eriboll is located in northwest Sutherland 4 miles (6.5 km) southeast of Durness and 9 miles (14 km) west of Tongue. On its western shore is Laid, a linear crofting township. In the late 19th century lime was produced from the local Durness limestone at Ard Neakie on the eastern shore and limekilns remain extant. The German U-Boat fleet surrendered in the loch in May 1945. The loch marks the northern extent of the Moine Thrust, and part of the eastern shore of the loch is protected as a Site of Special Scientific Interest (SSSI) for its geological importance.

Ericht, Loch *Highland/Perth and Kinross* A loch at an altitude of 351 m (1153 ft) above sea level in the Grampians, Loch Ericht straddles the boundary between Highland and Perth and Kinross council areas. It occupies a valley that is aligned northeast–southwest and is 15 miles (24 km) long and about 0.75 mile (1 km) wide. With a surface area of 18.6 sq. km (7.2 sq. miles), Loch Ericht is the tenth-largest freshwater loch in Scotland. Ben Alder rises to 1148 m (3766 ft) to the west, and at the loch's northern end is the village of Dalwhinnie. From its dammed southern end the loch is linked to a power station on Loch Rannoch by the 4-mile/6.5-km-long River Ericht.

Ericht, River *Perth and Kinross* A stream in eastern Perth and Kinross, the River Ericht is formed at the meeting of the Black Water and the River Ardle 5 miles (8 km) north of Blairgowrie. It meanders southwards for 10 miles (16 km) through Blairgowrie and Rattray before joining the River Isla 2 miles (3 km) northeast of Coupar Angus. Its principal tributary is the Lornty Burn.

Ericht, River *Perth and Kinross* A 4-mile/6.5-km-long stream in Highland Perth and Kinross, the River Ericht links the dammed southern end of Loch Ericht to a power station on the north side of Loch Rannoch. The river enters Loch Rannoch at Bridge of Ericht.

Erisgeir *Argyll and Bute* Located 2 miles (3 km) northwest of the headland of Rubha nan Goirteanan and 3 miles (5 km) south of the island of Little Colonsay, Erisgeir is a small rocky islet lying off the western coast of Mull, Argyll and Bute. Relatively flat, it is occasionally used for sheep grazing.

Eriskay *Western Isles* Situated in the Outer Hebrides between South Uist and Barra, the island of Eriskay (Gael: *Eirisgeigh*) is perhaps best known for the songs it has inspired, including the *Eriskay Love Lilt*, and its association with Bonnie Prince Charlie, who first set foot on Scottish soil here on 23 July 1745 when he was put ashore from the French ship *Du Teillay*. Sir Compton MacKenzie's book *Whisky Galore*, which was later filmed on the neighbouring island of Barra, was inspired by the sinking of the 12,000-tonne steamship *The Politician* in the Sound of Eriskay on 5 February 1941 en route to New York from Liverpool. Its cargo of 264,000 bottles of whisky was 'rescued' by the islanders, some of whom were later arrested and imprisoned in Inverness. A barren island of rocky moorland, Eriskay has an area of 759 ha (1862 acres) and rises to a height of 185 m (607 ft) at Ben Scrien. Haunn (also Haun), the chief settlement, lies at the head of a shallow bay on the north coast which is the terminal for the car-ferry link with South Uist. The distinctive Eriskay pony that stands at 12 to 13 hands high was used to carry peat and seaweed. The people of Eriskay fish for prawn and lobster, and produce shawls and jerseys with local patterns. A £9.4 million causeway, linking Eriskay with South Uist, was opened in 2001.

Erisort, Loch *Western Isles* A sea loch on the east coast of the isle of Lewis in the Western Isles, Loch Erisort (Gael: *Loch Eireasort*) extends 8 miles (13 km) from west to east, opening out into the Minch, 7 miles (11 km) south of Stornoway.

Erncrogo Loch *Dumfries and Galloway* A small loch in Dumfries and Galloway, Erncrogo Loch lies a mile (1.5 km) to the east of Crossmichael. It is linked to the River Dee to the west by the Mill Burn.

Erraid *Argyll and Bute* A small island to the west of the Ross of Mull, Erraid lies at the southern end of the Sound of Iona and is separated from the island of Mull by the Sound of Mull. An uninhabited island of approximately 3 sq. km (1 sq. mile) in area, it is referred to in the novel *Kidnapped* (1886) by Robert Louis Stevenson (1850–94).

Errochty, Glen *Perth and Kinross* The basin of Loch Errochty and the Errochty Water in Highland Perth and Kinross, Glen Errochty extends 12 miles (19 km) from west to east, joining Glen Garry between Blair Atholl and Calvine.

Errochty, Loch *Perth and Kinross* Located 4 miles (6.5 km) north-northeast of Kinloch Rannoch in Perth and Kinross, this reservoir forms part of the Tummel Hydro-Electric Power Scheme.

Errol *Perth and Kinross* The second-largest settlement in the Carse of Gowrie, Errol lies on the Firth of Tay, 10 miles (16 km) east of Perth and 10 miles (16 km) southwest of Dundee. The parish of Errol was the traditional fiefdom of the earls of Errol, and the kirkton of Errol achieved burgh status in 1648. It retains an unusual winding main street, and several buildings with clay wall construction. Described as the 'Cathedral of the Carse', the square-towered parish church of Errol, built by James Gillespie Graham in 1831–3, dominates the skyline. The kirkyard of the old parish church remains and nearby is one of the early Free Church Disruption kirks of 1843. A fountain and market cross can be found in the square at the centre of the village. Many of the 19th-century buildings are constructed using local bricks made from estuarine clays laid down in the carse after the last Ice Age. The Errol Brick Company continues the 200-year tradition of brick making at Inchcoonans to the northwest of Errol. A former wartime airfield to the northeast of the village is now occupied by an industrial estate that includes the Tayreed Company, which supplies thatch for roofing from nearby reed beds on the Tay estuary. These reed beds were planted in the 1780s by an enlightened landowner in an attempt to prevent erosion of the river bank. Errol station to the north of Errol, which operated between 1842 and 1985, was reopened in 1990 as a railway heritage centre by the Errol Station Trust.

Ersary An alternative name for Earsary in the Western Isles.

Erskine *Renfrewshire* A small town on the south side of the River Clyde, Erskine is situated 5 miles (8 km) north of Paisley. Developed by the Scottish Special Housing Association, it was one of the first postwar new towns. Erskine House (1828) to the northwest of the town, home of the lords of Blantyre, became the Princess Louise Hospital for Limbless Sailors and Soldiers during World War I and is today a hospital for ex-servicemen and women. Inscribed in the Old Erskine Parish Church (1813–14) is the motto of the Blantyre family: *Sola juvat virtus* ('Virtue alone delights'). The lands of Erskine were first owned by Henry de Erskine in the 13th century. Sir John Hamilton of Orbiston held the estate in the 17th century and in 1703 the property was acquired by the Blantyre family.

Erskine Bridge *Renfrewshire* The Erskine Bridge crosses the River Clyde near the villages of Erskine to the south and Old Kilpatrick to the north, linking Renfrewshire to West Dunbartonshire. It extends the M898 from the M8 on the south to the A82 (Great Western Road) on the north. Built between 1967 and 1971 by Freeman Fox, it was opened by the Princess Royal on 2 July 1971, and was carrying approximately 7000 crossings per day until the tolls were lifted in April 2006, a figure that has held steady since the late 1980s. This box-girder bridge with cable stays is 524 m (1720 ft) in length, not including the two approach spans of 68 m (224 ft) each. The masts of the main span are 38 m (125 ft) high, while the steelwork weighs some 11,000 tonnes and runs over 1310 m (4300 ft).

Esk, Glen *Angus* A glen in the Braes of Angus, Glen Esk occupies the valley of the River North Esk. The village of Edzell lies at the mouth of the glen.

Esk, Loch *Highland* A small corrie loch in the Grampians, Loch Esk lies near the summit of Broad Cairn and is a source of one of the headstreams that form the River South Esk.

Esk, River *Dumfries and Galloway* A river of Dumfries and Galloway that crosses into Cumbria in England, the River Esk is formed at the junction of the Black Esk, which rises on the northeast slope of Jock's Shoulder, and the White Esk, which rises on the southern slopes of

Ettrick Pen. The two headstreams meet in Castle O'er Forest at the southeast corner of Eskdalemuir before continuing as the River Esk through Bentpath and Langholm, then on for a total length of 22 miles (35 km) on its way to the head of the Solway Firth. Its principal tributaries are Megget Water, Wauchope Water, Ewes Water, Tarras Water and Liddel Water.

Esk, River *East Lothian* The River Esk is one of the main rivers of East Lothian. Formed by the merging of the River North Esk with the River South Esk, the River Esk is formed a mile (1.5 km) north of the settlement of Dalkeith. Flowing northwards to the Firth of Forth, it passes the settlements of Whitecraig and Inveresk before entering the firth at Musselburgh.

Eskdale *Dumfries and Galloway* The easternmost of the three historic districts of Dumfriesshire, Eskdale comprises the basin of the River Esk in Dumfries and Galloway. The parishes of Eskdalemuir, Westkirk, Langholm and Canonbie all lie within Eskdale which was until 1455 the domain of the Douglas family. Feudal powers of regality, exercised until 1747, passed from the Douglases through the Maxwells to the Scotts of Buccleuch.

Eskdalemuir *Dumfries and Galloway* A locality in Eskdale, Dumfries and Galloway, Eskdalemuir lies in the Southern Uplands, 14 miles (22 km) northwest of Langholm. Situated within the Eskdalemuir Forest, it has a meteorological station that also monitors the geomagnetic field in the UK. Scotland's first Buddhist temple, the Tibetan Samye Ling, was established here in 1967.

Ess of Glenlatterach *Moray* A waterfall on the Leanoch Burn in Moray, the Ess of Glenlatterach lies 4 miles (6.5 km) south of Elgin.

Essan, Loch *Stirling* A small loch in the Breadalbane Hills, Stirling Council area, Loch Essan lies 2 miles (3 km) to the north of Loch Dochart. It is the source of the Allt Essan, which flows southeastwards past Auchessan to join the River Dochart opposite the north-facing slopes of Ben More.

Estra-Hanet An alternative name for Annandale in Dumfries and Galloway.

Ethie Castle *Angus* Once the property of Arbroath Abbey and a residence of Cardinal Beaton in the 1530s and 1540s, Ethie Castle lies 2.5 miles (4 km) southeast of Inverkeilor in Angus. The property was granted to Sir Robert Carnegie of Kinnaird in 1549, eventually passing to Sir John Carnegie, who was created Lord Lour (1639) and Earl of Ethie (1647). These titles were later exchanged for others, including the Earl of Northesk and Baron Rosehill and Inglismaldie, and the property remained in the Carnegie family until the 20th century.

Ethie Haven *Angus* An old fishing hamlet on the North Sea coast of Angus, Ethie Haven lies in a secluded location at the south end of Lunan Bay, 6 miles (10 km) northeast of Arbroath. Once a thriving fishing village occupied by line fishers and salmon netters, Ethie Haven is now a quiet retreat with renovated holiday homes. To the south stands Ethie Castle.

Etive, Loch *Argyll and Bute* A sea loch between the Lorn and Benderloch districts of Argyll and Bute, Loch Etive is fed from the northeast by the River Etive which meets the loch at Kinlochetive. The loch extends 10 miles (16 km) southwest towards Bonawe, where it turns west for 8 miles (13 km) before entering the Firth of Lorn at Ledaig Point via the Connel rapids and Ardmucknish Bay.

Etive, River *Highland* A river in southern Highland Council area, the River Etive rises out of Lochan Mathair Etive on Rannoch Moor. It flows just over 15 miles (24 km) west-southwest past Kingshouse to enter the head of Loch Etive. On its passage through Glen Etive, it passes the high peaks of Buachaille Etive Mòr at the eastern entrance to Glen Coe.

Ettrick *Scottish Borders* A settlement in a parish of the same name in Scottish Borders, Ettrick once formed a remote, self-contained community hemmed in by hills 16 miles (26 km) southwest of Selkirk. The name is also given to the more extensive Ettrick Forest, which once covered most of the former county of Selkirk between Tweeddale and Teviotdale. A favourite hunting ground of the Scottish kings, grants of land in Ettrick Forest were made to the great Border abbeys. The poet James Hogg, known as the 'Ettrick Shepherd' (1770–1835), was born here and lies buried in the churchyard.

Ettrick Bay *North Ayrshire* Located on the western side of the island of Bute and overlooking the Kyles of Bute to Ardlamont Point, Ettrick Bay forms a wide inlet, 3 miles (5 km) west of Rothesay.

Ettrick Pen *Dumfries and Galloway* A summit in the Southern Uplands, Ettrick Pen rises to a height of 692 m (2270 ft) on the border between Dumfries and Galloway and Scottish Borders. The headwaters of the White Esk rise on its slopes.

Ettrick Water *Scottish Borders* A river of Scottish Borders, the Ettrick Water rises on Capel Fell to the east of Moffat. It flows nearly 33 miles (53 km) northeastwards through Ettrick, Ettrickbridge and Selkirk to join the River Tweed 3 miles (5 km) west of Melrose.

Ettrickbridge *Scottish Borders* A settlement in the Ettrick district of Scottish Borders, Ettrickbridge lies on the Ettrick Water 7 miles (11 km) southwest of Selkirk. The village has a primary school, inn, post office and sports facilities.

Euchan Water *Dumfries and Galloway* A stream in Dumfries and Galloway, the Euchan Water rises on the slope of Blacklorg Hill to the south of New Cumnock. It flows just over 9 miles (14 km) northeastwards to join the River Nith at Sanquhar.

Euchar, River *Argyll and Bute* A river of Lorn in Argyll and Bute, the Euchar flows west and northwest from Loch Scamadale, through Glen Euchar before emptying into Loch Feochan at Kilninver, 5 miles (8 km) south of Oban.

Eun, Loch nan *Perth and Kinross* A small loch in the Grampians in Highland Perth and Kinross, Loch nan Eun lies to the west of the Glen Shee ski slopes between the peaks of Beinn Lutharn and Mam nan Carn.

Euphort, Loch *Western Isles* A sea loch that penetrates deeply from the east coast of North Uist, Loch Euphort (also Loch Euphoirt) lies 3 miles (5 km) south of Lochmaddy. From a narrow mouth, the loch extends westwards for 8 miles (13 km). It contains several small islands and rocks, and its complex coastline opens into several embayments and other lochs, the largest of which is Loch Langais. The settlement of Locheport lies on its southern shore, 2 miles (3 km) from its head.

Eurocentral *North Lanarkshire* A road-rail interchange, distribution hub and manufacturing centre located at

Mossend, to the south of the A8/M8 and east of the M74. One of Scotland's largest commercial developments, the site extends to more than 263 ha (650 acres) and is strategically located close to the motorway network between Glasgow and Edinburgh. The site developed in association with Scotland's Channel Tunnel Rail Freight Terminal, which opened in 1994. Eurocentral, which offers Enterprise Zone status, has attracted several major international manufacturers and distribution/logistics companies.

Evan Water *South Lanarkshire* A river of South Lanarkshire and Dumfries and Galloway, the Evan Water rises in Crawford parish and flows southwestwards for 12 miles (19 km) to join the River Annan at Three Waters Foot near Beattock.

Evanton *Highland* A village in Easter Ross, Highland Council area, Evanton lies close to the north shore of the Cromarty Firth between Dingwall and Invergordon. To the west is Foulis Castle, the seat of the chiefs of the Clan Munro. On the summit of Fyrish Hill to the west stands a monument erected in 1781 by tenants of the Novar Estate to commemorate the victory of Sir Hector Munro of Novar at the Battle of Seringapatam in India. The village, which lies between the River Glass and the River Sgitheach, was created by Evan Fraser of Balernie in 1810 and populated by people cleared from the straths to the west. An airfield, established in the 1920s and used by the Fleet Air Arm, was converted for use as an industrial estate in the 1970s with steel-scrap, fence-making, textile and North Sea oil-related industries.

Evelix, River *Highland* A river of southern Sutherland in Highland Council area, noted for its salmon and sea trout, the River Evelix issues from Loch an Lagain, 4 miles (6.5 km) northeast of Bonar Bridge. It flows southeast and then turns southwest at Evelix before reaching the artificial Loch Evelix and then entering the Dornoch Firth through Poll na Caorach.

Evertown *Dumfries and Galloway* A hamlet in southeastern Dumfries and Galloway, Evertown, lies 2.5 miles (4 km) west of Canonbie.

Ewe, Loch *Highland* A sea loch on the coast of Wester Ross, Highland Council area, Loch Ewe is 10 miles (16 km) long and lies between two peninsulas, with the settlement of Poolewe at its head. The Isle of Ewe lies opposite Aultbea. Inverewe Gardens, created by Osgood Mackenzie, lie on an inlet to the east of Poolewe. Loch Ewe receives the River Ewe, which flows northwestwards for just over 3 miles (5 km) from Loch Maree.

Ewes Water *Dumfries and Galloway* A tributary of the River Esk in Dumfries and Galloway, the Ewes Water rises in two headstreams called the Blackhall and Mosspaul Burns and from their junction continues southwards for 8 miles (13 km) before joining the Esk at Langholm.

Eye *Western Isles* A peninsula in the Western Isles, known locally as Point, which lies 4 miles (6.5 km) east of Stornoway. It is connected to Lewis by a slender strip of land between Loch a' Tuath and Loch Braigh na h-Aoidhe. The peninsula extends northeastwards out into the Minch for 7 miles (11 km), terminating at Tiumpan Head. Its maximum width is 3 miles (5 km) and includes a number of scattered crofting settlements.

Eye Water *Scottish Borders* A river of Berwickshire in Scottish Borders, the Eye rises on Monynut Edge near Oldhamstocks. It flows 20 miles (32 km) east-southeast then north-northeast before entering the North Sea at Eyemouth.

Eyebroughy *East Lothian* A tiny island in the Firth of Forth. Eyebroughy lies 200 m (218 yd) off the East Lothian coast, 2.5 miles (4 km) north-northeast of Gullane and 3 miles (5 km) west of North Berwick. The island is noted for a colony of cormorants and is a designated Royal Society for the Protection of Birds (RSPB) Reserve. Geologically, Eyebroughy is formed from a sheet of intrusive trachyte of Lower Carboniferous age.

Eyemouth *Scottish Borders* A village of Berwickshire in Scottish Borders, Eyemouth is situated at the mouth of the Eye Water, 8 miles (13 km) north of Berwick-upon-Tweed. This fishing and holiday resort town on the North Sea coast became a burgh of barony in 1597 and was the port for Coldingham Priory. The town prospered through the 19th-century herring trade and the railway, now gone. Its narrow and intersecting alleys are said to have given smugglers a good chance of slipping past Customs men in the 18th and 19th centuries. The harbour (1768) was extended in the late 19th century and deepened in 1964, providing shelter for one of Scotland's mid-sized fleets (126 vessels in 1997). In 1881 disaster hit Eyemouth when a gale sank half its fleet, leaving 129 drowned.

Eynhallow *Orkney* The 'holy island' of Eynhallow lies in the Orkney Islands between the Mainland of Orkney and Rousay. Surrounded by reefs and shoals, the island extends to 75 ha (185 acres) and is today a nature reserve noted for its bird life. At its centre stand the ruins of a chapel that may have formed part of an early Christian monastic settlement. Uninhabited since the late 19th century, it had a population of 26 in 1841.

Eynort, Loch *Highland* A sea loch forming a large inlet on the west coast of the island of Skye to the west of the Cuillins, Loch Eynort is fed by the River Eynort which rises on Beinn Bhreac.

Eynort, Loch *Western Isles* A sea loch on the east coast of South Uist in the Outer Hebrides, Loch Eynort extends for 6 miles (10 km) before opening into the Minch.

Fad, Loch *Argyll and Bute* A long narrow loch on the island of Bute in Argyll and Bute, Loch Fad extends southwestwards for nearly 3 miles (5 km) along the line of the Highland Boundary Fault to the south of Rothesay. The ruins of St Mary's Chapel, once part of the bishopric of Man, lie near the northern end of the loch.

Fada, Loch *Argyll and Bute* The largest loch on the island of Colonsay in Argyll and Bute, Loch Fada lies between Kiloran and Scalasaig. It is a narrow loch with three distinct basins extending 2 miles (3 km) from northeast to southwest.

Fada, Loch *Argyll and Bute* A small loch at the northern end of the island of Coll in Argyll and Bute, Loch Fada lies 4 miles (6.5 km) northeast of the settlement of Arinagour and a mile (1.5 km) southwest of Sorisdale.

Fada, Loch *Western Isles* A small loch located with several others in low-lying land on the west coast of South Uist, Loch Fada lies immediately to the east of Peninerine and a half-mile (1 km) southwest of Howbeg, 9 miles (14 km) north-northwest of Lochboisdale. It is a mile (1.5 km) in length, but rarely more than an eighth of a mile (200 m) wide.

Faifley *West Dunbartonshire* A settlement of southeast West Dunbartonshire, Faifley lies nearly 2 miles (3 km) north of Clydebank and northwest of Drumchapel.

Fail *South Ayrshire* Sitting on the Water of Fail, a tributary of the River Ayr, the hamlet of Fail is located a mile (1.5 km) northwest of the settlement of Tarbolton in South Ayrshire. A monastery of Red Friars was established here in the 13th century.

Failford *South Ayrshire* The village of Failford is located 3 miles (5 km) west of Mauchline and 2 miles (3 km) southeast of Tarbolton in South Ayrshire. It lies on the north bank of a meander of the River Ayr at its confluence with the Water of Fail.

Fairburn Tower *Highland* A ruined five-storey tower in Easter Ross, Highland Council area, Fairburn Tower overlooks the River Orrin, just over 2 miles (3 km) southeast of Contin. It was built in the mid-16th century as a stronghold of the Mackenzies. The Brahan Seer foretold the demise of the Mackenzies of Fairburn and the abandoning of the tower, adding that a cow would give birth to a calf in the uppermost chamber. This prophecy was fulfilled.

Fairgirth *Dumfries and Galloway* A locality on the southeastern edge of Dalbeattie Forest, Dumfries and Galloway, Fairgirth lies in the parish of Colvend and Southwick, 4 miles (6.5 km) southeast of Dalbeattie.

Fair Isle *Shetland* One of the most isolated inhabited islands in Britain, Fair Isle is fringed by high red sandstone cliffs and is situated midway between the Shetland and Orkney island groups of the Northern Isles. With a population of 69 largely resident on croftland at the southern end of the island, Fair Isle is noted for its crafts, which include the manufacture of distinctive knitwear, fiddles, straw-backed chairs and model boats. The island has an area of 815 ha (2013 acres) and rises to a height of 217 m (712 ft) at Ward Hill. The ancient Feelie Dyke separates the northern hill-grazing from the southern croftlands, and the island's cliffs are home to large breeding colonies of sea birds. An airstrip is located in the centre of the island and a ferry connects Sumburgh on Mainland Shetland with the pier at North Haven. North Haven is overlooked by the Bird Observatory built in 1969. A museum is dedicated to the memory of George Waterston, who gained international recognition for the island by publicising its diverse birdlife. In 1948 he founded the Fair Isle Bird Observatory Trust and in 1954 he passed ownership to the National Trust for Scotland. Power on the island is augmented by two wind turbines, commissioned in 1982 and 1997, providing a combined output of 170 kW.

Fairlie *North Ayrshire* A residential and resort village with a pier on the coast of North Ayrshire, Fairlie lies 3 miles (5 km) south of Largs. Created a burgh of barony in 1601, Fairlie developed in the 19th century in association with boat building and tourism. Kelburn Castle and Country Centre lies just over a mile (1.5 km) to the north, and the ruined 16th-century Fairlie Castle, former seat of the Fairlies of that Ilk, lies on the Fairlie Burn, which rises to the east on Fairlie Moor and flows westwards to the coast. To the south of the Fairlie Burn the settlement comprises interwar bungalows and modern housing, and beyond is the Hunterston Development Complex developed since the 1960s.

Fairlie Roads *North Ayrshire* An arm of the Firth of Clyde, the Fairlie Roads separate the island of Great Cumbrae from the mainland of North Ayrshire.

Fairmilehead *City of Edinburgh* A residential suburb on the southern edge of the city of Edinburgh, Fairmilehead lies between the Braid Hills and the city bypass. It was developed largely in the latter half of the 20th century. Since 1936 the National Trust for Scotland has maintained the Caiy Stone, a 2.7-m/9-ft-tall prehistoric cup-marked stone also known as 'General Kay's Monument' or the 'Kel Stone'. The stone may mark the site of an ancient battle, possibly between the Picts and the Romans. The Princess Margaret Rose Hospital was built here in 1929, originally as a children's orthopaedic hospital, but closed in 1998.

Fairy Bridge *Highland* A locality in the parish of Duirnish on the island of Skye, the Fairy Bridge lies at a road junction, 3 miles (5 km) northeast of Dunvegan. There was formerly a cattle market here.

Fala *Midlothian* A village of Midlothian in the northern foothills of the Lammermuir Hills, Fala lies by the A68, 6 miles (10 km) southeast of Dalkeith. The village survived in the 19th century in association with the Blackshiels Inn and a smithy on the newly developed coaching route designed by Thomas Telford. Nearby, at Soutra Aisle, are the remains of a Red Friars Hospital founded in the 12th century.

Falkirk *Area: 293 sq. km (113 sq. miles)* A local government area midway between Glasgow and Edinburgh, Falkirk occupies a pivotal position between Edinburgh, Glasgow and Stirling in the valley of the River Forth. It comprises a flat lowland area that is watered by the River Carron and traversed by the Forth and Clyde Canal and Union Canal, and an upland region to the south through which flows the River Avon. Its deposits of coal, clay and ironstone have contributed to the economic wealth of the area and the development of the Falkirk and Grangemouth conurbations. In addition to traditional industries such as coach building, iron founding, paper making and saw milling, Falkirk has developed a number of high-tech business parks and industrial estates, and at Grangemouth on the River Forth is Scotland's leading petrochemical complex and container port. Formerly part of Stirlingshire, Falkirk was one of the three districts of Central Region between 1975 and 1996, after which it became a separate council area. The industrial development of Falkirk, Grangemouth and Bo'ness dates largely from the founding of the Carron Ironworks in the 1760s, and the opening in 1790 of the Forth and Clyde Canal which promoted trade with Glasgow in the west. The area is traversed by the Antonine Wall and several Roman sites have been excavated.

Falkirk *Falkirk* The administrative centre of Falkirk Council area, the town of Falkirk lies between the Forth and Clyde Canal and Union Canal in a pivotal position between Edinburgh and Glasgow. There are substantial remains of the Roman Antonine Wall, a ditched rampart fortification passing Callendar House. The house dates from the 14th century, when much of the area was granted by King Alexander II to the Livingstones. The descendants of that family became earls of Callendar and Linlithgow before forfeiting their lands during the first Jacobite Rising in 1715. On Callendar Ridge on 22 July 1298 was fought the first Battle of Falkirk, where

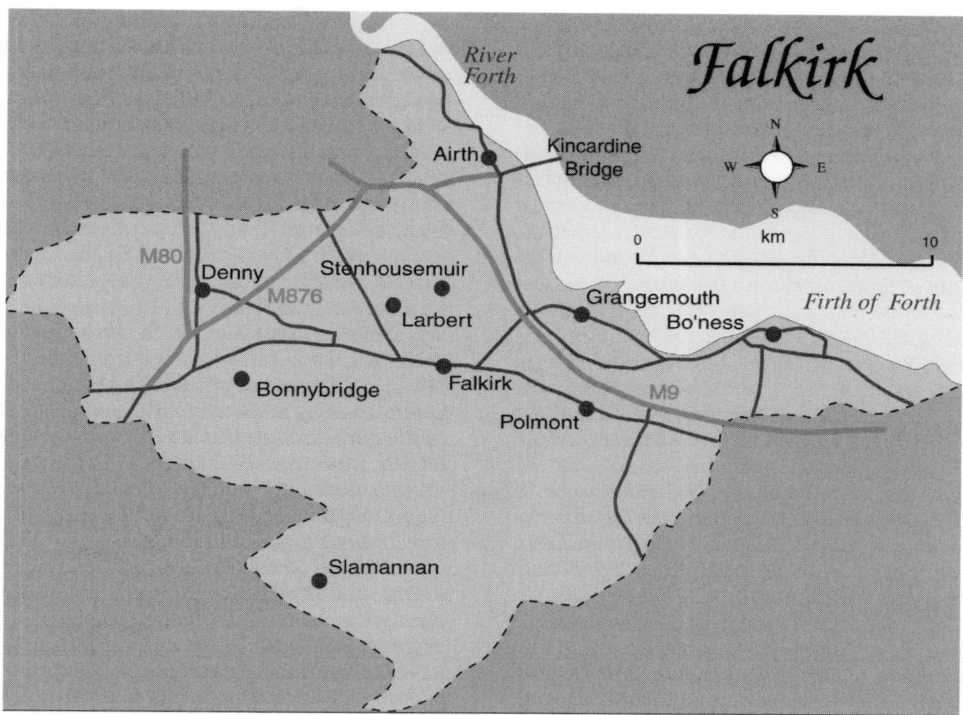

Edward I of England defeated William Wallace. The second Battle of Falkirk took place on 17 January 1746 when Prince Charles Edward Stewart (Bonnie Prince Charlie) defeated General Henry Hawley to the west of the town, near Bantaskine, where there is a monument. To the north, near Stenhousemuir, large numbers of cattle were sold at the Falkirk tryst or market after 1785, and from 1760 the surrounding area developed in association with local iron foundries and coal mining. Falkirk has football grounds, a greyhound racecourse and public parks, including Bellsmeadow, Dollar Park and Callendar Park. Callendar Square is its leading shopping centre. Buildings of note include The Steeple (1814), St Mordan's Parish Church (15th century), the Town Hall (1879) and St Francis Xavier's Roman Catholic Church (1960).

Falkirk Wheel *Falkirk* Located between Camelon and Bonnybridge, some 2 miles (3 km) west of Falkirk, the Falkirk Wheel is the world's only rotating boat-lift and was built to transfer boats between the Forth and Clyde and Union canals. Opened by Queen Elizabeth II during her Golden Jubilee tour of Scotland (2002), the wheel is 35 m (115 ft) in diameter and is the centrepiece of the £78 million Millennium Link project, which has seen both canals restored and reopened for use. A spectacular and stylish feat of engineering, the Falkirk Wheel comprises two counter-balanced tanks capable of moving 300 tonnes each (at least eight boats and the water in which they float) from one canal to the other, in approximately 15 minutes. It cost £17 million and occupies the site of an abandoned opencast mine. A 1.25-mile (2-km) extension to the existing Union Canal has been built, including a tunnel under the Antonine Wall, two aqueducts, three locks and a railway bridge. The extension replaced a long-demolished series of locks and a dock, which once linked the canals some 0.75 mile (1.25 km) to the east at Port Downie in Camelon. A visitor centre includes displays on the construction and operation of the wheel.

Falkland *Fife* A royal burgh lying in the northern foothills of the Lomond Hills, Falkland lies 8 miles (13 km) north of Glenrothes. Situated in a strategic location on a north–south route that opens out into the valley of the River Eden, it was the site of a castle built by Macduff, the Thane of Fife. The castle was destroyed by the English in 1337, although subsequently rebuilt. Robert Stewart (later Duke of Albany) purchased the property in the 14th century. In 1402, Stewart had his nephew David, Duke of Rothesay and heir to King Robert III, imprisoned in the castle and starved to death. In 1458, Falkland received its royal charter. Between 1501 and 1541 Falkland Palace was built by James IV and James V, who came to hunt deer and wild boar in the surrounding forests. Royal patronage of Falkland was not sustained after the Union of the Crowns (1603), although Charles II first constituted the Scots Guards here in 1650, but Falkland continued to prosper as a weaving town. In the early 1800s much of the town was improved by the Tyndall-Bruce family, which inherited the Falkland Estate. In 1970 one of the first conservation areas in Scotland was established in Falkland, whose palace and houses are now a major tourist attraction. The former textile and linoleum industries no longer exist but paper bags are still made in Falkland. The burgh has a nine-hole golf course.

Falkland Palace *Fife* Dominating the historic village of Falkland, the palace was originally built as a residence for King James IV in 1500, replacing an earlier 12th-century castle. It is a fortified but comfortable Renaissance-style residence and comprises ranges of buildings around an open courtyard. The south gatehouse range survives complete, while the east range is ruined, and only traces remain of the north range, which was burned during the occupation of Cromwell's troops in 1654. The Chapel Royal includes fine mullioned windows, a 16th-century oak screen and a beautifully painted ceiling that dates from 1633. There is also a gallery displaying fine tapestries. The Cross (or Croce) House contains the restored royal bedchamber, where King James V died in 1542. Adjacent to the palace is a garden, within which there is a royal (or real) tennis court dating from 1539. This is one of only two in the United Kingdom, the other being at Hampton Court. Mary, Queen of Scots and King James VI visited the palace, but royal patronage did not continue after the Union of the Crowns in 1603. King Charles I visited in 1633, and King Charles II in 1650–1. Despite a visit by King George IV in 1822, the palace deteriorated until 1887, when it was restored by the Marquess of Bute. The palace still belongs to the monarch, but has been maintained since 1952 by the National Trust for Scotland in its role as Deputy Keeper.

Fallin *Stirling* One of the three 'Eastern Villages' of Stirling Council area, Fallin is situated near a bend of the River Forth, 4 miles (6.5 km) east of Stirling. Formerly a coal-mining village, it is now largely a residential settlement.

Falloch, Falls of *Stirling* A scenic cascade on the River Falloch, the Falls of Falloch lie close to the main road midway between Crianlarich and the top end of Loch Lomond in Stirling Council area.

Falloch, Glen *Stirling/Argyll and Bute* A narrow valley in Stirling and Argyll and Bute council areas, Glen Falloch lies between Crianlarich and the top end of Loch Lomond. For the most part it follows the course of the River Falloch which rises on the north-facing slopes of Beinn a' Chroin and flows northwestwards into Glen Falloch where it turns sharply southwest before flowing 12 miles (19 km) into Loch Lomond. The river's principal tributaries are the Dubh Eas, Allt Fionn Ghlinne, Eas Eonan, Allt Criche, Allt a' Chuilinn and Allt Andoran. Both the A82 and the West Highland railway line north to Crianlarich pass through Glen Falloch.

Falls of Clyde Wildlife Reserve *South Lanarkshire* Located next to the world heritage industrial village of New Lanark, the Falls of Clyde Wildlife Reserve is owned and managed by the Scottish Wildlife Trust. A visitor centre can be found at the old dyeworks in New Lanark. Within the reserve are three of the waterfalls that form part of the Falls of Clyde, all lying upstream of New Lanark: Dundaff Linn, Corra Linn and Bonnington Linn. In the past, Dundaff Linn provided power for the New Lanark mills and the latter two are used as part of the Lanark Hydro-Electric Scheme.

Fannich, Loch *Highland* A large reservoir in Wester Ross, Loch Fannich lies to the north of Strath Bran, 18 miles (29 km) west of Dingwall. It is 7 miles (11 km) in length. To the north of the loch is the Fannich deer forest and a number of high peaks known as the Fannichs.

Fannichs, the *Highland* A range of mountains to the north of Loch Fannich in Wester Ross, the Fannichs are sometimes known as the Ross-shire Alps and represent wild and magnificent scenery. The range includes over a dozen peaks in excess of 914 m (3000 ft), from A' Chailleach in the west to Fionn Bheinn in the east. The highest summit is Sgurr Mòr, which rises to 1110 m (3641 ft).

Fara *Orkney* An island of the Orkney Islands, Fara is separated by the Gutter Sound from Hoy to the west and by the Weddel Sound from Flotta to the east. It rises to 43 m (141 ft) at Thomson's Hill at its centre and has an area of 295 ha (729 acres). Abandoned in the 1960s, the island had a population of 76 crofters in 1891.

Faray *Orkney* A small uninhabited island of the Orkney Islands, Faray and the Holm of Faray to the north form a ridge of middle old red sandstone that extends southwards from Weather Ness at the southern tip of the island of Westray. Rising to a height of 32 m (105 ft), Faray has an area of 180 ha (445 acres). In the early 1930s there were 40 people on the island earning a living from crofting and lobster fishing.

Farg, Glen *Perth and Kinross* A narrow glen in southern Perth and Kinross, Glen Farg extends the length of the River Farg, which rises in the Ochil Hills and flows north to join the River Earn east of Bridge of Earn. The village of Glenfarg (formerly Damhead) and the Beinn Inn are located in the glen.

Farigaig *Highland* A river in the Inverness district of Highland Council area, the River Farigaig rises to the east of Loch Ness. It flows just over 8 miles (13 km) southwestwards to join the loch at Inverfarigaig. There is a visitor centre with walks through the Farigaig Forest 17 miles (27 km) southwest of Inverness.

Farland Head *North Ayrshire* A headland on the North Ayrshire coastline, Farland Head extends into the Firth of Clyde 5 miles (8 km) northwest of Ardrossan.

Farnell *Angus* A village in an Angus parish of the same name, Farnell lies 3 miles (5 km) south of Brechin. Its Gothic-style church dates from 1806. Nearby Farnell Castle, a residence of the bishops of Brechin built in the 16th century, is said to stand on the site of an earlier building visited by King Edward I of England in 1296. The castle remained a property of the bishops until 1566 and eventually fell into the hands of the Carnegie family. To the north, within Kinnaird Deer Park, is Kinnaird Castle, the ancestral home of the Carnegie earls of Southesk since the early 15th century.

Farr *Highland* A township in a parish of the same name on the north coast of Sutherland, Highland Council area, Farr lies near the head of Farr Bay and northeast of Bettyhill.

Farragon Hill *Perth and Kinross* A hill rising to 780 m (2559 ft) between Loch Tummel and the River Tay, Farragon Hill lies to the west of Loch Derculich and 4 miles (6.5 km) north of Aberfeldy in Perth and Kinross.

Farrar, River *Highland* A river of Easter Ross, the River Farrar rises in the Monar area to the east of Loch Carron. It flows 25 miles (40 km) eastwards through Glen Strathfarrar to join the River Glass near Struy. It passes through reservoirs that form part of the Strathfarrar Hydro-Electric Scheme, including Loch Monar, Loch a' Mhuillidh and Loch Beannacharan.

Farroch, Loch *South Ayrshire* One of several small lochs in the uplands of Carrick district, South Ayrshire, Loch Farroch is situated 2 miles (3 km) northeast of Barrhill.

Fa'side Castle *East Lothian* Located 2 miles (3 km) southwest of Tranent in East Lothian, Fa'side (or Falside) Castle was built in the 14th century as a four-storey keep and was enlarged into an L-plan mansion in the 16th century. It was destroyed during the Battle of Pinkie in 1547 but underwent a comprehensive programme of restoration in the 1980s.

Faskally, Loch *Perth and Kinross* Located 1.5 miles (2.5 km) northwest of Pitlochry in Perth and Kinross, Loch Faskally is a man-made reservoir retained by the 16.5-m/54-ft-tall Pitlochry Dam which was built in 1947–50 as part of the North of Scotland Hydro-Electric Board's Tummel/Garry Power Scheme. Water is fed through two 7500 kilowatt generators. A salmon ladder attracts large numbers of visitors annually. An attractive riverside picnic area beside the loch includes the Clunie Arch, which is built to the exact dimensions of the tunnel that carries water from Loch Tummel to the Clunie Power Station.

Faslane *Argyll and Bute* A port and naval base on the east side of Faslane Bay at the head of the Gare Loch in Argyll and Bute, Faslane was built during World War II. In the 1960s the Clyde submarine base HMS *Neptune* became the controversial base of the Polaris nuclear submarine fleet. In 1996 Faslane became the naval headquarters for northern Britain. Shipbreaking was carried on here from 1950 and some of the UK's largest naval vessels were broken up here.

Fasnakyle *Highland* A deer forest in the Inverness-shire district of Highland Council area, Fasnakyle lies between Glen Affric and Glen Cannich.

Fasque House *Aberdeenshire* A four-storey neoclassical mansion, Fasque House is situated near Fettercairn on the northern edge of the Howe of the Mearns. It was built in 1809 for Sir Alexander Ramsay of Balmain to an earlier design by William Adam and replaced the former house of Faskie. Surrounded by a designed landscape of trees and rhododendrons, the building was extended by Sir John Gladstone (1764–1851), a wealthy Liverpool grain merchant who bought the estate in 1829. Gladstone's youngest son, William Ewart Gladstone (1809–98), grew up here and eventually became Britain's longest-serving prime minister. The name Fasque is derived from a Gaelic word that means 'shelter'.

Fast Castle *Scottish Borders* The ruined remains of Fast Castle (also known as Castle Knowe) are located next to the Wheat Stack headland, 4 miles (6.5 km) northwest of St Abb's Head and 5 miles (8 km) northwest of Coldingham in Scottish Borders. It was a meeting place of the Gowrie conspirators who plotted against James VI.

Fatlips Castle *Scottish Borders* A ruined former stronghold of the Turnbulls, Fatlips Castle stands on Minto Crags near the River Teviot in the Roxburgh district of Scottish Borders, between Hawick and Jedburgh.

Fatlips Castle *South Lanarkshire* A ruined castle in South Lanarkshire, Fatlips Castle stands on the edge of Tinto Hill, 2 miles (3 km) north-northeast of Wiston.

Fauldhouse *West Lothian* Located 9 miles (14 km) southwest of Livingston in West Lothian, Fauldhouse was first mentioned in 1523 as Fawlhous and began to prosper in the 18th century with the discovery of coal. In the late 18th century the discovery of ironstone by the Wilsontown Iron Company helped increase the population, as did the discovery in 1835 of the 'slatey ironstone' exploited by the Shotts Iron Company. Whinstone was also quarried here for Edinburgh housing, and a railway line was established in the 1860s.

Feall Bay *Argyll and Bute* An inlet at the southwestern end of the island of Coll, Argyll and Bute, Feall Bay lies to the north of a narrow neck of land that separates it from Crossapol Bay. It lies 6 miles (10 km) southwest of the settlement of Arinagour.

Fearn An alternative name for Fern in Angus.

Fearn *Highland* A settlement in Easter Ross, Fearn lies 2 miles (3 km) northwest of Balintore and 8 miles (13 km) northeast of Invergordon. Fearn Abbey, rebuilt in 1771, was originally erected here *c.*1238 by the Earl of Ross. Its roof collapsed in 1742, killing about 50 worshippers. Nearby is the small settlement of Hill of Fearn. Both villages comprise single-storey cottages with clay and boulder walls.

Fearnach, Gleann *Perth and Kinross* The valley of the Allt Fearnach in northeast Perth and Kinross, Gleann Fearnach extends a total length of 5 miles (8 km) from north to south. At its southern end the Fearnach meets the Brerachan Water to form the River Ardle.

Fearnach Bay *Argyll and Bute* An inlet at the head of Loch Melfort, a sea loch on the coast of Argyll and Bute, Fearnach Bay lies a mile (1.5 km) west of the settlement of Kilmelford.

Fearnan *Perth and Kinross* A crofting settlement on the north shore of Loch Tay 3 miles (5 km) west of Kenmore in Perth and Kinross, Fearnan lies at the junction of the road to Glen Lyon with the road from Kenmore to Killin. The lands of Fearnan passed back and forth between the Robertsons of Struan and the Campbells. In the early 1800s the Campbell Marquess of Breadalbane built an extension to the old settlement called Stron-fearnan.

Fell of Fleet *Dumfries and Galloway* A hill rising to 471 m (1545 ft) in Dumfries and Galloway, the Fell of Fleet is situated to the northeast of Cairnsmore of Fleet and to the south of the Queen's Way (A712) between New Galloway and Newton Stewart. It lies at the southern end of the Galloway Forest Park, to the south of the Black Water of Dee.

Fender, Loch *Perth and Kinross* A small loch in central Perth and Kinross, Loch Fender lies in the hills between the River Quaich and Glen Cochill, nearly 3 miles (5 km) northwest of Amulree. It is the source of the Glenfender Burn which flows southeastwards through Glen Fender to join the River Quaich.

Fender Burn *Perth and Kinross* A stream in highland Perth and Kinross, the Fender Burn rises in the southern Grampians on the slopes of Beinn a' Ghlo and flows 5 miles (8 km) southwestwards through Glen Fender to join the River Tilt near Fender Bridge, a mile (1.5 km) north of Blair Atholl.

Fenton Barns *East Lothian* A hamlet in East Lothian, Fenton Barns lies midway between Dirleton and Drem, 3 miles (5 km) southwest of North Berwick. The buildings associated with the former RAF airfield to the south at Drem are occupied by the Scottish Archery Centre and the Fenton Barns retail and leisure centre.

Fenton Tower *East Lothian* Immediately south of the hamlet of Kingston and 2 miles (3 km) south of North Berwick in East Lothian is Fenton Tower, built in 1550 for Patrick Whytelaw, son of Lord Ruthven. In 1587 the tower passed into the hands of Sir John Carmichael and in 1591 it was a refuge of King James VI, who had sailed across the Firth of Forth from Fife when faced by one of several attempts to usurp his power. James later gave the tower to his friend Sir Thomas Erskine who became Lord Dirleton (1604), Viscount Fenton (1606) and Earl of Kellie (1619). In 1631, the tower passed to Sir John Maxwell of Innerwick, who became Earl of Dirleton in 1646. In 1650 the Parliamentarian army of Oliver Cromwell invaded Scotland and destroyed many properties, including Fenton Tower and Dirleton and Tantallon Castles. The ruin passed to the Nisbets of Dirleton and Archerfield in 1663 and finally to the Simpson family around 1850. Having lain a ruin for 350 years, the castle was restored in 2000 to be used for premium holiday and business-meeting accommodation. Adjacent to the tower are the remains of a medieval chapel.

Fenwick *East Ayrshire* A sizeable dormitory village of central East Ayrshire, Fenwick lies on the Fenwick Water 3 miles (5 km) southeast of Stewarton and a similar distance northeast of Kilmarnock. By the early 1970s, Fenwick was bypassed to the west by the A77. Fenwick Kirk dates from 1643, when the villagers were strict adherents to the Covenanting cause. In the 18th century Fenwick was known for shoemaking and weaving, and the Fenwick Weavers' Society, formed in 1761, is claimed to be the world's first cooperative society.

Fenzie, Glen *Aberdeenshire* A narrow glen occupying the valley of the Glenfenzie Burn, a tributary of the River Gairn, Glen Fenzie lies 5 miles (8 km) northwest of Ballater.

Feoch Burn *South Ayrshire* The Feoch Burn starts as a runoff from Loch Crongart in South Ayrshire. The burn flows north and west to a point a mile (1.5 km) southeast of Barrhill, where it joins the River Duisk.

Feochan *Argyll and Bute* A stream in the Lorn district of Argyll and Bute, the Feochan rises in headstreams to the southeast of Oban. It flows 3 miles (5 km) north then west to join the River Nell before entering Loch Feochan. For part of its upper course it is called the Feochan Bheag before becoming the Feochan Mhòr.

Feochan, Loch *Argyll and Bute* A sea loch of the Lorn district of Argyll and Bute, Loch Feochan stretches 4 miles (6 km) from Barrnacarry Bay in the east to a mile (1.5 km) east of the settlement of Dunach. Oban lies 4 miles (6.5 km) to the north. The loch receives the River Nell from the east and the River Euchar which empties into the loch at Kilninver.

Fergusson Gallery *Perth and Kinross* Devoted to the artistic work of the Scottish Colourist painter John Duncan Fergusson (1874–1961), the Fergusson Gallery is located in Marshall Place, Perth, opposite the South Inch. Opened in 1992, the gallery occupies a neoclassical former waterworks designed in 1832 in the style of a Roman Doric temple by Adam Anderson, the rector of Perth Academy. In order to supply the town, fresh water was pumped by steam engine to a large domed cast-iron cistern from filter beds on Moncreiffe Island in the River Tay.

Ferindonald *Highland* The name of a district of Easter Ross in Highland Council area lying between Dingwall and Invergordon, Ferindonald refers to the territory of the Clan Munro in the parishes of Kiltearn and Alness to the west of the Cromarty Firth.

Ferintosh *Highland* A district of Easter Ross in Highland Council area, the former barony of Ferintosh lies at the head of the Cromarty Firth and east of the River Conon.

Fern *Angus* A locality on the edge of the Braes of Angus, Fern (or Fearn) lies to the north of the River South Esk, 7 miles (11 km) west of Brechin. Its church, rebuilt in 1806, is said to have been founded in the 7th century by Bishop Colman and dedicated to St Aidan. To the south, by the Noran Water, stand the ruins of Vayne Castle, a seat of the Montealto or Mowat family from the 12th century until the mid-15th century. In a sandstone rock close to the castle is the so-called Kelpie's Footmark.

Ferness *Highland* A small settlement in lower Strathdearn, eastern Highland Council area, Ferness lies in a forested area to the south of the River Findhorn, 8 miles (13 km) southeast of Nairn.

Fernie *Fife* A hamlet in Fife, Fernie is situated to the east of the village of Letham on the A92 to the Tay Bridge. Fernie Castle, now a hotel, is a 16th-century tower house once owned by the Balfour family.

Ferniegair *South Lanarkshire* A hamlet in South Lanarkshire, Ferniegair is located a mile (1.5 km) south of Hamilton and 2 miles (3 km) northwest of Larkhall. Nearby are Chatelherault Country Park and Hunting Lodge and Cadzow Castle.

Ferniehirst Castle *Scottish Borders* Ferniehirst Castle, the ancestral home of the Kerr family, is located a mile (1.5 km) south of Jedburgh in Scottish Borders. It was built in 1476 by Sir Thomas Kerr but was destroyed on several occasions over the next century. The castle was sacked by the English in 1523, attacked and retaken in 1549 with the help of the French and captured once again in 1570 by the English. In 1593 it was almost completely demolished by James VI to punish the then laird for assisting the king's enemies. Rebuilt in 1598 in a T-plan, it was occupied for two centuries before falling into decay. Between 1934 and 1984 it was leased by the Scottish Youth Hostel Association. In 1983, Peter Kerr, 12th Marquess of Lothian, purchased the castle and began major restoration, opening it to the public in 1986.

Fernybank *Angus* A locality in Glen Esk, Angus, Fernybank lies on the River North Esk, 8 miles (13 km) northwest of Edzell.

Ferryden *Angus* A former fishing village in Angus, Ferryden lies at the mouth of the River South Esk opposite Montrose. Until the river was bridged, it was the ferry station on the road from Aberdeen to Dundee.

Ferryport-on-Craig The former name of Tayport in Fife.

Feshie, River *Highland* Rising in the Grampians near the border between Highland and Perth and Kinross council areas, the River Feshie flows 23 miles (37 km) northwards through Glen Feshie to join the River Spey just northeast of Kincraig. There are fine stands of Scots pine in the glen and gliding and outdoor centres at Lagganlia near Feshiebridge to the east of Loch Insh.

Festival Theatre *City of Edinburgh* Located on Nicholson Street, the Festival Theatre occupies a site that has been a theatre since 1830. It was formerly the Empire Palace Theatre, opened in 1892. In 1911 a fire on stage killed eight people, including the illusionist Lafayette. Rebuilt and enlarged in 1928 as the Empire Theatre, to a design by W. and T. R. Millburn, it was a venue for music hall and variety and the main venue of the Edinburgh Festival from 1946 until 1963. It was subsequently used as a bingo hall before its major conversion in the early 1990s. Under the guidance of the architects Law and Dunbar Nasmith, the original frontage was replaced and the largest stage in Britain grafted onto the rear. The original auditorium was preserved and the new Festival Theatre opened in 1994.

Fetlar *Shetland* Described as the 'Garden of Shetland', the island of Fetlar in the Northern Isles contrasts markedly with the bleak and desolate neighbouring island of Yell. With an area of 4144 ha (10,236 acres), its name is thought to derive from the Old Norse for 'fat or prosperous land'. Over 200 species of wild flower have been identified, including rare sedges and orchids, and the island has a rich variety of bird life. Until 1967 Fetlar was the only UK breeding site of the snowy owl. The highest point of the island is Vord Hill which rises to 158 m (518 ft). There are many prehistoric remains, including the Stone of the Ripples, the Fiddler's Crus stone circles, the Haltadans ring of stones and the Finnigert (or Funzie Girt) Dyke which dates from the Bronze Age and divides the island in two halves. The Giant's Grave is thought to be the site of a Viking boat burial. In 1822 the first large-scale clearances in Shetland took place on the Lamb Hoga peninsula, where crofters were evicted by Sir Arthur Nicolson to make way for sheep. The population of the island has fallen from a total of 761 in 1841 to 86 in 2001. Buildings of interest include the Haa of Funzie fishing station; Brough Lodge, built *c.*1820 for the Nicolson family; Leagarth House, built in 1900 by Sir William Watson Cheyne (d.1932), a Fetlar man who was an assistant to James Lister, the pioneer of antiseptic surgery; and Aithbank, the home of the storyteller Jamesie Laurenson. The history of the island is told in the Fetlar Interpretive Centre at Houbie, the main settlement. The island can be reached via an airstrip northwest of Houbie or by a car ferry that links Oddista with Belmont on Unst and Gutcher on Yell.

Fetterangus *Aberdeenshire* A village of Buchan in northern Aberdeenshire, Fetterangus lies on the North Ugie Water, 2 miles (3 km) north of Mintlaw and east of the Forest of Deer.

Fettercairn *Aberdeenshire* Situated at the meeting of five roads in the Mearns of southern Aberdeenshire, Fettercairn is a quiet village of red-sandstone houses with a central square. Within the square are the Mercat Cross (1670) with its old-style ell measure and a fountain erected in 1869 in memory of Sir John Hepburn Stuart Forbes, Bt, of Pitsligo and Fettercairn. The road to the north heads over Cairn o' Mount towards Banchory and Royal Deeside, and 4 miles (6.5 km) to the east is Laurencekirk. At the entrance to the village from the south, a great archway commemorates a visit to Fettercairn made by Queen Victoria and Prince Albert, who stayed in the Ramsay Arms in September 1861. Whyte and Mackay's Fettercairn Distillery at Nethermill was founded in 1824 and claims to be the second-oldest licensed distillery. Its stables now house a visitor centre. To the north of the village are Fettercairn House, built in 1666 by the 1st Earl of Middleton (1610–73), whose family occupied land here for five centuries, and Fasque House. To the southwest is 16th-century Balbegno Castle, a Ramsay stronghold, and the vitrified fort of Green Cairn. At the beginning of July each year the villagers of Fetterie, as it is sometimes called, host the Fettercairn Cattle Show and Sports.

Fetteresso *Aberdeenshire* A village in southeastern Aberdeenshire, Fetteresso is situated on the Carron Water just over a mile (1.5 km) west of Stonehaven, from which it is separated by the main road to Aberdeen. Fetteresso Castle, rebuilt in the 1830s, was once the seat of the Earls Marischal of Scotland.

Fetternear *Aberdeenshire* A house and estate in Chapel of Garioch parish, Aberdeenshire, Fetternear lies near the River Don, just northwest of Kemnay. The estate was once owned by the bishops of Aberdeen, who had a summer lodge here, and a predecessor of the present church is said to have been founded in the early 12th century.

Feugh, Water of *Aberdeenshire* A stream in the eastern Grampians, the Water of Feugh rises in the Forest of Birse near the border between Aberdeenshire and Angus. It flows a short distance north to Ballochan where it is joined by the Burn of Corn. From here it flows eastwards to join the River Dee at Banchory. Its main tributaries are the Water of Aven and the Water of Dye.

Fiaray *Western Isles* An uninhabited island lying off the north coast of Barra in the Outer Hebrides, Fiaray (Gael: *Fiaraidh*) is located a quarter-mile (0.5 km) north of Scurrival Point on Barra, separated by the Sound of Fiaray. The island has an area of 41 ha (101 acres) and is for the most part low-lying, although two modest hills in the west rise to 30 m (98 ft).

Fiart, Loch *Argyll and Bute* Loch Fiart is located at the southern end of the island of Lismore, Argyll and Bute. The settlement of Achnacroish lies 3 miles (5 km) to the northeast of the loch.

Fidden *Argyll and Bute* The settlement of Fidden is located on the western coastline of the Ross of Mull, southwest Mull. Its beach extends into the Sound of Iona.

Fiddich, River *Moray* Rising in the uplands of Moray, the River Fiddich flows some 20 miles (32 km) northeast and northwest past Dufftown to join the River Spey at Craigellachie. In its upper reaches the river flows through Glen Fiddich, a name associated with a noted whisky produced at the Glenfiddich Distillery.

Fiddler's Crus *Shetland* The name given to three ancient stone circles, the Fiddler's Crus lies at the centre of the Shetland island of Fetlar between Vord Hill and Skutes Water.

Fidra *East Lothian* A small rocky island in the Firth of Forth, Fidra lies 300 m (328 yd) off Yellowcraig on the East Lothian coast, 2 miles (3 km) north of Dirleton and 2.5 miles (4 km) west-northwest of North Berwick. There is a lighthouse at North Dog and the remains of a chapel. Fidra is noted for its large colony of puffins, which can be viewed from the Scottish Seabird Centre in North Berwick. The island is a designated Royal Society for the Protection of Birds (RSPB) reserve. Fidra is described in Robert Louis Stevenson's novel *Catriona* (1893) and is geologically part of a basalt sill injected between the surrounding sedimentary rocks by volcanic activity some 335 million years ago.

Fife *Area: 1340 sq. km (517 sq. miles)* The 'Kingdom of Fife' in east-central Scotland forms a peninsula jutting out into the North Sea, with the Firth of Forth to the south and the Firth of Tay to the north. West Fife, between Dunfermline and Kirkcaldy, is the region's industrial and commercial heartland, while the picturesque old fishing villages of the East Neuk are popular with tourists. Its chief rivers are the Eden and the Leven, which flow eastwards to the sea from sources to the north and south of the Lomond Hills. The ancient city of St Andrews is at the eastern tip of Fife. Evidence from Tentsmuir on the sandy tip of the Fife peninsula shows that this part of Scotland was occupied by

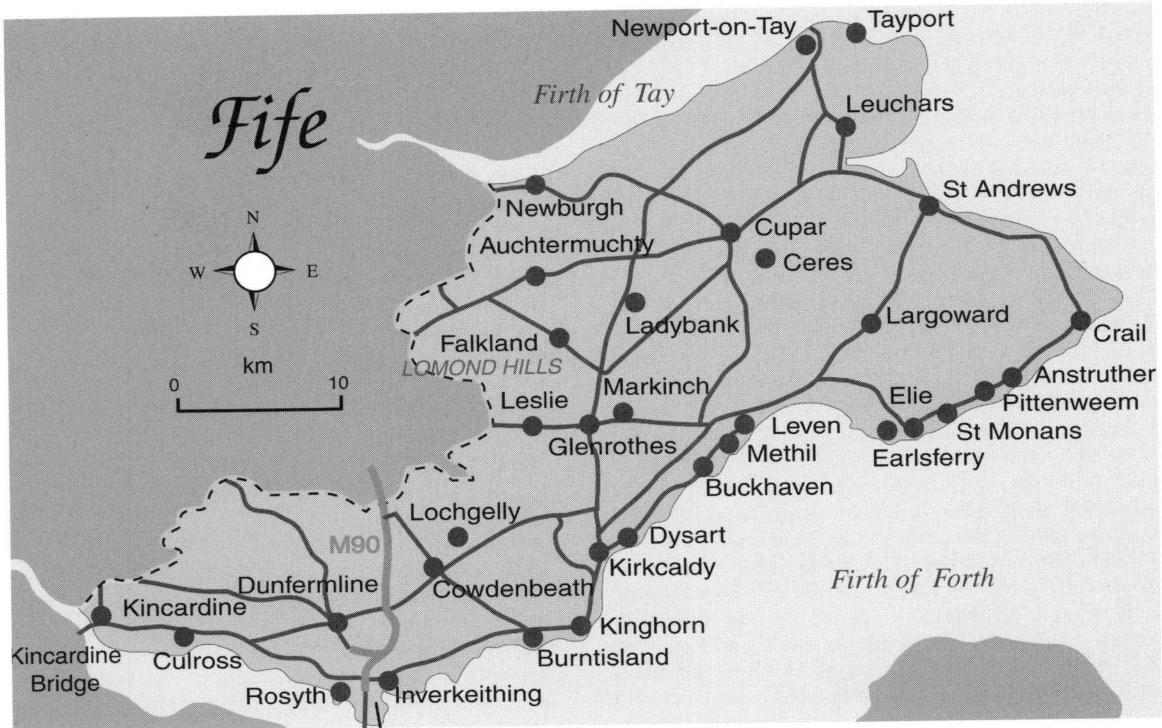

nomadic hunter-gatherer people over 8,000 years ago. The archaeological record, particularly burial sites and sites of ritual, suggests that Fife was well settled with a resident population around 4,000 years ago. The region has inherited a strong sense of identity that is derived partly from its sea- and firth-girt isolation and partly from its historic links with a regional kingdom of the Pictish confederation. The Pictish connection is still reflected in symbol stones, the remains of fortresses, and place names – particularly those including prefixes such as pit, meaning 'place of'. The region continued to be associated with royalty throughout the Middle Ages, with royal residences at Dunfermline and Falkland and royal charters granted to 18 of Fife's burgh towns. Of these royal burghs, 15 were ports whose trade with northern Europe was an important feature of Scotland's medieval economic growth and cultural development. The burgh of St Andrews became one of Scotland's greatest towns as a centre of the cult of St Andrew, the seat of the primacy of Scotland from 1472 until the Reformation, and the home of Scotland's oldest university (1412). Fife prospered from the 18th century, with improvements in agriculture, the expansion of fishing and boat building and the establishment of large-scale coal mining, textile and paper industries. The opportunities provided by the growth of the electronics industry and by the development of offshore oil and gas have significantly influenced the shape of the modern Fife economy. They have established the region as a centre of high-tech and information-based industries that have grown up alongside traditional long-established industries such as paper making, food processing, engineering, textiles and clothing. The tradition of manufacturing remains strong, employing almost 30 per cent of the workforce of 155,000, compared with 21 per cent nationally. Glenrothes is the administrative centre.

Fife Keith *Moray* A planned village built in 1817 by the Earl of Fife, Fife Keith lies on the left bank of the River Isla opposite Keith. It is built on a grid plan with a square at its centre.

Fife Ness *Fife* A sandstone headland at the eastern extremity of Fife, Fife Ness extends into the North Sea 2 miles (3 km) northeast of Crail and 9 miles (14 km) southeast of St Andrews. Close to a coastguard station are the remains of the village of Fife Ness which lies on the fairway of a golf course.

Fife Regional Park *Fife* Approximately 6475 ha (16,000 acres) of west-central Fife are divided into two areas – Fife Regional Park West and Fife Regional Park East. Fife Regional Park West stretches south from Benarty Hill and includes the Lochore Meadows Country Park. Fife Regional Park East, to the northwest of Glenrothes, extends over the largest upland area in Fife to include the peaks of East and West Lomond which are accessed from the Pitcairn Centre, Craigmead and East Lomond car parks.

Figgate Burn *City of Edinburgh* For most of its course, from its source in the Pentland Hills through the city of Edinburgh, the Figgate Burn is called the Braid Burn. It becomes the Figgate at Duddingston Mills, barely a mile (1.5 km) before draining into the Firth of Forth at Portobello, by the site of the old harbour. Northeast of Duddingston it passes the Figgate Pond, before entering Portobello at its western end. In 1882, the Portobello authorities forced Edinburgh to take action to clean up the burn, which had acted as an open sewer for parts of the city.

Fillan, River *Stirling* A headwater of the River Tay in northwest Stirling Council area, the River Fillan is formed at the meeting of headstreams to the south of Tyndrum. It flows southeastwards for 10 miles (16 km) through Strath Fillan before entering Loch Dochart 2 miles (3 km) east of Crianlarich.

Fillan, Strath *Stirling* The valley of the River Fillan, a headwater of the River Tay lying between Tyndrum and Loch Dochart, 2 miles (3 km) east of Crianlarich. The river and valley are named after St Fillan who was venerated by King Robert the Bruce and whose relics were paraded before the Scottish troops prior to the Battle of Bannockburn in 1314. The scant remains of St Fillan's Chapel are located by the farm of Kirkton to the north of the river, and a half-mile (1 km) up the valley is Linne Fhaolain (or St Fillan's Pool). Many cures are said to have resulted from taking the waters of this pool, which tradition asserts retained healing powers until a mad bull, pursued by dogs, plunged into it. The Healing Stones of St Fillan are preserved in the former mill at Killin which was reopened as the Breadalbane Folklore Centre in 1994.

Fin Glen *East Dunbartonshire* The Fin Glen, situated a mile (1.5 km) northwest of Lennoxtown in East Dunbartonshire, carries the Finglen Burn, a tributary of the Glazert Water which rises in the Campsie Fells. The Finglen Burn reaches the Glazert Water at Haughhead, south of Clachan of Campsie.

Finart, River *Argyll and Bute* A river of Argyll and Bute, the River Finart rises on Ben Bhreac between Loch Eck and Loch Long. It flows southeastwards through Glen Finart before entering Finart Bay, an inlet of Loch Long just north of Ardentinny.

Finavon Doocot *Angus* Lying alongside the A90 at Milton of Finavon, some 7 miles (11 km) northeast of Forfar in Angus, is the Finavon Doocot. It is believed to have been built for the Earl of Crawford in the 16th century and, with 2400 nesting boxes, is Scotland's largest dovecote. It is maintained by the National Trust for Scotland.

Fincastle House *Perth and Kinross* A mansion house in Glen Fincastle, Fincastle House overlooks the Fincastle Burn which flows from Lochan na Leathain through Allean Forest to join the River Tummel 4 miles (6.5 km) east of the Queen's View.

Fincharn Castle *Argyll and Bute* The ruined remains of the 16th-century tower house of Fincharn Castle are located on the eastern shore of Loch Awe, 2 miles (3 km) from the head of the loch, in Argyll and Bute. This castle was a stronghold of the Macdonald clan.

Findhorn *Moray* A seaport and resort in the Moray parish of Kinloss, Findhorn is situated on the east side of Findhorn Bay at the mouth of the River Findhorn. It is the third village of the same name, the original settlement to the west having been destroyed by the drifting of the Culbin Sands and its successor inundated by the sea in 1701. Once the principal port of Moray, its importance declined after the arrival of the railway in 1860. Thereafter the village developed as a holiday resort with marine leisure facilities. The community-based Findhorn Foundation, established here in 1962 by Eileen and Peter Caddy and Dorothy Maclean, erected the Universal Hall Arts and Conference Centre in Findhorn Park in 1974.

Findhorn, River *Highland* Rising in the Monadhliath Mountains in Highland Council area, the River Findhorn flows northeastwards for 62 miles (99 km), passing through Moray to join the Moray Firth at Findhorn Bay to the north of Forres.

Findhorn Bay *Moray* Before entering the Moray Firth, the River Findhorn flows into Findhorn Bay, a shallow estuary with a narrow channel that provides an outlet to the sea. To the west lie the Culbin Sands and near its outlet lies the village of Findhorn, whose harbour was once one of the busiest in Moray. Protected from the open sea, the bay is popular among yachting enthusiasts. The burgh town of Forres lies to the south.

Findhorn Viaduct *Highland* Located 500 m (550 yd) east of the village of Tomatin, some 14 miles (22 km) south-southeast of Inverness, the Findhorn Viaduct conveys the Perth–Inverness main railway line 49 m (160 ft) above the valley of the River Findhorn. Built between 1894 and 1897, this impressive curved viaduct is some 400 m (438 yd) long and consists of nine spans of lattice-steel structure supported on stonework piers. The viaduct was built by Sir John Fowler and Murdoch Paterson.

Findhu Glen *Perth and Kinross* A narrow valley in central Perth and Kinross, Findhu Glen extends 6 miles (10 km) south and southeast from Glen Artney.

Findlater Castle *Aberdeenshire* Located a mile (1.5 km) to the northwest of the village of Sandend in Aberdeenshire, the ruins of Findlater Castle sit atop a 15-m/50-ft-high cliff. Built by the Ogilvie family in 1455, the castle was besieged by Mary, Queen of Scots in 1562, during the Gordon Rebellion. The castle was abandoned in the 17th century and left to ruin. All that remains are the three-storey-high ruins and a nearby dovecote.

Findlay's Seat *Moray* A hill in Moray, Findlay's Seat rises to a height of 262 m (861 ft), just over 6 miles (10 km) southeast of Elgin, between the Glen of Rothes and the River Spey. Its eastern slopes are forested with the trees of Teindland Forest and the Wood of Dundurcas.

Findo Gask *Perth and Kinross* A locality with a church and school in a parish of the same name in Strath Earn, Perth and Kinross, Findo Gask lies on the Gask Ridge, 6 miles (10 km) southwest of Perth. There are the remains of a series of Roman signal stations along a Roman road that passes to the south. Trinity Gask Parish Church and manse date from the 1770s, and to the southwest is Gask House, built in 1801–05 for Laurence Oliphant of Gask. The Oliphants were associated with the Gask Estate for several centuries until the death of Kingston Oliphant in 1907. Although the house was forfeited after the Jacobite rising of 1745, the family returned to it in 1763. The celebrated lyricist Carolina Oliphant (1766–1845), later Lady Nairne, was born at Gask. Among her most famous songs were *The Laird o' Cockpen, Charlie is my darling* and *Will ye no come back again?*

Findochty *Moray* A resort and fishertown in the Moray parish of Rathven, Findochty is situated between two headlands on the Moray Firth coast between Buckie and Cullen. Known locally as Finechty, the 'Manor, port, customs and fisher lands' of Findochty existed as early as 1598, when they were acquired by the Ord family. But it was not until 1716, when Thomas Ord of Findochty Castle allegedly imported 13 men and four boys of Fraserburgh to fish, that the settlement began to grow into a fishertown. It developed with the white-fish and herring trade during the 19th century, but today David Stevenson's Hythe Harbour of the 1880s is largely frequented by leisure craft. The Gothic-style church (1863) on Long Head once acted as a beacon to fishermen, and to the west, at the end of a drained loch on Findochty Moor, stand the ruins of Findochty Castle, an L-plan keep dating from the 15th century. The moor was the scene of the Battle of the Bauds in AD 961 when the Norse, led by Eric of the Bloody Axe, were routed by the Scots. The King's Cairn marks the spot where Indulf, the Scottish king, fell in battle. The town has a watersports club and an 18-hole golf course.

Findon *Aberdeenshire* A cliff-top fishing and commuter village in Banchory Devenick parish, eastern Aberdeenshire, Findon (or Finnan) is situated on the North Sea coast, 8 miles (13 km) south of Aberdeen. The home of the 'Finnan Haddie', it is said to have been the first place to prepare the dried fish known as Findon or Finnan haddock.

Findon Ness *Aberdeenshire* A headland on the North Sea coast of Aberdeenshire, Findon Ness extends into the sea 6 miles (10 km) south of Aberdeen. The village of Findon lies to the west.

Findrack *Aberdeenshire* An estate and house in Lumphanan parish, Aberdeenshire, Findrack lies to the west of the Beltie Burn and just over a mile (1.5 km) east of Lumphanan. Built about 1700, the house has splendid views over the Dee Valley, and a walled garden.

Finegand *Perth and Kinross* A locality in Glen Shee, eastern Perth and Kinross, Finegand is situated by the Shee Water, 18 miles (29 km) north of Blairgowrie. The Clan MacThomas is associated with this part of the country.

Fingal's Cave *Argyll and Bute* A spectacular cave on the southern shore of the island of Staffa in the Inner Hebrides, which is part of the Mull Plateau Group, Fingal's Cave is one of the most famous locations in the Scottish islands. Surrounded by vertical basaltic columns representing lava flows that took place in the Tertiary period over 60 million years ago, the cave is 20 m (66 ft) in height with an opening of 13 m (42 ft). The massive regular columns at the base of the lava flow are overlaid by an upper tier of narrow, poorly developed columns topped by a slaggy flow. Fingal's Cave, named after the mythical giant Fin MacCoul, was first publicised by Sir Joseph Banks in 1772, resulting in a visit by Dr Johnson and his biographer, James Boswell, a year later. Sir Walter Scott described the cave in *The Lord of the Isles* (1815) following his visit in 1812, and in 1818 the composer Felix Mendelssohn was inspired by a visit to the cave to write his *Hebrides Overture*, or 'Fingal's Cave'.

Fingask *Aberdeenshire* A locality in the Formartine district of Aberdeenshire, Fingask lies midway between Daviot and Oldmeldrum. It comprises an estate with a mansion house built in 1834.

Fingask *Perth and Kinross* A 16th-century tower house in the Braes of the Carse on the southern flank of the Sidlaw Hills, Perth and Kinross, Fingask lies near the village of Rait, between Perth and Dundee. Originally a stronghold of the Bruces, Fingask was sold to the Threiplands, a Peeblesshire family who temporarily lost the property after the first Jacobite Rising in 1715. The building was restored in 1816. In the garden are fine examples of topiary.

Fingask Loch *Perth and Kinross* A small loch in the valley of the Lunan Burn, eastern Perth and Kinross, Fingask Loch lies a mile (1.5 km) to the southwest of Blairgowrie.

Fingland *Dumfries and Galloway* A hamlet of Eskdale in Dumfries and Galloway, Fingland lies on the White Esk, 18 miles (29 km) northwest of Langholm.

Fingland Burn *Dumfries and Galloway* A small stream in Eskdale, Dumfries and Galloway, the Fingland Burn is a tributary of the White Esk.

Fingland Lane *Dumfries and Galloway* A stream in Dalry parish, Dumfries and Galloway, the Fingland Lane rises on Fingland Hill and flows westwards to join the Black Water, a tributary of the Water of Ken.

Finglas, Glen *Stirling* A valley in the Trossachs district of Stirling Council area, Glen Finglas follows the course of the Finglas Water. It flows 8 miles (13 km) south and southeast from Creagan nan Sgiath before joining the Black Water between Loch Achray and Loch Venachar, a mile (1.5 km) to the west of Brig o' Turk. The Glen Finglas Reservoir, which is formed by the middle course of the river, also receives the Allt Gleann nam Meann and the Casaig Burn.

Finlaggan, Loch *Argyll and Bute* A loch at the north end of the island of Islay in the Inner Hebrides, Loch Finlaggan lies 3 miles (5 km) southwest of Port Askaig. The ruins of a castle of the Lords of the Isles stand on an islet, and on another small island close by the council of the Lords of the Isles met.

Finlarig *Stirling* A locality in Stirling Council area, Finlarig lies just north of Killin on a peninsula between the River Lochay and Loch Tay. In the grounds of the ruined 16th-century Finlarig Castle, a former stronghold of the Campbells, are the remains of a beheading pit.

Finlet Burn *Angus* A stream of Angus in the southern Grampians, the Finlet Burn rises between the River Isla and the Prosen Water. It flows south through Glen Finlet, eventually joining the River Isla as the Newton Burn.

Finnan An alternative name for Findon in Aberdeenshire.

Finnart *Perth and Kinross* A locality in Perth and Kinross, Finnart lies to the east of Bridge of Gaur at the western end of Loch Rannoch, where a stream flows down from Loch Finnart to enter the south side of Loch Rannoch. Finnart Lodge lies on a point at the eastern end of Finnart Bay, and to the west are the scattered settlements of Finnart and Little Finnart.

Finnarts Point *South Ayrshire* Finnarts Point is a headland of South Ayrshire at the mouth of Loch Ryan. Located on the northeast shore of Loch Ryan, Finnarts Bay lies a mile (1.5 km) to the south.

Finnich Burn *Stirling* Rising from Burncrooks Reservoir on Dumbarton Muir to the north of the Kilpatrick Hills, the Finnich Burn flows 5 miles (8 km) northeastwards to meet the Blane Water southwest of Killearn in southern Stirling Council area.

Finnieston Crane *Glasgow City* Located at the heart of Glasgow's former dockland, the Finnieston Crane is a cantilever crane built in 1932. It stands 59 m (195 ft) high and has a hammerhead jib of 46 m (152 ft). Although known as the Finnieston Crane, it actually stands on Stobcross Quay and was used to transfer boilers and engines into new vessels and load heavy machinery onto freighters. Now used only occasionally, it symbolises the past strength of Glasgow's heavy-engineering industry and is one of the city's best-known landmarks.

Finstown *Orkney* A village on Mainland Orkney,

Finstown lies at the head of the Bay of Firth, 6 miles (10 km) northwest of Kirkwall.

Fintray An alternative name for Hatton of Fintray in Aberdeenshire.

Fintray House *Aberdeenshire* Fintray House lies in the village of Hatton of Fintray on the River Don in Aberdeenshire. It was the home of the Forbes-Sempill family, who also possessed the barony of Craigievar and Craigievar Castle. Fintray House was rebuilt in the early 19th century to the designs of the architect William Burn (1789–1870) to become the primary home of the family. However, the house was requisitioned during World War II, and the family never returned.

Fintry *Stirling* Situated at the head of Strathendrick, the village of Fintry lies on the Endrick Water between the Fintry Hills and the Campsie Fells. It is a dormitory village for Glasgow, Stirling and Falkirk, with tourist facilities, hotels, caravan parks, local crafts, a leisure centre, a bowling club and a sports centre built by the local community. The parish church dates from 1823 and the former manse, Dunmore House, was built in 1723. Upstream from the picturesque Low Bridge of Gonacahan lie the ruins of the 15th-century castle of the Grahams of Fintry, and on a hill at the western end of the village is a well-preserved medieval motte and bailey. Fintry is a former winner of the 'Best Kept Small Village in Britain' and 'Britain in Bloom' competitions.

Fintry Hills *Stirling* Rising to a height of 512 m (1678 ft) at Stronend 2 miles (3 km) northeast of Fintry, the Fintry Hills form a western outlier of the Gargunnock Hills with steep west- and north-facing slopes. The Boquhan, Shelloch, Balmenach and Cammal Burns rise in the Fintry Hills.

Finzean *Aberdeenshire* A locality in the Aberdeenshire parish of Birse, Finzean lies 4 miles (6.5 km) southeast of Aboyne. To the southwest, on the Water of Feugh, stands the restored Finzean Bucket Mill with its craft shop and visitor centre.

Fionn Bheinn *Highland* Located south of Loch Fannich and north of Achnasheen in Wester Ross, Fionn Bheinn (or Fionaven), rises to a height of 933 m (3061 ft) with smooth grassy slopes to the south and steeper craggy flanks to the north. Its name is derived from the Gaelic for 'pale-coloured hill'.

Fionnphort *Argyll and Bute* A small hamlet and ferry port on the Ross of Mull, Fionnphort overlooks the Sound of Iona, 35 miles (56 km) west of Oban. A passenger ferry connects with Iona.

Firbush Point *Stirling* A locality in northern Stirling Council area, Firbush Point is located on the south shore of Loch Tay, 2 miles (3 km) east of Killin. A wood-built field centre operated by the University of Edinburgh is situated here.

Fishcross *Clackmannanshire* A village in central Clackmannanshire, Fishcross is situated to the north of Sauchie at a crossroads. A golf course and equestrian centre are located nearby and at Auchinbaird there is a fine example of a windmill built in the early 18th century to drain a coal pit and later converted to serve as a dovecote.

Fisherrow *East Lothian* A former fishing village on the Firth of Forth, Fisherrow lies to the east of Portobello and Joppa, and now forms part of Musselburgh in East Lothian. It sits on the left bank of the River Esk as it drains into the Firth of Forth. Fisherrow Harbour is preserved as a traditional fishing harbour and is used primarily by pleasure boats, although a few inshore fishing vessels remain.

Fisherton *South Ayrshire* Located a mile (1.5 km) north of Dunure, above the Heads of Ayr in South Ayrshire, Fisherton is a scattered community. To the south lie Dunure Castle and the Electric Brae, while to the north lies the town of Ayr.

Fishnish *Argyll and Bute* A locality on the east coast of the island of Mull in the Inner Hebrides, Fishnish lies on the Sound of Mull to the east of Fishnish Bay and Fishnish Point, 6 miles (10 km) southeast of Salen. A ferry connects Fishnish with Lochaline on the Morvern peninsula.

Fithie, Loch *Angus* A small loch in the valley of Strathmore, Angus, Loch Fithie lies between Rescobie Loch and Forfar. Restenneth Priory lies to the northwest. Prior to drainage in the 18th century the loch was much larger.

Five Sisters, the *Highland* A group of mountains to the east of Glen Shiel in Kintail, Wester Ross, the Five Sisters form a chain of peaks from Sgurr na Moraich (876 m/2873 ft) in the north through Sgurr nan Saighead (929 m/3047 ft), Sgurr Fhuaran (also Scour Ouran) (1067 m/3501 ft) and Sgurr na Carnach (1002 m/3287 ft) to Sgurr na Ciste Duibhe (1027 m/3369 ft) in the south. The Five Sisters of Kintail lie within a 7431-ha (18,362-acre) estate owned by the National Trust for Scotland.

Fivepenny *Western Isles* One of several closely associated crofting settlements in the Ness district at the northern tip of Lewis in the Outer Hebrides, Fivepenny (Gael: *Coig Peighinnean*) is located immediately to the east-southeast of Eorpie, a half-mile (1 km) north of Lionel and 1.25 miles (2 km) south-southeast of the Butt of Lewis.

Fladdabister *Shetland* A hamlet located above the Bay of Fladdabister on the east coast of the Mainland of Shetland, Fladdabister lies 6 miles (10 km) southwest of Lerwick.

Flanders Moss *Stirling* An extensive area of reclaimed land in the Carse of Stirling or upper valley of the River Forth, Flanders Moss was until the 18th century uncultivated peat moss. The agricultural improver Henry Home, Lord Kames (1696–1792), was the first local laird to attempt to remove the peat that covered a fertile bed of clay beneath. Improvement leases were offered to crofters from Balquhidder on condition that they worked to improve the land, and great volumes of peat were cut into sections and washed away using water from the River Teith. Within a few decades most of the former peat moss had been reclaimed and cultivated. Remnants of the moss north of Buchlyvie have been designated as a Site of Special Scientific Interest (SSSI).

Flannan Isles *Western Isles* A collection of seven islands and several smaller islets, arranged in three groups, the Flannan Isles (Gael: *Na h-Eileanan Flannach*) lie 21 miles (33 km) northwest of Gallan Head and 31 miles (50 km) west of Carloway in Lewis. Also known as the Seven Hunters, the islands are noted for their breeding sea birds, which include fulmars, gannets and puffins. The largest island, Eilean Mòr, has a small ruined chapel dedicated to the Irish bishop St Flann or St Flannan, and a lighthouse that was built in 1899 and automated in 1971. In December 1900 the three lighthouse keepers disappeared under mysterious circumstances. When a party arrived to determine why there was no light, they found a meal lying uneaten but no trace of the keepers. The incident is remembered in the poem *Flannan Isle* by English poet Wilfred Wilson Gibson (1878–1962).

Fleet, Islands of *Dumfries and Galloway* A group of small islands in Dumfries and Galloway, the Islands of Fleet lie at the mouth of Fleet Bay, an inlet of the Solway Firth. The principal islands in the group are Murray's Isle, Ardwall Island and Barlocco Isle.

Fleet, Loch *Dumfries and Galloway* A small loch in Dumfries and Galloway, Loch Fleet lies to the south of Fell of Fleet in Galloway Forest Park. It is the source of the Little Water of Fleet, a headstream of the Water of Fleet.

Fleet, Loch *Highland* An estuary and nature reserve of eastern Sutherland in Highland Council area, Loch Fleet lies between Skelbo and Littleferry, some 2.5 miles (4 km) southwest of Golspie. Bounded to the northwest by a causeway carrying the main A9 north, Loch Fleet receives the River Fleet which flows for 12 miles (19 km) southeastwards through Strath Fleet from its source near Lairg.

Fleet, Water of *Dumfries and Galloway* A river of Dumfries and Galloway, the Water of Fleet rises in Galloway Forest Park as the Big Water and Little Water of Fleet. The two headstreams meet 6 miles (10 km) north of Gatehouse of Fleet, from where the river flows southwards into Fleet Bay.

Fleet Bay *Dumfries and Galloway* An inlet of the Solway Firth, Fleet Bay lies at the mouth of the Water of Fleet, a mile (1.5 km) to the southwest of Gatehouse of Fleet. Where it receives the Skyre Burn, it is known as Skyreburn Bay.

Fleisirin *Western Isles* One of several contiguous crofting townships at the eastern end of the Eye peninsula on the east coast of Lewis in the Outer Hebrides, Fleisirin (sometimes Bail Ur na Fleisirin) is located immediately to the west of Cnoc Amhlaigh, 1.5 miles (2.5 km) southwest of Tiumpan Head.

Flemington *South Lanarkshire* A suburb of Strathaven in South Lanarkshire, Flemington is located about a mile (1.5 km) north of Strathaven Castle.

Fleoideabhagh The Gaelic name for Flodabay in the Western Isles.

Flisk *Fife* A sparsely populated rural parish on the shore of the Firth of Tay between Newburgh and Balmerino. It rises to 217 m (712 ft) at Glenduckie Hill and includes the ruins of Ballinbreich Castle, a former seat of the Leslie family.

Float Bay *Dumfries and Galloway* A small inlet on the west coast of the Rhinns of Galloway, Dumfries and Galloway, Float Bay lies 6 miles (10 km) southwest of Sandhead.

Flocklones *Perth and Kinross* A hamlet developed on the site of a farm in eastern Perth and Kinross, Flocklones is located a mile (1.5 km) north-northeast of Longforgan and comprises a handful of large detached houses built in 2003–04.

Flodabay *Western Isles* The southernmost of a string of connected settlements strung along the rocky east coast of South Harris in the Outer Hebrides, Flodabay (Gael: *Fleoideabhagh*) lies at the head of Loch Flodabay, to the west of Manish, 4.5 miles (7 km) northeast of Rodel.

Flodaigh The Gaelic name for Flodday in the Western Isles.

Flodaigh Beag The Gaelic name for Floddaybeg in the Western Isles.

Flodaigh Mòr The Gaelic name for Floddaymore in the Western Isles.

Floday *Western Isles* A small uninhabited island in the Outer Hebrides, Floday (Gael: *Floddaigh*) is located in West Loch Roag to the west of Little Bernera and the northwest of Great Bernera, 5 miles (8 km) west of Carloway on the island of Lewis. The island rises to 22 m (72 ft). Another larger island called Floday lies 5 miles (8 km) to the south-southwest.

Floday *Western Isles* An uninhabited island located in the Outer Hebrides, Floday (Gael: *Flodaigh*) is located in West Loch Roag, to the west of Vuia Beg, a mile (1.5 km) southeast of Uigen on the island of Lewis. The island rises to 48 m (157 ft) to the northeast. It was inhabited until the population was cleared for sheep in 1827. Another island named Floday lies 5 miles (8 km) to the north-northeast.

Flodday *Western Isles* An inhabited island in the channel that separates North Uist from Benbecula, Flodday (Gael: *Flodaigh*) lies a half-mile (1 km) southwest of Grimsay and is connected to Benbecula by a causeway.

Flodday *Western Isles* One of a group of uninhabited islands located off the northeast coast of Barra in the Outer Hebrides, Flodday (Gael: *Flodaigh*) has an area of 40 ha (99 acres) and rises to 42 m (137 ft) immediately to the east of Fuiay and a mile (1.5 km) south of Hellisay.

Flodday *Western Isles* A small uninhabited island in the Outer Hebrides, Flodday (Gael: *Flodaigh*) lies a mile (1.5 km) southwest of Vatersay, towards the southern end of the archipelago. Flodday comprises three parts; the largest, in the north, rises to 43m (141 ft).

Floddaybeg *Western Isles* A small island at the east end of the channel that separates North Uist from Benbecula, Floddaybeg (Gael: *Flodaigh Beag*) rises to 32 m (105 ft) just off the remote southeast coast of North Uist, a quarter-mile (0.5 km) northeast of the larger island of Floddaymore and 3 miles (5 km) northeast of Kallin on Grimsay.

Floddaymore *Western Isles* An island at the east end of the channel that separates North Uist from Benbecula, Floddaymore (Gael: *Flodaigh Mòr*) rises to 28 m (91 ft) off the remote southeast coast of North Uist, immediately to the east of the larger island of Ronay and 2.5 miles (4 km) northeast of Kallin on Grimsay. The island has three lochans.

Floddaigh The Gaelic name for Floday in the Western Isles.

Flodden Wall *City of Edinburgh* A defensive structure built around Edinburgh after the disastrous Battle of Flodden (1513) in which King James IV was killed. The construction was a response to threatened English invasion after a war started by James in support of the French and the 'Auld Alliance'. Although construction continued into the middle of the 16th century, the hurriedly conceived project offered little protection when Protector Somerset sacked Edinburgh during the 'Rough Wooing'. Its main effect, before being dismantled from the middle of the 17th century, was to restrict the southern development of Edinburgh's Old Town. Today, the wall is best inspected at two locations: in the Vennel to the west of the Grassmarket, and on the west side of the Pleasance turning up Drummond Street, where it originally enclosed the Blackfriars' Monastery.

Floors Castle *Scottish Borders* A magnificent stately home built between 1718 and 1725 for John Ker (c.1682–1740), 1st Duke of Roxburgh, Floors Castle lies just to the north of the River Tweed, a mile (1.5 km) west of Kelso in Scottish Borders. Designed by William Adam but greatly influenced by Sir John Vanbrugh, the castle was remodelled into a Tudor-style mansion by William Playfair between 1838 and 1849 for the 6th Duke of Roxburgh. It was visited by Queen Victoria and Prince Albert in 1867. Today, Floors is said to be the largest inhabited house in Scotland and remains the seat of the dukes of Roxburgh, originally the Kers of Cessford. A holly tree nearby marks the spot where King James II was killed by the accidental explosion of a large cannon, known as The Lion, while besieging Roxburgh Castle in 1460, at that time in English hands.

Floral Clock *City of Edinburgh* Located next to the foot of The Mound in West Princes Street Gardens, Edinburgh, is the oldest floral clock in the world. First created in 1903, the clock is replanted every spring in a topical design with thousands of colourful plants. The clock is 3.5 m (12 ft) in diameter and the hands, which are driven by an electrical mechanism, weigh more than 60 kg (130 lb). Overlooking the clock is a statue of the poet Allan Ramsay (c.1684–1758) by the sculptor Sir John Steell (1804–91).

Flosh *Dumfries and Galloway* A locality in Dumfries and Galloway, Flosh lies near the Solway coast between Ruthwell and Cummertrees, 5 miles (8 km) west of Annan.

Flotta *Orkney* Guarding the southern entrance to Scapa Flow in the Orkney Islands, the 'flat' island of Flotta, with an area of 976 ha (2411 acres), lies to the west of the Sound of Hoxa, which separates it from South Ronaldsay. During the 20th century it played two important maritime roles, first as a naval base during both World Wars and second as an oil terminal linked in 1974 by a 142-mile (230-km) pipeline to the Piper and Claymore fields in the North Sea. The island has an airfield as well as ferry links with Hoy and Mainland Orkney, and its population of 81 (2001) is associated with farming, fishing and the oil installation. The highest point on Flotta is West Hill at 58 m (190 ft). Pan Hope, a shallow bay to the east, was the site of saltpans during the 17th century.

Flow Country, the *Highland* The Flow Country is the name given to the blanket peat and wet lands that cover over 400,000 ha (988,400 acres) of Caithness and Sutherland. It is probably the largest area of blanket bog in the northern hemisphere and one of the most intact such areas in the world. 'Flows' is the local term for the intricate pattern of peat bogs and pool systems (or dubh lochans), but the term 'Flow Country' was coined by outsiders in the 1980s when conservationists mounted a sophisticated campaign to halt afforestation. The controversy ended with a judgement by the Secretary of State for Scotland dividing the Flow Country between forests and conservation, but by 1990 large-scale planting had ceased. The arguments in favour of conserving the Flows highlighted their landscape value, their significance as a biological resource and their wider scientific importance.

Fochabers *Moray* A small town in the Moray parish of Bellie, Fochabers is situated on high ground to the east of the River Spey, at the junction of the A98 and A96, 12 miles (19 km) east of Elgin. It was built on its present site on the line of the Aberdeen–Inverness road in 1776 by the 4th Duke of Gordon, replacing an earlier settlement close to Gordon Castle. The old burgh of Fochabers, which had been created in the late 16th century at a crossing on the Spey, was in a state of some decay when Johnson and Boswell passed through in 1773. The modern planned village is a spacious settlement built around a square dominated by a neoclassical steepled church (Bellie Church) of 1798 by John Baxter. Other buildings of interest include the Gothic-style Episcopal Chapel designed by Archibald Simpson in 1834, and Alexander Mackenzie's Elizabethan-style Milne's High School, founded in 1846 by Alexander Milne (1742–1839), a Scots emigrant who made his fortune in New Orleans. A viewpoint known as The Peeps can be reached by following the Winding Walk, and there are several woodland walks in the surrounding Speymouth Forest. Other features of the town include a folk museum and floral clock. Standing close to the probable site of a Roman camp, the original Gordon Castle, begun by George Gordon, 2nd Earl of Huntly, was developed into a great Renaissance palace by his grandson. In 1769 the Duke of Gordon invited John Baxter to rebuild the castle and in more recent times the central block was demolished and part of the remainder adapted to form a castellated mansion. Fochabers has tourist facilities, a folk museum and, on the opposite side of the river, the food-processing factory of Baxters of Speyside.

Fodragaigh The Gaelic name for Fodragay in the Western Isles.

Fodragay *Western Isles* A low-lying uninhabited island located among rocky islets in Bagh nam Faoilean to the southeast of Benbecula, Fodragay (Gael: *Fodragaigh*) is trimmed by rocks and it is possible to cross to the neighbouring island of Eilean na Cille at low tide. Wiay lies a half-mile (1 km) to the east.

Foinaven *Highland* A large mountain mass of northwest Sutherland, Foinaven (Gael: *Foinne Bhein*) rises steeply from the lochan-littered moorland to the east of Loch Inchard, 5.5 miles (9 km) northeast of Laxford Bridge. Composed of quartzite, the mountain sparkles spectacularly in the sunshine but is also of significant geological interest as an excellent exposure of the Moine Thrust. Its five summits are strung out along a 3-mile (5-km) ridge and reach a height of 914 m (2999 ft) at Ganu Mòr, which misses out on being classified as a Munro by only 0.3 m (1 foot), although some argue that the margin of survey error could mean it does actually meet the criterion. The other prominent top is Ceann Garbh at 902 m (2959 ft).

Fons Scotia An alternative name for Scotlandwell in Perth and Kinross.

Foodie Hill *Fife* A small hill rising to c.150 m (450 ft) 3 miles (5 km) northeast of Cupar in the parish of Dairsie. The farm of Foodie and the hamlet of Foodiecash lie to the southwest.

Footdee *Aberdeen City* A former fishing village, now part of Aberdeen, Footdee lies at the east end of the harbour.

Forbestown *Aberdeenshire* A small roadside village on the north bank of the River Don in Strathdon, Aberdeenshire, Forbestown lies just opposite Strathdon and to the east of Bellabeg, venue for the annual Lonach

Highland Gathering and Games. The village was founded by the Forbes family, one of whom, Sir Charles Forbes, is commemorated by a huge cairn erected on Lonach Hill to celebrate his elevation to a baronetcy.

Ford *Argyll and Bute* A hamlet in Argyll and Bute, Ford lies at the south end of Loch Awe, 4 miles (6.5 km) north-northeast of Kilmartin. Forestry, fishing and trout farming sustain a population of under 100.

Ford *Midlothian* A small village in Midlothian, Ford lies on the River Tyne to the west of Pathhead and south of Dalkeith.

Fordell *Fife* A former estate colliery village in western Fife, Fordell (formerly Fordel) is situated a mile (1.5 km) to the east of Crossgates. It was once linked by Scotland's first private railway to St David's Harbour on the Firth of Forth and comprised two squares known as Fordel Square and Wemyss Square. To the south is the late 16th-century Fordell Castle which belonged to the Henderson family for over 400 years and was restored by the late Sir Nicholas Fairbairn MP.

Fordoun *Aberdeenshire* A locality in the Howe of the Mearns, Aberdeenshire, Fordoun lies to the west of the A90 from Dundee to Aberdeen, 3 miles (5 km) north of Laurencekirk. Fordoun (or Fothirdun) lies in a parish of the same name, its kirkton being the village of Auchenblae. It is associated with the 14th-century chronicler, John of Fordoun.

Fordyce *Aberdeenshire* The village of Fordyce in Aberdeenshire lies 3 miles (5 km) southwest of Portsoy. Sitting in the shadow of Durn Hill, Fordyce dates from as early as 1272 and boasts its own castle. Now a conservation village, Fordyce is renowned as a centre of outstanding architectural and historical interest and has become a popular tourist resort. The Joiner's Workshop is one of the attractions of the village.

Forest Mill *Clackmannanshire* A hamlet in eastern Clackmannanshire, Forest Mill straddles the Black Devon River and the A977 from Kinross to Kincardine. The poet Michael Bruce (1746–67) taught at the primary school for several months prior to his death.

Forfar *Angus* The administrative centre of Angus and a royal burgh, Forfar is situated in the heart of the valley of Strathmore, 14 miles (22 km) north of Dundee. A conical mound known as Castlehill at the northeastern end of the town was the site of a royal residence dating from the time of Malcolm Canmore in the 11th century. This castle, which appears on the burgh's seal, was alleged by the historian Hector Boece to have been the meeting place of the parliament in 1057 at which surnames and titles were first conferred on the Scottish nobility. To the west lies Forfar Loch. Forfar was granted the status of a royal burgh by King David I (1084–1153), a charter reaffirmed by King Charles II in 1665. It was also the county town of Forfarshire. Once noted for its gloves, shoes and clothing, Forfar was a centre for tanning and the manufacture of coarse linen and jute in the 19th century. In addition to its present roles as an administrative centre and livestock market town, Forfar has dairy-produce, food-processing, textile, light-engineering and electronics industries. The town gives its name to the meat pasty known as a Forfar Bridie. The Meffan Gallery and Museum in the High Street illustrates the history, art and industry of Forfar. There is a leisure centre and 18-hole golf course at Cunninghill,

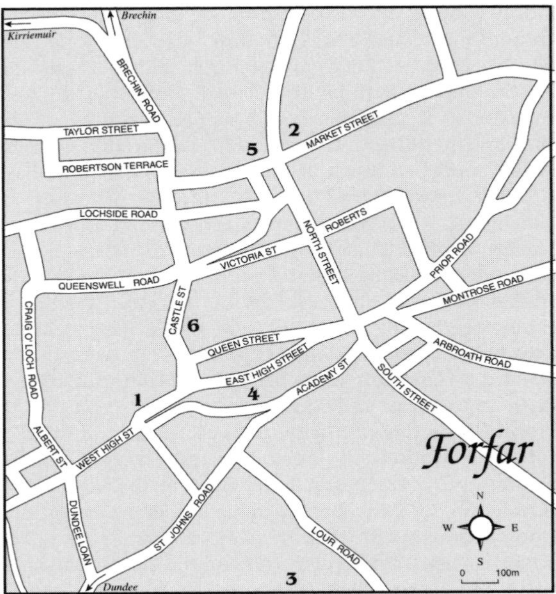

1 *Meffan Gallery and Museum*
2 *Market*
3 *Reid Park*
4 *Parish Church*
5 *County Buildings*
6 *Mercat Cross*

and each June the Forfar Highland Games are held at the Lochside.

Forfar Loch *Angus* Situated on the western outskirts of the Angus burgh town of Forfar, Forfar Loch forms the focal point of a 38-ha (93-acre) country park with a leisure centre at its eastern end. Much reduced by drainage in the 18th century, it was bought by the town in 1953. St Margaret's Inch, now occupied by a sailing club, was once the site of a prehistoric crannog, and local tradition suggests that a chapel of the Holy Trinity was founded here by Queen Margaret in the 11th century. The Dean Water flows westwards out of the loch.

Forgandenny *Perth and Kinross* A village of Perth and Kinross, Forgandenny lies a mile (1.5 km) south of the River Earn and 4 miles (6.5 km) southwest of Perth. Strathallan School, which was founded in 1912 and moved from Bridge of Allan to Freeland House in 1920, lies between the village and the river.

Forglen House *Aberdeenshire* A house and estate in Aberdeenshire, Forglen lies on the River Deveron, 2 miles (3 km) northwest of Turriff. The present house, built in 1842, is the successor to an earlier seat of the Abercromby family dating from the 15th century.

Forgue, Burn of *Aberdeenshire* A stream in northwest Aberdeenshire, the Burn of Forgue rises in the hills of Strathbogie to the southeast of Huntly. It flows north to join the River Deveron in a hollow known as the Howe of Forgue.

Formartine *Aberdeenshire* A district of Aberdeenshire, Formartine comprises the land between the Ythan and Don rivers and between the North Sea and the Deveron. The Formartine and Buchan Way from Parkhill near Dyce to Peterhead and Fraserburgh follows the route of a former railway that operated until 1979.

Forres *Moray* An ancient royal burgh and agricultural market town in northwest Moray, Forres lies on a ridge overlooking the River Findhorn midway between Elgin

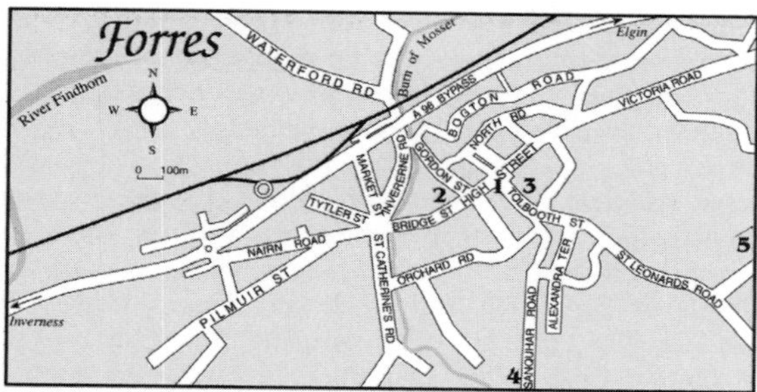

1 Tolbooth
2 St Laurence Church
3 Falconer Museum
4 Mechanics Institute
5 Nelson Tower

and Nairn. Situated in a strategic position on the route from Aberdeen to Inverness, Forres's western approaches were once defended by a royal castle. Forres retains much of its medieval layout and is now bypassed. Notable buildings include the Tolbooth, rebuilt by William Robertson in 1838; the Gothic-style St Laurence Church, built in 1904 to a design by John Robertson; the Mechanics Institute (1823); Nelson's Tower, an octagonal tower built in 1806 in memory of Lord Nelson to a design by Charles Stewart; Forres Academy, built in the 1960s to a design by Reiach and Hall; and the Falconer Museum (1869), built from a bequest by Alexander and Hugh Falconer to house a large collection of fossils. To the east of Forres is Sueno's Stone, a cross-slab that possibly dates from the 9th century and may commemorate a victory of the Picts over the Danes. To the south is the Dallas Dhu Distillery.

Forrestfield *North Lanarkshire* A scattered settlement located at the eastern edge of North Lanarkshire, Forrestfield lies a mile (1.5 km) to the east of the Hillend Reservoir and 3 miles (5 km) west of Blackridge.

Forsinard *Highland* A hamlet in eastern Sutherland, Forsinard lies in upper Strath Halladale. A railway station, opened here in 1874, is a request stop for passenger trains.

Forss *Highland* A small village on the north coast of the Caithness district of Highland Council area, Forss lies on the Forss Water where it meets the sea, 5 miles (8 km) west of Thurso. Nearby are Forss Mill, the ancient chapel of Crosskirk, and Brims Castle, a former stronghold of the Sinclairs of Dunbeath. The main road between Thurso and Tongue crosses the Bridge of Forss, and a US Navy satellite station was established here in 1987.

Fort Augustus *Highland* A settlement in the Great Glen, Highland Council area, Fort Augustus lies at the southern end of Loch Ness where the River Oich and the Caledonian Canal enter the loch. Barracks were built near the old township and church of Kilcummin in 1717, and in the 1730s the military road-builder General Wade constructed a road from Laggan via the Corrieyairick Pass and Glen Tarff to the fort, which was enlarged to hold over 300 men and renamed Fort Augustus. The fort was garrisoned until 1867, after which a Benedictine abbey and boarding school were founded by successive Lords Lovat. In 1890 the monks here established the first public electricity supply, but over a century later in 1998 the abbey closed. From 1820, following the construction of Telford's Caledonian Canal, a steamship operated between Fort Augustus and Inverness. Two years later, after the construction of five locks, a connection with Glasgow was established and the area was opened up to tourism. The steamer services ceased some time between 1927 and 1929 but the village remained an angling resort with an 18-hole golf course and hotel, and caravan and camping facilities, as well as the Fort Augustus Heritage Centre and Clansmen Centre with its re-creation of a Highland blackhouse.

Fort George *Highland* Located close to the village of Ardersier, on the shores of the Moray Firth, some 11 miles (18 km) east of Inverness, Fort George was built as a garrison fortress to house Government troops charged with policing the Highlands following the Jacobite Rising of 1745. Begun by William Adam in 1748, it took 21 years to complete, with John Adam continuing the work following his father's death. Fort George represents one of the largest construction projects ever undertaken in the Highlands, involving more than 1000 men, most of whom were drafted into the area from the Lowlands and beyond. Fort George is a substantial fortification and includes significant barrack accommodation and a chapel. Unlike its sister forts, Fort William and Fort Augustus, Fort George remains an operational military base today, the home of the Queen's Own Highlanders. The buildings are now in the care of Historic Scotland and open to the public.

Fort William *Highland* Located 105 miles (169 km) northwest of Glasgow and 145 miles (233 km) from Edinburgh, Fort William lies at the heart of the Lochaber district of Highland Council area. The first fort was built at the mouth of the River Lochy in 1645 by General George Monk, who named it Inverlochy. The adjacent village, established in association with the herring trade, was named Gordonsburgh. In 1690 the fort was enlarged and renamed Fort William, while the village underwent several name changes from Gordonsburgh to Maryburgh, then Duncansburgh, until by the 19th century it took the name of Fort William, at a time when the fort was being demolished to accommodate the railway. Fort William is a main station of the West Highland Line, which has operated from Glasgow to Mallaig via Fort William since it was opened in 1901. The introduction of the railway, the building of the Caledonian Canal and the arrival of the west-coast passenger steamers all contributed to making Fort William a busy tourist centre, and the town's proximity to the Nevis Range and the Aonach Mòr has made it a popular base for skiers, snowboarders and climbers. Ben Nevis, Scotland's highest peak, lies to the east. Visitor attractions include the West Highland Museum, which is located in the town's Cameron Square and houses a collection of Jacobite memorabilia, the Ben Nevis Distillery, the Lochaber Leisure Centre and an 18-hole golf course. Nearby attractions include 'The Treasures of the Earth' exhibition in Corpach, the ruins of Inverlochy Castle, and Neptune's Staircase, a series of locks on the Caledonian Canal completed in 1822. Distilling, fish processing and aluminium smelting are important industries, and divers are trained at the Underwater Centre.

Forter *Angus* A locality in Glen Isla, Angus, Forter lies to the west of the River Isla, 4 miles (6.5 km) northwest of Kirkton of Isla. Close by is the restored Forter Castle, a former stronghold of the Ogilvies that was stormed along with Airlie Castle by the Campbells of Inverewe in

1640 on the instructions of the Duke of Argyll. The Glen Isla Games are held in a field to the south of Forter each August.

Forteviot *Perth and Kinross* A village in Perth and Kinross, situated 3 miles (5 km) northeast of Dunning and 6 miles (10 km) southwest of Perth, Forteviot was rebuilt by the 1st Lord Forteviot, chairman of Dewar's Distillery, between 1925 and 1927 with attractive cottages and wide lawns laid out to a design by James Miller in the style of an English garden city. Forteviot is, however, much older than it seems. It was the ancient capital of the Pictish kingdom of Fortrenn and a favourite residence of Kenneth MacAlpin and Malcolm Canmore. Its church dates from 1778 and its village hall was opened by Sir Harry Lauder.

Forth *South Lanarkshire* A former mining village in South Lanarkshire, Forth lies 8 miles (13 km) northeast of Lanark at an elevation of 274 m (900 ft). It developed in the 19th century in association with the nearby Wilsontown Ironworks, which closed in 1942, and with housing developments in the 20th century.

Forth, River One of the principal rivers of central Scotland, the River Forth rises to the north of Ben Lomond in two headstreams, the Duchray Water and Avondhu, which meet a mile (1.5 km) west of Aberfoyle. The river meanders eastwards to Stirling, a strategic crossing point and tidal limit where the river begins to widen out into an estuary known as the Firth of Forth. The length of the river is usually quoted as 66 miles (106 km), but its full length including headwaters is 116 miles (187 km), of which 55 miles (88 km) is tidal. Its chief tributaries to the west of Stirling are the River Teith and the Allan Water.

Forth, Firth of The largest estuary on the east coast of Scotland, the Firth of Forth extends 55 miles (88 km) into the North Sea, with a maximum width of 19 miles (31 km) at its mouth. To the east of Stirling the River Forth opens out into an estuary that is crossed by the Kincardine Bridge and further east by the Forth Road Bridge, a sleek suspension bridge opened in 1964, and the world-renowned Victorian superstructure of the Forth Bridge. After passing the Queensferry Narrows to the east of Grangemouth and Rosyth, the Forth widens markedly as it passes Edinburgh. It narrows once more between North Berwick and Elie Ness before widening into the North Sea between Dunbar and Fife Ness. The Firth of Forth contains a number of small islands, including Inchgarvie, Inchmickery, Inchcolm and Cramond Island, which lie between Fife and the City of Edinburgh, and Fidra, Lamb, Craigleith, the Bass Rock and the Isle of May to the north of East Lothian. It remains an important shipping route serving major ports at Alloa, Bo'ness, Burntisland, Grangemouth, Granton, Leith and Methill, as well as the dockyard and ferry terminal at Rosyth, the oil terminal at Hound Point and the oil refinery at Grangemouth. Pittenweem on the Fife coast is a major centre of the fishing industry and numerous small harbours are frequented by leisure craft. In 1918 the fleets of Britain and the Allied Powers, totalling 201 warships, assembled at the mouth of the firth to meet the Imperial German High Seas Fleet (a further 70 ships) en route to internment in Scapa Flow.

Forth and Clyde Canal Stretching 35 miles (56 km) from Bowling on the River Clyde in the west of Scotland to Grangemouth on the River Forth, the Forth and Clyde Canal was built during the latter part of the 18th century, work beginning on 10 June 1768, and operated until 1 January 1963. The canal was re-opened by the Prince of Wales in 2001, having been the subject of a major restoration as part of the Millennium Link project. The centrepiece of this project is the Falkirk Wheel, a spectacular boat-lift built to transfer boats between the levels of the Forth and Clyde and Union Canals at Falkirk. The Forth and Clyde was the first canal built in Scotland, linking the two major estuaries of central Scotland for trade and transport, and providing an additional 3-mile (5-km) branch to central Glasgow at Port Dundas. Created to accommodate sea-going boats, its 39 locks are over 18 m (60 ft) long and nearly 6 m (20 ft) wide; its highest point of 48 m (156 ft) is between Banknock (Wyndford Lock) and Glasgow (Maryhill). The engineers who built the canal included John Smeaton (1768–73), Robert MacKell (1773–9) and Robert Whiteworth (1785–90), with no work being carried out in the period 1777–85 during much of the American Revolution. The first steamboat, the *Charlotte Dundas*, carried out trials in 1802 on the canal. One of the first canals to carry vehicles such as carts and railway wagons, the Forth and Clyde was bought by the Caledonian Railway in 1868. Its present owner is British Waterways.

Forth Bridge Located 9 miles (14 km) west of Edinburgh, the Forth Bridge (or Forth Railway Bridge) is a remarkable 19th-century cantilever structure, still regarded as an engineering marvel of its time and recognised the world over. The bridge was built to carry two tracks of the North British Railway a distance of 1.5 miles (2528 m) over the Firth of Forth between South Queensferry and North Queensferry, at a height of 46 m (150 ft) above the high tide. The structure, with its three massive cantilever towers each 104 m (340 ft) high, was designed by Sir John Fowler (1817–98) and Sir Benjamin Baker (1840–1907), and constructed by Sir William Arrol (1839–1913) at a cost of some £2.5 million. An earlier project, to be executed by Sir Thomas Bouch (1822–90), for which a foundation stone had been laid in 1873, was quickly cancelled following the collapse of his Tay Rail Bridge in 1879. Construction of the bridge began in 1883 and consumed 55,000 tonnes of steel, 18,122 cubic metres of granite and 8 million rivets. During building 57 lives were lost. At the opening ceremony on 4 March 1890, the Prince of Wales (later King Edward VII) drove home the last rivet, which was gold-plated and inscribed to record the event. The bridge remains in regular use, carrying the main east-coast line to Fife and onwards to Dundee and Aberdeen. The trains of today place much lower stresses on the bridge than did their heavier steam-powered predecessors.

Forth Road Bridge Located west of Edinburgh, the Forth Road Bridge spans the Firth of Forth between South Queensferry and North Queensferry. Work began on this suspension bridge in 1958, and it was opened by Queen Elizabeth II on 4 September 1964. It is a toll bridge for motorised traffic (free for pedestrians) and carries four lanes of traffic with two walkways. The bridge is nearly 1828 m (2000 yd) long, while its main span of 1005 m (3300 ft) is the tenth-longest in the world; its towers are over 150 m (500 ft) high. Traffic is heavy over the bridge, frequently exceeding 60,000 cars per day.

Fortingall *Perth and Kinross* Reputed to be the birthplace of Pontius Pilate, the ancient kirkton of Fortingall lies at the eastern end of Glen Lyon, Perth and Kinross, 8 miles (13 km) west of Aberfeldy and north of the River Lyon. A 3000-year-old yew tree in the churchyard is said to be the oldest living thing in Europe, and in a field to the south are three sets of stone circles dating from the 2nd millennium BC. The village comprises a number of thatched and slated cottages constructed largely since the 1880s, when the shipping magnate Sir Donald Currie initiated the transformation of the settlement to its present picturesque appearance. Glen Lyon House to the west dates from 1694 but was remodelled for Sir Donald, who used it as a shooting lodge. The parish church dates from 1900, although the first church on the site may have been built as far back as the 7th century, and is dedicated to St Cedd, patron saint of the parish of Fortingall. A Celtic handbell can be found in the church, and in the churchyard is the burial enclosure of the Stewarts of Garth.

Fortrose *Highland* A royal burgh in the Highland Council area parish of Rosemarkie, Fortrose lies on the Black Isle overlooking the Cromarty Firth opposite Fort George. In 1455 the two settlements of Chanonry and Rosemarkie were united as an ecclesiastical burgh under the Bishop of Ross, and in 1592 it was raised to the status of a royal burgh. Fortrose's red-sandstone cathedral was associated with a famous medieval school of divinity and was founded as the centre of a bishopric by King David I in 1124. Fortrose Academy was founded in 1791.

Forvie, Burn of *Aberdeenshire* A stream in eastern Aberdeenshire, the Burn of Forvie rises in hills to the north of Ellon. It flows southwards to join the River Ythan 2 miles (3 km) east of Ellon.

Forvie Ness An alternative name for Hackley Head in Aberdeenshire.

Foss *Perth and Kinross* The kirkton of Foss in Perth and Kinross lies on the Allt Kynachan which joins the southwest corner of Loch Tummel. Situated nearly 10 miles (16 km) west of Pitlochry, the settlement once enjoyed an annual fair in March. Close by is Foss House, built as a seat of the Menzies family.

Foss Mine *Perth and Kinross* A barytes mine in central Perth and Kinross, the Foss Mine lies 5 miles (8 km) northwest of Aberfeldy and south of Loch Tummel on the slopes of Meall Tairneachan, which rises to 787 m (2582 ft). Because of its high density, the mineral barytes is valued as a component of the lubricating 'mud' used in the oil-production industry. The 'mud' is pumped down at the wellhead and its weight counters the pressure of the upwelling oil.

Fossil Grove *Glasgow City* Located in Victoria Park to the west of Partick, Glasgow, the Fossil Grove is the remains of a 300-million-year-old forest discovered during the construction of a pathway in the park in 1887. The ten tree stumps are housed in a glass-roofed museum building.

Foswell *Perth and Kinross* A late 18th-century laird's house in Perth and Kinross, Foswell is located in the northern foothills of the Ochil Hills, just over a mile (1.5 km) to the southeast of Auchterarder.

Fothirdun An alternative name for Fordoun in Aberdeenshire.

Foula *Shetland* The most westerly island in the Shetland group of the Northern Isles, the rocky island of Foula lies 27 miles (43 km) west of Scalloway on Mainland Shetland. Noted for its stunning cliff scenery, the island has five peaks, rising to 418 m (1371 ft) at The Sneug and 376 m (1220 ft) at The Kame, which has the second-highest sheer cliff face in Britain. With an area of 1286 ha (3176 acres) and a population of 31 in 2001, Foula is one of the remotest inhabited islands in the UK. But for improved communications and the rebuilding of its school, the island might have become uninhabited. Over a century ago, in 1881, it had a population of 267, mostly employed in fishing. Today crofting as well as fishing are the main activities, half the population living at Hametoun in the southeast and the remainder to be found at Ham near Ham Voe on the east coast. Distinctly individual, the islanders still use the old Julian calendar, which the rest of Britain abandoned in 1753. Christmas Day is therefore celebrated on 6 January and New Year's Day on 13 January. There is an airstrip to the east of Hametoun and at Ham Voe a passenger ferry service links with Walls on Mainland Shetland.

Foulden *Scottish Borders* A village in a parish of the same name in the Berwickshire district of Scottish Borders, Foulden lies on the Whiteadder Water, midway between Chirnside and Berwick.

Foulford *Perth and Kinross* A locality in central Perth and Kinross, Foulford is situated near the head of the Sma' Glen, 3 miles (5 km) northeast of Crieff. An old drovers' inn sits opposite a section of the military road built by General Wade in the 1720s.

Foulis Castle *Highland* The seat of the chiefs of the Clan Munro, Foulis Castle overlooks the Cromarty Firth in Easter Ross. Built in the 1750s in the style of a large mansion house on the site of an earlier castle, Foulis Castle lies between Dingwall and Evanton.

Foulshiels *Scottish Borders* A locality in Scottish Borders, Foulshiels lies on the Yarrow Water, 3 miles (5 km) west of Selkirk. It was the birthplace of Mungo Park (1771–1806), the explorer of Africa.

Fountainhall A hamlet on the northern edge of Scottish Borders, Fountainhall lies on the Gala Water 3 miles (5 km) north of Stow.

Foveran *Aberdeenshire* A locality in a parish of the same name in eastern Aberdeenshire, Foveran lies on the Foveran Burn, 4 miles (6.5 km) southeast of Ellon.

Fowlis *Angus* A village in a parish of the same name in southwest Angus, Fowlis (also Fowlis Easter) lies 6 miles (10 km) northwest of Dundee. The lands of Fowlis were granted to William of Maule for his gallantry at the Battle of the Standard in 1138. To the south, at the head of the Den of Fowlis, stands Fowlis Castle. The parish church, a former collegiate church, was dedicated to St Marnan in 1242.

Fowlis Wester *Perth and Kinross* A typical Scottish fermetoun village in central Perth and Kinross, Fowlis Wester lies to the north of the road from Perth to Crieff, 4 miles (6.5 km) northeast of Crieff. Designated a conservation area, it is now largely a commuter settlement, but in its heyday it was the focal point of a parish that had a population in 1794 of 1224 weavers and farmers. At the centre of the village is the restored 13th-century church of St Bean, dedicated to an 8th-century Irish missionary who preached in this area. On display in the church are an 8th-century Pictish stone, carved to depict Jonah being swallowed by the whale, and a portion of MacBean tartan taken to the moon by US astronaut Alan McBean. A replica of another Pictish stone is located in the village square, and in the neighbourhood of the village can be found a Neolithic burial mound, a Bronze Age standing stone and stone circle, and an Iron Age hillfort.

Foyers *Highland* A small settlement in Highland Council area, Foyers lies on the River Foyers where it falls into Loch Ness, over 10 miles (16 km) northeast of Fort Augustus. The Falls of Foyers were used to power the first large-scale commercial hydro-electric scheme in the UK, created in 1896 by the North British Aluminium Company to reduce aluminium at a works located on the side of the loch. The aluminium smelter was closed in 1967 but the hydro-electric scheme was developed to combine conventional hydro and pumped storage, with a 305 megawatt capacity.

Foyers, River *Highland* A river rising in Stratherrick to the east of Loch Ness, the River Foyers flows 9 miles (14 km) northeast to enter Loch Ness near Foyers, 10 miles (16 km) northeast of Fort Augustus. The Falls of Foyers comprise two waterfalls of 27m (90 ft) and 9m (30 ft).

Fraoch Eilean *Argyll & Bute* A small island at the north end of Loch Awe in Argyll and Bute, Fraoch Eilean lies just over 2 miles (3 km) southwest of Kilchurn Castle. There are the remains of a stronghold of the Macnaughtons.

Fraserburgh *Aberdeenshire* A Moray Firth fishing port and resort town in the Buchan district of north Aberdeenshire, Fraserburgh is situated 43 miles (69 km) north of Aberdeen behind the rocky Kinnaird Head promontory at the west end of Fraserburgh Bay. Locally referred to as The Broch (a Scots word for burgh), it was originally known as Faithlie when it was founded in 1569, following a charter granted in 1564, by Sir Alexander Fraser of Philorth whose grandfather built the first harbour (later extended 1807–37, 1855–75 and 1881). In 1601 it was constituted 'a free port, free burgh of barony, and free regality, to be called in all time coming, the Burgh and Regality of Fraserburgh'. Its Mercat Cross dates from 1736, and its lighthouse (1786), the oldest in Scotland, sits on top of Fraser's Castle, a rectangular four-storeyed tower built in 1570. Nearby is the Wine Tower, the remains of a 16th-century watch tower built over a 30-m/100-ft-long cave known as the Selches Hole. Fraserburgh Academy dates from 1872, and the town's hospital was gifted by a local fish curer, Thomas Walker. The history of the settlement is told in the Fraserburgh Heritage Centre which is adjacent to the Scottish Lighthouse Museum. The short-lived Fraserburgh University was erected following a grant from the Scottish Parliament in 1595 but closed a decade later following the arrest of its first principal, who had incurred the displeasure of King James VI by taking part in the 1605 General Assembly. The college building erected by Alexander Fraser was, however, used for a short time in 1647 when King's College was forced to move from Aberdeen to Fraserburgh following an outbreak of the plague. Since the early 1800s the town's population has increased six-fold in response to the growth in the 19th century of the herring-fishing trade and in the 20th century to the development of white-fishing, food-processing and machine-tool industries. Fish canning and the manufacture of refrigerator vans are important modern industries. Fraserburgh was the home town of fashion designer Bill Gibb, polar explorer Dr Stewart Slessor and Thomas Baker Glover, who was responsible for opening up Japan in the 19th century and is thought to have given Puccini the idea for his opera *Madama Butterfly*.

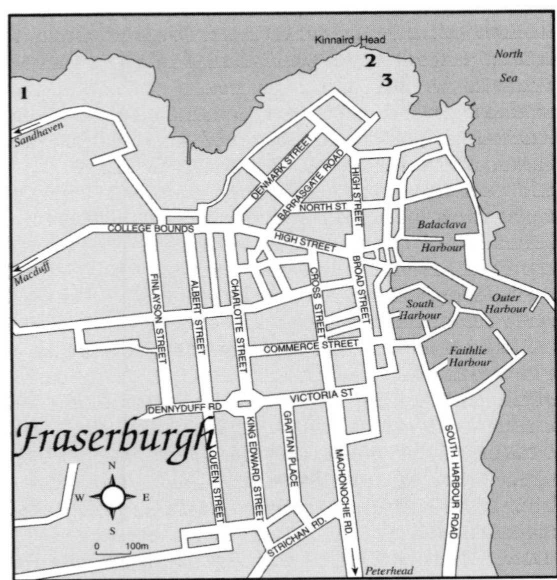

1 *Sandhaven Meal Mill Visitor Centre*
2 *Kinnaird Head Castle Lighthouse*
3 *Museum of Scottish Lighthouses*

Fraserburgh Bay *Aberdeenshire* An inlet of the Moray Firth on the Buchan coast, Aberdeenshire, Fraserburgh Bay lies to the east of the fishing port of Fraserburgh, between Kinnaird Head to the west and Cairnbulg Point to the east.

Frenchland Burn *Dumfries and Galloway* A small stream in Dumfries and Galloway, the Frenchland Burn is a tributary of the Moffat Water.

Freswick *Highland* The settlement of Freswick is located on the eastern coastline of Caithness district, Highland Council area, 4 miles (6.5 km) south of Duncansby Head. The area has had settlements for over 2000 years and is home to various brochs and cairns, and Viking and Norse settlements. Nearby stand the remains of Buchollie Castle.

Freuchie *Fife* A village in the Howe of Fife, Freuchie is situated 2 miles (3 km) east of Falkland. There are many interesting 18th- and 19th-century buildings, including a Victorian linen mill and a church built in 1875. It is said that French masons working on the construction of Falkland Palace lived here during the 16th century and that the village was a place of exile for disgraced courtiers, hence the old saying, 'Awa' tae Freuchie, whaur the Froggies live'.

Freuchie, Loch *Perth and Kinross* A loch in Glen Quaich, Highland Perth and Kinross, Loch Freuchie is located 2 miles (3 km) west of Amulree at an altitude of 264 m (867 ft) above sea level. Just over a mile (1.5 km) in length, Loch Freuchie lies on the course of the River Quaich, which rises to the northwest and flows out of the loch at its southeastern end, eventually meeting the Cochill Burn to form the River Braan.

Frigate *Unicorn Dundee City* Located within the Victoria Docks of Dundee City, the Frigate *Unicorn* is the oldest British-built warship still afloat. A 46-gun wooden warship, it was launched at Chatham in 1824. The exhibit now portrays life in the Royal Navy during the golden age of sail and complements Dundee's renowned Discovery Point.

Friockheim *Angus* An agricultural and commuter village in Angus, Friockheim is situated to the south of the Lunan Water, 6 miles (10 km) northwest of Arbroath. Probably the only example of a Gaelic-German placename, it was created as a set of feus for textile workers on the lands of Friock Mains in 1830. The German suffix was added by the local laird in recognition of the textile-manufacturing skills he had encountered in Germany. The prosperity of the village was enhanced with the arrival of the Arbroath and Forfar Railway in 1839 and the Aberdeen Railway in 1850, which made it a transit centre.

Frisa, Loch *Argyll and Bute* A loch in the northern part of the island of Mull, Argyll and Bute, Loch Frisa lies 4 miles (6.5 km) south of Tobermory. With a length of 5 miles (8 km), it is bordered on its southeastern flank by the Salen Forest and the peak of Speinne Mòr. The Ledmore River, which becomes the Aros River, flows from the southeastern end of the loch.

Frobost *Western Isles* A scattered crofting settlement on the west coast of South Uist in the Outer Hebrides, Frobost (more accurately North Frobost) lies to the west of the A865, a half-mile (1 km) south of Garryvaltos and 5 miles (8 km) northwest of Lochboisdale. South Frobost lies a half-mile (1 km) to the south.

Frostlie Burn *Scottish Borders* A stream of the southern Scottish Borders, Frostlie Burn is formed by the joining of the Linhope Burn and Comb Sike at Linhope. It flows north, receiving Corrie Sike, the Phaup Burn, the Limiecleuch Burn and the Binks Burn before emptying into the River Teviot immediately to the north of Teviothead, having completed a course of 2.5 miles (4 km).

Fruid Water *Scottish Borders* A river of Tweeddale in Scottish Borders, the Fruid Water rises on Hart Fell and flows northwards to join the Tweed to the southwest of Tweedsmuir. It was dammed to create a reservoir in 1969.

Fuaigh Beag The Gaelic name for Vuia Beg in the Western Isles.

Fuaigh Mòr The Gaelic name for Vuia Mòr in the Western Isles.

Fuar Bheinn *Highland* A mountain of the Lochaber district of Highland Council area, Fuar Bheinn lies 2 miles (3 km) north of Loch a' Choire, an arm of Loch Linnhe. It rises between the peaks of Glas Bheinn and Creach Bheinn to a height of 765 m (2509 ft).

Fuday *Western Isles* An uninhabited island lying a mile (1.5 km) off the northeast coast of Barra in the Outer Hebrides, Fuday (Gael: *Fuideigh*) has an area of 232 ha (573 acres) and rises steeply to 89 m (292 ft). It is separated from Barra by the Sound of Fuday, and Eriskay lies 3 miles (5 km) to the east. The island was inhabited until the early 20th century and is today owned by the Government.

Fuiay *Western Isles* One of a group of uninhabited islands located off the northeast coast of Barra in the Outer Hebrides, Fuiay (Gael: *Fuidheigh*) has an area of 84 ha (208 acres) and rises steeply to 107m (351 ft) at the mouth of North Bay immediately to the west of Flodday and a mile (1.5 km) southwest of Hellisay. The island was inhabited until the middle of the 19th century.

Fuidaigh The Gaelic name for Wiay in the Western Isles.

Fuideigh The Gaelic name for Fuday in the Western Isles.

Funtullich *Perth and Kinross* A locality in Glen Lednock, Perth and Kinross, Funtullich is situated near the River Lednock, 3 miles (5 km) northwest of Comrie.

Furnace *Argyll and Bute* A village of Argyll and Bute, Furnace lies on the shore of Loch Fyne, 9 miles (14 km) southwest of Inveraray. From 1755 to 1812 the Duddon Furnace Company of Furness in Cumbria operated an iron-smelting works here on a site originally named Craleckan. Porphyrite rock quarried nearby was used for making paving setts.

Fyne, Loch *Argyll and Bute* A sea loch of Argyll and Bute, Loch Fyne extends north from the Firth of Clyde and Kilbrannan Sound for just over 40 miles (64 km). It is fed from the north by the River Aray, the River Shira and the River Fyne, the latter of which rises near the border with Stirling Council area and flows 6 miles (10 km) southwards through Glen Fyne. The principal settlement on the loch's shore is Inveraray, which lies near its northern extremity.

Fyrish Hill *Highland* Also known as Cnoc Fyrish, Fyrish Hill rises to 453 m (1485 ft) to the north-northeast of Evanton and west of Alness in Easter Ross. On its summit is an unusual monument erected by General Sir Hector Munro of Novar in 1785 on his return from India.

Fyvie *Aberdeenshire* A village on the River Ythan in Aberdeenshire, Fyvie is situated 7 miles (11 km) southeast of Turriff. It was created a burgh of barony in 1673. In October 1644 it was the scene of the 'Skirmish of Fyvie', a battle between the Marquess of Montrose and the Duke of Argyll. Fyvie Castle, to the north of the village, is one of the great tower houses of northeast Scotland and was once part of a chain of royal fortresses throughout Scotland.

Fyvie Castle *Aberdeenshire* Fyvie Castle is located a mile (1.5 km) north of Fyvie in Aberdeenshire. It has parts that date back to the 13th century. Built in a Z-shape, it has undergone many additions corresponding to the wishes of each of its owners, and its five towers are named after them: Preston, Seton, Leith, Meldrum and Gordon. It is said that each family built one tower. The castle has many examples of the coat of arms of the ancestral Leiths and is noted for its Edwardian gallery and dining room. Also noted for its panelling and plaster ceilings, Fyvie Castle has within its walls the finest wheel stair in Scotland. Managed by the National Trust for Scotland since 1984, the castle contains a rich collection of portraits by artists including Raeburn, Gainsborough, Romney, Batoni, Opie and Hoppner. A stone figure on one of the towers depicts the Trumpeter of Fyvie, whose love for a miller's daughter is enshrined in Northeast balladry. Blowing a despairing love call from the top of Fyvie Castle, the broken-hearted trumpeter proclaimed that of all the bonnie lasses 'the flo'r o' them a' was in Fyvie, O.'

Gaa Sands *Angus* Located at the mouth of the Firth of Tay, the Gaa Sands form an offshore sandbank at the tip of Buddon Ness, southeast Angus.

Gabhsunn Bho Tuath The Gaelic name for North Galson in the Western Isles.

Gaick *Highland* A deer forest in the Badenoch district of Highland Council area, Gaick lies 10 miles (16 km) south of Kingussie.

Gair, Loch *Argyll and Bute* A loch in Argyll and Bute, Loch Gair forms an inlet on the western shore of Loch Fyne, with the settlement of Lochgair at its head.

Gair Loch *Highland* A loch on the coast of Wester Ross, Highland Council area, Gair Loch lies between Loch Torridon and Loch Ewe. The settlements of Port Henderson, Badachro, Shieldaig, Charlestown, Gairloch and Big Sand lie on its shores. The island of Eilean Horrisdale lies opposite Badachro.

Gairich *Highland* A mountain to the south of Loch Quoich in the Lochaber district of Highland Council area, Gairich rises to a height of 919 m (3015 ft). Its name is derived from the Gaelic for 'roaring'. The lower flanks of the peak are particularly rocky, and the summit is a broad ridge with a massive cairn.

Gairloch *Highland* A scattered settlement on the coast of Wester Ross, Highland Council area, Gairloch lies on the north shore of Gair Loch, 24 miles (38 km) northwest of Achnasheen, with which it was connected by road in 1843. A pier built at Flowerdale, an inlet near the township, prospered in association with fishing and a summer steamer service from Portree, Tobermory, Oban and Glasgow from 1850. Queen Victoria stayed at the Gairloch Hotel in 1878, and a golf course was laid out in 1898 for a growing number of tourists. The village has a school, and fish-processing and craft industries. The Gairloch Heritage Museum to the north of the village is located in a converted farmstead. It displays the history of this area from early Stone Age days through to the present and has exhibits including Pictish stones, geological and archaeological displays, an 18th-century croft-house room and a section devoted to the agriculture and fishing of the area.

Gairlochy *Highland* A small settlement in the Great Glen, Highland Council area, Gairlochy lies at the southern end of Loch Lochy, 3 miles (5 km) northwest of Spean Bridge. An overflow from Loch Lochy was created here during the building of locks on the Caledonian Canal, the diverted water plunging into the River Spean over artificial waterfalls that gave the hamlet its name, Gairlochy ('the roar of the Lochy'). The Mucomuir hydro-electric power station beside the falls was built in 1960. The Great Glen Cycle Route passes through Gairlochy.

Gairn, Glen *Aberdeenshire* A glen in the eastern Grampians of Aberdeenshire, Glen Gairn occupies the valley of the River Gairn, a tributary of the Dee.

Gairn, River *Aberdeenshire* Rising in headwaters on the slopes of Carn Eas and Ben Avon in the eastern Grampians of Aberdeenshire, the River Gairn flows eastwards through Glen Gairn to join the River Dee just west of Ballater.

Gairney, Water of *Aberdeenshire* A stream in the eastern Grampians, the Water of Gairney rises on Braid Cairn on the border between Aberdeenshire and Angus. It flows northeastwards through the Forest of Glen Tanar to join the Water of Allachy and then the Water of Tanar to form a tributary of the River Dee.

Gairney Bank *Perth and Kinross* A roadside settlement in Perth and Kinross, Gairney Bank is situated to the west of Loch Leven on the A90, a mile (1.5 km) south of Kinross. A tollhouse once operated here.

Gairney Water *Perth and Kinross* A stream in the Kinross area of Perth and Kinross, the Gairney Water rises to the southwest of Crook of Devon and flows 5 miles (8 km) east past the village of Cleish before entering Loch Leven a mile (1.5 km) to the northeast of Gairneybridge. Featured in the poetry of Michael Bruce (1746–67), its course was straightened in the early 19th century by local landowners.

Gairneybridge *Perth and Kinross* A locality in Perth and Kinross, Gairneybridge is situated on the Gairney Water, 2 miles (3 km) south of Kinross. A monument built in 1883 commemorates the founding of the Secession Church in a cottage near here in 1733, and a plaque celebrates the poet Michael Bruce (1746–67) who taught in a school here.

Gairnshiel Lodge *Aberdeenshire* A late 19th-century shooting lodge in Glen Gairn, Aberdeenshire, Gairnshiel Lodge lies on the River Gairn, 7 miles (11 km) northwest of Ballater.

Gairsay *Orkney* An island of the Orkney Islands, situated at the head of the Wide Firth between Mainland Orkney and Shapinsay, Gairsay is separated from the island of Wyre to the north by Gairsay Sound. Extending to 240 ha (593 acres), it rises to a height of 102 m (335 ft). The island, whose population of 71 in 1841 was reduced to five by 1931, is associated with the Viking Sweyn Asliefsson. During the 17th century a mansion house was built by Sir William Craigie at Langskaill on the site of Sweyn's drinking hall. There are piers at Langskaill and to the east of Millburn Bay, which is sheltered by the peninsula known as the Hen of Gairsay. The island is surrounded by small islets, reefs and skerries, including Sweyn Holm, Holm of Rendall, Grass Holm, Holm of Boray, Taing Skerry, Boray Skerries, Skertours and Little Seal Skerry.

Gaisgeir The Gaelic name for Gasker in the Western Isles.

Gaitnip Hill *Orkney* A hill overlooking the southeast coastline of the Orkney Mainland, Gaitnip Hill rises to a height of 85 m (279 ft) 3 miles (5 km) northwest of the settlement of St Mary's.

Gala Water *Scottish Borders* A river of east-central Scotland, the Gala Water rises in the Moorfoot Hills to the south of Gorebridge and flows 21 miles (33 km) southwards through Stow and Galashiels to join the River Tweed 2 miles (3 km) west of Melrose. Its main tributaries are the Heriot Water, Lugate Water and Cockholm Burn.

Galashiels *Scottish Borders* A town in Scottish Borders, Galashiels lies near the junction of the Gala Water with the River Tweed, 28 miles (45 km) southeast of Edinburgh and 5 miles (8 km) north of Selkirk. In medieval times there was a hunting tower near here at the heart of the royal forest of Gala and Leader, and huts or shiels by the river are said to have been used by pilgrims on their way to Melrose Abbey. Erected into a burgh of barony by the Pringles in 1599, Galashiels developed in association with the textile industry. The granting of the burgh charter is an event celebrated annually in early summer at the Braw Lads' Gathering. The town's coat of arms incorporates a fox attempting to reach plums on a tree, with the motto 'Sour Plums', an image that commemorates the story of a

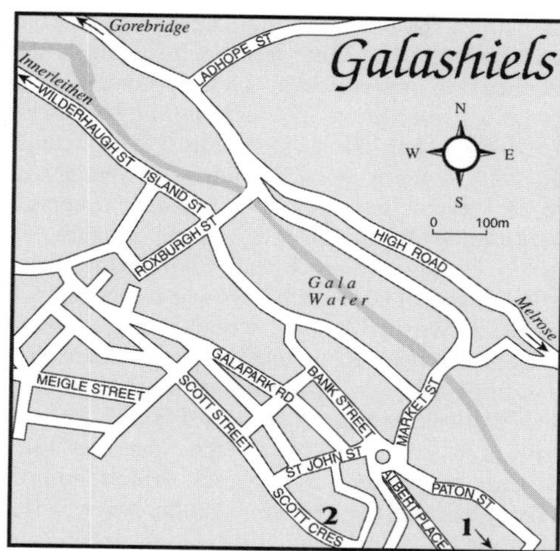

1 *Scottish College of Textiles* 2 *Old Gala House*

group of English soldiers killed in 1337 after stealing plums. About 1780 a new settlement closer to the river was laid out by the Scotts and new mills were built. By 1882 the population had risen to 17,000 and there were 21 mills in the town, which had been granted the status of a parliamentary burgh in 1868. In 1909 the Scottish Woollen Technical College – a campus of Heriot-Watt University from 1998 – was established, but by then the textile industry was in decline. The railway that had served Galashiels since 1849 was eventually closed in 1969, but food industries, electronics and the manufacture of leather goods provided employment from the 1970s. Buildings and monuments of note include Old Gala House (1583), a former residence of the lairds of Galashiels, the Peter Anderson Woollen Mill and Museum, and the fine equestrian statue of the Border Reiver by Thomas Clapperton (1879–1962), a native of Galashiels.

Gallan Head *Western Isles* A prominent headland on the west coast of Lewis in the Outer Hebrides, Gallan Head (Gael: *An Gallan Uigeach*) faces the Atlantic Ocean to the west of the entrance to West Loch Roag, 3 miles (5 km) north of Timsgarry. The hamlet of Aird Uig lies just below the headland and RAF Aird Uig, a NATO communications station, is located on the headland which rises steeply to 86 m (282 ft).

Gallatown *Fife* A northern district of Kirkcaldy, Fife, Gallatown was a separate village until 1876, when it was absorbed into the royal burgh. Originally called Gallowstown, it was the scene of public executions in medieval times. Nails were formerly manufactured here. Today it has its own industrial estate and an ice rink.

Galloway *Dumfries and Galloway* An area of southwest Scotland, now forming part of Dumfries and Galloway, Galloway until 1974 comprised the former counties of Wigtownshire and Kirkcudbrightshire stretching northwards from the Solway Firth into the Galloway Hills and including the hammerhead-shaped Rhinns of Galloway. Its much-forested uplands are a source of hydro-electric power and its lowlands are noted for farming, in particular dairy produce and cattle.

Galloway Forest Park A forest park extending over 595 sq. km (230 sq. miles) of South Ayrshire and Dumfries and Galloway in southwest Scotland, Galloway Forest Park stretches the full length of the Galloway Hills, from Loch Doon in the north to Gatehouse of Fleet in the south and from Barr in the west to Loch Ken in the east. One of the most heavily forested regions of Scotland, the principal woodlands and forests within the park are Bennan Wood, Castlemaddy Wood, Glen Trool Forest, Clatteringshaws Forest and Kirroughtree Forest, each of which has been developed since the 1930s to produce timber. In recent years the forests have also been managed for a wide range of amenity, conservation and recreational activities, and include over 200 miles (322 km) of waymarked routes for cyclists. There are visitor centres at Kirroughtree, Clatteringshaws and Glentrool in addition to a Red Deer Range and Goat Park on the Queen's Road (A712) near Talnotry.

Galloway Hills A range of hills in southwest Scotland, the Galloway Hills extend southwards into Dumfries and Galloway from Carrick in South Ayrshire. Rising to 843 m (2764 ft) at Merrick in the heart of Galloway Forest Park, the Galloway Hills include the Rhinns of Kells and Cairnsmore of Fleet ranges, and are the sources of rivers including the Dee and the Cree and a major source of water power.

Galloway Hydros Visitor Centre *Dumfries and Galloway* Located at Tongland Power Station, 2 miles (3 km) north of Kirkcudbright in Dumfries and Galloway, the Galloway Hydros Visitor Centre tells the story of the construction of the Galloway Hydros Scheme in the 1930s and the operation of the power station which contributes to the national electricity grid system. Nearby is the Tongland Dam and reservoir. Centred on the village of New Galloway, 12.5 miles (20 km) northwest of Castle Douglas, Galloway Hydro-Electric Power Scheme was the first large-scale hydro-electric power scheme in Scotland. Building began in 1929 and the scheme was fully operational by 1935. This is a modest scheme compared to those of the Highlands, with a total power-generation capacity of 106 megawatts. There are four power stations and the scheme makes use of Clatteringshaws Loch and Loch Ken.

Gallowgate, The *Glasgow City* The Gallowgate was one of Glasgow's four principal medieval streets, providing access to the city from the east and leading out towards the city gallows at Gallow Muir, a location some distance from the city centre. Today, the Gallowgate forms the northern edge of The Barras market and leads east towards Parkhead. The Barrowland Ballroom is located on the Gallowgate.

Galston *East Ayrshire* A small town in East Ayrshire, Galston lies on the Burn Anne where it meets the River Irvine, 5 miles (8 km) east of Kilmarnock. Settled by Huguenots in the 17th century, Galston developed in association with coal mining and the manufacture of footwear, paper, and wool, flax, silk and cotton textiles. It was designated a police burgh in 1862 and in the early 20th century produced blankets, muslin, lace and hosiery. Modern industries also include canning and engineering. A half-mile (1 km) to the north of Galston lies the shell of Loudon Castle, a former stronghold of the hereditary Campbell sheriffs of Ayr, which was rebuilt in 1811 by Archibald Elliott. Known as the 'Windsor of the north', its parkland was developed by Alexander Nasmyth (1758–1840). The castle was destroyed by fire in 1941, but its remains lie next to Loudoun Castle

Theme Park, which opened in 1996. Just to the southwest of the castle is Loudoun Academy, which has more than 1000 pupils. To the east of this school is Loudoun Gowf (Golf) Club, founded in 1909.

Galt, the The name given to the extreme northwest point of the island of Shapinsay in the Orkney Islands.

Gamrie An alternative name for Gardenstown in Aberdeenshire.

Gamrie Bay *Aberdeenshire* An inlet on the Moray Firth coast of Aberdeenshire, Gamrie Bay lies between Crovie Head and More Head. The village of Gardenstown (or Gamrie) lies in the shelter of the bay.

Gana Hill *South Lanarkshire* A summit of the Lowther Hills in South Lanarkshire, Gana Hill rises to a height of 668 m (2191 ft) 3 miles (5 km) southeast of Ballencleugh Law.

Gannochy Bridge *Angus* A locality on the border between Aberdeenshire and Angus, Gannochy Bridge lies on the River North Esk, a mile (1.5 km) north of Edzell. The bridge dates from 1732.

Gantocks *Argyll and Bute* A cluster of rocks in the Firth of Clyde, the Gantocks lie at the mouth of West Bay to the south of Dunoon and opposite Cloch Point.

Ganu Mòr *Highland* The summit of Foinaven, a significant mountain ridge of northwest Sutherland, Ganu Mòr is the second top along the ridge from the north. It is located 4 miles (6.5 km) east of the head of Loch Inchard and rises to 914 m (2999 ft).

Gaor Bheinn An alternative name for Gulvain in Highland.

Garadheancal *Highland* A largely seasonal settlement on Tanera Mòr, the largest of the Summer Isles off the west coast of Sutherland, Garadheancal lies to the south of The Anchorage, close to the island's pier.

Garbh Allt Falls *Aberdeenshire* Also known as the Garrawalt Falls, the Garbh Allt Falls are located on the Feindallacher Burn in Ballochbuie Forest, 4 miles (6.5 km) southeast of Braemar.

Garbh Chioch Mhòr *Highland* A mountain of Knoydart in Highland Council area, Garbh Chioch Mhòr rises to a height of 1013 m (3323 ft) at the head of Glen Dessarry.

Garbh Eileach *Argyll and Bute* The largest of the Garvellachs in the Firth of Lorn, Garbh Eileach is an uninhabited island with an area of 142 ha (351 acres). It rises to a height of 110 m (361 ft) and mainly comprises quartzite and limestone. There are the remains of an ancient fort and a burial ground.

Garbh Eilean Mòr *Western Isles* A small uninhabited island located between Grimsay and Ronay in the island-littered channel that separates North Uist and Benbecula, Garbh Eilean Mòr lies immediately offshore of Kallin.

Garbh Leac An alternative name for A' Chràlaig in Highland.

Garden *Stirling* A hamlet located on the A811, 12 miles (19 km) west of Stirling, Garden was the birthplace of mathematician James Stirling (1692–1770).

Gardenstown *Aberdeenshire* A fishing village on the Moray Firth coast of Aberdeenshire, Gardenstown is situated on Gamrie Bay, 6 miles (10 km) east of Macduff. It was founded in 1720 by Alexander Garden of Troup and rises from an older part on the water's edge to a newer part on higher ledges. Sometimes known as Gamrie, which is also the name of the parish, Gardenstown is a stronghold of the Plymouth Brethren.

Gare Loch *Argyll and Bute* A sea loch that flows south to open onto the Firth of Clyde, the Gare Loch is located 13 miles (21 km) northwest of Glasgow. The loch is 7 miles (11 km) long and a mile (1.5 km) wide. It is separated from Loch Long to the west by the Rosneath peninsula. The town of Helensburgh lies at its mouth, Greenock lies opposite and around the loch are the villages of Rhu, Shandon, Faslane, Garelochhead, Clynder and Rosneath. The deep water of Gare Loch has been associated with the navy since World War II, when a major base was developed at Rosneath and used by the Americans to train for landings in North Africa and on D-Day. In the 1950s British battleships were mothballed in the loch and by the 1960s it became the principal base for the UK's submarine-borne nuclear deterrent. Trident submarines remain at Faslane, the locus for regular peace protests.

Garelochhead *Argyll and Bute* A resort village and yachting centre of Argyll and Bute, Garelochhead lies at the head of the Gare Loch, 7 miles (11 km) northwest of Helensburgh. It developed from the 1820s with the advent of steamer cruising. Tourism was boosted with the opening of the West Highland Railway line to Oban in 1894, and in the late 20th century its prosperity was linked to the deep-water terminal at Finnart on Loch Long and the Faslane military port. Garelochhead Forest lies to the south.

Garenin *Western Isles* A crofting hamlet on the west coast of the isle of Lewis in the Outer Hebrides, Garenin (Gael: *Na Gearrannan*) lies 1.25 miles (2 km) northwest of Carloway. The oldest houses in the village, closest to the shore, have been designated a conservation area and restored as the Gearrannan Blackhouse Village, including a youth hostel, museum and interpretation centre.

Garf Water *South Lanarkshire* Rising to the north of Robert Law in South Lanarkshire, the Garf Water flows eastwards to meet the River Clyde at a point 2 miles (3 km) east of Wiston.

Gargunnock *Stirling* An historic village of Stirling Council area, Gargunnock lies between the northern edge of the Gargunnock Hills and the A811, 6 miles (10 km) west of Stirling. Formerly associated with distilling and the manufacture of tiles, it is now a commuter settlement with sawmilling and joinery industries. The focal point of the village is the Square, which lies adjacent to an 18th-century bridge over the Gargunnock Burn. Buildings of interest include the parish church (1626), Dunning House (formerly the manse), the Dissenters' Chapel (1843) and Gargunnock House (1580–1794).

Gargunnock Burn *Stirling* A stream rising in the Gargunnock Hills, Stirling Council area, the Gargunnock Burn flows northwards through the village of Gargunnock for a distance of nearly 4 miles (6.5 km) before meeting the River Forth.

Gargunnock Hills *Stirling* A range of hills in Stirling Council area, the steep north-facing slopes of the Gargunnock Hills look out over the valley of the River Forth. The Fintry Hills and Touch Hills form outliers to west and east. Carleatheran, rising to 486 m (1595 ft), is the highest point in the Gargunnock Hills.

Garioch, the *Aberdeenshire* A district of Aberdeenshire, the Garioch (pronounced 'geery') extends from the

Grampians into the lowlands of northeast Scotland, with Inverurie as its chief settlement. It is bounded by Mar to the west, Formartine to the east and northeast and Strathbogie to the northwest and west. Described as the 'granary of Aberdeenshire' it comprises fertile farmland watered by rivers such as the Urie. The Leslie and Forbes families dominated the area in medieval times, and two decisive battles in Scottish history were fought in east Garioch in 1307, when Robert the Bruce defeated the Comyns at Barra, and in 1411, when the Earl of Mar defeated the Lord of the Isles at Harlaw.

Garleton Hills *East Lothian* A range of hills in East Lothian, the Garleton Hills lie to the north of Haddington. They rise to 186 m (610 ft) at Skid Hill and include Bangly Hill, Byres Hill and Phantassie Hill. The Hopetoun Monument stands at the centre of the range, which comprises volcanic rocks of the Lower Carboniferous period formed as lava some 335 million years ago.

Garlieston *Dumfries and Galloway* A seaside village on Whithorn Bay, Dumfries and Galloway, Garlieston (formerly Garliestown) was created in 1746 by Lord Garlies, eldest son of the Earl of Galloway. His ancestral home near Whithorn had been destroyed by fire and a new house had been constructed at Rigg Bay, close to a village called Carswell. For his own privacy he removed the villagers of Carswell to Garlieston. For a while the village was a centre of boat building, sail making and rope making. Galloway House Gardens were created in 1740 by Lord Garlies, elder son of the 6th Earl of Galloway, and it was here that Captain Neil McEacharn learned to garden before moving to Italy to create the great gardens of Villa Taranto by Lake Maggiore. The garden contains a rare example of a handkerchief tree (*Davidia involucrata*).

Garlogie *Aberdeenshire* A roadside village in Aberdeenshire, Garlogie lies on the Leuchar Burn, 10 miles (16 km) west of Aberdeen and 2 miles (3 km) east of Echt. It developed in the 19th century as a textile-milling settlement, drawing water power from Loch of Skene to the north. Garlogie Mill features audiovisual presentations.

Garmond *Aberdeenshire* A late 18th-century planned village in the Aberdeenshire parish of Monquhitter, Garmond is situated just over a mile (1.5 km) north of Cuminestown and 7 miles (11 km) east of Turriff.

Garmouth *Moray* The village of Garmouth is located on the western banks of the mouth of the River Spey in Moray. Situated 8 miles (13 km) east of Elgin, Garmouth is linked to the village of Kingston, which lies directly to the north. Founded by the Innes family as a fishing centre and timber export port, it was here that Charles II returned from exile in 1650.

Garness, Head of *Aberdeenshire* A headland on the Moray Firth coast of Aberdeenshire, the Head of Garness lies 3 miles (5 km) east of Macduff.

Garnethill *Glasgow City* Garnethill is a traditional tenement area on the northwest edge of Glasgow city centre. Although predominantly residential, it is home to the Charles Rennie Mackintosh-designed Glasgow School of Art (1897–1909), the National Trust for Scotland-owned Tenement House and the McLellan Galleries. Its southern boundary is marked by Sauchiehall Street.

Garnkirk *North Lanarkshire* A scattered settlement of North Lanarkshire, Garnkirk is located a mile (1.5 km) southwest of Muirhead.

Garnock, River *North Ayrshire* A river of North Ayrshire, the Garnock rises on the slopes of the Hill of Stake in Clyde Muirshiel Regional Park. It flows 21 miles (33 km) southwards through Kilbirnie, Dalry and Kilwinning to enter the Firth of Clyde at Irvine.

Garrabost *Western Isles* A crofting township on the Eye peninsula of eastern Lewis in the Outer Hebrides, Garrabost lies 1.5 miles (2.5 km) northeast of Knock and 6 miles (10 km) east of Stornoway.

Garrison of Inversnaid *Stirling* A locality in Stirling Council area, Garrison of Inversnaid lies on the Snaid Burn, a mile (1.5 km) to the east of Inversnaid on Loch Lomond's western side. The farmstead of Garrison of Inversnaid incorporates the ruins of a military barracks built in 1718–19. It was the first in a series of barracks created after the Jacobite Rising of 1715 and was destroyed on more than one occasion by the Clan Macgregor.

Garroch Head *Argyll and Bute* The most southerly point on the island of Bute, Garroch Head overlooks the islands of Little Cumbrae to the southeast and Arran to the southwest.

Garron Point *Aberdeenshire* A headland on the North Sea coast of Aberdeenshire, Garron Point extends into the sea 2 miles (3 km) north of Stonehaven.

Garry, Glen *Highland* Lying in the Lochaber district of Highland Council area, Glen Garry extends in an easterly direction from the head of Loch Quoich towards the settlement of Invergarry. It carries the waters of the River Garry, which pass through Loch Garry en route to Loch Oich in the Great Glen.

Garry, Glen *Perth and Kinross* A valley of Atholl in Highland Perth and Kinross, Glen Garry extends the length of the River Garry from the Pass of Drumochter in the northwest to the Pass of Killiecrankie near Pitlochry in the southeast.

Garry, Loch *Highland* A loch in the Inverness district of Highland Council area, Loch Garry lies in Glen Garry to the west of the Great Glen. It receives water via the River Garry from Loch Quoich to the west and drains eastwards into Loch Oich at Invergarry. The Glengarry Forest lies to the south. Loch Garry and the River Garry form part of the Garry-Moriston Hydro-Electric Scheme which became fully operational in 1962 with a total capacity of 113 megawatts. The loch is dammed across a gorge at its outlet and a tunnel carries water to the 20-megawatt power station at Invergarry. In 1792, 150 Glen Garry crofters led by Alexander MacDonnell of Greenfield emigrated to Canada, settling in Glengarry County, Ontario.

Garry, Loch *Perth and Kinross* A loch of Highland Perthshire, Loch Garry lies to the south of the Pass of Drumochter and is separated from the much larger Loch Ericht to the west by the Craiganour Forest. It is almost 3 miles (5 km) in length and lies at an altitude of 397 m (1303 ft) above sea level.

Garry, River *Highland* A river in Lochaber to the west of the Great Glen, the River Garry rises in Loch Quoich and flows east through Loch Poulary and Loch Garry to join Loch Oich near Invergarry.

Garry, River *Perth and Kinross* Emerging from the north end of Loch Garry, the River Garry flows southeast for 22 miles (35 km) through Atholl in Highland Perth and Kinross before joining the River Tummel 2 miles (3 km) northeast of Pitlochry. On its course through the Pass of Drumochter and on to the Pass of Killiecrankie, the river falls nearly 300 m (1000 ft) and skirts the settlements of Calvine, Blair Atholl and Killiecrankie. It was described by Queen Victoria as 'very fine, rolling over large stones, and forming perpetual falls'. The principal tributaries of the Garry are the Edendon, Ender, Bruar, Tilt, Allt Girnaig and Errochty.

Garryhallie *Western Isles* A small crofting settlement on South Uist in the Outer Hebrides, Garryhallie (Gael: *Gearraidh Sheile*) is located on the A865 in the southwest of the island, a quarter-mile (0.5 km) north of Daliburgh.

Garrynamonie *Western Isles* A crofting township in southwest South Uist in the Outer Hebrides, Garrynamonie (Gael: *Gearraidh na Monadh*) lies 4 miles (6.5 km) southwest of Lochboisdale. A strikingly modern Roman Catholic church, Our Lady of Sorrows (built 1964), is located here.

Garryvaltos *Western Isles* A small crofting township amid machair on the west coast of South Uist, Garryvaltos (also Milton, Gael: *Gearraidh Bhailteas*) lies on the opposite side of the A865 from Mingarry and a mile (1.5 km) south of Kildonan.

Garscadden *Glasgow City* Garscadden is a residential area of Glasgow's West End, situated to the north of the River Clyde and bordered by Yoker, Scotstoun and Knightswood.

Gart Law *South Lanarkshire* A hill near the border with East Ayrshire, Gart Law rises to a height of 452 m (1483 ft) 5 miles (8 km) southwest of Glespin in South Lanarkshire. Tributaries of the Duneaton Water rise on its slopes.

Gartcosh *North Lanarkshire* A former industrial village of North Lanarkshire, Gartcosh lies nearly 3 miles (5 km) northwest of Coatbridge and west of the M73.

Garten, Loch *Highland* A small loch in the Strathspey district of Highland Council area, Loch Garten lies between the River Spey and the Cairngorm Mountains, 2 miles (3 km) southwest of Nethy Bridge. Surrounded by the birch and pine of the Abernethy Forest, it was the first osprey nesting site to be made accessible to the public. The loch is managed by the Royal Society for the Protection of Birds (RSPB) as a nature reserve.

Garthamlock *Glasgow City* A large postwar housing development to the east of Glasgow city centre, Garthamlock has a skyline dominated by three 18-storey tower blocks and large circular water towers.

Garth Castle *Perth and Kinross* Situated on the west side of the Strath of Appin in Perth and Kinross and overlooking the Keltney Burn, the square tower of Garth Castle dates from the 14th century. Partially rebuilt in the 1890s by Sir Donald Currie, it was formerly a stronghold of the Stewarts, the most notable of which was Alexander Stewart, Earl of Buchan, the so-called 'Wolf of Badenoch'. Garth House lies nearly 3 miles (5 km) to the south.

Garth House *Perth and Kinross* Rebuilt in 1838 to a design by Andrew Heiton senior, the Gothic-style Garth House is situated on the left bank of the River Lyon at the eastern end of Glen Lyon in Perth and Kinross. An earlier building on this site was the birthplace of Major-General David Stewart (1772–1829), Governor of St Lucia and author of *Sketches of the Highlanders*. It was later owned by Sir Archibald Campbell, Governor of New Brunswick, and Sir Donald Currie of the Union Castle shipping line.

Garthwhinzean *Perth and Kinross* A hamlet with a hotel on the western edge of Powmill in Perth and Kinross, Garthwhinzean lies on the A977, 5 miles (8 km) southwest of Kinross.

Gartmore *Stirling* A picturesque hillside village, Gartmore lies on the western edge of the Carse of Forth 18 miles (29 km) west of Stirling. It was built in the 18th-century as a planned village on the Gartmore Estate, whose last Graham owner was the noted writer, politician, co-founder of the Scottish Labour Party and first president of the Scottish National Party, Robert Bontine Cunninghame Graham (1852–1936). Nearby is Gartmore House, built by the Grahams in the early 18th century and enlarged in 1779–80 and again in the 1900s. To the north lie the ruins of the house's predecessor, Gartartan Castle, a 16th-century Z-plan tower. The cairn erected to the memory of Cunninghame Graham was moved by the National Trust for Scotland from its original site at Castlehill, Dumbarton, to Gartmore in 1981.

Gartmorn Dam Country Park *Clackmannanshire* A country park and local nature reserve to the east of Sauchie in Clackmannanshire, Gartmorn Dam Country Park includes the oldest man-made reservoir still operating in Scotland and incorporates facilities for picnicking, fishing, birdwatching and walking. The Gartmorn reservoir was built in 1713 by the Earl of Mar in an ambitious scheme to use water power to drive pumps in his coal mines.

Gartness *Stirling* A village in Stirling Council area, Gartness lies on the Endrick Water, a mile (1.5 km) west of Killearn. The Napier family owned an estate here.

Gartney, Strath *Stirling* A wide valley in the Trossachs district of Stirling Council area, Strath Gartney comprises the waters of Loch Katrine and its adjacent lands from Glengyle in the northwest to the Trossachs Pier in the southeast.

Gartocharn *West Dunbartonshire* A small village in West Dunbartonshire, Gartocharn lies to the northeast of Balloch and south of Loch Lomond. The conical Duncryne Hill, also known as The Dumpling, rises to 141 m (462 ft) on the nearby line of the Highland Boundary Fault, and at Ross Priory on the shore of Loch Lomond Sir Walter Scott (1771–1832) wrote parts of *The Lady of the Lake* (1810) and *Rob Roy* (1817).

Garvald *East Lothian* A picturesque linear village of East Lothian, Garvald lies 5 miles (8 km) southeast of Haddington and 4 miles (6.5 km) south of East Linton between the Papana Water and the Lammermuir Hills. Its church, rebuilt in 1829, dates from the 12th century, and among a number of listed 18th- and 19th-century buildings within a designated conservation area are the former school and schoolhouse. The Whiteadder Reservoir to the southeast supplies water to the settlements of East Lothian, and less than a mile (1.5 km) to the east of the village is the Cistercian community of Nunraw Abbey. An ambitious scheme by the North British Railway to extend a branch railway line from Gifford to Garvald and on to the east coast main line was never completed and trains stopped running to Gifford in 1948.

Garvan, Glen *Highland* A valley in the Lochaber district of Highland Council area, Glen Garvan carries the waters of the North Garvan River northeast to Loch Eil.

Garve *Highland* A small settlement of Easter Ross in Highland Council area, Garve lies to the northwest of Loch Garve, 10 miles (16 km) west of Dingwall.

Garve Island An alternative name for An Garbh-eilean in Highland.

Garvellachs *Argyll and Bute* The Garvellachs (or Isles of the Sea) are a group of small uninhabited islands in the Firth of Lorn between the islands of Lunga, to the southeast, and Mull, to the north. On the southernmost island of Eileach an Naoimh are the ruined remains of a Celtic monastery. The other islands of the group are A'Chuli, Garbh Eileach and Dun Chonnuill.

Garvock *Aberdeenshire* A locality with a church in a parish of the same name in south Aberdeenshire, Garvock lies 2 miles (3 km) east of Laurencekirk on the Hill of Garvock which forms an eastern edge to the Howe of the Mearns. A prominent feature nearby on the hill is a folly known as Johnston Tower which was built by James Farquhar in 1812 with stone left over from the building of his mansion house, Johnston Lodge.

Garyvard *Western Isles* A crofting township located in the South Lochs district of the island of Lewis in the Outer Hebrides, Garyvard (Gael: *Gearraidh Bhaird*) lies on the southern shore of Loch Erisort, 9 miles (14 km) southwest of Stornoway.

Garynahine *Western Isles* A small settlement on the Isle of Lewis in the Western Isles, Garynahine (also Garrynahine, Gael: *Gearraidh na h-Aibhne*) lies at the head of Loch Ceann Hulavig, an arm of East Loch Roag,, 14 miles (22.5 km) west of Stornoway.

Gask Ridge *Perth and Kinross* Stretching for a distance of 10 miles (16 km) between Perth and Crieff in the heart of Strath Earn, Perth and Kinross, the Gask Ridge is formed by rising ground that separates the Pow Water to the north from the River Earn to the south. It formed part of a Roman frontier system first constructed by Agricola in the AD 80s and comprising forts and watch towers along a road linking the Roman fort at Bertha near Perth and Camelon near Falkirk. Part of the Roman road can still be traced, and the site of a watch tower is marked near Ardunie.

Gasker *Western Isles* A remote uninhabited island in the Outer Hebrides, Gasker (Gael: *Gaisgeir*) lies in the Atlantic Ocean, 5 miles (8 km) west-southwest of Scarp on the west coast of North Harris. Rocky islets located a mile (1.5 km) to the southeast are known as Gasker Beg (Gael: *Gaisgeir Beag*).

Gass *South Ayrshire* A small village of South Ayrshire, Gass lies 2 miles (3 km) east of Straiton, on the road to Dalmellington.

Gatehead *East Ayrshire* A hamlet of southeast East Ayrshire on its border with South Ayrshire, Gatehead lies on the north bank of the River Irvine 1.25 miles (2 km) south of Crosshouse and 2 miles (3 km) northeast of Dundonald. The Kilmarnock–Troon railway runs through Gatehead, but its station has been closed for some years. There were once coal mines at Newfield and Fortacre to the south.

Gatehouse of Fleet *Dumfries and Galloway* A village in Dumfries and Galloway, Gatehouse of Fleet is situated near the mouth of the Water of Fleet, 6 miles (10 km) northwest of Kirkcudbright. It was founded in the 1760s as the estate village for Cally Estate by James Murray of Broughton and developed as a centre of tanning, brewing, boat building and cotton manufacturing. The village takes its name from the 'Gait-House' built by the Murrays in the 17th century, the 'gait' or road being the routeway from Dumfries to Creetown. Buildings of note include the Clock Tower (1871), the Murray Arms Hotel (1766) and the Mill on the Fleet (*c*.1790), formerly a cotton mill and now incorporating a visitor centre. Robert Burns composed the song *Scots Wha Hae* while riding from St Mary's Isle to Gatehouse of Fleet on 1 August 1793 and is thought to have written it down when he arrived at the Murray Arms Hotel.

Gatelawbridge *Dumfries and Galloway* A hamlet in Nithsdale, Dumfries and Galloway, Gatelawbridge lies in the southern foothills of the Lowther Hills, nearly 2 miles (3 km) northeast of Thornhill.

Gateside *Fife* A village in Strathmiglo parish, western Fife, Gateside lies 2 miles (3 km) west of Strathmiglo on the north bank of the River Eden and straddling the A91 to St Andrews. Once the site of the chapel of St Mary of Dungaitside, which belonged to the monks of Balmerino Abbey, it comprises the old fermetoun village of Gateside, the hamlet of Edensbank, and a 19th-century roadside settlement formerly known as Edentown or Edenshead. During the 19th century the Gateside Mills produced wooden bobbins and shuttles for weaving factories. Today these mills produce clothing, furniture and turned-wood components.

Gattonside *Scottish Borders* A village in the Roxburgh district of Scottish Borders, Gattonside lies on the north side of the River Tweed opposite Melrose and 4 miles (6.5 km) southeast of Galashiels. It is linked to Melrose by a metal suspension bridge.

Gauldry *Fife* A village in the parish of Balmerino linked with Wormit, northeast Fife, Gauldry is situated 2 miles (3 km) southwest of Wormit on a ridge north of the Motray Water. Once occupied by farmers, weavers and estate workers, Gauldry is now largely populated by commuters to Dundee and Cupar. In addition to being the base of a local coach company, it is the location of Balmerino Primary School and has a village hall (1896) and a park (Duncan Park) dedicated to a great-granddaughter of Admiral Viscount Duncan of Camperdown. Nearby are Naughton House (1793) and the ruins of Naughton Castle, built in the 16th century by the Hay family.

Gauldswell *Perth and Kinross* A locality in eastern Perth and Kinross, Gauldswell lies 3 miles (5 km) northwest of Alyth.

Gaulrig *Moray* The upland Moray farms of Easter and Wester Gaulrig overlook the left bank of the River Avon to the south of Tomintoul in the Grampian Mountains.

Gaur, River *Perth and Kinross* The River Gaur (or Gaoire) extends for 7 miles (11 km) in Perth and Kinross, linking Loch Laidon in the west with Loch Rannoch in the east via Loch Eigheach. It enters Loch Rannoch at Bridge of Gaur and receives en route the Abhainn Duibhe, Allt Chomraidh and Allt Chaldar.

Gavinton *Scottish Borders* A small village of Berwickshire in Scottish Borders, Gavinton lies 2 miles (3 km) southwest of Duns. It was built in 1760 to replace an earlier village called Langton and was named after its proprietor.

Geal Charn *Highland* A mountain in the Badenoch and Strathspey district of Highland Council area, Geal Charn rises to 1132 m (3714 ft) and is one of four peaks on the ridge between Strath Ossian and Loch Pattack. The name is derived from the Gaelic for 'white hill'.

Geal Charn *Highland* Rising to a height of 1049m (3442 ft) south of Loch Laggan in the Badenoch and Strathspey district of Highland Council area, Geal Charn has a flat summit and steep slopes that protect rare alpine plants from grazing animals. These alpines grow in lime-rich mica-schist.

Geal Charn *Highland* A mountain in the Monadhliath range in the Badenoch and Strathspey district of Highland Council area, Geal Charn rises to a height of 926 m (3038 ft) and is separated by Glen Markie from neighbouring Monadhliath tops.

Geal Charn *Highland* Located northwest of Laggan Bridge in Highland Council area, Geal Charn rises to a height of 917 m (3008 ft). It has a rounded peak with a broad ridge running southwest to northeast.

Geal Charn *Moray/Aberdeenshire* A mountain in the Grampians, Geal Charn rises to 683 m (1204 ft) at the northeast end of the Ladder Hills, on the border between Moray and Aberdeenshire and at the head of Glenbuchat. The River Livet rises between Geal Charn and Letterach to the west.

Gearraidh Bhailteas The Gaelic name for Garryvaltos in the Western Isles.

Gearraidh Bhaird The Gaelic name for Garyvard in the Western Isles.

Gearraidh na Monadh The Gaelic name for Garrynamonie in the Western Isles.

Gearraidh na h-Aibhne The Gaelic name for Garynahine in the Western Isles.

Gearraidh Sheile The Gaelic name for Garryhallie in the Western Isles.

Gearrannan Blackhouse Village *Western Isles* Located on the seaward side of Garenin, 1.25 miles (2 km) northwest of Carloway, the Gearrannan Blackhouse Village lies on the exposed Atlantic coast of the Isle of Lewis and comprises a unique group of traditional crofting houses dating from the late 19th century. These were restored by the Garenin Trust (Gael: *Urras nan Gearrannan*) between 1991 and 2001. Representing the last surviving group of black houses on Lewis, they were abandoned in 1974 and became derelict when the last residents moved to modern public housing nearby. The restored village was officially opened by the Princess Royal on 5 June 2001. Traditional methods were used to restore the houses sympathetically, with their drystone walls and thatched roofs, re-creating an authentic settlement offering visitors modern facilities discretely integrated into a historic environment. These include a museum and interpretation centre, craft shop, restaurant, and a simple youth hostel, which was opened by writer and broadcaster Magnus Magnusson. In this remote location, village life was traditionally hard; electricity arrived in the village only in 1952, and then was used only for lighting. It was not until the 1960s that piped water was available from a standpipe in the village street.

Geasgill Mòr *Argyll and Bute* Located off the southern coast of Ulva, near the entrance to Loch Na Keal, Argyll and Bute, Geasgill Mòr is little more than an offshore rock, one of many that lie off the coast of Mull. The smaller island of Geasgill Beag lies to the west.

Gedloch Burn *Moray* A stream in the uplands of Moray to the south of Elgin, the Gedloch Burn rises in boggy land known as the Gull Nest and flows northwest to join the River Lossie to the west of Easterton.

Geilston Gardens *Argyll and Bute* A property bequeathed in 1989 to the National Trust for Scotland, Geilston Gardens are associated with Geilston House, a small country house at the west end of Cardross on the banks of the River Clyde, 18 miles (29 km) northwest of Glasgow. The house and gardens were developed on the fortunes made from tobacco and other Glasgow-based industries. Among the many attractive features are a fruit and vegetable garden with a central 'dipping pond', a walled garden with traditional glasshouses, and a burn that winds through a wooded glen.

Geirnish *Western Isles* A linear crofting settlement lying on the south shore of Loch Bee on the island of South Uist in the Outer Hebrides, Geirnish (Gael: *Geirinis*) provides access to the range-head of the Hebrides Missile Range. The statue of Our Lady of the Isles sculpted by Hew Lorimer stands on Rueval a half-mile (1 km) to the south.

Gelder Burn *Aberdeenshire* A stream in the Balmoral Forest, Aberdeenshire, the Gelder Burn rises on the slopes of Conachcraig. It flows northwestwards through Glen Gelder to join the River Dee between Inver and Balmoral.

Geldie Burn *Aberdeenshire* A stream in the eastern Grampians of Aberdeenshire, the Geldie Burn rises between An Sgarsoch and Carn an Fhidhleir on the border between Aberdeenshire and Angus. It flows north then east into the upper reaches of the River Dee to the west of Linn of Dee. Cairn Geldie rises to 823 m (2508 ft) near the confluence of the two rivers.

Gellyburn *Perth and Kinross* A locality by Murthly on the edge of the Muir of Thorn, Perth and Kinross, Gellyburn lies on the Gelly Burn near its junction with the River Tay, 10 miles (16 km) north of Perth.

Gelston *Dumfries and Galloway* A village in Dumfries and Galloway, Gelston or Gilston lies 2 miles (3 km) south of Castle Douglas. The Adam-style Gelston Castle was built c.1805 for Sir William Douglas of Gelston (1745–1809), founder of Castle Douglas.

Geocrab *Western Isles* The northernmost of a string of connected settlements strung along the rocky east coast of the island of South Harris in the Outer Hebrides, Geocrab lies at the head of Loch Geocrab, to the northeast of Beacravik, 6 miles (10 km) northeast of Rodel.

George IV Bridge *City of Edinburgh* George IV Bridge represents an elevated street in Edinburgh, some 300 m (1000 ft) in length, which crosses the Cowgate and links Chambers Street with the Royal Mile. The bridge was built between 1829 and 1832 to a design by architect Thomas Hamilton (1784–1858), with a view to providing more effective access to the Old Town from the expanding south side of the city. Its construction required the demolition of two of the Old Town's traditional streets, namely the Old Bank Close and Liberton's Wynd. Only two of the arches supporting the bridge are visible, in the Cowgate and Merchant Street, but the others provide vaults and cellars for the tall buildings that rise from ground level to well above the street level of the bridge.

George Square *City of Edinburgh* A square in Edinburgh to the south of the Old Town, George Square lies to the west of Buccleuch Place and extends south towards The Meadows. It was originally laid out in 1766 by James Brown and was the first new development outside Edinburgh's overcrowded Old Town. The boyhood home of Sir Walter Scott (1771–1832) was at No. 25, and Thomas Carlyle (1795–1881) courted his wife Jane Welsh at No. 22. Lord Braxfield (1722–99), the model for Lord Hermiston in Robert Louis Stevenson's *Weir of Hermiston* (1896), had a house here, as did Henry Dundas, Viscount Melville (1742–1811), his nephew Robert Dundas of Arniston, Admiral Duncan, Viscount Camperdown (1731–1804), Elizabeth Leveson-Gower, the Countess of Sutherland (1765–1839), Henry Erskine, Lord Advocate, and the lexicographer the Revd John Jamieson (1759–1838). The original terraced houses survive on the west and northeast sides of the square, the remainder having been demolished in the 1960s to make way for modern buildings of the University of Edinburgh, including the University Library (designed by Sir Basil Spence), George Square Theatre, the Adam Ferguson Building and the William Robertson Building. The only building dating from the 19th century is the former George Watson's Ladies College (1876). The university first purchased property in the square in 1914 and began a major programme of redevelopment in 1949.

George Square *Glasgow City* Situated in the heart of Glasgow with the City Chambers on its eastern side, George Square is the main open space in the city centre, and is the site of the cenotaph and statues of Sir Walter Scott, Queen Victoria, Prince Albert, Robert Burns, Sir John Moore, Lord Clyde, Thomas Campbell, Dr Thomas Graham, James Oswald, James Watt, William Gladstone and Sir Robert Peel.

Georgian House *City of Edinburgh* Located on the north side of Charlotte Square in Edinburgh's New Town, the Georgian House is an 18th-century merchant's house built in the neoclassical architectural style synonymous with Robert Adam (1728–92). Dating from 1796, it is an example of the housing built for those who formerly occupied tenements in the Old Town. First owned by John Lamont of Lamont, it later became the town house of the Farquharsons of Invercauld (1816–45) and the home, until 1889, of the advocate Lord Neaves. The Georgian House was acquired by the National Trust for Scotland in 1966. The upper floors are the residence of the Moderator of the Church of Scotland.

Giffnock *East Renfrewshire* An outer suburb of the Greater Glasgow conurbation, Giffnock lies 5 miles (8 km) south of Glasgow city centre and just over a mile (1.5 km) south of Pollokshaws. Eastwood House, the former home of Viscount Weir, lies within the grounds of Eastwood Park and is used as a cultural and recreational venue. Giffnock benefits from a railway station, and nearby is Rouken Glen Park.

Gifford *East Lothian* A village of East Lothian, Gifford lies on the Gifford Water, 4 miles (6.5 km) south of Haddington. In 1708 Gifford replaced an earlier settlement that once stood close to Yester House near a collegiate church known as Bothans which was founded in 1421. The area has associations with the Gifford family that date from the 12th century, although their estates passed to the Hays by marriage. Given the family name Gifford, the village initially developed in association with textile and paper mills and had two annual fairs. The paper mill, which closed in the 1770s, produced Bank of Scotland notes. Buildings of interest include the Mercat Cross (1780), the Town Hall (1887) and the parish church (1710), which has a 15th-century bell and a 17th-century pulpit. In the church there is a memorial to the Revd John Witherspoon (1722–94) who was born in the village and emigrated to the United States of America where he became president of the New Jersey College, Princeton, and was a signatory to the American Declaration of Independence. The surrounding area is popular with golfers, hill walkers and pony trekkers.

Giffordtown *Fife* A 19th-century hamlet in Collessie parish, central Fife, situated in the Howe of Fife to the northwest of Ladybank. Also known as Gifferton, it has an equestrian centre.

Gigalum Island *Argyll and Bute* A small, uninhabited rocky island, Gigalum Island lies off the southeast coast of the island of Gigha in the Sound of Gigha, between Gigha and the Kintyre peninsula.

Gigha *Argyll and Bute* A small island of the Inner Hebrides, Gigha lies to the west of the Kintyre peninsula, from which it is separated by the Sound of Gigha. Ardminish on the east coast is linked by ferry to Tayinloan in Kintyre. Stretching 6 miles (10 km) from north to south and with an area of 1368 ha (3379 acres), Gigha largely comprises a ridge of volcanic and metamorphic rocks. The island was granted to the Lords of the Isles in the 14th century and passed to the MacNeills in the 1490s. In 1944 it was purchased by Sir James Horlick, who established a garden in the woodlands surrounding Achamore House with plants supplied by the National Trust for Scotland. The island was the subject of a community buy-out in 2002. To the south of the main settlement at Ardminish stand the ruins of the 13th-century chapel of Kilchattan.

Gigha, Sound of *Argyll and Bute* The Sound of Gigha is the name of the strait of water separating the island of Gigha from the west coast of the Kintyre peninsula.

Gighay *Western Isles* One of a group of uninhabited islands located off the northeast coast of Barra in the Outer Hebrides, Gighay (Gael: *Gioghaigh*) has an area of 96 ha (237 acres) and rises steeply to 95 m (311 ft) immediately to the northeast of Hellisay and 2.5 miles (4 km) southwest of Hellisay. Gighay is owned by the Scottish Ministers (the Government).

Gight Castle *Aberdeenshire* The ruined remains of the 16th-century L-plan tower house of Gight Castle are located on the north bank of the River Ythan, 4 miles (6.5 km) east of Fyvie in Aberdeenshire. The castle was associated with the Gordon family.

Gillfoot *Dumfries and Galloway* A locality in Dumfries and Galloway, Gillfoot lies 3 miles (5 km) to the north of New Abbey on the eastern edge of Mabie Forest. The mossland of the Kirkconnell Flow lies to the east.

Gillroanie *Dumfries and Galloway* A locality in Dumfries and Galloway, Gillroanie lies 3 miles (5 km) southeast of Kirkcudbright and 3 miles (5 km) west of Dundrennan.

Gills Bay *Highland* Gills Bay is located to the northeast of the Caithness settlement of Gills, 3 miles (5 km) west of John o' Groats in Highland Council area. The island of Stroma lies opposite. A ferry runs from Gills Bay to St Margaret's Hope in Orkney.

Gilmerton *Perth and Kinross* A village in central Perth and Kinross, Gilmerton is situated a mile (1.5 km) to the northeast of Crieff at the junction of the A85 from Perth to Crieff with the A822 heading north through the Sma' Glen to Aberfeldy. The neighbouring estate of Cultoquhey was owned by the Maxtone family for five centuries, their survival being attributed to the so-called Cultoquhey Prayer, written by an eccentric laird in the 1700s: 'From the greed of the Campbells, From the ire of the Drummonds, From the pride of the Grahams, And from the wind of the Murrays, Gude Lord preserve us'.

Gilmerton *City of Edinburgh* A district of Edinburgh, lying on a ridge to the south of the city centre, Gilmerton was originally a mining and quarrying village. The core of the old village, which was declared a conservation area in 1977, is centred on Drum Street, which retains a number of 18th-century houses. At the crossroads between Drum Street and Newtoft Street is Gilmerton Cove, a curious subterranean house excavated by a local blacksmith in 1720. Coal was mined to the south from the 17th century until the Gilmerton Pit closed in 1961. Limestone quarrying was also important in the 19th century.

Gilp, Loch *Argyll and Bute* An inlet extending northwards on the southwest shore of Loch Fyne, Argyll and Bute, Loch Gilp has the settlement of Ardrishaig on its western side, while at the head of the loch lies the settlement of Lochgilphead.

Gilsaigh The Gaelic name for Gilsay in the Western Isles.

Gilsay *Western Isles* One of a group of uninhabited islands in the middle of the eastern entrance to the Sound of Harris, Gilsay (Gael: *Gilsaigh*) rises to 28 m (91 ft) a half-mile (1 km) to the northeast of Lingay.

Gioghaigh The Gaelic name for Gighay in the Western Isles.

Giorra, Loch *Perth and Kinross* A former loch at the western end of Glen Lyon in Perth and Kinross, Loch Giorra merged with Loch an Daimh when it was dammed to form a reservoir.

Girdle Ness *Aberdeen City* A headland on the North Sea coast of Aberdeenshire, Girdle Ness extends into the sea at Aberdeen, separating Aberdeen Bay from Nigg Bay to the south. The shipmaster of Aberdeen demanded a lighthouse be built at Girdle Ness when the whaling ship *Oscar* was wrecked there in 1813 with only two survivors out of a crew of 45. The lighthouse was eventually built in 1833 by Robert Stevenson (1772–1850).

Girnock Burn *Aberdeenshire* A stream in Aberdeenshire, the Girnock Burn rises in hills to the south of the River Dee. It flows northwards through Glen Girnock to join the Dee at Ballhaloch, between Ballater and Crathie.

Girthon *Dumfries and Galloway* A hamlet on the south side of the Fleet Forest, Dumfries and Galloway, Girthon lies 2 miles (3 km) south of Gatehouse of Fleet.

Girvan *South Ayrshire* Situated on the South Ayrshire coast at the mouth of the Water of Girvan, the resort town of Girvan lies 21 miles (33 km) south of Ayr. Created a burgh of barony in 1668, Girvan developed in the 18th and early 19th centuries in association with shoemaking, weaving and fishing. The arrival of the railway in 1860 brought holidaymakers from Glasgow, attracted by the town's harbour and beach. Modern industries include distilling and the manufacture of textiles, chocolate, and alginate for food products.

Girvan, Water of *South Ayrshire* Rising in Loch Girvan Eye in South Ayrshire, the Water of Girvan flows north, entering and leaving Loch Bradan Reservoir. At Straiton it heads northwest until a point 2 miles (3 km) north of Crosshill, where it turns south and west before flowing past Dailly to enter the Firth of Clyde at Girvan.

Girvan Eye, Loch *South Ayrshire* Loch Girvan Eye is located 2 miles (3 km) northeast of the peak of Shalloch on Minnoch within the Glentrool Forest. It is the source of the Water of Girvan.

Gladhouse Reservoir *Midlothian* A reservoir lying 5 miles (8 km) south of Penicuik, in the shadow of the Moorfoot Hills to the southeast of Edinburgh, Gladhouse Reservoir is one of a network of reservoirs supplying the city with water.

Gladsmuir *East Lothian* A village of East Lothian, Gladsmuir lies 3 miles (5 km) west of Haddington. Now bypassed by the A1, it takes a linear form along the north side of the A199. The parish church was built in 1838 to a design by William Burn, replacing an earlier church now in ruins and dating from the 17th century. Professor William Robertson (1721–93), historian and principal of the University of Edinburgh, was parish minister here (1743–58), and the goldsmith George Heriot (1563–1624), who endowed George Heriot's School in Edinburgh, may have been born in Gladsmuir, which was the birthplace of his father. Gladsmuir developed as an industrial village associated with the working of coal and fireclay, and with an ironworks that operated in the latter half of the 19th century. A railway branch line once linked Gladsmuir to nearby Macmerry, and in the 1990s a science park was developed at Elvingston to the north.

Gladstone's Land *City of Edinburgh* Located in the Lawnmarket area of Edinburgh's Old Town, Gladstone's Land is a typical example of 17th-century tenement building. As space was at a premium and proximity to the Royal Mile important, the houses tended to expand and develop in terms of depth and height. Completed in 1620 and rising to a height of six storeys, Gladstone's Land contains furnishings typical of its period and paintings bought by the original owner, the Edinburgh burgess Thomas Gledstanes, a remote ancestor of prime minister William Gladstone (1809–98). Having been condemned by the city authorities, the property was saved and presented to the National Trust for Scotland in 1934. It was restored by Sir Francis Mears and Robert Hurd (1935–7) and leased to the Saltire Society until 1977. Thereafter it was opened to the public. The painted tempera ceilings are of particular note.

Glamaig *Highland* A mountain of the isle of Skye, Highland Council area, Glamaig lies 2 miles (3 km) east of the settlement of Sligachan and a mile (1.5 km) south of Loch Sligachan. The mountain has two peaks: Sgurr Mhairi, which rises to a height of 775 m (2542 ft), and An Coileach, which rises to 673 m (2208 ft).

Glamis *Angus* A village in the heart of Strathmore, Angus, Glamis lies 5 miles (8 km) southwest of Forfar. Nearby is Glamis Castle, the home of the earls of Strathmore who rebuilt the village in the 18th century. Several cottages have thatched roofs, and a row of six cottages gifted to the National Trust for Scotland in 1974 has been restored with 19th-century interiors as the Angus Folk Museum. In the churchyard are some fine

18th-century tradesmen's tombstones and in the garden of the village manse stands a Pictish cross slab known as the King Malcolm stone.

Glamis Castle *Angus* A castle on the outskirts of the village of Glamis in Angus, Glamis Castle is the home of the earls of Strathmore and Kinghorne. A royal hunting lodge existed as early as the 11th century, when Malcolm II (*c.*954–34) is thought to have been assassinated here. In the 15th century an L-plan castle was erected on lands that had earlier been granted to Sir John Lyon by his father-in-law King Robert II. Lyon's son, who became Lord Glamis in 1445, probably built the tower house. Lady Janet Douglas, widow of the 6th Lord Glamis, suffered from James V's persecution of the Douglas family and was imprisoned in Edinburgh Castle and burned as a witch on Castlehill in 1537. Her ghost is said to haunt the chapel at Glamis, which was subsequently confiscated by King James. The property was eventually restored to the Lyons, the 8th Lord Glamis (*c.*1544–77) entertaining Mary, Queen of Scots at the castle. His descendants were created Earl of Kinghorne in 1606 and Earl of Strathmore in 1677. The family fortunes suffered from their support of the royalist cause in the 17th century, but in the late 18th century their fortunes were revived when John, the 9th Earl (1737–76), married Mary Bowes (1749–1800), a Yorkshire heiress. The family home of Queen Elizabeth (1900–2002), wife of King George VI, Glamis Castle was the birthplace of Princess Margaret (1930–2002). Extended by the 2nd Earl in 1615 and remodelled in the late 17th century with policies landscaped by Capability Brown, Glamis Castle was visited in 1793 by Sir Walter Scott who was impressed by its splendour. Features of special interest include the Great Hall with its barrel-vaulted ceiling, the castle's many turrets and a 17th-century family chapel with wall paintings of biblical scenes by Jacob de Wet.

Glas Bheinn Mhòr Deriving its name from the Gaelic for 'big grey-green hill', Glas Bheinn Mhòr rises to a height of 997 m (3270 ft) to the southeast of the head of Loch Etive in Argyll and Bute. It has a symmetrical profile with a particularly steep north face. The so-called Robbers Waterfall lies east-northeast of the summit.

Glas Leathad Mòr *Highland* Located northeast of Garve, in the Ross and Cromarty district of Highland Council area, Glas Leathad Mòr is a summit of Ben Wyvis rising to a height of 1046 m (3431 ft).

Glas Maol *Angus* Located in the southwest corner of the Mounth plateau, Glas Maol lies on the border of Angus, Aberdeenshire and Perth and Kinross council areas. Its summit, which reaches 1068 m (3504 ft), is located in Angus.

Glas Tulaichean *Perth and Kinross* Located between Glen Shee and Glen Tilt in Perth and Kinross, Glas Tulaichean rises to a height of 1051 m (3448 ft).

Glascarnoch, Loch *Highland* Lying adjacent to the A835 to Ullapool, 14 miles (22 km) northwest of Strathpeffer, Loch Glascarnoch is a man-made reservoir that forms part of the Conon Hydro-Electric Scheme. It has a substantial dam, 28 m (92 ft) high and 510 m (1673 ft) in length.

Glasgow *Glasgow City Area: 175.1 sq. km (67.5 sq. miles)* The largest city in Scotland and a separate local government area since 1996, Glasgow straddles the River Clyde in west-central Scotland. It lies 44 miles (71 km)

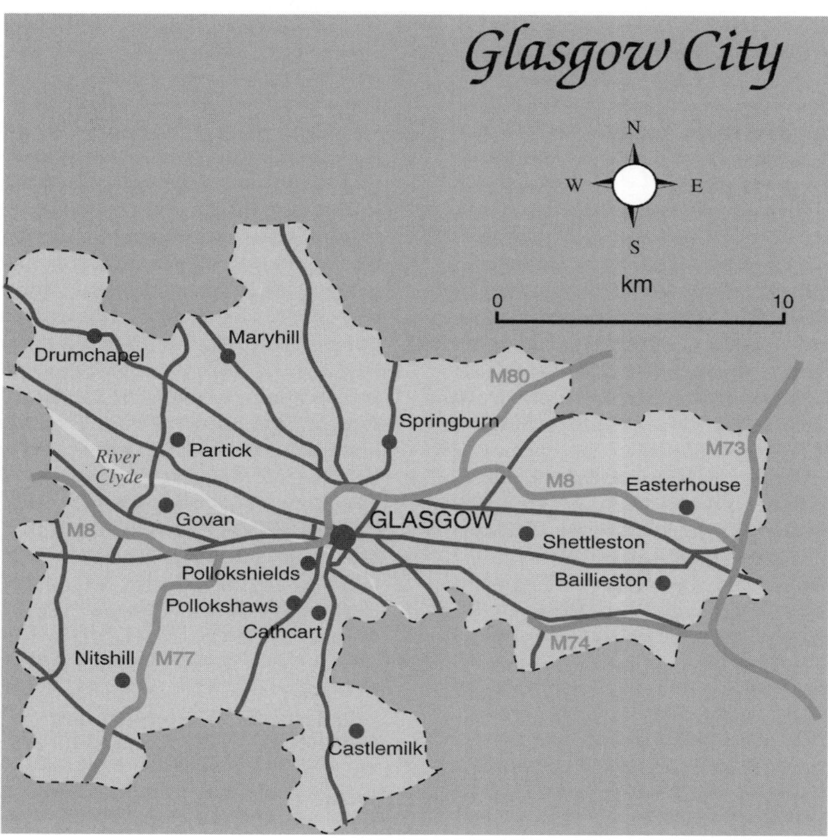

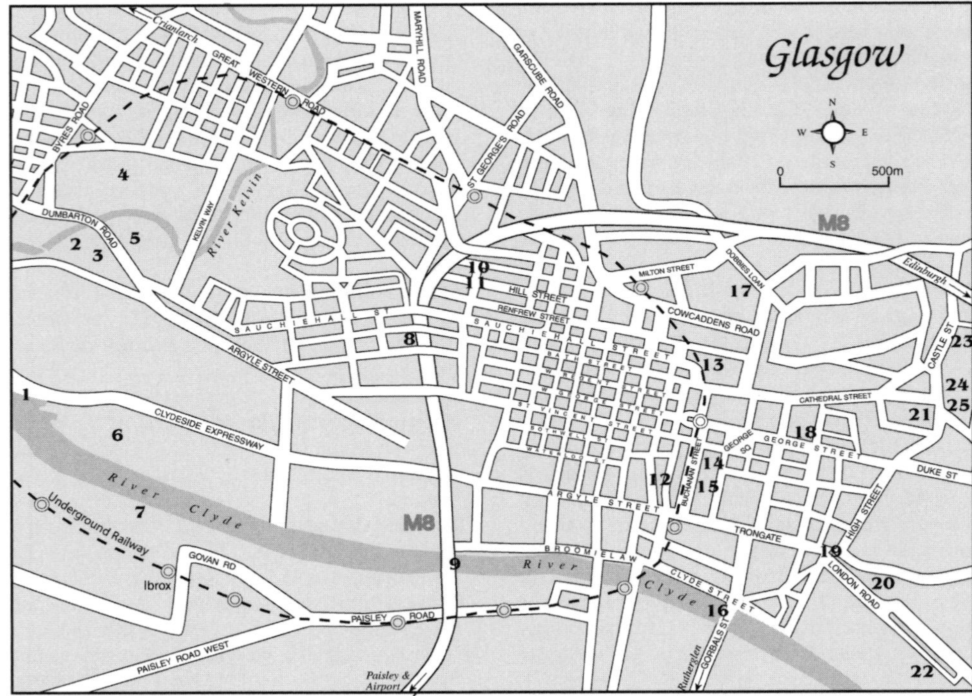

1 *Clyde Maritime Centre*
2 *Museum of Transport*
3 *Kelvin Hall*
4 *Glasgow University*
5 *Kelvingrove Art Gallery and Museum*
6 *Scottish Exhibition and Conference Centre*
7 *Glasgow Science Centre*
8 *Mitchell Library and Theatre*
9 *Kingston Bridge*
10 *Tenement House*
11 *Glasgow School of Art*
12 *The Lighthouse*
13 *Glasgow Royal Concert Hall*
14 *Gallery of Modern Art*
15 *Princes Square*
16 *Victoria Bridge*
17 *Glasgow Caledonian University*
18 *Strathclyde University*
19 *Tolbooth*
20 *Barras Market*
21 *Provand's Lordship*
22 *People's Palace Museum*
23 *Royal Infirmary*
24 *Glasgow Cathedral*
25 *St Mungo's Museum*

west of Edinburgh, 144 miles (232 km) southwest of Aberdeen and 397 miles (639 km) north of London. Its population, which reached a peak of over one million in the city's industrial heyday, has declined since the 1950s to 629,500 in 2001. The city, which is said to be founded on the site of a cell established by St Mungo (St Kentigern), developed from the 12th century in association with a cathedral erected between 1123 and 1136. The establishment of the Glasgow Fair and the later development of the settlement by merchants and craftsmen preceded the founding of a university in 1451. Glasgow was elevated to the status of a royal burgh in 1611 and a century later benefited from the opening up of trade with the New World, in particular the tobacco trade. Many fine buildings owe their origin to the fortunes made by the wealthy tobacco merchants of Glasgow and the banks that looked after their money. In 1814 Glasgow Green was laid out as Europe's first public park at a time when the city's population was expanding rapidly with immigration from the Highlands and Ireland in response to the growing textile, engineering and shipbuilding industries. The city expanded outwards, absorbing smaller communities on both sides of the River Clyde. In 1846 Anderston, Bridgeton, Calton, Gorbals, Kelvingrove and Woodside were added, and in 1891 Govanhill, Hillhead, Kelvinside, Maryhill and Pollokshields were brought within the city's bounds. Cathcart, Govan, Partick and Pollokshaws followed in 1912. Post-World War II planning initiatives involved the creation of numerous council-owned high-rise flats on the city's outskirts, the renewal of city-centre housing and the Glasgow Overspill Plan, which resulted in the movement of several hundred thousand people to nearby New Towns, such as East Kilbride, Cumbernauld and Irvine. The decline of heavy industry in the 20th century resulted in both a fall in the population and the initiation of urban-renewal projects, particularly the regeneration of riverside locations. In recent years Glasgow has reinvented itself as a city of commerce, enterprise and culture with three universities – the University of Glasgow, the University of Strathclyde and Glasgow Caledonian University. Designated European City of Culture in 1990 and UK City of Architecture and Design in 1999, major initiatives have included the building of the Scottish Exhibition and Conference Centre (SECC), the Glasgow Science Centre and the Glasgow Royal Concert Hall, as well as major shopping centres such as the St Enoch Centre, Princes Square, Braehead and the Buchanan Galleries. Museums, galleries and buildings of historic interest include Provand's Lordship, the Burrell Collection, Kelvingrove Art Gallery and Museum, Glasgow Cathedral, the House for an Art Lover, the Hunterian Museum, Hutchesons' Hall, the Lighthouse, the St Mungo Museum of

Religious Life and Art, the Tall Ship at Glasgow Harbour, the Tenement House, Pollok House, the Museum of Transport, the People's Palace, Glasgow City Chambers, the McLellan Galleries and the Museum of Piping. Notable sporting venues include the National Football Stadium at Hampden Park, Celtic Park and Ibrox Stadium.

Glasgow International Airport *Renfrewshire* Located due north of Paisley and 6 miles (10 km) west of Glasgow, Glasgow Airport is one of seven in the UK operated by the British Airports Authority, BAA plc. Between 1943 and 1963 a Fleet Air Arm airfield operated at Abbotsinch. In 1966, this base was opened as Glasgow Airport. It is Scotland's busiest airport, with more than 8.6 million passengers and 93,000 take-offs and landings annually and has two terminals and two runways that are 2658 m (8720 ft) and 1088 m (3570 ft) in length.

Glasgow Bridge *Glasgow City* Glasgow Bridge in the centre of the city of Glasgow carries Bridge Street, between Jamaica Street and Eglinton Street, over the River Clyde. The first bridge here was opened in 1772 but by the early 1830s traffic had increased to such an extent that a new bridge designed by Thomas Telford (1757–1834) had to be constructed. By the late 19th century a larger bridge was again required, and a remodelled bridge retaining the basic structure of Telford's bridge was opened in 1899 with a length of 170 m (560 ft).

Glasgow Cathedral *Glasgow City* Glasgow Cathedral, built on the site of the 6th-century cell of St Mungo (Kentigern), lies at the north end of the High Street to the east of Glasgow city centre. Building work in the 12th century by Bishop Jocelyn was completed in the 13th century, and major renovation work was undertaken in the 15th century, which included the construction of the central tower and the chapter house. Again repairs were needed in the 18th century, although unfortunately the western towers were removed before it was realised that there was no money to rebuild them. In the 20th century the area surrounding the Cathedral was improved, with the construction of a visitors' centre, the creation of St Mungo's Museum of Religious Art and Life and a piazza to the west.

Glasgow Cross *Glasgow City* A locality in Glasgow city centre, Glasgow Cross lies at the point where the High Street is crossed by Argyle Street. To the south, towards the River Clyde, is the Saltmarket. This area was the focal point for the development of mercantile Glasgow in the neighbouring Gallowgate and Trongate.

Glasgow Green *Glasgow City* Lying on the north bank of the River Clyde, Glasgow Green extends from Saltmarket in the west to Bridgeton in the east. An area of common land, Glasgow Green was sold by the city during the 16th and 17th centuries to alleviate the city's debt, only to be bought back during the 18th century. Since the late 18th century it has remained at its present size of 55 ha (136 acres). In 1814 it was established as Europe's first public park. More a functional space than ornate parkland, the Green has been used for grazing cattle, washing and drying of clothes, recreation and for speeches and demonstrations. Its western entrance is dominated by the McLellan Arch, while within the park can be found the Doulton Fountain, Collins Fountain and the 43.5-m/143-ft-tall Nelson's Obelisk. On the northwest edge of the park are the People's Palace and the Templeton Business Centre.

Glasgow, Paisley and Johnstone Canal Little remains of the Glasgow, Paisley and Johnstone Canal, which once extended 11 miles (18 km) from Johnstone to Port Eglinton (which no longer exists but lay close to Eglinton Street, some half a mile (1 km) south of Glasgow Bridge). Promoted and partially funded by Hugh Montgomerie of Coilsfield, the 12th Earl of Eglinton (1739–1819), the canal cost some £130,000 to build. The engineers John Rennie (1761–1821) and Thomas Telford (1757–1834) were involved in planning the canal, and John Ainslie (1745–1821) surveyed the route. Originally designed to reach the Ayrshire coast at Ardrossan, the canal was built only as far as Johnstone before funds ran out. The canal was taken over by the Glasgow and Southwestern Railway Company in 1869 and was eventually closed by Act of Parliament in 1881. In that year a railway track was laid along the section between Glasgow and Paisley, a route now linking Glasgow Central to Paisley Canal station. The Blackhall Aqueduct survives as a railway bridge, but it is in the environs of the Ferguslie Thread Works in Paisley that the canal is best preserved.

Glasgow Science Centre, The *Glasgow City* A Millenium Commission Lottery-funded project, the Glasgow Science Centre occupies a futuristic building on the southern bank of the River Clyde, on the site of the 1988 Garden Festival. The Centre comprises Scotland's first Imax Cinema, a 122-m/400-ft fully rotating tower with viewing platform and a four-storey, titanium-clad Science Mall which includes a range of interactive displays and exhibitions. The centre was opened by Queen Elizabeth II in July 2001. Across the river lie the Clyde Auditorium and Scottish Exhibition and Conference Centre.

Glasgow Underground *Glasgow City* The Glasgow Underground runs over a 6-mile (10-km) route under the city. There are fifteen stations on a circular route, with inner and outer loops of track, allowing a service to run clockwise, while another runs anti-clockwise. The distinctive little orange trains, which run on a 4-foot (1.2-m) gauge, have given rise to the network's sobriquet, the 'clockwork orange'. The trains climb and dip markedly, with the depth of the line below the surface varying from only 2.1 m (7 ft) to 35 m (115 ft). Opened on 14 December 1896, the service was originally privately financed but run by Glasgow Corporation from 1923. The system was completely modernised during the 1970s, with new stations, track and rolling stock and re-opened by Queen Elizabeth II on 1 November 1979. Today, it is operated by Strathclyde Passenger Transport Executive, which manages integrated transport within and around Glasgow. The 'clockwork orange' remains the only public underground transport system in Scotland.

Glass, River *Highland* A river of Easter Ross, the Glass issues from Loch Glass which lies in the shadow of Ben Wyvis to the west of the Cromarty Firth. Formerly known as the Allt Grande, it flows southeastwards past Evanton to join the Cromarty Firth 6 miles (10 km) northeast of Dingwall. A gorge near the mouth of the river is known as the Black Rock.

Glass, River *Highland* A river of the Inverness-shire district of Highland Council area, the River Glass is formed at the confluence of the Affric and Cannich rivers near Cannich. It flows northeastwards through Strathglass to join the River Farrar near Struy, where it becomes the River Beauly.

Glasserton *Dumfries and Galloway* A locality in a parish of the same name in Dumfries and Galloway, Glasserton lies nearly 2 miles (3 km) southwest of Whithorn. Former residences of the earls of Galloway and a mansion designed by Robert Adam in the 1790s once stood here. Glasserton Parish church dates from 1732.

Glassford *South Lanarkshire* Located 2 miles (3 km) northeast of Strathaven in South Lanarkshire, Glassford is a small farming community in a parish of the same name.

Glasshaugh Windmill *Aberdeenshire* Located at the eastern edge of Sandend in Aberdeenshire, the Glasshaugh Windmill was built in 1761. Only the ruins of the building remain, and as such are protected as a building of architectural and historical importance. Owing to its unusual shape, it is known locally as the Cup and Saucer.

Glassie, Loch *Perth and Kinross* A small loch in central Perth and Kinross, Loch Glassie lies at an altitude of 366 m (1200 ft) above sea level in the hills to the north of Aberfeldy. It drains southeastwards to the River Tay.

Glen Barry *Aberdeenshire* A locality in northwest Aberdeenshire near the Moray border, Glen Barry lies 11 miles (18 km) southwest of Banff in a glen of the same name between Knock Hill and Barry Hill. It originally developed in association with a station on the Great North of Scotland Railway.

Glen Ord Distillery *Highland* Located near the village of Muir of Ord, 3 miles (5 km) north of Beauly in Ross and Cromarty, Highland Council area, the Glen Ord Distillery dates from 1838 when it was built to a design by Robert Johnson and D. Maclennan. It produces a Highland malt that is regarded as the 'Whisky from the Black Isle'.

Glenapp Castle *South Ayrshire* Glenapp Castle is located a mile (1.5 km) south of Ballantrae in South Ayrshire. Built in 1870 by David Bryce for James Hunter, the Deputy Lord Lieutenant of Ayrshire, the castle was purchased in 1917 by James Lyle Mackay, and his descendants owned the castle until 1984. Since 1994 it has been used as a country house hotel.

Glenartney, Forest of *Perth and Kinross* A deer forest in central Perth and Kinross, Glenartney Forest lies in Comrie parish, between Loch Earn and Glen Artney.

Glenavon, Forest of *Moray* A deer forest in the Grampian Mountains, the Forest of Glenavon lies between the upper reaches of the River Avon to the north and the peaks of Ben Avon to the south.

Glenbarr *Argyll and Bute* A small settlement of Argyll and Bute, Glenbarr lies on the Barr Water near the west coast of the Kintyre peninsula, 10 miles (16 km) northwest of Campbeltown.

Glenbervie *Aberdeenshire* A village at the northern end of the Howe of the Mearns in Aberdeenshire, Glenbervie lies between the larger villages of Auchenblae and Drumlithie. Ancestors of the poet Robert Burns who farmed at Clochnahill are buried in the churchyard at Glenbervie. These tombstones were restored by the Glenbervie Burns Memorial Committee and re-dedicated in 1968. Also of interest in the churchyard are the remains of the ancient Douglas aisle. The church was rebuilt in 1826. Nearby is Glenbervie House, which dates from the 17th century. There is a local food-processing industry.

Glenboig *North Lanarkshire* A former industrial hamlet lying on both sides of a railway junction in North Lanarkshire, Glenboig is located 2 miles (3 km) north of Coatbridge. Its station closed c.1960, and its coal mine and fireclay works had gone by 1980, leaving considerable desolation.

Glenbrittle *Highland* Situated to the west of the Black Cuillins in the west of the isle of Skye, the hamlet of Glenbrittle lies in Glen Brittle, which provides access to the Cuillins for walkers and mountaineers. The Glen Brittle Hut, Glenbrittle House and a mountain rescue post are located here.

Glenbuchat Castle *Aberdeenshire* The ruined remains of Glenbuchat Castle stand near the junction of the Water of Buchat with the River Don, 4 miles (6.5 km) east-northeast of the village of Strathdon. Built by John Gordon in 1590, it is a random rubble structure in a Z-shape with four turrets. The castle was owned by the Gordons until 1738, when it was forfeited by John Gordon for his Jacobite sympathies. In ruins since the roof was removed in 1840, it has been in the care of Historic Scotland since 1948.

Glencairn Castle An alternative name for Maxwelton in Dumfries and Galloway.

Glencaple *Dumfries and Galloway* A coastal village in Caerlaverock parish, Dumfries and Galloway, Glencaple lies on the River Nith near its mouth, 5 miles (8 km) south of Dumfries. It was once a trading port for Dumfries.

Glencaple Burn *South Lanarkshire* A tributary of the Glengonnar Water, which is itself a tributary of the River Clyde, Glencaple Burn rises in the foothills of Peat Hill and flows 3 miles (5 km) north. It joins the Glengonnar Water a mile (1.5 km) south of Abington, South Lanarkshire.

Glencarse *Perth and Kinross* A settlement in the Carse of Gowrie, Glencarse is situated by the A85, 4 miles (6.5 km) east of Perth. Laid out as an estate village, it follows the line of the old Perth–Dundee road. Glencarse House was built for Thomas Hunter in 1790 to a design by Robert and James Adam, and All Saints Episcopal Church was built in 1878.

Glencoe *Highland* Also known as Bridge of Coe, the village of Glencoe lies at the south end of Glen Coe near the head of Loch Leven. Nearby are a National Trust for Scotland visitor centre and the Glencoe and North Lorn Folk Museum.

Glencorse *Midlothian* A parish to the north of Penicuik in Midlothian, Glencorse lies in the eastern foothills of the Pentland Hills to the south of Edinburgh. Nearby at Milton Bridge is Glencorse Barracks, headquarters of the Army Training Regiment. Dating from 1803, when the buildings were first used to hold prisoners during the Napoleonic Wars, the only surviving structure from that period is the former guardroom (now the clock tower). A memorial gateway to the Royal Scots Regiment marks the entrance to the barracks. Glencorse Reservoir, which supplies water to Edinburgh, was created 1819–28. Submerged beneath the waters of the reservoir is St Catherine's Chapel.

Glencoul, Loch *Highland* A sea loch in the Assynt district of western Sutherland, Loch Glencoul widens out from the smaller Loch Beag at the mouth of Glen Coul. Combining with Loch Glendhu at Unapool, the loch opens into Loch a' Chàirn Bhàin to the west of Kylesku, eventually draining into Eddrachillis Bay.

Glencraig *Fife* A former mining village in the Fife parish of Ballingry, Glencraig lies between Crosshill and Lochgelly. The estate of Glencraig, comprising Inchgall, Contle, Clune and Templelands, came into being about 1830.

Glendale *Highland* A locality forming part of a crofting township on the island of Skye, Glendale lies 4 miles (6.5 km) west of Dunvegan Castle, by the Hamara River which flows through Glen Dale into Loch Pooltiel. In 1904 Glendale was bought from the landlord by the Board of Agriculture and resold to the crofters who became the first crofter landowners in Scotland. The renowned Gaelic lyricists Donald MacLeod and his sons John and Neil were born at Glendale.

Glendaruel *Argyll and Bute* A valley on the Cowal peninsula of Argyll and Bute, Glendaruel lies to the north of Loch Riddon and is occupied by the River Ruel. The Clachan of Glendaruel lies at the south end of the glen.

Glendevon *Perth and Kinross* A village at the head of Glen Devon in central Perth and Kinross, Glendevon lies 2 miles (3 km) north of Yetts o' Muckhart, just to the north of the Castle Hill Reservoir. Glendevon Castle was a stronghold of the Douglas family, and close to Glendevon church and manse is an 18th-century humpback bridge across the River Devon. A footpath over the Ochil Hills connects with Dollar in Clackmannanshire.

Glendoe Forest *Highland* An area of deer forest to the south of Glen Doe, the valley of the Allt Doe, Glendoe Forest lies 4 miles (6.5 km) southeast of Fort Augustus in the Monadhliath Mountains.

Glendoick *Perth and Kinross* A settlement in the Carse of Gowrie, Glendoick is situated on the A85 between Perth and Dundee, 5 miles (8 km) east of Perth. Glendoick House dates from c.1747 and Glendoick school and schoolhouse are early 19th century.

Glenduckie *Fife* A small hamlet in northern Fife, Glenduckie lies on the southern slopes of Glenduckie Hill which rises to a height of 218 m (715 ft) 3 miles (5 km) east of Newburgh to the north of the A914 to Cupar.

Gleneagles *Perth and Kinross* Although most commonly associated with a well-known hotel in the heart of Perth and Kinross, the name Gleneagles is more anciently associated with a narrow valley within which are located a mansion house, a castle, an estate, a station and a chapel. Situated a mile (1.5 km) to the southwest of Auchterarder, Gleneagles Hotel has become one of the world's leading golfing venues, the King's and Queen's courses having been laid out between 1910 and 1919 by James Braid, five times British Open Champion. The hotel itself was conceived by Donald Mathieson of the Caledonian Railway and completed in 1925, the nearby Gleneagles Station being built in 1919 to welcome holidaymakers to the smart new railway hotel. Gleneagles House at the northern entrance to Gleneagles, comprises a 1750 extension to an earlier 17th-century building that is approached by an avenue of lime trees planted to commemorate the Battle of Camperdown (1797). The 2005 G8 summit was held at the Gleneagles Hotel. Little remains of Gleneagles Castle, the early 16th-century tower house of the Haldanes, but close by is the restored 16th-century Gleneagles Chapel, a private chapel, probably of greater antiquity, that gives the valley its Gaelic name which means 'the glen of the church'. Halfway up the glen, a 19th-century tollhouse has been restored as a private dwelling.

Glenegedale *Argyll and Bute* A locality on the island of Islay in the Inner Hebrides, Glenegedale is the site of the island's airport.

Glenelg *Highland* A village in a parish of the same name in the Inverness-shire district of Highland Council area, Glenelg lies on Glenelg Bay, an inlet at the northern end of the Sound of Sleat opposite Skye. Nearby are the Bernera Barracks.

Glenesslin Burn *Dumfries and Galloway* A stream in Dumfries and Galloway, the Glenesslin Burn rises on the south slopes of Bogrie Hill to the south of Dalmacallan Forest. It flows eastwards for 5 miles (8 km) before joining the Cairn Water southwest of the village of Dunscore.

Glenfarclas *Moray* A distillery in Moray founded in 1837 by Robert Hay, the Glenfarclas Distillery at Ballindalloch near the junction of the Avon and Spey rivers was acquired by J. and G. Grant in 1865. There is a visitor centre with an audiovisual display.

Glenfarg *Perth and Kinross* A village in the parish of Arngask, Perth and Kinross, Glenfarg lies on the River Farg, 8 miles (13 km) south of Perth. Formerly known as Damhead, its name was changed in the 1890s when the newly completed railway through Glen Farg brought tourists to the area. Now bypassed by the M90, Glenfarg is the venue for a folk festival.

Glenfiddich *Moray* A single-malt distillery at the northern end of Dufftown in Moray, Glenfiddich was established by William Grant in 1887 using stills from the Cardow Distillery. Still managed by the Grant family, it lies at the heart of an area once noted for its many small illicit stills and is the only distillery in the Highlands where malt whisky is bottled on the premises. The distillery, which was enlarged in 1955 to become one of the largest in Scotland, welcomes visitors with an audiovisual programme and guided tour.

Glenfiddich Lodge *Moray* A shooting lodge in the Grampian uplands of Moray, Glenfiddich Lodge lies on a bend of the River Fiddich to the west of the Cabrach Road from Dufftown to Rhynie.

Glenfinnan *Highland* A scattered settlement at the head of Loch Shiel, Glenfinnan lies 18 miles (29 km) northwest of Fort William on the road to Mallaig. Looking out onto Loch Shiel is the Glenfinnan Monument, which was erected in 1815 by Alexander Macdonald of Glenaladale as a tribute to the clansmen who died fighting for the cause of Prince Charles Edward Stewart (Bonnie Prince Charlie). Although the Prince's standard was raised here in 1745, the campaign to reinstate the Stewarts to the throne of Great Britain met with defeat in 1746 on the battlefield at Culloden. There is a station on the West Highland railway line, and to the northeast the Glenfinnan Viaduct crosses the River Finnan, which flows south through Glen Finnan into Loch Shiel.

Glengainoch Burn *Dumfries and Galloway* A stream of Dumfries and Galloway, the Glengainoch Burn rises on the eastern slopes of Fell of Fleet. It flows eastwards to meet the Airie Burn before joining the Black Water of Dee.

Glengarnock *North Ayrshire* An industrial hamlet of North Ayrshire, Glengarnock lies to the southwest of Kilbirnie Loch, a half-mile (1 km) southeast of Kilbirnie and 2 miles (3 km) southwest of Beith. Textile mills developed in the late 18th century, followed by coal mines and most notably the Glengarnock Iron Works, which opened in 1843 using the local coal and ironstone in its blast furnaces. The village grew rapidly as a result. By the early 20th century, the Glengarnock Iron and Steel Company employed thousands. However, by 1978 the industry was in terminal decline and was gone completely by 1985, bringing unemployment and economic collapse. New light industries have been established and few traces remain of the old industrial complex. Glengarnock has a primary school and a station on the railway line from Glasgow and Paisley to Kilwinning Junction. The ruined 15th-century Glengarnock Castle lies 2 miles (3 km) north of Kilbirnie.

Glengavel Water *South Lanarkshire* Rising in the foothills of Auchingilloch, the Glengavel Water flows south then north, passing through the Glengavel Reservoir before heading north to meet the Avon Water 5 miles (8 km) east of Darvel.

Glenglass Burn *Dumfries and Galloway* A stream in Dumfries and Galloway, the Glenglass Burn is a small tributary of the Euchan Water 5 miles (8 km) southwest of Sanquhar.

Glengonnar Water *South Lanarkshire* Rising in the Lowther Hills to the east of Leadhills, the Glengonnar Water flows north for 4 miles (6.5 km) to merge with the Glencaple Burn before emptying into the River Clyde.

Glengorm Castle *Argyll and Bute* A castle situated to the north of Tobermory on the northern coastline of the island of Mull, Glengorm was built in 1860 for James Forsyth, who is associated with the clearance of the crofting tenants of Dervaig. Now providing holiday accommodation, its gardens are a major source of vegetables on the island. To the west lie the ruins of Dun Ara Fort.

Glengoyne Distillery *Stirling* Established in 1833, the Glengoyne Distillery lies near Dumgoyne in Strathblane, 15 miles (24 km) north of Glasgow. Taking its name from nearby Glen Guin ('glen of the wild goose'), it is regarded as the southernmost of the Highland malt whisky distilleries in an area that once boasted 18 illicit stills.

Glengyle *Stirling* A locality in Strathgartney, Stirling Council area, Glengyle lies on the northwest shore of Loch Katrine. The Glengyle Water flows southeastwards through Glen Gyle to join Loch Katrine near here. Once a possession of the Macgregors, Glengyle is particularly associated with Rob Roy Macgregor who was born here in 1671. Glengyle House dates from the 18th century.

Gleniffer Braes Country Park *Renfrewshire* Located 3 miles (5 km) southwest of Paisley, the Gleniffer Braes Country Park forms part of the 526 ha (1300 acres) of woodland and moorland that make up the Gleniffer Braes in Renfrewshire. The park has waymarked and guided walks as well as play areas and views over Paisley and Glasgow.

Glenkens, The *Dumfries and Galloway* A district of Dumfries and Galloway, The Glenkens is the name given to the valley of the Water of Ken and its headwater, the Water of Deugh. It stretches from Carsphairn in the north to New Galloway and Loch Ken in the south.

Glenkiln Burn *Dumfries and Galloway* A stream in Dumfries and Galloway, the Glenkiln Burn is a tributary of the Water of Ae, which it joins after flowing southwards through the Forest of Ae from its source on Minnygap Height.

Glenkiln Reservoir *Dumfries and Galloway* A reservoir in Kirkpatrick Irongray parish, Dumfries and Galloway, Glenkiln lies at the head of the Old Water, to the northwest of Shawhead and 6 miles (10 km) west of Dumfries. In the open landscape to the west and south stand sculptures by Auguste Rodin, Henry Moore and Sir Jacob Epstein erected by local landowner Sir William Keswick from the early 1950s. There are walks in the neighbourhood reaching the top of Bishop Forest Hill.

Glenkinchie *East Lothian* An East Lothian hamlet centred on a distillery of the same name, Glenkinchie is located 1.25 miles (2 km) south of Pencaitland. The Kinchie Burn runs past the settlement, and the hamlet of Peastonbank lies immediately to the south. The distillery was established in 1837 by brothers John and George Rate. Disused between 1853 and 1880, it was rebuilt in 1890 and again in the 1920s. Following World War II the distillery manager bred prize-winning cattle, feeding them on the spent grain.

Glenlair *Dumfries and Galloway* A hamlet in the old county of Kirkcudbrightshire in Dumfries and Galloway, Glenlair lies 12 miles (19 km) west of Dumfries. The physicist James Clerk Maxwell (1831–79) spent his childhood here.

Glenlatterach *Moray* Located 6 miles (10 km) south of Elgin, the settlement of Glenlatterach lies a mile (1.5 km) northeast of Glenlatterach Reservoir and 2 miles (3 km) northwest of the peak of Pikey Hill.

Glenlatterach, Ess of *Moray* A waterfall on the Leanoch Burn of Moray, the Ess of Glenlatterach lies a mile (1.5 km) south of the confluence of the Leanoch with the River Lossie.

Glenlatterach Reservoir *Moray* The Glenlatterach Reservoir lies 6 miles (10 km) south of Elgin and a mile (1.5 km) west of Glenlatterach. The Leanoch Burn, which rises in the foothills of nearby Pikey Hill, passes through the reservoir before joining the River Lossie.

Glenlee Hill *Dumfries and Galloway* A hill in Dumfries and Galloway, Glenlee rises to a height of 271 m (888 ft) a mile (1.5 km) to the west of the Water of Ken and 2 miles (3 km) southwest of St John's Town of Dalry. To the west rises the Back Hill of Glenlee and to the north and south respectively, the Glenlee Burn and the Craigshinnie Burn flow eastwards to join the Water of Ken.

Glenlivet *Moray* A scattered upland settlement on the west bank of the River Livet, 9 miles (14 km) southwest of Dufftown, Glenlivet gives its name to a noted malt whisky produced here in the heart of the Grampian Mountains. In an area once noted for its whisky smugglers, the first legal distillery was opened in the valley of Glenlivet in 1824 by George Smith of Drumin (1792–1871), that distillery moving from Upper Drumin to its present site in 1858. Blairfindy Castle (1586) to the south was a hunting lodge of the earls of Huntly and to the east, near the Allt a' Choileachain, the Catholic earls of Huntly and Erroll defeated a Protestant army led by the Earl of Argyll at the Battle of Glenlivet on 3 October 1594.

Glenlochar *Dumfries and Galloway* A hamlet in

Dumfries and Galloway, Glenlochar lies on the River Dee just west of Townhead of Greenlaw and 3 miles (5 km) northwest of Castle Douglas. During the 1st and 2nd centuries AD the Romans occupied forts in the neighbourhood. A hydro-electric barrage of the Galloway Water power scheme was built here in the 1930s.

Glenlomond *Perth and Kinross* A village in Perth and Kinross, Glenlomond lies just north of Wester Balgedie in the shadow of the Lomond Hills. During World War I a hospital was established here, but since the 1980s the location has developed as a residential settlement with a nursing home. The old road to Gateside and Strathmiglo, known as the Dryside Road, passes the village. Nearby is Bishop Hill with views over Loch Leven.

Glenluce *Dumfries and Galloway* An agricultural village of Dumfries and Galloway, Glenluce lies at the mouth of the Water of Luce where it enters Luce Bay, 9 miles (14 km) east of Stranraer. Glenluce Abbey to the northwest of the village was founded in 1192 by Roland, Earl of Galloway, for the Cistercian order. Castle of Park, a former stronghold of the Hays, dates from 1590. There is a motor museum and an 18-hole golf course. An airship base operated near here during World War I.

Glenmavis *North Lanarkshire* A village of North Lanarkshire, Glenmavis lies 2 miles (3 km) north-northwest of Airdrie. Once surrounded by coal mines, these had closed by the 1970s, but Glenmavis managed to retain its community. Rochsoles Park was the site of a castle recorded on Timothy Pont's map of 1592, later replaced by a mansion that has subsequently been demolished. The stable block (1839) survives, and housing was developed on the park in the 1980s, extending the village to the east. The Glenmavis Liquefied Natural Gas (LNG) Storage Facility, a key node in the national gas transmission network, lies a half-mile (1 km) to the northwest.

Glenmore Forest Park *Highland* A recreational forest park in Strathspey, Glenmore Forest Park extends over an area of 3480 ha (8600 acres) between the River Spey and the Cairngorm Mountains. Established in 1948, it was the second forest park created by the Forestry Commission in Scotland on land acquired in 1923. It comprises an important remnant of native pinewood surrounding Loch Morlich and is approached from Coylumbridge to the east of Aviemore. The park, which attracts over 250,000 visitors each year, also includes the national outdoor training centre at Glenmore Lodge, the Loch Morlich Watersports Centre, the Glenmore Visitor Centre and the Cairngorm Reindeer Centre. A project to encourage the regeneration of the native pinewood has also led to the creation of a footpath through the woodland linking Glenmore village and the Coire Cas providing access to the mountains.

Glenogil *Angus* A small settlement in Glen Ogil in the Braes of Angus, Glenogil is situated on the Noran Water a half-mile (1 km) south of the Glenogil reservoir and 7 miles (11 km) northeast of Kirriemuir.

Glenprosen *Angus* A hamlet in Glen Prosen, Angus, Glenprosen lies at the junction of the Burn of Inchmill with Prosen Water, 10 miles (16 km) north of Kirriemuir.

Glenquey *Perth and Kinross* A reservoir in the Ochil Hills, Glenquey lies to the east of Innerdownie Hill and southwest of Glendevon village. A hill track extends over the hills from Glendevon to Dollar, and the outlet from the reservoir flows northwards into the River Devon.

Glenrothes *Fife* The administrative capital of Fife, Glenrothes is a New Town situated on the River Leven between Leslie and Markinch. Developed during the 1950s and 1960s on the principles of a 'Garden City' layout of well-landscaped, low-rise suburban housing, its planners originally envisaged a target population of 32,000. The town grew up adjacent to existing paper mills but by the 1970s had gained a 'Silicon Glen' reputation for its hi-tech industries. A wide range of food-processing, engineering and hi-tech industries are located on its Whitehill, Viewfield, Queensway and Southfield industrial estates, and a major town centre retail complex has been developed at the Kingdom Centre. In 1975 Glenrothes superseded Cupar as administrative capital of Fife. To the north of the River Leven, Greater Glenrothes incorporates the districts of Formonthills, Coul, Pitcairn, Collydean, Balgeddie, Whinnyknowe, Leslie Parks, Forester's Lodge, Pitcoudie, Balfarg, Cadham, Mount Frost, Balbirnie Burns and Prestonhall. To the south of the river lie the districts of Macedonia, South Parks, Queensway, Auchmuty, Woodside, Eastfield, Pitteuchar, Viewfield, Rimbleton, Caskieberran, Tanshall, Newcastle, Goatmilk, Whitehill, Southfield, Finglassie, Stenton, Bankhead and Bankhead West. The town is well endowed with playing fields and parks. There is a 23-ha (56-acre) airfield at Goatmilk, a swimming pool and sports centre adjacent to Glenrothes College at Viewfield, the Lomond Community Recreation Centre at Woodside, and two 18-hole golf courses at Goatmilk and Balbirnie.

Glensaugh *Aberdeenshire* A locality in the Braes of Angus, south Aberdeenshire, Glensaugh, or the Glen of the Willows, lies 3 miles (5 km) to the north of Fettercairn in the Howe of the Mearns. Now the site of a livestock research station, Glensaugh includes the man-made Loch Saugh, which is a fishing loch.

Glenshanna Burn *Dumfries and Galloway* A stream in Westkirk parish, Dumfries and Galloway, the Glenshanna Burn is a headwater of the Meggat Water rising between Grey Hill and Dod Fell.

Glentoo Loch *Dumfries and Galloway* A small loch in Dumfries and Galloway, Glentoo Loch lies to the west of the River Dee, 4 miles (6.5 km) west of Castle Douglas.

Glentress Forest *Scottish Borders* An area of plantation forest in Scottish Borders, Glentress Forest lies to the north of the River Tweed, 2 miles (3 km) east of Peebles. Established by the Forestry Commission in the 1920s, it was one of the first State forests in Scotland and now has a series of world-class mountain-biking trails.

Glentrool Forest Stretching from the northern part of Galloway Forest Park, Dumfries and Galloway, to the Carrick area of South Ayrshire, Glentrool Forest is centred on Glen Trool and offers forest trails, picnic sites and camp sites for visitors. Newton Stewart is located 11 miles (18 km) to the south.

Glentrool Village *Dumfries and Galloway* A settlement in Glentrool Forest in the Galloway Forest Park, Glentrool Village lies at the western end of the Glen of Trool, 11 miles (18 km) north of Newton Stewart.

Glenwhappen Rig *Scottish Borders* A hill 2 miles (3 km) northwest of Tweedsmuir, Glenwhappen Rig rises to 600 m (1968 ft) between Gathersnow Hill and Coomb Hill in the district of Tweeddale in Scottish Borders.

Glenwhilly *Dumfries and Galloway* A locality in Dumfries and Galloway, Glenwhilly lies on the Cross Water of Luce, 10 miles (16 km) northeast of Stranraer.

Glenzier Burn *Dumfries and Galloway* A stream in Dumfries and Galloway, the Glenzier Burn rises on the south-facing slopes of Kerr Height, 4 miles (6.5 km) southwest of Langholm. It flows southeastwards past Evertown and Glenzierfoot to join the River Esk just beyond the English frontier, 3 miles (5 km) south of Canonbie.

Gleouraich *Highland* A mountain in the Lochaber district of Highland Council area, Gleouraich rises to a height of 1035 m (3396 ft) to the north of Loch Quoich.

Glespin *South Lanarkshire* A hamlet of South Lanarkshire, Glespin lies on the Douglas Water 2.5 miles (4 km) southwest of Douglas. Hagshaw Hill Wind Farm is located 2 miles (3 km) to the northwest and the Glespin Burn joins the Douglas Water a mile (1.5 km) to the east.

Glespin Burn *South Lanarkshire* A river of South Lanarkshire, the Glespin Burn rises 2 miles (3 km) south of Mosscastle Hill and 3 miles (5 km) west of Crawfordjohn. Flowing north to the small settlement of Glespin to the southwest of Douglas, it joins the Douglas Water, a tributary of the River Clyde.

Glib Cheois The Gaelic name for Keose Glebe in the Western Isles.

Glimps Holm *Orkney* A small 55-ha (136-acre) island of the Orkney Islands, situated between Mainland Orkney and the island of Burray, Glimps Holm is linked by the Churchill Barriers to Burray in the south and Lamb Holm to the northeast.

Glomach, Falls of *Highland* Located 18 miles (29 km) east of Kyle of Lochalsh in the Kintail district of Highland Council area, the Falls of Glomach are one of the highest waterfalls in the United Kingdom. Located in a steep cleft in remote countryside they form a cascade of 113 m (370 ft) on the Glomach Burn or Allt a' Ghlomaich, which issues from Loch a' Bhealaich.

Gloraig Tharansaigh The Gaelic name for Taransay Glorigs in the Western Isles.

Gloup *Shetland* A small settlement in the Shetland Islands, Gloup lies on the west side of Gloup Voe on the island of Yell.

Gloy, Glen *Highland* Glen Gloy is located in the Lochaber district of Highland Council area, lying southeast of and running parallel to Loch Lochy. It carries the waters of the River Gloy, which empty into the loch at Invergloy.

Goatfell *North Ayrshire* Rising to a height of 874 m (2866 ft), Goatfell is the highest peak on the island of Arran. Its peak lies 4 miles (6.5 km) north of the settlement of Brodick and access for walkers is via Brodick Country Park or from Cladach on the A841 Brodick–Lochranza road. The remnants of a volcano dating from the Tertiary period some 60 million years ago, Goatfell and the neighbouring mountainous countryside were gifted in 1958 to the National Trust for Scotland by Lady Jean Fforde, daughter of Mary, Duchess of Montrose.

Goatmilk *Fife* The former name for the village of Kinglassie in Fife, Goatmilk is the name of a farm and district in southwest Greater Glenrothes. In Celtic and medieval times there was a territory known as Gaitmilkshire.

Gob Sgurabhal The Gaelic name for Scurrival Point in the Western Isles.

Goil, Loch *Argyll and Bute* A sea loch of Argyll and Bute, Loch Goil is an arm of Loch Long, striking to the north about halfway up that loch's western shore and surrounded by the Argyll Forest Park. The village of Lochgoilhead lies at the head of the loch and the hamlet of Carrick lies close to the mouth of the loch on its western shore. The defence contractor QinetiQ maintains a facility to assess the noise signatures of navy vessels on the loch at Douglas Pier.

Golly, Glen *Highland* A valley in the Sutherland district of Highland Council area, Glen Golly carries the waters of the River Golly southeastwards to join the southern end of Strath More.

Golspie *Highland* A small town on the east coast of Sutherland in Highland Council area, Golspie lies between Dornoch and Brora at the mouth of the Golspie Burn. It developed as a fishing village in the 18th century, and following the construction of a pier in the 19th century it prospered as a ferry terminal. The coming of the railway in 1868 brought tourists, and a golf club was opened in 1889. Between 1975 and 1996 Golspie shared Sutherland District's administration with Dornoch. Nearby are the Carn Liath Iron Age broch and Dunrobin Castle.

Gometra *Argyll and Bute* An island off the northwest coast of the island of Ulva to the northwest of Mull, Gometra has been uninhabited since the 1980s. There are the remains of Gometra House, the former schoolhouse and a number of cottages.

Goodie Water *Stirling* A stream in Stirling Council area, the Goodie Water issues from the southeast corner of the Lake of Menteith, flowing 11 miles (18 km) southeastwards across Flanders Moss before joining the River Forth near Easter Frew.

Goosey, Loch *South Ayrshire* Located 4 miles (6.5 km) east of Barrhill and a mile (1.5 km) northeast of Eldrick, Loch Goosey is the source of a tributary of the River Cree. It is one of many small lochs in the area, including Drumlamford Loch and Loch Crongart.

Gorbals *Glasgow City* Originally a crossing place on the south side of the River Clyde and the site of Glasgow's leper hospital in medieval times, the Gorbals developed in the 17th century in association with coal mining and weaving, and in the late 18th century became a fashionable suburb of Glasgow. In 1661 it was the first area to the south of the Clyde to be absorbed into the city of Glasgow, and in 1806 the neoclassical Laurieston House was built as part of the stylish Carlton Place terraced housing development. In the 19th century the Gorbals came to be associated with tenement flats built to house an expanding industrial population totalling 40,000, mostly drawn from Irish, Jewish, Indian and Pakistani immigrant communities. Postwar housing developments in the 20th century, including high-rise flats designed by Sir Basil Spence, addressed the need to improve environmental and social conditions in an area experiencing industrial decline that had become associated with poor housing. In the 1990s low-rise housing replaced much of the high-rise buildings of the 1960s. Both the Citizens' Theatre and the Central Mosque and Islamic Centre are located in the Gorbals. The Blessed John Duns Scotus

Church holds what are said to be the remains of St Valentine. John Robertson, who built the engine for the *Comet* steamship, was born in the Gorbals in 1782. Another native of the Gorbals was Allan Pinkerton, born in 1819, who emigrated to the USA where he founded a famous private detective agency.

Gordon *Scottish Borders* A small village of Berwickshire in Scottish Borders, Gordon lies 8 miles (13 km) northwest of Kelso. It developed in the 19th century in association with road and rail transport. Mellerstain House, built in 1725 for George Baillie to a design by William Adam, lies 3 miles (5 km) south, and to the west is Greenknowe Tower

Gordon Castle *Moray* A palace built for the dukes of Gordon near Fochabers in Moray, Gordon Castle was designed by John Baxter in 1769 for the 4th Duke of Gordon. It replaced an earlier castle that had been built by George Gordon, 2nd Earl of Huntly, in the 1470s and enlarged by his grandson into a magnificent Renaissance palace. The 18th-century reconstruction was described as 'the most magnificent edifice north of the Forth'.

Gordonsburgh *Moray* Situated on the Moray Firth, Gordonsburgh is one of a series of old fishing villages that lie on a 3-mile (5-km) stretch of shoreline to the east of Buckie.

Gordonstown *Aberdeenshire* A village in northwest Aberdeenshire, Gordonstown is situated between the Kirktown of Auchterless and Rothienorman on the slopes of Gordonstown Hill, which rises to 177 m (582 ft).

Gorebridge *Midlothian* A settlement of Midlothian, Gorebridge lies 12 miles (19 km) southeast of Edinburgh and north of the Moorfoot Hills. It developed in the 17th and 18th centuries in association with coal mining, limeworks and the manufacture of gunpowder, which was produced at Stobs Mill until 1875. The last local mine was closed in the 1960s and the railway, which had operated a through route from Edinburgh to Hawick since 1847, closed in 1969. In the 19th century the village's spectacular views and the beautiful Arniston Glen made Gorebridge a popular tourist resort. Nearby are Borthwick Castle, Newbyres Castle and an ancient hillfort on Camp Wood Hill.

Gorgie *City of Edinburgh* A former village on the Water of Leith, Gorgie now forms a suburb of Edinburgh 3 miles (5 km) southwest of the city centre. The village developed in association with the tanning industry and is now the location of Gorgie City Farm which was established in 1982 by the local community on land formerly used as a waste depot and later for civil-defence training.

Gormack Burn *Aberdeenshire* A stream in Aberdeenshire, the Gormack Burn rises on the Hill of Fare to the southwest of Echt. It flows north then east to join the Leuchar Burn, a tributary of the River Dee, just west of Peterculter.

Gosford Bay *East Lothian* A west-facing inlet on the East Lothian coast of the Firth of Forth, Gosford Bay lies to the north of Gosford Estate, whose mansion was built in the 1790s to a design by Robert Adam for the 6th Earl of Wemyss. The village of Aberlady lies a mile (1.5 km) to the northeast of the bay.

Gosford House *East Lothian* Home to the earls of Wemyss and March, this extensive mansion, designed by Robert Adam (1728–92), lies on Gosford Bay, 2 miles (3 km) north-northeast of Longniddry. Erected between 1790 and 1800 Gosford House has been much altered. The 8th Earl of Wemyss did not like the style of Adam's wings and had them demolished, leaving only the main block until 1890, when new wings were built by architect William Young. Young also created the stunning Italianate marble hall in pink alabaster, employing Sir William Arrol (1839–1913) to create the steelwork to support the enormous central dome. The house was badly damaged by fire during World War II and later by dry rot, but despite these problems it remains the residence of the 12th Earl.

Gott *Shetland* A hamlet in the Tingwall district of the Shetland Mainland, Gott lies at the head of the Lax Firth, 4 miles (6.5 km) northwest of Lerwick. Tingwall Airport is located a mile (1.5 km) to the southwest.

Gour, Glen *Highland* A valley of the Lochaber district of Highland Council area, Glen Gour carries the waters of the River Gour, which rises in the foothills of Sgurr nan Cnamh, to a point to the west of the headland of Sallachan Point on Loch Linnhe.

Gourdon *Aberdeenshire* An historic seaport and fishing village on the North Sea coast of Aberdeenshire, Gourdon lies a mile (1.5 km) to the south of Inverbervie and 10 miles (16 km) north of Montrose. Fish houses and curing sheds line the quay of this still-thriving settlement, whose fishermen trawl for whitefish, gill-net for cod and fish with the creel for shellfish. An old salthouse, where salt from Cheshire was stored for use in the preservation of herring, is decorated with a mural by local schoolchildren. Nearby is the Farquhar Monument, erected to the memory of Lieutenant William Farquhar RN, who was lost at sea off the coast of China in 1864. Gourdon harbour was built in two phases, the first to a design by Thomas Telford in 1819, the second seaward extension being added in 1842. At that time Gourdon was also a busy port exporting grain and importing coal and lime. A lifeboat station operated here from 1878 until 1969, and between 1865 and 1966 the village was linked to Montrose and Inverbervie by railway. The last working flax-spinning mill in mainland Britain operated in the village's Selbie Works until 1997. Gourdon flax yarns were used to make high-quality linen goods and tarpaulins, and jute yarns were used in a wide range of products from car seats to carpets.

Gourock *Inverclyde* A small town in Inverclyde, Gourock lies 3 miles (5 km) west of Greenock and 26 miles (42 km) west of Glasgow on Gourock Bay, an inlet of the Firth of Clyde. Created a burgh of barony in 1694, Gourock lay on the road to Cloch Point, where a ferry once crossed to Dunoon. It developed in association with rope making (a trade that eventually moved to Port Glasgow), copper mining, textile weaving and the production of kippers (cured herring). In 1820 a pier was opened with a direct ferry service to Dunoon, and later that century Gourock became a popular holiday resort largely frequented by day-trippers from Glasgow travelling 'doon the watter' by steamboat. Today Gourock has electronics industries and is the headquarters of the Cal Mac ferry company. Car ferries operate services to Dunoon and Hunter's Quay, and there are passenger ferries linking with Helensburgh and Kilcreggan. The Cloch lighthouse, first illuminated in 1796, is still in operation, and overlooking Gourock Bay is Granny Kempock's Stone, a 1.8-m/6-ft-high prehistoric stone said to offer protection to shipping and good luck to young couples seeking 'Granny's blessing'. There are fine views of the Firth of Clyde from above the town, and an 18-hole golf course to the west.

Govan *Glasgow City* A district of Glasgow situated 3 miles (5 km) west of Glasgow city centre, Govan lies on the south side of the River Clyde opposite the mouth of the River Kelvin. A Columban monastery was founded here by King Constantine in the 6th century, and later the settlement developed in association with the Govan ferry, which linked with Partick and was used seasonally by cattle drovers. In the 18th and 19th centuries weaving and coal mining were important, and in the early 19th century shipbuilding emerged as a leading industry. Gaining burgh status in 1862, Govan became Scotland's fifth-largest burgh, before being absorbed into the city of Glasgow in 1912. Formerly divided into Meikle Govan and Little Govan, the latter came to be known as the Gorbals. With the decline of shipbuilding in the 20th century, the Govan Initiative was established in 1986 to boost the economy and attract new housing. Local tradition survives in the form of the annual Govan Old Fair and the Govan Old Victualling Society, said to be the oldest cooperative society in the UK.

Govanhill *Glasgow City* A residential suburb of Glasgow, Govanhill lies on the south side of the River Clyde between Govan and Crosshill, 2 miles (3 km) south of Glasgow city centre. Extending to 57 ha (140 acres), its territory was disputed by two burghs prior to it achieving burgh status in 1877. In 1891 Govanhill was absorbed into the city of Glasgow.

Gowkhall *Fife* A small village in Carnock parish, western Fife, Gowkhall is situated to the north of the A907, 3 miles (5 km) west of Dunfermline.

Gowrie *Perth and Kinross* An ancient district of Perthshire, Gowrie lies between Stormont and the River Tay, to the north of Perth.

Grabhair The Gaelic name for Graver in the Western Isles.

Graddoch Burn *Dumfries and Galloway* A stream in Dumfries and Galloway, the Graddoch Burn rises on the western face of Cairnsmore of Fleet. It flows southwestwards to join the Palnure Burn close to that stream's confluence with the River Dee 3 miles (5 km) southeast of Newton Stewart.

Graemsay *Orkney* An island in the western approaches to Scapa Flow in the Orkney Islands, Graemsay lies between the Mainland of Orkney and the island of Hoy. Rising to a height of 62 m (203 ft) at West Hill, the island has an area of 409 ha (1011 acres) and a population of 27 crofters and fishermen. Graemsay is linked by ferry to Stromness and Hoy, its pier being located on the east coast southeast of the Hoy High Lighthouse on the Taing of Sandside. Both the Hoy High and Low lighthouses were built in 1851 to safeguard the herring fleet sailing the dangerous waters of Hoy Sound. On New Year's Day 1866 the ship *Albion* was wrecked off Point of Oxan, the island's northwest extremity. Although its school was closed in 1996, Graemsay still has a post office and a shop.

Grampian Mountains A series of mountain ranges extending southwest to northeast and lying north of the Highland Boundary Fault and south of Strathspey, the Grampian Mountains (also the Grampians) rise to a height of 1309 m (4295 ft) at Ben Macdui in the Cairngorm Mountains. They were formerly known as the Mounth, a name still preserved in the Cairn o' Mounth pass in Aberdeenshire and the plateau called the White Mounth to the south of the River Dee. The term Grampians was first applied by the Aberdeen historian Hector Boece in 1520 in reference to Mons Grampius, the site of Agricola's defeat of the Picts *c.*86 AD.

Grandtully *Perth and Kinross* Situated adjacent to Little Ballinluig in Strathtay, the settlement of Grandtully (pronounced Grantly) developed in association with a former railway station that lay midway between Aberfeldy and Ballinluig at a crossing of the River Tay. Today Grandtully is a noted centre for white-water canoeing on the Tay. Grandtully Castle to the west, a former stronghold of the Stewarts, dates from the 15th century with later additions. The lands of Grandtully were held in the 14th century by Sir John Stewart, Lord of Innermeath and Lorn, a descendant of Alexander, Lord High Steward of Scotland. St Mary's Church near to the castle was founded *c.*1533 by Sir Alexander Stewart to serve the township of Pitcairn. A fine example of a long, low pre-Reformation chapel, it is noted for its ecclesiastical painted ceilings.

Grange, The *City of Edinburgh* A residential district on the south side of Edinburgh, The Grange comprised the church lands of the Grange of St Giles, an estate later held by the Dick-Lauder family who lived in Grange House (demolished in 1936). On the corner of Beaufort Road and Kilgraston Road is the Grange Cemetery, which was was laid out in 1847 for the Southern Cemetery Company by architect David Bryce (1803–76). Famous Scots interred here include the naturalist and stonemason Hugh Miller (1802–56), publishers Thomas Oliver (1775–1853) and Thomas Nelson (1780–1861), the first Moderator of the Free Church of Scotland, Thomas Chalmers (1780–1847), veteran of the Indian Mutiny, General Sir James Hope Grant (1808–75), and the reformer Thomas Guthrie (1803–73).

Grangemouth *Falkirk* An industrial settlement and port in Falkirk Council area, Grangemouth is situated on the Firth of Forth at its junction with the Grange Burn, River Carron and the eastern end of the 35-mile/56-km-long Forth and Clyde Canal. The Dundas family was central to the foundation of the town. Formerly known as Sealock, Sir Lawrence Dundas (1712–81) developed Grangemouth as the link between the canal and the River Forth. The completion of the canal in 1790 created a boom in trade with Glasgow in the west, and Sir Lawrence's son, Sir Thomas, continued the expansion of the town. In 1867 Grangemouth received a further boost when the docks and canal were acquired by the Caledonian Railway Company. A large new complex of docks came into operation in 1906 and in 1924 the first deep-water oil jetty was commissioned. In April 1966 the first fully containerised deep-sea liner service from any UK port was inaugurated here. It continues as a major port facility, handling oil, forest products, coal, clay, sand, soda ash, bauxite and other bulk loads. BP's Grangemouth oil refinery pipes oil directly from the North Sea oil field. Grangemouth Museum tells the stories of the making of one of Scotland's earliest planned industrial towns and the building in 1803 of the world's first steamship, the *Charlotte Dundas*.

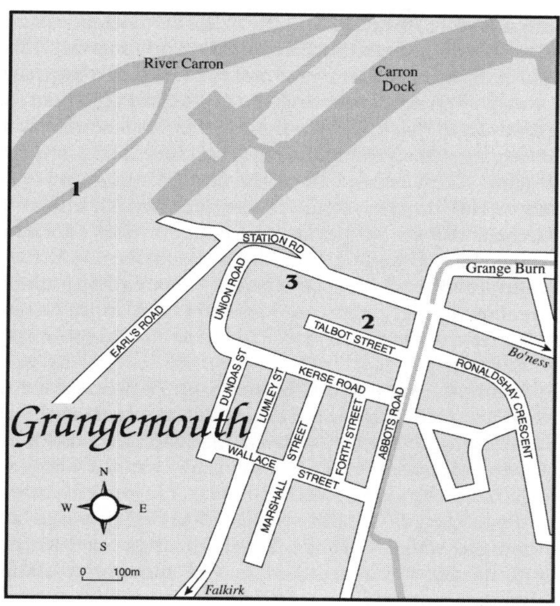

1 *Forth and Clyde Canal*
2 *Grangemouth Museum*
3 *Grangemouth Heritage Centre*

Grange of Lindores *Fife* A hamlet to the west of Lindores Loch in northern Fife, Grange of Lindores is situated 2 miles (3 km) southeast of Newburgh, just off the B936 to Auchtermuchty.

Grannoch, Loch *Dumfries and Galloway* A loch in Dumfries and Galloway, Loch Grannoch lies to the northeast of Cairnsmore of Fleet. Two miles (3 km) in length from north to south, it is the source of the Pullaugh Burn which flows north to join the River Dee.

Granny Kempock's Stone *Inverclyde* Resembling an old woman, Granny Kempock's Stone is a 1.8-m/6-ft-high prehistoric stone that stands on a hill in Gourock overlooking Kempock Point on the Firth of Clyde. A talisman to sailors and newlyweds, a group of women accused of witchcraft were burned to death here in 1662.

Granton *City of Edinburgh* A seaport suburb of Edinburgh, Granton lies on the Firth of Forth, 2.5 miles (4 km) to the north of the city centre. Its development as a seaport dates from 1836, when the building of a harbour was initiated by Walter, 5th Duke of Buccleuch (1806–84), on his Caroline Park property. Designed by the engineer Robert Stevenson, the harbour provided an important link with Fife and the north, the world's first train-ferry, the *Leviathan*, operating between Granton and Burntisland from 1850. Designed by Sir Thomas Bouch (1822–90), builder of the ill-fated Tay Rail Bridge, the complex series of ramps created to load and unload carriages had to accommodate the sizeable tidal range of the Firth of Forth. A coaling jetty was built in 1937 and car and passenger ferry services continued until the building of the Forth Road Bridge in 1964. The home of the Royal Forth Yacht Club, Granton was once the base for a large fishing fleet. The Granton Gas Works industrial complex, which now receives gas from the North Sea, dates from 1898, its massive gasometers being erected in 1902, 1933 and 1966. The redundant gasometers were demolished in 2004.

Grantown-on-Spey *Highland* A village of Strathspey in Highland Council area, Grantown-on-Spey lies on the River Spey, 13 miles (21 km) northeast of Aviemore. It was laid out as a planned village in 1766 by Sir James Grant of Grant, whose intention was to create a market town and industrial centre at the heart of his Strathspey estate. Castle Grant, the former seat of the Grants of Grant lies 2 miles (3 km) to the north. By 1841 the village had 1000 inhabitants, but it was not until the arrival of the railway in 1863 that the town began to develop as a fashionable holiday resort linked to fishing, shooting and hill walking. After the railway closed in 1965, the development of skiing helped to maintain Grantown-on-Spey as an all-year resort. There are sporting facilities, hotels and a museum.

Grantshouse *Scottish Borders* A small village of Berwickshire in Scottish Borders, Grantshouse lies on the Eye Water, 8 miles (13 km) west of Eyemouth. The settlement developed in association with a local mill and a railway station that remained open from 1846 to 1965.

Grassic Gibbon Centre *Aberdeenshire* Dedicated to the life and times of the writer James Leslie Mitchell (1901–35), who wrote under the name Lewis Grassic Gibbon, the Grassic Gibbon Centre is located adjacent to the parish hall in the village of Arbuthnott, at the heart of The Mearns district of Aberdeenshire. Built by the community as an educational centre in 1991, it is located close to the farm where the author was brought up. Nearby, in the graveyard of Arbuthnott's 13th-century church, Lewis Grassic Gibbon's ashes were interred.

Grassmarket *City of Edinburgh* A 210-m/230-yd-long former market place in central Edinburgh, the Grassmarket lies to the south of Edinburgh Castle at the western end of the Cowgate. A weekly market was held here from 1477 to 1911, livestock entering the Grassmarket via the West Port, a gateway in the city's ancient Flodden Wall. It was also the site of public hangings, most notably the execution in the late 17th century of Covenanters who are comemmorated by a monument erected in 1937. A public house is named after Maggie Dickson, the subject of an unsuccessful attempt at judicial hanging in 1728, and the Last Drop public house is a reminder of a grim past. The Grassmarket's role as a market place and coaching terminus has given rise to numerous inns such as the 18th-century Whitehart Inn and the 19th-century Beehive Inn. Buildings around the square date from the 17th century to the present and include the former Mountbatten Building of Heriot Watt University (1968), converted into a hotel in 1996. Dance Base, the Scottish National Centre for Dance, occupies a modern building with a traditional frontage built in 2001 in the shadow of Edinburgh Castle.

Graven *Shetland* A settlement on Mainland Shetland, Graven lies at the head of Garths Voe to the south of Sullom Voe.

Graver *Western Isles* An extended crofting settlement of the Park district of eastern Lewis in the Outer Hebrides, Graver (or Gravir; Gael: *Grabhair* or *Grabhir*) lies around the head of Loch Ouirn, 11 miles (18 km) south of Stornoway. The Pairc Primary School is located here.

Great Bernera *Western Isles* An island of the Outer Hebrides, Great Bernera (Gael: *Bearnaraigh*), 2240 ha (5532 acres), lies off the west coast of Lewis, a mile (1.5 km) northwest of Callanish. In 1874, Great Bernera was the site of a crofters' land revolt, and this event is remembered by a cairn in the centre of the island. A bridge linking it with the island of Lewis, built in 1953 at a cost of £70,000, was one of the earliest to be built of pre-stressed concrete. The Bernera Museum is located at Breaclete in the centre of the island. Salmon farming and shellfish processing make important contributions to the local economy.

Great Cumbrae *North Ayrshire* Located within North Ayrshire, a mile (1.5 km) off the mainland, immediately to the north of Little Cumbrae and east of Bute, Great Cumbrae has an area of 1155 ha (2854 acres). The island has a population of 1393 and is the most densely populated in Scotland. The highest point of the island is at Barbary Hill, centrally situated and rising to a height of 127 m (417 ft). It is claimed that the Viking King Haakon used the island and specifically the northern end at Tormont End as a base before the Battle of Largs (1263). The island's principal settlement is Millport, located on the southern shore, although early settlement occurred at Kirkton to the west. Once popular as a holiday destination during the heydays of the Clyde, the island still attracts day-trippers, although not nearly in the same numbers. The island is crossed by a number of geological dykes, one of which forms a prominent feature known as the Lion Rock. A marine laboratory and museum, operated jointly by the University of Glasgow and University College, London, were established in the 1890s, and a ferry links the Cumbrae Slip to the north of Millport with Largs.

Great Glen *Highland* Also known as Glen Mòr or Glen Albyn, the Great Glen forms a valley 60 miles (96 km) long, extending from Inverness in the northeast to Fort William in the southwest. Following a natural geological fault line that was later deeply eroded by ice, the glen contains Loch Ness, Loch Oich and Loch Lochy, each of which is linked by the Caledonian Canal which was opened in 1822. The Great Glen cycle route extends the full length of the glen.

Great Glen Fault One of the major geological features of Scotland, the Great Glen Fault extends southwest to northeast for a distance of at least 300 miles (480 km). It can be observed from Colonsay in the Inner Hebrides to Shetland in the Northern Isles. The fault splits the Highlands into the northern Highlands, to the northwest, and the Grampian Highlands in the southeast. The Great Glen Fault is a tear or strike-slip fault with a displacement estimated at 64 miles (104 km). A zone of shattered rock along the length of the fault is prone to erosion and this has given rise to the development of the most extensive valley in Scotland, the Great Glen (Glen Mòr). From Colonsay, the fault clips the southeast edge of Mull before proceeding across the Firth of Lorn, Lismore and Loch Linnhe to Fort William. It continues through Loch Lochy and Loch Ness, past Inverness and then cuts along the northern shore of the Moray Firth before curving northwards to Shetland where it appears as the Walls Boundary Fault. The fault may have developed as long as 1000 million years ago but was certainly active in the Devonian Period (370 million years ago) and reactivated in the Middle Jurassic (170 million years ago). Very limited movement still occurs on the fault, evidenced by occasional small earthquakes.

Great Western Road *Glasgow City* Great Western Road extends from St George's Cross in the east to Anniesland Cross in the west, a distance of over 3 miles (5 km). It is Glasgow's longest and straightest road and was originally built as a toll road following an 1816 Act of Parliament. It is lined for much of its length by terraced houses and villas, separated from the road by trees. The Glasgow Botanic Gardens (1891) lie to the north.

Green Hill *Angus* A hill in the southern Grampians, Green Hill rises to 865 m (2838 ft) above Glen Clova in Angus. Loch Brandy lies on its western slopes.

Green Lowther *South Lanarkshire* The highest peak in the Lowther Hills in the Southern Uplands, Green Lowther rises to 732 m (2403 ft) 2 miles (3 km) southeast of Leadhills.

Greenbank House and Gardens *East Renfrewshire* An elegant Georgian house in East Renfrewshire, Greenbank lies to the south of Clarkston and north of Newton Mearns. It was built in 1764 by a wealthy Glasgow merchant who also created a 1-ha (2.5-acre) walled garden and 6 ha (15 acres) of designed policies that now include woodland walks. Greenbank was gifted in 1976 to the National Trust for Scotland by Mr and Mrs William Blyth.

Greengairs *North Lanarkshire* A village of North Lanarkshire that developed in the 19th century in association with coal mining and quarrying, Greengairs mostly comprises public housing and lies 3 miles (5 km) southeast of Cumbernauld and a similar distance north-northeast of Airdrie. The village of Wattston lies immediately to the west. From 1990, former opencast workings to the south were developed into one of the largest landfill sites in the UK. Methane drawn from the biodegradable content in the infill powers the 3.8-megawatt Greengairs Power Station, which opened in 1996.

Greenhill *Falkirk* A village in Falkirk Council area, Greenhill lies to the south of Bonnybridge and adjacent to the main Edinburgh–Glasgow railway line. It has a small industrial park at its western end.

Greenhill *Dumfries and Galloway* A hamlet in Annandale, Dumfries and Galloway, Greenhill lies on the River Annan, 2 miles (3 km) southwest of Lockerbie. Greenhill is one of the Royal Four Towns of Lochmaben.

Greenknowe Tower *Scottish Borders* Erected in 1581 by James Seton of Touch, the ruined remains of Greenknowe Tower lie outside Gordon in Scottish Borders. Occupied until the 1850s, it was passed to Historic Scotland in 1937 by the then owners, the Dalrymple family.

Greenlaw *Scottish Borders* Located 7 miles (11 km) southwest of Duns and 12 miles (19 km) northwest of Coldstream, on the Blackadder Water, Greenlaw was built in the late 17th century and functioned as the county town of Berwickshire for 207 years until 1903, a title it shared with Duns after 1853. Its market cross (1696) and kirk (1675) are its oldest structures, although the cross was removed for most of the 19th century and is now west of the kirk. The last public hanging in Scotland took place at Greenlaw Kirk in 1834. The Greek-revivalist Greenlaw Town Hall was erected in 1829. Hume Castle (13th century), 3 miles (5 km) south of Greenlaw, was the seat of the Home family. It was destroyed in the 17th century and restored in the late 18th century.

Greenlea *Dumfries and Galloway* A village in the Annandale district of Dumfries and Galloway, Greenlea lies between the Lochar Water and the Linns Burn, 4 miles (6.5 km) east of Dumfries.

Greenloaning *Perth and Kinross* A locality in Strathallan, southwest Perth and Kinross, Greenloaning lies by the Allan Water and the Stirling–Perth railway line, a mile (1.5 km) to the south of Braco and 5 miles (8 km) north of Dunblane.

Greenock *Inverclyde* A large town on the south side of the Firth of Clyde, Greenock lies 23 miles (37 km) west of Glasgow. Originally a small fishing village with a castle built in the 16th century, Greenock took advantage of its deep offshore waters to develop as a port and shipbuilding centre with associated rope, sail cloth and malting industries. It became a burgh of barony in 1635 and a sizeable harbour was built *c.*1710 as the home base of the west of Scotland's largest herring-fishing fleet. James Watt, who perfected the steam engine, was born in Greenock in 1736, and shipowner Abram Lyle, whose name later came to be associated with sugar refining, was born here in 1820. In the 19th century, in addition to pottery, textile, shipbuilding, sugar refining, distilling, paper making, barrel making and engineering industries, Greenock became the principal departure point for emigrants. The decline of heavy industries since the 1960s has been partly offset by the development of electronics, computer, polythene and service industries mostly located in the nearby Spango Valley. There are fine views over the Clyde from Lyle Hill, and buildings of note include the James Watt Museum, McLean Museum, the Custom House and hammerhead crane at the James Watt Dock. There are two 18- and one nine-hole golf courses. Since 1993, James Watt College has been linked with Paisley University.

Greosabhagh The Gaelic name for Grosebay in the Western Isles.

Gress *Western Isles* A crofting township in the Outer Hebrides, Gress (Gael: *Griais*) lies to the north of the village of Back, 7 miles (11 km) northeast of Stornoway on the east coast of Lewis.

Gretna (Gretna Township) *Dumfries and Galloway* The modern village of Gretna (or Gretna Township) is located about a mile (1.5 km) northwest of the Scottish/English border, a similar distance south of Gretna Green and 8 miles (12 km) east of Annan in Dumfries and Galloway Council Area. The first 20th-century government-sponsored new town in Britain, Gretna was a social experiment, built from 1915 on 'garden city' principles to accommodate workers employed in an immense munitions factory lying around the village. A self-contained community, it was laid out by notable architects of the day, Raymond Unwin and Courtney Crickmer, complete with a central meeting hall, school, cinema, churches and shops. Different classes of houses were built for workers of differing status, but all had electricity, running water and inside toilets. The public houses in the area were all government-controlled, operated by the Carlisle State Brewery until the 1970s. The village became the model for the 'Homes Built for Heroes' programme after the war but today Gretna is predominately a commuter village. A mile (1.5 km) to the southwest is the Lochmaben Stane (or Clochmabenstane) dating from the second or third millennium BC.

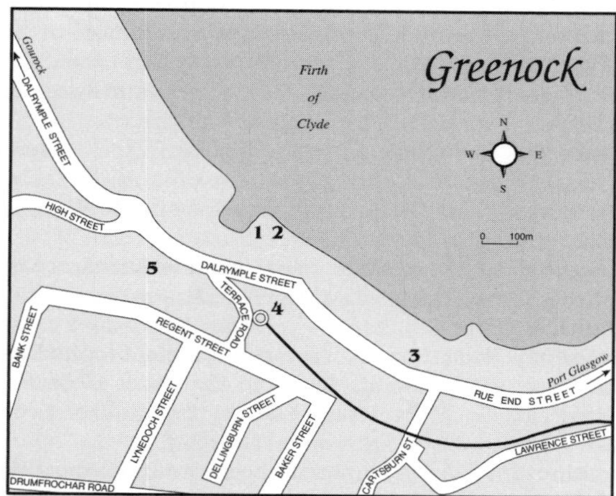

1 *Waterfront Leisure Complex*
2 *James Watt College*
3 *Police Station*
4 *Railway Station*
5 *Town Hall*

Gretna Green *Dumfries and Galloway* A village in Dumfries and Galloway, Gretna Green stands on the border with England near the northeast shore of the Solway Firth. The original small village of Gretna Green was popular with couples from south of the border seeking quick marriages under the more lenient Scots Law, a situation that lasted from 1573 to 1940. The place is still popular for weddings, a new Register Office being built in 1991. Buildings of note include the Old Toll Bar, the first house in Scotland across the border, and the Old Blacksmith's Shop where marriages were occasionally performed and which is now a museum.

Greyfriars' Bobby *City of Edinburgh* A memorial to the Skye terrier dog known as Greyfriars' Bobby lies on the junction of George IV Bridge and Candlemaker Row in Edinburgh, opposite the entrance to Greyfriars Kirk. The dog was owned by John Gray, a farmer, who came into the Grassmarket each market day. When Gray died in 1858, he was buried in Greyfriars kirkyard. Greyfriars' Bobby made his home by his master's grave. Local residents fed the dog and even built him a shelter, and the Lord Provost of Edinburgh was so touched by the dog's loyalty that he personally paid the annual dog licence. Awarded the Freedom of the City, Greyfriars' Bobby maintained his vigil until his death some 14 years later. Visitors came from around the country to see the dog, and one of these, Baroness Burdett-Coutts, was instrumental in ensuring that when the dog died a permanent memorial was built in recognition of his loyalty. Erected in 1872, the memorial comprises a life-sized bronze of the dog by sculptor William Brodie (1815–87), mounted on a granite plinth. Greyfriars' Bobby was buried in the kirkyard which he had made his home.

Greyfriars Kirk *City of Edinburgh* Situated just inside the Flodden Wall on the southernmost edge of the Old Town of Edinburgh, Greyfriars Kirk was built on the site of the 13th-century Grey Friars (Franciscan) Monastery, which had been sacked by a Calvinist mob in 1558. Completed in 1620, Greyfriars was the first post-Reformation church to be built in Edinburgh. The western section, added as a separate church in 1721, was damaged by fire in 1845 and reinstated by David Bryce

(1803–76). The original church was also subject to a fire in 1857 and restored by David Cousin (1809–78). The two buildings and their congregations were united in 1938. The National Covenant, which had been drawn up in Tailor's Hall, was signed at Greyfriars in 1638. So large was the crowd that it was taken out into the churchyard and spread on a gravestone to allow those who had been unable to get into the packed church to add their names. The Covenant was a reaction against the Anglicisation of the Presbyterian Church and was signed by thousands at churches across Scotland. Today, Greyfriars kirkyard has the best collection of 17th-century monuments in Scotland and is the last resting place of many notables, including architect William Adam and two of his sons, poet Allan Ramsay, geologist James Hutton, architect James Craig, historian William Robertson, and George Mackenzie, prosecutor of the Covenanters. The Martyrs' Monument (1706) remembers Mackenzie's victims, who were executed nearby in the Grassmarket.

Grey Mare's Fall *Highland* A spectacular stream of water, the Grey Mare's Fall (or Grey Mare's Tail Waterfall) is located just to the north of Kinlochleven in Highland Council area. It is said to have been so named by King Edward VII and, at 61 m (200 ft), is one of the highest waterfalls in Britain.

Grey Mare's Tail *Dumfries and Galloway* A spectacular 61-m (200-ft) waterfall in the Moffat Hills of Dumfries and Galloway, the Grey Mare's Tail lies 10 miles (16 km) northeast of Moffat. The surrounding area, which is rich in wild flowers and geological interest, is associated with the Covenanters who sought refuge here in the late 17th century. In 1962 870 ha (2151 acres) extending as far as Loch Skeen and White Coomb were acquired by the National Trust for Scotland, which subsequently opened a visitor centre with CCTV views of a peregrine falcon nesting site.

Greystone *Angus* A hamlet of east-central Angus, Greystone is located in Strathmore 3 miles (5 km) south of Letham and 6 miles (10 km) west-northwest of Arbroath.

Griais The Gaelic name for Gress in the Western Isles.

Gribloch *Stirling* A mansion house in the Gargunnock Hills of Stirling Council area, Gribloch lies half a mile (1 km) southwest of the village of Kippen. A white two-storey building with a flat roof, it was built in 1938–9 for the Glasgow steel magnate John Colville to a 'modern movement' design by Sir Basil Spence (1907–76). Internal features include elements of Regency style as well as modern conveniences such as an early example of an American-style fitted kitchen inspired by Colville's wife, who came from San Francisco.

Grim Brigs *Aberdeenshire* A rocky headland on the North Sea coast of Aberdeenshire, Grim Brigs lies close to Muchalls, 12 miles (19 km) south of Aberdeen.

Griminish *Western Isles* A linear crofting settlement located among lochans in the low-lying southwest of the island of Benbecula in the Outer Hebrides, Griminish (Gael: *Griminis*) lies 1.25 miles (2 km) north of Liniclate and 2 miles (3 km) south of Balivanich. Benbecula Parish Church is located here in a building originally erected as a Free Church in 1886.

Grimister *Shetland* A hamlet in the Shetland Islands, Grimister is situated on the island of Yell on the south side of Whale Firth.

Grimmet *South Ayrshire* A settlement in South Ayrshire, Grimmet is located a mile (1.5 km) east of Maybole.

Grimsay *Western Isles* An island in the Western Isles, Grimsay (Gael: *Griomasaigh*) lies between Benbecula and North Uist, to which it is linked by a causeway completed in 1960. It has a harbour at Kallin, which is the base to a sizeable shellfish industry. Kallin is also home to The Boatshed, a marine repair facility promoting traditional skills and housing a museum. There is a fine example of an Iron-Age wheelhouse on the northeast coast of the island.

Grimsay *Western Isles* A significant but low-lying island in Bagh nam Faoilean to the southeast of Benbecula, Grimsay (Gael: *Griomasaigh*) provides a stepping-stone between causeways conveying the B891 en route to the jetty at Peter's Port. The island rises gently to 20 m (65 ft) and supports a few crofts. A much larger Grimsay lies to the north between Benbecula and North Uist.

Grimshader *Western Isles* A linear crofting village of the Lochs district on the island of Lewis, Grimshader (Gael: *Griomsidar, Grimsiadar* or *Griomsiadair*) is strung out along a minor road to the north of Loch Grimshader, 5 miles (8 km) south-southwest of Stornoway.

Grimshader, Loch *Western Isles* A small sea loch on the east coast of Lewis in the Outer Hebrides, Loch Grimshader (Gael: *Loch Griomsiadair*) opens into the Minch 4.5 miles (7 km) south of Stornoway. For the most part it takes the form of a narrow channel, then opens to a larger hammerhead-shaped water body at its head, with the settlement of Grimshader to the north and Ranish to the south. The island of Buaile Mhòr lies at the head of the loch.

Griomasaigh The Gaelic name for Grimsay in the Western Isles.

Griomsidar The Gaelic name for Grimshader in the Western Isles.

Groatay *Western Isles* A small uninhabited island lying to the northeast of North Uist, Groatay (Gael: *Grodaigh*) rises steeply from the sea to the southwest of Hermetray and 5 miles (8 km) northeast of Lochmaddy. The ruins of Dun Mhic Laitheann (MacLean's Fortress) lie on a rocky islet adjoining Groatay to the southwest.

Groay *Western Isles* One of a group of uninhabited islands in the middle of the eastern entrance to the Sound of Harris, Groay (Gael: *Grodhaigh*) rises to 26 m (85 ft) a quarter-mile (0.5 km) to the west-northwest of Lingay and a mile (1.5 km) southwest of Gilsay.

Grodaigh The Gaelic name for Groatay in the Western Isles.

Grodhaigh The Gaelic name for Groay in the Western Isles.

Grogport *Argyll and Bute* A settlement on the east coast of the Kintyre peninsula, Grogport lies 4 miles (6.5 km) north of Dippen.

Grosebay *Western Isles* A small settlement located on the east coast of South Harris in the Outer Hebrides, Grosebay (Gael: *Greosabhagh*) lies at the head of Loch Grosebay, 5 miles (8 km) south of Tarbert.

Gruting *Shetland* A hamlet in the west of the Sandsting district of the Walls peninsula, in the west of the Shetland Mainland, Gruting lies 13.5 miles (22 km) northwest of Lerwick.

Gruinard Bay *Highland* An inlet of the sea on the coast of Wester Ross, Gruinard Bay lies between Loch Ewe and Little Loch Broom. It receives the Gruinard and Little Gruinard rivers. Gruinard Island had restricted access for many years following its contamination with anthrax during wartime military experiments.

Gryfe, River *Renfrewshire* Rising in hills to the south of Greenock in Inverclyde, the River Gryfe flows north into the Gryfe Reservoirs. From there it flows south and east down Strath Gryfe towards Bridge of Weir in Renfrewshire. It then travels east, joining the Black Cart Water at a point 3 miles (5 km) northeast of Bridge of Weir and 3 miles (5 km) northwest of Paisley.

Guardbridge *Fife* A village in Leuchars parish, eastern Fife, Guardbridge lies at the head of the River Eden estuary 3 miles (5 km) northwest of St Andrews. The six-arched Old Guard Bridge or Gaire Brig was built in the 15th century by Bishop Henry Wardlaw of St Andrews and repaired a century later by Archbishop James Beaton. The village developed at crossings over the River Eden and Motray Water, and during the Middle Ages it is said that pilgrims used to gather here before making the final journey under guard to the holy shrine at St Andrews. A distillery founded here by William Haig in 1810 was converted to a paper mill in 1873. The manufacture of paper is still the leading local industry.

Guay *Perth and Kinross* A small settlement in Strathtay, Perth and Kinross, Guay lies 6 miles (10 km) north of Dunkeld between Dowally and Kindallachan. There was formerly a railway station here.

Guildtown *Perth and Kinross* A linear village in Perth and Kinross, Guildtown lies on the A93, 6 miles (10 km) north of Perth. Guildtown was founded in 1818 by the Guildry Incorporation of Perth. To the east of Guildtown there is a Bronze Age stone circle of ten stones.

Guillamon Island *Highland* A small uninhabited island of the Inner Hebrides, Guillamon Island lies to the south of the larger island of Scalpay and east of the island of Skye. Little more than a rocky outcrop rising to 24 m (79 ft) it is occupied by large colonies of sea birds.

Gulberwick *Shetland* A small village at the head of the inlet of Gulber Wick on the east coast of the Mainland of Shetland, Gulberwick lies 2.5 miles (4 km) southwest of Lerwick.

Gullane *East Lothian* A resort village on the Firth of Forth coast northeast of Aberlady, Gullane lies 4 miles (6.5 km) southwest of North Berwick. Subjected to shifting sands, its 12th-century parish church of St Andrew, now ruined, had links with Dryburgh Abbey and was eventually abandoned in 1612. Described in Robert Louis Stevenson's novel *Catriona* (1893) as a well-to-do village with several golf courses and home to many wealthy and artistic Scots, Gullane's sandy shore, partly stabilised by tree planting, is overlooked by fine homes. A golf course was laid out on Gullane Links in 1880, and in 1891 the Honourable Company of Edinburgh Golfers established themselves at Muirfield, which became a championship course. The adjacent mansion house of Greywalls, now a hotel, was built c.1901 to a design by Edwin Lutyens for the sportsman Alfred Lyttleton.

Gullane Bay *East Lothian* A north-facing inlet of the Firth of Forth on the coast of East Lothian, Gullane Bay is separated from Aberlady Bay to the west by Gullane Point.

Gullane Bents *East Lothian* Gullane Bents is the name given to an area of heathland and grassland which lies between Gullane Bay and the town of Gullane in East Lothian. Situated near the coastline of the Firth of Forth, it is 4 miles (6.5 km) southwest of North Berwick.

Gulvain *Highland* A mountain in the Lochaber district of Highland Council area, Gulvain rises to a height of 987 m (3238 ft) to the south of Loch Arkaig. Its massive peak is composed of banded granite that forms steep slabs on its western flank, and its name is possibly derived from the Gaelic gaor bheinn, meaning 'filthy hill'.

Gunna *Argyll and Bute* An uninhabited island of the Inner Hebrides, Gunna lies between Tiree and Coll, from which it is separated by a shallow rocky passage that is crossable with care. The island, which is is used to graze sheep from Coll, comprises 68 ha (168 acres) and rises to a height of 35 m (115 ft).

Guthrie *Angus* A hamlet in an Angus parish of the same name, Guthrie lies on the upper reaches of the Lunan Water, 7 miles (11 km) east of Forfar. The Church of St Mary originally belonged to Arbroath Abbey and was rebuilt in 1826. Nearby Guthrie Castle, dating from the 15th century, was built by Sir David Guthrie of Kincaldrum, Treasurer to James III, whose son, Sir Alexander Guthrie, died at the Battle of Flodden in 1513. The castle was enlarged in 1848 to a design by David Bryce.

Haaf Gruney Island *Shetland* An uninhabited island of Shetland, Haaf Gruney lies a mile (1.5 km) to the southeast of Unst.

Habbies Howe *Scottish Borders* A locality on the western edge of the Pentland Hills of Scottish Borders, Habbies Howe lies on the River North Esk, a half mile (1 km) northeast of Carlops.

Habost *Western Isles* One of a collection of crofting townships lying in the Ness district at the northern tip of Lewis in the Outer Hebrides, Habost (Gael: *Tabost*) is located immediately to the southwest of Lionel and to the northeast of Swainbost. The Ness Heritage Centre and the Taigh Dhonnchaidh Gaelic Arts and Music Centre can be found here.

Habost *Western Isles* A scattered crofting township located in the South Lochs district of the Isle of Lewis in the Outer Hebrides, Habost (Gael: *Tabost*) lies on the southern shore of Loch Erisort, a mile (1.5 km) west of Kershader and 11 miles (18 km) southwest of Stornoway.

Hacklete *Western Isles* A scattered crofting township on the south coast of Great Bernera in the Outer Hebrides, Hacklete (Gael: *Tacleit*) lies a half-mile (1 km) northwest of the Great Bernera Bridge and 4 miles (6.5 km) west-northwest of Callanish on Lewis.

Hacklett *Western Isles* A scattered crofting township on the southeast coast of Benbecula in the Outer Hebrides, Hacklett (Gael: *Haclait*) lies a mile (1.5 km) east of Creagorry and 5 miles (8 km) south-southwest of Balivanich.

Hackley Head *Aberdeenshire* A headland on the North Sea coast of Aberdeenshire, Hackley Head (or Forvie Ness) forms a point on the Sands of Forvie between Collieston and the mouth of the River Ythan. Hackley Bay lies to the north.

Hackness *Orkney* A small settlement in the Orkney Islands, Hackness lies at the northeast end of South Walls, Hoy. Nearby is a Martello Tower built during the Napoleonic Wars to protect Baltic convoys gathering in Longhope inlet.

Haclait The Gaelic name for Hacklett in the Western Isles.

Haco's Ness *Orkney* A headland at the southeast end of the Orkney island of Shapinsay, Haco's Ness extends into Shapinsay Sound.

Haddington *East Lothian* A burgh town and administrative centre of East Lothian, Haddington lies on the River Tyne between the Garleton Hills and the Lammermuir Hills, 18 miles (29 km) east of Edinburgh. One of Scotland's earliest royal burghs (created some time between 1124 and 1153), it formerly gave its name to the county of Haddingtonshire. At its core it still has a medieval street plan with many buildings of interest, including the Town House, Jane Welsh Carlyle House, Haddington House, the Corn Exchange, and the 14th-century red-sandstone Church of St Mary, often referred to as the 'Lamp of the Lothian' and Scotland's largest parish church. In medieval times Haddington was an important religious centre on the pilgrimage route between St Andrews and Santiago de Compostela in Spain. The Church of St Mary became a collegiate church, attracting religious scholars. The ruin of St Martin's, on the edge of Nungate, represents the only visible remnant of a great Cistercian nunnery founded in 1178 by Ada de Warenne, who had been given the town as a wedding present by her father-in-law, David I. In 1503, the young Margaret Tudor stayed here on her way to marry James IV. Edward III of England destroyed the nunnery, church and St Mary's in 1356. From the 12th century to 1242 the town had a royal palace, which was the birthplace of Alexander II (1198–1249). John Knox (c.1513–72) was a native of Haddington, which was also the birthplace in 1801 of Jane Welsh Carlyle, wife of the writer Thomas Carlyle, and in 1812 of the author and reformer Samuel Smiles. Surrounded by rich agricultural land, Haddington has long been an important market town and agricultural service centre. It had the first significant grain market in Scotland and developed in association with malting, tanning and textile industries. Electrical and electronic goods are also manufactured. The 18th-century granary and maltings at Poldrate Mill are now a community centre, and there is an 18-hole golf course nearby at Amisfield Park.

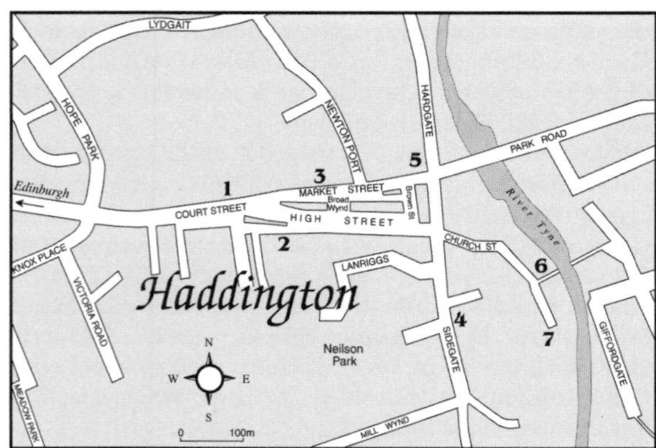

1 *Town House*
2 *Jane Welsh Carlyle House*
3 *Mitchell's Close*
4 *Haddington House*
5 *Kinloch House*
6 *The Nungate Bridge*
7 *Church of St Mary*

Haddo House *Aberdeenshire* Located 6 miles (10 km) northwest of Ellon in Aberdeenshire, Haddo House was built on the site of an older house between 1732 and 1735 by the architect William Adam (1689–1748) for William Gordon (1679–1746), 2nd Earl of Aberdeen. It lies amid a sizeable estate. George Hamilton Gordon (1784–1860), the 4th Earl and prime minister, significantly enlarged the house and landscaped the estate. James Hamilton Gordon (1847–1934), 1st Marquess and 7th Earl, was laird for 64 years, and together with his wife, Ishbel Marjoribanks, developed Haddo into a model estate. Haddo House, used as a maternity hospital during World War II, was acquired by the National Trust for Scotland in 1978 and opened to the public a year later. The adjacent country park, run by Aberdeenshire Council, was also opened in 1979.

Hadyard Hill *South Ayrshire* A hill in South Ayrshire, Hadyard Hill rises to 323 m (1059 ft) 6 miles (10 km) east of Girvan.

Haggersta *Shetland* A sizeable hamlet located at the head of the finger-like peninsula of Strom Ness, Haggersta lies between Weisdale Voe and the Loch of Strom, 6 miles (10 km) northwest of Lerwick.

Haggs *Falkirk* A locality in the west of the Falkirk Council area, Haggs lies immediately to the south of Longcroft on the opposite side of the A80 trunk road from Banknock.

Haghill *Glasgow City* A suburb of Glasgow, Haghill lies 3 miles (5 km) east of the city centre in Dennistoun district. It largely comprises 1930s' housing, some of which has been demolished.

Hagshaw Hill *South Lanarkshire* A hill rising to a height of 469 m (1540 ft), 5.5 miles (9 km) south-southwest of Lesmahagow, Hagshaw Hill is the site of a 15.6-megawatt wind farm established in 1995. Each of its 26 turbines can produce 600 megawatts of power.

Hailes Castle *East Lothian* Located on the south bank of the River Tyne, 1.5 miles (2.5 km) southwest of East Linton, Hailes Castle is an extensive ruin dating from the 13th century. Built originally by the de Gourlay family, Hailes was enlarged by the Hepburns in the 15th century. In the 16th century the castle was owned by James Hepburn, 4th Earl of Bothwell (1536–78), the third husband of Mary, Queen of Scots. Hailes was reduced to ruins by Oliver Cromwell in 1650. Later the castle was sold to Sir David Dalrymple (d.1721) of a noted legal family, whose grandson became Lord Hailes. The castle was given to the nation in 1926 by its then owner, the former Prime Minister Arthur Balfour, and is now in the care of Historic Scotland.

Halbeath *Fife* A former colliery village in western Fife, Halbeath is situated between Dunfermline and the M90. Between 1783 and 1867 a wagonway for the transport of coal operated between Halbeath and Inverkeithing. Today its development is linked to a retail park and its location at a motorway junction. The Calais Muir Wood lies to the south.

Halkirk *Highland* A village in the Caithness district of Highland Council area, Halkirk stands on the banks of the River Thurso, 6 miles (10 km) south of Thurso. In the early 13th century the Bishop of Caithness moved his residence or hall to Halkirk from Scrabster, but his successor moved south to Dornoch where a cathedral was built. Developed in the 18th and 19th centuries in association with whisky distilling and the quarrying of flagstones at nearby

Banniskirk and Spittal, the village was remodelled in a grid plan in the 1790s. Braal Castle, built in the 15th century, stands close by on the west bank of the river. Local industries include the quarrying of flagstones, and mechanical engineering and building.

Hall Bay *Aberdeenshire* A small inlet on the North Sea coast of Aberdeenshire, Hall Bay lies midway between Muchalls and Stonehaven.

Hall of Clestrain *Orkney* A derelict Georgian house located on the Orkney Mainland, 2.5 miles (4 km) east of Stromness, the Hall of Clestrain (sometimes the Hall of Clestran) looks out onto the island of Graemsay over the Clestrain Sound. Built in 1769 for Patrick Honeyman of Graemsay, a wealthy trader, this three-storey Grade B-listed structure was exceptionally grand for its time. It is noted as the birthplace, in 1813, of Arctic explorer Dr John Rae. Unoccupied since 1952, it has been used as a farmbuilding with a piggery in its basement. Plans have been drawn up to restore the hall to become the Orkney Boat Museum, and it featured in the BBC television series *Restoration* (2004).

Halladale River *Highland* A river in the Caithness district of Highland Council area, the Halladale River rises 4 miles (6.5 km) southeast of Forsinard. It flows northwards through Strath Halladale before entering the Pentland Firth at Melvich Bay.

Hallbar, Tower of *South Lanarkshire* A former stronghold of the Lockharts of Lee, the five-storey Tower of Hallbar is situated near Crossford in South Lanarkshire. Built in 1581, the building was restored by the Vivat Trust and re-opened as holiday accommodation in 2000.

Halliman Skerries *Moray* Lying a half mile (1 km) north of the coast of Moray and a mile (1.5 km) northwest of Lossiemouth, the Halliman Skerries form a small group of islands. A lighthouse was built on the nearby Covesea Skerries in 1846.

Hallival *Highland* A mountain on the island of Rum, Hallival rises to 723 m (2371 ft) 2 miles (3 km) south of Kinloch.

Hallyburton House *Perth and Kinross* An Elizabethan-style mansion house in Strathmore, eastern Perth and Kinross, Hallyburton House is situated 3 miles (5 km) southeast of Coupar Angus near the village of Kettins. Built in the 1680s to replace the old castle of Pitcur, it was remodelled in the 18th and 19th centuries. A dining-room wing designed by Robert Lorimer was added in 1903.

Haltadans *Shetland* A prehistoric stone circle, Haltadans is situated at the centre of the Shetland island of Fetlar between Vord Hill and Skutes Water. There is an outer circle of 38 serpentine stones and a lower inner earth bank.

Ham *Shetland* The main settlement on the Shetland island of Foula, Ham lies near Ham Voe on the island's east coast where there is a ferry link with Walls.

Ham *Highland* A settlement on the Caithness coast of Highland Council area, Ham lies 3 miles (5 km) southeast of Dunnet Head.

Ham *Shetland* A settlement on the Shetland island of Bressay, Ham lies on the Voe of Learaness, a mile (1.5 km) southeast of Lerwick on the opposite side of Bressay Sound.

Hamars Ness *Shetland* A headland on the northwest corner of the Shetland island of Fetlar, Hamars Ness lies to the north of the ferry pier at Oddsta.

Hamilton *South Lanarkshire* A town in South Lanarkshire, Hamilton lies to the west of Motherwell and the M74, 11 miles (18 km) southeast of Glasgow, near the junction of the Avon Water with the River Clyde. Chartered as a burgh of barony in the 15th century, Hamilton developed around the site of a college established by Lord Hamilton in 1451. The fortunes of the town were closely linked to the Hamilton family, who became the earls of Arran, dukes of Chatelherault and eventually dukes of Hamilton. They owned both the 13th-century Hamilton Castle and the nearby Cadzow Castle, another 13th-century fortress built originally for King Alexander II. The former was rebuilt as the grand edifice of Hamilton Palace in 1695, but was eventually demolished in the 1920s. The town expanded in the 18th and 19th centuries in association with the manufacture of textiles and the mining and engineering industries. Notable buildings include the neoclassical Town House, which was the headquarters of Hamilton District Council (1975–96), and the old parish church designed by William Adam in 1732, which has a Celtic cross in the churchyard. Close to the site of the former palace lies Mote Hill, an ancient site of justice, and the Hamilton Mausoleum, built 1842–58 for the 10th Duke of Hamilton as a chapel and tomb. Above the town is Chatelherault, the former hunting lodge of the dukes of Hamilton, also built by William Adam, which lies within Chatelherault Country Park. Several streams flow through the town, including Meikle Burn, Cadzow Burn, Wellshaw Burn, Park Burn and Earnock Burn. There are railway stations at West and Central, and Hamilton has several business parks in addition to the Hamilton Park Race Course, the Hamilton Water Palace leisure centre (1995), two golf courses and the Low Parks Museum, which incorporates the museum of the Cameronian Regiment. To the east, beyond the River Clyde, is Strathclyde Country Park.

Hamilton House *East Lothian* A mansion house on the southern margin of Prestonpans in East Lothian, Hamilton House was built in 1626 for Sir John Hamilton, brother of Thomas Hamilton (1563–1637), the 1st Earl of Haddington. Sometimes referred to as Lord Magdalen's House, after the Hamilton law lord of that name, this two-storey house was bought by the National Trust for Scotland in 1937 and subsequently restored.

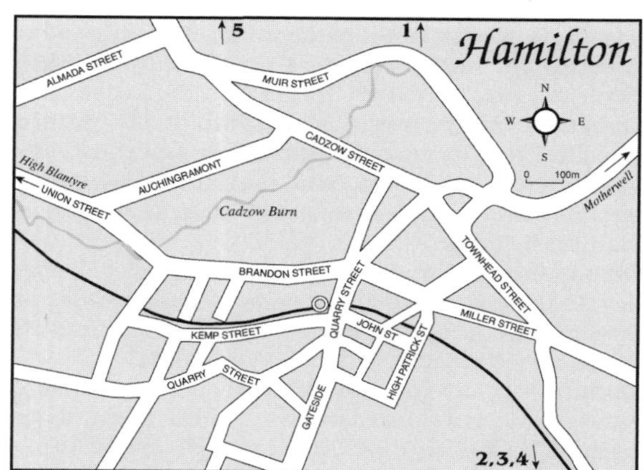

1 Hamilton Mausoleum
2 Chatelherault Hunting Lodge
3 Chatelherault Country Park
4 Cadzow Castle
5 Hamilton Park Racecourse

Hamilton Mausoleum *South Lanarkshire* Located in the Low Parks, Hamilton, the Hamilton Mausoleum has a dome that rises to 36 m (120 ft). Begun by David Hamilton in 1842, the mausoleum was completed by David Bryce and Alexander Richie in 1858 as a family chapel and tomb for the 10th Duke of Hamilton. Despite damage by subsidence, which sealed the fate of the neighbouring Hamilton Palace, the mausoleum remains as an extraordinary memorial to the Hamilton family.

Hamnavoe *Shetland* A small settlement at the head of Hamna Voe, an inlet at the southern end of Yell in the Shetland Islands.

Hamnavoe *Shetland* A settlement on the western side of Lunna Ness, a peninsula at the northeast end of Mainland Shetland.

Hamnavoe *Shetland* A fishing port occupying a natural harbour at the northern end of the Shetland island of West Burra, Hamnavoe lies 3 miles (5 km) southwest of Scalloway. It was the birthplace in 1740 of John Williamson (also known as Johnny Notions) a weaver, blacksmith and joiner who, during an epidemic of smallpox, developed a highly effective inoculation and successfully treated several thousand islanders.

Hampden Park (The National Stadium) *Glasgow City* A football stadium in southern Glasgow City, Hampden Park lies to the south of the River Clyde and west of Rutherglen. The home ground of Scottish League football team Queen's Park and the Scottish Claymores American Football team, it is the venue, as the National Stadium, for Scotland's home football internationals. Built in 1903, Hampden was designed in the same oval shape as Glasgow's Ibrox Stadium and Celtic Park, and following the construction of the North Stand in 1937 it became the largest stadium in the world with a capacity of 180,000. An intimidating place for travelling supporters, the noise generated by the home crowd came to be known as 'The Hampden Roar'. Between 1981 and 1986 the North Stand was demolished and the East terracing was replaced. These stands were further refurbished in 1994 and a new south stand was built in 1996–8. The resulting 52,000-seat stadium was opened in 1999 with extensive conference facilities and a museum dedicated to football.

Handa *Highland* An uninhabited island separated from the northwest coast of Sutherland by the Sound of Handa, Handa lies north of the village of Scourie and is accessed by a regular summer boat service from Tarbet. With an area of 309 ha (764 acres), the island is a designated nature reserve in the care of the Scottish Wildlife Trust. Its dramatic Torridonian sandstone cliffs in the north rise sheer from the Atlantic, providing nesting sites for sea-bird colonies that are the largest in northwest Europe.

Happas *Angus* A locality of south-central Angus, Happas lies to the east of the A90, 3 miles (5 km) northeast of Tealing and 5.5 miles (9 km) south of Forfar. There are farms at North, South, East and West Happas.

Harburn *West Lothian* A settlement and mansion house built in 1804 and situated in West Lothian, Harburn lies 15 miles (24 km) southwest of Edinburgh and 2 miles (3 km) southeast of West Calder.

Hardengreen *Midlothian* A former railway junction, Hardengreen lies a half mile (1 km) south of Eskbank in Midlothian. Closed in 1969, the junction lay at the meeting of the Peebles line with the main route south through the Borders from Edinburgh. The settlement has an industrial estate and large supermarket.

Hardgate *Dumfries and Galloway* A village of Dumfries and Galloway, Hardgate lies just northeast of Haugh of Urr, 4 miles (6.5 km) north of Dalbeattie.

Hare Cairn *Angus* A mountain in the southeast Grampians, Hare Cairn rises to 516 m (1692 ft) to the northwest of the Backwater Reservoir, 2 miles (3 km) northeast of Kirkton of Glenisla.

Hare Hill *East Ayrshire* A hill rising to 590 m (1935 ft), 2.5 miles (4 km) southeast of New Cumnock in East Ayrshire, Hare Hill is the site of a 13-megawatt wind farm comprising 20 Danish turbines opened in 2000.

Harelaw *Dumfries and Galloway* A hamlet in Eskdale, Dumfries and Galloway, Harelaw is situated nearly 3 miles (5 km) northeast of Canonbie. A limestone quarry operated here from 1714 to 1996.

Harelaw Reservoir *East Renfrewshire* A small reservoir in East Renfrewshire, Harelaw Reservoir is located a mile (1.5 km) northwest of Barrhead.

Harlosh Island *Highland* A small uninhabited island in the Inner Hebrides, Harlosh Island lies in Loch Bracadale opposite the headland of Harlosh Point on the west coast of the isle of Skye.

Harmony Garden *Scottish Borders* Located opposite the abbey in Melrose in Scottish Borders, Harmony Garden was named after the Jamaican pimento plantation called Harmony, from which the Melrose joiner Robert Waugh made his fortune. The garden surrounds a 19th-century house, which is closed to the public, and is characterised by lawns, mixed and herbaceous borders and displays of spring bulbs. The garden was bequeathed to the National Trust for Scotland in 1996.

Haroldswick *Shetland* A settlement on the island of Unst in the Shetland Islands, Haroldswick lies 2 miles (3 km) north of Baltasound at the head of Harold's Wick, a southeast-facing bay that opens out into the North Sea. Named after King Harald of Norway who landed here in 875 to annexe the Shetland Islands, it became Scotland's most northerly village. RAF Saxa Vord was established near here in the 1960s. A fishing-boat museum in the settlement and a heritage centre to the west have been created by the community.

Harperleas *Fife* A reservoir in the Lomond Hills near the head of the Lothrie Burn, Harperleas was created in 1880 to supply fresh water to the towns of Kirkcaldy and Dysart on the south coast of Fife.

Harperrig Reservoir *West Lothian* A reservoir in West Lothian, Harperrig lies to the west of the Pentland Hills, 4 miles (6.5 km) south of Mid Calder.

Harport, Loch *Highland* A sea loch on the west coast of the island of Skye in the Inner Hebrides, Loch Harport is an arm of Loch Bracadale. Rarely more than 900 m (984 yd) wide, the loch extends from Drynoch at the western end of Glen Drynoch for 6 miles (10 km) in a northwesterly direction to open into Loch Bracadale to the east of the islands of Wiay and Oronsay. Settlements along the southern shore of the loch include Merkadale, Carbost (with the Talisker Distillery) and Portnalong.

Harrapool *Highland* A scattered settlement on the southeast coast of the isle of Skye, Harrapool (or Harrabol) lies immediately east of Broadford.

Harray, Loch of *Orkney* A large loch on the Mainland of Orkney, the Loch of Harray lies between Dounby in the north and the Neolithic sites of the Ring of Brodgar, the Standing Stones of Stenness and Maes Howe in the south.

Harrietfield *Perth and Kinross* A village in Glen Almond, central Perth and Kinross, Harrietfield lies to the north of the River Almond, 8 miles (13 km) northwest of Perth. A Free Church here, closed in 1995, was the charge of John Watson (1850–1907), who wrote under the name Ian Maclaren. His book of Perthshire tales published in 1894 and entitled *Beside the Bonnie Brier Bush* opens with the couplet: 'There grows a bonnie brier bush in our kail-yard, And white are the blossoms on't in our kail-yard.' It was the word 'kailyard' spotted here by the critics that subsequently came to be applied to a whole genre of Scottish writing characterised by an idealised representation of rural life.

Harris *Western Isles* Forming the southern part of the 'Long Island' of Lewis-with-Harris, Harris (Gael: *Na Hearadh*) is itself divided into North Harris and South Harris, which are separated by a narrow neck of land less than half a mile (1 km) wide. Largely separated from Lewis by a broad barrier of hills that rise to 799 m (2622 ft) at Clisham, Harris has contrasting east and west coasts. In the east, bare gneiss is indented by some 30 bays, each of which has a township at its head. In the west, eight sandy beaches backed by machair leading onto grassy hills are divided by spurs of rock. The port of Tarbert, with its ferry link to Uig in Skye and Lochmaddy in North Uist, is the chief settlement, and the island of Scalpay in East Loch Tarbert is a fishing centre.

Harrow, Loch *Dumfries and Galloway* A small loch in Dumfries and Galloway, Loch Harrow lies on the eastern slopes of the Rhinns of Kells. It is the source of the Polharrow Burn which flows eastwards to join the Water of Ken between Carsfad Loch and Earlstoun Loch.

Hart Fell *Dumfries and Galloway/Scottish Borders* A hill on the boundary between Dumfries and Galloway and Scottish Borders, Hart Fell rises to a height of 808 m (2651 ft) in the Ettrick Hills, 6 miles (10 km) northeast of Moffat.

Hartaval *Highland* A peak of the Trotternish peninsula of the island of Skye, Highland Council area, Hartaval rises to a height of 668 m (2191 ft) a mile (1.5 km) northwest of The Storr.

Harthill *North Lanarkshire/West Lothian* A former mining village in central Scotland, Harthill lies on the River Almond near the M8, 2 miles (3 km) west of Whitburn. The village was divided between the two local government areas of West Lothian and North Lanarkshire in 1978. With the building of the M8 in the 1960s, Scotland's first motorway service station was built at Harthill. Food distribution and the manufacture of plastics are local industries.

Hartshorn Pike *Scottish Borders* A summit of the Cheviot Hills in Scottish Borders, Hartshorn Pike rises to 545 m (1788 ft) on the Scottish–English border, 3 miles (5 km) east of Singdean.

Hartwood *North Lanarkshire* A hamlet, with a railway station, of North Lanarkshire, Hartwood is located a half-mile (1 km) north of Allanton and 1.25 miles (2 km) southwest of Shotts. The station opened in 1869 on the Caledonian Railway line between Glasgow Central and Edinburgh. The Hartwood Asylum was built immediately to the northwest in the 1890s and became the largest psychiatric hospital in Scotland. Closed in 1998, the site was offered for sale in 2004. Hartwoodhill Hospital, which was developed to the east close to Shotts, remains.

Harviestoun *Clackmannanshire* An estate at the foot of the Ochil Hills in Clackmannanshire, Harviestoun lies due east of Tillicoultry. In 1787 the poet Robert Burns stayed at Harviestoun Castle, which was demolished in 1973. Beer is brewed locally.

Hatston *Orkney* A settlement located 1.25 miles (2 km) northwest of Kirkwall on the Mainland of Orkney, Hatston was the site of a Royal Naval Air Station established at the start of World War II and known as HMS *Sparrowhawk*. Aeroplanes from here attacked the German cruiser *Konigsberg* on 10 April 1940. After the war the station continued as the island's main airport but it was soon found to be too small. It continued to be used by the Orkney Flying Club until 1957 when it became an industrial estate. A memorial records the previous use of the site.

Hatton *Aberdeenshire* A village of Buchan in Aberdeenshire noted for its bakeries, Hatton lies on the Water of Cruden, 2 miles (3 km) west of Cruden Bay. Originally known as the Free Kirkton of Cruden, the village developed after the founding of Cruden Free Church here in 1844.

Hatton Castle *Aberdeenshire* Located 3 miles (5 km) southeast of the settlement of Turriff in Aberdeenshire, Hatton Castle is a 15th-century castle incorporating the ancient remains of the castle of Balquholly.

Hatton of Fintray *Aberdeenshire* Sometimes just referred to as Fintray, the Aberdeenshire village of Hatton of Fintray lies in Fintray parish, immediately north of the River Don, 8 miles (13 km) northwest of Aberdeen. Once a textile village, its church dates from 1821, and to the southwest, at Boat of Hatton, a ferry crossed the River Don.

Haugh of Glass *Aberdeenshire* A hamlet in western Aberdeenshire, Haugh of Glass lies on the Markie Water close to its junction with the River Deveron, 6 miles (10 km) west of Huntly.

Haugh of Urr *Dumfries and Galloway* A village of Dumfries and Galloway, Haugh of Urr lies on the Urr Water, 3 miles (5 km) northeast of Castle Douglas.

Haughhead *East Dunbartonshire* The settlement of Haughhead is located to the south of Clachan of Campsie, 2 miles (3 km) northwest of Lennoxtown, on the Glazert Water, a tributary of the River Kelvin.

Haughs of Cromdale *Highland* The fertile low-lying haugh lands between the River Spey and the Hills of Cromdale in Highland Council area are known as the Haughs of Cromdale. These lands were acquired by the Grants in 1609 and subsequently erected into a burgh of barony with a view to developing a market centre. Overshadowed by the creation of the new town of Grantown-on-Spey in the 18th century, the old township of Kirktown of Cromdale eventually dwindled to nothing, although the hamlet of Cromdale survived thanks to the expansion of tree planting on the Strathspey Estate. On 1 May 1690 a Highland army under General Buchan was overwhelmed by the dragoons of Sir Thomas Livingstone in the Battle of the Haughs of Cromdale, an event that brought to an end James VII and

II's hopes of retaining the thrones of England and Scotland with Scottish support.

Haun *Western Isles* The eastern part of an agglomeration of townships that form the major settlement on the island of Eriskay in the Outer Hebrides, Haun (Gael: *Haunn*) lies in the northwest of the island 5 miles (8 km) south of Lochboisdale on South Uist. A causeway crossing the Sound of Eriskay to link with South Uist lies immediately to the west and the township of Rubha Bàn beyond.

Hawick *Scottish Borders* A textile-manufacturing town in Scottish Borders, Hawick lies at the confluence of the Slitrig Water with the River Teviot. It developed close to a medieval motte and has a church dating from the early 13th century. Gaining burgh status in 1511, the town's importance was enhanced by the presence of a tower built by the powerful Douglas family in the 16th century. From the 17th century Hawick developed as a centre of textile, hosiery and knitwear manufacture, eventually becoming one of the leading textile centres of Scotland. The Hawick hand-frame knitting industry, pioneered in 1771 by local magistrate John Hardie, peaked in the 1840s with 1200 looms in operation, nearly half of all the frames in Scotland. The burgh has a long tradition of civic independence that is reinforced annually in June with the Common Riding or inspection of the marches, the largest event of its kind in the Borders. A month of celebrations marks the events of 1514, when a group of youths (callants) defeated an English force at Hornshole and captured their standard. Sites of interest include a museum and gallery, a monument to Border horsemen and a statue of motorcyclist James Guthrie. The Border College is based in Hawick, which from 1975 to 1996 was the administrative headquarters of Roxburgh District Council. Hawick was the birthplace in 1895 of the soprano singer Isobel Baillie. It was also the birthplace of the composers John McEwan (1868–1948) and Francis George Scott (1880–1958).

Hawthornden Castle *Midlothian* Hawthornden Castle is located a mile (1.5 km) east of Roslin in Midlothian. Dramatically situated on the north bank of the River North Esk, Hawthornden was the home of poet William Drummond, who built a new house (completed in 1638) around a ruined 15th-century tower. Visitors to the castle included the English playwright Ben Jonson, Dr Samuel Johnson and James Boswell. The caves beneath the castle are said to have given shelter to Robert the Bruce. The castle, which remained home to the Drummond family until 1970, is now a private retreat for writers.

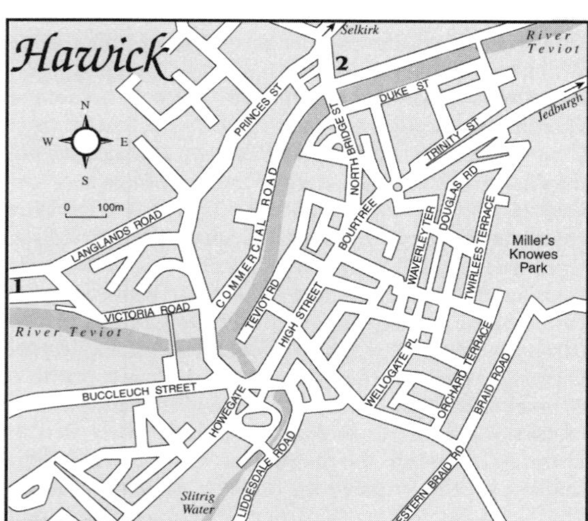

1 *Hawick Museum and the Scott Gallery* 2 *Leisure Centre*

Haymarket Station *City of Edinburgh* A railway station in west-central Edinburgh, Haymarket Station was built in 1840–42 as the terminus and head office of the Edinburgh and Glasgow Railway. Within four years trains ran on to what was to become Waverley Station and Haymarket took on a less important role. In 1866, the Edinburgh and Glasgow Railway was taken over by the North British Railway and in 1894 the platforms were redesigned.

Hazelton Walls *Fife* A hamlet in northern Fife, Hazelton Walls lies at a minor road junction on high ground overlooking the Firth of Tay, 5 miles (8 km) north of Cupar.

Hazlehead Park *Aberdeen City* A large park on Groats Road in Aberdeen, Hazlehead Park comprises floral displays, a small animal zoo, the Queen Mother Rose Garden, play and sporting areas and the Piper Alpha Memorial Garden.

Hearadh The Gaelic name for Harris in the Western Isles.

Heart of Midlothian, the *City of Edinburgh* A heart-shape set into the cobblestones of the High Street in Edinburgh marks the site of the 15th-century Tolbooth, which was demolished in 1817. Located close to St Giles Kirk, it earned the title 'Heart of Midlothian', the former county of Midlothian incorporating the city of Edinburgh until 1974. The Tolbooth features in Sir Walter Scott's novel *Heart of Midlothian* (1818) and gives its name to an Edinburgh football club.

Heathhall *Dumfries and Galloway* A locality in Dumfries and Galloway, Heathhall lies on the A701 between Dumfries and Locharbriggs. Dumfries and Galloway College is located here. One of Malcolm Campbell's speed record *Bluebird* cars was built at the Arrol-Johnson motor works in Heathhall in the 1930s.

Heaval *Western Isles* A mountain of Barra in the Western Isles, Heaval rises to a height of 383 m (1180 ft) a mile (1.5 km) northeast of the settlement of Castlebay.

Hebrides, the A scattered group of nearly 500 sparsely populated islands off the west coast of Scotland, the Hebrides were called 'Hebudes' by Pliny the Elder in AD 77. The Outer Hebrides, or Western Isles, consist of a chain of islands extending 130 miles (208 km) from the Butt of Lewis in the north to Barra Head in the south, the principal islands being Lewis and Harris, North and South Uist, Benbecula and Barra. Separated from the Outer Hebrides by the Minch, the Inner Hebrides include numerous islands, the largest of which are Skye, Mull, Islay and Jura. Microliths found on Jura date the earliest settlement of the Hebrides to the Mesolithic period *c.*6000 BC, while the impressive megalithic standing stones at Callanish on Lewis indicate a ritual landscape dating from around 3000 BC. From *c.* AD 300, monastic sites were established by the Celtic Church introduced by the Gaels from Ireland. The most important of these sites was the foundation established by St Columba on Iona. Viking settlement from the 8th century introduced Scandinavian placenames, and all the Hebrides came under the rule of the royal house of Man which owed allegiance to the Norwegian Crown. By the middle of the 12th century much of the Inner Hebrides had been restored to Gaelic control under Somerled, whose descendants, the MacDonald Lords of the Isles, held sway for over 300 years after the Hebrides had been ceded to the Scottish Crown by Norway in 1266. The Lordship of the Isles, whose administrative seat was at Finlaggan on Islay, was eventually forfeited in 1493. Today the Hebrides form outliers of the local government areas of the Western Isles, Argyll and Bute and Highland Council area.

Hebrides, Sea of the The Sea of the Hebrides is the body of water to the south of the Minch that separates Barra in the Outer Hebrides from the Small Isles of Canna, Eigg, Rum and Muck in the Inner Hebrides. It is bounded to the south by Tiree and Coll.

Heck *Dumfries and Galloway* A hamlet of east-central Dumfries and Galloway, Heck lies 2 miles (3 km) south-southeast of Lochmaben. Lochmaben Castle Loch lies a half-mile (1 km) to the northwest and the River Annan a similar distance to the east. Along with Hightae, Smallholm and Greenhill, Heck is one of the Royal Four Towns of Lochmaben.

Hecla *Western Isles* A mountain on the island of South Uist in the Outer Hebrides, Hecla rises to 606 m (1988 ft) to the southeast of Loch Druidibeg.

Heglibister *Shetland* A small linear hamlet on the west coast of the Mainland of Shetland, Heglibister lies on the western shore of Weisdale Voe, close to its head, 8 miles (13 km) northwest of Lerwick.

Heisker Islands *Western Isles* The Heisker Islands are a group of five larger islands and several associated islets, lying 6 miles (10 km) west of North Uist in the Western Isles. They are alternatively known as the Monach Islands and the group extends over some 4.5 miles (7 km) west-to-east and comprises the islands of Shillay, on which stands a lighthouse, Ceann Iar, Shivinish and Ceann Ear, which are connected by sandbanks at low tide, and the tiny Stockay, closest to North Uist. Once supporting more than 100 people, the island group is now uninhabited. In 1810, the islands had to be abandoned because of over-grazing. Later, people returned, but the islands were abandoned once again in the 1940s. The islands are separated from North Uist by the Sound of Monach.

Heiton *Scottish Borders* A village in the Roxburgh district of Scottish Borders, Heiton lies 2.5 miles (4 km) south-southwest of Kelso. Nearby are a championship golf course created in the 1990s and Sunlaws House, now a hotel, built by the dukes of Roxburgh in the 1890s.

Heldon Hill *Moray* Rising to a height of 234 m (768 ft) on the eastern edge of Monaughty Wood, Heldon Hill lies 6 miles (10 km) southwest of Elgin. Heldon Wood lies to the south.

Helensburgh *Argyll and Bute* A town on the northern shore of the Firth of Clyde, Helensburgh lies close to the Highland Boundary Fault, 8 miles (13 km) northwest of Dumbarton. Established in 1777 by Sir James Colquhoun of Luss and named after his wife, Lady Helen Sutherland, Helensburgh was designated a burgh of barony in 1802. It developed as a fashionable summer tourist resort with a ferry link from Greenock and later, in 1857, a rail link with Glasgow. It later became a dormitory settlement for Glasgow as well as a yachting centre. Helensburgh was the home of Henry Bell, builder of the *Comet*, the world's first paddle steamer. It was also the birthplace of John Logie Baird (1888–1946), the pioneer of television, the film stars Deborah Kerr (b.1921) and Jack Buchanan (1891–1957), and the Scottish entertainer Jimmy Logan (1928–2001). The most notable building in Helensburgh is the Hill House (1903), designed by Charles Rennie Mackintosh for the publisher W. Blackie and now in the care of the National Trust for Scotland.

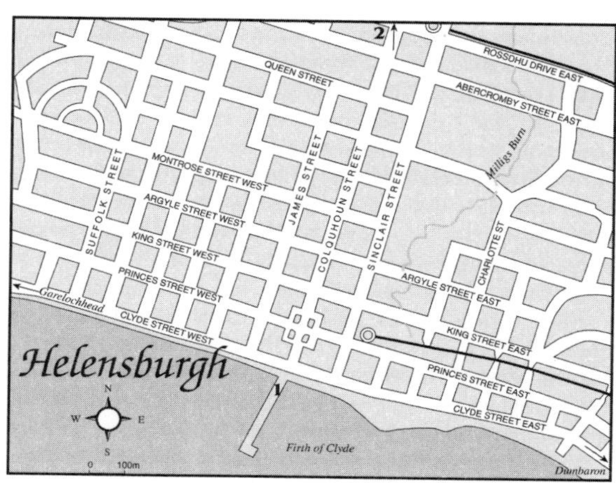

1 *Summer Ferry Terminal* 2 *The Hill House*

Hellisay *Western Isles* An uninhabited island of Lewisian gneiss in the Outer Hebrides, Hellisay lies to the northeast of Barra and adjacent to Gighay. With an area of 142 ha (351 acres) it rises to a height of 79 m (259 ft), at Meall Meadhonach, which falls steeply into the sea at Rubha na h-uamh. Most of the island's former inhabitants were evacuated to Eriskay in the 1840s.

Hellister *Shetland* A hamlet with a jetty on the west coast of the Mainland of Shetland, Hellister lies on the eastern shore of Weisdale Voe, 7.5 miles (12 km) northwest of Lerwick. The Loch of Hellister lies immediately to the northeast.

Hell's Glen *Argyll and Bute* A narrow steep-sided valley in Argyll and Bute, Hell's Glen (or Gleann Beag) is occupied by a headstream of the River Goil to the east of Loch Fyne and northwest of Loch Goil. A road through the glen provides access to Lochgoilhead.

Helmsdale *Highland* A village on the eastern coast of Sutherland in Highland Council area, Helmsdale lies at the mouth of the River Helmsdale, 11 miles (18 km) northeast of Brora. A planned fishing village was established here by the Sutherland Estates in 1814 to house some of the 15,000 tenants 'cleared' from the interior of the estate to make way for sheep farming. A harbour was constructed in 1818, and a bridge across the river was built by the engineer Thomas Telford. The settlement subsequently developed in association with fishing, fish processing, coastal trade, tourism and railway engineering, and in 1982 the Timespan Heritage Centre was created in a ruined cooperage. The River Helmsdale is one of Europe's finest fly-fishing rivers, and overlooking the harbour stand the remains of a castle built in the 15th century as a hunting seat of the Sutherland family.

Hensol House *Dumfries and Galloway* A Tudor-style

granite mansion house in Dumfries and Galloway, Hensol House lies on the Black Water of Dee close to its junction with Loch Ken. Built in 1822, it was designed by Robert Lugar for John Cunninghame of Lainshaw. Nearby are a lodge and bridge, also possibly designed by Lugar.

Heriot *Scottish Borders* A village in a parish of the same name on the south side of the Moorfoot Hills in Scottish Borders, Heriot lies on the Heriot Water, 7 miles (11 km) northwest of Stow and west of the A7 from Edinburgh to Galashiels. A settlement developed here in the 20th century in association with the railway which closed in 1969.

Herma Ness *Shetland* The wild northernmost peninsula of the Shetland island of Unst, Herma Ness is a designated nature reserve protecting 183-m (600-ft) cliffs that are home to many species of sea bird.

Herman Law *Scottish Borders* A hill in the Ettrick district of Scottish Borders, Herman Law rises to 614 m (2014 ft) to the south of St Mary's Loch.

Hermetray *Western Isles* The largest of a number of uninhabited islands lying to the northeast of North Uist, Hermetray (Gael: *Thernatraigh*) extends to 72 ha (178 acres) and rises to 35 m (114 ft) at Compass Knoll (Gael: *Cnoc a' Chombaiste*). The island lies 5.5 miles (9 km) northeast of Lochmaddy and was the site of a government-sponsored fishing station in the 17th century.

Hermitage, the *Perth and Kinross* A beautiful wooded area in the Atholl district of Perth and Kinross, the Hermitage straddles the gorge of the River Braan, a mile (1.5 km) to the west of Dunkeld. Overlooking the gorge is a picturesque folly known as Ossian's Hall, built secretly in 1758 by a nephew of the 2nd Duke of Atholl as a surprise for the duke who had set aside the woodland for the planting of exotic trees. In 1783 the interior of the folly was decorated with mirrors designed to create a dramatic effect. Notable visitors to the Hermitage have included the poet Wordsworth, the composer Mendelssohn and the author of children's books, Beatrix Potter. In 1944 the folly and 13 ha (32 acres) were gifted to the National Trust for Scotland by the widow of the 8th Duke of Atholl. Also of interest are one of Scotland's tallest Douglas fir trees and another romantic folly called Ossian's Cave, a place designed to evoke the atmosphere of the cell occupied by the legendary 3rd-century bard Ossian who sang of the deeds of his father, the great Celtic warrior Fingal.

Hermitage Castle *Scottish Borders* A ruined castle of Liddesdale in Scottish Borders, Hermitage lies 4 miles (6.5 km) north of Newcastleton by the Hermitage Water, a tributary of the Liddel Water. The oldest part of the building dates from the mid-14th century, when it was held by the Dacre family. Subsequently held as a stronghold by the Hepburns of Bothwell and then the Crown, it was abandoned in the mid-17th century. In the care of the State since 1930, its main features are the towers at each of its four corners, and the huge archways on the east and west facades.

Hermitage of Braid *City of Edinburgh* Designated a local nature reserve in 1993 along with neighbouring Blackford Hill, the Hermitage of Braid lies between Blackford Hill and the Braid Hills at the west end of a valley linking Comiston to Liberton, on the south side of Edinburgh. There are walks through mixed broad-leaf woodland and grassland rich in wildlife. Hermitage House, gifted to the city in 1938 and now a visitor centre, was completed in 1785 by architect Robert Burn (1752–1815) for Charles Gordon of Cluny.

Heron, Loch *Dumfries and Galloway* A small loch in Dumfries and Galloway, Loch Heron lies between Loch Ronald and the Black Loch, 6 miles (10 km) northeast of Glenluce.

Hestan Island *Dumfries and Galloway* An island of Dumfries and Galloway, Hestan Island lies at the mouth of Auchencairn Bay, an inlet of the Solway Firth.

Hewk Burn *Dumfries and Galloway* A small stream in Annandale, Dumfries and Galloway, the Hewk Burn flows westwards from Hallhills Loch to join the Dryfe Water.

Hielanman's Umbrella *Glasgow City* That part of Argyle Street beneath the railway bridge leading to Central Station in Glasgow acquired the nickname Hielanman's Umbrella when it came to be used as a rendezvous for exiles from the Highlands and Islands.

High Glenling *Dumfries and Galloway* A locality in the Machars, Dumfries and Galloway, High Glenling lies at a road junction on the Glenling Moss between Elrig Loch and Mochrum Loch.

High Valleyfield *Fife* A former mining village in western Fife, High Valleyfield is situated midway between Dunfermline and Kincardine. It sits on a hill overlooking Low Valleyfield on the coast of the Firth of Forth and was formerly part of the Valleyfield Estate purchased by the East Fife Coal Company in 1907.

Highland *Area: 25,784 sq. km (9,955 sq. miles)* Highland is the largest of Scotland's local government areas. Stretching from Appin on Loch Linnhe in the south to the northern tip of Caithness, and from the island of Skye in the west to Strathspey in the east, Highland Council area encompasses the northwest Highlands of Scotland, some of the islands of the Inner Hebrides and a deeply indented fjord-like coastline. Bisected by the Great Glen Fault, within which lie the Caledonian Canal and Loch Ness, the area includes some of the oldest rocks in Scotland and a landscape dominated by mountain and moorland. Britain's highest mountain, Ben Nevis, rises to the east of Fort William near the southern end of the region. Less than 2.5 per cent of the land, mostly in Caithness and Easter Ross, is devoted to arable farming, while more than 26 per cent comprises heather moorland and peatland. While the Gulf Stream on the northwest coast creates a surprisingly mild climate, rainfall can vary from 2500 mm in the west to less than 500 mm in the east. This is one of the least populated regions of Europe, having fewer than 10 inhabitants per sq. km, a consequence of the hard environment combined with land clearance and emigration during the 18th and 19th centuries. Inverness, however, is a fast-growing commercial centre in addition to being the administrative centre of the council area. Other centres of population include Nairn, Fort William, Kingussie, Newtonmore, Aviemore, Grantown-on-Spey, Dingwall, Strathpeffer, Invergordon, Brora, Lairg, Dornoch, Wick, Thurso, Lochinver, Ullapool, Kyle of Lochalsh and Portree. Created in 1975 as Highland Region, the present single-tier council area dates from local government reorganisation in 1996.

Highland Boundary Fault A significant geological discontinuity, the Highland Boundary Fault traverses

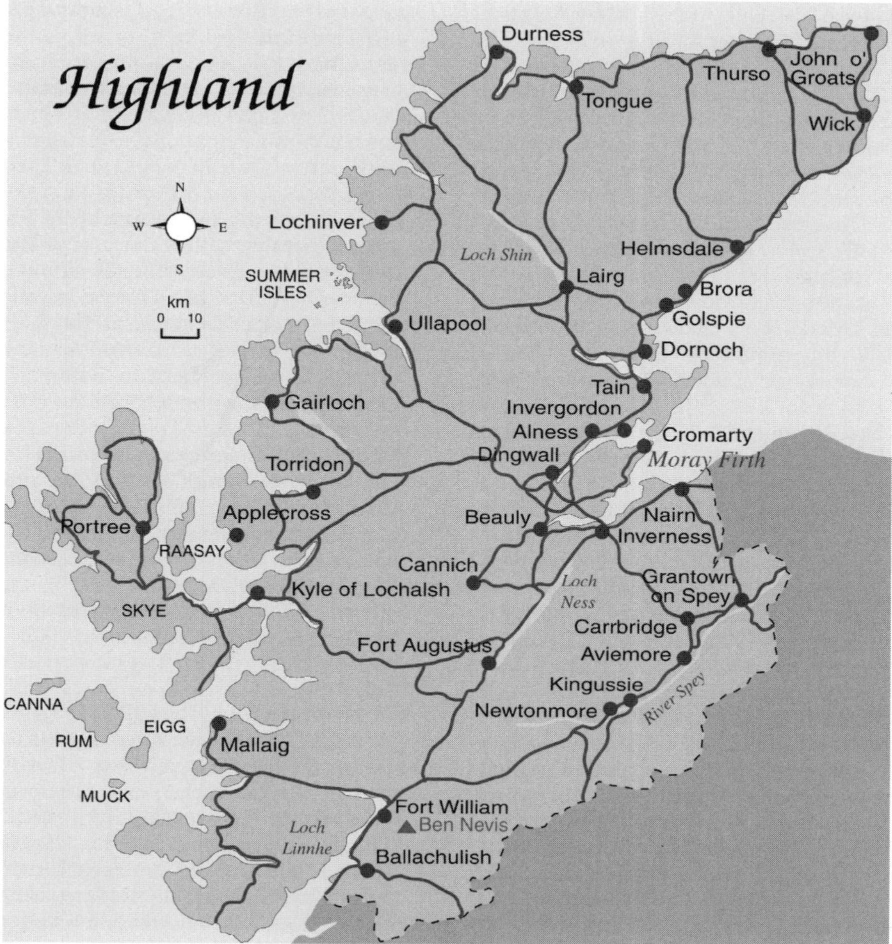

Scotland from the island of Arran in North Ayrshire to Stonehaven in Aberdeenshire, separating two distinctly different physiographic regions, namely the Highlands and the Midland Valley. To the north and west lie hard Pre-Cambrian and Cambrian metamorphic rocks of the Dalradian group and to the south and east are softer sedimentary rocks of the Devonian and Carboniferous periods, principally Old Red Sandstone. The fault runs southwest-northeast from Lochranza on Arran, across the Firth of Clyde, via Helensburgh, Loch Lomond, Aberfoyle and the Menteith Hills to Callander, Comrie and Crieff. It then forms the northern boundary of Strathmore before reaching the east coast at Stonehaven. Active during the Caledonian mountain-building episode, a plate tectonic collision that took place from the mid-Ordovician to mid-Devonian periods (520 to 400 million years ago), the Highland Boundary Fault allowed the Midland Valley to descend as a major rift or graben by as much as 4000 m (13,123 ft). This earlier vertical movement was later replaced by horizontal shear. A complementary fault, the Southern Uplands Fault, forms the southern boundary of the Midland Valley.

Highlands A name given to that part of Scotland northwest of a line approximating to the Highland Boundary Fault that stretches from Helensburgh in the southwest to Stonehaven in the northeast, the Highlands is a term that can be used in a geographical or cultural context. Geographically, it comprises the upland areas of Scotland in the Grampians and the northwest Highlands, which are separated from each other by the Great Glen. Culturally, the lower eastern margin from Caithness round the Moray Firth to Moray and Aberdeenshire can also be included in the Highlands.

Hightae *Dumfries and Galloway* A village of Annandale in Dumfries and Galloway, Hightae lies to the west of a bend on the River Annan, 2 miles (3 km) south of Lochmaben. Hightae Mill Loch lies a mile (1.5 km) to the north. Along with Heck, Greenhill and Smallholm, Hightae is one of the Royal Four Towns of Lochmaben.

Hildasay *Shetland* Possibly named after the battle goddess of Norse mythology, the oval-shaped 108-ha (267-acre) island of Hildasay lies to the west of the Mainland of Shetland and to the north of the smaller islands of Papa and Oxna. The island rises to 32 m (105 ft) and includes two lochs – West Loch and East Loch. To the southeast lies the smaller island of Linga. Uninhabited since the beginning of the 20th century, Hildasay had a population of 30 in 1891, at a time when its red granite was quarried and a curing station for herring was in operation.

Hill End *Fife* A small hamlet to the northeast of Saline in western Fife, Hill End lies below Wether Hill at the western end of the Cleish Hills where a minor road from Saline meets the A823 from Dunfermline to Crieff.

Hill House, the *Argyll and Bute* Situated in Helensburgh, Argyll and Bute, 23 miles (37 km) northwest of Glasgow, the Hill House is generally regarded as the finest of Charles Rennie Mackintosh's domestic buildings. Built for the Glasgow publisher Walter Blackie in 1902–04, the Hill House sits, as the name suggests, atop a hill and has commanding views of the Clyde estuary. The Hill House came into the care of the National Trust for Scotland in 1982.

Hill o' Many Stanes *Highland* A locality in eastern Caithness, the Hill o' Many Stanes is a Neolithic or Bronze Age site with around 200 stones set out in 22 parallel lines, 3 miles (5 km) northeast of Lybster and 8 miles (13 km) south of Wick.

Hill of Barra, The *Aberdeenshire* The Hill of Barra is a low, grassy hill rising to a height of 193 m (633 ft) just south of Oldmeldrum in Aberdeenshire. It is ringed by the ramparts of a prehistoric hillfort dating from the 1st millennium BC.

Hill of Beath *Fife* A former mining village in Beath parish, western Fife, Hill of Beath is situated between Cowdenbeath and Crossgates. It lies at the foot of the Hill of Beath, which rises to 242 m (786 ft). Mining was developed here by the Fife Coal Company, which acquired the local colliery in 1887.

Hill of Christ's Kirk *Aberdeenshire* A hill in Aberdeenshire, the Hill of Christ's Kirk rises to 311 m (1021 ft) a mile (1.5 km) west of Insch, opposite Dunnideer Hill. There are the remains of a prehistoric hillfort on its summit.

Hill of Crogodale *Highland* The Hill of Crogodale lies 2 miles (3 km) south of Duncansby Head on the eastern coastline of Caithness in Highland Council area. Lying a mile (1.5 km) southeast of John o' Groats, it rises to a height of 81 m (266 ft).

Hill of Dudwick *Aberdeenshire* A small hill in the Buchan district of Aberdeenshire, the Hill of Dudwick rises to 174 m (571 ft), 4 miles (6.5 km) north of Ellon.

Hill of Fare *Aberdeenshire* A hill range in Aberdeenshire, the Hill of Fare rises to 470 m (1545 ft) to the north of Banchory. On 28 October 1562, a skirmish between the followers of Mary, Queen of Scots under the Earl of Moray and forces of the Earl of Huntly took place in the marshy hollow of Corrichie on its southern slopes.

Hill of Foudland *Aberdeenshire* A hill in the Strathbogie district of Aberdeenshire, the Hill of Foudland rises to 467 m (1531 ft) 6 miles (10 km) southeast of Huntly. Its steep east-facing slopes are known as the Skirts of Foudland. Its slate used to be quarried extensively. To the north, the Glen Water flows through the Glens of Foudland.

Hill of Menmuir *Angus* A hill of northeast Angus, the Hill of Menmuir rises to a height of 271 m (889 ft) 1.25 miles (2 km) northwest of Kirkton of Menmuir and 5.5 miles (9 km) northwest of Brechin. The hill extends along a ridge overlooking the Paphrie Burn to the northwest.

Hill of Neap *Shetland* The Hill of Neap lies on the eastern coast of the Shetland Mainland. Rising to a height of 47 m (154 ft) it is located some 9 miles (14 km) north of the island's principal town of Lerwick.

Hill of Stake *North Ayrshire* The Hill of Stake rises to a height of 522 m (1712 ft) and is located to the northeast of Largs in North Ayrshire.

Hill of Tarvit *Fife* An Edwardian mansion house with 202 ha (500 acres) of garden, forest and farmland in eastern Fife, Hill of Tarvit is situated near the A916, 2.5 miles (4 km) south of Cupar. Built in 1696 and attributed to Sir William Bruce, the house at Hill of Tarvit was originally called Wemyss Hall. In 1904 it was bought by Mr F. B. Sharp and rebuilt to a design by Sir Robert Lorimer to form a suitable setting for his collection of French, Chippendale and vernacular furniture, Dutch paintings, Flemish tapestries and Chinese porcelain. In 1949 the property was bequeathed to the National Trust for Scotland by Miss E. C. Sharp. Today the house displays this significant collection among fine Edwardian interiors, and the grounds contain formal gardens also by Lorimer.

Hill of Three Stones Also known as Threestone Hill, the Hill of Three Stones rises to 632 m (2073 ft) in the Grampian uplands of Moray on the border between Moray and Aberdeenshire. The Water of Buchat rises on its southern slopes, to the south of the Cabrach Road from Dufftown to Rhynie.

Hill of Tillymorgan *Aberdeenshire* A hill in Strathbogie, Aberdeenshire, the Hill of Tillymorgan rises to 381 m (1250 ft) to the north of Kirkton of Culsalmond.

Hill of Towie *Moray* The Hill of Towie rises to a height of 339 m (1111 ft) to the southwest of Keith and the north and west of the River Isla in Moray. It lies in Rosarie Forest, with the Moor of Auchenacie on its northern slope.

Hill of Wirren *Angus* A hill in the southern Grampians, the Hill of Wirren rises to 677 m (2221 ft) in the Braes of Angus to the west of Glen Esk. To the northwest, West Wirren reaches a height of 628 m (2060 ft).

Hillend *Fife* A small village in western Fife, Hillend straddles the A921 coastal road a mile (1.5 km) to the east of Inverkeithing. There is an industrial park with industries producing electronics, electrical goods, plastic goods, optical components and building materials, and to the north at Fordell Firs is the Scottish Scouts Association National Camping and Training Centre.

Hillfoot *East Dunbartonshire* A locality to the north of Glasgow in East Dunbartonshire, Hillfoot is a district of Bearsden. There are the remains of a Roman bathhouse situated nearby

Hillfoots, The *Clackmannanshire* The settlements between the River Devon and the foot of the steep south-facing slopes of the Ochil Hills from Blairlogie to Yetts of Muckhart, including Menstrie, Alva, Tillicoultry, Dollar and Pool of Muckhart, have come to be known as the Hillfoot Villages. Many owe their development to 18th- and 19th-century textile mills driven by water power derived from fast-flowing streams that drop down from the hills to the valley of the River Devon.

Hillhead *Glasgow City* A residential district of Glasgow, Hillhead is located northwest of the city centre, with the River Kelvin to the south and east and the University of Glasgow main campus to the east. Hillhead was designated a police burgh in 1869 before being incorporated into the city of Glasgow in 1891.

Hillhead *Stirling* A locality in Stirling Council area, Hillhead lies to the south of the Bannock Burn, 2 miles (3 km) south of Stirling.

Hillington *Glasgow City* A suburb of Glasgow, Hillington lies on the south side of the River Clyde, 4 miles (6.5 km) southwest of the city centre. Immediately to the southeast is Cardonald, and to the northeast is the Hillington Industrial Estate.

Hills of Cromdale Situated between the River Spey and the River Avon, the Hills of Cromdale rise up on the northern edge of the Grampian Mountains to heights in excess of 700 m (2297 ft). The highest tops, which lie on the border between Moray and Highland council areas, include Creagan a' Chaise (722 m/2366 ft) Charn a' Ghille Chearr (710 m/2329 ft) and Carn Tuairneir (693 m/2278 ft)

Hillside *Angus* A village in Angus, Hillside lies 3 miles (5 km) to the northwest of Montrose. Situated on sloping ground with fine views, it developed in the 19th century as a summer retreat for the residents of Montrose who built villas there. Sunnyside Royal Hospital was originally founded in 1757 as Sunnyside Asylum and was a pioneering establishment in the treatment of mental illness. It is now a museum.

Hillswick *Shetland* A sheltered fishing village on the Mainland of Shetland, Hillswick is situated 35 miles (56 km) north-northwest of Lerwick on a bay of the Ura Firth which opens out into St Magnus Bay. Built of Scots pine in Norway and re-erected in Hillswick at the beginning of the 20th century, the St Magnus Bay Hotel was the Shetland terminal of the old North of Scotland Shipping Company.

Hillwell *Shetland* A hamlet in the Dunrossness district in the far southwest of the Mainland of Shetland, Hillwell lies a mile (1.5 km) north of the Bay of Quendale and 2.5 miles (4 km) northwest of Sumburgh Airport.

Hilton of Cadboll *Highland* A 19th-century fishing village in Easter Ross, Hilton of Cadboll overlooks the Moray Firth, 6 miles (10 km) northeast of Cromarty. A replica of the 9th-century Hilton of Cadboll Pictish cross slab, now in the Museum of Scotland, Edinburgh, was erected in 2000. Buildings of interest include Hilton of Cadboll Chapel and the remains of the 14th-century Cadboll Castle.

Hiort An alternative name for Hirta in the St Kilda group of islands.

Hirn *Aberdeenshire* A village in central Aberdeenshire, Hirn lies 4 miles (6.5 km) northeast of Banchory and southeast of the Hill of Fare.

Hirsel, the *Scottish Borders* Situated 2 miles (3 km) northwest of Coldstream, the Hirsel has been the seat of the Home family since the 12th century. The 14th Earl of Home, Sir Alec Douglas Home, gave up his title in 1963 to become prime minister, and in 1974 left the House of Commons with a life peerage as Lord Home of the Hirsel. The estate includes nature trails, the Hirsel Lake wildfowl sanctuary, Dundock Wood and Hirsel Homestead Museum and Craft Centre.

Hirta *Western Isles* The largest of the remote island group of St Kilda, Hirta (or Hiort) lies in the Atlantic Ocean 40 miles (64 km) northwest of the Outer Hebrides. Owned by the National Trust for Scotland, its dramatic stacks and towering cliffs of gabbro and granite provide a backdrop to the sheltered village on Village Bay which was abandoned in 1930 when the island's people were evacuated to the mainland. The highest peak is Conachair, which rises to 430 m (1400 ft).

Hobkirk *Scottish Borders* A small settlement to the south of Teviotdale in Scottish Borders, Hobkirk lies on the Rule Water, a half-mile (1 km) south of Bonchester Bridge and 6 miles (10 km) southeast of Hawick.

Hobseat *Aberdeenshire* A locality on the Cowie Water in southeast Aberdeenshire, Hobseat lies 8 miles (13 km) west of Stonehaven in Fetteresso Forest.

Hoddom Cross *Dumfries and Galloway* A hamlet of Annandale in Dumfries and Galloway, Hoddom Cross lies near the junction of the Mein Water with the River Annan, a mile (1.5 km) southwest of Ecclefechan. Nearby Hoddom Castle was built *c*.1568 by John Maxwell, 4th Lord Herries, as his chief stronghold on the West March.

Hogganfield *Glasgow City* A northeastern suburb of Glasgow, Hogganfield was incorporated into the city in 1931 along with Carntyne and other smaller parts of the East End. A residential area, it includes Hogganfield Loch Park, an area of land with recreational facilities extending to 50 ha (124 acres) acquired by the city in 1920.

Hogh Bay *Argyll and Bute* A sandy bay on the northern coast of the island of Coll in the Inner Hebrides, Hogh Bay lies to the southwest of the settlement of Ballyhaugh and is overlooked by Ben Hogh to the northeast.

Hogha Gearraidh The Gaelic name for Hougharry in the Western Isles.

Hoil, Loch *Perth and Kinross* A small loch in Perth and Kinross, Loch Hoil lies in the hills between Strath Braan and Strath Tay, 4 miles (6.5 km) south of Aberfeldy. It is the source of the Cochill Burn.

Hollanders' Grave *Shetland* A hillock overlooking Ronas Voe at the northern end of the Mainland of Shetland, Hollander's Grave is said to be the site where Dutch seamen were buried in 1674 following the capture by the English of the East-Indiaman the *Wapen van Rotterdam* which had sheltered there.

Hollanders' Knowe *Shetland* A locality on the Mainland of Shetland 3 miles (5 km) west of Lerwick, Hollander's Knowe was once a Dutch trading post.

Hollows *Dumfries and Galloway* A locality in Eskdale, Dumfries and Galloway, Hollows lies on the River Esk just over a mile (1.5 km) north of Canonbie.

Hollybush *East Ayrshire* A village of East Ayrshire, Hollybush lies at a road junction 3 miles (5 km) northwest of Patna. It developed in association with local mills and with road and rail transport, a rail link with Ayr being established in 1856.

Holm *Dumfries and Galloway* A hamlet in Eskdale, Dumfries and Galloway, Holm lies on the White Esk, just north of Eskdalemuir.

Holm *Western Isles* A small settlement with a jetty on the east coast of Lewis in the Outer Hebrides, Holm (Gael: *Thuilm* or *Tolm*) is located 2.5 miles (4 km) southeast of Stornoway. The surrounding area is also known as Holm, with Holm Bay and Holm Island lying a half-mile (1 km) to the southwest and Holm Point beyond. The Beasts of Holm, dangerous rocks lying just offshore at the entrance to Stornoway Harbour, brought the demise of the HMS *Iolaire* in 1919, with the loss of 205 souls. A memorial on Holm Point commemorates the disaster.

Holm of Papa *Orkney* A small island of the Orkney Islands, Holm of Papa is situated to the east of Papa Westray, from which it is separated by the bay of South Wick. The most notable feature on the island is a prehistoric long cairn 35 m (114 ft) in length and 16.8 m (55 ft) broad.

Holme House *Dumfries and Galloway* The remains of an early Doric mansion house in Dumfries and Galloway, Holme House lies a mile (1.5 km) to the northwest of Balmaclellan. The greater part of the house was demolished in the 1970s, leaving a single-storey service court and lodge.

Holmwood House *East Renfrewshire* Designed in 1858 by Alexander 'Greek' Thomson, Holmwood House lies to the south of Greenbank House and Garden, Clarkston, East Renfrewshire, and is regarded as Thomson's finest domestic building. Built for James Coupar, who owned the Millholm Paper Mill on the White Cart Water, it is classically inspired with ornately designed rooms in plaster, marble and wood. Holmwood House was acquired by the National Trust for Scotland in 1994.

Holy Island *North Ayrshire* An island in Lamlash Bay off the eastern coast of Arran, Holy Island has an area of 263 ha (625 acres) and rises to 314 m (1030 ft) at Mullach Mòr. It provides shelter to the bay, which is one of Scotland's finest naval anchorages. The island is associated with the 6th-century Irish missionary St Mo Las who occupied a cave on the western shore near a spring known as St Mo Las' Well. This cave contains runic and early Christian inscriptions. Formerly owned by the Duke of Hamilton, the island was purchased in 1991 by Scottish Buddhists of the Samye Ling Tibetan Centre. Native plants, trees and shrubs have been introduced to the island, which is a designated nature reserve, and there are populations of Soay sheep and feral goats.

Holy Loch *Argyll and Bute* An inlet of the Firth of Clyde on the Cowal peninsula of Argyll and Bute, Holy Loch opens out into the firth 2 miles (3 km) north of Dunoon. A submarine base of the US Navy operated here from 1961 to 1992.

Holyrood *City of Edinburgh* A district at the eastern end of the Royal Mile in the city of Edinburgh, Holyrood owes its origins to an abbey founded by David I in 1128 after he had been attacked by a stag during a hunting expedition. James II was born in the abbey lodgings and he, as well as James III, James IV and Queen Mary, were married in the abbey. James V and Charles I were crowned here, and David II, James II, James V and Lord Darnley were buried here. Damaged during the Reformation, the abbey was abandoned in 1768 following its collapse. Adjacent to the ruined abbey is the Palace of Holyroodhouse, the official residence of the monarch in Scotland. Holyrood Park, at 260 ha (650 acres), extends eastwards and incorporates Arthur's Seat and Salisbury Crags as well as Dunsapie Loch and St Margaret's Loch, two artificial lochs created in the 19th century. Originally a royal hunting estate, the park was enclosed by James V *c.*1540. The Scottish Parliament situated opposite the Palace of Holyroodhouse was opened in 2004.

Holytown *North Lanarkshire* A large village in the Bothwell parish of North Lanarkshire, Holytown lies 2 miles (3 km) northeast of Hamilton. It developed in the 18th century in association with coal mining, and a railway junction station named Holytown was opened at nearby New Stevenston in 1869.

Holywood *Dumfries and Galloway* A former milltown village in Dumfries and Galloway, Holywood lies 4 miles (6.5 km) northwest of Dumfries. A railway station operated here from 1849 to 1953. Nearby, in the valley of the Cairn Water, is a prehistoric stone circle known as the Twelve Apostles, close to which a Premonstratensian abbey was founded in the 13th century.

Hope, Loch *Highland* A loch in the Sutherland district of Highland Council area, Loch Hope lies due east of Loch Eriboll to which it is joined by the River Hope. The loch is fed from the south by the Abhainn nan Strath Mòr which flows through Strath More. To the southeast, Ben Hope rises to 927 m (3041 ft).

Hopeman *Moray* Founded in 1805 by the 'improving' laird William Young of Inverugie, the fishertown of Hopeman lies on the Moray coast between Burghead and Lossiemouth. After Young had moved to the Strath of Kildonan to engage in the infamous Clearances, the settlement was expanded with the building of a harbour in 1865 by Admiral Archibald Duff of Drummuir. Hopeman stone from the nearby Greenbrae and Clashach quarries was shipped from the harbour. The development of fishing and quarrying resulted in a three-fold expansion of the population from 445 in 1831 to 1323 in 1881. Buildings of interest include Hopeman Lodge (*c.*1840), built as a seaside pavilion for Young of Inverugie; a 19th-century icehouse for storing fish; Inverugie House, built in 1864 to a design by Alexander Reid; and the church (1854), with a Tudor Gothic-style tower gifted in 1923 by Elgin distiller Innes Cameron. The rich agricultural land beyond Hopeman was reclaimed by landowners such as William Young, with the gradual drainage of Loch Spynie which once stretched from Lossiemouth to Burghead.

Hopes Water *East Lothian* A river rising in the Lammermuir Hills of East Lothian, Hopes Water rises to the east of Lammer Law before passing through the Hopes Reservoir and flowing northwards. It joins the Gifford Water at a point a mile (1.5 km) southeast of Gifford.

Hopetoun House *West Lothian* More a palace than a country house, Hopetoun House lies within 40 ha (99 acres) of parkland, 2.5 miles (4 km) west of South Queensferry and 11 miles (18 km) west of Edinburgh. Originally built in 1699 for the Hope family by the architect Sir William Bruce, it was enlarged in 1721 by William Adam for the 1st Earl of Hopetoun. Adam, ably assisted by his sons Robert and John, added flanking wings, colonnades and pavilions to the north and south, as well as a grand entrance. In 1822 King George IV knighted the artist Henry Raeburn at Hopetoun during his visit to Scotland and was appropriately impressed by the grandeur of the house. Maintained by the Hopetoun Preservation Trust, Hopetoun House is the home of the Marquess of Linlithgow.

Hopetoun Monument *East Lothian* Located on Byres Hill, a summit of the Garleton Hills in East Lothian, the Hopetoun Monument was built in 1824 in memory of Sir John Hope, the 4th Earl of Hopetoun (1765–1823). Hope was a hero of the Peninsular Wars (1808–14) and, among various properties, owned Luffness House and its associated estates to the northwest.

Hopetoun Monument *Fife* On Mount Hill, about 3 miles (5 km) northwest of Cupar, is the conspicuous 29-m (95-ft) column erected in 1824 in memory of Sir John Hope, the 4th Earl of Hopetoun (1765–1823), hero of the Peninsular Wars.

Horn, Loch *Highland* A small loch in the Sutherland district of Highland Council area, Loch Horn lies 4 miles (6.5 km) northwest of Golspie at the head of Dunrobin

Glen, through which flows the Golspie Burn. To the east, Ben Horn rises to 521 m (1709 ft).

Horse Island *Highland* One of the Summer Isles situated off the northwest coast of the Scottish mainland, Horse Island lies to the south of Achiltibuie in the Coigach district of Sutherland. It has an area of 141 ha (350 acres).

Horse Isle *North Ayrshire* An uninhabited island and bird sanctuary in the Firth of Clyde, Horse Isle lies a half-mile (1 km) offshore from Ardrossan.

Hosh *Perth and Kinross* A locality in Strath Earn, Perth and Kinross, Hosh lies on the River Turret, a mile (1.5 km) to the northwest of Crieff.

Hosta *Western Isles* A small township on the west coast of North Uist in the Outer Hebrides, Hosta lies to the southwest of Loch Hosta and a mile (1.5 km) south of Balmartin. Hosta is regularly the site of the North Uist Highland Games, and to the northwest there are sandy beaches which are favoured by surfers.

Hoswick *Shetland* A hamlet at the head of Hos Wick, an inlet on the east coast of the Shetland Mainland, Hoswick lies a quarter-mile (0.4 km) west of Stove and 12 miles (19 km) south-southwest of Lerwick. Shetland tweed is produced here.

Hough Bay *Argyll and Bute* A large sandy bay on the northwest coast of the island of Tiree in Argyll and Bute, Hough Bay lies to the north of the headland of Rubha Chraiginis.

Hougharry *Western Isles* A crofting settlement on the west coast of North Uist in the Outer Hebrides, Hougharry (Gael: *Hogha Gearraidh*) is located to the north of the Balranald Nature Reserve and a mile (1.5 km) east of Aird an Runair.

Hound Hillock *Aberdeenshire* A summit in the eastern Grampians of Aberdeenshire, Hound Hillock rises to 516 m (1693 ft) to the northwest of Fettercairn and west of the Cairn o' Mount Road.

Hound Point *City of Edinburgh* A headland on the south shore of the Firth of Forth, Hound Point lies on the Dalmeny Estate, 1.5 miles (2.5 km) east of the Forth Rail Bridge and South Queensferry. It is the site of an offshore tanker berth and oil-handling facility, with pipelines extending to a storage site 2 miles (3 km) to the southwest near the village of Dalmeny.

Hourn, Loch *Highland* A sea loch to the north of Knoydart on the west coast of Highland Council area, Loch Hourn extends eastwards from Kinloch Hourn, opening out into the Sound of Sleat opposite the island of Skye.

House for an Art Lover *Glasgow City* Located within Bellahouston Park in Glasgow, the House for an Art Lover, or *Haus eines Kunstfreundes*, was built in 1989–96 to designs created by Charles Rennie Mackintosh in 1901. It was his best-known and most influential design, and would certainly have won the German design competition it was created for, if only it had been entered on time. It did, however, win a special prize and was widely praised by his peers.

House of Dun *Angus* A Georgian mansion house in Angus, situated to the west of Montrose overlooking the Montrose Basin, the House of Dun was designed by William Adam in 1730 for David Erskine, Lord Dun. The house, which has superb plasterwork by Joseph Enzer, has associations with Lady Augusta Kennedy-Erskine, a natural daughter of William IV and Mrs Jordan. The property, including 361 ha (893 acres) of woodland and farm land, was bequeathed to the National Trust for Scotland in 1980 by Mrs M. A. A. Lovett.

House of Pitmuies *Angus* Situated off the A932 between Forfar and Friockheim in Angus, the House of Pitmuies is a classically styled mansion house dating from the 18th century. Recently restored, its associated Home Farm buildings and garden are of special interest.

House of the Binns *West Lothian* Located 3 miles (5 km) east of Linlithgow and 5 miles (8 km) west of South Queensferry, the House of the Binns has been the home of the Dalyell family since 1612. The name derives from two hills, or binns, on which the house is situated. The Royalist General Tam Dalyell (1615–85) extended the Binns, adding the first of several towers said to have been built to prevent the devil blowing the house away. The Binns was further extended in the mid-18th century, and again around 1810 by the architect William Burn, who added towers and battlements in Scottish baronial style. In 1944, the Binns was the first mansion to be acquired by the National Trust for Scotland under its Country Houses Scheme. The grounds include a woodland walk with views over the Firth of Forth.

Housetter *Shetland* A hamlet overlooking Colla Firth on the east coast of the Northmavine district of the Shetland Mainland, Housetter is located 10 miles (16 km) north of Brae. The Loch of Housetter lies just to the north, the Ness of Housetter to the south and the hills of the Beorgs of Housetter lie to the northwest.

Houston *Renfrewshire* A large village located 6 miles (10 km) northwest of Paisley, Houston derives its name from 'Hew's town', a 13th-century village associated with the castle of Hugo de Kilpeter. In 1781 the castle was partly demolished and a new town of 35 houses was erected. The Crosslee Mill (demolished 1986) was built for cotton spinning in 1793, but in 1916–17 a new factory was constructed for spinning cordite fuses. The Mercat Cross has a sundial dating from the early 18th century, with a shaft that may be 14th-century. Houston House and Barochan House (both 17th century) are other notable buildings.

Houton *Orkney* A settlement on the south coast of the Orkney Mainland, Houton lies 5 miles (8 km) southeast of Stromness. A ferry crosses Scapa Flow from here bound for Hoy and Flotta. Houton was a seaplane base in World War I, and civilian flying boats bound for North America used Houton between the wars.

Howbeg *Western Isles* A small scattered hamlet near the west coast of South Uist in the Outer Hebrides, Howbeg (Gael: *Tobha Beag*) lies on the northeast shore of Loch Roag, a half-mile (1 km) south of Howmore.

Howe of Alford, The *Aberdeenshire* A district of Aberdeenshire, the Howe of Alford occupies the middle reaches of the River Don, with the village of Alford at its centre.

Howe of Fife *Fife* The name given to the fertile farming area of central Fife in the valley of the River Eden between Strathmiglo and Cupar.

Howe of Strathmartine *Angus/Dundee City* The broad valley of the Dighty Water to the north of Dundee, the Howe of Strathmartine crosses the border between Angus and Dundee City. Once rich farmland, much of the valley is now occupied by the peripheral housing estates of Dundee, including Downfield, Trottick, Fintry, Douglas and Angus, Whitfield and Balmossie.

Howe of the Mearns A district of southeast Aberdeenshire, the Howe of the Mearns forms a hill-girt basin at the northeast end of the wide valley of Strathmore beyond Brechin. It is separated from the North Sea by volcanic lava hills that culminate in Bruxie Hill (216 m/710 ft). To the north, the Howe is overlooked by Strathfinella Hill (414 m/1357 ft). Drained by the Luther Water and its tributaries, the chief town of the Mearns is Laurencekirk.

Howff, the *Dundee City* The Howff is the name given to the historic graveyard that occupies the garden of the former Greyfriars monastery in Dundee. Gifted to the city by Mary, Queen of Scots, it was the meeting place for the Nine Trades of Dundee, whose signs and symbols are inscribed on the gravestones. The monuments date from the 16th to the 19th centuries.

Howgate *Midlothian* A settlement in Midlothian, Howgate lies to the south of Edinburgh between Auchendinny and Leadburn. Its inn dates from c.1743.

Howie, Loch *Dumfries and Galloway* A small loch in Dumfries and Galloway, Loch Howie lies on the eastern edge of Corriedoo Forest to the south of the A702 between Moniaive and St John's Town of Dalry.

Howmore *Western Isles* A township near the west coast of South Uist in the Western Isles, Howmore (or Tobha Mòr) lies to the southwest of Loch Druidibeg, 1.5 miles (2.5 km) south-southwest of Stilligary and 10 miles (16 km) north-northwest of Lochboisdale. The white-harled Church of Scotland dating from 1858 is a notable landmark, and a cluster of ruined ancient and medieval chapels are of historical interest. A rustic youth hostel is located here, run by the Gatliff Trust. Haarsa rises to 139m (456 ft) to the east, with Hecla beyond, rising to 606m (1988 ft). Immediately to the south is the smaller settlement of Howbeg.

Hownam *Scottish Borders* A village in the Roxburgh district of Scottish Borders on the north side of the Cheviot Hills, Hownam lies on the Kale Water 8 miles (13 km) east of Jedburgh. To the north, Hownam Law rises to 449 m (1472 ft).

Howwood *Renfrewshire* A small village 6 miles (10 km) southwest of Paisley, Howwood derives its name from 'hollow wood'. There are some remnants of the Midtownfield Bleachworks (1835–40) to the south, and one wall remains of 15th-century Elliston Castle.

Hoy *Orkney* With an area of 14,375 ha (35,518 acres), the island of Hoy is the second-largest of the Orkney Islands. It takes its name from the Old Norse *haey* ('high island'), being hilly in the north and west where upper Old Red Sandstone has been weathered into steep and craggy uplands. Rising to 479 m (1570 ft) at Ward Hill, the highest hill in the Orkney Islands, Hoy is noted for its wildlife and its sandstone sea cliffs, which include the famous rock pinnacle the Old Man of Hoy at 137 m (450 ft), first climbed in 1966. The island, with a crofting population of 392, was sold in 1973 to the Hoy Trust, which has tried to encourage resettlement. Crofters have, since then, been able to purchase their landholdings and the RSPB has acquired North Hoy Nature Reserve which is noted for its colonies of arctic and great skuas, as well as the only mountain hares in the Orkney Islands. Buildings of interest include Melsetter House, a laird's house enlarged in the 19th century, and two Martello towers which flank the entrance to Long Hope. To the south of Ward Hill and overlooked by crags named the Dwarfie Hamars stands a large block of red sandstone known as the Dwarfie Stone. This is thought to be the only example in the UK of a rock-cut chamber tomb of the Neolithic or early Bronze Age. To the west is the crofting township of Rackwick, which stands beside a fine sand and boulder-strewn beach. To the northeast of Rackwick is Berriedale Wood, the most northerly woodland in Britain, and at St John's Head can be found the highest vertical cliff in the UK, rising to over 300 m (1000 ft). A passenger ferry service links Moness pier near the village of Hoy with Stromness on Mainland Orkney and there are car ferry services to Houton from Lyness, opposite the island of Fara, and the secluded natural harbour of Long Hope. The Longhope Lifeboat Station at Brims in South Walls, which is now a museum, has a remarkable record for daring rescues and is remembered for the loss of an entire crew when its lifeboat went to assist the stricken Liberian cargo ship *Irene* in 1969. Lyness once supported the shore facilities for the Navy base of Scapa Flow, and many remnants of that base, together with a naval cemetery, remain.

Huisinis The Gaelic name for Hushinish in the Western Isles.

Humbie *East Lothian* A small rural East Lothian village on the west bank of the Humbie Water, Humbie lies 4 miles (6.5 km) east of Pathhead and a similar distance south of Pencaitland, in the shadow of the Lammermuir Hills. The T-plan parish church, situated a half-mile (1 km) north of the village, was built in 1800 and remodelled by architect David Bryce in 1866. The Children's Village (1905), once a residential complex for children with learning difficulties, lies to the southeast of Humbie. Humbie Mill sits on the Humbie Water, and the 18th-century Humbie House lies a mile (1.5 km) to the northeast.

Hume *Scottish Borders* A village in the Berwickshire district of Scottish Borders, Hume lies 3 miles (5 km) south of Greenlaw and 6 miles (10 km) north of Kelso. On a hill nearby stands the 13th-century Hume Castle, a former stronghold of the Hume or Home family who moved to The Hirsel near Coldstream after the castle was destroyed by Cromwell's troops in 1651.

Hunda *Orkney* An island of the Orkney Islands lying west of Burray, to which it is linked by a causeway built over the Hunda Reef. Rich in birdlife, Hunda has an area of 100 ha (247 acres).

Hunterian Art Gallery, The *Glasgow City* Located on University Avenue and within the University of Glasgow, the Hunterian Art Gallery is based on the collection of William Hunter (1718–83). This purpose-built gallery was opened in 1980, with art works being transferred from the Hunterian Museum. The collection includes paintings by Hockney, Picasso, Rembrandt and Reynolds, together with those of Allan Ramsay (1713–84) and the largest European collection of the works of James Whistler (1834–1903). Most notable is the Charles Rennie Mackintosh collection, the world's largest, comprising over 80 pieces of furniture and 700 watercolours, designs and drawings.

Hunterian Museum *Glasgow City* Opened in 1807 as Scotland's first public museum, the Hunterian Museum is located on the campus of the University of Glasgow, 1.5 miles (3 km) west of the centre of Glasgow. The museum was endowed by William Hunter (1718–83), the noted obstetrician. On his death he gave the university the substantial sum of £8000 to create a building to hold his extensive and broad collection of anatomical specimens, works of art, coins, minerals, books and manuscripts. The original museum was situated on Glasgow's High Street, but it moved with the university to a new site on the western side of the city in 1870. The art collection was subsequently transferred to a purpose-built art gallery in 1980.

Hunter's Quay *Argyll and Bute* A locality with a ferry terminal on the Cowal peninsula, Hunter's Quay lies on the west side of the Firth of Clyde at the entrance to Holy Loch.

Hunterston *North Ayrshire* A locality on the North Ayrshire coast, Hunterston looks out onto the Firth of Clyde, 5 miles (8 km) south of Largs. Hunterston Castle, a former stronghold of the Hunter family dating from the 13th century, is the centre for the Clan Hunter Association. The Hunterston Terminal, which handles coal, was originally built in the 1970s by the former British Steel Corporation to land coal for the Ravenscraig steelworks in Motherwell which closed in 1992. The Hunterston A Nuclear Power Station, opened in 1964, eventually closed in 1990, and Hunterston B Nuclear Power Station, which dates from 1976, produces 1200 megawatt of power from two advanced gas-cooled (AGR) reactors.

Hunt Hill *Moray* Situated 3 miles (5 km) southwest of the settlement of Rothes in Moray, Hunt Hill rises to a height of 365 m (1197 ft). To the west of the hill lies the peak of Cairn Cattoch and to the north the Burn of Rothes.

Hunt Hill *Angus* A peak in Angus, Hunt Hill lies 3 miles (5 km) northwest of the settlement of Runtaleave and separates the heads of the valleys of Glen Prosen and Glen Clova. It rises to a height of 734 m (2408 ft).

Huntingtower Castle *Perth and Kinross* Built by the Ruthven family in the 15th century, Huntingtower Castle is located in Huntingtower, 3 miles (5 km) northwest of Perth. Comprising two separate towers, the original Ruthven Castle was the eastern tower, the western tower being an early 16th-century build. An infill building adjoining the two was built in the 17th century. Confiscated by the Crown in 1600, following the Gowrie Conspiracy, the name Ruthven was proscribed and the castle passed into the hands of the Murray family in 1663.

Huntly *Aberdeenshire* A livestock market town in Strathbogie, northwest Aberdeenshire, Huntly is situated at the confluence of the River Bogie and the River Deveron on the main road and rail route to Inverness. Occupying a strategic position on a low-lying plain surrounded by hills, it lies at the junction of ancient routes linking Moray with Strathdon and Aberdeen. The town developed around a defensive site that became the power centre of the Catholic Clan Gordon and was given burgh status in 1545. From 1776 Huntly was extended by the Duke of Gordon who laid it out in a regular grid pattern. There are tourist and sporting facilities, including an 18-hole golf course, a library and museum, a livestock market and walkways out of town to Ba'hill, Battlehill and Clashmach Hill. St Margaret's Catholic

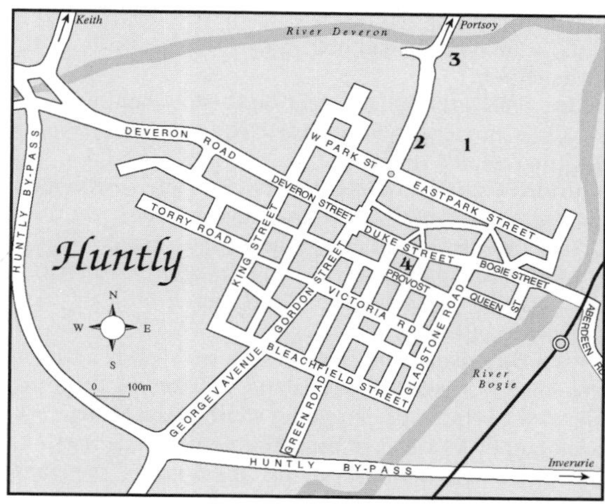

1 *Golf Course*
2 *Community Centre*
3 *Huntly Castle*
4 *Brander Museum*

Church (1834) has fine Spanish decorative panels, and on the south bank of the River Deveron stand the remains of Huntly Castle with its 12th-century Norman motte and bailey, medieval L-plan tower house and defensive earthworks dating from the Civil War. Destroyed by the Earl of Moray in 1452, the castle was rebuilt in a new 'palace' style that was not completed until 1602 when George Gordon, the 1st Marquess of Huntly, returned from exile after supporting the Catholic rebellion against James VI in 1594. It was subsequently abandoned in the 17th century when the Duke of Gordon moved to Fochabers.

Huntly Burn *Perth and Kinross* A stream rising in the Sidlaw Hills, eastern Perth and Kinross, the Huntly Burn flows down through the Braes of the Carse onto the Carse of Gowrie, entering the Tay estuary just west of Kingoodie. Castle Huntly lies close to the burn.

Hurich, Glen *Highland* A valley in the Lochaber district of Highland Council area, Glen Hurich carries the waters of the River Hurich south and west from the settlement of Resourie at Lochan Dubh to Loch Doilet.

Hurlet *Glasgow City* A district in the Nitshill area of Glasgow, Hurlet lies 3 miles (5 km) southeast of Paisley and 6 miles (10 km) southwest of Glasgow city centre.

Hurlford *East Ayrshire* A former railway junction and mining and foundry town, Hurlford is located 2 miles (3 km) east of Kilmarnock near the River Irvine. Now a residential centre, it was once part of the former Barony of Riccarton, which was associated with Clan Wallace during the lifetime of William Wallace (*c.*1272–1305). Local industries include whisky blending and bottling, and the manufacture of clothing.

Hushinish *Western Isles* A locality in the far west of North Harris in the Western Isles, Hushinish (Gael: *Huisinis*) lies to the north of Hushinish Bay (Gael: *Bagh Huisinis*), an inlet at the mouth of West Loch Tarbert, 5 miles (8 km) west of Amhuinnsuide at the end of the B887, and 15 miles (24 km) northwest of Tarbert. Hushnish Point (Gael: *Rubha Huisinis*) extends to the southwest.

Hutton *Scottish Borders* A village in a parish of the same name in the Berwickshire district of Scottish Borders, Hutton lies between the Whiteadder Water and the River Tweed, 6 miles (10 km) west of Berwick-upon-Tweed. To the northwest is Hutton Castle (alternatively Hutton Hall), a former stronghold of the Homes, built in the 16th century.

Huxter *Shetland* A settlement on the Shetland island of Whalsay, Huxter lies to the north of Loch Huxter, a mile (1.5 km) east of Symbister.

Hyndford Bridge *South Lanarkshire* A small settlement located at a crossing on the River Clyde, Hyndford Bridge lies 3 miles (5 km) southeast of Lanark.

Hyndland *Glasgow City* An area in the Partick district of the city of Glasgow, Hyndland lies 3 miles (5 km) northwest of the city centre.

Hynish Bay *Argyll and Bute* A wide and sandy beach on the southeast coast of the island of Tiree in the Inner Hebrides, Hynish Bay stretches south and west from the headland of An t-Ard to the settlement of Balemartine.

Hyvots Bank *City of Edinburgh* A suburb of the city of Edinburgh, Hyvots Bank lies 4 miles (6.5 km) southwest of the city centre.

Ianstown *Moray* Situated on the Moray Firth coast, Ianstown lies adjacent to the settlements of Gordonsburgh and Portessie and is one of a number of old fishing villages that lie on a 3-mile (5-km) stretch of shoreline to the east of Buckie.

Ibrox Stadium *Glasgow City* Located 3 miles (5 km) southwest of Glasgow city centre, Ibrox Stadium is the home of Rangers Football Club. Established in 1873, the club first played at Ibrox in 1890–91. The stadium can hold over 50,400 people, although before seating was installed the record capacity was 118,567 for a League game against Celtic in 1939.

Idoch Water *Aberdeenshire* A river of northern Aberdeenshire, the Idoch Water rises near New Byth then flows southwest through Cuminestown before turning northwest to run on to meet the River Deveron at Turriff. It is over 10 miles (16 km) in length.

Idrigill *Highland* A small settlement on the island of Skye in the Inner Hebrides, Idrigill (or Idrigil) lies on the west side of the Trotternish peninsula, a mile (1.5 km) west of Uig. Ru Idrigill (Gael: *Rhubha Idrigil*) forms a headland to the west at the entrance to Uig Bay.

Idrigill *Highland* A locality at the southern end of the Duirinish peninsula on the western side of the isle of Skye in the Inner Hebrides, Idrigill lies to the east of Ben Idrigill (340 m/1115 ft) and north of Idrigill Point, which extends into the mouth of Loch Bracadale.

Imachar *North Ayrshire* A scattered settlement on the island of Arran in North Ayrshire, Imachar lies on the western coastline of the island, overlooking the Kilbrannan Sound. Pirnmill lies 2 miles (3 km) to the north. Imachar Point extends into the Kilbrannan Sound to the south of Pirnmill.

Inaccessible Pinnacle An alternative name for Sgurr Dearg on the isle of Skye in Highland Council area.

Inch Kenneth *Argyll and Bute* An uninhabited island lying off the west coast of Mull, Inch Kenneth is 55 ha (136 acres) in area and is named after St Kenneth, a contemporary of St Columba. An important ecclesiastical centre, Inch Kenneth was second only to Iona, the monks of Iona farming the island to provide grain. The ruined remains of a chapel and burial ground are located in the southern half of the island.

Inchaffray Abbey *Perth and Kinross* Nothing remains of Inchaffray Abbey in central Perth and Kinross save a mound on the Pow Burn, 6 miles (10 km) east of Crieff. The original abbey stood on an island surrounded by a lake that was famous for its eels. Maurice, Abbot of Inchaffray, was chaplain to King Robert the Bruce and carried the relics of St Fillan before the Scottish army at the Battle of Bannockburn in 1314. A later abbot, Laurence Oliphant, was killed at the Battle of Flodden in 1513, but by this time the abbey's importance was in decline.

Inchard, Loch *Highland* A sea loch on the northwest coast of Sutherland in Highland Council area, Loch Inchard lies to the south of Kinlochbervie with Rhiconich at its head.

Inchbae *Highland* A deer forest in Easter Ross, Inchbae lies to the east of Loch Vaich, 6 miles (10 km) north of Garve.

Inchbare *Angus* A village in the Angus parish of Stracathro, Inchbare lies on the West Water tributary of the River North Esk, 3 miles (5 km) north of Brechin.

Inchbraoch An alternative name for Rossie Island in Angus.

Inchbuie *Stirling* A small island in the River Dochart, Stirling Council area, Inchbuie (or *Innes Buidhe*) is situated by the bridge over the Falls of Dochart in Killin. This was the burial place of the Clan MacNab, which occupied Glen Dochart and Strath Fillan for 800 years.

Inchcailloch *Stirling* A wooded island at the southeast end of Loch Lomond, Inchcailloch lies opposite Balmaha and the mouth of the Endrick Water at the southwest extremity of Stirling Council area. On the island are the ruins of a church in use until 1621 and dedicated to St Kentigern who is said to have lived there. The island is now part of a nature reserve.

Inchcape An alternative name for the Bell Rock in Angus.

Inchcolm *Fife* An island in the Firth of Forth off the south coast of Fife opposite Braefoot Bay, Inchcolm is separated from the mainland by a stretch of water known as Mortimer's Deep. It was the home of a religious community linked with St Colm or St Columba, the 6th-century Abbot of Iona. Alexander I was storm-bound on the island for three days in 1123 and in recognition of the shelter given to him by the hermits promised to establish a monastic settlement in honour of St Columba. Although the king died before the promise could be fulfilled, his brother, David I, later founded a priory here for monks of the Augustinian order. This was eventually erected into an abbey in 1223. The well-preserved abbey and ruins of the 9th-century hermit's cell attract visitors to the island, which can be approached by boat from Aberdour and South Queensferry.

Inchconnachan *Argyll and Bute* A small island of Loch Lomond, Inchconnachan lies to the east of Inchtavannach and to the north of Inchmoan, within Argyll and Bute. The island is mostly forested.

Inchcruin *Stirling* The 'round island' of Inchruin is situated at the southeast end of Loch Lomond, Stirling Council area, immediately west of the larger island of Inchfad.

Inchfad *Stirling* The 'long island' of Inchfad in Stirling Council area is situated at the southeast end of Loch Lomond to the northwest of Inchcailloch and opposite Arrochymore Point.

Inchgalbraith *Argyll and Bute* An islet located in the Argyll and Bute section of Loch Lomond, Inchgalbraith lies between the island of Inchmoan to the northeast and Rossdhu House, located a mile (1.5 km) southwest. There are the remains of a castle.

Inchgarvie Island *City of Edinburgh* Inchgarvie Island lies in the Firth of Forth beneath the Forth Bridge, where the river channel narrows to just a mile (1.5 km) wide between North and South Queensferry. The island occupies a key location for the defence of the upper reaches of the Firth of Forth and a castle was built here c.1490 by James IV. This served as a State prison between 1519 and 1671. Inchgarvie was fortified again in 1779 following the appearance of John Paul Jones' Franco-American fleet in the estuary. Its defences were reconstructed once more to protect the Forth Bridge and the nearby Rosyth Dockyard from air-attack during both World Wars. Inchgarvie was seen as a key staging point in various plans to bridge the River Forth. Foundations for a railway bridge designed by Sir Thomas Bouch (1822–90) were laid on the island in 1878, but following the Tay Bridge disaster and Bouch's disgrace, building was suspended. When, in 1882, work began on a re-designed bridge by William Arrol (1839–1913), Benjamin Baker (1840–1907) and John Fowler (1817-98), one of the huge cantilevers was centred immediately to the west of Inchgarvie and a pier built to allow foundations to be sunk and the structure constructed. Offices, workshops and sleeping accommodation were built on the island to support the construction of the bridge. Today, Inchgarvie is known for its bird life, which includes fulmars, roosting cormorants and grey herons.

Inchinnan *Renfrewshire* A village in Renfrewshire, Inchinnan lies between the River Clyde and the M8, 3 miles (5 km) north of Paisley. The village and parish of the same name are said to take their name from St Inan, a disciple of St Mungo. Inchinnan was an important base in aircraft manufacture.

Inchkeith *Fife* An island in the Firth of Forth, Inchkeith is situated 2 miles (3 km) south of the Fife coastal town of Kinghorn and 4 miles (6.5 km) north of Leith. Capped by a lighthouse first erected in 1803, it is a mile (1.5 km) long and rises to a height of 60 m (190 ft). The island is named after Robert de Keith, to whom it was granted in 1010 by Malcolm II in return for his efforts in fighting off marauding Danes. Later, between 1549 and 1560, it was known to French soldiers garrisoned there as L'Isle des Chevaux ('The Island of Horses'). James IV trained his hawks on Inchkeith and in 1497 the island was used as a refuge for victims of the plague transported from Edinburgh. Thereafter, until the end of World War II, it was used as a military base. Inchkeith was visited in 1773 by Boswell and Johnson, Johnson stalking 'like a giant among the luxuriant thistles and nettles', and in 1817 by Thomas Carlyle who described it as 'prettily savage'.

Inchlaggan *Highland* A scattered settlement of Glen Garry in the Lochaber district of Highland Council area, Inchlaggan lies on the northern shore of Loch Garry 8 miles (13 km) west of Invergarry.

Inchlonaig *Argyll and Bute* The most northerly of the large islands of Loch Lomond, Inchlonaig lies a half-mile (1 km) east of the settlement of Luss. Situated in the Argyll and Bute section of Loch Lomond, the island is predominantly forested. It reaches a high point of 62 m (203 ft).

Inchmahome *Stirling* The largest of the two islands in the Lake of Menteith, Stirling Council area, the wooded Inchmahome is dominated by the ruins of a priory founded in 1238 by Walter Comyn, Earl of Menteith, for the Augustinian order. The priory church built shortly afterwards is dedicated to St Colmoc. In the choir can be found the 13th-century effigies of Sir Walter Stewart, Earl of Menteith, and his wife Mary, and the graveslab of Sir John Drummond (d.1300). Also buried on the island is the noted aristocrat, author, politician and horseman, Robert Bontine Cunninghame Graham (1852–1936). The exotic trees, flowers and bushes that adorn the island were probably planted by the earls of Menteith, who created a pleasure ground on the island that can be approached by boat from Port of Menteith.

Inchmarlo *Aberdeenshire* A mansion house in Royal Deeside, Inchmarlo is situated on the north bank of the River Dee, nearly 2 miles (3 km) west of Banchory.

Inchmarnock *Argyll and Bute* An island in the Firth of Clyde, Inchmarnock is located a mile (1.5 km) to the west of St Ninian's Point, off the west coast of the island of Bute from which it is separated by Inchmarnock Sound. Covering an area of 253 ha (625 acres), the island is relatively flat, the highest point on a central ridge being 60 m (197 ft). Inchmarnock is home to the largest colony of herring gulls in the Firth of Clyde and is a wintering ground for greylag geese. Little remains of the chapel of St Marnoc at Midpark in the centre of the island. A Bronze Age cairn discovered at Northpark held the remains of 'The Queen of the Inch', a 3500-year-old woman decorated in a jet bead necklace and with a dagger.

Inchmarnock Sound *Argyll and Bute* Inchmarnock Sound is the name given to a stretch of water that separates the island of Inchmarnock from the western coastline of the island of Bute. The sound is a mile (1.5 km) across at its widest point.

Inchmarnock Water *Argyll and Bute* The Inchmarnock Water is the name given to the expanse of water that lies to the west of the island of Inchmarnock, Argyll and Bute. It stretches from the island westwards to the Kintyre peninsula.

Inchmickery *City of Edinburgh* An islet of the Firth of Forth, Inchmickery lies 2 miles (3 km) northwest of Granton, a mile (1.5 km) northeast of Cramond Island and a mile (1.5 km) southeast of Inchcolm. It is now an RSPB reserve and was established to protect its breeding terns.

Inchmoan *Argyll and Bute* The island of Inchmoan lies to the south of the islands of Inchtavannach and Inchconnachan within the Argyll and Bute section of Loch Lomond. Between the island and the chapel at Rossdhu House on the western shore of Loch Lomond lies the islet of Inchgalbraith.

Inchmurrin *West Dunbartonshire* An island at the southern end of Loch Lomond, Inchmurrin is the largest and most southerly of the islands in the loch. Formerly used as a deer park by the dukes of Montrose, the island is the site of a ruined former stronghold of the earls of Lennox and the site of a chapel dedicated to St Mirrin.

Inchnadamph *Highland* A village in the Sutherland district of Highland Council area, Inchnadamph lies at the head of Loch Assynt 9 miles (14 km) east of Lochinver. A mile (1.5 km) to the northwest stand the ruined remains of Ardvreck Castle, while to the east lies the Inchnadamph Forest. An extensive system of limestone caves lies a mile (1.5 km) to the east of the village.

Inchnadamph Forest *Highland* A deer forest of the Sutherland district of Highland Council area, the Inchnadamph Forest lies to the east of the settlement of Inchnadamph. The peaks of Ben More Assynt and Conival lie to the southeast of the forest.

Inchrory *Moray* A hunting lodge in the uplands of Moray, Inchrory lies in a remote corner of the Grampians close to the River Avon near its junction with the Burn of the Little Fergie. The lodge dates from 1847, but a hundred years earlier it was the site of a military camp designed to prevent cattle smugglers using Glen Avon as a routeway over the hills.

Inchtalla *Stirling* The small island of Inchtalla in the Lake of Menteith, Stirling Council area, is entirely occupied by the remains of a castle that was a seat of the earls of Menteith during the 16th and 17th centuries.

Inchtavannach *Argyll and Bute* Inchtavannach is one of the larger islands of Loch Lomond, Argyll and Bute. The island is located on the western side of the loch and faces the settlement of Aldochlay. It is privately owned and mostly wooded. The Inchtavannach Channel separates the island from the western shore of the loch.

Inchture *Perth and Kinross* A village in the Carse of Gowrie, southeast Perth and Kinross, Inchture lies 8 miles (13 km) southwest of Dundee. Derived from the Gaelic innis-tuir, meaning 'island of the tower', there was little evidence of either when the village was rebuilt on the line of a new toll road in the early 19th century. Until 1916 there was a horse-drawn tram link between the Dundee–Perth railway and Inchture from Inchture Station. To the north of Inchture is Rossie Priory, the home of the Kinnaird family, one of whom, Douglas Kinnaird, was banker and literary agent for Lord Byron.

Inchtuthill *Perth and Kinross* The site of a Roman fortress, Inchtuthill lies on the north side of the River Tay, a mile (1.5 km) southeast of Spittalfield. It dates from about AD 83.

Inchvuilt *Highland* A scattered settlement of the Inverness district of Highland Council area, Inchvuilt lies on the course of the River Farrar, 2 miles (3 km) east of the dam at the head of Loch Monar.

Inchyra *Perth and Kinross* A locality at the southern edge of the Sidlaw Hills, southeast Perth and Kinross, Inchyra Estate lies to the north of the River Tay, 4 miles (6.5 km) east of Perth. Inchyra House was built *c.*1810 for Edinburgh lawyer John Anderson, its frontage resembling that of the Commercial Bank in Edinburgh's New Assembly Close. Southwest of the house is a Bronze Age burial mound known as the Witch Knowe.

Indaal, Loch *Argyll and Bute* A large sea loch on the west coast of Islay, Loch Indaal extends inland from the northwest of Laggan Bay and lies to the east of the Rhinns of Islay. Almost splitting the island in half, its main settlements are Bridgend and Bowmore.

Ingale Skerry *Orkney* A rocky islet of the Orkney Islands, Ingale Skerry lies off the south coast of the island of Stronsay, a mile (1.5 km) southwest of Lamb Head and a mile (1.5 km) southeast of Tor Ness. To the north, separating the islet from Stronsay, is the Ingale Sound, while to the south is the Auskerry Sound.

Inga Ness *Orkney* A headland of the west coast of the island of Westray in the Orkney Islands, Inga Ness lies 4 miles (6.5 km) south of Noup Head.

Inganess Bay *Orkney* A bay located on the northeast coastline of the Orkney Mainland, Inganess Bay lies 2 miles (3 km) east of Kirkwall. At the head of the bay is Kirkwall Airport.

Ingleston *Dumfries and Galloway* A locality in Dumfries and Galloway, Ingleston lies to the south of the New Abbey Pow near its confluence with the River Nith, 10 miles (16 km) south of Dumfries. Criffel rises to the southwest.

Inglismaldie *Aberdeenshire* A house in the Howe of the Mearns, southeast Aberdeenshire, Inglismaldie lies close to the River North Esk and the border between Aberdeenshire and Angus, 4 miles (6.5 km) west of Marykirk. Built in the late 16th century, it was erected on the church lands of St Maldie, which were acquired in 1635 by Sir John Carnegie, Sheriff of Forfar and Earl of Northesk. The original Eccles Maldie, or Chapel of St Maldie, was replaced by a 19th-century extension to the house.

Ingliston *City of Edinburgh* A locality and former estate lying 7 miles (11 km) west of Edinburgh, Ingliston lies a half-mile (1 km) southwest of Edinburgh Airport and is home to a motor-racing circuit and also the permanent showground for the annual Royal Highland Show.

Inishail *Argyll and Bute* An island at the north end of Loch Awe, Inishail lies opposite Ardanaiseig at the point where the northwest-running arm of the loch that reaches the Pass of Brander joins the main loch. A ruined church dedicated to St Pindoca stands on the island.

Inkstack *Highland* A small settlement in Caithness, Inkstack lies on the northern coast 4 miles (6.5 km) northeast of Castletown.

Innellan *Argyll and Bute* A village and holiday resort of Argyll and Bute, Innellan lies on the western shore of the Firth of Clyde, 4 miles (6.5 km) south of Dunoon and directly opposite Wemyss Bay.

Inner Hebrides The name given to the inner islands off the west coast of Scotland in Highland and Argyll and Bute council areas. The chief islands are Skye, Mull, Islay, Jura, Raasay, Canna, Rum, Eigg, Muck, Coll, Tiree, Iona, Colonsay and Gigha. They are separated from the Outer Hebrides by the Sea of the Hebrides, the Little Minch and the Minch. There are also numerous smaller islands, islets and rocks.

Inner Holm *Orkney* An islet of the Orkney Islands, Inner Holm lies on the eastern side of Stromness Harbour on the southwest coastline of the Orkney Mainland. The islet of Outer Holm lies to the south.

Inner Sound The body of water that separates the island of Raasay from Wester Ross.

Innerleithen *Scottish Borders* A large village in Scottish Borders, Innerleithen lies 7 miles (11 km) east of Peebles and 11 miles (18 km) west of Galashiels at the confluence of the River Tweed and Leithen Water. Innerleithen developed as an important woollen, spinning and knitwear centre and is most famous for its medicinal spring, made famous in Sir Walter Scott's novel *St Ronan's Well* (1823) and refurbished in 1826. Malcolm IV is thought to have given the church to the monks of Kelso in 1159 and to have included the right to sanctuary, allegedly in honour of a son who drowned in the river. Innerleithen holds the annual Border Games, which began in 1827 and include the 'Cleikum Ceremony' in which St Ronan drives out the devil. Robert Smail's Printing Works in the High Street of Innerleithen (founded 1837) was acquired by the National Trust for Scotland in 1986. Nearby Traquair House is Scotland's oldest inhabited house.

Innerleven *Fife* Situated at the mouth of the River Leven on the coast of Fife, the settlement of Innerleven lies between Methil in the west and Leven in the east. Also known as Dubbieside, Innerleven is linked to the town of Leven by the Bawbee Brig, which crosses the River Leven here. The Methil Power Station and Industrial Estate lie adjacent.

Innermessan *Dumfries and Galloway* A locality in Dumfries and Galloway, Innermessan lies to the east of Loch Ryan, 3 miles (5 km) northeast of Stranraer. The site of a much larger ancient settlement and a World War II prisoner-of-war camp, its castle was a stronghold of the Agnews of Lochnaw.

Innerpeffray *Perth and Kinross* A locality close to the River Earn in the Strathearn district of Perth and Kinross, Innerpeffray lies 3 miles (5 km) southeast of Crieff. Innerpeffray Library, founded *c.*1680 by David Drummond, 3rd Lord Maddertie, was for centuries the oldest free lending library in Scotland. The Collegiate Chapel of St Mary adjacent to the library was rebuilt in 1507–08 by the Drummond family. Also adjacent is an old school building erected *c.*1680 and rebuilt in 1847. In 1762 the library was moved from the loft of the chapel to its present location, the collection of rare books being administered from 1694 by a private trust. Although lending ceased in 1968, the Innerpeffray Library continues as a reference library. Nearby are the ruins of Innerpeffray Castle, probably built for John Drummond in the mid-15th century and heightened for James Drummond, 1st Lord Maddertie, in 1610.

Innerwick *East Lothian* A village built on two adjacent ridges on the North Sea coast of East Lothian, Innerwick lies 4 miles (6.5 km) southeast of Dunbar near the Torness Nuclear Power Station. A designated conservation area with a parish church dating from 1784, many of its buildings are in a distinctive pink sandstone with orange pantiled roofs. Innerwick Castle, which lies close by on the Thornton Burn, was a stronghold of the Stewarts and then the Hamiltons, but was captured and destroyed by Edward Seymour, Duke of Somerset, in 1548.

Innerwick *Perth and Kinross* A locality in Glen Lyon, Perth and Kinross, Innerwick lies by the River Lyon, 7 miles (11 km) west of Fortingall. The church here is an example of a Thomas Telford-designed Parliamentary church dating from the 1820s. In its porch is a Celtic bell from an earlier church that existed at nearby Bridge of Balgie.

Innishewan *Stirling* A locality in Glendochart, Stirling Council area, Innishewan House lies immediately north of the River Dochart near the main road from Killin to Crianlarich. The MacNabs of Innishewan are buried in an enclosure here.

Innocent Railway, the The Innocent Railway linking Edinburgh and Dalkeith, the first railway line to be built in Edinburgh, derived its name from its record for safety. Built in 1831, the traction was still provided by horses when the line was sold to the North British Railway in 1845. Planned by engineer Robert Stevenson for a group of investors led by Walter, 5th Duke of Buccleuch (1806–84), the line ran south from St Leonards Station and Goods Yards (closed in 1968) through a tunnel to Duddingston, Craigmillar, Niddrie, Newcraighall and on to Dalkeith. With an extension from Niddrie to Leith, which opened in 1838, the line linked the Midlothian coalfield with the city of Edinburgh and the port of Leith. Parts of the line, including this latter section, are still in operation today. The Craigmillar–St Leonards section was converted into a walking and cycling route in the 1980s.

Insh *Aberdeenshire* A village of Badenoch and Strathspey, Insh lies 4 miles (6.5 km) east of Kingussie in the upper valley of the River Spey to the west of the Cairngorm Mountains. The nearby Insh Marshes are one of the most extensive river marshes in the UK, with abundant wetland and woodland birdlife protected by the RSPB.

Insh, Loch *Highland* A loch in the middle reaches of the River Spey, Loch Insh lies immediately south of Kincraig and 5 miles (8 km) northwest of Kingussie. A significant watersports centre was established on the east shore of the loch in 1969. Inshriach Forest lies to the east and the village of Insh lies on the south side of the Spey 2 miles (3 km) to the south. The Insh Marshes between Kingussie and Kincraig comprise the most important area of natural floodplain wetland in Britain. Extending to 837 ha (2068 acres), the Insh Marshes were designated a National Nature Reserve in 2003.

Insh Island *Argyll and Bute* An uninhabited island in the Firth of Lorn in Argyll and Bute, Insh Island lies a mile (1.5 km) northeast of Seil, from which it is separated by the Sound of Insh.

Inver *Aberdeenshire* A small roadside settlement in Royal Deeside, Inver is located on the A93, 3 miles (5 km) west of Crathie. It is the site of an old coaching inn.

Inver *Highland* A small village of Easter Ross, Inver lies 6 miles (10 km) east of Tain on Inver Bay, an inlet on the southern side of the Dornoch Firth.

Inver *Highland* A locality on the east coast of Caithness, Inver lies to the northeast of Dunbeath.

Inver *Perth and Kinross* A village in Strathtay, Perth and Kinross, Inver lies on the south side of the River Tay near its junction with the River Braan, a mile (1.5 km) from Dunkeld. A ferry once operated here and a former coaching inn still dominates the village square. Inver was the birthplace of the gifted musician Charles Mackintosh (1839–1922) and the renowned Scottish fiddler Neil Gow (1727–1807). Nearby is a woodland walk leading to a folly known as The Hermitage.

Inver, River *Highland* A river in the Assynt district of Sutherland, Highland Council area, the Inver flows west from Loch Assynt to Loch Inver, a sea loch on the west coast with the village of Lochinver at its head.

Inverailort *Highland* A location in the Moidart district of Highland Council area, Inverailort lies just south of the village of Lochailort at the head of Loch Ailort. During World War II, Inverailort House was one of several country houses in the area used as a training base by agents of the Special Operations Executive prior to being landed in occupied Europe on missions of sabotage.

Inveraldie *Angus* A small village of southern Angus, Inveraldie lies on the site of buildings once associated with RAF Tealing, a World War II training base situated a half-mile (1 km) south of Tealing and 4 miles (6.5 km) north of Dundee.

Inveralligin *Highland* A locality in Wester Ross, Inveralligin lies on the north shore of Upper Loch Torridon.

Inverallochy *Aberdeenshire* A fishing village in Aberdeenshire, Inverallochy lies on the Buchan coast, 3 miles (5 km) southeast of Fraserburgh. Within the village, Maggie's Hoosie is a survival of an early 19th-century fisher-wife's cottage, and to the south are the ruins of Inverallochy Castle, a stronghold of the Comyn family.

Inveramsay *Aberdeenshire* A locality in the Garioch district of Aberdeenshire, Inveramsay lies on the Urie Water, 2 miles (3 km) northwest of Inverurie, and comprises Inveramsay Farm, Milton of Inveramsay and Mains of Inveramsay.

Inveran *Highland* A locality in the Sutherland district of Highland Council area, Inveran lies at the junction of the rivers Shin and Oykel. It is the site of the Shin Hydro-Electric Power Station.

Inveraray *Argyll and Bute* A small town of whitewashed houses in Argyll and Bute, Inveraray lies near the head of Loch Fyne opposite St Catherines to which it was once linked by a ferry. Created a burgh of barony in 1474 and a royal burgh in 1753, Inveraray was rebuilt from 1744 to a regular plan conceived by Roger Morris and William Adam to allow the 3rd Duke of Argyll to build a new castle on the site of the old town. The castle, built between 1744 and 1789, was originally also designed by Morris and William Adam, but after their deaths in 1748 was completed by John Adam and Robert Mylne, both of whom also worked on the design of the town, along with Robert's brother, William. Buildings of interest include the Great Inn (1755), the Dubh Loch Bridge (1757), Inveraray Courthouse and Jail, and the two-part parish church (1802) where English and Gaelic services were conducted side-by-side. The town, which developed in association with linen weaving, herring fishing and tourism, was the administrative centre of the former county of Argyll until 1975. Steamer excursions from Gourock visited Inveraray until the 1960s, and in 2000 a steel-hulled schooner was moored at the pier as a marine heritage centre. Inveraray was the birthplace of the novelist Neil Munro (1864–1930), author of the *Para Handy* stories.

Inverarity *Angus* A locality in an Angus parish of the same name, Inverarity and its wide-bodied church lie on the Kerbet Water, 8 miles (13 km) north of Dundee and 4 miles (6.5 km) south of Forfar.

Inverarnan *Stirling* A roadside location with a drovers' inn in Stirling Council area, Inverarnan is situated by the River Falloch at the south end of Glenfalloch, near the head of Loch Lomond and nearly 9 miles (14 km) north of Tarbet.

Inverbeg *Argyll and Bute* A small settlement on the west side of Loch Lomond, Inverbeg lies 3 miles (5 km) north of Luss at the entrance to Glen Douglas. There is a passenger ferry link with Rowardennan.

Inverbervie *Aberdeenshire* A royal burgh in the southern Aberdeenshire parish of Bervie, Inverbervie is situated at the mouth of the Bervie Water on the A92, 12 miles (19 km) north of Montrose. Also known locally as Bervie, the town received its first royal charter in 1362 from David II, over 20 years after he landed here on returning from exile in France. The king is said to have been shipwrecked at the base of Bervie Brow, a headland flanking the northern shore of Bervie Bay with placenames that include King's Step, Kinghornie Farm and Craig David. A Carmelite friary once stood at Friar's Dubh near Bervie Bridge, and on the shore of Bervie Bay stands Hallgreen Castle, a 14th-century stronghold of the Dunnets that passed to the Rait family in the 15th century. Inverbervie developed from a market town to an industrial centre following the establishment of Scotland's first flax mill here in 1788, and today has textile and food-processing industries. In 1969 Sir Francis Chichester unveiled a memorial to Inverbervie's most famous son, Hercules Linton (b.1831), builder of the *Cutty Sark* tea clipper.

Inverboyndie *Aberdeenshire* A village in northwest Aberdeenshire, Inverboyndie lies at the mouth of the Burn of Boyndie, a mile (1.5 km) west of Banff.

Invercauld *Aberdeenshire* A locality at the western end of Royal Deeside, Invercauld lies on the north side of the River Dee, 2 miles (3 km) east of Braemar. An earlier castle on this site was a seat of the earls of Mar. The building was extended by the Farquharsons during the 19th century, and in its garden is a heather-thatch summerhouse. Old Invercauld Bridge, built in 1753 by Major Caulfield to link Blairgowrie with Corgarff, was superseded in 1859 by a new bridge built at the expense of Prince Albert to a design by J. F. Beattie.

Inverchoran *Highland* A settlement in the valley of the River Meig in the northwest Highlands, Inverchoran lies to the east of Loch Beannachan, 8 miles (13 km) southeast of Achnasheen.

Inverclyde *Area: 163 sq. km. (63 sq. miles)* A local government area in west-central Scotland, Inverclyde occupies a coastal plain on the Firth of Clyde backed by hilly moorland. It is bounded to the west and north by the Firth of Clyde, to the east and southeast by Renfrewshire, and to the southwest by North Ayrshire. Inverclyde is the third-smallest council area in size, the eighth-smallest in population and the ninth-highest in population density, with 68 per cent of its land used for agriculture, most of which is grassland and peatland. About one-sixth of its territory is developed, primarily for urban use. The population of Inverclyde is largely concentrated in the coastal settlements of Greenock (administrative centre), Gourock, Port Glasgow, Inverkip and Wemyss Bay, and the inland settlements of Kilmalcolm and Quarrier's Village. Ferry terminals offer access to the Highlands and islands, and port facilities handle both cruise ships and container transport. The upland interior forms part of the Clyde-Muirshiel Regional Park, and the main bodies of water are Loch Thom and the Gryfe Reservoirs, to the south of which rises Creuch Hill (441 m/1446 ft), the highest point in the council area. Inverclyde was created as a district of Strathclyde Region in 1975 from the burghs of Gourock, Greenock and Port Glasgow and from a part of the old Renfrewshire County. In 1996 it became a separate local government area. In addition to tourism, shipbuilding and port trade, there are major electronics and computer-based industries.

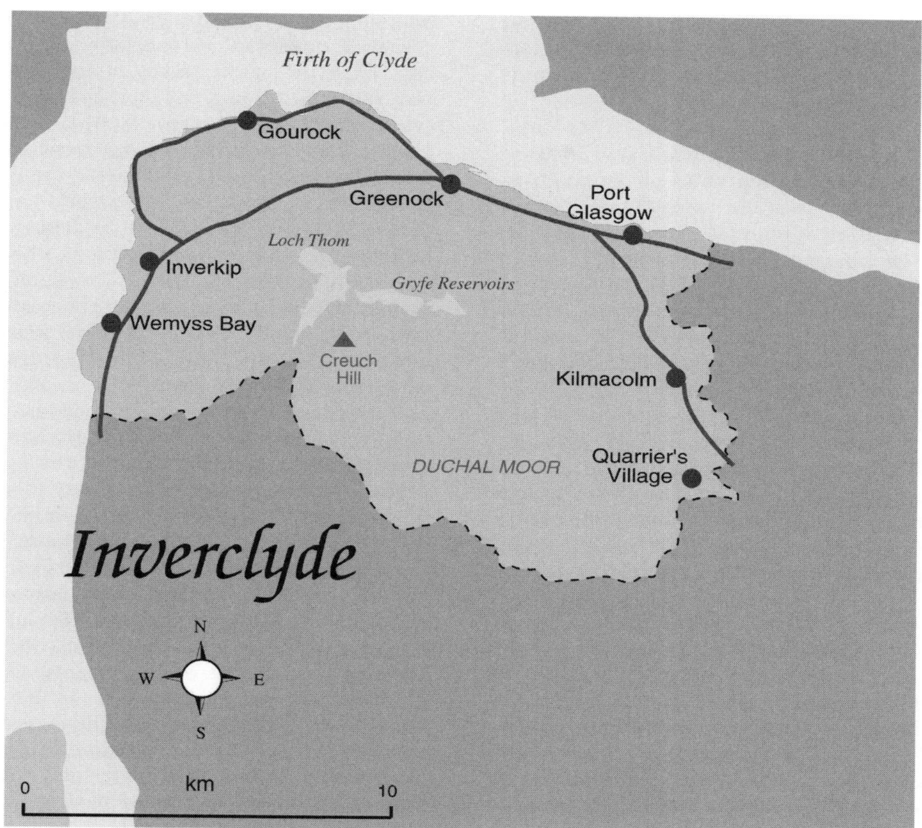

Inverdruie *Highland* A hamlet in the Strathspey district of Highland Council area, Inverdruie lies near the mouth of the River Druie, a mile (1.5 km) southeast of Aviemore. There is a fish farm, visitor centre and the small Episcopalian Chapel of St John, designed by the architect Sir Ninian Comper and dedicated in 1930.

Inverernan *Aberdeenshire* A mansion house in the Strathdon district of Aberdeenshire, Inverernan lies close to the River Don near its junction with the Ernan Water, 2 miles (3 km) southwest of Strathdon.

Inveresk *East Lothian* An historic village in East Lothian, Inveresk lies on the River Esk to the south of Musselburgh, of which it is now a suburb. The remains of both a 1st-century AD settlement and fort are of considerable archaeological interest. The village, which comprises a remarkable collection of 18th- and 19th-century listed buildings, is a designated conservation area. Noteworthy buildings include St Michael's Church, Inveresk Lodge and Garden (1683) and the 18th-century Inveresk House, built around a 16th-century core and later used by Oliver Cromwell as his headquarters in 1650. There is an industrial estate occupying former mills and to the east is Edenhall Hospital.

Inverewe *Highland* A house and 20-ha (50-acre) garden near Poolewe in Wester Ross, Inverewe Garden was laid out by Osgood Mackenzie from 1862 on a site by Loch Ewe that benefits from the warming effect of the Gulf Stream. Palm trees and giant yuccas grow alongside agapanthus from South Africa, American avalanche lilies, beds of the giant Chatham Island forget-me-not, Chilean flame flowers, Chinese magnolias, eucalypts from Tasmania, Japanese hydrangeas, oleria from New Zealand and rhododendrons from the Himalayas. Seeds were obtained from noted plant collectors such as George Forrest (1873–1932). The Scottish baronial Inverewe House was destroyed by fire and rebuilt in 1935 by Mackenzie's son-in-law. On his death in 1922, Osgood Mackenzie bequeathed the gardens at Inverewe to the National Trust for Scotland.

Inverey *Aberdeenshire* A hamlet in Crathie parish, Aberdeenshire, Inverey lies to the south of the River Dee opposite Mar Lodge and 4 miles (6.5 km) west of Braemar. The Ey Burn flows through the settlement to meet the River Dee.

Inverfarigaig *Highland* A settlement on the southeast shore of Loch Ness, Inverfarigaig lies at the mouth of the River Farigaig, 2 miles (3 km) northeast of Foyers. There are hydro-electric works and a forest exhibition centre nearby.

Invergarry *Highland* A village in the Lochaber district of Highland Council area, Invergarry lies at the foot of Glen Garry by the River Garry near where it enters Loch Oich. Nearby Invergarry Castle was the seat of the Macdonalds of Glengarry. Nearby is the Tobar nan Ceann or Well of the Seven Heads, a monument erected in 1815 to commemorate an incident known as the Keppoch murders, associated with local clan feuds.

Invergelder *Aberdeenshire* A locality in Royal Deeside, Aberdeenshire, Invergelder lies at the junction of the Gelder Burn with the River Dee, 2 miles (3 km) southwest of Crathie.

Invergeldie *Perth and Kinross* A locality in Glen

Lednock, Perth and Kinross, Invergeldie Lodge sits close to the Invergeldie Burn, which joins the River Lednock as it flows down towards the River Earn and the village of Comrie 4 miles (6.5 km) to the southeast.

Invergordon *Highland* A town in Easter Ross, Invergordon lies 11 miles (18 km) northeast of Dingwall adjacent to the sheltered deep water of the Cromarty Firth. The modern town was laid out in the 18th century by Sir William Gordon of Embo, who replaced the older settlement of Inverbreakie (or Innerbrachie). A harbour built in 1828 was expanded in 1857 and the town developed in association with port trade, whisky distilling and coaching travel. Boosted by the arrival of the railway in 1863, Invergordon subsequently became a fuelling and repair base for naval cruisers during World War I. During World War II flying boats were based here and during the 1960s and 1970s whisky distilling, aluminium smelting and oil-rig construction brought prosperity to Invergordon. The smelter closed in 1981 but cargo trade and the berthing of summer cruise liners continue to supplement whisky distilling, food processing and microelectronics as major sources of employment.

Invergowrie *Perth and Kinross* A dormitory village on the north shore of the Firth of Tay to the west of Dundee, Invergowrie was formerly incorporated with the City of Dundee. Said to have been a royal point of embarkation at which Alexander I planned to build a palace, Invergowrie was gifted to the monks of Scone in the Middle Ages. Its church was allegedly founded by St Bonifacius in the 8th century, and in the ancient churchyard are two large stones known as the Ewes (or Yowes) of Gowrie. Thomas the Rhymer predicted in the 13th century that 'When the Yowes o' Gowrie come to land, The day o' judgement's near at hand.' Another stone to the north of Invergowrie is associated with a local tale describing how the Devil flung a huge boulder from Fife with the intention of destroying the church. Invergowrie tollhouse stands nearby on the south side of the former Perth–Dundee turnpike road. The Scottish Crop Research Institute operates a facility here.

Invergowrie Bay *Perth and Kinross/Dundee City* A bay on the north side of the Firth of Tay, Invergowrie Bay lies between Invergowrie and Dundee, straddling the border between Perth and Kinross and Dundee City.

Inverhadden *Perth and Kinross* A locality in Perth and Kinross, Inverhadden (or Innerhadden) House lies a mile (1.5 km) to the southeast of Kinloch Rannoch. Close by are the remains of a prehistoric burial mound known as Seomar na Stainge ('chamber of the ditch').

Inverharity *Angus* A hamlet in Glen Isla, Angus, Inverharity lies to the east of the River Isla, 2 miles (3 km) north of Kirkton of Glenisla. Nearby are Forter Castle, Glen Isla House and a field in which the annual Glen Isla Games are held.

Inverie *Highland* A hamlet of Knoydart in Highland Council area, Inverie lies on the northern shore of Loch Nevis, northwest of Mallaig.

Inverie River *Highland* A small river on the Knoydart peninsula in the west Highlands, the Inverie River flows westwards out of Loch an Dubh-Lochain for a distance of 3 miles (5 km) to enter Loch Nevis at Inverie Bay.

Inverkeilor *Angus* A village in an Angus parish of the same name, Inverkeilor lies on the Lunan Water, 6 miles (10 km) north of Arbroath. Its asymmetrical church with a row of carved stone coats of arms has a kirkyard containing the ornate tombs of the Carnegie, Bruce-Gardyne, Lindsay, Raitt and Ramsay families.

Inverkeithing *Fife* A royal burgh in western Fife, Inverkeithing is situated on a hill overlooking the Inner Bay of Inverkeithing Bay, an inlet of the Firth of Forth. Given royal charters by William the Lion in 1139 and Robert III in 1399, it is one of the oldest royal burghs in Scotland, with historical associations that date back to Roman times. Agricola, Roman Governor of Britain, is thought to have set up a camp here between AD 78 and 87. Little remains of the town's medieval walls which were demolished in the 16th century, but notable historic landmarks include St Peter's Kirk, dating from the 5th century AD when a church was founded here by St Erat, a follower of St Ninian; the Scottish baronial Fordell Lodging, home of the Hendersons, who were hereditary provosts of Inverkeithing; the Friary (housing a local museum) and Friary Garden; the Town House (1770); the Mercat Cross (c.1400); Thomsoun's House (1617) with its cap-housed stair tower; and the Civic Centre (1962). The building in the High Street now known as the Royal Hotel was the birthplace in 1735 of Samuel Greig, 'The Father of the Russian Navy', and a cottage in Heriot Street was the home of the parents of the Scottish missionary Robert Moffat, who was the first man to translate the Bible into an African language and whose daughter married David Livingstone. Inverkeithing once held five annual fairs, of which the only one to survive is the August Lammas Fair, an event that still features the traditional Hat and Ribbon Race. Now a centre of paper making, engineering and quarrying with a commuter railway station, Inverkeithing's Inner Bay was for many years a centre of shipbreaking.

Inverkeithny *Aberdeenshire* A village of western Aberdeenshire, Inverkeithny lies at the junction of the Burn of Forgue with the River Deveron, 7 miles (11 km) west of Turriff and 3 miles (5 km) south of Aberchirder.

Inverkip *Inverclyde* A coastal village of Inverclyde, Inverkip is situated at the mouth of the River Kip where it enters the Firth of Clyde, 6 miles (10 km) southwest of Greenock. Its lands were granted to the monks of Paisley Abbey in the 12th century. The village was also a centre for fishing and smuggling and, in the 17th century, was the scene of witch hunts. It developed as a seaside resort with the arrival of the railway in the 1860s and is today a yachting centre. Notable buildings include Inverkip Castle (on the Ardgowan Estate), home of the Shaw Stewart family, and Ardgowan House (1748). Inverkip Power Station, Scotland's first oil-fired power station, lies between Inverkip and Wemyss Bay.

Inverleith *City of Edinburgh* A district of Edinburgh, Inverleith lies between Canonmills and Trinity, with Warriston to the east. Inverleith House lies within the grounds of the Royal Botanic Garden, less than a half mile (1 km) north of the New Town. The house was built in 1774 for James Rocheid, his family having owned the Inverleith Estate since 1665. Part of the estate was purchased for the Botanic Garden c.1820. The garden was extended and the house became the residence of its Regius Keeper. Inverleith House was the home of the National Gallery of Modern Art from 1960 until 1984. Inverleith Park, with an area of 22 ha (54 acres), is one of Scotland's largest urban parks. It was purchased by the city in 1889 and laid out to include playing fields, tree-lined walkways and a sizeable pond. The northwest quadrant of the park was later given over to small allotment gardens, which are rented by the city to local residents for growing fruit and vegetables. The park is the venue of the Edinburgh Children's Festival held each May.

Inverlochlarig *Stirling* A hamlet on the River Larig, east of the head of Loch Lomond in Stirling, Inverlochlarig lies 6 miles (10 km) southeast of Crianlarich and is believed to be the place where Rob Roy Macgregor died in 1734.

Inverlochlarig Burn *Stirling* Rising in the Braes of Balquhidder to the northwest of Loch Voil, Stirling Council area, Inverlochlarig Burn flows south through Inverlochlarig Glen to join the River Larig at Inverlochlarig, 10 miles (16 km) west of Balquhidder village.

Inverlochy Castle *Highland* Situated a mile (1.5 km) to the north of Fort William at the southwest end of the Great Glen, Inverlochy Castle was built by the Comyn family and dates from the mid-13th century. It is one of the oldest stone castles in Scotland. Built as a square courtyard with round corner towers, it was also held by the Clan Gordon. It now lies in a ruinous state. A new castle was built a mile (1.5 km) to the northeast in 1863 by Lord Abinger. Visited by Queen Victoria in 1873, this building is now a country house hotel.

Invermark Castle *Angus* Situated in a remote location in the Grampians, Invermark Castle lies at the head of Glen Mark where it meets Glen Esk, just to the east of Loch Lee, 16 miles (26 km) northwest of Laurencekirk. The castle was built *c*.1526 by the Lindsay family. It sheltered David Lindsay after he had killed Lord Spynie in Edinburgh in 1607 following a long-standing quarrel, and James Carnegie, Lord Balnamoon, who was being sought by Government troops after the Battle of Culloden in 1746. Invermark shooting lodge is situated nearby on the Dalhousie Estate.

Invermay *Perth and Kinross* An estate on the northern edge of the Ochil Hills, central Perth and Kinross, Invermay lies in the wooded glen of the Water of May, a mile (1.5 km) southeast of Forteviot. Invermay House dates from the late 18th century and nearby are some interesting outbuildings that include a neo-Gothic gazebo (1804), a U-plan stable block, a thatched dairy and dovecote (1803) and two West Lodges (1803). The 16th-century old house of Invermay faces the new house. Set within an attractive wooded landscape and the subject of a ballad entitled *The Birks of Invermay*, Invermay was described in the *Old Statistical Account* (1798) as 'one of the most romantic and pleasant spots in this part of Perthshire'. A deep gully known as the Humble Bumble was a focal point for the designs of landscape gardeners such as Walter Nicol, who in 1802 laid out a new approach to the house and other features. Sir Walter Scott (1771–1832) stayed here after crossing the Ochils by the Wallace Road.

Invermoriston *Highland* The village of Invermoriston is located on the River Moriston, a mile (1.5 km) from its mouth on Loch Ness, 8 miles (13 km) north of Fort Augustus and within Highland Council area. The village is famed for the waterfalls of the River Moriston and for the old Telford Bridge, built in 1813, which, although partially ruined, can still be used by pedestrians.

Invernaver *Highland* A hamlet near the north coast of the Sutherland district of Highland Council area, Invernaver lies at the mouth of the River Naver a mile (1.5 km) south of Bettyhill. The Invernaver National Nature Reserve designated in 1960 is nearby.

Inverness *Highland* Situated near the mouth of the River Ness, 157 miles (253 km) north of Edinburgh, Inverness was designated a city in the year 2000. The administrative centre of Highland Council area, it lies at a strategic location in the communications network of the Highlands at the northern end of the Caledonian Canal. Inverness became the centre of a sheriffdom with royal burgh status in the 12th century, and a Dominican priory was founded here in 1233. The town developed from the 18th century in association with malting, the manufacture of textiles, coaching trade and port trade. The building of the Caledonian Canal was a boost to Inverness, and a steamer service linking the town with Glasgow commenced in 1824. In 1855 the railway reached Inverness, bringing with it industry and tourism. Buildings of interest include Balnain House, Abertarff House (1592), Inverness Museum and Art Gallery, and Eden Court Theatre (1978). The University of the Highlands and Islands, based in Inverness, went online in 1997 as a centre of distance learning. As the 'Capital of the Highlands', Inverness continues to expand as a centre of local government, tourism, market trade and industry. Inverness Airport lies 10 miles (16 km) to the east.

Inverness-shire Formerly the largest county in Scotland, Inverness-shire included a section of the Highlands and parts of the Inner and Outer Hebrides. Its county town was Inverness. In 1974 it was divided between the Western Isles Authority and Highland Region, the latter containing the

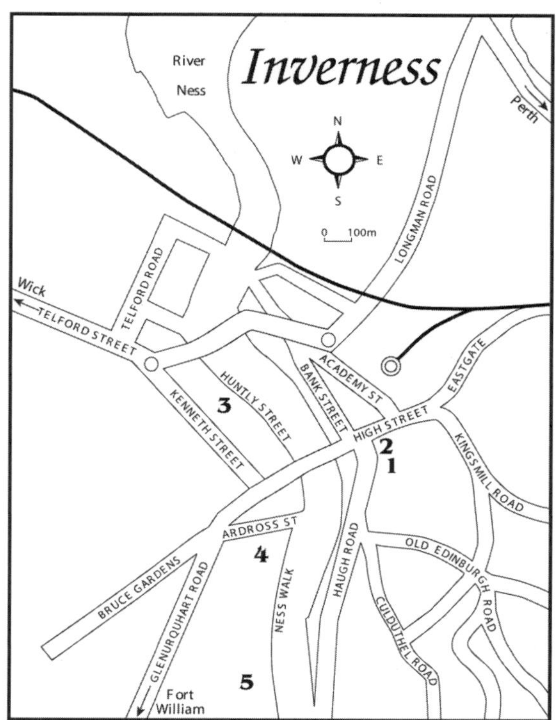

1 *Inverness Castle*
2 *Inverness Museum and Art Gallery*
3 *Balnain House*
4 *Eden Court Theatre*
5 *Bught Park*

much smaller Inverness District. In the local government reorganisation of 1996 it remained divided between the Western Isles and Highland Council Areas.

Inverpolly *Highland* A National Nature Reserve in the Assynt district of Highland Council area, Inverpolly occupies a remote area of bog, moorland, woodland and mountain peaks to the south of Lochinver. There is a geological centre at Knockan Cliff. Designated in 1961, the reserve covers an area of 10,857 ha (26,827 acres).

Inverquharity *Angus* A locality on the edge of the Braes of Angus, Inverquharity lies between the River South Esk and Quharity Burn, 3 miles (5 km) northwest of Kirriemuir. Inverquharity Castle, which dates from the 15th century and was restored in the 1960s, was a stronghold of the Ogilvies until the early 18th century.

Invershin *Highland* A scattered settlement with a railway station in southern Sutherland, Invershin lies just over 6 miles (10 km) south of Lairg on the River Shin near its junction with the River Oykel. The motte of the ancient Invershin Castle can be seen to the west.

Inversnaid *Stirling* A hamlet with a hotel, Inversnaid is situated on the eastern shore of Loch Lomond. There are spectacular views across the loch to the Arrochar Alps and nearby are the rock pools and waterfalls of the Snaid Burn. The locality provided inspiration for the poets William Wordsworth and Gerard Manley Hopkins, and Sir Walter Scott passed this way in 1792 and 1828. Rob Roy Macgregor acquired land at Inversnaid, and a barracks was erected here in 1719 to control the Jacobite districts after the 1715 Rising. Inversnaid is located 20 miles (32 km) northwest of Aberfoyle. It is linked by road to Stronachlachar on Loch Katrine, and to the east is a farmstead known as the Garrison of Inversnaid, which incorporates the remains of the military barracks. The West Highland Way passes through Inversnaid, and a mile (1.5 km) to the north by the lochside is Rob Roy's Cave, a refuge often used by Rob Roy Macgregor.

Inverugie *Aberdeenshire* A village of Buchan in Aberdeenshire, Inverugie lies on the River Ugie, a mile (1.5 km) northwest of Peterhead. The lands of Inverugie were granted by William the Lion to Bernard le Cheyne whose descendants Reginald and his brother Henry respectively became Chamberlain of Scotland and Bishop of Aberdeen. The original castle of the Cheynes, which lay on the coast at the mouth of the Ugie, was visited by Thomas the Rhymer who prophesied 'Inverugie by the sea, Lordless shall thy landis be'. Closer to the village a castle, whose motte still survives, was built in the 14th century and completed by the 5th Earl Marischal who founded Marischal College in Aberdeen.

Inveruglas *Argyll and Bute* A settlement on the northwest shore of Loch Lomond, Inveruglas lies at the mouth of the Inveruglas Water, which flows southeast from Loch Sloy and forms part of a major hydro-electric scheme. On Inveruglas Island in the loch are the ruins of a Macfarlane castle.

Inveruglas Water *Argyll and Bute* The Inveruglas Water rises in Loch Sloy, Argyll and Bute, and flows southeast for 2 miles (3 km) before emptying into Loch Lomond at the settlement of Inveruglas.

Inverurie *Aberdeenshire* An ancient royal burgh in eastern Aberdeenshire, Inverurie is situated on the A96 at the confluence of the River Don and the River Urie, 17 miles (27 km) northwest of Aberdeen. The main town of the old lordship of Garioch and former administrative centre of Gordon District, Inverurie is said to have been founded by David of Huntingdon, Earl of the Garioch, brother of Malcolm IV and great-great-grandfather of Robert the Bruce, who later defeated the Comyns nearby at the Battle of Barra on Christmas Eve 1307. The town's earliest known charter dates from 1558, but its modern development occurred after the building of the Aberdeen Canal linking Port Elphinstone with Aberdeen Harbour in 1806. To the east is The Bass, a medieval motte and bailey, and Kinkell Hall which includes a portion of the older Caskieben Castle associated with the Johnston family. To the south lie the ruins of the 16th-century parish church of Kinkell dedicated to St Michael, with its richly ornamented sacrament house dated 1524. There are several prehistoric stones in the area, most notably the East Aquorthies Stone Circle and the Brandsbutt sculptured stone. The town has a library, museum, community centre, and sporting facilities that include bowling, fishing, tennis, football, a swimming pool and an 18-hole golf course. A centre of locomotive engineering between 1902 and 1968, Inverurie is now a paper-making town with food-processing, refrigeration, glass-fibre and water-treatment equipment industries located on two industrial estates.

Invery House *Aberdeenshire* A country house in Royal Deeside, Aberdeenshire, Invery House lies on the Water of Feugh, a mile (1.5 km) south of Banchory.

Inzie Head *Aberdeenshire* A headland on the North Sea coast of Aberdeenshire, Inzie Head lies just southeast of St Combs and nearly 5 miles (8 km) southeast of Fraserburgh.

Iochdar *Western Isles* The largest of a series of settlements on the north coast of South Uist, the crofting township of Iochdar (sometimes Iochda or Eochdar, Gael: *Iochdair*) lies a mile (1.5 km) to the west of the A865, 1.25 miles (2 km) west-southwest of the causeway linking the island to Benbecula. The Iochdar Primary school is located to the east at Bualadubh. Fishing on numerous lochs nearby and the manufacture of jewellery are important contributions to the local economy.

Iona *Argyll and Bute* A small windswept island of the Inner Hebrides, Iona lies off the Ross of Mull, from which it is separated by the narrow Sound of Iona. With an area of 855 ha (2112 acres), it rises to a height of 100 m (328 ft) at Dun I. Much of the island comprises Lewissian gneiss, including the famous Iona marble which was quarried on the south coast. Inhabited during the Iron Age, the island is especially associated with the Irish monk Colum Cille or Columba who landed here in AD 563 and established a monastery that became a centre of learning and a site of pilgrimage famous throughout the world. The celebrated *Book of Kells* was probably written on Iona at the same time as a group of high crosses were created. A Benedictine abbey of pink granite was founded at the turn of the 12th and 13th centuries by Somerled. The seat of the bishopric of the Isles, this structure was largely rebuilt in the 1500s. Now in the care of the Iona Cathedral Trust, the abbey was restored by the Church of Scotland in the early 20th century and later maintained by the Iona Community which was founded by the Revd George MacLeod. Other buildings of interest include St Oran's Chapel and the Nunnery of St Mary. The village of Baile Mòr on St Ronan's Bay faces the Sound of Iona and has a pier that handles ferries bringing over half a million visitors each year. There is a regular passenger ferry service from Fionnphort on Mull.

Iona, Sound of *Argyll and Bute* The Sound of Iona forms a channel separating the island of Iona from the Ross of Mull, southwest Mull, Argyll and Bute.

Iorsa, Loch *North Ayrshire* A small loch in Glen Iorsa, on the island of Arran, North Ayrshire, Loch Iorsa lies on the course of the Iorsa Water.

Iorsa Water *North Ayrshire* The Iorsa Water rises in the western foothills of Caisteal Abhail on the island of Arran, North Ayrshire. Flowing south, it passes through the valley of Glen Iorsa and Loch Iorsa before heading west towards Dougarie. It empties into the Kilbrannan Sound at the northern end of Machrie Bay. A tributary stream flows from Loch Tanna.

Ireland *Shetland* A settlement on the west coast of the Mainland of Shetland, Ireland lies 9 miles (14 km) north of Sumburgh Head.

Irish Law *North Ayrshire* A hill in North Ayrshire, Irish Law rises to 484 m (1588 ft), 4 miles (6.5 km) east of Largs.

Ironmacannie *Dumfries and Galloway* A locality in Glenkens, Dumfries and Galloway, Ironmacannie lies on the Shirmers Burn, 2 miles (3 km) southeast of New Galloway.

Irvine *North Ayrshire* One of Scotland's five New Towns (designated in 1966), the burgh of Irvine is situated 7 miles (11 km) west of Kilmarnock and 12 miles (19 km) north of Ayr in North Ayrshire. It straddles the River Irvine as it flows into Irvine Bay in the Firth of Clyde. Originally a harbour town, it received its charter in 1308 from Robert I (and possibly earlier c.1240 from Alexander II). The royal burgh of Irvine functioned as the chief port for Glasgow until the 18th century when the River Clyde was deepened and Port Glasgow developed. It exported coal and chemicals, while its industries have included shipbuilding, engineering, chemicals, foundries and sawmills. Robert Burns lived in Glasgow Vennel in Irvine (1781–3), and the town was the birthplace of the author John Galt (1779–1840), the poet James Montgomery (1771–1854), and the sect leader Elizabeth Buchan (1738–91). Buildings of interest include Seagate Castle, the Scottish Maritime Museum, and the Magnum Centre, the largest sports centre in Scotland.

Irvine, River A major river of Ayrshire, the River Irvine rises on the border of East Ayrshire and South Lanarkshire to the north of Loudon Hill. It flows south and then west to be joined by the Glen Water at Darvel. It continues west past Newmilns and Galston and is joined by the Cessnock Water just to the northeast of Hurlford. It then passes Crookedholm before receiving the Kilmarnock Water towards the south of that town. It then forms the boundary between East Ayrshire and South Ayrshire as it flows past Gatehead, where it begins to meander. The river briefly forms the boundary between North Ayrshire and South Ayrshire before entering the former council area and receiving the Carmel Water. It passes Dreghorn and is joined by the Annick Water to the south of Irvine. It then meanders around the south and west of that town and receives the wide estuary of the River Garnock just before entering Irvine Bay, having completed a course of almost 30 miles (48 km).

Irvine Bay *North Ayrshire* A large bay on the west coast of North Ayrshire, Irvine Bay extends from Saltcoats south to Troon. It receives the River Irvine and the River Lugton.

Isay *Highland* An uninhabited island once occupied by a thriving fishing community, Isay lies off the northwest coast of the isle of Skye, in Highland Council area. Covering an area of 60 ha (148 acres), it is now used for grazing sheep.

Isbister *Shetland* A village on the Shetland island of Whalsay, Isbister is situated on the shore of Loch Isbister near the east coast.

Isbister *Shetland* The most northerly township on the Mainland of Shetland, Isbister lies at the northern end of the A970, to the north of the larger settlement of North Roe.

Isla, Glen *Angus* One of the more significant and the most westerly of the Angus glens, Glen Isla forms a wide valley in the southern Grampians between Glen Shee and Glen Prosen. Located on the border with Perth and Kinross, the head of the glen lies close to the border with Aberdeenshire. The River Isla flows south and then southeast through the glen into Strathmore. Part of the glen was once the property of the abbey of Coupar Angus which passed to the Campbells of Argyll after the Reformation. Other parts of the glen were the property of the Ogilvies of Airlie, the two families feuding from the late 16th century. This feud reached a climax in 1640 with the burning of Forter Castle in the Glen. A road from Alyth passes through the lower and middle reaches of the glen to connect with the A93 in Glen Shee.

Isla, River *Moray/Aberdeenshire* A river principally of Moray, the Isla rises to the northeast of Milltown of Auchindoun. It flows northeastwards for 18 miles (29 km) through Strath Isla, separating Keith from Fife Keith, and then forms the boundary between Moray and Aberdeenshire for a short distance before joining the River Deveron near Rothiemay.

Isla, River *Angus/Perth and Kinross* A river of Angus and Perth and Kinross, the Isla rises in the southern Grampians on the border between Angus and Aberdeenshire. Its headstreams, the Caenlochan and Canness Burns, flow down from the 1064-m (3491-ft) Cairn of Claise, and on its course southwards to the valley of Strathmore it is joined by the Newton Burn, the Burn of Kilry, the Cromie Burn, the Dean Water and the Burn of Alyth. Before it meets the River Tay near Cargill, the Isla is joined by the Ericht to the northeast of Coupar Angus and by the Lunan Burn to the east of Meikleour. Its total length through Glen Isla and Strathmore is 46 miles (74 km).

Islay *Argyll and Bute* Thought to have been named after a Norse princess, the island of Islay lies in the Inner Hebrides to the west of the Kintyre peninsula and southwest of the island of Jura, from which it is separated by the Sound of Islay. It is the third-largest and southernmost island of the Inner Hebrides. Noted for its whisky distilleries which utilise the island's extensive areas of peat, Islay's chief settlements are Port Ellen, Port Askaig, Bowmore, Bridgend and Port Charlotte. With an area of 61,497 ha (151,898 acres), the island rises to a height of 491 m (1610 ft) at Beinn Bheigeir. Settled by the Irish in the 3rd century AD, Islay was part of the ancient kingdom of Dalriada before the Norse invasions of the 9th century. For nearly four centuries from the 12th century, Islay was the headquarters of the powerful Lords of the Isles, whose seat was at Loch Finlaggan near Port Askaig. The island was subsequently granted to the Campbells, one of whom, John Francis Campbell (1822–85), spent his life recording the legends and traditions of the island. Islay is noted for its bird life, in particular the large number of overwintering geese, and a national nature reserve at Duich Moss was designated in 1993. Monuments of historic interest include the 9th-century Celtic cross at Kildalton and the 14th-century cross at Kilchoman, Dunyvaig Castle, and the chapel at Kilchiaran founded by St Columba. The Rinns of Islay form a hammerhead peninsula to the west, and to the west of Port Ellen the granite cliffs of The Oa peninsula are popular with climbers and feral goats. On the Mull of Oa is a memorial to those who lost their lives when the *Tuscania* was torpedoed in February 1918 and the *Otranto* was wrecked a year later. Ferries connect Port Ellen and Port Askaig with Jura and the mainland, and an airstrip lies to the north of Port Ellen at Glenegedale on the shell-sand beach of Laggan Bay.

Islay, Sound of *Argyll and Bute* The Sound of Islay is the name given to the stretch of water that separates the island of Islay from the island of Jura, Argyll and Bute. At its narrowest point a car ferry crosses from Feolin Ferry on Jura to Port Askaig on Islay.

Isle Martin *Highland* An uninhabited island off the northwest coast of Wester Ross, Isle Martin is an outlier of the Summer Isles group lying 3 miles (5 km) northwest of Ullapool. It has an area of 240 ha (593 acres).

Isle of May *Fife* Lying 5 miles (8 km) off the Fife coast, the Isle of May is the largest of the islands of the Firth of Forth. It is a mile (1.5 km) long and a quarter-mile (0.5 km) wide, and among naturalists is noted for its colonies of sea birds, its migrant birds and its colony of grey seals. Designated a national nature reserve in 1956, it is now recognised as an important sea-bird research centre. The island is the breeding ground for 20,000 pairs of puffins, 8000 pairs of guillemots and nearly 2000 razorbills, along with fulmars, shags and common and arctic tern. The island is accessed during the spring and summer when a regular boat service operates from Anstruther and Crail to the landing at Kirkhaven. Weekly stays are possible in the bird observatory by prior arrangement. Close to the Kirkhaven landing stand the ruins of the Chapel of St Aidan, which are all that remain of a priory built in the 12th century and dedicated to the Christian missionary who was killed on the island by marauding Danes in AD 875. The Isle of May was an important religious centre until its monks moved to Pittenweem in the 16th century, but the island remained inhabited until the early 18th century. In 1636 Alexander Cunningham built a lighthouse beacon, the first permanently manned lighthouse in Scotland, and in 1844 a subsidiary 'Low Light' was built on the eastern side of the island. During both World Wars the island was under military occupation, and in 1989 the Main Lighthouse became fully automated prior to the ownership of the island passing from the Northern Lighthouse Board to the Nature Conservancy Council, now Scottish Natural Heritage.

Isle of Noss *Shetland* A small uninhabited island and bird sanctuary in the Shetland Islands, the Isle of Noss lies to the east of the island of Bressay, from which it is separated by the Noss Sound.

Isle of Stenness *Shetland* A small island situated off the south end of Esha Ness on Mainland Shetland, the Isle of Stenness lies to the southwest of Stenness.

Isle of Whithorn *Dumfries and Galloway* A seaside village in the Machars district of Dumfries and Galloway, Isle of Whithorn lies at the head of a small inlet of Wigtown Bay, 3 miles (5 km) southeast of Whithorn. The 13th-century St Ninian's Chapel is most likely a successor to the Candida Casa (White House) established in the late 4th century AD by St Ninian, whose remains were removed from here to Whithorn when the church of the monastery was built there. Excavations have revealed a later Norse settlement here. Situated on a peninsula before land's end at Burrow Head, the Isle of Whithorn is not, in fact, an island, although it does claim to be the southernmost village in Scotland.

Isle Ornsay *Highland* A small uninhabited island off the east coast of the Sleat peninsula on the isle of Skye, Isle Ornsay lies opposite the village of Eilean Iarmain, also known as Isleornsay.

Isle Ristol *Highland* One of the Summer Isles group of islands, Isle Ristol lies off the coast of Wester Ross. It has an area of 225 ha (560 acres).

Isles of the Sea An alternative name for the Garvellachs in Argyll and Bute.

Islesteps *Dumfries and Galloway* A locality in Nithsdale, Dumfries and Galloway, Islesteps lies on the Cargen Pow near its confluence with the Nith, 3 miles (5 km) south of Dumfries.

Islivig *Western Isles* A small and remote crofting settlement located in the far west of the island of Lewis in the Outer Hebrides, Islivig (Gael: *Islibhig*) lies a mile (1.5 km) north of Brenish and 6 miles (10 km) southwest of Timsgarry.

Italian Chapel *Orkney* Two prisoner-of-war Nissen huts on the small island of Lamb Holm in the Orkney Islands were converted for use as a chapel by Italian soldiers captured in North Africa during World War II and sent to work on the construction of the Churchill Barriers. The interior murals were painted by one of the prisoners, Domenico Chiocchetti (1910-99), who also created a statue of St George slaying the dragon from barbed wire covered with cement. Chiocchetti also painted above the altar a representation of the Madonna and Child based on a famous work by Niccolo Barabino (1832–91), and from his home town of Moena in Italy there came the gift of a carved figure of the crucified Christ which was erected as a wayside shrine beside the chapel in 1961. Since the war the chapel has been maintained by a POW Chapel Preservation Committee and is now a popular tourist attraction.

Iubhair, Loch *Stirling* A loch in Glen Dochart, Stirling Council area, Loch Iubhair lies in the shadow of Ben More, immediately east of Loch Dochart and 4 miles (6.5 km) east of Crianlarich. The River Dochart flows through the loch and on to Loch Tay.

Jackton *South Lanarkshire* A small farming community in South Lanarkshire, Jackton lies 2 miles (3 km) east of Eaglesham and 3 miles (5 km) west of East Kilbride. The training and recruitment centre for Strathclyde Police is located here.

Jamestown *Highland* A small settlement of Easter Ross in Highland Council area, Jamestown lies a mile (1.5 km) to the south of Strathpeffer.

Jamieson's Point *Dumfries and Galloway* A small headland on the western shore of Loch Ryan in the Rhinns of Galloway, Jamieson's Point lies nearly 2 miles (3 km) north of Kirkcolm.

Janetstown An alternative name for Latheronwheel in Highland Council area.

Jardine Hall *Dumfries and Galloway* A hamlet of Annandale in Dumfries and Galloway, Jardine Hall lies on the River Annan, 5 miles (8 km) northwest of Lockerbie. The estate buildings are all that remain of the mansion house of Jardine Hall which was built in 1814 to a design by James Gillespie Graham.

Jarlshof *Shetland* Situated near Sumburgh Airport at the southern end of the Mainland of Shetland are the ruins of the ancient settlement of Jarlshof, which was rediscovered in 1905 when a violent storm eroded the south face of a great mound to reveal sections of a huge stone wall. First settled in 2000 BC, the site was successively occupied by Bronze Age dune dwellers, Iron Age broch builders, Pictish wheelhouse people and Vikings. The name Jarlshof, originally associated with a ruined medieval farmhouse, was coined by Sir Walter Scott (1771–1832) in his novel *The Pirate* (1822).

Jed Water *Scottish Borders* A river of Roxburghshire in Scottish Borders, the Jed Water rises as the Raven Burn on Carlin Tooth in the Cheviot Hills. It flows nearly 22 miles (35 km) north to join the River Teviot near Jedfoot Bridge, 2 miles (3 km) north of Jedburgh. The Jed Forest once occupied the valley of the Jed Water.

Jedburgh *Scottish Borders* A small town in Scottish Borders, Jedburgh lies on the Jed Water, 12 miles (19 km) northeast of Hawick and 11 miles (18 km) southwest of Kelso. Situated at a strategic location near a river crossing at the southern end of Lauderdale, the original settlement of Old Jedward, Jeddart or Jethart is thought to have been a post-Roman capital of the Geddewrd. The present town developed in association with an Augustinian priory for French monks from St Quentin in Picardy founded by David I in 1138. Elevated to the status of an abbey in 1147, it became one of the most powerful religious centres in the Scottish Borders. Although destroyed by the English in 1544, its ruins remain one of the architectural gems of the Scottish Borders. The settlement became a royal burgh in the 12th century and later became the county town of Roxburghshire until it was replaced by Newtown St Boswells in 1899. In medieval times Jedburgh defended itself against frequent Border raids, the local men deftly handling the famous Jeddart staff, a long pole tipped by a metal hook. The castle, which once stood on the site of the Jedburgh Castle Jail and Museum (1832), was ceded to England under the Treaty of Falaise in 1174 but was finally destroyed in 1409 by order of the Scottish Parliament. The ancient ball game known as Jethart Hand-ba supposedly derives from the Jedburgh men playing with the heads of English soldiers. Today the game is played at Candlemas and Easter E'en by two opposing teams. In addition to the abbey, buildings of note include Mary, Queen of Scots' House, where she stayed in October 1566, and the houses on the Castlegate, one of which was occupied by Prince Charles Edward Stewart (Bonnie Prince Charlie) on his way to England in 1745. Born in Jedburgh were the surveyor John Ainslie (1745–1834), the mathematician Mary Somerville (1780–1872) and the scientist Sir David Brewster (1781–1868), inventor of the kaleidoscope.

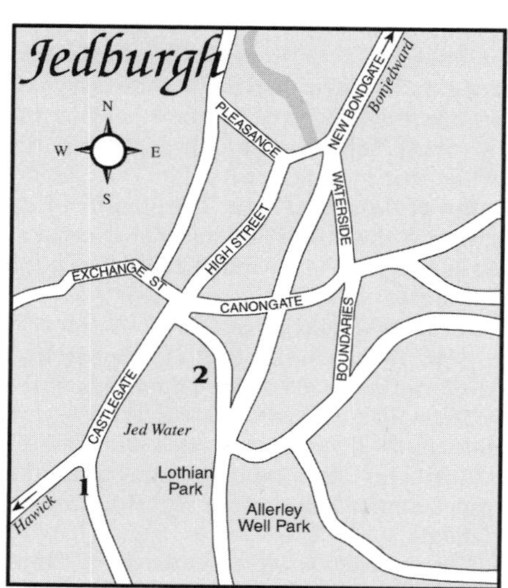

1 *Jedburgh Castle Gaol* 2 *Jedburgh Abbey*

Jemimaville *Highland* A village in the Black Isle parish of Resolis, Jemimaville lies on Udale Bay, an inlet on the south side of the Cromarty Firth, 5 miles (8 km) west of Cromarty. Founded as an estate village in 1822, it is named after Jemima Poyntz, the Dutch wife of a local Munro laird of nearby Ardoch, later renamed Poyntzfield.

Jericho *Angus* A hamlet in Strathmore, Angus, Jericho lies a mile (1.5 km) to the east of Glamis.

Jock's Lodge *City of Edinburgh* A district of Edinburgh and formerly a village of South Leith parish, Jock's Lodge lies to the northeast of Arthur's Seat, between central Edinburgh and Portobello.

Jock's Road *Angus* A routeway in the southern Grampians, Jock's Road links Glen Doll at the head of Glen Clova with Braemar in Royal Deeside.

John Muir Country Park *East Lothian* Established in 1976 to commemorate the conservationist and founder of the US national park movement, John Muir (1838–1914), the John Muir Country Park extends over 733 ha (1811 acres) of the East Lothian coastline around Belhaven Bay to the west of Dunbar where Muir was born. The park has a range of habitats, including cliffs, dunes, woodlands, salt marshes, scrub and permanent grassland, all of which support a rich variety of wildlife. Dunbar Castle lies within the country park.

John o' Groats *Highland* Situated at the northernmost extremity of mainland Scotland, although not the most northerly point, the settlement of John o' Groats lies 1.5 miles (2.5 km) west-southwest of Duncansby Head, 17 miles (27 km) north of Wick in Caithness, and 876 miles (1410 km) from Land's End at the southern tip of Britain. It is named after the Dutch settler Jan de Groot who operated a ferry to Orkney from here in the 15th century after the Orkney Islands were annexed to Scotland in 1472. A mound and flagpole mark the site of his octagonal house, allegedly built in that shape to placate his eight sons. When the railway arrived in Wick and Thurso in 1874, tourists started to arrive. John o' Groats remains a small farming, fishing and tourist settlement with a museum and a craft centre with knitwear, candle-making and pottery outlets.

Johnshaven *Aberdeenshire* A fishing village in southeast Aberdeenshire, Johnshaven lies at the foot of a cliff on the North Sea coast, 4 miles (6.5 km) southwest of Inverbervie. In 1722 it was reckoned to be 'amongst the first fishing towns of Scotland' according to the author of the *Statistical Account of the Parish of Benholm*. By the 1770s the number of Johnshaven fishermen had been reduced as a result of a disaster at sea and locals being press-ganged to join the Navy. In the 1790s a sail-cloth factory was established and locals earned additional income from spinning thread from flax and knitting stockings from wool. Today, the lobster and crab landed here find their way to restaurants around the world. Nearby Lathallan School, a prep school transferred here from Fife in 1951, occupies Brotherton Castle, which was built in 1850 by a Dundee jute manufacturer.

Johnstone *Dumfries and Galloway* A locality in Eskdale, Dumfries and Galloway, Johnstone lies at the junction of the Woodlaw Burn with the White Esk, 7 miles (11 km) south of Ettrick.

Johnstone *Renfrewshire* A small town situated on the Black Cart Water, 3 miles (5 km) west of Paisley, Johnstone developed as a textile town in the late 18th century, its Old End cotton mill being the largest in Scotland when it was built in 1782. A planned village with two open squares was laid out for the mill workers by George Houston not far from Johnstone Castle, and by 1841 Johnstone had a population of 7000 and 16 mills. Between 1811 and 1885 it was the terminus of the Glasgow, Paisley and Ardrossan Canal, which was surveyed by Thomas Telford but never completed. The town later expanded in association with coal mining, quarrying and the manufacture of machine tools, iron, brass, chemicals and paper. Buildings of note include the ruins of Johnstone Castle, once visited by the composer Frederick Chopin, Johnstone Mill (1782), Cartside Mill (1780), the octagonal and high-spired High Parish Church (1792–4) and nearby Cochrane Castle, a former stronghold of the earls of Dundonald dating from c.1592.

Johnstonebridge *Dumfries and Galloway* A small village of Annandale in Dumfries and Galloway, Johnstonebridge lies close to the River Annan, 8 miles (13 km) north of Lockerbie. Named after the Johnstones of Annandale who lived at nearby Raehills, its bridge was built by Thomas Telford in 1820. Johnstone Parish Church, dating from 1745, was enlarged in 1818.

Johnston Gardens *Aberdeen City* Situated on Viewfield Road in Aberdeen, Johnston Gardens is a small park with streams, ponds, a waterfall and a rustic bridge.

Johnston's Point *Argyll and Bute* A rocky headland with outliers on the southeast coast of the Kintyre peninsula, Argyll and Bute, Johnston's Point lies about a half-mile (1 km) to the south-southwest of the headland of Ru Stafnish.

Joppa *City of Edinburgh* An eastern suburb of Portobello in the city of Edinburgh, Joppa lies on the Firth of Forth adjacent to a sandy beach. It became a fashionable resort and residential area in the late 19th century.

Joppa *South Ayrshire* A hamlet of South Ayrshire, Joppa is located a mile (1.5 km) west of Coylton and a mile (1.5km) east of Belston on the A70 from Ayr to Cumnock.

Jordanhill *Glasgow City* A largely residential district of northwest Glasgow comprising tenement flats and villas, Jordanhill lies to the south of Anniesland and east of Knightswood. It grew in association with its northern neighbours and was centred on Jordanhill House, a 16th-century mansion house rebuilt by the Smith family in 1782 and now housing the University of Strathclyde's Jordanhill Teacher Training College.

Juniper Green *City of Edinburgh* A residential suburb on the western outskirts of the city of Edinburgh, Juniper Green lies on the left bank of the Water of Leith between Currie and Colinton. A settlement developed here from the 16th century in association with flax, grain, paper and snuff mills, the last of these in operation being the Woodhall Grain Mill. In 1874 the Caledonian Railway opened a single-track line between Slateford and Balerno which provided a passenger train service until 1943, the line eventually closing in the 1960s. Juniper Green was absorbed into the city of Edinburgh in 1920.

Jura *Argyll and Bute* An island of the Inner Hebrides, Jura is separated from the Knapdale district of Argyll and Bute to the east by the Sound of Jura, and from the island of Islay to the southwest by the narrow Sound of Islay. To the north, the Strait of Corryvreckan, with its notorious whirlpools, separates Jura from the island of Scarba. Extending 27 miles (43 km) northeast–southwest and 8 miles (13 km) at its widest, the island rises to a height of 785 m (2571 ft) at Beinn an Oir, one of the three distinctive conical peaks known as the Paps of Jura. Jura is nearly bisected by Loch Tarbert. Noted for its raised beaches and large caves, the island's geology comprises a mixture of granite, blue slate, micaceous sandstone and the largest area of metamorphic quartzite in the Highlands and islands. Covered in extensive areas of blanket bog, the total area of Jura is 36,543 ha (90,261 acres). Most of the island's population of 188 live in Craighouse, which sits on a bay on the east coast protected by a string of islets known as the Small Isles. A 19th-century distillery here was re-opened in 1963. Sold by the Clan Donald to the Campbells of Argyll in 1607, the island of Jura was a centre for the breeding of Highland cattle in the 18th and 19th centuries. The island is also associated with the Clan Maclean. In 1767 the depopulation of the island began when 50 of the island's 1100 crofters sailed from Jura to settle in Canada. After the introduction of sheep in the 1840s, population decline accelerated. Today, much of the land is given over to deer stalking. The island is linked by ferry to Port Askaig, Port Ellen and Kennacraig, and a single road follows the east coast as far north as Inverlussa. A track continues northwards past Barnhill, where the novelist George Orwell (1903–50) stayed while writing *1984* (1949).

Jura, Sound of *Argyll and Bute* The Sound of Jura is the name given to the stretch of water that separates the island of Jura from the Knapdale district of Kintyre of Argyll and Bute.

Kailzie Gardens *Scottish Borders* A 7-ha (17-acre) garden near Kirkburn in Scottish Borders, Kailzie Gardens lie in the Tweed valley 2.5 miles (4 km) east of Peebles. The walled garden dates fom 1812.

Kaim Hill *North Ayrshire* Located 4 miles (6.5 km) southeast of Largs and 2 miles (3 km) south of Kelburn Castle and Country Centre, Kaim Hill rises to a height of 387 m (1269 ft).

Kaimes *City of Edinburgh* A suburb of Edinburgh, Kaimes lies in Liberton parish, 4 miles (6.5 km) south of the city centre.

Kaims Castle *Perth and Kinross* The site of a Roman fortlet and camp in southwest Perth and Kinross, Kaims Castle lies 2 miles (3 km) north-northeast of Braco.

Kale Water *Scottish Borders* Rising as the Long Burn on Leap Hill in the Cheviot Hills, the Kale Water flows north to Hownam and Morebattle before turning west to meet the Teviot 4 miles (6.5 km) south of Kelso. It is just over 20 miles (32 km) in length.

Kalnakill An alternative name for Callakille in Highland Council area.

Kames *Argyll and Bute* A locality on the western side of Loch Fyne, Kames lies 5 miles (8 km) east of Lochgilphead.

Kames Bay *Argyll and Bute* An inlet of the Kyles of Bute, Kames Bay lies between the settlements of Port Bannatyne and Ardmaleish on the east coast of the island of Bute. The town of Rothesay lies 2 miles (3 km) to the south.

Kames River *Argyll and Bute* Rising on the slopes of An Suidhe to the east of Loch Awe, the Kames River flows north before heading west and emptying into Loch Awe, a mile (1.5 km) northeast of Eredine. The river is 3 miles (5 km) long.

Kamesburgh An alternative name for Port Bannatyne in Argyll and Bute.

Kanaird, Strath *Highland* A small valley in the Coigach district of Wester Ross, Strath Kanaird (also Strath Canaird) is located 4 miles (6.5 km) north of Ullapool. The valley contains the hamlet of Strathcanaird and carries the River Kanaird from Loch a' Chroisg to Loch Kanaird, a sea loch and inlet of Loch Broom.

Katrine, Loch *Stirling* The largest of the scenic lochs in the Trossachs district of Stirling Council area, Loch Katrine lies within the valley of Strath Gartney to the east of Loch Lomond. The loch derives its name from the Gaelic *cateran*, meaning a Highland robber, the most notorious of which was Rob Roy Macgregor who was born at Glengyle House at the northern end of the loch. Sir Walter Scott's best-selling poem *The Lady of the Lake* (1810) popularised the loch and in particular the romantic wooded islet known as Ellen's Isle. Queen Victoria sailed up the loch in September 1869. Much earlier it inspired the poets Samuel Coleridge and William Wordsworth, whose sister Dorothy took a less romantic view of the loch, which she described as being 'like a barren Ulswater [*sic*] – Ulswater dismantled of its grandeur, and cropped of its lesser beauties'. A source of pure water for the city of Glasgow since 1859, Loch Katrine is still visited by large numbers of tourists, who either walk or cycle the road on the north side of the loch or take the steamship *Sir Walter Scott*, which was launched in 1899 and still plies from the Trossachs Pier. The loch is 8 miles (13 km) long and has an area of 1238 ha (3059 acres).

Keal, Loch na *Argyll and Bute* Located on the western coastline of the island of Mull, Argyll and Bute, Loch na Keal forms a large sea loch that extends far inland, almost bisecting the island as it reaches a point only 3 miles (5 km) from the island's eastern coast. At the northwestern head of the loch lies the island of Ulva, while at its southwest head lies Inch Kenneth. The island of Eorsa lies within the loch.

Kearstay *Western Isles* A small uninhabited island located immediately off the north coast of the much larger island of Scarp, Kearstay (Gael: *Cearstaigh*) is located off the west coast of North Harris in the Outer Hebrides. The island rises steeply to 51 m (167 ft).

Kearvaig *Highland* A locality on the northwest coast of Sutherland, Kearvaig lies 2 miles (3 km) southeast of Cape Wrath. The Kearvaig stream, which rises in Loch na Gainmhich, enters an inlet of the sea near Kearvaig, and to the north Stac Clo Kearvaig forms a headland extending into the Pentland Firth.

Keava *Western Isles* An uninhabited island in East Loch Roag, Keava (Gael: *Ceabhagh*) lies off Kirkibost on the southeast coast of Great Bernera a mile (1.5 km) west-southwest of Breasclete on the Isle of Lewis. The island is approximately a half-mile (1 km) in length. The larger Eilean Kearstay lies a quarter-mile (0.5 km) to the south.

Kebock Head *Western Isles* A steep, rocky and isolated headland on the east coast of the Isle of Lewis in the Outer Hebrides, Kebock Head (or Cabag Head; Gael: *A' Chabag*) overlooks the Minch on the south side of the mouth of Loch Ouirn, 12 miles (19 km) south of Stornoway.

Keen of Hamar, The *Shetland* A small hill on the Shetland island of Unst, the Keen of Hamar lies on the east coast of the island between Baltasound and Haroldswick. A 30-ha (74-acre) nature reserve protects barren stony scree that supports a unique collection of plants adapted to a rare serpentine rock debris, including Edmonston's chickweed which is found nowhere else in the world.

Keig *Aberdeenshire* A village in an Aberdeenshire parish of the same name, Keig lies to the west of Castle Forbes and just north of the River Don, 3 miles (5 km) northeast of Alford.

Keil *Argyll and Bute* A hamlet on the south coast of the Kintyre peninsula of Argyll and Bute, Keil lies 10 miles (16 km) south-southwest of Campbeltown.

Keil *Highland* A small settlement in the Appin district of southwest Highland Council area, Keil lies on the southeast shore of Loch Linnhe between Glen Duror and Salachan Glen. It is the burial place of James Stewart, who was wrongly hanged for the Appin Murder of 1752.

Keillour *Perth and Kinross* A locality in central Perth and Kinross between Glen Almond and Strath Earn, Keillour comprises Keillour Castle, Parks of Keillour, Green of Keillour and Wester Keillour, all of which lie 3 miles (5 km) west of Methven in the heart of the Keillour Forest. Keillour Castle was built in the 1870s on the site of an earlier tower house.

Keills Chapel *Argyll and Bute* Situated 6 miles (10 km) southwest of Tayvallich on a narrow stretch of land between Loch Sween and the Sound of Jura in Argyll and Bute, Keills Chapel contains a collection of ancient graveslabs as well as the Keills Cross.

Keir Hills *Dumfries and Galloway* A range of hills in the Nithsdale district of Dumfries and Galloway, the Keir Hills rise to a height of 357 m (1171 ft) between Moniaive and Thornhill.

Keir House *Stirling* The ancestral seat of the Stirlings of Keir since the 15th century, although no longer owned by that family, Keir House stands on high ground looking out over the Carse of Lecropt, 3 miles (5 km) northwest of Bridge of Allan. In its policies stand the ruins of Arnhall Castle, a former seat of the Dow family. Born here was Lieutenant-Colonel Sir David Stirling (1915–90), who founded the Special Air Service (SAS).

Keir Mill *Dumfries and Galloway* A small village of Nithsdale, 1.5 miles (2.5 km) southeast of Penpont, Keir Mill was founded in the late 18th century. Its mill dates from 1771 and its church from 1815.

Keiravagh Islands *Western Isles* A group of small uninhabited islands connected by rocks at low tide, the Keiravagh Islands (Gael: *Eileanan Chearabhaig*) lie adjacent to the southeast coast of Benbecula in the Outer Hebrides. They rise to 23 m (75 ft) between Loch Keiravagh to the north and Loch a' Laip to the south. The island of Wiay is located a quarter-mile (0.5 km) to the south.

Keiss *Highland* The village of Keiss is located on the east coast of Caithness, 6 miles (10 km) north of Wick in Highland Council area. The area is noted for its crab fishing and the harbour is still in use.

Keith *Moray* A small agricultural town in Moray, Keith is situated at a crossing of the River Isla on the route from Aberdeen to Inverness. The original settlement of Old Keith, which was used by the abbots of Kinloss as a centre for agriculture and distilling, was rebuilt in the 1750s by the Earl of Findlater, who laid out on moorland to the east the regularly planned New Keith with its large central square (Reidhaven Square). Its three parallel streets – Moss Street, Mid Street and Land Street – are interconnected by a series of narrow lanes. Built to a similar design, the village of Fife Keith on the opposite side of the river was created in 1817 by the Earl of Fife. Until the 1750s the only way of crossing the Isla was by the packhorse bridge (1609) which survives close to the kirkyard of Old Keith. The roadbridge was built in 1770 above a pool known as the Gaun's Pot where witches were drowned. Whisky is manufactured nearby at the Strathisla Distillery (1786), said to be the oldest working distillery in Scotland. Prominent among the town's buildings are the Milton Tower, built by the Ogilvies in 1480, and the Italianate St Thomas's Roman Catholic Church (1831–2), which contains Francois Dubois's painting *The Incredulity of St Thomas*, donated by King Charles X of France. There is an 18-hole golf course in Fife Keith.

Keith Inch *Aberdeenshire* A peninsula on the eastern side of Peterhead Harbour, Aberdeenshire, Keith Inch was the site of the original fishing village of Keith Inch which predates Peterhead.

Keithick *Perth and Kinross* A locality in Strathmore, Perth and Kinross, Keithick House, Mains of Keithick and Little Keithick lie between Coupar Angus and Woodside to the southwest. The neoclassical Keithick House was built in 1818–23 for W. E. Collinswood. Its drawing room was decorated in a fine Adam Revival style by Morant.

Kelburn *North Ayrshire* A castle and country centre with spectacular views over the Firth of Clyde, Kelburn lies east of Fairlie to the south of Largs. Kelburn Castle, the historic home of the earls of Glasgow, dates from 1581 with later additions and is surrounded by forest and farmland on which a wide range of activities from walking to adventure training take place.

Kelhead *Dumfries and Galloway* A locality in Annandale, Dumfries and Galloway, Kelhead lies 4 miles (6.5 km) northwest of Annan by the Kelhead Moss Plantation.

Kellas *Angus* A hamlet of southern Angus, Kellas (formerly known as the Hole of Murroes) lies a mile (1.5 km) north of the boundary with Dundee and 1.25 miles (2 km) southwest of Wellbank. The Sweet Burn flows past the village to the east and then onwards to Murroes, a half-mile (1 km) beyond.

Kellas *Moray* A small village overlooking the River Lossie in Moray, Kellas lies to the southwest of Elgin, 3 miles (5 km) northeast of Dallas.

Kellie Castle *Fife* Situated 3 miles (5 km) northwest of Pittenweem in the East Neuk of Fife, Kellie Castle is a Jacobean tower house, largely dating from the 16th and early 17th centuries. Mentioned in a charter of David I *c.*1150, Kellie was owned by the Oliphant family from 1360 to 1613, when it was purchased by Sir Thomas Erskine, a childhood friend of James VI who created him Earl of Kellie (1619). Originally a simple tower house, the lower part of what is now the northwest tower is the oldest part of the castle, probably dating from 1360. A second larger tower was built to the southwest by 1573 and in 1606 a new range was completed connecting these two towers. Subsequently the castle has developed into a T-plan structure, comprising a complex collection of sheer gables, corbelled towers, turnpike stairs and chimneys, which is a fine example of Scottish domestic architecture. After being abandoned for many years, the castle was restored by James Lorimer, Professor of Law at the University of Edinburgh, who had rented it from the Earl of Mar and Kellie in the 1870s. His son, the architect Sir Robert Lorimer, was responsible for laying out the gardens when he was aged just 16. Later Robert continued his father's restoration work, designing magnificent plaster ceilings, painted panelling and furniture for the castle. Sir Robert's son, the sculptor Hew Lorimer, acquired the castle in 1948 and subsequently gave it, together with its Victorian walled garden, to the National Trust for Scotland in 1970.

Kello Water *Dumfries and Galloway* A stream of Dumfries and Galloway, the Kello Water rises on the northern slope of Blacklorg Hill to the east of Afton Reservoir. It flows nearly 9 miles (14 km) east to meet the River Nith 2.5 miles (4 km) northwest of Sanquhar.

Kelloholm *Dumfries and Galloway* A settlement adjacent to Kirkconnel in Nithsdale, Dumfries and Galloway, Kelloholm was created in 1921 as a model village to house miners. It expanded after World War I.

Kelloside *Dumfries and Galloway* A locality in Nithsdale, Dumfries and Galloway, Kelloside lies just south of Kirkconnel and the River Nith. Old Kelloside lies on the Kello Water, which joins the Nith a mile (1.5 km) to the east.

Kelso *Scottish Borders* A small town in Scottish Borders, Kelso lies on the north bank of the River Tweed near its junction with the Teviot, 19 miles (31 km) east of Selkirk and 10 miles (16 km) southwest of Coldstream. Described by Sir Walter Scott, who studied here as a child, as the 'prettiest, if not the most romantic village in Scotland', Kelso initially developed in association with a Benedictine abbey founded in 1128 by David I. It was raised to the status of an ecclesiastical burgh in the early 13th century and remained one of the wealthiest and most important religious centres in the Scottish Borders until the abbey was destroyed in 1545 during the Reformation. James III was crowned as an infant in the abbey, which passed as a ruin into the hands of the earls of Roxburghe, the owners of nearby Floors Castle, in

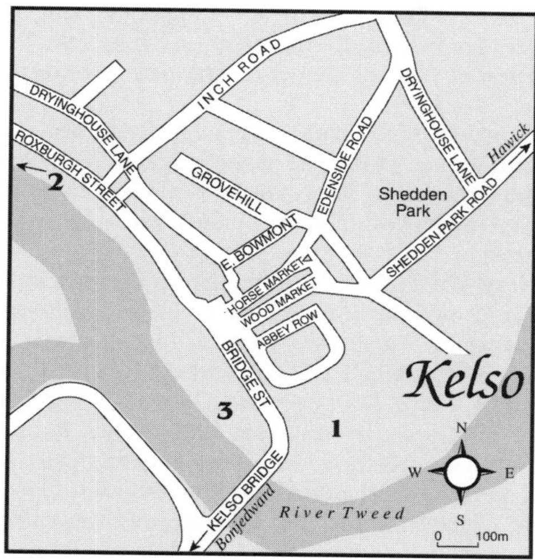

1 *Kelso Abbey*
2 *Floors Castle*
3 *Kelso Museum*

1607. Destroyed on a number of occasions, the town was designated a burgh of barony in 1644 and thereafter developed as a market town with brewing, shoe making and textile industries. Two bridges across the Tweed erected in 1754 and 1800–03 made Kelso an important centre of communication. Cattle were traded here until 1930 and an annual ram market is still held in September in addition to the Border Union Agricultural Show which takes place each July. Modern industries include tourism and the manufacture of agricultural machinery, soft drinks, plastics and electronics. Buildings of interest include the Italianate Town Hall (1816), the Corn Exchange (1855), octagonal parish church (1771–3) and Ednam House (1761). Scott's first major work, *The Minstrelsy of the Scottish Border*, was published by James Ballantyne of Kelso in 1802–03.

Keltie Water *Stirling* Rising in mountains to the east of Loch Lubnaig in Stirling Council area, the Keltie Water flows southeast and south for 10 miles (16 km) before joining the River Teith a mile (1.5 km) to the southeast of Callander, from where a woodland walk leads to the attractive Bracklinn Falls.

Keltneyburn *Perth and Kinross* A hamlet at the eastern end of Glen Lyon, Perth and Kinross, Keltneyburn lies near the junction of the Keltney Burn with the River Lyon, 7 miles (11 km) west of Aberfeldy. It comprises a picturesque group of cottages and former mills, with a village hall built c.1895 as a reading room by shipping magnate Sir Donald Currie, owner of the estate. The settlement is dominated by a statue of the military and Highland historian Major-General David Stewart of Garth (1772–1829), built in 1925. Close by is the Coshieville Hotel, which housed the officers of General Wade's military road-making force in the 1720s.

Kelton *Dumfries and Galloway* A scattered settlement of Nithsdale in Dumfries and Galloway, Kelton lies near the mouth of the River Nith, 3 miles (5 km) south of Dumfries. Its parish church, dating from 1805, was remodelled by R. Rowand Anderson in 1879. In a wood to the north of the church is the unusual Egypto-Grecian mausoleum of improving landowner Sir William Douglas (1745–1809), founder of Castle Douglas and Newton Stewart.

Kelton Hill An alternative name for Rhonehouse in Dumfries and Galloway.

Kelty *Fife* A former mining town in western Fife, situated immediately east of the M90, 2 miles (3 km) north of Cowdenbeath. The settlement was developed after 1872 when the Fife Coal Company was established.

Kelty Water *Stirling* A stream rising in Loch Ard Forest to the east of Loch Lomond, the Kelty Water flows eastwards for 12 miles (19 km) before joining the River Forth in Flanders Moss.

Kelvin, River *Glasgow City* A northern tributary of the River Clyde, the River Kelvin rises in the Kilsyth Hills, 3 miles (5 km) east of Kilsyth. It flows southwest for 21 miles (33 km) before joining the Clyde at Partick, 2 miles (3 km) west of Glasgow city centre. It passes through the residential suburb of Kelvinside. The Botanic Gardens, the University of Glasgow, the Kelvin Hall and the Kelvingrove Art Gallery and Museum all lie on its banks.

Kelvin Hall *Glasgow City* Situated opposite the Kelvingrove Art Gallery and Museum in the West End of Glasgow, the Kelvin Hall was built in 1927 to replace a previous building burned down in 1925. It housed large-scale exhibitions and during World War II was used to produce barrage and convoy balloons. Converted in 1987, it now houses the Museum of Transport and the Kelvin Hall International Sports Arena.

Kelvingrove Art Gallery and Museum *Glasgow City* Partly financed by the International Exhibition of 1888, the Kelvingrove Art Gallery and Museum was built in 1901 by the English architects Sir J. W. Simpson and Milner Allen. Following the Glasgow tradition of red sandstone buildings, it was built in a Spanish Baroque style. Originally intended to house a concert hall and an art school, it was opened in 1902. Major redevelopment of the building took place 2003–06.

Kelvingrove Park *Glasgow City* Located in Glasgow's West End, Kelvingrove Park lies between Charing Cross to the east, Park Circus to the north, Glasgow University to the west and to the south the Kelvin Hall and the Museum of Transport. Extending over an area of 34 ha (85 acres), it was created by Sir Joseph Paxton in 1852 as the West End Park. It was the site of the 1888 International Exhibition, the profits from which paid for the Kelvingrove Art Gallery and Museum, the 1901 International Exhibition and the 1911 Scottish Exhibition. The park has many statues and monuments, the largest of which is the Stewart Memorial Fountain, built to commemorate the achievement of Lord Provost Robert Stewart in promoting the Loch Katrine Act which provided the city with fresh water from the Trossachs. There are also statues commemorating Lord Kelvin, Lord Lister, Lord Roberts and Thomas Carlyle.

Kemback *Fife* A small village in eastern Fife, Kemback is situated 2.5 miles (4 km) east of Cupar, to the south of the River Eden. Although the parish of Kemback has ancient associations with St Salvator's College in St Andrews, the village was largely created during the 19th century for those working in the flax mills powered by the adjacent Ceres Burn, which flows down to the Eden through the deep wooded Dura Den Gorge. It was thus also known as Kemback Mills.

Kemnay *Aberdeenshire* A village in an Aberdeenshire parish of the same name, Kemnay lies on the River Don, 14 miles (22 km) northwest of Aberdeen. It developed during the second half of the 19th century after the opening of granite quarries by Aberdonian entrepreneur John Fyfe. Stone from Kemnay was used in the making of the Thames Embankment in London and the foundations of the Forth Bridge.

Kemp's Walk *Dumfries and Galloway* The name given to a promontory fort on the coast of the Rhinns of Galloway in Dumfries and Galloway, Kemp's Walk is situated at the end of Labrax Glen, west of Stranraer. It is thought to date from the 1st millennium BC.

Ken, Loch *Dumfries and Galloway* A loch in The Glenkens district of Dumfries and Galloway, Loch Ken forms an expansion of the lower course of the Water of Ken between New Galloway and its junction with the River Dee. Loch Ken is a centre for watersports, fishing and birdwatching.

Ken, Water of *Dumfries and Galloway* A stream of Dumfries and Galloway, the Water of Ken rises on the southern slopes of Blacklorg Hill to the northeast of Cairnsmore of Carsphairn. It flows southwestwards into The Glenkens valley through Carsfad Loch and Earlstoun Loch, passing St John's Town of Dalry and New Galloway before expanding in width to form Loch Ken. To the west of Castle Douglas it joins the River Dee, a total of 28 miles (45 km) from its source. A bridge over the Water of Ken near New Galloway was designed by the engineer John Rennie (1761–1821).

Kenly Water *Fife* A stream in eastern Fife, the Kenly Water rises in headstreams from the Cameron Reservoir and Kinaldy Burn which flow northeast to join the North Sea near Boarhills, 4 miles (6.5 km) southeast of St Andrews.

Kenmore *Argyll and Bute* A settlement on the western shore of Loch Fyne, Kenmore lies 4 miles (6.5 km) southwest of Inveraray. It was the birthplace of the Gaelic poet Ewan MacColl (1808–98).

Kenmore *Perth and Kinross* A village in highland Perth and Kinross, Kenmore lies at the east end of Loch Tay, 9 miles (14 km) west of Aberfeldy. Kenmore was created as a model village by the 3rd Earl of Breadalbane, who built cottages on either side of the square in 1760 and a bridge over the Tay in 1774 to replace the earlier settlement of Inchadney which lay at a ford over the Tay. The 4th Earl demolished the nearby Castle of Balloch in 1799 and replaced it with Taymouth Castle, which was completed in 1842 in time for the visit of Queen Victoria and Prince Albert. The estate and castle were eventually sold by the Campbells of Breadalbane in 1920. At the nearby Scottish Crannog Centre (Croft na Caber) on Loch Tay a crannog, or lake dwelling, has been reconstructed to a design based on the findings from the excavation of the 2500-year-old Oakbank Crannog located off the village of Fearnan. Today Kenmore is a tourist resort and centre of watersports and golf.

Kenmore *Western Isles* A remote locality on the eastern shore of Loch Seaforth, Kenmore (Gael: *Ceann Mòr*) is located in the Park district of the Isle of Lewis in the Outer Hebrides, 5 miles (8 km) northeast of Tarbert on Harris.

Kenmure Castle *Dumfries and Galloway* The 16th-century tower house of Kenmure Castle is located a mile (1.5 km) to the south of New Galloway in Dumfries and Galloway and was a seat of the Gordon family.

Kennacraig *Argyll and Bute* A hamlet on the southeast coast of West Loch Tarbert at the northern end of the Kintyre peninsula, Kennacraig lies 5 miles (8 km) southwest of Tarbert. There is a ferry link with the island of Islay.

Kennagary *Western Isles* A small crofting township in the southeast of North Harris, Kennagary (Gael: *Ceann a' Gharaidh*) overlooks the island of Scalpay, a half-mile (1 km) west-northwest of Kyles Scalpay and 3 miles (5 km) southeast of Tarbert.

Kennavay *Western Isles* A hamlet on the west coast of the island of Scalpay in the Outer Hebrides, Kennavay (Gael: *Ceann a Bhaigh*) lies 5.5 miles (9 km) southeast of Tarbert, overlooking East Loch Tarbert.

Kennedy's Cairn *Dumfries and Galloway* Situated on top of a hill at the southern end of the Rhinns of Galloway, Dumfries and Galloway, Kennedy's Cairn looks down onto the southern cliffs of the Mull of Galloway.

Kennet *Clackmannanshire* A former mining village in Clackmannanshire, Kennet lies a mile (1.5 km) southeast of Clackmannan. Nearby Kennet House was built in the early 19th century by the family of Bruce, which later acquired the title of Balfour of Burleigh.

Kennethmont An alternative name for Kirkhill of Kennethmont in Aberdeenshire.

Kennetpans *Clackmannanshire* A small settlement in Clackmannanshire, Kennetpans is situated on the north bank of the River Forth 2 miles (3 km) northwest of Kincardine. It once had an active harbour and took advantage of the local supplies of grain and fuel to produce spirit for the London gin market. The ruins of a distillery built about 1780 survive.

Kennoway *Fife* A former weaving village in southern Fife, Kennoway lies a mile (1.5 km) north of Windygates and 2 miles (3 km) northwest of Leven. Situated on lands that once belonged to the Priory of St Andrews, its pre-Reformation church was dedicated to St Kenneth. The present church of the parish of Kennoway (1850) is home to the oldest communion cup (1671) in Scotland. To the south is the Pictish motte of Maiden Castle and to the west is the Kennoway Den with its sandstone cliffs. Now largely a dormitory settlement, the village prospered on the old route from Pettycur ferry on the Firth of Forth to Tayport on the Firth of Tay and had malting and brewing industries. Its importance waned with the development of the New Inn route to the west, but during the 19th century the building of the turnpike road and the expansion of weaving and shoe making industries led to renewed growth. The village was designated a conservation area in 1977. Local industries, which include haulage facilities, are largely located in the Sandy Brae Industrial Estate at the south end of the village, and stone is extracted from the nearby Langside Quarry. There are playing fields, a primary school, a community centre and a bowling green.

Kennox Water *South Lanarkshire* Rising in forested land 3 miles (5 km) east of Cairn Table, the Kennox Water flows east then northeast and finally north to flow into the Douglas Water. It joins the Douglas Water a mile (1.5 km) southwest of Glespin, South Lanarkshire.

Kentallen *Highland* A hamlet in the Lochaber district of southwest Highland Council area, Kentallen lies on Kentallen Bay on the east side of Loch Linnhe, 3 miles (5 km) southwest of Ballachulish. It is associated with a rare rock type known as Kentallenite.

Kentra *Highland* A hamlet on the Ardnamurchan

peninsula of Highland Council area, Kentra lies on the eastern side of Kentra Bay, 4 miles (6.5 km) northwest of Salen.

Keose *Western Isles* A crofting township in the North Lochs district on the east coast of the Isle of Lewis in the Outer Hebrides, Keose (Gael: *Ceos*) lies on the north shore of Loch Erisort opposite Garyvard and 1.25 miles (2 km) east of Laxay. Keose Glebe lies immediately to the east and Loch Keose (Gael: *Loch Cheois*) is located a half-mile (1 km) to the east-northeast.

Keose Glebe *Western Isles* A small settlement in the North Lochs district of the isle of Lewis in the Outer Hebrides, Keose Glebe (Gael: *Glib Cheois*) lies on the north shore of Loch Erisort immediately to the east of Keose and 8 miles (13 km) southwest of Stornoway. Loch Keose is located just to the north.

Kepculloch *Stirling* A locality in Stirling Council area, Kepculloch lies on the A811, 2 miles (3 km) southwest of Buchlyvie.

Keppoch *Highland* A settlement in the Kintail district of western Highland Council area, Keppoch lies near the northeast shore of Loch Duich, 2 miles (3 km) southeast of Dornie.

Keppoch *Highland* A locality in Kilmonivaig Parish, Highland Council area, Keppoch lies to the east of the River Spean near its junction with the Roy, 16 miles (26 km) north-northeast of Fort William. A battle between the Macintoshes and the MacDonells in 1688 is said to have been the last clan battle to take place in Scotland.

Kerloch *Aberdeenshire* A hill in eastern Aberdeenshire, Kerloch rises to 535 m (1755 ft) to the east of Glen Dye and 6 miles (10 km) south of Banchory.

Kerran, Glen *Argyll and Bute* A small valley located at the southern end of the Kintyre peninsula, Argyll and Bute, Glen Kerran extends southwestwards to join the Conie Glen a mile (1.5 km) north of Keprigan.

Kerrera *Argyll and Bute* An island of the Inner Hebrides, Kerrera lies off the coast of the district of Lorn, from which it is separated by the Sound of Kerrera. With a geology that comprises basalt, schist and red sandstone rocks, its northern end provides protection to Oban Bay. The island, whose total area is 1234 ha (3048 acres), rises to 189 m (620 ft) at Carn Breugach. Associated with the Clan MacDougall since the 12th century, Kerrera's population has declined to its present level of 42 from a peak of just under 200 in the early 19th century. King Alexander II died on Kerrera and King Haakon of Norway mustered his fleet here before the Battle of Largs in 1263. Gylen Castle at the southern end of the island, built in 1587 by Duncan MacDougall of Dunollie, was destroyed by General Leslie in 1647 during the Covenanting Wars. Access to the island is by passenger ferry from Gallanach, 2 miles (3 km) south of Oban.

Kerry, River *Highland* A river in Wester Ross, the Kerry rises in hills to the southwest of Loch Maree. It flows northwest through the Pass of Kerrysdale and past Kerrysdale before joining the Gair Loch.

Kerrycroy *Argyll and Bute* A village on Kerrycroy Bay on the east coast of the island of Bute, Kerrycroy lies 2 miles (3 km) southeast of Rothesay. It was designed as a model village by Maria North, wife of the 2nd Marquess of Bute.

Kershader *Western Isles* A settlement in the South Lochs district of the Isle of Lewis in the Outer Hebrides, Kershader (Gael: *Cearsiadar*) lies on the south shore of Loch Erisort opposite Laxay, a half-mile (1 km) northeast of Habost and a mile (1.5 km) west of Garyvard. A youth hostel, located in a former school building, is owned and run by the local community. The Park War Memorial, unveiled in 1923, served the settlements of Kershader, Habost, Garyvard and Caversta until 2002, when a grant from the War Memorials Trust allowed 62 names of individuals from other villages in the Park district to be added.

Kessock Bridge *Highland* A road bridge carrying the A9 across the narrow strait between the Moray and Beauly firths, the Kessock Bridge links Inverness with North Kessock on the Black Isle. It was modelled on a bridge over the River Rhine near Dusseldorf and has a span of 1052 m (3450 ft). Work began in 1976 and it was opened in 1982.

Kettins *Perth and Kinross* A village in Strathmore, eastern Perth and Kinross, Kettins lies a mile (1.5 km) to the southeast of Coupar Angus. Formerly in Angus, Kettins has a school, old coaching inn, airfield, and a church on the site of a chapel built by a nearby Columban monastery. The present church was built in 1768 and enlarged in 1870 and 1891. In the churchyard stands a Flemish bell named Maria Troon which was cast in Belgium in 1519.

Kettlebridge *Fife* A village in the Howe of Fife, Kettlebridge is situated to the south of the River Eden on the A914 between Glenrothes and Cupar. Formerly known as Holekettle, it developed after the building of the turnpike road *c.*1800 and the opening of the railway to Cupar in 1847. Its bridge was built in 1831. Kettlebridge and neighbouring Kingskettle were centres of the linen trade, while coal, lime and stone were worked nearby.

Kettleholm *Dumfries and Galloway* A hamlet of Annandale in Dumfries and Galloway, Kettleholm lies on the Water of Milk, 3 miles (5 km) south of Lockerbie. It was built in the 19th century as an estate village for nearby Castlemilk. Its neat village hall dates from 1908, and St Mungo's Parish Church, dating from 1875, was designed by David Bryce. There are the remains of two earlier parish churches nearby, the earliest at Kirklands with a churchyard containing interesting tombstones.

Kiessimul Castle An alternative name for Kisimul Castle in the Western Isles.

Kilbagie *Clackmannanshire and Fife* A paper-making settlement straddling the border between Clackmannanshire and Fife, Kilbagie is situated a mile (1.5km) to the north of Kincardine. It is the headquarters of the Inveresk paper-making company and nearby is a stone quarry operated by Tillicoultry Quarries. In 1787 the first threshing machine in Scotland was erected by George Mackie on the farm at Kilbagie, and in the latter part of the 19th century the Kilbagie distillery was reckoned to be one of the largest in Scotland. It was connected by canal and tramway with Kennetpans.

Kilbarchan *Renfrewshire* A village situated 5 miles (8 km) west of Paisley, Kilbarchan was a religious centre named after the 7th-century St Barchan. In the 18th and 19th centuries weavers operated about 800 hand looms and a Weaver's Cottage (National Trust for Scotland) can be visited at the Cross. On the Kilbarchan Steeple (1755) is a bronze statue of 'Habbie' Simpson, a famous piper in the 16th century.

Kilberry Head *Argyll and Bute* A headland on the west

coast of the Knapdale district of Argyll and Bute, Kilberry Head lies a mile (1.5 km) west of the settlement of Kilberry and immediately to the north of Kilberry Bay. At Kilberry Castle there is a fine collection of medieval sculptured stones.

Kilbirnie *North Ayrshire* A village of North Ayrshire, Kilbirnie lies on the River Garnock, 10 miles (16 km) north of Irvine. It developed in association with linen and flax spinning and the manufacture of fishing nets and ropes. There is a 15th-century parish church constructed for the Crawford and Cunningham families.

Kilblaan Burn *Argyll and Bute* A small stream of Argyll and Bute, the Kilblaan Burn rises on Clachan Hill, 2 miles (3 km) north of the settlement of Clachan. Flowing south and then west, it joins the waters of the River Shira at a point in Glen Shira a half-mile (1 km) north of the village of Kilblaan.

Kilbrannan Sound *Argyll and Bute* The Kilbrannan Sound is the channel that separates the island of Arran from the Kintyre peninsula in Argyll and Bute. It has a length of 20 miles (32 km) and a maximum width of 8 miles (13 km).

Kilbride *Western Isles* A small settlement on the southeast coast of South Uist in the Outer Hebrides, Kilbride (Gael: *Cille Bhrighde*) comprises the adjacent communities of West Kilbride and East Kilbride 1.25 miles (2 km) south of Garrynamonie.

Kilbryde Castle *Stirling* A former seat of the Graham earls of Menteith and the Campbells of Aberuchill, Kilbryde Castle is situated on a rocky promontory on the banks of the Ardoch Burn, 3 miles (5 km) northeast of Doune, Stirling Council area. Close by in an ancient graveyard is the Kilbryde Chapel, created in 1864 as a memorial to the Campbells of Aberuchill.

Kilbucho *Scottish Borders* A hamlet in the Peeblesshire district of Scottish Borders, Kilbucho lies on the Kilbucho Burn, 2 miles (3 km) southwest of Broughton.

Kilchattan *Argyll and Bute* A settlement on the island of Bute, Kilchattan lies on Kilchattan Bay, an inlet on the east coast of the island, 2 miles (3 km) north of Garroch Head. The ruined 12th-century Romanesque St Blane's Church lies a mile (1.5 km) to the southwest.

Kilchiaran *Argyll and Bute* A settlement of the Rhinns of Islay, Kilchiaran lies close to Kilchiaran Bay, which forms an inlet on the western coastline of the island.

Kilchoan *Highland* A scattered village with a small harbour on the southern coast of the Ardnamurchan peninsula in the west Highlands, Kilchoan is located 6 miles (10 km) north of Tobermory on Mull. Its notable buildings include a hotel, community centre, primary school, the Ardnamurchan Free Church (dating from 1877) and the Ardnamurchan Parish Church, built by architect William Burn in 1829. The Old Parish Church of St Congan was built in 1763 on the site of an earlier medieval church, but is now a roofless ruin. Nearby are two graveslabs dating from the 14th or 15th century. A vehicle ferry operates between Mingary Pier, immediately to the south, and Tobermory. Mingary Castle lies a mile (1.5 km) to the southeast and dates from the 13th century.

Kilchrenan *Argyll and Bute* A village of Argyll and Bute, Kilchrenan lies 6 miles (10 km) southeast of Taynuilt. The Kilchrenan Burn, which rises in Loch Tromlee, passes through the village before emptying into Loch Awe.

Kilchurn Castle *Argyll and Bute* Located on an islet in Loch Awe to the west of Dalmally in Argyll and Bute, the ruined remains of the Campbell stronghold of Kilchurn Castle date from the mid-15th century. The castle was extended in the 17th century when it was used as a garrison, and the roof was removed in 1770 when the building was abandoned.

Kilconquhar *Fife* An attractive village in the East Neuk of Fife, Kilconquhar is situated on a knoll on the north shore of Kilconquhar Loch just north of Elie. Comprising the once separate neighbouring villages of Barnyards and Kilconquhar, the village is said to derive its name from the kil, or cell of the hermit Connacher. The old name for the village is perpetuated in the 18th-century Kinneuchar Inn, which more closely reflects its local pronunciation. The Gothic-style parish church dates from the 1820s. An earlier church here was cared for during the Middle Ages by the nuns of North Berwick. The parish church overlooks Kilconquhar Loch, where witches are said to have been drowned and where today the game of curling occasionally takes place when the water is frozen. To the east of the village is Kilconquhar House (a former seat of the earls of Lindsay) and the remains of a castle built in 1547 by Sir John Bellenden, Lord Justice Clerk in the reign of James V.

Kilcoy *Highland* A locality in Easter Ross, Kilcoy lies 8 miles (13 km) northwest of Inverness. Nearby is the restored Kilcoy Castle, a former stronghold of the Mackenzies.

Kilcreggan *Argyll and Bute* Situated at the southern end of the Rosneath peninsula, between Gare Loch and Loch Long, Kilcreggan has grown as a small holiday resort accessible from Glasgow via the Clyde port of Gourock. Three miles (5 km) northwest of the town stands Knockderry Castle, which stands over the dungeons of an ancient tower and is associated with Knock Dunder in Sir Walter Scott's *The Heart of Midlothian* (1818).

Kildalloig *Argyll and Bute* A small village on the Kintyre peninsula, Kildalloig lies 2 miles (3 km) east of Campbeltown by Kildalloig Bay.

Kildalton *Argyll and Bute* A locality on the southeast coast of the island of Islay in the Inner Hebrides, Kildalton lies 6 miles (10 km) to the northeast of Port Ellen. The 9th-century Christian wheel cross beside the chapel of Kildalton is the finest of its kind outside Iona. Within the chapel, which was revived by the Lords of the Isles in the 14th century, are displayed late-medieval carved graveslabs.

Kildary *Highland* A hamlet in Easter Ross, Kildary lies on the Balnagown River, 5 miles (8 km) northeast of Invergordon.

Kildavanan *Argyll and Bute* A small settlement on the west coast of the island of Bute, Kildavanan is situated to the north of Ettrick Bay just north of Kildavanan Point, which overlooks the Kyles of Bute.

Kildean *Stirling* A locality in Stirling Council area, Kildean lies on the River Forth on the northern edge of Stirling. Said to be the site of the original Stirling Bridge, it is now the location for a cattle market. The restored Kildean Mill dates from 1697.

Kildermorie Forest *Highland* A deer forest in Easter Ross, Kildermorie Forest lies to the northwest of Alness and west of Loch Morie. Kildermorie Lodge lies near the head of Loch Morie.

Kildonan *North Ayrshire* A settlement with a coastguard station on the southeast coast of the island of Arran, Kildonan lies 3 miles (5 km) south of Whiting Bay. It is said to be associated with St Donan who trained at Whithorn. The ruined Kildonan Castle dates from the 14th century and nearby are Drimla Lodge (1896) and the Lagg Hotel. Kildonan looks out over the Sound of Pladda to the island of Pladda, on which stands a lighthouse built in 1790 by Thomas Smith.

Kildonan *Western Isles* A small settlement amid machair on the west coast of South Uist, Kildonan (Gael: *Cill Donnain*) lies next to Loch Kildonan at the head of Glen Kildonan. The ruins of a 12th-century church can be seen here, and a sizeable museum (Taigh-tasgaidh Chill Donnain) is located in a former school on the eastern side of the A865. The birthplace of Jacobite heroine Flora Macdonald (1722–90) lies a half-mile (1 km) to the south.

Kildonan, Loch *Western Isles* A low-lying loch in the machair of South Uist, Loch Kildonan (Gael: *Loch Chill Donnain*) is located at the mouth of Glen Kildonan, 6 miles (10 km) northwest of Lochboisdale. The loch, split in two by a causeway, is known as Upper Loch Kildonan (Gael: *Loch Chill Donnain Uarach*) to the north and Loch Kildonan to the south.

Kildonan, Strath of *Highland* A broad valley in the Sutherland district of Highland Council area, the Strath of Kildonan extends in a southeasterly direction from Kinbrace to Helmsdale on the North Sea coast. It carries the water of the Helmsdale River, the railway and the A897, which passes Kildonan Lodge, a shooting lodge erected in 1896. A bridge was erected at Kilphedir in 1820 during a period of road improvement following extensive evictions from the Sutherland Estates that took place in the strath in 1813, when many tenants emigrated to Canada. There are a number of ancient hut circles, cairns and broch sites in addition to old Kildonan Parish Church, which dates from 1788. A plaque in the church commemorates George Bannerman, whose great-grandson, J. D. Diefenbaker, became prime minister of Canada. The Strath of Kildonan was the scene of a gold rush in 1869, bringing an influx of prospectors who set up a temporary settlement named Baile-an-Or ('town of gold') by the Kildonan Burn.

Kildrochet House *Dumfries and Galloway* A mansion house in the Rhinns of Galloway, Dumfries and Galloway, Kildrochet lies to the south of the Piltanton Burn, 3 miles (5 km) southeast of Stranraer.

Kildrummy *Aberdeenshire* A hamlet in mid-Aberdeenshire, Kildrummy lies close to the River Don, 7 miles (11 km) west of Alford. Kildrummy Kirk, which dates from 1805 and is of an unusual rectangular, bow-fronted shape, stands close to the remains of the earlier old kirk of St Bride. Nearby Kildrummy Castle, a former stronghold at a central point in the earldom of Mar, is one of the few great stone castles to have survived from the 13th-century peak of European castle-building. Originally said to have been built for King Alexander II, the castle was held in 1306 by Nigel Bruce, brother of Robert the Bruce, while besieged by Prince Edward of Caernarvon. Kildrummy was under siege again in 1335, burned in 1530 and taken by Cromwell in 1654. It became the headquarters of the Earl of Mar during the 1715 Jacobite Rising, after which it was abandoned and dismantled.

Kilfinan *Argyll and Bute* The village of Kilfinan is located on the eastern side of Loch Fyne, Argyll and Bute, 4 miles (6.5 km) northwest of Tighnabruaich. The Kilfinan Burn passes to the north of the village before emptying into Kilfinan Bay on Loch Fyne.

Kilfinichen Bay *Argyll and Bute* A large rocky inlet on the north shore of Loch Scridain on the west coast of Mull, Kilfinichen Bay is bordered on its eastern extreme by the headland of Aird Kilfinichen. The area known as Ardmeanach lies to the west of the bay.

Kilkerran *South Ayrshire* The estate and associated 15th-century keep at Kilkerran are located 4 miles (6.5 km) east of Maybole in South Ayrshire.

Kilkerran Castle *Argyll and Bute* A ruin on the coast of the Kintyre peninsula, Kilkerran Castle lies half a mile (1 km) southeast of Campbeltown. It was built in 1490 by James IV for the purpose of subduing the Clan MacDonald.

Killantringan Bay *Dumfries and Galloway* A bay on the west coast of the Rhinns of Galloway in Dumfries and Galloway, Killantringan Bay lies to the north of Black Head, nearly 2 miles (3 km) north of Portpatrick. Killantringan Lighthouse was built *c.*1900 by D. A. Stevenson.

Killean *Argyll and Bute* The settlement of Killean is located a half-mile (1 km) south of Tayinloan on the western side of the Kintyre peninsula. The village overlooks the islands of Gigha and Cara. The remains of a medieval church are located to the west of the village.

Killearn *Stirling* A dormitory village near the Endrick Water 17 miles (27 km) north of Glasgow, Killearn lies at the north end of Strathblane and northwest of the Campsie Fells. The historian and scholar George Buchanan (1506–82) was born near here.

Killegray *Western Isles* A significant island in the Sound of Harris, Killegray (Gael: *Ceileagraigh*) lies to the south of Ensay 3 miles (5 km) southwest of Leverburgh on Harris. The island rises to 45 m (148 ft) and extends to 176 ha (435 acres). It supported a small permanent population until just before World War II. The 19th-century Killegray House was renovated as holiday accommodation in the early 1990s. A jetty lies on the northeast coast opposite Killegray House, and the remains of an ancient chapel and graveyard lie on the coast to the north.

Killellan *Argyll and Bute* A locality and estate at the southern end of the Kintyre peninsula, Killellan lies to the north of Conie Glen, 4 miles (6.5 km) southwest of Campbeltown.

Killichonan *Perth and Kinross* A village on the north side of Loch Rannoch, Perth and Kinross, Killichonan lies at the mouth of the Killichonan Burn, 6 miles (10 km) west of Kinloch Rannoch. The kirkyard was the burial place of the Macgregors and of St Congan or Conan.

Killiechronan *Argyll and Bute* The village of Killiechronan (also Killichronan) lies at the head of Loch na Keal on the island of Mull, Argyll and Bute. The River Bà, which is a run-off stream from Loch Bà, flows to the south and east of the village before emptying into Loch na Keal.

Killiecrankie *Perth and Kinross* The village of Killiecrankie in Perth and Kinross lies at the northern end of the Pass of Killiecrankie above the River Garry, 4 miles (6.5 km) northwest of Pitlochry. On 27 July 1689 a Jacobite army led by Graham of Claverhouse ('Bonnie Dundee') defeated Government forces under General Hugh Mackay at the Battle of Killiecrankie. A spot known as the Soldier's Leap commemorates a spectacular jump across the Garry by a soldier desperate to evade capture. The wooded gorge here was much admired by Queen Victoria in 1844 and today 16 ha (40 acres) of oak and mixed deciduous woodland are preserved by the National Trust for Scotland which acquired the property in 1947 as a gift. A visitor centre tells the story of the battle, and birdlife in the woodland can be observed via a remote camera.

Killin *Stirling* A village in northwest Stirling Council area, Killin is situated at the west end of Loch Tay, where it is joined by the River Dochart and the River Lochay. In 1694 Sir John Campbell of Glenorchy, 1st Earl of Breadalbane, erected a burgh of barony close to Finlarig Castle, which takes its name from early associations with St Fingal. Killin is now a service centre for the surrounding rural community and a centre of tourism, with hotels, sporting facilities and the Breadalbane Folklore Centre, a former mill re-opened in 1994 as a visitor attraction. At the south end of the village are the scenic Falls of Dochart, and nearby is the Moirlanich Longhouse, a rare surviving example of a Scottish longhouse, maintained by the National Trust for Scotland.

Killinallan *Argyll and Bute* A small settlement near the northern coastline of the island of Islay in the Inner Hebrides, Killinallan lies a half-mile (1 km) southeast of Killinallan Point, looking west onto Loch Gruinart. Bridgend lies 5 miles (8 km) to the south.

Killunaig *Argyll and Bute* A small settlement on the southern shore of Loch Scridain on the island of Mull, Killunaig is situated directly opposite Kilfinichen Bay, a mile (1.5 km) west of Pennyghael.

Kilmacolm *Inverclyde* A dormitory village in a parish of the same name in the interior of Inverclyde, Kilmacolm (also Kilmalcolm) lies on the Gryfe Water, 7 miles (11 km) southeast of Greenock. The parish church (1833) stands on the site of an earlier foundation dating from the 12th century and dedicated to St Columba. The village developed in the 19th century as a hydropathic centre following the arrival of the railway in 1869. Many fine Victorian villas were erected, including Windyhill, which was designed by Charles Rennie Mackintosh. There is an 18-hole golf course.

Kilmahog *Stirling* A hamlet situated on the River Leny a mile (1.5 km) to the west of Callander at the junction of the Trossachs and Lochearnhead roads, Kilmahog was the site of an early 19th-century tollhouse and later a tweed mill.

Kilmalieu An alternative name for Cilmalieu in Highland Council area.

Kilmany *Fife* An old fermetoun village in northeast Fife, Kilmany is situated on the A92, 3 miles (5 km) north of Cupar. Dr Thomas Chalmers, church leader and first moderator of the Free Church after the Disruption of 1843, was minister (1803–15) of Kilmany parish church, which dates from 1768. The church was originally a rectory of St Salvator's College in St Andrews, and in its churchyard lies buried the Earl of Melville who supported William and Mary's claim to the throne in 1689. To the east stands the tower of Kinnear which lies on land occupied by the Kinnear family for over 700 years.

Kilmarnock *East Ayrshire* A town in the Cunninghame district of East Ayrshire, Kilmarnock lies on the Kilmarnock Water and River Irvine, 12 miles (19 km) northeast of Ayr. Said to have been established in the 7th century by the Irish missionary Mernoc, or St Ernan, Kilmarnock developed in medieval times around the Laigh Kirk. Nearby Dean Castle, built c.1300 by the earls of Kilmarnock, later fell into the hands of the Boyd family to whom Kilmarnock was chartered as a burgh in 1591. The town expanded in association with the manufacture of knives, clothes and shoes, and by the mid-18th century it was regarded as the leading centre of Scottish woollens in Scotland. Coal mining, iron founding, engineering, malting and the manufacture of carpets later became important. In 1820 a licensed grocery was established by John Walker, whose company adopted the whisky brand name Johnnie Walker in 1907. Engineering, packaging, spinning, blending and bottling, and the manufacture of shoes are still important industries. Places of interest include Kay Park with its monument to Robert Burns (1879), Laigh Park, the Dick Institute and Dean Castle. The first edition of the poetic works of Robert Burns was published in 1786 in Kilmarnock, which was the birthplace of a number of poets and authors, including John Goldie (1717–1809), Gavin Turnbull (1758–1801), George Campbell (1761–1818), James Thomson (1775–1832), John Kennedy (1789–1833) and Alexander Smith (1829–67). The artists James Tannock (1784–1863) and William Tannock were also born here, as was the documentary film-maker John Grierson (1898–1972).

Kilmarnock Water A river in the Cunninghame district of East Ayrshire, the Kilmarnock Water forms to the north of Kilmarnock at the confluence of the Fenwick Water and the Craufurdland Water which both have their headwaters to the east of Fenwick. After following a course of only 2 miles (3 km) through Kilmarnock it joins the River Irvine a mile (1.5 km) south of the town.

Kilmaron Hill *Fife* Rising to the northwest of Cupar in Fife, Kilmaron Hill overlooks the valley of the River Eden. On its south-facing slopes can be found Kilmaron Den, Kilmaron Farm and the remains of Kilmaron Castle, which was built to a design by J. Gillespie Graham c.1820 for the Dundee manufacturer and benefactor Sir David Baxter (1793–1872).

Kilmartin *Argyll and Bute* A village in the Lorn district of Argyll and Bute, Kilmartin lies on the Kilmartin Burn which joins the River Add between Crinan Loch and Loch Awe, 10 miles (16 km) north of Lochgilphead and 28 miles (45 km) south of Oban. In the surrounding area there are the remains of a number of prehistoric standing stones, stone circles and chambered cairns, as well as the restored Kilmartin Castle and the ruined Carnassarie Castle, which was built for Bishop Carswell of Argyll and the Isles. The ruined Poltalloch House nearby was built for the Malcolm family in the mid-19th century. Kilmartin Church has a fine collection of 13th–17th-century gravestones, as well as a group of crosses. The manse is now occupied as the Centre for Archaeology and Landscape, and Kilmartin House Museum of Ancient Culture highlights the remarkable archeology of the area.

Kilmaurs *East Ayrshire* A village in the Cunninghame district of North Ayrshire, Kilmaurs lies to the east of the Carmel Water, 2 miles (3 km) northwest of Kilmarnock.

Kilmaurs Place was the seat of the earls of Glencairn who established a collegiate church in the village, which became a burgh of barony in 1527. It developed in association with grain milling and the manufacture of cutlery, bonnets, boots and hosiery. Modern industry includes the manufacture of dairy produce and knitwear. The village's old tolbooth remains.

Kilmelford *Argyll and Bute* A small village in the Lorn district of Argyll and Bute, Kilmelford (also Kilmelfort) lies near the head of Loch Melfort, 13 miles (21 km) south of Oban. A gunpowder works was established here in the late 19th century by the proprietors of the Bonawe Ironworks, and in the 20th century the settlement developed in association with tourism, forestry and local hydro-electric schemes. A pier on Loch Melfort attracts yachts, and to the southwest are the 8-ha (20-acre) gardens of Arduaine.

Kilmeny *Argyll and Bute* A scattered settlement on the island of Islay in the Inner Hebrides, Kilmeny lies immediately south of Ballygrant and a half-mile (1 km) south of the Ballygrant Burn, midway between Port Askaig, on the island's northeastern coast, and Bridgend, at the head of Loch Indaal.

Kilmichael *Argyll and Bute* Lying to the east of the Back Water, Kilmichael is 2 miles (3 km) northwest of Campbeltown on the Kintyre peninsula of Argyll and Bute.

Kilmichael Glassary *Argyll and Bute* A small settlement in the Lorn district of Argyll and Bute, Kilmichael Glassary lies immediately northeast of Bridgend at a crossing on the River Add, 4 miles (6.5 km) north of Lochgilphead. An early Christian centre associated with nearby Dunadd, Kilmichael Glassary was later the scene of a cattle market. There are prehistoric cup-and-ring marked stones close by.

Kilmichael of Inverlussa *Argyll and Bute* A settlement on the east side of Loch Sween, in the Knapdale district of Argyll and Bute, Kilmichael of Inverlussa lies 5 miles (8 km) south of Crinan. The waters of the River Lussa flow through the settlement before emptying into Loch Sween.

Kilmorack *Highland* A hamlet in Easter Ross, Kilmorack lies on the River Beauly 11 miles (18 km) west of Inverness. The Strathfarrar–Kilmorack section of the Affric–Beauly Hydro-Electric Scheme includes a dam, and a power station with a fish ladder.

Kilmore *Argyll and Bute* Kilmore is a small, scattered village on the course of the Feochan Mhòr, which flows through Glen Feochan to empty into Loch Nell. Kilmore lies 4 miles (6.5 km) southeast of Oban.

Kilmory *Argyll and Bute* Located on the west coast of the Knapdale district of Argyll and Bute, Kilmory lies on the course of the Kilmory Burn as it heads towards Kilmory Bay, to the north of the Point of Knap. Dating from the 13th century, the medieval Kilmory Knap Chapel houses fine 8th–16th-century stone carvings. Kilmory Castle Gardens, created in the 1770s, are noted for their rhododendrons.

Kilmuir *Highland* A scattered crofting settlement towards the northwest of the Trotternish peninsula on the isle of Skye, Kilmuir is known for the Museum of Island Life and the grave of Jacobite heroine Flora Macdonald (1722–90), which both lie to the northeast.

Kilmuir *Highland* A former fishing hamlet on the Moray Firth coast of the Black Isle, Kilmuir is located 2.5 miles (4 km) north of Inverness and 1.25 miles (2 km) northeast of the Kessock Bridge. Ord Hill lies just to the southwest. The parish church of Kilmuir Wester is in ruins, although the churchyard remains in use. Not to be confused with another Kilmuir and the parish of Kilmuir Easter which lie 15 miles (24 km) to the northeast.

Kilmun *Argyll and Bute* A linear village hugging the northern shoreline of Holy Loch, Kilmun is located on the Cowal peninsula, 2 miles (3 km) northwest of Strone. Strone Point lies a mile (1.5 km) to the southeast of the village.

Kiln Burn *Dumfries and Galloway* A stream in Nithsdale, Dumfries and Galloway, the Kiln Burn rises 3 miles (5 km) to the northeast of Kirkconnel. It flows southeastwards for nearly 2 miles (3 km) to join the Crawick Water.

Kilnave *Argyll and Bute* A settlement to the west of Loch Gruinart at the north end of the island of Islay in the Inner Hebrides, Kilnave lies 6 miles (10 km) northwest of Bridgend.

Kilninian *Argyll and Bute* The scattered community of Kilninian lies on the northern side of Loch Tuath on the island of Mull. The village, which is divided by the Allt Hostarie stream, lies 4 miles (6.5 km) south of Calgary.

Kilninver *Argyll and Bute* The village of Kilninver lies 6 miles (10 km) south of Oban on the southern shore of Loch Feochan and on the course of the River Euchar, which empties into the narrows at the mouth of Loch Feochan.

Kiloran *Argyll and Bute* A village on the island of Colonsay in the Inner Hebrides, Kiloran lies at the north end of the island to the south of Kiloran Bay. There are noted gardens at Kiloran House, the home of Lord Strathcona.

Kilpatrick *Argyll and Bute* Little more than a collection of farm buildings, Kilpatrick lies a half-mile (1 km) southeast of Torosay Castle, overlooking Duart Bay on the eastern coast of the island of Mull in the Inner Hebrides. Craignure lies 2 miles (3 km) to the northwest.

Kilpatrick Hills *West Dunbartonshire* A range of hills to the north of the River Clyde in west-central Scotland, the Kilpatrick Hills extend east from the Vale of Leven to Strathblane. The highest point is Duncolm at 401 m (1316 ft).

Kilpheder *Western Isles* A scattered crofting township in the southwest of South Uist in the Outer Hebrides, Kilpheder (Gael: *Cille Pheadair*) is located 1.25 miles (2 km) southwest of Daliburgh and a similar distance north of North Boisdale. An Iron Age wheelhouse was excavated here in 1952, although there is little to be seen today. In 1997, a Norse settlement comprising the remains of 11 stone buildings was uncovered at Fairy Point (Gael: *Sithean Biorach*), a half-mile (1 km) to the northwest. The machair here is designated a Special Protection Area (SPA).

Kilravock Castle *Highland* Built as a stronghold of the Rose family in 1460, Kilravock Castle is located by the River Nairn between Croy and Clephanton, 5 miles (8 km) southwest of Nairn and 10 miles (16 km) east of Inverness.

Kilrenny *Fife* A village in the East Neuk of Fife, Kilrenny lies to the northeast of Anstruther. It was formerly known as Upper Kilrenny to distinguish it from Nether or Lower Kilrenny which is now known as Cellardyke. A church was founded here in AD 864 by the Celtic Culdees who dedicated the place to St Ethernan. In 1578 the village became a burgh with rights to hold a weekly fair. The present parish church, whose square tower was known to fishermen as 'St Irnie', dates from the 15th century and was extended in 1808 and renovated in 1933. In the churchyard are to be found the Scott of Balcomie Mausoleum, the Beaton Burial Enclosure and Lumsdaine's Burial Enclosure. Innergellie House, a former home of the Beatons and part of the marriage dowry of King Robert III's wife Annabella Drummond, was rebuilt in a Baroque style in 1740. Nearby is the Skeith Stone, a medieval boundary, and further up the coast are the Caiplie Caves, which are associated with Iron Age settlement and with St Adrian and St Ethernan. A conservation area was established in Kilrenny in 1977.

Kilry *Angus* A locality in the Braes of Angus, Kilry lies on the Kilry Burn and to the west of the River Isla, 4 miles (6.5 km) north of Alyth. The parish church of Kilry dates from the 1870s.

Kilspindie *Perth and Kinross* A hamlet in the Braes of the Carse, eastern Perth and Kinross, Kilspindie lies on a minor road at the mouth of a glen that opens out into the Carse of Gowrie, 7 miles (11 km) east of Perth. The seat of the Douglases of Kilspindie probably stood on the site of the present farmhouse, near to which are an old school (1821), a ruined dovecote and a parish church rebuilt *c.*1815. In the kirkyard is the Stuart of Rait Mausoleum (1822).

Kilsyth *North Lanarkshire* A former mining town in the Strathkelvin district of North Lanarkshire, Kilsyth lies to the south of the Kilsyth Hills near the River Kelvin and the Forth and Clyde Canal, 12 miles (19 km) northeast of Glasgow. Laid out in the 1670s by the 2nd Viscount Kilsyth, the town developed on the routeway connecting Glasgow with Stirling and later in association with coal mining, quarrying, paper making and the manufacture of textiles and hosiery. The billiard tables for RMS *Queen Mary* were made in Kilsyth, which was a 'dry' or alcohol-free town from 1923 to 1967. Nearby are the Townhead Reservoir and the remains of Colzium Castle and Colzium House, which dates from 1575. The Battle of Kilsyth, an encounter between Covenanters and the army of Montrose, was fought near here in 1645. There is a heritage museum in the town.

Kilsyth Hills *East Dunbartonshire/North Lanarkshire* A range of hills in central Scotland, the Kilsyth Hills form a southeastern outlier of the Campsie Fells to the north of Glasgow, extending across the border between East Dunbartonshire and North Lanarkshire. The town of Kilsyth lies to the south of the hills, which rise to a height of 458 m (1502 ft) at Garrel Muir. Other peaks include Tomtain (453 m/1486 ft) and Laird's Hill (425 m/1394 ft). The Garrel Burn and River Kelvin rise in the Kilsyth Hills.

Kiltarlity *Highland* A village of Easter Ross, Kiltarlity lies 3 miles (5 km) south of Beauly.

Kilwinning *North Ayrshire* A town and railway junction in the Cunninghame district of North Ayrshire, Kilwinning lies near the mouth of the River Garnock, 3 miles (5 km) north of Irvine. In the 8th century a church is said to have been founded here by St Winning. A later Benedictine abbey linked to Kelso became an important religious centre with a market. Kilwinning was a noted centre of archery in medieval times and later developed in association with coal mining, quarrying, ironfounding and textile manufacture. Modern industries include whisky blending and bottling, and the manufacture of plastics and electronics. In 1966 Kilwinning was included within the designated New Town of Irvine. Kilwinning Abbey Tower, now a heritage centre, was built in 1851 by David Hamilton to replace a previous tower that had been destroyed by lightning in 1809. Surrounding the tower are the remains of the 12th-century abbey.

Kinaldie *Aberdeenshire* A locality in the Aberdeenshire parish of Kinellar, Kinaldie lies on the River Don, nearly 10 miles (16 km) northwest of Aberdeen and southwest of Hatton of Fintray.

Kinbrace *Highland* A settlement in the Sutherland district of Highland Council area, Kinbrace lies 15 miles (24 km) northwest of Helmsdale at the head of Strath Halladale.

Kinbuck *Stirling* A small linear dormitory village with a primary school, Kinbuck is situated on the banks of the Allan Water near Ashfield, 4 miles (6.5 km) north of Dunblane.

Kincaldrum *Angus* A locality in south-central Angus, Kincaldrum lies a half-mile (1 km) northwest of Gateside and 3 miles (5 km) southeast of Glamis. The Guthries of Guthrie originated here, and later Kincaldrum House was the seat of the Baxter family. Kincaldrum Hill rises to 278 m (912 ft) to the southwest.

Kincaple *Fife* An attractive small dormitory village in eastern Fife, Kincaple lies to the south of the Eden estuary and the A91, 2 miles (3 km) northwest of St Andrews. Originally an old farming settlement, its inhabitants eventually found work in the paper mills, brickworks and maltbarns of nearby Guardbridge.

Kincardine *Fife* A village at the western extremity of Fife, Kincardine (known fully as Kincardine-on-Forth) is situated on the River Forth in Tulliallan parish. Dominated by the high-rise flats of Ramsay, Kincairne and Sandeman Courts, Kincardine was founded as a burgh of barony on reclaimed marshland in 1663. It developed as a river port trading in salt and as a centre of shipbuilding and quarrying. Its attractive old town, which has many fine 17th- and 18th-century houses and a mercat cross, is largely bypassed by the A985, which crosses the Forth over the Kincardine Bridge, built between 1932 and 1936 to a design by Alexander Gibb and Partners. The Gothic-style Tulliallan Parish Church built in 1833 replaced an older parish kirk with a tower dating from 1675, and Tulliallan Castle (1817–20), designed by William Atkinson, has been the home of the Scottish Police College since 1954. The Unicorn Inn was the birthplace of the physicist and chemist Sir James Dewar (1842–1923) who was the inventor of the vacuum flask, the first man to liquefy hydrogen gas and co-inventor of the explosive cordite. Kincardine Power Station, the chimney of which was once a notable landmark, opened in 1962 but was demolished in 2001. Longannet Colliery, the last deep mine in Scotland, lay 1.25 miles (2 km) to the southeast but closed in 2002. The Longannet Power Station continues to operate. Kincardine has an 18-hole golf course, a primary school, library and community centre.

Kincardine *Highland* A settlement on the south shore of the Dornoch Firth, Kincardine lies on the Allt Eiteachan, a half-mile (1 km) south-southeast of Ardgay and 1.25 miles (2 km) south of Bonar Bridge.

Kincardine *Highland* A parish in Strathspey, Kincardine lies on the River Spey northeast of Aviemore.

Kincardine Castle *Aberdeenshire* The ruined remains of the former royal residence of Kincardine Castle are located 2 miles (3 km) northeast of Fettercairn in Aberdeenshire.

Kincardine Castle *Perth and Kinross* More a mansion house than a castle, Kincardine Castle was built in the 19th century on the Ruthven Water, a mile (1.5 km) south of Auchterarder in Perth and Kinross. To the southwest lie the ruins of a 14th-century keep that was dismantled in 1645.

Kincardine O'Neil *Aberdeenshire* A hamlet in Deeside, southern Aberdeenshire, Kincardine O'Neil lies on the north side of the River Dee, 7 miles (11 km) west of Banchory. The settlement was founded by St Erchan whose holy well was enclosed in 1858. In 1228 the lands of Onele were granted to Thomas Durward who built a bridge here and whose son established a hospice for travellers. Buildings of interest include the old parish church (14th century), tollhouse, the Episcopal Church (1866), two terraces built *c.*1802 and Kincardine House (1897).

Kincardineshire *Aberdeenshire* A former county of Scotland on the northeast coast, Kincardineshire (or The Mearns) was bounded on the north by Aberdeenshire, from which it was separated by the River Dee, and on the south by Angus, from which it was divided by the River North Esk. Bounded to the west by the Grampians and the east by the North Sea, its coastline extended 32 miles (51 km) from north to south. Its county town was Stonehaven. In 1975 it became part of Grampian Region and in 1996 it formed the southern part of Aberdeenshire.

Kinclaven *Perth and Kinross* A locality in a Perth and Kinross parish of the same name, Kinclaven lies in a bend of the River Tay opposite its confluence with the River Isla, 10 miles (16 km) north of Perth. Directly opposite the mouth of the Isla stand the ruins of 13th-century Kinclaven Castle, which was a favourite haunt of Alexander II. The six-arched bridge over the Tay here was built 1903–05 and is the last roadbridge before Perth. The parish church, rebuilt in 1848, is approached through an attractive War Memorial Lych Gate erected in 1919, and in the kirkyard is an elaborate memorial to Alexander Cabel, Bishop of Brechin, completed *c.*1608.

Kincraig *Highland* A village in the Badenoch district of Highland Council area, Kincraig lies on the River Spey 6 miles (10 km) northeast of Kingussie.

Kincraigie *Perth and Kinross* A hamlet in Strathtay, Perth and Kinross, Kincraigie lies to the west of the River Tay, 5 miles (8 km) northwest of Dunkeld. Immediately to the north is Kinnaird Castle (Kinnaird House), built *c.*1770 by the Duke of Atholl and extended *c.*1900 and in 1928–9. Now a hotel, it has a notable drawing room with panels containing Highland scenes painted in French rococo style. During 1823–4 Kinnaird House was tenanted by the Buller family whose tutor, Thomas Carlyle (1795–1881), wrote most of his *Life of Schiller* here.

Kindallachan *Perth and Kinross* A hamlet in Strathtay, Perth and Kinross, Kindallachan lies on the A9 trunk road to the east of the River Tay, 6 miles (10 km) northwest of Dunkeld.

Kindar, Loch *Dumfries and Galloway* A small loch in Dumfries and Galloway, Loch Kindar lies a mile (1.5 km) to the south of New Abbey. It receives the Glen Burn, which flows down the northern slopes of Criffel, and from it the Drum Burn flows southwards before entering the Solway Firth.

Kindrochit Castle *Aberdeenshire* A ruined 14th-century castle, Kindrochit lies on the Clunie Water to the south of Braemar in Aberdeenshire. Once a royal stronghold, it was granted to Sir Malcolm Drummond in 1390. The castle was ruined by 1618.

Kindrogan Field Centre *Perth and Kinross* An early 19th-century house at Enochdhu in Kirkmichael parish, Perth and Kinross, was converted into the Kindrogan Field Centre in 1963 for the Scottish Field Studies Association. It is a base for field studies, conferences and natural-history excursions, and lies 7 miles (11 km) northeast of Pitlochry.

Kinerarach *Argyll and Bute* The farm building of Kinerarach and associated lands lie in the northern part of the island of Gigha in the Inner Hebrides. East Tarbert Bay lies a half-mile (1 km) to the south.

Kinfauns *Perth and Kinross* A village at the western end of the Braes of the Carse, southeast Perth and Kinross, Kinfauns overlooks the River Tay, 3 miles (5 km) east of Perth. The ruined pre-Reformation church of Kinfauns dates from the 15th century but stands on the site of a chapel of Scone Abbey that existed as early as 1226. The more modern parish church dates from 1869, the manse (Kinfauns House) from 1799 and a T-plan schoolhouse from 1832. The Gothic-style Kinfauns Castle Hotel to the west was designed 1820–26 by Sir Robert Smirke for Francis, 14th Lord Gray.

King's College Chapel *Aberdeen City* One of the best examples in Scotland of a collegiate church, King's College Chapel, situated on the King's College Campus of Aberdeen University, with its distinctive crown tower, was built in 1500. The interior retains its original ceiling, intricate chain stalls and rood screen, while the windows largely date from the 19th and 20th centuries. The crown tower fell and was restored in 1633. William Elphinstone, Bishop of Aberdeen (1431–1514) and founder of King's College, lies buried in the chapel. A near replica of the original tomb, which was damaged by Covenanters in the 17th century, stands outside the chapel. In 2000 the university organised a traditional Latin Mass in the chapel to celebrate its 500th anniversary, only the second time Mass has been held here since the Reformation.

King's Park *Glasgow City* A residential district of Glasgow, King's Park is situated between Cathcart and the South Lanarkshire settlement of Burnside, to the south of the city centre. The King's Park, extending to 40 ha (99 acres), was acquired by the city in 1930 and included Aikenhead House, built in 1806 by David Hamilton.

Kingarth *Argyll and Bute* A small village at the southern end of the island of Bute, Argyll and Bute, Kingarth lies on Kilchattan Bay, 8 miles (13 km) south of Rothesay and 3 miles (5 km) north of Garroch Head.

Kingennie Fishings *Angus* A settlement of southern

Angus, Kingennie Fishings was developed in 2003–04 as a greenfield housing development around a sport fishing centre of the same name, a half-mile (1 km) southeast of Wellbank and 3 miles (5 km) north of Broughty Ferry. The fishing centre comprises four ponds created next to the Buddon Burn, together with a clubhouse and holiday accommodation. The complex hosted the Scottish National Coarse Fishing Championships in 2003 and attracts around 10,000 anglers annually.

Kinghorn *Fife* A former ferryport in Fife, Kinghorn is situated on the north shore of the Firth of Forth between Burntisland and Kirkcaldy. Created a royal burgh in 1170, Kinghorn's former castle was frequently visited by the Scottish Court, the town's name being included in the title of the earldom of Strathmore and Kinghorne and the offices of Constable of Kinghorn and Keeper of the King's Door. During the Middle Ages the town had a hospice for the poor. In addition to its ferry link with the Lothians, Kinghorn developed into a thriving centre of spinning and shipbuilding, and is today a popular holiday resort for caravanners. There are many attractive 18th-century pantiled houses, the 17th-century Cuinzie Neuk, a railway viaduct built in 1847, and Kinghorn Parish Church (1774) with a Sailors' Aisle from an earlier church. To the west of Kinghorn a roadside cross erected in 1886 commemorates Alexander III, the last of Scotland's Celtic kings, who fell to his death from the cliff top here in March 1286. Kinghorn has a lifeboat station, primary school, leisure centre, football ground, sailing club and 18-hole golf course.

Kingie, Glen *Highland* Carrying the waters of the River Kingie northwest to join the western end of Loch Garry within Glen Garry, Glen Kingie lies in the Lochaber district of Highland Council area. To the north of the glen lies Loch Quoich and the peak of Gairich.

Kinglas, Glen *Argyll and Bute* A valley to the east of the head of Loch Fyne, Glen Kinglas carries the Kinglas Water for 6 miles (10 km) to enter Loch Fyne at the settlement of Cairndow. Located to the south of the glen, at its junction with Glen Croe, is the highest point on the old military road from Arrochar known as 'The Rest and be Thankful'.

Kinglas Water *Argyll and Bute* Rising as the Allt Uaine to the west of Loch Sloy, the Kinglas Water flows 6 miles (10 km) in a westerly direction through Glen Kinglas. It empties into Loch Fyne at the settlement of Cairndow, near the head of the loch.

Kinglass, Glen *Argyll and Bute* A valley to the east of Loch Etive, Glen Kinglass carries the water of the River Kinglass south and then west from the peak of Meall Garbh, where it merges with the Allt Hallater to empty into Loch Etive at the settlement of Ardmaddy. The sides of the glen are steep and forested.

Kinglass, River *Argyll and Bute* Rising to the south of Glas Bheinn Mhòr and east of Loch Etive, the River Kinglass flows south before turning west through Glen Kinglass. It enters Loch Etive at the settlement of Ardmaddy and has a total length of 10 miles (156 km).

Kinglassie *Fife* Formerly known as Goatmilk, the village of Kinglassie lies to the north of the Lochty Burn, 3 miles (5 km) southwest of Glenrothes in Fife. It was given to the monks of Dunfermline by Alexander I, but little of antiquity remains except for the Dogton Stone with its Celtic cross situated in a field a mile (1.5 km) to the south. For many years Kinglassie was a weaving village, but in the 19th and 20th centuries it developed as a mining town. It has a primary school, Mitchell Hall (1896), library and Miners' Welfare Institute (1931). Fife Airport lies a mile (1.5 km) to the north, and on a hill overlooking the farm of Redwells stands Blythe's Folly, a 15.6-m/52-ft-high tower built in 1812 by an eccentric Leith shipowner.

Kingledores Burn *Scottish Borders* A river rising on the slopes of Coomb Dod, 3 miles (5 km) west of Tweedsmuir, the Kingledores Burn flows northeast to meet the River Tweed.

Kingoodie *Perth and Kinross* A hamlet in the Carse of Gowrie, Perth and Kinross, Kingoodie lies on the River Tay estuary, 4 miles (6.5 km) west of Dundee. The village owes its origin to nearby quarries that supplied fine building stone for several centuries. The stone was particularly valued for harbour works and constructing sea walls. A small harbour here was used in the 19th century to export stone and import coal.

Kingsbarns *Fife* A village in eastern Fife, Kingsbarns lies 6 miles (10 km) southeast of St Andrews. The barns, now long gone, that gave the place its name supplied the royal residences at Crail and Falkland in medieval times. Little now remains of the harbour built c.1810 by the Earl of Kellie to ship grain and potatoes to Newcastle and London, as well as import coal and field-drainage tiles for the local farming community. There are several fine 18th- and 19th-century buildings, including Kingsbarns House, built in 1794 by John Corstorphine, and a primary school dating from 1822, which is the oldest still in use in Fife. The village was designated a conservation area in 1973. To the south is Cambo House and Garden.

Kingseat *Perth and Kinross* A locality in the Forest of Alyth, east Perth and Kinross, Kingseat lies at the mouth of a narrow glen that opens out into Glen Shee, 7 miles (11 km) north of Blairgowrie. On the slopes of the Hill of Kingseat to the northeast there is an ancient settlement and field system.

Kingseat *Fife* A former mining village in western Fife, Kingseat is situated just over a mile (1.5 km) north of Halbeath and south of Loch Fitty.

Kingshouse *Highland* A locality with a hotel at the western end of Rannoch Moor, Kingshouse lies to the north of the road leading into Glen Coe.

Kingshouse *Stirling* A roadside location of Strathyre in Stirling Council area, Kingshouse lies at the junction of the A84 with the road leading west to Balquhidder and Loch Voil. It owes its origin to military road-building between the two Jacobite Risings of 1715 and 1745, when its 'kingshouse', or military inn, was used by Government soldiers.

Kingskettle *Fife* A commuter village and market garden centre in the Howe of Fife, Kingskettle is situated to the south of the River Eden and east of the A92 between Glenrothes and Cupar. Known locally as Kettle (the name of the parish), it is said to take its name from the *cathel*, or battle, that took place here between Scots and Danes. The village developed in the 19th century with the creation of the turnpike road c.1800 and the opening of the railway to Cupar in 1847, linen weaving and the working of coal and lime being major sources of employment.

Kingsmuir *Angus* A village in Angus, Kingsmuir lies on the B9128 from Forfar to Carnoustie, nearly 2 miles (3 km) southeast of Forfar.

Kingsmuir *Fife* An estate and mansion house situated in Crail parish, eastern Fife, Kingsmuir lies to the west of the B9131 from Anstruther to St Andrews. Associated with the Hannay family, Kingsmuir was once a source of peat to surrounding communities. The ruined keep of the old castle of Pitarthue lies to the northwest.

Kingston *East Lothian* A hamlet in East Lothian, Kingston lies 2 miles (3 km) south of North Berwick. The former Board School (1878) has been converted into a bakery. To the south is Fenton Tower, which was restored in 2000 having lain derelict for 350 years, and to the east is a Ministry of Defence navigation facility.

Kingston *Moray* Situated on the left bank of the River Spey where it flows into the Moray Firth, the Moray village of Kingston (or Kingston-upon-Spey) was founded in 1784 by Messrs Dodsworth and Osborne of Kingston-upon-Hull, who were contracted by the Duke of Gordon to handle timber from the duke's estates in upper Speyside. Boats of up to 500 tonnes were constructed in its dockyard, and for nearly a hundred years timber that had been floated down the Spey from the Forest of Glenmore was exported from here. In 1829 nearly all the houses were swept away by the great flood known as the 'Muckle Spate'.

Kingston Bridge *Glasgow City* Built between 1967 and 1970, the Kingston Bridge links the eastern and western sections of the M8 motorway in the centre of Glasgow. When built, it was the longest pre-stressed concrete bridge in Scotland. This part of the M8 is recorded as being one of the busiest sections of road in Europe.

Kingswells *Aberdeen City* A commuter village of Aberdeen with agricultural-engineering industries, Kingswells is situated to the north of the A944, 5 miles (8 km) west of Aberdeen city centre. Nearby are fine examples of immense Consumption Dykes created in the 19th century during a period of agricultural improvement to 'consume' rocks and boulders littering fields. The small Gothic-style Free Church was constructed in 1857 using boulders gathered from local fields.

Kingussie *Highland* A village in the Badenoch district of Highland Council area, Kingussie lies on the Allt Mhòr in the upper valley of the River Spey, 70 miles (113 km) north of Perth. The Cairngorm Mountains rise to the east and the Monadhliath Mountains to the west. Created a burgh of barony in 1464, Kingussie was laid out in its present form as a planned village in 1799 by the Duke of Gordon. The arrival of the Highland Railway in 1863 stimulated tourism, and an 18-hole golf course was created in 1890. Three years later the Camanachd Association, which regulates the game of shinty, was formed here. Between 1974 and 1996 Kingussie was the administrative centre of the Badenoch and Strathspey District of Highland Region. Bone china, precision instruments and whisky are produced here, and the Highland Folk Museum highlights the history of country life in the Highlands.

Kinhoulavig, Loch *Western Isles* A sea loch on the northwest coast of the Isle of Lewis in the Western Isles, Loch Kinhoulavig (Gael: *Loch Ceann Hulavig, Loch Ceann Hulabhig* or *Loch Thulabhig*) lies immediately to the south of the settlement of Callanish and 12 miles (19 km) west of Stornoway. It connects with the Atlantic Ocean through East Loch Roag.

Kinkell Bridge *Perth and Kinross* A hamlet in Strathearn, Perth and Kinross, Kinkell Bridge lies on the River Earn, 2 miles (3 km) north of Auchterarder. A grand four-arched bridge over the River Earn was built *c.*1793, and alongside is a former tollhouse. A United Presbyterian church built in 1782 survives, as do the nearby ruins of the former parish church of Kinkell which dates from the 16th century. Dedicated to St Bean, the ancient parish church was abandoned when the parishes of Kinkell and Trinity Gask were united.

Kinloch *Perth and Kinross* A hamlet in Strathmore, eastern Perth and Kinross, Kinloch lies due north of the Loch of Drumellie (or Marlee Loch), 2 miles (3 km) west of Blairgowrie. Kinloch Parish Church dates from 1794, and the 17th-century white-harled Marlee House incorporates an earlier tower house. To the west is the ivy-clad Kinloch House Hotel, built *c.*1850.

Kinloch Castle *Highland* A mansion house on the east coast of the island of Rum in the Inner Hebrides, Kinloch Castle overlooks Loch Scresort. Built in 1901 by the wealthy industrialist George Bullough in a Gothic style, its stones were brought over from Arran, hence its distinctive reddish hue. The castle now operates as a youth hostel run by Scottish Natural Heritage who own both the castle and the island.

Kinloch Laggan *Highland* A locality at the head of Loch Laggan, Kinloch Laggan lies 11 miles (18 km) southwest of Newtonmore.

Kinloch Rannoch *Perth and Kinross* A village of grey stone houses in Perth and Kinross, Kinloch Rannoch lies at the eastern end of Loch Rannoch, 18 miles (29 km) west of Pitlochry. The village has a Telford-designed Parliamentary church built in 1829, and a bridge over the River Tummel (here known as Dubhaig) built in 1764 at the expense of estates forfeited after the 1745 Jacobite Rising. The village, now a centre for tourism and outdoor pursuits, was also created by the Commissioners for the Forfeited Estates. At the centre of the village is a memorial to the Gaelic poet Dugald Buchanan (d.1763).

Kinlochaline Castle *Highland* The ruined remains of Kinlochaline Castle sit at the head of Loch Aline in the Lochaber district of Highland Council area, overlooking the Sound of Mull. Built in the 15th century as a square turreted tower, the castle has lain in ruins since the late 17th century after numerous raids during the campaigns of James Graham, 1st Marquess of Montrose (1612–50). It is now privately owned and under restoration.

Kinlochard *Stirling* A hamlet at the head of Loch Ard, 4 miles (6.5 km) west of Aberfoyle in Stirling Council area, Kinlochard is surrounded by fertile farmland lying to the north of the Queen Elizabeth Forest Park.

Kinlochbervie *Highland* A scattered village on the west coast of Sutherland, Kinlochbervie lies on the north side of Loch Inchard, 4 miles (6.5 km) northwest of Rhiconich. Its T-plan Free Presbyterian church was built in 1829 by Thomas Telford. Kinlochbervie has a harbour that is a centre for handling fish. Engineering and mussel farming are also important.

Kinlochewe *Highland* A village of Wester Ross, Kinlochewe lies 2 miles (3 km) southeast of the head of Loch Maree, near the foot of Beinn Eighe. The surrounding area is associated with the Cameron and Mackenzie clans.

Kinlochleven *Highland* A village in the Lochaber district of southwest Highland Council area, Kinlochleven is situated at the head of Loch Leven. It lies on the River Leven, which flows west from the Blackwater Reservoir to Loch Leven. The settlement initially developed as a stopping place on the military road to Fort William built in the 1740s, and in 1909 a company village was created here in association with an aluminium-smelting plant. Although production was run down and the smelter eventually closed in 2000, hydro-electricity is still generated for another smelter at Fort William, with the excess sold to the national grid. The Kinlochleven Visitor Centre and Library incorporates an audiovisual display tracing the history of aluminium smelting. Also in the village is the Ice Factor, said to be the biggest indoor ice-climbing facility in the world, and nearby is the Grey Mare's Falls, one of the highest waterfalls in Britain.

Kinloss *Moray* A village near the head of Findhorn Bay in Moray, Kinloss is situated on the Kinloss Burn 2 miles (3 km) southeast of Findhorn and northeast of Forres amid rich agricultural land. Little remains of the former Cistercian abbey founded by David I in 1150 and one of the best-endowed religious houses in Scotland. One of its most notable abbots was Robert Reid (d.1558), who later became Bishop of Orkney. Responsible for running a school in which many Highland chiefs were educated, he is credited with the introduction into Moray from France of the art of grafting fruit trees. After the property came into the hands of Brodie of Lethen in 1643, the abbey stone was quarried for other buildings, including the local church and Inverness Castle. To the north of the village is an RAF station established in 1939 to train heavy-bomber crews.

Kinmount House *Dumfries and Galloway* A neoclassical mansion house in Dumfries and Galloway, Kinmount House lies amid wooded parklands to the north of Cummertrees between Dumfries and Annan. It was built in 1812 for the Marquess of Queensberry to a design by Sir Robert Smirke.

Kinmuck *Aberdeenshire* A hamlet in Keithhall and Kinkell parish, mid-Aberdeenshire, Kinmuck (or Kinmuick) lies 3 miles (5 km) southeast of Inverurie.

Kinnaber *Angus* A locality in northeast Angus, Kinnaber lies on the south side of the River North Esk, 2 miles (3 km) north of Montrose. An icehouse on the Kinnaber Estate was erected as part of a commercial salmon fishery at the mouth of the river. Kinnaber was at one time a railway junction.

Kinnabus *Argyll and Bute* A small settlement on the island of Islay in the Inner Hebrides, Kinnabus lies a half-mile (1 km) west of Loch Kinnabus on The Oa peninsula, 5 miles (8 km) southwest of Port Ellen.

Kinnaird *Perth and Kinross* A village in the Braes of the Carse, Kinnaird lies at the mouth of a glen that opens out into the Carse of Gowrie, 8 miles (13 km) northeast of Perth. Forming an attractive cluster of houses, Kinnaird has a rose garden in addition to a number of buildings of interest, including the parish church (1815), the former manse (now Delford House) dating from 1831, and an old school (1834), the latter two buildings being designed by the Perth architect William Mackenzie. On the hill slope above the village stands the four-storeyed, 15th-century Kinnaird Castle, which was a stronghold of the Threiplands of Fingask. An earlier tower house on this site was built by the Crown in the 12th century.

Kinnaird *Perth and Kinross* A hamlet in Perth and Kinross, Kinnaird lies on the Kinnaird Burn due east of Moulin and a mile (1.5 km) to the northeast of Pitlochry.

Kinnaird Castle *Angus* A 19th-century mansion house located 3 miles (5 km) southeast of Brechin in Angus, Kinnaird Castle stands on the site of earlier castles and was enlarged in 1854–60 by the architect David Bryce (1803–76). It was a property of the Carnegies from the 15th century. The castle offers views over Strathmore and the Grampians, and is surrounded by a large deer park, woodland, trout farms and arable land. The castle is famed for its art collection, including works by Jamesone, Raphael, Murillo, Dürer, Van Dyck, Raeburn, Landseer and Lucas Cranach.

Kinnaird Head *Aberdeenshire* A headland on the Moray Firth coast of Aberdeenshire, Kinnaird Head forms a peninsula extending into the sea at Fraserburgh. The Kinnaird Head Castle Lighthouse was built in 1787 by Thomas Smith (1752–1815) for the Board of Northern Lighthouses, their first in Scotland. The lighthouse was created from the existing 16th-century Kinnaird Castle, which had been a Fraser ancestral home. The lighthouse was decommissioned in 1991 and today forms part of the Museum of Scottish Lighthouses. A new light was built in 1990.

Kinneff *Aberdeenshire* A small scattered rural settlement within the parish of Kinneff and Catterline in southeast Aberdeenshire, Kinneff lies 2 miles (3 km) northeast of Inverbervie with fine views over the North Sea. A church dedicated to St Anthony and consecrated in 1242 was superseded in 1738 by the present building which had a north aisle added to it in 1876. It is an episode in the 16th century associated with the Old Church of Kinneff that gives the place its claim to fame. In September 1651 Cromwell's army laid siege to Dunnottar Castle further up the coast near Stonehaven and its garrison commander, George Ogilvy of Barras, realised that its capture was imminent. Earlier in the year the Scottish Parliament had ordered the Honours of Scotland, which comprised the Crown, Sceptre and Sword of State, to be moved north to Dunnottar for safe keeping. Now under threat of capture by Cromwell's forces, the Royal Regalia were smuggled out of the castle by the wives of the garrison commander and the parish minister of Kinneff. The 'Honours Three' were then buried under a stone in front of the pulpit of Old Kinneff Church, where they lay for the nine years of Cromwell's Commonwealth. At the Restoration in 1660 the Honours of Scotland were returned to Charles II and placed in Edinburgh Castle, but with the dissolution of the Scottish Parliament in 1707 they were locked in a chest in the Crown Room. There they remained forgotten until rediscovered in 1817 by Sir Walter Scott, who had obtained royal permission for a search to be made. No longer used for regular Sunday worship, the Old Church of Kinneff has been maintained since the 1970s by the Kinneff Old Church Preservation Trust.

Kinneil *Falkirk* An area of parkland with recreational facilities adjacent to Bo'ness in Falkirk Council area, Kinneil comprises Kinneil Wood; the ruined 12th-century Kinneil Church and the site of a medieval village; an Antonine Wall Roman fortlet; and Kinneil House, built by the dukes of Hamilton in the 16th–17th centuries and later leased to John Roebuck, a partner in the Carron Ironworks, and Dugald Stewart, the philosopher. Kinneil Museum displays examples of cast-iron objects and locally produced pottery; and the workshop cottage of the inventor James Watt, a joint patent-holder with John Roebuck of an improved steam engine to pump water from the Bo'ness coal pits. The Kinneil Estate was acquired by the Hamiltons in 1323. After World War I, the former Bo'ness Town Council purchased the woodland and surrounds of Kinneil House under the Public Parks Act. The estate is now owned by Falkirk Council.

Kinnell *Angus* A hamlet in an Angus parish of the same name, Kinnell lies on the Lunan Water 8 miles (13 km) southwest of Montrose. The parish church was rebuilt in 1855.

Kinnel Water *Dumfries and Galloway* A stream in Dumfries and Galloway, the Kinnel Water rises in the Lowther Hills to the north of Queensberry and flows southwards for more than 20 miles (32 km) before joining the River Annan to the east of Lochmaben. It passes through the village of St Ann's and is joined by the Water of Ae.

Kinnernie *Aberdeenshire* A locality in mid-Aberdeenshire to the west of Dunecht and 8 miles (13 km) west of Aberdeen, Kinnernie comprises Kinnernie, West Kinnernie and Old Kinnernie, which lies on the Kinnernie Burn. The former parish of Kinearny was divided in 1743 between the parishes of Midmar and Cluny.

Kinnesswood *Perth and Kinross* Formerly known by its Gaelic name, Kinaskit, the village of Kinnesswood in southern Perth and Kinross lies on the west-facing lower slopes of the Bishop Hill, overlooking Loch Leven. Now largely a commuter settlement, it was formerly a weaving village and before that an agricultural township. It is linked to Scotlandwell and Portmoak Moss by a pathway known as the Tetley Trail, and on its southern edge is the nine-hole golf course of the Bishopshire Golf Club (1903). Many of its older buildings date from the 18th and 19th centuries, among these being the birthplace of the 'Gentle Poet of Lochleven', Michael Bruce (1746–67), now maintained as a village museum. Also born in the village was the renowned meteorologist Alexander Buchan (1829–1907).

Kinning Park *Glasgow City* Located at the eastern end of Govan district in Glasgow, Kinning Park has developed as an industrial suburb. With the opening of the Kingston and Prince's docks, its importance as a workplace increased. It was originally a police burgh, before becoming part of the city in 1905.

Kinnordy *Angus* A hamlet and estate lying 2 miles (3 km) northwest of Kirriemuir in Angus, Kinnordy was the birthplace of geologist Sir Charles Lyell (1797–1875).

Kinnordy, Loch of *Angus* A nature reserve managed by the RSPB, the Loch of Kinnordy lies to the west of Kirriemuir in Angus.

Kinnoull Hill *Perth and Kinross* A prominent summit overlooking the River Tay at the southwest end of the Sidlaw Hills, Kinnoull Hill rises to 222 m (721 ft) a mile (1.5 km) east of Perth. A folly tower was built on the edge of the cliff by one of the earls of Kinnoull to simulate one of the romantic German castles perched above the Rhine. There are woodland walks.

Kinord, Loch *Aberdeenshire* A small loch in Royal Deeside, Aberdeenshire, Loch Kinord lies between Loch Davan and the River Dee, 5 miles (8 km) east of Ballater. Also known as Cannor, it is said to have taken its name from a hunting seat of Malcolm Canmore that was located on the largest of its islets.

Kinpurney Hill *Angus* A summit rising to 345 m (1132 ft) on the north side of the Sidlaw Hills, Angus, Kinpurney Hill looks down onto the valley of Strathmore at Newtyle. It is topped by an 18th-century observation tower and the ramparts of an ancient hillfort.

Kinross *Perth and Kinross* A town in Perth and Kinross, situated by Loch Leven 16 miles (26 km) south of Perth. The former county town of Kinross-shire, Kinross developed in medieval times in association with a royal hostelry that occupied a convenient stopping-off place en route between major royal residences. Lochleven Castle was a royal stronghold until the end of the 14th century, when it was given to the Douglas family, and the town was designated a burgh of barony in 1540. In 1675 the Kinross Estate was sold to Sir William Bruce (1630–1710), architect royal to Charles II, who built the imposing Kinross House, one of Scotland's first country houses. Kinross developed in the 18th and 19th centuries as a coaching centre, textile town, railway junction and administrative centre. It was also noted for its cutlery trade, which survived from 1680 to 1820, and its summer Jooley Fair. Today, without its former railway, it is largely a commuter settlement with a motorway service centre, leisure centre, cashmere spinning mill, Sunday market and light industries. Buildings and locations of interest

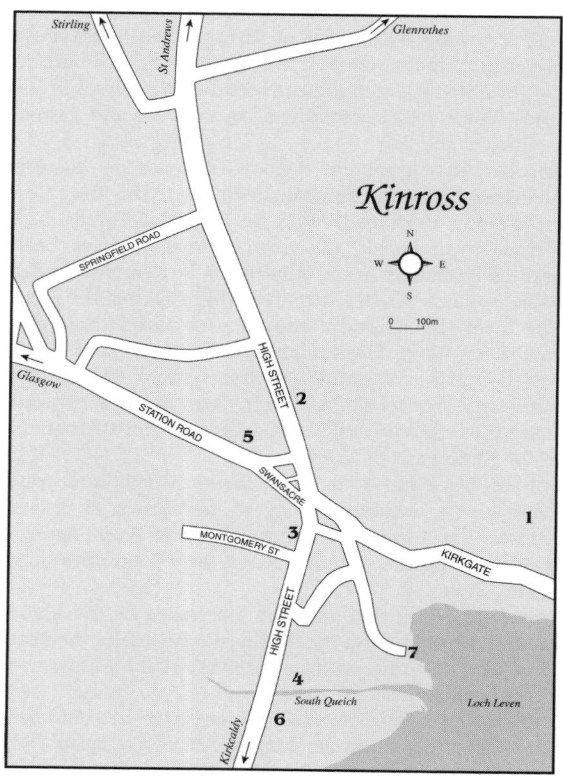

1 Kinross House
2 County Buildings
3 Town Hall
4 Auction Market
5 Parish Church
6 Lochleven Mill
7 Fishing Pier

in the town include the County Buildings, Old Tolbooth, Town Hall and Steeple, the Market Cross, Kinross House Gardens and the Hayfield Garden. The Kinross Agricultural Show is held annually in August.

Kinrossie *Perth and Kinross* A small linear village in Strathmore, Perth and Kinross, Kinrossie lies in the parish of Collace, 6 miles (10 km) northeast of Perth. It retains several reed-thatched cottages and a market cross dated 1686. In 1962 a former Free Church built in 1843 was converted into a village hall.

Kinross-shire A former county, until 1974, in central Scotland, Kinross-shire now forms the southern part of Perth and Kinross. Its county town was the burgh of Kinross.

Kintail *Highland* A district of Wester Ross between Loch Duich and Loch Long, Kintail is one of the finest stretches of mountain scenery in northwest Scotland. An area of 7431 ha (18,362 acres), including Morvich, has been owned by the National Trust for Scotland since 1944 and includes the Falls of Glomach and the Five Sisters of Kintail, four of which rise to heights in excess of 914 m (3000 ft). Historically Kintail is associated with the Mackenzies, who were lords of Kintail before they became earls of Seaforth, and with the Macraes who were the hereditary keepers of Eilean Donan Castle.

Kintessack *Moray* Situated between the Muckle Burn and Culbin Forest, the Moray village of Kintessack lies nearly 3 miles (5 km) northeast of Forres.

Kintillo *Perth and Kinross* Claiming to be the oldest village in Scotland, Kintillo with its neat thatched 18th-century cottages has now been largely subsumed as a southern suburb of Bridge of Earn, 3 miles (5 km) south of Perth. Immediately west is Kilgraston School built in 1793 by Francis Grant and converted into a school in the 1930s. There are the remains of an icehouse and a small Gothic chapel.

Kintore *Aberdeenshire* A small town in eastern Aberdeenshire, Kintore is situated close to the River Don on the A96, 13 miles (21 km) northwest of Aberdeen. A former royal burgh, the town is said to have been granted its charter in the 9th century by Kenneth II after its inhabitants assisted him in his fight against the Picts. The town has a library, caravan park and 18-hole golf course. Its Town House dates from 1737–47, and in its parish churchyard stands a Pictish symbol stone of the 6th or 7th century AD. A mile (1.5 km) to the southwest stand the ruins of Hallforest Castle, a former stronghold of the Keith earls of Kintore.

Kintour *Argyll and Bute* A settlement near the southeast coast of the island of Islay in the Inner Hebrides, Kintour lies 8 miles (13 km) northeast of Port Ellen on the banks of the Kintour River, which empties into nearby Aros Bay.

Kintra *Argyll and Bute* A small settlement on the island of Mull, Kintra lies on the northern coastline of the Ross of Mull, a half-mile (1 km) southwest of the Rubha nan Cearc headland.

Kintraw *Argyll and Bute* A settlement at the head of Loch Craignish, 10.5 miles (17 km) north of Lochgilphead, Kintraw lies to the south of the Barbeck River which empties into the loch closeby. A cairn and standing stone lie immediately to the south.

Kintyre *Argyll and Bute* A district of Argyll and Bute, Kintyre largely comprises a peninsula extending southwards from Knapdale, to which it is linked by a narrow neck of land between East Loch Tarbert and West Loch Tarbert. Just over 42 miles (67 km) in length and between 4 miles (6.5 km) and 11 miles (18 km) wide, it rises to a height of 454 m (1489 ft) at Beinn an Tuirc to the west of Carradale. Its southernmost tip is known as the Mull of Kintyre, which was known to Ptolemy as the *Epidium Promontorium*. A lighthouse here was built by Thomas Smith in 1788 and renovated by his stepson Robert Stevenson. Close by is a cairn commemorating those killed in a Chinook helicopter crash on 2 June 1994. The principal settlement of Kintyre is Campbeltown which has an airport to the west at Machrihanish.

Kinuachdrachd *Argyll and Bute* Located to the west of the headland of Aird of Kinuachdrachd and immediately to the north of Kinuachdrachd Harbour, this scattered settlement lies at the northeast corner of the island of Jura in the Inner Hebrides.

Kippen *Stirling* A picturesque dormitory village, Kippen lies at the foot of the Fintry Hills, 10 miles (16 km) west of Stirling. The surrounding parish is known as the 'Kingdom of Kippen', a name that originated in the 16th century when the local laird adopted John Buchanan as a baby in order to prevent his estate from being acquired by the king. The title 'The King of Kippen' was later bestowed upon John Buchanan by James V. The famous Kippen Vine, planted in 1891, was said to be the largest in the world, covering some 455 sq. m (5000 sq. ft) of roof space. The vineyard was sold in 1964 and the vine broken up. The home of Scottish clay pigeon shooting, Kippen was the venue for the 1986 Commonwealth Games shooting events. The village has rural industries as well as clockmaking and local crafts. Kippen Parish Church (1824) was modernised in 1924 under the guidance of the artist Sir D. Y. Cameron.

Kippenrait Glen *Stirling* Considered to be one of the best areas of mixed woodland on mineral-rich soils associated with rocky slopes, Kippenrait Glen straddles the Wharry Burn which flows down from the Ochil Hills to meet the Allan Water between Dunblane and Bridge of Allan in Stirling Council area.

Kippford *Dumfries and Galloway* Also known as Scaur, the village of Kippford lies at the mouth of the Urr Water on the Solway coast of Dumfries and Galloway, 5 miles (8 km) south of Dalbeattie. Now a resort village, it was once a centre of shipbuilding and granite quarrying.

Kippo Burn *Fife* A small stream in eastern Fife, the Kippo Burn flows northeast from its source near Kippo Farm to enter the North Sea at Cambo Ness near Kingsbarns.

Kirbuster *Orkney* A locality on the Orkney Mainland, Kirbuster lies on the Burn of Kirbuster, between the Loch of Boardhouse and the Loch of Hundland, 2 miles (3 km) southeast of Birsay. Kirbuster Hill rises to 103 m (335 ft) to the north. The notable Kirbuster Museum complex incorporates a central hearth homestead dating from the 16th century and an 18th-century farmhouse with traditional byres.

Kirclachie Burn *Dumfries and Galloway* A stream in Dumfries and Galloway, the Kirclachie Burn rises on the southern slope of Braid Fell, 4 miles (6.5 km) northwest of Stranraer. It flows southwestwards into Loch Ryan near Innermessan.

Kirk Cleuch *Dumfries and Galloway* A small stream in

Eskdale, Dumfries and Galloway, the Kirk Burn flows down from the Great Hill to join the River Esk at Bentpath.

Kirk Hill *South Ayrshire* Kirk Hill rises to a height of 249 m (817 ft) 2 miles (3 km) north of Dailly in South Ayrshire.

Kirk o' Shotts *North Lanarkshire* A locality in North Lanarkshire, Kirk o' Shotts (or Kirk of Shotts) lies to the south of the M8, 2.5 miles (4 km) northwest of Shotts and 5 miles (8 km) east-southeast of Airdrie. It was here that the first television transmitter station was established in Scotland in 1952. Television and radio transmitters are still located on Black Hill and Hirst Hill nearby.

Kirk of Mochrum An alternative name for Mochrum in Dumfries and Galloway.

Kirk Yetholm *Scottish Borders* A small village on the north side of the Cheviot Hills, Kirk Yetholm lies on the Bowmont Water 8 miles (13 km) southeast of Kelso. Once famous as the home of Scottish gypsies, it lies at the northern end of the Pennine Way long-distance footpath.

Kirkandrews *Dumfries and Galloway* A hamlet in Dumfries and Galloway, Kirkandrews sits on Kirkandrews Bay, an inlet of Wigtown Bay, 6 miles (10 km) southwest of Kirkcudbright.

Kirkbean *Dumfries and Galloway* A village of Dumfries and Galloway, Kirkbean lies at the southeast foot of Criffell, 5 miles (8 km) south of New Abbey. A largely 19th-century estate village for Arbigland to the southeast, Kirkbean was the birthplace of John Paul Jones (1747–92), founder of the US Navy. Jones's father was head gardener at Arbigland Gardens.

Kirkbuddo *Angus* A locality in Angus, Kirkbuddo is centred on a crossroads 5 miles (8 km) southeast of Forfar. To the west lies Kirkbuddo House, and at Haerfaulds on the Muir of Lour are traces of a Roman marching camp occupied during the Severan campaigns of AD 209–11.

Kirkcaldy *Fife* Known as the Lang Toun, Kirkcaldy stretches in a wide sweeping arc along the north shore of the Firth of Forth. It is the largest town in Fife and was the administrative centre of Kirkcaldy District from 1975 to 1996. Gifted to the monks of Dunfermline Abbey in 1364, the town's status as a royal burgh was confirmed by Charles II in 1661. Kirkcaldy grew up around its harbour near the mouth of the East Burn and expanded rapidly in the 19th century with the development of textile, linoleum and coal industries. Adam Smith (1723–90), the political economist and author of *The Wealth of Nations*, came from Kirkcaldy, and the novelist John Buchan spent part of his early youth here. Buchan's sister Anna, the novelist O. Douglas, was born in Kirkcaldy, and Thomas Carlyle taught here between 1816 and 1819. Other famous sons of Kirkcaldy include the architect Robert Adam (1728–92), the African missionary Dr John Philp (1775–1851) and Sir Sandford Fleming (1827–1915), who became chief engineer of the Canadian Pacific Railway and invented the Standard Time used internationally from 1883. Today Kirkcaldy encompasses the former burghs of Dysart, Linktown and Pathhead, as well as the villages of Sinclairtown and Gallatown and part of the Raith Estate. Its town centre was designated a conservation area in 1980. Among many interesting buildings are the Old Parish Church with its Norman tower, 15th-century Ravenscraig Castle, 17th-century Sailor's Walk, Kirkcaldy Art Gallery and Museum (1925), the Adam Smith Centre (1894–9), the Nordic-style Town House designed in 1937 by David Carr, Dunnikier House (built in the 1790s and now a hotel), Balwearie Community School dating from the 1960s, and St Brycedale Church (1877–81), which rises to 60 m (200 ft) and takes its name from Kirkcaldy's patron saint. Kirkcaldy has one of Scotland's largest indoor markets, and Fife College of Further and Higher Education has five campuses in the town.

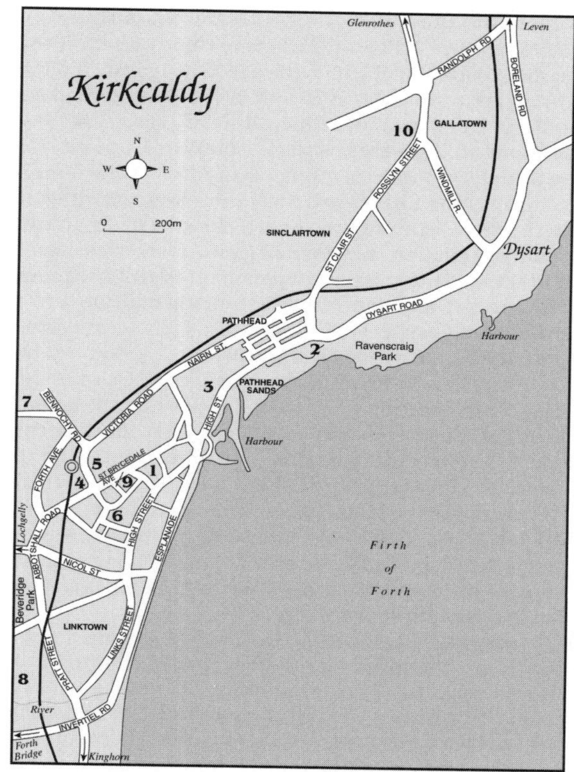

1 *Old Parish Church*
2 *Ravenscraig Castle*
3 *Sailor's Walk*
4 *Kirkcaldy Art Gallery and Museum*
5 *Adam Smith Centre*
6 *Nordic Style Town House*
7 *Kirkcaldy High School*
8 *Balwearie Community School*
9 *St Brycedale Church*
10 *Kirkcaldy Ice Rink*

Kirkchrist *Dumfries and Galloway* A locality in Dumfries and Galloway, Kirkchrist lies west of the River Dee, a mile (1.5 km) northwest of Kirkcudbright.

Kirkcolm *Dumfries and Galloway* A village at the north end of the Rhinns of Galloway, Dumfries and Galloway, Kirkcolm lies on a hillside sloping down to Loch Ryan, 6 miles (10 km) north of Stranraer. Originally named Stewarton, it was created a burgh of barony in 1613. In the 1780s it was rebuilt on its present location as a planned village. In the churchyard of Ervie and Kirkcolm Parish Church (1824) is the 10th-century Kirkcolm Celtic cross.

Kirkconnel *Dumfries and Galloway* A village of Nithsdale in Dumfries and Galloway, Kirkconnel lies on the River Nith, 30 miles (48 km) northwest of Dumfries. The village developed close to the site of the ancient church of St Connel in association with the manufacture of textiles and coal mining, the last pit closing in 1980. Its parish church dates from 1728 and nearby is a Miners' Memorial by Tom Sandilands erected in 1984.

Kirkconnel Burn *Dumfries and Galloway* A stream in Dumfries and Galloway, Kirkconnel Burn rises on the eastern slope of Bail Hill in the parish of Tynron. It flows 4 miles (6.5 km) eastwards to join the Shinnel Water 2 miles (3 km) northwest of the village of Tynron.

Kirkconnell *Dumfries and Galloway* A locality in Nithsdale, Dumfries and Galloway, Kirkconnell comprises the Kirkconnell Merse and Kirkconnell Flow by the River Nith and Kirkconnell House, 6 miles (10 km) south of Dumfries. Kirkconnell House is an extension of a tower house that was a stronghold of the Maxwells. An 18th-century addition to the house was built of bricks made on the estate.

Kirkconnell *Dumfries and Galloway* A locality in Dumfries and Galloway, Kirkconnell lies just west of the Tarff Water, nearly 2 miles (3 km) northwest of Ringford to the southwest of Castle Douglas. Kirkconnell Moor and the Towers of Kirkconnell are to the south, and to the north, on a stream flowing eastwards out of Loch Mannoch, are the waterfalls of Kirkconnell Linn.

Kirkcowan *Dumfries and Galloway* A village with a single street in Dumfries and Galloway, Kirkcowan is situated just north of the River Bladnoch, 8 miles (13 km) southwest of Newton Stewart.

Kirkcudbright *Dumfries and Galloway* A charming royal burgh in Dumfries and Galloway, Kirkcudbright is located 28 miles (45 km) southwest of Dumfries at the mouth of the River Dee, which flows into Kirkcudbright Bay near here. The town developed in the 14th century as a burgh of regality of the Douglas lords of Galloway and was a major centre of trade in wool and cloth. A Franciscan friary and Cistercian nunnery were established here. Destroyed by Manx raiders in 1507, the town's trade declined, but in the 19th century Kirkcudbright became a fashionable resort, and in the 20th century several notable artists, including Sir James Guthrie, E. A. Hornel, Jessie M. King, W. Y. McGregor, S. J. Peploe and E. A. Taylor, came to live in the town. Notable buildings include 16th-century MacLellan's Castle, the Sheriff Court (1866-8), the Town Hall (1878–9), and the Stewartry Museum. Broughton House, acquired by the National Trust for Scotland in 1997, was the mid-18th-century home of the Murrays of Broughton, and of the artist E. A. Hornel during the period 1909–33. Kirkcudbright's 17th-century Tolbooth was the model for the prison in Sir Walter Scott's novel *Guy Mannering* (1815), and the town features in Dorothy L. Sayers' mystery novel *Five Red Herrings* (1931). John Paul Jones, founder of the US Navy, was imprisoned here, charged with the death of a ship's carpenter who died after being flogged.

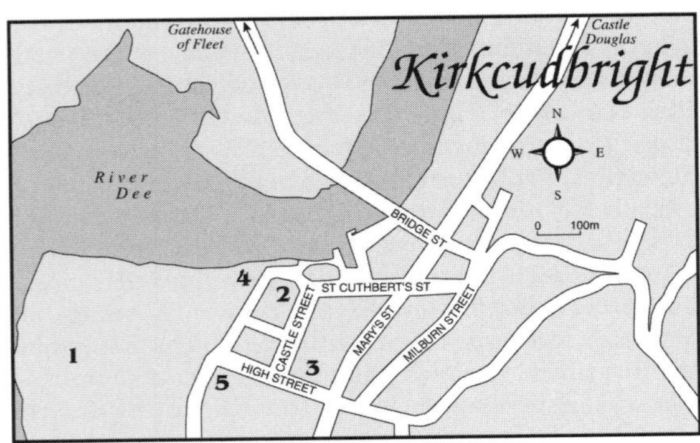

1 *Kirkcudbright Castle*
2 *MacLellan's Castle*
3 *Stewartry Museum*
4 *Broughton House*
5 *Tolbooth*

Kirkcudbright Bay *Dumfries and Galloway* An inlet of the Solway Firth on the coast of Dumfries and Galloway, Kirkcudbright Bay extends 6 miles (10 km) southwards from Kirkcudbright and the mouth of the River Dee. Little Ross Island lies at its mouth, and at its head are extensive tidal sands.

Kirkcudbrightshire A former county of southern Scotland, Kirkcudbrightshire was incorporated into Dumfries and Galloway in 1974. With an area of 2331 sq. km (900 sq. miles), it included territory stretching from the Solway Firth northwards into the Galloway Hills. Its chief towns were Kirkcudbright (the former county town), Castle Douglas, Dalbeattie, Gatehouse of Fleet and New Galloway. Also known as the Stewartry, the old county of Kirkcudbright was ruled by a steward, first appointed by the lords of Galloway in the late 14th century.

Kirkdale House *Dumfries and Galloway* A mansion house in Dumfries and Galloway, Kirkdale House lies on Wigtown Bay, 5 miles (8 km) southeast of Creetown. It was built in 1788 by Robert Adam for the wealthy merchant Sir Samuel Hannay of Mochrum. Nearby can be found a well-preserved sawmill with water wheel, icehouse, Egyptian-style bridge and the remains of the old parish church of Kirkdale with Sir Samuel Hannay's mausoleum.

Kirkfieldbank *South Lanarkshire* A village in a parish of the same name, Kirkfieldbank lies in the Clyde Valley opposite the junction of the Mouse Water with the River Clyde, a mile (1.5 km) west of Lanark. The waterfalls of Stonebyres Linn lie just downstream and the heritage village of New Lanark lies a mile (1.5 km) upstream.

Kirkgunzeon *Dumfries and Galloway* A village of Dumfries and Galloway, Kirkgunzeon is situated on the Kirkgunzeon Lane burn 8.5 miles (15 km) southwest of Dumfries.

Kirkgunzeon Lane *Dumfries and Galloway* A stream in Dumfries and Galloway, Kirkgunzeon Lane rises from Lochaber Loch in Mabie Forest to the southwest of Dumfries. It flows southwestwards for over 10 miles (16 km) before joining the Urr Water at Dalbeattie.

Kirkhill *Highland* A village in Easter Ross, Kirkhill lies 10 miles (16 km) west of Inverness where the Moniack Burn enters the Beauly Firth. Wine is produced at the 17th-century Moniack Castle, and fine soaps are manufactured locally. The Wardlaw Mausoleum was built on the site of the old church by the Frasers of Lovat in 1634.

Kirkhill of Kennethmont *Aberdeenshire* A village with a distillery in the Aberdeenshire parish of Kennethmont, Kirkhill of Kennethmont lies 7 miles (11 km) south of Huntly on the B9002 to Inverurie. To the north of the village is Leith Hall, which was bequeathed to the National Trust for Scotland by the Leith-Hay family in 1945.

Kirkhope *Scottish Borders* A hamlet in a parish of the same name in the Ettrick district of Scottish Borders, Kirkhope lies on the Ettrick Water a mile (1.5 km) southwest of Ettrickbridge and 8 miles (13 km) southwest of Selkirk. To the north is Old Kirkhope and Kirkhope Tower, a former stronghold of the Scotts of Harden, built in the 16th century.

Kirkhope Cleuch *South Lanarkshire* A stream of South Lanarkshire, the Kirkhope Cleuch rises between Rodger Law and Hirstane Rig in the Lowther Hills, 7 miles (11 km) west of Moffat and 8 miles (13 km) northeast of Thornhill. Flowing in a northeasterly direction, it empties into the southern end of the Daer Reservoir.

Kirkiboll An alternative name for Tongue in Highland Council area.

Kirkibost *Western Isles* A crofting township on the southeast coast of Great Bernera, Kirkibost (Gael: *Circebost*) is located 2 miles (3 km) northwest of Callanish, overlooking East Loch Roag. There is a pier at the northern end of the settlement for the landing of crustacea harvested from the sea loch.

Kirkinch *Angus* A hamlet in Strathmore, Kirkinch lies 2 miles (3 km) east of Meigle in Angus.

Kirkinner *Dumfries and Galloway* A village in the Machars of Dumfries and Galloway, Kirkinner lies 3 miles (5 km) south of Wigtown. Inside the parish church (1828) is the 10th-century Kirkinner Cross, and in the kirkyard is a mausoleum of the Van Agnews of Barnbarroch, an estate 1.5 miles (2.5 km) to the west. A mile (1.5 km) to the north stand the remains of Baldoon Castle, a former seat of the Dunbar family that inspired Sir Walter Scott's *The Bride of Lammermoor* (1819).

Kirkintilloch *East Dunbartonshire* The administrative centre of East Dunbartonshire, Kirkintilloch lies on the Forth and Clyde Canal near the junction of the Luggie Water with the River Kelvin. It developed near the site of a fort on the Roman Antonine Wall and became a royal burgh in the 12th century. Its growth was stimulated in the 18th century by the manufacture of textiles, coal mining and the opening of the eastern part of the canal. Brass founding and the manufacture of electrical circuits, nails and bottle closures emerged as modern industries. Thomas Johnston (1881–1965), Secretary of State for Scotland during World War II, was born in Kirkintilloch. The town's population rapidly expanded in the 1960s when it accommodated Glasgow's overspill, and from 1974 to 1996 Kirkintilloch was the administrative centre of the Strathkelvin District of Strathclyde Region. Buildings of interest include the Church of St Mary (1644), which is now a museum.

Kirkland *Dumfries and Galloway* A village of Nithsdale in Dumfries and Galloway, Kirkland lies on the Cairn Water, 2 miles (3 km) east of Moniaive. It has some 19th-century Tudor-style cottages. In the kirkyard of the Gothic-style Glencairn Parish Church (1836) stand the ruins of an earlier church and the mausoleum of the Gillespies of Parton.

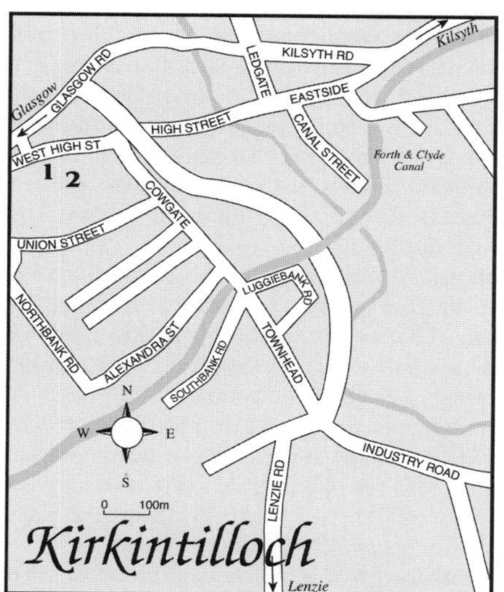

1 *Auld Kirk Museum* 2 *Barony Chambers Museum*

Kirkland Hill A hill in the parish of Kirkconnel, Dumfries and Galloway, Kirkland Hill rises to 509 m (1670 ft) near the border with East Ayrshire, 2 miles (3 km) north of Kirkconnel.

Kirkliston *City of Edinburgh* A dormitory settlement of Edinburgh, Kirkliston lies to the west of the city on the River Almond, 3 miles (5 km) south of South Queensferry. Created a burgh of barony in 1621, the village developed in association with the manufacture of textiles, quarrying and distilling. The Drambuie liqueur is blended here.

Kirkmabreck *Dumfries and Galloway* A locality in Dumfries and Galloway, Kirkmabreck lies to the east of Wigtown Bay, just over a mile (1.5 km) to the south of Creetown. Granite has been quarried here for some time, a quay on the bay serving to assist the export of stone. The remains of Kirkmabreck Old Parish Church stand on the Kirkbride Burn.

Kirkmadrine *Dumfries and Galloway* A locality to the south of Sandhead in the Rhinns of Galloway, Dumfries and Galloway, Kirkmadrine is the site of a 19th-century burial chapel, attached to which is a porch containing early Christian stones dating from the 5th century AD. Thought to be dedicated to bishop-priests, the stones are among the oldest Christian monuments in Scotland.

Kirkmaiden *Dumfries and Galloway* A small kirkton village at the southern end of the Rhinns of Galloway in Dumfries and Galloway, Kirkmaiden lies 14 miles (22 km) south of Stranraer between Port Logan and Drummore. Its church, one of the oldest in Galloway, contains the burial vault of the McDoualls of Logan. An unusual lighthouse monument in the kirkyard commemorates the son of a keeper of the Mull of Galloway lighthouse who died here in 1852.

Kirkmichael *Perth and Kinross* The village of Kirkmichael is located in the valley of Strathardle, 9 miles (14 km) east of Pitlochry in Perth and Kinross. Settlement here is believed to date from about 200 BC, with relics from this time discovered in the 1930s. Like many of the villages of the area it has had a turbulent past. Oliver Cromwell stationed his army here in 1653, and a battle subsequently took place in the grounds of the church, while in 1715, clans sympathetic to the Jacobite cause gathered here before marching south.

Kirkmichael *South Ayrshire* A village in a parish of the same name in South Ayrshire, Kirkmichael is situated on the Dyrock Burn 3 miles (5 km) east of Maybole. Nearby stands Kirkmichael House.

Kirkmuirhill *South Lanarkshire* A settlement in the valley of the River Nethan, South Lanarkshire, Kirkmuirhill lies adjacent to Blackwood, 6 miles (10 km) west of Lanark.

Kirknewton *West Lothian* A dormitory settlement in West Lothian, Kirknewton lies to the west of the Pentland Hills, 10 miles (16 km) southwest of Edinburgh. It developed in the late 19th century in association with quarrying and oil-shale mining. A military airfield established during the World War II is now used as a gliding school.

Kirkney Water *Aberdeenshire* A stream in Aberdeenshire, the Kirkney Water rises to the east of Cabrach. It flows north and northeast through Clashindarroch Forest to join the River Bogie at Culdrain, 4 miles (6.5 km) northeast of Rhynie.

Kirkoswald *South Ayrshire* A village in South Ayrshire, Kirkoswald lies nearly 2 miles (3 km) from the coast and 4 miles (6.5 km) southwest of Maybole. Associated with the ancient church of St Oswald, its parish church was rebuilt in 1777 to a design by the architect Robert Adam. In its churchyard are buried Douglas Graham and John Davidson who were immortalised by Robert Burns, who stayed in the village in 1778, as Tam o' Shanter and Souter Johnnie. Souter Johnnie's Cottage, the home of John Davidson, the village souter (shoemaker), was acquired by the National Trust for Scotland in 1932.

Kirkpatrick *Dumfries and Galloway* A hamlet of Nithsdale in Dumfries and Galloway, Kirkpatrick lies to the east of the River Nith, nearly 4 miles (6.5 km) southeast of Thornhill.

Kirkpatrick Durham *Dumfries and Galloway* A village of Dumfries and Galloway, Kirkpatrick Durham lies 6 miles (10 km) north of Castle Douglas. It was founded in 1783 by the Revd David Lamont, minister of the parish of Kirkpatrick Durham, who used a legacy to buy land that could be feued on good terms to handloom weavers. The village comprises two streets of one- and two-storey houses.

Kirkpatrick Fleming *Dumfries and Galloway* A village in Dumfries and Galloway, Kirkpatrick Fleming is situated just north of the Kirtle Water, 4 miles (6.5 km) northwest of Gretna.

Kirkstile *Dumfries and Galloway* A hamlet of Dumfries and Galloway, Kirkstile lies on the Ewes Water, 4 miles (6.5 km) north of Langholm.

Kirkton *Dumfries and Galloway* A village of Nithsdale in Dumfries and Galloway, Kirkton lies to the north of the River Nith, 4 miles (6.5 km) north of Dumfries. The settlement of Holywood lies to the southwest while to the northwest lie the remains of a Roman fortress.

Kirkton Head *Aberdeenshire* A small headland on the North Sea coast of Aberdeenshire, Kirkton Head lies 2 miles (3 km) northwest of Peterhead.

Kirkton of Airlie *Angus* A locality with a church in Angus, Kirkton of Airlie lies in Strathmore, 5 miles (8 km) southwest of Kirriemuir. Airlie Castle, a seat of the Ogilvies, lies to the northwest at the junction of the Melgam Water with the River Isla. It was built by Walter Ogilvy of Lintrathen following a grant made to him in 1432 by James I.

Kirkton of Auchterhouse *Angus* A village with a church at the centre of the Angus parish of Auchterhouse, Kirkton of Auchterhouse is located 5 miles (8 km) northwest of Dundee. Rebuilt in 1775, the parish church contains the nave of an earlier medieval building. Auchterhouse Hill rises behind the village to the north and 20th-century housing is arranged in terraces along its slopes up to the former Sidlaw Sanitorium, which has been converted into flats. Quarrying was once an important industry, and impressive stone walls around some of the houses are a reminder of this activity. The hamlet of Auchterhouse lies a mile (1.5 km) to the southwest.

Kirkton of Bourtie *Aberdeenshire* A small hamlet in Aberdeenshire, Kirkton of Bourtie lies a mile (1.5 km) to the south of Oldmeldrum. The Hill of Barra which rises to the north is capped by a hillfort dating from the 1st millennium BC. The parish church of Bourtie, which dates from 1806, has a Pictish stone fragment set into its south wall.

Kirkton of Cleish An alternative name for Cleish in Perth and Kinross.

Kirkton of Collace *Perth and Kinross* A small settlement with a church in the parish of Collace, Perth and Kinross, Kirkton of Collace lies at the foot of the western slopes of Dunsinane Hill, due east of Kinrossie and 6 miles (10 km) northeast of Perth. In the churchyard of the parish church (1813) is the Nairne Mausoleum, constructed using stone from an earlier church dedicated in 1242.

Kirkton of Culsalmond *Aberdeenshire* A hamlet with a church in the Garioch district of Aberdeenshire, Kirkton of Culsalmond lies on the Glen Water, 3 miles (5 km) north of Insch and 12 miles (19 km) northwest of Inverurie.

Kirkton of Durris *Aberdeenshire* Situated to the south of the River Dee, 14 miles (22 km) west of Aberdeen, the village of Kirkton of Durris lies on the Burn of Sheeoch near its junction with the Dee. To the east of the village are a medieval motte and Durris House dating from the 17th century. To the south, Durris Forest covers the slopes of Cairn-mon-earn, which rises to 378 m (1241 ft).

Kirkton of Glenbuchat *Aberdeenshire* A village with a church in the Strathdon district of western Aberdeenshire, Kirkton of Glenbuchat lies to the south of the Water of Buchat, which joins the River Don at Bridge of Glenbuchat. Originally dedicated to St Peter, the parish church was rebuilt in 1629. To the east, near Mains of Glenbuchat, stand the ruins of Glenbuchat Castle, which was built in 1590 by John Gordon of Glenbucket (Glenbuchat) in the style of a defensive laird's house. At the head of Glenbuchat, near Badenyon, the Earl of Fife built a shooting lodge in 1843.

Kirkton of Glenisla *Angus* A hamlet with a church in Glen Isla, Angus, Kirkton of Glenisla lies on the River Isla, 8 miles (13 km) north of Alyth.

Kirkton of Kingoldrum *Angus* A village in the Angus parish of Kingoldrum, Kirkton of Kingoldrum lies at the foot of Kirkton Hill on the Crombie Burn, 4 miles (6.5 km) west of Kirriemuir. The parish church was built in 1840, and to the south of the village stand the ruins of Balfour Castle, a former stronghold of the Ogilvies of Balfour, said to have been erected in the 16th century by Cardinal Beaton for his mistress, Marion Ogilvy, and their children.

Kirkton of Kinnettles *Angus* A small hamlet at the centre of the parish of Kinnettles in central Angus, Kirkton of Kinnettles (or simply Kirkton) lies a half-mile (1 km) southeast of Douglastown and 3 miles (5 km) southwest of Forfar. The parish church dates from 1812, although an earlier structure was dedicated by Bishop David de Bernham in 1241. The Duncan Hall was built as the United Free Church in 1843 and served in this capacity until 1919. Kinnettles House, a fine Scottish baronial mansion, lies to the northeast.

Kirkton of Largo An alternative name for Upper Largo in Fife.

Kirkton of Logie Buchan *Aberdeenshire* A hamlet with

a church in the Formartine District of eastern Aberdeenshire, Kirkton of Logie Buchan lies to the south of the River Ythan, a mile (1.5 km) east of Ellon. Alexander Arbuthnott (1538–83), the first Protestant principal of King's College, Aberdeen, was minister here from 1568 until his death. The present parish church dates from 1787.

Kirkton of Menmuir *Angus* A locality with a church in Menmuir parish, Angus, the Kirkton of Menmuir is situated on the edge of the Braes of Angus, 5 miles (8 km) northwest of Brechin.

Kirkton of Rayne *Aberdeenshire* A hamlet in mid-Aberdeenshire, Kirkton of Rayne lies a mile (1.5 km) to the northeast of Old Rayne at the heart of the parish of Rayne, which once belonged to the bishops of Aberdeen. The parish church, known as the 'white kirk of Rayne', was built in 1789. The 14th-century poet John Barbour, author of *The Bruis*, was priest here.

Kirkton of Skene *Aberdeenshire* A village to the east of Loch Skene in central Aberdeenshire, Kirkton of Skene lies 6 miles (10 km) west of Aberdeen. The parish church of Skene, which gives the settlement its fuller name, was originally dedicated to St Bride and rebuilt in 1801.

Kirkton of Strathmartine *Angus* A kirkton village in Angus, Strathmartine lies nearly 4 miles (6.5 km) north-northwest of Dundee.

Kirkton of Tealing *Angus* A hamlet with a church in the Angus parish of Tealing, Kirkton of Tealing lies a half-mile (1 km) west of Tealing village and 4 miles (6.5 km) north of Dundee. Its pre-Reformation church, now unused, was built in 1806. Revd John Glass (1695–1773), the founder of the Glassite movement, was minister of Tealing from 1719 until he was deposed from the ministry of the Church of Scotland in 1728 for advocating that congregations and their elders were subject to no jurisdiction other than that of Jesus Christ. The remains of the former RAF Tealing, a World War II training base, lie a quarter-mile (0.4 km) to the south.

Kirktown of Alvah *Aberdeenshire* A hamlet with a church in northwest Aberdeenshire, Kirktown of Alvah lies between the Hill of Alvah (176 m/578 ft) and the River Deveron, 2 miles (3 km) south of Banff. To the northwest is St Colme's Well, a holy well that used to supply water to Banff.

Kirktown of Auchterless *Aberdeenshire* A hamlet with a church in the Aberdeenshire parish of Auchterless, Kirktown of Auchterless lies in the northeast foothills of the Grampians, 5 miles (8 km) south of Turriff. Situated close to the River Ythan, the settlement lies in a valley here known as the Howe of Auchterless, a name remembered in a traditional 17th-century ballad that claimed there was 'many a bonnie lass in the Howe of Auchterless'. Today the most eye-catching feature is a neo-Gothic red-sandstone church built 1877–9, with a spire added in 1896. This building replaced the earlier St Drostan's Church whose ruins to the southwest retain a birdcage bellcote with a bell dated 1644. There are marble tablets dedicated to the Duff family in the old kirk, and in the new churchyard stands the Duff of Hatton Mausoleum built in 1877. The farm of Chapel of Seggat to the northeast is associated with a former chapel adjacent to the Well of Our Lady and with Peter Garden who allegedly outlived ten monarchs, dying in 1775 at the grand old age of 131. The novelist James Leslie Mitchell (1901–35) was born at the nearby farm of Hillhead of Seggat. Better known as Lewis Grassic Gibbon, he lived here for the first seven years of his life and used the name Seggat in the first volume of *A Scots Quair* (1932). Chief among the many prehistoric antiquities in the surrounding parish of Auchterless are the quartzite kerb cairns at Logie Newton which date from the 2nd millennium BC.

Kirktown of Clatt An alternative name for Clatt in Aberdeenshire.

Kirktown of Deskford *Moray* A kirkton settlement in Moray, Kirktown of Deskford lies 2 miles (3 km) south of Cullen on the Burn of Deskford. It was created a burgh of barony in 1698. The former Deskford Tower was a seat of the earls of Findlater and Seafield. Its church dates from 1551. A new village was built in the 1760s but industry failed to prosper and the village, now largely occupied by commuters, never expanded.

Kirktown of Mortlach *Moray* A village on the Dullan Water adjacent to Dufftown, Kirktown of Mortlach has long been a religious site associated with St Moluag of Bangor in Ireland, who came here in the 6th century. Its church dates from the 13th century and in its churchyard stands the Battle Stone, a monument said to mark the final defeat of the Danes by Malcolm Canmore in 1010. In the vestibule of the church is an earlier Pictish symbol stone known as the Elephant Stone. Mortlach Distillery lies downstream.

Kirktown of Slains *Aberdeenshire* A small settlement with a church (1806) in the Formartine district of Aberdeenshire, Kirktown of Slains lies immediately north of the coastal village of Collieston, 4 miles (6.5 km) east of Ellon.

Kirkwall *Orkney* The capital of the Orkney Islands, Kirkwall stands on a narrow neck of land that divides east and west Mainland. It was established by the Norse in the 11th century on the site of a natural harbour, and in 1137 gained city status with the founding of the Cathedral of St Magnus. Close to the cathedral are the Bishop's Palace, a 16th-century reconstruction of a 12th-

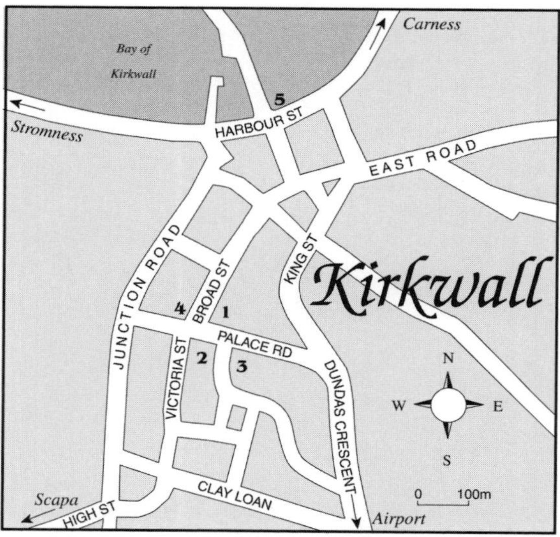

1 *Cathedral of St Magnus*
2 *Bishop's Palace*
3 *Earl's Palace*
4 *Tankerness House Museum*
5 *Orkney Ferries*

century building, and the 16th-century Earl's Palace, the former home of the earls of Orkney. Kirkwall was made a royal burgh by James III in 1486, 17 years after the Orkney and Shetland Islands passed into Scottish possession. Today it is a centre for administration, knitwear and craft production, fishing, food processing and the distilling of whisky, the Highland Park Distillery being the northernmost distillery in the UK. Among the burgh's local events are the St Magnus Festival, which has been held in Kirkwall every June since 1976, and The Ba', a football game that takes place in the main street on New Year's Day. Kirkwall Airport is situated on the A960, 3 miles (5 km) southeast of Kirkwall.

Kirn *Argyll and Bute* Kirn is the name given to a northeasterly extension of the town of Dunoon that lies on the western shore of the Firth of Clyde, Argyll and Bute.

Kirriemuir *Angus* A red-sandstone town in the valley of Strathmore in Angus, Kirriemuir is situated on the Gairie Burn 5 miles (8 km) northwest of Forfar. Described as the 'Gateway to the Glens', its settlement dates back at least to medieval times. Once a centre of handloom weaving and later jute processing, it now lies at the heart of rich farming land and has textile and milling industries. Its most famous son is the playwright and novelist J. M. Barrie (1860–1937), whose birthplace is now maintained by the National Trust for Scotland. There is a fascinating small aviation museum, and a camera obscura on Kirrie Hill, which was gifted to the town by Barrie. Kirriemuir was also the birthplace of the film star David Niven (1909–83) and the rock star Bon Scott (1946–80). The town has a leisure centre with a swimming pool, and in September holds a weekend festival.

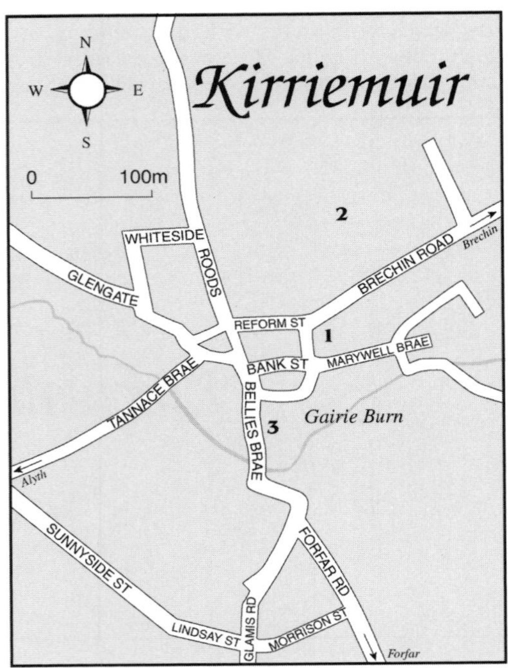

1 *J. M. Barrie Birthplace* 3 *Aviation Museum*
2 *Camera Obscura*

Kirriereoch Hill A hill rising to 786 m (2565 ft) on the border between South Ayrshire and Dumfries and Galloway, Kirriereoch lies just to the north of Merrick and east of the Glentrool Forest.

Kirroughtree Forest *Dumfries and Galloway* An area of woodland, Kirroughtree Forest lies to the northeast of Newton Stewart in Dumfries and Galloway.

Kirtle Water *Dumfries and Galloway* A stream in Dumfries and Galloway, the Kirtle Water rises on the southern slopes of Haggy Hill to the west of Langholm. It flows southwestwards through Kirtleton to Kirtlebridge then southeastwards to enter the head of the Solway Firth at Kirtlefoot near Gretna. The Winterhope Reservoir lies near its source and its total length is just over 16 miles (26 km).

Kirtlebridge *Dumfries and Galloway* A village of Annandale in Dumfries and Galloway, Kirtlebridge lies at a crossing of the Kirtle Water and on the railway from Carlisle to Glasgow, 9 miles (14 km) southeast of Lockerbie. To the southeast is Bonshaw Tower, a former stronghold of the Corrie and Irvine families.

Kishorn, Loch *Highland* A sea loch to the north of Loch Carron on the coast of Wester Ross, Loch Kishorn opens out into the Inner Sound opposite Skye. It is fed by the River Kishorn. A construction yard for deep-water oil platforms was established here in 1975 and a village was created for 2000 workers. The 600,000-tonne concrete Ninian Central Platform, the world's largest movable structure, was constructed here in 1978. The yard closed in 1987.

Kisimul Castle *Western Isles* Located on the tiny islet of Kisimul (or Kiessimul) in Castle Bay on the south coast of the island of Barra in the Western Isles, Kisimul Castle is the seat of the MacNeils of Barra and is believed to date back to 1120, although some accounts date construction to post-1427. What is not in doubt is that by the mid-18th century it was abandoned and burned. It remained in a ruinous state until restoration work was undertaken by Robert Lister MacNeil in the period 1938–70. Occupying the whole of the islet, the castle takes the shape of the shoreline and encompasses a courtyard, chapel, north tower, great hall and the Tanist House. It is home to Clan MacNeil memorabilia.

Kittochside *South Lanarkshire* Situated towards the north of South Lanarkshire on the northwest edge of East Kilbride, Kittochside is the site of the Museum of Scottish Country Life, which is jointly managed by the National Trust for Scotland and the National Museums of Scotland. The gift of Wester Kittochside to the NTS in 1992 included the contents of the farm and steading which reflect the history of ownership of the land by ten generations of the Reid family. The purpose-built exhibition erected on land acquired in 1997 also houses the National Country Life Collection. It was opened in 2002.

Knap, Point of *Argyll and Bute* The Point of Knap is the name given to a headland lying on the western coastline of the district of Knapdale, Argyll and Bute. Extending into the Sound of Jura, the headland lies on the western entrance to Loch Caolisport.

Knap of Howar *Orkney* The site of a Neolithic settlement on the island of Papa Westray in the Orkney Islands, the Knap of Howar was occupied more than a thousand years before the Egyptians started building the Great Pyramid. Situated on the west coast of the island, a half-mile (1 km) west of Holland House, its buildings are the oldest in Europe. It comprises two houses excavated in the early 1930s and again in the 1970s.

Knapdale *Argyll and Bute* A district of Argyll and Bute, Knapdale lies to the north of the Kintyre peninsula and south of the Crinan Canal, which separates it from the district of Lorn. It includes Loch Sween, Loch Caolisport and the Knapdale Forest to the north. Its principal settlement is Ardrishaig. Knapdale was associated with the Macneill and Macmillan clans.

Kneep *Western Isles* A settlement in western Lewis in the Outer Hebrides, Kneep (Gael: *Cnip*) looks out onto the Sound of Pabay immediately to the southeast of Valtos. Kneep is the site of an Iron Age wheelhouse complex and a Viking cemetery.

Knightswood *Glasgow City* A residential district of Glasgow, Knightswood lies to the northwest of the city centre, south of Drumchapel and west of Anniesland. It was developed as the largest of Glasgow's inter-war housing schemes and comprises cottages and cottage flats laid out along avenues and crescents.

Knock *Moray* A distillery and railway village in Moray, Knock lies on the Shiel Burn 8 miles (13 km) south of Portsoy. The farms of Knock and Nethertown of Knock lie to the north and south respectively.

Knock *Western Isles* A crofting village located on the Eye peninsula of eastern Lewis in the Outer Hebrides, Knock (Gael: *An Cnoc*) lies 5 miles (8 km) east of Stornoway. The settlement benefits from two churches, a post office and a primary school.

Knock Bay *Dumfries and Galloway* A bay on the west coast of the Rhinns of Galloway, Knock Bay lies beyond Black Head, 2 miles (3 km) north of Portpatrick.

Knock Castle *Aberdeenshire* A former stronghold of the Gordons on Deeside, Aberdeenshire, Knock Castle lies on the south side of the River Dee opposite Ballater. Dating from the early 17th century, it guarded the entry to Glen Muick.

Knock Fell *Dumfries and Galloway* A hill in Dumfries and Galloway, Knock Fell rises out of the Knock Moss, 6 miles (10 km) southeast of Glenluce.

Knock Head *Aberdeenshire* A headland on the Moray Firth coast of Aberdeenshire, Knock Head extends into the sea at the western end of Boyndie Bay, 2 miles (3 km) west of Banff and immediately north of Whitehills.

Knock Hill *Moray* Rising to 430 m (1412 ft) to the west of Glen Barry in Moray, Knock Hill lies 6 miles (10 km) to the southeast of Portsoy.

Knock of Braemoray *Moray* A hill in the uplands of Moray, the Knock of Braemoray rises to 456 m (1493 ft) to the east of the Dorback Burn, northeast of Lochindorb and north of Dava Moor, midway between Grantown-on-Spey and Forres.

Knockaird *Western Isles* One of several closely associated crofting townships in the Ness district at the northern tip of Lewis in the Outer Hebrides, the settlement of Knockaird (Gael: *An Cnoc Ard*) is located immediately to the southeast of Fivepenny, a mile (1.5 km) south of the Butt of Lewis. The former stronghold of the Morrisons of Ness on the islet of Dun Eistean lies a quarter-mile (0.5 km) to the north.

Knockan Crag *Highland* Described as one of the world's most important geological sites, Knockan Crag (or Knockan Cliff) is located near Elphin in the Assynt district of western Sutherland, 12 miles (19 km) north of Ullapool. During the Caledonian mountain-building period some 480 million years ago, internal pressure split the earth's crust along gently sloping faults, forcing other rocks upwards and westwards over younger rocks. This overthrust, known as the Moine Thrust, runs up the west coast of Sutherland and is clearly visible at Knockan. The feature baffled 19th-century geologists until Ben Peach and John Horne put forward an explanation of its origin. The site was designated a National Nature Reserve in 2004. It is owned by Scottish Natural Heritage, which opened an interpretation centre here in 2001.

Knockandhu *Moray* A hamlet with an inn in Moray, Knockandhu lies on the road from Tomintoul to Dufftown, 8 miles (5 km) northeast of Tominoul. A road from here leads into the Braes of Glenlivet towards the settlement of Chapeltown and the Church of Our Lady of Perpetual Succour.

Knockando *Moray* A distillery settlement on the left bank of the River Spey, Knockando lies 3 miles (5 km) southwest of Archiestown in Moray. The former Knockando Station is used as a visitor centre by the Tamdhu Distillery, and in the kirkyard of Knockando Church (1757) are three weathered Pictish stones. There is also a woollen mill with some of the oldest working machinery in the country. Knockando Distillery, which dates from 1898, was the first to install electric light.

Knockando Wool Mill *Moray* Located in the village of Knockando, the Knockando Wool Mill lies close to the River Spey and is mainland Scotland's last small spinning and weaving mill. The structure is A-listed and is said to represent industrial heritage of international significance. Built around 1784, the mill has been in continuous production for more than 200 years and still makes tweeds and blankets. Originally water-powered, electricity was installed in 1948 and, although its water wheel no longer turns, it is still visible on the side of the main building. The Knockando Woolmill Trust was created in 2000 to protect the structure, with the vision of a full restoration providing a tourist attraction as well as an education and training resource. The mill featured in the BBC television programme *Restoration* in 2004.

Knockdolian *South Ayrshire* A hill of South Ayrshire, Knockdolian rises to 265 m (869 ft) 2 miles (3 km) northeast of Ballantrae and overlooks Ballantrae Bay.

Knockentiber *East Ayrshire* A village located close to the western boundary of East Ayrshire, Knockentiber lies a quarter-mile (0.5 km) north-northeast of Crosshouse and 2 miles (3 km) northwest of Kilmarnock. Coal mining was once an important activity and a railway junction lay at the north end of the village. The Carmel Water flows just to the east.

Knockespock House *Aberdeenshire* A country house in the Aberdeenshire parish of Clatt, Knockespock lies on the northern edge of the Correen Hills, a mile (1.5 km) to the south of the village of Clatt.

Knockfarril *Highland* A conical hill topped by a vitrified fort in Easter Ross in Highland Council area, Knockfarril rises to 190 m (579 ft) to the east of Strathpeffer. It forms the summit of a ridge called Druim Chat (Cat's Back).

Knockfin Heights *Highland* An area of marshland with numerous small lochs on the border between the Sutherland and Caithness districts of Highland Council area, Knockfin Heights lies at an altitude of 438 m (1404 ft) northeast of Kinbrace.

Knockhill *Fife* A motor-racing circuit in western Fife, situated on the A823 to the north of Dunfermline in the shadow of Knock Hill, which rises to 362 m (1189 ft). Established on a farm in 1974, it has become Scotland's leading centre for motor sports, with an international licence up to Formula 3. In recent years major events in the racing calendar have included rounds of both the Scottish Motor Racing Club and British Touring Car championships.

Knockinaam Lodge *Dumfries and Galloway* A house in the Rhinns of Galloway, Dumfries and Galloway, Knockinaam Lodge lies close to the coast, nearly 2 miles (3 km) south of Portpatrick. During World War II, British prime minister Winston Churchill and American General Eisenhower stayed here.

Knocklea *Dumfries and Galloway* A small settlement in The Glenkens district of Dumfries and Galloway, Knocklea lies to the east of the Water of Ken between New Galloway and Balmaclellan.

Knocksting Loch *Dumfries and Galloway* A small loch in Dumfries and Galloway, Knocksting Loch lies to the west of Castlefairn Water, 5 miles (8 km) southwest of Moniaive.

Knowe *Dumfries and Galloway* A locality in the Bladnoch valley, Dumfries and Galloway, Knowe lies 8 miles (13 km) northwest of Newton Stewart on the Beoch Burn which drains south from Loch Ochiltree.

Knowe of Yarso *Orkney* The site of a prehistoric chambered tomb, the Knowe of Yarso is situated on a terrace 105 m (344 ft) above sea level on the south coast of the Orkney island of Rousay. Excavated in 1934, it has three compartments divided by upright slabs.

Knowehead *Dumfries and Galloway* A locality in The Glenkens district of Dumfries and Galloway, Knowehead lies on the eastern side of Kendoon Loch, 4 miles (6.5 km) southeast of Carsphairn.

Knoweside *South Ayrshire* A village of South Ayrshire, Knoweside lies a half-mile (1 km) south of the Electric Brae and 3 miles (5 km) northwest of Maybole.

Knoydart *Highland* A peninsula and district of Highland Council area, the so-called 'Rough Bounds' of Knoydart lie between Loch Nevis and Loch Hourn and are separated from the Sleat peninsula of the isle of Skye by the Sound of Sleat. Knoydart's mountainous nature has maintained its isolation, with no roads entering the area, although minor roads towards the west of the peninsula connect Inverie, the only village, with hamlets at Airor and Inverguseran. Inverie is connected by ferry to Mallaig. The main peaks of Knoydart are Ladhar Bheinn (1020 m/3346 ft), Meall Buidhe (946 m/3104 ft), Luinne Bheinn (939 m/3081 ft) and Beinn Bhuidhe (855 m/2804 ft). The Knoydart Estate, which once covered the entire peninsula, was the scene of a land raid in 1948 by the 'Seven Men of Knoydart', who are regarded as pioneers of the land-reform movement in Scotland. The estate was acquired by the Knoydart Foundation on behalf of the local community in 1999.

Kyle One of three ancient districts or 'regalities' of the old county of Ayrshire, Kyle is the middle of the three, between Cunninghame to the north and Carrick to the south. Today the district covers parts of East Ayrshire and South Ayrshire and comprises some 984 sq. km (380 sq. miles) of land between the River Irvine and the River Doon. Its principal settlements are Ayr itself, Prestwick, Troon, Mauchline, Auchinleck and Cumnock. The name is thought to have originated from the forests that once covered the area (Gael: *coille*). Still used locally, it was formally resurrected as the Kyle and Carrick District of Strathclyde Region between 1975 and 1996. Kyle Castle lies 5 miles (8 km) east of Cumnock.

Kyle Akin *Highland* Kyle Akin is the narrow stretch of water that separates the isle of Skye at the village of Kyleakin, from the village of Kyle of Lochalsh on the Scottish mainland. Once crossed by a ferry, it is now traversed by the Skye Bridge.

Kyle of Lochalsh *Highland* A village of Wester Ross, Kyle of Lochalsh lies on the shore of Loch Alsh opposite the island of Skye. It maintained a ferry link with Kyleakin on Skye until the opening of the Skye Bridge in 1995 and is the terminus of the scenic West Highland Railway from Inverness, which formerly provided an important freight link after it was established in 1897. Mailboats operated a service from here to Stornoway in the Outer Hebrides until 1973.

Kyle of Sutherland *Highland* A body of water at the head of the Dornoch Firth to which it is joined by a narrow channel, the Kyle of Sutherland extends nearly 3 miles (5 km) northwest from Bonar Bridge and is fed by the River Oykel.

Kyle of Tongue *Highland* A large inlet on the north coast of Sutherland, the Kyle of Tongue extends 6 miles (10 km) southwest from Tongue Bay. The village of Tongue lies to the east.

Kyle Rhea *Highland* A narrow stretch of water separating the island of Skye from the mainland, Kyle Rhea links the Sound of Sleat in the south with Loch Alsh to the north. There is a ferry link from the mainland to the settlement of Kylerhea on Skye, 4 miles (6.5 km) southeast of Kyleakin.

Kyleakin *Highland* A village at the southeast tip of the isle of Skye, Kyleakin was the main ferry terminal linking the island with Kyle of Lochalsh on the mainland until the opening of the Skye Bridge across Kyle Akin in 1995. The village was laid out in 1811 and later received steamers. In the 20th century it developed as a fishing and ferry port. The campaigning *West Highland Free Press* was established in Kyleakin in 1972. The former MacKinnon stronghold of Caisteal Maol, which dates from the 15th century, lies at the eastern end of the village.

Kyles of Bute *Argyll and Bute* A narrow channel separating the northern part of the island of Bute from the Cowal peninsula, the Kyles of Bute extend southwards in two arms from the mouth of Loch Riddon.

Kyles Scalpay *Western Isles* A crofting township in the far southeast of North Harris in the Outer Hebrides, Kyles Scalpay (Gael: *Caolas Scalpaigh*) is located 4 miles (6.5 km) southeast of Tarbert. Kyles Scalpay was the northern terminus of the ferry that crossed the Sound of Scalpay to the island of Scalpay, and now provides the landing point for the Scalpay Bridge which opened in 1997.

Kyles Stockinish *Western Isles* A small hamlet on the east side of the mouth of Loch Stockinish in South Harris, Kyles Stockinish (or simply Stockinish; Gael: *Caolas Stocinis*) looks out onto Stockinish Island, 5.5 miles (9 km) south of Tarbert.

Kylesknoydart *Highland* A hamlet of the Knoydart district of Highland Council area, Kylesknoydart lies on the north side of the narrow neck of Loch Nevis opposite Kylesmorar.

Kylesku *Highland* A small fishing hamlet, with a hotel, in the Assynt area of northwest Sutherland where Loch Glencoul and Loch Glendhu join to form a narrow passage that leads into Eddrachillis Bay via Loch a' Chairn Bhain. The Kylesku narrows, formerly crossed by a ferry, are now traversed by a curving five-span continuous pre-stressed concrete hollow bridge opened in 1984. Boats from Kylesku travel Lochs Glendhu and Glencoul, the latter visiting Britain's highest waterfall, Eas a' Chuail Aluinn (201 m/658 ft). The settlement of Kylestrome lies to the north.

Kymah Burn *Moray* A stream that flows northeast then northwest from the Ladder Hills in the uplands of Moray, the Kymah Burn joins the River Livet at the southern end of Glen Suie, 11 miles (18 km) south-southwest of Dufftown.

Kype Water *South Lanarkshire* Rising in the Kype Reservoir in South Lanarkshire, the Kype Water flows north then northwest before joining the Avon Water a mile (1.5 km) southeast of Strathaven.

Labost *Western Isles* A settlement near the northwest coast of the isle of Lewis, Labost lies a mile (1.5 km) north of Bragar.

Lacasaigh The Gaelic name for Laxay in the Western Isles.

Lacasdail The Gaelic name for Laxdale in the Western Isles.

Lacklee *Western Isles* A small hamlet on the eastern shore of Loch Stockinish on the southeast coast of South Harris in the Outer Hebrides, Lacklee (Gael: *Leac a' Li*) lies a half-mile (1 km) north of Kyles Stockinish and 5 miles (8 km) south-southwest of Tarbert.

Ladder Burn *Moray/Aberdeenshire* A short headstream of the Blye Water that flows northwards into the Livet Water in the uplands of Moray, the Ladder Burn rises in the Ladder Hills on the border between Moray and Aberdeenshire.

Ladder Hills *Moray/Aberdeenshire* A range of hills in the Grampians, the Ladder Hills rise to 804 m (2637 ft) at Carn Mòr to the south of Glenlivet on the border between Moray and Aberdeenshire.

Ladeddie *Fife* A hamlet in eastern Fife, 5 miles (8 km) west of St Andrews, Ladeddie is situated on high ground between Ladeddie Hill to the east and Kinninmonth Hill to the west. To the north on lower ground is the farm of Backfield of Ladeddie.

Ladhar Bheinn *Highland* Located west of Loch Quoich in the heart of Knoydart, Lochaber district, Highland Council area, Ladhar Bheinn comprises numerous ridges, corries and peaks, the highest of which rises to 1020 m (3345 ft). The northern part of the mountain is owned by the John Muir Trust, which is endeavouring to regenerate the native pine woods on its slopes.

Lady Bank *Angus* A sandbank in the Tay estuary, the Lady Bank lies to the south of the Monifieth Sands between Broughty Ferry and Monifieth in Angus.

Lady Isle *South Ayrshire* A small island with a lighthouse in the Firth of Clyde, Lady Isle is located in Ayr Bay, 3 miles (5 km) west of Troon.

Lady's Holm *Shetland* A small uninhabited island of the Shetland Islands, Lady's Holm lies off the southern coast of the Shetland Mainland, 2 miles (3 km) northwest of Sumburgh Head.

Lady's Rock *Argyll and Bute* An uninhabited islet in the Firth of Lorn, Lady's Rock lies between the islands of Lismore and Mull. It is said that one of the Macleans of Duart left his wife on this rock to be drowned by the rising tide.

Ladybank *Fife* A railway town in the Howe of Fife, Ladybank lies to the north of the River Eden, 5 miles (8 km) southwest of Cupar. It developed during the latter half of the 19th century at a railway junction built on land drained during the 18th century and formerly known as the Moss of Monegae or Our Lady's Bog. Lady's Bog was changed to the more elegant Ladybank. The name Monkstown, which is applied to the southern quarter of the town, is the only part of the settlement that predates the building of the railway in the 1850s. It is a reminder of the days when the monks of Lindores Abbey used to cut peat here. The town was designated a burgh in 1878 and developed linen and maltings industries. Its railway station is reckoned to be the oldest unaltered station in Scotland. Ladybank has an 18-hole golf course and there are forest walks in the neighbouring Heatherhall Wood. Sand and gravel are extracted at Melville Gates.

Ladykirk *Scottish Borders* A small village in the Berwickshire district of Scottish Borders, Ladykirk is located on the River Tweed, 7 miles (11 km) southwest of Berwick-upon-Tweed, opposite Norham in Northumberland, and 6 miles (10 km) northeast of Coldstream. Originally named Upsettlington, it was a popular crossing point between Scotland and England for armies long before its bridge was built in 1839. James IV nearly drowned here and, as a mark of thanks for his survival, erected a church, thus changing the village's name. Ladykirk House, built for William Robertson in 1797, was rebuilt after being demolished in 1966.

Ladylea Hill *Aberdeenshire* A hill in Aberdeenshire, Ladylea Hill rises to 609 m (1998 ft) 3 miles (5 km) north of Strathdon.

Lael, River *Highland* A river that rises on the north slope of Beinn Dearg, the River Lael flows northwest then west through Inverlael Forest into Loch Broom near Inverlael. Lael Forest Garden, 6 miles (10 km) south of Ullapool, was established in 1933 for interesting and ornamental plants.

Lag, Point of *Dumfries and Galloway* A headland of the Machars district of Dumfries and Galloway, the Point of Lag extends into Luce Bay at the southern end of Monreith Bay, 3 miles (5 km) southeast of Port William.

Laga *Highland* A small settlement on the southeastern coastline of the Ardnamurchan peninsula of Lochaber district in Highland Council area, Laga lies a mile (1.5 km) east of Glenborrodale and a mile (1.5 km) southwest of Ben Laga.

Laga, Loch *Highland* A small loch on the Ardnamurchan peninsula, Loch Laga lies to the northeast of Glenborrodale in the shadow of Ben Laga.

Lagain, Loch an *Highland* A small loch of the Sutherland district of Highland Council area, Loch an Lagain lies 4 miles (6.5 km) northeast of Bonar Bridge. The An Uidh flows into the loch from Loch Laro to the northwest.

Lagavulin *Argyll and Bute* A whisky-distilling settlement on the south coast of the island of Islay in the Inner Hebrides, Lagavulin lies 2 miles (3 km) east of Port Ellen, between the distilling villages of Laphroaig and Ardbeg. Claiming to be the oldest in Scotland, the distillery was opened in 1816.

Lagg *Argyll and Bute* A settlement on the east coast of the island of Jura in the Inner Hebrides, Lagg is situated on Lagg Bay to the southeast of Loch Tarbert. It used to be linked by ferry to northern Knapdale.

Lagg *North Ayrshire* A small settlement near the south coast of Arran, Lagg lies 7 miles (11 km) southwest of Lamlash. Its inn dates from 1791.

Lagg *South Ayrshire* A settlement on the Ayrshire coast of the Firth of Clyde, Lagg lies 2 miles (3 km) northeast of Dunure near the Heads of Ayr headland at the southern end of Ayr Bay. A mile (1.5 km) south lies Dunduff Castle.

Lagg Bay *Argyll and Bute* A small bay on the east coast of the island of Jura in the Inner Hebrides, Lagg Bay lies immediately to the south of Tarbert Bay, 3 miles (5 km) south of the head of Loch Tarbert.

Laggan *Argyll and Bute* A settlement on the island of Islay in the Inner Hebrides, Laggan lies at the north end of Laggan Bay, 4 miles (6.5 km) southwest of Bowmore. The River Laggan joins the bay near here.

Laggan *Highland* A small settlement in the Great Glen, Laggan lies between Loch Lochy and Loch Oich, 3 miles (5 km) southwest of Invergarry and 9 miles (14 km) southwest of Fort Augustus. The Laggan Cut is the highest section of the Caledonian Canal. The Laggan Swing Bridge lies a half-mile (1 km) to the north.

Laggan *Highland* A scattered village in the Badenoch district of Highland Council area, Laggan lies in the upper valley of the River Spey, 7 miles (11 km) southwest of Newtonmore.

Laggan, Loch *Highland* A loch to the east of Glen Spean in the Badenoch district of Highland Council area, Loch Laggan extends 7 miles (11 km) southwest from Kinloch Laggan. It was dammed in 1926 to form a reservoir providing hydro-electric power for the aluminium smelter at Fort William.

Laggan, River *Argyll and Bute* A river of the island of Islay in Argyll and Bute, the River Laggan rises near the eastern coastline of the island and flows southwestwards for 12 miles (19 km) to empty into Laggan Bay, a mile (1.5 km) southeast of the settlement of Laggan.

Laggan Bay *Argyll and Bute* Situated at the southeastern entrance to Loch Indaal on the southern coastline of the island of Islay in the Inner Hebrides, Laggan Bay stretches for 5 miles (8 km) from Laggan Point in the north to the headland of Rubha Mòr in the south.

Laggan Bay *Argyll and Bute* A bay on the west coast of the island of Mull, Laggan Bay forms an inlet at the southeastern end of Loch Tuath opposite Ulva. The settlement of Lagganulva lies on the bay.

Laggan Point *Argyll and Bute* A headland on the coast of the island of Islay in the Inner Hebrides, Laggan Point extends westwards into Loch Indaal at the north end of Laggan Bay. The settlement of Bowmore lies 3 miles (5 km) to the northeast.

Laggangarn *Dumfries and Galloway* A locality with ancient standing stones in Dumfries and Galloway, the Laggangain (also Laggangairn) stones form a prominent marker on the Southern Upland Way, 5 miles (8 km) northeast of New Luce. Dating from the 2nd millennium BC, the stones were incised with crosses some time during the 7th–9th centuries AD.

Lagganlia *Highland* A locality in the Badenoch district of Highland Council area, Lagganlia lies near Feshiebridge, 2 miles (3 km) southwest of Kincraig. There is an outdoor centre gifted to Edinburgh City Council by rubber planter Boyd Anderson and opened by the Duke of Edinburgh in 1970. There is a glider airfield nearby at Blackmill.

Lagganulva *Argyll and Bute* A small settlement on the west coast of the island of Mull in Argyll and Bute, Lagganulva lies on Laggan Bay at the southeastern end of Loch Tuath, 4 miles (6.5 km) west of Killiechronan. It looks out onto the island of Ulva.

Laid *Highland* A linear crofting township in the Sutherland district of Highland Council area, Laid lies on the western shore of Loch Eriboll, 5 miles (8 km) south of Durness.

Laide *Highland* A small settlement in the Ross and Cromarty district of Highland Council, Laide lies on the south shore of Gruinard Bay, 5 miles (8 km) southeast of Greenstone Point. The island of Gruinard lies 3 miles (5 km) across the bay.

Laidon, Loch *Perth and Kinross/Highland* A narrow loch on Rannoch Moor, Loch Laidon (or Lydon) straddles the border between Perth and Kinross and Highland council areas. It lies to the northeast of Loch Bà and 6 miles (10 km) west of the head of Loch Rannoch. Rannoch railway station lies at the northeastern end of the loch.

Laig *Highland* A settlement on the north coast of the island of Eigg in the Inner Hebrides, Laig looks onto the Bay of Laig. Cleadale lies a mile (1.5 km) to the northeast.

Laig, Bay of *Highland* A bay at the north end of the island of Eigg in the Inner Hebrides, the Bay of Laig opens out into the Sound of Rum. The settlement of Laig lies on its shore.

Laird's Burn *South Lanarkshire* Rising in forested land to the south of Cairn Table in South Lanarkshire, the Laird's Burn flows northeast to join the Duneaton Water a half-mile (1 km) south of Gart Law.

Laird's Hill *Stirling* A summit of the Kilsyth Hills, Laird's Hill rises to 425 m (1394 ft) 2 miles (3 km) northwest of Kilsyth.

Laird's Seat *South Lanarkshire* A hill of South Lanarkshire, Laird's Seat rises to 361 m (1184 ft) close to the border with East Renfrewshire. Eaglesham lies 4 miles (6.5 km) to the north and Strathaven 5 miles (8 km) to the east.

Lairg *Highland* A village in central Sutherland, Lairg lies at the southern end of Loch Shin, 11 miles (18 km) north of Bonar Bridge. It lies at the junction of five roads built in the early 19th century and developed in association with road and rail transport, limestone quarrying, angling and the marketing of livestock. The Ferrycroft Countryside Centre features displays on the many prehistoric sites in the surrounding area. Lairg was the birthplace of the entrepreneur James Matheson (1796–1878) who made his fortune in China.

Lairig Cheile, Lochan *Stirling* A small loch at the head of Glen Ogle in Stirling Council area, Lochan Lairig Cheile (also Loch Lairig Eala) is 3 miles (5 km) northwest of Lochearnhead and 3 miles (5 km) southwest of Killin. Between the road and the lochan is the line of a former railway.

Lairig Ghru *Highland* A mountain pass through a U-shaped glaciated valley in the Cairngorm Mountains, the Lairig Ghru links Glen More in Strathspey with Glen Dee and upper Deeside, connecting Aviemore with Braemar, a distance of 19 miles (31 km). Braeriach and Ben Macdui rise to the west and east respectively.

Lamachan Hill *Dumfries and Galloway* A hill in the Galloway district of Dumfries and Galloway, Lamachan Hill rises to 716 m (2350 ft) and sits 6 miles (10 km) north of Newton Stewart. It lies in the Galloway Forest Park between Glen Trool in the north and Kirroughtree Forest in the south.

Lamancha *Scottish Borders* A scattered settlement in Scottish Borders, Lamancha straddles the A701, 5 miles (8 km) southwest of Penicuik.

Lamb Head *Orkney* A headland on the southeast coast of the Orkney island of Stronsay, Lamb Head lies to the east of the Bay of Houseby.

Lamb Hoga *Shetland* A headland on the south coast of the island of Fetlar in the Shetland Islands, Lamb Hoga lies between the Wick of Tresta to the east and Colgrave Sound to the west.

Lamb Holm *Orkney* A small island of the Orkney Islands, Lamb Holm lies between Mainland Orkney and the island of Burray. It has an area of 40 ha (99 acres) and is linked by the Churchill Barriers to Mainland Orkney in the north and Glimps Holm to the southwest. Italians, who had been captured in North Africa during World War II and sent to work on the construction of the Churchill Barriers, converted two Nissen huts on the island into a chapel. The interior of the Italian Chapel still features the paintings of one of the prisoners, Domenico Chiocchetti.

Lamb Island *East Lothian* A small island off the coast of East Lothian, the Lamb or Lamb Island lies between Fidra and Craigleith, a mile (1.5 km) northwest of North Berwick. The island is noted for its sea birds, including cormorants, shags, guillemots and herring gulls, and is a designated Royal Society for the Protection of Birds (RSPB) Reserve. Geologically, the Lamb is part of the same Lower Carboniferous basalt sill as Fidra.

Lamba Island *Shetland* An uninhabited island of the Shetland Islands, Lamba Island lies in Yell Sound, a mile (1.5 km) from the entrance to Sullom Voe.

Lamba Ness *Shetland* Lamba Ness is a headland on the northeast coast of the island of Unst in the Shetland Islands.

Lambden *Scottish Borders* A small hamlet of Scottish Borders, Lambden lies 2 miles (3 km) northwest of Eccles.

Lamberton *Scottish Borders* A settlement of Scottish Borders, Lamberton lies 3 miles (5 km) northwest of Berwick-upon-Tweed, just to the north of the Scottish–English border.

Lambhill *Glasgow City* A suburb of Glasgow, Lambhill lies 2 miles (3 km) north of the city centre.

Lambhoga Head *Shetland* A headland on the southeast coast of the Shetland Mainland, Lambhoga Head lies at the southern entrance to the inlet of Voe, a mile (1.5 km) southeast of Boddam.

Lamington *Highland* A village in Easter Ross, Lamington lies 3 miles (5 km) southwest of Tain.

Lamington *South Lanarkshire* A small estate village in Clydesdale, South Lanarkshire, Lamington lies 6 miles (10 km) southwest of Biggar, on the eastern bank of the upper River Clyde. In 1848 a station of the Caledonian Railway was opened here. The Cowgill Reservoirs lie 2 miles (3 km) to the southeast.

Lamington Burn *South Lanarkshire* Rising in the foothills of Hadrig Head, the Lamington Burn flows north and then west for 3 miles (5 km) before emptying into the River Clyde at Lamington, a village located 6 miles (10 km) southwest of Biggar, South Lanarkshire.

Lamlash *North Ayrshire* A resort village on the east coast of the island of Arran, Lamlash lies on Lamlash Bay, 4 miles (6.5 km) south of Brodick. A steamer pier was built in 1883 and an 18-hole golf course opened in 1892. There is a factory producing delicatessen products.

Lamlash Bay *North Ayrshire* A deep and wide bay on the east coast of the island of Arran in North Ayrshire, Lamlash Bay is bounded by the headlands of Clauchlands Point to the north and Kingscross Point to the south. Sheltered by Holy Island, the bay has provided an important anchorage for naval vessels. The wreck of the *Derwent*, which went down in 1880, rests in the bay.

Lammer Law *East Lothian* The second-highest of the Lammermuir Hills in East Lothian, Lammer Law rises to 527 m (1729 ft) towards their western margin, 3 miles (5 km) south-southwest of Gifford.

Lammermuir Hills A range of hills that form the southern boundary of East Lothian, the Lammermuir Hills rise to 535 m (1755 ft) at Meikle Says Law. These rolling hills rise up from the plains of East Lothian and extend down into Scottish Borders, representing a change in geology along the Southern Upland Fault. They link with the Moorfoot Hills in the west and run to the coast between St Abb's Head and Cockburnspath.

Lanark *South Lanarkshire* A market town in South Lanarkshire, Lanark lies at the confluence of the Mouse Water with the River Clyde, 32 miles (51 km) southeast of Glasgow. It developed as a kirkton around the ancient church of St Kentigern close to the royal hunting forest of Mauldslie, and became a royal burgh and centre of a sheriffdom in the mid-12th century. In the 14th century a Franciscan friary was founded here by Robert I. A centre for the manufacture of cotton, woollens and stockings in the 18th century, Lanark established a thriving livestock market in the 1850s. In the 20th century the manufacture of clothing and biscuits provided employment in addition to the town's role as an agricultural service centre and administrative centre of the former county of Lanark and, from 1974 to 1996,

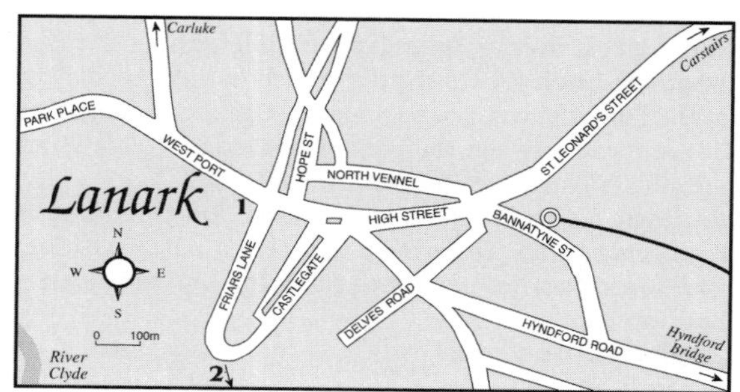

1 *Lanark Museum*
2 *New Lanark World Heritage Centre*

Lanark District of Strathclyde Region. Notable buildings include the 13th-century Church of St Kentigern, where William Wallace (*c.*1272–1305) may have been married, and the Church of St Nicholas (1774), which includes a statue of Wallace by local sculptor Robert Frost. The town has a museum.

Lanark Hydro-Electric Scheme *South Lanarkshire* Opened in 1927, the Lanark Hydro-Electric Scheme comprises two power stations on the River Clyde taking water from the Falls of Clyde. Stonebyres Power Station, which is located 2 miles (3 km) west of Lanark and draws water from above the Stonebyres Linn waterfall with a head of 30 m (98 ft), generates 5 megawatts of power. Bonnington Power Station is located a half-mile (1 km) south of New Lanark below the Corra Linn waterfall. It draws water from above the Bonnington Linn waterfall with a head of 51 m (167 ft), and generates 11 megawatts of power. For approximately five days between April and October each year, Bonnington Power Station is switched off and the Falls of Clyde can be seen to full effect.

Lanarkshire A former county of central Scotland between Glasgow and Edinburgh, Lanarkshire formed the greater part of the basin of the River Clyde, whose sheltered valleys were a centre of fruit growing and whose boundaries contained the greater part of Scotland's population and industry. It was formerly divided into three wards: lower (Glasgow), middle (Hamilton) and upper (Lanark). The much smaller district of Lanark in Strathclyde Region was created in 1974, and in 1996 the council areas of North and South Lanarkshire were established, the two together forming what is termed a 'supercounty'.

Landhallow *Highland* A small village on the east coast of the Caithness district of Highland Council area, Landhallow lies immediately west of Latheron.

Lang Craig *Angus* A headland on the Angus coast, Lang Craig extends into the North Sea at the southern end of Lunan Bay, 3 miles (5 km) east of Inverkeilor.

Langass *Western Isles* A locality with a hotel in North Uist, Langass (Gael: *Langais*) is situated 5.5 miles (9 km) southwest of Lochmaddy. It lies below Ben Langass (Gael: *Beinn Langais*) which rises to 90 m (295 ft) and overlooks Loch Langass to the southeast. The hotel was once the lodge of the surrounding sporting estate. Nearby are a stone circle and Neolithic burial chamber.

Langavat, Loch *Western Isles* A loch of South Harris in the Outer Hebrides, Loch Langavat (Gael: *Loch Langabhat*) lies 2 miles (3 km) northeast of Leverburgh.

Langavat, Loch *Western Isles* A loch on the Isle of Lewis, Loch Langavat (Gael: *Loch Langabhat*) lies to the west of Loch Erisort and the road from Stornaway to Tarbert. It is over 7.5 miles (12 km) in length.

Langavat, Loch *Western Isles* A loch in the Ness district of the Isle of Lewis, Loch Langavat (Gael: *Loch Langabhat*) lies midway between the Butt of Lewis and Tolsta Head, 12 miles (19 km) northeast of Stornoway.

Langavat, Loch *Western Isles* A loch on the island of Benbecula in the Outer Hebrides, Loch Langavat (Gael: *Loch Langabhat*) lies just over 4 miles (6.5 km) southeast of Ballivanich.

Langbank *Renfrewshire* A dormitory village in Renfrewshire, Langbank lies on the south side of the River Clyde, opposite Dumbarton and 3 miles (5 km) northwest of Bishopton. Its name is said to derive from the long dyke built in the Clyde in the 18th century for the purpose of keeping the channel open by encouraging tidal scour. The settlement developed after the opening of a railway station in 1841 and the arrival of tourists. Nearby Finlaystone House, the home of the earls of Glencairn for four centuries, is the seat of the chief of Clan Macmillan.

Langdyke *Fife* A hamlet 2 miles (3 km) northwest of Kennoway, Langdyke sits on hill ground to the north of Carriston and Donald Rose reservoirs in central Fife.

Langholm *Dumfries and Galloway* A small and remote burgh town in the Eskdale district of Dumfries and Galloway, Langholm lies at the confluence of the River Esk and Ewes Water, 30 miles (48 km) east of Dumfries. James II defeated the Douglases here in 1455 and a burgh was created in 1621. The gridiron pattern on the west side of the Esk was laid out in 1778 by the Duke of Buccleuch, who founded the planned village of New Langholm. The town became a regional wool centre, with several mills in production from the mid-19th century onwards. Its industries have also included cotton manufacture, brewing and distilling. The engineer Thomas Telford, born nearby at Westerkirk in 1757, served his apprenticeship as a mason in Langholm. The poet Hugh MacDiarmid (C. M. Grieve) was born near here in 1892 and is celebrated by a memorial in the form of an open book and a cairn on Whita Hill a mile (1.5 km) to the east, where there is also an obelisk commemorating General Sir John Malcolm. Notable buildings include the library (1875–8), the town hall (1811–12), the ruins of Langholm Castle, the mansion house of Langholm Lodge (1786–9) built by James Playfair, the 17th-century mercat cross and the Boatford Bridge (*c.*1871). A museum was established in 1997.

Langlee *Scottish Borders* A small village of Scottish Borders, Langlee lies 2 miles (3 km) south of Jedburgh.

Langshaw *Scottish Borders* A small village of Lauderdale in Scottish Borders, Langshaw lies 2.5 miles (4 km) northeast of Galashiels.

Langside *Glasgow City* A district on the south side of Glasgow near the River Cart, Langside was one of the city's 19th-century planned extensions. A feu plan developed by Neale Thomson, who acquired the site in 1852, resulted in the building of villas and terraced houses on crescents and avenues. The original village of Langside survived until the mid-1890s, when it was replaced by tenement housing. Langside was the site of a battle in 1568 in which the forces of Mary Queen of Scots, who had escaped from Loch Leven, were defeated by troops loyal to her half-brother James Stewart, 1st Earl of Moray and Regent of Scotland.

Langside *Perth and Kinross* Lying on the banks of the River Knaik in western Perth and Kinross, the village of Langside is situated 8 miles (13 km) north of Dunblane.

Langwell *Highland* A small village of Strath Oykel in the Sutherland district of Highland Council area, Langwell lies on the southern banks of the River Oykel, 2 miles (3 km) east of Oykel Bridge.

Langwell House *Highland* A locality near Berriedale in the Caithness district of Highland Council area, Langwell comprises an estate with an 18th-century house and walled garden, a forest and the Langwell Water, which rises in the forest and flows east to the North Sea coast at Berriedale.

Langwell Water *Highland* A river of the Caithness district of Highland Council area, the Langwell Water flows for a distance of 12 miles (19 km) in an easterly direction from its source in Loch Scalabsdale in the heart of the Langwell Forest before emptying into the North Sea at Berriedale.

Laniewee Burn *Dumfries and Galloway* A stream in Dumfries and Galloway, the Laniewee Burn rises in the uplands of Glentrool Forest and flows southwest towards the River Cree.

Lanrick Castle *Stirling* A family seat of the Haldanes demolished in 2002, Lanrick Castle lay close to the River Teith, 4 miles (6.5 km) northwest of Doune in Stirling Council area. For a short time in the 19th century it was known as Clan Gregor Castle, and within the policies the MacGregor Monument, consisting of a tree built in dressed stone capped by a Doric rotunda, can still be found.

Lanton *Scottish Borders* A village of Teviotdale in Scottish Borders, Lanton lies 2 miles (3 km) northwest of Jedburgh.

Laphroaig *Argyll and Bute* A distillery settlement on the south coast of the island of Islay in the Inner Hebrides, Laphroaig lies a mile (1.5 km) east of Port Ellen and overlooks the island of Texa to the south. To the east are the whisky villages of Lagavulin and Ardbeg. Whisky distillation has been undertaken here since the early 19th century and the whisky produced is characterised by its peaty, 'iodine-like' aroma. The name Laphroaig is said to be derived from the Gaelic for 'the beautiful hollow by the broad bay'.

Larachbeg *Highland* A settlement in the Lochaber district of Highland Council area, Larachbeg lies on the eastern boundary of Fiunary Forest, near the head of Loch Aline and 3 miles (5 km) north of the settlement of Lochaline. The gardens of Ardtornish lie immediately to the north, while to the south lie the ruined remains of Kinlochaline Castle.

Larbert *Falkirk* A settlement in Falkirk Council area, Larbert is situated to the north of the River Carron and west of Stenhousemuir. It developed from a village during the 19th century in association with local foundries, hospitals and the Larbert railway junction. Local industries today include transport services, metal casting and machining, engineering and the manufacture of plastics, chemicals and household goods. The Scottish explorer Sir James Bruce of Kinnaird (1730–94), who discovered the source of the Blue Nile, lies buried in Larbert Old Parish Churchyard.

Larg Hill *Dumfries and Galloway* A hill of Dumfries and Galloway, Larg Hill rises to a height of 675 m (2214 ft) to the south of Lamachan Hill in the centre of the Galloway Forest Park, nearly 6 miles (10 km) north of Newton Stewart.

Largiemore *Argyll and Bute* A small settlement on the southeastern shore of Loch Fyne in Argyll and Bute, Largiemore lies 5 miles (8 km) east of Lochgilphead on the opposite side of the loch.

Largo Bay *Fife* A wide bay of the Firth of Forth on the south coast of Fife, Largo Bay extends from Buckhaven and Methil in the west to Kincraig Point in the east.

Largo Law *Fife* A conical hill, the remains of a volcanic plug, Largo Law rises to 290m (965 ft) to the north of Upper Largo in the East Neuk of Fife.

Largoward *Fife* A former mining village in eastern Fife, Largoward is situated in a rural setting at a road junction 4 miles (6.5 km) northeast of Upper Largo. Falkland Palace was supplied with coal from mines that operated here until the 1920s. It has an inn and a church (1835).

Largs *North Ayrshire* A resort town and ferry port in the Cunninghame district of North Ayrshire, Largs is situated on Largs Bay, an inlet of the Firth of Clyde, 18 miles (29 km) southwest of Greenock in North Ayrshire. The defeat of Haakon IV of Norway by King Alexander II in 1263 at the Battle of Largs resulted in Norway giving up the Hebrides and the Isle of Man to the Scots. Largs became a burgh of barony in 1629 but only developed as a resort following the construction of a steamer pier in 1834 and the arrival of the railway in 1885. Places of interest include Largs Museum; the Park, which has a hillfort and burial chamber; the Pencil Tower (1910), commemorating the Battle of Largs; the Skelmorlie Aisle, a Renaissance mausoleum (1636) once part of the old parish church; the Three Sisters, stone columns erected in the 19th century by the astronomer General Sir Thomas Brisbane, who gave his name to the city in Queensland, Australia; the Prophet's Grave, erected in memory of the 17th-century minister William Smith who died of the plague; and the Christian Heritage Museum at the Benedictine Monastery. Ferries link with the island of Great Cumbrae. The Royal Largs Yacht Club was established in 1882 and a large yachting marina was created to the south of Largs in the 1980s.

Largue *Aberdeenshire* A locality in Aberdeenshire, Largue lies on the slopes of the Hill of Denmoss, 12 miles (19 km) northwest of Oldmeldrum.

Largybeg *North Ayrshire* A settlement on the southeast coast of the island of Arran, Largybeg lies at the southern end of Whiting Bay, 2 miles (3 km) northeast of Kildonan and 5 miles (8 km) south of Lamlash. The headland of Largybeg Point lies immediately to the east.

Largymore *North Ayrshire* A small village on the east coast of the island of Arran, Largymore lies on Whiting Bay a mile (1.5 km) north of Largybeg and 4 miles (6.5 km) south of Lamlash. The waters of Glenashdale Burn empty into Whiting Bay to the north of the village.

Larig, River *Stirling* Rising on the slopes of Beinn Chabhair on the western border of Stirling Council area, the River Larig flows 12 miles (19 km) eastwards past Inverlochlarig before entering Loch Doine in the vicinity of Balquhidder.

Larkhall *South Lanarkshire* A town of South Lanarkshire, Larkhall lies 4 miles (6.5 km) southeast of Hamilton between the Avon Water to the west and the M74 to the east. Formerly known as Laverockhall, Larkhall developed in the 18th and 19th centuries in association with mining, weaving, brick making and engineering industries, and in the 1840s was settled by Irish immigrants. Modern industries on the Larkhall and Strutherhill industrial estates include the manufacture of clothing, electronics, electrical goods and plastics. The Morgan Glen railway viaduct forms a notable landmark.

Laro, Loch *Highland* A small loch in the Sutherland district of Highland Council area, Loch Laro lies 4 miles (6.5 km) north of Bonar Bridge and 2 miles (3 km) east of the Falls of Shin.

Larriston Fells *Dumfries and Galloway* An area of high, open ground in Scottish Borders close to the border with England, the Larriston Fells lie 4 miles (6.5 km) west of Kielder, on the west side of the Kielder Forest Park. Burns flow from the western end of the fells into Larriston Burn. The highest point of the fells is at 512 m (1679 ft).

Lassintullich *Perth and Kinross* A mansion house of central Perth and Kinross, Lassintullich lies on the southern shore of the Dunalastair Reservoir, 3 miles (5 km) southeast of Kinloch Rannoch.

Lassodie *Fife* A former mining village in western Fife, Lassodie lies between Loch Fitty and the Blairadam Forest 4 miles (6.5 km) northeast of Dunfermline.

Lasswade *Midlothian* A village of Midlothian, Lasswade lies on the River North Esk, 9 miles (14 km) southeast of Edinburgh, between Dalkeith and Loanhead. It developed in the 18th and 19th centuries in association with paper making, flour milling, coal mining, carpet making and the textile industry. In 1929, Lasswade merged with Bonnyrigg. Buildings of interest include the ruined old parish church which dates from the 13th century and 18th-century Barony House, which was known as Lasswade Cottage when Sir Walter Scott rented it (1798–1804) and was visited here by the writer James Hogg (the 'Ettrick Shepherd') and the Wordsworths. Nearby Polton was the residence of the writer Thomas de Quincey until his death in 1859. The poet William Drummond of Hawthornden (1585–1649) is buried in the old parish church graveyard.

Latheron *Highland* A small village in a parish of the same name near the east coast of Caithness in Highland Council area, Latheron lies at the junction of the A99 coastal road to Wick with the A9 north to Thurso, 15 miles (24 km) southwest of Wick. The 17th-century Baldoo Bell on a nearby hilltop used to summon people to the old parish church, which is now the Clan Gunn Heritage Centre.

Latheronwheel *Highland* A linear village on the east coast of Caithness in Highland Council area, Latheronwheel lies a mile (1.5 km) to the southwest of Latheron. It was established in 1835 by local landowner Captain Robert Dunbar, whose wish was that the village be named Janetstown after his wife, but the older name, which was linked to a crossing place on the Burn of Latheronwheel, has survived. Its harbour sheltered over 50 vessels at the peak of the herring fisheries. Latheronwheel House, which dates from the early 18th century, was enlarged in Scottish baronial style by the architect David Bryce in the 1850s.

Lathones *Fife* The remnants of a former mining village in eastern Fife, Lathones lies a mile (1.5 km) northeast of Largoward and 6 miles (10 km) southwest of St Andrews.

Lauder *Scottish Borders* A village in the Lauderdale district of Scottish Borders, Lauder lies on the Leader Water 22 miles (35 km) southeast of Edinburgh. Created a royal burgh in the 14th century and again in 1502, it developed at a river crossing and near to a fort and water mills on the main route north to Edinburgh. Enlarged in 1672 for the Duke of Lauderdale, the fort was renamed Thirlestane Castle. Lauder was the site in 1482 of the hanging of six favourites of James III by Archibald Douglas, Earl of Angus. Buildings of interest include the parish church (1673), which is shaped like a Greek cross and was built by Sir William Bruce for the Duke of Lauderdale, and the 18th-century Town Hall, used as a prison until 1843.

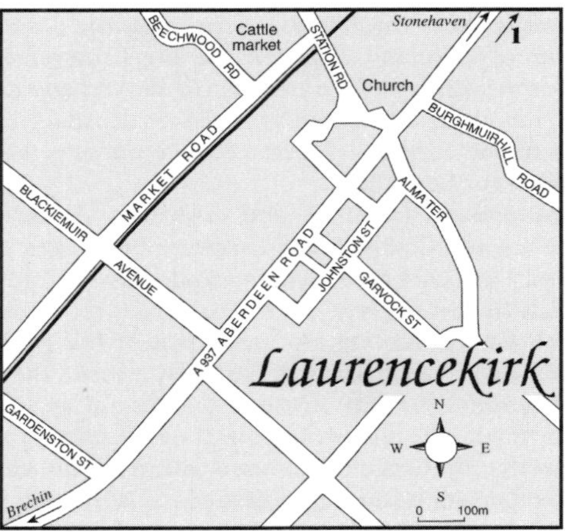

1 *The Grassic Gibbon Centre*

Lauderdale *Scottish Borders* A district of Scottish Borders comprising the basin of the Leader Water, Lauderdale extends southwards from the Lammermuir Hills to the valley of the River Tweed at Newtown St Boswells.

Laurencekirk *Aberdeenshire* The principal town of the Howe of the Mearns in southern Aberdeenshire, Laurencekirk is situated amid rich agricultural land in the valley of the Luther Water, 30 miles (48 km) south of Aberdeen. The original Kirkton of Conveth or St Laurence, with its church dedicated to St Laurence of Canterbury, was transformed into a planned village in the 1770s following the purchase of the estate of Johnston by Francis Garden, Lord Gardenstone, a successful lawyer, Sheriff of the Mearns and Court of Session judge. Lord Gardenstone introduced handloom weaving and the manufacture of snuffboxes to the town, and built an inn, the Gardenstone Arms, which he furnished with a library that impressed Samuel Johnson who passed this way in 1773. The status of the town was raised to that of a burgh of barony in 1779. Today, Laurencekirk has a large cattle market in addition to agricultural-engineering, handloom-weaving and craft industries.

Laurieston *Dumfries and Galloway* An attractive village of mainly 19th-century white-painted houses in Dumfries and Galloway, Laurieston lies on the Camelon Lane Burn, 10 miles (16 km) south of New Galloway. There is a monument to the novelist S. R. Crockett (1860–1914), author of *The Raiders* (1894) and *The Men of the Moss Hags* (1895), who was born at Balmaghie Farm and educated in Laurieston.

Laurieston *Falkirk* A commuter village and southeastern suburb of Falkirk, Laurieston lies a mile (1.5 km) east of Falkirk town centre and 2 miles (3 km) southwest of Grangemouth. A Roman fort of the Antoine Wall is located to the east of the settlement.

Lauriston Castle *City of Edinburgh* A 16th-century tower house extended in the 19th century, Lauriston Castle lies amid wooded grounds 4 miles (6.5 km) west-northwest of Edinburgh city centre and less than a mile (1.5 km) southeast of Cramond village. With fine views overlooking the Firth of Forth, the original tower house was built c.1590 by Sir Archibald Napier of Merchiston, father of John Napier (1550–1617), inventor of logarithms. Later, it was the home of the banker John Law (1671–1729). In 1827, Thomas Allan, a banker and mineralogist, commissioned William Burn (1789–1870) to extend the house in the Jacobean style. The last private owner, William Reid, acquired Lauriston in 1902 and installed modern plumbing and electricity. A cabinet-maker and avid collector of fine furniture and *objets d'art*, Reid and his wife bequeathed their home to the nation on the condition that it should be preserved unchanged. Since 1926 the City of Edinburgh has cared for Lauriston, which offers a fascinating glimpse of Edwardian life in a Scottish country house. Its furnishings include a notable collection of ornaments carved from the banded mineral blue john.

Law *South Lanarkshire* A village on the northern boundary of South Lanarkshire, Law lies 2 miles (3 km) northwest of Carluke in the shadow of Law Hill, which rises to 202 m (663 ft). It developed in association with coal mining from the 1790s and with a railway station established in 1848. A hospital was built nearby during World War II but closed in 2001. Mauldslie Castle, built in the 1790s by Robert Adam for the 5th Earl of Hyndford, was demolished in 1959.

Law Ting Holm *Shetland* An islet at the north end of Tingwall Loch on the Mainland of Shetland, Law Ting Holm is linked to the shore by a causeway. This was said to be the site of the Althing or Parliament, an annual gathering of all the local tings, or assemblies of Shetland.

Lawers *Perth and Kinross* A hamlet on the north side of Loch Tay in Perth and Kinross, Lawers lies on the Lawers Burn, 8 miles (13 km) northeast of Killin. Ben Lawers rises to 1214 m (3984 ft) to the north. The ruins of old Lawers Church, dating from 1669, lie by the lochside, with the later Lawers Church built in 1833 for the Society for Propagating Christian Knowledge by the 1st Earl of Breadalbane. An early 19th-century grain mill and a smithy of the same period survive in the hamlet.

Lawers Burn *Perth and Kinross* Rising from a small loch on the northeast slopes of Ben Lawers, the Lawers Burn flows for 5 miles (8 km) east then south to empty into Loch Tay to the southeast of Lawers.

Lawgrove *Perth and Kinross* A locality in Perth and Kinross, Lawgrove lies by the River Almond, nearly 2 miles (3 km) north of Perth.

Lawnmarket *City of Edinburgh* An area of the Old Town of Edinburgh lying to the east of the castle, the Lawnmarket comprises that part of the Royal Mile connecting Castlehill to the north end of the High Street. Its name is derived from a corruption of 'land market', a place where the produce from the hinterland of the burgh was sold. A cloth market was established here by James III in 1477. In this area are to be found the best remaining examples of medieval close, courtyard and 'land' developments in Edinburgh. Notable among these are James Court, Gladstone's Land, Riddle's Court and Mylne's Court, which was restored by the University of Edinburgh in the late 1960s. The infamous Major Thomas Weir, who confessed to being a wizard, lived close by in West Bow with his sister Jane, who herself was convicted of witchcraft.

Lax Firth *Shetland* An inlet on the east coast of the Shetland Mainland, Lax Firth lies 5 miles (8 km) north of Lerwick. The settlement of Laxfirth lies at the head of the inlet.

Laxadale Lochs *Western Isles* A series of three interconnected lochs in North Harris in the Western Isles, the Laxadale Lochs lie to the north of the settlement of Urgha. A stream rising on the slopes of Sgaoth Aird flows through the lochs to enter East Loch Tarbert at Urgha.

Laxay *Western Isles* A village on the east coast of the Isle of Lewis in the Outer Hebrides, Laxay (Gael: *Lacasaigh*) lies on the north side of Loch Erisort.

Laxay, River *Western Isles* Rising in Loch Trealaval and other nearby lochs and lochans on the Isle of Lewis, the River Laxay flows 3 miles (5 km) southeastwards to empty into Loch Erisort at Laxay.

Laxdale *Western Isles* A village on the Isle of Lewis in the Outer Hebrides, Laxdale (Gael: *Lacasdail* or *Lacasdal*) lies immmediately to the north of Stornoway at the head of the River Laxdale estuary. To the east lie the Nelbost Sands and Loch a' Tuath. Laxdale benefits from a sizeable primary school.

Laxdale, River *Western Isles* Rising on the southern slopes of Beinn Mholach on the Isle of Lewis in the Western Isles, the River Laxdale flows in a southeasterly direction for 5 miles (8 km), passing through the village of Laxdale and emptying into Loch a' Tuath.

Laxfirth *Shetland* A hamlet in the North Nesting district of the Shetland Mainland, Laxfirth overlooks Dury Voe 11 miles (18 km) north of Lerwick.

Laxford, Loch *Highland* A large sea loch of the western coastline of the Sutherland district of Highland Council area, Loch Laxford lies 4 miles (6.5 km) northeast of Scourie. Within the loch lie many small islands, and it is fed by the run-off from the River Laxford. At the head of the loch lies Laxford Bridge.

Laxford, River *Highland* A river of northwest Sutherland, the River Laxford rises in Loch Stack and flows northwestwards for 3 miles (5 km) to empty into Loch Laxford at Laxford Bridge.

Laxford Bridge *Highland* A locality centred on a bridge over the River Laxford on the northwest coast of Sutherland, Laxford Bridge sits at the head of Loch Laxford, 6 miles (10 km) south of Kinlochbervie. Here the A894 from Scourie meets the A838 from Lairg to Durness.

Leabaidh an Daimh Bhuidhe *Aberdeenshire/ Moray* Located on the border of Aberdeenshire and Moray, Leabaidh an Daimh Bhuidhe is the highest of the tops of Ben Avon, rising to 1171 m (3842 ft). There are a number of interesting geomorphological features on Ben Avon, including tors, the largest being Leabaidh an Daimh Bhuidhe which forms the summit. Its name is derived from the Gaelic for 'bed of the yellow stag'.

Leac a' Li The Gaelic name for Lacklee in the Western Isles.

Leacann, Loch *Argyll and Bute* A small loch in Argyll and Bute, Loch Leacann lies 3 miles (5 km) northwest of Furnace on the western side of Loch Fyne. The River Leacann flows southwestwards from the loch to empty into Loch Fyne at Furnace.

Leachkin *Highland* A small settlement in the Inverness district of Highland Council area, Leachkin lies 2 miles (3 km) west of Inverness. The Caledonian Canal passes to the southeast.

Leac na Hoe *Western Isles* A headland on the eastern

coastline of North Uist in the Western Isles, Leac na Hoe lies 3 miles (5 km) east of Lochportan. It is the most easterly point on the island.

Leadburn *Midlothian* A hamlet in southern Midlothian, Leadburn lies at the junction of the A701 with the A703 and A6094, 3 miles (5 km) south of Penicuik and 11 miles (18 km) south of Edinburgh.

Leaderfoot *Scottish Borders* A village in the Lauderdale district of Scottish Borders, Leaderfoot lies at the confluence of the Leader Water with the River Tweed, 2 miles (3 km) east of Melrose.

Leader Water *Scottish Borders* Rising in the southern foothills of the Lammermuir Hills in Scottish Borders, the Leader Water flows south through Lauderdale and the settlements of Lauder, Birkhill and Earlston before joining the River Tweed at Leaderfoot, 2 miles (3 km) east of Melrose.

Leadhills *South Lanarkshire Pop. 300* A village of upper Clydesdale, Leadhills is situated at an altitude of 395 m (1296 ft) in the Lowther Hills, 6 miles (10 km) southwest of Abington. One of the oldest lead-mining areas in Scotland, lead was mined here from the 12th century. The industry was developed on a large scale by the Hope family in the 16th century, and by the mid-1800s large smelting complexes were in operation in Leadhills and nearby Wanlockhead, which is now the location of the Museum of Scottish Lead Mining. Lead, silver and gold mining eventually ceased in the late 1920s. The village has a golf course and a revived railway established by the Lowther Railway Society on the line of the former light railway crossing the Hillhead summit from Elvanfoot. The poet Allan Ramsay (c.1686–1758) was born in Leadhills.

Lealt *Highland* A village on the isle of Skye, Lealt lies on the west coast of the Trotternish peninsula, 11 miles (18 km) north of Portree. The Lealt River, which rises in the foothills of Hartaval, flows through the village before emptying into the Sound of Raasay.

Leana Mhòr *Highland* A peak in the Lochaber district of Highland Council area, Leana Mhòr rises to 684 m (2244 ft) to the west of Glen Roy and east of Glen Gloy and Loch Lochy, 4 miles (6.5 km) north of Roybridge.

Leanoch Burn *Moray* A river rising in the uplands of Moray, the Leanoch Burn flows 4 miles (6.5 km) northwards through Glen Latterach to join the River Lossie to the north of Leanoch. On its way, it forms a waterfall at the Ess of Glenlatterach.

Leathaid Bhuain, Loch an *Highland* A loch in western Sutherland, Loch an Leathaid Bhuain lies in the Glendhu Forest, 3 miles (5 km) east of Kylestrome. Connected to Loch na Creige Duibhe to the northeast, it empties at its southern end into Loch Glendhu.

Leathan, Loch *Argyll and Bute* A small loch of Argyll and Bute, Loch Leathan lies 6 miles (10 km) north of Lochgilphead. It empties north into Loch Ederline and Loch Awe.

Leathan, Loch *Highland* A loch and reservoir on the Trotternish peninsula of the isle of Skye, Loch Leathan lies immediately to the north of Loch Fada and 5 miles (8 km) north of Portree. It empties into Bearrnaig Bay on the Sound of Raasay.

Leaths *Dumfries and Galloway* A locality in Dumfries and Galloway, Leaths lies a mile (1.5 km) to the east of Castle Douglas.

Lecht *Moray* One of the five prinicpal ski centres in Scotland, the Lecht Ski Centre is located at an altitude of 640 m (2090 ft) in the Grampians on the Cock Bridge to Tomintoul A939 which is also known as the Lecht Road. It is an all-year resort, providing in the winter 20 runs and a permanent snowboarding park. In the summer there are go-karts, tubing and quad bikes, as well as summer skiing and snowboarding on a 200-m (219-yd) dry slope.

Leckgruinart *Argyll and Bute* A small village of the island of Islay in the Inner Hebrides, Leckgruinart lies on the western shore of Loch Gruinart, 4 miles (6.5 km) south of Ardnave Point.

Leckie *Stirling* A locality in Stirling Council area, Leckie lies in the northern foothills of the Gargunnock Hills, 7 miles (11 km) west of Stirling. Leckie House, a mile (1.5 km) west of the village of Gargunnock, was built c.1836.

Leckmelm *Highland* A small settlement in Wester Ross, Leckmelm lies on the eastern shore of Loch Broom, 4 miles (6.5 km) southeast of Ullapool. A woodland garden planted in the 1870s and restored in 1984 is open to the public.

Ledaig *Argyll and Bute* A village on the island of Mull, Ledaig adjoins the southern edge of Tobermory.

Ledaig Point *Argyll and Bute* A rocky headland at the northern entrance to Loch Etive in Argyll and Bute, Ledaig Point extends into Ardmucknish Bay at its southern end. The Benderloch settlements of Ledaig and South Ledaig lie to the north.

Ledbeg *Highland* A small village in the Sutherland district of Highland Council area, Ledbeg lies 6 miles (10 km) south of Inchnadamph on the River Ledbeg, which empties into the Cam Loch a mile (1.5 km) to the west.

Ledmore *Highland* A small village in the Sutherland district of Highland Council area, Ledmore lies 6.5 miles (11 km) south of Inchnadamph and a half-mile (1 km) south of Ledbeg at the junction of the A837 from Lairg with the A835 from Ullapool to Scourie.

Lednock, Glen *Perth and Kinross* A valley of central Perth and Kinross lying between Breadalbane and Strath Earn, Glen Lednock extends north–south and carries the waters of the River Lednock south from its source in the southern foothills of Ruadh Mheall through Loch Lednock Reservoir to the River Earn at Comrie. The Falls of Lednock lie on the course of the river at Deil's Caldron.

Lee *Argyll and Bute* A small settlement on the southwest coast of the island of Mull, Lee lies 2 miles (3 km) east of Bunessan and immediately north of Loch Assapol on the Ross of Mull.

Lee, Glen *Angus* A valley of Angus, Glen Lee carries the waters of the Water of Lee eastwards through Loch Lee to its confluence with the Water of Mark where it becomes the River Esk.

Leebotten *Shetland* A village in the Sandwick district on the east coast of the Mainland of Shetland, Leebotten overlooks the Wick of Sandsayre 10 miles (16 km) south-southwest of Lerwick. Copper was mined here in the 19th century.

Leetown *Perth and Kinross* A linear settlement in the Carse of Gowrie, Perth and Kinross, Leetown lies in the parish of Errol, nearly 5 miles (8 km) east of Perth.

Leet Water *Scottish Borders* A river of Scottish Borders, the Leet Water rises between the settlements of Blackadder and Whitsome, and flows nearly 14 miles (22 km) southwestwards past The Hirsel before emptying into the River Tweed at Coldstream.

Leffnoll Point *Dumfries and Galloway* A headland of the Rhinns of Galloway on the east shore of Loch Ryan, Leffnoll Point lies just over 3 miles (5 km) northeast of Stranraer.

Left Law *South Lanarkshire* A summit at the southwest end of the Pentland Hills, Left Law rises to 360 m (1181 ft) 2 miles (3 km) northwest of Dunsyre.

Legerwood *Scottish Borders* A small village in the Lauderdale district of Scottish Borders, Legerwood lies 4 miles (6.5 km) southeast of Lauder.

Leireag, Gleann *Highland* A glen in the Assynt district of Sutherland, Gleann Leireag extends in a northwesterly direction from Spidean Coinich to the south of Quinag. It carries the waters of the River Leireag, which passes through Loch an Leothaid before emptying into Loch Nedd, an inlet of Eddrachillis Bay.

Leitfie *Perth and Kinross* A hamlet in Strathmore, eastern Perth and Kinross, Leitfie lies in the valley of the River Isla, 2 miles (3 km) west of Meigle.

Leith *City of Edinburgh* The principal port of the City of Edinburgh, Leith lies at the mouth of the Water of Leith where it enters the Firth of Forth. It became Edinburgh's official port in 1329 and was fortified by Mary of Guise in 1557. Leith was created a burgh in 1636 and was separated from Edinburgh from 1833 until 1920, when it was finally reincorporated into the city. In addition to its function as a port, Leith developed in association with shipbuilding, rope making, saw milling, flour milling and the manufacture of chemicals. Today, following an extensive regeneration programme, Leith has become a fashionable residential area with a wide range of shops and restaurants. Cruise liners call at Ocean Terminal, and the Scottish Executive occupies a new building at Victoria Quay. The former royal yacht *Britannia* is anchored at Leith. Notable buildings include the Customs House (1812), the Citadel Gate (1656–7), the Sikh Temple (1843, formerly St Thomas's Church), the Vaults (17th-century home of the Scotch Malt Whisky Society), Andrew Lamb's House (1587), the Shore, the former Leith Bank (1804), the Corn Exchange (1809), and the 9.1-m/30-ft-high Martello Tower (1809).

Leith, Water of *West Lothian/City of Edinburgh* Rising in Harperrig Reservoir in the Pentland Hills to the southwest of Edinburgh, the Water of Leith flows northeast for 18 miles (29 km) through West Lothian and the City of Edinburgh before entering the Firth of Forth at Leith. The river was a source of power for a succession of mills dating back to the 13th century. At their peak there were more than a hundred mills in operation, including meal, corn and paper mills at Balerno, paper and snuff mills at Currie, a grain mill (still operational) at Juniper Green, a sawmill at Colinton, and further mills at Stenhouse, Dean Village, Canonmills (where the river is known as the Puddocky Burn), Bonnington and Leith. At Colinton and Dean Village the Water of Leith runs through steep post-glacial gorges that cut down through sedimentary rocks of Lower Carboniferous age. The Water of Leith Walkway, first recognised for its amenity value in 1949, was formally designated in 1973 and today forms a picturesque and tranquil route for 13 miles (21 km) through the city.

Leith Hall *Aberdeenshire* A mansion and garden with woodland walks at Kennethmont, south of Huntly in Aberdeenshire, Leith Hall was erected by the Leith family and has been home to the Leith-Hays since 1650. Within the house are displays of Jacobite memorabilia, tapestries, needlework, portraits and antique furniture. Leith Hall was gifted to the National Trust for Scotland by the Hon. Mrs Leith-Hay in 1945.

Leith Walk *City of Edinburgh* Leith Walk forms a wide boulevard linking Edinburgh city centre to the port of Leith, and follows an ancient route that became the line of a defensive embankment thrown up in 1650. Most of its buildings were erected in the early 19th century, with Pilrig Street, approximately halfway down, representing the former boundary between the City of Edinburgh and the old Burgh of Leith.

Leithen Water *Scottish Borders* Rising in the southwest foothills of the Moorfoot Hills 3 miles (5 km) east of Eddleston, the Leithen Water flows south to join the River Tweed at Innerleithen.

Leitholm *Scottish Borders* A village in Scottish Borders, Leitholm lies 4 miles (6.5 km) northwest of Coldstream.

Lempitlaw *Scottish Borders* A hamlet in Scottish Borders, Lempitlaw lies 3 miles (5 km) east of Kelso and 2 miles (3 km) west of the Scottish-English border.

Lemreway An alternative name for Limervoy in the Western Isles.

Lendalfoot *South Ayrshire* A village on the Ayrshire coast of the Firth of Clyde, Lendalfoot lies 6 miles (10 km) southwest of Girvan in South Ayrshire.

Lendrick *Stirling* A locality in the Trossachs district of Stirling Council area, Lendrick lies on the north side of Loch Venachar, 6 miles (10 km) west of Callander.

Lenie *Highland* The settlements of Upper and Lower Lenie lie on the northwest shore of Loch Ness in the Inverness district of Highland Council area, 2 miles (3 km) south of Drumnadrochit and 2 miles (3 km) southwest of Castle Urquhart.

Lennel *Scottish Borders* Situated on the Scottish-English border, Lennel lies a mile (1.5 km) northeast of Coldstream on the course of the River Tweed. The Coldstream Museum lies to the southwest.

Lennox An ancient district of central Scotland that became an earldom in the 12th century, Lennox comprised much of present-day East and West Dunbartonshire and Renfrewshire, as well as parts of Stirling and Perth and Kinross council areas.

Lennox Hills A range of hills in central Scotland, the Lennox Hills extend northeast from Dumbarton to Stirling, taking in the Kilpatrick Hills, Campsie Fells, Kilsyth Hills, Fintry Hills and Gargunnock Hills, rising to 578 m (1896 ft) at Earl's Seat.

Lennox Plunton *Dumfries and Galloway* A small hamlet in Dumfries and Galloway, Lennox Plunton lies 3 miles (5 km) south of Gatehouse of Fleet within a mile (1.5 km) of the coast of Wigtown Bay.

Lennoxlove House *East Lothian* An historic 14th-century house, home of the Duke of Hamilton, Lennoxlove lies a mile (1.5 km) south of Haddington. Originally known as Lethington, it was the home of William Maitland (1525–73), Secretary of State to Mary, Queen of Scots, and remained in the family until after the death of John Maitland, 1st Duke of Lauderdale (1616–82). Many of the family are buried in the Lauderdale Aisle in nearby St Mary's Church. The house takes its name from

Frances Stuart, Duchess of Lennox, who bought the house *c.*1702. It subsequently passed to her nephew, Lord Blantyre. Gilbert Burns (1760–1827), brother of the poet, was appointed factor here in 1804. The 12th Lord Blantyre died without male heirs in 1900 and the house passed to his daughter and her husband Sir David Baird of Newbyth, a descendant of the noted soldier of the same name. In 1912, their son employed architect Sir Robert Lorimer to undertake a major restoration, and in 1946 Lennoxlove and the surrounding 926-ha (2287-acre) estate were acquired by the 14th Duke of Hamilton. The interior of the house ranges from medieval to Georgian in style, incorporating an important collection of portraits, furniture, porcelain and other artefacts, many of which came from Hamilton Palace in South Lanarkshire prior to its demolition in the 1920s. The Lennoxlove collection includes the boulle cabinet given to the Duchess of Lennox by Charles II, and a silver casket and sapphire ring belonging to Mary, Queen of Scots, together with her death mask. Among other memorabilia are a map and compass carried by Rudolf Hess, Adolf Hitler's deputy, who flew to Lanarkshire on 10 May 1941 in an attempt to involve the Duke of Hamilton in negotiating peace between Britain and Germany.

Lennoxtown *East Dunbartonshire* A town in East Dunbartonshire, Lennoxtown lies by the Glazert Water in the southern foothills of the Campsie Fells, 3 miles (5 km) north of Kirkintilloch. Long associated with the Lennox family, it developed from the late 18th century as a planned village (also known as Newton of Campsie) in association with cotton manufacture, calico printing, coal and limestone mining and the manufacture of alum and nails. A hospital was established 2 miles (3 km) to the north in the grounds of Lennox Castle, which was built 1837–41. One of the few remaining modern industries is the bottling of spring water. Craigend, 2.5 miles (4 km) west of Lennoxtown, was the birthplace of the explorer Sir Thomas Livingstone Mitchell (1792–1855).

Lentran Point *Highland* A headland on the Beauly Firth in Highland Council area, Lentran Point extends into the firth near the small settlement of Lentran, 5 miles (8 km) west of Inverness.

Leny, River *Stirling* The River Leny emerges from the south end of Loch Lubnaig in Stirling Council area, flowing southeastwards for 4 miles (6.5 km) through the narrow Pass of Leny before joining the Eas Gobhain to form the River Teith at Callander. The Falls of Leny form an attractive cascade on the river.

Lenzie *East Dunbartonshire* A commuter village in East Dunbartonshire, Lenzie lies immediately south of Kirkintilloch and 3 miles (5 km) northeast of Bishopbriggs. It developed on open moor after the opening in 1842 of a railway station serving Kirkintilloch on a site laid out by the Edinburgh and Glasgow Railway Company. Lenzie Academy and a mental hospital opened in the 1890s, and the village gradually expanded as a dormitory settlement for Glasgow.

Leochel-Cushnie *Aberdeenshire* A locality within a parish of the same name in the Howe of Alford, Aberdeenshire, Leochel-Cushnie is a scattered settlement with a church at the mouth of the Glen of Cushnie, 7 miles (11 km) southwest of Alford.

Leodhas The Gaelic name for the Isle of Lewis in the Western Isles.

Leonach Burn *Highland* The Leonach Burn rises in the northern foothills of Carn an t-Sean-liathanaich to the southwest of Lochindorb and flows north to join the River Findhorn near Dulsie, 4 miles (6.5 km) southwest of Ferness. On its lower course there are a series of waterfalls.

Lephin *Highland* A small hamlet of northwest Skye, Lephin lies 5 miles (8 km) west of Dunvegan.

Lephinmore *Argyll and Bute* A small settlement in Argyll and Bute, Lephinmore lies on the east shore of Loch Fyne opposite Minard Castle, 12 miles (19 km) north of Tighnabruaich.

Lerags *Argyll and Bute* A scattered community in the Lorn district of Argyll and Bute, Lerags lies to the north of Loch Feochan, 3 miles (5 km) south of Oban.

Lerwick *Shetland* The capital of the Shetland Islands and the northernmost town of the British Isles, Lerwick is situated on the Mainland of Shetland on a natural harbour sheltered to the east by the island of Bressay and is 225 miles (362 km) from Bergen and 702 miles (1130 km) from Reykjavik. Probably founded by Norsemen who are known to have gathered a huge fleet here in 1263, Lerwick was largely developed in the early 17th century by the Dutch as a fishing base. In 1653, Cromwell tried to oust the Dutch and lay claim to the surrounding fishing grounds by landing troops who built Fort Charlotte, the only surviving Cromwellian building in Scotland and the first permanent building in the town. During the 18th and 19th centuries, Lerwick gradually expanded as a centre of the herring- and cod-fishing industries and Arctic whaling. Merchants, exporting fish, oil, hides, meat and woollen goods, built waterfront houses with warehouses and piers known as lodberries – buildings that are still a feature of the town today. By 1901, it was reckoned that 2000 boats were active in Shetland waters, and during the two World Wars Lerwick's geographical position in the North Sea made it an important and strategic maritime base. During the 1950s there was little industrial activity, but in the 1960s Lerwick became a focal point for the revitalised traditional industries of fishing and knitwear, as well as the dynamic new North Sea oil industry. Between 1962 and 1981 the town's population grew from 6000 to 7000 in association with the development of pipeyards, oil-supply depots and

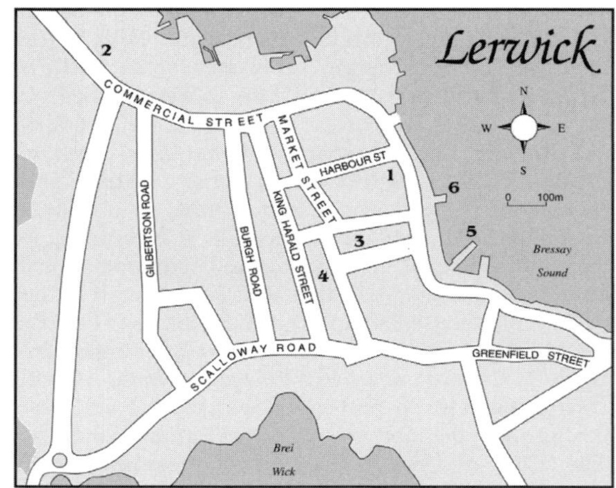

1 *Fort Charlotte*
2 *County Buildings*
3 *Town Hall*
4 *Museum and Library*
5 *Victoria Pier*
6 *Ferry Pier*

harbour improvements. First served by a regular steamer service in 1868, Lerwick is still linked to Aberdeen, Stromness and Bergen by ferry from the Holmsgarth Ferry Terminal. Smaller ferries from the Esplanade link with Bressay and the Out Skerries. Notable buildings include the County Buildings (1875), Town Hall (1882) and Museum and Library. The town's chief festival, Up-Helly-Aa, is held annually on the last Tuesday of January.

Leslie *Aberdeenshire* A hamlet in Aberdeenshire, Leslie straddles the Gadie Burn, 4 miles (6.5 km) southwest of Insch and 11 miles (18 km) northwest of Inverurie. The ruined Leslie Castle, built in 1661 by William Forbes of Monymusk, was one of the last of the fortified houses of the northeast. The surrounding barony of Leslie had been acquired through the marriage of William Forbes's father with the widow of one of the last of the Leslies who had held sway here since the 12th century.

Leslie *Fife* A burgh town in central Fife, Leslie sits on a ridge overlooking the River Leven to the west of Glenrothes. Originally known as Fettykill, its name was changed to Leslie in 1283 when Norman de Leslie obtained a grant of land here. Leslie House, designed by Sir William Bruce, was built by John Leslie, who was Lord Chancellor in the reign of Charles II and was created Duke of Rothes. The town flourished as a centre of spinning, bleaching and paper making in the 19th century, much of its industrial activity taking place by the River Leven. Created a burgh of barony in 1458, Leslie's ridge-top medieval layout is still visible. To the west, the Prinlaws quarter of town was developed for factory workers by the enlightened industrialist John Fergus and to the east, outside Christ's Church on the Green, stands the Bull Stone, a relic of bull-baiting at medieval fairs. Leslie is still a centre of paper making.

Lesmahagow *South Lanarkshire* A former mining village in upper Clydesdale, Lesmahagow lies to the west of the M74 on the River Nethan, 6 miles (10 km) southwest of Lanark. Named after St Machutus (Mahego), a 6th-century missionary, the site developed in association with a priory linked to Kelso Abbey founded in 1140 by David I. Well-known for its fruit-growing industry in medieval times, the surrounding area is still a fertile farming area. Though the priory was destroyed in the Reformation, there are remains near the present parish church (1803). Lesmahagow became a burgh of barony in 1668 and subsequently developed in association with coal mining. It has a high school and a hospital.

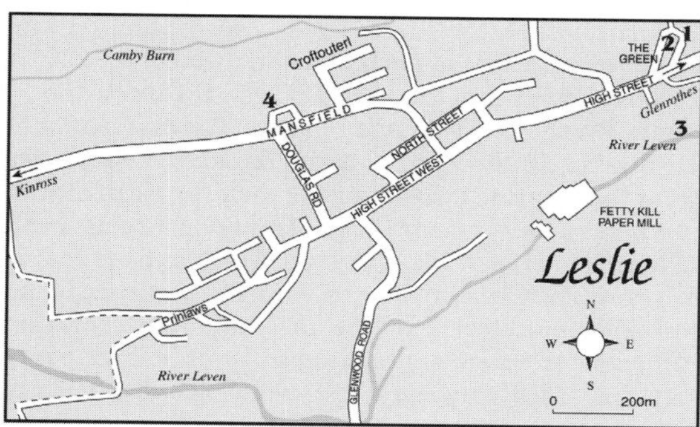

1 Christ's Church on the Green
2 Bull Stone
3 Leslie House
4 Maryfield House

Leswalt *Dumfries and Galloway* A village of the Rhinns of Galloway in Dumfries and Galloway, Leswalt lies 3 miles (5 km) northwest of Stranraer. To the west of this village of largely modern housing is Lochnaw Castle, the seat of the Agnews of Lochnaw, whose burial vault and loft can be found in the remains of the old parish church at Leswalt. To the northwest of the village, on top of the Tor of Craigoch, stands a four-storey tower built in memory of Sir Andrew Agnew.

Letham *Angus* A village in central Angus, Letham lies on the Vinny Water, 6 miles (10 m) east of Forfar. It was planned in 1788 as a textile village designed to enhance the economy of the Dunnichen Estate owned by the improving laird George Dempster. By 1850 the power looms of nearby towns had killed the cottage weaving industry, but it survives today as a commuter settlement which forms the largest village in Angus. At nearby Dunnichen Church, also built by George Dempster in 1802, stand a replica of a 7th-century Pictish stone and a cairn to commemorate the Battle of Nechtansmere in 685 at which the Picts defeated the Northumbrians.

Letham *Falkirk* A former mining village in Falkirk Council area, Letham is situated on carseland to the south of Airth, immediately north of the M876. The village is divided into two parts: Letham Cottages, arranged around three sides of an area of land once occupied by a colliery and coal bing, and Letham Terraces, which form a distinct linear development. The village was designated a conservation area in 1978.

Letham *Fife* An attractive village in Monimail parish in northeast Fife, Letham lies 4 miles (6.5 km) west of Cupar. The heart of the old village is approached by a row of 18th- and 19th-century cottages. Sand and gravel are extracted from the nearby Mountcastle Quarry.

Letham Grange *Angus* A commuter settlement and sporting resort of eastern Angus, Letham Grange is a greenfield development located 2.5 miles (4 km) north of Arbroath on the former Letham Grange Estate, part of which was once the property of 'Honest George' Dempster of Dunnichen (1732–1818). Housing development since 1982 surrounds a 19th-century country house, now a hotel, set in fine parkland. Sporting facilities include two golf courses, and an indoor curling rink that operates in the winter months.

Lethendy *Perth and Kinross* A locality in the Stormont district of eastern Perth and Kinross, Lethendy comprises the 16th-century Lethendy Tower, 18th-century Lethendy Bank farmhouse, the Kirkton of Lethendy with its ruined church abandoned in 1929, and the chapel of Lethendy, all lying between the Lunan Burn and the River Tay, 6 miles (10 km) east of Dunkeld.

Lethnot, Glen *Angus* A valley in northeast Angus, Glen Lethnot is located to the northwest of Brechin between Glen Clova in the west and Glen Esk in the east. The glen, which seems to have lost its name on the majority of modern maps, contains the Water of Saughs, which becomes the West Water in its lower reaches. The Glen extends east and then southeast from Ben Tirran (896 m/2941 ft) to meet Strathmore to the southeast of Edzell.

Letterewe *Highland* A small settlement on the western shore of Loch Maree in the Ross and Cromarty district of Highland Council area, Letterewe lies 7 miles (11 km) northwest of Kinlochewe. To the north is the extensive Letterewe deer forest.

Letterfearn *Highland* Situated on the western shore of Loch Duich in the Lochalsh district of Highland Council area, Letterfearn lies 5 miles (8 km) northwest of Shiel Bridge and 2 miles (3 km) south of Eilean Donan Castle.

Letterfourie House *Moray* Designed by Robert Adam and built in 1773, Letterfourie House in Moray lies in a beautiful setting above the Burn of Buckie, a mile (1.5 km) to the east of the village of Drybridge. In its grounds stands a folly known as the Craigmin Bridge (1779).

Lettermorar *Highland* A small hamlet of Arisaig in the Lochaber district of Highland Council area, Lettermorar lies on the southern shore of Loch Morar, 4 miles (6.5 km) southeast of the settlement of Morar.

Letters *Highland* Situated on the western shore of Loch Broom in the Ross and Cromarty district of Highland Council area, the settlement of Letters lies 2 miles (3 km) from the head of the loch and 5 miles (8 km) south of Ullapool.

Lettershaws *South Lanarkshire* A small settlement in upper Clydesdale, Lettershaws lies on the Glengonnar Water on the road to Wanlockhead in the Lowther Hills, 3 miles (5 km) southwest of Abington.

Lettoch *Highland* A small settlement in the Strathspey district of Highland Council area, Lettoch lies 2 miles (3 km) southeast of Nethy Bridge.

Leuchar Burn *Aberdeenshire/Aberdeen City* A stream rising in Loch Skene in Aberdeenshire, the Leuchar Burn first flows south but then turns southeast to form the boundary between Aberdeenshire and Aberdeen City. The stream then turns south once again before becoming the Culter Burn, which joins the River Dee at Peterculter.

Leuchars *Fife* A village in northeast Fife, Leuchars is situated 6 miles (10 km) northwest of St Andrews. Lying to the south of the Castle Knowe where Leuchars Castle once stood, it developed following the drainage of the surrounding area in the 18th century and the coming of the railway in 1848. The prosperity of Leuchars was further ensured with the establishment first of a Royal Navy (1917) and then a Royal Air Force (1920) station. Each September there is a Battle of Britain airshow at RAF Leuchars. The 12th-century Parish Church of St Athernase has been described as 'the second-finest piece of Norman work in the whole of Great Britain'. Nearby are Earlshall Castle and Tentsmuir Forest.

Leumrabhagh The Gaelic name for Limervoy in the Western Isles.

Leum Uilleim *Highland* A mountain in the Lochaber district of Highland Council area, Leum Uilleim rises to 906 m (2972 ft) to the northwest of Rannoch Moor and 3 miles (5 km) south of the head of Loch Treig, between Loch Ossian, Loch Eilde Mhòr and the Blackwater Reservoir.

Leurbost *Western Isles* A village in the Lochs district of the Isle of Lewis in the Western Isles, Leurbost (Gael: *Liurbost*; formerly *Luirbost*) lies 6 miles (10 km) southwest of Stornoway, near the head of Loch Leurbost (Gael: *Liurboist*; formerly *Luirboist*).

Leven *Fife* A town on the north side of the Firth of Forth, Leven lies at the mouth of the River Leven, forming an extensive urban area with the Fife coast burghs of Methil and Buckhaven. It is the only town in the parish of Scoonie, whose church was gifted in the 11th century to the Celtic Culdees of Loch Leven at the source of the River Leven. By the 16th century a harbour and village had emerged close to the church, the settlement being elevated to the status of a burgh of barony. During the next 300 years its industries expanded to include weaving, bleaching, spinning, coal mining, salt extraction, fishing and the manufacture of rope. During the 19th century its port activity declined with the silting up of its harbour and the building of the Methil Dock to the south of the River Leven, but with the arrival of the railway the town began to develop as a holiday centre. The town has a swimming pool and sports complex, several bowling greens, playing fields and two 18-hole golf courses. Industry, which is mainly located in the Banbeath Industrial Estate, Hawkshaw Trading Estate, Burnmill Industrial Estate and Levenmouth Business Centre, includes sawmilling, iron founding, printing, boatbuilding, whisky blending, engineering, industrial-plant fabrication, computer supplies and the manufacture of knitwear and plastics. Leven is linked to Innerleven on the other side of the River Leven by the Bawbee Brig. This was built in 1957 to replace the original bridge of 1840, which itself replaced a ferry crossing that cost the traveller a halfpenny or 'bawbee'.

Leven, Loch *Highland* A loch in the Lochaber district of Highland Council area, Loch Leven extends eastwards for 11 miles (18 km) from Kinlochleven, eventually opening out into Loch Linnhe. It is crossed by a bridge at Ballachulish.

Leven, Loch *Perth and Kinross* A loch of Perth and Kinross, Loch Leven has a circumference of 10 miles (16 km) and is the largest lowland loch in Scotland. Located immediately to the east of Kinross, the loch is famed for its brown and rainbow trout fishing. Created a national nature reserve in 1964, the loch is a wintering ground for many types of migrating birds and one of Europe's most important wildfowl breeding sites. On the largest island, St Serf's Island, are the remains of a priory, and on Castle Island stand the ruins of Lochleven Castle, in which Mary, Queen of Scots was imprisoned for 11 months during 1567–8. The loch was lowered in 1830 as part of a major drainage scheme that involved the straightening of the River Leven, which drains the loch to the Firth of Forth at Leven.

Leven, River *Highland* A river in the Lochaber district of Highland Council area, the River Leven flows from the western end of the Blackwater Reservoir for 4 miles (6.5 km) to empty into Loch Leven at Kinlochleven.

Leven, River *West Dunbartonshire* A river of West Dunbartonshire, the River Leven flows 7 miles (11 km) south from the foot of Loch Lomond through the Vale of Leven to empty into the Firth of Clyde at Dumbarton.

Leven, River *Fife/Perth and Kinross* The only outlet of Loch Leven in the Kinross basin, the River Leven flows from the southeast corner of the loch for a distance of just over 16 miles (26 km) before emptying into the Firth of Forth at Leven. A fall of over 90 m (300 ft) from source to sea made it attractive to millowners, particularly the textile manufacturers of the 18th and 19th centuries. Although its waters are today used by only three paper factories, a distillery and a hydro-electric scheme, there were in the 1820s some 40 mills between Strathenry and Leven. Between 1828 and 1832 the meandering upper course of the river between Loch Leven and Auchmuir Bridge was straightened with the creation of a 4-

mile/6.5-km-long 'cut' or channel. This was part of a scheme designed to reclaim land around Loch Leven and provide a regular supply of water to manufacturers on the river. The water flowing out of Loch Leven into the river passes through sluice gates controlled by the River Leven Trustees.

Leven Wick *Shetland* A bay on the west coast of the Shetland Mainland, Leven Wick lies 9 miles (14 km) north of Sumburgh Head.

Levencorroch *North Ayrshire* A settlement on the south coast of the island of Arran in North Ayrshire, Levencorroch lies 2 miles (3 km) northwest of Kildonan.

Levenish *Western Isles* An islet of the St Kilda group located 35 miles (56 km) west of North Uist in the Western Isles, Levenish lies 2 miles (3 km) southeast of Hirta. It is a haunt for sea birds.

Levenwick *Shetland* A village on the east coast of Mainland Shetland, Levenwick lies on the west side of Leven Wick, an inlet opposite Cumlewick Ness, 12.5 miles (20 km) south of Lerwick

Leverburgh *Western Isles* Also known as Obbe (Gael: *An t-Ob*), the crofting township of Leverburgh in South Harris was named in 1923 in honour of Cheshire soap manufacturer Lord Leverhulme, who bought Lewis-with-Harris in 1918 and invested in the building of piers, kippering sheds, houses and new roads. He appreciated the potential wealth of the Hebridean waters and chose the site at Leverburgh because it gave equal access to the waters of the Minch and the Atlantic, and his boats could always find sheltered fishing waters. His plans to turn Leverburgh into a large fishing port, however, where abruptly terminated with his death in 1925 and the subsequent abandonment of the island estate by his executors. Houses on the left of the street leading to the pier were built for his managers. Today Leverburgh retains a post office, a handful of shops and a ferry link with North Uist and Berneray.

Levern Water *East Renfrewshire/Glasgow City* A river rising in the Long Loch in East Renfrewshire on the border with North Ayrshire, the Levern Water flows northwest through Harelaw Dam and Commore Dam before turning northeast. It flows past Neilston and Barrhead, beyond which for a short distance it forms the boundary with Glasgow City. It then enters that council area at Nitshill to join the White Cart just over 3 miles (5 km) east-southeast of Paisley, having completed a course of 9 miles (14 km).

Lewis, Butt of *Western Isles* The Butt of Lewis is the name given to the headland with a lighthouse at the northernmost tip of the Isle of Lewis in the Western Isles.

Lewis, Isle of *Western Isles* The Isle of Lewis forms the northern part of the 'Long Island' of Lewis-with-Harris in the Outer Hebrides. Separated from Harris to the south by a range of hills, Lewis is dominated by the extensive Black Moor, a low peatland that gives the island its name in Gaelic (*Leodhas*). Crofting townships are spread around the coast, the island's chief settlement being Stornoway, the only town in the Outer Hebrides and administrative centre of the Western Isles. Southern Lewis is deeply indented, with half a dozen sea lochs penetrating the east coast, and sandy beaches can be found on the west coast especially at Uig and Valtos.

Lewiston *Highland* A village in the Great Glen, Lewiston lies at the east end of Glen Urquhart, directly south of Drumnadrochit, a mile (1.5 km) west of Urquhart Bay, an inlet on the west shore of Loch Ness. The village was created by the Grant family in the late 18th century, its inn at one time housing a brewery.

Lews Castle *Western Isles* Overlooking the Inner Harbour of Stornoway on the east coast of the Isle of Lewis in the Western Isles, Lews Castle was built in 1848 as a country house for Sir James Matheson (1796–1878), who made his fortune in the Far East and bought the Isle of Lewis in 1844. Surrounded by woodland policies, Lews Castle is an impressive three-storey Tudoresque fort, complete with towers and battlements. Soap baron William Lever, Lord Leverhume (1851–1925), bought the building, along with the island, in 1918 and in 1923 gifted land, including the castle and its policies, to the people of Lewis. Used as a naval hospital during World War II, it became the Lews Castle College in 1953. When the college moved to a modern building in the grounds in the 1970s, the castle was given over to Lews Castle School which occupied the building until 1988.

Leysmill *Angus* A dormitory village in Angus, Leysmill lies 5 miles (8 km) northwest of Arbroath and 2 miles (3 km) southeast of Friockheim. Its former inhabitants worked in a nearby quarry and a local flax mill.

Lhanbryde *Moray* The village of Lhanbryde is located 4 miles (6.5 km) east of Elgin and 4 miles (6.5 km) west of Fochabers in Moray. Nearby stands Coxton Tower.

Liathach *Highland* A mountain massif in the Torridon Forest, Wester Ross, Liathach rises to 1054 m (3456 ft) to the northeast of Torridon, at the western end of Glen Torridon. The massif comprises two summits, the smaller named Mullach an Rathain, the larger to the east being Spidean a' Choire Leith. Liathach lies in an extensive mountainous area cared for by the National Trust for Scotland.

Libberton *South Lanarkshire* A village of South Lanarkshire, Libberton lies 2 miles (3 km) south of Carnwath and a mile (1.5 km) southeast of the confluence of the Rivers Medwin and Clyde.

Liberton *City of Edinburgh* A residential suburb of Edinburgh, Liberton lies 3 miles (5 km) south of the city centre and is perhaps best known for Liberton Brae, a steep ascent on the main A701 out of the city. Formerly a scattered village, it comprised the settlements of Kirk Liberton, Liberton Dams (where the Braid Burn crosses between Liberton Brae and Mayfield Road), Nether Liberton (at the foot of Gilmerton Road) and Over Liberton (on the south slope of Blackford Glen). To the west, towards the Braid Hills, is the early 16th-century Liberton Tower. Liberton Parish Church, situated on the Kirkgate, was built in 1818 by J. Gillespie Graham (1776–1855) and replaced an earlier church destroyed by fire. Next to Alnwickhill is the public water supply treatment works, which receives water from the Midlothian reservoirs and delivers it to the residents of southeast Edinburgh.

Libo, Loch *East Renfrewshire* The source of the Lugton Water, Loch Libo lies 3 miles (5 km) southwest of Neilston and a half-mile (1 km) northwest of Uplawmoor, on the western edge of East Renfrewshire.

Liddel Water *Scottish Borders/Dumfries and Galloway* A river of Scottish Borders and Dumfries and Galloway, the Liddel Water is formed by the meeting of the

Caddroun, Wormscleuch and Peel Burns in the Dead Water Bog near Saughtree in Liddesdale. It flows just over 15 miles (24 km) southwestwards along the Scottish/English Border to join the River Esk 12 miles (19 km) north of Carlisle.

Liddesdale *Highland* A village in the Lochaber district of Highland Council area, Liddesdale lies on the southern shore of Loch Sunart, 3 miles (5 km) southwest of Strontian.

Liddesdale *Scottish Borders* The name given to the valley of the Liddel Water in Scottish Borders, Liddesdale extends southwestwards from the western end of the Cheviot Hills, crossing the Scottish/English border between Gretna and Carlisle where the Liddel enters the Solway Firth. Newcastleton is the principal settlement.

Liever, Glen *Argyll and Bute* A valley in the heart of the Inverliever Forest to the west of Loch Awe, Glen Liever carries the waters of the River Liever south to enter Loch Awe opposite Fincharn Castle.

Liff *Angus* A village in the parish of Liff and Benvie, eastern Angus, Liff lies nearly 5 miles (8 km) northwest of Dundee. To the north are the settlements of Muirhead of Liff and Backmuir of Liff. In private grounds to the south stands the House of Gray, which was built to a design by Alex McGill and John Strachan for the 12th Lord Gray in 1716.

Lilliesleaf *Scottish Borders* A small village of Scottish Borders, Lilliesleaf lies 7 miles (11 km) north of Hawick. The River Ale passes to the north.

Lilly Loch, the *North Lanarkshire* A small loch of North Lanarkshire, the Lilly Loch lies a half-mile (1 km) south of Caldercruix.

Limekilnburn *South Lanarkshire* A scattered settlement of South Lanarkshire, Limekilnburn lies 3 miles (5 km) south of Hamilton.

Limekilns *Fife* A coastal settlement of western Fife, Limekilns is situated on the Firth of Forth to the west of Rosyth. Its harbour was developed as a port by the medieval merchants of Dunfermline who exported lime, salt and coal and imported wood, wine, and glassware here. Brucehaven Harbour was built much later in c.1750 especially for the coal trade. The oldest building in Limekilns is the 16th-century King's Cellar in Academy Square, originally built by the monks of Dunfermline in the 14th century for storing wine and other imported goods. The village, which was also associated with brewing and the manufacture of soap and rope, was designated a conservation area in 1984. The neoclassical-fronted Limekilns Parish Church was built in 1825, and to the west are limekilns built into the cliff face c.1780.

Limerigg *Falkirk* A remote upland village in the south of Falkirk Council area, Limerigg is situated at the south end of the Slamannan Road at its junction with the Avonbridge–Caldercruix Road. It is a T-shaped village, dominated by the Mannan Forest plantation and divided into High and Low Limerigg.

Limervoy *Western Isles* A remote hamlet located at the end of the B8060 in the South Lochs district of the Isle of Lewis, Limervoy (also Limervay and Lemreway, Gael: *Leumrabhagh*) looks out onto Eilean Iuvard at the mouth of Loch Shell, 14 miles (22 km) south-southwest of Stornoway. Limervoy has a pier, post office and a Church of Scotland. The smaller settlement of Orasay lies a mile (1.5 km) to the west.

Linaclate An alternative name for Liniclate in the Western Isles.

Lincluden *Dumfries and Galloway* A locality in Nithsdale, Dumfries and Galloway, Lincluden lies on the northwest outsksirts of Dumfries at the junction of the Cluden Water with the Nith. The ruins of a medieval collegiate church stand on a mound by the Cluden Water. Founded in the 12th century as a convent for Benedictine nuns, Lincluden was converted into a collegiate church at the end of the 14th century by Archibald, Earl of Douglas.

Lindean *Scottish Borders* A small village of Scottish Borders, Lindean lies 2 miles (3 km) northeast of Selkirk.

Lindores *Fife* A village in Abdie parish, northern Fife, Lindores lies 2 miles (3 km) southeast of Newburgh at the head of Lindores Loch and at the junction of the A913 and B937. A castle of the Macduff earls of Fife once stood at the east end of the village, and a mansion house beside the loch was built by Admiral Sir Frederick Maitland (1777–1839) who received Napoleon on board the *Bellerophon* after the Battle of Waterloo. The title of Lord Lindores was acquired in 1600 by the Leslie family, but became dormant on the death of the seventh holder in 1775. Nearby are the Den of Lindores, Lindores Abbey and Abdie Church.

Lindores Abbey *Fife* The ruins of a foundation of the Benedictine Order established in 1178, Lindores Abbey is situated on the eastern outskirts of Newburgh in northwest Fife. The monks who cultivated fruit growing in the area were ousted during the Reformation in the 16th century. Since then the greater part of the abbey's red sandstone has been plundered for local house building.

Lindores Loch *Fife* A freshwater trout-fishing loch in northern Fife, Lindores Loch lies 2 miles (3 km) southeast of Newburgh. It extends over an area of 44 ha (109 acres) and has an average depth of 1.5 m (5 ft).

Linfern Loch *South Ayrshire* A small loch of Carrick, the Linfern Loch lies 4 miles (6.5 km) south of Straiton in South Ayrshire. A stream issuing from the loch joins the Stinchar River.

Ling, River *Highland* A river in the Lochalsh district of Highland Council area, the River Ling rises in the foothills of Aonach Buidhe and flows in a circular route to empty into the head of Loch Long, an inlet of Loch Duich.

Ling Ness *Shetland* A headland on the east coast of the Shetland Mainland, Ling Ness lies a mile (1.5 km) east of the settlement of Skellister, and is attached by a small narrow strip of land to the area known as South Nesting.

Linga *Shetland* A small, narrow, uninhabited island in the Shetland Islands, Linga lies at the southern end of the Bluemull Sound, which separates Yell from Unst. It has an area of 45 ha (111 acres) and has a long low ridge that rises to 26 m (85 ft) near its southern end. The island is separated from Yell by Linga Sound. A ruined chapel bears evidence of former settlement, but today the island's only inhabitants are sheep.

Linga *Shetland* An island located to the east of Mainland Shetland, Linga rises to 40 m (131 ft) in Yell Sound between Swinster Voe and Firths Voe, 3 miles (5 km) south of the island of Yell.

Linga Holm *Orkney* A tiny uninhabited island of the Orkney Islands, Linga Holm lies to the west of the much larger island of Stronsay from which it is separated by

Linga Sound. Extending to 57 ha (140 acres), it is noted as a wintering ground for Greenland white-fronted geese and as a breeding ground for grey seals. Its grassy swards are also grazed by the rare North Ronaldsay sheep. Archaeological remains include prehistoric cairns and a Pictish house.

Linga Sound *Shetland* A channel in the Shetland Islands, Linga Sound separates the island of West Linga from Whalsay to the east.

Lingay *Western Isles* A small island in the Outer Hebrides, Lingay (Gael: *Liungaigh*) lies in the Sound of Harris, midway between South Harris and North Uist. It is located among a group of small islands with Gilsay, Scaravay and Groay. Uninhabited, it rises to 28 m (92 ft).

Lingay *Western Isles* An island off the north coast of North Uist in the Outer Hebrides, Lingay (Gael: *Lingeigh*) lies 2 miles (3 km) southeast of Boreray and a similar distance southwest of Berneray. Uninhabited, it rises to 33 m (108 ft).

Lingay *Western Isles* A small uninhabited island in the Outer Hebrides, Lingay (Gael: *Lingeigh*) lies in the Sound of Pabbay to the south of Barra, 1.25 miles (2 km) north of Pabbay and 2.5 miles (4 km) west-southwest of Sandray. Lingay is oval in shape and rises steeply to 84 m (275 ft). There is a cave on its southeast coast.

Lingay *Western Isles* An islet trimmed by rocks in Bagh nam Faoilean, between Benbecula and South Uist in the Outer Hebrides, Lingay (Gael: *Lingeigh*) rises to 19 m (62 ft) immediately to the southwest of Wiay and a mile (1.5 km) southeast of Fodragay.

Linhouse Water *West Lothian* A stream of West Lothian, the Linhouse Water rises in the Pentland Hills and flows north through the Crosswood Reservoir to merge with the River Almond west of Livingston.

Liniclate *Western Isles* A scattered hamlet in southern Benbecula in the Outer Hebrides, Liniclate (Linaclate or Gael: *Lionacleit*) lies a mile (1.5 km) northwest of Creagorry and 4 miles (6.5 km) south of Balivanich. Liniclate has a modern hotel lying adjacent to a large secondary school that opened in 1988 and serves all the southern islands. The school incorporates community sporting facilities and a local authority museum, the Museum nan Eilean, which focuses on the social history of the islands south of Berneray.

Linicro *Highland* Situated on the western coastline of the Trotternish peninsula at the northern end of the isle of Skye, Linicro lies 2 miles (3 km) north of Uig.

Linklet Bay *Orkney* A wide bay on the east coast of North Ronaldsay in the Orkney Islands, Linklet Bay extends from Dennis Head in the north to Bride's Ness in the south.

Linktown *Fife* A western suburb of Kirkcaldy in Fife, Linktown was formerly a burgh of regality incorporated into the seaport and royal burgh of Kirkcaldy in 1876. The extension of Kirkcaldy into Linktown has contributed to the waterfront development of what has come to be known as 'the lang toon'.

Linlithgow *West Lothian* An ancient and royal burgh of West Lothian, Linlithgow lies between the Union Canal to the south and the M9 to the north, 18 miles (29 km) west of Edinburgh. A Roman fort and later a castle occupied the site which was, for three centuries, an important centre of the Anglians of West Lothian. Chartered by David I in the early 12th century and later made the seat of a sheriffdom, it developed important links with Church and State during the Middle Ages, particularly from the 14th century when it was re-chartered. These links, together with its commercial privileges contributed to Linlithgow's grandeur and important role in history, as it became one of Scotland's four leading burgh towns and a favourite home of royalty. Linlithgow Palace, which replaced the fort in the 12th century, was rebuilt in the 15th century by James I and later extended by James V whose daughter, Mary, Queen of Scots, was born here in 1542. Adjacent is the striking St Michael's Church, consecrated in 1242, rebuilt in 1424 after a fire, and restored in the 1890s. It is topped by a timber and aluminium flèche erected in 1964. Linlithgow's role declined after the Reformation and the Union of the Crowns in 1603. The palace was abandoned in 1746 after being destroyed by fire, although the town continued as a centre for tanning, brewing, distilling and the manufacture of textiles, shoes, paper and soap. Linlithgow Academy was founded in 1894. The prize-winning redevelopment of the town centre was the work of the architectural practice of Rowand Anderson, Kininmonth and Paul (1967), but today it lies incongruously next to historic buildings. Linlithgow remains a picturesque town; the National Trust for Scotland restored houses in the High Street, and the palace is a popular attraction. The story of the building of the Union Canal in 1817–22 is told in the Linlithgow Canal Centre which opened in 1977, and the history of the burgh is featured in a museum in Annet House opened in 1993. Linlithgow Loch is a bird sanctuary with canoeing, sailing, windsurfing and fishing. The town holds an annual festival of The Marches in June.

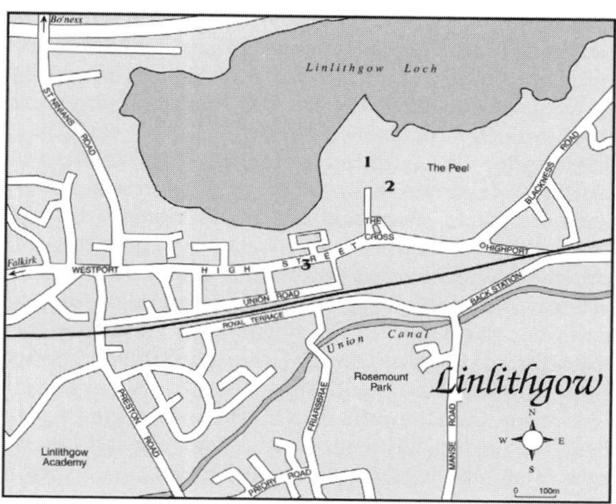

1 *Linlithgow Palace*
2 *St Michael's Church*
3 *The Linlithgow Story*

Linlithgow Bridge *West Lothian* Taking its name from the crossing over the River Avon, Linlithgow Bridge lies to the west of Linlithgow in West Lothian. The Battle of Linlithgow Bridge (1526) followed the murder of John Stewart, 3rd Earl of Lennox, by Sir James Hamilton of Finnart.

Linlithgow Palace *West Lothian* One of the most magnificent of Scotland's ancient monuments, Linlithgow Palace stands on a promontory jutting into Linlithgow Loch with vistas northwards to the M9. The palace, which was a royal residence from the 12th to the late 16th centuries, was occupied in 1298 by Edward I of England on his way to the Battle of Falkirk. In 1301 he returned to establish the town as his headquarters for the campaign of 1301–2, erecting a new castle and reinforcing the palace's defences. This castle was partially destroyed soon after in an ambush led by farmer William Bunnock, but it was restored by 1334. Following the Battle of Bannockburn (1314), David II razed the English fortifications and built a royal manor, destroyed by fire in 1424. The construction of the present building was begun in 1425 for James I and completed over the next century. Among those born in the palace were James V (b.1512) and Mary, Queen of Scots (b.1542). Following the Union of the Crowns in 1603, the palace fell into neglect, although Charles I was the last king to stay there briefly in 1633. The Scottish Parliament met in the palace several times, the last occasion being in 1646. Other notable visitors have included Oliver Cromwell, and Prince Charles Edward Stewart (Bonnie Prince Charlie) in 1745. The Duke of Cumberland, in pursuit of Jacobites, also occupied the palace in 1745, his Government troops destroying much of the inside of the building.

Linn of Tummel *Perth and Kinross* A locality in Perth and Kinross comprising 16 ha (40 acres) of woodland at the junction of the Tummel and Garry rivers, nearly 3 miles (5 km) northwest of Pitlochry. Through the woods, a pathway leads to the Linn of Tummel where an obelisk commemorates a visit by Queen Victoria in 1844. The Tummel used to drop dramatically down to meet the River Garry here, but in 1950 the fall became the Linn (Gaelic, *Linne*, a pool) when the level of both rivers was raised by a hydro-electric scheme that created Loch Faskally. The Linn, which was gifted to the National Trust for Scotland in 1944 by Dr G. F. Barbour of Bonskeid, can be approached through the Pass of Killiecrankie from the visitor centre or from the Garry Bridge car park.

Linn Park *Glasgow City* An area of parkland in Glasgow, Linn Park lies to the south of the River Clyde on the White Cart River north of Clarkston. It was acquired by Glasgow City Corporation in 1919 and comprises a mix of traditional formal gardens and woodland with nature trails. Covering an area of 86 ha (211 acres), it is the second-largest park in Glasgow after Pollok Park. The 14th-century Cathcart Castle lies within the park.

Linnhe, Loch A large sea loch in west-central Scotland, Loch Linnhe separates the Morvern and Ardgour peninsulas to the west from the districts of Appin and Benderloch and parts of Lochaber to the east. Stretching 22 miles (35 kms) from northeast to southwest, it forms a southern extension of the Great Glen that opens out into the Firth of Lorn with the islands of Lismore, Shuna, Bernera and Eileann Balnagowan at its southern end. Its greatest width is nearly 6 miles (10 km), while its narrowest point lies just north of the mouth of Loch Leven at the Corran Narrows. At its northern end are the town of Fort William and the entrance to the Caledonian Canal. A major quarry was opened at Glensanda on the western shore of the loch opposite Lismore in 1986.

Linshader *Western Isles* A small crofting settlement on the west coast of the Isle of Lewis in the Outer Hebrides, Linshader (Gael: *Linsiadar*) overlooks a narrow channel separating East Loch Roag from Loch Kinhoulavig, opposite Callanish.

Linsidemore *Highland* A small settlement in the Sutherland district of Highland Council area, Linsidemore lies 6 miles (10 km) northwest of Bonar Bridge in the valley of the River Oykel.

Lintlaw *Scottish Borders* A small village in the Berwickshire district of Scottish Borders, Lintlaw lies 4 miles (6.5 km) northeast of Duns.

Linton *Scottish Borders* A small settlement in a parish of the same name in the Roxburgh district of Scottish Borders, Linton lies in the northern foothills of the Cheviot Hills, a mile (1.5 km) northwest of Morebattle and 6 miles (10 km) south-southeast of Kelso. The Kale Water flows to the south of the village, and Linton Hill rises to 286 m (926 ft) nearby.

Linton, Bay of *Orkney* A small inlet on the east coast of the island of Shapinsay in the Orkney Islands, the Bay of Linton lies between the headlands of Ness of Ork to the north and the Foot to the south.

Lintrathen, Loch of *Angus* A nature reserve and water reservoir in the Braes of Angus, the Loch of Lintrathen is situated at the southern end of Glen Isla. Surrounded by farmland, the loch is visited by large numbers of wildfowl, wintering geese, whooper swans and the occasional osprey.

Linwood *Renfrewshire* An industrial town in Renfrewshire, Linwood lies on the Black Cart Water 2 miles (3 km) west of Paisley. Formerly a small hamlet, it developed initially in association with cotton milling in the 1790s when a planned village was laid out. Soap and paper were manufactured in the 19th century, but it was not until 1961 that the settlement expanded significantly with the opening of the Hillman car factory, which employed 4,800 people at its peak. The factory closed in 1981 and the site was subsequently developed as the Phoenix Retail Park, Linwood becoming a dormitory village for Glasgow and Paisley.

Lionacleit The Gaelic name for Liniclate in the Western Isles.

Lionel *Western Isles* One of a collection of crofting townships in the Ness district at the northern tip of the Isle of Lewis in the Outer Hebrides, Lionel (Gael: *Lional*) is located immediately to the northeast of Habost and to the southwest of Port of Ness.

Lion's Head *Aberdeenshire* A small rocky headland on the Moray Firth coast of Aberdeenshire, the Lion's Head lies midway between the village of Pennan and Troup Head. A hollow known as Hell's Lum is found here.

Lismore *Argyll and Bute* An island at the southwest end of Loch Linnhe, Lismore has an area of 2244 ha (5543 acres) and rises to a height of 127 m (417 ft) at Barr Mòr at the southern extremity of the island. Sheltered from the extremes of the Atlantic Ocean and with an underlying limestone geology, Lismore has a rich flora. During the 19th century limestone was quarried and exported from Eilann nan Caorach, Port Ramsay and Inn Island on the west coast. The island's population has fallen to its present level of around 150 from a peak of 1500 in the mid-19th century, most of the population today being employed in farming or fishing. Places of interest include the ruined remains of Coeffin Castle and Achadun Castle. St Moluag established a monastery in the mid-6th century and for a time the island was an important ecclesiastical centre. St Moluag's pastoral staff is still held by the Livingstones of Bachuil. John Stuart McCaig, the man responsible for building the folly above Oban, was born on Lismore. There are ferry links with Oban and Port Appin.

Little Bernera *Western Isles* A small island situated off the west coast of the Isle of Lewis in the Outer Hebrides, Little Bernera (Gael: *Bearnaraigh Beag*) lies between the sea lochs of West and East Loch Roag, immediately to the north of Great Bernera. The island rises to a height of 42 m (137 ft) and has an area of 138 ha (341 acres).

Little Brechin *Angus* A village in northeast Angus, Little Brechin lies 2 miles (3 km) northwest of Brechin.

Little Colonsay *Argyll and Bute* A small island off the west coast of Mull, Little Colonsay lies 2 miles (3 km) west of Inch Kenneth and a half-mile (1 km) south of the island of Ulva. It has an area of 88 ha (217 acres) and has been uninhabited since the 1940s.

Little Creich *Highland* A village of the Sutherland district of Highland Council area, Little Creich lies on the northern shore of the Dornoch Firth, 2 miles (3 km) southeast of Bonar Bridge.

Little Cumbrae *North Ayrshire* A sparsely populated island in the Firth of Clyde, Little Cumbrae lies to the south of the island of Great Cumbrae, between the coast of Ayrshire and the southern tip of the island of Bute. It has an area of 313 ha (773 acres) and rises to 123 m (403 ft) at Lighthouse Hill, which was the site of an open-fire warning beacon that operated before the creation of the lighthouse on the western shore of the island. Privately owned, the island's principal building is Little Cumbrae House, which lies on the east side of the island overlooking Castle Island. Little Cumbrae is a designated nature reserve.

Little Dunkeld *Perth and Kinross* A locality in Perth and Kinross, Little Dunkeld lies to the south of the River Tay between Dunkeld and Birnam. The white-harled Little Dunkeld Parish Church dates from 1798, its kirkyard containing memorials to the noted local musicians Neil Gow and Charles Macintosh. In addition to a school, there are modern housing estates at Kirkfield and Willowbank.

Little France *City of Edinburgh* A district of Edinburgh, Little France lies on the Old Dalkeith Road near Craigmillar Castle, 2.5 miles (4 km) southeast of the city centre. It derives its name from having housed the servants and courtiers of Mary, Queen of Scots on her return from France. Little France is the site of Edinburgh's new Royal Infirmary.

Little Green Holm *Orkney* A small, uninhabited islet of the Orkney Islands, Little Green Holm lies to the south of Muckle Green Holm, from which it is separated by the Sound of the Green Holms.

Little Gruinard *Highland* A small village in Wester Ross, Little Gruinard lies on the south shore of Gruinard Bay, 3 miles (5 km) southeast of Laide. Across the bay to the north lies the island of Gruinard, while passing through the village are the waters of the Little Gruinard River.

Little Havra *Shetland* A small uninhabited island in the Shetland Islands, Little Havra lies off the west coast of South Havra.

Little Holm *Shetland* A rock islet in the Yell Sound in the Shetland Islands, Little Holm lies 3 miles (5 km) southeast of Burra Voe.

Little Johns Haven *Aberdeenshire* A small inlet on the North Sea coast of southeast Aberdeenshire, Little Johns Haven forms a bay to the south of Kinneff.

Little Linga *Orkney* A small islet of the Orkney Islands, Little Linga lies in the waters off the Links Ness, at the northwestern point of the island of Stronsay.

Little Linga *Shetland* One of a number of small, uninhabited islands and islets, Little Linga lies in the waters between West Linga and the Shetland Mainland.

Little Loch Broom *Highland* A sea loch in the Ross and Cromarty district of Highland Council area, Little Loch Broom lies between Gruinard Bay to the west and Loch Broom to the east, with the settlements of Badcaul, Ardessie and Dundonnell close to its shores.

Little Loch Roag *Western Isles* A long narrow sea loch in the Western Isles, Little Loch Roag extends 5 miles (8 km) southwards from the southwest corner of West Loch Roag, on the west coast of the Isle of Lewis in the Outer Hebrides.

Little Loch Shin *Highland* A small reservoir in central Sutherland, Little Loch Shin lies to the south of Loch Shin. It is part of the Shin Hydro-Electric Power Scheme and is used to maintain a minimum level in the River Shin while passing water to the Shin Power Station at Inveran.

Little Minch A body of water separating the Western Isles from the isle of Skye, the Little Minch is 15 miles (24 km) wide at its narrowest.

Little Rack Wick *Orkney* A bay on the west coast of the island of Hoy in the Orkney Islands, Little Rack Wick lies 3 miles (5 km) southeast of Sneuk Head.

Little Roe Island *Shetland* An uninhabited island of the Shetland Islands, Little Roe Island lies at the southern end of the Yell Sound, 2 miles (3 km) east of Ollaberry on the east coast of the Shetland Mainland. It has an area of 70 ha (30 acres).

Little Ross *Dumfries and Galloway* A small island on the Solway coast of Dumfries and Galloway, Little Ross lies at the west side of the mouth of Kirkcudbright Bay. Its lighthouse dates from 1843.

Little Scares *Dumfries and Galloway* A group of tiny islets, the Little Scares form a rocky reef at the centre of Luce Bay, a major inlet of the Solway Firth in Dumfries and Galloway.

Little Scatwell *Highland* A small village in Easter Ross, Little Scatwell lies at the confluence of the rivers Meig and Conon, a mile (1.5 km) east of Loch Meig and a mile (1.5 km) south of the head of Loch Luichart.

Little Skerry *Orkney* The Little Skerry is the most southerly of the Pentland Skerries, a group of uninhabited small islands at the eastern end of the Pentland Firth.

Little Sypland *Dumfries and Galloway* A locality in Dumfries and Galloway, Little Sypland lies 3 miles (5 km) northeast of Kirkcudbright on the road to Gelston. Meikle Sypland lies a mile (1.5 km) to the south and west of the Balgreddan Burn.

Little Water *Aberdeenshire* A stream of Buchan in northeast Aberdeenshire, the Little Water rises to the east of Cuminestown and flows south to join the River Ythan at Chapelhaugh, 5 miles (8 km) east of Fyvie.

Little Water of Fleet *Dumfries and Galloway* A stream in Dumfries and Galloway, the Little Water of Fleet rises out of Loch Fleet in the Galloway Hills and flows southwards for 6 miles (10 km), joining the Big Water of Fleet 3 miles (5 km) northwest of Gatehouse of Fleet to form the Water of Fleet.

Little Wyvis *Highland* A mountain in Easter Ross, Little Wyvis rises to a height of 764 m (2506 ft) 3 miles (5 km) northeast of the settlement of Garve.

Littleferry *Highland* A small village on the east coast of Sutherland, Littleferry lies at the northern entrance to Loch Fleet, 3 miles (5 km) southwest of Golspie.

Littlemill *East Ayrshire* A village of East Ayrshire, Littlemill lies 2 miles (3 km) south of Drongan on the course of the Water of Coyle.

Littlemill *Highland* A small village in the Nairn district of Highland Council area, Littlemill lies 4 miles (6.5 km) south of Nairn.

Liungaigh The Gaelic name for Lingay in the Western Isles.

Liurbost The Gaelic name for Leurbost in the Western Isles.

Liursaigh Dubh The Gaelic name for Luirsay Dubh in the Western Isles.

Liursaigh Glas The Gaelic name for Luirsay Glas in the Western Isles.

Livet, River *Moray* A river rising in headwaters in the Grampian uplands of Moray to the south of Dufftown, the River Livet flows 11 miles (18 km) northwestwards through Glen Livet to meet the River Avon at Drumin.

Livingston *West Lothian* Located 13 miles (21 km) west of Edinburgh in the Almond Valley between the M8 and the A71. Scotland's fourth New Town of Livingston was created in 1962 around a large oil-shale village and now extends over an area of 22.9 sq. km. (10 sq. miles). The town, which lies at the centre of Scotland's 'Silicon Glen', has a distinctive grid layout that was designed for motor transport and for pedestrians, with Greenway paths separating the two. Developed from east to west along the Almond Valley, the new town's housing style changed from high-rise buildings in the 1960s to low-density 'low-rise' in the late 1980s and early 1990s. The original village at Livingston Peel comprises 18th-century cottages, a village green and the parish kirk (1732). Other notable buildings include the Almond Valley Heritage Centre, the Old Tollhouse (c.1800), St Andrew's Roman Catholic Church (1968), the Old Cameron Ironworks, and Alderstone House, an early 17th-century structure incorporating parts of an early 16th-century tower. Howden House, associated with the family of the painter Henry Raeburn, was built in the 18th century and lies at the heart of Howden Park Centre with community facilities. There are five principal industrial parks with textile, leisurewear, electronics and precision-engineering industries, and the Kirkton Campus on the north side of Livingston supports high-technology training. Livingston is noted for its roundabout sculptures, and the entry from the M8 is marked by the Norgate Sculpture in the form of a whalebone arch.

Lix *Stirling* A locality in Stirling Council area, Lix comprises the scattered settlements of Wester Lix, Mid Lix, Easter Lix and Lix Toll which lie at the junction of the A85 from Glen Ogle to Crianlarich and the A827 to Killin and Loch Tay. Early clachan settlements here were excavated in the 1960s by Horace Fairhurst of Glasgow University.

Loanan, River *Highland* A river of northwest Sutherland, the River Loanan flows from Loch Awe northwards to empty into Loch Assynt.

Loanhead *Midlothian* A former mining and paper making settlement in Midlothian, Loanhead lies 5 miles (8 km) southeast of Edinburgh. Coal was mined here from the late 17th century by the Clerks of Penicuik, who built miners' houses in 1736. Oil shale was worked from the 1880s until 1909, and limestone was quarried in the vicinity. Nearby Bilston Glen Colliery, opened in the 1950s, was closed in the late 1980s, and the Bilston Glen viaduct was restored in 1999. The modern Pentlands Industrial Estate has food-processing, packaging and light-engineering industries. Nearby Mavisbank House was built in 1723–7 by William Adam for Sir John Clerk. It was used as a hospital for a time and was badly damaged by fire in 1973.

Loans *South Ayrshire* A village of South Ayrshire, Loans lies 2 miles (3 km) east of Troon.

Loans, the *Falkirk* A small village in Falkirk Council area, the Loans forms a ribbon of development on the Avonbridge–Linlithgow Bridge road, close to the entrance to Muiravonside Country Park.

Loch Fell *Dumfries and Galloway* A hill in Dumfries and Galloway, Loch Fell rises to 688 m (2256 ft), 4 miles (6.5 km) east of Moffat.

Loch na Madadh The Gaelic name for Lochmaddy in the Western Isles.

Lochaber *Highland* An administrative district of Highland Regional Council between 1974 and 1995, Lochaber is an ancient territory that extends eastwards from Loch Linnhe to Loch Laggan. It includes Ben Nevis as well as Glen Spean, Glen Roy, Glen Gloy and parts of Rannoch Moor, and its principal settlement is Fort William.

Lochaber Loch *Dumfries and Galloway* A small loch in Dumfries and Galloway, Lochaber Loch lies in Mabie Forest, 3 miles (5 km) southwest of Dumfries. It is the source of the stream known as Kirkgunzeon Lane.

Lochailort *Highland* A settlement with a railway station on the West Highland Line, Lochailort is located at the head of Loch Ailort, 10.5 miles (17 km) southeast of Mallaig. There has been an inn here since at least the mid-17th century and the small whitewashed Roman Catholic church of Our Lady of the Braes (1874) is a notable landmark. Fish farming provides an important contribution to the local economy.

Lochaline *Highland* A small settlement on the south coast of the Morvern peninsula, Lochaline lies at the mouth of Loch Aline, looking out over the Sound of Mull. Silica has been mined locally, and a ferry links with Fishnish on the island of Mull.

Lochan Burn *Dumfries and Galloway* A stream in Dumfries and Galloway, the Lochan Burn rises in headstreams on the western slopes of Hart Fell to the north of Moffat. It flows southwest for 3 miles (5 km) before joining the River Annan.

Lochans *Dumfries and Galloway* A village of the Rhinns of Galloway, Lochans lies on the Piltanton Burn, 2 miles (3 km) south of Stranraer.

Locharbriggs *Dumfries and Galloway* A small town of Dumfries and Galloway, Locharbriggs lies 2 miles (3 km) northeast of Dumfries on the Lochar Water. It was one of several villages that stood on the edge of the extensive

Lochar Moss before it was drained and reclaimed in the 19th century, and is noted for the quarrying of distinctive red sandstone that has been used for buildings in towns and cities including Dumfries, Glasgow and Edinburgh. The stone has also been exported further afield, most notably to be used to create the steps of the Statue of Liberty in New York Harbour. Although only one quarry remains active, the quarries produced enormous quantities of stone throughout the 19th and early 20th centuries.

Lochar Moss *Dumfries and Galloway* An area of low flat land in Dumfries and Galloway, Lochar Moss lies in the valley of the Lochar Water to the east of Dumfries. It stretches from Locharbriggs in the north to the Solway Firth in the south and is 2–3 miles (3–5 km) wide. The first civil-engineering project of John Smeaton (1724–92), designer of the Eddystone Lighthouse, was the drainage of Lochar Moss.

Lochar Water *Dumfries and Galloway* A stream in Dumfries and Galloway, the Lochar Water rises as the Park Burn to the north of Dumfries and flows 18 miles (29 km) southwards to join the Solway Firth near Ruthwell. At low tide it traverses a further 5 miles (8 km) of sand flats.

Lochar Water *South Lanarkshire* Rising as the Feeshie Burn, the Lochar Water flows northwest from Lambhill to join the Avon Water, 3 miles (5 km) southeast of Strathaven, South Lanarkshire.

Lochavich *Argyll and Bute* A locality on the north shore of Loch Avich, between Loch Melfort and Loch Awe, Lochavich lies 6 miles (10 km) east of Kilmelford.

Lochawe *Argyll and Bute* A village at the north end of Loch Awe, Lochawe lies 3 miles (5 km) west of Dalmally. It has a railway station and steamer pier in addition to the Scottish baronial-style St Conan's Chapel built in 1883. Cruachan Hydro Power Station lies to the west.

Lochay, River *Stirling* A river of Breadalbane in northern Stirling Council area, the River Lochay rises about 6 miles (10 km) north of Crianlarich and flows north between Ben Challum and Beinn nan Imirean before turning east to flow the length of Glen Lochay. At Killin it meets the River Dochart as it enters the western end of Loch Tay.

Lochboisdale *Western Isles* The ferry port and village of Lochboisdale (Gael: *Loch Baghasdail*) is the chief settlement of South Uist in the Outer Hebrides and the only village on the east coast of the island. It lies at the head of a sheltered bay at the southeast end of the island where a car ferry links the island with Barra, Mallaig and Oban.

Lochbuie *Argyll and Bute* A village on the south coast of the island of Mull, Lochbuie lies at the head of the broad bay of Loch Buie. It had a ferry link with Oban until the 1790s and is surrounded by antiquities, including prehistoric standing stones and the ruined Castle Moy, a former stronghold of the Macleans.

Lochcarron *Highland* A village in Wester Ross, Lochcarron lies on the natural harbour of Slumbay on the northern shore of Loch Carron, 2 miles (3 km) northeast of its mouth. Formerly a crofting and fishing community, it developed in the 1960s in association with the oil-rig yard at Kishorn. It is today a tourist resort with a nine-hole golf course.

Lochdon *Argyll and Bute* A small scattered village on the southeast coast of Mull, Lochdon lies 2 miles (3 km) south of Craignure.

Lochearnhead *Stirling* Situated at the western end of Loch Earn and at the foot of Glen Ogle, Lochearnhead lies 31 miles (50 km) northwest of Stirling. It developed from the 18th century in association with road and rail transport, and is now a centre for tourism and watersports on the loch.

Lochee *Dundee City* A residential district of Dundee adjacent to Balgay Hill, Lochee was for many years a separate town. It developed during the 18th century in association with handloom weaving and in the 19th century as a centre of spinning, bleaching, dyeing and linen manufacture. The Camperdown Works of Messrs Cox Brothers, built 1849–64, was said to be the largest jute factory in the world, with 820 power looms, 150 hand looms and 5000 employees. Cox's Stack, the 86-m/282-ft-high campanile-style factory chimney, survives. Lochee Park was gifted by the Cox family to the city in 1871 for the benefit of millworkers. Sandstone from a quarry at Lochee was used in the construction of Dundee Harbour.

Lochenbreck Loch *Dumfries and Galloway* A small loch in Balmag parish, Dumfries and Galloway, Lochenbreck Loch lies 3 miles (5 km) to the west of Laurieston.

Lochend The former name for Beeswing in Dumfries and Galloway.

Lochend *City of Edinburgh* A residential area in the district of Restalrig in Edinburgh, Lochend lies adjacent to Lochend Loch and is centred on Lochend Park. The park, which contains a 16th-century beehive dovecote, is overlooked by Lochend House, a former home of the Logans of Restalrig. Built in 1820, it replaced an earlier castle destroyed at the end of the 16th century. The Doo'cot has a stonework collar around its top, a most unusual feature that is thought to have been a chimney related to the use of the building to burn infected clothing during the plague of 1645.

Lochend *Highland* A settlement in the Caithness district of Highland Council area, Lochend lies on the eastern shore of Loch Heilen, 4 miles (6.5 km) southeast of Dunnet.

Locheport *Western Isles* A linear crofting settlement drawn out along the southern shore of Loch Euphort on North Uist in the Outer Hebrides, Locheport (also Loch Euphort, Euphoirt or Locheuphort) is located 5.5 miles (9 km) southwest of Lochmaddy.

Locherben *Dumfries and Galloway* A locality in the Lowther Hills, Dumfries and Galloway, Locherben lies in the valley of the Garroch Water to the southwest of Queensberry.

Locheuphort An alternative name for Locheport in the Western Isles.

Lochfoot *Dumfries and Galloway* A hamlet in Dumfries and Galloway, Lochfoot lies on moorland at the north end of Lochrutton Loch, 5 miles (8 km) southwest of Dumfries. To the southeast is Hills Tower, a 16th-century stronghold of the Maxwell family.

Lochgair *Argyll and Bute* A village of Argyll and Bute, Lochgair lies on Loch Gair, an inlet on the western shore of Loch Fyne, 4 miles (6.5 km) northeast of Lochgilphead.

Lochgarthside *Highland* A small settlement on the eastern edge of the Great Glen in the Inverness district of Highland Council area, Lochgarthside lies on the western shore of Loch Mhòr, 2 miles (3 km) southeast of Foyers.

Lochgelly *Fife* A former coal-mining town in western Fife, Lochgelly sits on a ridge between Loch Ore and Loch Gelly. Situated on the railway line linking Dunfermline with Dundee, Lochgelly was once a small agricultural market centre. It prospered as a mining town between the granting of mineral rights to the Lochgelly Iron and Coal Company in the 1830s and the closure of local pits in the 1960s. Lochgelly is the highest town in Fife and was designated a burgh in 1876. 'The Lochgelly' was the name once given to the locally manufactured leather belt or tawse formerly used to administer corporal punishment in schools. Lochgelly has a modern community high school built in 1986, a community centre (1976), an 18-hole golf course, and an industrial estate with industries that include engineering, sawmilling, the manufacture of animal feed and rubber goods, and the supply of building materials.

Lochgilphead *Argyll and Bute* The administrative centre of Argyll and Bute since 1975, Lochgilphead lies at the head of Loch Gilp, an inlet on the western shore of Loch Fyne. Originally a small fishing village, it was laid out as a planned settlement following the construction of a new road linking Campbeltown with Inveraray in the 1780s. It subsequently served the Crinan Canal, which opened in 1801 and whose eastern terminus lies to the south at Ardrishaig. Lochgilphead developed as the county town of Argyllshire, a tourist resort and a centre servicing the surrounding rural area. Forestry, construction and the manufacture of knitwear are important local industries.

Lochgoilhead *Argyll and Bute* A small village of Argyll and Bute, Lochgoilhead lies on the River Goil where it enters Loch Goil, an arm of Loch Long, at the northern end of the Cowal peninsula. It is linked by road to Inveraray via Gleann Beag (Hell's Glen) and developed in the 19th century in association with the manufacture of textiles and the steamer trade.

Lochgoin Reservoir *East Renfrewshire/East Ayrshire* Straddling the borders of East Renfrewshire and East Ayrshire, Lochgoin Reservoir is situated 4 miles (6.5 km) southwest of Eaglesham. To the northeast are Dunwan Dam and Melowther Hill.

Lochhill *East Ayrshire* A small village of East Ayrshire, Lochhill lies 2 miles (3km) northwest of New Cumnock and 3 miles (5 km) southeast of Cumnock. There is a 9-hole golf course.

Lochindorb *Highland* A loch of Highland Council area, Lochindorb lies amid open moorland, 6 miles (10 km) northwest of Grantown-on-Spey and 8 miles (13 km) northeast of Carrbridge. The ruins of a 13th-century castle lie on an island in the loch.

Lochinvar *Dumfries and Galloway* A small loch in Dumfries and Galloway, Lochinvar lies in the hills to the east of The Glenkens, 3 miles (5 km) northeast of St John's Town of Dalry. The Lochinvar Burn flows south towards the Water of Ken and on an islet in the loch stand the ruins of a former stronghold of the Gordons of Lochinvar, one of whom was featured as Young Lochinvar in Lady Heron's song in Sir Walter Scott's *Marmion* (1808).

Lochinver *Highland* A resort and fishing village in the Assynt district of Sutherland, Lochinver lies at the head of Loch Inver 30 miles (48 km) northwest of Ullapool. Once a major herring-fishing port, it still ranks alongside Kinlochbervie as one of the busiest fishing ports on the west coast, with a new pier and fish-processing factory established in the early 1990s. In addition to fish farming, salmon and trout fishing for sport are also important in local rivers and lochs. The present Culag Hotel was originally built for the Duke of Sutherland and there is a visitor centre and local crafts. To the southeast, the Inverpolly National Nature Reserve and the rocks of Knockan Crag are of interest. The dramatic Torridonian sandstone peak of Suilven rises to a height of 731 m (2398 ft) to the east.

Lochluichart *Highland* A small village in the Ross and Cromarty district of Highland Council area, Lochluichart lies on the northwest shore of Loch Luichart, 4 miles (6.5 km) west of Gorstan.

Lochmaben *Dumfries and Galloway* A royal burgh in the Annandale district of Dumfries and Galloway, Lochmaben lies in the valley of the River Annan between Castle Loch, Kirk Loch and Mill Loch, 9 miles (14 km) northeast of Dumfries. Designated a royal burgh in 1440, its castle was the home of Robert the Bruce when Lord of Annandale. Lochmaben developed in association with lime quarrying and the manufacture of textiles, and today has industries producing dairy products. Notable buildings include the parish church (1818), town hall (early 18th and late 19th centuries), and Edward VII Memorial Fountain (1910–11). There is an 18-hole golf course and a sailing club.

Lochmaddy *Western Isles* Looking out onto a sea loch of the same name, Lochmaddy (Gael: *Loch na Madadh*) is the chief settlement and port of North Uist in the Outer Hebrides. Situated on the east coast, it has a court house, a cottage hospital and a factory producing alginates from seaweed. Visitor attractions include the Uist Outdoor Centre and the Tiagh Chearsabhagh Museum and Arts Centre. Lochmaddy developed in the 18th and 19th centuries as a fishing centre and port frequented by ships from as far afield as Ireland and the Baltic.

Lochnagar *Aberdeenshire* A mountain rising to a height of 1155 m (3789 ft) on the Balmoral Estate to the south of the River Dee, Lochnagar is a major peak of the northeast Grampians.

Lochnaw Castle *Dumfries and Galloway* The ancestral seat of the Agnews of Lochnaw, one-time hereditary sheriffs of Galloway, Lochnaw Castle is situated by Lochnaw in the Rhinns of Galloway, 5 miles (8 km) northwest of Stranraer. Largely dating from the 16th century, its 19th-century extensions were mostly demolished. Ruins of the original castle stand on a small islet in the loch.

Lochore *Fife* A former mining town in western Fife, Lochore takes its name from the adjacent 105 ha (260 acre) Loch Ore which was partially drained in the 1790s. Before its development as a mining town, Lochore lay on a major route linking the Firth of Forth with Perth and formed part of the barony of Lochoreshire in the ancient province of Fothrif.

Lochore Meadows *Fife* Encompassing Loch Ore and its surrounding area of reclaimed coal-mining waste-land, the 486-ha (1200-acre) Lochore Meadows Country Park lies at the heart of Fife Regional Park West, with Lochore, Crosshill and Glencraig on its eastern edge. It is the main centre for outdoor and environmental education in Fife and comprises a nature reserve, park centre, outdoor pursuits centre, adventure play area, picnic and barbecue areas and nature trails. Activities in the park include windsurfing, horse riding, orienteering and fishing, in addition to a nine-hole golf course and putting green. The ruins of Lochore Castle and the remains of the Mary Pit coal workings are also in the park.

Lochportan *Western Isles* A small fishing and crofting community on the northeast coast of North Uist in the Outer Hebrides, Lochportan (also *Lochportain*) lies on the sea loch Loch Portain, 2.5 miles (4 km) northeast of Lochmaddy and has a post office.

Lochranza *North Ayrshire* A small ferry port and yachting resort village at the north end of the island of Arran, Lochranza lies on the sea inlet of Loch Ranza, 13 miles (21 km) northwest of Brodick. The village developed in association with a castle, and later with salt extraction, coal mining and fishing. In 1995, a whisky distillery opened to the south of the village. A steamer pier was erected in 1886 and a ferry link to Claonaig in Kintyre was created in 1972. The Highland Boundary Fault passes to the northeast of the village, revealing a disjunction between the rock beds, one of the most famous of the three unconformities discovered by James Hutton (1726–97).

Lochrutton Loch *Dumfries and Galloway* A small loch in Dumfries and Galloway, Lochrutton Loch lies within a parish of the same name, 5 miles (8 km) southwest of Dumfries. The loch receives the Minnin Burn and the Under Brae Lane, and on its north shore sits the village of Lochfoot.

Lochs *Western Isles* A district and parish of the Isle of Lewis in the Western Isles, Lochs lies on the east coast of the island centred on Loch Erisort. North Lochs (Gael: *Lochan a Tuath*) extends north from here to Stornoway, while South Lochs (Gael: *Lochan a Deas*) extends south to a line between the head of Loch Seaforth and Loch Ouirn, where it meets the district of Park (part of the parish of Lochs).

Lochsie, Glen *Perth and Kinross* A valley of Perth and Kinross, Glen Lochsie carries the waters of the Glenlochsie Burn 5 miles (8 km) to join the Shee Water at the head of Glen Shee at Spittal of Glenshee.

Lochton *South Ayrshire* A small village of South Ayrshire, Lochton lies in the upper reaches of the River Duisk, 2 miles (3 km) southeast of Barrhill.

Lochty *Fife* A settlement in the East Neuk of Fife, Lochty is situated 4 miles (6.5 km) northwest of Anstruther and 7 miles (11 km) west of Crail. In 1966 the Fife Railway Preservation Society began to operate a private railway as a working steam railway museum on a remnant of the 15-mile/24-km-long Lochty branch line, which had opened in 1898 to serve the farms and coal pits in the area. To the north stand the ruins of Pittarthie Castle, a 17th-century fortified house associated with the Bruce family.

Lochty Burn *Fife* A stream that rises on Benarty Hill in Ballingry parish in western Fife, the Lochty Burn flows 10 miles (16 km) eastwards to join the River Ore just south of Coaltown of Balgonie. It passes through Ballingry and to the south of Kinglassie and Glenrothes, and at its source is Gruoch's Well, one of only a few places to be named after the wife of Macbeth.

Lochuisge *Highland* A small village in the Morvern district of Highland Council area, Lochuisge lies to the northwest of Loch Uisge, 8 miles (13 km) northeast of Ardtornish.

Lochwinnoch *Renfrewshire* A small town in Renfrewshire, Lochwinnoch sits on the Calder River on the southwest side of Castle Semple Loch, 10 miles (16 km) west of Paisley. Now a dormitory village, it developed in the 18th century in association with the textile industry and later with cabinet making and silk weaving and printing. Castle Semple, a former stronghold of the Sempill family, was rebuilt as a mansion. Castle Semple Loch is a water park for water-skiing, sailing and surfing, with an RSPB visitor centre on its shores. Notable buildings in the vicinity include the remains of 16th-century Barr Castle, a folly known as The Temple (1770), The Peel (*c.*1550), a collegiate church (1504–05) with the tomb of John, 1st Lord Sempil, and the Lochwinnoch Community Museum (1984).

Lochy, Burn of *Moray* Rising as headstreams that flow down from the Hills of Cromdale and the Cairngorm Mountains, the Burn of Lochy flows a short distance through Glen Lochy before joining the River Avon at Milton.

Lochy, Loch *Highland* A loch in the Great Glen, Loch Lochy lies between Loch Linnhe to the southwest and Loch Oich in the northeast. Ten miles (16 km) in length, with the settlements of Gairlochy and Laggan at either end, Loch Lochy forms part of the Caledonian Canal.

Lochy, River *Argyll and Bute* A river of Argyll and Bute, the Lochy rises in a small loch to the west of Tyndrum. It flows west through Glen Lochy to merge with the River Orchy, 2 miles (3 km) east of Dalmally.

Lochy, River *Highland* A small river of the Lochaber district of Highland Council area, the River Lochy flows a short distance in a southwesterly direction, linking Loch Lochy with Loch Linnhe in the Great Glen.

Lockerbie *Dumfries and Galloway* Founded in the early 18th century by the Johnstones of Lockerbie, Lockerbie in Dumfries and Galloway is located 14 miles (22 km) east of Dumfries and just east of the River Annan, by the M74. Scotland's largest lamb fair was held here in the 18th century, in 1847 the railway arrived and in 1863 Lockerbie became a burgh. Tragedy struck the town on 21

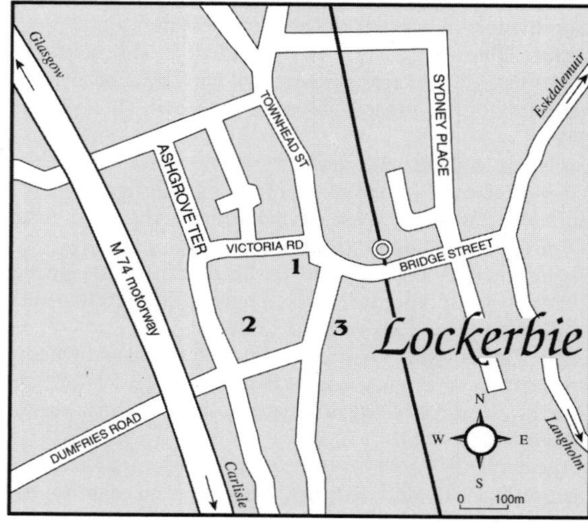

1 *Lockerbie Library*
2 *McJerrow Park*
3 *Lockerbie Town Hall*

December 1988 when a terrorist bomb destroyed a PanAm Jumbo Jet flying overhead, killing all 285 passengers and 11 people in the town. In medieval times the town was the focus of much feuding between the Johnstone and Maxwell families, giving rise to the term 'Lockerbie Lick' (a slashed face).

Loder Head *Shetland* A headland on the east coast of the island of Bressay in the Shetland Islands, Loder Head extends into the sea to the southeast of Aith Ness. The Isle of Noss lies to the southeast.

Logan *East Ayrshire* A village of East Ayrshire, Logan lies a mile (1.5 km) to the east of Cumnock and immediately to the south of the course of the Lugar Water.

Logan, Mull of *Dumfries and Galloway* A headland in the Rhinns of Galloway, southwest Dumfries and Galloway, the Mull of Logan lies to the northwest of Port Logan, separating Port Logan Bay from Drumbreddan Bay.

Logan Water *Dumfries and Galloway* A stream in Eskdale, Dumfries and Galloway, the Logan Water rises in the hills to the south of the River Esk. It flows generally southwards to join the Wauchope Water which flows into the Esk.

Logan Water *South Lanarkshire* A river rising in the shadow of Spirebush Hill in South Lanarkshire, the Logan Water flows into Logan Reservoir then eastwards to join the River Nethan, a tributary of the River Clyde.

Loganlea *West Lothian* A former mining village of West Lothian, Loganlea lies just to the south of the Breich Water, between Bents and Addiewell, 2 miles (3 km) south of Blackburn.

Loganlea Reservoir *Midlothian* A reservoir in the Pentland Hills supplying water to the City of Edinburgh to the north, Loganlea lies on the Logan Burn 3 miles (5 km) northwest of Penicuik.

Logie *Angus* A small village in the northeast corner of Angus, Logie lies to the west of the North Esk River, 4 miles (6.5 km) north of Montrose.

Logie *Fife* A hamlet situated in 'a hollow among hills', Logie lies in a parish of the same name on a minor road to the west of Balmullo in northeast Fife. James West (1756–1817), clergyman and author of a *System of Mathematics*, was the son of a minister of Logie parish. Sir Walter Scott (1771–1832) immortalised one of the local landowners in his ballad *The Laird of Logie*.

Logie, Glen *Angus* A narrow glen in the southern Grampian Mountains of Angus, Glen Logie occupies a tributary of the Prosen Water on the north side of Glen Prosen.

Logie Coldstone *Aberdeenshire* A settlement in the Cromar district of Aberdeenshire, Logie Coldstone lies 7 miles (11 km) northeast of Ballater on the road from Dinnet on Deeside to Strathdon.

Logie Head *Aberdeenshire* A headland on the Moray Firth coast of Aberdeenshire, Logie Head extends into the sea a mile (1.5 km) east of Cullen.

Logie Pert *Angus* A hamlet in a parish of the same name in northeast Angus, Logie Pert lies 5 miles (8 km) northwest of Montrose and nearly 2 miles (3 km) west of Marykirk.

Logiealmond *Perth and Kinross* A settlement in Glen Almond, Perth and Kinross, Logiealmond lies on the River Almond, 8 miles (13 km) northwest of Perth. It developed in association with textile industries and slate quarrying.

Logierait *Perth and Kinross* A village in a large parish of the same name in Highland Perth and Kinross, Logierait lies at the confluence of the Tay and Tummel rivers, due west of Ballinluig. There are Pictish crosses in the parish church and churchyard. Close by are a memorial to the 6th Duke of Atholl built to a design by Robert Rowand Anderson in 1866, a former railway viaduct by Joseph Mitchell (1865) and a museum of childhood at Cuil-an-Darach, a former poorhouse built in 1864. For many years Logierait was the seat of justice in the regality of Atholl. Adam Ferguson (1723–1816), Professor of Natural Philosophy at Edinburgh University at the height of the Enlightenment, was the son of the minister of Logierait.

Loin, Burn of *Moray* Rising in the Cairngorm Mountains as the Allt Chriosdain, the Burn of Loin flows southeastwards through Glen Loin before turning south to join the upper reaches of the River Avon.

Loin, Glen *Argyll and Bute* A valley of Argyll and Bute, Glen Loin carries the waters of the River Loin south to empty into the head of Loch Long.

Lomond, Loch The largest inland water body in the United Kingdom, Loch Lomond lies within the council areas of Argyll and Bute, Stirling and West Dunbartonshire and has an area of 71 sq. km. (27.4 sq. miles) and a shoreline 96 miles (153 km) in length. It extends 24 miles (38 km) from Ardlui in the north to Balloch in the south and, although narrower to the north, the loch widens in the south. Of the loch's 38 islands, the largest are Inchmurrin, Inchcailloch, Inchmoan, Inchtavannach and Inchlonaig. Its proximity to central Scotland makes it a popular centre for day trips, the loch and its surrounding area offering opportunities for watersports, fishing, golfing, walking and camping. It is now the focal point of Scotland's first national park, the Loch Lomond and Trossachs National Park, which covers an area of 440 sq. km (170 sq. miles) with a retail, leisure and visitor centre at Loch Lomond Shores. The chief settlements adjacent to the loch are Balloch, Balmaha, Luss, Tarbet and Inveruglas. Around Loch Lomond are some of the most accessible glacial landscape features in Scotland, including corries, hanging valleys and drumlins. Evidence of the Loch Lomond Readvance (or Stadial), a period of renewed glaciation occurring around 10,000 BC, can be seen at the southern end of the loch.

Lomond Hills Dominating the skyline for miles around, the Lomond Hills separate the Kinross basin in the west from Fife in the east. The two highest peaks, which are of volcanic origin, are West Lomond (522 m/1712 ft) and East Lomond (424 m/1391 ft). The western scarp slope of the Bishop Hill, which overlooks Loch Leven, rises to 461 m (1492 ft) and is capped by a volcanic sill of quartz dolerite overlying layers of sandstone and limestone of Carboniferous age. A freestanding column known as Carline Maggie is a feature of the quartz-dolerite outcrop. Limestone has been quarried, most notably at the Clatteringwell Quarry, and there are numerous examples of old limekilns. The Glen Burn flows northwestwards through Glenvale to join the River Eden at Burnside, and the Arnot, Lothrie and Conland Burns flow southeastwards to enter the River Leven. Between 1865 and 1914 a number of reservoirs (Harperleas, Ballo, Drumain, Holl and Arnot) were created in the Lomond Hills to provide fresh water for the rapidly expanding towns of west Fife. Iron Age remains have been found on West and East Lomond and a fine example of a hillfort can be found midway between the two at Maiden Castle. Included in Fife Regional Park, the hills are accessible from Pitcairn Centre (where park staff are based), Craigmead and East Lomond car parks.

Lòn Mòr *Highland* A river of the Trotternish peninsula at the north end of the isle of Skye in the Inner Hebrides, Lòn Mòr rises in the western foothills of the Storr and flows southwestwards to merge with the River Haultin before emptying into Loch Eyre, an eastern spur of Loch Snizort Beag.

Lonan, River *Argyll and Bute* A river of Argyll and Bute, the River Lonan rises in the foothills of Beinn Ghlas and flows for 7 miles (11 km) westwards through Glen Lonan before emptying into the head of Loch Nell, 3 miles (5 km) east of Oban.

Lonbain *Highland* A small coastal village in Wester Ross, Lonbain lies on the mainland shore of the Inner Sound, 6 miles (10 km) north of Applecross.

Londubh *Highland* Lying on the southern shore of Loch Ewe, in Wester Ross, the settlement of Londubh is situated between the village of Poolewe to the southwest and Inverewe Garden immediately to the north.

Lonemore *Highland* A small village in the Sutherland district of Highland Council area, Lonemore lies on the north shore of the Dornoch Firth and overlooks the Dornoch Sands to the south. The town of Dornoch lies 2 miles (3 km) to the east.

Long, Loch *Argyll and Bute* A sea loch to the east of the Cowal peninsula in west-central Scotland, Loch Long extends 17 miles (27 km) south from Arrochar to meet the Firth of Clyde.

Long Craig *Angus* A small rocky peninsula on the North Sea coast of Angus, Long Craig extends into the sea 2 miles (3 km) south of Montrose.

Long Haven *Aberdeenshire* An inlet on the North Sea coast of Aberdeenshire, Long Haven forms a bay a mile (1.5 km) to the southwest of Boddam.

Long Hermiston *City of Edinburgh* A southwestern suburb of the City of Edinburgh, Long Hermiston lies 5 miles (8 km) from the city centre.

Long Hope *Orkney* A natural harbour in the Orkney Islands, Long Hope lies between the island of South Walls and the south end of Hoy, to which it is joined by a causeway. Signifying a 'long bay', it was formerly an assembly point for naval convoys, its entrance being protected during the Napoleonic Wars by two Martello towers which still survive. The Hackness (south) Tower is open to the public. The former Longhope Lifeboat Station lies at the southern tip of Hoy and a memorial to the crew of the lifeboat lost with all hands in the Pentland Firth on 17 March 1969 stands on South Walls.

Long Loch *East Renfrewshire* Situated to the southeast of Harelaw Dam on the western edge of East Renfrewshire, Long Loch lies 3 miles (5 km) south of Neilston. It is the source of a tributary of the Annick Water.

Long Taing of Newark *Orkney* A promontory on the eastern coastline of the island of Sanday in the Orkney Islands, the Long Taing of Newark extends eastwards between the bays of Newark and Lopness.

Longa *Highland* An uninhabited island on the west coast of Ross and Cromarty, Longa lies at the mouth of Gair Loch, a mile (1.5 km) south of Rubha Bàn. It has an area of 126 ha (311 acres) and rises to 70 m (230 ft) at Druim am Eilean. The island once had a small fishing community.

Longannet *Fife* Located 2 miles (3 km) southeast of Kincardine in western Fife, on the shores of the Firth of Forth, Longannet is the site of a 2304-megawatt coal-fired power station established in 1970. For a time it was the largest power station in Europe. Ash, produced by the power station at a rate of up to 4350 tonnes per day, is piped as slurry to Preston Island by Low Valleyfield, where it is deposited in artificial lagoons as part of a coastal land-reclamation scheme. The Longannet coal mine to the north of Kincardine, which closed in 2002, was the last deep coal mine in Scotland.

Longay *Highland* An uninhabited island in the Inner Hebrides, Longay lies in the Inner Sound to the east of Scalpay and north of Pabay. It has an area of 50 ha (124 acres) and although once heavily forested is now used to pasture sheep. It was associated with pirates in the 16th century and its name is said to signify the 'longship island'.

Longcastle *Dumfries and Galloway* A locality in the Machars, Dumfries and Galloway, Longcastle (or Kirkland of Longcastle) lies on the A714, 6 miles (10 km) southwest of Wigtown. The former Dowalton Loch near here was completely drained in 1862 by local landowners. On its shore once stood Longcastle, a stronghold of the McDougalls.

Longcroft *Falkirk* A village of Falkirk Council area, Longcroft lies 4 miles (6.5 km) northeast of Cumbernauld.

Longforgan *Perth and Kinross* A village in a parish of the same name in the Carse of Gowrie, southeast Perth and Kinross, Longforgan lies 5 miles (8 km) west of Dundee. It was created a burgh of barony in 1672 and developed in association with Castle Huntly to the southwest.

Longformacus *Scottish Borders* A village in the Berwickshire district of Scottish Borders, Longformacus lies on the Dye Water on the south side of the Lammermuir Hills, 6 miles (10 km) northwest of Duns. Longformacus House was built in the 18th century by William Adam or James Smith, and a parish church with medieval foundations was rebuilt in 1730. The Watch Water Reservoir to the west was created in the 1960s. The Southern Upland Way long-distance footpath passes through the village.

Longhope *Orkney* An important hamlet and ferry port on the South Walls peninsula of the island of Hoy, Longhope lies on South Ness facing north onto an inlet of the same name. Longhope has been associated with the navy since trading ships heading for the Baltic were assembled into convoys here to avoid privateers during the Napoleonic Wars. The Longhope Hotel became the headquarters of the Scapa Flow Naval Base, home to the British Grand Fleet between 1914 and 1919, when it moved to Lyness, 3 miles (5 km) to the north. King George V visited in 1915, knighting Vice-Admiral Sir Stanley Colville (Admiral Commanding Orkney and Shetland) at the hotel, and Edward VIII (then Prince of Wales) visited later the same year. Longhope receives a ferry from Houton via Lyness and the island of Flotta. The Longhope lifeboat has been providing a rescue service in the dangerous Pentland Firth since 1874. Disaster struck on 17 March 1969 when the boat, *TGB*, was lost with its crew of eight in a force-9 gale while trying to reach the cargo ship *Irene*. The lifeboat station was originally located on Aith Hope, 2 miles (3 km) to the southwest, but in 1999 a new boat was brought into service from Longhope pier.

Longleys *Perth and Kinross* A hamlet in Strathmore, eastern Perth and Kinross, Longleys lies 2 miles (3 km) to the southwest of Meigle.

Longmanhill *Aberdeenshire* A roadside crofting settlement in the Aberdeenshire parish of Gamrie, Longmanhill lies on the A98 to Fraserburgh, 3 miles (5 km) southeast of Macduff. It was founded for crofters in 1822 by the Earl of Fife. Nearby is the prominent Neolithic long cairn known as Longman Cairn.

Longman Point *Highland* A shingle point on the southern shore of the Moray Firth, Longman Point lies immediately to the north of Inverness.

Longmorn *Moray* A distillery settlement in Moray, Longmorn lies on the line of a former railway, 2 miles (3 km) south of Elgin.

Longnewton *Scottish Borders* A small village of Scottish Borders, Longnewton lies 3 miles (5 km) south of Newtown St Boswells.

Longniddry *East Lothian* A commuter village near the coast of East Lothian, Longniddry lies 12 miles (19 km) east of Edinburgh. It developed initially in association with nearby Redhouse Castle and later in association with weaving, coal mining and the quarrying of stone in the vicinity. Its railway station was opened in 1845. Longniddry expanded in 1916 with the building of 20 cottages by the Scottish Veterans' Garden Cities Association. Buildings of interest include Longniddry House (early 18th-century), the Golf Club House (1929), and Gosford House, home of the Earl of Wemyss, which was built in 1790 by Robert Adam. There is a long (6219-yd) 18-hole golf course at Links Road.

Longridge *West Lothian* A small village of West Lothian, Longridge lies 2 miles (3 km) south of Whitburn.

Longriggend The former name for Upperton in North Lanarkshire.

Longside *Aberdeenshire* A linear, tree-lined commuter settlement in the Buchan district of Aberdeenshire, Longside is situated 6 miles (10 km) west of Peterhead. It was rebuilt in 1801 as a planned village by James Ferguson of Pitfour and developed in association with weaving and the quarrying of granite at Cairngall.

Longstone *City of Edinburgh* A district of the City of Edinburgh, Longstone lies 3 miles (5 km) southwest of the city centre.

Longyester *East Lothian* A hamlet in East Lothian, Longyester lies to the north of the Lammermuir Hills, 2 miles (3 km) southeast of Gifford.

Lonmay *Aberdeenshire* A settlement and parish of the Buchan district of northeast Aberdeenshire, Lonmay lies 2 miles (3 km) southeast of Rathen and 9 miles (14 km) northwest of Peterhead. Lonmay once had a station on the Formartine and Buchan Railway, but this closed in 1965 and today it is the Formartine and Buchan Way which follows the route of the former railway past Lonmay.

Lonmore *Highland* A small village on the isle of Skye in the Inner Hebrides, Lonmore lies a mile (1.5 km) southeast of Dunvegan and 2 miles (3 km) southeast of Dunvegan Castle.

Lop Ness *Orkney* A headland on the east coast of the island of Sanday in the Orkney Islands, Lop Ness extends into the sea at the eastern end of the Bay of Lopness, 2 miles (3 km) west of Start Point.

Lora, Falls of *Argyll and Bute* A series of rapids at the mouth of Loch Etive in the Lorn district of Argyll and Bute, the Falls of Lora or Falls of Connel are spanned by a bridge 5 miles (8 km) north of Oban.

Lord Lovat's Cave *Argyll and Bute* A cave on the island of Mull, Lord Lovat's Cave is located on Lord Lovat's Bay, a small inlet to the east of the entrance to Loch Buie.

Lorgill *Highland* A small crofting township on the northwest coast of the isle of Skye in the Inner Hebrides, Lorgill lies 6 miles (10 km) northwest of Idrigill Point.

Lorn *Argyll and Bute* A district of Argyll and Bute extending south from Loch Leven to Loch Awe and eastwards from Loch Linnhe to Rannoch Moor, Lorn (also Lorne) was an ancient lordship of the MacDougalls and the Stewarts before falling into the hands of the Campbells. The district gives its name to the courtesy title Marquess of Lorn held by the eldest son of the Duke of Argyll.

Lorn, Firth of *Argyll and Bute* A wide estuary to the southwest of Loch Linnhe, the Firth of Lorn (also Lorne) lies between the southeast coast of the island of Mull and the Argyll coastline of the Scottish mainland.

Lorn, Lynn of *Argyll and Bute* The Lynn of Lorn (also Lorne) is a strait separating the island of Lismore from the district of Benderloch in Argyll and Bute.

Lornty *Perth and Kinross* A settlement in the Stormont district of Perth and Kinross, Lornty lies a mile (1.5 km) to the north of Blairgowrie at the confluence of the Lornty Burn with the River Ericht.

Losgaintir The Gaelic name for Luskentyre in the Western Isles.

Lossie, River *Moray* A river of Moray that rises in headstreams to the southwest of Elgin, the River Lossie flows north and northeast for 31 miles (50 km) to join the sea at Lossiemouth. It passes through Elgin and has as its main tributaries the Leanoch Burn and the Back Burn.

Lossie Forest *Moray* An area of forest land on the north coast of Moray, the Lossie Forest lies to the east of the town of Lossiemouth. The Spynie Canal and Innes Canal both pass through the forest.

Lossiemouth *Moray* A fishing port and resort town in the Moray parish of Drainie, Lossiemouth is situated on the Moray Firth at the mouth of the River Lossie, 6 miles (10 km) north of Elgin. It incorporates the communities of Old Lossiemouth, a fishing village laid out by the merchants of Elgin in 1764, the fishing village of Stotfield, and Branderburgh, laid out on a cliff top to a design by George MacWilliam *c.*1830 and named after Colonel Brander of Pitgaveny. The original port, which was moved from Spynie to its present position in 1698 after the mouth of Spynie Loch had become closed with shingle, owed its early growth to its role as Elgin's seaport, but later, with the coming of the railway, developed as a marine resort. Ramsay MacDonald (1866–1937), Britain's first Labour prime minister, who was born in Lossiemouth, is buried in Old Spynie churchyard. Lossiemouth has golf courses and a

Fisheries and Community Museum. To the southwest at Kinnedar stand the ruins of an ancient castle of the bishops of Moray built on a site associated with St Gernadius, and to the west is RAF Lossiemouth, the one-time Royal Naval Air Station of HMS *Fulmar*.

Lossit Bay *Argyll and Bute* A small bay on the west coast of the Rinns of Islay on the island of Islay in the Inner Hebrides, Lossit Bay lies 3 miles (5 km) north of Rinns Point.

Lost *Aberdeenshire* A locality in Strath Don, western Aberdeenshire, the farm of Lost lies to the north of the River Don near its junction with the Water of Nochty, a mile (1.5 km) northwest of Strathdon. The local authority contemplated changing the name in 2004 because the signpost, a popular spot for tourist photographs, was regularly being stolen.

Loth, Glen *Highland* A valley in the Sutherland district of Highland Council area, Glen Loth carries the waters of the Loth Burn from the foothills of Beinn Mhealaich to the settlement of Lothbeg. It is joined by Glen Sletdale from the west.

Lothbeg Point *Highland* A headland on the east coast of Sutherland, Lothbeg Point lies a mile (1.5 km) southeast of Lothbeg.

Lothrie Burn *Fife* A stream that rises on the southern slopes of West Lomond, the Lothrie Burn flows 4 miles (6.5 km) generally southeastwards to join the River Leven east of Leslie. Its upper course was dammed during the late 19th and early 20th centuries to create the Harperleas, Ballo and Holl reservoirs.

Loudon Hill *East Ayrshire* A prominent hill of East Ayrshire, close to the boundary with South Lanarkshire, Loudon Hill rises to 316 m (1037 ft) 2.5 miles (4 km) east of Darvel. The River Irvine turns west as it flows past the hill. Two battles of the Wars of Independence took place nearby: William Wallace beat the English in 1296, and Robert the Bruce repeated this feat in 1307.

Loup of Fintry *Stirling* A dramatic series of waterfalls on the Endrick Water in the Fintry Hills, the Loup of Fintry is located to the east of Fintry by the B818 Denny road.

Louther Skerry *Orkney* One of the Pentland Skerries of the Orkney Islands, the small islet of Louther Skerry lies between Little Skerry and Clettack Skerry.

Low Ballevain *Argyll and Bute* Situated at the northern end of Machrihanish Bay on the west coast of the Kintyre peninsula, the small village of Low Ballevain (also Ballivain) lies 5 miles (8 km) northwest of Campbeltown.

Low Craighead *South Ayrshire* A small village of South Ayrshire, Low Craighead lies 3 miles (5 km) northeast of Girvan and a mile (1.5 km) north of Killochan Castle.

Low Parks *South Lanarkshire* Part of the estates of the former Hamilton Palace, the Low Parks lie to the northeast of Hamilton, opposite Motherwell. Today the Low Parks include the Hamilton Park Race Course, as well as golf and sports facilities and retail development. Buildings of historic interest include the Hamilton Mausoleum and the Hamilton Palace Riding School, which forms part of the Low Parks Museum.

Low Torry *Fife* A former mining village of western Fife, Low Torry lies on the north shore of the Firth of Forth between Torryburn and Newmills. The art collector and soldier Sir James Erskine of Torrie (1772–1825) lived at nearby Torrie House.

Low Valleyfield *Fife* A village in western Fife, Low Valleyfield is situated on the Firth of Forth, a mile (1.5 km) east of Culross and west of the Bluther Burn. Formerly part of the Valleyfield Estate, it is older than the 20th-century mining village of High Valleyfield which lies to the north. The nearby Valleyfield Colliery, which operated between 1908 and 1978, was the scene of a mining disaster in 1939 when 35 miners lost their lives. Valleyfield Woodland Park lies to the east.

Lower Breakish *Highland* A small settlement on the isle of Skye in the Inner Hebrides, Lower Breakish lies on the shore of the Ob Breakish, an inlet on the east coast 2 miles (3 km) east of Broadford.

Lower Kilrenny An alternative name for Cellardyke in Fife.

Lower Largo *Fife* A resort village in the East Neuk of Fife, Lower Largo is situated adjacent to Lundin Links at the foot of a cliff on Largo Bay. It was for centuries a prosperous fishing village noted for its manufacture of nets and knitwear. At the east end of the village, Temple Hill is said to mark the site of land owned by the medieval Knights Templar, who were brought to Scotland in the 12th century by David I. Daniel Defoe visited Lower Largo in 1706 and was inspired to write *The Life and Surprising Adventures of Robinson Crusoe* after visiting the birthplace of Alexander Selkirk, who was marooned on the island of Juan Fernandez for four years. There is a statue commemorating 'Robinson Crusoe' on the site of the house where Selkirk was born in 1676. Known fully as Seatown of Largo, its harbour was linked by steamboat to Newhaven on the south coast of the Firth of Forth during the 19th century. Lower Largo, with its fine sandy beach, eventually became a popular tourist centre after the arrival of the railway in 1856. It was designated a conservation area in 1978.

Lower Polmaise *Stirling* A locality in Stirling Council area, Lower Polmaise lies on a bend of the River Forth immediately north of Fallin and 4 miles (6.5 km) southeast of Stirling.

Lowes, Loch of *Perth and Kinross* A small loch at the northern edge of the valley of Strathmore in Perth and Kinross, the Loch of Lowes lies adjacent to the Loch of Butterstone and the Loch of Craiglush, a mile (1.5 km) northeast of Dunkeld. Noted for its breeding ospreys, it is managed as a nature reserve by the Scottish Wildlife Trust.

Lowes, Loch of the *Scottish Borders* A small loch in the Ettrick district of Scottish Borders, the Loch of the Lowes lies immediately south of St Mary's Loch from which it is separated by a narrow neck of land.

Lowes Loch *Dumfries and Galloway* A tiny loch in Dumfries and Galloway, Lowes Loch lies to the west of Garcrogo Forest, 9 miles (14 km) northwest of the village of Crocketford and 5 miles (8 km) east of New Galloway.

Lowlands A general term referring to all of Scotland outwith the Highlands and Islands, the Lowlands is sometimes more specifically used to delineate land between the Highlands and the Southern Uplands, the Central Lowlands being applied to that part of the Lowlands occupying the Midland Valley between Fife and the Lothians in the east and the Firth of Clyde in the west.

Lowlandman's Bay *Argyll and Bute* An inlet on the east coast of the island of Jura, Lowlandman's Bay lies 4 miles (6.5 km) southwest of Lagg. A rocky promontory to the southwest almost encloses the bay.

Lowther Hill *South Lanarkshire/Dumfries and Galloway* Located on the border of South Lanarkshire and Dumfries and Galloway, Lowther Hill gives its name to a range of hills that form part of the Southern Uplands. Located 7 miles (11 km) east of Sanquhar, it is the second-highest peak within the Lowther Hills, rising to a height of 725 m (2378 ft).

Lowther Hills *South Lanarkshire/Dumfries and Galloway* A range of hills straddling the border between South Lanarkshire to the north and Dumfries and Galloway to the south, the Lowther Hills rise to 732 m (2407 ft) at Green Lowther. Other principal peaks include Lowther Hill (725 m/2378 ft), Queensberry (697 m/2285 ft), and Ballencleuch Law (691 m/2267 ft), all lying in the watershed between Annandale to the east and Nithsdale to the west. The Elvan, Snar, Wanlock, Crawick, Mennock, Enterkin, Portrail and Daer waters rise in the Lowther Hills, the source of the Daer Water forming a reservoir. Three roads traverse the Lowther Hills from southwest to northeast via the Dalveen Pass, Mennock Pass and Crawfordjohn, and upland villages at Wanlockhead, Leadhills and Elvanfoot, among the highest settlements in Scotland, owe their origins to lead mining in the vicinity.

Loy, Glen *Highland* A valley in the Lochaber district of Highland Council area, Glen Loy carries the waters of the River Loy southeast to merge with the River Lochy at Strone.

Loy, Loch *Highland* A small loch in the Nairn district of Highland Council area, Loch Loy lies 3 miles (5 km) east of Nairn.

Loy, River *Highland* A river in the Lochaber district of Highland Council area, the River Loy rises in the Locheil Forest and flows in a southeasterly direction through Glen Loy before emptying into the River Lochy, 2 miles (3 km) southwest of Gairlochy.

Loyal, Loch *Highland* A loch in the Caithness district of Highland Council area, Loch Loyal extends southwards for 4 miles (6.5 km) from Loch Craggie, to which it is joined by a narrow neck, 4 miles (6.5 km) south of Tongue.

Loyne, Glen *Highland* A valley to the west of the Great Glen, Glen Loyne extends eastwards to the head of Glen Moriston following the course of the River Loyne which widens into Loch Loyne.

Loyne, River *Highland* Rising in foothills between the peaks of Gleouraich and Spidean Mialach in the Lochaber district of Highland Council area, the River Loyne flows north and east through Glen Loyne to empty into the western end of Loch Loyne.

Lubcroy *Highland* A small village of Glen Oykel in Highland Council area, Lubcroy lies at the confluence of the Garbh Allt with the River Oykel.

Lubnaig, Loch *Stirling* A loch to the north of the Trossachs in Stirling Council area, Loch Lubnaig extends northwards for 4 miles (6.5 km) from the Pass of Leny to Strathyre. The road from Callander to Lochearnhead follows the eastern shore, while Ben Ledi rises to a height of 879 m (2883 ft) to the west. The River Balvag drains from Loch Voil into the top end of Loch Lubnaig, and from its southern end emerges the River Leny.

Luce, Water of *Dumfries and Galloway* A stream of Dumfries and Galloway, the Water of Luce rises in two headstreams, named the Main Water of Luce and the Cross Water of Luce, which meet at New Luce before flowing southwards for 3 miles (5 km) through the Rhinns of Galloway into Luce Bay.

Luce Bay *Dumfries and Galloway* A large inlet of the Solway Firth on the southern shore of Dumfries and Galloway, Luce Bay separates the southern peninsula of the Rhinns of Galloway from the Machars peninsula to the east. It receives the Water of Luce which flows southwards through Glenluce into the bay.

Ludag *Western Isles* A village of the southern coastline of the island of South Uist in the Western Isles, Ludag lies 3 miles (5.5 km) south of Lochboisdale. A car ferry once left from the jetty here for the island of Eriskay to the south but was replaced by a causeway that opened in 2002 and makes landfall a quarter-mile (0.5 km) to the east.

Luffness *East Lothian* A village in East Lothian, Luffness lies on the southern shores of the Firth of Forth to the northeast of Aberlady and 5 miles (8 km) southwest of North Berwick. To the west of the village are 16th-century Luffness House, Aberlady Bay and Luffness Convent.

Lugar *East Ayrshire* A village in East Ayrshire, Lugar lies on the Lugar Water 2 miles (3 km) northeast of Cumnock. It developed in the 1840s in association with the Eglinton Iron Company. Buildings of interest include the parish church (1867), the Lugar Institute (1892) and fine examples of foundry foremen's housing in Craigston Square.

Lugar Water *East Ayrshire* A river of East Ayrshire, the Lugar Water is formed by the merging of the Glass and Glenmuir Waters at Lugar. Passing through Cumnock and by Ochiltree, it joins the River Ayr a mile (1.5 km) south of Mauchline.

Lugate Water *Scottish Borders* A river of Scottish Borders, the Lugate Water rises in headstreams to the west of Stow and flows southeastwards into the Gala Water, a mile (1.5 km) south of Stow.

Luggate *East Lothian* An agricultural hamlet of East Lothian, Luggate lies 2 miles (3 km) south of East Linton and a similar distance west of Stenton. The hamlet of Luggate Burn lies a half-mile (1 km) to the southeast.

Luggate Burn *East Lothian* A hamlet of East Lothian, Luggate Burn is located 2 miles (3 km) south of East Linton and 1.5 miles (2.5 km) west of Stenton. Whittinghame House is a half-mile (1 km) to the south and the hamlet of Luggate lies a quarter-mile (1 km) to the northwest.

Luggiebank *North Lanarkshire* A district of the new town of Cumbernauld in North Lanarkshire, Luggiebank lies a mile (1.5 km) south of the town centre.

Luggie Water Rising in hills to the south of Cumbernauld in North Lanarkshire, the Luggie Water flows past Luggiebank and Cumbernauld before entering East Dunbartonshire, where it joins the River Kelvin at Kirkintilloch.

Lugton *East Ayrshire* A small village in the Cunninghame district of Ayrshire, Lugton lies 4 miles (6.5 km) north of Stewarton, close to the border with Renfrewshire. The village developed as a road and rail junction and in association with the quarrying of limestone.

Lui, Glen *Aberdeenshire* A glen in Aberdeenshire, Glen Lui occupies the valley of the Lui Water, a tributary of the River Dee to the west of Braemar.

Lui Water *Aberdeenshire* A tributary of the River Dee in Aberdeenshire, the Lui Water is formed by the meeting of the Derry Burn and the Luibeg Burn. It flows down through Glen Lui to join the Dee just east of the Linn of Dee.

Luib *Highland* A small settlement on the isle of Skye in the Inner Hebrides, Luib lies on the south shore of Loch Ainort.

Luib *Stirling* A locality in Glen Dochart, northwest Stirling Council area, Luib lies on the main road from Killin to Crianlarich.

Luibeg Burn *Aberdeenshire* A stream in the eastern Grampians of Aberdeenshire, the Luibeg Burn rises between Ben Macdui and Derry Cairngorm. It flows southeast to meet the Derry Burn at Derry Lodge, there forming the Lui Water, a tributary of the River Dee.

Luichart, Loch *Highland* A loch and reservoir in the Ross and Cromarty district of Highland Council area, Loch Luichart lies 6 miles (10 km) west of Strathpeffer. Extending 6 miles (10 km) in a northwest–southeast direction, it is dammed to provide hydro-electric power.

Luing *Argyll and Bute* An island off the coast of Argyll, Luing lies to the southwest of Oban immediately south of Seil, from which it is separated by the Cuan Sound. A long narrow island with an area of 1440 ha (3557 acres), Luing rises to 94 m (308 ft) at Beinn Furachail. The island is surrounded by many tidal islands, the largest of these being Torsay which lies to the northeast. The chief settlements on the island are Cullipool, Ardinamir (or Ardinamar) and Toberonochy. There are numerous Iron Age forts on the island, which was at one time a source of slate.

Luing, Sound of *Argyll and Bute* A channel off the Argyll coast, the Sound of Luing separates the islands of Scarba and Lunga from the island of Luing.

Luinga Mhòr *Highland* An uninhabited island off the coast of southwest Highland Council area, Luinga Mhòr lies 3 miles (5 km) west of the village of Arisaig.

Luinne Bheinn *Highland* A mountain in the Knoydart district of southwest Highland Council area, Luinne Bheinn rises to a height of 939 m (3081 ft) to the north of Loch Nevis. It comprises a narrow ridge running west from Mam Unndalain, with steep slopes to the north and south. The true summit is the western top, marked by a small cairn.

Luirbost A former Gaelic name for Leurbost in the Western Isles.

Luirsay Dubh *Western Isles* A small uninhabited island located off the northeast coast of South Uist, Luirsay Dubh (Gael: *Liursaigh Dubh*) lies among a number of rocky islets looking out onto the Minch between Loch Skiport and Loch Carnan. The smaller Luirsay Glas lies immediately to the east.

Luirsay Glas *Western Isles* A small uninhabited island located off the northeast coast of South Uist, Luirsay Glas (Gael: *Liursaigh Glas*) rises to 28 m (91 ft) immediately to the east of Luirsay Dubh, looking out on the Minch.

Lumphanan *Aberdeenshire* A village in an Aberdeenshire parish of the same name, Lumphanan lies 3 miles (5 km) northwest of Torphins and 27 miles (43 km) west of Aberdeen. It developed as a railway settlement in the 19th century, but its church, rebuilt in 1762 and enlarged in 1851, is thought to have been originally dedicated to St Finan in pre-Reformation times. To the southwest is the Peel of Lumphanan, a flat-topped mound or motte on which there once stood a 13th-century fortification and a 15th-century manor house called Halton House which remained standing until 1782. On 21 July 1296, Edward I of England is thought to have received the submission of Sir John de Malevill at the Peel of Lumphanan. A cairn known as Macbeth's Cairn, situated between Lumphanan and Perkhill to the northwest, marks the spot where Malcolm Canmore is said to have killed Macbeth.

Lumphinnans *Fife* A former mining town in western Fife, Lumphinnans lies between Cowdenbeath and Lochgelly. The lands of Lumphinnans were first mentioned in a charter of 1242, but the town owes its existence to the development of the local mines in the 19th century by the Cowdenbeath Colliery Company.

Lumsden *Aberdeenshire* An Aberdeenshire village founded on barren moorland about 1825, Lumsden is situated at the western foot of the Correen Hills, 3 miles (5 km) south of Rhynie. The Lumsden valley here marks the division between the watersheds of the River Bogie to its north and the River Don to the south.

Lunan *Angus* A hamlet in an Angus parish of the same name, Lunan lies close to the mouth of the Lunan Water where it enters Lunan Bay, 4 miles (6.5 km) southwest of Montrose. The parish church was rebuilt in 1844, one of its priests in the 16th century being Walter Mill (1476–1558), one of the last of the Scottish martyrs to be burned at St Andrews. Near Lunan House are the ruins of a dovecote and an icehouse.

Lunan Bay *Angus* A large inlet of the North Sea on the coast of Angus, Lunan Bay lies to the south of Montrose between Boddin Point and the Lang Craig. The Lunan Water enters the bay near the hamlet of Lunan.

Lunan Burn *Perth and Kinross* Rising on Craig More in Perth and Kinross, 3 miles (5 km) north of Dunkeld, the Lunan Burn flows south and then east, through the lochs of Lowes, Butterstone, Clunie and Drumellie, before joining the River Isla 2 miles (3 km) west of Coupar Angus.

Lunan Water *Angus* A river of Angus, the Lunan Water issues from the eastern end of Rescobie Loch. It flows 13 miles (21 km) eastwards to enter Lunan Bay to the south of Montrose.

Lunanhead *Angus* A village in Angus, Lunanhead lies nearly 2 miles (3 km) northeast of Forfar on the road to Aberlemno. Now largely a dormitory suburb of Forfar, it is said to owe its origin to a medieval plague, this site being chosen for an isolation hospital when the plague reached Forfar. Lunanhead is sometimes called The Barracks, because it was used from time to time as a military base for Government troops.

Luncarty *Perth and Kinross* A dormitory village in central Perth and Kinross, Luncarty lies on the River Tay, 4 miles (6.5 km) north of Perth. It was founded in 1752 by William Sandeman to house workers at his bleach fields, an enterprise that was among the largest of its kind in Scotland at that time.

Lundie *Angus* A village in an Angus parish of the same name, Lundie lies in the Sidlaw Hills, 8 miles (13 km) northwest of Dundee. Largely altered in 1786, the parish church was originally erected in the 12th century by the Durward family who dedicated it to St Lawrence the Martyr. Its kirkyard is the burial place of the Duncans of Lundie, who eventually became the earls of Camperdown.

Lundie, Loch *Highland* A loch in Wester Ross, Loch Lundie lies to the west of Glen Shieldaig and south of Loch Torridon. Applecross lies 3 miles (5 km) to the southwest.

Lundie, Loch *Highland* A loch and small reservoir to the west of the Great Glen, Loch Lundie lies to the east of Loch Garry and north of the mouth of Glen Garry, 2 miles (3 km) northwest of Invergarry.

Lundin Links *Fife* A resort and dormitory town in the East Neuk of Fife, Lundin Links is situated on Largo Bay adjacent to Lower Largo. It largely developed as a 19th-century suburban extension of Lower Largo accommodating holiday-makers, but takes its name from the Lundin family who were granted land here in the 12th century. In addition to a fine beach, Lundin Links has tennis courts, bowling greens, a putting green and 18-hole and nine-hole golf courses. Within the grounds of the Lundin Ladies' Golf Club are located the three Lundin Links standing stones that date from the 2nd millennium BC.

Lundy, River *Highland* A river in the Lochaber district of Highland Council area, the River Lundy flows west into the River Lochy, 2 miles (3 km) northeast of Fort William.

Lunga *Argyll and Bute* A barren island in the Firth of Lorn, Lunga lies immediately north of the island of Scarba and west of Luing near the Argyll coast. It has an area of 254 ha (628 acres) and rises to 80 m (262 ft) at Bidein na h-Iolaire. To the north of the island are a group of tidal islands, the largest being Rubha Fiola. The island's population of two is located on the east coast on the only part of Lunga not covered in rocks and bog.

Lunga *Argyll and Bute* An uninhabited basalt island in the Inner Hebrides, Lunga lies off the northwest coast of Mull. The largest of the Treshnish Isles, it has an area of 81 ha (200 acres) and has been designated a Site of Special Scientific Interest (SSSI) because of its abundance of rare plant life, seals and sea birds. There are the remains of a village abandoned in 1857.

Lunga *Argyll and Bute* A small village of Argyll and Bute, Lunga lies 3 miles (5 km) south of Arduaine near Craobh Haven and 14 miles (22 km) south of Oban.

Lungard, Loch *Highland* A small loch in Glen Cannich, Loch Lungard lies at the east end of Loch Mullardoch to which it is joined.

Lunna Holm *Shetland* An uninhabited island in the Shetland Islands, Lunna Holm lies beyond the tip of the Lunna Ness headland on the northeast coast of Shetland Mainland.

Lunna Ness *Shetland* A headland on the northeast coastline of the Shetland Mainland, Lunna Ness lies at the southeast end of Yell Sound. The settlement of Lunna lies at the southwest end of the headland, while off the northeast coast lies the uninhabited island of Lunna Holm.

Lunnasting *Shetland* A small district and old parish located in the northeast of the Shetland Mainland, Lunnasting lies 15 miles (24 km) north of Lerwick.

Lunning Sound *Shetland* A channel in the Shetland Islands, the Lunning Sound separates the Shetland Mainland from the island of West Linga to the east, 11 miles (18 km) north of Lerwick and immediately south of the settlement of Lunning.

Lurgainn, Loch *Highland* A loch in the Coigach district of Wester Ross, Loch Lurgainn lies 8 miles (13 km) north of Ullapool and south of Inverpolly Forest. To the north, Stac Pollaidh rises to 613 m (2018 ft).

Lurg Hill *Moray* A hill to the south of Kirktown of Deskford in Moray, Lurg Hill rises to a height of 313 m (1028 ft).

Lurg Mhòr *Highland* A remote featureless mountain in Wester Ross, Lurg Mhòr rises to 986 m (3235 ft) between Strathcarron and Loch Monar.

Luskentyre *Western Isles* A locality in South Harris in the Western Isles, Luskentyre (Gael: *Losgaintir*) lies 5 miles (8 km) south-southwest of Tarbert. The magnificent sands of Luskentyre Bay (Gael: *Tràigh Losgaintir*) occupy an inlet of the Sound of Taransay.

Luss *Argyll and Bute* An attractive grey-slate village located on the western shore of Loch Lomond, Luss lies 8 miles (13 km) south of Tarbet. Originally named Clachan Dubh, meaning 'the dark village', it is believed to have taken the name Luss from the Gaelic for a plant. Developed by the Colquhouns of Luss who lived at nearby Rossdhu House, Luss pier was developed as an outlet for slate from nearby quarries and as a steamer landing for tourists. It is now a conservation village with cottages built to house cotton mill and slate workers in the 18th and 19th centuries. A visitor centre for the Loch Lomond and the Trossachs National Park is located in the village, and to the south at Rossdhu is a championship golf course designed by Tom Weiskopf.

Luss, Glen *Argyll and Bute* A valley of eastern Argyll and Bute, Glen Luss lies within the Loch Lomond and Trossachs National Park, 6 miles (10 km) north of Helensburgh. Glen Luss is 7 miles (11 km) long and contains the Luss Water, which flows east into Loch Lomond.

Lussa Loch *Argyll and Bute* A reservoir surrounded by forest in the centre of the Kintyre peninsula, Lussa Loch is located 5 miles (8 km) west of Saddell and 6 miles (10 km) north of Campbeltown. It receives the Bordadubh Water and the Strathduie Water and is the source of the Glen Lussa Water. The Lussa Power Station, which opened in 1952 and generates 2.4 megawatts of electricity, is part of the Sloy-Awe Hydro-Electric Power Scheme.

Lusta *Highland* A village on the Vaternish peninsula of the isle of Skye in the Inner Hebrides, Lusta overlooks Loch Bay to the southeast and Mingay Island and Isay to the west.

Luthermuir *Aberdeenshire* A village in the Aberdeenshire parish of Marykirk, Luthermuir lies a mile (1.5 km) to the north of the River North Esk, 8 miles (13 km) northwest of Montrose. Once dependent on farming and weaving, it is situated on the Luther Muir to the north of the Luther Water. To the west there are Bronze Age long barrows at Capo and Dalladies.

Luther Water *Angus* A river in the Howe of the Mearns, Aberdeenshire, the Luther Water rises in Drumtochty Forest to the northwest of Auchenblae. It flows 13 miles (21 km) south and southwest past Laurencekirk to join the River North Esk west of Marykirk. Its chief tributaries are the Ducat Water, Black Burn and Dourie Burn.

Luthrie *Fife* A village of northeast Fife, Luthrie lies some 6 miles (10 km) north of Ladybank, just off the A92 from Kirkcaldy to the Tay Bridge, to the north of the Parbroath crossroads. At one time Luthrie station (closed in 1951) was one of the most important stops on the North British Railway's North Fife line.

Lybster *Highland* A fishing village on the east coast of Caithness, Lybster lies off the A99, 10 miles (16 km) southwest of Wick. Established in 1802 by General Patrick Sinclair, its long Main Street overlooks the harbour. Sinclair's son continued to expand the village, naming the four sides of the square after Whig politicians of the 1830s. By then Lybster was the third-largest herring port in Scotland after Wick and Fraserburgh.

Lydon, Loch An alternative name for Loch Laidon.

Lynchat *Highland* A settlement in the Badenoch district of Highland Council area, Lynchat lies on the River Spey, 2 miles (3 km) northeast of Kingussie. Ruthven Barracks are 2 miles (3 km) southwest and the Highland Wildlife Park 2 miles (3 km) northeast.

Lyne *Moray* A former township of Strathavon in Moray, Lyne overlooks the River Avon 2 miles (3 km) south of the entrance to Glenlivet.

Lyne *Scottish Borders* A village of Scottish Borders to the south of the Meldon Hills, Lyne lies on the course of the Lyne Water, 3 miles (5 km) west of Peebles.

Lyne of Skene *Aberdeenshire* A village in mid-Aberdeenshire, Lyne of Skene lies on reclaimed moorland a mile (1.5 km) northeast of Dunecht and 7 miles (11 km) west of Aberdeen.

Lyne Water *Scottish Borders* Rising from headstreams and from the Baddinsgill and West Water reservoirs in the Pentland Hills, the Lyne Water flows south through West Linton, Romannobridge and Lyne to join the River Tweed 3 miles (5 km) west of Peebles.

Lyness *Orkney* A small settlement on the east coast of the Orkney island of Hoy, Lyness looks out across the Gutter Sound to the island of Fara. It was home to thousands of military personnel during both World Wars, when it was the headquarters for the Scapa Flow naval base. The base closed in 1957, but a naval cemetery and a visitor centre remain.

Lynwilg *Highland* A small settlement in the Badenoch district of southern Highland Council area, Lynwilg lies on the edge of Loch Alvie, 2 miles (3 km) southwest of Aviemore.

Lyon, Glen *Perth and Kinross* A valley of western Perth and Kinross, Glen Lyon carries the River Lyon eastwards from Loch Lyon to the River Tay, 4 miles (6.5 km) west of Aberfeldy.

Lyon, Loch *Perth and Kinross* A loch and reservoir of western Perth and Kinross, Loch Lyon lies close to the border with Argyll and Bute, at the head of Glen Lyon. The River Lyon flows from its eastern end towards the River Tay. Loch Lyon forms part of the Breadalbane Hydro-Electric Power Scheme.

Lyon, River *Perth and Kinross* A river of Perth and Kinross, the River Lyon rises in Loch Lyon and flows east through the Stronuich Reservoir before turning north and then east through Glen Lyon past Fortingall to join the River Tay 4 miles (6.5 km) west of Aberfeldy. Along its route it passes through the settlements of Moar and Bridge of Balgie.

Lyth *Highland* A settlement in northeast Caithness, Lyth lies 6 miles (10 km) southeast of Castletown near the Burn of Lyth. The Old School and Schoolhouse now serve as an arts centre.

Lyth, Burn of *Highland* Rising in Loch Heilen in the Caithness district of Highland Council area, the Burn of Lyth flows southeastwards for 8 miles (13 km) through the Loch of Wester before emptying into Sinclair's Bay, an inlet of the North Sea to the east of Quoys of Reiss.

Lythmore *Highland* A settlement in the Caithness district of Highland Council area, Lythmore lies 4 miles (6.5 km) southwest of Thurso and a half-mile (1 km) east of the Forss Water.

Maaruig *Western Isles* A settlement in North Harris in the Outer Hebrides, Maaruig (also Maruig, Gael: *Maraig*) is located on the north shore of Loch Maaruig, an inlet on the west side of Loch Seaforth, 4.5 miles (7 km) northeast of Tarbert.

Maaruig, Loch *Western Isles* An inlet on the western shore of Loch Seaforth, a sea loch on the eastern coastline of North Harris in the Western Isles, Loch Maaruig (Gael: *Maruig*) lies between Seaforth Island and the mouth of Loch Seaforth.

Maberry, Loch *Dumfries and Galloway* A small loch in Dumfries and Galloway, Loch Maberry lies at the head of the River Bladnoch, 10 miles (16 km) northwest of Newton Stewart.

Mabie Forest *Dumfries and Galloway* One of the forests of Solway in Dumfries and Galloway, Mabie Forest lies between Dumfries and New Abbey. Purchased by the Forestry Commission in 1943, it incorporates the 19th-century landscaped policy of Mabie House. There are a number of waymarked cycle routes, two of which pass through the Forest Nature Reserve of Lochaber Loch noted for its butterflies and old oak trees.

Macduff *Aberdeenshire* A resort town in the northern Aberdeenshire parish of Gamrie, Macduff is situated on the Moray Firth coast at the mouth of the River Deveron opposite Banff. It was originally known as the 'sea toune' of Doune but early attempts to develop the site as a seaport failed despite its designation as a burgh of barony in 1528. Economic growth eventually came in 1783 when James Duff, Lord Macduff and later Earl of Fife, built a harbour and changed the settlement's name to Macduff. Lord Fife's planned burgh town outgrew neighbouring Banff and today has thriving fishing, boatbuilding, soft-drink, fish-processing and tourist industries. The Customs House dates from 1884, when it was transferred across the River Deveron from Banff.

Macduff's Castle *Fife* A ruined castle standing on cliffs immediately to the east of East Wemyss in Fife, Macduff's Castle is said to have been originally constructed by the Macduff earls of Fife in the 11th century. The surrounding estates passed to the Wemyss family and the present structure was built in the 16th century as their seat. The castle was abandoned by the mid-17th century, when the family moved to Wemyss Castle 2 miles (3 km) to the southwest. Wemyss Caves lie below the castle.

Macduff's Cross *Fife* Thought to be the remains of an ancient stone cross, the base of Macduff's Cross stands in a field above Newburgh overlooking the Firth of Tay. It is believed to have been used as a place of sanctuary by the Clan Macduff.

Machany Water *Perth and Kinross* Rising to the west of Culloch, the Machany Water flows 14 miles (22 km) east before joining the River Earn at the settlement of Millearne. The Falls of Ness form a cascade a mile (1.5 km) to the west of the settlement of Machany.

Macharioch *Argyll and Bute* A small settlement on the Kintyre peninsula of Argyll and Bute, Macharioch is situated 3 miles (5 km) east of Southend, overlooking the Sound of Sanda and the island of Sanda to the south.

Machars, the *Dumfries and Galloway* A district of Dumfries and Galloway comprising famland, heathland and shoreline, the Machars is the name given to the low and flat peninsula of Galloway lying between Wigtown Bay and Luce Bay and to the south of the Galloway Hills. Its chief towns are Wigtown and Whithorn, and its southernmost point on the Solway Firth is Burrow Head. Machars is a Scots word meaning a flat area of land.

Macherie An alternative name for Cairnryan in Dumfries and Galloway.

Machir Bay *Argyll and Bute* A wide, sandy bay on the west coast of the island of Islay in the Inner Hebrides, Machir Bay forms an inlet to the south of Coul Point. The settlement of Kilchoman overlooks the bay.

Machrie *Argyll and Bute* A locality on the island of Islay, Machrie lies at the southern end of Laggan Bay 3 miles (5 km) northwest of Port Ellen. The Machrie River flows southwest through Glen Machrie into Laggan Bay. To the north is Islay Airport at Glenegedale, and to the south a notable hotel and golf course lie on machair land bordered by the sandy dunes of Tràigh a' Mhachaire.

Machrie *North Ayrshire* A scattered village on the west coast of the island of Arran in North Ayrshire, Machrie lies 4 miles (6.5 km) north of Blackwaterfoot overlooking Machrie Bay to the west.

Machrie Bay *North Ayrshire* A wide, sandy bay on the west coast of Arran in North Ayrshire, Machrie Bay forms an inlet of the Kilbrannan Sound, 4 miles (6.5 km) northwest of Blackwaterfoot. The Machrie Water rises on the northern slopes of An Tunna and flows 7 miles (11 km) west to empty into the Kilbrannan Sound at Machrie Bay.

Machrihanish *Argyll and Bute* A village on the west coast of the Kintyre peninsula, Machrihanish lies at the southern end of Machrihanish Bay, 5 miles (8 km) west of Campbeltown. The village was once linked by narrow-gauge railway to Campbeltown, although this was closed in the 1930s. South of the village lies the ruined village of Craigaig, and close by are Machrihanish (Campbeltown) Airport and an RAF air station.

Machrins *Argyll and Bute* A small settlement on the west coast of the island of Colonsay in Argyll and Bute, Machrins lies a mile (1.5 km) west of Scalasaig.

MacLellan's Castle *Dumfries and Galloway* Built in 1582 by Sir Thomas MacLellan of Bombie to an L-shaped plan, MacLellan's Castle is located within Kirkcudbright, Dumfries and Galloway. It is claimed that it was never really finished as the MacLellans fell on hard times, losing most of their estates by 1664 and deserting the castle in 1700. The ruined remains were taken into State care in 1912.

MacLeod's Maidens *Highland* Located to the south of Idrigill Point off the southwest coast of the isle of Skye in the Inner Hebrides, MacLeod's Maidens take the form of three prominent outlying basalt rocks.

MacLeod's Tables *Highland* A distinctive pair of hills on the Duirnish peninsula in the far west of the isle of Skye. MacLeod's Tables comprise MacLeod's Table South (Gael: *Healabhal Bheag*) reaching 489 m (1605 ft) and MacLeod's Table North (Gael: *Healabhal Mhòr*) which rises to 469 m (1540 ft). Although not high, these hills are distinctive because of their steep sides yet perfectly flat tops, and represent the remains of lava flows from the tertiary volcanoes that once erupted to form much of Skye. Steeped in folklore, the hills were said to have been used by MacLeod of Dunvegan to serve a grand feast to visitors.

Macmerry *East Lothian* A former mining village in East Lothian now bypassed by the A1, Macmerry lies 2 miles (3 km) east of Tranent. It developed in the 19th century in association with the Gladsmuir Ironworks but is now largely residential, the greater part of the village comprising housing erected by the local authority and the National Coal Board. Between 1868 and 1960 Macmerry was the terminus of a branch-line railway serving local coal mines. Opencast coal mines still operate to the northeast between Macmerry and Tranent, and there is an industrial estate to the east of the village.

Macphee's Hill *Western Isles* A hill on the island of Mingulay at the southern end of the Western Isles, Macphee's Hill rises to 224 m (735 ft).

Macquarie Mausoleum, The *Argyll and Bute* A mausoleum near Gruline on the island of Mull, the Macquarie Mausoleum is the burial place of Major General Lachlan Macquarie of Ulva (1761–1824), the first Governor of New South Wales and 'Father of Australia'. The site is maintained by the National Trust of Australia.

Macringan's Point *Argyll and Bute* A headland on the east coast of the Kintyre peninsula, Macringan's Point lies at the northern entrance to Campbeltown Loch opposite Davaar Island.

Madadh, Loch na The Gaelic name for the sea loch Loch Maddy and the associated settlement of Lochmaddy in the Western Isles

Madderty *Perth and Kinross* A locality in a parish of the same name in Strath Earn, Perth and Kinross, Madderty lies to the south of the Pow Water, at the site of a former railway station on the line between Perth and Crieff.

Maddiston *Falkirk* A settlement in Falkirk Council area, Maddiston lies on the Manuel Burn to the south of the Union Canal.

Maddy, Loch *Western Isles* A large sea loch on the east coast of North Uist in the Western Isles, Loch Maddy (Gael: *Loch na Madadh*) is dotted with many small, uninhabited islands and islets. The principal settlement on its shores is Lochmaddy, which has a ferry link with Uig on the isle of Skye.

Maes Howe *Orkney* One of the most outstanding Neolithic tombs in Great Britain, Maes Howe is situated near the southeast end of the Loch of Harray, just off the main road between Kirkwall and Stromness in the Orkney Mainland. Measuring 35 m (115 ft) in diameter at the base and 7.3 m (24 ft) in height, the tomb is surrounded by a broad ditch. The entrance leads through a passage way to a lofty inner chamber, the entire structure being built of large stones weighing up to 30 tonnes. The tomb was constructed before 2700 BC, but it contains two dozen runic inscriptions dating from a much later period of Viking occupation.

Magus Muir *Fife* A locality in eastern Fife, Magus Muir lies 3 miles (5 km) west-southwest of St Andrews. It was the scene of the murder of Archbishop James Sharp on 3 May 1679 by Covenanters.

Mahaick, Loch *Stirling* A small loch in the Braes of Doune, Stirling Council area, Loch Mahaick lies 6 miles (10 km) northwest of Doune. It is the source of the Ardoch Burn, which flows southeastwards to join the River Teith.

Maich Water *Renfrewshire/North Ayrshire* Rising on the western edge of Renfrewshire on the slopes of Misty Law, the Maich Water flows southeastwards along the border between Renfrewshire and North Ayrshire before emptying into Kilbirnie Loch.

Maiden Pap *Highland* A hill in the Caithness district of Highland Council area, Maiden Pap rises to 484 m (1588 ft) 3 miles (5 km) east of Morven and 6 miles (10 km) west of Dunbeath.

Maidens *South Ayrshire* A fishing village of Carrick in South Ayrshire, Maidens lies at the southern end of Maidenhead Bay, 2 miles (3 km) north of Turnberry and 5 miles (8 km) west of Maybole. A series of coastal rocks known as The Maidens of Turnberry form a natural harbour.

Main Water of Luce *South Ayrshire/Dumfries and Galloway* The westernmost of the two principal headwaters of the Water of Luce in Dumfries and Galloway is the Main Water of Luce, which rises in South Ayrshire 6 miles (10 km) southeast of Ballantrae. It flows generally southwards for 10 miles (16 km) to the village of New Luce where it is joined by the Cross Water of Luce before continuing southwards as the Water of Luce on its course to Luce Bay.

Mains Castle *Dundee City* A fortified house situated in Caird Park, Dundee, Mains Castle was built in 1550 by Sir David Graham, whose family owned the castle until the early 19th century. Overlooking a ravine and wooded glen through which flows the Gelly Burn, Mains Castle lies to the north of Kingsway on the northeastern outskirts of Dundee. On the opposite side of the burn is the old graveyard of Mains with the Graham family mausoleum. There are footpaths through the park, which also has 18- and nine-hole golf courses.

Mainsriddle *Dumfries and Galloway* A village in Dumfries and Galloway, Mainsriddle lies 3 miles (5 km) southwest of Kirkbean and nearly 8 miles (13 km) southeast of Dalbeattie.

Maisgeir *Argyll and Bute* An island of Argyll and Bute, Maisgeir lies off the southwest coast of the island of Gometra, which lies to the west of Mull.

Makerstoun *Scottish Borders* An estate and parish in Scottish Borders, Makerstoun lies to the north of the River Tweed, 4 miles (6.5 km) west of Kelso.

Mallaig *Highland* A fishing and ferry port in the North Morar district of Highland Council area, Mallaig lies on the Sound of Sleat near the mouth of Loch Nevis and opposite the Sleat peninsula of southwest Skye. It is one of the main west coast ports and lies at the terminus of the West Highland Railway. Car ferries link Mallaig with Armadale on Skye, Castlebay on Barra and with the Small Isles of Rum, Eigg, Muck and Canna. It developed in the 1890s as a herring-fishing port, its rail terminus opening in 1901. More recently it has become a centre for white-fish, prawn and lobster fishing, its prawn fleet being the largest in Scotland. A Sea Life Centre and museum were opened in the 1990s, and in 2000 a new community hall was erected. In 1746, Prince Charles Edward Stewart (Bonnie Prince Charlie) landed here on his flight from Skye. The hill of Carn a' Ghobhair rises about 3 miles (5 km) east of the town with splendid views towards Lochs Morar and Nevis, and over the Sound of Sleat to Skye and the Small Isles.

Mallaigvaig *Highland* A small village in the North Morar district of Highland Council area, Mallaigvaig lies a mile (1.5 km) to the northeast of Mallaig at the mouth of Loch Nevis.

Mallart River *Highland* A river of Caithness, the Mallart River rises in Loch Choire and flows east then north to join the River Naver a half-mile (1 km) east of the head of Loch Naver.

Malleny *City of Edinburgh* A house and garden at Balerno, 6 miles (10 km) southwest of Edinburgh, Malleny has been in the care of the National Trust for Scotland since 1968. The house, which dates from c.1589, was the home of the Hamiltons of Kilbrackmont until 1634, when the estate was acquired by Sir James Murray of Kilbaberton, architect to Charles I. In 1647 the estate passed to Edinburgh lawyer William Scott, and in 1882 Malleny was acquired by Archibald Primrose, 5th Earl of Rosebery, who became prime minister. The 1.2-ha (3-acre) walled garden, which is open to the public, is dominated by four 400-year-old yew trees, originally twelve in number and known as 'The Apostles'. The garden also includes a large collection of old-fashioned roses and fine herbaceous borders. The National Bonsai Collection for Scotland is also to be found at Malleny.

Mallie, River *Highland* A river in the Lochaber district of Highland Council area, the River Mallie rises on the lower slopes of Gulvain and flows east through Glen Mallie and the Locheil Forest before emptying into Loch Arkaig at Inver Mallie.

Malzie, Water of *Dumfries and Galloway* A stream in the northern Machars of Dumfries and Galloway, the Water of Malzie rises to the east of Mochrum Loch. It flows southeast then northeast to join the River Bladnoch 4 miles (6.5 km) west of Wigtown.

Mam na Gualainn *Highland* A mountain in the Lochaber district of Highland Council area, Mam na Gualainn rises to 796 m (2611 ft) on the north side of Loch Leven, 4 miles (6.5 km) west of Kinlochleven.

Mam Sodhail *Highland* One of the highest mountains north of the Great Glen, Mam Sodhail (or Mam Soul) rises to 1181 m (3875 ft) between Glen Cannich and Glen Affric.

Mamlorn, Forest of *Stirling* A deer forest in the Breadalbane district of northern Stirling Council area, the Forest of Mamlorn lies at the western end of Glen Lochay, between Loch Lyon to the north and Glen Dochart to the south.

Mamore Forest *Highland* A mountainous area of the Lochaber district in Highland Council area, the Mamore Forest lies between Glen Nevis to the north and Kinlochleven to the south. The mountain peaks within the Mamore Forest are generally referred to as the Mamores.

Mamores, the *Highland* The name given to the range of peaks to the north of Loch Leven and the Mamore Forest, The Mamores comprise nearly a dozen summits, the highest of which is Binnein Mòr (1130 m/3707 ft).

Manais The Gaelic name for Manish in the Western Isles.

Mandally *Highland* A scattered settlement in the Lochaber district of Highland Council area, Easter and Wester Mandally lie on the south side of the River Garry opposite Invergarry.

Manderston *Scottish Borders* A country house in the Berwickshire district of Scottish Borders, Manderston lies 1.5 miles (2.5 km) east of Duns and 9 miles (14 km) north of Coldstream. Originally built in the 1790s, Manderston was re-created between 1890 and 1905 in the Adam Revival style by architect John Kinross for Sir James Millar, known as 'Lucky Jim' because of his success on the race-track. Millar's father had bought the estate in 1860. Sir James married Evelyn Curzon, sister of the Viceroy of India, and her family home, Kedleston in Derbyshire, an 18th-century masterpiece by Robert Adam (1728–92), provided the model for Manderston. Surrounded by 23 ha (56 acres) of garden, it is now the home of Lord Palmer.

Maneight *East Ayrshire* A small village in East Ayrshire, Maneight lies at the foot of the Maneight Hill, 4 miles (6.5 km) northeast of Dalmellington.

Mangaster *Shetland* A small settlement on the western coastline of Shetland Mainland, Mangaster lies on the northern shore of the Mangaster Voe, an inlet of St Magnus Bay, 3 miles (5 km) northwest of Brae.

Mangersta *Western Isles* A settlement on the far west coast of the Isle of Lewis in the Outer Hebrides, Mangersta (Gael: *Mangurstadh*) lies 2.5 miles (4 km) north-northeast of Islivig and 3 miles (5 km) southwest of Timsgarry. The sandy beach here has been identified as being of geomorphological importance and is popular with surfers. A communications mast on Ard More Mangersta, 1.25 miles (2 km) to the north, was established during World War II and now services the British air-traffic control system.

Mangurstadh The Gaelic name for Mangersta in the Western Isles.

Manish *Western Isles* One of a succession of scattered settlements strung along the rocky east coast of South Harris in the Outer Hebrides, Manish (Gael: *Manais*) lies between Flodabay and Ardslave, 5 miles (8 km) northeast of Rodel.

Mannal *Argyll and Bute* A small settlement on the island of Tiree, Mannal (or Mannel) lies on Hynish Bay a half-mile (1 km) south of Balemartine.

Mannofield *Aberdeen City* A suburb of Aberdeen, Mannofield lies 2 miles (3 km) southwest of the city centre. The missionary Robert Laws was born in Mannofield in 1851.

Manor Water *Scottish Borders* A river of Scottish Borders, Manor Water rises in the Ettrick Forest 2 miles (3 km) southeast of Dollar Law and flows in a northerly direction to merge with the River Tweed a mile (1.5 km) southwest of Peebles.

Mansewood *Glasgow City* A suburb of Glasgow, Mansewood lies 3 miles (5 km) southwest of the city centre.

Maoile Lunndaidh *Highland* An isolated mountain in the western Highlands, Maoile Lunndaidh rises to a height of 1007 m (3304 ft) between Glen Carron, Glen Strathfarrar and Strath Conon.

Maol Bàn *Argyll and Bute* A mountain on the island of Mull in the Inner Hebrides, Maol Bàn rises to 338 m (1109 ft) 3 miles (5 km) southwest of the headland of Rubha nan Sailthean. It overlooks the Firth of Lorn.

Maol Chean-dearg *Highland* A mountain of Wester Ross, Maol Chean-dearg rises to 933 m (3061 ft) in the Coulin Forest to the south of Torridon. Its name is derived from the Gaelic for 'bald red head'.

Maol Chinn-dearg *Highland* One of seven peaks on the South Glen Shiel ridge in the western Highlands, Maol Chinn-dearg rises to 981 m (3218 ft) in the middle of the range.

Maol Domhnaich The Gaelic name for Muldoanich in the Western Isles.

Maovally *Highland* A hill in northwest Sutherland, Maovally rises to 299 m (981 ft) 3 miles (5 km) northwest of the mouth of the Kyle of Durness.

Mar *Aberdeenshire* An ancient district of southwest Aberdeenshire, Mar occupies territory at the western end of Royal Deeside, extending north from the River Dee towards the River Don. It is subdivided into Braemar, Midmar and Cromar and gives its name to an earldom.

Mar Lodge Estate *Aberdeenshire* A 29,380-ha (72,598-acre) estate in southwest Aberdeenshire, Mar Lodge extends from the valley of the River Dee northwards to the high peaks of the Cairngorms to the west of Tomintoul and Braemar. It includes much of the upper watershed of the River Dee, four of the highest peaks in the UK and important remnants of native pine forest. The estate was purchased by the National Trust for Scotland in 1995. Mar Lodge was built in 1895 by Alexander Duff, 1st Duke of Fife, and was designed to look like a German hunting lodge. It is situated close to the River Dee, 5 miles (8 km) west of Braemar. The original Mar Lodge, built in the late 18th century, was badly damaged by the 'Muckle Spate' of 1829 and later demolished. New Mar Lodge, also known as Corriemulzie Cottage, was built on higher ground in the mid-19th century. Much of this building was destroyed by fire in 1895. On either side of the present building, which was designed by the Aberdeen architect A. Marshall Mackenzie, stand an Episcopalian chapel and a ballroom decorated with 2500 deer skulls. Mar Lodge is approached over Victoria Bridge, a lattice-girder structure built across the Dee in 1905.

Maraig The Gaelic name for Maaruig in the Western Isles.

Maragan, Loch *Stirling* A small loch in the hills of Breadalbane, Loch Maragan lies beyond Creag Liaragan, 2 miles (3 km) due north of Loch Dochart at the western end of Glen Dochart.

Marbhig The Gaelic name for Marvig in the Western Isles.

Marchburn *Dumfries and Galloway* A locality in Dumfries and Galloway, Marchburn lies on the River Nith between Sanquhar and New Cumnock, close to the border with East Ayrshire.

Marchmont *City of Edinburgh* A district of Edinburgh, Marchmont lies a mile (1.5 km) south of the city centre. It is characterised by its desirable Victorian flats in fine sandstone tenement blocks. Marchmont is 'home' to Inspector Rebus, the detective in the novels of Ian Rankin (b.1960).

Marchmont House *Scottish Borders* A mansion house in the Berwickshire district of Scottish Borders, Marchmont House is situated amid extensive policies just over 4 miles (6.5 km) southwest of Duns. It was built in 1754 for Hugh Hume, 3rd Earl of Marchmont (1708–94), by Thomas Gibson and was later renovated and remodelled by architects William Burn (1834) and Sir Robert Lorimer (1913–20). The house is noted for its ornamental plasterwork in the hallway and panelling in the music room. Marchmont is today used by the Sue Ryder Foundation as a care home.

Marcus *Angus* A locality in Angus, the farms of Marcus and Easter Marcus lie on the course of the South Esk River, a mile (1.5 km) northeast of Finavon. The Finavon Doocot lies to the southwest. The Mill of Marcus lies on the Noran Water to the north of Easter Marcus.

Maree, Loch *Highland* A long, narrow loch with several islets in Wester Ross, Loch Maree extends 12 miles (19 km) in a northwesterly direction between Kinlochewe and Poolewe, where it empties via a short river into Loch Ewe. The loch has a maximum depth of 112 m (367 ft). The mountains of Liathach and Ben Eighe rise to the south.

Margnaheglish *North Ayrshire* A small resort village on the east coast of the island of Arran, Margnaheglish lies to the northeast of Lamlash, looking south onto Lamlash Bay. Noted for its fine beach, it developed in the 19th century as a holiday resort with a steamer pier.

Marischal College *Aberdeen City* Founded in 1593 by George Keith, 5th Earl Marischal of Scotland (*c.*1553–1623), Marischal College was created as a Protestant alternative to King's College in Old Aberdeen. Situated on Broad Street, Marischal College is the second-largest granite building in the world. The Gothic-style tower was extended to its present height of 85 m (279 ft) in 1895, and a granite facade was added in 1906. Marischal Museum has displays on the heritage of northeast Scotland.

Marishader *Highland* A small village on the Trotternish peninsula of the isle of Skye in the Inner Hebrides, Marishader lies a mile (1.5 km) southwest of Loch Mealt and 3 miles (5 km) south of Staffin Bay.

Marjoriebanks *Dumfries and Galloway* A locality in Annandale, Dumfries and Galloway, Marjoriebanks lies immediately north of Lochmaben.

Mark *Dumfries and Galloway* A hamlet in the Rhinns of Galloway, Dumfries and Galloway, Mark lies to the southeast of Soulseat Loch, nearly 4 miles (6.5 km) southeast of Stranraer.

Mark, Glen *Angus* A valley carrying the Water of Mark, Glen Mark extends northeast then southeast to join the head of the River North Esk 3 miles (5 km) west of Tarfside.

Mark, Water of *Angus* A headwater of the River North Esk in the southern Grampians, the Water of Mark rises on the border between Angus and Aberdeenshire on the Black Hill of Mark. It flows north past the Sheilin of Mark then southeast through Glen Mark to meet the Water of Lee and the Burn of Branny to form the River North Esk.

Markie, Glen *Highland* A valley in the Badenoch and Strathspey district of southern Highland Council area, Glen Markie carries the waters of the Markie Burn southwards from Carn Dearg to meet the upper reaches of the River Spey, a mile (1.5 km) west of Laggan Bridge.

Markie Water *Aberdeenshire* A stream in northwest Aberdeenshire, the Markie Water rises in hills to the southeast of Dufftown. It flows northeast to join the River Deveron at the Haugh of Glass.

Markinch *Fife* A small town in central Fife, Markinch lies to the north of the River Leven, 2 miles (3 km) east of Glenrothes and 6 miles (10 km) north of Kirkcaldy. Markinch is said to have been capital of Fife when it was one of the seven provinces of Pictland, and in medieval times it was the burgh of barony of Dalgynch. Terraces on Markinch Hill are thought to be either medieval or Roman in origin, and on the northern outskirts of the town beside the East Lodge of Balbirnie House stands the ancient Celtic Stob Cross which may have marked the limits of sanctuary of Markinch Church. The parish church stands on the site of a preaching station said to have been established towards the end of the 6th century by St Drostan, a nephew of St Columba. It overlooks the centre of Markinch, which was designated a conservation area in 1973. There is a Tudor Italianate railway station dating from the opening of the first railway through Fife in 1847, and a town house built in 1899. The town has two recreation parks, one of which is dedicated to Provost John Dixon who presented it to the burgh in 1919. The population of Markinch reached a peak of 6800 in 1901 as a result of the development of paper making, textile, coal mining, distilling and building industries. Paper making is still an important local employer, along with a wide range of industries mainly located on the industrial estates of neighbouring Glenrothes.

Marnoch *Aberdeenshire* A hamlet in Aberdeenshire, Marnoch lies on the left bank of the River Deveron, 2 miles (3 km) southwest of Aberchirder. The river is crossed near here by the two-span Bridge of Marnoch built in 1806. Its parish church dates from 1792.

Marr Burn *Dumfries and Galloway* A tributary of the River Nith in Dumfries and Galloway, the Marr Burn rises to the west of Drumlanrig Castle. It flows through Drumlanrig Woods before joining the Nith 2 miles (3 km) northwest of Thornhill.

Marsco *Highland* A mountain on the isle of Skye in the Inner Hebrides, Marsco rises to 736 m (2415 ft) to the east of the Cuillins, 3 miles (5 km) southwest of the head of Loch Ainort.

Martnaham Loch *East Ayrshire/Dumfries and Galloway* A loch of Carrick in southwest Scotland, Martnaham Loch straddles the border between East Ayrshire and Dumfries and Galloway, 5 miles (8 km) southeast of Ayr. The remains of a castle lie on an islet within the loch.

Martyrs' Monument *Fife* A monument at the western end of The Scores, St Andrews, the Martyrs' Monument commemorates the Protestant reformers Patrick Hamilton, George Wishart, Paul Craw, Henry Forrest and Walter Myln who were martyred around the time of the Reformation in the 16th century.

Maruig An alternative name for Maaruig in the Western Isles.

Marvig *Western Isles* A hamlet on the east coast of the Isle of Lewis in the Outer Hebrides, Marvig (occasionally Marthig, Gael: *Marbhig*) lies on the southern shore of Loch Marvig, in the South Lochs district, 9.5 miles (15 km) south of Stornoway.

Marvig, Loch *Western Isles* A sea loch of the east coast of the Isle of Lewis in the Western Isles, Loch Marvig (also Loch Mariveg, Gael: *Loch Mharabhig*) lies to the north of the settlement of Marvig.

Marwick Head *Orkney* A headland skirted by cliffs located 10 miles (16 km) north of Stromness on the Orkney Mainland, Marwick Head faces northeast into the North Atlantic Ocean. It was off Marwick Head that the cruiser HMS *Hampshire* struck a mine in a storm on 5 June 1916 while transporting Field Marshal Lord Kitchener, the British Minister of War, and his staff to a conference in Russia. A total of 643 men lost their lives, including Kitchener. An attempt to maintain secrecy resulted in the navy blocking access to the area which undoubtedly prevented more survivors being picked up. The Kitchener Monument, located at a height of 87 m (285 ft) on top of the cliffs, commemorates the incident.

Marybank *Highland* A small village of Easter Ross, Marybank lies south of the River Conon, 3 miles (5 km) south of Strathpeffer and 6 miles (10 km) southwest of Dingwall.

Marybank *Western Isles* A hamlet on the western outskirts of Stornoway on the Isle of Lewis in the Outer Hebrides, Marybank (Gael: *Bruach Mairi*) lies a mile (1.5 km) northwest of Lews Castle and 1.25 miles (2 km) northwest of the town centre. Stornoway golf course lies just to the east.

Maryburgh *Highland* A small village of Easter Ross, Maryburgh looks out onto the head of the Cromarty Firth, 2 miles (3 km) south of Dingwall.

Maryburgh *Perth and Kinross* A village in the Kinross part of Perth and Kinross, Maryburgh lies near the border with Fife, a mile (1.5 km) north of Kelty. It was laid out as a planned estate and mining village in the 1730s by the architect William Adam of Blairadam, but never completed. It takes its name from Adam's wife, Mary.

Maryculter *Aberdeenshire* A village in an Aberdeenshire parish of the same name, Maryculter (or more fully Kirkton of Maryculter), lies to the south of the River Dee, 5 miles (8 km) southwest of Aberdeen. Little remains of the old kirk close to Maryculter House by the Dee. Dedicated to St Mary and a dependent chapel of the church at St Peter Culter, now Peterculter, Maryculter was held by the Knights of St John of Jerusalem in medieval times, a link remembered in local names such as Templars Park. In the new church, built in 1782, are carved effigies of Thomas Menzies and his wife, Marion. It was the Menzies family that acquired the estate of Maryculter in the 14th century, the last of this name, John Menzies, gifting land in 1829 to the Catholic bishops for the founding of nearby Blairs (St Mary's) College.

Marygold *Scottish Borders* A small village of Scottish Borders, Marygold lies 4 miles (6.5 km) northeast of Duns.

Maryhill *Glasgow City* A district of Glasgow, Maryhill lies on the River Kelvin near its junction with the River Clyde, 3 miles (5 km) northwest of the city centre. It was established by Robert Graham in the late 18th century and was named after his wife, Mary Hill. The first temperance society in Britain was founded here in 1829 after their daughter Lilias Graham became teetotal. By the mid-19th century Maryhill had developed into an industrial village producing textiles, paper, lumber, boats and iron. In 1856 it became a police burgh and in 1912 it was incorporated into the City of Glasgow. The locks on the Forth and Clyde Canal here were referred to as the Botany Locks since prisoners are said to have been able to choose between transportation to Botany Bay, Australia, and manual work on the construction of the canal. Charles Rennie Mackintosh designed Maryhill's Queens Cross Church (1899), which is now home to the Charles Rennie Mackintosh Society.

Marykirk *Angus* A village in southeast Aberdeenshire, Marykirk lies close to the River North Esk, 5 miles (8 km) northwest of Montrose. The four-arched bridge and tollhouse were designed by the engineer John Smeaton in 1815. Originally dedicated to the Virgin Mary and consecrated in 1242, the parish church was rebuilt in 1806. Marykirk gives its name to the parish, which is also known as Aberluthnott, possibly because the River Luther joins the North Esk midway between Marykirk and Luthermuir, the other village in the parish. In the centre of the village can be found a market cross and the gate lodges at the entrance to the former Kirktonhill House.

Marypark *Moray* A village in Strathspey, Marypark lies 4 miles (6.5 km) southwest of Charlestown of Aberlour in the valley of the River Spey. To the east is Glenfarclas Distillery, which was founded by Robert Hay in 1836. Ben Rinnes rises to the southeast.

Maryport *Dumfries and Galloway* A hamlet situated on a bay of the same name at the southern end of the Rhinns of Galloway, Maryport lies nearly 3 miles (5 km) north of the Mull of Galloway.

Maryport Bay *Dumfries and Galloway* A bay on the Solway Firth coast of Dumfries and Galloway, Maryport Bay lies just over a mile (1.5 km) to the south of Dundrennan and a mile (1.5 km) northeast of Abbey Burnfoot. Nearby is 18th-century Maryport House. Mary, Queen of Scots left Scotland for the last time from Maryport.

Maryton *Angus* A locality in northeast Angus, Maryton lies in a parish of the same name to the south of the Montrose Basin, 3 miles (5 km) southwest of Montrose. Originally a chapel of the cathedral at Brechin and named St Mary's of Old Montrose, the kirk of Maryton was established as a separate parish church in 1649. The remains of a small medieval motte occupy a strongly defensive site on a headland projecting northeastwards towards the Montrose Basin from Maryton Law.

Marywell *Angus* A village in eastern Angus, Marywell lies on the road from Arbroath to Montrose, 2 miles (3 km) north of Arbroath.

Mas Sgeir *Western Isles* An islet in the Western Isles, Mas Sgeir lies off the west coast of the Isle of Lewis, 2 miles (3 km) north of Great Bernera.

Mashie, River *Highland* Rising on the slopes of Meall Cruaidh in the southern Grampians, the River Mashie flows in a northerly direction past Beinn Eildhe to merge with the River Spey, 8 miles (13 km) southwest of Newtonmore.

Massan, Glen *Argyll and Bute* A valley on the Cowal peninsula, Glen Massan carries the waters of the River Massan in a southeasterly direction before meeting the River Eachaig just south of Loch Eck and 2 miles (3 km) northwest of the head of Holy Loch.

Mathair Eite, Lochan *Highland* A small loch in the Lochaber district of Highland Council area, Lochan Mathair Elite lies 5 miles (8 km) southeast of the dam at the Blackwater Reservoir.

Mauchline *East Ayrshire* A village in the Kyle district of East Ayrshire, Mauchline is situated northeast of the River Ayr, 10 miles (16 km) east of Ayr and 10 miles (16 km) southeast of Kilmarnock. The settlement was established as an ecclesiastical centre linked to Melrose in the 12th century and became a burgh of barony in 1510. In the 19th century it developed in association with coal mining, sandstone quarrying, and the manufacture of textiles and finely painted boxes of polished sycamore that came to be known as Mauchline Ware. Modern industries include the manufacture of plastics, dairy products, glassware and curling stones. Ballochmyle viaduct across the River Ayr near Mauchline was built in 1846–8 to a design by John Miller for the Glasgow and Southwestern Railway. Mauchline is most noted for its associations with Robert Burns (1759–96). The house occupied by Burns and his wife Jean Armour, a Mauchline native, is now a museum, and nearby Poosie Nansie's tavern is associated with the poet's setting of *The Jolly Beggars*. Also in Mauchline is the National Burns Memorial Tower. Burns was a tenant for nine years at nearby Mossgiel Farm to the north.

Maud *Aberdeenshire* A livestock market and agricultural service centre of Buchan in Aberdeenshire, Maud lies on the South Ugie Water, 13 miles (21 km) west of Peterhead. Originally known as Bank of Behitch after a raised piece of ground where carters are said to have unhitched their horses, Maud lies at a junction of six roads and was formerly part of the Auldmaud (Old Maud) Estate. It developed as a livestock market, and with the arrival of the Great North of Scotland Railway in 1861 that function was enhanced by its location at a junction for trains to Fraserburgh in the north and Peterhead in the east. At this point the settlement was rechristened Brucklay, after the nearby Brucklay Estate, but before long it was renamed New Maud, the 'New' later being dropped. The railway station closed in 1979 and the Buchan Line Walkway along the route of the former railway passes through the village. Because of its location, Maud was chosen in 1869 as the site for the Buchan Combination Poorhouse, a building that later became a hospital for the elderly. Its Gothic-style church dates from 1876. Today Maud continues to be the 'meeting place' that is said to be the origin of its name.

Mauld *Highland* A small village in Strathglass in the Inverness district of Highland Council area, Mauld lies on the eastern banks of the River Glass, 6 miles (10 km) northeast of Cannich.

Mauricewood *Midlothian* A northern extension of the town of Penicuik, Mauricewood comprises a late 20th-century private housing development at the foot of the Pentland Hills. The district takes its name from a modest Victorian mansion built in 1836 and extended in 1897 by Dr Joseph Bell (1837–1911), the Edinburgh surgeon who inspired Arthur Conan Doyle (1859–1930) to create Sherlock Holmes. The house also gave its name to the former Mauricewood Pit, which was the site of a mining disaster on 5 September 1889 when an underground fire killed 63 miners.

Mavis Grind *Shetland* The gateway to the rugged and spectacular district of Northmavine at the northern end of the Mainland of Shetland, Mavis Grind – the 'gateway of the narrow isthmus' – is the name given to the narrow neck of land where the island is reduced to a strip little more than 100 m (328 ft) wide to the west of Brae. Here St Magnus Bay and the Atlantic in the west are separated from Ell Wick, Sullom Voe and the North Sea in the east. It is thought that the Vikings dragged their boats across Mavis Grind to avoid sailing dangerous waters to the north of Shetland, and fishermen did the same until the 1950s to move quickly between fishing grounds.

Mavisbank House *Midlothian* The ruined remains of a Palladian mansion house in Midlothian, Mavisbank overlooks the River North Esk to the south of Loanhead. It was built between 1723 and 1727 by William Adam (1689–1748) for Sir John Clerk of Penicuik (1676–1755), who himself had prepared the initial designs. After the Clerk family sold the house in 1815, it was extended by adding two sizeable wings in the 1840s. The house fell into disrepair and the 19th-century wings were demolished in 1954. Mavisbank was gutted by fire in 1973, its bare shell avoiding demolition only after an intervention by the Secretary of State for Scotland in 1987. The Mavisbank Trust has been set up to protect and renovate the structure, and Mavisbank appeared in the BBC television programme *Restoration* in 2003.

Maxton *Scottish Borders* A village in the Roxburgh district of Scottish Borders, Maxton lies 2 miles (3 km) southeast of Newton St Boswells and a further 3 miles (5 km) southeast of Melrose. The River Tweed flows to the north.

Maxwelltown *Dumfries and Galloway* An eastern suburb of Dumfries in Dumfries and Galloway, Maxwelltown lies to the west of the River Nith. Buildings of interest include Dumfries Mill, now the Burns Heritage Centre, Dumfries Museum and Observatory, the Sinclair Memorial, the former Dominican Convent of St Benedict, the Sheriff Court, Dumfries Prison, the former Maxwelltown Court House and Queen of the South football ground.

Maxwelton *Dumfries and Galloway* A locality in Dumfries and Galloway, Maxwelton House and its associated Mains and Chapel lie to the east of the Cairn Water, 3 miles (5 km) east of Moniaive. Originally named Glencairn Castle, Maxwelton was bought by Stephen Laurie who changed the name of the property, which dates from the 17th century and includes the bedroom of Annie Laurie, made famous in a song by Robert Burns. The Gothic-style Maxwelton Episcopal Chapel was built in 1868 as a memorial to John Minet Laurie.

May, Water of *Perth and Kinross* A river of Perth and Kinross, the Water of May rises in the western Ochil Hills and runs in a northerly direction into the River Earn, 5 miles (8 km) southwest of Perth.

May Craig *Aberdeenshire* A rocky islet on the North Sea coast of Aberdeenshire, the May Craig lies in the sea just north of Portlethen, 5 miles (8 km) south of Aberdeen.

May Wick *Shetland* A small north-facing bay on the west coast of the Shetland Mainland, May Wick forms an inlet of the sea a mile (1.5 km) southeast of South Havra.

Mayar *Angus* The most southerly hill of the Mounth plateau in Angus, Mayar rises to a height of 928 m (3045 ft).

Maybole *South Ayrshire* A commuter town in the Carrick district of Ayrshire, Maybole lies 9 miles (14 km) south of Ayr and 12 miles (19 km) northeast of Girvan between the Water of Girvan and the Ayrshire coast. Under the Kennedy family, which occupied Cassilis Castle 3 miles (5 km) to the northeast, it developed in medieval times as the administrative centre of Carrick and had a small monastic hospital. Maybole Castle, another Kennedy stronghold, dates from the 16th century, and its church was extended as a collegiate establishment in the 14th century. Crossraguel, 2 miles (3 km) to the southwest, was raised to the status of an abbey in 1286. Maybole was designated a burgh of barony in 1516 and developed in the 18th and 19th centuries in association with the manufacture of textiles, leather, farm tools and footwear. The parents of Robert Burns, William Burnes and Agnes Broun, came from Maybole.

Mayen House *Moray* A late-Georgian villa dating from 1788, Mayen House lies in a bend of the River Deveron to the east of Milltown of Rothiemay in Moray.

Mayfield *Midlothian* A dormitory settlement in Midlothian, Mayfield lies a half-mile (1 km) east of the former mining town of Newtongrange. It was largely developed in the 1950s to house miners working in the nearby Blinkbonny, Easthouses and Lingerwood Collieries, many of whom had relocated from the west of Scotland. Although there is no deep mining, opencast mining continues at Blinkbonny, 1.5 miles (2 km) to the south.

Mazeran, Glen *Highland* A valley in the Inverness district of Highland Council area, Glen Mazeran carries the waters of the Mazeran Water in an easterly direction to join the valley of Strath Dearn, 5 miles (8 km) southwest of Tomatin.

McArthur's Head *Argyll and Bute* A headland with a lighthouse on the east coast of the island of Islay in the Inner Hebrides, McArthur's Head extends into the sea at the southern end of the Sound of Islay.

McCaig's Tower *Argyll and Bute* A prominent landmark on the hillside overlooking Oban, McCaig's Tower was commissioned by John Stuart McCaig (1824–1902), a local banker. Built in the style of the Roman Colosseum, the folly acts as a memorial to both McCaig and his family. McCaig promoted the project in order to provide work for local stonemasons during the winter months between 1895 and 1902. He had planned a more elaborate structure, containing a museum and art gallery, but his death brought an end to funding and construction stopped with only the outer walls completed.

McEwan Hall *City of Edinburgh* Located in Bristo Square, Edinburgh, adjacent to the University of Edinburgh's Medical School, the McEwan Hall was built by Sir Robert Rowand Anderson between 1888 and 1897 in Italian Renaissance style. It was originally planned as part of the university's new Medical School (completed some 10 years earlier), but the government of the time refused to fund a graduation hall that they considered frivolous. Thus the university turned to the brewer William McEwan who contributed the necessary funding (£115,000) to create this ostentatious building. McEwan specified lavish decoration, by the artist William Palin, which includes panels depicting the academic disciplines, the virtues and even included himself presenting the hall. The decoration took more than three years to complete. The hall is used by the University of Edinburgh for graduations, concerts, meetings and examinations.

McLennan Arch *Glasgow City* Originally built in 1792 as the facade of Robert and James Adam's Assembly Rooms in the centre of Glasgow, the McLennan Arch was reconstructed at the northeast end of Greendyke Street by John Carrick in 1892. It was moved to its present site on Glasgow Green in 1922.

McManus Galleries *Dundee City* The McManus Galleries are located in the upper floor of the Albert Institute in Albert Square, Dundee, which was built in 1867 by Sir George Gilbert Scott to a Victorian Gothic architectural style. The main galleries are the Victoria Gallery, which houses a collection of 19th-century Scottish art, the McKenzie Gallery, which houses Scottish art from the period 1880–1950, the Costume Gallery, housing textiles and costumes from Dundee and around the world, and the Albert Hall, which houses fine and decorative art from Scotland's national collections.

Meabhaig The Gaelic name for Meavaig in the Western Isles.

Meadail, Gleann *Highland* A valley in the Knoydart district of southwest Highland Council area, Gleann Meadail carries the waters of the River Inverie west from Loch an Dubh-Lochain to Inverie Bay, an inlet of Loch Nevis.

Meadhonach, Gleann *Highland* A valley on the Sleat peninsula on the isle of Skye in the Inner Hebrides, Gleann Meadhonach carries the waters of the Dalavil westwards through Loch a' Ghlinne to enter the Cuillin Sound at Inver Dalavil.

Meadie, Loch *Highland* A loch in the northwest Highlands, Loch Meadie lies between Ben Hope and Loch Naver, 5 miles (8 km) northwest of Altnahara in Caithness.

Meadie, Loch *Highland* A narrow loch near the north coast of Caithness, Loch Meadie lies a mile (1.5 km) south of Kirtomy. It is 2 miles (3 km) long.

Meadowbank *City of Edinburgh* A locality in northeast Edinburgh, Meadowbank is noted for its sports centre which is the largest in the city. Built for the 1970 Commonwealth Games and used again as the principal venue when the Games returned to Edinburgh in 1986, it regularly hosts sporting events at international level.

Meadows, the *City of Edinburgh* Parkland on the south side of the city of Edinburgh, the Meadows lie to the south of George Square and the former Royal Infirmary buildings on Lauriston Place. It was originally called Hope Park after Thomas Hope of Rankeillor, who in the 1740s drained the Borough (Burgh) Loch, or South Loch, which had previously occupied the site. The South Loch had provided a supply of water for the city, while the Nor' Loch to the north of the Old Town served a purely defensive function before being transformed into Princes Street Gardens. The Meadows were laid out as parkland, with tree-lined walks and avenues, bisected by Melville Drive. The tall pillars, topped by a lion and a unicorn, at the west end of Melville Drive were designed by Sir James Gowans (1821–90) for the Edinburgh International Exhibition of 1886, which was held in an immense exhibition hall built in the Meadows. Gowans built the pillars using specimen stone from a number of Scottish quarries, the name of the quarry being carved into each stone. The pillars at the east end of Melville Drive were built in 1881 by the grateful Nelson brothers after the city provided them with alternative accommodation for their printing works which were destroyed by fire in 1878. The whale's jaw-bone arch, which lies on the north side of Melville Drive opposite Marchmont Road, came from Shetland for the International Exhibition.

Mealabost The Gaelic name for Melbost in the Western Isles.

Mealabost Bhuirgh The Gaelic name for Melbost Borve in the Western Isles.

Mealasta Island *Western Isles* An uninhabited island in the Outer Hebrides, Mealasta Island lies a half-mile (1 km) off the west coast of the Isle of Lewis, 3 miles (5 km) south of Breanais.

Mealisval *Western Isles* A mountain in the Outer Hebrides, Mealisval rises to a height of 574 m (1883 ft) on the west coast of the Isle of Lewis, 3 miles (5 km) west of the southern end of Loch Suainaval.

Meall a' Bhuachaille *Highland* A peak in the Badenoch and Strathspey district of Highland Council area, Meall a' Bhuachaille rises to 810 m (2657 ft) at the northern edge of the Glenmore Forest Park, 5 miles (8 km) north of Cairn Gorm. Its name is derived from the Gaelic for 'hill of the cowherd'.

Meall a' Bhuiridh *Highland* Rising to 1108 m (3635 ft) at the eastern end of Glen Coe, Meall a' Bhuiridh is most famous for its northeast corrie, Corrie Pollach, which has been one of Scotland's principal skiing centres since 1960, when chairlifts were installed. Located southeast of the River Etive, Meall a' Bhuiridh together with Creise forms a horseshoe ridge looking onto Rannoch Moor.

Meall a' Chaorainn *Highland* A mountain of the Ross and Cromarty district of Highland Council area, Meall a' Chaorainn rises to 705 m (2313 ft) 2 miles (3 km) northwest of Achnasheen.

Meall a' Chaorainn *Highland* A peak in the Ross and Cromarty district of Highland Council area, Meall a' Chaorainn rises to 632 m (2073 ft) to the southwest of Gleann Mòr, 8 miles (13 km) north of the Aultguish Inn.

Meall a' Choire Bhuidhe *Perth and Kinross* A mountain to the south of Glen Lochsie in the southern Grampians of Perth and Kinross, Meall a' Choire Bhuidhe rises to 868 m (2847 ft) 3 miles (5 km) northwest of Spittal of Glenshee. Ben Earb rises to the southeast.

Meall a' Choire Leith *Perth and Kinross* A peak at the western end of the Ben Lawers range, overlooking Lochan na Lairige in Perth and Kinross, Meall a' Choire Leith rises to 926 m (3038 ft). Popular for early-season skiing, its name is derived from the Gaelic for 'hill of the grey corrie'.

Meall a' Chrasgaidh *Highland* A rounded summit with steep heathery slopes in the Fannichs of Wester Ross, Meall a' Chrasgaidh rises to 934 m (3064 ft). Its name is derived from the Gaelic for 'hill of the crossing'.

Meall a' Chrathaich *Highland* A peak in the Inverness district of Highland Council area, Meall a' Chrathaich rises to 679 m (2227 ft) west of Loch Ness, 11 miles (18 km) southwest of Drumnadrochit.

Meall a' Ghiubhais *Highland* A peak in the Ross and Cromarty district of Highland Council area, Meall a' Ghiubhais rises to 878 m (2880 ft) in the Inchbae Forest, 2 miles (3 km) west of the head of Loch Maree.

Meall a' Mhuic *Perth and Kinross* A mountain in central Perth and Kinross, Meall a' Mhuic rises to 745 m (2444 ft) between Glen Lyon and Loch Rannoch, 2 miles (3 km) south of Rannoch Station.

Meall a' Phubuill *Highland* A mountain peak in the Lochaber district of Highland Council area, Meall a' Phubuill rises to 774 m (2539 ft) in Locheil Forest, 5 miles (8 km) northeast of Kinlocheil.

Meall a' Phuill *Perth and Kinross* A mountain of central Perth and Kinross, Meall a' Phuill rises to 878 m (2880 ft) a mile (1.5 km) to the north of the eastern end of Loch an Daimh.

Meall an Fhuarain *Highland* A mountain in the Ross and Cromarty district of Highland Council area, Meall an Fhurain rises to 578 m (1896 ft) 4 miles (6.5 km) west of Strath Oykel and southeast of Loch Urigill.

Meall an Fhuarain *Highland* A mountain in the Sutherland district of Highland Council area, Meall an Fhuarain rises to 473 m (1551 ft) 4 miles (6.5 km) southwest of Altnaharra.

Meall an Fhudair *Argyll and Bute* A peak in Argyll and Bute, Meall an Fhudair rises to 764 m (2506 ft) 7 miles (11 km) northeast of the head of Loch Fyne and northwest of the head of Loch Lomond.

Meall an t-Seallaidh *Stirling* A summit in northwest Stirling Council area, Meall an t-Seallaidh rises to 852 m (2795 ft) 3 miles (5 km) west of Lochearnhead.

Meall Blair *Highland* A peak in the Lochaber district of southwest Highland Council area, Meall Blair (Gael: *Meall a' Bhlair*) rises to 656 m (2152 ft) to the north of Loch Arkaig, 4 miles (6.5 km) northeast of the settlement of Murlaggan.

Meall Buidhe *Perth and Kinross* A mountain rising to 932 m (3058 ft) to the north of Loch an Daimh in central Perth and Kinross, Meall Buidhe is the highest point on a ridge between Glen Lyon and Loch Rannoch.

Meall Buidhe *Highland* A mountain with two summits in the Knoydart district of Highland Council area, Meall Buidhe rises to 946 m (3104 ft) between Loch Nevis and Loch Hourn. The ridge to the summit is narrow and particularly rocky in places.

Meall Buidhe *Stirling* A summit of Glen Ogle in northern Stirling Council area, Meall Buidhe rises to 719 m (2359 ft) 3 miles (5 km) north of the western end of Loch Earn and 4 miles (6.5 km) south of Killin.

Meall Chuaich *Highland* A prominent mountain in the Badenoch district of Highland Council area, Meall Chuaich rises to 951 m (3120 ft) to the northeast of Dalwhinnie.

Meall Corranaich *Perth and Kinross* A summit in central Perth and Kinross, Meall Corranaich rises to 1069 m (3507 ft) to the west of Ben Lawers.

Meall Dearg *Highland* The lower of the two peaks on the 2-mile (3-km) Aonach Eagach ridge in Glen Coe, Meall Dearg rises to 953 m (3127 ft). It was the last summit to be climbed by Revd A. E. Robertson, the first person to climb all the Munros, or mountains over 914 m (3000 ft) high. Its name is derived from the Gaelic for 'red hill'.

Meall Dearg *Perth and Kinross* A peak to the west of Glen Cochill in central Perth and Kinross, Meall Dearg rises to 690 m (2263 ft) to the east of Loch Fender, 5 miles (8km) southeast of Aberfeldy.

Meall Doire Faid *Highland* A peak in the Ross and Cromarty district of Highland Council area, Meall Doire Faid rises to 730 m (2395 ft) a mile (1.5 km) northeast of the Corrieshalloch Gorge and 5 miles (8 km) south-southeast of the head of Loch Broom.

Meall Dubh *Highland* A mountain in Wester Ross, Meall Dubh rises to 642 m (2106 ft) 2 miles (3 km) east of Leckmelm on the southeastern shore of Loch Broom.

Meall Fuar-mhonaidh *Highland* A peak in the Inverness district of Highland Council area, Meall Fuar-mhonaidh rises to 699 m (2293 ft) on the northwest side of Loch Ness, 6 miles (10 km) southwest of Drumnadrochit.

Meall Garbh *Perth and Kinross* One of four peaks in a range that forms a horseshoe-shaped continuous ridge to the north of Glen Lyon in central Perth and Kinross, Meall Garbh rises to 968 m (3169 ft).

Meall Garbh *Perth and Kinross* A mountain in central

Perth and Kinross, Meall Garbh rises to 1118 m (3668 ft) to the northeast of Ben Lawers.

Meall Garbh *Argyll and Bute* A summit to the east of Glen Kinglass in Argyll and Bute, Meall Garbh rises to 701 m (2301 ft) 6 miles (10 km) north of Dalmally.

Meall Ghaordie *Perth and Kinross/Stirling* A mountain on the border between Perth and Kinross and Stirling Council areas, Meall Ghaordie rises to 1039 m (3409 ft) to the south of the Stronuich Reservoir between Glen Lochay and Glen Lyon.

Meall Glas *Stirling* A flat-topped mountain in the Breadalbane district of northwest Stirling Council area, Meall Glas rises to 959 m (3146 ft) northeast of Crianlarich.

Meall Gorm *Highland* A summit on the main Fannich ridge in Wester Ross, Meall Gorm rises to 949 m (3113 ft) to the north of Loch Fannich.

Meall Greigh *Perth and Kinross* A peak in central Perth and Kinross, Meall Greigh rises to 1001 m (3284 ft) to the northeast of Ben Lawers.

Meall Lighiche *Highland* A mountain in the Lochaber district of Highland Council area, Meall Lighiche rises to 772 m (2532 ft), 4 miles (6.5 km) southwest of Glen Coe, close to the border with Argyll and Bute.

Meall Meadhonach *Highland* A mountain in the Sutherland district of Highland Council area, Meall Meadhonach rises to 422 m (1384 ft), 3 miles (5 km) south of Durness.

Meall Mheinnidh *Highland* A mountain in Wester Ross, Meall Mheinnidh rises to 720 m (2362 ft), 2 miles (3 km) northwest of Letterewe on the eastern shore of Loch Maree.

Meall Mòr *Stirling* A mountain in northwest Stirling Council area, Meall Mòr rises to 747 m (2450 ft) a mile (1.5 km) to the north of the head of Loch Katrine.

Meall Mòr *Highland* A mountain in Easter Ross, Meall Mòr rises to 738 m (2421 ft) between Loch Morie and Loch Glass.

Meall Mòr *Highland* A summit in the Lochaber district of Highland Council area, Meall Mòr rises to 676 m (2217 ft) at the northwest end of Glen Coe, 3 miles (5 km) south of Glencoe village.

Meall na Faochaig *Highland* A mountain to the south of Strath Bran in the Ross and Cromarty district of Highland Council area, Meall na Faochaig rises to 680 m (2230 ft) a mile (1.5 km) north of Inverchoran and a mile (1.5 km) northeast of Loch Beannachan.

Meall na h-Aisre *Highland* A summit at the southwest end of the Monadhliath Mountains, Meall na h-Aisre rises to 862 m (2827 ft), 10 miles (16 km) southeast of Fort Augustus.

Meall na Leitreach *Perth and Kinross* A peak of Highland Perth and Kinross, Meall na Leitreach rises to 775 m (2542 ft) to the east of Loch Garry.

Meall na Teanga *Highland* A summit to the west of Loch Lochy in southern Highland Council area, Meall na Teanga rises to a height of 918 m (3012 ft).

Meall nam Gabhar *Highland* A small uninhabited island of the Summer Isles off the coast of Wester Ross, Meall nam Gabhar lies at the mouth of Loch Broom, to the north of Horse Island.

Meall nan Aighean *Highland* Meall nan Aighean (also known as Creag Mhòr) is one of four peaks in a range that forms a horseshoe-shaped ridge extending for 5.5 miles (9 km) from east to west on the north side of Glen Lyon in southern Highland.

Meall nan Caorach *Perth and Kinross* A summit in central Perth and Kinross, Meall nan Caorach rises to 623 m (2043 ft) between Strathbraan and Glen Almond, 9 miles (14 km) northeast of Crieff.

Meall nan Ceapraichean *Highland* A mountain in Wester Ross, Meall nan Ceapraichean rises to 977 m (3205 ft) to the southeast of Ullapool and north of Loch Glascarnoch.

Meall nan Damh *Highland* A summit on the Ardgour peninsula to the east of Loch Shiel, Meall nan Damh rises to 723 m (2371 ft) to the north of Cona Glen, 4 miles (6.5 km) south of Glenfinnan.

Meall nan Eagan *Highland* A mountain in the Badenoch district of Highland Council area, Meall nan Eagan rises to 656 m (2152 ft) 3 miles (5 km) northwest of Dalwhinnie.

Meall nan Eun *Argyll and Bute* A mountain at the northeast end of the Ben Starav ridge in Argyll and Bute, Meall nan Eun rises to 928 m (3045 ft) to the east of Loch Etive.

Meall nan Eun *Highland* A mountain in the Knoydart district of Highland Council area, Meall nan Eun rises to 666 m (2184 ft) between Glen Barrisdale and Loch Hourn.

Meall nan Subh *Perth and Kinross/Stirling* A mountain on the border between Perth and Kinross and Stirling council areas, Meall nan Subh rises to a height of 804 m (2637 ft) between Loch Lyon and Glen Lochay.

Meall nan Tarmachan *Perth and Kinross* A summit rising to 1044 m (3425 ft) to the north of Loch Tay in the Breadalbane district of Perth and Kinross, Meall nan Tarmachan is the tallest peak in the Tarmachan range.

Meall Odhar *Stirling* A peak in the Breadalbane district, northwest Stirling Council area, Meall Odhar rises to 656 m (2152 ft) to the south of Glen Lochy, 2 miles (3 km) west of Tyndrum.

Meall Onfhaidh *Highland* A mountain in the Lochaber district of southwest Highland Council area, Meall Onfhaidh rises to 681 m (2234 ft) between Loch Arkaig and Loch Eil, 6 miles (10 km) northwest of Corpach.

Meall Reamhar *Perth and Kinross* A mountain in central Perth and Kinross, Meall Reamhar rises to 620 m (2034 ft) 8 miles (13 km) northeast of Crieff. A summit of the same name rises to 506 m (1660 ft) 6 miles (10 km) to the north in the hills between Aberfeldy and Dunkeld.

Meall Tairbh *Argyll and Bute* A mountain in northeast Argyll and Bute, Meall Tairbh rises to 665 m (2182 ft) to the north of Glen Orchy, 3 miles (5 km) southwest of Bridge of Orchy.

Meall Tairneachan *Perth and Kinross* A mountain in central Perth and Kinross, Meall Tairneachan rises to 787 m (2582 ft) 3 miles (5 km) northwest of Aberfeldy.

Meall Uaine *Perth and Kinross* A mountain in the southern Grampians, Perth and Kinross, Meall Uaine rises to 794 m (2604 ft) 2 miles (3 km) south of Spittal of Glenshee.

Meallach Mhòr *Highland* A mountain in the Badenoch and Strathspey district of Highland Council area, Meallach Mhòr rises to 769 m (2522 ft), 6 miles (10 km) south of Kingussie.

Meallan Liath Coire Mhic Dhughaill *Highland* A mountain peak in the Reay Forest, northern Sutherland, Meallan Liath Coire Mhic Dhughaill rises to 801 m (2627 ft), 2 miles (3 km) northeast of Loch More. It derives its name from the Gaelic for 'little grey hill of McDougall's corrie'.

Meallan a' Chuail *Highland* A mountain in the Sutherland district of Highland Council area, Meallan a' Chuail rises steeply to 750 m (2460 ft) to the north of Loch Dubh a' Chuail, 2 miles (3 km) east of Beinn Leoid.

Meallan nan Uan *Highland* A summit to the south of Strath Bran in the Ross and Cromarty district of Highland Council area, Meallan nan Uan rises to 840 m (2755 ft) 3 miles (5 km) above Loch Beannachan. It derives its name from the Gaelic for 'little hill of the lambs'.

Mealt, Loch *Highland* A small loch near the east coast of the Trotternish peninsula at the north end of the isle of Skye in the Inner Hebrides, Loch Mealt lies 7 miles (11 km) east of Uig.

Mearnskirk *East Renfrewshire* A suburb of Newton Mearns in East Renfrewshire.

Meaul *Dumfries and Galloway* A summit at the northern end of the Rhinns of Kells in Dumfries and Galloway, Meaul rises to 695 m (2281 ft) to the south of Loch Doon, near the border with East Ayrshire.

Meavaig *Western Isles* A small settlement on the southwest coast of North Harris, Meavaig (Gael: *Miabhaig* or *Miabhag*) lies on a sea loch of the same name which forms an arm of West Loch Tarbert, 5 miles (8 km) northwest of Tarbert. Another Meavaig lies 7 miles (11 km) to the southeast.

Meavaig *Western Isles* A small settlement on the northeast coast of South Harris, Meavaig (Gael: *Miabhaig* or *Meabhag*) lies on the south coast of Loch Ceann Dibig, an embayment in East Loch Tarbert, 2.5 miles (4 km) south of Tarbert. Another Meavaig lies 7 miles (11 km) to the northwest.

Meavaig, Loch *Western Isles* A sea loch in the Outer Hebrides, Loch Meavaig (Gael: *Loch Mhiabaig*) forms an inlet on the north shore of West Loch Tarbert in North Harris. It receives the Meavaig River, which rises in a small loch to the north.

Medwin Water *South Lanarkshire/Scottish Borders* One of two rivers in South Lanarkshire by this name, the Medwin Water rises on the slopes of White Craig, a peak of the Pentland Hills. Flowing southwards, it forms the boundary between South Lanarkshire and Scottish Borders before turning west where, with the addition of other streams, it becomes the South Medwin River.

Medwin Water *South Lanarkshire* One of two rivers in South Lanarkshire by this name, the Medwin Water is formed at the confluence of the South Medwin River and North Medwin River. It flows west to join the River Clyde a mile (1.5 km) south of Carnwath.

Meet Hill *Aberdeenshire* A small conical hill in Buchan, Aberdeenshire, Meet Hill rises to a height of 55 m (181 ft) to the west of the small coastal fishing village of Burnhaven. Thought to have been a seat of justice in medieval times, the hill is topped by a tower built to celebrate the passing of the Reform Bill of 1832.

Meggat Water *Dumfries and Galloway* A stream in Eskdale, Dumfries and Galloway, the Meggat Water rises on the slopes of Loath Knowe, 3 miles (5 km) north east of Eskdalemuir. It flows southwards for 4 miles (6.5 km) to join the River Esk a mile (1.5 km) northwest of Bentpath.

Megget Reservoir *Scottish Borders* A reservoir in the Ettrick district of Scottish Borders, the Megget Reservoir lies on the course of the Megget Water, 2 miles (3 km) west of Cappercleuch and St Mary's Loch and 2 miles (3 km) east of Talla Reservoir.

Megget Water *Scottish Borders* A river in the Ettrick district of Scottish Borders, the Megget Water rises on Broad Law and flows southeast then northeast through the Megget Reservoir before emptying into St Mary's Loch to the south of Cappercleuch.

Megginch Castle *Perth and Kinross* A former stronghold of the Hay family dating from the 15th century, Megginch Castle lies in the Carse of Gowrie, 12 miles (19 km) east of Perth and 2 miles (3 km) north of Errol. Much extended in the 18th and 19th centuries, the building was used as a location in the 1994 film *Rob Roy*.

Meig, Loch *Highland* A reservoir of Easter Ross in Highland Council area, Loch Meig lies on the course of the River Meig, a mile (1.5 km) west of the confluence of the Meig and Conon rivers and a mile (1.5 km) south of the head of Loch Luichart.

Meigle *Perth and Kinross* A village in Strathmore, eastern Perth and Kinross, Meigle lies just south of the River Isla, 4 miles (6.5 km) southeast of Alyth. A collection of Pictish stones and cross-slabs which were found in the vicinity are now housed in Meigle Museum. Belmont Castle, previously owned by the British prime minister Sir Henry Campbell-Bannerman (1836–1908), is now run by the Church of Scotland as a retirement home. Campbell-Bannerman is buried in Meigle Parish Kirkyard.

Meikledale Burn *Dumfries and Galloway* A stream in Eskdale, Dumfries and Galloway, the Meikledale Burn flows south from its source to join the Ewes Water near Arkleton, 4 miles (6.5 km) north of Langholm.

Meikle Earnock *South Lanarkshire* A former village of Lanarkshire, Meikle Earnock is now a southern suburb of the town of Hamilton.

Meikle Kilmory *Argyll and Bute* A small village on the island of Bute, Meikle Kilmory lies 3 miles (5 km) southwest of Rothesay.

Meikle Kinord *Aberdeenshire* A locality in Deeside, Aberdeenshire, Meikle Kinord lies on the Muir of Dinnet by Loch Kinord, 4 miles (6.5 km) west of Aboyne.

Meikle Mackie *Aberdeenshire* A small island on the North Sea coast of Buchan, Aberdeenshire, Meikle Mackie is situated to the north of Buchan Ness, opposite the village of Boddam.

Meikle Millyea *Dumfries and Galloway* A hill rising to 746 m (2448 ft) in Dumfries and Galloway, Meikle Millyea lies at the southern end of the Rhinns of Kells, to the northwest of New Galloway.

Meikle Obney *Perth and Kinross* A locality in central Perth and Kinross, Meikle Obney lies on the eastern slopes of the Obney Hills, 2 miles (3 km) south of Dunkeld. Nearby are the farms of Nether and Upper Obney.

Meikle Ross *Dumfries and Galloway* A headland on the Solway Firth coast of Dumfries and Galloway, Meikle Ross lies at the western entrance to Kirkcudbright Bay and is separated from the island known as Little Ross by The Sound.

Meikle Says Law *East Lothian/Scottish Borders* The highest of the Lammermuir Hills, Meikle Says Law rises to 535 m (1755 ft) on the boundary between East Lothian and Scottish Borders, 5 miles (8 km) southeast of Gifford.

Meikle Wartle *Aberdeenshire* A hamlet in the

Formartine district of Aberdeenshire, Meikle Wartle lies just south of the A920 from Culsalmond to Oldmeldrum. Nearby is Warthill House and to the south is the Mill of Wartle.

Meikleour *Perth and Kinross* Located 5 miles (8 km) south of Blairgowrie, just to the north of the confluence of the Rivers Tay and Isla in Strathmore in Perth and Kinross, Meikleour is noted for its tall beech hedge which screens Meikleour House from the main road. The hedge was planted in 1746 and is now 26 m (85 ft) high and 0.3 mile (0.5 km) long. It is said the hedge grows towards the heavens because the men who planted it were killed at Culloden. Meikleour House itself was built by David Bryce in 1870, and is now owned by the Marquess of Lansdowne. The village, which was designated a burgh of barony in 1665, has an old market cross and coaching inn.

Mein Water *Dumfries and Galloway* A stream in Annandale, Dumfries and Galloway, the Mein Water rises in the hills to the east of Lockerbie. It flows southwards through Torbeckhill Reservoir near its source, turning southwest just north of Eaglesfield where it continues for 3 miles (5 km) before entering the River Annan at Meinfoot, a mile (1.5 km) to the north of Brydekirk.

Meith Bheinn *Highland* A mountain in South Morar, Meith Bheinn rises to 710 m (2329 ft) between Loch Beoraid and Loch Morar.

Melbost *Western Isles* A crofting township on the east coast of the Isle of Lewis in the Outer Hebrides, Melbost (Gael: *Mealabost*) lies 2.5 miles (4 km) east of Stornoway at the head of an isthmus connecting with the Eye peninsula. Stornoway Airport is located here.

Melbost Borve *Western Isles* A crofting township on the northwest coast of the Isle of Lewis in the Outer Hebrides, Melbost Borve (Gael: *Mealabost Bhuirgh*) lies a mile (1.5 km) north of Borve, midway between Barvas and the Butt of Lewis.

Melby, Holm of *Shetland* A small, uninhabited island of the Shetland Islands, the Holm of Melby lies in the Sound of Papa between the Ness of Melby and the island of Papa Stour.

Melby, Ness of *Shetland* A headland on the west coast of the Shetland Mainland, the Ness of Melby extends into the Sound of Papa to the northwest of the village of Melby. The island of Papa Stour lies opposite.

Meldrum *Stirling* A hamlet in Stirling Council area, Meldrum lies to the northwest of Blair Drummond, nearly 2 miles (3 km) south of Doune.

Melfort *Argyll and Bute* A small village of Argyll and Bute, Melfort lies at the head of Loch Melfort, a mile (1.5 km) northwest of Kilmelford.

Melfort, Loch *Argyll and Bute* An inlet on the coast of Argyll and Bute, Loch Melfort opens out towards the islands of Luing and Shuna to the west, 9 miles (14 km) southwest of Oban. The settlements of Melfort and Kilmelford lie at the head of the loch, and Arduaine Gardens lie on its southwestern shore. The loch provides shelter for yachts.

Melgam Water *Angus* A river of western Angus, formed of two parts, the Melgam Water is a continuation of the Back Water which issues from the Backwater Reservoir. It becomes the Melgam Water at Dykend and flows southeast to enter the Loch of Lintrathen after 2 miles (3 km). It leaves the loch and flows southeast through Bridgend of Lintrathen. It then turns south and finally southwest at Kenny, receiving the Cromie Burn. Three miles (5 km) after leaving the loch, the Melgam Water joins the River Isla near Airlie Castle. The Loups of Kenny are the best known of three sets of waterfalls on the lower stretch of this river.

Melgarve *Highland* A small settlement in the Badenoch district of southern Highland Council area, Melgarve lies on the upper reaches of the River Spey, to the east of the Corrieyairick Pass and 10 miles (17 km) northwest of Kinloch Laggan.

Melgund Castle *Angus* A castle in Strathmore, Angus, Melgund lies 4 miles (6.5 km) southwest of Brechin near the village of Aberlemno. It was built in 1543 by Cardinal David Beaton for his mistress, Marion Ogilvy.

Mell Head *Highland* A headland at the southwest end the island of Stroma in the Pentland Firth, Mell Head extends into the sea at the western end of the Inner Sound.

Mellerstain *Scottish Borders* A mansion house in the Berwickshire district of Scottish Borders, Mellerstain lies 7 miles (11 km) northwest of Kelso. The seat of the earls of Haddington, it has the external appearance of a fort and was built in two stages. William Adam was commissioned by George Baillie of Jerviswood and his wife Lady Grisel Baillie to build two wings in 1725. In 1770, his son Robert built the main block linking his father's wings. Mellerstain is particularly noted for its delicate plasterwork, which includes large Wedgewood-esque plaques portraying classical themes by Zucci. Mellerstain passed through marriage to the Hamiltons, who in 1858 acquired the title of Earl of Haddington. In 1909 the 11th Earl of Haddington commissioned Sir Reginald Blomfield to refine the landscaping of the policies.

Mellon Charles *Highland* A small settlement in Wester Ross, Mellon Charles lies on the northern shore of Loch Ewe, opposite the Isle of Ewe and 2 miles (3 km) northwest of Aultbea.

Mellon Udrigle *Highland* A small settlement in Wester Ross, Mellon Udrigle lies on the western shore of Gruinard Bay, 3 miles (5 km) southeast of Greenstone Point.

Melness *Highland* A linear crofting township on the north coast of Sutherland, Melness lies to the west of the Kyle of Tongue opposite Coldbackie. Settled by crofters moved from the township of Ribigill to the south of Tongue, many of its cottages are roofed with slate quarried at Talmine to the northwest.

Melowther Hill *East Renfrewshire* A hill in the Eaglesham Moors, East Renfrewshire, Melowther Hill rises to 301 m (987 ft) 2 miles (3 km) south of Eaglesham.

Melrose *Scottish Borders* A small town in the Roxburgh district of Scottish Borders, Melrose lies in the valley of the River Tweed, 3 miles (5 km) southeast of Galashiels and 37 miles (60 km) southeast of Edinburgh. A monastery established to the east at Old Melrose and associated with St Aidan, St Boswell and St Cuthbert was overshadowed by the founding of a Cistercian abbey at Melrose by David I in 1136. An offshoot of Rievaulx in Yorkshire, Melrose Abbey attained great wealth through trade in wool. Frequently damaged in cross-border raids, it was destroyed in 1385 but was rebuilt in the 15th century. Further damaged in 1544 and 1545 and abandoned after the Reformation, it was partially repaired in 1822 with assistance from Sir Walter Scott and the Duke of Buccleuch. A later duke gave the abbey to the nation in 1918. Alexander II is buried here, and it is alleged that the heart of Robert the Bruce lies buried beneath the abbey's high altar. The town of Melrose developed in association with the abbey and became a burgh of barony in 1605. Brewing, flour milling and the manufacture of woollens and linen continued until the late 18th century, and with the arrival of the railway in 1849 Melrose became a tourist resort. In addition to the impressive ruined abbey, buildings of interest include Darnick Tower (1425), the 15th-century Commendator's House and the Mercat Cross (1642). Priorwood Garden and Harmony Garden are owned by the National Trust for Scotland, and nearby Abbotsford House was built by Sir Walter Scott in 1817–24. The game of Rugby Sevens originated in Melrose.

Melsetter *Orkney* A small village on the south coast of the island of Hoy in the Orkney Islands, Melsetter lies at the head of North Bay, a mile (1.5 km) northeast of Tor Ness.

Melvaig *Highland* A small village on the coast of Wester Ross in Highland Council area, Melvaig lies 3 miles (5 km) south of the headland of Rubha Reidh to the west of Loch Ewe and 10 miles (16 km) northwest of Gairloch.

Melvich *Highland* A village of the north coast of Sutherland, Melvich lies near the mouth of the River Halladale where it enters Melvich Bay, 15 miles (24 km) west of Thurso.

Melville Castle *Midlothian* Melville Castle, situated a mile (1.5 km) northeast of Lasswade in Midlothian, was built between 1786 and 1791 by the architect James Playfair (1755–94) for Henry Dundas, Lord Melville (1742–1811), Scotland's virtual ruler in the late 18th and early 19th centuries. Visitors have included Queen Victoria and George IV. Once derelict, it has been renovated for use as a hotel.

Melville House *Fife* A large mansion house by Monimail on the edge of the Howe of Fife, Melville House lies 2.5 miles (4 km) north of Ladybank. Thought to have been built in 1697 by the architect James Smith for George, 1st Earl Melville, it incorporates the 14th-century Monimail Tower. The H-plan house, with its pioneering neo-Palladian facade, was regarded as the finest in Fife, and the surrounding designed landscape once included the longest avenue in Scotland. Since World War II, when it was used as a billet for Polish troops, it has variously served as a boys' school and a home for the handicapped.

Memsie *Aberdeenshire* A village of Buchan in Aberdeenshire, Memsie is situated at a crossroads 3 miles (5 km) southwest of Fraserburgh. To the east on Cairn Muir is the Bronze Age Cairn of Memsie, a round cairn dating from the 2nd millennium BC. Sand and gravel are excavated from the nearby Cairnmuir Quarry.

Memus *Angus* A hamlet in northern Angus, Memus lies on the White Burn 4 miles (6.5 km) northeast of Kirriemuir. To the east are the farms of West Memus and East Memus.

Men of Mey *Highland* Located in the Pentland Firth off the north coast of Caithness, the Men of Mey form a small group of offshore rocks 2 miles (3 km) northeast of Mey Bay and directly opposite the headland of St John's Point.

Mendick Hill *Scottish Borders* A summit of the Pentland Hills in Scottish Borders, Mendick Hill rises to 451 m (1469 ft), 2 miles (3km) southwest of West Linton.

Menie House *Aberdeenshire* A locality in eastern Aberdeenshire, Menie House is situated near the North Sea coast, 7 miles (11 km) north of Aberdeen. The Mill of Menie lies close by, and both house and mill are separated from the sea by Menie Links.

Mennock *Dumfries and Galloway* A village of Dumfries and Galloway, Mennock lies 2 miles (3 km) southeast of Sanquhar at the confluence of the Mennock Water and River Nith. Wanlockhead is 5 miles (8 km) to the northeast.

Mennock Water *Dumfries and Galloway* A stream in Dumfries and Galloway, the Mennock Water rises in the Lowther Hills near Wanlockhead. It flows 6 miles (10 km) southwestwards through the Mennock Pass to join the River Nith at Mennock.

Menstrie *Clackmannanshire* A Hillfoot village in Clackmannanshire, Menstrie is situated at the western end of the Ochil Hills between Alva and Blairlogie. The Menstrie Burn, which divides Dumyat from Myretoun Hill, falls down to meet the River Devon here. Sixteenth-century Menstrie Castle was the birthplace c.1567 of Sir William Alexander, 1st Earl of Stirling, who founded Nova Scotia in Canada, and General Sir Ralph Abercromby (1734–1801), who defeated the French at Aboukir Bay. Formerly a centre for the weaving of blankets and other woollens, the nearby Glenochil Distillery was founded in 1760. Today distilling and the manufacture of yeast products by United Distillers are the main industries.

Menteith, Lake of *Stirling* Located just south of the Highland Boundary Fault in Stirling Council area, the Lake of Menteith is the only natural expanse of water in Scotland usually to be called a lake. Known as the Loch of Menteith until the 19th century, its modern name may be a Victorian alteration reflecting its English parkland setting. The lake is drained southeastwards towards the River Forth by the Goodie Water, and on its northeast shore is the village of Port of Menteith. Its two principal islands are Inchmahome, on which stand the remains of an Augustinian priory built in 1238, and Inchtalla, a castle island of the former earls of Menteith. The lake, which is stocked with trout, is favoured for angling competitions, and in winter, when the ice is thick enough, it is the venue for traditional outdoor curling competitions or 'bonspiels'.

Menteith Hills *Stirling* A range of hills rising to 427 m (1289 ft) on the Highland Boundary Fault, the Menteith Hills extend northeastwards from Aberfoyle to Loch Venachar in the Trossachs district of Stirling Council area.

Meoble *Highland* A location in South Morar, Meoble lies on the east bank of the River Meoble, 3 miles (5 km) northeast of Lochailort. During World War II, Meoble Lodge was used as a training base by French agents of the Special Operation Executive before they returned home to perform acts of sabotage.

Meoble, River *Highland* A river of South Morar in Highland Council area, the River Meoble rises in Loch Beoraid and flows for 2 miles (3 km) northwest, passing Meoble Lodge before emptying into Loch Morar.

Merchant City *Glasgow City* An area of Glasgow city centre to the west of the old High Street, the Merchant City developed with the expansion of city trade in the

18th and early 19th centuries beyond the old trading communities at Saltmarket and Bridgegate. The initial expansion of the Merchant City as far west as Buchanan Street, the home of many merchants and tradesmen, although regular in layout, was unplanned. Warehouses, banks and public buildings emerged in an area that was to prosper until 1969, when the fruit market moved out of the city centre to purpose-built premises to the north. The subsequent decay of many of its fine buildings has been countered since the 1980s in an attempt to regenerate the area as a centre for businesses, shops, restaurants and residential properties.

Merchiston *City of Edinburgh* A residential district of southwest-central Edinburgh, Merchiston is centred on the early 15th-century Merchiston Castle, which now forms part of the campus of Napier University and was the birthplace of the mathematician John Napier (1550–1617), inventor of logarithms. In 1833 Charles Chalmers founded Merchiston Castle School, which moved to its present site at Colinton in 1924.

Merkadale *Highland* A small settlement on the isle of Skye in the Inner Hebrides, Merkadale lies on the southern shore of Loch Harport, 2 miles (3 km) southeast of Carbost.

Merrick *Dumfries and Galloway* A hill in Dumfries and Galloway, Merrick rises to 843 m (2764 ft) in the Rhinns of Kells. The highest hill in the Southern Uplands, it is one of five summits in the so-called Range of the Awful Hand, a group of peaks that form the shape of a hand in the heart of the Galloway Forest Park. On the southeast face of Merrick is a rocky outcrop in the shape of a man's face known as the Grey Man of Merrick.

Merse *Dumfries and Galloway* An area of marshy wetland in Dumfries and Galloway, the Merse lies on the north coast of the Solway Firth, to the east of the mouth of the River Nith. Caerlaverock Castle and the settlement of Blackshaw lie to the north.

Merse *Scottish Borders* A low-lying area in the Berwickshire district of Scottish Borders, the Merse lies between the Lammermuir Hills to the north and the River Tweed on the English border. Centred on the town of Duns, the Merse lands or March lands formed an ancient earldom on the eastern march or border with England. Its chief town in medieval times was Berwick-upon-Tweed.

Merton Hall *Dumfries and Galloway* A house and estate in the northern Machars of Dumfries and Galloway, Merton Hall lies 2 miles (3 km) west of Newton Stewart. The house dates from 1767.

Methil *Fife* A town on the south coast of Fife, Methil lies on the Firth of Forth to the west of the mouth of the River Leven between Buckhaven and Leven. It forms the core of the industrial communities of Leven, Innerleven, Kirkland, Aberhill, Methilhill, Denbeath, Muiredge and Buckhaven, and owes its modern development to the docks that were established in the 1870s for the export of Fife coal. Lower Methil Heritage Centre (1995) features a changing programme of exhibitions focusing on the town's local industrial history. In addition to its three docks, Methil is the site of a coal slurry-fired power station built in 1965 and an industrial estate with industries producing machinery, clothing, bricks, plastic piping, animal feed and fertilisers.

Methilhill *Fife* A community at the western edge of the Buckhaven–Methil–Leven urban area in southern Fife, Methilhill is situated between Methil and the River Leven. It has a primary school, bowling green and community centre.

Methlick *Aberdeenshire* A commuter village in an Aberdeenshire parish of the same name, Methlick lies on the River Ythan, 6 miles (10 km) northwest of Ellon. The solo percussion player Evelyn Glennie was born in the village in 1966. To the southeast of Methlick is Haddo House, which was designed for the 2nd Earl of Aberdeen by William Adam in 1732, and has been managed by the National Trust for Scotland since 1979. The adjacent Haddo Country Park, run by Aberdeenshire Council, was also opened in 1979.

Methven *Perth and Kinross* A village in central Perth and Kinross, Methven is situated between the River Almond and the Pow Water, 5 miles (8 km) west of Perth. A collegiate church, of which only a fragment remains, was founded here in 1433 by Walter Stewart, Earl of Atholl, and in the churchyard is a magnificent mausoleum built in the form of a Greek temple to a design by James Playfair in 1793. Nearby is the restored Methven Castle, where Margaret, widow of James IV, died in 1540. The village, which largely comprises a single main street, developed in the 19th century as a jute- and linen-manufacturing settlement and a railway junction.

Mey *Highland* A village on the north coast of Caithness, Mey lies 6 miles (10 km) west of John o' Groats and a half-mile (1 km) southeast of the Loch of Mey. From the 1850s local flagstone was exported from its pier. The Castle of Mey, a former home of the earls of Caithness and of Queen Elizabeth the Queen Mother (1900–2002), lies a mile (1.5 km) to the northeast overlooking Mey Bay, an inlet of the Pentland Firth.

Mhoicean, Loch *Highland* A small loch in the Lochalsh district of Highland Council area, Loch Mhoicean lies to the east of the Killilan Forest, between the peaks of Aonach Buidhe and An Socach, 2 miles (3 km) northwest of Loch Mullardoch.

Mhòr, Loch *Highland* A reservoir to the east of the Great Glen, Loch Mhòr lies 2 miles (3 km) east of Loch Ness above Foyers. It was created in 1896 by the British Aluminium Company, which joined two small lochs to form a source of water for its hydro-electric power plant at Foyers. Loch Mhòr is now the upper reservoir of the Foyers Hydro-Electric Power Scheme which is primarily a pumped-storage scheme. In 1973, while the water level was lowered to permit reconstruction, a crannog, or ancient loch dwelling, was discovered in Loch Mhòr.

Mhuilinn, Loch a' *Highland* A small loch in central Caithness, Loch a' Mhuilinn lies 2 miles (3 km) southeast of Altnabreac Station. A run-off stream from the loch feeds the upper reaches of the River Thurso.

Mhuillidh, Loch a' *Highland* A small loch in Glen Strathfarrar in the Inverness district of Highland Council area, Loch a' Mhuillidh lies on the course of the River Farrar, 4 miles (6.5 km) downriver from Loch Monar and immediately to the west of Loch Beannacharain.

Miabhaig The Gaelic name for Meavaig in the Western Isles.

Miabhaig, Loch The Gaelic name for Loch Meavaig in North Harris in the Western Isles.

Miavaig *Western Isles* A small settlement in the far west of the Isle of Lewis in the Outer Hebrides, Miavaig (Gael:

Miabhaig or *Miabhig*) lies at the eastern end of Glen Valtos, on the shore of West Loch Roag, 2 miles (3 km) east of Timsgarry.

Mid Burn *Dumfries and Galloway* A headstream of the Big Water of Fleet in Dumfries and Galloway, the Mid Burn rises on the eastern slopes of Cairnsmore of Fleet.

Mid Calder *West Lothian* A settlement in West Lothian, Mid Calder lies on the left bank of the River Calder, a mile (1.5 km) southeast of Livingston and 12 miles (19 km) west of Edinburgh. Until 1974 it lay in Midlothian. Larger than the settlements of West Calder and East Calder, Mid Calder developed in the 18th century as a service centre at the junction of five roads, and from the 1860s until the 1930s in association with the production of shale oil. Overshadowed by the new town of Livingston, Mid Calder is now a residential conservation village with notable buildings including the 16th-century Kirk of Calder (St John's Parish Church) and 16th-century Calder House, the former seat of the Sandilands family, later the Lords Torphichen, from 1350. In 1556, John Knox celebrated communion according to Presbyterian rites for the first time at Calder House. The Almondell and Calderwood Country Park extends along the Linhouse Water to the southeast of Mid Calder.

Mid Clyth *Highland* A former fishing village close to the east coast of Caithness, Mid Clyth lies 2 miles (3 km) northeast of Lybster and 9 miles (14 km) southwest of Wick. Barytes was mined nearby during World War I, and a mile (1.5 km) to the northeast are the prehistoric standing stones at the Hill o' Many Stanes.

Mid Yell *Shetland* The chief settlement of the island of Yell in the Shetland Islands, Mid Yell lies to the south of Mid Yell Voe (formerly Reafirth) at the centre of the island. Now an active fishing port, it has two fish factories, a leisure centre and a boating club. There is access by road to Ulsta at the southern tip of the island, which has a ferry link with Mainland Shetland.

Middle Bank *Dumfries and Galloway* A sandbank in the Solway Firth, Dumfries and Galloway, the Middle Bank lies near the head of the firth opposite the mouth of the Lochar Water.

Middle Kames *Argyll and Bute* A settlement in Argyll and Bute, Middle Kames lies on the west shore of Loch Fyne, 3 miles (5 km) northeast of Lochgilphead.

Middlebie *Dumfries and Galloway* A hamlet in Dumfries and Galloway, Middlebie lies on the Middlebie Burn, nearly 2 miles (3 km) east of Ecclefechan. Immediately south of Middlebie, on the banks of the Mein Water, are the remains of Birrens Roman Fort.

Middlebie Burn *Dumfries and Galloway* A stream in Annandale, Dumfries and Galloway, Middlebie Burn rises to the east of Burnswark Hill to the north of Ecclefechan. It flows south through Purdomstone Reservoir and the hamlet of Middlebie to join the Mein Water.

Middlefield Law *East Ayrshire* A hill in East Ayrshire, Middlefield Law rises to 466 m (1528 ft) 2 miles (3 km) north of Muirkirk.

Middlequarter *Western Isles* A small settlement overlooking Vallay Strand on the north coast of North Uist in the Outer Hebrides, Middlequarter (Gael: *Ceathramh Meadhanach*) is located between Malaclate and Sollas, 7.5 miles (12 km) northwest of Lochmaddy.

Middleshaw *Dumfries and Galloway* A locality in Annandale, Dumfries and Galloway, Middleshaw lies to the east of the Water of Milk, 4 miles (6.5 km) south of Lockerbie.

Middleton *Argyll and Bute* A small settlement on the west side of the island of Tiree in the Inner Hebrides, Middleton lies 2 miles (3 km) southeast of the headland of Rubha Chraiginis.

Middleton *Midlothian* A small village in Midlothian, Middleton lies in the northern foothills of the Moorfoot Hills, 2.5 miles (4 km) southeast of Gorebridge and 1.25 miles (2 km) southwest of Borthwick. The early 18th-century Middleton Hall lies in a parkland estate immediately to the east. The village of North Middleton lies on the A7 a half-mile (1 km) to the north.

Middleton *Perth and Kinross* A small settlement in Perth and Kinross, Middleton lies a mile (1.5 km) to the north of Milnathort on the southern edge of the Ochil Hills.

Middleyard *East Ayrshire* A small settlement in East Ayrshire, Middleyard lies on the B7037, 3 miles (5 km) south of Galston.

Midhowe *Orkney* The site of an enormous prehistoric chambered cairn and a later Iron Age broch on the west coast of Rousay in the Orkney Islands. Excavated between 1930 and 1933 by W. G. Grant, the chambered tomb measures 32.5 m (107 ft) long by 13 m (43 ft) wide. The broch, which survives to a height of 4.3 m (14 ft), may be one of the oldest in the Orkney Islands.

Midland Ness *Orkney* A headland on the south coast of the Orkney Mainland, Midland Ness extends into the Bring Deeps, which separates the Mainland from Hoy to the southwest.

Midland Valley One of the three main physiographic divisions of Scotland, the Midland Valley lies between the Highlands and the Southern Uplands. It is separated from the former by the Highland Boundary Fault and the latter by the Southern Uplands Fault. The Midland Valley represents an immense block of the earth's crust which descended more than 4000 m (13,123 ft) between the Late Silurian and Carboniferous periods (410 and 320 million years ago). Geologically the valley is filled with sedimentary rocks, primarily Old Red Sandstone which was deposited under desert conditions contemporaneously as the valley descended and Carboniferous sediments and coal measures were deposited in coastal or shallow marine conditions. The volcanoes and volcanic intrusions from Carboniferous times have pushed through the sediments, surviving in the form of steep volcanic plugs such as Abbey Craig northeast of Stirling, Castle Rock in Edinburgh and North Berwick Law. Fertile soils ensure that the Midland Valley includes much of Scotland's prime agricultural land, for example Strathmore, the Mearns, East Lothian, the Forth and Clyde Valleys and Ayrshire. Eighty per cent of Scotland's population, and much of its industry, lies in the Midland Valley.

Midlem *Scottish Borders* A small village in the Roxburgh district of Scottish Borders, Midlem lies to the north of the Langhope Burn, 4 miles (6.5 km) southeast of Selkirk.

Midlock Water *South Lanarkshire* A river of South Lanarkshire, the Midlock Water rises on Clyde Law near the border with Scottish Borders and flows just over 5 miles (8 km) northwest into the River Clyde near Crawford.

Midlothian *Area: 355 sq. km (137 sq. miles)* Situated in the east-central Lowlands between Edinburgh and Scottish Borders, landlocked Midlothian lies to the east of the Pentland Hills and north of the Moorfoot Hills. Once heavily dependent on coal mining, the region is now a centre of light industry and residential development within commuting distance of Edinburgh. Its main settlements are Dalkeith (administrative centre), Bonnyrigg, Loanhead, Lasswade, Penicuik and Newtongrange, and its principal rivers are the North Esk and South Esk. Of the total area of Midlothian, 61 per cent is open countryside containing fertile farmland, woodland, and reservoirs feeding water to the city of Edinburgh. Also known as Edinburghshire, the former county of Midlothian was incorporated as a district of Lothian Region from 1974 to 1996, prior to it regaining unitary authority status. Places of interest include Rosslyn Chapel, Dalkeith Palace, Borthwick Castle, Crichton Castle, the Scottish Mining Museum at Newtongrange and Newbattle Abbey, which was originally founded by David I in 1140. Coal, which was extracted by the monks of Newbattle as early as the 13th century, was mined extensively in the 19th and 20th centuries. The quarrying of limestone, heavy engineering and the manufacture of gunpowder, carpets and paper have largely been replaced by modern glass-making, light-engineering and research industries. Europe's longest artificial ski slope was established at the Hillend Ski Centre on the northern edge of the Pentland Hills Regional Park. Sir Walter Scott (1771–1832) lived near Lasswade for several years, and the writer Thomas De Quincey lived in nearby Polton for almost 20 years before his death in 1859.

Midmar *Aberdeenshire* Located to the north of the Hill of Fare, 3 miles (5 km) west of Echt in Aberdeenshire, the agricultural parish of Midmar comprises Midmar Forest, Midmar Moss, 16th-century Midmar Castle and Midmar Kirk. In the graveyard of the church is a stone circle dating from the 3rd millennium BC.

Midpark *Argyll and Bute* The principal settlement of the island of Inchmarnock in Argyll and Bute, Midpark lies on the island's eastern coastline 4 miles (6.5 km) southwest of Rothesay on the island of Bute.

Midtown *Highland* A settlement in Caithness, Midtown lies close to Melvich on the western shore of the Kyle of Tongue, an inlet of the northern coast. Coldbackie lies 2 miles (3 km) southeast across the inlet.

Migdale, Loch *Highland* A small loch in southeast Sutherland, Loch Migdale lies a mile (1.5 km) east of Bonar Bridge.

Migvie *Aberdeenshire* A hamlet in the Cromar district of Aberdeenshire, Migvie lies 3 miles (5 km) northwest of Tarland and 8 miles (13 km) northwest of Aboyne. Nearby are the ruins of Migvie Castle, a stronghold of the Fraser family, and in the churchyard stands a 9th-century Pictish cross-slab known as the Migvie Stone.

Milesmark *Fife* A former mining village of western Fife, Milesmark is situated 2 miles (3 km) northwest of Dunfermline on the A907 to Alloa. It lies immediately

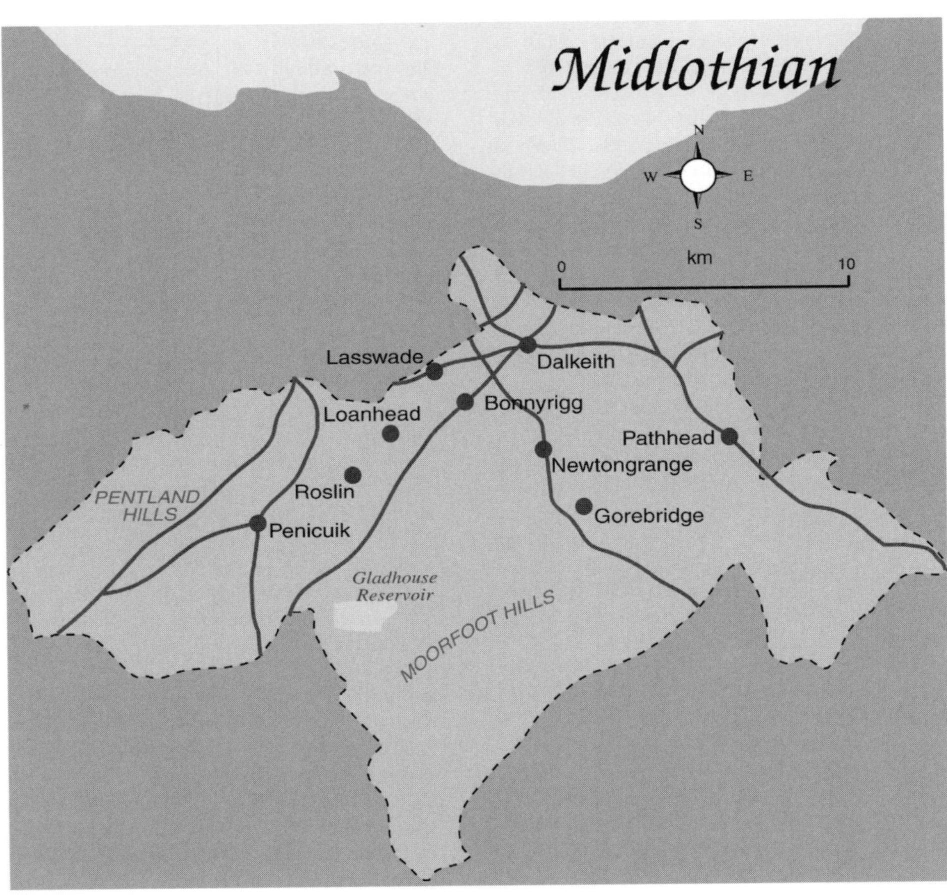

east of Parkneuk and adjacent to the former Elgin Colliery.

Milk, Water of *Dumfries and Galloway* A river of Annandale in Dumfries and Galloway, the Water of Milk rises in hills to the south of Castle O'er Forest. It flows generally southwest to join the River Annan 3 miles (5 km) west of Ecclefechan. Its chief tributary is the Corrie Water.

Mill Bay *Orkney* A wide and sandy bay on the east coast of the island of Stronsay in the Orkney Islands, Mill Bay extends south from Grice Ness to Odness.

Mill Burn *South Lanarkshire* A stream in South Lanarkshire, Mill Burn rises on Wildshaw Hill and flows southeast under the M74 to join the Duneaton Water, 2 miles (3 km) northwest of Abington.

Mill Loch *Dumfries and Galloway* A small loch in Annandale, Dumfries and Galloway, the Mill Loch lies adjacent to the northwest corner of Lochmaben.

Mill of Drummond *Perth and Kinross* A locality in Perth and Kinross, Mill of Drummond lies on the Machany Water, 2 miles (3 km) to the west of Muthill.

Mill of Fortune *Perth and Kinross* A locality near the mouth of Glen Artney, Perth and Kinross, Mill of Fortune lies to the south of the River Earn, just over a mile (1.5 km) to the southeast of Comrie.

Millarston *Renfrewshire* Millarston is a western suburb of the town of Paisley in Renfrewshire.

Millerhill *Midlothian* A settlement in Midlothian, Millerhill lies a mile (1.5 km) north of Dalkeith and 2 miles (3 km) east of Liberton. The Millerhill Freight Depot to the north primarily services coal trains at the junction with a former main line south to Scottish Borders.

Millerston *Glasgow City* A northern residential suburb of the city of Glasgow, Millerston lies between Provan and Springburn, to the north of Hogganfield Loch and the M8. The Tower is a 19th-century reproduction of a 17th-century tower house.

Milleur Point *Dumfries and Galloway* A headland at the northern tip of the Rhinns of Galloway, Milleur Point extends into the sea on the west side of the mouth of Loch Ryan, 9 miles (14 km) north of Stranraer.

Millfire *Dumfries and Galloway* A mountain rising to a height of 716 m (2349 ft) in Dumfries and Galloway, Millfire lies at the centre of the Rhinns of Kells to the northwest of New Galloway.

Millfore *Dumfries and Galloway* A mountain in Dumfries and Galloway, Millfore rises to 656 m (2146 ft) in Galloway Forest Park, 7 miles (11 km) northeast of Newton Stewart.

Millheugh *South Lanarkshire* Millheugh is a western suburb of the settlement of Larkhall in South Lanarkshire.

Millhouse *Argyll and Bute* A settlement on the Cowal peninsula between Loch Fyne and the Kyles of Bute, Millhouse lies due east of Asgog Loch and 3 miles (5 km) southwest of Tighnabruaich.

Millhousebridge *Dumfries and Galloway* A village of Annandale in Dumfries and Galloway, Millhousebridge lies on the River Annan, 4 miles (6.5 km) northwest of Lockerbie.

Millikenpark *Renfrewshire* Millikenpark is a southwestern suburb of Johnstone in Renfrewshire.

Millport *North Ayrshire* A resort town on the south coast of the island of Great Cumbrae in the Firth of Clyde, Millport is the only settlement of any size in the isles of Cumbrae. It developed from the former settlements of Kirkton and Kames in the 18th century after the building in 1745 of a barracks known as The Garrison commanding the approaches to the Firth of Clyde. From the 1830s Millport expanded in association with the steamer trade bringing tourists. The Episcopal Cathedral of Argyll and the Isles, built in 1849 and consecrated in 1876, is said to be the smallest cathedral in Europe. The Keppel Pier (1888) near the Marine Biological Station was the scene of the official welcome home in July 1904 of the SY *Scotia*, the research ship of the Scottish National Antarctic Expedition.

Milltimber *Aberdeen City* A village in the Aberdeen City parish of Peterculter, Milltimber lies on the A93 Deeside road, 6 miles (10 km) southwest of Aberdeen. It developed in the 19th century in association with a station on the Deeside railway.

Milltown *Dumfries and Galloway* A small settlement of Dumfries and Galloway, Milltown lies on the River Sark, 2 miles (3 km) north of the English border and 4 miles (6.5 km) west of Canonbie.

Milltown of Auchindoun *Moray* A hamlet in Moray, Milltown of Auchindoun lies on the River Fiddich, 2 miles (3 km) east of Dufftown. Nearby are the ruins of the 15th-century Gordon stronghold of Auchindoun Castle, which was destroyed in 1592 to avenge the murder of the Bonnie Earl of Moray. The old mill was the site of illicit whisky distilling until the first decade of the 20th century.

Milltown of Edinvillie *Moray* A scattered rural community in Moray, Milltown of Edinvillie, or 'the Milltown', lies on the Lour Burn, 2 miles (3 km) south of Aberlour. The ruins of an old mill lie on the Lour Burn and the focal points of the village are its primary school and community hall. Agriculture, building contractors and the Benrinnes and Glenallachie distilleries offer employment in the area.

Milltown of Rothiemay *Moray/Aberdeenshire* A granite-built village on the border of Moray and Aberdeenshire, Milltown of Rothiemay (or Rothiemay) lies on the River Deveron 5 miles (8 km) north of Huntly. The noted 17th-century cartographer John Gordon officiated in St Dunstan's Church, which was replaced in 1807 by a plain whinstone kirk. Rothiemay Castle once stood to the east and a kiln barn is thought to have been associated with whisky distilling in the 17th century. A bridge across the Deveron designed by John Willet was built in 1872, and an earlier bridge known as Queen Mary's Bridge dates from the mid-16th century.

Milnathort *Perth and Kinross* A village in the Kinross part of Perth and Kinross, Milnathort is situated at the foot of the Ochil Hills a mile (1.5 km) north of the burgh town of Kinross. Formerly a market town associated with nearby Burleigh Castle, once the stronghold of the Balfours of Burleigh, its meal mill was driven by water from the Fochy Burn. Nineteenth-century woollen and spinning mills were established to the south of the village centre on the North Queich, a development that resulted in the settlement extending southwards. The settlement is situated at a crossroads and its form is closely linked to the development of turnpike roads in the early 19th century. The churchyard of the Parish Church of Orwell, which was moved from its original site by Loch Leven in

1729, is the burial place of the Secession minister the Revd Thomas Mair, whose epitaph is in the form of an acrostic. The poet Walter Chalmers Smith was Free Church minister from 1853 to 1858 and another poet, James Logie Robertson (Hugh Haliburton), was born here in 1846. Now largely a residential settlement, Milnathort has a golf course and computer, craft, trailer-manufacture and agricultural-service trades.

Milngavie *East Dunbartonshire* A dormitory town in the Strathkelvin district of west-central Scotland, Milngavie (pronounced 'mil-guy') lies near the confluence of the Allander Water with the River Kelvin, 7 miles (11 km) northwest of Glasgow city centre. It developed at a river crossing and road junction in association with textile mills and, following the arrival of the railway in 1863, expanded as a residential settlement. Milngavie lies at the southern end of the West Highland Way and nearby are Bardowie Loch, Bardowie Castle, Tannoch Loch, Mugdock Country Park and Mugdock and Craigmaddie reservoirs.

Milovaig *Highland* A township on the isle of Skye in the Inner Hebrides, Milovaig lies on the west coast of Loch Pooltiel, 6 miles (10 km) west of Dunvegan.

Milton An alternative name for Garryvaltos in the Western Isles.

Milton *Dumfries and Galloway* A small village of Dumfries and Galloway, Milton lies adjacent to the Milton Loch, 2 miles (3 km) southeast of Crocketford.

Milton *Dumfries and Galloway* A small settlement of Dumfries and Galloway, Milton lies 2 miles (3 km) southeast of Glenluce.

Milton *Highland* A small dormitory settlement in Easter Ross, Milton lies to the north of Nigg Bay, 4 miles (6.5 km) northeast of Invergordon. The village, bypassed by the A9 in 1991, developed in the 1970s in association with aluminium smelting at Invergordon and North Sea oil-related industries.

Milton *Moray* The scattered settlement of Milton is located 3 miles (5 km) south of Cullen in Moray. The Burn of Deskford passes through the settlement as it flows north to join the Moray Firth.

Milton *Stirling* A village in the Trossachs district of Stirling Council area, Milton lies on the upper reaches of the River Forth near the eastern end of Loch Ard, a mile (1.5 km) to the west of Aberfoyle. The derelict Milton Mill, with its 4-m (14-ft) cast-iron wheel, dates from 1667.

Milton *West Dunbartonshire* A village of West Dunbartonshire, Milton lies between the Kilpatrick Hills and the Firth of Clyde, 2 miles (3 km) east of Dumbarton.

Milton Bridge *Midlothian* A small village in Midlothian, Milton Bridge lies on the Glencorse Burn, 2 miles (3 km) northeast of Penicuik. The village developed in the 19th century in association with paper mills and the Glencorse Barracks, an army training depot.

Milton Loch *Dumfries and Galloway* A small loch in Dumfries and Galloway, Milton Loch lies just south of the village of Crocketford, 8 miles (13 km) southwest of Dumfries.

Milton Morenish *Perth and Kinross* A locality on the north side of Loch Tay, in the Breadalbane district of Perth and Kinross, Milton Morenish lies 2 miles (3 km) northeast of Killin.

Milton Ness *Aberdeenshire* A headland on the North Sea coast of southeast Aberdeenshire, Milton Ness extends into the sea midway between the mouth of the River North Esk and the village of Johnshaven.

Milton of Abercairny *Perth and Kinross* A locality in central Perth and Kinross, Milton of Abercairny lies on the A85 from Perth to Crieff, 3 miles (5 km) northeast of Crieff.

Milton of Auchinhove *Aberdeenshire* A hamlet in the Cromar district of Aberdeenshire, Milton of Auchinhove lies to the west of the Peel of Lumphanan and to the south of Corse Hill, 1.5 miles (2 km) southeast of Corsehill.

Milton of Balgonie *Fife* A village in south-central Fife, Milton of Balgonie lies on the north bank of the River Leven, 2 miles (3 km) southeast of Markinch. It grew up as a riverside mill town near Balgonie Castle, its population in the 18th and 19th centuries engaging in coal mining, weaving, spinning and brick making. In addition to a meal mill and two spinning mills, a flax mill employing 265 people in 1841 operated from 1806 to 1885. There is a Miners' Institute (1926), a primary school (1823), a church (1836) and a playing field. To the south of the river lie the foundations of Balfour House, the birthplace of Cardinal James Beaton and of Mary Beaton, one of the 'Four Maries' who were ladies-in-waiting to Mary, Queen of Scots.

Milton of Buchanan *Stirling* A locality in Stirling Council area, Milton of Buchanan lies to the northwest of Buchanan Castle, 2 miles (3 km) northwest of Drymen and a mile (1.5 km) to the east of the southeast corner of Loch Lomond.

Milton of Campsie *East Dunbartonshire* A dormitory village in East Dunbartonshire, Milton of Campsie lies on the Glazert Water at the foot of the Campsie Fells, 2 miles (3 km) north of Kirkintilloch and 9 miles (14 km) north of Glasgow. A former milltown settlement, it developed in the late 18th and early 19th centuries in association with a printworks. An infectious-diseases hospital was erected in the early 1950s, and watches were assembled in Milton of Campsie until the mid-1980s.

Milton of Carmyllie An alternative name for Carmyllie in Angus.

Milton of Clova An alternative name for Clova in Angus.

Milton of Cushnie *Aberdeenshire* A hamlet on the Cushnie Burn in Aberdeenshire, Milton of Cushnie lies in the Howe of Alford, 6 miles (10 km) southwest of Alford.

Milton of Dalcapon *Perth and Kinross* A hamlet in Perth and Kinross, Milton of Dalcapon is situated on the Lochbroom Burn near its junction with the River Tay, 2 miles (3 km) north of Ballinluig.

Milton of Finavon *Angus* A hamlet in Angus, Milton of Finavon lies just south of the River South Esk, 4 miles (6.5 km) northeast of Forfar. A hillfort to the southeast dates from the mid-1st millennium BC and a ruined castle nearby was the chief stronghold of the Lindsay earls of Crawford. Near the road from Milton of Finavon to Oathlaw is the Finavon Dovecote, which is believed to be the largest double-chambered lectern-style dovecote in Scotland.

Milton of Leys *Highland* A dormitory village overlooking the Moray Firth, Milton of Leys lies on high ground 3 miles (5 km) southeast of Inverness. It has developed largely since the 1990s as a residential settlement.

Milton of Murtle *Aberdeen City* A village in the Aberdeen City parish of Peterculter, Milton of Murtle lies between Bieldside and Milltimber on the A93 Deeside road, 5 miles (8 km) southwest of Aberdeen. The Murtle Burn joins the River Dee near here.

Milton of Ogilvie *Angus* A hamlet of central Angus, Milton of Ogilvie lies in Glen Ogilvie, 2 miles (3 km) south of Glamis. The Glen Ogilvie Burn flows through the settlement.

Miltonise *Dumfries and Galloway* A locality in western Dumfries and Galloway, Miltonise (or Miltonish) lies in the Galloway Hills on the Cross Water of Luce, 5 miles (8 km) north of New Luce.

Minard *Argyll and Bute* A small village in Argyll and Bute, Minard lies on the western shore of Loch Fyne, 4 miles (6.5 km) southwest of Furnace. Minard Castle lies a mile (1.5 km) to the south. Granite stone setts and road chippings were quarried locally. Crarae Gardens lie a mile (1.5 km) to the northeast.

Minch, the A wide body of water off the northwest coast of Scotland, the Minch (or North Minch) lies between the mainland and the northern end of the Outer Hebrides and is 22–45 miles (35–72 km) wide. The Little Minch to the southwest separates the isle of Skye in the Inner Hebrides from the middle part of the Outer Hebrides and is 14–20 miles (22–32 km) wide.

Minch Moor *Scottish Borders* A hill in Scottish Borders, Minch Moor rises to 567 m (1860 ft) in the Elibank and Traquair Forest, 2 miles (3 km) southeast of Innerleithen.

Mingarry *Western Isles* A small crofting settlement on South Uist in the Outer Hebrides, Mingarry (Gael: *Minngearraidh*) lies to the east of the A865 opposite Garryvaltos and a mile (1.5 km) south of Kildonan. The birthplace of Jacobite heroine Flora Macdonald lies a quarter-mile (0.5 km) to the northwest.

Minginish *Highland* An area of central Skye in the Inner Hebrides, Minginish extends south fom Loch Harport and west of the River Sligachan, including the high peaks of the Cuillin Hills.

Mingulay *Western Isles* Once owned by the MacNeils of Barra, the island of Mingulay (Gael: *Miughalaigh*) is the largest of the small group of islands in the Outer Hebrides known as the Bishop's Isles. It measures 2.5 miles (4 km) by 1.5 miles (2.5 km), has an area of 640 ha (1581 acres) and takes its name from the Norse for a 'big island'. Largely comprising gneiss rock, the island has impressive rock stacks and cliffs rising to over 150 m (492 ft). At Gunamul on the southwest coast there is a huge natural arch. Mingulay has a long history of settlement, with many archaeological sites in evidence, but its population rapidly declined from a total of 140 inhabitants in 1901 to two in the 1930s. Two buildings still stand: the Schoolhouse, which was built in the 1880s by the Free Church Ladies' Association and later used as a sheep farmer's bothy; and the Chapel House, a Catholic priest's house built in 1898. An important breeding ground for sea birds such as kittiwakes and guillemots, Mingulay is grazed by some 500 sheep throughout the year. The island's chief landing place and anchorage is on the east coast in Mingulay Bay. Composed in 1938 by Hugh Roberton for his Glasgow Orpheus Choir, the haunting *Mingulay Boat Song* was never sung by the island's inhabitants.

Mingulay, Sound of *Western Isles* A channel in the Outer Hebrides, the Sound of Mingulay separates the island of Mingulay from Pabbay to the northeast.

Minishant *South Ayrshire* A small village in the Carrick district of South Ayrshire, Minishant lies to the west of the River Doon and the village of Dalrymple, 3 miles (5 km) northeast of Maybole. Once a granary for the monks at Crossraguel Abbey to the southwest of Maybole, it was later an important wool-production centre with a waulk mill that is now a village hall.

Minngearraidh The Gaelic name for Mingarry in the Western Isles.

Minnigaff *Dumfries and Galloway* A village of Dumfries and Galloway, Minnigaff lies on the east side of the River Cree opposite Newton Stewart. The Penkiln Burn joins the Cree here. Before the development of Newton Stewart, Minnigaff was a prominent market centre. Cumloden House to the north was built in 1875 for Sir William Stewart and became a summer retreat for the earls of Galloway, and to the east in the grounds of Kirroughtree House Hotel (1719) stand an icehouse and an octagonal dovecote. The Wood of Cree Reserve to the east is one of southern Scotland's largest remaining ancient broad-leaved woodlands.

Minnoch, Loch *Dumfries and Galloway* A small loch on the eastern slopes of the Rhinns of Kells in Dumfries and Galloway, Loch Minnoch lies between Loch Harrow and Loch Dungeon, 7 miles (11 km) northwest of St John's Town of Dalry. It is the source of the Mid Burn which flows east and northeast to join the Polharrow Burn.

Minnoch, Water of *South Ayrshire/Dumfries and Galloway* A river of southwest Scotland, the Water of Minnoch rises in Carrick Forest, South Ayrshire. It flows southwards into the Galloway Forest Park, Dumfries and Galloway, before joining the River Cree, 5 miles (8 km) north of Newton Stewart. Its chief tributaries are the Shalloch Burn, Kirriemore Burn and Water of Trool.

Mintlaw *Aberdeenshire* A dormitory village of Buchan in Aberdeenshire, Mintlaw lies in the valley of the South Ugie Water, 8 miles (13 km) west of Peterhead. It was laid out at a road junction in 1810 by James Ferguson of Pitfour and further expanded after the arrival of the railway in 1861. The settlement expanded rapidly as a commuter settlement in the 1970s in association with North Sea oil-related industries. In addition to Mintlaw Academy, which dates from the late 1980s, there is a village swimming pool.

Minto *Scottish Borders* A small village in the Roxburgh district of Scottish Borders, Minto lies between the River Teviot and the Minto Hills, 5 miles (8 km) northeast of Hawick and 3 miles (5 km) west of Jedburgh. Nearby Minto House, designed by the architect William Adam and now derelict, was built in 1738–43 for Lord Minto. A member of that family, Jean Elliot (1727–1805), wrote the famous lament *The Flowers of the Forest.*

Mio Ness *Shetland* A headland of the Shetland Mainland, Mio Ness extends into the southern end of Yell Sound, a mile (1.5 km) northwest of the settlement of Brough. To the west lies the inlet of Orka Voe.

Mirkady Point *Orkney* A headland of the southeast Orkney Mainland, Mirkady Point extends into Deer Sound, 4 miles (6.5 km) southwest of Mull Head.

Misty Law *North Ayrshire/Renfrewshire* A hill on the border between North Ayrshire and Renfewshire in the

Clyde Muirshiel Country Park, Misty Law rises to 510 m (1673 ft) 6 miles (10 km) northeast of Largs.

Mither Tap *Aberdeenshire* The highest peak of the Bennachie Hills, the Mither Tap rises to 518 m (1733 ft) to the north of the River Don, 6 miles (10 km) northeast of Alford.

Miughalaigh The Gaelic name for Mingulay in the Western Isles

Moan, Loch *Dumfries and Galloway/South Ayrshire* A small loch in Dumfries and Galloway, Loch Moan lies in the Galloway Forest Park on the border with South Ayrshire, 8 miles (13 km) northeast of Barrhill. The River Cree drains to the southwest and the loch has two principal islets named the Black and White Islands.

Mochrum *Dumfries and Galloway* A hamlet in the western Machars of Dumfries and Galloway, Mochrum (or Kirk of Mochrum) lies a mile (1.5 km) to the north of Port William and 8 miles (13 km) southwest of Wigtown. The medieval Druchtag Motte lies to the northeast.

Mochrum Fell *Dumfries and Galloway* A hill in Dumfries and Galloway, Mochrum Fell rises to 197 m (646 ft) to the south of Mochrum Loch and nearly 2 miles (3 km) northwest of Elrig.

Mochrum Loch *Dumfries and Galloway* A loch in Dumfries and Galloway, Mochrum Loch lies on the Gargrie Moor, 2 miles (3 km) north of Elrig. At the northern end of the loch stand the 15th–16th-century towers of the Old Place of Mochrum, which were restored after 1873 by successive marquesses of Bute.

Moffat *Dumfries and Galloway* A small town in the Annandale district of Dumfries and Galloway, Moffat lies on the River Annan, 19 miles (31 km) northeast of Dumfries. In existence in the 12th century, it developed as a spa town from the mid-17th century following the discovery of mineral springs. The Moffat Well and Hartfell Spa attracted visitors including Robert Burns. The fabric of the town mostly dates from the late 18th century when its main street, said to be the widest in Scotland, was broadened. It expanded rapidly as a spa resort with the opening of a railway station at nearby Beattock in 1847. Moffat is now a sheep-farming centre and resort town with tourist attractions including a museum and the Tweedhope Sheepdogs, which offers demonstrations of shepherding. Notable structures include the Colvin Fountain (1875), the old parish church with a medieval fragment, 13th-century St Cuthbert's Chapel, the Proudfoot Institute (1885), the Town Hall (1827) – originally Moffat Baths, a war memorial, and Moffat House, which was built in 1767 to a design by John Adam for the Earl of Hopetoun. Famous residents have included James Macpherson, author of *Ossian*, and Lord Dowding, Air Chief Marshal during the Battle of Britain.

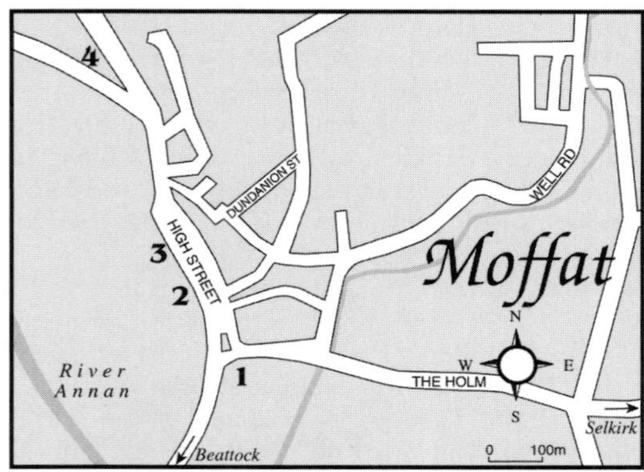

1 *Moffat Museum*
2 *Moffat Town Hall*
3 *Moffat Library*
4 *Beechgrove Park*

Moffat Water *Dumfries and Galloway* A stream in north Dumfries and Galloway, the Moffat Water rises in headwaters on the slopes of White Coomb near the border with Scottish Borders. It flows southwestwards, entering the River Annan 2 miles (3 km) south of Moffat.

Moidart *Highland* A mountainous area of Lochaber in southwest Highland Council area, Moidart lies to the west of Loch Shiel and to the south of Loch Eilt. The sea lochs of Ailort and Moidart lie on its western coastline and its highest peak is Beinn Odhair Bheag, which rises to 882 m (2893 ft).

Moidart, Loch *Highland* A sea loch on the west coast of Moidart in the Lochaber district of Highland Council area, Loch Moidart opens out to the south of the Sound of Arisaig. It is fed by the River Moidart which rises to the northeast and flows through Glen Moidart to meet the loch at the settlement of Kinlochmoidart. The island of Eilean Shona almost fills the mouth of the loch as it widens.

Moin, the *Highland* An extensive area of moorland in the northwest Highlands, The Moin (or A' Mhoine) lies between Loch Hope and the Kyle of Tongue in northwest Sutherland.

Moine Thrust *Highland* An extensive geological discontinuity of the northwest Highlands, the Moine Thrust is the easternmost and oldest of a series of low-angle faults that comprise a thrust zone up to 6 miles (10 km) in width within which older sheets of rock (or nappes) are piled up over younger sequences. The thrust trends south-southwest for 120 miles (192 km) from Loch Eriboll in the north, past Glencoul, Knockan Crag, Ullapool, Kinlochewe, Kishorn and Lochalsh to the Sleat peninsula of Skye. Formed during the Caledonian mountain-building episode between 500 and 430 million years ago, the structure generally involves Pre-Cambrian schists and and gneisses being pushed above a sequence of limestones, quartzites and shales of Cambrian and Ordovician age but has been much complicated by later deformation. The thrust zone defines the western margin of the Caledonian mountain belt in Europe. Since the thrust belt was first identified in the late 19th century, it has become a classic site for the study of structural geology, and its mode of formation has been reinterpreted several times as understanding of the science developed.

Moirlanich Longhouse *Stirling* Described as an outstanding example of a traditional cruck-frame cottage and byre, Moirlanich Longhouse has been little altered since it was built in the mid-19th century. Situated a mile (1.5 km) to the northwest of Killin in Stirling Council area, it was purchased by the National Trust for Scotland in 1992. It was home to at least three generations of the Robertson family, who lived there until 1968. In an adjacent building there is an exhibition of clothes and an interpretation of the history and restoration of the building.

Mol-chlach *Highland* The principal settlement on the island of Soay which lies to the south of the isle of Skye in the Inner Hebrides, Mol-chlach is situated to the west of the Camas nan Geall inlet, 3 miles (5 km) west of Elgol.

Mollinsburn *North Lanarkshire* A small commuter village of North Lanarkshire, Mollinsburn lies 4 miles (6.5 km) southwest of Cumbernauld.

Mona, Port *Dumfries and Galloway* A small bay on the west coast of the Rhinns of Galloway, Dumfries and Galloway, Port Mona lies over 3 miles (5 km) northwest of the Mull of Galloway.

Monach, Sound of *Western Isles* The Sound of Monach forms a channel in the Outer Hebrides separating the western coastline of North Uist from the Heisker Islands.

Monach Islands An alternative name for the Heisker Islands in the Western Isles.

Monachylemore *Stirling* A locality in the Balquhidder district of Stirling Council area, Monachylemore lies at the foot of the Monachyle Glen, between Loch Voil and Loch Doine. Meall Monachyle rises to 647 m (2123 ft) in the Braes of Balquhidder to the north, and to the east are the Ruveag Falls on the Monachyle Burn.

Monadhliath Mountains *Highland* An extensive range of mountains between the Great Glen and upper Strathspey, the Monadhliath Mountains rise to 945 m (3100 ft) at Carn Dearg, 16 miles (26 km) south of Inverness.

Monadh Mòr *Aberdeenshire/Highland* A mountain in the southern Cairngorms, Monadh Mòr rises to 1113 m (3651 ft) on the border between Aberdeenshire and Highland council areas and to the south of Loch nan Stuirteag. Deriving its name from the Gaelic for 'big hill', it is connected to Beinn Bhrotain by a col named Adha nam Fiann.

Monamenach *Angus/Perth and Kinross* A peak on the border between Angus and Perth and Kinross, Monamenach rises to 807 m (2647 ft) 4 miles (6.5 km) east of Spittal of Glenshee.

Monar, Loch *Highland* A loch at the centre of Highland Council area, Loch Monar lies between Glen Carron and Glen Cannich, to the south of the East and West Monar Forests. Dammed at its eastern end to form a reservoir, it extends 8 miles (13 km) east–west.

Monaughty Wood *Moray* An area of woodland in Moray, Monaughty Wood lies 5 miles (8 km) east of Forres and 6 miles (10 km) southwest of Elgin, extending from Califer in the southwest to Miltonduff in the northeast.

Monboddo *Aberdeenshire* A 17th-century house in the Howe of the Mearns, southeast Aberdeenshire, Monboddo House lies a mile (1.5 km) to the southeast of Auchenblae in the parish of Fordoun. Extended in Scottish baronial style in the 1880s, the house was the home of the judge James Burnett, Lord Monboddo (1714–99), author of *The Origin and Progress of Man and Language*, a study of evolution that predated Darwinian theory. James Boswell, travelling with Dr Johnson in the 1770s, described Monboddo as 'a wretched place, wild and naked with a poor old house'. Robert Burns, however, was much impressed by Lord Monboddo's daughter 'Fair Eliza' while staying there in 1786.

Moncreiffe Hill *Perth and Kinross* A hill of Perth and Kinross, Moncreiffe Hill rises to a height of 221 m (725 ft) 2 miles (3 km) southeast of Moncreiffe.

Moncreiffe Island *Perth and Kinross* An island in the River Tay that lies opposite the South Inch of Perth, Moncreiffe Island divides the Tay into two channels as it flows through Perth. It is the site of the King James VI Golf Course. The railway bridge, which conveys the Dundee line east through the Carse of Gowrie, crosses the river via the northern tip of the island.

Monega Hill *Angus* A summit in the southeast Grampians, Monega Hill rises to 908 m (2978 ft) to the south of Caenlochan Glen and 2 miles (3 km) southeast of the Glenshee Ski Centre.

Moness, Falls of *Perth and Kinross* A series of waterfalls on the Urlar Burn in Perth and Kinross, the Falls of Moness lie a mile (1.5 km) south of Aberfeldy.

Moness Burn *Perth and Kinross* An extension of the Urlar Burn in Perth and Kinross, the Moness Burn is a small river which flows for 1.25 miles (2 km) north from the Falls of Moness and through the Birks of Aberfeldy before dividing the village of Aberfeldy. It enters the River Tay 250m (273 yards) north of the village.

Moneydie *Perth and Kinross* A locality in central Perth and Kinross, Moneydie lies to the south of the Shochie Burn, 5 miles (8 km) northwest of Perth.

Moniaive *Dumfries and Galloway* A village in Dumfries and Galloway, Moniaive lies on the Dalwhat Water, 7 miles (11 km) southwest of Thornhill and 15 miles (24 km) northwest of Dumfries. Designated a burgh of barony in 1636, it was popular with artists and holiday-makers in the 19th century. Maxwelton House, the birthplace of Annie Laurie, lies 3 miles (5 km) east of the village.

Monifieth *Angus* A residential town in southeast Angus, Monifieth lies on the north shore of the Firth of Tay, 2 miles (3 km) east of Broughty Ferry. It developed in association with the industries of Dundee as a dormitory settlement. Its parish church, built in 1812, is said to have been built on the site of an earlier chapel that was the final resting place of St Andrew. An Art Deco war memorial built in 1922 is surrounded by an impressive annual floral display. Monifieth is a noted golfing centre, its links course serving as a qualifier for the Open golf championship.

Monikie *Angus* A village in a parish of the same name in Angus, Monikie is situated 4 miles (6.5 km) north of Monifieth and adjacent to Monikie Country Park, which includes two reservoirs formerly serving Dundee. Also in the parish are the settlements of Craigton, Newbigging and Kirkton of Monikie. Nearby is Affleck Castle, which is associated with the Lindsay and Auchinleck families, and on Downie Hill, near the site of the former Panmure House, stands the Panmure Testimonial, which was built by grateful tenants in the 19th century to commemorate the generosity of the Earl of Panmure. The Monikie Reservoirs, which date from 1847–53 and were last used as a source of water in April 1981, were developed into a 57-ha (140-acre) country park that was opened in August 1981.

Monimail *Fife* A hamlet in a parish of the same name in northern Fife, Monimail lies on the northern edge of the Howe of Fife on a minor road between the villages of Collessie and Letham. It once had a meal mill, smithy and brewhouse, but its origin is probably closely associated with a precursor of Monimail Tower (1578), a residence of the bishops of St Andrews. The last cleric to reside here was Archbishop Hamilton, who allegedly was cured of asthma by the Italian astrologer Cardan who advised him to drink water from a well nearby, now known as Cardan's Well. The tower is incorporated into the garden wall of Melville House, which was built between 1697 and 1703 by the 1st Earl of Melville to a design by James Smith. Monimail parish church (1794–7) has a four-stage Gothic-style tower built in 1811 by Robert Hutchison.

Monkland Canal Opened in 1793 at a cost of £120,000, the Monkland Canal was created under the direction of the engineer James Watt from 1770 to serve the coal mines of North Lanarkshire. It extended 12 miles (19 km) from Woodhall to Monkland basin at Port Dundas near Glasgow Cathedral, and connected with the Glasgow branch of the Forth and Clyde Canal. In the first half of the 19th century it was the most profitable waterway in Scotland, playing a strategic role in the industrial development of Glasgow. Between 1850 and 1887, barges were raised and lowered along a steam-driven inclined plane at Blackhill. The Monkland Canal merged with the Forth and Clyde Canal in 1867 when the Caledonian Railway Company took over the management of both waterways. As the coal mines and iron-stone quarries near the canal became exhausted, the use of the canals declined until 1935 when traffic ceased. Thereafter, the canal continued to supply water to the Forth and Clyde Canal, sections of the canal subsequently being infilled until the 1960s. The route of the canal later provided a useful corridor for the M8 motorway to enter the city of Glasgow. Today remnants of the canal are best seen in Drumpellier Country Park in Coatbridge.

Monklands A district in the neighbourhood of Airdrie and Coatbridge to the east of Glasgow, the Monklands were first recorded in the 14th century when these lands were held by the Cistercian monks of Newbattle Abbey near Edinburgh. After the Reformation, the name survived in the parishes of Old and New Monkland. When Scottish local government was reorganised in 1975, the old burghs of Airdrie and Coatbridge, along with other rural districts of Lanarkshire, were replaced by Monklands District. The Monkland Canal, commenced in 1770, linked the Forth and Clyde Canal with the North Calder Water, with branches linking with various ironworks.

Monkstadt *Highland* A scattered township on the Trotternish peninsula of the isle of Skye in the Inner Hebrides, Monkstadt lies 3 miles (5 km) north of Uig.

Monkton *South Ayrshire* A village in the Kyle district of Ayrshire, Monkton lies to the northeast of Prestwick Airport and 6 miles (10 km) north of Ayr. It developed as a weaving settlement in the 18th century and in association with road and rail transport in the 19th century. In 1935 an airport, flying-training school and aircraft-construction facilities were established nearby at Prestwick which became an international airport in 1946. The village, which still has aero-engineering industries, was bypassed in the 1970s.

Monreith *Dumfries and Galloway* A small 19th-century estate village in the western Machars of Dumfries and Galloway, Monreith lies on the east shore of Luce Bay, 10 miles (16 km) southwest of Wigtown. Monreith House to the north was built for the Maxwells of Monreith in 1791 to replace the earlier Myreton Castle whose ruins still stand in the grounds. To the south, above the remains of Kirkmaiden church, is a monument to the author Gavin Maxwell (1914–69) who was born nearby at the House of Elrig.

Monreith Bay *Dumfries and Galloway* An inlet on the east coast of Luce Bay, Dumfries and Galloway, Monreith Bay lies 2 miles (3 km) southeast of Port William. It is bounded north and south respectively by the headlands of Barsalloch Point and Point of Lag.

Montcoffer House *Aberdeenshire* A former seat of the earls of Fife, Montcoffer House stands on Montcoffer Hill overlooking the River Deveron, 3 miles (5 km) south of Banff in northern Aberdeenshire. The present building was erected in 1680 by Peter Russell.

Montgarrie *Aberdeenshire* A village in the Howe of Alford, Aberdeenshire, Montgarrie lies on the north bank of the River Don, a mile (1.5 km) north of Alford.

Montgreenan *North Ayrshire* A hamlet of North Ayrshire, Montgreenan lies 2 miles (3 km) east of Kilwinning. The former Montgreenan Castle was replaced by a mansion in 1817, and a railway station opened in 1878. Coal was mined at the nearby Fergushill Colliery until the early 1950s.

Montrave *Fife* An estate and hamlet in eastern Fife, Montrave lies 4 miles (6.5 km) north of Leven on the A916 from Kennoway to Cupar adjacent to Praytis Country Park. Associated with the Gilmour family, the mansion house dates from 1836. A hoard of English silver coins from the reigns of Edward I and Edward II was uncovered here in 1877.

Montrose *Angus* A coastal resort town and royal burgh in Angus, Montrose is situated between the mouths of the North and South Esk rivers, 38 miles (61 km) northeast of Dundee. It lies to the north of Montrose Basin, a large tidal inlet fed by the South Esk, and drains into the North Sea. Designated a royal burgh in the early 12th century, Montrose developed in medieval times in association with trade in skins, hides, salt and cured salmon. A castle built in the 12th century was occupied in 1296 by Edward I of England and destroyed a year later by William Wallace. Later in the 13th century a

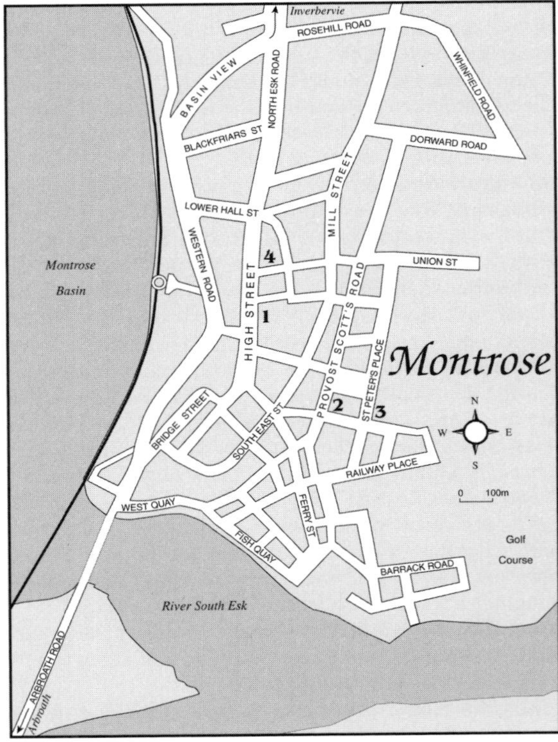

1 *Town House or Ba Hoose*
2 *Museum and Art Gallery*
3 *Montrose Academy*
4 *William Lamb Memorial Studio*

Dominican friary was established and the port became one of Scotland's four chief outlets for wool. The town later prospered as a centre of fishing, brewing, shipbuilding and the manufacture of textiles. Today the town's economy is based on the tourism, food-processing, chemicals, engineering and oil-related industries. It has the widest High Street in Scotland, and buildings of note include the Town House or Ba Hoose, Montrose Museum and Art Gallery, and Montrose Academy (1815). It is said that Lord James Douglas embarked from here in 1330 on a crusade against the Moors carrying the embalmed heart of King Robert the Bruce. Prince James Edward Stewart, the Old Pretender, also sailed from here at the close of the 1715 Jacobite Rising.

Montrose Basin *Angus* A virtually enclosed tidal inlet, Montrose Basin forms the wide estuary of the South Esk River, which flows out to the North Sea south of Montrose. A 750-ha (1850-acre) nature reserve managed by the Scottish Wildlife Trust, its waters and mud flats provide a rich feeding ground for thousands of resident and migrant birds, including curlews, oystercatchers, eider ducks and pink-footed and greylag geese. There is a wildlife centre at Rossie Braes overlooking the basin.

Monymusk *Aberdeenshire* A planned village in mid-Aberdeenshire, Monymusk lies just south of the River Don, 7 miles (11 km) west of Kintore and 17 miles (27 km) northwest of Aberdeen. In 1170 a community of Augustinian canons was established here by Gilchrist, Earl of Mar, on the site of an earlier Celtic foundation said to have been founded by Malcolm Canmore in 1078 while on a military mission against the rebels of Moray. The present Church of St Mary dates from the late 12th–early 13th centuries and contains monuments to successive Grant lairds, as well as a Pictish symbol stone known as the Monymusk Stone. Sir Archibald Grant of Monymusk replaced the old Kirkton of Monymusk in the 18th century with a planned village designed for estate workers and craftsmen. It was almost entirely rebuilt in 1840.

Monynut Edge *East Lothian/Scottish Borders* A ridge forming a watershed in the Lammermuir Hills, Monynut Edge lies on the border between East Lothian and Scottish Borders, 7 miles (11 km) south of Dunbar. The Monynut Water, which flows to the west, joins the Whiteadder Water near Abbey St Bathans.

Monzie *Perth and Kinross* A settlement in Perth and Kinross, Monzie lies on the Shaggie Burn, 2 miles (3 km) north of Crieff. Monzie Castle combines an early laird's house dating from 1634 with a late 18th-century neo-Gothic building with corner towers designed by John Paterson for General Alexander Campbell. The white-harled parish church of Monzie was rebuilt in 1831.

Mooa *Shetland* A small, uninhabited island of the Shetland Islands, Mooa lies off the east coast of Whalsay, 2 miles (3 km) south of the headland of Skaw Taing.

Moodiesburn *North Lanarkshire* A small town of North Lanarkshire, Moodiesburn lies 4 miles (6.5 km) southwest of Cumbernauld and a mile (1.5 km) to the west of the junction of the A80 with the M73. Situated at a road junction, it developed in the early 20th century in association with coal mining and Stoneyetts Hospital. The manufacture of collagen film for wrapping meat products developed as a major industry from the 1960s.

Moodlaw Burn *Dumfries and Galloway* A stream in Dumfries and Galloway, the Moodlaw Burn rises in headstreams that join to the west of Dumfedling Knowe, 5 miles (8 km) southwest of Craik Forest. The burn flows southwestwards into the White Esk, a mile (1.5 km) north of Eskdalemuir.

Moodlaw Loch *Dumfries and Galloway* A small loch in Dumfries and Galloway, Moodlaw Loch lies close to the border with Scottish Borders, 6 miles (10 km) northeast of Eskdalemuir.

Moonzie *Fife* A hamlet with a farmsteading, house (formerly the manse) and church on high ground, Moonzie lies within a parish of the same name 2 miles (3 km) northwest of Cupar. It lies on a pilgrimage route from Perth to St Andrews, the whitewashed parish church (*c.*1625) serving as a landmark for ships in St Andrews Bay.

Moorfoot Hills *Midlothian/Scottish Borders* A range of grass-covered rolling hills traversing the border between Midlothian and Scottish Borders, the Moorfoot Hills extend northeast from Peebles to Tynehead, rising to 659 m (2162 ft) at Windlestraw Law.

Mòr, Gleann *Highland* A steep and remote valley at the head of Strath Carron, Gleann Mòr lies to the west of the Glencalvie Forest and contains the Abhainn a' Ghlinne Mhoir. The valley extends for 6 miles (10 km) southwest from Alladale Lodge to meet Gleann Beag to the south of Bodach Mòr (822 m/2696 ft).

Mòr, Loch *Highland* A small loch on the west coast of the isle of Skye in the Inner Hebrides, Loch Mòr lies 7 miles (11 km) west of Dunvegan.

Mòr na Caorach, Loch *Highland* A small loch in Caithness, Loch Mòr na Caorach lies 3 miles (5 km) east of Achargary in Strathnaver.

Moraig, Loch *Perth and Kinross* A small loch of Perth and Kinross, Loch Moraig lies in the southern Grampians, 3 miles (5 km) northeast of Blair Atholl.

Morangie *Highland* A small whisky-distilling settlement in Easter Ross, Morangie lies a mile (1.5 km) northwest of Tain and overlooks the Dornoch Firth to the northeast. The Morangie Forest lies to the southwest.

Morar *Highland* A small village in the Morar district of Lochaber in southwest Highland Council area, Morar lies 2 miles (3 km) south of Mallaig at the western end of Loch Morar. It developed following the opening of the West Highland Railway in 1901, and from the late 1940s in association with the generation of hydro-electricity, tourism and boatbuilding.

Morar, Loch *Highland* A long, narrow loch in the Morar district of Lochaber in southwest Highland Council area, Loch Morar forms the divide between North and South Morar to the southeast of Mallaig. The deepest lake in the United Kingdom at 310 m (1017 ft), it extends east for 12 miles (19 km). The power of the Morar River, which falls to the sea from the western end of the loch, has been used to generate electricity since the late 1940s.

Moray *Area: 2238 sq. km (864 sq. miles)* Stretching from the Cairngorm Mountains northwards to a coastal lowland plain known as the Laigh of Moray, Moray is bisected by the River Spey, which flows northwards to empty into the North Sea. The council area is renowned for its many whisky distilleries, and its chief towns are Elgin (administrative centre), Forres, Buckie, Fochabers, Keith, Dufftown and Tomintoul. Nearly 60 per cent of the land of Moray is in agricultural use, and fishing as

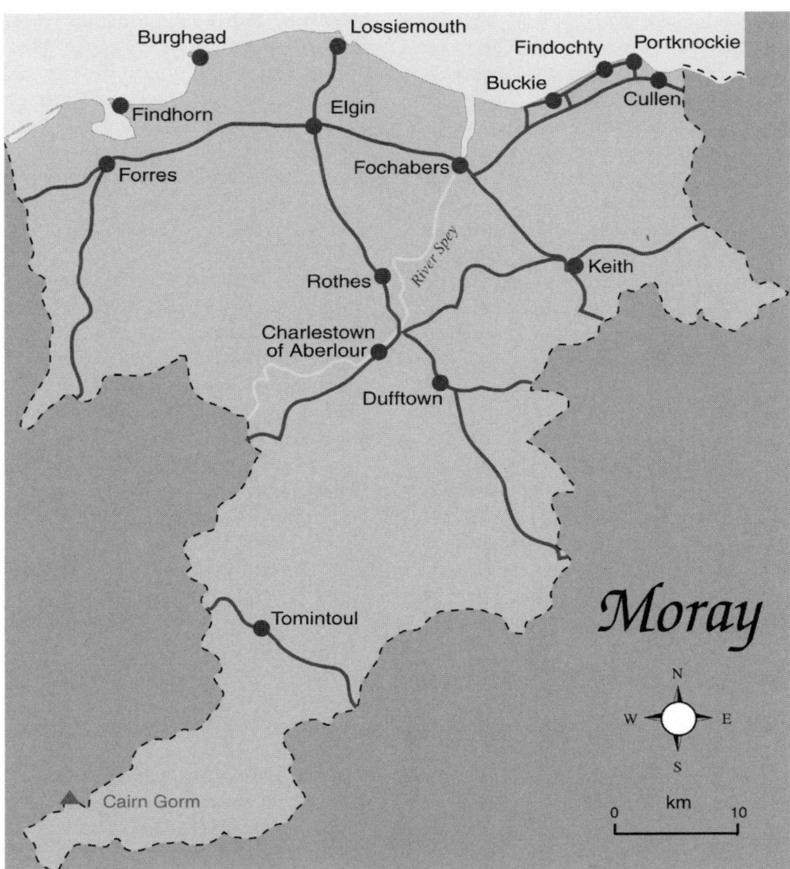

well as tourism and the manufacture of textiles are also important. It is thought that the promontory between Lossiemouth and Burghead was the centre of a Pictish kingdom and that the Pass of Grange might have been the site of the battle of Mons Graupius between Agricola and the Picts. The Province of Moray, separated from the rest of Scotland by mountain ranges, was semi-independent until the early Middle Ages, when the Crown asserted its authority by planting feudalism in the area. Its history thereafter is dominated by the bishops and earls of Moray, and great families such as the Comyns, Grants, Gordons and Duff earls of Fife. Moray has its fair share of planned villages dating from the period 1750–1850, and isolation finally ended with the coming of the railway in the 19th century.

Moray Firth An arm of the North Sea forming a triangular shape with its apex at the mouth of the Beauly Firth to the north of Inverness, the Moray Firth extends northwards beyond the mouths of the Cromarty Firth and Dornoch Firth to Duncansby Head and eastwards along the Moray and Aberdeenshire coast to Fraserburgh. The waters of the Inner Moray Firth, which includes the Inverness Firth between Inverness and Fort George, stretch out as far as Helmsdale to the north and Buckie to the east, and receive the waters of the rivers Spey, Lossie, Findhorn and Nairn. The Outer Moray Firth beyond includes Smith Bank and the Beatrice Oilfield. Bounded on two sides by over 500 miles (800 km) of coastline, the Moray Firth has a diverse array of coastal landscapes, an abundance of wildlife and an economy that thrives on tourism, fishing and the oil industry. In 1996 the Moray Firth Partnership was created, bringing together a wide range of people and organisations with a view to developing an integrated management plan for the complex area of sea, shoreline and coastal hinterland that makes up this so-called 'super-firth'.

More, Glen *Argyll and Bute* A high valley cutting across the centre of the island of Mull in the Inner Hebrides, Glen More extends for approximately 12 miles (19 km) from Loch Scridain in the west to Loch Don in the east. The valley reaches a watershed at just over 200 m (656 ft) 3 miles (5 km) north of Loch Buie, casting off the River Lussa to the east and the Coladoir River to the west.

More, Strath *Highland* A valley in northwest Sutherland, Strath More extnds south from Loch Hope and contains the Strathmore River, otherwise known as the River Hope. Ben Hope rises to 927 m (3041 ft) in the east.

More Barvas, Loch *Western Isles* A loch on the Isle of Lewis in the Outer Hebrides, Loch More Barvas (Gael: *Loch Mòr Bharabhais*) lies on the island's northwest coastline, immediately to the west of the village of Barvas and at the foot of Glen More Barvas.

More Head *Aberdeenshire* A headland on the Moray Firth coast of northern Aberdeenshire, More Head extends into the sea at the west end of Gamrie Bay near Gardenstown.

Morebattle *Scottish Borders* A village of Scottish Borders, Morebattle lies on the Kale Water, 6 miles (10 km) southeast of Kelso and 7 miles (11 km) northeast of Jedburgh. It once had a number of mills and now lies on the St Cuthbert's Way long-distance footpath. A half-mile (1 km) southeast of the village is 16th-century Corbet Tower, a former stronghold of the Kerrs.

Moredun *City of Edinburgh* A suburb of Edinburgh near Gilmerton, Moredun lies 3 miles (5 km) southeast of the city centre.

Morefield *Highland* A small settlement of Wester Ross in Highland Council area, Morefield lies on the northern shore of Loch Broom, a mile (1.5 km) northwest of Ullapool.

Morenish *Perth and Kinross* A locality on the north side of Loch Tay, Morenish lies 2 miles (3 km) northeast of Killin on the lower slopes of Meall nan Tarmachan. The hill ground of Morenish was acquired by the National Trust for Scotland in 1996 for its outstanding nature conservation value.

Morgan Glen Viaduct *South Lanarkshire* A landmark of the town of Larkhall, the six-span Morgan Glen railway viaduct is one of the highest railway bridges in Scotland, at 45 m (148 ft). Erected in 1904, it served a branch line linking Larkhall and Stonehouse which closed in 1964.

Morham *East Lothian* A small village of East Lothian, Morham lies 3 miles (5 km) southeast of Haddington.

Morie, Loch *Highland* A loch of Easter Ross in Highland Council area, Loch Morie lies 8 miles (13 km) northwest of Alness. It is one of the sources of the River Alness.

Moriston, River *Highland* A river in the Inverness district of Highland Council area, the River Moriston flows eastwards from the eastern end of Loch Cluanie through Glen Moriston and past the forests of Inverwick, Dundreggan and Portclair before emptying into Loch Ness a mile (1.5 km) southeast of Invermoriston.

Morlich, Loch *Highland* A loch of Badenoch in the Cairngorms National Park, Loch Morlich lies 4 miles (6.5 km) northwest of Cairn Gorm and 5 miles (8 km) southeast of Aviemore. It is a centre for water sports.

Mormond Hill *Aberdeenshire* Rising to a height of 234 m (768 ft) in northeast Aberdeenshire and topped by communication masts, Mormond Hill forms an eminence in the centre of flat farmland in the district of Buchan. It has two summits and was a landmark to sailors. On its southwest slope, overlooking Strichen, there is a prominent white-quartz rock image of a white horse created in the early 19th century by the tenants of Strichen Estate to commemorate the war-horse of Lord Lovat. On the seaward side of the hill, the rock was exposed in the form of a stag in 1870.

Morningside *City of Edinburgh* An affluent residential district of Edinburgh, Morningside lies 1.5 miles (2.5 km) southwest of the city centre and extends from Holy Corner in the north to Cluny and Braid in the south. It was a small village until the 19th century, when its expansion was encouraged by the opening of the Edinburgh Suburban Railway in 1885. The distinguished judge Francis Garden, Lord Gardenstone, lived in Morningside House, which has been demolished. Sir Reginald Johnston (1874–1938), tutor to the last Emperor of China, was born in Morningside, which was also the birthplace in 1961 of the impressionist Rory Bremner.

Morrone *Aberdeenshire* A hill at the northern end of Glen Clunie in western Aberdeenshire, Morrone rises to 859 m (2818 ft) at the junction of the Clunie Water with the River Dee by Braemar.

Morsgail, Loch *Western Isles* A small loch on the Isle of Lewis in the Western Isles, Loch Morsgail lies a mile (1.5 km) south of the head of Little Loch Roag.

Mortlach *Aberdeenshire* A parish in Aberdeenshire, Mortlach lies on the Whisky Trail to the south of the River Spey, with the planned village of Dufftown its largest settlement. The old Kirkton of Mortlach lies on the southern outskirts of Dufftown.

Mortlich *Aberdeenshire* A hill in the Cromar district of Aberdeenshire, Mortlich rises to 380 m (1248 ft) just over a mile (1.5 km) to the north of Aboyne in Royal Deeside.

Morton Castle *Dumfries and Galloway* The remains of a former Douglas stronghold near Carronbridge in Nithsdale, Dumfries and Galloway, Morton Castle is situated on the edge of Morton Loch, 3 miles (5 km) north of Thornhill. It was built in the 13th century.

Morton Hall *East Ayrshire* Morton Hall in Newmilns, East Ayrshire, was built in 1896 for William Morton before being gifted to the burgh two years later. It was used as a meeting place for the local community as well as being home to the local court for a period and the administrative centre for the burgh. Now under the administration of East Ayrshire Council, it was built to show the prosperity of the area.

Morton Lochs *Fife* Three lochs in northeast Fife, the Morton Lochs (North, South and West) lie a mile (1.5 km) south of Tayport and northwest of Tentsmuir. They were created for fish rearing in the early 20th century by diverting the Ninewells Burn into existing wet hollows among the sand dunes. Wildfowl and breeding birds are attracted from the nearby coast and Tay estuary, and in 1952 the lochs were designated a National Nature Reserve.

Moruisg *Highland* A mountain in Wester Ross, Highland Council area, Moruisg rises to 928 m (3045 ft) on the south side of Glen Carron in the Glencarron and Glenuig Forest.

Morven *Aberdeenshire* A round-topped hill in Aberdeenshire, Morven rises to a height of 871 m (2858 ft) just over 5 miles (8 km) north of Ballater. In 1859 it was climbed by Queen Victoria, who described the view from it as 'more magnificent than can be described'. Morven Lodge is situated on the Morven Burn, which descends the western slope of the hill to join the River Gairn, a tributary of the Dee. The name Morven, derived from the Gaelic for 'great mountain', is often used in Ossianic legend to describe the Highlands or that part of the Highlands with the greatest number of remote peaks.

Morven *Highland* A mountain in eastern Caithness, Morven rises to 706 m (2316 ft) 9 miles (14 km) north of Helmsdale.

Morvern *Highland* A peninsula and parish in the Lochaber district of southwest Highland Council area, Morvern is bounded by Loch Sunart, the Sound of Mull and Loch Linnhe. Its principal settlements are the ferry port of Lochaline and Fiunary, and its highest points are Fuar Bheinn (785 m/2511 ft) and Beinn Mheadhoin (739 m/2423 ft) in the east. Lead and copper ore were formerly mined at Lurg in Glen Dubh and Ternate.

Morvern, Lynn of *Highland* A channel in Loch Linnhe, the Lynn of Morvern separates the southern coast of Morvern in the Lochaber district of Highland Council area from the island of Lismore.

Morvich *Highland* A small village in Easter Ross,

Morvich lies on the northeast side of the River Fleet, 5 miles (8 km) west of Golspie.

Moscow *East Ayrshire* A dormitory village in the Cunninghame district of East Ayrshire, Moscow lies 4 miles (6.5 km) northeast of Kilmarnock

Moss *Argyll and Bute* A scattered township on the island of Tiree in the Inner Hebrides, Moss lies 2 miles (3 km) northwest of Crossapol.

Mossat *Aberdeenshire* A hamlet in Aberdeenshire, Mossat lies on the Mossat Burn at a road junction 7 miles (11 km) northwest of Alford and a mile (1.5 km) north of Kildrummy.

Mossbank *Shetland* A settlement on the northeast coast of the Shetland Mainland, Mossbank overlooks Yell Sound and the island of Samphrey to the northeast. It developed from the 1970s in association with North Sea oil-related industries.

Mossblown *South Ayrshire* A village of South Ayrshire, Mossblown lies to the north of the River Ayr, a mile (1.5 km) north of Annbank and 4 miles (6.5 km) northeast of Ayr.

Mossburnford *Scottish Borders* A small settlement in the Roxburgh district of Scottish Borders, Mossburnford lies to the east of the Jed Water, 3 miles (5 km) south of Jedburgh.

Mossdale *Dumfries and Galloway* A village of Dumfries and Galloway, Mossdale lies just north of the Black Water of Dee, 4 miles (6.5 km) south of New Galloway.

Mossend *North Lanarkshire* A settlement of North Lanarkshire, Mossend lies at the northeast edge of Bellshill, 2 miles (3 km) northwest of Strathclyde Country Park and 3 miles (5 km) north of Hamilton. The Eurocentral Rail Terminal lies to the north of the village.

Mossgiel *East Ayrshire* A small settlement of East Ayrshire, Mossgiel lies near the border with South Ayrshire, a mile (1.5 km) northwest of Mauchline.

Mossmorran *Fife* The site of a petrochemical processing plant, Mossmoran lies on the edge of a mossy tract of land to the south of Cowdenbeath in western Fife. Liquid gas is piped to Mossmorran from the North Sea, broken down to form ethane and then converted into ethylene, which is a basic hydrocarbon building block of the petrochemical industry. Developed since 1985 by the Shell–Exxon partnership, the site's products are piped 3 miles (5 km) to the Braefoot Bay Marine Terminal and fed into tankers and gas carriers for markets on the continent and in the USA. Ethane and ethylene are also piped to the BP plant at Grangemouth on the southern shore of the Firth of Forth and into the UK pipeline grid.

Mosspeeble Burn *Dumfries and Galloway* A small stream in Dumfries and Galloway, Mosspeeble Burn is a tributary of the Ewes Water rising between Pike Fell and Arkleton Hill, 5 miles (8 km) northeast of Langholm.

Moss-side *Highland* A settlement in Highland Council area, Moss-side lies on the north bank of the River Nairn, 2 miles (3 km) southwest of Nairn.

Mosstodloch *Moray* A village in Moray, Mosstodloch lies on the west bank of the River Spey, just over a mile (1.5 km) northwest of Fochabers. In 1916 the firm of Baxters began to manufacture preserved food here.

Mote of Mark *Dumfries and Galloway* Situated on a hill overlooking the Urr estuary 5 miles (8 km) south of Dalbeattie, the Mote of Mark is a hillfort dating from the 5th century AD. It takes its name from Mark, King of Dumnonia, who features in the tragic story of Tristan and Isolde.

Motherwell *North Lanarkshire* A former industrial town in the Clyde Valley, Motherwell is situated to the southeast of Glasgow between the River Clyde and the South Calder Water. Originally a weaving village, Motherwell developed as an important centre for coal mining, engineering, construction industries and the manufacture of iron and steel following the arrival of the railway in 1848. It gained burgh status in 1865, and in 1871 and 1881 respectively David Colville's ironworks and steelworks were established. The town's heavy industries declined during the 1980s, the extensive Ravenscraig Steelworks eventually closing in 1992. Other steelworks were developed nearby at Dalzell and Flemington. Buildings of interest include the Town Hall (1887), Motherwell Heritage Centre (1996) and the churches of Dalzell North and Dalzell High. To the west of the main railway is the site of the Lady Well, the town's namesake, which supplied water into the mid-19th century. Between 1975 and 1996 Motherwell was the administrative centre of Motherwell District, Strathclyde Region. It is now the administrative centre of North Lanarkshire. A Civic Centre and Technical College were established in the 1960s. Nearby are New Jerviston House, Dalzell House, Strathclyde Country Park and Dalzell Country Park.

Motte of Urr *Dumfries and Galloway* A medieval earthwork in Dumfries and Galloway, the Motte of Urr lies on the Urr Water to the northwest of Dalbeattie. Dating from the 12th century, it covers an area of about 2 ha (6 acres) and has been described as one of the most impressive motte-and-bailey castle sites in Scotland.

Moulin *Perth and Kinross* A village in a parish of the same name in Perth and Kinross, Moulin lies a mile (1.5 km) to the north of Pitlochry on the road to Kirkmichael. Formerly the largest settlement in the area, the village, now a conservation area, declined after the military road was rerouted in 1727. It has an early 18th-century inn, a church rebuilt in 1831 and again after a fire in 1873, and close by the remains of the 13th-century Black Castle of Moulin, said to have been destroyed c.1500 for fear of the plague.

Moulinearn *Perth and Kinross* A locality in Perth and Kinross, Moulinearn lies sandwiched between the A9 and the River Tay, 2 miles (3 km) southwest of Pitlochry. Once noted for its Atholl brose porridge, Moulinearn is the site of a former government inn or kingshouse, built during the mid-18th century to house travellers on the newly created military road. The explorer Sir Alexander Mackenzie (1764–1820), who gave his name to the Mackenzie River in Canada, died here.

Mound, the *City of Edinburgh* A road in central Edinburgh linking Princes Street in the New Town with the High Street in the Old Town, the Mound was created in 1763 as an artificial earthen bank over the Nor' Loch which extended over the area now occupied by Princes Street Gardens. The roadway was improved in 1835 by Thomas Hamilton and William Burn, and in 1959 an electric heating element was embedded in the road surface to prevent ice forming in winter. Buildings of note on the Mound include the Royal Scottish Academy (1835), the National Gallery of Scotland (1859), the Headquarters of the Bank of Scotland, the New College of the University of Edinburgh and the Assembly Hall of the Church of Scotland,

Mound, the *Highland* A locality in eastern Sutherland, The Mound lies at the mouth of the River Fleet, 5 miles (8 km) north of Dornoch. A passenger ferry once crossed the river here, and in 1818 a new bridge and embanked road known as the Mound was completed by Thomas Telford. In 1902 a light railway to Dornoch was established on this route.

Mounie Castle *Aberdeenshire* A castle in the Formartine district of Aberdeenshire, Mounie Castle lies 3 miles (5 km) west of Oldmeldrum, near the village of Daviot.

Mountain Cross *Scottish Borders* A hamlet in Scottish Borders, Mountain Cross lies close to the border with South Lanarkshire, a mile (1.5 km) south of Romannobridge.

Mount Alexander An alternative name for Dunalastair in Perth and Kinross.

Mount Annan *Dumfries and Galloway* A house and estate in Annandale, Dumfries and Galloway, Mount Annan lies to the east of the River Annan, a mile (1.5 km) to the north of the town of Annan.

Mount Battock *Angus/Aberdeenshire* A hill in the southern Grampians, Mount Battock rises to a height of 778 m (2552 ft) on the border between Angus and Aberdeenshire to the north of Glen Esk. The Burn of Turret flows southwards from Mount Battock to meet the River North Esk.

Mount Blair *Angus/Perth and Kinross* A mountain in the southeast Grampians on the border between Angus and Perth and Kinross, Mount Blair rises to 744 m (2440 ft) between Glen Shee and Glen Isla, a mile (1.5 km) southwest of Forter.

Mount Hill *Fife* A hill rising to 221 m (681 ft) northwest of Cupar in northeast Fife, Mount Hill has on its summit a 29-m (95-ft) monument to Sir John Hope of Rankeillor, 4th Earl of Hopetoun. The Mount on its eastern slopes was the birthplace of Sir David Lindsay who served at the courts of James IV and James V and wrote the famous satirical play *Ane Pleasant Satyre of the Thrie Estaitis*, first performed in Cupar in 1535.

Mount Keen *Angus/Aberdeenshire* A cone-shaped summit in the eastern Grampians, Mount Keen rises to 939 m (3081 ft) on the border between Angus and Aberdeenshire, 7 miles (11 km) east of Loch Muick and a similar distance south-southeast of Ballater. Approaching the summit, Queen Victoria is said to have stopped for refreshment at the Queen's Well.

Mount Stuart *Argyll and Bute* An impressive Gothic-style mansion on the east coast of the island of Bute, Mount Stuart lies within a large estate, 4 miles (6.5 km) south-southeast of Rothesay. The seat of the Stuarts of Bute, Mount Stuart was originally built by Alexander McGill in 1716. It was remodelled in 1780 by George Paterson and completely rebuilt in the style of a Venetian palace between 1879 and 1903 following a fire to a design by Robert Rowand Anderson (1834–1921). The church-like interior, together with the touches of the occult in the Horoscope bedroom with its Egyptian-influenced furniture, reflect the tastes of John Crichton-Stuart, 3rd Marquess of Bute. Unique features of the house include the magnificent hall, incorporating contrasting marble of the finest quality and lit through beautiful stained glass, the chapel in white marble, detailed carved and painted ceilings in many rooms and a vaulted Gothic swimming pool in the basement. Bronze railings around the gallery are copies of those at the tomb of the Emperor Charlemagne in Aachen. The house also incorporates a fine collection of 17th- and 18th-century furniture and paintings collected by John Stuart (1713–92), 3rd Earl of Bute, founder of Kew Gardens and British Prime Minister. The 6th Marquess of Bute (1933–93) undertook a major renovation programme at Mount Stuart, transferring ownership to a charitable trust.

Mount Vernon *Glasgow City* A residential suburb of Glasgow, Mount Vernon lies to the east of the city centre, between Baillieston and Shettleston. Because of its position on a commanding ridge, it was originally named Windy Edge. It was renamed Mount Vernon after a house built by Glasgow merchant George Buchanan in 1755. A century later, villas were built and a suburban rail line established.

Mountblairy *Aberdeenshire* A scattered settlement in northwest Aberdeenshire, Mountblairy comprises Mountblairy, Newton of Mountblairy, Bridgend of Mountblairy, Hill of Mountblairy and Hillhead of Mountblairy, all lying to the west of the River Deveron, 6 miles (10 km) south of Banff.

Mounth, The An alternative name for the Grampian Mountains derived from the Gaelic *monadh*, meaning 'moor' or 'heath'. It also came to signify a pass over the Grampians such as the Cairn-a'-Mounth, Capel Mounth, Elsick Mounth, Cowie Mounth, Builg Mounth and Stock Mounth. The Mounth Plateau lies in the centre of the Grampians around the White Mounth (1068 m/3503 ft) and Lochnagar (1155 m/3789 ft).

Mousa *Shetland* The 60th parallel, which passes through Cape Farewell, Oslo and St Petersburg, bisects the small island of Mousa in the Shetland Islands. The 180-ha (445-acre) uninhabited island is separated from the Mainland of Shetland by the Mousa Sound. On its west shore stands the Broch of Mousa, a circular drystone tower described as the best-preserved Iron Age fortification of its kind in the British Isles. Built of local slate, the broch is 13 m (43 ft) tall with a diameter of 15 m (49 ft) at ground level tapering to an upper diameter of 12 m (39 ft). Storm petrels and rock doves nest on Mousa, and there is also a breeding colony of arctic tern. In summer a boat provides access to Mousa from Leebotten on the Shetland Mainland.

Mousa Sound *Shetland* A channel in the Shetland Islands, Mousa Sound separates the island of Mousa from the Shetland Mainland to the west.

Mouse Water *South Lanarkshire* A river in South Lanarkshire, the Mouse Water rises 2 miles (3 km) northeast of Forth and flows south and west to join the River Clyde to the west of Lanark.

Mouswald *Dumfries and Galloway* A village of Nithsdale in Dumfries and Galloway, Mouswald lies 6 miles (10 km) southeast of Dumfries. The steading of Mouswald Grange to the northwest incorporates the tower of an 18th-century windmill designed to grind oatmeal.

Mowhaugh *Scottish Borders* Located on the upper reaches of the Bowmont Water in Scottish Borders, the settlement of Mowhaugh lies 4 miles (6.5 km) southeast of Morebattle and 5 miles (8 km) northwest of the Scottish/English border.

Moy *Highland* A scattered hamlet and former railway station of Strath Dearn in the Inverness district of Highland Council area, Moy lies on the western shore of Loch Moy, 9 miles (14 km) southeast of Inverness. Moy Hall, seat of the Clan Mackintosh, was visited by Prince Charles Edward Stewart on the eve of the Battle of Culloden in 1746.

Moy *Highland* A small settlement in Glen Spean, Moy lies on the northern shore of Loch Moy, Highland Council area, 9 miles (14 km) west of Kinloch Laggan.

Moy *Highland* A locality in the Great Glen, Moy lies on the Caledonian Canal, a mile (1.5 km) southwest of Loch Lochy. The Moy Bridge crossing the canal is a double-leaf swingbridge.

Moy, Loch *Highland* A loch in the Strathdearn Forest in the Inverness district of Highland Council area, Loch Moy lies to the east of the A9, 9 miles (14 km) southeast of Inverness. The Moy Burn flows through the loch before merging with River Findhorn a half-mile (1 km) southwest of Ruthven.

Moy, Loch *Highland* A loch in Glen Spean, Loch Moy lies to the west of the larger Loch Laggan, to which it is connected by a river. Dammed at its western end by the Laggan Dam to form a reservoir, Loch Moy is the source of the River Spean, which flows west through Glen Spean past Roybridge.

Moy Burn *Highland* Rising in the foothills of Carn nan Tri-tighearnan in the Badenoch and Strathspey district of Highland Council area, the Moy Burn flows southwest then southeast through Loch Moy before merging with the River Findhorn a half-mile (1 km) southwest of Ruthven.

Moy Forest *Highland* A forest and upland area of the Badenoch and Strathspey district of Highland Council area, the Moy Forest lies to the north of Loch Laggan and Loch Moy and south of the Corrieyairack Forest.

Mu Ness *Shetland* A headland on the western coastline of the Shetland Mainland, Mu Ness extends into the sea 4 miles (6.5 km) south of Melby.

Muasdale *Argyll and Bute* A village on the west coast of the Kintyre peninsula, Muasdale lies 3 miles (5 km) north of Glenbarr overlooking the Sound of Gigha with views towards the islands of Islay, Jura, Cara and Gigha.

Muchalls *Aberdeenshire* A former fishing village on the North Sea coast of Aberdeenshire, Muchalls occupies a cliff-top location 4 miles (6.5 km) north of Stonehaven. To the west of the village stands Muchalls Castle, a former stronghold of the Burnett family, and nearby is the Episcopal Church of St Ternan, built in 1831 to replace earlier churches dating back to 1624.

Muck *Highland* A sparsely populated island in the Small Isles group of the Inner Hebrides, Muck lies 3 miles (5 km) southwest of the island of Eigg, from which it is separated by the Sound of Eigg. It has an area of 559 ha (1381 acres) and rises to 137 m (451 ft) at Beinn Airein. The chief settlement and harbour is at Port Mòr on the south coast.

Muck Water *South Ayrshire* A river of South Ayrshire, the Muck Water rises in the Drumneillie Hills and flows south and west to join the River Duisk a half-mile (1 km) southeast of Pinwherry. The Duisk meets the River Stinchar a mile (1.5 km) to the southwest.

Mucklabrek, Wick of *Shetland* The Wick of Mucklabreck forms a wide inlet on the southwest coast of the island of Foula in the Shetland Islands.

Muckle Flugga *Shetland* A small uninhabited island in the Shetland Islands, Muckle Flugga lies immediately north of the island of Unst. Its lighthouse, which was automated in 1995 and is the northernmost in the British Isles, was built in 1858 by David Stevenson.

Muckle Green Holm *Orkney* A small uninhabited island of the Orkney Islands, Muckle Green Holm lies to the southwest of the island of Eday from which it is separated by a channel known as the Fall of Warness. To the south is the smaller island of Little Green Holm.

Muckle Holm *Shetland* A small uninhabited island in the Shetland Islands, Muckle Holm lies in Yell Sound between the northern tip of the Shetland Mainland and the island of Yell. The island is a designated nature reserve.

Muckle Ness *Shetland* A headland on the east coast of the Shetland Mainland, Muckle Ness extends into the sea to the south of Dury Voe.

Muckle Ossa *Shetland* The larger of two rocks located off the northwest coast of the Shetland Mainland, Muckle Ossa lies immediately to the north of Little Ossa and 2 miles (3 km) west of the headland of The Faither.

Muckle Roe *Shetland* A small circular red-granite island in the Shetland Islands, Muckle Roe lies to the west of the Shetland Mainland. The root of a 350 million-year-old volcano, it is linked to the Shetland Mainland by a road bridge. The island, which extends over an area of 1730 ha (4273 acres), is noted for its abundant plant life and its magnificent cliff scenery in the northwest, particularly at Hams. There are crofts in the east and southeast, the rest of the island comprising lochan-studded moorland.

Muckle Skerry *Orkney* The largest of the skerries of the Pentland Firth, Muckle Skerry is an islet with three lochans and a rectangular-shaped northern promontory known as the Tenniscourt. From a landing point in Scartan Bay a road leads towards a lighthouse built in 1794 and automated in 1994. Now uninhabited, the islet had a population of 17 in 1881.

Muckle Skerry of Neapaback *Shetland* An outlier rock of the Shetland Islands, Muckle Skerry of Neapaback lies off the headland of Heoga Ness on the southeast coastline of the island of Yell.

Mudale, River *Highland* A river of northern Sutherland, the Mudale rises in headstreams to the west of Altnaharra. It flows west past the settlement of Mudale to join the west end of Loch Naver.

Mudle, Loch *Highland* A small loch on the Ardnamurchan peninsula in the Lochaber district of Highland Council area, Loch Mudle lies 4 miles (6.5 km) northwest of Kilchoan.

Mugdock *Stirling* The so-called 'three towns' of Mugdock – Eastertown, Middletown and Westertown – once occupied a strategic location between Glasgow and the north, with a great vista south towards Glasgow. Westerton, now the modern village of Mugdock, is situated in Stirling Council area, 2 miles (3 km) north of Milngavie and 10 miles (16 km) north of Glasgow. Mugdock Castle, which lies to the northwest, dates from the 14th century. It was a stronghold of the Grahams of Montrose who built a mansion here in the 17th century before abandoning the site in favour of Buchanan Castle to the north. Partially restored in the 1880s, the castle and its policies now form part of the 303-ha (750-acre) Mugdock Country Park, which lies on the West Highland Way.

Mugdrum Island *Fife* Located in the Firth of Tay in Fife, Mugdrum Island is a low-lying, narrow island that lies northwest of Newburgh. The waters to the north and south are known as the North and South Deep respectively.

Mugeary *Highland* A small settlement on the isle of Skye in the Inner Hebrides, Mugeary lies near the head of Glenmore and close to the upper reaches of the River Snizort, 4 miles (6.5 km) southwest of Portree.

Muice, Gleann na *Highland* A valley to the east of Loch Maree in Wester Ross, Gleann na Muice carries the waters of Abhainn Gleann na Muice south from Loch Gleann na Muice at the southern end of Lochan Fada to merge with the waters of Abhainn Bruachaig at the Heights of Kinlochewe.

Muick, Glen *Aberdeenshire* A glen in the Braemar district of Aberdeenshire, Glen Muick occupies the valley of the River Muick, which rises in the mountains to the west of Loch Muick and flows northeastwards to join the River Dee opposite Ballater. Buildings of note in the glen include the mid-19th-century Mill of Sterin, the House of Glenmuick (formerly Braickley House), built in 1898 for Sir Alan Mackenzie, and Birkhall, built by Charles Gordon of Abergeldie in 1715 and later purchased by Prince Albert.

Muick, Loch *Aberdeenshire* A loch in the Grampian uplands of Aberdeenshire near the border between Aberdeenshire and Angus, Loch Muick lies at the head of Glen Muick and is largely fed by streams that rise on the White Mounth and Lochnagar. The River Muick flows into it from the west and emerges from its northern end, and near to the loch are the royal shooting lodges of Glasallt-Shiel (1862) and Allt-na-Guibhsaich (1849).

Muick, River *Aberdeenshire* A river in south Deeside, Aberdeenshire, the River Muick rises on Carn an t-Sagairt Mòr near the border between Aberdeenshire and Angus at an altitude of 1021 m (3350 ft). It flows rapidly downwards through Dubh Loch to join Loch Muick. It issues from the north end of the loch and continues to flow northeastwards through Glen Muick to join the River Dee opposite Ballater. It forms a waterfall at the Linn of Muick.

Muir of Dinnet *Aberdeenshire* An area of moorland and birch forest designated as a nature reserve on the north side of the River Dee in Aberdeenshire, the Muir of Dinnet lies between Ballater and Aboyne to the west and east, and Loch Kinord and the River Dee to the north and south. Dinnet House nearby was built in 1890 for the MP Charles Wilson, later Lord Nunburnholme. Dinnet Church was built in 1899 for Sir William Cunliffe Brooks.

Muir of Kinellar *Aberdeenshire* A hamlet in the Aberdeenshire parish of Kinellar, Muir of Kinellar lies on the A96 from Aberdeen to Inverurie, a mile (1.5 km) west of Blackburn.

Muir of Lownie *Angus* A linear hamlet of south-central Angus, Muir of Lownie (or Lownie Moor) lies 2 miles (3 km) southeast of Forfar and 3 miles (5 km) west of Letham. The farm of Cottown of Lownie lies to the east-southeast.

Muir of Ord *Highland* A large village in Easter Ross, Muir of Ord lies on the western edge of the Black Isle, 3 miles (5 km) north of Beauly and 14 miles (22 km) northwest of Inverness. It developed in the 19th century in association with whisky distilling and road and rail transport, superseding the former hamlet of Tarradale. The geologist and geographer Sir Roderick Impey Murchison (1792–1871) was born on the Tarradale Estate, and founder of Loganair, Willie Logan (1913–66), whose construction company built the Tay Road Bridge, was born in Muir of Ord. Tourism, distilling, construction and metal fabrication are the chief industries.

Muir of Thorn *Perth and Kinross* An area of forested moorland in Perth and Kinross, the Muir of Thorn lies to the south of the River Tay and southeast of Dunkeld. It is traversed north–south by the A9 and west–east by the Gelly Burn, which enters the Tay near Murthly.

Muiravonside Country Park *Falkirk/West Lothian* A country park in Falkirk and West Lothian council areas, Muiravonside straddles the River Avon, 3 miles (5 km) southwest of Linlithgow. Extending to 69 ha (170 acres), it comprises gardens, woodland and parkland, the last of which includes a disused mine shaft.

Muirfield *East Lothian* A locality to the east of Gullane on the Firth of Forth coast of East Lothian, Muirfield is the site of one of Scotland's most noted championship golf courses. The Honourable Company of Edinburgh Golfers moved from Musselburgh to this links site in 1891.

Muirhead *Angus* Also known as Muirhead of Liff, this settlement lies on the border of Angus and the City of Dundee. Camperdown Park is close by, the dormitory settlement of Birkhill is adjacent, and Backmuir of Liff lies to the southwest.

Muirhead *Fife* A village in the parish of Kettle, central Fife, Muirhead lies near the junction of the A92 and A914, 2 miles (3 km) north of Glenrothes.

Muirhead *North Lanarkshire* A former kirkton village of North Lanarkshire, Muirhead lies at the eastern edge of the council area, 4 miles (6.5 km) northwest of Coatbridge and a mile (1.5 km) south of Chryston. It developed in association with coal mining, brick making and distilling, and is now a dormitory settlement for Cumbernauld and Glasgow.

Muirhouse *City of Edinburgh* A residential suburb of northwest Edinburgh, Muirhouse lies to the west of Pilton and takes its name from a Tudor Gothic-style mansion built on Marine Drive in 1832 for the Davidson family, wealthy merchants trading in Rotterdam. Developed since 1953, it became associated with social and environmental deprivation and was the subject of urban renewal from the 1980s.

Muirhouses *Falkirk* A residential village in Falkirk Council area, Muirhouses lies to the south of the Carriden Burn, immediately east of Bo'ness. Built in the 1860s as a model village for workers on the Carriden House Estate, the original cottages were designated a conservation area in 1975. Little Carriden to the north comprises a section of cottage-style local authority housing, and close by are Carriden House and the sites of a Roman camp and fort.

Muirkirk *East Ayrshire* An isolated village in East Ayrshire, Muirkirk lies on the upper reaches of the River Ayr, 9 miles (14 km) northeast of Cumnock. It takes its name from a moorland church founded in 1650 and developed in association with coal mining, ironworks and tar production. John Loudon McAdam was manager of the

British Tar Company's works near here from 1789. During the 20th century, industry went into steep decline.

Muirmill *Stirling* The settlement of Muirmill is located to the east of Carron Valley Reservoir, a mile (1.5 km) west of Carron Bridge in Stirling Council area.

Muirneag *Western Isles* A hill on the Isle of Lewis in the Outer Hebrides, Muirneag rises to 248 m (813 ft) 6 miles (10 km) west of Tolsta Head.

Muirton *Perth and Kinross* A locality on the northern edge of Strathmore, Perth and Kinross, Muirton lies a mile (1.5 km) to the west of Alyth.

Muirton *Perth and Kinross* A northern residential suburb of the city of Perth, Muirton lies between the Dunkeld Road and the River Tay, a mile (1.5 km) north of the centre of Perth.

Muirton of Ardblair *Perth and Kinross* A locality in Strathmore, Perth and Kinross, Muirton of Ardblair lies at the southwest edge of Blairgowrie.

Mulben *Moray* A settlement in Moray, Mulben lies on the Burn of Mulben, 4 miles (6.5 km) west of Keith. It developed following the arrival of the railway in 1858, its station eventually closing in 1964. The Glentauchers Distillery to the east was opened in 1898, and in 1974 the Auchroisk Distillery to the west came into production.

Muldoanich *Western Isles* A small uninhabited island located towards the southern end of the chain of islands comprising the Outer Hebrides, Muldoanich (Gael: *Maol Domhnaich* or 'Sunday Isle') rises steeply from the Minch to 153 m (501 ft). The island lies 2 miles (3 km) east of Vatersay and 3 miles (5 km) south-southeast of Castlebay, providing a conspicuous landmark for the ferry approaching Barra. The island has an area of 78 ha (193 acres).

Mull *Argyll and Bute* An island in the Inner Hebrides, Mull lies off the coast of Argyll and opposite the Morvern peninsula at the western entrance to the Firth of Lorn and Loch Linnhe. Largely of volcanic origin, its physical landscape comprises granite, gabbro and extensive basalt lava flows, Ben More (966 m/3168 ft) being the highest example of Tertiary basalt in Great Britain and the only Munro peak in the Scottish islands. The Ross of Mull forms an extensive peninsula at the southwest end of the island which is deeply indented with sea lochs and has an area of 89,111 ha (220,104 acres). Controlled from 1266 by the Lords of the Isles, Mull came to be associated with the Macdougall, Macdonald, Mackinnon and Maclean clans. The island's chief settlements are Tobermory, Salen, Calgary and Craignure, and there are ferry links between Craignure and Oban on the mainland and between Fishnish on the Sound of Mull and Lochaline in Morvern. Ferries also connect with the islands of Iona and Ulva. Places of interest include 13th-century Aros Castle, former home of the Lords of the Isles; Torosay Castle, a Scottish baronial-style castle designed in 1856 by David Bryce, with terraced gardens laid out by Sir Robert Lorimer in 1899; Duart Castle, seat of the Macleans of Duart; ruined Moy Castle, a former stronghold of the MacLaines of Lochbuie; and the Macquarie Mausoleum, the burial place of Lachlan Macquarie (1762–1824), Governor of New South Wales, Australia, who was born on Ulva. At its peak in the 1820s, the population of Mull was 10,600; it is now 2667. Crofting, fishing, sheep farming and tourism are the main industries.

Mull, Sound of *Highland* A channel separating the island of Mull in the Inner Hebrides from the mainland peninsula of Morvern, the Sound of Mull is 18 miles (29 km) long and has a maximum width of 3 miles (5 km).

Mull and West Highland Railway, The *Argyll and Bute* Located on the eastern coast of the island of Mull, Argyll and Bute, this railway is the only island tourist railway in Scotland. A 260-mm (10-in) gauge railway, it runs from the village of Craignure to Torosay Castle, a distance of a mile (1.5 km), and offers views over the Sound of Mull, the Glencoe hills and the island of Lismore.

Mullach an Rathain *Highland* A sandstone summit of the 5-mile (8-km) Liathach ridge in Wester Ross, Mullach an Rathain rises to 1023 m (3356 ft) northeast of Torridon.

Mullach Charlabhaigh The Gaelic name for Upper Carloway in the Western Isles.

Mullach Clach a' Bhlair *Highland* A summit in the northern Cairngorm Mountains, Mullach Clach a' Bhlair rises to 1019 m (3343 ft), 8 miles (13 km) southwest of Ben Macdui. Its name is associated with a rock outcrop known as Clach a' Bhlair. Red deer frequent the high stony ridge of Moine Mhòr that connects this peak to Sgor Gaoith.

Mullach Coire Mhic Fhearchair *Highland* A remote summit to the north of Kinlochewe in Wester Ross, Mullach Coire Mhic Fhearchair rises to a height of 1018 m (3340 ft) and is capped by Cambrian quartzite.

Mullach Coire nan Geur-oirean *Highland* A mountain in the Lochaber district of Highland Council area, Mullach Coire nan Geur-oirean rises to 727 m (2385 ft) in the Locheil Forest, 4 miles (6.5 km) southeast of the head of Loch Arkaig.

Mullach Fraoch-choire *Highland* A mountain to the north of Loch Cluanie in the Inverness district of Highland Council area, Mullach Fraoch-choire rises to 1102 m (3615 ft) in Glenaffric Forest. Its pointed summit lies at the meeting of three ridges and its name is derived from the Gaelic for 'heather-corrie peak'.

Mullach Mòr *Highland* A hill on the island of Rum in the Small Isles, Mullach Mòr rises to 304 m (997 ft) 2 miles (3 km) northwest of Kinloch.

Mullach na Dheiragain *Highland* A summit in the Inverness district of Highland Council area, Mullach na Dheiragain rises to 982 m (3221 ft) to the north of Loch Cluanie.

Mullach nan Coirean *Highland* A mountain in Lochaber district of Highland Council area, Mullach nan Coirean ('summit of the corries') rises to 939 m (3080 ft) at the western end of the Mamore ridge, to the south of Fort William.

Mullardoch, Loch *Highland* A reservoir in Glen Cannich, Loch Mullardoch lies between Loch Affric and Loch Monar, 7 miles (11 km) west of the village of Cannich.

Mull Head *Orkney* A headland in the Orkney Islands, Mull Head extends into the sea on the northern coastline of Papa Westray.

Mull Head *Orkney* A headland of the Orkney Mainland, Mull Head lies on the island's eastern coastline to the east of Deer Sound and 8 miles (13 km) east of Kirkwall.

Mull of Galloway, The *Dumfries and Galloway* A headland at the southern tip of the Rhinns of Galloway peninsula, the Mull of Galloway is the most southerly point in Scotland. Its cliffs are home to breeding colonies of sea birds, and the strong tidal currents around the Mull provide a perfect feeding ground for gannets. The lighthouse here stands 82 m (269 ft) above sea level and is 18.3 m (60 ft) tall. It was built in 1828 by Robert Stevenson, grandfather of Robert Louis Stevenson. Kennedy's Cairn tops a hill to the west of the southern cliffs, and ancient earthworks link the bays of East and West Tarbert which pinch the peninsula. Boats are said to have been dragged across this narrow neck in preference to negotiating the strong currents around the headland.

Mull of Kintyre *Argyll and Bute* A headland at the southwest extremity of the Kintyre peninsula, the Mull of Kintyre extends into the sea 10 miles (16 km) southwest of Campbeltown and 6 miles (10 km) west of Southend. It is the nearest point of Scotland to Ireland.

Mullwharchar *East Ayrshire* A hill in East Ayrshire, Mullwharchar rises to 692 m (2270 ft) to the south of Loch Doon, 3 miles (5 km) west of the summit of Corserine.

Mulzie, Strath *Highland* A valley in the northwest Highlands, Strath Mulzie lies 9 miles (14 km) east of Ullapool, between the Rhidorroch and Freevater Forests. The waters of the Corriemulzie flow northeastwards through the valley to merge with the Rappach Water to form the River Einig, a tributary of the Oykel.

Muness Castle *Shetland* Muness Castle is located at the southeast corner of the Shetland island of Unst and is the most northerly castle of the British Isles. Built in 1598 by the Perthshire laird Laurence Bruce, a half-brother of Robert Stewart, Earl of Orkney, this Z-plan castle is now in ruins. It was burned by Dunkirk pirates in 1627 and abandoned by 1750 after being used by the Dutch East India Company in 1713 as storage for cargo salvaged from the wreck of the *Rynenburgh*.

Munga Skerries *Shetland* The Munga Skerries form a group of sea rocks off the northwest coast of the Shetland Mainland, 2 miles (3 km) northeast of the entrance to Ronas Voe.

Munlochy *Highland* A small settlement on the east coast of the Black Isle in Ross and Cromarty, Munlochy lies 6 miles (10 km) north of Inverness at the head of Munlochy Bay, an inlet of the inner Moray Firth. It developed in the 19th century in association with the Fortrose branch of the Highland Railway, and stone for the military barracks at Fort George was quarried nearby.

Munnoch *North Ayrshire* A small settlement in North Ayrshire, Munnoch lies 3 miles (5 km) west of Dalry and 3 miles (5 km) east of West Kilbride. To the south lies the Munnoch Reservoir.

Murdoch Head *Aberdeenshire* A headland on the North Sea coast of Aberdeenshire, Murdoch Head forms a promontory at the south end of Long Haven, 4 miles (6.5 km) south of Peterhead.

Murieston *West Lothian* A suburb of the new town of Livingston, Murieston lies 2 miles (3 km) south of the town centre on the Murieston Water, a tributary of the River Almond.

Murkle *Highland* A small settlement on the north coast of Caithness, Murkle lies 3 miles (5km) east of Thurso and overlooks Murkle Bay to the north and Dunnet Bay to the northeast.

Murlaggan *Highland* A small settlement in Glen Spean in the Lochaber district of Highland Council area, Murlaggan lies to the north of the River Spean, 6 miles (10 km) east of Spean Bridge and 3 miles (5 km) west of the head of Loch Moy.

Murlaggan *Highland* A small settlement of Locheil, Murlaggan lies on the north shore of Loch Arkaig, 12 miles (19 km) northwest of Fort William.

Murray's Isles *Dumfries and Galloway* A small group of islets in Wigtown Bay, Dumfries and Galloway, Murray's Isles form part of the Islands of Fleet at the mouth of Fleet Bay. The islands are host to a colony of cormorants and are an important site for breeding gulls. The islands were gifted to the National Trust for Scotland in 1991 by Mrs Murray Usher of Cally.

Murrayfield *City of Edinburgh* A western suburb of the City of Edinburgh, Murrayfield lies 2 miles (3 km) from the city centre. Murrayfield Stadium, opened in 1925, is the home of the Scottish Rugby Union. Following significant upgrading in 1982 and 1989, the stadium now seats 67,500.

Murroes *Angus* A village in an Angus parish of the same name, Murroes lies on the Murroes Burn, 3 miles (5 km) northeast of the centre of Dundee. Murroes Castle, a tower house dating from the 16th century, is associated with the Fotheringham family, on whose vault the parish church was built in 1848.

Murthly *Perth and Kinross* A village in Perth and Kinross, Murthly lies to the south of the River Tay, 5 miles (8 km) southeast of Dunkeld. The Murthly Estate, including its 15th-century castle, was acquired by Sir William Stewart of Grandtully in 1615. A new castle was built in 1827–32 in the style of a Jacobean palace for Sir John Stewart but was never completed internally. That building was destroyed in 1949, the stone subsequently being used to build the dam and hydro-electric station at Pitlochry. Sir William Drummond Stewart, who inherited the estate from his brother in 1838, travelled extensively in America, returning to Scotland with two native Indians who lived in the 17th-century Garden House in the policies of Murthly Castle. Sir William, after being nursed back to health by Jesuits, converted to Catholicism and built the Chapel of St Anthony the Eremite at Murthly in 1846. Restored in the 1990s, this building was designed by James Gillespie Graham, probably in collaboration with A. W. N. Pugin.

Museum of Transport *Glasgow City* Glasgow's Museum of Transport is located within the Kelvin Hall complex, a building that also houses the Kelvin Hall International Sports Arena. Originally housed in the tramcar depot of Albert Drive (now the Tramway Theatre), it was transferred to the larger premises at the Kelvin Hall in 1987. There are exhibits on Glasgow's shipbuilding, locomotive building and car manufacturing history, as well as collections of cars, bicycles, buses, tramcars, railway engines, carriages and model ships. There is also a reproduction of a 1939 Glasgow street. The museum intends a further move to a purpose-designed building in Glasgow's waterfront redevelopment in 2009.

Musselburgh *East Lothian* Originally named Eskmouth, Musselburgh lies near the mouth of the River Esk, 6 miles (10 km) east of Edinburgh. As early as the 12th century, when the Scottish barons assembled here to swear loyalty to Alexander, the infant son of William the Lion, it had taken the name 'Muschelburgh' after a mussel bank at the mouth of the Esk. It earned its nickname, 'the Honest Toun', when its citizens disclaimed any reward for honouring the body of Robert the Bruce's nephew, the Earl of Moray, who died here in 1332. Created a burgh of barony in the early 14th century, Musselburgh was granted by David I to the abbey of Dunfermline as part of the parish of Inveresk. A chapel and hermitage dedicated to Our Lady of Loretto were founded in the late 15th–early 16th centuries and became a place of pilgrimage. Musselburgh became a burgh of regality in 1562 but its attempt to become a royal burgh in 1632 was challenged by Edinburgh, the rivalry between the two towns prompting the rhyme 'Musselburgh was a burgh when Edinburgh was nane, And Musselburgh will be a burgh when Edinburgh has gane'. There is evidence of a Roman fort at Inveresk, but the settlement developed from medieval times in association with fishing, textile weaving, paper making and trade through the small harbour at Fisherrow, which had closed to all but small vessels by the early 19th century as a result of severe silting. Today Musselburgh is a dormitory and market town with a horse-racing course which moved from Leith Sands to Musselburgh Links in 1816. The Links were also said to have been used as a golf course by James IV in 1504 and were the home of the Honourable Company of Edinburgh Golfers from 1836 to 1891, prior to moving to Muirfield. Buildings of interest include the Tolbooth (1590), which incorporates stonework from the chapel of Our Lady of Loretto, and Pinkie House, first built in the 16th century by an abbot of Dunfermline and now part of Loretto School. The wounded of the Battle of Pinkie, fought between Scots and English nearby in 1547, were brought to Pinkie House. There is an 18-hole golf course at Monktonhall and a monument to Dr D. M. Moir, the 19th-century poet and novelist. Formerly in Midlothian, Musselburgh has been part of East Lothian since 1975.

Mutehill *Dumfries and Galloway* A locality in Dumfries and Galloway, Mutehill lies nearly 2 miles (3 km) south of Kirkcudbright on the east side of Manxman's Lake, an inlet of Kirkcudbright Bay.

Muthill *Perth and Kinross* A village in central Perth and Kinross, Muthill is situated in the heart of Strath Earn on the A822, 3 miles (5 km) south of Crieff. Largely destroyed by Jacobites in 1716, Muthilll rose from the ashes in 1742 with the building of a military road by General Wade. One landmark that survived unscathed was the parish church with its 11th-century tower. Designated a conservation area, the village has nearly 100 listed buildings, which include some of the finest examples of 18th-century Scottish vernacular architecture. The Highlandman's Green is a relic of the area's cattle-droving days, this being a resting stance en route to the Falkirk Tryst. At its southern corner is the Dog's Head Well with its ogee top and sculpted dog's head. Local residents have included the 17th-century Doune gunmaker Thomas Cadell and the minor poet David Malloch (1703–63). Muthill has a bowling green and a nine-hole golf course. Nearby is Drummond Castle with its magnificent Italian-style garden.

Mybster *Highland* A small settlement in northeast Caithness, Mybster lies 2 miles (3 km) northwest of the Loch of Toftingall and 5 miles (8 km) west of Watten.

Myres Castle *Fife* Situated to the south of the village of Auchtermuchty in northwest Fife, Myres Castle was built as a Z-plan fortress in 1530 and has had many alterations and additions since. Owned by many families over the years, it is now run as a country-house hotel.

Na Buirgh The Gaelic name for Borve on South Harris in the Western Isles.

Na Cuiltean *Argyll and Bute* A group of rocky islets with a lighthouse in the Sound of Jura, the Na Cuiltean rocks lie off the southeast coast of the island of Jura, a mile (1.5 km) southeast of the Rubha na Caillich headland.

Na Gearrannan The Gaelic name for Garenin in the Western Isles.

Na Gruagaichean *Highland* A mountain in the Mamore range in the Lochaber district of Highland Council area, Na Gruagaichean rises to 1055 m (3456 ft) to the northeast of Kinlochleven.

Na h-Eileanan Flannach The Gaelic name for the Flannan Isles.

Na Hearadh The Gaelic name for Harris in the Western Isles.

Na Stacan Dubha The Gaelic name for the Stack Islands in the Western Isles.

Naast *Highland* A settlement in Wester Ross, Naast lies to the west of Loch Ewe, 3 miles (5 km) northwest of Poolewe.

Nairn *Highland* The former county town of Nairnshire, Nairn lies at the mouth of the River Nairn where it empties into the Moray Firth, 16 miles (26 km) east of Inverness. In medieval times it developed in association with a royal castle and was designated a royal burgh in 1189 and the centre of a sheriffdom shortly after. When piers were built at the river mouth by Thomas Telford in the 1820s, Nairn became an important fishing port. Following the arrival of the railway in 1855, it developed as a resort town, its fine climate, sandy beaches, covered swimming pool and two 18-hole golf courses making it a popular destination. In the 20th century an auction market was opened, and between 1975 and 1996 Nairn was the administrative centre of the district of Nairn in Highland Region. Its harbour, rebuilt in the 19th and 20th centuries, is used by pleasure craft, and there are two museums established in the 1980s.

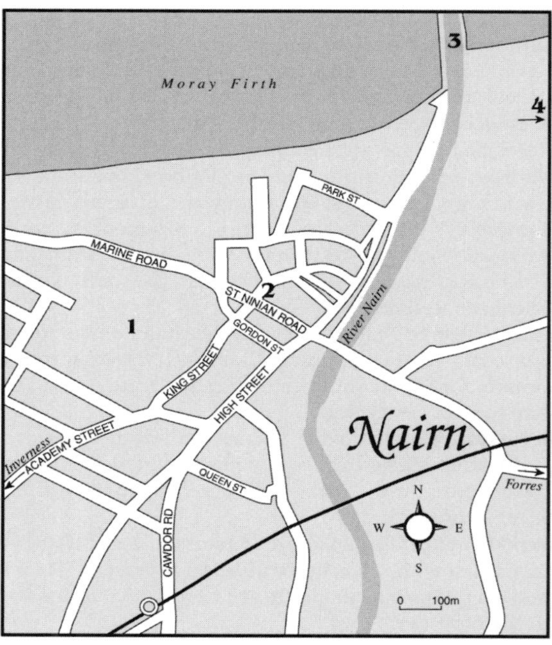

1 *Nairn Museum*
2 *Fishertown Museum*
3 *Piers*
4 *Culbin Sands*

Nairn, River *Highland* A river to the east of Loch Ness, the Nairn rises in headstreams on the slopes of Carn Ghriogair in the Monadhliath Mountains and flows northeastwards through Strathnairn for 38 miles (61 km) to empty into the Moray Firth at Nairn.

Nairnshire An ancient county and earldom of northern Scotland, Nairnshire was a district of Highland Regional Council between 1975 and 1996. Its chief town was Nairn.

Nant, Glen *Argyll and Bute* A glen to the northwest of Loch Awe in the Lorn district of Argyll and Bute, Glen Nant carries the River Nant northwards for 4 miles (6.5 km) from Loch Nant before entering Loch Etive at Airds Bay.

Narachan Burn *Argyll and Bute* A headstream of the Carradale Water on the Kintyre peninsula, the Narachan Burn rises on Narachan Hill to the west of Sunadale.

Narrows, the *Highland* The narrowest point on Loch Linnhe, the Narrows form a narrow neck between Ardgour and that part of Lochaber to the south of Fort William. The Corran Ferry crosses the loch here.

National Gallery of Scotland A neoclassical building at the foot of The Mound in Edinburgh, the National Gallery of Scotland was designed by W. H. Playfair and completed in 1854. The gallery incorporates Scotland's foremost collection of paintings, drawings and prints from the early Renaissance to the late 19th century, including the work of leading Scottish artists as well as European masters such as Constable, El Greco, Poussin, Raphael, Rembrandt, Reynolds, Rubens, Titian, Turner, Van Dyck, Velazquez and Vermeer. In 1995 Canova's *The Three Graces* was a controversial acquisition by the National Gallery of Scotland, which includes the Scottish National Gallery of Modern Art and the Scottish National Portrait Gallery, together with outstations at Duff House in Aberdeenshire and Paxton House in Scottish Borders.

National Library of Scotland *City of Edinburgh* The foundations of the main building of the National Library of Scotland on George IV Bridge, Edinburgh, were laid in 1939, but it was not until 1956 that the building was completed. Its frontage is decorated with sculpture by Hew Lorimer (1907–93), representing the arts and sciences. Founded in 1925, the core of the National Library's collection was derived from the Advocates' Library, which was established in 1680 by Sir George Mackenzie (1636–91). In 1989 the National Library's Map Library was relocated to a building at Causewayside designed by Sir Basil Spence.

National Monument *City of Edinburgh* A notable landmark on the skyline of Edinburgh, the National Monument stands on Calton Hill. Modelled on the Greek Parthenon, it was built to designs by C. R. Cockerell and William Playfair as a memorial to the Scottish soldiers and sailors who died in the Napoleonic Wars. A huge 6-tonne foundation stone was laid by George IV during his visit to Scotland in 1822, but building came to a halt in 1829 owing to a lack of funds. The unfinished monument came to be known as 'Edinburgh's Disgrace'.

National Stadium, the An alternative name for Hampden Park in Glasgow.

Nave Island *Argyll and Bute* A small uninhabited island in the Inner Hebrides, Nave Island lies off the northwest coast of the island of Islay, to the north of Ardnave Point.

Naver, Loch *Highland* A loch in Caithness, Loch Naver extends eastwards from Altnaharra for 6 miles (10 km). The River Naver emerges from the east end of the loch and flows north for 15 miles (24 km) through Naver Forest and Strathnaver before emptying into Torrisdale Bay on the north coast.

Navidale *Highland* A hamlet in eastern Caithness, Navidale lies a mile (1.5 km) northeast of Helmsdale.

Navity *Highland* A small hamlet in Easter Ross, Navity lies on the Black Isle, 2 miles (3 km) south of Cromarty.

Neaty, Loch *Highland* A small loch to the east of Strathglass, Loch Neaty lies 3 miles (5 km) southeast of Struy and a mile (1.5 km) northwest of the western end of Loch Bruicheach.

Neaty Burn *Highland* A river to the north of Glen Strathfarrar, the Neaty Burn rises on Beinn a' Bha'ach Ard and flows south for 5 miles (8 km) to join the River Farrar to the west of the Culligran Falls.

Neave Island *Highland* An uninhabited island off the north coast of Sutherland, Neave Island (also Coomb Island) lies opposite the settlement of Skerray, 3 miles (5 km) northwest of Torrisdale.

Neban Point *Orkney* A headland on the west coast of the Orkney Mainland, Neban Point extends into the sea 3 miles (5 km) northwest of Stromness.

Nechtansmere *Angus* The alleged site of a decisive battle between the Picts and Northumbrians in AD 685, Nechtansmere (occasionally Nechtanesmere) is located on low ground known today as Dunnichen Moss, situated at the foot of Dunnichen Hill, 4 miles (6.5 km) east-southeast of Forfar. Here Brude MacBeli, King of the Picts, defeated Ecgfrith, King of Northumbria. The battle is thought to be commemorated on Pictish symbol stones at Aberlemno to the north.

Necropolis, The *Glasgow City* Glasgow's answer to the Père Lachaise cemetery in Paris, The Necropolis lies to the east of the Royal Infirmary and Glasgow Cathedral. First used in 1833, it contains impressive tombs and headstones in Greek, Roman, Egyptian, Italian, Moorish and Gothic styles. Many notable Glasgow citizens lie buried in the Necropolis, including industrial chemist Charles Tennant (1768–1838).

Nedd *Highland* A crofting township in the Assynt district of Sutherland, Nedd lies at the head of Loch Nedd, an inlet of Eddrachillis Bay, 2 miles (3 km) southeast of Drumbeg.

Neidpath Castle *Scottish Borders* Located on a dramatic site on the bend of the River Tweed, a mile (1.5 km) west of Peebles, Neidpath Castle was built as a stronghold of the Hays in the late 14th century. It remained in their ownership for over 300 years until 1686 when it passed to William Douglas, 1st Duke of Queensberry, and after a time it became neglected. In 1810 it was acquired by the Earl of Wemyss, whose heirs have the title of Lord Neidpath.

Neilston *East Renfrewshire* A former textile village in Renfrewshire, Neilston lies on the Levern River 2 miles (3 km) southwest of Barrhead and 9 miles (14 km) southwest of Glasgow. It became a centre for bleaching cotton and calico printing in the 18th century, and continued printing and spinning cotton into the 20th century. John Robertson, who built the engine for the steamship *Comet* in 1811, was born in Neilston in 1782.

Neilston Pad *East Renfrewshire* A hill in Renfrewshire, Neilston Pad rises to 260 m (853 ft) a mile (1.5 km) south of Neilston.

Neist Point *Highland* The most westerly point on the isle of Skye in the Inner Hebrides, Neist Point forms a headland between Oisgill Bay and Moonen Bay, 8 miles (13 km) west of Dunvegan.

Neldricken, Loch *Dumfries and Galloway* A loch in Dumfries and Galloway, Loch Neldricken lies in hills to the east of Glentrool Forest, 11 miles (18 km) north of Newton Stewart.

Nell, Loch *Argyll and Bute* A loch in the Lorn district of Argyll and Bute, Loch Nell lies 2 miles (3 km) southeast of Oban. It receives the River Lonan from the northeast and drains southwestwards into Loch Feochan.

Nelson Monument *City of Edinburgh* A monument to Admiral Lord Nelson on Calton Hill in Edinburgh, the Nelson Monument was completed in 1807. In 1854 a time ball was set up on a mast at the top of the tower by the astronomer royal, Charles Piazzi Smyth (1819–1900). Falling at precisely 1.00 pm each day, it served as a time signal by which ships' chronometers were set in the Port of Leith.

Nemphlar *South Lanarkshire* A village in Clydesdale, Nemphlar lies to the north of the River Clyde, 2 miles (3 km) northwest of Lanark.

Nenthorn *Scottish Borders* A small village in Scottish Borders, Nenthorn lies to the south of Sweethope Hill, 3 miles (5 km) northwest of Kelso.

Nereabolls *Argyll and Bute* A locality on the island of Islay in the Inner Hebrides, Nereabolls (or Nerabus) is situated on the Rinns of Islay, 3 miles (5 km) southwest of Port Charlotte.

Nerston *South Lanarkshire* A settlement in South Lanarkshire, Nerston lies 2 miles (3 km) north of East Kilbride. Robert Wiseman Dairies, one of the largest commercial milk producers in the country, is based in Nerston.

Ness *Western Isles* An area of crofting townships at the northern tip of the Isle of Lewis in the Western Isles, Ness (Gael: *Nis*) lies to the south of the Butt of Lewis. Over 90 per cent of the people speak Gaelic.

Ness, Loch *Highland* Known the world over for its legendary monster, Nessie, Loch Ness lies in the Great Glen between Fort Augustus and Inverness. It is second only to Loch Lomond in area but double its volume and has a total length of 23 miles (37 km), an average depth of 182 m (600 ft) and a maximum depth of 230 m (754 ft) to the southwest of Urquhart Castle. The loch forms a major part of the Caledonian Canal, which links Loch Linnhe with the Moray Firth. During the construction of the canal, the level of the loch was raised by 3 m (9 ft) to ease navigation. St Columba (521–79) is said to have subdued a mysterious 'water beast', but it was not until 1932 that a spate of sightings focused media attention on Loch Ness.

Ness, River *Highland* The River Ness flows northeastwards from Loch Dochfour at the northeast end of Loch Ness in the Great Glen, emptying into the Moray Firth at South Kessock.

Ness Glen *East Ayrshire* A steep-sided gorge in East Ayrshire, Ness Glen carries the River Doon from Loch Doon 2 miles (3 km) northwards to Bogton Loch at Dalmellington.

Ness Head *Highland* A headland on the east coast of Caithness, Ness Head extends into the North Sea on the south side of Freswick Bay, 5 miles (8 km) south of Duncansby Head.

Ness of Burgi *Shetland* An exposed cliff-edged headland at the southern tip of the Mainland of Shetland, the Ness of Burgi lies to the west of Sumburgh Head and the West Voe of Sumburgh. On top of its low cliffs stands an Iron Age fort.

Nesting *Shetland* A locality on the east coast of Mainland Shetland, Nesting comprises North Nesting and the South Nesting peninsula 12 miles (19 km) north of Lerwick. South Nesting Bay forms a large inlet to the north of South Nesting.

Nethan, River *South Lanarkshire* A tributary of the River Clyde, the Nethan rises 2 miles (3 km) north of Glenbuck and flows 13 miles (21 km) northeast through Lesmahagow to join the Clyde at Crossford.

Nether Blainslie *Scottish Borders* A small hamlet in Lauderdale, Nether Blainslie lies 3 miles (5 km) southeast of Lauder.

Netherbow Port *City of Edinburgh* Once the principal gateway into the medieval burgh of Edinburgh, the Netherbow Port afforded an entry through the city wall from the Canongate to the east. The location of the gateway is marked on the road with brass plates and the name survives in the Netherbow Arts Centre, the home of the Scottish Storytelling Centre, which was established in 1995. The original Netherbow Bell has been re-hung in the open courtyard behind the Netherbow Arts Centre and John Knox's House. The Netherbow well-head outside John Knox's House is one of a number of enclosed wells erected *c.*1685 to supply water to the public.

Netherburn *South Lanarkshire* A small village in Dalserf parish, South Lanarkshire, Netherburn lies 3 miles (5 km) north of Blackwood.

Nether Dalgliesh Burn *Dumfries and Galloway* A small stream in eastern Dumfries and Galloway, the Nether Dalgliesh Burn rises on the slopes of the Cauld Face and flows southeastwards to join the Tima Water 4 miles (6.5 km) south of Ettrick.

Nether Kinmundy *Aberdeenshire* A hamlet in the Buchan district of Aberdeenshire, Nether Kinmundy lies on the edge of the Moss of Kinmundy, 6 miles (10 km) southwest of Peterhead and a mile (1.5 km) east of the Forest of Deer.

Nethermill *Dumfries and Galloway* A village in Dumfries and Galloway, Nethermill lies between the Kirkland Burn and the Garrel Water, 4 miles (6.5 km) northwest of Lochmaben.

Nethermuir *Aberdeenshire* A locality in the Buchan district of Aberdeenshire, Nethermuir lies 3 miles (5 km) south of Maud.

Netherthird *East Ayrshire* A village in East Ayrshire, Netherthird lies a mile (1.5 km) southeast of Cumnock.

Netherton *North Lanarkshire* A small village in North Lanarkshire, Netherton lies a mile (1.5 km) southwest of Wishaw.

Netherton *Perth and Kinross* A locality in southern Perth and Kinross, Netherton lies a mile (1.5 km) to the northeast of Milnathort near the southern entrance to Glenfarg.

Netherton *Perth and Kinross* A picturesque settlement 5 miles (8 km) northwest of Blairgowrie, eastern Perth and Kinross, Netherton lies on the Black Water near its confluence with the River Ericht. Its mill, smithy, cottages and neo-Gothic Free Church Mission date from the 19th century.

Netherton *Stirling* A locality in Stirling Council area, Netherton lies to the west of Bridge of Allan near the junction of the Allan Water with the River Forth.

Nether Wellwood *East Ayrshire* A small village in East Ayrshire, Nether Wellwood lies on the south bank of the River Ayr, 3 miles (5 km) southwest of Muirkirk.

Netherwood *East Ayrshire* A small village of East Ayrshire, Netherwood lies on the banks of the Greenock Water, 2 miles (3 km) northwest of Muirkirk.

Nethy, River *Highland* A tributary of the River Spey in its middle reaches, the River Nethy rises in the Cairngorm Mountains and flows north through Abernethy Forest to join the River Spey 4 miles (6.5 km) southwest of Grantown-on-Spey.

Nethy Bridge *Highland* A small village in Strathspey, Nethy Bridge lies on the River Nethy, 5 miles (8 km) south of Grantown-on-Spey. It developed in the 18th century in association with sawmilling, and during the late 19th century attracted tourists following the arrival of the railway in 1865. There is a school, hotel, outdoor centre and nine-hole golf course.

Nevie, Burn of *Moray* A small stream in Moray, the Burn of Nevie flows down the western slopes of Cairn Muldonich to the east of Tomnavoulin to meet the River Livet opposite Blairfindy.

Nev of Stuis *Shetland* A headland on the west coast of the island of Yell in the Shetland Islands, the Nev of Stuis extends into the sea on the west side of the entrance to the Whale Firth.

New Abbey *Dumfries and Galloway* An attractive village in Dumfries and Galloway, New Abbey lies near the mouth of the New Abbey Pow, 6 miles (10 km) south of Dumfries. Its situation in the lee of Criffell attracted Cistercian monks to establish here in 1273 a daughter foundation of Dundrennan Abbey, called Sweetheart Abbey. This was erected at the insistence of Devorgilla, widow of John Balliol, the founder of Balliol College in Oxford. The village largely comprises a single winding street, and buildings of interest include the late 18th-century New Abbey Corn Mill, beside which is a fish pond used to keep carp to provide fish for the monks.

New Aberdour *Aberdeenshire* A planned village in the Buchan district of northeast Aberdeenshire, New Aberdour lies just south of the Moray Firth coast, 7 miles (11 km) west of Fraserburgh. It was founded in 1798 to replace a former kirktown and comprises a long main street that stretches southwards from a road junction.

New Alyth *Perth and Kinross* A village in Strathmore, eastern Perth and Kinross, New Alyth lies on the A926, immediately south of the town of Alyth. It was laid out in a grid pattern in 1833.

New Byth *Aberdeenshire* A planned village in northern Aberdeenshire, New Byth lies 3 miles (5 km) north of Cuminestown and 8 miles (13 km) east-northeast of Turriff. It was founded in 1764 by James Urquhart of Byth, and its church, first built in 1793, was rebuilt in 1851.

New College *City of Edinburgh* New College, perched above The Mound in Edinburgh, houses the Faculty of Divinity of the University of Edinburgh. Originally the Free Church College, established following the Disruption in the Church of Scotland in 1843, the building was designed by W. H. Playfair and completed in 1850. Following the reuniting of the United Free Church with the Church of Scotland in 1929, the university's Faculty of Divinity, which trained ministers for the Church, relocated to the College building in 1935. The Assembly Hall is the venue for the annual General Assembly of the Church of Scotland, and from 1999 until 2004 provided a temporary debating chamber for the new Scottish Parliament.

New Cumnock *East Ayrshire* Founded as a mining village in the late 17th century, New Cumnock lies at the confluence of the Afton Water and the River Nith, 6 miles (10 km) southeast of Cumnock. It developed in association with limeworks and the mining of lead, antimony and coal, the last collieries closing in the 1970s. Opencast coal mining developed in the 1980s with a rail link to Ayr. In 2000, Britain's first unsubsidised wind farm was established on Hare Hill, 3 miles (5 km) south of New Cumnock.

New Deer *Aberdeenshire* The settlement of New Deer in Buchan is located 6 miles (10 km) west of Old Deer and 14 miles (22 km) southwest of Fraserburgh. The village was established in the late 18th century by James Ferguson of Pitfour and is the largest of the four settlements he created.

New Galloway *Dumfries and Galloway* A village in the Glenkens district of Galloway, New Galloway lies at the head of Loch Ken and at the eastern end of the Queen's Way, 19 miles (31 km) north of Kirkcudbright. It was built in the mid-17th century by Viscount Kenmure, who developed the site as a market centre for the Glenkens. Though it was created a royal burgh in 1630 it was not well served by its location and has remained the smallest burgh in Scotland. Nearby stand the remains of the 15th-century Kenmure Castle, the former seat of the Gordons of Lochinvar. Mary, Queen of Scots stayed here in 1563 on a tour, and was assisted by the family during her flight from Scotland. There is a nine-hole golf course,

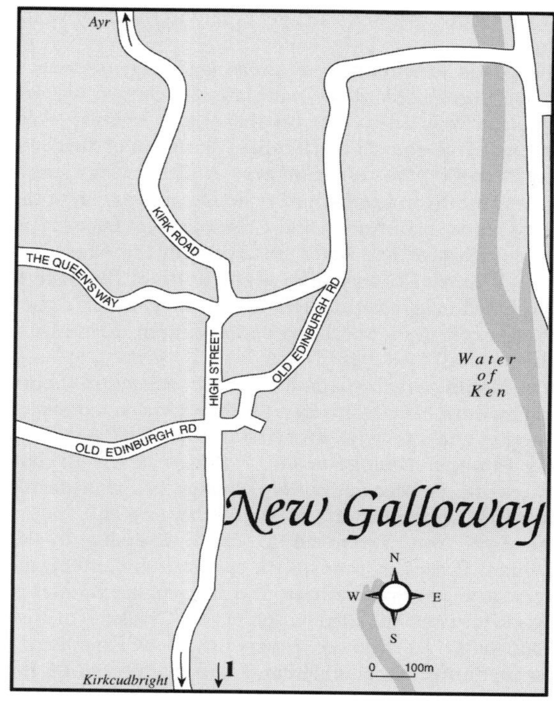

1 *Kenmure Castle*

and to the northwest is the Glenlee hydro-electric generating station built in 1933.

New Gilston An alternative name for Backmuir of New Gilston in Fife.

New Kelso *Highland* A small village in Wester Ross, New Kelso lies 3 miles (5 km) northeast of Lochcarron.

New Kilmarnock An alternative name for Barassie in South Ayrshire.

New Lanark *South Lanarkshire* A World Heritage Site situated in a picturesque gorge by the River Clyde, the planned 18th-century industrial village of New Lanark lies a half-mile (1 km) south of Lanark. Following the closure of the mills in 1967, the buildings were restored and are now preserved by the New Lanark Preservation Trust. In 1784, Glasgow textiles entrepreneur David Dale and industrial spinning pioneer Richard Arkwright identified the location as ideal for industrial development, with an excellent head of water to power cotton mills. They purchased the site from local landowner Lord Braxfield, the notorious 'hanging judge'. By 1793, Dale had built four mills, making New Lanark the largest industrial complex of its time, together with housing and a school. A total of 1157 people worked in the village, of whom 70 per cent were children, drawn from village families and orphanages as far afield as Glasgow and Edinburgh. Dale was noted for his good treatment of these orphans, remarkable for the time. They were well-fed, clothed and educated, and good standards of hygiene were maintained. In 1799, Robert Owen (1771-1858), Dale's son-in-law, purchased New Lanark and built on Dale's foundation to create a community where education and social justice were pre-eminent. Today, New Lanark comprises an award-winning visitor centre (opened in 1990), a hotel, youth hostel and housing for a community of around 150 people engaged in craft industries and small businesses. The Falls of Clyde and Falls of Clyde Wildlife Reserve are close by.

New Leeds *Aberdeenshire* A planned village of Buchan in Aberdeenshire laid out in the late 18th century by Lord Strichen, New Leeds lies on the A92, 8 miles (13 km) south of Fraserburgh and 2 miles (3 km) east of Strichen.

New Luce *Dumfries and Galloway* A village with a single street of 18th- and 19th-century houses in a parish of the same name in Dumfries and Galloway, New Luce lies at the junction of the Water of Luce with the Cross and Main Waters of Luce, 5 miles (8 km) north of Glenluce. It developed in association with lead mining, which ceased in the early 1950s, and has a parish church dating from 1821.

New Mains *South Lanarkshire* A village in South Lanarkshire, New Mains lies a mile (1.5 km) northeast of Douglas and a mile (1.5 km) west of the M74.

New Pitsligo *Aberdeenshire* A village in the Buchan district of Aberdeenshire, New Pitsligo lies amid fertile farmland on the eastern slope of Turlundie Hill and on the A950 from Peterhead to Banff. Founded by Sir William Forbes of Monymusk in the 18th century, the present village was built around the smaller hamlet of Cyaak, a name still used by the native 'Cyaakers' of New Pitsligo. At its peak of prosperity the village had a population of 2000 inhabitants and claimed to be the largest village in Scotland. It then had four churches, two of which survive, and earned a reputation for the production of lace, a manufacture introduced to the village in the 1820s. The art of lacemaking continues to be passed down from one generation to the next without written instructions. Nearby are the Northfield Farm Museum, and Bonnykelly Dam with trout fishing.

New Prestwick *South Ayrshire* A suburb of Ayr in South Ayrshire, New Prestwick lies 2 miles (3 km) northeast of Prestwick town centre.

New Sauchie *Clackmannanshire* Once a small village of Clackmannanshire, New Sauchie is now a northeastern suburb of Alloa.

New Scone The former name for Scone in Perth and Kinross.

New Stevenston *North Lanarkshire* Lying 2 miles (3 km) northeast of Motherwell, New Stevenston is one of a number of small villages that have merged to form a wider urban area including Holytown, Mossend, Newarthill and Carfin.

New Town *City of Edinburgh* The New Town of Edinburgh, which lies to the north of Princes Street Gardens, was built from the 1760s to replace the cramped and squalid conditions of the old medieval burgh. Promoted by the city's Lord Provost George Drummond (1687–1766), a design competition held in 1766 was won by James Craig (1744-95) with a patriotic plan of three parallel streets running between two grand squares. George Street, named in honour of George III, with Queen Street to the north and Princes' Street (the king's first three sons born by 1766) to the south, were designed to create a symbolic link between Scotland and England connecting St Andrew's Square in the east with St George's Square in the west. The latter was renamed Charlotte Square in honour of the queen and their first daughter before it was laid out by Robert Adam in 1791. Further symbolism was added with the creation of Rose Street and Thistle Street in 1781. The New Town continued to expand until 1830, the whole creating a grid plan of parallel streets, elegant squares and crescents. It was designated a World Heritage Site in 1995.

New Town *East Lothian* A village in East Lothian, New Town lies 3 miles (5 km) southeast of Tranent and a mile (1.5 km) northeast of Pencaitland.

New Valley *Western Isles* A linear crofting settlement on the Isle of Lewis in the Outer Hebrides, New Valley (Gael: *An Gleann Ur*) lies in a small valley to the southwest of the River Laxdale, a half-mile (1 km) west of Laxdale and 1.25 miles (2 km) northwest of Stornoway.

New Winton *East Lothian* A small village of 19th-century terraced cottages with a green in East Lothian, New Winton lies 1.25 miles (2 km) southeast of Tranent and a similar distance northwest of Pencaitland. Expanded as a residential settlement in the 20th century, its centre is a designated conservation area.

Newark Bay *Orkney* A sandy bay on the south coast of the Orkney Mainland, Newark Bay forms an inlet 2 miles (3 km) west of the Point of Ayre.

Newark Castle *Inverclyde* The remains of a castle on the south side of the River Clyde, Newark Castle lies to the east of Port Glasgow. Built in the 15th and 16th centuries, it was a stronghold of the Maxwell family and took its name from the nearby settlement of Newark, which was later renamed Port Glasgow.

Newark Castle *Scottish Borders* The ruined remains of 15th-century Newark Castle, a stronghold of the

Douglases, stand on the banks of the Yarrow Water, 3 miles (5 km) west of Selkirk in Scottish Borders.

Newarthill *North Lanarkshire* A former mining village in North Lanarkahire, Newarthill lies to the south of the Legbranock Burn, 3 miles (5 km) northeast of Motherwell. The construction engineer Sir Robert McAlpine (1847–1934) was born here.

Newbattle *Midlothian* A village in Midlothian, Newbattle lies on the left side of the River South Esk between Bonnyrigg and Dalkeith. Newbattle Abbey was founded as a monastery of the Cistercian order by David I in the 12th century. The abbey derived its income from sheep farming, coal mining and salt production, and was damaged during English raids in the 14th and 15th centuries. The last abbot, Mark Kerr, made a timely conversion to Protestantism and was able to retain the lands around the abbey. His son, also Mark, who became Lord Newbattle (1596) and Earl of Lothian (1606), built a house on the site of the abbey. It was later remodelled in turn by John Mylne (1650), William Burn (1836) and David Bryce (1858), the great drawing room being created by Thomas Bonnar *c.*1870. Newbattle Abbey remained the home of the marquesses of Lothian until 1937, when the building was given to the nation by Phillip Kerr, the 11th Marquess, to be used as a college of education.

Newbie *Dumfries and Galloway* A terraced village in Annandale, Dumfries and Galloway, Newbie lies on the west bank of the River Annan opposite Annan. It was built in 1898 to house boilerworkers at the nearby Newbie Mill.

Newbigging *Angus* A small village in southeast Angus, Newbigging lies 1.25 miles (2 km) south of Monikie and 2 miles (3 km) east-southeast of Wellbank. Stone is quarried nearby and there are souterrains to the east at Carlungie and to the south at Ardestie.

Newbigging *Angus* A hamlet in southern Angus, Newbigging lies immediately to the east of the A90, a half-mile (1 km) southeast of Tealing and 4 miles (6.5 km) north of Dundee.

Newbigging *Fife* A hamlet in the Fife parish of Auchtertool, Newbigging is an eastern extension of the village of Auchtertool.

Newbigging *South Lanarkshire* A hamlet 2 miles (3 km) east of Carnwath in South Lanarkshire, Newbigging is noted for its Old Cross dating from 1693. Newbigging railway station lay a half-mile (1 km) to the south on a branch line closed by the 1960s.

Newbridge *City of Edinburgh* A locality to the west of Edinburgh, Newbridge is situated at the junction of the M9 and M8, 3 miles (5 km) south of the Forth Road Bridge. There is a large industrial estate and the Newbridge Roundabout road hub.

Newbridge *Dumfries and Galloway* A hamlet of Nithsdale, Newbridge is located at the crossing of the Cluden Water, 2 miles (3 km) northwest of Dumfries.

Newburgh *Aberdeenshire* A dormitory village in the Aberdeenshire parish of Foveran, Newburgh lies on the south bank of the River Ythan, 4 miles (6.5 km) southeast of Ellon. It developed as a fishing village and port trading in grain, coal, timber and lime, and during the 12th and 13th centuries had a hospice that was an outpost of Deer Abbey. The first lifeboat station in Scotland to be provided by the RNLI was established here in 1828. There is an 18-hole golf course.

Newburgh *Fife* A town in northwest Fife, Newburgh lies on the south side of the Firth of Tay. Under the patronage of Lindores Abbey, whose ruins stand to the east, Newburgh was created a burgh of barony in 1266 by Alexander III. It was confirmed as a royal burgh in 1631 and developed as a port and market town for the surrounding area. During the 18th century the town was one of the two main ports in Fife handling flax, and in the 19th century the town prospered as a centre of salmon fishing and linen, jute and linoleum manufactures. Today, industry includes civil engineering, the manufacture of clothing and the extraction of aggregates at the nearby Clatchard Quarry. There is a small industrial estate to the east of the village. The Laing Museum, first opened in 1896, was gifted to the town by Alexander Laing (1808–92), who had made a collection of local and foreign antiquities. Designated a conservation area in 1969, Newburgh has a bowling club and a sailing club.

Newbyth *East Lothian* A hamlet in East Lothian, Newbyth lies on the Peffer Burn, 2 miles (3 km) north of East Linton. Newbyth House, which dates from 1817, was almost completely destroyed by fire in 1972 but was subsequently restored. Home of the Baird family, it was the birthplace of General Sir David Baird of Newbyth (1757–1829), a hero of military campaigns in India and during the Napoleonic Wars who was given a baronetcy in 1809.

Newcastleton *Scottish Borders* A village in Liddesdale, Newcastleton is situated on the Liddel Water, 20 miles (32 km) south of Hawick and 7 miles (11 km) east-northeast of Langholm. The village of Castleton was originally associated with Liddel Castle, which was built in the 12th century. In 1793, the Duke of Buccleuch built a new village on a grid plan for handloom weavers, naming it Newcastleton.

Newcraighall *City of Edinburgh* A former mining village and suburb of Edinburgh, Newcraighall lies to the east of the city centre, a mile (1.5 km) southeast of Portobello. Its row of miners' cottages and associated brickworks were developed in the 1890s, the Newcraighall colliery eventually closing in 1968. In the 1990s a retail park and cinema complex were created nearby.

Newfield *Dumfries and Galloway* A locality in Dumfries and Galloway, Newfield lies on the Kirkgunzeon Lane, 2 miles (3 km) northeast of Dalbeattie. Culloch Hill rises to the west.

Newfield *Highland* A small village in Easter Ross, Newfield lies 3 miles (5 km) south of Tain.

Newhailes *East Lothian* A fine Palladian mansion house near Newcraighall, Edinburgh, Newhailes lies a mile (1.5 km) west of Musselburgh and 4.5 miles (7 km) east of Edinburgh city centre. Known as Whitehill when it was built *c.*1686 by architect James Smith, it was from 1707 the home of the Dalrymple family who renamed it after Hailes Castle in East Lothian. The house was extended by William Adam and a notable library was created. Described by Dr Samuel Johnson as 'the most learned room in Europe', its collection of books passed to the National Library of Scotland following the death of Sir Mark Dalrymple in 1971. In 1996, Newhailes was acquired by the National Trust for Scotland.

Newhaven *City of Edinburgh* A former fishing port and shipbuilding centre to the west of Leith on the Firth of

Forth, Newhaven is now a district of northern Edinburgh. It was founded in 1500 by James IV as a royal dockyard to permit the building of much larger ships than was possible at Leith. Houses were built for French, Dutch and Flemish shipbuilders, and the Chapel of St Mary and St James, of which a fragment survives, was established in 1505. The immense *Great Michael*, the biggest vessel of its time, was launched from Newhaven in 1511. It was 73 m (240 ft) long, 11 m (36 ft) wide and had a hull of oak some 3 m (10 ft) thick, with a crew of 420 and the capacity to carry a thousand troops. Newhaven was the premier oyster port of Scotland from 1572 to *c*.1890, and the herring trade was important in the late 18th century. Edinburgh's first fish market was established here in the late 19th century, and photographers David Hill (1802–70) and Robert Adamson (1821–48) made a unique record of the Newhaven fisherfolk in 1843, one of the first uses of photography in the field of social history. The Society of Free Fishermen of Newhaven, which remains active today, gained its Royal Charter from James VI in 1573. Newhaven fishwives, with their cries of 'Caller Ou' and 'Caller Herrin', were a common sight on the streets of Edinburgh from the Middle Ages until the last one retired in 1974. Known today for its fish restaurants, Newhaven still retains the atmosphere of a fishing community whose story is told in the Newhaven Heritage Museum, opened on the site of the former fish market in 1993.

Newhouse *North Lanarkshire* A scattered settlement in North Lanarkshire, Newhouse lies to the south of the M8 between Glasgow and Edinburgh, 4 miles (6.5 km) southeast of Airdrie. It was created in the late 18th century at the junction of newly built turnpike roads but developed only from the 1930s following the construction of the A8 trunk road which attracted industry to the hamlet. An industrial estate was developed to the west of Newhouse on a site that attracted engineering, chemical and electronics industries. Legbranock close by was the birthplace of James Keir Hardie (1856–1915), a mineworker who founded the Labour Party.

Newington *City of Edinburgh* A district on the south side of Edinburgh, Newington lies between Dalkeith Road in the east and Causewayside and Mayfield Road in the west. The Grange lies to the west, Prestonfield to the east and Liberton to the south. Situated on a south-facing slope, its character differs on either side of Salisbury Road/Salisbury Place. To the north the streets are dominated by shops and Victorian tenement flats, while to the south is a leafy suburb characterised by large villas. The development of housing dates from 1805, when Newington House was erected by Edinburgh surgeon Dr Benjamin Bell (1749–1806). After Bell's death, the area around his house was developed for elegant town housing, exclusivity being maintained by gates that were locked each evening. A railway station served the community until 1962. Notable residents have included publishers William Blackwood (1776–1834) and Thomas Nelson (1780–1861), the infamous surgeon Dr Robert Knox (1791–1862) and photographer David Hill (1802–70). The Jewish synagogue on Salisbury Place was built in 1931, and the former Longmore Hospital is now the headquarters of Historic Scotland. The map-making firm of John Bartholomew and Son Ltd operated from the Geographical Institute in Duncan Street from 1911 to 1995, and in 1989 an extension of the National Library of Scotland housing its Map Library was opened on Causewayside. The Royal Commonwealth Pool on Dalkeith Road was opened prior to the Commonwealth Games held in Edinburgh in 1970, and to the east are the University of Edinburgh's Pollock Halls of Residence, built in the late 1960s.

Newkirk *Aberdeenshire* A village in the Cromar district of central Aberdeenshire, Newkirk lies 3 miles (5 km) west of Tarland amid a wooded landscape.

Newlandrig *Midlothian* A small village in Midlothian, Newlandrig lies 2 miles (3 km) northeast of Gorebridge and to the west of the upper reaches of the Tyne Water. Vogrie Country Park lies a mile (1.5 km) to the northeast.

Newlands *Scottish Borders* A small village on the upper reaches of the Hermitage Water in Liddesdale, Newlands lies 4 miles (6.5 km) north of Newcastleton.

Newlaw Hill *Dumfries and Galloway* A hill in Dumfries and Galloway, Newlaw Hill rises to 183 m (601 ft), a mile (1.5 km) to the northwest of Dundrennan.

Newmachar *Aberdeenshire* A dormitory village in eastern Aberdeenshire, Newmachar lies on the A947 from Aberdeen to Oldmeldrum, 9 miles (14 km) northwest of Aberdeen and midway between Dyce and Oldmeldrum. Cattle and horse fairs used to be held at the New Machar Inn to the north of the village, and Kinmundy to the south was the birthplace of the cartographer Robert Gordon of Straloch (1580–1661). Newmachar lies on the line of the former Formatine and Buchan Railway, which was closed in 1979 and subsequently developed as the Formartine and Buchan Way. There is an 18-hole golf course at Hawkshill to the south of the village.

Newmains *North Lanarkshire* A small town in North Lanarkshire, Newmains lies between the Garrion Burn and the South Calder Water, 2 miles (3 km) east of Wishaw. The settlements of Cambusnethan and Bonkle lie respectively to the southwest and northeast. It developed in the 19th century in association with coal mining and ironworks. The nearby Chapel Colliery was closed in the early 1960s and a decade later Newmains was bypassed by the new A71. Modern industries include opencast coal mining, the manufacture of concrete products and a motor auction.

Newmarket *Western Isles* A village on the Isle of Lewis in the Western Isles, Newmarket lies 2 miles (3 km) north of Stornoway and immediately to the north of Laxdale, from which it is separated by the River Laxdale.

Newmill *Moray* Founded *c*.1759 by the earls of Fife, the planned village of Newmill to the north of the River Isla was established as a rival to New Keith. Situated a mile (1.5 km) north of Keith, it consists of a main street which leads into a central square that is dominated by a War Memorial Clock Tower built in 1923.

Newmill *Scottish Borders* A small village of Teviotdale in Scottish Borders, Newmill lies at the confluence of the Allan Water with the River Teviot, 4 miles (6.5 km) southwest of Hawick.

Newmills *City of Edinburgh* A suburb of the City of Edinburgh, Newmills lies to the north of Balerno on the opposite side of the Water of Leith.

Newmills *Fife* A village in western Fife, Newmills lies on the north shore of the Firth of Forth between the Bluther Burn and Torryburn. It looks out over Torry Bay and takes its name from an important mill that once stood on the burn here. Operated by monks in medieval times, the mill dominated the local grain trade. On its main street are the 19th-century castellated gateway, flanking arches and neo-Gothic lodge that were once the impressive entrance to the former Torrie Estate.

Newmiln *Perth and Kinross* A small village of Strathmore in Perth and Kinross, Newmiln lies on the course of a tributary of the River Tay, 3 miles (5 km) north of Scone.

Newmilns *East Ayrshire* Said to have been established by the Campbells of Loudon in 1490, Newmilns lies on the River Irvine 7 miles (11 km) east of Kilmarnock. Newmilns Tower, dating from 1530, was a stronghold of the Campbells. Newmilns is one of a group of settlements, including Galston and Darvel, known as the 'valley burghs' and has associations with the 17th-century Covenanting movement. In the 19th century the village developed as a textile centre producing muslin, lace and curtain fabrics. In the 20th century its industries included the manufacture of textiles and light engineering. For its written support of the Union cause during the American Civil War in the 1860s, the US Congress later presented the village with an American flag.

Newport *Highland* A small village of the east coast of Caithness, Newport lies 4 miles (6.5 km) southwest of Dunbeath.

Newport-on-Tay *Fife* A town in northeast Fife, Newport-on-Tay lies on the Firth of Tay opposite Dundee and between the Tay Road and Rail bridges where it forms an urban area that includes Wormit and Woodhaven. It owes its existence to a ferry that crossed the firth here from at least the 12th century from a site once called Seamylnes. The town expanded during the 19th century, firstly with the building of a new harbour in the 1820s to a design by Thomas Telford, and secondly with the development of a fashionable residential commuter settlement for wealthy Dundee jute manufacturers. Formerly known as New Dundee, the greater part of this settlement was built on the Tayfield Estate of the Berry family and includes many interesting examples of Victorian architecture. The 2-mile/3.5-km-long Tay Rail Bridge, designed by W. H. Barlow and Sons and opened in 1887, replaced the earlier bridge of Thomas Bouch which collapsed in 1879, a year after its completion. To the east, the Tay is crossed by the 1.25-mile/2-km-long concrete multispanned Tay Road Bridge designed by Fairhurst and Partners and opened in 1966.

Newstead *Scottish Borders* A village in the lower reaches of Lauderdale in Scottish Borders, Newstead lies on the River Tweed, a mile (1.5 km) east of Melrose. To the east lie the ruined remains of the Roman fort of Trimontium.

Newton *Argyll and Bute* Situated on Newton Bay, an inlet on the south shore of Loch Fyne, the small village of Newton lies directly opposite Furnace.

Newton *Dumfries and Galloway* A small village in Annandale, Newton lies to the east of the M74, 7 miles (11 km) south of Moffat.

Newton *Scottish Borders* Situated at the northeast end of Teviotdale in Scottish Borders, Newton lies 3 miles (5 km) west of Jedburgh. The River Teviot flows to the north.

Newton *South Lanarkshire* A former mining village of South Lanarkshire, Newton lies between Cambuslang and Burnside, 5 miles (8 km) southeast of Glasgow city centre.

Newton *West Lothian* A small village on the south coast of the Firth of Forth, Newton lies 2 miles (3 km) west of the Forth Road Bridge.

Newton Mearns *East Renfrewshire* A small town in East Renfrewshire, Newton Mearns lies 7 miles (11 km) southwest of Glasgow. Possibly dating from the 14th century, it was created a burgh of barony in 1621 not far from Mearns Castle, a former stronghold of the Maxwells. The settlement is largely residential and has three 18-hole golf courses and one of Scotland's few synagogues. Newton Mearns was bypassed in 1996 by the M77.

Newton of Balcanquhal *Perth and Kinross* A locality in Arngask parish, Perth and Kinross, Newton of Balcanquhal lies on a minor road a mile (1.5 km) to the east of Glenfarg.

Newton of Falkland *Fife* A village in the Howe of Fife, Newton of Falkland lies between Falkland and Freuchie. The disused Bonthrone Maltings date from the 19th century.

Newton on Ayr *South Ayrshire* A northern suburb of Ayr established as a burgh of barony in the mid-14th century, Newton on Ayr developed in the late 18th century in association with coal mining and later with the expansion of the royal burgh of Ayr.

Newton Stewart *Dumfries and Galloway* A town in western Dumfries and Galloway, Newton Stewart lies on the River Cree 7 miles (11 km) north of Wigtown and 25 miles (40 km) east of Stranraer. The town was founded in the late 17th century by William Stewart of Castle Stewart and became an important local wool market centre at a river crossing. A bridge built over the Cree in 1745 was replaced by one constructed by John Rennie. The town's name changed to Newton Douglas in the 1770s when Sir William Douglas of Gelston became its superior, but his attempts at carpet manufacturing failed and the original name was reinstated in 1813. Newton Stewart has a livestock market and mohair-wool manufacturing industry. There is an 18-hole golf course and a museum.

Newton Wamphray *Dumfries and Galloway* A village of Annandale in Dumfries and Galloway, Newton

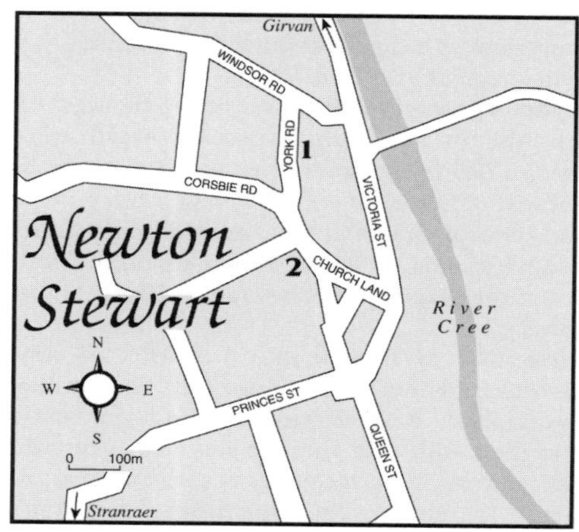

1 Newton Stewart Museum 2 Parish Church

Wamphray lies on the River Annan, 5 miles (8 km) south of Beattock.

Newtonferry An alternative name for Port nan Long in the Western Isles.

Newtongrange *Midlothian* A former mining village in eastern Midlothian, Newtongrange lies to the east of the River South Esk, 3 miles (5 km) south of Dalkeith. It developed as a colliery village from the 1830s, and by the 1890s had become Scotland's largest mining settlement following the sinking of the Lady Victoria Colliery with a shaft over 488 m (1600 ft) deep. Closed in 1981, the colliery buildings now house the Scottish Mining Museum. The ruined 12th-century Cockpen Old Parish Church and 15th-century Dalhousie Castle are to the southwest.

Newtonhill *Aberdeenshire* A commuter village in eastern Aberdeenshire, Newtonhill (formerly Skaterow) lies on the North Sea coast, 5 miles (8 km) northeast of Stonehaven and 10 miles (16 km) south of Aberdeen.

Newtonmore *Highland* A village in the upper reaches of the River Spey, Newtonmore lies on the Laggan Road linking Badenoch with Lochaber, 5 miles (8 km) southwest of Kingussie, 46 miles (74 km) northeast of Fort William and 38 miles (61 km) north of Pitlochry. It developed from a hamlet in the early 19th century, accommodating familes cleared from their crofts and unable to find space in the new planned village of Kingussie. Originally known as Stronemuir, its name was changed in 1828 to Newtonmore ('the big new town'). It developed as a resort town, local attractions now including the Waltzing Waters Light and Water Show (1992), the Highland Folk Park and Museum of Highland Sport (1995) and the Clan Macpherson Museum. There are sawmilling and whisky-blending industries.

Newtown St Boswells *Scottish Borders* A settlement in Scottish Borders, Newtown St Boswells is situated on the Bowden Burn above its confluence with the River Tweed, 3 miles (5 km) southeast of Melrose. The town developed as an important railway junction and market centre close to St Boswells' Green. Although the railway is long gone, Newtown St Boswells thrives as an administrative centre. From 1975 to 1996 it was the centre of the Ettrick and Lauderdale District and of Borders Region. It is now home to the headquarters of Scottish Borders Council.

Newtyle *Angus* A planned village in Angus, Newtyle is situated on the northern slopes of the Sidlaw Hills 5 miles (8 km) east of Coupar Angus. Founded in 1832 in connection with the development of a railway, it is laid out in a regular grid plan.

Newyork *Argyll and Bute* A locality on the west shore of Loch Awe in the Lorn district of Argyll and Bute, Newyork lies in the Inverliever Forest 11 miles (18 km) southeast of Oban.

Nibon, Isle of *Shetland* An uninhabited island in the Shetland Islands, the Isle of Nibon lies off the northwest coast of the Mainland of Shetland, 3 miles (5 km) west of Sullom.

Niddrie *City of Edinburgh* A district of southeast Edinburgh, Niddrie lies between Craigmillar and Newcraighall. It developed in the 19th century in association with coal mining and the manufacture of bricks, and in the 20th century was expanded as part of a scheme to rehouse residents from Edinburgh's Old Town. It occupies land formerly part of the Niddrie Marischal Estate.

Niddry *West Lothian* A locality to the east of the village of Winchburgh in West Lothian, Niddry comprises the farms of Niddry and Niddry Mains on the Niddry Burn. The L-plan Niddry Castle dating from c.1500 was a stronghold of the Setons.

Nigg *Highland* A small village in Easter Ross, Nigg lies on the east side of Nigg Bay, 6 miles (10 km) northeast of Invergordon. An oil-rig platform yard opened in the 1970s to the south on Nigg Bay and has continued to promote growth in the area. To the south, Nigg Ferry has made a connection to Cromarty on the Black Isle for at least eight centuries.

Nigg Bay *Aberdeen City* A small sandy beach on the North Sea coast, Nigg Bay forms an inlet between the headlands of Girdle Ness and Greg Ness, 2 miles (3 km) southeast of Aberdeen city centre. The mouth of the River Dee lies to the north and Duthie Park to the south.

Nine Mile Burn *Midlothian* A small hamlet in southern Midlothian, Nine Mile Burn lies 4 miles (6.5 km) southwest of Penicuik, between the North Esk Reservoir and the River Esk.

Ninemile Bar An alternative name for Crocketford in Dumfries and Galloway.

Nis The Gaelic name for Ness in the Western Isles.

Nisbet *Scottish Borders* A small village in Teviotdale, Nisbet lies on the River Teviot, 4 miles (6.5 km) northeast of Jedburgh. The Waterloo Monument, erected by the Marquess of Lothian to commemorate victory at the Battle of Waterloo, stands immediately to the northwest.

Nista *Shetland* A small, uninhabited island in the Shetland Islands, Nista lies off the east coast of Whalsay, a mile (1.5 km) south of Skaw Taing.

Nith, River *East Ayrshire/Dumfries and Galloway* A river of southwest Scotland, the Nith rises in East Ayrshire between Enoch Hill and Prickeny Hill at an altitude of 425 m (1400 ft) above sea level. It flows generally southeastwards for 71 miles (112 km) before falling into the Solway Firth 14 miles (22 km) south of Dumfries, where it forms a 10-mile (16-km) estuary. Its principal tributaries are the Afton Water, Kello Water, Crawick Water, Euchan Water, Minnick Water, Enterkin Burn, Carron Water, Cample Water, Scar Water, Duncow Burn, Cluden Water, Cargen Pow and Newabbey Pow.

Nith Bridge *Dumfries and Galloway* A locality in Nithsdale, Dumfries and Galloway, Nith Bridge lies at a crossing of the River Nith to the west of Thornhill. In a field to the west of the river stands an Anglian sculptured cross-shaft dating from the 10th century.

Nithsdale *East Ayrshire/Dumfries and Galloway* The name given to the valley of the River Nith, Nithsdale is the westernmost of the three ancient divisions of Dumfries-shire and was sometimes referred to as Strathnith or Stranith. It stretches from East Ayrshire to the Solway coast and includes the settlements of Dumfries, Thornhill, Closeburn, Sanquhar and Kirkconnel.

Nitshill *Glasgow City* A southwest district of Glasgow, Nitshill lies between the Levern Water to the west and the M77 to the east, 5 miles (8 km) from the city centre. It developed in the 19th century in association with various mineral industries and coal mining, and has an industrial estate with light-engineering and textile industries.

No Ness *Shetland* A promontory on the east coast of the Shetland Mainland, No Ness forms a headland at the southern entrance to Mousa Sound, which separates Mainland Shetland from the island of Mousa.

Noddsdale Water *North Ayrshire* A river of North Ayrshire, Noddsdale Water rises in the Clyde Muirshiel Regional Park and flows 7 miles (11 km) southwestwards to empty into the Firth of Clyde a half-mile (1 km) north of Largs.

Noe, River *Argyll and Bute* Rising on Stob Diamh, 3 miles (5 km) northwest of Lochawe in Argyll and Bute, the River Noe flows 5 miles (8 km) northwest through Glen Noe to empty into Loch Etive, a mile (1.5 km) west of the settlement of Glennoe.

Noir, Loch *Moray* A small loch in the uplands of Moray to the southwest of Dallas, Loch Noir is the source of the Burn of Clasgour which flows north and east to join the River Lossie.

Noltland Castle *Orkney* A Z-plan castle on the island of Westray in the Orkney Islands, Noltland Castle lies to the west of Pierowall. Begun in 1560, it was built by Gilbert Balfour.

Noness Head *Shetland* A headland on the east coast of the Shetland Mainland, Noness Head forms a promontory between the mouths of the Colla Firth and Swinning Voe.

Nor Wick *Shetland* A bay on the northeast coastline of the island of Unst in the Shetland Islands, Nor Wick lies 5 miles (8 km) northeast of Baltasound.

Noranside *Angus* A small village in Angus, Noranside lies by the Noran Water, 3 miles (5 km) northwest of Finavon. The open prison of Noranside lies to the northeast.

Noran Water *Angus* A river of Angus that rises in headstreams in the southern Grampians, the Noran Water flows southwards to the valley of Strathmore through Glen Ogil in the Braes of Angus, forming a reservoir in the glen and then a cascade at the Falls of Drumly Harry. It turns southeast at the Den of Ogil and flows on to meet the River South Esk west of Brechin.

Norman's Law *Fife* A summit at the eastern extremity of the Ochil Hills, Norman's Law rises to 285 m (936 ft) in the parish of Dunbog, 5 miles (8 km) northeast of Newburgh. On its rocky summit are the remains of an extensive Iron Age fort.

North Ayrshire *Area: 888 sq. km (342 sq. miles)* A local government area in west-central Scotland, North Ayrshire lies on the Firth of Clyde and includes the Cunninghame district of Ayrshire as well as the islands of Arran, Great Cumbrae and Little Cumbrae. It is bounded by East Ayrshire, East Renfrewshire, Inverclyde, Renfrewshire and South Ayrshire council areas, and the Firth of Clyde. Its main towns are Irvine (administrative centre), Ardrossan, Saltcoats, Largs, Dalry, Stevenston and Kilwinning. The area includes mountains and part of Clyde Muirshiel Regional Park in the north. Its chief rivers include the Garnock, Dusk Water and Noddsdale Water. There are ferry links with islands in the Firth of Clyde from Ardrossan and Largs. Places of interest include Brodick Castle, the North Ayrshire Museum in Ardrossan and Kelburn Country Centre near Largs.

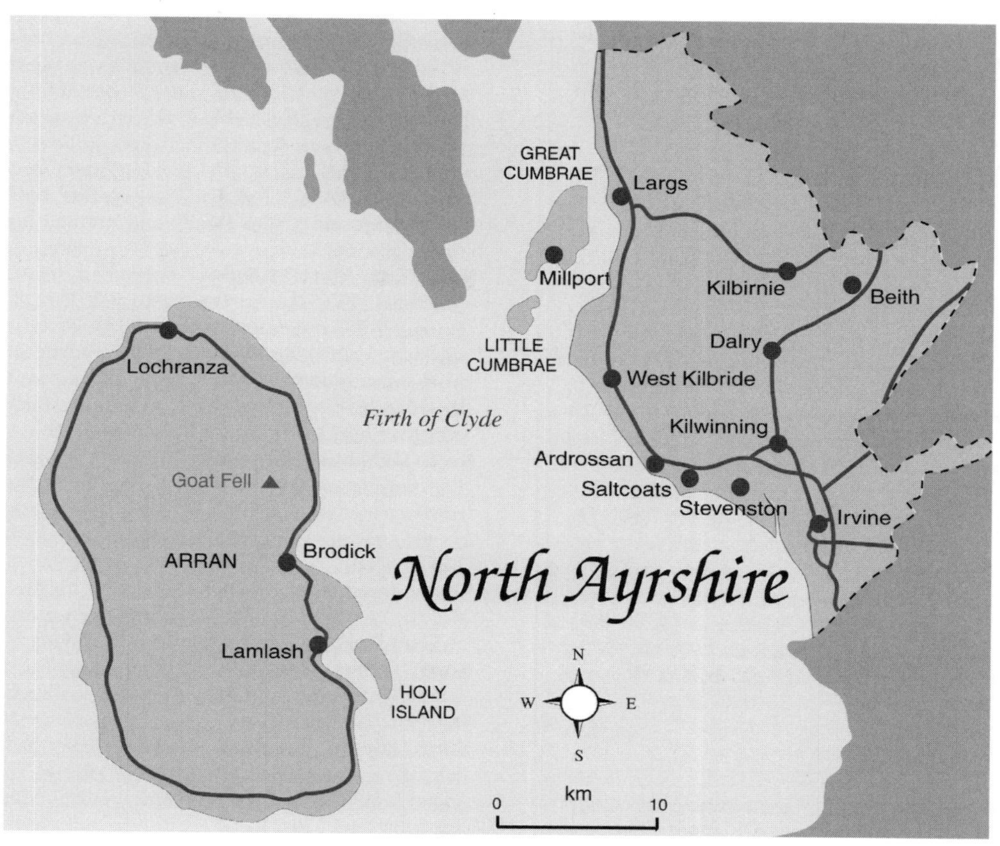

North Ballachulish *Highland* A village on the northern shore of Loch Leven in the Lochaber district of Highland Council area, North Ballachulich lies 8 miles (13 km) west of Kinlochleven opposite South Ballachulish.

North Balloch *South Ayrshire* Located 4 miles (6.5 km) east of Barr in South Ayrshire, the settlement of North Balloch lies on the north bank of the Stinchar River a half-mile (1 km) north of South Balloch.

North Bay *Orkney* A bay on the southern coastline of the island of Hoy in the Orkney Islands, North Bay forms an inlet to the north of the Ayre, the strip of land that connects South Walls to Hoy.

North Bay *Orkney* A large bay on the west coast of the island of Sanday in the Orkney Islands, North Bay is separated by the headland of Ness of Brough from the Bay of Brough to the south.

North Bay *Western Isles* A sizeable inlet on the northeast coast of Barra in the Outer Hebrides, North Bay (Gael: *Bagh a Tuath*) lies 4.5 miles (7 km) northeast of Castlebay. There are a number of islands at the mouth of North Bay, the largest being Fuiay and Flodday.

North Berwick *East Lothian* A residential and resort town on the south shore of the Firth of Forth, North Berwick lies 25 miles (40 km) east of Edinburgh. North Berwick, called this to distinguish it from Berwick-upon-Tweed which was sometimes known as South Berwick, belonged to the earls of Fife in the 12th century and was a staging point for pilgrims on their way to St Andrews. It was founded as a burgh in 1373 and raised to the status of a royal burgh c.1425. In the 19th century North Berwick developed as a fishing port, its harbour being well protected by outlying rocks, and with the arrival of the railway in 1850 came tourists. It it is still a holiday, golfing, sailing and angling centre, and has a sports centre with a swimming pool opened in 1996. The Scottish Seabird Centre was opened in 2000. Buildings of interest include a 12th-century Cistercian nunnery, the ruined 17th-century Old Parish Church, the 18th-century Lodge and Town House, North Berwick Museum and the pink sandstone art deco Playhouse Cinema built in the 1930s.

North Berwick Law *East Lothian* Topped by a whale-jaw arch, North Berwick Law rises to 187 m (613 ft) to the south of North Berwick. It comprises the remains of a volcanic plug dating from the Lower Carboniferous period around 335 million years ago. During the last Ice Age a crag-and-tail feature was formed.

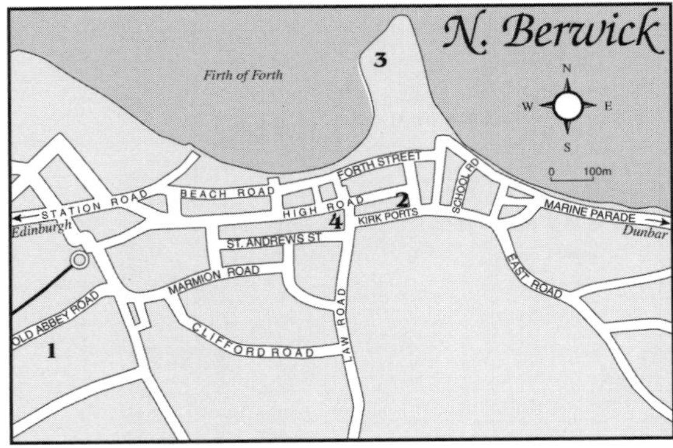

1 *North Berwick Abbey*
2 *North Berwick Museum*
3 *Scottish Seabird Centre*
4 *Old Parish Church*

North Boisdale *Western Isles* A linear crofting settlement on the southwest coast of South Uist in the Outer Hebrides, North Boisdale (Gael: *Baghasdal*) is located 3 miles (5 km) west-southwest of Lochboisdale. South Boisdale lies immediately to the southeast.

North Burnt Hill *North Ayrshire/Renfrewshire* A hill in Clyde Muirshiel Regional Park, North Burnt Hill rises to 431 m (1414 ft) on the border between North Ayrshire and Renfrewshire, 6 miles (10 km) northeast of Largs.

North Calder Water A river largely in North Lanarkshire, the North Calder Water rises in the Black Loch 4 miles (6.5 km) west-northwest of Armadale. It flows 16 miles (26 km) southwest through Hillend Reservoir, Caldercruix, Airdrie and Calderbank before joining the River Clyde near Broomhouse, a mile (1.5 km) northwest of Uddingston.

North Carr Rock *Fife* Situated in the North Sea off the coast of Fife, the North Carr Rock lies a mile (1.5 km) north of the headland of Fife Ness. A warning beacon is located on the rock.

North Connel *Argyll and Bute* A hamlet in the Benderloch district of northern Argyll and Bute, North Connel lies on the north shore of Loch Etive, just to the west of the Connel Bridge, 4.5 miles (7 km) northeast of Oban. Connel Airfield lies immediately to the west.

North Craigs *Dumfries and Galloway* A hamlet in Dumfries and Galloway, North Craigs lies on the Kirtle Water, 3 miles (5 km) northeast of Eaglesfield.

North Dell *Western Isles* A township located towards the northern end of the Isle of Lewis in the Western Isles, North Dell (Gael: *Dail bho Thuath*) lies 3 miles (5 km) south of the Butt of Lewis, between the settlements of South Dell and Cross.

North Esk, River *Angus* A river of Angus, the North Esk is formed in the southern Grampians by the meeting of the Water of Mark and the Water of Lee. It flows east and southeast through Glen Esk, falling down through the Braes of Angus to Strathmore, where it flows onwards to enter the North Sea 4 miles (6.5 km) north of Montrose. Its chief tributaries are the Water of Tarf, Luther Water, West Water and Craick Water, and its total length is 29 miles (47 km).

North Esk, River *Midlothian* A river in the Midlothian, the North Esk rises in the North Esk Reservoir in the Pentland Hills, a mile (1.5 km) north of the village of Carlops. It flows northeast to join the River South Esk a mile (1.5 km) north of Dalkeith. At this point it becomes the River Esk and flows north to join the Firth of Forth at Musselburgh.

North Galson *Western Isles* The scattered settlement of North Galson (Gael: *Gabhsunn Bho Tuath*) lies on the northwest coast of the Isle of Lewis in the Western Isles, 7 miles (11 km) southwest of Port of Ness. South Galson lies adjacent.

North Head *Highland* A headland on the coast of Caithness, North Head extends into the sea on the north side of Wick Bay, 2 miles (3 km) east of Wick.

North Holms *Shetland* A small, uninhabited rocky island in the Shetland Islands, North Holms lies off the west coast of Unst.

North Isle of Gletness *Shetland* The uninhabited island of North Isle of Gletness is one of two islands located off the east coast of Mainland Shetland, to the south of Glet Ness.

North Kessock *Highland* A village in Easter Ross, North Kessock lies on the northern shore of the Beauly Firth opposite Inverness, to which it is connected by the Kessock Bridge which superseded the ferry in 1982.

North Lanarkshire *Area: 476 sq. km (184 sq. miles)* A local government area to the east of Glasgow in central Scotland, North Lanarkshire extends southwards from the Kilsyth Hills to the River Clyde. It is bounded by South Lanarkshire, Glasgow, Falkirk, East Dunbartonshire, Stirling and West Lothian, and its chief towns are Airdrie, Coatbridge, Cumbernauld, Kilsyth, Motherwell (administrative centre), Shotts and Wishaw. Formerly with coal-mining, engineering and steel industries, its modern industries are linked to the rest of Europe via the Eurocentral freight facility at Mossend. Places of interest include Drumpellier Country Park and Summerlee Heritage Trust in Coatbridge, and Palacerigg Country Park in Cumbernauld.

North Lee *Western Isles* A hill in the Outer Hebrides, North Lee rises to 250 m (820 ft) on the island of North Uist.

North Middleton *Midlothian* A small village in eastern Midlothian, North Middleton lies 2 miles (3 km) southeast of Gorebridge and a half-mile (1 km) southwest of Borthwick. The village of Middleton lies a half-mile (1 km) to the south and the early 18th-century Middleton Hall lies to the southeast.

North Morar *Highland* A mountainous area of southwest Highland Council area, North Morar lies between Loch Morar and Loch Nevis. Its chief settlement is Mallaig.

North Ness *Orkney* A headland in the southeast of the island of Hoy in the Orkney Islands, North Ness lies on the northern side of Longhope. A small settlement of the same name, with a jetty, is located here and the hamlet of Longhope lies opposite.

North Queensferry *Fife* A former ferry port on the River Forth, opposite South Queensferry, North Queensferry lies between the northern ends of the Forth Rail and Road Bridges. The ferry crossing is said to derive its name from Queen Margaret, who regularly crossed the river here travelling to and from her chapel at Edinburgh Castle. On her death in 1093 the queen made her last crossing on the royal ferry to her final resting place at Dunfermline Abbey, which was subsequently given the ferry rights by her son David I. In medieval times the route became popular with pilgrims to the shrines of St Andrew and St Margaret. Between 1867 and 1893, the ferry crossing was controlled by the North British Railway, which built the Forth Bridge (1890). Ferries continued to operate between North and South Queensferry until 1964, when the Forth Road Bridge was opened to traffic. The Town Pier was built by John Rennie in 1810–18 and extended for steamships by John Telfer in 1828. The Railway Pier, dating from 1877, was later used by car ferries. At the Pierhead is the Signal Tower, with its hexagonal copper-domed lantern (*c.*1810).

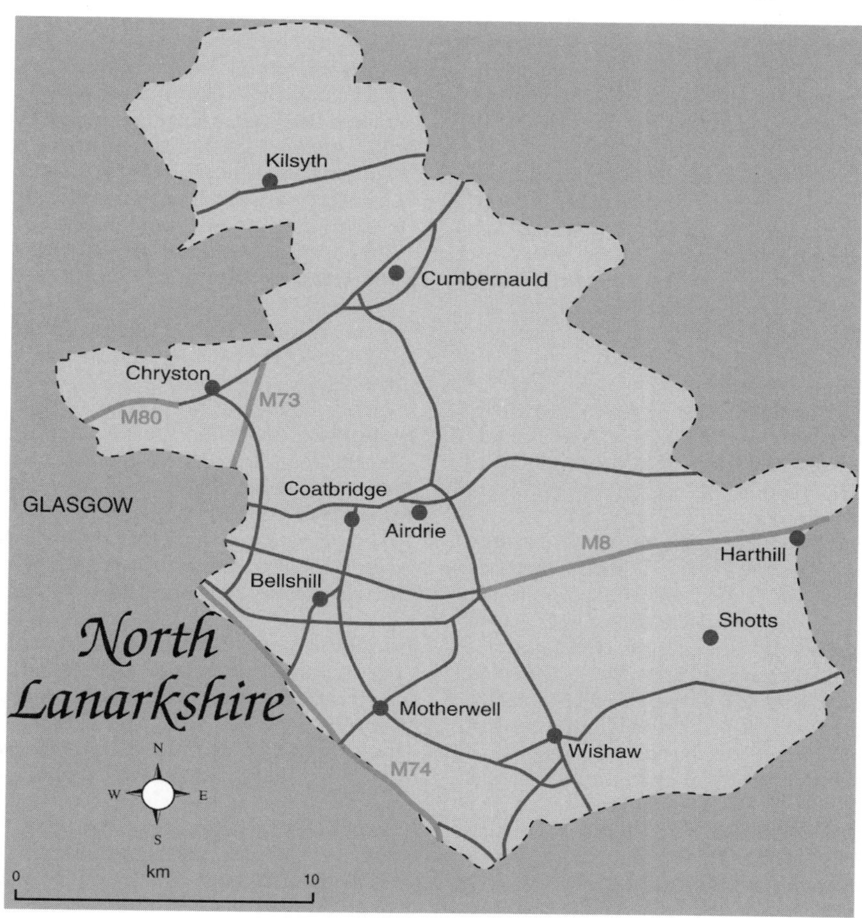

Designated a conservation area in 1984, North Queensferry is now largely a dormitory village. Its chief attractions are the views of the two bridges and the Deep-Sea World marine aquarium.

North Queich River *Perth and Kinross* A river of Perth and Kinross, the North Queich River is formed by the merger of headstreams that rise on the Ochil Hills. It flows in an easterly direction to enter Loch Leven to the northwest of Kinross.

North Roe *Shetland* A village and locality at the northern end of Mainland Shetland, North Roe lies to the north of Burra Voe.

North Ronaldsay *Orkney* The northernmost island of the Orkney Islands, North Ronaldsay is further north than the southern tip of Norway, although the Gulf Stream gives it an average temperature that is 5.5 °C warmer. Old traditions, such as the custom of communal grazing of the seaweed-eating North Ronaldsay sheep on the seashore, prevail here, and Orcadian surnames predominate in this, the remotest of the Orkney Islands. Owned for over 200 years by the Traill family, the island has an area of 780 ha (1927 acres) and a population that has fallen from 547 in 1881 to 70 in 2001. Though a small island, North Ronaldsay has a rich flora and a wide range of migrant birds. At 33 m (109 ft), the New Lighthouse built at Dennis Head in 1854 is the tallest land-based lighthouse in the UK. Sites of archaeological interest include the Broch of Burrian, Tor Ness, the Brae of Stennabreck and Muckle Gersty dykes. The island has an airstrip and there is a weekly ferry service from South Bay to Mainland Orkney. The island is separated from Sanday by North Ronaldsay Firth.

North Shian *Argyll and Bute* A scattered settlement in Argyll and Bute, North Shian lies on the northern shore of Loch Creran, directly opposite South Shian.

North Third *Stirling* A locality in Stirling Council area, North Third lies by the Bannock Burn, 4 miles (6.5 km) southwest of Stirling. The North Third Reservoir has been created by damming the Bannock Burn here.

North Tolsta *Western Isles* A settlement in the Outer Hebrides, North Tolsta (Gael: *Tolastadh bho Thuath*) lies on the east coast of the Isle of Lewis, 2 miles (3 km) west of Tolsta Head.

North Ugie Water *Aberdeenshire* A river of Aberdeenshire, the North Ugie Water rises on the eastern side of Windyheads Hill and flows in a southeasterly direction to merge with the South Ugie Water, a mile (1.5 km) northeast of Longside. At this point the rivers become the River Ugie.

North Uist *Western Isles* Measuring 12 miles (19 km) by 16 miles (26 km), the low-lying island of North Uist (Gael: *Uibhist a Tuath*) in the Outer Hebrides has fertile croftland on the west and a heavily indented coastline in the east that is deeply penetrated by Loch Maddy and Loch Euphort. Its total area is 34,464 ha (85,126 acres) and its principal settlement is the ferry port of Lochmaddy. The island economy is based on crab and lobster fishing, scallop farming, crofting, weaving and knitting, bulb growing and the production of alginates from seaweed. The Macdonalds from Sleat, who succeeded the MacRuaraidhs and eventually evicted many crofting tenants, owned the island from 1495 until 1855. Notable landmarks include the pre-Reformation church of St Columba in Clachan Sands, the ruins of the medieval monastery and college of Teampull na Trionaid at Carinish and the adjacent Teampull Clan A' Phiocair, the chapel of the Macvicars who taught at the college. At the northern tip of the island a ferry service from Port nan Long connects with Berneray and Leverburgh in South Harris.

Northbay *Western Isles* A crofting township on the east coast of Barra in the Outer Hebrides, Northbay (also Bayhirivagh or Bayherivagh, Gael: *Bagh Shiarabhagh*) lies around the head of Bay Hirivagh, an inlet of North Bay, 4 miles (6.5 km) northeast of Castlebay.

Northfield *City of Edinburgh* A residential suburb of the City of Edinburgh, Northfield lies to the west of Portobello, 2 miles (3 km) east of the city centre. Northfield was the birthplace of the champion boxer Ken Buchanan (b.1945).

Northfield House *East Lothian* A 17th-century house with a walled garden on the south side of Prestonpans, Northfield House was built in 1580–90 and later extended by Joseph Marjoribanks, an Edinburgh burgess, who acquired the property in 1607. In 1954 the architect W. Schomberg Scott purchased Northfield and commenced extensive conservation work.

Northmavine *Shetland* A peninsula, district and old parish, Northmavine lies in the far northwest of the Mainland of Shetland, separated by the narrow neck of land known as Mavis Grind.

Northton *Western Isles* A small village of South Harris in the Western Isles, Northton (Gael: *Taobh Tuath*) lies on the western coastline, 4 miles (6.5 km) southeast of Toe Head.

Northwaterbridge *Angus* A small village of Angus, Northwaterbridge lies on the course of the River North Esk and lies 5 miles (8 km) southwest of Laurencekirk.

Noss *Shetland* A settlement at the southern end of Mainland Shetland, Noss lies to the west of Loch Spiggie, 4.5 miles (7 km) northwest of Sumburgh. Noss Hill rises to 112 m (367 ft) to the south of Noss and to the west are the cliffs of the Noup o' Noss.

Noss Head *Highland* A headland on the east coast of Caithness, Noss Head extends into the North Sea at the southern end of Sinclair's Bay, 3 miles (5 km) northwest of Wick. A Stevenson lighthouse stands on the cliffs of Noss Head. The ruins of Girnigoe Castle and Castle Sinclair lie due west.

Noss Head *Shetland* A headland of the Isle of Noss in the Shetland Islands, Noss Head lies on the island's eastern coastline.

Noss Sound *Shetland* Noss Sound is the name given to the narrow sea channel that separates the Isle of Noss from Bressay to the west. At the end of the headland are the sheer cliffs of a large stack known as the Noup of Noss.

Nostie *Highland* A small village in the Lochalsh district of Highland Council area, Nostie lies at the northwestern end of Loch Alsh, 2 miles (3 km) west of Dornie.

Noup Head *Orkney* A headland with overhanging cliffs and a lighthouse, Noup Head extends into the sea at the northwest end of the island of Westray in the Orkney Islands. Automated in 1964, the Noup Head lighthouse was the first to use a system of mercury flotation in the revolving carriage.

Novar Hill *Highland* A hill in Easter Ross, Novar Hill

rises to the west of the Cromarty Firth, 5 miles (8 km) northwest of Evanton. Novar Wind Farm, comprising 34 turbines, occupies an area of 300 ha (741 acres) to the north of Glen Glass.

Nunraw *East Lothian* A locality in East Lothian, Nunraw lies a half-mile (1 km) southeast of Garvald and 7 miles (11 km) southwest of Dunbar. Nunraw Abbey is home to the only Cistercian monastic community in Scotland. Founded *c.*1158 by the nuns of Haddington, Nunraw or Nuns' Row developed into a thriving medieval village. In the 16th century a Z-plan tower house was erected to defend the community against English raids, and in 1548 the Scottish Parliament met there to decide on sending the young Mary, Queen of Scots to France. After the Reformation, Nunraw became a residence of the Hepburns. The original castle was incorporated into a baronial mansion built in the same red sandstone by the Dalrymple family in 1860. In 1946, Cistercian monks returned to Scotland for the first time since the Reformation, making Nunraw their home. In 1952, the monks began building the Sancta Maria Abbey, now one of three Cistercian abbeys in Britain. The original part-medieval, part-Victorian house is now the monastic guesthouse. In the grounds of Nunraw Abbey are a large walled garden, a beehive dovecote, a sundial and an arched gateway incorporating a lodge. The monks labour on Nunraw's 500-ha (1235-acre) farm, originally a mixed arable farm, now specialising in fattening beef cattle.

Nuns' Pass *Argyll and Bute* A pass on the south coast of the island of Mull in the Inner Hebrides, the Nuns' Pass lies between Beinn Chreagach and Creachan Mòr to the west of Carsaig Bay.

Nunton *Western Isles* A small settlement on the west coast of Benbecula in the Outer Hebrides, Nunton (Gael: *Baile nan Cailleach*) is located 1.25 miles (2 km) south of Balivanich. The much-altered Nunton House dates from the 14th century and was the home of the MacDonalds of Clanranald. Prince Charles Edward Stewart (Bonnie Prince Charlie) is said to have hidden here in 1746 and was given clothes to disguise himself by Lady Clanranald before heading 'over the sea to Skye' with Flora Macdonald (1722–90). Nunton is also the site of a ruined chapel, Teampall Mhoire, an old burial ground and a modern cemetery.

Nutberry Moss *Dumfries and Galloway* A flat area situated on the northern shore of the Solway Firth in Dumfries and Galloway, Nutberry Moss lies 3 miles (5 km) west of Gretna.

Oa, the *Argyll and Bute* A peninsula to the west of Port Ellen in the southwest corner of the island of Islay in the Inner Hebrides, the Oa gives us one of Scotland's shortest place names. Approximately 5 miles (8 km) in length and in breadth, The Oa is sparsely populated and characterised by moorland vegetation grazed by wild goats and by sheer cliffs. On the Mull of Oa, a headland at its western extremity, a cliff-top monument commemorates American servicemen who died when the *Tuscania* and *Otranto* troopships went down off the coast in 1918.

Oakbank *West Lothian* A settlement in West Lothian, Oakbank lies on the Linhouse Water, a half-mile (1 km) south of Mid Calder.

Oakley *Fife* A village in western Fife, Oakley is situated on the A907 at the meeting of the Comrie, Blair and Carnock Burns, 4 miles (6.5 km) west of Dunfermline. Originally developed in association with the Oakley Ironworks, which were established in 1846, the settlement was revitalised in the 1930s after the opening of the nearby Comrie coal mine. The white-harled Church of the Most Holy Name, notable for its magnificent stained-glass windows and carved Stations of the Cross, was built to the south of the village in 1956–8 for Roman Catholic miners who had moved from Lanarkshire to work in the more prosperous coalfields of western Fife. The village is overlooked by a folly known as Blair Tower.

Oakwood Tower An alternative name for Aikwood Tower in Scottish Borders.

Oathlaw *Angus* A locality in a mid-Angus parish of the same name, Oathlaw lies to the west of the Lemno Burn, 3 miles (5 km) north of Forfar. The parish church dates from 1815, and on Battledykes Farm to the southwest are the remains of a Roman marching camp of the Severan campaigns of AD 209–11.

Oatridge *West Lothian* A locality in West Lothian, Oatridge lies just over a mile (1.5 km) north-northwest of Uphall. An agricultural college was established here in 1972.

Oban *Argyll and Bute* The former county town of Argyllshire and the main port for the Hebrides, the resort town of Oban is situated on the sheltered anchorage of Oban Bay in the district of Lorn, 38 miles (61 km) north of Lochgilphead. Said to have been founded in 1713 by a trading company from Renfrew, a custom house was opened in 1765 prior to the site's development in the latter half of the 18th century in association with brewing, distilling, tanning and port trade encouraged by the Duke of Argyll. A year after gaining burgh status in 1811, a new road to Lochgilphead opened the settlement up to the interior. During the 19th century Oban became a major ferry terminal, with regular steamer services to Glasgow via the Crinan Canal bringing large numbers of tourists. The arrival of the railway in 1880 assisted in the development of the town as a road, rail and sea hub, and by 1890 it had a population in excess of 5000. In addition to a livestock market, modern industries include fishing, distilling and the manufacture of glassware and knitwear. On a headland to the north of Oban stand the remains of Dunollie Castle, an ancient stronghold of the MacDougall lords of Lorn built in the 12th century. On a hill overlooking the town is McCaig's Tower, a folly erected by local builder John Stuart McCaig as a job-creation scheme. There is an airfield and heliport at North Connel to the north of Oban. The Argyllshire Gathering is held in Oban each September.

Obbe An alternative name for Leverburgh in the Western Isles.

Obisary, Loch *Western Isles* A loch on the east coast of the island of North Uist in the Western Isles, Loch Obisary forms a southern arm of Loch Euphort to the southeast of Sidinish.

Obney *Perth and Kinross* A locality in Perth and Kinross, Obney comprises the farming settlements of Meikle Obney, Nether Obney and Upper Obney, all lying on the lower slopes of the Obney Hills, which rise to 403 m (1322 ft) 2 miles (3 km) south of Dunkeld and 2 miles (3 km) northwest of Bankfoot.

Occumster *Highland* A small settlement on the east coast of Caithness, Occumster lies a half-mile (1 km) northeast of Lybster and 12 miles (19 km) south of Wick.

Ocean Terminal *City of Edinburgh* A waterfront location on the shore of the Firth of Forth at Leith, Ocean Terminal comprises the redeveloped central section of the Leith Docks complex. In addition to facilities for ocean-going liners, Ocean Terminal, developed as Edinburgh's largest retail, restaurant and tourist complex plus a 12-screen cinema to a design by the architect Sir Terence Conran, opened in 2001. The complex is centred on the Britannia Visitor Centre, which provides access to the former royal yacht, now permanently berthed at Leith. The former Britannia Visitor Centre, located close by, now serves as the cruise-ship terminal, with the expectation of more than 60 visiting liners each year.

Ochil Hills A range of hills in Central Scotland, the Ochil Hills extend for more than 24 miles (38 km) eastwards from Dunblane and Bridge of Allan in Stirling Council area, through Clackmannanshire, Perth and Kinross and into Fife where it tails off eastwards along the south side of the River Tay. Largely comprising volcanic andesite from the Devonian period, the highest point in the range is Ben Cleuch, which rises to 721 m (2363 ft). The steep-sided north-facing slopes of the range above the hillfoot towns of Menstrie, Alva, Tillicoultry and Dollar are the result of the Ochil Hills' geological fault which caused the subsidence of land now forming the Clackmannanshire plain, an area comprising younger sediments including coal. Associated with the volcanic rocks of the Ochil Hills are deposits of copper and silver, as worked at Bridge of Allan and Sterling Glen. Largely given over to hill farming, the Ochil Hills is the largest area of remote land in central Scotland. The main access routes traversing the range from south to north are through Glen Farg and Glen Eagles.

Ochiltree *East Ayrshire* A village in the Kyle district of East Ayrshire, Ochiltree is situated 4 miles (6.5 km) west of Cumnock, close to the confluence of the Burnock Water with the Lugar Water. It developed from the 1890s in association with coal mining, a sawmill and a tileworks. Following the demise of deep mining in the surrounding area, Ochiltree turned to treating opencast coal for delivery to power stations. George Douglas Brown (1869–1902), author of *The House with the Green Shutters*, was born in Ochiltree. It was also the birthplace of the industrial chemist Charles Tennant (1768–1838).

Ochiltree *West Lothian* A small settlement with a restored castle in West Lothian, Ochiltree lies 3 miles (5 km) southeast of Linlithgow. The building is associated with the Stirlings of Keir and the Hamiltons of Finnart.

Ochiltree, Loch *Dumfries and Galloway* A loch in Dumfries and Galloway, Loch Ochiltree lies between the A714 and B7027, 6 miles (10 km) northwest of Newton Stewart. It is connected at its southern end to the Loch of Fyntalloch and by the Beoch Burn to the River Bladnoch.

Ochtertyre *Perth and Kinross* A house and estate in Strath Earn, Ochtertyre lies a mile (1.5 km) to the west of the Falls of Turret and 2 miles (3 km) northwest of Crieff. Associated with the Murray family, the ruins of Castle Cluggy and the later Ochtertyre House overlook Loch Monzievaird. Built in 1784–90, the house was a venue for theatrical performances in the 1970s.

Ochtertyre *Stirling* A locality in Stirling Council area, Ochtertyre lies on the River Teith, 3 miles (5 km) northwest of Stirling. Ochtertyre Moss between the Rivers Teith and Forth was reclaimed in the 18th century and Ochtertyre House, which dates from the 1760s, was the home of the celebrated diarist John Ramsay of Ochtertyre (1736–1814).

Ochtow *Highland* A small settlement of Strath Oykel in the Sutherland district of Highland Council area, Ochtow lies on the River Oykel, 9 miles (14 km) southwest of Lairg.

Ockle *Highland* Situated a half-mile (1 km) southeast of Ockle Point on the north coast of the Ardnamurchan peninsula, Ockle lies 6 miles (10 km) northeast of Kilchoan and 8 miles (13 km) east-northeast of Ardnamurchan Point.

Ockran Head *Shetland* A headland on the northwest coastline of the Shetland Mainland, Ockran Head lies a mile (1.5 km) southwest of The Faither headland. This coastline has many caves and natural archways.

Od, Point of *Orkney* A headland in the Orkney Islands, the Point of Od extends into St Peter's Bay, an inlet of the Deer Sound at the southern end of the Orkney Mainland, 7 miles (11 km) southeast of Kirkwall.

Odhairn, Loch The Gaelic name for Loch Ouirn in the Western Isles.

Odin Bay *Orkney* A wide bay on the east coast of the island of Stronsay in the Orkney Islands, Odin Bay extends from Burgh Head at its southern extremity to the headland of Odness. Within the bay lies the Vat of Kirbuster, a dramatic opening or 'gloup' spanned by the finest natural arch in Orkney.

Odin Ness *Orkney* A headland on the northwest coast of the island of Gairsay in the Orkney Islands, Odin Ness overlooks Gairsay Sound.

Odness *Orkney* A headland on the east coast of the island of Stronsay in the Orkney Islands, Odness lies at the northern end of Odin Bay.

Odness, Holm of *Orkney* A rocky islet in the Orkney Islands, the Holm of Odness lies off the headland of Odness on the east coast of the island of Stronsay.

Ogil *Angus* A locality at the end of Glen Ogil in north-central Angus, Ogil lies 6 miles (10 km) north of Forfar and comprises the farms of Milton of Ogil, Easter Ogil and Mains of Ogil, with the Den of Ogil Reservoir located a half-mile (1 km) to the west. HM Prison Noranside lies a mile (1.5 km) to the east.

Ogil, Glen *Angus* A narrow glen in the southern Grampians, Glen Ogil occupies the course of the Noran Water which cuts down through the Braes of Angus to the north of Tannadice.

Ogilvie, Glen *Angus* A glen in the eastern Sidlaw Hills, Angus, Glen Ogilvie (occasionally Glen Ogilvy) occupies the valley of a tributary of the Dean Water to the south of Glamis.

Ogle, Glen *Stirling* A deeply cut valley extending northwestwards for 7 miles (11 km) to Lix Toll from Lochearnhead in Stirling Council area, Glen Ogle contains within its narrow bounds the River Ogle, the main A85 road to Oban and Fort William, and the remains of a railway line that used to extend to Crianlarich. At the head of the glen is Lochan Lairig Cheile. The present road supersedes an older military road built in 1749 by Major Caulfield, a successor to the road-building General Wade.

Ohirnie, Port *Argyll and Bute* A small bay on the southeast coast of the island of Mull in the Inner Hebrides, Port Ohirnie is 2 miles (3 km) east of the entrance to Loch Buie. Frank Lockwood's Island lies a half-mile (1 km) to the southwest.

Oich, Loch *Highland* A narrow loch in the Lochaber district of Highland Council area, Loch Oich is situated in the Great Glen between Loch Lochy and Loch Ness, where it forms the summit level of the Caledonian Canal. It is 4 miles (6.5 km) long and no more than a half-mile (1 km) wide and is fed from the west by the River Garry which enters the loch near the settlement of Invergarry. Loch Oich is connected by the River Oich to Loch Ness which lies 7 miles (11 km) to the northeast.

Oich, River *Highland* The River Oich rises at the northern end of Loch Oich in the Great Glen and flows 7 miles (11 km) northeast to enter the head of Loch Ness at Fort Augustus. It forms part of the Caledonian Canal.

Oigh Sgeir *Highland* A group of rocky islets in the Inner Hebrides, the Oigh Sgeir (or Hyskeir) are located 9 miles (14 km) west of the island of Rum.

Oisgill Bay *Highland* An inlet on the northwest coast of the isle of Skye in the Inner Hebrides, Oisgill Bay is situated 7 miles (11 km) west of the settlement of Dunvegan.

Oisinneach Mòr, Lochan *Perth and Kinross* A small loch of Perth and Kinross, Lochan Oisinneach Mòr lies 4 miles (6.5 km) northeast of Ballinluig

Olavat, Loch *Western Isles* A small loch at the northern end of the island of Benbecula in the Western Isles, Loch Olavat lies 3 miles (5 km) east of Balivanich and 3 miles (5 km) southeast of Benbecula Airport.

Old Aberdeen *Aberdeen City* Now a northern suburb of Aberdeen, Old Aberdeen was once an independent burgh. The King's College Campus of the University of Aberdeen and St Machar's Cathedral are located in Old Aberdeen.

Old Barr *Dumfries and Galloway* A locality in Nithsdale, Old Barr lies on the Euchan Water, a mile (1.5 km) southwest of Sanquhar.

Old Bridge of Urr *Dumfries and Galloway* A hamlet in Dumfries and Galloway, Old Bridge of Urr lies on the Urr Water, nearly 4 miles (6.5 km) north of Castle Douglas. The river is crossed here by a two-span bridge bearing two panels dating from 1580. Downstream is the Mill of Urr, complete with water wheel, millstones and corn-drying kiln.

Old Buittle *Dumfries and Galloway* A tower house and castle in Dumfries and Galloway, Old Buittle lies a mile (1.5 km) west of Dalbeattie. It was here that John Balliol, the 13th-century King of Scots, held court. Old Buittle Tower, dating from the 15th century, was built for the Gordons of Lochinvar.

Old Calton Burial Ground *City of Edinburgh* A cemetery on Calton Hill in Edinburgh, the Old Calton Burial Ground was opened in 1718 for the burial of tradesmen and merchants. It was extended in 1767 but was divided by the building of Waterloo Place in 1818. The larger part of the cemetery lies to the south of Waterloo Place and includes a number of grand memorials. An enormous obelisk by Thomas Hamilton (1784–1858) commemorates the political martyrs of 1793 who were transported for sedition. The neoclassical monument to philosopher David Hume (1711–76) was built in 1777 by Robert Adam (1728–92), and the Emancipation Monument (1893), comprising a bronze of Abraham Lincoln with a grateful freed slave, honours the Scottish soldiers who fought in the American Civil War (1861–5). The latter was the first monument portraying Lincoln built outside the United States. Other notable personalities interred in Old Calton Burial Ground include the painter David Allan (1744–96), the architect Robert Burn (1752–1815), the publisher Archibald Constable (1774–1827) and the sculptor Sir John Steell (1804–91).

Old Coalburn *East Ayrshire* A locality in East Ayrshire, Old Coalburn lies to the north of the River Nith, 3 miles (5 km) west of New Cumnock.

Old Craighall *East Lothian* A former mining village at the western extremity of East Lothian, Old Craighall lies in a greenbelt area a mile (1.5 km) south of Musselburgh and 5 miles (8 km) east of Edinburgh city centre, between the A1 to the northeast and the A720 Edinburgh bypass to the southeast. At the southern end of the village is 17th-century Monkton House and to the northwest is Newcraighall.

Old Cumnock The former name for Cumnock in East Ayrshire.

Old Dailly *South Ayrshire* A small village of South Ayrshire, Old Dailly lies to the south of the Water of Girvan, 3 miles (5 km) east of Girvan. It developed in association with farming and quarrying. Camregan Castle, Killochan Castle, Penkill Castle and the emparked mansion of Bargany are closeby. The painter John Thomson was born in the parish in 1778.

Old Deer *Aberdeenshire* The settlement of Old Deer is located on the south side of the Forest of Deer, 10 miles (16 km) west of Peterhead in Aberdeenshire. St Columba is said to have founded the Abbey of Deer where the famous *Book of Deer* was produced between the 9th and 12th centuries. This volume contains some of the earliest-known writing in Gaelic. In 1218, the new Abbey of St Mary was established for Cistercian monks by the Earl of Buchan. Noted for its cattle fairs, the village was largely rebuilt in the 19th century. Although smaller than New Deer, Old Deer is regarded as the 'capital' of the area. Situated on the Formartine and Buchan Way, Old Deer has camping and caravan facilities and an agricultural heritage centre.

Old Graitney *Dumfries and Galloway* A small settlement of Annandale in Dumfries and Galloway, Old Graitney lies immediately southwest of Gretna and overlooks the mouth of the Liddel Water as it enters the Solway Firth.

Old Hall Bay *Aberdeenshire* A small bay of Aberdeenshire, Old Hall Bay lies 1.5 miles (2.5 km) to the south of Stonehaven. The headland to the north of the bay is the site of Dunnottar Castle.

Old Head *Orkney* A headland at the southeast corner of the island of South Ronaldsay in the Orkney Islands, Old Head is situated 2 miles (3 km) southeast of Burwick. To the northwest is the Tomb of the Eagles museum.

Old Hill *Western Isles* A small, uninhabited island in the Western Isles, Old Hill lies 2 miles (3 km) southwest of Great Bernera and west of the Isle of Lewis.

Old Kilpatrick *West Dunbartonshire* A small commuter village on the north bank of the River Clyde, Old Kilpatrick lies on the Forth and Clyde Canal, 10 miles (16 km) west of Glasgow. A Roman fort occupied this site which lies at the western end of the Antonine Wall. Said to have been the birthplace of St Patrick, Old Kilpatrick was the location of a medieval hospital and ferry crossing. The Erskine Ferry ceased to operate when the Erskine Bridge was opened in 1972. The settlement subsequently developed in association with textile industries and shipbuilding and in the 20th century became an oil depot.

Old Man of Hoy *Orkney* Rising dramatically out of the Atlantic to a height of 137 m (450 ft), the Old Man of Hoy is a rock stack that has been separated by the erosive power of wind and wave from the northwest coast of the Orkney island of Hoy. It lies to the north of Rora Head and is one of Scotland's most noted landmarks, as well as being a challenge to rock climbers

Old Monkland *North Lanarkshire* Once a distinct hamlet, Old Monkland now forms a southern suburb of Coatbridge, lying on the River North Calder in a parish of the same name. James Baird (1802–76), a founder of William Baird and Company, which became the largest producer of iron in Britain, was born on a farm nearby.

Old Philpstoun *West Lothian* A small settlement in West Lothian, Old Philpstoun lies to the east of Philpstoun between the M9 and the Union Canal. The Binns lies to the northwest and Philpstoun House, which was built in 1676 for John Dundas, is located to the east.

Old Polmont *Falkirk* An attractive residential village in Falkirk Council area, Old Polmont is situated at the junction of the Bo'ness Road and Grange Road, to the north of the M9 which separates it from Polmont. The line of the Antonine Wall runs to the south, and to the east are Polmont Woods. The old church, now a ruin, was built in 1731.

Old Rayne *Aberdeenshire* A village in the Garioch district of Aberdeenshire, Old Rayne lies on the River Urie, to the east of the A96 from Aberdeen to Huntly. Once a burgh of barony, the village has a 17th-century market cross and was the scene of the Lawrence Fair. The bishops of Aberdeen who owned the parish of Rayne once had a residence here. Today, Old Rayne has timber industries.

Old Sauchie *Stirling* A 16th-century tower house in Stirling Council area, Old or Little Sauchie lies 3 miles (5 km) southwest of Stirling. It was built in 1541 by James Erskine, with additions in the 17th and 18th centuries. The Battle of Sauchie, also known as the Battle of Sauchieburn, was fought near here on 11 June 1488 between James III and his rebellious nobles. The king's army was defeated and the king was himself murdered at a nearby mill after falling from his horse in flight. To the east is the Howietoun Fish Farm, which was established in the 1870s by Sir James Maitland as a pioneering experiment.

Old Scone *Perth and Kinross* The site of a former settlement in Perth and Kinross, Old Scone lies in the grounds of Scone Palace, a mile (1.5 km) north of Perth. The capital of Pictavia, the ancient kingdom of Kenneth I (d.858), Old Scone lay close to the Moot (or Mote) Hill where Scottish kings from Kenneth I in 838 to Charles II in 1651 were crowned. The hill is said to have been created from soil brought by clan chiefs paying homage to their new king, who would have been crowned while seated on the Stone of Destiny (or Stone of Scone). In 1296, the stone was removed to Westminster Abbey by Edward I, a replica now being on show in the chapel on Moot Hill. An abbey founded here by Alexander I in the 12th century was ransacked by a mob in 1559 following a rousing sermon given by the Reformation preacher John Knox in Perth. Although a few remnants of the village can be seen, including the mercat cross and a section of the church, most of it was demolished in 1805 to make way for a designed landscape associated with the reconstruction of Scone Palace by the Earl of Mansfield. The population was relocated to Scone, a planned village 2 miles (3 km) to the east.

Old Water *Dumfries and Galloway* A stream in Dumfries and Galloway, the Old Water rises in the Glenkiln Reservoir 5 miles (8 km) west of Dumfries and flows southeast then north to join the Cluden Water to the east of Drumpark.

Oldany Island *Highland* An uninhabited island off the Assynt coast of Sutherland, Oldany Island lies at the southwest entrance to Eddrachillis Bay, 2 miles (3 km) northwest of Drumbeg and 7 miles (11 km) north of Lochinver. It has an area of 200 ha (494 acres).

Oldhamstocks *East Lothian* Lying 6 miles (10 km) southeast of Dunbar and 2 miles (3 km) west of Cockburnspath near the eastern extremity of East Lothian, Oldhamstocks is situated on a hillside overlooking the North Sea. Built primarily in a distinctive purple stone, the name Oldhamstocks means 'old dwelling place'. The late-medieval parish church, later altered in 1701 and 1930, was extended with the addition of the Hepburn Aisle in 1581. A mercat cross and water pump can be found on the green at the centre of the village.

Oldmeldrum *Aberdeenshire* A town in the parish of Meldrum, central Aberdeenshire, Oldmeldrum is situated at a road junction, 17 miles (27 km) northwest of Aberdeen. Created a burgh of barony in 1672, Oldmeldrum was the main burgh of the medieval lordship of Garioch until the 19th century, when it was superseded by Inverurie 5 miles (8 km) to the southwest. Known mostly as Meldrum, its narrow streets reflect the irregular plan of the old medieval market town, which is centred on the Market Square with its fine Town Hall of 1877. A centre of the hosiery trade in the 18th century with a distillery founded in the 1790s, Oldmeldrum has a library, pleasure park and nine-hole golf course. Modern industries include engineering, whisky distilling, farm industries and trading in farm machinery. The parish of Meldrum within which it is situated was known as Bethelnie until 1684. Meldrum House to the north of the town is associated with the Seton and Urquhart families. Oldmeldrum was the birthplace of Sir Patrick Manson (1844–1922), a pioneer of tropical medicine who discovered how mosquitos transmit malaria.

Oldshore Beg *Highland* A small settlement on the northwest coast of Sutherland, Oldshore Beg lies 3 miles (5 km) northwest of Kinlochbervie and overlooks the uninhabited island of Eilean an Ròin Mòr to the west.

Oldshoremore *Highland* A small village on the northwest coast of Sutherland, Oldshoremore (also Oldshore More) lies a mile (1.5 km) southeast of Oldshore Beg and 2 miles (3 km) northwest of Kinlochbervie.

Olginey, Loch *Highland* A loch in the Caithness district of Highland Council area, Loch Olginey lies immediately to the south of Loch Calder and 3 miles (5 km) southwest of Halkirk.

Oliver *Scottish Borders* A small village of Tweeddale in Scottish Borders, Oliver lies on the west bank of the River Tweed, a mile (1.5 km) northeast of Tweedsmuir.

Ollaberry *Shetland* Situated on the northern shore of a bay of the same name, the scattered fishing village of Ollaberry lies on the northeast coastline of the Shetland Mainland, 4 miles (6.5 km) north of Sullom. A pier at Collafirth to the north serves large fishing vessels.

Ollay Lochs, the *Western Isles* A group of three small lochs named West, Mid and East Loch Ollay, the Ollay Lochs lie 3 miles (5 km) east of the Rubha Ardvule headland on the west coast of South Uist in the Western Isles.

Olna Firth *Shetland* A sea loch on the western coastline of the Shetland Mainland, Olna Firth lies 3 miles (5 km) south of Brae. The island of Muckle Roe lies at the mouth of the loch, while at its head lies the village of Voe.

Olrig *Highland* A location close to the north coast of Caithness, Olrig lies 1.5 miles (2.5 km) southwest of Castletown. The Old Kirk of Olrig, burned to the ground in 1745, has a burial ground with many fine tombs. Olrig House dates from the mid-19th century, and to the south the Hill of Olrig rises to 141 m (462 ft).

Onich *Highland* A village in the Lochaber district of Highland Council area, Onich lies on the northern shore of Loch Leven, 2 miles (3 km) west of North Ballachulish.

Oosta An alternative name for Out Stack in Shetland.

Opinan *Highland* A hamlet in Wester Ross, Opinan lies a mile (1.5 km) southwest of Port Henderson and 4 miles (6.5 km) southwest of Gairloch.

Orasay *Western Isles* One of a large number of small islands off the northeast coast of North Uist in the Outer Hebrides, Orasay (Gael: *Orasaigh*) lies in Loch Aulasary 3.75 miles (6 km) northeast of Lochmaddy. Another Orasay, of similar size, lies a half-mile (1 km) to the east.

Orbliston *Moray* A railway settlement in Moray, Orbliston lies to the west of the River Spey, 7 miles (11 km) southeast of Elgin and 3 miles (5 km) southeast of Lhanbryde.

Orbost *Highland* A scattered settlement on the west coast of the isle of Skye in the Inner Hebrides, Orbost lies 3 miles (5 km) south of Dunvegan.

Orchardton Bay *Dumfries and Galloway* An inlet on the Solway Firth coast of Dumfries and Galloway, Orchardton Bay lies to the northeast of Auchencairn. It is separated by headlands from Auchencairn Bay and Rough Firth and receives the Orchardton Burn and Potterland Lane. Orchardton House, built in 1761 and enlarged for William Robertson-Douglas in 1881, overlooks the bay near the mouth of the Orchardton Burn. Orchardton Tower near Palnackie is the only example of a round tower-house in Scotland. It is believed to have been built in the 1450s for John Cairns and passed to the Maxwell family in 1633. Its most famous resident was Sir Robert Maxwell, who featured in Sir Walter Scott's novel *Guy Mannering* (1815).

Orchy, River *Argyll and Bute* Rising in Loch Tulla to the southeast of Glen Coe, the River Orchy flows south past Bridge of Orchy and southwest through Glen Orchy and the Strath of Orchy before emptying into the head of Loch Awe, to the north of Kilchurn Castle. It has a total length of 12 miles (19 km).

Ordhead *Aberdeenshire* A hamlet in Aberdeenshire, Ordhead lies 3 miles (5 km) southwest of the village of Monymusk on the A944 from Aberdeen to Huntly via Dunecht.

Ordie *Aberdeenshire* A village in the Cromar district of Aberdeenshire, Ordie lies 6 miles (10 km) northeast of Ballater on Royal Deeside.

Ordie, Loch *Perth and Kinross* A small loch in the Forest of Clunie in northeast Perth and Kinross, Loch Ordie lies 4 miles (6.5 km) southeast of Ballinluig.

Ordie Burn *Perth and Kinross* Rising in the hills of southeast Strathbraan, to the west of Bankfoot, the Ordie Burn flows in a southeasterly direction for 8 miles (13 km) before joining the River Tay to the northeast of Luncarty, 4 miles (6.5 km) north of Perth.

Ord Point *Highland* A coastal headland on the border between Sutherland and Caithness, Ord Point extends into the sea 3 miles (5 km) northeast of Helmsdale. The granite hill known as the Ord of Caithness rises from the sea to 198 m (652 ft).

Ore, Loch *Fife* A small loch lying to the southwest of Lochore in Fife, Loch Ore lies 2 miles (3 km) north of Cowdenbeath. Lochore Meadows forms part of Fife Regional Park.

Ore, River *Fife* Rising in Loch Ore, the River Ore flows 17 miles (27 km) east before joining the River Leven between Milton of Balgonie and Cameron Bridge. It separates Auchterderran from Cardenden and passes through the southern end of Thornton. The water of the river is rich in iron in its lower course, a problem that was particularly marked during the 1960s and 1970s as a result of minewater discharge from the Westfield opencast coal site into its tributary the Lochty Burn.

Oreval *Western Isles* A mountain of North Harris in the Outer Hebrides, Oreval rises to 662 m (2171 ft) in the heart of the Forest of Harris, a mile (1.5 km) north of Cleiseval.

Orfasay *Shetland* A small uninhabited island of Shetland, Orfasay lies to the south of the island of Yell from which it is separated by the Sound of Orfasay.

Ork, Ness of *Orkney* A headland of the island of Shapinsay in the Orkney Islands, the Ness of Ork lies on the island's northern coastline where it extends into the Stronsay Firth.

Orka Voe *Shetland* An inlet on the north coast of the Shetland Mainland, Orka Voe lies at the southern end of Yell Sound, 6 miles (10 km) northeast of Brae.

Orkney *Area: 1025 sq. km (395.7 sq. miles)* Six miles (10 km) north of the mainland of Scotland, beyond the Pentland Firth, lie the 70 islands of the Orkney archipelago. Twenty of these islands are inhabited and most are formed by rock of the Middle Old Red Sandstone period, except for the hills of Hoy which consist of rocks from Upper Old Red Sandstone. The geology gives rise to sandstones and flagstones that split easily along bedding planes and are therefore ideal for building. A fertile land of well-cultivated, gently rolling hills rising to spectacular sheer cliffs along the west and north coasts, the Orkney Islands lie at the meeting point of the Atlantic Ocean and North Sea where fresh coastal waters are rich in plankton and fish. Sea cliffs, moors and marshland are home to over a million sea birds during the summer, making the islands a mecca for ornithologists. Some 85 per cent of the people in the Orkney Islands live on the Mainland (or Pomona), the

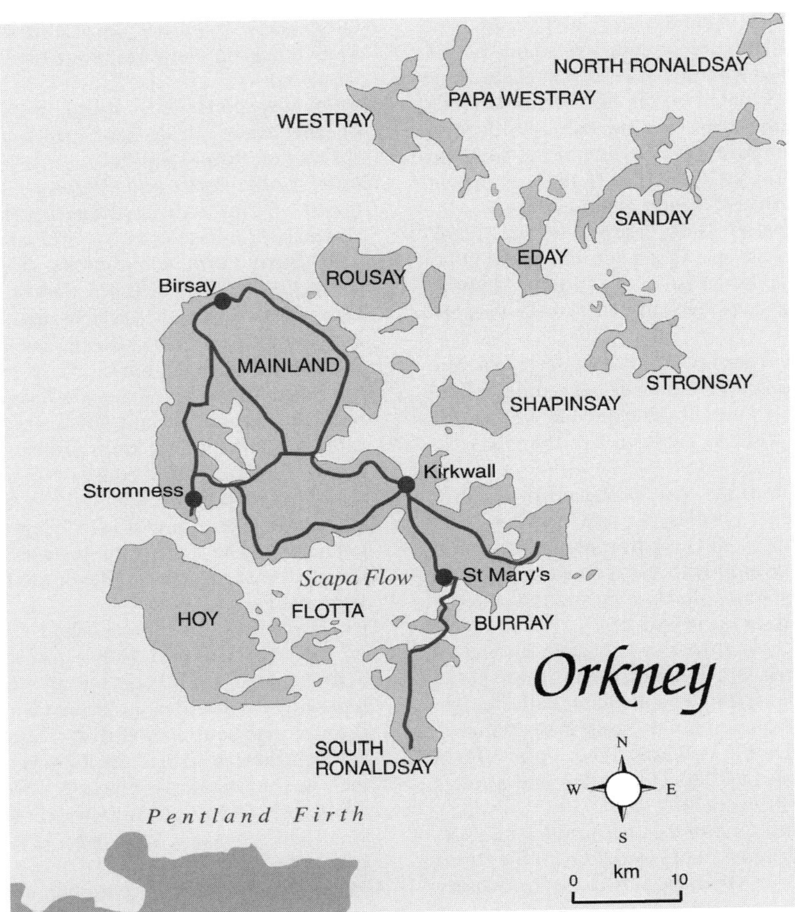

remainder of the population living on 16 smaller islands ranging from Westray with a population of over 700 to Gairsay with a single family. Orkney Mainland has an area of 50,340 hectares (124,390 acres) and a population of 15,315 in 2001. Kirkwall is the main administrative and shopping centre of the Orkney Islands and the focus of the annual St Magnus Festival. Thought to derive its name from the Icelandic for 'the seal islands', Orkney has been settled since prehistoric times when its fertile soils and rich coastal waters attracted early man. A wealth of exceptional archaeological sites survive, indicating that small communities began to settle in Orkney during the middle of the 4th millennium BC. During the late 1st millennium AD the Norse came to dominate Orkney, an influence that lasted until 1468, when the islands were pledged to James III of Scotland as security for the dowry of Margaret of Norway, his queen. The Old Norse language was subsequently replaced by English, Gaelic never having been spoken in Orkney. Employing over 2000 workers, the main industry in Orkney today is farming, in particular beef farming. Of a total area of 1025 sq. km (395.7 sq. miles), 48 sq. km (18.5 sq. miles) is under crops, 468 sq. km (180.7 sq. miles) under grass and 278 sq. km (107.3 sq. miles) given over to rough grazing. Other major employers are Orkney Islands Council, Orkney Health Board and the oil terminal at Flotta. Manufacturing as an industry in Orkney is relatively small, depending on food products, distilling, and craft goods such as textiles, jewellery and the famous Orkney chair. There are air links from mainland Scotland to Kirkwall Airport, as well as daily roll-on/roll-off ferry connections between Scrabster and Stromness and a passenger ferry connecting John o' Groats to Burwick in South Ronaldsay. There are ferries to most of the inhabited islands and airfields servicing local flights on Flotta, South Walls, Westray, Papa Westray, Eday, North Ronaldsay, Sanday and Stronsay.

Ormiscaig *Highland* A small village on the coast of Wester Ross, Ormiscaig lies on the northern shore of Loch Ewe, overlooking the Isle of Ewe to the west. Aultbea lies a mile (1.5 km) to the southeast.

Ormiston *East Lothian* Located south of Tranent, Ormiston was one of the first planned villages to be built in Scotland in the 18th century. Replacing a small mill settlement, it was laid out in 1735 in the style of an English village by one of the initiators of the Agricultural Revolution, John Cockburn of Ormiston (1685–1758). In addition to a brewery, distillery and cottages for textile workers, one of Scotland's first bleach fields was established here. Cockburn did not achieve the expected return on his investment and sold the village in 1747 to the Earl of Hopetoun. Ormiston later developed as a mining village, the last mines in the area closing in the mid-1960s. Sites of interest include Ormiston Hall, built for Cockburn (1745–8) and later extended for the Earl of Hopetoun, the pre-Reformation St Giles' Parish Church and the 15th-century Mercat Cross, unusual for its simple cruciform shape. The Reforming preacher George Wishart was captured by Bothwell while hiding here in 1545, and there is a monument to the missionary Dr Robert Moffat (1795–1883) who was born here.

Ormsaigmore *Highland* A small village on the south coast of the Ardnamurchan peninsula in the Lochaber district of Highland Council area, Ormsaigmore lies a mile (1.5 km) southwest of Kilchoan and overlooks Kilchoan Bay to the southeast.

Ormsary *Argyll and Bute* A small village of Knapdale in Argyll and Bute, Ormsary lies on the eastern shore of Loch Caolisport, 4 miles (6.5 km) southwest of Achahoish.

Ornish *Western Isles* A small uninhabited island in the Western Isles, Ornish lies off the east coast of South Uist, near the entrance to Loch Sgioport.

Oronsay *Argyll and Bute* Possibly deriving its name from St Oran, a disciple of St Columba, the rocky island of Oronsay lies immediately south of the island of Colonsay in the Inner Hebrides. Connected to Colonsay at low tides by a sandy causeway, the island is sparsely populated. Mesolithic shell mounds dating from *c*.4000 BC provide one of the earliest records of human settlement in Scotland, and the Iron Age fort of Dun Domhnuill stands on a high elevation. In the mid-14th century an Augustinian priory was founded under the patronage of the Lords of the Isles. It was the location of a workshop producing intricately carved grave-slabs and stone crosses until *c*.1500. The Oronsay Cross stands within the remains of the priory. Nearby is a small airstrip.

Oronsay *Western Isles* An uninhabited and low-lying island in the Western Isles, Oronsay lies in a bay on the north coast of North Uist to which it is connected by sands at low tide. The islands of Lingay and Boreray lie to the north.

Orosay *Western Isles* A small uninhabited island in the Western Isles, Orosay lies off the northeast coast of the island of Barra, to the east of the Tràigh Mhòr or Cockle Strand, from which it is separated by the Sound of Orosay (Gael: *Caolas Orasaigh*).

Orosay *Western Isles* A small island near the mouth of Castle Bay, on the south coast of the island of Barra in the Western Isles, Orosay faces the island of Vatersay across the Sound of Vatersay.

Orosay *Western Isles* A small uninhabited island of the Western Isles, Orosay lies off the southwest coast of South Uist, 5 miles (8 km) southwest of Lochboisdale.

Orphir *Orkney* A locality and parish on the Mainland of Orkney overlooking Scapa Flow, Orphir is associated with the Norse crusader Earl Hakon Paulsson who died in 1122 and who had a seat here. The remains of Scotland's only circular medieval church survive. Dating from the 12th century, it derives its shape from the Church of the Holy Sepulchre in Jerusalem, which was visited by Earl Hakon. Excavated remains close to the church may be the remains of the earl's residence or Bu, which is described in the *Orkneyinga Saga* as standing next to the church. Orkney's Norse heritage is featured in the Orkneyinga Saga Centre.

Orrin, Glen *Highland* A valley in the Ross and Cromarty district of Highland Council area, Glen Orrin carries the River Orrin from its source in headwaters to the north of Loch Monar 26 miles (42 km) east through Loch na Caoidhe, Am Fiar Loch and the 5-mile/8-km-long Orrin Reservoir to join the River Conon near Urray to the southwest of Conon Bridge. As the river enters Strathconan it cascades over the Falls of Orrin.

Orroland *Dumfries and Galloway* A locality in Dumfries and Galloway, Orroland lies on the Solway coast a mile (1.5 km) to the southeast of Dundrennan. It comprises the Orroland Heugh, Orroland Lodge and the farm of Orroland.

Orsay Island *Argyll and Bute* A small uninhabited island off the southeast coast of the island of Islay in the Inner Hebrides, Orsay lies a half-mile (1 km) southwest of the settlement of Portnahaven at the southwest extremity of the Rhinns of Islay. There are the remains of a chapel and a Stevenson lighthouse built in 1825.

Orval *Highland* A mountain on the island of Rum in the Small Isles, Orval rises to a height of 571 m (1873 ft) 4 miles (6.5 km) west of Kinloch.

Orwell *Perth and Kinross* A parish in the Kinross-shire district of Perth and Kinross, Orwell lies between Loch Leven and the Ochil Hills. Its chief settlement is the village of Orwell. Two prehistoric stones, known as the Standing Stones of Orwell, are located in a field on the farm of Orwell.

Ose, Glen *Highland* A valley on the west coast of the isle of Skye in the Inner Hebrides, Glen Ose carries the waters of the River Ose from its source in Loch Connan southwestwards into Loch Bracadale.

Osgaig, Loch *Highland* A loch in the Coigach district of Sutherland, Loch Osgaig (or Loch Owskeich) lies to the west of Inverpolly Forest, a mile (1.5 km) south of Enard Bay and 2 miles (3 km) northeast of Achiltibuie.

Oskaig *Highland* A small village on the west coast of the island of Raasay in the Inner Hebrides, Oskaig lies to the east of Oskaig Point at the southern end of Holoman Bay, 3 miles (5 km) from the southern tip of the island.

Osnaburgh A former name for Dairsie in Fife.

Ospisdale, Loch *Highland* An artificial loch in southeast Sutherland, Loch Ospisdale was created by philanthropist Andrew Carnegie (1835–1918) in the grounds of Skibo Castle, 4 miles (6.5 km) west of Dornoch.

Oss, Loch *Stirling* A corrie lochan situated between Ben Oss and Beinn Dubhchraig, Loch Oss lies 6 miles (10 km) southwest of Tyndrum. It is drained by the Allt Oss which flows southeastwards into Glen Falloch.

Ossian, Loch *Highland* A loch of eastern Lochaber on the 'Road to the Isles', Loch Ossian lies in the southwest Grampians between Loch Treig and Loch Ericht. It is surrounded by the Corrour Forest which contains many exotic tree species and rhododendrons planted by Sir John Stirling Maxwell in the early 20th century. A shooting lodge stands at the northeast end of the loch, which empties northwards through Strath Ossian towards Glen Spean via the River Ossian. On its course the Ossian widens to form Loch Guilbinn before continuing north as the Abhainn Ghuilbinn to empty into the eastern end of Loch Moy.

Ossian's Cave *Highland* Located on the northern face of Aonach Dubh, one of the Three Sisters of Glen Coe, Ossian's Cave takes its name from the legendary warrior Ossian who is said to have been born at nearby Loch Achtriochtan.

Ossian's Grave *Perth and Kinross* A large stone associated with the legendary Ossian, Ossian's Grave is situated by the River Almond in Perth and Kinross, 5 miles (8 km) south of Amulree and 6 miles (10 km) northeast of Crieff.

Ossian's Hall *Perth and Kinross* The name given to a summerhouse built in a scenic location in the Hermitage by the Duke of Atholl, Ossian's Hall overlooks the River Braan to the northwest of Dunkeld.

Otter Burn *Scottish Borders* A tributary of the Eye Water in the Berwickshire district of Scottish Borders, the Otter Burn rises in the Lammermuir Hills and joins the Eye near Grantshouse.

Otter Ferry *Argyll and Bute* A small village and former ferry port in Kilfinan parish on the eastern shore of Loch Fyne, Otter Ferry lies 5 miles (8 km) southeast of Lochgilphead and 12 miles (19 km) north of Millhouse. A small ferry once linked the settlement with Port Ann or West Otter Ferry in Knapdale, and steamers stopped here in the early 20th century. A pedestrian ferry operated until the late 1940s.

Otter Rock *Argyll and Bute* The southernmost rocky islet of the Torran Rocks group in the Inner Hebrides, Otter Rock lies 4 miles (6.5 km) southwest of the Ross of Mull.

Otters Wick *Orkney* A large inlet on the north coast of the island of Sanday in the Orkney Islands, Otters Wick has wide sandy beaches.

Otters Wick *Shetland* A bay on the east coast of the island of Yell in the Shetland Islands, Otters Wick opens out towards the southern end of the Colgrave Sound. The settlement of Otterswick lies at its head and to the west the Ward of Otterswick, Yell's highest peak, rises to 205 m (673 ft).

Ouirn, Loch *Western Isles* A remote sea loch on the east coast of the Isle of Lewis in the Outer Hebrides, Loch Ouirn (Gael: *Loch Odhairn*) lies in the South Lochs district midway between Loch Erisort and Loch Shell. The loch opens into the Sound of Shiant. Kebock Head lies on the south side of its mouth and the settlement of Graver is located on its north shore.

Ousdale *Highland* A settlement near the east coast of Caithness, Ousdale lies on the Ousdale Burn, 4 miles (6.5 km) southwest of Berriedale. The remains of the Ousdale Broch, which dates from the 1st century BC, are located at the mouth of the burn.

Ouse, The *Orkney* A bay on the northeast coast of the island of Westray in the Orkney Islands, The Ouse opens out into the Bay of Skaill and Papa Sound opposite the island of Papa Westray.

Out Head *Fife* A headland on the south side of the River Eden estuary, Out Head lies 2 miles (3 km) north of St Andrews. The golf courses of the St Andrews Links, comprising the Old, New, Jubilee, Eden and Strathtyrum 18-hole courses and the nine-hole Baldove Course lie on and to the south of this headland.

Out Skerries *Shetland* A group of islands and rocky islets in the Shetland Islands, the Out Skerries are situated 6 miles (10 km) northeast of Whalsay and 24 miles (38 km) northeast of Lerwick. The three main islands of Housay (West Isle), Bruray (East Isle) and the uninhabited island of Grunay all surround a natural harbour. The islanders, of whom there are 90, earn their living from fishing and salmon farming. The local school is Britain's smallest secondary school. Bound Skerry, with its Stevenson lighthouse (1858), is Shetland's easternmost point. A passenger ferry links the Out Skerries to Vidlin and Lerwick on the Shetland Mainland, and a small airstrip was opened in 1974.

Out Stack *Shetland* The northernmost island of the British Isles, Out Stack (or Oosta) lies 2 miles (3 km) north of the island of Unst in the Shetland Islands. In 1849, Lady Franklin landed here to pray for her husband, Sir John Franklin, who had not returned from his expedition to find the Northwest Passage.

Outer Booth *Shetland* A rocky islet off the north coast of the Shetland Mainland, the Outer Booth lies between the Point of Fethaland and the bird sanctuary island of Gruney.

Outer Flaess *Shetland* A rocky islet off the northeast coast of the island of Unst in the Shetland Islands, Outer Flaess lies to the north of the Holm of Skaw.

Outer Holm *Orkney* Outer Holm is one of two uninhabited islets that shelter the harbour of Stromness on the Orkney Mainland. The other islet is the Inner Holm.

Outer Holm of Skaw *Shetland* A rock outlier off the northeast coast of the island of Whalsay in the Shetland Islands, the Outer Holm of Skaw lies beyond the Inner Holm of Skaw.

Outshore Point *Orkney* A headland on the northeast coast of the Orkney Mainland, Outshore Point lies 2 miles (3 km) south of Marwick Head and 3 miles (5 km) north of the Bay of Skaill.

Outsta Ness *Shetland* A headland on the north coast of the island of Yell in the Shetland Islands, Outsta Ness lies to the east of the Wick of Breckon, a mile (1.5 km) northwest of the settlement of Greenbank.

Over Ardoch *Perth and Kinross* A small settlement in Perth and Kinross, Over Ardoch lies on the course of the River Knaik, a mile (1.5 km) north of Braco.

Over Dalgleish Burn *Dumfries and Galloway* A stream in northeast Dumfries and Galloway, the Over Dalgleish Burn is a tributary of the Tima Water, rising on the slopes of Nether Craig.

Over Rankeilour *Fife* A locality in central Fife, Over Rankeilour lies 3 miles (5 km) west of Cupar and 2 miles (3 km) north of Ladybank. A mansion house was built here by General Sir John Hope, whose monument stands on a nearby hill. The steading at Over Rankeilor has been converted to a retail outlet and Deer Centre.

Overtown *North Lanarkshire* A village of Clydesdale in North Lanarkshire, Overtown lies to the west of the River Clyde and a mile (1.5 km) south of Wishaw. It developed in the 19th century as a mining village with railways serving nearby collieries. Its population declined after the closure of the mines and the railway in the early 1950s.

Ox Rock *East Lothian* A rocky headland on the southern shore of the Firth of Forth, the Ox Rock extends into the estuary at Prestonpans.

Oxan, Point of *Orkney* The most northerly headland on the island of Graemsay in the Orkney Islands, the Point of Oxnan extends into Hoy Sound.

Oxcars *Fife* A small, rocky islet with a lighthouse (1884) in the Firth of Forth, Oxcars lies a half-mile (1 km) southeast of Inchcolm and a half-mile (1 km) north of Inchmickery.

Oxenfoord Castle *Midlothian* A castle in Midlothian, Oxenfoord lies a mile (1.5 km) north of Pathhead and 9 miles (14 km) southeast of Edinburgh. Built in the 16th century as an L-plan tower house by the MacGill family, Oxenfoord passed to the Dalrymples in 1779. The architect Robert Adam enlarged and modernised the house in 1780–2 to create an early example of the Scottish baronial style. A new castellated house completely encased the old tower, incorporating grand public rooms, including the dining room which survives today. Above the entrance Adam added statues of an ox and a horse. When the family inherited the Earldom of Stair in 1840 William Burn was employed to upgrade the building. Burn replaced Adam's porch and added a low block of reception rooms, also creating a magnificently decorated library and drawing room. Now a hotel, Oxenfoord was used as a private school between 1931 and 1993. The original 1.4-ha (3.5-acre) walled garden has been open to the public since 1965. The bridge over the Tyne Water carrying the driveway to the castle was built around 1783 by Alexander Stevens and later castellated by William Burn.

Oxgangs *City of Edinburgh* A residential suburb developed on the south side of Edinburgh in the 20th century, Oxgangs lies on high ground 4 miles (6.5 km) to the south of the city centre and west of Fairmilehead.

Oxna *Shetland* Now uninhabited, the Shetland island of Oxna lies to the west of Papa. With an area of 68 ha (168 acres) and rising to 38 m (125 ft) at Muckle Ward, the island is linked by a reef to the rocky Hoggs of Oxna which are, in turn, separated from three islets to the north known as the Cheynies by Bulta Sound. The ruins of the former main settlement, which was abandoned after World War I, are located at Sandy Voe.

Oxnam *Scottish Borders* A small settlement in a parish of the same name in Scottish Borders, Oxnam lies on the Oxnam Water, 4 miles (6.5 km) southeast of Jedburgh.

Oxnam Water *Scottish Borders* Rising in the Cheviot Hills, the Oxnam Water flows north for 13 miles (21 km), passing through Oxnam, to join the River Teviot near the village of Crailing.

Oxton *Scottish Borders* A small village in the Lauderdale district of Scottish Borders, Oxton lies on the Leader Water, 4 miles (6.5 km) northwest of Lauder. A half-mile (1 km) to the northwest of the village lie the ruined remains of a Roman camp.

Oyce of Huip *Orkney* A small bay on the north coast of the island of Stronsay in the Orkney Islands, the Oyce of Huip is an inlet of the Bay of Franks. It is partially enclosed by rocks at low tide.

Oykel, River *Highland* A river in Sutherland and Ross and Cromarty, the Oykel rises in the Ben More Forest to the southeast of Inchnadamph. It flows southeast through Loch Ailsh and Glen Oykel before turning east to continue through Strath Oykel, passing the villages of Langwell, Brae and Rosehall. It merges with the River Shin before entering the Kyle of Sutherland at the head of the Dornoch Firth, 4 miles (6.5 km) northwest of Bonar Bridge. Its total length is 35 miles (56 km).

Oykel Bridge *Highland* A locality in Sutherland, Oykel Bridge lies on the River Oykel, 12 miles (19 km) southwest of Lairg. An inn was built here to serve travellers on the road to Assynt completed in 1831. Its hotel is popular with anglers.

Oyne *Aberdeenshire* A village in the Garioch district of mid-Aberdeenshire, Oyne lies in a parish of the same name, 7 miles (11 km) northwest of Inverurie and 20 miles (32 km) northwest of Aberdeen. Kirkton of Oyne and the ruins of Harthill Castle lie a mile (1.5 km) to the east. The historian John Leslie, who was later Bishop of Ross, became a parson here in 1559. Oyne is home to the 16-ha (40-acre) Archaeolink Prehistory Park, a tourist attraction which interprets the numerous archaeological remains in the area and includes historical re-enactments.

Pabaigh The Gaelic name for Pabbay in the Western Isles.

Pabaigh Mòr The Gaelic name for Pabay Mòr in the Western Isles.

Pabaigh Beag The Gaelic name for Pabay Beag in the Western Isles.

Pabay *Highland* A small uninhabited island in the Inner Hebrides, the 'priest island' of Pabay lies in the Inner Sound to the northeast of the isle of Skye opposite Broadford Bay. With an area of 122 ha (301 acres), the low-lying island plateau of Pabay is predominantly limestone. There are the remains of a chapel and burial ground to the east of the jetty. Pabay is one of a few British islands licensed to issue its own postage stamps.

Pabay, Sound of *Western Isles* A channel on the west coast of the Isle of Lewis in the Outer Hebrides, the Sound of Pabay (Gael: *Caolas Phabaigh*) is the name given to the stretch of water that separates the islands of Pabay Mòr and Vacasay from Lewis. The village of Valtos overlooks the channel.

Pabay Beag *Western Isles* A small uninhabited island in the Outer Hebrides, Pabay Beag (Gael: *Pabaigh Beag*) lies within West Loch Roag on the west coast of the Isle of Lewis. The island rises to 42 m (137 ft) immediately to the north of Pabay Mor and 1.25 miles (2 km) northeast of Valtos.

Pabay Mòr *Western Isles* An uninhabited island of the Outer Hebrides, Pabay Mòr (Gael: *Pabaigh Mòr*) lies within West Loch Roag, a large sea loch on the west coast of the Isle of Lewis, a half-mile (1 km) northeast of Valtos and 3 miles (5 km) east of Gallan Head. The island extends to 101 ha (250 acres) and rises to 68 m (223 ft). Cleared of its population to allow for grazing in 1827, Pabay Mòr has subsequently supported only a seasonal population associated with fishing and tending sheep. The island was bought in 1983 by a London professional, who restored two black houses to provide a holiday residence.

Pabbay *Western Isles* An uninhabited island of 250 ha (618 acres) at the southern end of the Western Isles, Pabbay (Gael: *Pabaigh*) lies between Sanday and Mingulay. It is one of a small group of islands known as the Bishop's Isles and rises in the southwest to a height of 171 m (561 ft) at The Hoe. In early Christian times there was a cell or hermitage on the island. A symbol stone, cross-slab and chapel site still survive above the white shell-sand beach of Bagh Bàn. On 1 May 1897 all the able-bodied men of the island lost their lives at sea while long-line fishing, and by 1911 the island's population had dwindled to 11.

Pabbay *Western Isles* An uninhabited island in the Western Isles, Pabbay (Gael: *Pabaigh*) lies in the Sound of Harris between North Uist and South Harris. Situated to the north of Berneray, from which it is separated by the Sound of Pabbay, it lies 5 miles (8 km) southwest of Toe

Head and has an area of 820 ha (2026 acres). Rising to 196 m (642 ft) at Beinn a'Charnain, its only settlement was Baile-na-Cille.

Padanaram *Angus* A hamlet of central Angus, Padanaram is located 2 miles (3 km) west-northwest of Forfar and 3 miles (5 km) southeast of Kirriemuir. The Scottish Midland Junction railway line, which ran immediately to the south, closed in 1967.

Paddockhole *Dumfries and Galloway* A locality in Dumfries and Galloway, Paddockhole lies on the Water of Milk, 6 miles (10 km) east of Lockerbie.

Paddy's Market *Glasgow City* An outdoor market in and around the Briggait (or Bridgegate) in Glasgow, Paddy's Market sells mainly second-hand clothes and furniture. The haphazard arrangement of its stalls is a byword for anything that appears untidy or disorganised.

Paible *Western Isles* A locality on the west coast of North Uist in the Outer Hebrides, Paible (Gael: *Paibeil* or *Phaibeil*) lies 3 miles (5 km) southeast of the headland of Aird an Runair and 2 miles (3 km) northwest of Kirkibost Island. Located to the east of Loch Phaibeil, Paible comprises the hamlet of Bayhead, which includes the Gaelic-medium Paible School, together with the crofting townships of Knockaline (Gael: *Cnoc a Lin*), Kyles Paible (Gael: *Caolas Phaibeil*), Balmore (Gael: *Baile Mòr*), Knockintorran (Gael: *Cnoc an Torrain*) and Paiblesgarry (Gael: *Paiblesgearraidh*).

Pairc The Gaelic name for Park in the Western Isles.

Paisley *Renfrewshire* Situated 7 miles (11 km) west of Glasgow and 53 miles (85 km) west of Edinburgh, Paisley is the largest town in Scotland. The original settlement of Oakshaw sat at the lowest fordable point on the White Cart River on an important route to Ayrshire via the Lochwinnoch Gap. It took advantage of its location at the highest navigable point upriver from the Clyde as well as its proximity to the Hammils waterfall, which provided a source of water power. St Mirin (or Mirren) is said to have founded a church here in the 6th century, and in the 12th century the site was chosen for a Cluniac priory established by Walter Fitzalan, the first hereditary High Steward of Scotland and a forebear of the Royal House of Stewart. The priory was elevated to the status of an abbey in 1219 and is said to be the burial place of Marjorie Bruce, daughter of Robert the Bruce. The abbot secured burgh of barony status for the settlement in 1488, and in 1587 the town was designated a burgh of regality. The rapid expansion of Paisley in the 18th century was associated with distilling and the manufacture of textiles, the name Paisley coming to be associated with the Paisley Pattern, a Kashmiri pattern of curving shapes printed on silk and cotton fabric introduced to the shawl industry in 1805. The early development of the town was promoted by the Hamilton and Cochrane families, and in the 19th century the major thread-making mills of the Coats and Clark families dominated the town alongside engineering and chemical industries. Following the decline of traditional manufacturing industries, Paisley developed from the 1960s as a service centre with a College of Technology founded in 1950 and raised to the status of a university in 1992. Buildings of interest include the Town Hall (1879–82), Paisley Museum and Art Gallery, the Coats Observatory (1883), the John Neilson Institute (1849–52), the Sma' Shot Cottages, Paisley Arts Centre (formerly the Laigh Kirk) and St Mirin's Roman Catholic Cathedral. There are recreational facilities at the Lagoon Leisure Centre, Phoenix Park and Barshaw Park, and on the edge of town is the Gleniffer Braes Country Park. The songwriter Robert Tannahill (1774–1810) and the bird painter Alexander Wilson (1766–1813) were born in Paisley.

Paithnick, Burn of *Moray* Rising in Aultmore parish to the south of Kirkton of Deskford in Moray, the Burn of Paithnick flows southwards to join the River Isla west of Davoch of Grange.

Palace of Spynie *Moray* The Palace of Spynie is located 2 miles (3 km) north of Elgin and to the south of Lossiemouth in Moray, and is the remains of a grand medieval palace of the bishops of Moray. Built on a headland jutting out into Spynie Loch, this fortified palace was constructed over a period of two centuries after Bishop Richard temporarily established the Cathedral of Moray on this site before its relocation to Elgin 24 years later. Its principal feature is David's Tower, which was built in the 15th century by Bishop David Stewart and which gives views over the nearby Spynie Loch and Moray Firth.

Palacerigg Country Park *North Lanarkshire* Situated

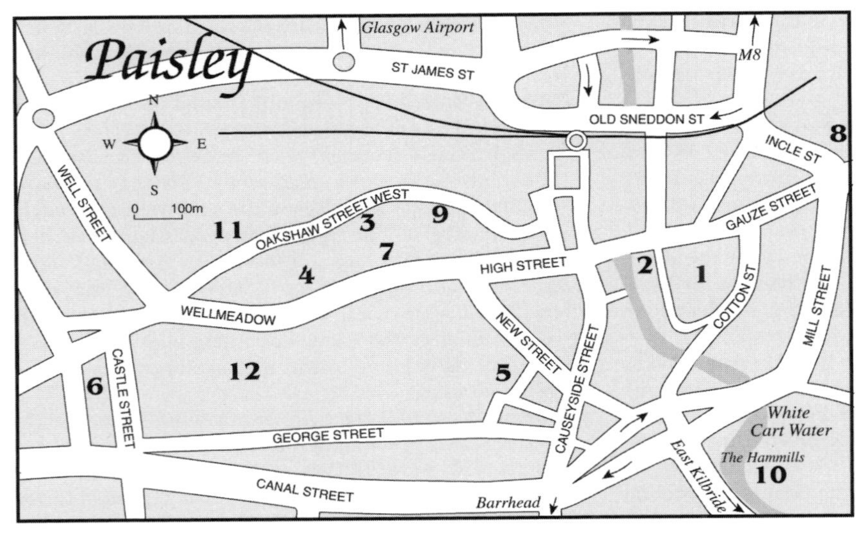

1 *Paisley Abbey*
2 *Town Hall*
3 *Coats Observatory*
4 *Thomas Coats Memorial Church*
5 *Sma' Shot Cottages*
6 *Tannahill Cottages*
7 *Museum and Art Gallery*
8 *St Mirin's RC Cathedral*
9 *Oakshaw Trinity (High Church)*
10 *Anchor Mills*
11 *John Nelson Institute*
12 *University of Paisley*

on the southern outskirts of Cumbernauld in North Lanarkshire, Palacerigg Country Park was created in the mid-1970s on the site of a former upland farm. With an area of 40 ha (99 acres), the park is planted with native plants, shrubs and trees to provide a natural habitat for populations of rabbit, hare, badger, fox and roe deer, as well as owls and hawks. Located within the grounds of the park are a Children's Farm, a Wildlife and Rare Breeds Collection, nature trails, a tree-top walkway and a centre for weekend training courses.

Palnackie *Dumfries and Galloway* A river port in Dumfries and Galloway, Palnackie is situated on a muddy estuary near the mouth of the Urr Water, 3 miles (5 km) south of Dalbeattie. Its wooden-piled harbour dates from the 1850s, and in the 18th and 19th centuries, before the development of railway communications, it was the port for Castle Douglas. The houses are built of local granite. Immediately north is the Scottish baronial-style Barlochan House.

Palnure *Dumfries and Galloway* A locality in Dumfries and Galloway, Palnure lies on the Palnure Burn, 3 miles (5 km) southeast of Newton Stewart.

Palnure Burn *Dumfries and Galloway* A stream in Dumfries and Galloway, the Palnure Burn rises 7 miles (11 km) northeast of Newton Stewart. It flows southwest and south for 8 miles (13 km) through Bargaly Glen before joining the River Cree 3 miles (5 km) southeast of Newton Stewart.

Panbride *Angus* A dormitory settlement in southeast Angus, Panbride and Newton of Panbride lie just north of Carnoustie in a parish of the same name. The barony of Panbride once belonged to the ancestors of the noted historian Hector Boece (*c.*1465–1536). The Gothic-style parish church dates from 1851.

Panmure *Angus* A ruined castle and estate near Monikie in Angus, Panmure gives its name to the earldom of Panmure, which was created in 1646. Old Panmure Castle, which stands on a promontory that projects into the valley of the Monikie Burn near Muirdrum, was a stronghold of the Maule family. Held in the 12th century by a chamberlain of William the Lion, the lands of Panmure passed to the Maules in 1224. The 'New' Castle of Panmure was begun in 1666 to plans by John Mylne, the Royal Master Mason in Scotland. Designed as a Renaissance palace, the building was enlarged by the Earl of Panmure and Dalhousie in 1852. The demolition of this building in 1955 has been described as 'one of the greatest acts of officially sanctioned vandalism of its type in Scotland'. The stable block remains.

Panmure House *City of Edinburgh* A building adjacent to the Royal Mile in Edinburgh, Panmure House was built in 1690 as the city home of the earls of Panmure. The economist Adam Smith (1723–90), whose grave is in the nearby Canongate Churchyard, stayed here when he was Commissioner of Customs. Restored in 1957, the building is now occupied by the Social Services Department of City of Edinburgh Council.

Pannanich *Aberdeenshire* A locality in Royal Deeside, Aberdeenshire, Pannanich lies on the south side of the River Dee, 2 miles (3 km) east of Ballater. About 1760, four wells here were discovered to have medicinal value and an inn was built as a form of spa. Queen Victoria tasted the water of Pannanich Wells on 3 October 1870, noting in *More Leaves from the Journal of a Life in the Highlands* (1884) that John Brown 'formerly stayed here for a year as servant'.

Pap of Glencoe *Highland* A mountain overlooking Loch Leven and the village of Glencoe in the Lochaber district of Highland Council area, the Pap of Glencoe (Gael: *Sgorr na Ciche*) rises to 742 m (2434 ft) at the west end of Glen Coe.

Papa *Shetland* One of Shetland's 'holy' islands, the uninhabited island of Papa lies to the west of Mainland Shetland and to the north of West Burra. It has an area of 59 ha (146 acres) and rises to 32 m (105 ft). Papa's coastline is deeply indented and a tidal channel joins it to the West Head of Papa. Occupied by early Christian missionaries, the island had a population of 36 in 1901 before being abandoned in the early 1930s.

Papa, Holm of *Orkney* The Holm of Papa is a small uninhabited island located off the east coast of Papa Westray in the Orkney Islands. The island is home to a number of prehistoric cairns, the largest of which has 14 separate chambers.

Papa, Sound of *Shetland* A sea channel of the Shetland Islands, the Sound of Papa lies to the northwest of the Shetland Mainland, separating it from the nearby island of Papa Stour.

Papa Little *Shetland* Situated at the head of Aith Voe on the west coast of Mainland Shetland, the 226-ha (558-acre) peat-covered island of Papa Little is protected from the Atlantic wind by the islands of Vementry and Muckle Roe. It has two small lochans, Mill Loch and Little Loch, as well as several hills, the largest of which is North Ward (82 m/269 ft). Papa Little was last inhabited in the 1840s, when it had a population of 11.

Papa Sound *Orkney* A sea channel of the Orkney Islands, Papa Sound separates the island of Westray from Papa Westray to the northeast.

Papa Sound *Orkney* A sea channel of the Orkney Islands, Papa Sound separates the island of Stronsay from Papa Stronsay to the northeast.

Papa Stour *Shetland* Papa Stour – 'the great island of the priests' – was an early base for Christian missionaries in the Shetland Islands. Separated from Mainland Shetland by the Sound of Papa, the fertile island of Papa Stour lies at the southern edge of St Magnus Bay. The island's coastal stacks and inlets support large colonies of nesting sea birds, and Kirstan's (or Christie's) Hole is reckoned to be one of Britain's finest sea caves. Rising to 87 m (285 ft) at Virda Field in the northwest, Papa Stour has an area of 883 ha (2181 acres). Probably occupied since 3000 BC, the island was later settled by early Christian missionaries and Norsemen, including, in the 13th century, Duke Haakon who later became king of Norway. Chambered cairns, burned mounds and the remains of homesteads provide a wealth of archaeological evidence of early settlement. Looking onto Housa Voe, Papa Stour's oldest settlement is known as Biggings. Reached by boat from West Burrafirth, the island has seen its population decline, falling from a total of 351 in 1871 to 23 today.

Papa Stronsay *Orkney* A low, flat island of the Orkney Islands, Papa Stronsay lies to the northeast of the island of Stronsay, from which it is separated by Papa Sound. It covers an area of 83 ha (205 acres). Situated opposite the Stronsay village and ferry port of Whitehall which it shelters, Papa Stronsay once had five fish-curing stations and luxuriant crops of grain and vegetables. Archaeological remains include a burned mound, two cairns and derelict crofts. Thought to have been a hermitage for early Christian monks, the island's population fell from 28 in 1841 to 3 in 1971, before it was abandoned. It was purchased in May 1999 to become an island monastery with a population of 10.

Papa Westray *Orkney* A 'priest' island of the Celtic monks in the Orkney Islands, Papa Westray lies to the east of the larger island of Westray on roughly the same latitude as Stavanger in Norway. With an area of 840 ha (2076 acres), Papa Westray is 4 miles (6.5 km) long and a mile (1.5 km) wide, rising steadily along a central ridge towards the North Hill (48 m/157 ft). In contrast to the rocky Atlantic-facing north and west coasts, the island's eastern and southern shores have fine sandy bays. Most of the northern end of Papa Westray is occupied by the North Hill Nature Reserve, while in the south the landscape is dominated by the Loch of St Tredwell. Archaeological sites of interest include the 5000-year-old Knap of Howar, which is thought to be northwest Europe's oldest standing house. Featuring in the *Orkneyinga Saga*, Papa Westray is said to have been the burial place in 1046 of Earl Rognavald Brusasson, after he was murdered by his uncle, although the site of his grave is not known. Between 1881 and 2001 the population of Papa Westray fell from 345 to 65, but since 1978 the island's community cooperative has attempted to encourage settlement and sustain the island's facilities, which include a shop, youth hostel, post office, guesthouse, an airstrip and ferry services to Mainland Orkney. The flight between Westray and Papa Westray represents the world's shortest scheduled route, taking just two minutes.

Paphrie Burn *Angus* A stream in the Braes of Angus, the Paphrie Burn rises in the southern Grampians, 3 miles (5 km) north of Tannadice. It flows northeastwards behind the Hill of Menmuir to join the West Water which flows on to meet the River North Esk.

Papil *Shetland* A settlement at the southern end of the island of West Burra, which lies to the west of the south Shetland Mainland. The ruined St Laurence's Church at Papil stands on the site of an earlier church which may have been the principal church of south Shetland in pre-Norse times. Several fine examples of Pictish sculptured stones have been found in the churchyard, including the 'Papil Stone', the side-slab of an altar depicting a procession of monks

Papple *East Lothian* A small village of East Lothian, Papple lies to the west of the Whiteadder Water, 3 miles (5 km) south of East Linton.

Paps of Jura, The *Argyll and Bute* A name given to prominent peaks on the west side of the island of Jura in the Inner Hebrides, the Paps of Jura rise to 785 m (2571 ft) at Beinn an Oir. Other peaks include Beinn a' Chaolais and Beinn Shiantaidh.

Parbroath *Fife* A locality in eastern Fife, Parbroath comprises a hamlet and farm at a major road intersection 4 miles (6.5 km) northwest of Cupar and 5 miles (8 km) north of Ladybank.

Park *Dumfries and Galloway* A village of Annandale in Dumfries and Galloway, Park lies 2 miles (3 km) southeast of Closeburn. It was built to serve the nearby limeworks which, during the 18th and 19th centuries, were the largest in Dumfries and Galloway.

Park *Western Isles* A district of the Isle of Lewis in the Western Isles, Park (Gael: *Pairc*) lies to the southeast of the island and is bordered by Loch Seaforth to the west and north. Only the north of Park is now inhabited, the south having been cleared in the 19th century by the landowner Sir James Matheson (1796–1878). The area was maintained as a deer park and is associated with the 19th-century struggle of crofters to retain their rights to land.

Park, Loch *Moray* A small narrow loch between Dufftown and Keith in Moray, Loch Park lies at the head of Strath Isla.

Park Circus *Glasgow City* An elegant locality in the centre of Glasgow, Park Circus lies on a ridge overlooking the University of Glasgow, between Charing Cross and the top of Kelvingrove Park. Dominated by Trinity Tower (1856–61), erected by Charles Wilson as Trinity College, Park Circus was developed in a French style following the natural contour of the land between 1855 and 1863.

Parkgate *Dumfries and Galloway* A hamlet in Dumfries and Galloway, Parkgate lies on the Clatterstanes Burn, 9 miles (14 km) northeast of Dumfries. Barony College is to the south.

Parkhall *West Dunbartonshire* A western suburb of Clydebank in West Dunbartonshire, Parkhall lies 2 miles (3 km) northwest of the town centre.

Parkhead *Glasgow City* A district of Glasgow, Parkhead originally developed as a weaving village around the site of an inn at a crossroads to the east of the city centre. It later expanded in association with coal mining and engineering, the famous Parkhead Forge founded in 1837 later producing high-grade steel for the shipbuilding industry. The forge, which was taken over by William Beardmore in 1879, closed in 1983. Modern industries include the manufacture of soft drinks, the famous Barr's Irn Bru being launched here in 1901. Celtic Football Club, which originated in Bridgeton in 1887, moved to Parkhead in 1888 and its present site at Celtic Park in 1892.

Parkside *North Lanarkshire* A small village of North Lanarkshire, Parkside lies 3 miles (5 km) north of Wishaw.

Parliament Square *City of Edinburgh* Located to the south of Edinburgh's High Street, behind St Giles Kirk, Parliament Square was built on the kirkyard of St Giles where the religious reformer John Knox (*c*.1513–72) lies buried. The square was created in the early 19th century while Robert Reid (1774–1856) was working on a new frontage for the adjacent old Parliament House. Now the home of the High Court, this building incorporates the 17th-century Parliament Hall, the Signet Library and the Advocates' Library. In the centre of the square is a lead statue of Charles II mounted on a horse, one of the earliest equestrian statues in Britain (*c*.1685) and probably of Dutch origin.

Parph, the *Highland* An area of remote moorland between Cape Wrath in the far northwest of Sutherland and the Kyle of Durness in the east, the Parph extends over 20,700 ha (51,150 acres). Much of the area is given over to military ranges and training grounds, but public access is possible when firing is not taking place. The Clo Mòr cliffs, the highest sea cliffs in Britain, lie on the north coast.

Partick *Glasgow City* A former burgh which now forms

a northwestern district of Glasgow lying between the River Kelvin and the Clyde Tunnel, Partick was the site of a royal palace of the ancient kingdom of Strathclyde given to the Bishop of Glasgow as a retreat in 1136 by David I. Situated on the River Kelvin, it developed in the 18th and 19th centuries in association with water-powered mills spinning cotton and producing flour, paper, flint and silt-iron. From the 1830s, shipyards were erected on both sides of the River Kelvin, an industry that survived until the 1960s. Partick became a police burgh in the mid-19th century and was incorporated into the city of Glasgow in 1912. Four years after the founding of Partick Thistle Football Club in 1868, the world's first international football match between Scotland and England was played at the West of Scotland Cricket Ground located in Partick.

Parton *Dumfries and Galloway* A village of the Glenkens in Dumfries and Galloway, Parton lies midway along the eastern shore of Loch Ken, 6 miles (10 km) northwest of Castle Douglas. Its neat row of terraced houses was laid out in 1901 as an estate village for Parton House, which was demolished in 1964. In the churchyard of Parton parish church (1832) stand the remains of an earlier church and a monument to the physicist James Clerk Maxwell (1831–79), whose country house was at nearby Glenlair.

Paterson's Rock *Argyll and Bute* A rocky outlier with a lighthouse, Paterson's Rock is situated in the Firth of Clyde, a mile (1.5 km) east of the island of Sanda which lies off the southeast coast of the Kintyre peninsula.

Path of Condie *Perth and Kinross* A locality in the Ochil Hills, Perth and Kinross, Path of Condie overlooks the Water of May, 3 miles (5 km) southeast of Dunning. Robert Burns is said to have inscribed his name with a ring on the window of the school at Path of Condie after a visit to Invermay House.

Pathhead *East Ayrshire* A small settlement in East Ayrshire, Pathhead is situated on the River Nith to the north of New Cumnock.

Pathhead *Fife* A former village on the south coast of Fife, Pathhead is now a suburb of Kirkcaldy. It was originally situated at the top of a steep path that led up from the mouth of the Den Burn. In the 18th century Pathhead was a noted centre for the production of nails, and in 1807 Alex Robertson in Pathhead invented a spring-loaded flax-heckling device. Pathhead Hall (1883) was converted into a leisure centre in 1995.

Pathhead *Midlothian* A small village in Midlothian, Pathhead lies on the eastern bank of the Tyne Water, 4 miles (6.5 km) southeast of Dalkeith. The settlement developed on a main routeway linked by a path to a ford on the Tyne that was replaced by a bridge in 1831. The village developed in association with road transport, sawmilling and the quarrying of lime.

Pathstruie *Perth and Kinross* A locality in the Ochil Hills, Perth and Kinross, Pathstruie lies in the deeply cut valley of the Water of May, 3 miles (5 km) southeast of Dunning.

Patna *East Ayrshire* A former mining village in East Ayrshire, Patna is situated on the River Doon, 5 miles (8 km) northwest of Dalmellington. The village was named in the early 19th century by local landowner William Fullarton of Skeldon, who was born in the Indian city of Patna. Originally a scattered community, the village developed in the 19th century in association with coal mining and the ironworks in Dalmellington. Villagers in nearby Lethanhill and Benquhat were relocated to Patna in the mid-20th century.

Pattack, Loch *Highland* A small loch in the Badenoch district of Highland Council area, Loch Pattack lies to the southeast of Loch Laggan and northwest of Loch Ericht. The Ben Alder Forest is to the southwest. The River Pattack rises in the loch and flows north and west to enter Loch Laggan at Kinloch Laggan.

Pattiesmuir *Fife* A small dormitory village to the west of Rosyth in western Fife. Formerly an agricultural settlement, it was designated a conservation area in 1974.

Paxton *Scottish Borders* A village in the Berwickshire district of Scottish Borders, Paxton lies on the Whiteadder Water near the border with England, 4 miles (6.5 km) west of Berwick-upon-Tweed. The Palladian-style Paxton House, a half-mile (1 km) to the south, was built in 1758 for Patrick Home to a design by John and James Adam. Situated amid 32 ha (80 acres) of gardens, parkland and woodland, Paxton House contains a fine collection of furniture and paintings. In 1811 a picture gallery designed by Robert Reid was added to the house, which since 1993 has been an outstation of the National Galleries of Scotland. In the policies are a restored Victorian boathouse and a fisheries museum.

Pean, Glen *Highland* A valley in the Lochaber district of Highland Council area, Glen Pean carries the waters of the River Pean from its source on Sgurr nan Coireachan east to join the River Dessarry, a half-mile (1 km) to the west of the head of Loch Arkaig.

Pearsie *Angus* A small village in Glen Prosen, Pearsie lies to the west of the Prosen Water, 4 miles (6.5 km) northwest of Kirriemuir.

Pease Bay *Scottish Borders* A small sandy bay on the North Sea coast of Scottish Borders, Pease Bay lies a mile (1.5 km) east of Cockburnspath. At its southern end is Siccar Point, noted for its geology.

Peaston *East Lothian* A small village of East Lothian, Peaston lies 3 miles (5 km) south of Pencaitland.

Peaston Bank *East Lothian* A hamlet lying in the valley of the Kinchie Burn, Peaston Bank lies immediately south of the Glenkinchie Distillery and a mile (1.5 km) south of Pencaitland.

Peat Inn *Fife* A hamlet in eastern Fife, the Peat Inn sits at the junction of the B940 and B941, 6 miles (10 km) southwest of St Andrews. The inn here is noted for its cuisine.

Peathill *Aberdeenshire* A village on the north coast of Aberdeenshire, Peathill lies a mile (1.5 km) southeast of Rosehearty. The 15th-century Pitsligo Castle lies to the northwest.

Peden Burn *South Lanarkshire* Served by the waters of the Big Windgate Burn, the Craigs Grain and the Stow Gill, Peden Burn flows east then south before emptying into the Portrail Water at Peden, a settlement 3 miles (5 km) south of Elvanfoot.

Peebles *Scottish Borders* A town in Scottish Borders, Peebles lies at the junction of the Eddleston Water (the Cuddy) with the River Tweed, 23 miles (37 km) south of Edinburgh and 18 miles (29 km) west of Galashiels. The county town of Peeblesshire until 1975 and headquarters of Tweeddale District Council (1975–96), Peebles was designated a royal burgh in 1125 and was the residence of

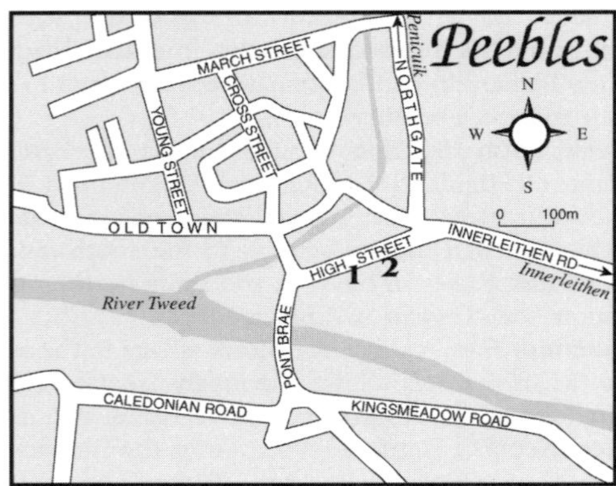

1 *Tweedale Museum Gallery* 2 *Chambers Institution*

kings while hunting in nearby Ettrick Forest. It flourished at a crossing point on the Tweed and had several religious houses, including the Trinitarian Cross Kirk which dates from 1261. During the 18th and 19th centuries it developed as a textile and brewing centre. Following the arrival of the railway in the 1850s and the building of the Peebles Hydropathic in 1881, Peebles flourished as a popular holiday destination. Today it remains a market town and centre of tourism, with fishing, golfing, tennis and pony-trekking in the surrounding area. The Beltane Festival (Riding of the Marches) is held on the last Saturday of June. Buildings of interest include the parish church (1887), St Andrew's Church (1195), the elaborate Chambers Institution (c.1859), the 14th-century Mercat Cross and the 15th-century Tweed Bridge. The philosopher, poet and historian John Veitch (1829–94) and the publishers William Chambers (1800–83) and Robert Chambers (1802–71) were born in Peebles. The explorer Mungo Park (1771–1806) lived here for two years before leaving on his final trip to Africa in 1805.

Peebles-shire A former county in the Southern Uplands of southeast Scotland, Peebles-shire occupied the area known as Tweeddale in the upper reaches of the River Tweed. Its county town was Peebles at the junction of the Tweed with the Eddleston Water. In 1974 it was incorporated into the new Borders Region as Tweeddale District and in the local government reorganisation of 1996 remained part of the Scottish Borders Council Area.

Peel Fell *Scottish Borders* A summit in the Cheviot Hills, Peel Fell rises to 602 m (1975 ft) 4 miles (6.5 km) north of Kielder on the border with Northumberland in England.

Peel of Gartfarren *Stirling* An ancient homestead situated within a bank and ditch enclosure, the Peel of Gartfarren lies at the western edge of Flanders Moss, 3 miles (5 km) northwest of Buchlyvie in Stirling Council area.

Peffer Burn *East Lothian* The Peffer Burn rises in the Garleton Hills a mile (1.5 km) north of Haddington. It flows northeastwards to join the North Sea 4 miles (6.5 km) northwest of Dunbar. Another Peffer Burn rises 2 miles (3 km) to the north and flows westwards into Aberlady Bay.

Peffermill *City of Edinburgh* A district of southeast Edinburgh, Peffermill lies immediately to the southeast of Prestonfield and to the west of Craigmillar. Traversed by the Southern Suburban railway and the Braid Burn, it includes high-rise modern housing, a small industrial estate, the playing fields of the University of Edinburgh and 17th-century Peffermill House.

Pegal Bay *Orkney* An inlet on the east coast of the island of Hoy in the Orkney Islands, Pegal Bay lies directly opposite the island of Rysa Little. The Pegal Burn rises on the Knap of Trowieglen, in the centre of the island, and flows east into Pegal Bay.

Peighinn nan Aoireann The Gaelic name for Peninerine in the Western Isles.

Peinchorran *Highland* A small village on the isle of Skye in the Inner Hebrides, Peinchorran lies on the north shore of Loch Sligachan, 8 miles (13 km) southeast of Portree. The peak of Ben Lee rises a mile (1.5 km) to the west

Peinlich *Highland* A small settlement on the Trotternish peninsula at the northern end of the isle of Skye in the Inner Hebrides, Peinlich lies on the River Hinnisdal 3 miles (5 km) south of the settlement of Uig.

Pencaitland *East Lothian* A dormitory village with pantile-roofed 18th- and 19th-century cottages, Pencaitland lies on the Tyne Water, 6 miles (10 km) southwest of Haddington. The Tyne separates Easter and Wester Pencaitland, which are joined by an early 16th-century bridge with three arches. The Mercat Cross in Wester Pencaitland takes the form of a sundial, and the parish church includes a chapel that is thought to date from the late 13th century. The school, built from a donation by Lady Ruthven, is in a heavily ornate style. Winton House to the east of the village, forfeited by the Seton family in 1715, is a fine example of the Anglo-Scots Renaissance style of the 17th century. Fountainhall (formerly Woodhead) to the southwest was built by the Pringles before being passed in 1685 to Sir John Lauder, later Lord Fountainhall.

Penicuik *Midlothian* A town in Midlothian, Penicuik lies on the River North Esk, 10 miles (16 km) south of Edinburgh. It was originally laid out as a planned village in 1770 by Sir James Clerk of Penicuik and subsequently developed in association with cotton mills, coal mining, paper making and the manufacture of glassware. Buildings of note include the French Prisoners' Monument (1830), the remains of the 17th-century St Kentigern's Church in the graveyard of the parish church (1771), the Episcopal church of St James the Less (1882) and Penicuik South Church (1862), a 'master work' by F. T. Pilkington. Nearby are Uttershill Castle (c.1510), Brunstane Castle, and Penicuik House, home to the Clerk family, which was gutted by fire in 1899.

Penifiler *Highland* A small village on the isle of Skye in the Inner Hebrides, Penifiler lies on the south shore of Loch Portree, a mile (1.5 km) south of Portree.

Peninerine *Western Isles* A small crofting settlement on low-lying land on the west coast of South Uist, Peninerine (Gael: *Peighinn nan Aoireann*) is located between Loch Altabrug and Loch Fada, a half-mile (1 km) southwest of Howbeg and a similar distance north of Stoneybridge.

Peninver *Argyll and Bute* Located on the east coast of the Kintyre peninsula of Argyll and Bute, the village of Peninver lies 4 miles (6.5 km) northeast of Campbeltown.

Penkill *South Ayrshire* A small village in South Ayrshire, Penkill lies a mile (1.5 km) south of Old Dailly and 3

miles (5 km) northeast of Girvan. To the south of the village is the 16th-century Penkill Castle and to the southeast is the Penwhapple Reservoir.

Penkiln Burn *Dumfries and Galloway* A stream in Dumfries and Galloway, the Penkiln Burn rises 6 miles (10 km) northeast of Newton Stewart. It flows south and southwest to join the River Cree at Minnigaff.

Pennan *Aberdeenshire* A fishing village of Buchan on the north coast of Aberdeenshire, Pennan lies on Pennan Bay, 2 miles (3 km) southeast of Troup Head. This picturesque village was the setting for Bill Forsyth's film *Local Hero* (1983). Pennan Head extends into the sea to the west of the bay.

Penninghame House *Dumfries and Galloway* A Jacobean-style country house in Dumfries and Galloway, Penninghame House lies on the west bank of the River Cree, 4 miles (6.5 km) northwest of Newton Stewart. Built in 1864 for the Stopford-Blair family, it is now used as an open prison.

Pennyghael *Argyll and Bute* A scattered settlement on the island of Mull in the Inner Hebrides, Pennyghael lies on the south shore of Loch Scridain, 9 miles (14 km) east of Bunessan. The waters of the River Leidle flow to the east.

Pennyglen *South Ayrshire* A small settlement in South Ayrshire, Pennyglen lies 2 miles (3 km) west of Maybole and 3 miles (5 km) northeast of Culzean Castle.

Pennygown *Argyll and Bute* A small village on the northeast coast of the island of Mull in the Inner Hebrides, Pennygown overlooks the Sound of Mull 2 miles (3 km) east of Salen.

Penpont *Dumfries and Galloway* A small village formerly associated with limestone quarrying in Dumfries and Galloway, Penpont lies in the valley of the Scaur Water, 3 miles (5 km) west of Thornhill and 16 miles (26 km) north of Dumfries. The geologist and explorer Joseph Thomson was born here in 1858. Inventor of the bicycle Kirkpatrick Macmillan, who was a blacksmith at Keir Mill, was born nearby in 1813.

Pentland Firth A strait separating the Orkney Islands from the Scottish mainland, the Pentland Firth extends 14 miles (22 km) from Dunnet Head in the west to Duncansby Head in the east and has a maximum width of nearly 8 miles (13 km). The Pentland Skerries and the Island of Stroma lie within the firth.

Pentland Hills A range of hills extending 16 miles (26 km) southwestwards from a point 3 miles (5 km) southwest of the centre of the city of Edinburgh, the Pentland Hills extend across the City of Edinburgh, West Lothian, Midlothian, South Lanarkshire and Scottish Borders council areas. Comprising 400 million-year-old sandstone and volcanic rocks of Devonian age, the hills rise to a height of 579 m (1898 ft) at Scald Law, a mile (1.5 km) northeast of Penicuik. The West Water, Baddinsgill, North Esk, Loganlea, Threipmuir, Harlaw and Glencorse reservoirs supply water to Edinburgh. In 1984 the area was designated as a regional park with headquarters at Boghall Farm. There is an artificial ski slope at Hillend at the north end of the range and a Ministry of Defence shooting range at Castle Law. Much of the land is given over to forestry, sheep farming and grouse moor.

Pentland Skerries *Orkney* A group of four uninhabited islands to the north of Caithness in the eastern Pentland Firth, the Pentland Skerries lie 3 miles (5 km) south of

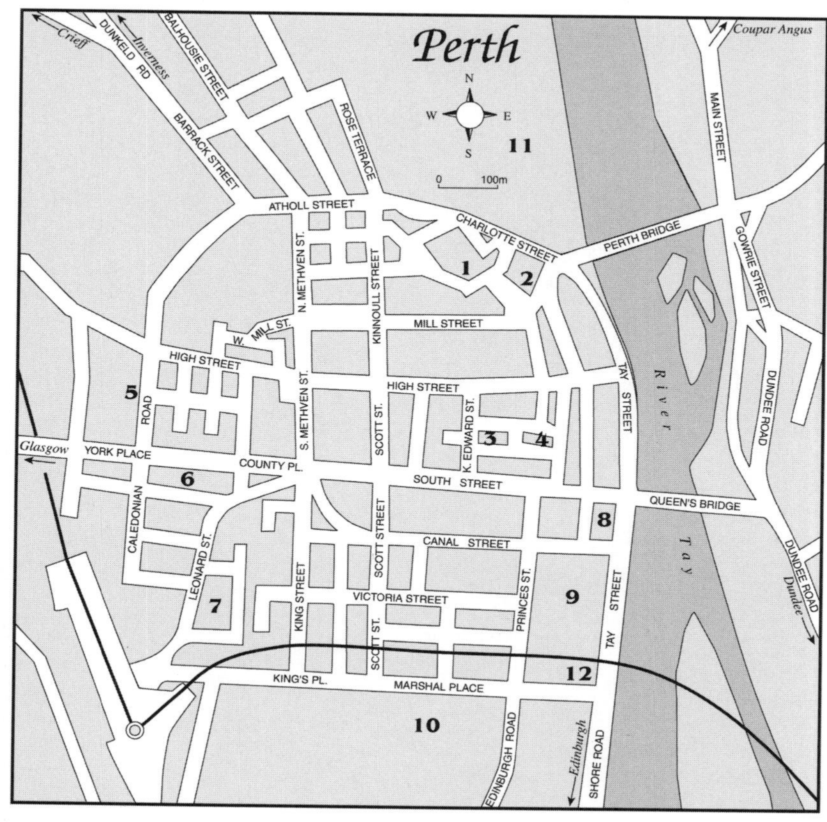

1 *Fair Maid's House*
2 *Museum and Art Gallery*
3 *City Hall*
4 *St John's Kirk*
5 *Cattle Market*
6 *Library*
7 *Bus Station*
8 *Sheriff Court*
9 *Greyfriars Church Yard*
10 *South Inch*
11 *North Inch*
12 *Fergusson Gallery*

South Ronaldsay and comprise the islands of Muckle Skerry, Little Skerry, Louther Skerry and Clettack Skerry.

People's Palace, the *Glasgow City* Opened on Glasgow Green in 1898, the People's Palace is home to a museum dedicated to the social and political life of the city. Constructed in red sandstone, it is French Renaissance in design and was built by the city architect of the time, A. B. MacDonald. The rear of the building comprises a huge winter garden that is four times the size of the museum.

Perceton *North Ayrshire* Perceton is an eastern suburb of the new town of Irvine in North Ayrshire.

Perth *Perth and Kinross* The administrative centre of Perth and Kinross, Perth is situated at the heart of Scotland, 22 miles (35 km) west of Dundee and 45 miles (72 km) north of Edinburgh. The town owes its existence to its location at an important crossing of the River Tay at the highest point of the tidal water and was occupied by the Romans who established a camp at Bertha to the north of the present city. Trading in salmon, wool and other agricultural products, Perth developed into a strong fortified commercial centre, eventually gaining the status of a burgh during the reign of David I (1124–53). In 1126, the Kirk of St John the Baptist was built and for a time the city was known as St Johnstoun. It remains a river port, agricultural market town and rail and road hub. The River Tay is crossed by the concrete Queen's Bridge and the red sandstone Perth Bridge built by John Smeaton in 1771. Known as the 'Fair City', Perth has two large parklands named the North and South Inch and is overlooked to the east by Kinnoull Hill, which rises to 222 m (729 ft). Among Perth's main tourist attractions are the Fair Maid's House, Perth Museum and Art Gallery, the Black Watch Museum, the Fergusson Gallery, St John's Kirk, Bell's Cherrybank Gardens, Branklyn Garden and Caithness Glass Factory and Visitor Centre. Perth has numerous sporting facilities, including a National Hunt racecourse at Scone Park (opened in 1908 and the UK's most northerly racecourse), McDiarmid Park football stadium (home to St Johnstone FC) and four 18-hole golf courses. In addition to the St John's Shopping Centre in the heart of the city, there are retail parks to the west and industrial estates at Inveralmond and on the Shore Road. Agricultural chemicals, farm machinery, soft drinks, furniture, glassware, clothing and textiles are the chief manufactures in addition to distilling, insurance, civil-engineering and printing industries. Annual events include Perth Festival of the Arts in May, Perth Agricultural Show in June and Perth Highland Games in August. Perth was the birthplace of photography pioneer D. O. Hill (1802) and of author and statesman John Buchan, 1st Baron Tweedsmuir (1875). An airfield (Perth Airport) was opened in 1934 at Scone, 4 miles (6.5 km) northeast of Perth.

Perth and Kinross *Area: 5,406 sq. km (2,087 sq. miles)* The former counties of Perthshire and Kinross-shire, which formed the Perth and Kinross District of Tayside Region from 1975 to 1996, combined to form this largely rural council area straddling the boundary between the Highlands and Lowlands of Scotland. It stretches from the famous trout-fishing waters of Loch Leven in the south to the Grampian Mountains beyond Blair Atholl in the north, and from Loch Tay in the west

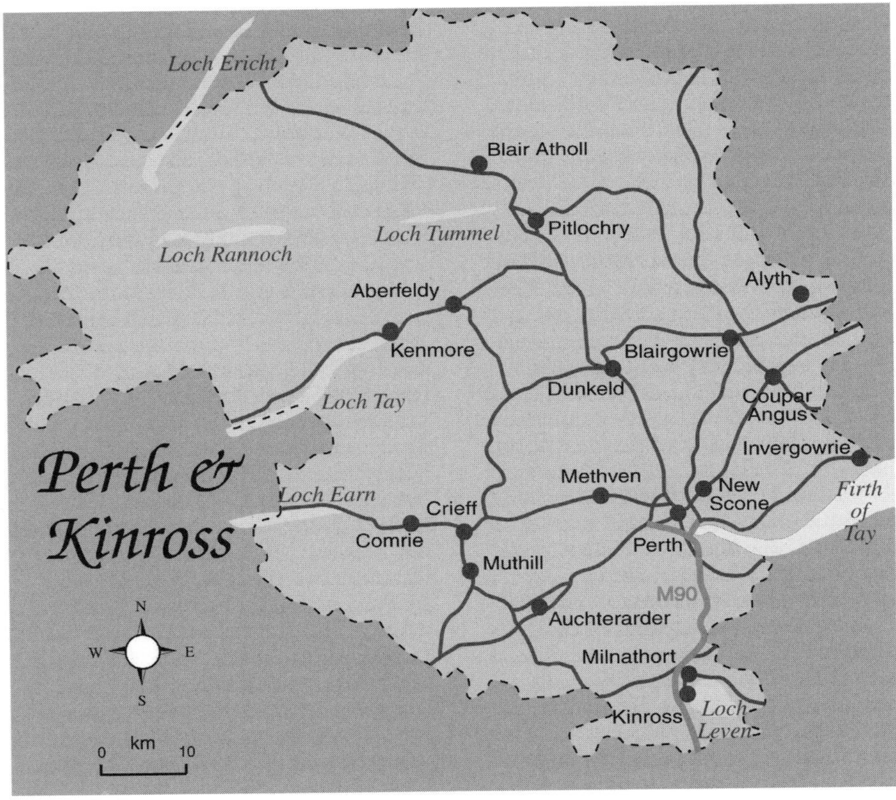

to the Lomond Hills in the east. Watered by the Tay, Earn, Tummel, Garry and Isla Rivers, its leading towns are Perth (administrative centre), Crieff, Coupar Angus, Blairgowrie, Auchterarder, Comrie, Aberfeldy, Pitlochry and Kinross. In the south the Kinross basin, with Loch Leven at its focal point, comprises a valley surrounded by Benarty and the Lomond, Cleish and Ochil Hills. To the north of the Tay the fertile river plain of the Carse of Gowrie is separated by the Sidlaw Hills from the equally fertile Strathmore valley, which is the centre of Scotland's fruit-growing industry. Highland Perthshire is characterised by a series of river valleys of varying width that in general trend west–east or southwest–northeast from Strath Allan in the south to Glen Garry in the north. Some of these contain the region's largest lochs, including Loch Tay, Loch Earn, Loch Rannoch and Loch Tummel. The principal valleys are those of the River Tay (Strathtay), which is Scotland's longest river, and the River Earn (Strath Earn). Beyond these valleys the southern outliers of the Grampians rise up through the Braes of Angus and the Forest of Atholl. Tourism, knitwear, crafts, distilling, farming, fruit growing and forestry are the leading industries.

Peterculter *Aberdeen City* A village of Aberdeen City, Peterculter is situated on the A93, 8 miles (13 km) southwest of Aberdeen city centre and north of the River Dee where it is joined by the Culter Burn. Developed around a paper mill established in 1751 but now largely a commuter settlement for Aberdeen, its parish church was originally dedicated to St Peter. Nearby is Culter House, which is associated with the Cumming and Duff families, and overlooking the main street of the village is a statue of Rob Roy Macgregor.

Peterhead *Aberdeenshire* A fishing port and resort town on the North Sea coast of Aberdeenshire, Peterhead is situated on a peninsula at the most easterly point of Scotland, 32 miles (51 km) north of Aberdeen. Largely built of red granite from nearby Stirling Hill, the town was founded by George Keith, 5th Earl Marischal, following the granting of a charter creating a burgh of barony in 1593. Until then, the only settlement in existence had been the fishing village of Keith-Inch (Caikinche), situated on an island separated from the mainland by a narrow channel that was filled in with stones in 1739 to create a causeway known as the Queenzie. The port's south harbour was built in 1773 by the engineer John Smeaton, and the north harbour was begun in 1818 to designs by Thomas Telford. In 1850 a canal was created across the peninsula linking the two harbours so that boats could be moved when one or other harbour was windbound. Towards the end of the 18th century Peterhead became a fashionable spa, its Wine Well and other springs attracting people to the town. Also associated with the former whaling and herring-fishing industries, Peterhead is today Europe's leading white fishing port with capacity for a fleet of some 300 vessels. It is also a service base for the North Sea oil industry and has a heliport to the west near Longside. Peterhead Maritime Heritage and the Arbuthnot Museum tell the story of the town's fishing and whaling industries. There are nine- and 18-hole golf courses in addition to a sailing club.

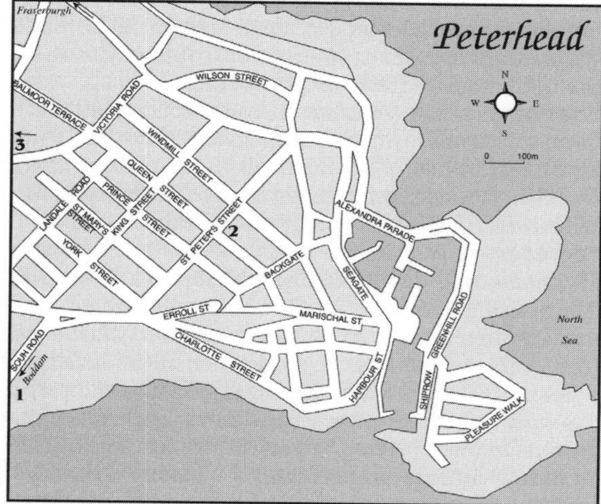

1 *Peterhead Marine Heritage*
2 *Arbuthnot Museum*
3 *Aberdeenshire Farming Museum*

Peterhead Bay *Aberdeenshire* Peterhead Bay lies to the south of the town of Peterhead in Aberdeenshire and forms a natural harbour for the town. At its northern extreme, it is bounded by the headland of Keith Inch, while to the south lies the settlement of Burnhaven.

Peter's Port *Western Isles* A locality with a pier on Eilean na Cille in Bagh nam Faoilean, Peter's Port (Gael: *Port Pheadair*) lies at the remote end of the B891, which extends from the extreme southeast of Benbecula over the island of Grimsay and various rocky islets to Eilean na Cille. The pier was built in 1896, at a cost of £2100, in response to demands for a new Hebridean port, but poor planning and political compromise saw a location chosen that was both inaccessible by road and difficult to enter from the sea. A new road was built, but little could be done to improve access from the sea and thus the use of the port has always been limited. The area is popular with bird-watchers.

Petershill Wildlife Reserve *West Lothian* Situated on the eastern outskirts of Bathgate in West Lothian, Petershill Wildlife Reserve was designated a Regionally Important Geological Site in 1999. The site comprises a limestone reef formed in the Carboniferous era, some 330 million years ago, and contains abundant fossils. Lime was quarried here from 1768 until two of the workings were converted into drinking-water reservoirs in 1886 and 1905. These reservoirs, declared redundant in 1981, were subsequently drained and the 5.4-ha (13.3-acre) site was gifted to the Scottish Wildlife Trust in 1990 as a nature reserve.

Pettinain *South Lanarkshire* A small village of Clydesdale, Pettinain lies to the south of the River Clyde, 2 miles (3 km) south of Carstairs Junction.

Pettycur *Fife* A resort village of southern Fife on the north shore of the Firth of Forth, Pettycur sits on a headland between Kinghorn and Burntisland. It was, until the development of the Newhaven–Burntisland railway ferry in 1848, the northern terminal of the Forth ferry, with road links via Cupar to the Tay ferry at Woodhaven.

Phabail The Gaelic name for Bayble in the Western Isles.

Phaibeil The Gaelic name for Paible in the Western Isles.

Phantassie *East Lothian* A hamlet and farm in East Lothian, Phantassie lies to the east of East Linton. A beehive dovecote containing 544 nest boxes was gifted to the National Trust for Scotland in 1961 by Mr W. Hamilton of Phantassie Farm. It was here that engineer John Rennie (1761–1821) was born and his mentor Andrew Meikle (1719–1811), millwright and inventor of the threshing machine, had his workshop. Rennie's elder brother George (1749–1828), well known for many innovations in farming practice, extended the 18th-century Phantassie farmhouse in 1820.

Phearsain, Loch a' *Argyll and Bute* A small loch in Argyll and Bute, Loch a' Phearsain lies to the northeast of Kilmelford. It drains into Loch Melfort.

Philiphaugh *Scottish Borders* An estate in Scottish Borders, Philiphaugh lies to the north of the confluence of the Yarrow and Ettrick waters, 2 miles (3 km) west of Selkirk. To the east is the site of the Battle of Philiphaugh, scene of the defeat of James Graham, the Marquess of Montrose, by the Covenanting General David Leslie on 13 September 1645.

Philorth, Water of *Aberdeenshire* A small river of the Buchan district of northeast Aberdeenshire, the Water of Philorth rises on the northern slopes of Waughton Hill (234 m/768 ft) to the south of Fraserburgh. It flows northeast for 8 miles (13 km), receiving the Water of Tyrie, and enters the North Sea at the eastern end of Fraserburgh Bay.

Philpstoun *West Lothian* A small village in West Lothian, Philpstoun (occasionally Philipstoun) lies to the north of the Forth and Clyde Canal, 3 miles (5 km) east of Linlithgow.

Phones *Highland* A small settlement in the Badenoch district of Highland Council area, Phones lies at the northeast end of Glen Truim, 3 miles (5 km) south of Newtonmore.

Phuill, Loch a' *Argyll and Bute* Located at the western end of the island of Tiree in the Inner Hebrides, Loch a' Phuill lies between the settlements of Balephuil in the south and Barrapoll in the north. It empties into Balephuil Bay.

Physgill House *Dumfries and Galloway* A late 17th-century three-storey country house in the southern Machars of Dumfries and Galloway, Physgill House overlooks Port Castle Bay on the Solway Firth, 2 miles (3 km) southwest of Whithorn.

Pickletillem *Fife* A hamlet with an inn in northeast Fife, Pickletillem lies on the A914, 2.5 miles (4 km) north of Balmullo and 2 miles (3 km) south of Newport-on-Tay.

Pierowall *Orkney* A village on the Orkney island of Westray, Pierowall is situated at the head of a bay that forms an inlet at the south end of Papa Sound. It is the largest settlement on the island and has ferry links with Papa Westray and Kirkwall. Westray Heritage Centre occupies a 19th-century school at the centre of the village. A large Viking cemetery was discovered in the sand dunes of the Bay of Pierowall in the 19th century, and it was to this anchorage that Earl Rognald and his men came in 1136 at the beginning of the subjugation of the Orkney Islands. The *Orkneyinga Saga* notes that Earl Rognald attended a service at the church here. The oldest part of the church that survives at Pierowall dates from the 13th century, most of the building representing 17th-century alterations. A mile (1.5 km) to the west of Pierowall stands Noltland Castle, which dates from the 16th century.

Pikey Hill *Moray* Located 4 miles (6.5 km) northwest of the settlement of Rothes in Moray, the Pikey Hill rises to a height of 355 m (1164 ft). The Leanoch Burn rises here.

Pilgrim's Way, The *Dumfries and Galloway* Signposted by the Whithorn Pilgrimage Trust, The Pilgrim's Way follows a route southwards from the Southern Upland Way through the Machars region. It passes through New Luce and by the early Christian holy sites of Glenluce, Whithorn, Isle of Whithorn and St Ninian's Cave. The main part of the route from Glenluce to Whithorn is 25 miles (40 km) long and passes the remains of the Cistercian abbey of Glenluce, where monks treated lepers en route to the nearby medieval leper colony of Liberland. From Stair Haven the route turns inland, passing the House of Elrig, which was the home of Gavin Maxwell, author of *Ring of Bright Water*.

Pilrig *City of Edinburgh* A northeastern suburb of Edinburgh, Pilrig is located a mile (1.5 km) from the city centre.

Piltanton Burn *Dumfries and Galloway* A stream in the Rhinns of Galloway, the Piltanton Burn rises to the northwest of Stranraer. It flows southeast to Lochans then east before entering Luce Bay nearly 2 miles (3 km) west of Glenluce.

Pilton *City of Edinburgh* A district of northwest Edinburgh, Pilton lies 2 miles (3 km) from the city centre. Its public housing largely dates from the 1930s.

Pinkie *East Lothian* An estate in the East Lothian parish of Inveresk, Pinkie is located to the east of the River Esk, between Musselburgh and Wallyford. Pinkie House, originally a country seat of the Abbots of Dunfermline, was enlarged by the Seton family in the early 17th century and is said to have been occupied by Prince Charles Edward Stewart (Bonnie Prince Charlie) about the time of the Battle of Prestonpans. Noted for its fine ceilings, the King's Room was specially created for Charles I who stayed here on his journey north to be crowned in 1637. Since 1951 the building has been used as a boarding house by Loretto School. On 10 September 1547 a battle took place nearby at Pinkie Cleugh during an episode known as the 'Rough Wooing'. A Scottish army, led by the 2nd Earl of Arran, was defeated by English forces under the Duke of Somerset.

Pinminnoch *South Ayrshire* A small settlement in South Ayrshire, Pinminnoch lies 3 miles (5 km) south of Girvan.

Pinmore *South Ayrshire* A small settlement in South Ayrshire, Pinmore lies 5 miles (8 km) south of Girvan on the north bank of the River Stinchar.

Pinwherry *South Ayrshire* A settlement in South Ayrshire, Pinwherry lies 8 miles (13 km) south of Girvan near the confluence of the Duisk Burn and the River Stinchar. Nearby stand the remains of Pinwherry Castle, a former stronghold of the Kennedy family.

Piperdam *Angus* A settlement of southwest Angus, Piperdam was developed from 1998 as a greenfield housing development associated with Piperdam Golf and Country Park, 4.5 miles (7 km) northwest of Dundee. The golf and country park includes an 18-hole golf course, a 16-ha (40-acre) trout loch, clubhouse and lodge. Piperdam Loch has attracted fishing ospreys since the 1980s, and the Piperdam Osprey Centre was constructed to provide an observation facility for visitors via CCTV.

Piperhill *Highland* A small settlement in the Nairn district of Highland Council area, Piperhill lies 4 miles (6.5 km) south of the town of Nairn.

Pirnhall *Stirling* Now a service location at the junction of two motorways in Stirling Council area 2 miles (3 km) south of Stirling, Pirnhall was once a centre for making pirns, or weavers' reels. Pirnhall Inn dates from the 18th century.

Pirnmill *North Ayrshire* A small settlement on the west coast of the island of Arran, Pirnmill lies 6 miles (10 km) southwest of Lochranza and looks westwards over the Kilbrannan Sound towards the Kintyre peninsula.

Pitagowan *Perth and Kinross* Situated in Glen Garry where the glens of Bruar and Errochty meet, the small village of Pitagowan lies at the confluence of the River Garry with the Bruar Water, 3 miles (5 km) west of Blair Atholl. The Falls of Bruar lie to the north of the settlement.

Pitcairn *Fife* A residential district of northern Glenrothes, Pitcairn is situated to the east of Collydean, between Western Avenue and Pitcairn Avenue. Pitcairn Outdoor Centre is located here, and most of the streets and courts are named after Scottish artists.

Pitcairn *Perth and Kinross* A small settlement of Perth and Kinross, Pitcairn lies a mile (1.5 km) southeast of Dunning, on the northern slopes of the Ochil Hills.

Pitcairngreen *Perth and Kinross* An 18th-century planned industrial village, Pitcairngreen lies to the north of Almondbank, 4 miles (6.5 km) northwest of Perth. It was laid out around a green in 1786 by the Duke of Atholl's factor, James Stobie, for Thomas Graham, a textile manufacturer. The rivalry with Manchester textile factories is recorded in a verse by Hannah Cowley (1786) that begins: 'Go Manchester and weep thy slighted loom, Its arts are cherished now in Pitcairne Green.'

Pitcalnie *Highland* A small hamlet of Easter Ross, Pitcalnie lies 2 miles (3 km) north of the entrance to the Cromarty Firth.

Pitcaple *Aberdeenshire* A hamlet in the Garioch district of central Aberdeenshire, Pitcaple lies on the River Urie, 4 miles (6.5 km) northwest of Inverurie. Nearby Pitcaple Castle was visited by Mary, Queen of Scots, James IV and Charles II, and restored by William Burn in 1830.

Pitcox *East Lothian* Situated to the south of the Biel Water in East Lothian, the settlement of Pitcox lies 3 miles (5 km) southwest of Dunbar.

Pitcur *Perth and Kinross* A hamlet in the Sidlaw Hills, Pitcur lies 2.5 miles (4 km) southeast of Coupar Angus in Perth and Kinross. Situated alongside the A923 from Dundee, Pitcur is known for its ruined 16th-century castle.

Pitfichie *Aberdeenshire* A locality with a restored castle in Aberdeenshire, Pitfichie lies by the River Don, a mile (1.5 km) north of Monymusk. Associated with the Covenanting General Hurry, the castle was later acquired by the Forbes family of Monymusk.

Pitgrudy *Highland* A small settlement of Easter Ross in Highland Council area, Pitgrudy lies a mile (1.5 km) northwest of Dornoch.

Pitkeathly Wells *Perth and Kinross* A hamlet in Perth and Kinross, Pitkeathly Wells lies to the north of the Ochil Hills, 2 miles (3 km) southeast of Bridge of Earn. The springs here were once noted for their healthy minerals and were partly responsible for the development of Bridge of Earn as a spa town in the 19th century. Schweppes took over the springs in 1910 but after a fire in 1927 water bottling came to an end and in 1949 the wells ceased to function as a spa.

Pitkevy *Fife* A settlement in central Fife, Pitkevy lies 3 miles (5 km) northwest of Glenrothes town centre and 3 miles (5 km) south of Falkland.

Pitlessie *Fife* A village in the Howe of Fife, Pitlessie is situated on the River Eden 4 miles (6.5 km) southwest of Cupar. It is the only village in the parish of Cults and largely developed during the 19th century in association with the Priestfield Maltings and nearby limeworks. Its former cattle fair was the scene depicted in a famous painting by Sir David Wilkie, who was born at Cults manse in 1785 and went to school in Pitlessie.

Pitlochry *Perth and Kinross* A resort town in Highland Perth and Kinross, Pitlochry is situated on the River Tummel 28 miles (45 km) north of Perth. Well provided with hotels, guesthouses, caravan and camping parks, Pitlochry's fame as a holiday resort dates from the 1860s. Its chief attractions are the Pitlochry Dam and Fish Ladder, created during the 1950s when the River Tummel was dammed for hydro-electric purposes. The fish ladder allows fish to bypass the dam and enter the man-made Loch Faskally. Additional attractions include the Pitlochry Festival Theatre, Blair Atholl Distillery (1798) and Visitor Centre, and Edradour Distillery, which claims to be the smallest whisky distillery in Scotland. The town has craft workshops, a curling rink, a leisure centre, an 18-hole golf course and bowling greens.

Pitlurg *Aberdeenshire* A locality in Aberdeenshire, Pitlurg lies to the east of the Burn of Forvie, 5 miles (8 km) northeast of Ellon.

Pitmedden *Aberdeenshire* A village in the Formartine district of Aberdeenshire, Pitmedden lies on the Bronie Burn, 4 miles (6.5 km) southwest of Ellon. Pitmedden Garden, with its formal parterres, herb garden and wildlife garden, was originally laid out in 1675 by Sir Alexander Seton, 1st Baronet of Pitmedden. In 1952, the property was given to the National Trust for Scotland by Major James Keith. In 1978 the trustees of William Cook of Little Meldrum handed over to the trust a collection of agricultural and domestic artefacts that were used to form the nucleus of the Museum of Farming Life. Also nearby is Udny Green, with its castle and churchyard containing an unusual mort house.

Pitmuies An alternative name for House of Pitmuies in Angus.

Pitroddie *Perth and Kinross* A locality in the Carse of Gowrie, eastern Perth and Kinross, Pitroddie lies surrounded by fertile farmland, 6 miles (10 km) east of Perth.

Pitscottie *Fife* A village in Ceres parish, eastern Fife, Pitscottie is situated on the Ceres Burn at a road junction to the south of Dura Den, 3 miles (5 km) southeast of Cupar. It was the home of Robert Lindsay of Pitscottie who wrote the first vernacular prose history of Scotland entitled the *Historie and Cronicles of Scotland, 1436–1565*. The nearby Pitscottie Moor was a favourite meeting place of Covenanters during the late 17th century, and during the 1820s the village became a centre of flax spinning. There is an 18th-century bridge over the Ceres Burn.

Pitsligo Castle *Aberdeenshire* The ruined remains of the 15th-century Pitsligo Castle stand on the Buchan coast of Aberdeenshire a half-mile (1 km) southeast of Rosehearty. The castle was a Fraser stronghold and later owned by the Forbes family. In 1633, Alexander Forbes was created Baron Forbes of Pitsligo, a title forfeited after the 1745 Jacobite Rebellion.

Pittencrieff Park *Fife* A 31 ha (76 acre) park in Dunfermline, western Fife, Pittencrieff Park is known locally as The Glen. It was formerly part of the privately owned Pittencrieff Estate. In 1902 the house and estate were bought by the industrialist and philanthropist Andrew Carnegie, who donated the whole property to the town as a public park. It is said that as a child he had been forbidden to play in the grounds of the lairds of Pittencrieff. Today the beautifully landscaped park has within its bounds a statue of Andrew Carnegie, the Pittencrieff House Museum, the remains of Malcolm Canmore's Tower, nature trails, paddling pools, playgrounds and an animal centre.

Pittendreich *Moray* A scattered settlement of Moray, Pittendreich lies a mile (1.5 km) southwest of Elgin. The Black Burn flows through Pittendreich on its way to join the River Lossie south of Aldroughty.

Pittenweem *Fife* A fishing village in the East Neuk of Fife, Pittenweem is situated on the Firth of Forth between St Monans and Anstruther. Designated a burgh of regality in 1452 and a royal burgh in 1541, Pittenweem developed a prosperous trade with the Low Countries in medieval times. Its harbour, which succeeded the earlier Boat Haven, was first built in stone *c*.1600 and many of its houses have been restored by the National Trust for Scotland under its Little Houses Improvement Scheme. Interesting buildings include the parish church, which largely dates from the 16th century; Kellie Lodging, the restored 16th-century town house of the earls of Kellie; and the ruins of Pittenweem Priory, a foundation of the Augustinian canons who came from the Isle of May in the 13th century. In the cliff face beneath the priory is St Fillan's Cave, which was the alleged retreat of St Fillan in the 7th century. Pittenweem, which still has a thriving fish market, also has bowling and tennis facilities, and an annual arts festival in August.

Pitteuchar *Fife* A southeastern suburb of Glenrothes in Fife, Pitteuchar is situated to the north of the Lochty Burn. Prior to the building of the new town of Glenrothes in the 1950s, there existed the farms of Wester and Easter Pitteuchar. Glenrothes Technical College, the Glamis Centre and the Crystals Arena Bowling and Ice Centre are all located in Pitteuchar.

Pittodrie *Aberdeenshire* A locality in the Garioch district of Aberdeenshire, Pittodrie lies to the south of the River Urie, a mile (1.5 km) west of Chapel of Garioch. Bennachie rises to the southwest. To the north of the mansion of Pittodrie stands the Maiden Stone, a pink granite cross-slab dating from the 9th century AD that takes its name from the legend of the daughter of the laird of Balquain who died trying to elope.

Pittodrie Stadium *Aberdeen City* The home ground of Aberdeen Football Club, Pittodrie Stadium is located at the northern end of Union Street, the main thoroughfare of Aberdeen city centre. Established in 1881, the club was created by 12 individuals, most of whom were teachers (hence the team nickname 'The Dons'). The land they occupied as tenants was named Pittodrie Park after the owner, Mr Knight Erskine of Pittodrie. In 1903, Orion and Victoria United Football Clubs were united with Aberdeen Football Club, and in the 1960s the modern stadium with a seating capacity of 21,634 was developed.

Pittrichie *Aberdeenshire* A mansion in Udny parish, Aberdeenshire, Pittrichie lies 2 miles (3 km) southeast of Oldmeldrum.

Pittulie *Aberdeenshire* A fishing village in the Aberdeenshire parish of Pitsligo, Pittulie lies on the Moray Firth coast immediately west of Sandhaven and 2 miles (3 km) west of Fraserburgh. Pittulie Castle was a former stronghold of the Frasers of Philorth was and enlarged by the Cumines.

Pityoulish, Loch *Highland* A small loch in the Strathspey district of Highland Council area, Loch Pityoulish lies to the east of the River Spey, 2 miles (3 km) northeast of Aviemore.

Pladda *North Ayrshire* A small uninhabited island of volcanic rock, Pladda (also *Fladda*) lies in the Firth of Clyde to the south of the island of Arran, from which it is separated by the Sound of Pladda.

Plaidy *Aberdeenshire* A locality in northwest Aberdeenshire, Plaidy lies on a tributary of the River Deveron, 6 miles (10 km) south of Macduff. A railway station once existed here, and to the south are the farms of Bogs of Plaidy and Back Plaidy.

Plains *North Lanarkshire* A small village in North Lanarkshire, Plains lies 2 miles (3 km) northeast of Airdrie and a mile (1.5 km) west of Caldercruix.

Plasterfield *Western Isles* A settlement in eastern Lewis in the Outer Hebrides, Plasterfield (Gael: *Raon na Creadha*) lies immediately to the east of Stornoway and a mile (1.5 km) west of Stornoway Airport. Plasterfield developed as 'prefab' public housing to meet the demand for homes for troops returning after World War II.

Plean *Stirling* One of the three 'Eastern Villages' of Stirling Council area, Plean lies 3 miles (5 km) southeast of Bannockburn. Plean was formerly a mining village but the last coal pit closed in January 1963. The neighbouring Plean Estate has been opened to the public as a country park. Its neoclassical country mansion, which was built in the late 18th century by William Simpson, a wealthy East India trader, was last occupied in 1970.

Pleasance *Fife* A hamlet in north-central Fife, Pleasance is situated on the A893 a half-mile (1 km) to the north of Auchtermuchty.

Plewlands House *City of Edinburgh* A 17th-century house in the centre of South Queensferry, the three-storey L-plan Plewlands House was built in 1641 for Samuel Wilson and his wife Anna Ponton, whose initials are carved above the entrance along with the motto '*Spes Mea Christus*' (My hope is in Christ). The building was restored in 1955 by the National Trust for Scotland.

Plockton *Highland* A picturesque lochside village in the Lochalsh district of Highland Council area, Plockton lies on the southern shore of Loch Carron 5 miles (8 km) northeast of Kyle of Lochalsh. It was founded in the late 18th century as a fishing and crofting settlement. Nearby Duncraig Castle, later used as a college, was built in 1866 for Sir Alexander Matheson to designs by Alexander Ross. The estate of Balmacara to the south was acquired by the National Trust for Scotland in 1953. The popular 1990s television series *Hamish Macbeth* was filmed in and around Plockton.

Pluscarden Abbey *Moray* Situated in the shadow of Heldon Hill, 6 miles (10 km) southwest of Elgin, Pluscarden Abbey is the only medieval monastery in Scotland still occupied by monks. The original Cistercian abbey was founded in 1230 by Alexander II and in 1345 came under the authority of the Bishop of Moray, whose seat at Elgin Cathedral had also been founded by Alexander in 1224. Dedicated to St Mary, St John and St Andrew, it was one of only three Valliscaulian foundations in Scotland linked to the Priory of Val des Choux in Burgundy. Badly damaged following an assault by Alexander Stewart, the 'Wolf of Badenoch', in 1390, Pluscarden was taken in hand by the Benedictine order in 1454 on its union with the Priory of Urquhart, 4 miles (6.5 km) east of Elgin. After the Reformation the buildings fell into ruin, passing through various hands before being restored by the Roman Catholic antiquarian John, 3rd Marquess of Bute, at the end of the 19th century. In 1943, the restored buildings were returned by his son, Lord Colum Crichton-Stuart, to the Benedictine community of Prinknash Abbey in Gloucestershire, England. The monks, who now welcome visitors, took up residence in 1948 and continued the restoration of the 13th-century church. Occupied by nearly 30 monks, priests and novices, Pluscarden Priory was raised to the status of an abbey in 1974.

Pocan Smoo *Highland* A rocky outlier in the sea off the north coast of Sutherland, Pocan Smoo lies a mile (1.5 km) east of Durness and to the northeast of Smoo Cave.

Pochriegavin Burn *South Ayrshire/Dumfries and Galloway* A stream on the border between South Ayrshire and Dumfries and Galloway, the Pochriegavin Burn rises on the slopes of Ben Brack. It flows eastwards to join the Water of Deugh.

Point of Graand *Orkney* A headland on the island of Egilsay in the Orkney Islands, the Point of Graand extends into the sea at the south end of the island.

Polbain *Highland* A small coastal settlement in the Coigach district of Wester Ross, Polbain lies on Badentarbat Bay, an inlet on the north shore of Loch Broom, 2 miles (3 km) northwest of Achiltibuie.

Polbaith Burn *East Ayrshire* A stream in East Ayrshire, the Polbaith Burn rises on the eastern slopes of Sneddon Law and flows southwest to join the River Irvine a mile (1.5 km) west of Galston.

Polbeth *West Lothian* A village of West Lothian, Polbeth lies 3 miles (5 km) southwest of Livingston and a mile (1.5 km) northeast of West Calder.

Polglass *Highland* A village in the Coigach district of Wester Ross, Polglass lies on the north side of Loch Broom, a mile (1.5 km) southeast of Achiltibuie and 9 miles (14 km) northwest of Ullapool.

Polgown *Dumfries and Galloway* A locality in Dumfries and Galloway, Polgown lies near the head of the Scaur Water, 6 miles (10 km) southwest of Sanquhar.

Polharrow Burn *Dumfries and Galloway* A stream in Dumfries and Galloway, the Polharrow Burn rises in Loch Harrow and flows eastwards to join the Water of Ken 2 miles (3 km) northwest of St John's Town of Dalry. Its chief tributaries are McAdam's Burn and Crummy Burn.

Polkemmet *West Lothian* A moorland in West Lothian, Polkemmet lies to the west of Whitburn.

Poll a' Charra The Gaelic name for Pollachar in the Western Isles.

Polla *Highland* A settlement at the northern end of Strath Beag in Sutherland, Polla lies at the head of Loch Eriboll and east of the mountain Cranstackie.

Pollachar *Western Isles* A locality with an inn on the southwest coast of South Uist, Pollachar (also *Polochar*, Gael: *Poll a' Charra*) lies a quarter-mile (0.5 km) west of Kilbride and 4 miles (6.5 km) southwest of Lochboisdale.

Polliwilline Bay *Argyll and Bute* Situated at the southern end of the Kintyre pensinsula, Polliwilline Bay forms an inlet 7 miles (11 km) south of Campbeltown.

Polloch *Highland* A settlement in the Sunart district of southwest Highland Council area, Polloch lies on the River Polloch just east of an inlet on the south shore of Loch Shiel.

Pollok *Glasgow City* A residential suburb of Glasgow, Pollok lies 4 miles (6.5 km) southwest of the city centre and east of the M77. The 146-ha (361-acre) Pollok Country Park, which is bisected by the White Cart Water and includes Pollok House and the Burrell Collection, was created by the owner of Pollok Estate, Sir John Stirling Maxwell (1866–1956), a founder member of the National Trust for Scotland. He realised the importance of maintaining green areas within cities and gave the people of Glasgow access to part of his estate from 1911. He entered into a conservation agreement with the National Trust for Scotland in 1939, both parties agreeing to maintain the land as open space in perpetuity. Between 1747 and 1752 the neo-Palladian Pollok House was built on the banks of the White Cart for Sir John Maxwell to a design by William Adam, the Maxwell family having owned the estate since the mid-13th century. From 1911 Stirling Maxwell created the gardens around the house, which was used as a military hospital during World War I. In 1966 his daughter, Mrs Anne Maxwell Macdonald, gave the house, including her father's art collection and the surrounding estate, to the City of Glasgow. The management of Pollok House was transferred to the National Trust for Scotland in 1998.

Pollokshaws *Glasgow City* A former weaving village, now a residential suburb of Glasgow, Pollokshaws lies on the White Cart Water to the south of the River Clyde. Designated a burgh of barony in 1813, it developed in association with linen printing, cotton milling, paper making and iron founding. It had one of the earliest printworks in Scotland in 1742, and its cotton mill was the first in the country to be lit by gas. A daughter of the poet Robert Burns, Betty Johnstone, is buried in the Kirk Lane Burying Ground. Gaining a reputation for working-class militancy, Pollokshaws was the birthplace of the socialist MP James Maxton (1885–1946). Redeveloped in the 1960s, Pollokshaws comprises a mixture of old tenement flats and new low- and high-rise flats.

Pollokshields *Glasgow City* A residential suburb on the south side of Glasgow, Pollokshields lies to the east of the M77 and south of the M8. Originally two separate burghs, Pollokshields West and Pollokshields East, Pollokshields was incorporated into the City of Glasgow in 1891 following the designation of the two settlements as police burghs in 1876 and 1880. While Pollokshields East developed in association with retail and industry, conditions of the feus of Pollokshields West prohibited shops, and trade limited the types of housing. To the southwest, near Pollok Country Park, is Haggs Castle (1585).

Polly Bay *Highland* An inlet of Enard Bay on the coast of Wester Ross, Polly Bay (or Loch Polly) lies to the east of the headland of Rubh' a' Choin. It receives the River Polly, which flows west from Loch Sionascaig.

Polmaddie *Dumfries and Galloway* A locality in The Glenkens district of Dumfries and Galloway, Polmaddie lies at the junction of the Polmaddy Burn with the Water of Ken, 4 miles (6.5 km) southeast of Carsphairn.

Polmaddie Hill *South Ayrshire* A hill in the Carrick district of South Ayrshire, Polmaddie Hill rises to 565 m (1853 ft) 6 miles (10 km) northeast of Barrhill.

Polmaddy Burn *Dumfries and Galloway* A stream in Dumfries and Galloway, the Polmaddy Burn rises on the slopes of Polmaddy Gairy in the Rhinns of Kells. It flows north and east to join the Water of Ken at Polmaddie to the south of Dundeugh Hill.

Polmadie *Glasgow City* An industrial suburb of Glasgow, Polmadie lies 2 miles (3 km) south of the city centre, close to Govanhill.

Polmaise *Stirling* A former rural estate owned by the Murray family and situated on flat carselands by the River Forth to the east of Stirling, Polmaise developed as a centre of coal mining during the 20th century when shafts were sunk. Polmaise colliery eventually closed in 1984.

Polmont *Falkirk* A dormitory village in Falkirk Council area, Polmont is situated to the south of Grangemouth between the M9 and the Union Canal. It developed in the 18th and 19th centuries in association with coal mining and the canal. A young offenders' institute is located nearby.

Polmoody *Dumfries and Galloway* A locality in the Moffat valley, Dumfries and Galloway, Polmoody lies on the Moffat Water, 7 miles (11 km) northwest of Moffat.

Polnoon *East Renfrewshire* A scattered settlement on the eastern edge of East Renfrewshire, Polnoon lies a mile (1.5 km) east of Eaglesham.

Polochar An alternative name for Pollachar in the Western Isles

Poltalloch *Argyll and Bute* A small village in the Argyllshire parish of Kilmartin, Poltalloch lies to the northeast of Crinan Loch, 7 miles (11 km) northwest of Lochgilphead. The Poltalloch Estate is associated with the Malcolm family.

Polton *Midlothian* A village in Midlothian, Polton lies on the North Esk River, a mile (1.5 km) southeast of Loanhead and a mile (1.5 km) southwest of Bonnyrigg. Mavisbank House was built in 1723–7 by William Adam for Sir John Clerk. It was was badly damaged by fire in 1973 and featured in the BBC television programme *Restoration* in 2003. Poltonhall lies adjacent to Bonnyrigg and comprises later 20th-century private and military housing. Polton was home to 'opium-eating' author Thomas De Quincey (1785–1859).

Polwarth *Scottish Borders* A village in a parish of the same name in the Berwickshire district of Scottish Borders, Polwarth lies 4 miles (6.5 km) southwest of Duns.

Polwhat Burn *Dumfries and Galloway* A stream in Dumfries and Galloway, the Polwhat Burn rises on Polwhat Rig and flows northwestwards through the Carsphairn Forest to join the Water of Deugh 6 miles (10 km) southeast of Dalmellington.

Ponesk Burn *East Ayrshire* Rising on the slopes of Priesthill Height, the Ponesk Burn flows south to join the River Ayr 2 miles (3 km) east of Muirkirk.

Ponfeigh Burn *South Lanarkshire* Rising in high land a mile (1.5 km) south of Rigside in South Lanarkshire, the Ponfeigh Burn flows north for 3 miles (5 km) before passing through the settlement of Douglas Water, where it enters the Douglas Water.

Pool of Muckhart *Clackmannanshire* A village in the Clackmannanshire parish of Muckhart, Pool of Muckhart lies in the valley of the River Devon, 3 miles (5 km) northeast of Dollar and near the entrance to Glen Devon.

Poolewe *Highland* A village in Wester Ross, Poolewe lies at the head of Loch Ewe, 4 miles (6.5 km) northeast of the Gair Loch and 2 miles (3 km) from the head of Loch Maree to the southeast. The surrounding area is owned by the National Trust for Scotland. To the north lie the trust's gardens of Inverewe.

Pooltiel, Loch *Highland* A sea loch on the northwest coast of the isle of Skye in the Inner Hebrides, Loch Pooltiel lies 3 miles (5 km) northwest of Colbost and 4 miles (6.5 km) southwest of Dunvegan Head.

Port Appin *Argyll and Bute* A small settlement in the Appin district of Argyll and Bute, Port Appin looks out onto Loch Linnhe and the island of Lismore, to which it is linked by a ferry

Port Arnol *Western Isles* A bay on the northwest coast of the Isle of Lewis in the Outer Hebrides, Port Arnol lies a mile (1.5 km) northwest of Arnol village. The bay is separated from More Bragar by a headland.

Port Askaig *Argyll and Bute* A village and ferry port on the east coast of the island of Islay, Port Askaig lies at the narrowest point on the Sound of Islay which separates the island from Jura to the east. A steamer service from Glasgow first operated in 1821. Today there are ferry links with Feolin Ferry on Jura, Kennacraig on West Loch Tarbert on the west coast of the Kintyre peninsula, Scalasaig on the island of Colonsay, and Oban.

Port Bàn *Argyll and Bute* A small inlet on the north coast of the island of Tiree in the Inner Hebrides, Port Bàn lies 2 miles (3 km) northeast of Gott Bay.

Port Bannatyne *Argyll and Bute* A resort village on the east coast of the island of Bute, Port Bannatyne is situated to the north of Ardbeg Point on Kames Bay, 2 miles (3 km) north of Rothesay. It has fine views over the Kyles of Bute to the Cowal peninsula. Originally named Kamesburgh after the estate on which it was established, it was created by the Bannatynes of Kames Estate as a planned village in an attempt to rival Rothesay. Kames Castle lies on the western outskirts of the village.

Port Castle Bay *Dumfries and Galloway* An inlet on the Solway Firth coast of Dumfries and Galloway, Port Castle Bay lies 3 miles (5 km) southwest of Whithorn between Burrow Head and the Point of Cairndoon.

Port Charlotte *Argyll and Bute* A small linear village on the island of Islay in the Inner Hebrides, Port Charlotte lies on the Rhinns of Islay to the west of Loch Indaal. It was laid out in 1828 by the Revd Maclaurin on the site of two former clachans to provide accommodation for local distillery workers. The distillery closed in 1929, its malt barns later being occupied by the Islay Creamery. The village has a youth hostel, field centre and Museum of Islay Life.

Port Donain *Argyll and Bute* Lying a mile (1.5 km) south of Loch Don, Port Donain is a small bay that lies on the southeastern coast of the island of Mull, Argyll and Bute.

Overlooking the Firth of Lorn, the bay lies a mile (1.5 km) northeast of the headland of Rubha na Faoilinn.

Port Driseach *Argyll and Bute* A small village on the Cowal peninsula, Port Driseach lies on the western shore of Loch Riddon a half-mile (1 km) northeast of Tighnabruaich.

Port Dundas *Glasgow City* A district of north-central Glasgow, Port Dundas lies a mile (1.5 km) to the north of the city centre. It developed in the 1790s in association with the linking of the Glasgow branch of the Forth and Clyde Canal with the Monkland Canal. In the 19th century, the emergence of textile mills, chemical works, grain mills, distilleries, glassworks, iron foundries and engineering works turned the site into a flourishing industrial location. By the late 1960s many of these industries had declined, the original Port Dundas basin being drained and the M8 motorway constructed. The basin was restored in 2006.

Port Edgar *City of Edinburgh* A small harbour and yachting marina on the south shore of the Firth of Forth on the western border of the City of Edinburgh, Port Edgar lies a half-mile (1 km) west of South Queensferry.

Port Ellen *Argyll and Bute* A small port and distillery town on the south coast of Islay in the Inner Hebrides, Port Ellen lies on the shore of Loch Leodarnais, an inlet of Kilnaughton Bay. It is the island's second-largest settlement and only deep harbour, with ferry links to the mainland and an airport 4 miles (6.5 km) to the northwest at Glenegedale. Port Ellen was established in 1821 by Walter Frederick Campbell, who named the settlement after his wife. Nearby are the ruined remains of the 14th-century Dunyveg Castle, a former stronghold of the MacDonald Lords of the Isles.

Port Elphinstone *Aberdeenshire* A village of central Aberdeenshire, Port Elphinstone lies on a bend of the River Don opposite Inverurie. It originally developed as a port at the northwest end of the Aberdeenshire Canal which linked it with the city of Aberdeen between 1807 and 1854. It later developed as an industrial suburb of Inverurie with a railway station.

Port Erroll *Aberdeenshire* A small harbour settlement in east Aberdeenshire, Port Erroll lies immediately southeast of Cruden Bay, where the Water of Cruden enters the Bay of Cruden, an inlet of the North Sea between Aberdeen and Peterhead. Formerly known as the Ward of Cruden, its harbour was developed in the 19th century for shipping corn and importing coal and other goods.

Port Fada *Argyll and Bute* A bay on the east coast of the Kintyre peninsula, Port Fada forms an inlet 2 miles (3 km) southwest of Claonaig and 2 miles (3 km) northeast of Crossaig.

Port Glasgow *Inverclyde* A seaport on the south side of the Firth of Clyde, Port Glasgow lies 4 miles (6.5 km) east of Greenock and 20 miles (32 km) northwest of Glasgow. The second-largest town in Inverclyde, Port Glasgow was originally associated with Newark Castle, a stronghold of the Maxwells. In 1668 Glasgow Corporation, in search of a port with deeper water, acquired the Newark Estate and created Port Glasgow. By the mid-18th century Port Glasgow had become Scotland's leading port, with rope making, sugar refining and brewing. As the Clyde was deepened, the port focused on shipbuilding, the first Cunarder, *Britannia*, being built here in 1840. Following the decline in shipbuilding in the 20th century, clothing and electronics industries were introduced. Finlaystone House and Garden to the east of the town comprise 4 ha (10 acres) of woodland with walks and recreational facilities.

Port Henderson *Highland* A village in Wester Ross, Port Henderson lies on the south shore of Gair Loch, 4 miles (6.5 km) southwest of Gairloch.

Port Logan *Dumfries and Galloway* A village in the Rhinns of Galloway, Port Logan overlooks Port Logan Bay, 11 miles (18 km) south of Stranraer. The village comprises a row of houses along the shore established in the early 19th century by Colonel McDouall of Logan in an attempt to create an improved port facility. It has a harbour built in 1818–22 and a circular granite lighthouse dating from the 1830s. Rock-cut steps lead into the 15-m/50-ft-diameter Logan Fish Ponds which are enclosed with crenellated walls and guarded by a castellated cottage. The ponds were originally stocked by the McDoualls with carp. Described as 'the most exotic garden in Scotland', the nearby Logan Botanic Garden features many plants that thrive in the exceptionally mild climate of southwest Scotland. It is a specialist garden of the Royal Botanic Garden Edinburgh. Also close by are the remains of Balzieland Old Castle, a former stronghold of the McDoualls of Logan.

Port Logan Bay An alternative name for Port Nessock Bay.

Port Mholair The Gaelic name for Portvoller in the Western Isles.

Port Mòr *Highland* A small village in the Small Isles, Port Mòr is situated on the southeast side of the island of Muck.

Port More Bragar *Western Isles* A bay on the northwest coast of the Isle of Lewis in the Outer Hebrides, Port More Bragar (Gael: *Port Mhòr Bhragair*) lies a mile (1.5 km) north of Bragor.

Port na Craig *Perth and Kinross* A settlement in Logierait parish, Perth and Kinross, Port na Craig is situated on the River Tummel opposite Pitlochry.

Port nan Long *Western Isles* A settlement on the north coast of the island of North Uist in the Western Isles, Port nan Long (or Newtonferry) lies a mile (1.5 km) north of Beinn Mhòr.

Port Nessock Bay *Dumfries and Galloway* An inlet on the west coast of the Rhinns of Galloway, Dumfries and Galloway, Port Nessock Bay lies between the Mull of Logan and Cairnywellan Head. Also known as Port Logan Bay, the village of Port Logan lies on its shore.

Port Nis The Gaelic name for Port of Ness in the Western Isles.

Port of Menteith *Stirling* A village on the northeast shore of the Lake of Menteith, Port of Menteith lies 8 miles (13 km) southwest of Callander and 6 miles (10 km) east of Aberfoyle. Situated at the heart of the ancient earldom of Menteith and lands of the Clan Graham, it is the main access point for the island of Inchmahome. Created a burgh of barony in 1467 by James III, it is surrounded by fertile farming land overlooked by the Menteith Hills. It is also a centre for anglers.

Port of Ness *Western Isles* A settlement at the northern tip of the Isle of Lewis in the Western Isles, Port of Ness (Gael: *Port Nis*) lies in the Ness district, 2 miles (3 km) southeast of the Butt of Lewis.

Port of Spittal Bay *Dumfries and Galloway* An inlet on the west coast of the Rhinns of Galloway, Dumfries and Galloway, Port of Spittal Bay is nearly 2 miles (3 km) southeast of Portpatrick.

Port Pheadair The Gaelic name for Peter's Port in the Western Isles.

Port Ramsay *Argyll and Bute* A settlement on the northwest coast of the island of Lismore in Loch Linnhe, Port Ramsay developed in association with its natural deep harbour and local limeworks.

Port Seton *East Lothian* A resort town on the south coast of the Firth of Forth, Port Seton is now part of the combined burgh of Cockenzie and Port Seton which lies to the east of Prestonpans.

Port Wemyss *Argyll and Bute* A small village of the island of Islay in the Inner Hebrides, Port Wemyss lies at the southern end of the Rhinns of Islay immediately to the south of Portnahaven and 2 miles (3 km) to the south of the Rubha na Faing headland. Despite its lack of harbour facilities, it developed as a fishing village in the 19th century, occupied by crofters cleared from the land.

Port William *Dumfries and Galloway* A harbour village of the western Machars in Dumfries and Galloway, Port William lies on the Killantrae Burn, which here flows into Luce Bay, 11 miles (18 km) southwest of Wigtown. Largely remodelled as a planned village in the 1770s by Sir William Maxwell of Monreith, after whom it is named, its harbour was originally built for trading ships. Today the harbour is frequented by fishing boats and pleasure craft.

Portachoillan *Argyll and Bute* A village on the west coast of the Kintyre peninsula, Portachoillan lies on the southeast shore of West Loch Tarbert, at its seaward end. The village of Clachan lies a mile (1.5 km) to the south.

Portankill *Dumfries and Galloway* A bay on the southeast coast of the Rhinns of Galloway, Dumfries and Galloway, Portankill lies to the north of the Mull of Galloway.

Portavadie *Argyll and Bute* A settlement on the Cowal peninsula, Portavadie lies on the east shore of Loch Fyne, 4 miles (6.5 km) southwest of Tighnabruaich. During the 1970s, a controversial and short-lived oil rig platform yard was constructed here, taking advantage of the site's deep water offshore. A ferry across the loch links the village with Tarbert on the Kintyre peninsula.

Portencalzie *Dumfries and Galloway* A locality in Dumfries and Galloway, Portencalzie lies close to the northern tip of the Rhinns of Galloway, 9 miles (14 km) north of Stranraer.

Portencross *North Ayrshire* A locality in the Cunninghame district of Ayrshire, Portencross lies on the Firth of Clyde 5 miles (8 km) northwest of Ardrossan. The ruined 14th-century Portencross Castle was a stronghold of the Rosses and then the Boyds. It comprises an oblong structure of three storeys, built in red sandstone, with an attached four-storey wing to the east. It was used in the 18th century to house French prisoners of war, but lost its roof in a storm in 1739. Although now uninhabited and ruined, it still stands to its full height. The castle was featured in the BBC television series *Restoration* (2004).

Porterstown *Dumfries and Galloway* A locality in Nithsdale, Dumfries and Galloway, Porterstown lies to the west of the River Nith and at the foot of the Keir Hills, just over a mile (1.5 km) southeast of Keir Mill.

Portessie *Moray* Situated on the Moray Firth coast, Portessie is one of a number of old fishing villages that lie on a 3-mile (5-km) stretch of shoreline to the east of Buckie. Originally known as Rottinslough, it was established as a fishing station in 1727. Most of its cottages date from the 19th century.

Portgordon *Moray* A fishing village in Moray, Portgordon lies on the Moray Firth coast, 2 miles (3 km) southwest of Buckie and 12 miles (19 km) east of Elgin. It was founded in 1797 by the 4th Duke of Gordon and in its heyday maintained over 80 fishing boats employing over 250 men and boys. Its harbour was rebuilt in the 1870s.

Portgower *Highland* A former fishing village with an inn on the east coast of Sutherland, Portgower lies 2 miles (3 km) southwest of Helmsdale. Its old schoolhouse dates from 1892.

Portincaple *Argyll and Bute* A settlement on the eastern shore of Loch Long, Portincaple lies at the head of the Gare Loch, a mile (1.5 km) to the north of Garelochhead.

Portinnisherrich *Argyll and Bute* A scattered village on the eastern shore of Loch Awe, Portinnisherrich lies 8 miles (13 km) southwest of Portsonachan directly opposite Dalavich.

Portknockie *Moray* A fishing village in the Moray parish of Rathven, Portknockie is situated on a cliff top at the western end of Cullen Bay on the Moray Firth coast between Buckie and Cullen. It dates from 1677 when its natural harbour attracted fishermen from Cullen. There is an 18-hole golf course.

Portlethen *Aberdeenshire* A small town in eastern Aberdeenshire, Portlethen is located between the A90 trunk road and the mainline railway 6 miles (10 km) south of Aberdeen. The town developed quickly in the 1970s in conjunction with the oil industry and as a commuter settlement. Its industries include a large abattoir and oilfield services, and the town also benefits from a station (which re-opened in 1985, having previously closed in 1963), primary and secondary schools (Portlethen Academy has a roll of 850 pupils), a golf club and swimming pool. The original cliff-top fishing community, now known as Portlethen Village, lies separately a half-mile (1 km) to the east.

Portling Bay *Dumfries and Galloway* A small bay on the Solway Firth coast of Dumfries and Galloway, Portling Bay lies to the south of the Dalbeattie Forest, 2 miles (3 km) east of Rockcliffe.

Portmahomack *Highland* A village on the Tarbat peninsula in Easter Ross, Portmahomack is situated on the south shore of the Dornoch Firth, 2 miles (3 km) southwest of Tarbat Ness. In the 10th century a chapel was built here by St Colmac, who gave his name to the settlement. The village developed in association with fishing, and a pier was erected in 1810. A nine-hole golf course was laid out in 1908 and the village has a visitor centre, hotels and a caravan site.

Portmoak *Perth and Kinross* A parish in southeast Perth and Kinross, Portmoak lies to the east and south of Loch Leven. The former farm of Portmoak near the southeast corner of the loch was purchased by the Scottish Gliding Union in 1967 for the purpose of developing an airfield. Situated in the parish of Portmoak, the farmstead stands next to the site of an ancient churchyard, at the centre of which stood a chapel dedicated to St Moak. A thousand-year-old Celtic cross-slab (the Portmoak Stone) found here in 1976 is now located within the modern parish church of Portmoak which stands on higher ground between the villages of Scotlandwell and Kinnesswood. This church, rebuilt in 1832, replaced the earlier chapel in 1661, and in its kirkyard is a monument to the 'Gentle Poet of Lochleven', Michael Bruce (1746–67).

Portmore Loch *Scottish Borders* A small loch in Scottish Borders, Portmore Loch is situated on the western edge of the Moorfoot Hills, 2 miles (3 km) northeast of Eddleston.

Portnacroish *Argyll and Bute* Located on Loch Laich, an inlet on the shore of Loch Linnhe, the Appin village of Portnacroish lies 2 miles (3 km) northeast of Port Appin. Opposite the village is Castle Stalker, which stands on a small island.

Portnaguran *Western Isles* A village on the east coast of the Isle of Lewis in the Western Isles, Portnaguran lies at the northern end of the Eye peninsula, a mile (1.5 km) southwest of Tiumpan Head.

Portnahaven *Argyll and Bute* A small village on the island of Islay in the Inner Hebrides, Portnahaven lies at the southern end of the Rhinns of Islay peninsula, immediately to the north of Port Wemyss and a mile (1.5 km) to the south of the Rubha na Faing headland. It developed as a fishing village in the early 19th century, absorbing crofters cleared from the land. It is now a resort village with a school, pier and wave- and wind-powered generators.

Portnalong *Highland* A small settlement on the west coast of the isle of Skye in the Inner Hebrides, Portnalong lies 2 miles (3 km) northwest of Carbost, between Loch Harport and Fiskavaig Bay.

Portobello *City of Edinburgh* A settlement on the Firth of Forth, Portobello lies 3 miles (5 km) east of Edinburgh city centre. It is said to have developed from a single thatched cottage in the mid-18th century held by a veteran of the 1739 campaign at Puerto Bello in Panama. By the end of the century it had become a fashionable bathing resort for Edinburgh's well-to-do. It also developed in association with industries producing bottles, bricks, glass, lead, paper, pottery, soap and mustard. The town was designated a burgh in 1833 and was incorporated into Edinburgh in 1896. Notable buildings include the Old Parish Church (1809), the multi-spired St John's Church (1909) and the early 19th-century villas along Regent Street. Noted residents of the town have included geologist Hugh Miller (1802–56), who shot himself at his home in the High Street, physicist Sir David Brewster (1781–1868), music-hall artist Sir Harry Lauder who was born here in 1870, and the polar explorer Dr William Speirs Bruce (1867–1921).

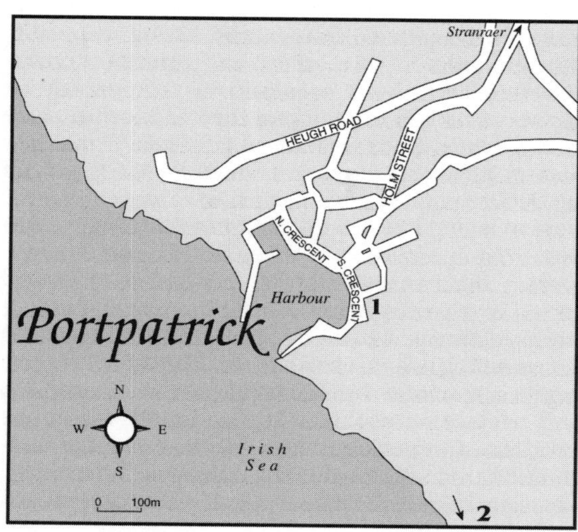

1 *Southern Upland Way* 2 *Dunskey Castle*

Portpatrick *Dumfries and Galloway* Overlooking the Irish Sea on the west side of the Rhinns of Galloway, the small holiday resort of Portpatrick lies 8 miles (13 km) southwest of Stranraer. From 1661 to 1849 it was the main harbour for the crossing to Northern Ireland but was superseded by steamships using Stranraer. Nearby stand the ruins of 15th-century Dunskey Castle.

Portree *Highland* The chief settlement on the isle of Skye in the Inner Hebrides, Portree is situated on Loch Portree, a sheltered natural harbour opening out into the Sound of Raasay. It lies 34 miles (55 km) northwest of Kyle of Lochalsh and was called Kiltragleann prior to it being renamed Port an Righ after the visit of James V during his 1540 tour of the Highlands. An important fishing port in the 19th century, Portree still has a small lobster and crab fleet in addition to knitwear, tourism and local agriculture and forestry industries. The Isle of Skye Highland Games are held at the beginning of August. In June 1746, Prince Charles Edward Stewart (Bonnie Prince Charlie), disguised as 'Betty Burke', arrived at Portree with Flora Macdonald while on the run after the Battle of Culloden. A room in the Royal Hotel was the scene of their parting as he fled to Raasay.

Portskerra *Highland* A small settlement on the north coast of Caithness, Portskerra overlooks Melvich Bay, a mile (1.5 km) northeast of Melvich.

Portslogan *Dumfries and Galloway* A locality in Dumfries and Galloway, Portslogan lies in the Rhinns of Galloway, 5 miles (8 km) west of Stranraer.

Portsoy *Aberdeenshire* A coastal resort town in the northern Aberdeenshire parish of Fordyce, Portsoy is situated on the A98 between Banff and Cullen. Created a burgh of barony in 1550, it looks out onto Links Bay, an inlet of the Moray Firth into which flows the Burn of Durn. Its old harbour was built by Patrick Ogilvie of Boyne in order to ship out local 'Portsoy marble', a beautiful variety of serpentine that is greenish or reddish in hue. In the 18th century much of this stone was exported to France where Louis XIV used it in the making of two chimneypieces at the Palace of Versailles. A new harbour was built in 1825–8 by the Earl of Seafield to enhance the town's commercial trade and fishing industry. Destroyed by a storm in January 1839, the harbour was reconstructed in 1884 to accommodate an expanding herring fleet of 56 boats. After the arrival of the railway in 1859, the burgh developed as a resort. Today it has a sailing club and craft industries. To the east, beyond the wooded ravine of the Burn of Boyne, stand the ruins of Boyne Castle, a former stronghold of the Ogilvy family.

Portuairk *Highland* A settlement at the western end of the Ardnamurchan peninsula, Portuairk lies 2 miles (3 km) east of the Point of Ardnamurchan and overlooks Sanna Bay.

Portvoller *Western Isles* One of several contiguous settlements located at the eastern end of the Eye peninsula on the east coast of the Isle of Lewis in the Outer Hebrides, Portvoller (Gael: *Port Mholair*) lies to the south of Cnoc Amhlaigh, a half-mile (1 km) east of Broker and a mile (1.5 km) southwest of Tiumpan Head. The bay, Bagh Phort Bholair, lies to the south.

Portyerrock *Dumfries and Galloway* A hamlet in the Machars of Dumfries and Galloway, Portyerrock lies 2 miles (3 km) southeast of Whithorn on a bay of the same name, an inlet on the western shore of Wigtown Bay.

Possilpark *Glasgow City* A northern district of Glasgow, Possilpark lies to the north of the River Clyde and to the east of Maryhill. It was laid out by Walter MacFarlane and Company of the Saracen Foundry in Anderston, which acquired the Possil Estate in 1867, and developed in association with coal mining, ironworks, railway engineering and pottery works. At the time it was regarded as one of the best laid-out and planned areas within the city. In the 1950s and 1960s the area was blighted by industrial decline, and today very few of its industries have survived. Civic improvements have been generated since the mid-1980s by a local housing cooperative. The former Possil Loch is now a nature reserve.

Post Rocks *Argyll and Bute* A small cluster of outlying rocks off the north coast of Islay in the Inner Hebrides, the Post Rocks lie a mile (1.5 km) offshore and 2 miles (3 km) west of Rubh' a' Mhail.

Potarch *Aberdeenshire* A locality in Aberdeenshire, Potarch lies on the south side of the River Dee, 2 miles (3 km) south of Kincardine O'Neil. The three-arched Bridge of Potarch, which crosses the Dee here, was built in 1812.

Potrail Water *South Lanarkshire* Potrail Water rises close to the border between South Lanarkshire and Dunfries and Galloway on Ballencleuch Law in the Lowther Hills. It flows north and east to join the Daer Water, 2 miles (3 km) south of Elvanfoot.

Pots of Gartness *Stirling* A series of rocky pools on the Endrick Water, the Pots of Gartness lie to the west of Killearn.

Potterton *Aberdeenshire* A village of Aberdeenshire, Potterton lies 2 miles (3 km) southwest of Balmedie and 6 miles (10 km) north of Aberdeen city centre. To the southwest is Corby Loch.

Pouton *Dumfries and Galloway* A locality in the south Machars of Dumfries and Galloway, Pouton lies just west of Galloway House Park near Garlieston.

Pow Burn *Stirling/Falkirk* A stream that forms part of the border between Stirling and Falkirk council areas, the Pow Burn rises to the west of the M9 and flows northeast to empty into the Firth of Forth a half-mile (1 km) northwest of the Kincardine Bridge.

Powderhall *City of Edinburgh* A small residential district on the north side of the city of Edinburgh, Powderhall is the site of a former athletic stadium and dog-racing track. The Powderhall Waste Transfer Station, modernised in 1970, was originally built by the city engineer in 1893 as an incinerator. The plant compacts refuse into containers that are then conveyed by rail to a landfill site located in disused limestone workings at East Barns near Dunbar. The original stable block and offices (1893) now house a visitor centre, which was opened in 1999.

Powfoot *Dumfries and Galloway* A village in Dumfries and Galloway, Powfoot lies on the Solway Firth at the mouth of the Pow Water, just southeast of Cummertrees and 12 miles (19 km) southeast of Dumfries. During World War II an explosives factory was built to the east.

Powmill *Perth and Kinross* A settlement in southern Perth and Kinross, Powmill lies on the Pow Burn and straddles the A977 from Kinross to the Kincardine Bridge

Praytis Country Park *Fife* A country park with recreational facilities, Praytis lies on the A916 between Kennoway and Cupar in eastern Fife.

Press Castle *Scottish Borders* A 17th-century mansion house in the Berwickshire district of Scottish Borders, Press Castle stands on the Ale Water, 2 miles (3 km) west of Coldingham.

Pressendye *Aberdeenshire* A hill in Aberdeenshire, Pressendye rises to 619 m (2030 ft) 3 miles (5 km) north of Tarland.

Pressmennan Loch *East Lothian* A narrow man-made loch of East Lothian, Pressmennan (also Pressman) Loch (or Pressmennan Lake) lies in a steep ravine at the eastern end of the Lammermuir Hills, a mile (1.5 km) southeast of Stenton. Created in 1819, the reservoir is 1.25 miles (2 km) in length and surrounded by mixed woodland, part of which is said to represent one of the last traces of Scotland's ancient native woodland.

Preston *East Lothian* A hamlet of East Lothian, Preston is situated immediately to the northeast of East Linton. The 18th-century Preston Mill, a National Trust property, is located here, with the Phantassie dovecote a short walk over the River Tyne.

Preston *Scottish Borders* A small village in Scottish Borders, Preston lies 2 miles (3 km) north of Duns, on the northern banks of the Whiteadder Water.

Preston Hall *Midlothian* Preston Hall is a fine late-18th-century mansion that lies 0.75 mile (1.5 km) north of Pathhead in Midlothian. Located in scenic parkland bordering the Tyne Water, the current structure is the second on this site. The first Preston Hall was built c.1700 and extended in 1738 by William Adam for the dowager Duchess of Gordon. It was later home to her son General Lord Adam Gordon (c.1726–1801). The present house was begun shortly after Alexander Callander bought the estate in 1789, having returned to Scotland with a fortune made in India. The architect was Robert Mitchell, whose seven-bay structure presents fine elevations both to the entrance front and garden at the rear. Mitchell appears to have retained Adam's pavilions and modified these to fit his design for the new main block. The rebuilding was completed c.1794.

Preston Island *Fife* A small island in Torry Bay, western Fife, Preston Island lies to the south of Low Valleyfield. During the 17th century the Prestons of Valleyfield mined coal here to fire saltpans which were said to have operated throughout the night, acting as a beacon to homecoming sailors. The ruins of saltpans and the mine complex developed by Sir Robert Preston around 1800 still exist. After the 1823 repeal of salt duties, the saltworks declined and were abandoned by the mid-1850s. The old saltpans are being filled by ash slurry from Longannet Power Station as part of a land-reclamation project.

Preston Mill *East Lothian* One of the oldest

mechanically intact water-driven meal mills in Scotland, Preston Mill lies on the River Tyne a half-mile (1 km) northeast of East Linton. The mill was acquired by the National Trust for Scotland in 1950. With its rustic conical-roofed kiln and millpond, Preston Mill forms an idyllic composition for artists and photographers.

Prestonfield *City of Edinburgh* A residential district on the south side of Edinburgh, Prestonfield lies between Duddingston and Newington, 2 miles (3 km) southeast of the city centre. Prestonfield House was built in 1687 by Sir William Bruce for Sir James Dick, Lord Provost of the city, to replace a previous house burned down by demonstrators during the No Popery Riot of 1681. The house was visited by Dr Samuel Johnson in 1773. Since 1958 it has been a hotel and a part of its grounds are occupied by Prestonfield golf course.

Prestongrange *East Lothian* A locality in East Lothian associated with coal mining since the 12th century, Prestongrange is situated at Morison's Haven, 1.5 miles (2.5 km) west-southwest of Prestonpans. The Prestongrange Industrial Heritage Museum occupies the former Prestongrange Colliery, which closed in 1952, and has a restored beam engine built in 1874 to pump water from the mine.

Prestonmill *Dumfries and Galloway* A locality in Dumfries and Galloway, Prestonmill lies on the Prestonmill Burn which rises on Craigtappock, a summit of the Criffell massif. The village of Kirkbean is nearly 2 miles (3 km) to the northeast.

Prestonpans *East Lothian* A settlement on the south coast of the Firth of Forth, Prestonpans lies to the east of Edinburgh between Musselburgh and Cockenzie. Founded as a 'Priest-Town' by monks in the 12th century, it was designated a burgh in 1552 and a harbour was built four years later. Incorporating the villages of Aldhamer, Preston and Cuthill, it developed in association with coal mining, fishing, saltworks, pottery works and brickworks. The Guild of Chapmen (pedlars) met annually here until the late 19th century to elect their 'King'. The early post-Reformation parish church (1596, enlarged 1774) has an 18th-century painting of a fishing scene. Other sights include the mercat cross, the ruined 15th-century Preston Tower (a former stronghold of the Hamiltons), the war memorial (1921), two large dovecotes, 17th-century Hamilton House and 17th-century Northfield House. Nearby is the site of the Battle of Prestonpans, where the Jacobites defeated Hanoverian troops in 1745. Local festivals include the annual Fisherman's Walk to celebrate the return of the boats, and the Miners' Gala. There is an 18-hole golf course at Preston Grange House.

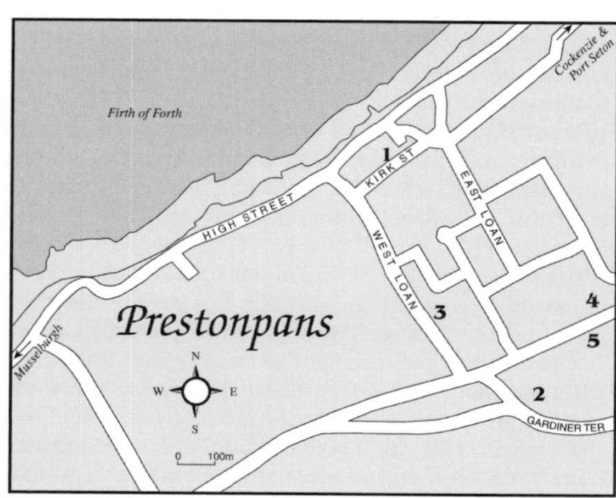

1 *Parish Church*
2 *Mercat Cross*
3 *Preston Tower*
4 *Hamilton House*
5 *Northfield House*

Prestrie *Dumfries and Galloway* A locality in the Machars of Dumfries and Galloway, Prestrie lies on the pilgrimage route between Whithorn and Isle of Whithorn.

Prestwick *South Ayrshire* A burgh town on the Ayrshire coast, Prestwick is situated at the north end of Ayr Bay, 2 miles (3 km) north of Ayr. Designated in 1170 as one of Scotland's first burghs of barony, it had a leprosy hospital said to have been visited by Robert the Bruce. A golf course laid out in 1851 was the scene of the first Open Championship in 1860. The town subsequently developed as a resort and, because it is fog-free, an international airport was sited here in 1946.

Priest Island *Highland* An outlying island, one of the Summer Isles, Priest Island (Gael: *Eilean a' Chleirich*) lies off the coast of Coigach in Wester Ross. Covering an area of 122 ha (301 acres), it is owned by the Royal Society for the Protection of Birds (RSPB). In addition to wild bird colonies, there are populations of grey seals, pygmy shrews and otters. The island, which was an early Christian retreat, also has a number of prehistoric stone circles.

Priesthill Height *South Lanarkshire/East Ayrshire* Located on the border between South Lanarkshire and East Ayrshire, Priesthill Height rises to 492 m (1614 ft) 4 miles (6.5 km) northeast of Muirkirk. The Greenock Water rises on the hill.

Priestland *East Ayrshire* One of the valley settlements of Ayrshire, Priestland is situated a mile (1.5 km) east of Darvel.

Priestside *Dumfries and Galloway* A locality on the Solway coast of Dumfries and Galloway, Priestside lies a mile (1.5 km) to the south of Ruthwell. To the east is the peatland of the Priestside Flow and to the south the coastal sands of the Priestside Bank stretching out to the Rough Scar rocks that mark the meeting of the Lochar Water and River Eden channels.

Princes Street *City of Edinburgh* Edinburgh's principal shopping street. It was originally to be called after St Giles. However, following an objection from George III, who knew St Giles only as a slum area in London, it was named in honour of the three royal princes born by the time of James Craig's plan for the New Town (1766), of which it forms the southern boundary. It was planned to have no building on its southern side, so the residents could enjoy the view to the castle and Old Town. However, over the years this proved difficult to enforce, with Acts of Parliament required to maintain the integrity of Princes Street Gardens. Among a tedious string of chain stores and melange of architectural styles, only a few of the original frontages survive at street level. The street has undergone almost continuous redevelopment from Victorian times to the present day. Jenners department store, which was rebuilt in grand style following a devastating fire in 1892, and the Waverley Market are the only more interesting retailing experiences. The Waverley Market was originally a vegetable market, built 1874–6, and demolished in 1974 to be replaced by a prize-winning shopping centre in 1984. Triangular granite prisms rise above street level, while floors of small shops around a large atrium descend below. Alongside is the Balmoral Hotel, once the railway hotel for the adjoining Waverley Station. Also on the south side of Princes Street are the Royal Scottish Academy and, behind, the National Gallery of Scotland, at the bottom of The Mound. At the west end are St John's and St Cuthbert's Churches. The other notable feature of the south side of Princes Street are its monuments and statues, all actually located in Princes Street Gardens. Most obvious among them is the Scott Monument.

Princes Street Gardens *City of Edinburgh* Princes Street in Edinburgh was planned to have no building on its southern side, so the residents could enjoy the view to the castle and Old Town. Thus Princes Street Gardens were developed initially as private gardens for the residents, but from 1876 as a public park. Located on the site of the old Nor' Loch, a significant health hazard as it took the sewage from the Old Town, the gardens are divided by The Mound. East Princes Street Gardens cover 3.5 ha (8.5 acres) to Waverley Bridge and West Princes Street Gardens extend 12 ha (29 acres) to St John's and St Cuthbert's churches in the west. Over the years preventing development proved difficult, with Acts of Parliament required to maintain the integrity of the gardens. Controversy came when the railway was extended through the gardens in 1846, the eventual compromise requiring it to be hidden at the back of the gardens, with W. H. Playfair (1789–1857) undertaking the design of the stone-walled cutting. Within the gardens, along the south side of Princes Street are statues and monuments. Most obvious is the enormous Scott Monument (built 1846) in the East Gardens, along with statues of explorer David Livingstone (1813–73), publisher Adam Black (1784–1874) and essayist Professor John Wilson (1785–1854). In the West Gardens are statues of poet Allan Ramsay (1681–1758), reformer Thomas Guthrie (1803–73) and obstetric pioneer James Young Simpson (1811–70), together with monuments to the Royal Scots Greys, the Royal Scots and Dean Edward Ramsay (1793–1872), plus the Scottish American War Memorial and the exhuberant Ross Fountain. Also here is the famous Floral Clock, and the Ross Bandstand which hosts summer concerts.

Prior Muir *Fife* A hamlet in eastern Fife, Prior Muir lies 3 miles (5 km) southeast of St Andrews straddling the B9131.

Priorwood Garden *Scottish Borders* A garden in Melrose, Priorwood is a specialist centre for the craft of dried-flower arranging. Once the property of the Curle family, owners of Priorwood House (now Melrose Youth Hostel), Priorwood Garden was purchased by the National Trust for Scotland in 1974.

Prosen, Glen *Angus* A glen in the southern Grampians, Glen Prosen occupies the valley of the Prosen Water in the Braes of Angus. There is a memorial cairn at the foot of the glen dedicated to the memory of the Antarctic explorers Captain Robert Falcon Scott (1868–1912) and Dr Edward Wilson (1872–1912) who used to visit this locality. The cairn was erected in 1981 on the site of a memorial fountain put there in 1919 and accidentally destroyed in 1979. Glenprosen village sits on the slopes of the Hill of Spott. Overlooking the Prosen Water on Tulloch Hill is the Airlie Monument, a copy of one of the towers of Airlie Castle, erected to the memory of David Ogilvy, 9th Earl of Airlie, who was killed in the Boer War.

Prosen Water *Angus* A river in the southern Grampians, the Prosen Water rises in the Braes of Angus between Glen Isla and Glen Clova. It flows 18 miles (29 km) southeastwards before joining the River South Esk on the northern edge of the valley of Strathmore, 3 miles (5 km) northeast of Kirriemuir.

Protstonhill *Aberdeenshire* A roadside hamlet in the Aberdeenshire parish of Gamrie, Protstonhill lies on the B9031 between Gardenstown and Pennan.

Provand's Lordship *Glasgow City* Located at the top of Castle Street and opposite the Cathedral and Royal Infirmary in Glasgow, Provand's Lordship is regarded as Glasgow's oldest house and is believed to date from 1471. It was built as the manse for the Cathedral's clergy and was one of the more prominent buildings of the city, located at the junction of the old town's principal streets, High Street and Rottenrow.

Provost Ross's House *Aberdeen City* Situated on Shiprow between Union Street and the Harbour, Provost Ross's House was built in 1593. It is the second-oldest dwelling house in the City of Aberdeen.

Provost Skene's House *Aberdeen City* Situated in Guestrow off Broad Street in the centre of Aberdeen, Provost Skene's House is the oldest surviving town house in the city. The house is named after its most notable owner, Sir George Skene, who was a rich merchant engaged in trade with the Baltic and was Provost of Aberdeen from 1676 to 1685. Built in the early 16th century, the house was occupied by the Duke of Cumberland in 1746. Much later it became a hostel for the homeless. Provost Skene's House was threatened with demolition in 1940, but a long-running campaign saved it. Restoration began in 1951 and it was opened as a museum in 1953. Today, it is a museum illustrating wealthy merchant city life from Jacobean to Victorian times. Of interest to visitors are the painted ceilings, furnished period rooms and local history displays.

Pulcree *Dumfries and Galloway* A locality in the valley of the Water of Fleet, Dumfries and Galloway, Pulcree lies on the Pulcree Burn, 2 miles (3 km) northwest of Gatehouse of Fleet.

Pullaugh Burn *Dumfries and Galloway* A stream in Dumfries and Galloway, the Pullaugh Burn rises in Loch Grannoch. It flows north for nearly 2 miles (3 km) to meet the River Dee on the edge of the Cairn Edward Forest.

Pulrossie *Highland* A small village of Easter Ross, Highland Council area, Pulrossie lies on the northern shore of the Dornoch Firth 5 miles (8 km) east of Dornoch and across a small bay from Skibo Castle.

Pulteneytown *Highland* A planned village to the south of Wick in Caithness, Pulteneytown (or Old Wick) was laid out in 1786 by Thomas Telford for the British Fisheries Society on 390 acres of land obtained from Sir Benjamin Dunbar of Hempriggs. The town was named after Telford's patron Sir William Pulteney, a former governor of the British Fisheries Society.

Pulwhirrin Burn *Dumfries and Galloway* A stream in

Dumfries and Galloway, the Pulwhirrin Burn rises to the west of Kirkcudbright and flows southwest into Kirkandrews Bay on the coast of Wigtown Bay.

Pumpherston *West Lothian* A village of West Lothian, Pumpherston lies to the south of Uphall and adjoins the New Town of Livingston on its northeast boundary. It developed in association with oil-shale works initiated in 1883.

Putachie The former name for Castle Forbes in Aberdeenshire.

Pyke *Moray* A small settlement in southeast Moray, Pyke lies in the valley of the River Deveron between Inverharroch and Tomnaven.

Pykestone Hill *Scottish Borders* A mountain in Scottish Borders, Pykestone Hill rises to a height of 737 m (2417 ft) in Tweeddale, 3 miles (5 km) southeast of Drumelzier.

Quaich, River *Perth and Kinross* Rising in the eastern hills of Breadalbane, the River Quaich flows east and then south through Glen Quaich to enter Loch Freuchie. It continues east to the village of Amulree before joining with the Cochill Burn to form the River Braan.

Quair Water *Scottish Borders* The Quair Water rises between Dun Rig and Deuchar Law in the Ettrick district of Scottish Borders. It flows north and east past Traquair to join the River Tweed a mile (1.5 km) south of Innerleithen.

Quanter Ness *Orkney* A headland on Mainland Orkney, Quanter Ness extends into the Wide Firth 3 miles (5 km) northwest of Kirkwall. The Quanterness Skerry, a rocky outlier in the firth, lies a half-mile (1 km) from the headland.

Quarrier's Village *Inverclyde* A settlement in eastern Inverclyde, Quarrier's Village lies 2 miles (3 km) south of Kilmacolm and 2 miles (3 km) northwest of Bridge of Weir. Also known as Quarrier's Homes, it was built in the late 19th century by the philanthropist William Quarrier who aimed to care for 'destitute children', mainly from Glasgow. It also became a care centre for people with epilepsy. Today, about 200 people are cared for by the Quarrier's Homes. There is a craft centre, coffee house, museum and heritage trail for visitors.

Quarry Head *Aberdeenshire* Located on the northern coastline of Aberdeenshire, the headland of Quarry Head is located 2 miles (3 km) southwest of Rosehearty and 6 miles (10 km) west of Fraserburgh. To the west of the headland lies Aberdour Bay.

Quarry Hill *Aberdeenshire* Quarry Hill in western Aberdeenshire rises to a height of 440 m (1443 ft) close to the boundary with Highland Council area, 4 miles (6.5 km) west of the settlement of Gartly and 7 miles (11 km) southwest of Huntly.

Quarter *North Ayrshire* A small linear settlement on the North Ayrshire coast, Quarter overlooks the Firth of Clyde 2 miles (3 km) north of Largs.

Quarter *South Lanarkshire* A small settlement in South Lanarkshire, Quarter lies southwest of Chatelherault Country Park, 3 miles (5 km) east of Larkhall and 3 miles (5 km) south of Hamilton.

Queen Elizabeth Forest Park *Stirling* Extending westwards to Loch Lomond from Loch Venachar in the Trossachs district of Stirling Council area, the Queen Elizabeth Forest Park comprises 16,780 ha (41,454 acres) of moorland and plantations. It was purchased by the State in 1928 and designated a National Forest Park in 1953, the year of Elizabeth II's coronation. The park includes Loch Ard Forest, Ben Lomond and the headwaters of the River Forth, all lying within the Loch Lomond and the Trossachs National Park.

Queen Street *City of Edinburgh* A street in the centre of Edinburgh with Georgian tenements to the south and gardens to the north, Queen Street formed the northern edge of James Craig's mid-18th-century plan for Edinburgh's first New Town. Mirroring Princes Street to the south and named after Queen Charlotte, wife of George III, it has fine views north over the Firth of Forth and is noted as the longest parade of 18th-century architecture in Edinburgh. Queen Street was originally laid out in blocks between 1768 and 1792, the first house (No. 8) being designed by the noted architect Robert Adam. This house is now occupied by the General Medical Council in Scotland. Other notable buildings include the Royal College of Physicians, designed by Thomas Hamilton in 1833; No. 19, the home of Sydney Smith (1771–1845), co-founder of the *Edinburgh Review*; Simpson House (No. 52), the home of obstetrician James Young Simpson (1811–70); No. 62, home of the noted judge Lord Jeffrey (1773–1850); and No. 66, built for General Sir Ralph Abercromby (1734–1801). At the eastern end is York Place, on the south side of which is the Venetian-Gothic-style Scottish National Portrait Gallery.

Queen Street Station *Glasgow City* Originally named Dundas Street Station, Queen Street Station is the oldest railway station in Glasgow. It was built in 1842 as the western terminus of the Edinburgh and Glasgow Railway. The station was unique in that it was approached from the north via the Cowlairs Incline, a steep incline of 1.5 miles (2.5 km) up which trains were hauled from the station by means of a steam-driven winding cable. In 1878, a low-level station was erected and an iron and glass roof added.

Queen's Drive *City of Edinburgh* A road that largely encircles the hills within Edinburgh's Holyrood Park, the Queen's Drive rises sharply from its lowest point to the east of the Palace of Holyroodhouse onto the southern and eastern flanks of Arthur's Seat. The road provides spectacular views over the city.

Queen's Gallery, the *City of Edinburgh* Located next to the Palace of Holyroodhouse at the eastern end of the Royal Mile in Edinburgh's Canongate is the Queen's Gallery. Opened by Elizabeth II in November 2002 as part of her Golden Jubilee celebrations, the gallery represents the first permanent exhibition space in Scotland for the Royal Collection. This collection includes artworks, jewellery and furniture of international importance. The gallery was built by architect Benjamin Tindall in the shell of the former Holyrood Free Church and Duchess of Gordon's School, and its construction was funded entirely by the Royal Collections Trust. The Duchess of Gordon's School was built in Scots Renaissance style by architect Archibald Simpson in 1846. The Holyrood Free Church was also endowed by Elizabeth, Duchess of Gordon, and built on an adjacent site in 1850 by local church architect John Henderson (1804–62).

Queen's Hall, the *City of Edinburgh* Located on the west side of Clerk Street, in the Newington district of Edinburgh, the Queen's Hall is the principal venue on the south side of the city for concerts. Built in 1823 as the Hope Park Chapel of Ease, the building has a two-storey villa frontage, with a tall and slender neoclassical steeple. Converted into a concert hall in 1979 and opened by Elizabeth II, the 850-seat auditorium still strongly reflects its ecclesiastical origins, although the pulpit has been replaced by an early 19th-century chamber organ. Painted 18th-century panels displaying the Commandments and the Lord's Prayer, which were brought from the former Buccleuch Parish Church in 1950, can be seen on the stairs.

Queen's View *Perth and Kinross* From the high vantage point of the Queen's View in the heart of the Tay Forest Park there is a spectacular view westwards to the conical summit of Schiehallion along the full length of Loch Tummel. Situated 4 miles (6.5 km) west of Pitlochry, the Queen's View has, in addition to the viewpoint, tourist facilities including an exhibition on Scottish forestry. Although the site was visited by Queen Victoria in 1866, the name is much older.

Queen's View *Stirling* A viewpoint on the north-facing scarp slope of the Kilpatrick Hills in Stirling Council area, the Queen's View can be approached from a car park on the A809 west of Strathblane. Auchineden Hill rises to 357 m (1171 ft) to the southwest, and to the west is the rocky landslip feature known as The Whangie.

Queen's Way, the *Dumfries and Galloway* The Queen's Way is the name given to the route of the A712 between New Galloway and Newton Stewart in Dumfries and Galloway. It passes Clatteringshaws Loch, Bruce's Stone, Goat Park and a hilltop monument to oriental linguist Alexander Murray.

Queen's Well *Angus* Located at the head of Glen Esk, where it joins Glen Mark, and just east of Loch Lee, is the Queen's Well. The unusual crown-shaped monument was built over a natural spring in 1861 in honour of Queen Victoria. After staying at the nearby Invermark Lodge, Victoria and Prince Albert are said to have stopped here to drink before travelling on to Balmoral.

Queens Park *Glasgow City* Extending over an area of 60 ha (146 acres) on the south side of Glasgow, Queens Park is one of the oldest parklands within the city. Dating from 1857, it was named after Mary, Queen of Scots, whose forces were defeated by those of Regent Moray at the Battle of Langside in 1568 on a site believed to be within the park. An artificial mound was built at the highest point, offering magnificent views to the north. Langside Hall, formerly a bank situated in Queen Street in the city centre, was re-erected in the park in the early 20th century.

Queensberry *Dumfries and Galloway* A hill in Dumfries and Galloway, Queensberry rises to a height of 697 m (2285 ft) at the southern end of the Lowther Hills, 5 miles (8 km) southwest of Moffat.

Queensberry House *City of Edinburgh* Located on Edinburgh's Royal Mile in the burgh of Canongate, Queensberry House was built in 1681. Purchased five years later by the 1st Duke of Queensberry, it is best remembered in association with an incident involving James Douglas, the deranged Earl of Drumlanrig (1697–1715) who escaped confinement to roast and devour a kitchen-boy in 1707. The house was extended in the 18th century and was sold to the government by the Queensberry family in 1801. In 1808, the building was converted to a barracks and the gardens were turned into a parade ground. More recently, Queensberry House was used as a geriatric hospital, which closed in 1995. It was then restored and has been incoporated into the new Scottish Parliament complex.

Queensferry An alternative name for South Queensferry in the City of Edinburgh.

Queenside Hill *Renfrewshire* Rising to a height of 424 m (1391 ft) to the south of Queenside Loch in the Queenside Muir, Queenside Hill lies at the heart of the Clyde Muirshiel Regional Park in the northwest corner of Renfrewshire.

Queenslie *Glasgow City* A suburb of Glasgow to the east of the city centre near Easterhouse, Queenslie was originally developed as an industrial estate in the post-war years.

Queenzieburn *North Lanarkshire* A village in North Lanarkshire, Queenzieburn lies 2 miles (3 km) west of Kilsyth and 3 miles (5 km) northeast of Kirkintilloch. The Roman Antonine Wall and the River Kelvin pass to the south of the village. To the southwest is a small nature reserve.

Quendale *Shetland* A settlement in the Dunrossness district at the south of the Mainland of Shetland, Quendale lies on the Bay of Quendale, a half-mile (1 km) south of Hillwell and 2 miles (3 km) northwest of Sumburgh Airport.

Quendale, Bay of *Shetland* A wide sandy inlet at the southern end of the Shetland Mainland, the Bay of Quendale lies to the east of Garths Ness. The settlements of Hestingott and Toab lie to the southeast.

Quey Firth *Shetland* An inlet of Yell Sound on the northeast coast of the Shetland Mainland, the Quey Firth lies to the south of the Colla Firth from which it is separated by the Ness of Queyfirth.

Queyon, Ness of *Shetland* A headland on the east coast of the island of Yell in the Shetland Islands, the Ness of Queyon extends into the Colgrave Sound to the north of Otters Wick.

Quharity Burn *Angus* A stream in the southern Grampians, the Quharity Burn rises on the eastern slopes of Milldewan Hill between Glen Prosen and Glen Isla. It flows southwards to join the Melgam Water at the Loch of Lintrathen.

Quharity Burn *Angus* A stream rising in the Braes of Angus in the southern Grampians, the Quharity (or *Carity*) Burn flows north from the northeast slopes of Strone Hill, a half-mile (1 km) to the northeast of the Loch of Lintrathen. It turns eastwards and flows past Inverquharity and Inverquharity Castle. The Quharity Burn joins the River South Esk just southeast of that river's junction with the Prosen Water, 3 miles (5 km) northeast of Kirriemuir, having completed a course of 8 miles (13 km). Another Quharity Burn passes a half-mile (1 km) to the west, flowing south to enter the Loch of Lintrathen.

Quidan Ness *Shetland* A headland on the northeast coast of Mainland Shetland, Quidan Ness lies on the west coast of the Lunna Ness peninsula.

Quidinish *Western Isles* A small settlement on the southeast coast of South Harris in the Outer Hebrides, Quidinish (Gael: *Cuidhtinis*) is located 1.25 miles (2 km) south of Flodabay and 4 miles (6.5 km) northeast of Rodel.

Quien, Loch *Argyll and Bute* A loch on the island of Bute, Loch Quien lies to the southwest of Loch Fad on the line of the Highland Boundary Fault. It drains southwestwards into Scalpsie Bay, an inlet of the Sound of Bute.

Quinag *Highland* A mountain massif in the Assynt district of western Sutherland, Quinag rises to 808 m (2650 ft) at Sàil Gharbh, 2 miles (3 km) north of Loch Assynt and 4 miles (6.5 km) northwest of the settlement of Inchnadamph. Secondary peaks to the southwest rise to heights of 745 m (2444 ft), 713 m (2339 ft) and 764 m (2507 ft) at Spidean Coinich. To the north another summit, Sàil Gorm, rises to 776 m (2545 ft).

Quinish *Argyll and Bute* An area on the north coast of Mull in the Inner Hebrides, Quinish lies between Mornish to the west and Mishnish to the east, 5 miles (8 km) west of Tobermory. The rocky headland of Quinish Point extends into the Sea of the Hebrides.

Quirang *Highland* A locality on the Trotternish peninsula of northeast Skye in the Inner Hebrides, the Quirang lies 2 miles (3 km) northwest of Staffin Island and 6 miles (10 km) southeast of the headland of Rubha Hunish. A landscape dominated by landslide features created when Jurassic sediments buckled under the weight of a large volume of lava, the Quirang occupies an area of 8.5 sq. km (3.3 sq. miles) and extends 2.2 km (1.4 miles) from the scarp crest to the sea. The Quirang landslide is the largest in Britain.

Quoich, Glen *Aberdeenshire* A valley in the Braemar Forest of Aberdeenshire, Glen Quoich carries the Quoich Water from its source on Beinn a' Bhuird south to join the River Dee 2 miles (3 km) west of Braemar. The river cascades over the Linn of Quoich near Allanaquoich.

Quoich, Loch *Highland* A loch to the east of Knoydart in the Lochaber district of Highland Council area, Loch Quoich lies at the head of Glen Garry. The River Quoich flows southwards into the loch through Glen Quoich, and the Glenquoich Forest lies between the loch and Loch Loyne.

Quoy *Orkney* A locality on the South Walls peninsula of the island of Hoy in the Orkney Islands, Quoy lies a mile (1.5 km) east of the settlement of Longhope.

Quoy Ness *Orkney* A headland located on the east coast of the island of Flotta in the Orkney Islands, Quoy Ness lies at the southern entrance to Pan Hope. The settlement of Bow lies a mile (1.5 km) to the west.

Quoynalonga Ness *Orkney* A headland in the Orkney Islands, Quoynalonga Ness extends into the sea on the west coast of the island of Rousay. A prominent natural arch feature is located at Scarba Head, a half-mile (1 km) to the south.

Quoyness *Orkney* The site of a spectacular prehistoric chambered tomb, Quoyness lies on the Quoy Ness peninsula on the south coast of the Orkney island of Sanday. Excavated in 1867 and again in 1952, the tomb has a main chamber and six smaller cells.

Quoyness *Orkney* A linear settlement on the north coast of the island of Hoy in the Orkney Islands, Quoyness lies to the east of the Bay of Quoys, an inlet opposite the island of Graemsay.

Quoys, Ness of *Highland* A small headland on the northern Caithness coast, the Ness of Quoys extends into the Inner Sound at the eastern end of Gills Bay opposite the Island of Stroma, 2 miles (3 km) northwest of the settlement of Huna.

Raasay *Highland* An island in the Inner Hebrides, Raasay lies to the east of the isle of Skye, from which it is separated by the Sound of Raasay and the Narrows of Raasay. Largely State-owned since 1922, Raasay is occupied by crofters. Its population has fallen from over 900 in the early 1800s to a total of 163 in 1991, the island having the lowest proportion of children of all the Scottish islands. Extending to 6282 ha (15,522 acres), the highest point on the island is Dun Caan, which rises to 443 m (1453 ft) to the east of Loch na Mellich. The main settlement on the island is Inverarish, which is located on the southwest coast, a mile (1.5 km) north of the ferry terminal at Suisnish. Locations of interest include the 15th-century Brochel Castle, Dun Borodale broch, the 7th-century Pictish Ogam stone on Temptation Hill, The Battery, site of an early 19th-century cannon emplacement, and Raasay House, which is built on the site of a Macleod family home and now used as an outdoor centre. Once known for its pipers, Raasay was the birthplace of the poet Sorley MacLean (1911–96).

Rabbit Islands *Highland* A group of three small uninhabited islands located in Tongue Bay, an inlet on the north coast of Sutherland, the Rabbit Islands lie 5 miles (8 km) north of the settlement of Tongue.

Rachan Mill *Scottish Borders* A locality in Tweeddale in Scottish Borders, Rachan Mill lies 5 miles (8 km) southeast of Biggar at the junction of the A701 from Edinburgh to Dumfries and the B712, which runs northeast past Drumelzier alongside the River Tweed. A corn mill once operated where the Holms Water joins the Tweed here. Rachan Hill rises to the southeast. Rachan House, a Georgian mansion, was demolished in 1965. In a garden is the Piper's Stone, a large block of whinstone associated, according to local tradition, with Bertram the Cobbler, who is a said to have been granted land after playing the pipes so well when the king passed by.

Racks *Dumfries and Galloway* A hamlet of Nithsdale in Dumfries and Galloway, Racks lies just east of the Lochar Water, 5 miles (8 km) southeast of Dumfries on the railway from Carlisle to Glasgow.

Rackwick *Orkney* A scattered village on the island of Hoy, the southernmost island of the Orkney Islands, Rackwick lies 3 miles (5 km) from the north end of the island in a bay enclosed by sandstone cliffs. The local school, closed in 1958, is now a museum, and a youth hostel stands on a location once described as 'the most beautiful place in Orkney'. Nearly 2.5 miles (4 km) east is a large stone slab known as the Dwarfie Stane.

Radernie *Fife* A hamlet in Cameron parish, eastern Fife, Radernie lies to the west of the A915, 5 miles (8 km) south of St Andrews. The settlement is all that remains of a former mining village whose mines once provided coal to the royal palace of Falkland. These mines operated until the 1920s and provided employment to the villagers of Radernie, Largoward and Lathones.

Rae Burn *Dumfries and Galloway* A stream in Eskdalemuir, Dumfries and Galloway, the Rae Burn is a tributary of the White Esk.

Raeberry Castle *Dumfries and Galloway* A former stronghold of the Maclellans on the Solway coast of Dumfries and Galloway, little remains of Raeberry Castle, which is situated on a cliff top just over 6 miles (10 km) southeast of Kirkcudbright.

Raeburnfoot *Dumfries and Galloway* The site of a 1st-century AD Roman fort in Dumfries and Galloway,

Raeburnfoot is located at the junction of the Rae Burn with the White Esk, a mile (1.5 km) north of Eskdalemuir. It probably lies close to the point where the Roman road to Newstead crossed the Esk during the Antonine period.

Raehills *Dumfries and Galloway* A Tudor-style country house in Johnstone parish, Dumfries and Galloway, Raehills stands on the Kinnel Water, 10 miles (16 km) northwest of Lockerbie. It was built in 1786 by James, 3rd Earl of Hopetoun, and extended in 1834 for John James Hope Johnstone of Annandale.

Raemoir *Aberdeenshire* A locality in mid-Aberdeenshire, Raemoir comprises the Mill of Raemoir and the Raemoir House Hotel, which are situated just over a mile (1.5 km) to the north of Banchory on Royal Deeside. Raemoir House was formerly owned by the Innes family.

Raerinish Point *Western Isles* A headland on the east coast of the Isle of Lewis in the Western Isles, Raerinish Point lies 2 miles (3 km) east of Crossbost and 6 miles (10 km) south of Stornoway. The headland separates Loch Grimshader to the north from Loch Leurbost to the south.

Raffin *Highland* A crofting settlement on the Stoer Peninsula, western Sutherland, Raffin lies 2 miles (3 km) northwest of Clashnessie.

Rafford *Moray* A small settlement in Moray, Rafford lies 2 miles (3 km) southeast of Forres. Nearby are 16th-century Blervie Castle and Blervie House (1910).

Raggra *Highland* A scattered crofting settlement in Caithness, Raggra lies between the A9 and Loch of Yarrows, 5 miles (8 km) southwest of Wick. There are a number of traditional long houses surviving.

Rahoy *Highland* A settlement on the Morvern peninsula of Highland Council area, Rahoy lies a mile (1.5 km) northwest of Kinloch on the northeast shore of Loch Teacuis, a southern inlet of Loch Sunart.

Raiders' Road, the *Dumfries and Galloway* The Raiders' Road is the name given to a 10-mile (16-km) forest road in Dumfries and Galloway that links the Queen's Way (A712) with the A762 near Mossdale. The route was popularised by the writer S. R. Crockett (1860–1914) in his novel *The Raiders* (1894), a story of cattle rustling and Border intrigue.

Rainberg Mòr *Argyll and Bute* A mountain on the island of Jura, Rainberg Mòr rises to 453 m (1486 ft) at the north end of the island, 4 miles (6.5 km) west of Lussagiven.

Rait *Perth and Kinross* The old village of Rait lies in the Braes of the Carse at the mouth of the Glen of Rait where it opens out into the Carse of Gowrie. There are a number of reed-thatched cottages and the remains of a pre-Reformation church, abandoned when Rait parish united with Kilspindie in 1619.

Raitcastle *Highland* A hamlet situated between the River Nairn and Laiken Forest, Raitcastle lies 2.5 miles (4 km) south of Nairn. To the southeast is Rait Castle, a ruined 13th-century hall house built by the de Rait family and later held by the Cummings, Mackintoshes and Campbells of Cawdor. The Duke of Cumberland is said to have stayed here before defeating the Jacobites at the Battle of Culloden in 1746.

Raith *Fife* An estate in Fife, Raith lies a mile (1.5 km) west of Kirkcaldy. The estate was acquired in the 17th century by the Fergusons, who built Raith House in 1694. Raith Tower to the west of Raith House is a 19th-century folly. Robert Ferguson of Raith (1767–1840), an MP and Lord Lieutentant of Fife, is remembered for having a scandalous affair with Lady Elgin and being successfully sued for £10,000 by her husband Lord Elgin, of Elgin Marbles fame. Raith lends its name to Raith Rovers, a local football club whose home ground is at Stark's Park in Kirkcaldy.

Raitts Burn *Highland* Rising in the foothills of Meall a' Chocaire in Badenoch, the Raitts Burn flows south to join the River Spey at Lynchat, 2 miles (3 km) northeast of Kingussie.

Ramasaig *Highland* A small township on the west coast of the isle of Skye in the Inner Hebrides, Ramasaig lies 8 miles (13 km) south of Dunvegan Head on the south side of Ramasaig Bay.

Ramnageo, Ness of *Shetland* A headland on the south coast of the island of Unst in the Shetland Islands, the Ness of Ramnageo lies 2 miles (3 km) east of Uyeasound.

Ramna Stacks *Shetland* A nature reserve in the Shetland Islands, Ramna Stacks form a group of small islands and rocks that lie immediately to the north of Gruney and a mile (1.5 km) north of the Point of Fethaland, the most northerly point on the Shetland Mainland.

Ramornie *Fife* A hamlet in Fife, Ramornie lies a mile (1.5 km) east of Ladybank and a half-mile (1 km) west of Pitlessie. Ramornie Mill is close by. The hamlet and surrounding estates are associated with the Heriot and Haig families.

Rams Ness *Shetland* A headland on the south coast of the island of Fetlar in the Shetland Islands, Rams Ness extends into the sea at the southern end of the Lamb Hoga peninsula.

Ramsay Garden *City of Edinburgh* An elegant group of tenement houses at the top of Edinburgh's Royal Mile, Ramsay Garden forms a prominent feature on the skyline adjacent to the Esplanade of Edinburgh Castle. Built in 1892–3 around the house of poet Allan Ramsay (1686–1758) to the design of innovative town planner Sir Patrick Geddes, the development was intended to bring Edinburgh University staff and students into contact with Edinburgh citizens in a residential setting. Scottish baronial and English cottage styles are combined with distinctive red sandstone and whitewash on a steeply sloping site that gives spectacular views over the New Town.

Ramseycleugh *Scottish Borders* A hamlet in the Ettrick district of Scottish Borders, Ramseycleugh lies on the Ettrick Water, 5 miles (8 km) southeast of St Mary's Loch.

Ramscraigs *Highland* A small settlement on the east coast of Caithness, Ramscraigs lies 2 miles (3 km) southwest of Dunbeath.

Rangag, Loch *Highland* A small loch in Caithness, Loch Rangag lies 5 miles (8 km) northwest of Lybster, between Loch Stemster and Loch Ruard.

Ranish *Western Isles* A linear crofting village of the Lochs district on the Isle of Lewis, Ranish (Gael: *Ranais*) is strung out at the end of the B897 to the south of Loch Grimshader, at the neck of the Aird Ranish peninsula, 5.5 miles (9 km) south-southwest of Stornoway. Facilities include the Lochs Free Church and a jetty on Loch Grimshader.

Rankinston *East Ayrshire* A former mining village in East Ayrshire, Rankinston lies 3 miles (5 km) northeast of Patna near the Water of Coyle, a tributary of the River Ayr.

Rankle Burn *Scottish Borders* A river in Scottish Borders, the Rankle Burn rises on the slopes of Black Knowe in the Craik Forest and flows north for 7 miles (11 km), passing through Buccleuch and merging with the Ettrick Water at Cacrabank.

Rannoch, Loch *Perth and Kinross* A loch in eastern Perth and Kinross, Loch Rannoch extends 10 miles (16 km) from Kinloch Rannoch in the east to Bridge of Gaur in the west. It has an area of 19.1 sq. km (7.4 sq. miles) and reaches a depth of 134 m (440 ft). The loch is dammed at its eastern end and forms part of a major hydro-electric scheme. The ancient pine forest known as the Black Wood of Rannoch lies to the south, and Rannoch Moor extends westwards to Glen Coe.

Rannoch Moor *Highland/Perth and Kinross* An upland plateau to the north of Breadalbane and east of Glen Coe, Rannoch Moor comprises an extensive area of moorland dotted with lochans and peat bogs occupying an area of 5180 ha (12,800 acres) in southern Highland Council area and western Perth and Kinross. It reaches an elevation of over 384 m (1260 ft) and is surrounded by mountains that rise to heights in excess of 914 m (3000 ft) to the southeast and west and 610 m (2000 ft) to the north. Forming an immense watershed, Rannoch Moor is underlain by granite and has been shaped by glaciation during the last Ice Age, when it formed the focal point of a glacial re-advance 12,500 years ago. Although traversed in a north–south direction by the A82 from Glasgow to Fort William and by the West Highland Railway, there is no west–east crossing of the moor, which is regarded as one of the last truly wild places in Scotland. The major lochs of Rannoch Moor include Loch Laidon, Loch Bà and Lochan na h-Achlaise. In his novel *Kidnapped* (1886). Robert Louis Stevenson noted that 'A wearier looking desert a man never saw'.

Rannoch River *Highland* A river on the Morvern peninsula, Rannoch River rises in Loch nan Clach and flows west, passing through Loch Tearnait to empty into the head of Loch Aline at Ardtornish.

Rannoch Station *Perth and Kinross* Situated on the railway line from Glasgow to Fort William, the isolated Rannoch Station lies at the road end, 5 miles (8 km) west of Loch Rannoch in Perth and Kinross. Rannoch Station itself was built *c.*1890. At the north end of the platform is the sculpted head of J. H. Renton, whose financial support ensured the completion of the West Highland Railway line across Rannoch Moor. The railway line was constructed by 5000 Irish labourers, who laid the track on a floating bed of turf, brushwood and ash. To the south is the 208 m (227 yd) nine-span concrete Rannoch Viaduct built by Sir Robert McAlpine.

Ranochan *Highland* A small village of South Morar in Highland Council area, Ranochan lies on the northern shore of Loch Eilt, 3 miles (5 km) east of Lochailort. The West Highland Railway line passes to the south of the loch.

Ranza, Loch *North Ayrshire* A sea loch forming an inlet of the Kilbrannan Sound on the north coast of the island of Arran, Loch Ranza lies 8 miles (13 km) northwest of Brodick. A summer ferry connects the village of Lochranza with Claonaig on the Kintyre peninsula. Lochranza Castle is nearby.

Raon na Creadha The Gaelic name for Plasterfield in the Western Isles.

Raploch *Stirling* A district of Stirling, Raploch lies to the northwest of the Castle Rock, a mile (1.5 km) from the centre of the town. Formerly a separate community, very little survives of the old village. The houses of Raploch council estate facing the Drip Road were designed in 1920 by E. S. Bell to resemble small Scottish palaces, complete with towers and turreted roofs.

Rapness Sound *Orkney* A channel of water in the Orkney Islands, Rapness Sound separates the island of Faray from the southern end of Westray to the north.

Rappach Water *Highland* A river of Wester Ross, the Rappach Water rises in headstreams in the Rhidorroch Forest and flows east to be joined first by Abhainn Poiblidh and then by the Corriemulzie Water to become the River Einig which flows through Glen Einig to meet the River Oykel near Oykel Bridge.

Rascarrel *Dumfries and Galloway* A locality in Dumfries and Galloway, Rascarrel lies on the Solway coast, 2 miles (3 km) south of Auchencairn from which it is separated by Rascarrel Moss. Rascarrel Bay is an inlet of the Solway Firth between Airds Point in the east and Castle Muir Point in the west.

Ratagan *Highland* A small settlement with a youth hostel in the Skye and Lochalsh district of western Highland Council area, Ratagan lies on the southwest shore of Loch Duich, a mile (1.5 km) northwest of Shiel Bridge.

Rathen *Aberdeenshire* A hamlet in the Buchan district of Aberdeenshire, Rathen lies in a parish of the same name, 4 miles (6.5 km) south of Fraserburgh. Mormond Hill rises to the southwest, and the Water of Philorth passes to the north on its way to Fraserburgh Bay. A spired church built in 1868 replaced an earlier kirk whose churchyard was the burial place of the grandparents of the Norwegian composer Edvard Grieg (1843–1907).

Rathillet *Fife* A small village with a primary school and parish hall in Kilmany parish, northeast Fife, Rathillet is situated on the A92, 3 miles (5 km) north of Cupar. In medieval times the lands of Rathillet supported the Dominican priory in Cupar and in 1679 one of its inhabitants, David Hackston, was one of the Covenanting murderers of Archbishop James Sharp. To the north lies the beautifully landscaped Mountquhanie Estate, once the property of the earls of Fife.

Ratho *City of Edinburgh* A commuter village 8 miles (13 km) west of Edinburgh, Ratho lies to the south of the M8 by the Union Canal. An inn was built by the canal in 1822, and an 18-hole golf course was established to the east at Ratho Park in 1928. The sculptor William Grant Stevenson, who carved notable statues of Robert Burns and William Wallace, was born here in 1849. The Adventure Centre, home of the National Rock Climbing Centre and the world's largest indoor climbing arena, was opened in 2003 on the site of a quarry to the west of the village.

Ratho Station *City of Edinburgh* A commuter settlement to the west of Edinburgh, Ratho Station lies on the old A8 Glasgow–Edinburgh road to the north of the M8 and a mile (1.5 km) north of Ratho. Ingliston, the Ingliston Motor Racing Circuit and the Royal Highland Showground all lie immediately to the east.

Rathven *Moray* A village to the east of Buckie in Moray, Rathven was the centre of the parish of Rathven before the development of the coastal settlements of Findochty and Portknockie. In medieval times it was the centre of a leper colony. Rathven Church dates from 1794 and in its churchyard is the burial aisle of the Hays of Rannas (1612).

Rattar *Highland* A settlement on the north coast of Caithness, Rattar lies on the southern shore of the Loch of Mey, a mile (1.5 km) southwest of the Castle of Mey. Dunnet Head extends into the Pentland Firth 4 miles (6.5 km) to the northwest.

Rattray *Perth and Kinross* A village and parish in Strathmore, Perth and Kinross, Rattray is situated on the River Ericht opposite Blairgowrie. It comprises the villages of Old Rattray and New Rattray which developed in the 19th century in association with flax and jute spinning.

Rattray Bay *Aberdeenshire* A wide, sandy inlet on the east coast of Aberdeenshire, Rattray Bay extends 3 miles (5 km) between Rattray Head to the north and Scotstown Head to the south. Peterhead lies 4 miles (6.5 km) to the southeast.

Ravelston *City of Edinburgh* A residential suburb of Edinburgh, Ravelston lies 2 miles (3 km) west of the city centre. The Dean Gallery, Scottish Gallery of Modern Art and Daniel Stewart's and Melville College is located here.

Ravenscraig Castle *Fife* The ruined remains of Ravenscraig Castle stand on a rocky cliff overlooking the Firth of Forth to the east of Kirkcaldy. Acquired by Lord Sinclair in 1470, as part of a deal with James III who conferred on him the Earldom of Orkney, it remained in Sinclair possession until 1898, finally passing into State care in 1955.

Ravenstruther *South Lanarkshire* A small hamlet in the Clydesdale valley, Ravenstruther lies to the north of the River Clyde, 3 miles (5 km) northeast of Lanark.

Raw Camps *West Lothian* Once associated with Scotland's largest limestone quarry, the former village of Raw Camps lay a mile (1.5 km) east of East Calder adjacent to the village of Camps. Little remains of the settlement, although there is still evidence of the limestone industry that was operated by the Earl of Morton from the 1760s. The quarries reached peak production in the 1880s under the ownership of the Coltness Iron Company, lime being transported on the Union Canal from the nearby Linn's Mill and later by the North British Railway. The lime mortar produced at Raw Camps was used in the building of Edinburgh's New Town.

Rearquhar *Highland* A township in Sutherland, Rearquhar lies in the valley of the River Evelix, 4 miles (6.5 km) northwest of Dornoch.

Reawick *Shetland* A settlement on the Shetland Mainland, Reawick lies on Rea Wick bay, 2 miles (3 km) south of Garderhouse.

Reay *Highland* A village on the north coast of Caithness, Reay (or New Reay) lies on the Reay Burn where it enters Sandside Bay, 10 miles (16 km) west of Thurso. Built around a village green, it replaced the former settlement of Old Reay, which was submerged by the sea. The market cross from the earlier village stands on the green. The spire of the parish church, which dates from 1739, was a landmark for sailors.

Reay Forest *Highland* A large deer forest in northwest Sutherland, Reay Forest extends northeastwards from Kylestrome. This area has long been associated with the Mackay lords of Reay.

Red Castle *Angus* A 15th-century red sandstone castle on an elevated mound overlooking Lunan Bay on the North Sea coast of Angus, Red Castle is situated just over 2 miles (3 km) northeast of Inverkeilor. The lands of Inverkeilor were granted to Walter de Berkeley, the royal chamberlain of William the Lion, and passed on his death c.1194 to the Balliol family, the probable builders of the first stone castle. During the Wars of Independence the castle was granted to Donald Campbell who sold the lands to the Stewarts who built the later tower house.

Red Cuillins, the *Highland* A mountain range on the isle of Skye in the Inner Hebrides, the Red Cuillins rise to 732 m (2401 ft) at Beinn na Caillich the east of Glen Sligachan. Volcanic in origin, the red granite of the Red Cuillins contrasts with the dark gabbro of the Black Cuillins to the west.

Red Head *Angus* A headland on the North Sea coast of Angus, Red Head is located to the south of Lunan Bay between Lang Craig and Prail Castle.

Red Head *Highland* A headland on the west coast of the Island of Stroma in the Pentland Firth, Red Head extends into the sea a mile (1.5 km) northwest of Uppertown.

Red Head *Orkney* Red Head is the most northerly headland on the island of Eday in the Orkney Islands.

Red Holm *Orkney* A small islet in the Orkney Islands, Red Holm lies at the northern end of the Sound of Faray, between the islands of Eday and Faray.

Red Well, the *Aberdeenshire* Located to the east of the village of Whitehills on the north coast of Aberdeenshire, the Red Well is sheltered under a beehive-shaped building that, it is claimed, was built in Roman times. It contains a spring that runs red and is believed to have curative properties.

Redburn *Highland* A small settlement in Easter Ross, Redburn is situated on the River Glass in Glen Glass, 2 miles (3 km) west of Evanton.

Redcastle *Dumfries and Galloway* A locality in the valley of the Urr Water, Dumfries and Galloway, Redcastle lies nearly a mile (1.5 km) to the southeast of the village of Haugh of Urr.

Redcastle *Highland* A small village in Easter Ross, Redcastle lies on the north shore of the Beauly Firth, 4 miles (6.5 km) east of Muir of Ord. The ruined 16th-century Redcastle, a former stronghold of the Mackenzies, stands on a mound at the head of the Beauly Firth on a site where the original castle of Edradour is thought to have been built by William the Lion in the 12th century. There is a fine range of late 18th-century stables in parkland near the castle, and the Gothic-style Redcastle Church by the firth was rebuilt from 1800.

Redding *Falkirk* A settlement in Falkirk Council area, Redding is situated between Polmont and Falkirk to the north of the Union Canal.

Reddingmuirhead *Falkirk* A village in Falkirk Council area, Reddingmuirhead lies on the Gardrum Burn to the south of the Union Canal and southeast of Falkirk.

Redford Barracks *City of Edinburgh* Located on Colinton Road in Edinburgh, Redford Barracks represent the largest military installation built in Scotland since Fort George (1748). Built by local contractors for the War Office between 1909 and 1915, the barracks provide military accommodation together with offices and training facilities. Facing Colinton Road is a massive Cavalry Barracks, with a large clock tower in the centre.

Redgorton *Perth and Kinross* A locality in Perth and Kinross, Redgorton is situated to the west of the A9 and the River Tay, 4 miles (6.5 km) north of the centre of Perth. Scottish Natural Heritage maintains an administrative building and conference centre immediately to the north at Battleby.

Redhythe Point *Aberdeenshire* A headland on the north coast of Aberdeenshire, Redhythe Point extends into the sea a mile (1.5 km) west of Portsoy, to the east of Sandend Bay.

Redland *Orkney* A hamlet on the north coast of the Orkney Mainland, Redland lies a mile (1.5 km) south of the Broch of Gurness and 3 miles (5 km) northwest of Tingwall.

Redpath *Scottish Borders* A small village of lower Lauderdale in Scottish Borders, Redpath lies on the east bank of the Leader Water, 3 miles (5 km) east of Melrose.

Redpoint *Highland* A small township on the coast of Wester Ross, Redpoint lies 3 miles (5 km) south of Port Henderson, between Loch Torridon in the south and Gair Loch in the north.

Redstone *Perth and Kinross* A locality between the Sidlaw Hills and the River Tay in Perth and Kinross, Redstone lies on the A94 midway between Balbeggie and Burrelton.

Reed Point *Scottish Borders* A rocky headland on the North Sea coast of Scottish Borders, Reed Point lies a mile (1.5 km) northeast of Cockburnspath and a mile (1.5 km) northwest of Pease Bay.

Reef *Western Isles* A small scattered settlement on the west coast of the Isle of Lewis in the Outer Hebrides, Reef (Gael: *Riof*) overlooks the islands of Vuia Beg and Floday in Loch Roag, 3 miles (5 km) east of Timsgarry and 6 miles (10 km) west of Callanish.

Reekie Linn *Angus* A waterfall on the course of the River Isla in Angus, Reekie Linn is located immediately southeast of the village of Bridge of Craigisla, 4 miles (6.5 km) north of Alyth.

Reelig Glen *Highland* A steep-sided wooded valley in eastern Highland, Reelig Glen lies to the south of Reelig House, a half-mile (1 km) southeast of Moniack Castle and 3 miles (5 km) southeast of Beauly. The glen contains part of the course of the Moniack Burn and is known for its stand of Douglas Fir trees, all more than 100 years old and 50m (164 ft) in height. One specimen, measured in 2000 and known locally as Dughall Mòr, is one of the tallest trees in Britain at 62m (204 ft). The glen was long the property of the Fraser family, with traveller James Baillie Fraser (1783–1856) having planted many of the trees but was purchased by the Forestry Commission in 1949.

Rees, Wells of the *Dumfries and Galloway* A locality on the Southern Upland Way between the Tarf Water and Craigmoddie Fell, the Wells of the Rees are possibly of religious significance on the old pilgrimage route to Glenluce Abbey and Whithorn. Three dome-shaped drystone structures cover wells where water seeps from the ground.

Reidh Eilean *Argyll and Bute* A small uninhabited islet to the west of the island of Mull in the Inner Hebrides, Reidh Eilean lies 2 miles (3 km) northwest of the island of Iona.

Reinigeadal The Gaelic name for Rhenigidale in the Western Isles.

Reiss *Highland* A small village in Caithness, Reiss lies 2.5 miles (4 km) northwest of Wick at the junction of the A99 to John o' Groats with the B876 to Castletown and Dunnet Bay. It has views over the sands of Sinclair's Bay and lies to the south of Quoys of Reiss.

Relugas House *Moray* A ruined former seat of the Comyn family in Moray, Relugas House is situated on the Logie Estate near the junction of the River Findhorn and River Divie, 5 miles (8 km) southwest of Forres. It was described by Elizabeth Grant of Rothiemurchus as 'about the prettiest place ever lived in', and by marriage became the home of Sir Thomas Dick Lauder (1784–1848), the author of *The Moray Floods, Highland Legends* and other books. Close by is Randolph's Leap and two markers on the banks of the River Findhorn indicating the flood level reached during the 'Muckle Spate' of 1829.

Remony *Perth and Kinross* A locality on the south side of Loch Tay, Perth and Kinross, Remony lies a mile (1.5 km) to the southwest of Kenmore.

Renfrew *Renfrewshire* The county town of Renfrewshire in west-central Scotland , Renfrew lies at the junction of the White Cart and Black Cart Rivers on the south side of the River Clyde, 3 miles (5 km) northeast of Paisley and 5 miles (8 km) west of Glasgow. Created a royal burgh in the 12th century, it became the seat of a sheriffdom in 1414 and was associated with a Cluniac abbey that later moved to Paisley, with a ferry and with trade to Ireland. The town developed initially in association with textile and soap manufactures and later with shipbuilding, engineering and the manufacture of steel, furniture and rubber. An aerodrome operated nearby from World War I until 1966. Hillington Industrial Estate, opened in 1938, was one of the first of its kind to be created in Scotland. The large Braehead shopping centre was opened in 1999. Buildings of note include the remains of a royal castle, the parish church with 15th-century effigies and the Town Hall (*c.*1871) with a tower 32 m (105 ft) high. Renfrew was the birthplace of the poet Andrew Park (1807) and the minister William Barclay (1907).

Renfrewshire *Area: 261 sq. km (101 sq. miles)* A council area and former county in west-central Scotland situated to the south of the River Clyde between Glasgow and the Firth of Clyde, Renfrewshire became a district of Strathclyde Region in 1975 and a separate local government area once again in 1996. Renfrewshire is bounded by the Firth of Clyde to the north, East Renfrewshire to the south, Inverclyde to the west, North Ayrshire to the southwest and Glasgow City to the east. Its main towns include Paisley (its administrative centre), Renfrew, Bishopton, Johnstone and Linwood, and it possesses a large rural hinterland with smaller settlements such as Kilbarchan, Bridge of Weir and Lochwinnoch. In the early 20th century coal, fire clay and oil shale were worked in the Linwood area west of Paisley. Small lochs within the council area include Castle Semple Loch, Barr Loch, Kilbirnie Loch and Whitliemuir Loch (a reservoir). Renfrewshire is drained by the Calder, Gryfe, Black Cart Water, White Cart Water and Locher Water. The highest point is Misty Law (510 m/1673 ft) on the border with North Ayrshire, and its territory includes much of the Clyde-Muirshiel Country Park. Renfrewshire is the ninth-smallest council area in

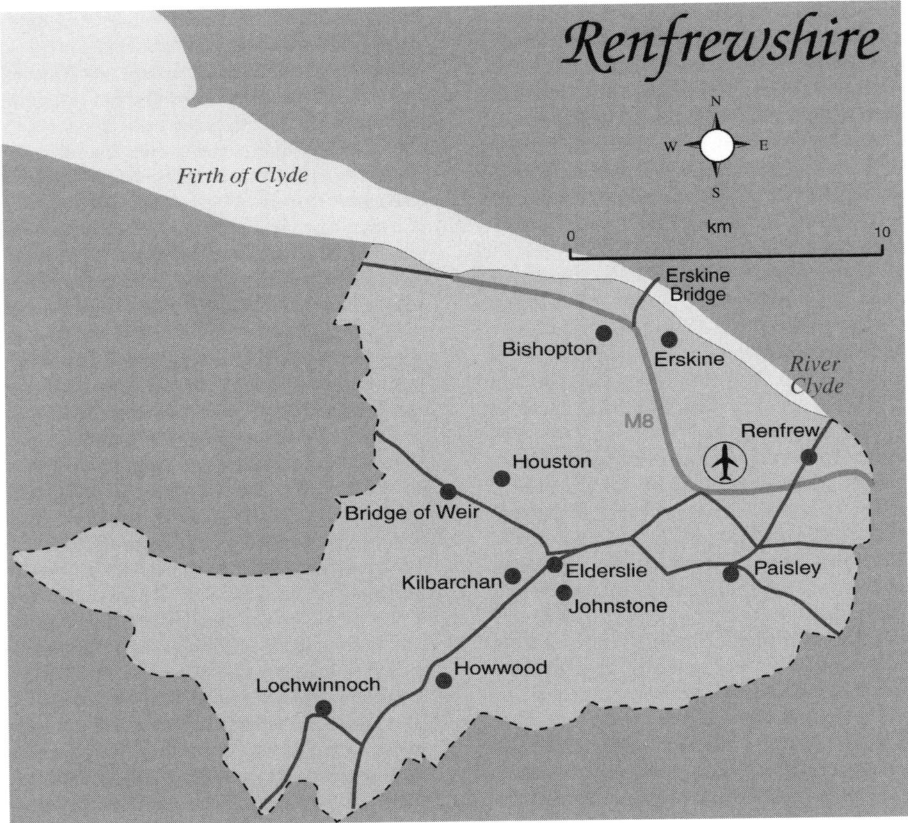

size, the ninth-largest in population and the sixth-highest in density, with 54 per cent of its land used for agriculture, most of which is grassland and peatland. About one sixth of its territory is developed, primarily for urban use. Renfrewshire has a diverse economy that has benefited from the presence of substantial employers such as Glasgow International Airport, the Royal Ordnance, and electronics, engineering, service and food-production industries. Places of interest include Castle Semple Water Country Park, Gleniffer Braes Country Park and Paisley Abbey.

Rennibister *Orkney* The site of a Pictish earth house or souterrain which was discovered in 1926 in the farmyard at Rennibister on Mainland Orkney, 4 miles (6.5 km) northwest of Kirkwall.

Renton *West Dunbartonshire* A settlement in the Vale of Leven, Renton lies on the west bank of the River Leven just south of Alexandria and 2 miles (3 km) northwest of Dumbarton. It developed from the 18th century in association with the printing, dyeing and bleaching of textiles, the earliest manufactory being the Dalquhurn Works (1715). The town itself was created in 1782 by Mrs Smollett of Bonhill, who named it after her daughter-in-law, one of the Rentons of Lammerton. The novelist Tobias Smollett (1721–71), who was born at Dalquhurn near Renton, is commemorated by an 18-m/60-ft-high monument.

Rescobie Loch *Angus* A loch in the valley of Strathmore in Angus, Rescobie Loch lies to the east of Forfar in a parish of the same name. It is a noted fishing loch and is 1.25 miles (2 km) in length with a depth of up to 6 m (20 ft). Turin Hill rises to the north and Dunnichen Hill to the south. The Lunan Water flows from the foot of the loch.

Resipole *Highland* A hamlet in Sunart, Resipole lies 2 miles (3 km) east of Salen. To the east, Beinn Resipol rises to 845 m (2774 ft) between Loch Shiel to the north and Loch Sunart to the south.

Resolis *Highland* A small settlement in Easter Ross, Resolis is situated on the northwest shore of the Black Isle, looking out onto the Cromarty Firth, 9 miles (14 km) west of Cromarty.

Resort, Loch *Western Isles* A sea loch on the west coast of the 'long island' of the Outer Hebrides, Loch Resort forms part of the boundary between Lewis and Harris, pressing inland for 5.5 miles (9 km). Located between rocky hills carpeted in heather moorland, Loch Resort is isolated, the nearest road terminating at the few houses that form the settlement of Hushinish, 2.5 miles (4 km) south of its entrance. The island of Scarp lies opposite this entrance.

Rest and be Thankful *Argyll and Bute* A road in Argyll and Bute between Loch Long and Loch Fyne, the Rest and be Thankful rises to 262 m (860 ft) 4 miles (6.5 km) west of Arrochar. It takes its name from the inscription on a rough stone bench at its summit, probably inscribed by William Caulfield who built the first military road over the pass 1746–8.

Restalrig *City of Edinburgh* A district and former village of eastern Edinburgh, Restalrig lies between Meadowbank and Craigentinny. In the 12th century Restalrig (Lestalric) was designated a barony of the Logan family. Restalrig House was demolished in 1963 to make way for a tower block, which was given the same name. Hawkhill House, an 18th-century mansion designed by John Adam (1721–92), was demolished in 1971. The 16th-century Craigentinny House survives on the north side of Loaning Road, despite being hit by a German bomb during World War II. The core of old Restalrig survives around the historic St Margaret's Parish Church, next to which is the 15th-century St Triduana's Well. On 27 August 1784, James Tytler, a local journalist and polymath, made the first manned balloon flight in Britain. Taking off from Abbeyhill, he rose to a height of 105 m (350 ft) before safely landing at Restalrig. Hibernian football club was founded here by local Irishmen in 1875.

Restenneth *Angus* A parish to the northeast of Forfar in Angus, Restenneth is noted for its ruined priory, which was probably a Pictish foundation. Its square tower with octagonal spire forms a prominent landmark. From the 12th century until the Reformation it was an Augustinian priory.

Reston *Scottish Borders* A village of Berwickshire in Scottish Borders, Reston is situated in the valley of the Eye Water, 2.5 miles (4 km) southwest of Coldingham. It developed from the farms of East and West Renton into a small settlement that prospered in association with travel between northeast England and Edinburgh. In 1832, the English reformer and traveller William Cobbett described the Houndwood Inn, 2 miles (3 km) north of Reston, as 'a place for changing horses convenient and clean'. The railway arrived a decade later and Reston became a centre of the livestock trade. Despite the closure of the railway station in the 1960s and the livestock market in 2001, the village retains its hotels, a primary school and agricultural contracting companies.

Rhenigidale *Western Isles* A small settlement on the remote east coast of North Harris in the Outer Hebrides, Rhenigidale (Gael: *Reinigeadal*) lies at the mouth of Loch Seaforth, 5 miles (8 km) east of Tarbert. A youth hostel was established here in 1962, but it was not until 1990 that a road was built to Rhenigidale. It is also accessible by a spectacular footpath from the southwest.

Rhiconich *Highland* A settlement at the head of Loch Inchard on the west coast of Sutherland, Rhiconich lies 11 miles (18 km) southwest of Durness. The River Rhiconich rises in the Reay Forest and flows northwest through the village into Loch Inchard.

Rhidorroch *Highland* A settlement in Wester Ross, Rhidorroch lies on the north side of Loch Achall, 3 miles (5 km) east of Ullapool. The Rhidorroch River flows west into Loch Achall through Rhidorroch Forest.

Rhinns of Islay, the A peninsula on the west side of the island of Islay in the Inner Hebrides, the Rhinns of Islay (also Rinns of Islay) extend northwards for c.10 miles (16 km) from Rhinns Point in the south and is separated from the eastern half of the island by Loch Indaal.

Rhinns of Kells, the *Dumfries and Galloway* Situated at the eastern edge of the Galloway Hills, the Rhinns of Kells (also Rinns of Kells) is a north–south ridge that forms part of the Kells range of mountains. Summits include Corserine (the second-highest hill in Galloway), Millfire and Meikle Millyea.

Rhinns of Galloway, the *Dumfries and Galloway* A district of western Dumfries and Galloway forming a prominent peninsula of southwest Scotland, the Rhinns (also Rinns), or more fully the Rhinns of Galloway, extends from Milleur Point and Corsewall Point in the north to the Mull of Galloway some 27 miles (43 km) to the south, and stretches inland to the Water of Luce. Its chief towns are Stranraer and Portpatrick. Fishing, agriculture and tourism are important industries, in addition to connections by sea with Ireland.

Rhonehouse *Dumfries and Galloway* A village of Dumfries and Galloway, Rhonehouse (also known as Kelton Hill) lies to the east of the River Dee, 2 miles (3 km) southwest of Castle Douglas. The hill of Kelton Hill rises to the northeast.

Rhu *Argyll and Bute* A yachting resort on the east side of Gare Loch in Argyll and Bute, Rhu lies 2 miles (3 km) northwest of Helensburgh. It is the home of the Royal Northern and Clyde Yacht Club. Nearby are the gardens at Glenarn.

Rhum An alternative name for Rum in the Inner Hebrides.

Rhynd *Perth and Kinross* A hamlet in a parish of the same name in Perth and Kinross, Rhynd lies between the River Tay and Moncreiffe Hill, 4 miles (6.5 km) southeast of Perth. A Tudor-Gothic-style parish church dating from 1842 replaced an earlier church whose ruins can be found at Easter Rhynd, near the confluence of the Earn and the Tay. In addition to its 19th-century cottages, the hamlet of Rhynd has Scotland's only K3 telephone kiosk, produced from 1929 to designs by Sir Giles Gilbert Scott. To the north at Elcho, overlooking the Tay, stands Elcho Castle, a former stronghold of the Wemyss family.

Rhynie *Aberdeenshire* A village in an Aberdeenshire parish of the same name, Rhynie lies between Ord Hill and the Water of Bogie, 14 miles (22 km) northwest of Alford. A former market centre, the village was also known as Muir of Rhynie. In the old kirkyard of Rhynie are three Pictish symbol stones dating from the 6th–7th century AD. Two more Pictish stones stand in the village square, and at the entrance to the school is a cast of the Rhynie Man, taken from a stone now located at Woodhill House, Aberdeen. A mile (1.5 km) to the northwest, on the Tap o' Noth (564 m/1849 ft) is a spectacular hillfort occupied on at least two occasions between the 1st millennium BC and the early 1st millennium AD. The Old Red Sandstone of Rhynie has provided some of the best fossil specimens of the primitive *Rhynia*, one of the earliest land plants dating from the Devonian period.

Rhynie *Highland* A small settlement in Easter Ross, Rhynie lies to the southeast of Loch Eye, between the Cromarty Firth and Dornoch Firth. Hill of Fearn lies 1.25 miles (2 km) to the southwest.

Riccarton *East Ayrshire* A southern suburb of Kilmarnock in East Ayrshire, Riccarton lies on the south side of the River Irvine. Once noted for its market, it was connected to Kilmarnock with the building of a bridge in 1726, and in 1909 was absorbed into the burgh town. There is an oil depot, and automotive parts industries.

Riccarton *City of Edinburgh* A locality on the western outskirts of the city of Edinburgh, Riccarton lies a mile (1.5 km) to the north of Currie. The campus of Heriot-Watt University is located to the west of Riccarton Mains.

Riccarton Hills *West Lothian* A small range of hills in West Lothian, the Riccarton Hills rise to 254 m (833 ft) southeast of Linlithgow.

Riddon, Loch *Argyll and Bute* A sea loch at the southern end of the Cowal peninsula, Loch Riddon extends southwards for 4 miles (6.5 km) before opening out into the two arms of the Kyles of Bute.

Riddrie *Glasgow City* An eastern suburb of the city of Glasgow, Riddrie lies to the north of Carntyne. It was created as a low-density housing estate in the 1920s and is the location of Barlinnie Prison.

Riechip *Perth and Kinross* A locality in the Stormont district of eastern Perth and Kinross, Riechip is situated on a tributary of the Buckny Burn, a mile (1.5 km) north of Butterstone and 4 miles (6.5 km) northeast of Dunkeld.

Rig *Dumfries and Galloway* A locality in Dumfries and Galloway, Rig lies on the A76 near the border with East Ayrshire, between New Cumnock and Sanquhar.

Rigg *Dumfries and Galloway* A village in Dumfries and Galloway, Rigg lies on the west bank of the Kirtle Water, a mile (1.5 km) west of Gretna.

Rigg Bay *Dumfries and Galloway* An inlet of Wigtown Bay on the eastern Machars coast of Dumfries and Galloway, Rigg Bay lies just south of Garlieston. It is also known as Cruggleton Bay.

Rigside *South Lanarkshire* A former mining village in South Lanarkshire, Rigside lies on the Douglas Water 5 miles (8 km) south of Lanark. The early 19th-century Folkerton Mill survives complete with water wheel and machinery. A railway line connected with coal pits near here between 1864 and 1969, and in 1997 an opencast mine was opened.

Ring of Brodgar, The *Orkney* An impressive prehistoric stone circle lying between the Loch of Stenness and the Loch of Harray on Mainland Orkney, the Ring of Brodgar originally comprised 60 stones set six degrees apart starting from geographical north. Only 36 stones now remain in position within the confines of a deep ditch broken by two opposing causeways. Thought to have been a lunar observatory, its construction is likely to date from before 1500 BC.

Ringford *Dumfries and Galloway* A small village of Dumfries and Galloway, Ringford lies just east of the Tarf Water at a road junction 5 miles (8 km) north of Kirkcudbright.

Rinnes, Glen *Moray* A narrow glen to the east of Ben Rinnes in Moray, Glen Rinnes stretches southwest from Dufftown to form the valley of the Dullan Water

Riof The Gaelic name for Reef in the Western Isles.

Risay, Loch *Western Isles* An inlet in East Loch Roag in the Outer Hebrides, Loch Risay (Gael: *Loch Riosaigh*) lies on the northeast coast of Great Bernera, a half-mile (1 km) east of Breaclete. A restored Norse mill lies on its western shore and the loch contains a number of islets.

Risga *Highland* An islet near the mouth of Loch Sunart in Lochaber, Risga lies close to the north shore between the islands of Carna and Oronsay.

Rispain *Dumfries and Galloway* An earthwork on the slopes of Camp Hill in the Machars of Dumfries and Galloway, Rispain Camp is located to the southwest of Whithorn. Long believed to have been a Roman camp, it has been identified as a native homestead dating from about 60 BC. It has a surrounding ditch 5.8 m (19 ft) deep.

RM Condor *Angus* A Royal Marines base located 2 miles (3 km) northwest of the centre of Arbroath in eastern Angus, RM *Condor* began as a Fleet Air Arm facility, established in 1938, and later became a Royal Naval Air Station, known as HMS *Condor*. The home of 45 Commando regiment since 1971, *Condor* has a complement of almost 900 military and civilian personnel. An airfield is maintained for operational purposes, including use as a drop-zone for parachute training, but it is also regularly used by a civilian gliding club.

Roadside of Cookston *Aberdeenshire* A locality in the Aberdeenshire parish of Banchory-Devenick, Roadside of Cookston lies on the A92, 6 miles (10 km) south of Aberdeen.

Roag, Loch *Western Isles* A large sea loch littered with islands on the west coast of Lewis in the Outer Hebrides, Loch Roag (Gael: *Loch Ròg*) is divided by Great Bernera into West Loch Roag and East Loch Roag. The name Loch Roag is itself applied to two distinct bodies of water: the first lies to the southwest of Great Bernera and narrows to form Little Loch Roag (Gael: *Loch Ròg Beag*); the other lies to the south and west of Eilean Kearstay, to the southeast of Great Bernera, at the mouth of Loch Kinhoulavig. These are separated by the Great Bernera Bridge and another arm of the loch referred to as Loch Barraglom.

Roan, Loch *Dumfries and Galloway* A small loch in Dumfries and Galloway, Loch Roan lies to the east of the River Dee, just over a mile (1.5 km) northeast of Crossmichael.

Roan Fell *Dumfries and Galloway/Scottish Borders* A hill in southern Scotland, Roan Fell rises to 568 m (1863 ft) on the border between Dumfries and Galloway and Scottish Borders, 4 miles (6.5 km) northwest of Newcastleton.

Robert Law *South Lanarkshire* A hill rising to 406 m (1332 ft) 3 miles (5 km) northeast of Douglas in South Lanarkshire, Robert Law lies to the east of the M74. The Garf Water flows east from its source on Robert Law to join the Clyde near Biggar.

Roberton *Scottish Borders* A hamlet in a parish of the same name in southwest Scottish Borders, Roberton lies on the north bank of the Borthwick Water 5 miles (8 km) west of Hawick.

Roberton *South Lanarkshire* A hamlet in Clydesdale, Roberton lies on the River Clyde to the north of Abington. Chartered as a burgh of barony in 1631, it once prospered near a river crossing.

Roberton Burn *South Lanarkshire* A stream in South Lanarkshire, the Roberton Burn rises between Wildshaw Hill and Scaur Hill and flows east to join the River Clyde near Roberton.

Robert Smail's Printing Works *Scottish Borders* Situated on the High Street in Innerleithen, Robert Smail's Printing Works operated as a printing and stationery firm from 1847 to 1985. It was purchased and restored by the National Trust for Scotland in 1986. Visitors can watch the printing process and view items that give an insight into this historic Borders town.

Robgill Tower *Dumfries and Galloway* A tower house situated by the Kirtle Water in Dumfries and Galloway, Robgill Tower lies a mile (1.5 km) to the southeast of Kirtlebridge. Built in the 16th century by the Irvine family, the tower was substantially altered in the 19th century.

Robroyston *Glasgow City* A northeastern suburb of the city of Glasgow, Robroyston lies to the west of Stepps, 4 miles (6.5 km) northeast of the city centre. A hospital was erected here in the early 20th century. Robroyston

House, which stood on the routeway to Kirkintilloch, was demolished in the 1960s.

Rockall *Western Isles* A rock stack in the Atlantic Ocean, Rockall (the 'Sea-rock of Roaring', Gael: *Sgeir Rocail*) lies 186 miles (300 km) west of St Kilda. It is the furthest outlier of the British Isles and gives its name to a shipping-forecast area that is bounded to the north by Bailey, northeast by Hebrides, east by Malin and south by Shannon. It rises to c.19 m (63 ft) and has a navigation light, installed in 1972.

Rockcliffe *Dumfries and Galloway* A resort village in Dumfries and Galloway, Rockcliffe lies at the mouth of the Urr Water on the eastern shore of the Rough Firth, 6 miles (10 km) south of Dalbeattie. The Mote of Mark, a hillfort of the 5th century AD, is located to the northwest on Mark Hill, the name Mark being associated with the king of ancient Dumnonia who was the husband of Isolde in the story of Tristan and Isolde. The Jubilee Path along with the Muckle Lands form an extensive area of coastland between Rockcliffe and Kippford.

Rock Hall *Dumfries and Galloway* An early 17th-century laird's house in Dumfries and Galloway, Rock Hall is situated near Woodside, 5 miles (8 km) east of Dumfries.

Rodel *Western Isles* A settlement at the southern tip of Harris in the Outer Hebrides, Rodel (Gael: *Roghadal*) has a hotel and harbour. Nearby is St Clement's Church, which contains some fine medieval tombs, including the burials of the standard bearers of the MacLeods.

Rodger Law *South Lanarkshire* A summit in the Lowther Hills, Rodger Law rises to 688 m (2257 ft) 7 miles (11 km) south of Elvanfoot in South Lanarkshire.

Rodney Stone, the *Moray* A Pictish symbol stone situated by the drive leading to Brodie Castle in Moray, the Rodney Stone is decorated with a cross on one side and fish-monsters, an elephant and double-disc and Z-rod symbols on the other. On the roll mouldings at the edge of the stone there are examples of Ogam script. The stone, which was found while digging out foundations at the church in the nearby village of Dyke, was set up in the village in honour of Admiral George Rodney's victory over the French in the West Indies in 1782. It was moved to its present site in 1842.

Rogart *Highland* A village in eastern Sutherland, Rogart is situated in the valley of Strath Fleet, 9 miles (14 km) west of Golspie. It developed in association with a railway station, meal mill, woollen mill and auction market.

Roghadal The Gaelic name for Rodel in the Western Isles.

Rogie Burn *Highland* A stream in Ross and Cromarty, the Rogie Burn flows south from Carn Gorm to join the Black Water 3 miles (5 km) west of Strathpeffer.

Rogie Falls *Highland* A waterfall on the course of the Black Water in Ross and Cromarty, Rogie Falls are located 2 miles (3 km) west of Strathpeffer.

Roineval *Highland* A hill on the isle of Skye in the Inner Hebrides, Roineval rises to 439 m (1440 ft) 3 miles (5 km) north of the head of Loch Harport and 7 miles (11 km) southwest of Portree.

Roineval *Western Isles* A hill on the Isle of Lewis in the Outer Hebrides, Roineval rises to 281 m (922 ft) 2 miles (3 km) west of the settlement of Baile Ailein and 14 miles (22 km) southwest of Stornoway.

Roinn a' Bhuic *Western Isles* A headland on the northwest coast of Lewis in the Outer Hebrides, Roinn a' Bhuic lies immediately to the west of the settlement of Melbost Borve.

Romach Loch *Moray* Situated on the north side of Romach Hill in Moray and surrounded by the Newtyle Forest, Romach Loch lies 3 miles (5 km) south of Forres.

Rommanobridge *Scottish Borders* A village in the Peeblesshire district of Scottish Borders, Romannobridge lies on the Lyne Water, 3 miles (5 km) south of West Linton. On a hill nearby are medieval cultivation terraces.

Rona *Highland* An island of ancient Lewissian gneiss with an area of 1047 ha (2587 acres) in the Inner Hebrides, Rona (also South Rona) lies to the east of the isle of Skye and to the north of Raasay, from which it is separated by Kyle Rona. The Sound of Raasay lies to the west and the Inner Sound to the east. Before the islanders were removed at the onset of World War II, the island had a permanent crofting population of 176 in 1881. In the postwar years, the NATO base at the north end of the island was manned by Royal Navy personnel. Owned by the Macleods until 1843, Rona passed through several hands before being purchased by the Government in 1922. It returned to private ownership in 1992 and two residents were recorded in the 2001 census. The island rises to a height of 125 m (410 ft) at Meall Acarseid. The ruins of the former main settlement, Acarseid Mhòr, are situtated due north on a bay of the same name. The other chief settlement on the island was at Doire na Guaile, close to an early church site at An Teampull. Before the island church was built in 1912, the people of Rona worshipped in the Church Cave.

Rona *Western Isles* A remote uninhabited island in the Atlantic Ocean, Rona (also North Rona) lies 10 miles (16 km) east of Sula Sgeir and 44 miles (70.5 km) northeast of the Butt of Lewis. It has an area of 209 ha (269 acres) and rises to 108 m (354 ft) at Toa Rona. St Ronan's Chapel is one of the oldest buildings of the Celtic Church. At one time it was occupied by a single family, the last member of which left the island in 1844. Today, Rona is grazed by sheep. It is a designated National Nature Reserve and a breeding place for Atlantic grey seals.

Ronachan Point *Argyll and Bute* A headland on the west coast of the Kintyre peninsula, Ronachan Point lies on the south side of the entrance to West Loch Tarbert at the northern end of the Sound of Gigha. The settlement of Ronachan lies close by.

Ronaigh The Gaelic name for Ronay in the Western Isles.

Ronald, Loch *Dumfries and Galloway* A loch in western Dumfries and Galloway, Loch Ronald lies to the east of the Tarf Water, 6 miles (10 km) northeast of Glenluce.

Ronas Hill *Shetland* Rising to 450 m (1476 ft) at the north end of Mainland Shetland, Ronas Hill is the highest hill in the Shetland Islands. At its summit overlooking Ronas Voe to the south are the remains of an ancient chambered cairn as well as spectacular views westwards to the Atlantic and eastwards to Yell Sound.

Ronay *Western Isles* A significant island facing the Little Minch at the eastern end of the channel between North Uist and Benbecula, Ronay (Gael: *Ronaigh*) extends to 563 ha (1391 acres) in area. This craggy island has a highly indented coastline and rises to 115 m (377 ft) at Beinn a' Charnain. Once supporting a population exceeding 150, Ronay's impoverished land resulted in most of the people being cleared by the 1870s. By the 1930s the island was uninhabited.

Roneval *Western Isles* A hill in the Outer Hebrides, Roneval rises to 201 m (659ft) 4 miles (6.5 km) southeast of Lochboisdale in South Uist.

Roneval *Western Isles* A hill in the Outer Hebrides, Roneval rises to 459 m (1509 ft) to the east of Leverburgh in South Harris.

Rora *Aberdeenshire* A hamlet in the Buchan district of Aberdeenshire, Rora lies between the River Ugie to the south and Rora Moss, 5 miles (8 km) northwest of Peterhead. Middleton of Rora lies to the south and the Mill of Rora to the west on the Ugie.

Roromore *Perth and Kinross* A locality in Glen Lyon, Perth and Kinross, Roromore lies to the south of the River Lyon, 6 miles (10 km) west of Fortingall.

Rosal *Highland* The remains of a former township in Strathnaver, Sutherland, Rosal lies within Naver Forest, 9 miles (14 km) northeast of Altnaharra. Rosal supported 70–80 people until it was cleared in 1816. The site was excavated in the 1960s under the direction of Dr Horace Fairhurst and is now interpreted on-site by the Forestry Commission. Opposite Rosal, on the east bank of the River Naver, is a memorial to Donald Macleod, a stonemason who observed the clearing of the township.

Rosebery *Midlothian* Rosebery, the estate from which the earls of Rosebery take their title, lies a mile (1.5 km) southwest of Temple in Midlothian. Clerkington House, owned by the Hepburn family, was rebuilt here for Archibald Primrose, 4th Earl of Rosebery, by William Atkinson in 1812. Its impressive steading with a clock tower and spire dates from *c.*1805.

Rosebery Reservoir *Midlothian* A deep reservoir lying in a sheltered valley 4 miles (6.5 km) southwest of Gorebridge, to the south of Edinburgh, Rosebery Reservoir is one of a network of reservoirs supplying the city with water.

Roseburn *City of Edinburgh* A western residential suburb of Edinburgh, Roseburn lies 2 miles (3 km) west of the city centre near Murrayfield and Gorgie. Roseburn House dates from 1562.

Rosehearty *Aberdeenshire* A fishing village in the northern Aberdeenshire parish of Pitsligo, Rosehearty is situated on a promontory jutting into the Moray Firth 6 miles (10 km) west of Fraserburgh. It is said to be one of the oldest seaports in Scotland, dating from the 14th century, when a small group of shipwrecked Danes settled among local crofters and taught them to fish. A burgh of barony was created in 1681, and during the peak of the herring trade in the 1880s its harbour accommodated 88 fishing boats. During the 20th century Rosehearty developed as a tourist resort and today has a nine-hole golf course and a heritage centre. Nearby stand the ruins of Pitsligo Castle and the castle of Pittullie. The Jacobite Alexander Forbes, 4th and last Lord Pitsligo, hid in the Cave of Cowshaven to the west of Rosehearty while a fugitive after the 1745 Rebellion.

Roseisle *Moray* A locality on the north coast of Moray, Roseisle lies 2 miles (3 km) southeast of Burghead. Roseisle Forest lies to the west, bordering Burghead Bay.

Rosemarkie *Highland* A village in Easter Ross, Rosemarkie lies on the Moray Firth coast of the Black Isle opposite Fort George and a mile (1.5 km) northeast of Fortrose. The Groam House Museum in the village is home to 15 Pictish stones that were found in the local area and date back to the 8th century. In the same building is the nationally important George Bain collection of Celtic art.

Rosemount *Perth and Kinross* A southeast extension of Blairgowrie in eastern Perth and Kinross, Rosemount lies to the south of the River Ericht.

Rosewell *Midlothian* A former mining village in Midlothian, Rosewell lies 2.5 miles (4 km) southeast of Loanhead and 3 miles (5 km) northeast of Penicuik. The majority of the village was laid out *c.*1891 by the coal baron Archibald Hood to house miners for his Whitehill Colliery, which lay just to the southwest of the village. The workers were housed in neat rows of brick-built terraced cottages, each with its own garden, an innovation at the time. The overseers were housed in semi-detached villas nearby. Bricks were manufactured at Hood's Whitehill Brickworks, which made use of fire clay removed from the coal workings. Hood took a detailed interest in every aspect of the running of his village, ensuring the establishment of churches, schools, a cooperative store and a system to put the profits from the public house back into community projects. Notable buildings include the parish church (1871), the Rosewell Institute (1917) and St Matthew's Roman Catholic Church (1925). Nearby are Rosslynlee Hospital; Whitehill House, built in 1844 by architects William Burn and David Bryce; Midfield House, renovated by Robert Lorimer (1918); and 15th-century Hawthornden Castle.

Roslin *Midlothian* A dormitory village in Midlothian, Roslin lies 2 miles (3 km) south of Loanhead. Roslin (or Rosslyn) Castle, a former stronghold of the St Clair family built in the 14th century, stands on a steep promontory above the River North Esk which flows through the Roslin Glen Country Park. The village was designated a burgh of barony in 1456 and developed in association with mining, quarrying and the manufacture of textiles and gunpowder. Modern industries include the manufacture of pharmaceuticals in association with research in animal husbandry, the Roslin Institute conducting the world's first cloning of a sheep named Dolly. Rosslyn (or Roslin) Chapel, a collegiate church containing some of the finest stone carving in Scotland, was erected near here in 1446–85 by Sir William St Clair. James Gillespie, founder of a hospital that later became a noted Edinburgh school, was born in Roslin in 1726.

Rosneath *Argyll and Bute* A village on a peninsula of the same name in southern Argyll and Bute, Rosneath lies on the west shore of the Gare Loch opposite Rhu and 2 miles (3 km) west of Helensburgh. The village was known for boatbuilding and became an important naval base during World War II, which was shared with the Americans in the lead-up to amphibious landings in North Africa and on D-day. The 16th-century Rosneath Castle was destroyed by fire and replaced by a fine neoclassical mansion that became home to Princess Louise, daughter of Queen Victoria and wife of the 9th Duke of Argyll. This was itself gutted by fire in 1947 and demolished in 1961. Today the village is a tourist centre with boating facilities.

Rosneath Peninsula *Argyll and Bute* Lying between the Gare Loch and Loch Long in Argyll and Bute, on the north shore of the Firth of Clyde, the Rosneath peninsula is 6 miles (10 km) long and between a mile (1.5 km) and 2.5

miles (4 km) wide. Its settlements are Garelochhead, Clynder, Rosneath, Kilcreggan, Cove and Coulport. The Royal Naval Armament Depot at Coulport provides storage facilities for the Trident nuclear weapons that arm the submarines based at nearby Faslane.

Ross *Dumfries and Galloway* A locality in Dumfries and Galloway, Ross lies at the southern end of a peninsula extending into the Solway Firth 5 miles (8 km) southwest of Kirkcudbright. Situated at the head of Ross Bay, an inlet of Kirkcudbright Bay, the cairn-topped Mull of Ross rises to the west. To the south of Ross Bay, the Meikle Ross forms a headland that is separated from the island of Little Ross by the Sound and Ross Roads.

Ross, the *Perth and Kinross* A locality at the western edge of Comrie in Perth and Kinross, the Ross lies to the south of the River Earn and is accessed by a picturesque bridge built in 1792. The House of Ross (1908), the Bobbin Mill (c.1830), Drumearn (late 19th century), Auchenross (c.1910) and the Earthquake House (1869) are buildings of interest here.

Ross and Cromarty A former county in the Scottish Highlands stretching from the Moray Firth to the Minch, Ross and Cromarty formed a district of Highland Region between 1975 and 1996 with its administrative centre in Dingwall. Its area was 4952 sq. km (1913 sq. miles).

Ross of Mull *Argyll and Bute* The granite rock Ross of Mull forms a peninsula facing Iona at the southwest end of the island of Mull in the Inner Hebrides. Its chief settlement is Bunessan.

Rossdhu *Argyll and Bute* An estate with a mansion house on the west shore of Loch Lomond, Rossdhu lies 2 miles (3 km) south of the village of Luss. Formerly the seat of the Colquhouns of Luss, it is now a major centre for golf.

Rossend Castle *Fife* Built in 1119 and extended in 1382 and 1563, the restored Rossend Castle overlooks the Firth of Forth at the western end of Burntisland. It was visited by many of the kings and queens of Scotland, including Mary, Queen of Scots, and was said to have been the hiding place of the relics of Queen Margaret.

Rossie Castle *Angus* Built in 1800, Rossie Castle in Angus lies just south of Montrose Basin on the edge of Rossie Moor.

Rossie Island *Angus* A southern district of Montrose, Rossie Island (or Inchbraoch) lies on the south side of the River South Esk as it leaves Montrose Basin. It provides a staging point for both the A92 and railway to enter Montrose from the south.

Ross-shire An ancient county of Highland Scotland, Ross-shire extended from the Moray Firth in the east to Lewis in the Outer Hebrides. It was unusual in that it contained a number of outlying tracts of the neighbouring Cromarty, with which it was united in 1889 to form the county of Ross and Cromarty. Its county town was Dingwall. In 1974 the county was divided between the new Western Isles Authority and Highland Region, the latter including the smaller Ross and Cromarty District. In the local government reorganisation of 1996, Ross-shire remained divided between the Western Isles and Highland Council Areas.

Rosyth *Fife* A town and dockyard complex on the south coast of Fife, Rosyth lies due west of Inverkeithing. Taking advantage of the deep, tidal-free water off St Margaret's Hope, the Admiralty decided in 1903 to build a naval base and dockyard here. The town of Rosyth was planned as a 'garden city' to house the workers, and construction of the dockyard and naval base, which extends over 505 ha (1248 acres) of reclaimed land, began in 1909. The first vessel to be repaired was *HMS Zealandia*, which entered No. 1 Dock in March 1916. During the Cold War years after World War II the dockyard and its associated naval base were developed as a refitting centre for conventional and nuclear Polaris submarines as well as frigates, minesweepers and offshore protection vessels. Babcock International, which had taken over management of the facility in 1987, acquired the site in 1997, making the Rosyth Royal Dockyard the first privatised naval dockyard in Britain. Notable modern buildings in the town include the domestic housing on Queensferry Road (1919), the Anglican Church of St Margaret (1969) and St John's Primary School (1989). Rosyth, now an important ferry port linking Scotland to Europe, has additional industries such as the manufacture of drilling equipment and weighing equipment located on the Primrose and Belleknowes Industrial Estates.

Rothes *Moray* A whisky-making town in Moray on the Malt Whisky Trail, Rothes lies to the west of the River Spey, 10 miles (16 km) south of Elgin. It was founded by the Earl of Findlater in 1766, replacing an earlier settlement. Its first whisky distillery, Glen Grant, was founded in 1840 by James and John Grant. Nearby stand the ruins of Rothes Castle, built in the 15th century by the Leslie Earl of Rothes. The town has two nine-hole golf courses.

Rothes, Burn of *Moray* A stream in the uplands of Moray, the Burn of Rothes rises in Elchies Forest and flows eastwards through the town of Rothes to meet the River Spey.

Rothes, Glen of *Moray* The Glen of Rothes lies immediately northwest of the town of Rothes in Moray where the Broad Burn flows down towards the River Spey. The A941 from Rothes to Elgin, part of the Malt Whisky Trail, passes this way.

Rothesay *Argyll and Bute* Situated on a sheltered bay on

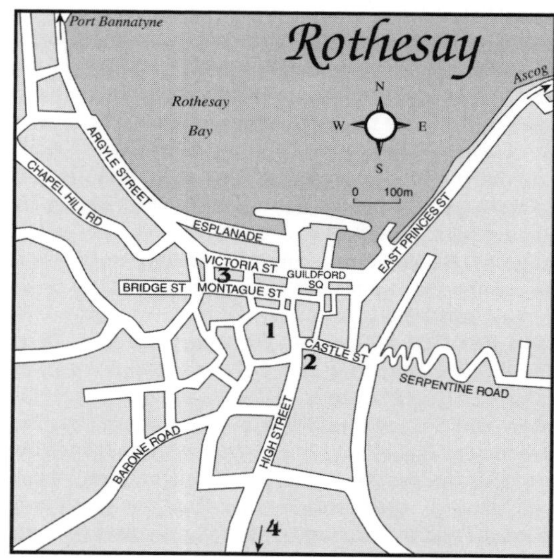

1 *Rothesay Castle*
2 *Bute Museum*
3 *Winter Garden*
4 *Mount Stuart*

the east coast of the island of Bute, Rothesay is a 30-minute ferry journey from Wemyss Bay on the mainland. Chartered as a royal burgh in 1401, its 12th-century castle was the favourite residence of King Robert III. Rothesay developed in association with the manufacture of textiles and fishing and became a popular seaside destination for Victorian Scots, particularly day-trippers from Glasgow by steamship. Architecture associated with Rothesay's heyday as a tourist centre includes its Winter Gardens (1924), Pavilion (1936), Promenade and Pier which were built on reclaimed land. The Royal Northern Yacht Club of Rothesay was founded here in 1824.

Rothie An alternative name for Rothienorman in Aberdeenshire.

Rothiemay An alternative name for Milltown of Rothiemay in Moray.

Rothiemurchus *Highland* An estate and forest in the Badenoch and Strathspey district of Highland Council Area, Rothiemurchus lies between the Cairngorm Mountains and the River Spey. Owned by the Grant family for nearly five centuries, the estate comprises native pinewood and moorland extending southwards along Gleann Einich and eastwards to Loch Morlich. There is a visitor centre at Inverdruie, hotel and camping facilities at Coylumbridge and facilities for fishing, clay-pigeon shooting, mountain biking and wildlife watching. There are numerous footpaths, including a walk round Loch an Eilein.

Rothienorman *Aberdeenshire* A village in the Aberdeenshire parish of Fyvie, Rothienorman lies on the Fordoun Burn, 8 miles (13 km) northwest of Oldmeldrum. Often referred to simply as Rothie, it is an agricultural service centre producing dairy products.

Rotten Calder *South Lanarkshire* The lower reaches of the Calder Water in South Lanarkshire.

Rottinslough An alternative name for Portessie in Moray.

Roucan *Dumfries and Galloway* A locality in Nithsdale, Dumfries and Galloway, Roucan lies on the A709 road between Torthorwald and Dumfries.

Rough Bounds of Knoydart An alternative name for the district of Knoydart.

Rough Castle *Falkirk* Lying just over a mile (1.5 km) to the southeast of Bonnybridge, Rough Castle is the best preserved of the Roman Antonine forts. The Antonine Wall was built c.AD 143 and stretched from Bo'ness on the River Forth to Old Kilpatrick on the River Clyde. Located immediately to the south of the wall, this fort was relatively small, extending to 0.4 ha (1 acre) in size and enclosed within ditches and a rampart. The 90-ha (222-acre) Roughcastle Community Woodland to the south was created on the site of an opencast coal mine that operated until 1996.

Rough Firth *Dumfries and Galloway* An inlet of the Solway Firth, Dumfries and Galloway, the Rough Firth lies 3 miles (5 km) south of Dalbeattie. It receives the Urr Water and is separated from Orchardton Bay and Auchencairn Bay by a peninsula that extends from Castle Hill to Almorness Point. The 8-ha (20-acre) Rough Island in the bay is a noted bird sanctuary that was given to the National Trust for Scotland by John and James McLellan in 1937 in memory of their brother, Colonel William McLellan CBE of Orchard Knowes. The resort village of Rockcliffe looks out onto the bay from the east.

Rouken Glen Park *East Renfrewshire* An area of parkland in Giffnock, Rouken Glen is one of the largest public parks in Scotland. Established in 1906 following a gift from Lord Rowallan, the area of the park was eventually increased to 92 ha (227 acres). It has grasslands, lawns, a boating pond and a Highland Glen complete with falls, cliffs and crags.

Roundstonefoot *Dumfries and Galloway* A locality in the Moffat Hills, Dumfries and Galloway, Roundstonefoot lies at the junction of the Roundstone Burn with the Moffat Water, 4 miles (6.5 km) northeast of Moffat.

Rousay *Orkney* A hilly island in the Orkney Islands, Rousay lies to the north of the Mainland of Orkney, from which it is separated by Eynhallow Sound. It rises to 250 m (821 ft) at Blotchnie Fold and has an area of 4805 ha (11,873 acres). In the southeast lies the Trumland RSPB Reserve where merlin, short-eared owl, red-throated diver and golden plover can be seen. The island also has a wealth of archaeological sites, including the Midhowe Broch and Cairn, burial cairns at the Knowe of Yarso, Blackhammer, Taversoe Tuick and the Knowe of Lairso, the Neolithic village of Sourin and the crannogs of the Loch of Wasbister. Once sustaining a population of nearly 1000, Rousay had a total of 212 people living and working on its narrow agricultural margin in 2001. There is car ferry link with Tingwall on Mainland Orkney.

Row *Stirling* A locality in Stirling Council area, the scattered settlement of Row which lies to the north of the River Teith, a mile (1.5 km) to the southeast of Doune, comprises Row, Easter Row and Hillside of Row. The house at Row and the farmhouse, steading and horsemill at Hillside of Row were designed by J. L. Fogo, who is noted for his work on additions to the Royal and Ancient Clubhouse at St Andrews.

Rowallan Castle *East Ayrshire* Built by the Mures family in the 16th century but with later additions, Rowallan Castle is located near Kilmaurs, 3 miles (5 km) north of Kilmarnock in East Ayrshire. Subsequently held by the earls of Glasgow, earls of Loudoun and the Corbett lords Rowallan, it is now cared for by Historic Scotland.

Rowanburn *Dumfries and Galloway* A former mining village of Eskdale in Dumfries and Galloway, Rowanburn lies a mile (1.5 km) to the northeast of Canonbie. It was established in the late 19th century to house miners working in the Canonbie coalfield. To the south is the Riddings Viaduct, a nine-span railway viaduct built in 1864 for the Border Union Railway.

Rowardennan *Stirling* A locality in the Loch Lomond and the Trossachs National Park, Rowardennan lies on the east shore of Loch Lomond, nearly 10 miles (16 km) north of Balloch. Situated within the Queen Elizabeth Forest Park and Ben Lomond Memorial Park, with Ben Lomond rising to the east, Rowardennan sits on the West Highland Way and has a youth hostel, a hotel and a summer ferry link with Inverbeg on the west side of Loch Lomond.

Roxburgh *Scottish Borders* A small village in Teviotdale, Roxburgh lies to the west of the River Teviot, 3 miles (5 km) southwest of Kelso. Created a royal burgh in the early 12th century, its castle (Marchmount) was a royal residence. As a member of the Court of the Four Burghs in the 13th century, Roxburgh was regarded as the fourth most populous and important town in Scotland. The castle later passed back and forth between the Scots and the English and was eventually destroyed. James II was killed in 1460 during a siege of the castle when a cannon exploded beside him. A nearby viaduct dates from 1847 and its graveyard is the burial vault of the Kers of Chatto.

Roxburghshire A former county in the south of Scotland largely lying within the drainage basin of the River Teviot, Roxburghshire was a district of the Borders Region from 1975 to 1996. Its administrative centre was Newtown St Boswells.

Royal and Ancient Golf Club *Fife* Formed in 1754 as the Royal and Ancient Society of St Andrews Golfers for the purpose of organising an annual competition, the society changed its name to the Royal and Ancient Golf Club eight years later. In 1854, a clubhouse designed by George Rae was built on the edge of the Links in St Andrews and c.1897 the club became the governing body for the game of golf in all countries except the USA, Canada and Mexico. It has a membership of about 1800.

Royal Botanic Garden Edinburgh *City of Edinburgh* Situated in the Inverleith district of Edinburgh to the north of the New Town, the Royal Botanic Garden comprises 28 ha (70 acres) of gardens, hothouses, research laboratories, a herbarium with over two million specimens and the UK's oldest botanical library with over 100,000 volumes. The garden moved to its present location on the Inverleith Estate in 1824 and owes its origins to a 'physic garden' established in 1671 by Sir Robert Sibbald (1641–1722) and Andrew Balfour (1630–94) near Holyrood Abbey. A second garden was established at Trinity College Church, on the site of present-day Waverley Station, the two original gardens being relocated to a site on Leith Walk by Dr John Hope (1725–86) in 1763. Inverleith House, now used to house exhibitions, was not acquired until 1877. There are satellite gardens at Benmore in Argyll and Bute, Dawyck in Scottish Borders and Port Logan in Dumfries and Galloway.

Royal Deeside *Aberdeenshire* A name applied to the middle reaches of the valley of the River Dee in Aberdeenshire since the 1850s when Balmoral Castle became a favourite residence of Queen Victoria. The subsequent development of the railway into Deeside brought tourists to settlements such as Banchory, Ballater and Aboyne.

Royal Highland Centre *City of Edinburgh* The Royal Highland Centre is Scotland's largest exhibition venue and showground. Located at Ingliston, 8 miles (13 km) west of Edinburgh, it hosts a wide range of events, including trade exhibitions, rock concerts and the annual Royal Highland Show. It is the home of the Royal Highland Agricultural Society of Scotland, which was founded in 1784. The site at Ingliston was acquired by the Society in 1958.

Royal Mile, the *City of Edinburgh* Edinburgh's most famous and historic thoroughfare, which has formed the heart of the Old Town since medieval times, is known as the Royal Mile. It extends from Edinburgh Castle to the Palace of Holyroodhouse, and includes Castlehill, Lawnmarket, Canongate and Abbey Strand.

Royal Observatory of Edinburgh *City of Edinburgh* Located 3 miles (5 km) south of the centre of Edinburgh on Blackford Hill, the red sandstone Royal Observatory of Edinburgh was built in 1892–6 to a design by W. W. Robertson. It replaced the former observatory on Calton Hill, which was by then affected by pollution. A visitor centre was opened in 1981 and the University of Edinburgh's Institute for Astronomy is located here, the Astronomer Royal holding a professorship in Astronomy.

Royal Scottish Academy *City of Edinburgh* A grand neoclassical temple situated at the foot of The Mound on the south side of Edinburgh's Princes Street, the Royal Scottish Academy was built in 1826 to a design by W. H. Playfair (1789–1857). It is often confused with the National Gallery of Scotland, which is a similar building lying behind. However, the academy is in the Doric style and was completed in 1826, some 28 years before the Ionic-styled National Gallery. The building was commissioned by the Board of Manufactures, an arm of Government which at the time was responsible for public works. The building was enlarged in 1831–6 and a statue of Queen Victoria designed by Sir John Steell was later added to the frontage. Opened as the Royal Institution, it was formerly occupied by the Society of Antiquaries of Scotland (until 1890) and the Royal Society of Edinburgh (until 1909). A major refurbishment of 2001–03, the Playfair Project, provides a link with the National Gallery of Scotland and new galleries underground.

Royal Yacht Britannia, the *City of Edinburgh* Now permanently berthed at Ocean Terminal on the regenerated western side of the Port of Leith, the Royal Yacht *Britannia* was built on the Clyde in 1953. In 1997, after sailing over a million miles (1.6 million km) in the service of the royal family the ship was decommissioned in Portsmouth. Formerly crewed by 230 men and 20 officers, the yacht provided a travelling focus for British trade and diplomacy and played a leading role in some of the defining moments of recent history. Now managed by the Royal Yacht *Britannia* Trust, the ship is a major tourist attraction.

Roybridge *Highland* A small village at the head of Glen Roy, where it meets Glen Spean, Roybridge lies at the confluence of the rivers Roy and Spean in the Lochaber district of Highland Council area. Spean Bridge lies 3 miles (5 km) to the west.

Ruadh-stac Mòr *Highland* A mountain peak in Wester Ross, Ruadh-stac Mòr is the highest of the nine summits of the Beinn Eighe range. It rises to 1010 m (3313 ft) to the west of Kinlochewe.

Ruadh Stac Mòr *Highland* Rising to 918 m (3012 ft) to the east of Loch Maree in the centre of the Letterewe wilderness area in Wester Ross, Ruadh Stac Mòr is one of the most remote of Scotland's peaks. Its summit is 8 miles (13 km) north of Kinlochewe.

Ruaig *Argyll and Bute* A small village on the northeast coast of the island of Tiree in the Inner Hebrides, Ruaig lies 2 miles (3 km) southwest of Rubha Dubh headland.

Ruard, Loch *Highland* A small loch in southeast Caithness, Loch Ruard lies 8 miles (13 km) northwest of Dunbeath.

Ruathair, Loch an *Highland* A loch in eastern Sutherland, Loch an Ruathair lies in Achentoul Forest, 3 miles (5 km) north of Kinbrace.

Rubers Law *Scottish Borders* A hill in Teviotdale in Scottish Borders, Rubers Law rises to 424 m (1392 ft) 2 miles (3 km) southeast of Denholm.

Rubha Bàn *Western Isles* The larger part of an agglomeration of townships forming the main settlement on the island of Eriskay in the Outer Hebrides, Rubha Bàn lies in the northwest of the island

5 miles (8 km) south of Lochboisdale on South Uist. The Eriskay Primary School is located here, and the causeway that links with South Uist lies immediately to the east. The township of Haun is beyond and the township of Balla lies to the south.

Rubha Bocaig *Western Isles* Rubha Bocaig forms a headland on the east coast of the island of South Harris in the Western Isles. It is the most easterly point on the island and lies 3 miles (5 km) east of the settlement of Grosebay.

Rubha Dubh Tigh a Ghearraidh *Western Isles* A headland on the west coast of the island of North Uist in the Western Isles, Rubha Dubh a Tigh Ghearraidh lies to the southeast of Aird an Runair, the westernmost point on the island. The small settlement of Tigharry (Gael: *Tigh a' Ghearraidh*) lies to the southeast.

Rubha Hunish *Highland* A headland on the north coast of the isle of Skye in the Inner Hebrides, Rubha Hunish lies at the northern end of the Trotternish peninsula, 9 miles (14 km) north of Uig. The islands of Gearran, Gaeilavore and Fladda-chuain lie 3 miles (5 km) to the northwest.

Rubha Mòr *Highland* A significant peninsula in Wester Ross, Rubha Mòr lies to the northwest of Coigach, 8 miles (13 km) southwest of Lochinver. Enard Bay lies to the northeast, while Isle Ristol and the Summer Isles lie in Loch Broom to the southwest.

Rubha na Faing *Argyll and Bute* Extending into the sea on the west coast of the island of Islay, the headland of Rubha na Faing lies at the southwest end of the area known as the Rhinns of Islay, a mile (1.5 km) north of the settlement of Portnahaven.

Rubha na Faoilinn *Argyll and Bute* A headland on the southeast coast of Mull in the Inner Hebrides, Rubha na Faoilinn extends into the Firth of Lorn at the mouth of Loch Spelve.

Rubha nam Brathairean *Highland* A headland on the northeast coast of the isle of Skye in the Inner Hebrides, Rubha nam Brathairean extends into the sea at the northern end of the Sound of Raasay, 8 miles (13 km) east of Uig.

Rubha Reidh *Highland* A headland on the coast of Wester Ross, Rubha Reidh extends into the Minch, 10 miles (16 km) northwest of Poolewe.

Rubha Robhanais The Gaelic name for the Butt of Lewis in the Western Isles.

Rubislaw Quarry *Aberdeen City* Lying to the west of Aberdeen is Rubislaw Quarry, an immense void that once provided stone for the 'Granite City' as well as buildings much further afield, from public works in London to docks at Sebastopol and even a temple in Japan. The quarry forms a 142-m/465-ft-deep chasm, and is said to have produced some six million tonnes of granite over 230 years. Architects John Smith (1781–1852) and Archibald Simpson (1790–1847) used the stone to great effect in their creation of the fine buildings of Aberdeen from the early 19th century, and mineralogist Matthew Forster Heddle (1828–97) noted fine specimens of the minerals tourmaline and beryl here. Now flooded to a depth of 55 m (180 ft), the quarry was closed in 1970.

Ruchill *Glasgow City* A northern suburb of Glasgow, Ruchill lies 2 miles (3 km) north of the city centre to the west of Possilpark. Ruchill Park, opened in 1892, lies adjacent to a hospital, now closed and partially demolished, that was established in 1900 as Glasgow's second fever hospital. An artificial hill in the park was created from 24,000 cartloads of material excavated during the building of the hospital and given the name 'Ben Whitton' after the director of parks at that time.

Ruchill, Water of *Perth and Kinross* Formed by the merging of streams in southwest Perth and Kinross, the Water of Ruchill flows northeast through Glen Artney to join the River Earn at Comrie.

Ruddons Point *Fife* A headland on the south coast of Fife, Ruddons Point extends into the Firth of Forth to the east of Largo Bay, 2 miles (3 km) west of Earlsferry.

Ruel, River *Argyll and Bute* A river on the Cowal peninsula, the Ruel flows south through Glendaruel for 9 miles (14 km), passing the settlements of Clachan of Glendaruel and Ormsdale before emptying into marshland at the head of Loch Riddon.

Rueval *Western Isles* A hill at the northern end of the island of South Uist in the Outer Hebrides, Rueval (Gael: *Ruabhal*) is also known as The Hill of Miracles. On its summit stands the 9-m (30-ft) granite statue of Our Lady of the Isles designed by Hew Lorimer and erected in 1957.

Ruisgarry An alternative name for Rushgarry in the Western Isles.

Ruisigearraidh The Gaelic name for Rushgarry in the Western Isles.

Rule Water *Scottish Borders* A river in Scottish Borders, the Rule Water flows north from Bonchester Bridge to join the River Teviot, 4 miles (6.5 km) west of Jedburgh.

Rullion Green *Midlothian* A locality on the slopes of Carnethy Hill on the eastern edge of the Pentland Hills, a mile (1.5 km) northwest of Penicuik, Rullion Green was the scene of a battle in 1666 at which a force of Covenanters were defeated by General Sir Thomas Dalyell (1615–85).

Rum *Highland* The largest of the Small Isles in the Inner Hebrides, Rum (also Rhum) lies to the south of the isle of Skye between Canna to the northwest and Eigg to the southeast. It is a mountainous, diamond-shaped island with an area of 10,826 ha (26,740 acres) and rises to 812 m (2663 ft) at Askival in a range called the Cuillin. Predominantly composed of red Torridonian sandstone, the island is fringed with sea cliffs. Small areas of arable land exist near the settlements of Kilmory, Kinloch and Harris. The island has been inhabited since 7000 BC and was held by the Norse until 1266. Later held by the Macleans, 300 of the islanders were persuaded to emigrate to Canada and the United States to make way for sheep farming in the 19th century. In 1888, Rum was purchased by John Bullough of Oswaldtwistle, a Lancastrian MP who used the island as a holiday retreat. His son, George Bullough, built Kinloch Castle on the east side of the island and a Greek-style mausoleum at Harris on the southwest coastline. The castle featured in the BBC series *Restoration* in 2003. Now managed by Scottish Natural Heritage, Rum was designated a National Nature Reserve in 1957. There are anchorages at Kilmory Bay, Loch Scresort and Camas na h-Atha.

Rumble, the *Shetland* A rocky outlier in the Shetland Islands, the Rumble lies off the east coast of the island of Whalsay, 3 miles (5 km) east of Clett Head.

Rumbling Bridge *Clackmannanshire* A hamlet in Clackmannanshire, Rumbling Bridge is situated 4 miles (6.5 km) east of Dollar close to a spectacular gorge of the River Devon. The river at this point descends in a series of waterfalls through a deep and narrow gorge, the best known of which are the Devil's Mill and the Cauldron Linn. The river is crossed by two bridges built one above the other. The lower of the two bridges, 24.3 m (80 ft) above the bed of the river, was built in 1713. A later crossing was built 36.5 m (120 ft) above the Devon in 1816. There are footpaths with viewpoints through the gorge linking with Crook of Devon to the east.

Rumbling Bridge *Perth and Kinross* A locality in Strath Braan, central Perth and Kinross, Rumbling Bridge is situated by a deep gorge on the River Braan, 2 miles (3 km) southwest of Dunkeld.

Rumford *Falkirk* A settlement in Falkirk Council area, Rumford is situated to the south of Brightons, Polmont and the Union Canal.

Rumsdale Water *Highland* A river of Caithness, the Rumsdale Water rises on Cnoc Cromuillt and flows generally east to join the River Thurso at Dalganachan, 4 miles (6.5 km) southwest of Loch More.

Rumster *Highland* An area of forest land in eastern Caithness, Rumster lies to the northwest of Lybster, between the Reisgill Burn and the A9 to Thurso.

Rushgarry *Western Isles* A scattered settlement in the northeast of the island of Berneray in the Outer Hebrides, Rushgarry (also *Ruisgarry*, Gael: *Ruisigearraidh*) lies a mile (1.5 km) northeast of Borve and 8 miles (13 km) north of Lochmaddy on North Uist. Berneray harbour lies just to the south.

Rusk Holm *Orkney* A small uninhabited island in Rapness Sound in the Orkney Islands, Rusk Holm lies midway between the headland of Fers Ness at the northern corner of the island of Eday to the southeast and the Point of Huro at the southern tip of Westray to the northwest.

Ruskie *Stirling* A locality on the northern edge of Flanders Moss in Stirling Council area, Ruskie lies midway between Thornhill in the east and Port of Menteith in the west. Loch Rusky lies a mile (1.5 km) to the northwest on the edge of Torrie Forest.

Rusko *Dumfries and Galloway* A small village of Dumfries and Galloway, Rusko lies in the valley of the Little Water of Fleet, 2 miles (3 km) northwest of Gatehouse of Fleet.

Russa Ness *Shetland* A headland of the Shetland Mainland, Russa Ness is steep in aspect and lies on the western side of the entrance to Weisdale Voe, 7 miles (11 km) northwest of Lerwick.

Rutherford *Scottish Borders* A small village in the Teviotdale district of Scottish Borders, Rutherford lies to the south of the River Tweed, 6 miles (10 km) southwest of Kelso.

Rutherglen *South Lanarkshire* A settlement forming a southeastern suburb of the greater Glasgow conurbation, Rutherglen lies to the south of the River Clyde, 2 miles (3 km) east of the city centre and northwest of Cambuslang. Chartered in 1126 as one of the first of Scotland's royal burghs, Rutherglen developed as an important trading centre at the head of navigation. By the late 13th century it was overshadowed by Glasgow but was known for its horse fairs. It later developed in association with mining, weaving, shipbuilding, soap making and the manufacture of steel. Modern industries include milk bottling and the manufacture of household products, duvets, glassware and ceramics. It was here, suggests the chronicler Blind Harry, that Sir John Menteith agreed to betray William Wallace (*c*.1272–1305), and where the Scottish Parliament met in 1300. On 29 May 1679, the Declaration of Rutherglen was read out here by a band of armed Covenanters. Three days later they defeated John Graham of Claverhouse at the Battle of Drumclog. Rutherglen was incorporated into Glasgow in 1975 but became part of South Lanarkshire in 1996. Notable buildings include the ruined parish church of St Mary and Rutherglen Town Hall, built in 1862 to a design by Charles Wilson.

Ruthrie, Linn of *Moray* A cascade on the Aberlour Burn, the Linn of Ruthrie is located a mile (1.5 km) south of the village of Charlestown of Aberlour.

Ruthven *Angus* A hamlet in an Angus parish of the same name, Ruthven lies near the junction of the Burn of Alyth with the River Isla, just over 2 miles (3 km) north of Meigle. Ruthven House to the southeast stands near the site of Ruthven Castle, which was a stronghold of the Lindsay earls of Crawford.

Ruthven, Loch *Highland* A loch to the east of Loch Ness in the Inverness district of Highland Council area, Loch Ruthven lies 4 miles (6.5 km) south of Dores between Loch Duntelchaig and Loch a' Choire to the north and Loch Mhòr to the southwest.

Ruthven Barracks *Highland* The ruined remains of Ruthven Barracks in Badenoch and Strathspey stand on a mound to the east of the River Spey, a mile (1.5 km) south of Kingussie. Completed in 1721 as one of a network of military barracks built by the government to maintain control over the Jacobite population of the Highlands, Ruthven Barracks stands on the site of the ancient Ruthven Castle. It housed a garrison of 120 troops in two barrack blocks with stabling for 28 horses and lay at the meeting point of three military roads built by General Wade. In February 1746, the garrison fell to Jacobite troops, and on 17 April 1746, the day after the defeat of the Jacobite army at the Battle of Culloden, 2000 Highlanders gathered here intending to battle on. However, after a message from Bonnie Prince Charlie was relayed to the troops to 'save themselves as best they could', the Jacobites set fire to the barracks before dispersing.

Ruthvenfield *Perth and Kinross* An 18th-century textile village in Perth and Kinross, Ruthvenfield lies to the south of the River Almond, 2 miles (3 km) northwest of Perth city centre. Ruthven House to the north was built *c*.1800. Close by are the Huntingtower Bleachworks (1866) and 15th-century Huntingtower, a former stronghold of the Ruthven family.

Ruthven Water *Perth and Kinross* A river of southern Perth and Kinross, the Ruthven Water rises in Glen Eagles and flows north for 9 miles (15 km) to join the River Earn just north of the village of Aberuthven.

Ruthwell *Dumfries and Galloway* An agricultural settlement near the Solway coast of Dumfries and Galloway, Ruthwell lies 10 miles (14 km) southeast of Dumfries. The world's first commercial savings bank was established here by Dr Henry Duncan in 1810. Inside Ruthwell Parish Church can be found the Ruthwell Cross, one of the best examples in Scotland of an Anglican sculptured cross from the 8th century AD.

Ryan, Loch *South Ayrshire/Dumfries and Galloway* A sea loch of southwest Scotland providing a natural sheltered anchorage, Loch Ryan lies between the northern arm of the Rhinns of Galloway and that part of the South Ayrshire and Dumfries and Galloway coast stretching from

Finnarts Point southwards past Cairnryan to Stranraer, which is one of the main ferry ports linking Scotland with Larne and Belfast in Northern Ireland. The loch extends just over 8 miles (13 km) from north to south and measures nearly 3 miles (5 km) at its maximum width. A sandbank called the Scar runs down the west side of the loch opposite Kirkcolm, and on its eastern shore is a small headland called Cairn Point, on which stands Cairnryan. Loch Ryan lighthouse was erected on this point in 1847.

Rye Water *North Ayrshire* A river of North Ayrshire, the Rye Water rises in Camphill Reservoir to the west of Kilbirnie and flows south to merge with the River Garnock at Dalry.

Rysa Little *Orkney* An uninhabited island in the Orkney Islands, Rysa Little lies to the east of Hoy, from which it is separated by Rysa Sound.

Sacquoy Head *Orkney* A headland in the northwest corner of the Orkney island of Rousay, Sacquoy Head extends into the Westray Firth at the northernmost tip of the island.

Saddell *Argyll and Bute* A settlement on the east coast of the Kintyre peninsula, Saddell lies 5 miles (8 km) south of Carradale and 8 miles (13 km) north of Campbeltown on Saddell Bay, an inlet of the Kilbrannan Sound that receives the Saddell Water. There are the remains of a Cistercian abbey founded in 1160 by Somerled, whose descendants were MacDonald Lords of the Isles. The community was noted in medieval times for its stone carving, some of which features in the grounds of the abbey. The castle at Saddell, built in 1508 by the Bishop of Argyll, was later a stronghold of the Clan Donald.

Saddell Water *Argyll and Bute* Formed at the meeting of the Guesdale Water and the Ifferdale Burn on the Kintyre peninsula, the Saddell Water flows southeastwards for 2 miles (3 km) to the village of Saddell, where it empties into Saddell Bay, an inlet of the Kilbrannan Sound.

Saddle, the *Highland* A mountain straddling the Lochaber and Lochalsh districts of Highland Council area, the Saddle rises to 1010 m (3313 ft) 4 miles (6.5 km) to the south of Shiel Bridge.

Saddle Yoke *Dumfries and Galloway* A summit in the Moffat Hills, Saddle Yoke rises to 735 m (2411 ft) to the east of Hart Fell and the Blackhope Burn, 5 miles (8 km) northeast of Moffat.

Saighdinis The Gaelic name for Sidinish in the Western Isles.

Sàil Chaorainn *Highland* A summit in Glen Affric Forest, Sàil Chaorainn rises to 1002 m (3287 ft) to the north of Loch Cluanie and 4 miles (6.5 km) south of the head of Loch Affric.

Saileag *Highland* One of the Five Sisters of Kintail, Saileag rises to 956 m (3136 ft) to the north of Glen Shiel.

Sailfoot Burn *Dumfries and Galloway* A small stream in northern Dumfries and Galloway, the Sailfoot Burn rises on Sailfoot Law, 4 miles (6.5 km) northeast of Moffat. It flows down to the Moffat Water, running parallel to the Sailfoot Linn to the north.

Sàil Mhòr *Highland* One of the peaks of Beinn Eighe in Wester Ross, Sàil Mhòr rises to 981 m (3218 ft) between Loch Maree and Glen Torridon.

Sàil Mhòr *Highland* A mountain of Wester Ross, Sàil Mhòr rises to 767 m (2516 ft) to the south of Little Loch Broom and west of Dundonnell.

Sailm, Loch na *Argyll and Bute* Loch na Sailm is one of a series of small inland lochs located a mile (1.5 km) northeast of the settlement of Kilmelford in Argyll and Bute.

St Abbs *Scottish Borders* A picturesque resort and fishing village on the Berwickshire coast of Scottish Borders, St Abbs lies 3 miles (5 km) northeast of Eyemouth. Clear waters offshore make it a centre for underwater diving, and stunning cliffs to the north at St Abb's Head form part of a 77-ha (190-acre) nature reserve designated in 1983 to protect a large colony of nesting sea birds. The offshore waters form part of Scotland's first marine nature reserve. A nunnery was founded at St Abbs in the 7th century by St Ebba (or Ebbe), daughter of Ethelfred, and local buildings of interest include a lighthouse built c.1861 by the Stevensons, a 14th-century chapel at Kirk Hill, and Renton House, an early Georgian mansion. Fast Castle, situated on a cliff top 3 miles (5 km) northwest, was the meeting place of the Gowrie conspirators who plotted against James VI. This location was described as the keep of Wolf's Crag in Sir Walter Scott's novel *The Bride of Lammermoor* (1819). The castle was destroyed in 1515 and rebuilt six years later; it had a drawbridge over a chasm 7.3 m (24 ft) wide.

St Andrew Square *City of Edinburgh* An elegant Georgian square in the New Town of Edinburgh, St Andrew Square (often St Andrew's Square) lies at the east end of George Street. It mirrors Charlotte Square at the western end of James Craig's planned New Town and dates from 1768. The intention had been to erect St Andrew's Church on its east side with a view along George Street to its twin, St George's Church, on Charlotte Square which was laid out in 1792. However, Sir Lawrence Dundas, a wealthy businessman, preferred the site for his home and bought the ground before Craig's plan could be implemented. St Andrew's Church was eventually built on George Street, and its place on St Andrew Square was taken by Dundas House which was built by Sir William Chambers (1723–96). This building is the headquarters of the Royal Bank of Scotland. The former headquarters of the British Linen Bank and the National Bank of Scotland were both in St Andrew Square, which is now largely occupied by financial institutions. In the centre of the square is a monument erected to the memory of Henry Dundas, 1st Viscount Melville (1742–1811). Famous residents of St Andrew Square have included philosopher David Hume (1711–76), who lived at No. 8, and politician and inventor Henry Brougham (1778–1868), who lived at No. 21. No. 35 was built by Robert Adam (1728–92) and is the oldest house in the square. This building was subsequently the Douglas Hotel, which was patronised by Sir Walter Scott, Queen Victoria and Empress Eugenie, wife of Napoleon III, while she consulted the surgeon Sir James Simpson. To the east of the square is Edinburgh's principal bus station and a major shopping complex.

St Andrew's House *City of Edinburgh* An Art Deco-style building on Regent Road, Edinburgh, St Andrew's House is the principal office of the Scottish Executive. It was built in 1939 to a design by Thomas Tait and until 1999 housed the Scottish Office. To the rear of St Andrew's House, next to the Old Calton Burial Ground, is the Governor's House, a turreted structure that was part of the former municipal prison.

St Andrew's Suspension Bridge *Glasgow City* A

footbridge in Glasgow, the St Andrew's Suspension Bridge crosses the River Clyde at Bridgeton. It was built in 1856 to a design by the engineer Neil Robinson and was intended to replace the ferry that transported workers from their homes on the south side of the Clyde to their work in Calton and Bridgeton. Its most striking features are the Corinthian columns that stand approximately 6 m (20 ft) high.

St Andrews *Fife* The ancient university city of St Andrews, once the ecclesiastical capital of Scotland and now a golfing and tourist mecca, lies at the eastern extremity of the Fife peninsula where the North Sea coastline is characterised by sweeping sandy bays on either side of a rocky headland. The city grew from a small religious settlement founded on the headland of Kinrimund ('Head of the King's Mount') where, *c.* AD 345, St Rule is said to have landed with the bones of St Andrew, the patron saint of Scotland. By the mid-8th century the site had become a place of pilgrimage and Scotland's leading religious centre. In the 12th century a cathedral was built, in 1411 a university was founded and in the 15th century Pope Sixtus IV erected the see of St Andrews into an archbishopric. St Andrews University, the oldest in Scotland, was quickly recognised as one of the leading universities of Europe, and by the late Middle Ages had three endowed colleges: St Salvator's (North Street), founded in 1450; St Mary's (South Street), founded in 1537; and St Leonard's, founded in 1512. Bishop James Kennedy, who built St Salvator's collegiate church (1450–60), and his niece Katherine have been remembered since 1849 in an end-of-term student rag known as the Kate Kennedy Pageant. St Andrews was the first university to enrol women (1862), the first to have a students' union and the first to have a marine laboratory (1882). Among its famous graduates have been the 15th–16th-century poets William Dunbar and Sir David Lindsay of the Mount, James Graham, Marquess of Montrose (1612–50), and John Napier of Merchiston (1550–1617), the inventor of logarithms. Its rectors have included Andrew Carnegie, Sir James Barrie and the explorer Fridjof Nansen; one of its principals, Sir David Brewster, invented the kaleidoscope in 1817 and went on to play an important part in the development of photography. First granted a royal charter c.1140 by David I, the town developed as a centre of trade, its merchant burgesses building for themselves fine houses with elegant forestairs, crow-stepped gables and pantiled roofs. In the post-Reformation years of the 17th and 18th centuries, prosperity declined and the castle and cathedral fell into ruin. But with the development of fishing, agriculture and tourism in the 19th century, the town's harbour once more came alive with herring boats, ships exporting coal and iron, as well as grain and potatoes, and ferries linking St Andrews with ports such as Dundee and Leith. St Andrews is internationally famous as the 'home of golf' and the frequent venue of championship events. The game has been played here at least since 1553, when the archbishop allowed its townsfolk to play golf and other games on the links, and in 1754 the Royal and Ancient Society of St Andrews Golfers was set up to organise an annual competition. There are now five 18-hole courses (Old, New, Strathtyrum, Jubilee and Eden) and one nine-hole course (Balgove), as well as many golf shops, manufacturers of golf clubs and a British Golf Museum. Other places of interest include the remains of the medieval castle, cathedral, city wall and Black Friars Monastery, the Church of the Holy Trinity, St Andrews Museum in Kilburn House (1855), St Andrews Preservation Trust Museum (North Street), St Andrews Aquarium and St Andrews Botanic Garden, which was established in 1889 by Dr John Wilson and moved to its present site in 1960. The older part of St Andrews rests on the beach of a former shoreline some 23 m (70 ft) above the present mean sea level, and at the North Haugh the newer university buildings stand on a lower raised beach eroded by the sea. Between the West Sands and East Sands, which look onto the North Sea, are sandstone, mudstone and limestone cliffs with some coal seams. The earldom of St Andrews is a royal title held by the eldest son of the Duke of Kent.

St Ann's *Dumfries and Galloway* A settlement in Dumfries and Galloway, St Ann's lies on the Kinnel Water, 14 miles (22 km) northeast of Dumfries.

St Anthony's Chapel *City of Edinburgh* The remains of St Anthony's Chapel overlook St Margaret's Loch on the north side of Arthur's Seat in Holyrood Park. Thought to date from the mid-15th century, the chapel is said to be associated with the Knights Hospitallers of St Anthony of Leith and was positioned so that they could see ships arriving in the Firth of Forth and welcome them with a light in the tower.

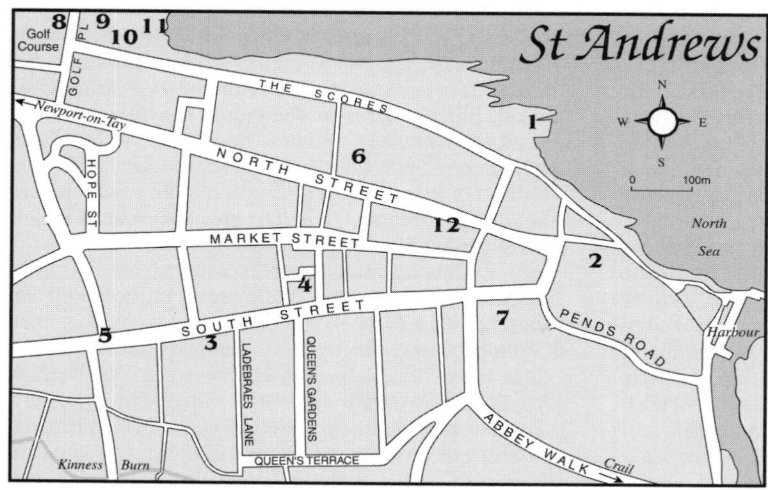

1 *St Andrews Castle*
2 *St Andrews Cathedral and St Rule's Tower*
3 *Blackfriars Chapel*
4 *Holy Trinity Church*
5 *West Port*
6 *College of St Salvator*
7 *College of St Leonard*
8 *Royal and Ancient Club House*
9 *British Golf Museum*
10 *Martyrs Monument*
11 *Sea Life Centre*
12 *St Andrews Preservation Trust Museum*

St Boswells *Scottish Borders Pop: 1128* A village of Roxburghshire in Scottish Borders, St Boswells lies on the River Tweed opposite Dryburgh Abbey, 3 miles (5 km) southeast of Melrose. Once known as Lessuden and possibly named after St Bosiel, the village is noted for its former cattle and wool markets and for its 16-ha (40-acre) green, which is the largest in Scotland. Notable buildings include the early-19th-century pink sandstone kennels of the Buccleuch Hunt, the sandstone villas of the Croft (1870s), Braeheads House (c.1908) by F. William Deas, and 17th-century Lessuden House, the family home of the Scotts of Raeburn. A chain suspension bridge, the first in Britain, was erected over the Tweed near Mertoun in 1817. Hiltonshill to the south was the birthplace in 1844 of the physician Thomas Brunton, author of one of the first extensive works on pharmacology.

St Catherines *Argyll and Bute* A small settlement on the east shore of Loch Fyne, St Catherines lies 5 miles (8 km) north of Strachur, opposite Inveraray. A passenger ferry service operated from here until the 1960s.

St Catherines Wells *Aberdeenshire* A locality in the Buchan district of Aberdeenshire, St Catherines Wells lies in the valley of the Gonar Burn, 2 miles (3 km) northwest of New Pitsligo.

St Combs *Aberdeenshire* A dormitory village on 'the outermost edge of Buchan' in Aberdeenshire, St Combs lies on the North Sea coast, 4 miles (6.5 km) southeast of Fraserburgh. Associated with the ancient church of St Columba or Colm, it developed as a fishing village in the 18th century, replacing the old Fishtown of Corskelly.

St Cuthbert's Church *City of Edinburgh* A church at the west end of Princes Street Gardens in Edinburgh, St Cuthbert's Church lies behind St John's Episcopal Church and is accessed from Lothian Road. Also known as the West Kirk, the present building was erected 1892–5 to a design by Hippolyte J. Blanc. This building stands on the site of earlier church foundations possibly dating back to the 8th century. The interior of the church, which was subject to restoration in 1990, is notable for its sumptuous furnishings and decoration. Of particular interest is a representation of *David and Goliath* in stained glass by Tiffany of New York and a monument to John Napier (1550–1617), the inventor of logarithms. Poet Thomas De Quincey (1785–1859), artist Alexander Nasmyth (1758–1840) and George Kemp (1795–1844), designer of the Scott Monument, lie buried in the graveyard.

St Cuthbert's Way *Scottish Borders* A long-distance walk linking Melrose in Scottish Borders with Lindisfarne in Northumberland, St Cuthbert's Way follows a 62-mile (99-km) route over the Eildon Hills and along the Roman Dere Street. St Cuthbert was a prior of Lindisfarne who spent his early days in Melrose during the mid-7th century.

St Cyrus *Aberdeenshire* Formerly known as Ecclesgreig, the village of St Cyrus in southeast Aberdeenshire lies close to the North Sea coast, 4 miles (6.5 km) north of Montrose. Its earlier name is linked to a chapel last used in 1632 that once stood on the site of the Nether Kirkyard to the south of the village. A centre for agriculture, arts and crafts, St Cyrus is also associated with salmon fishing, the salmon moving along this part of the coast on their way towards the mouth of the River North Esk. St Cyrus National Nature Reserve, which lies between the village and the sea, protects beach, dune, grassland and cliff environments, and includes a breeding area for tern immediately south of a visitor centre that is the main access to the reserve.

St David's *Perth and Kinross* A small linear hamlet in Madderty parish, central Perth and Kinross, St David's lies 4 miles (6.5 km) north of Auchterarder.

St David's Harbour *Fife* A modern residential housing development on the Firth of Forth between Inverkeithing and Dalgety Bay, St David's Harbour was largely developed for commuters in the 1990s. The original harbour was built in 1752 by Sir Robert Henderson as an outlet for coal brought by rail from mines at Fordell. Originally, horse-drawn wagons ran on wooden rails, although by 1870 steam trains were operating on the line. The railway was closed in 1946. Today there is an adjacent business park and residential development at St David's Bay.

St Enoch Square *Glasgow City* Located in central Glasgow, St Enoch Square lies between the River Clyde and Argyle Street. Created in 1783 and originally used for grazing sheep, the St Enoch Railway Station was erected on the site in 1876. Closed in 1974, the site was developed for retail, with the St Enoch Shopping Centre, Europe's largest glass-covered shopping centre, opening in 1990. St Enoch Underground Station was built in 1896 by James Miller.

St Fergus *Aberdeenshire* A village in the Buchan district of Aberdeenshire, St Fergus lies a mile (1.5 km) from the North Sea coast and 3 miles (5 km) northwest of Peterhead. It comprises an old Kirktown to the west and a Newtown to the east, and takes its name from an Irish bishop who built a basilica here in the early 8th century. Since 1977 St Fergus has been one of the most important terminals handling gas from the Frigg Field in the North Sea.

St Fillans *Perth and Kinross* A village at the eastern end of Loch Earn in Perth and Kinross, St Fillans is situated 4 miles (6.5 km) west of Comrie on the A85. Now a tourist and boating centre, it was in the 18th century a small clachan known as Port of Lochearn or Meikleport. In 1817 it was renamed St Fillans by Lord Gwydyr, the husband of Clementina Drummond, heiress to the Drummond Estate. The pre-Reformation church (St Fillan's Chapel), whose kirkyard is the traditional burial place of the Stewarts of Ardvorlich, lies to the south of the River Earn, between St Fillans and Dundurn (also St Fillan's Hill or Dunfillan), on top of which is an Iron Age hillfort. It is said that the Irish missionary St Fillan lived on this hill. Not far from the foot of the hill is a stream called Allt Ghoinean, which is claimed to be the Gonan or Monan of Sir Walter Scott's poem *The Lady of the Lake* (1810): 'The stag at eve had drunk his fill, where danced the moon on Monan's rill.' The golf course at St Fillans was created in 1903 by Willie Auchterlonie. To the east of the village is a natural rock known as The Crocodile. Painted in bright colours and formerly known as the Pig Rock, it is said to lie on a ley line.

St Fillan's Cave *Fife* A cave in the sandstone cliff face at Pittenweem ('the place of the cave') in the East Neuk of Fife, St Fillan's Cave is associated with St Fillan, an early Christian missionary from Ireland whose bell and crozier are still preserved in the Royal Museum of Scotland in Edinburgh. It was perhaps one of these relics that was carried by the abbot of Inchaffray into the Battle of Bannockburn (1314), after which the Scots attributed their victory to the support of St Fillan. Many miracles of healing were attributed to the saint and to holy wells associated with him. One of these wells is to be found within the cave, which was rededicated as a shrine in 1935 by the bishop of St Andrews and is still a place of worship.

St Giles' Kirk *City of Edinburgh* Situated on the Royal Mile in the Old Town of Edinburgh, St Giles' Kirk (or Cathedral) was built by Alexander I in 1120 and much restored by William Burn in the 19th century. In 1560 the Protestant reformer John Knox was appointed minister of the kirk, which today contains the tomb of James Graham, 1st Marquess of Montrose, and memorials to Robert Burns (1759–96) and Robert Louis Stevenson (1850–94). Within the cathedral is the Thistle Chapel, created in 1911 by Robert Lorimer for the Most Ancient and Most Noble Order of the Thistle, Scotland's foremost order of chivalry. Founded by James VII in 1687, the order comprises the monarch and 16 knights.

St John's Church *City of Edinburgh* Located at the west end of Princes Street, Edinburgh, St John's Episcopal Church was built in high neo-Gothic style in 1816–18 to a design by William Burn. Its interior is modelled on St George's Chapel, Windsor, and in its churchyard are buried the artist Sir Henry Raeburn (1756–1823), Sir Walter Scott's mother and James Donaldson, founder of Donaldson's School.

St John's Town of Dalry *Dumfries and Galloway* A village in The Glenkens district of Dumfries and Galloway, St John's Town of Dalry overlooks the Water of Ken, 3 miles (5 km) north of New Galloway. Situated on an old pilgrimage route and named after the Knights of St John, a medieval settlement here was extended and developed as a planned village from the late 18th century by the Earl of Galloway. Its Town Hall dates from 1859. The Southern Upland Way passes through the churchyard of the Gothic-style Dalry Parish Church which was built 1830–2. Two miles (3 km) to the north, on the east side of Earlstoun Loch, stands Earlstoun Castle, a former stronghold of the Gordons of Earlstoun.

St Kilda *Western Isles* A remote island group in the Atlantic, St Kilda comprises the main island of Hirta together with Dun, Soay and Boreray, all lying 40 miles (64 km) west of North Uist in the Outer Hebrides and 100 miles (160 km) from the Scottish mainland. This volcanic archipelago offers spectacular landscapes and some of the highest cliffs in Europe, providing a refuge for colonies of nesting sea birds. Declared a National Nature Reserve (1957), a Site of Special Scientific Interest (1981), a Biosphere Reserve (1976), a World Heritage Site (1986) and a Special Protection Area (1992), the islands support their own sub-species of woodmouse and wren, together with the world's largest gannet colony, largest British colony of fulmars and half of Britain's puffins. The islands have a great wealth of archaeology, including evidence of Bronze Age and Viking settlement. Thought to have been occupied continuously for 2000 years, St Kilda's population was finally evacuated in 1930 from the main settlement at Village Bay. Owned by the Macleods of Macleod for over 800 years, St Kilda was acquired by the National Trust for Scotland in 1957. Managed by Scottish Natural Heritage, a small part of Hirta is leased by the Ministry of Defence, which operates a radar station.

St Machar's Cathedral *Aberdeen City* Named after a disciple of St Columba, St Machar's Cathedral in Old Aberdeen was said to have been founded on a spot where a river, as it approached the sea, described the curve of a bishop's crozier. Extensive restoration was undertaken in the 14th and 15th centuries, William Elphinstone, Bishop of Aberdeen (1431–1514), eventually completing the central tower which later collapsed in 1688. The ceiling of panelled oak bears 48 heraldic shields placed there in 1520 by Bishop Gavin Dunbar. The font was sculpted by Hew Lorimer in 1953 and the organ, by Henry Willis, was installed in 1891.

St Madoes *Perth and Kinross* A parish at the western end of the Carse of Gowrie, Perth and Kinross, St Madoes lies due east of Perth opposite the confluence of the rivers Earn and Tay. Its parish church (1799) is dedicated to a 4th-century French missionary called Madoch. The Pictish cross-slab originally located in the kirkyard is now in Perth Museum.

St Magnus Cathedral *Orkney* The Cathedral of St Magnus in Kirkwall on Mainland Orkney is the most northerly and one of the smallest cathedrals in Britain. Built in the Romanesque style, work began in 1137 following a vow made by Earl Rognvald, while the islands were still ruled by Norway. It is one of the finest examples of polychrome stonework, with red and yellow locally quarried sandstone used together in the doorways. The cathedral is dedicated to Magnus, Earl of Orkney, who was canonised in 1135. Inside the cathedral are a number of interesting tombstones moved inside from the graveyard, a memorial to the men who died when the HMS *Royal Oak* was torpedoed and sunk in Scapa Flow in 1939 and the neo-Gothic tomb of Arctic explorer John Rae (1813–93). Unusually, the cathedral includes a dungeon.

St Margaret's Cave *Fife* A cave in the centre of Dunfermline, St Margaret's Cave is associated with Queen Margaret who came to meditate and pray here in the 11th century. Located near the Glen Bridge Car Park, it is one of Scotland's holy shrines.

St Margaret's Chapel *City of Edinburgh* Located at the very centre of Edinburgh Castle and at the highest point of Castle Rock is a tiny Norman chapel dedicated to St Margaret (1045–93), wife of Malcolm III (*c.*1031–93). The chapel was most likely completed between 1110 and 1120 by her youngest son, David I, but there is some evidence that it was built on top of an earlier chapel in which Margaret herself may have worshipped. St Margaret's Chapel measures only 5 m by 3 m (17 ft by 11 ft), with a simple nave separated by a distinctly Norman arch from a stone-vaulted semicircular apse. The chapel survived many attacks on the castle but was altered in the 17th century for use as a gunpowder store. In 1845, the antiquarian Sir Daniel Wilson rediscovered the chapel, and it was restored on the orders of Queen Victoria in 1853. Further restoration work was undertaken in 1886 by the French architect Hippolyte J. Blanc. Stained-glass windows portraying Saints Andrew, Columba, Margaret and Ninian, together with patriot William Wallace, were inserted in 1922. The chapel was rededicated in 1934 and a new doorway created on the north side five years later. Today the simply decorated chapel is still in use and members of the castle garrison have the right to be married in it.

St Margaret's Hope *Fife* A sheltered bay to the west of North Queensferry on the Fife coast of the Firth of Forth, St Margaret's Hope is said to be the place where Margaret, queen of Malcolm III, landed when she first came to Scotland in the 11th century. The bay forms a natural deep-water harbour within which the Rosyth dockyard and naval base were developed from 1909.

St Margaret's Hope *Orkney* A picturesque village at the northern end of the island of South Ronaldsay in the Orkney Islands, St Margaret's Hope looks out onto a bay that forms an inlet of Water Sound. A former fishing station and landing place for boats from mainland Scotland, it takes its name from the Maid of Norway who died here in 1290. In addition to a school and post office, the village has craft shops and a museum featuring wireless history since the 1930s.

St Margaret's Well *City of Edinburgh* A late-medieval well with a vaulted chamber, St Margaret's Well is situated in Holyrood Park, Edinburgh, in the shadow of Salisbury Crags. The well was originally located at Jock's Lodge and was moved stone by stone in 1859 to allow the St Margaret's Workshops to be extended for the North British Railway Company. The workshops were subsequently replaced by St Margaret's House, a government office, but the original site of the well is marked by a monument in the form of a boulder.

St Martin's *Perth and Kinross* A hamlet in a parish of the same name in Perth and Kinross, St Martin's lies between the River Tay and the Sidlaw Hills, 5 miles (8 km) northeast of Perth. Balbeggie and Guildtown are the largest settlements in the parish, which is said to take its name from St Martin of Tours. The parish church was rebuilt 1791–3 and again in 1842. Edinburgh lawyer William Farquharson McDonald built the classical-style St Martin's Abbey to the east, with the adjoining chapel added in 1843. Plans to extend the building in the style of a French chateau in the 1860s were never executed.

St Martin's Church *East Lothian* The late 12th-century church of St Martin lies on the eastern outskirts of Haddington. Thought to be one of the oldest surviving churches in Scotland, St Martin's was originally part of a Cistercian abbey founded in 1178 by Ada, daughter-in-law of David I. Although nothing of the abbey itself remains, the ruined nave of St Martin's Church can still be found on the edge of Nungate.

St Mary's *Orkney* A township at the southern tip of the eastern section of Mainland Orkney, St Mary's lies 6 miles (10 km) south of Kirkwall, at the northern end of the Churchill Barriers, which link the mainland with Burray and South Ronaldsay.

St Mary's Collegiate Church *East Lothian* Located to the southeast of the centre of Haddington, on the west bank of the River Tyne, St Mary's Collegiate Church is the longest parish church in Scotland. Construction, which began in the late 14th century, was completed in 1462, the church being consecrated around 1400. St Mary's was one of three great pre-Reformation churches in the Lothians, the others being St Giles' in Edinburgh and St Michael's in Linlithgow. It was known as 'The Lamp of Lothian', such was its beauty and spiritual significance. The church was badly damaged during the siege of Haddington (1548–9) but at the request of John Knox, a native of the town, the nave was restored and used as the parish church for 400 years, while the choir and transepts remained open to the elements. A major restoration in the 1970s returned the church to its former glory. Today the church maintains a tradition of ecumenicalism, exemplified by the Lauderdale Aisle, an Episcopal chapel within the church, with strong Roman Catholic and Orthodox influences. This is the burial place of the earls and duke of Lauderdale. The Lammermuir pipe organ, built locally at Oldhamstocks, was installed in 1990, and new bells from Dunnecht House near Aberdeen were installed in 1999, replacing those removed by the English army in 1548.

St Mary's Episcopal Cathedral *City of Edinburgh* A neo-Gothic building in Palmerston Place at the west end of the New Town of Edinburgh, St Mary's Episcopal Cathedral is said to be the largest church constructed in Scotland since the Reformation. Built by Sir George Gilbert Scott in 1879, it is topped by enormous twin towers in the west and a central tower in the east that rises to 84 m (275 ft). The church, which has a Father Willis organ, is a member of the Anglican communion.

St Mary's Isle *Dumfries and Galloway* A narrow peninsula 2 miles (3 km) southwest of Kirkcudbright in Dumfries and Galloway, St Mary's Isle separates Manxman's Lake to the east from Goat Well Bay to the west. To the west, the River Dee flows out into Kirkcudbright Bay.

St Mary's Loch *Scottish Borders* A loch in the Ettrick district of Scottish Borders, St Mary's Loch lies midway between Selkirk and Moffat. It receives eight streams including the Megget Water and Kirkstead Burn. The River Yarrow issues from its northern end, and Tibbie Shiels Inn and the Loch of the Lowes lie at the southern end of the loch. The loch is 3 miles (5 km) long and a half-mile (1 km) wide, with the Southern Upland Way running along its eastern shore. Noted for its trout fishing, St Mary's Loch features in the poetry of William Wordsworth (1770–1850), Sir Walter Scott (1771–1832) and James Hogg (1770–1835), whose monument stands at the southern end of the loch.

St Mary's Roman Catholic Cathedral *City of Edinburgh* Located between Leith Street and York Place at the top of Leith Walk in Edinburgh, St Mary's Roman Catholic Cathedral was built in 1813 by James Gillespie Graham. It was the first new Roman Catholic chapel to be consecrated in Edinburgh since the Reformation, the site being chosen in 1801 by a bishop who had seen his chapel in Blackfriars' Wynd burned by a mob. In 1830, the deposed Charles X of France and his family worshipped here. St Mary's was elevated to the status of a cathedral in 1878 and remains the cathedral Church of the Archdiocese of St Andrews and Edinburgh. The handsome gable front, surmounted by pinnacles 21 m (70 ft) high, is all that remains of the original chapel. Rebuilding behind the frontage began following a fire in 1891. In 1932, the roof was raised to create a greater feeling of space and, in the 1970s, a new porch was built on the site of the old Theatre Royal which once lay next to the cathedral until it burned down in 1946. The inside is unusual, with a wide nave and a spectacular roof. A painting of the *Coronation of the Blessed Virgin Mary as Queen of Heaven* by the Belgian artist Louis Beyart hangs above the sanctuary arch. Within the altar are two relics of St Andrew, one acquired in 1879, the other gifted by Pope Paul VI in 1969. Pope John Paul II visited the cathedral on 31 May 1982, during his tour of Scotland at the invitation of Cardinal Gordon Gray. A succession of archbishops of St Andrews and Edinburgh and other senior clergy lie buried in the vaults below the cathedral. In front of the cathedral are three large sculptures by Sir Eduardo Paolozzi erected in 1991. They symbolise the links between Scotland and Italy.

St Michaels Inn *Fife* A hamlet with an inn in northeast Fife, St Michaels Inn lies a mile (1.5 km) northwest of Leuchars at the junction of the A914, A919 and B945.

St Moluag's Chapel *Western Isles* A restored medieval chapel situated on raised ground a short walk northeast of Eorpie in the Ness district of northern Lewis, St Moluag's Chapel (Gael: *Teampall Mholuaidh* or *Teampull Mholuidh*) most likely dates from the 12th–14th centuries. The first building on this site was thought to have been erected by the Vikings, and here an ancient cult once celebrated the sea-god Shony by offering ale on All Saints' Day. The chapel was restored in 1911–12 to provide a venue for worship for the Scottish Episcopalian Church. Although it was little used for many years, regular services were revived in 1994 despite a lack of heating and lighting, which makes worship here impossible in the winter when alternative premises in Tong are used. Outside is a war memorial in the form of a Celtic cross.

St Monans *Fife* A fishing village in the East Neuk of Fife, St Monans (or St Monance) lies on the Firth of Forth between Elie and Pittenweem. Originally known as Inverin, Inverie or Inweary, its present name is derived from a shrine to St Moineinn established on the shore by early Christian missionaries. The version of the name ending in 'ce' is a possessive form as in once, twice, etc. In the 1890s there was a dispute as to the most appropriate version of the placename. St Monance, which appears on many maps, was favoured until more recent times, when St Monans has found its way back into use. The village grew up around a well dedicated to the saint, its water being used to wash fishermen's nets and lines for many centuries. In 1362, David II gave thanks here after surviving a shipwreck in the Firth of Forth and in gratitude ordered a church to be built. Restored 1826–8 by William Burn, this building is a prominent feature in the landscape. In addition to many fine pantiled 17th- and 18th-century houses, there are the remains of saltpans overlooked by a restored windmill that was used to pump water up from the sea. On the coastal walk to the west of the settlement are a restored 16th-century beehive dovecote and the ruins of Newark Castle, which was remodelled by David Leslie (later Lord Newark) in 1649. Salt, coal and fishing were the chief industries of St Monans for many years, but during the 20th century it has largely been a centre of tourism and boatbuilding, a trade that has been associated with the town for more than 200 years. Additional small industries such as the production of smoked fish are located on the Netherton Industrial Estate.

St Mungo Museum of Religious Life and Art *Glasgow City* The first museum in the world to be dedicated to the study of religious art and life, the St Mungo Museum in Glasgow is located on Castle Street next to Glasgow Cathedral. Opened in 1993, it contains works of art depicting the world's six major religions including Salvador Dali's *Christ of St John of the Cross.*

St Ninians *Stirling* Also known as St Ringans, the ancient village of St Ninians lies a mile (1.5 km) south of the centre of Stirling, to which it is now adjoined. During the 18th and 19th centuries it was a centre of coal mining and tartan weaving. The prominent tower of the parish church of St Ninians dates from 1734, this being the only part of the kirk to survive an explosion in 1745 when the building was being used by Jacobites as an arsenal. The church was rebuilt in 1751 on a separate site to the north. Some interesting buildings dating from the 17th and 18th centuries survive in Kirk Wynd.

St Ninian's Bay *Argyll and Bute* An inlet on the west coast of the island of Bute, 4 miles (6.5 km) southwest of Rothesay, St Ninian's Bay looks out over Inchmarnock Sound towards the island of Inchmarnock. On St Ninian's Point, a headland at the north end of the bay, stand the ruins of an ancient chapel.

St Ninian's Cave *Dumfries and Galloway* A cave near Physgill at the southern end of the Machars of Dumfries and Galloway, St Ninian's Cave is said to have been used by the early Christian missionary St Ninian as a devotional retreat. Incised crosses on the rock face suggest that the site has been venerated by pilgrims since the 8th century.

St Ninian's Chapel *Moray* Situated at Tynet, just north of the A98 between Fochabers and Portgordon in Moray, the white-harled St Ninian's Chapel is the oldest post-Reformation Catholic church still in use in Scotland. Originally a sheep cote with a thatched roof and no glazed windows, it was given by a local Gordon laird to the Catholic community in 1755 for use as a meeting place at a time when Catholics were viewed with some suspicion.

St Ninian's Isle *Shetland* A small islet of the Shetland group, St Ninian's Isle lies off the southwest coast of Mainland Shetland, to which it is linked by a tombolo of pure white sand opposite Bigton. An early Christian monastic settlement existed here and in 1958, during an excavation, a Shetland schoolboy uncovered a hoard of Celtic monastic silver comprising 28 objects. The St Ninian's Isle Treasure, described as 'the most important single discovery in Scottish archaeology', is now located in the Royal Museum of Scotland in Edinburgh. A slab with a Pictish Ogam inscription on one edge, found in 1876, is also in the museum.

St Quivox *South Ayrshire* A small settlement in South Ayrshire, St Quivox lies to the east of Prestwick, 3 miles (5 km) northeast of Ayr. Nearby is the Scottish Agricultural College and Research Institute at Auchincruive.

St Rule's Tower *Fife* A 35-m/115-ft-high medieval square tower prominent on the skyline of St Andrews, St Rule's Tower is all that remains of the church of St Rule or St Regulus which was probably built in the 11th century. It stands immediately southeast of the ruins of St Andrews Cathedral, which succeeded it in the 12th century. The tower is dedicated to the Greek monk St Rule who is said to have brought the relics of St Andrew, Scotland's patron saint, from Patras *c.* AD 345 to prevent them from being taken to Constantinople by the Emperor Constantine.

St Serf's Island *Perth and Kinross* An island in Loch Leven, St Serf's Island is also known as The Inch. Now a noted wildfowl-breeding site and wintering ground for migrant geese, the island was occupied by priors of the Augustinian order until the Reformation. This religious house succeeded an earlier foundation of the Celtic Church and came to be noted for its literary output, including Prior Andrew Wyntoun's *Oryginale Cronykil of Scotland*, completed at the beginning of the 15th century. Little remains of the priory except a ruined chapel that survived as a shepherd's bothy after the island was enlarged by the lowering of the level of the loch 1828–32. Excavations in 1877 revealed two graves, thought to be those of the Abbot St Ronan and Archbishop Patrick Graham (d.1478).

St Triduana's Well *City of Edinburgh* An ancient well in the Restalrig district of Edinburgh, St Triduana's Well lies adjacent to St Margaret's Parish Church. It was built by the Logan family for James III *c.*1477 and comprised a lower rib-vaulted wellhouse and an upper chapel that no longer exists. Water from the wellhouse was used to treat diseases of the eye, following St Triduana's ability to heal the blind. The lower floor was later used as a burial vault by the Logan family, which possessed the barony of Restalrig. The wellhouse, which had become entirely buried, was exposed and subjected to a major restoration in 1906.

St Vigeans *Angus* A village in Angus, St Vigeans lies on the Brothock Burn, a mile (1.5 km) to the north of Arbroath. Named after a 7th-century Irish saint, Fechin or Vigianus, the village is noted for its collection of early-Pictish carved stones that are housed in a converted cottage at the foot of the knoll on which the church stands. Nearby is the Kirkton Industrial Estate, opposite which is RM *Condor*, a former Royal Naval Air Station established in 1938 and now occupied by Royal Marines. A civilian gliding club operates from the *Condor* airstrip.

Salachail *Argyll and Bute* A small settlement in Glen Creran, Salachail lies on the River Creran, 5 miles (8 km) south of Ballachulish.

Salachan Burn *Highland* A burn of Lochaber district in Highland Council area, the Salachan Burn flows northwestwards down Salachan Glen to empty into Loch Linnhe opposite Eileann Balnagowan.

Salen *Argyll and Bute* A village on the east coast of the island of Mull in the Inner Hebrides, Salen lies on Salen Bay, an inlet of the Sound of Mull opposite Morvern and 9 miles (14 km) southeast of Tobermory. On the north side of Salen Bay stands Aros Castle, built in the 13th century by the Lords of the Isles and later held by Maclean of Duart. From the 1850s until superseded by Craignure Pier in the 1950s, Salen was served by steamers from Oban. An airstrip was opened nearby in 1966.

Salen *Highland* A scattered settlement at the eastern end of the Ardnamurchan peninsula, Salen lies on Salen Bay, an inlet on the north shore of Loch Sunart, 3 miles (5 km) south of Acharacle. Formerly a port of call for Clyde steamers with a pirn factory and an inn, it survived as a fishing resort and boating centre in the 20th century.

Saligo Bay *Argyll and Bute* An inlet on the west coast of the island of Islay in the Inner Hebrides, Saligo Bay lies due west of Loch Gorm.

Saline *Fife* A former weaving village in western Fife, Saline has many interesting 18th-century cottages that have survived despite the extensive development of mining in the neighbourhood during the 19th and 20th centuries. Running parallel to the Saline Burn, the main street stretches down a slope that looks towards the Ochil Hills, with Saline Hill rising to a height of 359 m (1178 ft) to the northeast. Held for many years by the earls of Mar, Saline was often visited by Sir Walter Scott (1771–1832) who stayed at nearby North Kinneddar, the home of his friend William Erskine, Lord Kinneddar, to whom he dedicated the Third Canto of his poem *Marmion* (1808). The village has a nine-hole golf course, a community leisure centre, a primary school (built as Saline Public School in 1875) and a parish church (Saline and Blairingone Church) built in 1810 to a Tudor-Gothic-style design by William Stark.

Salisbury Crags *City of Edinburgh* The cliff face of Salisbury Crags looks westwards over the rooftops of central Edinburgh from Holyrood Park. This dolerite intrusion represents the glaciated remains of a Carboniferous sill injected between sedimentary rocks, which formed in a shallow sea some 340 million years ago. Tilted by later earth movements and eroded by ice, the crags were a source of stone used to pave the streets of London in the 19th century. At Hutton's Section, the geologist James Hutton (1726–97) recognised that the rock now forming the crags had been injected in a molten state. He was able to use this evidence to disprove the suggestion of the influential German Abraham Werner, that all rocks had crystallised from a supposed primordial sea.

Sallachan *Highland* A small village of Ardgour in southwest Highland Council area, Sallachan is situated at the mouth of the Gour River on the western shore of Loch Linnhe. It looks out over Sallachan Point towards the Corran Narrows.

Sallachy *Highland* A small village in the Lochalsh district of Highland Council area, Sallachy lies on the north shore of Loch Long, 5 miles (8 km) northeast of Eilean Donan Castle and 10 miles (16 km) east of Kyle of Lochalsh.

Salsburgh *North Lanarkshire* A village in the North Lanarkshire parish of Shotts, Salsburgh lies to the south of the M8, 5 miles (8 km) southeast of Airdrie and 3 miles (5 km) northwest of Shotts. It developed in association with coal mining and quarrying at the end of the 19th century.

Salt Ness *Orkney* A headland on the west coast of the island of Shapinsay in the Orkney Islands, Salt Ness extends into the Wide Firth 2 miles (3 km) north of Balfour.

Salt Pans Bay *Dumfries and Galloway* An inlet on the west coast of the Rhinns of Galloway, Salt Pans Bay lies 3 miles (5 km) north of Black Head below Larbrax Moor.

Saltburn *Highland* A village of Easter Ross, Saltburn lies on the north shore of the Cromarty Firth, a mile (1.5 km) northeast of Invergordon. This village, like Invergordon, developed in association with North Sea oil industries.

Saltcoats *North Ayrshire* A resort town in the Cunninghame district of North Ayrshire, Saltcoats lies on the Firth of Clyde immediately southeast of Ardrossan. Chartered as a burgh of barony in the 16th century, it developed as a port trading in coal, salt and fish after the building of a harbour in the 1680s. In the 18th century a shipyard was opened and from the 1790s Saltcoats developed as a resort town. Although the railway brought tourists from Glasgow from the 1840s, neighbouring Ardrossan superseded Saltcoats as the principal port of trade from the 1850s. The North Ayrshire Museum is located in the town.

Saltmarket, the *Glasgow City* A street in Glasgow, The Saltmarket extends south from Glasgow Cross towards the River Clyde. A popular place to live for early 18th-century Glaswegian merchants, it was formerly known as the Waulcergait and was associated with fullers (scourers of woollen cloth).

Saltoun See East Saltoun and West Saltoun.

Salum *Argyll and Bute* A scattered settlement on the island of Tiree in the Inner Hebrides, Salum lies on the island's northern coastline on a bay of the same name, 5 miles (8 km) northeast of Crossapoll and 2 miles (3 km) west of the headland of Rubha Dubh.

Samala *Western Isles* A small settlement on the northeast coast of the island of Baleshare, which lies off the west coast of North Uist in the Outer Hebrides, Samala (Gael: *Samhla*) is located at the western end of the Baleshare Causeway, which gives access to the island, 9 miles (14 km) southwest of Lochmaddy.

Samalaman Island *Highland* A small island off the coast of Moidart, Samalaman Island lies at the southern entrance to the Sound of Arisaig, 3 miles (5 km) west of Roshven and 7 miles (11 km) southwest of the settlement of Lochailort.

Samalan Island *Argyll and Bute* A small island in the Inner Hebrides, Samalan Island lies on the west side of the island of Mull to the northeast of Inch Kenneth, at the mouth of Loch Na Keal.

Samhla The Gaelic name for Samala in the Western Isles.

Samphrey *Shetland* An uninhabited island of the Shetland Islands, Samphrey is situated to the north of the Shetland Mainland and south of the island of Yell, at the entrance to Yell Sound. The island has an area of 66 ha (163 acres).

Samuelston *East Lothian* Situated on the north bank of the River Tyne in East Lothian, the village of Samuelston lies 3 miles (5 km) southwest of Haddington and 2 miles (3 km) west of Lennoxlove House.

Sanaigmore *Argyll and Bute* A crofting village on the north coast of Islay in the Inner Hebrides, Sanaigmore lies 8 miles (13 km) northwest of Bridgend on a bay of the same name. The headland of Tòn Mhòr is 2 miles (3 km) northwest.

Sand Wick *Shetland* An inlet on the northwest shore of the Shetland Mainland, Sand Wick opens out into St Magnus Bay to the west of the settlement of Hillswick.

Sand Wick *Shetland* A south-facing bay on the east coast of the Shetland Mainland, Sand Wick opens out into the sea 11 miles (18 km) south of Lerwick. The settlement of Sandwick lies at the head of the bay.

Sand Wick *Shetland* An inlet on the east coast of the island of Unst in the Shetland Islands, Sand Wick forms a wide sandy bay between Brough Taing and Mu Ness.

Sanda Island *Argyll and Bute* An uninhabited island of 127 ha (314 acres) in the Firth of Clyde, Sanda Island lies 2 miles (3 km) southeast of the Kintyre peninsula, from which it is separated by the Sound of Sanda. Privately owned and used for grazing, the island was once home to a thriving fishing community. The ruins of St Ninian's Chapel are located in the sheltered centre of the island, which rises to 123 m (403 ft) in the east. Surrounded by dangerous skerries, the island has a lighthouse (1850) which stands on the Ship Rock. To the north are the rocky islet of Glunimore Island and Sheep Island.

Sandaig *Highland* Situated at the western end of Knoydart, Sandaig lies at the head of Sandaig Bay on the north shore of Loch Nevis, 5 miles (8 km) northeast of Mallaig.

Sandaig *Highland* A small settlement in the Lochalsh district of Highland Council area, Sandaig lies on the east shore of the Sound of Sleat, 4 miles (6.5 km) southwest of Glenelg. It looks westwards to the Sandaig Islands and the isle of Skye.

Sanday *Highland* An island of the Inner Hebrides, Sanday lies in the Inner Sound immediately to the south of the island of Canna to which it is joined at low tide. Sanday is 2 miles (3 km) long and a half-mile (1 km) wide. At low tide the northern coastline of Sanday forms the southern shore of Canna harbour.

Sanday *Orkney* An irregularly shaped, fertile island of the Orkney Islands group, Sanday lies 24 miles (38 km) northeast of Kirkwall, with which it is linked by car ferry and by air. It is a low-lying island rising to 65 m (213 ft) at the Wart and has an area of 5306 ha (13,111 acres). Interesting archaeological finds on the island have included the chambered cairn at Quoyness, a Viking ship-burial near Scar and a group of burial mounds at Tofts Ness. Kelp was the main industry in the 18th century, Sanday providing one-quarter of Orkney's total production. Today, its population of 478 is engaged in the production of knitwear, in the farming of beef cattle and sheep, and in fishing for crab, lobster and scallops. The island also has its own electronics factory. Sanday is separated from the island of Stronsay by the Sanday Sound.

Sandbank *Argyll and Bute* A dormitory settlement with a business park on the Cowal peninsula, Sandbank lies on the south side of the Holy Loch, 2 miles (3 km) northwest of Dunoon. Immediately east is the settlement of Ardnadam, from which it is separated by Lazaretto Point. Noted as a centre of yacht building and sail making, Sandbank once had two boatyards, one of which, Robertsons, built yachts for the Americas Cup challenges.

Sandend *Aberdeenshire* A settlement on the northwest coast of Aberdeenshire, Sandend lies on the west side of Sandend Bay, between Portsoy and Cullen. Dating from the early 17th century, its harbour was developed for fishing in the 19th century. Although no longer a fishing village, it still has fish-processing industries. Findlater Castle and Logie Head lie to the west.

Sandford *South Lanarkshire* Situated 2 miles (3 km) southeast of Strathaven in South Lanarkshire, the small village of Sandford lies on the Kype Water, a half-mile (1 km) south of its confluence with the Avon Water.

Sandford Bay *Aberdeenshire* An inlet on the northeast coast of Aberdeenshire, Sandford Bay lies 2 miles (3 km) south of Peterhead, between the settlements of Burnhaven to the north and Boddam to the south.

Sandgarth, Bay of *Orkney* A bay on the south coast of the island of Shapinsay in the Orkney Islands, Sandgarth opens out into Shapinsay Sound. The village of Sandgarth lies to the east.

Sandhaven *Aberdeenshire* A fishing village in the Buchan district of Aberdeenshire, Sandhaven lies at the west end of Phingask Shore, 3 miles (5 km) west of Fraserburgh. It has a harbour built in 1840 and is a centre of boat building. There is a restored water-powered meal mill at the east end of the village.

Sandhead *Dumfries and Galloway* A village of the Rhinns of Galloway, Dumfries and Galloway, Sandhead lies on Sandhead Bay, a broad sandy inlet at the head of Luce Bay, 6 miles (10 km) south of Stranraer. Nearby Balgreggan House, demolished in 1966, was built in 1730 for John McDowall to a design by William Adam.

Sandholm *Scottish Borders* A locality in Liddesdale in Scottish Borders, Sandholm lies on the Liddel Water at its junction with the Hermitage Water, just over a mile (1.5 km) northeast of Newcastleton.

Sandness *Shetland* A scattered settlement in the most westerly district of Mainland Shetland, Sandness lies 29 miles (46 km) northwest of Lerwick near the end of the Trona Scord road (A971). It comprises a group of crofting townships including Norby, Huxter and Melby. A mile (1.5 km) offshore is the island of Papa Stour.

Sandoyne, Bay of *Orkney* An inlet on the southwest coast of the Orkney Mainland, the Bay of Sandoyne opens out into Scapa Flow to the west of the settlement of St Mary's.

Sandquoy, Bay of *Orkney* An inlet on the northeast coast of the island of Sanday in the Orkney Islands, the Bay of Sandquoy lies at the mouth of the larger inlet of Otters Wick. The settlement of Sandquoy lies on the east side of the bay.

Sandray *Western Isles* An uninhabited island at the southern end of the Western Isles, Sandray (Gael: *Sanndraigh*) lies to the south of Vatersay, from which it is separated by the Sound of Sandray. It is separated from Pabbay to the southwest by the Sound of Pabbay. The island has an area of 400 ha (988 acres) and rises to 207 m (679 ft) at Cairn Galtair.

Sandside Bay *Highland* An inlet on the northern coast of Caithness, Sandside Bay opens out into the sea a mile (1.5 km) north of Reay. Sandside Burn flows north for 6 miles (10 km) into the bay, which lies 2 miles (3 km) southwest of Dounreay Nuclear Power Station. Sandside Head forms a headland to the west. Sandside Harbour and associated fishing store and cottages were built *c.*1830 by Major William Innes of Sandside. There are a number of Pictish stones in the area, and Sandside House dates from 1751.

Sandsting *Shetland* A district and old parish forming a southern arm of the Walls peninsula, Sandsting lies 12 miles (19 km) west-northwest of Lerwick. Its main settlement is Skeld and the district of Aithsting is located to the north.

Sandwick *Shetland* A settlement on the east coast of Mainland Shetland, Sandwick lies 15 miles (24 km) south of Lerwick at the head of the Sand Wick. Once a major fishing centre, it has offshore oil-service industries and a secondary school serving the southern Mainland of Shetland. Shetland tweed is produced in the nearby township of Hoswick, and to the north at Leebotten copper was mined during the 19th century. During the summer a ferry takes tourists to the nearby Broch of Mousa.

Sandwick *Western Isles* A village on the eastern coast of the Isle of Lewis in the Western Isles, Sandwick (Gael: *Sanndabhaig*) is situated on Stornoway Harbour, a mile (1.5 km) southeast of Stornoway. Stornoway Airport is to the northeast.

Sandwood Bay *Highland* A wide sandy inlet on the northwest coast of Sutherland, Sandwood Bay lies 6 miles (10 km) southwest of Cape Wrath. Sandwood Loch to the southeast drains into the bay, which forms part of the Sandwood Estate, a reserve owned by the John Muir Trust. The estate, which also includes the crofting townships and grazings of Sheigra, Oldshore Beg and Oldshoremore to the south, is noted for its glacially eroded peatland landscape, dynamic sand dunes and dramatic cliffs.

Sandyford *Dumfries and Galloway* A locality in Castle O'er Forest, Dumfries and Galloway, Sandyford lies on the Black Esk, 10 miles (16 km) northeast of Lockerbie.

Sandyhills *Dumfries and Galloway* A locality on the Solway coast of Dumfries and Galloway, Sandyhills lies 3 miles (5 km) east of Rockcliffe. Here the Fairgirth Lane flows into Sandyhills Bay, an inlet of the Solway Firth facing onto the Mersehead Sands.

Sango Bay *Highland* A picturesque sandy bay on the north coast of Sutherland, Sango Bay is located by the village of Durness, 4 miles (6.5 km) west of Loch Eriboll. Extending to a half-mile (1 km) in width, Sango Bay offers camping and caravan sites and is popular with surfers. Surrounded by low cliffs, it is also of interest to geologists, providing some classic exposures of the Moine Thrust. The settlement of Sangomore lies to the southwest and the Smoo Cave is a half-mile (1 km) to the southeast.

Sangobeg *Highland* A township on the north coast of Sutherland, Sangobeg lies 2 miles (3 km) southeast of Durness and a mile (1.5 km) southeast of Smoo Cave.

Sangomore *Highland* A linear crofting township on the north coast of Sutherland, Sangomore lies immediately southeast of Durness.

Sanna Bay *Highland* A sandy inlet at the western end of the Ardnamurchan peninsula, Sanna Bay lies between the headlands of Sanna Point to the north and the Point of Ardnamurchan to the south.

Sanndabhaig The Gaelic name for Sandwick in the Western Isles.

Sanndraigh The Gaelic name for Sandray in the Western Isles.

Sannick, Bay of *Highland* An inlet on the northeast coast of Caithness, the Bay of Sannick opens out into the Pentland Firth between Duncansby Head and the Ness of Duncansby, to the northeast of John o' Groats.

Sannox, Glen *North Ayrshire* A broad U-shaped glaciated valley in northeast Arran, Glen Sannox extends northeastwards from the high peaks, draining into Sannox Bay on the east coast of the island. Barytes was mined here in the 19th century. The hamlet of Sannox lies at the foot of the glen.

Sanquhar *Dumfries and Galloway* A burgh town in upper Nithsdale, Sanquhar lies to the west of the Lowther Hills on the River Nith near its confluence with the Crawick Water and the Euchan Water, 26 miles (42 km) northwest of Dumfries. Created a burgh of barony in 1484 and a royal burgh in 1598, it first developed as a market town in association with its castle. From the 18th century it prospered in association with coal mining and the manufacture of textiles, in particular the Sanquhar Pattern of knitwear. Modern industries have included the manufacture of fireworks, bricks, clothing, carpets, aluminium and plastics. There are many ancient remains in the area, including the Sean Caer or 'old fort', said to give the town its name, which is pronounced 'sanker'. Buildings of note include the remains of Sanquhar Castle (15th century); the Town House and Tolbooth, both designed in 1735 by William Adam for the 3rd Duke of Queensbury; and 'Britain's oldest Post Office', which opened in 1763. In 1680, local schoolteacher Richard Cameron and an armed band of Covenanting followers signed the Declaration of Sanquhar as an act of rebellion against Charles II. The survivors founded the Cameronian Regiment. Sanquhar has a museum and a nine-hole golf course.

Sarclet *Highland* A linear crofting township on the east coast of Caithness, Sarclet lies 5 miles (8 km) south of Wick. Once a safe natural harbour for local fishing boats, the cliff-top settlement was developed in the early 19th century by David Brodie of Hopeville, a tenant of Sir John Sinclair of Ulbster (1754–1835). Sarclet Head extends into the sea a half-mile (1 km) to the southeast.

Sark, River *Dumfries and Galloway* A river in Dumfries and Galloway, the Sark flows south through Half Morton and Gretna parishes to enter the channel of the River Esk by Gretna. For much of its course it follows the border with Cumbria. The Black Sark is a smaller stream to the west.

Saturness Point, Satterness Point Alternative names for Southerness Point in Dumfries and Galloway.

Sauchen *Aberdeenshire* A village with a working smithy in the mid-Aberdeenshire parish of Cluny, Sauchen lies 3 miles (5 km) west of Dunecht and 10 miles (16 km) west of Aberdeen.

Saucher *Perth and Kinross* A hamlet between the Sidlaw Hills and the River Tay in Perth and Kinross, Saucher lies to the north of Kirkton of Collace, 2 miles (3 km) south of Burrelton.

Sauchie *Clackmannanshire* A former mining and textile-weaving village in central Clackmannanshire, Sauchie is situated on high ground between Alloa and Tillicoultry. The parish church of Sauchie and Coalsnaughton dates from 1841. Many of the older cottages are built of red sandstone. Sauchie Tower (or Old Sauchie), which dates from the early 15th century, was built by the Shaws, one of whom was ambassador to Edward IV of England and later Governor of Stirling Castle. Built in 1865, the Sauchie Beam Engine House was used to pump water from the former Devon Colliery. There are annexes of Clackmannan College in Sauchie, and the Carsebridge Business Centre is the focal point for electronic, textile and construction industries. The housing estate of New Sauchie was built nearby in the 1920s.

Sauchiehall Street *Glasgow City* One of the city of Glasgow's most noted thoroughfares, Sauchiehall Street extends westwards from Buchanan Street to Charing Cross and on into the West End. Created in 1807, its name describes the 'hollow of the willows' that once existed here. It developed as the city's main shopping street in the 19th century and was part-pedestrianised in the late 20th century. The Glasgow Royal Concert Hall and McLellan Galleries are located on Sauchiehall Street.

Sauchinford *Stirling* A village in southeast Stirling Council area, Sauchinford lies just west of the A9, between Bannockburn and East Plean.

Saughs, Water of *Angus* A headstream of the West Water in the southern Grampians, the Water of Saughs rises between Glen Esk and Glen Clova.

Saughton *City of Edinburgh* A suburb of Edinburgh, Saughton lies 3 miles (5 km) southwest of the city centre. HM Prison Edinburgh (or Saughton Prison) lies on the southern margin of the district.

Saughtree *Scottish Borders* A locality in the Roxburgh district of Scottish Borders, Saughtree lies on the Liddel Water, 8 miles (13 km) northeast of Newcastleton.

Saviskaill Bay *Orkney* An inlet on the north coast of the island of Rousay in the Orkney Islands, Saviskaill Bay lies between the headlands of Saviskaill Head and Farraclett Head and looks out over the Westray Firth. The scattered community of Saviskaill lies along the bay.

Saxa Vord *Shetland* The hill of Saxa Vord rises to 285 m (935 ft) on the north coast of the island of Unst in the Shetland Islands. Communications masts relating to the early warning station of RAF Saxa Vord lie on its slopes.

Scadabay *Western Isles* A hamlet located on the east coast of South Harris in the Outer Hebrides, Scadabay (Gael: *Scadabhagh*) lies around the head of the narrow inlet of Loch Scadabay, 1.25 miles (2 km) east of Grosebay and 5 miles (8 km) south of Tarbert.

Scad Head *Orkney* A headland on the north coast of the island of Hoy in the Orkney Islands, Scad Head lies 4 miles (6.5 km) east of Ward Hill, the highest point on the island.

Scalan *Moray* Situated on a track beyond Chapeltown in the remote Braes of Glenlivet in upland Moray is an 18th-century farm building converted for use as a Roman Catholic college. From 1719 to 1799, over 100 Catholic priests were trained at the remote College of Scalan, which takes its name from the Gaelic *sgalan* or 'turf shieling'. The original building was destroyed on several occasions by Government troops, the present building dating from 1767. The college eventually moved in 1799 to Aquhorthies near Inverurie in Aberdeenshire.

Scalasaig *Argyll and Bute* The principal settlement of the island of Colonsay in Argyll and Bute, Scalasaig lies on the east coast and has ferry links with Oban to the north and Port Askaig to the south.

Scalaval *Western Isles* A hill on the Isle of Lewis in the Western Isles, Scalaval rises to a height of 260 m (853 ft), 3 miles (5 km) south of the head of Little Loch Roag.

Scald Law *Midlothian* A summit of the Pentland Hills overlooking Loganlea Reservoir, Scald Law rises to 579 m (1898 ft) 3 miles (5 km) west of Penicuik.

Scalloch, Loch *South Ayrshire* A small loch in South Ayrshire, Loch Scalloch lies 3 miles (5 km) south of Barr.

Scalloway *Shetland* A fishing port and yachting centre on Mainland Shetland, Scalloway lies 5 miles (8 km) to the west of Lerwick around a sheltered harbour that opens out into the East Voe of Scalloway. The capital of Shetland in the 17th century, its castle was built in 1600 by Patrick Stewart, Earl of Orkney, to replace an earlier dwelling at Sumburgh to the south. This was the landing place for Norse landowners attending Shetland's annual parliament or ting, held on the Law Ting Holm in Tingwall Loch 2 miles (3 km) to the north. Scalloway Museum features displays on local history, fishing and the wartime exploits of Norway's 'Shetland Bus' heroes who made the village their base. At Port Arthur, beyond the yachting marina, is the North Atlantic Fisheries College.

Scalp, the *Moray* A hill in Moray, the Scalp rises to a height of 487 m (1597 ft) 3 miles (5 km) southeast of Dufftown.

Scalpay *Highland* An island in the Inner Hebrides, Scalpay is located to the northwest of Pabay, off the northeast coast of the isle of Skye. It has an area of 2483 ha (6135 acres) and rises to 396 m (1299 ft) at Mullach na Carn. The principal lochs of the island, all lying in the northeast, are Loch an Leoid, Loch Dubh and Loch a' Mhullinn. Red deer are farmed in a 1600-ha (3954-acre) enclosure that forms part of a programme established by the former Highlands and Islands Development Board.

Scalpay *Western Isles* A small island in the Outer Hebrides, Scalpay (Gael: *Scalpaigh*) lies off the east coast of Harris, 6 miles (10 km) southeast of Tarbert. It rises to 104 m (341 ft) at Beinn Scorabhaig and since 1997 has been linked to Harris by the 300-m/328-yd-long Scalpay Bridge which forms part of an EU-funded programme of road- and bridge-building designed to enhance the economic development of the Outer Hebrides. Although the bridge was in use from December 1997, when Scalpay's oldest resident the 103-year-old Mrs Kirsty Morrison led the first cars across, it was officially opened in 1998 by Tony Blair, the first serving British Prime Minister to visit the Western Isles. A lighthouse was erected in 1789 at Eilean Glas at the eastern end of the island. A former haven for herring fishers, the island's economy is centred on knitwear, prawn fishing and salmon farming.

Scalpsie Bay *Argyll and Bute* An inlet on the southwest coast of the island of Bute, Scalpsie Bay looks out towards the Sound of Bute and Arran, 3 miles (5 km) northwest of Kingarth.

Scamadale *Argyll and Bute* A small village in the Lorn district of Argyll and Bute, Scamadale lies on the north shore of Loch Scamadale, 6 miles (10 km) south of Oban.

Scamodale *Highland* Situated on the southeast shore of Loch Shiel, Scamodale lies 6 miles (10 km) southwest of Glenfinnan in the Lochaber district of Highland Council area.

Scapa *Orkney* A small settlement with an anchorage in the Orkney Islands, Scapa lies on the Orkney Mainland at the head of Scapa Bay, a half-mile (1 km) south of Kirkwall.

Scapa Flow *Orkney* An expanse of deep water in the Orkney Islands, Scapa Flow is enclosed by a ring of islands, the largest of which are Mainland Orkney to the north, Burray and South Ronaldsay to the east and southeast, and Flotta and Hoy to the west and southwest. Its anchorages have sheltered fishing and naval vessels, and it was here, near the small island of Cava, that the captured German fleet of more than 200 vessels was scuttled on 21 June 1919. Although most of these ships were removed for salvage, seven remain. The east end of Scapa Flow was blocked by the building of the Churchill Barriers after the sinking of HMS *Royal Oak* by a German submarine on 14 October 1939.

Scar Nose *Moray* A rocky headland on the Moray Firth coast, Scar Nose projects into the sea immediately to the east of the cliff-top fishing village of Portknockie.

Scaraben *Highland* A mountain in Caithness, Scaraben rises to 626 m (2053 ft) in the Langwell Forest, 4 miles (6.5 km) northwest of Berriedale.

Scaravay *Western Isles* A small uninhabited island in the Western Isles, Scaravay (Gael: *Sgarabhaigh*) lies in the Sound of Harris, 4 miles (6.5 km) off the northeast coast of North Uist. The island rises to 23 m (75 ft).

Scarba *Argyll and Bute* An uninhabited island in the Inner Hebrides, Scarba lies to the north of the island of Jura, from which it is separated by the Strait of Corryvreckan. With an area of 1474 ha (3642 acres), the island has the appearance of a mountain top rising from the seabed to a height of 449 m (1473 ft). Scarba was the site of an early Christian settlement and once had a population of 50 people. The remains of an ancient chapel and crofts are all that remain on the east coast near Kilmory. The only permanent buildings that survive are Kilmory Lodge, the occasional home of the owner of the island, and an outward-bound centre located at Bagh Gleann a' Mhaoil to the south. Predominantly covered in heather, the island has a sizeable population of red deer, wild goats and otters, in addition to the domestic sheep and Luing cattle that are grazed here.

Scardroy *Highland* A settlement in the North West Highlands, Scardroy lies 5 miles (8 km) southeast of Achnasheen on the River Meig which flows into the western end of Loch Beannachan to the south of Strath Bran.

Scares, the *Dumfries and Galloway* A group of rocky islets at the mouth of Luce Bay between the Mull of Galloway and Burrow Head, Dumfries and Galloway, The Scares comprise the Little Scares to the north and Big Scare to the southwest.

Scarfskerry *Highland* A linear settlement on the north coast of Caithness, Scarfskerry overlooks an inlet of the Pentland Firth, 7 miles (11 km) west of John o' Groats and 2 miles (3 km) west of the Castle of Mey. The ferry house dates from the early 19th century.

Scarinish *Argyll and Bute* The principal village on the island of Tiree in the Inner Hebrides, Scarinish lies on the south coast between Hynish Bay to the southwest and Gott Bay to the northeast. Its harbour, now used by lobster fishers, was built in 1771, and nearby is a ferry terminal with links to Oban and Coll.

Scarp *Western Isles* An uninhabited island lying off the west coast of North Harris in the Western Isles, Scarp has an area of 1045 ha (2582 acres) and rises to 308 m (1010 ft) at Sròn Romul. The island was occupied by crofters in 1823 but the population gradually declined, the last two families leaving Scarp on 2 December 1971.

Scatsta *Shetland* A hamlet in the Shetland parish of Delting at the northern end of the Shetland Mainland, Scatsta lies to the southwest of the Voe of Scatsta on the east side of Sullom Voe. Located some 24 miles (38 km) north-northwest of Lerwick and 5 miles (8 km) southwest of the oil terminal at Sullom Voe, is Scatsta Airport.

Scaur An alternative name for Kippford in Dumfries and Galloway.

Scaur Water *Dumfries and Galloway* A river of Nithsdale in Dumfries and Galloway, the Scaur (or Scar) Water rises in hills to the southwest of Sanquhar. It flows east and southeast for more than 18 miles (29 km) past Penpont before entering the River Nith 2 miles (3 km) south of Thornhill.

Scavaig, Loch *Highland* A sea loch on the southwest coast of the isle of Skye in the Inner Hebrides, Loch Scavaig opens out into the Cuillin Sound to the south of the Cuillins. The island of Soay lies to the west and the Strathaird peninsula to the east.

Scaven, Loch An alternative name for Loch Sgamhain in Highland.

Scawd Law *Dumfries and Galloway* A summit in the Lowther Hills, Scawd Law rises to 660 m (2167 ft) to the east of Durisdeer. Little Scawd Law to the northwest rises to 589 m (1933 ft).

Schiehallion *Perth and Kinross* Rising to 1083 m (3547 ft) southeast of Kinloch Rannoch in Perth and Kinross, the quartzite summit of Schiehallion appears to have a perfect conical appearance from the west and east, whereas from the north and south it takes the form of a whale-backed ridge. From 1774 to 1776 the Astronomer Royal, Nevil Maskelyne (1732–1811), measured the deflection of a plumb line on the slopes of the mountain to determine the mean density of the earth. The mountain was purchased by the John Muir Trust in 1999.

Schivas *Aberdeenshire* A locality in Aberdeenshire, Schivas lies to the north of the River Ythan, 6 miles (10 km) northwest of Ellon. Built about 1640, the mansion house at Schivas was a seat of the Gray family.

Sciennes *City of Edinburgh* A residential district of Edinburgh, Sciennes lies between Newington and Marchmont on the south side of the Meadows, a mile (1.5 km) south of the city centre. It takes its name from the Convent of St Catherine of Siena, which was dedicated in 1517 on a site now occupied by St Catherine's Place. Sciennes Hill House, part of which remains today, was the home of the Biggar family. The only meeting between the poet Robert Burns (1759–96) and the novelist Sir Walter Scott (1771–1832) took place here at a dinner hosted by Adam Ferguson (1723–1816). The Royal Edinburgh Hospital for Sick Children, which lies on Sciennes Road, was completed in 1895 by architect George Washington Browne (1853–1939). In Sciennes House Place is a tiny Jewish Cemetery, opened in 1816.

Scone *Perth and Kinross* A village in Perth and Kinross, Scone lies to the east of the River Tay, 2 miles (3 km) northeast of Perth. Known as New Scone until 1997, it was built as a planned village by the Earl of Mansfield in 1805, replacing Old Scone, which had grown up in the vicinity of the early monastic buildings at Scone Palace. Present-day Scone Palace, 1.25 miles (2 km) to the west, was built in 1802 to a design by William Atkinson. Perth Airport was established nearby in 1934, and at Murrayshall there is an 18-hole golf course. There are several examples of prehistoric standing stones and stone circles nearby. Perth Racecourse is located at Scone Park.

Scone Palace *Perth and Kinross* Scone Palace is located at Old Scone, 1.5 miles (2 km) north of Perth, and is the family home of the earls of Mansfield. Despite its historic setting, the palace was built in 1802 by English architect William Atkinson. Originally the site of a 6th-century Celtic church which was replaced in the 12th century by an Augustinian abbey and a bishop's palace that provided lodgings for the kings of Scots, both the palace and abbey were destroyed in 1559 by a Perth mob incited by the preacher John Knox. The lands then passed to the Earl of Gowrie who built a new house. After the Gowrie Conspiracy, an attempt to kidnap James VI in 1600, the estates were forfeited and given to Sir David Murray who was created Lord Scone. Murray built a new palace in 1618 and it was here in 1651 that Charles II stayed before being crowned on the nearby Moot Hill, the site of royal coronations since the time of Kenneth MacAlpin (d.858). Charles was the last king to be crowned here. Other notable visitors have included Prince James Francis Edward Stewart) (The Old Pretender) in 1715 and his son Prince Charles Edward Stewart (Bonnie Prince Charlie) in 1745. Murray's descendants became the viscounts Stormont (1602) and then earls of Mansfield (1776). The 1st Earl spent his time in London and the 2nd Earl found the old palace too damp. Thus it was David Murray, becoming the 3rd Earl at only 19, who commissioned the rebuilding of the palace as the splendid castellated Tudor-Gothic-style edifice in red sandstone that we see today. It houses fine collections of furniture, paintings, ivory and porcelain, together with historically important royal heirlooms belonging to James VI and his mother, Queen Mary. The grounds include a Douglas fir tree planted in 1825 from seed collected by botanist David Douglas (1799–1834), a former gardener at the palace.

Sconser *Highland* A settlement on the isle of Skye in the Inner Hebrides, Sconser lies on the south side of Loch Sligachan, 11 miles (18 km) northwest of Broadford. Once an important staging post in the mail service, Sconser has been the main ferry link with Raasay since 1976.

Scoonie *Fife* A northeastern suburb of the town of Leven on the south coast of Fife, Scoonie takes its name from the parish whose church was granted to the Culdees of Loch Leven by Tuadal, Bishop of St Andrews in the 1060s. Abandoned in 1769 when a new parish church was built in Leven, the ruins of this church lie in a cemetery adjacent to the A915 to Largo. There is a golf course and bowling club.

Scoraig *Highland* A small crofting township in Wester Ross, Scoraig lies on the northeast shore of Little Loch Broom, 2 miles (3 km) southeast of Cailleach Head.

Score Bay *Highland* A wide inlet on the northwest coast of the Trotternish peninsula on the isle of Skye in the Inner Hebrides, Score Bay (Gael: *Lub Score*) is bounded by Rubha Hunish to the north and Ru Bornaskitaig to the south.

Scorrodale, Glen *North Ayrshire* A valley at the southern end of the island of Arran, Glen Scorrodale extends 8 miles (13 km) southwestwards from Lamlash to Sliddery on the southwest coast of the island.

Scotland's Secret Bunker *Fife* Located at Troy Wood in the East Neuk of Fife, 3 miles (5 km) north of Anstruther and 5 miles (8 km) southeast of St Andrews, Scotland's Secret Bunker was an underground command bunker built for use by the Government during the Cold War. It was designed to accommodate 300 people and withstand nuclear attack. Originally built as a radar station during World War II, it was completely rebuilt as part of the Rotor early-warning system in the 1950s. However, this localised system quickly became obsolete and the bunker was redeveloped once again to act as the Scottish Government Headquarters in 1973. Kept a secret for many years, it was opened to the public for the first time in 1995. It comprises a labyrinth of tunnels and operations rooms on two levels 30 m (100 ft) below ground and encased in 4.5 m (15 ft) of reinforced concrete. The accommodation and dining rooms, power plant, communications centre, emergency broadcasting studios and computer room are all preserved with largely authentic artefacts. Entry is through an innocuous-looking bungalow on the surface.

Scotlandwell *Perth and Kinross* A village in the parish of Portmoak, Perth and Kinross, Scotlandwell lies to the east of Loch Leven and at the foot of the Bishop Hill, 3 miles (5 km) west of Leslie. A hospital established here on the site of an early Celtic foundation was gifted to the Red Friars in the 13th century. Described in early charters as Fons Scotia, the hospital and village became a centre of pilgrimage, the friars using spring water to cure an assortment of diseases. Robert the Bruce, who came to be cured of leprosy, held a parliament here and in 1858 a canopy was built over the well that gives the village its name. Little remains of the Red Friars' Hospital except for a few foundations and a handful of gravestones. Buried here in an enclosure are the wife, mother and children of the Revd Ebenezer Erskine, father of the Secession Church, who was minister of Portmoak Parish between 1703 and 1730. There are a number of 18th- and 19th-century weavers' houses and the remnants of a wash house, bleaching green and garden which, with the well, formed part of a mid-19th-century village amenity scheme designed by David Bryce for Thomas Bruce of Arnot. On the hillside above the village are the remnants of a medieval runrig field system known locally as the Crooked Rigs. A mile (1.5 km) to the south of Scotlandwell is the Portmoak Airfield of the Scottish Gliding Union.

Scotstarvit Tower *Fife* A five-storey 16th-century keep overlooking the Howe of Fife, Scotstarvit Tower lies a mile (1.5 km) northwest of Craigrothie in east-central Fife. During the early 17th century it was occupied by Sir John Scott of Scotstarvit, a noted antiquarian and topographer who compiled a directory of contemporary politicians and administrators entitled *The Staggering State of Scots Statesmen*. The tower was abandoned in 1696.

Scotstoun *Glasgow City* A district to the northwest of Glasgow city centre, Scotstoun lies to the north of the River Clyde and south of Jordanhill. Scotstoun House and surrounding estate was the home of the Oswald family. By 1861, the westward march of the shipbuilding yards had reached Scotstoun, with the opening of Connell's Scotstoun Yard. Portions of land were subsequently sold for housing, industrial development and the creation of Victoria Park. The southern part of Scotstoun is characterised by late 19th- and early 20th-century tenement housing, while the north is mostly inter- and postwar local authority housing.

Scotstown *Highland* A village in the Sunart district of Highland Council area, Scotstown lies a mile (1.5 km) north of Strontian.

Scott Monument *City of Edinburgh* Built between 1840 and 1846 as a memorial to the writer Sir Walter Scott (1771–1832), the Scott Monument was designed by architect George Kemp (1795–1844) who won a competition with his design. Its Gothic cathedral-like spire dominates the south side of Edinburgh's Princes Street and has an internal staircase with 287 steps. The sandstone used in the construction of the monument was excavated from Binny Quarry near Uphall in West Lothian. This quarry was especially re-opened for a major restoration of the monument in 1998–9.

Scott's View *Scottish Borders* A spectacular vantage point on Bemersyde Hill, Scott's View looks out over the River Tweed towards the three peaks of the Eildon Hills, 2 miles (3 km) northeast of Newtown St Boswells. The view was much loved by the author Sir Walter Scott (1771–1832).

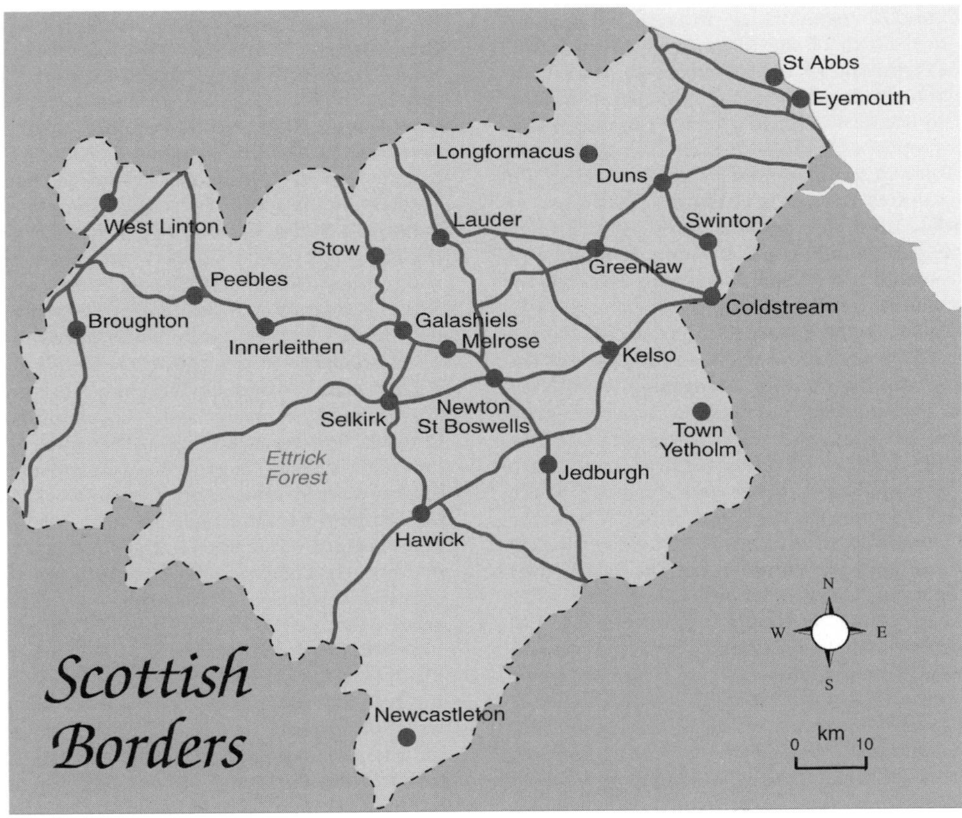

Scottish Borders *Area: 4727 sq. km (1825 sq. miles)* Occupying that part of Scotland adjacent to the frontier with England, Scottish Borders council area stretches from Tweedsmuir in the west to the North Sea in the east. The sixth largest of Scotland's 32 local government areas, Scottish Borders comprises the eastern half of the Southern Uplands of southeast Scotland. It is bounded to the east by the North Sea, to the north by East Lothian and Midlothian, to the west by South Lanarkshire and Dumfries and Galloway, and to the south by the English border regions of Northumberland and Cumbria. It is watered by the River Tweed and its many tributaries, and includes rolling moorland, rich agricultural plains and rocky coastline. Among its leading towns, which serve as centres of agriculture, light industry and textile manufacturing, are Peebles, Innerleithen, Selkirk, Galashiels, Kelso, Melrose, Lauder, Hawick, Jedburgh, Duns and Coldstream. Its administrative centre is Newton St Boswells. Generally characterised by folded sedimentary rocks, Scottish Borders comprises four distinct physiographic regions: an upland rim that separates it from the Lothians and includes the Moorfoot, Lammermuir, Tweedsmuir and Cheviot Hills; a series of river valleys or dales that provide access routes from south to north; the Merse or plain of the River Tweed, which extends from Berwick-upon-Tweed in the east to Galashiels in the west; and the Berwickshire coast, which includes fine beaches and high cliffs. Fed by the Gala, Leader, Ettrick Water, Yarrow, Teviot and Till, the River Tweed flows eastwards from its source west of Peebles to join the North Sea at Berwick-upon-Tweed in Northumberland. St Mary's Loch is the largest natural water body. Some 26 per cent of the area is rough grass or moorland, 18 per cent arable land and 16 per cent woodland. Settlement in the Borders has been dated to 3000 BC and the finding of a longbow from around 3640 BC suggests the presence of hunters at an even earlier period. During their brief expeditions into Scotland, the Romans built forts and fortlets at Newstead (Trimontium) and Lyne, and in succeeding years the local population built fortified settlements, notably multiple-rampart hillforts and fortified farmsteads. Invaded by the Danes in AD 886 and constantly fought over by Scots and English raiders or 'reivers', Scottish Borders has many fine castles in addition to its famous abbeys at Melrose, Dryburgh, Jedburgh and Kelso. The novelist Sir Walter Scott (1771–1832) made his home at Abbotsford. Today the area is noted for its local festivals, common ridings and passion for the game of rugby. Formerly comprising the counties of Berwickshire, Selkirkshire, Roxburghshire and Peeblesshire, Scottish Borders region was created in 1975 and survived the 1996 local authority reorganisation. It is administered from Newtown St Boswells. Fishing, now focused at Eyemouth, farming and forestry play an important part in the rural economy, while the textile industry remains a significant employer in Galashiels, Hawick, Innerleithen, Jedburgh, Peebles, Selkirk and Walkerburn. Lately, light engineering and electronics have made a vital contribution to the Scottish Borders' economy, in addition to increased tourism.

Scottish Exhibition and Conference Centre, the *Glasgow City* Opened in 1985 and built at a cost of £36 million, the Scottish Exhibition and Conference Centre (SECC) is situated on the site of the former Queen's Dock, 1.25 miles (2 km) west of Glasgow city centre and on the northern bank of the River Clyde. Comprising five interlinked halls, with a total area of 19,000 sq. m (204,500 sq. ft), the SECC comprises the main Scottish venue for pop concerts and trade exhibitions. Nearby stands the Clyde Auditorium (The Armadillo) while across the Bell's Bridge over the River Clyde is the Glasgow Science Centre.

Scottish National Gallery of Modern Art *City of Edinburgh* Located on Belford Road, northwest of Edinburgh's New Town and opposite the Dean Gallery, is the Scottish National Gallery of Modern Art. The gallery, which is part of the National Galleries of Scotland, houses a collection of more than 5000 items, dating from the late 19th century to the present day, including important Surrealist and German Expressionist works, with paintings by Giacometti, Hockney, Matisse and Picasso, along with an unrivalled collection of 20th-century Scottish art. The Greek Doric building was designed by William Burn and completed in 1825 as the John Watson School for the 'fatherless children of the professional classes'. It takes the form of a five-bay neoclassical frontage, with a grand six-columned portico. The building, with its classrooms and dormitories, has been successfully adapted (1981–4) to its new function, providing bright and spacious rooms. The extensive surrounding parkland provides a setting for works of sculpture and landscaping by, for example, Jenck, Caro, Hepworth and Moore, and also includes the remains of an early 18th-century windmill.

Scottish National Portrait Gallery *City of Edinburgh* Located in a fine red sandstone edifice towards the east end of Edinburgh's Queen Street, the Scottish National Portrait Gallery forms part of the National Galleries of Scotland. It houses a large collection of portraits of famous Scots, together with the national collection of photography, including important works by Robert Adamson (1821–48) and David O. Hill (1802–70). The building mixes Italian and Gothic styles and was constructed between 1885 and 1890 by Sir Robert Rowand Anderson (1834–1921) as the National Museum of Antiquities. There are great similarities between this building and Mount Stuart, completed by Anderson for John Crichton-Stuart, 3rd Marquess of Bute, in 1880. It is constructed from red Dumfries-shire sandstone, and the facade includes statues of famous Scots by sculptors such as Pittendrigh MacGillivray (1856–1938) and W. Birnie Rhind (1853–1933). The building and museum were a gift to the nation from John Richie Findlay (1824–98), who owned the *Scotsman* newspaper at the time and gave £50,000 for its construction. The National Museum of Antiquities, as part of the Royal Museum of Scotland, shared the building with the Portrait Gallery until its collection was relocated to the new Museum of Scotland in Chambers Street in 1999. The library of the Society of Antiquaries of Scotland remains on the second floor.

Scottish Parliament *City of Edinburgh* A modern building at the foot of the Royal Mile in Edinburgh, the Scottish Parliament building was designed by Spanish architects Enric Miralles and Benedetta Tagliabue in partnership with the Edinburgh firm of Robert Matthew Johnson-Marshall after the site was chosen in 1998. There was considerable controversy relating to the final cost of the building, which exceeded initial estimates by more than ten times. The building was opened by Queen Elizabeth II on 9 October 2004. A theme of boat-shaped buildings starts with the Debating Chamber, on the east side of the complex, and continues through the towers and garden lobby. The Debating Chamber comprises a semi-circular bank of seats facing the Presiding Officer and provides the focus of debates involving the 129 MSPs. Galleries for the public, press and guests also provide views over Salisbury Crags. The building includes an education centre, exhibition areas, restaurant and shop. The five tower buildings lie around the Debating Chamber and house media facilities, committee rooms and offices for Government ministers and support staff. MSPs' offices lie at the west end of the site and feature vaulted ceilings and unique projecting windows incorporating 'contemplative space'. Kemnay granite and Caithness stone feature in several of the buildings. More traditional are the administration offices in Queensberry House, once home to the Dukes of Queensberry, and supporting offices on the Canongate located behind existing facades. A garden lobby, which provides an informal meeting space, links the buildings and features unique leaf-shaped roof lights. Complex landscaping connects the Parliament to Holyrood Park. The Scottish Parliament had its origins in the 12th century but had no fixed meeting place until 1641. Parliament House, behind St Giles' Church in Edinburgh's Old Town, provided a base until it was suspended following the Act of Union in 1707. Following its re-institution in 1999, the Scottish Parliament occupied temporary accommodation around the Lawnmarket, while awaiting the completion of its permanent home, the temporary debating chamber being located in the Church of Scotland Assembly Hall at the top of the Mound.

Scourie *Highland* A small village on the west coast of Sutherland, Scourie lies at the head of Scourie Bay, 7 miles (11 km) southwest of Laxford Bridge. Now bypassed, the village developed in association with an inn in the mid-19th century. Scourie House was built in the 1840s for the Sutherland Estate factor. The village is a popular centre for walkers, anglers and birdwatchers making the trip to the nearby island of Handa.

Scousburgh *Shetland* A hamlet in the Dunrossness district at the southern end of the Mainland of Shetland, Scousburgh overlooks the Bay of Scousburgh, 5 miles (8 km) north-northwest of Sumburgh Airport. The Ward of Scousburgh rises to 263 m (862 ft) to the northeast and the settlement of South Scousburgh lies a quarter-mile (0.4 km) to the south.

Scrabster *Highland* A 19th-century fishing port on the north coast of Caithness, Scrabster lies beneath a cliff on the west side of Thurso Bay, 2 miles (3 km) northwest of the town of Thurso. It is built on the site of a much older Norse homestead, its 13th-century castle being a former stronghold of the bishops of Caithness. Scrabster House dates from 1834. From the large harbour, constructed c.1850, ferries connect with Orkney, Shetland and the Faroe Islands. Flagstone quarries nearby were worked until the early 20th century, and a lighthouse at Holborn Head was first lit in 1862. A BP oil depot was established in 1978 and the harbour was enlarged in the 1990s to handle large ocean-going fishing boats in addition to Scrabster's lifeboat and coastguard cutter. Scrabster has a business park with a call centre and hi-tech industries.

Screel *Dumfries and Galloway* A locality in Dumfries and Galloway, Screel lies at the eastern foot of Bengairn near the head of Orchardton Bay, an inlet of the Solway Firth. Dalbeattie is 6 miles (10 km) to the northeast.

Scrape, the *Scottish Borders* A hill in the Ettrick district of Scottish Borders, the Scrape rises to 715 m (2347 ft) 7 miles (11 km) southwest of Peebles.

Scridain, Loch *Argyll and Bute* A long sea loch on the west coast of Mull in the Inner Hebrides, Loch Scridain is 12 miles (19 km) in length and 3 miles (5 km) at its widest. It lies between Ardmeanach to the north and the Ross of Mull to the south. The Aird of Kinloch at its head separates Loch Scridain from the small Loch Beg, which receives the River Coladoir.

Scuir Vuilinn An alternative name for Sgurr a' Mhuilinn in Highland Council area.

Scurdie Ness *Angus* A headland on the coast of Angus, Scurdie Ness extends into the North Sea to the south of the mouth of the River South Esk, a mile (1.5 km) east of Montrose. It shelters the entrance to Montrose Basin and is marked by a Stevenson-built lighthouse.

Scurrival Point *Western Isles* The most northerly point on the island of Barra in the Western Isles, Scurrival Point looks out over the Sound of Barra towards Fiaray and South Uist.

Scuthvie Bay *Orkney* A large wide bay in the Orkney Islands, Scuthvie Bay forms an inlet on the northeast coast of the island of Sanday, to the west of Start Point and 5 miles (8 km) northeast of Overbister.

Sea of the Hebrides A stretch of sea between the Inner and Outer Hebrides, the Sea of the Hebrides extends westwards from the isle of Skye to South Uist.

Seafar *North Lanarkshire* A central district of the new town of Cumbernauld.

Seafield *City of Edinburgh* A northeastern district of the city of Edinburgh, Seafield forms a suburb between Leith and Portobello. The Eastern General Hospital is located here.

Seafield *Moray* A former parish in Moray, now included in Rathven parish, Seafield gave its name to the title of the earls of Seafield, whose estates stretch from the coast of the Moray Firth southwards into Strathspey and the Cairngorm Mountains.

Seafield *South Ayrshire* A southern suburb of the town of Ayr, Seafield lies at the southern end of Ayr Bay.

Seafield *West Lothian* A small village in West Lothian, Seafield lies 1.5 miles (2.5 km) east of Blackburn and 2 miles (3 km) southeast of Bathgate, between the River Almond to the south and the M8 to the north.

Seaforth, Loch *Western Isles* A sea loch on the east coast of North Harris in the Outer Hebrides, Loch Seaforth opens out into the Sound of Shiant. Seaforth Island, with an area of 273 ha (675 acres), rises sheer out of the loch to 217 m (712 ft). The loch gives its name to an extinct branch of the Clan Mackenzie, founders of the Earldom of Seaforth, and a regiment, the Seaforth Highlanders, which was created in 1881 on the amalgamation of the 72nd and 78th Highlanders, the 78th having been founded in 1778 by the Earl of Seaforth.

Sealg, Loch The Gaelic name for Loch Shell in the Western Isles.

Seamab Hill *Clackmannanshire* A summit in the Ochil Hills, Seamab Hill rises to 439 m (1442 ft) 3 miles (5 km) northeast of Dollar near the entrance to Glen Devon.

Seamill *North Ayrshire* A resort in the Cunninghame district of North Ayrshire, Seamill lies on the Firth of Clyde immediately south of West Kilbride. Originally built as a mill town, it developed in the late 19th century as a hydropathic centre for convalescents.

Seana Bhraigh *Highland* A mountain in Ross and Cromarty, Seanna Bhraigh rises to 926 m (3041 ft) to the southeast of Ullapool. It consists of a high plateau with the impressive Luchd Choire on its northern flanks.

Seaton Cliffs *Angus* A nature reserve with spectacular cliffs, sea stacks and caves, Seaton Cliffs look out onto the North Sea on the Angus coast immediately northeast of Arbroath. The cliffs have many breeding sea birds and from the car park in Victoria Park it is possible to follow a 3-mile (5-km) nature trail.

Seatown of Largo An alternative name for Lower Largo in Fife.

Seil *Argyll and Bute* A small island on the east side of the Firth of Lorn, Seil lies on the Argyllshire coast 7 miles (11 km) southwest of Oban. It has an area of 1405 ha (3472 acres) and rises to 146 m (479 ft) at Meall Chaise. Its deposits of slate were quarried for nearly 300 years until 1965. At one time slate was transported by boat through the Crinan Canal from the small port of Easdale. The chief settlements are at Clachan Bridge, Easdale, Balvicar and Cuan, where a ferry connects with the island of Luing. Seil Sound, a narrow passage of water separating the island from the mainland, is traversed by the Clachan Bridge, built by Thomas Telford in 1792 and often referred to as the 'Bridge over the Atlantic'.

Seilebost *Western Isles* A village in South Harris in the Outer Hebrides, Seilebost lies 6 miles (10 km) southwest of Tarbert overlooking a sandy inlet.

Seisiadar The Gaelic name for Sheshader in the Western Isles.

Selcoth Burn *Dumfries and Galloway* A stream in northern Dumfries and Galloway, the Selcoth Burn flows down the west-facing slope of Loch Fell to join the Moffat Water, 4 miles (6.5 km) northeast of Moffat.

Selkirk *Scottish Borders* A former county town in the Ettrick valley of Scottish Borders, Selkirk lies on the Ettrick Water, 11 miles (18 km) north of Hawick and 19 miles (31 km) west of Kelso. In 1113 David I erected a Tironensian monastery on the site of an earlier foundation, but in 1128 the monks left to take up residence in the larger abbey at Kelso. In the early 14th century a royal castle known as Selkirk Peel was erected on Peel Hill and the town was chartered as a royal burgh. Noted in medieval times for its shoemakers (souters), Selkirk later developed in association with the manufacture of tweed and woollens, industries that have now largely been replaced by modern fabrics and electronics. Notable buildings include The Haining (1794), a neoclassical house; Halliwell's House Museum; Bowhill (1708); and the Court House, within which are displayed items belonging to Sir Walter Scott, who served as Sheriff from 1803 to 1832. A statue by Thomas Clapperton (1913) commemorates Selkirk's sole survivor at the Battle of Flodden (1513), after which the English destroyed the town. In 1645, the Covenanters under David Leslie massacred Royalists under the command of the Marquess of Montrose at nearby Philiphaugh. The explorer Mungo Park was born nearby at Foulshiels (1771) and Robert Burns wrote his *Epistle to Willie Creech* in Selkirk in 1787. Selkirk's Common Riding is the second-largest boundary festival in Scottish Borders.

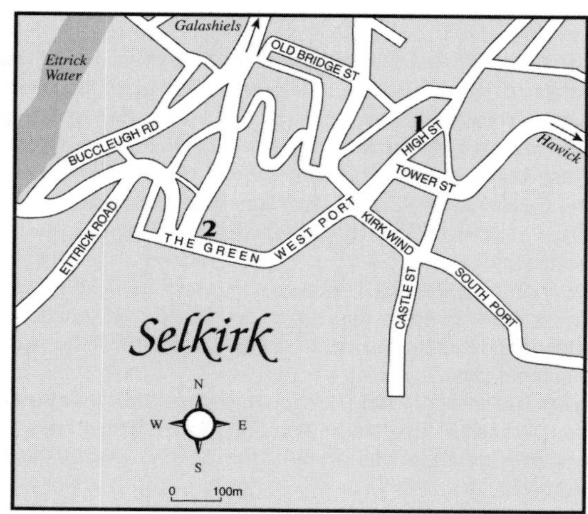

1 *Scottish Borders Council Museum* 2 *Halliwell's House Museum*

Selkirkshire A former Scottish county extending over the valleys of the Ettrick, Yarrow and Tweed and the basin of St Mary's Loch, Selkirkshire was absorbed into the larger Borders Region in 1974. Its county town was Selkirk.

Seton Collegiate Church *East Lothian* Founded in 1470 as a college by Lord Seton, Seton Collegiate Church lies a mile (1.5 km) southeast of Cockenzie. It incorporates sections of an earlier parish church (1248) and was abandoned after the Reformation.

Seton Mains *East Lothian* A hamlet in East Lothian, Seton Mains lies 1.5 miles (2.5 km) east of Port Seton and a half-mile (1 km) south of Seton Sands. Seton Collegiate Church and Seton House are located a half-mile (1 km) to the west.

Setter, Stone of *Orkney* Described as Orkney's finest standing stone, the Stone of Setter is a prehistoric standing stone situated to the north of Mill Loch on the island of Eday in the Orkney Islands.

Sgairneach Mhòr *Perth and Kinross* A mountain in highland Perth and Kinross, Sgairneach Mhòr rises to 991 m (3250 ft) between the Pass of Drumochter and Loch Ericht.

Sgamhain, Loch *Highland* A small loch in Ross and Cromarty, Loch Sgamhain (also Loch Scaven) is situated in Glen Carron, 4 miles (6.5 km) southwest of Achnasheen.

Sgarabhaigh The Gaelic name for Scaravay in the Western Isles.

Sgarbh Breac *Argyll and Bute* A hill in the northeast corner of the island of Islay in the Inner Hebrides, Sgarbh Breac rises to 364 m (1194 ft) 6 miles (10 km) northwest of Port Askaig.

Sgeir a' Chaisteil *Argyll and Bute* An island in the Inner Hebrides, Sgeir a' Chaisteil is one of the Treshnish Isles group, lying a half-mile (1 km) north of Lunga, to which it is connected by a spit called Corran Lunga.

Sgeir an Eirionnaich *Argyll and Bute* A small island in the Inner Hebrides, one of the Treshnish Isles, Sgeir an Eirionnaich lies a mile (1.5 km) northeast of Lunga.

Sgeir Dremisdale *Western Isles* A rocky outcrop in the

sea off the west coast of the island of South Uist in the Western Isles, Sgeir Dremisdale is connected to the mainland at low tide.

Sgeir Dubh *Western Isles* Sgeir Dubh is the name given to a group of rock outliers in the Sound of Harris, a mile (1.5 km) southwest of the island of Ensay in the Western Isles.

Sgeir nam Feusgan *Highland* A skerry off the coast of Wester Ross, Sgeir nam Feusgan lies to the northwest of Eilean a' Bhuic in the Summer Isles.

Sgeir Rocail An alternative name for Rockall.

Sgiath Chuil *Stirling* A mountain of Breadalbane, Sgiath Chuil rises to 921 m (3022 ft) on the north side of Glen Dochart, 6 miles (10 km) west of Killin.

Sgiogarstaigh An alternative name for Skigirsta in the Western Isles.

Sgioport, Loch *Western Isles* A sea loch in the Outer Hebrides, Loch Sgioport (also Loch Skiport) opens out into the Little Minch on the northeast coast of North Uist. The settlement of Loch Sgioport lies at its head.

Sgitheach *Highland* A river in Easter Ross, the Sgitheach (also Skiack) flows eastwards from the slopes of Ben Wyvis through Strath Sgitheach before emptying into the Cromarty Firth just south of Evanton.

Sgor an Lochain Uaine *Aberdeenshire* A summit of the southern Grampians, Sgor an Lochain Uaine, sometimes referred to as Angel's Peak, rises to 1258 m (4127 ft) northwest of Cairn Toul. The ridge running from Lochan Uaine to this peak is one of the few arretes in the Cairngorms. Sgor an Lochain Uaine derives its name from the Gaelic for 'peak of the little green loch'.

Sgor Gaibhre *Highland/Perth and Kinross* A mountain on the border between Highland and Perth and Kinross, Sgor Gaibhre rises to 955 m (3133 ft) 4 miles (6.5 km) south of Ben Alder. With Carn Dearg it forms a number of open corries that contain some of the largest gatherings of red deer in Scotland.

Sgor Gaoith *Highland* A mountain in Badenoch at the western end of the Cairngorms, Sgor Gaoith rises to 1118 m (3667 ft) to the east of Glen Feshie, 6 miles (10 km) southeast of Kincraig. Below the summit two features dominate the skyline, a sharp pinnacle called A' Chailleach (old woman) and the nearby pillar Am Bodach (old man).

Sgor na h-Ulaidh *Highland* Often referred to as the 'lost mountain' of Glen Coe, Sgor na h-Ulaidh rises to 994 m (3261 ft) to the south of the glen.

Sgorr Dhearg *Highland* A mountain rising to 1024 m (3359 ft) to the west of Glen Coe and south of Ballachulish, Sgorr Dhearg forms the eastern part of the Beinn a' Bheithir range with Sgorr Dhonuill. Above the treeline, the landscape consists of a number of pink quartzite boulders that probably gave rise to its Gaelic name, which can be translated as 'red peak'.

Sgorr Dhonuill *Highland* Rising to 1001 m (3284 ft) to the south of Ballachulish and west of Glen Coe, Sgorr Dhonuill forms part of the Beinn a' Bheithir range with Sgorr Dhearg.

Sgorr nam Fiannaidh *Highland* Rising to 967 m (3172 ft) to the north of the Pass of Glencoe, Sgorr nam Fiannaidh is the higher of the two peaks forming the 2-mile (3-km) Aonach Eagach ridge.

Sgorr Ruadh *Highland* A mountain in Wester Ross, Sgorr Ruadh rises to 962 m (3156 ft) to the south of Torridon in the Coulin Forest.

Sguman Coinntich *Highland* A mountain in the Lochalsh district of Highland Council area, Sguman Coinntich rises to a height of 879 m (2883 ft) in the Killilan Forest, a mile (1.5 km) southeast of Ben Killilan and 3 miles (5 km) east of the head of Loch Long.

Sgurr a' Bhealaich Dheirg *Highland* One of the Five Sisters of Kintail, Sgurr a' Bhealaich Dheirg rises to 1036 m (3399 ft) to the north of Glen Sheil.

Sgurr a' Chaorachain *Highland* A mountain in the West Monar Forest, Sgurr a' Chaorachain rises to 1053 m (3455 ft) between the western end of Loch Monar and Glen Carron.

Sgurr a' Choire Ghlais *Highland* One of the four peaks of the North Strathfarrar Ridge, Sgurr a' Choire Ghlais rises to 1083 m (3553 ft) between Glen Strathfarrar to the south and Strathconon Forest to the north.

Sgurr a' Ghreadaidh *Highland* A summit of the Cuillin Hills on the isle of Skye, Sgurr a' Ghreadaidh rises to 973 m (3192 ft). It is the highest peak on the northern part of the Cuillin ridge.

Sgurr a' Mhadaidh *Highland* Sgurr a' Mhadaidh forms a summit with four well-defined tops in the Cuillins on the isle of Skye. It rises to 918 m (3011 ft) at 'peak of the fox'.

Sgurr a' Mhaim *Highland* One of four peaks in the 'Ring of Steall', a horseshoe-shaped range around Coire a' Mhail at the western end of the Mamore Forest in Lochaber, Sgurr a' Mhaim rises to 1099 m (3606 ft) to the south of Glen Nevis. Its summit is capped with quartzite and to the south is a sharp arrete known as the Devil's Ridge.

Sgurr a' Mhaoraich *Highland* A remote mountain in Lochaber, Sgurr a' Mhaoraich rises to 1027 m (3369 ft) to the north of Loch Quoich.

Sgurr a' Mhuilinn *Highland* A mountain in central Ross and Cromarty, Sgurr a' Mhuilinn (also Scuir Vuilinn) rises to 879 m (2883 ft) to the south of Strath Bran.

Sgurr Alasdair *Highland* A peak in the Cuillins on the isle of Skye, Sgurr Alasdair rises to a height of 993 m (3258 ft). It is named after Alexander Nicolson, who was a native of Skye and one of the earliest explorers in the Cuillins.

Sgurr an Airgid *Highland* A mountain in the Lochalsh district of Highland Council area, Sgurr an Airgid rises to 841 m (2758 ft) a mile (1.5 km) north of the head of Loch Duich.

Sgurr an Doire Leathain *Highland* One of the seven peaks of the South Glen Shiel Ridge, Sgurr an Doire Leathain rises to 1010 m (3314 ft) between Sgurr an Lochain and Maol Chinndearg.

Sgurr an Lochain *Highland* One of the seven peaks of the South Glen Shiel Ridge, Sgurr an Lochain rises to 1004 m (3294 ft) to the northwest of Sgurr an Doire Leathain.

Sgurr Bàn *Highland* A remote mountain in Wester Ross, Sgurr Bàn rises to 989 m (3245 ft) to the north of Kinlochewe. Its summit is composed of Cambrian quartzite rock.

Sgurr Breac *Highland* The most westerly of the Fannich mountains in Ross and Cromarty, Sgurr Breac rises to 999 m (3278 ft) to the north of the western end of Loch Fannich.

Sgurr Choinnich *Highland* A mountain in the West Monar Forest, Sgurr Choinnich rises to 999 m (3278 ft) to the north of the western end of Loch Monar.

Sgurr Chòinnich Mòr *Highland* A mountain in Lochaber, Sgurr Chòinnich Mòr rises to 1094 m (3589 ft) to the east of Ben Nevis.

Sgurr Dearg *Highland* A summit in the Cuillins on the isle of Skye, Sgurr Dearg rises to 986 m (3234 ft) in the centre of the range. Reaching its summit involves a difficult ascent of the 24 m (79 foot) Inaccessible Pinnacle.

Sgurr Dhomhnuill *Highland* A mountain in Ardgour to the west of Loch Linnhe, Sgurr Dhomhnuill rises to 888 m (2913 ft) 6 miles (10 km) northeast of Strontian. The Strontian River rises on its slopes.

Sgurr Dubh Mòr *Highland* A summit of the Cuillins on the isle of Skye, Sgurr Dubh Mòr rises to 944 m (3096 ft) to the southeast of Sgurr Alasdair.

Sgurr Eilde Mòr *Highland* A mountain at the eastern end of the Mamore Ridge, Sgurr Eilde Mòr rises to 1008 m (3307 ft) to the north of Loch Eilde Mòr and northeast of Kinlochleven.

Sgurr Fhuaran *Highland* The highest peak of the Five Sisters of Kintail, Sgurr Fhuaran rises to 1067 m (3501 ft) to the north of Glen Shiel.

Sgurr Fhuar-thuill *Highland* A remote mountain on the North Strathfarrar Ridge, Ross and Cromarty, Sgurr Fhuar-thuill rises to a height of 1049 m (3442 ft) to the north of Glen Strathfarrar.

Sgurr Fiona *Highland* One of the peaks of An Teallach in Wester Ross, Sgurr Fiona rises to 1059 m (3474 ft) to the southwest of Dundonnell.

Sgurr Mhic Choinnich *Highland* A summit in the Cuillins on the isle of Skye, Sgurr Mhic Choinnich rises to 948 m (3110 ft). It is named after John Mackenzie, a local guide and one of the earliest explorers of the Cuillins.

Sgurr Mhòr *Highland* The highest of the summits of Beinn Alligin in Wester Ross, Sgurr Mhòr rises to 985 m (3231 ft) northwest of Torridon.

Sgurr Mòr *Highland* The highest summit of the Fannich Ridge in Ross and Cromarty, Sgurr Mòr rises to 1110 m (3642 ft) to the north of Loch Fannich.

Sgurr Mòr *Highland* A remote mountain peak in Lochaber, Sgurr Mòr rises to 1003 m (3291 ft) to the south of the west end of Loch Quoich.

Sgurr na Banachdich *Highland* A peak of the Cuillins on the isle of Skye, Sgurr na Banachdich rises to 965 m (3166 ft) due east of the Glen Brittle Memorial Hut. The main summit can be reached by the western ridge from Coir' an Eich.

Sgurr na Carnach *Highland* One of the Five Sisters of Kintail, Sgurr na Carnach rises to 1002 m (3287 ft) to the north of Glen Shiel.

Sgurr na Ciche *Highland* A mountain in the so-called 'Rough Bounds' of Knoydart, Sgurr na Ciche rises to 1040 m (3412 ft) between Loch Nevis and Loch Quoich.

Sgurr na Ciste Duibhe *Highland* One of the Five Sisters of Kintail, Sgurr na Ciste Duibhe rises to 1027 m (3369 ft) to the north of Glen Shiel. The south face of this peak is one of the steepest in Scotland, rising 1000 m (3280 ft) in a horizontal distance of a mile (1.5 km).

Sgurr na Feartaig *Highland* A mountain ridge in Ross and Cromarty, Sgurr na Feartaig rises to 862 m (2827 ft) 3 miles (5 km) northwest of the western end of Loch Monar. Achnashellach Forest swathes its lower north-facing slopes overlooking Glen Carron.

Sgurr na Lapaich *Highland* A mountain at the head of Glen Affric in the Inverness district of Highland Council area, Sgurr na Lapaich rises to 1036 m (3398 ft) between Loch Mullardoch and Loch Affric.

Sgurr na Lapaich *Highland* A remote mountain to the north of Glen Cannich, Sgurr na Lapaich rises to 1150 m (3773 ft) between Loch Mullardoch and Loch Monar.

Sgurr na Ruaidhe *Highland* A summit at the eastern end of the North Strathfarrar Ridge, Sgurr na Ruaidhe rises to 993 m (3258 ft) to the north of Glen Strathfarrar.

Sgurr na Sgine *Highland* A mountain in Kintail, Sgurr na Sgine rises to 946 m (3101 ft) to the south of Glen Shiel.

Sgurr nan Ceannaichean *Highland* A mountain of Wester Ross, Sgurr nan Ceannaichean rises to 915 m (3002 ft) to the south of Glen Carron.

Sgurr nan Ceathreamhnan *Highland* A remote mountain at the head of Glen Affric, Sgurr nan Ceathreamhnan rises to 1151 m (3776 ft) to the west of Loch Affric.

Sgurr nan Clach Geala *Highland* A summit at the centre of the Fannich Ridge in Ross and Cromarty, Sgurr nan Clach Geala rises to 1093 m (3586 ft) to the north of Loch Fannich. The Coire Mhoir face has impressive mica-schist buttresses.

Sgurr nan Coireachan *Highland* A mountain in Lochaber, Sgurr nan Coireachan rises to 956 m (3136 ft) to the north of Glenfinnan.

Sgurr nan Coireachan *Highland* A mountain in Lochaber, Sgurr nan Coireachan rises to 952 m (3123 ft) at the head of Glen Dessarry and to the south of the western end of Loch Quoich.

Sgurr nan Conbhairean *Highland* A mountain peak in Lochaber, Sgurr nan Conbhairean rises to 1109 m (3638 ft) to the north of Loch Cluanie.

Sgurr nan Each *Highland* A summit at the centre of the Fannich Ridge in Ross and Cromarty, Sgurr nan Each rises to 923 m (3028 ft) to the north of Loch Fannich. The summit ridge of the mountain falls steeply to the east at Coire Mhoir.

Sgurr nan Eag *Highland* A summit of the Cuillins on the isle of Skye, Sgurr nan Eag rises to 924 m (3031 ft) above Coire na Laogh.

Sgurr nan Gillean *Highland* A mountain peak in the Cuillins on the isle of Skye, Sgurr nan Gillean rises to 965 m (2932 ft) at the eastern extremity of the range overlooking Glen Sligachan.

Sgurr nan Gillean *Highland* A mountain on the island of Rum in the Inner Hebrides, Sgurr nan Gillean rises to 764 m (2506 ft) a mile (1.5 km) northeast of the southern headland of Rubha nam Meirleach.

Sgurr Thuilm *Highland* A flat summit in Lochaber, Sgurr Thuilm, rises to 963 m (3159 ft) 4 miles (6.5 km) southwest of the head of Loch Arkaig. It is said that Bonnie Prince Charlie spent a night on the peak following his defeat at Culloden.

Shalloch on Minnoch *South Ayrshire* A summit in the Carrick district of South Ayrshire, Shalloch on Minnoch rises to 769 m (2522 ft) 9 miles (14 km) south of Straiton.

Shader *Western Isles* A township on the northwest coast of the Isle of Lewis in the Outer Hebrides, Shader (also Shadar; *Gael: Siadar* or *Siadair*) lies midway between Barvas and the Butt of Lewis, 1.25 miles (2 km) southwest of Borve. The townships of Lower and Upper Shader

(Gael: *Siadar Iarach* and *Siadar Uarach*) lie closeby and to the west stand the remains of Teampall Pheadair. To the east are the Steinacleit chambered cairn and standing stones.

Shandon *Argyll and Bute* A small village of Argyll and Bute, Shandon lies on the east shore of Gare Loch, 3 miles (5 km) southeast of Garelochhead and 3 miles (5 km) northwest of Helensburgh.

Shandwick *Highland* A small settlement in Easter Ross, Shandwick lies on Shandwick Bay, a small inlet of the Moray Firth a half-mile (1 km) south of Balintore and 12 miles (19 km) northeast of Invergordon. Shandwick is the site of an ornate Pictish stone.

Shapinsay *Orkney* The green and fertile island of Shapinsay lies at the centre of the Orkney Islands group to the north of the eastern section of Mainland Orkney. Six miles (10 km) in length and generally flat, it rises to a height of 64 m (210 ft) at Ward Hill in the centre. Largely made of middle Old Red Sandstone rock, the island's most interesting features include its 'ayres' or storm beaches, which are strips of sea water shut off from the ocean by narrow necks of land. The island is intensively cultivated. Its anchorage at Elwick was used by King Haakon's fleet in 1263 before sailing south to Largs on the Firth of Clyde. Mill Dam in the east is an RSPB nature reserve which is home to many breeding birds, including the water rail, pintails, waders and black-headed gulls. In 1805 the minister of Shapinsay first noted here the Orkney vole, *Microtus arvalis*, a sub-species of the European vole. Sites of archaeological interest include Odin's Stone, Mor Stein standing stone, Castle Bloody chambered cairn and the Broch of Burroughston. Buildings of note include Balfour Castle, Elwick Mill, 12th-century Linton Chapel and Shapinsay Heritage Centre, which is located in an old smithy. Quholm in the northeast was the birthplace of the father of American writer Washington Irving. The population of the island fell from just over 900 in 1891 to 300 by 2001, most of the islanders now being engaged in the farming of sheep and cattle, boat building, knitwear production and craft industries such as wood carving. Shapinsay, which is linked to Kirkwall by car ferry, is separated from the Orkney Mainland by Shapinsay Sound.

Shawbost *Western Isles* A crofting township with tweed mills on the northwest coast of the Isle of Lewis in the Outer Hebrides, Shawbost (Gael: *Siabost*) is situated on the Shawbost River between Carloway and Barvas, 13 miles (21 km) northwest of Stornoway. The township has a folk museum and a community school with a public sports hall and swimming pool. Shawbost includes the linear extensions of North Shawbost (Gael: *Siabost bho Thuath*), South Shawbost (Gael: *Siabost bho Dheas*) and New Shawbost (Gael: *Pairc Shiaboist*).

Shawhead *Dumfries and Galloway* A village in the Dumfries and Galloway parish of Kirkpatrick Irongray, Shawhead lies on the Old Water, 7 miles (11 km) west of Dumfries.

Shawlands *Glasgow City* A southern suburb of Glasgow, Shawlands lies between Pollokshaws and Crossmyloof, 3 miles (5 km) southwest of the city centre.

Shawsholm *Dumfries and Galloway* A locality in Nithsdale, Dumfries and Galloway, Shawsholm lies between Closeburn and the River Nith.

Shearington *Dumfries and Galloway* A locality in Nithsdale, Dumfries and Galloway, Shearington lies between the Lochar Water and the Solway Firth, 7 miles (11 km) southeast of Dumfries.

Shebster *Highland* A settlement in northern Caithness, Shebster lies to the west of the Forss Water, 3 miles (5 km) south of Lybster and 7 miles (11 km) southwest of Thurso.

Sheddens *East Renfrewshire* A suburb of Clarkston in East Renfrewshire, Sheddens lies between Clarkston and Busby to the east.

Shee, Glen *Perth and Kinross* A valley in eastern Perth and Kinross, Glen Shee carries the Shee Water southwards from Spittal of Glenshee to its junction with the River Ardle at Bridge of Cally. To the north, beyond the Devil's Elbow, is the Glenshee Chairlifts and Ski Centre. Glenshee Church dates from 1831, and the humpbacked Glenshee Bridge was constructed during the building of the military road in 1749–63.

Sheep Island *Argyll and Bute* A small uninhabited island lying a half-mile (1 km) north of the island of Sanda to the east of the Kintyre peninsula in Argyll and Bute, Sheep Island is used for grazing livestock. Major geological features include a cave and a natural stone arch.

Sheigra *Highland* A remote township in northwest Sutherland, Sheigra lies 4 miles (6.5 km) northwest of Kinlochbervie.

Shell, Loch *Western Isles* A sea loch of the east coast of the Isle of Lewis in the Outer Hebrides, Loch Shell (Gael: *Loch Sealg*) is located to the southwest of Kebock Head, in the area known as Park. At the mouth of the loch lies the island of Eilean Iuvard.

Shennanton *Dumfries and Galloway* A locality in western Dumfries and Galloway, Shennanton lies on the River Bladnoch, 6 miles (10 km) southwest of Newton Stewart. The Tudor-style Shennanton House was built in 1908 to a design by H. E. Clifford.

Shennas *Dumfries and Galloway* A locality in western Dumfries and Galloway, Shennas lies to the west of the Main Water of Luce, 11 miles (18 km) northwest of Glenluce.

Sheriffmuir *Stirling* A desolate moor on the northwest-facing western edge of the Ochil Hills, Sheriffmuir lies 2 miles (3 km) northeast of Dunblane. In November 1715 an indecisive battle was fought here between the Jacobites under the Earl of Mar and Government forces led by the Duke of Argyll, who was determined to prevent the Jacobites reaching the River Forth. Despite the Jacobites' greater numbers, Mar was forced to retreat to Perth, losing many Highlanders who deserted en route. While the Government force suffered greater casualties, the Jacobites never recovered momentum and the rebellion crumbled. Still visible are the great burial mounds, and a gathering stone from where the Duke of Argyll is said to have watched the opposing Jacobite army gather.

Sheshader *Western Isles* A crofting township on the Eye peninsula on the east coast of the isle of Lewis in the Outer Hebrides, Sheshader (Gael: *Seisiadar*) overlooks Sheshader Bay and the Minch 1.25 miles (2 km) southwest of Aird and 7.5 miles (12 km) east of Stornoway.

Shetland *Area: 1468 sq. km (567 sq. miles)* The northernmost islands of the British Isles, Shetland comprises over a hundred islands, of which 15 are inhabited. These windswept islands stretch for over 95 miles (152 km) from Muckle Flugga in the north to the

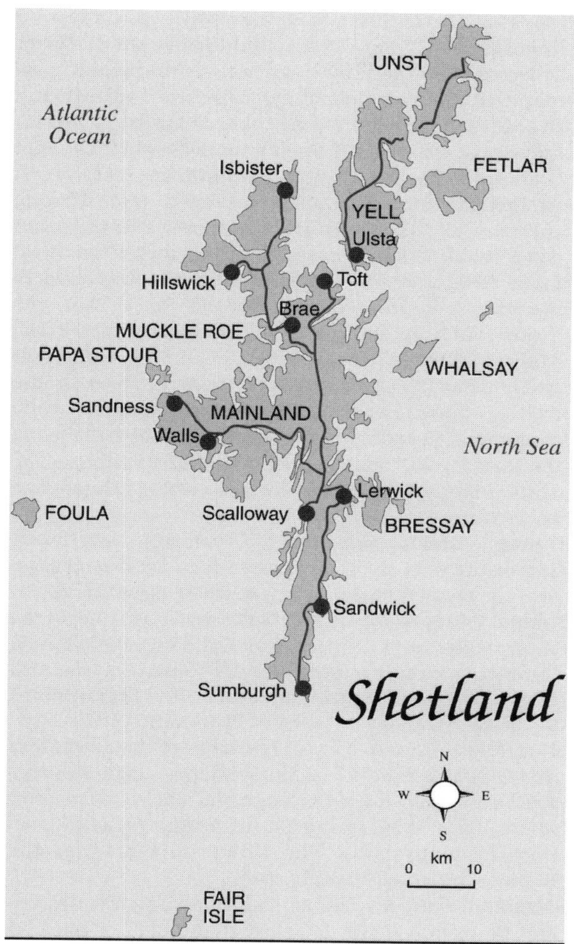

Fair Isle in the south, the longest of the islands being the Mainland which is 55 miles (88 km) long and 20 miles (22 km) wide at its broadest point. It has an area of 96,997 ha (239,680 acres) and a population of 17,550 (2001). Geologically, the islands are the tops of a range of drowned hills whose Precambrian and Dalradian rocks seldom decompose into fertile soil but give rise to bleak landscapes of blanket peat interspersed with rocky outcrops. Granite and gneiss are common in the north, while in the south and east grey-brown flagstones give a distinctive appearance to buildings. Many of the islands are fringed by steep cliffs that are home to large colonies of nesting birds, and much of the island archipelago's 1450-km (900-mile) coastline is indented, long inlets or voes leading to low shingle shores that often rise up to long, whale-backed hills. The climate of Shetland is oceanic, mild in winter and cool in summer, the North Atlantic Drift bringing a milder climate than might be expected to this northerly latitude (60 °N). In the summer when the days are long, the sky barely darkens between the midnight hour and dawn, a time that gives rise to the 'Simmer Dim'. Strong winds and saltspray combine to limit vegetation growth to a stunted state, trees being a rare sight among the isles. The Shetland Islands, occupying a maritime crossroads where the North Sea meets the Atlantic Ocean, have been continuously inhabited for at least 5500 years, since the arrival of the first Neolithic farmers. The first settlers would have encountered a kinder climate and low, scrubby forest, a landscape subsequently altered by grazing, clearance of woodland and climatic change. The archaeological remains of these early Neolithic and Bronze Age farming communities are among the most outstanding in Europe, as are the more prominent Iron Age fortifications which include the Mousa Broch. The sites of almost 100 of these brochs have been found in the islands. Christianity first arrived among the Pictish people of Shetland during the 6th century AD and several early churches from this period have been found, the most notable being that on St Ninian's Isle whose ruins yielded a rich hoard of Celtic church silver in 1958. The subsequent arrival of the Vikings during the 8th century left an indelible mark on the culture, language and place names of Shetland that remains to this day. Under Norse control for nearly five centuries, the islands were eventually pledged to the Scottish Crown in 1469 under the marriage treaty of James III and Princess Margaret of Denmark. Every year the midwinter festival of Up Helly-Aa is a reminder of the islanders' Scandinavian past. Taking advantage of their strategic position, the islands played an important role in both World Wars, after which the fishing industry was revitalised and sheep farming extended to provide the basis of a growing knitwear industry. The tourist trade subsequently developed with the arrival of regular air and ferry services to the islands, and in the 1970s the Shetland economy was given a dramatic boost with the establishment of air and sea bases, most notably at Sumburgh and Sullom Voe, to service the North Sea oil industry. Fish processing, knitwear and marine engineering, all largely based in the administrative centre, Lerwick, are the chief manufacturing industries, while fishing, fish farming, agriculture and oil-related activities are the main primary industries. The fiddle music and knitwear of Shetland are known throughout the world.

Shettleston *Glasgow City* An eastern district of the city of Glasgow, Shettleston lies to the north of Tollcross and east of Parkhead, 3 miles (5 km) east of the city centre. As early as the 13th century Shettleston Cross was a collecting point for tolls, and from the 18th century it developed in association with coal mining, weaving and agriculture. In the 19th century its populace supplied a workforce for local ironworks and the manufacture of rope, bottles and textile machinery.

Shian Bay *Argyll and Bute* An inlet on the west coast of the island of Jura in the Inner Hebrides, Shian Bay is sheltered by Shian Island to the northeast. It receives the Shian River which flows northwest from Loch Righ Mòr.

Shiant Islands *Western Isles* A group of uninhabited islands in the Minch, the Shiant Islands are separated from North Harris in the Outer Hebrides by the Sound of Shiant. A geological outlier of the isle of Skye, the Shiant Islands comprise a group of two islands and several islets and skerries. Garbh Eilean, the northernmost part of the largest island, is connected to Eilean an Tigh in the south by a narrow neck of pebbles. To the east is Eilean Mhuire (or Mary's Island), an elevated plateau surrounded by steep cliffs. The columnar basalt rock formations are similar to Staffa and the Giant's Causeway (Ireland), rising to heights in excess of 150 m (492 ft). Both islands have evidence of occupation but today are given over to sheep grazing. Sailors tell stories of the legendary 'Blue Men' of the Minch who are said to live between the Shiant Islands.

Shibhinis The Gaelic name for Shivinish in the Western Isles.

Shiel, Loch *Highland* A narrow loch in Lochaber, Loch Shiel extends 11 miles (18 km) southwest from Glenfinnan to Acharacle, between Moidart and Sunart.

Shiel, River *Highland* A river in the Lochalsh district of Highland Council area, the Shiel rises in mountains to the south of Glen Shiel and flows northwestwards through the glen to enter Loch Duich at Shiel Bridge.

Shiel Bridge *Highland* A locality in Wester Ross, Shiel Bridge lies at the mouth of Loch Shiel and the head of Loch Duich.

Shiel Burn *Moray* Rising in hills to the east of Glen Barry in Moray, the Shiel Burn flows southwestwards to join the River Isla to the south of Nethermills.

Shiel Hill *Dumfries and Galloway* A summit in the Galloway Hills, Dumfries and Galloway, Shiel Hill rises to 478 m (1568 ft) to the southwest of Sanquhar.

Shieldaig *Highland* A settlement in Wester Ross, Shieldaig lies at the head of Loch Shieldaig, an inlet of the Gair Loch, 2 miles (3 km) south of Gairloch.

Shieldaig *Highland* A linear village of whitewashed cottages in Wester Ross, Shieldaig lies on the east shore of Loch Shieldaig, an inlet of Loch Torridon, 14 miles (22 km) west-southwest of Kinlochewe. Built in the 18th century as a planned village, it looks onto the 13 ha (32 acre) Shieldaig Island, which was acquired by the National Trust for Scotland in 1970.

Shieldhill *Dumfries and Galloway* A locality in Dumfries and Galloway, Shieldhill lies to the east of the River Dee, 6 miles (10 km) northwest of Castle Douglas.

Shieldhill *Falkirk* A former mining village in Falkirk Council area, Shieldhill lies on a ridge top, 3 miles (5 km) south of Falkirk.

Shiellahill *Dumfries and Galloway* A locality in Dumfries and Galloway, Sheillahill lies 4 miles (6.5 km) northeast of Kirkcudbright on the road to Gelston.

Shillay *Western Isles* The most westerly of the Heisker or Monach Islands, Shillay is today uninhabited and lies 8 miles (13 km) southwest of Aird an Runair, on the west coast of North Uist in the Western Isles. The island is separated from Ceann Iar by the Sound of Shillay. In medieval times, monks living on the island maintained a light to guide sailors. Today there are two lighthouses, the older being built in 1864 and decommisioned in 1948. A new automated light was built in 1997 to delimit the deep-water route designated for the safe navigation of large tankers. The Natural Environment Research Council established a research-oriented nature reserve on the island in 1966.

Shillford *East Renfrewshire* A hamlet near the border between East Renfrewshire and Glasgow, Shillford lies close to Barrhead.

Shin *Highland* A loch and river in central Sutherland, Loch Shin extends northwestwards for 17 miles (27 km) from Lairg, the River Shin flowing southwards from its southern end for 7 miles (11 km) before joining the River Oykel at Inveran. The Shin Hydro-Electric Power Scheme, which is the most northerly of its kind in Scotland, is centred on Loch Shin and Little Loch Shin (on the River Shin), together with the diverted headwaters of the Cassley and Brora rivers. Water collected from the River Cassley feeds the remote 0.45-megawatt power station at Duchally, from where water is diverted through a 2.5-mile (4-km) tunnel to the 10-metawatt Cassley Power Station on the western shore of Loch Shin. Loch Shin, the main storage reservoir, is retained by the Lairg Dam, some 427 m (1400 ft) long and 12 m (40 ft) high, which is built over a 3.5-megawatt power station. Water passes to the smaller reservoir of Little Loch Shin immediately below, which is used to maintain a minimum level in the River Shin, the majority of water being routed through a 5-mile (8-km) tunnel to the 24-megawatt Shin Power Station at Inveran. Further water is diverted from the River Grudie to this power station. The scheme became fully operational in 1960, when a fish ladder was installed at the Lairg Dam to allow for the migration of salmon. The Linn of Shin or Shin Falls forms a notable salmon leap on the river.

Shinary, Strath *Highland* A valley in northwest Sutherland, Strath Shinary descends to Sandwood Loch near the coast, 6 miles (10 km) south of Cape Wrath.

Shinnel Water *Dumfries and Galloway* A tributary of the Scaur Water in Dumfries and Galloway, the Shinnel Water rises in hills to the north of Moniaive. At the Aird Linn near Tynron it forms a waterfall. The Shinnel joins the Scaur at a point just west of Penpont.

Shira, Glen *Argyll and Bute* The valley of the River Shira in Argyll and Bute, Glen Shira extends 5 miles (8 km) southwestwards from Lochan Shira and Lochan Sròn Mòr to Loch Shira, an inlet at the northern end of Loch Fyne near Inveraray. The River Shira receives the Brannie Burn and the Kilblaan Burn.

Shiresmill *Fife* A small agricultural hamlet in western Fife, Shiresmill is situated close to the Bluther Burn on the B9037 midway between Blairhall and Culross.

Shirmers Burn *Dumfries and Galloway* A stream in the Glenkens district of Dumfries and Galloway, the Shirmers Burn rises to the northeast of Balmaclellan and flows southwards to enter Loch Ken.

Shivinish *Western Isles* A low-lying uninhabited island of the Heisker (or Monach) Islands, which lies to the west of North Uist in the Western Isles. Shivinish (Gael: *Shibhinis*) lies between the larger Ceann Iar and Ceann Ear, and is linked to both at low tide. It has an area of 28 ha (69 acres).

Shotts *North Lanarkshire* A former industrial town in central Scotland, Shotts lies to the south of the M8, 6 miles (10 km) northeast of Wishaw. Replacing the original isolated village of Kirk o' Shotts, it developed in the 19th century in association with coal and ironstone mining, as well as engineering, ironworks and steel-founding industries. There is a heritage centre in the local library, and in 1990 Shotts Prison was opened as an extension of the Barlinnie Special Unit.

Shougle *Moray* The small settlement of Shougle lies 4 miles (6.5 km) southeast of Forres in Moray.

Shulishader *Western Isles* A crofting township on the north coast of the Eye peninsula on the east coast of the Isle of Lewis in the Outer Hebrides, Shulishader (Gael: *Sulaisiadar* or *Siulaisiadar*) is located a mile (1.5 km) northwest of Sheshader, 1.25 miles (2 km) northeast of Garrabost and 7 miles (11 km) east of Stornoway.

Shuna *Argyll and Bute* An island in the Firth of Lorn, Shuna lies off the Argyllshire coast, between the island of Luing and the mainland near the mouth of Loch Melfort. It has an area of 451 ha (1114 acres) and rises to 90 m (295 ft) at Druim na Dubh Ghlaic. Limestone was once quarried from the island, which is privately owned and grazed with livestock. Shuna House stands on the northeast coast. In 1841, the island had a population of 69.

Shuna *Argyll and Bute* An uninhabited limestone island in Loch Linnhe, Shuna is separated from the mainland of Appin by the Sound of Shuna. Privately owned, it has an area of 155 ha (383 acres) and rises to 71 m (233 ft) at the table-topped Tom an t-Seallaidh to the northeast of Loch Shuna. The remains of 16th-century Castle Shuna, a former stronghold of the Stewarts of Appin, stand at the southern end of the island.

Siabost The Gaelic name for Shawbost in the Western Isles.

Siadar The Gaelic name for Shader in the Western Isles.

Sibster *Highland* A small farming community in northeast Caithness, Sibster lies 3 miles (5 km) northwest of Wick. The Square of Sibster farmsteading to the west comprises an 18th-century kiln-barn, stables and a 19th-century hexagonal engine house.

Siccar Point *Scottish Borders* A rocky peninsula on the North Sea coast of Scottish Borders, Siccar Point juts into the sea east of Cockburnspath and Pease Bay. It is well known to geologists for its angular unconformity, a feature first recognised by the noted Scottish geologist James Hutton (1726–97). The fact that rock strata laid down 425 million years ago could appear in a younger sequence laid down 345 million years ago led Hutton to the conclusion that the earth was not made in six days and that faulting and folding were important processes in the evolution of the landscape.

Sidinish *Western Isles* A crofting settlement drawn out along the southern shore of Loch Euphort in North Uist in the Outer Hebrides, Sidinish (Gael: *Saighdinis*) lies immediately to the east of the settlement of Locheport, 5 miles (8 km) southwest of Lochmaddy.

Sidlaw Hills *Perth and Kinross/Angus* A range of hills in Perth and Kinross and Angus council areas, the Sidlaw Hills extend northeastwards to Forfar from Kinnoull Hill near Perth. The Sidlaws separate Strathmore from the Carse of Gowrie and the Firth of Tay, and rise to 455 m (1492 ft) at Craigowl Hill to the south of Glamis.

Sighthill *City of Edinburgh* A western suburb of Edinburgh, Sighthill lies between South Gyle to the north and Wester Hailes to the south. Stevenson College and the Scottish regional office of the Ordnance Survey are located here.

Sighthill *Glasgow City* A northern district of Glasgow, Sighthill lies to the north of the M8, between St Rollox and Springburn. It developed as a rail freight depot. In Sighthill Cemetery is a monument to John Baird and Andrew Hardie, who were involved in the so-called Radical Rising of 1820.

Signet Library, the *City of Edinburgh* A building in Edinburgh's Old Town, the Signet Library lies adjacent to Parliament House, which opens out onto Parliament Square to the south of St Giles' Kirk. Originally built for the Faculty of Advocates, the Library comprises the grandiose Upper Library, Lower Library and West Wing. The Upper Library, designed by Robert Reid (1774–1856), has interiors by William Stark and was completed in 1822. George IV, who saw the Upper Library in the year it was completed, is said to have described it as the most beautiful room he had ever seen. The Upper and Lower Libraries are linked by a grand staircase designed by William Burn, with a screen dating from 1819 by William Playfair. The Lower Library is divided into reading bays, each with its own dome.

Silver Glen *Clackmannanshire* A narrow glen in the Ochil Hills, the Silver Glen is situated between the Middle and Wood Hills behind the Hillfoot village of Alva. In 1712, a silver mine was opened here by Sir John Erskine.

Silverknowes *City of Edinburgh* A residential district of Edinburgh, Silverknowes lies 3 miles (5 km) northwest of the city centre to the east of Cramond. Land surrounding Silverknowes Farm, which formerly lay on the Muirhouse Estate, was developed from the 1920s, streets being laid out in a series of concentric semicircles divided by Silverknowes Road. There are fine views north over the Firth of Forth and closeby is Lauriston Castle. There is an 18-hole municipal golf course.

Silvermills *City of Edinburgh* A district to the north of Edinburgh's New Town, Silvermills lies near the Water of Leith. Silvermills House (*c.*1760) and East and West Silvermills Lane are all that remain of the old village where mills refined a silver ore brought from mines near Livingston in West Lothian. The yield of silver prompted King James VI to buy the mine and the mills for £5000. Around 1812, a tannery was established here. Silvermills was the birthplace of the artist Robert Scott Lauder (1803–69).

Sinclair's Hill *Scottish Borders* A settlement in the Berwickshire district of Scottish Borders, Sinclair's Hill lies 3 miles (5 km) southeast of Duns.

Sinclairtown *Fife* Formerly a village in the parish of Dysart, Fife, Sinclairtown is now an eastern suburb of Kirkcaldy, situated between Kirkcaldy harbour and Gallatown to the north.

Sionascaig, Loch *Highland* A loch in Wester Ross, Loch Sionascaig lies to the north of Stack Polly and west of Cul Mòr in the Inverpolly Forest.

Skae, Loch *Dumfries and Galloway* A small loch in Dumfries and Galloway, Loch Skae lies a mile (1.5 km) to the south of the road between Moniaive and New Galloway, in the shadow of Fell Hill. The Loch Skae Burn flows down to meet the Blackmark Burn.

Skara Brae *Orkney* In 1850 a severe storm stripped the grass from a high dune on the west coast of Mainland Orkney in the south corner of the Bay of Skaill to reveal the ruins of ancient dwellings buried to the tops of surviving walls in a huge heap of refuse comprising ash, shells and broken bones. Once the site had been excavated, Skara Brae (or Skeroo Brae) was recognised as the best-preserved prehistoric village in northern Europe. The remains consist of a cluster of six self-contained houses and a workshop, connected by passageways. It is suggested that the site was occupied during two periods between 3100 and 2500 BC.

Skateraw *Aberdeenshire* A former fishing village with a harbour in Fetteresso parish, southeast Aberdeenshire, Skateraw lies on the North Sea coast by Newtonhill at the mouth of the Burn of Elsick, 6 miles (10 km) north of Stonehaven.

Skaw *Shetland* A hamlet in the northeast of the island of Whalsay in the Shetland Islands, Skaw overlooks Skaw Voe 5 miles (8 km) northeast of Symbister. Whalsay Airport is located here and the headland of Skaw Taing lies a mile (1.5 km) to the northeast.

Skeabost *Highland* A township on the isle of Skye in the Inner Hebrides, Skeabost lies at the head of Loch Snizort Beag, 19 miles (31 km) east of Dunvegan. There is a nine-hole golf course and hotel.

Skeabrae *Orkney* A locality in the Sandwick district of the Orkney Mainland, Skeabrae lies 1.25 miles (2 km) northwest of the Loch of Harray and a similar distance west of Dounby. A naval airfield, established here at the beginning of World War II and taken over by the Royal Air Force as a fighter base in 1940, closed shortly after the end of the war and was eventually sold in 1957. The remains of several-air force buildings can still be seen on the site.

Skeen, Loch *Dumfries and Galloway* A hill loch in northern Dumfries and Galloway, Loch Skeen (or Skene) lies to the north of White Coomb, nearly 10 miles (16 km) northeast of Moffat. The Tail Burn flows southeastwards from Loch Skeen to join the Moffat Water, en route forming a spectacular 61-m (200-ft) waterfall, the Grey Mare's Tail. In 1962, land extending to Loch Skeen was purchased by the National Trust for Scotland, which established a visitor centre with facilities for viewing peregrine falcon nest sites.

Skelbo Castle *Highland* A ruined castle in Sutherland, the remains of Skelbo Castle stand on a hilltop overlooking Loch Fleet, 5 miles (8 km) north of Dornoch. Old Skelbo House, just below the castle, was built *c.*1600.

Skeld *Shetland* Located on the south side of the west Mainland of Shetland, 11 miles (18 km) west-northwest of Lerwick, Skeld comprises the small settlement of Wester Skeld and a mile (1.5 km) to the northeast the larger Easter Skeld lying on Skelda Voe. Easter Skeld has a pier, primary school, community hall, post office and small industrial estate with a smokehouse producing smoked fish.

Skellister *Shetland* A hamlet in the South Nesting district on the east coast of the Mainland of Shetland, Skellister lies on the East Voe of Skellister, 8 miles (13 km) north of Lerwick. The Hill of Skellister lies a half-mile (1 km) to the northwest.

Skelmorlie *North Ayrshire* A red sandstone village on the North Ayrshire coast, Skelmorlie lies on the Firth of Clyde, nearly 5 miles (8 km) north of Largs. It developed as a residential resort after the building of a hydropathic hotel in 1868. Skelmorlie Castle, which dates from the early 16th century, was a stronghold of the Montgomery family.

Skelston *Dumfries and Galloway* A locality in Dumfries and Galloway, Skelston lies to the southeast of Dalmacallan Forest, 9 miles (14 km) northwest of Dumfries. It comprises Skelston Moor and the farms of East and West Skelston which lie on the Skelston Burn, a tributary of the Cairn Water.

Skene *Aberdeenshire* A parish and locality in Aberdeenshire, Skene lies 8 miles (13 km) west of Aberdeen. It comprises the settlements of Lyne of Skene and Kirkton of Skene, together with the Loch of Skene and Skene House.

Skerrow, Loch *Dumfries and Galloway* A loch in Dumfries and Galloway, Loch Skerrow lies to the south of the River Dee and 7 miles (11 km) north of Gatehouse of Fleet. Fed by the Loch Lane, it is the source of the Airie Burn which flows north to join the Dee.

Skerryvore *Argyll and Bute* A dangerous reef in the Inner Hebrides, Skerryvore lies 11 miles (18 km) south-southwest of the island of Tiree. Skerryvore lighthouse, which can be seen for more than 20 miles (32 km), was designed and constructed by Alan Stevenson in 1844. Built of granite, it is 41.75 m (137 ft) in height, with walls 3 m (9.5 ft) thick at the base. It took 150 men seven years to build the lighthouse, which was described by the Institute of Civil Engineers as 'the finest combination of mass with elegance to be met within architectural or engineering structures'.

Skibo *Highland* A mansion house and estate in southeast Sutherland, Skibo lies 4 miles (6.5 km) east of Dornoch. Skibo Castle, incorporating a Scottish baronial-style house of 1880, was extended between 1899 and 1903 to a design by Alexander Ross for philanthropist Andrew Carnegie. It stands on the site of a castle owned by the bishops of Caithness from 1224 to 1565, and has terraced gardens laid out in 1904 by Thomas Mawson. The estate comprises two farms, grouse moors and forests extending into the adjacent Flow Country. Between the castle and the Dornoch Firth is landscaped parkland incorporating a championship-standard 18-hole golf course and the artificial Loch Ospisdale. Now an exclusive hotel owned by English millionaire Peter de Savary, Skibo Castle has hosted a number of celebrity weddings and wedding parties in modern times, among the most famous being those of pop star Madonna, golfer Sam Torrance and film stars Robert Carlyle and Ewan MacGregor.

Skigersta *Western Isles* The easternmost of a collection of settlements at the northern tip of the Isle of Lewis in the Outer Hebrides, Skigersta (also Skegirsta or Gael: *Sgiogarstaigh*) is located just over 3 miles (5 km) southeast of the Butt of Lewis.

Skinflats *Falkirk* A village in Falkirk Council area, Skinflats is situated to the east of Carronshore and north of the River Carron. It was named by Dutch engineers brought here to reclaim land in the 18th century. They dubbed their achievement 'beautiful plains', the Dutch words being corrupted to create a name that has been described as the ugliest in Scotland.

Skipness *Argyll and Bute* A village on the northeast coast of the Kintyre peninsula, Skipness looks out onto the Kilbrannan Sound, 15 miles (24 km) southeast of Tarbert. Skipness Castle dates from the 13th century, and an ancient chapel is dedicated to St Brendan. A ferry once linked Skipness to the island of Bute.

Skiport, Loch An alternative name for Loch Sgioport in the Western Isles.

Skirling *Scottish Borders* A small commuter village at the northern end of Tweeddale, Skirling lies 3 miles (5 km) northeast of Biggar. The village, which became a burgh of barony in 1592, at one time had a famous horse market.

Skye *Highland* The largest of the islands of the Inner Hebrides off the west coast of Scotland, Skye takes the shape of a series of lobate peninsulas, divided by sea lochs, the most prominent being Snizort, Dunvegan, Bracadale, Eynort, Brittle, Scavaig, Eishort, Slapin, Scavaig, Ainort, Sligachan and Portree. It contains some of the most spectacular scenery and varied geology in the British Isles, ranging from rolling plateaux to the serrated heights of the Black Cuillin. With an area of 1637 sq. km (632 sq. miles), the island rises steeply to 992 m (3255 ft) at Sgurr Alasdair in the Cuillins, which represent the exposed heart of Tertiary volcanoes associated with the formation of the Atlantic Ocean over 60 million years ago. Here the coarse, crystalline gabbro of the Black Cuillin Hills contrasts with the granite that dominates the Red Cuillins to the east. There are notable landslip features at The Storr, the highest point on the Trotternish escarpment, and at Quirang at the north end of the Trotternish peninsula. Along the Trotternish escarpment are some of the lowest ice-carved corries in Scotland. From Rubha Hunish in the north to Point of Sleat in the south is a distance of nearly 45 miles (72 km). The chief settlements on Skye are Portree and Broadford, with crofting, fishing, fish farming and tourism the most significant economic activities. The noted Gaelic-language college, Sabhal Mòr Ostaig, is located by Kilbeg on the Sleat peninsula, and the great tradition of the pibroch is associated with Boreraig and Dunvegan in the northwest. The population of the island declined sharply through the 19th century, having been subject to successive clearances. More recently it has been growing again, from 7269 in 1981 to 9232 in 2001. There is access to the island by the Skye Bridge from Kyle of Lochalsh, or via vehicle ferries sailing from Glenelg to Kylerhea and Mallaig to Armadale. Ferries also link Uig with the Outer Hebrides. Opened in 1995, the Skye Bridge is 570 m (623 yd) long, although the complete crossing, which includes the Carrich Bridge and the island of Eilean Bàn, extends to 1.5 miles (2.5 km). The main span of this free-cantilever structure is 250 m (273 yd) long.

Skyre Burn *Dumfries and Galloway* A stream in Dumfries and Galloway, the Skyre Burn rises in headwaters on the slopes of Meikle Bennan and Pibble Hill. It flows southeastwards for nearly 5 miles (8 km) to enter Skyreburn Bay, an inlet at the head of Fleet Bay, 2 miles (3 km) southwest of Gatehouse of Fleet. It is joined by the Glen, Arkland, Cauldside, Whiteside and Black Burns.

Slains Castle *Aberdeenshire* The atmospheric and substantial ruins of New Slains Castle stand on the clifftop overlooking the North Sea a half-mile (1 km) east of Port Errol in Aberdeenshire. This structure replaced the earlier Old Slains Castle, located 6 miles (10 km) to the southwest, which had been the property of the Hay family, Earls of Errol. The old castle having been destroyed in 1594, New Slains was erected in 1597 by Francis Hay, the 9th Earl of Errol (c.1564–1631), on the site of the former Bowness Castle. The castle was built around a courtyard and extended over the years to form a massive structure. It was rebuilt and faced with granite in 1836 to form a modern country house. However, it fell into disuse after death duties forced its sale by the 20th Earl in 1916 and had its roof removed for reasons of safety in 1925. Dr Samuel Johnson (1709–84) and James Boswell (1740–95) visited in 1773 and it is said that this building gave Bram Stoker the inspiration for Count Dracula's castle while staying at nearby Cruden Bay in 1895.

Slamannan *Falkirk* The largest village in rural Falkirk Council area, Slamannan is situated on the Culloch Burn in an upland area 6 miles (10 km) south of Falkirk. It is the chief settlement of the parish of Slamannan, which was known as the parish of St Laurence in pre-Reformation times. During the 19th century the village developed as a mining settlement.

Slateford *Edinburgh* A district of southwest Edinburgh, the former village of Slateford lies on the Water of Leith.

Slattadale *Highland* A settlement in Wester Ross, Slattadale lies on the south shore of Loch Maree, 12 miles (19 km) northwest of Kinlochewe. The Slattadale Forest extends southwards into mountainous country.

Sleat *Highland* A peninsula at the southwest end of the isle of Skye in the Inner Hebrides, Sleat is separated from the mainland of Scotland by the Sound of Sleat. There are ferry links between Armadale and Mallaig. The Clan Donald Centre is located at Armadale. The peninsula's southernmost headland is the Point of Sleat. The Sabhal Mòr Ostaig Gaelic-language college was established in the 1970s in former farm buildings at Ostaig.

Sletdale, Glen *Highland* An arm of Glen Loth in eastern Sutherland, Glen Sletdale lies 5 miles (8 km) north of Brora. Carrying the waters of the River Sletdale from the slopes of Meallan Liath Beag, Glen Sletdale extends 4.5 miles (7 km) southeast and then east to merge with Glen Loth.

Sliddery *North Ayrshire* A small settlement on the southwest coast of the island of Arran, Sliddery lies on the Sliddery Water at the southwest end of Glen Scorrodale, 8 miles (13 km) southwest of Lamlash.

Sligachan, Glen *Highland* A narrow valley on the isle of Skye in the Inner Hebrides, Glen Sligachan lies to the east of the Cuillins, from where it carries the River Sligachan east and north to join Loch Sligachan at Sligachan, 9 miles (14 km) south of Portree. The Sligachan Inn on the main road between Broadford and Portree was built in the 1880s near the bridge over the River Sligachan. There is a mountain rescue post in the hotel.

Slioch *Aberdeenshire* A locality in the Aberdeenshire parish of Drumblade, Slioch lies 2 miles (3 km) southeast of Huntly. Robert the Bruce is said to have camped here in 1307 during his campaign against the Comyns.

Slioch *Highland* A mountain to the east of Loch Maree in Wester Ross, Slioch rises to 981 m (3218 ft) 4 miles (6.5 km) north of Kinlochewe.

Slitrig Water *Scottish Borders* A river in the Roxburgh district of Scottish Borders, the Slitrig Water rises between Teviotdale and Liddesdale and flows 11 miles (18 km) north to join the River Tweed at Hawick.

Slochd *Highland* A deep hollow on the high ridge between Carrbridge and Inverness, the Slochd Pass is traversed by the main northbound road and railway line, which rise to 405 m (1328 ft) at its summit.

Slogarie *Dumfries and Galloway* A locality in Balmaghie parish, Dumfries and Galloway, Slogarie lies at the foot of Slogarie Hill, 3 miles (5 km) northwest of Laurieston.

Sloy, Loch *Argyll and Bute* A freshwater loch and reservoir in Argyll and Bute, Loch Sloy lies to the west of the northern end of Loch Lomond, between Ben Vorlich and Ben Vane. The Inveruglas Water drains southeastwards into Loch Lomond, which also receives water from the reservoir via a tunnel supplying the Sloy-Awe Hydro-Electric Power Station at Inveruglas. Fully operational since 1959, the part of the scheme centred on Loch Sloy discharges into the northern end of Loch Lomond and the headwaters of Loch Fyne, and includes the Alt-na-Lairig dam, the first significant pre-stressed concrete dam to be built in western Europe, together with a complex system of aqueducts and tunnels.

Slug Road *Aberdeenshire* A road rising to 230 m (757 ft) in southeast Aberdeenshire, the Slug Road links Stonehaven with Banchory on the River Dee, 13 miles (21 km) to the northwest.

Sma' Glen *Perth and Kinross* A picturesque glen in central Perth and Kinross through which flows the River Almond, the Sma' Glen lies 5 miles (8 km) north of Crieff to the west of Glen Almond. Only 4 miles (6.5 km) in length, it was once part of a major routeway linking Strath Earn to Strathtay. The glen was of strategic importance to the Romans who built a fort and watch tower at Fendoch, and in the 18th century General Wade built a military road through the Sma' Glen. Bones found beneath Ossian's Stone, a large stone removed to its present site by Wade's road-builders, were thought to be those of the legendary hero Ossian.

Sma' Shot Cottages *Renfrewshire* Located in Paisley, Renfrewshire, the Sma' Shot Cottages are the only buildings left on what was formerly Shuttle Street. They were built between 1735 and the early 1750s, and today, as a museum, tell the story of hand-loom weaving,

Smailholm *Scottish Borders* A village in the Roxburgh district of Scottish Borders, Smailholm lies 4 miles (6.5 km) northwest of Kelso. To the southwest stands Smailholm Tower, a former stronghold of the Pringle family built in the 15th century. Repeatedly attacked by the English in the 16th and 17th centuries, the castle later passed to the Scott family. The writer Sir Walter Scott (1771–1832) spent part of his childhood at nearby Sandyknowe Farm.

Smallholm *Dumfries and Galloway* A hamlet of Annandale in Dumfries and Galloway, Smallholm lies on the west bank of the River Annan, nearly 4 miles (6.5 km) south of Lochmaben. With Hightae, Heck and Greenhill, Smallholm is one of the Royal Four Towns of Lochmaben.

Small Isles *Argyll and Bute* A group of uninhabited islands in the Inner Hebrides, the Small Isles lie to the southeast of the island of Jura, between the headlands of Rubh an Leanachais in the north and Rubha na Caillich in the south. From south to north they are Eilean nan Gabhar, Eilean nan Coinein, Eilean Diomhain, Pladda and Eilean Bhride.

Small Isles *Highland* A group of islands forming a parish in the Inner Hebrides, the Small Isles lie to the south of the isle of Skye. They comprise the islands of Canna, Rum, Eigg and Muck.

Smerclate *Western Isles* A scattered hamlet on the southwest coast of South Uist, Smerclate (Gael: *Smercleit* or *Smeircleit*) lies among small lochans a half-mile (1 km) south of Garrynamonie and a similar distance north of Pollachar. North Smerclate lies around the B888, while the remainder of the settlement is located to the southwest amid machair that forms part of a Special Protection Area noted for its breeding corncrakes.

Smercleit The Gaelic name for Smerclate in the Western Isles.

Smithton *Highland* A commuter village of eastern Highland Council area, Smithton lies immediately to the southwest of Culloden, close to the southern shore of the Moray Firth and 2.5 miles (4 km) east of Inverness.

Smoo Cave *Highland* A large limestone cave on the north coast of Sutherland, the Smoo Cave lies a mile (1.5 km) southeast of Durness. The Allt Smoo falls into a loch in an inner cavern. The cave, which is 15 m (50 ft) high and 30 m (100 ft) broad, was made famous by Sir Walter Scott following a visit in 1814, and by a Daniell print.

Snade *Dumfries and Galloway* A locality in Dumfries and Galloway, Snade lies on the Cairn Water, nearly 3 miles (5 km) northwest of Dunscore. There are earthworks and the remains of a castle nearby, and to the north on the Cairn Water is Snade Mill.

Snaid Burn *Stirling* A stream rising to the east of Loch Lomond, the Snaid Burn flows south from the slopes of Beinn a' Choin to join with waters flowing westwards out of Loch Arklet before entering Loch Lomond at Inversnaid. There is an attractive cascade known as the Falls of Inversnaid.

Snar Water *South Lanarkshire* The Snar Water rises on the northern slopes of Wanlock Dod, approximately a half-mile (1 km) north of the South Lanarkshire settlement of Wanlockhead. Flowing northwards, it joins the Duneaton Water, a tributary of the River Clyde, a mile (1.5 km) southwest of Crawfordjohn.

Snizort, Loch *Highland* A sea loch on the northwest coast of the isle of Skye in the Inner Hebrides, Loch Snizort lies between the Vaternish and Trotternish peninsulas and is fed via Loch Snizort Beag by the River Snizort, which flows northwards from headwaters in hills to the east of Bracadale.

Soa *Argyll and Bute* A small island in the Inner Hebrides, Soa lies 2 miles (3 km) southwest of Iona and 3 miles (5 km) from the island of Erraid to the west of the Ross of Mull.

Soa *Argyll and Bute* A small island off the coast of Tiree in the Inner Hebrides, Soa lies to the east of Gott Bay and the settlement of Scarinish. At low tide the island is connected to Tiree by sandbanks.

Soa *Argyll and Bute* A small rocky island off the south coast of Coll in the Inner Hebrides, Soa lies 2 miles (3 km) southwest of Crossapol Bay at the mouth of Loch Breachacha.

Soaigh The Gaelic name for Soay in the Western Isles.

Soaidh Beag The Gaelic name for Soay Beag in the Western Isles.

Soaidh Mòr The Gaelic name for Soay Mòr in the Western Isles.

Soay *Highland* A sparsely inhabited island in the Inner Hebrides, Soay lies to the west of Loch Scavaig on the west coast of the isle of Skye, from which it is separated by Soay Sound. It extends over an area of 1036 ha (2560 acres) and rises to 141 m (462 ft) at Beinn Bhreac. The main settlement is at Mol-chlach. Formerly held by the MacLeods of Dunvegan, Soay was owned for three years from 1946 by the author Gavin Maxwell, who engaged in commercial fishing for basking sharks. In 1850, there were 150 people living on the island. The world's first solar-powered telephone exchange was established here in 1978.

Soay *Western Isles* An uninhabited island in the St Kilda group, Soay (Gael: *Soaigh*) lies to the northwest of Hirta, the main island in the group. Trimmed by cliffs, it rises steeply to 378 m (1240 ft) at Cnoc Glas and extends to 99 ha (245 acres). With the other islands, it is owned by the National Trust for Scotland, managed by Scottish Natural Heritage as a nature reserve and is included in the St Kilda World Heritage Site. It is unlikely that this island ever had permanent habitation.

Soay Beag *Western Isles* A small uninhabited island in West Loch Tarbert in the Outer Hebrides, Soay Beag (Gael: *Soaidh Beag*) lies adjacent to the larger Soay Mòr, off the southwest coast of North Harris, from which it is separated by the Soay Sound. The island is round in shape and rises to 37 m (121 ft).

Soay Mòr *Western Isles* An uninhabited island in West Loch Tarbert in the Outer Hebrides, Soay Mòr (Gael: *Soaidh Mòr*) lies off the southwest coast of North Harris, from which it is separated by the Soay Sound. The island extends to 45 ha (111 acres), rises to 37 m (121 ft) and provides shelter for a fish farm located to the northeast. The smaller Soay Beg lies immediately to the northwest and is accessible from Soay Mòr at low tide.

Socach Burn *Argyll and Bute* A stream located between Loch Awe and Loch Fyne, the Socach Burn rises in Loch Gaineanhach, 7.5 miles (12 km) north-northeast of Lochgilphead. It flows 3 miles (5 km) west to join the Clachandubh Burn, a stream draining from Loch Leathan.

Sodom An alternative name for Sudheim in Shetland.

Soldier's Leap *Perth and Kinross* A locality on the River Garry in the Pass of Killiecrankie, Soldier's Leap marks the spot on the narrow wooded gorge where, it is said, a soldier avoided capture by jumping 5.5 m (18.5 ft) across the river during the Battle of Killiecrankie on 27 July 1689.

Sole Burn *Dumfries and Galloway* A stream in the Rhinns of Galloway, western Dumfries and Galloway, the Sole Burn is formed by headwaters that rise to the north of Lochnaw. It flows southeast and east to enter Loch Ryan due east of Leswalt at Soleburn Bridge.

Sollas *Western Isles* A crofting township at the northern end of North Uist in the Western Isles, Sollas (Gael: *Solas*) lies 5 miles (8 km) east of Griminish Point.

Solway Firth *Dumfries and Galloway* Opening out into the Irish Sea, the Solway Firth forms an estuary on the southwest coast of Scotland on the border between Scotland and England. It is fed from the north by numerous rivers, including the Nith, Annan, Urr Water and Lochar Water, and from England by the River Eden and Liddel Water. One of the least industrialised and most natural large estuaries in Europe, the Solway Firth comprises a range of coastal and marine habitats, including salt marshes, mud flats and sand flats. It contains the third-largest area of continuous littoral mudflats and sandflats in the UK. The ever-changing pattern of channels and mudflats, coupled with the moderately strong tidal currents, can be dangerous. From 1869 to 1935 the Solway Firth was spanned by the Solway Viaduct, the longest railway viaduct in Europe when first built.

Solwaybank *Dumfries and Galloway* A locality in Dumfries and Galloway, Solwaybank lies by the Woodside Burn, 6 miles (10 km) north of Gretna Green.

Sonachan, Loch *Argyll and Bute* Loch Sonachan is one of a number of small freshwater lochs that lie in the Lorn district of Argyll and Bute, some 7 miles (11 km) southeast of Oban and on the southwest slopes of Beinn Ghlas.

Soray *Western Isles* A tiny uninhabited islet in the Flannan Islands group, Soray (Gael: *Soraidh*) lies a half-mile (1 km) south of Eilean Mòr and Eilean Tighe, the larger islands of the group.

Sorbie *Dumfries and Galloway* A village in the Machars of Dumfries and Galloway, Sorbie lies to the west of Wigtown Bay, 5 miles (8 km) south of Wigtown. It was established as a planned village in the late 18th century by the 7th Earl of Galloway and was once famous for its manufacture of damask. The mausoleum of the earls of Galloway (1735) stands in the kirkyard of the old parish church. A mile (1.5 km) to the east of the village stand the ruins of the Old Place of Sorbie, a 16th-century tower that was a stronghold of the Hannay family. The minor poet Robert Cowper (1750–1818) was born at Balsier Farm to the south.

Sorn *East Ayrshire* A village in East Ayrshire, Sorn lies 4 miles (6.5 km) east of Mauchline. Sorn Castle, a former stronghold of the Hamiltons and then the Campbells of Loudon, dates from the early 15th century. Also formerly known as Dalgain, the village of Sorn developed in association with farming, coal mining and its location at a crossing on the upper reaches of the River Ayr.

Sorne Point *Argyll and Bute* A headland to the west of Ardmore Bay on the north coast of the island of Mull in the Inner Hebrides, Sorne Point flooks out over the Sound of Mull to the Ardnamurchan peninsula.

Soulseat Loch *Dumfries and Galloway* A loch in the Rhinns of Galloway, Soulseat (also *Saulseat*) Loch lies 3 miles (5 km) southeast of Stranraer. It is joined to the Piltanton Burn to the south by the Soulseat Burn. A Premonstratensian abbey was built on a promontory in the loch in 1148.

Souter Johnnie's Cottage *South Ayrshire* A small cottage museum in the village of Kirkoswald, 4 miles (6.5 km) southwest of Maybole, Souter Johnnie's Cottage was the home of John Davidson, the village shoemaker (souter) who was immortalised in Robert Burns's poem *Tam o' Shanter*. The cottage contains a restored souter's workshop and in the garden are life-sized figures of Tam, Souter, the innkeeper and his wife. The cottage was acquired by the National Trust for Scotland in 1932.

South Alloa *Falkirk* A linear village in Falkirk Council area, South Alloa lies on the south bank of the River Forth at the former ferry crossing point to Alloa. Alloa Inches, a wetlands area to the northwest, is a Site of Special Scientific Interest (SSSI).

South Ayrshire *Area: 1230 sq. km (475 sq. miles)* A local government area of southwest Scotland created in 1996, South Ayrshire rises eastwards from the Firth of Clyde into the western Southern Uplands and includes part of the area traditionally known as Carrick. Its principal settlements – Ayr (the administrative centre), Troon, Maybole, Girvan, Prestwick and Ballantrae – lie on its coastal plain, but the region is perhaps best known for its associations with the national bard Robert Burns (1759–96) who was born in the village of Alloway. Key locations in South Ayrshire linked to transport and tourism are its

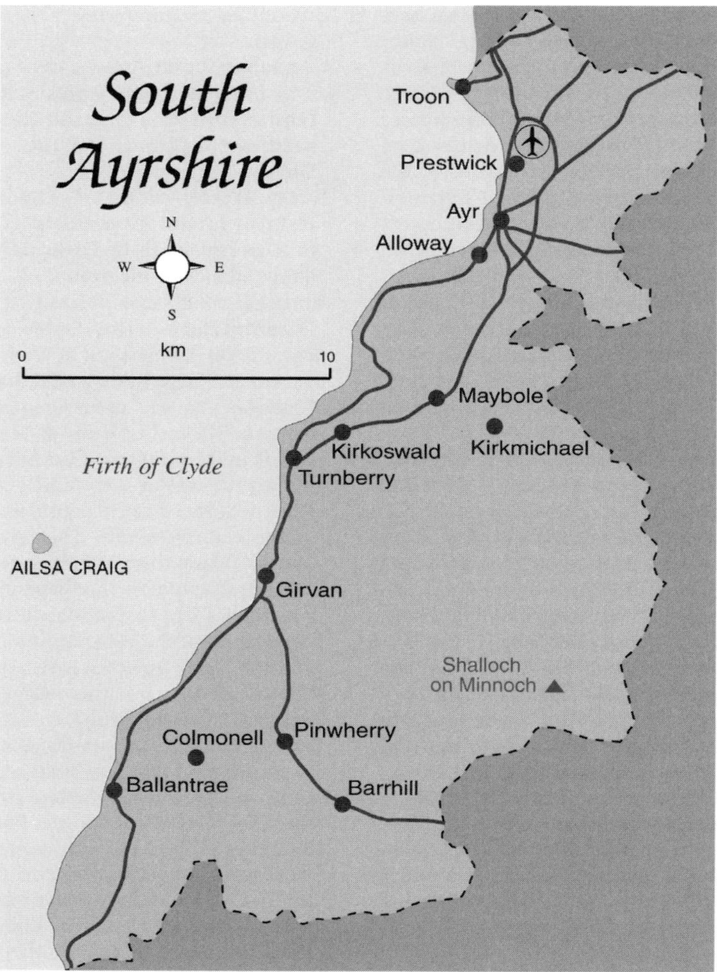

international airport at Prestwick, its championship golf courses at Turnberry and Troon, and Scotland's first country park at Culzean Castle. Nearly 50 per cent of South Ayrshire is improved grassland, rough pasture and moorland. Agriculture is a major economic activity in the uplands. To the north of Ayr and Prestwick there are aerospace and hi-tech industries.

South Balloch *South Ayrshire* Located 3 miles (5 km) northeast of Barr in South Ayrshire, South Balloch lies on the southern banks of the Stinchar River, a half-mile (1 km) south of the settlement of North Balloch.

South Boisdale *Western Isles* A scattered crofting settlement on the southwest coast of South Uist in the Outer Hebrides, South Boisdale (Gael: *An Leth Meadhanach*) is located 3 miles (5 km) to the west southwest of Lochboisdale. North Boisdale lies immediately to the northwest, and Loch an Eilean to the south separates South Boisdale from Garrynamonie.

South Calder Water *North Lanarkshire* Rising in the hills east of Shotts in North Lanarkshire, the South Calder Water flows in a westerly direction, passing to the north of Motherwell and then through Strathclyde Loch in Strathclyde Country Park, before emptying into the River Clyde.

South Dell *Western Isles* A crofting township at the northern end of the Isle of Lewis in the Western Isles, South Dell (Gael: *Dail Bho Dheas*) lies on the left bank of the Dell River, 3 miles (5 km) south of the Butt of Lewis and a half-mile (1 km) southwest of North Dell.

South Devon An alternative name for the Black Devon in Clackmannanshire and Fife.

South Esk, River *Aberdeenshire/Angus* A river of Angus, the South Esk rises in the southern Grampians on the border between Angus and Aberdeenshire. Its headstreams flow from the slopes of Broad Cairn and Cairn Bannoch and include the small corrie lochan of Loch Esk. In its upper reaches it is joined at Braedownie by the White Water which flows through Glen Doll. The river continues its southeast course through Glen Clova and is joined near the mouth of the glen by the Prosen Water. Flowing from the Braes of Angus into the wide valley of Strathmore, the South Esk meanders eastwards past Brechin before entering Montrose Basin through which it flows outwards to the North Sea by a narrow channel between Montrose and Ferryden. The total length of the river is almost 49 miles (79 km).

South Esk, River *Midlothian* A river of Midlothian, the South Esk rises at the southernmost extremity of the council area, on the western slopes of Blackhope Scar (651 m/2136 ft), the highest of the Moorfoot Hills. The river flows north through Gladhouse and Rosebery Reservoirs, and through the village of Temple, before receiving the Redside Burn close to Arniston House. It is joined by the Gore Water and then the Dalhousie Burn, just to the west of Newtongrange, before passing Newbattle Abbey. It proceeds through Dalkeith before merging with the North Esk a quarter-mile (0.5 km) north of Dalkeith Palace, having completed a course of 19 miles (31 km). The River Esk continues north-northeast to enter the Firth of Forth at Musselburgh.

South Galson *Western Isles* The scattered settlement of South Galson (Gael: *Gabhsunn Bho Dheas*) lies on the northwest coast of the Isle of Lewis in the Western Isles, 7 miles (11 km) southwest of Port of Ness. North Galson lies adjacent and to the north.

South Harris See Harris.

South Havra *Shetland* Last inhabited in 1923, the 59-ha (146-acre) island of South Havra lies to the west of the south Mainland of Shetland, south of the Burras. It rises to a height of 42 m (138 ft), its summit being capped by a 19th-century corn-grinding mill, the only one in Shetland. Surrounded by a rocky shoreline with caves and natural arches, South Havra was the home of Olaf Sinclair, who was the 'foud' or magistrate of all Shetland in the 16th century. Nearby is the smaller islet of Little Havra and adjacent skerries and reefs

South Kingennie *Angus* A hamlet comprising agricultural holdings in southern Angus, South Kingennie lies a half-mile (1 km) north of the boundary with Dundee, a similar distance east of Murroes and 1.25 miles (2 km) south of Wellbank.

South Lanarkshire *Area: 1777 sq. km (686 sq. miles)* A unitary authority in central Scotland bordering Dumfries and Galloway, East Ayrshire, East Renfrewshire, Glasgow City, North Lanarkshire, Scottish Borders and West Lothian, South Lanarkshire stretches from the Lowther Hills in the Southern Uplands northwards towards Blantyre, Rutherglen, Cambuslang, East Kilbride, Larkhall, Carluke and Hamilton (the administrative centre) on the southern outskirts of Glasgow. It is bisected from south to north by the M74, which links the north of England to Glasgow. Beyond the urban settlements of Greater Glasgow, it is a largely rural area with a handful of market towns, including Strathaven, Lanark and Biggar. Over 70 per cent of the land area is upland pasture and moorland. Tourism is concentrated on the picturesque valley of the upper Clyde, and places of interest include the former home of the missionary-explorer David Livingstone in Blantyre, Calderglen Country Park, Chatelherault Country Park and the New Lanark World Heritage Village which has associations with the industrial philanthropist Robert Owen.

South Lee *Western Isles* A hill of North Uist in the Western Isles, South Lee rises to 281 m (922 ft) 2 miles (3 km) southeast of the settlement of Lochmaddy.

South Lochboisdale *Western Isles* A linear settlement drawn out along the southern shore of Loch Boisdale on South Uist in the Outer Hebrides, South Lochboisdale (Gael: *Taobh a' Deas Loch Baghasdail* or *Ceann a' Deas Loch Baghasdail*) lies 1.25 miles (2 km) southwest of Lochboisdale, the principal settlement of the island.

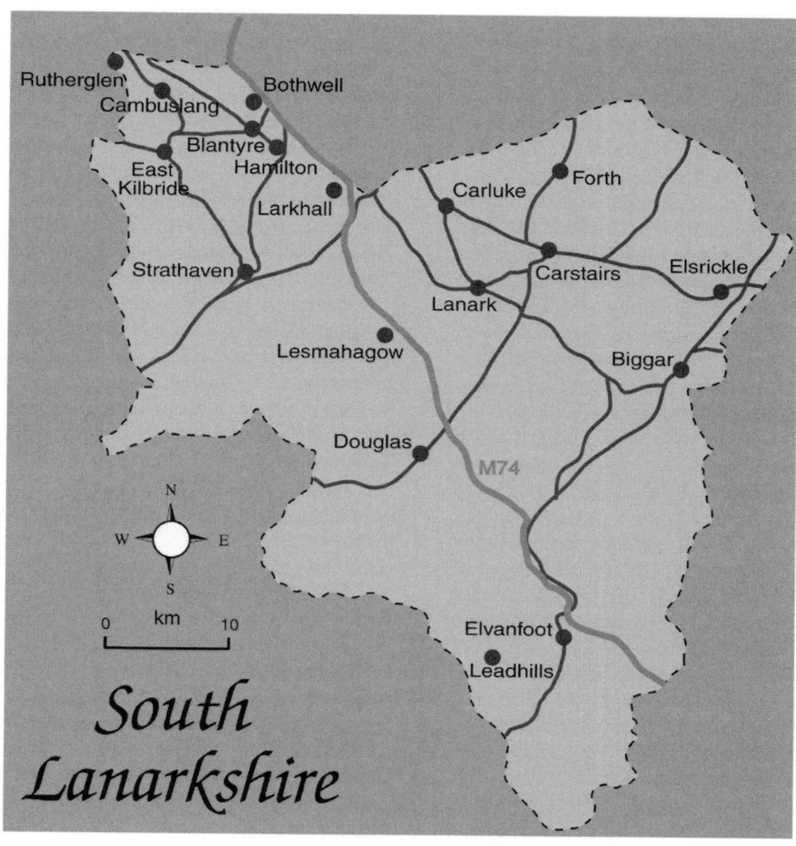

South Ness *Orkney* A small headland on the northern shore of the South Walls peninsula in the south of the island of Hoy. The hamlet of Longhope is located here.

South Portland Street Suspension Bridge *Glasgow City* Built in 1853, the South Portland Street Suspension Bridge in Glasgow was designed by Alexander Kirkland and built by George Martin. It replaced an earlier wooden bridge erected in 1833. Renovated in 1870, its decks and hangers were renewed in 1926.

South Queensferry *City of Edinburgh* Formerly in the county of West Lothian, South Queensferry (or simply Queensferry) lies on the south shore of the Firth of Forth, 10 miles (16 km) west of Edinburgh. It has been an important crossing since at least 1071, when Malcolm III granted free passage at the 'Queen's Ferry' for pilgrims on their way to St Andrews. A ferry service operated until 1964, the year the Forth Road Bridge was opened. South Queensferry was created a burgh of regality in the 13th century and made a royal burgh in 1636. It traded actively with Europe in the 17th century. Buildings dating from this period include Laburnum House, the Hawes Inn, the Tolbooth Tower, the Black Castle, the Old Parish Church and Plewlands House. St Mary's Episcopal Church (from 1441) was a monastery and hospice before the Reformation. The Hawes Inn features in Robert Louis Stevenson's novel *Kidnapped* (1886). Today, South Queensferry is a dormitory village and yachting centre with electronics, oil-storage and whisky industries.

South Ronaldsay *Orkney* The southernmost island of the Orkney Islands, South Ronaldsay is linked to Mainland Orkney via Burray by the Churchill Barriers, which were constructed during World War II to prevent German U-boats from entering Scapa Flow. Rising to a height of 118 m (387 ft) at Ward Hill, the island has an area of 4973 ha (12,288 acres), most of which is given over to the production of beef, dairy cattle, sheep, pigs and goats. The principal settlement is St Margaret's Hope, where there was once a chapel dedicated to St Margaret, Malcolm III's queen. It was off the coast of South Ronaldsay that the Longhope lifeboat was lost in March 1969 with the loss of all on board. Each year in August the Sand o' Right in Widewall Bay is the scene of a unique 'tidal' Ploughing Match involving boys under 15 years old using miniature ploughs. The population of South Ronaldsay has fallen from 2557 in 1881 to 854 in 2001, most of the islanders engaging in farming, fishing, boatbuilding and knitwear production, and crafts such as pottery and gold and silversmithing. Some are also employed in the oil industry on the neighbouring island of Flotta, the oil pipeline from the North Sea to the Flotta oil terminal passing through the north end of the island.

South Scousburgh *Shetland* A hamlet in the Dunrossness district at the southern end of the Mainland of Shetland, Scousburgh lies just to the east of the Loch of Spiggie, 5 miles (8 km) north-northwest of Sumburgh Airport. The settlement of Scousburgh lies a quarter-mile (0.4 km) to the north.

South Uist *Western Isles* The second-largest island in the Outer Hebrides, with an area of 32,094 ha (79,304 acres), South Uist (Gael: *Uibhist a Deas*) is 20 miles (32 km) long by 6 miles (10 km) wide. The island is penetrated on the east coast by the sea lochs of Loch Skiport, Loch Eynort and Loch Boisdale and ranged down its east side are the hill-ridges of Hecla (606 m/1988 ft), Beinn Mhòr (620 m/2034 ft) and Stulaval (374 m/1227 ft). Its western side is characterised by a large number of freshwater lochans set behind an unbroken beach of white-shell sand backed by dunes and machair grasslands. That part of the machair west of West Gerenish and Loch Bee was given over to a Royal Artillery range originally established by the Ministry of Defence in 1961 to test the Corporal missile. Lochboisdale, the only village on the east coast, is the island's ferry port link with Oban, Mallaig and Barra. In the north the island is connected to Benbecula by the South Ford Causeway (1983). Notable landmarks on South Uist include a cairn marking the birthplace of Flora Macdonald, the prehistoric chambered cairn and ring of pillar stones at Barpa Mhingearraidh on the slope of Reineval, the ruins of 18th-century Ormiclate Castle and the statue of Our Lady of the Isles on the slope of Rueval, the Hill of Miracles. Loch Druidibeg National Nature Reserve, extending over 1678 ha (4145 acres) of sandy shore, loch, machair and peat moorland, is noted for its wildlife and flora. After the Norse occupation, South Uist was held by the MacDonalds of Clanranald until 1838, when Colonel Gordon of Cluny bought the island and initiated clearances to make way for sheep farming. The population of South Uist fell from a total of 5093 in 1841 to 1818 in 2001.

South Walls *Orkney* A peninsula in the Orkney Islands, South Walls is attached by a narrow neck to the south end of the island of Hoy. Its chief settlement is Longhope, which looks out onto an inlet of the same name. Flotta lies to the northeast.

Southend *Argyll and Bute* A village at the southern tip of the Kintyre peninsula, Southend lies at the foot of Conie Glen, 7.5 miles (12 km) south of Campbeltown. St Columba is believed to have first set foot on Scottish soil near here, and at nearby St Ciaran's Cave a stone table and water basin mark the site of Scotland's first church. Dunaverty to the west was the seat of the kings of Dalriada until the 8th century.

Southern Upland Way *Dumfries and Galloway/Scottish Borders* A long-distance footpath in southern Scotland, the Southern Upland Way stretches across the Southern Uplands from Portpatrick in Dumfries and Galloway to Cockburnspath on the North Sea coast to the south of Dunbar. Opened in 1984, it has a total length of 212 miles (340 km) and is the longest of Scotland's long-distance footpaths. The route is managed by Countryside Ranger Services based at Harestanes and Dumfries. Passing through most of the habitats and landscapes of Southern Scotland, it takes between 10 and 20 days to walk the entire route.

Southern Uplands *Dumfries and Galloway/ Scottish Borders* The rolling uplands of southern Scotland in Dumfries and Galloway and Scottish Borders are known as the Southern Uplands. They lie to the south of the Southern Uplands Fault which extends from the northern tip of the Rhinns of Galloway to Dunbar on the east coast, separating the Border country from the industrialised landscapes of the Midland Valley to the north. The Southern Uplands comprise several ranges of hills, including the Lammermuir Hills, Moorfoot Hills, Lowther Hills, Tweedsmuir Hills, Moffat Hills, Ettrick Hills, Carsphairn Hills, Galloway Hills and Roxburgh and Cheviot Hills, as well as deeply incised river valleys such as Nithsdale, Annandale, Eskdale, Teviotdale, Liddesdale, Tweeddale and Lauderdale, all of which form important routeways. Dominated by sedimentary rocks of the Ordovician and Silurian periods, the hills of the Southern Uplands are generally rounded and often covered with peat. The highest peak is Merrick, which rises to 843 m (2764 ft). Prominent granite features resulting from Caledonian igneous intrusions include the Rhinns of Kells, Criffell and Cairnsmore of Fleet in Galloway.

Southern Uplands Fault One of the major geological features of Scotland, the Southern Uplands Fault stretches from the northern tip of the Rhinns of Galloway, in the west, across the mouth of Loch Ryan, trending east-northeast to the south of Ballantrae and eventually reaching Dunbar on the coast of East Lothian. It marks the southern boundary of the Midland Valley, the rift valley that runs across the centre of the country comprising primarily sedimentary rocks of Devonian and Carboniferous age deposited in desert and shallow marine conditions. To the south are older Silurian and Ordovician sediments deposited in a deep ocean environment. The Southern Uplands Fault permitted the Midland Valley to descend as a major rift or graben by as much as 4000 m (13,123 ft).

Southerness Point *Dumfries and Galloway* A headland on the Solway coast of Dumfries and Galloway, Southerness (also Satterness or Saturness) Point lies at the eastern end of the Mersehead Sands, 9 miles (14 km) south of New Abbey. A lighthouse was built here in 1748 by Dumfries Town Council for the direction of shipping coming into the River Nith. At this point the coast suddenly bends in a westerly direction. The small coastal village of Southerness was established 4 miles (6.5 km) south of Kirkbean in the late 18th century by Richard Oswald of Auchencruive, who hoped to find coal in the area.

Southwick House *Dumfries and Galloway* A country house in Southwick parish, Dumfries and Galloway, Southwick House lies close to the Southwick Burn near where it empties into the Solway Firth and on the southern slopes of Criffell, 4 miles (6.5 km) west of Kirkbean. It was built c.1750. There are a fine home farm, stable, mill and lodge buildings associated with the house, in addition to a bridge (1789) and the attractive mid-19th-century Tudor Shawfoot Cottage. On the opposite side of the Southwick Burn stands Southwick Parish Church, a Romanesque-style kirk built in 1891.

Soutra Aisle *Scottish Borders* Located on the western flank of Soutra Hill, 2 miles (3 km) southeast of Fala is the noted Soutra Aisle. It lies just to the northwest of Dun Law, with its wind farm, and just within Scottish Borders at its boundary with Midlothian. Soutra Aisle is all that remains of a grand hospital, monastery and church which occupied a location half-way between Edinburgh and the Borders abbeys, from its foundation by King Malcolm IV in the 12th century until the 17th century. The House of the Holy Trinity at Soutra, as the medieval hospital was formally known, was run by Augustinian monks to minister to the poor, sick and pilgrims. Soutra Aisle is just a fragment of the church, surviving only because it became the burial place of the Pringles of Soutra in 1686.

Spalefield *Fife* A small settlement in the East Neuk of Fife, Spalefield sits at the junction of the B9131 and B9171, 2 miles (3 km) north of Anstruther.

Spallander Reservoir, Loch *South Ayrshire* Loch Spallander Reservoir lies 6 miles (10 km) east of Maybole in South Ayrshire. It is the source of the Spallander Burn that joins the Water of Girvan a mile (1.5 km) northeast of Kirkmichael.

Spango Water *Dumfries and Galloway* A stream in northern Dumfries and Galloway, the Spango Water rises in hills to the north of Kirkconnel. It flows eastwards to join the Crawick Water at Spango Bridge. To the north Spango Hill rises to 424 m (1392 ft).

Spean, Glen *Highland* Located in Lochaber, Glen Spean runs westwards from Loch Moy and carries the waters of the River Spean towards Spean Bridge. It also stretches south from here to Fort William, and carries the River Lochy between Loch Linnhe and Loch Lochy.

Spean Bridge *Highland* A village in Lochaber to the east of the Great Glen, Spean Bridge lies on the River Spean, 3 miles (5 km) southeast of the foot of Loch Lochy. A bridge over the river designed by Thomas Telford was erected in 1819 and a road up Glen Spean was subsequently built. A monument erected in 1952 a mile (1.5 km) west of Spean Bridge commemorates the commandos who trained in the area during World War II.

Spedlins Tower *Dumfries and Galloway* A former stronghold of the Jardines of Applegarth, Spedlins Tower is situated by the River Annan near Jardine Hall, 4 miles (6.5 km) northwest of Lockerbie. A 15th-century building remodelled in 1605 and re-roofed in 1988–9, Spedlins Tower had been a seat of the Jardines since the late 12th century. The tower became a ruin after the Jardines built a new mansion for themselves nearby.

Speinne Beag *Argyll and Bute* A hill on the island of Mull in the Inner Hebrides, Speinne Beag rises to 354 m (1161 ft) 7 miles (11 km) south of Tobermory.

Speinne Mòr *Argyll and Bute* A hill to the north of Salen Forest on the island of Mull in the Inner Hebrides, Speinne Mòr rises to 444 m (1456 ft) 3 miles (5 km) south of Tobermory.

Spelve, Loch *Argyll and Bute* A sea loch on the southeast coast of the island of Mull in the Inner Hebrides, Loch Spelve is entered through a narrow inlet connecting with the Firth of Lorn. The settlement of Kinlochspelve lies at its western end.

Spey, River *Highland/Moray* Rising in the Monadhliath Mountains to the west of Laggan in Highland Council area, the River Spey flows 100 miles (160 km) east and northeast into Moray, where it joins the sea at Speymouth. It has a catchment area of 3367 sq. km (1300 sq. miles) and on its route to the Moray Firth it passes the towns of Newtonmore, Kingussie, Aviemore, Grantown-on-Spey, Charlestown of Aberlour, Craigellachie, Rothes and Fochabers. The Spey is the second-longest river in Scotland after the Tay and its headwaters (but the longest with a single name), the seventh-longest in the UK, and in terms of volume of water discharged into the sea it ranks eighth in Britain. Both the upper and lower reaches of the river are fast-flowing with steep gradients. In its middle reaches, the river passes through the wide alluvial plain of Strathspey. Here the gradient flattens out and the river has a slow and meandering form. The mouth of the river has always been subject to change, with the formation of shingle spits and the cutting of new outlets. Relatively free from pollution and obstruction, the River Spey supports a major spawning population of the Atlantic salmon (*Salmo salar*) and is one of the most important salmon-fishing rivers in the north of Scotland. The sea lamprey (*Petromyzon marinus*) spawns throughout the lower and middle reaches of the river, and the more inaccessible deep-water areas sustain one of the largest populations of fresh-water pearl mussels in Scotland. The principal tributaries of the Spey in its upper reaches are the Truim, from Loch Ericht, and the Calder. After widening into Loch Insh, the Spey is joined by the Feshie and the Nethy which flow down from the Cairngorms, and the Dulnain which flows down from the Monadhliath Mountains west of Carrbridge. Below Grantown-on-Spey the river is joined by right-bank tributaries including the Avon, Livet, Aberlour, Rinnes and Fiddich. During the 18th and 19th centuries, timber was floated downriver to Kingston and Garmouth from the forests of Glenmore, Rothiemurchus and Strathspey.

Spey Bay *Moray* A wide bay on the coast of the Moray Firth, stretching from Lossiemouth in the west to Findochty in the east, Spey Bay lies at the mouth of the River Spey which flows down through Moray to meet the sea here. A windswept village of the same name with a golf links to the east lies to the east of the river mouth. This settlement was once the principal salmon-fishing station on the River Spey. Of interest in the vicinity are the reedy estuary of the river, an enormous shingle ridge, a metal-trussed railway bridge, a driftwood summerhouse, the Tugnet Icehouse and the Moray Firth Wildlife Centre.

Speymouth *Moray* Speymouth is the name given to the small estuary at the mouth of the River Spey lying between the settlements of Kingston and Spey Bay. It is noted as the landing place on 23 June 1650 of Charles II on his way to be crowned king of Scots.

Spidean a' Choire Leith *Highland* The highest of the peaks of the Liathach ridge in Wester Ross, Spidean a' Choire Leith rises to 1054 m (3456 ft) to the northeast of Torridon.

Spidean Dhomhuill Bhric *Highland* A mountain peak in northern Lochaber district, Spidean Dhomhuill Bhric rises to 940 m (3083 ft) to the west of The Saddle, 4 miles (6.5 km) south of Shiel Bridge.

Spidean Mialach *Highland* A mountain in Lochaber, Spidean Mialach rises to 996 m (3268 ft) to the north of the eastern end of Loch Quoich.

Spinningdale *Highland* A hamlet in eastern Sutherland, Spinningdale lies on the north shore of the Dornoch Firth, 8 miles (13 km) west of Dornoch. A large spinning mill, eventually destroyed by fire in 1806, was established here in 1793 by industrial entrepreneurs David Dale and George Dempster.

Spittal *Dumfries and Galloway* A locality in the Machars, Dumfries and Galloway, Spittal lies at a crossroads by the River Bladnoch, 5 miles (8 km) northwest of Wigtown.

Spittal of Glenshee *Perth and Kinross* Situated at the head of Glen Shee, eastern Perth and Kinross, Spittal of Glenshee lies at the junction of two burns that flow down Gleann Beag and Glen Lochsie to form the Shee Water. A travellers' inn or hospice has been located here for several centuries, and today the hamlet is a centre for tourism, outdoor activities and winter sports. The road heads north from here towards the ski slopes of the Cairnwell, bypassing the notorious Devil's Elbow on the old road to Braemar from Blairgowrie.

Spittalfield *Perth and Kinross* A planned weaving village laid out around a large green in 1766, Spittalfield lies between Caputh and Meikleour on the A984, 6 miles (10 km) east of Dunkeld.

Spothfore Burn *Dumfries and Galloway* A stream in Dumfries and Galloway, the Spothfore Burn rises on the eastern slopes of Cocker Hill, 5 miles (8 km) northwest of Sanquhar. It flows eastwards for more than 2 miles (3 km) to join the Crawick Water.

Spott *East Lothian* The picturesque small village of Spott lies in a sheltered location in a parish of the same name among the foothills of the Lammermuir Hills, 2 miles (3 km) south of Dunbar in East Lothian. Most of its buildings date from the 19th century, but the small parish church is late 18th-century with an early example of a watch tower in its kirkyard. Spott House to the southeast was rebuilt in 1830 by architect William Burn.

Springboig *Glasgow City* An eastern suburb of Glasgow, Springboig lies to the north of Shettleston and east of Carntyne. It comprises late 19th-century terraced and semidetached housing, and postwar three-storey tenements inspired by German and Viennese styles. Lightburn Hospital and Greenfield Park lie to the south of the Edinburgh Road.

Springburn *Glasgow City* A district of Glasgow, Springburn lies to the north of the M8 and east of Possilpark. It developed in the 19th century in association with railway engineering and the nearby Cowlairs depot, industries highlighted in Springburn Museum, Glasgow's first community museum.

Springfield *Fife* A village in the Howe of Fife, Springfield lies to the north of the River Eden, 3 miles (5 km) southwest of Cupar. Said to take its name from the numerous springs that fed into a small lake that once existed at nearby Stratheden, Springfield originally grew up around a corn mill on the River Eden. The village developed after the arrival of the railway in 1847 and became a prosperous industrial centre, at various times producing bricks, tiles and textiles. To the north lies Stratheden Hospital (1850).

Springfield *Dumfries and Galloway* A village in Dumfries and Galloway, Springfield lies on the River Sark, a mile (1.5 km) to the east of Gretna Green.

Springholm *Dumfries and Galloway* A village in Dumfries and Galloway, Springholm lies on the Spottes Burn, a mile (1.5 km) east of Kirkpatrick Durham and 6 miles (10 km) northeast of Castle Douglas. Established c.1800 as a planned village, it comprises a single street of 19th-century cottages surrounded by 20th-century housing.

Springkell *Dumfries and Galloway* A house and estate in Kirkpatrick Fleming parish, Dumfries and Galloway, Springkell lies to the east of the Kirtle Water opposite Eaglesfield. The house was built in 1734 and enlarged in 1818 by the Maxwell family, proprietors of the Barony of Kirkconnel and Springkell since 1609.

Springside *North Ayrshire* A village on the southeast border of North Ayrshire, Springside lies 1.5 miles (2.5 km) west of Crosshouse and 3 miles (5 km) east of Irvine. The Garrier Burn flows immediately to the east of the village. There was once a railway station in Springside and a coal mine to the north, but both were gone by the 1970s.

Spuir *Western Isles* An uninhabited rocky outlier in the Outer Hebrides, Spuir lies to the north of Boreray, from which it is separated by the Sound of Spuir.

Spynie, Loch *Moray* A loch in Moray, Loch Spynie lies midway between Elgin and Lossiemouth. The remains of the pre-Reformation Bishop's Palace of Spynie stand to the southwest, and to the northeast Lossie Forest stretches along the Moray Firth coast. The loch was much reduced in size as a result of drainage operations executed by Thomas Telford between 1808 and 1812.

Sròn a' Choire Ghairbh *Highland* The highest peak of the Loch Lochy hills, Sron a' Chòire Ghairbh rises to 935 m (3068 ft) to the west of Loch Lochy. It forms part of a horseshoe-shaped ridge around Coire Glas.

Stack Islands *Western Isles* A small group of islands at the southern end of the Outer Hebrides, the Stack Islands (Gael: *Na Stacan Dubha*) lie in the Sound of Barra, just off the south coast of the island of Eriskay. They comprise the larger Eilean Leathan to the south, together with several rocky islets to the north. The island of Gighay lies 2 miles (3 km) to the southwest.

Stack Polly *Highland* A distinctive steep-sided mountain in the Assynt district of Wester Ross, Stack Polly (*Gael: Stac Pollaidh* or 'peak of the pools') rises to 613 m (2009 ft). Its summit lies on a craggy ridge. Easily accessible and popular with hillwalkers, not least for the spectacular views it provides of the surrounding area, Stack Polly lies 11 miles (18 km) north of Ullapool within the Inverpolly National Nature Reserve.

Stadhlaigearraidh The Gaelic name for Stilligary in the Western Isles.

Staffa *Argyll and Bute* One of the most celebrated of the small uninhabited islands of the Inner Hebrides, Staffa comprises 33 ha (82 acres) of columnar basalt located to the northwest of the island of Mull. The hexagonal columns result from the slow cooling of basalt lava created during volcanic activity 60 million years ago as the Atlantic Ocean was formed. Its most famous feature is Fingal's Cave, to the east of which is the Colonnade or Great Face, a vast area of columns that rise 17 m (56 ft). Other notable caves include the Boat Cave, Cormorant Cave and Mackinnon's Cave, the latter two being connected by an internal passageway. Following a visit by the noted scientist Sir Joseph Banks in 1772, the island became a curiosity and was visited by Sir Walter Scott (1810), John Keats (1818), J. M. W. Turner (1830), William Wordsworth (1833), Queen Victoria and Prince Albert (1836), Jules Verne (1839) and the composer Felix Mendelssohn (1829), whose *Hebrides Overture* was inspired by the noise of the sea in Fingal's Cave. The island, which is a National Nature Reserve, was given to the National Trust for Scotland in 1986 and can be accessed by tour boats from Mull, Iona and Oban.

Staffin *Highland* A hamlet on the isle of Skye in the Inner Hebrides, Staffin lies on the shore of Staffin Bay, 17 miles (27 km) north of Portree. The Columba 1400 Community and International Leadership Centre is based here. Prehistoric dinosaur footprints have been discovered in Mesozoic sedimentary rocks nearby.

Stair *East Ayrshire* A hamlet in a parish of the same name in the Kyle district of Ayrshire, Stair lies on the River Ayr, 7 miles (11 km) east of Ayr. The Stair Bridge over the Ayr was built in 1745 and the Gothic-style Stair Church dates from 1864. Stair House near the church was built in the 17th century by the Dalrymple family. It was John Dalrymple, Earl of Stair, who sanctioned the Massacre of Glencoe in 1692.

Stair Haven *Dumfries and Galloway* A locality in Dumfries and Galloway, Stair Haven lies on the east shore of Luce Bay at the mouth of the Milton Burn, 2 miles (3 km) south of Glenluce.

Standburn *Falkirk* A 19th-century mining village in southern Falkirk Council area, Standburn is situated on the B825, 2 miles (3 km) northeast of Avonbridge.

Stanley *Perth and Kinross* A planned industrial village sited on a dramatic bend of the River Tay in Perth and Kinross, Stanley lies 5 miles (8 km) north of Perth. It was founded next to an old corn mill by George Dempster of Dunnichen and laid out in a grid pattern by James Stobie, factor to the Duke of Atholl, in 1784. The adjacent Stanley Mills, which operated between 1784 and 1850, were in their time the largest industrial complex in Scotland. The first of these great cotton mills, Bell Mill, was designed by Richard Arkwright and completed in 1790. Drawing water power from the Tay through a 243-m/800-ft-long tunnel, two other mills (East Mill and Mid Mill) formed additional massive ranges. The settlement of Stanley provided housing for the mill workers. The mill buildings were restored in 1995. Stanley is named after Lady Amelia Stanley, wife of the 1st Marquess of Atholl.

Stanydale *Shetland* A township on the west Mainland of Shetland, Stanydale lies 3 miles (5 km) to the east of Walls. Nearby is an outstanding archaeological site comprising a variety of remains, including the Stanydale Temple, a double-sized version of the common prehistoric house and the only truly megalithic structure to have survived from prehistoric Shetland. The temple was probably built between 2500 and 2000 BC.

Staoinebrig A Gaelic name for Stoneybridge in the Western Isles.

Staoinebric A Gaelic name for Stoneybridge in the Western Isles.

Staosnaig, Loch *Argyll and Bute* A sea loch on the east coast of the island of Colonsay in the Inner Hebrides, Loch Staosnaig forms a bay a mile (1.5 km) to the southwest of Scalasaig.

Star *Fife* A village in central Fife, Star lies 2 miles (3 km) northeast of Markinch. Known more fully as Star of Markinch, it is situated on raised ground at the centre of former swamp land which is said to give the village its name. Its crooked main street reflects its evolution from a collection of farmsteadings into a nucleated settlement, and its schoolhouse was the home in the 1880s of the Scottish novelist who wrote under the pen name of Annie S. Swan (1859–1943).

Staxigoe *Highland* A small settlement on the east coast of Caithness, Staxigoe is situated on a narrow inlet 2 miles (3 km) northeast of Wick. It has a quay and 18th-century warehouses used for storage of incoming and outgoing goods transported by small boats that formerly ran back and forth to larger ships anchored at sea. Today, creel and pleasure boats still use the pier.

Steall, Falls of *Highland* A waterfall on the Water of Nevis, the Falls of Steall drop 106 m (350 ft) in Glen Nevis, 6 miles (10 km) southeast of Fort William.

Steelend *Fife* Situated just east of Saline in western Fife, the small mining village of Steelend was created by the Wilson and Clyde Coal Company which opened a colliery nearby. Its houses are largely of the postwar Cruden council-house style, and the village has a miners' welfare club and football club. Steelend takes its name from a farm on Saline Hill to the north.

Steinish *Western Isles* A small crofting township on the east coast of Lewis in the Outer Hebrides, Steinish (Gael: *Stenis*) overlooks the Sands of Tong immediately to the west of Stornoway Airport and 1.25 miles (2 km) east of Stornoway.

Steisay *Western Isles* An islet in Bagh nam Faoilean, between Benbecula and South Uist in the Outer Hebrides, Steisay (Gael: *Steisaigh*) rises to 18 m (59 ft) a quarter-mile (0.4 km) south-southwest of Lingay and a mile (1.5 km) southwest of Wiay. Steisay is trimmed by rocks that connect to a group of rocky islets to the northwest, the largest of which is Cleit Steisay.

Stenhouse *Dumfries and Galloway* A locality in Dumfries and Galloway, Stenhouse lies on the Shinnel Water just west of the village of Tynron.

Stenhousemuir *Falkirk* A settlement in Falkirk Council area, Stenhousemuir lies to the north of the River Carron between Larbert and Carron. Great cattle trysts or markets took place on the neighbouring common, now a golf course, from 1785 until the demise of cattle droving in the 19th century. There are a football ground, library and recreational facilities in Crownest Park.

Stenis The Gaelic name for Steinish in the Western Isles.

Stenness, Loch of *Orkney* A shallow loch on Mainland Orkney, the Loch of Stenness lies between Stromness and the Loch of Harray. In the vicinity there are prehistoric remains at the Ring of Brodgar, Maes Howe and the Stones of Stenness.

Stenness, Stones of *Orkney* Situated on the southeast shore of the Loch of Stenness on Mainland Orkney, the Stones of Stenness form a prehistoric monument probably constructed in the early 3rd millennium BC. Surrounded by a ditch, there were 12 stones in the original plan.

Stennies Water *Dumfries and Galloway* A stream in Eskdale, Dumfries and Galloway, Stennies Water rises in Westerkirk parish to the east of Eskdalemuir. It flows southwestwards to join the Meggat Water.

Stenton *East Lothian* A picturesque agricultural village in East Lothian, Stenton (the 'stone town') lies 4.5 miles (7 km) southwest of Dunbar and 2.5 miles (4 km) southeast of East Linton. Designated a conservation area in 1969, it has many buildings of architectural and historic interest. Weekly cattle and sheep markets were held here between 1681 and 1862. The restored mercat post and scales on the East Green are a reminder of these markets. Community facilities include a primary school, shop and post office, village hall and bowling green. The Gothic-style Parish Church, built in 1829 to a design by William Burn, replaced the 16th-century Old Parish Church whose remains stand to the northeast. To the southwest are 17th-century Ruchlaw House and 19th-century Whittingehame House, former family home of British Prime Minister Arthur Balfour (1848–1930).

Steornabhagh Alternative Gaelic name for Stornoway in the Western Isles.

Stepps *Glasgow City* A northeastern suburb of Glasgow, Stepps lies on the Cumbernauld Road to the north of Garthamlock. It developed following the arrival of the railway in 1831 and later in association with brass sounding, whisky blending and the Cardowan Colliery, which operated until 1984. The Buchanan Business Park was developed here in the 1990s.

Stevenson House *East Lothian* A largely 17th-century three-storey house with gardens in East Lothian, Stevenson House lies a mile (1.5 km) east of Haddington. Associated with the Sinclair family, it was built around a square open courtyard. The building was squared off and extended in the early 19th century and restored in the 1950s. The interior is mostly late-17th century and 18th century, although corridors around the inner sides of the courtyard were added *c.*1820 and lined with wood panelling taken from the former Red Star liner SS *Columbia* in 1934.

Stevenston *North Ayrshire* A town in the Cunninghame district of Ayrshire, Stevenston lies immediately east of Saltcoats and 5 miles (8 km) northwest of Irvine. Named after a 12th-century landowner, Stephen Loccart, it initially developed in association with a market. In the 17th century, coal was mined nearby and a canal was built to carry it to Saltcoats. In 1849, the large Ardeer Ironworks were established, and in 1873 the chemist Alfred Nobel built a nitroglycerine and dynamite factory here. Later owned by ICI, this facility produced plastics, polyesters, nylon and silicon. There is an 18-hole golf course at Ardeer and a nine-hole course at Auchenharvie.

Stewarton An alternative name for Kirkcolm in Dumfries and Galloway.

Stewarton *East Ayrshire* Situated on the Annick Water 5 miles (8 km) north of Kilmarnock in East Ayrshire, the town of Stewarton developed from the 16th century, specialising in the manufacture of bonnets and 'regimental headgear', particularly Tam o' Shanter bonnets, which earned it the nickname 'The Bonnet Town'. From the 19th century, it produced other textiles such as woollens, lace and hosiery. Stewarton has also engaged in engineering and copper production. The industrialist David Dale (1739–1806) was born in Stewarton.

Stewartry, the More fully, the Stewartry of Kirkcudbright, the Stewartry was the name of a former Scottish county now forming part of the Dumfries and Galloway local government area. The term 'stewartry' was once applied to any area of Crown property in Scotland administered by a steward rather than a sheriff. The Stewartry of Kirkcudbright was annexed to the Crown in 1455 by James II in his bid to break the power of the Douglas lords of Galloway. Between 1974 and 1996, Stewartry was the name of one of the four districts of Dumfries and Galloway. The Stewartry Museum is located in Kirkcudbright in a building erected in 1891.

Stichill *Scottish Borders* A small settlement in the Roxburghshire district of Scottish Borders, Stichill (or Stitchel) lies in a parish of the same name in the valley of the River Tweed, 2 miles (3 km) north of Kelso.

Stilligary *Western Isles* A crofting township on the west coast of South Uist in the Outer Hebrides, Stilligary (Gael: *Stadhlaigearraidh*) lies 1.25 miles (2 km) southwest of Rueval and 12.5 miles (20 km) north-northwest of Lochboisdale. Loch Stilligary lies immediately to the south.

Stinchar, River *South Ayrshire* A river of Carrick in

South Ayrshire, the Stinchar rises in the northern part of the Glentrool Forest Park to the east of Barr. It flows north then west through North Balloch and Glengennet before turning south past Barr, Pinwherry and Colmonell to enter the sea at Ballantrae Bay to the south of Ballantrae, a distance of nearly 30 miles (48 km).

Stirling *Area: 427 sq. km (165 sq. miles)* A local government area in central Scotland, Stirling extends northwards from the River Forth to Loch Tay and Breadalbane in the Highlands. Within its bounds lie the Trossachs, Braes of Balquhidder and several lochs, including Katrine, Lubnaig, Voil, Venachar, Achray, Ard, Arklet, Chon, Drunkie and Dochart, Glen Finglas Reservoir and the Lake of Menteith. The headwaters of the Tay and Forth rivers are located in Stirling Council area, and among its highest peaks are Ben More (1174 m/3852 ft), Stob Binnein (1165 m/3822 ft), Ben Lui (1130 m/3707 ft) and Ben Lomond (974 m/3195 ft). Just over 20 per cent of the land is woodland or forest, and 10.5 per cent is arable farmland. The remainder, apart from 1.6 per cent of urban or rural settlement, is rough grazing, improved pasture, wetland or moorland. With a relatively sparse population density of 38 per sq. km, Stirling carries 1.6 per cent of Scotland's total population and 2.8 per cent of its land cover. The larger settlements are concentrated within a small southeast corner of the council area, the remaining rural settlements being spread from Strathblane and Killearn in the southwest to Killin and Tyndrum in the north. Straddling the great divide between the Highlands and Lowlands of Scotland, Stirling played a key role in directing the course of Scottish history. Until it was drained and reclaimed in the 18th and 19th centuries, the Carse of Forth restricted north–south movement, forcing travellers to pass through the royal burgh of Stirling whose castle guarded a strategic routeway and crossing of the River Forth. The Trossachs, which were immortalised by artists and writers such as Sir John Lavery (1856–1941), William Wordsworth (1770–1850) and Sir Walter Scott (1771–1832), eventually become one of Scotland's leading tourist areas. The former county of Stirlingshire, which also included Falkirk, was absorbed into Central Region in 1975 as one of three districts. In 1996, Stirling once again became a separate local government area. Tourism, forestry and farming are the chief sources of employment, and the main towns are Stirling (the administrative centre), Bridge of Allan, Dunblane, Doune, Callander, Aberfoyle, Killin and Crianlarich.

Stirling *Stirling* Scotland's sixth city and the largest settlement and administrative centre of Stirling Council area, Stirling lies between the River Forth and the prominent 122-m/400-ft-high crag on top of which sits Stirling Castle. Situated midway between the east and west coasts of Scotland at the lowest crossing point on the River Forth, it was for long a place of great strategic significance. To hold Stirling was to hold Scotland. In 843 Kenneth Macalpine defeated the Picts near Cambuskenneth; in 1297 William Wallace defeated the English at Stirling Bridge; and in June 1314 Robert the Bruce routed the English army of Edward II at Bannockburn. For fully 500 years, from the reign of Alexander I to that of James VI, Stirling Castle was a principal residence of the kings of Scots. Under the shadow of the castle there developed one of Scotland's earliest royal burghs with its market cross, Tolbooth, Parish Kirk and 'ludgings' of wealthy merchants and nobles of the court. Buildings of historic and architectural interest include 15th-century Stirling Bridge, the Church

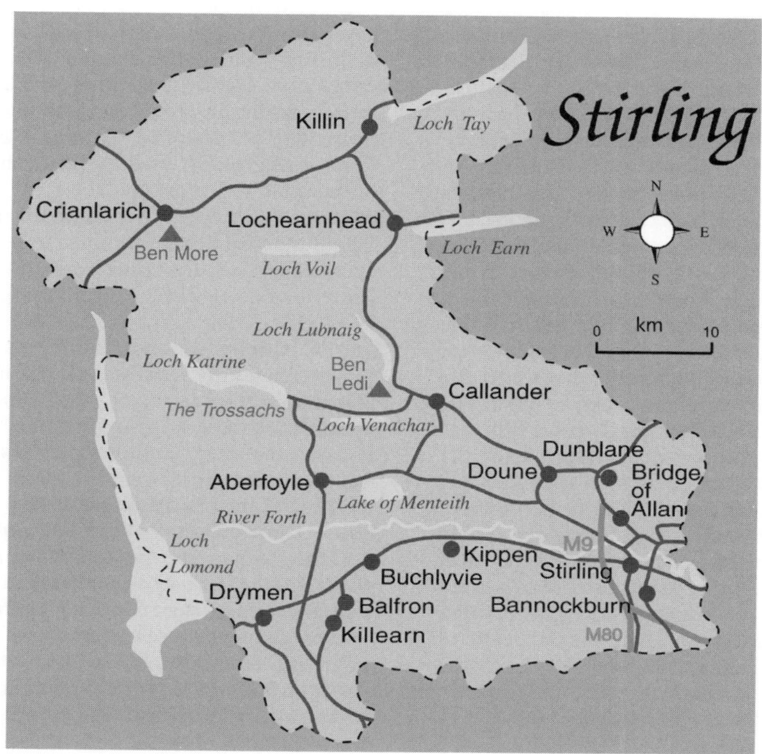

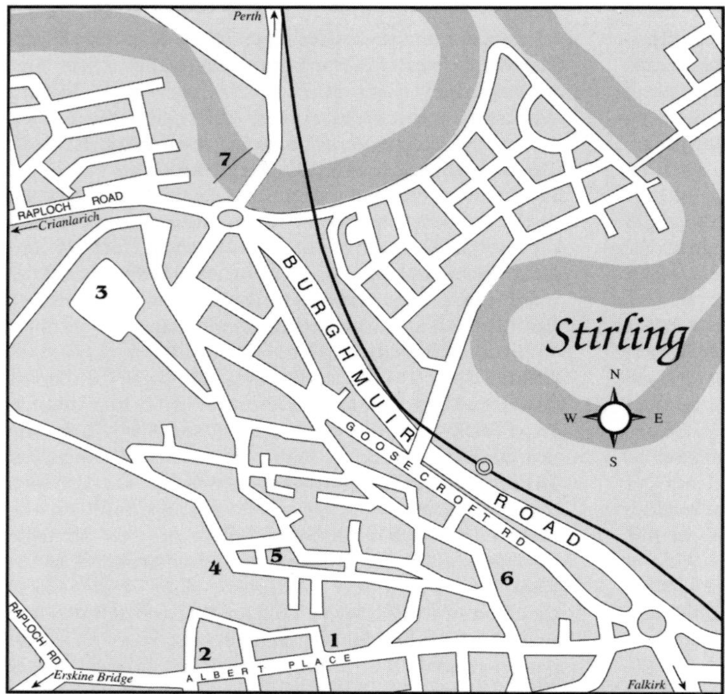

1 *Albert Hall*
2 *Art Gallery and Museum*
3 *Stirling Castle*
4 *Church of the Holy Rude*
5 *Tolbooth*
6 *Thistle Centre*
7 *Stirling Bridge*

of the Holy Rude (from 1456), the Tolbooth (1703–5), Argyll's Lodging (c.1630), Mar's Wark (1569), Cowane's Hospital (1639–49), the Old Town Jail, Darnley House, Norie's House (1671), Erskine Church (1824–6) and the Municipal Buildings (1914). The Smith Art Gallery and Museum was founded in 1874 with a legacy from the painter and collector Thomas Stuart Smith. Today, Stirling is a leading centre of commercial and retailing industries and tourism, retaining much of its historic character. Founded in 1967, the University of Stirling is located near Bridge of Allan on the other side of the River Forth. The Scottish Environmental Protection Agency (SEPA) has its headquarters in the Castle Business Park to the west of the town. Stirling was named Scotland's sixth city in 2002 in honour of Elizabeth II's Golden Jubilee, Her Majesty presenting the 'letters patent' in May of that year.

Stirling Castle *Stirling* Often considered the greatest of Scotland's castles, Stirling Castle dominates the skyline above the city of Stirling. It occupies a strategic location at the lowest crossing point and the highest navigable point of the River Forth, and was for many years the chief royal residence. Destroyed by Robert the Bruce after the Battle of Bannockburn, it was rebuilt in 1333 by Edward III of England. The present building largely dates from the 15th and 16th centuries, a prominent feature being the Renaissance palace created by James V in 1540. A chapel was founded by Alexander I, who died in the castle in 1124. William the Lion also died here in 1214, and in 1452 James III was born in the castle. James IV built the Great Hall in 1500 and the gatehouse in 1510, and Mary, Queen of Scots was crowned in the chapel in 1543. Her son, James VI, who was baptised here in 1566, built the Chapel Royal for the baptism of his first son, Prince Henry. Stirling Castle remained in use as a barracks until 1964, its links with the Argyll and Sutherland Highlanders being featured in a museum display.

Stirlingshire A former county in central Scotland, Stirlingshire extended from the Campsie, Kilsyth and Fintry Fells in the south to the River Forth in the north and Loch Lomond in the west. Its county town was Stirling. In 1974 it was incorporated into the new Central Region as the much-enlarged Stirling District, gaining parts of southern Perthshire but losing Falkirk, Grangemouth and the surrounding area. In the local government reorganisation of 1996 this District emerged as Stirling Council Area.

Stob, Hill of *Moray* The Hill of Stob lies 4 miles (6.5 km) west of Rothes in Moray and rises to a height of 308 m (1010 ft). The peaks of Carn na Cailliche and Cairn Cattoch rise nearby, while to the north flows the Burn of Rothes.

Stob, the *Stirling* A mountain in the Braes of Balquhidder in Stirling Council area, The Stob rises to 752 m (2467 ft), 3 miles (5 km) north of Loch Voil. The Luib Burn flows down its north-facing slope to join the River Dochart.

Stob a' Choire Mheadhoin *Highland* One of two mountains jointly known as the Easains, Stob a' Choire Mheadhoin rises to 1105 m (3625 ft) to the west of Loch Treig in Lochaber. A long ridge called Meall Cian Dearg leads to the stony summit, to the west of which is a steep-walled corrie. Its name is derived from the Gaelic for 'peak of the middle corrie'.

Stob a' Choire Odhair *Argyll and Bute/Highland* Stob a' Choire Odhair, the 'peak of the dun-coloured corrie', rises to 945 m (3100 ft) on the border between Argyll and Bute and the Lochaber district of Highland Council area, 5 miles (8 km) northwest of Bridge of Orchy. Its satellite top, Beinn Toaig, rises to 834 m (2736 ft) to the southeast.

Stob an t-Sluichd *Moray* A mountain in the Grampians, Stob an t-Sluichd rises to 1106 m (3628 ft) 6 miles (10 km) east of Loch Avon.

Stob Bàn *Highland* Rising to a height of 999 m (3278 ft) at the west end of the Mamore Ridge to the north of Loch Leven, Stob Bàn derives its name from the Gaelic for 'light-coloured peak'. This is appropriate since the cone-shaped summit is composed of quartzite crystals which from a distance make the peak look snow-covered.

Stob Bàn *Highland* A mountain in Lochaber, Stob Bàn rises to 977 m (3205 ft) to the east of Ben Nevis.

Stob Binnein *Stirling* A mountain rising to 1165 m (3822 ft) 4 miles (6.5 km) to the southeast of Crianlarich, Stob Binnein (also Stobinian or Ben A' An) lies to the south of Ben More.

Stob Choire Claurigh *Highland* A mountain peak in Lochaber, Stob Choire Claurigh rises to 1177 m (3862 ft) in the Grey Corries range to the east of Ben Nevis.

Stob Coir' an Albannaich A mountain with a sharp-pointed summit, Stob Coir' an Albannaich rises to 1044 m (3425 ft) to the east of Ben Starav and to the east of Glen Etive on the border between Highland and Argyll and Bute. At its summit there is a particuarly large cairn, a relic of early theodolite triangulation by the Ordnance Survey.

Stob Coire a' Chairn *Highland* One of four peaks collectively known as the Ring of Steall, Stob Coire a' Chairn rises to 982 m (3218 ft) in the Mamore range to the north of Kinlochleven.

Stob Coire an Laoigh *Highland* A mountain in Lochaber, Stob Coire an Laoigh rises to 1116 m (3660 ft) 10 miles (16 km) south of Spean Bridge.

Stob Coire an Lochain *Highland* A mountain in Lochaber, Stob Coire an Lochain rises to 1066 m (3496 ft) to the southeast of Stob Binnein, 3 miles (5 km) southeast of Crianlarich.

Stob Coire Easain *Highland* Rising to a height of 1116 m (3660 ft) to the west of Loch Treig in the Lochaber district of Highland, Stob Coire Easain is linked to Stob a' Choire Mheadhoin to the northeast by a high bealach or pass at 960 m (3050 ft).

Stob Coire nan Lochan *Highland* A mountain in Glen Coe, Stob Coire nan Lochan rises to 1115 m (3657 ft) to the south of Loch Triochatan.

Stob Coire Raineach *Highland* A mountain in Lochaber to the southeast of Glen Coe, Stob Coire Raineach rises to 924 m (3031 ft) at the northeast end of Buachaille Etive Beag.

Stob Coire Sgreamhach *Highland* A mountain linked to Bidean nam Bian to the southwest of Glen Coe, Stob Coire Sgreamhach rises to a height of 1072 m (3517 ft).

Stob Coire Sgriodain *Highland* A mountain in Lochaber, Stob Coire Sgriodain rises to 976 m (3201 ft) between Loch Treig and Chno Dearg.

Stob Cross *Fife* A Celtic stone cross on the northern edge of Markinch in central Fife, the Stob Cross stands by the East Lodge of Balbirnie House. It is thought to have marked the limit of sanctuary associated with Markinch Church.

Stob Dearg *Highland* A mountain at the eastern end of Glen Coe, Stob Dearg rises to 1022 m (3352 ft) on the Buachaille Etive Mòr ridge.

Stob Diamh *Argyll and Bute* A mountain peak in the Ben Cruachan massif, Stob Diamh rises to 998 m (3274 ft) to the north of the Pass of Brander. Together with two satellite peaks, it forms part of an east-facing horseshoe-shaped ridge known as the Dalmally Horseshoe.

Stob Dubh *Highland* Rising to a height of 958 m (3142 ft) at the eastern end of Glen Coe, Stob Dubh is the higher of the two peaks of Buachaille Etive Beag.

Stob Ghabhar *Highland/Argyll and Bute* A granite mountain rising to 1087 m (3565 ft) between Glen Etive and Glen Orchy, Stob Ghabhar lies on the border between Highland and Argyll and Bute.

Stob na Broige *Highland* The lower of the two peaks of Buachaille Etive Mòr, Stob na Broige rises to 956 m (3136 ft) to the southeast of Glen Coe.

Stob na Cruaiche *Perth and Kinross/Highland* A mountain on the border between Perth and Kinross and Highland Council areas, Stob na Cruaiche rises to 739 m (2424 ft) between the Blackwater Reservoir and Loch Laidon, in the heart of the Black Corries.

Stob Poite Coire Ardair *Highland* A mountain peak to the northeast of Creag Meagaidh, between Loch Laggan and the Corrieyairack Forest, Stob Poite Coire Ardair rises to 1053 m (3454 ft) to the northwest of Lochan a' Choire.

Stobhall *Perth and Kinross* The estate and home of the Earl of Perth, Stobhall lies 7 miles (11 km) northeast of Perth.

Stobo *Scottish Borders* A hamlet in Tweeddale, Stobo lies in a parish of the same name 5 miles (8 km) west of Peebles on the B712 to Drumelzier. There was an early-Celtic church at Stobo. Stobo Castle, now a residential health resort, was built for the Montgomery family in 1805–11 to a design by J. and A. Elliot.

Stockay *Western Isles* The easternmost of the Heisker Islands, Stockay (Gael: *Stocaidh*) is a tiny uninhabited islet lying 4.5 miles (7 km) west of North Uist and a half-mile (1 km) east of Ceann Ear.

Stockbridge *City of Edinburgh* A district of Edinburgh, Stockbridge lies to the northwest of the New Town. It developed as a small village adjacent to a pedestrian bridge over the Water of Leith, erected in 1786. The painter Sir Henry Raeburn (1756–1823) owned adjacent lands at Deanhaugh and St Bernard's, which he developed with the assistance of architect James Milne, who was responsible for the fine St Bernard's Church (1823) in Saxe Coburg Street. Poet James Hogg (1770–1835) lodged in Deanhaugh Street, as did the surgeon Sir James Simpson (1811–70), who stayed in his brother's bakery. Ann Street, designed by Raeburn and named after his wife, is a rare example of a New Town street with front gardens. Here lived the publisher Robert Chambers (1802–71) and author and editor Professor John Wilson (1785–1854), who for a time had the writer Thomas De Quincey (1785–1859) as a lodger. The grand, sweeping St Bernard's Crescent, featuring facades replete with Doric columns, was inspired by Raeburn's acquaintance and fellow artist Sir David Wilkie (1785–1841). Landscape painter Horatio McCulloch (1805–67) lived opposite in Danube Street. By the river is St Bernard's Well, a mineral spring housed in a grandiose Doric temple, designed in 1788 by Alexander Nasmyth (1758–1840) and restored by publisher William Nelson (1816–87). To the north, between Glenogle Road and the Water of Leith, are the eleven parallel streets of the Stockbridge Colonies, built by the Edinburgh Cooperative Building Company from 1861 with the aim of providing low-cost housing for working people. The streets are named after those who founded the company, including geologist and writer Hugh Miller (1802–56). While retaining its village-like character, Stockbridge has become a popular and cosmopolitan residential area within the city.

Stockinish An alternative name for Kyles Stockinish in the Western Isles.

Stockinish Island *Western Isles* An uninhabited island in the Outer Hebrides, Stockinish lies at the entrance to Loch Stockinish on the southeast coast of South Harris, 6 miles (10 km) south of Tarbert.

Stockval *Highland* A mountain on the isle of Skye in the Inner Hebrides, Stockval rises to 416 m (1364 ft) a mile (1.5 km) east of Talisker.

Stoer *Highland* A scattered crofting settlement in a parish of the same name in the Assynt district of western Sutherland, Stoer lies near the shore of the Bay of Stoer, 5 miles (8 km) southeast of Point of Stoer and 6 miles (10 km) northwest of Lochinver. The Point of Stoer at the northern tip of Stoer Head on the Assynt peninsula is composed of Torridonian sandstone and is a noted landmark to sailors. There are the remains of Pictish brochs nearby, and the lighthouse at Stoer Head dates from 1870.

Stoer Peninsula *Highland* A significant peninsula in western Sutherland, the Stoer Peninsula lies 6 miles (10 km) northwest of Lochinver, between Clashnessie Bay and the Bay of Stoer. It terminates at the Point of Stoer in the northwest. Several small settlements are located on the peninsula, including Achnacarnin, Balchladich, Culkein and Raffin, with Clashnessie and Stoer at its neck.

Stonebyres Linn *South Lanarkshire* A waterfall on the River Clyde, Stonebyres Linn forms a cascade a mile (1.5 km) downstream of Lanark. It is 21 m (69 ft) high and is a source of hydro-electric power generated by the Stonebyres Power Station.

Stonehaven *Aberdeenshire* A resort town on the coast of Aberdeenshire, Stonehaven lies 15 miles (24 km) south of Aberdeen in a sheltered position where the Carron Water and the Cowie Water empty into the North Sea. Formerly the county town of Kincardineshire, Stonehaven lies adjacent to a deeply indented bay surrounded on three sides by higher land between Downie Point and Garron Point. The harbour, consisting of two basins, was improved in the 1820s by the engineer Robert Stevenson and became an important centre of the 19th-century herring trade. During the 20th century the town changed from being a predominantly fishing settlement to a holiday resort, with a variety of recreational and sporting facilities, including a leisure centre, swimming pool and 18-hole golf course. Stonehaven is bypassed by the A92 and has light industry, including furniture making, building, printing and packaging, some of which is located on the Spurryhillock Industrial Estate. Each new year is seen in with the swinging of fireballs in a celebration that is said to have originated in the 19th century as a fishermen's festival.

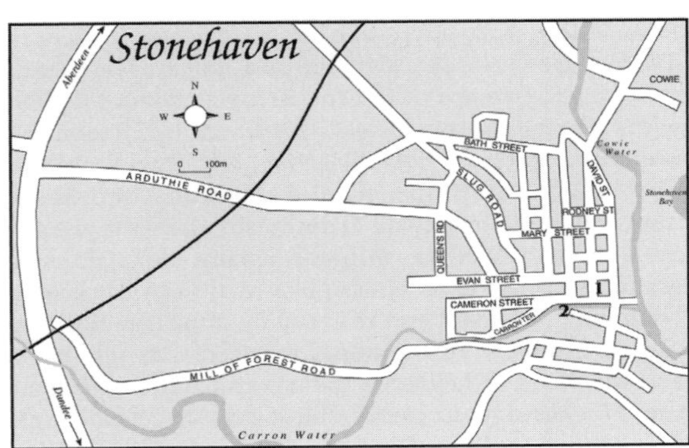

1 *Market Square*
2 *St James's Church*

Stonehouse *South Lanarkshire* A former weaving village in Clydesdale, Stonehouse lies 3 miles (5 km) south of Larkhall. Stone cists found in the grounds of St Ninian's Church indicate early settlement but the village developed in more modern times in association with textile weaving and then coal mining, the Candlerigg Colliery eventually closing in 1958. The weavers' cottages at the centre of the village are now part of a conservation area. Sites of interest nearby include Sodom Hill, scene of a Covenanters' battle in 1679, an Iron Age fort at Double Dyke, and St Ninian's Church, where The Bloodstone with a seam of red ochre running through it is a memorial to one of the martyrs of the Battle of Drumclog (1679).

Stoneybridge *Western Isles* A scattered hamlet located amid machair on the west coast of South Uist, Stoneybridge (Gael: *Staoinebrig* or *Staoinebric*) lies a mile (1.5 km) north of Ormiclate and 9 miles (14 km) north-northwest of Lochboisdale. Stoneybridge benefits from a community hall and Gaelic-medium primary school.

Stoneyburn *West Lothian* A former mining village in West Lothian, Stoneyburn lies 4 miles (6.5 km) south of Bathgate.

Stoneykirk *Dumfries and Galloway* A small 19th-century village in the Rhinns of Galloway, Stoneykirk lies nearly 5 miles (8 km) southeast of Stranraer. Its parish church dates from 1827, and in woods to the south are the remains of an 18th-century windmill.

Stoneywood *Aberdeenshire* A settlement in Aberdeenshire, Stoneywood lies on the River Don nearly 5 miles (8 km) northwest of Aberdeen. It developed in association with paper making.

Stonybreck *Shetland* The main settlement on Fair Isle, Stonybreck lies towards the south of the island, a half-mile (1 km) north of South Harbour.

Stormont *Perth and Kinross* A district in Perth and Kinross, Stormont lies to the north of Perth and is bounded by the rivers Ericht, Isla and Tay. The district gave its name to the title Viscount Stormont created in 1621.

Stormont Loch *Perth and Kinross* A small loch in Perth and Kinross, Stormont Loch (also Loch Bog) lies 2 miles (3 km) southeast of Blairgowrie.

Stornoway *Western Isles* The administrative centre and only town of the Western Isles, Stornoway (Gael: *Steornabhagh*) lies at the head of a sheltered harbour that opens out onto the North Minch. Made a burgh of barony by James VI, Stornoway developed to its present size only with the rise of fishing in the 19th century. It became the main centre of the Scottish herring-fishing industry in 1912, but as fishing declined during the 20th century, the people of the town turned to the weaving of tweed which flourished especially after World War II. In the 1960s, Stornoway mills employed 1000 workers and distributed yarn to 1500 mainland weavers. Today

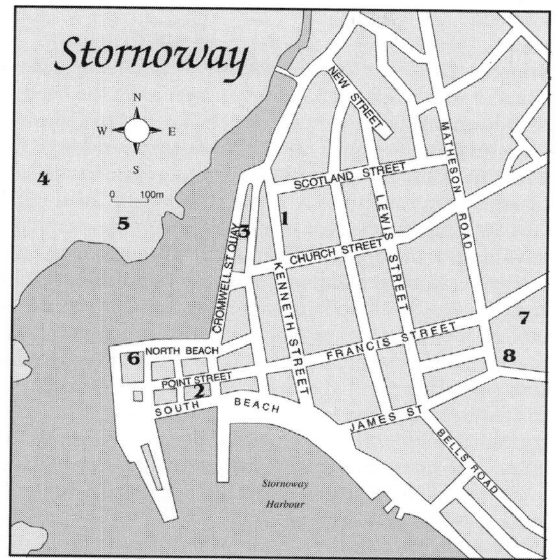

1 *Western Isles Museum*
2 *Town Hall*
3 *Lewis Loom Centre*
4 *Lews Castle College*
5 *Lews Castle*
6 *Fishmarket*
7 *Nicolson Institute*
8 *Sports Centre*

tourism, textile, seafood and offshore oil industries are important to the town. Visitor attractions include the Western Isles Museum, An Lanntair Art Gallery, the Lewis Loom Centre and numerous craft and knitwear outlets. Lews Castle College is situated in the grounds of Lews Castle which was built by Sir James Matheson shortly after he bought the island in 1844. Other buildings of interest include the Town House, Old Town Hall (1905), St Peter's Episcopal Church (1839) and 19th-century Amity House, formerly the custom house and now the offices of the Pier and Harbour Commission. Martin's Memorial Church, named after the Revd D. J. Martin, stands on the site of the house in which Sir Alexander Mackenzie was born. In 1793, Mackenzie was the first European to cross the North American continent, giving his name to the Mackenzie River, which he followed to the Arctic Ocean. The 1500-pupil Nicholson Institute, the only secondary school in the Western Isles, was founded in 1873 as a result of a bequest by Alexander Morrison Nicholson, an engineer. An airport links Stornoway internally with Benbecula and Barra, and with Glasgow and Inverness on the mainland. Roll-on/roll-off car-ferry services have operated since 1973 between Stornoway and Ullapool.

Storr, the *Highland* The highest point on the Trotternish escarpment on the isle of Skye in the Inner Hebrides, the Storr rises to 719 m (2260 ft), forming a landscape of huge rock buttresses and pinnacles 7 miles (11 km) north of Portree. The name derives from the Old Norse for 'great' or 'big', and the Storr probably formed a landmark for Viking seafarers. The Storr landslide is among the most spectacular landslide features in Britain, the entire southeast face of the mountain having collapsed 6500 years ago to produce a great hollow, Coire Faoin, bounded to the southwest and northwest by sheer basalt cliffs 200 m (650 ft) high. Among the shattered ridges and pinnacles the most impressive is the Old Man of Storr, which rises to 49 m (160 ft).

Storr, Old Man of *Highland* The most impressive of the pinnacles of the Storr (Norse: *big*), the highest point on the Trotternish escarpment to the north of Portree on the isle of Skye, the Old Man of Storr forms part of a spectacular landslide feature that is one of the most extensive in Britain. It is 49 m (160 ft) high and was probably a landmark for Viking seafarers.

Stotfield Point *Moray* A point or headland on the Moray Firth coast at Branderburgh, Stotfield Point was chosen by the burghers of Elgin as the site for a new fishing harbour in 1834. Developed hand in hand with Branderburgh (the new town of Lossiemouth) the harbour was designed for the Stotfield and Lossiemouth Harbour Company by James Bremner of Wick to cope with a large herring-fishing fleet. Constructed between 1837 and 1839, the harbour was enlarged in 1852 when a railway link with Elgin was opened. At its peak it was frequented by 120 herring-fishing boats, and it was here in 1879 that the first of the Zulu class of fishing boats was built. An Edwardian extension to Lossiemouth, Stotfield comprises large guesthouses and hotels along a ridge to the west of the town.

Stove *Shetland* A hamlet in the Sandwick district, close to the east coast of Mainland Shetland, Stove lies immediately to the west of Houlland and a quarter-mile (0.4 km) east of Hoswick. The Sandwick Junior High School, with a roll of 270 pupils, opened here in 1984.

Stow *Scottish Borders* A village in Scottish Borders to the south of the Moorfoot Hills, Stow lies on the Gala Water, 7 miles (11 km) north of Galashiels. Formerly one of Scotland's original seats of sanctuary and a summer residence of the bishops of St Andrews, Stow's 15th-century Old Kirk was built around the Church of St Mary, consecrated in 1242 and supposedly holding one of her relics. An even older Chapel of Our Lady was built to the south near the Lady's Well, allegedly by King Arthur. A more recent church was built in the 1870s. The mid-17th-century packhorse bridge was constructed with a low parapet to allow burdened horses to cross in safety. Stow developed in the late 18th century in association with weaving, the turnpike road and the river crossing. Nearby are Bowland (1811), a castellated mansion, and Bow Castle, an ancient broch similar to Torwoodlee (also in Stow parish) and Edin's Hall near Abbey St Bathans. Stow was transferred from Midlothian to Borders Region in 1975.

Stracathro *Angus* A locality and old parish in the Howe of the Mearns, Stracathro lies on the Cruick Water near its junction with the North Esk, 3 miles (5 km) southeast of Edzell, close to the border with Aberdeenshire. It is the site of a Roman fort, a school, a church and Stracathro House, a neoclassical mansion (*c.*1840) by the Aberdeen architect Archibald Simpson, which was converted for use as a hospital in 1939. The first patients were the victims of a wartime air raid on Montrose. It later became a noted teaching hospital with specialised departments including orthopaedic surgery and a hi-tech surgical appliance unit, and continues as a general hospital for northeast Angus. In 1130 an army of David I defeated Angus, Mormaer of Moray, at a battle at Stracathro, and it was in the parish church here that Edward I of England humiliated John Balliol by depriving him of his kingship in 1296.

Strachan *Aberdeenshire* A village in Aberdeenshire, Strachan is situated at a crossing on the Water of Feugh, 2 miles (3 km) south of Banchory in Royal Deeside. The road from Fettercairn over Cairn o' Mount crosses the river here on its way to Banchory.

Strachur *Argyll and Bute* A village in Argyll and Bute, Strachur (also Clachan Strachur) lies on Strachur Bay, an inlet on the eastern shore of Loch Fyne. A church built in 1789 dominates the village, while on a nearby hill stands the Caillaich Bheir ('the old wife of thunder'), a stone that is believed to have the power to move from hilltop to hilltop. A ferry across Loch Fyne once operated from Creggans, where an inn built in 1863 still stands, and Strachur developed in association with forestry and tourism. Strachur House, the former home of soldier and author Sir Fitzroy Maclean (1911–96), was built in the 1780s. A blacksmith's smiddy operated from the 1790s to the 1950s.

Strae, River *Argyll and Bute* Rising to the northeast of Beinn Mhic-Mhonaidh in Argyll and Bute, the River Strae flows southeast to enter the head of Loch Awe, 2 miles (3 km) northeast of the settlement of Lochawe. The river flows through Glen Strae.

Straiton *Midlothian* A locality on the northern boundary of Midlothian, which transferred from the City of Edinburgh to Midlothian after the local authority reorganisation of 1996. Lying immediately to the south of the A720 Edinburgh bypass and just to the northwest of Loanhead, Straiton is dominated by a large retail park.

Straiton *South Ayrshire* A picturesque village in the Kyle district of South Ayrshire, Straiton lies on the Water of Girvan, 6 miles (10 km) southeast of Maybole. It was laid out as a linear planned village c.1760 by Thomas, Earl of Cassillis, and was virtually rebuilt c.1900 by Sir Edward Hunter Blair of Blairquhan. The village is characterised by a narrow main street flanked by low single-storey cottages on either side, buildings of note including the Black Bull Inn (1766), Traboyack (1795) and the church (1758, restored 1901), which contains a pre-Reformation chantry chapel founded in 1350 and enlarged in the 15th century. Straiton developed in association with forestry.

Straloch *Perth and Kinross* A locality in Kirkmichael parish, Perth and Kinross, Straloch lies near the confluence of the Allt Fearnach with the River Ardle, a mile (1.5 km) north of Kindrogan Field Centre and 8 miles (13 km) northeast of Pitlochry.

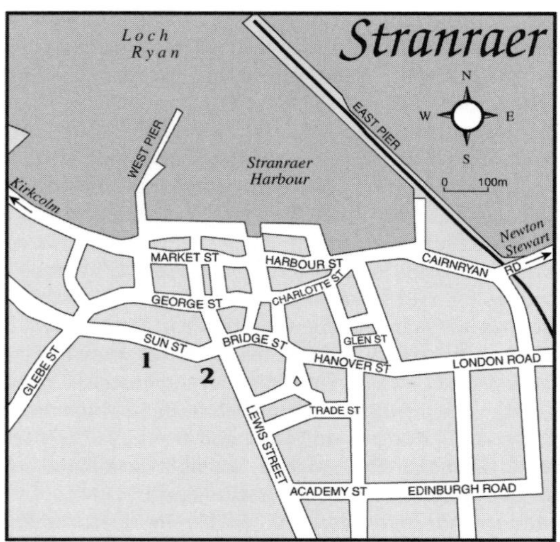

1 *Castle of St John* 2 *Stranraer Museum*

Strannda The Gaelic name for Strond in the Western Isles.

Stranraer *Dumfries and Galloway* A port and holiday resort in southwest Scotland, Stranraer lies at the head of Loch Ryan on the eastern side of the Rhinns of Galloway peninsula. It developed as a market town and was the principal trading centre in western Galloway. It was made a burgh of barony in 1595 and a royal burgh in 1617. In 1831, Stranraer was served by regular steamers, eventually becoming a major ferry port with links to Larne and Belfast in Northern Ireland. Notable buildings include the Old Castle of St John, associated with Graham of Claverhouse in 1632; the North West Castle, now a hotel but previously a residence of the Arctic explorer Sir John Ross (1777–1856); and the Stranraer Museum, which was erected in 1776 as the town hall.

Strathaird *Highland* An estate on the isle of Skye in the Inner Hebrides, Strathaird lies south of Blaven and southeast of the Cuillins, forming a peninsula between Loch Scavaig and Loch Slapin.

Strathallan *Perth and Kinross* The valley of the Allan Water in southwest Perth and Kinross, Strathallan lies between Blackford and Bridge of Allan. Strathallan School, founded at Bridge of Allan in 1912, transferred to Freeland House by Forgandenny in Strathearn. The Strathallan Estate was associated with the Drummond family, William, 1st Viscount Strathallan, allegedly introducing the thumbscrew to Scotland.

Strathallan *Perth and Kinross* A castle in Strathearn, Strathallan is situated near the Machany Water, 3 miles (5 km) northwest of Auchterarder. Dating from 1818, it replaced an earlier building remodelled by Robert Smirke for MP James Drummond, who was later to become Viscount Strathallan.

Strathaven *South Lanarkshire* A dormitory town in the South Lanarkshire parish of Avondale, Strathaven (pronounced 'Strayven') lies in the valley of the Avon Water, 7 miles (11 km) southwest of Hamilton. Designated a burgh of barony in 1450, it has a medieval layout with a town green where the market was held. The village developed in the 19th century in association with engineering, brewing, weaving and the manufacture of silk and hosiery. In the 20th century, knitwear and rayon goods were produced. Notable buildings include Dungavel House, Avondale Castle, the Town Mill Arts Centre, and Lauder Ha', the home of Sir Harry Lauder (1870–1950). In 1679, when Strathaven was a Covenanting stronghold, Government troops attacked Convenanters at nearby Drumclog, a battle commemorated in the John Hastie Museum.

Strathbeg, Loch of *Aberdeenshire* A loch in Buchan, the Loch of Strathbeg lies 6 miles (10 km) southeast of Fraserburgh, just west of Strathbeg Bay on the North Sea coast. The loch is noted for its bird life.

Strathblane *Stirling* A dormitory village for Glasgow, Strathblane lies in a parish of the same name adjacent to Blanefield on the A81 at the southern extremity of Stirling Council area. The Strath Blane valley lies between the village and Dumgoyne, with the Strathblane Hills to the east. The Blane Water and West Highland Way pass through the valley.

Strathbogie *Aberdeenshire* A district of western Aberdeenshire, Strathbogie stretches east and west of the River Bogie with the town of Huntly at its centre. It forms an outlier of the Grampians, with fertile valleys running out into the northeast lowlands. In medieval times, Strathbogie was a lordship controlling strategic routes to the north.

Strathbungo *Glasgow City* A southwestern suburb of Glasgow, Strathbungo lies between Shawlands and Pollokshaws.

Strathcarron *Highland* A valley in Easter Ross, Strathcarron carries the water of the River Carron eastwards from Glen Alladale to the head of the Dornoch Firth at Bonar Bridge.

Strathclyde A former kingdom of west and southwest Scotland, Strathclyde was founded by the Britons during the Roman occupation of Britain. It extended south from the Antonine Wall into Cumbria and eastwards to the Lothians, its principal stronghold being Dumbarton Rock on the north shore of the River Clyde. In the 5th and 6th centuries, the Britons were converted to Christianity by St Patrick and St Mungo, founder of Glasgow. From AD 870 the kings of Strathclyde were subservient to the Scots, and some time between 960 and 1018 the kingdom's independence came to an end, the last king, Owen the Bald, helping Malcolm II defeat the English at Carham. The name was revived in 1975 with the creation of Strathclyde Region, a local government region comprising 19 districts with Glasgow as its capital. The region, which had an area of 13,503 sq. km (5215 sq. miles) and a population (1991) of 2,218,230, survived until 1996, when it was abolished during another round of local-government reform. The name, however, was retained by a number of organisations, including Strathclyde Police, Strathclyde Passenger Transport and Strathclyde University, which was established as Glasgow's second university in 1964 through the amalgamation of the Royal College of Science and Technology (1796) and the Scottish College of Commerce (1845).

Strathclyde Country Park *North Lanarkshire* Lying adjacent to the River Clyde in North Lanarkshire, between the towns of Motherwell and Hamilton and to the northeast of the M74, Strathclyde Country Park is regarded as one of the principal centres for outdoor pursuits in central Scotland. Comprising 445 ha (1100 acres) of mature woodland, parkland and wetlands, the park surrounds Strathclyde Loch, which is the focal point of many of the park's outdoor activities. The loch was artificially created in the 1970s, flooding the area of Bothwellhaugh, including the former mining village of the same name, to occupy an area of 81 ha (200 acres). Used for the water events of the 1986 Commonwealth Games, the Watersports Centre on the west side of the loch provides facilities for rowing, canoeing, windsurfing, dingy sailing and water-skiing. On land, there are facilities for football, hockey, riding, cycling and mountain biking, coarse fishing, jogging and cross-country running. To complement these activities, a hotel, bar, restaurant and theme park have been created at the northwest end of the park, while nearby are a caravan and camping site. The area of the park has a long and rich history illustrated by a Roman fort and bathhouse that have been excavated. However, little remains of the former industrial landscape associated with extensive coal mining here between the 1880s and 1970s. Formerly part of the Hamilton Palace Estate, the area was reclaimed as parkland in the 1970s.

Strathdon *Aberdeenshire* A locality in the valley of Strathdon in western Aberdeenshire, Strathdon lies near the junction of the Water of Nochty with the River Don. Sometimes known as the Cathedral of the Strath, the large Church of Strathdon dates from 1851. The Lonach Highland Gathering and Games are held each August in the Bellabeg Park on the north bank of the Don.

Strathendrick *Stirling* The valley of the Endrick Water lies between the head of the Carron Valley in the east and Loch Lomond in the west. It is sometimes referred to in literature as 'Sweet Innerdale'.

Strathenry *Fife* A locality in Fife, Strathenry lies between the Lomond Hills and the River Leven to the west of Leslie. It comprises a house, castle and estate.

Stratherrick *Highland* A sparsely populated valley to the east of Loch Ness, Stratherrick runs parallel to the Great Glen for 13 miles (21 km), following the upper reaches of the River Foyers and extending east towards Loch Ruthven and the head of Strath Nairn. It includes the settlement of Whitebridge, where a bridge over the River Fechlin built in 1732 by General Wade survives.

Strathfarrar, Glen *Highland* The valley of the River Farrar in the Inverness district of Highland Council area, Glen Strathfarrar extends eastwards for 12 miles (19 km) from the head of Loch Monar to Strathglass. Loch a' Mhuillidh and Loch Beannacharan lie in the glen.

Strathglass *Highland* The valley of the River Glass in the Inverness district of Highland Council area, Strathglass lies to the west of Loch Ness. Formed by the meeting of the River Affric and the River Cannich, the River Glass flows northeast to join the River Farrar at Struy, where it continues on as the Beauly to empty into the Beauly Firth. Forestry, shooting and the generation of hydro-electric power are the main local activities.

Strathkinness *Fife* Situated to the north of the B939, 3 miles (5 km) west of St Andrews in eastern Fife, Strathkinness is a commuter village with origins that probably date back to the 12th century, when the surrounding lands were granted to the Priory of St Andrews. It was formerly an agricultural community that developed weaving in the 18th and 19th centuries in addition to the quarrying of stone, which was an important industry until the 20th century. To the south of Strathkinness on Magus Muir a cairn marks the spot where, on 3 May 1679, James Sharp, Archbishop of St Andrews, was murdered by nine Presbyterians.

Strathmiglo *Fife* A town at the western end of the Howe of Fife, Strathmiglo is situated on the River Eden just south of the A91 to St Andrews. A medieval burgh of barony with districts once owned by the Church and the Knights Templar, its merchants once supplied nearby Falkland Palace with goods and services. During the 18th and 19th centuries, the town developed as a textile centre but also became famous for its 'Fife boots' first manufactured by A. T. Hogg (1858–1927). Strathmiglo High Street is dominated by the Tolbooth with its open forestair and octagonal spire. Outside the parish church stands a Pictish symbol stone dating from c.AD 700.

Strathmore Strathmore (the 'Great Glen') forms a wide valley between the southern Grampians and the Sidlaw Hills, extending from Perth in the southwest to Stonehaven in the northeast and including the districts in the northeast known as the Mearns and the Howes of Angus. Its principal rivers are the Tay, Isla, Dean Water,

North Esk and South Esk, and its chief settlements include Perth, Coupar Angus, Blairgowrie, Forfar, Brechin, Kirriemuir, Alyth, Laurencekirk and Stonehaven. Glamis Castle is the seat of the earls of Strathmore.

Strathnaver *Highland* A broad, fertile valley in northern Sutherland, Strathnaver carries the water of the River Naver 19 miles (31 km) north from the foot of Loch Naver to the sea at Torrisdale Bay to the west of Bettyhill. Once heavily populated, the strath was systematically cleared of population by the Sutherland Estate between 1807 and 1822 to make way for sheep farms. The Rosal township, cleared in 1816 and excavated in the 1960s under the direction of Dr Horace Fairhurst, is interpreted on-site by the Forestry Commission.

Strathpeffer *Highland* A former spa town in Easter Ross, Strathpeffer lies on the River Peffery, 4 miles (6.5 km) west of Dingwall. Several local springs supply water rich in sulphur and iron whose curative properties were noted in 1777 by a local minister. By 1819 Strathpeffer was regularly frequented by visitors seeking cures, and after the arrival of the railway in 1885 it developed as a popular resort with fine hotels and villas built of grey metamorphic stone. Still a tourist centre, Strathpeffer's station and pump room have been converted for use as a shopping and tourist facility in addition to housing the Museum of Childhood. Nearby is Castle Leod, seat of the Mackenzie earls of Cromarty.

Strathspey *Highland* Strathspey is the name given to the middle reaches of the River Spey between Aviemore and Craigellachie where the river widens out into a broad alluvial plain composed of silts, sands and gravels. It is the homeland of the Clan Grant, whose seat is at Castle Grant near Grantown-on-Spey. In the 18th and 19th centuries, the Strathspey Estate of the chiefs of the Clan Grant extended over some 72,846 ha (180,000 acres), encompassing the parishes of Duthil, Cromdale, Abernethy and part of Kincardine. Between 1975 and 1996, neighbouring Badenoch along with Strathspey formed an administrative district of Highland Region, its chief town being Kingussie. The area gave its name in the 18th century to a dance form played in 4/4 time known as the Strathspey Reel.

Strathtay *Perth and Kinross* A village in Strath Tay, central Perth and Kinross, Strathtay lies to the north of the River Tay, 5 miles (8 km) west of Ballinluig. It comprises a number of settlements scattered along the roadside.

Strathy *Highland* A village on the north coast of Sutherland, Strathy lies a half-mile (1 km) southeast of the mouth of the River Strathy where it enters Strathy Bay, and 8 miles (13 km) east of Bettyhill. Buildings of interest include the Strathy Parliamentary Church and manse, built by Thomas Telford in 1828, a Free Church (c.1845) and manse (1862), a Free Presbyterian Church (c.1900) and the Church of Scotland and its manse (1910–11). Strathy Bridge, a concrete girder bridge built in the 1920s by Sir Owen Williams, spans the River Strathy. Strathy Point Lighthouse (1958) was the first all-electric lighthouse in Scotland.

Strathyre *Stirling* Originally located on the route of an old drove road on the opposite side of the River Balvag, modern Strathyre developed on its present site on an access route to the Highlands, especially with the coming of the railway and later in association with forestry. Situated in the heart of Stirling Council area, 24 miles (38 km) northwest of Stirling, it is a centre for exploring Balquhidder and Rob Roy country.

Stravithie *Fife* A settlement in eastern Fife, Stravithie is situated within an estate of the same name on the Kenly Water, 3 miles (5 km) southeast of St Andrews. Stravithie was acquired by Margaret Erskine, wife of Sir William Douglas of Loch Leven, Mary, Queen of Scots' jailer in 1567–8. She passed the lands on to James Stewart, Earl of Moray, her son by James V. The estate later came to be associated with the Sprot family, one of whom, the Tory MP Sir Alexander Sprot, unseated the famous Liberal Prime Minister Herbert Asquith in 1918.

Strelitz *Perth and Kinross* A hamlet between the Sidlaw Hills and the River Tay, Strelitz lies a mile (1.5 km) to the southwest of Burrelton and 8 miles (13 km) north of Perth. It was originally designed in 1763 to house soldiers discharged from fighting at the end of the Third Silesian or Seven Years' War and takes its name from a Prussian town then noted for its manufacture of linen and other fabrics.

Strichen *Aberdeenshire* A village in the Buchan district of Aberdeenshire, Strichen lies on the North Ugie Water, 9 miles (14 km) southwest of Fraserburgh. Designated a conservation area in 1985, it was founded in 1764 by the Frasers of Strichen and was known as Mormond until the 1850s. The population of the new village expanded to 200 in 1790 and 681 in 1840, its development further boosted when the railway arrived in 1865. The two-storey Town Hall in the centre of the village dates from 1816, and the public library in the Anderson and Woodman Institute was opened in 1923. The parish church was originally built as a Free Church in 1893, and replaced an older building within the churchyard to the southwest of the village on the union of the Free Church with the Church of Scotland in 1929. The older building, which dates from 1798, was itself the successor to an earlier church built in 1620. Also in the old kirkyard is the Tolquhon Tomb, which was erected in 1589 for William Forbes of Tolquhon Castle and his wife Elizabeth Gordon. Other church buildings in Strichen include an Episcopal Church (1861) and a building thought to have been built in 1580 as a Roman Catholic chapel but never completed. Nearly a mile to the south of the village is a recumbent stone circle that dates from the 3rd–2nd millennia BC. Strichen House to the southwest of the village was designed in 1821 for Thomas Fraser of Strichen, who later became Lord Lovat. It was sold to the Bairds of Gartsherrie in 1855 and was later used as a shooting lodge, a hotel and an army billet before being gutted in 1954. The village of Strichen is the home of the Buchan Countryside Group, a conservation organisation established in the 1970s that is responsible for the development of the Formartine and Buchan Way, which follows the route of the old railway from Dyce to Fraserburgh via Strichen, last used in 1979.

String, the *North Ayrshire* A mountain road on the island of Arran, the String links Brodick with Blackwaterfoot, 11 miles (18 km) to the southwest. It rises to 233 m (768 ft).

Striven, Loch *Argyll and Bute* A long narrow sea loch at the southern end of the Cowal peninsula, Loch Striven opens out at its southern end into the Kyles of Bute. It extends 8 miles (13 km) from Strone Point on the Kyles of Bute to its head a half-mile (1 km) northeast of Craigendive.

Stroan Loch *Dumfries and Galloway* A loch of Dumfries and Galloway, Stroan Loch lies 4 miles (6.5 km) northwest of Laurieston. It is formed at a widening of the Black Water of Dee which flows eastwards here towards Loch Ken.

Stroma, Island of *Highland* An uninhabited island in the Pentland Firth, the Island of Stroma lies between the north coast of Caithness and the Orkney Islands. It is separated from Caithness by the Inner Sound. It has an area of 375 ha (927 acres) and rises to 53 m (174 ft) at Cairn Hill. Largely comprising Old Red Sandstone, the island is bisected north–south by a geological fault line. The ruins of Castle Mestag stand on Mell Head in the southwest, and in the north are the remains of an Iron Age fort. Nethertown and Uppertown mark the sites of former settlements. In the northwest is a deep hollow in the rock known as the Gloup. The island's population fell from 341 in 1881 to only five lighthouse keepers in 1981. The lighthouse at the north end of the island was automated in 1996, the lighthouse and pier having both been erected in the 1890s. Stroma is surrounded by turbulent seas with dangerous tidal races such as the Men of Mey and the Swilkie.

Stromay *Western Isles* One of the larger of a group of small uninhabited islands off the northeast coast of the island of North Uist in the Outer Hebrides, Stromay (Gael: *Stromaigh*) lies in Loch Aulasary, 4 miles (6.5 km) north of Lochmaddy.

Stromeferry *Highland* A locality in the Lochalsh district of Highland Council area, Stromeferry lies on the south shore of Loch Carron, 53 miles (85 km) west of Dingwall. On the opposite side of the loch is Strome Castle, a 15th-century fortified tower house built on a strategic promontory overlooking the mouth of the loch. A former stronghold of the earls of Ross, the Camerons of Lochiel and the MacDonells of Glengarry, the castle was destroyed after a long siege by the MacKenzies of Kintail in 1602. The ruin was acquired by the National Trust for Scotland in 1939. A ferry service was started at Stromeferry in 1819, following the completion of the road linking Kintail with Dingwall. A railway station bringing tourists to the pier was opened in 1870, but with the extension of the line to Kyle of Lochalsh in 1897 it became less important. The ferry was superseded with the completion of a road around the head of Loch Carron in 1973.

Stromness *Orkney* A town on Mainland Orkney, Stromness is the terminal for the ferry from Scrabster on the mainland of Scotland. Once a busy port servicing ships on the northern sailing routes, Stromness was a base for the Hudson Bay Company from 1670 to 1891, being the last port of call en route to Canada. The explorer Dr John Rae (1813–93) sailed for North America from Stromness in 1833, and the ships of Captain Cook and Sir John Franklin were serviced here. After the building of a wharf in 1764, Stromness became a major whaling centre and later a centre of the herring-fishing industry. It is still a fishing port with boat building and fish- and food-processing industries, and there are ferry links with Scrabster and the Orkney Islands of Hoy and Graemsay. Stromness, which has a natural history museum founded in 1837, was the home of the writer George Mackay Brown (1929–96).

Stronachlachar *Stirling* A locality on the western shore of Loch Katrine in Stirling Council area, Stronachlachar is a terminus for boat trips from Loch Katrine Pier on the SS *Sir Walter Scott*. It is situated 11 miles (18 km) northwest of Aberfoyle by road and is 4 miles (6.5 km) east of Inversnaid on the east shore of Loch Lomond.

Strond *Western Isles* A linear crofting settlement on the southwest coast of South Harris, Strond (Gael: *Strannda*) lies a mile (1.5 km) northwest of Rodel and 1.25 miles (2 km) north-northwest of Renish Point.

Strone Glen *Argyll and Bute* A narrow valley at the southern tip of the Kintyre peninsula, Strone Glen carries the Strone Water southeastwards to enter the Firth of Clyde at Carskey Bay.

Stronend *Stirling* Rising to a height of 512 m (1678 ft), Stronend is the highest point in the Fintry Hills of southern Stirling Council area.

Stron-fearnan *Perth and Kinross* A village on the north side of Loch Tay, Stron-fearnan lies 3 miles (5 km) west of Kenmore. It was built in the early 1800s by the Marquess of Breadalbane.

Stronsay *Orkney* A fertile low-lying island in the Orkney Island group, Stronsay's rich pastures, heather moorland, lochs and wetlands are home to a wide variety of rare plants and birds. The island has many fine sandy beaches, and on the east coast there are several dramatic rock stacks, including the Malme, Tam's Castle, Burgh Head and the Vat of Kirbister which boasts the finest natural arch in the Orkney Islands. Rising to a height of 46 m (154 ft) at Burgh Hill, the island has an area of 3532 ha (8728 acres). Whitehall, which is the main settlement and ferry port, takes its name from a house built in the 1670s by the pirate Patrick Fea. Protected from the open sea by Papa Stronsay, it was for two centuries one of the most active fishing ports in the northern Orkney Islands. The island's population has declined from 1234 in 1881 to 343 in 2001, most of the islanders now engaging in farming, fishing and fish processing. The island is linked by air with Kirkwall, Sanday and Westray, and there is a daily car-ferry service from Kirkwall to Whitehall.

Strontian *Highland* A crofting township in Sunart in southwest Highland Council area, Strontian lies on the north side of Loch Sunart near the head of the loch. In 1724, Sir Alexander Murray of Stanhope opened lead mines that were operated intermittently during the 18th and 19th centuries, and in 1808 the settlement gave its name to the natural element strontium which was first discovered here. The mines were last active in the 1920s, and in the 1970s a barytes quarry was opened to provide drilling muds for North Sea oil wells. In the 1960s, Strontian became a centre for local services, tourism and forestry on the route to Ardnamurchan from Corran Ferry. In 2003, the new Ardnamurchan High School opened in Strontian at the cost of £7 million.

Stroquhan *Dumfries and Galloway* A red sandstone country house in Glenesselin, Dumfries and Galloway, Stroquhan House lies nearly 2 miles (3 km) southwest of Dunscore to the west of the Cairn Water. It dates from the 18th century, with 19th-century additions.

Struan *Highland* A crofting township on the isle of Skye in the Inner Hebrides, Struan lies to the north of Loch

Harport, a mile (1.5 km) west of Bracadale. Nearby are Ullinish Lodge (1773) and Dun Beag Iron Age broch.

Struan *Perth and Kinross* A hamlet in Highland Perth and Kinross, Struan lies at the confluence of the River Garry and the Errochty Water near Calvine. This area is associated with the Robertson chiefs of the Clan Donnachaidh who are buried in Struan churchyard. Old Struan lies to the east on the opposite side of the Errochty Water.

Struie *Highland* A hill in Easter Ross, Struie rises to 371 m (1217 ft) to the south of the Dornoch Firth, 7 miles (11 km) northwest of Tain. The B9176 Struie to Bonar Bridge road is a former drove road developed 1810–15 by the Commission for Highland Roads and Bridges.

Struthers *Fife* A small settlement in east-central Fife, Struthers lies 3 miles (5 km) south of Cupar on the A916 from Kennoway to Cupar. Ruined Struthers Castle dates from the 14th century and was associated with the Ochter-Struthers family, the Keiths who were grand marischals of Scotland, the Lindsays and the Crawfords. In 1633, the title of Lord Struthers was given to the 1st Earl of Lindsay by Charles I, who is said to have been entertained at Struthers.

Struy *Highland* A hamlet in the Inverness district of Highland Council area, Struy lies at the northern end of Strathglass, 9 miles (14 km) southwest of Beauly. The Struy Bridge crosses the River Farrar to the northeast, and the hamlet lies a half-mile (1 km) west of the junction of this river with the River Glass.

Stuartfield *Aberdeenshire* A village in Buchan, Stuartfield (or Stewartfield) lies to the south of Old Deer, nearly 3 miles (5 km) southwest of Mintlaw and 10 miles (16 km) west of Peterhead. It was erected as a planned village in 1774 by John Burnett, the Laird of Crichie, who named it after his grandfather, Captain John Stuart.

Stuc a' Chroin *Perth and Kinross/Stirling* Stuc a' Chroin rises to 975 m (3198 ft) to the southwest of Ben Vorlich on the border between Perth and Kinross and Stirling Council areas.

Stuchd an Lochain *Perth and Kinross* A mountain at the head of Glen Lyon in western Perth and Kinross, Stuchd an Lochain rises to 960 m (3150 ft) to the south of Loch an Daimh.

Stulaval *Western Isles* A hill on South Uist in the Outer Hebrides, Stulaval rises to 374 m (1227 ft) 4 miles (6.5 km) northeast of Lochboisdale.

Stulaval *Western Isles* A hill in North Harris in the Outer Hebrides, Stulaval rises to 579 m (1899 ft) to the west of the southern end of Loch Langavat.

Stulaval, Loch *Western Isles* A loch in South Uist in the Outer Hebrides, Loch Stulaval lies 2 miles (3 km) north of Lochboisdale.

Stuley *Western Isles* An uninhabited 45-ha (111-acre) island in the Outer Hebrides, Stuley lies off the east coast of South Uist, 4 miles (6.5 km) northeast of Lochboisdale. Used as a grazing ground for sheep, the island is separated from South Uist by the Sound of Stuley.

Suainaval *Western Isles* A hill in the Outer Hebrides, Suainaval rises to 429 m (1407 ft) 6 miles (10 km) south of Gallan Head on the west coast of the Isle of Lewis. Loch Suainaval stretches 4 miles (6.5 km) from north to south to the west of Suainaval.

Suainebost The Gaelic name for Swainbost in the Western Isles.

Suardail The Gaelic name for Swordale in the Western Isles.

Sudheim *Shetland* A locality on the Shetland island of Whalsay, Sudheim lies between the port of Symbister and the Loch of Huxter. Derived from the Old Norse for 'south home', this place name has been anglicised to *Sodom* in more recent times. The poet Christopher Grieve (Hugh MacDiarmid) lived here from 1933 to 1942.

Sueno's Stone *Moray* Described as the 'tallest and most complex piece of early medieval sculpture in Scotland', Sueno's Stone stands over 6.4 m (21 ft) high at the east end of Forres in Moray, on the Forres to Kinloss road. Possibly built to commemorate a heroic battle between the men of Moray and the Norse, this 7.6 tonne slab of sandstone was probably brought inland from the coast to its present site. On its west face is carved a highly decorated cross, and on its east face four panels depict foot soldiers and horsemen in action.

Suie *Stirling* A locality in Glen Dochart, the Old House of Suie, an 18th-century laird's house, stands by the road from Killin to Crianlarich. The MacNabs of Innishewan are buried in an enclosure at nearby Innishewan House.

Suilven *Highland* A mountain of ancient Torridonian sandstone in the Assynt district of western Sutherland, Suilven rises from the surrounding moorland to form a distinctive twin-peaked saddle-shaped summit, 5 miles (8 km) southeast of Lochinver. Known as the 'sugar loaf mountain', its higher peak to the northwest reaches 731 m (2399 ft).

Sula Sgeir *Western Isles* A remote uninhabited island in the Atlantic Ocean, Sula Sgeir lies 41 miles (65 km) north of the Butt of Lewis in the Western Isles. Surrounded by smaller islets and rocks this area, together with North Rona, has been designated a National Nature Reserve for its internationally important populations of storm petrel, Leach's petrel, gannet and guillemot. The island used to be visited by the men of Ness in Lewis to collect young birds and eggs.

Sulaisiadar The Gaelic name for Shulishader in the Western Isles.

Sullom Voe *Shetland* A long inlet, or voe, on the Mainland of Shetland stretching southwards from Yell Sound to Ell Wick, Sullom Voe is perhaps best known because of its association with the Sullom Voe Oil Terminal which is situated at Calback Ness on a 400-ha (1000-acre) site. The terminal lies 29 miles (46 km) north of Lerwick and was established in the 1970s to service the North Sea oil industry. It is operated by BP Exploration Operating Company Ltd on behalf of nearly 30 companies participating in the Brent and Ninian pipeline groups. The first oil was pumped from the Dunlin oilfield to Sullom Voe through the Brent pipeline on 25 November 1978, and five days later the first oil was shipped out of the terminal by the Shell tanker *Donovania*. With an average throughput of 700,000 barrels of crude oil per day and a design capacity of 1.2 million barrels per day, the terminal employs a workforce of about 700 and was visited by up to 672 tankers in a year during peak production in the mid-1980s.

Sumburgh *Shetland* A settlement at the southern tip of the Mainland of Shetland, Sumburgh lies 25 miles (40 km) south of Lerwick. To the north is Sumburgh Airport, opened in 1979 to facilitate access to North Sea oil-service centres in Shetland. Sumburgh lighthouse at

Sumburgh Head was built in 1821 by Robert Stevenson, and close by is the archaeological site at Jarlshof, which was occupied for over 3000 years and rediscovered only in 1905 when a violent storm exposed sections of huge stone walls. There is a mailboat link with Fair Isle from Grutness nearby.

Summer Isles *Highland* A group of a dozen small islands at the mouth of Loch Broom on the coast of Wester Ross, the Summer Isles comprise a group of dispersed islands, including Tanera Mòr, Tanera Beg, Horse Island, Priest Island, Isle Ristol, Eilean Mullagrach, Glas-leac Mòr, Glas-leac Beag, Eilean Dubh, Bottle Island and Carn nan Sgeir. They acquired their name from the practice of local farmers using the islands for the summer grazing of livestock.

Sunadale *Argyll and Bute* A locality on the east coast of the Kintyre peninsula, Sunadale looks out over the Kilbrannan Sound to the island of Arran, 15 miles (24 km) north of Campbeltown.

Sunart *Highland* A sparsely populated district to the west of the Ardgour peninsula in southwest Highland Council area, Sunart lies to the south of Moidart and east of Ardnamaurchan. It is bounded to the south by Loch Sunart and to the north by Loch Shiel. Its chief settlement is Strontian.

Sunart, Loch *Highland* A sea loch in Highland Council area, Loch Sunart extends nearly 20 miles (32 km) westwards from the foot of Glen Tarbert, opening out into the Sound of Mull. It separates Ardnamurchan and Sunart to the north from Morvern in the south, and near its mouth are the islands of Oronsay, Carna, Risga and Eilean Mòr.

Sundaywell *Dumfries and Galloway* A locality in Glenesslin, Dumfries and Galloway, Sundaywell lies on the Glenesslin Burn, a tributary of the Cairn Water, 12 miles (19 km) northwest of Dumfries. There are the remains of a 16th-century tower in the farmhouse bearing the date 1651 and the initials of James Kirkoe and his wife Susan Walsh of Colliston.

Sunipol *Argyll and Bute* Situated on the northeast coast of the island of Mull in the Inner Hebrides, Sunipol lies a mile (1.5 km) east of the headland of Caliach Point.

Sunnylaw *Stirling* A locality in Strathallan, Sunnylaw is a northwestern residential suburb of Bridge of Allan overlooking the Allan Water.

Sunnyside Bay *Aberdeenshire* The deserted beach of Sunnyside Bay lies 1.5 miles (2.5 km) northwest of Sandend on Aberdeenshire's northern coast. Overlooked by Findlater Castle, the bay has a cave at its western edge that was home to a French hermit known as 'Charlie', who lived there before World War II.

Sursaigh The Gaelic name for Sursay in the Western Isles.

Sursay *Western Isles* One of the larger of a group of uninhabited islets and islands lying to the northeast of North Uist, Sursay (Gael: *Sursaigh*) lies 5 miles (8 km) northeast of Lochmaddy.

Sutherland *Highland* An ancient county and dukedom of northern Scotland, Sutherland was the 'South-land' of the Vikings and was under Norse rule until the 12th century when William the Lion claimed it for Scotland. It occupies about one-eighth of the land mass of Scotland and has an east, west and north coastline, backed by a sparsely populated landscape of mountain, moor and loch. Sutherland is bounded on the south by the Dornoch Firth, Strathcarron and Strath Oykel, on the north by the Pentland Firth separating the mainland from Orkney, on the east by Caithness and the North Sea, and on the west by the Atlantic Ocean and the North Minch. Its highest point is Ben More Assynt at 998 m (3247 ft). A district of Highland Region between 1975 and 1996, when it had a population (1991) of 13,740 and an area of 5865 sq. km (2264 sq. miles), its chief town is Dornoch. The archaeology of the past reveals Iron Age brochs, souterrains, burial sites and hillforts, as well as more recent townships cleared of their inhabitants in the early 19th century to make way for sheep farms. It was the most sparsely populated county in Scotland.

Sutors of Cromarty *Highland* Two opposing headlands in Easter Ross, the Sutors of Cromarty guard the entrance to the Cromarty Firth, rising to 147 m (486 ft) on the north and 140 m (463 ft) on the south. Sutor or soutar is a Scots word for a shoemaker.

Swainbost *Western Isles* A crofting hamlet located in the Ness district at the northern end of Lewis in the Western Isles, Swainbost (Gael: *Suainebost*) lies 2 miles (3 km) southwest of Port of Ness and 3 miles (5 km) south of the Butt of Lewis.

Swanston *City of Edinburgh* A picturesque village of 18th-century whitewashed cottages to the south of Edinburgh, from which it is separated by the A720 Edinburgh bypass, Swanston lies 4 miles (6.5 km) south of the city centre in the shadow of Caerketton Hill, the most northerly summit of the Pentland Hills. Built for workers on the Swanston Estate, the cottages were restored by the city in 1964 and are the only group in Lowland Scotland to be thatched with reed from the Firth of Tay. The author Robert Louis Stevenson spent his summers in Swanston Cottage between 1867 and 1880, and the village provides the setting for his novel *St Ives* (1897). A memorial bench commemorates the poet Edwin Muir (1887–1959) who also found peace in Swanston. Close to the village are Swanston and Lothianburn Golf Courses, a member of the latter club being the partially blind championship golfer Tommy Armour (1895–1968).

Swarta Skerry *Shetland* Rocky outliers off the west coast of the Shetland Mainland, Swarta Skerry lies to the east of The Deeps, 4.5 miles (7 km) west-southwest of Tingwall.

Sween, Loch *Argyll and Bute* A narrow sea loch on the Knapdale coast of Argyll and Bute, Loch Sween extends southwestwards to open into the southern end of the Sound of Jura. There are a number of islands in the loch, including the Ulva Islands and Eileann Loain. The settlement of Lochgilphead lies 6 miles (10 km) to the east of the head of the loch.

Sweetheart Abbey *Dumfries and Galloway* A late 13th- and early 14th-century Cistercian abbey at New Abbey, 5 miles (8 km) south of Dumfries, Sweetheart Abbey was founded by Devorgilla, Lady of Galloway, in memory of her husband John Balliol, the father of King John Balliol. Devorgilla is buried in the presbytery with a silver and ivory casket containing her husband's embalmed heart, which she had treasured after his death, hence the name 'sweet heart'.

Sweinna Stack *Shetland* A marine rock stack in Yell Sound, Sweinna Stack lies off the west coast of the island of Yell in the Shetland Islands.

Sweyn Holm *Orkney* Located to the north of the Orkney Mainland, the uninhabited island of Sweyn Holm lies off the northeast coast of Gairsay.

Sweyn Holm *Shetland* An uninhabited island, Sweyn Holm lies off the Shetland Mainland's western coast and to the south of St Ninian's Isle.

Swilkie Point *Highland* The most northerly point on the Island of Stroma in the Pentland Firth, Swilkie Point lies a half-mile (1 km) to the north of Nethertown. The Swilkie to the north is a dangerous tidal race.

Swiney *Highland* A settlement in eastern Caithness, Swiney lies a mile (1.5 km) west of Lybster. Swiney House, dating from *c.*1730, is a fine example of a laird's house.

Swinhill *South Lanarkshire* A small settlement in South Lanarkshire, Swinhill lies 2 miles (3 km) south of Larkhall and to the east of the M8.

Swining Voe *Shetland* A north-facing sea loch in the Shetland Islands, Swining Voe forms an inlet on the east coast of the Shetland Mainland, 2 miles (3 km) north of Dury Voe.

Swinton *Scottish Borders* A village in the Merse district of Berwickshire in Scottish Borders, Swinton lies 5 miles (8 km) north of Coldstream, on the road to Duns. The village is built around a large green. The Leet Water flows to the north.

Switha *Orkney* The tiny 41-ha (101-acre) island of Switha lies in the shadow of Flotta and South Walls in the southern approaches to Scapa Flow in the Orkney Islands. Sheep are grazed on the island, but there is little evidence of human settlement except for two standing stones and a cairn dating from Neolithic times. Its southernmost point is called The Ool, and in the southwest is a shallow cove known as The Pool.

Switha Sound *Orkney* The Switha Sound in the Orkney Islands forms a channel between the islands of Switha and Flotta.

Swona *Orkney* Uninhabited since 1974, the 92-ha (227-acre) island of Swona lies in the southern approaches to Scapa Flow, west of South Ronaldsay in the Orkney Islands. Rising to 41 m (134 ft) at Warbister Hill, its east coast is dominated by Old Red Sandstone cliffs. There are remains of prehistoric, early Christian, Viking and more recent crofting settlement, and a herd of feral cattle still grazes here.

Swordale *Western Isles* A crofting township in the southwest of the Eye peninsula on the Isle of Lewis in the Western Isles, Swordale (Gael: *Suardail*) lies immediately to the south of Knock and 2 miles (3 km) southwest of Garrabost. The settlement overlooks Loch Braigh na h-Aoidhe and the narrow isthmus that connects the peninsula to the rest of Lewis.

Swordly *Highland* A settlement on the north coast of Sutherland, Swordly lies 2 miles (3 km) east of Bettyhill and to the south of Kirtomy Bay.

Symbister *Shetland* The principal settlement and port of the Shetland island of Whalsay, Symbister has a ferry link with Mainland Shetland. There is a lighthouse at Symbister Ness. The granite Symbister House, which has served as a school since 1940, was built in 1823 by the Bruce family.

Symbister Ness *Shetland* A headland on the west coast of the island of Whalsay in the Shetland Islands, Symbister Ness lies a half-mile (1 km) west of the settlement of Symbister.

Symington *South Ayrshire* A kirkton settlement in the Kyle district of South Ayrshire, Symington lies 4 miles (6.5 km) northeast of Prestwick and 5 miles (8 km) southwest of Kilmarnock. Centred on a 12th-century Norman church, it developed as a weaving village. The ruinous 15th-century Craigie Castle was a stronghold of the Wallaces of Craigie.

Symington *South Lanarkshire* A village in Clydesdale, Symington lies in the shadow of Tinto Hill on the northern bank of the upper reaches of the River Clyde, 3 miles (5 km) southwest of Biggar. It developed from the 1860s at a railway junction, the railway eventually closing in 1966. The Culter Hills lie to the south and southeast.

Syre *Highland* A small settlement in Caithness, Syre lies in the heart of Strathnaver, 11 miles (18 km) south of Bettyhill.

Syre, Loch *Highland* A small loch in Caithness, Loch Syre lies 2 miles (3 km) east of the southern end of Loch Loyal and 11 miles (18 km) south of Bettyhill. The loch contains many small islands.

Tabhaigh More The Gaelic name for Tavay More in the Western Isles.

Tabost The Gaelic name for Habost in the Western Isles.

Tacleit The Gaelic name for Hacklete in the Western Isles.

Tahay *Western Isles* The most conspicuous and one of the largest of a number of uninhabited islands lying to the northeast of North Uist, Tahay (Gael: *Taghaigh*) lies 4.5 miles (7 km) northeast of Lochmaddy. The island extends to 53 ha (131 acres) and rises to 65 m (213 ft). It was occupied briefly in the mid-19th century but proved unable to sustain its population.

Tain *Highland* A small town in Easter Ross, Tain lies to the south of the Dornoch Firth, 10 miles (16 km) northeast of Invergordon. Thought to have been chartered in 1066 by Malcom Canmore, it was confirmed as a royal burgh in the 15th century. Tain was the birthplace *c.* AD 1000 of St Duthac, who gave his name to the Gaelic Baile Dhubhthaich ('Duthac's village'). A chapel known as the Girth of Tain, built on the site of his birth, became a centre of pilgrimage visited by several Scottish monarchs. The name Tain is thought to derive from the Scandinavian *ting* ('place of assembly'). In addition to being a market town and centre of pilgrimage on the old north road, Tain developed in the 18th century in association with linen spinning and the distilling of whisky at nearby Glenmorangie. Modern industries include distilling, agricultural engineering and the manufacture of cheese. Buildings of interest include a massive tolbooth (1730), Royal Academy (1812) and collegiate church (1371) with an associated museum. There is an 18-hole golf course.

Talbot Rice Art Gallery *City of Edinburgh* Located in Playfair's Georgian Gallery within the University of Edinburgh's Old College on South Bridge, Edinburgh, the Talbot Rice Art Gallery exhibits a collection of paintings and bronzes, among which is the Torrie Collection. This is a set of 16th- and 17th-century European works collected by Sir James Erskine of Torrie, including the bronzes *Anatomical Figure of a Horse* by Giambologna and *Cain and Abel* by De Vries. The Talbot Rice Art Gallery also holds the Hope Scott Collection, with works by Bonnard, Ernst, Picasso, Utrillo and Van Dongen, together with paintings by 20th-century

Scottish artists, including a significant collection of the works of William Johnstone (1897–1981). The gallery is named after David Talbot Rice (1903–72), Professor of Fine Art at the university between 1934 and 1972.

Talisker *Highland* A small village on the west coast of the isle of Skye in the Inner Hebrides, Talisker lies 4 miles (6.5 km) west of Carbost and 3 miles (5 km) southeast of the headland of Rubha nan Clach. The MacAskill brothers established a distillery here in 1843. Talisker Bay, which receives the River Talisker, forms an inlet of the Sea of the Hebrides.

Talla Bheith *Perth and Kinross* A country house in Perth and Kinross, Talla Beith lies on the northern shore of Loch Rannoch, 6 miles (10 km) west of Kinloch Rannoch. It lies in the centre of a game forest that carries the same name.

Talla Linnfoots *Scottish Borders* A small settlement in the Tweeddale district of Scottish Borders, Talla Linnfoots lies in Glen Talla, 2 miles (3 km) southeast of Tweedsmuir, at the southeast end of the 121-ha (300-acre) Talla Reservoir, which is fed by the Talla Water.

Talladale *Highland* A village in Wester Ross, Talladale lies on the southwest shore of Loch Maree, 8 miles (13 km) southwest of Gairloch.

Talmine *Highland* A village in northern Caithness, Talmine lies on Talmine Bay, an inlet on the western shore of Tongue Bay, 4 miles (6.5 km) north of Tongue.

Talnotry *Dumfries and Galloway* A locality in the Galloway Forest Park, Dumfries and Galloway, Talnotry lies on the Queen's Way from New Galloway to Newton Stewart. It sits at the foot of the Fell of Talnotry, near the junction of the Grey Mare's Tail Burn with the Palnure Burn. There is a camp site here and on a nearby hill stands Murray's Monument, a monument to Alexander Murray, a local shepherd's son who went on to become Professor of Oriental Languages at Edinburgh University in 1812 but died the following year, aged 37. Murray was born on 22 October 1775 in a cottage at Dunkitterick, a mile (1.5 km) east of Talnoltry. A path leads up to the Grey Mare's Tail waterfall, and nearby is the 61-ha (150-acre) Wild Goat Park created by the Forestry Commission in 1970.

Tamanavay, Loch *Western Isles* A sea loch on the west coast of North Harris in the Western Isles, Loch Tamanavay (Gael: *Tamnabhaigh*) lies to the north of Loch Resort. It receives the River Tamanavay.

Tanar, Glen *Aberdeenshire* A valley of Royal Deeside lying a mile (1.5 km) southwest of Aboyne, Glen Tanar carries the middle section of the Water of Tanar northeastwards towards Bridge of Ess. The glen includes the Forest of Glentanar and the Braeloine Visitor Centre.

Tanar, Water of *Aberdeenshire* A river of southern Aberdeenshire, the Water of Tanar rises close to the border with Angus and flows north and east, passing though Glen Tanar and Bridge of Ess, before emptying into the River Dee a mile (1.5 km) west of Aboyne.

Tanera Beg *Highland* An island in the Summer Isles group off the coast of Wester Ross, Tanera Beg lies at the mouth of Loch Broom to the west of the island of Tanera Mòr. It has an area of 66 ha (163 acres) and rises to 83 m (272 ft) in a central plateau.

Tanera Mòr *Highland* The largest of the Summer Isles, Tanera Mòr lies at the mouth of Loch Broom, a mile (1.5 km) west of the coast of Wester Ross opposite Badentarbat Bay. Occupying an area of 310 ha (766 acres) and rising to a height of 122 m (400 ft), Tanera Mòr was a successful herring-fishing port in the early 19th century but suffered the same decline as much of the Scottish herring fleet. There are two settlements on the island at Ardnagoine and Garadheancal, the majority of buildings being holiday homes.

Tang Head *Highland* A headland on the east coast of Caithness, Tang Head lies at the northern end of Sinclair's Bay, 7 miles (11km) north of Wick.

Tankerness *Orkney* A small, scattered community on the Orkney Mainland, Tankerness lies on the Deer Sound 2 miles (3 km) southwest of Rerwick Head and 5 miles (8 km) southeast of Kirkwall. Situated within the township is the Tankerness House Museum, while to the north is the Loch of Tankerness.

Tanna, Loch *North Ayrshire* A loch on the island of Arran, Loch Tanna lies 3 miles (5 km) east of the settlement of Pirnmill. It is the source of a headwater of the Iorsa Water.

Tannach *Highland* A settlement in northeast Caithness, Tannach lies 3 miles (5 km) southwest of Wick and to the west of Loch Hempriggs.

Tannadice *Angus* A village in an Angus parish of the same name, Tannadice lies on the River South Esk, 4 miles (6.5 km) north of Forfar. Nearby Tannadice House was built in 1805.

Tannadice Park *Dundee City* A football stadium on Tannadice Road in Dundee, Tannadice Park is the home ground of Dundee United Football Club (formerly Dundee Hibernian) which was established in 1909 as a focus for the Irish community of the area in circumstances similar to the establishment of Celtic Football Club in Glasgow and Hibernian Football Club in Edinburgh. The club was admitted into the Scottish League in 1910. The stadium has a seating capacity of 14,209.

Tannahill Cottages *Renfrewshire* A museum dedicated to the life and works of the Paisley-born poet Robert Tannahill (1774–1810), the Tannahill Cottages are located in the centre of Paisley. The Paisley Burns Club meets regularly here.

Tannochside *North Lanarkshire* Tannochside forms a northern suburb of Uddingston in North Lanarkshire.

Tantallon Castle *East Lothian* Occupying a dramatic cliff-top position with views towards the Bass Rock in the Firth of Forth, Tantallon Castle lies 3 miles (5 km) east of North Berwick. Built in the 14th century by William, 1st Earl of Douglas, the castle passed through his illegitimate son to the earls of Angus (the 'Red Douglases'). Tantallon was largely destroyed during a siege in 1651. It has a dovecote, earthwork defences, a dry moat, a massive 15-m (50-ft) curtain wall with flanking towers, and a gatehouse tower extended and remodelled in the 16th century by James V.

Taobh a' Chaolais *Western Isles* A small crofting township on the south coast of South Uist in the Outer Hebrides, Taobh a' Chaolais is located 3 miles (5 km) south-southwest of Lochboisdale.

Taobh a' Deas Loch Baghasdail The Gaelic name for South Lochboisdale in the Western Isles.

Taobh Tuath The Gaelic name for Northton in the Western Isles.

Taran Mòr *Western Isles* A hill on the west coast of Harris in the Western Isles, Taran Mòr rises to 303 m (994 ft) to the south of Loch Resort.

Taransay *Western Isles* An island in the Western Isles, the windswept island of Taransay (Gael: *Tarasaigh*) lies a mile (1.5 km) to the west of South Harris, from which it is separated by the Sound of Taransay. The island, which is 4 miles (6.5 km) long, has an area of 1475 ha (3645 acres) and rises to 267 m (881 ft) at Beinn Raah. It comprises a large and a small part linked by a narrow sand-dune neck. Taransay had a population of 76 in 1911 but was largely abandoned by 1942, the island's main settlement being at Paible close to the site of St Keith's Chapel and St Taran's Chapel. The island was used in 2000 by BBC Television as the setting for a survival programme called *Castaway*.

Taransay Glorigs *Western Isles* The Taransay Glorigs (Gael: *Gloraig Tharansaigh*) form a group of rocks lying 3 miles (5 km) northwest of the island of Taransay and 2 miles (3 km) southeast of Hushinish Point on North Harris in the Western Isles.

Tarasaigh The Gaelic name for Taransay in the Western Isles.

Tarbat Ness *Highland* A headland with a lighthouse (1830) on the coast of Easter Ross, Tarbat Ness extends into the sea between the Dornoch Forth and the Moray Forth, 10 miles (16 km) northeast of Tain.

Tarbert *Argyll and Bute* A fishing village at the northern end of the Kintyre peninsula, Tarbert lies on the narrow neck of land between East Loch Tarbert and West Loch Tarbert. The Norse King Magnus Barefoot carried a boat across this isthmus in 1093. In 1329, Tarbert was chartered as a royal burgh. It developed initially as a market centre in association with a castle of the sheriffs of Argyll, and later as a fishing port and centre for steamers operating on Loch Fyne. Tourism, fishing and yachting are locally important.

Tarbert *Argyll and Bute* A small settlement on the island of Jura in the Inner Hebrides, Tarbert lies on Tarbert Bay, an inlet of the Sound of Jura, 5 miles (8 km) southwest of Ardlussa.

Tarbert *Argyll and Bute* A locality on the island of Gigha in the Inner Hebrides, Tarbert lies at the northern end of the island, 2 miles (3 km) north of Ardminish.

Tarbert *Highland* A small village located in Sunart, Tarbert lies on the western shore of Sunart Bay, an inlet on the northern shore of Loch Sunart, a half-mile (1 km) southwest of Salen.

Tarbert *Western Isles* Surrounded by rocky hills, the village of Tarbert stands on the half-mile/1-km-wide narrow neck of land that links Harris with South Harris in the Western Isles. It is the main port for Harris and has car-ferry links with Uig in Skye and Lochmaddy in North Uist. The settlement developed in association with a steamer pier from the 1840s.

Tarbert, Glen *Highland* A glen in Sunart, Glen Tarbert carries the water of the River Tarbert, which rises in headwaters on Garbh Bheinn and flows east into Loch Linnhe.

Tarbert, Loch *Argyll and Bute* A sea loch on the west coast of the island of Jura in the Inner Hebrides, Loch Tarbert almost divides the island into two. The head of the loch lies a mile (1.5 km) west of the settlement of Tarbert, which lies on Tarbert Bay, an inlet on the island's east coast.

Tarbert Bay *Highland* A small bay on the south coast of the island of Canna in the Inner Hebrides, Tarbert Bay lies 3 miles (5 km) east of Garrisdale Point, facing southeast towards the island of Sanday.

Tarbet *Highland* A hamlet of North Morar, Tarbet lies on the southern shore of Loch Nevis, 7 miles (11 km) southeast of Mallaig, but is inaccessible by road. It is served by a passenger ferry from Mallaig via Inverie.

Tarbolton *South Ayrshire* A village in the Kyle district of South Ayrshire, Tarbolton lies 4 miles (6.5 km) west of Mauchline and 5 miles (8 km) east of Prestwick. Designated a burgh of barony in 1671, it developed initially in association with coal mining. In 1780 a debating society known as the Bachelors' Club was established by the poet Robert Burns and his friends. They met in a cottage in Sandgate Street acquired by the National Trust for Scotland in 1938.

Tarbrax *Angus* A locality in south-central Angus, Tarbrax lies immediately to the west of the A90, 2.5 miles (4 km) northeast of Tealing. There are farms at North, South and West Tarbrax.

Tarbrax *South Lanarkshire* A small village in the western foothills of the Pentland Hills, Tarbrax lies on the North Medwin River, 6 miles (10 km) northeast of Carnwath, close to the border with West Lothian.

Tarf, Falls of *Perth and Kinross* A waterfall on the course of the Tarf Water in Highland Perth and Kinross, the Falls of Tarf are located 11 miles (18 km) northeast of Blair Atholl near the head of Glen Tilt.

Tarf, Water of *Angus* A river with many tributaries in the southern Grampians of Angus, the Water of Tarf rises near the border between Angus and Aberdeenshire. It flows nearly 8 miles (13 km) southeastwards to join the River North Esk near Tarfside.

Tarf Water *Dumfries and Galloway* A river in western Dumfries and Galloway, the Tarf Water rises in New Luce parish to the west of Craigairie Fell. It flows generally southeastwards for most of its course, until a short distance beyond Tarf Bridge near Mark of Luce it turns northeastwards for just over 3 miles (5 km) before joining the River Bladnoch just east of Kirkcowan. Its total length is about 17 miles (27 km).

Tarf Water *Perth and Kinross* A river of Perth and Kinross, the Tarf Water rises in the foothills of Beinn Bhreac and flows eastwards for 9 miles (15 km), through the Falls of Tarf, and joins with other streams to become the River Tilt, 11 miles (18 km) northeast of Blair Atholl.

Tarff, Loch *Highland* A small loch in the Great Glen, Loch Tarff lies to the southeast of Loch Ness, 3 miles (5 km) east of Fort Augustus.

Tarff, River *Highland* A river in the southwest Monadhliath Mountains, the River Tarff rises between the Glendoe and Corrieyairack Forests. It flows west then north through Glen Tarff to empty into Loch Ness near Fort Augustus.

Tarff Water *Dumfries and Galloway* A river of Dumfries and Galloway, the Tarff Water rises in Laurieston Forest. It flows 9 miles (14 km) southwards to join the River Dee a mile (1.5 km) north of Kirkcudbright.

Tarfside *Angus* A hamlet in Glen Esk, Tarfside lies on the Water of Tarf near its junction with the River North Esk, 9 miles (14 km) northwest of Edzell. Tarfside is the principal village in the remote parish of Lochlee. An Episcopal church here was built in 1879 by Lord Forbes in memory of the Revd Alexander Forbes, Bishop of

Brechin. Today, St Drostan's Church incorporates a retreat centre run by the cathedral in Brechin. Tarfside has close associations with the principal landowners, the earls of Dalhousie. The 1st Lord Panmure built a Masonic Hall here in 1821, and later the Maule Memorial Church was built following the Disruption in the Church of Scotland (1843). While the 1st Lord Panmure was not sympathetic to the Free Church, Fox Maule Ramsay, the 2nd Lord Panmure and 11th Earl of Dalhousie (1801–74) gave the necessary land to his friend and leader of the Free Church, Dr Thomas Guthrie (1803–73). Both men are commemorated in the fine stained glass in the church. On the Hill of Migvie to the west is a cairn, known as the Rowan Tower, which was erected as a family memorial in 1866 by the 11th Earl of Dalhousie.

Tarken, Glen *Perth and Kinross* A valley in Perth and Kinross, Glen Tarken carries a small stream south to join Loch Earn, 2 miles (3 km) northwest of St Fillans.

Tarland *Aberdeenshire* A small village in the Cromar district of Aberdeenshire, Tarland is situated on the Tarland Burn, 5 miles (8 km) northwest of Aboyne. The Douneside Estate to the north is associated with the MacRobert family.

Tarmachan Range *Perth and Kinross* A mountain range in Breadalbane, the Tarmachan Range lies to the west of Ben Lawers and north of Loch Tay. It comprises four peaks, the highest being Meall nan Tarmachan (1044 m/3425 ft). The three other peaks are Meall Garbh, Beinn nan Eachan and Creag na Caillich. The narrow Tarmachan Ridge provides popular hillwalking, with views towards Ben Lawers.

Tarner Island *Highland* A small uninhabited island off the west coast of Skye in the Inner Hebrides, Tarner Island lies in Loch Bracadale, a mile (1.5 km) north of the island of Wiay.

Tarras Water *Dumfries and Galloway* A river of Eskdale in Dumfries and Galloway, the Tarras Water rises to the west of Roan Fell near the boundary with Scottish Borders. It flows more than 11 miles (18 km) south to join the River Esk 2 miles (3 km) south of Langholm opposite Auchenrivock.

Tarsan, Glen *Argyll and Bute* A glen on the Cowal peninsula, Glen Tarsan extends northeastwards from the head of Loch Striven. It carries a short stream down into the loch from Loch Tarsan.

Tarskavaig *Highland* A small village on the isle of Skye in the Inner Hebrides, Tarskavaig lies on Tarskavaig Bay, an inlet on the west coast of the Sleat peninsula, 5 miles (8 km) northwest of Armadale and 7 miles (11 km) north of the Point of Sleat.

Tarves *Aberdeenshire* A village in the Formartine district of Aberdeenshire, Tarves lies 4 miles (6.5 km) northeast of Oldmeldrum. Situated on the road from Aberdeen to Buchan, it developed in the 18th and 19th centuries as a market centre, coaching hub and agricultural service centre, many of its buildings being erected around a central square. To the north is Haddo House (1731) and to the east on a hilltop is a folly known as the Prop of Ythsie, built in 1862 to commemorate the 4th Earl of Aberdeen who was British Prime Minister at the time of the Crimean War.

Tarvie *Perth and Kinross* A locality in Kirkmichael parish, highland Perth and Kinross, Tarvie lies in Glen Brerachan, 6 miles (10 km) northeast of Pitlochry.

Tavay More *Western Isles* Tavay More (Gael: *Tabhaigh More*) is one of a group of islands and rocks that sit at the entrance to Loch Erisort on the eastern coastline of the Isle of Lewis in the Western Isles. The smaller island of Tavay Beag (Gael: *Tabhaigh Beag*) lies to the northeast.

Taversoe Tuick *Orkney* The site of an unusual two-storey prehistoric chambered tomb, Taversoe Tuick is located on the south coast of the Orkney island of Rousay, just west of Trumland. When the site was excavated, three stone burial cists were found.

Tay, Firth of An estuary on the east coast of Scotland at the mouth of the River Tay, the Firth of Tay extends eastwards from the confluence of the rivers Earn and Tay, opening into the North Sea beyond Buddon Ness in Angus and Tentsmuir Point in Fife. Its channel is 23 miles (37 km) in length and although quite narrow, because of sandbanks, has a maximum width of 3 miles (5 km) at Invergowrie to the west of Dundee. The Firth of Tay is crossed by the Tay Road Bridge and Tay Railway Bridge at Dundee, the principal port and settlement on the estuary.

Tay, Loch *Perth and Kinross/Stirling* A loch in the Breadalbane district of Perth and Kinross, but touching on Stirling Council area, Loch Tay extends northeastwards for 15 miles (24 km) from Killin to Kenmore, reaching a depth of over 155 m (508 ft) and a maximum width of just over a mile (1.5 km).

Tay, River The Tay is the longest river in Scotland, stretching a distance of 120 miles (193 km) from the northern slopes of Ben Lui to the Firth of Tay beyond Perth. It rises as the Fillan at the western end of Breadalbane and flows southeastwards through Strath Fillan to become the Dochart at Crianlarich. From there it continues eastwards through Loch Dochart and Loch Iubhair in Glen Dochart to join Loch Tay at Killin. Issuing from the eastern end of Loch Tay, the River Tay proper flows east and southeast past the settlements of Kenmore, Aberfeldy, Dunkeld and Perth before emptying into the Firth of Tay near its junction with the River Earn. It has the largest catchment of any Scottish river, some 6216 sq. km (2400 sq. miles).

Tay, Strath *Perth and Kinross* A broad valley in Perth and Kinross, Strath Tay carries the River Tay from the eastern end of Loch Tay to the Firth of Tay, passing Aberfeldy and Logierait before turning south at the confluence with the River Tummel towards Dunkeld and Perth.

Tay Forest Park *Perth and Kinross* Areas of coniferous and broadleaf woodland in Highland Perthshire, the Tay Forest Park extends from Craigvinean near Dunkeld in the east to Braes of Foss and South Rannoch in the west. It also includes areas of forest at Faskally near Pitlochry, Weem Forest near Aberfeldy, Drummond Hill near Kenmore and Allean by Loch Tummel. Notable views within the park include the Queen's View at the eastern end of Loch Tummel where there is a visitor centre.

Tay Railway Bridge Carrying the railway line from London and Edinburgh to Dundee and Aberdeen, the Tay Railway Bridge crosses the Tay estuary from Wormit in Fife to the city of Dundee. It was built by the North British Railway and opened on 11 July 1887, replacing an earlier bridge completed in 1878 to a design by Sir Thomas Bouch. Part of the former bridge collapsed during a storm on the night of 28 December 1879, killing the 75 passengers and crew of a train that was passing over the bridge at the time. The stumps of the original railway bridge can still be seen a few metres to the east of the present bridge, which is 3135 m (3429 yd) long and comprises two tracks.

Tay Road Bridge Opened by Queen Elizabeth, the Queen Mother on 18 August 1966, the Tay Road Bridge crosses the Tay estuary, linking Newport-on-Tay in northeast Fife with the city of Dundee. Designed by William Fairhurst and built at a cost of £6 million by the Muir of Ord-based construction company Duncan Logan Ltd, the bridge is 2253 m (2464 yd) long and crosses the Tay 10 m (32 ft) above water level. A 15.5-m/51-ft-high obelisk at the Fife end of the bridge commemorates Willie Logan (1913–66), director of the construction company, Robert Lyle, former town clerk of Dundee, and five men who died while the bridge was being built.

Tayinloan *Argyll and Bute* A village on the west coast of the Kintyre peninsula, Tayinloan lies 2 miles (3 km) south of Rhunahaorine Point opposite the island of Gigha, to which it is connected by a ferry.

Taymouth Castle *Perth and Kinross* A mansion house in Strath Tay, Taymouth Castle stands on the south bank of the River Tay, a mile (1.5 km) east of Kenmore. It was built by the earls of Breadalbane on the site of the Castle of Balloch between 1801 and 1842 and has an interior designed by the architect James Gillespie Graham. Queen Victoria and Prince Albert stayed here in 1842.

Taynish *Argyll and Bute* A scattered community in Knapdale in Argyll and Bute, Taynish lies on the western shore of Loch Sween at the entrance to Linnhe Mhuirich.

Taynuilt *Argyll and Bute* A village in the Lorn district of Argyll and Bute, Taynuilt lies to the south of Loch Etive on the A85 from Crianlarich to Oban, 6 miles (10 km) southeast of Connel. It developed in association with iron smelting at Bonawe and the building of the military road in the mid-18th century, and with the arrival of the railway in 1880. Tourism and the development of the hydro-electric power station at Inverawe enhanced the settlement in the 20th century. There is a nine-hole golf course.

Tayport *Fife* A dormitory town on the northeast coast of Fife, Tayport lies at the mouth of the Firth of Tay, 11 miles (18 km) north of St Andrews. Known as Ferryport-on-Craig until 1846, it was for many centuries a ferry port linking Fife with Dundee and Broughty Ferry. The town developed in the 19th century, firstly with the arrival of the railway and the creation of a railway ferry in the 1840s, and secondly with the opening of the Tay Rail Bridge in 1878. Its harbour was rebuilt by Thomas Grainger in 1847 for the Northern Railway Company to accommodate paddle steamers. Tayport has an 18-hole golf course (Scotscraig), and a tower on Hare Law to the west commemorating the defeat of Napoleon at Waterloo in 1815.

Tayvallich *Argyll and Bute* A village in Knapdale, Tayvallich ('the house in the valley') lies on Loch a' Bhealaich, a sheltered inlet on the western shore of Loch Sween. A small pier was built here in the early 19th century and the village developed in association with fishing, forestry and tourism.

Teacuis, Loch *Highland* A loch on the north coast of the Morvern peninsula, Loch Teacuis forms an inlet on the south side of Loch Sunart. At the mouth of the loch is the uninhabited island of Carna.

Tealasavay, Loch *Western Isles* A sea loch in the Outer Hebrides, Loch Tealasavay (Gael: *Loch Tealasbhaigh* or *Thealasbhaidh*) forms an inlet on the southwest coast of the Isle of Lewis, between Loch Resort and Loch Tamanavay.

Tealing *Angus* A small village in a parish of the same name in southern Angus, Tealing lies 4 miles (6.5 km) north of Dundee. In a field close by is an Iron Age earth house (souterrain) dating from the 1st century AD, discovered by a farmer in 1871. By the farmsteading is a rectangular dovecote built in 1595 with a lintel stone bearing the monogram of Sir David Maxwell of Tealing and his wife Helen. Also nearby are the remains of a World War II Air Force training base where in 1942 the Russian Foreign Minister, Molotov, landed en route to meet Winston Churchill to sign the Anglo-Russian Treaty. Kirkton of Tealing lies a half-mile (1 km) to the west.

Teampall Mholuaidh The Gaelic name for St Moluag's Chapel in the Western Isles.

Teangue *Highland* A village on the isle of Skye in the Inner Hebrides, Teangue lies on the east coast of the Sleat peninsula, a mile (1.5 km) southwest of Knock Castle and 4 miles (6.5 km) northeast of Armadale. It looks out onto Knock Bay, an inlet on the Sound of Sleat.

Teatle Water *Argyll and Bute* Rising on Beinn Bhalgairean to the south of Dalmally, the Teatle Water flows west to empty into the northeastern end of Loch Awe, 2 miles (3 km) south of Kilchurn Castle.

Teith, River *Stirling* A river of central Scotland, the Teith rises from Loch Venachar in the Trossachs as the Eas Gobhain. It is joined by the River Leny at Callander and flows for 16 miles (26 km) as the Teith southeastwards past Doune before joining the River Forth 3 miles (5 km) northwest of Stirling. The Ardoch and Annet Burns flow down from the Braes of Doune to join the River Teith on either side of Doune.

Tempar *Perth and Kinross* A locality on the south side of Loch Rannoch in Perthshire, Tempar lies 2 miles (3 km) southeast of Kinloch Rannoch.

Templand *Dumfries and Galloway* A village of Annandale in Dumfries and Galloway, Templand lies between the River Annan and the Kinnel Water, 5 miles (8 km) northwest of Lockerbie.

Temple *Midlothian* A village between Edinburgh and the Moorfoot Hills, Temple lies on the steep banks of the River South Esk, 2.5 miles (4 km) southwest of Gorebridge. It takes its name from the Knights Templar who were based here between the middle of the 12th century and their suppression in the early 14th century. The ruined old parish church, which possibly dates from the 12th century, is more likely to have been built by the Knights of St John soon after they succeeded the Templars in 1312. This is suggested by the inscription *VÆSAC MIHM* (*Vienne Sacrum Concilium Militibus Johannis Hierosolymitani Melitensibus* or 'The Sacred Council of Vienne to the Knights of St John of Jerusalem and Malta') on the gable end of the building. The kirkyard contains a number of fine 18th-century memorials, including one to the Revd James Goldie that includes his last will and testament. A later parish church dates from 1832. Elevated above the river is the main part of the village, which comprises 18th-century cottages along a single street. The painter Sir William Gillies (1898–1973) lived at No. 14. To the northeast is Arniston House and to the southwest Rosebery House.

Temple *Glasgow City* A suburb of Glasgow, Temple lies 4 miles (6.5 km) northwest of the city centre, close to Anniesland.

Templehall *Fife* A northwestern suburb of Kirkcaldy in Fife, Templehall lies to the south of the B981. It developed in the early 19th century in association with coal mining and limestone quarrying. The Central Fife Retail Park and John Smith Business Park are located nearby.

Templeton Business Centre *Glasgow City* Modelled on the Doge's Palace in Venice, the Templeton Carpet Factory was built in 1889 to a design by the architect William Leiper. It is characterised by multicoloured brickwork on the facade facing onto Glasgow Green. The factory was converted in 1984 for use as the Templeton Business Centre.

Tenement House, the *Glasgow City* A flat in a late-Victorian building in central Glasgow, the Tenement House is located at 145 Buccleuch Street in Garnethill to the north of Sauchiehall Street. Built in 1893 and retaining its original fittings, it was the home of Miss Agnes Toward from 1911 until 1975. During this period the house remained almost unchanged except for the installation of electric lighting. In 1982, the flat was acquired by the National Trust for Scotland.

Tennet, Burn of *Angus* A stream in the southern Grampians, the Burn of Tennet rises on the Hill of Cammie on the border between Angus and Aberdeenshire. It flows southwest through Glen Tennet to join the Tarf Water, a tributary of the River North Esk.

Tentsmuir *Fife* An area of forest in northeast Fife, Tentsmuir extends over 1500 ha (3700 acres) of coastal sand dunes between the estuaries of the Tay and the Eden. The land was acquired by the Forestry Commission in the 1920s and planted predominantly with Scots and Corsican pine. In addition to commercial forestry, careful management has created an interesting mixture of open spaces, ponds, trees and sand dunes that are rich in wildlife, including three species of roosting bat. Several forest walks begin at the Kinshaldy car park and picnic site, and of special interest is the 19th-century icehouse and pond built to keep locally caught salmon fresh. There is archaeological evidence that the site was occupied in Mesolithic times by hunters and fishermen who were among the earliest settlers in Scotland, and the name Tentsmuir is thought to be derived from the camps that used to be set up by local fishermen. During World War II, the army used the area for training, and discarded ammunition is an occasional hazard. The remains of coastal defences, particularly concrete blocks used to prevent the landing of armoured vehicles, litter the area. Tentsmuir Point, a headland at the entrance to the Firth of Tay, is the focal point of a 1043-ha (2577-acre) National Nature Reserve, which is an important roosting and feeding area for huge concentrations of sea duck, waders and wildfowl, as well as a haul-out area for over 2000 common and grey seals.

Terally *Dumfries and Galloway* A locality in the Rhinns of Galloway, Terally lies to the west of Terally Point at the southern end of Terally Bay, 2 miles (3 km) east of Port Logan.

Terregles *Dumfries and Galloway* A small dormitory village in Nithsdale, Dumfries and Galloway, Terregles lies 2 miles (3 km) northwest of Dumfries. The parish church incorporates the burial aisle (1588) of Agnes, Lady Herries, and nearby once stood Terregles House, built for William Constable-Maxwell in 1789 and demolished in 1964.

Terreglestown *Dumfries and Galloway* A locality in Nithsdale, Dumfries and Galloway, Terreglestown lies northwest of Dumfries and southeast of Terregles.

Teviotdale *Scottish Borders* A valley in Scottish Borders, Teviotdale carries the waters of the River Teviot northeastwards from Teviothead to Ancrum Bridge, a half-mile (1 km) to the west of Ancrum.

Teviothead *Scottish Borders* A small village in Teviotdale, Teviothead lies to the south of the headwaters of the River Teviot, 8 miles (13 km) southwest of Hawick. Its inns served travellers on the road to Hawick and a scattered farming community now much reduced in size.

Texa *Argyll and Bute* A small rocky uninhabited island in the Inner Hebrides, Texa lies to the south of the island of Islay, from which it is separated by Caolas an Eilein. Covering an area of 48 ha (119 acres), the island is said to be the place where St Kenneth found the pastoral staff blessed by St Columba. The remains of a ruined chapel and burial ground can be seen near the island's main landing point.

Thainstone *Aberdeenshire* A locality in mid-Aberdeenshire, Thainstone lies to the west of the River Urie, a mile (1.5 km) south of Inverurie. Once the seat of the Forbes-Mitchells, an earlier mansion house here was destroyed by the Jacobites in 1745. Thainstone Agricultural Centre provides industrial units for agricultural service industries.

Thankerton *South Lanarkshire* A hamlet in mid-Clydesdale, Thankerton lies to the west of the River Clyde, 4 miles (6.5 km) west of Biggar. It was formerly associated with mills and later survived in association with road and rail links.

Thealasbhaidh, Loch An alternative Gaelic name for Loch Tealasavay in the Western Isles.

Thernatraigh The Gaelic name for Hermetray in the Western Isles.

Thirlestane Castle *Scottish Borders* A turreted red sandstone castle in Lauderdale, Thirlestane Castle lies to the northeast of Lauder. The historic seat of the Maitland family, it was built between 1670 and 1676 for the 1st Duke of Lauderdale to a design by Sir William Bruce, who was assisted by royal mason Robert Mylne. Its central square tower-house, which dates from c.1590, was erected by John Maitland, younger brother of William Maitland of Lethington, to replace an earlier medieval castle on the same site. Wings were added to the building in 1840 by David Bryce, and both Bryce and William Burn were responsible for the Jacobean-style dining room. The Border Country Life Museum occupies the south wing.

Thom, Loch *Inverclyde* A reservoir in Inverclyde serving Greenock, Loch Thom lies to the west of the Gryfe Reservoirs. Named after the engineer Robert Thom who provided Greenock with drinking water in the 1820s, it is 12.8 m (42 ft) deep.

Thornhill *Dumfries and Galloway* A village in Nithsdale,

Thornhill lies on the River Nith, 14 miles (22 km) north of Dumfries. It was created as a planned village on the Queensberry Estate in 1714 and was situated on the new road from Dumfries to Glasgow. Notable structures include a monument to the explorer Joseph Thomson, a market cross (1714), the Buccleuch and Queensberry Hotel (1855, by Charles Howitt, on the site of a cobbler's shop patronised by Robert Burns), Thornhill Hospital (1900), and four churches built in the 18th and 19th centuries. Nearby are Drumlanrig Castle, Morton Castle and, at Nith Bridge, a 10th-century cross-shaft with carved panels.

Thornhill *Stirling* A linear village in the Menteith district of Stirling Council area, Thornhill lies 7 miles (11 km) west of Dunblane. Its long gardens extend down to former commons on the north and south sides of the village, which was built in the mid-18th century to house displaced Highlanders.

Thornliebank *East Renfrewshire* A suburb of Glasgow, Thornliebank lies 4 miles (6.5 km) southwest of the city centre, with Giffnock to the south and Pollokshaws to the north. It developed in association with calico-printing mills and bleachfields on the Auldhouse Burn and with the quarrying of stone used to build houses in the rapidly expanding Glasgow. In the 19th century it further developed in association with the railway and industries including food processing and the manufacture of household goods.

Thornton *Fife* A town in central Fife, Thornton lies between the Lochty Burn and the River Ore to the south of Glenrothes. Formerly an important staging post on a coaching route, it developed during the 19th century at a railway junction associated with the coalfields of western Fife. Its station was closed in 1969 and its Rothes Pit abandoned in the early 1970s. Thornton has an 18-hole golf course.

Thorntonhall *South Lanarkshire* A dormitory village in South Lanarkshire, Thorntonhall is situated 2 miles (3 km) southeast of Busby and 3 miles (5 km) west of East Kilbride.

Threave *Dumfries and Galloway* A flat 8-ha (20-acre) island on the River Dee in Dumfries and Galloway, Threave lies a mile (1.5 km) to the west of Castle Douglas. A large tower house was erected here by Archibald The Grim shortly after he was created Lord of Galloway by David II in 1369. The castle was besieged by James II in 1455 and after its capture remained a royal fortress for the rest of its life. Occupied by successive stewards of Kirkcudbright, the castle was again besieged by Covenanters for 13 weeks in 1640, and during the Napoleonic Wars its tower was used to accommodate French prisoners. It fell into ruin during the 19th century and was eventually placed in State care in 1913, before being handed over to the National Trust for Scotland in 1948 by Major A. F. Gordon. The nearby 26-ha (64-acre) Threave Gardens are renowned for their spring daffodil displays, colourful summer flower displays and splendid heather beds.The National Trust for Scotland's School for Practical Gardening is located in Threave House. Adjacent to Threave Gardens is the 492-ha (1215-acre) Threave Estate, which highlights the integrated approach to land management taken by the National Trust for Scotland, with emphasis on forestry, agriculture and nature conservation. There are important wetlands within the estate and these provide a refuge for various wildfowl. A 2-mile (3-km) nature trail leads through the estate to a visitor centre created in 1975.

Three Miletown *West Lothian* A hamlet of West Lothian, Three Miletown lies a mile (1.5 km) east of Bridgend and 2 miles (3 km) west of Winchburgh.

Three Sisters, the *Highland* A group of three mountain peaks on the south side of Glen Coe, the Three Sisters of Beinn Fhada, Gearr Aonach and Aonach Dubh form part of a dramatic volcanic landscape.

Threipmuir Reservoir *City of Edinburgh* A reservoir in the Pentland Hills supplying the city of Edinburgh, Threipmuir Reservoir lies 2 miles (3 km) southeast of Balerno.

Throsk *Stirling* A hamlet in southeast Stirling Council area, Throsk lies on a bend of the River Forth to the east of Fallin.

Throughgate *Dumfries and Galloway* A locality near Dunscore in Dumfries and Galloway, Throughgate was the site of a tollhouse in the 19th century.

Thrumster *Highland* A crofting township in Caithness, Thrumster lies 4 miles (6.5 km) south of Wick. Buildings of interest include Thrumster Church (1893), Thrumster House (c.1800) and Thrumster railway station (1903), which served the Wick and Lybster Light Railway.

Thuilm The Gaelic name for Holm in the Western Isles.

Thulabhig, Loch A Gaelic name for Loch Kinhoulavig in the Western Isles.

Thunga An alternative Gaelic name for Tong in the Western Isles.

Thurso *Highland* A town in northern Caithness, Thurso lies on the Thurso River where it enters Thurso Bay, an inlet of the Pentland Firth, 8 miles (13 km) east of Dounreay and 20 miles (32 km) west of John o' Groats. Thought to derive its name from the Norse *Thor's-a* or 'river of the god Thor', Thurso was the site of a castle of the Norse earls and a place trading with Scandinavia until the 12th century. It is situated on a bay that is sheltered to the west by Holborn Head and to the east by Clardon Head. Created a royal burgh in 1633, Thurso is the most northerly town on the British mainland. In 1719, the lands and burgh of Thurso were acquired by the Sinclairs of Ulbster. Old Thurso, a group of fishermen's houses on the east side of Thurso Bay, developed in the 17th and 18th centuries in a random street pattern.The new town was laid out in a regular grid pattern by Sir John Sinclair in 1798. In the second half of the 20th century, Thurso expanded in association with the development of the nuclear facility at Dounreay. Buildings of interest include Old St Peter's Church, the 19th-century Kippering-house in Shore Street, the Meadow Well (1818), Thurso Bridge (1887), Thurso High School (1958), Dunbar Hospital (1882), Davidson's Lane Public Library (formerly the Miller Institution), St Anne's Roman Catholic Church (1960), Tollemache House (1963), the Burgh Chambers (c.1860), and Pennyland House (1770), the home of Sir William Alexander Smith (1854–1914), founder of the Boys' Brigade. Thurso Castle was built by Sir Tollemache Sinclair in 1872–8 and Harold's Tower (1780–90) was erected by Sir John Sinclair to commemorate the Norse Earl Harold, killed in the Battle of Clairdon in 1195. Thurso Heritage Museum houses the Pictish Ulbster Stone and the herbarium of local baker Robert Dick (1811–66).

Tibbermore *Perth and Kinross* A hamlet on the north side of the Gask Ridge, Tibbermore lies in the valley of the Pow Water, 3 miles (5 km) west of Perth. In the churchyard of Tibbermore Parish Church is a monument to an eccentric local worthy named James Ritchie depicting his prize bull and curling gear. In 1644, the Marquess of Montrose defeated the Covenanters at the Battle of Tibbermore.

Tibbers *Dumfries and Galloway* A locality in Nithsdale, Dumfries and Galloway, Tibbers lies on a promontory of the Drumlanrig Estate in the midst of Tibbers Wood. A castle was built here in 1298 by Sir Richard Siward, Sheriff of Dumfries. The castle, which was visited by Edward I of England after his victory at the Battle of Falkirk, later passed to the Dunbar earls of March and then to the Maitlands of Auchen.

Tifty *Aberdeenshire* A locality in the Buchan district of Aberdeenshire, Tifty and Mill of Tifty lie a mile (1.5 km) to the north of Fyvie. A local ballad known as *Mill o' Tifty's Annie* recalls an Agnes Smith who died in 1678 of a broken heart, her father having locked her in her room to prevent her from eloping with the Trumpeter of Fyvie. A stone figure of the trumpeter can still be seen on one of the castle towers at Fyvie.

Tig, Water of *South Ayrshire* The Water of Tig rises in the Arecloch Forest and flows north and west to join the River Stinchar at a point a half-mile (1 km) west of the Mains of Tig.

Tigharry *Western Isles* A scattered crofting township on the west coast of North Uist in the Western Isles, Tigharry (Gael: *Tigh a' Gearraidh*) lies 2 miles (3 km) northeast of Aird an Runair, the most westerly point of the island, and 3 miles (5 km) north of Paible.

Tighnabruaich *Argyll and Bute* A resort village on the Cowal peninsula, Tighnabruaich lies on the west shore of the Kyles of Bute, 3 miles (5 km) southwest of the entrance to Loch Riddon. Developed in the 19th century as a village with a pier and marine villas, it has now become a popular centre for pleasure sailing and yachtbuilding. Specialist foods and liqueurs are produced locally. There is a wooded setting to the north, and spectacular views of the Kyles of Bute and islands of the Firth of Clyde are offered from a National Trust for Scotland viewpoint.

Tighvein *North Ayrshire* A summit on the island of Arran, Tighvein rises to 458 m (1502 ft) 3 miles (5 km) southwest of Lamlash.

Tillery *Aberdeenshire* A locality in eastern Aberdeenshire, Tillery House is situated in Foveran parish 3 miles (5 km) southeast of Pitmedden.

Tillicoultry *Clackmannanshire* A Hillfoot village in Clackmannanshire, Tillicoultry is situated to the north of the River Devon between Alva and Dollar. The Tillicoultry Burn, which flows down through the Mill Glen to meet the Devon, was the source of water power used by textile mills such as the Clock Mill, which was built by James and George Walker from Galashiels to manufacture blankets, plaids and tartan shawls. A walk into the glen from the top of Upper Mill Street leads to panoramic views of the Forth and Devon valleys. Interesting buildings include the Provost Thomas Murray Clock Tower and 'Howff for Aged Men' (1930), the Popular Institute (1859) with its tower (1878), and the Baker's Company Jubilee Fountain (1896). The Sterling Warehouse, Britain's largest furniture store, stands on the site of one of Tillicoultry's former woollen mills.

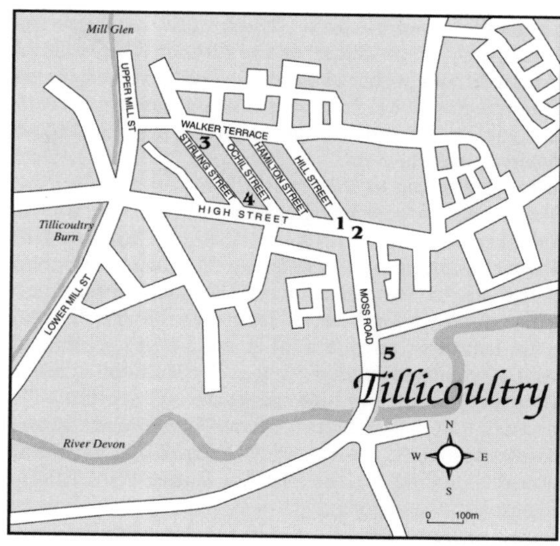

1 *The Howff*
2 *Clock Tower*
3 *Popular Institute*
4 *Jubilee Fountain*
5 *Sterling Warehouse*

Tillinamolt *Aberdeenshire* A locality in the Buchan district of Aberdeenshire, Tillinamolt lies a mile (1.5 km) to the northeast of New Pitsligo.

Tillyfour *Aberdeenshire* A hamlet in mid-Aberdeenshire, Tillyfour lies to the south of the Leochel Burn, 4 miles (6.5 km) south of Alford. Visited by Queen Victoria, Tillyfour Farm was the home of the noted 19th-century breeder of Aberdeen Angus cattle, William M'Combie (1805–80). Craigievar Castle lies to the southwest.

Tillyfourie *Aberdeenshire* A locality on the A944 in central Aberdeenshire, Tillyfourie lies on the Ton Burn at the foot of Tillyfourie Hill, 4 miles (6.5 km) southeast of Alford. It formerly lay on a railway line close to stone quarries.

Tillyminnate *Aberdeenshire* A locality on the edge of Clashindarroch Forest, Aberdeenshire, Tillyminnate lies near the junction of the Long Burn with the Kirkney Water, 4 miles (6.5 km) south of Huntly.

Tillyrie *Perth and Kinross* A locality in Orwell parish, Perth and Kinross, Tillyrie comprises the farms of Upper and Nether Tillyrie which lie on the south side of the Ochil Hills, a mile (1.5 km) to the northwest of Milnathort.

Tilt, Glen *Perth and Kinross* A valley of highland Perth and Kinross, Glen Tilt carries the waters of the River Tilt in a southwesterly direction to Blair Atholl, where the Tilt merges with the River Garry.

Timsgarry *Western Isles* A scattered hamlet on the west coast of the Isle of Lewis in the Outer Hebrides, Timsgarry (Gael: *Timsgearraidh*) forms the principal centre of the community of Uig. The hamlet is located to the northeast of Uig Bay at the end of Gleann Bhaltois, 24 miles (38 km) west of Stornoway. The Gaelic-medium Uig Primary School is located here.

Tingwall *Shetland* A district at the heart of the Shetland Mainland, Tingwall derives its name from the Norse for 'a field or place where courts or assemblies are held'. Here in the 'parliament valley', on the islet of Law Ting Holm in the Loch of Tingwall, annual gatherings were held bringing together representatives of all the local

Shetland assemblies, or tings. The settlement of Veensgarth at the centre of the district lies 6 miles (10 km) northwest of Lerwick, and an airstrip nearby is used to connect with neighbouring islands. Sites of interest in the locality include Tingwall Kirk and the Shetland Agricultural Museum.

Tinto *South Lanarkshire* A hill in South Lanarkshire, Tinto rises to 707 m (2319 ft) 3 miles (5 km) south of Thankerton and 3 miles (5 km) north of Dungavel Hill.

Tinwald *Dumfries and Galloway* A village overlooking Nithsdale in Dumfries and Galloway, Tinwald lies 4 miles (6.5 km) northeast of Dumfries. Its parish church dates from 1765, and Tinwald House a mile (1.5 km) to the southeast was designed in 1740 by William Adam for Charles Erskine, a lord advocate of Scotland. The politician and merchant William Paterson was born in Tinwald in 1658. He founded the Bank of England and was responsible for the ill-fated Darien Expedition to Panama in the 1690s.

Tiree *Argyll and Bute* A flat and treeless island, 8191 ha (20,232 acres), in the Inner Hebrides, Tiree lies to the west of the island of Mull and southwest of the island of Coll. Largely comprising a bedrock of schist and limestone (Tiree marble), the island has extensive sandy beaches and machair, with a dense cover of meadow flowers interspersed with numerous small lochans, the largest of which are Loch a' Phuill and Loch Bhasapoll. The highest points on the island are Ben Hynish (141 m/465 ft) and Ben Hough (119 m/393 ft), and the flat centre of the island is known as The Reef. There are no peat bogs and rainfall is low, Tiree being both the sunniest place in Britain and the windiest, its constant wind making it a venue for the International Windsurfing Championships. Settled for at least 3000 years, a monastery was founded at Sorobaidh by Baitheine, a cousin of St Columba. Tiree was later controlled by the Norse, the Kingdom of Man, the Lords of the Isles and the dukes of Argyll. In 1830 the island had a population of 4450. Fifty years later it had fallen by 2700 as a result of the potato famine and evictions. In 2001 it was 770. Today, the island's people are largely crofters who graze sheep and cattle as well as engage in some hi-tech and horticultural enterprises. Access is by air to a landing strip on The Reef, 2 miles (3 km) north of Crossapoll, or by ferry from Oban to Scarinish.

Tirga Mòr *Western Isles* A peak in the Outer Hebrides, Tirga Mòr rises to 679 m (2227 ft) in North Harris, in the heart of the Forest of Harris, 5 miles (8 km) southwest of the head of Loch Resort.

Tiumpan Head *Western Isles* A headland on the east coast of the Isle of Lewis in the Outer Hebrides, Tiumpan Head (Gael: *Rubha an t-Siumpain*) extends into the Minch at the southern entrance to Loch a' Tuath at the end of the Eye peninsula, 9 miles (14 km) east of Stornoway.

Toa Galson *Western Isles* A headland in the Outer Hebrides, Toa Galson extends into the Atlantic on the northwest coast of the Isle of Lewis, 6 miles (10 km) southwest of the Butt of Lewis.

Tobermory *Argyll and Bute* The largest settlement on the island of Mull in the Inner Hebrides, Tobermory ('St Mary's Well') lies on the north side of Tobermory Bay, an inlet of the Sound of Mull on the northeast coast of the island. Largely designed as a planned village, it was laid out in 1788 by the British Fisheries Society to provide housing for fishermen employed in the herring trade. A pier was built by Thomas Telford and in the 1820s Tobermory was linked by steamer service to Glasgow. It developed in the 19th century in association with fishing, tourism and the distilling of whisky. While its population declined in the 20th century, Tobermory remained a service centre for the surrounding community as well as a centre for tourism and pleasure yachting. It has a folk museum, a golf club, yacht club and lifeboat service. In 1588, a ship of the Spanish Armada sank in Tobermory Bay. A car ferry links the town with Kilchoan on the Ardnamurchan peninsula, and there is an airstrip (Tobermory Airport) to the southeast near Salen. Tobermory is the backdrop to the popular children's television programme *Balamory*.

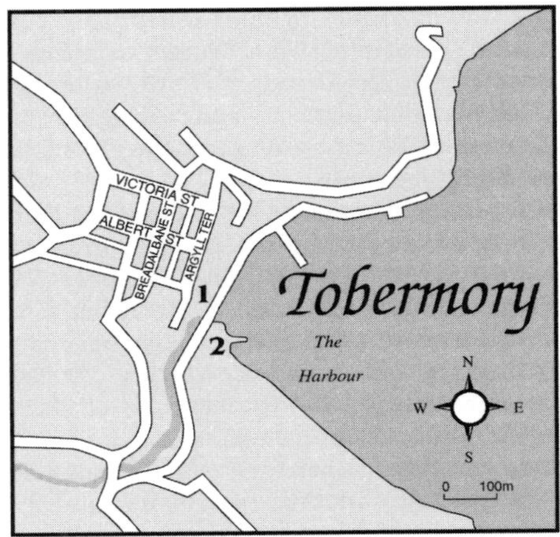

1 *Mull Museum* 2 *Tobermory Distillery*

Tobha Beag The Gaelic name for Howbeg in the Western Isles.

Tobha Mòr An alternative Gaelic name for Howmore in the Western Isles.

Tobson *Western Isles* A small settlement on the west coast of the island of Great Bernera off the west coast of Lewis in the Outer Hebrides, Tobson overlooks West Loch Roag and the island of Vacsay, 2 miles (3 km) northwest of Breaclete.

Toddun *Western Isles* A peak in North Harris in the Western Isles, Toddun rises to 528 m (1732 ft) 2 miles (3 km) northwest of the entrance to Loch Seaforth.

Toe Head *Western Isles* Toe Head, the most westerly point of South Harris in the Western Isles, extends into the Atlantic Ocean 6 miles (10 km) northwest of Leverburgh.

Toft *Shetland* A ferry port on Mainland Shetland, Toft lies 27 miles (43 km) north of Lerwick. It has a car-ferry link with Ulsta at the southern end of the island of Yell.

Tofts Ness *Orkney* A headland on the Orkney island of Sanday, Tofts Ness lies on the northeast coast and is the most northerly part of the island.

Tolastadh a' Chaolais The Gaelic name for Tolstachaolais in the Western Isles.

Tolastadh bho Thuath The Gaelic name for North Tolsta in the Western Isles.

Toll Creagach *Highland* A mountain in Glen Cannich, Toll Creagach rises to 1054 m (3458 ft) to the south of Loch Mullardoch.

Tollcross *Glasgow City* An eastern district of Glasgow, Tollcross lies between Shettleston and Bridgeton. Incorporated into the city in 1912, it was originally a small weaving village.

Tolm An alternative Gaelic name for Holm in the Western Isles.

Tolmount *Aberdeenshire/Angus* A mountain in the eastern Grampians to the south of Braemar on the border between Aberdeenshire and Angus, Tolmount rises to 958 m (3143 ft).

Tolquhon Castle *Aberdeenshire* A castle situated northwest of the village of Pitmedden in Aberdeenshire, Tolquhon Castle was built by the Forbes family from 1420, when the tower was erected. Extended in 1584–9 by William Forbes, it had been abandoned and was roofless by the end of the 19th century.

Tolsta *Western Isles* A locality on the east coast of Lewis in the Outer Hebrides, Tolsta (Gael: *Tolastadh*) lies to the west of Tolsta Head, 12 miles (19 km) northeast of Stornoway. The primary settlement is the crofting township of North Tolsta (*Tolastadh bho Thuath*), with the smaller township of New Tolsta (*Bail Ur Tholastaidh*) located just to the north. Glen Tolsta lies 1.25 miles (2 km) to the southwest. Until the 1960s, North Tolsta was known as South Tolsta and New Tolsta was North Tolsta.

Tolsta Head *Western Isles* A headland on the east coast of the Isle of Lewis in the Outer Hebrides, Tolsta Head extends into the Minch at the northern entrance to Loch a' Tuath, 12 miles (19 km) northeast of Stornoway.

Tolstachaolais *Western Isles* A hamlet on the west coast of the Isle of Lewis in the Outer Hebrides, Tolstachaolais (Gael: *Tolastadh a' Chaolais*) lies on the east side of a hammerhead-shaped peninsula that pushes out into East Loch Roag, 2.5 miles (4 km) north-northwest of Breaclete and a similar distance south of Carloway.

Tom a' Choinich *Highland* A mountain to the south of Glen Cannich and Loch Mullardoch, Tom a' Choinich rises to 1112 m (3648 ft).

Tom an Fhuadain *Western Isles* A small settlement on the southern shore of Loch Ouirn, on the east coast of the Isle of Lewis in the Outer Hebrides, Tom an Fhuadain lies opposite Graver, 12 miles (19 km) south of Stornoway.

Tom Buidhe *Angus* A mountain in the eastern Grampians, Tom Buidhe rises to 957 m (3140 ft) to the south of Braemar.

Tom na Gruagaich *Highland* One of the two summits of Beinn Alligin in Wester Ross, Tom na Gruagaich rises to 920 m (3018 ft) to the northwest of Torridon. Largely comprising ancient Torridonian sandstone, it is capped with quartzite.

Tomatin *Highland* A village in Strath Dearn, Tomatin lies on the north bank of the River Findhorn, 14 miles (22 km) southeast of Inverness. Situated at an altitude of 305 m (1000 ft), it lies on the edge of the Monadhliath Mountains which rise to the southwest. A former railway halt, the mainline railway to Inverness still runs to the east of the village and crosses the river over the grand Findhorn Viaduct (1897). The A9 trunk road, which now bypasses Tomatin to the east, is conveyed over the river by a modern bridge. The old road, which still services the village, crosses the river a half-mile (1 km) to the south using a rather more modest concrete bridge (1926), which replaced one built by Thomas Telford in 1833. The Tomatin Distillery (1897), the largest in Scotland, lies to the northwest of the village.

Tomb of the Eagles, the *Orkney* A stalled chamber tomb dating from c.3000 BC, the Tomb of the Eagles lies at the southeast end of South Ronaldsay in the Orkney Islands. It takes its name from the many eagles' claws found among the burials.

Tomintoul *Moray* A village in the Moray parish of Kirkmichael, Tomintoul lies in Strathavon 14 miles (22 km) southwest of Grantown-on-Spey. At an elevation of 354 m (1160 ft) and on the fringe of the Cairngorm Mountains, it is the highest village in the Highlands. Tomintoul was laid out as a planned village by the 4th Duke of Gordon, who in 1775 decided to create a manufacturing settlement as a focus for the communities scattered throughout his upland property. The proposed textile and quarrying industries never took off despite its strategic position on the military road from Strathdon and Deeside to Fort George via the Lecht. The village survived only with the arrival of tourists in the wake of Queen Victoria's visit in 1853, even though she thought it a 'tumbledown, miserable, dirty-looking place'. A long linear main street lined with stone or harled cottages opens into a central square. Buildings of interest include the Museum, Tomintoul Visitor Centre, Thomas Telford's Parliamentary Church (1826), the Catholic Chapel (1837) and Richmond Hall which was rebuilt as a Memorial Hall and Library after World War I. Tomintoul Distillery lies on the Malt Whisky Trail 6 miles (10 km) north of the village. Tomintoul, which is situated at the southern extremity of the Speyside walk, has a youth hostel in addition to several hotels. Immediately to the south at the Lecht are skiing facilities.

Tomnavoulin *Moray* A village of stone and white-harled cottages with a distillery in Glenlivet, Tomnavoulin lies on the River Livet, 5 miles (8 km) northeast of Tomintoul.

Tòn Mhòr *Argyll and Bute* A headland on the north coast of the island of Islay in the Inner Hebrides, Tòn Mhòr extends northwards into the sea, 4 miles (6.5 km) southwest of Ardnave Point and a half-mile (1 km) north of the settlement of Sanaigmore.

Tong *Western Isles* A crofting township of the Outer Hebrides, Tong (Gael: *Thunga or Tunga*) lies 2.5 miles (4 km) northeast of Stornoway on the east coast of the Isle of Lewis. The settlement extends east to the Aird of Tong (Aird Thunga) which lies above the rocky shore.

Tongland *Dumfries and Galloway* A village in Dumfries and Galloway, Tongland lies on the River Dee, 2 miles (3 km) northeast of Kirkcudbright. In the kirkyard of the parish church (1813) are the remains of an earlier church incorporating a doorway from Tongland Abbey (1218) whose last abbot, an Italian alchemist called Damian, attempted to fly from the parapets of Stirling Castle in the presence of James IV. Also in the churchyard is the granite mausoleum of the Neilsons of Queenshill, containing the busts of James Beaumont Neilson (1792–1865), inventor of the hot-blast system of iron smelting, and his son Walter Montgomerie Neilson, founder of Neilson and Company locomotive builders in Glasgow. During World War I, aero-engines were made in a factory that later produced Galloway motor cars, and in 1936 the Art Deco Tongland Power Station was erected as part of the Galloway Hydro-Electric Scheme. Tongland Bridge spanning the Dee was the work of Thomas Telford 1804–8 and was the first bridge in Britain to carry a road on spine walls rising from the arch rings.

Tongue *Highland* A village in northern Sutherland, Tongue (Old Norse *tunga*, 'a tongue of land') lies to the east of the Kyle of Tongue, 31 miles (50 km) north of Lairg. A seat of the Clan Mackay was established here in 1554 and a mansion, the House of Tongue, erected in 1678. In 1829 it passed to the Sutherland Estate. Other buildings of interest include Tongue Mains courtyard steading (1843), St Andrew's Church on the ancient site of St Peter's Chapel (Teampull Pheader), Tongue Hotel (1854) and Castle Varrich. An 18th-century crow-stepped boathouse is said to have housed Jacobite prisoners from the ship *Hazard*, sunk in 1746 just prior to the Battle of Culloden. A 184-m (603-ft) bridge was built over the Kyle of Tongue in 1971.

Torbrex *Stirling* A former weaving village in Stirling Council area, Torbrex lies a mile (1.5 km) to the southwest of Stirling, between Cambusbarron and St Ninians. Mainly comprising 19th-century cottages, it has among its older buildings Torbrex House (1721) and Williamsfield House, which was built in 1682 by William Wordie of Torbrex. Torbrex High School dates from 1962.

Torduff Point *Dumfries and Galloway* A headland on the Solway coast of Dumfries and Galloway, Torduff Point extends out towards the channel of the River Esk, 4 miles (6.5 km) southeast of Annan.

Tore *Highland* A locality on the Black Isle in Easter Ross, Tore lies 6 miles (10 km) northwest of Inverness close to a major junction on the A9 (Tore Roundabout) created following the building of the Kessock Bridge.

Torhousekie *Dumfries and Galloway* A locality on Torhousemuir near Little Torhouse in the Bladnoch valley, 3 miles (5 km) west of Wigtown, Torhousekie is the site of one of the best-preserved prehistoric stone circles in the country. Dating from the 2nd millennium BC, the circle comprises 19 granite boulders. In the centre is a row of three stones that have been referred to as 'King Galdus's Tomb'.

Torlum *Western Isles* A settlement located on low-lying land in the southwest of the island of Benbecula in the Outer Hebrides, Torlum lies a half-mile (1 km) south of Griminish and a similar distance north of Liniclate. Loch Fada lies just to the northwest.

Tornahaish *Aberdeenshire* A locality in western Aberdeenshire, Tornahaish lies on the Tornahaish Burn near its junction with the River Don, 4 miles (6.5 km) southwest of Strathdon. A Roman Catholic chapel was built here in 1880, and a hoard of silver coins was found in 1822 at Tom a' Bhuraich to the east.

Torness *East Lothian* A locality on the North Sea coast of East Lothian, Torness lies 5 miles (8 km) southeast of Dunbar. It is the site of a nuclear power station producing 1364 megawatts of electricity from two advanced gas-cooled reactors built between 1980 and 1988. With a staff of over 600, Torness is one of the largest employers in East Lothian. The power station has a visitor centre.

Torogay *Western Isles* A small uninhabited island with extensive reefs in the Outer Hebrides, Torogay lies in the Sound of Berneray to the north of North Uist and a half-mile (1 km) south of Berneray. It shelters Loch nam Bàn on the coast of North Uist.

Torosay Castle *Argyll and Bute* A Victorian castle in the parish of Torosay on the island of Mull in the Inner Hebrides, Torosay Castle lies to the southeast of Craignure to which it is connected by a narrow-gauge railway. Originally built in 1858 for John Campbell and known as Duart House, its name changed to Torosay after restoration work was carried out on Duart Castle. In 1868 the property was sold to the Guthrie family. The gardens at Torosay extend over 5 ha (12 acres) and include a Japanese garden, terraced gardens and a statue walk.

Torphichen *West Lothian* A village in central West Lothian, Torphichen lies 2 miles (3 km) north of Bathgate and nearly 5 miles (8 km) south-southwest of Linlithgow. Torphichen Preceptory to the north of the village was the Scottish seat of the Knights of St John of Jerusalem (the Knights Hospitallers), an order established in the 12th century. The church was finished in the mid-13th century, and some of it survives today. The estate surrounding the Preceptory church provided sanctuary to criminals and debtors. Other buildings in Torphichen include the parish kirk (1756), and mansions including Wallhouse (1840), Couston (early 17th century) and Bridge (15th century). To the west is Gowanbank (1842–62), the seat of architect Sir James Gowans (1821–90). It was built around an early 19th-century farmhouse erected by his father.

Torphins *Aberdeenshire* A village in an Aberdeenshire parish of the same name, Torphins lies on the Beltie Burn, 6 miles (10 km) northwest of Banchory. It developed as a railway settlement on the Deeside line during the 19th century.

Torr Point *Dumfries and Galloway* A headland in Dumfries and Galloway, Torr Point forms the southeastern extremity of a short peninsula separating Orchardton Bay to the north from Auchencairn Bay to the south. Beyond the Point, the Auchencairn Lane finds its way to the Solway Firth.

Torraigh The Gaelic name for Torray in the Western Isles.

Torran Rocks *Argyll and Bute* A scattered group of rocks in the Inner Hebrides, the Torran Rocks lie off the southwest coast of Mull, 5 miles (8 km) south of Iona. The group comprises Dearg Sgeir, Na Torrain, Ruadh Sgeir, McPhail's Anvil, Torran Sgoilte, Sgeir Ghobhlach and Otter Rock. To the west is the West Reef.

Torrance *East Dunbartonshire* A dormitory village in the parish of Campsie, Torrance lies on the River Kelvin a mile (1.5 km) east of the village of Balmore and 6 miles (10 km) north of Glasgow.

Torray Island *Western Isles* An uninhabited rocky island in the Outer Hebrides, Torray (Gael: *Torraigh* or *Eilean Thoraidh*) rises to 54 m (177 ft) off the east coast of the Isle of Lewis, 9 miles (14 km) south of Stornoway and 4 miles (6.5 km) north of Kebock Head.

Torridon *Highland* A mountainous area in Wester Ross, Torridon lies between Loch Maree and Loch Torridon. One of Scotland's finest scenic areas offering excellent climbing, it contains the nine peaks of Beinn Eighe, which rise to over 1000 m (3300 ft), the seven peaks of the Liathach ridge and, to the west, Beinn Alligin. The mountains here comprise 750-million-year-old Torridonian sandstone capped by 600-million-year-old white quartzite. Much of the area is included within the Torridon Estate, 5708 ha (14,100 acres) of which were passed to the National Trust for Scotland in May 1967 following the death of the 4th Earl of Lovelace. In 1968, the Trust received a further 810 ha (2000 acres) at Wester

Alligin, a gift in memory of Sir Charles and Lady Blair Gordon. A National Trust for Scotland Countryside Centre is situated at the junction of the A896 and the Diabaig road. There is also a deer park nearby. The village of Torridon lies at the head of Upper Loch Torridon, which receives the Torridon River via Glen Torridon.

Torrisdale *Highland* A hamlet in northern Sutherland, Torrisdale lies on Torrisdale Bay to the west of the River Borgie and 2 miles (3 km) west of Bettyhill.

Torry Bay *Fife* A bay on the coast of the Firth of Forth in western Fife, Torry Bay is overlooked by the settlements of Newmills and Torryburn. Its mud flats and salt marshes are important feeding grounds for wintering birds.

Torryburn *Fife* A settlement overlooking Torry Bay in western Fife, Torryburn is one of several old ports lying on the coast of the Firth of Forth between Culross and Inverkeithing. It developed as a mining settlement during the late 19th century. The parish church of Torryburn and Newmills, rebuilt c.1800, has an hexagonal corbelled bell tower. One of its ministers in the 17th century gained notoriety as a witch hunter. Torryburn has secondary and primary schools, and interesting buildings include Craigflower, a house remodelled in Scottish baronial style by David Bryce in 1862. Alison Cunningham, the nurse of Robert Louis Stevenson, was born here in 1822.

Torsay *Argyll and Bute* One of the Slate Islands off the coast of Argyllshire, Torsay lies at the southern end of Seil Sound between the islands of Seil and Luing.

Torthorwald *Dumfries and Galloway* A village in Dumfries and Galloway, Torthorwald lies to the east of the Lochar Water, midway between Lochmaben and Dumfries. Buildings of interest include the parish church (1782), a recently restored cruck-framed cottage with a thatched roof, and the ruins of a castle that was a stronghold of the Kirkpatrick and Carlyle families.

Torwood *Falkirk* A village in Falkirk Council area, Torwood lies 2 miles (3 km) north of Larbert. It is surrounded by woodland and farmland. Nearby Tappoch Broch and a Roman road are scheduled monuments, and to the south lie the ruins of 16th-century Torwood Castle.

Touch Hills *Stirling* A range of hills in the uplands of southern Stirling Council area, the Touch Hills form an eastern outlier of the Gargunnock Hills to the southeast of Gargunnock and west of Cambusbarron. Reservoirs occupy part of Touch Muir, and the Touch Burn flows northeastwards to meet the River Forth near Touch Home Farm. Touch House on the northeastern edge of the Touch Hills combines an old tower of the 16th–17th centuries with a fine neoclassical facade created for the Setons of Touch in 1747 by John Steinson.

Toward Point *Argyll and Bute* A headland with a lighthouse (1812) on the Cowal peninsula opposite Skelmorlie in North Ayrshire, Toward Point extends into the Firth of Clyde 8 miles (13 km) south of Dunoon. Nearby are the settlement of Toward and Castle Toward, a neo-Gothic mansion built in 1821 near the ruined castle of the Lamont lords of Cowal. Toward Hill rises to 345 m (1131 ft) to the north of the headland.

Towie *Aberdeenshire* A hamlet in an Aberdeenshire parish of the same name, Towie lies on the right bank of the River Don, 10 miles (16 km) south of Rhynie. Its church dates from 1803 and in its kirkyard is an interesting mortsafe. The Castle of Towie was a stronghold of a branch of the Forbes family.

Towie Barclay Castle *Aberdeenshire* An L-plan tower house in Aberdeenshire, Towie Barclay Castle was built in 1593 and lies to the south of Mains of Towie, 4 miles (6.5 km) south-southeast of Turriff. Restored in the 1970s, it was a stronghold of the Barclay family, one of whose line was the Russian general Prince Michael Barclay de Tolly (1759–1818).

Town Yetholm *Scottish Borders* A village on the northern edge of the Cheviot Hills, close to the English border, Town Yetholm lies on the Bowmont Water opposite Kirk Yetholm, 7 miles (11 km) southeast of Kelso. Once referred to as Little Egypt, it was the seat of the Faa family, who were kings and queens of the Scottish gypsies from the 16th century. The last queen of the gypsies, Esther Faa Blytte, died in 1883 and her son, crowned king in 1902, died a few years later. A Yetholm native, Jean Gordon, was the real-life Meg Merrilies of Sir Walter Scott's novel *Guy Mannering* (1815). Gordon died (c.1746) a day after being attacked by a Carlisle mob angered by her Jacobite sympathies.

Townhead *Dumfries and Galloway* A locality in Kirkmichael parish, Townhead lies near the junction of the Black Linn with the Water of Ae, just south of the Forest of Ae.

Townhead *Glasgow City* A locality on the north side of Glasgow city centre, Townhead lies between the campus of the University of Strathclyde and the M8. Formerly the northern extremity of the medieval city of Glasgow, it is today predominantly an area of medium- and high-rise housing with some businesses and warehouses.

Townhead of Greenlaw *Dumfries and Galloway* A crossroads village in Dumfries and Galloway, Townhead of Greenlaw lies to the east of the River Dee, 2 miles (3 km) northwest of Castle Douglas.

Townhill *Fife* A former colliery village in western Fife, Townhill lies 2 miles (3 km) north of Dunfermline. Known as Moncur in medieval times, its name was changed to Dunfermline Coaltown in the 18th century and then to Townhill in the early 19th century, reflecting its location at the top of a hill leading up from Dunfermline. In 1781–3 a wooden rail track was built to transport coal to Inverkeithing on the Firth of Forth. The village was once the site of the Dunfermline town gallows, and the Cairncubie Spring northeast of the village was an important source of drinking water for the town. The last remaining pit at Muircockhall was used for training until it closed in 1970. Townhill Country Park comprises two areas of amenity and recreational land to the east and west of the village. The eastern section includes Townhill Wood, while the western area is dominated by the Town Loch which is now a centre for both water skiing and breeding wildfowl. Once an active industrial area, there are the remains of a brickworks and power station by the loch, whose water was also used to power steam engines in two flax mills and a flour mill in Dunfermline.

Trades Hall *Glasgow City* The only surviving Robert Adam-designed building in Glasgow, the Trades Hall in Glassford Street was built between 1791 and 1794 to house the federation of Glasgow's 14 trades, collectively known as the Trades House.

Tràigh Mhòr The Gaelic name for Cockle Strand in the Western Isles.

Trailflat *Dumfries and Galloway* A hamlet of Annandale in Dumfries and Galloway, Trailflat lies to the south of the Water of Ae, nearly 3 miles (5 km) northwest of Lochmaben.

Tralaig, Loch *Argyll and Bute* A small loch and reservoir in the Lorn district of Argyll and Bute, Loch Tralaig lies 3 miles (5 km) northeast of the head of Loch Melfort.

Tramway, the *Glasgow City* A theatre and arts venue in a former tramcar depot, the Tramway is located in Pollokshields to the south of Glasgow city centre. The building housed the city's Transport Museum before it moved west to the Kelvin Hall complex and lay unused for a number of years before it was adapted for its current use.

Tranent *East Lothian* A small market town in East Lothian, Tranent lies 2 miles (3 km) southeast of Prestonpans and 9 miles (14 km) east of Edinburgh. Designated a burgh in 1541, it developed in association with the manufacture of textiles, the quarrying of stone and coal mining. In the 13th century the nearby 2.5-m/7-ft-thick coal deposits of the 'Great Seam' were mined by the monks of Newbattle, and in 1722 what may have been Scotland's first wagonway to carry coal was laid to Cockenzie on the coast. The 1797 Militia Act requiring local military recruiting quotas led to an incident known as the 'Massacre of Tranent' in which a number of miners were shot dead. Buildings of interest include the old parish church incorporating parts of a late 15th-century church, and the remains of the 16th-century Tranent Tower. Ross High School was opened in the 1950s, a civic centre was developed in 1968 and the town was bypassed in 1986. There are light industries, including precision engineering.

Traprain Law *East Lothian* A distinctive dome-shaped hill rising to 224 m (734 ft) 4.5 miles (7 km) east of Haddington, Traprain Law is a 335-million-year-old laccolith or igneous intrusion of the Lower Carboniferous age. Topped by an Iron Age hillfort that was occupied by the Votadini until the early 6th century and thought to be the ancient capital of Lothian, it forms a strong defensive position on the north side of the Lammermuir Hills. A hoard of silver was found nearby in 1919 and at its foot is the Loth Stone, which is said to mark the grave of the legendary King Loth after whom the Lothians were said to be named. On the northeast side of the hill is a disused road-metal quarry abandoned in the 1970s.

Traquair *Scottish Borders* A locality in Tweeddale, Traquair lies on the Traquair Water near its junction with the Tweed, a mile (1.5 km) south of Innerleithen. Traquair House, said to be the oldest inhabited house in Scotland, was built before 1107 as a royal hunting lodge. The charter establishing the city of Glasgow was signed at Traquair, and in 1469 James III gave the house to his favourite, William Rodgers. The house was shortly after restored to Stewart ownership when the king's uncle, the Earl of Buchan, forced Rodgers out and later hung him from Lauder Bridge. In 1566, Mary, Queen of Scots and Lord Darnley visited with their baby son, later James VI. The baby's crib can still be seen in the house, along with Mary's rosary, crucifix and purse. The original tower house was extended *c.*1641 by the 1st Earl of Traquair, who had been Lord High Treasurer of Scotland during the reign of Charles I. The 2nd Earl extended the house further and also reverted to Catholicism. A concealed room, where Mass was celebrated, dates from this time. The house retains its connection with the Stuart family and the Jacobite cause, the main Bear Gates being closed on the departure of Prince Charles Edward Stewart (Bonnie Prince Charlie), never to be opened until a Stewart is restored to the throne. The house includes a fine library, a museum and a brewery that has been producing a range of traditional ales since the 1960s.

Trealaval, Loch *Western Isles* A loch on the Isle of Lewis in the Outer Hebrides, Loch Trealaval lies 2 miles (3 km) northwest of Baile Ailein on the north side of Loch Erisort.

Treble, Burn *Moray* A stream to the east of Glen Fiddich in Moray, Burn Treble flows southeastwards alongside the Cabrach Road to join the River Deveron at Inverharroch.

Treehope Height *Dumfries and Galloway* A hill on the south side of the Mennock Pass, Treehope Height rises to 549 m (1802 ft) in the Lowther Hills.

Treig, Loch *Highland* Situated on the 'Road to the Isles' to the north of Rannoch Moor, Loch Treig extends just over 5 miles (8 km) south-southwest from Fersit in Glen Spean. It is fed by the Abhainn Rath and other streams and drains northwards via the River Treig into the River Spean. The West Highland Railway Line passes on its east side en route to Fort William. The hills to the east and west were planted with exotic trees and rhododendrons in the early 20th century by Sir John Stirling Maxwell, owner of the Corrour Estate.

Treshnish Isles *Argyll and Bute* A group of uninhabited basalt lava islands and rocky outliers in the Inner Hebrides, the Treshnish Isles lie to the west of the island of Mull. They include the distinctively shaped Bac Mòr or Dutchman's Cap, Lunga (the largest in the group), Fladda, Bac Beag, Sgeir an Eirionnaich, Sgeir na h-Iolaire, Sgeir an Fheoir, Cairn na Burgh More, Cairn na Burgh Beg and Sgeir a' Chaisteil.

Treshnish Point *Argyll and Bute* A headland on the northwest coast of Mull in the Inner Hebrides, Treshnish Point extends into the sea on the south side of Calgary Bay, a mile (1.5 km) west of the settlement of Treshnish. The headland looks out towards the Treshnish Isles to the southwest and the island of Coll to the west.

Tressait *Perth and Kinross* A locality in Perth and Kinross, Tressait lies on the north side of Loch Tummel, 5 miles (8 km) west of Pitlochry.

Trialabreck *Western Isles* A low-lying island in Bagh nam Faoilean to the southeast of Benbecula, Trialabreck (Gael: *Triallabreac*) is trimmed by rocks and washed by Loch Leiravag to the north.

Trimontium *Scottish Borders* The site of a Roman fort at the south end of Lauderdale in Scottish Borders, Trimontium is located near the village of Newstead to the east of Melrose. Garrisoned for about a hundred years, it was one of a series of forts on the great military road from Dover to Aberdeen. At its height the 6-ha (15-acre) fort housed 1500 Roman infantry and cavalry, and the 80-ha (200-acre) surrounding enclosures were occupied by a similar number of civilians.

Trinafour *Perth and Kinross* A locality at the western end of Glen Errochty in Highland Perth and Kinross, Trinafour lies on the Errochty Water, 6 miles (10 km) west of Calvine.

Trinity Gask *Perth and Kinross* A hamlet in a parish of the same name in Perth and Kinross, Trinity Gask lies on the Gask Ridge, 4 miles (6.5 km) northeast of Auchterarder. Trinity Gask Parish Church dates from 1770 and its old manse, Trinity Gask House, was built in 1779. A Roman road with signal stations traverses the ridge to the north.

Triuirebheinn *Western Isles* A hill on the island of South Uist in the Outer Hebrides, Triuirebheinn rises to 357 m (1171 ft) 2 miles (3 km) northeast of Lochboisdale.

Trochry *Perth and Kinross* A locality in Strath Braan, Perth and Kinross, Trochry and Little Trochry lie nearly 4 miles (6.5 km) southwest of Dunkeld on the road to Amulree and the Sma' Glen.

Trollamarig, Loch *Western Isles* A sea loch on the southeast coast of North Harris in the Outer Hebrides, Loch Trollamarig forms an inlet at the entrance to Loch Seaforth.

Tromie, Glen *Highland* A glen in the Badenoch district to the west of the Cairngorm Mountains, Glen Tromie carries the River Tromie north to join the River Spey, a mile (1.5 km) east of Kingussie.

Tromlee, Loch *Argyll and Bute* A small loch in the Lorn district of Argyll and Bute, Loch Tromlee lies a mile (1.5 km) north of Kilchrenan and 2 miles (3 km) west of Ardanaiseig.

Tronach Head *Moray* A headland on the Moray Firth coast, Tronach Head projects into the sea midway between Findochty and Portknockie.

Trondra *Shetland* An island to the west of Mainland Shetland, Trondra is connected by road bridges to the Mainland and the island of West Burra. It has an area of 271 ha (670 acres) and provides shelter to Scalloway harbour.

Tron Kirk *City of Edinburgh* Built between 1636 and 1647 by royal mason John Mylne, the Tron Kirk occupies a prominent position on the Royal Mile in Edinburgh's Old Town. The building, which has a fine hammerbeam roof, was truncated in 1785 when South Bridge and Hunter Square were developed. The original tower, lost in the great fire of 1824, was replaced in 1828 by a taller spire designed by R. and R. Dickson. The Tron Kirk ceased to function as a church in 1952, when it was acquired by Edinburgh City Council. In 1974, the remains of 16th-century Marlin's Wynd, including shops and cellars, were discovered beneath the church. Today, the Tron Kirk houses a visitor information centre for the Old Town of Edinburgh. The Tron Kirk was for long the traditional focus of New Year celebrations.

Trongate, the *Glasgow City* The Trongate, one of the four principal medieval streets of Glasgow, extends from Glasgow Cross to Argyle Street. Formerly known as St Thenew's Gait and named after the mother of Glasgow's patron saint, St Kentigern (St Mungo), it became an important residential and business area before the development of Sauchiehall Street and Buchanan Street to the west. The Glasgow Theatre Club was established in the Tron St Mary's Church in 1980. Opening as the Tron Theatre Club in 1982, it eventually became a public theatre, and in 1989 changed its name to the Tron Theatre. The theatre specialises in contemporary Scottish and international works.

Trool, Loch *Dumfries and Galloway* A loch in Galloway Forest Park, Loch Trool lies just over 8 miles (13 km) north of Newton Stewart in the heart of Glentrool Forest. It is 17 m (55 ft) deep and is drained by the Water of Trool, which flows southwestwards for 4 miles (6.5 km) through Glen Trool to join the Water of Minnoch.

Troon *South Ayrshire* A resort town on the coast of Kyle in South Ayrshire, Troon lies on a headland at the north end of Ayr Bay that extends into the Firth of Clyde 7 miles (11 km) north of Ayr and 35 miles (56 km) southwest of Glasgow. It developed initially on the south side of the headland in association with its natural harbour, and in 1808 the Duke of Portland began to build a harbour with docks on the north side. Connected to coal mines near Kilmarnock, it soon became Ayrshire's main coal port. A shipyard established in the 1860s was managed by the Ailsa Shipbuilding Company from 1885, and it was here that the SY *Scotia*, the research vessel of the Scottish National Antarctic Expedition of 1902–4, was refitted before sailing to the South Atlantic. The shipyard also built the Navy's first paddle minesweeper of the *Ailsa* class in 1916. A native of Troon, David MacIntyre, son of the owner of the Ailsa shipyard, jointly with the Marquess of Clydesdale and Douglas flew over Mount Everest (1933), founded Scottish Aviation (1935) and established the Prestwick Flying Training School. With the opening of a station in 1892 and the development of three 18-hole golf courses, Troon quickly developed as a resort in the late 19th and early 20th centuries. The Royal Troon Golf Club's Old Course founded on the links in 1878 first hosted the Open Championship in 1923. Piersland House, now a hotel, was built by Sir Alexander Walker (1869–1950), the grandson of the whisky magnate Johnnie Walker. Shipbuilding and repair ceased in the 1990s and the harbour became a focus for cruise-ship docking, a marina for pleasure craft, a lifeboat service and roll-on/roll-off ferry links with Ireland.

Trosairidh The Gaelic name for Trossary in the Western Isles.

Trossachs, the *Stirling* A picturesque area forming part of the Loch Lomond and the Trossachs National Park, the Trossachs was originally the name given to a pass extending from the head of Loch Achray to the end of Loch Katrine, with Ben An (463 m/1520 ft) to the north and Ben Venue (727 m/2386 ft) to the southwest. It is now loosely used to designate all the scenic area between Callander and Loch Lomond. The Trossachs, which featured in Sir Walter Scott's *Lady of the Lake* (1810) and in his novel *Rob Roy* (1817) are synonymous with Scotland's scenic beauty and the evolution of tourism from the early 19th century.

Trossary *Western Isles* A small settlement located in the southwest of the island of South Uist in the Outer Hebrides, Trossary (Gael: *Trosairidh*) lies just to the east of Garrynamonie, 3 miles (5 km) southwest of Lochboisdale. The remains of a chambered cairn, Dun Trossary, lie to the east and the modern Garrynamonie Roman Catholic Church is located immediately to the south.

Troston, Loch *Dumfries and Galloway* A small loch in Dumfries and Galloway, Loch Troston lies to the south of the Stroanshalloch Burn, 5 miles (8 km) west of Moniaive.

Trotternish Peninsula *Highland* A large lobate peninsula forming the northernmost part of the isle of Skye in the Inner Hebrides, Trotternish extends northwards from Portree to Rubha Hunish. Loch Snizort separates Trotternish from the Vaternish peninsula to the west, and to the east the Sound of Raasay separates Trotternish from the island of Raasay. Its geology is dominated by the Trotternish escarpment, which comprises a line of steep basalt cliffs rising to 719 m (2360 ft) at the Storr. The Storr and Quirang landslides are among the most spectacular in Britain.

Troup Head *Aberdeenshire* A headland on Aberdeenshire's northern coastline, Troup Head lies 9 miles (14 km) east of Banff and 11 miles (18 km) west of Fraserburgh.

Truim, Glen *Highland* A glen in the Badenoch area of southern Highland Council area, Glen Truim carries the River Truim northeastwards for 18 miles (29 km) from its source near the Pass of Drumochter to the River Spey, 5 miles (8 km) southwest of Kingussie. The Falls of Truim lie to the west of the A9 from Perth to Inverness, which passes through the glen.

Trushel Stone *Western Isles* A prehistoric standing stone on the northwest coast of the Isle of Lewis in the Outer Hebrides, the Trushel Stone (Gael: *Clach an Truiseil* or *Clach an Trushal*) lies in the crofting township of Ballantrushal. At 5.75 m (20 ft) in height, it is the largest monolith both in Scotland and in Europe. The site is said to have been the scene of the last major battle on Lewis, fought between the Morrisons of Nis and the MacAulays of Uig in the 16th century.

Trusty's Hill *Dumfries and Galloway* A hill near Gatehouse of Fleet, Trusty's Hill is topped by a hillfort occupied in the 1st and 2nd centuries AD, and later reoccupied in the 6th and 7th centuries. Pictish symbols were carved on a rock face here during the second period of occupation, reflecting the contact between the Britons of southwest Scotland and the Picts.

Tuath, Loch *Argyll and Bute* A sea loch on the northwest coast of the island of Mull in the Inner Hebrides, Loch Tuath separates the mainland of Mull from the islands of Gometra and Ulva. Ballygown Bay and Laggan Bay form inlets to the north of Ulva, and to the west of its mouth lie the Treshnish Isles.

Tugnet Icehouse *Moray* Erected at the mouth of the River Spey, 4 miles (6.5 km) north of Fochabers in Moray, the vast Tugnet Icehouse once formed part of a salmon-fishing station operated by the dukes of Richmond and Gordon. A complex of three brick-vaulted blocks was built in 1830 to replace an earlier structure, its function being to store salmon prior to it being packed in ice for the journey to southern markets. At the end of the 18th century this industry employed 150 people servicing two dozen London-bound vessels carrying salmon. The restored buildings include displays on the former salmon-fishing and boatbuilding industries at the mouth of the River Spey.

Tuilyies *Fife* The site of a 2.4-m/8-ft-high standing stone dating from the 2nd millennium BC, Tuilyies lies a half-mile (1 km) northeast of Torryburn in western Fife.

Tulla, Loch *Argyll and Bute* A loch in northeast Argyll and Bute on the edge of Rannoch Moor, Loch Tulla lies 2 miles (3 km) north of Bridge of Orchy. The loch is fed by streams including the Water of Tulla and drains southwards via the River Orchy.

Tullibardine *Perth and Kinross* A locality with an ancient chapel in central Perth and Kinross, Tullibardine lies in Strath Earn, 6 miles (10 km) southeast of Crieff and 2 miles (3 km) west of Auchterarder. The chapel, one of the most complete small medieval churches in Scotland, was founded in 1446 and rebuilt *c.*1500.

Tullibody *Clackmannanshire* A small town in Clackmannanshire, Tullibody is situated on high ground between the Forth and Devon valleys, 2 miles (3 km) northwest of Alloa. Although an old settlement, Tullibody developed during the 19th century in association with mining, distilling and textile manufacture. The old Parish Church of St Mungo dates from the 16th century, and the Bridge at Bridgend was built in 1697 by local masons Thomas and Tobias Bauchop. Erected on the site of a tannery business founded in the 18th century by shoemaker Alexander Paterson, the four-storey brick factory of John Tullis and Son Ltd (*c.*1880) is the largest surviving tannery building in Scotland. Today Tullibody is given over to public and private housing, with retailing and distilling the chief economic activities.

Tullich Hill *Argyll and Bute* A mountain in Argyll and Bute, Tullich Hill rises to 632 m (2073 ft) on the east side of Loch Long, 2 miles (3 km) south of Arrochar.

Tulliemet *Perth and Kinross* A hamlet in Strath Tay, Perth and Kinross, Tulliemet lies a mile (1.5 km) to the east of Ballinluig on the lower slopes of Creagan Ruathair.

Tulloch *Stirling* A locality in the Balquhidder district of Stirling Council area, Tulloch lies close to the north shore of Loch Voil, a mile (1.5 km) west of Balquhidder village.

Tullybelton *Perth and Kinross* A locality in central Perth and Kinross, Tullybelton comprises Tullybelton House, the farm of Little Tullybelton and Loch Tullybelton, all situated to the west of the A9, 8 miles (13 km) northwest of Perth.

Tullynessle *Aberdeenshire* A hamlet in the central Aberdeenshire parish of Tullynessle and Forbes, Tullynessle lies on the Suie Burn, 3 miles (5 km) northwest of Alford. The summits of the Correen Hills rise to the northwest and west, and nearby is Terpersie Castle, a former stronghold of a branch of the Gordon family. The present church dates from 1876.

Tummel, Loch *Perth and Kinross* A linear loch and reservoir in highland Perth and Kinross, Loch Tummel lies on the River Tummel in the heart of the Tay Forest Park 4 miles (6.5 km) northwest of Pitlochry. It is overlooked from the north by the Queen's View, and stretches 7 miles (11 km) from west to east. Its eastern end is dammed as part of the Tummel Hydro-Electric Scheme.

Tummel Bridge *Perth and Kinross* A locality in Perth and Kinross, Tummel Bridge lies on the River Tummel at the western end of Loch Tummel. A 35 mW hydro-electric power station, now part of the extensive Tummel Hydro-Electric Power Scheme, was established here in 1935.

Tundergarth *Dumfries and Galloway* A parish in Annandale, Tundergarth lies to the east of Lockerbie and the Water of Milk. Tundergarth Mains lies just south of the Water of Milk, 3 miles (5 km) east of Lockerbie.

Tunga An alternative Gaelic name for Tong in the Western Isles.

Turnberry *South Ayrshire* A village in the Kyle district of South Ayrshire, Turnberry lies to the west of Turnberry Bay, 6 miles (10 km) north of Girvan. It has close by 1.5

miles (2.5 km) of fine sandy beaches, championship golf courses and a notable hotel. There is a lighthouse on Turnberry Point, and Turnberry Castle is thought to be the birthplace of Robert the Bruce (1274–1329).

Turrerich *Perth and Kinross* A locality in Glen Quaich, Perth and Kinross, Turrerich lies at the northwest end of Loch Freuchie, nearly 3 miles (5 km) northwest of Amulree.

Turret, Burn of *Angus* A tributary of the River North Esk in Angus, the Burn of Turret rises on Mount Battock on the border between Angus and Aberdeenshire. It flows 4 miles (6.5 km) southwards to meet the North Esk at Millden.

Turret, Glen *Perth and Kinross* A glen in central Perth and Kinross, Glen Turret extends 5 miles (8 km) northeastwards from Crieff, culminating in the Loch Turret Reservoir which is the source of the Turret Water. The Glenturret Distillery at the Hosh dates from 1775 and claims to be Scotland's oldest distillery.

Turret, River *Highland* A small river in Lochaber, the River Turret rises to the southeast of Loch Oich in the Great Glen. It flows 3 miles (5 km) south through Glen Turret to join the River Roy at Turret Bridge, 8 miles (13 km) northeast of Roybridge.

Turriff *Aberdeenshire* A market town with red sandstone buildings 11 miles (18 km) south of Banff, Turriff is situated between the districts of Buchan and Banff on a hilltop overlooking the Burn of Turriff or Idoch Water, which meets the River Deveron nearby. Created a burgh of barony in 1511, Turriff is located on a major routeway linking the Moray Firth with the south. It is thought to have been the capital of Lathmon, a Pictish principality, and its ancient ruined church dating from the 12th century was dedicated to St Comgan who gave his name to the annual Cowan Fair. Given to Arbroath Abbey in 1214, a hospital was founded on the lands of Turriff in 1272 by Alexander Comyn, Earl of Buchan. Turriff figured briefly in the nation's history when in 1639 it was the scene of a famous encounter between Royalist and Covenanting forces at which it is alleged 'the first blood was spilt in the great civil war'. Much later, in 1913, a battle was fought against Lloyd George's National Health Insurance scheme by a local farmer, Robert Paterson, whose refusal to participate gave rise to the celebrated incident of 'the Turra Coo'. The town has a library, museum, community centre, swimming pool, and recreation and sporting facilities including an 18-hole golf course. There is a livestock market, and each August the town hosts the two-day Turriff Show, the largest agricultural show in northeast Scotland. There are also meat processing, agricultural engineering, printing and office-equipment industries. Places of interest nearby include Delgatie Castle (1570), home of the Clan Hay; Craigston Castle, built between 1604 and 1607 by John Urquhart, the Tutor of Cromarty, so called because he tutored the father of Sir Thomas Urquhart, the translator of Rabelais; Kinedar Castle, the main 13th-century stronghold of the Comyn earls of Buchan; and Towie Barclay Castle (1593), home of the Barclay family, one of whose line was the Russian general Prince Michael Barclay de Tolly (1759–1818).

Twatt *Shetland* A settlement on the west coast of Shetland, in an area known as the West Mainland, Twatt lies at the head of Bixter Voe, a northern inlet of Sandsound Voe, 11 miles (18 km) northwest of Lerwick. The Burn of Twatt flows to the west of the settlement, emptying into nearby Effirth Voe.

Twatt *Orkney* A settlement of Mainland Orkney, Twatt is located 3 miles (5 km) northwest of Dounby and immediately south of the Loch of Boardhouse. A military airfield (HMS *Tern*) was established beside the Loch of Isbister in 1940.

Twechar *East Dunbartonshire* A former mining and quarrying village in East Dunbartonshire, Twechar lies to the south of the River Kelvin, 2 miles (3 km) southwest of Kilsyth. The Roman Antonine Wall passes nearby.

Tweed, River Renowned for its salmon fishing, the River Tweed is the principal river of Scottish Borders and, at 97 miles (156 km) long, the fourth-longest river in Scotland. Its catchment area, the second-largest in Scotland, is 4843 sq. km (1840 sq. miles). The Tweed rises in the Southern Uplands at Tweed's Well, 6 miles (10 km) north of Moffat, and flows northeast through Tweeddale to Lyne, where it is joined by the Lyne Water and the Manor Water as it turns east through Peebles. It continues southeastwards past Innerleithen and Melrose, receiving the Ettrick and Gala Waters before turning northeastwards again through Kelso, where it is joined by the River Teviot, and along the border with England to enter the North Sea at Berwick-upon-Tweed.

Tweed's Well *Scottish Borders* The River Tweed rises at Tweed's Well in the Southern Uplands, 6 miles (10 km) north of Moffat and not far from the sources of the rivers Clyde and Annan.

Tweedbank *Scottish Borders* A small scattered settlement at the southern end of Lauderdale in Scottish Borders, Tweedbank lies 2 miles (3 km) west of Melrose.

Tweeddale *Scottish Borders* A name that was applied to the former county of Peebles, Tweeddale occupies the upper reaches of the River Tweed from its source south of Glenbreck to its confluence with the Lyne Water, 3 miles (5 km) west of Peebles. It gives its name to the title of Marquess of Tweeddale. The history of the area is featured in the Tweeddale Museum and Gallery located in the former Chambers Institution in Peebles, a building donated to the town in 1859 by the publisher Dr W. Chambers.

Tweedsmuir *Scottish Borders* A small settlement in Upper Tweeddale, Tweedsmuir lies on the River Tweed, 8 miles (13 km) south of Broughton. The Talla Reservoir lies a mile (1.5 km) to the southeast. The Scottish author and statesman John Buchan (1875–1940) took the title 1st Baron Tweedsmuir.

Twelve Apostles, the *Dumfries and Galloway* A prehistoric stone circle near Newbridge in Dumfries and Galloway, the Twelve Apostles comprise one of the largest stone circles in Britain. It is thought that as many as 18 stones formed this landscape at one time.

Twiness *Orkney* A headland on the island of Westray in the Orkney Islands, Twiness lies to the west of the Bay of Tofts.

Twynholm *Dumfries and Galloway* A village of Dumfries and Galloway, Twynholm lies to the west of the River Dee, 3 miles (5 km) northwest of Kirkcudbright. The parish church of Twynholm dates from 1818, while just over a mile (1.5 km) to the southeast is the Tudor-style mansion house of Cumstoun (formerly Compstone), built in 1829 for the Maitland family. Also southeast lie the ruins of

Cumstoun Castle, within whose walls the soldier-poet Alexander Montgomery composed *The Cherrie and the Slae* in 1595. The Formula One racing driver David Coulthard was born in Twynholm.

Tyndrum *Stirling* A small village in northwest Stirling Council area at the head of Strath Fillan, Tyndrum lies 37 miles (60 km) northwest of Stirling. It is a key service centre for tourism and the surrounding farming community and is situated just south of the junction of roads leading to Oban and Fort William that were initially built as military roads in the mid-18th century. Lead was first mined nearby in the 1740s by Sir Robert Clifton. In the 1870s Tyndrum became a railhead and then a railway hub, with two stations serving a growing number of anglers and hillwalkers.

Tyne, River *East Lothian* Formed at the confluence of the Tyne Water with the Birns Water a mile (1.5 km) east of Pencaitland, the River Tyne flows northeast through Haddington and East Linton before emptying into the North Sea 3 miles (5 km) west of Dunbar.

Tyne Water *East Lothian* One of the headstreams of the River Tyne, the Tyne Water rises on the northern slopes of the Moorfoot Hills and flows north and east through the settlements of Tynehead, Pathhead and Ormiston before joining the Birns Water at Pencaitland to become the River Tyne.

Tynecastle Stadium *City of Edinburgh* A football stadium near Gorgie Road in western Edinburgh, Tynecastle is the home ground of Heart of Midlothian Football Club which moved to a site close by from Powderhall in 1881. Five years later the club moved to its present location, which has a stadium seating capacity of 18,008.

Tynehead *Midlothian* A small settlement in Midlothian, Tynehead lies to the east of the Tyne Water, 3 miles (5 km) east southeast of Gorebridge and 6 miles (10 km) southeast of Dalkeith.

Tynet, Burn of *Moray* A river that rises in headstreams to the south of Portgordon in Moray, the Burn of Tynet flows north to join the Moray Firth between Portgordon and Spey Bay.

Tyninghame *East Lothian* A picturesque planned estate village in East Lothian, Tyninghame ('the hamlet on the Tyne') lies 2 miles (3 km) northeast of East Linton and 4 miles (6.5 km) west of Dunbar. The original village lay in front of Tyninghame House, the home of the earls of Haddington on the banks of the River Tyne. The village was demolished in 1761 and rebuilt a half-mile (1 km) to the southwest in order to accommodate space around the house for parkland. St Baldred's Church, dating from the 12th century, was subsequently used by the earls of Haddington as a private chapel. The original village is recorded as having been burned by the Danes in AD 941. Extended in the 19th century, the village was designated a conservation area in 1969. The red-sandstone Tyninghame House was built to a design by William Burn on the site of an earlier house in 1829 for the Earl of Haddington, whose family had acquired the property in 1628. Prior to the Reformation, the estate had been held by the archbishops of St Andrews.

Tynron *Dumfries and Galloway* A former kirkton settlement of Nithsdale in Dumfries and Galloway, Tynron lies in a hollow on the Shinnel Water, 2 miles (3 km) northeast of Moniaive. It comprises a single row of 19th-century cottages with a church, manse, former school and schoolhouse. At Tynron Doon, on a spur of nearby Auchengibbert Hill, there are a 16th-century tower and the ramparts and ditches of an Iron Age hillfort.

Tyrebagger Hill *Aberdeenshire* A hill in eastern Aberdeenshire, Tyrebagger Hill rises to 250 m (820 ft) in the Kirkhill Forest, a mile (1.5 km) east of Blackburn and a mile (1.5 km) west of Aberdeen (Dyce) Airport.

Tyrie *Aberdeenshire* A locality in the Buchan district of Aberdeenshire, Tyrie lies 4 miles (6.5 km) southwest of Fraserburgh. It comprises the settlements of Tyrie and Tyrie Mains on the Water of Tyrie. Tyrie Kirk has a Pictish stone known as the Raven Stone beside the vestry.

Uachdar *Western Isles* A crofting township on the north coast of Benbecula in the Outer Hebrides, Uachdar lies a half-mile (1 km) east of Benbecula Airport and a similar distance to the west of Gramisdale.

Uags *Highland* A settlement on the coast of Wester Ross, Uags looks out over the Caolas Mòr towards the Crowlin Islands and Skye, 6 miles (10 km) south of Applecross and 6 miles (10 km) north of Kyle of Lochalsh.

Uair, the *Highland* A river in northern Sutherland, the Uair rises in Loch nam Breac to the west of Strath Halladale and flows north for 9 miles (14 km) before joining the Strathy Water to the east of Strathy Forest.

Uamh, Loch nan *Highland* A sea loch on the Sound of Arisaig, Loch nan Uamh separates the Arisaig peninsula in the north from the Ardnish peninsula to the south. The Prince's Cairn commemorates the landing of Prince Charles Edward Stewart (Bonnie Prince Charlie) here in 1745.

Uamh Bheag *Stirling/Perth and Kinross* A mountain on the border between Stirling and Perth and Kinross council areas, Uamh Bheag rises to 664 m (2178 ft) 5 miles (8 km) northeast of Callander.

Uanagan, Loch *Highland* A small loch in the Great Glen, Loch Uanagan lies between Loch Oich and Loch Ness, a mile (1.5 km) southwest of Fort Augustus. It is bypassed by the Caledonian Canal to the north and the A82 following the route of one of General Wade's military roads to the south and east. The River Oich flows to the north and west, while to the east flows the River Tarff.

Udalain, Gleann *Highland* A glen in the Lochalsh district of Highland Council area, Gleann Udalain carries the waters of the Allt Gleann Udalain southwest towards Nostie on the northern shore of Loch Alsh, 3 miles (5 km) southeast of Stromeferry.

Udale Bay *Highland* An inlet on the south shore of the Cromarty Firth in Easter Ross, Udale Bay opens out into Cromarty Bay, 7 miles (11 km) west of Cromarty on the Black Isle directly opposite Invergordon. An extensive area of marsh, mud flats and wet grasslands, it is a wintering ground for large numbers of wildfowl and wading birds, and is protected as a nature reserve managed by the Royal Society for the Protection of Birds (RSPB).

Uddingston *South Lanarkshire* A small commuter town in South Lanarkshire, Uddingston lies 4 miles (6.5 km) southwest of Coatbridge, between the settlements of Tannochside to the north and Bothwell to the south, and lies between the M74 and the River Clyde. On the banks of the Clyde lie the ruined remains of Bothwell Castle. A former market town, Uddingston developed at a major road junction in the 18th century and in association with coal mining. Uddingston Cross was for a time a terminus for Glasgow's electric trams. Since 1890, Uddingston has been the home of Tunnock's Bakery which manufactures the famous caramel wafer.

Uddington *South Lanarkshire* A small settlement in South Lanarkshire, Uddington lies between the Douglas Water and the M74, 2 miles (3 km) northeast of Douglas.

Udny Green *Aberdeenshire* A hamlet in the Formartine district of Aberdeenshire, Udny Green lies immediately southwest of Pitmedden. Udny Castle is said to date from the 14th century, and in the kirkyard of Udny Parish Church (1821) is an unusual mort house built in 1832 to a design by Captain John Marr of Cairnbrogie.

Udny Station *Aberdeenshire* A small village in Formartine, Aberdeenshire, Udny Station lies 5 miles (8 km) east of Oldmeldrum and 5 miles (8 km) southwest of Ellon.

Udstonhead *South Lanarkshire* A small village in South Lanarkshire, Udstonhead lies 2 miles (3 km) northeast of Strathaven and 2 miles (3 km) southwest of Glassford.

Ugadale *Argyll and Bute* Little more than a farm and surrounding buildings, Ugadale is located west of Ugadale Point, to the north of Kildonald Bay on the Kintyre peninsula. It overlooks Kilbrannan Sound and the island of Arran.

Ugadale Point *Argyll and Bute* Located on the east coast of the Kintyre peninsula, Ugadale Point faces the island of Arran over the Kilbrannan Sound, and lies 2 miles (3 km) south of the settlement of Saddell and 6 miles (10 km) northeast of Campbeltown.

Ugie, River *Aberdeenshire* A river of Buchan in northeast Aberdeenshire, the Ugie is formed by the merging near Longside of the North and South Ugie Waters that rise near New Pitsligo. Flowing north and then south and east, it empties into the North Sea at Buchanhead to the north of Peterhead.

Uibhist a Deas The Gaelic name for South Uist in the Outer Hebrides.

Uibhist a Tuath The Gaelic name for North Uist in the Outer Hebrides.

Uidh *Western Isles* A small crofting settlement on a peninsula at the eastern end of the island of Vatersay in the Outer Hebrides, Uidh is located 2 miles (3 km) southwest of Castlebay on Barra and looks out over Vatersay Bay to the south.

Uig *Argyll and Bute* A small settlement on the island of Coll in the Inner Hebrides, Uig lies a mile (1.5 km) north of Loch Breachacha, a sea loch on the island's southern coast.

Uig *Highland* A settlement on the Trotternish peninsula at the northern end of the isle of Skye, Uig lies at the head of Uig Bay, an inlet of Loch Snizort. Accessed by a road from Portree in 1812, a pier was built in 1840 to service shipping links with the Outer Hebrides. A new ferry pier was erected in the 1960s to serve ferries connecting with Lochmaddy and Tarbert. Glen Uig carries the waters of the River Conon westwards to empty into Uig Bay to the east of Uig.

Uig *Western Isles* A remote and scattered community surrounding a beautiful sandy bay on the west coast of the Isle of Lewis, Uig lies 23 miles (37 km) west of Stornoway. Timsgarry is the principal township in the area. The ancient Dun Borranish fort looks out onto Uig Bay (Gael: *Camas Uig*) in whose sandy dunes were found in 1831 the three famous Lewis chessmen made of walrus ivory in the 12th century. There was a medieval Benedictine convent to the south at Mealasta.

Uig, Glen *Angus* A narrow valley in the southern Grampians in northwest Angus, Glen Uig is a western arm of Glen Prosen to the east of Glen Isla. The Burn of Glenuig flows through the glen which extends for 4 miles (6.5 km) to meet Glen Prosen at Easter Lednathie.

Uigen *Western Isles* A small settlement of western Lewis in the Outer Hebrides, Uigen looks out onto Loch Roag a half-mile (1 km) east of Miavaig and a mile (1.5 km) west of Reef.

Uiginish *Highland* A settlement on the isle of Skye in the Inner Hebrides, Uiginish lies a mile (1.5 km) northwest of Dunvegan across Loch Dunvegan. Uiginish Point forms a headland near the head of the loch.

Uigshader *Highland* A small settlement on the isle of Skye in the Inner Hebrides, Uigshader lies 2 miles (3 km) south of Skeabost and 4 miles (6.5 km) northeast of Portree. The River Snizort flows northwards to the east of the settlement.

Uisg, Loch *Argyll and Bute* A loch on the island of Mull in the Inner Hebrides, Loch Uisg lies on a narrow neck of land between Loch Buie and Loch Spelve, a half-mile (1 km) east of Lochbuie. It is just over 2 miles (3 km) in length.

Uisge, Loch *Highland* A small loch on the Morvern peninsula of southwest Highland Council area, Loch Uisge lies on the course of the Abhainn na Coinnich which flows 3 miles (5 km) southeastwards to enter Loch a' Choire, a western inlet of Loch Linnhe opposite Appin.

Uisgnaval Mòr *Western Isles* A mountain in North Harris in the Western Isles, Uisgnaval Mòr rises to 728 m (2391 ft), 2 miles (3 km) west of Clisham.

Ulbster *Highland* An area of scattered crofts on the east coast of Caithness, Ulbster lies 7 miles (11 km) south of Wick. It was the ancestral home of the Sinclairs who later moved to Thurso. Sir John Sinclair of Ulbster, the 'Good Sir John' (1754–1835), was the first President of the Board of Agriculture and instigator of *The Statistical Account of Scotland* published in the 1790s. The Ulbster burial ground, the site of medieval St Martin's Chapel, includes the Sinclair Mausoleum, erected in 1700 and restored in 1995. Mains of Ulbster farmhouse dates from the 18th century.

Ullapool *Highland* A village and ferry port in Wester Ross, Ullapool lies on the eastern shore of Loch Broom, 59 miles (95 km) northeast of Inverness, 225 miles (362 km) north of Glasgow and 214 miles (344 km) northeast of Edinburgh. It was laid out as a planned village in 1788 by the British Fisheries Society in an attempt to stem emigration, and subsequently became one of the principal west coast ports for the herring trade. Served by a weekly steamer from Glasgow from the 1880s, Ullapool never developed as an industrial centre and was never served by a railway. In the 20th century it developed in association with hydro-electric power and tourism, a new ferry link with Stornoway being established in 1973. Its large harbour continued to attract fishing boats, with many East European fish-factory ships lying offshore for a few years from the late 1970s. The Telford Parliamentary-style church built in 1829 was turned into a museum in 1995. In the same year a local radio station, Lochbroom FM, was started by local volunteers.

Ulsta *Shetland* A village near the southern tip of the Shetland island of Yell, Ulsta is linked by car ferry to Toft on Mainland Shetland.

Ulva *Argyll and Bute* A hilly island in the Inner Hebrides, Ulva lies off the west coast of Mull, covering an area with Gometra, to which it is linked by a short causeway, of 2415 ha (5968 acres). Lachlan Macquarie (1761–1824), the 'father' of Australia, was born on Ulva, which was also the home of explorer David Livingstone's family. The island's population, which reached 570 in 1841, was largely cleared in the late 1840s.

Ulzieside *Dumfries and Galloway* A locality in Nithsdale, central Dumfries and Galloway, Ulzieside is situated by the Euchan Water near its junction with the River Nith, a mile (1.5 km) southwest of Sanquhar.

Unapool *Highland* A hamlet in Assynt, western Sutherland, Unapool lies on the western shore of Loch Glencoul, 1.25 miles (2 km) southeast of Kylestrome. The Unapool Burn enters Loch Glencoul just to the south, and Loch Unapool lies a mile (1.5 km) southwest.

Unich, Water of *Angus* A stream in the eastern Grampians, the Water of Unich rises on the border between Angus and Aberdeenshire. It flows generally eastwards to join the Water of Lee just west of Loch Lee and is one of the headwaters of the River North Esk.

Union Canal Extending eastwards for 31 miles (51 km) from the Lochrin Basin in the Tollcross area of Edinburgh, the Union Canal joins the Forth and Clyde Canal at Falkirk. A contour canal following the natural lie of the land, it maintains the same height throughout its length and therefore does not require locks. Opened in 1822, it passes through a 640-m (2070-ft) tunnel near Falkirk, the only canal tunnel in Scotland, amd crosses the Avon Aqueduct, which is the longest and tallest aqueduct in Scotland at 247 m (810 ft) long and 26 m (86 ft) high. Of its three other aqueducts, the best known and most accessible is at Slateford in Edinburgh, a mere 152 m (500 ft) long and 23 m (75 ft) tall. The Union Canal is operated by British Waterways and, along with the Forth and Clyde Canal, was subject to a major renovation as a Millennium project. The centrepiece of the project has been the Falkirk Wheel, a 35-m/115-ft-diameter lift built to transport boats from the height of the Union Canal down to the Forth and Clyde Canal and vice versa using state-of-the-art mechanical, electronic and hydraulic engineering. The Union Canal links Edinburgh, Ratho, Broxburn, Winchburgh, Linlithgow and Falkirk. An extension planned by engineer Robert Stevenson (1772–1850), which would have taken the canal on to Leith Docks via what is now Princes Street Gardens, was never built.

Unst *Shetland* The home of many of Shetland's 'tows' (trolls) and giant 'Saxis' of folklore, Unst is the most northerly inhabited island of the British Isles. Rectangular in shape and with a deeply indented coastline, it has an area of 12,557 ha (31,028 acres). Unst, with its cliff scenery and peat moorland, is ecologically one of the most interesting of the Shetland Islands. Rare species of plants such as the Norwegian sandwort and the Shetland mouse-ear chickweed have been found in the Keen of Hamar National Nature Reserve, the former being discovered by locally born Thomas Edmonston, author of *A Flora of Shetland* published in 1845. In the far north, Herma Ness National Nature Reserve protects 183-m (600-ft) cliffs that are home to many species of sea bird. Rising to 285 m (935 ft), Saxa Vord is the highest point on the island. At the Ministry of Defence installations around Saxa Vord, an unofficial wind speed record of 177 mph (285 kph) was recorded in 1962. Sites of archaeological interest include the excavated Norse settlement of Sandwick, and Bordastubble, the island's largest standing stone. Buildings of note include the ruined Muness Castle, Britain's northernmost castle, built in 1598 by the tyrannical Laurence Bruce of Cultmalindie in Perthshire, and the medieval Kirk of Lund which was last used for worship in 1785. The island's chief settlement is Baltasound, and to the northeast at Haroldswick is the site of a building that was Britain's most northerly post office. Britain's northernmost dwelling house, a croft farmhouse, is further north still at Wick of Skaw. Most of Unst's population of 720 are crofters and fishermen. The island can be reached by air to Baltasound Airstrip or by car ferry to Belmont from Gutcher on Yell.

Unstan *Orkney* The site of a prehistoric chambered tomb, Unstan lies 2 miles (3 km) northeast of Stromness on Mainland Orkney. It was excavated in 1884 by Orkney antiquarian R. S. Clouston and is remarkable for the number of pottery bowls (Unstan Ware) uncovered.

Unthank Burn *Dumfries and Galloway* A small stream of Eskdale in eastern Dumfries and Galloway, the Unthank Burn flows down to meet the Ewes Water 6 miles (10 km) north of Langholm.

Uphall *West Lothian* A village in West Lothian, Uphall lies on the Brox Burn, 1.5 miles (2 km) west of Broxburn and 13 miles (21 km) west of Edinburgh. Formerly known as Strathbrock ('valley of badgers', which is also the meaning of Broxburn), it developed in the 19th century in association with quarrying, shale mining and paraffin production. Notable buildings include the Oatridge Hotel (*c.*1800), Middleton Hall (*c.*1700), the 12th-century old parish church with its bell of *c.*1500, and Houston House which was built *c.*1600 for Sir Thomas Shairp, advocate.

Uplawmoor *East Renfrewshire* A commuter village in East Renfrewshire, Uplawmoor lies 3 miles (5 km) southwest of Neilston on a routeway linking Glasgow with the Ayrshire district of Cunninghame. It developed in the 19th century in association with mining and a railway station. Nearby are Loch Libo, Auchenbathie Tower and Caldwell House, which was for a time used as a hospital. There is an 18-hole golf course.

Upper Carloway *Western Isles* A linear crofting township close to the west coast of the Isle of Lewis, Upper Carloway (Gael: *Mullach Charlabhaigh*) lies a quarter-mile (0.5 km) to the northeast of Carloway and a similar distance to the southeast of Garenin.

Upper Kilchattan *Argyll and Bute* A township on the island of Colonsay in the Inner Hebrides, Upper Kilchattan lies 2 miles (3 km) northwest of Scalasaig and a half-mile (1 km) west of Loch Fada. Lower Kilchattan lies immediately to the south.

Upper Kilrenny The former name of Kilrenny in Fife.

Upper Knockando *Moray* A small village in Moray, Upper Knockando lies a mile (1.5 km) northwest of Knockando. The Burn of the Cowlatt flows to the east of the village, while to the south flows the Allt Arder.

Upper Largo *Fife* An ancient village in the East Neuk of Fife, Upper Largo lies to the north of Lower Largo. Also known as Kirkton of Largo, the village is centred on its 12th-century parish church of Largo, which was given to the Cistercian nunnery at North Berwick by Earl Duncan of Fife. A Pictish symbol stone and the headstone of the family of Alexander Selkirk (on whom Daniel Defoe based the novel *Robinson Crusoe*) are to be found in the churchyard, and inside the church is a model of the *Yellow Caravel*, the ship of the Scottish admiral Sir Andrew Wood, a Largo native who defeated the English fleet in 1498. North of the church is the Jacobean-style Wood's Hospital or Wood's House, founded in 1665 and rebuilt in 1830.

Upper Mumbie *Dumfries and Galloway* A locality in Eskdale, eastern Dumfries and Galloway, Upper Mumbie, Nether Mumbie and Mumbie Cottages lie just east of the River Esk, 3 miles (5 km) south of Langholm.

Upper Rusko *Dumfries and Galloway* A locality in central Dumfries and Galloway, Upper Rusko lies on the west bank of the Water of Fleet, nearly 2 miles (3 km) northwest of Gatehouse of Fleet. To the north lie the farms of Nether Rusko and Upper Rusko, and by a bend in the Water of Fleet stands Rusko Castle, built in the 16th century by the Gordon family and restored in the 1970s.

Upperton *North Lanarkshire* A small village in North Lanarkshire, Upperton lies 5 miles (8 km) northeast of Airdrie. Until 2002 it was known as Longriggend, but the villagers wished to change the name of the settlement which had associations with the nearby remand centre, closed in 2000.

Ura Firth *Shetland* A large inlet of St Magnus Bay on the west coast of Mainland Shetland, Ura Firth is separated from Ronas Voe to the north by a narrow neck of land a mile (1.5 km) wide.

Ure, Glen *Argyll and Bute* A glen in the Appin district of Argyll and Bute, Glen Ure carries the River Ure westwards to join the River Creran in Glen Creran, 3 miles (5 km) northeast of the head of Loch Creran. Beinn Sgulaird rises to 932 m (3022 ft) to the south of the glen.

Urgha *Western Isles* A locality on the south coast of North Harris in the Outer Hebrides, Urgha lies 1.25 miles (2 km) east of Tarbert. The location comprises the small settlements of Urgha and, to the northwest, Urgha Beg (Gael: *Urgha Beag*). The Urgha River (Gael: *Abhainn Urgha*) flows through Glen Lingadale (Gael: *Gleann Lingeadail*) and Urgha Beg before entering Urgha Beg Bay (Gael: *Bagh Urgha Beag*). Urgha Bay (Gael: *Bagh Urgha*) forms a smaller inlet to the southeast of Urgha.

Urie, River *Aberdeenshire* A river in the Garioch district of north-central Aberdeenshire, the Urie rises to the south of Largie and flows in a southeasterly direction for 20 miles (28 km). It passes the hamlets of Old Rayne, Pitcaple and Milton of Inveramsay before joining the River Don a mile (1.5 km) southeast of Inverurie.

Urie Loch *North Ayrshire* A small loch on the island of Arran, Urie Loch lies 3 miles (5 km) northwest of Whiting Bay.

Urlar Burn *Perth and Kinross* A small river of Perth and Kinross which rises 3 miles (5 km) southeast of Kenmore, the Urlar Burn flows northeast to become the Moness Burn at the Falls of Moness, a mile (1.5 km) south of Aberfeldy. The Moness Burn joins the River Tay just beyond that village.

Urquhart *Moray* Situated to the north of Lhanbryde in Moray, the village of Urquhart lies at the heart of fertile agricultural land where once there stood a Benedictine priory founded by David I in 1125. A carved wheel cross in the wall of the church hall is all that remains of this foundation whose priors were expelled in 1460 by the monks of Pluscarden Abbey.

Urquhart, Glen *Highland* A narrow glen to the west of Loch Ness, Glen Urquhart carries the River Enrick eastwards through Loch Meikle to enter Urquhart Bay, an inlet on the west shore of Loch Ness by Drumnadrochit. At the glen's western end is a prehistoric chambered cairn at Corrimony and at its eastern extremity Castle Urquhart looks out over Loch Ness.

Urr, Loch *Dumfries and Galloway* A loch in central Dumfries and Galloway, Loch Urr lies between the Craigmuie Moor and the Craigenvey Moor, 4 miles (6.5 km) south of Moniaive. The Urr Water drains southwards from the loch to enter the Rough Firth, an inlet of the Solway Firth.

Urray *Highland* A scattered settlement in Easter Ross, Urray comprises Easter, Old and Wester Urray lying 2 miles (3 km) northwest of Muir of Ord.

Usan *Angus* A locality on the east coast of Angus, 2 miles (3 km) south of Montrose, Usan comprises Fishtown of Usan, Seaton of Usan, Mains of Usan and Usan House. The Fishtown of Usan, a single row of 28 cottages, was created in 1822 by local landowner George Keith. A square tower was built as a landmark for shipping, and an icehouse and saltpans are reminders of the former salmon fishery and a saltworks that operated between 1794 and 1820. Today all that remains are the tower and the ruins of the cottages.

Usher Hall *City of Edinburgh* A baroque-style concert hall in west-central Edinburgh, the Usher Hall lies to the east of Lothian Road. It was the gift of brewer and distiller Andrew Usher (1826–98), who gave £100,000 for its construction in 1896 by J. Stockdale Harrison of Leicester. The foundation stone was laid by George V and Queen Mary in 1911, and the hall opened in 1914. Situated on a triangular site between Grindlay Street and Cambridge Street, the building is round, with an ashlar frontage and low copper-domed roof. The front is decorated with sculptures by Birnie Rhind, Crosland McLure and H. S. Gamley. Managed by the City of Edinburgh Council, it has an audience capacity of 2900.

Uskavagh, Loch *Western Isles* A large sea loch in the Outer Hebrides, Loch Uskavagh (Gael: *Uisgebhagh*) opens out into the Minch on the east coast of the island of Benbecula. The settlement of Uisgebhagh lies at the southern entrance to the loch.

Uyea *Shetland* The uninhabited Shetland island of Uyea lies to the south of the much larger island of Unst, from which it is separated by the Skuda Sound. The island has an area of 205 ha (507 acres) and rises to 50 m (164 ft) at the Ward. At the northern end of the island is a chambered cairn and on the central ridge stands 'The Hall', the home of Sir Basil Neven-Spence, MP for Orkney and Shetland from 1935 to 1950. Sir Basil lies buried in an old chapel overlooking Brei Wick – the 'broad bay'.

Uyeasound *Shetland* A small and scattered village on the south coast of Unst in the Shetland Islands, Uyeasound lies around a bay at the junction of Uyea Sound and Skuda Sound, looking to the island of Uyea. The village has a small primary school and a harbour.

Uynarey *Shetland* An uninhabited island of the Shetland Islands, Uynarey lies in the Yell Sound, off the southwest coast of Yell, a mile (1.5 km) west of Ulsta.

Vaa, Loch *Highland* A small loch in Strathspey, Loch Vaa lies 3 miles (5 km) north of Aviemore.

Vacasay Island *Western Isles* A small uninhabited island in the Outer Hebrides, Vacasay Island (Gael: *Eilean Bhacasaigh*) lies in East Loch Roag, a sea loch on the west coast of the Isle of Lewis. It rises to 29 m (95 ft) off the east coast of Great Bernera and 1.25 miles (2 km) west-northwest of Breaclete.

Vaccasay *Western Isles* One of the larger of a group of uninhabited islands lying to the northeast of North Uist, Vaccasay (Gael: *Bhacasaigh*) rises to 18 m (59 ft) a half-mile (1 km) northwest of Hermetray and 5 miles (8 km) northeast of Lochmaddy.

Vacsay *Western Isles* A small uninhabited island in the Outer Hebrides, Vacsay (Gael: *Bhacsaigh*) lies in West Loch Roag, on the west coast of the Isle of Lewis in the Outer Hebrides. Vacsay extends to 41 ha (101 acres) and rises to 34 m (112 ft), a half-mile (1 km) southeast of Pabay Mòr, 1.25 miles (2 km) east of Valtos and 1.5 miles (2.5 km) to the west of Great Bernera.

Vagastie, Strath *Highland* A valley in Sutherland, Strath Vagastie carries the waters of the Allt a' Chraisg northeast from Crask Inn to the head of Loch Naver near Altnaharra.

Vaich, Loch *Highland* A narrow loch in Ross and Cromarty, Loch Vaich extends 4 miles (6.5 km) from north to south to the northeast of Loch Glascarnoch. It is linked to the Black River via Strath Vaich.

Vaila *Shetland* An island of 327 ha (808 acres), Vaila provides shelter to the small port of Walls on the west Mainland of Shetland, from which it is separated by the Wester and Easter Sounds which form entrances to Vaila Sound. The island comprises peat and heather moorland fringed by a rocky coastline that provides nesting for large numbers of sea birds. There are two round hills, East Ward at 95 m (312 ft) and West Ward at 81 m (266 ft). An ancient watch tower known as Mucklaberry Castle was restored in the 1890s by the island's owner, the Yorkshire millowner Herbert Anderton. Anderton also built Vaila Hall in 1895. The largest house of its kind in Shetland, it incorporated a former laird's house built in the 17th century by James Mitchell. Vaila's previous owner was the Shetland-born shipowner and philanthropist Arthur Anderson (b.1792), a co-founder of the shipping company that became Peninsular and Oriental (P&O).

Vale of Leven *West Dunbartonshire* The broad valley of the River Leven which flows southwards for 5 miles (8 km) from Loch Lomond to the River Clyde is known as the Vale of Leven. It includes the settlements of Balloch, Alexandria, Bonhill and Dumbarton.

Valigan, Loch *Perth and Kinross* A small loch in the Grampians, Loch Valigan lies 3 miles (5 km) south of the summit of Beinn a' Ghlo, between the peaks of Meall Breac and Ben Vuirich.

Vallay Island *Western Isles* A small island off the north coast of North Uist in the Western Isles, Vallay Island is connected to the main island by the sand banks of Vallay Strand at low tide. Covering an area of 260 ha (642 acres), there are duns, standing stones and chapel ruins in addition to Vallay House, which was built by Erskine Beveridge, a Fife linen manufacturer.

Valley, Loch *Dumfries and Galloway* A loch in Galloway Forest Park, Dumfries and Galloway, Loch Valley lies nearly 2 miles (3 km) northeast of Loch Trool, to which it is linked via the Gairland Burn.

Valleyfield *Dumfries and Galloway* A locality in Dumfries and Galloway, Valleyfield lies a mile (1.5 km) to the southwest of Ringford near the meeting of the Spout Burn with the Tarff Water.

Valleyfield *Fife* A village of western Fife, Valleyfield lies a mile (1.5 km) to the east of Culross and comprises the settlements of High Valleyfield and Low Valleyfield.

Valleyfield Woodland Park *Fife* Opened in 1990, Valleyfield Woodland Park in western Fife lies to the northeast of Culross. It is traversed by the Bluther Burn and forms part of a landscape created in 1802 by Sir Robert Preston of Valleyfield Estate. It was the only commission of its kind in Scotland to be carried out by Humphrey Repton (1752–1818), the famous English landscape gardener. Although the mansion house was demolished and much of Repton's landscape was lost after the estate was taken over by the East Fife Coal Company in 1917, there are still remains of the walled flower garden, an icehouse, ornamental pond, beech avenue and ha-ha. The park is entered from the south by the Bluther Burn at Newmills, and from the north near Shiresmill.

Valtos *Highland* The scattered community of Valtos is located on the west coast of the Trotternish peninsula at the northern end of the isle of Skye in the Inner Hebrides. Kilt Rock, a series of vertical grooves and columns in the cliff face resembling the pleats of a kilt, lies 2 miles (3 km) to the north.

Valtos *Western Isles* A small township on the Isle of Lewis in the Outer Hebrides, Valtos (Gael: *Bhaltos*) lies on the west shore of West Loch Roag, 3 miles (5 km) southeast of Gallan Head.

Vane Farm *Perth and Kinross* A nature reserve on the south side of Loch Leven in southeast Perth and Kinross, Vane Farm is managed by the Royal Society for the Protection of Birds (RSPB). It comprises low-lying wetland, farmland, and heather- and tree-clad hillside (Vane Hill). It is noted for its migrating geese in winter.

Varragill, Glen *Highland* A glen on the isle of Skye in the Inner Hebrides, Glen Varragill carries the Varragill River southwards through the Portree and Glen Varragill Forests to empty into Loch Sligachan. The main A87 to Portree passes through the glen.

Vasa Point *Orkney* A small headland on the west coast of the island of Shapinsay in the Orkney Islands, Vasa Point extends into the sea at the southern end of the Bay of Furrowend.

Vastray, Point of *Orkney* A headland on the northeast coast of the Orkney Mainland, the Point of Vastray extends into the Eynhallow Sound, which separates the mainland from the island of Rousay to the north. The settlement of Tingwall is located 2 miles (3 km) to the southeast.

Vat Burn *Aberdeenshire* Rising to the southeast of Culbean Hill in central Aberdeenshire, the Vat Burn flows east for a mile (1.5 km) to empty into Loch Kinord.

Vaternish *Highland* A basalt peninsula of northwest Skye in the Inner Hebrides, Vaternish (or Waternish) lies to the west of Loch Snizort. At its northern tip, Vaternish Point extends into the Minch.

Vatersay *Western Isles* An island in the Outer Hebrides, Vatersay (Gael: *Bhatarsaigh*) lies to the southwest of Barra, to which it is linked over the Sound of Vatersay by a 250 m (819 ft) causeway created between 1989 and 1991 with

220,000 tonnes of rock. The highest point on the island is Heishival Mòr at 190 m (623 ft). In 1906 crofters, who came to be known as the Vatersay Raiders, landed on the island and laid claim to land. Fishing and sheep and cattle farming are the main occupations.

Vatersay Bay *Western Isles* A significant bay on the east coast of the island of Vatersay, the most southerly inhabited island in the Outer Hebrides, Vatersay Bay (Gael: *Bagh Bhatasaigh*) is separated from West Bay (Gael: *Bagh Siar*) by a narrow isthmus of sand dunes that links the northern and southern parts of the island. The settlement of Vatersay lies immediately to the southwest.

Vatten *Highland* A settlement on the isle of Skye in the Inner Hebrides, Vatten lies on the east shore of Loch Vatten, an inlet at the head of Loch Bracadale. The village of Dunvegan lies 3 miles (5 km) to the northwest.

Vaul *Argyll and Bute* A settlement on the north coast of the island of Tiree in the Inner Hebrides, Vaul lies at the western end of Vaul Bay, 2 miles (3 km) north of Scarinish. The ruins of the Iron Age Dun Mor Vaul lie to the northwest.

Ve Skerries *Shetland* The Ve Skerries are a group of outlying rocks located 3 miles (5 km) northwest of the island of Papa Stour, itself located off the west coast of the Shetland Mainland.

Veantrow Bay *Orkney* A wide bay on the north coast of the island of Shapinsay in the Orkney Islands, Veantrow Bay lies between The Galt in the west and Holm Taing in the east.

Veensgarth *Shetland* A small village in the Tingwall district in the centre of Mainland Shetland, Veensgarth is located a half-mile (1 km) southeast of Tingwall Airport.

Veilish Point *Western Isles* A headland on the north coast of the island of North Uist in the Outer Hebrides, Veilish Point lies 2 miles (3 km) north of the settlement of Sollas.

Vementry *Shetland* An uninhabited island in the Shetland parish of Aithsting, Vementry lies to the north of the west Mainland of Shetland, from which it is separated by the Cribba and Uyea Sounds. It has an area of 370 ha (914 acres) and rises to 90 m (295 ft) at Muckle Ward, which is capped by a circular chambered cairn, one of the best preserved in Shetland. The Swarback Minn separates Vementry from the island of Muckle Roe to the north.

Venachar, Loch *Stirling* A loch in the Trossachs district of Stirling Council area, Loch Venachar extends a distance of 6 miles (10 km) between Callander and Brig o' Turk. The Black Water empties from Loch Achray into the western end of Loch Venachar and at its eastern end emerges the River Teith, which carries the name Eas Gobhain before it merges with the River Leny at Callander. On the loch's south shore stands the mansion of Invertrossachs, which was visited by Queen Victoria in 1869.

Vennel, the *City of Edinburgh* A narrow medieval lane in Edinburgh, the Vennel links the Grassmarket with Lauriston Place via Heriot Place. It formerly provided access to the city wall, part of which remains.

Venniehill *Dumfries and Galloway* A hill with a viewpoint in Gatehouse of Fleet, Dumfries and Galloway, Venniehill is partially surrounded by earthworks that may have formed an ancient defence or early settlement. The site was gifted to the National Trust for Scotland by Mary Usher of Cally in 1981.

Verdant Works *Dundee City* A textile heritage centre housed in an old jute mill in West Henderson's Wynd, Dundee, the Verdant Works were built for the flax-spinner and merchant David Lindsay in 1833. Later owned by canvas manufacturer John Ewan in the 1850s, it had by 1864 three engines driving 70 power looms and a workforce of 500. Operating until 1899, it was one of 61 spinning and power-loom works in Dundee. The works, which are the headquarters of the Dundee Heritage Trust, reopened as a museum in 1996 and were awarded European Industrial Museum of the Year in 1999.

Vere, the *Shetland* The Vere is an outlying rock situated a mile (1.5 km) northwest of the headland of Mu Ness on the southeast coast of the island of Unst.

Vest Ness *Orkney* A headland at the southwest end of the island of Papa Westray, Vest Ness lies to the west of the Bay of Moclett.

Veyatie, Loch *Highland* A long narrow loch in the Assynt district of western Sutherland, Loch Veyatie lies 7 miles (11 km) southwest of Inchnadamph and 3 miles (5 km) west of Ledmore. It is 4 miles (6.5 km) long.

Victoria Bridge *Glasgow City* The oldest surviving bridge over the River Clyde in Glasgow, Victoria Bridge was built in 1854 to replace the former Bishop's Bridge. In its time it was the second-widest bridge in Britain.

Victoria Dock *Dundee City* A quay in Dundee opening out onto the Firth of Tay to the east of the Tay Road Bridge, Victoria Dock was begun in 1833 to a design by Thomas Telford. Occupying some 4.3 ha (10.7 acres), this was one of the largest enclosed docks in Scotland. Anchored in the dock is HMS Frigate *Unicorn*, the oldest British-built ship afloat and the most completely original preserved wooden sailing ship in the world. Scotland's only example of a warship from the golden age of sail, the 46-gun *Unicorn* was built for the Royal Navy in the Royal Dockyard at Chatham and launched in 1824. After service there and at Woolwich, she came to Dundee in 1873 as drill-ship for the Royal Naval Reserve, remaining in service as RNVR/RNR Tay Division Headquarters ship until 1968. The ship has been maintained since then by the Unicorn Preservation Society.

Victoria Falls *Highland* Named after Queen Victoria, who visited in 1877, the Victoria Falls in Wester Ross lie on the course of a stream that flows north from Loch Garbhaig into Loch Maree.

Victoria Park *Glasgow City* Located in the West End of Glasgow, the 25-ha (62-acre) Victoria Park was opened to the public in 1886, the year of Queen Victoria's Golden Jubilee. In 1911 the park, which includes the Fossil Grove, was incorporated into the city along with Partick.

Vidlin *Shetland* A small fishing settlement on the east coast of the Shetland Mainland, Vidlin lies at the head of Vidlin Voe, 4 miles (6.5 km) east-northeast of Voe. Lunna House nearby was the home of the Norwegian resistance movement during World War II. There are ferry links with Whalsay and the Out Skerries.

Viewpark *North Lanarkshire* A settlement to the east of the M74 in North Lanarkshire, Viewpark lies just northwest of Bellshill, 3 miles (5 km) southwest of Coatbridge. It stands on a south-facing escarpment overlooking the North Calder Water. It developed in association with the railway.

Village Bay *Western Isles* A sheltered bay on the south coast of the island of Hirta in the St Kilda Group, Village Bay was formerly known as Loch Hirta. The island's former main settlement overlooks the bay.

Vinny Water *Angus* A stream in Angus, the Vinny Water (also Vinney Water or Vinny Burn) rises to the south of Forfar and flows eastwards through Letham before joining the Lunan Water at Friockheim.

Voe *Shetland* An inlet at the southern end of the Shetland Mainland, Voe opens out into the sea to the north of Lambhoga Head. The settlement of Boddam lies at the head of Voe.

Voe *Shetland* A picturesque small settlement on the west coast of the Shetland Mainland, Voe lies at the head of Olna Firth, 14 miles (22 km) north of Lerwick. Formerly a herring and whaling station, it is popular with pleasure craft and has tweed weaving.

Voe *Shetland* A settlement at the northern end of the Shetland Mainland, Voe lies at the head of Ronas Voe, 8 miles (13 km) north of Brae.

Vogrie Country Park *Midlothian* A country park to the southeast of Edinburgh, Vogrie lies 3 miles (5 km) northeast of Gorebridge. Vogrie Burn flows through the park, which offers nature trails, a walled garden, ponds, a golf course and a model railway. Vogrie House, which was built in 1875 for the Dewar family of whisky distillers, is in a light form of the Scottish baronial style. The architect was Andrew Heiton (1823–94) of Perth, and this is said to be his finest surviving work. The house and estate were given to Midlothian Council in the 1980s to form the park.

Voil, Loch *Stirling* A loch in the Balquhidder district of Stirling Council area, Loch Voil extends 5 miles (8 km) from east to west. It drains water from the much smaller Loch Doine immediately to the west and the Monachyle Burn, which descends from the Braes of Balquhidder to meet the loch at its western end. The village of Balquhidder lies at the eastern end of the loch where the River Balvag emerges en route to Loch Lubnaig through Strathyre.

Vord Hill *Shetland* A hill on the island of Fetlar in the Shetland Islands, Vord Hill rises to 158 m (518 ft).

Vorran Island *Western Isles* A rocky islet in the Outer Hebrides, Vorran Island (Gael: *Eilean Bheirean*) lies 1.5 miles (2.5 km) west of Peninerine, off the west coast of the island of South Uist, to which it is connected at low tide.

Voshimid, Loch *Western Isles* A small loch in the Outer Hebrides, Loch Voshimid lies 3 miles (5 km) south of the head of Loch Resort in North Harris.

Votersay *Western Isles* One of the larger of a group of uninhabited islets and islands lying to the northeast of North Uist, Votersay (Gael: *Bhotarsaigh*) lies 4.5 miles (7 km) northeast of Lochmaddy.

Vrotachan, Loch *Aberdeenshire* A small loch in the eastern Grampians, Loch Vrotachan lies a half-mile (1 km) to the northeast of The Cairnwell and immediately east of the Glen Shee Chairlifts and Ski Centre.

Vuia Beg *Western Isles* An uninhabited island in a sea loch on the west coast of the Isle of Lewis in the Outer Hebrides, Vuia Beg (Gael: *Fuaigh Beag*) is located in West Loch Roag, a half-mile (1 km) southwest of Vuia Mòr and 2 miles (3 km) southwest of Great Bernera. The island rises to 69 m (225 ft).

Vuia Mòr *Western Isles* An uninhabited island located on the west coast of the Isle of Lewis in the Outer Hebrides, Vuia Mòr (Gael: *Fuaigh Mòr*) is located in West Loch Roag, a mile (0.8 km) to the west of Great Bernera and 3 miles (5 km) southeast of Valtos on Lewis. The island extends to 84 ha (208 acres) and rises to 48 m (157 ft). It supported a population of around 50 until the middle of the 19th century when the islanders were evicted to make way for sheep.

Wadbister *Shetland* A settlement in Tingwall parish on the east coast of the Shetland Mainland, Wadbister lies 5 miles (8 km) north-northwest of Lerwick on the south side of Wadbister Voe. Wadbister Ness separates Wadbister Voe from Lax Firth.

Walbutt *Dumfries and Galloway* A locality in Dumfries and Galloway, Walbutt lies between the River Dee and the Urr Water, a mile (1.5 km) to the northeast of Crossmichael.

Walkerburn *Scottish Borders* A small village in Tweeddale, Walkerburn lies on the north side of the River Tweed where it is joined by the Walker Burn (formerly Priesthope Burn), 2 miles (3 km) east of Innerleithen. It developed in association with the Tweedvale and Tweedholm woollen mills established here in the 1850s and 1860s. Its population of nearly 1300 in 1891 halved during the 20th century as the textile industry declined, leaving only a Scottish Museum of Woollen Textiles.

Wallace Monument *Stirling* Standing on top of the wooded Abbey Craig, a volcanic crag-and-tail feature to the east of Stirling, the Wallace Monument is a prominent landmark of Stirling Council area. It was erected between 1861 and 1869 in honour of Scotland's national hero Sir William Wallace (d.1305), at a total cost of £15,000. Built of freestone quarried on and around the craig and rising to 67 m (220 ft), the monument was designed by John T. Lochead of Glasgow in the Scottish baronial style. On show is the gigantic two-handed sword with which Wallace 'made great room about him'.

Wallacestone *Falkirk* A village in Falkirk Council area situated 1.5 miles (2.5 km) southwest of Polmont, Wallacestone lies to the south of the Union Canal and Reddingmuirhead, from which it is separated by the Polmont Burn.

Wallaceton *Dumfries and Galloway* A locality in central Dumfries and Galloway, Wallaceton lies on the Cairn Water, 5 miles (8 km) southeast of Moniaive.

Wallacetown *South Ayrshire* A northern suburb of Ayr, Wallacetown was established on the Park of Newton as a coal-mining village by the Wallaces of Craigie.

Walls *Shetland* A crofting and fishing township in the most westerly district of Mainland Shetland, Walls lies 25 miles (40 km) northwest of Lerwick. It is situated at the head of two voes or bays that open out into Vaila Sound, overlooking a natural harbour well sheltered by the island of Vaila. Taking its name from the Old Norse for 'voes', its spelling was anglicised to its present form because it sounded like 'was', the Scottish pronunciation of 'walls'. A pier was established in the 18th century. From the late 18th century, Walls was a centre of fishing and fish curing operated by the Shetland Fishery Company, which was managed for a time by Arthur Anderson, a co-founder of the P&O shipping company. The ferry to the island of Foula sails from Walls.

Walls Peninsula A bulbous peninsula on the west coast

of Shetland, the Walls Peninsula is located 12 miles (19 km) northwest of Lerwick and is heavily indented by sea lochs. Its major settlements are Aith, Skeld, Walls and Sandness.

Wallyford *East Lothian* A former mining village in Inveresk parish, East Lothian, Wallyford lies 1.5 miles (2.5 km) east of Musselburgh. Following the closure of the colliery, the village was revitalised as a commuter settlement by the opening of a new dual-carriageway bypass in the early 1980s and the opening of a rail link with Edinburgh in 1994. Wallyford was the birthplace in 1828 of the novelist Margaret Oliphant. Immediately southwest is the site of the Battle of Pinkie (1547), the culmination of the 'Rough Wooing' campaign.

Walston *South Lanarkshire* A small village in a parish of the same name, Walston lies at the southern end of the Pentland Hills, 5 miles (8 km) east of Carnwath and 6 miles (10 km) north of Biggar.

Walton, Loch *Stirling* A small loch at the southeast end of the Fintry Hills in the uplands of southern Stirling Council area, Loch Walton drains into the nearby Endrick Water.

Walton Park *Dumfries and Galloway* A locality in the valley of the Urr Water, central Dumfries and Galloway, Walton Park lies at the junction of the Coldstream Burn with the Urr, 2 miles (3 km) west of Kirkpatrick Durham.

Wamphray Water *Dumfries and Galloway* A stream of Annandale in Dumfries and Galloway, the Wamphray Water rises on Loch Fell, 4 miles (6.5 km) east of Moffat. It flows southwestwards for 7 miles (11 km) to join the River Annan. At the confluence of the Lemoir Burn and Wamphray Water stand the remains of a tower house of the Johnstones and an earlier motte and bailey.

Wamphraygate *Dumfries and Galloway* A locality in Annandale, Dumfries and Galloway, Wamphraygate lies on the Wamphray Water near its junction with the River Annan, 7 miles (11 km) south of Moffat. In 1848 a railway station was opened at Wamphraygate, which was shortened to Wamphray, and today the main line passes a half-mile (1 km) to the west.

Wandel *South Lanarkshire* A small settlement of Clydesdale, Wandel lies to the south of the junction of the Wandel Burn with the River Clyde, 3 miles (5 km) northeast of Abington.

Wanlock Dod *South Lanarkshire* A summit in the Lowther Hills, Wanlock Dod rises to 550 m (1807 ft) a half-mile (1 km) north of Wanlockhead in Dumfries and Galloway. The Snar Water rises on the north side of the hill, and on the south side are the remains of former lead mines.

Wanlock Water *Dumfries and Galloway* A stream in the Lowther Hills of northern Dumfries and Galloway, the Wanlock Water rises by Wanlockhead and flows northwestwards to join the Crawick Water near Spango Bridge.

Wanlockhead *Dumfries and Galloway* An isolated village in the Lowther Hills of northern Dumfries and Galloway, Wanlockhead lies on the Wanlock Water, nearly 2 miles (3 km) southwest of Leadhills. Formerly a lead-mining village, it is situated at c.500 m (1500 ft) above sea level and is Scotland's highest village. A trail through the village from Wanlockhead Museum follows the route of a former narrow-gauge railway to the Loch Nell Mine, which was first opened in 1710 when the Quaker Company leased the land and rebuilt the village. Wanlockhead was rebuilt again after 1842, when the dukes of Queensberry took a direct interest in the running of the mines and the welfare of the miners. A water-powered beam engine used to pump water out of the Straitsteps Mine is the only one of its kind in Britain to have survived virtually intact. A beam engine built at Wanlockhead in 1875, and now part of the museum, is an example of a 19th-century wooden water-balance pump used to drain water from nearby lead mines until 1945.

War Ness *Orkney* Located on the island of Eday in the Orkney Islands, War Ness is the most southerly headland of the island. It overlooks the Fall of Warness to the south and Muckle Green Holm to the southwest.

Ward Hill *Orkney* The highest point on the island of Hoy in the Orkney Islands, Ward Hill rises to 479 m (1570 ft) at the northern end of the island.

Ward Hill *Orkney* A hill on the Orkney Mainland, Ward Hill rises to 268 m (879 ft) 3 miles (5 km) north of Orphir Bay.

Ward Hill *Shetland* The highest point on Fair Isle, Ward Hill rises to 217 m (712 ft) at the northern end of the island. There are the remains of a wartime radar station on its summit, and to the east is a modern radio mast. On the coast to the west is the rock stack known as the Tower of Ward Hill.

Ward Holm *Orkney* A small islet of the Orkney Islands, Ward Holm lies a mile (1.5 km) west of the island of Copinsay.

Wardhouse *Aberdeenshire* An estate and mid-18th-century Palladian mansion situated 2 miles (3 km) northeast of Kennethmont in northern Aberdeenshire, Wardhouse was the birthplace of naval commander James Alexander Gordon (1782–1869). Known as the 'Spanish Gordons', this family moved to Spain rather than renounce the Roman Catholic faith. Alfonso XIII of Spain and his queen, Victoria Eugenia, spent their honeymoon here in 1906, but by the 1950s the mansion had fallen into disrepair.

Wardie *City of Edinburgh* A suburb of Edinburgh, Wardie lies between Inverleith and Granton, 2 miles (3 km) to the north of the city centre. The former Wardie Muir extended from Inverleith as far as the shore of the Firth of Forth.

Wardrop's Court *City of Edinburgh* A courtyard in the Old Town of Edinburgh, Wardrop's Court lies to the north of the Lawnmarket and east of Lady Stair's Close. Following the demolition of tenements in the 1890s, the town planner Sir Patrick Geddes created the courtyard. Among the buildings demolished was the house in which Robert Burns (1759–96) lodged during his first visit to the city. To the north of Wardrop's Court is Blackie House, a 17th-century tenement named after Professor J. S. Blackie (1809–95) and refurbished by Geddes as a student residence for the University of Edinburgh, later sold in the 1950s as private flats.

Warmanbie *Dumfries and Galloway* A locality and a hotel in Annandale, Dumfries and Galloway, Warmanbie lies on the River Annan, just over a mile (1.5 km) north of the town of Annan.

Warrender *City of Edinburgh* A small district with Victorian tenement crescents and streets on the south side of Edinburgh, Warrender lies next to Marchmont on the south of The Meadows and east of Bruntsfield. It takes its name from a family that occupied a mansion here.

Warriston *City of Edinburgh* A northern district of Edinburgh, Warriston lies on the Water of Leith to the east of Inverleith, a mile (1.5 km) north of the city centre. Warriston Crematorium stands alongside Warriston Cemetery (1843), which was the burial place of the surgeon Sir James Young Simpson (1811–70) and the artist Horatio McCulloch (1805–67).

Wart Holm *Orkney* An outlying rock in the Orkney Islands, Wart Holm lies a half-mile (1 km) west of the Point of Huro at the southern end of the island of Westray.

Watch Water *Scottish Borders* A river in Scottish Borders, the Watch Water rises in the Lammermuir Hills and flows east to merge with the Dye Water at a point just west of Longformacus.

Water Beck *Dumfries and Galloway* A stream of Annandale in Dumfries and Galloway, the Water Beck rises on Grange Fell, 7 miles (11 km) east of Lockerbie. It flows south through the village of Waterbeck to join the Kirtle Water, a tributary of the River Annan.

Water Sound *Orkney* A narrow strait in the Orkney Islands, Water Sound separates the islands of South Ronaldsay and Burray.

Waterbeck *Dumfries and Galloway* A village of Annandale in Dumfries and Galloway, Waterbeck lies to the west of the Kirtle Water, 3 miles (5 km) northeast of Ecclefechan.

Waterfoot *East Renfrewshire* A village in East Renfrewshire, Waterfoot lies on the west bank of the White Cart Water, a mile (1.5 km) south of Busby and 2 miles (3 km) east of Newton Mearns. Formerly associated with a mill and smithy, it developed in the late 20th century as a green-belt dormitory village for affluent commuters.

Waterloo *Highland* Overlooking Broadford Bay on the east coast of the isle of Skye in the Inner Hebrides, the settlement of Waterloo lies a mile (1.5 km) east of Broadford.

Waterloo *North Lanarkshire* A small village in Cambusnethan parish, North Lanarkshire, Waterloo lies a mile (1.5 km) southeast of Wishaw and 3 miles (5 km) northwest of Carluke.

Waterloo *Perth and Kinross* A settlement in Strath Tay, Waterloo lies on the B867, a mile (1.5 km) northwest of Bankfoot.

Waternish An alternative name for Vaternish on the isle of Skye.

Waterside *Aberdeenshire* A locality in eastern Aberdeenshire, Waterside is situated on the east bank of the River Ythan near its mouth.

Waterside *East Ayrshire* A former industrial village in the valley of the River Doon, Waterside lies 3 miles (5 km) northwest of Dalmellington. In 1847, a large ironworks employing over 2000 men was established here by the Dalmellington Iron Company and seven years later a railway station was opened. The ironworks closed in 1921 and in 1936 the Dunaskin Brickworks was built on the site of the iron furnaces. Waterside's housing was largely cleared and the brickworks eventually closed in 1976. In 1998, the Dunaskin Open-Air Museum celebrating the industrial heritage of Ayrshire was opened.

Waterside *East Ayrshire* A hamlet of northern East Ayrshire, Waterside lies on the Dunton Water, 1.25 miles (2 km) east of Fenwick and 5 miles (8 km) northwest of Kilmarnock.

Waterside *East Dunbartonshire* A settlement in East Dunbartonshire, Waterside is situated on the Luggie Water, 2 miles (3 km) southeast of Kirkintilloch.

Waterstein Head *Highland* A hill on the west coast of the isle of Skye in the Inner Hebrides, Waterstein Head rises in steep cliffs to a height of 296 m (967 ft) above Moonen Bay, 6 miles (10 km) west of Dunvegan.

Watten *Highland* A small village to the south of Loch Watten in northeast Caithness, Watten lies 8 miles (13 km) northwest of Wick on the A882 to Thurso. The settlement developed in the 19th century at a road junction and had an oatmeal mill (Achingale) in operation until the 1960s. Achingale Bridge was built by Thomas Telford in 1812–17, and Alexander Bain (1810–77), inventor of the electric clock and electric telegraph, was born nearby on a croft at Houstry.

Watten, Loch *Highland* A loch in central Caithness, Loch Watten is located north of the village of Watten and 9 miles (14 km) northwest of Wick. The loch is 2.5 miles (4 km) long and about a half-mile (1 km) wide. The railway from Georgemas Junction to Wick runs along its northern shore.

Wattston *North Lanarkshire* A former mining village of North Lanarkshire, Wattston lies 3 miles (5 km) south-southeast of Cumbernauld and a similar distance north-northeast of Airdrie. The village of Greengairs lies immediately to the east. Although the coal pits had closed by the 1950s, opencast mining is still carried on to the south.

Wauchope Burn *Scottish Borders* A stream rising in the Wauchope Forest in the Cheviot Hills near the border with England, the Wauchope Burn is a headwater of the Rule Water which flows north to join the Teviot near Bedrule.

Wauchope Water *Dumfries and Galloway* A stream of Eskdale in Dumfries and Galloway the Wauchope Water rises in headwaters to the west of Langholm. It flows northeastwards to join the River Esk in Langholm.

Waughslea *Dumfries and Galloway* A locality in southeast Dumfries and Galloway, Waughslea lies 4 miles (6.5 km) northeast of Kirkpatrick Fleming.

Waulkmill Bay *Orkney* A large sandy bay on the south coast of the Orkney Mainland, Waulkmill Bay lies to the east of Ve Ness.

Waverley Station *City of Edinburgh* The principal railway station in Edinburgh, Waverley Station lies in the heart of the city beneath the North Bridge and extends from Waverley Bridge in the west to Calton Hill in the east. Covering an area of 10 ha (24 acres), with a 5-ha (12-acre) glass roof, Waverley is the second-largest station in Britain. It was built originally as three separate stations in the 1840s on the site of the former Nor' Loch which had been drained in the 18th century and was named after Sir Walter Scott's first historical novel (1814). The present structure dates from 1868, when the North British Railway amalgamated the three stations.

Weather Ness *Orkney* A headland in the Orkney Islands, Weather Ness extends into Rapness Sound at the southeast end of the island of Westray, 2 miles (3 km) southeast of Stanger Head.

Weaver's Cottage, the *Renfrewshire* Located in the

village of Kilbarchan, 2 miles (3 km) west of Johnstone, the Weaver's Cottage is a museum dedicated to the handloom weavers who worked in the village during the 19th century. A typical weaver's cottage, it is furnished with period fittings, and houses the last working loom of more than 800 that were at work in the village in the 1830s. The property was acquired by the National Trust for Scotland in 1954.

Weaver's Point *Western Isles* A headland with a lighthouse on the northeast coast of North Uist in the Outer Hebrides, Weaver's Point extends into the Minch on the north side of the mouth of Loch na Madadh.

Wedder Holm *Shetland* A small, uninhabited island in the Shetland Islands, Wedder Holm lies off the southeast coast of the island of Uyea.

Wedderlairs *Aberdeenshire* The settlement of Wedderlairs is located a mile (1.5 km) northwest of Tarves in central Aberdeenshire.

Weem *Perth and Kinross* A settlement in Strathtay, central Perth and Kinross, Weem lies to the north of the River Tay, a mile (1.5 km) northwest of Aberfeldy. The old parish church of Weem now forms the Menzies Mausoleum, and the Weem Hotel boasts associations with the 18th-century military road-builder General Wade. To the west of the village is 16th-century Castle Menzies, restored by the Clan Menzies Society from the 1960s.

Weisdale *Shetland* A district of central Mainland Shetland, Weisdale lies at the head of Weisdale Voe, which receives the Burn of Weisdale. The centre of the community lies 11 miles (18 km) north of Lerwick. Formerly a crofting area, it was transformed in the 1970s by North Sea oil housing. Weisdale was the birthplace in 1786 of John Clunies Ross, who became 'king' of the Cocos Islands in the Indian Ocean. At Kergord near the head of the voe stands the largest plantation of trees in the Shetland Islands.

Well of the Lecht, the *Moray* A white stone plaque erected in 1754 records the fact that five companies of the 33rd Regiment built the military road 'from here to the Spey'. The plaque is located above a natural spring by the A939 Cock Bridge to Tomintoul road, about a mile (1.5 km) north of the Lecht summit.

Wells of the Rees, the *Dumfries and Galloway* A locality on the Southern Upland Way in Dumfries and Galloway, The Wells of the Rees lie to the east of the Tarf Water at the southern foot of Craigairie Fell. Situated on an old pilrimage route to Whithorn, the three stone-capped wells probably have some religious significance.

Wellbank *Angus* A village of southern Angus, Wellbank is located 2 miles (3 km) north of the boundary with Dundee and a similar distance southwest of Monikie. Flax spinning was once an important industry, but more recently quarrying provided significant employment. Wellbank expanded greatly during the 20th century with the building of public housing.

Welldale *Dumfries and Galloway* A locality in Annandale, Welldale forms a western suburb of the town of Annan on the River Annan.

Wells of Ythan *Aberdeenshire* A village in the Strathbogie district of western Aberdeenshire, Wells of Ythan lies at the source of the River Ythan, 8 miles (13 km) southwest of Turriff. A mile (1.5 km) to the east are the remains of a Roman marching camp.

Wellwood *Fife* A northern suburb of Dunfermline in western Fife, Wellwood lies to the west of the Town Loch on the A823 heading northwards. A community centre and playing fields lie adjacent to the Canmore Golf Course.

Wemyss Bay *Inverclyde* A dormitory village in the Cunninghame dstrict of Inverclyde, Wemyss Bay lies on the coast of the Firth of Clyde 8 miles (13 km) southwest of Greenock and 31 miles (50 km) west of Glasgow. It developed from 1865 as a resort settlement following the opening of a railway terminal and pier to serve steamer services to Arran and Bute, and later to Ardrishaig and Tarbert. In 1903, the station was rebuilt to elegant designs by James Miller and Donald Mathieson. Part of Anthony Trollope's novel *Barchester Towers* (1857) was written at nearby Castle Wemyss, a 19th-century mansion.

Wemyss Caves *Fife* A series of natural caves in sandstone cliffs on the north shore of the Firth of Forth, Wemyss Caves lie to the northeast of East Wemyss. Some of the caves contain notable examples of Pictish art dating from the 1st millennium AD. Those containing carved artwork include the Court Cave, Dovecot Cave, Jonathan's Cave (Factor's Cave) and the Sliding or Sloping Cave. First described by obstetrician Professor James Young Simpson who explored the caves in 1865, some of the carvings were illustrated in the second edition of John Stuart's *Sculptured Stones of Scotland* (1867).

Wemyss Point *Inverclyde* A headland on the Inverclyde coast of the Firth of Clyde, Wemyss Point extends into the firth to the north of Wemyss Bay.

West Affric *Highland* An area of wild and rugged landscapes extending over an area of 3642 ha (9000 acres) to the west of Loch Affric and 22 miles (35 km) east of Kyle of Lochalsh, West Affric was acquired by the National Trust for Scotland in 1993. It adjoins the Trust's Kintail and Glomach properties to the west and includes east–west pathways once used by drovers travelling from Skye to the markets of Dingwall. There is a youth hostel at Alltbeithe and a bothy at Camban.

West Arthurlie *East Renfrewshire* West Arthurlie is a suburb of Barrhead in East Renfrewshire.

West Barns *East Lothian* A small village in East Lothian, West Barns lies a mile (1.5 km) west of Dunbar and immediately southwest of Belhaven.

West Burra *Shetland* One of two long green islands in the Shetland Islands known as the Burras, West Burra lies to the west of the south Mainland of Shetland and has an area of 790 ha (1952 acres). Road bridges link West Burra with East Burra and Trondra, the island's main settlements being located at Bridge End and the fishing port of Hamnavoe. At Papil in the south stand the ruins of St Laurence's Church, in whose churchyard have been found several Pictish sculptured stones, including the famous Papil Stone.

West Burra Firth *Shetland* An inlet on a western arm of Mainland Shetland, West Burra Firth opens out into St Magnus Bay, 4 miles (6.5 km) east of Melby. The settlement of West Burrafirth, with a pier built in the 1980s, lies to the east of the inlet, and there are several Iron Age brochs and prehistoric remains in the vicinity. There is a ferry link to the island of Papa Stour.

West Calder *West Lothian* Located in an upland area 16 miles (26 km) southwest of Edinburgh, West Calder originally developed as a roadside hamlet but in the 19th

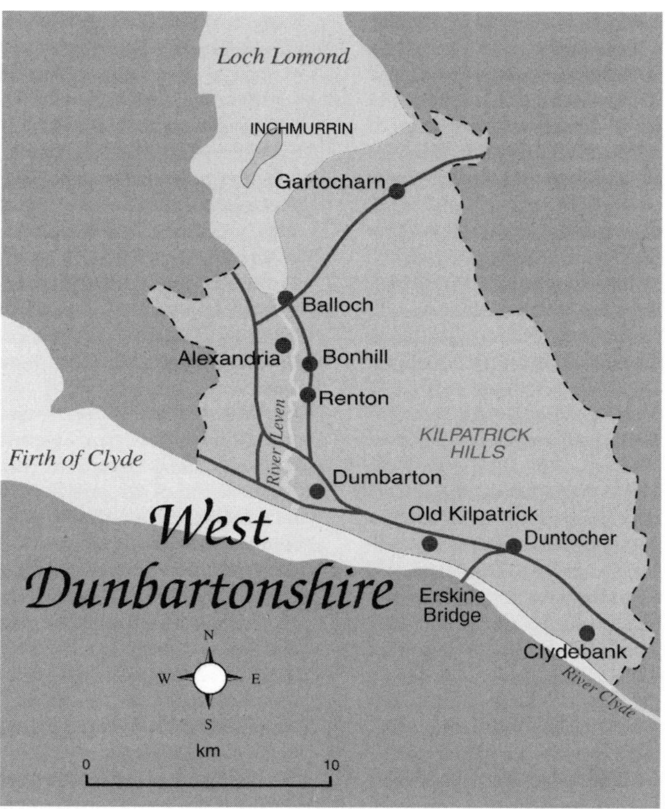

century expanded as a centre of the oil-shale industry. In the 20th century textile, civil-engineering, road-transport and construction industries were attracted to the village.

West Canisbay *Highland* A settlement close to the north coast of Caithness, West Canisbay lies to the west of Canisbay and 2 miles (3 km) west of John o' Groats.

West Croachy *Highland* A settlement to the east of Loch Ness, West Croachy lies adjacent to East Croachy, 5 miles (8 km) southeast of Dores.

West Dunbartonshire *Area: 176 sq. km (68 sq. miles)* A local government area in central Scotland, West Dunbartonshire lies to the northwest of Glasgow between Loch Lomond and the River Clyde. Formerly comprising the districts of Dumbarton and Clydebank, its chief settlements are Dumbarton (administrative centre), Alexandria, Balloch and Bonhill which lie in the Vale of Leven, and Clydebank, Old Kilpatrick and Bowling which lie on the northwestern periphery of Greater Glasgow. The River Leven flows south from Loch Lomond to the Clyde, and the Kilpatrick Hills rise in a series of lava flows to the north of Old Kilpatrick. The Erskine Bridge spans the River Clyde linking West Dunbartonshire to Renfrewshire, and in the north is the southwest tip of the Loch Lomond and the Trossachs National Park.

West Dunnet *Highland* A small settlement in northeast Caithness, West Dunnet overlooks Dunnet Bay, a half-mile (1 km) northwest of Dunnet.

West End *South Lanarkshire* A settlement in Clydesdale, West End lies to the north of the River Clyde, a mile (1.5 km) west of Carnwath and 2 miles (3 km) north of Carstairs Junction.

West Gerinish *Western Isles* A crofting township in the Outer Hebrides, West Gerinish (Gael: *Geirninis*) lies on the south side of Loch Bee at the northern end of South Uist.

West Highland Railway Line A scenic railway line 140 miles (225 km) in length, the West Highland Line links Craigendoran (near Helensburgh) with Mallaig via Rannoch Moor and Fort William. The line, which posed considerable engineering problems during its construction, comprises 350 viaducts and several tunnels. The West Highland Line was constructed in two phases by Sir Robert McAlpine (1847–1934), who used concrete, a novel material at the time. The section from Fort William to Craigendoran was built in 1889–94, and the extension to Mallaig was begun in 1897 and opened in 1901. The most significant engineering works are the Glenfinnan Viaduct (380 m/418 yd), the Rannoch Viaduct (208 m/227 yd) and the Loch Treig Tunnel (127 m/139 yd). The railway brought new industries to the West Highlands, and accessibility permitted easier transportation of fish and agricultural produce to the markets of Glasgow. Closure was proposed in 1963, but the line survived as an important scenic route for tourists and railway enthusiasts who occasionally travel on steam-hauled services.

West Highland Way, the A long-distance walking route opened in 1980, the West Highland Way extends 95 miles (152 km) from Milngavie in the south to the foot of Ben Nevis just north of Fort William. The route follows old drove roads, coaching routes and military roads built by General Wade in the 18th century, passing along the east side of Loch Lomond.

West Hill *East Lothian/Scottish Borders* A hill straddling the border between East Lothian and Scottish Borders, West Hill rises to 451 m (1479 ft) at the western end of the Lammermuir Hills, 4 miles (6.5 km) southeast of Fala.

West Kilbride *North Ayrshire* A small town in the Cunninghame district of North Ayrshire, West Kilbride lies a mile (1.5 km) east of Seamill and 4 miles (6.5 km) northwest of Ardrossan on the Firth of Clyde. It developed as a weaving village in the 18th century and became a dormitory settlement after the arrival of the railway in 1878. Its mild climate and fine views have made West Kilbride a popular place to retire to. To the west are 14th-century Portencross Castle (featured on the BBC Television series *Restoration* in 2004) and an Iron Age fort, and to the northwest is the Hunterston Nuclear Power Station. There is a museum and 18-hole golf course nearby.

West Kip *Midlothian* A summit of the Pentland Hills, West Kip rises to 550 m (1804 ft) 3 miles (5 km) north of Carlops and 3 miles (5 km) west of Penicuik.

West Linga *Shetland* An uninhabited island in the Shetland Islands with an area of 127 ha (314 acres), West Linga lies between the northeastern coastline of the Shetland Mainland, from which it is separated by the Lunning Sound, and the island of Whalsay, from which it is separated by the Linga Sound.

West Linton *Scottish Borders* A picturesque dormitory village in the southeastern foothills of the Pentland Hills, West Linton lies on the Lyne Water, a tributary of the Tweed, 15 miles (24 km) southwest of Edinburgh. Known as Lyntoun Roderyck until the 12th century and as Lintoun until the 19th century, when 'West' was added, it was the birthplace of Bernard of Lintoun who drafted the Declaration of Arbroath in the 14th century. One of the oldest market settlements in Scotland, it was the scene of large sheep markets and in the 17th century was associated with silver and lead mining as well as stone carving largely created by local laird James Gifford. The village was served by a railway between 1864 and 1933 and is now a conservation area. An annual celebration held in June is associated with the old horsemen's mutual aid society, the Whipmen, founded in 1803.

West Loch Roag *Western Isles* A large sea loch on the west coast of the Isle of Lewis in the Outer Hebrides, West Loch Roag is separated from East Loch Roag by the island of Great Bernera. Islands in the loch include Pabay Mòr, Vacsay, Vuia Beg, Vuia Mòr and Floday. The long narrow Little Loch Roag opens into the loch from the south.

West Loch Tarbert *Argyll and Bute* A sea loch in Argyll and Bute, West Loch Tarbert is separated from East Loch Tarbert by a narrow isthmus linking Knapdale to the northern end of the Kintyre peninsula. The settlement of West Tarbert lies at its head. It was here in 1098 that, according to legend, Magnus Barelegs, son of King Olaf of Norway, had his men drag his ship across the isthmus, thereby claiming Kintyre as an island and therefore a Viking possession.

West Loch Tarbert *Western Isles* A sea loch in the Outer Hebrides, West Loch Tarbert forms a broad inlet almost separating South Harris from North Harris. It is separated from East Loch Tarbert by a narrow isthmus on which stands the village of Tarbert. The islands of Soay Mòr, Soay Beg and Isay lie at the mouth of the loch, which is sheltered in the southwest by Taransay.

West Lomond *Fife* The highest summit in the Lomond Hills, West Lomond rises to 522 m (1712 ft) 3 miles (5 km) south of Strathmiglo and 4 miles (6.5 km) west of Falkland. Its rounded top forms the remains of a volcanic plug dating from the Carboniferous period.

West Lothian *Area: 428 sq. km (165 sq. miles)* A local government area in central Scotland, West Lothian lies to

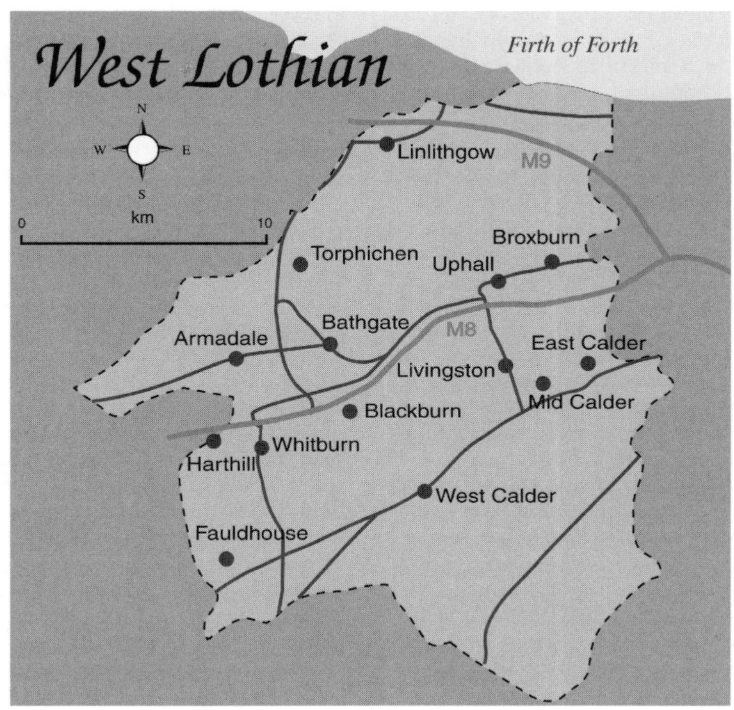

the west of Edinburgh and east of Falkirk, with a short coastline on the Firth of Forth. Traversed from east to west by the M8, it also lies adjacent to Scottish Borders, North Lanarkshire and South Lanarkshire, and rises from the coast to uplands which include the Bathgate Hills and part of the Pentland Hills. Most of the area is underlain by Carboniferous sedimentary rocks which include a large shale-oil field greatly exploited in the 19th and early 20th centuries, and large red shale bings dominate the landscape around Broxburn, Livingston and West Calder. The west-central band of sedimentary and basalt rocks supplies silica sand, while the area to the west around Armadale and Whitburn lies within the Central Scotland coalfield. The chief rivers and waterways are the River Almond, River Avon, Niddry Burn and Union Canal. Two-thirds of West Lothian are agricultural, and its chief settlements are Bathgate, Armadale, Whitburn, Mid Calder, West Calder, Broxburn and the new town of Livingston (administrative centre). The region has attracted inward investment from world-leading hi-tech firms and has industrial estates catering for a wide range of small- and medium-sized businesses that have easy access to Edinburgh Airport. Historic monuments include Cairnpapple Hill, Torphichen Preceptory, the Binns and Linlithgow Palace, the birthplace of Mary, Queen of Scots (1542–87). Formerly known as Linlithgowshire, West Lothian became a district of the larger Lothian Region in 1975. In 1996 its status as a unitary authority was restored as the 20th-largest of the 32 local government areas.

West Monar Forest *Highland* A deer forest in Ross and Cromarty, the West Monar Forest lies at the head of Loch Monar and includes the peaks of Lurg Mhòr, Bidean a' Choire Sheasgaich, Beinn Tharsuinn, Sgurr Choinnich and Sgurr a' Chaorachain.

West Morriston *Scottish Borders* A small settlement to the east of the Lauderdale district of Scottish Borders, West Morriston lies 3 miles (5 km) southwest of Gordon. Legerwood Hill rises to 281 m (922 ft) to the northwest.

West Ness *Fife* A rocky headland in the East Neuk of Fife, West Ness looks out onto the Firth of Forth to the southwest of Crail.

West Pilton *City of Edinburgh* A residential district of northern Edinburgh, West Pilton lies to the north of Ferry Road between Pilton and Muirhouse. Public housing was first built here 1936–7 but not completed until the mid-1950s. The area has been the subject of urban renewal since the mid-1980s.

West Port *Fife* The West Port or entry to the ancient burgh of St Andrews dates from 1589 and is the best example of its kind in Scotland. Situated at the west end of South Street, it comprises a central archway flanked by semi-octagonal 'rounds'. It was reconstructed 1843–5 with the addition of relief panels on either side carrying the arms of the city and of David I (1084–1153).

West Reef *Argyll and Bute* A small group of rocky outliers in the Inner Hebrides, the West Reef lies to the west of the Torran Rocks, just southwest of the Ross of Mull.

West Saltoun *East Lothian* A dormitory village to the west of its near neighbour East Saltoun, West Saltoun lies to the east of the Birns Water, 2 miles (3 km) southeast of Pencaitland. The village was served by a branch-line railway until 1933, the former line now serving as a cycle track. Saltoun Hall, a half-mile (1 km) to the north, was built in Gothic style in 1817 by William Burn.

West Sandwick, Holm of *Shetland* A small uninhabited island in the Shetland Islands, the Holm of West Sandwick lies in the Sound of Yell a half-mile (1 km) west of the headland of the Ness of West Sandwick.

West Sandwick, Ness of *Shetland* A headland on the west coast of the island of Yell in the Shetland Islands, the Ness of West Sandwick extends into the Sound of Yell a mile (1.5 km) south of West Sandwick Bay.

West Tarbert *Argyll and Bute* A small hamlet at the north of the Kintyre peninsula, West Tarbert lies near the head of West Loch Tarbert, a mile (1.5 km) southwest of Tarbert.

West Tofts *Perth and Kinross* A locality in central Perth and Kinross, West Tofts lies to the west of the River Tay, a mile (1.5 km) to the north of the village of Stanley.

West Voe *Shetland* A body of water in the Shetland Islands, West Voe separates the islands of West Burra and East Burra.

West Voe of Sumburgh *Shetland* A bay at the southern tip of Mainland Shetland, West Voe of Sumburgh lies between the two peninsulas that terminate in the Ness of Burgi and Sumburgh Head. The archaeological site at Jarlshof lies on its sandy eastern shore.

West Water *Angus* A river in the Braes of Angus, the West Water rises in headstreams between Glen Esk and Glen Clova. It flows east and southeast to join the River North Esk at Stracathro.

West Wemyss *Fife* A village on the north shore of the Firth of Forth, West Wemyss lies 2 miles (3 km) northeast of Kirkcaldy. Created a burgh of barony in 1511, the 'Haven Town of Wemyss' developed first as a port with salt pans and later as a mining settlement. It was designated a conservation area in 1985 and has many picturesque buildings, including an 18th-century Tolbooth, Wemyss Castle (*c*.1420) and many salters' and colliers' houses.

Wester, Loch of *Highland* A small loch in northeast Caithness, the Loch of Wester lies 6 miles (10 km) northwest of Wick. The waters of the Burn of Lyth flow through the loch before emptying into Sinclair's Bay.

Wester Balgedie *Perth and Kinross* A commuter village in Perth and Kinross, Wester Balgedie (formerly Meikle or Mickle Balgedie) lies 4 miles (6.5 km) east of Kinross with views over Loch Leven. It is a nucleated settlement, formerly an agricultural and weaving fermetoun that for the most part sits off the main road to Kinross. At a fork in the road stands the Balgedie Toll Tavern, which dates from the early 19th century.

Wester Craiglockhart Hill *City of Edinburgh* A hill in Edinburgh, Wester Craiglockhart Hill rises to 175 m (575 ft) 2.5 miles (4 km) southwest of the city centre. On the hill are the Craiglockhart Golf Course and the Craiglockhart Campus of Napier University, previously the Craiglockhart College of Education and originally built as the Craiglockhart Hydropathic Institution. On the summit there are the remains of an Iron Age fort that was largely destroyed when gun emplacements were erected during World War I.

Wester Fearn Burn *Highland* A stream in Easter Ross, the Wester Fearn Burn rises in the foothills of Meall Bhenneit and flows northeast for 7 miles (11 km) to empty into the Dornoch Firth at Wester Fearn Point, 3 miles (5 km) southeast of Bonar Bridge.

Wester Fintray *Aberdeenshire* A small settlement in eastern Aberdeenshire, Wester Fintray lies on the northern bank of the River Don, a mile (1.5 km) east of Kintore.

Wester Hailes *City of Edinburgh* A modern residential district of southwest Edinburgh, Wester Hailes lies to the east of the A720 city bypass. Its public housing was erected in the late 1960s. In the 1990s part of the route of the Union Canal filled in during the construction of the estate was restored.

Wester Hoevdi *Shetland* A headland on the west coast of the island of Foula in the Shetland Islands, Wester Hoevdi extends into the sea below The Sneug, 3 miles (5 km) west of the settlement of Ham.

Wester Newburn *Fife* A settlement in eastern Fife, Wester Newburn lies to the east of Largo Law on the A915, 3 miles (5 km) northeast of Lower Largo.

Wester Quarff *Shetland* A small settlement on the west coast of the Shetland Mainland, Wester Quarff lies on the West Voe of Quarff, a small inlet of the Clift Sound, a mile (1.5 km) southwest of Easter Quarff and 7 miles (11 km) southwest of Lerwick. To the southwest lie the islands of East Burra and West Burra.

Wester Ross *Highland* A rugged and sparsely populated mountainous area of the North West Highlands with a deeply indented coastline, Wester Ross comprises the western part of the former county of Ross and Cromarty. It stretches westwards from a point 9 miles (14 km) northwest of Dingwall and includes Beinn Eighe National Nature Reserve, Kinlochewe Forest and the settlements of Ullapool, Poolewe, Aultbea and Dundonnell.

Westerdale *Highland* A small scattered settlement in Caithness, Westerdale lies on the River Thurso, 5 miles (8 km) south of Halkirk. Buildings of interest include 18th-century Dale House with walled garden and dovecote, Westerdale Free Churh (1844) and Westerdale Bridge (1834).

Western Isles (Na h-Eileanan Siar, Na H-Eileanan an Iar) *Area: 3080 sq. km (1189 sq. miles)* The windswept Western Isles, or Outer Hebrides, comprise the 'long island' of Lewis and Harris and islands to the south including North Uist, South Uist and Barra. Here the topography is shaped by the underlying ancient Lewisian gneiss, much of which is covered with a thin layer of peat that is still used as a major source of fuel for

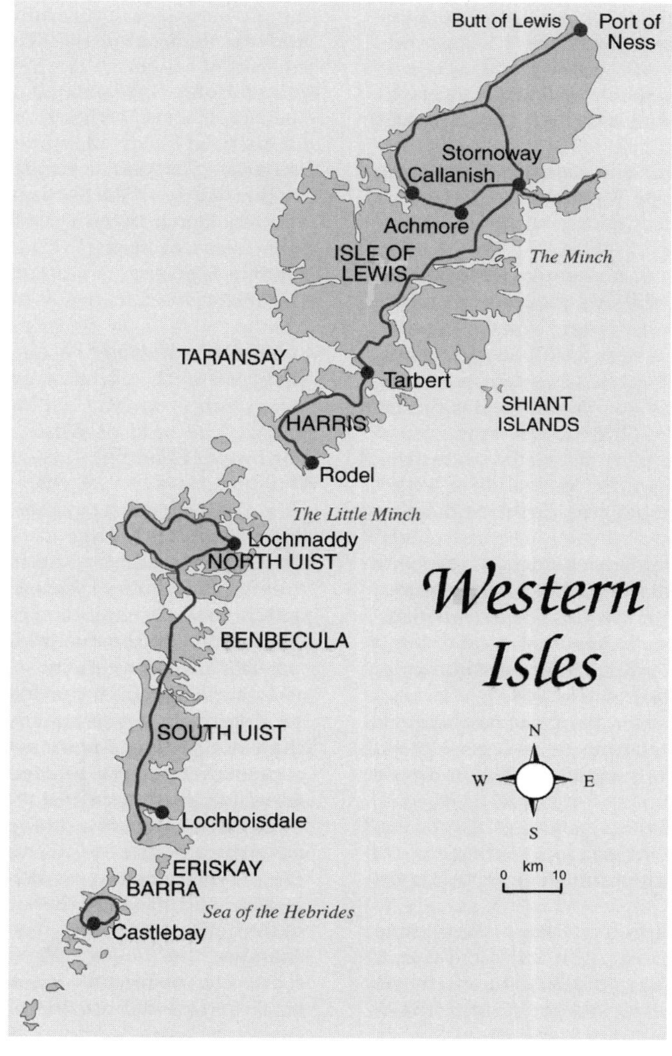

winter fire. Nearly half the islands' households live on croft land, and farming, fishing, fish farming and the manufacture of Harris tweed are the chief economic activities. Some 68 per cent of the people speak the Gaelic language. The main towns and ferry ports are Stornoway (administrative centre), Tarbert, Leverburgh, Lochmaddy, Lochboisdale and Castlebay. The local government area is administered by the Western Isles Council (Comhairle nan Eilean Siar).

Westfield *Fife* An industrial location in western Fife, Westfield lies 1.5 miles (2.5 km) east of Ballingry and 2 miles (3 km) northwest of Auchterderran, close to the border with Perth and Kinross. A former opencast coal mine here was the deepest excavation of its kind in the UK at 215 m (705 ft). The Westfield site has developed as an energy park with a biomass plant producing electricity and fertiliser from poultry litter. A 400-megawatt gas-fired power station is also being constructed there.

Westfield *North Lanarkshire* A western suburb of Cumbernauld, Westfield lies 2 miles (3 km) west of the town centre.

Westfield *West Lothian* A small settlement in West Lothian, Westfield lies 3 miles (5 km) northwest of Bathgate at the junction of the Logie Water with the River Avon. It developed in association with a paper mill established in the early 19th century and a railway branch line opened in 1855. A railway viaduct crosses the Avon close by, and to the south is the 14th-century Bridge Castle.

Westfields of Rattray *Perth and Kinross* A locality in eastern Perth and Kinross, Westfields of Rattray is situated on the River Ericht at the northern edge of Rattray.

Westhill *Aberdeenshire* A commuter settlement in eastern Aberdeenshire, Westhill lies 3 miles (5 km) east of the Loch of Skene and 6 miles (10 km) west of Aberdeen. It was created in 1968 as a new town and was rapidly developed in the 1970s to meet housing demand during the early days of North Sea oil development. It expanded to include the settlement of Elrick and became a centre for construction, timber and oil-related industries. There is an 18-hole golf course as well as a library, schools, swimming pool, shopping centre and tennis and bowling facilities.

Westhill *Highland* A commuter settlement to the south of the Moray Firth, Westhill lies 3 miles (5 km) southeast of Inverness and 2 miles (3 km) southwest of Culloden.

Westmuir *Angus* A village in Angus, Westmuir lies 2 miles (3 km) southwest of Kirriemuir, straddling the A926 from Kirriemuir to Blairgowrie.

Westport *Argyll and Bute* A locality at the northern end of Machrihanish Bay, an inlet on the west coast of the Kintyre peninsula, Westport lies 5 miles (8 km) northwest of Campbeltown.

Westquarter *Falkirk* A southern suburb of the town of Falkirk, Westquarter lies 2 miles (3 km) southeast of the town centre. Buildings of interest include a 17th-century dovecote.

Westray *Orkney* An island in the Orkney Island group, Westray has an area of 4792 ha (11,841 acres) and rises to a height of 169 m (554 ft) at Fitty Hill. Known as the 'Queen of the North Isles', Westray has a diverse landscape that includes the Noup Cliffs Nature Reserve. Automated in 1964, the Noup Head lighthouse was the first to use a system of mercury flotation in the revolving carriage. The chief settlement of Westray is Pierowall, which has a ferry link with Papa Westray and a heritage centre with a permanent exhibition on the island's history. The main ferry terminal is at Rapness in the far south, and at the northern tip of the island is an airstrip (Westray Airport) at Aikerness with links to Kirkwall. Buildings of historic interest include St Mary's Parish Church, the 16th-century Balfour stronghold of Noltland Castle, Cross Kirk and Norse settlement near Tuquoy, and the Knowe o' Burristae Broch. The island's population declined from 2200 in 1881 to 563 in 2001, most of its inhabitants now engaging in farming, fishing and the production of knitwear.

Westray Firth *Orkney* A body of water in the Orkney Islands, the Westray Firth is bounded by Westray to the north, Faray and Eday to the east, Egilsay and Rousay to the south and by open water to the west.

Westrigg *West Lothian* A small village in West Lothian, Westrigg lies just east of Blackridge, close to the border with North Lanarkshire and 2 miles (3 km) north of Harthill.

Westruther *Scottish Borders* A remote upland village on the southern edge of the Lammermuir Hills, Westruther lies near the head of the Blackadder Water, 7 miles (11 km) east of Lauder.

Wether Holm *Shetland* An uninhabited island in the Shetland Islands, Wether Holm lies off the east coast of the Shetland Mainland, 2 miles (3 km) southeast of Firth.

Wethersta *Shetland* A hamlet on the west coast of the Delting district of the Shetland Mainland, Wethersta lies on a headland between Busta Voe and Olna Firth, 2 miles (3 km) south of Brae.

Weydale *Highland* A scattered settlement in northern Caithness, Weydale lies 3 miles (5 km) southeast of Thurso.

Whale Firth *Shetland* A long narrow sea inlet on the west coast of the island of Yell in the Shetland Islands, Whale Firth, with Mid Yell Voe, almost splits the island in two. The head of Whale Firth lies a mile (1.5 km) northwest of Mid Yell.

Whaligoe *Highland* A narrow cleft enclosed by steep cliffs between two headlands, Whaligoe ('whale geo' or 'inlet of whales') forms an inlet on the east coast of Caithness, 6 miles (10 km) northeast of Lybster and 7 miles (11 km) south of Wick. From the cliff top 365 steps, built in the 17th century and representing each day of the year, descend to the inlet which was a landing place for fishermen. Boats were winched up to the top of the cliffs and lashed down in bad weather. On the cliff top stands a 19th-century herring station.

Whalsay *Shetland* Known as the 'bonny isle', Whalsay is a peat-covered, loch-studded island in the Shetland Islands, situated to the east of the Mainland of Shetland. It rises to a height of 119 m (390 ft) at Ward of Clett and has an area of 2111 ha (5214 acres). Its population largely earns a livelihood from fishing. The island's port is located at Symbister in the south and its airstrip at Skaw in the north.

Whangie, the *Stirling* A rock feature comprising a spectacular 10-m/33-ft-high and 3-m/10-ft-wide slab of basalt separated from the adjacent cliff by a narrow chasm, the Whangie (meaning 'cut' or 'slice') is located on the north-facing scarp slope of the Kilpatrick Hills in southwest Stirling Council area. Older blocks of stone, in various stages of collapse, occur on the downslope side of the slab, providing evidence of a landslide produced by the sliding of the surface basalt rocks over the underlying sandstones. Local legend attributes these features to the devil, who is reputed to have sliced the chasm with his tail while flying by. The Whangie can be accessed from the Auchineden (Queen's View) car park on the A809.

Wharral, Loch *Angus* A small corrie lochan in the southern Grampians, Loch Wharral lies on the upper slopes of Ben Tirran in Glen Clova.

Whauphill *Dumfries and Galloway* A village in the Machars district of southwest Dumfries and Galloway, Whauphill lies at a road junction 4 miles (6.5 km) southwest of Wigtown.

Whim *Scottish Borders* A small hamlet in Peeblesshire, Whim lies close to the Midlothian border, 2 miles (3 km) southwest of Leadburn. Whim House, now a retirement home, was built by the Duke of Argyll in the 18th century.

Whing Burn *Dumfries and Galloway* A stream of Nithsdale in Dumfries and Galloway, the Whing Burn rises on Weltrees Tappin, nearly 4 miles (6.5 km) southwest of Sanquhar. It flows northeastwards to join the Euchan Water, a tributary of the River Nith.

Whinnieliggate *Dumfries and Galloway* A hamlet in central Dumfries and Galloway, Whinnieliggate lies between the Balgreddan Burn and the B727 from Castle Douglas to Kirkcudbright.

Whinnyfold *Aberdeenshire* A small settlement on the coast of Aberdeenshire, Whinnyfold lies a mile (1.5 km) west of The Skares and 2 miles (3 km) south of the village of Cruden Bay.

Whinyeon, Loch *Dumfries and Galloway* A loch in Glengap Forest, south-central Dumfries and Galloway, Loch Whinyeon lies 3 miles (5 km) northeast of Gatehouse of Fleet in the shadow of Bengray.

Whita Hill *Dumfries and Galloway* A hill to the east of Langholm in eastern Dumfries and Galloway, Whita Hill rises to a height of 355 m (1163 ft). Nearby is a memorial to the poet Hugh MacDiarmid (1892–1978).

Whitburn *West Lothian* One of the principal towns of West Lothian, Whitburn is situated on the River Almond and to the south of the M8, 8 miles (13 km) southwest of Livingston. Originally a crossroads settlement, it developed as a coal- and iron-mining town in the 19th and 20th centuries, particularly in association with the Polkemmet Colliery, sunk in 1915 and operated from 1922 until the mid-1980s. The Baillie family, founders of the Baillie Institute community centres, were associated with the now demolished Polkemmet House. There is a nine-hole golf course at nearby Polkemmet Country Park, and notable buildings include the parish church (1729), the Burgh Hall (*c.*1830) and Whitburn Academy (1967). In the churchyard there is a memorial to Elizabeth Burns, daughter of the poet Robert Burns.

White Bridge *Perth and Kinross* A locality between Loch Tummel and Loch Tay, White Bridge lies 3 miles (5 km) to the south of Tummel Bridge on the line of General Wade's 18th-century military road.

White Cart Water The White Cart Water rises on the East Renfrewshire and South Lanarkshire border and flows through Busby, Cathcart, Pollokshaws and Pollok Country Park, before joining the Black Cart Water in Paisley. Between Eaglesham and Netherlee, the White Cart Water forms the boundary between East Renfrewshire and South Lanarkshire, and then East Renfrewshire and Glasgow City council areas.

White Caterthun *Angus* Described as one of the finest prehistoric ruins in Britain, the White Caterthun is an Iron Age hillfort located on the Hill of Menmuir, 5 miles (8 km) northwest of Brechin. It comprises a complex of defences representing several phases of development.

White Coomb *Dumfries and Galloway* A summit of the Moffat Hills, White Coomb rises to 822 m (2696 ft) 8 miles (13 km) northeast of Moffat.

White Esk *Dumfries and Galloway* A river of eastern Dumfries and Galloway, the White Esk rises on Ettrick Pen, 8 miles (13 km) east of Moffat. It flows generally southwards and in Castle O'er Forest is joined from the west by the Black Esk to form the main course of the River Esk, which flows through Langholm to the Solway Firth.

White Hart Inn *City of Edinburgh* Located in the Grassmarket in Edinburgh, the White Hart Inn first welcomed travellers in the early 18th century and claims to be the oldest public house in Edinburgh. Robert Burns stayed here in 1791 during his last visit to Edinburgh, and it was also visited by the Wordsworths in 1803. The building exhibits wallhead gables to the front and semi-octagonal stair towers to the rear.

White Hill of Vatsetter *Shetland* A hill on the Shetland island of Yell, the White Hill of Vatsetter rises to 32 m (105 ft) near the Gamla headland on the east coast of the island.

White Horse Close *City of Edinburgh* A picturesque close at the eastern end of the Royal Mile in the Old Town of Edinburgh, White Horse Close was from the 17th century the site of an inn that was the terminus of the coach service to London. Formerly the site of the Palace of Holyroodhouse stables, it may have been named after the favourite white mount of Mary, Queen of Scots. In 1745, Prince Charles Edward Stewart's officers were quartered here, and in 1889 the close was rebuilt to provide housing for working men. In 1961–4 the close was completely reconstructed in the vernacular style by Frank Mears and Partners. William Dick (1793–1866), founder of the Royal (Dick) School of Veterinary Science, was born in White Horse Close.

White Loch *Dumfries and Galloway* A loch in the Rhinns of Galloway, the White Loch lies 2 miles (3 km) east of Stranraer. It is separated from the Black Loch to the north by a narrow spit of land on which stand Lochinch Castle and the remains of Castle Kennedy.

White Loch *Dumfries and Galloway* A small loch in the Machars of Dumfries and Galloway, the White Loch lies by the Auchness Moss, 3 miles (5 km) south of Whauphill. Close by is Ravenstone Castle, built *c.*1560, a former stronghold of the Maclellans and later the Stewarts.

White Loch *Dumfries and Galloway* A small loch in southern Dumfries and Galloway, the White Loch is located to the north of Colvend, 1.25 miles (2 km) north of the Solway Firth coast and a similar distance northeast of Rockcliffe and the Rough Firth.

White Loch of Myrton *Dumfries and Galloway* A small loch in the Machars of Dumfries and Galloway, the White Loch of Myrton lies a mile (1.5 km) to the east of

Port William on the east coast of Luce Bay. Monreith House and Castle lie to the south.

White Ness *Shetland* A long narrow peninsula on the west coast of the Shetland Mainland, White Ness separates Whiteness Voe in the east from Stromness Voe in the west. There are the remains of an Iron Age broch and prehistoric standing stones.

White Water A headwater of the River South Esk in the southern Grampians, the White Water rises on the slopes of Tom Buidhe on the border between Angus and Aberdeenshire. It flows southeastwards through Glen Doll to join the River South Esk as Braedownie.

Whiteadder Water *Scottish Borders* Rising on the slopes of Clint Dods in the Lammermuir Hills, the Whiteadder Water flows southeastwards, passing through the Whiteadder Reservoir (opened 1968) and on through the eastern part of Scottish Borders, before emptying into the River Tweed near Berwick-upon-Tweed in England. On its course it passes the settlements of Cranshaws, Abbey St Bathans, Chirnside and Paxton.

Whitebridge *Highland* A settlement in northeast Caithness, Whitebridge lies on the northern trunk road (A836), 2 miles (3 km) southwest of the Castle of Mey and to the southwest of the Loch of Mey. Skarfskerry lies a mile (1.5 km) to the northwest.

Whitebridge *Highland* A hamlet in Stratherrick, Whitebridge lies at the confluence of the River Fechlin and Allt Breineag, 2.5 miles (4 km) southeast of Loch Ness.

Whitecraig *East Lothian* A former mining village in western East Lothian, Whitecraig lies 2 miles (3 km) south of Musselburgh and 6 miles (10 km) southeast of Edinburgh.

Whitecrook *Dumfries and Galloway* A locality in the Rhinns of Galloway, Whitecrook lies on the A75 trunk road nearly 2 miles (3 km) west of Glenluce.

Whitecross *Falkirk* A village in eastern Falkirk Council area, Whitecross is situated on the Manuel Burn 1.5 miles (2.5 km) west of Linlithgow between the line of the Edinburgh–Glasgow railway and the B825 Avonbridge–Linlithgow Bridge road. A Bernardine convent was established here in the 12th century, and in the 15th century Almond Castle was built nearby. The village developed in the early 20th century in association with coal mining and the manufacture of firebricks.

Whiteface *Highland* A scattered settlement in eastern Sutherland, Whiteface lies close to the north shore of the Dornoch Firth, 5 miles (8 km) west of Dornoch. Skibo Castle lies to the east.

Whitefaulds *South Ayrshire* Whitefaulds is a western suburb of the settlement of Maybole in South Ayrshire.

Whitefield Castle *Perth and Kinross* A ruined castle in Strath Ardle, eastern Perth and Kinross, Whitefield Castle is situated 9 miles (14 km) east-northeast of Pitlochry. It was built in 1577 by the Spalding family.

Whitefield Loch *Dumfries and Galloway* A small loch in southwest Dumfries and Galloway, Whitefield Loch lies 2 miles (3 km) southeast of Glenluce.

Whitehall *Orkney* The chief village and ferry port of the Orkney island of Stronsay, Whitehall is situated on the Grice Ness peninsula between Mill Bay and Papa Sound. Once a prosperous fishing settlement, it took its name from a house built in the 1670s by the privateer Patrick Fea.

Whitehills *Aberdeenshire* A coastal village in northwest Aberdeenshire, Whitehills lies 2 miles (3 km) northwest of Banff. It was founded in 1681 as a fishing village and developed for a while in association with a brick and tile works and whisky distilling. Whitehills harbour is popular for mooring yachts.

Whitehouse *Argyll and Bute* A small hamlet at the northern end of the Kintyre peninsula, Whitehouse lies on the south shore of West Loch Tarbert, 6 miles (10 km) southwest of Tarbert.

Whitehouse *Aberdeenshire* A roadside hamlet in the Howe of Alford, central Aberdeenshire, Whitehouse lies on the A944, 2 miles (3 km) southeast of Alford. It formerly lay on a railway line.

Whiteinch *Glasgow City* A suburb of Glasgow situated between Scotstoun and Partick, Whiteinch was originally an island or inch, connected to the north bank of the River Clyde by a silt causeway. In the 18th century it formed part of the farm of the Smiths of Jordanhill. Dredging of the River Clyde resulted in it being joined permanently to the river bank. The site was developed initially for industry and housing and later in the construction of roads approaching the Clyde Tunnel.

Whitekirk *East Lothian* A small kirkton settlement in East Lothian, Whitekirk lies 2.5 miles (4 km) north of East Linton. In the 13th century the site was developed as a pilgrimage resort drawing on the curative powers of the Holy Well of Our Lady, situated 200 m (220 yd) east of the parish church. Linked to Holyrood Abbey in Edinburgh, the shrine is said to have attracted over 15,000 pilgrims in 1413. James I placed the church under his personal protection and built hostels for the growing number of pilgrims. In 1338, the church was pillaged by Edward III's troops during their invasion of the Lothians. In 1453, the shrine was visited by Aeneas Silvius Piccolomini, an Italian diplomat on a mission to Scotland who later became Pope Pius II. James IV regularly made the journey to Whitekirk, but his son James V gave the site to the Sinclair family who built a rare example in Scotland of a tithe barn with stone from the former pilgrims' hostel. In 1678, the Covenanting preacher John Blackadder (1615–86) held his last coventicle on the hill behind Whitekirk Church. Following agricultural drainage in the 19th century, the holy well dried up and in 1914 suffragettes set fire to the church, which was subsequently restored by Sir Robert Lorimer.

Whitemill Point *Orkney* A headland on the north coast of the island of Sanday in the Orkney Islands, Whitemill Point lies at the western entrance to Otters Wick.

Whiteness Sands *Highland* A vast expanse of sandy beach on the south shore of the Dornoch Firth, the Whiteness Sands extend eastwards from the settlement of Tain to Inver Bay, encircling small islets including Innis Mhòr and Innis Bheag.

Whiten Head *Highland* A headland on the north coast of Sutherland, Whiten Head extends into the sea to the east of the entrance to Loch Eriboll, 6 miles (10 km) east of Durness.

Whiterashes *Aberdeenshire* A hamlet in the Formartine district of Aberdeenshire, Whiterashes lies at a road junction 3 miles (5 km) southeast of Oldmeldrum.

Whiterow *Highland* A hamlet in northeast Caithness, Whiterow lies a mile (1.5 km) to the southwest of Wick and a mile (1.5 km) to the northeast of Loch Hempriggs. The Castle of Old Wick lies to the southeast.

Whiteside *West Lothian* A settlement with an industrial estate in West Lothian, Whiteside lies a mile (1.5 km) to the southwest of Bathgate.

Whithorn *Dumfries and Galloway* A village in the Machars district of Galloway, Whithorn lies 15 miles (24 km) south of Wigtown. This ancient trading settlement came to be associated with St Ninian, who is said to have returned to Whithorn from Rome to establish a monastery and church known as *Candida Casa*. A major centre of pilgrimage for over 1100 years, a cathedral and priory were built here in the 12th century. It became a burgh in 1325 and was raised to the status of a royal burgh in 1511. Pilgrimages were banned in 1581 and Whithorn lost its religious significance. A museum opened in 1957 houses several early Christian stones, including the 7th-century St Peter Stone and the Latinus Stone (AD 450), said to be the oldest Christian monument in Scotland. Whithorn was the terminus of a railway from Newton Stewart that operated from 1877 to 1950.

Whiting Bay *North Ayrshire* A village on the east coast of the island of Arran, Whiting Bay lies 3 miles (5 km) south of Lamlash. The original crofting settlement on a raised beach at Kiscadale was cleared of its tenants in the 1830s, and in the years that followed Whiting Bay developed as a fishing village with a ferry link to Saltcoats on the Ayrshire coast. From 1860 a new ferry bringing tourists from Ardrossan encouraged the building of villas and holiday homes, and the laying out of an 18-hole golf course in 1895. Despite the closure of the pier in 1957, Whiting Bay continued to thrive as a tourist resort with a summer ferry service to Holy Island.

Whiting Ness *Angus* A headland on the North Sea coast of Angus, the red sandstone cliffs of Whiting Ness are located due northeast of Arbroath.

Whitletts *South Ayrshire* A suburb of Ayr, Whitletts lies to the northeast of the town centre.

Whitsome *Scottish Borders* A hamlet in the Berwickshire district of Scottish Borders, Whitsome lies between the River Tweed and the Whiteadder Water, 4 miles (6.5 km) south of Chirnside and 8 miles (13 km) southeast of Duns.

Whittingehame *East Lothian* A parish to the north of the Lammermuir Hills, Whittingehame lies to the east of Haddington and southwest of Dunbar. Drained by the Whittingehame Water, its most notable buildings are 15th-century Whittingehame Tower, Whittingehame Parish Church (1722) and Whittinghame House (1817). There are memorials in the church to Arthur James Balfour (1848–1930), owner of the Whittinghame Estate and British prime minister (1902–5).

Wiay *Highland* An uninhabited island in the Inner Hebrides, Wiay lies in Loch Bracadale off the west coast of the isle of Skye. Owned by the Clan Macleod, it has an area of 148 ha (366 acres). Last occupied in the 19th century, Wiay has two large herring gull colonies.

Wiay *Western Isles* Separated from the southeast coast of the island of Benbecula by Loch a' Laip, the uninhabited island of Wiay (Gael: *Fuidaigh*) has an area of 375 ha (927 acres). Rocky and barren, it rises to 102 m (334 ft).

Wick *Highland* A town and port on the east coast of Caithness, Wick lies on the Wick River where it enters Wick Bay, 21 miles (33 km) southeast of Thurso and 95 miles (153 km) north of Inverness. The name Wick or *vic* is Old Norse for 'bay'. A royal burgh from 1589, the ancient town grew up on the north bank of the Wick River, its street layout reflecting various attempts to bridge the river. The town's modern development began *c*.1805 when Thomas Telford, in the employ of the British Fisheries Society, began work on the building of a harbour and new town, Pultneytown, on the south side of the river. Pultneytown was eventually incorporated into Wick in 1902. Wick grew rapidly during the 19th century to become the largest herring-fishing port in Europe and was linked to Inverness by rail in 1874. Buildings of interest include the Bridge of Wick (1877), the Town Hall and Tolbooth (1828), the Old Parish Church (1830), Caithness General Hospital (1986), Wick Railway Station (1874), Lifeboat House (1915) and Wick Heritage Centre, which was opened by the Wick Society in 1981 and comprises a dwelling house, curing yard and cooperage. Wick Airport, 2 miles (3 km) north of the town centre, was opened in 1933. In addition to fishing, tourism, boat building, food processing and whisky distilling, Wick was noted for the production of glassware.

Wick River *Highland* A river in Caithness, the Wick River rises in Loch Watten and flows southeast for 10 miles (16 km) before emptying into Wick Bay at Wick.

Wide Firth *Orkney* A body of water in the Orkney Islands, the Wide Firth separates the Orkney Mainland from the island of Shapinsay to the northeast.

Wideford Hill *Orkney* Wideford Hill is the site of a prehistoric chambered tomb, situated at a height of 100 m (328 ft) above sea level, 2.5 miles (4 km) west of Kirkwall on Mainland Orkney. The cairn comprises a circular mound of stones with an entry passage leading to a main rectangular chamber and three subsidiary cells.

Widewall Bay *Orkney* A large bay in the Orkney Islands, Widewall Bay forms an inlet on the west coast of the island of South Ronaldsay. The settlements of Quindry and Herston lie on the bay.

Wife Geo *Highland* A small inlet on the northeast coast of Caithness, Wife Geo is located 3 miles (5 km) south of Duncansby Head.

Wigtown *Dumfries and Galloway* The county town of Wigtownshire until 1975, Wigtown lies just north of the River Bladnoch where it joins Wigtown Bay, 7 miles (11 km) south of Newton Stewart. A church was established

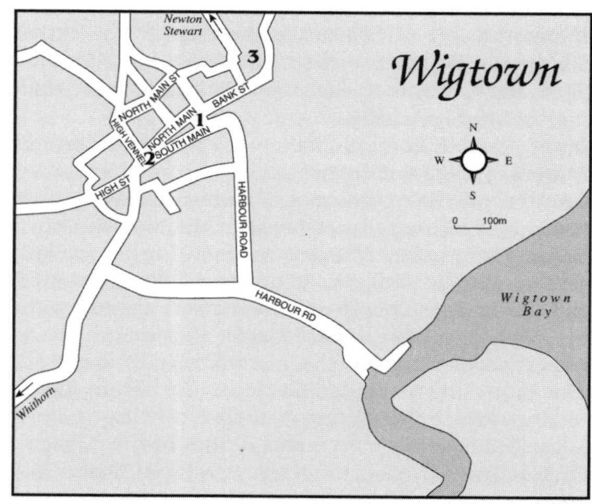

1 *County Buildings*
2 *Martyrs' Monument*
3 *Wigtown Parish Church*

here as early as the 6th century, and in the early 13th century Devorgilla Balliol founded a Dominican friary. Designated a royal burgh in 1292, Wigtown was the centre of a sheriffdom embracing west Galloway. Little remains of its royal castle. Wigtown's port silted up in the late 17th century. A new harbour was built in the late 18th century and the town developed in association with textile mills, whisky distilling and port trade. In 1998 Wigtown was launched as 'Wigtown Book Town' with numerous bookshops. There are two market crosses (1738, 1816), a fine French Gothic-style County Buildings (1863) and the remains of the pre-16th-century Old Parish Church. There is a museum, and nearby are the Torhousekie stone circle, Wigtown Bay Local Nature Reserve and the Galloway Forest Park.

Wigtown Bay *Dumfries and Galloway* An inlet on the north coast of the Solway Firth, Wigtown Bay forms a large bay receiving the River Cree, River Bladnoch and Water of Fleet. Its chief headlands are the Cairn Head and Meikle Ross.

Wigtown Sands *Dumfries and Galloway* A sandbank in Wigtown Bay, Dumfries and Galloway, Wigtown Sands lie to the east of Wigtown at the junction of the channels of the River Bladnoch and the River Cree.

Wigtownshire A former county in southwest Scotland, Wigtownshire was incorporated into Dumfries and Galloway in 1974. With an area of 1261 sq. km (487 sq. miles), it included the Rhinns of Galloway and the valleys of the Cree, Bladnoch and Luce rivers. Its chief towns were Wigtown (the former county town), Newton Stewart, Whithorn, Stranraer and Portpatrick.

Wildmanbridge *South Lanarkshire* A small settlement in Clydesdale, Wildmanbridge lies 2 miles (3 km) northwest of Carluke.

Wildshaw Hill *South Lanarkshire* A hill in South Lanarkshire, Wildshaw Hill rises to 374 m (1227 ft) 4 miles (6.5 km) southeast of Douglas.

Wilkhaven *Highland* A small settlement on the coast of Easter Ross, Wilkhaven lies on the Moray Firth a mile (1.5 km) south of Tarbat Ness.

Wilkieston *West Lothian* A village in West Lothian, Wilkieston lies to the north of the upper reaches of the Gogar Burn, 2 miles (3 km) southwest of Ratho and 3 miles (5 km) east of Livingston.

Willowbrae *City of Edinburgh* A suburb of the city of Edinburgh, Willowbrae lies to the west of Willowbrae Road and adjacent to Holyrood Park, a mile (1.5 km) southwest of Portobello.

Wilton *Scottish Borders* Wilton is a western suburb of Hawick in Scottish Borders.

Winchburgh *West Lothian* A dormitory village in West Lothian, Winchburgh lies between the M8 and M9, 3 miles (5 km) north of Broxburn and 6 miles (10 km) southeast of Linlithgow. It developed in association with its ancient church and in the 19th century with the opening of the Union Canal, the arrival of the railway, quarrying and the manufacture of shale oil. The 15th-century Niddry Castle of the Setons lies a mile (1.5 km) to the southeast, and a new village known as the Niddry Rows was created in 1901 by the Oakbank Oil Company. In 1960, the Niddry Castle Oil Works, the last to produce shale oil in Scotland, were closed leaving behind a landscape of shale-oil waste known as bings.

Windhill *Highland* A small settlement in Easter Ross, Windhill lies a mile (1.5 km) south of Muir of Ord and the same distance north of Beauly.

Windlestraw Law *Scottish Borders* The highest peak in the Moorfoot Hills, Windlestraw Law rises to 659 m (2162 ft) 4 miles (6.5 km) northeast of Innerleithen.

Windrow Burn *South Lanarkshire* A stream in South Lanarkshire, the Windrow Burn rises on Windrow Hill and flows south and east to join the Douglas Water a half-mile (1 km) southwest of Douglas.

Windy Gyle *Scottish Borders* A summit in the Cheviot Hills, Windy Gyle rises to 619 m (2030 ft) near the border with England, 15 miles (24 km) south of Coldstream.

Windy Standard *Dumfries and Galloway* A summit in the Galloway Hills, Dumfries and Galloway, Windy Standard rises to 698 m (2290 ft) to the northeast of Cairnsmore of Carsphairn, on the border with East Ayrshire. The hill is capped by one of the largest wind farms in Europe, extending over an area of 350 ha (865 acres) and comprising 36 turbines.

Windygates *Fife* A village in central Fife, Windygates lies to the north of the River Leven, between Markinch and the town of Leven. Situated at the junction of the A911, A915 and A916, Windygates was once an important staging post on the coach route linking north and central Fife with the Pettycur ferry across the Firth of Forth. Still a major road junction, the centre of the village is now bypassed by a dual carriageway. Windygates has haulage and fencing-supply industries. At nearby Cameron Bridge is a distillery established by the Haig family in the early 19th century.

Winless *Highland* A scattered settlement in northeast Caithness, Winless lies to the southeast of the Loch of Winless, 4 miles (6.5 km) northwest of Wick.

Winton House *East Lothian* A mansion house in East Lothian, Winton House lies a half-mile (1 km) north-northwest of Pencaitland. It has at its core Wintoun Castle, a 15th-century stronghold of the Seton family. Destroyed in 1544 by the Earl of Hertford during the 'Rough Wooing', the castle was reconstructed and extended for George, 8th Earl of Seton, in 1619 by architect William Wallace, Master Mason to James VI. Winton was extended to the north and west in the Gothic-baronial style by architect John Paterson in 1805. A fine example of Anglo-Scots Renaissance architecture, Winton House faces south onto a terraced garden.

Wishaw *North Lanarkshire* A town in Clydesdale, Wishaw lies 3 miles (5 km) southeast of Motherwell and 15 miles (24 km) southeast of Glasgow. Built on the line of a Roman road, the original weaving village of Wishawtoun developed in the 19th and 20th centuries in association with coal mining, iron smelting, whisky distilling and the manufacture of steel, lorries, clocks, rolling stock, sports goods and electronics. In 1920 Wishaw was incorporated with Motherwell as the burgh of Motherwell and Wishaw. The ironworks and steelworks had closed by 1992. Notable mansion houses nearby include Cambusnethan Priory (1819), Coltness House and Wishaw House, a seat of Lord Belhaven of Biel. The suburb of Gowkthrapple was developed in the 1970s.

Wiston *South Lanarkshire* Situated on the Garf Water, a tributary of the upper River Clyde, Wiston lies 7 miles (11 km) southwest of Biggar in South Lanarkshire.

Wolfelee *Scottish Borders* A small settlement between

Teviotdale and the Cheviot Hills, Wolfelee lies a mile (1.5 km) south of Hobkirk and 6 miles (10 km) southeast of Hawick.

Wolfhill *Perth and Kinross* A village near the source of the Burrelton Burn in Perth and Kinross, Wolfhill lies between the Sidlaw Hills and the River Tay, 2 miles (3 km) northeast of Guildtown and 7 miles (11 km) northeast of Perth.

Wood Wick *Orkney* A bay on the northeast coast of the Orkney Mainland, Wood Wick lies a mile (1.5 km) north of Tingwall and overlooks to the east the Eynhallow and Gairsay Sounds.

Wood Wick *Shetland* A small bay on the west coast of the island of Unst, Wood Wick is located 3 miles (5 km) northwest of Baltasound.

Woodend *Highland* A small hamlet in Strath Dearn in the Inverness district of Highland Council area, Woodend lies 2 miles (3 km) southwest of Tomatin to the north of the River Findhorn.

Woodend *Highland* A settlement in Sunart, Woodend lies 2 miles (3 km) west of Strontian on the northern shore of Loch Sunart.

Woodhall Loch *Dumfries and Galloway* A loch in Balmaghie parish, Dumfries and Galloway, Woodhall Loch lies a mile (1.5 km) to the north of Laurieston. It is just over a mile (1.5 km) in length and drains northwards into the Black Water of Dee.

Woodhaven *Fife* A settlement forming part of Newport-on-Tay on the Firth of Tay in northeast Fife, Woodhaven lies between Wormit and Newport and was for many centuries the leading ferry port on the south side of the River Tay. It later became the northern terminus for the coaching route across Fife to the ferry port of Pettycur on the Firth of Forth.

Woodhead *Aberdeenshire* A hamlet in the Buchan district of northeast Aberdeenshire, Woodhead lies a mile (1.5 km) to the east of Fyvie and just north of the River Ythan.

Woodhouselees *Dumfries and Galloway* A locality in Eskdale, southeast Dumfries and Galloway, Woodhouselees lies a mile (1.5 km) to the south of Canonbie.

Woodlands *Dumfries and Galloway* A locality in Annandale, southeast Dumfries and Galloway, Woodlands lies 3 miles (5 km) south of Lochmaben and just west of the River Annan.

Woodside *Aberdeen* A northwestern suburb of Aberdeen between Old Aberdeen and Bucksburn, Woodside developed as a separate village from the late 18th century in association with cotton spinning, bleaching, paper making and iron founding. In 1891, Woodside was incorporated into the city of Aberdeen.

Woodside *Dumfries and Galloway* A locality in Nithsdale, southeast Dumfries and Galloway, Woodside lies on the A75 between Collin and Mouswald, 4 miles (6.5 km) east of Dumfries.

Woodside *Fife* An eastern suburb of Glenrothes in central Fife, Woodside lies on the Bighty Burn to the south of the River Leven and east of the A92 from Kirkcaldy to Cupar. The former village of Woodside was expanded in 1950 as a residential area for the accommodation of Glenrothes Development Corporation staff. This was the first phase of the development of the new town of Glenrothes, the first house being opened here on 4 July 1951 by Lady McNeill, wife of the Chairman of the Development Corporation.

Woodside *Perth and Kinross* A settlement between the Sidlaw Hills and the River Tay in eastern Perth and Kinross, Woodside is a northern extension of the village of Burrelton on the A94.

Work, Head of *Orkney* A headland on the Orkney Mainland to the north of the Bay of Work, the Head of Work overlooks the Sound of Shapinsay and the island of Shapinsay, and lies 3 miles (5 km) northeast of Kirkwall.

Wormit *Fife* A settlement on the Firth of Tay in northeast Fife, Wormit lies at the southern end of the Tay Rail Bridge at the western end of the Newport-on-Tay urban area. It developed as a Dundee commuter settlement after the opening of the Tay Bridge in 1887. Wormit, which claims to have been the first village in Scotland to install electricity, has a bowling club and a boating club.

Wormit Bay *Fife* An inlet on the north coast of Fife, Wormit Bay opens out into the Firth of Tay to the west of the settlement of Wormit.

Wrath, Cape *Highland* A headland on the northwest coast of Sutherland 11 miles (18 km) northwest of Durness, Cape Wrath is the most northwesterly point on the British mainland. A granite lighthouse built in 1827 stands on cliffs 121 m (400 ft) above sea level. The surrounding area has been designated a Site of Special Scientific Interest and a Special Protection Area (SPA) for birds.

Wren's Egg, the *Dumfries and Galloway* The name given to a glacial erratic stone near Port William in Dumfries and Galloway, The Wren's Egg is located near Blairbuie farmsteading. Close by are two standing stones dating from the 3rd–2nd millennia BC.

Wyre *Orkney* The island of Wyre in the Orkney Islands is situated to the southeast of the larger island of Rousay, from which it is separated by Wyre Sound. It is a small flat island with an area of 311 ha (768 acres) and a small hill rising to 32 m (105 ft) at its centre. To the north of the hill stand the ruins of Cubbie Roo's Castle and St Mary's Chapel, the latter dating from the 12th century. Wyre was the birthplace in 1887 of the poet Edwin Muir. The island is accessed by ferries linking with Egilsay, Rousay and Tingwall on Mainland Orkney.

Yardie *Moray* Situated on the Moray Firth coast, Yardie is one of a number of old fishing villages to be found on the shoreline to the east of Buckie.

Yardstone Knowe *Scottish Borders* A hill to the south of the Moorfoot Hills in Scottish Borders, Yardstone Knowe rises to 513 m (1683 ft) to the west of the Gala Water, a mile (1.5 km) southwest of Stow.

Yarehouse, Loch of An alternative name for Loch of Yarrows in Caithness.

Yarrow *Scottish Borders* A village in the Ettrick district of Scottish Borders, Yarrow lies on the Yarrow Water, 9 miles (14 km) west of Selkirk. Its original church was built *c.*1640 by the Covenanters and restored after a fire in 1922. Sir Walter Scott attended church here while he lived at Ashiestiel (1804–12), and a sundial contains the instruction 'Watch and Pray, Tyme is Short'. An early Christian stone lies about a half-mile (1 km) southwest of the village with a faint Latin inscription that possibly names members of a British Christian dynasty in the 5th or 6th centuries AD. Yarrow has inspired numerous poems and ballads, such as *The Dowie Dens of Yarrow*, and featured in Sir Walter Scott's collection of Border minstrelsy (1802–03). Other authors associated with the area include William Dunbar, James Hogg, Christopher North and William Wordsworth. The African explorer Mungo Park (1771–1805) was born nearby at Foulshiels.

Yarrow Feus *Scottish Borders* A small settlement in the Ettrick district of Scottish Borders, Yarrow Feus lies on the Yarrow Water a mile (1.5 km) southwest of Yarrow and 7 miles (11 km) west of Selkirk.

Yarrow Water *Scottish Borders* A river of Ettrick in Scottish Borders, the Yarrow Water rises from the northeast end of St Mary's Loch and flows 13 miles (21 km) northeastwards through the settlements of Yarrow Feus, Yarrow, Yarrowford and Selkirk before emptying into the Ettrick Water 2 miles (3 km) southwest of Selkirk.

Yarrows, Loch of *Highland* A loch in northeast Caithness, the Loch of Yarrows (or *Yarehouse*) lies a half-mile (1 km) northeast of the Hill of Yarrows (212 m/695 ft) and 5 miles (8 km) southwest of Wick.

Yarrowford *Scottish Borders* A hamlet in the Ettrick district of Scottish Borders, Yarrowford lies on the Yarrow Water 3 miles (5 km) northeast of Yarrow and 4 miles (6.5 km) northwest of Selkirk. There is a youth hostel.

Yell *Shetland* Described as the 'Gateway to the Northern Isles', Yell is the second-largest of the Shetland Islands. Shaped like a rectangle that is almost cut in half by two voes (Whale Firth and Mid Yell), it comprises 21,629 ha (53,437 acres) of lochan-studded blanket peat, mire and croft land with a rocky indented coastline. In summer the moorland is alive with breeding birds such as whimbrel, golden plover, dunlin, eider duck, Arctic skua, great skua, red-breasted merganser, red-throated diver and merlin, Britain's smallest bird of prey. Many of these birds can be seen on the Lumbister Reserve, which extends over an expanse of moorland that includes the Lochs of Lumbister. Yell is also one of the best places in Europe to see otters, which thrive on the rich food in the offshore shallows. Yell's highest hill is the Ward of Otterswick, which rises to 205 m (673 ft). Mid Yell is the island's main settlement and, save for West Sandwick, the majority of the island's hamlets and crofts are to be found on the east coast. These include Gloup, Cullivoe, Sellafirth, Aywick and Burravoe. Early prehistoric remains can be found scattered around the island's coast, including the ancient settlement at Birrier and the Iron Age broch at Ness of Burraness which is one of 12 broch sites on Yell. Historic buildings include the Old Haa of Burravoe (1637), the haunted Windhouse, the ruined whale station at Grimister, and the Kirk of Ness, which has been deserted since 1750. At the head of Gloup Voe in the far north stands the Fishermen's Memorial commemorating the 58 fishermen who were drowned on 21 July 1881. The island's population has fallen from 2611 in 1841 to 957 in 2001. There are car ferries linking Toft on the Mainland with Ulsta at the south end of the island, Belmont on Unst with Gutcher, and Oddsta on Fetlar with Gutcher.

Yell Sound *Shetland* A channel in the Shetland Islands, Yell Sound separates the island of Yell from the Shetland Mainland.

Yellowcraig *East Lothian* A nature reserve with trails on the rocky shore of the Firth of Forth, Yellowcraig lies to the west of North Berwick.

Yester Castle *East Lothian* Located 1.5 miles (2.5 km) southeast of Gifford in East Lothian, Yester Castle was built in 1297 by Hugo de Gifford, the so-called 'Wizard of Yester'. Beneath is the sizeable Goblin Ha', where Gifford is said to have made magic. This name is echoed in a small hotel in the village of Gifford, and the goblins were immortalised in Sir Walter Scott's *Marmion* (1808). The castle passed to the Hay family through marriage in the 14th century, and in a similar fashion to so many others it was abandoned after the Hays moved to the more comfortable surroundings of a new home on the site of the present Yester House. Today the castle lies a ruin on the margins of the Yester Estate, acquired by the Italian composer Gian Carlo Menotti (b.1911) in 1972.

Yester Chapel *East Lothian* Located close to Yester House, southeast of the East Lothian village of Gifford, Yester Chapel, the family chapel and burial place of the Hays of Yester, was originally a 15th-century Collegiate Church of St Cuthbert. When the original village of Bothans was re-sited by the 2nd Marquess of Tweeddale (1645–1713) to the model village of Gifford in the late 17th century, public worship moved to the new Yester Parish Church, which was designed by architect James Smith and completed in 1710. The Hay family commissioned the architects John and Robert Adam to remodel the exterior of the old church as their private chapel in 1753.

Yester House *East Lothian* A mansion house on the Yester Estate, Yester House lies a mile (1.5 km) southeast of the village of Gifford. It was built by the architect James Smith (1645–1731) for John Hay, 2nd Marquess of Tweeddale (1645–1713). Smith was assisted by his partner Alexander MacGill. Although work began in 1697, progress was slow and the house was not completed for more than 20 years. By 1729, the 4th Marquess was already planning modernisation. He turned to William Adam (1689–1748), who provided a new roof and some exterior detail in addition to remodelling the interior. The Saloon by William, John and Robert Adam was described by the painter Gavin Hamilton (1723–98) as 'the finest room at least in Scotland'. None of Smith's original interior remains today, but the Adam work is of remarkable quality. Robert Adam was commissioned once again to restyle the exterior in 1789, but only the north side was completed because of Adam's death in 1792. The architect Robert Brown reworked the interior in the 1830s, moving the main entrance to the west. To achieve this, the west wing was demolished. The original entrance was converted to a dining room and the garden parlour turned into a fine drawing room. The architect Robert Rowand Anderson made further changes in 1877. The house and estate were acquired in 1972 by Gian Carlo Menotti (b.1911), the Italian operatic composer.

Yetholm *Scottish Borders* A parish in Scottish Borders adjacent to the border with England, Yetholm's chief settlements are the twin villages of Town Yetholm and Kirk Yetholm, which lie on either side of the Bowmont Water 7 miles (11 km) southeast of Kelso. Yetholm was for a long time the home of the Faa family, the 'royal house' of Scottish gypsies, the last of whom, 'Queen' Esther Faa Blythe, was buried here in 1883. Sir Walter Scott based his character Meg Merrilies in *Guy Mannering* (1815) on Jean Gordon, a native of Yetholm and wife of Patrick Faa.

Yetholm Loch *Scottish Borders* A small loch in Scottish Borders, Yetholm Loch lies a mile (1.5 km) to the west of Kirk Yetholm.

Yett *South Ayrshire* A locality in the Kyle district of

South Ayrshire, Yett lies to the north of the River Ayr, 4 miles (6.5 km) southwest of Mauchline.

Yetts o' Muckhart *Clackmannanshire* A village in the Clackmannanshire parish of Muckhart, Yetts o' Muckhart lies adjacent to Pool of Muckhart, 4 miles (6.5 km) northeast of Dollar near the entrance to Glen Devon. A tollhouse was established here in the early 19th century on a road used by cattle drovers and coaches.

Yieldshields *South Lanarkshire* A settlement in South Lanarkshire, Yieldshields lies 2 miles (3 km) to the east of Carluke.

Yinstay Head *Orkney* A headland on the Orkney Mainland, Yinstay Head extends into Shapinsay Sound 2 miles (3 km) west of Rerwick Head. The rocky island of Skerry of Yinstay lies offshore to the west.

Yoker *Glasgow City* A western suburb of Glasgow at the eastern end of Clydebank, Yoker lies on the north bank of the River Clyde, 5 miles (8 km) northwest of the city centre. From the 14th century a ferry linked Yoker with Renfrew on the south bank. A whisky distillery was established here in the late 18th century and in 1877 Napier Shanks and Bell opened the 'Yoker Old' shipyard. The arrival of the railway and the deepening of its offshore waters from the 1880s encouraged the building of larger vessels. Motor vehicles and tramcars were also manufactured in Yoker, which is now an operations centre for Glasgow's suburban rail service. By the 1980s shipbuilding had largely disappeared, but the last remaining Clyde ferry still crosses from Yoker to Renfrew, a ferry having operated this route since the 14th century.

Yorkhill *Glasgow City* A small district of Glasgow, Yorkhill lies just to the north of the River Clyde and is today divided by the Clydeside Expressway. Originally the site of a mansion and estate, which was named Yorkhill after being bought by Andrew Gilbert in 1813. In 1868, Yorkhill Quay was built on the river and Yorkhill Basin added c.1907. In 1916, the first of several hospitals replaced the original mansion and today the area is principally known for its hospitals, namely the Royal Hospital for Sick Children (built 1971) and the Queen Mother's Maternity Hospital (built 1964). The district becomes residential to the east and includes the Kelvin Hall to the north.

Yorkston *Midlothian* A small settlement in Midlothian, Yorkston lies on the River South Esk near Rosebery Reservoir, 6 miles (10 km) south of Bonnyrigg.

Younger Botanic Garden *Argyll and Bute* A formal garden near Benmore in the dramatic setting of the Eachaig Valley on the Cowal peninsula, the Younger Botanic Garden lies 5 miles (8 km) north of Dunoon. It is an outstation of the Royal Botanic Garden Edinburgh and is noted for its viewpoints looking out to the Holy Loch and for its collections of trees and rhododendrons. An avenue of giant redwood trees, planted in 1863, are now among highest trees in Britain, exceeding 40 m (131 ft) in height. The garden, which extends over 50 ha (124 acres) on the slopes of Benmore Hill with tree planting dating from 1820, was gifted to the nation by Harry George Younger in 1925. There is an outdoor pursuits centre at Benmore Lodge.

Ythan, River *Aberdeenshire* A river in eastern Aberdeenshire, the Ythan rises in the Wells of Ythan, 7 miles (11 km) east of Huntly. It flows east to Bruckhills, northeast to Mains of Towie and then south to Fyvie, from where it meanders generally southeastwards to Ellon. It then continues south before entering the North Sea at Newburgh Bar, 12 miles (19 km) north of Aberdeen.

Ythanwells *Aberdeenshire* A village in Strathbogie, northeast Aberdeenshire, Ythanwells lies in the eastern Grampians, 7 miles (11 km) east of Huntly. The River Ythan rises nearby at the Wells of Ythan.

Ythsie *Aberdeenshire* A locality in the Formartine district of Aberdeenshire, Ythsie comprises the farms of North Ythsie, South Ythsie, Little Ythsie and Milltown of Ythsie, all of which lie to the east of Tarves. On a hill nearby stands a folly known as the Prop of Ythsie, built in 1862 to commemorate the 4th Earl of Aberdeen, prime minister during the Crimean War.

Zetland A form of the name Shetland now seldom used, Zetland was the official name of Zetland County Council until 1975. It still survives in the title of the earldom of Zetland, created in 1838 for Laurence Dundas and superseded in 1892 by the marquisate awarded to his grandson. The Norse *hjaltland* ('high land') for Scotland's most northerly group of islands is variously rendered in Scots and English as Hetland, Yetland, Zetland and Shetland.

Selected Bibliography

Adams, I.H. (1976) *Agrarian Landscape Terms: A Glossary for Historical Geography*. Institute of British Geographers Special Publication No. 9, Edinburgh

Alexander, Derek (ed.) (1996) *Prehistoric Renfrewshire. Papers in honour of Frank Newall*. Renfrewshire Local History Forum, Edinburgh

Anon (1877) *Old Edinburgh: with notes on its Ecclesiastical Antiquities*. T. Nelson & Sons, Edinburgh

Anon (1937) *W. & A.K. Johnston's Gazetteer of Scotland*. W. & A.K. Johnston, Edinburgh

Anon (1959) *The History of Dundee*. Scottish Advertisers Ltd, Dundee

Anon (1960) *The Complete Scotland: A Ward Lock Tourist Guide*. Ward, Lock & Co. Ltd, London

Anon (1981) *Buildings of Architectural and Historic Interest in Clackmannan District*. Planning Department, Clackmannan District Council, Alloa

Anon (1995) *The New Councils Statistical Report*. Government Statistical Service, HMSO, Edinburgh

Anon (1997) *Scottish Atlas and Gazetteer*. Collins, London

Anon (1998) *Aberdeen City Council Official Guide*. Aberdeen City Council

Anon *Classic Landforms Series*. Geographical Association, Sheffield

Automobile Association (1960) *Illustrated Road Book of Scotland*. Automobile Association, London

Baird, W.J. (1991) *The Scenery of Scotland*. NMS, Edinburgh

Baird, William (1898) *Annals of Duddingston and Portobello*. Andrew Elliot, Princes Street, Edinburgh

Baldwin, John (1997) *Exploring Scotland's Heritage: Edinburgh, Lothians and Borders*. (2nd edn) The Royal Commission on the Ancient and Historical Monuments of Scotland & The Stationery Office, Edinburgh

Banks, F.R. (1977) *The Borders*. B.T.Batsford, London

Barry, G. (1805) *The History of the Orkney Islands*.

Bearhop, Derek A. (ed.) (1997) *Munro's Tables and other tables of lower hills*. Scottish Mountaineering Trust, Edinburgh

Beaton, Elizabeth (1992) *Ross and Cromarty: An Illustrated Architectural Guide*. RIAS, Edinburgh

Beaton, Elizabeth (1995) *Sutherland: An Illustrated Architectural Guide*. The Rutland Press, Edinburgh

Beaton, Elizabeth (1996) *Caithness: An Illustrated Architectural Guide*. The Rutland Press, Edinburgh

Bennet, D.J. & Strang, T. (1994) *The Northwest Highlands*. Scottish Mountaineering Trust, Edinburgh

Bennet, Donald (ed.) (1991) *The Munros - Scottish Mountaineering Club Hillwalkers Guide. Vol 1*. Scottish Mountaineering Trust, Edinburgh

Bennet, Donald J. (1991) *The Southern Highlands*. Scottish Mountaineering Trust, Edinburgh

Bennett, G.P. *The Great Road Between Forth and Tay from early times to 1850*. Markinch Printing Company, Markinch

Bennett, G.P. *The Past at Work Around the Lomonds*. Markinch Printing Company, Markinch

Bisset, Alexander M. (1906) *History of Bathgate and District. An account of the parishes of Bathgate, Torphichen, Livingston and Whitburn, in the county of Linlithgow*. West Lothian Printing & Publishing Co., Bathgate

Bluck, B.J. (ed.) (1973) *Excursion Guide to the Geology of the Glasgow District*. Geological Society of Glasgow

Blundell, Nigel (1996) *Ancient Scotland*. Promotional Reprint Company Ltd, London

Boyd, J. Morton & Boyd, Ian L. (1996) *The Hebrides: A Mosaic of Islands*. Birlinn Ltd, Edinburgh

Boyd, J. Morton & Boyd, Ian L. (1996) *The Hebrides: A Habitable Land*. Birlinn Ltd, Edinburgh

Boyle, Anne, Dickson, Colin, McEwan, Alasdair & MacLean, Colin (1985) *Ruins and Remains: Edinburgh's neglected heritage*. Scotland's Cultural Heritage, University of Edinburgh, Edinburgh

Branigan, Keith & Foster, Patrick (2002) *Barra and The Bishop's Isles: Living on the Margin*. Tempus Publishing Ltd, Stroud

Breeze, David J. (2002) *Historic Scotland: People and Places*. B.T. Batsford Ltd, London & Historic Scotland, Edinburgh

Britannica.com Inc. (ed.) (2000) Encyclopaedia Britannica Online. http://www.britannica.com/

Brogden, W.A. (1986) *Aberdeen: An Illustrated Architectural Guide*. Scottish Academic Press & RIAS, Edinburgh

Bruce, William Scott (1980) *The Railways of Fife*. Melvin Press, Perth

Buchan, David (1990) *Old Ecclesiastical Buildings of Alloa*. Clackmannan District Libraries (reprint from 1920 edition)

Burgher, Leslie (1991) *Orkney: An Illustrated Architectural Guide*. RIAS, Edinburgh

Campbell, Malcolm (1999) *The Scottish Golf Book*. Lomond Books, Edinburgh

Campbell, Robin N. (ed.) (1999) *The Munroist's Companion*. Scottish Mountaineering Trust, Edinburgh

Cant, Malcolm (1999) *Villages of Edinburgh: An Illustrated Guide*. Malcolm Cant Publications, Edinburgh

Cant, R.G. (ed.) (1975) St Andrews, *The Handbook of the St Andrews Preservation Trust to the city and its buildings*. St Andrews Preservation Trust, St Andrews

Cant, Ronald G. & Lindsay, Ian G. (1948) *Old Stirling*. Oliver and Boyd, Edinburgh

Cant, Ronald G. (1976) *Historic Crail: an illustrated survey*. Crail Preservation Society, Crail

Chambers, Robert (1868) *Traditions of Edinburgh*. W. & R. Chambers, Edinburgh

Chambers, William *Historical Sketch of St Giles' Cathedral*. W. & R. Chambers, Edinburgh

Clark, Sylvia (1988) *Paisley: A history*. Mainstream, Edinburgh

Close, Rob (1992) *Ayrshire and Arran: An Illustrated Architectural Guide*. RIAS, Edinburgh

Close-Brooks, Joanna (1995) *Exploring Scotland's Heritage: The Highlands*. (2nd edn) The Royal Commission on the Ancient and Historical Monuments of Scotland & HMSO, Edinburgh

Collard, Mark (1998) *Lothian: A historical guide*. Birlinn, Edinburgh

Coltart, J.S. (1936) *Scottish Church Architecture*. The Sheldon Press, London.

Connachan-Holmes, J.R.A. (1995) *Country Houses of Scotland*. House of Lochar, Isle of Colonsay, Argyll

Cooper, Derek (1995) *Skye*. Birlinn Ltd, Edinburgh

Coventry, Martin (2001) *The Castles of Scotland*. Goblinshead, Musselburgh

Cowling, David (1997) *An Essay for Today. The Scottish New Towns, 1947 to 1997*. Edinburgh, Rutland Press

Craig, G.Y. & Duff, P.McL.D. (1975) *The Geology of the Lothians and South East Scotland.* Scottish Academic Press, Edinburgh

Craig, G.Y. (ed.) (1983) *Geology of Scotland.* Second Edition, Scottish Academic Press, Edinburgh

Daiches, David (1977) *Glasgow.* Andre Deutsch, London

Dennison, E. Patricia & Coleman, Russel (2000) *Historic Linlithgow.* Historic Scotland, Edinburgh

Devine, T.M. & Jackson, Gordon (eds.) (1995) *Glasgow. Vol. I: Beginnings to 1830.* Manchester University Press, Manchester

Doak, A.M. & Young, Andrew McLaren (eds.) (1977) *Glasgow at a Glance.* Robert Hale Limited, London

Dorward, David (2001) The Glens of Angus: Names, Places, People. The Pinkfoot Press, Balgavies

Dow, James L. (1957) *Greenock.* Greenock Corporation

Dowds, Thomas J. (2003) *The Forth and Clyde Canal: A history.* Tuckwell Press, Phantassie, East Lothian

Durie, Alastair J. (1993) *Bridge of Allan, 'Queen of the Scottish Spas': 19th-century development as a health resort.* The Forth Naturalist & Historian, Vol 16, pp 91-103

Dysart Trust, *The The Dysart Trail: A guide to places of interest in the conservation area of Dysart.*

Editor, The (1923) *The Councillor's Manual: being a guide to Scottish Local Government in Burghs, Parishes, and Counties.* 10th Edition, W. Green and Son Ltd, Edinburgh

Edwards, Brian (1986) *Scottish Seaside Towns.* BBC, London

Evans, David J.A. & Hansom, James D. (1998) *The Whangie and the landslides of the Campsie Fells.* Scottish Geographical Magazine, vol 114, no 3, pp 192-96

Eyre-Todd, George (1921) *Scotland: Picturesque and Traditional.* Gowans & Gray Limited, Glasgow

Fabian, D.J., Little, G.E. & Williams, B.N. (1989) *Islands of Scotland including Skye.* Scottish Mountaineering Trust, Edinburgh

Falkland Society, The (1988) *A Falkland Guide.*

Fenton, Alexander (1978) *The Northern Isles: Orkney and Shetland.* John Donald Publishers Ltd, Edinburgh

Fenwick, H. (1986) *Scottish Baronial Houses.* Robert Hale, London.

Ferguson, Keith (1982) *A History of Glenrothes.* Glenrothes Development Corporation, Glenrothes

Fife Regional Council (1996) *The Kingdom of Fife.* The British Publishing Company

Finlayson, Clarence (1979) *The Strath: The Biography of Strathpeffer.* The Saint Andrew Press, Edinburgh

Finnie, Mike (1990) *Shetland: An illustrated architectural guide.* Mainstream & RIAS, Edinburgh

Fisher, Joe (1994) *Glasgow Encyclopedia.* Mainstream, Edinburgh

Fojut, Noel & Pringle, Denys (1993) *The Ancient Monuments of Shetland.* HMSO, Edinburgh

Ford, Donald (1999) *The Great Scottish Courses.* Donald Ford, South Queensferry

Fotheringham, Norman (1997) *Charlestown: Built on lime.* Carnegie Dunfermline Trust, Dunfermline

Fotheringham, Norman (1997) *The Story of Limekilns.* Charlestown Lime Heritage Trust

Fraser, W. Hamish & Maver, Irene (eds.) (1996) *Glasgow. Vol. II: 1830-1912.* Manchester University Press

Fyall, Aitken (1999) *St Monans: History, Customs and Superstitions.* The Pentland Press, Edinburgh

Galashiels History Committee (ed.) (1983) *Galashiels: A Modern History.* Galashiels History Committee & Ettrick and Lauderdale District Council, Galashiels

Gemmell, Alastair (1998) *Discovering Arran.* John Donald Publishers Ltd, Edinburgh

Gibb, Andrew (1983) *Glasgow. The making of a city.* Croom Helm, London

Gibson, W. (1883) *Reminiscences of Dollar and Tillicoultry.* Strong Oak Press

Gifford, John (ed.) (1988) *The Buildings of Scotland: Fife.* Penguin, London

Gifford, John, McWilliam, Colin& Walker, David (eds.) (1991) *The Buildings of Scotland: Edinburgh.* Penguin, London

Gifford, John (ed.) (1992) *The Buildings of Scotland: Highland and Islands.* Penguin, London

Gifford, John (ed.) (1996) *The Buildings of Scotland: Dumfries and Galloway.* Penguin, London

Gifford, John & Walker, Frank Arneil (eds.) (2002) *The Buildings of Scotland: Stirling and Central Scotland.* Yale University Press, New Haven and London

Gillen, Con (2003) *Geology and Landscapes of Scotland.* Terra Publishing, Harpenden

Goodlad, C. A. (1971) *Shetland Fishing Saga.* Shetland Times, Lerwick

Gordon, John E. (ed.) (1997) *Reflections on the Ice Age in Scotland.* Scottish Association of Geography Teachers & Scottish Natural Heritage

Gow, Ian (1977) *Scottish Houses and Gardens from the archives of Country Life.* Aurum Press Limited, London

Gow, Ian & Rowan, Alistair (eds.) (1995) *Scottish Country Houses 1600–1914.* Edinburgh University Press, Edinburgh

Green, C.R. (1908) *Haddington, or East Lothian.*

Groome, Francis H. (ed.) (1882) *Ordnance Gazetteer of Scotland.* Vols 1-6. Thomas C. Jack, Grange Publishing Works, Edinburgh

Haddington History Society (ed.) (1997) *Haddington: Royal Burgh - A history and a guide.* Tuckwell Press, Phantassie, East Lothian

Hamilton, Alan (1978) *Essential Edinburgh.* Andre Deutsch, London

Hannah, Ian C. (1913) *The County Coast Series: The Berwick and Lothian Coasts.* T. Fisher Unwin, London

Haswell-Smith, Hamish (1996) *The Scottish Islands.* Canongate, Edinburgh

Haynes, Nick (2000) *Perth & Kinross: An illustrated architectural guide.* The Rutland Press, Edinburgh

Henderson, Frances L. *Rambles round Edinburgh.* W. & A.K. Johnston, Edinburgh

Henderson, I.A.N. (1996) *Discovering Angus and the Mearns.* John Donald Publishers Ltd, Edinburgh

Hendrie, William F. (1988) *The History of Livingston.* Livingston Development Corporation

Hendrie, William F. (1989) *Linlithgow. Six hundred years a Royal Burgh.* Edinburgh, John Donald

Hendrie, William F. (1996) *Discovering the River Forth.* John Donald Publishers Ltd, Edinburgh

Hewison, W.S. (2000) *Scapa Flow in War and Peace.* Bellavista Publications. Kirkwall

Historic Scotland *The Sites to See: A guide to over 300 historic sites spanning 5000 years.* Historic Scotland, Edinburgh

Hodgkiss, Peter (1994) *Central Highlands: Scottish Mountaineering Club District Guidebook.* Scottish Mountaineering Trust, Edinburgh

Hume, John R. (1976) *The Industrial Archaeology of Scotland. Vols 1 & 2.* B.T. Batsford Ltd, London & Sydney

Jacobsen, J. (1936) *The Place-Names of Shetland.* London & Copenhagen

Jamieson, John (1902) *Bell the Cat; or, who destroyed the Scottish abbeys?* Eneas Mackay, Stirling

Jaques, Richard & McKean, Charles (1994) *West Lothian: An illustrated architectural guide.* The Rutland Press, Edinburgh

Kay, Billy (ed.) (1995) *The Dundee Book: An Anthology of Living in the City.* Mainstream, Edinburgh

Keay, John & Keay, Julia (eds.) (1994) *Collins Encyclopedia of Scotland.* HarperCollins Publishers, London

Keith, Alexander (1987) *A Thousand Years of Aberdeen.* Aberdeen University Press, Aberdeen

Kersting, Anthony F. & Lindsay, Maurice (1981) *The Buildings of Edinburgh.* B.T. Batsford Ltd, London

King, David (1991) *The Complete Works of Robert and James Adam.* Butterworth Architecture, Oxford

Knight, John & Gifford, John (1992) *East Lothian Villages.* East Lothian District Library

Knox, Susan A. (1984) *The Making of the Shetland Landscape.* John Donald Publishers Ltd, Edinburgh

Lamont-Brown, Raymond (1988) *Discovering Fife.* John Donald Publishers Ltd, Edinburgh

Lang, Theo (1951) *The Kingdom of Fife and Kinross-shire.* Hodder & Stoughton, London

Lang, Theo (ed.) (1952) *The Queen's Scotland: Edinburgh and the Lothians.* Hodder & Stoughton, London

Lang, Theo (ed.) (1957) *The Queen's Scotland: The Border counties.* Hodder & Stoughton, London

Lindsay, Jean (1968) *The Canals of Scotland.* David & Charles, Newton Abbot

Lindsay, Maurice (1994) *The Castles of Scotland: A Constable Guide.* Constable & Company Ltd, London

Lindsay, Maurice (ed.) (1996) *The Burns Encyclopaedia.* Robert Hale Ltd / http://www.robertburns.org/encyclopedia/

Linklater, E. (1965) *Orkney and Shetland. An Historical, Geographical, Social and Scenic Survey.* Robert Hale, London

Linlithgow Community Council (ed.) (1988) *Linlithgow Town Guide.* Linlithgow Community Council & West Lothian District Council

Livingstone, Sheila (1997) *Scottish Festivals* . Birlinn, Edinburgh

Lythe, S.G.E. (1938) *The origin and development of Dundee: a study in historical geography.* Scottish Geographical Magazine Vol. 54, pp. 344-57

MacDougall, Carl (1990) *Glasgow's Glasgow: The Words and The Stones.* Glasgow

MacGibbon, David & Ross, Thomas (1887) *The Castellated and Domestic Architecture of Scotland.* David Douglas, Edinburgh

MacGregor, A.R. (1968) *Fife & Angus Geology.* William Blackwood & Sons, Edinburgh, for the University of St Andrews

MacInnes, Ranald, Glendinning, Miles & MacKechnie, Aonghus (1999) *Building a Nation: The story of Scotland's Architecture.* Canongate Books Ltd, Edinburgh

MacLehose, Alexander (1936) *Historic Haunts of Scotland.* Alexander MacLehose & Company, London

Mackay, A.J.G. (1890) *History of Fife and Kinross.* County History Series

Mackie, J.D. (1978) *A History of Scotland.* Penguin Books Ltd, Harmondsworth.

Macleod, Innes & Gilroy, Margaret (1996) *Discovering the River Clyde.* John Donald Publishers Ltd, Edinburgh

Mair, Craig (1988) *Mercat Cross and Tolbooth.* John Donald Publishers Ltd, Edinburgh

Marren, Peter (1990) *Grampian Battlefields.* Mercat Press, Edinburgh

Marshall, J.S. (1986) *The Life and Times of Leith.* John Donald Publishers Ltd, Edinburgh

Marshall, T.H. (1849) *History of Perth.*

Martin, Paula (1991) *A Guide to St Monans.*

Martin, Paula (1992) *What to see in Newburgh: A guided walk.*

Martin, Paula *St Monans: Salt pans and the lost industrial landscape.* Fife Regional Council, Glenrothes

Martine, Roddy (1983) *Royal Scotland.* Paul Harris Publishing, Edinburgh

Marwick, H. (1947) *The Place-Names of Rousay.*

Marwick, H. The Place-Names of North Ronaldsay, *Proceedings of the Orkney Antiquarian Society,* I:53-64.

Maxwell, Rt. Hon. Sir Herbert (1916) *Edinburgh: A historical study.* Williams and Norgate, London

Mays, Deborah (ed.) (1997) *The Architecture of Scottish Cities.* Tuckwell Press, East Linton

McCarthy, James (1994) *Scotland, Land and People, An Inhabited Solitude.* Luath Press Ltd, Edinburgh

McConnell, Rodger & Gulliver, Stuart (1998) *Glasgow's Renewed Prosperity. Glasgow's economic position statement.* Glasgow City Council / Glasgow Development Agency

McDowall, William (1986) *History of Dumfries.* (4th rev edn) T.C. Farries, Dumfries

McKean, Charles, with Walker, David (1982) *Edinburgh: An illustrated architectural guide.* RIAS Publications, Edinburgh

McKean, Charles & Walker, David (1984) *Dundee: An illustrated introduction.* RIAS & the Scottish Academic Press, Edinburgh

McKean, Charles (1985) *Stirling and the Trossachs: An illustrated architecural guide.* Scottish Academic Press & RIAS, Edinburgh

McKean, Charles (1987) *The District of Moray: An illustrated architectural guide.* Scottish Academic Press & RIAS, Edinburgh

McKean, Charles, Walker, David & Walker, Frank (1989) *Central Glasgow: An illustrated architectural guide.* RIAS, Edinburgh

McKean, Charles (1990) *Banff and Buchan: An illustrated architectural guide.* Mainstream and RIAS, Edinburgh

McKirdy, Alan & Crofts, Roger (1999) *Scotland the Creation of its Natural Landscape: A Landscape Fashioned by Geology.* Scottish Natural Heritage, Edinburgh

McNeill, P. (1883) *Tranent and its Surroundings.* John Menzies & Co, Edinburgh & Glasgow

McNeill, P. (1902) *Prestonpans and Vicinity: Historical, Ecclesiastical and Traditional.* Tranent

McNeill, Peter G.B. & MacQueen, Hector L. (eds.) (1996) *Atlas of Scottish History to 1707.* The Scottish Medievalists and the Department of Geography, University of Edinburgh, Edinburgh

McNeish, Cameron (1999) *The Munros: Scotland's highest mountains.* Lomond Books, Edinburgh.

McWilliam, Colin (ed.) (1978) *The Buildings of Scotland: Lothian except Edinburgh.* Penguin Books Ltd, Harmondsworth, Middlesex

Millar, A.H. (1895) *Fife, Pictorial and Historical, its People, Burghs, Castles and Mansions.*

Miller, James (2000) *Scapa.* Birlinn Ltd, Edinburgh

Miller, James (2002) *The Dam Builders: Power from the Glens.* Birlinn Limited, Edinburgh

Millman, R.N. (1975) *The Making of the Scottish Landscape.* B.T. Batsford, London & Sydney

Milton of Balgonie Primary School (1986) *Village History and Walks Around Milton of Balgonie.*

Mitchell, Ian (2004) *Isles of the West.* Birlinn Ltd, Edinburgh

Moisley, H.A. & Thain, A.G. (eds.) (1975) *The County of Renfrew,* The Third Statistical Account of Scotland. vol. XI

Moncrieffe of that Ilk, Bart., Sir Iain (1963) *The Royal Palace of Falkland.* The National Trust for Scotland, Edinburgh

Montgomery-Massingberd, H. & Sykes, C.S. (1997) *Great Houses of Scotland.* Lawrence King Publishers

Morrison, Ian A. (1985) *Landscape with Lake Dwellings: The Crannogs of Scotland.* Edinburgh University Press

Morton, H.V. (1929) *In Search of Scotland.* Methuen & Co. Ltd, London

Morton, H.V. (1933) *In Scotland Again.* Methuen & Co. Ltd, London

Muir, Meta (1963) *The Royal Mile.* Oliver and Boyd, Edinburgh

Muirison, W. (1910–) *Cambridge Country Geographies Series.* The University Press, Cambridge

Mullay, Sandy (1996) *The Edinburgh Encyclopaedia.* Mainstream, Edinburgh

Mullay, Sandy (2002) *The Illustrated History of Edinburgh's Suburbs.* The Breedon Books Publishing Company, Derby

Munro, David (1994) *Loch Leven and the River Leven: A Landscape Transformed.*

Munro, R.W. (ed.) (1973) *Johnston's Gazetteer of Scotland.* Johnston & Bacon, Edinburgh & London

Murray, Sir John & Pullar, Laurence (eds.) (1908) *Bathymetrical Survey of the Fresh-water Lochs of Scotland.* Edward Stanford and The Royal Geographical Society, London

Murray, W.H. (1993) *Scotland's Mountains.* The Scottish Mountaineering Club Trust

Naismith, Robert J. (1985) *Buildings of the Scottish Countryside.* Victor Gollancz Ltd, London

Neale, Christopher (1985) *Dunfermline Heritage.* Carnegie Dunfermline Trust, Dunfermline

Northern Lighthouse Board, The (ed.) (2003) *Lighthouse Library.* http://www.nlb.org.uk/ourlights/library.htm

O'Dell, A.C. (1939) *The Historical Geography of the Shetland Islands.* T. & J. Manson, Lerwick

Old Town Renewal Trust & City of Edinburgh District Council Planning Department (1996) *Edinburgh Old Town Action Plan 1996-1997.* Edinburgh Old Town Renewal Trust, Edinburgh

Oram, Richard (1996) *Angus and the Mearns: A Historical Guide.* Birlinn, Edinburgh

Oram, Richard D. (1996) *Moray & Badenoch: A Historical Guide.* Birlinn Ltd, Edinburgh

Pacione, Michael (1995) *Glasgow: the socio-spatial development of the city.* Wiley, Chichester

Palsson, Hermann & Edwards, Paul (eds.) (1978) *Orkneyinga Saga, The History of the Earls of Orkney.* Penguin Classics

Park, Brian A. (1984) *The Woollen Mill Buildings in the Hillfoots Area.* Forth Naturalist & Historian, Stirling

Parry, M.L. & Slater, T.R. (eds.) (1980) *The Making of the Scottish Countryside .* Croom Helm, London

Paterson, James (1857) *History of The Regality of Musselburgh.* James Gordon, Musselburgh.

Pattullo, Nan (1967) *Castles, Houses and Gardens of Scotland.* William Blackwood & Sons Ltd, Edinburgh and London

Peck, Edward H. (1983) *Avonside Explored: A guide to Tomintoul and Glenlivet.*

Peden, Allan (1992) *The Monklands: An illustrated architectural guide.* RIAS, Edinburgh

Penny, George (1836) *Traditions of Perth.*

Piggott, Stuart (1982) *Scotland before History.* Edinburgh University Press, Edinburgh

Prentice, Robin (ed.) (1978) *The National Trust for Scotland Guide.* 2nd Edn, Jonathan Cape, London

Pride, Glen L. (1990) *The Kingdom of Fife: An illustrated architectural guide.* RIAS, Edinburgh

RCAHMS (1992) *Dundee on Record - Images of the past.* Royal Commission on the Ancient and Historical Monuments of Scotland & HMSO, Edinburgh

Rae, William & The City of Edinburgh District Council (1994) *Edinburgh: The new official guide.* City of Edinburgh District Council & Mainstream, Edinburgh.

Reed, Peter (ed.) (1993) *Glasgow: The forming of the city.* Edinburgh University Press, Edinburgh

Richardson, J.S. & Wood, Marguerite (1929) *Edinburgh Castle – Official Guide.* HMSO, Edinburgh

Riddell, John (2000) *The Clyde: The making of a river.* John Donald Publishers Ltd, Edinburgh

Ritchie, Anna & Ritchie, Graham (1978) *The Ancient Monuments of Orkney.* HMSO, Edinburgh

Ritchie, Anna (1997) *Exploring Scotland's Heritage: Shetland.* 2nd edn, The Royal Commission on the Ancient and Historical Monuments of Scotland & HMSO, Edinburgh

Ritchie, Anna & Ritchie, Graham (1998) *Scotland: An Oxford Archaeological Guide.* Oxford University Press, Oxford

Ritchie, Graham & Harman, Mary (1996) *Exploring Scotland's Heritage: Argyll and the Western Isles.* 2nd edn, The Royal Commission on the Ancient and Historical Monuments of Scotland & HMSO, Edinburgh

Robertson, D.M. (1993) *Longniddry.* East Lothian District Library

Robertson, George & Crawford, George (1818) *A General Description of the Shire of Renfrew.* Paisley

Robertson, John F. (1985) *Story of Galloway.* Lang Syne Publishers, Newtongrange

Robertson, W. (1979) *Old Dunfermline.*

Rodger, Johnny, with photographs by John Niall McLean (2001) *Edinburgh: A Guide to Recent Architecture.* Ellipsis, London

Rogers, Laurie (1996) *Walks into History: Nine walks around the Forfar area.* Angus District Council Library & Museum Services

Ross, David (1998) *Scotland: History of a Nation.* Lomond Books

Rowntree Bodie, W.G. (1960) *Glenrothes and its Environs in Days Gone By.* Fifeshire Advertiser, Kirkcaldy

Rowntree Bodie, W.G. (1968) *Some Light on the Past Around Glenrothes.* University Press, St Andrews

Russell, John (1922) *The Story of Leith.* Thomas Nelson & Sons Ltd, London

Scotland's Churches Scheme & illustrated by Hume, John R. (eds.) (2004) *Churches to Visit in Scotland.* NMS Publishing, Edinburgh

Scott, Alan (ed.) (2002) *Rampant Scotland.* http://www.rampantscotland.com

Scott, Ian & Ferguson, James (1993) *Larbert Old Parish Church: A short history.* Falkirk

Scott-Moncrieff, George (ed.) (1938) *The Stones of Scotland.* B.T. Batsford Ltd, London

Scott-Moncrieff, George (1939) *The Face of Britain: The Lowlands of Scotland.* B.T. Batsford Ltd, London

Scottish Civic Trust (ed.) (1981) *New Uses for Older Buildings in Scotland. A Report for the Scottish Development Department.* HMSO, Edinburgh

Scottish Natural Heritage (ed.) (2002) *Facts and Figures 2001-2002.* Scottish Natural Heritage, Edinburgh, http://www.snh.org.uk/publics/docs/factsandfigures/

Scottish Natural Heritage *The Isle of May National Nature Reserve.*

Scottish Parliament Corporate Body, The (ed.) (2004) *Holyrood Building.* http://www.scottish.parliament.uk/holyrood/hbuilding.html

Shairp, J.C. (ed.) (1974) *Recollections of a Tour made in Scotland A.D. 1803, by Dorothy Wordsworth.* The Mercat Press / James Thin, Edinburgh

Shaw, Carol P. & Fyfe, Alastair (1995) *Famous Scots* (Collins Gem). HarperCollins, Glasgow

Shaw, James E. (1942) *Local Government in Scotland.* Oliver & Boyd, Edinburgh

Shepherd, Ian (1994) *Gordon: An Illustrated Architectural Guide.* The Rutland Press, Edinburgh

Shepherd, Ian (1996) *Exploring Scotland's Heritage: Aberdeen and North East Scotland.* The Royal Commission on the Ancient and Historical Monuments of Scotland & HMSO, Edinburgh

Shepherd, Thomas H. (1831) *Modern Athens: Edinburgh in the Nineteenth Century.* Jones and Co, London

Sibbald, Sir Robert (1710) *The History, Ancient and Modern of the Sheriffdoms of Fife and Kinross.*

Silver, Owen (1987) *The Roads of Fife.* John Donald Publishers Ltd, Edinburgh

Simpson, Eric (1992) *Discovering Banff, Moray and Nairn.* John Donald Publishers Ltd, Edinburgh

Smart, Aileen (2002) *Villages of Glasgow: North of the Clyde.* John Donald Publishers Ltd, Edinburgh

Smith, Janet (1989) *The Empty Shore: The Story of Cowie, Kincardineshire* .

Smith, Robert (1988) *Discovering Aberdeenshire.* John Donald Publishers Ltd, Edinburgh

Smith, Robert (1989) *The Granite City: A History of Aberdeen.* John Donald Publishers Ltd, Edinburgh

Smith, Robert (1996) *Buchan: Land of Plenty.* John Donald Publishers Ltd, Edinburgh

Smith, Robin (2001) *The Making of Scotland.* Canongate Books Ltd, Edinburgh

Smith, Ronald (ed.) (2002) *Linlithgow Old and New.* Linlithgow Civic Trust

Smout, T.C. (1963) The Erskines of Mar and the development of Alloa. *Scottish Studies*, Vol.7, pp. 57-64

Snoddy, T.G. (1937) *Round About Greenock. A sketch-book of West Renfrewshire and North Cunninghame.* Arbroath

Snoddy, T.G. (1950) *Afoot in Fife.* Serif Books, Edinburgh

Spence, Alan (1992) *Discovering the Borders* Vols 1 & 2. John Donald Publishers Ltd, Edinburgh

Stavert, Marion L. (1992) *Perth: A Short History.* Perth and Kinross District Libraries, Perth

Stell, Geoffrey (1996) *Exploring Scotland's Heritage: Dumfries and Galloway.* Second Edition, The Royal Commission on the Ancient and Historical Monuments of Scotland & HMSO, Edinburgh

Stevenson, J.B. (1985) *Exploring Scotland's Heritage: The Clyde Estuary and Central Region.* The Royal Commission on the Ancient and Historical Monuments of Scotland & HMSO, Edinburgh

Stevenson, Jack (1995) *Exploring Scotland's Heritage: Glasgow, Clydeside and Stirling..* Second Edition, The Royal Commission on the Ancient and Historical Monuments of Scotland & HMSO, Edinburgh

Stevenson, Robert Louis (1879) *Edinburgh Picturesque Notes.* Seely, Jackson & Halliday, London

Strang, Charles Alexander (1994) *Borders and Berwick: An illustrated architectural guide to the Scottish Borders and Tweed Valley.* The Rutland Press, Edinburgh

Sutherland, Robertson (1974) *Loanhead: The development of a Scottish burgh.* Macdonald Publishers, Loanhead

Swan, Adam (1987) *Clackmannan: An illustrated architectural guide.* Scottish Academic Press & RIAS, Edinburgh

Tabraham, Chris (2000) *Scottish Castles and Fortifications.* Historic Scotland, Edinburgh

Taylor, James (1859) *A Pictorial History of Scotland from the Roman Invasion to the Close of the Jacobite Rebellion (A.D. 79–1746).* James S. Virtue, London

Thomas, Jane (1995) *Midlothian: An Illustrated Architectural Guide.* The Rutland Press, Edinburgh

Thompson, Francis (1990) *Discovering Speyside.* John Donald Publishers Ltd, Edinburgh

Thomson, Rev. Thomas (ed.) (1872) *A Biographical Dictionary of Eminent Scotsmen*, New Edition (originally edited by Robert Chambers). Blackie & Sons, Glasgow

Tranter, Nigel (1979) *Portrait of the Lothians.* Robert Hale, London

Tranter, Nigel (1986) *The Fortified House in Scotland – Volume 2: Central Scotland.* The Mercat Press, Edinburgh

Troup, J.A. & Eunson, F. (1967) *Stromness, 150 years a burgh, 1817-1967.*

Tulloch, P.A. (1974) *A Window on North Ronaldsay.*

Walker, Bruce & Ritchie, Graham (1987) *Exploring Scotland's Heritage: Fife and Tayside.* The Royal Commission on the Ancient and Historical Monuments of Scotland & HMSO, Edinburgh

Walker, Bruce & Ritchie, Graham (1996) *Exploring Scotland's Heritage: Fife, Perthshire and Angus.* 2nd edn, The Royal Commission on the Ancient and Historical Monuments of Scotland & HMSO, Edinburgh

Walker, Frank Arneil (1986) The *South Clyde Estuary. An Illustrated Architectural Guide to Inverclyde and Renfrew.* Scottish Academic Press & RIAS, Edinburgh

Walker, Frank Arneil (1992) *Phaidon Architecture Guide: Glasgow.* Phaidon Press Limited, London

Walker, Frank Arneil, with Sinclair, Fiona (1992) *The North Clyde Estuary: An illustrated architectural guide.* RIAS , Edinburgh

Walker, Frank Arneil (ed.) (2000) *The Buildings of Scotland: Argyll and Bute.* Penguin, London

Wallace, Joyce M. (1998) *The Historic Houses of Edinburgh.* John Donald Publishers Ltd, Edinburgh

Watney, John (1994) *Perthshire Walks.* Ordnance Survey and Jarrold

Watson, Adam (1992) *The Cairngorms, Lochnagar and the Mounth.* Scottish Mountaineering Trust, Edinburgh

Wheater, Hilary (1981) *Aberfeldy and Glenlyon.* The Tamdhu Guide

Wheater, Hilary (1982) *Kenmore and Loch Tay.* The Tamdhu Guide

White, Dennis B. (1990) *Exploring Old Duddingston and Portobello: A local history.* Mainstream, Edinburgh

Whittington, G.W. and I.D. Whyte (eds.) (1983) *An Historical Geography of Scotland.* Academic Press, London

Whyte, Donald (1970) *West Lothian, The Eastern District: Official tourist guide.* Kirkliston and Winchburgh District Council

Whyte, Ian & Whyte, Kathleen (1988) *Discovering East Lothian.* John Donald Publishers Ltd, Edinburgh

Wickham-Jones, C.R. (2001) *The Landscapes of Scotland.* Tempus, Stroud

Wilkie, James (1919) *Historic Musselburgh.* William Blackwood & Sons, Edinburgh

Williams, David (1989) *A Guide to the Southern Upland Way.* Constable & Company, Edinburgh

Williamson, Elizabeth, Riches, Anne & Higgs, Malcolm (eds.) (1990) *The Buildings of Scotland: Glasgow.* Penguin, London

Williamson, George (1888) *Old Greenock.* Paisley

Williamson, Rev. Alex. (1895) *Glimpses of Peebles.* George Lewis & Co, Selkirk

Willis, Douglas (1997) *Discovering the Black Isle.* John Donald Publishers Ltd, Edinburgh

Wills, Elspeth M. (1996) *Livingston: The Making of a Scottish New Town.* The Rutland Press & the Livingston Development Corporation

Wilson, James (1850) *Annals of Hawick 1214–1814.* Thomas George Stevenson, Edinburgh

Wilson, John J. (1985) *The Annals of Penicuik.* Spa Books, Stevenage

Withers, C.W.J. (1998) *Introduction to 'A Description of the Western Isles of Scotland ca 1695 and a Late Voyage to St. Kilda'.* Birlinn, Edinburgh

Wood, Rev. Walter (1887) *The East Neuk of Fife.* David Douglas, Edinburgh

Youngson, A.J. (1966) *The Making of Classical Edinburgh (1750–1840).* Edinburgh University Press, Edinburgh

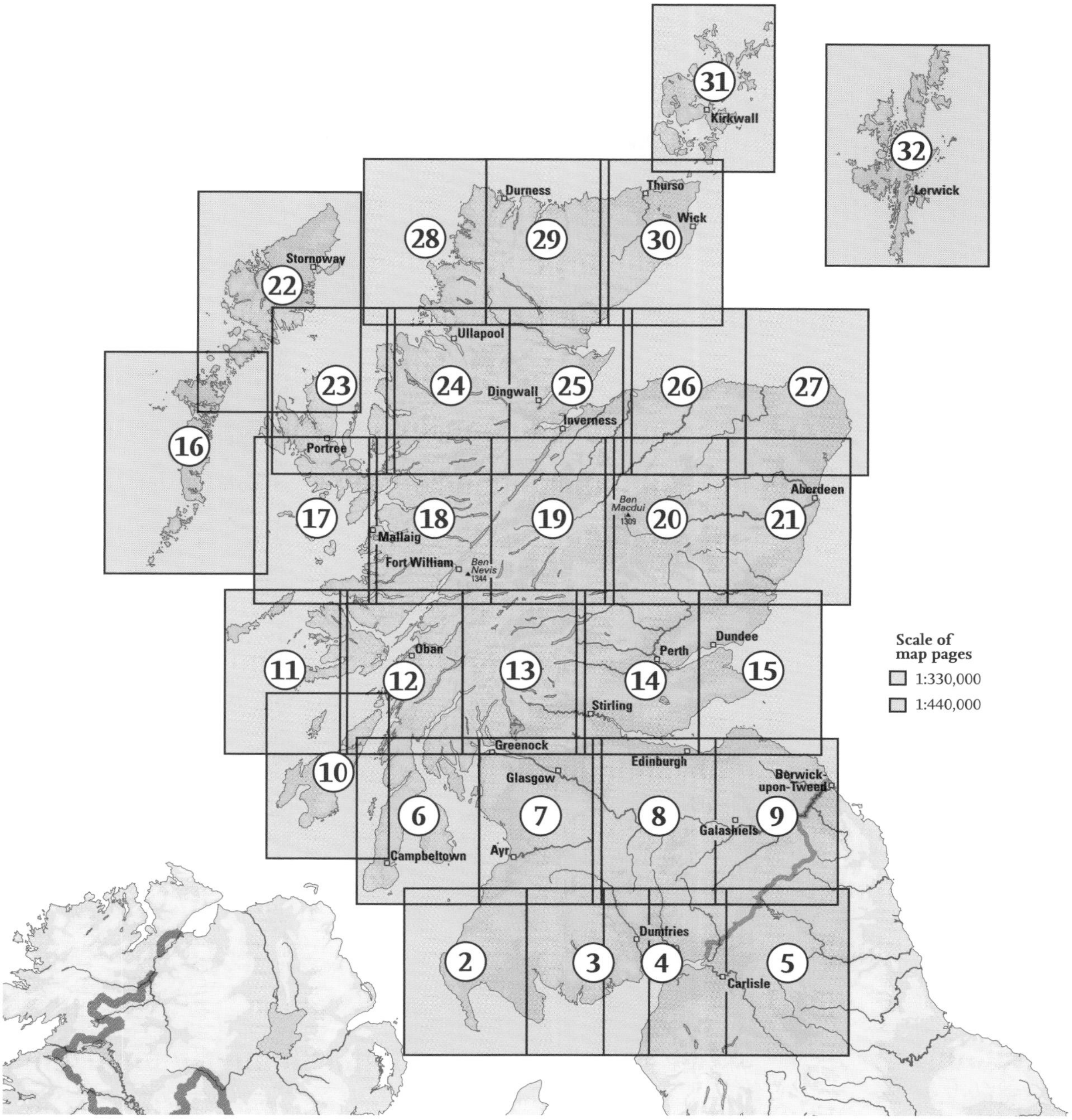

31 Kirkwall
32 Lerwick
Durness
Thurso
Wick
28
29
30
Stornoway
22
Ullapool
23
24
Dingwall
25
Inverness
26
27
16
Portree
17
18
Mallaig
Fort William
Ben Nevis 1344
19
Ben Macdui 1309
20
21
Aberdeen
11
Oban
12
13
Perth
14
Stirling
Dundee
15
Greenock
10
Glasgow
6
Campbeltown
7
Ayr
Edinburgh
8
Galashiels
Berwick-upon-Tweed
9
2
3
Dumfries
4
Carlisle
5

Scale of map pages
1:330,000
1:440,000

Key to map section

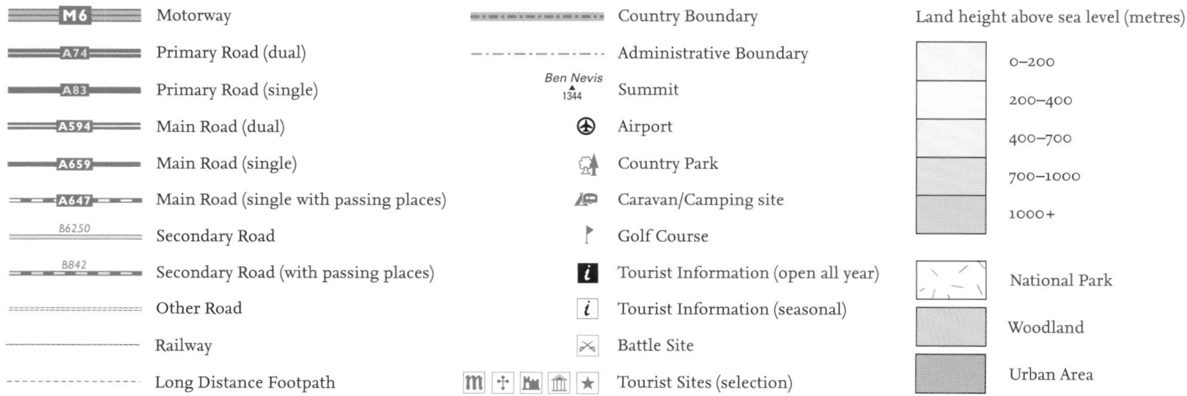

2
N
O
P
Q
R
S
63
64
65
66
67
68
69
70
Ailsa Craig
Dowhill
Wallacetown
Kilkerran
Dipple
Low
Craighead
Chapeldonan
Killochan
Dailly
Bargany
Grangeston
Old Dailly
Penkill
Hadyard Hill
324
Garleffin Fell
429
Girvan
Houston
Saugh Hill
296
Glendoune
Penwhapple Reservoir
Glengennet
North Balloch
Black Neuk
South Balloch
Glendrissaig
Ardwell
Barr
Pinminnoch
Kennedy's Pass
Grey Hill
297
A714
SOUTH
Changue Forest
Nick of the Balloch Pass
341
CARRIC
565
Polmaddie Hill
Stinchar
Pinmore
B734
479
12
Lendalfoot
Motte
Water of Lendal
AYRSHIR
Carleton Fishery
Aldons
Daljarrock
Poundland
Pinwherry
Muck Water
Bennane Head
A77
Colmonell
B734
Dalreoch
Glenduisk
Knockdolian
265
Stinchar
Craigneil
A714
Black Clauchrie
Loch Moan
Cree
Garwall Hill
349
Ballantrae Bay
B7044
Mains of Tig
Ballochmorrie
Water of Tig
Duisk
Barrhill
Ballantrae
Auchairne
Shiel Hill
230
Loch Goosey
Geoch Burn
Eldrick
Glenapp Castle
Balkissock
Lochton
Corwar House
22
Downan Point
Smyrton
A714
Kilantringan Loch
Craigie Fell
Beneraird
439
Glentrool
Cross Water
Drumlamford Loch
323
Carlock Hill
Milljoan Hill
403
Chirmorrie
Drumlamford Ho.
Altimeg Hill
Loch Dornal
Loch Ochiltree
Bargrennan
Glen App
Main Water of Luce
Loch Maberry
Clachaneasy
Finnarts Point
Markdhu
Standing Stones
Polbae
Milleur Point
Southern Upland Way
Miltonise
Corsewall Point
Cross Water of Luce
Glenwhilly
Knowe
Knockville
LOCH RYAN
Barnhills
Dalnigap
17
North Cairn
DUMFRIES AN
Urrall Fell
184
Penninghame
B738
South Cairn
Cairnryan
B7027
Main Water of Luce
Black Burn
Glenrazie
Dounan Bay
Kirkcolm
Corsewall
Airies
Ervie
Loch Connell
Artfield Fell
Carseriggan
Cairn Point
235
Braid Fell
B738
A718
A77
Beoch Burn
Black Burn
Portobello
St Mary's Croft
B798
Balminnoch
213
Culvennan Fell
Knocknain
Leswalt
Soleburn
New Luce
Tarf Bridge
Loch Ronald
Benfield
Innermessan
Shennanton
A75
Lochnaw
B7043
THE RINNS OF GALLOWAY
Auchmantle
Galdenoch
A77
Lochinch Castle
Black Loch
Craig Fell
164
15
Linn of Barhoise
B738
A751
Castle Kennedy
White Loch
Carscreugh
Barlae
Craighlaw
Kirkcowan
Broadsea Bay
Stranraer
Castle Kennedy
A75
B733
Bladnoch
Portslogan
Southern Upland Way
Loch Magillie
A75
Abbey
Whitecairn
Dunragit Moor
Soulseat Loch
Dunragit
Glenluce
Spittal
Whiteleys
Lochans
Piltanton Burn
10
Dernaglar Loch
Black Head
Kildrochet House
Genoch
Whitecrook
Castle of Park
Knock Moss
175
Knock Fell
Cairn Pat
182
B7077
Whitefield Loch
Fell Loch
Old Place of Mochrum
Dinvin
6
Colfin
Genoch Square
B7084
Castle Loch
A77
A716
B7084
Milton
Culmalzie
Portpatrick
Dunskey
Awhirk
Stoneykirk
Sands of Luce
Crow's Nest
8
Mochrum Loch
Water of Malzie
B7042
Auchenmalg
Port of Spittal Bay
11
Cairngarroch Bay
Sandhead
Auchenmalg Bay
Culshabbin
B7005
Balgreggan
A747
Alticry
Elrig Loch
Loch Head
Money Head
Kirkmadrine Stones
Chapel Finian
Elrig
A716
Clachanmore
Ardwell House
6
Motte of Druchtag
Ardwell Bay
Ardwell
Barr Point
Mochrum
14
Chapel Rossan
LUCE BAY
Standing Stones
Drumbreddan Bay
Logan
Balgowan
Port William
Logan Botanic Gardens
New England Bay
Mull of Logan
Danger Zone
Barsalloch Point
Fort
Monreith Bay
Port Logan
Terally
B7065
A716
Clanyard Bay
Kilstay
Kirkmaiden
Drummore
Laggantalluch Head
Damnaglaur
Cailiness Point
B7041
Maryport
Crammag Head
Dunman
160
Portankill
Nick of Kindram
East Tarbet
West Tarbet
Mull of Galloway
0 2 4 6 miles
0 2 4 6 8 10 km
N
O
P
Q
R
S

3
T
U
V
W
X
Y
Craigengillan
Maratz Hill
Windy Standard
698
Dalgonar
Countam
475
478
Cairnkinna Hill
552
Enterkinfoot
Breconside
Durisdeer
Gateslack
Wedder Law
666
Craighoar Hill
Earncraig Hill
610
Queensberry
697
Benbrack
448
Eriff
Alhang
Dodd Hill
498
Colt Hill
598
Countam
500
Holm of Drumlanrig
Drumlanrig
Morton Loch
Rashy Height
380
Wee Queensberry
512
Minnygap Height
399
Cairnsmore of Carsphairn
797
Drumjohn
Loch Doon
A713
Black Shoulder
688
Auchenbrack
Benbuie
516
Bail Hill
Torbraehead
400
Auchenhessnane
Carronbridge
Dabton
Thornhill
Gatelawbridge
Loch Bradan Reservoir
Waterhead
Craiglee
523
Loch Doon
Lamloch
Coran of Portmark
622
Brochloch
Craig of Knockgray
Garryhorn
Starr
Loch Head
Knockgray
Carsphairn
Marscalloch Hill
381
Southern Upland Way
Wether Hill
Cornharrow Hill
Carroch
Bennan
Burnhead
Penpont
Keir Mill
Clonrae
Tynron
A702
Keir Hills
Closeburn
Croalchapel
Loch Ettrick
Great Hill
353
Forest of Ae
Hole
63
Meaul
695
Bardennoch
Kendoon Loch
B729
Craigdarroch
Moniaive
Crawfordton
Kirkland
Dalshangan
19
Polmaddy Burn
Glencrosh
Crossford
Barndennoch
Dalswinton Common
Ae Village
Kirkland
A70
GALLOWAY FOREST PARK
Carlin's Cairn
Rhinns of Kells
Corserine
813
Forrest Lodge
Loch Harrow
Burnhead
Wether Hill
385
Castlefairn
Holmhead
Bogrie Hill
432
Glenhead
Blackwood
Auldgirth
Millfire
716
Meikle Millyea
746
Knocknalling
A713
Earlstoun Loch
B7000
13
A702
Lochurr
Loch Urr
Waterhead
Sundaywell
Crawston Hill
217
Milton
Stroquhan
Dunscore
Allanton
Friars Carse
Dalswinton
Duncow
Glenae
64
Craignaw
Loch Neldricken
Loch Valley
Garroch
Corriedoo
St John's Town of Dalry
406
Blackcraig Hill
Loch Howie
Craigenputtock
Speddoch
14
A76
Kirkton
Amisfield Town
Holywood
Tinwald
Darrou
Glenlee
Bogue
Blackcraig
Drumwhirn
Newtonairds
Gribton
Clatteringshaws Loch
Bennan
381
Bruce's Stone (NTS)
New Galloway
A762
A712
Balmaclellan
Garcrogo Forest
Knocklearn
Slongaber
Skeoch Hill
Glenkiln Resr
New Bridge
Lincluden Coll
Locharbriggs
A701
Lochar Moss
Craigencallie
Darnaw
Clatteringshaws
493
Cairnsmore of Dee
Kenmure
A713
Gibbshill
282
Largliar Hill
15
Corsock
Corsock Loch
Margreig
398
Glen
Scaur
Shawhead
Terregles
DUMFRIES
Collin
Millfore
656
Forest Drive (summer only)
Dee (Black Water of Dee)
Galloway Deer Range
A712
Merkland
A712
Crofts
Brooklands
Henderland
A75
9
Cargenbridge
Lochfoot
Camera Obscura
Robert Burns
65
445
Wild Goat Park
19
Round Fell
402
Fell of Fleet
471
Shaw Hill
385
Bennan Cottage
Drumrash
Glenlair
Square Point
Auchenreoch Loch
Crocketford or Ninemile Bar
Milton Loch
Brae
Dalskairth
Goldielea
Kingholm Quay
GALLOWAY
601
Toll
Mossdale
Parton
Walton Park
Kirkpatrick Durham
8
Milton
Cargen
A710
Netherwood
Dallash
Craignelder
Loch Grannoch
Loch Fleet
Auchencloy Hill
209
Airie Hill
291
Slogarie
13
A713
Loch Roan
Springholm
Lochaber Loch
Mabie
Whinny Hill
Gillfoot
Kelton
A712
Cairnsmore of Fleet
711
Loch Skerrow
Craig
14
Auchendolly
Old Bridge of Urr
Crossmichael
Hermitage
Stonehouse
Tower
Beeswing
Loch Arthur
14
321
Lotus Hill
Glencaple
Kirkconnell
Shambellie
Bargaly
Newton Stewart
Blackcraig
Cairnsmore
Door of Cairnsmore
White Top of Culreoch
344
Laurieston
Glenlochar
Clarebrand
Townhead of Greenlaw
A75
Mollance
Haugh of Urr
Kirkgunzeon
A711
Kinharvie
Corn Mill
New Abbey
Sweetheart Abbey
66
Palnure
6
A75
Darngarroch
A762
Threave
Hillowton
Motte of Urr
B794
Cuil Hill
Loch Kindar
16
Baltersan
Spittal
Castramont
Loch Whinyeon
4
Castle Douglas
Buchan
Carlingwark Loch
A745
Craignair
6
Dalbeattie
Loch Fern
Criffell
569
A710
Carse Bay
Barholm Mains
Gem Rock Museum
Creetown
Glenquicken Moor
Rusko
Low Barlay
Glengap
Bridge of Dee
Rhonehouse (Kelton Hill)
Breoch
A710
Dalbeattie Forest
B793
Kirkbean
Carsethorn
Cavens
Wigtown Sands
Cassencarie
Martyrs' Monument
Wigtown
Glen
Lauchentyre
Cairnharrow
456
Anworth
Gatehouse of Fleet
Ringford
2
Dildawn
Argrennan House
Gelston
Palnackie
Barnbarroch
Caulkerbush
Southwick
Borron Point
Mainsriddle
Carsluith
Chambered Cairns
Ardwall
Cardoness Castle
Valleyfield
Barcaple
6
A711
Netherthird
Tongland Loch
Airieland
Screel Hill
343
Kippford (Scaur)
Orchardton Tower
10
Fairgirth
Sandyhills
A710
Preston Merse
Southerness
67
Bladnoch
Carsluith
13
Cardoness
Girthon
A75
Twynholm
Cumstoun
Tongland
Dam
391
Bengairn
A711
Mote of Mark (NTS)
Rough Firth
Colvend
Rockcliffe
Port o' Warren
Mersehead Sands
Southerness Point
Baldoon Sands
Kirkdale House
A75
Sandgreen
Fleet Bay
Barharrow
A755
Langlands
7
Broughton Ho
Kirkcudbright
Stewartry Museum
Maclellan's Castle (ruin)
Auchencairn
18
Auchencairn Bay
Castlehill Point
Almorness Point
Barnhourie Sands
Kirkinner
Orchardton Bay
Murray's Isles
Lennox Plunton
High Borgue
Bombie
Bankhead
Hazlefield
Hestan Island
Balcary Point
Stewarton
Innerwell Port
A746
Ardwall Island
Islands of Fleet
Barlocco Island
Knockbrex
B727
Borgue
St Mary's Isle
Auchnabony
Dundrennan
A711
Rascarrel
Rascarrel Bay
Eggerness
B7004
B7052
Garlieston
Galloway House
Kirkandrews
Townhead
Abbey
Orroland
Barlocco Bay
12
Senwick
Kirkcudbright Bay
WIGTOWN BAY
Ringdoo Point
Borness
Ross
Balmae
Port Mary
Cruggleton Bay
Cults
(ruin)
B7063
Little Ross
Abbey Head
68
Port Allen
Whithorn
Priory
A746
Portyerrock
B7004
Isle of Whithorn
St Ninian's Chapel
Kidsdale
Cutcloy
Devil's Bridge
SOLWAY FIRTH
Maryport
69
5
Flimby
A596
Seaton
Great Clifton
Stainburn
WORKINGTON
A597
Schoose
A596
3
A595
High Harrington
Branthwaite
70
Distington
A595
6
Howgate
Low Moresby
Parton
Moresby Parks
WHITEHAVEN
0 2 4 6 miles
0 2 4 6 8 10 km

4
DUMFRIES AND GALLOWAY
SOLWAY FIRTH
LAKE DISTRICT NATIONAL PARK
DUMFRIES
WORKINGTON
Cockermouth
Maryport
Wigton
Annan
Gretna
Lockerbie
Lochmaben
Dalbeattie
Keswick
Silloth
Aspatria
Thornhill
Langholm
0 2 4 6 miles
0 2 4 6 8 10 km

5
NORTHUMBERLAND NATIONAL PARK
KIELDER FOREST PARK
CHEVIOT HILLS
LIDDESDALE
Kershope Forest
Kielder Water (Reservoir)
Kielder Water Experience
Kielder
Kielder Forest
Newcastleton
Newcastleton Forest
Kershopefoot
Hermitage
Saughtree
Larriston Fells
Wark Forest
Spadeadam Forest
Danger Zone
Bewcastle
Falstone
Greenhaugh
Bellingham
Otterburn
Otterburn 1388
Rochester
Byrness
Catcleugh Reservoir
Harwood Forest
Elsdon
Raylees
West Woodburn
Ridsdale
Kirkwhelpington
Redesmouth
Wark
Birtley
Simonburn
Chollerton
Humshaugh
Chollerford
Hadrian's Wall
Housesteads (Vercovicium) (NT)
Vindolanda
Once Brewed Visitor Centre
Birdoswald (Camboglanna)
Gilsland
Greenhead
Haltwhistle
Melkridge
Henshaw
Bardon Mill
Haydon Bridge
Hexham
Corbridge
Acomb
Fourstones
Newbrough
Brampton
Lanercost Priory
Walton
Naworth
Irthington
Crosby-on-Eden
Hayton
Warwick Bridge
Wetheral
Great Corby
Corby Castle
Cumwhinton
Carlatton
Cumrew
Castle Carrock
Talkin
Talkin Tarn
Hallbankgate
Tindale
Midgeholme
Halton Lea Gate
Coanwood
Featherstone Castle
Lambley
Plenmeller Common
Langley
Allen Banks (NT)
Whitfield
Catton
Allendale Town
Ninebanks
Slaggyford
Knarsdale
Kirkhaugh
Alston
Nenthead
Killhope Lead Mining Centre
Killhope Moor
Garrigill
Cowshill
Wearhead
St John's Chapel
Westgate
Eastgate
Stanhope
Rookhope
Allenheads
Carr Shield
Blanchland
Edmundbyers
Slaley
Slaley Forest
Penrith
Eamont Bridge
Brougham
Brocavum Roman Fort
Yanwath
Stainton
Penruddock
Dacre
Pooley Bridge
Ullswater Steamers
Askham
Lowther
Lowther Castle
Lowther Wildlife Park
Hackthorpe
Clifton
Temple Sowerby
Culgaith
Acorn Bank (NT)
Langwathby
Edenhall
Melmerby
Ousby
Skirwith
Kirkoswald
Lazonby
Glassonby
Great Salkeld
Little Salkeld
Plumpton
Inglewood Forest
Armathwaite
Ainstable
Croglin
Renwick
Hartside Height
Cross Fell
Great Dun Fell
Dufton
Appleby-in-Westmorland
Long Marton
Brampton
Crackenthorpe
Kirkby Thore
Cow Green Reservoir
Widdybank Fell
Cauldron Snout
High Force
Forest-in-Teesdale
Newbiggin
Holwick
Lune Forest
Grassholme Reservoir
Selset Reservoir
Balderhead Reservoir
Hury Reservoir
Romaldkirk
Middleton Common
Eggleston
Barnard Castle
Lartington
Cotherstone
Hamsterley Forest
Alston Moor
Milburn Forest
Geltsdale Middle
King's Forest of Geltsdale
0 2 4 6 miles
0 2 4 6 8 10 km

6
L
M
N
O
P
Q
55
56
57
58
59
60
61
62
Tarbert
Tarbert Bay
Keillmore
New Ulva
Ulva Islands
Taynish
Dunardry
Auchbraad
Lagg
Rubh' a' Chamais
Gate House
Danna Island
Sween
Loch Sween
Achamore
Corr Eilean
Eilean Mòr
Eilean Mòr Chapel
Kilmory
Chapel
Ellary
St Columba's Cave
Ardmenish
An Dùnan
Rubh' an Leim
Sròn Garbh
Rubh' an Leanachais
Point of Knap
Loch Caolisport
Achahoish
Clachbreck
Ballyaurgan
Baile Boidheach
Ormsary
Druimdrishaig
Larach na Gaibhre
Loch nan Torran
Cretshengan
Coulaghailtro
Kilberry
Kilberry Head
Crosses
Cruach Airde
213
Carse
Dunmore
Rubha Cruitiridh
Ardpatrick
Achadh-chaorrunn
Ardpatrick Point
Portachoillan
Quinhill
Clachan
Ronachan Point
Ronachan
Corriechrevie
Ballochroy
Auchinafaud
Rhunahaorine Point
Rhunahaorine
Tayinloan
Killean
Beacharr
Muasdale
Achaglass
Glenacardoch Point
Belloch
Arnicle
Glenbarr
Bellochantuy Bay
Bellochantuy
Killocraw
Corrylach
Tangy
Tangy Loch
Westport
Low Ballevain
Skeroblingarry
Drumgarve
Glen Lussa
Calliburn
Kilchenzie
Peninver
Ardnacross Bay
East Darlochan
Machrihanish Bay
Kilmichael
CAMPBELTOWN (MACHRIHANISH)
Drumore
Machrihanish
Campbeltown
Campbeltown Loch
Davaar Island
Dalivaddy
Witchburn
Drumlemble
Mus
Davaar
Kilkerran
Glenramskill
New Orleans
Chiscan
Knocknaha
Beinn Ghuilean
352
Oatfield
Kilchrist
Eraradale Point
385
The Slate
Conie Water
Killellan
312
Arinarach Hill
446
Cnoc Moy
Largybaan
273
Cnoc Reamhar
Dùin Bhàin
Cnoc Odhar
277
Conie Glen
Glen Kerran
Feochaig
Ru Stafnish
Sheanachie
Glen Breackerie
Brecklate
Kepprigan
Kildavie
Strone Glen
Beinn na Lice
428
Carrine
Macharioch
Polliwilline Bay
Keil
Southend
Garveld
Carskey Bay
Feorlan
Borgadelmore Point
Mull of Kintyre
Sanda Sound
Sheep Island
Sanda Island
0 2 4 6 miles
0 2 4 6 8 10 km
A846
A83
B8024
B8025
B8001
B842
B843
A841
B880
A886
A8003
A844
A815
A880
B836
B878
B881
B8000
ARGYLL AND BUTE
KNAPDALE
KINTYRE
ARRAN
NORTH AYRSHIRE
SOUND OF JURA
SOUND OF GIGHA
SOUND OF BUTE
KILBRANNAN SOUND
LOCH FYNE
FIRTH OF CLYDE
Achaglachgach Forest
Cruach a' Phubuill
477
Stob Odhaim
562
Meall Mòr
471
Cnoc a' Bharaille
Loch Fuar Bheinne
Loch Chaorunn
Meall Reamhar
480
Dubh Chreag
329
Erines
Srondoire
Barmore Island
Stonefield
Barfad
Ashens
East Loch Tarbert
Tarbert
West Tarbert
Escart
Mealdarroch Point
Dubhchladach
Cruach an t-Sorchain
343
Corranbuie
Achadacaie
Cruach Doire Leithe
377
Cnoc a' Bhaile-shios
422
Kennacraig
Redhouse
Whitehouse
West Loch Tarbert
Coire nan Capull
334
Gartavaich
Gartnagrenach
Glenrisdell
Cruach nam Fiadh
269
Claonaig
Skipness
Skipness Point
Auchameanach
Rockfield
Escart Farm
Port Fada
Loch Ciaran
Loch Garasdale
Crossaig
248
Cruach Mhic-Gougain
Cnoc an t-Samhlaidh
264
Cour Bay
Cour
Narachan Hill
285
Cnoc Reamhar
203
Sunadale
Grogport
Deucheran Hill
329
Cruach Mhic-an-t-Saoir
364
Cruach nan Gabhar
354
Carradale Forest
Diollaid Mhòr
362
Carradale East
Beinn Bhreac
426
Rhonadale
Carradale
Dippen
Carradale Garden
Carradale Bay
Beinn an Tuirc
454
Torrisdale
Bord Mòr
408
Whitestone
Meall Buidhe
374
Abbey (ruins)
Saddell
Saddell Bay
Saddell Forest
Sgreadan Hill
397
Bunlarie
Lussa Loch
Ugadale Point
Ballochgair
Port Mòr
West Tarbert Bay
East Tarbert Bay
Tarbert
Creag Bhan
100
Ardailly
Druimyeon Bay
Gigha
Ardminish
Ardminish Bay
Achamore Gardens
Craro Island
Grob Bagh
Cara Island
Mull of Cara
Caolard Rubha
Eilean Mòr
Ballimore
Auchalick
Fearnoch
Rubha Beag
Kilfinan Bay
Lindsaig
Kilfinan
Otter
Port Leathan
Drum
Auchalick Bay
Lower Auchalick
Melldalloch
Craignafeoch
Derybruich
Portavadie
Tighnabruaich
Port Driseach
Acharosson
Beinn Bhreac
454
Beinn Capuill
438
West Glen
Auchenlochan
Kames
Millhouse
Blair's Ferry
207
Cnoc na Carraige
Kilbride Farm
Low Stillaig
Asgog Bay
Kilbride Bay
Carry
Ardlamont
Ardlamont Bay
Ardlamont Point
Rubha Lagganroaig
Camas na Ceardaich
Culindrach
Ballochandrain
Craigendive
Ormidale
458
Cruach nan Caorach
Auchenbreck
Ard a' Chapuill
Springfield
Fearnoch
Buttock Point
Colintraive
Rhubodach
Shalunt
Stuck
Kames Hill
Ardmaleish
Ardmaleish Point
Ardyne Point
Glenmore
Glecknabae
Kilbride
Drumachloy
Port Bannatyne
St Colmac
Ardbeg
Ardbeg Point
Rothesay
Craigmore
Bogany Point
Ardencraig Gardens
Bute Museum
Ascog
Loch Ascog
St Mary's Chapel
Kerrycroy
Ettrick Bay
Upper Ardroscadale
Straad
Loch Fad
St Ninian's Point
Meikle Kilmory
Meikle Grenach
Inchmarnock
Midpark
Loch Quien
Ambrismore
Mount Stuart
Ardscalpsie
Scalpsie Bay
Stravanan
Stravanan Bay
Piperhall
Kingarth
Kilchattan Bay
Dunagoil Bay
St Blane's Church
Garrochty
Garroch Head
Tòrr Mòr
146
Strone Point
Knockdow
Innellan
Toward
Toward Point
Glenkin
Sandbank
Hunter's Quay
Dunloskin
Bishop's Seat
504
Inverchaolain
Corlarach Hill
419
Beinn Ruadh
323
Kilmarnock Hill
365
Blairbuie
Coustonn
South Hall
Glaic
Troustan
Black Craig
522
Beinn Bhreac
507
Invervegain
Cruach nan Capull
568
Leacann nan Gall
611
Cruach Neuran
607
Ardtaraig
Dalinlongart
Clachaig
Ardnadam
Great Cumbrae
Millport
Little Cumbrae
Hunterston
Gull Point
Portencross
Farland Head
Tomont End
Cock of Arran
Newton
Loch Ranza
Lochranza
Catacol Bay
Catacol
Glen Chalmadale
Rubha Airigh Bheirg
Craw
Lenimore
Thundergay
Glen Catacol
Beinn Bhreac
711
554
Beinn Tarsuinn
573
523
Caisteal Abhail
859
North Glen Sannox
Glen Sannox
Sannox
Sannox Bay
Cioch-na-h-Oighe
661
Cir Mhòr
798
Auchamore
Pirnmill
Beinn Bhreac
Mullach Buidhe
721
715
Beinn Bharrain
Loch Tanna
Beinn Tarsuinn
825
792
Goat Fell
874
Corrie
Whitefarland Point
Imachar
Balliekine
Beinn Nuis
Glen Iorsa
Glen Rosa
Dougarie Point
Dougarie
Brodick (NTS)
Merkland Point
Brodick Castle and Garden (NTS)
Brodick Bay
Heritage Mus
Brodick
Strathwhillan
Chambered Cairn
361
An Tunna
Glencloy
Auchgallon Stone Circle
Glaister
Tarrnacraig
512
Machrie Bay
Machrie
Machrie Water
Ard Bheinn
512
A'Chruach
South Corriegills
Clauchlands Point
Machrie Moor Stone Circles
Beinn Bhreac
503
Ballymichael
Benlister Glen
Margnaheglish
Lamlash
Lamlash Bay
Holy Island
Tormore
King's Cave
Hut Circles
Shiskine
Cnoc a' Chapuill
417
Glenkiln
Torbeg
Fort
Blackwaterfoot
Drumadoon Bay
Kilpatrick
458
Tighvein
Knockenkelly
Kingscross Point
Kingscross
Kiscadale
Whiting Bay
Brown Head
Glen Scorrodale
Glen Ashdale
Largymore
Corriecravie
Sliddery
Torr a' Chaisteal
Largybeg
Largybeg Point
Dippen
Kilmory Water
Kilmory
Levencorroch
Dippin Head
Lagg
Chambered Cairns
Shannochie
Kildonan
Bennan Head
Sound of Pladda
Pladda
Ailsa Craig
14
5
16
33
17
11
25
13
10
6
7
4
3
12
8
1
2

7
Rosneath
Helensburgh
Alexandria
Balloch
Jamestown
Bonhill
Renton
Cardross
GREENOCK
Port Glasgow
DUMBARTON
WEST DUNBARTONSHIRE
Kilpatrick Hills
Milton
Bowling
Old Kilpatrick
Erskine
Bishopton
Clydebank
Milngavie
Bearsden
Strathblane
Lennoxtown
Lennox Forest
EAST DUNBARTONSHIRE
CAMPSIE FELLS
Kilsyth Hills
Kilsyth
Milton of Campsie
Kirkintilloch
Lenzie
Moodiesburn
Cumbernauld
INVERCLYDE
CLYDE MUIRSHIEL REGIONAL PARK
Kilmacolm
Houston
Bridge of Weir
Renfrew
Inchinnan
Linwood
PAISLEY
Johnstone
Elderslie
GLASGOW
Rutherglen
Coatbridge
Airdrie
Chryston
Muirhead
Glenboig
Glenmavis
Chapelhall
Holytown
Bellshill
Uddingston
Bothwell
Blantyre
MOTHERWELL
HAMILTON
EAST KILBRIDE
Carfin
Newarthill
Cleland
Wishaw
Overtown
Larkhall
Quarter
Law
Ashgill
RENFREWSHIRE
Howwood
Lochwinnoch
Kilbirnie
Beith
Barrhead
Neilston
Uplawmoor
EAST RENFREWSHIRE
Waterfoot
Mearns
Eaglesham
Thorntonhall
Carmunnock
Strathaven
Chapelton
Glassford
Stonehouse
Blackwood
Kirkmuirhill
Lesmahagow
SOUTH LANARKSHIRE
Dalry
Kilwinning
Ardrossan
Stevenston
Saltcoats
Stewarton
Dunlop
Fenwick
Kilmaurs
CUNNINGHAME
IRVINE
Dreghorn
Springside
KILMARNOCK
Crosshouse
Galston
Newmilns
Darvel
Priestland
Irvine Bay
Dundonald
Symington
Troon
Barassie
Craigie
Crosshands
Mauchline
Catrine
Sorn
Tarbolton
PRESTWICK INT
Prestwick
Monkton
Mossblown
Ayr Bay
AYR
Annbank
Auchinleck
Cumnock
Muirkirk
Glespin
Douglas
Coalburn
KYLE
EAST AYRSHIRE
Ochiltree
Drongan
Coylton
Heads of Ayr
Alloway
Dalrymple
Maybole
Kirkoswald
SOUTH AYRSHIRE
Patna
Dalmellington
New Cumnock
Kirkconnel
Sanquhar
Crosshill
Straiton
Dailly
Lady Isle

8
X
Y
Z
AA
BB
CC
55
56
57
58
59
60
61
62
Firth of Forth
EDINBURGH
Dean Gallery
Edinburgh Castle
Edinburgh University
Murrayfield
Our Dynamic Earth
Palace of Holyroodhouse
FALKIRK
Grangemouth
Larbert
Bo'ness
Linlithgow
WEST LOTHIAN
LIVINGSTON
Bathgate
Armadale
Whitburn
Broxburn
Queensferry
Kirkliston
Musselburgh
Dalkeith
Penicuik
Loanhead
Bonnyrigg
Newtongrange
Gorebridge
MIDLOTHIAN
PENTLAND HILLS REGIONAL PARK
PENTLAND HILLS
Shotts
Wishaw
Carluke
Lanark
New Lanark
Carstairs
Carnwath
Biggar
West Linton
Peebles
Innerleithen
Lesmahagow
Douglas
SOUTH LANARKSHIRE
Abington
Crawford
Leadhills
Wanlockhead
LOWTHER HILLS
Moffat
Tweedsmuir
Megget Reservoir
ETTRICK FOREST
Craik Forest
Eskdalemuir
NITHSDALE
Thornhill
TWEEDDALE
MOORFOOT HILLS
M8
M9
M74
A74(M)
A70
A701
A702
A708
A72

0 2 4 6 miles
0 2 4 6 8 10 km
DD
EE
FF
GG
HH
II
55
56
57
58
59
60
61
62
Gullane Point
Gullane Bay
Gullane
Scoughall
Dirleton
North Berwick Law
Aberlady
Fenton Barns
Whitekirk
St Baldred's Cradle
Tyninghame House
John Muir
Tyne Mouth
Belhaven Bay
Luffness
Craigielaw
Drem
East Fortune
Museum of Flight
Tyninghame
Dunbar
Preston Mill & Phantassie Dovecot (NTS)
Chesters Hill Fort
Preston
Gosford House
Ballencrieff
EAST
Athelstaneford
East Linton
West Barns
Broxburn
Barns Ness
Spittal
Longniddry
Garleton Hills
Traprain
Pitcox
Dunbar 1650
Skateraw
Skateraw Harbour
Elvingston
Haddington
St Mary's Church
Hailes
Luggate
Church
Spott
Doonhill Homestead
Brunt Hill
Thorntonloch
Gladsmuir
Traprain Law Fort
Luggate Burn
Stenton
Innerwick
Macmerry
LOTHIAN
Penston
Pressmennan Lake
Halls
Bilsdean
Dunglass Church
Reed Point
Cove
Pease Bay
Siccar Point
Fast
Wheat Stack
New Winton
Lennoxlove
Papple
Whitelaw Hill
Deuchrie Dod
Cocklaw Hill
319
Oldhamstocks
Cockburnspath
Telegraph Hill
174
New Town
Samuelston
Bolton
Garvald
Bransly Hill
397
Pencaitland
Carfrae
Nunraw Abbey
Dunbar Common
St Abb's Head
Lumsdaine
Coldingham Loch
Gifford Church
Clints Dod
398
Ecclaw
Meikle Black Law
Northfield
St Abbs
West Saltoun
Gifford
Danskine
White Castle
Monynut Edge
Heart Law
391
Ecclaw Hill
277
Coldingham Moor
East Saltoun
Rangely Kip
400
Spartleton Edge
Southern Upland Way
Coldingham Bay
Peastonbank
Gilchriston
Peaston
Longyester
Newlands Hill
423
LAMMERMUIR HILLS
Gamelshiel
Blackburn Rig
Grantshouse
Coldingham
Priory
Laughing Law
307
Press
Houndwood
Mus
Eyemouth
Humbie
Whiteadder Reservoir
Penshiel Hill
Abbey St Bathans
Trout Farm
Horseley Hill
262
Cairncross
Lammer Law
528
Hopes Resr
Meikle Says Law
535
Cranshaws Hill
379
Cranshaws
Drakemire
Reston
Ayton
Burnmouth
Fala
Crib Law
509
Seenes Law
513
Ellemford
Cockburn Law
325
Edin's Hall Broch
Auchencrow
Millerton Hill
132
Ayton Hill
199
Hilton Bay
Lamberton Beach
West Hill
451
Meikle Law
467
Wrunk Law
364
Marygold
Soutra Hill
368
Dun Law
394
Hunt Law
495
Blythe Edge
LAMMERMUIR
Longformacus
Lintlaw
Tithe Barn
Lamberton
Mordington Holdings
Marshall Meadows
Needles Eye
Gilston
Turf Law
Preston
Blanerne
Edrom
Norman Arch
Chirnside
Chirnsidebridge
Foulden
Clappers
Halidon Hill
Hogs Law
448
Watch Water Reservoir
Dirrington Great Law
398
Duns
Manderston
Allanton
Hutton
Paxton
Berwick-upon-Tweed
Ravensdowne Barracks
Oxton
Carfraemill
Dirrington Little Law
363
Gavinton
Whitelaw
Blackadder
Sunwick
Paxton House
Fishwick
Collie Law
381
Scoured Rig
363
Choicelee
Polwarth
Sinclair's Hill
Whitsome
Union Bridge
East Ord
Redshin Cove
Inchkeith Hill
365
Edgarhope Wood
Westruther
Hule Moss
Greenlaw Moor
Fogo
Fogo Church
Horndean
Lady Kirk Church
Horncliffe
Longridge Towers
Scremerston
Thirlestane
Lauder
Thirlestane
Houndslow
Fogorig
Swinton
Swinton Quarter
Ladykirk
Thornton Park
Murton
Thornton
Torquhan
Lauder Common
Whiteburn
Greenlaw
Swintonmill
Upsettlington
Norham
Shoreswood
West Allerdean
Shoresdean
Killochyett
Stow
Nether Blainslie
Purves Hall
Leitholm
Simprim
Grindon
Ancroft
Berrington
Torsonce
Legerwood
Greenknowe Tower
Felkington
Duddo
Huntlywood
Gordon
Easter Howlaws
Orange Lane
Bowsden
Birkhill
East Morriston
West Morriston
Hume
Humehall
Lambden
Eccles
The Hirsel
Lennel
Castle Heaton
William Law
401
Fans
Legars
Coldstream Museum
Barmoor Lane End
Buckholm
Langshaw
Mellerstain
Sweethope Hill
223
Bingham
Coldstream
Cornhill on Tweed
New Heaton
Etal
Lowick
Earlston
Stichill
Carham
Wark
Crookham Eastfield
Crookham
Galashiels
Glendearg
Nenthorn
Ednam
West Learmouth
East Learmouth
Pallinsburn House
Branxton
Mardon
Ford
Meigle Hill
423
Woollen Mill
Drygrange
Redpath
Smailholm
Hendersyde Park
Kelso
Hadden
Pressen
Flodden 1513
Flodden
Kimmerston
Caddonfoot
Gattonside
Leaderfoot
Smailholm Tower
Sprouston
Downham
Milfield
Fenton
Gala Hill
Abbotsford
Melrose
Newstead
Scott's View
Floors
Mindrummill
Mindrum
Howtel
Housedon Hill
267
Yair Hill Forest
Boleside
Darnick
Priorwood (NTS)
Eildon
Bemersyde
Wallace Monument
Kelso Abbey
Pawston
Kilham
Nesbit
Eildon Hills
422
Dryburgh
Clintmains
Makerstoun
Trows
Maxwellheugh
Lempitlaw
Ewart
Doddington
Newtown
Peat Law
426
Cauldshiels Hill
328
Newtown St Boswells
Dryburgh Abbey
Mertoun
Kilham Hill
328
Lanton
Coupland
Homildon Hill
Lindean
St Boswells
Roxburgh
Blakelaw
Vencher Hill
269
Westnewton
Yeavering
Selkirk Glass
Bowden
Maxton
Rutherford
Heiton
Kirknewton
Akeld
Selkirk
Sir Walter Scott's Courtroom
Charlesfield
Yetholm Mains
Coldsmouth Hill
416
361
Humbleton
Wooler
Bowmont Forest
Linton Hill
282
Gipsy Palace
Yeavering Bell
Philiphaugh
Halliwell's House Mus
Longnewton
Fairnington
Frogden
Town Yetholm
Kirk Yetholm
Hethpool
Newton Tors
Fredden Hill
347
Earle
Haugh Head
Midlem
Ancrum Moor 1545
Waterloo Monument
Peniel Heugh
237
Kale Water
Linton
White Law
Middleton Hall
Lilliesleaf
New Belses
Nisbet
Eckford
Crookedshaws Hill
306
Preston Hill
526
Cold Law
452
North Middleton
South Middleton
Clerklands
Riddell
Old Belses
Ancrum
Harestanes Woodlands Centre
Crailing
Morebattle
The Curr
564
The Schil
601
Ilderton
Chesters
Bonjedward
Cessford
Gateshaw
Hownam Law
449
Langleeford
Langlee Crags
Woll
Ashkirk
Minto Hills
Lanton
Jedburgh
Hartrigge
Crailinghall
Mowhaugh
Sourhope
The Cheviot
815
Hassendean
Minto
Newton
Mary Queen of Scots House
Shibden Hill
307
Hownam Mains
Groundistone Heights
Drinkstone Hill
318
Horsleyhill
Knowetownhead
Dunion Hill
Abbey
Hownam
Craik Moor
Hedgehope Hill
714
Dunmoor Hill
567
Clarilaw
Denholm
Bedrule
Hundalee
Oxnam
Chatto
Esdale Law
356
Ashybank
Appletreehall
Langlee
Comb Fell
652
Hawick Mus & Scott Gallery
Rubers Law
424
Swinside Hall
Swanlaws
Cook Law
Windy Gyle
619
Hawick
Cavers
Bairnkine
Mossburnford
NORTHUMBERLAND NATIONAL PARK
Roberton
Hallrule
Faw Hill
331
Bloodybush Edge
610
Shill Moor
528
Cochrane
Drumlanrig's Tower
Kirkton
Abbotrule
Mervinslaw
Camptown
Falla
Beefstand Hill
562
Cushat Law
616
High Knowes
394
Branxholm Bridgend
White Hill
301
Woden Law
422
Loft Hill
460
Nettlehope Hill
475
Wether Cairn
563
Prendwick
Branxholme
Bonchester Bridge
Hobkirk
Bonchester Hill
Philip Law
414
Blindburn
Hazelton Hill
476
Alnham
Newmill
Cleuch Head
Chesters
Bell Hill
491
Scrainwood
Southdean
Wolfelee
Wolfelee Hill
Huntford
Deerlee Knowe
Leithope Forest
Arks Edge
Grindstone Law
468
Makendon
Woolbist Law
433
Chew Green
Elilaw
Netherton Northside
Netherton Burnfoot
Broadhaugh
Teviot
Northhouse
Berryfell Hill
393
Redeswire Fray 1575
Leap Hill
471
Ravens Knowe
527
Shillmoor
Clennell
Biddlestone
Netherton
Linbriggs
Newton
Alwinton
Burradon
Carter Bar
418
Catcleugh Shin
544
Hungry Law
501
Windy Crag
491
Crigdon Hill
377
Linshiels
Danger Zone
Hyndlee
Shankend
Green Law
368
Blackkip
445
Harbottle
Sharperton
High Trewhitt
The Pike
462
Wyndburgh Hill
507
Wauchope Forest
Carter Fell
556
Catcleugh
Catcleugh Reservoir
Lady's Well
Plainfield
Skelfhill Pen
532
Note o' the Gate
376
Carlin Tooth
551
Knox Knowe
Fanna Hill
514
Needs Law
444
Girdle Fell
530
Byrness
Holystone Common
Holystone
Caistron
Flotterton
Maiden Paps
511
Sandy Edge
Hartshorn Pike
545
Ellis Crag
497
Redesdale Forest
North Yardhope
Corby Pike
368
Hepple
Little Tosson
Cauldcleuch Head
608
Greatmoor Hill
599
Singdean
Kielderhead Moor
Toll
Sills
Bickerton
Millstone Edge
565
Tudhope
599
Saughtree Fell
434
Peel Fell
602
Oh Me Edge
Blakeman's Law
Hindhope Law
425
Rochester
Rushy Knowe
325
Tosson Hill
440
Simonside
429
Saughtree
Forest Drive
Davyshiel Common
Billsmoor Park
Dough Crag
Hermitage
Arnton Fell
Wether Hill
496
Horsley
Blakeman's
Otterburn
Geordie's Hill
529
Roman Road
Rothbury

H
I
J
K
L
G
53
54
55
56
57
58
59
an Naoimh
Monastery (ruin)
Lunga
Guirasdeal
Cruach Scarba
449
Scarba
Str. of Corryvreckan
Beinn nan Capull
252
Cruach na Seilcheig
296
Dubh Artach
Eilean Dubh
Balnahard Bay
Rubh' a' Geodha
Kiloran Bay
Balnahard
Loch an Sgoltaire
Kiloran Gardens
Port Ceann a' Gharraidh
Kiloran
Colonsay House
Upper Kilchattan
Lower Kilchattan
Port Mòr
Loch Fada
B8086
B8087
Scalasaig
COLONSAY
Machrins
Port Lotha
Loch Staosnaig
B8085
Baleromindubh
Rubha Dubh
Sguide an Leannal
Garvard
Balerominmore
Eilean Mhucaig
Dubh Eilean
Priory
Rubha Bàn
Oronsay
Caolas Mòr
Eilean Ghaoideamal
Eilean nan Ron
Glengarrisdale Bay
Bàgh Gleann Speireig
Glengarrisdale
Glendebadel Bay
Ben Garrisdale
365
Cruach Ionnastail
295
Lealt Burn
Lealt
Corpach Bay
Beinn Bhreac
467
Dubh Bheinn
J U R A
Tramaig Bay
Shian Bay
Rainberg Mòr
453
Cruach Sganadail
Ardlussa
Lussagiven
Inverlussa
Lussa Point
Eilean an Rubha
Gleann Dorch
Gleann Aoistail
Sgeir Mhòr a' Bhrein- phuirt
Loch Righ Mòr
Beinn Sgaillinish
190
Barrahormid
Rubh' an t- Sàilein
Rubh' a' Chrois-aoinidh
Loch Tarbert
Creag Nam Fiadh Mòr
262
Tarbert
Tarbert Bay
Keillmore
Rubh' a' Mhàil
Rubha Bholsa
Glenbatrick
Scrinadle
506
Beinn Bhreac
439
Beinn Tarsuinn
416
Lagg
Rubh' a' Chamais
Gate House
Danna Island
Sgarbh Breac
364
Jura Forest
Achamore
Corr Eilean
Na Peileirean
Nave Island
Ardnave Point
Gortantaoid Point
283
Margadale Hill
Beinn an Oir
785
Beinn Shiantaidh
755
A846
24
Ardmenish
Eilean Mòr
Kilmory
Eilean Mòr Chapel
Kilmory Bay
A R G Y L L
Ardnave
Killinallan Point
Loch a' Chnuic Bhric
Beinn a' Chaolais
734
Corran
An Dùnan
Carraig Bhàn
Giur-bheinn
316
Bunnahabhain
Loch an t-Siob
Paps of Jura
Rubh' an Leim
Point of Knap
Ton Mhòr
Tayovullin
Kilnave
Killinallan
Beinn Bhreac
286
Ardnahoe
Loch Staoisha
Knockrome
Leargybreck
Sanaigmore
Ardnave Loch
Loch Gruinart
Glas Bheinn
561
Sròn Garbh
Rubh' an Leanachais
Loch na Mile
Eilean Mòr
Braigo
Balulive
Feolin
Rubha Lamanais
Leckgruinart
Keills
Port Askaig
Feolin Ferry
Eilean Bhride
Smaull
Aoradh
Loch Finlaggan
Dubh Bheinn
530
Keils
Small Isles
Ballinaby
Carnduncan
Craigens
Craighouse
Eilean nan Gabhar
Saligo Bay
B8017
Grainel
Ballygrant
I S L A Y
A N D
Rubha na Caillich
Loch Cam
Loch Ballygrant
Brat Bheinn
342
Crackaig
Coul Point
Loch Gorm
Aruadh
B8018
Foreland
Lyrabus
A846
Kilmeny
Loch Lossit
Esknish
Moin'a'choire
Machrie
Rockside
A847
Blackrock
Islay Ho.
Cabrach
Na Cùiltean
Machir Bay
Kilchoman
Conisby
Redhouses
Beinn Dubh
267
Ardfin
Sannaig
Jura Ho.
Am Fraoch Eilean
Rubha na Tràille
Bridgend
Cachlaidh Mhòr
Brosdale Island
Kilberry Head
Crosses
Bruichladdich
Neriby
Sgorr nam Faoileann
429
Kilchiaran
Gartnatra
Bowmore
Barr
Cattadale
B U T E
Kilchiaran Bay
Gearach
15
Port Charlotte
Ronnachmore
Cruach
Cluanach
Glas Bheinn
471
Beinn na Caillich
337
McArthur's Head
Rubha Cruitiridh
Tormisdale
Gartbreck
Kilennan
Proaig
Ardpa
Lossit
Beinn Tart a' Mhill
232
Carn
Laggan
Beinn Bhan
471
Beinn Bheigeir
491
Rubha Liath
Kelsay
Laggan
Duich
B8016
RINNS OF ISLAY
LOCH INDAAL
Nerabus
Ardtalla
Port Mòr
Rubha na Faing
Easter Ellister
A847
13
Beinn Uraraidh
454
Claggain Bay
West Tarbert Bay
East Tarbert Bay
Portnahaven
A846
Laggan Bay
Loch Uraraidh
Kintour
Trudernish
Tarbert
Creag Bhan
100
Port Wemyss
Orsay
Rinns Point
Glenegedale
Sgorr Bhogachain
Loch Uigeadail
Kintour
Ardmore Point
Ardaily
Druimyeon Bay
Machrie
Beinn Sholum
347
Kildalton Church & Crosses
Ardmore
Gigha
Rhunahaorine Point
Rubha Mòr
Machrie
Kintra
Leorin Lochs
Leorin
Eilean a' Chuirn
Ardminish
Ardminish Bay
A83
Eilean Bhride
Craro Island
Achamore Gardens
Maol Buidhe
165
Cornabus
Port Ellen
3
Lagavulin
Ardbeg
Rubha na Gainmhich
Carnmore
A846
Laphroaig
Grob Bagh
THE OA
The Ard
Caolas an Eilein
Texa
Cara Island
Mull of Cara
Killean
Tayinl
Lower Killeyan
Risabus
Port Chubaird
Beacharr
Mull of Oa
Loch Kinnabus
Inerval
Muasdale
Rubha nan Leacan
SOUND OF GIGHA
SOUND OF JURA
SOUND OF ISLAY
KINTYRE
Glenacardoch Point
33
Belloch
A83
Barr Water
Glenbarr
Bellochantuy Bay
Bellochantuy
Corrylach
Killocraw
Tangy Loch
Tangy
Westport
Skeroblingarry
Low Ballevain
Kilchenzie
Machrihanish Bay
Darlochan
A83
Kilmichael
CAMPBELTOWN (MACHRIHANISH)
Machrihanish
Drumore
0 2 4 6 miles
0 2 4 6 8 10 km

COLL
Sorisdale
Eilean Mòr
Clabhach
Ben Hogh
Arinagour
Loch Eatharna
Feall Bay
Crossapol Bay
Gunna
Urvaig
TIREE
Balephetrish Bay
Salum Bay
Vaul
Caolas
Ruaig
Rubha Dubh
Kenovay
Gott Bay
Soa
Scarinish
Kilkenneth
Crossapoll
Baugh
Hynish Bay
Balemartine
Balephuil
Hynish
The Hynish Story
Rinn Thorbhais
INNER HEBRIDES
Treshnish Isles
Lunga
Fladda
Bac Mòr (Dutchman's Cap)
Staffa
Staffa (NTS)
Little Colonsay
Gometra
ULVA
Eorsa
Loch Na Keal
Inch Kenneth
Chapel
Balnahard
Ben More
966
MULL
Ardmeanach
Burg (NTS)
Loch Scridain
Kilchoan
Ormsaigmore
Ardmore Point
Bloody Bay
Tobermory
Mishnish
Quinish
Caliach Point
Croig
Mornish
Calgary
Art in Nature
Dervaig
Calgary Bay
Loch Frisa
Speinne Mòr
444
Carn Mòr
342
Salen Forest
Burg
Kilninian
Port Burg
Fanmore
Loch Tuath
Beinn na Drise
424
Lagganulva
IONA
Dun I
100
Iona Abbey
Maclean's Cross
Baile Mòr
Ruanaich
Iona (NTS)
Sound of Iona
Rubha nan Cearc
Kintra
Fionnphort
Loch na Lathaich
Ardtun
Bunessan
Lee
Port an Aird Fhada
Brolass
Ross of Mull
Ardalanish
Ardchiavaig
Soa Island
Erraid
Rubha nam Bràithrean
Malcolm's Point
Torran Rocks
Dubh Artach
Eilean Dubh
Balnahard Bay
Rubh' a' Geodha
Kiloran Bay
Balnahard
Loch an Sgoltaire
Kiloran Gardens
Port Ceann a' Gharraidh
Kiloran
Colonsay House
Upper Kilchattan
Lower Kilchattan
Port Mòr
Loch Fada
Scalasaig
COLONSAY
Machrins
Loch Staosnaig
Port Lotha
Balerominndubh
Sguide an Leanna
Garvard
Rubha Dubh
Balerominmore
Eilean Mhucaig
Dubh Eilean
Priory
Rubha Bàn
Oronsay
Eilean Ghaoideamal
Caolas Mòr
Eilean nan Ron
Shian Bay
Sgeir Mhòr a' Bhrein- phuirt
Rubh' an t- Sailein
Rubh' a' Chrois-aoinidh
Loch Tarbert
Rubh' a' Mhàil
Sgarbh Breac
Scrinadle
Glenbatrick
A849
B8070
B8071
B8072
B8065
B8066
B8067
B8068
B8069
B8073
B8035
B8085
B8086
B8087
0 2 4 6 miles
0 2 4 6 8 10 km
E F G H I J
47 48 49 50 51 52 53 54

12
Glenbeg
Ben Laga
512
Loch Sunart
Ardery
Anaheilt
Garbh Bheinn
885
Keppanach
Natural History Centre
Glenborrodale
Ardnastang
Strontian
Glen Tarbert
Onich
North Ballachulish
Mingary
Oronsay
Carna
Meall a' Bhroin
303
Liddesdale
A861
A884
A82
Inversanda Bay
Bloody Bay
Auliston Point
Beinn Ghormaig
452
Loch Teacuis
Beinn Iadain
571
Fuar Bheinn
765
Kilmalieu
B8043
Kentallen
Ballachulish
Sgorr Dhonuil
1001
Sgorr Dhearg
1024
Tobermory
Calve Island
M O R V E R N
Lochuisge
Beinn Na Cille
651
Duror
Beinn a' Bheithir
A828
Drimnin
Beinn Chlaonleud
475
Loch Arienas
Camasnacroise
APPIN
B849
Sidhean na Raplaich
550
Rhemore
Beinn Mheadhoin
739
Alltachonaich
Meall Ban
655
Salachail
Glen Creran
Speinne Mòr
444
Ardnacross
Killundine
Beinn an t-Sruthain
267
Fiunary Forest
Claggan
Larachbeg
Kinlochaline
Ardtornish
Meall Damh
339
Shuna Island
Portnacroish
Stalker
Invercreran
Beinn Sgulaird
932
Salen Forest
Sound of Mull
Fiunary
Loch Teàrnait
Kingairloch
Loch Linnhe
Glen Aros
Aros
Glais Bheinn
479
Port Ramsay
Port Appin
Creagan
Druimavuic
Beinn na Drise
424
Salen
A848
A849
Pennygown
Fishnish
Lochaline
Ardtornish Point
Buchuill
Clachan
Eriska
Dallachulish
Creach Bheinn
810
Killiechronan
Kellan
Gruline
Knock
Beinn Bhuidhe
412
Garmony
Lynn of Morven
Achnacroish
Loch Creran
Barcaldine
Scottish Sealife Sanctuary
Loch Ba
Gaodhail
Rubha an Ridire
Bernera
Achadun (ruin)
Lismore
Lynn of Lorn
Kilcheran
Benderloch
Ledaig
Loch Na Keal
Salen Forest
Craignure
Mull & West Highland Railway
Dun da Ghaoithe
766
Torosay Castle
Duart
North Connel
Black Crofts
Ardchattan Priory
714
Beinn Mheadhonach
Cadderlie
Loch Etive
B8035
M U L L
Beinn Talaidh
761
Sgurr Dearg
741
Lochdon
Dunstaffnage
Connel
Achnacloich
Bonawe
Ben More
966
Corra-bheinn
704
Glen More
A R G Y L L
Dunollie
A85
Black Lochs
Fearnoch Forest
Bonawe Furnace (iron works)
Taynuilt
Ben Cruachan
1126
Ardura
Oban
Barguillean Garden
Pass of Brander
Loch Scridain
A849
Pennyghael
Loch Fuaron
Ben Buie
717
Beinn na Croise
503
Croggan
Loch Spelve
Balliemore
Kerrera
Sound of Kerrera
L O R N
Gylen
A816
Kilbride
Cleigh
Kilmore
Loch Nell
515
Beinn Ghlas
Falls of Cruachan
Cruachan Station
Ardanaise
Lochbuie
Loch Uisg
Loch Buie
A N D
Loch Feochan
Brolass
Carsaig
Firth of Lorn
Kilninver
Loch Scamadale
Loch Nant
Kilchrenan
Annat
Portsonachan
Malcolm's Point
Insh Island
B U T E
Seil
Easdale
An Cala Garden
Clachan-Seil
Balvicar
B844
B8003
Easdale Folk Museum
515
Beinn Chapuill
Inverinan
Inverinan Forest
B840
Loch Awe
Melfort
Kilmelford
Loch Melfort
Kilchoan
Cullipool
Garvellachs
Garbh Eileach
Isles of the Sea
Eileach an Naoimh
Monastery (ruin)
Eilean Dubh Mòr
Lunga
Sound of Luing
Luing
Arduaine Garden (NTS)
Arduaine
Loch Avich
Dalavich
Carn Duchan
491
Inverliever Forest
Eredine
Beinn Bhreac
526
Inveraray
Toberonochy
Shuna
Barravullin
Craobh Haven
Lunga
Guirasdeal
Douglas Water
Wildlife Park
Dalchenna
Eredine Forest
Beinn Dearg
482
Cruach Scarba
449
Scarba
Ardfern
Ford
Fincharn
B840
A83
Auchindrain
Museum of Country Life
Rubha Righinn
Corryvreckan Whirlpool
Str. of Corryvreckan
Craignish
B8002
Carnassarie
Carnasserie
Beinn nan Capull
252
Rèisa an t-Sruith
Sculptured Stones
Kilmartin
Beinn Bhan
319
Barmolloch
Carron
Beinn Ghlas
420
Furnace
Stuckreoch
Glengarrisdale Bay
Cruach na Seilcheig
296
Kinuachdrachd
Kinuachdrachd Harbour
Island Macaskin
Stone Circle
Slockavullin
Ri Cruin Cairn
Kilmartin House
Baluachraig
Knockalava
Gleann Airigh
Crarae Woodland Garden
Feorlin
Crarae
Newton
Leacnach
Loch Fyne
Bàgh Gleann Speireig
Glengarrisdale
Poltalloch Monuments
Minard Forest
Leckuary
Minard
Tullochgorm
Lachlan
Garbhallt
A886
Glendebadel Bay
Ben Garrisdale
365
Crinan Loch
Crinan
Drimvore
Kilmichael Glassary
Loch Glashan
Birdfield
Cruach an Lochain
508
Ardnoe Point
Duhadd Fort
Bridgend
Minard Castle
Barnacarry
Lephinmore
Cruach Ionnastail
295
Lealt Burn
Bellanoch
B8025
Achnashelloch
Cup & Ring Marks
Achnabreck Cup & Ring Marks
24
Caol Ghlas
Corpach Bay
Beinn Bhreac
467
Lealt
Lussa
Cnoc Reamhar
265
Moine Mhòr
B841
Asknish
Kilbridemore
Dunans
Dubh Bheinn
Ardnackaig
Gallchoille
Gariob
Cairnbaan
Badden
Lochgair
Lephinchapel
J U R A
Tramaig Bay
SOUND OF JURA
Carsaig Island
Carsaig Bay
Knapdale Forest
Auchindarroch
Middle Kames
Loch Gair
B8000
Garvie
Conchra
Rainberg Mòr
453
Cruach Sganadail
Shian Bay
Ardlussa
Inverlussa
Lussa Point
Lussagiven
Eilean Dubh
Tayvallich
Seafield
Achnamara
Lochgilphead
Carrick
Cruach Chuilceachan
435
Ardacheranmor
Eilean an Rubha
Turbiskill
Eilean Loain
Kilmichael of Inverlussa
Brackley
Achnaba
Camquhart
Cruach nan Cuilean
432
Loch Righ Mòr
Gleann Dorch
Gleann Aoistail
Beinn Sgaillinish
190
Kilmory
Ashfield
Ardrishaig
Beinn Bheag
331
A83
Loch Gilp
Castleton
Otter Ferry
Ardachearanbeg
Clachan of Glendaruel
Loch Tarsan
Rubh' an t-Sailein
A846
Barrahormid
Taynish
Daltote
Ballimore
Ballochandrain
Craigendive
Ardtaraig
Tarbert
Ulva Islands
Auchnaha
Ormidale
Rubh' Loch Tarbert
Creag Nam Fiadh Mòr
262
Tarbert Bay
Keillmore
New Ulva
Dunrostan
Auchbraad
Inverneil
Fearnoch
Cruach nan Caorach
458
Auchenbreck
Loch Striven
Glenbatrick
Beinn Bhreac
439
Lagg
Rubh' a' Chamais
Loch na Cille
Loch Sween
Sween
B8024
Srondoire
Rubha Beag
Kilfinan Bay
Lindsaig
Otter
Kilfinan
Ard a' Chapuill
Springfield
Beinn Bhreac
454
Scrinadle
506
416
Gate House
Danna Island
Corr Eilean
Abhainn Mòr
Loch Fuar Bheinne
Cruach a' Phubuill
477
Fearnoch
Beinn Bhreac
507
Jura Forest
Achamore
Ellary
Achahoish
Drum
Beinn Capuill
Port Leathan
A886
A8003
B836
K
L
M
N
O
P
47
48
49
50
51
52
53
54
0 2 4 6 miles
0 2 4 6 8 10 km

13
Kinlochleven
Glen Coe
Blackwater Reservoir
Black Corries
Rannoch Moor
RANNOCH
Loch Rannoch
Kinloch Rannoch
TAY FOREST PARK
PERTH AND KINROSS
Glen Lyon
Black Mount
Bridge of Orchy
Glen Orchy
Glen Lochy
Tyndrum
Crianlarich
Glen Dochart
Killin
Loch Tay
BREADALBANE
Lochearnhead
Loch Earn
St Fillans
Glen Falloch
Balquhidder
Strathyre
LOCH LOMOND & THE TROSSACHS NATIONAL PARK
STIRLING
Loch Katrine
Callander
Aberfoyle
QUEEN ELIZABETH FOREST PARK
Glen Fyne
Glen Kinglas
Arrochar
Tarbet
Loch Lomond
Luss
Balmaha
Drymen
Killearn
Balfron
Kippen
Gargunnock Hills
Fintry Hills
CAMPSIE FELLS
Garelochhead
Helensburgh
Alexandria
Balloch
Gourock
GREENOCK
DUMBARTON
WEST DUNBARTONSHIRE
Lennoxtown
Kilsyth
Strathblane
Q
R
S
T
U
V
47
48
49
50
51
52
53
54

14
Glen Errochty
TAY FOREST PARK
Tressait
Aldclune
Killiecrankie
Pass of Killiecrankie
Ben Vrackie
841
Glen Brerachan
Ennochdhu
Mount Blair
744
Folda
Dunalastair
Tummel Bridge
Foss
Loch Tummel
Queen's View Centre
Moulin
Edradour Distillery
Pitlochry
Kirkmichael
Bridge of Brewlands
Blacklunans
Kirkton of Glenisla
Bellaty
Lassintullich
Dunalastair Reservoir
Loch Faskally
Hydro-Electric Visitor Cen & Fish Ladder
Strathardle
Forest of Alyth
Dykends
Schiehallion
1083
Farragon Hill
780
Dunfallandy Stone
Ballintuim
Loch Derculich
Deer Park
Creag nam Mial
561
Strathtay
Grandtully
STRATH TAY
Ballinluig
Balduff Hill
425
Bridge of Craigisla
Carn Mairg
1042
Black Watch Memorial
Little Ballinluig
Tulliemet
Netherton
Balnaguard
Logierait
Forest of Clunie
Loch Ordie
Bridge of Cally
Bamff
Creag Mhòr
981
Menzies
Grandtully
Coshieville
Camserney
Dull
Weem
Aberfeldy
Balmacneil
Kindallachan
Blackcraig Forest
Lyon
Ancient Yew
Wade's Bridge
Deuchary Hill
509
Loch Benachally
Alyth
Fortingall
Falls of Moness
Dowally
Riechip
Middleton
New Alyth
Parkhill
Fearnan
Kenmore
Taymouth
Craigvinean Forest
Dalguise
Butterstone
Loch of Clunie
Kinloch
Rattray
Blairgowrie
Acharn
Scottish Crannog Centre
Falls of Acharn
Scotston
Loch of the Lowes
Dunkeld
Loch of Butterstone
Craigie
Muirton of Ardblair
Rosemount
Loch of Drumellie
Little Dunkeld
Birnam
Kirkton of Lethendy
Arthurstone
The Hermitage (NTS)
PERTH
Dunkeld & Birnam Sta
Caputh
Spittalfield
Coupar Angus
Quaich
Garrow
Milton
Trochry
Obney Hills
403
Gellyburn
Meikleour
Kinclaven
Kettins
Loch Tay
Ardtalnaig
Loch Freuchie
Strathbraan
Amulree
AND
Murthly
Ardoch
Woodside
Burrelton
Pitcur
Creagan na Beinne
888
Meall nam Fuaran
805
Waterloo
Bankfoot
Cargill
Ardeonaig
Corrymuckloch
Meall nan Caoraich
623
Airntully
West Tofts
Little Glenshee
Tullybelton
Stanley
Wolfhill
Creag Uchdag
879
Auchnafree
KINROSS
Strathord Forest
Guildtown
Kinrossie
Abernyte
Ben Chonzie
931
Glen Almond
Meall Tarsuinn
648
Sma' Glen
Logiealmond
Chapelhill
Newmiln
St Martins
Loch Lednock Reservoir
Loch Turret Reservoir
Harrietfield
Luncarty
Pickston
Glen Almond
Buchanty
Kinnaird
Invergeldie
Glen Lednock
Glen Turret
Falls of Monzie
Pitcairngreen
Old Scone
Scone Palace
Creag Liath
499
Falls of Keltie
Monzie
Fowlis Wester
St Bean's Church
Braegrum
Methven
Almondbank
Huntingtower
Scone
Rait
Braes of the Carse
St Fillans
Deil's Caldron
Melville's Mon
Ochtertyre
Falls of Barvick
Huntingtower
Kilspindie
Megginch Castle
Kinfauns Forest
Ardtrostan
Falls of Turret
Hosh
Glenturret Distillery
Gilmerton
Sculptured Stone
Keillour Forest
Tibbermore
PERTH
Branklyn (NTS)
Kinfauns
Glendoick
Comrie
Dalginross
Quoig
Crieff
Stuart Strathearn Crystal
Madderty
Inchaffray Abbey
Chapelhill
Leetown
Errol
Glencarse
St Madoes
Strath Earn
Ross
Crieff Visitors Centre
St David's
Clathy
Milltown of Aberdalgie
Elcho
Rhynd
Torlum
393
Water of Ruchill
The Balloch
Culloch
Drummond Castle Gardens
Innerpeffray Library
Forgandenny
Bridge of Earn
Newburgh
Lindores Abbey
Glen Artney
Dalchruin
Muthill
Muthill Church
Millearne
Machany
Aberuthven
Forteviot
Kintillo
Abernethy
Grange of Lindores
Machany Water
Falls of Ness
Tullibardine Chapel
Dron
Aberargie
Round Tower
Westerton
Roman Road
Auchterarder
Dunning
Pitmedden Forest
Beinn Odhar
632
Knaik
Garrick
Gleneagles Hotel
Glenfarg Reservoir
Balvaird
Auchtermuchty
Colless
Uamh Bheag
665
Slymaback
Roman Fort
Gleneagles
Path of Condie
Bullie Burn
Braco
Blackford
Glenfarg
Dunshalt
Strathmiglo
Muckle Burn
Gleneagles House
Steele's Knowe
485
Dochrie Hill
356
Gateside
FIFE REGIONAL PARK
Falkland Palace
Drummond
Kincardine
Greenloaning
Innerdouny Hill
497
Falkland
West Lomond
522
Lomond Hills
Freuch
Braes of Doune
Glendevon Reservoirs
Glendevon Forest
Milnathort
Burleigh
Wester Balgedie
Kinbuck
Sheriff Muir
Glen Devon
Glendevon
North Queich
South Queich
Dalqueich
Kinnesswood
Ashfield
Sheriffmuir 1715
Carnbo
Kinross
Kinross House
Scotlandwell
Leslie
Doune
Deanston
Blairdenon Hill
631
Ben Cleuch
720
Yetts o' Muckhart
Pool of Muckhart
Loch Leven
Priory
GLENROTHES
Blair Drummond
Dunblane
Cath
Pisgah
Cauldhame
King's Seat Hill
648
Drum
Crook of Devon
Kinglassie
Safari Park
CLACKMANNANSHIRE
Campbell (NTS)
Rumbling Bridge
Powmill
Bridge of Allan
Mill Trail Visitor Centre
Tillicoultry
Dollar
Cleish
Benarty Hill
356
Ballingry
Nyadd
Menstrie
Alva
Sterling Mills
Blairingone
Wether Cleish Hills
Blairadam Forest
Lochore Meadows
Lochore
Crosshill
Auchterderran
Gargunnock
Drip Moss
Wallace Monument
Tullibody
Fishcross
Coalsnaughton
Cult Hill
379
Kelty
Cardenden
Smith Art Gallery & Museum
Cambuskenneth
Gartmorn Dam
Hill End
Knock Hill
364
Butterchurn Restaurant & Crafts
Lochgelly
Argyll & Sutherland Highlanders Mus
Touch Hills
STIRLING
Cambus
Sauchie
Forest Mill
Kirkcaldy
Cambusbarron
Royal Burgh of Stirling Visitor Cen
Alloa
Clackmannan
Bluther Burn
Balgonar
Saline
Knockhill
Lassodie
Cowdenbeath
Museum & Art Gallery
Fallin
Bannockburn Heritage Cen (NTS)
Bannockburn
Tower
Bogside
Bowershall
Auchtertool
North Third
Earl's Hill
441
Cowie
Dunmore
Blairhall
Comrie
Gowkhall
Townhill
Crossgates
Donibristle
The Pineapple (NTS)
Kincardine
Oakley
Carnock
Milesmark
Halbeath
Wellwood
Fordell
North Third Reservoir
Airth
Valleyfield
Crossford
Dunearn
Loch Coulter Reservoir
Bowtrees
Town House (NTS)
Culross
Low Torry
Torryburn
Cairneyhill
DUNFERMLINE
Abbey
Burntisland
Plean
Easter Buckieburn
South Bellsdyke
Culross Palace (NTS)
Crombie
Aberdour
Muirmill
Dunipace
Stenhousemuir
Charlestown
St Bridget's
Carron Bridge
Tomtain
453
Fankerton
Denny
Skinflats
Grangemouth
Bo'ness & Kinneil Railway
Limekilns
Rosyth
Hillend
Dalgety Bay
Inchcolm
Larbert
Inverkeithing
Inverkeithing Bay
St Davids
St Colm's Abbey
Bonnybridge
Dennyloanhead
FALKIRK
Carriden
Muirhouses
St Margaret's Hope
Deep Sea World
North Queensferry
Inchmickery
Banton
Banknock
Longcroft
Bo'ness
Blackness
Hopetoun
Forth Road Bridge
Forth Bridge
Inch Garvie
Hound Point
Cramond Island
Royal Yacht Britannia
Kilsyth
Haggs
High Bonnybridge
Laurieston
Champany
Dalmeny
Abercorn
Newton
Queenzieburn
Roman Fort
Glen Village
Brightons
Reddingmuirhead
Linlithgow
Philpstoun
South Queensferry
EDINBURGH
Dullatur
Shieldhill
Maddiston
W
X
Y
Z
AA
BB
47
48
49
50
51
52
53
54

CC
DD
EE
FF
GG
HH
47
48
49
50
51
52
53
54
Falls of Drumly Harry
Cruick Water
Little Brechin
Pathhead
Fern
Trinity
Hillside
Kinnaber
Brechin
House of Dun (NTS)
Noran Water
Dykehead
Cortachy
Careston
Memus
Tannadice
Round Tower
A935
Tayock
Montrose
Bridge of Dun
Caledonian Rly
Montrose Basin
Montrose Museum & Art Gallery
Finavon
Doocot (Dovecot) (NTS)
South Esk
Netherton
Oathlaw
Ferryden
Inchbraoch
Kirkton of Craig
Kirkton of Kingoldrum
Northmuir
Farnell
Sculptured Stones
Aberlemno
Montreathmont Forest
A934
Fishtown of Usan
Barrie's House (NTS)
Turin Hill
252
Kirriemuir
Westmuir
A926
Lunanhead
Restenneth Priory
Rescobie
Reswallie
Lunan
Braehead of Lunan
Lunan Bay
Red Castle
Redcastle
Padanaram
St Orland's Stone
Forfar
A932
Milldens
Guthrie
Craigton
Meffan Institute
Middleton
Friockheim
Inverkeilor
Kingsmuir
685
Dunnichen
Letham
Chapelton
Ethie Mains
A928
Glamis
Douglastown
Leysmill
B965
A92
Eassie Sculptured Stone
A94
Kinnettles
Craichie
Angus Folk Museum (NTS)
Kirkton
Vinny Burn
Parkhill
Charleston
Eassie
Inverarity
Whigstreet
Redford
Colliston
A933
Marywell
Auchmithie
Gateside
Kirkbuddo
St Vigeans
Milton
B9127
ANGUS
Gallow Hill
379
Gallowfauld
Hayhillock
Carmyllie
Elliot Water
Abbey
Craigowl Hill
455
Crombie
Arbirlot
Arbroath
Wormiehills
Kirkton of Tealing
Tealing
Monikie
B9128
Kirkton of Auchterhouse
Dovecot & Earth House
B978
Monikie
Craigton
Barry Mill (NTS)
Muirdrum
A92
Bridgefoot
A90
Newbigging
Panbride
Baldovan
Dundee United FC
Kellas
East Haven
Clatto
Barry
Carnoustie
Birkhill
Camperdown
B961
A930
Liff
Dundee FC
Monifieth
Dundee Contemporary Arts
DUNDEE
Broughty
Buddon Ness
Kingoodie
Tayport
DUNDEE
Discovery Point & R.R.S. Discovery
B946
Newport-on-Tay
TAY
Wormit
Tentsmuir Forest
B945
Balmerino
Abbey (NTS)
A914
Gauldry
St Michaels
A919
Kilmany
Leuchars
Eden Mouth
Creich
Rathillet
R.A.F. Memorial
Balmullo
Earlshall
Guardbridge
St Andrews Bay
A91
Dairsie
Kincaple
British Golf Mus
St Andrews Aquarium
St Andrews
A913
Strathkinness
St Andrews
Cupar
Kemback
B939
Craigtoun
A917
Boarhills
B9131
Hill of Tarvit (NTS)
Pitscottie
Kingsbarns
Ceres
Fife Folk Museum
A915
Dunino
Scotstarvit Tower
Craigrothie
B940
Radernie
Kippo Burn
Fife Ness
Kinaldy Burn
Kingsmuir
Pitlessie
A916
B940
Crail
New Gilston
Kettlehill
Montrave
Largoward
Carnbee
B9171
B941
FIFE
Largo Law
290
Arncroach
Kilrenny
Kellie (NTS)
Anstruther
Colinsburgh
Scottish Fisheries Museum
Lundin Links
Lower Largo
St Monans
Pittenweem
Windygates
Leven
Kilconquhar
Largo Bay
Balgonie
Innerleven
Earlsferry
Elie
Isle of May
Methil
Chapel
Buckhaven
Macduff's Castle
East Wemyss
Coaltown of Wemyss
West Wemyss
FIRTH OF FORTH
North Berwick
Yellowcraig
Scottish Seabird Centre
Tantallon
Muirfield
A198
Dirleton
Auldhame
Scoughall
Gullane Bents
Dirleton
Gullane Point
Gullane
Kingston
Whitekirk
St Baldred's Cradle
Aberlady Bay
Fenton
Aberlady
Luffness
Barns
Drem
Tyninghame House
Tyne Mouth
John Muir
Belhaven Bay
Craigielaw
B1377
East Fortune
Craigielaw Point
Mungoswells
Chesters Hill Fort
Tyninghame
Dunbar
Gosford Bay
Preston Mill & Phantassie Doocot (NTS)
Preston
Barns Ness
Longniddry Bents
Ballencrieff
A1087
Cockenzie
Church of Plaque
Athelstaneford
East Linton
Broxburn
Collegiate
Longniddry
A6137
A199
Carleton Hills
A1
Dunbar 1650
Skateraw
0 2 4 6 miles
0 2 4 6 8 10 km

A
B
C
D
E
F
G
34
35
36
37
38
39
40
41
42
43
44
Sound of Shillay
Northton
(Taobh Tuath)
(CEANN A DEAS NA HEARADH)
Geocrab
Cluer
(Cliuthar)
Pabbay
Leverburgh
(An t-Ob)
Roneval
459
Quidinish
(Cuidhtinis)
Ensay
Sound of Pabbay
Cairminis
A859
Ceann a' Bhàigh
Killegray
Strannda
Rodel
(Roghadal)
St Clement's Church
Boreray
Berneray
(Ellean Bhearnaraigh)
Renish Point
Borgh
Groay
SOUND OF HARRIS
Lingay
Port nan Long
Griminis Point
Vallay
Sollas
(Solas)
Grenitote
(Greinetobht)
A865
Baile Mhartainn
Hosta
Hermetray
Loch Fada
Hogha Gearraidh
NORTH UIST
Lochportain
Knockintorran
(Cnoc an Torrain)
Ceann a' Bhàigh
Loch Scadavay
(UIBHIST A TUATH)
Lochmaddy
(Loch na Madadh)
Loch na Madadh
Sound of Monach
A867
North Lee
250
Kirkibost Island
Locheport
(Locheuphort)
South Lee
281
Vaternish P
Monach Islands
(Heisker)
Islands
Teanamachar
Saighdinis
Carinish
(Cairinis)
Baleshare
Teampull na Trionaid
Eaval
347
LITTLE MINCH
Trump
Baile Glas
Grimsay
(Griomasaigh)
Dunvegan Head
Isay
Balivanich
(Baile a'Mhanaich)
Uachdar
Ceallan
Ronay
(Ronaigh)
Rueval
124
Ben Skriaig
307
Galtrigill
Borerai
BENBECULA
(BEINN NA FAOGHLA)
Griminish
(Griminis)
Torlum
Loch Uisgebhagh
Feriniquarrie
Totaig
Uiskevagh
(Uisgebhagh)
Milovaig
Linaclate
(Lionacleit)
Creagorry
(Creag Ghoraidh)
Colbost Croft Museum
Ardivachar Point
Aird a' Mhachair
Iochdar
Bagh nam Faoileann
Wiay
Moonen Bay
OUTER HEBRIDES
A865
Loch a' Charnain
Ramasaig
Geirinis
WESTERN ISLES
Groigearraidh
Loch Sgioport
Drimsdale
(Dreumasdal)
Stilligarry
(Stadhlaigearraidh)
Homore
(Tobha Mòr)
Loch Druidibeg
Hecla
606
SOUTH UIST
Staoinebrig
(UIBHIST A DEAS)
Beinn Mhòr
620
Rubha Ardvule
Flora Macdonald's Birthplace
Minngearraidh
Loch Eynort
Stulaval
374
Stuley
Askernish
(Aisgernis)
Dalabrog
Pictish Wheel House
Lochboisdale
(Loch Baghasdail)
Cille Pheadair
Dughaill
Crois
Baghasdal
Leth Meadhanach
Gearraidh na Monadh
Cille Bhrighde
Ludag
Lingay
Sound of Eriskay
Bunmhullin
Ben Scrien
185
Fiaray
Sound of Barra
Balla
Eriskay
(Eiriosgaigh)
Scurrival Point
Eolaigearraidh
Fuday
Cille-Bharra
Orosay
Oitir Mhòr
Stack Islands
Greian Head
Ardmhòr
Gighay
Northbay
Bayherivagh
Hellisay
BARRA
(Barraigh)
Bruernish
Flodday
Borgh
A888
Heaval
383
Fuiay
Earsairidh
Brevig
Castlebay
(Bàgh a'Chaisteil)
Heishival Mòr
190
Castle Bay
Vatersay
(Bhatarsaigh)
Muldoanich
Sound of Sandray
Cairn Galtair
207
Lingay
Sandray
(Sanndraigh)
Sound of Pabbay
Pabbay
(Pabaigh)
Sound of Mingulay
Carnan
273
Mingulay
(Miughalaigh)
Berneray
0 2 4 6 8 miles
0 2 4 6 8 10 12 km

17
SKYE
RAASAY
Portree
Aros Experience
Penifiler
Ben Tianavaig
413
Camastianavaig
Glenmore
Mugeary
Dun Caan
443
385
Oskaig
Clachan
Inverarish
East Suisnish
Narrows of Raasay
INNER
Milton
Camusteel
Applecross
Toscaig
Crowlin Islands
Ramasaig
Orbost
Roag
Vatten
Harlosh
488
Healabhal Bheag (Macleod's Table South)
Loch Caroy
Ose
Ebost
Dun Beag
Bracadale
Coillore
Ullinish
Loch Bracadale
Wiay
Ardtreck Point
Portnalong
Fernilea
Loch Harport
Rubha nan Clach
Carbost
Drynoch
Merkadale
Talisker Bay
Talisker
A863
A87
B885
B883
B8009
Peinchorran
Sconser
Loch Sligachan
Glamaig
775
Sligachan
Kyle More
Scalpay
Mullach na Carn
396
Longay
Pabay
Dunan
Loch Ainort
Luib
570
Glas Bheinn Mhòr
Beinn Bhreac
445
Eynort
Minginish
Loch Eynort
Cuillin Hills
Sgurr nan Gillean
965
Marsco
736
Sgurr a Ghreadaidh
973
Sgurr Dearg (Inaccessible Pinnacle)
986
Glenbrittle
993
Sgurr Alasdair
924
Sgurr nan Eag
Loch Brittle
Garbh-bheinn
806
928
Bla Bheinn (Blaven)
Strathaird
Beinn na Caillich
732
Broadford
BROADFORD
Corry
Waterloo
Lower Breakish
Upper Breakish
A851
Torrin
B8083
Kilmarie
Loch Slapin
Heast
Beinn Seamraig
561
Drumfearn
SEA OF THE HEBRIDES
Rubh' an Dùnain
Soay Sound
Loch Scavaig
Soay
Mol-chlach
Elgol
Glasnakille
Rubha na h-Easgainne
Loch Eishort
Ord
Isleornsay (Eilean Iarmain)
Isle Ornsay
Dunsgaith
Tokavaig
Tarskavaig
Tarskavaig Bay
Achnacloich
Teangue
Knock
Kilmore
Ferrindonald
Sleat
Sound of Sleat
Armadale Castle Gardens & Museum
Armadale
Armadale Bay
Calligarry
Ardvasar
Aird of Sleat
Point of Sleat
Airor
Sandaig
Rubha Raonuill
CUILLIN SOUND
Carn a' Ghaill
210
Garrisdale Point
Canna (NTS)
A'Chill
CANNA
Sanday
Sound of Canna
Kilmory
Rubha na Roinne
Kinloch
Orval
571
National Nature Reserve
RUM
Harris
Askival
812
781
Ainshval
Rubha nam Meirleach
Oigh-sgeir
INNER HEBRIDES
Mallaigvaig
Mallaig
Glasnacardoch
Beoraidbeg
Morar
Bracora
A830
Portnaluchaig
Bunacaimb
Back of Keppoch
B8008
ARISAIG
Arisaig
599
Druimindarroch
The Prince's Cairn
Loch nan Uamh
Sound of Arisaig
Sound of Rum
Cleadale
Bay of Laig
Rubha an Fhasaidh
Laig
EIGG
An Sgurr
393
Kildonnan
Galmisdale
Sound of Eigg
Eilean nan Each
Beinn Airein
137
Port Mòr
Muck
0 2 4 6 miles
0 2 4 6 8 10 km
Smirisary
Glenuig
300
Glenuig Hill
Roshven
Eilean Shona
MOIDART
Kinlochmoidart
Ardmolich
Tioram
Ardtoe
Shielfoot
Kentra
Kentra Bay
A861
Dalnabreck
Fascadale
Kilmory
Ockle
Sanna Bay
Achnaha
Point of Ardnamurchan
Achosnich
Port Min
Gorteneorn
Acharacle
ARDNAMURCHAN
Salen
Loch Sunart
B8007
Kilchoan
Ben Hiant
528
Ormsaigmore
Mingary
Natural History Centre
Glenbeg
Ardslignish
Glenborrodale
Ben Laga
512
303
Meall a' Bhroin
Eilean Mòr
Sorisdale
B8072
B8071
Ben Hogh
104
Arinagour
Ardmore Point
Bloody Bay
Auliston Point
Oronsay
Carna
452

18
M
N
O
P
Q
R
Milton
Applecross
Bealach na Ba
626
776
710
792
Camusterrach
Meall Gorm
Ardarroch
Lochcarron
Strathcarron Sta
Strathcarron
Achintee
A896
A890
Attadale
Attadale Forest
Achintraid
Toscaig
Loch Kishorn
Loch Carron
Stromemore
Strome (NTS)
Ardaneaskan
Ardnarff
Stromeferry
Achmore
Plockton
Duirinish
Drumbuie
Erbusaig
Kyle of Lochalsh
Balmacara Estate (NTS)
Balmacara
Kyleakin
Caisteal Maol
Loch Alsh
Auchtertyre
Kirkton
Nostie
Conchra
Loch Long
Camus-luinie
Killilan
Sallachy
Killilan Forest
Ardelve
Bundalloch
Dornie
Eilean Donan
Keppoch
Carnach
Falls of Glomach (NTS)
Crowlin Islands
Longay
Pabay
Broadford
Lower Breakish
Upper Breakish
A851
A87
Sgurr na Coinnich
739
Kyle Rhea
Kylerhea
Ardintoul
Letterfearn
Loch Duich
Inverinate
Sgurr an Airgid
841
Morvich
Ratagan
339
Ault a' chruinn
Shiel Bridge
Galltair
Bernera Barracks
Glenelg
Eilanreach
Glenelg Brochs
Glen More
Beinn na Seamraig
561
Beinn a' Chapuill
742
Beinn Sgritheall
981
Beinn nan Caorach
773
Isleornsay
Isle Ornsay
Knock
Ferrindonald
Arnisdale
Corran
Loch Hourn
Sound of Sleat
Airor
Beinn na Caillich
785
Ladhar Bheinn
1020
Barrisdale
Kinloch Hourn
Roinn na Beinne
441
Sandaig
Knoydart
Sgurr Coire na Coinnich
796
Inverie
Luinne Bheinn
939
913
Sgurr a' Choire-bheithe
Loch an Dubh Lochain
Druim Chòsaidh
Rubha Raonuill
Mallaigvaig
522
Sgurr an Eilein Ghiubhais
Mallaig
946
Meall Buidhe
Loch Nevis
Camusrory
Stoul
Morar
Bracora
Bracorina
Tarbet
Kylesmorar
North Morar
Swordland
Loch Morar
A830
South Morar
Back of Keppoch
Arisaig
599
Sidhean Mòr
Meith Bheinn
710
Meoble
Loch Beoraid
Ardnish
Lochailort
Inverailort
A861
Loch nan Uamh
Prince's Cairn
An Stac
814
Druim Fiaclach
869
Roshven
Rois-Bheinn
882
Glenuig
300
Croit Bheinn
663
Beinn Odhar Bheag
882
Glenfinnan
Glenfinnan Monument (NTS)
Loch Eilt
Beinn Gaire
666
Glenaladale
Moidart
Kinlochmoidart
Ardmolich
Loch Shiel
Sgurr an Tarmachain
756
Dalnabreck
Polloch
Sunart
845
Beinn Resipol
Resipole
Scotstown
Ardery
Anaheilt
Ardnastang
Strontian
Loch Sunart
303
Meall a' Bhroin
Liddesdale
A884
Glen Tarbert
Garbh Bheinn
885
Carn na Nathrach
786
Sgurr Dhomhnuill
888
Ardgour
Glen Gour
Glen Scaddle
Cona Glen
Druim Leathad nam Fias
Sgurr na h-Eanchainne
730
Stob Coire a' Chearcaill
770
Aryhoulan
Clovullin
Corran (Ardgour)
Inversanda Bay
Onich
North Ballachulish
Ballachulish
Kentallen
Keppanach
Glenrigh Forest
Sgurr an Airgid
West Monar Forest
East Monar Forest
Loch Monar
Sgurr Choinnich
Bidean a' Choire Sheasgaich
986
Lurg Mhor
An Gead Loch
Beinn Dronaig
797
Loch an Iasaich
Loch an Tachdaidh
Sgurr na Lapaich
1150
1129
An Riabhachan
Carn nan Gobhar
992
Glencannich Forest
1069
An Socach
Aonach Buidhe
899
Loch Mullardoch
Glen Cannich
Beinn Fhionnlaidh
1005
Carn Eighe
1183
1111
Tom a' Choinich
Toll Creagach
1054
Beinn a' Mheadhoin
611
Mullach na Dheiragain
982
1180
Mam Sodhail
Sgurr na Lapaich
1036
Sgurr nan Ceathreamhnan
1151
An Socach
920
A' Ghlas-bheinn
918
Loch Gaorsaic
Loch a' Bhealaich
Loch Affric
Glen Affric
Loch Beinn a' Mheadhoin
Beinn Fhada (Ben Attow)
1032
Kintail Forest
Five Sisters
Sgurr Fhuaran
1068
Sgurr na Ciste Duibhe
1027
Glen Shiel
Aonach Shasuinn
889
Ciste Dhubh
982
Mullach Fraoch-choire
1102
Sgurr a' Bhealaich Dheirg
1038
959
Saileag
A'Chralaig
1120
Sàil Chaorainn
1002
Ceannacroc Forest
1003
Aonach Meadhoin
Sgurr nan Conbhairean
1110
The Saddle
1010
Glenshiel
1719
Sgurr na Sgine
945
Creag nan Damh
918
Sgurr an Lochain
1004
22
Glen Cluanie
Cluanie Forest
957
Carn Ghluasaid
Carn nam Feuaich
732
Tomchrasky
Roderick Mackenzie's Memorial
Loch Cluanie
Buidhe Bheinn
879
Sgurr an Doire Leathain
1010
981
Maol Chinn-dearg
Aonach air Chrith
1021
Druim Shionnach
987
947
Creag a' Mhaim
Beinn Loinne
Bunloinn Forest
Meall Dubh
788
Glen Loyne
Loch Loyne
Beinneun Forest
1027
Sgurr a' Mhaoraich
Glenquoich Forest
Gleouraich
1035
996
Spidean Mialach
Druim na h-Achlaise
540
Highland
14
Loch Quoich
Inchlaggan
Loch Garry
Coille Mhorgil
Tomdoun
Glen Garry
Greenfield
Gairich
919
Glen Kingie
Sgurr Mòr
1003
Sgurr na Ciche
1040
1013
Garbh Chioch Mhòr
Sgurr nan Coireachan
953
Sgurr Mhurlagain
880
Sgurr Choinnich
747
Meall Coire nan Saobhaidh
821
Glengarry Forest
Sròn a' Choire Ghairbh
935
Meall na Teanga
917
Lochaber
Glendessary
Strathan
Murlaggan
Loch Arkaig
Ardechvie
Achnasaul
Great Glen Way
Loch Lochy
Clunes
Invergloy
Bunarkaig
Inver Mallie
Glen Mallie
Loch Eil Forest
Sgurr nan Coireachan
956
Sgurr Thuilm
963
Gulvain
987
962
Beinn Bhan
796
Gairlochy
Stronaba
Spean Bridge Woollen Mill
Commando Memorial
Spean Bridge
A86
Inverroy
Killiechonate
Glen Loy
Druim Fada
Strone
Caledonian Canal
Leanachan Forest
Kinlocheil
Corribeg
Fassfern
Loch Eil Outward Bound
11
Locheilside Sta
Garvan
Loch Eil
Duisky
Blaich
Neptune's Staircase
Banavie
Torlundy
Aonach Mòr Mountain Gondola & Nevis Range Ski Centre
Corpach
Caol
Achaphubuil
Jacobite Steam Train
Trislaig
1431 & 1645
Old Inverlochy
Fort William
Killiechonate Forest
Carn Mòr Dearg
1219
1223
Aonach Mòr
Achintee
West Highland Museum
Glen Nevis
1344
Ben Nevis
1238
Aonach Beag
Stob Coire an Laoigh
1115
1095
Sgurr Choinnich Mòr
Loch Linnhe
A82
Druimarbin
Blarmachfoldach
Nevis Forest
Water of Nevis
Achriabhach
An Gearanach
982
Sgurr a' Mhaim
1098
Binnein Beag
940
Binnein Mòr
1128
Blar a' Chaorainn
939
Mullach nan Coirean
Stob Ban
999
1001
Sgorr an Iubhair
981
Stob Coire a' Chairn
1032
Am Bodach
1008
Sgurr Eilde Mòr
1005
Na Gruagaichean
Loch Eilde Mòr
Mamore Forest
Lairigmor
Mam na Gualainn
796
Kinlochmore
Kinlochleven
Caolasnacon
West Highland Way
Loch Leven
Garbh Bheinn
867
Glencoe
Sgorr nam Fiannaidh
Meall Dearg
951
Glen Coe
Glencoe (NTS)
Altnafeadh
B863
B8004
B8005
B8007
Abhainn Rath
39
40
41
42
43
44
45
46

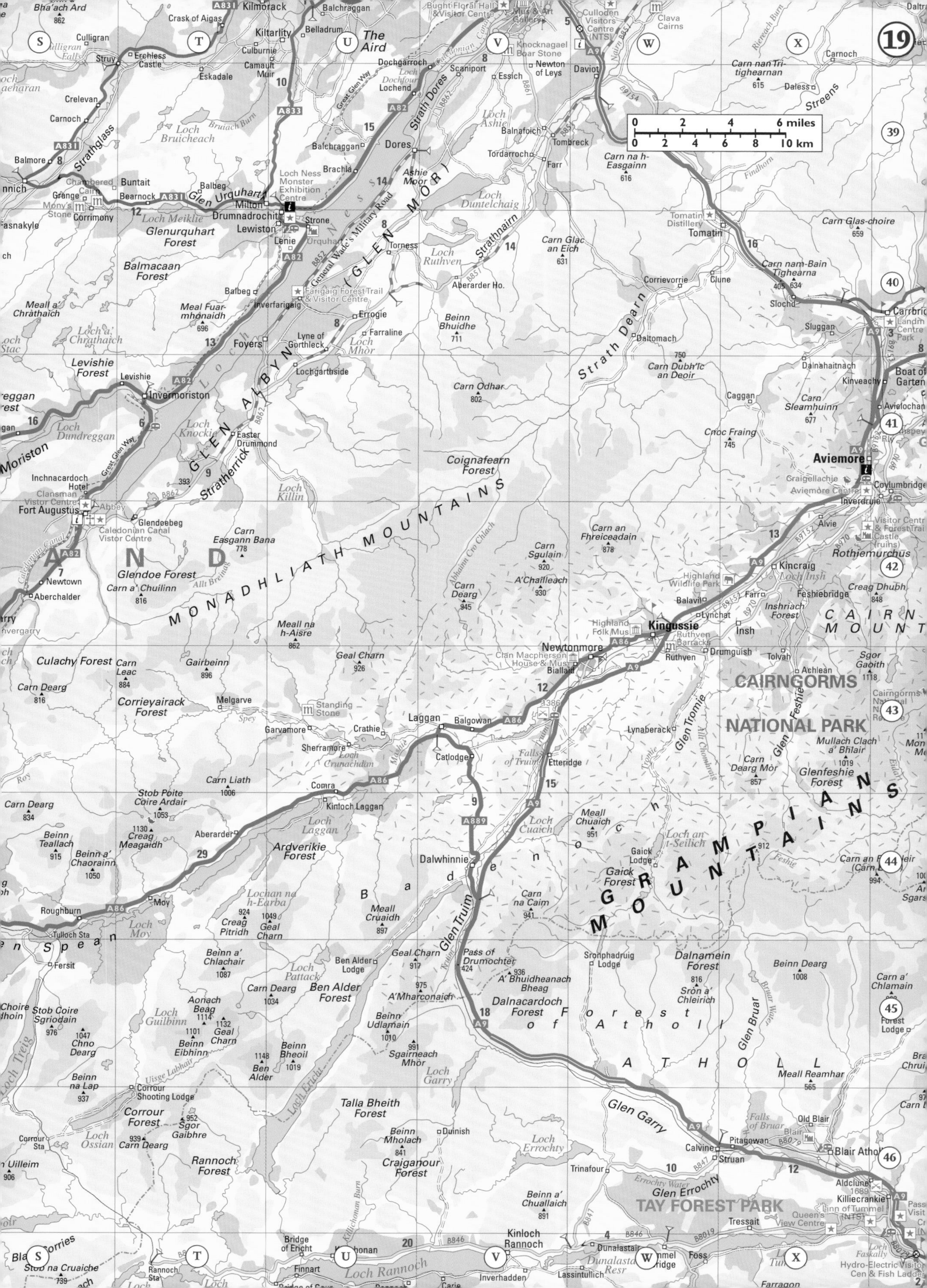
19
0 2 4 6 miles
0 2 4 6 8 10 km
Kilmorack
Balchraggan
Crask of Aigas
Kiltarlity
The Aird
Belladrum
Culligran
Struy
Erchless Castle
Eskadale
Culburnie
Camault Muir
Crelevan
Carnoch
Loch Bruicheach
Strathglass
Balmore
Buntait
Chambered Cairn
Grange
Corrimony
Bearnock
Glen Urquhart
Milton
Drumnadrochit
Loch Meiklie
Glenurquhart Forest
Lewiston
Strone
Lenie
Balmacaan Forest
Balbeg
Inverfarigaig
Meall Fuar-mhonaidh
696
Loch Ness Monster Exhibition Centre
Dochgarroch
Loch Dochfour
Lochend
Great Glen Way
Strath Dores
Scaniport
Essich
Dores
Balchraggan
Brachla
Ashie Moor
General Wade's Military Road
GLEN MOR
Farigaig Forest Trail & Visitor Centre
Errogie
Farraline
Lyne of Gorthleck
Loch Mhòr
Foyers
Levishie Forest
Levishie
Invermoriston
Lochgarthside
GLEN ALBYN
Loch Knockie
Easter Drummond
Stratherrick
Dundreggan
Moriston
Inchnacardoch Hotel
Clansman Vistor Centre
Fort Augustus
Abbey
Glendoebeg
Caledonian Canal Vistor Centre
Newtown
Aberchalder
Invergarry
Bught Floral Hall & Visitor Centre
Mus & Art Gallery
Knocknagael Boar Stone
Newton of Leys
Culloden Visitors Centre (NTS)
Clava Cairns
Daviot
Loch Ashie
Balnafoich
Tombreck
Tordarroch
Farr
Loch Duntelchaig
Torness
Loch Ruthven
Strathnairn
Aberarder Ho.
Beinn Bhuidhe
711
Carn Glac an Eich
631
Carn na h-Easgainn
616
Carn nan Tri-tighearnan
615
Daless
Carnoch
Streens
Findhorn
Tomatin Distillery
Tomatin
Carn Glas-choire
659
Carn nam-Bain Tighearna
634
Corrievorrie
Clune
Slochd
Carrbridge
Landmark Centre
Sluggan
Strath Dearn
Daltomach
750
Carn Dubh'Ic an Deoir
Dalnahaitnach
Kinveachy
Boat of Garten
Caggan
Carn Sleamhuinn
677
Aviemore
Cnoc Fraing
745
Carn Odhar
802
Coignafearn Forest
Loch Killin
MONADHLIATH MOUNTAINS
Carn Easgann Bana
778
Glendoe Forest
Carn a' Chuilinn
816
Carn an Fhreiceadain
878
Carn Sgulain
920
A'Chailleach
930
Carn Dearg
945
Craigellachie
Aviemore Centre
Coylumbridge
Inverdruie
Alvie
Visitor Centre & Forest Trail
Castle (ruins)
Rothiemurchus
Kincraig
Loch Insh
Highland Wildlife Park
Feshiebridge
Creag Dhubh
848
Balavil
Lynchat
Inshriach Forest
Insh
Highland Folk Mus
Kingussie
Ruthven Barracks
Newtonmore
Clan Macpherson House & Mus
Ruthven
Drumguish
Tolvah
Achlean
Sgor Gaoith
1118
CAIRNGORMS NATIONAL PARK
CAIRN MOUNT
Meall na h-Aisre
862
Geal Charn
926
Culachy Forest
Carn Leac
884
Gairbeinn
896
Carn Dearg
816
Corrieyairack Forest
Melgarve
Standing Stone
Spey
Garvamore
Crathie
Laggan
Balgowan
Sherramore
Loch Crunachdan
Catlodge
Falls of Truim
Etteridge
Lynaberack
Glen Tromie
Glen Feshie
Carn Dearg Mòr
857
Mullach Clach a' Bhlair
1019
Glenfeshie Forest
Carn Liath
1006
Stob Poite Coire Ardair
1053
Carn Dearg
834
Comra
Kinloch Laggan
Loch Laggan
Ardverikie Forest
Aberarder
Creag Meagaidh
1130
Beinn Teallach
915
Beinn a' Chaorainn
1050
Dalwhinnie
Loch Cuaich
Meall Chuaich
951
Loch an t-Seilich
Gaick Lodge
Gaick Forest
GRAMPIAN MOUNTAINS
Badenoch
Carn an Fhidhleir
994
Moy
Roughburn
Tulloch Sta
Spean
Loch Moy
Lochan na h-Earba
Creag Pitridh
924
Geal Charn
1049
Meall Cruaidh
897
Glen Truim
Carn na Caim
941
Fersit
Beinn a' Chlachair
1087
Loch Pattack
Ben Alder Lodge
Geal Charn
917
Pass of Drumochter
424
A' Bhuidheanach Bheag
936
Sronphadruig Lodge
Dalnamein Forest
Beinn Dearg
1008
Carn a' Chlamain
Carn Dearg
1034
Ben Alder Forest
975
A'Mharconaich
Dalnacardoch Forest
Forest of Atholl
Sròn a' Chleirich
816
Glen Bruar
Forest Lodge
Stob Coire Sgriodain
976
Chno Dearg
1047
Aonach Beag
1114
Loch Guilbinn
Beinn Eibhinn
1101
Geal Charn
1132
Beinn Udlamain
1010
Sgairneach Mhòr
991
Ben Alder
1148
Beinn Bheoil
1019
Loch Garry
ATHOLL
Meall Reamhar
565
Loch Treig
Beinn na Lap
937
Uisge Labhair
Corrour Shooting Lodge
Loch Ericht
Talla Bheith Forest
Glen Garry
Corrour Forest
Sgor Gaibhre
952
Carn Dearg
939
Corrour Sta
Loch Ossian
Beinn Mholach
841
Duinish
Loch Errochty
Falls of Bruar
Old Blair
Blair
Blair Atholl
Calvine
Pitagowan
Struan
Craiganour Forest
Rannoch Forest
Trinafour
Glen Errochty
Errochty Water
Aldclune
1689
Killiecrankie
Pass of Killiecrankie Visitor Centre
TAY FOREST PARK
Beinn a' Chuallaich
891
Tressait
Queen's View Centre
Glen of Tummel (NTS)
Kinloch Rannoch
Dunalastair
Dunalastair Resr
Tummel Bridge
Foss
Loch Faskally
Hydro-Electric Visitor Cen & Fish Ladder
Bridge of Ericht
Kinlochonhan
Killichonan Burn
Loch Rannoch
Finnart
Rannoch Sta
Stob na Cruaiche
739
Inverhadden
Lassintullich
Carie
Farragon
A831
A833
A82
A86
A889
A9
B852
B862
B851
B861
B8019
B846
B847
B9152
B970
39
40
41
42
43
44
45
46
S
T
U
V
W
X

20
HIGHLAND
MORAY
ABERDEEN
PERTH AND KINROSS
ANGUS
GRAMPIAN MOUNTAINS
CAIRNGORM MOUNTAINS
CAIRNGORMS NATIONAL PARK
GLENMORE FOREST PARK
STRATHSPEY
BRAEMAR
Aberlour (Charlestown of Aberlour)
Dufftown
Grantown-on-Spey
Aviemore
Tomintoul
Ballater
Braemar
Pitlochry
Carrbridge
Boat of Garten
Nethy Bridge
Cromdale
Bridge of Avon
Ballindalloch
Glenlivet Distillery & Visitor Centre
Tomnavoulin
Cock Bridge
Corgarff
Strathdon
Crathie
Balmoral
Blair Atholl
Kirkmichael
Spittal of Glenshee
Glenshee Chairlifts & Ski Centre
Lecht Ski Centre
Clova
Kirkton of Glenisla
Cortachy
Dykehead
Killiecrankie
Lochnagar 1155
Ben Macdui 1309
Cairn Gorm 1245
Braeriach 1296
Ben Avon
Morven 871
Mount Keen 939
Ben Rinnes 840
Ben Vrackie 841
Beinn a' Ghlo
Loch Muick
Glen Clova
Glen Prosen
Glen Isla
Glen Shee
Glen Dee
Glen Avon
Abernethy Forest
Rothiemurchus
Balmoral Forest
Glenfeshie Forest
Glen Ey Forest
A9 A93 A95 A97 A939 A941 A944 A924
Y Z AA BB CC DD
39 40 41 42 43 44 45 46

21
EE
FF
GG
HH
II
JJ
Huntly
Drumblade
Brideswell
Ythanwells
Kirktown of Auchterless
Badenscoth
Gordonstown
Fyvie
Fyvie (NTS)
Woodhead
Cottown
Cairnorrie
Auchnagatt
Kinnadie
Nether Kinmundy
Blackhill
Moss of Cruden
Aldie
Ardallie
Hill of Dudwick
174
Arthrath
Hatton
Cruden Bay
Bullers of Buchan
Chapel Hill
Port Erroll
Bay of Cruden
Toll of Birness
Bogbrae
Kiplaw Croft
Whinnyfold
Methlick
Fisherford
Rothienorman
St Katherines
Earlsford
Haddo House (NTS)
Barthol Chapel
Thornroan
Tarves
Ythsie
Ellon
Auchmacoy
Kirkton of Logie Buchan
Kirktown of Slains
Collieston
Waterside
Sands of Forvie
Newburgh
Foveran House
Drums
Skares
Kirkton of Culsalmond
Colpy
Largie
Newseat
Folla Rule
Meikle Wartle
Upper Boddam
Leith Hall (NTS)
Kennethmont
Picardy Stone
Insch
Kirkton of Rayne
Old Rayne
Loanhead Stone Circle
Durno
Daviot
Glengarioch Distillery
Oldmeldrum
Tolquhon
Pitmedden (NTS)
Pitmedden
Udny Green
Pettymuick
Ardlair
Duncanston
Rothney
Ardoyne
Westhall
Oyne
Pitcaple
Clatt
Kirkton
Leslie
Auchleven
Archaeolink Prehistory Park
Maiden Stone
Chapel of Garioch
Balhalgardy
Kirkton of Bourtie
Whiterashes
Whitehaugh Forest
Muckletown
Garioch
Easter Aquorthies Stone Circle
Inverurie
Port Elphinstone
Burnhervie
Kinmuck
Newmachar
Glenton
Montgarrie
Grampian Transport Mus
Haughton House
Alford
Howe of Alford
Pitfichie Forest
Pitmunie
Monymusk
Kemnay
Kinkell Church
Tavelty
Kintore
Hatton of Fintray
Cothall
Whitecairns
Belhelvie
Balmedie
Whitehouse
Todlachie
Craigearn
Leylodge
Dyce Symbol Stones
Blackburn
Dyce
ABERDEEN
Stoneywood
Cushnie
Muir of Fowlis
Tillyfourie
Little Ley
Ordhead
Sauchen
Craigievar (NTS)
Leochel-Cushnie
Kintocher
Fraser (NTS)
Lyne of Skene
Craibstone
Bridge of Don
Aberdeen Exhibition & Conference Centre
St Machar's Cath
Dunecht
Kirkton of Skene
Fairley
Westhill
Elrick
Kingsford
Loch of Skene
Aberdeen FC
Aberdeen Maritime Museum
Provost Skene's House
Aberdeen Art Gallery
Craiglich
476
Drumlasie
Tornaveen
Lumphanan
Echt
South Kirkton
Garlogie
Hazlehead
Gordon Highlanders Regimental Mus
Nigg Bay
David Welch Winter Gardens
Loirston
Altens
Milton of Auchinhove
Peel Ring
Hill of Fare
471
Midmar Forest
Landerberry
Cullerlie Stone Circle
1562
The Birks
Milton of Cullerlie
Torphins
Hardgate
Bridge of Dee
Charlestown
Banchory-Devenick
Cove Bay
Mid Beltie
Milton of Campfield
Kincardine O'Neil
Drum (NTS)
Peterculter
Storybook Glen
Kirkton of Maryculter
Hillside
Findon
Portlethen
Aboyne
Glassel
Cordach
Bridge of Canny
Crathes (NTS)
Crathes
Birse
Kirkton of Durris
Marywell
Blackhall Forest
Banchory
Auchattie
Denside
Cammachmore
Downies
Netherley
Newtonhill
Durris Forest
Cairn-mon-earn
378
Muchalls
Drumhead
Strachan
Water of Feugh
Westerton
Mongour
376
Peter Hill
617
Rickarton
Mowtie
Garron Point
Cowie
Glendye Lodge
589
Clachnaben
Fetteresso Forest
Stonehaven
Kirktown of Fetteresso
Mount Battock
778
Bridge of Dye
Dunnottar
Newmill
Drumlithie
Cairn o'Mount
455
Drumtochty Forest
Glenbervie
Mill of Uras
Crawton
Fernybank
Auchenblae
Catterline
Clatterin Brig
Strathfinella Hill
Fasque House
Fordoun
Parkneuk
Arbuthnott
Roadside of Kinneff
Thainston
Arbuthnott House
Kinneff
Auchmull
Fettercairn
Howe of the Mearns
Inverbervie
Laurencekirk
Gourdon
Witton
Gannochy
Balfield
Edzell
Luthermuir
Dunlappie
Brown Caterthun (fort)
Feus of Caldhame
Johnshaven
Inchbare
Pert
Ecclesgreig
Stracathro
Marykirk
Lochside
St Cyrus
Tigerton
Little Brechin
Pathhead
Trinity
Brechin
Hillside
House of Dun (NTS)
Kinnaber
Tayock
Round Tower
Bridge of Dun
Montrose
Montrose Basin
Montrose Museum & Art Gallery
Caledonian Rly
Netherton
Inchbraoch
Ferryden
Farnell
0 2 4 6 miles
0 2 4 6 8 10 km
39
40
41
42
43
44
45
46

E
F
G
H
I
J
K
26
27
28
29
30
31
32
33
34
35
36
0 2 4 6 8 miles
0 2 4 6 8 10 12 km
OUTER HEBRIDES
Butt of Lewis
(Rubha Robhanais)
Teampull Mholuidh
Eoropaidh
Còig Peighinnean
Swainbost
(Suainebost)
Port of Ness
(Port Nis)
Lionel (Lional)
North Dell
South Dell
(Dail Bho Dheas)
Harbost
(Tabost)
Cross
(Cros)
Sgiogarstaigh
Gabhsunn Bho Dheas
Gabhsunn Bho Thuath
Ness
Broch
Melbost Borve
(Mealabost)
A857
Siadar Iarach
Borve
(Borgh)
Steinacleit Cairn & Standing Stones
Loch Langavat
Cellar Head
Loch Mòr Bharabhas
Black House
Barvas
(Barabhas)
Labost
Fibhig
Arnol
Brue
(Brù)
Bragar
Muirneag
248
Tolastadh
Tolsta Head
Shawbost
(Siabost)
A858
Pairc
Loch Urrahag
Loch Breivat
Dail Beag
Dail Mòr
Gearrannan
20
11
12
Beinn Bragar
261
Borghastan
Loch Carlabhagh
Carloway
(Carlabhagh)
Cirbhig
Carloway Broch
ISLE OF LEWIS
Bac
Gress
(Griais)
B895
Col
Col Uarach
Breibhig
Tiumpan Head
(Rubha an t-Siumpain)
Gallan Head
West Loch Roag
Tobson
East Loch Roag
Great Bernera
Tolastadh a' Chaolais
Beinn Mholach
292
Tunga
Aird Thunga
Portnaguran
(Port nan Giùran)
Broker
Aird Uig
Bhaltos
Breascleit
(EILEAN LEODHAIS)
Newmarket
Laxdale (Lacasdal)
Loch a' Tuath
10
Aird
Timsgearraidh
Miavaig
(Miabhaig)
Kirkibost
(Cìcebost)
Callanish (Calanais)
Callanish Standing Stones
New Valley
Marybank
Stornoway
(Steornabhagh)
Siulaisiadar
Seisiadar
A866
Eye Peninsula
(An Rubha)
Camas Uig
Cairisiadar
Iarsiadar
Garrynahine
(Gearraidh na h-Aibhne)
13
Lews Castle
Bayhead
Garrabost
Melbost
Sandwick
(Sanndabhaig)
St Columba's Church
Cnoc
Upper Bayble
(Pabail Uarach)
Lower Bayble
(Pabail Iarach)
Mangurstadh
Eadar dha Fhadhail
Suainaval
429
Geisiadar
B8011
B8059
5
Linsiadar
3
A858
Eitshal
223
Suardail
Ceann na Circ
Stornoway Harbour
16
Loch Suainaval
Islibhig
Mealisval
574
Einacleit
Scealascro
B8011
Achadh Mòr
A859
Arnish Moor
4
6
Leurbost
(Liurbost)
Grimshader
(Griomsiadar)
Breanais
WESTERN ISLES
Loch Grunavat
Giosla
Loch an Fhir Mhaoil
Loch Airigh na h-Airde
Loch Fadagoa
Crosbost
Loch Leurbost
Ranish
(Ranais)
Mealasta Island
Loch Cairigerod
Roineval
281
Balallan
(Baile Ailein)
Loch Trealaval
12
Keose
(Ceos)
Loch Erisort
Cromore
Loch na Craobhaig
Lacasaigh
Scalaval
260
Loch Strandavat
Cearsiadar
B8060
13
Loch Benisval
Morsgail Forest
Loch Resort
Airidh a' Bhruaich
Malasgair
172
Scarp
Loch Langavat
A859
Mòr Mhonadh
401
Loch Sgibacleit
Grabhair
Loch Odhairn
Kebock Head
Gasker
Huisinis
NORTH HARRIS
Tirga Mòr
679
18
Park
Leumrabhagh
Hushinish Point
B887
Forest of Harris
Aird a' Mhulaidh
Seaforth Island
Beinn Mhòr
572
Loch Shell
12
(CEANN A TUATH NA HEARADH)
Abhainnsuidhe
Cleiseval
511
Clisham
799
Loch Seaforth
Crionaig
470
Loch Claidh
Loch Bhrollum
WEST LOCH TARBERT
Bun Abhainn Eadarra
Maraig
(Maaruig)
Rhenigidale
(Reinigeadal)
Taransay
(Tarasaigh)
Aird Asaig
3
Beinn a' Chaolais
Taobh Siar
Tarbert
(An Tairbeart)
Beesdale
Losgaintir
287
Ùrgha
Kyles Scalpay
(Caolas Scalpaigh)
Sound of Taransay
South Harris Forest
East Loch Tarbert
Scalpay
Scalpay
(Eilean Scalpaigh)
Shiant Islands
SOUND OF SHIANT
Toe Head
Seilebost
23
Na-Buirgh
SOUTH
A859
Miabhag
Drinisiader
Kennavay
Chaipaval
365
A859
An Coileach
386
Sgarasta Mhòr
HARRIS
Greosabhagh
Scadabhagh
Lacklee
(Leac a' Li)
Geocrab
Loch Grosebay
Shillay
Sound of Shillay
Northton
(Taobh Tuath)
(CEANN A DEAS NA HEARADH)
Cluer
(Cliuthar)
Loch Stockinish
Loch Langavat
Loch Fleòideabhagh
Pabbay
Aird Mhighe
Roneval
459
Quidinish
(Cuidhtinis)
Leverburgh
(An t-Ob)
Ensay
Sound of Pabbay
SOUND OF HARRIS
Cairminis
A859
Ceann a' Bhàigh
Loch Finsbay
Killegray
Strannda
Rodel
(Roghadal)
St Clement's Church
Boreray
Berneray
(Eilean Bhearnaraigh)
Borgh
Renish Point
Groay
Fladda-chuain
Lingay
Sound of Berneray
Port nan Long
3
B893
Eilean Trodday
Rubha Hunish
Duntulm
Kilmaluag Bay
Kilmaluag
35
Loch nan Geireann
Hermetray
Score Bay
Skye Cottage Museum
19
Flodigarry
Eilean Flodigarry
Loch Fada
A865
Lochportain
NORTH UIST
Bornisketaig
Quiraing
543
Staffin Bay
Lochmaddy
(Loch na Madadh)
Loch na Madadh
A855
Digg
Staffin Island
Kilvaxter
Monkstadt
Balgown
Meall na Suiramach
Stenscholl
Staffin
A867
8
North Lee
250
Vaternish Point
Totscore
Linicro
Whitewave Activities
A855
South Lee
281
Elishader
Idrigil
Ascrib Islands
Marishader
Carinish
(Cairinis)
Saighdinis
Eaval
347
Ben Geary
284
Geary
Uig
Uig Bay
Beinn Edra
611
Balnaknock
Garros
Culnaknock
Earlish
Lealt
Trumpan
Vaternish
LOCH SNIZORT
Trotternish
Halistra
Baile Glas
Grimsay
(Griomasaigh)
Ceallan
Ronay
Dunvegan Head
Isay
Hallin
Rubha Maol
Ben Galtrigill
Lusta
Greshornish
Kingsburgh
Beinn a' Ruadh
637
11
13
A855
The Storr
RONA
THE MINCH

0 2 4 6 miles
0 2 4 6 8 10 km
Leumrabhagh
Crionaig
470
Rhenigidale
(Reinigeadal)
Kyles Scalpay
Scalpay
(Eilean Scalpaigh)
SOUND OF SHIANT
Shiant
Islands
THE MINCH
Fladda-
chuain
Eilean
Trodday
Rubha
Hunish
Duntulm
Kilmaluag
Bay
Kilmaluag
Score
Bay
Skye Cottage
Museum
Borniesketaig
Flodigarry
Eilean
Flodigarry
Quiraing
543
Digg
Meall na
Suiramach
Staffin
Bay
Staffin
Island
Stenscholl
Staffin
A855
Kilvaxter
Balgown
Monkstadt
Linicro
Totscore
Whitewater
Activities
Idrigil
Uig
Uig Bay
Ellishader
Marishader
Beinn Edra
611
Garros
Balnaknock
Culnaknock
Earlish
Lealt
Ascrib
Islands
LOCH
SNIZORT
Trotternish
Baca
Ruadh
637
Kingsburgh
The Storr
719
Romesdal
Eyre
Kensaleyre
Carn Liath
Ben
Dearg
552
Loch
Leathan
Loch
Fada
HIGHLAND
Ben
Geary
284
Geary
Vaternish
Halistra
Hallin
Rubha
Maol
Lusta
Loch
Bay
Beinn
Chreagach
326
Greshornish
Claigan
327
Beinn
Bhreac
Dunvegan
Flashader
Edinbane
A850
Bernisdale
Peinmore
Borve
Skeabost
Carbost
Drumuie
Dunvegan
Roskhill
A863
Roag
Orbost
Vatten
Harlosh
Ose
Glengrasco
B885
Portree
Aros
Experience
Penifiler
Torvaig
Glenmore
Ben
Tianavaig
413
Camastianavaig
Mugeary
Dun
Beag
Bracadale
Ebost
Coillore
Ullinish
Loch
Bracadale
Wiay
Ardtreck
Point
Portnalong
Rubha
nan Clach
Fernilea
Carbost
Drynoch
SKYE
A87
B883
Peinchorran
Sconser
A863
Loch Sligachan
Glamaig
775
Sligachan
Merkadale
Talisker Bay
Talisker
Beinn Bhreac
445
Eynort
Sgurr nan
Gillean
Luib
570
Narrows of Raasay
Kyle More
Loch Ainort
Dunan
RONA
Kyle Rona
SOUND OF RAASAY
Loch
Arnish
Arnish
Brochel
RAASAY
385
Dun
Caan
443
Oskaig
Clachan
Inverarish
East Suisnish
Scalpay
Mullach
na Carn
396
INNER SOUND
Crowlin
Islands
Longay
Rubha
Reidh
Cove
An
Cuaidh
296
B8057
Melvaig
Aultgrishan
B8021
North Erradale
Big Sand
Strath
Gairloch
Longa
Island
Gair Loch
Port Henderson
Badachro
Opinan
B8056
Shieldaig
South
Erradale
Red Point
LOCH TORRIDON
Lower
Diabaig
Upper
Diabaig
Fearnmore
Fearnbeg
Cuaig
Arinacrinachd
Kenmore
Callakille
Lonbain
An Fur
387
Loch
Lundie
Applecross
Forest
Sgurr a' Chaorachain
Beinn
Bhan
Milton
Applecross
Camusteel
Camusterrach
Bealach
na Ba
626
776
710
792
Meall Gorm
Toscaig
Ardarroch
Loch Kishorn
Ardaneaskan
Plockton
Duirinish
Drumbuie
Erbusaig
Balmacara
Estate (NTS)
Balmacara
Kyleakin
Caisteal
Maol
Kirkton
A87

24
Ullapool
Loch Broom
Summer Isles
Isle Ristol
Achiltbuie
Priest Island
Isle Martin
Greenstone Point
Gruinard Island
Gruinard Bay
Laide
Aultbea
Isle of Ewe
Loch Ewe
Poolewe
Gairloch
Charlestown
Kerrysdale
Badachro
Shieldaig
Loch Maree
Talladale
Kinlochewe
Beinn Eighe
Beinn Alligin
Liathach
Torridon
Upper Loch Torridon
Shieldaig
Annat
Glen Torridon
Achnasheen
Strath Bran
Lochcarron
Loch Carron
Strathcarron
Attadale
Stromeferry
Plockton
Dornie
Balmacara
Loch Monar
Loch Mullardoch
Glen Cannich
Cannich
Strathconon Forest
Loch Fannich
Fannich Forest
Dirrie More
Loch Glascarnoch
Braemore
Dundonnell
An Teallach
Fisherfield Forest
Rhidorroch Forest
Strath Canaird
Coigach
Elphin
Ledmore
Knockan
Drumrunie
Inverpolly Forest
W E S T E R   R O S S
H I G H L A N D S
N O R T H   W E S T
0 2 4 6 miles
0 2 4 6 8 10 km

Ben Sgeireach
Airde
Dalmichy
Achnairn
Sithean Achadh nan Eun
317
Cnoc Leamhnachd
Lothmore
Portgower
T
U
V
W
X
Y
Col-bheinn
538
Badintagairt
Dalchork
Grumby Rock
299
Lothbeg
11
Colaboll
Strath Brora
Sciberscross
Gordonbush
Lothbeg Point
Saval
A836
Sallachy
West Langwell
Loch Brora
Savalbeg
Knockarthur
Lairg
Ben Horn
521
Farlary
East Langwell
West Clyne
Cnoc a' Choire
402
14
32
Muie
Clynelish
Torroble
Gruids
Strath Fleet
Lairg Sta
Ardachu
Brora
Oykel Forest
Rogart
Beinn Lunndaidh
446
8
Invercassley
A839
Achany
Pittentrail
Dunrobin Castle Sta
Backies
Shin Forest
Rogart Sta
Morvich
7
A9
Brae
Doune
Altass
A836
Dunrobin Castle
Achinduich
Culmaily
9
B864
Linsidemore
Shin Falls
A839
Golspie
8
Achnahanat
A837
Kirkton
Little Torboll
Loch Fleet
Skelbo
Littleferry
Carbisdale
InversHin Sta
Clashban
33
Culrain
4
Skelbo
Achvaich
Skelbo Street
1650
A836
Rearquhar
Badninish
Embo
Strathcarron
Tulloch
6
Kyle of Sutherland
Croick
Wester Gruinards
Lower Gledfield
Bonar Bridge
Evelix
Embo Street
The Craigs
Ardgay
Loch Migdale
Evelix
Amat Forest
Dounie
Spinningdale
A949
8
1
2
Cath
Clashmore
Dornoch
Kincardine
Craft Centre
Dornoch Point
Tarbat Ness
Carn Bhrain
635
Ardchronie
4
Wilkhaven
Easter Fearn
A836
Struie Hill
3
A9
Portmahomack
9
D O R N O C H
F I R T H
34
Diebidale Forest
Carn Chuinneag
838
Edderton
Rockfield
Tain
Inver
Carn Cas nan Gabhar
602
Morangie Forest
St Duthus's Chapel
Aultnamain Inn
Tarrel
R
R
O
S
S
5
B9176
Rhynie
Beinn Tharsuinn
692
Kildermorie Forest
Braeantra
Fearn Sta
Hill of Fearn
B9165
Loch Morie
Tullich
Fearn Abbey
Beinn nan Eun
742
Balnagown
Hilton of Cadboll
Strath Rusdale
B9166
Balintore
L
A
N
D
14
A9
35
Meall Mòr
738
Shandwick
Ankerville
Kildary
Ardross
Meall an Tuirc
625
Boath
Dalnavie
Milton
Easter Ardross
B9175
Tullich Muir
Loch Glass
Achandunie
Barbaraville
Kilmuir
Nigg Bay
Nigg
Rhicullen
Wyvis Forest
Tomich
B817
Alness
12
Saltburn
Balnapaling
Glas Leathad Mòr
1046
Castlecraig
Dalmore
Invergordon
North Sutor
Cromarty
Black Rock Gorge
B817
Alness Bay
Cromarty Court House
Ben Wyvis
Hugh Miller's Cottage (NTS)
Balblair
Redburn
Swordale
Evanton
Balconie Point
Resolis
Sutors of Cromarty
5
Cromarty Firth
Newton
Little Wyvis
764
B9163
Cullicudden
Jemimaville
B9163
M O R A Y F I R T H
36
Findhorn
The Den
Glenurquhart
10
Culbin Forest
Heights of Brae
Mountgerald
4
Millbuie Forest
187
Wellhill
Town House
A862
Findon Mains
Culbo
A832
Kintessack
Auchterneed
B9160
Rogie Falls
Fodderty
Dingwall
Culbokie
Janefield
Whiteness Head
The Bar
Springfie
Tarvie
A834
7
Forres
A835
Strathpeffer
A9
Killen
Dyke
2
Rosemarkie
Black Isle
Fort George
Fort George
Nairn
Brodie (NTS)
Strathpeffer
1411
Lochussie
Alcaig
Fortrose
Boath Dovecot (NTS)
Contin
Loch Ussie
Maryburgh
Corntown
Duncanston
Knockbain
Easter Suddie
Cath
Tradespark
Findhorn
Old Military Road
1
Conon Bridge
Bogbuie
Ardersier
B9092
10
Auldearn
37
Easter Kinkell
4
Avoch
B9039
B9006
Auldearn 1645
Darnaway
Whitemire
Marybank
A832
4
8
A96
Moss-side
Strathconon
A835
Munlochy
15
A939
5
A832
B9090
B9091
Laiken Forest
Conicavel
INVERNESS
Balvaird
Tore
Piperhill
Darnaway Forest
Falls of Orrin
Kilcoy
Fisherton
Cawdor
Regoul
Presley
B9169
Newton
Muir of Ord
Faebait
6
B9161
Littlemill
Milton
Redcastle
A9
Tornagrain
Croy
Cawdor
Kilmuir
Randolph's Leap
15
Newton
10
Culloden Forest
Aultvaich
A862
Charlestown
Craigton
Moray Firth
Relugas
4
Beauly Firth
Redburn
Beauly
North Kessock
INVERNESS
Balloch
Assich Forest
B9007
Made in Scotland
Battle of Culloden 1746 (NTS)
Cantraydoune
Priory
Kirkhill
Rhinduie
10
A862
Bunchrew
Cath
Cumberland Stone
Ardclach Bell Tower
38
B9164
Smithton
Ferness
A831
Kilmorack
Drumchardine
Leachkin
A940
Balchraggan
Bught Floral Hall & Visitor Centre
Culloden Visitor Centre (NTS)
Clava Cairns
Daltra
Findhorn
Crask of Aigas
Belladrum
Mus & Art Gallery
B851
Rierach Burn
The Aird
5
6
Knock of Braemore
456
9
Kiltarlity
Caledonian Canal
Knocknagael Boar Stone
Dulsie
A939
Culburnie
Camault Muir
Newton of Leys
A9
Carnoch
Nairn
Dochgarroch
8
Scaniport
Drummossie Muir
Carn nan Tri-tighearnan
615
Aitnoch
Eskadale
A833
Loch Dochfour
Daviot
Daless
B9007
Essich
B9154
Dava
10
Lochend
B861
Lochindorb
Strath Dores
Streens
Bruiach Burn
15
A82
Findhorn
Lochindorb
484
Loch Bruicheach
Loch Ashie
Balnafoich
B851
39
Carn Ruigh Charrach
Auchn
Balcbraggan
Tombreck
Moy
Loch Moy
Dores
B862
Tordarroch
Carn na h-Easgainn
616
Brachla
Farr
7
A939
Ashie Moor
Cottartown
Loch Ness Monster Exhibition Centre
Ness
12
Balbeg
General Wade's Military Road
Loch Duntelchaig
HIGHLAND
A831
Glen Urquhart
Milton
Drumnadrochit
R
8
B851
Bearnock
14
Glenurquhart Forest
1
Strone
M
Tomatin Distillery
Carn Glas-choire
659
Urquhart
Lewiston
Tomatin
A9
Grantown-on-Spey
Lenie
631
16
Carn Glac an Fich
Torness
Loch Ruthven
14
Carn nam-Bain Tighearna
Dulnain
3

Lossiemouth
Elgin
Forres
Keith
Buckie
Cullen
Huntly
Rothes
Aberlour (Charlestown of Aberlour)
Dufftown
Fochabers
MORAY
Strath Isla
STRATHBOGIE
SPEY

FF
GG
HH
II
JJ
KK
0 2 4 6 miles
0 2 4 6 8 10 km
32
33
34
35
36
37
38
39
Knock Head
Troup Head
Rosehearty
Kinnaird Head
Museum of Scottish Lighthouses
Fraserburgh
Fraserburgh Bay
Boyne
Boyndie Bay
Whitehills
Macduff
Banff
Duff House
Gamrie Bay
Crovie
Gardenstown
Melrose
Pennan
Sandhaven
Pitsligo
Peathill
Cairnbulg
Inverallochy
St Combs
Longmanhill
Dubford
New Aberdour
Upper Boyndlie
Mid Ardlaw
Memsie
Memsie Cairn
Cairness
Strathbeg Bay
Kirktown of Alvah
Keilhill
Ladysford
Rathen
Loch of Strathbeg
Nether Glasslaw
Lonmay
Crimonmogate
Rattray Head
Eden
Craigmaud
Mormond Hill
Crimond
Strichen
Blackhill
Plaidy
Craigston
New Pitsligo
Rattray Bay
Gas Terminal
Fintry
New Byth
New Leeds
Aberchirder
Bonnykelly
North Ugie Water
Backfolds
Garmond
Adziel
Fetterangus
Denhead
Rora Moss
St Fergus
Bogton
Turriff
Delgatie
Oldwhat
Forest of Deer
Kirktown
Kirkton
Cuminestown
Rora
Bridgend
B U C H A N
Aberdeenshire Farming Mus
Arbuthnot Mus
Maud
Deer Abbey
Mintlaw
Longside
Inverugie
Peterhead
Mill of Colp
Darra
New Deer
Drymuir
Old Deer
Aden
Peterhead Maritime Heritage Centre
Inverkeithny
A B E R D E E N S H I R E
Glendronach Distillery
Fortrie
Maryhill
Stuartfield
Millbreck
Peterhead Bay
Burnhaven
Towie Barclay
Clola
Sandford Bay
Nether Kinmundy
Boddam
Kinnadie
Blackhill
Buchan Ness
Kirktown of Auchterless
Cottown
Cairnorrie
Auchnagatt
Moss of Cruden
Aldie
Badenscoth
Fyvie (NTS)
Ardallie
Ythanwells
Gordonstown
Woodhead
Hill of Dudwick
Bullers of Buchan
Fyvie
Methlick
Hatton
Cruden Bay
Fisherford
Rothienorman
Arthrath
Chapel Hill
Slains (ruins)
Port Erroll
St Katherines
Earlsford
Toll of Birness
Bogbrae
Bay of Cruden
Haddo House (NTS)
Kiplaw Croft
Barthol Chapel
Kirkton
Newseat
Folla Rule
Thornroan
Whinnyfold
Colpy
Tarves
Meikle Wartle
Auchmacoy
Upper Boddam
Kirkton of Rayne
Ythsie
Ellon
Tolquhon
Kirkton of Logie Buchan
Loanhead Stone Circle
Kirktown of Slains
Old Rayne
Durno
F o r m a r t i n e
Ardoyne
Daviot
Glengarioch Distillery
Pitmedden (NTS)
Pitmedden
Collieston
Waterside
Pitcaple
Westhall
Oldmeldrum
Ythan
A98
A97
A947
A950
A981
A90
A952
A948
A920
A975
B9031
B9033
B9032
B9105
B9093
B9121
B9025
B9170
B9027
B9024
B9029
B9106
B9030
B9001
B9005
B992
B9139
B9000
B9005
B9170
1639
230
174
1308

M
N
O
P
Q
R
24
25
26
27
28
29
30
31
0 2 4 6 miles
0 2 4 6 8 10 km
THE MINCH
Sandwood Loch
Strath Shinary
Creag Riabhach
Sheigra
Blairmore
Balchrick
Oldshore Beg
Kinlochbervie
B801
Loch Inchard
Achriesgill
Achlyness
Rhiconich
Fanagmore
Tarbet
Loch Laxford
Handa Island
Sound of Handa
Foindle
A838
Laxford Bridge
Loch nam Breac
Badnabay
A894
Scourie
Badcall
Ben Stack
721
19
Ben Strome
426
Point of Stoer
Oldany Island
Eddrachillis Bay
Kylestrome
Loch a' Chairn Bhain
Unapool
Culkein
Clashnessie Bay
Drumbeg
Achnacarnin
21
B869
Loch Poll
Nedd
Clashnessie
Loch Glencoul
Balchladich
Loch Poll Dhaidh
Quinag
808
Stoer
Clachtoll
Loch Crocach
Loch Beannach
Spidean Coinich
764
5
9
Glas Bheinn
776
A837
Loch Assynt
Achmelvich
Ardroe
Baddidarach
Lochinver
Beinn Gharbh
540
Ardvreck (ruin)
Inchnadamph
Badnaban
Strathan
Inverkirkaig
Glencanisp Forest
Suilven
731
Canisp
846
Falls of Kirkaig
Enard Bay
Fionn Loch
Cam Loch
Brae of Achnahaird
Reiff
Loch Sionascaig
Loch Veyatie
Ledmore
Drumrunie
Inverpolly Forest
Elphin
Isle Ristol
Polbain
Loch Osgaig
Forest
Knockan
Loch Bad a' Ghaill
Cul Beag
Inverpolly
The Hydroponicum
Achiltibuie
Ardnagoine
Loch Lurgainn
Loch Urigill
Summer
516
NORTH WEST HIGHLAND

29
S
T
U
V
W
X
24
25
26
27
28
29
30
31
Faraid Head
Durness Old Church
Balnakeil
Durness
Craft Village
Smoo Cave
Keoldale
Leirinmore
Sangobeg
A838
Rispond
Eilean Hoan
Beinn Ceannabeinne
383
422
Meall Meadhonach
15
Loch Eriboll
Port-na-Con
19
Heilam
Lochside
22
Beinn Spionnaidh
772
Cranstackie
802
Polla
Eriboll
Loch Hope
Strath Dionard
An Lean-charn
521
Creag Dionard
778
Ben Hope
927
Creag Riabhach Bheag
463
Whiten Head
Ben Hutig
408
Midfield
Talmine
Midtown
Moine Ho.
Achuvoldrach
Kyle of Tongue
Tongue Bay
Tongue
Ribigill
A836
Coldbackie
Skullomie
Torrisdale
Skerray
Eilean nan Ron
Caol Raineach
Farr Point
Torrisdale Bay
Strathnaver Museum
Farr
Swordly
Kirtomy
Armadale
28
Bettyhill
Invernaver
Leckfurin
Loch Meadie
Skelpick
Achargary
B871
Borgie Forest
Loch Slaim
Loch Craggie
Beinn Stumanadh
527
Ben Loyal
764
Lettermore
Loch Loyal
Loch an Dherue
17
Rhifail
Skail
Strathnaver
Syre
B873
Meall a' Chuirn
777
Glen Golly
Strath More
Alltnacaillich
Dun Dornaigil Broch
Allnabad
HIGHLAND
Loch Meadie
Meallan Liath Coire Mhic Dhughaill
801
Loch More
Aultanrynie
Kinloch
Ben Hee
873
Mudale
Altnaharra
Klibreck
Loch Naver
Ben Klibreck
Strath Vagastie
Meall Ailein
721
Meall nan Con
961
Loch Choire Forest
Loch Choire Lodge
Mallart
Loch Rimsdale
Loch nan Clar
Loch Badanloch
Loch Truderscaig
Gearnsary
Loch an Alltan Fhearna
Badanloch Lodge
Strathy Point
Totegan
Brawl
Baligill
Strathy
Melvich
Portskerra
Bighouse
Golval
Bowside Lodge
Beinn Ruadh
254
A897
Achiemore
Craigtown
Dalhalvaig
Trantlemore
Trantlebeg
Forsinain
Sletill
280
Strath Halladale
Forsinard
Loch Druim a' Chliabhain
Ben Griam Beg
580
Beinn a' Mhadaidh
403
Ben Griam Mhòr
590
Achentoul Forest
Loch an Ruathair
Lochside
Knockfin Heights
438
Achentoul
Kinbrace
Cnoc an Liath-bhaid Mhòir
474
Beinn Leoid
792
Loch Merkland
Loch Fiag
A838
Cnoc a' Ghriama
372
Loch a' Ghriama
Corrykinloch
Fionn Loch Mòr
34
Glen Fiag
Cnoc an Alaskie
312
Loch a' Bhealaich
Meall a' Bhata
581
Meall nan Aighean
694
Loch Choire
Creag a' Choire Ghlais
704
266
Crask Inn
Cnoc a' Ghiubhais
346
Strath Tirry
18
Creag Mhòr
713
Ben Armine Forest
Altanduin
Creag nam Fiadh
387
Kildonan
Craggie
Maovally
512
Ben More Assynt
Loch Shin
Creag Riabhach na Greighe
461
Meallan Liath Mòr
461
Strath na Seilge
Black Water
Strath Skinsdale
Duchally
Rhian
Dalbreck
Meall a' Phiobaire
372
Dalnessie
Brora
Arscaig
The Airde
Shinness Lodge
Dalmichy
Achnairn
Ben Sgeireach
476
Sithean Achadh nan Eun
317
Cnoc Leamhnachd
293
Grumby Rock
299
Strath Brora
Sciberscross
Gordonbush
Ben Uarie
623
Meallan Liath Beag
479
Col-bheinn
538
Loch Ailsh
Glen Cassley
Badintagairt
Dalchork
Colaboll
Sallachy
Saval
Savalbeg
3
Beinn an Eòin
544
West Langwell
Knockarthur
Loch Brora
Glen Oykel

Y
Z
AA
BB
CC
DD
24
25
26
27
28
29
30
31
0 2 4 6 miles
0 2 4 6 8 10 km
Heldale Water
B9047
Longhope
Melsetter
Tor Ness
Cantick Head
South Walls
Bow
Hope
Herston
Widewall Bay
B9044
B9042
Lythes
SOUTH RONALDSAY
A961
Ward Hill
118
Swona
Burwick
Brough Ness
PENTLAND FIRTH
Muckle Skerry
Island of Stroma
Mell Head
Dunnet Head
B855
Castle of Mey
Scarfskerry
Brough
Hunspow
Ham
Rattar
Mey
Gills Bay
Gills
Kirkstyle
Ness of Duncansby
Duncansby Head
Huna
John o' Groats
Canisbay
A99
Warth Hill
124
Skirza
Tofts
Freswick
Freswick Bay
Ness Head
Auckengill
Keiss
Dunnet Bay
Dunnet
St John's Loch
Barrock
Inkstack
Loch Heilen
Lochend
Slickly
Brims Ness
Clett
Holborn Head
Scrabster
St Mary's Chapel
Crosskirk
Thurso Bay
Thurso
A836
Murkle
Castletown
Bridge of Forss
Dounreay
Nuclear Power Exhibition
Buldoo
Portskerra
Fresgoe
Bighouse
Reay
Isauld
Shebster
Golval
Newlands of Geise
Westfield
Lieurary
Olrig House
Alterwall
Bowermadden
Lyth
Sortat
Howe
Bowertower
Sordale
Knockdee
B874
B876
B870
Loch Calder
Broubster
Braal Castle
Halkirk
Roadside
Halcro
Gillock
Hastigrow
Mireland
Kirk
Westerloch
Georgemas Junc. Sta
Loch Scarmclate
North Watten
A897
Achiemore
Craigtown
Smigel Burn
Brawlbin
Scotscalder Sta
Loch Shurrery
Spittal Hill
176
A882
Loch Watten
Mains of Watten
Killimster
Sinclair's Bay
Dalhalvaig
Trantlebeg
Beinn Nam Bad Mòr
290
Dorrery
Olgrinmore
Spital
Houstry of Dunn
Watten
Bilbster
Ackergill Tower
Girnigoe
Noss Head
Reiss
Ackergill
Sinclair
Staxigoe
Loch Caluim
Mybster
Westerdale
Strath
Sibster
Caithness Glass
Janetstown
Wick
HIGHLAND
Badlipster
Castle of Old Wick
Tannach
Loch Hempriggs
Forsinain
Strath Halladale
Sletill Hill
280
Thurso
Altnabreac Sta
Lochdhu Hotel
Loch More
Camster Burn
Achairn Burn
Grey Cairns of Camster
Thrumster
Sarclet
Hill of Yarrows
213
Forsinard
Achavanich
Cnoc an Earrannaiche
211
Cairn of Get
Ulbster
Roster
Prehistoric Stones
Dalganachan
Ben Alisky
349
Halladale
Upper Lybster
Ben-a-chielt
287
Rumster Forest
Glutt Water
Swiney
Occumster
Lybster
Knockfin Heights
438
Achentoul
Houstry
Latheron
Latheronwheel
Kinbrace
Laidhay Croft Museum
Heritage Centre
Gobernuisgeach
Braemore
Berriedale Water
Knockally
Dunbeath
Morven
706
Cnoc an Eireannaich
517
Meall na Caorach
396
Ramscraigs
Scaraben
626
Langwell Forest
Borgue
Newport
Creag Scalabsdale
555
Langwell House
Berriedale
Langwell Water
Kildonan Lodge
A9
Creag Thoraraidh
404
Ousdale
Kilphedir
Torrish
Eldrable Hill
416
Marrel
Navidale
Ben Uarie
623
628
Beinn Dhorain
West Helmsdale
Gartymore
Helmsdale
Portgower
479
Lothmore
Col-bheinn
538
Lothbeg
Lothbeg Point
Craggie
6
9
11
15
16
17
20
22

BB
CC
DD
EE
FF
GG
0 2 4 6 miles
0 2 4 6 8 10 km
17
18
19
20
21
22
23
24
Mull Head
North Hill
Papa Westray
St Boniface Kirk
Bow Head
Knap of Howar
Holland
Chambered Cairn
St Tredwell's Chapel
Noup Head
Rackwick
Noltland
Pierowall
St Mary's Medieval Church
WESTRAY
B9067
Midbea
Skelwick
B9066
Cross Kirk
Berst Ness
Stanger Head
Rapness
THE NORTH SOUND
Point of Sinsoss
North Ronaldsay
Hollandstoun
Strom Ness
North Ronaldsay Firth
Tofts Ness
Linklet Bay
Sandquoy
Otters Wick
Burness
B9069
Start Point
Newark
Roadside
Broughtown
B9068
B9070
SANDAY
B9069
Kettletoft
Quoy Ness
Tres Ness
Elsness-Quoyness Chambered Tomb
Calf of Eday
Vinquoy Hill Chambered Cairn
Faray
Calfsound
Stone of Setter
Guith
Millbounds
B9063
Braeswick
SANDAY SOUND
Loth
Spur Ness
EDAY
Eday Sound
Backaland
WESTRAY FIRTH
Sacquoy Head
ROUSAY
Wasbister
B9064
Sourin
Costa Head
Midhowe Broch and Cairn
Westness
Knowe of Yarso Chambered Cairn
Brinian
B9064
St Magnus Church
Egilsay
Brough Head
Earl's Palace
Brough of Birsay
Birsay
Standing Stones
A966
Costa
Eynhallow Church
Loch of Swannay
Kitchener's Monument
Marwick Head
Marwick
A967
Kirbuster
Loch of Hundland
Evie
Broch of Gurness
Redland
St Mary's Chapel
Cubbie Roo's Castle
Wyre
Gairsay Sound
Twatt
Loch of Boardhouse
B9057
Isbister
Woodwick
B9056
Click Mill
Tingwall
Gairsay
Quoyloo
Dounby
ORKNEY
Skara Brae
Skaill
Corrigall Farm Museum
Settiscarth
A986
A967
Loch of Harray
Bimbister
A966
Yesnaby
B9055
Voy
MAINLAND
Ring of Brodgar
Loch of Stenness
Stones of Stenness
Maes Howe
Finstown
Wide Firth
Bay of Firth
A965
Chambered Cairn
Rennibister Earth House
A965
Chambered Cairn
Stromness
Museum and Pier Arts Centre
Hoy Sound
Ward Hill
268
Loch of Kirbister
Kirbister
A964
Clestrain
A964
Greenigo
Hobbister
Houton
Gyre
Orphir Round Church and Earl's Bu
Graemsay
Linksness
Bring Deeps
Ward Hill
479
B9047
Dwarfie Stane
Man of Hoy
Rackwick
Knap of Trowieglen
399
Rora Head
Rack Wick
HOY
Cava
Rysa Little
SCAPA FLOW
Sneuk Head
Lyness Naval Base & Interpretation Centre
Lyness
Fara
Oil Terminal
Flotta
Heldale Water
Bow
B9047
Martello Tower
Longhope
Melsetter
Cantick Head
Tor Ness
South Walls
Swona
PENTLAND
Papa Stronsay
Linga Holm
Whitehall
B9062
STRONSAY
STRONSAY FIRTH
Rothiesholm
B9061
Aith
Everbay
Grobister
B9060
Burgh Head
Lamb Head
Edmonstone
B9058
SHAPINSAY
Balfour
Balfour
Sandgarth
Auskerry
Shapinsay Sound
Rerwick Head
Grainbank Earth House
Kirkwall
Tankerness House Museum
St Magnus Cathedral
Scapa
Inganess Bay
Mull Head
The Gloup
Skaill
Toab
A961
A960
Gritley
Point of Ayre
B9052
Upper Sanday
Graemshall House
St Mary's
Italian Chapel
Cornquoy
Copinsay
Rose Ness
Hunda
Burray
Southtown
St Margaret's Hope
Grim Ness
Widewall Bay
B9044
Herston
Widewall
B9042
Lythes
SOUTH RONALDSAY
118
Ward Hill
A961
Burwick
Cleat
Tomb of the Eagles
Brough Ness
Old Head

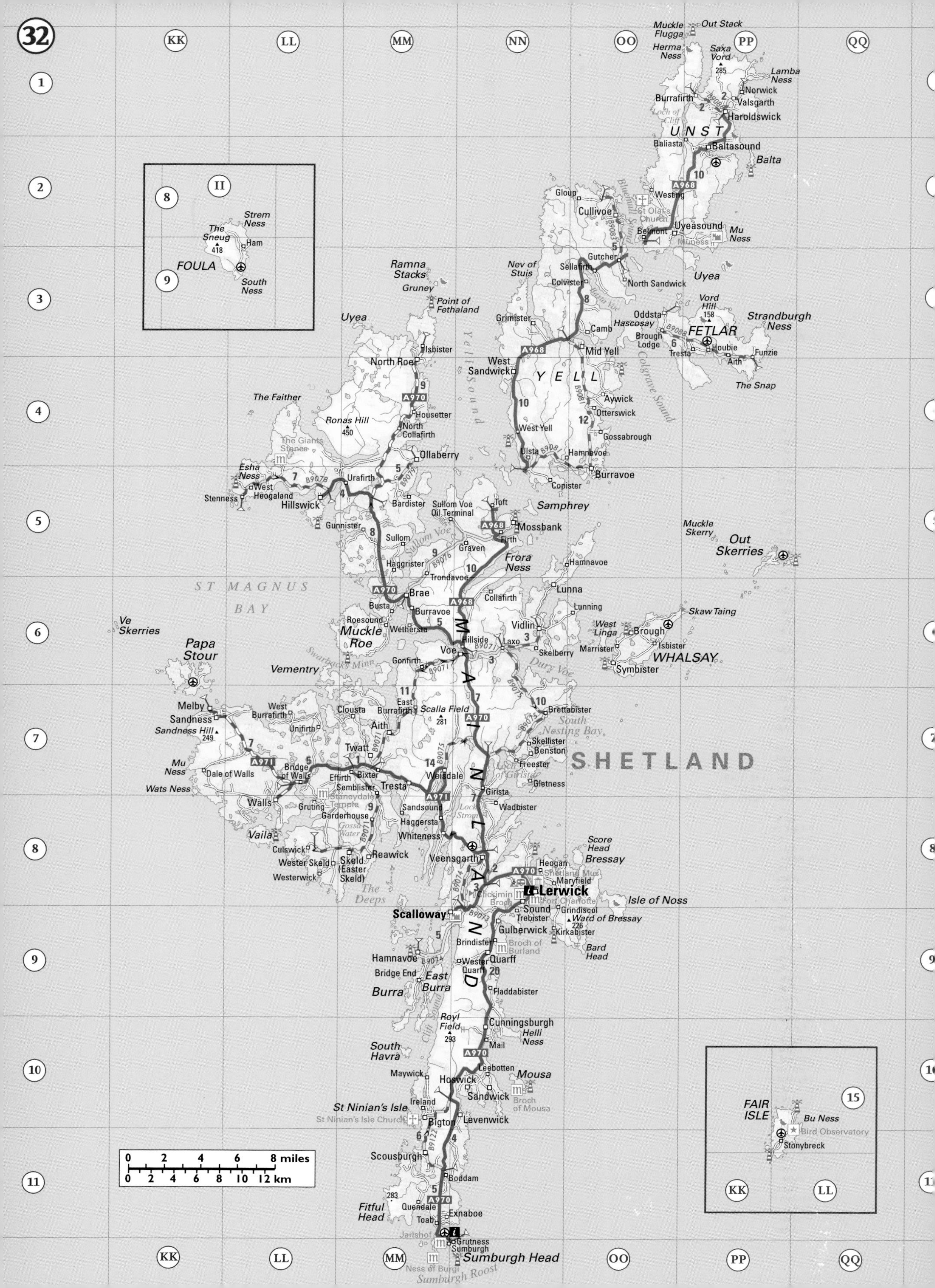

KK
LL
MM
NN
OO
PP
QQ
1
2
3
4
5
6
7
8
9
10
11
II
8
9
Strem Ness
The Sneug
418
Ham
FOULA
South Ness
Muckle Flugga
Out Stack
Herma Ness
Saxa Vord
285
Lamba Ness
Norwick
Burrafirth
Valsgarth
Loch of Cliff
Haroldswick
UNST
Baliasta
Baltasound
Balta
A968
Westing
Gloup
Cullivoe
Bluemull Sound
St Olaf's Church
Belmont
Uyeasound
Muness
Mu Ness
Gutcher
Sellafirth
North Sandwick
Uyea
Nev of Stuis
Colvister
Basta Voe
Ramna Stacks
Gruney
Point of Fethaland
Uyea
Vord Hill
158
Strandburgh Ness
Oddsta
Hascosay
Brough Lodge
FETLAR
Houbie
Funzie
Tresta
Aith
The Snap
Grimister
Camb
Mid Yell
Isbister
North Roe
West Sandwick
Yell Sound
YELL
Colgrave Sound
Aywick
Otterswick
The Faither
A970
Housetter
Ronas Hill
450
North Collafirth
The Giants Stones
West Yell
Gossabrough
Ollaberry
Ulsta
Hamnavoe
Burravoe
Copister
Esha Ness
West Heogaland
Stenness
Urafirth
Hillswick
Bardister
Sullom Voe Oil Terminal
Toft
Samphrey
Mossbank
Firth
Gunnister
Sullom
Sullom Voe
Graven
Muckle Skerry
Out Skerries
Frora Ness
Haggrister
Hamnavoe
Trondavoe
ST MAGNUS BAY
Brae
Collafirth
Lunna
Busta
Lunning
Roesound
Burravoe
Skaw Taing
Ve Skerries
Muckle Roe
Wethersta
Vidlin
West Linga
Brough
Papa Stour
Hillside
Laxo
Marrister
Isbister
Swarbacks Minn
Voe
Skelberry
WHALSAY
Symbister
Vementry
Gonfirth
Dury Voe
Melby
West Burrafirth
Clousta
East Burrafirth
Scalla Field
281
Brettabister
Sandness
Sandness Hill
249
Unifirth
Aith
South Nesting Bay
Skellister
Benston
Twatt
SHETLAND
Mu Ness
Dale of Walls
Bridge of Walls
Effirth
Bixter
Weisdale
Loch of Girlsta
Freester
Wats Ness
Sembister
Tresta
MAINLAND
Gletness
Girlsta
Walls
Gruting
Staneydale Temple
Sandsound
Wadbister
Garderhouse
Gossa Water
Haggersta
Loch of Strom
Vaila
Whiteness
Score Head
Bressay
Culswick
Reawick
Veensgarth
Wester Skeld
Skeld (Easter Skeld)
Heogan
Shetland Mus
Westerwick
Maryfield
Clickimin Broch
Lerwick
The Deeps
Fort Charlotte
Isle of Noss
Scalloway
Sound
Grindiscol
Trebister
Ward of Bressay
226
Gulberwick
Kirkabister
Brindister
Broch of Burland
Bard Head
Hamnavoe
Wester Quarff
Quarff
Bridge End
East Burra
Burra
Fladdabister
Royl Field
293
Cliff Sound
Cunningsburgh
Helli Ness
South Havra
Mail
Maywick
Leebotten
Mousa
Hoswick
Sandwick
Broch of Mousa
St Ninian's Isle
Ireland
St Ninian's Isle Church
Bigton
Levenwick
Scousburgh
Boddam
283
Fitful Head
Quendale
Exnaboe
Toab
Jarlshof
Grutness
Sumburgh
Sumburgh Head
Ness of Burgi
Sumburgh Roost
FAIR ISLE
Bu Ness
Bird Observatory
Stonybreck
15
0 2 4 6 8 miles
0 2 4 6 8 10 12 km

Index to map section.

This index lists a selection of places and features shown on the map section of the Encyclopedia.

Entries, other than those for towns and cities, will usually include a descriptor indicating the type of geographical feature, the name of the region in which the feature is located and a reference correlating to the map page and grid square in which the feature can be found. An explanation of descriptors used is on the right.

Some geographical features (such as bays and river estuaries), which cross more than one administrative region have been left without any specific regional locator.

Descriptor abbreviations used in the index:

admin. div.	administrative division	*mt.*	mountain
b.	bay	*mts*	mountains
coastal area	coastal area (inc. beach, dunes)	*nat. park*	national park
est.	estuary, firth	*nature res.*	nature reserve
h.	hill	*path*	footpath
hd	headland	*pen.*	peninsula
hills	range of hills	*pt*	point
i	island	*r.*	river
inlet	sea inlet, sea loch	*railway sta.*	railway station
is	islands	*reg.*	region
isth.	isthmus	*resr*	reservoir
l.	loch	*resrs*	reserviors
moorland	moorland (inc. lowlands)	*sea chan.*	sea channel, straight
		val.	valley

A

B

C

D

H

I

J

K

L

M

N

O

P

Q

R

S

T

U